THE OXFORD ENCYCLOPEDIA OF
THEATRE & PERFORMANCE

THE OXFORD ENCYCLOPEDIA OF

THEATRE &

PERFORMANCE

EDITED BY

Dennis Kennedy

VOLUME 2 · M–Z

OXFORD
UNIVERSITY PRESS

OXFORD
UNIVERSITY PRESS

Great Clarendon Street, Oxford OX2 6DP

Oxford University Press is a department of the University of Oxford.
It furthers the University's objective of excellence in research, scholarship,
and education by publishing worldwide in

Oxford New York

Auckland Cape Town Dar es Salaam Hong Kong Karachi Kuala Lumpur
Madrid Melbourne Mexico City Nairobi New Delhi Taipei Toronto
Shanghai

With offices in

Argentina Austria Brazil Chile Czech Republic France Greece
Guatemala Hungary Italy Japan South Korea Poland Portugal
Singapore Switzerland Thailand Turkey Ukraine Vietnam

Oxford is a registered trade mark of Oxford University Press
in the UK and in certain other countries

Published in the United States
by Oxford University Press Inc., New York

British Library Cataloguing in Publication Data
Data available

Library of Congress Cataloging in Publication Data
Data available

ISBN-13: 978-0-19-860174-6 (set)
ISBN-10: 0-19-860174-3 (set)

ISBN-13: 978-0-19-860672-7 (Vol. 1)
ISBN-10: 0-19-860672-9 (Vol. 1)

ISBN-13: 978-0-19-860671-0 (Vol. 2)
ISBN-10: 0-19-860671-0 (Vol. 2)

3 5 7 9 10 8 6 4

Typeset in Pondicherry, India, by
Alliance Interactive Technology
Printed and bound in China through
Phoenix Offset

CONTENTS

VOLUME 1

VOLUME 2

NOTE TO THE READER

Alphabetic arrangement. Entries are arranged alphabetically letter by letter in the order of their headwords, except that 'Mc' and 'St' are treated as if spelled 'Mac' and 'Saint'. The one numerical headword (the company called 7:84) is listed as if spelled out. In order to avoid an unhelpfully long series of entries that begin with a form of the word 'theatre', most such entries are recorded under the next significant word (e.g. theatre of the oppressed is placed under 'oppressed', Théâtre du Soleil under 'Soleil', Teatro Nacional D. Maria II under 'Nacional'). Exceptions include institutions commonly known by their initials (Théâtre National Populaire, Theatre Communications Group) or items that it would be confusing to list otherwise (Theatre Guild, theatre studies, Theatre Workshop).

Names and romanization. Names of persons used as headwords are those the figure is best known by. They follow the form of the relevant country or language; thus Chinese, Japanese, and Korean names, whether in headwords or text, are normally given with the family name first followed by the given name without a separating comma (e.g. Gao Xingjian and Ninagawa Yukio). All accents are included for languages with Roman alphabets. In transliterating other alphabets the standards of the Library of Congress on romanization have been followed and diacritical marks have normally been left out. The major exceptions are Japanese and Korean, where the macron or long mark has been used because of its significance in establishing meaning (e.g. kyōgen and nō in Japanese, *kamyŏnguk* in Korean). Chinese terms and names in headwords are given first in the *pinyin* system, followed by the Wade-Giles system in parenthesis: *canjun xi* (*ts'an chün hsi*), Gao Ming (Kao Ming).

Dates of plays and translation of titles. Dates of plays are of first production, unless otherwise noted. Foreign play titles follow the most commonly seen version when an English translation of the work is known to exist, but often there is no standard translated title, and more often no translation at all. In such circumstances the contributor has given a translation designed to convey the sense and quality of the original title.

Cross-references. An asterisk (*) in front of a word signals a cross-reference to a relevant entry. Any reasonable form of the referenced headword is marked in the text ('*naturalist' for 'nat-uralism', '*political drama' for 'politics and theatre'). When the mention in the text is not directed towards the content of the entry by that name, however, the word is usually not marked as a cross-reference ('actor', 'critic', and 'director', which appear very frequently, are tagged only when they refer to the substance of the entries on acting, criticism, and directing). It has seemed unnecessary to mark the many occurrences of the name Shakespeare. Cross-references are indicated the first time they appear in an entry only. '*See*' and '*see also*' followed by a headword in small capitals are used to draw attention to relevant entries that have not been specifically mentioned in the text.

Contributor signatures are given as initials at the end of each entry. A key to these begins on p. xxxv of volume 1, and brief biographies of the editors and contributors begin on p. xxxvii of volume 1.

Thematic contents. All works in dictionary format suffer from the tyranny of the alphabet. As a guide to the entries contained in the work, a Thematic Table of Contents appears in the front of the first volume, offering a topical method of approaching the entries in the Encyclopedia.

Bibliographies Brief bibliographies have been appended to most longer entries, and a general bibliography ('Further Reading') is placed near the end of the second volume. It should be noted that a number of contemporary theatre institutions have websites, most of them easy to find. We have chosen not to list them in bibliographies, or those of any other Internet reference sources, because web addresses change too frequently to be of long-term use.

Reader's comments. Every effort has been made to ensure that the information in this Encyclopedia is accurate. But minor errors and inconsistencies are inevitable, and readers are invited to call attention to any they discover, or comment on the entries, by writing to:

> Joanna Harris, Trade and Reference Department, Academic Division, Oxford University Press, Great Clarendon Street, Oxford, ox2 6dp, UK

Readers' comments will be passed on to the editor.

·M·

MABOU MINES

American experimental company, based in *New York, formed in 1970 by JoAnne *Akalaitis, Lee *Breuer, and Ruth *Maleczech. Previously the company members had worked with Herbert *Blau's *Actor's Workshop in *San Francisco. (The company was named after a small town in Nova Scotia where the founders created their first piece.) Additional members have included Philip *Glass, David Warrilow, William Raymond, and Frederick Neumann. Mabou Mines has developed a multiform style that includes the use of traditional psychological *acting played within a highly imagistic stage. Although the performance aesthetics of the company are diverse, reflecting the interests of different directors, unifying elements include the use of mixed media and new technologies including holograms in *Imagination Dead Imagine* (1985), and televisual performers in *Hajj* (1983). *Text development includes traditional playwriting of company members, *collective *devising, and adaptations. Major productions have included Breuer's *The Red Horse Animation* (1970), *Dressed Like an Egg* (1977), *Dead End Kids* (1982), *Kroetz's *Through the Leaves* (1984), *The Gospel at Colonnus* (1988), *Lear* (1990), and *Peter and Wendy* (1996). Mabou Mines has produced eight works by *Beckett, six of which have been world premières of texts not originally written for the theatre, which have led to the company's recognition as among the foremost interpreters of Beckett's work. *See also* MULTIMEDIA PERFORMANCE.   MDC

MacARTHUR, CHARLES (1895–1966)

American playwright. MacArthur's best work was in collaboration with Ben *Hecht, with whom he shared a background as a *Chicago reporter. Their *farce-*melodrama *The Front Page* (1928) brought them wide attention and invitations to Hollywood, which they soon accepted. Though much of their work (both together and separately) would thereafter be in *film, they collaborated on five more stage works, including the farce-melodrama *Twentieth Century* (1932) and the *circus *musical extravaganza *Jumbo* (music and lyrics by Richard *Rodgers and Lorenz *Hart), produced at *New York's *Hippodrome in 1935. MacArthur's outstanding solo work for theatre was the 1942 political *satire *Johnny on a Spot*. MacArthur was married to actress Helen *Hayes. His later years were less productive, due to a long struggle with alcoholism.   MAF

McBURNEY, SIMON (1958–)

English director, actor, and writer. McBurney developed an early interest in comedy (performing at the Comedy Store in 1979), and in 1983 founded the *collective *devising company Theatre de *Complicité, with classmates from Jacques *Lecoq's school, Annabel Arden, Marcello Magni, and Fiona Gordon. Early on they were a hit at the *Edinburgh Festival with *More Bigger Snacks Now* (1985). McBurney's abilities as a physical performer were evident in *text-based work at the Royal *National Theatre, *The Street of Crocodiles* (1992) and *Brecht's *Caucasian Chalk Circle* (1997), which he directed and performed in. Since 1992 he has been the sole director of Complicité (renamed in 2000), where his directing work has increasingly combined physical devising, literary adaptation, and *multimedia devices. McBurney played the choirmaster in the BBC *television series *The Vicar of Dibley*, directed comedy duo French and Saunders, and has acted in the *films *Morality Play* and *The Furnace*. *See also* PHYSICAL THEATRE.   KN

McCANN, DONAL (1943–99)

Irish actor. Born in *Dublin, he trained at the Abbey School of Acting. Early successes included Vladimir in *Beckett's *Waiting for Godot* at the *Abbey Theatre with Peter *O'Toole. McCann excelled in subtle and ambivalent roles and played in Irish and European classics as well as in contemporary work. The depth of his concentrated presence onstage reflected his complex and troubled personality. He embodied the intelligence, spirituality, excessiveness, and dangerous sensitivity of Frank Hardy in Brian *Friel's *Faith Healer* (1980), and his Captain Boyle in *O'Casey's *Juno and the Paycock* at the *Gate Theatre, Dublin, was full of complexity and bravado. On *film he worked several times with the director John Huston, most notably playing Gabriel in the adaptation of Joyce's 'The Dead'. McCann's last, and to many his most moving performance before his death from cancer, was in Sebastian *Barry's *The Steward of Christendom* (1995) in *London and Dublin.   CAL

McCARTHY, LILLAH (1875–1960)

English actress and *manager. After eight years of world *touring with Wilson *Barrett, she created the role of Ann Whitefield in *Shaw's *Man and Superman* at the *Royal Court Theatre in *London in 1905, playing opposite Harley Granville *Barker, whom she soon married. She became central to Barker's reforming project, excelling in roles for passionate, dominating women, including some Shaw wrote for her. She also went into management with her husband at a number of London theatres. Shaw thought she gave 'performances of my plays which will probably never be surpassed'; she was also notable as Jocasta in *Reinhardt's monumental *Oedipus the King* at Olympia, in Barker's revivals of *Euripides, and in his three Shakespeare productions at the *Savoy in 1912 and 1914 (as Hermione in *The Winter's Tale*, Viola in *Twelfth Night*, and Helena in *A Midsummer Night's Dream*). They divorced in 1917, to her dismay; at first she continued acting but without Barker's direction her career was effectively over. She married the Oxford botanist Sir Frederick Keeble in 1920.   DK

McCLENDON, ROSE (1884–1936)

*African-American actress. In 1916 McClendon studied acting in order to coach children's drama at St Mark's Episcopal church in Harlem. A series of major professional roles followed, including *Galsworthy's *Justice* in 1919, a revival of *Roseanne* in 1924, and *Greene's *In Abraham's Bosom* in 1926. Her graceful performance in *Deep River* that same year caused Ethel *Barrymore to remark that watching her was a lesson in distinction. The next year she appeared in the *Heywards' play *Porgy*. Her last role was in Langston Hughes's *Mulatto* (1935). With Dick Campbell, McClendon formed the Negro People's Theatre to give *training and opportunity to black actors. When it merged in 1935 with the Negro Theatre Unit of the *Federal Theatre Project, she held a leadership post until her death soon after.

                                                        BBL

McCLINTIC, GUTHRIE (1893–1961)

American director and producer. Though he began his career in 1914 as an actor, McClintic became one of the most admired directors of his era, directing 94 productions between 1921 and 1952. Twenty-eight of his productions featured his wife Katharine *Cornell. Born in Seattle, McClintic studied at the *American Academy of Dramatic Arts in *New York and acted small roles until 1921, when he made his New York directing debut with *The Dover Road* and married Cornell. Their careers reached simultaneous zeniths in the 1930s and 1940s with a series of productions noted for their intelligent *casting, elegant design, and literary quality, including *The Barretts of Wimpole Street* (1931), *Romeo and Juliet* (1933), *Ethan Frome* (1936), *Hamlet* (1936), *High Tor* (1937), *Candida* (1937), *The Doctor's Dilemma* (1941), and *Medea* (1949).   MAF

McCOWEN, ALEC (1925–   )

Restrained and intelligent English actor who trained at the *Royal Academy of Dramatic Art and worked with *regional repertory theatres in Birmingham and York in the 1940s. His first major role in *London was Daventry in Roger MacDougall's *Escapade* (1953). He joined the *Old Vic in 1959 and was quickly established as a versatile actor in both the classic and modern repertoire: *A Comedy of Errors* and *King Lear* (both 1964), *After the Rain* (1967), and *Hadrian VII* (1969). He was well cast in Christopher *Hampton's *The Philanthropist* (1970), as Alceste in John *Dexter's production of *The Misanthrope* (1972), and as a witty and urbane Higgins in the West End revival of *Pygmalion* (1974). He began performing his *one-person shows *St Mark's Gospel* in 1978 and *Kipling* in 1984. At the *National Theatre he was a moving Crocker-Harris in Michael *Rudman's revival of *The Browning Version* (1980) and a thoughtful and caring Vladimir in his production of *Waiting for Godot* (1987). In 1991 he appeared as Jack in the West End production of Brian *Friel's *Dancing at Lughnasa* and the following year was the English hostage in the *Hampstead Theatre Club production of Frank *McGuinness's *Someone Who'll Watch over Me* (1992).

                                                        AS

McCULLOUGH, JOHN (1832–85)

Irish-American actor. Son of an Irish farmer, McCullough arrived in *Philadelphia as an illiterate 15-year-old. Largely self-taught, he made his professional debut in 1857, playing Thomas in *The Belle's Stratagem* at the *Arch Street Theatre. By 1861 he was performing at the *Walnut Street Theatre and within a year he had been hired by Edwin *Forrest to play major supporting roles. In 1869, after several years *touring the country, he joined Lawrence *Barrett in *San Francisco as *manager of the California Theatre. But the financial panic that swept the country in the 1870s eventually forced McCullough back on the road as a star, playing many of Forrest's former roles.   PAD

McDONAGH, MARTIN (1971–)

English playwright, born in London, but writing in the idiom of his Irish heritage. Hailed as a cross between J. M. *Synge and *film director Quentin Tarantino, McDonagh's carefully constructed *melodramas feature acute observations of the obsessions and innate violence of Irish country life in *farcical situations. His comic sensibility and manipulation of *audience emotions and expectations made his first play *The Beauty Queen of Leenane* (1996) a huge popular success in both Ireland and abroad. The première production (the first of the 'Leenane Trilogy', together with *A Skull in Connemara* and *The Lonesome West*) by the *Druid Theatre, Galway, and *Royal Court Theatre, *London, went on to win four Tony *awards. London's Royal National Theatre premièred a fourth play, *The Cripple of Inishmaan* (1997). *The Lieutenant of Inishmore*, premièred by the *Royal Shakespeare Company (2001), featured paramilitary violence in a graphic black comedy.   BRS

McEWAN, GERALDINE (1932–)

English actress. Early in her career McEwan was in the company of the *Shakespeare Memorial Theatre, appearing as Jean Rice in *Osborne's *The Entertainer* (1957), Olivia (1957, 1960), Beatrice, and Ophelia (both 1961). She has a particular reputation for Restoration *comedy, where her roles have included Lady Teazle (1962), Lady Brute (1980), Mrs Malaprop (1983), and Lady Wishfort (1995). She appeared opposite *vaudevillian Jimmy Jewel in Michael *Bogdanov's revival of the *Kaufman and *Hart *musical *You Can't Take It with You* (1993), and in 1998 played the Old Woman in Simon *McBurney's production of *Ionesco's *The Chairs*. On *television she appeared as the brittle and eccentric *heroine in *The Prime of Miss Jean Brodie* (1978) and the monstrous mother in *Oranges Are Not the Only Fruit* (1990).   AS

McGEE, GREG (1950–)

New Zealand playwright. Nearly all his writing is centrally concerned with the loss of collective values and individual altruism in an increasingly materialist and selfish society. *Foreskin's Lament* (1980), his first and most successful play, employs an intense mixture of locker-room humour and passionate soul-searching to turn New Zealand's national religion of rugby into a metaphor for the loss of innocence in a post-colonial society. The massive civil upheaval provoked by a 1981 South African apartheid-regime rugby tour to New Zealand rendered the play prophetic, and gave it an influence far beyond the theatre. *Tooth and Claw* (1983) used the law as a metaphor similar to rugby in *Foreskin's*

Lament to portray a bleak future of urban civil war between haves and have-nots. From the late 1980s McGee has mainly written for *television and *film, but always with a strong social critique.   DC

MacGOWAN, KENNETH (1888–1963)

American *producer and *critic. Educated at Harvard, Macgowan reviewed plays for major newspapers and *Theatre Arts* magazine. *The Theatre of Tomorrow* (1921) and *Continental Stagecraft* (with Robert Edmond *Jones, 1922) made him a leading proponent of the New Stagecraft and experimental techniques in playwriting. Macgowan was appointed head of the *Provincetown Players in 1923, but managed in a 'Triumvirate' with Eugene *O'Neill and Jones. In 1924 operations were reorganized as the Experimental Theatre, Inc., and staged *The Great God Brown* and other works by O'Neill. In the early 1930s Macgowan became a major *film producer in Hollywood and professor at the University of California, Los Angeles.   MAF

MacGOWRAN, JACK (1918–73)

Irish actor. Born in *Dublin, educated at Christian Brothers' School, Synge Street, he worked in insurance until part-time acting brought him to professional attention. Notable early stage performances were in Irish-language *geamaireachta* (*pantomimes) at the *Abbey Theatre (1947–9); he also directed for the Abbey Experimental Theatre. He was much praised as the Dauphin in *Shaw's *St Joan* (*Gate Theatre, 1953), Nicola in Shaw's *Arms and the Man* (Queen's, 1955), and Joxer in *O'Casey's *Juno and the Paycock* to Peter O'Toole's Boyle (*Gaiety, 1966), all in Dublin. He was in John Ford's *film *The Quiet Man* (1952), Polanski's *Dance of the Vampires* (1967), and Lean's *Ryan's Daughter* (1970). He was acclaimed in the first English-language productions of four plays by Samuel *Beckett: Tommy in *All that Fall* (1957), Clov in *Endgame* (1958), Henry in *Embers* (1959), and Joe in *Eh Joe* (1956). *Awards included British TV actor of the year for Vladimir in *Waiting for Godot* (1961) and New York Critics' for his Beckett compilation *Beginning to End* (1971). His brooding presence and lugubrious countenance produced an extraordinary effect, at once tragic and comic.

          CFS

McGRATH, JOHN (1935–2002)

British (of Irish descent) writer, director, *producer, and cultural activist, who was a distinctive cultural presence since the 1950s, working across theatre, *television, and *film. He came to critical attention as one of the new writers promoted by the *English Stage Company in the late 1950s, and as a principal creator of *Z Cars*, the legendary *television police drama series, whilst a director at the BBC in the early 1960s. McGrath had further success in the theatre, with *Events While Guarding the Bofors Gun* (1965), and as a screenwriter with *Billion Dollar Brain* (1967). In the early 1970s with his wife Elizabeth McLennan he established *7:84 and 7:84 (Scotland), *touring companies committed to performing socialist popular theatre to working-class *audiences. 7:84 (Scotland)'s *The Cheviot, the Stag and the Black, Black Oil* (1973) became one of the most influential post-war *political plays and was televised by the BBC in 1974. McGrath reflected critically on his work, popular theatre generally, and cultural politics in *A Good Night Out* (1981), and *The Bone Won't Break* (1990). Thereafter he continued to produce theatre (mainly in Scotland) and films for television through his company, Freeway Films.   SWL

McGUINNESS, FRANK (1953–)

Irish playwright, born in County Donegal, McGuinness is renowned for an exceptional sensitivity for the traditions, beliefs, and sensibilities of others. His representation of Protestants, most notably in *Observe the Sons of Ulster Marching towards the Somme* (Peacock Theatre, *Dublin, 1985), interrogates their loyalism to England and loyalties to each other in the First World War in an *expressionistic, moral stage battle. *Mutabilitie* (Royal *National Theatre, *London, 1997), washes up William Shakespeare in an Ireland governed by Edmund Spenser and pits the brutalities of opposing ideologies with the loves of good men. In 1999, *Dolly West's Kitchen* (*Abbey Theatre) broke a host of taboos by questioning Ireland's neutrality in the Second World War, and permitted Irish nationalism to embrace homosexuality. His most commercially successful play, *Someone Who'll Watch over Me* (London, Dublin, and *New York, 1992) features the plight of three Western hostages in an unnamed Middle Eastern country. All his work provides for tortuous paths through tolerance in bold challenges to *realism.
                                        BRS

MACH

Traditional theatre form of Madhya Pradesh, *India. Originating at the end of the eighteenth century, it shares characteristics with other north Indian theatrical forms like *nautanki* and *khayal*. Based on religious, historical, romantic, and social themes, *mach* (stage) is a lyrical musical form played on a two-level platform in the *open air. The performance opens with humorous pieces from low-class *characters like the *bhishti* (water carrier) and the *farrasa* (carpet spreader), following which the *vandana* (invocation) is made to deities like Ganesh and Bhairav. After all the actors assemble on stage with stylized walks and postures, they are systematically introduced and the play proper begins. Sher Khan, a jester-like character, links the different vignettes to topical events. Apart from its delicate and evocative verse, *mach* is also known for musical structures

called *rangats*, which combine the classical and folk melodies of the region. Despite the infusion of social subject matter, the *mach* struggled to survive at the end of the twentieth century, its traditional rural *audiences turning to *television.   KJ

MACHIAVELLI, NICCOLÒ (1469–1527)

Florentine political theorist and playwright. A devoted student of classical literature, Machiavelli was the author of two original prose *comedies in the new humanist style, and one translation from *Terence. *The Mandrake* (c. 1518) is regarded by many as the masterpiece of *commedia erudita*: it deals in single-minded fashion with a *plot to seduce a virtuous wife with the cooperation of her incredibly stupid husband and a corrupt friar. The wife herself is not a willing collaborator (unlike the *heroines of most traditional comic adultery tales), and modern *audiences might be uncomfortable with the way in which her role is treated, but the play contains some devastating moments of black comedy. *Clizia* (1525) shows the resourceful wife Sofronia foiling her husband's erotic designs on their young ward: the play thus has a socially acceptable *denouement, which in the end became more common in this *genre of comedy.
                                        RAA

McINTYRE, JAMES (1857–1937) AND THOMAS HEATH (1852–1938)

American blackface *minstrels. Together for 60 years, McIntyre and Heath were the longest-paired act in minstrelsy. Rumoured to have been raised in the south (McIntyre was born in Wisconsin and Heath in Philadelphia), they met and partnered in San Antonio, Texas, in 1874. Heath was the rotund straight man, and McIntyre his thin, whiny dupe. They developed several classic minstrels sketches, including 'The Ham Tree' (later developed into a 1905 *musical), 'Chickens' (with McIntyre dressed in drag), and 'Back to the Stable'. Their 'Rabbit' song, danced with the buck-and-wing step, was reputed by McIntyre to have originated ragtime music. They conducted a farewell *tour in 1924, and made another farewell appearance with Rudy Vallee on the *radio in 1929.   AB

MACINTYRE, TOM (1935–)

Irish playwright, poet, and fiction writer. From County Cavan, MacIntyre has been a restless experimenter in different styles and media, including an early *political play *Eye-Winker, Tom Tinker* (1972). His most significant contribution to Irish theatre has been a series of image- and movement-based plays of the 1980s, staged at the *Abbey in collaboration with the director Patrick *Mason and the actor Tom Hickey. These included *The Bearded Lady* (1984), centred on the writings of Swift, and *Rise* *up Lovely Sweeney* (1985), based on Irish mythological material. The most outstanding of them, however, was the adaptation of Patrick Kavanagh's long poem *The Great Hunger* (1983). Working from certain central images in Kavanagh's bleak evocation of the sexual and spiritual repressions of mid-century rural Ireland, MacIntyre choreographed a drama of *lighting, *mime, and movement. More recent plays, *Sheep's Milk on the Boil* (1994), and *Good Evening Mr Collins* (1995), have been more conventionally language based.   NG

MacIVOR, DANIEL (1962–)

Canadian actor, director, and writer. *Artistic director of the *Toronto theatre company da da kamera, he has created a number of theatre pieces in collaboration with other artists, notably the director/creator Daniel Brooks. They include his *one-person shows *House* (1992), *here lies henry* (1995), and *Monster* (1998), and shows for larger casts, such as *Never Swim Alone* (1991), *This Is a Play* (1992), *The Soldier Dreams* (1997), *Marion Bridge* (1998), and *In on It* (2001). In MacIvor's work, the presence/absence of the performer signifies the fragility of identity, relationships, and life itself.   RCN

MACK, WILLARD (CHARLES WILLARD McLAUGHLIN) (1887–1934)

Canadian playwright. Active in American theatre and early *film (1914–34), Mack wrote over 40 plays. The majority of his energetic if *melodramatic adaptations of popular fiction played on Broadway, *toured Canada and the USA, and often became movies. While the Ontario-born Mack once lived in Alberta (1911–14), his four 'Canadian' works owe more to popular stereotypes of the Mountie, native, or trapper than to actual experience. Still his *Tiger Rose* (1917), which achieved 384 performances in *New York, England, Australia, and Canada gave international *audiences a rare if highly romanticized glimpse of the Canadian north-west.   MJD

MacKAYE, PERCY (1875–1956)

American theorist and playwright. Son of Steele *MacKaye and the writer Mary Keith Medbery, MacKaye was educated at Harvard and began writing on commission for the actor E. H. *Sothern. MacKaye's *Jeanne d'Arc* was premièred by Sothern and Julia *Marlowe in 1906 and *The Scarecrow* was a *New York success in 1911. Seeing theatrical activity as a pathway to meaning in an increasingly mechanized world, MacKaye wrote several influential books encouraging 'participatory drama', including *The Civic Theatre in Relation to the Redemption of Leisure* (1912) and *Community Drama* (1917). His mass *spectacles put these principles to use, such as a 'masque' celebrating the

150th anniversary of the founding of St Louis, performed in the open air with a cast of 8,000. When the vogue for pageantry faded during the First World War, MacKaye turned to *folk drama based on research in Kentucky and New England and wrote plays commemorating *historical events. *See also* COMMUNITY THEATRE, USA; LITTLE THEATRE MOVEMENT.   MAF

MacKAYE, STEELE (1842–94)

American actor, playwright, acting teacher, theatre architect, and inventor. After studying with François *Delsarte in *Paris in 1869, McKaye opened a Delsartian *acting school in *New York in 1871. He made his professional debut as actor and writer the following year in *Monaldi*, but his first major writing successes did not come until an adaptation, *Rose Michel* (1875), and his original piece *Won at Last* (1877). His insistence upon *realistic *acting and natural *dialogue are evident even in *historical romances such as *Anarchy* (1887). McKaye's best play, *Hazel Kirke* (1880), ran for more than a year at his *Madison Square Theatre. His interest in theatrical modernization was evident in this venue, which introduced elevator stages and folding chairs, both of McKaye's own design, and an electrical *lighting system designed by Thomas Edison. McKaye subsequently opened the *Lyceum Theatre complex, which incorporated innovative firefighting equipment, rising orchestra pit, and rooms for an acting school. At his death McKaye was working on a 'Spectatorium' for the 1893 *Chicago World's Fair, a monumental venue intended for the staging of his epic story of Columbus' adventures, *The World Finder*.   GAR

McKELLEN, IAN (1939–)

English actor. Graduating from Cambridge in 1961, McKellen worked in Coventry, the West End, and at the *National Theatre before his performances for *Prospect Theatre Company as Shakespeare's Richard II on *tour in 1968, and as a camp extrovert incarnation of *Marlowe's Edward II in 1969, brought him to national prominence as a brilliant classical actor, sensitive to language, complex in characterization, powerful in effect. He was a founder member of the Actors' Company in 1972, an attempt to diminish directors' power. In 1974 he began working for the *Royal Shakespeare Company, moving from a romantic Romeo to a tortured Macbeth (both 1976). In Martin Sherman's *Bent* (1979, 1989) he used the role as part of his campaign for *gay rights. He toured his *one-person show *Acting Shakespeare* from 1980 to 1983. From 1984, his seasons at the RNT included *Chekhov's Platonov (1986), a physically powerful and socially vulnerable Coriolanus (1984), and a 1930s fascist Richard III (1989); the last formed the basis of a powerful *film adaptation (1995) which he wrote and starred in. His search for *realism in Shakespeare generated a paranoid and punctilious Iago (RSC, 1989), while dislike of the major companies led him to a season at West Yorkshire Playhouse (*The Seagull*, Prospero, and *Coward's Garry Essendine, 1998–9). Other film roles include the wizard Gandalf in *The Lord of the Rings* (2001). He was knighted in 1991.   PDH

McKENNA, SIOBHÁN (1922–86)

Irish actress. Born in Belfast, her stage career began in the Irish language at An Taibhdhearc Theatre in Galway in 1940, where she played Lady Macbeth and St Joan (1941). She was at the *Abbey Theatre in *Dublin (1943–6), and starting in 1947 established a career in *London and *New York. Her appearances in *Shaw's *St Joan* (this time in English) and as Pegeen in *Synge's *Playboy* (*filmed in 1961) were highly acclaimed. A candid and earthy energy and poetic verve drove these performances; she also excelled in the painfully vulnerable title role in Brian *Friel's *The Loves of Cass Maguire* (1967). She first played her *one-person show *Here Are Ladies* (1970) in Oxford. Subsequently *televised in Ireland, the work illustrated her extraordinary range from high *comedy to Molly Bloom's soliloquy from Joyce's *Ulysses*. Tom *Murphy wrote the part of Mommo in *Bailegangaire* (1985) for her; she gave an unforgettable performance as an obsessive, bedridden storyteller, which was, sadly, her last.   CAL

McKERN, LEO (1920–2002)

Australian actor. Most famous for his creation of a very English *character, Rumpole of the Bailey in the *television series written by John *Mortimer, McKern had a long and successful stage career. After acting in *radio and as an *amateur for May Hollingworth's *Sydney Metropolitan Theatre, McKern left Australia for the UK in 1946, following, and then marrying, the actress Jane Holland. Tyrone *Guthrie directed him in *Molière's *The Miser* at the *Old Vic in *London, where he stayed for a number of years, and he also took major roles (including Iago) for the *Shakespeare Memorial Theatre *tour of Australia in 1952–3. Despite his extensive British career, in Australia McKern played the iconic role of Ned Kelly, in Douglas Stewart's poetic drama of the same name (1956), and had great commercial success with the *one-person show *Boswell for the Defence* by Patrick Edgeworth, which toured extensively 1988. He also played the lead in the 1987 Australian film of David *Williamson's *Travelling North*.   EJS

MacKINTOSH, CAMERON (1946–)

English *producer. Born in north *London, he fell in love with *musical theatre as a child. After stints as a stagehand and *stage manager, he began producing shows in 1969 but did not have a real hit until the 1976 London production of *Side by Side by Sondheim*. He reached the top of the profession when he produced Andrew *Lloyd Webber's *Cats* (1981), followed by *Boublil and Schönberg's *Les Misérables* (1985) and *Miss Saigon* (1989), and Lloyd Webber's *The Phantom of the Opera* (1986). He has produced hundreds of musicals—new and old, large and small—becoming the world's most successful theatre entrepreneur. 'It's called show *business*,' he has said, and he has revolutionized that business, largely by keeping tight supervisory control (some might say 'franchising') over all productions of his shows, assuring a standard of quality in every venue. A respected but hard-nosed businessman, he notably displayed his toughness in 1990 when American Equity (*see* TRADE UNIONS, THEATRICAL) declined to permit Jonathan *Pryce to re-create his role of the Eurasian Engineer in the Broadway production of *Miss Saigon*, arguing that an Asian actor should play the role. Mackintosh, despite $35 million in advance sales, cancelled the *New York production, relenting only when the union reversed its decision. He has contributed substantial sums to the Royal *National Theatre to permit them to produce large-scale musicals, in each of which he retains co-producer interest, supervising subsequent commercial transfers. He owns seven West End theatres, and in 1996 was knighted for services to British theatre.   JD

MACKLIN, CHARLES (1699–1797)

Irish actor and playwright, one of the most famous and longest-lived actors of eighteenth-century Britain. He capitalized on the *Drury Lane actors' rebellion of 1733, making his *London debut there during the absence of the regular company. He became an invaluable *stage manager for Charles Fleetwood and began to acquire more roles. His greatest triumph was as Shylock in 1741. Macklin revolutionized the play by restoring Shakespeare's *text and by abandoning the standard, treating the *character as fiercely malevolent in a *realistic manner, and adapting the *costuming to a more historically correct style. His range was not great: he was at his best in cantankerous old man roles, such as Sir Gilber Wrangle in *Cibber's *The Refusal*. As a playwright Macklin tended to write similar roles for himself, like Sir Archy MacSarcasm in *Love à la Mode* (1759) and Sir Pertinax MacSycophant in *The Man of the World* (1781). Famously litigious, he made important legal strides for actors and authors, defending his plays from pirated editions and performances (*see* COPYRIGHT), successfully prosecuting *audience members for conspiring to have him fired from *Covent Garden in 1773, and then the *managers for firing him. Macklin's hot temper meant persistent problems with managers and a career marked by travel and uncertainty. He died famous, but not rich, just a few years shy of 100.   MJK

McLAREN, ROBERT (1942–)

South African director and actor. In the late 1960s he helped set up a multiracial theatre group, Workshop 71, which created such celebrated devised productions as *Crossroads*, about eviction of blacks from a *Cape Town township, *Zzip!*, a *musical entirely in African languages, and *Survival*, a combative anti-apartheid play. Using the *nom de guerre* Mshengu Kavanagh, McLaren was the prime initiator of a radical drama magazine, *S'ketsh*. In 1976 he went into exile. After doctoral studies at the University of Leeds, he lectured in drama at the University of Addis Ababa (1980–4). Since 1984 he has worked in Zimbabwe, where he was instrumental in staging influential plays such as *Mavambo* and *The Adamant Eve*. He helped form the community theatre group Zambuko/Izibuko, *devising plays about the South African struggle for freedom such as *Katshaa! Song of the AK*, *Nelson Mandela: the spirit of no surrender*, and *Chris Hani, Revolutionary Fighter*. Other work focused on Zimbabwean issues, notably the anti-IMF polemic *Simuka Zimbabwe!* (1994). McLaren's activism has also included organizational work with groups such as *Zimbabwe Association of Community Theatre and the Children's Performing Arts Workshop. He is the author of *Theatre and Cultural Struggle in South Africa* (1985), a manual for *community theatre workers, and has edited an influential collection, *South African People's Plays* (1980).   DaK

MacLÍAMMÓIR, MICHEÁL (1899–1978)

Irish actor, designer, and writer. Born Alfred Willmore in London, he visited Ireland as a child actor in *Peter Pan*, studied art and the Irish language in London, and following an Irish Shakespearian *tour with Anew *McMaster settled in *Dublin in 1927. He was instrumental in founding the Irish-language theatre An Taibhdhearc in Galway in 1928, the year in which he co-founded Dublin *Gate Theatre Productions with Hilton *Edwards; their production style derived largely from romantic German *expressionism. His most admired roles were Speaker/Emmet in Denis *Johnston's *The Old Lady Says, 'No!'*, Brack in *Ibsen's *Hedda Gabler*, Dan in Maura Laverty's *Tolka Row*, and the title parts in *Pirandello's *Henry IV* and Shakespeare's *Richard II* and *Hamlet*—all produced several times, the latter also at Elsinore. His *one-person show *The Importance of Being Oscar* was seen in nineteen countries from 1960 to 1975. The most enduring of his eight plays are *Diarmuid agus Gráinne* (1927), *Where Stars Walk* (1940), and *Ill Met by Moonlight* (1946). Among his autobiographical works are *All for Hecuba* (1946) and *Put Money in thy Purse* (1952). He was awarded the Gregory Medal for literature in Irish, a doctorate in laws from Dublin University, and the freedom of the city of Dublin.   CFS

McMAHON, GREGAN (1874–1941)

Australian actor and director, awarded the CBE in 1938 for services to Australian theatre. McMahon began acting with the Sydney University Dramatic Society while studying for an arts degree. He acted professionally in Robert Brough's Comedy Company (1900–1), and William Hawtrey's company (1901–6). From 1911 to 1917, McMahon established and ran the mostly *amateur Melbourne Repertory Theatre Company, and remained centrally involved in the repertory theatre movement until his death. He introduced the literary drama of *Shaw, *Galsworthy, *Chekhov, and *Ibsen to Australian *audiences, and championed Australian playwrights, staging thirteen new Australian plays in six years, including work by Louis Esson, Helen Simpson, and Arthur Adams. McMahon's professional directing career included working for J. C. *Williamson's company (1920–8 and 1935–41), running their repertory companies in *Sydney and *Melbourne, and continuing his joint policies of producing the best British intellectual drama and encouraging new Australian writing.   KMN

McMASTER, ANEW (1891–1962)

Irish *actor-manager. Of Ulster descent, he was born in Birkenhead (biographies wrongly give Monaghan in 1894). At 19 Anew (Andrew) forsook a banking career for the stage; his first major success came in 1920 as Jack O'Hara in *Paddy the Next Best Thing* at the *Savoy. He *toured Australia in this and other plays, and in 1925 formed his own company to tour Shakespeare, chiefly in Ireland but also in Britain and Australia, continuing until the early 1960s. At the *Shakespeare Memorial Theatre in Stratford he appeared as Hamlet, Coriolanus, Macduff, Leonato, Escalus, and Petruchio (1933). His greatest acknowledged roles were Othello and Shylock, adding Lear in 1952. He toured the United States as James Tyrone in *O'Neill's *Long Day's Journey into Night* in 1956. The possessor of 'a great organ voice', Harold *Pinter, who acted in his company in Ireland, described him as 'evasive, proud, affectionate, shrewd, merry'. He married Marjorie Willmore, actress and designer, a sister of Micheál *MacLíammóir.   CFS

McNALLY, TERRENCE (1939–)

American playwright. *And Things That Go Bump in the Night* (1964) was a quick flop, but the young Texan continued to write, eventually succeeding in serious drama, *comedy, and *musical comedies. McNally began on Broadway, although much of his later work was done *Off-Broadway, and, starting in 1987 with *Frankie and Johnny in the Clair de Lune*, found an artistic home at the *Manhattan Theatre Club, from which many of his plays were transferred into commercial Broadway or Off-Broadway engagements (*Lips Together, Teeth Apart*, 1991; *A Perfect Ganesh*, 1993; *Love! Valour! Compassion!*, 1994). His *Master Class* (1995) achieved immense popularity, while his 1997 *Corpus Christi*, which featured a gay Jesus-like figure and his disciples in modern-day Texas, aroused storms of protest and controversy at each production. McNally was also a musical comedy librettist:

The Rink (1984), his first musical, was regarded as a weak vehicle for stars Chita Rivera and Liza Minelli. Rivera also starred in *Kiss of the Spider Woman* (1990). McNally's librettos for *Ragtime* (1997) and *The Full Monty* (2000) were better received. His early plays deal, often comically, with *characters battling uncaring power figures or structures. After the mid-1980s, his attention shifted to the redeeming power of love and of art, and his work in the late 1980s and early 1990s was also heavily influenced by the AIDS epidemic, which features directly or indirectly in several of his most important plays. McNally has been active as an officer in the *Dramatists Guild.   AW

McPHERSON, CONOR (1971–)

Irish dramatist. After study at University College, *Dublin, he founded Fly by Night Theatre Company which produced his early work, including *This Lime Tree Bower* (1995), which transferred to *London's *Bush Theatre where he became writer-in-residence (1996). His 1997 commission by the *Royal Court Theatre, *The Weir*, ran for over two years and transferred to Broadway, winning a host of *awards. There followed another Royal Court commission in 2000, *Dublin Carol*, and for the *Gate Theatre, Dublin, *Port Authority* (2001), first performed at the New Ambassadors, London. He has also written two screenplays, *I Went Down* (1997) and *Saltwater* (2000). His theatre writing is characterized by evocative storytelling in *monologue form.   BRS

MACREADY, WILLIAM CHARLES (1793–1873)

English actor and *manager. Born in London, the son of William McCready, manager of the Birmingham circuit, Macready was not intended for the stage but for the law, and went to school at Rugby. In 1808, however, he left to assist his father, whose circuit was in severe financial difficulties. Reluctantly, Macready then went on stage, and this reluctance to be an actor remained with him for the rest of his career. In 1816 he made his *London debut as Orestes in Ambrose Phillips's *tragedy *Orestes*, and soon established himself as a major actor. Before his first period of management Macready had played many leading Shakespearian roles and was indisputably at the head of his profession. His managements at *Covent Garden (1837–9) and *Drury Lane (1841–3) were financially unrewarding, but distinguished and influential. A dedicated, hard-working manager, Macready *rehearsed as thoroughly as he could, given the size of his repertory, searched endlessly for new plays of merit, worked extensively with inexperienced dramatists on their scripts, as with *Bulwer-Lytton on *Richelieu* (1837), introduced the pictorial illustration of Shakespeare's *texts through *scenery and *spectacle, and used large numbers of crowd scenes with a skill not witnessed previously on the London stage. He respected the text, and restored the Fool to Shakespeare's *King Lear*, not seen since Nahum *Tate's 1681 version. Stressing unity and coherence in production, Macready operated with high standards of artistic integrity. He led the way; *Phelps, Charles *Kean, and *Irving followed.

Macready's problems were largely those of personality and temperament. Regarding himself as a gentleman, he disliked actors, but felt he must carry on for the sake of his family, to which he was devoted. His friendships with the literary elite—*Dickens, Browning, Forster, Talfourd, etc.—made him overprotective of the worth of the *legitimate drama, and too indulgent to new legitimate plays which usually failed disastrously when he staged them. As an actor, he was a great Lear and Macbeth, and strong in any role, such as Virginius in Sheridan *Knowles's *Virginius* (1820), involving a father–daughter relationship. He retired in 1851, doffing the *costume of Macbeth at Drury Lane and giving his farewell speech from the stage in the plain black clothes of a Victorian gentleman. His years of retirement were spent at Sherborne, Dorset, and then at Cheltenham, where he died.   MRB

McVICKER, JAMES H. (1822–96)

American *actor and *manager. Born in *New York, McVicker began as a comic actor specializing in 'Yankee' *characters. He *toured the south and Midwest, joining the company at John B. Rice's Randolph Street Theatre in *Chicago in 1848. By 1857 he had raised $84,000 and built his own theatre on Madison Street, initiating a long and successful career as manager. He was especially renowned for his revivals of *comedies by Shakespeare and *Sheridan. Among the stars he attracted were Edwin *Booth, Charles *Kean, and James *O'Neill. His *stock company was regarded as one of the best in the country and McVicker's Theatre reigned as Chicago's premier *playhouse.   PAD

MADÁCH, IMRE (1823–64)

Hungarian playwright and poet. Madách graduated as a lawyer and was a Member of Parliament from 1861. In the same year he published his masterpiece *Az ember tragédiája* (*The Tragedy of Man*), a great success that gained him entrance to literary circles and the Hungarian Academy of Sciences. Although he wrote poems and fiction, and was an acknowledged journalist and orator, his main interest lay in drama. His work includes *historical plays such as *Commodus* (1839) and *Nápolyi Endre* (*Andrew of Naples*, 1841–2) and a *comedy, *A civilizátor* (*The Civilizer*, 1859) in the style of *Aristophanes. *The Tragedy of Man*, a sweeping philosophical play about the destiny of mankind, was influenced by *Goethe's *Faust* and seems to look forward to *Ibsen's *Peer Gynt*. The three *characters, Adam, Eve, and Lucifer, each embody a general type of human behaviour and a related philosophical concept. The work was not staged until 1883 and received international recognition in 1892. It has been translated into many languages and produced frequently in Central Europe. *The Tragedy of Man* remains central to the Hungarian repertoire; the new National Theatre in *Budapest opened with it in 2002.   HJA

MADANGŬK

Modern Korean open-space theatre. Returning to roots became a major trend in South *Korea in the 1970s, with playwrights and directors drawing upon traditional lore for contemporary purposes. The country was governed almost continuously by military dictatorships after 1961, and during the 1970s and 1980s *madangŭk* played an important role in the anti-government *political theatre movement, flourishing in college areas and industrial complexes that were under severe *censorship. *Madangŭk* employs ingredients from Korean masked dance-drama (*kamyŏngŭk)—such as *stock characters, episodic scenes, *satiric *dialogue, *dances, songs, and *rituals—but mixes these folk elements with Western *documentary theatre and *epic theatre. Characteristically performed in open spaces, the form normally demands *audience participation.   JOC

MADANI, IZZEDINE (1938–   )

Short-story writer and playwright, the most popular Tunisian dramatist of the 1970s and 1980s. His dramatic career began when Ali *Ben Ayed produced *The Revolt of the Man on the Ass* (*Tunis, 1970). Madani has written nine further plays, which have been produced widely: in Casablanca, Tayeb *Saddiki directed *Al-Ghofran* (*Forgiveness*, 1976); in *Cairo, Samir Asfouri staged *Attarbii wa Attadwir* (*To Round and to Square*, 1985); in Tunis and *Paris, Cherif Khaznadar directed *Al Halladj* (*The Voyage*, 1985). The most important period of Madani's career, however, was in tandem with Moncef Souissi, director of the regional Tunisian company El Kef. Taking *Brecht as a point of reference, Madani wrote plays about revolutions and *characters drawn from Arabic and Islamic history.   MMe

MADDY, YULISA AMADU (1936–   )

Sierra Leonean dramatist, actor, director, and dancer. After drama study in *London (1962–4), his first play, *Yonkon*, was broadcast by the BBC. Other work followed in abundance, including *Life Everlasting, Alla Gba, Take Tem Draw Di Rope, Naw We Yone Dehn See, Big Berrin, A Journey into Christmas*, and *Drums, Voices and Worlds*. Back in Freetown in 1968 as head of *radio drama, he also directed national *dance troupes there and in Zambia and founded his long-lived theatre company Gbakanda Afrikan Tiata. Never one to duck confrontation, Maddy was imprisoned in Sierra Leone in 1977, possibly in connection with his play *Big Berrin*, and on his release moved

to London where he directed Alem Mezgebe's *Pulse* (1979). Maddy has since carried his high ideals for *African theatre to Ibadan in 1980, where he directed *Pulse, Jero*, and *Big Breeze*, and, over a twenty-year period, to Britain and the USA. Maddy's own *texts embody a radical voice of protest in a variety of styles. His attempts to achieve professional levels of production with his Gbakanda have not always succeeded, but the qualities of *Pulse* were recognized by a Fringe First *award at the *Edinburgh Festival (1979).   JMG

MADISON SQUARE THEATRE

Erected as the 5th Avenue Theatre in 1862 in *New York, converted into the 5th Avenue Opera House by the Christy Minstrels in 1865, then leased by a *burlesque company until renovated by James Fisk for John *Brougham. Renaming it the 5th Avenue Theatre and mounting a high-toned *legitimate repertoire, Augustin *Daly made it into the city's most fashionable *playhouse from 1869 until it burned in 1873. Rebuilt in 1877 as the Madison Square Theatre, the structure gained fame again when Steele *MacKaye installed technical innovations beginning in 1879, including an air cooling system, folding chairs, more sophisticated gas *lighting, and, most famously, a double *stage mounted on elevators to facilitate quicker *scene shifting. Subsequently the theatre was *managed by Albert M. Palmer from 1885 to 1891, became (Charles) *Hoyt's Theatre until 1899, and then was rented out per play until demolition in 1908.

KM

MADRID

Located far from the coast and major commerce, this city was an unlikely candidate as an important theatre centre until Philip II moved his court there in 1561. The first permanent public theatres, the Corral de la *Cruz (1579) and the Corral del *Príncipe (1582), were open-air performance spaces created in the patios between existing buildings and were managed by religious brotherhoods that shared their profits with the city's hospitals. The Italian *actor-manager *Ganassa drew large *audiences in the early years with *commedia dell'arte* pieces and was instrumental in improving performance conditions. By the time Lope de *Vega codified the new three-act Spanish dramatic form known as the *comedia* in his *New Art of Writing Plays* (1609), he was already the dominant figure among numerous Spanish playwrights who wrote prolifically to supply the demand for new plays. Although the theatres were closed periodically because of a royal death or royal whim, the local citizens' craze for theatrical experiences did not diminish. Spain's second great Golden Age dramatist, *Calderón de la Barca, arrived on the scene just as Lope's career was ending and continued to refine the *comedia* with verbal subtleties and philosophical depth. Calderón abandoned the public theatres years before his death in 1681 and devoted himself to *allegorical *autos sacramentales for *Corpus Christi street performances and to elaborate productions at the court of Philip IV where the Italian stage engineer Cosme Lotti had designed a palace theatre. (See also EARLY MODERN PERIOD IN EUROPE.)

When the Bourbon dynasty took over the Spanish throne in 1700, French influence increased and academic playwrights attempted to emulate *neoclassicism, while audiences showed a distinct preference for 'magical theatre', a thriving *genre filled with apparitions and scenic effects calculated to astound. The two *corrales that had been the cradle of the comedia now became enclosed theatres called coliseos, with performances lit by candles. By the end of the eighteenth century a struggle had developed between the new impresarios and the traditional beneficiaries and *managers of Madrid's most important theatres, and actors were beginning to demand a greater voice for their profession. Although the nineteenth century would bring political upheavals and periods of stultifying *censorship, it was also a time of remarkable theatrical fecundity and diversity in Spain. *Moratín's enduring neoclassical comedy When a Girl Says Yes was premièred in 1806, and Madrid's most prominent actor, Isidoro Máiquez, returned from France after studies with *Talma to introduce a more *naturalistic style of *acting to the next generation of Spanish performers. After the turmoil of the Napoleonic invasion, adaptations of Golden Age plays and translations of French *melodramas dominated the stage until the belated premières of works by Spanish *romantics, following the death of the repressive Fernando VII. During the 1840s private theatres sponsored by 'dramatic societies' offered an alternative to the principal theatres under municipal control. These clubs spurred the building of new theatres, and the introduction of gas *lighting in 1845 enhanced the theatrical experience as *bourgeois theatre began to thrive in Madrid. Following the success of the playwright Gertrudis *Gómez de Avellaneda, other women writers gained a foothold in a profession previously controlled by men. Future Nobelist José *Echegaray dominated the Spanish stage for several decades and achieved international recognition for plays that were later ridiculed for their excessive passions.

By the end of the century, Galdós had sucessfully introduced *realism to Spain and the young Jacinto *Benavente was at the beginning of a prosperous 50-year career. An important contributor to the success of these writers' works was the actress-impresario María *Guerrero, who set a standard for professionalism at a time when leading actors were often erratic and self-indulgent. In the 1920s, *Valle-Inclán, *García Lorca, and a large group of young playwrights were breaking with the traditional modes of drama even as the theatres still remained conservative and catered to conventional tastes. Catalan actress Margarita *Xirgu became director of the Teatro *Español in 1933 under the republic and staged such notable premières as those of Valle-Inclán's Divine Words and Lorca's Yerma,

with the collaboration of the leading actor Enrique Borrás and director Cipriano Rivas Cherif. During the Civil War theatre offerings were hardly diminished, and propaganda plays joined the mix of popular entertainments. Production resumed immediately after the fall of the city to Franco's troops in 1939, but some of the most important talent had chosen exile. Lorca had been tragically murdered by a posse in Granada. In a devastated economy, sets and *props were recycled to accommodate new plays as the theatres themselves became increasingly decrepit.

When the annual Lope de Vega Prize for new plays was revived in 1949, the winner turned out to be a recent political prisoner named Antonio *Buero-Vallejo. His Story of a Stairway, staged by the Teatro Español's director Cayetano Luca de Tena, quickly became a symbol of theatrical renewal, and was followed by a student production of another innovative play, Alfonso *Sastre's Condemned Squad (1953), whose abrupt closing by the military gave it political import it might otherwise not have had. Censorship was relaxed somewhat in the 1960s and in the twilight of the dictatorship the wealth of new talent became increasingly apparent. Production standards were by no means uniform, and in any season superior stagings existed alongside others with substandard acting, sets, or lighting. Euphoria accompanied the elimination of censorship following the death of Franco in 1975, as previously forbidden plays were staged and nudity became almost obligatory in productions for several years. Under the socialist government, the Theatre for New Tendencies was founded as an adjunct to the Teatro *National María Guerrero and a former commercial venue, the Teatro de la Comedia, became the home of the new Centre for Classical Drama. Appointed director of the María Guerrero in 1983, Lluis *Pasqual brought new theatrical excitement and scenic daring with major stagings of *Brecht's version of *Marlowe's Edward II (1983), Valle-Inclán's Bohemian Lights (1984), and Lorca's The Public (1986). *Alternative theatres multiplied in the final decades of the twentieth century and provided venues for experimentation and production that drew increasing *critical and public attention.   MPH

GIES, DAVID THATCHER, The Theatre in Nineteenth Century Spain (Cambridge, 1994)

HOLT, MARION P., The Contemporary Spanish Theatre: 1949–1972 (Boston, 1974)

McKENDRICK, MELVEENA, Theatre in Spain: 1490–1700 (Cambridge, 1989)

MAETERLINCK, MAURICE (1862–1949)

Belgian *symbolist playwright and poet, championed by French directors Paul *Fort and *Lugné-Poe at the end of the nineteenth century. Fort directed two of Maeterlinck's early *one-acts at the Théâtre d'*Art, The Intruder (1891) and The Blind (1892), productions which gave rise to the term 'static theatre'. In these plays actors barely move, as the spirit world is evoked through atmosphere and the performers' reactions. *The Blind* features a split *stage dividing the human race by sex, and a host of blind *characters who have been led into a forest by a priest. They cannot see that the priest is lying dead and that they have been abandoned. The *verse is incantatory and liturgical, the fear is vague but palpable, presaging *Beckett's early plays and other *absurdist dramas. Death is a tangible presence, and perhaps even the play's greatest (though unseen) character.

Pelléas and Mélisande, first directed by Lugné-Poe in 1893, and set to music by Debussy in 1902, frees characters from stasis and permits spatial and temporal progression in a retelling of the story of Paolo and Francesca. Maeterlinck's duo face misfortune and death with inertia and resignation. Gone is the pleading for mercy of *The Blind* as Pelléas has a foreboding that he might be murdered by the jealous Golaud for loving Mélisande. But the eponymous tragic *heroes lack psychological motivation: Maeterlinck's symbolism brings metaphysical undercurrents to the fore and uses them as characters and *plot devices. Life, like the course of his dramas, is determined by unknown forces; his characters are led to their deaths but fail to understand their predicament or fate, even at their final moments. Maeterlinck believed his work was not best performed by human actors— though this was not the case in practice— and in 1894 wrote three plays specifically for *puppets (*Alladine et Palomides, Intérieur, La Mort de Tintagiles*). Other notable later works include *Monna Vanna* (directed by Lugné-Poe, 1902), and the much *filmed *L'Oiseau bleu* (*Blue Bird*), first produced by *Stanislavsky at the *Moscow Art Theatre in 1908. Most of Maeterlinck's later career was as an essayist and poet. He was awarded the Nobel Prize for Literature in 1911.

BRS

MAFFEI, FRANCESCO SCIPIONE (1675–1755)

Italian scholar, literary critic, playwright, and librettist. Attributing the decadence of Italian theatre to a dependence on French writers such as *Corneille, the rationalist Maffei urged a return to the tradition of sixteenth-century Italian *tragedy. He enlisted Luigi and Elena *Riccoboni, who were in the service of the Duke of Modena, to present contemporary tragedies specifically written for them, as well as sixteenth- and seventeenth-century works such as *Trissino's *Sofonisba,* *Tasso's *Torrismondo,* and his own extremely successful tragedy *Merope* (1713). Considered an ideal of *neoclassical simplicity and verisimilitude, this play inspired *Voltaire's of the same title.

JEH

MAGAÑA, SERGIO (1924–90)

Mexican playwright, novelist, and theatre critic. A member of the so-called Generation of 1950, his first successful piece, *The*

Signs of the Zodiac (1951), is still considered among the best twentieth-century Mexican plays. Set in a *vecindad* or tenement building in the older part of *Mexico City, the *text explores the daily comings and goings of the lower middle class whose lives are determined by the physical and psychological restrictions of their cramped quarters; *The Small Case of Jorge Lívido* (1958) deals with similar subject matter. While a critic of the social inequities of Mexican society, Magaña also struck a patriotic note in *historical plays such as *Moctezuma II* (1954), an attempt at modern *tragedy which, like many of his plays, was a popular success. His *Frozen Rents* (1960) is one of a handful of modern Mexican *musicals.

KFN

MAGDALENO, MAURICIO (1906–86)

Mexican playwright and *filmmaker. He wrote ardent criticisms of a Mexico in revolutionary transition. His major play *Pánuco 137* (1931) is a scathing expose of the oil industry and capitalist rapacity. After the 1930s Magdaleno abandoned the theatre for a successful career in film.

KFN

MAGGI, CARLOS (1922–)

Uruguayan playwright, scriptwriter, and novelist. A lawyer with a highly visible public persona, Maggi began to write in the 1950s and became the most renowned Uruguayan playwright of his generation. His work scrutinizes the social, political, and intellectual conditions of the nation, drawing upon strategies related to *expressionism, the *absurd, and the *grotesque. Major early plays include *La biblioteca* (*The Library,* 1959), *Esperando a Rodó* (*Waiting for Rodó,* 1961), and *El pianista y el amor* (*The Pianist and Love,* 1965). During Uruguay's dictatorial period (1973–85) Maggi was persecuted and stopped writing for the theatre, but he reappeared with *Don Frutos* (1985), a look at the life of President Fructuoso Rivera, and a number of new works in the 1990s.

JCC

MAGIC SHOWS

In the third century AD the Roman Alciphron recorded street performers offering the 'cup and ball' trick, making pebbles disappear and reappear under dishes and cups, and out of spectators' noses and ears. The Latin name for conjuror was *acetabularius,* derived from wine-cup or goblet, the Greeks had *psephopaikteo,* referring to the pebbles used by illusionists, and the cup and ball illusion, requiring enormous skill and dexterity, remains a standard table trick. Street conjurors were a common sight in the medieval fairs of Europe. By the eighteenth century more lavish conjuring *fairground booths, such as that of Isaac Fawkes, were found at Bartholomew Fair; Fawkes's great illusion was a tree that bore ripe apples in less than a minute. By the nineteenth century magic and spectacular effects were important features of popular drama. The 'transformation scene' became a standard element of *pantomime, and *Pepper's ghost (an apparition created by projecting an image onto a tilted mirror) enlivened otherwise unremarkable dramas. *Illusion was frequently dissected in popular magazines, with cutaways showing stage effects and techniques. The availability of simple conjuring apparatus in the second half of the nineteenth century, and the publication of magicians' manuals such as Professor Hoffman's *Modern Magic* (1876) and Professor Kunard's *Conjuring for Amateurs* (reprinted c.1900), prompted growth in amateur conjuring.

Robert-Houdin (1805–71), the 'father of modern magic', rose from watchmaker to *manager of the Théâtre des Soirées Fantastiques in the *Palais Royal in *Paris (1845). His levitation trick called 'Ethereal Suspension'—in which his son was supposedly rendered weightless by the inhalation of ether—was typical of his fascination with mechanics and technology. Another watchmaker, John Nevil Maskelyne (1839–1917), and his friend George Alfred Cooke (cabinetmaker and cornet-player), successfully debunked popular spiritualist acts (the Davenport Brothers in particular), whilst establishing themselves at the forefront of British magic in the Egyptian Hall in *London's Piccadilly, England's 'Home of Mystery' for almost 30 years (1873–1904). Maskelyne incorporated illusions into short dramatic playlets: a box escape, for example, became 'Will, the Witch and the Watch'.

*Music-hall and *variety entertainment encouraged magicians such as David Devant (1868–1941) and P. T. Selbit, who specialized in short and sensational programmes. Selbit promoted the involvement of the female magician's assistant, variously chained, impaled, and dismembered in a series of torture effects. Infamous on the variety stage was Carl Hertz, an American conjuror specializing in disappearing canaries; in 1921 he was forced to play before a House of Commons Select Committee on Performing *Animals to prove that he did not kill a bird each time he made it disappear. Though the Committee was satisfied, there is little doubt that Hertz's skill in substituting a lookalike bird saved his reputation and his act. Harry *Kellar, who joined spiritualism with escape, was enormously popular in America at the turn of the twentieth century. But Harry *Houdini, as flamboyant and self-promoting as Hertz, was the great escapologist, 'The Handcuff King'. Most of his sensational escapes were performed in public: manacled, laced, and chained, he was confined within the embalmed body of a whale in *Boston in 1911, when the fumes from the embalming fluid were, he claimed, more potent than the cold waters of the East River. William Robinson (1861–1918), known as Chung Ling Soo, also risked personal injury in his extraordinary bullet-catching illusion; he died when he was hit by one of the two bullets he purportedly caught.

In the latter part of the twentieth century, magic underwent a major *television revival, with the extravagant performances of conjurors like David Copperfield, who memorably made the Concorde aircraft disappear. David Blane, in a determinedly streetwise approach, continues to appeal to the younger television *audience, offering variations on card tricks, levitation, and spectacularly sealing himself in a block of ice for three days in *New York's Times Square.   AF

MAGNANI, ANNA (1908–73)

Italian actress. She performed in *variety shows in 1934, excelling for her aggressive and picturesque personality, and in 1941 began a career alongside the Neapolitan comedian Totò. She was offered her first *film role by Vittorio de Sica in *Teresa Venerdì*, reprising the type of lower-class and defiant Roman *chorus girl she had successfully played on stage. Magnani turned to film after the war, and is particularly remembered for Rossellini's neorealist *Roma città aperta* (1945), Visconti's *Bellissima* (1951), and Renoir's *La carrozza d'oro* (1953). She made her Hollywood debut in the film version of Tennessee *Williams's *The Rose Tattoo* (1955), which won her an Oscar.   DMcM

MAGNES (fl. c.472 BC)

Greek *comic dramatist. In the *Poetics* *Aristotle mentions Magnes and Chionides as the earliest Athenian comic poets. Magnes won eleven victories at the City *Dionysia, though the titles of only eight plays are known.   RWV

MAGÓN, RICARDO FLORES (1873–1922)

Mexican journalist, anarchist, and occasional playwright. After his death in a United States federal penitentiary, friends published his writings in 1924, among them *Executioners and Victims*, a play about workers' rights and bourgeois corruption (written in 1917–18, first performed in 1955 by workers in union halls).   KFN

MAHELOT, LAURENT (fl. 1625–40)

French designer. Mahelot, whose non-professional life remains a mystery, probably succeeded Georges Buffequin in the late 1620s as resident scenic designer–stage director at the *Hôtel de Bourgogne in *Paris. He is known to us exclusively through the manuscript workbook-memorandum commonly called the *Mémoire de Mahelot*, a document to which he was the first of three contributors. Mahelot's section—notes describing the production requirements of 71 plays in the company's repertory in the early 1630s, plus ink-and-wash sketches of his settings for 47 of them—illustrates the *medieval tradition of multiple staging, as it moved onto the enclosed end-*stage of the seventeenth-century *playhouse. The various scenic elements representing the locations required by a play's *action—prisons, palaces, caves, temples, shops, and gardens, all chosen from stock—are arranged on three sides of a central, unoccupied acting space. While he rarely attempted to compose these individual elements into homogeneous stage pictures similar to *Serlio's famous scenes, Mahelot's frequent use of *perspective, either on backdrops or in the symmetrical arrangement of the elements, reflects the influence of distinctively Italian *early modern practice. The *Mémoire* records the moment at which the medieval and the early modern collide, and the irregularity of baroque symbolism capitulates to a *neoclassical striving for scenic *illusion.   JG

MAHENDRAVIKRAMAVARMAN (580–630)

Sanskrit poet, playwright, and musician. His father Simhavishnuvarman, the founder of the Pallava dynasty, established an extensive kingdom in south *India between the rivers Krishna and Kaveri, with Kanchipuram as the capital. Mahendravikramavarman's many accomplishments are chronicled by honorific inscriptions on south Indian rock temples, where he is called *Chaityakara* (builder of temples), *Chitrakarappuli* (tiger among artists), *Purushottama* (most renowned among men), and *Mattavilasa* (one who revels in intoxication). The last is the title of his best-known play (*Drunken Reveller*), which belongs to the *prahasana* (*farce) category in Sanskrit drama. *Bhagavadajjukiyam* (*Hermit and Harlot*) is sometimes attributed to him, though not entirely on conclusive evidence.

Mattavilasa, which dramatizes the degeneration of religious sects in ancient India, bears sufficient testimony to Mahendravikramavarman's unique place in Sanskrit literature and confirms his status as a great religious reformer. In this irreverent play we encounter a Kapalin, or Saivite mendicant, who goes through the streets of Kanchi visiting liquor shops along with Devasoma, his attractive female companion. In their drunken revelry Kapalin loses his begging bowl. Later he picks a quarrel with a Buddhist monk whose begging bowl he claims as his own. A devotee of Lord Siva tries in vain to arbitrate the dispute, and finally a madman retrieves the bowl from a dog's mouth, proving himself more sane than the others. The *characters in this farce, drawn from contemporary life, are all degenerate in one form or another, regardless of their religious beliefs, and the royal author, an ardent Saivite himself, vehemently *satirizes them.   KNP

MAILLET, ANTONINE (1923–)

French-Canadian dramatist and novelist. Born in Acadia, the first enduring French colony on the North American mainland, she is the most eloquent chronicler and defender of Acadian popular culture, history, and language. Her first major success was *La Sagouine* (*The Slattern*, 1971), the play for which she is still best known. A series of sixteen poignant *monologues in the archaic Acadian dialect, spoken by an elderly cleaning woman, it reflects with mordant but balanced humour on the injustices to which she, her social class, and indeed all Acadians have been subject. It was an instant success in Canada, on stage and *television, in more than 700 performances. Published in France in 1976, it has been staged there and in other European countries. Maillet's other plays (some fifteen), although often successful, have not received such acclaim. Typical is *Évangeline Deusse* (*Evangeline the Second*, 1976), an impassioned rejection of Longfellow's passive, tearful *heroine. Also a major novelist, she received France's prestigious Prix Goncourt in 1979 for her novel *Pélagie-la-Charrette*, a semi-historic recounting of the Acadian nation's return from exile.   LED

MAIMO, SANKIE (1935–)

Cameroon playwright and fiction writer, the most important figure in English-speaking drama in the country. His first play, *I Am Vindicated* (1959), was written while he was a teacher at the Mayflower College in Ikot Ikpene, western Nigeria. This was followed by *Sov Mbang, the Soothsayer* (1968), *The Mask* (1970), *Succession in Sarkov* (1981), *Sasse Symphony* (1989), and *Retributive Justice* (1992). With the exception of *Sasse Symphony*, a *documentary drama about his education, his plays treat the conflicts between tradition and modernity.

HNE

MAIRET, JEAN (1604–86)

French dramatist. A contemporary and rival of Pierre *Corneille, Mairet is generally regarded as responsible for the introduction of the three *unities into serious French drama, first in a preface to *Silvanire*, a *pastoral *tragedy of 1630, then in practice in his masterpiece *Sophonisbe* (1634), the first play to illustrate the *bienséances* (*decorum) as well as the unities, thereby achieving the fourth unity—that of tone—which was to be the hallmark of French tragedy throughout the *neoclassical period. Mairet, a protégé of Cardinal *Richelieu and for a time a member, with Corneille, of the 'cinq auteurs' who composed plays under the Cardinal's direction, wrote one of the most hostile attacks on Corneille's *Le Cid* (acting, it is assumed, on Richelieu's orders); indeed, the 'Quarrel of the *Cid*' can fairly be regarded as a controversy originating in, and kept alive by, the vanity and touchiness of both Corneille and his principal adversary.

WDH

MAKE-UP

Cosmetics applied to the face or body, one of several means by which performers transform themselves. Some performers build characterization around a distinctive or traditional make-up. Crude body colours and more sophisticated decorative patterns were used from prehistory for *ritual and ceremonial reasons. Women, and some men, improved upon nature by using cosmetics. The colourful, painted faces of Greek and Roman *masks were merely exaggerations of what could be seen in daily life. Roman satirists and Christian moralists criticized this practice as false and vain. The ability to enhance features (eyes, cheeks, lips), to disguise poor skin, or to offer a simulacrum of youthfulness or age was (and remains) an important skill for unmasked performers.

The use of white or gold paint for the face and hands of God or Christ in *medieval religious dramas was symbolic and awe-inspiring in much the same way as the use of powdered white chalk was for the faces of *ghosts and murderers in post-seventeenth-century theatre. The lead content in pigments used for make-up, especially white and yellow, was dangerous, and the use of make-up was not considered essential. Leone de' *Sommi, writing in the mid-1560s, thought that appropriate *costume was enough of a *disguise 'without changing the appearance of [performers'] faces'. Over 100 years later the English actress Elizabeth *Barry was admired because her expressive face was not rendered immobile by 'Cosmetic trowl'd on'. The French actress Mlle *Clairon recommended 'a little art' to assist nature but decried 'thick enamel' as injurious to health and an enemy to the animation and expression of face that an intelligent performer needed. Actors were rarely as skilful as David *Garrick, who transformed himself from a young to an old man by subtle application of Indian ink and pencil to simulate lines and wrinkles.

In the nineteenth century, when the larger gaslit theatres demanded make-up, early acting manuals gave instruction on its use. Such books passed on established procedures; a manual of 1827 praised French subtlety in creating wrinkles, explained the technique, but warned against crude and ineffective applications. From the 1820s to the 1870s actors experimented by mixing powdered colours with other non-toxic substances to form a lasting make-up. Ludwig Leichner, a German *opera singer, founded the eponymous firm in 1873 to produce sticks of greasepaint. By 1900 greasepaint was widely used, often in conjunction with powdered colours, but less make-up was needed to enhance or disguise once electric *lighting became usual. Late twentieth-century manuals gave step-by-step illustrated instruction on the differing make-ups needed for stage, *film, and *television, and recommended which types of make-up were appropriate. Modern ranges offer make-up and body colour for performers with differing skin colours, and provide information on prosthetics and other materials for disguising face and body.

In some forms of theatre in *China, *India, and *Japan the skin and features are overlaid with a heavy make-up and the features exaggerated, coloured, or stylized to suit specific roles. (See, for example, NŌ; KABUKI; KATHAKALI; JINGJU.) Such mask-like make-ups are occasionally used in Western *intercultural theatre.

VLC

MAKHÉLÉ, CAYA (1952–)

Novelist, dramatist, and director from the Congo (formerly Zaire). His first theatre group, founded in Brazzaville in 1983, created school plays which sought inspiration from Congolese urban life. *Coup de vieux* (*A Touch of Age*, 1988, written with Sony *Labou Tansi) was followed by *La Danse aux amulettes* (*Dance with Amulets*, 1997), a ceremonial play which Makhélé produced in France. *La Fable du cloître des cimetières* (*The Cloister of Cemeteries*) explores the world of the torturer and executioner in civil war. *La Veillée des mondes* (*Worlds in Vigil*) was presented in *Avignon in 1999, and *Les Travaux d'Ariane* (*The Labours of Ariadne*, 2000), has been successful in the schools and the working-class districts of *Paris.

PNN trans. JCM

MAK YONG

Ancient Malay *dance-drama from the Malay-speaking regions in southern *Thailand and the state of Kelantan in *Malaysia, associated with the myth of Semar, the ancient Javanese deity, his sons, or the spirit of rice, known as *mak hiang* in Malay. *Ritual elements still reflect its archaic origin, such as building the theatre (the *bangsal* or *panggung*) to specific cardinal alignments and designs, *buka panggung* and *tutup panggung* (formal opening and closing of the performance), and the blessing of musicians and their instruments prior to the *buka panggung*. *Mak yong* is still performed in healing ceremonies and exorcism. Aside from ritual components, the form is characterized by stylized dance and *acting, songs, instrumental music, and *improvised spoken text for the narrative. The most exquisite part of the performance is the *tarian menghadap rebab* (dancing in front of the *rebab* or spike fiddle), an opening section accompanied by the *lagu menghadap rebab* (singing in front of the *rebab*). A heterophonic duet between the lead actor, played by a woman, and the *chorus of dancers singing melismatic tunes accompanied by interlocking drum parts, gongs, and the *rebab*, creates a massive proliferation of pitches and dance movements as preparation for the dance-drama.

MA

MALAYSIA

Independent from Britain since 1957, this South-East Asian nation currently comprises the Malay peninsula (except *Singapore) as well as Sabah, Sarawak, and the Federal Territory of Labuanon in north-western Borneo. Of its 22 million inhabitants, the majority are ethnically Malay while about one-third are Chinese and Indian immigrants who have preserved many of their overseas performance traditions (*see* CHINA; INDIA). The range of extant Malaysian theatre forms reflects the disparate cultural traditions historically traced to the region. For example, a pre-Islamic shamanist practice of spirit conjuring underlies the healing ceremony *main puteri* from the eastern province of Kelantan and is believed to be the origin of the *mak yong *dance-drama as well. At the same time, Islam (the official state religion) provides the source and inspiration for other performances such as *dabus, where the recitation of sacred Islamic texts (*zikir*), combined with music and martial arts, sends the dancers into trance. Several similar but distinct forms are also found in *Indonesia (for instance *ketoprak and *reog) and influences from neighbouring *Thailand are clearly evident in the *folk theatre called *nora. Seeds for modern theatre were sown at the turn of the twentieth century with the creation of *bangsawan, an urban commercial show modelled after *touring *Parsi troupes. From this developed *amateur *sandiwara companies which used written scripts for the first time.

Modern Malay-language theatre based on Western conventions began in earnest in the 1940s. The development of modern theatre has been centred primarily in the capital, Kuala Lumpur, a sprawling metropolis with an ethnically diverse population. The 1950s and 1960s saw the emergence of several important playwrights and directors including Shaharom *Husain, Usman *Awang, and Mustapha Kamil *Yassin. Since the 1970s the Ministry of Culture, Arts, and Tourism has implemented programmes and institutions designed to preserve and promote traditional Malay performance and to encourage modern Malay-language theatre. Unfortunately this focus on Malay arts has neglected theatrical practices in the non-Malay communities, where many traditions are in danger of extinction. Several successful modern companies and *training centres performing in Malay and English have been active since the 1980s, including the Five Arts Centre, the Actors Studio Malaysia, the Instant Café, Dramalab, and Sutra Dance Theatre. In 1994 the Ministry inaugurated the National Arts Academy which grants degrees in traditional and modern theatre, dance, creative writing, and music. Courses in *mak yong*, *wayang kulit*, and *bangsawan* were made compulsory in the hope that the students would become either practitioners or scholars of these endangered traditional forms. The long-awaited Istana Budaya (Cultural Complex) opened in 1999, becoming home to the National Theatre Company and the National Symphony Orchestra. It touts itself as the most technologically advanced theatre complex in Asia.   CRG

MALECZECH, RUTH (1939–)

American actor and director. After work with the *San Francisco Mime Troupe and the San Francisco Tape Music Center, Maleczech travelled in Europe where she acted in *Beckett's *Play* (1965) and studied with *Grotowski. With JoAnne

*Akalaitis, Lee *Breuer, David Warrilow, and Philip *Glass, she formed *Mabou Mines in 1969. Maleczech insisted in 1970 that the production budget cover child care; she and Akalaitis founded the Children's Liberation Day Care Center. Maleczech acted in five productions at the *New York Shakespeare Festival, including *Dead End Kids* by Akalaitis (1980), a play about nuclear power, and Breuer's poetic performance piece *Hajj* (1983). She acted the role of a submissive butcher in *Kroetz's *Through the Leaves*; played the title role in a cross-gendered *Lear*, set by Breuer in the 1950s American south-east (1987); and performed Winnie in Beckett's *Happy Days* (1997). Though she writes and directs, her focus remains on *acting, where her meticulous, straightforward approach and wide-ranging experimental techniques make her a major artist.   FL

MALE IMPERSONATION

Women cross-dressing to represent men or boys, within a context of public performance, does not appear to have the long history or the roots in *ritual practice that could be said to legitimize cross-dressing by men (*see* FEMALE IMPERSONATION). Nor does it have the same range of meanings, and such difference may account for its relative rarity. Historically, male cross-dressing is a commonplace of performance, accommodated relatively comfortably within both social hierarchies and the conventions of *gender ordering. Not so for women. Their gradual appearance on European professional stages during the sixteenth and seventeenth centuries led at once to their performing in male clothes (*see* BREECHES ROLE; WOMEN AND PERFORMANCE), but such appearances were usually defused of any possible threat by being sexualized in a mode which emphasized the femininity of the performer, if simply by the physical exposure of wearing the breeches. Only in the later nineteenth century in Britain and America did the 'impersonation' of men, in the sense of an *illusionistic and sometimes *satirical intent to replicate their dress and physical demeanour, become a popular performance speciality. It has not remained so; since the coming of a general awareness in the early twentieth century of possible challenges to white male definitions of masculinity and of *lesbian meanings in such performance, the psychological discomforts and social transgressiveness of being or of seeing a woman dressing up (as opposed to a man dressing down) in their performance of gender have stood in the way of widespread male impersonation for entertainment.

The flowering of male impersonation was on the nineteenth-century stage, in *vaudeville and *music hall. The habit of simple cross-playing, girls representing boys in dramatic sketches simply for convenience, survived unchecked, and there were also still *dancers who used elements of male dress simply to display their own bodies with a freedom denied by voluminous skirts; but singers, especially, had begun to use a more thoroughgoing gender transformation on stage.

According to physical type, ability, and temperament, they might represent slender youths in fashionable dress and especially in attractive uniforms (Vesta *Tilley, Bessie Bonehill, Hetty King are examples of this mode) or heavyweight roistering swells or dudes (early examples were Annie Hindle and Ella Wesner in America, Fanny Robina in England, Louise Rott in Germany, and later the Australian Ella *Shields, and the black vaudeville 'bull dagger' Gladys Bentley). There were many variations in *realism of representation: Robina wore corsets under her tail-coated *costume, while Tilley was so immaculately androgynous that she was supposed to have set male fashions. But she had a soprano voice. How far the gender play extended, that is, whether their representation of masculinity was mocking or idealized, and whether the personae projected and received were sexually ambiguous or romantically innocent, must have varied not only between individual performers but between venues, and been differently read even across parts of the house, by working men and middle-class loungers; and certainly the response must have differed between men and women in the *audience. Such an absence of common agreement about how to understand the act of full-dress male impersonation is arguably the reason for its fading, rather than becoming an established and acceptable form of gender play: it is too uncomfortable for a general audience.

Twentieth-century examples of its use endorse that conclusion in two distinct ways. In 1914 Kobayashi Ichizō organized an all-girl acting company in a small town in *Japan, from which the *Takarazuka took its name. Still thriving, and with a huge following of Japanese women, this lavishly mounted song-and-dance entertainment is characterized by young women playing otoko-yaku, idealized young men, more perfect than any male self-representation. Their material typically draws on Western music and cultural icons, and their polished routines present a perfect simulacrum of glamorous romantic relationships whose remoteness from real life guarantees a safe sub-sexual thrill which is in no way challenging or unsettling. On the other hand, some Western *feminist performers have taken up male impersonation as an explicit challenge to patriarchal hegemony. Peggy Shaw's performances such as A Menopausal Gentleman openly explore gender boundaries and transgressive experience (see SPLIT BRITCHES); while some British *television *satire, such as the representation of Prime Minister Margaret Thatcher in the *puppet show Spitting Image, or the disgusting sexism of the fat middle-aged working men in sketches presented by Dawn French and Jennifer Saunders, make male impersonation a route to explicit critique of masculine attitudes and supremacy. Since there is still no generally understood and easy way of integrating such performance into light entertainment in the West, such acts remain a minority interest, and an aggressive statement. See also QUEER THEORY. JSB

SENELICK, LAURENCE, The Changing Room: sex, drag and theatre (London, 2000)

American director, actor, playwright, and activist. Born in Germany, she emigrated with her family to the USA and trained as an actor and director with Erwin *Piscator at the New School in *New York. In 1947 she founded the *Living Theatre with her husband Julian *Beck, and promoted an experimental approach to their work with productions of *avant-garde playwrights such as *Stein, *Cocteau, *Brecht, and *Pirandello. Malina's anarcho-pacifist beliefs led the Living Theatre to explore new forms of theatre-making through structuring the company as a *collective, developing performances through collective creation and *improvisation, while developing an aesthetic of physicality and confrontation. She performed throughout Europe and the Americas in such landmark productions as Mysteries and Smaller Pieces (1964), Frankenstein (1965), Antigone (1967), and Paradise Now (1968). She won eight Obie *awards, including one for best actress in her translation and adaptation of Brecht's Antigone (1969). After Beck's death in 1985, Malina continued the work of the Living Theatre with her partner Hannon Resnikov, performing new works throughout the world. As an actress she has appeared in such *films as Dog Day Afternoon (1975), Radio Days (1987), The Addams Family (1991), and Looking for Richard (1996). MDC

MALI PUPPET THEATRE

Performed by rural and urban youth associations in south-central Mali. Originating in the pre-colonial era, it is now performed mainly by five ethnic groups: the Boso and Sòmonò fishermen, and the Bamana, Maraka, and Maninka farmers. Young men are the puppeteers and drummers; young women are the singers. Performances consist of youth association dances followed by the *puppet theatre. The drama is organized into discrete sequences which are separated by short intervals of song and *dance. These sequences consist of mimed dance presentations of individual *characters, generally voiceless, who are accompanied by songs and drumming. There may be well over twenty puppet acts in a single evening's festivities. The theatre includes rod puppets, rod and string puppets, dummy heads, and helmet and face masks. Rod puppets dominate, made of large carved wooden heads to which a rod is attached through the puppet's body, itself a *costumed armature under which the puppeteer is hidden. Characters are drawn from a stock of bush and water animals. Troupes also perform a range of conventionalized human types representing neighbouring ethnic groups and different classes of people within their own group. There are also spirits, imaginary beasts, personages drawn from epics, and others inspired by contemporary experience. Each ethnic group maintains its own performance, singing, and drum styles, though all groups share certain characters and a common sculptural method. (See illustration p. 1084.) MJA

MALKOVICH, JOHN (1953–)

American actor. Malkovich joined the *Steppenwolf Theatre Company in *Chicago in 1976 and subsequently appeared in *Shepard's *True West* (1982), Lanford *Wilson's *Burn This* (1987), and directed his own adaptation of Don DeLillo's *Libra* (1994). He played Biff in Dustin *Hoffman's 1984 Broadway revival of *Death of a Salesman*. His *film roles include Mr Will in *Places in the Heart* (1984), Al Rockoff in *The Killing Fields* (1984), Basie in *Empire of the Sun* (1987), Tom in *The Glass Menagerie* (1987), the Vicomte de Valmont in *Dangerous Liaisons* (1988), Lennie in *Of Mice and Men* (1992), Mitch Leary in *In the Line of Fire* (1993), and himself in *Being John Malkovich* (1999). He has appeared in several films released by European companies, some in French. His *television credits include Deeley in *Old Times* (1991) and Kurtz in *Heart of Darkness* (1994). JDM

MALONE, EDMUND (1741–1812)

Irish author, educated at Trinity College, Dublin, the greatest editor of Shakespeare in the eighteenth century. He brought a lawyer's zeal for fact and method to a job that had hitherto been the province of creative writers. His 1790 edition was the first to account for the chronology of Shakespeare's plays; it restored the sonnets to the 1609 text, complete with notes; and it corrected and supplemented many aspects of Shakespeare's biography. A friend of Dr *Johnson, Boswell, and other London writers, Malone's was the decisive voice that exposed the forgeries of Thomas Chatterton, and of *Ireland's Shakespeare papers in 1796. MJK

MALOYA

Traditional song and dance of Réunion island, imported by African and Malagasy slaves. Unlike its secular cousin the *séga, however, it was long banned by the civil and religious authorities because of its association with animist beliefs and *rituals. Rediscovered in the 1970s by the Catholic worker-priest Christian Fontaine, *maloya* was taken up by the poets of the creole revival and inspired several internationally successful performers. Gramoune Lélé used its traditional forms, for example; Danyel Waro made it a vehicle for politically committed poetry; and the group Ziskakan fused *maloya* with electronic and world music influences. PGH

MALVERN FESTIVAL

Summer drama *festival held annually from 1929 to 1939, revived briefly in the 1940s and 1960s, and re-established as a more general annual arts festival in 1977. Barry *Jackson founded the festival in 1929 as a forum for British drama.

The first season included the British première of *The Apple Cart* by George Bernard *Shaw, the festival's patron. His works continued to feature prominently, but the festival also presented the work of dramatists ranging from Thomas *Heywood, Ben *Jonson, and John *Dryden to Arthur *Pinero, James *Bridie and J. B. *Priestley, and offered rarely performed plays such as *Ralph Roister Doister* (1932) and *Gammer Gurton's Needle* (1933). VRS

MALY THEATRE (MOSCOW)

The city's oldest theatre, which grew out of a university-based theatre group, created in 1756, and granted imperial status in 1806. Between 1815 and 1824 the company acquired a galaxy of outstanding actors, including Pavel *Mochalov and Mikhail *Shchepkin—the Edmund *Kean and David *Garrick of their day—and, more importantly, the present building in central *Moscow. It was here that *Griboedov's great comedy *Woe from Wit* was premièred in 1831. Shchepkin brought about a one-man revolution in truth-to-life *realism, while the *romantic tradition was continued by Mochalov, whose 1837 *Hamlet* created a sensation. The next great phase of the theatre's existence is associated with the work of Aleksandr *Ostrovsky, 47 of whose plays were given premières here, beginning with his first in 1853, and establishing the acting reputations of Prov *Sadovsky and Glikeria *Fedotova. The 1880s saw productions of plays which had previously been banned, such as *Pushkin's *Boris Godunov* (1880), and *Turgenev's *A Month in the Country* (1881), in the latter of which Maria Savina made a strong impact as Verochka. The 1890s saw Maria *Ermolova begin to impress as a tragic actress; her stage partners Aleksandr *Lensky, Aleksandr Yuzhin, Aleksandra *Yablochkina, Aleksandr Ostuzhev, and Olga Sadovskaya were no less outstanding. Nationalized after the revolution, the theatre was awarded the title 'Academic', in 1920, and responded by staging *Lunacharsky's *Oliver Cromwell*, followed by a number of productions of contemporary Soviet plays with Civil War themes, the most notable of which was *Trenyov's *Lyubov Yarovaya* in 1926, with Vera Pashennaya in the title role. The 1930s saw a whole range of fairly undistinguished Soviet plays but also a notable production by Sergei *Radlov in 1935, *Othello* with Aleksandr Ostuzhev. The theatre staged a number of patriotic plays during the 1940s and, after the war, was refreshed by the acquisition of distinguished acting talent in the shape of former *Meyerhold actors Igor *Ilinsky and Mikhail Tsaryov. The Maly also benefited from the directorial input of Aleksei Diky, Boris Babochkin, and Boris Ravenskikh, the last of whom directed a powerful production of *The Power of Darkness*, with Ilinsky as Akim, in 1956. In 1962, *Lermontov's *Masquerade* was presented in homage to the rehabilitated *Meyerhold, with Tsaryov repeating the role of Chatsky which he had acted in Meyerhold's revised 1930s production. Sadly little of distinction was staged here in the last quarter of the twentieth century.　　　NW

MALY THEATRE (ST PETERSBURG)

Established in 1895 by Aleksei Suvorin and others as the Literary-Artistic Theatre Society in *St Petersburg. Pavel *Orlenev, Lydia Yavorskaya, and other outstanding actors performed here in the theatre's pre-revolutionary heyday. The present Maly Drama Theatre, seating about 460 people and situated in a block of flats on Rubinshtein Street, was founded in 1944 and by the 1990s had a company of some 50 actors and 150 supporting staff. When Lev *Dodin became *artistic director in 1983, the company was transformed into a distinctive *collective renowned for its intensive *rehearsal methods and socially committed work. During the 1980s and 1990s productions were seen in most European capitals, in *Japan, and in the USA, drawing high praise from *audiences and theatre *critics alike. The first production to make an impact was of Aleksandr *Galin's *Stars in the Morning Sky*, which encapsulated the spirit of glasnost in the Soviet theatre. This was followed by powerful ensemble work based on *improvisation: *Gaudeamus*, which offered an honest glimpse of Soviet military training methods, and *Claustrophobia*, an intensely realized response to post-Soviet regional conflicts, set in a lunatic asylum. *Brothers and Sisters*, based on Fyodr Abramov's tetralogy of novels about Soviet peasant life, was a riveting six-hour production in two parts. An equally mammoth three-part version of Dostoevsky's *The Devils* came next, and more normally proportioned versions of *Chekhov's *The Cherry Orchard* and *Platonov*. In the first a pond featured prominently, and in the second, an entire lake in which the actors swam, made love, and met their deaths.　　　NW

MAMBÍ, TEATRO

Concept applied by critic Rine Leal to Cuban theatre committed to the independence struggles from 1868 to 1898, named after the guerrilla soldiers who fought against Spain. In 1869 a clandestine journal published the first insurgent drama, José *Martí's *Abdala*. Other works were written in exile: Alfredo Torroella's *El mulato* (*The Mulatto*, 1870), Juan Ignacio de Armas's *Alegorías cubanas* (*Cuban Allegories*), Luis García Pérez's *El grito de Yara* (*The Yara Proclamation*), Diego Vicente Tejera's *La muerte de Plácido* (*The Death of Plácido*). Military troops improvised entertainments and shows about the war of independence, though little is known about battlefront production methods.　　　MMu

MAMET, DAVID (1947–)

American writer and director. Born and raised in *Chicago, Mamet returned there in 1973 after studying and then teaching at Goddard College in Vermont, and joined the vibrant Off-Loop theatre scene as a playwright and co-founder of the St Nicholas Theater Company. Early influences included the plays of *Pinter, a year of *Meisner training at the *Neighborhood Playhouse in *New York, and Chicago's Second City comedy club, where he worked as a busboy one summer. In Chicago he met the director Gregory *Mosher, who would direct many Mamet plays, starting with the 1975 première of *American Buffalo* at the *Goodman Theatre. After winning an Obie *award *Off-Broadway in 1976, the play opened on Broadway in 1977 and thrust Mamet into the national spotlight, partly for its earthy and liberal use of profanity. Its taut *naturalistic tale of three lowlifes who botch the theft of a coin collection introduced some of Mamet's enduring themes: *characters caught in cycles of trust and betrayal, vernacular speech as a desperate effort to achieve meaning, the rough-and-tumble intimacy of machismo, and the spiritual vacuity of post-industrial capitalist culture.

These themes were advanced in two major works of the 1980s, the Pulitzer Prize-winning *Glengarry Glen Ross* (1984), about a group of unscrupulous Chicago real-estate agents, and *Speed-the-Plow* (1988), about two Hollywood insiders and the innocent woman who comes between them. *Oleanna*, Mamet's provocative take on political correctness and sexual harassment, sparked controversy when it premièred in 1992. His subsequent plays, including the quasi-autobiographical *The Cryptogram* (1994) and *Boston Marriage* (1999), effected a more serene, and sometimes even relaxed, demeanour. In the 1990s the prolific Mamet concentrated more on his *film and prose careers. He began writing screenplays for hire in the 1980s (*The Postman Always Rings Twice*, 1981; *The Verdict*, 1982; *The Untouchables*, 1987) and directing his own scripts (*House of Games*, 1987; *Things Change*, 1988). Later films written and directed by Mamet include *The Spanish Prisoner* (1997), an adaptation of *Rattigan's *The Winslow Boy* (1999), and *State and Main* (2000). All told, he has written more than two dozen screenplays and directed nearly a dozen films. *Writing in Restaurants* (1986), his first collection of essays, memoirs, and occasional pieces, was followed by more than half a dozen other volumes. He also published novels, collections of poetry, and children's stories, but his status as playwright remains high. For the idiomatic rhythms of his *dialogue, the desperate bravado of his characters, and the menacing immediacy of his *plots, he ranks as one of the most important American dramatists of the twentieth century.　　　STC

MAMONTOV, SAVVA (1841–1918)

Russian industrialist and patron of the arts. After some years in Italy studying singing and the history of the visual and expressive arts, in 1870 Mamontov bought the estate of Abramtsevo near *Moscow, where he formed an artistic colony whose members included the painters Vrubel, Serov, *Simov, Levitan, and the brothers Vasnetsov and Korovin. He also gave private operatic performances at his Moscow house in which *Stanislavsky took part and where the *scenery was designed by members of the colony. In 1885 Mamontov opened a private *opera theatre in Moscow and managed to attract Fyodor Chaliapin from the Imperial Mariinsky Theatre. Productions were marked by a new approach to operatic acting and staging and the importance of *scenography was evident in the contribution of artists mentioned above. Productions included work by Glinka, Dargomyzhsky, Mussorgsky, Borodin, Tchaikovsky, Rachmaninov, and Anton Rubinstein. Apart from Chaliapin, singers during the Lent seasons of 1889–92 included such masters of bel canto as Mazzini, Tamagno, Marie von Zandt, and Silva. The theatre was forced to close in 1904 because of financial difficulties, Mamontov, whose money was in railways, having been bankrupted in 1899.   NW

MAMOULIAN, ROUBEN (1898–1987)

Russian-born American director. When his studies at *Vakhtangov's Third Studio in *Moscow were disrupted by the Russian Revolution, he co-founded a theatre in his native *Tbilisi. He emigrated to *London in 1921 where he directed Russian émigrés at the Macaroff Theatre; his West End debut came in 1922. Mamoulian headed the *opera programme at the Eastman School of Music in Rochester, New York, from 1923 to 1925, and the *Theatre Guild's *acting school in 1926. He staged nine Guild productions, including *Porgy* (1927), *Marco Millions* (1928), *Wings over Europe* (1928), the American première of *A Month in the Country* (1930), and the *musicals *Porgy and Bess* (1935), *Oklahoma!* (1943), and *Carousel* (1945). His musicals were notable for advancing the seamless integration of elements. Among other significant shows directed by Mamoulian, who also directed a number of *films, were *St Louis Woman* (1946) and *Lost in the Stars* (1949).   SLL

MANAGER

Generally speaking, the person responsible for organizing the practical necessities of bringing a theatrical performance into being, including the choice of play, the selection and/or hiring of personnel (and often the *casting of actors), the procurement of an appropriate venue, and the controlling of the *finances. Functioning at the juncture of art and business, managers find their roots in both theatre and commerce. Managers drawn from the world of *playwrights, *actors—and later, *directors—appeared in England and France at the end of the sixteenth century, usually as the leading members of acting troupes in which all shared the risk and the profits (*see* COMPANY ORGANIZATION IN EUROPE, 1500–1700). A more markedly entrepreneurial model emerged when managers were able to control the *playhouse as

well as the acting company, a profitable combination that began in England in the 1590s and continued in England and then America through most of the nineteenth century. The 'sharer' system broke down completely in the seventeenth century, and was replaced by a system in which risk and profit were taken by managers (and external investors) and the actors were salaried. Management at times fell to businessmen with little or no theatrical experience or competence, but this in itself was not necessarily detrimental to the enterprise.

Nevertheless the period from the mid-eighteenth century to the First World War in both England and America was the era of the *actor-manager, many of whom—William *Macready, Madame *Vestris, Beerbohm *Tree—strongly influenced theatrical style. In France and the German-speaking lands, the entrepreneurial role of the manager was made largely redundant by the *early modern system of court theatres, and then by the introduction of state funding in the early nineteenth century, which released managers to concentrate on theatrical art, but which also brought state supervision. In Germany, the state-appointed theatrical manager (*Intendant*) was considered in some cases an impediment to the artistic enterprise as late as the 1960s, though many major German directors in the later twentieth century succeeded in that role at high levels of creativity and originality. In the English-speaking theatre the manager's twofold function has devolved onto (*a*) the *artistic director, a theatrically trained manager who supervises the production, protected in varying degrees from the vicissitudes of the market-place by state or philanthropic funding, boards of directors, and legal contracts; and (*b*) the *producer, an entrepreneur who markets stars and theatrical productions within the context of 'show business'. Between these extremes, managerial functions are served by persons with a variety of titles.   RWV

MANAKA, MATSEMELA (1956–98)

South African director and playwright, born in *Johannesburg. While working as a teacher, the 1976 Soweto student uprising provoked his theatrical career. He founded the Soyikwa African Theatre group, which developed satirical plays in response to current events. Between 1977 and 1991 Manaka wrote fourteen plays in the workshop context, as well as the important essays 'Theatre of the Dispossessed' and 'Theatre as a Physical Word'. Committed to the Pan-African and Black Consciousness movements, his work integrated European and African forms of *dance, *music, and *physical theatre to explore issues of apartheid and post-colonial Africa, including rural poverty, urbanization, detribalization, migrant labour, forced removals, social disintegration in the townships, and crime. His plays include *Egoli: city of gold* (1978), *Imbumba* (1979), *Vuka* (1980), *Pula* (1982), *Children of Asazi* (1984), and *Gorée* (1989).   YH

MANCHESTER

Situated in the populous north-west of England, Greater Manchester possesses the largest number of *playhouses of any UK city outside *London. As one of Britain's first Industrial Revolution urban centres, Manchester acquired a variety of big and small theatres through the course of the nineteenth century. But its national prominence was established in 1907 when Annie *Horniman opened a repertory theatre in the refurbished *Gaiety Theatre, the first such theatre in mainland Britain and one that set in motion the burgeoning *repertory theatre movement. The Gaiety also helped to foster an identifiable 'Manchester school' of playwrights, consisting of writers such as Elizabeth *Baker, Harold *Brighouse, Stanley *Houghton, and Allan *Monkhouse, noted for their use of contemporary *realism, industrial working-class settings, and Lancashire dialect. After the First World War other ventures came and went, including the Rusholme Rep and, notably, a number of pioneering radical left-wing theatre groups, the best known of which was Ewan MacColl's and Joan *Littlewood's Theatre of Action, which re-formed after the Second World War to become *Theatre Workshop in London.

Today, Manchester's major playhouses include the *Royal Exchange Theatre, based from 1976 in an impressive theatre-in-the-round (*see* ARENA AND IN-THE-ROUND) inside the old Cotton Exchange and specializing in high-definition productions of the classic and modern classic repertoire, with an occasional world première; the city-run Library Theatre, a more intimate space especially suited to the staging of contemporary drama; the Bolton Octagon and Oldham Coliseum Theatres, offering programmes that reflect the characteristics of their diverse communities; and Contact Theatre on the university campus, reopened in 1999 with a specific brief to appeal to young people, including those from the city's ethnic minority cultures, as active participants as well as *audiences. Large-scale *touring is provided by several major commercial houses and by the vast new Lowry Centre in Salford Quays, opened in 2000, containing art gallery, large *opera house, and *studio theatre, while small-scale work is found in a variety of *fringe venues, a lively university drama scene, and in the work of touring companies such as M6 Theatre (theatre for *youth and *theatre-in-education).

ARJ

MANHATTAN THEATRE CLUB

American company founded in 1970. Manhattan Theatre Club's many transfers to Broadway, including *Crimes of the Heart*, *Ain't Misbehaving*, and *Proof*, have made it what *critic Mel Gussow calls the *Off-Broadway equivalent of the *Theatre Guild; it is also a playwrights' theatre with a mainstream *audience and a number of *New York venues. Occasionally criticized for conservatism and clubbiness, MTC produces the work of new writers from America and abroad, as well as its favourites A. R. *Gurney and Terrence *McNally. Tony *Kushner describes MTC, run by *artistic director Lynne *Meadow with *producer Barry Grove, as favouring 'a certain kind of narrative *realism on stage that has some *political overtones but isn't bitingly political'. It received unwanted attention in 1998 when it first cancelled McNally's tale of a gay Christ-like figure, *Corpus Christi*, after receiving bomb threats, but reversed its decision following protests from artists and civil liberties groups. MTC's many *awards include six Tonys and three Pulitzer prizes.

GAO

MANIM, MANNIE (1942–)

South African designer and *manager. He began in commercial theatre, designing and *stage managing productions for the Brian Brooke company and the Cockpit Players. While with the state-subsidized Performing Arts Council of the Transvaal he became involved with the Phoenix Players at Dorkay House in 1960, through contact with Athol *Fugard. As the Black Consciousness movement gained impetus and black performers were less willing to collaborate with whites, Manim and Barney *Simon formed the Company (1974) and the *Market Theatre (1976), which Manim managed. They aimed to shift *Johannesburg away from the European classics and *avant-garde to theatre created locally. Manim has remained committed to supporting new African theatre as the manager of the Baxter Theatre in *Cape Town, and facilitates South African productions abroad with Mannie Manim Productions. YH

MANIPURI THEATRE

Sequestered in north-east *India on the border of Burma (*Myanmar), Manipur is linked geopolitically to South-East Asia and on cultural and linguistic levels to the traditions of *Tibet and Burma. An independent kingdom until it came under British control in 1891, Manipur was formally annexed to post-independence India in 1949. Numerous secessionist and insurgent groups still view this as neocolonial domination by India, and their battles both with the Indian army and within their own ranks intensified during the last decades of the twentieth century. Against this political background, the sheer density and range of Manipur's cultural activities are striking, both in the traditional and contemporary sectors. Rapturous performances of *ras lila* and *nata sankirtana*, which are themselves part of the legacy of the Vaishnavite Hindu movement in the eighteenth century, coexist with *rituals celebrating pre-Vaishnavite practices relating to agriculture and ancestor worship, as in the ancient festival of the *lai-haraoba*. Martial arts like *thang-ta* have provided the foundations of actor *training in the contemporary theatre of Manipur, while the enormously popular tradition of *shumang lila* (courtyard play), with its

Ratan Thiyam's production of *Chakravyuha* (1984) with his Chorus Repertory Theatre from Imphal, Manipur, India (seen here at the Edinburgh Festival, 1987). Thiyam's work draws upon traditional epics and **Manipuri** performance modes, including the martial art *thang-ta*, to create sophisticated spectacle.

vibrant entertainment and social commentary, continues to thrive in rural areas.

Theatre companies began to emerge in the semi-urban capital of Imphal from the 1930s onwards—Manipur Dramatic Union (1931), Aryan Theatre (1935), Society Theatre (1937), and Rupmahal (1943). Associated with the Society Theatre was one of Manipur's most beloved theatre practitioners and playwrights, G. C. Tongbra (1913–96), a veteran of over 70 plays, who regaled *audiences over the years with a *satirical humour reminiscent of *Shaw. His plays, which exposed injustice, corruption, double standards, and nepotism, included hits like *Indiada Nambo Thaba* (*The Woes of India*), *Luda Mi Changba* (*Man in the Trap*), *Mister Damncare, Miss Bottle, Ngabong Khao* (*The Flesh Trap*), and *Leibak Houba Andolan* (*Agitation of the People*), which was *censored by the government for sedition in 1960. By this time political ferment in Manipur was on the rise with the pan-Mongoloid movement demanding an 'autonomous Meitei state'. Among the first leaders of the anti-India revolutionary movement was the playwright Somorendra Arambam, who was to play a vital role in the social *realist plays of the Aryan Theatre, and who was shot dead by unknown assailants while attending a drama seminar in 2000. A strong advocate of

shumang lila, he was one among numerous playwrights— P. Shamu, Athokpam Tomchou, Shri Biren, B. K. Wahengba, W. Kamini—who explored new plays strongly influenced by a *surreal, metaphysical, and *symbolist *dramaturgy.

Around the time that Manipur was declared a full-fledged state of the Indian union in 1972, the theatre in Imphal was beginning to assert its modernity in startlingly inventive ways. One influence was provided by Badal *Sircar, the Bengali founder of the non-*proscenium and physically oriented 'Third Theatre' movement, which attracted Manipuri theatre workers like Heisnam *Kanhailal and Lokendra Arambam. Another important influence was the *National School of Drama in New Delhi, which trained a number of Manipuri students who later became prominent figures. While Kanhailal did not complete his study there, others like Harokcham 'Sanakhya' Ebotombi returned to Imphal to start the National Theatre School, while Ratan *Thiyam returned to form the Chorus Repertory Theatre in 1976, which has since become India's most internationally recognized theatre group.

Unlike Kanhailal in his lyrical chamber theatre (*Pebet, Memoirs of Africa*) and Thiyam in his spectacular epics (*Chakravyuha, Uttarapriyadarshi*), Lokendra Arambam initiated *documentary drama in his productions of *1891*, about Manipur's War of Independence, and *Irabot*, about the life of the communist peasant leader of the Manipur Kisan Party. From the 1980s onwards, he drew on tribal myths to create a contemporary ritual piece, *Phou-oibi Langol*, which was followed by metaphysical reinterpretations of classics like *Tagore's *Raja* and Shakespeare's *Macbeth* (performed on water on a floating stage). As director of the Forum for Laboratory Theatres of Manipur, funded by the Ford Foundation, Arambam has attempted to coordinate the activities of dynamic young directors and theatre artists, like Nongthombham Premchand, R. K. Tombisana, Loitongbam Dorendra, Lourembam Kishworjit, and Yungnam Rajendra. Today Manipuri theatre is faced with the challenge of articulating a present that is caught between the militarism of the Indian state and the violence of insurgency, and between the reality of poverty and the dubious agendas underlying foreign and state funding for the arts.   RB

BHARUCHA, RUSTOM, *The Theatre of Kanhailal: 'Pebet' and 'Memoirs of Africa'* (Calcutta, 1992)

MANITOBA THEATRE CENTRE

The oldest of Canada's regional theatres, in Winnipeg. Inspired by the founding of the *Stratford Festival (1953) and Canada Council (1957), the MTC was created in 1958 in a merger of the *amateur Winnipeg Little Theatre and a fledgling semi-professional company called Theatre 77. The new company was headed by *artistic director John *Hirsch and administrative director Tom Hendry; this structure of dual leadership, reporting to a community-based volunteer board, became a model for Canadian professional theatre. The MTC now produces about ten plays per year in two spaces, the 785-seat mainstage (built 1970) and the 274-seat Warehouse.   DWJ

MANN, DIETER (1941–)

German actor and director. After serving an apprenticeship in industry Mann trained at the East *Berlin state acting academy. In 1964 he joined the *Deutsches Theater and quickly became a member of the regular ensemble. He achieved recognition throughout Germany for his title role in Ulrich Plenzdorf's *Die neuen Leiden des jungen W.* (1972), a version of *Goethe's novel *The Sorrows of Young Werther*, adapted to the German Democratic Republic. From 1984 to 1991 he was *Intendant* of the Deutsches Theater. A highly versatile actor, he became a household name in the GDR for numerous parts in *television dramas and *films.   CBB

MANN, THEODORE (1924–)

American *producer and director. Along with José *Quintero, Mann founded *Circle in the Square Theatre in 1951, and their production of *Summer and Smoke* (1952) is credited with legitimizing the *Off-Broadway movement. His producing of *O'Neill's plays, directed by Quintero, including *The Iceman Cometh* (1956), *Long Day's Journey into Night* (1956), and *A Moon for the Misbegotten* (1968), led to the revival of O'Neill's reputation. Mann led Circle in the Square's expansion and move to Broadway in 1972, and, after Quintero's departure, directed many of the productions until the theatre closed in 1997.
                                                            WFC

MANNHEIM COURT THEATRE

Erected in 1742 by Alessandro Galli-*Bibiena, the spectacular baroque *playhouse, seating over 2,000 spectators, had two significant periods. Under Bibiena it became a leading centre for *opera and occasionally for French drama, which was popular at German courts in the eighteenth century; in the 1750s the French plays were personally supervised by *Voltaire. Its second notable phase began in 1777, when the director Count von Dalberg renamed it 'Nationaltheater' (1779), and assembled a fine *acting troupe including Seyler and *Iffland, who developed a distinctive *realist style conducive to new plays such as *Schiller's *The Robbers*, which was premièred there (1782). The original building was destroyed by Austrian cannon fire in 1795. In 1839 the rebuilt theatre became the first German house to come under municipal administration.   CBB

MANOHAR, R. S. (1925–)

Actor and director from Tamil Nadu in the south of *India who joined the Tamil *film industry as an actor in 1950. Inspired by Nawab Rajamanickam Pillai's spectacular historical extravaganzas, Manohar strayed into the theatre and became a major star and impresario. In 1954 he founded a company called the National Theatre, which specialized in plays on social themes that exploited the patriotic fervour of post-independence India. In collaboration with the Tamil writer Thuraiyur Murthy, Manohar went on to direct *Inba Naal* (*The Happy Day*, 1954), a play celebrating love and equality, also acting the main role. His major breakthrough was his shrewd retelling of the Hindu epic *Ramayana* in his own play *Ilankeswaran* (*The God of Lanka*, 1956), which replaced the role of Rama with Ravana, the alleged *villain of the epic who abducts Sita. In three decades of active work, Manohar has produced, directed, and acted the lead roles in 29 major productions. His company employs 60 actors and has given close to 8,000 performances all over India and in many other Asian countries. Most of these productions drew on legendary figures, sensationalized in a *mise-en-scène packed with tricks and special effects. Experimenting with the first stereo sound system in *Tamil theatre, Manohar also drew heavily on the technology and conventions of the popular

*Parsi theatre, and is remembered as the most popular mainstream Tamil theatre artist of his time.   PR/RB

MANSFIELD, RICHARD (1854–1907)

English-American *actor-manager and playwright. Born in Berlin to a British father and German mother, he was raised in England, and began his theatrical career in New England (1876), chiefly with the works of *Gilbert and *Sullivan. After a period of only modest success, he created a sensation as a dissolute roué in A Parisian Romance (*New York, 1883). He first played Shakespeare in *London (Richard III, 1889), then returned to America, where his major career was shaped in the 1890s with Beau Brummell (1890), The Scarlet Letter (1892), Arms and the Man (1894), Cyrano de Bergerac (1898), and Beaucaire (1901). He married Beatrice Campbell, his leading lady, in 1892, having managed her in A Doll's House at matinées during his *tour in 1890. He premièred *Ibsen's Peer Gynt in the United States (1906). He wrote several plays, none of which remained long in his repertory. Mansfield prepared carefully and thoroughly for his roles, striving to find appropriate and individual physical and vocal patterns. He gave many interviews expounding his ideas of art and theatrical creativity, and often responded sharply and publicly to perceived *critical malice. Possibly as a result, he was widely regarded as eccentric, both in personality and in performance. His supporters found his performances intensely individual in their *realism, marking a sharp break with traditional *acting style; his voice was termed 'golden' in its richness and resonance. His detractors, by contrast, characterized his work as idiosyncratic and highly mannered, with artificial and arbitrary vocal choices.
          AW

MANSION

In the simultaneous settings used in *medieval theatre a mansion or 'house' was any area which contained a structure. The structure might be a building, like the sepulchre or a prison, or the symbolic presentation of a location, like *heaven or *hell, or even the cross itself, representing Golgotha. There was often a 'station' adjacent to the mansion in which *characters related to it stood.   JWH

MANTEGNA, JOE (1947–)

American actor. He studied at DePaul University, played Berger in Hair (*Chicago, 1969), co-wrote the Organic Theatre's Bleacher Bums (1977), and made his Broadway debut in Working (1978). His subtly caustic wit suits fellow Chicagoan David *Mamet well. Mantegna appeared in the *Goodman Theatre première of Mamet's A Life in the Theatre (1977) as well as three of Mamet's *films, played Gould in Speed-the-Plow (1988), and won a Tony *award as Ricky Roma in Glengarry Glen Ross (1984). His *film roles include George Raft in Bugsy (1991), Lawrence Oberman in The Water Engine (*television, 1992), Fred in Searching for Bobby Fischer (1993), Andy in Forget Paris (1995), and Gomez in The Wonderful Ice Cream Suit (1998).   JDM

MANTELL, ROBERT B. (1854–1928)

British-American actor. Born in Scotland, Mantell acted in *amateur productions as a teenager before making his professional debut in 1876, followed by extensive *touring in the provinces. Throughout his career he was one of the few actors to adhere to an old-fashioned unrestrained style with plenty of bombast and exaggerated gesturing—which impressed some and dismayed others. But there was no denying his extraordinary personal magnetism. From 1882 on, he performed almost entirely in America, not just in *New York but all over the country in large cities and small towns. His first important Broadway vehicle was The Romany Rye (1882), followed the next year by *Sardou's Fedora. He achieved stardom as a matinée idol in the *melodrama Tangled Lives (1886). Starting in 1904 he concentrated almost entirely on Shakespeare, performing Richard III and Othello, and adding Iago, King John, Brutus, and Hamlet. He was at his best as Shylock, Macbeth, and Lear—performing Lear more than 500 times.   CT

MANTLE, ROBERT BURNS (1873–1948)

Longtime *critic for the *New York Daily News (1922–43), Mantle worked as a drama critic from the age of 15 when he began at the Denver Times (1898). A practical critic who appreciated innovation in playwriting, Mantle edited his annual The Best Plays series from 1919 to 1948. These volumes, 'The Year Book of the Drama in America', included synopses and extensive excerpts from Mantle's selection of the ten best Broadway plays of the year, essays assessing the season, and a cast and staff listings for all Broadway productions.   MAF

MANUEL, NIKLAUS (c.1484–1530)

Swiss dramatist and painter. During the early years of the *Reformation, Manuel wrote several plays attacking Catholic institutions and practices. His best-known play, The Pardon Pedlar (1525), which echoes the *Fastnachtsspiel in its setting and language, was played in Ann Arbor in 1983.   RWV

MANZONI, ALESSANDRO (1785–1873)

Italian writer. Author of the famous novel I promessi sposi (The Betrothed, 1825–7), Manzoni was a leader of the Italian *romantic movement that manifested itself about 1815 in a yearning for political independence from Austria, freedom from the French *neoclassical tradition, and a new national literature. Inspired by Shakespeare and the German romantics, Manzoni's *verse *tragedies, *Il conte di Carmagnola* (1828) and *Adelchi* (1843), take local history as their tragic subject, defy the *unities, and employ a language that departs from the neoclassical rhetorical tradition. While these tragedies have not met with much success in the theatre (though *Adelchi* was directed in 1960 by Vittorio *Gassman), excerpts from *Adelchi* served as *monologues for the great Italian actors like Gustavo *Modena. Manzoni's *Preface* to *Carmagnola* and his *Lettre à M. C[hauvet]* (1823) are important *theoretical documents of Italian romanticism.   JEH

MAORI THEATRE

The oral culture of the indigenous Maori of Aotearoa (New Zealand) incorporates performative elements in formal oratory and traditional songs, and *haka* (*dance) has both *ritual and entertainment uses; recent research has revealed pre-European *whare tapere* (houses of entertainment), although details are uncertain. Maori forms evolved quickly in the nineteenth century, with *haka poi* (poi dance), for instance, now a virtuosic women's dance manipulating a light fibrous ball on a cord, moving in the 1880s from a game to a symbol of resistance to colonial rule, and then (like *waiata-a-ringa*, 'songs using the hands') into a significant entertainment form in the twentieth century for *kapa haka* (formation dancing) troupes, who often adopted popular Western music. The biennial Aotearoa Traditional Performing Arts Festival (founded 1972) concentrates on cultural tradition, but the Takitimu Performing Arts School and others incorporate modern dance and Western theatre techniques.

Colonial drama largely depicted Maori in a stereotypical manner, and reserved major roles for European actors in blackface. Bruce *Mason was the first playwright to write substantial *characters for Maori actors. Harry Dansey's *Te Raukura* (1972), in English but incorporating Maori *dialogue and song, was the first play by a Maori. Maori plays of the 1970s and 1980s attacked racial inequality and a century of grievances, as in Rori Hapipi's *Death of the Land* (1976), and dislocation of Maori values by the dominant urban colonial culture, as in Roma Potiki's *Whatungarongaro*, devised with her troupe He Ara Hou (1990). A syncretic *dramaturgy developed, yoking European-derived spoken drama to Maori spiritual values and rhetorical and performative modes. A specifically nationalist bicultural theatre, Taki Rua, was established as a collective in the 1980s to produce Maori plays (some in Maori) and to create opportunities for Maori directors, designers, and other theatre workers. The design for the first production of Hone Kouka's *Nga Tangata Toa: the warrior people* (1994), an adaptation of *Ibsen's *The Vikings at Helgeland*, reproduced the physical arrangements of a *marae* (meeting house), and the play includes a *mihi* (greeting) to the *audience. Later plays, such as *When Sun and Moon Collide* (2000) by Briar Grace-Smith, are often less self-consciously Maori in their thematic concerns. Nevertheless, the Maori context has become a fundamental part of New Zealand theatre.

DC

MAPA TEATRO

Colombian theatre group founded in 1984 by Heidi and Rolf Aberhalden Cortés. After working with companies in Europe like Théâtre du *Soleil, they returned in 1986 with *Casa tomada* (*Occupied House*), based on a short story by Julio Cortazar. *De Mortibus: réquiem para Samuel Beckett* (1990), *Medeamaterial* (1991) by Heiner *Müller, and *Orestea ex machine* (1995) established Mapa as an experimental group interested in *spectacles and *rituals of body, gestures, and ceremonial artefacts. *El león y la domadora* (*The Lion and the Woman Tamer*, 1998), by Antonio Orlando Rodríguez, on the Cuban *diaspora, and a new translation of Shakespeare's *Richard III* (2000), have also met with significant success.

BJR

MAPONYA, MAISHE (1951–)

South African dramatist and director. Born in *Johannesburg, his family was forcibly removed to Soweto. His early work includes *The Cry* (1976) and *Peace and Forgive* (1978), followed by *The Hungry Earth* (Soweto, 1979), which looks at the lives of three miners in rural and urban settings, and *Umongikazi* (*Nurse*, *Market Theatre and townships, 1983), about apartheid in hospitals. *Gangsters* and *Dirty Work* (Market, 1984) form a diptych on the security state and its agents. His plays are multilingual, using *agitprop and *physical theatre techniques. Maponya won the 1985 Standard Bank Young Artists award, and works as an executive of the Johannesburg Southern Metroplitan Council.

YH

MARAINI, DACIA (1936–)

Italian writer. Maraini has helped found three theatre companies: Blu (1967), whose aim was to give Italian authors access to the stage, Centocelle (1970), named after the Roman housing estate where it performed *street theatre, and finally La Maddalena, an all-women troupe. Maraini is one of Italy's leading *feminists and her own plays focus largely on the problems of women in society. Some were written in support of specific campaigns, others highlight wider aspects of a culture hostile to women (*Dialogue of a Prostitute with a Client*, 1976), and others again reassess classical myths (*The Dreams of Clytemnestra*, 1979).

JF

MARAIS, THÉÂTRE DU

*Paris's second public *playhouse, a converted *tennis court, was opened in 1634. Rebuilt after a *fire in 1644, the Marais measured 34.4 m (113 feet) by 11.7 m (38 feet), its raked stage was 9.7 m (32 feet) deep, with a practicable upper *stage at the rear. Around a standing pit, the *auditorium was fitted with two tiers of *boxes, parallel to the walls, a *paradis* above the seven side boxes, and a tiered *amphithéâtre* behind the four rear boxes. In the 1650s and 1660s the Marais's fortunes were maintained by the success of spectacular machine-plays, the accommodation of which required extensive remodelling: the stage was extended and equipped with machinery, the *auditorium boxes realigned into an Italianate horseshoe, and the *amphithéâtre* relocated to the rear of the pit. But the Marais had little future. Its leading actors were forced in 1673 to merge with those of the recently deceased *Molière at the *Guénégaud, after which it briefly housed a *puppet troupe in 1677 and then disappeared from the records.   JG

MARATHI THEATRE

Maharashtra is one of the largest states in *India, extending from the Konkan coast on the west to the Deccan plateau in south-central India. Like other regions of the country it has numerous traditional forms like *tamasha, *powada, and *dashavatar, though it is also identified with some of the most important interventions in the creation of modern Indian theatre. The first Marathi play, *Sita Swayamvar* (*The Marriage of Sita*), was performed in 1843 in Sangli, a small princely state in southern Maharashtra. The author, Vishnudas Bhave (c.1820–1905), an engineer-poet in the service of Raja Chintamanrao Patwardhan, wrote plays based on the *Ramayana*. A typical Bhave play included a *sutradhara (narrator-conductor), who sang introductions to the *characters and events of the story accompanied by a group of musicians. The actors enacted and *danced this narration. On the rare occasions they spoke, the *dialogue was extempore. A *vidushaka (jester) provided the comedy, always irreverent, and the highlights were noisy battle scenes between gods and demons. Forced by the death of the Raja of Sangli to *tour with his troupe, Bhave staged the first *ticketed show of Marathi theatre in Bombay (*Mumbai) in 1853.

By the mid-1870s the popularity of Bhave-style plays was waning. Balwant Pandurang Kirloskar, who had written many such plays himself, realized the potential of speech and music theatre when he saw *Indra Sabha*, a *Parsi theatre production in Pune. His *Shakuntal*, an adaptation of *Kalidasa's Sanskrit classic *Abhijnanashakuntala* (*Shakuntala Recognized*), staged in 1880 in Pune, was his first experiment with the new form. His *sutradhar* only introduced the theme of the play, and thereafter the actors spoke and sang their parts. The new form, called *sangeet natak*, dominated the Marathi stage for the next 50 years, achieving its full glory with the legendary singer-actor *Balgandharva, who played female roles.

Chief amongst Kirloskar's followers was G. B. Deval (1855–1916), whose *Sangeet Sharada* (1899) was the first independent play on a social theme. In a more nationalist register, Krishnaji Prabhakar Khadilkar (1872–1948) used a story from the *Mahabharata* to allegorize the repressive regime of the Viceroy, Lord Curzon; *Keechaka Vadh* (*The Killing of Keechaka*, 1907) was declared seditious and banned in 1910. Several *musical plays of the time promoted the reformist cause. *Ekach Pyala* (*One Glassful Only*, 1919), by Ram Ganesh Gadkari (1885–1919), demonstrated the tragic results of alcoholism. Anti-reform plays against new ideas like education for women were also written but have not entered the canon, and despite Maharashtra's progressivism, women were barred from appearing on stage until 1933, although all-women troupes from low-caste communities had existed since the 1870s.

Shripad Krishna Kolhatkar (1871–1934) made a conscious departure from Kirloskar-style plays by rejecting their mix of *folk, traditional, and classical melodies. He preferred the jaunty, modern tunes of the Parsi theatre. But very few of those songs have survived in the people's memory. *Kunjavihari* (1908), the first play by Bhargavaram Vitthal Warerkar (1983–1964), was another attempt at copying Parsi-Gujarati theatre. It was a huge success, but its author was too interested in social and *political issues to continue in that style. His *Sonyacha Kalas* (*The Golden Spire*, 1931), about labour relations, was staged despite *censorship from the Home Department.

By 1933 educated young people had become aware of *Ibsen. *Andhalyanchi Shala* (*The School for the Blind*, 1933), by the newly founded company Natyamanwantar, was a somewhat naive attempt at Ibsenist *realism, and used women in women's roles for the first time. The advent of sound *film around this time, and the effects of war soon after, made it difficult to sustain theatre, and *touring companies folded one by one. *Playhouses were taken over by cinema. During the next twenty years or so, only two playwrights were popular—P. K. Atre (1898–1969), whose most successful plays were adaptations of European *comedies, and playwright-director-producer M. G. Rangnekar (1907–94), who wrote sentimental, mildly progressive family drama. They both incorporated songs into their plays to keep *audiences happy.

The 100th anniversary of Marathi theatre was celebrated on a large scale in Bombay and Sangli in 1943, prompting renewed interest and giving new impetus to theatre activity. Alongside the mainstream theatre represented by Bal Kolhatkar, Baban Prabhu, Atmaram Bhende, Vidyadhar Gokhale, Madhusudan Kalelkar, and others, an *alternative theatre movement was gathering momentum, led by young practitioners like Vijaya Mehta, Vijay *Tendulkar, Shreeram Lagoo, Satyadev Dubey, and Amol Palekar. Vijaya Mehta's theatre laboratory, Rangayan, staged *Elkunchwar's *Holi*, an adaptation of *Ionesco's *Chairs*, among other new works. Arvind and Sulabha Deshpande split from the group in the early 1970s to form their own company, Awishkar, one of their most ambitious productions a translation of Girish *Karnad's *Tughluq*. Pune's Progressive Dramatic Association, headed by Bhalba Kelkar, also explored new themes and forms. One of the group's most acclaimed productions was Vasant Kanetkar's *Vedyacha Ghar Unhat* (*The Madman's House Is in the Sun*, 1957).

The Deshpandes found an inexpensive space in Chhabildas School, Dadar, which became synonymous with experimental plays until the facility was withdrawn in the late 1980s. The Progressive Dramatic Association also split over the production of Tendulkar's *Ghashiram Kotwal* (*Police Chief Ghashiram*, 1972). When the old guard objected to the lewd characterization of the much admired chancellor of the Peshwas, Nana Phadnavis, the younger members of PDA split from the group to form the Theatre Academy, touring *Ghashiram Kotwal* abroad with great success. In the 1970s Maharashtra became acquainted with the work of Badal *Sircar, Mohan *Rakesh, and Girish Karnad, whose plays were adapted in Marathi along with Ionesco, *Beckett, and *Brecht. Simultaneously there were self-conscious experiments in forging a post-colonial Indian identity through an adaptation of traditional Indian forms and theatrical conventions. Satish Alekar's *Mahanirvan* (*The Great Death*, 1973), for instance, used the *keertan* (traditional musical sermon) to make an ironic comment on the death rites of Hindus.

In the mid-1980s, with the intensification of communal politics led by the Shiv Sena, a militant Hindu party based in Maharashtra, the Marathi theatre turned its focus on Mahatma Gandhi, who has always been a target of attack in middle-class Marathi circles for his allegedly pro-Partition stand. In this context, Ajit Dalvi's play *Gandhi Viruddha Gandhi* (*Gandhi Versus Gandhi*, 1996), which critiqued Gandhi as an unjust father, proved to be a big success. A more blatantly communal play, *Mee Nathuram Godse Boltoy* (*This is Nathuram Godse Speaking*, 1999), by a minor playwright, Pradeep Dalvi, vindicated Nathuram Godse's assassination of Mahatma Gandhi. Violent protests by Congress Party workers led to its banning. Santosh Pawar's *Yadakadachit* (*Perhaps*, 2000), an energetic *satire using *Mahabharata* characters, was also censored by the Shiv Sena before it could be performed. Growing cultural terrorism by sectarian groups, aggravated by Mumbai's predatory capitalism and rampant consumerism, soon made experimental theatre in the city unviable. Former fringe playwrights now write for the mainstream theatre. Amongst the more significant are Prashant Dalvi, Premanand Gajvi, and Shafaat Khan, whose plays *Char Chaughi* (*Four Ordinary Women*, 1991), *Gandhi Ani Ambedkar* (*Gandhi and Ambedkar*, 1997) and *Shobhayatra* (*The Show Parade*, 1999), respectively, are among some of the more noteworthy productions. Meanwhile, Rangvardhan, an organization formed in 1998 to network experimental theatre groups across

the state, has been organizing an annual *festival of plays that travels to theatre centres all over Maharashtra.   SGG

GOKHALE, SHANTA, *Playwright at the Centre: Marathi drama from 1843 to the present* (Calcutta, 2000)

RANADE, ASHOK D., *Stage Music of Maharashtra* (New Delhi, 1986)

MARAZBAN, ADI (1914–87)

Indian playwright, director, editor, and *radio and *television broadcaster. Trained at the *Pasadena Playhouse in the early 1950s, Marazban began writing plays in Parsi-Gujarati on his return to Bombay (*Mumbai). He wrote as he *rehearsed, improvising, reducing, or enlarging roles to suit the talents of his predominantly *amateur cast. *Comedy, *farce, and *revue were his strengths. A fine ballroom dancer, amateur conjuror, and ventriloquist, he trained his actors in these skills to add more energy to his hugely popular shows. The English-language theatre in Bombay was poorly attended, but Marazban's *manager, Pesi Khandalawala, would run on even unsuccessful plays to keep them in the public eye. The strategy paid off with the phenomenal success of their production of Ron Clark and Sam Bobricks's *Ah Norman* (1972), which played for hundreds of performances. The Marazban–Khandalawala team was also the first in *amateur theatre to pay actors and technicians, distributing *box-office returns equally, providing a model for 'semi-professionalism' in *Indian theatre. Above all he is remembered as one of the greatest humorists of the Parsi community. Collaborating with his wife, he exposed Parsi eccentricities in numerous radio programmes, including *Buddhi Dhanshak Mandal* (*Old Woman's Curry Club*) and *Avo Maari Saathe* (*Come Along with Me*).   SGG

MARBER, PATRICK (1964–)

English playwright, actor, and director. Marber emerged initially as a comic writer and actor, contributing to the unsettlingly brilliant news *parodies *On the Hour* and *The Day Today* for BBC *radio and *television respectively. His first play, *Dealer's Choice* (1995), uses the *rituals of the all-male poker game to investigate the bluffs and gambles of masculinity in crisis. This piece was developed at the *National Theatre, which also staged *Closer* (1997), a searing portrait of contemporary male–female relationships and the caverns that open up between sex and understanding. Both plays transferred to the West End. *Howard Katz* (2001), directed like the first two by Marber himself, concerns a successful actor's agent falling from success to squalid loneliness; its anguished ethical concerns chimed with a turn towards moral investigation in British theatre. Marber has also directed well-received productions of *Potter's *Blue Remembered Hills* (1996), *Mamet's *The Old Neighbourhood* (1998), and *Pinter's *The Caretaker* (2002).   DR

MARCEAU, MARCEL (1923–)

French *mime. Son of a kosher butcher killed at Auschwitz, Marcel Mangel became Marcel Marceau when he moved to *Paris in 1944 from Limoges, where he and his brother worked for the Resistance. He first studied with Étienne *Decroux in Charles *Dullin's school, and in 1946 joined Jean-Louis *Barrault's company to perform in the *Baptiste* pantomime Barrault created following the success of his starring role in the *film *Les Enfants du paradis*. In 1955, after years of European *touring, Marceau's six months of sold-out performances in *New York, and his coincidental *television appearances, made him a household word. He defined the art of mime for millions of people who never knew it existed. Finally more influenced by silent film actors and by the nineteenth-century whitefaced silent pantomime of Jean-Gaspard *Deburau than by the radical and austere *modernism of Decroux, Marceau's stage persona Bip has become synonymous with mime and with himself. He toured internationally for half a century, and his school in Paris attracts students from everywhere in the world.

TL

MARCH, FREDRIC (FREDERICK McINTYRE BICKEL) (1897–1975)

American actor. He made his debut in a David *Belasco production of Sacha *Guitry's *Deburau* (1920) and played his first major role in J. E. Goodman's *melodrama *The Law Breaker* (1922). He then acquired his stage name and performed in several plays before meeting Florence Eldridge in summer *stock. They married in 1927, *toured with the *Theatre Guild Repertory Company, and continued to act together. After 1928 March worked in *films before returning to Broadway with Eldridge to co-star in *Yr. Obedient Husband* (1938). Commuting between Hollywood and *New York, he played Mr Antrobus in *Wilder's *The Skin of our Teeth* (1942), Major Joppolo in Paul *Osborn's *A Bell for Adano* (1944), Nicholas Denery in *Hellman's *The Autumn Garden* (1951), James Tyrone in *O'Neill's *A Long Day's Journey into Night* (1956), and the Angel in *Chayefsky's *Gideon* (1961). His performance of Tyrone was the masterpiece of his stage career. He made 69 films.

FL

MARCHESSAULT, JOVETTE (1938–)

Québec playwright, novelist, painter, sculptor. Largely self-taught, her radical *feminist perspectives are evident in all that she produces, most of it intended to provoke patriarchal reaction. Her first stage success was *La Saga des poules mouillées* (*The Saga of the Wet Hens*, 1981), in which four female writers reject oppressive male authority. Similar themes are explored in plays such as *La Terre est trop courte, Violette Leduc* (*The Earth is Too Small, Violette Leduc*, 1982), and *Anaïs dans la queue de la comète* (*Anaïs [Nin] in the Comet's Tail*, 1985), dealing with famous lesbian writers of the past. *See also* LESBIAN THEATRE.

LED

MARCOS, PLÍNIO (1935–99)

Brazilian playwright. The most censored dramatist during the worst period of the dictatorship (1964–79), Marcos has nonetheless attracted a wide range of production interest from student, *alternative, *amateur, and professional companies. Writing about *São Paulo's most abjectly dispossessed, his plays focus on pivotal moments in the lives of the criminals and outcasts: prostitutes, transvestites, homosexuals, pimps, small-time crooks, conmen, prisoners, and addicts. His hyper-*naturalistic and often brutal *dialogue nonetheless creates an imagistic stage language that stands in contrast to the grim themes. This is notably apparent in his searing AIDS play *Mancha roxa* (*Scarlet Mark*, 1989), an *allegory about the redemptive powers of community in a women's penitentiary, in which factions, friendships, enmities, love, and sexual relationships realign as the women *characters discover or betray the wounds that join or separate them. Its large cast is unusual for Marcos, whose works generally are duets or trios of desperate persons who shift back and forth from victims to victimizers, as in *Navalha na carne* (*Knife through Flesh*, 1967).

LHD

MARCUS, FRANK (1928–)

English actor, dramatist, director, and critic. Marcus was born in Germany and migrated to Britain in 1939. In 1952 he adapted *Schnitzler's *Reigen* as *Merry-Go-Round*. His first West End success was *Formation Dancers* (1964), followed by *Cleo* (1965). In the same year, *The Killing of Sister George*, about the lesbian relationship of an actress playing a district nurse in a BBC *radio soap opera, broke new ground. Premièred by the *Bristol Old Vic Company, it was made into a *film in 1969. Subsequent plays included the less successful and somewhat underrated *Mrs Mouse Are You Within*, premièred in Bristol in 1968, and *Notes on a Love Affair* (1972). From 1968 to 1980 Marcus was also the theatre critic of the *Sunday Telegraph* (*see* CRITICISM).

JTD

MARDZHANOV, KONSTANTIN (1872–1933)

Georgian/Soviet director. From 1910 to 1913 Mardzhanov worked as assistant director at the *Moscow Art Theatre, collaborating with *Stanislavsky and *Craig on *Hamlet* and with *Nemirovich-Danchenko on *Peer Gynt* and *The Brothers Karamazov*. He left to found his own Free Theatre in *Moscow in 1913, where he specialized in *operetta, *pantomime, and the work of *Offenbach. Mardzhanov was fascinated by the notion of the *carnivalesque and staged a production of Lope de *Vega's

Fuente Ovejuna in *Kiev in 1919, followed by a number of *mass performances of revolutionary *spectacles, and planned a production of *Mayakovsky's *Mystery-Bouffe* on top of a mountain. In 1922, Mardzhanov became virtual founder of a Soviet Georgian theatre when he staged productions at the Rustaveli Theatre in *Tbilisi of plays by Georgian writers as well as *The Merry Wives of Windsor, Hamlet*, and *Synge's *The Playboy of the Western World*. In 1928 he created a second Rustaveli Theatre in Kutaisi, which later transferred to Tbilisi (after his death it was rechristened the Mardzhanov Theatre). Here he staged *Toller's *Hoppla, We're Alive!* (1928), plays by Georgian and Soviet playwrights, and *Shelley's *The Cenci* (1930).   NW

MARÉCHAL, MARCEL (1937–)

French playwright, actor, and director. Known for his successful collaborations with playwrights Jacques *Audiberti, Jean *Vauthier, and Louis Guillot, his Marseille-based Compagnie Marcel Maréchal became a Centre Dramatique National in 1972. Producing a classical and contemporary repertoire, including Shakespeare, *Molière, *Beckett, and *Brecht, he was celebrated for his flamboyant *directorial style in such productions as *The Three Musketeers* (1980). Since 1995 the company has been located at the renovated Théâtre du Rond Point in *Paris, where Maréchal has, among many other projects, continued championing the American playwright David *Mamet.

                                                                 DGM

MARGULES, LUDWIK (1933–)

Mexican director who arrived in Mexico from Poland in 1957 and established himself as a premier director of European and North American dramatists. His 1978 adaptation of *Chekhov's *Uncle Vanya* was especially praised. Another success was the 1990 adaptation of Nicholas Wright's *Mrs Klein*.   KFN

MARIJNEN, FRANZ (1943–)

Flemish director and *manager. After study in *Brussels, Marijnen spent a *training period at Jerzy *Grotowski's *Polish Laboratory Theatre in Wrocław. Invited to work at *La Mama in *New York in 1970, he established Camera Obscura in Jamestown, New York, in 1973, where he created a number of tense, highly physical productions in which Grotowski's influence was apparent. *Oracles* (1973) gradually developed from the exchange of personal experiences and from *improvisation about the Oedipus myth (*see* DEVISING; COLLECTIVES AND COLLECTIVE CREATION). *Measure for Measure* (1974) was a personal reinterpretation of Shakespeare's play in which power games and sex were central concerns. In 1977 Marijnen became *artistic director of the Rotterdam Ro Theater, where he developed a far more spectacular and exuberant style. He took over the Royal

Flemish Theatre in Brussels in 1993, where his *King Lear* of that year marked a return to interiority and *textual integrity.

                                                                 JDV

MARINETTI, FILIPPO TOMMASO (1876–1944)

Italian poet, playwright, *theoretician, and literary manager, best known as the founder of *futurism. As a late *symbolist poet in turn-of-the-century *Paris he shocked *audiences with his anarchist poetry declamations and *Jarry-inspired productions of *Le Roi Bombance* and *Poupées électriques* (both 1909). Creating theatre scandals became a favoured method of the early futurist movement, which Marinetti set up in various Italian cities. He published several theatre manifestos and wrote a large number of playlets for the new dramatic *genres he created in the 1910s and 1920s (Synthetic Theatre, Theatre of Surprise, Tactile Theatre). When futurism began to have an impact on the conventional *playhouses and found some congenial directors and designers in the established theatre, Marinetti wrote several full-length plays that were staged in Italy and abroad: *Il tamburo di fuoco* (1922), *Bianca e Rosso* (1923), *Prigionieri* (1925), *Vulcano* (1926), *L'oceano del cuore* (1927), *Il suggeritore nudo* (1929), *Simultanina* (1931). As a champion of modern technology and scientific modernity he immediately seized upon the new invention of *radio and wrote several dramas for this medium. He was equally fascinated by early experiments with *television and wrote a manifesto on *Il teatro aeroradiotelevisivo* (1931). Marinetti also tried his hand at architectural design and took Gropius' *total theatre as a starting point for his own project of a *Teatro totale per masse* (1933). As a member of the Italian Academy and secretary of the Writers' Union he used his influence to promote *avant-garde drama in Italy, to improve the technical installations of Italian theatres, and to institute modern *training courses for actors and designers.   GB

MARIONETTE

The term arose in France in the seventeenth century as a generic word for *puppets, but was little used before the nineteenth. In English it refers uniquely to puppets operated from above by strings, rods, or wires. Most marionettes are jointed, usually at the neck, shoulder, elbows, hips, and knees. In *China even the fingers may be jointed, but in Rajasthan unjointed figures are used. Jointed figures survive from classical antiquity. Europe favoured operation by a rod or wire to the head, and one or more ancillary strings. The success of the widely travelled Holden Company from England in the 1870s ensured the abandonment of the head rod in most of Europe. Strings may be held directly in the hand (Rajasthan) or attached to a control bar or bars, with additional ones held in the hand (*Myanmar, China). In modern times carefully balanced and highly elaborate controls have developed.   JMcC

MARIVAUX, PIERRE CARLET DE CHAMBLAIN DE (1688–1763)

French dramatist and man of letters. Equally well known to contemporaries for his novels *La Vie de Marianne* (1731–41) and *Le Paysan parvenu* (1735–6), and for his journalism (for instance *Le Spectateur français*, an imitation of *Addison's *Spectator*), Marivaux started writing for the theatre under the influence of the Italian players in *Paris (*see* COMÉDIE ITALIENNE), for whom he produced two comedies in 1720 as well as a *tragedy for the *Comédie-Française. Thereafter his dramatic output was shared between the two theatres; though his most original work is found in plays written for the Italians, where his inspiration was the *stock roles of the naive valet Arlequin (played by Visentini, followed by Carlin) and the more astute Trivelin, together with the leading lady Silvia (played by Zanetta-Rosa Benozzi) and the young leading man or *jeune premier* Lélio (played by Romagnesi). Reliance on tradition regarding *character, and preference for simplicity in terms of plot, helped Marivaux to produce the subtlety of *dialogue by which he is best known. For instance, in what has remained his most popular play, *Le Jeu de l'amour et du hasard* (*The Game of Love and Chance*, 1730), the *plot has something in common with that of *She Stoops to Conquer*, but the misunderstandings are handled with a light-hearted subtlety that is quite foreign to *Goldsmith's play. At first used disparagingly by contemporaries, who criticized what they saw as a new form of preciosity, the term 'le marivaudage' has survived as an appreciative definition of the mixture of wordplay, psychological exploration, and revelation which marks the author's distinctive comic style, as in *La Double Inconstance* (*The Double Inconstancy*, 1723) or *Les Fausses Confidences* (*Misleading Confessions*, 1737). Since its rehabilitation in the nineteenth century, the term has entered the critical vocabulary used by students of the language of modern drama, cinema, and novel; and to write of the 'marivaudage' of *Giraudoux, for instance, is not the paradox it might appear. The tragedy *Annibal*, a failure in 1720, was again unsuccessful when revived at the Comédie-Française in 1747, after Marivaux's election to the Académie Française.

Meanwhile he had tried his hand with mixed success outside the formula he inherited from the Italians. *La Mère confidente* (1735) was not only popular with contemporary *audiences, but its theme of confidence and trust between mother and daughter—replacing conventional disapproval and rebellion—is handled in a manner anticipating that of *Diderot's *drame bourgeois*. Another new departure is seen in a group of fantasies based on provocative philosophical ideas. *L'Île des esclaves* (*Island of Slaves*, 1725), presenting an island community where social equality rules, enjoyed the longest opening run of any Marivaux play; but in *L'Île de la raison; ou, Les Petits Hommes* (*Island of Reason; or, The Little Men*, Comédie-Française, 1727)—exploiting the popularity of the recently translated *Gulliver's Travels* by the notion that one's rational qualities are reflected in one's stature (the castaway Europeans all being reduced to 'petits hommes')—the *illusion proved so unconvincing that the public much preferred a *parody staged at the Italians. Whereas the adoption by the Comédie-Française of plays that had been premièred by the Italians was not immediately successful (the *acting styles of the two companies militated against an easy transfer), by the end of the century, especially under Mlle *Contat's influence, Marivaux had been well assimilated to the repertory of the national theatre. The process continued throughout the next century, and in the post-1950 period Marivaux was to become, after *Molière, the French classical dramatist most frequently performed on the French stage. Pride of place during this period should perhaps go to the company founded by Jean-Louis *Barrault and Madeleine *Renaud at the Marigny Theatre, Paris, in 1946. Productions here, and foreign tours by the company (*Edinburgh Festival, *London, *New York), brought Marivaux to a new worldwide audience. His work is now frequently performed outside France.   WDH

McKEE, KENNETH N., *The Theater of Marivaux* (New York, 1958)

MARKET OF AFRICAN PERFORMING ARTS (MARCHÉ DES ARTS DU SPECTACLE AFRICAIN)

Founded in 1993 by the Inter-governmental Agency for Francophone Affairs, MASA is a festival that brings together makers and consumers of the performing arts from all regions of Africa, to encourage a wider distribution of work within Africa and internationally, and to organize *training sessions for practitioners. The eight-day festival, which takes place in Abidjan in the Ivory Coast, showcases the best African dramatic, *dance, and musical performances, chosen on the basis of creativity in *scenography, *mise-en-scène, and *dramaturgy. Festivals have taken place in 1993, 1995, and 1999, with an average attendance of 400 artists from nineteen countries.   SVA trans. JCM

MARKET THEATRE

Established in 1976 in *Johannesburg's Indian Fruit Market by Barney *Simon and Mannie *Manim, the Market has become South Africa's most famous theatre. Its spaces include the main Market Theatre, the Theatre Upstairs, the Laager, the Warehouse, two art galleries, a jazz bar, a *cabaret and music venue, a bookshop, two restaurants, a shopping mall, and a Saturday flea market. The trustees contravened the Group Areas

John Kani and Winston Ntshona in Athol Fugard's *The Island* at the **Market Theatre**, Johannesburg, 1986, directed by the author.

Act from the start by making it a multiracial venue, and evaded *censorship mainly through the theatre's national and international visibility. It has hosted innumerable South African practitioners, offering militant, contestatory theatre and more traditional Western plays. As one of the few non-segregated public spaces in the country, the Market offered pre-1994 South Africa a glimpse of a social, political, and cultural alternative to apartheid. Many significant South African plays by the Company, *Junction Avenue Theatre, and established artists have been developed and premièred there, despite the tensions created by its location in the metropolitan centre (as opposed to a township) and its reliance on capital from private white companies in Johannesburg. The Laboratory facilitates exploration and exchange between artists and community groups. One of the Market's greatest achievements has been the encouragement of black artists, like directors Francis and Alan Joseph, performers James Mthoba, Winston *Ntshona, John *Kani, and Sam Williams, and Black Consciousness playwrights like Matsemela *Manaka and Maishe *Maponya.

YH

MARK TAPER FORUM
American *regional theatre. Started at the University of California, *Los Angeles, as the Theatre Group, in 1967 it became the resident theatre in the new Los Angeles Music Center, where, along with the Ahmanson Theatre (a larger, more commercial house), it makes up the Center Theatre Group. Under the continuing leadership of *artistic director Gordon *Davidson since 1967, the Taper became the flagship of institutional theatres in Los Angeles and played an instrumental role in the development of many new American plays, including *The Kentucky Cycle*, *Kushner's *Angels in America*, and *Smith's *Twilight: Los Angeles, 1992*. Though hampered by the lack of a permanent second stage, the theatre has promoted new play development and produced new work over the years through various programmes at temporary off-site facilities. In the 1990s it diversified its artistic staff, expanded its multicultural programming, and created advocacy groups and developmental workshops for *Chicano, *Asian-American, *African-American, and disabled playwrights and performers.   STC

MARLOWE, CHRISTOPHER (1564–93)
English dramatist. The eldest son of a debt-ridden Canterbury shoemaker, Marlowe was awarded a scholarship to the King's School in that city in 1578, and later earned a second scholarship to Corpus Christi College, Cambridge. At this time he was possibly looking forward to a career in the Church; though he completed the BA and some requirements for the MA, his interests were elsewhere. By the time he left Cambridge he had probably written one or two plays. (Some theatre historians believe that *Dido, Queen of Carthage* is from the Cambridge period, although others place it in the middle or at the end of Marlowe's career.) Despite the vigorous theatrical scene in Cambridge there is no evidence that Marlowe acted in or wrote plays that were performed there. By 1587, however, his *Tamburlaine the Great, Part I* had taken *London by storm. The play was so successful that its author was immediately commissioned to write a sequel; and the actor who memorialized the lead role, the young Edward *Alleyn, went on to make his career in other Marlowe plays. Marlowe followed the *Tamburlaine* plays with four others: *Dr Faustus* (c.1588), *The Jew of Malta* (1589–90), *The Massacre at Paris* (c.1591–2), and *Edward II* (c.1591–2). The first three were performed at the *Rose playhouse by the Lord *Admiral's Men, and Marlowe's work became the mainstay of the company for generations. *Edward II* was

Faustus, standing within a magician's circle in his study, conjures the devil Mephistophiles in **Marlowe**'s *Doctor Faustus* (c.1588) in the costume and amid material signifiers of a scientist or academic. This woodcut is taken from a 1636 edition of the play.

The Tragicall Histoy of the Life and Death

of Doctor Fauſtus.

With new Additions.

Written by *Ch. Mar.*

LONDON,
Printed for *Iohn Wright*, and are to be ſold at his ſhop without
Newgate, at the ſigne of the Bible. 1620.

performed by the Earl of Pembroke's Men at an indeterminable theatre.

Marlowe seems to have been a turbulent personality. On 30 May 1593 he journeyed to a tavern in Deptford with two acquaintances who, some think, were government spies working in association with the Elizabethan secret police. A fight broke out over the payment of the bill, and Marlowe was stabbed to death and buried with dispatch in Deptford. This odd meeting has fuelled many popular theories concerning Marlowe's involvement in espionage. Furthermore, it has—in combination with *Edward II* and selections from Marlowe's poems—prompted some scholars to conclude that Marlowe's sexuality was ambiguous; that he, in fact, lived many double lives. Yet his professional life had an enormous impact on the drama of his contemporaries. The main *characters in his plays tend to be distinguished by what their author referred to as 'high astounding terms' and what literary critics characterize as 'overreaching'. So different are his plays from those of his predecessors that some theatre historians go so far as to credit Marlowe with single-handedly launching the most prominent period of Elizabethan drama (*see* EARLY MODERN PERIOD IN EUROPE). It is clear that the playgoers who first heard Marlowe's 'mighty line' were astonished by its resonance.

Stage productions of *Dr Faustus*, *Tamburlaine the Great* (both parts), and *The Jew of Malta* were plentiful in the 1590s, with *Faustus* and *Tamburlaine* retaining their popularity until the third quarter of the seventeenth century. During the eighteenth and nineteenth centuries Marlowe's plays were virtually absent from the stage, both in England and America; they began to be performed again on a more regular basis in the early part of the twentieth century. *Faustus* was seen in England in 1904 and 1925, and the *Old Vic (which had moved to the *Liverpool Playhouse during the war) produced the play in 1944. *Faustus* was at the *Shakespeare Memorial Theatre (1946–7), and the Old Vic (back in London) revived it in 1948. A BBC *radio version had been broadcast in 1934, and a *television version aired in 1947. Orson *Welles directed a production (and played Faustus) for the *Federal Theatre Project in the USA in 1937, and again took the part in *Paris in 1950 in his own version, which featured Eartha Kitt as Helen and music by Duke Ellington.

Productions of *Tamburlaine the Great* have been fewer. An abridged version was directed by Tyrone *Guthrie at the Old Vic (1951), noted for its emphasis on horrifying bloodlust and wild gaiety. Peter *Hall inaugurated the Olivier stage at the new *National Theatre in London with a relatively full-length but more restrained version of both parts in 1976, with Albert *Finney in the title role, Susan Fleetwood as Zenocrate, and Barbara *Jefford as Zabina. At the *Royal Shakespeare Company's *Swan Theatre (Stratford-upon-Avon, 1992) Terry *Hands returned to the savage *spectacle of earlier productions. The *text was again abridged, with Antony *Sher emphasizing the spectacle and

physicality of Tamburlaine by swinging down from the galleries and at one point climbing to the ceiling on the rope from which hung Bajazeth's cage.

The Jew of Malta was revived first in America, in a production at Williams College, Massachusetts (1907). In 1923 the Phoenix Society gave two performances at Daly's Theatre, London, and Yale Dramatic Association performed the play in 1940. Since then performances on both sides of the Atlantic have been steady, with seven productions in the 1960s in England alone. The best known of these was Clifford *Williams's for the RSC, which opened at the *Aldwych Theatre, London, in 1964, with Clive Revill (Barabas), Ian *Richardson (Ithamore), Glenda *Jackson (Bellamira), and Tony Church (Ferneze); it played in Stratford the following year with a new cast, including Eric *Porter as Barabas.

Most interesting has been the increasing popularity of *Edward II*, now distinguished as a gay classic (*see* QUEER THEORY). The play seems to have been performed only sporadically in its own day, but it has been produced steadily in the twentieth century with special attention to its homosexual themes. Toby Robertson's production (1969) starred Ian *McKellen, and Simon Russell *Beale played the role for the RSC in 1990. There have also been numerous radio versions. A *film version by Derek Jarman (1993) has become a cult classic, and in 1995 the play became a ballet by David Bintley in Stuttgart.

SPC

NICOLL, CHARLES, *The Reckoning* (London, 1992)

ROWSE, A. L., *Christopher Marlowe* (New York, 1964)

URRY, WILLIAM, *Christopher Marlowe and Canterbury* (London, 1988)

MARLOWE, JULIA (1866–1950)

Anglo-American actress. She was born Sarah Francis Frost in England, and at 4 emigrated to the state of Ohio, where she was known as Fanny Brough. In 1876 she first appeared on stage in a nine-month *tour of *HMS Pinafore*. In 1882 she went to *New York for several years of arduous coaching and singing lessons, during which time she chose her new stage name. Her New York debut came in the starring role of Parthenia in *Ingomar* (1887), which was enthusiastically received. This propelled her into her chief love—Shakespeare—beginning with Juliet (which *Duse proclaimed the greatest in her experience) and Viola, and proceeding to Rosalind, Beatrice, Imogen, even Prince Hal, Ophelia, Portia, Katherine, Cleopatra, and Lady Macbeth (often opposite the distinguished actor E. H. *Sothern, whom she married in 1911). Her moral standards led her to avoid *Ibsen and *Shaw, though she did act successfully in some *historical dramas: the title roles in *The Countess Valeska* (1898), *Colinette* (1899), and *Barbara Frietchie* (1899), and Mary Tudor in *When Knighthood Was in Flower* (1901, a huge hit). She was lauded for her velvety contralto voice and magnetic charm. She and Sothern retired permanently from the stage in 1924.   CT

MAROWITZ, CHARLES (1934–   )

American director, dramatist, and critic. Born in New York, Marowitz moved to Britain in the 1950s. He worked with Peter *Brook on *King Lear* (1962) and on the Theatre of *Cruelty season in 1963, and was *artistic director of the small Open Space Theatre in *London (1968–79). The company's many experimental productions included new plays by *Hare, *Brenton, *Griffiths, and *Shepard; Marowitz's own 'collage' variations on Shakespeare, including *Hamlet*, a *feminist *Shrew*, and a Black Power *Othello*; and *environmental productions such as *Fortune and Men's Eyes*, for which the theatre was transformed into a prison. His work, partly influenced by *Artaud, was notable for rapidly changing images and *lighting, and verbal and visual shocks. In 1980 he moved to California, where he has taught in universities and directed at the Los Angeles Theatre Center and at the Malibu Stage Company, which he founded in 1990. *Sherlock's Last Case* (1984), which he called a pot-boiler, was successfully produced on Broadway. He has always written lively and polemical journalism, and has published some two dozen books of plays, *criticism, reflections on *acting, and autobiography.   EEC

MARQUÉS, RENÉ (1919–79)

Puerto Rico's most important twentieth-century dramatist. Marqués conquered the national stage in 1953 with *La carreta* (*The Oxcart*). Performed in Spanish in *New York the same year, it encouraged Puerto Rican theatrical activity in the USA, enlarged when the Puerto Rican Travelling Theatre presented it in English (1967); American critics called it the Puerto Rican national drama. The play depicts the movement of Puerto Ricans from the countryside to deprived urban outskirts to the American metropolis, ending with a utopian return to the motherland to rescue national identity. In 1958 *Los soles truncos* (*Broken Suns*), directed by Victoria Espinosa, had huge success at the Puerto Rican Theatre Festival and was staged in *Chicago in 1959 as part of the cultural activities of the Pan American Games. Marqués followed with *La casa sin reloj* (*The House without a Clock*, 1961), *Un niño azul para esa sombra* (*A Blue Boy for that Shadow*, 1962), *El apartamiento* (1964), and *Marina; o, El alba* (*Mariana; or, The Dawn*, 1966). *Carnaval afuera, carnaval adentro* (*Carnival Outside, Carnival Inside*) was written in 1960 and performed in *Havana in 1962, but banned at home until 1979 because of its commitment to Puerto Rican independence. A constant experimenter, Marqués turned to parables in the 1970s with *Sacrificio en el Monte Moriah* (*Sacrifice on Mount Moriah*), *Titus y Bernice*, and *David y Jonathan*, the last two still unperformed at the end of the century.   JLRE

MARS, MLLE (ANNE-FRANÇOISE-HIPPOLYTE BOUTET) (1779–1847)

French actress. Born into the world of the theatre as the illegitimate daughter of the actor Monvel, Mlle Mars was admitted to the *Comédie-Française as a *sociétaire* with a part share in 1799, gaining a full share in 1807. She made her reputation in the comic theatre of *Molière and *Marivaux, impressing *audiences by her perfectly modulated diction, as well as by the elegance and refinement of her manner, attributes she used to good effect outside the theatre, becoming a leader of fashion in her own salon, where she set an example of style and good taste. Adapting badly to the *romantic revolution, she played an important part in the events leading up to the 'bataille d'Hernani' (*see* HERNANI RIOTS). Cast as the young heroine Doña Sol (at the age of 51), she spearheaded the opposition to *Hugo in matters of staging, versification, and imagery. In the case of Hugo's *Angelo*, hostility towards the author was accompanied by a personal vendetta against Marie *Dorval, recently brought in from the *boulevard theatre. Mlle Mars retired from the stage in 1841, and her funeral cortège six years later was reportedly followed by 50,000 mourners.   WDH

MARSH, NGAIO (1895–1982)

New Zealand director, teacher, and writer. After art school in Christchurch Marsh *toured with the Allan Wilkie Shakespearian Company in 1919–20, but soon turned to directing and teaching at a time when there was almost no professional theatre in New Zealand. International success as a crime writer enabled her to continue this work. She applied a wide experience of English theatre to her much admired Christchurch Shakespeare productions in the 1940s, and to *training many successful young actors. Her short-lived British Commonwealth Theatre Company in 1951 was a harbinger of the creation of New Zealand-based professional theatre. In 1965 she became New Zealand's first DBE for services to literature.   DC

MARSHALL, NORMAN (1901–80)

English director and *manager, born in India, educated at Oxford. He emerged as a director with Terence *Gray's *Cambridge Festival Theatre in the 1920s. In 1932, under his own management, he directed *O'Neill's *Marco Millions*, and in 1934 took over the *Gate Theatre (*London), where he produced and directed a range of plays from *Aristophanes' *Lysistrata* to Steinbeck's *Of Mice and Men*. He also staged the annual Gate *revues. He served in the army in 1940–2, then returned to directing with *Sherwood's *The Petrified Forest* (1942). In 1950 he *toured in *India with abridged versions of Shakespeare's plays. Throughout the 1950s and 1960s he continued to direct. He was chairman of the British Council's Drama

Committee (1961–8) and served with *Olivier as joint chairman of the National Theatre Building Committee. His book *The Other Theatre* (1947) is an important treatment of the British *alternative theatre movement of the first half of the twentieth century.   TP

MARSTON, JOHN (1576–1634)

English playwright. After receiving his BA at Oxford in 1594, Marston moved to the Middle Temple in *London, where he published fashionable satiric and erotic poetry. Around 1599, soon after the Children of Paul's resumed acting, he provided the troupe with self-consciously innovative plays. *Antonio and Mellida* (1602) and *Antonio's Revenge* (1602) are absurdist plays marked by flamboyant linguistic inventiveness and by the use of child actors to *burlesque the adult world and to *parody plays performed by adult companies (*see* BOYS' COMPANIES; BOY ACTOR). In *Jack Drum's Entertainment* (1601), he mocked other Paul's plays as 'the mustie fopperies of antiquity'. In *Satiromastix* (1602), co-authored with Thomas *Dekker, and *What You Will* (1607), he traded caricatures with Ben *Jonson in 'the War of the Theatres'.

After 1603 he wrote for the children's troupe at *Blackfriars, and may have been involved in its directorate. That troupe produced *The Malcontent* (1604), his revenge *comedy stolen by Shakespeare's troupe; *Eastward Hoe* (1605), the *city comedy he wrote with Jonson and *Chapman and which landed the authors in jail; *The Dutch Courtesan* (1605), a warning to gallants about prostitutes; *The Fawn* (1606), an Italianate anti-court *satire; and *Sophonisba* (1606), the *tragedy of a virtuous Roman matron. Several of his satires offended the ecclesiastical authorities, and he was often in legal difficulties. In 1609 he became a country clergyman, abandoning a play about an aristocratic nymphomaniac later completed by William Barkstead under the title of *The Insatiate Countess* (1613). Aside from a few productions in the twentieth century, the stage history of Marston's work is quite meagre.   MS

MARTHALER, CHRISTOPH (1951–)

Swiss-German composer and director. One of the most original (and idiosyncratic) German-speaking directors, Marthaler worked initially as a theatre musician and composer (but also trained as an actor with *Lecoq). His productions include original works, classics, and *opera. They are invariably dominated by rhythm, *music, and protracted periods of non-verbal humorous *action unmotivated by the *text. His most successful production, *Stunde Null* (*Year Zero*, 1995), a collage commenting on 50 years of the Federal Republic of Germany, has *toured successfully throughout Europe for many years. He was appointed *artistic director of the *Zurich Schauspielhaus in 2000.   CBB

MARTÍ, JOSÉ (1853–95)

Cuban writer, political theorist, and advocate of the unification of American peoples 'to the south of the Rio Bravo'. Having organized the 'necessary war' leading to Cuba's independence from Spain, he died in combat. In 1869 he wrote *Abdala*, a patriotic dramatic parable, and in 1872 the drama *Adúltera* (*Adulterous*). His *comedy *Amor con amor se paga* (*Paying Back Love with Love*) was premièred in Mexico in 1875. In *Patria y libertad* (*Fatherland and Liberty*), written in 1877, he heralded a modern Latin American epic. The unfinished *Chac-mool*, dated around the 1880s or early 1890s, is most original: conceived as a 'synthesis of American Civilisation', the *plot—revolving around the statue of a Mayan god discovered by a US scientist who attempts to steal it—is impressive for its fragmentation and emphasis on *ritual. As a critic he stressed the link between theatre and history, together with the importance of the 'natural', understood as what is vital and non-artificial. Written in a prose of amazing modernity, his *Combat Diary* was staged in 1970 by director Roberto Blanco.   MMu

MARTIN, KARL HEINZ (1888–1948)

German director, one of the earliest proponents of *expressionism. He staged Carl *Sternheim in Frankfurt and Georg *Kaiser's *From Morn to Midnight* in Hamburg (1918), which he also directed as a *film. Martin was a founding member of the expressionist theatre Die Tribüne in *Berlin, where he directed Ernst *Toller's *Transfiguration* (1919), a breakthrough production for the author. The bare stage, striking *acting from Fritz *Kortner, and innovative *lighting effects defined the aesthetics of the movement. Throughout the Weimar Republic, Martin worked at major theatres in Berlin, *Munich, and *Vienna. After 1933 he was mainly in the film industry, returning to the Berlin theatre during the war, chiefly at the *Volksbühne. From 1945 to 1948 he was *artistic director of the Hebbeltheater in Berlin.
                                                                                       CBB

MARTIN, MARY (1913–90)

American *musical comedy actress-singer, who broke into show business in 1935 as a *radio and nightclub singer. Her Broadway debut was in *Leave It to Me* (1938), where her striptease-like number 'My Heart Belongs to Daddy' made her a star. This led to a series of mostly forgettable *films for Paramount in the early 1940s. She returned to Broadway for *One Touch of Venus* (1943), moved on to *Lute Song* (1946), appeared in *London in *Pacific 1860*, and *toured the United States in *Annie Get your Gun* (1947). Her signature role came with *Rodgers and *Hammerstein's *South Pacific* (1949), when she played the spirited military nurse Nellie Forbush, washing her hair nightly onstage as she sang 'I'm Gonna Wash That Man Right Outa my Hair'.

Martin played Nellie for two years in London (1951–3). She was on Broadway in *Kind Sir* (1953), toured Europe and the United States in *The Skin of our Teeth* (1955), and starred in various *television specials, most memorably in *Peter Pan* (1954) following its brief Broadway run. Martin's lithe figure, youthful face, wholesomeness, and ebullient personality often allowed her to play roles much younger than her age, which held true of her performance as the novice nun in *The Sound of Music* (1959). Other major shows included *Hello, Dolly!*, performed on tour to GIs in Asia (1965) before opening in London, Broadway's two-character *I Do, I Do* (1966), co-starring Robert Preston, and *Do You Turn Somersaults?* (1978). Her final show, *Legends* (1986), co-starring Carol *Channing, closed out of town. SLL

MARTINELLI FAMILY

Mantuan *commedia dell'arte* actors. **Drusiano** is known to have appeared with various companies: his brother **Tristano** (1557-1630) was far more famous, as interpreter of the role of Arlecchino or *Harlequin. It seems increasingly likely that a Martinelli actually invented this mask for the theatre, basing it on a demonic figure from French legend; and that Tristano adapted it as a lowlife role for Italian *comedies, one which later became assimilated to other 'servant' or *Zanni stereotypes. Like all improvising performers, Martinelli has left us few clues as to his material and manner, though roles in two comedies by Giovan Battista *Andreini may capture some of his aggressive style. Correspondence by and about Martinelli shows him as a selfish, obsessed performer who changed companies frequently, adapted badly to the new corporate discipline of the *arte* troupes, and was constantly seeking autonomous star status together with a star income. RAA

MARTÍNEZ, GILBERTO (1934–)

Colombian playwright, director, actor, theoretician, and cardiologist, who has helped establish many groups in his home town of Medellín, including Corporación Casa del Teatro (founded 1987), which he still heads. Among his best-known plays are *El grito de los ahorcados* (*The Dead Man's Agony*, 1965), *El zarpazo* (*The Smash*, 1974), and *La guandoca* (*The Jail*, 1994), a work celebrating the life of movie maker Gabriela Samper, who was unjustly incarcerated in 1972 and died a year later. A versatile director with a penchant for *realism, Martínez has staged plays by *Brecht, *Genet, Dario *Fo, and Alfonso *Sastre, among others. His books include *Hacia un teatro dialéctico* (1975), *Teatro, teoría y práctica* (1986), and *Teatrario* (1994). BJR

MARTÍNEZ, JOSÉ DE JESÚS (1929–91)

Panamanian playwright and director, born in Nicaragua, educated in Mexico City, Madrid, and Heidelberg, who became professor of philosophy and mathematics at the University of Panama and a close friend of General Torrijos. His work shows a growing interest in French existentialist and *absurdist drama, accenting the meaninglessness of life and the relationship of human beings to the universe. This is most apparent in *El juicio final* (*The Last Judgement*, 1962), in which a deceased bureaucrat attempts to convince God about the virtue of his past life. Other plays include *La mentira* (*The Lie*, 1955), *Caifás* (*Caiaphas*, 1961), and *La guerra del banano* (*Banana War*, 1974), a biting critique of the international banana trade. EJW

MARTÍNEZ SIERRA, GREGORIO (1881–1948)

Spanish stage and *film director and theatre *manager. Although widely known as a playwright, he collaborated with his wife María de la O Lejárraga on most of the titles that bear his name. *The Cradle Song* (1911) and *The Kingdom of God* (1915) were performed internationally. In England, Helen and Harley Granville *Barker were champions of their plays and Eva *Le Gallienne's *Civic Repertory Theatre staged *The Cradle Song* in *New York in 1927. As a director, Martínez Sierra was instrumental in introducing new European and *avant-garde Spanish works through his Teatro Eslava in the 1920s, and staged *García Lorca's first play. In 1930 he went to Hollywood, where he wrote scripts in the Spanish divisions of several studios and oversaw the filming of several productions. After the victory of Franco, he lived in Argentina, his long career virtually at an end. MPH

MARTIN-HARVEY, JOHN (1863–1944)

English *actor-manager, knighted in 1921. He began his *London career with *Irving's *Lyceum company (1882–96), and in 1898 he appeared with Mrs Patrick *Campbell in *Maeterlinck's *Pelléas and Mélisande*. The following year he became a popular star in *melodrama when he appeared as Sydney Carton in *The Only Way*, a dramatization of *Dickens's *A Tale of Two Cities*. Work in several melodramas and Shakespeare culminated in a successful *Hamlet* in 1904. In 1912 he played Oedipus in *Reinhardt's London production of *Oedipus Rex*, and during the 1920s he made a successful *tour of North America; back in London he performed in *Shaw, including *The Devil's Disciple*; for the rest of his career he was featured mainly in revivals of his famous roles. His wife Nina de Silva was his leading lady. He published an autobiography in 1933. TP

MARTOGLIO, NINO (1870–1921)

Italian director and author. In 1902 Martoglio took charge of the Catania-based Compagnia Dialettale Siciliana (Sicilian Dialect

Theatre Company), which included actors Angelo *Musco and Giovanni *Grasso. He encouraged Sicilian authors, including his friend the novelist Luigi *Pirandello, to write for the theatre in Sicilian dialect. Martoglio's company thus produced Pirandello's first plays: *Pensaci, Giacuminu!* (*Think It Over, Giacomino!*, 1916), *Liolà* (1916), and *'A birritta cu' i ciancianeddi* (*Cap and Bells*, 1917). The two friends collaborated on several works, including *'A vilanza* (*The Scales*, 1917). Martoglio succeeded in expanding the scope of the Sicilian repertoire beyond its *verismo themes of passion and revenge, and wrote a number of plays himself, including the *comedies *San Giuvanni decullatu* (*St John Decapitated*, 1908) and *L'aria del continente* (*Continental Airs*, 1915), which Pirandello had begun. Martoglio's Sicilian dialect companies and their offshoots received international recognition, and he is also remembered for directing two important *films: *Sperduti nel buio* (*Lost in the Dark*, 1914) and *Teresa Raquin* (1915).   ATS

MARTYN, EDWARD (1859–1923)

Irish playwright. With *Yeats and Lady *Gregory he co-founded the *Irish Literary Theatre (1899–1901), whose efforts he backed financially. His plays *The Heather Field* and *Maeve* were staged in the first two seasons but a third contribution (*The Tale of a Town*) occasioned harsh criticism from Yeats and George *Moore (who redrafted it as *The Bending of the Bough*). Martyn seceded from the group, creating in the Theatre of Ireland (1906) a rival venture to what became the *Abbey. Martyn's plays quickly reveal his influences: *Ibsen's structuring and use of organizing symbols; *Maeterlinck's building up of threatening but enigmatic atmospheres.   RAC

MARX BROTHERS

American comic performers. The three eldest Marx brothers—**Chico** (Leonard) (1887–1961), **Harpo** (Adolph Arthur) (1888–1964), and **Groucho** (Julius Henry) (1890–1977)—formed the core and substance of the *family *variety act that went on to Broadway musical *revues, Hollywood *films, and iconic status in twentieth-century Western culture. **Gummo** (Milton) (1892–1977), and **Zeppo** (Herbert) (1901–79) each served as comic foil at different times during the performing brothers' incubation period in *vaudeville, and Zeppo appeared in films up to *Duck Soup* (1933). It was, however, the trio of Groucho, Chico, and Harpo which imprinted itself indelibly on the face of American comic performance with a *surreal, anarchic humour.

The young Marxes started as musical entertainers but found their inclinations toward silliness and horseplay much more crowd-pleasing. By the time of their early successes on Broadway in the 1920s, they had adopted their trademark guises: Groucho wore a greasepaint moustache and walked with a stoop; Chico spoke with an Italian accent; Harpo wore a red fright wig and became known as the silent one. The Marx Brothers' Broadway shows hung songs and routines on the bones of a romantic *plot. The formula served just as well for the movies, and from the mid-1920s to the late 1930s the comics traced a legendary arc of success. Stage productions like *The Cocoanuts* (1925) and *Animal Crackers* (1928), were subsequently translated to the screen; *Monkey Business* (1931) was their first film written directly for Hollywood. In the 1940s, the brothers began turning to individual pursuits, though they did reunite for several more films. They each appeared variously on the rapidly growing medium of *television, and Groucho made the most of his wisecracking persona as host of the quiz series *You Bet your Life*, which aired on *radio and then television between 1947 and 1961. Martin Esslin observed that the Marx Brothers 'bridge the tradition between the *commedia dell'arte* and vaudeville, on the one hand, and the theatre of the *absurd, on the other'. *Artaud and *Beckett are among the figures who drew inspiration from their zany and often disturbing physical and verbal comedy.   EW

MARXISM *See* MATERIALIST CRITICISM.

MASAS, TEATRO DE

'Mass theatre', a Mexican propaganda form from the 1920s. Promoted by the government after the Mexican Revolution, *teatro de masas* reoriented elements of *religious *folk drama towards an understanding of Mexican history, promoting progress informed by the goals and ideals of the revolution and the revolutionary government. These plays were gigantic *pantomimes utilizing thousands of actors. They rejected colonial notions of history and attempted to resuscitate an Aztec nobility of spirit as the foundation for the nation's new life.   AV

MASEFIELD, JOHN (1878–1967)

English poet and playwright. Along with Gordon *Bottomley and John *Drinkwater, Masefield laboured to revive poetic drama in pre-First World War England. His plays include the *melodramas *The Campden Wonder* (1907) and *The Witch* (1910), the Shavian *historical drama *The Tragedy of Pompey the Great* (1910), the *kabuki-inspired *The Faithful* (1914), and a *Racine adaptation, *Esther* (1921). Masefield achieved *critical success with *The Tragedy of Nan* (1908), directed by Harley Granville *Barker and featuring Lillah *McCarthy. Masefield's plays have been little performed since their premières, suffering as they do from the tendency of *verse drama towards untheatrical stasis. After the First World War, Masefield moved away from commercial theatre and formed the Hill Players, an *amateur group devoted to verse drama. He became Poet Laureate in 1930.   MDG

MASK AND MASKING

Masking carries with it a double notion of hiding and of transforming identity. A potent force in theatrical *performance, its uses can also range from religious *ritual to architectural embellishment. The mask can become a physical representation of a god or ancestor figure and, divorced from a human wearer, it can bring spiritual potency to Buddhist temples, Maori houses, or *Native American totem poles. Medieval Christian iconography represented the entrance to *hell as a huge and savage mouth. The compelling power of the stone heads on Easter Island shows the inherent strength of the giant mask.

The mask occurs in virtually every culture. Commonly perceived as an object that covers all or part of the face, the mask usually must be seen in the full context of an accompanying *costume. In some cases a costume itself can transform the wearer and be a mask without needing to cover the face (ceremonial robes, uniforms, *carnival costumes, or even sportswear). Indians of the American north-west coast wore frontlets on top of the head which were halfway between a mask and a heraldic crest. In *Africa many masks are worn on top of the head, with the actor concealed by the costume, whilst in Melanesia the wearer enters totally into a woven fibre structure.

Origins and sacred function. The earliest use of the mask was probably in the context of animist magic. By wearing a skin or other animal attribute a man might take on some of the qualities of that animal; large animal figures with concealed performers are still used in initiation ceremonies in Mali. Masks were elements of most early religions. Shamans employed masks so as to become vehicles for a spirit. In certain cultures in Africa and Asia today the donning of a mask allows the wearer to enter into a state of trance. Where cult made way for theatrical representation the mask began to lose its shamanic and seasonal or ritual functions, but could retain ambivalent status. *Nō masks in *Japan are still idealized forms, intended as vehicles for the spiritual and not as *realistic portrayals of *characters, and are treated with reverence. The Balinese *topeng pajegan* dancer may run through a series of masked characters in a 'secular' performance for tourists, but when he uses the priestly mask he reverts to a shamanic role and may go into trance.

The Aztecs used stone masks to cover the faces of the dead, and beaten gold ones had a similar function. The Etruscans placed masks over the faces of dead heroes, whilst the Romans preserved death-masks of family members and produced them on special occasions (the Latin word *larva* applied to both a ghost and a mask). In some cultures masks were preserved over long periods of time as religious objects and brought out regularly for performance. Native Americans of the north-west have an important mask culture associated with ancestor worship. They were used in *dances and initiation rites, but possession of a prized mask was more important than wearing it. The *hahoe*

masks of *Korea (*see* KAMYŎNGŬK), made in a variety of materials, including gourds, papier mâché, fur, and occasionally wood, relate to a local shamanistic ritual designed to celebrate moments of the agricultural year and to drive away evil spirits. Many African initiation masks are kept in a special place until required for the ceremonies. In other cultures the mask was not kept, but burned after use to dispose of any evil spirits it might have attracted, as in Melanesia.

Wild man. The wild man, a hirsute counterpart of 'civilized' man clad in animal accoutrements, erupts in a context of carnival. Ancient *Greek *satyr-plays took over the wild man, and slave masks likewise reflected uncivilized man, while *Atellan farces continued the idea. The Christian Church perceived links between masks and pagan practices, and this may explain the proscription on masquerading in *medieval England. Hallow'en (the Celtic new year) was the festival of the dead, when those from the underworld were thought to roam, prompting bands of young men to go through the countryside, often disguised as wild men. A popular figure from Austria was *Harlequin (Hellequin). When he appeared as a stage servant in northern Italy in the sixteenth century, *audiences would have immediately recognized the diabolical and animalistic associations suggested by his black leather mask. Even where masks were not used, the blackened face was common to many *mumming traditions. In Anatolia mummers went from house to house with blackened faces, some wearing goat or animal skins or animal masks. The Bilmawn masqueraders of the Atlas mountains visit houses, turning everything topsy-turvy and presenting a series of crude and sexually explicit sketches. The central figure wears a goat's head and is dressed in uncured skins.

The sixteenth- and seventeenth-century court *masque in England, and the closely related French *ballet de cour*, originated in popular mummings and *disguisings, but lifted them to the level of courtly *allegory. The *grotesque antimasque elements, often performed by professional entertainers, related in a contained way to carnival and the wild man tradition. The fantastic creations of the court masque, and later the *opera, required huge papier mâché masks. Later such masks were the stock in trade of the nineteenth-century theatrical extravaganza, and similar masks continue to be employed in street carnival, especially in Iberia. In the twentieth century the carnival use of the mask, because of its power and visibility, was adopted for *political theatre by Russian *agitprop groups of the 1920s, and this idea was repeated in the 1960s and 1970s, most notably by the *Bread and Puppet Theatre in the USA.

The theatrical mask. The mask is often seen as an emblem of theatre, and theatrical performance in most cultures can involve masks. All masks carry signifiers and when transposed to theatrical performance these signifiers become part of a code that audiences read and relate to other elements of the performance. In the second century AD Julius *Pollux attempted to classify the reinforced linen masks of Greek *New Comedy as old men, young men, slaves, and women. In Korea a similar typology was prevalent, and nō masks likewise fall into a limited number of types. At its most complex and abstract are the painted faces of Chinese opera (*see*, for example, JINGJU; KUNQU), where colour and design convey highly specific information about different characters.

Performance masks can cover just the face, or a part of it, or the whole head (Greek satyr masks). Thai *khon dancers originally wore full head masks but today only Hanuman and the various demons do. The nō mask originated in the *gigaku dance, which also covered the entire head, but then became a smaller than life-size wooden visor, thus drawing attention to the fact that it is a mask. In *kathakali in south *India the actor's face itself is built up with rice paste until it becomes virtually a mask. Various form of traditional Indian theatre have shown how the actor, with supreme control over the facial muscles, can model his own face into a mask. *Mime artist Marcel *Marceau developed this skill, as did Jerzy *Grotowski, and the Japanese *butoh theatre.

The notion of a performer changing masks to present different characters to an audience is quite widespread. Apart from the *topeng* peformer, it can be found in the *tragedies of *Euripides and in the *comedies of Menander, where the three male actors each played several roles. In contrast, a *commedia dell'arte* performer developed a close relationship with a single mask, and the mask itself became a *stock character. Bertolt *Brecht used the mask to emphasize the gap between the actor and the persona presented.

Reacting against the *naturalism of the nineteenth century, *modernist European theatre returned to the masks of *commedia dell'arte* and Asian theatre. Jacques *Copeau used the mask for actor *training because of the emphasis on the whole body as a means of expression, whilst W. B. *Yeats tried to create a repertoire for the masked performer. Already in 1896 Alfred *Jarry attempted to codify the ways the mask could express emotion through different head angles. Antonin *Artaud, drawing on the cultural and sacred origins of the mask, was amongst the practitioners to recommend giant masks. Masking the human body was the aim of many *futurist artists and also of the *Bauhaus. Fernand Léger designed costumes which turned the dancer into a modernist abstract sculpture. In the 1970s the Swiss company Mummenschanz devised a form of body mask that concealed actors totally within abstract amorphous shapes which they brought to life. *Interculturalism in late twentieth-century theatre has drawn heavily on different masking traditions. Sometimes worn, sometimes carried, sometimes completely divorced from the live performer, sometimes superimposed on stages or performers by techniques of projection (*see* MULTIMEDIA PERFORMANCE), the mask is now extensively used in visual and *physical theatre.   JMcC

BIHALJI-MERIN, OTO, *Masks of the World* (London, 1971)
EMIGH, JOHN, *Masked Performance* (Philadelphia, 1996)

MACK, JOHN (ed.), *Masks: the art of expression* (London, 1994)
SMITH, SUSAN H., *Masks in Modern Drama* (Berkeley, 1984)
WILES, DAVID, *The Masks of Menander* (Cambridge, 1991)

MASON, BRUCE (1921–82)

New Zealand playwright. Mason's lifelong crusade against New Zealand philistinism was evident in his bleakly *realist 1950s *one-act plays for Wellington's Unity Theatre (modelled on *London's socialist *Unity), but his idealism was more evident in the romantic, almost operatic, *dramaturgy of his full-length plays, several on the then unusual topic of Maori and bicultural issues, especially *The Pohutukawa Tree* (1957; BBC *television 1959), which became the first New Zealand play to be a set text for schools. With the collapse of the *New Zealand Players in 1960, he turned to *radio and solo performance as the only avenues for a professional playwright; and his nearly 2,000 performances of *The End of the Golden Weather*, many in small towns, displayed his gifts of rhetoric and mimicry (over 40 *characters) to the full. An ardent supporter of the new professional theatres in the late 1960s, and a drama and music critic proclaiming cultural values, all his writing was a crusade against the casual destruction of sensitivity and aspiration by bland and ignorant conformism.   DC

MASON, MARSHALL W. (1940–)

American director. Born in Amarillo, Texas, Mason graduated from Northwestern University in 1961. He moved to *New York and began directing *Off-Off-Broadway (notably at the *Caffe Cino, starting in 1962) and *Off-Broadway (*Little Eyolf*, 1964). In 1965 he directed the première of Lanford *Wilson's *Balm in Gilead*, which led to a collaboration between the two that extended to some twenty plays, including *The Hot l Baltimore* (1973), *The Fifth of July* (1978), the Pulitzer Prize-winning *Talley's Folly* (1979), *Burn This* (1987), and *Redwood Curtain* (1992). In 1969 Mason became the founding *artistic director of the *Circle Repertory Company, remaining at its helm until 1987, and staging not only a dozen Wilson plays but also works by Shakespeare, *Schiller, David *Storey, Jules Feiffer, Corinne Jacker, and Romulus *Linney. He has also directed on Broadway, in *regional theatre, and abroad. He served as president of the Society of Stage Directors and Choreographers (1983–5), and in 1994 began a professorship at Arizona State University.

CT

MASON, PATRICK (1951–)

Irish director. Born in Britain, Mason lectured in drama at Manchester University before embarking on a career as a director. For over twenty years he has been an important figure in Irish theatre. From 1992 to 1999 he was *artistic director of the Irish

National Theatre (*Abbey Theatre), where he achieved a high degree of stability in a troubled institution, and gained international recognition for his productions of new plays. Before heading the National Theatre he directed many notable premières there including an adaptation of Patrick Kavanagh's poem *The Great Hunger* (1983), Frank *McGuinness's *Observe the Sons of Ulster Marching toward the Somme* (1985), and, to international critical acclaim, Brian *Friel's *Dancing at Lughnasa* (1990), which won him a Tony *award in *New York. As artistic director he continued a strong repertoire of new work, directing the premières of Thomas *Kilroy's *The Secret Fall of Constance Wilde* (1997), Marina *Carr's *By the Bog of Cats* (1998), and McGuinness's *Dolly West's Kitchen* (1999). All his work manifests a strong sense of symbolism appropriate for his subsequent work as a director of *opera.   BRS

MASQUE

A stylized form of drama performed in the sixteenth and seventeenth centuries at the English court and aristocratic country houses. According to the chronicler Edward Hall, the masque was 'a thing not seen afore in England' when, on Twelfth Night 1513, King Henry VIII and eleven of his courtiers arrived at Greenwich in *disguise and asked the ladies to *dance. Though the English court had often revelled in fancy dress since the fourteenth century, this event had a new, quasi-dramatic quality centring on the arrival of the masquers, who effectively combined their real court personas with the fictional identities conferred by their *costumes. Later Tudor masques incorporated narrative elements which 'explained' the characters' visit, and by Elizabeth I's reign they were scripted as well as choreographed. The *genre reached its full formal development in the early seventeenth century, combining elaborate pageantry with literary and musical virtuosity; court masques of this period were usually written and designed by established professional figures such as the poet-dramatists Samuel *Daniel and Ben *Jonson, and the architect Inigo *Jones.

A typical masque would feature *allegorical or mythological *characters, often all of the same gender, either enacting some simple fable or visiting the performance venue for some benevolent purpose. Everything would lead up to a sequence of stately figure dances, after which the masquers would 'take out' members of the *audience for livelier, more sexually charged dancing, and the dramatic fiction would dissolve into the social reality of a court revel; finally the masquers would make their departure. This recognized format was extended in 1609 when Queen Anne asked Jonson to provide *The Masque of Queens* with 'some dance or show that might precede hers', and he wrote an antimasque of witches, a threatening presence banished by the arrival of the masquing queens. Thereafter the antimasque became a standard feature, counterpointing the main masque's elegance with *grotesque figures, and later grew increasingly

prominent and disconnected from the central action: for example, the antimasque of Jonson's *News from the New World Discovered in the Moon* (1620), *satirizing newsmongers, reads like a *revue sketch, racy, demotic, and quite at odds with the formality of the briefer masque speeches and dances which follow.

Masques took place indoors in the evening, and dancing usually went on until the small hours; Jonson's *Oberon, the Fairy Prince* (1611) is designed to end as dawn breaks. Though antimasque roles were often played by professional actors, the main performers in a masque were always *amateurs, usually courtiers (of either sex) or members of the *Inns of Court; audiences regularly included foreign ambassadors (and where they sat in relation to one another was an issue of some diplomatic delicacy). *Music was an important feature of the performance, from the loud wind consort which played as the King arrived to the closing song and dance; some later masques, probably beginning with Jonson's *The Vision of Delight* (1617), also had speeches 'spake in song' in the Italian *recitative style, a development associated with the composer Nicholas Lanier. The survival of masque music is haphazard (no complete score exists for any performance), but we are better served for the visuals: the *costume and scenic designs by Inigo Jones, supplemented by the court's financial records, give us a good sense of the events' sheer *spectacle (*see* SCENOGRAPHY). Beginning with Jones's *Masque of Blackness* (1605; libretto by Jonson), the action took place on a stage set at one end of the hall (earlier masques ranged more freely through the room); an open space between the stage and the audience's seating was reserved for the dancing. There was elaborate architectural *scenery, sometimes solid and sometimes mechanically sophisticated: some masques, such as *The Essex House Masque* (1621), assign the performers places on hopefully sturdy structures, while others incorporate spectacular effects requiring apparently fixed scenery to open or otherwise transform itself (*see* SCENE SHIFTING). Costumes, too, were flamboyant, made of costly, luxurious materials like taffeta, silk, and cloth of gold. Female masquing costumes were often sexually provocative, exposing the performer's nipples or legs: one innocent, unmarried courtier remarked that he never knew women *had* legs before seeing the Queen's when she appeared in Daniel's *The Vision of the Twelve Goddesses* (1604).

A masque's ostensible purpose was to celebrate a special occasion such as an aristocratic wedding, a calendar festival like Shrovetide or Christmas, or a state event such as the investiture of Prince Henry as Prince of Wales in 1610. Its latent *political significance was complex. Early in Elizabeth's reign there were several attempts to co-opt the nascent masque form in support of radical Reformation politics, but the Queen's disapproval ensured that, for the rest of the sixteenth century, such events remained strictly non-committal on specific issues. Under the early Stuart monarchs, however, masques were seen as latent expressions of the royal will, and so were scrutinized by ambassadors and politicians seeking to decode the King's intentions; Jonson called them 'court hieroglyphics'. Most fundamentally, though, the genre was political in that it existed to praise and support the ruling elite. A typical masque narrative develops towards hierarchical order and harmony (also figured metaphorically in the dancing), which is not so much established as confirmed by the action, so effortlessly are the discordant forces expelled; this proclaimed a more than fictitious state of affairs because the courtier performers' actual identities were never entirely effaced by their roles. The performance, too, worked to honour the most exalted member of the audience: the King was sometimes expected to intervene in the *action as the agent of its concluding concord; even the *perspective scenery was designed to ensure that the image was least distorted when seen from his canopied throne of state. Even the expense of the occasion was an assertion and display of the power of the crown—in 1610, for instance, James I authorized unlimited expenditure on Daniel's *Tethys' Festival*; its actual cost was in excess of £2,000—and in the *early modern court culture of gifts and compliments, some masques were financed by prominent politicians seeking to declare their devotion, and so cement their own status, by extravagant expenditure. Naturally sceptical commentators, in the seventeenth century and later, felt that the genre was, as *Beaumont and *Fletcher put it in 1611, 'tied to rules of flattery'. (*See* STATE DISPLAYS.)

There are several surviving examples of masque *texts performed at country houses in England, Wales, and Ireland. They followed the same formal structure as their cousins at court, but were typically less ambitious in their visual and scenic effects, though several used machinery to effect the descent of a goddess. Many of them, including *The Coleorton Masque* (1618) and John Clavell's *Introduction to the Sword Dance* (1632), are more overtly concerned with sexual politics than with matters of state, though they have also been seen as an attempt to assert an alternative set of aristocratic 'country' values using the theatrical language of the court.

Masques were a recognized feature of court life in the early seventeenth century, and some commercial playwrights used miniature inset masques as an element of court settings: sometimes they merely represented a social practice, but in *tragedies they are often a powerful metaphor for duplicity and corruption, used as a cover for one or more murder plots. There was also some cross-fertilization between masques and plays: in the early 1610s, some textual and choreographic elements of specific masques were reused in King's Men (*see* CHAMBERLAIN'S MEN, LORD) plays soon afterwards (notably Shakespeare and Fletcher's *The Two Noble Kinsmen* and *Webster's *The Duchess of Malfi*), and it has been speculated that the company also acquired masque costumes for similar purposes. The last court masque was William *Davenant's *Salmacida Spolia* (1640); there are some later masques written for private performance during the Interregnum, notably James *Shirley's *Cupid and Death* (1653), but the genre did not return with the Stuart monarchy in 1660. Some of its features are seen, however, in Restoration drama and early English *opera.

Sometimes masques were repeated, either for reasons of economy or because they were considered exceptionally enjoyable (*The Running Masque* was performed at least six times in early 1620), but fundamentally they were designed as single-occasion events: when librettos were published, it was as an account of what had happened, with the staging described in the past tense. Accordingly, most individual masques have no subsequent stage history beyond antiquarian reconstruction attempts, and even those are inhibited by the dispersal of the component parts—text, score, design, and choreography. However, *Milton's *Comus* (1634) has a strong enough narrative to sustain occasional amateur revival, and in the twentieth century the genre had a brief revival when the future Queen Elizabeth II visited Oxford in 1948, and the university entertained her with a new masque written by the theatre-minded don Nevill Coghill. *See also* BALLET DE COUR.

MJW

LINDLEY, DAVID (ed.), *The Court Masque* (Manchester, 1984)

ORGEL, STEPHEN, and STRONG, ROY, *Inigo Jones: theatre of the Stuart court* (London, 1973)

SPENCER, T. J. B., and WELLS, STANLEY (eds.), *A Book of Masques* (Cambridge, 1973)

WALLS, PETER, *Music in the English Courtly Masque, 1604–1640* (Oxford, 1996)

MASRAH AL-JADID, AL-

When the 'New Theatre' was founded in *Tunis in 1975 by Fadhel Jaibi, Fadhel Jaziri, Mohamed Driss, Jalila Baccar, and Habib Masrouki, it marked a turning point in Tunisian cultural life. The organizers, realizing that work within university and publicly supported theatres was too limiting, established Al-Masrah al-Jadid as the first independent company in the country with a well-defined aesthetic, intellectual, and professional programme. Free of established ideas, the group produced *The Wedding*, *Heritage* (both 1976), *The Instruction* (1977), and *Autumn Rain* (1979). Masrouki's suicide during the preparation of *Lam* (1982) signalled the beginning of the end. Jaziri and Jaibi wrote and directed *Arab* (1987) and *El Awada* (1989) collaboratively, but with Jaziri's departure thereafter the venture closed. As a result of the founders' example, however, ten independent companies were operating in Tunisia at the start of the new millennium.

MMe

MASRAH AL-KASABA

Important Palestinian company founded by George Ibrahim in Jerusalem in 1970. Located in theatres in the centre of the city (since 1989) and in Ramalah (since 1998), the troupe was known under various names before settling on its current title. It has staged over 50 plays since its founding, including some fifteen plays for *youth. Work by *Arabic dramatists such as Tawfiq el-*Hakim, Alfred *Farag, Elias Khouri, and Fathi Radwan has appeared side by side with *Marivaux, *Dürrenmatt, *Camus, *Sartre, and *Kleist. Striving to be in harmony with the Palestinian public and the Palestinian cause, Masrah al-Kasaba tends to adapt European *texts to local circumstances.   MMe

MASRAH EL KALAA (CITADEL THEATRE)

Founded in *Algiers in 1989 by the director Ziani Cherif-Ayad with the collaboration of the playwright Mohamed Benguettaf and the actress Sonia. During its first six years the company produced nine plays and enjoyed a remarkable success in Algeria and elsewhere, with work such as *El Ayta* (*The Cry*, 1989), *Fatma* (1990), *The Repetition* (1994), and *Compulsory Stop* (1996). The first contemporary company to break away from the subsidy of the public sector (in 1989; *see* FINANCE), and especially to counter the near monopoly of Théâtre National Algérien, Masrah el Kalaa started the development of independent theatre companies based on initiative and freedom of expression.   MMe

MASRAH EL YAOUM (THEATRE OF TODAY)

Independent Moroccan company, founded in Casablanca in 1987 by the director Abdelouahed Ouzri and the actress Touria Jabrane. This small troupe has sought to create a new Arabic drama concerned with contemporary Moroccan issues. Its work, which *tours widely in the country, has included important productions of *Tales without Borders* by the Syrian dramatist Maghout (1987), *Boughaba*, an adaptation of *Brecht's *Puntila and his Man Matti* (1989), *The Insane Are among Us* (1990), *Souirti Moulana* (1992), *Berrechid's *Namroud in Hollywood* (1991), Abdelatif Laabi's *The Sun Fails* (1999), and Youssef Fadhel's *Days of Glory* (1994).   MMe

MASSEY, RAYMOND (1896–1983)

Canadian actor. Best known for portraying Abraham Lincoln in Robert *Anderson's *Abe Lincoln in Illinois* (1938, *filmed 1941), Massey had a long career as an actor and occasional director on both sides of the Atlantic. Appearing in numerous *London productions between the wars, he was mainly associated with the London Everyman Theatre, where he also directed. Massey made his *New York debut in *Hamlet* (1931), followed by *Ethan Frome* (1936) and *Idiot's Delight* (1938). He also appeared with Katharine *Cornell in *The Doctor's Dilemma* (1940) and *Candida* (1942). After the war, Massey spent most of the rest of his career in America, where his roles included Brutus and

Prospero for the *American Shakespeare Theatre (1955) and Mr Zuss in Macliesh's *JB*, directed by Elia *Kazan (1957). Massey featured in the long-running *television drama *Dr Kildare*. His numerous films include *Fire over England* (1936), *Arsenic and Old Lace* (1944), *Mourning Becomes Electra* (1947), and *East of Eden* (1955). Massey's children Anna and Daniel both became actors.   MDG

MASSINGER, PHILIP (1583–1640)

English playwright. Born in Salisbury, he studied at Oxford and then moved to *London, where he may have been an actor before writing for the stage. Attached to the King's Men (*see* CHAMBERLAIN'S MEN, LORD) for all of his dramatic career (except for a short interval in 1623–5, when he wrote for the Queen's Men), he collaborated with John *Fletcher on a number of plays (most notably *The Tragedy of Sir John van Olden Barnavelt*, 1619) before succeeding him as resident dramatist in 1625. Not quite as popular as Fletcher with the *audience of the *Blackfriars, he also had to face the competition of court playwrights like Carew and *Davenant, who were gaining ground at the expense of professional dramatists like *Ford, *Shirley, and *Brome. Massinger was a protégé of the Herbert family, who were active in supporting opposition artists throughout the 1620s, and most of his plays deal with controversial topical issues. The *tragicomedy *The Bondman* (1623), for instance, is an attack on Buckingham, Charles I's protégé and a favourite target of the opposition, while *The Maid of Honour* (*c.*1621) uses its Sicilian setting to deal with English foreign policy. Massinger's best-known *comedy, *A New Way to Pay Old Debts* (*c.*1621), is a combination of topical and general *satire against court greed and corruption, while his most famous *tragedy, *The Roman Actor* (1626), is an outspoken defence of the freedom of the stage, which he considered as an agent of social reformation.   PCR

MASS MEDIA

The combination of print, *radio, *film, *televisual, electronic, and Internet communications capable of delivering information to local, national, and world *audiences. The effects of mass media on the construction of identity and culture are profound and have been analysed by cultural theorists as an ideological apparatus for the production of multinational capital and globalization. Jean Baudrillard has argued that the flow of information through mass media has led to a world state of simulation wherein all elements of the real are replaced by signs of the real. In this way, mass media are capable of regulating and controlling the creation of the real for the world audience of media information. In a more materialist critique, the mass media are noted for product placement and promotion which strives to establish an American cultural norm through Hollywood cinema and American broadcast television. The mass media often override local culture, which is challenged and reconfigured as information and ideological perspectives filter through multiple levels of society. The field of media studies, which is closely linked with *performance studies, attempts to understand the ways in which meaning, culture, and identity are constructed and manipulated through the flow of information of the mass media. Theatre and *performance artists (Stelarc, Orlan, *Gómez-Peña) have recently begun to respond to the effects of mass *media and performance on culture and identity through new aesthetics and research in *multimedia performance and *cyber theatre.   MDC

MASS PERFORMANCES

Large-scale Soviet theatrical presentations, usually in the *open air and involving large numbers of participants. Their origins reach back to primitive *rituals and mass festivities, such as the *Greek dramatic festivals, as well as the *medieval theatre's *mysteries and *cycle plays, May Day ceremonies, holiday and *civic festivals. Such presentations began to take on a political coloration in the wake of the French Revolution, and a mass pageant was staged on the Field of Mars in *St Petersburg as early as 1790. In Russia, mass performances were associated with agricultural and harvest festivals in medieval times, but they assumed massive scale and popularity in the wake of the October Revolution of 1917. One of the first of its kind was presented in 1918 by the Red Army in Petrograd in honour of the Third International. In May the following year, Yury *Annenkov staged The Mystery of Liberated Labour, in Petrograd, and this was followed by Towards the World Commune, staged by Sergei *Radlov, Adrian Piotrovsky, Nikolai Petrov, and Konstantin *Mardzhanov on the steps of what had been the Petersburg Stock Exchange.

To commemorate the October Revolution, Nikolai *Evreinov staged the most famous of these mass performances in 1920, The Storming of the Winter Palace, with a cast of thousands and involving units of the Soviet armed forces. The attack on the actual palace was signalled by blank shells fired from the cruiser Aurora moored on the Neva River. A *film was made of this (which still survives) and may well have influenced *Eisenstein's own film October (1926); the fictional reconstruction of the seizure of the Winter Palace is often excerpted in newsreels as if it were *documentary footage. In his home town of Irkutsk in Siberia, Nikolai *Okhlopkov presented a mass *spectacle in the town square, The Struggle between Labour and Capital (1921), and *Meyerhold's direction of *Tretyakov's *montage text Earth Rampant (1923) was re-created as a mass spectacle in the open air on Moscow's Lenin Hills, involving thousands of troops. Meyerhold also planned another mass spectacle, with designs by Lyubov *Popova and Aleksandr Vesnin, Struggle and Victory, which never came to fruition. Evgeny *Vakhtangov

planned to direct episodes of the Bible in an open-air *arena, whilst the tradition of the medieval mystery play informed *Mayakovsky's celebration of the revolution in his play Mystery-Bouffe (which Mardzhanov planned to place on Mount Ararat). Annual May Day demonstrations, and the ceremonial military parades in Red Square each 7 November, kept the tradition alive. So did reconstructions of the wartime defence of Sevastopol in 1961; and the following year in Smolensk the momentous events of 1812 were re-created with all the fervour and pyrotechnics of Tchaikovsky's celebratory overture. See also STATE DISPLAYS.   NW

MASTER OF THE REVELS

English official of the royal household during the sixteenth and seventeenth centuries, responsible for organizing the court's dramatic entertainment, and later for the *licensing and *censorship of plays. The mastership was established as a permanent office with the appointment of Sir Thomas Cawarden in 1545, and, since court performances were lucratively rewarded, carried considerable powers of patronage which helped shape the institutional development of the *London theatre. The corresponding powers of censorship grew during the tenure of Cawarden's successor Sir Thomas Benger, who eventually previewed all plays intended for court performance, and were formalized in 1581 when Edmond Tilney (1536–1610; Master from 1578) was named the official licenser of plays for the realm. Acting companies would routinely submit prompt books for the Master's perusal, along with a fee, and he would return them marked up with any amendments required, and a performance licence written on the back. The principal objective was to delimit plays' *political content, but successive incumbents had other sensitivities too: Sir George Buc (Master 1610–22) excised *satire aimed at courtiers, and Sir Henry Herbert (Master 1623–73) disliked swearing. Although restrictive, the licensing system also gave the acting companies a degree of protection from ad hoc criticism. See also LORD CHAMBERLAIN   MJW

MATERIALIST CRITICISM

A wide umbrella term for forms of *criticism which share a concern with the mode of production of the object under scrutiny; an analysis of the socio-historical relationships between the object, its moment of production, and its moment of reception; and a reliance on the material, or concrete, substance and effects of its existence. The term 'materialism' comes from philosophy, and denotes the belief that matter is the fundamental reality; it is also associated with Marxist cultural theory, from which materialist criticism derives many of its concepts. In practice, materialist criticism offers an account of how works of art make their meanings in relation to the basic economic conditions of their creation, on the one hand, and to the historicoideological struggles surrounding the work on the other. In contrast to formalist criticism, which searches for the enduring features of a work unrelated to context, materialist criticism often explores historical change as productive of new meanings and forms of aesthetic practice.

In the modern period, Bertolt *Brecht, Georg Lukács, and Walter Benjamin laid the groundwork for the applications of these ideas to theatre. An emphasis on the dialectical processes of the relationship between the work of art and society marks their theories, in spite of many significant differences between them. Lukács, while Marxist, is often characterized as Hegelian (therefore idealist) in contrast to Brecht and Benjamin. However, Lukács used the nineteenth-century novel to work out an analysis of the link between the emergence of this realistic genre and the moment in which socio-economic contradictions were producing the bourgeois state. Through his theory of types, which held that *characters stand for both individual experience and also characteristic types of individuals produced in a given period, he provided a dynamic historical basis for understanding *realism. His *Studies in European Realism* (1950) and *History and Class Consciousness* (1972) were outstanding examples of materialist criticism. In his preface to the first book he writes, 'Every great historical period is a period of transition, a contradictory unity of crisis and renewal of destruction and rebirth; a new social order and a new type of man always come into being in the course of a unified though contradictory process.'

It is to Brecht and Benjamin, however, that most theatre scholars turn for their pioneering ideas about materialist culture. Brecht famously wanted art to demonstrate its own mode of production-in-the-making, and Benjamin insisted on the enormous consequences of the new technologies of reproduction, not only for art forms, but also for epistemology in a new age of mass consumption. Contemporary materialist performance criticism almost always returns to one or the other of these revolutionary thinkers. The key texts are Brecht's *A Short Organum* (1948); or, more generally, Brecht's *theoretical writings translated into English by John Willett, *Brecht on Theatre* (1964), and Benjamin's 'Art in the Age of Mechanical Reproduction' (1936). Brecht's emphasis on a theatre which described material conditions in order to change them gave rise to his particular *dramaturgy and style: 'We need a type of theatre which not only releases the feelings, insights and impulses possible within the particular historical field of human relations in which the action takes place, but employs and encourages those thoughts and feelings which help transform the field itself.' For Benjamin, able to foresee and articulate the immense changes technologies of reproduction would bring to the twentieth century, the very conditions of knowing, the apparatus of perception, would also change. 'During long periods of history, the mode of human sense perception changes with humanity's entire mode of existence. The manner in which human sense perception is organized, the medium in which it is accomplished, is

determined not only by nature but by historical circumstances as well.' Reproduction destroyed the aura of the original object and led to an epistemological crisis, which contemporary performance theorists such as Philip Auslander (*Liveness*, 1999) argue has resulted in a totally media-saturated and commodified stage.

Raymond Williams (1921–88) was one of the most influential critics writing in English under the banner of materialist criticism. Responding to changes in the understanding of the relationship of the base to the superstructure (the classical Marxist notion of the subordination of artistic and other cultural practices to the economic base), Williams argued in *Problems in Materialism and Culture* (1980) for a broader understanding of the processes of cultural production and for a new valuation of superstructure 'towards a related range of cultural practices, and away from a reflected, reproduced or specifically dependent content'. Williams was a sociologist who wrote widely on drama, *television, and other *mass media, and has been especially influential in materialist performance *criticism.

In the last decades of the twentieth century, materialist feminist criticism has been one of the most vital and prevalent forms of this critical practice. Sue-Ellen Case (*Feminism and Theatre*, 1988) and Jill Dolan (*The Feminist Spectator as Critic*, 1988) were two early proponents of materialism's contribution to *feminism. Dolan wrote, 'Materialist feminism deconstructs the mythic subject Woman to look at women as a class oppressed by material conditions and social relations.' This view rejects essentialism, stressing that women have been subject to differences of class, *race, and sexuality, which are themselves historically conditioned and subject to change.

A wide range of writing can be considered under the rubric of materialist criticism. As some critics have chosen to distance themselves from classical Marxism, the primacy of class has somewhat given way to an elaborate examination of the concomitant aspects of economic, social, and political life that shape the apparatuses of performance. Following Williams (and also the thought of Antonio Gramsci on hegemony), the instability of social formations and the struggle over particular meanings or 'readings' of performance have been emphasized. Studies that might be considered materialist range in topic from David Román's consideration of the evolution of representations of AIDS, *Acts of Intervention: performance, gay culture, and AIDS* (1998), to Harry Elam's history of the *African-American and *Chicano social protest theatres of the 1960s (*Taking It to the Streets*, 1997). Feminist critics continue to apply and transform materialist analysis, evident in Sue-Ellen Case's *The Domain-Matrix* (1998), treating *lesbian representation and the new cyberculture (*see* CYBER THEATRE), and owing a great deal to both Brecht and Benjamin. Lest these studies seem to limit materialist criticism to issues of identity politics, one might mention that Bruce McConachie's *Melodramatic Formations: American theatre and society 1820–1870* (1992) and Baz

Kershaw's *The Politics of Performance* (1992) also clearly exemplify materialist criticism. *See also* STRUCTURALISM AND POST-STRUCTURALISM.

JGR

McCONACHIE, BRUCE, 'Historicizing the Relations of Theatrical Production', in J. Reinelt and J. Roach (eds.), *Critical Theory and Performance* (Ann Arbor, 1992)

MATHEWS, CHARLES (1776–1835)

English actor and dramatist, the virtual originator of the *one-person show. Mathews made his debut in *Dublin in 1794, rising to become a principal comedian with Tate *Wilkinson's company at York. In 1803 he appeared at the *Haymarket in *London, later acting at *Drury Lane and *Covent Garden, distinguishing himself for eccentric *comedy in a decade when the London stage was blessed with excellent comedians. Many of his parts were especially written for him, but he also played Falstaff in *Henry IV* and Sir Peter Teazle in *The School for Scandal*. Mathews was a superb, protean mimic, and he devised the notion of an entertainment in which he would play all, or most of the parts. The first such entertainment was *The Mail Coach Adventure* (1808), and the idea evolved into a unique series entitled *Mr Mathews at Home*, which he performed in London during the season and the provinces in the summer, as well as in America. These energetic entertainments, to which comic writers contributed scripts tailored to Mathews's talents, featured him as a player of widely different eccentric *characters, quick-change artist, singer of comic songs, speaker of rapid patter, and storyteller. He is sometimes referred to as Charles Mathews the Elder in distinction to his son, Charles James *Mathews.

MRB

MATHEWS, CHARLES JAMES (1803–78)

English actor and dramatist, the son of Charles *Mathews the Elder. Trained as an architect, he did not act professionally until 1835, when he joined Madame *Vestris's *Olympic company, marrying his *manager in 1838. They then assumed the management of *Covent Garden (1839–42) and the *Lyceum (1847–55). Both managements were financially disastrous, and Mathews was twice imprisoned for debt. Vestris died in 1856, and Mathews married the American actress Lizzie Davenport, spending much of the rest of his career—he acted until his death—*touring, both abroad and at home. Mathews was the leading light comedian of his time, although he did not regard himself as belonging to a particular *line of business. On stage he was brisk and lively, with a rapid and distinctly enunciated delivery. Like his father he was an excellent and versatile mimic. These talents showed themselves in his own *farce, *Patter versus Clatter* (1838), which is a virtual *monologue in several impersonations, and his elegant man-about-town Dazzle in *Boucicault's *London Assurance* (1841). Of his nearly 40 plays

he wrote many farces and comediettas for his own inimitable style of performance; when he died his repertory died with him.

MRB

MATKOWSKY, ADALBERT (1857–1909)

German actor, a leading player at the *Berlin Royal Theatre from 1889 until his death from exhaustion. He made his debut in 1877 at the Dresden Court Theatre in classical roles (*Schiller, Shakespeare), which remained the focus of his acting. Strikingly handsome and equipped with a powerful voice, he epitomized the German court actor (*Hofschauspieler*) but had little interest or success in the modern repertoire.

CBB

MATSUI SUMAKO (1886–1919)

Japanese actress in *shingeki*. Born in Nagano prefecture, Matsui entered the *training programme of *Tsubouchi Shōyō's newly created Bungei Kyōkai (Literary Society) and soon appeared with particular success in 1911 as Ophelia in *Hamlet* and as Nora in *Ibsen's *A Doll's House*, a production that made her famous. In *kabuki women's roles are played by men, so that Matsui can be said to be the first actress in the history of modern Japanese theatre. (She had a predecessor in Sada Yacco (1872–1946), a former geisha who performed in bowdlerized Japanese *historical plays in Europe at the turn of the century.) Matsui had a powerful temperament, and her love affair with Shōyō's associate, the writer and director Shimamura Hōgetsu (1871–1918), was the scandal of the decade. The pair withdrew from the Literary Society and began their own company in 1915, when Matsui had her greatest triumph as Katsusha in Shimamura's adaption of *Tolstoy's novel *Resurrection*. Shimamura fell ill and died in 1918; Matsui, distraught, committed suicide a short time later, ending a brilliant if unstable career.

JTR

MATTES, EVA (1954–)

German actress. Although she began working professionally while still at school, Mattes first became widely known for her performance of the handicapped girl Beppi in *Kroetz's *Stallerhof* (Hamburg, 1972). There followed major roles in theatre (Desdemona in Peter *Zadek's *Othello*, Hamburg, 1976) and in *films by *Fassbinder, Hauff, Herzog, and Schlöndorff. She has had a close working relationship with Zadek and is one of the most accomplished actresses of her generation.

CBB

MATTHEWS, BRANDER (1853–1929)

American scholar, critic, and playwright. Raised in *New York, Matthews attended Columbia University and in 1891 began teaching there. In 1902 he became professor of dramatic literature, the first such position in the country. Active as a critic from 1875 until 1895, he wrote for the *Nation*, a liberal weekly. Among his plays were the popular (if now forgotten) *Margery's Lovers* (1884), *A Gold Mine* (1889), and *On Probation* (1889). He wrote over two dozen books on the theatre, including the five-volume *Actors and Actresses of Great Britain and the United States* (with Laurence Hutton, 1883), *Development of the Drama* (1903), *A Book about the Theatre* (1916), *Principles of Playmaking* (1919), and *Rip Van Winkle Goes to the Play* (1926). A founder of the *Players Club, he retired in 1924, having established a place for *theatre studies in the American academy. TFC

MATTHISON, EDITH WYNNE (1875–1955)

English actress. Matthison began her professional career with Ben *Greet's company, playing, among other roles, Portia in *The Merchant of Venice* and Queen Katherine in *Henry VIII*, which she later reprised opposite Henry *Irving (1904) and Herbert Beerbohm *Tree (1916). Her first public acclaim came when at short notice she played Violet Oglander in H. A. *Jones's *The Lackey's Carnival* (1900), but her sustained reputation rested upon classical roles from *Greek *tragedy to Shakespeare. Her success in William *Poel's *London production of the *medieval *morality play *Everyman* (1902)—she played the title role cross-dressed—led to an American performance the same year. Thereafter she spent almost equal time working on opposite sides of the Atlantic. She was married to Charles Rann Kennedy, in whose plays she occasionally appeared, and she worked frequently with Granville *Barker. TK

MATURA, MUSTAPHA (1939–   )

Trinidadian playwright of Indo-*Caribbean heritage. Matura left at the age of 21 for *London, where he has had a highly successful career as a dramatist at the *Royal Court, the *National Theatre, and elsewhere. He writes about Trinidad, as in *Play Mas* (1974), and about the tensions of West Indian exiles in Britain, as in *As Time Goes By*, which won him the George Devine and the John Whiting *awards for the most promising playwright of 1971. His output of over twenty plays includes *Rum and Coca Cola* (1976), about a calypsonian whose relationship with his assistant turns violent, *Welcome Home, Jacko* (1979), which deals with the alienation of West Indian adolescents in Britain, and *The Coup* (1991), a bitterly funny portrayal of a bungled revolution, partly based on the 1970 Black Power uprising in Trinidad. His work has been widely produced in English-speaking countries. He is also a director, and a founder of the Black Theatre Cooperative in London. His interest in the details of West Indian culture was underscored in the production of *Play Mas* designed by Peter Minshall, a well-known Trinidadian *carnival band designer, who drew upon carnival images, espe-

cially in *costume. In 1984 Matura adapted *Synge's *comedy as *The Playboy of the West Indies*, and *Chekhov's *The Three Sisters* as *Trinidad Sisters*. His scripts for British *television include *Bakerloo Line* (1972), the series *No Problem* (1983), and *Black Silk* (1985). AS

MAUDE, CYRIL FRANCIS (1862–1951)

English *actor-manager. One of the best comic actors of the Edwardian period, Maude was adept at light *comedy and in elderly roles. He first appeared in *London in 1886, and in 1890 began his long association with eighteenth-century comedies, playing Joseph Surface in *Sheridan's *The School for Scandal*. He went on to play Sir Benjamin Backbite in the same play in 1890 and 1896, and the ageing Sir Peter Teazle in 1900 at the age of 38. He played opposite Charles *Wyndham at the Criterion and George *Alexander at the *St James's in the 1890s. Between 1896 and 1905, together with Frederick Harrison, he *managed the *Haymarket Theatre, reviving *Goldsmith's *She Stoops to Conquer*, Sheridan's *The Rivals* (both in 1900), and *Colman and *Garrick's *The Clandestine Marriage* (1903), as well as appearing in plays by *Barrie and H. A. *Jones. After 1913 he went on extended *tours of North America and Australia with occasional returns to England, and went into semi-retirement in 1932. VEE

MAUGHAM, SOMERSET (1874–1965)

English writer. Most of Maugham's tightly constructed *comedies, like his novel *Of Human Bondage* (1915), depict enslavement to marriage and society. He had early success with lightweight comedies, with four running in the West End in 1908. *Penelope* (1909) and *The Unattainable* (1916) were directed by the younger Dion Boucicault. In *The Circle* (1921), his most revived play, a young woman on the verge of leaving her stodgy marriage comes into contact with her mother-in-law, who had deserted her own husband, with subversive romantic results; Rex *Harrison starred in a 1989 Broadway revival. *The Sacred Flame* (*New York, 1928; *London, 1929) deals with euthanasia, while *For Services Rendered* (1932) pessimistically examines England after the First World War by focusing on one family. In *Sheppey* (1933), adapted from his own short story 'A Bad Example', a lottery-winning barber models himself after Christ while his family plot to have him committed. The play's bitterness and its mixture of comedy, social commentary, and *allegory confused *audiences and critics alike, and Maugham stopped writing plays. GAO

MAUVOIS, GEORGE (1922–   )

Martinican playwright, best known for biting social *satires such as *Agénor Cacoul* (1966) and *Misyé Molina* (1988). His works use both French and creole, and his translations and adaptations, such as his creole version of Molière's *Don Juan* (1966), have done much to enhance the standing of creole theatre. Many of his plays have not been produced, though they have all been published. *See also* CARIBBEAN THEATRE, FRANCOPHONE.

AR

MAY, ELAINE (1932–)

American actress, director, and playwright. May began performing as a child with her father, the *Yiddish actor Jack Berlin. After studying *acting with Maria *Ouspenskaya in *New York, she moved to *Chicago where she met Mike *Nichols. With others, they formed an *improvisational theatre group in 1954 at the Compass Theatre (a forerunner to Second City). The two refashioned themselves as the comedy duo Nichols and May, moved to New York in 1957, and achieved quick fame after *television appearances. In 1960 they created a successful stage version, *An Evening with Mike Nichols and Elaine May*, which they revised and performed off and on until 1965. May also wrote three plays: *A Matter of Position* (1962), *Not Enough Rope* (1962), and *Adaptation* (1969), which she also directed. Primarily a screenwriter since then, she appeared with Nichols in a revival of *Who's Afraid of Virginia Woolf?* in 1980 at New Haven's *Long Wharf Theatre.

JAB

MAYAKOVSKY, VLADIMIR (1893–1930)

Russian/Soviet poet, dramatist, painter, propagandist, and co-founder in 1913 (with David Burlyuk and others) of the Russian *futurist movement. That same year he made his stage debut at the Luna Park Theatre, *St Petersburg, in his own *'tragedy', *Vladimir Mayakovsky*, in a double bill with Kruchonykh's futurist extravaganza *Victory over the Sun*. In 1917 he was one of only four artists, including *Blok and *Meyerhold, to answer *Lunacharsky's call to artists and writers to rally in support of the Russian Revolution. Mayakovsky and Meyerhold between them staged what has become known as 'the first Soviet play', *Mystery-Bouffe* (St Petersburg, 1918), with decor by Kazimir Malevich, in which Mayakovsky played the role of 'Man, Pure and Simple' (Chelovek Prosto). He subsequently revised the play for a production in honour of the Third Communist International, staged by Meyerhold in 1921. Like Meyerhold, Mayakovsky was drawn to traditional forms of *popular entertainment such as the medieval *mystery play, *commedia dell'arte*, *pantomime, and *circus. Although most of his energies during the 1920s were devoted to writing poetry and acting as spokesperson for LEF (the Left Front of the Arts), he found time to write short propaganda plays for circus performance as well as *film scripts. He had previously starred in three films during 1918, one of which, *The Lady and the Hooligan*, remains extant. In 1928, Meyerhold persuaded Mayakovsky

to return to dramatic writing. His *satire on the New Economic Policy period and the new Soviet bourgeoisie, *The Bedbug*, with music by Shostakovich for firemen's band (1929), got a mixed reception, even seeming anti-Soviet to some critics, while his dystopian satire on future prospects for the Soviet Union, *The Bathhouse* (1930), although written and staged in a genuinely comradely spirit, proved too much for his major antagonists, who included members of the Association of Proletarian Writers, an organization which Mayakovsky had recently joined. A combination of overwork, hostile *criticism, a failed love affair with a Russian émigrée in *Paris, and an apparently increasing sense of disillusionment with the direction the Russian Revolution was taking led him to shoot himself.

NW

MAYAKOVSKY THEATRE

Situated on Herzen Street in *Moscow, it began life in 1922 as the Theatre of the Revolution and was briefly headed by *Meyerhold. Between 1931 and 1935 it came under the direction of Aleksei *Popov and was then managed by a *collective. In 1943 it was rechristened the Moscow Theatre of Drama, headed by Nikolai *Okhlopkov, and renamed the Mayakovsky Theatre in 1954; after Okhlopkov's death in 1967, Andrei Goncharov assumed artistic control. The theatre played an important role during the period of glasnost in bringing productions to places like *London's Royal *National Theatre, which demonstrated the Soviet Union's willingness to be frank and open about hitherto suppressed aspects of the nation's past. Goncharov's production of *Tomorrow Was War*, invited to London in October 1987, surprised *audiences and *critics alike with its revelations about Stalinist oppression and the extent of Soviet losses in the Second World War.

NW

MAYO, FRANK (1839–96)

American actor, *manager, and playwright. Born to Irish immigrants in *Boston, Mayo sought his fortune in California's gold fields of the early 1850s, but found his way onto the *San Francisco stage. After supporting such *touring stars as Laura *Keene and Junius Brutus *Booth throughout California, he returned to Boston as a leading man in 1865. While he played Shakespearian roles opposite such stars as Edwin *Booth, his greatest initial success came as Badger in *Boucicault's *The Streets of New York*. In 1872 Mayo secured the rights to Frank *Murdoch's *Davy Crockett*, the play that gave him his signature role for more than two decades. He eventually felt trapped by the role that made him famous, but a chance 1894 meeting with old friend Mark Twain led to Mayo's enormously successful adaptation of Twain's *Pudd'nhead Wilson* (1895), which he was touring when he died.

GAR

MA ZHIYUAN (MA CHIH-YÜAN) (1260–1325)

Chinese playwright. Ma was ranked among the finest dramatists of his age and fully half of his sixteen known *zaju* plays have survived in complete or partial versions. Suffused with an otherworldly outlook, his work tends to stress the futility of fame and fortune. Ma collaborated with actors affiliated with the court entertainment bureau on the *Yellow Millet Dream*, the sort of deliverance play that may have been performed on *ritual occasions at local temples or at court. For early Ming imperial drama enthusiasts, Ma's work was admired because it resonated with their own interest in Taoist immortality, while in the late Ming the literati approved his handling of the conflict between private sentiments and public duty. The definitive literati *zaju* anthology, *The One Hundred Yuan Plays*, gave pride of place to Ma's tale of love lost to political exigency, *Autumn in the Han Palace*, and included six of his other plays, including *Yellow Millet Dream* and *Tears on the Blue Gown*.

PS

MBARI CLUBS

Nigerian arts institutions. The Mbari Club in Ibadan, founded in 1961 (and partly funded through the CIA), was a meeting place for artists, an organization for publishing ventures, and a venue for performance. Travelling theatre troupes performed there and in 1962 Wole *Soyinka directed both *Brother Jero* (1962) and *Clark-Bekederemo's *Song of a Goat* there. Other Mbari Clubs followed, including Mbari Mbayo in Oshogbo (1962). Mbari Mbayo saw the première of *Ladipo's first *opera, *Oba Moro* (*Ghost-Catcher King*), and subsequently his *Oba Koso* and *Oba Waja*. As in Ibadan, the premises were a point of contact between artists of various kinds, particularly painters and performers.

JMG

MBOWA, ROSE (1943–99)

Ugandan actress, director, and playwright. She began her career with the Makerere Travelling Theatre in the 1960s. After an MA from Leeds she worked for *Serumaga's Abafumi Theatre, Radio Uganda, and Jimmy Katumba before becoming director of the department of music, dance, and drama at Makerere University. Her most influential play is *Mother Uganda and her Children* (1987) about Uganda's devastation through ethnic politics and the rebuilding of the nation on the principles of cultural diversity. She produced *Mine by Right* for the investigations of human rights violations, and works with her students in a variety of theatre for *development projects. She was last seen on stage as Mother Courage in a Luganda adaptation of *Brecht's classic (*Maama Nalukalala Ne'zzade Lye*).

EB

MDA, ZAKES (1948–)

South African playwright, novelist, and artist. Born in the eastern Cape, he lived in Lesotho from 1963. He has written many literary and theatre for *development plays which call for community social action, particularly with the Lesotho-based Maratholi Travelling Theatre Company, foregrounding the complexities of southern African issues. In 1978 *We Shall Sing for the Fatherland* won his first Amstel Playwright of the Year Award, which he won again in 1979 for *The Hill*. Other plays include *Dead End, Dark Voices Ring* (both 1979), *The Road* (1982), *And Girls in their Sunday Dresses* (*Edinburgh Festival, 1988), *Joys of War* (1989), and *Broken Dreams* (1995). *The Nun's Romantic Story* (1995), about the relationship between Church and state in an unnamed *post-colonial country, has been performed in South America as well. He also wrote *Banned* (BBC *radio, 1982), *The Final Dance* (a 'cinepoem'), and the textbook *When People Play People: Development Communication through Theatre* (1993).

YH

MEADOW, LYNNE (1946–)

American director and *manager, *artistic director of the *Manhattan Theatre Club since 1972. Her directing credits include Charles Busch's *The Tale of the Allergist's Wife*, Donald Margulies's *The Loman Family Picnic*, and Alan *Ayckbourn's *A Small Family Business*, the first play MTC co-produced specifically for Broadway (1992). When Meadow took over MTC at the age of 24 it was a struggling *Off-Off-Broadway theatre in the Bohemian Club, on the Upper East Side of *New York; under her leadership it has become a successful *Off-Broadway theatre with many Broadway transfers. Meadow's mentor was Joe *Papp; like him she nurtures new playwrights and offers a home to established writers; her directing style is considered insightful and unobtrusive. She has been the recipient of many *awards.

GAO

MECHANE

A large crane used by 435 BC in the Athenian Theatre of *Dionysus for the sudden airborne entrances of divinities or the magical transportation of tragic and para-tragic comic *heroes. *Euripides was said to rely excessively upon the 'god from the machine' (*deus ex machina*) for the resolution of his plots.

EGC

MECKLER, NANCY (1941–)

American director. Meckler pursued a freelance directing career in England from the late 1960s, founding Freehold Theatre Company, and moved on to be associate director for *Hampstead Theatre and the Leicester Haymarket. In 1981 she became the first woman to direct a mainhouse production at the *National Theatre (*Albee's *Who's Afraid of Virginia Woolf?*). Since 1988 she has been the *artistic director of Shared Experience, making highly physical and actor-based productions of classic drama and literary adaptations, including co-directing world *tours of *The Mill on the Floss* and *Anna Karenina*. For *film she directed *Sister my Sister* (1994) and *Alive and Kicking* (1997).

KN

MEDIA AND PERFORMANCE *see page 825*

MEDICINE SHOW

Itinerant presentation composed of huckstering, crude salesmanship, and quack remedies, practised largely in America during the nineteenth century. Taking advantage of a rural and poorly educated population, and a cultural inclination for the new-found benefits of science, charlatans and mountebanks travelled the American *frontier selling balms, elixirs, and medicinal salves claiming to cure all maladies. Travelling alone or with small companies, they attracted potential customers by performing brief sketches, comic scenes, and *magical feats, often from the back of a wagon. The form developed a discernible structure by the end of the century, combining elements of *minstrelsy, *Chautauqua, *vaudeville, and lecture to create a simple *variety show. Independent operators were the norm, presenting short acts and selling home-brewed concoctions. But there were larger operators as well, who dealt in mass-produced products and carefully mounted productions. Among the biggest manufacturers were Hamlin's Wizard Oil Company of *Chicago, the Kickapoo Indian Medicine Company of New Haven, and the Oregon Indian Medicine Company, each sponsoring elaborate road shows. With the promulgation of the Pure Food and Drug Act in 1906, followed by the establishment of the Food and Drug Administration in 1923, medicine shows declined in popularity, replaced by *film and commercially sponsored *radio shows.

PAD

MEDIEVAL THEATRE IN EUROPE

1. Dramatic forms and genres; 2. Biblical plays; 3. Morality plays; 4. Staging: principles and practice; 5. Modern revivals

1. Dramatic forms and genres

Drama usually serves to reinforce the beliefs and customs of its *audience, and medieval drama was no exception. At the most basic level *folk plays affirmed the continuity and future well-being of the community, by enacting life-affirming *rituals like the death and resurrection of the spirit of the corn, or the triumph of spring sunlight over the darkness of winter, while 'lords of misrule' were appointed to supervise winter revels that briefly inverted and mocked authority to reaffirm its importance by its temporary withdrawal: for instance a boy bishop from the choir would replace his superior for a day during which the sacred ceremonies and teachings of the Church were often shamelessly mocked by the clergy. These rituals were certainly theatrical because they displayed important aspects of life using *characters, often *masked, that symbolized forces which profoundly affected people's lives. However, it is doubtful whether such performances yet contained the element of tension which would render them dramatic.

There were similar celebrations of a courtly kind—civic *entries, *mummeries, and later *disguisings and *masques—which are sometimes grouped together as *the theatre of social recreation*. These reaffirmed the values of aristocrats and rich townsmen rather than peasants. The civic entry greeted a monarch returning from a great victory or the successful wooing of a foreign princess. It was an occasion when no expense was spared, and the streets were decorated with triumphal arches and platforms from which the grateful citizens addressed flattering speeches to their ruler as he passed, while the city fountains often flowed with wine. Mummeries were the courtly version of the 'first footing' at New Year when strangers representing Dame Fortune arrived to play a dice game (mumchance) with the owners of the house, the dice being weighted so that the owners would always win the prize, and thus confirm their future good luck. After this there would be social dancing, at which the ambassadors of Fortune always danced apart from the householders.

Later came the disguisings, like those presented at Westminster Hall by Henry VII on the occasion of the marriage of his eldest son Arthur to Catherine of Aragon in 1501. These involved two groups of aristocratic dancers, one male and the other female, who entered the hall accompanied by elaborate pageants representing mountains, ships, or castles. The *action of disguisings was limited and always symbolic. For instance, the men from the ship would besiege the ladies in the castle and eventually lure them out, symbolizing successful courtship. Then the two groups would mingle to perform the latest and most fashionable dances, after which the floor was thrown open for social dancing, though again the disguisers did not mingle with the spectators. However, soon in Italy the spectators and performers were allowed to mix, and this converted the disguising into a masque, and led to a freedom of intercourse between young people that scandalized some of the older spectators. In England, predictably, it was Henry VIII who introduced this innovation during the Christmas of 1512.

At any important banquet, the guests might be treated to a dramatic *dance or rudimentary *ballet. For instance, at the famous Feast of the Pheasant given by the Duke of Burgundy in 1454, a piece was presented which gave an account of Jason's

(continued on p. 826)

MEDIA AND PERFORMANCE

The relation of recording and electronic media and live *performance is complex and has helped to reconfigure perceptions of performance as strictly a live and present phenomenon. Their convergence has led to the development of *multimedia theatre, which combines various media in a single work, and *cyber theatre forms, which incorporate new media and computer technologies with some element of live performance. Thus both the *theory of performance and the practice of theatre have been greatly altered by the effects of media. In turn, theatre and *performance art are offering useful analyses and critiques of the ways in which media construct culture and identity.

The effects of media on culture and subjectivity are profound. The *mass media, whose network of electronic, *televisual, *film, *radio, and print constructs a datasphere of information flow surrounding the world, are the primary apparatus for the spread of globalization, multinational capitalism, and the 'Americanization' of culture. World culture is subject to a mediated colonialism in which multinational capital delivered through the media creates world consumers in a hyper-commodified exchange system. The media are both the channel for capitalism, but also the product. As Marshall McLuhan argued, the medium is the message. The delivery of information through the mediated signs of live video and electronic data streams is marked by its speed and simulation of the real, which allow for certain manipulations of the ways in which events are represented. The real becomes subject to the technologies of representation of the media. In addition, vigorous systems of surveillance are present worldwide adding a new dimension to the levels of control inherent in mediatized cultures.

In technologized cultures human subjectivity is undergoing similar changes as individuals with access to the media flow view, collect, and at times interact with the information. Theorists such as Haraway, Avital Ronell (*The Telephone Book*, 1989), and N. Katherine Hayles (*How We Became Posthuman*, 1999) have articulated the ways in which new models of identity are activated in mediated environments. Haraway uses a 'fictive theory' of the cyborg to argue that the old boundaries of biology and *gender are circumvented in technologized culture. Ronell suggests that there is no off switch to technology and thus we must answer its call. Hayles argues that even within a posthuman culture, which is driven by the development of televisual and virtual technologies, embodiment and materiality matter and inevitably form the basis of any cultural construction. The consensus is that in virtual and electronic environments,

identity is liquid and the presentation of the self assumes a freedom of *performativity unknown in previous generations.

The ontology of performance and the nature of 'liveness' in mediatized cultures was widely discussed during the 1990s in Western academic circles. Peggy Phelan (*Unmarked*, 1993) argues that performance is defined through its non-reproducibility. Performance happens only once, disappears, and is unrecordable. When recorded, performance is no longer performance. The essence of performance corrupts as it is engaged in technological reproduction. Philip Auslander disputes Phelan, suggesting that the live is an artefact of mediatization. Liveness exists not as a prior condition, but as a result of mediatization. The theses of Phelan and Auslander mark the cornerstones of contemporary debate on the nature of performance in technologized cultures, yet both are problematic. Phelan disregards any effect of technology on performance and draws a non-negotiable, essentialist border between the two media. Auslander's material theory and legalistic argument overlooks the most material aspect of the live, namely death.

The theoretical debate on performance and the changes in culture and identity under the influence of mediated technologies (including speed, ubiquitousness, and surveillance) demands a theatre vocabulary capable of responding to and critiquing these phenomena. Performance has traditionally been bounded by its temporal and spatial configuration of the here and now: in other words, its presence. The supplementing of live performance with mediated technologies of representation creates a system which can alter the spatio-temporal system through being present and absent simultaneously. What is created in contemporary mediated performance is a theatre which mimics or embodies the tropes of media by incorporating its technologies. Much of the highly mediated performance works of contemporary artists and companies such as Stelarc and Company in Space (both from Australia) and the *Wooster Group (USA) foreground the possibilities of live performance to interrupt the flow and control of media with embodied and politicized information. The performance artist Stelarc creates performative sculptures of hybrids of human and machine, which interface with electronic and Internet communications. Control of the performance is often in the hands of telepresent spectators linked through computers, or from a self-contained technological response system reading the information flow of the Internet. The body is present yet not in control—it is only an element, not the centre of the performance. The stages of the Wooster Group and Company in Space include live and mediated performers. Neither the biological nor machine performer is offered privilege over the other. The technological and the biological signify uniquely and remain discrete, but are placed within a *mise-en-scène that denies a fully human focus.

The collision of embodied information in live performance and the technologies of mechanical reproduction suggests that even as identity is subsumed and altered within the dominant and repressive representation of media, the body is still resistant and the material persists, and performance is the manner in which it is presented. However, in the final analysis, it may be that in the convergence of media and performance neither has priority and the distinctions of mechanical reproduction and live presence are as suspect as gender and *race differences. *See also* MODERNISM AND POSTMODERNISM. MDC

AUSLANDER, PHILIP, *Liveness: performance in a mediatized culture* (London, 1999)
HARAWAY, DONNA, 'A manifesto for cyborgs: science, technology and socialist feminism in the 1980s', *Socialist Review*, 15 (1985)

quest for the golden fleece. Here we have the introduction of the narrative element essential to *drama. When such pieces became longer in France and began to employ elaborate *costumes and *scenery, they were called *ballets du cour*, but the simpler early versions generally tended to be grouped together with disguisings under the general title of *moriscos*.

Other forms of social recreation became dramatic by containing an element of identification that could create tension. For example, the *tournament, which was originally a simple battle exercise, gradually evolved into a social occasion, with elaborate introductions for the competitors, particularly in Italy, where they would often be wheeled in triumphally on elaborate pageant wagons, wearing decorative armour which was so heavy that it had to be exchanged for more practical equipment before the jousting began. Then, at tournaments in France, the *pas d'armes* appeared where, in imitation of the knights of Charlemagne or Arthur, a challenger would ride into the hall and proclaim that he would hold a ford, or a well, or some other perilous passage against all comers for the love of his lady—or, if he was playing a *villain, he would challenge the knights present to defeat him and release a lady whom he was holding captive. Everybody would then repair to the tiltyard, where a wooden castle or some other appropriate device had been erected, and the principal knight would be challenged to combat by various opponents. After the tournament there would be a grand banquet in the hall with dancing and other entertainments, and the lady of the castle would award prizes to the most successful competitors. In the *pas d'armes* we have the introduction of either a *hero, whom the audience want to win, or a villain whom they want to lose.

There was also one type of professional drama that had outlasted the fall of the *Roman Empire. This was the *farce, which continued to be played by troupes of travelling players called *mimes who roamed Europe, as they had done ever since Greek times, playing to *audiences at markets, fairgrounds, archery contests, and tournaments, and sometimes even at the local monasteries, despite their reputation for *satirizing the clergy. Some of these travelling entertainers expanded their performances by teaming up with minstrels, whose heroic recitals were the favourite pastime of the Romans' barbarian successors, and these became known as *jongleurs, but many of them chose not to. These 'usual masked players', as one Beverley observer calls them, probably continued to perform farces throughout the whole medieval period, but we lose sight of them from about 960 until the late twelfth century, when we once again have descriptions of French jongleurs acting the parts of drunkards, fools, and whores. Then in the late thirteenth century scripted farces begin to appear, like the three-handed English piece called 'The Interlude of the Clerk and the Maiden', which involves a clerk, a maiden, and Mother Heloise, who advises the young man on how to get the girl to sleep with him. Later, in the fifteenth century, came the French *sotties (fooleries) where jesters in fools' costumes raised riotous laughter by sharp satirical sallies, and similar performances, known as *Faschinge* or *Fastnachtsspielen* (*carnival comedies), occurred in Germany.

Against this background of general entertainments, a new serious drama slowly developed, for which the age is best remembered. This consisted essentially of two branches. First there were *biblical plays, which began with simple episodes sung and enacted in Latin to accompany the daily services (*liturgical drama) and ended with large-scale presentations on public holidays of selected material from the Old and New Testaments delivered in the local language (*Passion plays, Creed plays, or *cycle plays). Later came the other main dramatic development, *morality plays, sometimes strongly influenced by farces, which cast a spotlight on the everyday shortcomings of humanity, and generally illustrated a standard of behaviour acceptable to the Church. These new forms of theatre served to instruct and emotionally engage the audience and reinforce their faith in the standards established by their leaders. They were fully theatrical in their use of costumes, *props, staging, and structural scenic items, and fully dramatic because they contained characters with whom the audience identified and whose adventures therefore enabled the dramatist to manipulate the story to produce the rising and falling patterns of tension that drama usually requires.

2. Biblical plays

By the early ninth century the continued use of classical Latin, which most people now found difficult to understand, began to cause daily services to lose their impact. This worried many senior churchmen, and Amalarius, the bishop of Metz, attempted to counter the decline by promoting a more dramatic rendering of the mass by the priests who presented it. This proved very popular and it was not long before drama itself began to appear on a small scale in the major religious establishments, where a relevant biblical incident would be enacted either before or after the service on the occasion of important holy feasts, to make the occasion more vivid. (*See* BIBLICAL PLAYS.) This simple liturgical drama was based around tropes—musical treatments of prose passages written in simple Latin that were used to make what was happening clear to the congregation. The earliest trope to be dramatized was the *Quem Quaeritis, which was sung at Easter. The Latin words mean 'Who are you looking for?' and they occurred in an enactment by clergymen of the visit of the two Marys to the sepulchre on Easter morning. A simple structure representing the sepulchre was usually erected near the altar and this contained the chalice and paten holding the wine and bread, which represented the newly sacrificed body of Christ (the Host). These had been consecrated before Easter but withheld from the congregation as a mark of mourning for Christ's death. The two clergymen representing the Marys approached the sepulchre, where they were greeted by another clergyman playing an angel with the words, 'What are you looking for in the tomb, Christian women?', to which they replied, 'Jesus of Nazareth who was crucified, heavenly one.' 'He is no longer here,' declared the angel; 'He has risen as he predicted. Go! Proclaim the news that he is risen from the tomb.' The Host was then brought out of the structure to symbolize the Resurrection and the Marys proclaimed, 'The Lord has truly risen, alleluia!' The earliest surviving version of this simple play dates from about 925 and comes from the monastery of Saint-Martial at Limoges, but it was soon being replicated at important religious centres all over Europe, and by about 970 the version used by the Benedictine monks at Winchester already contained instructions to help the actors with their performance. By the end of the tenth century, versions of the *Quem Quaeritis* trope were being used on Christmas Day, when the angel's question was, 'Who are you looking for in the manger?' and at the festival of the Ascension when the question was 'Who have you just seen ascending to the stars?'

It was at Christmas and not Easter that more developed plays first began to appear, probably because Christ's birth was not so solemn an occasion as the Resurrection and the writers felt less constrained. In the eleventh century the Christmas trope developed into a play where three clergymen, representing the shepherds, travelled up from the west end of the church to the altar to visit the manger—probably the same structure that had been used for the sepulchre—which now contained an image of the Virgin and child, or sometimes a living actor holding a doll. To this was added a play of *The Wise Men (Magi)*, on 6 January, representing the visit of the Three Kings to worship Christ, and a play about King Herod and the slaughter of the innocents which was performed on 28 December, the traditional date of the massacre. Later the first play appeared that ran a number of separate incidents together, combining the Three Kings' visit to King Herod with the adoration of the Christ child in the manger by both kings and shepherds. This play must, for the first time, have freed the performance from the date of a specific festival.

Towards the end of the eleventh century a new piece appeared called *Ordo Prophetarum* (*The List of Prophets*), based upon a popular sermon which itemized the prophecies that anticipated Christ's birth. Each prophet was represented by a separate clergyman who stepped forward, delivered his prophecy, and then retired. The twelfth century at last saw a shift of dramatic focus from Christmas to the central festival of Easter. Now the Marys' visit to the tomb (*Visitatio Sepulchri*) frequently acquired the Virgin Mary's lament on her way to view her son's body, and her triumphant affirmation of his sacrifice after his Resurrection. To this were added related incidents, such as Mary Magdalene's lamentation at the loss of her beloved Saviour's body, the meeting where she mistakes him for the gardener, the race of John and Peter to the tomb when they hear that Christ's body is no longer there, and, on the Continent, the Marys' visit to an ointment seller (*unguentarius*), from whom they purchase spices to help preserve Christ's body—the first non-biblical incident.

In the following centuries the material covered by liturgical plays expanded to include additional incidents from both the Gospels and the Old Testament, such as the raising of Lazarus, where Christ's recall of Lazarus from the tomb was always seen as an anticipation of his own Resurrection; or the story of the three Jewish children who were thrown into the burning fiery furnace by Nebuchadnezzar and preserved by a godly figure who joined them there (identified by Christians with Christ). These incidents can all be seen as demonstrations of Christ's power and his constant concern for mankind. Later still other material was used, such as an account of the Virgin Mary's Presentation at the Temple as a young child, taken from the apocryphal Gospels.

The next development, in the latter part of the twelfth century, was the appearance of plays in the vernacular, the language of the people, instead of Latin. These dealt with selected material from the Old and New Testaments and were usually performed outside the church building. They can be seen as elaborations of the two 'lessons' read in the daily service to broaden the congregation's awareness of biblical history. They were selected and arranged in several ways. In France, Italy, and Catholic Germany the plays concentrated mainly upon the Gospel accounts of Christ's Passion (suffering); in Protestant Germany and particularly England they often reviewed the history of salvation as a cycle; and in any of these countries a shortened version of the Passion and Last Judgement might be achieved by presenting episodes that illustrated clauses of the Apostles' Creed (a Creed play).

Behind all these forms lay the idea, borrowed by Christians from the Jews, that God had a plan for Man—to allow him to show his obedience by the exercise of free will. First, the revolt of Lucifer, the brightest of the angels, against his creator introduced the possibility of wrongdoing into the world. This enabled Adam's obedience to be tested. He failed the test by eating fruit from the forbidden tree with the encouragement of his wife Eve, and they were both cast out of Paradise. Man's sin deepened with Cain's murder of his brother Abel, and eventually God prepared to destroy all mankind with a flood, but preserved the obedient Noah and his family. Noah's descendants soon began to sin again, but when Abraham was ordered by God to sacrifice his only son, he proved loyal, and at the last minute God substituted a ram for the boy. God then caused his own son to be born to the Virgin Mary, who by his self-sacrifice on the cross taught men the way to escape sin and death through faith and obedience, and he was appointed to return on the Last Day to judge mankind and assign the persistent sinners to hell and the truly good to heaven.

The most complete treatment of this theme was in the English cycle plays. Study of the *texts from Chester, York, and Wakefield, and the 'N-Town' cycle (which is probably from Bury St Edmunds), together with a list of plays from Beverley, has revealed that there were two principles that governed the material chosen: first, *figura* (reflection), which is best described as an anticipation or echoing of some aspect of Christ's life which is found elsewhere in biblical history; secondly, the division of biblical history into a number of ages, each of which is heralded by a great spiritual leader.

Examples of *figura* already existed in the biblical material. Noah's preservation of his family in the ark was seen as a prefiguration of Christ preserving the faithful from the flood of damnation on the Last Day within the structure of the Church—the comparison is made by Jesus himself. The additional comic figure of Mrs Noah, who squabbles with her husband and refuses to enter the ark, is seen as a reflection of the disobedient Eve; but when she enters the ark (the Church) she becomes wholly obedient, like the Virgin Mary. Similarly, Abraham's readiness to sacrifice his only son is seen as a prefiguration of God's free gift of his own son to save mankind, and Moses' leading of God's chosen people out of Egypt is compared with Christ leading his own chosen people out of the state of sin into salvation. God's instruction to kill and eat a pure lamb and mark the doorposts with its blood so that the Angel of Death will pass over the house during the last plague is compared to the sacrifice of Christ, the lamb of God, the eating of his body and blood (the bread and wine) in the mass, and the power of his blood to save mankind.

The alternative idea of seeing biblical history as a series of ages came originally from St Matthew, who found that there seemed always to be fourteen generations between the important events in Jewish history—the birth of Abraham, the birth of King David (Christ's ancestor), the Babylonian Captivity (then the most miserable event of Jewish history), and the birth of Christ. St Augustine tried to extend this system by using the records in the book of Genesis, but without success. However, he noticed that in the generations listed there, Noah fell exactly midway between Adam and Abraham, and he observed that all three of these men were presented with a 'covenant' or contract by God, although Adam broke the agreement by his disobedience. This led Augustine to propose a system of seven ages, echoing the seven days of creation, which were heralded respectively by the births of Adam, Noah, Abraham, David, the Babylonian Captivity, the birth of Christ, and Christ's Second Coming to judge mankind. This remained more or less the norm, except that later Moses was substituted for the Babylonian Captivity which had no great leader, while King David tended to slip back into the *List of Prophets*. The two concepts of *figura* and 'ages' reinforced the 'God's plan' pattern and provided it with extra coherence. In several cycles apocryphal stories of the life and ascension to heaven of the Virgin Mary were added to the sequence as a kind of post-figuration of Christ's life and Ascension.

The principles of *figura* and ages were recognized on the continent of Europe too, but most of the dramatists there had much less interest in presenting historical cycles, and from the very first the vernacular plays tended to be biographical accounts of Christ's life with emphasis upon his Passion and very little use of Old Testament material. For example Arnoul *Greban wrote a huge Passion play in which only 1,500 lines out of 30,000 dealt with the Old Testament, and those covered only *The Creation*, *The Fall of Man*, and *The Murder of Abel*.

Large-scale *open-air presentations of vernacular plays seem to have grown up quite quickly during the early fourteenth century, mainly as a result of Pope Clement V instituting the new feast of Corpus Christi (the Body of Christ) in 1311, although many communities preferred to perform the pieces at Whitsun. The feast of Corpus Christi arose because Christianity was passing through a phase when the common people felt starved of the presence of Christ by the excessive mediation of the priesthood, and the Pope wanted to defuse the situation by parading the Host round the streets for all to see before it was taken into the church. Since this was an outdoor festival a date in summer was chosen—the Thursday after Trinity Sunday—and the feast was a great success, attracting large and elaborate parades in the cities, which involved the mayor, the council, and representatives of all the trade *guilds and local religious foundations. Banners or models representing incidents from the Bible, like Noah's ark, were usually carried in these processions, and some of the participants dressed up as biblical figures.

It was not long before the parades became the most important part of the festival, and it seems that as a result the banners and models began to be replaced by plays in some of the more important towns, although the evidence is fragmentary. From at least 1313, the Parisians were using actors in living tableaux to tell the story of the Passion. Speech is first found in Innsbruck in Austria in 1391 where Adam, Eve, the Disciples, the Prophets, the Three Kings, and others delivered 30 short speeches which seem ideally suited to being presented during the procession at prearranged stopping places. By 1394 complete plays were being performed on pageant wagons in York. (*See* CORPUS CHRISTI PLAYS.)

The remarkable and sudden explosion of all kinds of religious drama in the fourteenth century may well have been accelerated by the presence of the Black Death, which first appeared in Europe in 1347 and destroyed a quarter of the population by 1350. Many performances of religious cycles or passions were first staged as an act of thanksgiving for delivery from the plague. Ironically, it also made such performances possible, because the shortage of skilled labour it created gave the trade guilds a stronger bargaining position and made them rich, and the presentation of religious plays at Corpus Christi or Whitsuntide was a good way for them to thank their Saviour for his kindness, repay the townspeople for their support, and display their wealth and importance.

The performances of vernacular plays continued until they were deliberately suppressed. This occurred in England at the time of the *Reformation at the hands of zealots like Matthew Hutton, the dean of York, who considered the plays popish propaganda and therefore gathered in the manuscripts for 'revision' and did not return them. Cities were forbidden to present the plays and when they continued to do so, to benefit their innkeepers and publicans, mayors were called before the authorities to justify their action. On the Continent, the Passion plays came into question at the Counter-Reformation, partly because the Catholic Church did not want to be associated with material that now seemed childish and outdated, but much more because of a running fire of opposition from the Calvinists. Calvinists controlled most of the big city councils, which is why the Freiburg Whitsun play and the Nuremberg Good Friday play were banned after 1523, and why, in 1548, we find the *Paris *parlement* forbidding the city's Brotherhood of the Passion (*Confrérie de la Passion) from presenting any sacred *mysteries. This trend had spread to most towns in France by 1565. In Catholic areas of Germany, however, some biblical plays continued to be performed until 1770 when the archbishop of Salzburg suppressed those remaining—with the single exception of the play at *Oberammergau (a very late piece dating from 1634) which was saved by the personal intervention of the Emperor Maximilian.

3. Morality plays

Plays analysing and investigating moral subjects were an important and popular form of drama in both the late Middle Ages and the *early modern period. Like biblical plays they taught

that God had given every man the free will to choose between good and evil, and they fulfilled the basic functions of a sermon: to advise by good example, to dissuade people from sinful behaviour by showing what might happen if they did not reform, and to encourage them to examine their own lives.

The first moralities were simple exemplary pieces about the lives of saints, which are known as *miracle plays, and show the saints' triumphs over temptation and persecution, but the later *morality plays were distinguished by the use of *allegory. Their characters personified a wide range of internal and external forces that influence the life of man, such as *political and *religious institutions (kingdom, Church, synagogue), social classes (nobility, merchants, peasants), mental and moral faculties (soul, wit, wisdom), sinful impulses (lust, envy, covetousness), virtuous impulses (faith, hope, love, mercy), and other abstract concepts (truth, justice). This made possible the analysis of many situations ranging from current political problems to the moral life of the average citizen, or from the effect of a particular moral failing, like malicious gossip or gluttony, to the way in which one should prepare oneself for death, by confession and repentance.

However, most moralities are centred around an 'Everyman' figure who undergoes a process of spiritual death and resurrection. This pattern is first seen in a piece called *The King of Life* in the early fourteenth century, where King Life arrogantly challenges Death to a duel and is slain, after which his Soul is first seized by devils, and then saved by the Virgin Mary who intercedes for him, after which he is allowed to ascend to heaven. This kind of play, with its pattern of fall and redemption, develops into either large-scale moralities dealing with the whole life of man, which are broken up into a series of ages, each threatened by its own particular sin—youth by lechery, middle age by pride, age by covetousness—or moralities dealing with just one particular age and its related sins. Often the Seven Deadly Sins are invoked as a paradigm of the shortcomings to which mankind is subject.

Morality plays started as substantial community plays with a wholly serious purpose, but when they fell into the hands of professional actors in the fifteenth century they soon became shorter and introduced humorous and bawdy elements, including a central comic character called the Vice who was leader of the sins and embodied many of them himself. They were useful plays for small professional troupes to perform because many of the characters could be *doubled. The central Everyman character was worked upon alternately by sins trying to tempt him to damnation and virtues trying to bring him to heaven and, since these forces never directly met, each of the other actors could double up as a sin and a virtue, playing two characters. By the sixteenth century, moralities, now called *interludes, were usually quite short and seem to be thought of mainly as entertainments to accompany a banquet. Professional productions of moral interludes disappeared at the time when permanent companies like Shakespeare's began to perform in *London, which suggests that they could not compete with the new drama. They continued to be written, however, for *amateurs to perform in schools and universities until about 1610 (see UNIVERSITY AND SCHOOL DRAMA).

The great appeal of morality plays, in comparison with the biblical plays, was their unpredictability. The audience knew that good deeds would be rewarded and bad deeds punished, but they never knew whether the central character would succeed in making his act of repentance in time, and this enabled the authors to create dramatic tension. Sometimes the audience could be surprised by a central character who did not even try to reform: in one late French piece a son murders his parents for their money and remains unrepentant to the end. Moralities can be very powerful in performance still. The serious scenes provide strong visual images and provoke reflection, while the comic scenes provide a constant display of new characters and are very entertaining, so it is not surprising that they had a considerable effect on the emerging Elizabethan drama.

4. Staging: principles and practice

The staging of medieval drama had a very simple objective, to get its message over to the audience. To do this it always tried to achieve clarity and leave the spectators with memorable images to match those painted on the church's walls or worked into the stained glass of its windows. The images also drew upon a sense of symbolism, which had become instinctive to medieval people.

For instance, liturgical plays used the church building as their *playhouse, and its structure was seen to possess a spiritual dynamic. On the main axis lay first the high altar to the east, which represented heaven and the Resurrection; then came the cross formed by the junction of the two transepts with the body of the church, which was often referred to as 'the centre of the church' and was where actors representing the Christian community gathered; next came the nave, which was often called 'Galilee', and was considered a very worldly space; and finally there was the great western door, which was viewed as the gateway to death and hell, with the lobby beyond it, if there was one, representing the grave. The axial significance was combined with a lateral one which gave specific meaning to the north and south sides of the church. When the priest officiated at mass in the early church he stood behind the altar table facing the congregation, representing Christ at the last supper. The north side of the church, which lay on his right hand as he faced westwards, was considered good, and the south side, which lay on his left hand, was considered bad, because the ancient Romans believed that the left (sinister) hand was ill-omened.

This dichotomy was usually reflected in performances. An example is a twelfth-century play from Rouen called Peregrinus (The Pilgrim) about the meeting with Christ on the road to Emmaus. Here the house at Emmaus was represented by a platform in the centre of the nave, with a table and chairs upon it. The two subdeacons playing disciples entered from the 'worldly' western door and, not yet knowing that Christ had risen, advanced slowly up the southern, negative side of the nave. A priest representing the risen Christ then entered from the western door, which in his case represented the sepulchre, and advanced up the positive, northern side of the church. They met at the centre of the nave, where Christ told the disciples about the Resurrection. They invited him to share their meal and all three of them mounted the platform representing the house. As Christ took and blessed the bread, they recognized him. At that point he suddenly stepped back and vanished—in fact, a contemporary woodcut shows him tiptoeing away eastwards towards the altar. The two pilgrims followed him and encountered a priest representing the Virgin Mary at the centre of the church together with the choir, who represented the other disciples. She showed them the winding cloths from the grave and proclaimed that Christ had risen, and they all retired eastwards to the altar singing songs of praise.

Everything in the presentation of liturgical drama was achieved as simply as possible. A platform was usually provided in the nave for the main action and a large chair placed on this could represent a throne, or the spice-seller's shop, or even a town like Jerusalem. The costuming of the pieces was achieved by modifying the usual clerical vestments. The actors might shed their outer cope to represent poverty or humility, or carry a wallet and staff to show that they were travelling. They might wear an amice knotted round their head to look like a woman's headscarf, or don a richly embroidered dalmatic robe to imply their importance, but all was achieved with the minimum of fuss.

The *acting, on the other hand, seems to have been thoroughly rhetorical, according to the instructions in a thirteenth-century text from Cividale del Friuli. The actors underlined the meaning of what was said with large, clear, symbolic gestures, and often actually pointed to what was being spoken about—the actor himself, Christ, the cross, the wound in Christ's side, and so on. Other texts imply that at less serious moments villains could act rather more realistically, but the style involved was still large and pantomimic.

The staging of vernacular plays was more complex and could be very elaborate. One play from the latter part of the twelfth century, called the Seinte Resurrection (Holy Resurrection) has detailed instructions about staging which make the method employed quite clear—and it is a method that we find used in all presentations that are not acted upon wagons. The principle employed is décor simultané, or simultaneous staging. This involves having all the locations that a play will need visible from the beginning, with the actors moving between them as necessary. In the Seinte Resurrection the text clearly establishes three different types of location: 'places' (lius) where

The setting for the first of the 25 days of performance of the Valenciennes mystery play in 1547, one of a series of illustrations made 30 years later by Hubert Cailleau, who had designed the production. With heaven on stage right (i.e. to the left of the picture) and hell mouth on stage left, this arrangement for simultaneous staging also shows mansions identified as Nazareth, the Temple, Jerusalem, Pontius Pilate's palace, the Sea of Galilee, and limbo, among other locations.

things happen; 'stations' (*estals*) where groups of characters stand when they are not directly involved in the action; and 'houses' (*mansions) which are areas containing a structure, like the sepulchre, or Christ's cross. The layout is semicircular, consisting of five mansions, and observes the principle of stage right and stage left being respectively good and evil, as do most medieval settings. The cross stands centrally at the back of the curve. To its left, on the sinister side, stands first a prison, and then, nearest the audience, *hell. To its right is first the sepulchre counterbalancing the prison, and then the mansion of *heaven, counterbalancing hell. In front of each of these houses is a station. In front of heaven stand the good Joseph of Arimathea and Nicodemus, in front of the sepulchre stand the disciples and the Marys, in front of the prison stand Caiaphas and a party of Jews, and in front of hell stand Pontius Pilate and his knights. Nobody originally stands in front of the cross, but there are two places in front of it where important actions occur, one nearer to the audience than the other. In this way a spiritual plan identifying the moral roles of each of the characters is presented to the audience from the very beginning of the play.

When we come to the historical cycles, it is only possible to give examples of the most common ways in which they were presented. A circular arrangement was popular, probably because people naturally gather around anything of interest. Often the performance took place in a 'round' or 'playing-place', where bulls and bears were *baited and wrestling matches occurred.

These were common in towns and villages all over Europe; the *Cornish mystery plays, for instance, were presented in a large, well-built round. Alternatively a special arena could be created. *The Martyrdom of St Apollonia*, dating from about 1460, shows a semicircular arrangement of high scaffolds topped with mansions. Richer members of the audience and musicians have seating interposed between the mansions occupied by the actors, or share the mansions with them, while the poorer people sit on the ground below the scaffolds. The main action is plainly occurring in the central acting area, or 'place' (from Latin *platea*, 'a flat area'). Heaven and hell are in their usual opposed positions, with the Emperor, whose throne is vacant because he is currently involved in the central action, set midway between them. What is on the side we are looking from is not shown. However, the arrangement is more likely to have been circular than semicircular, and it is probable that St Apollonia's mansion was on a scaffold facing the Emperor, contrasting spiritual with earthly power. A 'styteler' or 'stickler' (a marshal carrying a white rod of authority) seems to be prompting the actors, even though it is a performance. Members of the audience were inclined to invade the platea, and to stop this we often find it ringed round with a low hedge or palisade or even sometimes by a ditch full of water, while the round as a whole often seems to have been surrounded with a high wattle fence to exclude those who had not paid an entrance fee. (*See* illustration on p. 908.)

A drawing of the Valenciennes mystery play of 1547 shows the various houses arranged in a single row on a long platform. As usual, heaven is on stage right, and on stage left is an elaborate *hell mouth, which could open and close its jaws, with a prison behind it where the souls of the righteous pre-Christians are waiting to be saved by Christ when he 'harrows' hell. In between these extremes lie three other structures: the Jewish temple to right of centre, with the Muslim crescent on it (because Christians tended to lump all their enemies together); Pontius Pilate's judgement hall in the centre, with a prison below it; and to the left a large cistern of water representing the Sea of Galilee with a real boat upon it. Between heaven and the temple are a row of hurdles representing the sheepfold at Bethlehem. A few alterations were made to this setting on the other 24 days of performance, but they were minor. *The Play of St Lawrence* (*Laurentius*) at Cologne in 1581 reveals an interesting later development, where all the mansions and plateas are located on a high scaffold which is enclosed at the back and sides, suggesting a trend towards the picture-frame stage that was soon to arise in Italy, although this show has no *proscenium arch.

Then there were large-scale presentations in market places, like the two-day event in the wine market at Lucerne in 1583. This was an impressive show using the whole square. Heaven was on the balcony of a large house at the eastern end, with Paradise below it. The western end was occupied by a large platform, which carried the manger on the first day and witnessed Christ's trial on the second. To stage left of the platform was an elaborate hell mouth. On the north (the good) side was the table where the Last Supper took place, and on the south the Jewish temple with its usual Islamic crescent. In the middle of the square were altars for the sacrifices of Cain and Abel and Abraham's sacrifice of Isaac, a house for the Annunciation near heaven, Moses' golden calf on a pillar, and so on. Action on the first day moved basically westwards towards the manger, and on the second day basically eastwards towards heaven, with the Crucifixion occurring on the spot where Adam ate the apple. Seating was provided for the richer members of the public, probably behind the western stage, but it is possible that non-seated members of the crowd physically followed the actors from place to place, and gathered around them and, if the seating was high enough and the marshals prevented the people from crowding too close, this should not have blocked the sitters' sight lines.

An alternative to these set pieces, in some of the richer cities, was the presentation of the plays on *pageant wagons, as happened at York, Chester, and Wakefield. The wagons are described as 'very large and high' with an enclosed lower section in which the actors dressed themselves. They seem to have been pushed around the city from one playing station to another, each pageant following the one before it as the next playing station became available. It is likely that the performance did not take place solely upon the wagon, for there is evidence from Chester and Coventry that wheeled scaffolds were driven out to the playing places and pitched there the day before the performance, and the pageants probably drew up behind these platforms allowing the actors to perform on them. This may explain why one of the York wagons had hangings for the back and sides of the pageant, which suggest that it was mainly a decorative back piece to the platform where the action occurred. Stands for the public were also erected at the playing places and presumably people paid for seats on them, because at York the right to build them was auctioned off to the highest bidder, the money going to help defray the costs of production. Sometimes there were many pageants involved. At Chester there were 24, each shown at four or five stations in the town over the course of three days, which seems reasonable, but at York there were at least 48, each reputedly shown at twelve or more stations in a single day. This seems most unlikely in view of the fact that, with only about two dozen pageants at Coventry, the concluding *Doomsday* could not be played at the first station in 1457 for lack of light.

The evidence suggests that both the pageant wagons and the set-piece stagings were elaborately finished. French records show that only the most expensive materials were used and that skilled craftsmen were involved at every stage, and descriptions of the English pageants include items like wainscot panelling, which required oak imported from Russia. In any case, one of the city guilds took responsibility for each pageant and they would not want to show anything that was shoddy, particularly on a public occasion when there were large crowds present, including representatives from other cities. So we may safely assume that each guild hired in specialists from other guilds to do the painting, cloth-hanging, carriage-building, and so on. This may have been one reason why each guild tended to perform a play in which their craft was significant. For instance, the goldsmiths would present *The Magi* because of the kings' golden gifts, the bakers and vintners *The Last Supper* because of the food and drink, the armourers', cutlers', bowyers', and fletchers' plays involving armed men like *The Betrayal of Christ*, and the skinners' *The Fall of Man* because of the fine-leather body-suits that Adam and Eve wore when 'naked'.

In many productions *trapdoors and tunnels were used to make characters appear and disappear, and allow souls to rise at the beginning of the *Doomsday*, while pageants sometimes had lifts to carry God up and down. On the Continent quite elaborate machinery was sometimes used, involving heavens that revolved, clouds that rose and fell and opened up to show the actor, and rockets that travelled down wires to set model buildings on fire, representing lightning from heaven. Music was used more sparingly in these outdoor performances than in the church, but it was certainly important. The local organist and choir would provide the heavenly music, and the city's official band would provide fanfares for kings and emperors and the unharmonious accompaniment for devils. One continental director also wrote an instruction warning the band to be ready to fill in if there was any hold-up in the action.

The costumes seem to have been very colourful, and the colours were often symbolic, such as white and black for good and evil, red for passion, yellow for wealth, and blue for good reputation. Actors would also wear or carry emblems that defined their function—the King or Emperor his crown, St Peter the keys of heaven and hell, the risen Christ a small cross, Death his dart, and Justice a sword. Many of the simpler costumes were provided by the actors themselves, but the more elaborate costumes of kings, emperors, devils, and angels would be commissioned from the local tailors and cutters' guild, and any hats from the cappers. These special costumes were carefully guarded during *rehearsals and performance because they had to be returned to the guild wardrobe after the show. It is not clear which guild would provide the 'heads' (masks), but these were certainly used for devils, and often for King Herod, who seems to have been presented as an ogre. A golden mask was also sometimes used for God.

Occasional hints suggest that the acting of the historical biblical plays was more *realistic than that of liturgical drama. There must, however, still have been a large rhetorical aspect to it, partly because it was being delivered in the open air to a large and noisy crowd—which tried the patience of some medieval *directors—and partly because the objective was to leave the audience with a number of posed visual images, like Eve offering the apple to Adam, Noah steering his ark with his family beside him, and Christ on the cross with John and the Virgin at its foot—the same moments of frozen high drama that we see in so many Renaissance paintings.

Some care was taken to ensure that the actors were competent. At York, for instance, one or two experienced performers were appointed to *audition all those who were to be involved. In a pageant presentation these would usually be members of the guild presenting the pageant, who were paid for their services, but in other productions it would be any citizen who was interested and willing to give time for free. However, there were fines at York for actors who forgot their lines or did not make themselves heard clearly. The use of rhyme helped here, because it makes lines more memorable, and the audience would more easily pick up the verbal echoes. We have evidence of a number of semi-professional producers who were paid to present plays for guilds other than their own, and also of semi-professional actors who played several parts and were therefore presumably skilful. This will have helped greatly because most of the plays were put on with only one or two rehearsals, usually held in the early morning before work began.

The responsibility for production was often taken over by a local 'Brotherhood of the Passion' which had been formed specifically for the purpose—particularly on the Continent—but there were always 'commissioners' or pageant masters appointed as well to keep a check on expenses. The money to mount the performances came from many sources: the city council, taxes levied on guilds or the citizens, a proportion of the tithes gathered by local churches and religious communities, gifts from wealthy citizens, house-to-house collections, bring-and-buy sales, and so on. There were, however, occasional cases of private enterprise like the show at Valenciennes, which was expensive to mount, but actually made money for its backers.

The large-scale early moralities were staged in the same way as the popular religious plays. For instance we have a contemporary diagram and detailed instructions for the staging of *The Castle of Perseverance* in the form of a round. The notes show the castle standing on long legs in the middle of two concentric circles. Between the circles is written: 'This is the water about the Place, if any ditch may be made where it shall be played; or else that it be strongly barred all about . . .', suggesting that the play was intended to be *toured. Outside the two concentric circles, stressing the fact that they enclose the platea, the position of five scaffolds is marked: heaven to the east, the unspiritual world to the west, Belial (lust) to the north, and the corruptible flesh to the south, while to the north-east is the scaffold of Covetyse (Covetousness) an especially important character. Most of the action takes place in the centre, on or beneath the Castle, but characters also travel out from the centre to the different scaffolds and return, or vice versa. The playtext, which has also been preserved, reveals that this piece, like the cycle plays, was a communal effort involving a large number of performers.

Later pieces written for professionals, like *Mankind*, show a very different pattern. The play needs only five performers, and could easily be produced by travelling players on a simple booth stage, raised on trestles and backed by a curtain through which the actors could make their entrances and exits—a type of stage that became popular at about the time the play was written. Only one actor needs to double—Mercy, the friar, who advises Mankind at the beginning and saves him at the end, clearly doubles with the devil Tittivillus, who leads him astray, and the actor is given plenty of time to don his new clothes and an impressive mask while the sins move amongst the audience collecting money to persuade the devil to reveal himself, thus implicating them in the mischief which is to come.

Many professional pieces involved much more doubling, and this had the advantage of constantly presenting the audience with new characters, despite the small size of the company. The popular morality pattern that involves a central Everyman character, who is first assailed by sins and then helped by virtues, allows each of the other actors to play a sin and a virtue by turns. As mentioned above, the exception was the Vice, where he exists, who was usually too busy to double his role, though he

The Last Judgement in a contemporary performance of the York cycle of Corpus Christi or mystery plays, on a stationary stage set before the ruins of the abbey in York, 1988. One of the chief promoters of the revival of medieval theatre, the city of York presents selected plays from the cycle at regular intervals.

might provide a *prologue and *epilogue. The actors' changes of costume offstage were covered by either the Everyman character reflecting on his fortune or, more entertainingly, by stand-up comedy from the Vice. Changing costume openly on stage had a different meaning, suggesting a change of attitude in the character involved, as in *Mankind* where the central character's sensible cloak is progressively cut down to a fashionable cape which cannot even keep him warm.

When professional moral interludes were presented at banquets, they were originally acted in the centre of the hall, with or without the benefit of a stage, but later they were sometimes performed on a narrow transverse stage that spanned the hall with an audience on both sides, or more often on a low platform set up in front of the doorways to the kitchen area, which were curtained and became entrance points for the actors. There was usually a musicians' gallery above the doorways and this was occupied by the more important members of the audience, while the rest sat round the stage below—arrangements that anticipate the Elizabethan stage. In both this form of presentation, and on the *booth stage, making entrances from the back of the acting area simplified the staging and usually freed

the action by removing the need for specific mansions, although one play of *Susannah and the Elders* had a simultaneous setting that spread out to include the whole hall. Though the comic acting in morality plays seems to have remained broad and farcical, the actors' performances in the professional pieces must have required subtler interpretation because of the closeness of the audience. In such a context, however, it was also possible to present more complex speeches, because the actor could be more easily heard.

5. Modern revivals

It was the Oberammergau play that brought about the modern revival of medieval drama, which seems to be mainly an Anglo-Saxon preoccupation. With the rise of tourism after 1850 the play's ten-yearly performance became a focus for pious visitors, who were greatly impressed by its solemnity and good taste, and the fact that it was mounted by 'simple God-fearing peasants'. By that time the play had been extensively rewritten, and the eight-hour performance occurred on a specially built *neoclassical stage, with a Greek-style *chorus which sang its words to *Mozart-like melodies, using tableaux from the Old Testament

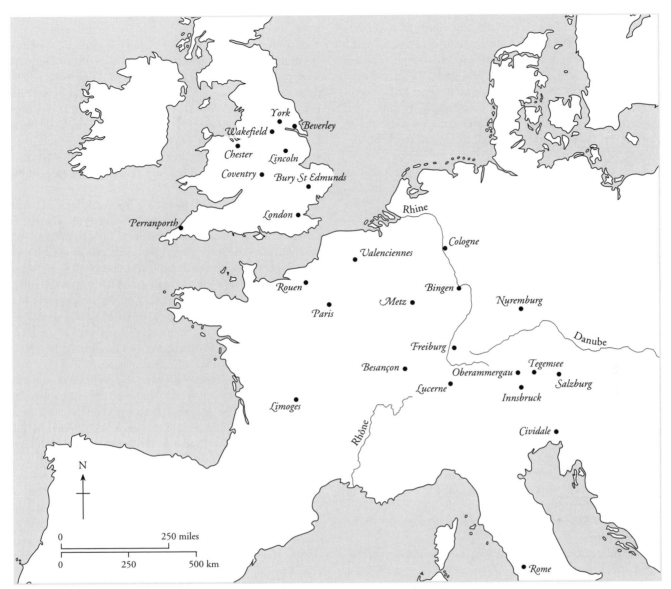

Major locations in England and Western Europe for the performance of biblical and other plays in the medieval period.

to precede each of its eighteen *acts, and words taken directly from the Bible. The scourging and nailing occurred behind a *curtain which was then drawn to reveal Christ on the cross, and the staging deliberately reflected the great Italian painters. While the English cycle plays were seen as vulgar and indecent and quite unproduceable, there were proposals to imitate the Oberammergau play in England or even transport the complete production from Bavaria. Any such move was resolutely opposed by the *Lord Chamberlain, then the *censor of plays, who eventually ruled that neither God nor Jesus might appear on the stage or take a speaking part. America, with no censor, produced an imitation of the play at the *San Francisco *opera house in 1879, but not without protest.

William *Poel was the next stimulus. In 1901 he produced *Everyman*, which had not been seen on stage since the late fifteenth century, for the *Elizabethan Stage Society, together with *The Sacrifice of Isaac* from Chester. Since this was a private performance by a society for its members, the censor had no power over it. The 'appearance' of God as a voice offstage caused some comment, but the production was very reverential, although *Isaac* was generally judged unworthy of performance. In 1909, Nugent Monck, a disciple of Poel, prepared to present a selection of plays from the N-Town cycle, then wrongly associated with Coventry, on the public stage, but he was arrested before the show could begin and the performance was stopped. By 1929, though, attitudes had radically changed and the Religious Drama Society was formed, under the presidency of George Bell, bishop of Chichester, who in 1930 appointed E. Martin *Browne as director of religious drama for the diocese. By that time many churches were presenting Nativity plays from the cycles, and in 1931 Browne produced the plays dealing with the life of the Virgin from the N-Town cycle in the garden of the bishop's palace.

For the Festival of Britain in 1951, the government encouraged cities to revive their plays. Chester produced its cycle in the cathedral and, more importantly, York made its plays the central element of what was to become a four-yearly *festival. The first production used professional actors in the main parts, and a professional production team headed by Browne. The plays were staged against the ruins of a former Benedictine abbey in the museum gardens, which provided arches at a high level that could be used to frame some scenes, while houses were constructed below them to back the rest. The general inspiration of the staging was the play at Valenciennes. In subsequent years innovations were made to this setting, which became increasingly more modern, and some producers introduced *Brechtian effects which aroused local opposition. In 1969 the city council took over the festival and since then all the roles except Christ have been filled by local amateurs, although the production team remains professional.

Processional productions on wagons were slow to arrive, though they had been pioneered by Jane Oakshott in Leeds,

using the York cycle, as early as 1975. In the early days at York a single play on a pageant wagon had often accompanied the festival, but it was not until 1988 and 1992 that several plays were performed in this way, and it was 1994 before a wholly pageant-based production of the plays took place at some of the original sites in the city. This was so successful that it was repeated in 1998, being partly financed by the city guilds who had asked to be involved. A special millennial performance of a version of the plays took place in York Minster itself in 2000, but this had to rely very much on visual impact because of the difficult acoustics.

Chester has produced its cycle at five-yearly intervals since 1951. Complete productions of the N-Town cycle occurred at Coventry in 1962, and of the Wakefield cycle at Bretton Hall near Wakefield in 1967. Since 1969 a selection of the N-Town cycle has been given in or around Lincoln Cathedral, and since 1980 the Wakefield cycle has been presented at its home town. Most strikingly, a production of the Cornish cycle of plays (the *Ordinalia*) was given in 1969 by Bristol University's drama department in the large and impressive 'round' that still exists at Piran near Perranporth, with mansions erected around the playing area in the traditional medieval manner.

Productions of cycle plays have also occurred on the professional stage for many years. The most impressive was the performance of *The Mysteries* from York, adapted by Tony *Harrison into modern Yorkshire speech and directed by Bill *Bryden, at the Royal *National Theatre in 1985, which later transferred to the *Lyceum. The plays were presented as 'people's theatre' in a *promenade performance, the venue was decorated with objects associated with the rural and industrial working classes, like oil-heaters, lanterns, pitchforks, and dartboards. The audience stood or moved freely around the area in which the plays took place, and the actors moved through them, clearing their own spaces in which to perform. Adam and Eve played naked, but the rest wore modern clothes; God, in particular, wore overalls and a hard-hat for *The Creation* and was elevated on a fork-lift truck. A repeat production of these plays was mounted in 2000.

William Poel's *Everyman* revived an interest in morality plays as well. It had a woman, Edith Wynne *Matthison, playing the central role, and an elegant Pre-Raphaelite style of presentation that appealed to contemporary audiences. The production was later promoted by Charles *Frohman and proved very successful both in America and England, though the presence of God in the play presented problems, which were overcome sometimes by screening him with latticework and sometimes by making him a voice offstage. Max *Reinhardt was greatly impressed by *Everyman* and had the poet Hugo von *Hofmannsthal prepare a German version, called *Jedermann*, that he staged in front of the cathedral when he established the *Salzburg Festival in 1920. It subsequently became an annual event.

A new impulse was given to morality plays in Britain by the success of Tyrone *Guthrie's production of *Ane Plesant Satyre of the Thrie Estatis*, translated into modern Scots, at the *Edinburgh Festival in 1948. This is a vigorous and very funny political morality, written in 1540, in which Johne the Common Weill eventually wins out over the Establishment (Temporalitie), Business (Merchant), and the Church (Spirituality), the latter being shamelessly mocked. In 1966 the Poculi Ludique Societas (Society of Drinks and Plays) was founded at the University of *Toronto as the by-product of a seminar. Since then it has engaged in a very ambitious set of medieval revivals using amateur players, performing moralities, cycle plays, and interludes. In 2000 it was a successful independent company with a website. In England, the Medieval Players were formed in the early 1980s, and toured productions of moral interludes and other early dramas with great success, mostly to universities, enhancing their productions with excellent early *music, and sometimes—more questionably—with stilt-walking, fire-eating, and other *circus acts, but sadly this lively company is now defunct.   JWH

BEADLE, RICHARD (ed.), *The Cambridge Companion to Medieval English Theatre* (Cambridge, 1994)

ECKEHARD, SIMON (ed.), *The Theatre of Medieval Europe: new research in early drama* (Cambridge, 1991)

ELLIOTT, JOHN R., *Playing God: medieval mysteries on the modern stage* (Toronto, 1989)

HARRIS, JOHN WESLEY, *Medieval Theatre in Context* (London, 1992)

ROSSITER, A. P., *English Drama: from early times to the Elizabethans* (London, 1950)

TYDEMAN, WILLIAM, *The Theatre in the Middle Ages* (Cambridge, 1978)

MEDINA, LOUISA (c.1813–38)

Spanish-American playwright. Little is known of Medina's life outside a five-year period from 1833 to 1838, when she produced numerous successful plays. Born in Europe, she emigrated to the United States in 1831 or 1833, quickly establishing herself as an able theatrical adapter and working most often for Thomas S. Hamblin, the *actor-manager of *New York's *Bowery Theatre. Medina's three published plays—*The Last Days of Pompeii* (1835) and *Ernest Maltravers* (1838), both adapted from novels by *Bulwer-Lytton, and *Nick of the Woods* (1838), derived from Robert Montgomery *Bird's novel—reflect her versatility. Ranging from classical *spectacle to European domestic *melodrama to *frontier adventure, the plays suggest a writer whose success was grounded in her ability to meet the Bowery *audience's tastes.   GAR

MEDWALL, HENRY (fl. 1495)

English playwright. Medwall was chaplain to Cardinal John Morton, archbishop of Canterbury, and both of his *interludes are assumed to have been performed at the Great Hall at Lambeth, where the young Thomas More also served. *Nature* (c.1495), a *morality play in two parts, retains the conventions of the form, including the fall and redemption pattern and *farcical vices. Of more interest is *Fulgens and Lucrece* (c.1497), the earliest extant secular play in English. In it a debate on birth versus worth between Lucrece's two suitors in ancient Rome is made relevant to Medwall's aristocratic *audience through the device of a framing *plot featuring two pages who emerge from the audience, not only to comment on the action, but to take part in a comic parallel wooing of Lucrece's maid. Both plays are indebted to the popular theatrical tradition and were probably performed by professionals.   RWV

MEE, CHARLES L. (1938–   )

American playwright and historian. In the middle of a career as an editor and an author of books on American political history, Mee resumed an interest in theatre in 1986 when he provided the *texts for Martha *Clarke's *Vienna Lusthaus*. He went on to create a series of radical reconstructions of *Greek *tragedies or modern classics that led to collaborations with such experimental directors as Anne *Bogart, Robert *Woodruff, Tina Landau, and David Schweizer. Inspired by the collage techniques of Max Ernst and Robert Rauschenberg, Mee often borrows excerpts from wide-ranging sources and includes them verbatim in the *dialogue of his plays. Productions at *New York Theatre Workshop and En Garde Arts led to relationships with a number of *regional theatres, including *Steppenwolf and *American Repertory Theatre, each of which produced *Full Circle*, Mee's take on *Brecht's *Caucasian Chalk Circle*. *Actors Theatre of Louisville premièred two of his plays, *Big Love* (2000), which went on to the Next Wave Festival at the Brooklyn Academy of Music, and *bobrauschenbergamerica* (2001) written for Bogart's SITI Company.   STC

MEI LANFANG (MEI LAN-FANG) (1894–1961)

World-famous Chinese actor of *jingju (Beijing opera). Beginning his career as a *qingyi* ('black robe' or singing female) at the age of 8, Mei had become one of the chief actors of the *dan* (female) category before he was 20. After 1915 he gradually formed his own style through reforms in singing, *costume, and *make-up, and by creating his own repertoire. He also merged the once rigid division between *qingyi*, pantomime (*huadan*), and dance and acrobatic (*wudan* and *daomadan*) roles. The result was a new category he called *huashan* (colourful robe). In 1927 Mei was chosen the best *dan* actor in *China by popular vote. He made three *tours to *Japan between 1919 and 1924, and in 1930 he performed in the USA for about half a year, including two months on Broadway. His 1935 tour to the Soviet Union received high praise from *Stanislavsky, *Meyerhold,

*Eisenstein, and *Brecht. Some scenes from his repertoire were captured on film during these tours. During the Sino-Japanese War Mei remained in Hong Kong; when the Japanese occupied the city in 1942 he grew a moustache and abandoned the stage. He returned to China and resumed performance after the war.
SYL

MEILHAC, HENRI (1831–97) AND LUDOVIC HALÉVY (1834–1908)

A prolific partnership of *Parisian playwrights under the Second Empire; during their long joint career they wrote journalism, novels, and more than 50 plays and librettos. They are now mainly remembered for the lively and witty librettos for *Offenbach's *operettas, including *Orpheus in the Underworld* (Halévy alone, 1861), *La Belle Hélène* (1864), *La Grande Duchesse de Gérolstein* (1867), and *La Vie parisienne* (1867). They also wrote a successful *tragicomedy, *Froufrou* (1869), in which Sarah *Bernhardt had great success; and Halévy wrote the libretto for Bizet's *Carmen*. W. S. *Gilbert adapted *Les Brigands* and *Le Réveillon* (as *On Bail*).
EEC

MEININGEN PLAYERS

German theatre company. Although the court theatre in Meiningen, a small town in Thuringia, was founded in 1831, the fame of the Meiningen players (known in Germany as 'Die Meininger') is linked with Duke Georg II of Saxe-Meiningen (1826–1914), who assumed direct responsibility for the company in 1870. Under his direction, a provincial court theatre developed into one of the most influential theatres in Europe in the late nineteenth century. His first reform had been the abolition of *opera four years earlier so as to concentrate resources entirely on drama. Although the Duke did not assume the official position of *director—this task was carried out by Ludwig *Chronegk—his control of central aspects of production effectively made him one. His overriding artistic principle was historical authenticity in the manner of *historicist painting (*see* ANTIQUARIANISM). To achieve this end, he conducted extensive research into the cultural, historical, and archaeological context of the plays to be staged. Innovations in staging techniques included *realistic *sound effects and the creation of a three-dimensional stage with a system of steps and rostra to create more dynamic spatial arrangements for crowd scenes. Another innovation was the creation of a true ensemble, in which even famous actors had to take turns playing smaller parts. The Meiningen Players demonstrated their new style on extended *tours throughout Europe. Between 1874 and 1890 they visited 38 cities and gave a total of 2,591 performances. Their influence was considerable, particularly on the *naturalistic theatre of the

1890s. Their admirers included Henry *Irving, Otto *Brahm, André *Antoine, and Konstantin *Stanislavsky.
CBB

MEISL, KARL (1773–1853)

Austrian playwright. Meisl was a Slovenian, who studied philosophy in Laibach (Ljubljana), before moving to *Vienna where he worked in the War Department until his retirement. He belonged to a group of dramatists that included Adolf *Bäuerle and Joseph *Gleich who wrote for the Viennese popular theatre after the Congress of Vienna (1815). Between 1818 and 1830 he wrote on average seven plays a year. He became famous for his brilliant settings of classical myths in modern Vienna and *parodies of serious drama. Most of his plays feature a comic figure, an updated successor of *Hanswurst, who holds together the loosely structured *scenes. Due to their strong local flavour, very few of his plays were performed outside Vienna.
CBB

MEISNER, SANFORD (1905–97)

American *acting teacher who exerted wide influence. A native of Brooklyn, Meisner studied traditional approaches to voice and movement at the *Theatre Guild School of Acting and made his Broadway debut with the Guild in 1924. Sensitive and idealistic, Meisner joined the *Group Theatre in 1931 and studied the competing interpretations of *Stanislavsky taught by Lee *Strasberg and Stella *Adler. Like Adler, Meisner distrusted Strasberg's use of 'emotional memory' and developed his own methods centring on pursuit of an *action in relation to another person. For Meisner, a focus on action liberated the actor's instinct for truth. On the wall of his classroom at the *Neighborhood Playhouse in *New York, where he taught from 1935 to 1959 and 1964 to 1989, were the mottoes, 'Act before You Think' and 'An Ounce of Behavior Is Worth a Pound of Words'. Meisner's students included *film actors Joanne Woodward, Gregory Peck, and Robert Duvall, and playwright David *Mamet.
MAF

MELBOURNE

Although this city has produced two of the biggest names in Australian playwriting—Ray *Lawler and David *Williamson—initially the emphasis was not on home-grown theatre. Theatre in Melbourne began to flourish as the city grew in size under the influence of the gold rushes of the mid-nineteenth century, and stars from abroad performed as part of their *tours of Australasia. Some localized work was produced, such as *Marvellous Melbourne* (1889), a *melodrama featuring many city locations, and the premières of *The Sunny South* by George Darrell (1883) and *Robbery under Arms* by Alfred Dampier and Garnet Walch (1890). The tendency for Melbourne talents such as Nellie Melba and Geelong-born Oscar *Asche to depart for work, fame, and fortune overseas was repeated many times, although both Melba and Asche returned on star tours to their homeland.

The fight to produce distinctively Australian drama, as opposed to accepting imports from the UK or the USA, was initially taken up by *amateur groups such as the Pioneer Players, founded in 1922 by Louis *Esson, Vance Palmer, and Stewart Macky, who sought to follow the example of the *Abbey Theatre, *Dublin, in fostering the work of home-grown and nationalistic playwrights. Gregan *McMahon's Melbourne Repertory Theatre Company tended to produce *Ibsen, *Chekhov, and *Shaw, but also found space for Australian plays. For over 30 years of the late nineteenth and early twentieth centuries, however, Melbourne theatre was dominated by J. C. *Williamson, an American-born entrepreneur who promoted star tours, and who held there was no market for plays about Australia. Away from the glossy production values of Williamson's commercial tours, pioneering work was done by amateur theatres such as the New Theatre, a left-wing theatre group founded in the 1930s to present the best of international, *politically committed theatre, as well the work of local playwrights.

Melbourne's professional theatre received a great boost early in the 1950s when the Union Theatre Repertory Theatre, initially part of Melbourne University, began its transition into a fully professional theatre company (renamed the Melbourne Theatre Company or MTC in 1968). This company was founded, built up, and run by John *Sumner from 1953 to 1955 and again from 1959 to 1987; it is now the major subsidized theatre company in Melbourne and one of the main occupants of the high-profile Victorian Arts Centre. Its early success was immeasurably helped by the production of Ray Lawler's *Summer of the Seventeenth Doll* (1955), a play which was indubitably Australian in subject matter and set in Carlton, in inner-city Melbourne. A smash hit in Australia, it travelled successfully to the *Royal Court in *London.

During the nationalistic period of the late 1960s and 1970s MTC was criticized for following the theatrical lead of London and several alternative theatre groups appeared in the city. *La Mama, a tiny experimental theatre space, was opened in 1967 by Betty Burstall, who had been impressed by Café *La Mama in *New York and wanted to stimulate new, risk-taking work in Melbourne. La Mama still thrives as a venue which welcomes new work, new practitioners, and new ideas. In its early days it was often home to the *Australian Performing Group, a radical, nationalistic, and left-wing theatre group which set about proclaiming alternative lifestyles, breaking performance taboos, and shocking *audiences with exciting and confrontational theatre. APG nurtured many major talents, including David Williamson, whose first major play, *The Removalists*, suited the anti-authoritarian house style. Other APG graduates include the actor-directors Lindy Davies and Graeme Blundell, actors Max Gillies and Peter Cummins, and playwrights Jack *Hibberd and John *Romeril. The group also fostered artists as diverse

as Circus Oz, founded in 1977, and the director Jenny Kemp. This period of intense and nationalistic theatrical activity also saw the foundation in 1976 of the Victorian College of the Arts, a *training institution, originally emphasizing inventive Australian theatre-makers. Playbox theatre company, which started life as Hoopla productions, was also founded in 1976, by Blundell, Garrie Hutchinson, and Carillo Ganter, primarily to showcase Australian work, acquiring a permanent home in 1990. At the end of the twentieth century Melbourne was still visited by star tours, especially by the international juggernauts like *Les Misérables* and *Phantom of the Opera*, but its alternative theatre scene continues to thrive. *See also* SYDNEY.

EJS

MELMOTH, CHARLOTTE (1749–1823)

English and American actress. After acting in *Dublin and *London, Melmoth made her American debut at *New York's *John Street Theatre in 1793. Her addition to the Old American Company caused friction between *Hodgkinson, who promoted her, and other members. William *Dunlap considered her the best tragic actress in New York at the time. She was particularly known for playing Elizabeth I in Henry Jones's *The Earl of Essex*. Melmoth became obese in later years, and because of her appearance her performances of tragic roles were sometimes subjected to ridicule. She retired from the stage in 1812.

AHK

MELO, JORGE SILVA (1948–)

Portuguese actor, playwright, and director, co-founder with Luís Miguel *Cintra of the company Teatro da Cornucópia in 1973. He acted in and directed both classical and contemporary plays there, but left in 1979 to take up *film directing. He graduated from Lisbon University, attended the *London Film School, worked with Peter *Stein and Giorgio *Strehler in the early 1980s, and later joined Jean Jourdheuil in France. Back in *Lisbon in the 1990s, he combined film, cultural *criticism in newspapers, and theatre activity as director of Artistas Unidos, a company he founded in 1996 that is devoted mainly to contemporary work. Committed to *Brecht's and *Müller's idea of theatre as a 'poetry of politics', he is the author of three provocative plays—*António, a Young Man from Lisbon* (1995), *The End; or, Have Mercy on Us*, and *Prometheus* (both 1997)—focusing, in a tragic atmosphere, on the problems and fears of young men in modern society (violence, drugs, unemployment) and the question of *political revolution.

MHS

MELODRAMA *see page 840*

MELODRAMA

The term 'melodrama' originally meant a performance blending *music and *action, with or without speech, to tell a story (see MÉLODRAME). It has sometimes been used merely as a formal description, denoting a drama of simple moral imperatives in which embattled goodness eventually triumphs. Such a category may then be used alongside *comedy and *tragedy in describing representations from all periods: it has been suggested that the mixed *genre to which *Corneille's *Le Cid* (1636) belongs, or the domesticated horrors of *Arden of Feversham* (1590), or indeed the moral structure of *Macbeth*, ending unequivocally with the death of the *villain, qualify these plays as melodrama rather than tragedy. But the term is more useful when confined to a particular kind of staged fiction whose conventions and sensibilities began to develop in Europe in the late eighteenth century, marked by new formal characteristics which were the result of cultural shifts expressed through new emphasis upon technical interactions between theatre arts. Rather than being chiefly realized in the actors' performance of a writer's work, melodrama calls on all theatre systems, weaving its complexity from music, *mime, comedy, and *spectacle. New technical capabilities in the theatre—larger *stages, ever increasing possibilities of *lighting and *scenery, as well as large casts and orchestras—were used to explore radical ideas and often to democratize moral assumptions.

The melodramatic stage embodied the newly conceptualized inner world of *romantic psychology and the resulting changed perception of the outer world of natural wonder and exotic sensation. It was organized by the new, anthropocentric moral order of personal sensibility, nationalism, prescriptive *gender roles, and family values. The result is a genre that externalizes conflicts and personifies cultural meanings in iconic roles—*hero, heroine, villain—within an *action rendered through the entire repertoire of physical performance. Thus music is an essential part of high melodrama, as is athletic, expressive movement; stage setting will strive for visual and aural excitement to match the size and importance of the issues dramatized. The internal and external discoveries of the post-revolutionary years—exotic distant places, and inner psychological depths—are rendered visible and sensationally present; and to keep the *audience both engaged and protected, the extreme *theatricality of the genre continually advertises and refers to itself, in heroic, comic, and ironic interplay.

Exactly how the emergence of melodrama correlated with late eighteenth-century upheavals in European society and revolutionary politics is a vexed question. The link was certainly felt to be very real at the time: *Schiller's *The Robbers* (1781) was banned; Europe-wide performances of *Masaniello*, about the rise and fall of a humble man, were suspected of contributing to the revolutions of 1830–1; strict *censorship was enforced on the *London stage, where the only apparent consensus between many contending interests was that *politics should never be allowed in drama. Modern scholarship is divided. Peter Brooks's very influential view is that melodrama was a creative expression of French revolutionary culture, asserting its democratic character which, however, he argues to have deteriorated rapidly after the beginning of the nineteenth century. On the other hand the analysis initiated by Anne Ubersfeld and taken up by Frederick Brown (*Theatre and Revolution*, 1980) regards melodrama as emerging from the tradition of the French *drame bourgeois* and corroborating its values.

There is less debate about whose plays were the first melodramas proper: in Germany August von *Kotzebue built successful popular plays out of the revolutionary sentiments, extreme situations, and new morality first expressed on stage by Schiller. In France Guilbert de *Pixérécourt renounced the dominant *neoclassicism of the stage in favour of a form of writing avowedly aimed at offering to those who could not read sensational stories illustrating the new moral world of the post-revolutionary republic. Radical British writers, excited by the new continental modes, soon generated a frightened backlash when translations of 'sickly German tragedies' deluged the London stage, to the delight of audiences. In 1802, significantly during the brief truce of Amiens between Britain and France, the radical Thomas *Holcroft brought a Pixérécourt play, *Cœlina* (1800), to *Covent Garden as *A Tale of Mystery*, and the model for the first generation of British melodramas was established. The picturesque setting of this play and its imitations, in a remote Gothic time and place, should not distract us from the contemporaneity of its romantic structure of feeling, in which innocence makes itself triumphantly known in the language of the heart— silent gesture and expressive music—and self-sacrificing love is powerful enough to overcome and convert both aristocratic selfishness and bourgeois caution. It is significant, too, that in the English version honest simplicity and right feeling are also embodied in Paulina, a woman servant, who adds comedy to the mix of music, spectacle, and mime.

Gothic-romantic melodrama, with its evocation of the sublime and picturesque through massive sets, violent action, and expressive music, and its egalitarian sentiments, was for a time high fashion. In England, as political reaction set in during the post-Napoleonic period, Walter Scott's novels provided a conservative turn to *plots and setting. In France a further generation of dramatists—Victor *Hugo, Alexandre *Dumas *père*—developed the genre poetically; the addition of a literary dimension was facilitated by the legal situation in French theatre, which paid writers well for their work (*see* ROYALTIES). In England writers of the next generation who had a natural bent towards melodrama, such as Charles *Dickens, were called away from the stage by the much greater rewards of the novel. Nevertheless, by the time Victoria came to the throne in 1837, the melodramatic had become established as simply the perceived story of today, the universal way of reading modern life. High comedy and classic tragedy had ceased to speak to the general audience; as Louis James has it, melodrama was the modality of the Victorians. And as the basic pattern for theatre, melodrama rapidly developed differentiation according to national and class tastes.

In Britain after Scott and the turn to history, the most significant shift was to settings in modern England. Douglas *Jerrold and other middle-class reformist writers sought to dramatize more explicitly the sufferings of the poor and the injustices of pre-Reform governments. *Black-Ey'd Susan* (1829) was his most successful championing of the honest Briton against all oppressions, since the sailor was already a national hero (*see* NAUTICAL MELODRAMA); more hard-hitting in their class critique were his *Press Gang* (1830) and *The Rent Day* (1832), the latter shifting to the significant locale of an idealized rural England, but this time in the present, menaced by enclosure and industrialization. Class confrontation in such plays was always important, and was personalized: evil systems, whether of landlordism or factory production, tended to be personified in the wicked mill owner or absentee lordling, and solved by the individual virtue of the heroine, the pluck of the sailor, or the sufferings of a humble family. This does not necessarily imply a failure to grasp the depth of the change in social relations consequent on the growth of capitalism: the simple solutions offered by the claptraps of heroism and repentance were undercut in the mode of melodrama by the ever present irony of the comic characters and their cheerfully pragmatic view of life, often cowardly, normally stoic, and always undeceived.

In the 1850s and 1860s the sensational strand of the melodramatic resurfaced, expressed first in the work of women writers, and therefore as novels. Harriet Beecher Stowe's *Uncle Tom's Cabin* (1852; *see* TOM SHOWS), Mary Braddon's *Lady Audley's Secret* (1862), and Ellen Wood's *East Lynne* (1861) were rapidly dramatized. Their huge success on both sides of the Atlantic was followed up by writers for the stage who produced dramas of crime and madness, the nightmare underside of the now strongly established and potentially suffocating Victorian dispensation: crime melodramas like Charles *Reade's *It's Never Too Late to Mend* (1853), Tom *Taylor's *The Ticket-of-Leave Man* (1863), and eventually Henry *Irving's star vehicle *The Bells* (by Leopold Lewis, 1871) explored panic, pressure, guilt, and punishment for a middle-class audience. Dion *Boucicault was the master of sensational melodrama, and his Irish plays in particular, but also his exploitation of the human costs of the growth of the cities, British imperialism, and interracial strife, were successful across the English-speaking world. The strength of such pieces was their heightening deployment of all possible theatre systems, exploding the internalized tensions of modern life into actualization by highly expressive *acting, feats of physical performance—mime, *disguise, fighting—in impressive settings. Sensation melodrama was modern life illuminated and expanded by new technologies of gaslight and hydraulics.

Such dramas, pursued seriously by middle-class audiences as theatregoing became a fashionable pastime again in the 1870s, led on to the sophistications of A. W. *Pinero and H. A. *Jones, and writer's theatre reasserted itself as *copyright laws in England were established; increasingly full-blooded histrionics were left to the large suburban and East End houses. The West End exception was *Drury Lane, where an annual spectacular melodrama with amazing stage effects—sinking ships, steaming trains, or racing horses—purveyed the cruder heroics of empire to a large and various audience. In America the same development occurred; and on both sides of the Atlantic, therefore, the spectacular stage drama was ready to take up the next technical development—the cinematograph. *Birth of a Nation* (1915) and *Ben-Hur* (1925) feed melodrama through to Indiana Jones and James Bond; naval battles staged in real water and horse races run on revolves are the forerunners of daredevil stunts and digitally enhanced imaging on *film.

In the silent years of film, not only visual spectacle and music remind us of earlier melodrama: mute acting reached a new flowering, and in such films as *The Wind* (1928) we may glimpse the scope of bodily expression possible within such a performance genre. In film criticism, however, the term has been shifted to denote not the big action movie, which is arguably the nineteenth-century play's most direct descendant, but the 'woman's film', especially the self-conscious saturation with high colour and emotion found in such work as Douglas Sirk's in the 1950s. This manifestation shares with stage melodrama the externalization of intensity into the *semiotic systems of music, colour, and extremity. Some commentators credit these films with a camp sensibility, but explicitly at least they seem to have lost the important ironizing influence of the comic dimension of Victorian melodrama, which was in many ways the element which added complexity to the high drama of right and wrong.

*Modernism's disdain for the arts of mass appeal discounted any serious appreciation of melodrama, especially when it found new vitality in the early twentieth century by spreading from the popular stage to popular film. Critical commentary on the genre during most of the twentieth century was either derogatory or, at best, defensive. This has at last given way to a deeper interest, the result of a postmodern realization that melodrama is not 'the *realism of dreams' (Bentley), but precisely a non-realist dramatic form, suited to a sophisticated interactive relationship between writer, performers, and audience. *See also* OPERA.   JSB

BENTLEY, ERIC, *The Life of the Drama* (New York, 1974)
BRATTON, J. S., et al. (eds.), *Melodrama: stage, picture, screen* (London, 1994)
BROOKS, PETER, *The Melodramatic Imagination* (New York, 1985)
HAYS, MICHAEL, and NIKOLOPOULOU, ANASTASIA (eds.), *Melodrama: the cultural emergence of a genre* (New York, 1996)
REDMOND, JAMES (ed.), *Themes in Drama 14: melodrama* (Cambridge, 1992)

MÉLODRAME

French dramatic *genre, current *c.*1800 to 1840. The literal translation of *mélodrame* (music drama) is misleading, as is the English term *melodrama derived from it. The freeing of controls on *Paris theatres in 1791 led to a proliferation of small houses, in which new dramatic forms flourished: the *musical accompaniment, deriving from 'la pantomime' (a popular development of the 1770s) was a relatively unimportant feature of this movement, which has been variously defined as '*tragedy for popular audiences' (Geoffroy), 'a product of the development of *drame bourgeois* (Gaiffe), and even 'the logical end-term of the evolution of the whole eighteenth-century theatre' (Marsan). Other theatre historians have rightly emphasized the lack of any cultural background on the part of the new *audiences produced by the revolution; hence their appetite for sensational *action, simplistic *characterization based on the Manichaean opposition of good and evil, and countless variations on the theme of innocence persecuted. It is not surprising that this new class of spectators should share so many characteristics with the audiences of the early silent *film a 100 years later; while there is an undoubted continuity between *le mélodrame* and the *romantic drama of the 1830s, despite the literary pretensions of the latter.   WDH

MENANDER (*c.*342–*c.*291 BC)

Athenian comic playwright, the only writer of *New Comedy whose work has survived. Until the twentieth century he was known mainly by reputation or through quotations. Substantial fragments of his plays then turned up in Egypt and elsewhere through a series of lucky accidents. In 1957 Martin Bodmer published *Dyskolus* (*The Bad-Tempered Man*, sometimes translated as *The Malcontent* or *The Grumbler*), which is all but complete, and in 1969 *The Woman from Samos*, 85 per cent of which survives. From these, and substantial sections of at least three other plays, *The Arbitration*, *The Shorn Girl* (*The Rape of the Locks*), and *The Shield*, it became possible to uncover some of the reasons for Menander's huge popularity in the ancient world. Aristophanes of Byzantium considered him the supreme realist: 'O Menander and Life! Which of you imitated the other?' Plutarch, comparing him with the playwright *Aristophanes, wondered why anyone would ever want to go to the theatre

except to see a play by Menander. The two virtually complete plays demonstrate a radical departure from the *political bite of Aristophanes. Menander's plays are social *comedies in which the *characters are recognizably human and ultimately humane. Cnemon, the central figure of *The Bad-Tempered Man*, tries to live as a recluse, and to shelter his daughter from the outside world. When the wealthy Sostratus falls in love with her he has to resort to all manner of subterfuge to try to gain her hand. Cnemon himself is far more than a cardboard caricature. Menander reveals himself as less the harbinger of *commedia dell'arte* than the forebear of *Molière, *Chekhov, and Alan *Ayckbourn. The careful mix of *farcical comedy and genuine feeling is explored more deeply in *The Woman from Samos*, where misunderstandings that arise out of people trying to avoid hurting one another's feelings almost result in Demeas losing both the woman and the adopted son he loves. Most twentieth-century productions of Menander have been imaginative, if improbable, reconstructions from earlier fragmented *texts. When *The Bad-Tempered Man* was first unearthed it was presented on BBC *radio, as was *The Woman from Samos*, which was also used in the 1970s by Luigi Bernabò Brea to initiate experiments in the re-creation of a set of New Comedy *masks found in Lipari. The balance of the comic and the potentially heart-wrenching was finely brought out in a production in 1994 at the Getty Museum in Malibu which demonstrated admirably how Menander can be simultaneously funny and moving.   JMW

WALTON, J. MICHAEL, and ARNOTT, PETER D., *Menander and the Making of Comedy* (Westport, Conn., 1996)
WILES, DAVID, *The Masks of Menander: sign and meaning in Greek and Roman performance* (London, 1991)

MENDES, SAM (1965–   )

English director. Precocious success with *award-winning productions in *Chichester led Mendes quickly to the West End, where his *Cherry Orchard* (1989) with Judi *Dench revealed a talent for working harmoniously with famous actors and a response to *text that was clear and decisive. In 1990 he directed *Troilus and Cressida* for the *Royal Shakespeare Company at the *Swan Theatre, a production brutal in tone, virtuosic in manner. His highly developed skills in creating exciting theatre in small spaces were shown in *Jonson's *The Alchemist* and in *Richard III*

(1992, RSC at the Other Place), though he was less successful in large theatres at the RSC and Royal *National Theatre. In 1992 he became *artistic director of the *Donmar Warehouse in *London, combining a flair for attracting major stars with an interest in less familiar plays, for instance in reviving *Sondheim's previously unsuccessful *musical *Assassins* (1992) and directing Nicole Kidman in *The Blue Room* (1998). Though remaining at the Donmar, Mendes's Oscar-winning success with the *film *American Beauty* (1999) has led him away from *directing in the theatre.   PDH

MÉNDEZ BALLESTER, MANUEL (1909–2002)

Puerto Rican playwright. *El clamor de los surcos* (*Outcry of the Furrows*) won the 1938 theatre contest sponsored by Puerto Rican Athenaeum and is considered the beginning of Puerto Rican modern theatre. Performed in 1939, the play strongly objected to land monopolizing by sugar refineries and the resulting impoverishment of the farming class. The *tragedy *Tiempo muerto* (*Dead Season*, 1940) established Méndez Ballester as the leading playwright of his generation; the production was enhanced by a neo-*naturalistic set that established new standards for the national stage. He next turned to *comedy with *Un fantasma decentito* (*A Decent Ghost*, 1950), *El milagro* (*The Miracle*, 1961), *Bienvenido, don Goyito* (1965), *Arriba las mujeres* (*Hail to the Women*, 1968), and *El circo* (*The Circus*, 1979), which received critical and public acclaim. His late work *Tambores en el Caribe* (*Caribbean Drums*) was staged at the Fine Arts Centre in 1996.   JLRE

MENDOZA, HÉCTOR (1932–)

Mexican playwright, director, and educator. After the success of his first play, *Simple Things* (1953), Mendoza turned to *directing, becoming celebrated for his adaptations of classical *texts and his innovative use of performance spaces. His production of *Tirso de Molina's *Don Gil of the Green Breeches* (1966) in the handball courts of the National Autonomous University won him accolades from fellow innovators and brickbats from conservatives. His 1983 production with the title of *Hamlet, for Example*, staged in the small performance space of the Convent of St Catherine, was influenced by the *Living Theatre and *Grotowski's *Polish Laboratory Theatre.   KFN

MENG JINGHUI (MENG CHING-HUI) (1965–)

Chinese director, playwright, and actor. After receiving his master's degree in *directing from Beijing's Central Academy of Drama in 1991, Meng became a director at the Central Experimental Theatre in Beijing. He rose to prominence with his 1993 production of *The World of the Mortals Beckons*—an adaptation of a little-known work by an anonymous writer of the Ming Dynasty (1368–1644) combined with Boccaccio's *The Decameron*. Naughty, playful, wicked, the production made experimental theatre at once fascinating and accessible to the *audience. Since then he has become a major figure in the *avant-garde movement in *China. Particularly memorable are his productions of *I Love XXX* (1994) and his pop-music experimental drama *Rhinoceros in Love* (1999). He also continues to use adaptation as a creative tool, most successfully in *Faust: a pirated version* (1999) and *Twelfth Night* (2000). He has participated in theatre *festivals in Germany, Brussels, *Japan, and *Hong Kong with his works, including productions of *Waiting for Godot* (1993) and *King Lear* (2000). His 1998 production of Dario *Fo's *Accidental Death of an Anarchist* went on a world *tour in 2000 to enthusiastic reviews.   MPYC

MENSHIKOV, OLEG (1960–)

Soviet/Russian actor. After graduating in 1982 from the Shchepkin Theatre School, Menshikov worked in a number of theatres in *Moscow and was particularly noted for his roles as the dictator Caligula (1991), the dancer Nijinsky (1993), and the poet Sergei Esenin in the *London production of *When She Danced . . .* (1992, with Vanessa *Redgrave). In 1998 he made his debut as a director with a production of *Griboedov's *Woe from Wit*, in which he also played Chatsky; this was followed in 2000 with *Kurochkin's *The Kitchen*. He has acted in cinema since 1986.   BB

MERCADÉ, EUSTACHE (d. 1440)

Lawyer and playwright. Mercadé is best known for *La Passion d'Arras*, first of the great French *Passion plays, performed over four days at Metz in 1437 but also incorporated into the Valenciennes production of 1547. Mercadé established the pattern of dramatized events later followed by Arnoul *Greban and Jean *Michel. *See* BIBLICAL PLAYS.   RWV

MERCER, DAVID (1928–80)

English playwright. Born into working-class Yorkshire, Mercer became a successful writer of witty yet substantial stage and *television plays in the 1960s, often dealing with social alienation and class loyalties. These themes appear in Mercer's first successful play, *Ride a Cock Horse* (1965), as well as in *After Haggerty* (1970), an ironic *comedy in which a theatre critic, lecturing about the British theatrical revolution of 1956 in the face of real, political revolutions, must also confront his offensive working-class father. Mercer specialized in creating vivid, eccentric (and sometimes insane) *characters such as the artist Morgan in *A Suitable Case for Treatment* (broadcast 1962;

*filmed 1965, with David *Warner) and the renegade vicar in *Flint* (1970) who burns down his church. Other plays include *Belcher's Luck* (1966), *Duck Song* (1974), and *Cousin Vladimir* (1978).   MDG

MERCHANT, VIVIEN (ADA THOMPSON) (1929–82)

English actress. Playing cool, sexually charged *characters, Merchant was best known as an interpreter of Harold *Pinter, to whom she was married. She originated the role of Ruth, the trophy-wife-turned-prostitute, in *The Homecoming*, directed by Peter *Hall for the *Royal Shakespeare Company (1965), a role she reprised in the 1973 *film version. She appeared as Anna in Pinter's *Old Times* (1971), also directed by Hall for the RSC. Her non-Pinter work for the RSC includes *Macbeth* (1967), David *Mercer's *Flint* (1970), and James Joyce's *Exiles* (1970). Her films include *Alfie* (1966), *The Accident* (1967, scripted by Pinter), Alfred Hitchcock's *Frenzy* (1970), and *Genet's *The Maids* (1974). Merchant's career suffered after the break-up of her marriage with Pinter in the mid-1970s.   MDG

MERCIER, LOUIS-SÉBASTIEN (1740–1814)

French playwright. Mercier was a pre-*romantic iconoclast. A staunch opponent of elitism who sought to abolish the *neoclassical tradition, he was an Anglophile, who championed the *drame bourgeois* with its scenic *realism as the appropriate forum for debating moral, social, and *political issues. His *Le Déserteur* (*The Deserter*, 1770), for example, pleads against the mandatory death penalty for army deserters, and *La Brouette du vinaigrier* (*The Vinegar-Seller's Barrow*, 1775), answering *Diderot's wish that the stage portray all professions, urges the tolerance of marriage across class lines. His adaptations of Shakespeare have a similar naive optimism, cloying sentiment, and rhetorical tone. In *Les Tombeaux de Vérone* (*The Tombs of Verona*, 1782) he campaigns for freedom of choice in marriage and protests against female oppression. Accepted at small theatres, at fairgrounds, in the provinces, and abroad, Mercier was *persona non grata* at the *Comédie-Française: not only does his passionate manifesto *Du théâtre* (*On the Theatre*, 1773) attack the entrenched privilege of the state theatre, and extol Shakespearian heterogeneity over neoclassical regularity, but it demands the comfort of a seated pit for ordinary spectators (*see* BOX, PIT, AND GALLERY). Moreover, Mercier supported *Beaumarchais's campaign against the Comédie for authors' rights. In 1792, as a deputy to the revolutionary Convention, he voted against the execution of Louis XVI. Subsequently imprisoned, he was saved from the guillotine by the fall of Robespierre in 1794.   JG

MERCOURI, MELINA (1923–94)

Greek actress and politician. Mercouri studied in the *acting conservatory of the *Greek National Theatre in *Athens and made her first appearance in 1944 in Alexis Solomos's *Path of Freedom*. In 1949 her interpretation of Blanche Dubois in the Art Theatre's production of *A Streetcar Named Desire* established her as a leading actress. She made her screen debut in 1955 in Michalis Kakogiannis's *Stella*. In 1960 she shared the award for best actress at the Cannes Film Festival (with Jeanne Moreau) and was nominated for an Academy award for *Never on Sunday*, directed by her husband, the American expatriate Jules Dassin. She also starred in Dassin's *films *Phaedra* (1961) and *Topkapi* (1964), and in Norman Jewison's *Gaily, Gaily* (1969). During the 1966–7 season she made her *New York debut in Dassin's *Ilya Darling*, a stage adaptation of *Never on Sunday*. She actively opposed the military dictatorship in Greece (1967–74) while in exile abroad. In 1976 she played Medea for the State Theatre of Northern Greece. She was elected to Parliament on the socialist ticket in 1977 and became Greece's Minister of Culture in 1981.   KGo

MERCURY THEATRE

Company founded in 1937 by Orson *Welles and John *Houseman in *New York. When the *Federal Theatre Project's production of Marc *Blitzstein's leftist *opera *The Cradle Will Rock* was stifled due to political pressures, Welles led his company and *audience through the streets to the Venice Theatre, where the actors performed the piece from the *auditorium while Blitzstein accompanied at a piano onstage. A reconstituted version later that year launched the Mercury Theatre, conceived by Welles and Houseman as a repertory focusing on classics. The company, with Welles its creative genius and Houseman his practical conscience, staged innovative and critically hailed productions of *Julius Caesar* (1937), *Dekker's *The Shoemaker's Holiday* (1938), and *Shaw's *Heartbreak House* (1938). Precarious *finances and Welles's spontaneous leadership style caused the company to close down in its second season. Despite widespread *publicity resulting from the *radio broadcast of *The War of the Worlds* in October 1938 (which many took as a real Martian invasion), audiences avoided *Büchner's *Danton's Death* and Welles failed to attract financing to bring *The Five Kings* (his reworking of Shakespeare's history plays) to New York. Welles took the Mercury name to Hollywood and used part of the company in his first *film, *Citizen Kane* (1940).   MAF

MEREZHKOVSKY, DMITRY (1865–1941)

Poet, dramatist, historical novelist, translator of *Greek *tragedy, essayist, and religious philosopher, who popularized French *symbolism in Russia and was married to the noted symbolist poet Zinaida Gippius. Influenced by the ideas of Nietzsche, Vladimir Solovyov, and Vasily Rozanov, Merezhkovsky sought a religious revival based on a struggle between paganism and Christianity, the flesh and the spirit. His trilogy of works on early nineteenth-century history include a play, *Paul I*, whilst his 1906 essay '*Gogol and the Devil*' is said to have exercised a strong influence on *Meyerhold's famous 1926 production of *The Government Inspector*.   NW

MERMAID THEATRE

Opened in 1959 at Puddle Dock, Blackfriars, in *London, the single-block, 500-seat, *open-stage *auditorium united actors and *audience in a brick-walled continuity, the outcome of Bernard *Miles's experiments with Elizabethan staging erected first in his garden in 1951. Despite success for Bill *Naughton's *Alfie* and Peter Luke's *Hadrian VII*, there were chronic *financial problems. Rebuilding in the early 1980s, which enlarged capacity, did not save the Mermaid from sale in 1984, after which it went into decline. In 2001 a campaign was launched to save it from demolition.   CEC

MERMAN, ETHEL (1909–84)

American singer and actress. Born Ethel Zimmerman, the former stenographer was vaulted to fame in the *Gershwins' *Girl Crazy* (1930), in which she introduced 'I Got Rhythm'. With her brassy personality, clarion voice, and immaculate enunciation, she remained a sure-fire *box-office star in the *musical theatre for three decades. Star vehicles were created for her by Cole *Porter (*Anything Goes* and four others, all big hits) and Irving *Berlin (*Annie Get your Gun, Call Me Madam*). Her final original role was perhaps her greatest—Mama Rose in *Gypsy* (1959). The title role in *Hello, Dolly!* was written for her, but she chose not to create it, although she was Broadway's final Dolly in 1970. While her outsize stage persona was generally too large for *film, she still made several motion pictures, repeating her stage role in the film of *Call Me Madam*. A dedicated performer, she typically stayed with her shows for their entire runs, and nearly all of them made a profit. 'Broadway has been awfully good to me', she noted on her retirement, 'but then I've been awfully good to Broadway.'   JD

MERON, HANNAH (1923–   )

Israeli actress, leading lady of the *Cameri Theatre, of which she was a founding member in 1945. Born in *Berlin, she was a child star, appearing on screen in Fritz Lang's *M* before moving to Palestine in 1933. On stage she projected a modern and sophisticated presence, always recognized by her uniquely rasping voice. She has played nearly 60 roles, representing a wide spectrum of native Israeli, classical, and modern plays: Shamir's *He Walked in the Fields*, *Shaw's *Pygmalion*, Shakespeare's *As You Like It*, *Schiller's *Mary Stuart*, and *Ibsen's *Hedda Gabler*. Always eager for new challenges, she left the Cameri for the freedom to work in experimental productions as well as commercial *musicals such as *Hello, Dolly!* and *My Fair Lady*. She appeared with various orchestras, in *film and *television, and taught and directed at Tel Aviv University. In 1970 she lost a leg in an Arab machine gun attack at Munich airport.   EN

MERRICK, DAVID (1912–2000)

American producer. Merrick, originally a lawyer, began producing with *Fanny* (1954), and was responsible for 88 Broadway plays and *musicals, many imported from *London, some of them challenging and provocative. His distinguished contributions to *New York include *The Matchmaker* (1955), *Look Back in Anger* (1957), *The Entertainer* (1958), *The World of Susie Wong* (1958), *Gypsy* (1959), *A Taste of Honey* (1960), *Stop the World I Want to Get off* (1962), *Oliver!* (1963), *Oh! What a Lovely War* (1964), *Hello, Dolly!* (1964), *Marat/Sade* (1965), *I Do, I Do* (1966), *Rosencrantz and Guildenstern are Dead* (1967), *Promises, Promises* (1968), *Play It Again, Sam* (1969), *Travesties* (1975), and *42nd Street* (1981). Merrick also produced four *films. Dubbed the 'abominable showman', he employed outrageous *publicity stunts, such as paying an *audience member to slap an actor onstage in *Look Back in Anger*, advertising rave quotes for *Subways Are for Sleeping* (1961) signed by men with the same names as the leading *critics, and, on *42nd Street*'s opening day, keeping secret news of director Gower *Champion's death so that he could announce it during the *curtain call. He often feuded with New York's critics. Following a disabling stroke in 1983, Merrick remained active but had no new hits.   SLL

MERRY, ANNE BRUNTON (1769–1808)

English and American actress and *manager. Recruited by *Wignell for his New American Company, Merry first appeared in the United States in 1797, with Thomas A. *Cooper and William *Warren. Praised for her sweet voice, gracefulness, and simplicity of manner, she became a popular performer in the outstanding company at the *Chestnut Street Theatre in *Philadelphia, playing both tragic and comic roles. In 1801, she gave guest performances in *New York's *Park Theatre, at *Dunlap's invitation. She married Wignell in 1803, but he soon died and she co-managed the company with Alexander Reinagle until, in 1806, she married William *Warren.   AHK

MERSON, BILLY (1881–1947)

English *pantomime and *variety artist. Born in Nottingham, he was briefly a *circus *clown and part of a *music-hall double act called Keith and Merson. An *acrobat, he was noted for his

'Crocodile Walk' speciality—walking up and down stairs on his forearms, his feet above his head. Going solo, he turned to *acting and songwriting. His songs were witty and often bizarre, the most famous being 'The Spaniard that Blighted my Life'. At the height of his variety career he would amaze the *audience by hanging on to the *curtain when it rose and fell, but after a brief and disastrous sortie into *actor-management he died impoverished in Charing Cross Hospital.

AF

MESGUICH, DANIEL (1952–)

Algerian-French actor and director. Born in Algeria, Mesguich studied under Antoine *Vitez at the *Conservatoire in *Paris, where he has himself taught since 1983. After founding Théâtre du Miroir in 1974, he headed the Théâtre Gérard-Philipe (1986–9) and Théâtre National de Lille, renamed La Métaphore (1991–8). Like Vitez, Mesguish is interested in the role of *verse in the classical repertoire and is known for his reinterpretations of Shakespeare and *Racine, often based on ideas gained from his reading of French literary and cultural *theory. He has directed several productions at the *Comédie-Française, including a popular version of *Offenbach's La Vie parisienne (1997), Shakespeare's The Tempest (1997), and Racine's Mithridate and Andromaque (1999). His *opera stagings have been seen at the *Opéra, the *Opéra-Comique, and the Théâtre Royal de la Monnaie in *Brussels. As an actor Mesguich has appeared on *television and in many *films by noted directors, including Costa-Gavras, Truffaut, *Mnouchkine, and James Ivory.

DGM

MESSEL, OLIVER (1904–78)

English artist and designer. A student of the Slade School of Art, Messel's style tended towards a *romantic, imaginative, and sometimes sinister aesthetic. His work for C. B. *Cochran between 1926 and 1932 included macabre *masks for Noël *Coward's This Year of Grace (1928) and a striking white-on-white setting for Max *Reinhardt's Helen (1932). Among his designs were a tulle and gauze Victorian pastiche for Tyrone *Guthrie's A Midsummer Night's Dream (1937), and a delicate, innovatively constructed Winter Garden for Peter *Brook's Ring round the Moon (1950). His designs for *ballet included the celebrated and lavish Sleeping Beauty at *Covent Garden (1946), and for *opera, a light and elegant La Cenerentola at Glyndebourne (1952). His rich, colourful, painterly style was appropriate to stagings which used backcloths and *flats rather than more *modernist presentations.

VRS

METASTASIO (1698–1782)

Metastasio's misfortune is that he was uncontested master of melodramma, a form which has no modern proponents or exponents. The *genre is a form of *musical drama which employs poetic language and the heroic style, but its pursuit of pathos or grandiloquence makes it appear merely overwrought to modern tastes. The emotional dilemmas of Dido and Aeneas, Alexander the Great, Cato of Utica, and the Emperor Hadrian all feature in Metastasio's works. In his own time, no man was more highly esteemed. The composers who vied to write music for his works included Vivaldi, Pergolesi, Scarlatti, Salieri, and Albinoni. *Mozart used his Clemenza di Tito, albeit adapted by Carlo Mazzolà, for his *opera of the same name.

Metastasio was christened Pietro Trapassi. The precocious talent which saw him write his first *tragedy at 14 years led to his adoption by G. V. Gravina, who gave him the Grecian name by which he is known. Gravina was among the founders of Arcadia, a literary academy responsible for unleashing the myth of pastoral simplicity, and his impact was lasting. Metastasio's Didone abbandonata, a classic tale of unrequited love and descent into madness, was produced in *Naples in 1724 and five years and five melodrammi later he was summoned to *Vienna as court poet in succession to Apostolo Zeno, the other great eighteenth-century writer of melodramma.

Like *Goldoni with *comedy and *Maffei with *tragedy, Metastasio was afflicted by the eighteenth-century urge to reform. His programme was aimed at eliminating from melodramma baroque excess, giving less prominence to design and more to the lyrics and *music, reducing the role of the *chorus, attaining a sober simplicity of style, and ensuring that the resultant work was imbued with high moral standards. He considered his best work to be Attilio Regolo, composed in 1740 but only produced a decade later, though his most enduring script is Olimpiade (1733), a poetic reworking of ancient legends of a child found abandoned as a consequence of prophecies of patricide. Metastasio was admired by Stendhal, who wrote a biography, but enjoyment of his work requires an unusual level of suspension of disbelief and a willing immersion in a dimension of heroic fantasy.

JF

METATHEATRE

Self-reflexive drama or performance that reveals its artistic status to the *audience. The reflexivity may be embedded in a script's structure by the *playwright, when it can be called metadrama, or superimposed in production by the *director or designer. In either instance, aesthetic self-consciousness is often presented in both artistic and metaphysical terms, especially in works that speculate on alternative versions of reality, including the artifice of representation. The play-within-the-play in Hamlet (c.1600) set the standard for the elevation of *theatricality to metaphysical proportions in Western drama. As Lionel Abel observed, because the play-within-the-play seems to have been scripted by Hamlet himself, he is the 'first stage figure with an acute awareness of what it means to be staged'. While it can be argued that some ancient *Greek plays also lean in this direction, it is certain that Shakespeare's concern with *performativity resurfaced often, most tellingly in one of his last plays, *The Tempest* (1611), when Prospero comments on his devotion to theatrical magic. No wonder the work is a favourite of modern directors such as Giorgio *Strehler, whose 1978 production infused *text and *mise-en-scène with a concern with directorial and *scenographic artifice.

Self-consciously dramatic *characters are also apparent in *early modern Spanish dramatists, some of whom extended a baroque preoccupation with artifice to themes not traditionally associated with aesthetics. In *Lo fingido Verdadero* (*What's Feigned Is True*, *c.*1608), a play about the martyrdom of the ancient *Roman actor St Genesius, Lope de *Vega compares the levels of fervour required of actors and the spiritually devout. Like Shakespeare, Lope's observations on performance presaged eighteenth-century *acting *theory; *Diderot made Hamlet's advice to the actors on speech the template for a rationalist approach that would ultimately transform acting styles to the *illusionist model he and other Enlightenment figures preferred. But from the standpoint of metaphysics *Calderón's *Life Is a Dream* (*c.*1629) is widely acknowledged as the precursor to the deployment of metatheatre in *modernism. Abel noted that if the play-within-the-play in *Hamlet* rationalized characters 'of a certain imaginative size who would not be at home in *tragedy or *comedy', Calderón's characters 'rewrite a preordained tragedy' even as they traverse real, imagined, and dreamed states of consciousness (*see also* DREAMS AND THEATRE).

In the age of psychology in the late nineteenth and early twentieth centuries, preoccupation with the dynamics of personality would assume diverse forms, from *naturalism at one end to the exposure of the mechanisms of illusionism on the other. Bridging both impulses, *Strindberg in the preface to *Miss Julie* (1888) stipulated the theatrical correlatives of *Zola's objectivism, though he simultaneously defied them in his justification for an impressionist setting. Strindberg would subsequently explore the theatre's potential to mirror subjective processes in *A Dream Play* (1907), where *plot and scenography are material emanating from the unconscious mind of the dreamer/author (*see also* SYMBOLISM; EXPRESSIONISM). So prolific was *Pirandello's treatment of theatre-as-metaphor that the term 'Pirandellian' has come to refer to what Eric Bentley called 'the confrontation between form and life'. In the trilogy comprised of *Six Characters in Search of an Author* (1921), *Each in his Own Way* (1924), and *Tonight We Improvise* (1930), Pirandello builds tension among the constituents of theatrical events, pitting characters against playwrights, actors against characters, and performers against the audience. While the versatility of Pirandello's metatheatre would be absorbed by theatre and *film directors too numerous to count, special mention should be made of *Brecht, whose anti-illusionist techniques were intended to stimulate social change. Brecht and other modernists were influenced by traditional Asian theatre forms in which the illusionist impulse is non-existent and meaning is derived from the interplay of the myriad performance codes laid bare to the spectator.

Apart from formal ingenuity, what most links the metatheatre of the sixteenth with that of the late nineteenth and early twentieth centuries is the presumption of a cohesive, if not quite finite system of social values that may be compared (or reduced) to the theatrical realm. The metaphor of theatricality, in other words, implies that life itself is fixed on a stage of limited scope. The aestheticizing of social life characteristic of *neoclassicism can be viewed as a by-product of political and artistic constraints, as well as a sanctuary from their tyranny. Similarly, philosophical relativism—implicit in Calderón and explosive in Pirandello—is inseparable from its service to the hierarchies of power: Calderón became a court and religious playwright, while Pirandello, whatever he may have thought of Mussolini, was held in high esteem under *fascism. Conversely, if Brecht's anti-illusionist devices were the means by which he intended to expose the mechanisms of capitalism and totalitarianism, his *politics were as blatant as his theatrics.

It is the absence of such social givens that most typified versions of metatheatre after the Second World War. If the slipperiness of metaphor resides at the heart of *absurdist despair, the opening up of interpretative possibilities is one of its happier by-products, as can be seen from the metatheatrics of *Ionesco, *Genet, and *Beckett. The indeterminateness of meaning has been borne out in formal experimentation with metatheatre in some postmodern theatre, particularly in the work of Robert *Wilson, Richard *Foreman, Elizabeth *LeCompte, Pina *Bausch, and Robert *Lepage. And the solo activity of *performance art, often taking the body of the playwright-performer as the entire site of theatricality, suggests that metatheatre has transcended its status as metaphor by becoming a major representational mode, and one no longer confined to the theatrical realm.

DRP

ABEL, LIONEL, *Metatheatre* (New York, 1963)

MÉTELLUS, JEAN (1937–)

Haitian writer who fled the dictatorship of François Duvalier in 1959 to settle in France for medical studies. He published his first poems in 1978 and his first novel in 1981. He switched to the theatre with *Anacaona* (1986), *Le Pont rouge* (1991), and *Colomb* (1992), work which renewed the Haitian tradition of lyrical *historical drama. The action in his plays operates in two realms simultaneously: in the actual events represented on stage, and the unseen symbolic world created through poetic language. His work was much admired by the director Antoine *Vitez.

MLa trans. JCM

METHOD

A term usually applied to the acting techniques developed by Lee *Strasberg for the purpose of freeing and enabling the actor to create truthful behaviour on stage. Strasberg's Method was based on the System of Konstantin *Stanislavsky and additional ideas of Stanislavsky's student Eugeny *Vakhtangov. Strasberg first encountered the ideas while studying with *Moscow Art Theatre actors at the *American Laboratory Theatre in *New York in 1924 and over the course of his long teaching career, especially at the *Group Theatre in the 1930s and the *Actors Studio (1948–82), Strasberg developed his own exercises for accomplishing Stanislavsky's goals of relaxation, concentration, and creativity. Strasberg was sometimes criticized for his reliance on 'affective (or emotional) memory' and Vakhtangov's related technique of the 'adjustment'. Suggested by the Russians' reading of Pavlov, the techniques are designed to assist the actor in bringing to consciousness a set of feelings from a past event and then devising a physical or mental cue so that the recalled emotion can be brought forward during a performance. During the 1950s the Method became a matter of public controversy, accused by some of promoting self-absorbed and inarticulate performances (from Marlon *Brando, James Dean, and others) while praised by many as a reliable path into the variety of truth and away from theatrical clichés. The Method has worked well in the intimate and psychologically intense area of Hollywood *film drama.   MAF

METROPOLITAN OPERA HOUSE

In 1880 a committee of *New York patricians resolved to build an *opera house comparable with La *Scala, the *Paris *Opéra, and *Bayreuth. Josiah Cleaveland Cady's design offered a *proscenium opening 15 m (50 feet) square; a stage 32 m wide, 26 m deep, and 38 m high (106 by 86 by 125 feet); and an *auditorium measuring 32 m (104 feet) from the proscenium to the back of the centre box. The house sat 3,045 in two balconies, three tiers of *boxes, and a parquet; 70 box-holders contributed $17,500 each toward the cost of over $1.7 million. Located on the block between 39th and 40th streets, and Broadway and 7th Avenue, the Met opened in 1883 with Gounod's *Faust* sung in Italian. Caroline Astor and 'The Four Hundred' supported the Met as an emblem of New York pride, and in 1888–9 the company presented the first American rendition of *Wagner's *Ring* cycle. After an 1892 *fire, the capacity was expanded to 3,400 and electricity replaced gas *lighting. Met regulars subsequently included singers Nellie Melba, Enrico Caruso, Geraldine Farrar, Rosa Ponselle, Lawrence Tibbett, Lauritz Melchior, Ezio Pinza, Robert Merrill, and Richard Tucker, as well as conductors Gustav Mahler and Arturo Toscanini, and designer Joseph *Urban. Under general *manager Rudolf Bing, the Met moved to *Lincoln Center into a house with a proscenium 16 m (54 feet)

square and a capacity of 4,065, with an exterior of travertine and glass, interior decor of burgundy velour, and 32 crystal chandeliers. The new Met opened with the 1966 world première of Samuel Barber's *Antony and Cleopatra* and has firmly established its place as one of the world's leading opera companies.
                                                                    JDM

MEXICAN-AMERICAN THEATRE *See* CHICANO THEATRE.

MEXICO CITY

The cultural centre and capital of Mexico, one of the largest urban areas in the world, with a population of over 20 million in 2001. Under Spanish rule it was the seat of the viceroyalty of New Spain, where, with the support of Spanish nobles and their courts, the arts flourished. While most theatrical activity during the three centuries of Spanish domination was imported, baroque Mexico produced one of the greatest playwrights of all the Spanish-speaking world: the nun Sor *Juana Inés de la Cruz (1651–95), who was the equal of her renowned Iberian contemporaries. After gaining independence in 1821, Mexico suffered decades of instability which necessarily affected a fledgling theatre still in the process of freeing itself from antiquated Spanish models. Although more Mexicans were writing plays, they were not often lucky in production, as the stage was dominated by *touring groups from abroad, especially from Spain, Italy, and France. The armed phase of the Mexican Revolution (1910–20) was greatly disruptive for artists, with the city under siege and in constant political and economic turmoil.

After the gunpowder settled, Mexico City began to reconstruct itself and became the centre of a government-inspired revolutionary cultural project that included painting (the murals of Diego Rivera and José Clemente Orozco), music (the composer Carlos Chávez), and to a lesser, but still significant degree, theatre. During this period arts administration became highly concentrated in Mexico City, with the creation of the National Institute of Fine Arts (*INBA) in 1947. For the remainder of the century, the federal government was a major source of support for production costs, for leasing existing venues, and for building new ones like the numerous Social Security Theatres spread across the city to help expand *audiences. The government also provided joint funding for the professional theatres of the National Autonomous University, and continues to support the theatres of *SOGEM (General Society of Mexican Writers), which are dedicated solely to mounting Mexican plays. The newest subsidized arts complex in Mexico City, the National Centre for the Arts, boasts theatres comparable to the best anywhere. Over the years, the governmental infrastructure that oversees and funds these efforts has grown diversified and increasingly complex, if not cumbersome. Among important agencies engaged in subsidizing the theatre are the National Council for

Culture and the Arts, the Institute for Social Security, INBA, and the Institute for Security and Social Services for State Workers, all of them under the umbrella of a commission for *national theatre. While this funding has been basic for the vitality of theatre in Mexico City (with an average of 50 per cent of productions being wholly or partially funded by the government), it is also tied to the national economy and in times of crisis, such as Mexico experienced in the latter part of the twentieth century, it can be insufficient, irregular, and highly contested.

Mexico City also has many independent theatres, which tend to be driven by the *box office and cater to a traditional upper-middle-class audience with Broadway hits and other crowd pleasers. These are often staged in theatres privately owned by powerful impresarios such as the late Manolo Fábregas (1921–96). In an era of global economics, more businesses, such as banks and international corporations, have begun to sponsor these kinds of plays. There are also numerous *alternative venues for experimental theatre: bars, *cabarets, small chapels, cultural centres, museums, bookstores, cloisters. Among these the best known and most frequented is the Bar El Hábito and the Teatro de la Capilla, owned and *managed by the *performance artist Jesusa *Rodríguez. Audiences at these places tend to be university students, artists, and intellectuals.

Popular theatre (the equivalent of *vaudeville and *burlesque) and *political *revues also have a long tradition in Mexico City, dating from the Mexican Revolution and 'tent theatre' which transmitted news from the battlefields and critiqued the political situation. The comic *Cantinflas came from this tradition; one theatre in particular, the Blanquita, is identified with it and, although it has lost much of its original bite, it continues to attract large and enthusiastic audiences. Political skits and revues were much in evidence and much attended during the late 1990s, when corruption was rampant in Mexican politics. There is an active theatre for *youth in Mexico City, with one yearly festival and perhaps 50 plays and *puppet shows on the bill every week. There is also a small but growing *gay theatre movement (often performed in gay bars and cabarets), and a more developed tradition of performance art (in everyday places such as streets, plazas, and museums).

Every summer since 1989 the municipality has sponsored the Mexico City Festival, which hosts theatre groups, promoters, and performance artists from around the world, adding to the international flavour of dramatic arts in the capital. (*See also* LATIN AMERICA.) Unlike other major cultural centres such as *New York, *London, or *Buenos Aires, however, Mexico City has no clearly demarcated theatre district; venues are spread widely throughout the city, especially in the southern parts such as Coyoacan and University City, with a small cluster in the centre. Explosive growth of the metropolitan area in recent decades, with its consequent problems of traffic and crime, has meant that many theatres have difficulty filling the house. But theatre in Mexico City remains rich and varied. There are over 400 venues which in any given week offer programming from around the world, as well as by Mexico's best playwrights, at affordable prices.   KFN

MEYERHOLD, VSEVOLOD (1874–1940)

Russian/Soviet actor, director and *theorist of theatre who, as a protégé of *Nemirovich-Danchenko, was among the founding members of the *Moscow Art Theatre in 1898 and the original Konstantin there in *Chekhov's *The Seagull*. At first an enthusiastic admirer of *Stanislavsky and his methods, Meyerhold became attracted by the non-*naturalistic possibilities of the *symbolist theatre movement and left the MAT in 1902 to lead his own troupe in the Russian provinces where between 1902 and 1905 he staged over 170 productions. After returning briefly to the MAT in 1905, in order to assist Stanislavsky's own experiments in symbolist staging, Meyerhold was invited by Vera *Komissarzhevskaya to head her own theatre in *St Petersburg, a post which he held in 1906 and 1907, and where he staged groundbreaking productions of Aleksandr *Blok's classic symbolist play, *Balaganchik* (*The Fairground Booth* or *The Puppet Show*), as well as highly original, stylized versions of *Ibsen's *Hedda Gabler* and Leonid *Andreev's *The Life of Man*. Parting company with Komissarzhevskaya, somewhat acrimoniously, Meyerhold was invited to become head of the imperial theatres in St Petersburg and between 1908 and 1917 staged a range of significant *opera and theatre productions with many of the leading singers, actors, designers, and musicians of the day. As well as major productions of *Molière, *Ostrovsky, and *Lermontov, he also staged operas by *Wagner, Richard *Strauss, *Gluck, Stravinsky, and *D'Annunzio's *verse drama *La Pisanelle* for Ida Rubinstein in *Paris. He also found time to make two *films, the first of them *The Picture of Dorian Gray* in 1914, with himself as Lord Henry.

As significant as his work at the imperial theatres was his unofficial work in private and *fringe venues in St Petersburg, where he and a group of fellow enthusiasts staged a number of experimental productions based on conventions of theatre performance which went back to *Greek, *Roman, and pre-Renaissance theatre, and with a special debt to popular forms such as the *pantomime, the *circus, and the harlequinade. These productions experimented with ideas drawn from a number of sources, including *commedia dell'arte*, Asian theatre, the recent theories of Edward Gordon *Craig, Adolphe *Appia, Fyodor *Sologub, Georg *Fuchs, and Wagner (among others), foregrounding an overt sense of *theatricality plus a strong feeling for the *grotesque. The radicalism of Meyerhold's approach to theatre was reflected in his political acceptance of the October Revolution and led to his appointment, by *Lunacharsky, as head of the theatre section of the *Moscow Cultural Commissariat. Having staged what became known as 'the first Soviet play', *Mystery-Bouffe*, in collaboration with its author, Vladimir

Meyerhold's production of *The Bedbug*, Meyerhold Theatre, Moscow, 1929. Mayakovsky's satire (he called it a 'magnifying glass') about the new economic policy and rising Soviet bourgeoisie is chiefly a series of sketches, out of which Meyerhold created a fantasia on changing social conditions a decade or so after the 1917 Revolution.

*Mayakovsky, Meyerhold threw himself into the task of converting theatres to the communist cause with the kind of zeal that so alarmed his political superiors that he was rapidly relieved of his post. This had the effect of setting him free to pursue the revolutionizing of Soviet theatre on his own terms and in his own way.

At the various theatre workshops which he established in Moscow during and after the Civil War, Meyerhold surrounded himself with a remarkable group of actors and future directors, including Nikolai *Okhlopkov and Sergei *Eisenstein, and staged a number of outstanding productions which combined experimental forms of *constructivist staging with his own highly original actor-*training methods known as *biomechanics. Principal among these was the 1922 production of Crommelynck's farce *Le Cocu magnifique* (*The Magnanimous Cuckold*), with constructivist staging by Lyubov *Popova. Acquiring his own theatre in 1924, which became known as the Meyerhold Theatre (a distinction rarely conferred on a living practitioner and construed by his enemies as a typical sign

of his overweening arrogance), Meyerhold staged a number of brilliantly original productions during the 1920s, notably of *Ostrovsky's *The Forest* (1924) and *Gogol's *The Government Inspector* (1926). Never an easy person to work with, Meyerhold attracted violent antipathy and unqualified allegiance in equal measure, as did his wife Zinaida Raikh, who was given leading roles in many of his productions and who was considered by *critics to be either highly talented or grossly overused.

His association with Mayakovsky, *Tretyakov, and the Left Front of the Arts—and with that group's espousal of *modernist techniques deriving from Russian formalism, *futurism, constructivism, cubo-futurism, and German *expressionism—came under increasing scrutiny at the end of the 1920s and in the early 1930s, as Stalinist elements tightened their grip on power and began to insist on increasingly conservative forms of artistic production. Meyerhold's staging of Mayakovsky's *satirical plays *The Bedbug* and *The Bathhouse* in 1929 and 1930 (the first with music by the theatre's resident pianist, Dmitry Shostakovich) challenged bureaucracy and the betrayal of revolutionary ideals, only to be criticized as anti-Soviet, as were other productions which Meyerhold staged during the 1930s, such as *Olesha's *A List of Assets*. He sought to confirm the genuineness of his political allegiance with productions of *Vishnevsky's *The Last Decisive* (1931) and Yury German's *The Prelude* (1933), both of which had anti-fascist or anti-bourgeois themes, as did his lavishly conceived production of *Dumas *fils*'s *The Lady of the Camellias* (1934). By the mid-1930s, however, the writing was on the wall, and not even an attempt to stage *How the Steel Was Tempered* (1937), based on a novel by the conspicuously pro-Soviet writer Nikolai Ostrovsky, could save him. It was banned and his theatre closed in 1938. Notwithstanding painful efforts to justify himself and prove his pro-Soviet loyalties at a conference of directors in 1939, Meyerhold was arrested and imprisoned that June. Despite desperate appeals to high officials like Molotov, wherein he sought to refute the ludicrous charges brought against him of Trotskyism and espionage, Meyerhold was shot on 2 February 1940 and his body placed in a common grave. His name was then erased from public records, just as his image was airbrushed from photographs, until his posthumous rehabilitation by a Military Court of the USSR in 1955.

Meyerhold's main legacy has been less his theory than his practice. Crucially, he was the first to bring open theatricality back into play and to do so in a radically populist manner inspired by indigenous and broader European forms of public entertainment. His left-wing ideology and his foregrounding of 'the means of theatrical production' has enabled us the better to understand work of like-minded practitioners such as *Piscator and *Brecht, and to weigh the merits of socially and *politically oriented theatre against the more personal and psychological forms of Stanislavsky, or the therapeutic and spiritually convulsive intensities of *Artaud and *Grotowski. In terms which Peter *Brook has provided, Meyerhold may be said to have raised 'rough' theatre to 'holy' heights of achievement.

NW

BRAUN, EDWARD, *Meyerhold: a revolution in theatre* (London, 1995)
RUDNITSKY, KONSTANTIN, *Meyerhold the Director*, trans. G. Petrov (Ann Arbor, 1981)

MEZA, GUSTAVO (1938–)

Chilean actor, playwright, and director, founder of the group Teatro Imagen (1974). His best-known play is *El último tren* (*The Last Train*, 1978). *La reina Isabel cantaba rancheras* (*Queen Isabel Used to Sing Rancheras*, 1999), produced by Teatro Imagen under Meza's direction, became an instant hit. MAR

MÉZIÈRES, PHILIPPE DE (c.1327–1405)

Crusader, diplomat, and writer. Mézières in 1378 devised an elaborate entertainment depicting the capture of Jerusalem, and produced in 1385 an equally elaborate *liturgical play based on a ceremony from the Eastern Church, *The Presentation of the Virgin Mary*. His *Griselda* (c.1395) is an early example of a serious, non-religious French play. RWV

MHLANGA, CONT (1958–)

Zimbabwean playwright and director. In 1982 he founded Amakhosi Theatre in Makokoba Township, Bulawayo, which remains Zimbabwe's most famous theatre company. He remained playwright and *artistic director of the group until 1999, professionalizing its structures and expanding it into *film, *radio drama, and music. *Workshop Negative* (1986, published 1992) was Mhlanga's most controversial play, causing a nationwide debate on *race relations, reconciliation, and corruption. Other plays include *Nansi LeNdoda* (1985), *Stitsha* (1990), *Dabulap* (1992), and *Hoyayaho* (1994), the last a *musical on AIDS with predominantly *mimed *action. Mhlanga's plays, most of them written in what he calls 'ndenglish'—the typical township mixture of SiNdebele and English—and his direction have won several *awards at festivals run by the National Theatre Organization of Zimbabwe. He has also published a collection of short stories in SiNdebele, *Nga Kadengisazi*. From 1990 to 1995 he was chair of the Zimbabwe Writers' Union. MRo

MHLOPE, GCINA (1958–)

South African writer, director, and actress. Born in Kwa-Zulu Natal, she spent her teen years in Transkei. In the 1970s she published short stories including 'The Toilet' and 'Dear Madame'; her first play, *Have You Seen Zandile?* (1985), was collaboratively written, and she also collaborated with Barney *Simon on *Born in the RSA* the same year. In 1989 she became the in-house director of the *Market Theatre in *Johannesburg, where she wrote and directed *Somdaka* (*Proud to be Dark-Skinned*, 1989). She co-authored *The Good Person of Sharkeville* with Janet *Suzman (an adaptation of *Brecht, 1995) and her *Love Child* premièred in *Grahamstown in 1998. She founded Zanendaba Storyteller in 1992, a group that performs traditional stories for children and adults. She won best actress *awards in America for *Born in the RSA* (Obie, *New York, 1987) and *Have You Seen Zandile?* (Joseph Jefferson award, *Chicago, 1988). Her role in reclaiming and teaching oral performance forms, particularly in the urban context, has been profound; she made a recording with the vocal group Ladysmith Black Mambazo in 1994.

YH

MICHEL, JEAN (d. 1501)

Angevin physician and playwright. Michel fashioned a *Passion play by appropriating two-thirds of Arnoul *Greban's *Passion* (11,296 lines) and augmenting it to nearly 30,000 lines. The play was often performed and went through seventeen editions between 1488 and 1550. It was also incorporated into productions at Mons (1501) and Valenciennes (1547).   RWV

MICHELL, KEITH (1928–)

Australian actor, designer, and director. Michell left his native Adelaide to train at the *Old Vic in *London and achieved major successes in the UK. He had leading roles at Stratford in the 1950s, *toured Australia with the *Shakespeare Memorial Theatre in 1952–3, and was *artistic director of the *Chichester Festival from 1974 to 1977. He also worked in *musicals—*Robert and Elizabeth* (1964) and *La Cage aux folles* (1985), for example—but is most famous for his King Henry in the BBC *television series *The Six Wives of Henry VIII* (1970). He worked extensively in Australia as well, and wrote and acted in an Australianized version of *Peer Gynt* (*Pete McGynty and the Dreamtime*, *Melbourne, 1981). He began his career as a designer, has exhibited paintings, and illustrated the children's book *Captain Beaky* by Jeremy Lloyd, which inspired television spin-offs and a recording with Michell reading the poems.   EJS

MICKERY THEATRE

Dutch initiative developed in 1965 by the actor Ritsaert ten Cate, first at his farmhouse and from 1972 in a disused cinema in *Amsterdam, which became a leading institution for theatre reform in the Netherlands and worldwide. Mickery was a protest against conventional production with its rigid *repertory system and domination by the *director. It sought instead a *collective ideology of theatre-making and developed new views of theatrical space that broke down the physical separation of *audience and performers. Ten Cate invited *avant-garde companies from all over the world to experiment at various venues in Amsterdam, including *La Mama Experimental Theatre Club, the *Living Theatre, *Pip Simmons Theatre, the *People Show, *Mabou Mines, and *Bread and Puppet Theatre. Mickery had a formative influence on major innovators like *Terayama Shūji and Robert *Wilson; it became 'the headquarters of the international avant-garde, a kind of United Nations of world theatre' (Ian Buruma). Its collaboration with international companies tended to eclipse the excellent local work it produced, like *Fairground*, *Contempt Theatre*, *Folter Follies*, *Sweet Dreams*, and *Rembrandt and Hitler or Me*. Mickery was officially disbanded in 1991, and ten Cate moved on to found the Amsterdam School for Advanced Research in Theatre and Dance Studies (DasArts).   TH

MICKIEWICZ, ADAM (1798–1855)

Poet and playwright, considered the greatest Polish writer. As a student in *Vilnius, Mickiewicz joined the anti-Russian cause, was jailed, exiled, and eventually settled in Paris, where he was a professor at the Collège de France (1840–4). He died of cholera in Turkey, organizing a Polish military force. Among his masterworks is the *romantic *Forefathers' Eve*, a dramatic poem published in five parts (1823–32). Long and anarchic, it is an explosive call for Poland's spiritual and political freedom, prohibited in Poland in the nineteenth century and on several occasions *censored by the communist regime after 1945. It was staged for the first time by Stanisław *Wyspiański (*Cracow, 1901) in an adapted *text, and since then has remained central to Polish theatre, often seen in rich *spectacles with *music, monumental *scenery, crowd scenes, and powerful *acting. Leon *Schiller's production (Lvov, 1932; Vilnius, 1933; *Warsaw, 1934), designed by Andrzej Pornaszko, is remembered for its vast, open platform crowned with three crosses, equating the suffering of Poland with the suffering of Christ. *Forefathers' Eve* was frequently produced after the war, notably by Jerzy *Grotowski (Opole, 1961) and Konrad *Swinarski (Cracow, 1973).   KB

MIDDLE COMEDY

The transitional *comedy in Athens and the Greek world in the fourth century BC. The term covers the period from the last two plays of *Aristophanes, *Ecclesiazusae* (or *Women in the Assembly*, 392/1 BC) and *Plutus* (*Wealth*, 388 BC), to the first play of *Menander (c.323 BC). There are no other surviving plays from the period, only titles from a number of writers such as Alexis, Anaxilas, and Eubulus, which seem to suggest a mix of mythological theme and *character comedy, but without either the hard edge or the fantasy in which the previous century rejoiced. The two late Aristophanes comedies are noticeably different in tone and structure from his earlier work. The *choruses have far less influence on the *plot, and what they actually say, or sing, is often omitted in the received *text in favour of a *stage direction, 'chorou', which simply means 'choral interlude'. *Ecclesiazusae*, in which the women of Athens *disguise themselves as men in order to go to the Assembly and vote themselves into power, does have the feel of the authentic Aristophanes, complete with its directed *satire against Platonic social engineering. *Wealth* is social satire too in its story of the return to sight of the blind god of money. Neither, though, shows the exuberance or the personal attacks on living characters which made *Old Comedy seem both dangerous and volatile. In a time of political change in Athens there was no place for the comedy of the Peloponnesian War that had so fiercely mocked institutions and politicians. *See also* NEW COMEDY.   JMW

MIDDLETON, THOMAS (1580–1627)

English dramatist. A Londoner, he was educated at Oxford, and had begun to work in the theatre by 1601. In 1602, he contributed to a number of plays (all lost) for the *Henslowe companies, working with, among others, *Dekker and *Webster. A period of intense activity in 1604–6 produced a run of *satirical *comedies for the Paul's *boy company, including *A Mad World, my Masters*, *A Trick to Catch the Old One*, and *Michaelmas Term*. These plays adapt the characteristic preoccupations of sixteenth-century Italian comedy to a contemporary *London setting, with unscrupulous, predatory young men tricking their elders in a quest for money and sex (*see* CITY COMEDY). For the King's Men (*see* CHAMBERLAIN'S MEN, LORD) he began as a writer of sardonic *tragedies of sexual and political intrigue in foreign courts, notably *The Revenger's Tragedy* (1606) and *The Maiden's Tragedy* (1611); the former is a stage perennial which graced the *Royal Shakespeare Company's repertory from 1966 until 1970 in a long-running production by Trevor *Nunn. Some late twentieth-century scholarship claimed that Middleton was Shakespeare's collaborator on *Timon of Athens* and the reviser, after Shakespeare's retirement, of *Macbeth* and *Measure for Measure*.

Much of Middleton's early writing has the hard, intellectual brittleness of a young man's work, but the mid-Jacobean fashion for *romance tempered his satirical tendencies, beginning with his comedy, *No Wit, No Help Like a Woman's* (1611). The plays of this middle period are less harsh in tone, more *tragicomic in incident, and the presence of uncomplicatedly sympathetic figures, like the title *character of *A Chaste Maid in Cheapside* (1613), make the happy endings the more unreservedly joyous. The year 1613 also saw the first of a series of eight city *pageants, which he continued to write on and off for the rest of his life, and the beginning of a long-standing, intermittent collaboration with William *Rowley. Middleton's later work includes his great tragic studies of female psychology and sexuality, *Women Beware Women* (1621) and *The Changeling* (1622, with Rowley), which have proved his most enduring contributions to the repertory: both had notable twentieth-century revivals at the Royal Shakespeare Company, *Women Beware Women* directed by Anthony Page in 1962 and *The Changeling* by Terry *Hands in 1979. Middleton's last extant play is the *political satire *A Game at Chess* (1624), which uses its chessboard analogy to represent the worsening diplomatic relations between England and Spain, and played for nine consecutive days (the English theatre's first *long run) before it was closed by the authorities.

Opinions on Middleton's plays could not be more varied. In the early twentieth century, he was considered an almost anonymous writer, a *realist subsumed in the world he represents; but this was a judgement based on an incomplete canon. Later critics emphasized both the range and the narrowness of his work: though diverse in style and *genre, the plays return repeatedly to the same themes, events, and motifs. (This may help to explain why relatively few of his many plays were professionally revived in the twentieth century.) A Calvinist sense of damnation is never far away, and the plays enact an uncomfortable conjunction between the short-term material world of sex and commerce and another, eternal dimension of moral absolutes. By the twentieth century's end, Middleton's was recognized as one of the most distinctive personal styles of any Jacobean dramatist: reality was not so much represented as transformed by the workings of his peculiar imagination.

MJW

MIELZINER, JO (JOSEPH) (1901–76)

Pre-eminent American designer of the mid-twentieth century. Although trained as an easel artist, Mielziner became an early assistant and disciple of Robert Edmond Jones, when *Jones was insisting that the designer could provide a visual metaphor for the play to give it depth and meaning. Under the spell of Jones's New Stagecraft, Mielziner made his mark early with the *Theatre Guild production of *Molnár's *The Guardsman*, starring Alfred *Lunt and Lynn Fontanne, in 1924. Rising quickly to the top of his profession, for the next 50 years he matured into the finest set and *lighting designer of his time. Convinced that the designer should control all visual elements of a production, he served as *costume, lighting, and *scenery designer during the first few years of his career, relinquishing costume designing when it became too burdensome. The favourite not only of the Theatre Guild, but also of Katharine *Cornell's company, the Playwrights Company, *Rodgers and *Hammerstein, and a number of Broadway playwrights and *producers, he gained a reputation as a problem solver. He used the technology of the time creatively, often adding his own refinements to both scenery and lighting. His notable successes were *Annie Get your Gun* by Irving *Berlin (1946), *A Streetcar Named Desire* by Tennessee *Williams (1947), *Death of a Salesman* by Arthur *Miller (1949), *Guys and Dolls* by Frank *Loesser (1950), and *The King and I* by Rodgers and Hammerstein (1951). Chafing against the restrictions of Broadway, he sought to make changes in the design of *playhouses, and in the early 1960s he worked with Eero Saarinen on the design of the Vivian Beaumont Theatre in *Lincoln Center, and served as designer or consultant on a number of university theatres. *See also* SCENOGRAPHY. MCH

MIHURA, MIGUEL (1905–77)

Spanish playwright, director, and humorist. His first and most acclaimed play, *Three Top Hats*, was written in 1932 but not staged until 1952, initiating a career of almost two decades. At the end of the Spanish Civil War, he founded the popular satirical magazine *La Cordoniz*, which thrived in spite of *censorship restrictions. *Sublime Decision* (1955) and *The Fair Dorothea* (1963) rank with the best serio-comic plays of their time and illustrate his gift for brilliant, near *absurdist *dialogue. In *Carlota* (1954), one of his several crime plays, he anticipates postmodernism (*see* MODERNISM AND POSTMODERNISM) by inverting the conventions of the murder mystery *genre and denying his *audience a definitive ending. He directed brisk and stylish productions of many of his own plays in *Madrid's leading commercial venues.   MPH

MIKANZA, NOBERT MOBYEM (1944–94)

Congolese dramatist and choreographer. One of the founders of the National Theatre of Congo (formerly Zaire), he started his career with the Théâtre du Petit Nègre of Kikwit in 1967 after completing *theatre studies in the United States. His first production, *Mundele Ndombe*, an adaptation of *Molière's *The Would-Be Gentleman*, caricatured the behaviour of the Congolese bourgeoisie. *Allo Mangembo, keba!*, an adaptation of *Gogol's *The Government Inspector*, caused a furore for its treatment of the corruption of a press under the thumb of the country's single political party. *Ngembo* (1979), a *musical play within an elaborate choreography, contained appearances by popular music stars in Kinshasa. The *dancers of the National Ballet alternated with actors who *parodied the government's most important personalities. In this work Mikanza used the International Year of the Child celebrations to critique the regime's indifference to the plight of abandoned children.

                                                   PNN trans. JCM

MIKEY, FANNY (1931–)

Argentine-born actor, director, and *manager, who moved to Colombia at the end of the 1950s and became a member of the Teatro *Experimental de Cali. While acting in most of its productions, she organized five seasons of the highly successful Festival of the Arts in *Cali. In 1969 she moved to *Bogotá and worked for eight years with Teatro *Popular de Bogotá. Once on her own, she created a *café-concert* vogue with her *one-person shows *Véanme* and *Oíganme* (*See Me* and *Listen to Me*, 1975–6). In 1978 she founded the Teatro *Nacional, which she brought to a high level of success through a repertory that combined well-known contemporary plays with commercial work. With Ramiro Osorio, she founded the biennial Festival Iberoamericano de Bogotá in 1987.   BJR

MIKHOELS, SOLOMON (1890–1948)

Soviet Jewish actor and director who joined the Jewish Theatre Studio in *St Petersburg in 1919, from which emerged the Moscow Jewish Chamber Theatre and, later, the *Moscow State Yiddish Theatre which Mikhoels led from 1929. Mikhoels made a name for himself as an actor, mainly in plays by Sholem *Aleichem but most notably in Sergei *Radlov's 1935 production of *King Lear*, designed by Aleksandr Tyshler, and which Edward Gordon *Craig much admired on a visit to *Moscow.

Moments from this production survive on *film and reveal Mikhoel's characteristic style. His own approach to *acting was highly traditional and derived from forms of Jewish *folk theatre, allied with sophisticated forms of *expressionist performance based on stylized gesture and speech, together with exaggeratedly bold use of *mask-like *make-up redolent of the *grotesque. This style lent itself well to forms of folk *comedy but could also be refined, in Mikhoels's hands, to produce more poignant and subtly tragic creations, such as his Jewish 'Don Quixote' in *The Voyage of Veniamin III* (1927) and his Teve in Aleichem's *Tevye the Milkman* (1937). Mikhoels had a prominent public profile and did much to encourage popular interest in a state-sponsored Jewish theatre. He also appeared in films and was something of a roving ambassador abroad, visiting America in 1943. His death in a car accident in mysterious circumstances was rumoured to have been contrived at Stalin's behest in the year in which Mikhoels had also suffered the closure of his theatre. *See also* YIDDISH THEATRE.   NW

MILAN

Theatres were established in the ducal court of Milan at least by the late sixteenth century, and *touring *commedia dell'arte* troupes, including the *Fedeli, whose *capocomico* was the celebrated G. B. *Andreini, and the *Accesi made well-recorded visits to the city. One of the minor *stock characters of *commedia*, Meneghino, was presented as Milanese, and in the nineteenth century several actors, of whom Giuseppe Moncalvo was the most successful, attempted to make this boastful, wily figure as representative of Milan as was Pulcinella of *Naples.

    Even if Milan cannot, in the history of Italian theatre, rival Venice in the age of *Goldoni or Naples in the period astride the nineteenth and twentieth centuries for the production of original work, the impact of Milanese theatre-makers, including impresarios and directors, has been significant. By the early nineteenth century, Milan was firmly established as the economic and industrial capital of Italy, and so was ideally placed to became the centre of commercial, or *bourgeois, theatre. Although this term has acquired negative overtones, it was drama produced in Milan which most accurately reflected the political and social tensions and aspirations of Italy during the Risorgimento, as well as the disillusionment which attended the completion of the unification process. The city was made capital of the Cisalpine Republic after the invasion by the Napoleonic French, and the new atmosphere allowed a new theatre to flourish. A Society for Patriotic Theatre was established in 1798, and put on many plays, including works by *Metastasio and *Alfieri judged to be sufficiently patriotic in tone, and new works tied to immediate *political circumstances. *The Marriage of Brother Giovanni* by G. A. Ranza, advocating ecclesiastical reform, can be taken as typical of much that was produced at that time. If the reflection of contemporary interests meant that the works were unlikely to survive first production, the ambition for contemporary relevance and the desire to mirror the concerns of society became an enduring characteristic of Milanese theatre. In 1805, the Society changed its name to the Teatro dei Filodrammatici, but continued to enjoy the favour of the Viceroy Beauharnais, who also founded Italy's first state theatre in Milan in 1807.

Throughout the century, irrespective of French domination, Austrian rule, or the achievement of Italian unity, entrepreneurs established new theatres: the Carcano in 1803 was the last to be named after an aristocratic owner, while the Re in 1813 and the Fossati in 1853 took the names of the bourgeois entrepreneurs who had them built. The new capitalist ethic provided a driving force for the development of a theatre which was aware of its need to serve a new public and to keep in step with a new ethos. The Manzoni, the property of a limited liability company, appeared in 1870 but rapidly established itself as the most important theatre in Italy. Each theatre developed a character of its own and attracted its own *audience. The history of Milanese theatre in the nineteenth century is primarily a history of actors and impresarios, not of writers or directors. The great *actor-managers who were the dominant force in Italian theatre all played in Milan. Gustavo *Modena, who was briefly exiled in *London for his political views, played at the Carcano with the Lombard Dramatic Company, as did Ernesto *Rossi, Tommaso *Salvini, and Eleanore *Duse.

The Teatro Re hosted the première of Silvio Pellico's *Francesca da Rimini* (1815), which can be taken as marking a switch in public taste from *neoclassicism towards that combination of *romanticism and nationalism which was an important strand in Italian nineteenth-century theatre. The dominant figure in romanticism was Alessandro *Manzoni, himself a native of Milan, who wrote two *tragedies, *Il conte di Carmagnola* (1816) and *Adelchi* (1822), although these plays were no more intended for performance than were *Byron's. Manzoni wrote various *theoretical treatises on tragedy and on romanticism, but in drama, unlike in fiction, he did not attract followers who regarded themselves as forming a Lombard school. When Milanese schools appeared, they were grouped around nationalism or the aesthetic doctrines of Scapigliatura and *verismo. Nationalist enthusiasm was expressed by *Verdi in his *operas, and the same feelings found expression in drama, in both street performance and commercial theatre, especially after the Five Days in 1848 when Milan rebelled against the Austrians. However, the energy needed to achieve the aims of the Risorgimento was scarcely expended when a feeling of fatigue or disillusion began to be expressed. This took various forms. The Scapigliatura was one, an amorphous, inchoate, anti-bourgeois movement based in Milan and straddling all the arts, which flourished between 1860 and 1880, as was the drive towards dialect theatre. Cletto Righetti, a minor playwright, was the driving force behind the Academy of Milanese Theatre, established in 1870, which put on several plays in Milanese. The motivating spirit behind the

best of these works overlapped with verismo, the Italian version of *realism. *El Nost Milan* by Carlo Bertolazzi (1870–1916) was an enormous success with audiences and *critics. The first part, *La povera gent* (1893), took as its subject the proletariat, while the less successful sequel, *I sciori* (1895) examined the upper class. The same troupe produced *La guera* (1901) by Pompeo Bettini and Ettore Albini, an embittered examination of profiteering during the supposedly glorious Risorgimento. At around the same time, Marco *Praga offered the new middle class a view of themselves in works like *The Virgins* (1889), a reworking of the old theme of lost virginity as an insuperable obstacle to the marriage contract.

From the turn of the century until the rise of *fascism, the Teatro Manzoni was the natural arena for Milanese writers of bourgeois theatre and set standards for theatres all over Italy. Touring companies preferred to open there, while its premières included works by *D'Annunzio, *Pirandello, and Ugo *Betti. Its rule ended with *fascism, which imposed its own requirements, but with the Liberation Milan regained its pre-eminent position. The *Piccolo Teatro, Italy's first *teatro stabile*, offered a model which other cities were keen to imitate. Following the lead of the Piccolo, permanent theatres, subsidized by the city council, appeared in Turin, *Rome, and Genoa. The pioneering efforts of a new generation of directors, such as Luchino *Visconti and Giorgio *Strehler, meant that the balance of power inside Italian theatre was shifted away from the actors, and that the very nature of theatre production was revolutionized. In the 1960s Dario *Fo offered an alternative model, which found enthusiastic adherents elsewhere in Italy and abroad.

JF

MILES, BERNARD (1907–91)

English actor, director, writer, and theatre owner, Miles's diverse stage and *film career straddled high and popular art. Best loved by *audiences as Long John Silver and a *variety theatre 'Mummersetshire' rustic rogue, he played many classical roles including an acclaimed Iago in 1941. Supported by his wife, actress Josephine Wilson, he poured all his resources into fundraising, building, and running the *Mermaid Theatre in *London from 1959 until 1984. Despite some artistic misjudgement and ultimate *financial failure, major successes included *Lock up your Daughters*, his *musical adaptation of *Fielding's *Rape upon Rape*, which launched the Mermaid in 1959. He was knighted in 1969, and made a life peer in 1979.

CEC

MILET, JACQUES (c.1425–1466)

Playwright, author of *The Destruction of Great Troy* (1450–2). The requirement of four days for a performance and the use of multiple *mansions indicate Milet's debt to the *medieval religious drama. Trappings of fictional *romance and the use of minstrels to perform during intervals reflect the secular subject matter.   RWV

MILLER, ARTHUR (1915–)

American playwright and theorist. Beginning with *All my Sons* in 1947, Miller acquired a worldwide reputation and joined the ranks of Eugene *O'Neill and Tennessee *Williams as one of the most accomplished American dramatists. More than 25 Miller plays have been produced and several have entered the world repertory of serious drama: *All my Sons* (1947), *Death of a Salesman* (1949, Pulitzer Prize), *The Crucible* (1953), *A View from the Bridge* (1955), *After the Fall* (1964), *Incident at Vichy* (1964), and *The Price* (1968). Of the later work, *The Ride down Mount Morgan* (1991), and *Broken Glass* (1994) have seen major productions in *London and *New York. Miller's work began and to a degree continued within the modern *realistic tradition developed by *Ibsen—psychologically complex and logically motivated *characters move through strong *plots driven by external social pressures, the *protagonists finding resolutions which conclude the *action and deliver potent but satisfyingly ambiguous moral reflections. Nevertheless Miller stretched the realistic form by interweaving *dream states and subjective imaginings into the fabric of his dramatic world. In *Death of a Salesman*, widely regarded as his masterpiece and one of the outstanding English-language plays of the modern period, the playwright provides the objectively viewed realistic scenes of the present-day salesman Willie Loman—ageing, confused, and on the verge of disaster. The play also moves freely about in Willie's memory and imagination, mingling the 'real' *scenes of the present with Willie's replaying of scenes from his past as well as his present-time conversations with the imagined presence of a dead relative. The allure, necessity, and unreliability of memory in relation to one's own sense of moral responsibility is a persistent theme in Miller's work, as is the related issue of time and the ability of the human to 'bend' it through memory and art. Two Miller *one-act plays produced in New York (1987) and London (1988) bear the title *Danger! Memory!* and Miller's memoir, *Timebends*, was published in 1987.

Despite these interests, Miller is not a relativist. There is a truth to be found, and the struggle of human beings, with their limited capacities to find that truth, is the central drama of existence. The clearest model for Miller's lifelong project may be *After the Fall*, which takes place in the mind of its protagonist who, in Miller's words, 'turned at the edge of the abyss to look at his experience, his nature, and his time'. Like other Miller protagonists, Quentin experiences anguish over his social responsibility for both the whole world and those nearest him—his male friends and female lovers and wives—and seeks, if not exoneration, then at least insight, clarity, the kind of redemption that could come with understanding. *Broken Glass* in some ways fulfilled Miller's persistent search for a connection between private and public morality, with its female protagonist subtly oppressed by her husband and obsessed by reports of attacks on Jews in Europe. *Death of a Salesman* and *The Crucible* were criticized by some who felt that Miller over-articulated the message of the plays in their final scenes. Later works put greater trust in metaphor. As the final stage action of *Broken Glass*, the protagonist, who has been suffering from an apparent case of 'hysterical paralysis', rises from her bed and walks for the first time in the play. No character steps forward to guide our interpretation; Miller leaves his audience with what he has called 'the wordless darkness that underlies all verbal truth'.

Miller has been a major public figure and, at times, even a celebrity. He was associated with a number of pro-communist activities during the 1940s and became a focus of the House Un-American Activities Committee during the 1950s. *The Crucible* (1953), his *historically based play about witch trials in seventeenth-century Salem, Massachusetts, was widely interpreted as offering a parallel to tactics of congressional investigators, by which witnesses were intimidated into naming communists as a means of saving themselves, just as seventeenth-century colonists were frightened into naming witches. Miller became the focus of intense media scrutiny when at about the same time that he was called to testify before HUAC (1956), he announced his impending marriage to the *film star Marilyn Monroe. (They divorced in 1961.) Having refused to 'name names', the playwright was indicted for contempt of Congress (1957), but the conviction was overturned on appeal in 1958. From 1965 to 1969, Miller was international president of PEN (the organization of Poets, Essayists, and Novelists) and used this position to advocate freedom of expression for writers in totalitarian states of the left or the right. His 1969 travel journal *In Russia*, and his public attacks on the oppression of dissident writers, led to the banning of his works by the Soviet regime.

The Theater Essays of Arthur Miller (1978) include his influential 'Tragedy and the Common Man', first published in 1949. Miller argued that 'tragic stature' is achieved for modern audiences not in the *Greek sense of a 'person of high estate' whose fall affects the whole community, but rather through the commonality of the *hero, a shared status that allows the audience to identify with the protagonist.   MAF

BIGSBY, CHRISTOPHER (ed.), *The Cambridge Companion to Arthur Miller* (Cambridge, 1997)

BLOOM, HAROLD (ed.), *Modern Critical Views: Arthur Miller* (New York, 1987)

CENTOLA, STEVEN R. (ed.), *Arthur Miller in Conversation* (Dallas, 1993)

MILLER, HENRY (1859–1926)

Anglo-American actor, director, and *manager. Born in London, he moved in 1873 to *Toronto, where he played small parts. From 1876 he resided in *New York, making his debut there in

Cymbeline (1880). His gorgeous voice and restrained style made him a favourite leading man. He first achieved stardom in *Heartsease* (1897), and his reputation was secured when he *produced, directed, and starred in *Moody's *The Great Divide* (1906). He capped his career in 1918 by erecting his own handsome theatre—the first *playhouse with built-in air-conditioning—where he acted in many successes.   CT

MILLER, JONATHAN (1934–   )

English director. Trained as a doctor, Miller became known as a comedian through his part in *Beyond the Fringe* (with Alan *Bennett, Peter Cook, and Dudley Moore, 1961) but quickly moved to directing with John *Osborne's *Under Plain Cover* (*Royal Court, 1962). Since then, in classic drama and in *opera, though very rarely with new work, Miller has been sensitive to the psychology of *character (Lear's ageing or Ophelia as a latent schizophrenic) and the social implications of the *text. Often willing to direct the same play (he has done four productions of *King Lear*), his research interests and immense intellect have enabled him to theorize the practice of revivals, writing brilliantly about it in *Subsequent Performances* (1986). Miller's use of alternative period settings, for instance setting *The Merchant of Venice* in the late nineteenth century for the *National Theatre (1970), *Rigoletto* in the New York mafia of the 1930s (English National Opera, 1984), or *The Mikado* in a Victorian hotel (ENO, 1986), is always the consequence of careful examination of the text's original social context. In *The Taming of the Shrew* (*Royal Shakespeare Company, 1987), he made the play a detailed study of the emerging belief in companionate marriage. But intellectual justification never becomes arid in Miller's work: his productions have a freshness and energy which many directors envy. After an uncomfortable period as associate director of the National Theatre (1973–5), he has preferred to work in less pressured circumstances where his skilful explorations can be comfortably valued by performers and *audiences alike.   PDH

MILLER, MARILYN (1898–1936)

American singer and actress. Born Mary Ellen Reynolds, she began performing in *vaudeville as a child. Her appearance (beginning at the age of 16) as a *dancer in the *Shubert brothers' *Passing Show* *revues made her such a star that she was lured away to appear in the *Ziegfeld Follies of 1918*. Beginning with *Sally* in 1920, she starred in several hit shows designed specifically for her talents. A splendid dancer with a passable voice and enormous charm, the tiny, blonde Miller was arguably the most popular American *musical comedy star of the 1920s.
                                                              JD

MILLER, MAX (THOMAS SARGENT) (1895–1963)

English comedian. The 'Cheeky Chappie' began his career as an army entertainer during the First World War, followed by work in seaside concert parties and provincial *variety theatres. His steady climb up the variety ladder was as a solo performer, writing his own material and songs; by the 1930s he was one of the highest-paid variety entertainers. Miller was renowned for his outrageous clothes and blue jokes; in garish suits and kipper ties he would declare, 'I'm a commercial traveller, and I'm ready for bed.' His risqué gags about honeymoon couples and sex-starved girls were accompanied by a lascivious grin or sidelong glance, whilst leaning confidentially across the *footlights. Vigorously heterosexual, his flamboyant *costume and *make-up, and throwaway lines ('He's a boy, isn't he? I hope so!'), softened his otherwise aggressive sexual energy. He was a master of timing and *audience management, one of the greatest British stand-up comedians.   AF

MILLER, TIM (1958–   )

American *performance artist and gay rights activist. A native of Whittier, California, he moved to *New York in 1978, becoming part of the emerging performance art movement, and co-founding PS 122, a centre for experimentation in an abandoned former school. He attained notoriety as one of the 'NEA Four'—artists whose grants were cancelled in 1990 by the *National Endowment for the Arts for their sexual content. Miller became a leader in the effort to recognize gay partnerships later in the 1990s. *See* GAY THEATRE AND PERFORMANCE.   AW

MILLS, FLORENCE (1895–1927)

*African-American performer, who went on the stage as a child. In 1899 she was featured in Bert *Williams and Walker's *Sons of Ham*, singing 'Hannah from Savannah'. In *vaudeville, she *toured with her sisters Olivia and Maude and the Tennessee Ten, but took the lead in *Shuffle Along* in 1921 in *New York. Broadway loved her. She left to join Lew Leslie's *Plantation Review*, which was reworked for *London, and in 1924 she opened in *Dixie to Broadway*, refashioned from the London show. In 1926 she starred in Leslie's New York *revue called *Blackbirds*, which featured her famous song, 'I'm a Little Blackbird Looking for a Bluebird'. The show toured *Paris and London, where the Prince of Wales came so often he was labelled a 'repeat attender'.   BBL

MILLS, JOHN (1908–   )

English actor who began his career in *musical theatre but made his name playing plucky Brits in a succession of war *films that included *In Which We Serve* (1942), *This Happy Breed* (1944), and *Ice Cold in Alex* (1958). He made his *London debut in 1927 in the *chorus of *The Five O'Clock Review*, thereafter joining the repertory company the Quaints and *touring the Far East. In 1931 he appeared in *Coward's *Cavalcade*, and in 1938 he joined Tyrone *Guthrie's *Old Vic company. He made his Broadway debut in 1961 in *Rattigan's *Ross* and again appeared in a Rattigan play, *Separate Tables*, in London in 1977. Later stage roles include *Goodbye Mr Chips* (1982), *Little Lies* (1983), and *Pygmalion* (1987). His most successful film roles were Barrow in *Tunes of Glory* (1960) and Michael in *Ryan's Daughter* (1970). Mills was knighted in 1977. AS

MILNE, A. A. (ADAM ALEXANDER) (1882–1956)

English playwright and children's writer. Having established himself as a humorist with *Punch*, Milne's theatrical success came with *Mr Pim Passes By* in 1919 and continued with light *comedies such as *The Truth about Blayds* (1923) and *Michael and Mary* (1930). The whimsy of these plays has dated and they are rarely, if ever, produced. The same quality, however, has made Milne's 1929 adaptation of Kenneth Graham's *The Wind in the Willows*, entitled *Toad of Toad Hall*, a perennial Christmas favourite and Milne's most enduring play.

MDG

MILTON, JOHN (1608–74)

Poet in four languages, political and religious pamphleteer, historian, translator, and teacher. Milton was a Londoner, educated at St Paul's School and Cambridge, where he wrote and performed in college entertainments. His short pastoral entertainment (*Arcades*), set to music by his friend Henry Lawes, was followed in 1634 by a more elaborate *masque which members of the same family performed at Ludlow Castle, again with Lawes as composer, director, and performer; it was later called *Comus* by its editors. Milton, who saw himself as destined to write an English masterpiece, initially seems to have thought that it would be a classical drama on a subject from biblical or English history. It was only in the late 1640s that he decided that his chosen subject, the fall of man, should be an epic (*Paradise Lost*, 1667). *Dryden later adapted it as an *opera (*The State of Innocence*, published 1677). Milton's own classical *tragedy on a biblical theme, *Samson Agonistes*, was published in 1673, when its portrayal of the blind *hero must have seemed a self-vindication to the then blind writer. *Comus*, in a slightly modernized version with music by Thomas Arne, was performed with great success in 1738 by a double cast of singers and actors and held the stage for another hundred years. The original Lawes version has frequently been given in concert performance, as at the Folger Shakespeare Library in Washington in 2001. *Samson*, though Milton said it was 'never intended' for the stage, has been recorded and performed as a dramatic reading. LDP

MIME

Contemporary dictionaries define the verb 'to mime' as 'to play a part with gestures and actions, but usually without words'. This definition, however, suits only some theatre events which have called themselves mime. A more inclusive definition was proposed by the teacher and inventor of 'corporeal mime', Étienne *Decroux: mime is not mute theatre, but actor-centred theatre in which the expressive means (words included) are selected and arranged by actors. In 1931 he proposed that theatre become silent for 30 years, but this was to allow the presence of the *actor to displace literature from its central position. Decroux's revolutionary assertion that literature is the writer's art and theatre is the actor's art set the stage for a host of diverse and sometimes contradictory contemporary performance activities. Decroux suggested that the play be *rehearsed before it is written, that is, the actors should determine the spoken *text and physical text simultaneously, not begin with pre-existing script to interpret; decades later companies as different as Theatre de *Complicité and the *Odin Teatret did just that.

Decroux's definition helps us to understand history better. Records of Greek *mime and Roman *pantomime (the terms are often used interchangeably) mention that the actors spoke, or were accompanied by narrators or *chorus, but differed from other actors in that they did not use a text which had first been established by a *playwright. In *commedia dell'arte (c.1550–c.1750) actors also *improvised and developed their own *scenarios. As they relied heavily on gesture, *acrobatics, *masks, and facial expression, *commedia* performers could *tour in many countries while speaking only Italian. In *Paris they were prohibited from speaking on stage by Louis XIV in 1697, as they were competing with the two official French theatres (*see* Comédie Italienne). In order to survive they performed silent mime for the duration of the proscription, and their performances gave rise to the best-known pantomime performer of the nineteenth century, Jean-Gaspard *Deburau, who also played mute because of governmental restrictions on the fairground theatres where he performed. In the late 1940s Marcel *Marceau perfected his mute *character Bip, inspired by Jean-Louis *Barrault's portrayal of Deburau in the *film *Les Enfants du paradis* (1945); Marceau also admired the work of silent film* stars Charlie Chaplin and Buster Keaton. In these examples muteness was more an accident of history (or limited technology, as in the case of early cinema) than a prerequisite of mime.

Much *performance art and a host of activity generically entitled *physical theatre, despite dissimilarities, find certain common ground: none is mute, all are actor centred. Mime, instead of a light diversion for a child's birthday party or a simplistic street corner amusement, has become central to the work of contemporary theatre. Released from the stereotype of whitefaced charm and mute, entertaining *illusions, mime in the later twentieth century reclaimed its place as a powerful alternative to logocentric theatre.

We have only to look at the companies and individuals who are invited to perform annually at the two leading international mime *festivals—the Mimos Festival in Périgueux in south-west France, directed by Peter Bu, and the London International Mime Festival directed by Joseph Seelig—to find dictionary definitions of the form inadequate. The work at these two venues may include *puppetry, object animation, masks, acrobatics, *commedia*, *butoh, and myriad other forms and postmodern combinations thereof. For the most part performers use text and voice, in addition to very strong physical and gestural components; mime differs from mainstream theatre in that those who create it also perform it. What is rarely seen at the festivals is the mute, whitefaced, illusionist pantomime which tells stories through gesture, which seems to have reached its logical conclusion with Marceau. Students of the three great mime teachers of the twentieth century—Decroux, Marceau, and Jacques *Lecoq—are to be found in many parts of the world. While a few of Marceau's students carry on his tradition, for the most part mime has come to mean a postmodern blend of varied elements that does not begin with written text, nor exclude it.   TL

DECROUX, ÉTIENNE, *Words on Mime*, trans. Mark Piper (Claremont, Calif., 1985)
LEABHART, THOMAS, *Modern and Post-Modern Mime* (London, 1989)

MIME, GREEK

Mimos (imitator, imitation, hence actor, play), a form of *comic drama originating in Syracuse independently of the Athenian choral *drama, reached Athens in the early fourth century BC. Mime consisted of *monologue, *dialogue, and *dance featuring mythological *burlesque or scenes of everyday life. The treatment was topical, *farcical, and often indecent, with an element of *improvisation. Interest lay in *character and situation rather than in sustained dramatic *action. Performers were of either sex, and their skills could include juggling and acrobatics as well as singing. Male characters frequently wore *phalluses. Performing alone or as members of a small troupe, mime actors, who wore no *masks, relied on facial expression as well as gesture and voice. They initially performed in the marketplace or in private houses; only in the *Roman period did they appear in theatres. Among the writers of mimes were Sophron of Syracuse (fifth century BC) and Herodas (third century BC), whose eight mimes represent the bulk of those extant. (Theocritus' *Idyll 15* is in fact a mime, but its performance is doubtful.) Mimes may have influenced the Athenian drama, and they appear to be related to the *phlyakes* of southern Italy. On the Roman stage Latin mimes eventually replaced the *Atellan farce as afterpieces and interludes (*see* PANTOMIME, ROMAN). The mime tradition persisted into *medieval theatre.   RWV

MIMESIS

Although the term is used in earlier Greek critical studies, mimesis first assumes a central function in the writings of Plato. The basis of reality, according to Plato, is the realm of pure 'Ideas', dimly reflected in the material world and in turn copied by art. This copying, imitation, or mimesis, is viewed generally negatively, especially in Plato's *Republic*, since it creates a product twice removed from the reality sought by philosophy. *Aristotle, who viewed reality as a process in which the partially realized forms of the physical world were moving toward more complete realizations, saw mimesis in a much more positive light. His *Poetics* suggests that the poet's concern should not be imitating things 'as they are' but 'as they ought to be'. Through the influence of Aristotle, mimesis became a central, if often disputed, critical term in Western dramatic and literary *theory. During the *medieval and early Renaissance periods, the Latin term *imitatio* became much more associated with the imitation not of a Platonic or Aristotelian reality, but of existing and admired models, an emphasis that continued through the *early modern period, when classic authors were widely assumed to provide the ideal models for modern authors to imitate.

During the Enlightenment the term 'mimesis' generally gave way to 'imitation', and the focus shifted with the rise of modern bourgeois society away from imitation of abstract reality or earlier models to models of social action and self-understanding. Aristotle's concept of mimesis as a tool for looking toward a more fully formulated reality became interpreted on a much more social and even psychological level. The late eighteenth-century drama offered social and psychological mimetic models, and gradually the idea of society itself as mimetic role playing, suggested by such theorists as *Rousseau and *Diderot, began to become a part of modern social consciousness.

Mimesis regained popularity as a critical term in the twentieth century, though its historical association with *realism and models of social action led many critics, most notably Eric Auerbach in the best-known modern work on the subject (*Mimesis*, 1946), to apply it more commonly to discussions of the novel than of drama. Among theatre theorists, those same associations led socially engaged writers like Bertolt *Brecht and Augusto *Boal to distrust mimesis, seeing it as a device for encouraging acceptance of and conformity with the existing social order, while some *feminist critics asked if there could be a feminist use of the term. Elin Diamond in *Unmaking Mimesis* (1997), following Luce Irigaray, focused upon Plato's discomfort with mimesis as a destabilizing process, introducing difference into the consciousness. Instead of viewing mimesis as a strategy for reinforcing an established social system (the concern also of Boal and Brecht), Diamond advocated recapturing the mimesis Plato feared in its destabilizing and playful aspect, which she called mimicry. *See also* GREEK THEATRE, ANCIENT; MODERNISM AND POSTMODERNISM. MC

BOYD, JOHN D., *The Function of Mimesis and its Decline* (Cambridge, Mass., 1980)

GOLDEN, LEON, *Aristotle on Tragic and Comic Mimesis* (Atlanta, 1992)

MINETTI, BERNHARD (1905–98)

German actor. With a career spanning over 70 years (from 1927 until shortly before his death, aged 93) Bernhard was a living legend of German theatre. The stations of his life, from *training under *Jessner in the 1920s, to major roles at the *Berlin state theatre under *Gründgens and *Fehling in the 1930s and 1940s, to various theatres in the post-war period (Hamburg, Frankfurt, Düsseldorf), to a return to Berlin in 1965, provided Minetti with experience of most major aesthetic developments from *expressionism to postmodernism. He was equally at home in classical and contemporary roles and was particularly drawn to the plays of *Beckett and *Bernhard. The latter even wrote a play for him, called *Minetti* (1976). CBB

MINKS, WILFRIED (1930–)

German designer and director. Minks studied stage design at the Academy of Fine Arts in *Berlin. In Ulm (1959–62) and then in Bremen (1962–9) he began a fruitful cooperation with Kurt Hübner and Peter *Zadek. At Bremen, then one of the most innovative theatres in Germany, Minks's designs incorporated elements of *environmental staging as well as a new pictorialism, with citations from pop art and the media. His visual contributions were a crucial element of German director's theatre, particularly associated with Zadek (*Spring's Awakening* and *The Robbers*, both 1966), *Palitzsch (*Wars of the Roses*, 1967), and *Grüber (*The Tempest*, 1969). It was only logical that after 1971 Minks combined both functions. Productions he directed and designed, such as *Mary Stuart* (1972) and *The Maid of Orleans* (1973), were hailed as inaugurating a visual turn in German theatre, and since then Minks has seldom worked for other directors. His work has decisively influenced younger designers such as Erich Wonder and Karl-Ernst *Herrmann. CBB

MINOR THEATRES

*London theatres of the first 40 years of the nineteenth century operating under a special licence. At the end of the eighteenth century *playhouses in London holding a royal *patent—*Drury Lane and *Covent Garden—and the *Haymarket, with a special summer licence from the *Lord Chamberlain, were the only theatres, by the terms of the 1737 *Licensing Act, where the spoken word could be heard. By 1807 the Lord Chamberlain had issued seven further licences to new theatres. These 'minor' theatres were not allowed to play *legitimate drama—*tragedy, *comedy and *farce—but only the 'illegitimate': *melodrama, *spectacle, *pantomime, *burlesque, and almost anything with songs and *musical accompaniment. The minors, including the *Adelphi, the *Olympic, and the Surrey, tried to enlarge their privileges, even staging comedies and tragedies rewritten in doggerel *verse with a piano accompaniment. The 'majors'—Drury Lane and Covent Garden—resisted, and prosecuted theatres that strayed over admittedly ill-defined boundaries. However, the tide was turning in favour of the minors, which were increasing in number, and legislation was introduced into Parliament in 1833 to permit any theatre to perform the legitimate drama and centralize in the Lord Chamberlain all authority over theatres. It passed the House of Commons but was narrowly defeated in the Lords. In 1843 similar legislation was embodied in the Theatres Regulation Bill, which passed both houses with almost no opposition. All theatres were now technically equal before the law. The condition of the theatre did not, however, markedly improve after 1843. Before 1843 this same law was therefore responsible for some of the liveliest and most experimental theatre in London. In contrast to the generally parlous *financial and artistic condition of the major theatres from the 1820s, a few minor theatres were both handsomely profitable and artistically vigorous. MRB

MINSTREL SHOW

Minstrelsy was the most popular form of American entertainment from the middle to the end of the nineteenth century. Minstrel performers, mostly white males, many of them of Irish and Jewish descent, applied burnt cork as *make-up to change their racial appearance and sang, danced, played musical instruments, and told jokes as caricatures of the inept and inarticulate slave or free black. Also known as blackface, and performed on both national and international stages, minstrelsy developed the template for how the *racial other was portrayed as a juvenile halfwit not to be taken seriously. More often than not, minstrelsy was racially demeaning, but it also provided the point of entry into mainstream entertainment for *African-American performers.

The *genre evolved through three phases: early, solo, and group. Early minstrel performance originated in the eighteenth century, when blackface characters were included in *legitimate dramas such as *Othello* and *The Padlock*. Blackface acts were also associated with the *circus and performed as a diversion between acts in legitimate theatres. Women were among the first performers, but men soon predominated.

The solo minstrel performer emerged at the beginning of the nineteenth century. In the early 1820s Charles *Mathews, an English actor who came to *New York to perform at the prestigious *Park Theatre, created for performance in England a show called *A Trip to America*. It included a blackface act based on his visits to the *African Company, a Manhattan church service presided over by an emancipated preacher, and his observance of black workers on the New York streets. Around the same time, Edwin *Forrest, later the leading American Shakespearian actor, wore blackface to portray a black laundress in *Philadelphia and a male slave in Cincinnati. In the second half of the decade, George Dixon popularized a minstrel song called 'Long Tail Blue' about a fast-talking dandy nicknamed Zip Coon. Shortly thereafter, Thomas Dartmouth *Rice introduced a between-acts skit in which he mimicked the song and *dance of a disadvantaged black labourer. *Audiences went wild for his 'crippled step' routine. They were delighted by this depiction of black diminishment, and the name of Rice's borrowed song, 'Jim Crow', became an institution. Jim Dandy and Jim Crow, the urban image and the agricultural, became the bookends of black limitation in America. Subsequently these two were transmuted into 'endmen', the comic duo essential to the semicircle formed by minstrel performers onstage.

In its group phase, minstrelsy was headquartered in New York, where minstrel houses eventually lined both sides of lower Broadway. Two early groups, the Virginia Minstrels and the Christy Minstrels, both established in 1843, were extremely important. The initial New York appearance of the Virginia Minstrels, a troupe of four musician-actors led by Dan Emmett, a former blackface circus performer, was a sensation. For an audience enduring economic depression, laughing at merry darkies was just the ticket. By year's end they had been booked in England, where they were well received. The Christy Minstrels, however, had far longer tenure and greater impact. They featured the songs of Stephen Foster, pioneered *female impersonation, introduced the whitefaced mediator Mr Interlocutor to communicate with the endmen, and set the standard for the three-act minstrel form. The first act included songs and banter with the endmen, beginning with a cakewalk and the command, 'Gentlemen Be Seated'. The second act, called the olio, consisted of a *variety show and often concluded with a stump speech. The third act was a short drama set on the plantation or a *burlesque of a serious play, perhaps Shakespeare or a popular *melodrama.

By 1848 the Christy Minstrels, although still playing at Mechanics Hall, had been succeeded as the most popular troupe by the Ethiopian Serenaders, the first to include an African American, Henry Allen ('Juba') Lane. An extraordinary dancer, he is often considered the father of tap; his capabilities were applauded by *Dickens in *American Notes*. The popularity of Thomas Dilward, another African-American minstrel performer before the Civil War, was based on his height of less than 1 m

(3 feet). The unprecedented success of dramatized versions of *Uncle Tom's Cabin*, continuing virtually non-stop from the 1850s into the *film era, insinuated minstrel characterization still further into the American imagination, promoting a degraded image of African Americans (*see* TOM SHOW).

Minstrelsy's immense popularity was due in part to its unifying function, bringing whites of different ethnic, socio-economic, and historical backgrounds together in differentiation from racial outsiders. The African American was cast as beyond the norm, the one to be *parodied and victimized. Minstrelsy became so popular that white minstrels toured successfully throughout Britain and Australia, and later in Belgium, France, and Germany. After the Civil War, African-American performers began to enter the ranks of minstrelsy, gaining an arena to develop their own abilities and attain celebrity, although they were usually forced to wear the blackface mask, and so minstrelsy gradually became a repository and workshop for black humour and songs. W. C. Handy, Bert *Williams, Ma Rainey, and Jelly Roll Morton are among some of the many African-American performers who received early training on the minstrel stage.

Though live minstrel shows were in serious decline at the beginning of the twentieth century, their appeal continued in the recorded media, *variety shows, and early *musicals, including *Minstrel Misses* (1903), *A Snapshot of Dixie* (1904), and *Lulu Belle* (1926). In film, Al *Jolson blacked up in the first talkie, *The Jazz Singer* (1927), and so did Bing Crosby in *Dixie* (1943). While live minstrel productions continued at *Radio City Music Hall in New York in the 1930s and 1940s, it was in *radio (Jack Benny, Fred Allen, Tallulah *Bankhead) and *television (Ed Sullivan, Milton Berle, Dean Martin, and Jerry Lewis) that the tradition continued most forcefully. In Britain, the Black and White Minstrels enjoyed a two-decade tenure on television until 1978, when minstrelsy was finally perceived as unacceptable as the basis for entertainment. Yet *amateur productions flourished in American social, church, and school clubs, and in fraternal organizations as well, for much of the century. And at its end, the black film director Spike Lee signalled a renewed, revisionist interest in minstrelsy in *Bamboozled* (2000).   BBL

MIRACLE PLAY

Mimetic presentations or *spectacles of an unspecified kind were sometimes called *miracula* in medieval Latin. The Middle English equivalent, 'miracles', was most prominently used in the title of the fifteenth-century 'Tretise of Miracles Pleyinge' taken by some scholars to be 'the chief surviving *antitheatrical document from the Middle Ages', but it is impossible to determine the exact nature of the performances to which it refers. The Old French equivalent often appears in the title of plays dramatizing the lives and miraculous activities of the saints, as in the *Miracles de sainte Geneviève* and the *Miracles de Notre*

Dame. In 1800 an article translated from French appeared in *Archaeologia* which equated 'theatrical pieces called "*Miracles*"' with 'the martyrdom of some saint of the primitive church'. 'Miracle play' thus came to have the specific meaning of *saint's play in English scholarship and was also more widely used by some early twentieth-century writers to refer to any kind of *religious drama including *biblical plays. AFJ

MIRA DE AMESCUA, ANTONIO (*c.*1574–1644)

Spanish dramatist, active and highly regarded from *c.*1600 to 1632. An exuberant but somewhat erratic disciple of Lope de *Vega, he nevertheless foreshadowed *Calderón. His plays, though they include accomplished *comedies, are predominantly serious, on *religious, biblical, and *historical subjects. Several chart the rise and fall of favourites, like *La rueda de la fortuna* (*The Wheel of Fortune*), but the most famous and influential was his complex *melodrama *El esclavo del demonio* (*The Devil's Slave*), in which a hermit turns bandit and sells his soul, but is ultimately redeemed. VFD

MIRII, NGUGI WA (1951–)

Kenyan director, actor, playwright, and teacher. Trained as a social welfare officer, wa Mirii was a facilitator for the Kamariithu Community Cultural and Educational Centre (KCCEC) in his home village near Limuru. At the KCCEC's invitation wa Mirii and his cousin Ngugi wa *Thiong'o wrote a controversial play, *Ngaahika Ndeenda* (*I Will Marry When I Want*). The community built a theatre for the 1977 performances. After the play's banning and the detention of Thiong'o (*see* CENSORSHIP), wa Mirii tried to build Kamariithu into an egalitarian cultural centre. In 1981 the government ordered the destruction of the theatre and began a purge of intellectuals, whereupon wa Mirii, like several other Kenyan theatre activists, fled to Zimbabwe. He joined Foundation for Education with Production in 1983, and as director of the Zimbabwe Association of Community Theatres since 1986 has been active in promoting Zimbabwean community theatre and running numerous *training workshops and theatre for *development projects. DaK

MIRREN, HELEN (ILYENA LYDIA MIRONOFF) (1946–)

English actress. A classical actress of tremendous power and subtlety, Mirren established herself in theatre, *film, and *television. Performances with the *National Youth Theatre while still in her teens led to her appearance as a young Cleopatra at the *Old Vic in 1965. From 1967 to 1970 she performed in leading roles with the *Royal Shakespeare Company, including Cressida and *Strindberg's Miss Julie. In 1972 she joined Peter *Brook's *International Centre for Theatre Research and *toured *The Conference of Birds* throughout North Africa. Back in England, she made a remarkable impression as the rock singer in David *Hare's *Teeth and Smiles* (1975) as well as in frequent Shakespearian parts in the 1980s. In 1995 she received a Tony *award for her portrayal of Natalya Petrovna in *Turgenev's *A Month in the Country*, and was noted for her Lady Torrance in Tennessee *Williams's *Orpheus Descending* at the *Donmar Warehouse (2000). She has appeared in numerous films, including *Cal* (best actress at Cannes, 1984) and as Queen Charlotte in *The Madness of King George* (1994). On TV she created the role of Detective Chief Inspector Tennison in a series of episodes of *Prime Suspect*, receiving an Emmy award for *Prime Suspect: Scent of Darkness* (1998). TK

MISE-EN-SCÈNE

French for 'the placing or the setting of the scene'. Strictly speaking, when applied to the techniques of stage representation the term refers to painted *scenery, scenic effects, stage pieces, and *properties. But it has a more expansive meaning, signifying not only the stage setting but also *lighting, *costuming, and all other related aspects of the spatial and temporal order of a theatrical performance. In this more comprehensive meaning, mise-en-scène refers to what happens in the spatio-temporal continuum, including the actions and movements of all the performers (*actors, singers, or *dancers) who provide the dynamic rhythm of the production. In the modern period, the role of the *director is to organize all of these elements into a unified artwork. In this sense mise-en-scène and *Wagner's concept of the *Gesamtkunstwerk*, or total artwork, are related, both evoking all the features and principles of a theatrical presentation, from language, speaking, and *music, to gesture, movement, and design (*see* TOTAL THEATRE). Likewise, in *film theory mise-en-scène refers to all the elements before the camera: settings, costumes, behaviour of actors, *make-up, lighting, and properties. *See also* SCENOGRAPHY; VISION AND THE VISUAL. TP

MISHIMA YUKIO (1925–70)

Japanese novelist and playwright. Mishima's fiction, flamboyant life, and spectacular suicide have obscured his stature as a dramatist. A brilliant and widely read author, his works demonstrate a penetrating intelligence, a love of paradox, and a taste for the aristocratic, the artificial, the exotic, and the decadent. His first play, *The Burning House*, was performed by Haiyūza (the Actors' Theatre) in 1949, and he went on to write as many as 40 plays in a wide variety of styles. His *Modern Noh Plays* (1950–6), which helped establish Mishima's reputation abroad, were written for the *naturalistic *shingeki* stage. In contrast, his *kabuki plays, including one of his last works, *The Crescent Moon* (1969), were written in the classical language and baroque style of that theatre. Mishima's preoccupation with the tension between aesthetic contemplation and political action is reflected in dramas like *Rokumeikan* (1957) and *My Friend Hitler* (1968). In the same vein is his most famous play, *Madame de Sade* (1965); Ingmar *Bergman's celebrated production for the *Dramaten in *Stockholm (1989) subsequently toured *Tokyo, *London, and *New York. Mishima also directed and acted in a number of stage and screen productions.   CP

MISTINGUETT (JEANNE-MARIE BOURGEOIS) (1873–1956)

French actress, *dancer, and singer. Legendary queen of the *Parisian *music hall, she was renowned more for her beautiful legs than for her talent as a singer. She began her career at the Casino de Paris under the name 'Miss Tinguett', then made her debut in comic roles at the Trianon-Concert in 1885, followed by a ten-year engagement at the Eldorado (1897–1907). In 1909 she danced with Max Dearly at the *Moulin-Rouge, which propelled her to stardom. In 1912 she appeared in 'la valse renversante' at the *Folies-Bergère with Maurice *Chevalier, who was to become her partner and lover for several years. From 1919 to 1923 she enjoyed great success in *tours of both Americas in such *revues as *Paris qui danse* and *Paris qui jazz*. She also appeared in several *films, including *Les Misérables* in 1913 and *Rigolboche* in 1936. Mistinguett retired from the stage in 1951.   CHB

MITCHELL, ADRIAN (1932–   )

English playwright, translator, lyricist, and performance poet. Mitchell became an icon of the 1960s when he performed 'Tell Me Lies about Vietnam' at the 1965 Albert Hall Poetry Olympics. His plays, like the anti-racist *Man Friday* (1977), often reflect his committed left-wing views, or celebrate counter-cultural heroes such as Eric Satie (*Satie Day/Night*, 1986) and William Blake (*Tyger*, 1971, revised as *Tyger Two*, 1994). Mitchell's first theatre work was writing the lyrics for Peter *Brook's production of *Weiss's *Marat/Sade* (1964). As a translator, he was instrumental in introducing English-speaking *audiences to the Spanish Golden Age with versions of *Calderón (*The Mayor of Zalamea*, 1981; *Life Is a Dream*, with John *Barton, 1983) and Lope de *Vega (*Fuente Ovejuna*, 1989). An immensely prolific author, Mitchell has also written many plays for *youth, adapting children's classics such as *The Pied Piper* (1986), *The Lion, the Witch and the Wardrobe* (1999), and *Alice in Wonderland* (2001).   CDC

MITCHELL, JULIAN (1935–   )

English writer. Already known as a novelist, Mitchell began his playwriting career adapting novels for performance, starting with several Ivy Compton-Burnett works, including *Heritage and History* (1965), *A Family and a Fortune* (1966), and *Half-Life* (1977). For *television he adapted Austen's *Persuasion* (1971), Paul Scott's *Staying On* (1980), and Ford's *The Good Soldier* (1981). Of his original plays, his biggest success came with *Another Country* (1981), concerning the sexual and political tensions in an English public school in the 1930s, with a thinly disguised Guy Burgess as the main *character. The play displays Mitchell's talents as a writer of well-crafted, intelligent commercial dramas; it won the 1982 Society of West End Theatres *award for best play and was *filmed in 1984. Mitchell's other stage plays include *The Enemy Within* (1980), *Francis* (1983), and *After Aida* (1986). In 1998 he wrote the screenplay for *Wilde*.   MDG

MITCHELL, KATIE (1964–   )

English director. Productions for her company, Classics on a Shoestring, at the *Gate Theatre, *London, in the early 1990s— *Women of Troy*, *The House of Bernarda Alba*, and *Vassa Zheleznova*—bore the hallmarks of intimate, *acting-led ensemble work. *The Dybbuk* (1992), *Henry VI* (1994), and *The Phoenician Women* (1995) were influenced by Eastern European culture (she received a Winston Churchill Memorial Travelling Fellowship in 1989), and reflected the atrocities of Bosnia. *Sowerby's *Rutherford and Son* (1994) and *Toller's *The Machine Wreckers* (1995) at the Royal *National Theatre were painstakingly researched. From 1997 to 1999 Mitchell was *artistic director of the *Royal Shakespeare Company's Other Place, Stratford, where she directed *The Mysteries* and *Beckett pieces with a team of women designers. In the late 1990s she also began to work with living writers, directing Martin *Crimp's *Attempts on her Life* (*Piccolo Theatre, *Milan) and his translation of *The Maids* (*Young Vic). Mitchell has directed for *television (D. H. *Lawrence's *The Widowing of Mrs Holroyd*) and for the Welsh National *Opera.   KN

MITCHELL, LANGDON (1862–1935)

American playwright. Twelve of Mitchell's plays were staged during his lifetime, but his reputation was based for the most part on *The New York Idea* (1906), a *comedy of manners that satirized the superficiality of the urban social elite, especially in the areas of marriage and divorce. A highly successful vehicle for Minnie Maddern *Fiske, the play was compared to the work of *Shaw and *Wilde in its use of comedy for serious social purpose. Mitchell also wrote *Becky Sharp* (1899, adapted from Thackeray's novel *Vanity Fair*), which succeeded as a vehicle for Mrs Fiske; and the John *Drew vehicle *Major Pendennis* (1916) was based on Thackeray's *Pendennis*.   MAF

MITRA, DINABANDHU (1830–73)

Bengali dramatist. An employee of the colonial administration in *India, he wrote his first play *Nil Darpan* (*Indigo Mirror*, published 1860) under a pseudonym, because it dealt with British indigo planters' oppression of Indian peasants. Its translation into English by Michael *Dutt (1861) resulted in imprisonment and a fine for the Calcutta (*Kolkata) publisher, Revd James Long. The original, a watershed work, inspired innumerable scripts suffixed *darpan* (mirror), but its provocative content prevented a complete staging until 1872, when the National Theatre's historic production inaugurated professional *Bengali theatre. The script's *realism made it politically potent even after the British Raj, and many left-wing troupes exploited its anti-feudalism. Mitra's best *farce, *Sadhabar Ekadasi* (*The Wife's Ritual Fast*, 1868), gave the celebrated *actor-manager Girish *Ghosh one of his biggest hits. Its *satire of dissipated Anglophile Bengalis ensured revivals into the late twentieth century. Literary critics do not rate Mitra's plays highly, but that judgement never dampened their popularity. AL

MITRA, SOMBHU (1915–97)

Bengali actor and director. After an apprenticeship on Calcutta's (*Kolkata) commercial stage (1939–43), where he learnt the techniques of professional acting and production, he joined the leftist *Indian People's Theatre Association and co-directed the harbinger of the new drama movement, *Nabanna* (*New Harvest*, 1944) by Bijon *Bhattacharya. In 1945 he married Tripti *Mitra, who also acted in IPTA productions, and both left to eventually form their own group, Bohurupee, in 1948. Under Mitra's leadership, Bohurupee became one of the most influential Indian troupes. He directed several *Tagore classics, firmly refuting the notion that Tagore wrote *closet dramas because nobody since the author had successfully staged them. Mitra's imaginative vision gave him access to the poet's symbolism and *allegory. Interestingly his work with Tagore began with an adaptation of the novel *Char Adhyay* (*Four Chapters*, 1951), and continued with the plays *Rakta-karabi* (*Red Oleander*, 1954), *Muktadhara* (1959), *Bisarjan* (*Sacrifice*, 1961), and *Raja* (1964).

Mitra also directed *Ibsen (*An Enemy of the People*, 1952; *A Doll's House*, 1958), *Sophocles (*Oedipus the King*, 1964), Badal *Sircar's *Baki Itihas* (*Remaining History*, 1967) and *Pagla Ghora* (*Mad Horse*, 1971), and Vijay *Tendulkar (*Silence! The Court Is in Session*, 1971). His directorial work was marked by an emphasis on minute details which contributed to a composite design. He had tremendous stage presence as an actor, and played the *hero in most Bohurupee productions, exploiting his peculiar musical-recitative delivery and a finely tuned body to express the inner state of *characters. He worked under other directors as well, as Thakurda in Tagore's *Dakghar* (*The Post Office*, 1957), Chanakya in *Visakhadatta's *Mudrarakshasa* (*The Signet Ring of Rakshasa*, 1970), and the eponymous king in Girish *Karnad's *Tughlaq* (1972). Mitra turned reclusive after 1971, dissociating himself from Bohurupee, acting less and less. He wrote a few plays himself, of which the ambitious *Chand Baniker Pala* (*The Merchant Chand's Opera*, 1978) remains unstaged. He also wrote essays on Indian theatre, and scripted and directed an award-winning Hindi *film, *Jagte Raho* (*Stay Awake*, 1956). *See also* BENGALI THEATRE. AL

MITRA, TRIPTI (1925–89)

Bengali actress and director. She performed in plays by Bijon *Bhattacharya, some of them for the leftist *Indian People's Theatre Association, including his trailblazing *Nabanna* (*New Harvest*, 1944), co-directed by Sombhu *Mitra, whom she married the following year. She joined him to form the pioneering *Bengali troupe Bohurupee in 1947 and stayed on as its leading lady until 1979, mostly acting opposite her husband in a wide variety of classic roles from *Sophocles to *Tagore. Her virtuosity was unparalleled in mid-twentieth-century *Bengali theatre, but she particularly excelled in portraying Tagore's *heroines like Nandini in *Rakta-karabi* (*Red Oleander*, 1954) and Sudarshana in *Raja* (1964), and the new Indian women created by contemporary dramatists like Badal *Sircar and Vijay *Tendulkar. Her characterizations combined psychological depth, facial mobility, physicality, and vocal range—even in *one-person shows like *Aparajita* (1971). She directed occasionally, notably Tagore's *Dakghar* (*The Post Office*, 1957), and increasingly so after Sombhu Mitra distanced himself from the company. Her work included *Ionesco's *Rhinoceros* (1972), Tagore's *Ghare-Baire* (*The Home and the World*, 1974), Steinbeck's *Of Mice and Men* (1975), and Sircar's *Yadi ar Ek Bar* (*If Only Once More*, 1976). AL

MITTERWURZER, FRIEDRICH (1844–97)

German actor and director. Born and educated in Saxony, Mitterwurzer spent most of his professional life in *Vienna. After engagements in Hamburg and Leipzig in the 1860s, he joined the *Burgtheater in 1871 where he remained (with interruptions) until his death. He was appointed director of the Theater an der Wien (1875) and the Carlstheater (1884) but was less successful there. As an actor Mitterwurzer was renowned for his physical and facial expressiveness, and he was particularly famous for character roles such as Shylock, Richard III, and Mephisto. CBB

MITZI E. NEWHOUSE THEATRE *See* LINCOLN CENTER FOR THE PERFORMING ARTS.

MLAMA (MUHANDO), PENINA (1948–)

Tanzanian director and playwright. Like Ebrahim *Hussein, Mlama writes her plays in Swahili about the project of *Ujamaa* (an African form of socialism or communalism) and liberation. *Tambueni Haki Zetu* (*Recognize our Rights*, 1973), *Harakati za Ukombozi* (*Liberation Struggles*, 1982), and *Lina Ubani* (*An Antidote to Rot*, 1984) reveal a shift from enthusiasm for *Ujamaa* socialism to its critical appreciation. Her study *Culture and Development: the popular theatre approach* (1991) summarized the experiences of the theatre for *development movement that flourished in Tanzania from the 1980s. She advocated the change from *vichekesho* (*farce) to *ngonjera*, a performance style combining traditional *dance, song, and *mime with modern political issues.   EB

MNOUCHKINE, ARIANE (1939–)

French director, arguably the most celebrated woman director of the twentieth century. With a group of friends from the Sorbonne she formed the Théâtre du *Soleil in *Paris in 1964 along the lines of a workers' cooperative. Her early productions vacillated between the extremes of psychological *realism and *commedia dell'arte*, but it was *training at the École Jacques *Lecoq which proved to be the turning point of her career. An opening *mime sequence to her production of Arnold *Wesker's *realist drama *The Kitchen* (1967) brought her recognition, as well as demonstrating her leftist political affiliation and desire for a people's theatre. In subsequent productions she deliberately exposed the process of *acting and the machinery of theatre to make a political point about the conditions of labour (*see* POLITICS AND THEATRE). After the upheaval of May 1968 she felt unable to perform scripted plays from the canon, and thus developed a series of five productions dubbed 'créations collectives' (*collective creations), essentially *devised plays. During the process Mnouchkine found one of the German words for director, *Probenleiter* (leader of *rehearsals), more appropriate for her task.

The most famous of these was *1789; or, The Revolution Must Stop at the Perfection of Happiness* (1970), a *promenade, multi-focused *spectacle of popular theatre forms applied to French history. Throughout her early career, however, her interest in the theatre of Asia was to have the most enduring effect on her own practice. From 1981 onwards an oriental *interculturalism defined her practice with two major groups of European classics (a Shakespeare sequence, 1981–4, and the *Greek *tragedies *Les Atrides*, 1990–3), and contemporary Asian-themed plays by Hélène *Cixous. In these she developed a highly declamatory style of *acting ('jouer frontal'), *mask work, and Asian-inspired *dance and movement. Her only production of a play from the French canon, *Tartuffe* (1995), used *Molière's attack on fundamentalism as a template for an in-

vestigation of the politics of *gender. Since 1971 she has worked at the Cartoucherie in Vincennes outside of Paris, inventing an environment for each production, creating work of *physical and visual beauty which critiques colonialism and imperialism in all its manifestations. *See also* POST-COLONIAL STUDIES.
                                        BRS

MOBILE THEATRE (ASSAM)

*Touring troupes in Assam (*India), begun in the 1920s with the formation of the Moiramara Chaturbhuj Opera Party by Jibeswar Sarma and the Pathsala Natya Samity by Santa Ram Chaudhury. Significant contribution came from Braja Nath Sarma, who toured with his Kalika Opera Party and Assam Kohinoor Party. In 1963 Achyut Lahkar established Nataraj Theatre; its novelty and commercial success prompted further expansion, and by 2000 about 30 mobile groups were operating in the state. The theatre season is typically from July to April. After five or six weeks of *rehearsal the groups tour about 55 towns and villages, staying in one location for three to five days. They stage a different play each night, preceded by a *dance-drama, in a three-hour show. A group travels with 100 to 150 persons, including actors, musicians, dancers, carpenters, technicians, cooks, and *managers—accompanied by truckloads of modern *sound and *lighting equipment, generators, set materials, and provisions to accommodate about 1,800 spectators.

Mobile theatre has gained tremendous popularity because it brings appealing stories, dramatic excitement, and dazzling *special effects to remote locations. A villager without access to *films can watch the Titanic sink to the ocean floor, Lady Diana cruising in a motor boat, an anaconda writhing in the Amazon rainforests, or cars rolling downhill after a collision. In the 1980s and 1990s a number of important playwrights, directors, and actors joined mobile theatres. New plays have adapted familiar Western themes (Cleopatra, Hamlet, Napoleon) or Indian epics (*Mahabharata*, Sri Krishna), and have dealt with local history and literature and contemporary events and themes. Although mobile theatre has traditionally stressed mass entertainment and commercial success, it now also seeks higher artistic standards, using the form to address current social and political issues of Assamese and Indian society.   BNS

MOCHALOV, PAVEL (1800–48)

Russian actor. His *Moscow debut was in 1817 and he joined the *Maly Theatre in 1824, where he established a reputation as one of the finest actors of his generation. Many of the leading writers of the day wrote penetratingly about Mochalov's talent, including Aleksandr Herzen and Vissarion Belinsky, often contrasting his raw, inspirational style with the cooler, more studied style of *Karatygin. His major triumphs were in Shakespeare and *Schiller—as Othello (1837), Hamlet (1837), King

Lear (1839), Richard III (1839), Romeo (1841), Karl Moor (*The Robbers*, 1828), and Don Carlos (1829). He would also have been a superb Arbenin in *Lermontov's *Masquerade* had not the *censor intervened, but this was more than compensated by his Moscow première of Chatsky in *Griboedov's hitherto banned *comedy *Woe from Wit* (1831). His outstanding role was undoubtedly that of Hamlet, about which Belinsky wrote that everything in Mochalov's performance, apart from the 'To be or not to be . . .' speech and one other scene, 'was beyond any possible conception of perfection', and Pyotr Weinberg left a vivid account of the famous *soliloquy which was delivered 'in a state of extreme nervous excitement'. An actor 'of impulse and unruly inspiration', according to Herzen, Molchalov also had something of a drink problem which rendered the quality of his performances uneven. He frequently *toured in the provinces and it was on one of these tours that he died of a cold caught in Voronezh.   NW

MODENA, GUSTAVO (1803–61)

Italian *actor-manager and political activist. Modena's greatest roles were in *Saul* by *Alfieri and *Louis XI* by *Delavigne. From 1843 to 1846 he headed an extremely influential company; his teaching directly influenced Tommaso *Salvini and Ernesto *Rossi, and led to important reforms in the Italian theatre. He demanded that the recitation of *tragic *verse be based not on old declamatory techniques that approached those of *operatic singing but on solid *character analysis and psychological truth. He taught that the art of *acting demanded *political commitment, that theatre should have an educational and civic purpose, that it should open people's eyes, rid them of their prejudices and superstitions, and make them think. The company relied on recent French dramas—*Hugo, *Scribe, *Dumas *père*—for its repertory but introduced the new Italian *historical drama that featured *melodramatic *spectacle. His own political commitment to the Risorgimento, Mazzini, and the 'Young Italy' movement led him into direct confrontation with the Austrian rulers of the northern Italian states and to many years of exile.   JEH

MODERNISM AND POSTMODERNISM

Stylistic and chronological labels that are used across the arts to name a variety of movements. Although modernism was a term in use all through the twentieth century, by the twenty-first century the couplet modernism/postmodernism signalled a contrast. Let us look first at what is taken to be modern or modernist in theatre and performance and then move on to examine its postmodern 'other'. Unlike in adjacent fields, such as visual art, architecture, literature, and *dance, the terms 'modern' and 'modernist' do not have a unified or homogeneous meaning in *theatre and *performance. These terms do not even appear

in the indexes of some of the major textbooks in the field. They are sources of disagreement and contestation. Patrice Pavis points out that in theatre 'neither modernism nor what comes afterwards appears to correspond to specific historic movements or distinct *genres or aesthetics'.

Perhaps this difficulty of identifying what is modernist, or even modern, in theatre arises partly from the split between dramatic literature and theatrical performance. 'Modern drama' is the term often applied to sophisticated *realist plays, from the late nineteenth century onward, though some track this tendency back as far as the drama of *romanticism. (This designation is complicated by the fact that the term '*early modern', taken from the field of European history where the modern period—the period formerly labelled 'the Renaissance'—begins after the *medieval period, has now entered the field of literature. In this confusing concatenation of terms, *Ibsen, *Strindberg, *Chekhov, *Shaw, *O'Neill, and *Hansberry, despite some of their experiments with *symbolism and *expressionism, are 'modern' playwrights—and one might even call *Kleist an early 'modern' playwright, according to the old model; but according to the new model, Shakespeare is an 'early modern' playwright.)

On the other hand, 'modernist' drama may be seen as a term for experimental or non-realist literary works in the lineage of modernist writers like James Joyce, Virginia Woolf, and Ezra Pound. In this sense, plays by *Yeats, *Pirandello, *Eliot, *Wilder, *Stein, *Beckett, *Jean Genet are modernist. And 'modernist' theatre is a label sometimes applied to the non-realistic directorial practices allied to the European and American *avant-garde; various movements in avant-garde theatre and performance have been associated with cognate schools in the visual arts (for example, *futurism, *dada, *constructivism, and *surrealism). Thus *Meyerhold, for instance, who not only worked with constructivist designers but thought of his stage as a constructivist space and his technique as constructivist practice, whether staging a classic play or a contemporary play, may be seen as a modernist director. So may *Brecht, who began as an expressionist and whose mature work combined elements (such as 'baring the devices' and spare functionalism, as well as social criticism) of both constructivism and the movement called New Objectivity (*Neue Sachlichkeit*). The *Bauhaus theatre of Oskar *Schlemmer and others was an attempt to stage modernist principles of Bauhaus design in painting, sculpture, and architecture. *Artaud's visions of alternative theatre practices grew partly out of his affiliation with the surrealist movement.

In short, the term 'modernism' in theatre seems generally to be a synonym for 'avant-garde'—often allied to the various and non-converging avant-gardes in other art forms—rather than a unified movement in itself, like modern dance or modernist painting. Perhaps it is useful to think of theatrical modernism by analogy with modernist movements, especially in the visual arts. This sort of modernism obtains when artists or critics from one art form begin to imitate the strategies and language of another art form, where the relevant features in question in that other art form are already called 'modern' or 'modernist'. Modernism by analogy helps to explain why playwrights and directors who are typically called modernist have pursued radically different aesthetic, political, and social programmes. And yet *directing emerged almost entirely as a modern Western practice, dating back only to the mid-nineteenth century, so that both Saxe-*Meiningen and *Stanislavsky may be seen as modern (though not modernist) directors. Moreover, a modern movement in *scenography spearheaded by *Appia and *Craig searched, in a modernist vein (in the visual art and architectural senses), for the pure 'essence' of the theatre as a physical space.

Modern drama or modern theatre suggests a chronological framework connected to modern life, society, and politics after the Industrial Revolution. It is linked not only to the rise of *naturalism and realism in dramatic literature and on the stage at the end of the nineteenth century, and to the emergence of the director as an *auteur* controlling all the aspects of the production, but also to progressive or reform politics. It may also have engaged with themes and content concerning modern life, including the relationship between humans and machines, the search for self, the rights of women and other oppressed persons, and the ravages of both capitalism and its alternatives. Modernist drama or modernist theatre, however, suggests not only the chronological moment from the late nineteenth century up to the Second World War or so, but, more particularly, aesthetic ties with the modernist, anti-realist movements in the other arts—either literature, in the case of *drama, or the visual arts, in the case of theatre.

In its *primary* usage, postmodern or postmodernist art names what comes *after* modern or modernist art. But the difference between modern and postmodern is not only temporal. Postmodern art is also opposed to certain tenets of whatever is being called modern art. Thus postmodern architecture (by Robert Venturi, Michael Graves, James Stirling, Frank Gehry, and others) comes after what is called modern architecture (as exemplified by Le Corbusier), and it rejects the austere functionalism of the latter in favour of expressivity. Postmodern dance (by Yvonne Rainer and others) comes after modern dance (Mary Wigman, Martha *Graham, and others) and opposes its highly emotive address in favour of more ordinary or everyday movement. Likewise, postmodernist visual art (by Ron Kitaj, Barbara Kruger, Cindy Sherman, and others) comes after modernist visual art (such as minimalism) and eschews the brand of formalism that emphasizes art for art's sake reflexivity and, in contrast, aspires to incorporate content and culture, both high and low, in its address.

In its primary usage, the term 'postmodernism' is not merely the invention of critics. The artists who populate the relevant movements stand in an Oedipal relation to preceding movements that have already been labelled 'modern' or 'modernist', and they signal their rejection of their predecessors by calling themselves 'postmodern' or 'postmodernist'. Some might just as easily call themselves 'anti-modern' or 'anti-modernist'. In its primary usage, the label postmodern tracks the actual thinking processes of upcoming generations of artists as they seek to displace their modern or modernist predecessors.

This understanding of the 'postmodern' requires that there be some homogeneous notion of modernism for the postmoderns to repudiate. But this requirement raises certain problems in applying the modern/postmodern couplet to theatre. For though we sometimes hear of postmodern theatre or performance, it is by no means clear what the modernist target of its resistance might be, since, as we have suggested, the range of modern and modernist work in the theatre covers a vast, diverse spectrum of writing and staging practices. But if there is no readily identifiable, homogeneous modernist theatre for postmodernists to follow and to reject, how can one intelligibly apply the label 'postmodernist' to theatre? In fact, the range of what is called 'postmodern' drama or theatre by scholars and teachers ranges from plays by Beckett, *Pinter, *Mamet, *Shepard, *Handke, *Müller, Ntozake *Shange, Francisco *Nieva, Louis *Nowra, and Ginka Steinwachs to deconstructionist literary readings of *Goethe and Brecht to contemporary stagings of Shakespeare (from *New York to *London to *Tokyo) to *performance art and *cyber performance. It also includes deconstructions of canonical works of modern drama as well as the classics by directors such as Frank *Castorf, Luca *Ronconi, Ivo van Hove, Peter *Sellars, and Elizabeth *LeCompte.

There is also a secondary use of the term postmodernism, which we can call 'postmodernism by analogy'. Just as in modernism by analogy, postmodernism by analogy obtains when artists or critics from one art form imitate the strategies and language of another art form, where the relevant features in question in that other art form are already called 'postmodern' or 'postmodernist' (in the primary sense). So postmodernist painting is postmodernist in the primary sense. It rejects the purity of modernist painting and instead opts for pastiche and quotation. Filmmakers, who have no unified modernist *film movement against which to revolt, can nevertheless lay claim to being postmodernists by imitating the strategies of postmodernist painters, such as pastiche and quotation. Postmodernist theatre is in the same boat as postmodernist film. It is postmodern by analogy. It is not opposed to some antecedent, definable, and homogeneous movement called modernist theatre; rather it amounts to an ensemble of strategies that are analogous to ones found in other art forms that are postmodernist in the primary sense. Thus the most straightforward way to locate postmodernism in contemporary theatre is to list some of the strategies it shares with postmodernist practices in other arts, especially the fine arts (the fine arts are a particularly important source for postmodernism in theatre). The list that follows is not meant to be exhaustive, but only to point out some of the most salient manifestations of analogy postmodernism in recent theatre.

Borrowing from and adapting Roland Barthes's notion of 'the death of the author' and other poststructuralist concepts regarding literature, Elinor Fuchs announced the arrival of postmodernism in the American theatre in her 1983 article 'The Death of Character'. Fuchs alleges that in postmodern theatre, as in postmodern literature, the notion of *character—and of representation itself—dissolves, leaving a theatre that is ultimately about itself. Though she acknowledges that 'character has been dying for a hundred years', from the dramas of Strindberg and Pirandello to Brecht's *Verfremdungseffekt, Fuchs sees a radical shift, for instance, in the work of playwright-director Richard *Foreman, who creates a theatre where human subjectivity literally becomes a set of objects and where language, rather than character, rules the stage, thus thematizing theatrically the poststructuralist/postmodernist topic of 'the death of man'. For Fuchs, a 'post-literary', reflexive approach to *texts and performances in the works of both *Mabou Mines and the *Wooster Group makes them 'autopresentational', deconstructionist, and post-humanist.

On the one hand, what Fuchs describes might more accurately be characterized as high modernism or late modernism—art about art (see METATHEATRE). But on the other, the giddy dissolution of character into language and the recycling of artistic conventions, verging on *parody, as well as an antiformalist refusal of coherence and depth, correlates with strategies of postmodern fiction by American writers like John Barth, Thomas Pynchon, and Donald Barthelme. No longer seeking to 'make it new', postmodern theatre, like postmodern literature, reworks, rereads, and destabilizes the past, as in the Wooster Group's radical revisions of canonical plays like Wilder's Our Town (Route 1 & 9, 1981), *Miller's The Crucible (L.S.D (. . . Just the High Points . . .), 1983–4), and Chekhov's Three Sisters (Brace-Up!, 1991), in which quotations from the original texts constitute just a small part of a cacophony of words, images, and *actions. In their 'deconstructions' of works by modern playwrights, the Wooster Group may also be seen as postmodern in the primary sense, directly reacting against what was considered by some to be the canon of modern drama.

Through correspondence with postmodern literary strategies, Fuchs groups language playwrights Jeff Jones, Des McAnuff, and others with the postmodern movement in theatre practice, since their technique of language sampling allegedly decentres and questions the very notion of dramatic text, *plot, or character. Despite their titles, Robert *Wilson's *spectacles of the 1970s, such as The Life and Times of Joseph Stalin (1973) and Einstein on the Beach (1976), were devoid of plot and character and presented series of discontinuous, *dreamlike images and verbal texts, by analogy to literary strategies also appearing postmodern. There is a suggestive correlation between post-

modern theatre practice and poststructuralist theories of language, reading, textuality, and corporeality. Foreman, among other postmodern playwrights, directors, and choreographers, has explicitly cited poststructuralist influences, including Derrida and Heidegger.

The experimental theatre and drama Fuchs wrote about in the early 1980s had obvious analogies with American and French experimental fiction of the 1960s and 1970s—what some regard as the first phase of postmodern literature. American and European directors such as Andrei *Şerban, Liviu *Ciulei, Eugenio *Barba, Lee *Breuer, Ariane *Mnouchkine, Klaus Michael *Grüber, and Ivo Van Hove, as well as playwrights like Müller, have all employed strategies analogous to postmodern architecture: riving components of various periods or styles from their original historical or cultural contexts and reassembling them in an eclectic, quotational manner, in particular reworking classics through what architectural historian Charles Jencks calls a 'double coding' that combines specialized historical knowledge with pleasurably expressive effects. For example, in Şerban's production of *Beaumarchais's The Marriage of Figaro (1982), there were wheelchairs, rollerskates, a *circus swing, references to Hollywood gangsters and Dr Strangelove, eighteenth-century *costumes, and *acting styles taken from *melodrama, *commedia dell'arte, and Spanish dancing. Müller writes of layering a *Euripides play, Homer's Odyssey, a *Japanese *nō play, and Hitchcock's film The Birds.

By the late 1980s and 1990s new developments in the visual arts (and in the work of writers like Kathy Acker) offered additional strategies that theatre appropriated. Various critics have argued that the postmodern in theatre simply is performance art. Philip Auslander has stressed the way postmodern performance (and culture) is 'mediatized', created from and for mass culture. The breakdown between high art and popular or mass art supplies content, imagery, codes, and contexts for postmodern art, as in the work of visual artists Jeff Koons and Hans Haacke, both of whom recontextualize commercial art but to very different political ends, since Koons apolitically revels in commodity and kitsch culture and Haacke harshly criticizes the social and political forces of capitalism.

For Auslander, American performance artists like Laurie *Anderson, Spalding *Gray, and Eric *Bogosian are particularly notable examples of the postmodern breakdowns between avant-garde art and mass culture. They also exemplify what he sees as a turn from 'the politics of ecstasy' in the emancipatory and often participatory *political theatre in the 1960s (by companies including the *Living Theatre and the *Performance Group) to a postmodernist 'ecstasy of communication' that simultaneously participates in and criticizes the contemporary flow of information and imagery. In his examples, we can see that performance art becomes postmodern by following strategies analogous to those of visual art. Anderson has adopted the persona of a rock star, performing her songs live and on recordings and videos in a rock concert format, complete with back-up band, and she has had a hit single record ('O Superman', 1981). Gray's *monologues have been performed in avant-garde venues but also on *television, and he works as a character actor in mainstream films—an experience that finds its way back into his monologues. While not exactly a standard stand-up comic (he calls himself a 'sit-down comic'), Gray borrows from and manipulates that popular culture format. Bogosian's early performance art pieces, in which he challenged the notion of coherent character and subjectivity itself as he shifted rapidly from one stereotyped male persona to another, would fit with Fuchs's view of the death of character in postmodern theatre and performance (as, in a different way, would Anderson's and Gray's performances of themselves that border on but also challenge 'character') and yet, in terms of postmodernism, their relationship to popular culture seems most salient. Early in his career as a performance artist, Bogosian himself identified his approach more closely with visual artists like Robert Longo and Cindy Sherman than with theatre. As Sherman posed photographic images of femininity that alluded to popular culture, Bogosian recycled comparable images of violent masculinity in performance.

But this postmodern strategy of mixing high and low culture appears in theatre as well as performance art. Looking again at the language playwrights Fuchs discussed in 1983, at the pop-culture imagery and structures of Shepard's plays since the 1960s, and at more recent work—for instance that of Charles *Mee, who puts found texts from contemporary popular culture in the mouths of classical Greek characters, and Suzan-Lori *Parks, who mixes figures from American history, classical, biblical, and contemporary texts, and racial stereotypes—one is more likely to notice analogies with the mass-media 'image world' data bank of postmodern visual art and the high culture–low culture 'double-coding' of postmodern architecture than with formal dissolutions of literary conventions.

Performance itself as an all-inclusive, post-disciplinary, or anti-disciplinary genre seems to characterize postmodernism in the arts, which in part reacts against the idea (in visual art modernism and by analogy in other modernisms) of essentialism in regard to medium. The breakdown of boundaries between artistic disciplines and media creates uncertainty as to whether an artwork is a painting, a dance, a play, a music concert, a poetry reading, a film, or some other, unnamed genre. The interarts and mixed-media experiments of the 1960s internationally, including the Gutai Group, *happenings, Fluxus, the work of John Cage and Merce Cunningham, and other movements and individuals, seem to constitute an early phase of postmodern performance, characterized by indeterminacy and the breakdown of boundaries between art and life. However, performance in the 1980s and 1990s, once again polymorphous and mixing media, had a different tone. It was ironic about, rather than appreciative of, ordinary life; it was knowing

about artifice, rather than in search of authenticity; it saw the world as a forest of signs and art as a sign of signs (see SEMIOTICS). And it had a new, ambivalent, relationship to ideas of beauty—so long anathema to modernists. In these regards, too, it resembled postmodern gallery art.

Although much writing on postmodern theatre and performance focuses on experimental theatre groups and avant-garde directors, as suggested briefly above, postmodern architectural practice and Jencks's influential books on the subject have influenced design and directing in mainstream theatre and *opera as well (although sometimes to the point where postmodern design has simply come to stand for eclecticism in regard to period and style). Arnold Aronson argues that modern scenography (Appia, Craig, *Svoboda, and Ming Cho *Lee) challenged the *illusionism of romanticism and realism, creating sets that provided unified abstract, poetic, and also self-referential images of the drama's themes and structures, rather than the illusionistic representations of actual spaces, both indoors and out, of realist theatre and certain branches of earlier theatre. Postmodern scenography, in contrast, influenced partly by Brecht's theories of the incongruity that produces the *Verfremdungseffekt*, is dissonant, intertextual, and offers multiple references and viewpoints. As in postmodern architecture, it mixes historical references with contemporary entertainment.

Aronson's examples include the decor in Pina *Bausch's dance-theatre works by designers (including Rolf Borzik), which turns real objects—the water covering the stage in *Arien* (1979) and the damp sod in *1980*—into signs by including them onstage. Another example is John *Conklin's 1983 design for *The Rhinegold*, in which Valhalla was an amalgam of four specific pieces of architecture from the eighteenth and nineteenth centuries that made reference not only to themes in the *Ring* cycle but to *Wagner's biography, to recent German history, and to the institution of the opera house. In England, Maria *Björnson's designs for the *Royal Shakespeare Company have regularly mixed historical periods. Russian-born designer George *Tsypin observes that 'We live in a period in which all the myths and all classical literature is treated . . . as if it is happening right now' and says, therefore, that he tries to achieve not a juxtaposition but a fusion of styles and references.

Analogous to the boundary-blurring between genres and practices in the visual arts—as art museums, for instance, stage exhibitions about automobile design and record covers—one of the boundaries postmodern theatre practice has ultimately blurred is the line between experimental and mainstream theatre, opera, and dance. Postmodern directors have been hired to head major theatre companies in Europe and America; postmodern theatre directors regularly direct their versions of canonical operas in the world's leading houses; postmodern dancers have choreographed for major *ballet and modern dance companies internationally; and Shakespeare plays at theatres and *festivals worldwide (as well as in film and on TV) use designs that promiscuously mix periods and styles.

Robert Wilson's *Black Rider* (1990), first performed in Germany and intended as a homage to both German expressionism and German opera, is a perfect example of the various strategies of postmodernism by analogy in the theatre that we have discussed. Rather than creating a new performance text, as he did in his early spectacles, Wilson began with an old text—Carl Maria von Weber's *Der Freischütz* (1821), about a deal with the Devil and a magic bullet that tragically homes in on the hunter's beloved. But Wilson did not simply create a new production of an old opera. Instead, he intermingled its story and imagery with incongruous styles, genres, and historical periods. Working with the writer William Burroughs and the rock balladeer Tom Waits, he generated something in between an American *musical, a circus, a *magic show, a Weimar *cabaret, a German expressionist silent film, and *The Rocky Horror Picture Show*. *Black Rider* seemed both old and new, familiar and strange. It lived between two continents—between Old World and New World. It trafficked in both *tragedy and *comedy; sentimentality and parody; high art and low art; live performance, film, and painting and drawing. It explicitly mentioned contemporary deals with the Devil—from drug addiction to selling out in Hollywood. And it was both raucously vulgar and stunningly beautiful.

Though the label 'postmodern' generally functions as a local style descriptor in theatre discourse—as when Vito Taufer is called a 'postmodern director'—there is also a more global notion of postmodernism abroad according to which the present epoch is postmodern not only in terms of specific artistic practices but also in terms of economic, political, and social structures and leading intellectual and scientific trends. Popularized by the literary critic Fredric Jameson, this notion of global postmodernism rests on a neo-Marxist philosophy of history (*see* MATERIALIST CRITICISM) and a comprehensive theory of global capitalism as well as a reflection theory of the relation of art to society. Some theatre commentators use this global concept of postmodernism as a premiss in analysing the movement of theatrical styles and productions around the world, including the 'industrial' methods employed in *touring British mega-musicals and the tourism involved in international festivals and the reconstruction of the *Globe Theatre in London. However, whether the extremely ambitious claims (philosophical, economic, sociological, scientific, and political) that underwrite Jameson's picture of global postmodernism can be sustained, and whether his framework is necessary to explain such current theatre-specific trends, are open to reasoned theoretical debate.   SB/NC

ARONSON, ARNOLD, 'Postmodern design', *Theatre Journal*, 43 (1991)
AUSLANDER, PHILIP, *Presence and Resistance: postmodernism and cultural politics in contemporary American performance* (Ann Arbor, 1992)
CARROLL, NOËL, 'The concept of postmodernism from a philosophical point of view', in Douwe Fokkema and Hans Bertans (eds.), *International Postmodernism: theory and literary practice* (Philadelphia, 1997)
FUCHS, ELINOR, *The Death of Character: perspectives on theater after modernism* (Bloomington, Ind., 1996)
INNES, CHRISTOPHER, *Avant Garde Theatre: 1892–1992* (London, 1993)
KENNEDY, DENNIS, 'Shakespeare and cultural tourism', *Theatre Journal*, 50 (1998)
KRUTCH, JOSEPH WOOD, *'Modernism' in Modern Drama: a definition and an estimate* (Ithaca, NY, 1953)

MODJESKA, HELENA (1840–1909)

Polish actress. Born Helena Opid in *Cracow, Modjeska was married at an early age to Gustave Modrzejewski, whose name she kept after their separation in 1865, shortening it to Modjeska during her first appearance in the United States. Modjeska was a successful actress in Poland from 1861 until 1876, when she and her politically radical second husband Karol Bozenta Chlapowski emigrated to America with friends to establish a cooperative Polish colony in California. Modjeska first performed in the USA in 1877 as Adrienne Lecouvreur in *San Francisco. After a successful *tour of California, she opened as Adrienne in *New York later that year. She played in Poland in 1878, then returned to America. During subsequent successful tours of England, Poland, and the USA she played Nora in adaptations of *Ibsen's *A Doll's House*, among other roles.   LQM

MOELLER, PHILIP (1880–1958)

American director. A founding member of *New York's *Washington Square Players (1914–18), Moeller continued as frequent director with the reconstituted *Theatre Guild throughout the 1920s and early 1930s, directing 70 plays between 1915 and 1935. Admired for his stage composition, Moeller excelled in a wide variety of styles. Most notable were his concepts and staging for Eugene *O'Neill—including first productions of *Strange Interlude* (1928), *Mourning Becomes Electra* (1931), and *Ah, Wilderness!* (1933)—as well as the first American productions of *Shaw's *St Joan* (1923) and *Major Barbara* (1928).   MAF

MOHUN (MOONE), MICHAEL (d. 1684)

English actor. Mohun was a *boy actor at the *Cockpit before the closing of the theatres, and continued his career as an adult under Thomas *Killigrew at the Cockpit and later the Theatre Royal. He acted major roles in both Elizabethan revivals and contemporary dramas. Samuel *Pepys was ambivalent about Mohun's talent, but Nathaniel *Lee and Richard *Steele were impressed. Mohun ceased acting in 1682.   RWV

MOISEWITSCH, TANYA (1914–)

English designer who began her career working regularly for Hugh *Hunt's productions, particularly at the *Abbey Theatre, *Dublin, after 1935. For many years from 1953 she was associated with the *Stratford Festival, Ontario, designing the *thrust stage there to Tyrone *Guthrie's specifications, where the prime concern was to foster intimacy between actor and spectator; no one was to be more than 20 m (65 feet) from the stage, a problem she solved by creating an *auditorium sweeping through 220 degrees. The stage comprised a series of wide, rising platforms backed by a raised balcony that reached out to spectators like the prow of a ship. It was a stage for rapid transitions, challenging for a designer anxious to make a statement, but where design was calculated to support the actor. This is the hallmark of the many productions on which Moisewitsch has worked (they number in excess of 60, not including an early period (1941–4) working in repertory at Oxford Playhouse). A characteristic venture was the permanent setting for Shakespeare's history cycle at the *Shakespeare Memorial Theatre in 1951, where a *constructivist-style structure of wooden platforms and bridges could quickly be transformed by swags or arrangements of heraldic emblems, to avoid disrupting the rhythmic impetus of the action, creating evocative but unassuming environments for the actors' *dialogue to localize. Moisewitsch has designed *opera at *Covent Garden and the *Metropolitan, for Strehler's *Piccolo Teatro, and the *Habima, for the *Guthrie Theatre, Minneapolis, and for the Royal *National Theatre, *London, during *Olivier's directorship.

RAC

MOISSI, ALEXANDER (1880–1935)

Austrian actor. The son of an Albanian merchant and an Italian mother, Moissi came to *Vienna in 1897 to train as an *opera singer. While working as an extra at the *Burgtheater he was discovered by Josef *Kainz, and his first success was at the German theatre in *Prague. In 1903 he joined Max *Reinhardt in *Berlin where he became one of the most important actors in the ensemble. His notable roles before the war include Osvald in *Ibsen's Ghosts (1906), the title part in *Sophocles' Oedipus (1909), and, his most famous role, Fedjy in Lev *Tolstoy's The Living Corpse (1913). During the war Moissi was interned in Switzerland, though he was able to perform in that country until his release in 1917. After the war his fame waned. He performed principally in *touring productions and occasionally for Reinhardt in Vienna and at the *Salzburg Festival—he played the original Everyman in *Hofmannsthal's Jedermann (1922). Moissi's voice, with its strongly melodic, almost operatic range, was legendary. He specialized in troubled *characters whom he played with great introspection.

CBB

MOLANDER, OLOF (1892–1966)

Swedish director. Molander began his career as an actor at *Dramaten in *Stockholm (1914–19), but thereafter concentrated on *directing and was responsible for some 120 productions at Dramaten until his retirement in 1963. From 1934 to 1938 he was *artistic director of the theatre, directing epoch-making productions of *Strindberg's plays which gave *audiences a uniquely Swedish view of Strindberg's most complex work, including A Dream Play (1935) and To Damascus (1937). Previously, a Germanic, angst-ridden, and *expressionist view of Strindberg had prevailed in Swedish theatre, the legacy of Max *Reinhardt who had directed at Dramaten in the 1910s and 1920s. But Molander's production of A Dream Play stressed the sense of compassion and humanity running through the *text. He also made use of images from Strindberg's Stockholm projected onto the cyclorama to conjure up a *dreamlike reality. In his later career Molander returned repeatedly to A Dream Play, mounting guest productions in Denmark and Norway.

DT

MOLÉ, FRANÇOIS-RENÉ (1734–1802)

French actor. From 1760 for 40 years, Molé's charming elegance won him the adoration of *Comédie-Française *audiences. An exponent of *Diderot's *acting *theories, he gave energetic and tear-provoking performances in *tragedy and *bourgeois drama, and was equally impressive in high *comedy: he created *Ducis's version of Hamlet (1769) and *Beaumarchais's Almaviva (The Marriage of Figaro, 1784). Protesting his republicanism, he left the Comédie in 1791 and in 1795 became the first actor nominated to the Institut de France.

JG

MOLIÈRE see page 872

MOLINA, TIRSO DE See Tirso de Molina.

MOLNÁR, FERENC (1878–1952)

Hungarian playwright. Molnár began as a journalist and dramatic translator. His first original play, A doktor úr (The Doctor), was performed in 1902, but international fame came with Az ördög (The Devil) in 1907 and for many years thereafter a new work of his was performed almost annually in *Budapest. His *dramaturgy often follows the pattern of nineteenth-century French *comedies and *well-made plays, but his *dialogue and use of dramatic situation are unique. He often directed his own work, and was also successful as a writer for *cabaret. His most famous plays, including Liliom (1909), The Guardsman (1910),

(continued on p. 874)

MOLIÈRE (JEAN-BAPTISTE POQUELIN) (1622–73)

French actor, playwright, and *manager. Molière changed the face of French theatre and raised *comedy to a status almost equal to that of *tragedy, and he did this in a career in *Paris that lasted only fourteen years. He was born into the solid bourgeoisie in the heart of Paris; his father, an interior decorator like both grandfathers, had prospered greatly and secured an appointment at court. At the age of 21 he renounced his succession to the royal appointment (which, however, he subsequently regained) and joined a young company, headed by Madeleine *Béjart and her siblings, that rashly attempted to compete with the *Hôtel de Bourgogne and the Théâtre du *Marais. Bankruptcy followed, and Molière and the Béjarts disappeared into the provinces. Thirteen years later, in 1658, the company, now headed by Molière, returned to Paris. The king's brother secured them an *audition before the court; a tragedy by *Corneille was tepidly received, but Molière's *farce *afterpiece, now lost, was so successful that Louis XIV allowed the company to share the *Petit-Bourbon theatre with the *commedia dell'arte troupe of Scaramouche.

At this point Molière had written two competent comedies in five *acts and *verse, the obligatory format for 'regular' literary drama (see NEOCLASSICISM), and several *one-act farces, of which two survive. The troupe supplemented this material with old plays by other authors and with the personal repertory of *Jodelet, who soon joined from the Marais; it subsisted thus for over a year until Molière produced his first new play in Paris, the one-act afterpiece Les Précieuses ridicules (The Affected Damsels, 1659). This *satire on contemporary affectations was so unlike standard theatrical fare that it quadrupled receipts and made Molière a controversial celebrity; another successful new farce, Sganarelle; or, The Imaginary Cuckold (1660), solidified his position.

The demolition of the Petit-Bourbon forced the troupe to move to the derelict *Palais Royal, which, after repairs, opened in January 1661. Two weeks later Molière offered a project intended to establish him as an actor of serious roles: his 'heroic' play Dom Garcie de Navarre; or, The Jealous Prince. The failure was humiliating and complete, but it was followed in the same year by two great successes: The School for Husbands, a preview of the 'character comedies', and Les Fâcheux (The Bores), the first of the *comédies-ballets. This hybrid venture, commissioned by Foucquet to entertain the king, alternated a series of caricatures of courtly eccentrics, of whom Molière played four, with *dances by Beauchamps in an outdoor setting by *Torelli, his last project in France. Like most of the comédies-ballets that

followed, The Bores was later adapted for public performance at the Palais Royal.

Within three years of his arrival, Molière had learned that in tragic roles his vocal delivery was too choppy, his bearing too ungainly, his approach too conversational to gain favour with Paris *audiences. In comedy he was a revelation: he was admired for the expressiveness of his face (reputedly learned from Scaramouche), the sharp observation of contemporary social behaviour, and what was described rather helplessly as the naturalness of his acting. Still, for an actor and an author, comedy was inferior in prestige to tragedy, and the afterpiece was a minor form. His next work, sixteen months later, was a 'regular' five-act verse play standing alone on the bill: The School for Wives (1662). It was a novel treatment of a traditional *plot and a tour de force for himself, Mlle de *Brie, and *La Grange, the troupe's three best actors. Some moralists found the play indecent and impious; its popularity enraged the rival Hôtel de Bourgogne; and a flurry of pamphlets and polemical afterpieces ensued that lasted two years and raised attendance at both houses. Armande *Béjart, the 19-year-old sister or daughter of Madeleine, had married Molière earlier in the year; now she made her first appearances in the two plays that Molière contributed to the controversy, The Critique of the School for Wives and The Versailles Impromptu. *Montfleury, satirized in these plays, so far forgot himself as to accuse Molière of having married his own daughter; the king, to whom this complaint was addressed, responded by standing godfather to the couple's first child and by commissioning and dancing in Molière's second comédie-ballet, The Forced Marriage.

Molière was no longer a mere entertainer but a literary author to be taken seriously, a favourite of the king, and a man with enemies, who began working to suppress Tartuffe even before it was performed. The preliminary three-act version that was presented as part of a festival at *Versailles was banned within days, after pressure from the Archbishop of Paris and perhaps also the queen mother. The ban was not lifted until 1669, after five years of revisions and appeals. Meanwhile, after producing the first play of *Racine, the troupe presented a spectacle-play on a popular subject, Don Juan (1665), in which La Grange played the charming, amoral aristocrat. Denunciations from the pulpit were thunderous, focusing on the performance of Molière in the role of the nattering, moralistic valet. Attendance was excellent, but for reasons we can only guess at, the play abruptly and permanently vanished from the repertory.

The king's favour continued, however; in August 1665 he gave the company the title of the *Comédiens du Roi and an annual subsidy, and in September commissioned another *comédie-ballet*. In June 1666, after a lengthy illness which forced the theatre to close, Molière presented the third of his great plays on hypocrisy, *The Misanthrope*, with himself as Alceste and his wife as Célimène; the play drew puzzled admiration and reasonably good receipts.

The Misanthrope was a watershed in Molière's career: after it he wrote only one more 'regular' play, *The Learned Ladies* (1672), and prose, fantasy, and visual *spectacle dominated the second half of his career as verse and *realism had the first. The change has been attributed to various causes: bitterness at the attacks of his enemies; a crisis in his health or, notionally, in his marriage; the increasing burden of entertaining the king; or, taking a more positive view, the desire to experiment. Most of Molière's later plays defy traditional classification: even *The Doctor in Spite of Himself*, the next play after *The Misanthrope*, is a play-within-a-play, a *commedia* plot framed by a native French farce, while *The Tricks of Scapin* (1671), ostensibly a throwback to *commedia*, seems to ironize that *genre's conventions. *Amphitryon* (1668), his most poetic play, was written in free verse rather than traditional alexandrines; furthermore, it was a 'machine-play' like *Psyché* (1671), a 'tragedy-ballet' with settings by Carlo *Vigarani and *text by Molière, *Quinault, and Corneille that was transferred at vast expense from the *Tuileries to the Palais Royal, where it became the troupe's most reliable producer of income. Many of the *comédies-ballets* lose their meaning outside the matrix of court production: *George Dandin* (1668), shorn of its *pastoral interludes, is like an antimasque without the *masque. Two of Molière's most enduringly popular works, *The Would-Be Gentleman* (1670) and *The Hypochondriac* (1673), combine the characteristics of the *comédie-ballet* and character comedy; and each *denouement, instead of restoring the deluded central *character to reality, carries him off in a final *ballet sequence into the realms of permanent fantasy.

During that ballet in the fourth performance of *The Hypochondriac*, Molière was fatally stricken, finished the show, and died at home a few hours later. Implacable to the end, the church first refused burial, then permitted maimèd rites. At the end of the season, four actors defected to the Hôtel de Bourgogne and *Lully, composer for many of the *comédies-ballets*, seized the Palais Royal. The remaining members moved to the rue *Guénégaud and absorbed the Marais troupe; in 1680 a merger with the Hôtel de Bourgogne created what soon became known as the *Comédie-Française.

Molière's role was always the comic lead, a list that includes heavy fathers, clever or befuddled valets, hapless husbands, rustics, and foolish courtiers. The constant is what contemporaries called the 'naturalness' of his acting style. This term implied a contrast with his predecessors, who had achieved success by creating and satisfying audience expectations of a familiar stage persona with a recurrent name, *costume, and bag of tricks; Molière regularly defied expectation, and he individualized the name and costume of each character he played. In *scenography also, the setting, though it might use stock elements, was specific to the play and frequently situated the characters in their private interior environment, a practice that was then rare. The perceived naturalness of Molière's acting extended to the members of his loyal, well-trained company, who 'seemed to be born for all the characters they portray', and for most of them—La Grange, *Du Croisy, Mlle de Brie, Mlle Molière (Armande Béjart), *Hubert, *La Thorillière—Molière wrote at least one starring role.

The Comédie-Française is called the 'house of Molière' with some reason, but the boast of a continuous performance tradition is misleading. From the moment of its founding the Comédie jettisoned Molière's scenic reforms in favour of stock sets—it used the same decor for *Tartuffe* and *The Miser* as late as 1907—while Molière's own roles were parcelled out among several actors, Louis XIV himself directing that *Brécourt should play the valets. Thus the personal repertory of Molière became fragmented into various *lines of business which in the following centuries developed their own performance traditions, coloured by the work of later authors: Scapin, played by *Préville, became a variant of Crispin (*see* POISSON, RAYMOND) and Figaro, while for 40 years the Comédie presented *The Misanthrope* and *Dumas *fils*'s sententious *Demi-Monde* (1855) with the same male and female leads. Jean Provost, recruited from the boulevards in 1835, made it his mission to emphasize what he considered the tragic and tender aspects of the central characters in *The School for Wives*, *Tartuffe*, *The Hypochondriac*, and *The Miser*, an interpretation which he also enforced in his classes at the *Conservatoire.

Molière's modern status in the pantheon of French and world literature reflects a long critical tradition, symbiotic with the practices of the Comédie-Française, that concentrated on the 'serious' masterpieces, that saw him as the exponent of a benign, cautious moral philosophy, and that valued the dramatic over the theatrical and the verbal over the visual. The landmark productions of Molière in the twentieth century took place outside the Comédie: *Antoine's *Tartuffe* at the *Odéon (1907), *Jouvet's *School for Wives* at the Athénée (1936), *Planchon's *Tartuffe* at the *Théâtre National Populaire in Lyon (1962), *Vitez's 'tetralogy' at *Avignon (1978). Since the mid-1980s the Comédie has belatedly begun to embrace untraditional stagings. Some of these were merely repackaging of the standard reading of the plays as tragic autobiography, but some have achieved genuinely fresh interpretations. One of the Comédie's important actors, the Polish-trained Andrzej Seweryn, staged the relatively unfamiliar *Forced Marriage* as a mordant, surreal fable of modern despotism (1999), while Jean-Louis Benoit's production of the beloved *Would-Be Gentleman*

(2000), with a stunning design by Alain Chambon, rediscovered a balance between comedy and ballet, farce and fantasy, that honoured the seventeenth century while delighting audiences of the twenty-first.   RWH

BRAY, RENÉ, *Molière homme de théâtre* (Paris, 1954)
CARMODY, JAMES, *Rereading Molière* (Ann Arbor, 1993)
DESCOTES, MAURICE, *Les Grands Rôles du théâtre de Molière* (Paris, 1960)
HERZEL, ROGER, 'The decor of Molière's stage', *PMLA* 93 (1978)
—— ' "Much depends on the acting": the original cast of *Le Misanthrope*', *PMLA* 95 (1980)
HOWARTH, W. D., *Molière: a playwright and his audience* (Cambridge, 1982)

and *The Play's the Thing* (1926), were translated and frequently performed in *Vienna, *Paris, *London, and *New York, often provided vehicles for star actors (like the American *Lunts), and continued to be revived in Hungary and abroad. He also wrote *The Boys of Pál Street*, one of the best-known Hungarian juvenile novels, which has been adapted for the stage. His international success helped him to escape Nazism; he lived in the USA from 1939 with his actress wife Lili Darvas. The story of *Rodgers and *Hammerstein's *musical *Carousel* (1945) is borrowed from *Liliom*.   HJA

MONCRIEFF, GLADYS (1892–1976)

Australian singer known as 'Australia's Queen of song', and 'our Glad.' Moncrieff was contracted to J. C. *Williamson's company in 1911, and made her debut as Josephine in *HMS Pinafore* in 1914. She became a national star with *The Maid of the Mountains* in 1921. From 1926 Moncrieff starred in *London musicals, returning to Australia in 1928 for *The Chocolate Soldier* and a reprise of *The Maid of the Mountains*. Her status as national icon was confirmed by her work as entertainer in the Second World War and *Korea. After the wars, she was a popular performer live, on *radio, and later on *television.
                                                    KMN

MONCRIEFF, WILLIAM THOMAS (1794–1857)

English playwright and *manager. The author of over 100 *melodramas, *comedies, *burlettas, *farces, and adaptations of novels, the manager of several *minor theatres in *London, Moncrieff churned out plays to suit the taste of his mostly working and lower-middle-class *audiences. On the whole, his most popular plays were melodramas, among them *The Shipwreck of the Medusa* (1820), one of the many nineteenth-century plays based on well-known paintings; *The Lear of Private Life* (1820), a version of a novel by Amelia Opie; *The Cataract of the Ganges* (1823), a *Drury Lane play with an exotic setting and a real waterfall on stage; and *The Scamps of London* (1843), a lowlife play from the French. *Tom and Jerry; or, Life in London* (1821), a farcical burletta based on Pierce Egan's sketches *Life in London*, was his greatest comic success.
                                                    MRB

MONGITA, ALBERT LIKEKE (c.1916–1985)

Actor, dramatist, and painter from ex-Belgian Congo, a caricaturist of colonial society. Apart from short pieces and sketches for Belgian-Congolese *radio, he also acted in colonial plays. He left his mark with the production by his LIFOCO troupe (the League for Congolese Folklore) of *Mangengenge* (1956), set in fairyland on a mountain top, and *Ngombe*, about a conflict between a legendary king and a son fighting to abolish social practices that he finds abhorrent. *Ambeya* (1972) celebrates the military conquests of ancient warriors whose achievements he parallels with those of the then Congolese leader Mobutu. Using the myths and legends of his Ngombe people, Mongita highlighted folklore and local traditions in his work. Although some of his plays—*Soko Stanley* (1954), *Au fond je dois tout à ce garçon* (1958)—were written in French for the magazine *Voix du Congo*, they were all performed in Lingala, the lingua franca of the country's capital Kinshasa. Produced in theatres, stadiums, and other public spaces, his plays take on the air of village festivals, and were the inspiration for Congo's popular theatre.
                                              PNN trans. JCM

MONK, EGON (1927–)

German director. After training as an actor in *Berlin, Monk joined *Brecht at the *Berliner Ensemble in 1949 as an assistant director. Between 1949 and 1954 he was involved in some of Brecht's 'model' productions as well as directing himself (*Urfaust*, 1952; Brecht's *Señora Carrar's Rifles*, 1953). In 1953 he moved to West Germany, joining north German *radio as a *dramaturg. From 1960 to 1968 he headed *television drama there, producing acclaimed adaptations of Brecht's model productions. In 1968 he was appointed *artistic director of the Schauspielhaus in Hamburg but resigned after three months. He returned to television where he continued to make adaptations of Brecht's works. His memoirs of the Berliner Ensemble were published in 2001 (*Auf dem Platz neben Brecht*).
                                                    CBB

MONK, MEREDITH (1942–)

American composer, singer, filmmaker, and director/choreographer. She was a trained musician and contributor to the new era of postmodern *dance coming out of *New York's Judson

Church performance *collective during the mid-1960s. Monk founded her own company, the House, in 1968 and began creating large interdisciplinary, site-specific pieces which layered storytelling, visual imagery, movement, and *music into the creation of a 'new world . . . where the elements are not separated'. True to her intent, Monk's career has been consistently multidisciplinary, routinely crossing *genre boundaries as she explores the terrain of differing media. In the 1980s Monk's music-theatre pieces pioneered her 'extended vocal technique', a *ritualistic singing style evocative of found sounds but also filled with emotionality and imagery. She formed Meredith Monk & Vocal Ensemble in 1978 and has produced a series of recordings. Her *films and videos include *Quarry*, *Ellis Island*, and *Book of Days*. Major stage works from the 1980s and 1990s include *The Games* (1983), created with Ping *Chong, and *Atlas*, a full-length *opera commissioned by the Houston Grand Opera in 1991.   LTC

MONKHOUSE, ALLAN (1858–1936)

English playwright and critic. Less well known than his fellow Manchester school dramatists Harold *Brighouse and Stanley *Houghton, Monkhouse nevertheless had a number of plays produced at Annie *Horniman's *Gaiety Theatre, including *The Choice* (1910), *Mary Broome* (1911), and the backstage *farce about the Gaiety which featured Horniman herself, *Nothing Like Leather* (1913). Monkhouse's characteristic works are north-country domestic *tragedies of generational strife arising from intractable *characters. His biggest success, although more critical than commercial, came with his anti-war play *The Conquering Hero* (1924). He joined the *Manchester Guardian* in 1902 and remained for many years its respected drama *critic.
                                                    MDG

MONKHOUSE, BOB (1928–   )

English *television presenter, comedian, and actor. Educated at Dulwich College, he undertook national service in the Royal Air Force from 1946. His early career was in *variety theatre with summer seasons and variety bills in venues as diverse as the King's Southsea, the Blackpool Wintergardens, and the *Glasgow Alhambra. He has written material for Bob Hope, Frank Sinatra, Dean Martin, and Jerry Lewis. He appeared in *musicals and *revues including *Sauce Piquante* (1950) with Tommy *Cooper and Norman Wisdom, as well as in the original *London casts of Cole *Porter's *Aladdin* (1959) and *Rodgers and *Hart's *The Boys from Syracuse* (1963), where he played Antipholus of Syracuse to Denis *Quilley's Antipholus of Ephesus. He appeared in the first *Carry On* *film, *Carry on Sergeant* (1958). He has also appeared in numerous television and *radio variety shows, quiz shows, sitcoms, and dramas, and is a celebrated after-dinner speaker.   AS

MONODRAMA

A dramatic performance by a single *actor; a composition written for such a performance; sometimes called a *monologue. Examples, which can be drawn from nearly every period and culture, reflect four basic variations. (*a*) Single *character, single *action: a well-known *Chinese play from the eighteenth century, *Longing for Laity*, features a young nun yearning for love; *Chekhov's *On the Harmfulness of Tobacco* (1886) exploits the fiction of a lecture to involve the spectators as the fictive *audience. (*b*) Single character, multiple actions: Marcel *Marceau's *mime performances are of this type, as are many of Rowan Atkinson's *television performances as Mr Bean. (*c*) Multiple characters, single action: ancient *Greek rhapsodes and citharodes performed monodramas in this sense. Timotheus of Miletus' *The Persians* (fifth century BC) required the citharode to impersonate through tone and gesture several characters reacting to the battle of Salamis. (*d*) Multiple characters, multiple actions: a ninth-century *text speaks of a mime performing 'so that you would think many people spoke from one mouth'. A stage performance by the comic actor Bill Cosby routinely involves his impersonation of different characters in a variety of situations, as do the performances of Anna Deavere *Smith.

One-person—usually one character—plays are in fact a staple of the modern theatre. They are plays of character and sometimes exploit figures already known to the audience: Mark Twain, Harry Truman, John *Barrymore. At other times monodramas can be used to express themes of communication breakdown and individual alienation, as in *Beckett's *Krapp's Last Tape* (1958). Monodrama has also been used to designate a play, or a performance of a play, which is shaped by the perceptions of a single character. *Craig famously advocated that *Hamlet* be played through the eyes of the main character, a concept enacted in his production with *Stanislavsky (*Moscow Art Theatre, 1911–12). Nikolai *Evreinov's monodramas presented the dramatic world in terms of the *protagonists' perceptions in order for the audience to share the dramatic experience as the protagonist's alter ego.   RWV

MONOLOGUE

Most simply, a dramatic utterance that is not *dialogue; a speech of extended length and internal coherence, delivered by a single speaker, that does not include another's response. Monologues of *exposition, reflection, or deliberation can be addressed to the *audience, to another *character, to the speaker herself (an 'interior monologue'), or even to an inanimate object. They can be dramatically motivated or simply a theatrical convention, delivered from outside the *action by a *chorus figure or from inside the action by a character. A 'protatic figure', whose only function is to facilitate the monologue through brief interjections, is occasionally present. Monologue is sometimes used as a synonym for *soliloquy and *monodrama.

RWV

MONOPOLY, THEATRICAL See PATENT THEATRES.

MONSTROUS REGIMENT

English *touring company. Founded in 1975, and taking its name from John Knox's pamphlet 'The Blast of the Trumpet against the Monstrous Regiment of Women' (1558), the company was established as a socialist/feminist performers' collective which promoted new playwriting and sought new *audiences. By policy, women members outnumbered men and performances placed women's experience centre stage. *Scum: death, destruction and dirty washing* by Claire Luckham and Chris Bond was followed by Caryl *Churchill's *Vinegar Tom* (both 1976). Live music was a significant part of the company's performances, developing into women's *cabaret in *Floorshow* (1977) and *Time Gentlemen Please* (1978). Translations of European works, such as *Aquarium's *Shakespeare's Sister* (1980) and *The Fourth Wall* (1983) by Franca *Rame and Dario *Fo, formed part of the repertoire. The company stopped touring in 1993.   LT

MONTAGE

A technical and *theoretical term (in Russian, *montazh*) associated with the Soviet theatre and *film director Sergei *Eisenstein. It first appeared in his 1923 essay 'Montazh Attraktsionov' ('Montage of attractions') and referred to the *circus-style series of episodic 'turns' which characterized his reworked version of *Ostrovsky's *Enough Stupidity in Every Wise Man*, staged as a *satiric-political *clown show with *acrobatics, high-wire stunts, and filmed inserts. Eisenstein later adapted his ideas to the editing of film—the intercutting and juxtaposition of unrelated but emotive images which produce a heightened *political perception in the observer. Famous examples are the slaughter of an ox counterpointed with the slaughter of striking workers in *Strike* (1924); the Odessa Steps sequence in *Battleship Potemkin* (1925), where the descent of stamping military boots is intercut with the helpless downward trajectory of an occupied, untended pram; and in *October* (1927), where Kerensky's pause before the doors of power is intercut with the seemingly narcissistic posturing of a mechanical bird. In the original manifesto, an 'attraction' was defined as 'any aggressive moment in theatre, i.e. any element of it that subjects the *audience to emotional or psychological influence, verified by experience and mathematically calculated to produce specific emotional shocks in the spectator in their proper order within the whole. These shocks provide the only opportunity of perceiving the ideological aspect of what is being shown, the final ideological conclusion.' Eisenstein was clearly influenced by having worked as

*Meyerhold's assistant, and montage techniques are evident in Meyerhold's own work during the 1920s.   NW

MONTANSIER, MLLE (MARGUERITE BRUNET) (1730–1820)

French *manager. Born in Bayonne and educated by the Ursulines, she was an adventuress until an actor captured her heart and she turned to theatre at 33. Her success at running a theatre in Nantes led to her management of a virtual chain of theatres in northern France. As a protégée of Marie Antoinette from 1768, she directed court productions and the theatre of *Versailles. In 1790 she opened the Théâtre Montansier in *Paris and ran it from prison in 1793. Her post-revolutionary ventures proved less successful.   FHL

MONTANTIN, MICHÈLE (1943–)

Guadeloupean playwright, director, actor, and president of the Centre d'Action Culturelle de la Guadeloupe (1983–8). She organized four international theatre *festivals, the Rencontres Caribéennes, from which emerged the original staging of Simone *Schwarz-Bart's *Ton beau capitaine* (*Your Handsome Captain*, 1987) by Haitian director Syto Cavé. Montantin also wrote and directed *Vie et mort du Vaval* (*The Life and Death of Vaval*, 1991), based on traditional *carnival myths, and *Le Chemin des petites abymes*, which was staged by Michèle Césaire at Théâtre Racines in Fort de France.   AR

MONTCHRÉTIEN, ANTOINE DE (c.1575–1621)

French dramatist. A pioneer industrialist, Montchrétien also wrote several *tragedies. These mostly treat subjects from mythology, ancient history, or the Old Testament; but in *La Reine d'Écosse* (1601) he unusually took a contemporary subject, the relationship between Elizabeth and Mary, Queen of Scots. The play's non-performance was apparently due to diplomatic pressure from England.   WDH

MONTDORY (GUILLAUME) (1594–1653/4)

French *actor-manager. Montdory spent his early years as an itinerant actor with Valleran *Le Conte before settling in *Paris as leader of the company at the *Marais Theatre. Here he acted in Pierre *Corneille's earliest plays, including *L'Illusion comique*, where the role of Clindor, a young man of good family who has left home to become an actor, reflects the circumstances of Montdory's own life; and also playing Rodrigue in Corneille's masterpiece *Le Cid*. His prestigious career was soon cut short, however, when he suffered an apoplectic fit on stage while playing Herod in Tristan's *La Mariane* (evidence, perhaps, of a highly physical acting style). He retired from the stage with a generous pension from *Richelieu, a discerning patron of the theatre.   WDH

MONTERÍA, CORRAL DE LA

The last and best-known *playhouse of seventeenth-century Seville, inaugurated in 1626 and closed in 1679, when public theatre was banned in the city. Seven *corrales de comedias* broadly similar to those of *Madrid had been opened in Seville at various times between 1570 and 1600, the most important being the Corral de Doña Elvira (c.1570–1631). The Corral del Coliseo (1607–79), rebuilt four times, was in its second and fourth versions a large, sumptuous, semicircular theatre. The Montería, built in a patio of the Alcázar (royal palace), had an elegant elliptical *auditorium, entirely roofed, with a capacity of 1,400. The fairly small stage (7 m by 3 m; 23 by 10 feet) projected into the yard from a *tiring house with lower and upper balconies. There were two tiers of *boxes and a women's gallery on the third floor. The elliptical yard contained rows of chairs, with benches behind these and standing room at the back.

CD

MONTEVERDI, CLAUDIO (1567–1643)

Italian composer born in Cremona. Monteverdi's whole approach to composition can be described as loosely 'dramatic': his books of madrigals established a new manner of interpreting words and emotions through music, of which the *operas were then simply a natural extension. *Orfeo* (1607), composed for the dukes of Mantua, was the first ever masterpiece in the *genre: like the other earliest operas, it developed more out of *pastoral than from any other existing genre of theatre. It was followed by *Arianna* (1608), of which all is now lost except the Lament which was sung by Virginia *Andreini; and a number of semi-theatrical compositions, many also lost, which provided a fusion of words, *music, and *dance. He moved from Mantua to Venice in 1613. The later surviving operas—*Ulysses's Return to his Homeland* (1641) and *The Crowning of Poppaea* (1642)—are seen as showing a response to developing public taste and demands: critics discern clearer distinctions than in *Orfeo* between *recitative and aria, and between dramatic and decorative moments. From the *dramaturgical point of view, all early opera shows a readiness to leaven serious stories with scenes of a lighter touch—something which was dogmatically excluded from spoken *tragedy.   RAA

MONTEVIDEO

Now the capital of the small nation of Uruguay in *Latin America, Montevideo was established as a military base in 1726 as part of Spain's successful campaign to drive the Portuguese out of the area. Uruguay's theatrical history begins in Montevideo in 1791, when the colonial Governor, Antonio Olaguer Feliú, ordered the building of the Casa de Comedias, a venue for *touring companies from *Buenos Aires and Europe. An attempted invasion by England in 1806 sparked the start of nationalist sentiment in Uruguay, and several poets wrote dramatic poems which were read in the Casa de Comedias. The theatre was remodelled and renamed several times in the nineteenth century, but was eventually torn down in 1879 after it had been eclipsed by the Teatro Solís, built in 1856. The construction of the Teatro Solís signalled a break from the architecture of the colonial past, as the building's design shows the influence of French *neoclassical style. The theatre opened with *Verdi's *opera *Hernani*, and a number of international stars performed there, including Sarah *Bernhardt in 1886.

During the early nineteenth century native dramatists copied forms from Europe and from neighbouring Buenos Aires. Uruguay did not achieve independence from Spain until 1828, a few years after its neighbours, by which point European inhabitants had almost completely destroyed the indigenous population. The new country suffered throughout the nineteenth century, as many Latin American nations did, through *caudillo* warfare and divisive partisan politics. A few early writers wrote formulaic *melodramas for the Solís. Eduardo Gordon (1835–75) wrote in the *costumbrismo style, introducing the Montevideo middle-class *character to the stage, and *romantic writers like Pedro Pablo Bermúdez (1816–60) explored the genocide of the Charrúa people. The artists of Uruguay struggled, however, to find a national form until the early part of the twentieth century, when the government began to support the national theatre movement during the progressive presidency of José Batlle y Ordóñez. The native *costumbrismo* style mixed with *realism from Europe to create a drama which addressed important local issues, and was as much about class conflict as it was about the Montevideo bourgeoisie. The city also benefited from the presence of foreign artists, particularly exiles from the Spanish Civil War such as the Catalan actress and director Margarita *Xirgu, a circumstance that precipitated an explosion of theatrical activity during the 1930s and 1940s.

The *Comedia Nacional opened in 1947 at the Teatro Solís, mounting 50 dramas by national writers over the next twenty years. Under the direction of Xirgu, the repertoire of the company was strengthened by productions of the classics. Meanwhile, in the late 1940s and through the 1950s an independent theatre movement flourished as new directors, actors, and dramatists broke away from the conventional companies to establish theatres of their own. Most of these groups, such as El *Galpón and Teatro *Circular, were dedicated to social realism and to a type of *political theatre typified by the work of *Brecht. Economic hardship and political turmoil in the 1960s caused some companies to fold, and the military coup of 1973 shut down most of the rest (*see* CENSORSHIP).

With the end of the military dictatorship in 1984 several artists returned from exile or were released from prison. Old independent companies reopened and several new ones were formed. While some of the new drama examined the nation's history, such as Alberto Restuccia's *Salsipuedes* (*Leave if You Can*, 1985, about the extermination of the indigenous people), other plays took a more *surreal look at maintaining one's humanity under oppression, such as Mauricio *Rosencof's *El combate en el establo* (*Fight in the Stable*, 1985). The theatre of Montevideo picked up the threads of the past in the post-dictatorship period, examining issues of exile, imprisonment, and torture, and the prospect of rebuilding the nation.

EJW

MONTEZ, LOLA (1818–61)

Irish dancer and actress. Montez was an Irish-born beauty who made her stage debut in *London as a dancer in 1843 after the failure of her first marriage. She performed in Europe and was for a short time mistress of Franz Liszt and of King Ludwig I of Bavaria (1847–8) before making her debut in *New York in *Betley the Tyrolean* (1851). In 1852 she played the title role in a play written to capitalize on her European experiences by C. P. T. Ware, *Lola Montez in Bavaria*. She subsequently went to California, then in the throes of the gold rush, scandalizing *San Francisco *audiences with her spider *dance, performed on *tour in Australia in 1855. She also tutored the child actress Lotta *Crabtree. From 1856 she appeared on the lecture circuit. After a religious conversion in 1859 she became a recluse, dying in poverty on Long Island, New York.

JTD

MONTFLEURY (ZACHARIE JACOB) (c.1600–67)

French actor. Montfleury has the misfortune of being remembered chiefly for his worst features: he was lampooned by Cyrano de Bergerac for his spectacular obesity and by *Molière for his roaring delivery and shameless begging for *applause, and in retaliation he disgraced himself by attempting without success to denounce Molière for incest. The fact remains that, between the sudden retirement of *Montdory and the gradual emergence of *Floridor, Montfleury was the leading tragedian of mid-century. After making his early reputation in the provinces as a wildly emotional interpreter of the *tragicomedies and *pastorals of the 1630s, he joined the *Hôtel de Bourgogne in 1638, where he was a favourite of *Richelieu, the court, and the public, and where for three decades he was a fixture in roles of kings and emperors. However, his bellowing style seemed increasingly outlandish as playwriting and performance shifted towards greater restraint and *realism. *Racine tailored the role of Oreste in *Andromaque* to his talents, and he died

of his exertions in the mad scene. His son was a successful playwright; his daughter, Mlle d'Ennebaut, played the young *heroines in Racine's *Britannicus*, *Bajazet*, and *Phèdre*.

RWH

MONTGOMERY, ELIZABETH *See* MOTLEY.

MONTHERLANT, HENRY DE (1896–1972)

French writer. Already an established essayist and novelist, Montherlant did not come to the theatre until 1942 with the successful performance of *La Reine morte* (*The Dead Queen*) at the *Comédie-Française. This was followed by a series of contemporary and *historical dramas: *Fils de personne* (*No Man's Son*, 1943), *Celles qu'on prend dans ses bras* (*Those We Take in our Arms*, 1950), *Malatesta* (1946), *Le Maître de Santiago* (*The Master of Santiago*, 1948), and *Port-Royal* (1954). In post-war France Montherlant's works were admired for their subtle poetic style and for their glorification of the human soul, capable always of resisting the inherent fallibility of the material world. The last of his plays was *La Ville dont le prince est un enfant* (*The Town Whose Prince Is a Child*), which depicts the intimate yet ambiguous relationships between boys and priests at a Catholic seminary. Written in 1951, Montherlant did not allow its production until 1967. Afraid that he was losing his sight, he committed suicide.

CHB

MONTI, RICARDO (1944–)

Argentinian playwright and screenwriter. Although he has written less than many of his contemporaries (ten plays since 1970), he has been called Argentina's most important recent dramatist. Monti terms his aesthetic a 'broader *realism'. In his theatre, classical *tragedy fuses with Christian *Passion plays; history, myth, and *dreams converge; and the personal is both political and metaphysical. The mixture has created plays of dynamic, *metatheatrical tension. *An Evening with Mr Magnus and Sons* (1970) was one of the first Argentine plays to meld reflective realism with *avant-garde experimentation. *Tendentious History of the Argentine Middle Class* (1971) was openly political, and during the years of the dictatorship he produced *Visit* (1977), *Marathon* (1980), and *The Beaded Curtain* (1981), plays that poetically eluded the censor to examine the possibility of revolution under repression and individual complicity within history (*see* CENSORSHIP). Monti's post-dictatorship works (*A South American Passion*, 1989; *Asunción*, 1992; *The Obscurity of Reason*, 1993) cross national borders, locating themselves in a mythic 'America'. *Hotel Columbus* (1998) and *Finland* (1999, condensed from *South American Passion*) continue in the vein of 'broader realism', also exploring *gender construction.

Monti's work, which tends to deconstruct the tenets of *modernism, evades easy categorizing.   JGJ

MONTIGNY, ADOLPHE (c.1812–1880)

French actor, playwright, and *manager, also known under the name Lemoine-Montigny. He made his debut at the *Comédie-Française in 1829, although he never received much recognition on the national stage. He eventually moved to the *boulevard circuit, where he enjoyed some success in dramatic roles, particularly at the Nouveautés and the Ambigu. At the same time he wrote several dramas and *vaudevilles, including *Le Doigt de Dieu* (*The Finger of God*, 1834), *Amazampo; ou, La Découverte de quinquina* (*Amazampo; or, The Discovery of Quinine*, 1836), *Zarah* (1837), and *Samuel le marchand* (*Samuel the Merchant*, 1838), all of which he wrote in collaboration, and his solo work, *Un fils* (*A Son*, 1839). In 1841 he was appointed director of the *Gaîté with Horace Meyer, then in 1844 he took over the direction of the Théâtre du Gymnase, which had fallen onto hard times. He married actress-dancer Rose Chéri in 1845, and together they successfully brought the Gymnase back into fashion, with a repertoire that included works by Balzac, George Sand, *Dumas *fils*, and *Scribe. An extremely capable director, Montigny specialized in contemporary situational dramas and the *well-made play. He ran the Gymnase for 30 years, and was awarded the Légion d'Honneur in 1865. In his *Observations on the Théâtre-Français and the Secondary Theatres* (1847), Montigny examined what he considered to be the most serious problems of the Comédie-Française.   CHB

MONTRÉAL

Long the economic and cultural capital of French Canada, the city has also been an important centre of English-language theatre since the early nineteenth century. With more than 150 professional and *amateur companies performing regularly in French, English, and other languages, Montréal offers a broad scenic spectrum, from predictable classics (*Molière and Shakespeare are particularly favoured, the latter usually in Québécois 'tradaptation' (translation + adaptation) by authors as prominent as Antonine *Maillet, Michel *Tremblay, and Michel *Garneau) to modern international successes (*Albee, *Claudel, *Stoppard, *Brecht, *Pirandello), canonic Québécois dramatists (Marcel *Dubé, Tremblay, Marie *Laberge), and a dizzying panoply of experimental offerings that obscure traditional boundaries.

Prominent companies such as Théâtre du *Nouveau Monde and *Rideau Vert in French, the Centaur and the Saidye Bronfman Centre in English, offer eclectic fare with an international flavour, mixed with generally proven Québécois works, while the Théâtre d'*Aujourd'hui opts exclusively for local authors and many of the others incline in that direction.

Troupes such as Carbone 14 blend *dance, *music, *acrobatics, and innovative *lighting in felicitous experimentation, while Le Théâtre Omnibus specializes in *mime. The Other Theatre offers unpredictable *alternative theatre, while *puppetry—giant puppets inspired by Japanese *bunraku—is featured at the Théâtre Sans Fil. On another level La Nouvelle Compagnie Théâtrale has found a comfortable niche offering theatre for high-school students, while half a dozen others (notably Le Carrousel and Le Théâtre de la Marmaille) serve an even younger clientele. The National Theatre School/L'École Nationale du Théâtre, Canada's most important venue for *training actors, directors, designers and other stage professionals, is also located in Montréal, and several of the major theatre companies operate apprenticeship programmes there. Finally, as the principal site for *television and *film production in French, the city serves as a magnet for dramatists, scriptwriters, *actors, and those who have learned to appreciate their work.

For francophone theatre it was not always so; indeed, it was only after the Second World War that French-language production (apart from *variety and *burlesque of the American type) permanently superseded English-language offerings, although demographically anglophones had been a diminishing minority for more than a century. The roots underlying this anomaly plunge deep into the history of French Canada. There are no reliable reports of public theatre in Montréal under the French regime, and indeed it had been explicitly prohibited throughout New France since the 1690s. Some modest theatrical activity occurred in French immediately after the Conquest, much of it by British troops garrisoned there. But the enduring misgivings of the Catholic hierarchy regarding public performance ensured that French-language theatre remained sporadic and amateur until nearly the end of the nineteenth century.

English-language entertainment, on the other hand, encountered no such barrier. The *Theatre Royal, founded by anglophones in 1825, generally welcomed French-language activity, and there the first professionals from France performed in 1827. With improvements in transatlantic travel and the completion of a railway system linking Montréal to *New York, *Boston, and *Philadelphia, visits by *touring professionals became more common after mid-century and other theatres, also funded by anglophones, were built to receive them, such as the Academy of Music in the 1880s and Her Majesty's in the 1890s. Visits by professionals from France increased as well, exemplified by the eight Canadian tours of Sarah *Bernhardt. These frequently elicited hostile reaction by the clergy but led eventually to the Church's encouragement of local alternatives. The 1890s are often described as the 'golden age' of theatre in Montréal—a misleading designation, since most of the repertoire was imported (and less than 17 per cent was offered in French). A valiant attempt to replace suspect *Parisian fare with more wholesome entertainment was made in 1898, when church-approved 'Soirées de Famille' (Family Nights) were inaugurated at the *Monument National, but this ultimately proved ineffective as well.

Overall, the glitter quickly vanished, as American-style *vaudeville, burlesque, and silent *film conspired to displace traditional theatre. This tendency was heightened in the 1920s, when improvisational burlesque became the main attraction, with stars such as Olivier Guimond and Rose *Ouellette. In the next decade, 'talkies' and *radio arrived, spreading with unprecedented speed. Radio in particular became a nursery for local writers and actors, many of whom now passed easily from that medium to the traditional stage, notably Henry Deyglun, one of the founders of the Théâtre Stella, a rare beacon in a sea of general mediocrity.

But the seeds of a new, indigenous, professional theatre were already being sown in the 1930s, with the foundation of Émile *Legault's Compagnons de Saint-Laurent (a troupe of amateurs which would later provide a whole generation of theatre professionals), with the formation of the courageously bilingual Montreal Repertory Theatre, and with the advent of Gratien *Gélinas and his clever, irreverent *character Fridolin. Yet the inescapable fact is that in Montréal the best and most vigorous theatre provided before the end of the Second World War was produced and performed in English, often by touring professionals from the USA and the UK.

The unprecedented success, in French and English, of Gélinas's *Tit-Coq* in 1948 heralded the arrival of a new age, confirmed by the founding of Le Rideau Vert the same year, the Théâtre du Nouveau Monde (1951), the Théâtre de Quat'Sous (1955), the Comédie Canadienne (1958), and in the next decade a score of new companies, some ephemeral, others that endure and prosper (La Nouvelle Compagnie Théâtrale, 1964; the tri-theatre complex La Place des Arts, 1963; the Centaur, 1969). The heady 1970s and 1980s brought international attention to Montréal's theatre scene, heightened since 1985 by the Festival du Théâtre des Amériques, which annually attracts troupes from every continent. Successive generations of gifted dramatists have appeared, following in the wake of Michel Tremblay's groundbreaking *Les Belles-Sœurs* in 1968, their works directed, produced, and performed by native professionals, and frequently exported to major international centres. All this has been encouraged by dependable subsidies at the municipal, provincial, and federal levels, an important factor in stabilizing what had long been a precarious cultural sector. Stage arts in Montréal are now mature, secure, complex, and cosmopolitan.

LED

MONUMENT NATIONAL THEATRE

Built to house the cultural activities of Québec's nationalistic Société Saint-Jean-Baptiste in *Montréal, it opened in June 1893 with seating for 1,500. The 1890s have been termed the 'golden age' of theatre in Montréal, but most of its French-language offerings came from France, still morally suspect in the eyes of local clergy. To counter this the Church sanctioned programmes of 'wholesome' entertainment, the 'Soirées de Famille', beginning in 1898. The *playhouse has since been used by a succession of *amateur and professional troupes, notably Gratien *Gélinas's *Fridolinades*. Since 1971 it has housed the co-lingual National Theatre School/École Nationale du Théâtre.   LED

MOOCK, ARMANDO (1894–1942)

Chilean playwright and novelist who wrote an impressive number of sentimental and *realistic plays, mainly between 1915 and 1935, regularly produced in *Santiago and elsewhere. Although his first play *Crisis económica* (*Economic Crisis*, 1914) was a failure, starting with *Isabel Sandoval* (1915) he became the most accomplished playwright of his day. *Pueblecito* (*Little Town*, 1918), a drama of customs and manners that is a classic of Chilean theatre, focuses on the economic and cultural changes occurring in big cities and the countryside. In 1919 he emigrated to Argentina where he successfully continued his career in *Buenos Aires.   MAR

MOODY, WILLIAM VAUGHN (1869–1910)

American playwright. Born in Indiana and orphaned in his teens, Moody worked his way through Harvard College. While teaching at the University of Chicago (1895–1902) he published acclaimed lyric poetry and wrote *verse dramas. His 1906 prose drama *The Great Divide*, in which the untamed west is contrasted with eastern gentility as a metaphor for the battle of the sexes, ranks as a masterpiece of its era. A second prose play, *The Faith Healer* (1909), reached *New York in January 1910, nine months before its author died of a brain tumour.   FHL

MOORE, EDWARD (1712–57)

English playwright who began as a linen draper. His first work, *The Foundling* (1748), was a popular *comedy of the sentimental variety. Moore also found success with an adaptation of *Lesage's *Gil Blas* (1751), but his greatest achievement was the domestic *tragedy *The Gamester* (1753), which gave *Garrick one of his most affecting roles as the suicidal title character, Beverley. Although not immediately successful, the play was revived and remained influential throughout the century, later adapted by *Diderot.   MJK

MOORE, GEORGE (1852–1933)

Irish novelist who maintained a long-standing interest in theatre. If he was viewed with suspicion by *Yeats and the *Fays when he commented on weaknesses in *directing ('stage-management') at the *Abbey, it was Moore's involvement with English theatrical ventures they found suspect: Jimmy Glover's *touring *operetta company, which he had followed to furnish a necessary verisimilitude for his novel *The Mummer's Wife* (1885); George Sims, with whom he entered into a bet (1892) to write an unconventional play (*The Strike at Arlingford*) for *Grein's *Independent Theatre; the *London-based performers (Ben *Webster and May Whitty) whom he brought to *Dublin, when *Martyn despaired of Florence *Farr's directing skills during *rehearsals for the first season of the *Irish Literary Theatre (1899). Yeats's suspicions had developed during his attempts to collaborate in playwriting with Moore: *Diarmuid and Grania* (1901) demonstrated the absurdity of fusing Yeats's *symbolist tendencies with Moore's earthy *realism; and their second effort fared no better, though Yeats salvaged the basic idea for *Where There Is Nothing* (1902). Moore became a fierce critic of Abbey productions.   RAC

MOORE, MAVOR (1919–   )

Canadian actor, director, playwright, and *critic. The son of Canadian theatre pioneer Dora Mavor Moore, he co-founded two companies with her, the Village Players (1938) and the New Play Society (1946), and was a driving force behind the latter's annual *revue, *Spring Thaw* (1948–71). He was founding director of the Charlottetown Festival, of *Toronto's St Lawrence Centre, and of *television drama at the Canadian Broadcasting Company. He was a drama critic for the Toronto *Telegram* (1959–60) and an arts columnist for the *Globe and Mail* (1984–9). At York University he created the first course in Canadian theatre (1970), and later chaired the Canada Council (1979–83). In 1973 he was made an Officer of the Order of Canada; an autobiography appeared in 1994.   DWJ

MORALITY AND THEATRE See CENSORSHIP; RELIGION AND THEATRE.

MORALITY PLAY

A popular *genre of *medieval theatre in Europe. Although there are examples from the tenth century onwards, moral plays do not become frequent until the early fourteenth century, when their marked increase was probably a result of the Christian Church stressing the need for regular confession and penance to ensure God's forgiveness, reinforced by the presence of the Black Death, which threatened to snatch people away at any moment with their sins upon their heads. Indeed, the Plague's presence produced a drama called *The Dance of Death*, where Death comes to take away people of all ranks and ages, from the king to the labourer, the old man to the child. Such a *dance was performed at Besançon in 1453, and episodes of similar dances

were painted on the walls of many churches to remind the people to perform deeds of charity while they still could. The earliest moral plays to be written used the triumph of saints over temptation and persecution as an example for Christians to imitate. In the tenth century, we have a number written by *Hrotsvitha, an influential laywoman attached to the convent at Gandersheim, and the tradition was extended by twelfth-century writers to include the conversion of St Paul and plays dealing with the good deeds and miracles of popular saints like St Nicholas. Such plays became a distinctive form of morality, called the *miracle play, which could be applied to virtually any saint.

Miracle plays tended to use direct narrative, but the distinguishing mark of most morality plays was the use of allegorical *characters to represent the interplay of various positive and negative forces in human life. *Allegory of this type was invented by the late Roman writer Prudentius in his fourth-century epic called *Psychomachia* (*The Battle for the Soul*) where he provided a dramatic account of how the sins attacked a town representing the human soul and how the virtues defended it. Soon characters representing the soul, sins, and virtues came to be treated as forces acting within the human mind, thus making possible a simple form of psychological analysis. The first dramatic use of allegory in the West seems to have been a musical play called *Ordo Virtutum* (*The Way of the Virtues*) written by the Abbess *Hildegard von Bingen in about 1150 as the result of a vision. This showed the (female) Soul being saved from the Devil by characters that personified her virtues. The staging, too, was allegorical; the piece was presented on a staircase, using actors dressed in symbolically coloured *costumes who ascended and descended according to their level of goodness.

Allegorical figures were also used to analyse the weaknesses of men in the sphere of *politics. The first play of this kind was called *Antichristus* (*Antichrist*), and it was performed in the twelfth century at Tegernsee in Austria. It mixed together characters representing earthly power, like the Emperor, the Pope, and three European kings, with others representing contemporary religious forces, like the Synagogue and the Church, and abstract virtues, like Mercy and Justice. It deals very simply with the individual's conflicting duties to the Church and the state, and the need to be honest in politics even if deception seems to be more successful. As the range of characters in this play suggests, the application of the allegorical method could be very flexible. It could be used to analyse institutions, political situations, people's impulses and objectives, or particular problems like preparing oneself for death. Some French examples show that it could also be used to treat the two sides of a moral question, such as peace versus war (*Moralité de Paix et de Guerre*), or the effects of a particular failing like malicious gossip (*Moralité de Langue Envenimée*) or gluttony (*Moral joyeulx du Ventre*, where the belly is the central character).

However, most moralities are centred around an 'Everyman' figure, who undergoes a process of spiritual death and resurrection. This pattern is first seen in a piece called *The King of Life* in the early fourteenth century. King Life, who is protected by two bodyguards, Strength and Health, brags that he is immortal and challenges Death to a duel. When Death takes up the challenge, first the bodyguards and then the King himself are slain. As Life dies, his Soul is seized by devils and his Body and Soul dispute over where the blame should lie, but finally the Virgin Mary intercedes and his Soul is allowed to ascend to heaven. This play, with its bragging, death, and resurrection, has obvious parallels to the *folk plays involving the death and resurrection of St George.

Another popular morality pattern involves a central 'Everyman' figure being dragged to and fro between sins, who tempt him towards damnation, and virtues, who try to save his soul. This is often combined with the death and resurrection theme. Some of these plays represent the whole life of man as a series of different ages, each governed by a particular vice, while others, like *Lusty Iuventus*, deal with the sins of a specific age like youth. A good example of the 'whole life' morality is *The Castle of Perseverance*. This begins with Mankind's birth, already accompanied by good and bad angels. He wants to be rich but also to save his soul. The Bad Angel suggests he should accumulate riches first and consider salvation when he grows older. Mankind agrees and falls into the hands of the seven deadly sins, but his Good Angel summons a bevy of beautiful virtues who save him and bring him to refuge in the Castle of Perseverance. Undefeated, the Bad Angel tempts him out again, using Lechery, Gluttony, Idleness, and Covetousness, the last of which grows stronger as he grows older. Death comes unannounced and Mankind's Soul is carried off to hell. His Body and Soul debate over where the blame lies and the four daughters of God review his case. Mercy speaks in his favour but Justice and Truth oppose her. Peace finally suggests that they lay the case before God himself, and there Mercy persuades her father to forgive Mankind's Soul and send it to heaven. It is worth noting that the seven deadly sins (envy, anger, idleness, avarice, gluttony, lechery, and, most dangerous of all, pride) which appear in this play served in medieval times as a convenient checklist for anybody going to confession so that they could ascertain where their life had fallen short of the basic Christian requirements.

The sins are not always the central focus of a moral play, however. In the well-known morality play *Everyman*, printed in 1495, and adapted from a Flemish original, *Elkerlijc*, the subject is how best to prepare for death. The central character has to overcome his weaknesses in order to win a place in heaven, but no separate sins are specified. Summoned unexpectedly by Death, Everyman tries to find a companion to travel with him beyond the grave. He is rejected in turn by Fellowship, Kindred, and Goods, and then finally discovers his Good Deeds—but she cannot help him because she is bound hand and foot by his 'sin'.

However, she calls her sister Wisdom, who takes Everyman to Confession, and his repentance frees Good Deeds, who is the only one of his qualities that can follow him beyond the grave. All his physical powers then leave him one by one, but after his final descent into the earth an angel is heard confirming that he has achieved salvation.

During the fifteenth century, *Rederijkerskamers* (*Chambers of Rhetoric) in the Netherlands produced many moral pieces like *Everyman*, which is an example of the *Spelen van Sinne* ('meaningful' or serious plays). These could be varied, some having quite *realistic motivations and *actions in place of symbolic arguments; for instance, one is a direct account of the raising of Lazarus, and hence a *biblical play. Another, *Mariken of Nijmegen*, has a *heroine, 'who lived more than seven years with the Devil', but who is finally turned to repentance by seeing a play performed on a *pageant wagon where the Virgin Mary successfully appeals to God to forgive Mankind. More unusual examples are the early fourteenth-century *Abele Spelen* ('seemly' plays), which are often described as *romances because they deal with the world of chivalry, but which in fact centre upon moral questions of knighthood; for instance, in *Lancelot of Denmark* the hero, on his mother's advice, speaks vulgarly to the girl he loves just after he has seduced her and is rejected by her for a more considerate lover and left bitterly regretting his discourtesy.

Another kind of morality that appeared in the late fourteenth century was called the Pater Noster play, because it used the Lord's Prayer (*Pater Noster*, 'Our Father') as a reminder of the various sins that man could fall prey to. In England we only have descriptions of this kind of play, but the pattern is clear. A series of *scenes demonstrated each of the seven deadly sins in turn and the show was introduced and concluded by a master of ceremonies called something like 'Vicious'. *The Play of the Paternoster* that was popular in York was of this kind, and there are parallel examples from Beverley and the Netherlands.

Perhaps the most unusual of the serious moral plays are the *autos sacramentales* (sacred plays) of Spain, regularly presented on the feast of *Corpus Christi from the fifteenth century onwards. These employed allegorical figures to illustrate the main dogmas of the Catholic Church; using characters like Faith, Thought, and Grace to clarify the dogma involved and trace a movement towards understanding and acceptance within the central character's mind. These pieces were brought to a very high level by *Calderón in the seventeenth century, which shows how long the allegorical method continued to appeal.

Most early moral pieces are rather serious, but many later examples are humorous and bawdy, and often contain a new central character called the Vice. He is the leader and organizer of the sins, and also incorporates many of them in himself—which is why Prince Hal in Shakespeare's *Henry IV* calls Falstaff a 'reverend Vice'. He is a cynical commentator whose role could only be sustained by an accomplished comedian, and he probably appeared because the pieces were now being played by professional players who depended upon their *audience for their living. A good example of these later professional pieces is *Mankind* (1465). Its eponymous hero is a simple farmer, who is tempted to leave his work and take up a life of idleness and crime, despite the warnings of a friar called Mercy. He is misled by Mischief, who is the Vice, and his three fashionable followers, New Guise, Naught, and Nowadays, and they eventually drive him to despair—but he is saved from suicide by Mercy. In the course of the play the audience are tricked into singing an indecent song, and are persuaded to donate money to see the sensationally costumed devil Tittivillus—a clear indication that the play is intended for commercial presentation. In the Netherlands such humorous moralities were called *Esbatementen* ('revels' or *'farces'). A good example is *The Farce of the Apple Tree*, where God grants the prayer of Staunch Goodfellow and his wife Steadfast Faith that anybody who tries to steal fruit from their apple tree shall stick there until they free them. As a result the branches soon become heavy with would-be thieves: Insatiability, Riotous Living, Loose Wanton, the Devil, and even Death.

By the sixteenth century moralities were usually called *interludes and seem mainly to have been entertainments to accompany a banquet. They became shorter, and some authors were advising the actors to omit 'much of the sad matter' to make them lighter. The only pieces that remained long were political interludes, like *Skelton's *Magnificence* of about 1516 and *Bale's *King John* of 1536, which used allegorical figures to provide an interpretation of the workings of politics, showing rulers being misled by corrupt courtiers or the desire for wealth or power, and occasionally being saved by the good sense of wise counsellors. In these pieces the names of individuals are sometimes briefly attached to the allegorical forces and, in a very simple way, we begin to see the actions of real men spearheading the abstract forces in society—a pattern later elaborated by Shakespeare in his *histories. The moral plays also helped to lay a basis for Elizabethan *tragedies and *city comedies, the tragedies benefiting from the moral conflict of sins and virtues within the individual and the *comedies from the vivid and constantly varying catalogue of colourful types presented as the lesser actors changed quickly from role to role.

Professional moral interludes disappeared at the time when permanent companies like Shakespeare's began to perform in *London, so they clearly could not compete with the new drama (*see* EARLY MODERN PERIOD IN EUROPE). However, we know that Queen Elizabeth greatly enjoyed moral plays, and they continued to be written for *amateurs to perform in schools and universities until about 1610, when they finally died away.

JWH

CRAIK, T. W., *The Tudor Interlude* (Leicester, 1967)
POTTER, ROBERT, *The English Morality Play* (London, 1975)
HARRIS, JOHN WESLEY, *Medieval Theatre in Context* (London, 1992)

MORATÍN, LEANDRO FERNÁNDEZ DE (1760–1828)

Spanish poet and playwright. The son of a celebrated writer, he was exiled to Paris following the Spanish War of Independence, only to return to Spain in 1820 and, from an influential position in the theatre, to help implement the reforms of Carlos III. A confirmed *neoclassicist, Moratín's strict respect for the *unities of time, place, and *action was coupled with a *didactic conception of *comedy as the corrector of ignorant behaviour and outmoded or decadent customs. The marriage of convenience between an old man and an adolescent female was the target of *satire in *El sí de las niñas* (*The Maidens' Consent*) of 1806, while in the earlier *La comedia nueva o el café* (*The New Play; or, The Café*) (1792), Moratín had mounted a swingeing attack on contemporary Spanish theatrical tastes.

KG

MORECAMBE, ERIC (ERIC BARTHOLOMEW) (1926–84) AND ERNIE WISE (ERNEST WISEMAN) (1925–99)

English comedians. Both were early discoveries of Jack Hylton, Ernie *auditioning for his *radio show *Bandwagon* in 1938, aged 13, with the legendary Arthur *Askey, and Eric for Hylton's *revue *Youth Takes a Bow*, which Ernie joined two months later. Their double act, originally called Morecambe and Leeds, was established after the war. Their early career was on radio and in summer seasons in Blackpool; *television would claim them almost entirely from the 1960s. Announcements made in front of a plush curtain, the running gag of Ernie's 'plays what I wrote' featuring stage and screen actors of note (Glenda *Jackson, Flora *Robson, John *Mills), the referential nature of song-and-*dance routines, Ernie's efforts to sing a solo, catchphrases and catch-actions (the two-handed slap on the cheeks, the shoulder hug, Ernie's mythical toupé), all contributed to the clean, cosy, and safe reputation of the Morecambe and Wise Show, which attracted consistently high ratings. Their Christmas specials, rerun into the twenty-first century, have assumed national heritage status.

AF

MORENO, RITA (1931–)

American actress, *dancer, and singer, born Rosita Dolores Alverio in Puerto Rico. A Spanish dancer and entertainer by her early teens, Moreno made her Broadway debut in *Skydrift* (1945). At 17 she was signed to an MGM contract, appearing in many *films, including *Singin' in the Rain* (1952), though often *cast as an ethnic stereotype. Moreno's talent and range were given freer rein following her Oscar-winning performance as Anita in the film version of *West Side Story* (1961). She appeared in the *London première of *She Loves Me* (1962), then returned to

*New York to star in *The Sign in Sidney Brustein's Window* (1964). She later originated the role of Googie Gomez in *The Ritz* (1975), and played Olive Madison in Neil *Simon's *gender-reversed version of *The Odd Couple* (1985). She was featured on *The Electric Company* children's *television show in the 1970s, and has since made many other appearances on TV and film.

EW

MORESCA

Energetic and humorous *dance-drama, presumably Moorish in origin, that spread from post-Muslim Spain throughout Europe in the late fifteenth and early sixteenth centuries via companies of travelling performers. The dancers wore exuberant *costumes studded with bells, and after a brief spoken *prologue danced to fife and tabor, around bonfires, in villages, manors, and castles. Despite the complaints of the clergy, the *moresca* has persisted to this day, where it lives on as an ancient festival in parts of the Adriatic, as well as being a possible, if unproven, source of certain forms of *morris dance in England.

KG

MORETO Y CABAÑA, AGUSTÍN (1618–69)

The most representative dramatist of late seventeenth-century Spain. Almost all his works were indebted to earlier plays, restyled with restraint and disciplined craftsmanship. Some serious ones are distinguished, but he excelled in constructing comic intrigues, in which scheming, witty *graciosos* often take charge. *El lindo don Diego* (*The Dandy Don Diego*) is an hilarious *comedia de figurón, and *No puede ser* (*There's No Guarding a Woman*) an original treatment of the 'guardian-outwitted' theme, but his masterpiece is the high *comedy (much imitated abroad) *El desdén con el desdén*, whose *hero wins its disdainful heroine by feigning disdain himself.

VFD

MORIONES

A *festival which takes place annually during Holy Week on Marinduque Island in the *Philippines. Now a major tourist attraction, the *pageant was introduced in the late nineteenth century by a local parish priest to dramatize the legend of Longinus, the centurion who speared Jesus Christ on the cross. Drops of blood spurted out (John 31: 34), striking Longinus in his blind eye and miraculously restoring his sight. After witnessing the Resurrection, Longinus publicly professed his new faith and was beheaded. In Mogpog, the original version of the festival (*moryonan*) is performed as *mime. There are four critical events: (*a*) the crucifixion of Jesus, (*b*) the breaking of Longinus' spear into three pieces, symbolizing his final conversion to Christianity, (*c*) the chase of Longinus (*habulan*) throughout the community by roaming *moriones*, and (*d*) the climactic de-

capitation and martyrdom of Longinus (*pugután*). In Boac, a *Passion play (*sinakulo*) has been introduced. Although *masking has not played a significant role in indigenous Philippine culture, the *moriones* festival is famous for its elaborate *mascara* and headdresses (*turbante*), which look either saintly (*bulaklakan*) or fiercely grotesque ('Roman'). *Morion* actors perform under religious vow (*panata*), pledged as petition or thanksgiving.

NHB

MORISSEAU-LEROY, FÉLIX (1912–98)

Haitian playwright and poet. He began writing in French but switched to creole in 1953 for a collection of poems called *Dyakout* and for his masterful adaptation of *Sophocles in *Antigòn*. After its theatrical success he continued to write in creole even after he went into exile in 1959. *Téyat kreyòl* (*Creole Theatre*, 1997) brings together his principal plays, including *Wa Kreyòn*, a sequel to *Antigòn*, and his fine *comedy *Bouki ak Malis nan Nouyok* (1983). 'Every time there is an advance in theatre, the people progress,' he said, and he followed this social intent by adapting foreign subjects to Haitian culture. The staging and behaviour of his *characters are inspired by Haitian customs and beliefs, especially by *voodoo. Freed from the constraints of French, his plays inaugurated a new Haitian *realism. He died in Miami.

MLa trans. JCM

MORLEY, CHRISTOPHER (1937–   )

English designer. Following work (1960–5) at the Coventry Belgrade Theatre and the Leicester Phoenix Theatre, the powerful structural simplicity of Morley's *scenographic approach came to prominence in 1966 in his brightly lit golden box within a larger box created for William *Gaskill's controversial *Royal Court production of *Macbeth*. The same year his collaboration with Trevor *Nunn on *The Revenger's Tragedy* for the *Royal Shakespeare Company produced a grotesque *comedy played out in black and silver *costumes on a painted silver circle, luridly bathed in light. Appointed head of design for the RSC (1968–74), Morley continued to work with Nunn to create a company style stripped of extraneous detail. In 1969 Morley's great empty white box, illuminated from above with a huge cone of *lighting, provided the permanent frame for the whole season including a brilliant-white design for Nunn's *The Winter's Tale* and an atmospheric cage of latticed wicker for John *Barton's *Twelfth Night*. The new stage, operated on a system of hydraulics, which Morley designed for Nunn's season of the Roman plays in 1972 was less successful. He was made honorary associate artist of the RSC in 1984. In the 1970s and 1980s his other work in theatre and *opera included productions at *Birmingham Rep, most notably Peter Farago's British première of *Wesker's *The Merchant*, where Morley introduced back-projection screens into the box concept. He was head of the

Birmingham School of Theatre Design from 1980 until 1991.

CEC

MORRIS, CLARA (1846/8–1925)

American actress, born in Toronto. After growing up in poverty with her mother and apprenticing in Cleveland and Cincinnati, she joined Augustin *Daly's company at *New York's 5th Avenue Theatre in 1870, where she triumphed in *Man and Wife* and the more torrid *L'Article 47*, *Alixe*, and *Madeline Morel*. Chafing under Daly's autocracy, she broke her contract in 1874 and moved to Palmer's Theatre to become the greatest American Camille since Matilda *Heron, then to *Booth's for a controversially seductive Lady Macbeth, and, ultimately, to the head of her own company, reprising and expanding her signature repertoire of French domestic *melodrama. Dubbed 'Queen of Spasms' and 'Mistress of the Ductus Lachrymalis', Morris specialized in physically graphic portrayals of putatively genuine extreme emotion. She published three colourful if unreliable memoirs: *Life on the Stage* (1901), *Stage Confidences* (1902), and *The Life of a Star* (1906).

KM

MORRIS DANCE

References to morris dance are found in Britain as early as the fifteenth century, but they do not enable us to characterize the performance clearly. A pattern *dance with the brandishing of swords is common in surviving accounts, however. As with other *medieval *folk plays and performances, the morris dance carried social implications. The combative element, for example, would have altered its social meaning after the performances were banned from their traditional role at parish fundraising festivals and performed in defiance of the episcopacy. Morris dances continue into the twenty-first century in numerous locales within and without Great Britain, with great variety in their form and social setting. *See also* MUMMERS' PLAY.

JCD

MORTIMER, JOHN CLIFFORD (1923–   )

English playwright and novelist. A scriptwriter for the Crown Film Unit during the Second World War, Mortimer was a barrister and novelist when he turned to *radio and *television writing in the 1950s. Somewhat like Terence *Rattigan, Mortimer specialized in creating beleaguered middle-class *characters confronting their life-sustaining illusions. His first play for radio, *The Dock Brief* (1957), was his most successful, being reincarnated on television, stage, and *film. The play concerns a prisoner and his over-imaginative barrister whose incompetence ironically sets him free. In its stage version, *The Dock Brief* ran as a double bill with *What Shall We Tell Caroline?* (1958), set in a boys' school in which a teenage girl is the quiet centre of her

parents' complicated *ménage a trois* with the assistant headmaster. The full-length *The Wrong Side of the Park* (1960) focuses on a woman coming to terms with false fantasies of her first marriage which are impinging on her second. The play's thin *plot and final-act revelation, worthy of *Pinero, suggested that Mortimer was more comfortable with the *one-act format fitting radio and television. Indeed, his best-known work comes from television and includes *Brideshead Revisited* (1981) and the series *Rumpole of the Bailey*, which originated in 1978. Other notable plays include an adaptation of *Feydeau's *A Flea in her Ear* (1966) for the *National Theatre, *A Voyage round my Father* (1972), *I, Claudius* (the stage version, 1972) which starred David *Warner, and *Collaborators* (1973) with Glenda *Jackson.

MDG

MORTON, CHARLES (1819–1904)

*Music-hall proprietor, who opened the Canterbury Hall, Lambeth, in 1851, built as an annex to the Canterbury Arms. It was so profitable that he rebuilt it in 1854. In 1861 he opened the Oxford in Oxford Street, the first purpose-built music hall. Although he popularized music hall, he did not invent it—despite being known as the 'Father of the Halls' by the 1890s. Prosecuted several times by the *London theatre *managers for contravention of the Theatres Act in the 1860s (*see* LICENSING ACTS), he retained a respectable demeanour that 'would have done credit to a churchwarden'.

JTD

MORTON, MARTHA (c.1865–1925)

American playwright. Although not the first professionally produced woman playwright in *New York, Morton was regarded as a pioneer and called 'the doyen of women playwrights' for her persistence in overcoming obstacles to production (impelling her to *direct her own work) and for encouraging other women to write for the stage. Her successes included *A Bachelor's Romance* (1896) and *The Senator Keeps House* (1911). Unable to gain admission to the male playwrights' club, she founded the Society of Dramatic Authors in 1907. After the men petitioned for membership alongside her 30 women writers, Morton became vice-president of a consolidated organization, the Society of American Dramatists and Composers.

FHL

MORTON, THOMAS (c.1764–1838)

English dramatist. Morton's first play, the melodramatic *Columbus; or, A World Discovered*, was performed at *Covent Garden in 1792. He wrote two dozen plays altogether, almost all for Covent Garden. These are mostly *comedies, of which the best known in their time—none survives in the theatre today—are *The Way to Get Married* (1796), *A Cure for the Heart-Ache* (1797),

Speed the Plough (1800, containing the *character of the unseen but fearsome Mrs Grundy), *The School of Reform* (1805), and the *farce *A Roland for an Oliver* (1819). Morton's plays possess the striking features of late eighteenth- and early nineteenth-century English comedy. They are heavily sentimental, moralistic, anti-aristocratic, bustling with *plot, intensely idealistic about virtue and rural domestic life. They are full of low comedy as well as *melodrama, and the pathetic and potentially tragic elements are in equal balance with the comic and farcical. This type of comedy represented the most popular *legitimate drama of its age and established a distinctive pattern inherited by the Victorian theatre.   MRB

MOSCOW

Theatrical capital of the Russian Federation. The first theatrical performance in Russia was given at court in 1672 by a troupe led by a priest, Johann Gottfried Grigory. In 1702 Peter the Great invited a German *actor-manager, Johann Kunst, to train a group of Russians in the art of theatre and built premises on Red (Beautiful) Square where performances were given in both German and Russian. In 1742 Empress Elizaveta Petrovna ordered the construction of an *opera theatre and a German theatre in Moscow. A Russian Theatre was opened in 1759 by a group of entrepreneurs, including one Michael Maddocks (Mikhail Georgevich Medoks), an Englishman who in 1780 built his own Petrovsky Theatre, a 1,500-seater later known as the Teatr Medoksa (Maddocks Theatre), where he staged German and French classic plays and those of *Fonvizin, the first significant Russian dramatist. During the second half of the eighteenth century, *serf theatres began to proliferate, which the imperial court sought to control through the imposition of *censorship and, in 1827, through the restriction of performance rights to court-controlled imperial theatres, the first of which had been established in 1806. The most important Moscow Imperial Theatre, the *Maly, opened in 1824, a few months before the *Bolshoi in 1825, the latter becoming the venue for opera and *ballet productions, giving first performances of works by Glinka and Tchaikovsky.

The first successful challenge to the imperial monopoly was made when Anna Brenko established the Pushkin Theatre on Tverskaya Street in 1880, offering productions of serious plays as an alternative to the *operettas and other forms of light entertainment permitted under the monopoly. The imperial monopoly was finally rescinded in 1882, leading to the establishment of a number of private theatres, the most prominent of which were organized by Fyodor Korsh, Elizaveta Goreva, Maria Abramova, and Konstantin Nezlobin. In 1885 S. I. *Mamontov opened the first private opera theatre and proceeded to bring about a major revolution in opera production, in collaboration with Chaliapin, Rachmaninov, Rimsky-Korsakov, and a host of outstanding artists and theatre designers. During this period

Moscow *audiences also became familiar with actors and *touring companies from abroad, such as the Saxe-*Meiningen troupe, Sarah *Bernhardt, Eleanore *Duse, Tommaso *Salvini, Ernesto *Rossi, and Constant-Benoît *Coquelin. However, the theatrical event of the 1890s was undoubtedly the founding in 1897 of the *Moscow Art Theatre (MAT) by *Stanislavsky and *Nemirovich-Danchenko, who together revolutionized attitudes towards acting and stage production.

Following the 1917 Revolution, the former imperial theatres came under the auspices of the Moscow Theatre Section of the Commissariat of Enlightenment. At the same time a number of new theatres and groups sprang up, such as the Proletkult (in Prince Yusupov's former mansion on Kalinin Prospekt), the Meyerhold Theatre, the Theatre of Revolutionary Satire, the Theatre of the Revolution (later the Mossoviet Theatre), the *Moscow State Yiddish Theatre, the Gypsy Theatre (the Romany), *Blue Blouse collectives, and Theatres of Young Workers (*TRAM). Further *studios became attached to MAT, such as the Third Studio in 1921 (later the Vakhtangov Theatre, 1926), MAT 2, which opened in 1924, and a Fourth Studio in 1927, which later became the Realistic Theatre headed by Nikolai *Okhlopkov. With the promulgation of Lenin's New Economic Policy, in 1921, the state's grip on Moscow theatres loosened somewhat and, although they were closely supervised because dependent on state funding, a degree of self-*financing through box-office receipts was tolerated, until this policy was sharply rescinded with the creation of the state censorship body Glavrepertkom, and the complete nationalization of theatrical enterprises. The 1930s proved a fairly grim period for Moscow theatres as, one after another, they were either merged, closed down, or threatened with closure. *Meyerhold's theatre was closed in 1938, as was the Realistic Theatre when forced to merge with the Kamerny, while other theatres tended to play safe in the repressive artistic climate. The war, ironically, brought a period of respite during which many Moscow theatres were evacuated to the east. However, their return to the capital was marked by further repression as first the Yiddish Theatre, then the Kamerny, were officially closed down, in 1947 and 1950.

Because Moscow is the capital it also functions as the nation's theatre *training centre and it was from institutes such as the Shchukin Theatre School, as well as from the children's theatres, that the post-Stalin revival emerged. This was spearheaded by Oleg *Efremov at the *Sovremennik Theatre, founded in 1957, and by Yury *Lyubimov at the *Taganka Theatre, founded in 1964. During the Khrushchev era they seemed to herald a new dawn before the grey pall of Brezhnev's period of stagnation occluded it. The imminent collapse of the regime was signalled by a split in the Moscow Art Theatre, in 1987, between old-style and new-style communists, with the old guard occupying a new building on Tverskoy Boulevard and assuming the name of *Gorky, whilst the more progressive wing retained control of the old building, but rechristened it after *Chekhov. The collapse of communism in the early 1990s triggered a period of economic and cultural chaos but also led to the creation of a lively *fringe theatre along Western lines. A 1979 publication listed 28 mainstream theatres in Moscow, including three children's theatres and two *puppet theatres, of which only sixteen could be called mainstream drama theatres. By the 1990s a good 50 per cent of the venues for plays in Moscow had not even existed in 1979. In fact, a total of some 28 new venues were listed in the magazine *Plays International* by the end of the twentieth century. Moscow is also home to a number of theatre *museums, the most famous of which are the Moscow Art Theatre Museum and the Bakhrushin Theatre Museum, and of the All-Union Theatrical Society (VTO; rechristened the Union of Theatre Workers, STD), and the State Institute of Theatrical Art (GITIS) which trains both actors and directors.

NW

MOSCOW ART THEATRE

Russian company, founded by *Stanislavsky and *Nemirovich-Danchenko in 1897 in *Moscow. Like the free theatres of André *Antoine in *Paris (Théâtre *Libre) and Otto *Brahm in *Berlin (*Freie Bühne), the Moscow Art Theatre set out to correct the faults of existing theatre by creating a serious, contemporary repertoire, encouraging ensemble organization and playing, raising standards of design and production in the pursuit of authenticity (*see* NATURALISM), and educating a serious, more democratic *audience. The phrase 'open to all' (*obschedostupnyi*) figured in early publicity, late spectators were barred, only one play was performed per evening, the customary musical overture was dropped, and actors no longer courted *applause. MAT opened in 1898 with Aleksei *Tolstoy's previously banned historical play *Tsar Fyodor Ioannovich*. The production was admired for its historical accuracy, stunning sets, *costumes, and standards of *acting. From 1898 to 1905 the theatre consolidated its reputation for *realist drama in contemporary plays by *Chekhov (five), *Gorky (three), *Ibsen (six), and *Hauptmann (four). Nemirovich-Danchenko operated as literary manager, administrator, and *director, while Stanislavsky—sometimes acting, sometimes co-directing with Nemirovich-Danchenko—created a series of productions that are still admired and analysed for their skill. The Moscow Society of Art and Literature, Stanislavsky's Alma Mater, brought the performers Lilina, Andreeva, Luzhsky and Artem; and from the Music and Drama Institute of the Moscow Philharmonic Society, where Nemirovich-Danchenko taught, came *Knipper, *Moskvin, and *Meyerhold. Sets and costumes were designed by Viktor *Simov. After 1904 the MAT turned to the *modernists, *Maeterlinck, Hamsun, and *Andreev, causing some criticism, not least from Stanislavsky. Relations between the two directors deteriorated so that by 1908 Stanislavsky had resigned from

the board to develop his *theory of acting based on realist drama, his 'system'. The results were first visible in *Turgenev's *A Month in the Country* (1909). By this time Nemirovich-Danchenko had returned to classic realism, including the work of *Griboedov and Lev *Tolstoy. Meanwhile the earlier successes continued in the repertoire.

The first of the several studios associated with MAT was set up in 1913, for Stanislavsky to work on his theories with Leopold *Sulerzhitsky. This studio became known as MAT 2 in 1924 under the actor-director Michael *Chekhov (closed 1936). In 1920 the Third Studio was operated by *Vakhtangov, and a fourth was set up by actors from the mother company (1921). Nemirovich-Danchenko also established a studio for *music theatre in 1919. These studios enlarged the repertoire and bridged the gap between the founding members and the Soviet generation: MAT had to find its way with the new regime. In 1922–4 a second foreign *tour to Europe and America (the company visited Europe in 1906), led by Stanislavsky, secured the theatre's international reputation. Still working with Simov, Stanislavsky introduced new writers in the 1920s, notably *Bulgakov (*Days of the Turbins*, 1926) and Vsevolod *Ivanov (*Armoured Train 14–69*, 1927).

MAT's political standing was not helped by the pre-revolutionary productions still in the repertoire. Chekhov was readdressed (*Cherry Orchard*, 1927) and politically acceptable writers such as *Afinogenov (*Fear*, 1931) and *Kirshon (*Bread*, 1931) were embraced. With Gorky's new work (*Egor Bulychov and the Others*, 1934, and the revised *Enemies*, 1935) MAT demonstrated its conformity with *socialist realism. For much of the remaining Stalinist period, MAT supplied the *political fodder required, becoming not much more than a museum of earlier successes. Its reputation for authentic period realism denuded the early productions of their freshness and contemporaneity, but the company retained the thoroughness of its practices. By this time the founding members had gone, but the theatre school was the most highly regarded *training institution in Russia, and MAT's foreign tours in the 1950s and 1960s confirmed its international reputation. It became a national institution surviving by inertia rather then creativity, until revitalized by Oleg *Efremov with a programme of reform in 1970. His arrival caused the departure of the first Soviet generation and a new, younger company emerged. As well as fresh productions of the classics, a more international repertoire, and new writers such as Aleksandr *Gelman and Mikhail *Shatrov, brought a new lease of life. Allegiance to Stanislavsky's system was, and is still, strong.

A crisis in the wake of perestroika in 1987 forced a split in the company. Efremov's group called itself the Chekhov Art Theatre, while a group led by Tatyana Doronina became the Gorky Art Theatre. Efremov's productions of once-controversial writers, Bulgakov, Solzhenitsyn, and *Petrushevskaya, have been followed by restagings of classics by Chekhov, Griboedov, and

*Pushkin in tune with the 1990s. In 1997 the Chekhov Art Theatre laid formal claim to MAT's great heritage by holding the centenary of the foundation. *See also* STUDIO THEATRE MOVEMENT.

CM

SMELIANSKY, ANATOLY, *The Russian Theatre after Stalin* (Cambridge, 1999)

WORRALL, NICK, *The Moscow Art Theatre* (London, 1996)

MOSCOW STATE YIDDISH THEATRE

Referred to by its acronym GOSET, the theatre was founded in 1919 in Petrograd (*St Petersburg). It transferred to *Moscow in 1920 under Aleksandr Granovsky, who directed the first production in 1921, in which Solomon *Mikhoels made his mark. Mikhoels became *artistic director in 1929, shifting the repertoire away from time-honoured Jewish themes presented in a deliberately archaic style, towards a concern with contemporary plays of modern Jewish import, always performed in Yiddish. Despite this, the theatre's landmark production is still considered to be *King Lear* (1935), which exploited the traditions of *Yiddish theatre to powerful effect.

NW

MOSHER, GREGORY (1952–)

American director and producer. After seven years (1978–85) as *artistic director of the *Goodman Theatre in *Chicago, Mosher took over the dormant *Lincoln Center Theatre in 1985 and, with Bernard Gersten, transformed it into a successful operation that blurred the distinction between not-for-profit and commercial theatre in *New York. Productions included new plays, such as John *Guare's *Six Degrees of Separation*, and Broadway-minded revivals of *Anything Goes* and *Waiting for Godot*. As a director, he is best known for his association with David *Mamet and the premières of *American Buffalo* (1975), *Glengarry Glen Ross* (1983), and *Speed-the-Plow* (1988). He left Lincoln Center in 1991 to pursue an independent career.

STC

MOSKVIN, IVAN (1874–1946)

Russian/Soviet actor and founder member of the *Moscow Art Theatre, who starred as the simple-minded *protagonist in their opening production of *Tsar Fyodor Ioannovich* (1898), the public popularity of which ensured the theatre's *financial survival in its first season. Moskvin was also a memorably sanctimonious Luka in *Gorky's *The Lower Depths* (1902) and an hilariously pathetic Epikhodov in *Chekhov's *The Cherry Orchard* (1904). One of *Stanislavsky's favourite actors, Moskvin was equally at home in Russian classics, the *socialist realist repertoire, in comic and serious roles. He co-directed a number of productions and made several *film appearances.

NW

MOSTEL, ZERO (1915–77)

American actor. With soulful eyes, baggy face, and portly elegance, Mostel acquired a reputation for unpredictability onstage and off, an 'inspired lunatic' regarded by Samuel *Beckett as a *clown of Chaplinesque stature. A career that began auspiciously on Broadway in 1942 stalled by the early 1950s when Mostel became branded along with other Hollywood artists as a communist sympathizer. He eventually regained momentum, notably with a portrayal of Leopold Bloom in *Ulysses in Nighttown* (1958), which earned an Obie *award and first prize for acting at the Théâtre des Nations festival in *Paris. Although he performed in works by *Molière, *Brecht, and *Ionesco, Mostel's singular stamp remains associated with his Tony award-winning *musical roles: Pseudolus in *A Funny Thing Happened on the Way to the Forum* (1962) and Tevye in *Fiddler on the Roof* (1964). His *films include *The Producers* (1968) and *The Front* (1976). Poised to redefine himself as a tragedian in the title role of Arnold *Wesker's *Shylock* (originally named *The Merchant*), Mostel died during its pre-Broadway try-out in *Philadelphia.

EW

MOTA, JOÃO (1942–)

Portuguese actor and director. He attended Peter *Brook's *International Centre for Theatre Research in *Paris and has, since the early 1970s, devoted himself to teaching performance at the Conservatory while engaging in the artistic management of A Comuna, which he founded in *Lisbon in 1972. One of the major Portuguese companies with a certain international visibility, it has had considerable success in attracting young *audiences. Mota began his career as a child in *radio and *television, joined the Teatro *Nacional in Lisbon, but soon left for experiments with other practitioners eager to resist the commercial and institutional circuits. As a director he promoted *collective creation, and his style stresses physicality in performance (foregrounding *ritualistic features) and develops a spatial and affective complicity with the audience. Favouring a repertoire (both classical and contemporary) where *political awareness mingles with poetry (*Sophocles, Richard Demarcy, António Ferreira, Natália Correia), he has also had memorable success with satirical *cabaret on Saturday nights, staged in the bar of his theatre.

MHS

MOTLEY

English design firm, comprised of **Audrey** ('Sophie') **Harris** (1901–66), **Margaret** ('Percy') **Harris** (1904–2000), and **Elizabeth Montgomery** (1902–93). Formed at the behest of John *Gielgud, Motley got their start in 1932 at Oxford designing *scenery and *costumes for *Romeo and Juliet* under his direction. In 1933 their first big *London success, *Richard of Bor-

deaux by Gordon Daviot, starring Gielgud in the title role, pioneered the use of simple scenery and costumes from ordinary materials, such as felt treated with kitchen soap and paint in place of leather. The standards of simplicity and adherence to the script became emblems of Motley's work in future decades. After collaborating with Gielgud on some sixteen productions throughout the remainder of the 1930s, including his revival of *Romeo and Juliet* (London, 1935), the threesome created designs for many important classical and commercial productions, *musicals, *operas, and *ballets, in the West End, on Broadway, and in Hollywood. Elizabeth Montgomery created most of their work in the United States, beginning with the 1941 *Romeo and Juliet* of Laurence *Olivier and Vivien *Leigh, which she worked on with Sophie Harris. Among the musicals Motley designed were *South Pacific* (1949) and *Can-Can* (1953) in *New York, and the *film version of *Oklahoma!* (1955).

In 1966 Percy Harris founded the Motley Theatre Design course at *Sadler's Wells. The school later moved to Islington at the *Almeida Theatre, and its students have carried Motley design principles throughout the world. The firm was largely responsible for the establishment of ascetic visual style of the *Royal Court Theatre and the early *National Theatre. Among early productions by Motley at the Royal Court were a charming *The Country Wife* (1956) and a chilling *Requiem for a Nun* (1957). With George *Devine, who married Sophie Harris, Percy Harris worked to establish a permanent stage surround at the Royal Court. For the National's first season (1963–4) Motley designed Noël *Coward's *Hay Fever*. In 1997 Percy Harris received a special Olivier *award for lifetime achievement in the theatre.

TK

MOULIN-ROUGE, BAL DU

Originally called Bal de la Reine-Blanche, this café and *music hall was established in Montmartre in 1889 by Charles Zidler and Joseph Oller in an effort to offer the controversial 'quadrille naturaliste', the *dance of the cancan, to more respectable *audiences. A huge theatrical windmill dominated the entrance, providing the name by which this *café-concert* became legendary. Dancers like La Goulue, Nini Pattes-en-l'air, and Môme Fromage impressed the patrons with suggestive moves such as the 'porte-d'armes' and the 'grand écart'. The building burned in 1915, then reopened with a repertoire of cancans and dinner *revues. Some of the most famous international entertainers of the music-hall era have graced the stage, including *Mistinguett, Joséphine *Baker, Max Dearly, and Maurice *Chevalier. After 1929 the space was converted to a cinema. It reopened as a live entertainment venue in 1953, and continues today to offer upscale *burlesques and lavish *cabaret shows to visitors to *Paris.

CHB

MOUNET-SULLY (JEAN MOUNET) (1841–1916)

French actor. Though originally trained for the Protestant ministry, Mounet enrolled at the *Conservatoire, graduated in 1868, and worked for a minor *Paris theatre where his vocal accomplishments attracted the notice of the director of the *Odéon. At the end of the Franco-Prussian War, having adopted Mounet-Sully as his professional name, he was accepted into the company of the *Comédie-Française by Émile Perrin, the newly appointed administrator. Making his debut in *Racine's *Andromaque*, he was highly praised for his convincingly 'oriental' Orestes; as *Sarcey was later to record, this was 'a wholly new way of understanding the role and interpreting the *character'. He became a *sociétaire* in 1875, and from the early 1870s to the beginning of the twentieth century was the outstanding interpreter of the tragic repertoire at the Comédie-Française, particularly in partnership with Sarah *Bernhardt up to her stormy departure from the company in 1880. Their success in a revival of *Hugo's *Hernani* in 1878 was especially notable, as was Mounet-Sully's Hamlet; though his Oedipus (in an adaptation of *Sophocles' play) received some criticism for its 'excessive' violence. His younger brother Paul Mounet made his debut at the Comédie-Française in the title role in *Corneille's *Horace*.

WDH

MOU SEN (MOU SĒN) (1963–)

Chinese director. With no formal *training in theatre, Mou nevertheless managed to establish himself as a freelance director in Beijing with his 1987 production of *Ionesco's *Rhinoceros*. Since then he has been able to attract sponsorships—foreign and local—for his productions. They include translated plays such as Ramuz's *Histoire du soldat* (1988) and *O'Neill's *The Great God Brown* (1989), as well as controversial successes such as 'The Other Side' and a Discussion about Grammar in 'The Other Side' (1993), *Something to Do with AIDS* (1994), and *Yellow Flowers* (1995). In 1995, he took *File Zero*—an *avant-garde rendition of a long poem by his contemporary Yu Jian—on a highly successful international *tour, and he became a symbol of the *alternative theatre in *China. He concentrated on the making of documentary *films when his self-financed production of *Confession* (1997) was a *box-office disaster, but he has vowed to return to the stage sometime in the future.

MPYC

MOWATT, ANNA CORA (1819–70)

American playwright and actress. Mowatt was born Anna Ogden, daughter of an American merchant living temporarily in Bordeaux. She enjoyed family theatricals as a child and read Shakespeare extensively, but seemed destined for a conventional middle-class life when at 15 she married James Mowatt, an attorney. Her husband's subsequent debilitating illness led to her writing career. In 1845 she wrote *Fashion*, a spritely five-act *satire of American high society's pretension that has remained popular since its première. Needing more money than playwriting could provide, Mowatt became an actress, making her debut as Pauline in *Bulwer-Lytton's *The Lady of Lyons* in 1845. Although not professionally trained, Mowatt was attractive, had a good voice, possessed a ready intelligence, and abandoned herself to the emotions of her roles. It was a combination that engrossed *audiences, and she was highly successful until she abandoned the stage to marry William Ritchie in 1854. Her *Autobiography of an Actress* (1854) remains an invaluable source of information about American theatre in the 1840s and 1850s.

GAR

MOZART, WOLFGANG AMADEUS (1756–91)

Austrian composer. One of the most versatile composers in history, Mozart especially prized *opera. As a youth he showed himself adept in the conventional *genres of the day, *Idomeneo* (*Residenztheater, *Munich, 1781) being the most accessible of all *opera seria*. Mozart's greatness is revealed in the operas he wrote to librettos by Lorenzo *da Ponte. *The Marriage of Figaro* (*Burgtheater, *Vienna, 1786), still the most revived of all comic operas, has a vitality, pathos, and humanity that intensifies the revolutionary message of *Beaumarchais's original play. Mozart's masterpiece *Don Giovanni* (Tyl Theatre, *Prague, 1787) is perhaps the only successful *tragicomedy in the operatic repertoire; here music is used throughout to create an ironic perspective on *action and *character. *Così fan tutte* (Burgtheater, 1790) is a searching, ultimately painful *comedy on the instability of sexual desire. His two operas in the style of the *Singspiel, *The Abduction from the Seraglio* (Burgtheater, 1782) and the well-loved *The Magic Flute* (Theater auf der Wieden, Vienna, 1791), demonstrated his capacity to write in the popular styles of his time. Although Mozart's operas are divided into separate musical numbers linked by *recitative, the extended finales to the acts of his mature work did much to develop music as a continuous dramatic language.

SJCW

MROŻEK, SŁAWOMIR (1932–)

Polish playwright, cartoonist, and humorist. From 1963 he lived in the West before returning to Poland in the 1990s. In satirical *cabaret sketches—*Out at Sea* (1960), *Striptease*, and *Charlie* (both 1961)—Mrożek developed a parable form of drama using model situations to explore the operations of power. *Tango* (1964), in the guise of a family drama, charts the descent of liberal Europe into totalitarianism; its *absurd humour, *grotesque *characterization, and *slapstick precision made it the

most widely performed Polish play of the decade. Moving beyond the closed circle of political repression, *Vatzlav* (1970) and *Émigrés* (1974) examine the paradoxes of freedom and ironies of exile. *On Foot* (1981) offers a panorama of dislocated lives during the Second World War, including an apocalyptic artist patterned after *Witkiewicz; *Portrait* (1988) settles accounts with Stalin's poisoned heritage; *Widows* (1990) reinstates parable as an existential dance of death; and *Love in the Crimea* (1993) traces the collapse of Russia through a pastiche of *Chekhovian themes. Jerzy Jarocki's 1998 production *A History of People's Poland According to Mrożek*, based on a *montage of the author's plays, reaffirmed Mrożek's pre-eminence as chronicler of life in communist Poland and master *parodist of theatrical *genres and styles.

DG

MTONGA, MAPOPA (c.1945–)

Zambian choreographer, actor, and musician. As a youth Mtonga was initiated into the Chewa *Nyau* cult, where he learned drumming and dance techniques of the *Gule wa Mkulu* masquerade. He exploited these skills later in academic studies of the form and promotion of Zambian performance. From the late 1960s he choreographed important Zambian theatre productions and promoted African *dance worldwide. As head of the Arts Centre at the University of Zambia he helped revive *Chikwakwa Theatre in the 1990s by encouraging the integration of indigenous performance *genres with theatre for *development. He was also a prime mover in the formation of Zambian Popular Theatre Alliance (1992).

DaK

MTSHALI, THULANI (c.1963–2002)

South African writer, director, and *producer. Born in Kwa-Zulu Natal, he grew up in Soweto. He wrote or co-wrote nine plays, which include *Memories* (1981), *Prisons* (1985), *Burning Ambers* (*Edinburgh Festival, 1986), *Top Down* (1987), *Target* and *Devil's Den* (both 1994), *Golden Gloves* (*Grahamstown Festival's best of the fringe *award, 1993), *Sekoto* (1995), and *WEEMEN* (1996). From 1984 to 1986 Mtshali *trained at the Centre for Research and Training in African Theatre in *Johannesburg, acquiring skill in *improvisation, scriptwriting, poetry, movement, and research. In 1987 he co-founded Bachaki (Visitors) Theatre, through which he produced all his plays. It also creates *community theatre, involving *collective playmaking and praise poetry, a traditional southern African performance form of oral poetry, charged with emotion and a strong rhythm.

YH

MTWA, CREDO (c.1925–)

Zulu traditional healer and storyteller. Born in southern Natal, as a child he lived with his grandfather, a high priest, and later with his Catholic father, moving to Potchefstroom in 1928. He worked in the mines in *Johannesburg until 1958, when he returned to Zululand to train as a traditional healer. He is best known for *uNosilimela* (a girl's name, representing the children of Africa, 1973), a play which appealed to black South Africans to turn to the religion and civilization of their forefathers as they searched for self-knowledge and truth in the confusion of a colonial world. His essay 'Imlinganiso—The Living Tradition' supports the appeal to an authentic pre-colonial Africa. *Africa Is my Witness* and *Indaba, my Children* (traditional tales, 1985) illustrate his involvement in preserving oral history, tribal legends, customs, and religious beliefs.   YH

MTWA, PERCY (1954–)

South African actor and playwright, born on the Witwatersrand. As a member of one of Gibson *Kente's *touring companies he met Mbongeni *Ngema and together they formed the Earth Players and conceived *Woza Albert!* With the help of Barney *Simon the work was finalized for performance at the *Market Theatre in *Johannesburg (1981). The play's theme of the Second Coming of Christ to apartheid South Africa signals the emerging Black Theology movement. Mtwa also created *Bopha!* (Market, 1985), about the need for resistance to an oppressive South African government.   YH

MUA ROI NUOC

A unique form of water *puppetry (literally 'puppets dancing on water') originating in the Red River Delta of *Vietnam, records of which go back to 1121. It is traditionally performed by all-male guilds or *phuong* who, while deriving no income from the art, pursue it as a source of community pride and satisfaction, keeping their manipulation techniques strictly secret from outsiders and other *phuong*. In 1992 about 26 *phuong* were said to exist, of which eight were currently performing. *Mua roi nuoc* is traditionally performed in a village pond at festival time. A bamboo scene-house is erected in the centre of the pond, within which the puppeteers stand chest-deep in water and manipulate the puppets by means of controls hidden beneath the pond's surface. The *audience sits on the pond bank. The puppets are either mounted on long rods (*may sao*) or on wires stretched between posts hammered into the pond bed (*may day*). All puppet heads and most bodies are carved from wood and may be hollow to contain apparatus to move them. The appearance of the puppets reflects the iconography of traditional wooden statuary and most are about 30 to 50 cm (12–20 inches) tall. Performances centre on a series of *tich* or vignettes which are sometimes combined to form extended narrative or thematic sequences called *tich tro*. Subjects are distilled from aspects of Vietnamese rural life, mythology, legend, or history, usually connected with water. Such scenes have special resonance for their Vietnamese audiences since the Vietnamese word for 'nation' is the same as that for 'water', reflecting the country's deep affinity with its aquatic heritage. Over 200 different scenes have been recorded and an individual performance typically features about twenty scenes in a programme of some 40 minutes' duration.

Mua roi nuoc performances rely primarily on visual impact, percussive and some melodic accompaniment (produced by a variety of traditional *cheo* instruments), snatches of *verse and song, occasional pyrotechnics, and interaction with the audience. There is little spoken *dialogue. Performances are usually opened by *Chu Teu*, a comic *character with both adult and childlike traits, who engages the audience in repartee. Since 1957 state-supported professional puppeteers have taken an interest in water puppetry and by the late 1990s Vietnam had two professional city-based water puppetry troupes operating from specially built theatres and *touring abroad with tank-stages. Performing the traditional repertoire, these troupes differ from traditional *phuong* mainly in their internal organization, the regularity of their performances, their use of artificial *lighting, the presence of female puppeteers, and their cooperation with professional directors and musicians.   MJ

NGUYEN HUY HONG and TRAN TRUNG CHINH, *Vietnamese Traditional Water Puppetry* (Hanoi, 1992)

MUFWANKOLO

The oldest and, between 1974 and 1988, one of the most successful popular theatre groups in Lubumbashi in the Shaba province of ex-Belgian Congo. Founded by Citoyen Kyembe (stage name Mufwankolo), its performers were mostly *radio station (and therefore state) employees. In the context of their radio programme *The Zaire of Tomorrow* the troupe produced weekly, improvised, highly comic sketches on themes of urban life, domestic discord, or, allusively, politics. The sketches linked up into serials and thus created suspense for the following instalments. Performed in Shaba Swahili (the local lingua franca which guaranteed them a mass *audience), the sketches were notable for their overt moralizing (with an emphasis on respect for 'traditional' values), verbal dexterity, and (as is to be expected of actors who are state employees and yet suspicious of all authority) double meanings. They consist of two basic *characters—Mufwankolo ('English key') and his wife Bibikawa—whose domestic quarrels punctuated with moments of reconciliation, or whose misunderstandings with neighbours, all against a background of political upheavals, constitute the core of the *action.   PNN trans. JCM

MUGO, MICERE GITHAE (1942–)

Kenyan director and playwright. She participated in the Makerere Free Travelling Theatre and joined *Ruganda's Nairobi *University Travelling Theatre. She co-published plays in

the Shona language with Shimmer Chinodya, and co-authored *The Trial of Dedan Kimathi* with Ngugi wa *Thiong'o (Nairobi, 1977). *Kimathi* deals with the betrayal of the Mau-Mau freedom fighter, but implies the betrayal of the ideals of independence by the new leaders. Mugo cooperated with Ngugi on his Kamirithu project, a people's theatre that led to his detention and the escape of both into exile in 1982.　　　　　　　　EB

MÜLLER, HEINER (1929–95)

German playwright and director. Müller's plays mix *Brechtian, *Artaudian, and postmodern techniques (*see* MODERNISM AND POSTMODERNISM), and a vast range of reference to European literature, in blood-drenched collages of the catastrophes of European Enlightenment in general and German history in particular. Yet as his characteristically grim aphorism—'I am an optimist: I believe in the Fourth World War'—suggests, he extracted a utopian dialectic from these images of humanity's interlocking drives to self-destruction and survival. In the 1950s and early 1960s, plays such as *Der Bau* (*Construction*, 1964) subverted the heroics of *socialist realism with critical images of the German Democratic Republic's troubled transition from ;capitalism to socialism. Their production, when permitted at all, brought Müller repeated difficulties, such as exclusion from the national writers' organization in 1961; and his less direct criticism of the state through adaptations of *Greek classics and Shakespeare in the 1960s and 1970s did not protect his *Macbeth* (1972) from accusations of pessimism and escapism.

From the 1970s on Müller radically intensified his representations of conflict, rejecting linear progress and the self-determining subject and exploding *character and the *unities. In *Germania Tod in Berlin* (*Germania Death in Berlin*, 1978), *Die Schlacht* (*The Battle*, 1975), or *Germania 3* (1995), brutal yet grotesquely comic images of betrayal, dismemberment, or cannibalism link the GDR with the disasters of German history. Parallel scenes stress fateful links: between Hitler and Stalin, or the communist worker and his fascist brother. Other plays such as *Verkommenes Ufer*, *Medeamaterial*, and *Landschaft mit Argonauten* (*Desolate Shore*, *Medea Material*, and *Landscape with Argonauts*, all 1983) link patriarchy and colonialism in a radical indictment of the European legacy. Both in form and content, *Hamletmachine* (1978) dismantles the Enlightenment individual, paralleling the artistic subject as moulder of his material and the machine as symbol of dominance over nature.

Heiner **Müller**'s *Quartet*, American Repertory Theatre, Cambridge, Massachusetts, 1988, directed and designed by Robert Wilson. The hanging scene, in which Wilson visualized Müller's reflections on sexuality, shows Jennifer Rohn as Young Woman and Bill Moor as Valmont (centre) and Wilson's long-time collaborator Lucinda Childs as the Marquise de Merteuil to the right.

Meanwhile, in the 'ruins of Europe' Ophelia's resistance to *gender determination generates revolutionary energy. (Because of *censorship difficulties, the production dates listed often differ substantially from the dates of composition.)

Müller's texts are often *monologic; the drama of interacting subjects, whether bourgeois or proletarian, cannot express his vision of history's horrors. Thus non-verbal images are central; Müller admired the performance work of Robert *Wilson (with whom he cooperated on a production of *Hamletmachine* in 1986) and the *dance-theatre of Pina *Bausch. For Müller, aesthetic value emerged only from conflict, between *text and production, or production and *audience. His plays challenge the production process through unrealizable *stage directions or blocks of unattributed *dialogue.

His *directing work also sought to provoke, not elucidate. He avoided psychological *realism, favouring *montage, clownish exaggeration, fluid intertextuality, and often grandiose visual symbolism (as in his production of *Wagner's *Tristan and Isolde* at *Bayreuth, 1993). His *Hamlet*, whose conception, *rehearsal, and première in 1990 accompanied the GDR's rapid disintegration, dismembered and reassembled both Shakespeare's play and Müller's own *Hamletmachine*. The result was an eight-hour necrology for the decayed and doomed East German state but also for Müller's own work as subversive art. With designer Erich Wonder, Müller staged a complex visual metaphor for the state's collapse: grey gauze, cold *lighting, and a vast block of ice became, by the time the golden-headed, business-suited Fortinbras arrived, a parched desert: a characteristic example of Müller's allusive, unresolved juxtapositions of political *allegory and epochal symbolism.

　　　　　　　　　　　　　　　　　　　MMcG

MULTIMEDIA PERFORMANCE

Strategy combining varied media including juxtapositions of theatre, *dance, *music, projections of *film, video, and slides, computer technologies, virtual environments, plastic arts, and popular entertainments in a single performance. The history of multimedia performance may be seen as running concurrently with the history of the Euro-American *avant-garde. *Wagner's notion of *Gesamtkunstwerk* is a prototype for the convergence of varied art forms in one performance: dance, *acting, art, *light, theatre, poetry, and music (*see* TOTAL THEATRE). The *symbolists explored synaesthesia by using aromas and abstract lighting to heighten the performance. The *futurists, *dadaists, and *surrealists in their *cabarets combined a variety of popular and high art forms into a single presentation. However, the work of German director Erwin *Piscator marks some of the first experiments in combining media technologies and live performance. His 'living backdrop' created through film projections in a live performance attempted to redefine theatrical space and time through the addition of mechanical reproductions.

*Happenings, developed during the 1950s and 1960s by painters and sculptors (*Kaprow, Paik, Rauschenberg, Warhol), applied a form of multimedia performance through the addition of plastic art production, film, video, and daily activity in live art.

New media *performance artists such as *New York's *Wooster Group, Québec's Robert *Lepage, and *Japan's company called dumbtype employ extensive use of video and new technologies in live performances, extending the stage to combine both live and pre-recorded performers. A technological and multimedia stage of analogue and digital recording apparatus creates a performative space unrestricted by the spatio-temporal configuration of 'here and now', toward a live performance which can include a technological space of 'not here and not now'. Once the province of experimental and avant-garde theatre and performance, multimedia is now a tool of art performance and a popular entertainment as well. Currently multimedia performance can be seen in the popular entertainments of theme parks, rock concerts, and the *spectacles of Las Vegas, utilized in art installations and interactive sculptures, and as a common element in both traditional and experimental theatre. *See also* MEDIA AND PERFORMANCE; CYBER THEATRE.

MDC

MUMBAI (BOMBAY)

Capital of Maharashtra state, and commercial and industrial capital of *India, its cosmopolitan name 'Bombay' was officially changed to Marathi Mumbai in 1995 by chauvinistic politicians. Speaking a variety of languages, immigrant labourers, traders, shipbuilders, textile mill owners, and administrators settled in Mumbai in waves during the nineteenth century. Its population now comprises *Marathi-speaking Maharashtrians, along with Hindus, Parsis, and Muslims who speak Gujarati, *Urdu-speaking Muslims, English-speaking Catholics from Goa, and *Hindi-speaking Punjabis, all of whom, with the addition of Sindhis, Uttar Pradeshis, and Biharis, make Mumbai a cultural microcosm of India.

All four major language theatres of Mumbai—Marathi, Gujarati, Urdu/Hindi, and English—began their activities in the mid-nineteenth century. Vishnudas Bhave staged the first Marathi professional play at the Grant Road Theatre in 1853. The Parsi Theatrical Company's *amateur productions of plays in Gujarati and Urdu were staged a few months later, *Parsi theatre evolving into a professional theatre of *spectacle, jaunty songs, and trick scenes. English theatre began and ended with university student productions of Shakespeare and current *comedies.

Theatre suffered in the 1930s and 1940s from the economic depression and the arrival of sound *film, but picked up in the mid-1950s when the cultural organization Bharatiya Vidya Bhavan started intercollegiate drama competitions. The Bhavan *auditorium became the hub of an *alternative theatre movement in Marathi challenging mainstream sentimental family dramas, and encouraging theatre practitioners like Vijay *Tendulkar, Vijaya Mehta, Shreeram Lagoo, Arvind and Sulabha Deshpande, and Amol Palekar. Gujarati alternative theatre produced directors and actors like Mahendra Joshi, Kanti Madia, and Pravin Joshi, but petered out soon after the 1970s. Hindi had no mainstream. However, director-teacher Satyadev Dubey used Marathi actors in his plays, bringing new talent into the Marathi alternative stream. Again it was through the Hindi adaptations and translations directed by him that the work of playwrights like Mohan *Rakesh, Badal *Sircar, and Girish *Karnad came to Marathi *audiences. The Chhabildas school hall in central Mumbai remained the centre for the alternative theatre movement from the mid-1970s to the mid-1980s.

English theatre was dominated in the 1950s by Ebrahim *Alkazi's well-designed productions for Theatre Group. After he left in the early 1960s to become the first director of Delhi's *National School of Drama, Pearl and Alyque Padamsee began to direct the Theatre Group plays. Mostly they staged successful West End and Broadway productions like *The Crucible, Children of a Lesser God, Jesus Christ Superstar,* and *Evita*. The director Adi *Marazban contributed uniquely to both English and Parsi-Gujarati theatre. In the 1980s Bharat Dabholkar launched a series of immensely popular *revues beginning with *Bottoms Up*. The language of these plays about metropolitan life in Mumbai was and continues to be a mix of Indianized English, Hindi, and Marathi, and their comedy a mix of *slapstick, caricature, and sexual innuendo. Equally popular are bedroom *farces directed by Dinyar Contractor and more serious plays like Rahul Da Cunha's *I'm Not Bajirao*.

Marathi mainstream theatre is performed in nine *playhouses, each with at least two shows a day. Devendra Pem's *All the Best* ran for over 1,500 performances in five years during the 1990s by deploying three teams of actors to play at the same time in different venues. Gujarati and English theatre is presented at weekends only. Gujarati plays cater to the business class, which demands comedy, suspense, or sensation; actors must look good and be expensively *costumed. Hindi plays are confined to the 200-seat Prithvi Theatre in north Mumbai, committed to serious work during the week and subsidized by commercial plays at weekends.

Theatre is not restricted to the four main languages. *Yakshagana* troupes from Karnataka visit Mumbai every year to perform for the city's Kannada-speaking residents. Troupes from Uttar Pradesh arrive before the Dussehra festival to stage the nine-day *Ram lila*, the story of Ram, for thousands of spectators on Chowpaty beach and in Shivaji Park. Goa's traditional *tiatr* entertains the Catholic community with boisterous comedy, social themes, and musical interludes. By supporting such diverse cultural traditions, Mumbai asserts its multicultural character in the face of ongoing sectarian tensions and communal violence.

SGG

MUMMERS' PLAY

English *folk play. Traditionally divided into Hero Combats, Sword Dances, and Wooing plays, mummers' plays have in common performance by *disguised local *amateurs during the winter months in Britain, concluding with the demand for donations or drink. The earliest surviving *texts date from the eighteenth century, but similar dramatic elements in *medieval *morality plays suggest a much longer heritage. The troupe has traditionally been composed only of men and boys who visit private homes and public houses during a holiday period and perform a traditional text using loud and relatively uninflected voices. Movement within the playing space is likewise formal and restricted. *Costuming varies from *realistic dress for the *character to adoption of 'ribbon costumes' for the troupe, with strips of bright cloth or paper in many colours worn over the performers' own clothing. Plays typically mix the comic with the serious and even threatening (the demand for entrance by *masked visitors, combat to the death). Repeated *plot elements include combats between St George and a Turkish Knight, the competition to woo a wife, and the resurrection of a slain combatant from the dead; the theme of triumph over death, sterility, and destruction led early twentieth-century scholars to regard the plays as survivals of ancient seasonal *rituals. Later, interest shifted away from questions of *origin and turned to the function of the plays as community-affirming *rituals. In the early years of the twenty-first century, scholarship has looked at more specific historical dynamics; for example, local lords' sponsorship of such performances as a form of resistance to the centralizing agenda of the monarchy.   JCD

MUMMING

In England, a processional visitation by silent, *masked figures to a private house, where dice might be played or a gift bestowed, followed by music and *dancing. Mumming appears to have been the prerogative of the middle classes and was especially popular in the early fifteenth century. Authorities banned the activity in 1418, but further bans in 1479 and 1511 suggest that it continued in spite of their efforts. Nevertheless, with the addition of an *allegorical *text this *bourgeois entertainment became *disguising, a form indistinguishable from the aristocratic *momeria* or *entremets of Europe. *See also* MUMMERS' PLAY.
RWV

MUNDAY, ANTHONY (1560–1633)

English playwright. Munday, who wrote ballads, pamphlets, and Lord Mayor's pageants and translated several French chivalric *romances, was author or co-author of over a dozen plays, most of them commissioned by Philip *Henslowe for the Lord *Admiral's Men. Between 1590 and 1601 he collaborated with such dramatists as Chettle, *Dekker, Drayton, and *Middleton, as well as with Shakespeare and others, in writing *Sir Thomas More* (unpublished in its time but probably written c.1593). In 1598 Francis Meres described him as one of 'the best for comedy' and 'our best plotter'. The artisan acting troupe in his *John a Kent and John a Cumber* (unpublished but probably acted c.1594) invites comparison with Shakespeare's 'rude mechanicals' in *A Midsummer Night's Dream*. Munday also wrote two Robin Hood plays, *The Downfall of Robert Earl of Huntingdon* and *The Death of Robert Earl of Huntingdon* (both 1601).
MS

MUNDEN, JOSEPH (1758–1832)

English actor, singer, and *manager. He began acting in *London in 1779, but was not regularly engaged until he was hired by *Covent Garden in 1790. Despite serious disagreements with the managers, he remained at that theatre until 1811, usually acting at the *Haymarket or in the provinces during the summer. Although criticized for his buffoonery and grimace, he was famous for his expressive face and his skill at playing old men. Of his more than 200 roles, he was best as Old Dornton in *Holcroft's *The Road to Ruin* and Polonius, a part that *Byron said would die with Munden.
MJK

MUNFORD, ROBERT III (c.1737–c.1783)

American politician and playwright. Born into colonial Virginia's planter class, Munford studied classics in England and law in Virginia before becoming a gentleman planter. Between 1765 and 1780 he served twelve years in Virginia's House of Burgesses and House of Delegates. He early acknowledged colonial grievances against Parliament, but was suspicious of broad democracy. His first play, *The Candidates*, written after 1770, satirizes electioneering in rural Virginia, casting a sceptical eye on democracy's practices. *The Patriots* (composed 1777–9) anatomizes ethnic partisanship masquerading as patriotism. Neither play was produced in Munford's lifetime.   GAR

MUNI, PAUL (1896–1967)

American actor, born Muni Weisenfreund in Ukraine, to a family of itinerant actors who emigrated to the United States in 1901. Muni acted over 300 roles in *Yiddish theatres, specializing in old men. His English-language debut (*We Americans*, 1926) was as an old man; he first played a young role in *Four Walls* (1927). He moved to *films in the 1930s, starring in a series of major biographical films (*The Story of Louis Pasteur*, 1935—for which he received an Academy award—*The Life of Émile Zola*, 1937; *Juarez*, 1939), along with such successes as *Scarface* (1932), *The Good Earth* (1937), and his final film, *The Last Angry Man* (1958). He regularly appeared on Broadway

The vigour of theatre in **Munich** revealed in Shakespeare's *King Lear* at the Kammerspiele, 1992, directed by Dieter Dorn, designed by Jürgen Rose. The blinded Gloucester (Thomas Holtzmann) stands in a crucified pose above his son Edgar (Stefan Hunstein).

(*Counsellor-at-Law*, 1931, revived 1942; *Key Largo*, 1939; *Inherit the Wind*, 1955—winning a Tony *award). Muni was celebrated for his thorough and careful preparation, and his ability to vanish within the *character. Although remembered primarily as a serious actor, he also performed *comedy and appeared in *musicals, both in Yiddish and in English. He married Bella Finkel, of the famed *Tomashefsky theatrical *family, in 1921.

AW

MUNICH

Until well into the nineteenth century, theatre life in Munich was dominated by the Wittelsbach court, the ruling family of Bavaria since 1180. Theatrical activity in the *medieval period is poorly documented, although it can be assumed that the churches would have contributed the usual Christmas and Easter performances. The Munich court had close ties with Italy and there was considerable traffic between the two coun-

tries throughout the *early modern period. Well documented is the 1568 wedding of the Bavarian Crown Prince Wilhelm with Renata of Lorraine, which included one of the earliest reports of a *commedia dell'arte* performance north of the Alps.

In 1559 the *Jesuits established a theatre attached to their college in Munich which grew to become one of the major centres of the Counter-*Reformation in Germany. The theatre itself also had the function of a court theatre, as it was supported by the staunchly Catholic Wittelsbach court who provided their architects, musicians, and *painters for performances. The Jesuits in Munich specialized in spectacular *open-air productions involving hundreds of extras. The inauguration of Michaeliskirche in 1597 included the play *Triumph of St Michael*, a mass *spectacle, which climaxed with the dramatic 'fall' of 300 angels. Between 1590 and 1620 there were occasional visits by itinerant Italian and English troupes (*English Comedians) but their activities were curtailed by the outbreak of the Thirty Years War in 1618. Activity resumed with a vengeance in 1651 with the new Elector Ferdinand Maria, who made the Munich court a centre of European theatrical culture. The first *opera house in Germany was built in 1654 by Francesco Santurini, a pupil of *Torelli. Dramatic theatre was also supported. The most significant events in the late seventeenth and early eighteenth centuries were the court festivals such as *Applausus festivi* (1662), staged to commemorate birthdays and dynastic marriages. The Munich festivals were particularly elaborate and involved opera, *fireworks 'dramas', and dramatized *tournaments.

Theatre flourished throughout the eighteenth century with a succession of electors fostering both dramatic and musical theatre. Performances took place in the Residenz, the opera house, and at Nymphenburg Castle in a garden theatre. In 1745 Max III Josef constructed a Komödientheater within the Residenz for the French troupe. After it burnt down, it was replaced by the *Residenztheater, a rococo building which opened in 1751.

In the second half of the century German drama gained in importance. A Nationalschaubühne was instituted by the court in 1778; in 1795 the Residenztheater was renamed 'Court and National Theatre' and opened to the public. Throughout the eighteenth century the itinerant troupes also performed in the town hall and public houses. Towards the end of the eighteenth century a few smaller theatres sprang up on the outskirts of the old city but their number was strictly controlled. A major change came in 1806 when Napoleon declared Bavaria a kingdom, and a theatre commensurate with the new status was promptly built. The new Royal Court and National Theatre, which opened in 1818, was a monumental *neoclassical construction, seating 2,600 spectators in a city numbering only 55,000 inhabitants. Its style suited the architectural refashioning of the city under King Ludwig I (1825–48), who constructed mock Florentine and Classical Greek buildings. Its size, however, did not always match its artistic status. Its first real flowering came with the directorship of Franz von *Dingelstedt between 1851 and 1857, who revived the classics. His productions of *Greek *tragedies, *Antigone* (1851) and *Oedipus the King* (1852), were among the first in Germany.

Like most German cities Munich experienced an unprecedented period of modernization and economic expansion in the wake of unification after 1870. Between 1870 and 1914 the population quadrupled. Until 1873 Munich had only five theatres; by 1900 there were over 40. The largest expansion was in the private sector with the establishment of many popular *variety theatres, but also several highbrow dramatic societies. The most notable was the Academisch-Dramatischer Verein, founded in 1891 to promote *naturalist theatre. Influenced by the *Freie Bühne in *Berlin, it staged plays by *Hauptmann and *Ibsen which otherwise would have fallen foul of the *censor. The variety theatres (*Volkssängerbühnen*), located mainly in working-class districts, became an important feature of Munich's theatrical life and brought forth Karl *Valentin, who crossed the line between popular and *avant-garde performance. Munich also became a centre of the new *cabaret movement. The most important was the Eleven Executioners (1901–3) featuring Frank *Wedekind. By 1900 Munich had become a renowned artistic centre, with its bohemian suburb Schwabing hosting numerous theatres, art galleries, dramatists, and directors. The anti-naturalistic theatre reform movement in Germany had its centre here under the tutelage of the journalist Georg *Fuchs. His activities led to the building of the *Munich Art Theatre which was opened in 1908, the first theatre in Germany built on art nouveau principles.

The dominance of the court theatre was challenged with the establishment of the Munich Kammerspiele in 1911. Under the directorship of Otto *Falckenberg from 1917 to 1944 it became Munich's municipal theatre and a venue of national importance. After 1918 the court theatres (Residenztheater, Nationaltheater, and Prinzregentheater) came under state control. The abolition of censorship led to a more progressive repertoire here as well, but Munich lost its once predominant position to Berlin. Between 1933 and 1945 the theatres came under direct influence of the Nazis. Many artists went into exile, while those who stayed (such as Falckenberg) tried to steer an apolitical course in the face of massive interference. Since most of the major theatres were destroyed by the end of the Second World War, the late 1940s saw major improvisation and rebuilding. The Kammerspiele survived relatively unscathed and resumed operation in 1945. It hosted *Brecht before he took over the *Berliner Ensemble and established itself as the major dramatic theatre in the 1950s. The late 1960s saw the emergence of an active free theatre scene, although many of the artists such as R. W. *Fassbinder were quickly absorbed by the subsidized theatres. Today the free theatres, which number about 30, receive a modest subsidy from the city (*see* FINANCE). Munich theatrical life is still overwhelmingly dominated by the state and municipal theatres, which include two opera houses (Nationaltheater and Gärtnerplatz) and three dramatic theatres (Residenztheater, Kammerspiele, and the Volkstheater).

Under the directorship of Dieter *Dorn and a team including the designer Jürgen Rose, the Kammerspiele enjoyed a period of artistic continuity from the mid-1970s until 2001 unique in German theatre. It became home to the finest *acting ensemble in the country, its Shakespeare productions were major events, and it fostered contemporary Bavarian dramatists such as Franz Xaver *Kroetz and Herbert Achternbusch. The Bavarian State Theatre in the Residenztheater has had a more chequered history. A succession of *artistic directors, occasional political interference, and an unwieldy infrastructure have all contributed to its problems. In 2001 Dorn assumed directorship of the theatre, after Frank Baumbauer (previously in Hamburg) was appointed director of the Kammerspiele, so the history of rivalry between the two houses is set to continue.   CBB

Jelavich, Peter, *Munich and Theatrical Modernism: politics, playwriting and performance* (Cambridge, Mass., 1985)

Schläder, Jürgen, and Körner, Hans-Michael (eds.), *Münchner Theatergeschichtliches Symposium* (Munich, 2000)

MUNICH ART THEATRE

Designed by Max Littmann and opened in 1908, the Munich Art Theatre was the first *playhouse constructed according to art nouveau aesthetic. The main initiator was the journalist and dramatist Georg *Fuchs, who in 1907 founded a society in *Munich, the Verein Münchner Künstler-Theater, with the expressed aim of building a theatre according to 'artistic principles'. The theatre was built with a shallow *stage, apron (*see* FORESTAGE), and no orchestra pit. Seats were arranged in an *amphitheatre form. The most innovative feature was the 'relief stage' where the performer acted before a stylized backdrop. Although the first productions coordinated by Fuchs were not particularly successful, the building and the relief stage attracted a good deal of attention. In 1909 it was leased to Max *Reinhardt and finally closed in 1914. The building was destroyed during Second World War bombing.   CBB

MUNICIPAL GENERAL SAN MARTÍN, TEATRO

*Buenos Aires inaugurated the General San Martín Municipal Theatre in 1960. Located on Corrientes Street, in the heart of the theatre district, Argentina's largest theatre complex houses three theatres (seating 1,000, 500, and 200), a cinema, and several art galleries. During the 1960s the San Martín's seasons favoured canonical Western and Argentinian plays but by the early 1970s had expanded to include music and modern *dance. During the 1976–83 military dictatorship, offerings were severely modified and works by 'questionable' national playwrights excluded, even as a permanent acting company, a contemporary *ballet, and a *puppet group were created. The theatre's productions frequently represent Argentina at international *festivals, and it hosts many foreign companies. It coproduces in other theatres and cultural centres in the city, publishes play *texts and *Teatro* magazine, and organizes national and international *tours.   JGJ

MUNK, KAJ (1892–1944)

Danish playwright, one of the most controversial figures in modern Scandinavian drama. After his ordination as a priest in 1924, Munk pursued his other burning ambition to become a dramatist. His *miracle play *The Word*, written in 1925, was eventually performed in 1932. Copenhagen's *Kongelige Teater accepted his next play, *An Idealist*, for performance in 1928. Written in pastiche Shakespearian style, it shows King Herod defying all his foes, even God, and was violently attacked by the *critics. Following this shaky start, Munk went on to write a series of plays that echoed his fascination with superhuman figures, including King Henry VIII in *Cant* (1931) and King David in *The Chosen Ones* (1933). Munk's admiration for strong leaders even led him to write a Nazi adaptation of *Hamlet* in 1935, in which Fortinbras, dressed as a Danish Nazi, comes to liberate Denmark from democracy. As war threatened, Munk lost faith in the strong dictator figures of the age, reflected in *He Sits by the Melting Pot* (1938), and during the Nazi occupation of Denmark spoke out strongly against the Germans and their collaborators. He was murdered by Gestapo thugs.   DT

MUÑOZ, EUNICE (1928–   )

Portuguese actress. Born into a family of *variety artists, she began performing at the age of 4 and made her professional debut at the Teatro *Nacional D. Maria II, *Lisbon, when she was 13. She has worked with several companies and some of the most important Portuguese directors (António *Pedro, João *Lourenço, João *Mota, Ricardo *Pais), in a diversity of productions and styles, proving equally creative in *comedy, drama, *tragedy, and more popular forms, including *film. Over the years she has developed a technique that combines heightened intuition with a rare attention to detail and characterization. Amongst her most memorable roles are Maria in *Garrett's *Frei Luís de Souza* (1943), *Anouilh's Joan of Arc (*The Lark*, 1955), Shakespeare's Viola (1957), *Racine's *Phèdre* (1967), Claire in *Genet's *The Maids* (1972), *García Lorca's Bernarda Alba (1983), and *Brecht's Mother Courage (1986), widely considered her most accomplished performance. Her greatest triumph has been her ability to maintain a powerful relationship with successive generations of *audiences.   PEC

MURDOCH, FRANK H. (1843–72)

American actor and playwright. Best known for the romantic *melodrama *Davy Crockett* (1872), which he wrote as a vehicle for Frank *Mayo, Murdoch (born Hitchcock) was the nephew of actor James E. Murdoch, whose name he borrowed for the stage. He spent his entire career as a member of Louisa *Drew's company at the *Arch Street Theatre, *Philadelphia. He also wrote *Light House Cliff* (produced in California *c.*1870), thought to be the inspiration for James A. *Herne's *Shore Acres*, as well as *The Lottery of Art* (1872), a literary *satire, and *Only a Jew* (1873), a sentimental *comedy.   PAD

MURPHY, ARTHUR (1727–1805)

The Irish Murphy had a brief career as an actor and a long one as an essayist, playwright, and lawyer. He was introduced to the stage by Samuel *Foote and played Othello in 1754 at *Covent

Garden. Over the next two years he performed there and at *Drury Lane, acting competently in some major roles, such as Jaffeir in *Otway's *Venice Preserv'd* and Young Bevil in *Steele's *The Conscious Lovers*. But his theatrical *criticism in the *Gray's Inn Journal*, his biographies of *Fielding and *Garrick, and his plays constitute Murphy's important contributions. Of his plays, *The Grecian Daughter* (1772) and *Know your Own Mind* (1777) are among the best.   MJK

MURPHY, TOM (1935–)

Irish playwright. Coming from the Galway town of Tuam, having trained as a metalwork teacher, Murphy made his name with his first full-length play *A Whistle in the Dark* in 1961, produced in *London by the *Theatre Workshop. The uninhibited violence of this representation of an Irish emigrant family living in Coventry aroused some controversy, but the power of its theatrical energies was critically recognized and it went on to a successful West End run. The *naturalism of this early play, however, was to be replaced by more experimental styles in *Famine* (1968), an *expressionist rendering of the Irish potato famine, the fable-like *Morning after Optimism* (1971), and *The Sanctuary Lamp* (1975), which brought protests over its outspoken anticlericalism. Three plays of the 1980s represent the finest examples of Murphy's innovative *dramaturgy. *The Gigli Concert* (1983) counterpoints its three-actor drama with operatic arias; *Bailegangaire* (1985), which gave a last starring role to Siobhán *McKenna, makes imaginative theatrical use of traditional Irish storytelling; *Conversations on a Homecoming* (1985) brilliantly choreographs an uninterrupted night's drinking in a country pub. Murphy's preferred themes, the nullities of small-town life and the rootlessness of the emigrant, reappear in more recent plays, *The Wake* (1998) and *The House* (2000).
                                                                          NG

MURRAY, GILBERT (1866–1957)

Australian classicist, dramatist, and translator. Murray's play *Carlyon Sahib* (1889) had been championed by William *Archer before *London production by Mrs Patrick *Campbell, but it was his vivid translations, which used rhyme and decorative language to approximate the effect of the *verse of *Greek *tragedy, that most affected British theatre. Granville *Barker staged three of Murray's works at the *Royal Court (*Hippolytus*, 1904; *The Trojan Women*, 1905; *Electra*, 1906), using *modernist stage effects, and *Reinhardt used Murray's *Oedipus Rex* at *Covent Garden (1912). Barker toured America with *The Trojan Women* and *Iphigenia in Tauris* (1915; Lillah *McCarthy as Hecuba). Particularly influential to America's *Little Theatre and university theatre movements, Murray was *Shaw's model for Cusins in *Major Barbara*. Associated with the Cambridge School of Anthropo-

logists (*see* ORIGINS OF THEATRE), Murray's passion for civilization led to work with the League of Nations.   GAO

MURRAY, T. C. (THOMAS CORNELIUS) (1873–1959)

Irish schoolmaster who turned to playwriting as a hobby. Associating in Cork with Lennox *Robinson, who staged Murray's *comedy *The Wheel of Fortune* there (1909), doubtless helped Murray get a hearing at the *Abbey. *Birthright* (1910), *Maurice Harte* (1912), *Sovereign Love* (a revision of his comedy, 1913), *Spring* (1918), *The Serf* (1920), *Aftermath* (1922), *Autumn Fire* (1924), *The Pipe in the Fields* (1927), *The Blind Wolf* (1928), *Michaelmas Eve* (1932), all Abbey plays, many directed by Robinson, are remarkable for their patient *realism, which avoids any sensationalism in depicting rural lives knowing only desperation, penury, lovelessness, and greed. His best plays intimate situations resonant with mythical or biblical parallels, which bring tragic dignity to the *characters, while the minutiae of observed life which filter through the *dialogue endow them with a credible verisimilitude. When after 1930 Murray endeavoured to write of urban, middle-class life (*A Flutter of Wings*, *A Spot in the Sun*, *Illumination*) the results were disappointingly thin by comparison.   RAC

MURRELL, JOHN (1945–)

Canadian playwright. Born in the USA, Murrell settled in Calgary and left teaching to work as an actor, writer, and director. *Waiting for the Parade* (1977) intertwines the lives of women on the home front during the Second World War; its use of *music and space have made it popular in Canada and abroad. In *Memoir* (1978), Sarah *Bernhardt demands that her secretary replay scenes from her life. Siobhán *McKenna performed Bernhardt in the première at the Guelph Spring Festival, a French version had a lengthy run in *Paris (with Delphine Seyrig), and the work has been translated into 35 languages and performed in fifteen countries. Robin *Phillips directed *Farther West* (1982), *New World* (1984), and *Democracy* (1991). Other plays include *October* (1988) and translations of *Chekhov, *Ibsen, *Machiavelli, and *Racine. Murrell became *artistic director of theatre at the Banff Centre for the Arts in 1999.   FL

MUSCO, ANGELO (1871–1937)

Italian actor, a leading figure of Sicilian dialect theatre. *Pirandello wrote his first plays, in dialect, specifically for him. From the popular performance tradition, Musco took improvisational liberties with *text, which infuriated Pirandello who eventually cut his ties. Musco went on to achieve recognition in Italy and abroad.   ATS

MUSEUMS OF THEATRE

*Thespis introduced the *actor to the stage in the sixth century BC. Henry *Irving attained knighthood in 1895. In the centuries between, most societies censured or disdained those who trod the boards, and historians often frowned upon the theatre as unworthy of scholarly attention. The records of performances, past and present, were either ignored or neglected. Only the *drama and the literature of the stage (commentary, *criticism, and history) were considered to be of substantial interest. In the first quarter of the twentieth century, however, the aesthetic *theories of the *avant-garde brought a fresh consciousness to both Europe and America. It was then that collections of theatrical ephemera (*playbills and programmes, photographs and engravings, clippings, and designs), along with promptbooks, play scripts, stage memorabilia, *scenery, and stage machinery, took on new and exciting dimensions. The works of *Appia, *Craig, *Antoine, *Copeau, *Stanislavsky, and Robert Edmond *Jones lit up not only marquees throughout the world, but also exhibition cases in libraries, museums, and theatres.

Nevertheless, some theatre treasures had been preserved in Europe in many places and forms. The *Drottningholm Theatre near *Stockholm had its heyday during the reign of Gustav III (1772–92) when the Frenchman Louis-Jean Desprez was commissioned to design its *costumes and scenery. Now those renditions form one of the most important deposits in the Drottningholm Theatre Museum. The German actress and dramatist Clara Ziegler bequeathed her house and library to *Munich as a theatre museum, together with a legacy for the maintenance of a theatre collection. The Raymond Mander and Joe Mitchenson Theatre Collection in *London is one of the most notable private collections in the English-speaking world. Theatres themselves began to recognize the significance of their archives: La *Scala in *Milan, the *Opéra and *Comédie-Française in *Paris, the *Finnish National Theatre in *Helsinki, and the *Shubert Organization in *New York began to collect, preserve, and make available for study their extensive and valuable material. Nearly every major theatre in Russia developed a museum and library with government support, initially as a part of the national cultural and political programme.

By 1960 an acceleration of techniques for organizing, preserving, and cataloguing collections was encouraged and promoted in a number of locations. That year, under the auspices of the Société Internationale des Bibliothèques et des Musées des Arts du Spectacle, the volume *Performing Arts Libraries and Museums of the World* was published. During the next 30 years three revised editions appeared. In 1996 a more inclusive volume covering 170 countries emerged as the *SIBMAS International Directory of Performing Arts Collections* with all information entered into a comprehensive database allowing for continued updating and revision.

*London's Theatre Museum is a treasure house of British theatre history ranging from ephemera to costumes, manuscripts, statuary, and *objets d'art*. The theatre department of the Metropolitan *Toronto Library maintains the leading performing arts collection in Canada with special emphasis on production, staging, architecture, and Canadian theatre history. The Library of Congress in Washington lays claim to the largest collection of American drama in the world, due primarily to the deposit since 1870 of hundreds of thousands of published and unpublished scripts for *copyright registration. The Harvard Theatre Collection encompasses all aspects of the history of performance throughout the world, with emphasis on the English and American stage and the history of *ballet and *dance. The Museum of the City of New York contains an array of memorabilia illustrating the dramatic and musical events in the metropolis from colonial times to the present. The inception of the Billy Rose Theatre Collection of the New York Public Library for the Performing Arts, located at *Lincoln Center, dates back to 1919 when David *Belasco offered his archive with the proviso that it was to be the beginning of an ongoing collection. The Hoblitzelle Theatre Arts Library at the University of Texas in Austin restricts its collection policy to the American stage and such related areas as *circus, *film, *magic shows, and pugilism. The holdings of the Wisconsin Center for Film and Theatre Research consist of items relating to practitioners, film and *television writers, producers and motion picture companies.

Because performing arts collections continue to grow to surprising proportions and at a rapid rate, and because technology has advanced the methods of cataloguing and access, the holdings of lesser-known institutions can now be widely known—such as the Brunei Museum, the Kuwait National Museum, and the Oman Museum.   LAR

MUSICAL PLAY

(Also called musical comedy, musical theatre, or musical.) A play in which *music, usually in the form of songs, is essential to the narrative. A musical typically relies on the alternation of *dialogue and song, as opposed to the continuous music, sung speech (*recitative), and arias of *opera. Although the term 'musical comedy' generally connotes light humorous and/or romantic material, contemporary musical plays are diverse in both subject matter and style. As in related forms, such as *revues, *music hall, *vaudeville, opera, and *operetta, there is frequent use of *dance and a *chorus of singers or dancers, as well as featured performers and spectacular *scenography. This entry focuses on the broadly popular commercial productions that began to diverge from European opera in the eighteenth century and flourished in Europe and the United States from the late nineteenth century to the present. In the twentieth century, the focus will be primarily on the United States, where musicals developed most of their contemporary features.

The modern musical began to separate itself from opera in the early eighteenth century with the development of *ballad opera. Essentially a *comedy with popular songs and melodies inserted throughout, the form emerged in 1728 with the success in *London of John *Gay's *The Beggar's Opera*. Featuring criminals, whores, and beggars as *characters, it was a robust *parody of the mythological subjects and settings of serious opera. Combining topical *satire with vigorous lampooning of Italian opera, ballad operas became so popular that Parliament acted to stop satirical plays in 1737 (*see* LICENSING ACTS; CENSORSHIP). Nonetheless, ballad operas had significant influence on comic opera, operetta, *burlesque, and musical theatre in general. In 1735 the ballad opera *Flora* became the first professional musical theatre performance in America.

Throughout the eighteenth and early nineteenth centuries, light opera and operetta were the main musical theatre offerings in Europe and America. But despite a debt to extant forms, musical plays also developed by combining and differently emphasizing the various elements of performance and production (dance, design, staging and *costuming) and blending the popular stage and musical traditions of Europe and the United States. Musicals are avid borrowers from different periods and forms, frequently crossing borders and stealing from *variety, music hall, *pantomime, and pastiche, as well as from opera and its descendants.

In the mid-nineteenth century these multiple strains came together and developed unique native forms in the United States. Slavery, its aftermath, and the tremendous influx of immigration in the country from the late nineteenth to the early twentieth centuries produced the *minstrel show, vaudeville, and a distinctive form of American popular song. The minstrel show was an American blackface variety form that flourished from the 1840s through the 1870s with a combination of fast-paced comedy, song, dance, and crude *racial caricatures. Troupes were usually white men mocking *African-American speech and behaviour, although there were black minstrel troupes as well. As the first indigenous American popular musical entertainment, minstrelsy exerted a great influence on later developments in musical theatre by its fluid use of chorus and solo elements and the great exuberance of its performance.

From the mid-nineteenth century, musical theatre owed its evolving character to cross-pollination between Europe (particularly England and France) and the United States. Burlesque, music hall, light opera ballet, and *spectacle all converged in an 1866 production that changed the course of popular musical plays. *The Black Crook* was a *melodrama based on the Faust legend into which the producers inserted a French *ballet troupe. Its lavish sets, dancers in flesh-coloured tights, and interpolation of popular melodies made it a hit, spawning numerous imitations in *New York and London in the 1870s and 1880s.

By 1900 operetta, revues, and variety performance dominated both of those centres. It was then that American musical plays began to find their voice—musically and theatrically. George M. *Cohan, an Irish-American theatrical jack of all trades, began writing and starring in his own patriotically saturated shows such as *Little Johnny Jones* (1904). The development of ragtime piano by Scott Joplin and other American black musicians provided a driving rhythmic platform from which Irving *Berlin, George *Gershwin, and later songwriters fashioned a new popular music. Berlin followed his first hit, 'Alexander's Ragtime Band' (1911), with more than half a century of memorable songs and shows. A few years later, Jerome *Kern blended the European penchant for melody, the emerging American pulse of ragtime, and his own desire for musical plays with more fully integrated elements. The result was a series of 'Princess Theatre musicals', written with P. G. *Wodehouse and Guy *Bolton between 1915 and 1918, which set a new standard for the integration of song, dialogue, and character.

In the 1920s jazz and musical-theatre songs became the mainstays of popular music, as major songwriters turned their talents to Broadway. In addition to Kern and Berlin, George and Ira *Gershwin, Cole *Porter, Richard *Rodgers, and Lorenz *Hart were among the major forces in the United States. In England the musical productions of Noël *Coward and Ivor *Novello gained popularity. Lavish annual revues, such as Florenz *Ziegfeld's *Follies*, were sumptuously costumed and staged entertainments that have seldom been equalled. However, despite the innovations of Kern's Princess Theatre shows, 1920s musicals featured formulaic *plots, thin characterization, and little real integration of their elements.

Kern's *Show Boat* (1927, lyrics and *book by Oscar *Hammerstein II) provided a new model for the unification of song and story. Based on the novel by Edna Ferber, it spanned three generations of a *showboat family in the American south after the Civil War. The 1930s and 1940s saw the further development of more sophisticated musical plays. The satiric musicals of the Gershwin brothers (*Strike up the Band*, 1930; *Of Thee I Sing*, 1931; *Let 'Em Eat Cake*, 1933) were followed in 1935 by their most adventurous show, *Porgy and Bess*. This operatic work, set in a black community in Charleston, brought together the complex blend of jazz, blues, popular melodies, and classical influences that typified George Gershwin's unique style. Cole Porter brought urbane sophistication and playfulness to the music and lyrics for his shows, such as *Anything Goes* (1934) and *Kiss Me, Kate* (1948). The 1930s also saw experimentation with dance as a narrative element, as seen in choreographer George *Balanchine's work with Rodgers and Hart. Balanchine's 'Slaughter on 10th Avenue' in *On your Toes* (1936) was the first ballet conceived as an integral part of a musical comedy. Rodgers and Hart also blazed new trails with *Pal Joey* (1940), a dark, unsparing tale of a small-time nightclub host. By the late 1930s, musicals reached worldwide *audiences through the *films of choreographer Busby Berkeley (a former Broadway dance director) and Fred *Astaire, who had starred on Broadway in musicals by the Gershwins and by Porter.

The most significant production since *Show Boat* came in 1943 with *Oklahoma!*, the first collaboration between Rodgers and Hammerstein, who became the most influential creative team of the next two decades. Set in the last days of the American frontier, *Oklahoma!* employed dance to further plot and character. Forsaking lavish chorus lines and spectacle, Agnes *de Mille's choreography used *folk idioms, ballet, tap, and modern dance in a manner new to musical theatre. Rodgers and Hammerstein combined the exotic locales and *romanticism typical of operetta with the colloquial characters and dialogue of musical comedy to create plays of poetic depth, sophistication, and charm. Their shows were based on the premiss that songs, dance, staging, and design must flow from and serve the story and characters. Rather than stopping the action for a dance, song, or chorus sequence, their production numbers sprang directly from dialogue and situation. The success of *Oklahoma!* and other Rodgers and Hammerstein shows, such as *Carousel* (1945), *South Pacific* (1949), and *The King and I* (1951), became the touchstones for the development of subsequent musicals.

The late 1940s to the mid-1960s were a particularly rich and productive period. Among the practitioners who emerged after the Second World War was Frank *Loesser, whose range as a composer-lyricist was equalled only by Irving Berlin. Loesser's *Guys and Dolls* (1950) achieves a rare balance between comic and romantic elements. His 1961 *How to Succeed in Business without Really Trying* (written with his *Guys and Dolls* collaborator, the director-librettist Abe *Burrows) won the Pulitzer Prize (*see* AWARDS IN THE THEATRE). Other notable post-war composers include Jule *Styne, who (like Loesser) began his career writing film songs in Hollywood. Styne's shows include *Gentlemen Prefer Blondes* (1949), *Gypsy* (1959), and *Funny Girl* (1964). Lyricist Alan Jay *Lerner and composer Frederick Loewe gave romantic material a special wit and sophistication with *Brigadoon* (1947), *My Fair Lady* (1956), and *Camelot* (1960), among others. They managed in *My Fair Lady* a deft musicalization of *Shaw's *Pygmalion*, memorably performed by Rex *Harrison and Julie Andrews.

The post-war period also saw noteworthy contributions from composer Leonard *Bernstein, whose *West Side Story* (1957) was another advance in the integration of music, dialogue, dance, and staging. Working with choreographer-director Jerome *Robbins and librettist Arthur *Laurents, Bernstein's music served a novel retelling of *Romeo and Juliet* as a street-gang conflict on New York's Upper West Side. Robbins staged an opening number that established atmosphere, setting, and character dynamics before a word was uttered. The show also established Stephen *Sondheim, who wrote the lyrics, as a significant emerging talent. In Sondheim musical theatre found

both the culmination and extension of its traditions. Mentored by Hammerstein, Sondheim went on to write lyrics for Styne's *Gypsy* (1959) and music and lyrics for the broadly *farcical *A Funny Thing Happened on the Way to the Forum* (1962). He firmly established himself as an innovator with *Company* (1970), *Follies* (1971), and *A Little Night Music* (1973), which featured his most popular song, 'Send in the Clowns'.

In 1979 he blended operetta, spectacle, and *Grand Guignol in *Sweeney Todd*, which musicalized Christopher Bond's 1973 play. Imaginatively staged by Hal *Prince, the show remains controversial for both its content (the principal character, a barber, slits the throats of his customers which his associate bakes into meat pies) and stark satire. Sondheim's later work includes *Sunday in the Park with George* (1984), for which he won the Pulitzer Prize, and *Passion* (1994). The often acerbic tone of Sondheim's writing, seen by many critics as a weakness, gives his work a unique place in musical theatre. Eschewing the emphasis on romantic love, upbeat chorus numbers, traditional ballads, and happy endings favoured by Hammerstein, Sondheim's musicals nonetheless maintain the strong foundation in character and story typical of his mentor's collaborations with Rodgers. Sondheim's work also remained connected to the *genre's musical traditions at a time when rock and roll had become dominant in popular music and the cultural impact of theatrical musicals was waning.

Despite this, the 1960s and 1970s produced shows that stand in the first rank of modern musicals. *Fiddler on the Roof* (1964), by composer Jerry *Bock and lyricist Sheldon Harnick, brought the stories of Sholem *Aleichem vividly to life. That same year *Hello, Dolly!* began a run of 2,844 performances with stars like Carol *Channing, Pearl Bailey, and Ethel *Merman in the title role. Composer John *Kander and lyricist Fred Ebb created the hits *Cabaret* (1966) and *Chicago* (1975) that looked at the darker sides of *Berlin and *Chicago in the 1930s. In 1975 *A Chorus Line* started its fifteen-year run on Broadway. Director-choreographer Michael *Bennett developed the show from tape recordings of musical-theatre dancers talking about their lives.

The 1970s also saw the re-emergence of British influence through the work of Andrew *Lloyd Webber. While Sondheim placed a premium on innovation and seldom produced commercially successful shows, Lloyd Webber demonstrated a cagey awareness of both musical theatre and the business of popular music. With lyricist Tim *Rice, his first hit, *Jesus Christ Superstar* (1971), began life as a hugely successful sung-through pop-rock album prior to its first live performance. In 1978 the collaborators created *Evita*, which traced the rise of Eva Perón, wife of Argentine dictator Juan Perón. Like its predecessor, *Evita* was a study in power, stardom, and the ambition and charisma of those that achieve it. In 1981 Lloyd Webber, working with director Trevor *Nunn, adapted T. S. *Eliot's light poems *Old Possum's Book of Practical Cats* (1939). Essentially a revue with spectacular costumes, *make-up, choreography, and no dialogue, *Cats* became the longest running musical in the stage history of both New York and London. The show was equally popular in *Japan, and more than 200 different recordings have been made of its hit song 'Memory'.

The 1980s found spectacle reasserting itself with productions of *Les Misérables* (1985) and *Miss Saigon* (1989) by the French team Alain *Boublil and Claude-Michel Schönberg, Lloyd Webber's *Phantom of the Opera* (1986), and the entry of the Walt Disney Company into live production. Starting with a stage version of their animated film *Beauty and the Beast* (1993), Disney then presented an innovative staging of another animated hit, *The Lion King* (1998), directed and designed by *avant-garde luminary Julie *Taymor. Their most recent offering is a pop version of *Aida* (1999) with a score by Elton John and words by Tim Rice.

The 1990s also saw revivals of classic musicals by Porter, Berlin, Rodgers and Hammerstein, the Gershwins, and Loesser. Although new musicals were rarer each season, the decade produced *Rent* (1998), whose composer, Jonathon Larson, died shortly after opening, and *Ragtime* (1997), based on the novel by E. L. Doctorow. The comedy writer and director Mel Brooks took Broadway by storm in 2001 with a stage version of his 1968 satiric film *The Producers*, which at the start of the new millennium promised to be a *long-running hit. The modern musical is unlikely to return to the prominence it enjoyed from the 1940s to the 1960s when its songs were heard everywhere and cast albums topped the record charts. Yet it remains popular worldwide and will probably add a few shows each year to the canon of one of history's most widely enjoyed theatrical forms.

SN

BORDMAN, GERALD, *American Musical Comedy* (New York, 1982)
GANZL, KURT, *The Musical* (New York, 1998)
GREEN, STANLEY, *The World of Musical Comedy* (New York, 1980)
KISLAN, RICHARD, *The Musical* (New York, 1999)
MAST, GERALD, *Can't Help Singin'* (New York, 1987)
STEYN, MARK, *Broadway Babies Say Goodnight* (London, 2000)

MUSIC HALL

The music hall in Britain came into existence as Queen Victoria was crowned, flowered with her reign, and entered the twentieth century ready to decline; its heyday was roughly from 1890 to 1910. The first purpose-built halls began to be erected in numbers in the early 1840s, with forerunners such as the Star at Bolton which opened in 1832. Signs of the end were the 1907 performers' strike and the 1912 Royal Command performance, which signalled the arrival of the respectable *variety theatre. Over this period a fertile seedbed of small-scale entertainments, in converted or newly built rooms up and down the country, presided over by pub proprietors and semi-professional chairmen, yielded a crop of big businesses operating

under strictly enforced and eventually over-determining rules. At first the growth of the halls provided a leisure service to growing urban populations, and enabled talented individuals to develop star careers and fortunes. Cultural change and aspiration, the broadening of the *audience to include more segments of society, and concomitant moves to increase discipline and market control shifted power into the hands of business *managers and investors. They spent venture capital on large, sumptuous *auditoriums laid out as theatres rather than 'halls', transforming the audience–performer relationship; and they protected their investments by the *censorship of material and the contractual disciplining of performers to strict time limits on stage. They also bound them to work more or less on demand for the contracting syndicate, while forbidding appearances elsewhere. The transformation resulted not only in the shifting character of the large halls themselves, as they developed into 'variety theatres', but also the suppression of small independent halls. It eventually deracinated an institution which then failed to meet the challenge of further developments in the leisure industries.

Interpretations of this phenomenon begin as a popular success story of development 'from pot-house to palace', celebrating Charles *Morton, 'the Father of the Halls', and evoking the 'good old days' of sing-songs and class solidarity. From different twentieth-century perspectives music halls have been condemned as a seedbed of jingoism, racism, and misogyny, or given wry recognition as a 'culture of consolation' that kept the Victorian working man happy in his subservience. It would be more fruitful, perhaps, to discriminate between the social functions of provincial halls, which were often community centres and resources, *London East End and suburban halls, which served a local and predominantly working-class clientele, and the grand London West End establishments like the Empire and the Alhambra. Here the most highly paid music-hall turns shared the bill with lavish *dance *spectacles, and the attentions of the audience with high-class prostitution. These too had regular patrons, drawn from the ranks of civil and military servants of the British Empire. However its *politics are interpreted, music hall was an important element in the development of modern British culture.

Music hall was the primary, but not the only, Victorian home of professional entertainment. It shared the development of popular song and dance, especially comic and sentimental songs sung by *costumed performers 'in *character', with *musical theatre and *operetta in upper-class venues. Freaks and novelties, feats of strength and agility, and technical mastery continued to be exhibited in *circuses, fairs, and pleasure gardens as well as on the halls. Verbal and physical *clowning overlapped into *farce and *pantomime in popular theatres. After the 1843 Theatre *Licensing Act any performance containing narrative, whether expressed in *dialogue, song, or dance, was supposed to be the preserve of the theatres, and throughout the century charges were brought against individual halls for encroachments on this right in the form of *ballets d'action*, spectacular and melodramatic mini-dramas (called 'scenas'), or comic sketches. These were essentially proprietorial turf wars: performers continued to sell their services to whoever wanted them, and audiences chose where to see them in terms of the price, the company, and the other amenities on offer at various venues. The cultural politics of pleasure and leisure was a multi-layered and important discourse, then as now, touching upon many significant beliefs and practices; a concentration of financial, class, and *gender issues made the halls a prime focus of Victorian identity formation.

This is most obvious in the character songs and their singers, still recalled as the characteristic product of the halls. This is partly an accidental and unwarranted effect of the preservation of evidence, in the form of song sheets illustrated by famous Victorian lithographers like Alfred Concanen. These were sold at four shillings each for use in middle-class drawing rooms, and are therefore scarcely the most reliable evidence of what happened in the halls. However, they record particularly important aspects of music-hall culture. The songs of the 'lions comiques' like Alfred Vance and George Leybourne (whose version of urban masculinity celebrated good companionship, promoted the cheap pleasures of mass-produced fashion, set modern drinking habits, and mocked aristocratic exclusivity) became a model to which large swathes of the young male population aspired. Character songs setting female fashion, behaviour, and self-image suggest a range of class types: Jenny *Hill and Bessie Bellwood depicted working women, chiefly for their own amusement, while Marie *Lloyd evoked the fun had by a series of Daisies and Millies, lower-middle-class girls who were the working counterparts of the young men of the City. Some performers specializing in working-class depictions, like Gus Elan and Dan *Leno, were lionized by the West End, and translated, in Leno's case, to the famous Christmas pantomime at *Drury Lane, which was a ritual exposure to theatreland for the middle-class child. There are fewer song sheets that record one of the most significant turns unique to the music hall, the *male impersonators, presumably because there were fewer girls with pianos who would want to sing such songs themselves, however fascinated they were by Vesta *Tilley, Bessie Bonehill, Hetty King, or Ella *Shields on the stage. In any case the vivid imagery of the song sheets should not obscure the importance of other music-hall acts, like the ubiquitous clowning routines done in blackface (*see* MINSTREL SHOW), the surreal and uproarious playlets which could sometimes be of the most anti-establishment, counter-imperial character, or the feats of strength and agility and novelty acts that filled out every bill. The halls were an important and highly specific Victorian phenomenon which reverberated in the cultural imagination of Britain through most of the twentieth century.

JSB

BAILEY, PETER (ed.), *Music Hall: the business of pleasure* (Milton Keynes, 1986)

BRATTON, J. S. (ed.), *Music Hall: performance and style* (Milton Keynes, 1986)

KIFT, DAGMAR, *The Victorian Music Hall: culture, class and conflict* (Cambridge, 1996)

MUSIC IN THE THEATRE

Pure music is commonly regarded as an abstract language, but when it is used in the theatre it can take on highly specific meaning. Music can make more rather than less precise the *subtext of *dialogue and can give clarity to the shape of dramatic *action. Successful theatrical performance is closely aligned to music as it depends upon a highly developed sense of rhythm; some practitioners and theorists argue that rhythm is the prime means by which the attention of the *audience can be held. The phrase 'it's all in the timing' applies to more than just *comedy. Music was employed in the earliest phases of spoken theatre. Normally the *chorus in ancient *Greek theatre was visibly accompanied by a piper, playing the double pipes, as can be seen on many vases: he marked the rhythm of the *verse for its delivery and for *dancing. Most spoken dialogue in later periods of the theatre has been delivered without such rhythmic support, though it can be heard occasionally in the modern theatre in the revival of classical drama or in spoken dramas whenever there is an attempt to create an atmosphere of *ritual or grandeur.

Historically, theatrical performance has made liberal use of music. In the theatres of England, Italy, and Spain during the *early modern period, breaks between the *acts of spoken plays would usually provide the opportunity for interludes, *dances, songs, and other musical turns, a pattern of programming that lasted well into the eighteenth and, in some instances, the nineteenth century. Songs and dances were often incorporated into the action as well, as, for example, in several of Shakespeare's *comedies and the comic works of subsequent generations. In cities such as *London and *Paris, where the performance of spoken drama was the privilege of a few *patent theatres, plays were often staged in other theatres in conjunction with musical performances, under the pretence that the event was a concert with spoken interludes. Yet there were few systematic attempts to wed music and the spoken word until the latter half of the eighteenth century with the advent of *melodrama. Initially referring to the formal recitation of a spoken text to orchestral or instrumental accompaniment (*see* MÉLODRAME), melodrama by the beginning of the nineteenth century was recognized as a distinct theatrical *genre, of which music was an integral part. Much of the spoken dialogue in melodrama was delivered to orchestral accompaniment, particularly in passages designed to arouse an atmosphere of intense pathos or great tension and excitement. Usually, scripts would indicate where music should be played, so the dialogue was written with musical accompaniment in mind. This practice began to decline in the latter part of the nineteenth century and is rarely in use today. Frequently modern productions of spoken drama will employ recordings or live musicians to set the atmosphere, bridge scenes, or even divert audiences during particularly long scene changes, but melodrama itself is practised now only as a historical oddity. It does, however, still flourish in *film, where music is constantly used to intensify the emotional impact of the dialogue and to generate heightened dramatic tension.

Perhaps one reason why melodrama did not enjoy a longer tenure in the theatre of the nineteenth century was the growing popularity of various genres of *musical theatre, which still dominate the repertoire of commercial theatres in major cities around the globe. While the *operetta and its national sub-genres prevailed in the nineteenth century, in the twentieth century the musical has thrived. Both forms usually require orchestra and chorus, though generally the forces required for the operetta are larger. Usually both operettas and musicals originate in a spoken play in which passages of dialogue lead to formal musical numbers, solo songs, duets, larger concerted and choral pieces, and dance sequences. It is impossible to specify all occasions on which music is a more appropriate medium of expression than spoken words, but music is employed whenever the action reaches an emotional, sentimental, or dramatic highpoint, whenever festive occasions are represented on stage or set pieces are required to represent the social world of the drama. Music in the theatre tends to formalize and frequently idealize both social and personal experiences. In recent decades, some musicals have entirely dispensed with the spoken word, which brings them formally close to *opera.

Opera is the one genre in which, in the great majority of instances, solo, concerted, and choral singing to orchestral accompaniment is almost the sole medium of expression. Operatic music is best suited to representing the extremes of the human condition, so the *plots of operas often explore the most intimate recesses of the characters' emotions against a large-scale background of public affairs. Much of opera's history has been informed by the efforts of composers and librettists to devise a combination of poetry and music that most exactly represents the flow of human emotions and discourse without drawing undue attention to discrete musical form. Although certain composers such as *Gluck and *Wagner have the deserved reputation of revolutionizing music so as to make it into a flexible dramatic language, composers as diverse as *Monteverdi, *Mozart, Rossini, *Verdi, *Puccini, Richard *Strauss, and Berg constantly modified the musical and vocal forms of their time to achieve an unbroken continuity in their music.

Although the practice of performing music, songs, dances, and *acrobatics between the acts of spoken plays died out at the beginning of the twentieth century, compiling theatre programmes from a variety of acts continued, most notably in the *music halls of Great Britain and in *revues, which originated in Paris, but soon spread throughout Europe and the United States, where they continue still.

SJCW

MUSINGA, VICTOR ELAME (1943–   )

Cameroon playwright, director, actor, and *filmmaker. Though self-schooled, Musinga is the country's most prolific dramatist with some 22 plays to his credit, written in English. Best known for *The Tragedy of Mr No Balance* (1976), his other work includes *Accountant Wawah* (1968), *Madam Magrana* (1969), *Colofonco* (1970), *Night Marriages* (1972), *The Trials of Ngowo* (1973), *Lady Njoko* and *Njema* (both 1974), *Incredible Madam Etonde* (1974), *The Challenge of Yoe* (1975), and *Mr Director* (1977). Musinga principally writes social *satires about corruption, prostitution, and sorcery. He runs his own theatre company, the Musinga Drama Group, which has performed virtually all his plays, with the author invariably playing the lead role.

HNE

MUSSET, ALFRED DE (1810–57)

French poet and dramatist. The youngest, and arguably the most original, of the four principal *romantic playwrights (*Hugo, *Dumas, and *Vigny), Musset was little performed in his lifetime. After the failure of *La Nuit vénitienne* (*Odéon, 1830), he adopted the formula of 'armchair drama', many of his bittersweet *comedies, as well as his 'Shakespearian' *history play *Lorenzaccio*, being published under the title 'Spectacle dans un fauteuil' (1833–4; *see* CLOSET DRAMA). *Lorenzaccio* (1834) marks a complete break from French *neoclassical tradition, with its construction (39 separate *scenes), the wide social spread of its *characters, and above all the manner in which the *hero is presented. The clear-cut conflict or dilemma exhibited by *Corneille's Cinna or *Racine's Titus is replaced by Lorenzo's gradual development from an unsympathetic, if enigmatic, character to one whose motivation is laid bare in a series of emotionally charged scenes by flights of poetic fancy: small wonder that comparison with *Hamlet* has become a critical commonplace. When first produced, at the Renaissance Theatre in 1896, Musset's play was reshaped by Armand d'Artois on the neoclassical model: a separate single setting for each of the five *acts. Sarah *Bernhardt played Lorenzo, starting a tradition followed by Falconetti, Piérat, and Jamois. Indeed, the *Théâtre National Populaire at *Avignon saw the first major production with a male actor (Gérard *Philipe) in the role in 1952, well over 100 years after first publication. Musset's *comedy *Un caprice* had been performed at *St Petersburg by a French actress, Mme Allan, in 1837; and it was she whose performance in the same play on her return to *Paris in 1847 led to the belated recognition of Musset's *comedies. Some of these, slight *one-acts with a *realistic drawing-room setting, soon became well established as curtain raisers at the *Comédie-Française; among the more substantial full-length plays, *Les Caprices de Marianne* (1851) and *On ne badine pas avec l'amour* (*Don't Joke with Love*, 1861) suggest the *tragicomic mood of Shakespeare's *Measure for Measure*.   WDH

MUTHUSWAMY, NA (1936–   )

Playwright, director, and short-story writer, based in Chennai (Madras), Tamil Nadu, *India. From his breakthrough in 1979 with *Kalam Kalmaga* (*From Time Immemorial*), regarded as a landmark in modern *Tamil theatre, Muthuswamy has continued to explore the conflicting values of the urban metropolis in relation to non-modern cultural traditions. Working within a highly stylized and disjunctive narrative structure, in which multiple episodes are linked within a non-linear thematic logic, Muthuswamy is known for experimental plays that are marked by an extremely inventive use of the Tamil language, including *Undhichuzhi* (*Umbilical Cord*), *Suvarottigal* (*Wall Posters*), *Natrunaiyappan* (*A God*), *Ingilandhu* (*England*), *Cinemavil Oru Katchi* (*A Scene from the Movie*). As the *artistic director of the troupe Koothuppattarai (1979), re-established as a repertory company by 1986 with Ford Foundation funding, he has brought together diverse talents like Kannappa Thambiran and Sambandha from traditional *terukkuttu with contemporary painters, choreographers, *dancers, and *critics. Eclectic and iconoclastic, Koothuppattarai's hybrid interaction with diverse forms and disciplines has been complemented by its rewriting of traditional material. Muthuswamy's translation of a classical Sanskrit play by *Bhasa (*Dhuthagatothkajam*), for example, was matched by his reinterpretation of the 'Burning of the Khandava Forest' episode from the *Mahabharata*, where he strategized environmental issues within the traditional context of *terukkuttu*. Muthuswamy's capacity to connect the artistic vocabularies of tradition and modernity continues to fuel his work as organizer, director, and playwright.   PR/RB

MUTIYETTU

*Ritual theatre annually performed at specific Bhadrakali temples in central Kerala, *India, to propitiate Bhadrakali—the violent and ferocious manifestation of the goddess associated with the power of destruction and warfare. *Mutiyettu* is traditionally performed to ensure prosperity and happiness, and to protect devotees from smallpox or enemies. It is performed by families of Marar and Kurup, some of Kerala's many temple-service castes whose other duties include playing percussion instruments and singing as part of daily temple worship.

Mutiyettu dramatizes the story of the defeat of the demon Darika by Bhadrakali. Long ago there had been a fierce war between the gods and demons. When the demons were on the brink of defeat, Lord Brahma sired two demon sons who would take vengeance on the gods, Danavendra and Darika. Darika secured boons from Lord Brahma that made him invincible to men, demons, and gods. But he made one mistake—he did not ask that he be invincible to women. As Darika, Danavendra, and the demons continued to persecute both gods and sages. Siva, enraged by Darika's atrocities, opened the third eye of his forehead, giving birth to the fearsome woman Bhadrakali who, after hunting down Darika and Danavendra, presented their heads to Siva.

Seven *characters appear in the ritual drama: Siva, Narada, Darika, Danavendra, Bhadrakali; Kooli (a female comic character considered one of Siva's attending spirits) and Koimbidar (a Nayar martial arts practitioner carrying sword and shield) accompany Bhadrakali to battle. Prior to the performance proper, Bhadrakali's presence is first invoked into an elaborate, colourful, three-dimensional floor drawing of the goddess whose image is meant to be terrifying and awe inspiring—her body is gigantic and jet black in colour, her head reaches the sky, she has three red eyes that burn like fire, and her numerous arms hold sword, spear, club, bow, and trident, and Darika's bleeding head. When the performer playing Bhadrakali 'fastens' (*ettuka*) the crown (*muti*), he 'forgets himself', is possessed by Bhadrakali, and therefore literally manifests the presence of the deity—a state inspiring awe and fear in devotees, and allowing the performer to *dance for hours as he pursues and battles Darika, ultimately 'beheading' him and Danavendra.

PZ

MVET

A poetic *genre found among the Fang of Gabon and Cameroon. The word has three definitions: a rigorously structured epic *text (*nlan mvet*) whose performance can last more than 48 hours; the player of the instrument (*mbom mvet*), an initiate who recites and *mimes *actions; or the accompanying instrument, a cithara with four strings made from palm and bamboo sticks. The general subject of a *mvet* performance is man's power as an element of nature and his struggles against visible and invisible forces. Denouncing the abuse of power, the struggles pit mortals (the men of Oku) against immortals (the men of Engong). The origins of *mvet* are attributed to the migration narratives of the Fang, which centre around a mythical hero, Oyono Ada Ngono.   PNN trans. JCM

MWONDO THEATRE

A company founded in Chimbambo in Katanga Province of Congo. It expanded activities across Congo, later travelling to other African countries and the World Theatre Festival in Nancy in 1977. Blending dramatic with choreographic elements, Mwondo relied on simple effects like slides, *shadow puppets, song, *mime, and offstage narration. *Buhamba* is characteristic. In a sequence of *dances and mimes, the piece concerns the birth of twins, at first perceived as threatening and unnatural. Eventually the community is made to see that twins do not upset the natural order, and the performance ends with festivity and new social awareness.

PNN trans. JCM

MYANMAR

Formerly known as Burma, Myanmar (population 41 million) is located in mainland South-East Asia, bordered by *India, *China, *Bangladesh, *Thailand, *Malaysia, and *Laos. Yangon (Rangoon) is the capital and largest city. Burmans make up the ethnic majority, having migrated to the region between the eleventh and thirteenth centuries. Since independence from British colonial rule (1886–1948), a repressive Burman-led government has shaped Myanmar's cultural development except in the mountainous regions along the borders, areas which are home to more than 60 ethnic groups, including the Karen, the Shan, and the Mon, and which in practical terms function as independent states. Under the military government in power in 2001, all information is state controlled; strict *censorship prohibits freedom of expression. Since 1993 the Ministry of Arts has upheld the state's mandate to develop a Myanmar cultural heritage by sponsoring annual traditional performing arts competitions in order to prevent 'the penetration of neocolonial imperialistic cultural influences'. Traditional venues for political *satire and *comedy have been sanitized and co-opted by the state, including the a-nyeint, which features female *dances interspersed with *clown skits. Those who defy government edicts prohibiting social criticism are banned from performing or jailed. Amnesty International campaigned on behalf of two such comedians from the a-nyeint Moustache Brothers Troupe, who were imprisoned from 1996 to 2001.

The roots of popular theatre can be traced to eleventh-century pageants called nebhatkhin in which young devotees created silent *tableaux vivants depicting a story of the birth of Buddha, or zat (see JATAKA). By the mid-eighteenth century, *dialogue, *music, and song were added. During the same period, *yokthe pwe (*marionette theatre) appeared, combining zat tales with nat (spirit) worship in all-night performances. Adherents of Theraveda Buddhism, Myanmar's main religion, have traditionally performed propitiatory dances to 37 recognized spirits. At least two variations of these dances are still performed today as *nat pwe (spirit shows) and in the a-nyeint. Myai waing (earth circling performance) was another popular all-night event, performed on temporary dirt *stages surrounded by the *audience. *Ritual offerings and songs to the nat were followed by a drama enacted by mintha (male actors), minthamee (female actors), and lubyet (clowns). The origins of court theatre are less clear. Scholars do agree that following the capture of the Siamese city Ayutthaya in 1767, performances in the Konbaung court

appear to have been modelled on Thai forms. Stories from the Ramayana and the Thai Inao (based on *Panji) were often staged. In the nineteenth century original scripts were commissioned from court playwrights, including U *Kyin U and U *Pon Nya. Following the expulsion of the royal family by the British in 1885, former court performers sought employment with popular troupes, which became generally known as *zat pwe, although historical and fictional scripts were added to the repertoire. Famous actors, including *Po Sein, are credited with popularizing and modernizing zat pwe during the colonial period, and today it is accepted as part of Myanmar's cultural heritage programme.

CRG

MYSTERY PLAYS (MYSTÈRES)

The term mystère appears first in 1374 in the records of Rouen linked with *'miracle', where a confrérie of Rouen is commanded to play 'aucun vrai mistere ou miracle'. The terms seem to be interchangeable in late medieval French usage. Later French use of the term refers to *Passion plays, *biblical plays, *dumb shows, and even plays on profane subjects. Because one of the meanings of the French word mystère is 'craft', English scholars of the late nineteenth century applied the phrase 'mystery play' to works thought to have been performed by craft *guilds—particularly those sequences (or *cycles) that dramatize salvation history: the York, Chester, Towneley, N-Town plays, and the Cornish Ordinalia. See MEDIEVAL THEATRE IN EUROPE; CORPUS CHRISTI PLAYS. (See illustration p. 908.)

AFJ

MYTH STUDIES

A form of *criticism and interpretation which makes use of latent mythical patterns underlying performances. It came to prominence with literary critic Northrup Frye's groundbreaking Anatomy of Criticism (1957), but had been linked with drama through the work of Cambridge classicists James Frazer, Gilbert *Murray, Jane Harrison, and Francis Cornford in the early years of the twentieth century (the Cambridge School of Anthropology). The claims for the intertwining of myth and *ritual in the beginnings of early civilizations and, subsequently, in *Greek *tragedy, led both to hermeneutical practices of myth criticism and also to artists who worked self-consciously to interweave myth in their other dramatic materials. T. S. *Eliot is perhaps the most famous of these self-conscious myth-users, especially in his 'modern' plays such as The Cocktail Party (1939) and The Family Reunion (1949) which incorporate the Orestes and Alcestis myths, respectively. Closely related to these approaches, archetypal criticism developed from the ideas of Carl Jung, who believed that archetypes were original models or matters imprinted in the collective unconscious.

Frye's ambition in Anatomy of Criticism was no less than to provide 'a central hypothesis which, like the theory of evolution

in biology, will see the phenomena it deals with as parts of a whole'. Developing theories of modes, symbols, myths, and *genres, he attempted to provide a classificatory scheme which covered all of Western history and still identified permanent structures in its literature. Thus he asserts that myth is present in different historical modes, and in four mythoi (*comedy, *romance, tragedy, and irony). Displacement is the means by which raw or pure myth is reworked into *romantic and *realistic representations. Works of fiction have drawn on two metaphorical worlds, one desirable and one not, which Frye calls the apocalyptic and demonic spheres. Displacement of mythic patterns increases with historical progression through Frye's periodization into mythic, romance, high mimetic, low mimetic, and ironic modes which roughly correspond to classical, *medieval, and *early modern periods, the eighteenth century, and the nineteenth/twentieth centuries. While for Frye the whole system constituted its explanatory strength, various aspects of his scheme have been adopted by critics writing about myth.

Francis Fergusson's *The Idea of a Theatre* (1949) is a prior (to Frye) instance of myth criticism, acknowledging its debt to the Cambridge anthropologists, and reading mythic and ritual elements in *Oedipus the King*, *Hamlet*, *Tristan and Isolde*, *The Infernal Machine*, and *Murder in the Cathedral*. C. L. Barber brought these methods to Shakespeare in *Shakespeare's Festive Comedy* (1959) in which a saturnalian pattern in the 'green comedies' links the structure of comedy to seasonal myths and resembles Frye's approach. Through the 1970s, myth criticism was used productively to probe the underlying structures of canonical dramatists such as *Ibsen and *O'Neill. Thomas Porter's *Myth and Modern American Drama* (1969) is typical of these analyses, as is Harold Knutson's *Molière: an archetypal approach* (1976).

During the 1970s, *structuralism also made use of mythic analysis, especially in its reappropriation of the work of Vladimir Propp on classifying and organizing *folk tales, and Claude Lévi-Strauss's insistence that myth is structured like language and is a kind of code from the whole of a culture to its individual members. In *Structural Anthropology* he writes, 'The myth will be treated as an orchestra score would be if it were unwittingly considered as a unilinear series; our task is to re-establish the correct arrangement.' Post-structuralist critiques of ahistoricism and universalism began to diminish the strength of these approaches, charging that the emphasis on the universal aspects of myths belied cultural specificity and tended to revalidate a white Eurocentric ideology even while surveying the myths of widely divergent societies. Nevertheless, myth criticism has remained viable for some scholars; for example, Mary A. Doll's study *Beckett and Myth: an archetypal approach* appeared as late as 1988.

More central to late twentieth-century scholarship, however, were the studies of non-Western theatre forms which include elements of myth and ritual. Whether looking at *Myth in Indian Drama* (1994) by R. G. Joshi, or at African drama (*Ancient Songs Set Ablaze: the theatre of Femi Osofisan*, 1996) by Sandra Richards, the emphasis on evocation of myth and ritual in order to illuminate a universal literary or dramatic tradition has given way to a specific and often *materialist analysis of the relationships between societies, cultural practices, and theatrical representation. The product of particular historical and cultural situations, myths are often seen now as strong signifiers of traumatic or celebratory experiences for specific spectators rather than as terms of address for a universal mankind. In many *intercultural performances, they are woven into the materials used to draw upon the history and symbols of the source cultures. *See also* ORIGINS OF THEATRE.   JGR

French *mystère* or **mystery play** depicting the martyrdom of St Apollonia, c.1460, with a 'book holder' in evidence (right of centre, with round hat and raised stick). The arrangement of elevated mansions in a semicircle in the background seems characteristic of the performance of the biblical or cycle plays of medieval theatre, with heaven in its usual place on the left of the picture, hell mouth on the right.

N

NACIONAL, TEATRO

Colombian theatre company founded in *Bogotá in 1978 by Fanny *Mikey. It opened in a renovated cinema in 1981 with *The Hostage* by Brendan *Behan, with Mikey in one of the roles, directed by Argentine-born David Stivel. Thereafter it has maintained a repertory of contemporary national and international plays, which alternate with commercial productions. In 1992 it acquired another space, the Teatro de la Castellana, followed by a third, the Casa del Teatro Nacional, in 1994. It is also the host company for the prestigious Festival Iberoamericano de Teatro, founded in 1988 by Mikey, which has brought major companies from all over the world.   BJR

NACIONAL D. MARIA II, TEATRO

Opened in 1846 as Portugal's first national theatre, the D. Maria was the result of the new Liberal government's decision to further the 'civilization and moral perfection of the Portuguese nation'. Designed and built by the Italian architect Fortunato Lodi over the ruins of the old Paço dos Inquisidores in the heart of *Lisbon, the *playhouse's first director was Almeida *Garrett, who offered a repertoire of established Portuguese and foreign classics, oversaw the professional *training of actors, and founded an important theatre archive. With the coming of the republic in 1910, the theatre took the name of its founder, only to revert in 1939 to its original name. Under the Salazar dictatorship the theatre continued to offer a varied repertoire of local and foreign work, much of which was unfamiliar to *Lisbon *audiences. In 1964 a *fire destroyed all but the outer shell of the building and it would be another fourteen years before the theatre reopened in its present form. The *management of the theatre was, except for the period 1853–68 and after its recent reconstruction, in the hands of artistic guilds, headed by prestigious actors. A *sala experimental* or workshop theatre has been added recently for the production of new and less conventional work.   KG

NACIONAL MARÍA GUERRERO, TEATRO

Designed by Agustín Ortiz Villajos, who was also responsible for *Madrid's Teatro de la Comedia, the Teatro Princesa, as it was first known, opened in Madrid in 1885. Regular home to the actress María *Guerrero and the Guerrero-Díaz de Mendoza company from 1909—and named after her in 1928—the *playhouse was also the venue of Margarita *Xirgu's Madrid debut in 1914. Renovated and created a national theatre during the early years of the Franco regime, when it was run by Luis Escobar and Huberto Pérez de la Ossa, it presented a more adventurous repertory than its limited mandate might suggest, hosting visits from French companies like Jean Vernier's in 1942 and Louis *Jouvet's in 1950. Under the directorship of José Luis *Alonso in the early 1960s, it combined the world repertory with promotion of new Spanish playwrights. In 1978 the theatre was reconceived on the model of the French national theatre network as the Centro Dramático Nacional, and Lluis *Pasqual's tenure as *artistic director in the mid-1980s received international recognition.   MMD

NAEVIUS, GNAEUS (c.270–201 BC)

Roman playwright who specialized in *comedy but also wrote *tragedies and translated and adapted Greek plays into Latin versions. He created as a *genre plays on Roman history (*fabulae praetextae*). His comedies used *plot, language, and *characterization in a manner anticipating *Plautus. Titles of 37 works survive.   RCB

NAKAMURA UTAEMON VI (1917–2001)

Japanese *kabuki actor, *onnagata (woman's role specialist), and Living National Treasure. The son of Nakamura Utaemon V, he began performing at 5 years of age under the name of Kotarō and went through successive name changes as Fukusuke (1933) and Shikan (1941) before assuming the name Utaemon VI in 1951. Equally strong at dance roles and at playing courtesans, maidens, and princesses, Utaemon's style is elegant and subtle. In the 1950s and 1960s he was the favourite actor of *Mishima Yukio, who wrote several new kabuki plays for him. In 2000 Utaemon was the senior onnagata and a leader of the art, exerting strong influence on play selection and actor promotion. Although his adopted son Matsue is his nominal successor, Utaemon also *trained other leading onnagata actors.

LRK

NALOMA-TLON (NALOMA THEATRE)

A women's improvisational theatre performed primarily in Bamana rural communities and in some towns in Mali. Naloma-tlon means 'stupid person play' and the skits satirize aspects of male behaviour that Bamana interpret as degrading. Members of the troupe are generally older married or widowed women. They don men's clothing and are accompanied by male drummers. Initially the women crowd into the acting space and multiple improvisations develop simultaneously. Eventually the individual *improvisations coalesce into smaller, more focused scenarios that involve *stock characters such as the swaggering proud adolescent, the drunken man, and the insane man.

MJA

NAMIKI SŌSUKE (SENRYŪ) (1695–1751)

Japanese playwright. Born in *Osaka, he was a Buddhist priest before becoming a playwright at the Toyotake-za *puppet theatre in Osaka. He produced about 47 *bunraku and ten *kabuki plays, most written in collaboration under his direction. He became the senior playwright in 1727, after only one year with the troupe. He briefly went to Edo (*Tokyo) around the end of 1741, and then in 1742–5 wrote kabuki for Osaka theatres. In 1745 he moved to the Takemoto-za, and under the name Senryū collaborated with *Takeda Izumo II and Miyoshi Shōraku to produce ten works, including three famous plays, Sugawara and the Secrets of Calligraphy (1746), Yoshitsune and the Thousand Cherry Trees (1747), and Chūshingura: the treasury of loyal retainers (1748). In 1751 he returned to the Toyotake-za to write two works under the name Sōsuke; he died after completing Act III of The Battles at Ichinotani (1751). His works are known for their critical and tragic view of Tokugawa period society, and today he is considered the second greatest

Japanese playwright after *Chikamatsu Monzaemon.

CAG

KEENE, DONALD, Chūshingura: the treasury of loyal retainers (New York, 1971)

NANDIKESWARA

Author of Abhinayadarpana (The Mirror of Acting, possibly as early as the fifth century AD), a Sanskrit compendium of gestures, postures, and movements in classical *Indian *dance. His authority in the field is confirmed by none other than *Abhinavagupta, the greatest commentator on the *Natyasastra. Also known as Nandi, Nandikeswara provided dance with an autonomous status, apart from differentiating between the 'male' (and vigorous) mode of dance known as tandava and the 'female' (and more graceful) style of lasya. Although a theory of *rasa (aesthetic sentiments) is attributed to him, he is more readily recognized as an authority on music, erotic love, and *acting. The works on music attributed to him are Nandikeswara mate Taladhyay (The Chapter on Rhythm According to Nandikeswara) and Bharatarnava, a compilation of his own work and that of *Bharata dealing with dramatic gestures and tala (rhythm). Through Ananda Coomaraswamy's widely disseminated English translation (The Mirror of Acting, 1917), Nandikeswara's codifications of gesture provided an interesting reference for an *intercultural debate between Gordon *Craig and Coomaraswamy himself on the virtues and difficulties of transferring traditional techniques of non-Western acting to contemporary European theatre.

KNP

NANG

Ancient *puppet theatre from *Thailand, both *shadow and silhouette, first documented in 1385, which has resemblances to the *Indonesian *wayang and may be related to it. Nang yai, as the Thai form is known today, uses stiff, engraved, flat leather puppets, 1–2 m (3–6 feet) high, with two control sticks. The male puppeteers, each working a single puppet, dance in front of and behind a large white screen hanging above the stage. Coconut shells, which burn brightly and smokelessly, are the traditional *lighting source. The action in front of the screen depicts intimate scenes like a royal audience or hand-to-hand combat, while behind the screen the events tend to be distant ones like a journey or a full battlefield. A pipat ensemble, located on the ground in front of the screen, accompanies the performance, and the puppets are moved to the recitation by two chanters of episodes of the Indian epic the Ramayana (Ramakien in the Thai version). At designated moments the puppets dance set pieces that signify mood or thought. One episode may feature up to 250 puppets operated by twelve puppeteers. A performance usually begins around 9 p.m. and includes a musical prelude that pays homage to deities and gurus, fights between black and

A **nang yai** performance as depicted in murals from the early nineteenth century in Wat Phra Keo, Bangkok, Thailand. Two puppeteers perform in front of the screen, chanters on either side, with a *pipat* ensemble in the foreground.

white monkeys that pass along moral lessons to the audience, and finally the play proper, which is performed from midnight until dawn. *Nang yai* is also staged at cremation ceremonies in the afternoon, sometimes without a screen, when the puppets may be painted in various bright colours. *See also* NANG TALUNG.

SV

NANG SBEK THOM

*Cambodian *shadow-puppet theatre, now rare, in which large leather figures up to 1.8 by 1.2 m (6 by 4 feet) are danced in front of and behind a screen 10 m long and 4 m high (30 by 10 feet). Though its origin is obscure, the form may date from the ninth century when Jayavarman II returned from the *Indonesian archipelago with a model of Javanese *wayang kulit*. In the *devaraja* cult, which Jayavarman founded, courtiers would swear allegiance by enacting Hindu myths detailing how gods overcome demons and confirm Indra as divine ruler. A story from the *Ramayana* in which monkey *characters struggle with demons to affirm the kingship of Rama became entwined with this fealty *ritual, and courtiers began to perform episodes of the *Ramayana* (*Reamker*) using *puppets or *masks, leading to the allied arts of *nang sbek* and masked dance (*khol*). Performances at cremations and other court events became common, were preserved, and emulated in *Thailand (*see* NANG TALUNG).

In a contemporary performance, ten dancers carry intricately incised, opaque, mostly non-articulate leather panels which portray single-figure or multi-person scenes. Music is provided by the eight members of the *pinpeat* orchestra and the story is chanted by two narrators. The size of the images makes them among the world's largest shadow figures, and approximately 150 puppets make up a set. Their design reflects royal Khmer court dress and aesthetics similar to figures in Angkor Wat bas-reliefs. The *text, personnel, and performance technique are shared with the masked dance. While in former times it took three weeks to present the whole *Reamker*, today the story may be presented in three nights, or 90-minute excerpts may be shown for tourists or urban viewers. After the Khmer Rouge killed or forced court artists into exile (1975–9), a revival of the art took place in the late 1980s at the Fine Arts Academy

A few of the hundreds of leather comic figures for **nang talung**, a shadow puppet theatre from Thailand.

in Phnom Penh with the support of the Minister of Culture. Another puppet tradition similar to Thai *nang talung* is known in Cambodia as *nang sbek touch, nang kalung*, or *ayang*. Here, much smaller, articulate, single-character puppets are operated by a single puppeteer.   KFo

NANG TALUNG

Thai *shadow-puppet theatre. *Nang* (leather) is the term applied to both shadow puppet genres of *Thailand: *nang yai* (large leather figures), a court art borrowed in 1431 from Cambodian *nang sbek thom*; and *nang talung*, which means 'leather figures of Pattalung Province', a southern *folk genre of Pattalung and Songkhla believed to have developed in the seventeenth century. Small translucent images about 60 cm (2 feet) high are manipulated by a solo *puppet master and storyteller, called a *nang nai*, while a six-person orchestra accompanies the performance.

Presentations are given from a small screened hut. The stage area is set above the ground where spectators stand. As with the related Malay-Indonesian *wayang kulit, puppets are set on a banana-log stage and *rituals are linked with the perform-

ance. Today a puppeteer may use 50 of the 200 figures in his set to present the story, usually from the *Ramakien* (the Thai *Ramayana*) or local folk tales. Refined *characters speak central Thai dialect while clowns speak southern dialect, endearing these comic figures to the southern *audience. Despite the competition of new media, the comedy in *nang talung* kept it popular in 2000.   KFo

NANXI (NAN HSI)

Important form of *Chinese drama which developed in the early twelfth century. The Song Dynasty (960–1127) ended with the Mongol invasion, but the southern Song continued until 1279 and its drama had a longer period of development than that prevalent in the north. *Nanxi* plays are divided into role types, including principal male (*sheng*), principal female (*dan*), secondary male (*mo, wai*), secondary female (*tie*), and other 'strong men' or comic roles, each with its own tradition of performance. There was no restriction on the number of *scenes, and solo, duet, and ensemble singing were all allowed, in marked contrast to the strict four-act *zaju* form that developed in the north during the Mongol Yuan Dynasty (1280–1368). By the late

Yuan, however, the southern fashion spread northward and gradually metamorphosed into the characteristic drama of the Ming Dynasty (1368–1644), *chuanqi, which differed from the nanxi only in its increasingly stringent rules about the succession of tune types. Drama in the Song Dynasty can be generally regarded as having developed under the impetus of urban living. Records indicate that permanent *playhouses were available, roofed over to permit performances in all weathers, as well as *stages used by *puppeteers, comedians, ballad singers, and others, and it was from such a rich mix of entertainment possibilities that Song plays were developed.

From extant documents it seems clear that spoken and sung sections alternated in the course of performance, and that the *music used was borrowed or adapted from the distinctive *folk music then popular in the southern areas of the empire, which serves as one reason for the drama to be referred to as 'southern-style'. The *texts of these plays, usually composed by what were called 'writing societies', were often elaborate, and the titles of some 170 are known. A few texts are more or less complete, though most scripts have been lost. The plays might loosely be described as romantic *comedies or *melodramas. A number of the *plots concern scholar-officials who, in order to rise in influence, abandon wives and families, while other plays deal with corrupt Buddhist priests. Those who betray their wives or duties are usually caught and exposed. Plays of considerable literary distinction were composed when the form was revived at the end of the Yuan Dynasty, and the texts and the names of some authors are known. One of the most famous of these later plays in the southern sung style is the fourteenth-century Pipa ji (The Story of the Lute) by *Gao Ming. Much later adapted into various Western languages, it even formed the basis for a Broadway *musical starring Mary *Martin entitled Lute Song (1946).   JTR/KC

NAPIER, JOHN (1944–)

English designer. *London born, he *trained with Ralph *Koltai at the Central School of Arts and Crafts, but left to become head of design at the Phoenix Theatre, Leicester. Work for *Marowitz's Open Space and the *Royal Court led to appointment as associate designer for the *Royal Shakespeare Company (1974). He was part of the team that restructured the RSC main stage (1976) and achieved international recognition for The Greeks (1980) and a *constructivist Nicholas Nickleby (1980). Napier is associated with bravura West End *musicals such as Sunset Boulevard (1993). He rejects pictorial *realism; stripping the stage of decor, he replaces it with an evocative object such as the 'American dream' Cadillac in Miss Saigon (1989). His sets include the *audience as part of the design, requiring transformation of *auditorium and *stage space: seats were removed for skaters' tracks in Starlight Express (1984), and Cats (1981) extended its junkyard set into the *auditorium. Trevor *Nunn

praises Napier as 'an inventor. He makes machines to make the impossible happen.'   RVL

NAPLES

Italian city with a rich theatrical tradition dating back to *Roman theatre. The first vernacular works were *Atellan farces, originating in the city where Virgil wrote the Bucolics. These fables already contained some of the main characteristics of subsequent Neapolitan theatre: strong satirical elements and *stock characters, some of whom eventually became maschere (masks) of *commedia dell'arte. The penchant for *satire and polemic developed in Neapolitan theatre alongside a more complacent form of drama which celebrated the Spanish court which ruled the region. The eighteenth century was one of the most productive periods, especially in music, as the composers Pergolesi, Scarlatti, Trinchera, Paisiello, and Cimarosa wrote both comic and serious *operas which sometimes indirectly denounced the widespread social injustice that crippled Naples.

During the period of the Risorgimento in the early nineteenth century, a more openly revolutionary stance was taken in the operas of Bellini, and was apparent as well in the choice of many dramatists to write in Neapolitan dialect. As popular objections to the ruling class became more pronounced, theatre reflected the social divide. The Teatro San Carlo came to represent the status quo, staging operas and plays for an elite *audience, while the Teatro San Carlino catered for ordinary people with comic operas, satires, and *burlesques of the opera seria that appealed to the aristocracy. The split was not always heavily marked, however. The buildings were in the same poor area of Naples, facing each other, and often the nobles would cross the square from the San Carlo to the San Carlino to laugh at portrayals of themselves.

During the nineteenth and twentieth centuries the best-known Neapolitan playwrights, such as Antonio Petito, Raffaele *Viviani, Salvatore Di Giacomo, and Eduardo *Scarpetta, appealed to all social classes through representations of social injustice, before and after the unification of Italy. Their plays strongly suggest that ordinary people did not profit by the change of political power. Petito's famous Pulcinella became the symbol of the downtrodden Neapolitan, exploited, always hungry, the victim of injustice who must resort to a thousand tricks to keep alive. The tragic black mask of the *character hid the miserable conditions of the congenitally impoverished residents of the city. Scarpetta immortalized the downtrodden Neapolitan in his character Felice Sciosciammocca, a new Pulcinella, poor, hungry, dishonest out of necessity, but without the mask to hide his true nature. The character, which featured in many dramas, was most famously celebrated in Scarpetta's Miseria e nobiltà (Poverty and Nobility, 1888), which depicted the daily struggle for survival.

Scarpetta's son, Eduardo *de Filippo, inherited and expanded this rich tradition, starting in the 1920s and continuing until his death in 1984. Eduardo, as he was universally known, expressed social injustice in yet more open and sombre tones. His plays are sharp portrayals of the divide between rich and poor in a society where personal revenge, cheating, and even the Camorra (the Neapolitan equivalent of the Mafia) in *Il sindaco del rione sanità* (*The Local Authority*, 1960) are the result of an ingrained injustice which comes from centuries-long subjection to external power. All these writers used Neapolitan dialect (in more or less stage versions) to express *napoletanità*—the spirit of the underprivileged Neapolitan people. Dialect was not something picturesque; especially for Eduardo, it was a political choice, even if he shrank from overtly *political theatre. Neapolitan was seen as the language of the people, as opposed to the language of the ruling classes.

Contemporary Neapolitan theatre is profoundly linked to its past: *napoletanità*, dialect, and *verismo (a form of *realism) still form the basic tissue of drama, even when playwrights deal with current issues. Enzo Moscato (1947–   ), in works such as *Carciofolà* (1978), *Scannasuric* (1980), *Trianon* (1983), and *Pièce noire* (1985), mixes baroque and working-class idioms with foreign words which have entered daily speech through the *mass media. Annibale Ruccello (1956–86) was close to the popular tradition with *I gingilli indiscreti* and *L'osteria del Melograno*, but was inspired by the realist novel of the nineteenth century in his *Ferdinando* (1984), which addresses the complex history of Italy in the 1890s. Finally, Manlio Santanelli (1938–   ) maintains Neapolitan roots but, like Ruccello, looks beyond Naples to European modes. His plays are a mixture of popular theatre and the theatre of the *absurd (*L'isola di Sancho*, 1981; *Regina Madre*, 1985) and portray tormented family relationships reminiscent of Harold *Pinter.   DMcM

VIVIANI, VITTORIO, *Storia del Teatro Napoletano* (Naples, 1969)

NAQQAL

Punjabi *folk performer and performance type. From the Farsi word meaning to imitate, the *naqqal* is an impressionist and prankster who makes the *audience laugh by establishing a satirical point of view or deflating institutions or situations. Employed by the rulers of small feudal principalities in earlier times, the *naqqal* traditionally critiqued social conditions. Though urbanization has caused the decline of their art, the *naqqal* continue to entertain local communities during weddings and other auspicious occasions. Originally from the professional caste of *bazighars* or *acrobats, a *naqqal* troupe is composed of musicians, singers, *maskharas* (*clowns), and *dancers; men play the female roles. The performance starts with an invocation. Two actors then face one another, one of them holding a leather strap (*chomota*); at climactic moments this is brought

swishing to hit the open palm of the second actor, sending the crowd into a frenzy of *laughter. The remainder of the performance is a dramatization of a love legend or a myth, interspersed with dance and ribaldry. Most of the narrative is sung in *bait*, a form of poetic composition. The *costumes are a loosely tied sarong-like wrap and a short shirt, while the *female impersonators dress in glitzy nylon with garish designs.

NMSC

NARTOSABDHO (1925–85)

Javanese *dalang* (puppeteer) who rose from poverty to become one of the most influential masters of twentieth-century *wayang kulit purwa*, the *shadow-puppet theatre of *Indonesia. In 1945 he joined Nesti Pandawa, a *wayang orang* (*dance–drama) company, as a drummer, and began performing as a *puppet master in 1955. His troupe, Condong Raos, located in Semarang, rose quickly to prominence; though his innovations were rejected by conservative practitioners, his immense popularity with *audiences earned him many imitators. He introduced musical effects from Banyumas and west Java into the Javanese repertoire, highlighted humour, and added new twists to traditional plots.   KFo

NASCIMENTO, ABDIAS DO (1914–   )

Brazilian playwright, artist, and political activist, a founder of the Teatro Experimental do Negro in *Rio de Janeiro. TEN served as a *training ground for Afro-Brazilian actors who found little opportunity on the commercial stage, and promoted a *dramaturgy that would reflect black history, black culture, and issues of *race. The company's first production was the Brazilian première of *O'Neill's *Emperor Jones* (1945); its last was Nascimento's most important play, *Sortilégio: mistério negro* (*Sortilège: Black Mystery*, 1957).   LHD

NATA SANKIRTANA

A devotional ensemble performance held on *ritual occasions in the Meitei society of *Manipur in *India. The oldest form of *nata sankirtana* was *bangdesh pala*, introduced in 1709, followed by *manoharshai pala* (1850); two other variations are *dhrumel* and *dhap pala*. A typical performance is held in the courtyard of a house or a temple, with the *audience sitting on three sides of the sacred performing space. The head of the function (*mandap mapu*) ritually begins and ends the function, and the conch shell sounds to mark the conclusion of each phase. The performance proper is an action between the singer-dancers and the drum-dancers. The singers perform while standing, play rhythmic cymbals, and enact the meaning of the songs in expressive gestures, the lead singer often narrating parts of the story in speech. The drum-playing is accompanied by *dancing with vigorous jumps and *acrobatic turns. The songs, performed in archaic Bengali, concern the life of Lord Krishna and Lord Sri Chaitanya. An alternative tradition of *nata sankirtana*, emerging as part of a Meitei revival movement, uses songs in the Meitei language about the pre-Hindu gods and goddesses of Manipur.

SR

NATHAN, GEORGE JEAN (1882–1958)

American critic. A native of Fort Wayne, Indiana, Nathan began writing dramatic *criticism soon after his graduation from Cornell in 1904. Eric *Bentley described Nathan as 'the leading example of a whole lifetime principally and profitably dedicated to dramatic criticism'. Drama critic at the *Smart Set* from 1909 and its co-editor with H. L. Mencken (1914–23), Nathan joined Mencken to found the *American Mercury* in 1924, where he stayed until 1932, when he founded the *American Spectator*. After 1935 he reviewed for many weekly and monthly publications, including *Newsweek* and *Esquire*. Erudite and given to extended literary comparisons (under which the new playwright usually fared poorly), Nathan described his critical approach as 'intelligent emotionalism'. His early writing was instrumental in switching the critical emphasis away from *acting and onto the play. Quite the opposite from his contemporary Brooks *Atkinson, Nathan mingled enthusiastically with theatre people, dined out nightly at the 21 Club, and passed along scripts and *casting advice. Such actions were typified in Nathan's advancing the careers of Eugene *O'Neill and William *Saroyan.

MAF

NATION, THÉÂTRE DE LA *See* COMÉDIE-FRANÇAISE.

NATIONAL ARTS CENTRE

Canadian arts complex. Created by an Act of Parliament, the National Arts Centre opened in 1969 to assist the 'development of the performing arts' in the nation's capital of Ottawa and elsewhere in Canada. Ambitions to develop a bicultural theatre programme with resident French- and English-language companies *touring Canadian and international work were frustrated by severe funding cutbacks in the 1980s. However, the *opera theatre and studio complex, with its fine resident orchestra, has consistently showcased the performing arts in Canada, with over 16 million *ticket holders attending 22,000 events between 1969 and 1994.

MJD

NATIONAL ENDOWMENT FOR THE ARTS

A federal agency of the United States government responsible for endowing arts programming by public *finance. In the au-

tumn of 1965 President Lyndon B. Johnson signed a bill forming the National Endowment for the Arts in order to 'develop and promote a broadly conceived national policy' in support of the arts. The NEA is headed by a presidentially appointed chairman reporting to the National Council on the Arts, an advisory panel of fourteen citizens with recognized knowledge in the field. Since 1997 the Council is required by law to appoint six members of Congress to serve in an ex officio, non-voting capacity.

Debate over the use of public monies for the arts is longstanding in the American republic, rooted in late eighteenth-century concerns over the function of art in a democracy. While George Washington believed 'the Arts and Sciences essential to the Prosperity of the State', other founding fathers discouraged government patronage on the grounds that emphasis on the fine arts would lead to an excess of luxury (the court of *Versailles was the prime contemporary example). Though the debate continued, unsettled, throughout the nineteenth and early twentieth centuries, support for public art came in a variety of secondary ways: the commissioning of portraits and statues; the establishment of national museums; and ongoing international cultural exchanges. In 1935 Roosevelt's Works Progress Administration began sheltering the nation's first comprehensive federal arts programming (*see* FEDERAL THEATRE PROJECT), but it was discontinued in 1943.

Beginning with its first full-year appropriation of $8 million in 1967, the NEA has made grants to arts institutions, individual artists, and a series of enhancement initiatives that range from support for artists' housing (1965) to *touring programmes designed to bring performing arts to underserved communities (2000). Annual budget allocations have been as high as $176 million (1992). Since inception the agency has been at the centre of varying First Amendment controversies. A significant battle erupted in the summer of 1989, prompted by Senator Jesse Helms's charge that the government was funding 'blasphemy' and 'pornography' in the form of objectionable art and the work of *performance artists like Karen *Finley and Tim *Miller. Though the House of Representatives eventually rejected the Senate effort to end federal grants, a conference committee did pass a series of milder restrictions. Since then ongoing legislative conflagrations have occurred over everything from the fair administration of grants to the agency's continued existence. *See also* ARTS COUNCILS; NATIONAL THEATRE MOVEMENT, NORTH AMERICA.

LTC

NATIONAL SCHOOL OF DRAMA

Premier *training institute in New Delhi, *India, originating as the Asian Theatre Institute in 1958. In 1962 Ebrahim *Alkazi became director and extended the course to a three-year diploma with specializations in *directing, *acting, and stagecraft. A number of initiatives have expanded its mandate: a professional repertory company in 1968; a *theatre-in-education company in 1989; a regional resource centre in Bangalore in 1994 as a step towards decentralization; a National Drama Festival established in 1999. Though the NSD started with a model of Western training, methodology, and aesthetics, it moved towards indigenous work under the leadership of B. V. *Karanth from 1977. The NSD has played a seminal role in revitalizing experimental theatre through its interaction with traditional forms. Alumni actors and directors, including Naseeruddin Shah, Om Puri, Ratan *Thiyam, and Prasanna, have made major contributions to contemporary theatre and *film. For a culturally and linguistically diverse country, however, the NSD's approach has disadvantages, particularly in its acting programme. While the training attempts to be comprehensive, it is conducted primarily in Hindi and English, thereby marginalizing other linguistic and cultural traditions in India.   KJ

NATIONAL THEATRE MOVEMENT, BRITAIN

The movement for a British national theatre took more than a century to get anywhere, and its ends and means changed over time. Effingham Wilson in 1848 proposed a 'theatre wherein the works of Shakespeare, the "world's greatest moral teacher", may be constantly performed'. This edifice was to be purchased by national subscription and held in trust for the nation. In 1879 Matthew Arnold proposed state provision of a West End theatre building and state funding of a company, to play 'a repertory . . . taken out of the works of Shakespeare and out of the volumes of *Modern British Drama*' and to be fed by 'a school of dramatic elocution and declamation'. Arnold's concluding exhortation—'organize the theatre!'—resonated long and loud, but his notion that the state should supply and support the organizing was unrealizable in an economic culture of individual enterprise.

Veterans of 1890s *alternative theatre did, however, envisage a theatre organized on a scale grander than any of them could achieve. William *Archer and Harley Granville *Barker devised and costed a set of *Schemes and Estimates for a National Theatre*, which was privately circulated in 1904 and then published, with an initial statement of approval from four West End *managers and three established playwrights, in 1907. The following year, these and other proponents of a national theatre joined forces with a committee that already controlled a £3,000 bequest for a *London memorial—its form unspecified—to Shakespeare. An amalgamated Shakespearian Memorial National Theatre Committee set out to raise £500,000 in time for an opening in 1916, the tercentenary of Shakespeare's death. Barring the intermittent suggestion that land might be donated by the London county council, the expectation continued to be that a national theatre would be built and endowed by private philanthropy. By 1913, thanks mainly to a single philanthropist, enough had been raised to warrant the purchase of a site between the British Museum and the newly established *Royal Academy of Dramatic Art. That year, moreover, Parliament at least debated a bill proposing the establishment of 'a National Theatre, to be vested in trustees and assisted by the State, for the performance of the plays of Shakespeare and other dramas of recognized merit'. At this point, the apogee of the British Empire, the case for such a theatre in London could be made in terms of cultural imperialism, both as an expression of anglophone reverence for Shakespeare and as a beacon of theatrical excellence sparking provincial and indeed global imitators to reflect, and/or feed, the flame in the capital.

Suspended during the First World War, the Shakespearian Memorial National Theatre Committee were precariously placed in the inter-war years. At the beginning and end of the period they had a building site—the Bloomsbury one was sold in 1922–3 while another, at South Kensington, was bought in 1937—and architectural plans to match. Neither site was big enough for the bicameral building which Barker, revising his and Archer's earlier book under the title *A National Theatre*, recommended in 1930. They had funds, well invested, but nothing like the sum required for the project in the economic climate of the 1920s and 1930s. Yet there was enough in their trust to attract up-and-running ventures that could be designated 'Shakespeare memorial national theatre'. The New Shakespeare Company, presenting the annual festival at the *Shakespeare Memorial Theatre in Stratford-upon-Avon, was given a guarantee against loss for several years, but in 1925 this was deemed illegal. Legal obstacles also protected Shakespearian Memorial National Theatre Committee funds from being used when Lilian *Baylis extended operations from the *Old Vic to *Sadler's Wells. Populist from its inception as a temperance *music hall and prompt to secure the status of an educational charity (and consequent exemption from Entertainments Tax), the Old Vic appeared to embody the inter-war case for drama as means of mass education.

Parliament finally passed a National Theatre Bill in the winter of 1948–9. By then the London county council, planning to redevelop the South Bank, had taken the South Kensington site in exchange for two and a half riverside acres (1 hectare), enough for a tricameral national theatre. The bill authorized payment of £1,000,000 from the Treasury 'to the funds of the Shakespeare Memorial Trust, in respect of the cost of erecting and equipping a national theatre'. Running costs were not mentioned, but other sources of public money would be tapped for both direct and indirect subsidy by the nascent welfare state. (A brand new *Arts Council of Great Britain was already funding the Old Vic company.) The unprecedented socio-economic situation provided additional arguments for a national theatre, such as job creation and post-war recovery. And old reasons were reinvoked in new accents: moral elevation, professional improvement, metropolitan example, national honour, Commonwealth ties, English-speaking union, mass education, middle-class obligation, constructive use of leisure—altogether too much to expect of a single institution. Yet the bill gave no time frame: another fourteen years passed before the *National Theatre came into existence as a playing company, and thirteen more before its building opened. *See also* NATIONAL THEATRE MOVEMENTS, EUROPE; NATIONAL THEATRE MOVEMENT, IRELAND; NATIONAL THEATRE MOVEMENT, NORTH AMERICA; FINANCE; ROYAL SHAKESPEARE COMPANY.   MOC

ELSOM, JOHN, and TOMALIN, NICHOLAS, *The History of the National Theatre* (London, 1978)
WHITWORTH, GEOFFREY, *The Making of a National Theatre* (London, 1951)

NATIONAL THEATRE MOVEMENT, IRELAND

Before the final years of the nineteenth century, Ireland relied on the English stage for its repertoire. After the death of Parnell in 1891, political energies were substantially diverted into cultural nationalism. As part of this broader movement, signalled by the founding of the Gaelic League in 1893, the idea of a national theatre proposed the stage as a crucial site for the assertion and exploration of Irish cultural definition. Proto-*feminist and suffrage organizations, such as Inghinidhe na hEireann (Daughters of Ireland), founded in 1900 by Maud Gonne, created pageants and tableaux celebrating Irish mythic themes. The meeting of W. B. *Yeats, Augusta *Gregory, and Edward *Martyn in 1897 set in motion the establishment of the *Irish Literary Theatre (*Dublin, 1899) with productions of plays by Yeats, Martyn, George *Moore, and Alice Milligan. Parallel to this, Frank *Fay and W. G. *Fay founded the Irish National Dramatic Society, primarily an actors' company, which in 1902 produced Yeats and Gregory's *Cathleen Ni Houlihan*, amongst other plays. The combination of these two groups led to the Irish National Theatre Society in 1903, which toured to *London, attracting the sponsorship of Annie *Horniman. The Society found a permanent home in 1904 at the Mechanics' Institute in Abbey Street in Dublin, and the limited company known as the *Abbey Theatre was born there. The first directors were Yeats, Gregory, and J. M. *Synge. Highly talented members of the acting company, many of whom began as *amateurs, included the Fay brothers, Sara *Allgood, her sister Máire O'Neill (Molly Allgood), Máire nic Shiubhlaigh, Dudley Digges, and Arthur Sinclair. Independently, the Ulster Literary Theatre was founded in Belfast in 1904 and mirrored the aims of the Abbey. These were to create a theatre free of commercial pressures and of European realist trends (*see* REALISM AND REALITY; NATURALISM), an authentic expression of Irish life, myth, poetry, and history. The founding principles, as expressed by Gregory in *Our Irish Theatre* and by Yeats in the journal *Samhain*, bore a constantly changing relationship to the performance practice of the theatre, particularly in the 1920s. In 1925 the Abbey became one of the world's first national theatres to obtain subsidy from a democratically elected government.   CAL

NATIONAL THEATRE MOVEMENT, NORTH AMERICA

The idea of a national theatre reflected broader movements for national self-definition, especially after independence and during periods of social upheaval or revolution. National theatre debates in the United States and in Mexico did not play as central a cultural role as in Europe (*see* NATIONAL THEATRE MOVEMENTS, EUROPE), in part because linguistic differentiation from the former colonial power mattered less than political and economic independence, and in part because size and a relatively dispersed population diluted support for high culture in a remote capital. Calls for a national theatre in Québec, where polemics, institutions, and repertoires emerged under the aegis of *francophonie*, resembled European developments in part, while theatre in the anglophone 'rest of Canada' defined itself initially in opposition to American hegemony and only later as distinctly Canadian.

From the early republic to the Civil War, theatre in the United States reflected rivalry between American *actor-managers and European, mostly British, imports, rather than concern for a national repertoire—although local plays, such as Royall *Tyler's *The Contrast* (1787), introduced the popular theme of the honest American challenging the corrupt European. The founding of the National Theatre in Washington in 1835 and of rivals in *Philadelphia and *New York had less impact than the *Astor Place riot in 1849, when plebeian followers of the American actor Edwin *Forrest battled with police and patrician patrons of the English actor William *Macready, and which encouraged theatres to produce local work such as Harriet Beecher Stowe's *Uncle Tom's Cabin* at the New York National Theatre (1853). Unlike European national theatres, which attempted to combine indigenous repertoires with a standing company, official subsidy, and national legitimization, the American examples were all commercial *managements. Although patriotic themes drew *audiences to commercial theatres in the nineteenth century, and the 'art theatre' movement in the early twentieth generated debate about a national theatre for American dramatic art, subsidized theatre remained largely utopian. An important but short-lived exception, the *Federal Theatre Project (1935–9) subsidized classics, *farces, and a distinctively American form of the *living newspaper until defunded for allegedly un-American communism. Despite the *American National Theatre and Academy (founded 1935) and repeated calls for a national theatre, the twentieth century saw the growth of *regional and ethnically based theatres, partially subsidized by the *National Endowment for the Arts (1965) and equivalent state agencies. Although many of these theatres have national reputations, they do not claim to represent national unity.

In contrast, calls for a Canadian national theatre included pleas for national unity against external threats, especially the US *Theatrical Syndicate. The Théâtre National (*Montréal, 1900) represented Québécois responses to English cultural hegemony and American touring capital, staging Catholic spectacles such as La Passion (1902) and patriotic *historical drama like Laure Conan's Aux jours de Maisonneuve (1921). But, as in central Europe, *folk *revue furnished the central figures of theatrical nationhood; Gratien *Gélinas's Fridolin (1930s) and Tit-Coq (1940s) were hailed alike by popular audiences and intellectual contributors to L'Amérique française. Whereas national theatre projects in Québec were grounded from the outset in arguments for the province's distinct society, both francophone and New World, English-Canadian proposals remained in thrall to British hegemony until the mid-twentieth century. The British Canadian Theatre Organization (1911) resisted the power of the Syndicate by insisting in 1915 that the first National Theatre of Canada was 'British' and the founders of the *Stratford Festival in 1953, including its director, Tyrone *Guthrie, subordinated a 'distinctive Canadian style', along with the festival town and name, to the authority of Shakespeare and the English canon.

From mid-century, the Canada Council (established 1957) provided federal funding for theatre but, despite the National Arts Centre in Ottawa, the gap between francophone and 'English Canada' remained. While Québécois theatre moved from fervent to ironic nationalism with Michel *Tremblay's Les Belles-Sœurs (Sisters-in-Law, 1968) and Claude Levac and Françoise *Loranger's 'patriotic comedy' Le Chemin du Roy (The King's Highway, 1969), English-Canadian drama entered the mainstream only in 1967, the centennial year, and, in R. P. Knowles's view, developed distinctively in regional and local institutions and accents rather than in any nationalist programme 'under one flag [and] one proper accent'. Rapprochement in the late twentieth century happened under the aegis not of nationalism but of multinationalism, as public funding dwindled in favour of corporate sponsorship of festivals like Stratford and the Festival des Amériques, or production companies like Livent. Attempts, especially in Québec, to claim companies like Cirque de Soleil and Robert *Lepage's Ex Machina as national treasures fail against the transnationalization of capital and personnel.

Although shaped by different religious, linguistic, and political traditions, the elites of independent Mexico (after 1822) shared with their counterparts in the USA a taste for romantic nationalism. The Teatro Santa Ana, later Nacional (1844–1900), mixed Spanish and French imports with local romances and *history plays, but the repertoire was increasingly dominated by *zarzuelas. The revolution (1910–20) encouraged plays about peasant rebellion, such as La venganza de la gleba (The Revenge of the Peasant, 1904) by Federico *Gamboa, and, sponsored by Education Minister José Vasconcelos, mass patriotic *spectacles against the backdrop of pre-Columbian pyramids or the new murals he also commissioned. Enduring Mexican types emerged in the 1930s, especially the urban rogue *Cantinflas, as did experimental and socialist groups who challenged sentimental nationalism in the name of international *avant-gardes. National themes and avant-garde forms merged in the 'generation of 1950s', especially Rodolfo *Usigli's trilogy on Mexican mythology produced on a scale comparable to the murals of Rivera, Orozco, and Siqueiros, and by theatres sponsored by the universities and *INBA (National Institute for Fine Arts). Their authority was challenged by student and indigenist movements, whose demonstrations at moments of crisis such as 1968 and 1994 represented an alternative theatrical nationhood to central government institutions. See also FINANCE.   LK

BOURASSA, A., et al., Le Théâtre au Québec: 1825–1980 (Montréal, 1988)

KNOWLES, R. P., 'From nationalist to multi-national: the Stratford Festival, free trade, and the discourse of intercultural tourism', Theatre Journal, 47 (1995)

SALTER, D., 'The idea of a national theatre', in R. Lecker (ed.), Canadian Canons (Toronto, 1991)

VERSÉNYI, A., Theatre in Latin America (Cambridge, 1993)

NATIONAL THEATRE MOVEMENTS, EUROPE

The idea of the national theatre, the movements inspired by this idea, and the institutions established under its aegis in Europe since the eighteenth century have more often than not preceded the nation-state that they claimed to represent. The leaders of these movements and institutions were usually *actor-managers whose social status was ambiguous, or intellectuals who, as members of the educated middle classes, lacked political representation in the monarchies and principalities of the period, and saw in the theatre an institution and occasion for national representation. From the German principalities and the Austro-Hungarian Empire in the eighteenth century to the nineteenth- and early twentieth-century nationalist agitation against Prussian, Austrian, Russian, or Ottoman hegemony in Czech, Slovak, Magyar, Polish, and South Slavic-speaking territories, the founders of national theatres tried to cultivate national consciousness. They strove to create a national repertoire as opposed to the internationally dominant French *comedy and Italian *opera, a national *audience (or at least a public) as opposed to an aristocratic coterie, and a stable public institution in a capital or would-be capital city, as opposed to itinerant troupes, all of which might stand in for the as yet unconstituted nation-state. To be sure, public theatres had emerged earlier, primarily in monarchies whose ruling language was by and large also the language of trade and everyday life: in sixteenth-century Castilian Spain, with playwrights such as Lope de *Rueda and Lope de *Vega in *Madrid; in Elizabethan and Jacobean England, with playwrights from Christopher *Marlowe to Ben *Jonson, and the licensing of the *Queen's Men (1583) and later the King's Men (1603; see CHAMBERLAIN'S MEN, LORD) by the court-appointed *Master of the Revels in *London; in Bourbon *Paris, the *Comédie-Française received an exclusive patent for French drama from Louis XIV in 1680, as did the royal theatres of Denmark (1772) and Sweden (1773) for their respective languages, and, in the Netherlands, a rare republican example, the *Schouwburg opened in *Amsterdam in 1638.

These institutions, like the nation-states housing them, were exceptions in a pre-revolutionary Europe where princes and subjects did not often share a common, let alone national language. The rival regional attempts to create a national theatre, and thus at least the ideal of a nation, out of German-speaking areas divided by religion, dialect, and dynastic politics in the eighteenth century—rather than the single theatre in the capital sponsored by the monarchs of the seventeenth—became the model for nineteenth-century programmes of theatrical nationhood that would resist imperial hegemony (whether Napoleonic, Russian, Prussian, Austrian, or Danish) through national theatre. The first attempt to create a national theatre occurred not under princely patronage but in the free trading city-state of Hamburg (1765–9). The *Hamburg National Theatre founded by actor-manager Konrad *Ackermann, who had previously run a German theatre in Königsburg (now Russian Kalingrad), and the critic Johann Friedrich Löwen (1727–71), who published a defence of a national theatre in 1766, was supported *financially by Hamburg merchants and bankers and critically by the playwright Gotthold Ephraim *Lessing. His play Minna von Barnhelm dealt in part with the dignity of German gentry as against the French, and his *dramaturgical notes on replacing the still dominant French drama with a German national repertoire were published as the Hamburgische Dramaturgie in 1768 (Hamburg Dramaturgy; see CRITICISM). Later German-language national theatre projects in Prussia (Gotha, 1775; *Berlin, 1786; Breslau, 1797), Bavaria (Mannheim, 1777; *Munich, 1778), Saxony (*Weimar, 1791), or Austria (*Vienna, 1776) enjoyed princely patronage and some (as in Gotha or Vienna) suffered royal restrictions on modern themes in the repertoire. The most enterprising included new drama that poured national themes into fluid forms that combined Shakespeare with *Sturm und Drang and purportedly national *costume; The Robbers by Friedrich *Schiller, which had its première in Mannheim in 1782, was the first of a series of his plays on national themes, culminating with William Tell (Weimar, 1803). As the range of competing venues indicates, national theatre was vested less in the territory of a particular polity than in the claims of particular institutions to channel the unifying force of language and culture, especially in the face of outside invasion (by Napoleon). Despite *romantic elements in his plays, Schiller's influential

statement, 'What can a good stable theatre actually achieve?' (1784), rested on Enlightenment principles of moral education, advanced by Lessing and his mentor Denis *Diderot, of 'the stage as a moral institution', and argued that 'in a word, if we . . . have a national theatre . . . we should indeed become a nation'.

While Schiller distinguished between 'the jurisdiction of the stage' and that of 'secular law' to promote 'aesthetic education' of the 'thinking, better half of the people', his mentor Louis-Sébastien *Mercier argued in 1773 for a theatre that might 'illuminate and arm the people as a whole', and so bring together art and mass political action. Mercier's programme and Jean-Jacques *Rousseau's call for assembling the nation in the open air (1758) influenced the festivals that celebrated the anniversaries of the revolution in France (1790 and 1791), as well as the programme of the Théâtre de la Nation (as the Comédie-Française was renamed in 1789), and the other theatres, which benefited from the abolition in 1791 of the Comédie-Française's monopoly on the French repertoire since the seventeenth century and the new assignment of *copyright to authors. The plays and other *spectacles produced during the revolution, such as the five-act *tragedy Charles IX; ou, La Sainte-Barthélemy (1789) by Marie-Joseph *Chénier, Henry VIII (another anti-royalist play by Chénier, 1791), or the operatic setting of 'La Marseillaise', L'Offrande à la liberté, by François Gossec at the Théâtre de la République (formerly the *Opéra) in 1792, may not be canonical literary works, but they reflect a radical, if short-lived, transformation of the institution, the performance forms, and the audience address of theatrical nationhood.

This revolutionary programme would be revived by socialist reformers of the national theatre idea in the late nineteenth-century, such as Maurice Pottécher (1867–1960) of the Théâtre Populaire in Bussang, Louis Lumet (1872–1923) of the Théâtre Civique, and other promoters of théâtres populaires in working-class suburbs in Paris including Jean Jaurès, leader of the Socialist Party, Romain *Rolland, author of Le Théâtre du peuple (1903), and Firmin *Gémier, head of the first *Théâtre National Populaire (1920), which *toured France in a tent before playing the Trocadéro (now *Chaillot) in Paris. Although the first TNP did not last long, it and its predecessors introduced programmatic elements such as *decentralization and popularization by cheap, even free seats, and targeted solicitation of non-theatregoing audiences, which would inform the revived TNP under Jean *Vilar from 1951 and later Roger *Planchon at Villeurbanne in Lyon (1968), and would be copied by regional theatre movements abroad. The first TNP shared with the *Volksbühnen established in Germany in the 1890s, and to a degree with the state socialist theatres of the early Soviet Union, a commitment to transforming the audience as well as the forms of theatre, yet the French programme was understood as national as well as popular, explicitly invoking the revolutionary tradition as French patrimony. The commitment was especially apparent with *mass performances or spectacles like Rolland's *Danton* (staged by Lumet at the Maison du Peuple in Montmartre, 1900) or *The Taking of the Winter Palace* (1919) by Nikolai *Evreinov.

In the decades around the French Revolution, however, it was not the revolutionary subordination of theatre to politics, but rather Schiller's notion of the autonomous 'aesthetic state' that prevailed in Central and Eastern Europe, where national theatre movements challenged the hegemony of French, German, or Russian language and culture by dodging rather than dislodging the political power of the Napoleonic, Austrian, Prussian, and Russian empires. In Poland, the Polish Comedy Theatre was established in *Warsaw by King Stanislas Augustus in 1765 with a Polish adaptation of *Molière's play *The Bores*, but the theatre closed in 1767 and the regime itself fell to aristocratic collusion with the Russians in the first of three partitions of Poland among Russia, Prussia, and Austria in 1772. Only with the ascent of Wojciech Bogusławski (1757–1829), who left a military career for the stage and *managed the Warsaw Theatre on and off from 1783 to 1814, did the repertoire expand to include topical *comedy, such as *Powrót Posła* (*The Return of the Member of the Diet*) by Julius Niemcewics (1751–1841), first produced in 1791. Bogusławski, who was later to claim the Comedy Theatre the first Polish National Theatre (in his *History of the National Theatre*, 1820), wrote and produced *Krakowiacy i Górale* (*Cracovians and Highlanders*) about the Kościuszko uprising against Russian occupation in 1794, in which he also participated. The resulting controversy, and later Prussian occupation of Warsaw, led him to move part of the company to Lvov in then Austrian Poland. He returned in 1799 to Warsaw and the National Theatre, which received a national subsidy from the nominally independent duchy of Warsaw in 1807, including a national drama school from 1811. After the Congress of Vienna in 1815 replaced the duchy with the even weaker kingdom of Poland, the theatre was subject to severe *censorship, and, despite a charter mandating performances in Polish, was allowed only the name 'Warsaw Theatre'. The failed November uprising of 1830 sent thousands into exile, including the romantic poet-playwrights now known as the founders of modern Polish drama, Adam *Mickiewicz and Julius *Słowacki. Mickiewicz's *Dziady* (*Forefathers' Eve*), a messianic drama on Poland's destiny, was written in exile in 1832, but only with its production in 1901 in then Austrian *Cracow by Stanisław *Wyspiański, himself a playwright, could a Polish National Theatre re-emerge, culminating with the Teatr Polski in Warsaw in 1913, five years before the end of the First World War restored political sovereignty to Poland.

Compared to Poland, where the exile of a generation or more of intellectuals and the division of the nation-state among three empires produced a caesura in the national theatre movement, the Czech and Magyar (Hungarian) national theatres benefited from the loosening of German cultural hegemony within the Austro-Hungarian Empire over the course of the nineteenth century, but were nonetheless influenced by the German example. This was especially true in *Prague, where more German than Czech was spoken and where the first Czech production in a designated National Theatre—whose director, Josef von Brunian, knew of the theatre in Hamburg—was a translation of a German *farce, *Herzog Michel* by J. C. Krüger, in 1771. A rival theatre, known from 1797 by the revolutionary name 'Theatre of the Estates', produced the patriotic *Liberation of the Motherland* (1814) by Jan Štěpánek (1783–1844), but by 1846, J. K. *Tyl was still struggling to produce a Czech repertoire at this theatre, and, despite his promotion of a national theatre in the short-lived revolutionary government of 1848, it was not until 1868 that the foundation stone for a fully *Czech National Theatre was laid. In Hungary, the first public performance of a play in Magyar, György Bessenyei's *Tragedy of Agis* (1772), was an adaptation of a play by the German theatre reformer *Gottsched, produced in 1784, the same year that the Habsburgs made German the language of the empire, and the first National Theatre (1821) was not in *Budapest but in Kolozsvár (now Cluj, Romania), in the largely Magyar province of Transylvania. Liberalization of imperial control and the Age of Reform (1825–48) saw the construction of the Magyar Theatre of Pest in 1837, its legislation as National Theatre in 1840, a year after Magyar became the official language, and, in the years before the failed Revolution of 1848, many plays about the plight of the peasants by writers like Ignác Nagy (1810–54) and Ede Szigligeti (1814–78). After the compromise of 1867, which created the 'dual monarchy', Budapest became a major city, but the National Theatre under Szigligeti lapsed, like his own work, into the realm of *operetta. In Norway, a German actor established a permanent theatre in Christiania (Oslo) in 1771 but only with the Nordske Theater in 1850 (and, from 1852, its resident dramatist *Ibsen) did Norwegian replace the Danish imperial language on the stage. Theatre in Finland was influenced by German touring groups in the eighteenth century, when Finland was ruled by Sweden. Professional theatre in Finnish developed alongside Swedish in the nineteenth century, under Russian rule; the Finnish Theatre founded in 1872 became the *Finnish National Theatre in 1902, before political autonomy in 1917.

If nineteenth-century Europe saw the rise of national theatres established in anticipation of nation-states, which were established or re-established with the break-up of the Ottoman, Russian, and Austro-Hungarian empires after the First World War, Europe in the twentieth century, especially after the Second World War, maintained subsidized national theatres such as the TNP in France or the *Deutsches Theater in (East) Germany. It also witnessed the growth of theatre institutions and personalities with European if not international repertoires and reputations, even if the language of performance remained national, such as *Brecht's *Berliner Ensemble, *Grotowski's *Polish Laboratory Theatre, or Giorgio *Strehler's *Piccolo Teatro di Milano. In this post-war period, characterized above all by decolonization, the idea of national theatre was taken up by newly post-colonial nation-states, such as *India (where national theatre projects emerged in the anti-colonial movements of the 1930s) or Nigeria (where the Pan-African National Theatre represented, albeit briefly, Nigeria's confidence in its regional and international power as an oil-rich country in the 1970s), as a means of demonstrating cultural autonomy from the erstwhile imperial centres. In Europe, especially the affluent Western states of the European Union, the subsidy and thus legitimization of regional-language stages appeared to herald the ebb of the nationalist tide in favour of a balance between transnational political economy and regional culture. This is apparent in developments like the Catalan theatre in post-Franco *Barcelona since 1975, or of minority theatres within nation-states, such as Turkish-language theatre in Berlin, home to one of the largest Turkish-speaking populations in the world, since the 1980s. To be sure, the break-up of the Soviet Union and its sphere of influence have led to resurgent, even violent nationalist politics, especially in the Balkans, but the primary vehicles for this nationalism have been the *mass media and the music industry rather than the theatre, which has at least in part provided space for anti-nationalist as well as international performance.

Looking back at the eighteenth- and nineteenth-century national theatre movements through the prism of the international and regional developments of the late twentieth and early twenty-first centuries allows us not only to see the former as a historically grounded phenomenon, but also to perceive more clearly the boundaries and exclusions effected by national theatres in theory as well as in practice. Histories of national theatre in Central and Eastern Europe, for instance, focus on the resurgence of Slavic or Magyar culture against German- or Russian-language hegemony, but tend themselves to be nationalistic, focusing on the more dominant resurgent culture (such as Magyar) at the expense of marginalized minorities (such as Slovak). Even more striking is the almost total omission of the flourishing *Yiddish theatre whose repertoire and audience had international reach as well as regional variation in nineteenth- and early twentieth-century Europe, until the Holocaust left only remnants of Yiddish culture, mostly in the Americas (see also JUDIO, TEATRO). And while calls for a national theatre have been usually accompanied by attempts to produce a national dramatic canon, key performances for the development of the national theatre institution, particularly in revolutionary and socialist theatre in France, have often included farces or patriotic spectacles whose impact has little to do with literary value. As Wilmer suggests, the notions of geographic contiguity, linguistic and cultural homogeneity, and aesthetic consistency that underlie the idea of creating a unified nation through the theatre are often belied by the facts of heterogeneity, *diaspora, and inconsistency—if not outright division. It remains true, however, that ideas and programmes of national theatres flourished in the era of rising nationalism in Europe; the very lack of national unity fed the desire for theatrical nationhood as a substitute for as well as a harbinger of the nation-state, and both persist today despite their inconsistent, if not downright contradictory character. *See also* adjacent entries on NATIONAL THEATRE MOVEMENT, BRITAIN; NATIONAL THEATRE MOVEMENT, IRELAND; NATIONAL THEATRE MOVEMENT, NORTH AMERICA.   LK

BRANDT, G., and HOGENDOORN, W. (eds.), *German and Dutch Theatre, 1600–1848* (Cambridge, 1991)

HEMMINGS, F. W. J., *The Theatre and the State in France, 1750–1905* (Cambridge, 1994)

KRUGER, LOREN, *The National Stage: theatre and cultural legitimation in England, France, and America* (Chicago, 1992)

ROLLAND, ROMAN, *Le Théâtre du peuple* (Paris, 1903)

SENELICK, LAURENCE (ed.), *National Theatre in Northern and Eastern Europe, 1746–1900* (Cambridge, 1991)

WILMER, S. E., 'Reifying imagined communities: nationalism, post-colonialism and theatre historiography', *Nordic Theatre Studies*, 12 (1999)

NATIONAL THEATRE OF GREAT BRITAIN (ROYAL NATIONAL THEATRE)

Honouring Shakespeare and showing that Britain deserved a 'state' theatre like those of its European neighbours were strong motives for the founding of a National Theatre in *London. (The 'Royal' of its title was not approved until 1988, and in 2002 the company began to de-emphasize the regal designation in its *publicity.) Bringing the theatre to life was a long and tortuous process. In 1848 a publisher, Effingham Wilson, wrote a short pamphlet with the grand title *A House for Shakespeare: a proposition for the consideration of the nation*. This he sent to eminent persons whose reactions were mixed, state interference and competition with commercial theatres being among the objections. Effingham gave up hope, but in the 1870s the cause was taken up by Matthew Arnold and Henry *Irving, the man of letters making common cause with the *actor-manager. Their motives were different, however, and in succeeding years the theatre's history seldom ran smoothly, despite the existence of the *Shakespeare Memorial Theatre at Stratford-upon-Avon and the *Old Vic in London, and the efforts of Harley Granville *Barker and William *Archer in the early decades of the twentieth century. (See NATIONAL THEATRE MOVEMENT, BRITAIN.)

Many vicissitudes later, in 1948, both Houses of Parliament voted £1 million towards building a national theatre on the South Bank in London, but not until 1963 did a company, formed and led by Laurence *Olivier, open at the Old Vic with a production of *Hamlet*. Remaining there for over a decade, Olivier produced some highly acclaimed work on a small scale and with a sense of the temporary nature of the enterprise. A board of trustees had been established and a committee of theatre professionals was appointed to advise Denys Lasdun as architect for an impressive new building. He designed two major *auditoriums, the Olivier, with 1,160 seats curved fan shaped around a *thrust stage, and the Lyttelton, with 890 seats on two levels in almost straight rows facing a wide straight-fronted stage. The best of everything was prescribed, including the latest technical equipment that promised to reduce operating costs and make a frequently changing repertoire practicable. In a space originally left conveniently empty, a third auditorium, the Cottesloe, was created in which a stage and some 300 seats could be variously configured. The fittings of this theatre, intended for small-scale and experimental work, were much less luxurious.

Construction was slow and not until 1977 was the National in full occupation with Peter *Hall in charge, having replaced Olivier as director. A red, white, and blue poster, featuring a partially obscured Union Jack, proclaimed that 'The New National Theatre is yours', but it was to face harsh criticism, political manoeuvring, unofficial strikes, and shortage of funds. With the National mocked and envied as the 'establishment', a seemingly tireless Hall fought eloquently for the health and finance of the company. Attracting talented dramatists, directors, actors, designers, and technicians of all kinds, he was criticized for stripping other theatres of the personnel as well as the subsidy they needed. Inevitably, not everyone was pleased: some productions had to be withdrawn or their run curtailed; some of his appointees resigned, accompanied by squalls of publicity. From the start, Hall used a group of associates, including Michael *Blakemore, John *Bury, Jonathan *Miller, and Harold *Pinter, together with the composer Harrison Birtwistle and the *film director John Schlesinger, to meet regularly and advise him on planning and repertoire. In 1988, Hall handed over to Richard *Eyre, director of the National's *Guys and Dolls* and previously *artistic director of the Nottingham Playhouse, a much smaller organization in which he had developed new plays and reworked classics. In 1998 Trevor *Nunn succeeded Eyre, having previously run the *Royal Shakespeare Company and directed a string of successful West End *musicals. In 2001 Nicholas *Hytner was appointed to take over on the retirement of Nunn; he had directed several long-running productions on the National's main stages but had no experience as a director of a theatre building or theatre company.

With changes in leadership and in the political and cultural context, the National developed from a theatre maintaining a wide repertoire of new productions in its own theatres to a more diverse organization. During the first three weeks of September 1977, by which time all three theatres were in operation, nine productions were in the repertoire, four of them of new plays. In the same three weeks of 2001, the repertoire was one visiting production, one revival from a previous season, three new plays, and a UK première of an American double-bill, but that was only part of the National's activity. Three productions from earlier seasons were playing in the West End. In the 1999–2000 financial year, an education department had mounted small-

scale *touring productions, *youth theatre projects, in-service teacher training, workshops, school visits, and much else. The National's Studio, based in the former workshops of the Old Vic, was busy with master classes, *training, play readings and exploratory workshops, and productions. A fundraising development department had raised £2,077,000, or more than an eighth of the theatre's total income.

In common with many theatres, the National's financial situation has never been totally secure. In the 1970s amalgamation with the RSC was discussed informally. The deficit for 1977–8 was £129,971 and for 1999–2000, £291,000. Self-generated income has remained constant at around 50 per cent of expenditure; the other half comes from public subsidy and private sponsorship. In 1975, the *Arts Council commissioned the accountancy firm of Peat Marwick to inquire into the running of the National; a second inquiry followed in 1979. In 1985, Lord Rayner conducted the theatre's own 'scrutiny' of its cost effectiveness, income generation, marketing, organization, planning, and control. A British national theatre has proved as difficult to maintain as it was to establish. Change of direction or artistic director, drastic reduction of output, reliance on proved popular successes, or an increase of touring commitment have all, so far, failed to solve the problems of turning a grand idea into an assured reality.

See also FINANCE; NATIONAL THEATRE MOVEMENTS, EUROPE; NATIONAL THEATRE MOVEMENT, IRELAND; NATIONAL THEATRE MOVEMENT, NORTH AMERICA.   JRB

ELSOM, JOHN, and TOMALIN, NICHOLAS, *The History of the National Theatre* (London, 1978)

HALL, PETER, *Peter Hall's Diaries: the story of a dramatic battle* (London, 1983)

NATIONAL THEATRE SOCIETY *See* ABBEY THEATRE.

NATIONAL YOUTH THEATRE OF GREAT BRITAIN

Founded in 1956 by Michael Croft, the company of boys from Alleyn's School in *London where Croft taught was the first in what would become a UK-wide network of young people's drama groups known as *youth theatres. The first production was of *Henry V* at Toynbee Hall, but by 1960, when the company was recognized as a national organization and given a grant by the Ministry of Education, both boys and girls were applying to join from all over Britain. Initially focusing on Shakespeare, the first contemporary play was David *Halliwell's *Little Malcolm and his Struggle against the Eunuchs* (1966). Thereafter a relationship with playwright Peter Terson led to the commissioning of plays such as *Zigger Zagger* (1967), *The Apprentices* (1968), and *Fuzz* (1969). The first *Arts Council grant was awarded in 1969, and in 1971 the company acquired the Shaw Theatre as a home. The increasingly ambitious programmes developed in the 1970s, which included international *tours and the establishment of a professional company, came under threat when Arts Council funding was withdrawn in 1981. The company moved out of the Shaw Theatre but survived with commercial sponsorship; Croft died in 1986, and was replaced by former NYT actor Edward Wilson. With Arts Council funding restored, in 1998 a National Lottery grant enabled the refurbishment of headquarters in north London. The numerous actors who started their careers with the NYT include Simon Ward, Derek *Jacobi, Helen *Mirren, and Timothy Dalton.   CEC

NATIONS, THÉÂTRE DES

Conceived at a meeting of the *International Theatre Institute (ITI) in 1955, this biennial *festival of international theatre presents a varied programme by companies performing in their native languages. From 1957 until 1968 the festival was held at various theatres in *Paris, including the Théâtre Sarah-Bernhardt, the *Vieux-Colombier, and the *Odéon. Among the most influential companies that participated during the first few decades of the festival were the *Berliner Ensemble, who gave their first performance in the West at the Festival de Paris in 1954, *Milan's *Piccolo Teatro, the *Moscow Art Theatre, and the *Living Theatre. Since 1968 the festival has been itinerant, hosted by cities such as Caracas, Seoul, Baltimore, Venice, and Hamburg, with the participation of 20–30 companies from various nations. In 1998 the ITI established the Academy of the Theatre of Nations, offering workshops for young performing artists.   CHB

NATIVE AMERICAN PERFORMANCE

The ceremonial performances of Native American nations often include *dancing, music, *puppetry, storytelling, sacred *clowns, tricksters, potlatches, purification, and tests of physical endurance. Because there are over 500 Native American nations in the United States alone, the practices and meanings of these ceremonies are as distinct as the various nations who created them. For example, the ancient salt pilgrimage of the Pima or Papago people from Arizona consists of an elaborate four-day journey—complete with *ritual purification, speeches, and fasting—to the Pacific Ocean's salt deposits in California. Conversely, their Hopi neighbours in Arizona are visited yearly by Kachina (spirit messengers) who perform various ritual dances and songs, monitor the actions of adult Hopi people, and initiate Hopi children into the community's belief systems. Each ceremonial event has a specific context and must be understood within the conditions of each Native American nation's unique history, natural environment, spiritual belief system, and kinship structures. Conversely, the secular forms of Native American performance tend to be intertribal, or performed by people from various Native American nations. The *Wild West shows of the late nineteenth century often featured exaggerated versions of *dance forms from different tribal nations. Contemporary powwows, such as Oklahoma City's Red Earth Festival, are intertribal and feature many styles of drumming, singing, and dancing. For example, powwows often include the men's Southern Traditional 'Straight' Dance, which is connected to the Ponca, Osage, Kiowa, Comanche, and Kaw Nations, and the women's Fancy Shawl Dance, created in Northern America in the 1950s by young women who wanted a more colourful and fast-paced style of dance. Regardless of the origin of the dances, powwow dancers freely choose to perform the style they like best.

The history of Native American professional theatre is still being recovered. Although Buffalo Bill (William *Cody) is remembered for hiring Native Americans to perform in his shows, an Ojibwa man named Maungwudaus (George Henry) created his own Wild West production with Ojibwa performers who, between 1844 and 1845, *toured the United States, Great Britain, France, and Belgium. In the 1890s Pauline Johnson (Mohawk) gained minor celebrity by performing her poetry and short stories, which raised political questions about issues affecting Native American and biracial women. From 1919 through the 1980s, a classically trained actress named Te Ata (Chickasaw) created and performed *one-person shows that educated *audiences in the Americas and Europe about various Native American cultures. Also, the playwright Rollie Lynn Riggs (Cherokee) had success with *Green Grow the Lilacs* (1931), later adapted into the *musical *Oklahoma!* And Will *Rogers (Cherokee), who began as a lasso artist in Wild West shows, developed a droll comic persona that turned him into a major star of the stage (*Ziegfeld Follies*) and screen.

In 1956 Arthur Smith Junaluska (Cherokee) founded the American Indian Drama Company, the first modern group devoted to developing professional Native American playwrights and productions. Native American theatre gained momentum with the emergence of the Red Power Movement in the 1960s. In 1962 the Institute of American Indian Arts in Santa Fe was founded to support emerging Native American artists. In 1972 Hanay Geiogamah (Kiowa-Delaware) founded the *politically charged American Indian Theater Ensemble. Geiogamah has continued to devote his career to the development of Native American theatre through organizations such as UCLA's Project HOOP, founded in 1997. In 1975 *Spiderwoman Theater (Kuna/Rappahannock) began its legacy of creating productions that challenge representations of Native American women.

Native American theatre of the late twentieth and early twenty-first centuries is as diverse as the range of experiences encountered by people from various nations. Some plays adhere to a *realistic structure of *climax, while many others challenge the conventions of linear time and the consistency of space. Many plays, such as Marie Clements's (Metis) *Urban Tattoo*, are staged with the use of *film clips and overlapping projections. Other plays, like *Indian Radio Days* by LeAnne Howe (Choctaw) and Roxy Gordon (Choctaw), use an *improvisational style that fosters audience–performer interaction. Productions like Judy Lee Oliva's (Chickasaw) *musical *Te Ata* reclaim history for Native Americans; and other productions, like Victoria Nalani Kneubuhl's (Native Hawaiian/Samoan) *The Story of Susanna*, envision new rituals based upon traditional beliefs. A network of organizations, including the Native American Women Playwrights Archive at Miami University and Native Voices at the Autry Museum of Western Heritage, continues to support this growing theatre movement.   CLS

D'Aponte, Mimi Gisolfi (ed.), *Seventh Generation* (New York, 1999)
Geiogamah, Hanay, and Darby, Jaye (eds.), *American Indian Theater in Performance* (Los Angeles, 2000)

NAT PWE

Trance-dance in *Myanmar (Burma) based in indigenous animistic spirit worship. Besides Buddhism, ancient animistic *nat* spirit worship underlies religious beliefs in Burma. *Nats* encompass nature spirits, guardian spirits of Buddhism, and 37 spirits based on legendary or historical figures. The latter were officially canonized during the reign of King Anawaratha in the mid-eleventh century and they are the focus of *nat pwe* performances. Accompanied by a small orchestra of drums and gongs, a female or male shaman called *natkadaw* (spirit wife) goes into trance while dancing and assumes the character of the *nat* that is to be propitiated. The shaman thus functions as intermediary between the human and spirit realm as healer or oracle, giving offerings and in turn receiving protection for the community or individual that has commissioned the performance. A major festival of *nat pwe* is held in Taungbyon where numerous *nat pwe* groups gather for annual *rituals. The *dance of a female *nat* votaress constitutes an important opening sequence in most Burmese performing arts such as in *zat pwe* (classical dance-drama) and in *yokthe pwe* (*puppetry). In the latter, the dance is performed by a *natkadaw* *marionette.
                                                                    KP

NATURALISM

Although the term has come to be applied to any drama which depicts recognizable *characters in everyday situations, naturalism properly refers to a nineteenth-century European movement influenced by positivist sociology, natural history, and empirical scientific method. It is marked by a realistic representation of contemporary life, in *acting, writing and *mise-en-scène, with an emphasis on revealing the darker corners of social experience not usually acknowledged in bourgeois society. Although theatrical *realism was hardly new, it took on particular importance in *Paris in the 1880s. Émile *Zola's ad-

vocacy of naturalism in his own novels prepared the way for his polemical *Naturalism in the Theatre* (1881), which demanded that the naturalist experiment be repeated on stage, which was mostly given over to harmless entertainments in the tradition of the *well-made play. Henri *Becque's *Crows* (written 1876), about the sexual and financial corruption of a family, did not find a production for six years and then was coolly received. Meanwhile adaptations of Zola's novels, notably *Thérèse Raquin* (1867), *Nana* (1881), and *Germinal* (1888), compromised too readily with conventional dramatic forms, and the scientific scrutiny of the novels seemed cheapened as a result.

The first successful naturalist theatre was *Antoine's Théâtre *Libre (1887). The opening production included a short piece by Zola, *Jacques Damour*, and the company was soon celebrated for its intimate acting style and the detailed authenticity of its settings. Antoine removed the *footlights, dimmed the *auditorium, and experimented with stage *lighting. He championed foreign dramatists of a naturalist bent like *Tolstoy, *Ibsen, *Strindberg, and *Hauptmann. The Théâtre Libre sparked similar independent companies across Europe: *Brahm's *Freie Bühne in *Berlin (1889), *Grein's *Independent Theatre in *London (1891), Strindberg's *Intima Teatern in *Stockholm (1907). Italian realism, *verismo, produced important naturalist plays, such as *Giacosa's *Sad Loves* (1887) and *Like the Leaves* (1900), and *Capuana's *The Rosary* (1912); the movement's most acclaimed writer, Giovanni Verga, successfully adapted some of his stories for the stage, including *Cavalleria rusticana* (1884) and *The She-Wolf* (1896).

Antoine often spoke of his indebtedness to Zola, whose own inspiration lay not just in novels of Balzac and Stendahl but also in Darwin, Taine, and Comte. In his *Course in Positive Philosophy* (1830–42) Auguste Comte argued that the history of the human mind shows a progression from theological to metaphysical and finally to scientific (or positive) understanding of the world. In the preface to the second edition of *Thérèse Raquin* Zola's scientism is visible in his assertion that he is dissecting the behaviour of his *characters as dispassionately as a surgeon in an operating theatre. Hippolyte Taine's highly deterministic view of human behaviour, most clearly expressed in *History of English Literature* (1864), assumed that the human being is 'a machine with well-arranged cogs; he is a system'. Taine argued that behaviour was determined by *race* (inherited factors), *milieu* (social and political environment), and *moment* (the historical forces that bear upon the present). This displacement of morality and divinity from the field of human endeavour was still shocking to a society reeling from Charles Darwin's view of humanity created not by the invisible hand of God but by gradual adaptation to the environment. The application of Darwinian natural history to society (social Darwinism), fostered by writers like Herbert Spencer who saw society as a struggle between the weak and the strong, is a pervasive presence in naturalist writing.

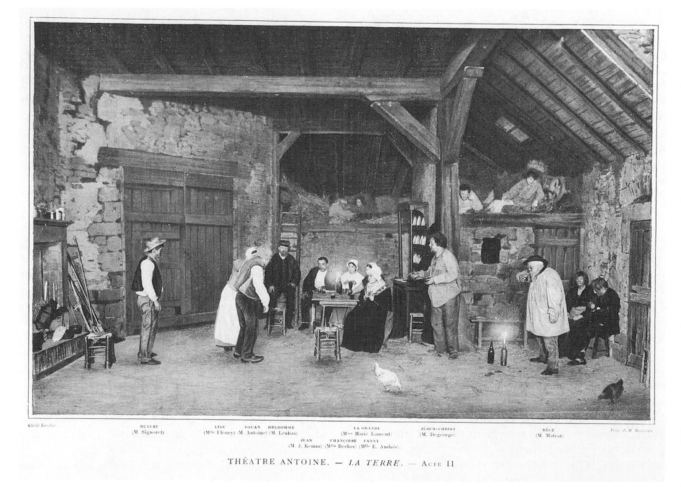

THÉATRE ANTOINE. — *LA TERRE.* — Acte II

A prime example of French **naturalism**, Zola's *La Terre* (*The Earth*), Théâtre Antoine, Paris, 1900. André Antoine's production brought the mundane material realities of the poor on stage, including a live chicken pecking at the ground. Three actors to the left (including Antoine as the old man) have their backs to the audience, a characteristic of Antoine's mise-en-scène that violated accepted principles of French acting.

Despite the broadly liberal or socialist views of many naturalists there is often a political ambiguity, notably in Ibsen's and Strindberg's work, between extreme individualism and its critique. There were considerable theatrical and philosophical anxieties in the naturalist enterprise as well, and the *audience's sense of the fictiveness of the theatrical event was in many ways heightened, rather than suppressed, by the highly theatrical innovations for which the naturalists were famous. The theatre's own techniques and traditions of representation also interfered with a naturalist playwright's single-minded apprehension of reality; not only are most naturalist plays visibly shaped, albeit unconsciously, by the structures and styles of *melodrama or the well-made play, but the collaborative nature of theatre makes it hard for a single vision to dominate. Indeed writers found themselves displaced by the *director in the very form they had so vehemently called for, as the demands of increased realism necessitated a single eye that could place

the script in a coherent visual structure (*see* SCENOGRAPHY). Naturalism's bequest to the theatre was not just a theatrical *genre but the figure of the director as well.

If naturalism had wished to follow Comte's abandonment of metaphysics it would have had to jettison many of the techniques that help shape aesthetic experience. In the most artistically successful plays of the naturalist period there is a tension between undiluted representation and *symbolism that suggests a struggle between materialism and idealism in late nineteenth-century European culture. In the prose plays of Ibsen, metaphors and imagery abound, eventually subsuming the realistic impulses within them. In *An Enemy of the People* (1883), Dr Stockmann discovers that the town's famous spas are infected with disease. He properly observes that this is not unlike the municipal corruption he encounters as he tries to expose it, yet the suspicion remains that the affinity is as much artistic as it is sociological. Throughout Ibsen's work metaphors seem to transcend the purely rational, from the fire at the orphanage in *Ghosts* (1882), which never entirely expels the implication of divine retribution, through the complex web of imagery behind the title of *The Wild Duck* (1884), right up to the white horses of *Rosmersholm* (1887), and the sexual guilt that mysteriously haunts the action of *Little Eyolf* (1895).

*Chekhov represents another approach to the naturalist experiment. In place of the psychological breakdowns of Strindberg and the political passions of Ibsen and Zola, Chekhov wrote with a detached calmness that put *action into the background. The intriguing authorial blankness of *Three Sisters* (1901) and *The Cherry Orchard* (1904) has allowed them to be appropriated as *boulevard *comedies by the English stage and as harbingers of the revolution by the Soviets. Chekhov's plays are witty and ironic, sometimes bleak, sometimes broadly comic in tone; yet his collaborating director, *Stanislavsky, developed a detailed naturalist mise-en-scène for them at the *Moscow Art Theatre. Stanislavsky's influential *theories of *acting tended towards an internalization of the actor's craft, and suited the *bourgeois, individualist aspects of naturalism more than they did its *political and critical role.

Naturalism in the theatre was always a tensile and fissured project. Despite its relatively short flowering, the theatre of the twentieth century was largely given to working out its contradictions. Strindberg's journey is instructive: naturalism was a short-lived phase in his work, and in plays like *The Father* (1887) and *Creditors* (1889) the project of uncovering truths about others pulls the *protagonists' minds apart, perhaps leading directly to the symbolist and proto-*expressionism of *A Dream Play* (1907), *To Damascus* (written 1898–1904), and *The Ghost Sonata* (1908). The symbolist theatres of Paris in the 1890s were indebted to naturalism as much as they turned away from its every principle. Naturalist devices continue to dominate the contemporary stage, even when *playwrights and directors— most searingly, *Brecht—rebel against its strictures. Although in some quarters it has become a byword for unimaginative and pedestrian acting, in its succession of controversies, innovations, and manifestos naturalism should be seen as a vitally experimental theatre, perhaps the first theatrical *modernism.

DR

BRAUN, EDWARD, *The Director and the Stage* (London, 1982)
CARTER, LAWSON A., *Zola and the Theatre* (Westport, Conn., 1977)
SCHUMACHER, CLAUDE (ed.), *Naturalism and Symbolism in European Theatre* (Cambridge, 1996)

NATYADHARMI

The stylized mode of *acting in *Indian performance traditions, as determined by the intricate codes and conventions of acting in ancient encyclopedic texts like the *Natyasastra. The word *natya* connotes more than drama insofar as it encompasses a simultaneous knowledge of music, *dance, literature, and all the mythic, emotional, and psychophysical resources associated with these disciplines. Drawing on different styles (*vritti*) of presentation—the graceful (*kaisiki*), the grand (*sattvati*), the energetic (*arabhati*), and the verbal (*bharati*)—natyadharmi relies on one of the most rigorously codified systems of gesture, movement, and voice in world theatre. *See also* ABHINAYA; LOKADHARMI.

LSR/RB

NATYASASTRA

Earliest known Sanskrit compendium on *Indian *dramaturgy, *dance, and *acting, attributed to the sage *Bharata. Allegedly written almost two millennia ago, this encyclopedic text has incorporated interpolations over the years which have been tacitly approved by generations of gurus and performers. In the opening chapters, the divine origin of drama is established with a graphic description of how the first play was enacted— and interrupted—in the presence of gods and demons by Bharata and his sons. The *open-air performance was later shifted to a *natyagriha* (*playhouse), which has three architectural models: *vikrista* (oblong), *caturasra* (square), and *tryasra* (triangular). Apart from prescribing how particular gods have to be worshipped on these stages, the *Natyasastra* also elaborates on the *purvaranga* (the preliminary scene) and the *ritualistic ceremonies preceding the performance.

Broadly dividing the art of acting into two different modes, *natyadharmi (stylized) and *lokadharmi (real), the *Nastyasastra* outlines numerous components of dance, drama, *music, and *spectacle. Apart from dealing with dance through a detailed description of *karanas* (movements of hands and limbs), *angaharas* (combinations of different *karanas*), and *recakas* (movements of limbs), it also outlines at least three kinds of *angikabhanaya (acting with body): *mughaja* (facial), *sarira* (related to limbs) and *cestakrita* (movements of the entire body). The nature of *nritta* (pure dance) in relation to *abhinaya (acting) is also dealt with through descriptions of *hastas (hand gestures), *caris* (leg movements), *sthanas* (body postures), and *gatis* (gaits) suitable for different *characters, situations, places, and occasions.

The *Natyasastra* attaches great importance to *rasas (aesthetic sentiments) in acting. There are eight *rasas*: *sringara* (erotic), *hasya* (comic), *karuna* (pathetic), *raudra* (furious), *vira* (heroic), *bhayanaka* (terrible), *bibhatsa* (odious), and *adbhuta* (marvellous). Later *shanta* (peace of being) was included as the ninth *rasa*. The respective *sthayibhavas* (dominant states of emotion) relating to the *rasas* are *rati* (love), *hasa* (mirth), *soka* (sorrow), *krodha* (anger), *utsaha* (energy), *bhaya* (terror), *jugupsa* (disgust), and *vismaya* (astonishment). There are also 33 *vyabhichari bhavas* (transient emotions), which together with the *vibhavas* (determinants of the emotional states) and the *anubhavas* (consequents) stimulate the dominant state of *rasa*.

NAUGHTON, BILL

Apart from *angikabhinaya*, the *Natyasastra* attaches great importance to **vacikabhinaya* (vocal acting), which outlines the differences between Sanskrit and the less refined regional languages of Prakrit; the fundamental aspects of *kavya* (poetry); the rules of dramatic composition; the characteristics of different metrical patterns and prosody. The chief characteristics of the ten kinds of plays (*dasarupaka*) and the *sandhis* (junctures in the action of a drama) are discussed elaborately in connection with different combinations of vocal and instrumental music.

In addition to physical and vocal acting, the *Natyasastra* also elaborates on **sattvikabhinaya* (acting of the innermost sentiments) and **aharyabhinaya*, which is concerned with the histrionic and visual possibilities of *costumes, *make-up, ornaments, weapons, and carriages. The geographic divisions of the acting area in relation to entries and exits, and the positions and postures of the actors, are dealt with in the section dealing with *kakshyavibhag* (zonal division). Ultimately, since the art of drama has to be appreciated by an *audience, the *Natyasastra* emphasizes the characteristics of an ideal *preksaka* (spectator) and the aesthetic preparation needed for the full appreciation of *rasa*.

The closing chapter of the *Natyasastra* deals with how *natya* (drama) descended to earth from heaven. In the course of time it appears that the sons of Bharata, intoxicated with their skills in acting, began to misuse the art. Consequently, they were cursed by angry sages, but later consoled and advised to go to earth and propagate the art of drama for the good of humanity. Reflecting a unity of purpose and integrated vision of dramaturgy with related arts, the *Natyasastra* remains an invaluable reference for all classically *trained artists in drama, music, and dance, as well as for contemporary Indian artists inspired by traditional resources.   KNP

GHOSH, MANMOHAN, *The Natyasastra Ascribed to Bharat Muni* (Calcutta, 1967)

NAUGHTON, BILL (1910–92)

English dramatist and novelist. His first stage successes, *All in Good Time* (1963) and *Spring and Port Wine* (1964), are gentle *comedies of Lancashire working-class life, adapted from earlier *radio plays. *Alfie* (1963) is a darker metropolitan comedy, and its 1966 *film version, scripted by Naughton and starring Michael Caine as the promiscuous antihero (*see* HERO), was an influential portrait of social and sexual change in the 1960s. Naughton's later work included the futurist *satire *He Was Gone When We Got There* (1966) and *Lighthearted Intercourse* (1971), which returned to the social comedy of his earlier work.   SF

NAUMACHIA

The most extensive form of dramatized punishment at Rome (*damnatio*) was the *naumachia*, a staged naval battle based upon a real or imaginary episode from Greek history that demonstrated the emperor's control over human resources and simultaneously his power to re-create history. In 46 BC Julius Caesar staged a historically unattested engagement between 'Tyre' and 'Egypt' on a custom-built lake at Rome; after his death the lake was filled in. In 2 BC Augustus dug an enormous lake in Trastevere so as to stage the battle of Salamis (480 BC) during the inaugural celebrations for the temple of Mars Ultor, which commemorated the avenging of Caesar's death. Excluding marines, 3,500 men were involved. The result was faithful to the historical outcome: 'Athens' won. In AD 52 Claudius used a *naumachia* as an advertisement for an engineering project by staging a sea battle between Rhodes and Sicily on the Fucine Lake just before he drained it in a land-reclamation scheme; 19,000 prisoners participated; some survived. Some emperors effected a miracle by flooding a venue associated with terrestrial displays: in AD 80 at the 100 days of celebrations to inaugurate the Colosseum a small *naumachia* was held in the Colosseum itself to re-enact a battle between Corfu and Corinth from the Peloponnesian War. An emperor might also rewrite the past. During the same inaugural celebrations Augustus' lake was the venue for a re-enactment of the Athenian expedition against Syracuse later in the war (414 BC), but this time history was reversed in that the 'Athenians' routed the 'Syracusans'. The island that stood in the middle of the lake was interpreted as Ortygia, the island outside Syracuse, and captured by the 'Athenians', thus combining a naval battle and an infantry engagement. Domitian (AD 81–96) and Trajan (AD 98–117) constructed their own lakes for *naumachiae*. The last recorded *naumachia* in the city was staged by Philip the Arab in AD 248 to celebrate Rome's millennium.
                                    KMC

NAUTANKI

*Hindi- and *Urdu-language theatre popular in the villages and towns of northern *India that combines sophisticated folk singing and drumming, *dancing by female artists and transvestites, and dramatic recitation of poetic tales. *Nautanki* belongs to the class of rural theatre forms originating in pre-modern South Asian contexts, like *jatra* of Bengal, *tamasha* of Maharashtra, and *bhavai* of Gujarat, that have become urbanized popular entertainments to varying degrees. *Nautanki* is performed at fairs, religious festivals, and weddings. Troupes may be sponsored by a patron (often a merchant or landlord) or booked for *ticketed performances, and the personnel come from a mixture of castes with artisan groups dominating. *Audiences are drawn from the semi-urban working class and agriculturalists, and include women and children (though they are often discouraged from attending).

Stories of romance are prevalent in the secular *nautanki*, with *plots frequently derived from legends of Arabic, Persian, or Indo-Islamic origin, for instance, *Laila Majnun* and *Shirin*

Farhad. The *genre is named for the Princess Nautanki, an alluring heroine famed for her delicacy and beauty. In these dramas pure love is pursued even unto death, though romance is also combined with ascetic virtue in cautionary tales that warn against the dangers of sensual attachment, and some plays (*Satyavadi Harishchandra*) laud saints who renounced sexuality. Martial prowess is another preoccupation: the tale of Amar Singh Rathor, an officer in Shah Jahan's army, shows Rajput chivalry in full flower. Many legends of the *Alha-Udal* epic, a heroic cycle from the Bundelkhand region of Uttar Pradesh, were dramatized as *nautanki* in the early twentieth century and local outlaws like Sultana the dacoit are also celebrated in the repertoire. Of particular interest are plays focusing on heroic women. The avenging warrior woman (*virangana*) may appear as Virmati, the Rani of Jhansi, or the bandit queen Phulan Devi.

In the nineteenth century *nautanki* was composed entirely of songs and recitative. Beginning in the early twentieth century, prose passages and comic skits were interpolated, and now an evening's show is generally introduced by dance and comedy. With the advent of the *mass media the frequency of *nautanki* performances began to decline, and shows in the mid-twentieth century incorporated songs, dances, and stories from Hindi *films. Yet several veteran artists, like Gulab Bai, have received national honours, and directors such as Habib *Tanvir, Bansi Kaul, Anuradha Kapur, and Urmil Thapaliyal have adopted its features into their productions or made successful adaptations of traditional *nautanki* stories for urban audiences.

KH

HANSEN, KATHRYN, *Grounds for Play: the nautanki theatre of north India* (Berkeley, 1992)

NAUTICAL MELODRAMA

Form of *melodrama popular in Britain and the USA (but not France) in the first half of the nineteenth century, reflecting the high reputation of the navy in the two anglophone countries after the Napoleonic Wars. The trend roughly coincided with the career of T. P. *Cooke, who created many of the great parts, including the faithful William in Douglas *Jerrold's *Black-Ey'd Susan* (1829). The *genre began in the 1790s with J. C. Cross's wordless melodramas at the Royal Circus, and continued with battles on stage with realistic ships at *Sadler's Wells after the installation of a large water tank; thereafter the popular figure of the British Tar fought Frenchmen, Americans, pirates, and wreckers on many stages, especially at the Surrey Theatre. The British Tar first clearly appeared as Will Steady in Cross's *The Purse; or, The Benevolent Tar* (1794). He was called something like Harry Hallyard or Jack Junk, and spoke in strange nautical metaphors; he was fearless, generous, patriotic, plain-spoken to his superior officers, and good at the hornpipe. *Gilbert and *Sullivan satirized many of these familiar characteristics in *HMS Pinafore* (1878), *The Pirates of Penzance* (1879), and

Ruddigore (1887); but nautical melodramas continued to surface from time to time until the end of the nineteenth century, when William *Terriss appeared as a sailor in *The Harbour Lights* (1885) and *The Union Jack* (1888).

EEC

NAVAJAS, ESTEBAN (1948–)

Colombian playwright and anthropologist, a founding member of Teatro *Libre Bogotá (1973). His greatest hit, *La agonía del difunto* (*The Dead Man's Agony*, 1997), has been performed in many countries and translated into several languages. In 1994 he was *awarded the best play prize at the Colombian National Playwriting Competition for *Fantasmas de amor que rondaron el veintiocho* (*Love Ghosts that Hover about the Twenty-Eight*).

BJR

NAVARRE, MARGUERITE OF (1492–1549)

French poet and dramatist. Sister of François I of France, consort of Henri II of Navarre, and author of the *Heptameron*, Marguerite also wrote four spiritual *comedies and several secular plays ('théâtre profane'), all acted, or intended to be acted, before aristocratic *audiences. The four *biblical plays are loosely modelled on *medieval *mysteries, the seven secular plays on contemporary *farce and *morality drama. *Most, Much, Little, Less* (1545–6) is a *satire on the clergy; *The Passing of the King* (1547) commemorates the death of François I; *Mont de Marsan* (1548) is a delightful examination of human and divine love.

RWV

NDAO, CHEIK ALIOU (1933–)

Senegalese writer. After study in France and Wales, he taught English in Senegal and became fascinated with the court life and traditions of its ancient kingdoms of Senegambia. His plays reimagine African *history in order to recover heroic figures of the past. *La Case de l'homme* (*The Lodge of the Initiate*, 1973) treats traditional customs, especially the initiation associated with circumcision *rituals. Three plays are devoted to the rehabilitation of heroes of anti-colonial resistance: *L'Exil d'Albouri* (*Albouri's Exile*, 1967), *Le Fils de l'Almamy* (*Almamy's Son*, 1973), and *Du sang pour un trône; ou, Gouye Ndiouly un dimanche* (*Blood for a Throne; or, Gouye Ndiouly one Sunday*, 1983). Two further works, *La Décision* (1967) and *L'Île de Bahila* (1975), treat American history. His work has been performed in many African countries and has earned him a reputation far beyond Senegal. He has also written two volumes of poetry and a number of novels. Although he publishes in French, Ndao remains a strong advocate of a literature in African languages, especially in Wolof, his mother tongue.

OD trans. JCM

NDÉBÉKA, MAXIME (1944–)

Congolese dramatist and novelist. He was introduced to *political theatre during his studies at Patrice Lumumba University in *Moscow, and in 1970 was appointed Director-General of Cultural Affairs in Congo (Zaire). In his first play, *Le Président*, produced in *Paris and published in 1973, he depicts the successive political crises his country experienced after independence. Imprisoned for involvement in a military plot against the government, he explored his incarceration in *Les Lendemains qui chantent* (*Brighter Tomorrows*, 1982) and *Equatorium* (1987). In the second play Ndébéka intersperses historical sequences with burial *rituals, enthronement, and divination ceremonies. After a brief return to the Ministry of Culture, he moved to France, where he devotes his time to writing and the theatre.

PNN trans. JCM

NEDERLANDER, JAMES (1922–)

American theatre owner and *producer. The Nederlander Organization started in Detroit under James's father. By the 1990s, with James long at the helm, it claimed to operate the largest chain of *legitimate theatres in the world. Though it later sold some to the new behemoth, Clear Channel/SFX/PACE, it remains second only to the *Shubert Organization on Broadway, where it controls nine theatres (such as the *Gershwin, *Palace, Lunt–Fontanne), with half a dozen more in *Los Angeles, Detroit, and *Chicago, and three in *London (*Aldwych, *Adelphi, Dominion). Following the increasing tendency for theatre owners to co-produce, the Nederlanders have been most successful with *musicals (*Nine, Applause, La Cage aux Folles*), imports (*The Dresser, Noises Off, Copenhagen*), and revivals.

CR

NEGRITO

*Character from the nineteenth-century Cuban *teatro* *bufo*, a vernacular figure of African descent, usually played by a white actor. Influenced by the North American *minstrel shows that *toured the island around the turn of the century, the *negrito* was a racist, pointedly satirical version of a member of the dispossessed classes.

AV

NEGRO ENSEMBLE COMPANY

*African-American theatre company, founded with the aid of a Ford Foundation grant in 1967 to fill a *racial void in the theatre. Charismatically led by the actor-playwright Douglas Turner *Ward, who had initially sparked its creation, the NEC became the home of African-American plays and actors, though it was occasionally criticized for locating outside Harlem in St Mark's church *Off-Broadway. Despite its fine work, five years after opening the future was uncertain, forcing the NEC in 1972–3 to eliminate its resident company, trim the staff, and produce only one play per season. Relief came with a series of *critical and *financial successes, including the Broadway transfers of Joseph Walker's *The River Niger* (1973), Charles *Fuller's *A Soldier's Story* (1981)—both of which won important *awards and were *filmed—and Sam-Art Williams's *Home* (1979). In 1980 NEC moved uptown to 55th Street, within reach of Broadway, but money again became troublesome; it abandoned the bigger house in 1988 for a series of rented theatres. Despite a history of national and international *tours and acclaim, by 1991 the company carried a half-million dollar debt, and was forced to reduce its output once more before closing its doors for good.

BBL

NEHER, CASPAR (1897–1962)

German designer, whose career was inextricably linked with that of his schoolfriend Bertolt *Brecht. From 1918 to 1922 Neher studied in *Munich. His first stage design was for *Kleist's *Das Käthchen von Heilbronn* (*Heilbronn's Casket*, *Berlin, 1923), and his collaborations with Brecht began with *The Life of Edward II* (Munich, 1923) and *Baal* (Berlin, 1926). Thereafter Neher worked closely with Brecht and his disciple Erich *Engel, designing the premières of *In the Jungle of the Cities* (Munich, 1923) and, most famously, *The Threepenny Opera* (1928). Neher also designed for Leopold *Jessner and Max *Reinhardt in Berlin, and from 1927 to 1932 was head of design for the municipal theatre in Essen. In the 1930s he began to design for *opera, and starting in 1940 had a productive collaboration with Oscar Fritz Schuh in *Vienna and in Hamburg, particularly with a series of *Mozart productions. From 1946 to 1949 Neher was at the *Zurich Schauspielhaus, working again with Brecht (*Antigone*, 1948); in 1949 they reunited in Germany at the *Berliner Ensemble, where Neher designed some of the most famous productions. Characteristic of Neher's style was a spare, anti-*illusionistic stage which stressed use of space rather than pictorial elements. Design elements frequently highlighted *theatricality, citing historical styles or *genres, sometimes employing projections. The famous, bare, *Brechtian stage was largely Neher's invention. *See also* SCENOGRAPHY.

CBB

NEIGHBORHOOD PLAYHOUSE

*Little Theatre opened on *New York's Lower East Side in 1915 by sisters Irene and Alice Lewisohn to house the Neighborhood Players, a *community theatre group originating in the sisters' social work at the Henry Street Settlement House from 1902. Working initially with large groups of poor immigrant children, the Lewisohns hoped to find 'symbolic imagery' that would unify and provide meaning to their actor-audiences from around the world. Organizing entire families through the children, the Lewisohns developed processions, *dances, and *rituals designed to awaken 'the creative play instinct' in the participants, sometimes numbering as many as 500. The sisters added a dramatic club in 1912 for older children, supplemented by volunteer actors from around the city, presenting short plays in libraries and other spaces. Encouraged by public interest in the idealism of the enterprise, the Lewisohns began in 1913 to plan their own theatre, visiting Max *Reinhardt's theatres in *Berlin and the *Dalcroze–*Appia Theatre at Hellerau. The 390-seat Neighborhood Playhouse opened in 1915. Their meticulously *rehearsed productions of short plays by such authors as John *Galsworthy, Lord *Dunsany, and Anton *Chekhov were supplemented by children's theatre, the cultural festivals, and classes in sewing, painting, and dance. A professional company was established in 1920 and staged 43 productions before folding in 1927. The Neighborhood Playhouse School of the Theatre survived the closing of the company and from 1935 was associated with Sanford *Meisner and his *Stanislavskian approach to *actor *training. *See also* YOUTH, THEATRE FOR.

MAF

NEKROŠIUS, EIMUNTAS (1952–)

Lithuanian director. Nekrošius trained under Andrei Goncharov at the State Institute for Theatre, *Moscow; after graduation he worked at the State Youth Theatre, *Vilnius, where he produced his own adaptation *Love and Death in Verona* (a rock *opera based on *Romeo and Juliet*, 1982) and Aitmatov's *A Day Longer than a Century* (1983). During the 1980s his productions focused on *characters close to death, experiencing a last burst of energy (Eliseeva's *The Square*, 1980; Korostylev's *Pirosmani, Pirosmani*, 1981). In his two *Chekhov productions (*Uncle Vanya*, 1986; *The Three Sisters*, 1995) Nekrošius offered fresh readings of plays often crippled by the restraints of psychological *realism. He directed *Pushkin's *Mozart and Salieri* (1994) and Shakespeare's *Hamlet* (1997) for the Lithuanian International Theatre Festival (LIFE). Since 1998 he has headed his own theatre in Vilnius, Menofortas, where he directed *Macbeth* (1999) and *Othello* (2000). His productions impress by their clarity and their closed system of visual references, where the narrative is created through a series of images and their variation.

BB

NELSON, RICHARD (1950–)

American playwright. After graduating from Hamilton College, Nelson received a fellowship to study drama in *Manchester. His early plays, *The Killing of Yablonski* (1975), *Conjuring an Event* (1976), and *Jungle Coup* (1978), reflect both Nelson's criticism of American political reportage and his enthusiasm for Sam *Shepard. Later Nelson entered what he called a 'classical' phase which emphasized elements of *Brecht and *Chekhov to create a more ironic *political drama. The first 'classical' work to appear was *Principia Scriptoriae* (1986), a play about two political

activists who were tortured in a Central American country. It failed in the United States, but won British acclaim in a *Royal Shakespeare Company production directed by David *Jones. Since then Nelson has written a series of plays exploring Anglo-American themes which have premièred in Britain, including *Some Americans Abroad* (1989), *Two Shakespearean Actors* (1990), *New England* (1994), *The General from America* (1996), and *Goodnight Children Everywhere* (1997). His adaptations include plays by *Molière, *Strindberg, Chekhov, and Dario *Fo. He is an honorary associate artist of the RSC.

JAB

NEMIROVICH-DANCHENKO, VLADIMIR (1858–1943)

Russian director, playwright, and *dramaturg. After a period as a *critic, he trained actors at the Moscow Philharmonic Society's Institute of Music and Drama from 1891 to 1902. His desire for a contemporary repertoire and better performance standards nurtured a union with *Stanislavsky, and together they founded the *Moscow Art Theatre (MAT) in 1897. Nemirovich-Danchenko's literary and organizational skills complemented Stanislavsky's success in *acting and *directing. They co-directed many early productions, with Stanislavsky often acting a major role, including the four *Chekhov plays (1898–1904), and *Gorky's *Philistines* and *The Lower Depths* (both 1902). As dramaturg, Nemirovich-Danchenko interested *Moscow in *Ibsen and *Hauptmann and directed *Julius Caesar* (1903) in a new historical *realist style. His hallmark as a director was a close reading of the *text to extrapolate authorial intention within an examination of social and historical context. His working relationship with Stanislavsky, under strain for several years, broke down as their differences built into opposition, causing Stanislavsky to resign from the MAT board in 1908. Nemirovich-Danchenko directed classic productions at this time, including *Griboedov's *Woe from Wit* (1906), *Pushkin's *Boris Godunov* (1907), and controversial new adaptations of Dostoevsky (*The Brothers Karamazov*, 1910; *Nikolai Stavrogin*, 1913). Nemirovich-Danchenko founded a musical *studio at MAT in 1919, producing *operas and *operettas by *Offenbach, Bizet, and *Verdi. In the 1930s he brought MAT back into political favour by staging *Gorky (*Egor Bulychov and the Others*, 1934, and the revised *Enemies*, 1935) as models for *socialist realism, but with MAT's exacting standards still in place.

CM

NEOCLASSICISM

Historical/critical term, describing European drama, literature, and the fine arts that acknowledged the influence of the literary culture of Greece and Rome. A fairly recent coining, it is absent from general dictionaries and from specialist works of reference until about 1930. In its most straightforward use, neoclassicism is interchangeable with 'classicism'—though this term, whose primary meaning was 'suitable for use in the classroom', was adopted only in the mid-eighteenth century. The movement now often known as neoclassicism is largely, though not exclusively, a French phenomenon. Seminal works like Du Bellay's *Défense et illustration de la langue française* (1549) argued that the way to eclipse Italian Renaissance (*see* EARLY MODERN PERIOD) achievement, and to establish French literature as the pre-eminent equivalent of that produced by the ages of Pericles and Augustus, was through close familiarity with the classical texts and faithful imitation of the models handed down by the ancients.

The head start gained by Italian Renaissance *theorists and commentators, and by playwrights in both *tragedy and *comedy, was already yielding to French competition by the turn of the century; and by the end of the 1630s, when *Mairet's *Sophonisbe*, *Corneille's *Médée*, and *Rotrou's *Hercule mourant* had proved to be successful embodiments of the classical formula, the force of example was able to ensure the victory of 'regular' tragedy based on the theoretical principles derived from *Aristotle and his Renaissance commentators. Irregular *tragicomedy had had its day, despite the success of Corneille's *Le Cid* (1637); and in his Roman plays from *Horace* (1640), *Cinna* (1640), and *Polyeucte* (1642) onwards, as well as in his theoretical writings, Corneille became his generation's leading practitioner of neoclassical tragedy. Its principal features were a five-act structure closely adhering to the *unities: a single setting (unity of place), a single, closely related series of events (unity of *action), and a concentration of this action into a single day (unity of time). The *Greek *chorus had by now been dispensed with; superfluous action took place offstage, and was narrated onstage by one of the small number of ancillary *dramatis personae: servants, messengers, or *confidants of the main *protagonists. This is what Lytton Strachey, writing about *Racine's *Bérénice* (1670), was to call the aesthetic of 'concentration', by contrast to the Shakespearian aesthetic of 'comprehension' illustrated in *Antony and Cleopatra*. Both in his plays on historical subjects (such as *Bérénice*) and in his adaptations of Greek mythological subject matter, of which *Phèdre* (1677) stands as the supreme example, Racine exploits to the full the possibilities of the neoclassical dramatic idiom. His contemporary *Molière was able to realize, in the no less testing medium of five-act *verse *comedy, a dramatic form capable of expressing both a sophisticated portrait of the society of his own day and a provocative theatre of ideas, as in *The Misanthrope* (1666), *Tartuffe* (1669), or *The Learned Ladies* (1672). By the time of Racine's retirement from the theatre after *Phèdre*, there was a growing feeling in France that the aims of the neoclassical crusade were well on the way to being achieved.

If we set the programme of the playwrights and poets of the seventeenth century in a broader context, it is no wonder that their cultural imperialism had come to be regarded as the counterpart—indeed, as an integral part—of the successful political imperialism of *Richelieu and Louis XIV, for courtier-poets were already flattering the King by comparing the Age of Louis to the Age of Augustus. When *Boileau published his magisterial *Art poétique* in 1674, his survey of the development of dramatic art in France was presented from the vantage point of one who was fortunate enough to be living in a period of cultural fulfilment; throughout the controversy between the 'Ancients' and the 'Moderns' towards the end of the century, the position held by Boileau and his allies was that the literature of the modern age was still far from establishing itself as the equal of that of the golden ages of antiquity, yet, paradoxically, the only way to strive for such equality was to imitate the masters of the remote past. While the regular tragedy, as established by Corneille and Racine, did not go unchallenged in the theatre, the creation of what was in effect a national theatre (the Théâtre Français, founded in 1680 under royal patronage; *see* COMÉDIE-FRANÇAISE) helped to maintain a hierarchy of *genres, in which the popular machine-plays (*see* SALLE DES MACHINES) and other mixed-genre forms took second place to the revivals of seventeenth-century tragic masterpieces, which were accompanied by the attempts of less gifted authors to produce new masterpieces through the application of increasingly mechanical formulas rather than through genuine inspiration. In comedy, the hierarchy was just as rigid, with the 'grandes comédies' (five *acts in verse) taking pride of place, even if the theatre-going public came more and more to prefer the freer compositions of the *Comédie Italienne and the fairground players.

Particularly in tragedy, when we come to the eighteenth century it seems that the guiding principles were no longer positive and creative but negative and restrictive, the 'rules' being overshadowed by the dead hand of the *bienséances* (*decorum), those conventions which governed what could and could not be shown on stage or expressed in verse. Reported offstage action, circumlocution, and the avoidance of the material and commonplace are features of the Racinian manner, but when these same features constantly recur in the work of less talented imitators, the term neoclassicism almost inevitably acquires a pejorative connotation. In *Voltaire (whom many contemporaries judged to be the equal in tragedy of Corneille, if not of Racine) we find a man of letters who was forward-looking and iconoclastic in his thinking, but a fervent supporter of the status quo in matters of dramatic composition; and nothing illustrates this better than the scorn he pours on the 'ignoble' phrase 'Not a mouse stirring', with which Shakespeare chooses to indicate the stillness of the night in *Hamlet*, as a feature quite incompatible with the dignity of tragedy. Voltaire in particular was prepared to use the neoclassical form to produce tragedy with a philosophical (especially an anticlerical) message; but his mind remained closed to any modification of the neoclassical aesthetic.

The dead hand of this aesthetic, hardly challenged at all at the ultra-conservative Comédie-Française through a good deal of the eighteenth century, was to be seen first and foremost in a declamatory *acting style, producing static (even statuesque) delivery; in derivative forms of writing, which shunned any suggestion of local colour in favour of abstract rhetoric; in *costume, where attempts at *realism in portrayal of historical period were regularly defeated by the determination of leading actors, male and (particularly) female, to show off their own sumptuous wardrobe; and in *mise-en-scène, where any call for greater realism in setting was frustrated by the presence of scores of onstage spectators. Voltaire was quite prepared to accept the status quo, dismissing English attempts at historical realism with the comment that a couplet of alexandrine verse was more effective on stage than a whole army of supernumeraries. However, the stage was freed from spectators in 1759, and the pioneering attitudes to costume of Mlle *Clairon and *Lekain did gradually achieve something of a breakthrough; but the language of tragedy remained an arcane idiom.

Elsewhere in Europe Shakespeare found a more ready acceptance and French cultural imperialism failed to sweep the board. Although the neoclassical formula was exported with some success to other European lands—in *Addison's *Cato*, *Johnson's *Irene*, *Gottsched's *Der sterbende Cato*, or some of the plays of *Maffei and *Alfieri—playwrights and their publics outside France on the whole remained much more eclectic in their choices. While *Goethe, for instance, produced in *Iphigenie* (1787) one of the most perfect neoclassical dramas of his time, as well as the most stirring embodiment of the century's 'Humanitätsideal', his *Götz von Berlichingen* (1773) looked towards Shakespeare for the form in which to express *Sturm und Drang* fervour. *Schiller was likewise capable of writing a play of wholly classical inspiration like *The Bride of Messina* (1803), alongside the sprawling history trilogy *Wallenstein* (1798–9). It is revealing that Constant, while writing an appreciative account of *Wallenstein*, nonetheless felt obliged to reduce it for a French public to the style and idiom of a Voltairian tragedy (*Wallstein*, 1809).

The cultural relativism of a new generation was to spell the end of the dominance of neoclassicism, even in France. Madame de Staël's *De la littérature* (1800) had shown the way; Guizot's *Shakespeare et son temps* (1821) and Stendhal's *Racine et Shakespeare* (1823) led to *Hugo's *Préface de Cromwell* (1827), before the final showdown occasioned by the production of *Hernani* in 1830. The 'bataille d'*Hernani*' was between two generations: the predominantly conservative establishment of the Comédie-Française and their diehard supporters, versus the young promoters of *romanticism who succeeded in carrying the day (*see* HERNANI RIOTS). Henceforward, dramatists might choose to write on 'classical' subjects, from Ponsard in *Lucrèce* (1843) down to *Cocteau in *La Machine infernale* (1934) and *Anouilh

in *Antigone* (1944), but the idiom of French neoclassical tragedy would never be resurrected.   WDH

JONES, THORA B., and DE BEAR NICOL, B., *Neo-classical Dramatic Criticism, 1560–1770* (Cambridge, 1976)

HOWARTH, W. D. (ed.), *French Theatre in the Neo-classical Era, 1550–1789* (Cambridge, 1997)

NEPALI THEATRE

Theatre in Nepal owes its origin to ancient myth, *folklore, and religious practices. Legend has it that the oldest Nepali *dance dates from the ninth century, composed by the Buddhist deity Vairochan. The Licchavi rulers of the Kathmandu valley (AD 200–879) were great patrons of the arts, and left behind a performance culture later adopted by the Malla Dynasty (1200–1767). King Pratap Malla 'Kabindra' of Kathmandu (1641–74) was a virtuoso of classical dance and performed frequently at Nyasal Chowk in Hanuman Dhoka. Many other Malla rulers were playwrights or choreographers.

Early performances in the valley were held on a *dabu* or *dabali*, a 60 cm (2 foot) stone platform, while every *chowk* (street junction) and *bahil* (courtyard) could have been used as a stage for dance and theatre troupes narrating tales of the gods and the demons. After the unification of Nepal under the Shah Dynasty in 1767, the Kathmandu valley performance, though it appeared insular, had absorbed some of the theatrical traditions of *India encountered earlier in the Malla era; one of the major influences was the romantic *Parsi theatre popular in north India.

When the Ranas assumed power in 1846 and controlled the monarchy, all public performances were banned (*see* CENSORSHIP), as well as public education, though religious performances continued among the indigenous communities of the Tarai plains and the hills. Ironically the Ranas, imitating European architecture and styles, imported the concept of *proscenium theatre for their private entertainment during the late nineteenth century. The plays performed in Hindi and Urdu were thoroughly influenced by styles prevalent in Indian theatre, and Calcutta (*Kolkata) became the port of call for *training, especially for the aristocracy. Despite the restrictions of the Rana, Moti Ram Bhatta adapted and staged *Shakuntala* (1892), thereby becoming the first recognized Nepali playwright and director. Eight years later, Manik Man Tuladhar, Nepal's first commoner theatre professional to be trained in Calcutta, returned to stage the play *Indar Sabha* (1900). Tuladhar attempted to institute a *ticket system and a fenced-in stage. But Chandra Sumsher Rana, then Prime Minister, fearing rebellion against the ruling class, summoned Tuladhar to run his private theatre at Singh Durbar which was the largest *playhouse in the country (until it was destroyed by *fire in 1973). By the early 1900s the resident envoys of the British Raj had built temporary stages for their private viewing, using European *scenography and stage effects; some of these techniques

Nepali dancers in heavy costumes and masks in a street performance in Mustang, Nepal, 1996.

were adopted for public performance by Kasai Paltan, a theatre troupe from the underprivileged community of Kathmandu.

Bal Krishna Sama, born into the Rana family, is recognized as the father of modern Nepali theatre. Sama was grandson of Dambar Shumsher, a Calcutta-trained drama expert, and found himself opposing his clan by writing plays for the populace. His first work, *Tansenko Jhari* (*Rain in Tansen*, 1923), inaugurated a golden age of the Nepali theatre; his fifteen plays, *comedies, *tragedies, and *historical dramas, remain the most influential in Nepali *dramaturgy. Gopal Prasad Rimal's *realistic play *Masan* (*Crematorium*, 1945), portraying social conflict and women's demand for social justice, set theatre in a new direction. After the establishment of democracy in 1951, Nepali society looked for reform in all the arts, and playwrights like Govinda Malla 'Gothale' and Vijaya Malla in the 1950s furthered the cause of realistic and *naturalistic plays.

In 1962, after implementing a no-party political system, King Mahendra, a poet and lyricist himself, began to institution-alize literature and the arts. In theatre, however, few major developments occurred until the arrival of *street theatre troupes like Sarwanam (1981), proscenium theatre practitioners like Arohan (1981), and the indigenous Maithili drama troupe, Janakpur-based Mithila Natya Parishad (1980). After the restoration of multi-party democracy (1990), theatre workers became development activists, performing plays under 'awareness' campaign banners (*see* DEVELOPMENT, THEATRE FOR). This sponsored work tended to restrict artistic progress, but with the opening of a chapter of the *International Theatre Institute in 2000, and the consequent links made with international companies, Nepali theatre has found encouragement for a new wave of experimentation.   SS

NEPTUNE THEATRE

The regional theatre of Halifax and the largest company in Atlantic Canada. It produces about six plays per season in a

480-seat former *vaudeville house and cinema; extensive renovations completed in 1997 added a 180-seat theatre, studios, and offices. The first production was *Shaw's *Major Barbara* (1963), which was repeated after the 1997 remodelling. Its general repertory, like most regional theatres, is a mix of classics, modern classics, recent successes from larger centres, and the occasional locally written play. The company was founded on the *Manitoba Theatre Centre model, with *artistic director Leon Major (1962–8) reporting to a community-based board. Other artistic directors have included John *Neville (1978–83) and Linda Moore (1990–2000). *Touring, especially to schools, has always been an important part of Neptune's mandate.

DWJ

NESBITT, CATHLEEN (1888–1982)

English actress. She first distinguished herself in 1912 with the *Abbey Irish Players, appearing in *New York and *London in the plays of *Synge and *Yeats. She also played Perdita in Granville *Barker's *The Winter's Tale* in 1912. During the First World War she acted in the USA, taking on roles in *Galsworthy and *Shaw, and returned to London in 1919 to play the lead in *Webster's *The Duchess of Malfi*. In the 1920s she performed mainly in modern works, and in 1935 played Katherine in *The Taming of the Shrew*. She *toured in Shakespeare with the *Old Vic company in 1939, and in 1940 played Goneril in *Gielgud's *King Lear*. During the Second World War she performed in England, but in 1950 shifted to America for the next two decades, notably in plays by T. S. *Eliot and Tennessee *Williams. On occasion she returned to London, appearing, for example, in Robin Maugham's *The Claimant* (1964). She continued to act into her nineties. In 1974 she published an autobiography.

TP

NESTROY, JOHANN NEPOMUK (1801–62)

Austrian actor and dramatist, who made his debut in 1822 as Sarastro in *Mozart's *The Magic Flute* at the *Vienna Court Opera House. Following successful engagements as a singer in *Amsterdam, *Brno (Brünn), and Graz, he returned to Vienna in 1831, where he quickly established himself as a popular comedian in the suburban theatres. His coarse and aggressive *acting affronted *bourgeois *audiences, however, and political authorities repeatedly intervened against his poignant criticism of Church and state. To avoid *censorship, he became a master of the extempore, for which he was several times imprisoned. He began writing plays in order to provide himself and his associates with adequate roles, and following the success of *The Evil Spirit Lumpazivagabundus* (1832) he became the most popular playwright in Vienna. Displeasure with the censor's interventions into his *texts forced him into dangerous high-wire acts of *improvisation and *mime, which made him an idol of the op-

position forces before the 1848 Revolution. Nestroy's style was the reverse of the pious, romantic, and apolitical plays of Ferdinand *Raimund, then the most admired Viennese writer for the popular stage. Nestroy's plays are full of caustic caricatures and acerbic commentaries on the social ills of the *Vormärz* era. He was an astute observer of the class conflicts of his time and of the effects industrialization had on the craftsmen and urban poor. He was also an adroit wordsmith, whose skill in both Viennese dialect and literary language was complemented by his sophisticated body language in performance. Despite his ironic scepticism he preserved a streak of human kindness, best expressed in his roles of social underdogs and nonchalant losers. Nestroy keenly observed the 1848 Revolution and exposed the political immaturity of the Viennese bourgeoisie in the *satirical *comedy *Freedom Comes to Krähwinkel*. Following the defeat of the revolution, he wrote some of his most melancholic works, including the bleak, dystopian *farce *Chief Zephyr; or, The Gruesome Banquet*. Of his more than 80 plays about a dozen are still regularly performed, some of these in adapted form also outside Austria, including *Der Talismann* (*The Talisman*), *Das Mädl aus der Vorstadt* (*The Girl from the Suburbs*), *Einen Jux will er sich machen* (adapted by Thornton *Wilder as *The Merchant of Yonkers* and *The Matchmaker*, and by Tom *Stoppard as *On the Razzle*), *Der alte Mann mit der jungen Frau* (*The Old Man with the Young Wife*).

GB

NETHERSOLE, OLGA (1863/1870–1951)

English actress and *manager. First appearing in *London in 1887, she gravitated toward the roles of fallen or unconventional women, beginning with a revival of *Sardou's *Diplomacy* in 1893. During the 1890s and 1900s she managed several London theatres for short periods, often performing plays by *Dumas *fils*, *Sudermann, and *Pinero. Her success as an emotional actress in siren roles carried her to *New York, where she was arrested in 1900 for the supposed moral indecency of Clyde *Fitch's *Sappho*. She won an acquittal and much fame, which made her a star in both New York and London. She retired in 1914.

TP

NEUBER, CAROLINE (WEISENBORN) (1697–1760)

German actress and *manager. The daughter of a lawyer, she eloped with the student Johann Neuber in 1717 to join an itinerant theatre troupe, eventually establishing their own company in Leipzig. Between 1727 and 1737 she was closely associated with the professor of literature and dramatist J. C. *Gottsched and together they initiated one of the most important reform projects in German theatre. Their changes were directed initially against the dramatic forms popular at the time, which were a mixture of *Haupt- und Staatsaktionen and *Hanswurst comic interludes. Neuber devoted her energies to improving the status of actors as well as purifying the repertoire. In 1737 she symbolically banned Hanswurst from the stage by burning a *puppet dressed as the comic figure. The gesture had more symbolic than immediate consequences, however; after falling out with Gottsched her influence waned and her troupe fell into disfavour. She died impoverished and largely forgotten.

CBB

NEVILLE, JOHN (1925–)

English actor and director. At the *Old Vic, he notably alternated as Iago and Othello with Richard *Burton (1955), played Romeo to Claire *Bloom's Juliet (1956), and Hamlet with Judi *Dench as Ophelia (1958). In the 1960s he worked at Nottingham Playhouse as actor, associate producer (1961–3), and joint director (1963–7). After moving to Canada in 1972, he became director of the Citadel Theatre, Edmonton (1973), where he invited Peggy *Ashcroft to appear in *Beckett's Happy Days (1977). He became director of the Neptune Theatre, Halifax (1978), and *artistic director of the *Stratford Festival (1986–9), where his productions included Hamlet (1986), Mother Courage (1987), and The Three Sisters (1989). VRS

NEW COMEDY

The *comedy of Greece and Rome from the late fourth to the second century BC. *Greek New Comedy emerged from the *Middle Comedy of the fourth century with the work of *Menander, but so vague is the nature of the transitional period that some commentators choose to refer only to *Old Comedy (fifth century BC Athens), and New Comedy (anything after the defeat of Athens in the Peloponnesian War in 404 BC). That the war had brought an effective end to *political comedy is beyond dispute, for Menander's world is one where the central issues are those of family life. Though only two of his plays have survived more or less complete—and those, The Bad-Tempered Man and The Woman from Samos, were not published until after 1957— substantial sections of others survive. *Plots revolve around love affairs and means of bringing them to successful conclusions in marriage; disputes over children and their legitimacy; misunderstandings over relationships. The location is usually Athens or the countryside of Attica, and the *characters are recognizable types distinguished in the main by age, class, and gender. Gods are reduced to the occasional *prologue and the *chorus to entr'actes which the manuscripts omit. The formula might seem constricting, especially as it was also adopted by Menander's main rivals, Philemon and Diphilus. But the plays of Menander were crafted with considerable skill. Though still acted in *masks and, for the most part, in the Theatre of *Dionysus now rebuilt in stone, the range of situation and character

is both complex and subtle, allowing for pathos and even tragic potential. Menander's plays are farcical in parts but look forward to the whole European tradition of serious comedy, serious in the sense that the characters are worth taking seriously.

After the death of Philemon in about 263 BC, New Comedy in Greece went into stagnation. It re-emerged in Rome with the work of *Plautus (c.250–184 BC) and *Terence (193 or 183–159 BC), both writing in Latin. Twenty plays of Plautus have survived, more than from any other playwright in the ancient world, and all six of those written by Terence, who drowned when still quite young. Both playwrights confessedly adapted their work from Greek Middle and New Comedy originals anything up to 200 years old. This *Roman comedy was known as *fabula palliata, 'comedy wearing the pallium', a short Greek cloak. The plays were set in Greece or a Greek city; the characters are Greek and live according to a Greek morality, in strong contrast to the staid and respectable world of the Roman Republic; even the metre and the ethos are Greek with 'citizens' meaning Athenians, anyone else being foreigners.

Borrowing from one or more plays by Menander and other Greek comic writers was known as contaminatio, but the plays of Plautus and Terence were much more than simple translations. Though no Greek play survives to compare with its Roman counterpart, there are enough indications in the prologues of Terence and elsewhere to show that the Latin playwrights prided themselves on the originality of their approach and, further, that plagiarism was a charge that might well be levelled at one playwright by a rival. There are many aspects of the work of both Plautus and Terence which are wholly un-Greek. The plays were presented on makeshift *stages—no permanent theatre was allowed in Rome until the first century BC—during Roman public festivals. They vied for attention with the alternative attractions of the fairground. There is a strong colouring from Roman public life in Plautus and in Terence; there are metatheatrical in-jokes; and especially a love of words and wordplay with puns, alliteration and, despite the metrical form, the argot of the street. In other ways Plautus and Terence are very different. Plautus was a writer of *farces with a strong enough *musical content for some to consider him the founder of comic *opera. Still performed in masks, they provide one strand of the Italian street tradition which, combined with the local comedy of the fabula atellana, would eventually turn into the improvised comedy of the *commedia dell'arte. Terence wrote more Menandrian comedy, less broad and with hardly any slapstick, but his characters are living and breathing. In the fourteenth century Petrarch revived the study of Terence, and an enthusiasm for both Terence and Plautus was confirmed by the rediscovery of a missing Plautine manuscript in 1428 and the commentary on Terence by Donatus five years later. Performances in translation were regularly presented at the court at Ferrara and, together with the commedia dell'arte, provided a platform for the whole European tradition of physical and character comedy.   JMW

HUNTER, R. L., *The New Comedy of Greece and Rome* (Cambridge, 1985)

SANDBACH, F. H., *The Comic Theatre of Greece and Rome* (London, 1977)

NEW LAFAYETTE THEATRE

*African-American company founded in *New York in 1967 by Robert Macbeth with major foundation support, which was lost in 1973. It encouraged black writers to avoid stereotypes, and gave impetus to the careers of playwrights Ed *Bullins and Richard Wesley, actors Roscoe Orman and Sonny Jim, and critic Larry Neal.   BBL

NEW THEATRE

Built as a philanthropic gesture by wealthy *New Yorkers to bring theatre to the masses, the New Theatre was designed in an ornate *neoclassical style that belied it as a people's theatre. It opened with *Antony and Cleopatra* in 1908. Subsidized for two more years by its well-meaning patrons, it was then leased (with a name change to the Century) to a succession of commercial *producers, who had no better luck in luring *audiences to Central Park West and 62nd Street. Sold in 1929 and torn down a year later, it was replaced by an apartment building.
                                                                MCH

NEWTON, CHRISTOPHER (1936–)

English-Canadian actor and director. Newton came from England to the USA for graduate studies and, after a brief academic career, began acting professionally in 1961 with the Canadian Players. After acting in regional theatres, in *New York, and for three seasons with the *Stratford Festival, in 1968 he was appointed founding *artistic director of Theatre Calgary. In 1973 he moved to another Canadian regional theatre, the *Vancouver Playhouse, where he revitalized the artistic fortunes of the company and established a prestigious professional *training school. In 1979 he was appointed artistic director of the *Shaw Festival, where he developed a highly skilled semi-permanent acting ensemble dedicated to the plays of Bernard *Shaw and his contemporaries. Newton is perhaps the world's leading interpreter of Shaw and *Coward, having directed at least twenty of their plays, including Shaw's *Misalliance* (1980, 1990), *St Joan* (1981), *Caesar and Cleopatra* (1983 and 2002), *Heartbreak House* (1985), *You Never Can Tell* (1988 and 1995), *Man and Superman* (1989), *Pygmalion* (1992), and *The Doctor's Dilemma* (2000). In 1995 he was made a Member of the Order of Canada. He left the Shaw Festival in 2002.   DWJ

NEW VAUDEVILLE

A strain of late twentieth-century American performer or performance, merging popular-entertainment traditions and a mischievous, *avant-garde sensibility. The term came into use in the 1980s to describe a new generation of artists using tried-and-true performance skills as vehicles for the critique of contemporary society and of performance itself. The *vaudeville reference may have been intended to evoke the *music-hall nature of skills employed—like *clowning, ventriloquism, *magic, and *juggling—as well as a consummate showmanship, even as the very foundations of *genre and performance underwent radical reinvention. However, Ron Jenkins's *Acrobats of the Soul* (1988), which might otherwise be considered a defining document for the movement, dismisses the New Vaudeville label, preferring to emphasize a self-deprecating clowning spirit with which virtuoso skills are wielded to puncture the conceits of post-industrial society. A marked recognition of the *audience's actual presence and expectations also characterizes the genre.

Often described as a thinking person's entertainment, New Vaudeville has been most readily associated with displays of physical mastery, including work by Bill *Irwin (clown and eccentric dancer), Michael Moschen (juggler), Paul Zaloom (ventriloquist), the Flying Karamazov Brothers (jugglers), and Penn and Teller (illusionists). The successful fusion of mass and high art, and the New Vaudevillians' ironic, self-referential preoccupations with technological society explain why they often surface in discussions of postmodern performance, along with other movements that seek to mix the popular with the experimental. *See* MODERNISM AND POSTMODERNISM.   EW

NEW YORK

The city's future pre-eminence as the theatre capital of America and one of the great theatrical centres of the world was not evident in the earliest years of its colonization. The Dutch, who founded and settled at the tip of the island, which they named New Amsterdam in the seventeenth century, were pious and hard-working, but had little in the way of theatrical heritage. In 1664, the settlement was gradually and peacefully integrated into the embryonic British Empire and renamed New York (after King Charles's brother James, Duke of York), and slowly became an integrated English village. With prosperity came social amenities and the spark to ignite culture. In 1699, one Richard Hunter petitioned the English governor John Nanfan for a licence to perform plays, but nothing more is known of his efforts. Other tantalizing bits of information suggest that there might have been *amateur theatrical activity during the early years of the eighteenth century, but the first hard evidence comes from the 1730s, when a map appeared showing a theatre on Broadway. There may have been two small rival theatres in operation during this period, one in Abraham Corbett's Tavern on Broadway and another in a building owned by Rip Van Dam, sometime acting governor of the colony, both evolving from the growing native disaffection with English rule.

1. 1700–1800; 2. 1800–1900; 3. Since 1900

1. 1700–1800

Historical and circumstantial evidence, as scanty as it is, has tended to support a theory that all theatrical activity during the first half of the eighteenth century was amateur and that the *playhouses were makeshift and temporary expedients. Certainly such activity was not encouraged either officially or from the pulpit, where it was roundly condemned as the devil's handiwork. The frequency of travel between the mother country and America would have exposed American visitors to Restoration theatre in *London, then very active and prolific. But if there was interest in the theatre during this period in the colony, it was very likely confined to drawing rooms or to large public rooms of taverns. Itinerant bands of *acrobats, *animal *circus acts, and *marionettes may also have made periodic stops in the developing city. Professional activity arrived at mid-century and brought in its wake the first theatres built specifically for the production of plays.

When the monopolizing effects of the *Licensing Act of 1737 in England began to take effect, actors and *managers became refugees from its strictures and sought out the English-speaking New World for venues. Little is known of the first troupes and their disappearance from the colonies is shrouded in mystery. Whether they arrived on the American continent from the island of Jamaica, which was proving to be a hospitable site to theatrical entertainers (see CARIBBEAN THEATRE, ANGLO-PHONE), cannot be ascertained but is probable. The appearance of an early troupe was heralded by an advertisement in the *New York Gazette-Weekly Post-Boy* for 20 February 1750, which announced that performances would be held in a 'convenient Room' in one of Rip Van Dam's buildings on Nassau Street, probably the same that had been fitted up for a theatre in 1732. The troupe played until the summer and returned in the autumn, this time listing the name of the managers of the company, Walter Murray and Thomas Kean, and departing in summer 1751 for other colonies. A list of their performances preserved through newspaper advertisements closely resembles a standard *repertory of a minor English company.

The next tenant of the theatre in Nassau Street was Robert Upton's company, which appeared not to have prospered as well as the Murray–Kean troupe, and also disappeared shortly after its stay in New York. Encouraged, however, by the seeming success of theatrical activity in America, a London manager, William Hallam, dispatched his brother Lewis at the head of the London Company of Comedians, landing in Virginia, then moving to New York in 1753 (see HALLAM FAMILY). With the persistent prejudices against theatre in the city, the company was unable at first to gain official permission to perform, but Hallam eventually obtained a licence, demolished the theatre in Nassau Street, and constructed a new one in its place. Their stay in New York lengthened to eight months, after which, in 1754, they transferred to Jamaica, where Lewis died.

Another transplanted English actor, David *Douglass, after marrying Hallam's widow, gathered up the remnants of the old London Company, augmented it with other English actors in exile, and sailed from Jamaica for New York in 1758, ready to begin fresh ventures. Finding no trace of the old Nassau Theatre, Douglass built the first of his three playhouses in New York on a wharf owned by John Cruger, Jr., in the ceremonial post of mayor, who was a supporter of Douglass's plans. Official difficulties prevented Douglass from playing more than a few months at the Cruger's Wharf Theatre, and the company decamped for *Philadelphia early in 1759.

In 1761, when he returned to New York, Douglass made sure to secure the proper licences, but things did not go smoothly for his company in the new theatre in Beekman Street, just north of the old Nassau Street playhouse. Sharper attacks from the pulpit against the immorality of the theatre (see ANTI-THEATRICAL POLEMIC), revulsion over the money spent on such frivolity, and growing anti-English sentiment led Douglass to suspend his activities in New York and move on to more hospitable colonial cities in 1762. When he again returned in 1767, he had changed the name of his troupe to the American Company of Comedians. He built his last and most ambitious playhouse, the *John Street Theatre, just east of Broadway, then the main thoroughfare and most prestigious address in the burgeoning city. Although the theatre was described later by William *Dunlap, a future chronicler of New York's theatrical history, as 'principally of wood, an unsightly object, painted red', it was to serve the city for the next 30 years. It survived use by the British occupation troops and the American Revolution, and was abandoned only when the city was ready for a structure of more elegance and comfort. When a ban was imposed in 1775 on all activities that did not serve the revolution, Douglass returned to Jamaica and lived out his days there. But unquestionably it was Douglass who laid the groundwork for the establishment of a permanent theatre in New York and the other colonial cities.

What Douglass did not do was to stimulate a native American theatre and a community of actors and playwrights who could interpret the American experience. *Audiences in the major cities Douglass visited were drawn from all walks of life—the only obstacle for admission was the price of the *tickets—and were content to patronize the troupes. American theatre as well as American civilization as a whole remained a pale reflection of life in the mother country, but two wars were to change all that. Douglass's selection included Shakespeare, of course, and Restoration *comedies by *Farquhar, *Gay, and *Vanbrugh, as well as the eighteenth-century *melodramas by

*Otway, *Home, and *Rowe, in what constituted a typical repertory for a British itinerant company.

In 1785, Lewis Hallam the Younger ventured back to New York at the head of a small troupe to reclaim the John Street Theatre and begin anew. He found a devastated city but a playhouse substantially intact. He also found a growing population with a thirst for entertainment after the arid war years. Actors continued to migrate to America from England to join the companies in the burgeoning cities, and the old Hallam–Douglass troupe at the John Street discovered that it could survive resident in its own theatre without travelling to other cities. On rare occasions, Douglass presented or tried to present works by Americans, the first probably being *The Prince of Parthia* by Thomas *Godfrey of Philadelphia, later produced in New York, in 1767. (Not until 1787 was another American play, *The Contrast* by Royall *Tyler, performed on the New York stage.) On even rarer occasions, an American actor briefly trod the boards, but by the end of the eighteenth century, every actor on the American stage was of British origin.

2. 1800–1900

New York was ready for a new and better playhouse in 1798, which materialized in the *Park Theatre, opposite City Hall, close to Broadway. For the next 50 years the Park, under a succession of managers, dominated the cultural life of the city, attracting competition with the building of other theatres and the importation of English stars. One of the Park's early managers, Stephen *Price, struggling to keep the theatre on a strong financial footing, decided that importing stars from England would create greater interest in the theatre and, hence, was responsible for creating the star system in America that has persisted to the present day. (It left little room for the development of an American *acting profession and an American acting style for many years.) The War of Independence and the War of 1812 served as spurs to create a truly indigenous theatre in New York but it was to be many years before American actors and American plays were routinely accepted by American audiences. New Yorkers who frequented the Park and other theatres continued to be diverse and democratic. The gallery in all New York's theatres remained the province of labourers, servant girls, mechanics, and the working classes in general. Eventually, New York's theatrical offerings became as diverse as the audiences for them.

For a time the newer and more elegant *Bowery Theatre, built in 1826, offered strong competition to the Park, while the smaller theatres springing up around both theatres offered popular-priced entertainment in the form of low comedies, melodramas, and light musical fare, frequently with a charismatic performer at the top of the bill. One of the most popular of these theatres was *Niblo's Garden, whose location many blocks north of the Park heralded the northward movement of the city. (It was at Niblo's Garden in 1866 that the landmark musical extravaganza *The Black Crook* opened and played for sixteen months.) Another was the Astor Place Opera House, built originally to satisfy the hunger for grand *opera, but also lent to presenters of Shakespeare and classical theatre. It was the site of the infamous *Astor Place riot in 1849, engendered by a rivalry between the American actor Edwin *Forrest and the visiting English star William *Macready, regarded as the standard-bearers for the pro-American and pro-British factions within the city. The clash cost 22 lives and an appraisal of the futility of such rivalry.

If Broadway, not the Bowery, was evolving at the mid-nineteenth century as a magnet for theatrical activity, the reasons were manifestly clear. It had become the city's prime thoroughfare, paved and lighted, fit for an evening stroll. It was well served by public transportation and imposing residences lined both sides of the street, interspersed with shops for all necessities. A new theatrical phenomenon, the *minstrel show, sparked a concentration of theatres along Broadway and beyond at mid-century. (In so doing, it also transformed the street into a commercial thoroughfare.) During the peak of popularity of the minstrel show, every available hall, *auditorium, and theatre was appropriated to satisfy the seemingly insatiable taste for minstrelsy for twenty years. From the Park Theatre to Niblo's Garden, all the playhouses were invaded by minstrelsy at least in some period of their histories. For anyone wanting more serious fare, there was Dion *Boucicault's *Winter Garden Theatre, which was carved out of a larger theatre built by the comedian William *Burton, and which presented popular melodramas along with an established repertory. Through the persistent efforts of opera aficionados, the Academy of Music was built in 1854 on 14th Street. Succeeding the Astor Place Opera House, it became the Mecca for opera (always considered more acceptable socially than drama), but its managers were forced to share its stage with *legitimate fare to survive. For a number of years, the Academy marked the northern end of the theatrical zone.

Just a block south and slightly west of the Academy was the most renowned theatre of its era. It was the second home of the *Wallack *family of actors, led originally by James W. Wallack, who had emigrated from England in 1818 for an engagement at the Park Theatre. Wallack was not only a gifted actor but an excellent manager. When in 1851 he took over a theatre which had been recently leased by John *Brougham, another popular English actor, he provided New Yorkers of more refined taste with a repertory of English and classic plays meticulously produced and acted. His son Lester eventually succeeded him and continued at *Wallack's Theatre until 1881, when he joined the movement northward to another burgeoning theatre district.

At the opposite end of the spectrum from Wallack's was the Theatre Comique, which presented the antics of Edward *Harrigan and Tony Hart in song, *dance, and story. Using *racial stereotypes as the meat of Harrigan's boisterous concoctions, the two comedians took over a succession of Broadway theatres during their immense popularity, until they separated in 1884 when their theatre on Broadway near 8th Street burned down. Harrigan and Hart represented quintessential New Yorkers, who tailored their fare to local audiences. Other comic teams (among them *Weber and Fields), aping their success, sprung up to appeal to other facets of New York life, sometimes creating *characters like 'Mose, the Bowery B'hoy', a favourite of audiences for many years.

From around 1870 to the last decade of the nineteenth century, Union Square, at Broadway and 14th Street, was the heart of New York's first theatre district. It encompassed not only theatres located in its immediate environs, holdovers to the south from previous eras, and theatres built to the north in the later years of the century, but, more importantly, most of the supporting activities of theatrical production. It became the headquarters of every kind of business that fed off the theatre, from book stores selling plays to *wigmakers, offices of managers and agents, boarding houses for actors, hotels for the visiting stars, printers of *playbills and *posters, and photographers: a centre for everything necessary for the industry that theatre had become. Streets and street corners in the area became a gathering place to do business, to book or cancel shows, schedule *tours, and to hire and fire.

From the post-Civil War era until the final years of the nineteenth century, the Union Square theatre district pervaded the life of every New Yorker. Within its environs every sort of entertainment was offered, from the waning but not dead minstrel show, to the antics of Harrigan and Hart, to *music halls and *variety shows, to rambunctious *burlesques, to plays offered in French and German, and to finely acted classical and contemporary dramas and drawing-room comedies. At a theatre on 14th Street, named after him, the former singer and circus performer Tony *Pastor purveyed a type of variety entertainment that became known as *vaudeville in America. Consisting of a variety of acts, it was wholesome and family oriented and persisted into the twentieth century. At the theatres under the aegis of the managers A. M. Palmer, Augustin *Daly, and Steele *MacKaye, the audience was drawn from the upper reaches of New York society. But the city itself was moving swiftly northward along the preordained gridiron of streets and avenues devised in 1811.

New York understandably became the Mecca for actors from all parts of the country and the era created the myth that only success in a New York theatre meant elevation to stardom. During the last decades of the nineteenth century, an American style of acting was being slowly developed, aided by innovative directors like MacKaye and David *Belasco and fostered by the *American Academy of Dramatic Arts, which was founded in 1884 by Belasco, MacKaye, and others.

While American letters developed rapidly during the early part of the nineteenth century, producing notable figures, American playwrights had a more difficult time establishing themselves. Like the actors, success in New York was important in their careers. Most of the plays produced by the early playwrights bore the influences of European melodramas even if the subjects were American. They depicted American *stock characters, which became stage Indians, backwoodsmen, slick Yankees, and other broad types, and which bore little resemblance to reality. Among the most perceptive of the early American dramas was *Fashion; or, Life in New York* (1845), written by Anna Cora *Mowatt, which offered a tart critique of parvenu American society.

In the early 1890s Broadway was at its apogee as the theatrical boulevard of the city. Stretching 25 blocks from Union Square to Herald Square at 34th Street, it stopped close to the threshold of Long Acre Square, an area at the confluence of Broadway and 7th Avenue. The first to locate his ventures northward was the manager Charles *Frohman, who built the *Empire Theatre in 1893 on Broadway and 40th Street, across from the new *Metropolitan Opera House, which was built in 1883 but did not immediately supplant the Academy of Music in public favour until the 1890s. The district was ripe for development. Within a few years theatre building leaped to 42nd Street, then to the side streets radiating from the Long Acre Square. The area eventually pulled along with it all the necessary supporting businesses to create another theatre district, anchored at the southern end by the new headquarters of the *New York Times* Company, which, in 1904, was rewarded by having its name given to the area, henceforth known as Times Square.

The enormous expansion of theatrical production and theatre building could be attributed to the huge growth in population from the tides of immigration which had begun at the mid-nineteenth century and continued unabated to the early decades of the twentieth. Other factors include improvement in public transportation (the subway system was inaugurated in 1904), the centralization of many industries, the recognition that the city was the financial hub of the country, and, finally, the lure of manifold cultural amenities and activities offered by the metropolis to business people and tourists alike. With the emergence of great native stars begun in the nineteenth century with Forrest, Edwin *Booth, and Charlotte *Cushman, New York theatre became renowned abroad as well as throughout the North American continent. By 1900 the city had joined the great cultural capitals of the world.

3. Since 1900

Not until the twentieth century did American playwriting come of age, not merely the discovery of an American psyche by writers, but also the result of external forces. The First World War turned the country inward by removing ready communication with the European continent for nearly five years. In 1915 Eugene *O'Neill emerged from an experimental group in Massachusetts, the *Provincetown Players, which later centred its activities in Greenwich Village in New York, to become America's leading playwright. Other groups were formed which produced plays and playwrights away from the white lights of Broadway. Within the next 50 years, New York's theatre became the seedbed for scores of dramatists who were for the first time examining the uniqueness of the American experience, sometimes with lacerating frankness, sometimes with crusty good humour. The new plays demanded new methods of production which resulted in extraordinary feats of stage design led by Robert Edmond *Jones, the founder of the 'New Stagecraft', and furthered by his many disciples, who included Jo *Mielziner and Donald *Oenslager.

Largely through the entrepreneurial acumen and the questionable business practices of several men, including Abraham L. Erlanger, Marc Klaw, Oscar *Hammerstein I, and the *Shubert brothers, theatre was transformed into an industry. They embarked on and stimulated an unprecedented era of building and play production that eventually encompassed, in New York alone, more than 80 playhouses within the overlapping theatre districts of Union and Times Squares. No longer resident in their own theatres, an enterprise under a manager or *'producer' became a company hired for a single production and booked into a rented theatre. Other 'duplicate' companies could take the same play on the road to thousands of theatres located coast to coast, most of which were controlled through theatre chains by Klaw and Erlanger and the Shuberts in New York.

At its peak in the first three decades of the twentieth century, the boundaries of Times Square theatre district stretched along Broadway and into its side streets from 39th to Columbus Circle and 59th Street, with the greatest concentration of playhouses fanning out from Times Square in the west 40s. During the 1920s more than 200 plays and *musicals were presented in these theatres, some of which bore generic names (Imperial, Majestic, Music Box, Gaiety, *Palace, Ritz, Ambassador, Century); others honouring their founders (Sam. S. Shubert, Klaw, Erlanger, *Belasco, Earl Carroll, *Ziegfeld, Selwyn); still others indicating place (New York, Broadway, Manhattan, Knickerbocker, Times Square, Hudson, New Amsterdam); and finally, others honouring great stars of the era (Ethel *Barrymore, Maxine Elliott, Julian *Eltinge, George M. *Cohan, and Al *Jolson). Time and changing owners renamed many of these houses.

By 1930 the boom that had engulfed all aspects of New York life, including its theatre, was over. The dire consequences of over-expansion and overproduction were brought into sharp focus with the collapse of the American economy brought about by the stock market crash of 1929. Empty theatres, *tickets unsold at any price, unemployed actors, bankrupt producers, unpaid mortgages on theatres, and the rise of *radio entertainment and the talking *films, all contributed to the pall that settled on Broadway in the 1930s. In the years to follow, the theatres which could not be drawn off by the movies or transformed into studios for radio were either demolished or converted to

other uses. In the mid-years of the 1930s, the *Federal Theatre Project, a government-sponsored and supported initiative to bring employment to actors, producers, and stage personnel at all levels, kept the lights on in some of the less desirable playhouses in the theatre district and brought work to part of the theatrical community, but it survived for only a few years. The attrition continued even with a spurt of renewed activity during the years of the Second World War, when New York was a Mecca for servicemen.

After the war theatre had a more potent enemy in its battle for survival. Although it had been sorely tested by the advent of entertainment radio in the late 1920s and nearly decimated by the encroachment of talking pictures and the flight of stars and writers to Hollywood during the 1930s, New York's theatre was unprepared for the rapid rise of a new popular medium in the 1950s: *television. During the next four decades, twenty theatres were converted to movies, television studios, nightclubs, or to other uses, and more than 30 had been razed. Thirty-five of the original 80 or so in the theatre district were still standing and actively presenting live theatrical fare. Government-sponsored initiatives over the years led to the creation of three new theatres in high-rise structures and the Landmarks Commission led the way for the preservation of most of the remaining structures. Twenty blocks to the north of the district, the privately subsidized complex *Lincoln Center provided two additional dramatic theatres during the 1960s, the Vivian Beaumont and the Mitzi E. Newhouse.

As if the attrition on Broadway caused by competing forms of electronic entertainment were not enough, the post-war years brought forth a movement in reaction to the dominance of commercial theatre in New York. Actors and playwrights fresh out of acting schools and theatre departments in American colleges and universities flocked to the city in search of a place to display their talents. Finding the commercial theatre inhospitable and unable to absorb them, they looked to other venues or created them for themselves in cafés, abandoned nightclubs, warehouses, and other empty spaces. The movement became known as *Off-Broadway, which soon spawned yet another theatrical subculture known as *Off-Off-Broadway. Within a few years, small bands, sometimes transitory, in out-of-the-way locations throughout Manhattan were beginning to siphon off some of the middle-class audiences that traditionally bought tickets to Broadway shows and were finding it more and more difficult to pay the advancing prices. From being regarded as a temporary aberration, both Off-Broadway and Off-Off-Broadway have persisted into the new millennium and show no signs of abatement.

During the 1970s, with relaxed moral standards and universal permissiveness pervading the land, New York's theatre district was invaded by the sinister industry of *pornography. Beginning on West 42nd Street, once the main thoroughfare of the theatre district, and spreading into the area surrounding

Times Square, theatre owners had few weapons to fight for the preservation of the district in the face of the rights of the purveyors of pornography. The forces for good relied on the city government to enact ordinances against their opponents, as had been done during the late 1930s when Mayor Fiorello LaGuardia fought off striptease burlesque (*see* SEX SHOWS AND DANCES) within the theatre district with a series of zoning edicts. Eventually the city prevailed, but it took more than twenty years of court skirmishes and questionable statutes to rid the theatre district of these tainted businesses.

In the 1990s, through the intervention of government on state and local levels (a far cry from earliest condemnations of theatrical enterprises), a partnership with private entrepreneurs was set up to develop and implement plans for conservation. One of the three original theatres on the block, the New Amsterdam, was reclaimed by the Disney Company; two were subsumed by a new theatre, the Ford Center for the Performing Arts; one, the New Victory, continues as a family-oriented theatre; and another, the former Selwyn (renamed the American Airlines Theatre), has been taken over by the Roundabout Theatre Company, a not-for-profit *regional theatre. Most of the theatres in the main district above 42nd Street continue to be controlled by three groups of owners or lessees: the Shubert, *Nederlander, and Jujamcyn organizations, which also support productions presented by independent producers from time to time.

The new millennium found the eternal invalid that is New York's theatre still functioning, albeit in a different setting. Once a human-scaled district of low-rise buildings, it has become overwhelmed by structures of imposing height and bulk. To stimulate almost a *carnival atmosphere in the area, the city government has encouraged façades of bright lights, neon signs, giant screens for televised and projected images, and has made the dropping of the New Year's Eve ball of light from the tower at the base of the district an international event. The district continues to be a magnet for tourists, some of whom seek out half-price tickets at a special booth for that purpose at the end of Times Square, and everyone else who is looking for a good time.

For the past 30 years, the main fare in the theatres has been the musical, whether home grown or imported. *Long runs, which in former times went from 100 performances to 1,000, are now counted in years. *A Chorus Line*, an American musical, and *Cats*, a British import, have established new records on Broadway, but there are others waiting in the wings to break those records. If New York's theatre and its attitude, both official and popular, have changed, so have the dynamics of the city, which has always been influenced by the economy, the political scene, the temper of the times, and myriad other factors. Although New York's theatre has been buffeted by the winds of change during its 250-year history, it has been remarkably resilient and will probably endure. MCH

BLOOM, KEN, *Broadway* (New York, 1991)
HENDERSON, MARY, *The City and the Theatre* (Clifton, NJ, 1973)
—— *Theater in America* (New York, 1986, 1996)
ODELL, GEORGE C. D., *Annals of the New York Stage*, 15 vols. (New York, 1927–49)

NEW YORK PUBLIC THEATRE *See* NEW YORK SHAKESPEARE FESTIVAL.

NEW YORK SHAKESPEARE FESTIVAL/ PUBLIC THEATRE

American company, the brainchild and lifetime project of Joseph *Papp, who first brought a group of actors together as the Shakespeare Workshop to perform scenes from Shakespeare's plays in an East Village church hall in 1954. In 1956 the renamed New York Shakespeare Festival presented free outdoor performances in the East River Park, which expanded to productions of Shakespeare around all five boroughs of *New York, transporting sets and actors in a flatbed truck. In 1962 the company opened its first *playhouse, the *Delacorte Theatre, in Central Park. Among the actors who performed Shakespeare with the festival in these early days were Colleen *Dewhurst, George C. *Scott, and Roscoe Lee Browne. Wanting to expand the theatre's repertoire and activities, Papp discovered the Astor Library on Lafayette Street, which had fallen into disuse and was scheduled for demolition. He persuaded the city to declare it a landmark, and it opened as the Public Theatre in 1967. Its first production, the *musical *Hair*, was a huge success and transferred to Broadway.

Papp framed the Public's artistic remit around his own tastes and passions: he was interested in locating and nurturing new talents from diverse backgrounds, and the Public became something of a haven for young playwrights, composers, directors, and actors. Papp championed the work of writers David *Rabe, John *Guare, Ntozake *Shange, and Miguel Pinero; actors Meryl Streep, Kevin *Kline, and Mandy Patinkin; and directors Wilfred Leach, A. J. *Antoon, and Michael *Bennett. The latter's behind-the-scenes musical about Broadway dancers, *A Chorus Line*, premièred at the Public in 1975 and then ran on Broadway for fifteen years. The revenue from *A Chorus Line* provided crucial *financial stability for the Public until 1990 and allowed Papp to expand his talent-development interests as well as bankroll the theatre's continuing summertime free Shakespeare productions. Among less successful experiments was a residency in *Lincoln Center's Vivian Beaumont Theater; the Public took over the perennially troubled space in 1973 and withdrew in 1977 because Papp found it a financial and artistic drain.

Throughout the 1980s Papp continued his spirited if idiosyncratic programming, founding an annual celebration of Latin American writing talent, Festival Latino, and producing a number of groundbreaking and lucrative shows including Larry

*Kramer's seminal AIDS play *The Normal Heart* (1985) and *The Pirates of Penzance* (Delacorte, 1980; Broadway, 1981) featuring pop stars Rex Smith and Linda Ronstadt. In 1990, secretly suffering from prostate cancer, Papp reorganized the theatre, appointing JoAnne *Akalaitis his artistic associate and David Greenspan, Michael Greif, and George C. *Wolfe resident directors. After Papp's death, Akalaitis took over the theatre, but her reign was troubled, and she was ousted by the theatre's board and succeeded by Wolfe in 1993, who continues as *artistic director.   KF

NEW ZEALAND FESTIVAL

Founded in 1986, the biennial Festival in Wellington is New Zealand's largest cultural and arts event. In addition to bringing major international theatre, *dance, and music to New Zealand (in cooperation with the *Hong Kong and Australian *festivals), in the mid-1990s it expanded its commissioning programme from an artistic centrepiece *opera to also producing several new plays for each festival, including *Maori and Pacific works. For example, Hone Kouka in *Waiora* (1996) surrounded a *realist story about family dislocation from rural tribal roots with *ritualized Maori performance. The play was subsequently well received at overseas festivals. The associated fringe festival presents predominantly new work.   DC

NEW ZEALAND PLAYERS

The only national company in New Zealand. Formed in 1953 by Richard and Edith Campion, it *toured from one end of the country to the other, including many one-night stands in small towns which otherwise never saw professional theatre. The repertoire included Shakespeare, *Shaw, *Coward, *Anouilh, *musical comedies, and the occasional New Zealand play such as Douglas Stewart's *Ned Kelly* and a workshop production of Bruce *Mason's *The Pohutukawa Tree*. The overstretched company collapsed in 1960, the year, ironically, government finally committed to public subsidy of the arts (*see* FINANCE). Regional rather than national theatre, however, became the professional norm for New Zealand.   DC

NGEMA, MBONGENI (1955–)

South African actor, playwright, musician, choreographer, and director, born in Natal. He began his career as a guitarist in the theatre, and his first play, *The Last Generation* (1978), was produced at the Stable Theatre in Durban. While working for Gibson *Kente, he met Percy *Mtwa and created *Woza Albert!* (1981) with him and Barney *Simon. Moving to the *Market Theatre in *Johannesburg, he created *Asinamali!* (*We Have No Money*, 1985) a *musical exploration of township rent strikes. *Sarafina* (1986), which celebrated the indomitable spirit of South African

youth, was produced internationally and won many *awards, enabling the formation of the Committed Artists at the Market in 1988, which *toured these two plays abroad in 1989. He unsuccessfully attempted *community theatre with *Sarafina 2* (1987), an AIDS play. In *Maria, Maria* (1997) he created a musical mixing the Christ story with that of Steve Biko.   YH

NGONJERA

A *didactic Tanzanian theatrical form developed in the 1960s, most notably by Mathias Mnyampala, as a *verse *dialogue accessible to a number of ethnic groups. Originally *ngonjera* consisted of disputes in Kiswahili between two people. One was politically 'correct', the other a 'fool' who would be won round to the more 'enlightened' view. The form was taken up by many politically committed intellectuals and diversified, encompassing both *monologues and disputes between several parties. *Ngonjera* had originally been around fifteen minutes long, but encouraged as a separate category in national arts competitions, productions grew in length and were often serialized on *radio.
                                                                    JP

NIBLO, WILLIAM (1789–1878)

Irish-American theatre *manager. Born in Ireland, Niblo emigrated to *New York as a youth, and apprenticed at and later took over a coffee house. In 1823 he turned a *circus site into a restaurant and concert garden. In 1829 he opened a new three-storey structure with shrubbery-lined corridors and named the complex Niblo's Garden and Theatre. At first he offered summertime concerts and *fireworks, but from the late 1830s he was also offering stage productions with eminent stars, such as Charles *Kean's Hamlet, Edwin *Forrest's Macbeth, Charlotte *Cushman in *Guy Mannering*, and J. H. *Hackett as Falstaff in *The Merry Wives of Windsor*. From 1842 to 1860 he regularly presented the Ravel family, a celebrated French troupe of five *acrobats and *dancers. The theatre burned in 1846, but Niblo put up a new building, which he opened in 1849 and ran until his retirement in 1861.   CT

NICHOLS, MIKE (1931–)

American stage and *film director, *producer, and actor. With five Tony *awards for best director between 1964 and 1984—for *Simon's *Barefoot in the Park*, *The Odd Couple*, *Plaza Suite*, and *The Prisoner of Second Avenue*, Murray Schisgal's *Luv*, and *Stoppard's *The Real Thing*)—and an Oscar for best director (*The Graduate*, 1967), Nichols is one of the most acclaimed directors in contemporary theatre. Born Michael Igor Peschkowsky, he fled to the USA from Nazi Germany with his family at the age of 8. After study with Lee *Strasberg at the *Actors Studio in *New York, in 1955 he formed an *improvisational comedy troupe called the Compass Players (later Second City), whose members included Elaine *May and Alan Arkin. *An Evening with Mike Nichols and Elaine May* (Broadway, 1960) brought socio-political *satire and wry observations about the sexes to a mainstream *audience. Though he is chiefly known for his success with *comedy, Nichols also directed serious works like David *Rabe's *Streamers* and Trevor *Griffiths's *Comedians* (both 1976). *Albee's *Who's Afraid of Virginia Woolf?* starring Elizabeth Taylor and Richard *Burton, was his *film debut, and *The Graduate* encapsulated a generation's alienation and longing. Other projects included *Beckett's *Waiting for Godot* on Broadway with Steve Martin, Robin Williams, J. Murray Abraham, and Bill *Irwin (1988), and many films. Nichols occasionally returns to acting, as in *The Designated Mourner* by Wallace *Shawn (London, 1997). He is married to news anchorwoman Diane Sawyer.

GAO

NICHOLS, PETER (1927–)

English playwright. Nichols acted in *regional theatre before turning to *television and *film writing (including the script for *Georgy Girl*, 1966). His first stage play, *A Day in the Death of Joe Egg* (1967), was a hugely successful black *comedy on the unlikely topic of a couple with a brain-damaged child. His next play, commissioned by Kenneth *Tynan, was *The National Health* (1969), a *parody of television soap operas tinged with an underlying bitterness, as is much of his work. *Forget-Me-Not Lane* (1971), a nostalgic family drama, has proven a continuing success with *regional theatres. After this string of successes, Nichols struggled with his next two works, the domestic drama *Chez Nous* (1974) and *The Freeway* (1974), an *allegory about a traffic jam that proved to be as popular as its topic. Nichols returned to success with the *musical *Privates on Parade* (1977), based on his RAF experiences in *Malaysia. *Passion Play* (1981), produced by the *Royal Shakespeare Company, was also a hit. The play's conventional topic, adultery, is enlivened by the addition of a second pair of performers acting as the *protagonists' alter egos. Nichols's second musical, *Poppy* (1983), a parody Victorian *pantomime, centred on the opium wars in *China. Perhaps as a result of this troubled production, Nichols announced in 1983 that he was giving up playwriting for novels, but returned to the stage in 1987 with *A Piece of my Mind*, about a novelist with writer's block.

MDG

NICOLL, ALLARDYCE (1894–1976)

Scottish theatre historian. Nicoll was one of the first British academics to understand that the study of drama and theatre were inextricably intertwined (*see* THEATRE STUDIES). His account of *The Development of the Theatre* (1927, frequently revised and expanded) long remained the standard history of the changes in *playhouse architecture, while his seven-volume history of Eng-

lish drama began publication in 1923 with the Restoration and ended in 1973 with the period from 1900 to 1930. His wide interests included popular forms of *early modern theatre as much as the high culture of Stuart court *masques, the relation of theatre to *film and to dramatic *theory, as well as the practice of *commedia dell'arte*. His histories are remarkable for their sheer breadth, their extraordinary calendars of drama, and their detailed archival data on theatre and performance. In 1948, while professor of English at Birmingham, he founded *Shakespeare Survey*, an annual journal for Shakespeare research, which he edited until 1966. In 1951 he created the Shakespeare Institute as a centre for postgraduate study in Stratford-upon-Avon.

PDH

NIEVA, FRANCISCO (1929–)

Spanish novelist, playwright, and designer. Closely associated in his youth with underground literary and artistic movements, Nieva has also acknowledged the influence on his work of classical Spanish authors such as Fernando de *Rojas and Quevedo, as well as of popular theatrical forms such as the *entremés and the *sainete. His earliest work for the stage, subdivided by the author into 'theatre of *farce and calamity' and the 'furious theatre' of pieces like *La carroza de plomo candente* (*The Molten Lead Carriage*) of 1971, are strongly anti-*naturalist plays which challenge the traditional idea of the stage as a site of reflection, analysis, or debate. In later plays like *Los baños de Argel* (*The Baths of Algiers*), for which he was *awarded the Premio Nacional de Teatro in 1980, Nieva combined *surrealist stage spaces with disruptions of the typical structures of *action and speech, in order to interrogate the basis of conventional morality. A refractory and often outspoken member of the Spanish intelligentsia, Nieva was nonetheless appointed to the Real Academia Española.

KG

NINAGAWA YUKIO (1935–)

Japanese director. Ninagawa began as a painter but became an actor after seeing a production of *Abe Kōbō's *The Uniform*. He founded the Contemporary People's Theatre in *Tokyo in 1968 and made his directorial debut the following year with *Shimizu Kunio's *Sincere Frivolity*. During the 1960s and early 1970s, Ninagawa's work (frequently with Shimizu) was experimental and *politically engaged, but since 1974 he has won a reputation for his commercial productions, often for the Tōhō Group, of Shakespeare and *Greek *tragedy. His productions of *Medea* (1979), *Macbeth* (1980), and *The Tempest* (1987) have *toured abroad to great acclaim. At the same time, he has been active cultivating younger talent with his Ninagawa Company. He also continues to direct contemporary Japanese drama, by Shimizu, *Akimoto Matsuyo, *Mishima Yukio, *Kara Jūrō, and *Terayama Shūji. His English-language production of Shimizu's *Tango at

Shakespeare's *Macbeth* was entitled *Ninagawa Macbeth* when directed by **Ninagawa** in Tokyo in 1980, a stunningly beautiful Japanning of the play that drew upon the visuals of the samurai era. The King (Masane Tsukayma) and queen (Komaki Kurihara) are in front of a screen in the 1987 tour to the National Theatre in London. Later Ninagawa productions of Shakespeare relied more heavily on intercultural elements.

the End of Winter, starring Alan Rickman, premièred at the *Edinburgh Festival in 1991. Ninagawa's productions are distinguished by their innovative and spectacular staging; set designer *Asakura Setsu frequently works with him. He has also directed *opera, notably *The Flying Dutchman* (1992), and an English-language production of *Peer Gynt* in 1994. His *Midsummer Night's Dream* (1994) and *Hamlet* (1995) both travelled to *London a few years after their Tokyo runs. In 1999 he staged Shakespeare in English for the first time, in a co-production of *King Lear* with the *Royal Shakespeare Company with Nigel Hawthorne in the lead, which opened in Tokyo and then played London and Stratford.   CP

NINASAM

Grass-roots theatre and cultural organization in Karnataka, south *India. Established in 1949 in the village of Heggodu in the Shimoga district, Ninasam began as an *amateur theatre group producing occasional plays for local *audiences. Its activities took a decisive turn in the 1970s when K. V. Subbanna

(1932–), a founding member, assumed leadership. Ninasam built a *playhouse at Heggodu (1972), conducted a festival of world *film classics for a rural audience (1979), leading to the formation of a rural film society, and in 1980 established a one-year *training programme in drama. Its graduates have been instrumental in spreading theatre to all parts of rural Karnataka. The organization formed Tirugata in 1985, a seasonal repertory company that *tours the region, and has also conducted theatre and cultural workshops for varied communities, including the Siddis, based in the forest settlements of Manchikeri. Ninasam's work is widely recognized and valued, and Subbanna received the prestigious Magsaysay *award in 1992. *See also* Kannada Theatre.   KVA

NIÑO, JAIRO ANÍBAL (1941–)

Colombian playwright, director, and teacher, author of one of the most widely staged Colombian plays, *El monte calvo* (*Bald Mountain*, 1966), about the aftermath of the country's senseless participation in the Korean War. Other works include *La*

Nō drama in performance in Japan, a print from 1848. The open-air simple stage is at the left, its canopy supported by four square pillars, with the obligatory large pine tree painted on the rear wall. Actors are downstage, with musicians and chorus upstage. The lower classes of spectator are on the ground (front left), the upper classes in covered spaces in the house facing the stage.

madriguera (*The Burrow*, 1975), *Los inquilinos de la ira* (*The Tenants of Wrath*, 1976), and *El sol subterráneo* (*The Subterranean Sun*, 1978), all of which portray historical events from the point of view of marginalized sectors of Colombia. He is also the author of several children's plays.   BJR

NISSEI THEATRE

One of the major theatres in *Tokyo for productions of *opera, *musicals, and contemporary drama. Opened by the Nippon Life Insurance Corporation in 1963 and managed by the Nissei Cultural Foundation, the theatre has staged dozens of Japanese and international productions of opera, starting with Beethoven's *Fidelio*. Asari Keita, founder of Gekidan Shiki (the Four Seasons Company), served as its first *artistic director until 1970, and the Nissei has continued to be the venue for productions by Four Seasons of such popular musicals as *Cats*, *Phantom of the Opera*, and *The Lion King*. Nissei Masterpiece Theatre invites schoolchildren free of charge to Four Seasons productions. The Nissei Opera was established in 1979, with a similar aim to introduce opera to younger *audiences; its first production was of Dan Ikuma's *Twilight Crane*, based on the play by *Kinoshita Junji.   CP

NIXTAYOLERO

Nicaraguan theatre for *youth (the name means 'morning star'), founded by Alan *Bolt in 1979. Located just outside of Matagalpa, Bolt offered a *training programme for young actors that often doubled as a sanctuary for homeless children. The young troupe often staged works that reflected Bolt's commitment to agricultural reform, sustainable agricultural practices, and other environmental issues. The group also staged works that dealt with current *political issues and events, and occasionally came under fire from the revolutionary government for its critical position. The collaborative performances continue to incorporate many popular traditions, Nicaraguan myths and legends, *music, and *masks, staged for a popular *audience.
                    EJW

NKASHAMA, PIUS NGANDU (1946–)

Prolific Congolese novelist, dramatist, and critic. Born in the former Zaire, he returned to teach there in 1975 after study at the University of Strasbourg. The author of a dozen novels and theatre *criticism, his four plays are *La Délivrance d'Ilunga* (*Ilunga's Deliverance*, 1977), *Bonjour Monsieur le Ministre* (1983), *L'Empire des ombres vivantes* (*The Empire of Living Shadows*, 1991), and *May Britt de Santa Cruz* (1993). In addition to acting in plays by Aimé *Césaire while at university, his practical theatre experience includes work with Mobyem *Mikanza at the National Theatre of Zaire, and in 1990 *training with the Théâtre Populaire Romand in Chaux-de-Fonds, Switzerland, where he conceived *L'Empire*. Césaire's influence is unmistakable in two of his plays, not only in their recourse to poetic prose and *radio announcements but also in the theme of the quest for liberty from political oppression. But unlike Césaire's, Nkashama's plays, especially *L'Empire*, tend to be isolated lyrical outpourings with little dramatic action.   JCM

NŌ (NOH)

*Japanese theatrical tradition which combines poetic *texts, *dance, and *music with elaborate *costumes and simple *props. Developed from earlier performing arts by *Kan'ami and *Zeami in the fourteenth and fifteenth centuries, nō maintains an unbroken performance tradition. From the early twentieth century, nō became an international art influencing theatre people everywhere. The nō *stage, a small architectural gem with an austere beauty that is never compromised by *scenery, developed in the seventeenth century. It is a raised and roofed structure, about 6 m (20 feet) square, with ceramic jugs strategically placed underneath the highly polished floor to add resonance to foot stamps. The back wall is decorated with the painting of a large pine tree, in front of which is a small area used by instrumentalists. At stage left another small area holds the *chorus. A bridgeway, approximately 2 m by 10 m (5 by 33 feet), leads obliquely from rear stage right to a curtained exit into the dressing rooms and serves as a secondary performing area. After any large props are carried in by stage attendants (*shite actors), the musicians and the chorus (eight to ten *shite* actors) enter the stage before the *waki, who generally introduces himself and travels to the site of the play's *action.

Most plays are in two *acts: the first introduces a narrative—the establishment of a shrine, the death of a warrior, the loss of a loved one—and the second presents some part or result of that story. A single player, normally the *shite*, performs most of the action and is the visual centre of interest. He is garbed in a large, brightly coloured costume and a carved, wooden *mask, both of which may be of museum quality. The *shite*, however, is always surrounded by supporting performers, a large number for such a small stage, and it is the interaction among the entire ensemble that creates the power and the beauty of the performance. Nō plays rarely focus on *character development or dramatic conflict; rather they explore an emotion (love, anguish, longing, regret, resentment); celebrate deities, poetry, longevity, fertility, or harmony; or exorcize external or internal ghosts and demons. Some plays feature a supernatural being or the *ghost of a human recalling its life on earth; others present real (but sometimes deranged) people living in the dramatic present. Nō plays are divided into five categories—deities, warriors, women, miscellaneous (including most living-people plays), and demons or strong characters—and one play from each group made up a traditional, formal programme with four *kyōgen plays performed between the nō. Since the Second World War, however, programmes have been shortened drastically, sometimes to a single nō play. The current nō repertory contains approximately 250 plays.

Nō texts are expressed in music and dance. A flute and two or three drums play in all nō performances. Drummers play two types of hand drums and one larger stick drum and issue calls (*yo, ho, yoi*), whose quality helps establish the mood of a piece and whose precise placement in the drum patterns is an important means of controlling the rhythm. A chorus chants large portions of the text, which may describe and comment on the settings and the characters' actions or feelings. *Dialogue plays a relatively minor role: the chorus sometimes speaks in the first person for a character; an actor is not restricted to remaining in character, and two actors or the *shite* and the chorus often share lines. All movement is choreographed, and the *shite* often dances during the chanting of the most intense sections of the text and usually performs a dance to instrumental music. Professional performers (approximately 1,500 actors and musicians currently) undergo intensive *training from childhood to early adulthood, and the discipline and control they develop are widely admired by their Western counterparts. To augment their performance fees, most performers give lessons in nō chanting and dancing to *amateurs, who in turn constitute a dedicated *audience.

Because the stage is sparsely decorated, costumes and masks provide most of the colour and visual beauty as well as indicating the age, gender, social status, and nature of the characters. Adult *shite* actors, except those playing ordinary, living male characters, wear masks whose expressions range from the serenity of a young woman to the diabolic features of a demon. The bulky, layered costumes of fine silks and brocades present multiple textures, colours, and designs. The sleeves are wide and long, emphasizing the gestures of the dance, and large *wigs and headdresses add height to the stage figures. Many hand props are used, including swords, branches, rosaries, nets, letters, bells, and drums, and the *shite* and *waki* carry spread-tip fans (*chūkei*) which may be used to pour sake, represent the wind, or point out the moon. Some plays use large stage props (boats, huts, gates, bell towers, wells), which are usually built in simple outline with bamboo and cloth for each performance.

In the twentieth century, nō has become an international art with its players performing throughout the world and playwrights using nō in new compositions. For example, Benjamin Britten's *Curlew River* and *Brecht's *Der Jasager* transformed the nō plays *Sumidagawa* and *Taniko* respectively into very different types of theatre. W. B. *Yeats's *At the Hawk's Well*, based on *Oimatsu*, has in turn been reworked into a more nō-like play by Japanese actors, and *Mishima Yukio's modern nō plays have been translated and performed in numerous countries. Nō actors (*Kanze Hisao is an example) have cross-trained in other performance traditions and worked with writers, amateurs, and even foreigners to create new types of nō, sometimes to participate with performers from other traditions to create a fusion theatre. In Japan traditional nō attracts large crowds at outdoor, torchlight performances (*takigi nō*), and at the turn of the twenty-first century elements of nō have entered Japanese pop culture in comics, animations, and youthful fashions.

KWB

BRAZELL, KAREN, *Twelve Plays of the Noh and Kyogen Theatre* (Ithaca, NY, 1988)

KOMPARU KUNIO, *The Noh Theatre: principles and perspectives* (New York, 1983)

TAMBA AKIRA, *The Musical Structure of Nō* (Tokyo, 1983)

TYLER, ROYALL, *Japanese Noh Dramas* (Harmondsworth, 1993)

NOAH, MORDECAI M. (1785–1851)

American playwright. Primarily a journalist, Mordecai Noah published several plays set during the American Revolutionary War. He achieved success only with *She Would Be a Soldier; or, The Plains of Chippewa*, produced in 1819 and performed regularly until 1868. *Melodramatic and patriotic, the play celebrates American yeomanry while ridiculing British foppery. It also provided a stirring *breeches role for its leading lady, who joins the army from patriotic and romantic motives. The play provided an early important role for Edwin *Forrest, who played a noble Native American chief in an 1825 Albany production. Noah's other plays were literary, rather than theatrical, successes.

AW

NOBLE, ADRIAN (1950–)

English director. After successful productions at the *Bristol Old Vic and *Manchester's *Royal Exchange Theatre, Noble began working at the *Royal Shakespeare Company in 1980, and was its *artistic director from 1991 to 2003. Almost all his work since 1982 has been for the company, with large-scale projects including *The Plantagenets* (from Shakespeare's histories) and *Sophocles' Theban plays. He was responsible for Kenneth *Branagh's first RSC season (including *Henry V* in 1983) and for reviving the career of Robert *Stephens (Falstaff in 1991 and King Lear in 1993). Unafraid of the largest stages, Noble created emotionally powerful productions comfortably within the traditions of British classical theatre. His control of the RSC in difficult economic circumstances (*see* FINANCE) removed the last traces of its leftist *political image. Noble sought to attract new family *audiences (with *The Lion, the Witch and the Wardrobe*, 1998). His reorganization of the RSC in 2001 abandoned the tradition of ensemble *repertory in favour of project-based companies and sought to find new American funding partnerships as well as planning new theatres for Stratford. PDH

NODA HIDEKI (1955–)

Japanese playwright, director, and actor. In 1976 he established his own theatre company, Yume no Yuminsha (Dream Idlers), while still an undergraduate at *Tokyo University. With their colourful sets, frenetic athleticism, and speedy delivery, Noda's fragmented and irreverent productions were a hallmark of the hedonistic spirit of the Japanese bubble economy of the 1980s. His plays are typically *surrealistic pastiches of elements derived from Japanese and Western popular culture, filled with gags, pratfalls, and puns. Watching one of his plays has been compared to channel surfing. His productions for Dream Idlers include *The Prisoner of Zenda* (1981) and *Descent of the Brutes* (1982); *Comet Messenger Siegfried* (1985) and *Half a God* (1986) have been performed in Europe and the USA. In 1992, Noda disbanded the Dream Idlers and took a sabbatical in England, returning the following year to found a new company called Noda Map. Recent productions include *Taboo* (1996). Noda is also famous for his riotous versions of Shakespeare, including *Richard III*, *Twelfth Night*, and *Much Ado About Nothing*.

CP

NOER, ARIFIN C. (1941–c.1996)

Indonesian playwright, filmmaker, and director. Best known for his masterwork *Moths* (1970), Arifin was a major influence on late twentieth-century theatre, *television, and *film in *Indonesia. Born in Cirebon, he studied in central Java where he began writing plays. In the 1960s he worked with *Rendra's Bengkel (Workshop) Teater and Teater Muslim in Yogyakarta. In 1968 he founded Teater Kecil (Little Theatre). He produced regularly at TIM (Taman Ismail Marzuki), the art centre in *Jakarta, doing both Western plays like *Caligula* and *Macbeth* and his own works like *Beloved Grandmother*, *Ozone* (set in a post-apocalyptic future), and *The Bottomless Well* (1964, 1989). His 25 scripts combined metaphysics, poetry, and deep self-questioning of society in the Suharto era. *Moths*, which has been performed internationally, is a *surreal play dealing with the light and darkness of human nature Films include *Suci, the Prima Donna* (1977) and *The Dawn* (1982). He was given Indonesia's national *award in the arts, the Anugerah Seni, in 1971. KFo

NOGUCHI, ISAMU (1904–88)

American sculptor and designer. Son of the Japanese poet Yone (Yonejirō) Noguchi and American writer Leonie Gilmour, Noguchi was born in Los Angeles but lived with his mother in *Japan from 1906 to 1918, when he was enrolled in a public school in northern Indiana in the Midwestern USA. He entered a pre-medical programme at Columbia University in New York in 1922, but left in 1924 to pursue a career in sculpture. Having received a Guggenheim Fellowship in 1927, he apprenticed with the sculptor Constantin Brancusi in *Paris. Noguchi's designs for smooth, abstract forms, many originally conceived as playground equipment, were first used as stage settings in *Frontier*, a 1934 Martha *Graham *dance piece. Noguchi developed a close friendship with Graham and collaborated with her repeatedly until 1966, including the influential *Appalachian Spring* (1944). Noguchi also designed for choreographers Merce *Cunningham and George *Balanchine. A rare design for spoken drama was *King Lear* at the *Shakespeare Memorial Theatre (1955, with John *Gielgud). MAF

NOGUERA, HÉCTOR (1938–)

Chilean actor and director, one of the most accomplished figures of his generation. He taught at the Theatre School of the Catholic University of Chile and founded and directed Teatro de Comediantes, Teatro Escuela Q, and Teatro Camino. His most successful acting roles were in *Calderón's *Life Is a Dream* (1974), *Theo and Vincent Wiped out by the Sun* (1990, an adaptation by Gustavo Meza of Jean Menaud's *Letters to Theo*), and *King Lear* (1992, translated by the Chilean poet Nicanor Parra). MAR

NOMURA MANZŌ VI (1898–1978)

*Kyōgen actor of the *Izumi school. The eldest son of Nomura Manzō V, Manzō VI succeeded to the Nomura *family headship in 1922 (Nomura Manzō I was active in the early 1700s). In 1920 Manzō VI joined his father and younger brother in founding the kyōgen performance series Yoiya-kai which produced some 200 all-kyōgen shows to 1944. In the post-war period Manzō organized three performance series that showcased his talents and those of his three sons. In 1963 Manzō went to the University of Washington as a visiting professor, and up to 1971 made frequent trips to Europe and America to perform and teach kyōgen. Early in his career his *acting was known for its rigidity and strictness, but it later evolved into a witty, unconstrained style. He garnered fans and supporters from many quarters and was largely responsible for the pre-eminence of his family in *Tokyo kyōgen. In 1955 he published *Kyōgen no Michi* and his writings are available in *Nomura Manzō Chōsakushō* (1982). LRK

NORA

*Folk theatre found in southern *Thailand and popular with Thai-speaking minorities in *Malaysia. Related to *lakon chatri*, *nora* traditionally enacts the Manora story, a tale of a half-bird, half-woman heroine known throughout Asia. *Nora* comes in two forms. Traditional *nora* is a *dance-drama similar to *lakon* but the play is replaced by a solo improvisation of *dancing and singing. Modern *nora* begins traditionally but is followed by a modern drama in which actors and actresses wear contemporary *costumes and sing both traditional and modern songs. SV/KP

NORMAN, MARSHA (1947–)

American playwright. Raised in Kentucky in a strict religious family, Norman said she felt invisible as a child and eventually wrote about people who would otherwise go unheard. Jon *Jory directed *Getting Out* (*Actors Theatre of Louisville, 1977), about an ex-convict who makes peace with her violent younger self, and *Third and Oak* (1978), comprised of two *one-acts (*The Laundromat* and *The Pool Hall*) intended as a single piece about loss. In *'night, Mother* (1982, Pulitzer Prize), a mother fails to prevent her middle-aged daughter's suicide; though some *feminists have questioned the canonization of this play, it has been produced in 36 countries and 23 languages. For the next eight years her new work, treating comedy, myth, and religious scepticism, was seen at American *regional theatres (*The Holdup*, 1983; *Traveler in the Dark*, 1984; *Sarah and Abraham*, 1988). Norman returned to Broadway with *books for the *musicals *The Secret Garden* (1991) and *The Red Shoes* (1993). She complained that she could not get a straight play accepted for production unless Jory had commissioned it, and preferred a life in musical theatre. Jory did present *Loving Daniel Boone* (1992), about hero worship, and *Trudy Blue* (1995), a *comedy about an author's midlife crisis as she faces the threat of cancer; it succeeded in *New York in 1999. FL

NORTON, THOMAS *See* SACKVILLE, THOMAS.

NOUVEAU MONDE, THÉÂTRE DU

French Canada's pre-eminent theatre company, founded in *Montréal in 1951 by actor-directors Jean *Gascon and Jean-Louis *Roux (who became, respectively, its *artistic director and secretary-general) along with French-born actor Guy Hoffman, and writers Éloi de Grandmont and Georges Groulx. After an initial uncertainty as to repertoire and clientele, the TNM found a successful formula balancing French and international classics with carefully chosen works by Québécois authors, all characterized by high standards of performance, *directing, design (usually by Robert *Prévost), and *music (usually by Gabriel Charpentier). The first Canadian professional company to perform in France, it was highly praised in its first appearance in *Paris in 1955 for its innovative interpretations of *Molière. It has since *toured frequently and extensively in Europe and America. Initially housed in the tiny Salle du Gesù, the TNM moved permanently to the much larger Comédie Canadienne in 1972. LED

NOVELLI, ERMETE (1851–1919)

Italian *actor-manager. A tall, lean man with a chiselled face and supple body, Novelli made his name in the Calloud-Diligenti

(1868–73) and the *Bellotti-Bon (1877–83) companies as a comic actor. He possessed natural powers of delivery and an extraordinary ability to change his persona to suit many roles in works by Italian (*Goldoni, *Ferrari, *Giacosa) and French playwrights (*Scribe, *Augier, *Sardou) and his own comic *monologues. In 1884 Novelli formed a company that toured Italy, Spain (1886–7), other European cities (1894–9), and South America (1890, 1894, 1899); and in 1898 he made an acclaimed *Parisian debut. While he expanded his vast comic repertory to include *tragedy and *drama in the late 1880s, he was more admired for his interpretative skill in roles requiring tragic and comic contrast, such as the title roles in *Shylock* (adapted from Shakespeare) and Aicard's *Papa Lebonnard*. When his attempt to create a regional theatre in *Rome called Casa di Goldoni (1900–1) failed, he returned to the nomadic *touring life.

JEH

NOVELLO, IVOR (DAVID IVOR DAVIES) (1893–1951)

Welsh composer, actor, dramatist, and impresario celebrated for his stylish performances and glamorous image as much as for his popular songs and romantic *musicals. In 1914 he wrote one of the First World War's most popular standards, 'Keep the Home Fires Burning', and 'We'll Gather Lilacs' (1945) was a similarly successful response to the next war. After serving in the Royal Naval Air Service he made his acting debut in *Duburau* (1921) in *London, and subsequently became an *actor-manager, beginning with *The Rat* (1924, written with Constance Collier). His many other plays include *Symphony in Two Flats* (1929) and *The Truth Game* (1930). Novello's musicals have simple, often *melodramatic *plots, and lush and sentimental scores; they include *Glamorous Night* (1935), *Careless Rapture* (1936), *Crest of a Wave* (1937), *The Dancing Years* (1939), *Arc de Triomphe* (1943), *Perchance to Dream* (1945), and *King's Rhapsody* (1949). Most had lyrics by Christopher Hassall. Novello also wrote original and adapted screenplays and acted in several *films.

AS

NOVO, SALVADOR (1904–74)

Mexican playwright, director, poet, and novelist. As a member of the experimental Teatro de *Ulises (1928), he sought to modernize the Mexican stage. A translator of *O'Neill, *Beckett, and *Synge, Novo was appointed the first director of the theatre section of the National Institute of Fine Arts (*INBA) in 1947. His first significant play was *The Cultured Lady* (1951), a rather vitriolic *satire of Mexican high society. *At Eight Columns* (1956) is a critique of the press and *The Third Faust* (1956) is one of the first Mexican plays to deal openly with homosexuality.

KFN

NOWRA, LOUIS (1950–)

Australian playwright. Nowra's earlier plays, such as *The Precious Woman* (1980), are historical fantasies set outside but still relevant to Australia. Later work focused on contemporary predicaments shaped by historical traumas, such as the effects of colonization—particularly for indigenous Australians—and class oppression, best exemplified in *The Golden Age* (1985). A prolific decade in the 1990s saw the production of semi-autobiographical *comedies such as *Cosi* (1992), Aboriginal-centred dramas such as *Radiance* (1993), and plays such as *The Temple* (1993) which offered *satires of contemporary situations. Nowra has an original dramatic style, and has also written for *film, *television, *radio, and *opera.

SBS

NTSHONA, WINSTON (c.1945–)

South African actor. From the Eastern Cape, Ntshona was working as a laboratory assistant in the Ford plant when John *Kani introduced him to Athol *Fugard and the Serpent Players in 1967, and by 1972 was a full-time professional performer. Classified as Fugard's domestic workers, Ntshona and Kani workshopped *Sizwe Bansi Is Dead* (1972) and *The Island* (1973) with him, based on their personal experiences of apartheid South Africa. The two were imprisoned in the Transkei for remarks criticizing the government's 'Bantustan policy' of total separation of blacks in *Statements after an Arrest under the Immorality Act* (1972), but released under pressure from Europe. Ntshona played Daan in the *film *Marigolds in August* (written by Fugard, 1979).

YH

NUEVO GRUPO, EL (CHILE)

Theatre troupe created in 1984 by the actors Julio Jung and María Elena *Duvauchelle and the producer Neda Rivas. The first production was Jaime Miranda's *Regreso sin causa* (*Return without a Cause*, 1984), a play about the problems of exile, which was performed during Pinochet's dictatorship and attracted a large *audience. The playwright was *awarded an important prize that was withheld by the authorities. Miranda's second work, *La ardiente paciencia* (*Burning Patience*, 1986), based on the life of Pablo Neruda and Allende's socialist government, was directed by Héctor *Noguera. Other works produced by Nuevo Grupo include *Telarañas* (*Spider Web*, 1985), written by the Argentine Eduardo *Pavlosky and directed by Jorge Loncón, and *El día en que me quieras* (*The Day You Love Me*, 1985) and *Acto cultural* (*Cultural Act*, 1987), both by the Venezuelan José Ignacio *Cabrujas.

MAR

NUEVO GRUPO, EL (VENEZUELA)

Troupe founded in 1967 by Isaac *Chocrón, Román *Chalbaud, and José Ignacio *Cabrujas. Their aim was to produce *text-based professional theatre with high-quality *acting and *scenography, without conforming to a particular aesthetic. Their own plays were produced alongside some 30 national and international authors, including Sam *Shepard, Lanford *Wilson, Edward *Albee, and Harold *Pinter. Notable directors included Ugo *Ulive and Antonio Constante. The organizers published the journal *Revista Nuevo Grupo* (1967–70) and six books. In 1974 they set up a prestigious competition for young authors, which brought Edilio Peña, Nestor Caballero, Jaime Miranda, Luis Chesney, and Omar Quiaragua to the national stage. Nuevo Grupo was *financed privately for its first seven years, after which it was state subsidized until 1988 when funding was withdrawn and the enterprise closed.

LCL trans. AMCS

NUÑEZ, JOSÉ GABRIEL (1937–)

Venezuelan playwright, screenwriter, and economist. His most important works are *Quedo igualito* (*I Remain the Same*, 1963), *La ruta de los murciélagos* (*The Bat Route*, 1964), *Los peces del acuario* (*Fish in the Aquarium*, 1967), *Bang bang* (1968), *Tú quieres que me coma el tigre* (*You Want the Tiger to Eat Me*, 1975), *Madame pompinette* (1980) and *Maria Cristina me quiere goberná* (*Maria Cristina Wants to Rule Me*, 1989). His dramatic world abounds with alienated people fighting a battle of wits to maintain their dignity. He draws on *realism, the *absurd, *epic theatre, and the *folkloric *costumbrismo approach to manners and customs, always with a touch of black humour.

LCL trans. AMCS

NUNN, TREVOR (1940–)

English director. After a successful undergraduate career in Cambridge, Nunn worked at the Belgrade Theatre, Coventry, from 1962 to 1965. Joining Peter *Hall's *Royal Shakespeare Company, Nunn made his mark with *The Revenger's Tragedy* (1966). By 1968 he was Hall's natural successor as *artistic director, a role he shared with Terry *Hands after 1978 and gave up in 1986. Under Nunn's control the company moved into the *Barbican Theatre as its *London home and developed two new spaces in Stratford (the Other Place and the *Swan Theatre) so that, inheriting a company with two theatres, he handed on a company with five. Nunn's own work throughout this period showed an extraordinary ability to adapt to every kind of space: his small-scale *Macbeth* (1976) was an intense study of the working of evil, while he rescued the company from the brink of *financial disaster with an eight-hour, two-part, large-cast, spectacular version of *Nicholas Nickleby* (1980) that explored the social conditions of Victorian England in a *Dickensian spirit. His best work, like *All's Well That Ends Well* in 1981, made a less familiar Shakespeare play into a masterpiece of social relations, emotional tension, and ambiguity of response. He was just as adept in establishing large-scale Shakespeare projects (such as the season of Roman plays in 1972) as in turning *The Comedy of Errors* into a *musical in 1976; the latter's success encouraged him towards musical theatre.

Hands's presence enabled him to work outside the RSC. His commercial productions of *Lloyd Webber's *Cats* (1981) and *Starlight Express* (1984), and of *Boublil and Schönberg's *Les Misérables* (1985, originally an RSC production), established a new model for theatre as a global product, with mountings all over the world contractually obliged to reproduce his originating version as exactly as possible (*see also* MACKINTOSH, CAMERON). If his work in classical theatre has never been marked by profound innovation or experimentation, the invention, freshness, and commercial acuity of these productions redefined musical theatre (and made Nunn by far the richest English director). It also provided a model for successful work in *opera (for example, *Porgy and Bess* at Glyndebourne in 1986). Returning to Shakespeare after a break in the mid-1980s for *Othello* (RSC, 1989), Nunn moved far from the broad strokes of his musical work by developing the style of minute social *realism he had used for *Porgy and Bess*, not only locating the play in a precise milieu but filling it with carefully observed social detail. Musicals apart, Nunn showed only limited interest in new work, though he directed the première of *Stoppard's *Arcadia* (1993). In 1997 he was a surprising choice to succeed Richard *Eyre as artistic director of the Royal *National Theatre, where he tried to recreate the RSC's ensemble company, long abandoned at the National. His own success with small-scale Shakespeare (*The Merchant of Venice*, 1999) and large-scale musicals (*My Fair Lady*, 2001) continued the best of his previous work but his period of rule was marked by a narrow repertoire and a failure to encourage young directors or writers. He was expected to leave the National in 2003. In 2002 he was honoured with a lifetime achievement *award at the annual Olivier Awards ceremony.

PDH

NUYORICAN THEATRE *See* HISPANIC THEATRE, USA.

O

OAKLEY, ANNIE (1860–1926)

American sharpshooter, who learned her skills providing game for restaurants near her Ohio home. As a young girl she defeated professional shooter Frank Butler. Eventually they married and he became her *manager. The diminutive performer joined Buffalo Bill *Cody's *Wild West show in 1885. Known as 'Little Sureshoot', a name given her by her friend and fellow Wild West star Sitting Bull, one of her tricks involved shooting holes in playing cards; by association, punched complimentary passes came to be known as 'Annie Oakleys'. With brief interruptions when she appeared in action-oriented *melodramas, Oakley *toured with the Wild West show for seventeen seasons until a disastrous 1901 railway accident, though she continued to perform occasionally over the next twenty years. Her career inspired the Irving *Berlin *musical *Annie Get your Gun* (1946).

RAH

OBERAMMERGAU

At the beginning of each decade between May and September the villagers of Oberammergau in Bavaria mount approximately 100 performances of a *Passion play that lasts all day, in fulfilment of a pledge made in 1633. The first *texts have not survived. In 1750 Ferdinand Rosner produced a baroque drama in rhyming couplets which remained in use until the early nineteenth century. In 1811 a new prose version by Othmar Weiss created a form in which dramatized *dialogue alternated with *tableaux illustrating the central moments of the Passion. Weiss depicted the Jews in a harsh light, making them responsible for Christ's death. This interpretation survived the 1860 revision by Daisenberger, the version which remained current until 2000, when a new text purged of all anti-Jewish sentiments was produced. The first performances presumably took place in the parish church and after 1700 on a temporary *open-air stage. After 1800 a *perspective stage was constructed which remained in use until the end of the century. The present theatre was built in 1928–9 and retains an outside stage, while the spectators sit in a covered *auditorium holding up to 4,700. By the end of the nineteenth century the play had already become a major tourist attraction, a function which has increasingly replaced its *religious significance.

CBB

OBERIU

Russian/Soviet organization and movement, an acronym for Obshchestvo real'nogo iskusstva (Association for Real Art). Founded by Daniil Kharms, Aleksandr Vvedensky, and others in 1927, its goal was to 'fight against hack art, against stagnation in form and feeling'. Even among the most radical *avant-garde artists in 1920s Russia it would be difficult to trace the influence of crucial European movements such as *surrealism and *dada. However, the work of Kharms and Vvedensky may be said to constitute the missing link between Soviet Russia and those influential aspects of European culture, and to anticipate the methods of the theatre of the *absurd. The Oberiu manifesto was published in 1928 in three sections, devoted to poetry, *film, and the theatre. The version of theatre proposed was to be *plotless and illogical. For example: 'A chair appears on the stage; on the chair is a samovar. The samovar boils. Instead of steam, naked arms rise up from under the lid.' The group's first show, *Three Left Hours*, was given in Leningrad (*St Petersburg) in 1928, and included a performance of Kharms's play *Elizaveta Bam*, a Kafkaesque work in which the central *character is besieged in her flat and accused of all crimes, including murder. Whilst the theme is sinister, the manner is that of *vaudeville, complete with songs and *dances, fights, and mock medieval jousting. The method is not unlike that of *Eisenstein's *montage (without the Marxist dialectic) with disconnected jump-cuts and calculated shocks which ricochet between theatrical *genres and moods. Vvedensky's *Christmas at the Ivanovs* is even more illogical, as if Kafka, *Jarry, Apollinaire, and *Ionesco had all conspired to compose a play both terrifying and hilarious. In a mixture of horror and *farce, a murdered woman engages in a conversation with her own severed head. Children of the same family, but with different surnames, have ages ranging from 1 to 82, the brightest being the 1-year-old. A psychiatrist is a raving lunatic. The parents of the murdered girl make love on a couch beside the coffin containing her dismembered corpse. According to Kharms, who numbered among his literary/artistic heroes and acquaintances *Gogol, Edward Lear, Sherlock Holmes, Kazimir Malevich, and Knut Hamsun, 'only two things in life are of great worth: humour and saintliness'. They were hounded during the 1930s, when both earned their living writing children's stories. Vvedensky took refuge in the Ukraine where he was arrested and died in 1941. Kharms was arrested in 1941 and died in a psychiatric prison the next year. Both were aged 37.   NW

OBEY, ANDRÉ (1892–1975)

French dramatist. Born in Douai, Obey studied law and literature in Lille. In *Paris from 1919, he wrote music and drama *criticism. After writing two plays with Denys Amiel, he met director Jacques *Copeau, whose skill at blending physicality and poetry influenced Obey's subsequent style. Obey's best plays resulted from his collaborative work with Copeau and disciples; *Noé*, *Le Viol de Lucrèce*, and *La Bataille de la Marne* were all produced at the Théâtre du *Vieux-Colombier in 1931. His *Huit cents mètres* (*Eight Hundred Metres*, 1941) was performed in a *sports stadium. Obey wrote three plays about Don Juan and translated or adapted works of *Aeschylus, Shakespeare, and Tennessee *Williams. As director of the *Comédie-Française (1945–7), he initiated reforms to allow production of contemporary works. Obey's skill at *mime-based storytelling is said to have influenced both Jean-Louis *Barrault and Thornton *Wilder.   FHL

OBLIGATORY SCENE *See* SCÈNE À FAIRE.

OBOLENSKY, CHLOE (1942–)

Greek designer, educated in England and France. She studied theatre design in *Paris, beginning her career as assistant to Lila de Nobili. She designed *Aristophanes' *Frogs* (directed by Karolos *Koun, Greek Art Theatre, 1967) and *Verdi's *Aida* (Franco *Zeffirelli, La *Scala), and productions at the *Comedie-Française and the Spoleto Festival with Gian Carlo Menotti. She is especially noted for her extensive work with Peter *Brook at the *Bouffes du Nord in *Paris, including *The Cherry Orchard*, *The Tragedy of Carmen* (both 1981), *The Mahabharata* (theatre 1985, and *film 1989), *The Tempest* (1990), *Impressions of*

Pelléas (1992), *Don Giovanni*, and *Hamlet* (2000). Her simplicity of colour and objects has been particularly suited to Brook's work. She has also designed the *opera *La Dame de Picques* (directed by Lev *Dodin, Paris, 1998) and *Chekhov's *The Seagull* (*Maly Theatre, *St Petersburg, 2001).   PH

OBRAZTSOV, SERGEI (1901–91)

Russian/Soviet *puppet master who trained as an artist and graphic designer before appearing as an actor in 1922. Obraztsov became involved in puppetry as early as 1920, and became *artistic director of the *Moscow State Central Puppet Theatre in 1931. He did much to elevate puppetry to a respectable place in Soviet theatre, improving its techniques and broadening its generic range to embrace political *satire and heroic *romance. A prominent figure on the international scene, he pioneered techniques of Eastern rod puppetry in the West and made several European *tours.   NW

O'BRIEN, TIMOTHY (1929–)

English designer. Born in India, he studied history at Cambridge University and design at the *Yale School of Drama with Donald *Oenslager. Head of design for ABC *television at the age of 27, he designed drama for director Ted Kotcheff. Not interested in *realism, he created kinetic stage units that evolve as working symbols of thematic concerns. His collaborations with Tazeena Firth at the *Royal Shakespeare Company in the 1960s and 1970s include *Richard II* (1973): two giant escalators conveying the hapless king offered a visual metaphor for his loss of power. *Evita* (1978) combined projection and mobile units into a self-described 'machine for presenting a play'. The tumult of *War and Peace* (Kirov Opera, *St Petersburg, 1991) was suggested by hinged walls, which reconfigured the stage and contrasted with an enduring Russian oak. For the endless journey of *Outis* (La *Scala, 1996), monolithic figures disappeared and appeared from the void of the revolve. A contributor to all *Prague Quadrenniales, he has twice captured its major *awards: the Gold Medal (1976) and Golden Triga (1991).   RVL

O'CASEY, SEAN (1880–1964)

Irish playwright and autobiographer. Born John Casey, he grew up in a lower-middle-class *Dublin Protestant family depressed into the working classes by the early death of his father. Though hardly as ill-educated as his heavily fictionalized *Autobiographies* suggest, he did live in poverty and deprivation, working as a navvy on the railways, and then as a union organizer. The alliance of the socialist Irish Citizen Army with the nationalist Volunteers disillusioned him with the 1916 Easter Rising, political views reflected in the three Dublin plays that brought him international success. The two-act *The Shadow of a Gunman*,

953

produced by the *Abbey in 1923, made an immediate impact with its comic vignettes of Dublin slum life and its tragic background of the just-ended Irish War of Independence. The vividness of inner-city working-class speech and manners, never before represented in the theatre, the topicality of the subject matter, the phenomenon of the self-educated worker playwright, all contributed to the play's appeal and that of its immediate successor, *Juno and the Paycock* (1924). This full-length play, set at the time of the Irish Civil War (1922–3), provided major starring roles for three of the Abbey's best actors, the veteran Sara *Allgood as the harassed mother Juno, Barry *Fitzgerald as the strutting husband Captain Boyle, and F. J. McCormick as his parasite friend Joxer. The play's rough mixture of *melodramatic situation and *character *comedy yielded a high voltage of theatrical energy.

The reception of *The Plough and the Stars* (1926), O'Casey's version of the Easter Rising itself, was strikingly different. Staged just ten years after the event that had come to be regarded as the iconic founding moment of the Irish Free State, it was felt to be intolerably provocative in its anti-heroic perspective. The second-act pub scene, with its satiric mockery of the political rhetoric of the executed leader Patrick Pearse and the scandalous appearance of the prostitute Rosie Redmond, was especially offensive. Once again, as with *Synge's *Playboy*, W. B. *Yeats for the Abbey management vehemently defended the play against the protesters.

O'Casey's situation as the Abbey's most successful, if controversial, playwright was dramatically changed with the theatre's humiliating rejection of his next play, *The Silver Tassie*, in 1928: the irascible O'Casey quarrelled loudly and publicly with the Abbey directors. Already living in *London where his earlier plays had been critically acclaimed, he cut his links with the Irish theatre. Though the experimental *Silver Tassie*, with its *expressionist dramatization of the Flanders trenches, had a *succès d'estime* when produced in London in 1929 with Charles *Laughton in the lead, and the more fully expressionist *Within the Gates* (1934) was well received in *New York, for the rest of his long life O'Casey never regained an assured position as a working dramatist in any theatre. His later plays, including *Red Roses for Me* (1943), *Cock-a-Doodle Dandy* (1949), and *The Drums of Father Ned* (1959), were fantasic in idiom, promoting a fervently socialist and anticlerical utopianism. O'Casey's Dublin 'trilogy', outstandingly popular and frequently revived in Ireland, has held its place on the world stage also. Though uneven in style and uncertain in formal control, the plays in the theatre retain the urgency and ambiguity of their *tragicomic mode.

NG

ODÉON

The Théâtre de l'Odéon, as it became in 1797, was originally built as the Théâtre-Français (*see* COMÉDIE-FRANÇAISE) by de Wailly and Peyre on the site of the former Hôtel de Condé. Opened in 1782, it was the first *playhouse in *Paris to be conceived as a significant free-standing architectural entity and the central feature of a major urban redevelopment. The building was enclosed by an open arcade, and from each side of its majestic Doric pillared façade bridges led to cafés incorporated into adjacent pavilions. Its circular *auditorium accommodated four tiers of *boxes, set in slight retreat, and—for the first time—a seated pit. Twice destroyed by *fire, in 1799 and 1818, and twice rebuilt, by Chalgrin in 1808 and Baraguey and Provost in 1819, the Odéon, now the Odéon-Théâtre de l'*Europe, still stands and, if bereft of its original setting, retains much of its original monumental austerity.

JG

ODEON

Ancient *Greek 'music hall'. The best known was in Athens, next to the Theatre of *Dionysus, and was built by Pericles and used for recitations of all kinds but also for other public functions. The term is used generally for the smaller roofed theatres that developed in Hellenistic times from the *ecclesiasterion* or assembly room; these were suitable for more intimate musical, rhetorical, and dramatic functions. However, very large roofed or partially roofed music halls were then constructed in many cities under the *Roman empire, such as the Odeon of Herodes Atticus in Athens and the Odeon of Domitian in Rome.

WJS

ODETS, CLIFFORD (1906–63)

American playwright and director. Odets was a minor actor with the *Group Theatre before he burst onto the *New York scene in 1935 with four plays on Broadway in one season. *Waiting for Lefty* (1935) was an hour-long episodic play which used the flashback technique to dramatize reasons behind the New York cab drivers' strike of 1934. Its Group Theatre production on an experimental Sunday evening bill at an obscure downtown theatre (6 January) was rapturously received by its left-wing *audience and it soon transferred to Broadway, paired with *Till the Day I Die*, an anti-Nazi *one-act hastily readied by Odets. But a month before *Lefty* got to Broadway, Odets's *Awake and Sing!*—a *realistic drama about a working-class Bronx family, and like *Lefty* specially crafted for the Group actors—opened there (in February), and in December *Paradise Lost*, a *character-driven family drama, appeared in the theatre which had just housed *Lefty*. Success brought Hollywood offers, and Odets would remain a Hollywood-based writer for the rest of his life. The Group produced three more plays, including *Golden Boy* (1937), before their 1940 dissolution, but Odets's relationship with them was strained. *Critics found his later work disappointing in light of his initial promise. *The Country Girl* (1950), about an alcoholic actor and his salvific wife, and *The Flowering Peach* (1954), a retelling of the Noah myth, were commercial successes in Broadway productions directed by Odets. The Marxist content of his early plays and his 1934 membership in the Communist Party led to Odets's 1952 questioning by the House Un-American Activities Committee. His limited cooperation with the committee kept him off the blacklist.

MAF

ODIN TEATRET

One of Europe's most important independent group theatres, founded and led by Eugenio *Barba. The company was formed in Oslo in 1964 and moved to Holstebro in Denmark in 1966, when it became a centre for performance research as well as a producing theatre company combined under the rubric of the Nordisk Teaterlaboratorium. As well as the company, the organization incorporates the International School of Theatre Anthropology, an archive of films and videos on *training and performances, and a research library. The company is decidedly international, having always consisted of actors from different countries who spend most of the year *touring, primarily in Europe and *Latin America. The Odin has mounted over 30 productions since 1964, ranging from large-scale works that include the entire troupe to *one-person pieces, 'barters', and workshop-demonstrations of performance and *training techniques. The company's pedagogical concerns have prompted it to spend a portion of each year teaching its physical, vocal, and *dramaturgical techniques both in Holstebro and abroad. *See also* ANTHROPOLOGY, THEATRE; INTERCULTURISM.　　IDW

OENSLAGER, DONALD (1902–75)

American designer and teacher. Born in Harrisburg, Pennsylvania, Oenslager first came into notice as a protégé of George Pierce *Baker, the founder of the Harvard 47 Workshop, who later hired him as stage design teacher at the newly founded *Yale School of Drama (1925). Oenslager balanced professional careers as Broadway set and *lighting designer and teacher throughout his life. A follower of Robert Edmond *Jones and the New Stagecraft, he designed for early experimental groups, notably the *Neighborhood Playhouse, and later for *regional theatre and such established institutions as the *Metropolitan Opera and the New York City Opera. Known for his ability to design interior *box sets that reflected the personalities of their inhabitants in their psychological detail, he was sought after by George S. *Kaufman, Garson *Kanin, Moss *Hart, Marc *Connelly, and other contemporary playwrights. He also designed *musicals and *revues: *Anything Goes* (1934), *Red, Hot, and Blue!* (1936), and *Three to Make Ready* (1946). Among his most notable achievements were *Of Mice and Men* (1937), *The Man Who Came to Dinner* (1939), *My Sister Eileen* (1940), *Born Yesterday* (1946), and *JB* (1958). The author of *Stage Design* (1975), his extensive collection of historic designs was deposited with the Morgan Library, *New York. *See also* SCENOGRAPHY.

MCH

ŒUVRE, THÉÂTRE DE L'

French company, formed in 1893 by Aurélien *Lugné-Poe after the demise of the Théâtre d'*Art, in whose productions he had acted. Set up as an 'aesthetic and dramatic society which aimed to perform the work of the great foreign playwrights and the plays of the young "idealists" ', its first production was *Maeterlinck's *Pelléas and Mélisande*, directed by Lugné-Poe. (The play had been abandoned by Paul *Fort at the Théâtre d'Art the year before.) Despite the *symbolist intentions of the enterprise, the first two seasons were filled with the new Scandinavian drama of *Ibsen, *Bjørnson, and *Strindberg. The most infamous of all productions was Alfred *Jarry's *Ubu roi* in 1896. L'Œuvre began life at the *Bouffes du Nord and moved to the 1,000-seat Nouveau-Théâtre, where Lugné-Poe offered free *tickets to most of the public, and only 100 to subscription holders—a far cry from Fort's elite circle of artists—and public order was sometimes seriously challenged. At the end of the 1897 season Lugné-Poe announced a break with symbolism and signalled the theatre's demise.　　BRS

OFF-BROADWAY

*New York movement, intended as an alternative to the commercial methods of Broadway. Off-Broadway emerged after the Second World War as the memory of earlier experiments in non-commercial theatre collided with the post-war reinvigoration from the European *avant-garde. The result was a cosmopolitan group of theatres dedicated to introducing modern European classics and new American playwrights to more sophisticated *audiences in the 1950s. Since that decade the Off-Broadway theatre has gone through phases of commercialization that made it a smaller version of Broadway or a mirror of *regional repertory theatres.

The movement started with New Stages' production of *Sartre's *The Respectful Prostitute* (1948) in Greenwich Village, and it was formalized the next year when five theatre companies formed the Off-Broadway Theatre League and struck a deal with Actors' Equity (*see* TRADE UNIONS) that permitted union members to work on a reduced pay scale. *Circle in the Square's revival of Tennessee *Williams's *Summer and Smoke* (1952), directed by José *Quintero, was Off-Broadway's first popular success and compelled the attention of major critics like Brooks *Atkinson, whose favourable reviews could mean a *long run or a transfer to Broadway. In 1957 the *Village Voice* newspaper initiated the Obie *awards to recognize the best new plays, performers, and productions Off-Broadway. Other important companies were the *Phoenix Theatre, the *Living Theatre, and the *New York Shakespeare Festival. By the end of the 1950s

Off-Broadway venues began to showcase a new generation of young American playwrights, with successes ranging from *Gelber's *The Connection* (1959) and *Albee's *The Zoo Story* (1960) to *Kopit's *Oh Dad, Poor Dad, Mamma's Hung You in the Closet and I'm Feelin So Sad* (1961). Albee's quick graduation to Broadway with his first full-length play, *Who's Afraid of Virginia Woolf?* (1962), suggested to audiences and producers alike that Off-Broadway was less an alternative to the commercial theatre than a place where theatregoers might see tomorrow's hits today. But as expectations and production values increased, the cost to mount an Off-Broadway show soared. Corporate foundations and public agencies like the *National Endowment for the Arts were soon enlisted to subsidize their seasons (*see* FINANCE).

The dramatic rise of *Off-Off-Broadway during the 1960s eventually distanced Off-Broadway from avant-garde theatre circles and pushed it toward the commercial mainstream. The long-running *musical *The Fantastiks*, which opened in 1960, remained Off-Broadway for 42 years. Joseph *Papp's Public Theatre, founded in 1966 as an extension of the New York Shakespeare Festival, used successful transfers to Broadway like *A Chorus Line* (1975) to underwrite more daring productions, particularly by racially marginalized playwrights such as Miguel Pinero, Ntozake *Shange, and David Henry *Hwang. Identity politics continued to fuel much of the best Off-Broadway theatre of the 1980s, reflected by institutions such as the *Negro Ensemble Company, the Jewish Repertory, and the Pan Asian Repertory. Varieties of *gay, *lesbian, and *feminist plays became a mainstay for such venues as the *Manhattan Theatre Club, the Roundabout Theatre Company, and the *American Place Theatre.

The economic boom of the 1990s was a mixed blessing for Off-Broadway. The redevelopment of Times Square brought record numbers of new tourist audiences, but escalating real-estate values and other costs meant that by the end of the century even a three-*character, one-set Off-Broadway play needed a capitalization of over $400,000. As a result New York companies increasingly co-produce shows with theatres outside the city, an arrangement that further blurs the distinction between Off-Broadway and the regional theatre movement.   JAB

BERKOWITZ, GERALD M., *New Broadways*, rev. edn. (New York, 1997)
LITTLE, STUART W., *Off-Broadway: the prophetic theater* (New York, 1972)

OFFENBACH, JACQUES (1819–80)

French *operetta composer of German birth. A talented instrumentalist and conductor, in 1855 Offenbach founded the Bouffes-Parisiens, a company devoted to the performance of satirical light *opera, which he directed until 1862. He was a prolific composer, turning out almost 100 stage works between 1847 and his death in 1880. He collaborated with some of the most talented librettists in *Paris at a time when the theatre was central to that city's social life. In his masterpieces—*Orpheus in the Underworld* (1858), *La Belle Hélène* (1864), *La Vie parisienne* (1866), and *La Périchole* (1868)—Offenbach's graceful, energetic, and tuneful music is a perfect foil to the witty *text. The works not only effectively satirized the Second Empire, they achieved a level of comic ebullience that has since guaranteed their survival. Offenbach's fortunes declined after the fall of Napoleon III in 1871, public taste no longer favouring his brand of *satire. In his final years, Offenbach was preoccupied with the composition of a romantic opera, *The Tales of Hoffmann*. Although he did not live to complete the work, the allure of its melodies, its poetic and bizarre setting, and its theme of the *poète maudit* have assured the opera's success.   SJCW

OFF-OFF-BROADWAY

A *critic for the *Village Voice* coined the term Off-Off-Broadway to describe a collection of bohemian performance spaces that were springing up in lower Manhattan in *New York in the early 1960s, marking them as distinct from the *Off-Broadway movement which was fast becoming commercialized. *Caffe Cino is credited with founding the new development in 1958. A coffee shop with a tiny stage, its owner, Joe Cino, offered a cheap venue for a wide range of performance that included poetry, *dance, music, and theatre. Ellen *Stewart's *La Mama Experimental Theatre Club (1962) and Ralph Cook's Theatre Genesis (1964) focused more directly on the theatrical side of this emerging arts counter-culture. Among the playwrights featured in early Off-Off Broadway houses were Megan *Terry, Sam *Shepard, Maria Irene *Fornés, Jean-Claude *Van Itallie, Lanford *Wilson, Ronald Tavel, Charles *Ludlam, Terrence *McNally, John *Guare, Ed *Bullins, Adrienne *Kennedy, Rochelle *Owens, and Israel *Horovitz. The *Open Theatre, founded by Joseph *Chaikin in 1963, may have best realized Off-Off Broadway's aesthetic tendency to incorporate dance, poetry, and the visual arts into theatrical performance. The most controversial production associated with the movement was the *ritualistic *Paradise Now* (1968), created by the *Living Theatre, formerly an Off-Broadway company. Other important Off-Off Broadway theatres and artists to emerge from the tumultuous 1960s were the *Performance Group, the New Federal Theater, *Mabou Mines, the *Ridiculous Theatrical Company, Andre *Gregory's Manhattan Project, Andrei *Şerban, Meredith *Monk, and Richard *Foreman.

'Experimental' describes the movement's early restlessness with traditional dramatic form. After the impact of the New Left, the Vietnam War, and the seminal influence of *Grotowski, anthropology became a more radical inspiration for some artists, like director and scholar Richard *Schechner, who increasingly sought to subordinate or eliminate dramatic *texts in favour of a more comprehensive principle of *performance. The result was often a war between *playwrights and *directors during the 1970s that led many dramatists to write for mainstream Off-Broadway and *regional theatres. The rise of identity politics in the 1980s gave Off-Off Broadway writing a new lease on life. *Gay and *lesbian artists, for example, found dramatic performance to be an effective rhetorical strategy for resisting the new cultural conservatism of the Reagan era as well as coping with the AIDS crisis.

Off-Off Broadway was increasingly vertically integrated into the commercial theatre system during the 1990s. 'Showcases'—limited-run performances primarily designed to place new actors in the eye of *casting directors—became increasingly important. At the same time Off-Off-Broadway theatres assumed a greater role in the development of new plays with commercial aspirations. Resolutely *avant-garde companies like the *Wooster Group and Foreman's *Ontological Hysteric Theatre have become the exception to a trend that is erasing the cultural-geographical distinctions that marked New York theatre from 1955 or so. By the start of the new millennium, *performance art and venues like Performance Space 122 in SoHo emerged as the heirs to the anti-establishment spirit of the 1960s and 1970s. Given the commercial success of older performance artists like Spalding *Gray, Laurie *Anderson, and Eric *Bogosian, it is not clear if the category 'Off-Off' will continue to be meaningful.   JAB

OGILVIE, GEORGE (1931–)

Australian director, actor, and teacher, who trained under *Lecoq in the early 1960s. An associate director of *Melbourne's Union Theatre Repertory Company from 1965, he left in 1972 to become the first *artistic director of the South Australian Theatre Company in Adelaide. Ogilvie has performed in the UK and Europe, and taught at the Central School of Drama in *London, but his career has chiefly been in freelance *directing in Australia, where he is renowned for exciting productions of the classics, scrupulous attention to detail, and adventurous exploration of *subtext.   EJS

OGUNDE, HUBERT (CHIEF) (1916–90)

Playwright, musician, and *manager, the 'father of Nigerian theatre'. While employed as a policeman, Ogunde produced an innovative 'native air opera' in Lagos, Garden of Eden and the Throne of God (1944), which started a 45-year career of more than 50 stage productions and several *films. Concerned chiefly with the Yoruba experience, his plays include Africa and God (1944), which explored the Yoruba oral tradition, Strike and Hunger (1946), The Tiger's Empire (1946), an attack on colonial rule in which women professionals appeared on the Nigerian stage for the first time, the nationalistic Herbert Macaulay (1946), and Bread and Bullet (1950), based on the Enugu miners'

strike. In the cauldron of post-independence *politics, Ogunde wrote Yoruba Ronu! (Yoruba Awake!, 1964), which, like Bread and Bullet, was banned (see CENSORSHIP).

The direct influence of Yoruba mask theatre on Ogunde's method of production can be seen in the 'Opening Glees' that continued the tradition of the ijuba or entrance song, and in his debts to Alarinjo theatre and Ilorin acrobat theatre. These were combined with rehearsed songs, *stock characters, *music-hall routines, and *slapstick in productions that were created through *improvisation. Ever alert to innovations, he incorporated trumpets and guitars and used filmed inserts in the manner of *documentary theatre. Not surprisingly, he was one of the first Nigerians to move into *film production. The financial outlay required provoked caution, and his films (such as Aiyé and Jaiyesimi) are relatively conventional. A compelling actor on screen as well as stage, Ogunde started shooting Mister Johnson, a major international film, just before he died. As a manager Ogunde stood aloof from the rivalries between other company leaders, and in a statesmanlike way played a key role in the settlement of disputes. He was largely responsible for the formation of the Union of Nigerian Dramatists and Playwrights, later known as the Association of Nigeria Theatre Practitioners. See also YORUBA POPULAR THEATRE.   JMG

OGUNMOLA, E. KOLA (1925–72)

Nigerian actor, director, and *manager. From the early 1950s Ogunmola struck observers as a subtle performer who created memorable roles by extracting the typical from *characters. As a director of works like Love of Money, he combined a moral imperative with emotion and humour. In 1960, benefiting from Rockefeller funding, Ogunmola was able to work with Demas Nwoko and others at the University of Ibadan on a dramatization of Amos Tutuola's The Palm-Wine Drunkard. Hubert *Ogunde subsequently *toured this production extensively, and it helped to establish his company on a professional, independent basis. Ogunmola's *film for the International Planned Parenthood Federation, My Brother's Children (1971), demonstrates the quality of his work, particularly of his *acting and *improvisational skills, though it only hints at the warmth with which his *audiences responded to his stage presence. See also YORUBA POPULAR THEATRE.   JMG

OGUNYEMI, WALE (1939–)

Nigerian dramatist, director, and actor. Since the mid-1960s his life has been, in his own words, 'write—produce—act, write—produce—act'. Deeply grounded in Yoruba verbal arts and performance, Ogunmola has been involved in theatre in Ibadan at almost every point. His output includes scripts for the stage, *radio, *television, and *film, and covers the mythological and historical, farcical and domestic, the adapted and the highly original. An actor with experience of the gamut of European forms, Ogunyemi has moved with assurance between English and Yoruba. He performed with Duro *Ladipo and Kola *Ogunmola, and has put his mark indelibly on several roles, including that of Dende in *Kongi's Harvest*. Ogunmola's *farce *The Divorce*, billed as 'a scintillating drama about matrimonial strife', was the first production of a groundbreaking professional group working in English, the Unibadan Performing Company (1980). JMG

OIDA YOSHI (1933–)

Paris-based Japanese actor and director. Oida studied both modern (*shingeki) and classical theatre in *Japan before being invited by Jean-Louis *Barrault to work with Peter *Brook at the Théâtre des *Nations *festival in *Paris in 1968. He played Ariel in a production of *The Tempest* directed by Brook that year, and later returned to Paris to join Brook's *International Centre for Theatre Research for such productions as *The Conference of the Birds* (1979), *The Ik* (1975), and *The Mahabharata* (1985). Oida has been active as an independent stage and film actor as well as director and teacher. His own productions include *Japanese Liturgical Games* and *The Divine Comedy*. He has also directed operas, notably Britten's *Curlew River* and Stravinsky's *The Nightingale*, and has written two books, *An Actor Adrift* (1992) and *The Invisible Actor* (1997). CP

O'KEEFFE, JOHN (1747–1833)

Irish playwright, actor, and theatrical memoirist. Born into a *Dublin Catholic family, O'Keeffe performed for twelve years with Henry Mossop's *Smock Alley company, until blindness forced him to retire from acting. Turning to playwriting, he had his first *London success with *Tony Lumpkin in Town* (1778), based on a *character by Oliver *Goldsmith. O'Keeffe's plays are often structured around innovative stage effects presenting exotic landscapes. For instance, *Omai* (*Covent Garden, 1785) was a showcase for designs by *Loutherbourg, whose South Pacific sets catered to public interest generated by the voyages of Captain Cook. Between 1766 and 1826, O'Keeffe wrote 64 *operas and *comedies, of which *Wild Oats; or, The Strolling Gentlemen* (1791) was revived successfully in 1976 by the *Royal Shakespeare Company. His most enduring legacies are his Irish plays, particularly *The Poor Soldier* (1782) and *The Wicklow Mountains* (1795). They combine spectacular landscape effects, songs, and *music within the framework of reconciliatory comic *plots, in which divisions of class and nationality are bridged by romantic love. Exceptionally popular in Ireland, England, and America until the 1820s, O'Keeffe's Irish plays established many of the basic conventions that would be developed by Dion *Boucicault and others into the Irish *melodrama, which in turn formed the basis for the earliest Irish *films. O'Keeffe is

thus a crucial transitional figure, and his *Recollections* (1826) a lively source for the study of the theatre of his time. ChM

OKHLOPKOV, NIKOLAI (1900–67)

Russian/Soviet actor and director who caused a stir with his first production, a *mass performance in Irkutsk (1921). Moving to *Moscow, Okhlopkov joined *Meyerhold's troupe, acting in *Tarelkin's Death* (1922), *Bubus the Teacher* (1925), and *Roar, China!* (1926). Deeply committed to the communist cause, and to the cause of overt *theatricality, Okhlopkov acquired the leadership of the Realistic Theatre in 1932 where, in company with the designer Yakov Shtoffer, he sought to implement, in the round and on a scale of intense intimacy, his idea of a communal theatre. Reconfiguring actor–*audience relationships so as to encourage and facilitate emotional involvement, whilst retaining overtly theatrical means and effects, Okhlopkov staged imaginatively visceral productions of plays on revolutionary and Civil War themes. He also staged an idealized version of Soviet prison camp life as moral reclamation therapy, which stretched the bounds of experimental staging (not to say credulity) to breaking point. Ironically the theatrical establishment rewarded him by closing his theatre and merging it with *Tairov's—the theatrical equivalent of chalk with cheese. Following *film appearances, which included one as peasant folk hero in *Eisenstein's *Aleksandr Nevsky*, Okhlopkov's career resumed its course when he took over the Mayakovsky Theatre, mounting a stage version of Fadeev's anti-fascist novel *The Young Guard* (1947) in a style of elevated romantic *realism, and a *Hamlet* (1954) in a famous cellular setting by Vadim Ryndin, reflecting Hamlet's sense of Denmark as a prison and constituting a surreptitious post-mortem examination of Stalin's Russia. NW

OKUNI (IZUMO NO OKUNI) (fl. 1590–1613)

*Japanese performer, prostitute, and legendary creator of *kabuki. Born c.1578, she began her career as a *miko* (shrine maiden), performing *music and *dances based on *nō, *kyōgen, and Shinto *rituals. In *Kyoto she devised in 1603 a hybrid dance-drama called kabuki, in which she combined sacred temple dances with sensual skits about samurai procuring prostitutes. Okuni became famous for her performances of *rōnin*, the masterless samurai warriors. Suffusing her roles with flamboyant sensuality by dressing in Portuguese men's trousers, kimono, a dangling crucifix, and samurai swords, she toyed with the icons of male authority and forged links between the supernatural, the dramatic, and the erotic, an attribute of kabuki that has continued to the present. By stamping the form with a lush and socially transgressive character, she prepared the way for women to become celebrities in the world of prostitution and performance. The government found this development dangerous: in 1629 female prostitution fell under official licensing and professional women performers were banned from the stage until the beginning of the twentieth century. *See also* MALE IMPERSONATION; WOMEN AND PERFORMANCE.   KMM

OLD COMEDY

The *festival *comedy of Athens during the fifth century BC. By the time of *Aristophanes, the only writer of Old Comedy whose work has survived, comedy held almost as important a position in Athens as did *tragedy. Plays were presented in competition at the Great, or City, *Dionysia and at the Lenaea, both held in honour of *Dionysus, god of the theatre. Comedy was first presented in competition at the Great Dionysia of 486 BC. The Lenaea was more closely associated with the presentation of Old Comedies but did not offer prizes for playwrights or actors until after 440 BC. The difference between the two festivals was dictated by the time of year at which they took place. The Great Dionysia was held in spring when the sailing season had resumed and Athens could play host to visiting traders, guests, and diplomats. The Lenaea was in the dead of winter and exclusive to Athenians and resident aliens. The difference for the comic writer is pointed out by Aristophanes himself who was successfully prosecuted by the politician Cleon after the production of *Babylonians* at the Great Dionysia in 426 BC. He responded with *Acharnians* the following Lenaea at which nobody could accuse him of 'defaming the state in the presence of strangers'. The organization of the festivals is not wholly clear and changed as the exigencies of the Peloponnesian War began to bite. Five comedies were probably presented at the Lenaea, and at least three, one after each set of tragic plays, at the Great Dionysia.

Old Comedy was played in *masks. It was topical and *political, but it was also social and *satirical fantasy in which gods and heroes from the mythological past could consort with celebrated contemporary figures and fictional *characters. The plays contained a fair sprinkling of scatological and sexual references, as well as explicit comic business, and in later centuries much of Aristophanes was banned from both schoolroom and public stage. The plays often feature a confrontation (*agon) between opposing parties and usually a *parabasis* in which the *chorus becomes a mouthpiece for the author, addressing the *audience directly on contemporary issues. Until recently this was thought to have made Aristophanes too parochial to have travelled outside fifth-century Athens, but there is evidence of a performance tradition in southern Italy during his lifetime, and the plays are frequently revived today. Singing and *dancing choruses of 24 members might represent the animal kingdom or some original theatrical conceit. Writers from the earlier part of the fifth century, and Aristophanes' own rivals, have survived only in fragments or by title. *Magnes, Crates, and *Eupolis wrote plays such as *The Gallflies*, *The Animals*, and *The Goats*, while Aristophanes' Old Comedies include *Clouds*, *Wasps*, *Birds*, and *Frogs*. The earliest comedians wrote on mythological themes, perhaps closer in style to the *satyr-play which concluded a group of tragedies. Aristophanes was celebrated as the finest comic playwright of his time, probably for his originality of approach and fresh comic inspiration. *See also* MIDDLE COMEDY.   JMW

OLDFIELD, ANNE (c.1683–1730)

English actress, who joined the *Drury Lane company in 1699. Her rise to fame began in 1703 when Susannah Verbruggen's parts became available following that actress's illness and sudden death. Oldfield's easy and spirited comic style was used to great effect in the creation of Lady Betty Modish in *Cibber's *The Careless Husband* (1704). Considered to be Anne *Bracegirdle's rival for *London's favour, Oldfield's career flourished when Bracegirdle retired (1707). Oldfield's popularity with the Drury Lane *audience made her the best-paid actress of her day.

GBB

OLD VIC THEATRE

*London *playhouse in the Waterloo Bridge Road, which opened as the Coburg Theatre (named for Princess Charlotte) in 1818. It was built as a *minor theatre but was a handsome building with a beautifully proportioned *auditorium. Renamed the Royal Victoria in 1833, it remained a local house with a popular and sensational repertoire until 1880, when it became the Royal Victoria Hall and Coffee Tavern, run by the temperance reformer Emma Cons. Her niece Lilian *Baylis joined her in 1898, and took over in 1912. In 1914 she started Shakespeare seasons which continued until 1941; from 1914 to 1923 she presented all the plays in the First Folio, at popular prices. Throughout the 1930s most leading English actors appeared at the theatre, and the directors included Tyrone *Guthrie and Michel *Saint-Denis. Baylis died in 1937, and the theatre was bombed in 1941. It was not fully repaired until 1950, though from 1947 to 1952 it housed Saint-Denis's influential Old Vic Theatre School (*see* TRAINING FOR THEATRE). Michael *Benthall also presented the entire First Folio between 1953 and 1958. In 1963 the *National Theatre Company under Laurence *Olivier took over, staging numerous important productions and establishing the Old Vic as one of the most important venues in the world. Olivier was followed by Peter *Hall from 1974 to 1976, when the National's move to its new complex on the South Bank was complete. Since then the Old Vic's status has been much debated. *Prospect Theatre took over until 1981, when the theatre went dark. It was bought in 1983 by 'Honest Ed' Mirvish, a *Toronto businessman, who paid for a major refurbishment, restoring the 1871 auditorium and reconstructing the façade. Mirvish subsidized productions until 1998, after which a charitable trust was established to purchase the building. In 2001 its future direction was not yet clear.   EEC

OLESHA, YURY (1899–1960)

Russian/Soviet poet, novelist, dramatist, screenwriter, best known for his experimental novel *Envy* (1927), which explores the conflict between the individual and the collective in the conditions of 1920s Soviet Russia, and which he later dramatized as *The Conspiracy of Feelings* (1929). His play *A List of Assets* (1931), staged by *Meyerhold, concerns a Soviet actress who, weighing the pros and cons of life in the Soviet Union, opts temporarily to live abroad, with unfortunate consequences. Olesha also wrote a play for children based on his story *Three Fat Men* (1928) and adapted Dostoevsky's *The Idiot* for the stage (1958).   NW

OLIMPICO, TEATRO

An *early modern theatre designed by *Palladio for the Olympian Academy in Vicenza, still in use. This circle of learned connoisseurs from various social classes, founded in 1555 with the aim of furthering humanistic and scientific studies, took an active interest in the revival of classical drama and organized performances both of ancient and modern plays. The temporary *stages erected by Palladio for these occasions were fairly sophisticated structures, but costly and restrictive. In 1580 the Academy acquired the site of an old prison building, where they had a permanent theatre built to Palladio's design. The architect died a few months after work began on 28 February 1580, and his son Silla was entrusted with supervising the completion of the building. *Scamozzi finished the theatre in 1584 in accordance with Palladio's design, except for the stage, which he extended behind the *scaenae frons on a plot of land purchased by the Academy in 1582. The *auditorium (*cavea*) had an elliptical plan rather than being arranged as a semicircle, in order to allow a better view of the stage. The stage proper (*pulpitum*) was a long and narrow rectangular (29 by 8 m; 95 by 26 feet) in front of an ornamented architectural façade. In its centre a large arch (*porta regia*) opened up, flanked on each side by two lesser doors (*portae minores*), and two further doors situated at the sides (*versurae*) of the *pulpitum*. Palladio's original idea had been to place *perspective *scenery or *periaktoi behind the arches; Scamozzi opened them up into alleyways with wood-and-plaster houses constructed in diminishing perspective. This setting thus fixed the prototypical urban scene, which *Serlio had constructed in painterly fashion, in a three-dimensional manner. *See also* PLAYHOUSE; SCENOGRAPHY; ANCIENT THEATRES.   GB

OLIVERA, CASA DE LA

The *playhouse of Valencia, Spain's most important theatrical centre after *Madrid and Seville, inaugurated in 1584, rebuilt in 1619, and finally closed in 1749. Valencia had had some earlier theatres, all short-lived. The first Olivera, founded by the General Hospital, was similar to the Madrid *corrales de comedias*: a rectangular *open-air yard behind a house, first-floor *boxes, and a second-floor women's gallery, though there were also chairs and benches in the yard, as well as standing room. The total capacity was perhaps 2,000. The second Olivera, or Casa Nova, built largely of masonry, was much more sophisticated, with a roofed, polygonal *auditorium approximating an extended semicircle, up to 392 chairs in the yard with benches behind, *gradas* (raked seating), first-floor boxes, a second-floor women's gallery, and a low, shallow, *thrust stage (9.5 m by 3.6 m; 31 by 12 feet), sometimes extended forward, projecting from a *tiring house with a balcony.   CD

OLIVIER, LAURENCE (1907–89)

English actor and *manager. The greatest heroic actor of his age, Olivier always made sure his performances were marked by extremes, whether in physical movement (his dying fall off a platform as Coriolanus at Stratford, 1959) or *make-up (false teeth to adjust his jaw line as Shylock at the *National Theatre, 1970), or often by giving inordinate emphasis to the wrong line in a speech ('Dishonour not your mothers' in Henry V's 'Once more unto the breach' at Harfleur). But he was also the most thrilling and daring of actors. His abilities were recognized early: Sybil *Thorndike dubbed his schoolboy performance in *The Taming of the Shrew* in 1922 'the best Kate I ever saw'. Like many others, after a number of walk-ons he worked with Barry *Jackson at the *Birmingham Rep, where from 1926 he learned his craft in a variety of classic and *stock roles. A long run as Ralph in *Coward's *Private Lives* (1930) brought him a measure of success and proved his skills in *comedy. But it was his Romeo and Mercutio opposite Peggy *Ashcroft (exchanging the roles with John *Gielgud during the run) that made him a star, helped by the production's move to *New York. Lacking Gielgud's sensitivity to the *verse, Olivier made his Romeo a dashing romantic *hero of great erotic charge.

With *Guthrie's *Old Vic company he played Hamlet, taking the performance to Elsinore in 1937, but also Macbeth, Henry V, Iago, Coriolanus, and Sir Toby Belch. His Hamlet was strongly influenced by a Freudian reading of the *character and he consulted Freud's disciple Ernest Jones to understand Iago, whom he played by underlining the character's homoerotic desire for Othello. But Olivier's style was less psychological study than sheer theatrical power and panache. It led to a spell in Hollywood as a matinée idol *film star (as Heathcliff in *Wuthering Heights*, 1939, and Maxim in *Rebecca*, 1940) and marriage to Vivien *Leigh (his first marriage, to the actress Jill Esmond, having just ended in divorce). The glamorous couple left Hollywood for Olivier to take up war service, initially in the navy but soon by making films, especially *Henry V* (1944), supported by the Ministry of Information and released on the eve of the Normandy invasion. Patriotism and a commitment to Shakespeare on screen combined perfectly, winning him a special Academy award for his work as actor, producer, and director. The concern to film Shakespeare subsequently led also to *Hamlet* (1947) and *Richard III* (1954).

With Ralph Richardson he ran the *Old Vic company at the New Theatre (1944–9), where he learned management, created an extraordinary ensemble, and extended his own range of work. The company's achievement was immense but Olivier's commitment to an actors' theatre investigating the classical repertory was crucial. As a brutally sardonic Richard III, tempestuous Hotspur, and tortured Oedipus, he confirmed his status as energetic hero, but was also brilliantly funny as Justice Shallow (*2 Henry IV*) and *Sheridan's Mr Puff in *The Critic* (which he played as a double bill with *Oedipus*). The Old Vic with its acting school (*see* TRAINING) could have formed a national theatre, but Olivier and Richardson were effectively sacked in 1948 while on *tour.

Olivier tried commercial theatrical management but it did not appeal and he returned to classical theatre. His Titus, directed by *Brook (*Shakespeare Memorial Theatre, 1955), was the first ever production of *Titus Andronicus* in Stratford and was an astonishing success, its tragic power matched by his eccentric Malvolio (1955) and deeply patrician Coriolanus (1959). But Olivier was also prepared to engage with the new forms of drama then emerging, quickly sensing both their significance and their opportunities for actors. As *Osborne's *music-hall comic Archie Rice in *The Entertainer* (*Royal Court, 1957) Olivier appropriated the role for an extraordinary display of *acting skills. He also played in *Ionesco's *Rhinoceros* (Royal Court, 1960) and *Anouilh's *Becket* (New York, 1960).

Olivier's marriage to Leigh collapsed as her mental health deteriorated and, after divorce in 1960, he married Joan *Plowright, whom he had met in the cast of *The Entertainer*. In 1962 he became director of the *Chichester Festival Theatre and planned the long-awaited *National Theatre, of which he became the first director in 1963 when it opened at the Old Vic. As at the New Theatre, Olivier assembled a genuine company of actors, not simply a galaxy of stars, encouraging younger actors including Derek *Jacobi, Robert *Stephens, and Colin *Blakely. Helped and provoked by Kenneth *Tynan, Olivier established a broadly based and often experimental *repertory of classical and new drama which won immediate and intense admiration. Though exhausted by illness, endless battles for subsidy (*see* FINANCE), and the delays in constructing the National's home on the South Bank, Olivier also gave some of his finest performances. His Othello (1964) was a colossus, for which he added lower octaves to his vocal range, the last great Othello by a white actor blacked up. As *Congreve's Tattle in *Love for Love* (1965), Edgar in *Strindberg's *Dance of Death* (1967), Chebutikhin in *Chekhov's *Three Sisters* (1969), and Tyrone in *O'Neill's *Long Day's Journey into Night* (1971), he showed his continuing determination to experiment, to create memorable stage images, and to steal almost every scene.

Olivier had been knighted in 1947 but his life peerage in 1970 (making him Lord Olivier of Brighton) was the first ever given to an actor, apt state recognition of his status in the profession. Struggling with illness, Olivier stopped acting and left the National Theatre in 1973, distressed by the secrecy which kept Peter *Hall's appointment as his successor from him. The largest *auditorium of the National Theatre was named after him—appropriately, in view of its difficult demands on actors. He was made a member of the Order of Merit in 1981. His last stage appearance was as a hologram projection in a *musical called *Time* (1986). But his film work had continued both in blockbusters and in recording his stage performances. He won a number of Academy awards, including a lifetime achievement award (1979). In 1984, though seriously ill, he played King Lear for a *television production in which, while the heroic fire was a pale shadow, the final scenes were profoundly moving. He published an autobiography, *Confessions of an Actor* (1982), and further thoughts *On Acting* (1986).   PDH

BRAGG, MELVYN, *Laurence Olivier* (London, 1984)

HOLDEN, ANTHONY, *Olivier* (London, 1988)

SPOTO, DONALD, *Laurence Olivier: a biography* (London, 1991).

OLIVIER THEATRE *See* NATIONAL THEATRE OF GREAT BRITAIN.

OLLANTAY

Quechua-language play from Peru. Though possibly pre-Columbian, its structure and language indicate that it was actually composed by Padre Antonio Valdés out of indigenous myths and legends. Around 1780 Valdés directed *Ollantay* for the Inca chieftain Tupac Amaru, who later rebelled against the Spanish.   AV

OLYMPIC THEATRE

A *London *playhouse off the Strand. The first theatre on the site, the Olympic Pavilion, was built and opened by Philip Astley in 1806. It was successfully *managed by Robert *Elliston (1813–18) with a programme of *melodrama, *farce, and *pantomime, and rebuilt in 1818. After a succession of managerial bankruptcies, the Olympic saw its best days under the important management of Madame *Vestris (1831–9), who redecorated the interior elegantly and tastefully, reduced the length of the bill, and appealed to the fashionable with a light entertainment repertory of *burlettas, extravaganzas, and genteel farce. The theatre was destroyed by *fire, rebuilt in 1849 and co-managed by William Farren and Frederick *Robson, who starred in *burlesque. A long series of managements then ensued, of no particular distinction, and the theatre was reconstructed in 1890. It closed in 1899 and was demolished in 1904 because of the Aldwych improvements. MRB

OMAHA MAGIC THEATRE

American theatre, founded by director Jo Ann Schmidman in 1968 after performing with the *Open Theatre in *New York. Her bold effort to establish an *avant-garde company with a *feminist bent in a conservative Nebraska city has proved surprisingly successful. By the 1990s OMT had staged well over 100 new plays and *musicals, many of them by Megan *Terry, who joined the company as playwright-in-residence in 1974. *Babes in the Bighouse* (1974), *Flat in Afghanistan* (1981), *Mollie Bailey's Traveling Family Circus, Featuring Scenes from the Life of Mother Jones* (1983), and other notable productions are documented in the pictorial book *Right Brain Vacation Photos* (1992). Geography, plus the company's blend of humanism and unapologetic aestheticism, failed to bolster its reputation with feminist critics, despite OMT's prolific exploration of *gender and sexual *politics. JAB

OMBRES CHINOISES *See* SHADOW-PUPPET THEATRE.

ONE-ACT PLAY

A dramatic composition complete in one *act, sometimes referred to as a one-acter. The act structure that informs Western playwriting may be *dramaturgically linked to ancient *Greek *tragedy, in which episodes containing the main *action were separated by *choral songs. During the *early modern period dramatic form was standardized into a five-act structure, the result of an emerging *neoclassicism that demanded uniformity on aesthetic grounds. Since then the standard number of acts deemed culturally necessary has steadily diminished, from four in the eighteenth and nineteenth centuries to three in the early twentieth century to two sometime after the Second World War. Though modern one-act plays were often considered special-category pieces and difficult to programme, many well-regarded playwrights experimented with the form's narrower focus and more economical dramaturgy, including *Strindberg (*Miss Julie*), *Pirandello (*The Man with the Flower in his Mouth*), *Glaspell (*Trifles*), *Ionesco (*The Chairs*), and *Beckett, in a number of plays. The proliferation of contemporary one-act plays is the result of a combination of influences, including shorter *audience attention span and the models of *film and *television drama. LTC

O'NEAL, FREDERICK (1905–92)

*African-American actor, co-founder of the American Negro Theatre in Harlem (1940–50) with playwright and actor Abram Hill.

Together they performed in Hill's *Striver's Row* (1939), revived the next year as the first production of the new company. O'Neal performed in a number of roles on Broadway and *Off-Broadway, including *Lost in the Stars* (1949), *House of Flowers* (1954), *Take a Giant Step* (1953; *film, 1958), and *Ballad for Bimshire* (1963). From 1964 to 1973 he was president of Actors' Equity Association (*see* TRADE UNIONS, THEATRICAL), the first African-American actor to rise to that office. BBL

O'NEIL, NANCE (1874–1965)

American actress. Born Gertrude Lamson in California, she was the epitome of the emotional, passionate performer. O'Neil made her debut (1893) at the Alcazar Theatre in *San Francisco, and acted in a wide range of parts, from Camille to Lady Macbeth, Nancy in *Oliver Twist*, *Leah the Forsaken*, *Giacometti's *Elizabeth, Queen of England*, and *Hedda Gabler* (which she *filmed in 1917). Tall and powerful, her emotional outbursts startled *audiences in *New York, as did her liberal use of stage blood and vivid death scenes. She remained a stage star until the 1930s, and made 24 movies, most notably *Cimarron* (1930). AW

O'NEILL, ELIZA (1791–1827)

Irish actress, daughter of the *actor-manager of Drogheda Theatre, where she made her debut. After seasons in Belfast and *Dublin, she was engaged at *Covent Garden (1814), where her statuesque physique and resonant voice were much admired till her early retirement in 1819 (*Hazlitt considering her a worthy successor to *Siddons). *Comedy was O'Neill's forte (her Lady Teazle was deemed exemplary), though she was admired too for roles like Juliet in romantic *tragedy. RAC

O'NEILL, EUGENE (1888–1953)

American dramatist. The only US playwright to win the Nobel Prize (1936), O'Neill was the first to bring native *tragedy to the American stage. Writing with a novelist's insights and drawing on his own turbulent life, he revolutionized Broadway in 1920 with *Beyond the Horizon*. Until then, the American theatre consisted mainly of artificial *melodrama, *farce, and *musical comedy; anything weightier came from abroad. With O'Neill's innovative tragedies—among them *The Emperor Jones* and *Anna Christie* (both 1920), *The Hairy Ape* (1921), *Desire under the Elms* (1924), *Strange Interlude* (1927), and *Mourning Becomes Electra* (1931)—he paved the way for an enlightened cadre of home-grown dramatists led by Arthur *Miller and Tennessee *Williams. Influenced by *Strindberg and German *expressionism, he adapted those concerns to native subjects.

O'Neill's father, the actor James *O'Neill, was born in Ireland during the potato famine and was brought to America at

6 by his parents in 1851. He began acting at 20 and soon was a matinée idol, ultimately achieving huge acclaim in his signature role in *The Count of Monte Cristo*. As a boy Eugene accompanied his father on *tour, absorbing the life of the theatre. His mother Ella Quinlan, the daughter of prospering Irish immigrants, found it increasingly difficult to endure the touring life, the dirty trains, shabby hotel rooms, the lack of a permanent home in which to raise her children. Her second son (Edmund) died of measles in infancy, while she was touring with her husband, and Eugene, her third child, was born in a hotel on Broadway. The birth was difficult, and the hotel doctor administered morphine, then a common pain reliever. Ella, depressed and guilty since Edmund's death, not wanting another child, found that the drug relieved her psychological pain as well. Her morphine addiction, coupled with Eugene's knowledge that he had been unwanted, became the defining facts of his life, material he turned to use in *Long Day's Journey into Night*. Written 'in tears and blood' in 1941, shortly before a crippling illness ended his writing career, and produced posthumously, the play is sometimes regarded as America's greatest drama. O'Neill's other masterworks, *The Iceman Cometh* (1939) and *A Moon for the Misbegotten* (1943), were also drawn from the events of his life.

When Eugene was 7 his parents sent him to a Catholic boarding school. While religious mysticism remained a strong influence, evidenced in many of his plays, at the age of 14 he refused to attend church any longer. His rejection of Catholicism coincided with his discovery of his mother's addiction. He escaped into reading: European novelists, philosophers, and playwrights, Eastern mystics, and *Greek tragedians. He entered Princeton at 18, but ignored his courses and was dismissed before the end of his freshman year. Pursuing what he liked to call 'life experience', he plunged into a six-year period of self-education that nearly killed him, but that also provided him with a rich store of material for his future work. By the time he began writing plays at 25, he had carelessly fathered a child he refused to acknowledge (until the boy was 11), spent almost two years drifting as a sailor and dock worker, and nearly drunk himself to death in *Buenos Aires and at a *New York saloon called Jimmy the Priest's, the basis for the setting of *The Iceman Cometh*. He worked briefly as a reporter and satiric poet on the New London *Telegraph* in Connecticut, and in 1912 suffered a bout of tuberculosis, after which he began to write *one-act plays. His enrolment in George Pierce *Baker's playwriting course at Harvard (1913–14) was followed by a mostly drunken year in Greenwich Village, at the end of which he found recognition through a group of *avant-garde writers and artists, the *Provincetown Players. They mounted his sea play *Bound East for Cardiff* at their ramshackle Wharf Theatre in Provincetown, Massachusetts, in 1916, and later that year in Greenwich Village.

By 1924 O'Neill had won two Pulitzer Prizes, for *Beyond the Horizon* and *Anna Christie* (he later won two more for *Strange Interlude* and *Long Day's Journey into Night*). By 1926 his marriage to Agnes Boulton had become problematic and he fell in love with the actress Carlotta Monterey, who had appeared in *The Hairy Ape*. They were married in France in 1929 as O'Neill was starting work on *Mourning Becomes Electra*. In the late 1930s he suffered from a nervous disorder that caused his hands and body to shake and eventually forced him to give up work on a cycle of eleven linked plays, collectively entitled *A Tale of Possessors Self-Dispossessed*, tracing the fortunes of an Irish-American family from 1754 to 1935. Unable to write, he vented his frustration on Carlotta, engaging her in battles that were not resolved until he was close to death. With Carlotta at his side he died in a Boston hotel of pneumonia. His last words: 'Born in a hotel room and—Goddammit—died in a hotel room!'

In performance O'Neill has become one of the most durable of twentieth-century playwrights. After the initial Broadway successes, Lawrence *Langner worked to bring O'Neill into the *Theatre Guild but overcame the reluctance of the board only in 1927, with *Strange Interlude*. It became a sensation, not least for its *Wagnerian length: it began at 5.15, breaking for dinner at 7.30, starting again at 9.00, and playing until 11.00. It ran through a hot summer with no air conditioning to sold-out houses. As Robert Benchley quipped, 'After all it's only an ordinary nine-act play.' Many *critics considered Nina to be the finest role ever undertaken by Lynne Fontanne (*see* LUNT, ALFRED), though she never liked the play or its author. The Guild also produced *Mourning Becomes Electra* and O'Neill's only *comedy, *Ah, Wilderness!* (1933), starring George M. *Cohan. All three productions were directed by Philip *Moeller.

Langner tried unsuccessfully to prise plays from O'Neill during the Second World War. When his dark work *The Iceman Cometh* was finally staged in 1946, it suffered from inadequate *acting and *directing and critics failed to appreciate the *text, though it has since become a staple in the world repertoire. The 1947 production of *A Moon for the Misbegotten* suffered a worse fate, as its weak road production kept it out of New York. Although O'Neill is now praised for his later plays, they achieved theatrical success only after his death, chiefly through the efforts of director José *Quintero and actor Jason *Robards, who became notably associated through the revival of *Iceman* and the première of *Long Day's Journey into Night* (both 1956). Their subsequent productions greatly enhanced O'Neill's international reputation as a major dramatist.   ANG/BSG/YS

GELB, ARTHUR, and GELB, BARBARA, *O'Neill: life with Monte Cristo* (New York, 2000)
—— —— *O'Neill* (New York, 1962)
SHEAFFER, LOUIS, *O'Neill, Son and Artist* (New York, 1990)

O'NEILL, JAMES (1845–1920)

Irish-American actor. Born in County Kilkenny during the potato famine, at the age of 6 he and his family emigrated to Buffalo, New York, where his father deserted them. At 20 James landed a minor acting role in Cincinnati and soon was supporting the era's great stars, including Charlotte *Cushman and Edwin *Booth. O'Neill achieved great fame in the late nineteenth century as Edmond Dantès in the stage adaptation of Alexander *Dumas *pere's* novel *The Count of Monte Cristo*, in which he *toured the United States for more than 30 years. Despite huge promise, O'Neill found himself trapped in the role;*audiences flocked when he played it, and stayed away when he took other parts. In 1877 he married the convent-educated Ella Quinlan, who later became addicted to morphine. She bore James three sons, among them the playwright Eugene *O'Neill. In his autobiographical *tragedy *Long Day's Journey into Night*, Eugene dramatized his mother's addiction and depicted his father as the actor James Tyrone, a man psychologically crippled by his terror of poverty.   ANG/BSG

ONE-PERSON SHOW

A solo theatre piece which foregrounds the abilities of the specific performer in a full-length exploration of *character, narrative, or theme. Although the essence of the one-person show may be found in the storytelling traditions of any culture, the form as such hails from eighteenth-century solo entertainments, like those of George Alexander Stevens, and the nineteenth-century 'platform' performance. Charles *Dickens, who read publicly from his own work throughout Britain and the United States, epitomized the *genre as a packaging of literary material, performative skill, and charismatic presence. In the USA, *Chautauqua and Lyceum circuits booked readings from stables of popular performers. By the twentieth century the one-person show had spread to the *music hall and theatre, and might feature songs, sketches, and impersonations. Ruth *Draper portrayed single characters, evoking a cast of imaginary listeners. In mid-century, Emlyn *Williams as Charles Dickens and Hal *Holbrook as Mark Twain became known for their nightly biographical incarnations.

In the latter part of the twentieth century, John *Gielgud revived the 'reading' form of the one-person show, with an acclaimed programme of Shakespearian excerpts. Spalding *Gray and Quentin Crisp built shows around autobiographical material, as have *touring performers from other countries, including *Africa and *India; Barry *Humphries *satirized British life in the guise of Dame Edna Everage. Lily Tomlin, Whoopi Goldberg, and Eric *Bogosian mounted notable solo productions, each embodying a variety of sharply observed characters. In the 1990s Anna Deavere *Smith used the one-person *genre to investigate controversial cultural events.   EW

ONG KENG SEN (1963–)

Singaporean director, *artistic director of TheatreWorks *Singapore. Ong's major initiative has been to revise traditional theatre forms in order to present Asian histories in the context of contemporary urban Asia. In 1994 he established the Flying Circus Project, a biennial workshop bringing performers from many Asian countries together for collaboration. His experimental productions use English as the most commonly shared language of the different cultures, but depend more on the visual and physical elements of performance, including *music, *ritual, *film, and *documentary, to create disjunctive perspectives on Asian identity. *Descendants of the Eunuch Admiral* (1995) focused on male sexuality and hierarchies, *Broken Birds* (1995) depicted Japanese prostitutes, and *Workhorse Afloat* (1997) juxtaposed foreign workers in nineteenth-century and contemporary Singapore. Ong's best-known works internationally are *Lear* (1997) and *Desdemona* (2000), which combined different performance forms and languages in an Asian *intercultural response to Shakespeare. *The Continuum: Beyond the Killing Fields* (2001) showcased traditional *Cambodian dancers speaking in Cambodian about their personal histories. Ong has also directed in the USA.   YLL

ONNAGATA

Male *actors in *kabuki who specialize in female roles. The term first appeared in *Japan after 1629, when women were banned from the public stage, and was used to designate boys playing female roles. The word is derived from the *Chinese characters *onna* (female) and *gata* or *kata* ('form' or 'person'). *Yoshizawa Ayame, along with Segawa Kikunojo I (1693–1748), created the physical techniques and iconography, Ayame establishing *onnagata* as an art of female-likeness, as recorded in his treatise 'Ayamegusa' ('The Words of Ayame' in *The Actors' Analects*). The 'gender acts' or *kata* that *onnagata* use to inhabit female roles were devised over time as elaborate methods of disguise and transformation, necessitated by government bans on eroticism and violence on stage. Major *onnagata* roles are classified by age and status: *yūjo* (courtesan), *himesama* (princess), *musume* (young girl), *jidainyōbō* (period wife), *sewanyōbō* (contemporary wife), *baba* (old woman or grandmother), and *akuba* (evil female). *Onnagata* have always held a lower status in kabuki troupes than the *tachiyaku*, the male-gender specialists. Contemporary *onnagata* include Nakamura Shikan VI, Nakamura Jakuemon IV, and *Bandō Tamasaburō V. Nakamura Ganjirō III is exceptional in that he plays both male and female roles. *See also* FEMALE IMPERSONATION; GENDER AND PERFORMANCE.
                                    KMM

ŌNO KAZUO (1906–)

Japanese *butoh dancer. Born in Hakodate, Ōno was inspired to study modern *dance by seeing a performance of the flamenco dancer La Argentina (Antonia Mercé) in 1929. He went on to study under the leaders of German *Neue Tanz* in *Japan, Ishii

Baku and Eguchi Takuya. Converted to Christianity in 1930, for much of his career he worked as a gymnastics teacher (and, later, janitor) at a private mission school in Yokohama. His first public performance was not until 1949; thereafter he or his son Yoshito collaborated with *Hijikata Tatsumi on a number of seminal butoh pieces, starting with *The Old Man and the Sea* (1959) and *Forbidden Colours* (1959). Since 1980 Ōno has regularly given performances and workshops around the world, sometimes with his son. In contrast to Hijikata's fascination for the darker side of life, Ōno's work is marked by its tenderness. His most famous pieces, *Admiring La Argentina* (1977) and *My Mother* (1981), feature him in women's dress.   CP

ONTOLOGICAL HYSTERIC THEATRE

Experimental American company, founded in 1968 in *New York by Richard *Foreman, who acts as writer, director, designer, and *producer for the company. His stated objective for the company is to present theatre which is non-emotive and promotes an understanding of a world as is, not as representation. The plays of Foreman often use the structure of a traditional triangular conflict, but attempt to foreground a metaphysical space as opposed to a *naturalistic one. His direction and design incorporate highly formalized stage pictures within a strict *proscenium configuration wherein objects in a forced *perspective setting are given as much focus as the bodies of the actors or words of the *text. Wires and strings are often stretched across the space to emphasize the construction of the theatrical space. *Lighting and *sound (flashes and alarms) are often used to interrupt the *action and disarm the *audience's gaze so as to turn the performance, self-reflexively, toward the theatre's technologies of representation and the ideologies of power present in the representations. Performers are often untrained and *acting consists of a presentational, non-*realist style that, like the *mise-en-scène, points towards its own form as opposed to representing something else. In the 1970s Kate Manheim acted in many of the Ontological Hysteric Theatre productions, originating the role of Rhoda in *Rhoda in Potatoland* (1975). Other productions have included *Bad Boy Nietzsche* (2000), *Perminant Brain Damage* (sic, 1996), *I've Got the Shakes* (1995), *My Head Was a Sledgehammer* (1994), and *Film Is Evil, Radio Is Good* (1988).   MDC

ONWUEME, OSONYE TESS (1955–)

Nigerian playwright and director. A prominent activist in Nigerian campus theatre in the 1980s, Onwueme left her country in 1990 to take up a series of academic appointments in the United States. While her earliest plays (for example, *The Broken Calabash*, 1984) deal with domestic issues such as obstructed love matches and incest, from the late 1980s her work focused increasingly on the unequal relations between the West and the rest of the world. Thus *The Desert Encroaches* explored the hypocrisies of global political and economic relations, while *Go Tell It to Women* (400 pages long, 1992) focused on distinctions between Western and non-Western *feminisms. Onwueme's plays are notable for an experimental diversity of form and their dazzling, caustic wordplay. They have been successfully produced in Nigeria and the USA, mostly by university-based groups (which does not, at least in Nigeria, imply an exclusively elite *audience). Yet they pose considerable challenges: the use of animal *masking (*Ban Empty Barn*) and the vast length of a *text such as *Shakara: dance-hall queen* (2000), which contains over 5,000 lines of *dialogue.   CPD

OPEN-AIR PERFORMANCE

The *Greeks and *Romans performed outdoors; the *medieval *cycle plays were held on fairgrounds or in the streets; in England and Spain much *early modern theatre was performed in closed but roofless spaces. Open-air performance, however, is subject to weather, street noise, and non-paying spectators, and from 1600 forward, as European theatre became more commercial and less communal, it moved indoors. Open-air performance in the West was revived in the twentieth century. The Open Air Theatre in Regent's Park in *London offered summer seasons of Shakespeare in 1933 and continues to flourish. A number of Midwestern cities in the USA built public outdoor theatres, such as the Municipal Opera in St Louis, and local communities perform annual *historical pageant-plays outdoors. Professional and university summer *Shakespeare festivals throughout the English-speaking world perform outdoors, and in the United States *musicals *tour through extensive circuits of large outdoor theatres, usually playing a week in each city. Because *ticket prices are relatively low and *audience behaviour informal, many children receive their first introduction to theatre at an open-air performance, brought by families enjoying a picnic before dark, the pleasant summer weather, and the virtuous feeling of passing on culture.   JB

OPEN STAGE

Originally the term in Britain for a *thrust or *arena *stage, 'open stage' became a general slogan for the *modernist *avant-garde, and performing without a *proscenium became a metaphor for closer contact with the *audience. Particularly associated with the Elizabethanist revival of Shakespeare performance, 'open staging' now might mean any arrangement in which audience and actors are reasonably close and not separated by barriers, as in the *playhouses designed or influenced by Tyrone *Guthrie (*see* STRATFORD FESTIVAL; GUTHRIE THEATRE; CHICHESTER FESTIVAL THEATRE).   JB

Maria Björnson's scenography for Leoš Janáček's **opera** *Kátya Kabanová* (first heard in Brno, 1921; libretto based on Ostrovsky's *The Thunderstorm*), in a production at the Royal Opera House, Covent Garden, London, 1994, directed by Trevor Nunn. The design created two stage levels visually connected by hanging cloth.

OPEN THEATRE

American experimental theatre *collective. Formed in 1963 by Joseph *Chaikin, the Open Theatre was organized to explore new *acting and performance strategies through *improvisation, body and voice *training, and workshop explorations of physically *devised collective creation. The company included actors Raymond Barry, Tina Shephard, and Paul Zimet, writers Jean-Claude *Van Itallie, and Susan Yankowitz, and *dramaturgs Gordon Rogoff and Richard Gilman. Productions included Megan *Terry's *Viet Rock* (1966), as well as *The Serpent* (1969), *Terminal* (1971), *The Mutation Show* (1973), and *Nightwalk* (1973). Similar to other American and European collectives of the 1960s, such as the *Living Theatre and Théâtre du *Soleil, the Open Theatre attempted to reconfigure the aesthetics and politics of theatre practice through ensemble devising. Workshop process superseded production *rehearsals as a means of developing techniques for freeing the body and voice of the actor while pursuing deep explorations of narratives that might lead toward a devised performance. Chaikin had earlier worked as an actor for the Living Theatre and many of the performers who formed the Open Theatre had studied with Nola Chilton, an acting teacher of the *Stanislavsky method. Chilton had begun to develop physicalized acting techniques in response to the demands of *absurdist drama and her exercises, in combination with the improvisation work of Viola Spolin, became the starting point for the Open Theatre's explorations of acting through sound and movement improvisation. The performance works of the Open Theatre were physically devised pieces developed with single authors around such themes as biblical myths in *The Serpent* (developed with Van Itallie), and death in *Terminal* (with Yankowitz). The performance aesthetic of the

Open Theatre included a focus on the presence, physicality, and art of the actor. Yet the *texts and the performances pursued a structure of narrative fragmentation, fluid subjectivities, and presentational theatrics. The Open Theatre has had a wide influence in the West and its techniques continue to be reworked in contemporary devised performance. The company disbanded in 1973 and the Open Theatre papers are housed at Kent State University. *See also* PHYSICAL THEATRE. MDC

OPERA

Dramatic work in which the *action is sung by solo singers and, in most works, a *chorus, to orchestral, instrumental, or keyboard accompaniment. Some operas include passages of spoken *dialogue or passages spoken over orchestral accompaniment. Opera by nature of its musical idiom is most suited to the representation of the extremes of human conduct. The actions of many operas, therefore, involve the spectacular *rituals, conflicts, and confrontations of political, social, and military life, but they also explore the most intimate human emotions. On the whole opera does not successfully represent the transactions of everyday life or easily incorporate dramatic actions that generate discursive ideas. Originating in Europe, opera has spread over the centuries to all parts of the world, though it remains primarily a Western form.

1. Seventeenth century; 2. Eighteenth century;
3. Nineteenth century; 4. Twentieth century

1. Seventeenth century

The first theatrical works that consistently explored music as a dramatic medium arose in different parts of Italy in the late sixteenth and early seventeenth centuries (*see* EARLY MODERN PERIOD IN EUROPE). In the courts of northern Italy, the operas of Jacopo Peri in Florence (*Dafne*, 1598; *Euridice*, 1600), *Monteverdi, and others were presented as revivals of the style of ancient *Greek *tragedy, though they were generically related to the *intermedi or intermezzi performed between *acts of plays and other musical and dramatic events staged during festivities at the courts of princes. In *Rome, a varied operatic tradition was founded on the patronage of rich families and wealthy princes of the Church, while from 1637 opera was performed in Venice on a vigorous commercial basis (at one time the city boasted seven opera houses). Monteverdi ended his career here while Cavalli—whose work, especially *Giasone* (1849), enjoyed an international vogue—first staged most of his works in Venice. Opera narratives were taken from a wide range of sources, including classical mythology, biblical stories, and history. By the end of the seventeenth century, opera had spread throughout Italy and to the major courts and larger cities of Europe. The Habsburg court in *Vienna became a noted centre after the performance of Cesti's extravagant *The Golden Apple* at an im-perial wedding in 1668, and although Italian opera was not popular at the French court when it was introduced in 1645, it laid the groundwork for the foundation of the *Opéra in 1669, where the *tragédies lyriques* of its director, Jean-Baptiste *Lully, were staged. This eclectic form, which incorporated elements from *neoclassical tragedy, *ballet, *pastoral, and symphonic and choric performances, dominated French opera until well into the eighteenth century.

2. Eighteenth century

The splendour of opera's music and the opportunities it offered for extravagant *spectacle made it the ideal vehicle by which European monarchs could manifest their wealth and symbolically give evidence of their power. In the course of the eighteenth century, royal governments of both large and small territories installed companies in specially constructed theatres to give opera performances, sometimes under the direct supervision of the monarch, on a regular rather than occasional basis. As the relatively peaceful conditions of eighteenth-century Europe led to an increase in trade and the growth of large cities, municipal communities were also able to support their own opera, sometimes under commercial auspices. All the larger cities of German-speaking Europe and Italy housed regular companies, some supporting two or more.

Several of the great opera houses that are still in use today, either in modified or rebuilt form, were built in the eighteenth century, including *Covent Garden, *London (1732), the Teatro San Carlo, *Naples (1737), the Teatro Communale, Bologna (1763), the Teatro alla *Scala, *Milan (1778), the Grand Théâtre, Bordeaux (1780), and the Teatro la *Fenice, Venice (1792). The *auditoriums of these *playhouses were built in the shape of a horseshoe, fronted by a *proscenium arch, beneath which was the orchestra pit. The parterre accommodated a good portion of the *audience, who might sit or stand, depending on the custom of the house. An equally large number of spectators were housed in tiers of *boxes that formed the walls of the auditorium. In the largest theatres, such as La Scala, there were six tiers. This configuration proved congenial to the function of opera. As opera-going became one of the pre-eminent social activities of the wealthier classes, patrons could mingle in the parterre or could entertain guests in their boxes, most of which were owned by prominent families in the community. They often engaged in card playing and lotteries, and the practice of prostitution was not infrequently encountered in the house. The auditorium was, in effect, a glorified drawing room. Nevertheless, audiences also came to observe the performance. The horseshoe shape allowed for near perfect acoustics and the side walls, which tapered toward the proscenium and continued the alignment of the *perspective *scenery, created good sight lines and a pleasing unity between *stage and auditorium. In court opera houses, the royal box would be situated in the most prominent part of the auditorium, either at the apex of the horseshoe or above the orchestra pit.

During the eighteenth century each season contained new pieces or pieces not previously heard in the theatre. This meant there was a constant demand for new material, so composers had to be extremely prolific. It was not unusual for a popular composer to write more than 80 operas in his career. By and large, Italian was the preferred language in Europe for most of the eighteenth century.

Most of the vast number of Italian operas written at this time can be assigned to one of two categories, *opera seria* and *opera buffa*. *Opera seria* (serious opera), a term which appeared only at the end of the century, was an action, usually based on ancient history and involving a small number of royal or aristocratic figures, in which such virtues as courage, fidelity, patriotism, and honesty were put to the test and invariably emerged triumphant in obligatory happy endings. Neo-*Aristotelian *unities were observed and *comedy rigorously eschewed. During the middle decades, when *seria* reached its apogee throughout Europe, an opera would generally be in three acts, constructed of a string of accompanied *da capo* arias, in ABA form, linked by dry *recitative. Accompanied recitative might be used for dramatic emphasis and ensembles (duet, trios, occasionally *choruses) often concluded the act. Many *opera seria* were based on the tightly constructed librettos of Pietro *Metastasio, which were also noted for the elegance of their poetry and were highly suitable for singing. Several of Metastasio's librettos were set many times; there were, for example, 90 settings of his most popular libretto, *Artaserse*, between 1730 and 1840. Among the most popular and prolific composers of *opera seria* were Nicola Porpora (1686–1768), Leonardo Leo (1694–1744), Johan Adolf Hasse (1699–1783), Baldassare Galuppi (1706–85), Nicoló Jommeli (1714–74), and Tommaso Traetta (1727–79). Although the operas of *Handel in England were characteristic of *opera seria*, they had little influence on the Continent. In mid-century, *Gluck breathed new life into *seria* with his so-called 'reform' operas, notably *Orpheus and Eurydice* (Vienna, 1762), and *Alceste* (Vienna, 1767), which drastically simplified the complex action of *seria*, dissolved differences between recitative and aria so that the music could more easily express the contour of the action and the emotions of the *characters, and intensified the dramatic impact. *Mozart recalled the earlier *seria* in *Idomeneo* (*Munich, 1781) and *La clemenza di Tito* (*Prague, 1791). The heroic dimensions of *seria* action required splendour in the settings and wealthier theatres especially devoted considerable resources to constructing grandiose *scenery representing in detail antique landscapes and cityscapes. In those theatres that could afford it, single perspective settings of the mechanical theatre were sometimes abandoned for scenery based on multiple or angled perspectives (*scena per angolo), a mode of design perfected by the noted *family of designers *Bibiena (*see also* SCENOGRAPHY).

Opera buffa (comic opera) originated in Naples in the early decades of the century, but swiftly moved northward. Less subject to convention than *seria* because more informal, *buffa* represented the everyday life of the bourgeoisie and peasantry. The successful collaboration of Galuppi and *Goldoni in Venice allows parallels to be drawn between *buffa* and sentimental comedy. By the end of the century, with the waning of audience interest in *seria*, *buffa* was the more widely practised form. Giovanni Paisiello (1740–1816) and Domenico Cimarosa (1749–1801) were the most successful practitioners, but the high point of *buffa* was reached in Mozart's ironic masterpieces *The Marriage of Figaro* (Vienna, 1786), *Don Giovanni* (Prague, 1787), and *Così fan tutte* (Vienna, 1790). *Buffa* gave rise to national comic opera *genres, notably the *Singspiel in German-speaking countries, the *opéra comique in France, the *zarzuela in Spain, and the *operetta internationally.

3. Nineteenth century

The Industrial Revolution and the increase of global trade led to the growth of immense cities in Europe and the United States in the course of the nineteenth century, demanding mass entertainment on an unprecedented scale. While opera did not expand as rapidly as other forms of theatre, it still maintained its cultural centrality. Indeed, as the bourgeoisie aspired to display its new wealth in the same way that the aristocracy it was displacing had done, opera's prestige was enhanced rather than diminished.

New opera houses were built to accommodate the major companies of the larger cities. In most cases the auditorium retained a horseshoe or semicircular shape, but the stage was equipped with increasingly complex and cumbersome machinery for *scene shifting. More space was given to foyers, staircases, and cloakroom facilities, to accommodate the enlarged social functions of the opera house. Major houses constructed in the nineteenth century include the *Bolshoi Theatre, *Moscow (1825), the court operas at Dresden (1841) and Vienna (1869), the Mariinsky Theatre, *St Petersburg (1860), the grandiose *Paris Opéra (1875), and the *Czech National Theatre in Prague (1881). Opera had been performed in the United States since colonial days but at the start of the nineteenth century only New Orleans could boast its own resident company, which mainly performed French works. Opera became increasingly a part of the *New York theatre scene but regular seasons were not given until the foundation of the *Metropolitan Opera in 1883. Most other American cities saw their opera in performance by travelling companies, though in the last decades of the century there were continuous seasons in *San Francisco.

As the century advanced, it became clear that the principle upon which the repertoire was formed was changing. Throughout the eighteenth century, opera seasons had been composed almost exclusively of new works, but by the middle of the nineteenth a canon had begun to develop, centred initially around Gluck, Mozart, Cimarosa, and Rossini. In the course of the century Bellini, Donizetti, *Verdi, and *Wagner would be added, along with single works by notable composers: Beethoven's *Fidelio* (Vienna, 1805), for example, Mussorgsky's *Boris Godunov* (St Petersburg, 1874), and Bizet's *Carmen* (Paris, 1875). Although some composers continued to produce as prolifically as in earlier generations, their rate slowed substantially in later decades.

The most characteristic operatic genre of the nineteenth century was grand opera, which originated at the Paris Opéra. A successor to *opera seria*, the action of grand opera was most frequently set during the European Middle Ages or the Renaissance. *Plots involved conflict between individuals, most frequently lovers from aristocratic and bourgeois backgrounds, and mighty historical forces that eventually destroyed them. Grand opera appealed to the audience's desire for spectacle and their need to acquire some sense of historical identity in a rapidly modernizing society. It required large casts, immense choruses, an enlarged orchestra, and elaborate scenery that reconstructed historical environments down to the tiniest detail (*see* ANTIQUARIANISM). The genre was defined by a few works all premièred in Paris—Auber's *The Mute Girl of Portici* (1828), Rossini's *William Tell* (1829), Meyerbeer's *Robert the Devil* (1831), *The Huguenots* (1834), and *The Prophet* (1849), and Halévy's *The Jewess* (1835)—which went on to have a huge success in Europe. But so ubiquitous was the appeal of grand opera that few, if any, composers were not influenced by it.

Although Italian composers contributed generously to the repertoire of grand opera, the dramatic focus of their work tended to be more upon individual experience. Early nineteenth-century Italian opera, still bearing the unmistakable traces of *seria* and *buffa*, is commonly referred to as bel canto (fine singing), a term that indicates beauty of voice is the prime interest in an operatic performance. In fact the operas of the great bel canto composers—Gioachino Rossini (1792–1868), Gaetano Donizetti (1797–1848), and Vincenzo Bellini (1801–1835)—effectively dramatize several of the prime concerns of *romanticism, though display of the virtuoso voice, especially of the coloratura soprano, was a major appeal of their ingratiatingly melodic work. All three explored the intricate dynamics of romantic love, and all three ended their careers in Paris, where Rossini and Donizetti especially made significant contributions to the repertoire of grand opera.

The modes of *bel canto* and grand opera were most effectively combined in the operas of Italy's greatest composer, Giuseppe Verdi. Verdi's reputation was built on work with extended choruses in grand operatic settings that seemed to articulate the aspirations of his countrymen for national unity. However, his unique capacity to use music to endow the heroic striving of the individual with theatrical credibility meant dramatic interest was focused on how characters face social and political coercion, with greater defiance than in Meyerbeer. Ultimately Verdi's operas articulate an individualist ethos in which the forces of history, the very motive power of grand opera, are called into question.

The other towering figure of nineteenth-century opera is the German Richard Wagner. Although skilled at grand opera, Wagner was profoundly alienated from the theatre of his time by what he considered to be too great an emphasis on the skills of performance and a total disjunction between music, design, and staging. In part, Wagner saw himself as an heir of Gluck, through-composing the action so that it was clearly articulated by the flow of the music. Although it is still possible to identify formal musical numbers such as arias, duets, and ensembles in his great tetralogy *The Ring of the Nibelung* (*Bayreuth Festival, 1876), the continuous music is structured on the repetition of myriad themes (leitmotifs) rather than on discrete musical forms, and the drama unfolds without hiatus for musical embellishment. Wagner's festival theatre at Bayreuth provided a viable alternative to the horseshoe-shaped auditorium of the Italian opera house, while the care with which his music dramas were prepared for production contrasted with the relatively slapdash practices of several European opera houses.

Nationalism in the nineteenth century was the prime ideology upon which states built their authority, and dissident groups used opera to give voice to their separatist ambitions. Opera was a great aid to both parties. Carl Maria von Weber's *Der Freischütz* (*The Freeshooter*, *Berlin, 1821) was the most widely performed of a number of works that brought to the stage the characteristically German rustic romanticism of forests and wicked magic. Weber appealed strongly to Wagner as a young man, who saw his operas as materializing fundamental aspects of the German character. Verdi was a rallying point for Italian independence and unity, a role he did not relish. In Bohemia, a province of the Habsburg (later Austro-Hungarian) Empire, the native language, Czech, was approaching extinction early in the century. However, growing demands for independence led to a revival, especially in the theatre, and the operas of Bedřich Smetana (1824–84) and Antonin Dvořák (1841–1904) were both composed to Czech librettos and dramatized themes taken from Bohemian history and *folklore. In Russia Modest Mussorgsky (1839–81) explored similar terrain, and Pyotr Ilyich Tchaikovsky (1840–93) earned international recognition for his dramatization of two of the iconic stories of Russian romanticism, *Eugene Onegin* (Moscow, 1881) and *The Queen of Spades* (St Petersburg, 1890). It was, however, the operas of Nikolay Rimsky-Korsakov (1844–1908) that most thoroughly mined Russian folklore.

4. Twentieth century

The large number of personnel required to perform opera, the large stipends that have, since its earliest days, been commanded by singers, and the spectacle that is usually more lavish than for spoken drama have meant that for most of its history opera has been difficult to produce commercially. It has traditionally depended upon the patronage of politically powerful or wealthy individuals and, in the modern age, upon heavy government subsidy (*see* FINANCE). *Ticket prices have always been considerably higher than for spoken theatre. Consequently opera has found it difficult to shed its reputation as an elitist art form and this has done it some damage during a century when egalitarian values have been widespread, especially among those who prize the fine and performing arts. Furthermore, the heroic dimensions of much operatic action, the tendency of opera to look back to the past with nostalgia, and the formal display that can still be found in the conduct of both singers and the well-heeled segments of the audience have given opera an unfortunate air of archaism and exclusiveness that potentially alienates newcomers to the genre. Nevertheless, after signs of decline in the middle decades of the twentieth century, opera at the start of the new millennium was undergoing a surprisingly vigorous revival, especially in the United States.

Although most major European companies were founded in the nineteenth century, if not earlier, in the United States they are of more recent origin. Operatic productions can now be seen in all American cities of any size and regular seasons of several months' duration are sponsored by the Metropolitan Opera, the San Francisco Opera (founded 1923), the Lyric Opera of *Chicago (1954), the Houston Grand Opera (1955), and the *Los Angeles Opera (1985). Smaller companies like the Seattle Opera (early 1960s) and *festivals such as Santa Fe (1956) and Glimmerglass (1975) attract international audiences. Larger cities in Europe and America can support several companies, many of which specialize in certain genres or national schools of opera; there are, for example, at least 23 sites in New York where opera is performed on an occasional or regular basis.

The canon has been substantially expanded in the twentieth century. The emotionally stirring and eminently theatrical *verismo operas of Giacomo *Puccini are among the most frequently performed works in the repertoire, while the post-Wagnerian compositions of Richard *Strauss, with their tortuous Freudian psychology, elaborate symbolism, and massive orchestration, are firmly placed in the repertoire. The tersely intense but moving operas on Moravian and Russian themes by the Czech Leoš Janáček (1854–1928) have also undergone a spectacular international renaissance since 1970. As in previous centuries, some composers have made their mark with one opera: Dmitry Shostakovich's *Lady Macbeth of the Mtsenk District* (Leningrad, 1924), Alban Berg's *Wozzeck* (Berlin, 1925), and Kurt *Weill's *The Rise and Fall of the City of Mahagonny* (*text by *Brecht, Leipzig, 1930) are regularly performed. These works have succeeded in part because they use music to articulate the experience of social alienation that was so salient a feature of serious theatre in the twentieth century. But it has not been easy for modern composers to find large audiences. The latest composer who regularly features in seasons is the Englishman Benjamin Britten (1913–76) and, while there are no objective means of measuring inclusiveness, it is still uncertain whether his works have become canonical. And, for good or ill, canonicity is a crucial factor in the operatic world. Toward the

end of the century, American composers were particularly productive: *Einstein on the Beach* (*Avignon, 1976), *Satyagraha* (Rotterdam, 1980), and *The Voyage* (New York, 1992) by Philip *Glass, *Nixon in China* (Houston, 1987) and *The Death of Klinghoffer* (*Brussels, 1991) by John Adams, and *Emmeline* (Santa Fe, 1996) by Tobias Picker have found enthusiastic audiences. But, however successful a new work may be at its première, the odds against it finding acceptance into the 60 or so works that form the core of the canon are overwhelming, whatever the quality of the musical drama.

The advent of long-playing records in the 1950s and compact discs during the 1980s has had some positive impact upon the repertoire. Recordings allow potential audiences to become familiar with a difficult work prior to seeing it in the theatre. They have also increased awareness of the depth of the historical repertoire. Some decades ago, for example, Rossini was represented mainly by a single work, *The Barber of Seville* (Rome, 1816). Now all his 39 operas have been recorded; several of his *buffa*, and even some of his *seria* operas, are regularly staged. Recordings may even have added a major composer to the canon. Only a decade or so ago, performances of Handel's operas were exceptionally rare; now companies may include a variety of his works in successive seasons. Nevertheless, in contrast to the spoken theatre or to *musical comedy, change in the composition of the operatic repertoire is glacial.

Under these circumstances, it might be puzzling why opera appeals to the theatregoing public today. The answer may lie as much in the interpreters as in the music. From its beginnings in the seventeenth century, singers with opulent voices and flamboyant personalities have found opera their natural medium. In the eighteenth century, the *castrati were the toast of Europe and audiences would flock to *opera seria* mainly to hear their extraordinary vocal acrobatics. As the castrati fell out of favour, the agile and highly trained voices of coloratura sopranos drew public acclaim, while in the second part of the nineteenth century, Verdi and Wagner placed the voices of lyrical and heroic tenors in special prominence. In the twentieth century, with the widespread popularity of recordings, audiences are as likely to be brought to opera through the voice of a single singer as through an actual visit to the theatre. Aficionados often argue that the golden age of singing always lies in the past and no one will dispute that Enrico Caruso (1873–1921), Fyodor Chaliapin (1873–1938), Lauritz Melchior (1890–1973), Kirsten Flagstad (1895–1962), Jussi Björling (1911–60), and Maria Callas (1923–77), to name just a handful of great singers, vastly enriched the form with the quality of their singing and through the myths generated by their personalities. Nevertheless, opera has voices of equal quality and stature today. At the start of the twenty-first century singers such as Cecilia Bartoli, Placido Domingo, Luciano Pavarotti, and Bryn Terfel sing to audiences far more numerous than those which attend live opera, and at the same time expand the audience for live performance.

Throughout the twentieth century, the public became increasingly interested, sometimes infuriated, by the manner in which operas are designed and staged. Opera offers stage *directors and designers challenges equal to those of the spoken theatre. In particular, given the limitations of the repertoire, directors have to devise ways to give theatrical life to operas which have been performed so frequently that most of the audience are likely to be intimately familiar with them. From the early 1900s the scenic abstraction associated with *symbolist drama gradually eroded the literalness of operatic sets, as did *expressionism, but it was not until the productions of Wolfgang and Wieland *Wagner at Bayreuth in the 1950s, influenced by *Appia, that symbolist principles were completely embraced. Since then the production not only of Wagner but of the whole operatic repertoire has been transformed. From the early to mid-1970s on, what can best be termed a postmodern (*see* MODERNISM AND POSTMODERNISM) approach to design and directing spread throughout the operatic world. Aesthetic unity was no longer a prime consideration; the production would highlight the social and political implications of the opera's action and frequently include onstage references to the work's own performance history. Now it is comparatively rare to see a production designed and directed in a style resembling its first staging, or its imagined staging by the librettist and composer. Noted contemporary directors include Jonathan *Miller, David Pountney, Graham Vick, and Keith Warner of Great Britain; Patrice *Chéreau of France; Dieter *Dorn, Peter Konwitschny, Harry *Kupfer, and Herbert Wernicke of Germany; Luca *Ronconi of Italy; Francesca Zambello, Peter *Sellars, and Robert *Wilson of the United States; and Robert Carsen of Canada. It is significant that a number of these directors (and others as well) have come from spoken theatre. Their work is highly individual and varies from production to production; and opera audiences, being of a somewhat conservative bent, have not always taken kindly to what they regard as unwarranted liberties with works dear to their hearts. Nevertheless, if modes of theatrical representation stagnate, the theatre itself will die. The vitality of opera in the present world is in part guaranteed by these directors' work.

SJCW

LINDENBERGER, HERBERT, *Opera: the extravagant art* (Ithaca, NY, 1984)

PARKER, ROGER (ed.), *The Oxford Illustrated History of Opera* (Oxford, 1994)

SADIE, STANLEY (ed.), *History of Opera* (London, 1989)

SOMERSET-WARD, RICHARD, *The Story of Opera* (New York, 2001)

WESTBROOK, RAY, BARFOOT, TERRY, and HEADINGTON, CHRISTOPHER, *Opera: a history* (New York, 1987)

OPÉRA (PARIS)

Founded in 1669, the Academy of Opera gave its inaugural production, Perrin and Cambert's *Pomone*, in 1671, at the Bouteille *tennis court in *Paris. From 1672, with an exclusive privilege to perform all drama set entirely to *music—upheld until the revolution and re-established by Napoleon shortly thereafter—*Lully took over the directorship of what had become the Royal Academy of Music. In 1673, with Lully's lyric *tragedies heading the repertoire, it moved into *Molière's Théâtre du *Palais Royal, and played there until dispossessed by *fire in 1763. Despite providing a prestigious public setting for the aristocracy, for much of the eighteenth century the institution was plagued by *financial difficulties and torn by artistic controversy. Administered by the city of Paris throughout most of the 1790s, the Opéra (a title first assumed in 1791) was taken over directly by Napoleon in 1802 and by Louis XVIII from 1814 to 1830, when it ceased to depend on the royal household and was reorganized as a private enterprise.

The Salle Le Pelletier, the Opéra's home from 1821 to 1873, saw the triumph of *romantic grand *opera, especially in the person of Giacomo Meyerbeer, whose heroic and spectacular *Robert the Devil* (1831) made him Europe's most celebrated composer. *Ballets were just as popular as opera throughout this period: Marie Taglioni made her debut in 1827, and a string of masterpieces followed, from Hérold's *La Fille mal gardée* (1828) to Delibes's *Coppélia* (1870). The period from 1870 to 1914 witnessed growing prosperity and prestige for the institution. Commissioned in 1860 by Napoleon III for Haussmann's renovated cityscape, Charles Garnier's new opera house, a neo-baroque, seventeen-storey masterpiece, with multicoloured marbles, lavish statuary, and grand staircase, was inaugurated in 1875. Many new titles appeared in the 1880s—*Verdi's *Aida* and *Rigoletto*, Massenet's *Le Cid*, and Gounod's *Roméo et Juliette*—and the 1890s saw Saint-Saëns's lavish *Samson et Dalila* and, a departure from classical or *historical themes, the *verismo of Alfred Bruneau's *Messidor*, based on *Zola. Particularly striking was the measure of popularity achieved by *Wagner: the *Ring* tetralogy reached the Palais Garnier in 1911. And the impact of *Diaghilev's *Ballets Russes, with Nijinsky and Pavlova, was sensational between 1909 and 1914.

Appointed in 1915, Jacques Rouche directed the Opéra through two world wars, until 1945. In a predominantly French post-romantic repertory, he produced Poulenc, Milhaud, and Stravinsky, and commissioned new work from composers such as Bruneau, Mariotte, and d'Indy. Between the wars he invited companies from *Vienna and *Berlin to sing Wagner and *Strauss in German. Although important creations were staged—notably Alban Berg's *Wozzeck* in 1963—the period 1950 to 1968 saw morale and work at the Opéra sink steadily to an all-time low. The institution was resurrected in 1973 by the appointment of Rolf Liebermann as director. With Georg Solti as his music adviser, Liebermann completely transformed the Opéra. His were golden days, with *Strehler's production of *Figaro*, and Placido Domingo and Kiri Te Kanawa making their singing debuts. But Liebermann's outstanding achievement was the world première of Berg's complete *Lulu* (1979), directed by *Chéreau. In 1982 plans were announced for a new opera house—the Paris Opéra's fourteenth in 330 years—and in 1990 Berlioz's *Les Troyens* inaugurated Carlos Ott's rigorously geometric Opéra Bastille.   JG

OPÉRA-COMIQUE

Destined to play an important part in eighteenth-century French theatre history, the name *opéra-comique* appears officially for the first time in 1715, applied to the distinctive productions of the fairground theatres. It became the generic term for various kinds of popular entertainment with musical accompaniment, produced under constant harassment from the official theatres, the *Comédie-Française and the *Opéra. In 1721, the *opéra-comique* took an important step towards official recognition, when a poor tax was levied on the fairground theatres, putting them on an equal footing with the monopoly companies. However, 1721 also saw competition from the Italian players, who took over one of the fairground sites, though they accepted defeat and withdrew after three years. The future of the *opéra-comique* remained precarious under a series of directors, and in 1745 the Opéra managed its complete closure. Reopening with a *privilège* from the Opéra in 1751, it prospered under the direction of Jean Monnet; and in 1762, after premises at the Saint-Germain fairground had been destroyed by *fire, the *opéra-comique* amalgamated with the *Comédie Italienne at the *Hôtel de Bourgogne, the joint company taking the official title in 1780 and moving into the present-day premises of the Théâtre de l'Opéra-Comique (the Salle Favart, off the boulevard des Italiens) in 1783. In the history of European opera, the French term *opéra-comique* has retained from its eighteenth-century origins a more technical meaning: a work containing spoken *dialogue, whether 'comic' in tone or not (thus Bizet's *Carmen* ranks as an *opéra-comique*).   WDH

OPERETTA

A light *opera in which musical numbers, songs, and *dances are linked by spoken *dialogue. Although the term dates from mid-eighteenth-century Italy, operetta is first recognizable as an independent *genre in 1850s *Paris. One-act stage works by *Offenbach were designated 'operettes', or 'little operas', while his full-length works were labelled 'opéra-bouffes'. Nevertheless, his great *satires—*Orpheus in the Underworld* (1858), *La Belle Hélène* (1864), *La Vie parisienne* (1866), and *La Périchole* (1868)—are, along with the flamboyant historical *burlesques of his associate Hervé (1825–92), acknowledged as the first operettas. Despite the local appeal of Offenbach's satire, his work found its way to other European capitals, but when Paris fell to the Prussians in 1870, the centre for operetta shifted to *Vienna. This did not mean the genre was dead in Paris. Several Parisian operettas, notably Charles Lecocq's *The Daughter of Mme Angot* (1872) and Robert Planquette's *The Bells of Corneville* (1877), were international hits, but Europe, and later America, found operetta in the Viennese idiom more attractive.

Viennese operetta provided the perfect antidotal entertainment for a society experiencing anxiety over modernization. The fairy-tale atmosphere of its *plots, usually set among the colourful peasantry and glamorous aristocracy of the Austro-Hungarian Empire, the seductive lilt of its waltzes, and the sentimental allure of melodies conjuring up dreams of Old Vienna had a potent appeal to Austrians and Europeans alike. Although Johann Strauss the Younger (1825–99) is regarded as the preeminent operetta composer, in fact he was more successful as a writer of concert waltzes. Of his nineteen stage works, only *Die Fledermaus* (*The Bat*, 1874) has achieved lasting popularity, his later *Night in Venice* (1883) and *Gypsy Baron* (1885) surviving more for the beauty of their music than for the dramatic qualities of their librettos. Perhaps the true father of Viennese operetta was Franz von Suppé (1819–95), who wrote close to 200 theatre scores over his 54-year career as a composer. Although best known today for his overtures, some of his works, in particular *The Beautiful Galathea* (1865), *Fatinitza* (1876), and *Boccaccio* (1879), still have a potent theatrical appeal. The third major composer in the first phase of Viennese operetta was Karl Millöcker (1842–99), whose *Beggar Student* (1882) is still regularly revived.

Operetta in *London was dominated by the partnership of William Schwenck *Gilbert and Arthur *Sullivan, whose 'Savoy Operas', named after the *Savoy Theatre specially built to house them, represent some of the highest achievements in the *genre. Gilbert, a successful commercial playwright, wrote comic songs with astoundingly versatile metre, ingenious rhymes, and spectacular vocabulary. Sullivan wished to compose grand opera and choral work, but his talents perfectly complemented Gilbert's as his graceful, lively music gave emphasis to the words rather than smothering them. Gilbert and Sullivan's most popular collaborations, such as *The Pirates of Penzance* (1879), *Patience* (1881), *Iolanthe* (1881), *The Mikado* (1885), *The Yeomen of the Guard* (1888), and *The Gondoliers* (1889), often satirized contemporary London life and burlesqued serious theatrical and operatic forms. Consequently only *The Mikado*, a comic masterpiece, found an international *audience. Later composers such as Sidney Jones (1861–1946), with the immensely popular *Geisha* (1896), and Edward German (1862–1936), with *Merrie England* (1902) and *Tom Jones* (1907), continued the Sullivanesque tradition, but, by the early twentieth century, the American *musical, with its greater emphasis on production values, was gaining in popularity with London audiences, so the tradition of operetta in Britain was short-lived.

Viennese operetta survived the convulsions of the First World War to remain a vital part of the city's theatrical culture. The pre-eminent composer in the twentieth century was Franz Lehár (1870–1948), whose *Merry Widow* (1905) has proved to be the most successful of all operettas. While Lehár is noted for his graceful waltzes and sinuously romantic melodies, he later expanded the dramatic range of operetta, occasionally moving into the field of social *realism or, in operettas written for the Austrian tenor Richard Tauber (1891–1948), into an intensity of expression characteristic of grand opera. His other hits included *The Count of Luxemburg* (1909), *Gypsy Love* (1910), *Paganini* (1925), and *The Land of Smiles* (1929). Lehár presided over a productive period in the Viennese operetta. Other noted composers of this time included Leo Fall (1873–1925), whose successes included *The Dollar Princess* (1907) and *Madame Pompadour* (1922), Oscar Straus (1870–1954), best known internationally for *The Chocolate Soldier* (1908), based on *Shaw's *Arms and the Man*, and Emmerich Kalmán (1882–1953) whose *Csárdás Princess* (1915) and *Countess Maritza* (1924) have remained staples of the repertoire. During the 1920s, in operetta as in theatre, the centre of gravity in German-speaking Europe moved from Vienna to *Berlin. Towards the ends of their careers, Viennese composers often had their operettas premièred in Berlin prior to production at home, but although Berlin had its own well-established operetta tradition, it contributed little original to the genre.

Viewed from the early twenty-first century, operetta looks like a genre that was always in transition. Emerging from the disparate traditions of *opéra-comique*, English burlesque, *Singspiel*, and even *opera buffa*, it achieved distinctive form only in the latter half of the nineteenth century, to be replaced in the early twentieth by the American musical. It contributed greatly to the development of the musical; distinct vestiges of its music can be heard in the work of Jerome *Kern, Richard *Rodgers, and Stephen *Sondheim. Yet it has survived as part of the repertoire only in Vienna, where one theatre, the Volksoper, is devoted largely to preserving it. Some of the operettas of Offenbach, Johann Strauss, and Lehár have been taken up by regular opera companies and are still regularly performed. And Gilbert and Sullivan are as popular as they ever were in the English-speaking world. However, as a genre operetta seems destined to remain a delightful but dated curiosity, whose works give us an intriguing, sometimes touching view of the playful fantasies and nostalgic yearnings of an earlier age.

SJCW

TRAUBNER, RICHARD, *Operetta: a theatrical history* (London, 1984)

OPPRESSED, THEATRE OF THE

A system of techniques designed to encourage the public to be participants ('spect-actors') in identifying and dramatizing the connections between socio-cultural problems, economic and political repression, and internal or personal oppressions. Gradually elaborated by the Brazilian Augusto *Boal in collaboration with numerous theatre and community projects since the 1970s, theatre of the oppressed in 2000 was practised in some 70 countries worldwide, according to Boal's estimate. Inspired by Paulo Freire's participatory teaching system developed in the drought- and poverty-stricken Brazilian north-east (*Pedagogy of the Oppressed*, 1970), Boal's first theoretical book, *Theatre of the Oppressed and Other Political Poetics* (published in Spanish in 1974, with subsequent translations into about 25 languages), argues that an oppressed people can learn to change their circumstances by actively discovering the nature of their oppressions, rather than being told what they are. 'You can only teach if you learn' is Boal's advice to *political theatre artists: do not show the people what is wrong with their world, use your skills to let them discover it themselves.

The basic techniques of the theatre of the oppressed have evolved in accord with Boal's engagement with specific communities since the early 1970s. The initial schemes were conceived in the climate of political dictatorship, in order to find new avenues for protest and social mobilization. The 'joker system', for example, sought to re-evaluate the need for national heroes: the *character of the Joker, acting as narrator, moderator, and interpreter of events on stage, gave perspective to the ideological underpinnings of historical realities and myths. In 'forum theatre', probably the most utilized technique, actors dramatize a problem common to the community, then represent the scene again with a community member taking over the *protagonist's role, improvising solutions in *dialogue with other spect-actors. 'Invisible theatre' arose from the need for anonymity: already in exile in Argentina, which had just itself suffered a military coup (1976), Boal knew it was too dangerous to mount overt protest; instead actors staged scenes in public places, such as racial or class discrimination in a restaurant, designed to provoke polemic while planted observers instigated and directed commentary.

In 1979, exiled in Europe and working mainly in *Paris with groups of social workers, therapists, educators, activists, and actors, Boal developed further variations, such as 'the cop-in-the-head', which focused on internalized oppression and psychological stresses. Since his return to Brazil in 1986 after redemocratization, he has developed 'legislative theatre' to address the legal codification of citizen rights and responsibilities. Both are articulated in his book *The Rainbow of Desire* (1995).

These varied practices have been adapted by groups worldwide to fit their community's concerns. For example, during the World Social Forum held in 2002 in Porto Alegre, Brazil, fifteen theatre of the oppressed troupes stimulated dialogue on themes ranging from family problems and land reform to ethical solutions to the mounting national debt. Theatre of the oppressed has generated much productive controversy internationally about how to reconceptualize political theatre within a globalized context. There are objectors, and some critics view the method as politically reductionist. They question the transferability of its techniques (for instance, from the 'Third World' to white middle-class *feminists), the politically counter-productive indulgence of its psychodrama aspects, and note that the emphasis on the protagonist's role reasserts the social hierarchies that theatre of the oppressed wishes to expose. Boal insists that the method promotes neither messages nor social *catharsis, but rather offers a theatrical language for the individual to investigate and externalize blockages that prohibit the full exercise of creativity and citizenship. *See also* BRECHTIAN; DEVELOPMENT, THEATRE FOR; THEORIES OF DRAMA, THEATRE, AND PERFORMANCE; COMMUNITY THEATRE. LHD

SCHUTZMAN, M., and COHEN-CRUZ, J. (eds.), *Playing Boal: theatre, therapy, activism* (London, 1994)

OP RIOTS

The Old Price *riots were *London's longest theatrical disruptions. When *Covent Garden reopened in 1809 after a *fire, the acting *manager John Philip *Kemble raised *box and pit prices and abolished the shilling (or upper) gallery. Protests occurred, fuelled by class antagonism and radical politics. For two months rioters shouted, waved banners, blew catcalls, danced a peculiar OP dance, and battled the management's hired bruisers, all the time demanding a public apology from Kemble, the old prices restored, fewer boxes, and the reinstitution of the shilling gallery. Finally, Kemble acquiesced to some, but not all, of these demands. MRB

ORCHESTRA

Greek for 'dancing place'. After *c.*330 BC the orchestra was a large, circular surface separating *theatron* (auditorium) and *skene* (stage building) in the *Greek theatre. Extant theatres that are definitively dated earlier (about seven in all) have rectilinear orchestras. The *chorus was generally confined to the orchestra, while actors moved freely between it and the *skene*. The *Roman stage (*pulpitum*) extended into the orchestra, reducing it to a semicircle. As Roman drama had no *chorus or a minimal chorus which the *pulpitum* could easily accommodate, the orchestra of Roman theatres was generally used for seating spectators of the senatorial class. *See* ANCIENT THEATRES. EGC

OREGON SHAKESPEARE FESTIVAL

The oldest continuing *Shakespeare festival in the USA was begun by Angus L. Bowmer for Ashland's 1935 Fourth of July celebration. Students from Bowmer's college classes performed *Twelfth Night* on 2 and 4 July, and *The Merchant of Venice* on 3 July, on a temporary outdoor *stage within the ivied walls of a long-abandoned *Chautauqua *auditorium. The city fathers advanced Bowmer $400 for the project, but, fearing financial loss, scheduled daytime boxing matches in the space. It was the boxing that lost money while the plays attracted about 500 people and showed a small profit. By 1940 the annual summer Shakespeare event had expanded to four plays and a total attendance of 2,000, but the Second World War necessitated a hiatus. Production resumed in 1947 in a rebuilt facility. The festival expanded steadily in production quality and length of season, completing the Shakespeare canon for the first time in 1958. Following Bowmer's 1970 retirement as producing director, OSF was led in turn by Jerry Turner (1970–91), Henry Woronicz (1991–6), and Libby Appel (1996–   ). It received the 1983 Tony *award for outstanding achievement in *regional theatre. Shakespeare remains at the core of each season, but other classics and contemporary fare, including new and commissioned plays, are also presented. OSF currently produces a nine-month season of eleven plays in its three theatres, playing to over 380,000 people at 95 per cent capacity. FHL

ORIENTACIÓN, TEATRO DE

Mexican company. Founded by the playwright Celestino *Gorostiza, it enjoyed a brief but productive life with programmes in 1932–4 and 1938–9. At a time of extreme Mexican nationalism, Orientación assembled an international repertoire that included *Cervantes, *Chekhov, *O'Neill, *Giraudoux, *Cocteau, and *Gogol, many of their *texts in translation by Gorostiza and other members of the group. With Orientación, Mexican theatre began to modernize: the *director took on added importance and autonomy, *actors were better trained in ensemble work, and new and more sophisticated *audiences were created. KFN

ORIGINS OF THEATRE *see page 975*

ÖRKÉNY, ISTVÁN (1912–79)

Hungarian writer and *dramaturg. After incarceration during the Second World War Örkény worked as a dramaturg in *Budapest. His first play, *Voronyezs*, was banned in 1948. Success came at the Thália Theatre with *Tóték* (*The Tóth Family*, 1967), an adaptation of his own novel. Thereafter he became known at home and abroad as the chief representative of the Hungarian theatre of the *absurd. The absurdity of his plays, however, is always based on sheer, recognizable reality. His best regarded works include *Macskajáték* (*Cat's Play*, 1971), *Vérrokonok* (*Blood Relatives*, 1974), and *Pisti a vérzivatarban* (*Stevie in the Bloodstorm*, 1979). HJA

(continued on p. 981)

ORIGINS OF THEATRE

The twentieth century was fascinated with the 'ritual theory of origin'. Itself of nineteenth-century origin and first proposed in scientific guise by the Cambridge School of Anthropology, the theory swiftly became a commonplace even beyond the circles of theatre scholarship. Although repeatedly refuted, the influence of the CSA is still felt in subsequent *theories. While alternative arguments have been suggested, the main thesis—that theatre originated in *ritual—remains firm.

Eventually this theory was also adopted by leading directors, such as Peter *Brook, Jerzy *Grotowski, Richard *Schechner, Ariane *Mnouchkine, and Eugenio *Barba, who attempted to restore the ritual elements they assumed had been lost and that they considered vital for the rejuvenation of theatre. Their created elements were not genuine ritual elements, however, but no more than inventions of stagecraft inspired by principles thought to underlie ritual behaviour in a constructed religious culture.

The grip of the ritual theory of origin is enigmatic, for it contradicts the rather obvious perception that ritual and theatre belong in different spheres of human activity. A ritual is a complex act, whose main purpose is to affect a divine sphere for the benefit of a community of believers. In contrast, theatre is a particular medium, a method of signification and communication based on images, mainly produced by human actors and imprinted on their own bodies, which affords a means for description of worlds, mostly fictional ones. In principle a ritual may be performed by means of a medium, such as natural language (for example, a prayer), or a non-verbal action (for example, the sacrifice of an animal). But theatre may be employed for any purpose, either similar to or conflicting with those of ritual: it might either reconfirm or refute common beliefs. The latter function cannot be imagined in any ritual. If ritual and theatre are indeed independent of each other, it is sensible to assume that ancient rituals may have included theatrical components, just as they equally well may have not.

1. The advent of ancient theatre;
2. The re-creation of theatre by the Church;
3. Egyptian coronation ritual; 4. Alternative theories

1. The advent of ancient theatre

Despite changing arguments, three major contributions to the theory of ritual origin can be discerned; in chronological order these are: the CSA theory, the shamanist theory, and Schechner's performance theory.

(*a*) **Cambridge School of Anthropology** In its scientific form, the theory that ancient *Greek *tragedy and *comedy originated in Dionysiac ritual was suggested by a group of English scholars known as the Cambridge School of Anthropology. Its leading proponents, Jane Harrison, Gilbert *Murray, and Francis McDonald Cornford, published their major works at the beginning of the twentieth century. Unfortunately they never unambiguously declared whether the object of their research was the origin of these dramatic *genres or the origins of theatre as a medium. They definitely focused on the former, although elements of the latter occasionally arose. Lack of distinction plagues even recent studies, not to mention textbooks of theatre history. The widespread implicit assumption is that these are two aspects of the same process. Their discussion should be separated, however: while genres differ according to the nature of their fictional worlds, the medium of theatre is shared by all of them.

The CSA accepted *Aristotle's account (in the *Poetics*) regarding the development of tragedy from dithyrambic poetry. However, in contrast to Aristotle, who was closest to the process, they argued for continuity—mediated by *dithyramb—between Dionysiac ritual and tragedy. Under the influence of James G. Frazer (*The Golden Bough*, 1890–1915), they also assumed the existence of an ur-worship of a Spring Daimon (*eniautos daimon*), meant to explain a variety of faiths reflecting the same mythical pattern of death and resurrection of a god—such as Osiris, Tamuz, and Adonis, and including *Dionysus—symbolizing the yearly cycle of death and resurrection of nature. Continuity was thus expanded to include this ur-ritual. But theatre could have originated in Dionysiac ritual without entailing such an ancestry.

The CSA thesis is that the traces of this mythical pattern demonstrate the origin of dithyramb and the dramatic genres in ritual. Murray suggested an apparently sophisticated method for detecting these traces, a pattern of recurrent narrative components featuring: *agon*, a struggle between the Spring Daimon and its enemy (winter); *pathos*, the ritual death of the Daimon; *messenger*, the report of death or display of corpse; *thrernos* or *lamentation*, the expression of grief; *anagnorisis*, the recognition of the dead Daimon; and *epiphany* or *theophany*, his resurrection and apotheosis. Cornford suggested a quite similar pattern for *Old Comedy, their differences being enigmatic, if the assumption is that both genres originated in the same ritual.

As early as 1927 Pickard-Cambridge challenged the existence of these narrative components in their stipulated order, and demonstrated that they are not to be found either in any known form of Dionysiac ritual or in dithyramb, tragedy, or comedy. Even in *Euripides' *The Bacchae*, the only extant tragedy that dramatizes an episode of Dionysus' life, there is no death and resurrection. In general, the application of this model involves intolerable flexibility. The reduction of all narratives to a single mythical pattern, in contrast to their manifest diversity, is obviously absurd. Death in tragedy is humanly final: no one resurrects.

According to the CSA, dithyramb (a sublime choral storytelling poem) was created within Dionysiac ritual from a *sacer ludus* (ritual *dance) representing the *aition* (mythical narrative) of Dionysus. Assumedly, tragedy inherited this pattern. In contrast, Pickard-Cambridge demonstrated that the link with Dionysiac ritual was severed prior to the advent of tragedy. Indeed, there is no known fragment or complete dithyramb that narrates this *aition*. Only short passages in the god's honour have been found. There is also ample evidence that dithyrambs featured narratives of gods and heroes typical of the Homeric tradition.

If the intention of the CSA was to discover the origin of the theatre medium, their main fallacy was to look for it in the fictional worlds of dithyramb, tragedy, and comedy. In principle, medium and fictional worlds are independent of each other. The same fictional world can be described by different media (for instance, literature and theatre); and the same medium is capable of describing different fictional worlds. Moreover, there is evidence for the existence of a theatre medium prior to these genres: pictures on early sixth-century BC vases and names of theatrical *burlesques. Aristotle suggests that Attic comedy developed from popular forms of comedy. Cornford accepts this account and quotes *Aristophanes' contemptuous remarks on earlier Megarean *farce. Cornford even claims that it is difficult to see how drama could develop from what is not, even in kernel, dramatic, but this is a regressive argument: if theatre could only develop from a previous theatrical form, the problem of its creation cannot be solved.

*Thespis, credited with the creation of tragedy, may have figured out the possibility of performing the Homeric narratives and sublime style typical of dithyramb in a medium that was already in existence, and that apparently had not been employed for this type of narrative before his time. Tragedy could have developed the dialogic element found in dithyramb itself, as in other forms of storytelling too. The moment Thespis, as a member of the dithyrambic *chorus, enacted *dialogue in *character, the theatre medium was employed and tragedy was born.

(*b*) **Shamanistic theory** Despite heavy criticism, the ritual thesis of origin remained firm. Ernest T. Kirby, attempting to replace obsolete arguments, suggested that theatre originated in the ecstatic nature of shamanism. In contrast to the CSA, he focuses on the shaman exhibiting another identity. Enacting a charac-

ter, allegedly shared by both shaman in the state of trance and actor on stage, indeed regards a crucial property of theatre.

The term 'shaman', of Siberian origin and originally employed in Siberian ethnography, is applied to medicine men in different cultures, who combine healing, magic, and mediumship. The shaman is believed to enter a state of trance, travelling other worlds, taking control of spirits and compelling them to cure people. While in trance, the shaman behaves as if possessed by a spirit, speaking in his voice. The spirit is in need of the shaman's body in order to reveal itself within the human world. For Kirby, this establishes him as the prototype of the *actor, because of his embodying an entity other than himself.

This is a fallacy, for it overlooks the internal viewpoint of the shaman's culture. From this perspective, the shaman is definitely not enacting a spirit but constitutes a means for its revelation in the world. The efficacy of the ritual depends on the community's belief that the spirit is real and operates through the shaman. If the shaman is suspected of impersonation, he is seen as a fraud and efficacy is impaired. In contrast, an actor genuinely enacts a character, a fictional entity that reaches existence only in the spectator's imagination. The actor consistently preserves the duality actor/character; thus the duality is not perceived as fraudulent but as essential to the art. Moreover, ecstasy cannot be a necessary condition of acting. Even in a state of extreme identification with a character, this basic duality is not and cannot be cancelled. At most, it can be an *illusion sought by a particular acting style such as that of *naturalism, which is a marginal style in the history of theatre.

The shaman officiates in front of a community of believers, on whose participation and faith the efficacy of his act depends. Although there is 'participation' in theatre too, its meaning is different. Whereas in ritual it means a community involved in a common effort to produce a change in the human world, in theatre it means an *audience sharing a form of thinking and experiencing the potentialities of human nature. The shaman also officiates in a well-delimited space, such as a hut or enclosed space, thus allowing the impression that he is 'performing' in a 'theatre' in front of an 'audience'. Accordingly, Kirby suggests that transition from ritual to theatre happens when belief in the shaman's powers dwindles. It is possible that, in decline, shamanism may engage in what he terms 'para-theatrical' acts in order to improve its grip on the community. The implication is, however, that theatre originates in disintegrating ritual.

In an attempt to devise a unitary theory, Kirby suggests that Dionysiac ritual was a particular form of shamanism. Although the ecstatic character of Dionysiac faith supports this thesis, the main features of shamanism are missing in it. By merely changing the CSA's line of argument, Kirby's theory infused new life into the thesis of ritual origin. Yet his change of emphasis was a critique of the CSA position in that by focusing on the performative element, Kirby created a genuine theory of theatre origins.

(c) **Performance theory** Richard Schechner's theory, inspired by Victor Turner's anthropological approach, reflects a sense of crisis regarding ritual theories of origin. While denying a generative link between ritual and theatre, Schechner suggests an even stronger bond: they are different manifestations of the single comprehensive category of *'performance', a combination of two ubiquitous elements of 'entertainment' and 'efficacy'. In varying proportions, which can be changed at will, these create the continuum of all kinds of performance: when entertainment overweighs efficacy, the result is 'aesthetic theatre'; and when efficacy overweighs entertainment, the result is 'ritual'. In contrast to previous theories, just as ritual can change into theatre, theatre can change into ritual. For Schechner, 'aesthetic theatre' achieved its peaks during periods in which the proportion between these elements was balanced.

Inclusion of such disparate activities as ritual, football (*see* SPORT), and theatre under 'performance' necessarily leads to an over-abstract definition: 'a performance is an activity done by an individual or group *in the presence* of and for the benefit of another individual or group.' Whereas this applies to almost any kind of human activity, including some kinds of work (for example, a fire brigade rescuing people from a fire in front of a gathering of curious observers), it excludes activities most akin to theatre, such as imaginative play, writing fiction, and making *films. Paradoxically, even ritual is excluded, because it does not include the community's performative participation. Moreover, whereas the category of 'performance' may correctly explain some shared characteristics of different domains, it cannot account for their specific differences. (*See* PERFORMANCE STUDIES.)

Schechner characterizes 'entertainment' and 'efficacy' by listing their contrasting elements. Most of these reiterate antinomies traditionally employed for distinguishing between theatre and ritual. His main innovation resides in distinguishing between 'fun' (a synonym of 'entertainment') and 'results' (a synonym of 'efficacy'). But this antinomy is not valid, because it contrasts a type of audience response with a type of effect in the sphere of the 'absent other', who is an additional addressee. Altogether the validity of these antinomies is dubious, because they presuppose what they should demonstrate: that ritual and theatre are activities in the same sphere. Furthermore, instead of unravelling the relationship between ritual and theatre, questions about it multiply. For example, does almost pure 'entertainment' exhaust the nature of 'aesthetic theatre'? Does the category of 'entertainment' apply to subversive kinds of theatre, whose main aim is to baffle and even shock audiences? In fact, by means of this category Schechner gives a reductive account of a medium which can serve any purpose. The notion of 'efficacy' raises similar difficulties: although it applies to both ritual and theatre, the meanings are different in each domain.

Schechner claims that a performance is an 'actual', in the sense of not representing anything, but being identical with itself, here and now. The 'actual' thus contrasts with the *'mimetic'. He also maintains that 'aesthetic theatre' reflects both representation and actuality; that is, they do not exclude each other, and may complement each other. Indeed, focusing attention on the mechanism of producing the stage *text, including actors, can highlight the 'actual' elements of theatre. In contrast, ritual is only an actual. Even if it employs systems of representation, it subordinates them to its nature. Schechner thus provides the ideology for creating *'performance art', which professedly aims at pure actuality. He also proposes what he calls 'transformational' acting as the 'actual' counterpart of 'mimetic' acting. But this contradicts the principle of 'enacting' characters, since only in the absence of acting would a performer refer *only* to himself. In contrast, an actor refers both to a character (mainly) and *also* to himself (as producer of a stage text). The audience's correlative of actual acting is a kind of ritual participation. Following his two-directional model, Schechner suggests that transition from theatre to ritual occurs when a group of individuals changes into a community of participants. These ideas reveal Schechner's attempt to reintroduce into theatre ritual elements that supposedly have been lost. Ritual acting and participation, however, can only be an ideal of specific theatrical styles, and probably never attained.

Schechner acknowledges his affinity to the CSA, despite its shortcomings, and mentions its profound influence on modern theatrical practice and reconsideration of the dramatic tradition. He also accepts central elements of the shamanistic theory, especially the shaman as the prototype of the performer, including the actor. Nonetheless, Schechner negates both schools: 'I am not going to replace the Cambridge origin theory with my own. Origin theories are irrelevant to understanding theater. . . . there is no reason to hunt for "origins" or "derivations".' His approach thus aims a deadly blow to all ritual theories of theatre origin, and reflects a need for an alternative theory. But he attempts to solve the problem by eliminating the useful distinction between 'ritual' and 'theatre', and suggesting instead a feeble distinction between 'entertainment' and 'efficacy', which conforms with neither intuition nor experience.

2. The re-creation of theatre by the Church

Controversy also surrounds the theory of re-creation of theatre *ex nihilo* within Christian ritual, about the tenth century, after a prolonged discontinuity from early *medieval theatre and the disappearance of any of its traces. This theory is of *romantic origin. In 1809 A. W. von *Schlegel declared that no theatre could be found in all of Europe throughout the Middle Ages. In 1839 Charles Magnin claimed, well prior to the CSA, that the new theatre was created from the festivals of the Christian Church during the tenth and eleventh centuries, exactly as it had been created from the religious festivals of ancient Greece. In 1849 Edélestand du Méril adopted this analogy and suggested the Church as the cradle of European theatre. In 1886 Leon

Gautier conjectured, most cautiously, that these origins resided in the dramatization of Easter tropes, especially those of the tenth century (tropes are non-official texts inserted in the sacred macro-text of the mass). He thus set the foundations for conceiving the *Quem Quaeritis* trope as the firstling of European theatre. In 1928 Gustave Cohen generalized this trend by claiming that 'all religions generate drama and all rituals willingly and spontaneously take dramatic and theatrical shape'. He published this 'law' a year after Pickard-Cambridge proved the CSA theory groundless. (*See* RELIGION AND THEATRE.)

In contrast, inspired by Edmund K. Chambers (*The Medieval Stage*, 1903), Hunningher claimed that the Church could not have re-created theatre for two reasons: an essential opposition existed between the nature of theatre and the Christian faith, and no break in the theatrical tradition took place. I take these points in order.

First, the essential disagreement between Christianity and theatre is not plausible because of their long partnership. Hunningher himself restricted his claim to the necessary conditions for its creation and, anticipating Kirby, suggested ecstasy as a crucial one. While endorsing the development of theatre from ecstatic Dionysiac ritual, he rejected re-creation within a non-ecstatic symbolic religion, which substituted prayer for sacrifice and the word for the deed. However, whereas Hunningher's claim that the Church could only have adopted theatre can be accepted, his line of argument cannot: there cannot be an essential opposition between a religion and a medium which can express any idea. More plausible is his rejection of the assumption (vehemently advocated by O. B. Hardison in *Christian Rite and Christian Drama in the Middle Ages*, 1965) that the mass features theatrical elements, on the grounds that in it there is no 'impersonation' in the sense of acting. In contrast to this assumption, which clearly supports re-creation, from the beginning the Christian faith considered the mass not as representing crucifixion and communion, but as re-experiencing it.

Second, the re-creation thesis requires demonstration of total discontinuity. It would appear that absence of documentation about any form of theatre unquestionably supports discontinuity. Paradoxically, from the third to the tenth centuries, the only sources on possible theatrical activity are decisions of the Church, which consistently denounced the art of the *mimes (mimi)* and their successors, and blamed even the clergy for indulging in this 'Satanic' activity. While the frequency of decisions clearly decreases during the tenth century, when the supposed re-creation took place, the relative silence of the Church can be interpreted as evidence of final disappearance, or as mitigation of hostility towards theatre, and even awareness of its educational potential.

It is not at all clear what were the actual professions of the 'mimes', a collective name for a variety of stage artists, such as magicians, *animal tamers, escape artists, ventriloquists, puppeteers, musicians, singers, dancers, and storytellers. It is uncertain whether or not these included actors. The Church probably objected to artists reflecting a heretical attitude to sacred matters. Hunningher considers drawings of mimes in the troparium of Saint-Martial as evidence of continuity and infiltration of mimes into the sacred service. However, these depict only musicians, dancers, and *jugglers. The Church was probably opposed not to theatre in itself, but to its pagan connotations.

A. M. Nagler, who published the scenario of the *Quem Quaeritis* trope in English translation, claims that 'in the *Concordia Regularis* [*c*.970], the birth of medieval drama from the spirit of liturgy lies clearly before us'. In contrast, for Hunningher it only bears witness to its adoption within a continuous dramatic tradition. Indeed, analysis of the text indicates that no aspect of theatre production has been overlooked. The scenario reveals a degree of acquaintance with theatre practice that definitely contradicts spontaneous re-creation.

Hunningher's main theoretical contribution resides in suggesting a model of rejection–adoption, in any order, rather than origin. This model presupposes an essential difference between theatre and ritual, while entailing the option of use by any ritual. A thousand years of rejection and a few centuries of cooperation support its validity. This model may also apply to rituals that supposedly originated theatre. The claim that theatre was created or re-created by a ritual that employed it—just as ritual employs other media—is as absurd as claiming that natural language, poetry, or music originated in ritual. *See also* LITURGICAL DRAMA; BIBLICAL PLAYS; CYCLE PLAYS.

3. Egyptian coronation ritual

In 1950 Theodor H. Gaster (*Thespis*) published an interpretation, couched in theatrical terms, of the *Ramesseum Dramatic Papyrus*, usually called the *Egyptian Coronation Drama*. The papyrus, discovered in 1896 by Quibel in the precinct of the Ramesseum at Thebes, was written during the reign of Sesostris (Senusret) I, a king of the Twelfth Dynasty (*c*.1970 BC). According to Sethe, who first published in 1928, it is a transcription of a papyrus written during the First Dynasty (*c*.3300 BC). If Gaster's interpretation is correct, it pre-dates the origins of Greek theatre by more than 2,000 years.

The text is meant to be narrated by a reader and is interspersed with dialogue. It relates Horus' victory over Seth, who had previously vanquished and killed Osiris, and Horus' installation as the god/king of united Upper and Lower Egypt. Dialogue was performed by the king and his followers: the king represented Horus, and his followers the other characters of the myth. An effigy probably represented the dead king, equated with Osiris. Seth was a mute character. The ritual was performed for the king's installation or annual reconfirmation as a descendant of Horus, and for the opening of the Nile for navigation. Identification with the divine ancestors was probably meant to attach a divine aura to the new king, and thus legitimize his power.

However, the mere assumption that the king was believed to be only enacting Horus would have destroyed the ritual nature of the event. Furthermore, it was not performed in front of an audience, but in the midst of a community of involved supporters and believers. Nonetheless, there are episodes that indicate use of theatrical principles; for instance, the combat between Horus and Seth was performed as 'a punching-match . . . staged between two champions'. These support the thesis that ritual can make use of the theatre as a medium.

Gaster views the fight between Horus and Seth, which is only related in a similar papyrus known as the *Memphite Drama*, as 'the typical Ritual combat between Old Year and New, Summer and Winter, Life and Death, Rain and Drought, etc., which we find in seasonal festivals everywhere'. However, a struggle between kings and the eventual unification of two realms hardly represent the alleged mythical struggle. Gaster meant to infuse new blood into the CSA thesis but repeated its main fallacy: seeking the origins of theatre in elements of the fictional world.

4. Alternative theories

The continued persistence and vitality of the main thesis of ritual origin, despite repeated criticism, is puzzling. What is its charm and its appeal in the eyes of theoretician, practitioner, and layman alike? A possible answer may lie in the romantic reason that the thesis lends theatre a numinous aura which it does not always possess otherwise.

The theoretical stalemate probably stems from the methodologies employed in researching the elusive question of origins. While theatre *historiography is limited by available documentation, theatrical phenomena probably hark back to prehistoric times which by and large have left scanty and deficient traces. Whereas the history of major theatrical genres can be determined on quite reliable grounds, the history of the medium is a black hole providing no historical data and inviting a great deal of speculation. Analogously, cultural anthropology is limited by its own presuppositions and constructs. In its quest for shared intercultural phenomena, it shows a clear tendency to broad categories which, based on extreme abstraction of singularities, allow almost uninhibited application and hardly fit any given culture. Yet these categories are supposed to apply to primeval cultures in which theatre was being created.

J. Huizinga (*Homo Ludens*, 1944) identified seven cultural domains—ritual, play, game, sport, dance, music, and theatre—and almost all of these have been suggested by scholars as ancestors of theatre. Huizinga himself made an attempt to demonstrate that they all originated in the spirit of play, characterized in terms of competitive game. His thesis can hardly be demonstrated for theatre, apart from the competitions of tragedies or comedies in ancient Greece. Friedrich Nietzsche's claim (*The Birth of Tragedy*, 1870–1) that tragedy was born from the spirit of music has similar shortcomings. Schechner basically accepts Huizinga's typology under the notion of 'performance', while adding that of 'social drama' too. He suggests an umbilical connection between 'social drama' and theatre, similar to the ritual–theatre model: 'the hidden structure of one is the visible structure of the other.' He disregards the existential gap between the world and thinking about it. Some other theories, however, are on more solid ground.

1. Karl Groos (*The Play of Man*, 1899) considers *imaginative play of children* as the source of theatrical drama. In order to enact fictional characters, such as mother, father, child, doctor, and patient, children produce images of human beings, imprint them on their own bodies, and attribute them to characters. But children do not distinguish between using their own bodies and manipulating dolls or tin soldiers (as in *puppet theatre) to represent people and, in many a case, they mix these media. Moreover, they may use their own bodies or other objects to represent the same referent: a child's own body or a matchbox might represent a car. The similarity of representation resides only in the way the body or the object is conventionally manipulated; for example, by imitating the typical sounds of a car in both cases. Children play for themselves, not for an audience. In contrast to Groos's concept of playful experimentation as pre-exercise of adult roles and skills, Jean Piaget (*Play, Dreams and Imitation in Childhood*, 1945) provides empirical evidence for considering it as an infantile form of representing and pondering past and possible experiences. Piaget thus views imagination as the faculty of producing and employing (imprinted) images as units of thinking.

2. *Children's imaginative drawing* also indicates use of imprinted images for the sake of reflecting on their own world. Their drawings are also not intended for spectators. *Realism (in the sense of extreme similarity) and beauty are not the children's concern, which suggests that the images are used for representation and thinking. For these purposes the limited drawing abilities of children are sufficient. Children may also play with drawings as with dolls. Psychoanalysis uses both play and drawing as indications of their thinking processes.

3. Harrison suggests a *ritual dance* in honour of Dionysus as the origin of drama. She traces the origins of mimetic dance back to the dawn of human culture, when people commemorated successful events, such as a good hunt or a victory at war, by redoing them, and anticipated such beneficial results by predoing them. Assumedly, they did so by imprinting images of these events on their own bodies. Kurt Sachs (*World History of Dance*, 1933) provides, in addition to archaeological evidence, examples of primitive 'image dances' performed even today. There is no limit to the objects of imitation, which include animals, plants, meteorological phenomena, and obviously fellow human beings, thus recalling the play of children. Human images usually represent typical activities, such as hunting, fishing, and harvesting. It is widely assumed that most primitive dances served a magic-ritual aim. Harrison relies on the

'mimetic' element to connect such ritual dancing to theatre, since 'all rites *qua* rites are mimetic'. She invokes the semantic kinship of the Greek words *dromenon* (ritual) and 'drama' (both from *dran*, the Doric word for 'to do'), and suggests thereby a similarity between theatre medium, which is a method of representation by means of doings on stage, and ritual, which is performing a doing, imbued with religious meaning.

4. *Rock and cave paintings* and engravings from the Stone Age are usually conceived as objects of ritual or depictions of ritual acts. Rock paintings and engravings at Tassili n'Ajjer (central Sahara, *c*.6000–3500 BC) display masked men, *masks, processions, dancing groups, and possibly jesters. Some masks, which represent heads of animals and later became associated with known rituals, are considered possible indications of shamanism and thus of theatre's origin (disregarding the fact that masks are not a necessary element of theatre). Images of jesters are considered to reflect possible elementary forms of acting. Indeed, physical distortion, long noses, and swollen bellies do call to mind comic actors in pictures of popular comedy in ancient Greece. However, jesting, although a possible element of ritual, does not necessarily indicate acting. In any case, lack of verbal description precludes definite interpretation. In its present state 'The Sorcerer' (*c*.14000 BC), discovered and possibly reconstructed by Breuil, reveals a man wearing a skin and head of a deer. Although different interpretations are possible, many scholars consider it as the earliest theatrical document. However, there is no indication of acting, unless an essential connection between *disguise and theatre is presupposed. Nonetheless, these pictures, especially the amazing cave paintings at Altamira (*c*.14000 BC) and Lascaux (*c*.18000 BC), reflect the use of imprinted images (although not on bodies) for signification and communication. Even if used for magic purposes, their descriptive function must be presupposed.

5. J. Michael Walton (*Greek Theatre Practice*, 1980) suggested *storytelling* as the source of acting. This is a verbal art, which naturally includes the verbal components of dialogue. If a story is written, the concomitant non-verbal aspects of dialogue are also described by words; but, if the story is performed orally, dialogue can be (and usually is) enacted by the storyteller himself, reflecting the fictional speakers' characterization. This element of acting in performed dialogue could have been the ground for transition from dithyrambic storytelling to tragic theatre. Against the background of the vital storytelling tradition in ancient Greece, Walton suggests that the actor developed directly from the bard or *rhapsode*, a performing storyteller, and bases his claim on analyses of passages in the *Odyssey* in which a bard enacts characters in dialogue. Indeed, the moment the oral storyteller performs dialogue 'in character' there is acting, that is, imprinting of images of direct speech on his own body.

6. For Sigmund Freud (*The Interpretation of Dreams*, 1900), from the viewpoint of their method of signification rather than their contents, *dreams* are a kind of mental theatre. He considers dreams to proceed from thoughts in waking life, to create a dream-text through a process of distortion. This process reflects the unconscious intention to disguise 'latent thoughts', and thus avoid upsetting consciousness and fulfil the central function of dream, which is to express a suppressed wish while protecting sleep. Distortion occurs in the initial symbolizing of (verbal) thoughts and the final 'regression' to images—the 'raw material' of human conceptual thinking. Images are thus regarded by Freud as units of unconscious thinking. The fact that these are uncoded units does not prevent their function in thinking, which is characterized by representation and abstraction.

While Freud was more interested in discovering the latent thoughts than in analysing dreams as self-contained texts, Carl C. Jung developed a text-oriented approach: 'The dream is a spontaneous self-portrayal, in symbolic form, of the actual situation of the unconscious.' Following Nietzsche's intuition, psychoanalysis conceived dreams as preserving an early stage in the development of human thinking. Moreover, their imagistic guise led Freud to conceive them as dramatized texts, in which the dreamer acts as *playwright, *director, performer, spectator, and ultimate referent. Obviously a dream is not a piece of theatre, but its affinity to theatre is quite discernible. Similar considerations apply to daydreams.

Some of the theories outlined above potentially testify to the existence of magic rituals that used various media, while subordinating them to their intentions and purposes. However, their mere use presupposes their meaningfulness. These media comprised oral storytelling, dance, music, design, sculpture, and architecture (even the use of caves for religious purposes reflects architectural considerations). Primeval ritual was probably a conglomerate of forms of representation, which eventually developed into independent media and/or arts and outlived the cults in which they were initially employed. It is plausible, therefore, that embryonic theatrical representation was also used in rituals of early humanity. Yet despite the use of all these rudimentary arts in primitive rituals, only theatre has been accorded the groundless privilege of originating in ritual.

The common denominator of all these approaches to the origin of theatre is not the often invoked instinct for impersonation, but rather the crucial role of imagination in all the domains: the propensity of the human brain to produce mental images and use them for thinking. Since theatre is a medium that operates by the use of imprinted images, it is sensible to search for its *roots* in elementary functions of the human brain. Such an approach circumvents the problems involved in determining its *origin* at a specific time and place. Whereas a history of theatre could determine the origins of particular theatrical genres in ancient Greece or medieval Europe, the quest for roots assumes that proto-theatrical activities may have emerged any time and anywhere. The roots of theatre must lie in the very structure of the human psyche. Antonio R. Damasio, a brain researcher, characterizes the mind as having 'the ability to display images internally and to order those images in a process called thought' (*Descartes' Error*, 1994). The brain thus carries out its primary mode of thinking in images, on which verbal thinking is grafted. Traces of this primary mode can be sought in primitive and infantile phenomena. Following the thesis that childhood replicates early stages in the development of humankind, it is plausible that children's play and drawing replicate principles embodied in primitive dance and rock and cave engravings and paintings.

Mental images, which are experienced in both awake and dream thinking, cannot be communicated unless they are imprinted materially. Children's imaginative play and drawing, rock and cave engraving and painting, image dance, oral storytelling, and theatre—all imprint images on matter. Theatre extends the principle of the similarity underlying images to the imprinting matter: that is, images of human beings are imprinted on human actors. Although this also applies to some kinds of play and dance, it is not a general principle in them. Despite similarities, however, none of these domains should be conceived as originating theatre; but all of them attest to common roots in the mental imagery spontaneously produced by the human psyche.

The imagistic method of representation, which was superseded by natural language and probably residually left as the 'language' of the unconscious, is socially permitted to re-enter verbal culture only within predetermined domains, mainly in the form of art. If that is so, we must assume both a primeval phase of spontaneous creation of imagistic media, and a subsequent phase of formalization, in which natural language fulfilled a crucial role, in order to conform with a mind conditioned by language. It is in this transitional phase in the development of culture, which assumedly conjoined imagistic thinking and incipient language, probably replicated in children's imaginative play and drawing, that the roots of the medium of theatre may be found. ER

ARISTOTLE, *The Poetics*, in *Aristotle's Theory of Poetry and Fine Art*, ed. and trans. S. H. Butcher (1902; London, 1952)

ELIADE, MIRCEA, *Shamanism: archaic techniques of ecstasy*, trans. W. R. Trask (1964; Princeton, 1974)

HARRISON, JANE E., *Ancient Art and Ritual* (1913; London, 1951)

HUNNINGHER, BENJAMIN, *The Origin of the Theater* (New York, 1961)

KIRBY, ERNEST T., *Ur-Drama; the origins of theatre* (New York, 1975)

MURRAY, GILBERT, 'Excursus on the ritual forms preserved in Greek tragedy', in J. E. Harrison, *Themis* (Cambridge, 1912)

PICKARD-CAMBRIDGE, ARTHUR W., *Dithyramb, Tragedy and Comedy* (Oxford, 1927)

ROZIK, ELI, *The Roots of Theatre* (Iowa City, 2002)

SCHECHNER, RICHARD, *Performance Theory* (1977; New York 1988)

ORLENEV, PAVEL (1869–1932)

Russian actor who studied at the *Maly Theatre School in *Moscow before cutting his teeth at various venues in the provinces. By virtue of his short stature and slight build, factors which did not lend themselves to leading roles, he succeeded in creating the type *character of the neurasthenic, which became very fashionable in turn-of-the-century Russia. Among his outstanding performances were stage incarnations of Raskolnikov in *Crime and Punishment* (1899), de *Musset's Lorenzaccio (1900), Arnold Kramer in *Hauptmann's *Michael Kramer*, Oswald in *Ibsen's *Ghosts* (1903), and Brand (1907). He *toured widely in Europe and America, visiting *London in 1905. NW

ORLIK, EMIL (1870–1932)

German-Czech artist and designer. Best known as a painter and graphic artist, Orlik, the son a Jewish tailor, received his training at the Academy of Fine Arts in *Munich in the 1890s where he was associated with the art nouveau movement. In *Berlin Orlik worked occasionally with Max *Reinhardt at the *Deutsches Theater, and his design for *The Winter's Tale* (1906) may have been the first major application of art nouveau aesthetics to *scenography. After seeing the production Gordon *Craig accused Reinhardt of plagiarism, which Orlik took as a compliment. His next design was for *Schiller's *The Robbers* (1908), after which he became more directly involved in staging and the entire visual effect. In 1900–1 Orlik had spent a year in *Japan studying artistic techniques. This experience was decisive in the construction of a *kabuki-style stage with a *hanamichi (ramp) for the *pantomime *Sumurun* (1910), a massive and wordless Reinhardt show performed in Berlin, *Paris, *London, and *New York. Other set designs for Reinhardt included *Oedipus the King* (1910). CBB

ORTON, JOE (1933–67)

English playwright. Before his violent murder at the hands of his lover, Joe Orton was one of the most promising young playwrights of the 1960s. Called by Ronald Bryden 'the Oscar Wilde of Welfare State gentility', Orton specialized in slightly *absurdist black *comedies in which his *characters' observation of social form and primness of speech clash spectacularly with their situations. Perhaps because he represents so much unfulfilled potential, his reputation remains high despite his slim output of only three full-length plays. Orton's first play, *Entertaining Mr Sloane*, was produced at the New Arts Theatre in 1964 and transferred to the West End. The situation of its *plot—a brother and sister blackmail their father's killer into becoming a sexual toy for both of them—inspired just enough controversy to ensure his notoriety and future as a playwright. His next play, *Loot*, won both the *Evening Standard* and *Plays and Players* *awards for best play of 1966. *What the Butler Saw*, more in line with traditional *farce than his earlier works, was still being revised by Orton at the time of his death. It received a posthumous West End production starring Ralph *Richardson in 1969, although it was not a great success. Orton's other dramatic works include the short plays *The Ruffian on the Stair* (1967), *The Erphingham Camp* (1967), *Funeral Games* (produced 1970), and several unfinished *television and *film scripts. His *Diaries*, edited by John Lahr, was published in 1986.   MDG

OSAKA

Japan's third largest city, located on Osaka Bay in western *Japan. The port town of Naniwa stood on the site from the seventh century, and in 1583 the national military ruler, Toyotomi Hideyoshi (1536–98), constructed Osaka Castle there. Osaka was Japan's centre of commerce and finance in the Tokugawa Period (1600–1867), a city dominated by merchants and a showcase for merchant culture. *Kabuki flourished in Osaka and the first great actors of male leading roles, Arashi San'emon I (1635–90) and *Sakata Tōjūrō I, began their careers there. Kabuki and *puppet theatres were located on Dotombori Street, still the entertainment centre of the city. Courtesans practised the arts of *dance, singing, and *shamisen* playing in the Shinmachi licensed pleasure district. Osaka became the chief city for puppet theatre (*bunraku) in 1684 when the chanter *Takemoto Gidayū opened his theatre there. Playwright *Chikamatsu Monzaemon joined him twenty years later, and puppet playwriting and staging flourished in the early 1700s thanks to competition between the Takemoto-za and the Tokyotake-za theatres. In the mid-eighteenth century great puppet chanters, puppeteers, and playwriting teams overshadowed the accomplishments of rival kabuki theatres. In the late 1700s puppet theatre fell into a decline and was revived early in the nineteenth century when a troupe from nearby Awaji Island opened the Bunraku Theatre in Osaka. Today Osaka is the site of the National Bunraku Theatre, three kabuki theatres, several *nō theatres, and many large concert halls and smaller theatres for contemporary performances of all sorts. The city has numerous Buddhist temples and Shinto shrines which sponsor festivals that include performances ranging from *bugaku* (archaic court dance) to parades of sacred palanquins and decorated boats, to amateur dancing and singing.   LRK

OSANAI KAORU (1881–1928)

Japanese playwright and director. Along with *Tsubouchi Shōyō, Osanai took a strong interest in introducing concepts of modern Western theatre and performance into *Japan (*see* SHINGEKI). Inspired by *Chekhov and *Ibsen, Osanai formed a theatre company to present such plays in *Tokyo, which he named Jiyū Gekijō (the Free Theatre), based on the model of *Antoine's Théâtre *Libre. Their first production was a translation of Ibsen's *John Gabriel Borkman* prepared by the great contemporary novelist Mori Ōgai. Osanai had available only *kabuki actors so that the women's roles were performed by men. A trip to Europe in 1912 helped him see what reforms were needed and his growing knowledge and enthusiasm resulted in the establishment of Tokyo's Tsukiji Shōgekijō (*Tsukiji Little Theatre) in 1924. It chiefly produced European plays in translation until his death, at which point the company split into literary and political factions. Osanai was a charismatic figure who inspired a generation of artists and intellectuals.   JTR

OSBORN, PAUL (1901–88)

American playwright and screenwriter. Osborn attended the University of Michigan and studied playwriting with George Pierce *Baker at Yale (1927). His play *Hotbed* was produced on Broadway in 1928, the first of ten. Osborn's 1939 *Mornings at Seven*, a gentle *comedy about four eccentric sisters in a small town, won a Tony *award as best revival when it was restaged on Broadway in 1980 and led to a renewed interest in the playwright's work. Osborn's other plays, some of them adaptations from novels by other writers, included *A Ledge* (1929), *The Vinegar Tree* (1930), *Oliver, Oliver* (1934), *Tomorrow's Monday* (1936), *On Borrowed Time* (1938), *The Innocent Voyage* (1943), *A Bell for Adano* (1944), and *Point of No Return* (1951). Osborn was well known as a screenwriter, with principal writing credit for, among others, *The Yearling* (1946), *East of Eden* (1955), and *South Pacific* (1958).   MAF

OSBORNE, JOHN (1929–94)

English playwright and actor. Osborne was working as a jobbing actor when his fourth play, *Look Back in Anger* (1956), was accepted by George *Devine at the new *English Stage Company at the *Royal Court. It marked a revolution in British theatre. Its antihero (*see* HERO AND ANTIHERO), Jimmy Porter, became the archetype of the 'angry young man', marking the arrival of a new generation of disenchanted, socially conscious, undeferential artists. The play does not bear the weight of its history well, but Jimmy's long speeches, lashing out at the world and people around him, have retained a bruised, searing eloquence. The apparent *realism of *Look Back in Anger* hung around Osborne's reputation, leading to misreadings of his subsequent work, which was often formally experimental. There are *Brechtian influences (always denied) in *The Entertainer* (1957), an extraordinary state-of-the-nation play about the decline of the empire which gave *Olivier one of his greatest parts, and *Luther* (1961), which equally suited Albert *Finney. In *Inadmissible Evidence* (1964), Osborne takes us into the mind of his *protagonist Bill

Maitland (played by Nicoll *Williamson), yet allows a complex structure of ironies to trouble the vicious hatreds and suspicions that rend Bill's mind. Even more daring is the *metatheatrical *A Sense of Detachment* (1972), seemingly designed to provoke *audiences into leaving. And in his last play, *Déjàvu* (1992), a sequel to *Look Back in Anger*, Jimmy is a curiously *Pirandellian *character, aware of his fictional status and burdened by his notorious eloquence.

Osborne's anger was initially thought to be left wing, and his eventual move to the right seemed to some like a betrayal. But in *Time Present, A Hotel in Amsterdam* (1968), and *West of Suez* (1971) his ambivalence towards the left was as evident as his hostility to the new radicals of the late 1960s. He wrote very little of substance in the last fifteen years of his life, except for his hilariously cruel autobiographies, *A Better Class of Person* (1981) and *Almost a Gentleman* (1991).   DR

OSOFISAN, FEMI (1946–   )

Nigerian writer and director. Educated at Ibadan and in *Paris, Osofisan is a prolific playwright and an industrious director; unlike many university-educated writers of his generation, he has remained based in Nigeria. His plays, written in English, are complex and multi-layered. He has taken the thematic challenges posed in villages by theatre for *development activists, and moved them to venues such as the Arts Theatre of the University of Ibadan. Influenced by Marx, Fanon, and Cabral, the *politically confrontational dimension of his work has been combined with an appreciation of Yoruba mythology and of Nigeria's colonial and neocolonial experience (*see* POST-COLONIAL STUDIES). Osofisan deploys a range of devices to make spectators self-aware, so that his theatre is a place of constant reinterpretation, interrogation, and subversion. He extended *Brecht's model for a reconsideration of history in works such as *The Chattering and the Song* (1976) and *Morountodun* (1979), and in those that embody challenges on social issues, such as *Once upon Four Robbers*. In his programme note for the première at Ibadan (1979), he wrote that he hoped the production would help 'to change our attitude from passive acceptance or sterile indignation to a more dynamic, more couraged determination to confront ourselves and our lives'. Searching for vehicles through which to bring about change, this dedicated reformer has also adapted *Gogol's *The Government Inspector* (as *Who's Afraid of Tai Solarin?*) and *Feydeau's *Paradise Hotel* (as *Midnight Hotel*).

Osofisan has worked with Wole *Soyinka but has adopted a radically different position from the Nobel laureate and the authors of an older generation. He critiqued Soyinka's *The Strong Breed* with his own *No Longer the Wasted Breed* (1981), insisting on the value of concerted action. He treated *Clark-Bekederemo's *The Raft* with a similar reply in *Another Raft* (1989). An experienced director who has worked in the United States and Ghana as well as Nigeria, Osofisan founded the Kakaun Sela Company, and in 2000 was appointed chief executive and general *manager of the National Theatre in Lagos.   JMG

OSTERMEIER, THOMAS (1968–   )

German director. In a very brief career Ostermeier has established himself as one of the most important directors in Germany. After study at the Ernst Busch theatre academy, he was invited in 1996 to run a small experimental stage attached to the *Deutsches Theater in *Berlin. Known as the Baracke, its repertoire of contemporary plays, especially by English authors such as Mark *Ravenhill and Sarah *Kane, soon attained cult status. He regards his commitment to contemporary drama as indicative of a 'new *realism' and a departure from the usual focus on the classics in German theatre. In 1999 he became co-director of the *Schaubühne in Berlin.   CBB

OSTROVSKY, ALEKSANDR (1823–86)

Russian dramatist. Widely acknowledged as Russia's greatest playwright, he was also the most prolific, producing 47 original dramas and 22 translations of foreign plays. Comparatively unknown in the West, his main subject is the manners and mores of the Russian merchant class, especially those who inhabited the Zamoskvoreche region of *Moscow. After studying law at Moscow University, Ostrovsky got a job as a *prompter at the Imperial *Maly Theatre at a time when the leading actor was Mikhail *Shchepkin and the reputation of the theatre as a force for cultural enlightenment led to its being hailed as Moscow's Second University. Most of Ostrovsky's work was premièred here. He sought to bring about substantial changes in the internal organization of the Russian theatre, campaigning for the removal of the imperial monopoly and seeking to develop the art of *acting by founding a new *training school. Ostrovsky's first play of note, *It's a Family Affair—We'll Settle It Ourselves* (1849) was banned because of its unflattering depiction of the merchant class, the Governor of Moscow placing Ostrovsky on a blacklist (*see* CENSORSHIP). However, his cause was taken up by the Slavophiles, who encouraged the composition of his first play to be staged in 1853, *Don't Sit in Another's Sleigh*. His next three plays were all substantial works and found critical success when published in the *Muscovite*, where they came to the attention of two important critics of the day, Chernyshevsky and Dobrolyubov. Of *The Poor Bride* (1851), Dobrolyubov noted its striking depiction of the contemporary position of Russian women, subjected to petty domestic tyranny. But another play, *Poverty Is No Crime* (1853), was criticized by Chernyshevsky for portraying the old order nostalgically.

In 1856 Ostrovsky volunteered to take part in an ethnological excursion to the more far-flung regions of Russia and was directed to the Upper Volga. This led to the composition of *The Thunderstorm* (published 1860), now generally considered to be his masterpiece. The central character, Katerina, is a compound of provincial backwardness and obscurantism, engendered by mystical religious beliefs, domestic tyranny, and sexual repression, which leads to rebellion, guilt, and suicide. Dobrolyubov's famous essay on the play, 'A Ray of Light in the Kingdom of Darkness', became a landmark of nineteenth-century *criticism. During the 1860s Ostrovsky turned to writing *historical dramas as well as producing articles on the state of Russian theatre. In 1870 he organized the Association of Russian Playwrights and later the Actors' Circle, a democratic institution which was open to women and anyone interested in serving the arts. During the 1870s and 1880s, Ostrovsky wrote some of his best plays. In the wake of *Enough Stupidity in Every Wise Man* in 1868, he wrote *The Forest* (1870) and *Talents and Admirers* (1881) which, alongside *The Thunderstorm*, are the plays best known abroad. His final days were spent working on a translation of *Antony and Cleopatra*, which he made with the help of an Englishman named Watson, who acted under the stage name of Dubrovin.   NW

O'SULLIVAN, VINCENT (1937–)

New Zealand playwright. Already an established poet and short-story writer, O'Sullivan's first play, *Shuriken* (1983), incorporates *realism, *expressionism, *nō, and newsreels to depict the cultural incomprehension surrounding a historical event (the death of 50 Japanese soldiers and one guard in a 1943 prisoner of war incident in New Zealand). Subsequent plays have similarly deployed non-*naturalist conventions, from classical Greek to *music hall, to portray *historical periods or people (for instance Katherine Mansfield, of whom O'Sullivan is a distinguished scholar, and Roger Casement). All O'Sullivan's plays display learning, sardonic wit, and a poet's concern for humane values of the heart.   DC

O T'AE-SŎK (1940–)

*Korean director and playwright. The author of over 30 plays, he has directed nearly all of them for the Mokhwa (Cotton) Theatre Company in Seoul. O T'ae-sŏk emerged in modern Korean theatre (*shingŭk) in the late 1960s. *Glass Tomb* (1973) characteristically dealt with the conflict between civilization and the primitiveness of Korean life; it was performed under the title *The Order* at *La Mama Experimental Theatre Club in *New York in 1974. In his directing, O has applied the *Gestus* of *Brecht's *epic theatre, and *Artaud's theatre of *cruelty, to indigenous themes. His representative plays, published in English in *The Metacultural Theatre of Oh T'ae-Sŏk* (1999), are *Lifecord* (1974), *Ch'un-p'ung's Wife* (1976), *Bicycle* (1983), and *Intimacy between Father and Son* (1987).   JOC

ŌTA SHŌGO (1939–)

Japanese playwright and director. Born in China and evacuated to *Japan after the Second World War, Ōta began writing plays in high school and was active in both theatre and politics for most of the 1960s. In 1968 he helped found Tenkei Gekijō (the Transformation Theatre) in *Tokyo for which he served as house playwright and *artistic director until the group was disbanded in 1988. His first major critical success was the *nō-inspired *Legend of Komachi* (1977). In contrast to the speed, noise, and garrulousness of much contemporary Japanese theatre, Ota's plays are distinguished by their austerity, silence, stillness, and glacial pace. The nature of being, rather than doing, is what informs his *dramaturgy. Ota's works reflect his 'desire to stage living silence' in order to capture the most basic elements of human experience. Hence many of his works, like *Water Station* (1981), have no *dialogue whatsoever. Since the 1970s he has regularly performed abroad. Other works include *Sarachi* (1992).
                                                            CP

OTHER PLACE *See* ROYAL SHAKESPEARE COMPANY.

OTOKODATE

A dashing male *hero in Japanese *kabuki or *bunraku plays who acts and dresses extravagantly and who sides with the commoner class against oppressive samurai in the service of the central authorities.   LRK

O'TOOLE, PETER (1932–)

Irish-born actor who spent his childhood in Leeds. His *London debut was in *Shaw's *Major Barbara* (*Old Vic, 1956), followed by *The Long and the Short and the Tall* (*Royal Court, 1958) and a season with the *Royal Shakespeare Company playing Shylock, Thersites, and Petruchio (1960). Thereafter his career, although focused on *London and *Dublin, became ever more international: productions included *Brecht's *Baal* (1963), *Hamlet* (1964), *O'Casey's *Juno and the Paycock* (1966), Shaw's *Man and Superman* (1967), and *Beckett's *Waiting for Godot* (1967). In 1984 he appeared as Higgins in *Pygmalion* in the West End, a role he revived on Broadway in 1987. In 1989 he appeared as the eponymous journalist in *Jeffrey Bernard Is Unwell*, a role he recreated in 1999 at the Old Vic. On screen, his gripping performance in David Lean's *Lawrence of Arabia* (1962) brought O'Toole huge international recognition and the first of seven Academy award nominations; other *films included *Becket* (1964), *The Lion in Winter* (1968), the remake of *Goodbye Mr Chips* (1969), *The Ruling Class* (1971), *The Stunt Man* (1979), and *My Favourite Year* (1982).   AS

OTTO, TEO (1904–68)

German designer. After study at the *Bauhaus in Weimar, Otto began designing *opera in Kassel. In 1927 Otto Klemperer engaged him for the Kroll Opera, *Berlin, and in 1931 he became chief designer at the Berlin State Theatre (*Berlin Royal Theatre). In 1933 he was forced to emigrate to Switzerland, where he was associated with the *Zurich Schauspielhaus. During this time Otto began a lasting collaboration with *Brecht, designing the first productions of *Mother Courage* (1941), *Galileo* (1943), and *The Good Person of Setzuan* (1943). After the war he became an internationally known designer for theatre and opera with productions in most major European cities and at *New York's *Metropolitan Opera. Besides Brecht, he worked with the leading directors of the early post-war period, including Gustav *Gründgens (*Faust*, 1957), Leopold Lindtberg, Fritz *Kortner, and Karl Heinz Stroux. He designed the premières of the plays of Max *Frisch and Friedrich *Dürrenmatt's *The Visit* (New York, 1958). He was appointed professor of stage design at the Academy of Fine Arts, Düsseldorf, a position he held until his death. Otto's designs, exceptionally varied stylistically, range from *realism to abstract stylization. (*See* illustration p. 986.)
CBB

OTWAY, THOMAS (1652–85)

English playwright. Clergyman's son, Oxford drop-out, and failed actor, Otway turned to playwriting with *Alcibiades* (1675), a moderately successful melodramatic *heroic tragedy, and followed it with two other plays in a similar vein: *Don Carlos* (1676), which adds individual psychology to the heroics, and *The History and Fall of Caius Marius* (1679), which grafts the pathos of *Romeo and Juliet* onto Roman political history. Otway's penchant for tragic pathos found expression in the two blank *verse *tragedies for which he is best known. *The Orphan* (1680) is a domestic *melodrama in which the inadequacies of human nature replace villainy in bringing about tragic suffering. *Venice Preserv'd* (1682), Otway's masterpiece, explores love, honour, and the pathos of undeserved suffering in the context of a political conspiracy. On the other hand, there is little pathos in Otway's *comedies. *Friendship in Fashion* (1678) is a bitter and violent social *satire. *The Soldier's Fortune* (1680) is an equally sardonic sex comedy that recognizes the real social problems underlying adulterous behaviour. *The Atheist* (1683) includes a dark view of the ugly reality that follows the romantic union with which conventional comedies end. Otway's *Titus and Berenice* (1676), a translation of *Racine's play, is significant only in that the author chose to augment its performance with the addition of the first post-Restoration *afterpiece, a translation of *Molière's *The Cheats of Scapin*.
RWV

OUELLETTE, ROSE (1903–96)

French-Canadian comic actress and *manager. As a child performer she acquired the nonsense nickname 'La Poune', which stuck with her throughout her long career in *variety theatre, in American-style *burlesque, and, later, in *television. The best-known, best-loved (and most frequently imitated) female entertainer of her day, she was also the first Québec woman to serve as an *artistic director. A capable administrator, she headed *Montréal's Cartier Theatre and the National Theatre during the heady but difficult era of burlesque in Canada, from the 1920s to the birth of television in the early 1950s.
LED

OUAGADOUGOU INTERNATIONAL PUPPET FESTIVAL (FITMO)

Burkina Faso event, founded in 1993, which succeeded the Ouagadougou Theatre Festival (established 1987). Directed by the playwright Jean-Pierre *Guingané, the *festival promotes theatre in Burkina Faso and encourages exchanges between local and international practitioners. *Puppetry is a major feature of the festival, which also stages conventional plays and organizes seminars on the performances and the annual theme. The 2000 festival on 'Theatre and Human Rights in *Africa' attracted practitioners from West Africa, *Japan, France, and the UK, and was dedicated to the memory of Sony *Labou Tansi.
JCM

OUSPENSKAYA, MARIA (1876–1949)

Russian-born actress and *acting teacher. Trained in the provincial theatre and then at the *Moscow Art Theatre, Ouspenskaya remained in *New York after the MAT *tour of 1923. She was retained in 1923 by Richard *Boleslavsky as principal acting teacher for the *American Laboratory Theatre, where she taught her version of the *Stanislavsky system. Two students—Stella *Adler and Lee *Strasberg—became key figures in the *Group Theatre and themselves influential acting teachers. Ouspenskaya was a sought-after character actress in New York from 1923 to 1936 and in Hollywood thereafter until her death.
MAF

OUTDOOR PERFORMANCE *See* OPEN-AIR PERFORMANCE.

OUYANG YUQIAN (OU-YANG YÜ-CHIEN) (1889–1962)

*Chinese actor, director, and playwright of both *jingju (Beijing opera) and the Western-style *huaju (spoken drama). As a student in Japan, he performed in the *Chunliu She (Spring Willow Society) production of *Uncle Tom's Cabin*, the first Western-style play in Chinese. After returning to *Shanghai in 1910

Teo **Otto**'s design for the first performance of Dürrenmatt's *The Visit*, Zurich Schauspielhaus, 1956, directed by Oskar Wälterlin. Therese Giehse is seated on the balcony.

he became active in the new drama movement, performing and writing *wenming xi (civilized drama). Meanwhile he also studied Beijing opera as a *dan* (female) actor, becoming professional in 1916; for over ten years he was the leading *dan* actor in Shanghai, where he enjoyed equal fame with *Mei Lanfang, who was based in Beijing. Ouyang also wrote some of the Beijing operas he performed, including *Pan Jinlian* (1927) in which he transformed a traditional loose woman into an individualist who lived and died for the sake of love. After leaving Shanghai and acting in 1927, he took various positions, teaching, directing, translating, and writing for both theatre forms as well as *film. Some of his better-known plays include: *Liang Hongyu* (1937), *Li Xiucheng, the Duke of Loyalty* (1941), and *The Peach Blossom Fan*, a *chuanqi play he adapted first into *jingju* (1937) and then *huajü* (1946). After 1949 he served as president of the Central Drama Conservatory in Beijing.   SYL

OWEN, ALUN (1925–94)

English playwright. A prolific writer for stage, screen, and *radio, Owen was appreciated for his precise ear for speech and his depiction of life in Liverpool. He began his career as an actor but turned in 1958 to writing with the *television play *The Rough and Ready Lot*. His reputation as a Liverpool playwright began with *Progress to the Park* (broadcast, 1958; staged by the *Theatre Workshop, 1959) which depicts two star-crossed lovers whose relationship is ruined by the religious bigotry of their elders. Other television and stage plays about Liverpool life include *No Trams to Lime Street* (1959), *Lena, Oh my Lena* (1960), *After the Funeral* (1960), and the book for Lionel *Bart's *musical *Maggie May* (1964). Owen is probably most popularly remembered as the screenwriter of the Beatles' *A Hard Day's Night* (1964).   MDG

OWENS, ROCHELLE (1936–)

American playwright and poet. Born Rochelle Bass in Brooklyn, Owens has been a leading exponent of *avant-garde drama, in which she mines the subconscious and unflinchingly puts it on stage with all its perversity, cruelty, violence, and repulsive imagery. Her most famous work is *Futz* (published in 1961 and given its first *New York production in 1967, winning an Obie *award). A farmer enjoys sodomizing his pet pig, whom he regards as his wife; and the reactions of outraged villagers result in several deaths. *Homo* (1966) deals with greed, xenophobia, and racial purity. The savage excesses of *Beclch* (pronounced 'beklek', 1966) lead to elephantiasis and self-strangulation. Owens occasionally turns to historical *characters—George and Martha Washington, Karl Marx (in a play with *music), Emma Goldman. Her works have been staged widely in Europe and translated into half a dozen languages. She has also published more than a dozen volumes of poetry.   CT

OWUSU, MARTIN (OKYERE) (1943–)

Ghanaian playwright, actor, and director. During the mid-1970s Owisu was director of the Oguaa Playhouse at the University of Cape Coast, and in the 1980s he founded and directed the Abibisunsum Theatre. He has been involved as actor or director with productions of many Ghanaian plays, including *Sutherland's *Edufa* and *de Graft's *Muntu*, as well as with Western classics such as *Oedipus the King*, *Tartuffe*, *Čapek's *RUR*, and *Priestley's *Dangerous Corner*. Since his pioneering *The Sun Shines Bright*, Owusu has firmly established himself as a major writer for Ghana *Television, with broadcast versions of his plays *The Story Ananse Told* (1967) and *Sasa and the King of the Forest* (1968). His other plays (some published in 1973) include *The Mightier Sword*, *The Sudden Return*, and *Python: the legend of Aku Sika*. *Blocks, Nails and Hammers: a time to build* (1997) was produced at the National Theatre of Ghana.   JMG

O YŎNG-JIN (1916–74)

*Korean playwright of Western-style theatre (*shingŭk). After the Second World War, the ideological disorder between the right and the left entangled the Korean theatre, newly liberated from Japanese colonial tyranny. Under these conditions, many playwrights sought to reflect the hope of the long-suffering nation for a better life. Of them, O Yŏng-jin took the unusual approach of drawing on *folklore to broaden the subject matter of *shingŭk* and introduce traditional culture to the form. Most of his twenty or so plays are *satiric *comedies that ridicule the social customs and politics of the time. Representative are *Wedding Day* (1943), *His Excellency Yi Chung-seng Is Still Alive* (1949), and *Tale of Hŏseng* (1970).   JOC

OYONO-MBIA, GUILLAUME (1939–)

Cameroon playwright. Writing in a style similar to *Molière, his plays in French include *Trois prétendants, un mari* (*Three Suitors, One Husband*, 1959), *Jusqu'à nouvel avis* (*Until Further Notice*, 1970), *Notre fille ne se mariera pas* (*Our Daughter Won't Marry*, 1973), *Le Train spécial de son Excellence* (*His Excellency's Special Train*, 1976) and *Le Bourbier* (1989). Some have been adapted into English by the author, and the first translated into a number of European languages. Despite his position as Cameroon's best-known and most popular dramatist, Oyono-Mbia has claimed to be the victim of parsimonious *publishers and theatre troupes, and announced he would abandon the stage.   HNE

OZEROV, VLADISLAV (1769–1816)

Russian dramatist. Beginning as a proponent of the *neoclassical school, Ozerov was among the first to embrace sentimentalism.

His first *tragedy, *Yaropolk and Oleg* (1798), imitated the style of *Sumarokov and *Knyazhnin, but his real success came with *Dmitry Donskoy* (1807), which celebrated Russia's victory over the Tartars. The play also mirrored Russia's struggle with Napoleonic France, and when first performed after Russia's defeat at the battle of Austerlitz, Dmitry's line 'The time has come to wreak vengeance on our foes' was greeted with excited *applause. After 1812 the play became even more popular. Whilst adhering to the three *unities, the play also makes concessions to the increasing taste for sentimentalism through the introduction of a love theme. Ozerov's drama was soon to be succeeded by that of *Shakhovskoy, and both Belinsky and *Pushkin were critical of his work. Yet his plays proved excellent vehicles for a certain style of *acting, and Aleksei Yakovlev and Ekaterina *Semyonova scored successes in *Oedipus in Athens* (1804), *Fingal* (1805), and *Polyxena* (1809).   NW

·P·

American actor and director. Born in *New York, Pacino studied at the *Actors Studio and the Herbert *Berghof Studio before making his *Off-Broadway debut in Jack *Gelber's *The Connection* (1961). In that decade Pacino, now associated with *Method acting, originated a series of intense and troubled *characters; he received an Obie *award in 1968 for best actor for his role as Murphy in *Horovitz's *The Indian Wants the Bronx*. Pacino achieved *film stardom during the 1970s for his performances in *The Godfather*, Parts I and II (1972, 1974), *Serpico* (1973), and *Dog Day Afternoon* (1975). He also received Tony awards for *Does the Tiger Wear a Necktie?* (1969) and David *Rabe's *The Basic Training of Pavlo Hummel* (1977). Pacino became an important interpreter of David *Mamet during the 1980s, appearing in an acclaimed revival of *American Buffalo* (1983) and in the film of *Glengarry Glen Ross* (1992). His long-term collaboration with *Boston-based director David Wheeler on Shakespeare and *Brecht culminated in *Looking for Richard* (1996), a film in which Pacino (as actor and director) examined American attitudes toward Shakespeare through a documentary collage of scene work from *Richard III*, interspersed with *rehearsal footage and interviews. He made his Off-Broadway directorial debut with *O'Neill's *Hughie* the same year. JAB

PACUVIUS, MARCUS (c.220–c.130 BC)

*Roman tragic playwright. Pacuvius was probably of Oscan origin, like his uncle and teacher, the playwright *Ennius. Supported at Rome by aristocrats associated with Scipio the Younger, he was admired as a writer of *tragedies, as an authority on Greek drama, and for his painting. Some 440 lines and the titles of thirteen works of his output survive; all but one of the plays were probably based upon the works of *Sophocles and other Greek tragedians. The exception, *Paullus*, was a Roman *historical play (*fabula praetexta*) commemorating the victory of Lucius Aemilius Paullus over Macedonia in 168 BC. RCB

PAGE, GERALDINE (1924–87)

American actress. The Missouri-born Page trained at *Chicago's *Goodman Theatre and made her *New York debut with *Off-Broadway's Blackfriars Guild in 1945. After years of summer and winter *stock, she joined Off-Broadway's *Circle in the Square, making her breakthrough as the spinster Alma Winemiller in a renowned revival of *Summer and Smoke* (1952) that demonstrated her affinity for Tennessee *Williams *heroines. In 1954, a year after her first appearance on Broadway, she had a hit as Lizzie in *The Rainmaker* (1954), which she also played in *London. She appeared in sixteen other Broadway plays, including *Sweet Bird of Youth* (1959); *Strange Interlude* (1963) and *The Three Sisters* (1964), both produced by the *Actors Studio, to which she belonged; *Black Comedy/White Lies* (1967); and *Agnes of God* (1982). Page acted in *regional theatres, on *television (she won two Emmys), and in 27 *films. After seven nominations, she won the Academy award for *The Trip to Bountiful* (1985). She and her husband, actor Rip Torn, founded Off-Broadway's Sanctuary Theatre in 1976, and she belonged to the Mirror Repertory Company from 1983. Although often cast as flighty neurotics, she had a wide range and could be convincingly glamorous or frumpy. SLL

PAGE, LOUISE (1955–)

English playwright. Page first received notice in 1978 with *Tissue*, a play about breast cancer. She was resident playwright at the *Royal Court Theatre (1982–3) and associate director of Theatre Calgary in Canada in 1987. Her best-known play, *Salonika* (1982), received the George Devine *award. Other major plays include *Real Estate* (1984), *Golden Girls* (1984), *Beauty and the*

Beast (1985), and *Diplomatic Wives* (1989). Page's work, which has been produced at the Royal Court, the *Tricycle, Stratford's Other Place, and the *Liverpool Playhouse, focuses on *gender and issues of ambition and choice in contemporary life.

AHK

PAGEANT

In modern usage 'pageant' usually means a spectacular procession or *tableau, but historically the term often meant either a scenic structure or a play, or both. Thus in a fifteenth-century document we find references to both 'a pageant with wheels' and 'the pageant called Doomsday'. As a structure, pageant most often designated a scenic float on wheels, commonly used in civic and religious processions, *tournaments, and in aristocratic entertainments such as *entremets. Less common was their use as *stages for dramatic performances. Pageants ranged in size and configuration from simple carts carrying a person to gigantic figures of human beings and exotic animals. They could represent ships, mountains, elaborate trees, castles, or towers. Those used for plays were of a 'cube-and-house' form, a platform with a roof on four corner posts, set on four wheels. In the north of England, pageants used in *medieval theatre were large, bi-level scenic structures, drawn by horses or pushed by men to various parts of the town. It is usually assumed that the pageants moved from station to station in sequence, each *biblical play being performed at each stop. Other possibilities are (*a*) that the performances went on simultaneously, (*b*) that at the conclusion of the procession the wagons gathered at a single large station for the performance, or (*c*) that following the procession the pageants were arranged in a round outside the town for the performance. These 'cube-and-house' structures were functionally similar to *booth stages or place-and-scaffold configurations. *See also* CYCLE PLAYS.

RWV

PAGNOL, MARCEL (1895–1974)

French dramatist and filmmaker. Pagnol's birth and early career as an English teacher were in the south of France, near Marseille, the setting for his dramatic trilogy *Marius* (1929), *Fanny* (1931), and *César* (1937, dramatized from his own 1933 *film). This poignant love story set in a seaport bar takes on a *folkloric quality with its local colour and its warm humour in the supporting *characters. Pagnol had taken a more satiric approach in his earlier stage successes: *Les Marchands de gloire* (1925, with Paul Nivoix) on war profiteering, *Jazz* (1926), indicting a modern Faust's neglect of human values, and *Topaze* (1928) on a naive schoolmaster who learns cynicism. With the advent of talking pictures, Pagnol formed a film company and wrote his own screenplays. Notable films include *Regain* (*Harvest*, 1937), *La Femme du boulanger* (*The Baker's Wife*, 1938), and *La Fille du puisatier* (*The Well-Digger's Daughter*, 1940). His 1946 elec-

tion to the Académie Française was the first for a filmmaker.

FHL

PAINTING OF SCENES

Since the *early modern period the European theatre has been a painter's theatre, from its picture-frame *proscenium to its painted *perspective to its adoption of styles and movements from easel painting. The ancient theatres sometimes used painted *scenery (*see* PINAKES; PERIAKTOI); *medieval stages sometimes had a painted arras; and there is much painting in the theatre traditions of *China and *India. But the European theatre of 1550–1900 emphasized painted scenery more than any other. Even at the beginning of the twenty-first century the need for realistic surfaces has kept scene painting a vital concern.

The scene painter's challenges are scale and speed. Theatrical sets are large, and perspective often requires a picture to be distributed across separated surfaces, so that the artist cannot simultaneously see the whole set and paint it. Furthermore, set painting requires a wide variety of texture effects to be achieved on a large scale, literally overnight. To solve the problem of scale, for each scenic piece a scale grid is normally pencilled onto the designers' elevation, and a corresponding grid is chalk-lined onto the piece. The elevation is then copied block by block. In the Anglo-American method, the piece is hung on a back wall, and many English-language theatres of the nineteenth century had flying bridges that facilitated this. In the continental method, pieces are secured to the floor. More recently, as projections have largely replaced gridding, the Anglo-American method has come to dominate. Dealing with large areas, elaborate detail, and short deadlines, scene painters feel none of the studio artist's bias toward a single technique with a single medium. Though the brush, sprayer, and roller are still used conventionally for most work, scene painters now often use dry brushing, spattering, scumbling, pouring, soap resists, translucent washes, and wet mixing. They apply paint with wet towels, squeeze bottles, sponges, insecticide sprayers, ropes, netting, artificial grass, bare hands, carpet scraps, and tennis balls, among many other tools. The mastery of hundreds of tactics and techniques takes many years, and thus scene painting has remained a highly respected craft in the theatre. *See also* SCENOGRAPHY.

JB

PAIS, RICARDO (1945–)

Portuguese director. Having discovered theatre at university under the direction of Víctor *García, Pais later trained as a director at the Drama Centre, *London. Back in *Lisbon in 1974, he was first associated with the company Os Cómicos, but soon began a highly personal and varied career. With a belief in the virtue of mixing various disciplines, as well as a deep awareness of the possibilities of technology (*see* MEDIA AND PERFORMANCE),

Pais has created seductive stage metaphors and powerful visual and aural landscapes, dominated by experiments with space, body, movement, and voice. He has directed classical and contemporary plays (*Vicente, *Machiavelli, Shakespeare, *Otway, *Garrett, *Wedekind, *Ionesco, *Bernhard) as well as creating productions, mostly written or conceived by him, in which *music or *dance play a leading role. His interpretation of *texts, allied to bold performance methods, transforms the stage into a place of 'unpredictable events'. His *Fausto. Fernando. Fragmentos* (1988, after Fernando Pessoa's 'impossible poem' on the Faust myth) remains one of the most imaginative and inspiring Portuguese productions of the last decades of the twentieth century. He has also been in charge of major cultural initiatives in Oporto, where he brought a radically new approach to the Teatro Nacional de S. João (1995–2000).   PEC

PAKISTAN

After the Partition of the Indian subcontinent in 1947, theatre failed to take root in Pakistan as it did in *India, or even in post-1971 *Bangladesh following its split from Pakistan. There were some exceptions: remnants of *folk theatre called *swang* lingered in western Punjab (*see also* PUNJABI THEATRE), as did some *Parsi theatre in Karachi (a confluence of slapstick Parsi humour and *musical plays in Gujarati, English, and Urdu). There are several reasons for the lack of development. Most obviously, the ruling Islamist ideology of Pakistan, the *raison d'être* of the state, is intrinsically hostile to theatre because of its potential to question all belief systems. Second, the commingling of the sexes in performance implies an exposure of the female body which is also against orthodox Islamic values. The third reason is political: Pakistan has been ruled by military dictatorships for most of its history, with brief interludes of civilian government that have been dominated by political coteries. As the director and actor Khalid Ahmad noted in 1997, neither of these types of regime 'can be expected to look upon serious cultural activities with favour since these lead to questioning and questioning can lead to change'. Finally, the Muslim middle class left behind in Pakistan after Partition had a profound anti-cultural bias which has resulted in a contempt for art forms such as *dance and theatre that are perceived as borrowing elements of Hindu culture; one of the chief Pakistani ideological imperatives was to carve out a cultural identity that was separate and distinct from the common heritage of South Asia. In such circumstances, it is no surprise that state and corporate funding for the theatre is non-existent (*see* FINANCE).

Despite such bleak circumstances, it is remarkable that several varieties of theatre have developed anyway. The largest and most faithful *audiences have been created by commercial urban theatre, the biggest centre for which is Lahore. Commercial theatre is an outgrowth of a genuine folk or *lok* theatre, which had its heyday in the Punjab during the 1940s and 1950s,

although its roots are steeped in traditions dating back centuries. *Lok* theatre originated in song and dance, the most popular instruments being the flute, lyre, and drum. *Touring theatre companies, most of them originating in Lahore, would set up tents (*shamianas*) for performances at village fairs (*melas*) during harvest season. Epics and ballads such as *Heer Ranjha, Mirza Sahibaan, Sohni Mahiwaal*, and *Sassi Punnu* were used to draw crowds, and the gate money was sufficient to make these ventures economically viable. Theatre owners and *managers stayed in business by exploiting their employees in various ways, especially the women. Some of the best-known theatres, all named after their owners, were Phaji Shah, Babu Kaley Khan, Maula Bakhsh, and Shah Jahan; the only enterprise operated by a woman was the Shama Theatre, owned by the legendary Bali Jati. The most popular performers were Bali herself, Inayat Hussain Bhatti, and Alam Lohar. By the end of the twentieth century commercial theatre had largely devolved into crude slapstick *comedy; its highly suggestive *dialogue makes use of lewd double entendres, much appreciated by the urban petty bourgeoisie that comprises its audience. These plays are performed in commercially operated theatre halls; well known in Lahore are the Tamaseel *auditorium and Rabia Theatre. The state-owned Alhamra Arts Council in Lahore also rents out its halls to commercial theatre groups.

The success of commercial theatre has rankled with those activists committed to protest or *political theatre (see below). Objections are also heard from those who, like the stage and TV actor Rahat Kazmi, believe in 'economically viable, yet meaningful theatre which is also aesthetically satisfying', such as the adaptations and Urdu-language plays by 'artistic' playwrights like Bano Qudsia and Intizar Hussain. In this view commercial theatre is a corruption of the traditions of folk theatre (which died out with the advent of *television and *film), and is inherently vulgar, catering to the basest tastes, relying on sexual innuendoes and double entendres contained in witty repartee (*juggat bazi*). While these charges are often justified, it is more significant that commercial theatre, as Shoaib Hashmi has said, has even in the face of huge opposition 'created an audience sizable enough to sustain the beginnings of a theatre'.

The college dramatic societies (such as the Government College Dramatics Club, and the Najmuddin Dramatics Society of Kinnaird College in Lahore under the direction of Perin Boga) have kept theatre alive through annual self-supported productions even during the most difficult of times. Though they cater to an English-speaking elite audience, some remarkable theatre personalities have emerged through these organizations. A few have moved beyond their elite training: Samina Ahmad, for example, is a well-known stage and TV actress and director, and also programme director of the Lahore Arts Council in recent years; Madeeha Gauhar is a leading actress of stage and television and founding director of the *alternative theatre group *Ajoka in Lahore.

Political theatre emerged in Pakistan in the late 1970s, primarily as a pro-democratic response to an increasingly repressive state apparatus. It takes the forms of *street theatre or alternative theatre (also called 'parallel' or protest theatre) and has contributed much to the growing debate around issues of human rights and gender equity (see POLITICS AND THEATRE). It had two predecessors. First, the protest theatre of the early years of the nation, when Marxist intellectuals and party workers affiliated with the Communist Party of Pakistan or the Mazdoor Kisan Party (Peasant Workers' Party) created political work for the 'masses'; in pre-Partition India some of these activists, like Ali Ahmad, Ismail Yusuf, Mansoor Saeed, and Khwaja Moinuddin, had been members of the leftist *Indian People's Theatre Association (IPTA) and carried their commitment to the new state. Second, the traditional *lok* theatre, rooted in an indigenous rural setting and using folk idioms: alternative theatre groups such as Ajoka and *Punjab Lok Rehas have aimed at producing politically aware theatre that also combines elements of folk traditions. They, as well as Tehrik-I-Niswan of Karachi, were founded in conjunction with political movements such as the Movement for the Restoration of Democracy and the Women's Action Forum, which sprang up in resistance to the repressive military regime of General Zia-ul-Haque in the late 1970s. They wanted to create plays written in the language of the people, Urdu or Punjabi, while simultaneously reviving folk traditions of song and dance. They have not escaped controversy, but have nevertheless contributed original work and innovative performance styles and have encouraged the growth of similar groups all over Pakistan, creating a rudimentary but genuine people's theatre that can be sustained at low cost. Some groups that started out performing street theatre, such as Ajoka, have become regular troupes committed to delivering socially meaningful and artistic theatre; others, such as Punjab Lok Rehas, have moved toward theatre for *development, borrowing from the methods of the Brazilian theatre practitioner Augusto *Boal. *See also* URDU THEATRE. FAK

PAK SŬNG-HŬI (1901–64)

Korean actor, director, producer, and playwright of modern commercial theatre (*shinp'agŭk). He was a founding member of the Towolhoe (Earth and Moon) group in 1922 while a college student in *Tokyo. After returning to *Korea, he led the group for over twenty years (it was dissolved in 1946), exhausting his inheritance to maintain its activities. He sought to revolutionize dramatic form by writing complete play scripts and abandoning the improvised *dialogue common in Korean theatre. His most successful play, *Arirang Pass* (1929), which was lost and reconstructed through the director's recollection, dealt with lovers forced to part because of family bankruptcy caused by Japanese exploitation. This play, which sentimentalized life under Japanese suppression, is still loved by contemporary Korean *audi-

ences. He wrote over 200 plays, including translations and adaptations; all but four were lost in a fire during the Korean War. Of those which survive, *Offspring* (1929) and *Hometown* (1933) also portray the repression of Korean life under the Japanese. JOC

PALACE THEATRE

*Playhouse at Broadway and 47th Street in *New York, which opened in 1913 and quickly became the premier showcase for *vaudeville entertainment and the flagship for the Keith–*Albee circuit of first-class vaudeville houses. Its stage saw the leading entertainers of the later 1910s and 1920s, including Sarah *Bernhardt, Harry *Houdini, W. C. *Fields, Eddie *Cantor, and the *Marx Brothers. With a capacity of 1,800, the theatre was highly profitable during the 1920s, but when vaudeville faltered in the Great Depression the venue was gradually converted to a cinema (1932). Live *musical-theatre performances returned in 1965 and it underwent a major renovation from 1987 to 1991. MAF

PALAIS ROYAL, THÉÂTRE DU

Seventeenth- and eighteenth-century *Paris *playhouse, or one of later theatres with the same name. The larger of two private *proscenium theatres constructed for Cardinal *Richelieu within his Parisian palace, it was originally supplied with an *auditorium of gently sloping steps and equipped with the latest Italianate stage machinery. Opening with Jean Desmarets's *Mirame* in 1641, it typically housed spectacular productions that explicitly glorified France. After Richelieu's death it passed into the control of the French royal family, who often used it for court performances. In 1660 Louis XIV granted the use of the theatre to *Molière's company, which shared the space with the King's Italian players throughout the height of the writer's career (see COMÉDIE ITALIENNE). After Molière's death in 1673, the theatre passed into the hands of his rival Jean-Baptiste *Lully, and afterwards remained the site of the *Opéra until it was destroyed by *fire in 1763. CJW

PALITZSCH, PETER (1918–)

German director who began his career at the end of the 1940s at the *Volksbühne in Dresden. In 1949 he joined *Brecht as assistant and *dramaturg at the *Berliner Ensemble. Between 1956 and 1959 he directed (with Manfred *Wekwerth) *Synge's *Playboy of the Western World*, *Vishnevsky's *Optimistic Tragedy*, and (with Ekkehard Schall) Brecht's *Arturo Ui*. In 1961 he left the German Democratic Republic to direct in West Germany, and became *artistic director at Stuttgart's State Theatre (1966–72), then co-director of the municipal theatre in Frankfurt (1972–80). Since 1980 Palitzsch has worked freelance in Germany and abroad, and in 1992 joined the board of the Berliner Ensemble. As a *Brechtian he had a major impact on West German theatre in the 1960s and 1970s, directing classics and contemporary work (*Frisch, *Pinter, *Beckett). His direction is characterized by precise dramaturgy and clarity, with theatrical wit balancing a dialectical and analytical approach. Eight of his productions were invited to the Berlin *Theatertreffen. CBB

PALLADIO, ANDREA (1508–80)

Italian architect, whose attempts to resurrect the architectural principles and methods of antiquity had a decisive influence on *neoclassical architecture throughout Europe. Most of his buildings can be found in Venice and the Veneto region. Through his patron *Trissino he became involved with the Olympian Academy in Vicenza, which took an active interest in the revival of classical drama. In 1556 he illustrated the *Vitruvius edition of Daniele Barbaro, which allowed him to develop a clearer picture of the theatre architecture of classical times (see ANCIENT THEATRES). In 1558 he constructed for the Academy a small stage for the performances of 'Olympic Games' (semi-scenic poetry recitations and play readings), and a few years later a temporary stage in the Palazzo della Ragione, complete with *scaenae frons and *perspective *scenery, which was used for productions of Piccolomini's *Amor costante* (Unceasing Love, 1561) and Trissino's *Sophonisba* (1562). In 1564 he constructed another temporary theatre for the Compagnia della Calza in Venice, probably in the courtyard of the Palazzo Dolfin, for a performance of Conte di Monte's *Antigono*, which *Vasari described as 'a wooden half-theatre in the style of the Colosseum'. These preparatory studies allowed Palladio to design his masterpiece, the Teatro *Olimpico in Vicenza, begun in February 1580, shortly before his death on 19 August of the same year, and completed by his pupil *Scamozzi in 1584. *See also* PLAYHOUSE. GB

PALLENBERG, MAX (1877–1934)

Austrian actor. After an initial career at provincial theatres in Austria and *Vienna, *Reinhardt engaged Pallenberg in 1914 for the *Deutsches Theater, *Berlin, where he remained for the rest of his career. His important roles included the leads in *Molnár's *Liliom* (1922) and *Hofmannsthal's *Der Unbestechliche* (Vienna, 1923), and the father in *Pirandello's *Six Characters in Search of an Author* (1924). He created the part of Schwejk in *Piscator's *The Adventures of the Good Soldier Schwejk* (1928), which remained one of his most important performances. Pallenberg's special gift for gesture, facial mimicry, and *improvisation enabled him to add political insight and critique to the petty bourgeois *characters he so often played. He is acknowledged as one of the greatest German-speaking actors of the Weimar period. His exceptional range spanned low comic roles to Mephisto in

Reinhardt's production of *Faust* (*Salzburg Festival, 1933). CBB

PANIKKAR, KAVALAM NARAYANA (1928–)

Indian playwright, director, poet, composer, and critic. Based in the state of Kerala in *India, Panikkar graduated in law from Madras University and later served as the secretary of the *Sangeet Natak Akademi in Kerala (1961–70). In 1968 he formed Kuthambalam, an experimental theatre in Alappuzha, and wrote and produced *Sakshi* (The Witness, 1964), *Daivattar* (The Revered God, 1973), and *Tiruvazhithan* (1974). Moving to Thiruvananthapuram, he renamed his troupe Tiruvarang, and it functioned under the umbrella of Sopanam, a centre for performing arts and research. His major productions in Malayalam were *Avanavankadamba* (One's Own Impediment, 1975) and *Karimkutty* (The Black Guy, 1983), noted for their use of regional *folk idioms and *acting methods. Panikkar is known for inventive productions of Sanskrit dramas which draw on the tenets of the *Natyasastra. They have included *Bhasa's *Madhyamavyayoga* (The Middle One, 1979), *Karnabhara* (Karna's Task, 1984), *Urubhanga* (The Broken Thighs, 1988), and *Swapnavasavadatta* (The Vision of Vasavadatta, 1990); *Kalidasa's *Shakuntala* (1982) and *Vikramorvasiya* (1981). Panikkar's ethnographic research on the *sopanam* music style and its application to *mohiniattam* *dance, theatre, and *film has been widely recognized. JoG

PANJI

Collections of *Indonesian tales about a legendary eleventh-century Javanese prince named Panji, which became popular dramatic material during the Majapahit era (1293–1520). Written in Kawi, the Javanese language of the tenth to fourteenth centuries, the literature spread throughout the Indonesian islands and Malaysia, and as far as *Thailand, *Cambodia, and *Laos, where the stories became localized under various names such as *Inao* or *Eynao*. Panji literature is used in several Indonesian *masked drama forms (*topeng), *dance-dramas (*wayang wong and *gambuh), *shadow-puppetry *genres (*wayang kulit), and operetta (*arja); Inao story material finds expression in classical Thai and Khmer dance-dramas and related *genres. The popular episodes follow the refined hero Panji on his adventurous search for his mysteriously vanished fiancée Chandra Kirana. In the Balinese version called *Malat*, Panji is shipwrecked in Bali and comes to the rescue of a Balinese princess in distress. KP

P'ANSORI

*Korean folk *opera. *P'ansori* (literally, 'story singing') utilizes a single singer-actor and a drummer. It needs no *props except a hand fan for the singer, a double-headed barrel drum (*pug*) for the drummer, and a straw rug on which the singer stands and the drummer sits. The fan can represent anything and the rug can stand for any location. Traditionally, *p'ansori* was performed almost anywhere: in a market-place, town square, a courtyard, or a king's palace. The singer-actor performs all the parts and produces all *sound effects. The performance contains three elements: singing in *verse (*sori* or *ch'ang*), *dialogue and narration in prose (*aniri*), and *acting and movement expressing emotion (*ballim*). The drummer sometimes employs gestures and exclamations (*ch'uimsae*) to augment the performance. The singer-actor, who can be male or female, undergoes years of vocal training.

Although the origin of the form is unclear, some scholars believe that shamanistic ritual songs prompted the art in the early eighteenth century, when twelve *p'ansori* works existed. The number fell to six in the late nineteenth century when Sin Jae-hyo (1817–84), a *p'ansori* master, set down the *texts which had previously existed only in oral tradition. Of these only five are popularly performed today: *Song of Ch'un-hyang*, on a wife's sincere feelings for her husband; *Song of Shim Ch'ŏng* on filial piety; *Song of Hŭng-bu* on virtue and vice; *Song of the Water Palace*, based on a animal fable; and *Song of the Red Cliff*, from *Chinese *folklore. The singer-actor memorizes the scripts, each of which lasts several hours in performance.   JOC

PANTOMIME, BRITISH *see page 995*

PANTOMIME, ROMAN

Ancient masked entertainment. There were two types, comic and tragic, both of which first appeared at Rome in the late first century BC, but remained hugely popular for centuries throughout the empire. The solo, silent performer, accompanied by an orchestra and *chorus, presented all the *characters of the drama using different *masks and *costumes. The immense skill required for such meticulous performances, as well as the physical beauty of the performers, brought great renown to certain stars, some of whom enjoyed the favour of emperors (and their wives), as well as popular adulation that frequently led to *riots. *See* ROMAN THEATRE.   RCB

PAPP, JOSEPH (1921–91)

American *producer and director. Born Joseph Papirofsky in Brooklyn, Joe Papp was the child of Eastern European Jewish immigrants. He trained as an actor in Hollywood, and worked behind the scenes in theatre and *television through the mid-1950s. In 1954 he formed the Shakespeare Workshop—the organization that became the *New York Shakespeare Festival in 1956—and directed its first productions. Papp was a brilliant organizer and fundraiser, and a tireless and inventive promoter

of his theatre. He was known to appear uninvited in newsrooms to harangue reporters and *critics; and in 1957 claimed the festival's flatbed truck broke down in the middle of Central Park so that the group could perform there (though no engine trouble was ever verified). In 1962, after Papp's aggressive lobbying with funders and city officials, the festival opened the *Delacorte Theatre in Central Park, and in 1967 opened its downtown home, the Public Theatre. Papp controlled all aspects of his theatre along with a tight group of deputies including his fourth wife Gail Merrifield, the company's literary manager. The Public was renamed the Joseph Papp Public Theater in 1992.   KF

PARADE

The *farces which figured prominently in the repertory of the fairground theatres in eighteenth-century *Paris owed their name to the practice of earlier mountebanks and charlatans, who attracted customers to their *booths by performing impromptu sketches at the entrance. Such ephemeral performances had developed by 1730 or thereabouts into a *genre of popular *comedy combining simplified versions of traditional *characters and *plot with a stylized rendering of Parisian speech patterns, seasoned with linguistic wordplay and much scatological and sexual innuendo. The liveliness and licence of the fairground theatres were much enjoyed by fashionable playgoers seeking a change from the more staid productions of the official houses; and the *parade* was soon appropriated as entertainment for the private *playhouses in aristocratic chateaux and Paris mansions. If the ancestry of the *parades* can be recognized in the *commedia dell'arte* origins of the fairground theatres from which they borrowed plot and characters, their progeny is much more specific: *Beaumarchais's debuts as a playwright can be seen in his offerings to the private theatre of the financier Lenormand d'Étiolles (husband of Madame de Pompadour) in the 1750s, and his own surviving *parades* provide a source for his *The Barber of Seville*.   WDH

PARADES AND PROCESSIONS

Events in which people move in groups through public spaces for purposes of display or *ritual celebration. Though in practice they often overlap, parades and processions differ essentially in their styles and functions. Parades (from Latin *parare*, to make ready, prepare, adorn, beautify, furnish) are designed primarily for presentation before an *audience, the energy directed outward to the spectators. Parades have many different functions, ranging from festive celebration to *civic festivals and *state displays and shows of power, the latter emphasized by the fact that in fifteenth-century Italy the term *parata* was used to define the process of training a horse to start and stop for show. In contrast, processions (ultimately from Latin *procedere*, to go forward) direct their energy into the processional group,

(continued on p. 998)

PANTOMIME, BRITISH

For above three centuries pantomime has been a continually mutating British theatrical *genre. During much of this span it has been characterized by rhyming doggerel *verse, orchestral *music, song, *dance, *allegorical or mythic *characters sharing the stage with comic roles, and spectacular scenic *illusions or 'transformations'. Despite the implications of its name, pantomime is not silent and is, in its later manifestations, highly verbal. It is an entertainment whose core remains largely persistent despite constant demands for novelty, yet, in response to taste and cultural pressures, pantomime's structure, purpose, frequency, and *audience have all changed dramatically. Today pantomime is a seasonal (Christmas) family entertainment, whereas it was, and is at heart, a *satirical drama intended for adults and meant to be offered at theatres year long. In the nineteenth century new pantomimes were produced at Easter, Whitsun, September, and near Guy Fawkes Day as well as the longer December–March season.

The first entertainments to be labelled pantomimes were seen in the public theatres of *London in the second decade of the eighteenth century, though the distinctive ingredients of these early examples are observable in the Jacobean *masque where startling transformations of *scenery coincided with simultaneous transformations of characters. In the masque, stage mountains and massed clouds removed the principal characters to bring forth the bizarre figures of the 'antimasque' gambolling in a grotesque *parody of the harmonious masque, often dressed in *commedia dell'arte-style *costumes.

The immediate ancestor of pantomime was created in 1702 when the police in *Paris suppressed illegal theatres performing dramas in commedia dell'arte style in fairgrounds near the city gates. Denied work in Paris and dispersed across Europe, a mixed handful of French and English actor-dancers, Sorin, the Alard brothers, Louis Nivelon, and Richard Baxter, sought work at London *playhouses. The French-speaking performers could be understood only when they danced and *mimed their roles, so the entertainments offered were commedia episodes transposed to the English environment and set to music. These were billed as 'night scenes' or 'Italian night scenes' and featured comic episodes in which, in familiar London settings, London tradesmen mingled with the commedia characters. In one such night scene a cooper, his wife, and his manservant met Scaramouche and Punch in a tavern. These two ate and drank prodigiously whilst the astonished Londoners gaped. The quick-witted strangers then left the slower Londoners to pay the bill.

By 1710 both *Drury Lane and *Lincoln's Inn Fields employed skilled dancing-masters to devise comic night scenes and to assist with the staging of serious musical diversions which resembled brief *operas with *balletic episodes. In such circumstances it was an inevitable step that these initially separate entertainments would fuse into a single piece. In 1716 John Weaver, the dancing master at Drury Lane, devised The Loves of Mars and Venus, which was advertised as a 'new Entertainment in Dancing after the manner of the Antient Pantomimes'. The 'pantomimes' referred to were those of the late Roman Empire (see PANTOMIME, ROMAN), but in England the term was first employed to dignify a serious narrative with dancers impersonating the Roman gods. Not to be outdone by this attraction, the rival Lincoln's Inn Fields offered its own 'pantomime' with characters from Roman mythology suddenly transformed into or replaced by characters from the night scenes, and the mythic setting transformed to modern London. Thus a pantomime was a drama in two halves: a mythic, musical opening, and a briefer comic modern knockabout segment.

The *manager at Lincoln's Inn Fields was John *Rich, whose talents lay in dancing and devising *spectacles. Under the stage name of Lun, Rich developed the role of *Harlequin and the range of traits which made this endlessly reusable stage character the *hero of the English harlequinade. Rich was agile and dexterous, able to sustain remarkable mime illusions, such as that of a chick-like Harlequin stirring, pecking through shell, and eventually hatching from an egg. Moreover, Rich gave his Harlequin the power to create stage *magic in league with offstage craftsmen who operated trick *scenery. Armed with a magic sword or bat (actually a *slapstick), Rich's Harlequin treated his weapon as a wand, striking the scenery to sustain the illusion of changing the setting from one locale to another. Objects, too, were transformed by Harlequin's magic bat.

As much to the point, under Rich's influence pantomimes acquired the structure that was to identify the form for the next 50 years. Rich's pantomimes began with a classical opening, that is, a *plot taken from Greek or Roman mythology to furnish characters, a narrative, and amorous complications. Later in the century the search for plots for the openings widened to include British *folk tales, popular literature, and, in the 1780s and 1790s, nursery tales. As the opening concluded, an enchantress with remarkable powers intervened to conduct the 'transformation scene'. Here the characters were transformed as if by magic to the identities of the harlequinade. In actuality, the performers' outer *costumes, often papier-maché *masks or 'big-heads', were removed by wires tugged by stagehands hidden in the wings. In the harlequinade were Harlequin, his female companion Columbine, Columbine's parent or guardian Pantaloon, and a miscellany of topical English characters. Harlequin and Columbine tried to elude the pursuing Pantaloon using Harlequin's magic to stave off capture, their flight meanwhile taking them in successive scenes to places currently in the news, offering wry comment on persons and events. Harlequinades featured topical satire, brief, visual—and, because visual rather than spoken, less provocative to government *censors. Pantomime spread to every corner of the United Kingdom to be enjoyed by adults of all classes. 'Panto' was available at *theatres royal and fit-up *fairground booth theatres, even at *puppet booths and primitive *circuses.

By 1800 the pantomime was a ubiquitous theatrical form. In the next 60 years it passed through a period of remarkable development and gradual decline, its growth due largely to the talents of a single performer, Joseph *Grimaldi, and to the astute showmanship of the actor and pantomime 'arranger' Charles Farley (1771–1859), its decline due to changing tastes of Victorian *audiences and to the vacuum left when Grimaldi, ill and dying, retired from the stage. By 1815 Grimaldi had deflected the centre of the harlequinade from Harlequin to *Clown, a new pantomime character chiefly created by himself. The overall structure of pantomime again changed to what was to be its most elaborate form, and pantomime was recognized by its champions as an effective mirror and running commentary on British life as the nation adjusted to the Industrial Revolution and the expansion of trade and empire, and coped with foreign conflicts and domestic crises.

In Thomas J. Dibdin's *Harlequin and Mother Goose; or, The Golden Egg* (1806), Grimaldi added the Clown to the knot of pursuers of the runaway lovers. In place of pursuit and trick work stood Clown's wry visual and musical comments on current follies. Grimaldi's Clown was loyal to no one and was anarchic in actions and values. In an age that respected strong and authoritarian figures and that severely punished even petty criminals, Clown was subversive, insulting figures of authority, ridiculing military preparations for the Napoleonic War, exposing pomposity and profiteering. In an age obsessed with manufacturing products and the market value of goods, Grimaldi smashed and robbed objects and built new fantastic apparatus from his stolen property, forcing social comment and relief when the society Clown menaced and ridiculed caught him and inflicted comic punishment.

With Grimaldi's success the long *allegorical or nursery pantomime opening began to dwindle and became little more than a pretext for determining the characters who were to be transformed into those of the harlequinade: the lovers were invariably Harlequin and Columbine, the old father or guardian was Pantaloon, the rival suitor or household cook or nurse was Clown. Harlequin always received his magic bat from a benevo-

lent agent or good fairy, thus signalling the start of a harlequinade which could extend for as many as ten or fifteen *scenes. Finally, in a scene set in a gloomy forest, cavern, or ruined castle—the 'dark scene'—Harlequin's attention wandered long enough for Clown or Pantaloon to seize the magic bat and render the lovers helpless. Again the benevolent agent appeared, restored Harlequin's power at the return of the bat, and effected a reconciliation in a final splendid scene. Grimaldi's individual approach had ossified into a national style and determined the form of pantomimes for the four decades to follow: clowns thereafter were called 'Joey'.

Pantomime has long featured cross-dressing. A cliché arms that 'The dame is a man, and the *principal boy is a girl'. Both dame and principal boy roles point to a long-existing and deep-seated anxiety about behaviour appropriate to the sexes. Both roles reveal efforts to control, if only in fantasy, female power and to limit the areas in which women may hold power. Both roles were found in the pantomime opening, the dame the earlier of the two. Grimaldi and other Clowns of the early nineteenth century created female characters who were a part of Pantaloon's household: queens, chaperones, widows, cooks, all middle-aged women depicted as grotesque and flirtatious. However, the dame did not emerge as a fully realized character until, in Grimaldi's absence, the openings began slowly to expand. Pantomimes from the Regency and Victorian periods offered biased stereotypes of ageing females: ugliness allied to misplaced vanity, sexual voracity paired with squeamishness, assertiveness, slovenly housekeeping, appalling taste in clothes, excessive curiosity, and chronic and indiscriminate gossiping.

The reasons for the implicit attacks on women are to be found in the character and history of the principal boy. Although attempted as early as 1819, the principal boy was not accepted into pantomime until the 1830s and even then was performed by adolescent or pre-pubescent girls, not by mature actresses. The principal boy appeared in the opening, as she does today—as the male lover courting the girl who will become Columbine. However, in the Victorian transformation scene, the principal boy was replaced by a male Harlequin. Only a real male was allowed Harlequin's potent weapon, the bat, and permitted to win Columbine. Further, the principal boy did not appear until women begin to compete with men for jobs in industries where the first 'factory girls' were children and adolescents. As the median age of female employment in factories rose through the 1860s, so the age and appearance of the principal boy changed, from immature adolescent to sexually mature woman with full hips and padded thighs.

As early as the 1830s Victorian taste was turning away from the assertive satire and anarchy of the Regency harlequinade. Although accepting its current structure, arrangers looked for means of enhancing a Grimaldi-less pantomime, and the following seven decades leisurely altered the flavour and structure of pantomime with infusions from two rival sources of entertainment: *burlesque and *music hall. In burlesque, as in pantomime, men undertook roles burlesquing older women, and shapely actresses took men's roles. Music was drawn from many sources, and new comic lyrics were fitted to these tunes. To continue to draw audiences, the settings and costumes of burlesques became increasingly lavish, and the term 'extravaganza' was coined to describe these lavish pieces. From the 1840s pantomime openings increasingly borrowed from burlesque/ extravaganza, the openings expanding to allow more jokes, songs, parodies, and greater spectacle. By the 1850s burlesque/ extravaganza had largely replaced pantomime at all seasons but Christmas. Concurrently, harlequinades lost popularity as topical jokes and songs moved forward into the opening. The transformation scene became an occasion, not for transforming characters, but for elaborate scenic display. Transformation scenes were increasingly fused with the final scene to provide an astonishing end to the pantomime. By the century's end, harlequinades were rarely more than half a dozen scenes in length. Reduced to episodes of knockabout violence and with so many property vegetables and fish thrown about, the harlequinade became known by the derisive label 'the spill and pelt'.

By the 1870s music-hall artistes were cast in pantomime opening roles and were contracted to perform their variety turns, regardless of the relevance of the material to the plot. With the advent of music-hall stars, strongly satiric topical jokes disappeared from pantomime. What the late Victorian and Edwardian pantomime did offer was exceptional lavishness. Even dazzling scenic effects were by the 1890s regarded as inadequate by competing managements, and pantomimes were decorated with quantities of supernumeraries in parade costumes. The Augustus *Harris management at Drury Lane in the early 1890s, and the Arthur Collins regime that followed into the first decade of the twentieth century, used as many as 300 walk-ons in the glittering transformation scene and related processions.

Pantomime continues to change. The structure that now survives is a confused residue of the Edwardian form: the 'dark' penultimate scene is now the 'dark opening' in which a Demon King arrives to spread blight on the happiness of a nursery tale character; the opening itself is swollen to great length; the final scene is wholly absorbed into the transformation scene; the harlequinade has vanished altogether. The once wide range of subjects has shrunk as well. The overwhelming preference is for *Cinderella*, followed by *Aladdin*, *Dick Whittington*, *Jack and the Beanstalk*, *Babes in the Wood*, *Mother Goose*, and *Robinson Crusoe*. Rarely, if ever, do we see a *Yellow Dwarf*, *Bluebeard*, *Cherry and Fair Star*, or any one of the hundreds of subjects from fairy tales and English folklore which formerly found their way into pantomimes. Changes came from other directions as well. Music-hall comediennes such as Nellie *Wallace tried the role of dame, but few other actresses have managed to be accepted in the role. On the other hand, male rock 'n' roll stars Tommy Steele and Cliff Richard were among the first male principal boys since the early 1830s; today the female principal boy is more likely to be found in regional and northern pantomimes than in the south of England.

With the twentieth century came the competing entertainments of *film, *radio, and *television. As the popularity of each new medium increased, it became commonplace for leading pantomime roles, especially those of the comics, principal boy, and female *ingénue, to be *cast from these rival media. It is not uncommon to find actors known to British audiences through Australian television serials, American situation comedy, and international professional athletics. Although such performers add a certain topicality, and although jokes identify the performer with her or his usual vehicle, pantomime has become more generalized in addressing comic subjects and much less specific in selecting targets for even mild satire. Sanctioned by economies of cost, some pantomimes are now planned for ten years of hard stage life: the new script, with fresh costumes, scenery, and music, is first performed in a major urban centre, then, with different casts, annually recycled to progressively smaller cities and lesser theatres until sets and costumes are threadbare. The other economically successful option is for a single performer to own and mount a pantomime in which he or she stars and periodically refurbishes. At the beginning of the twenty-first century the most successful of these is a *Mother Goose* owned by the comic actor John Inman, known to international audiences through the television serial *Are You Being Served?*

Shakespeare may be the national dramatist, but pantomime is still the British national entertainment. It accounts for approximately 20 per cent of all live performance, and approximately the same percentage of work for actors in live entertainments occurring between December and March. *See also* FÉERIE; MALE IMPERSONATION; FEMALE IMPERSONATION. DM

AVERY, EMMETT L., et. al., *Prefaces to the London Stage 1660–1800* (Carbondale, Ill., 1968)

BOOTH, MICHAEL (ed.), *English Plays of the 19th Century*, vol. v (Oxford, 1977)

MAYER, DAVID, *Harlequin in his Element: English pantomime 1806–1836* (Cambridge, Mass., 1969)

SCOTT, VIRGINIA, 'The infancy of English pantomime', *Theatre Journal*, 24 (1972)

which may be commemorating a religious or civil rite, or engaging in a festival occasion, or both. Whereas parades are ordinarily out of doors, in the street or on a designated parade ground, processions take place indoors as well as out. They are frequently characterized by a mood of solemnity lacking in parades.

Parades and processions manifest the human need to congregate for purposes of communal expression. They may celebrate the triumphs of military victories (Roman triumphal entries, tickertape parades following the twentieth-century world wars), or of *sporting events (championships, the parades of the nations in Olympic games). Processional *audiences may mourn collectively at times of local, regional, or national loss: for the funeral of French writer Victor *Hugo 3 million people massed in the streets of *Paris in 1885, for example, and fallen state leaders such as Abraham Lincoln (1865), Vladimir Lenin (1924), John Kennedy (1964), and François Mitterrand (1996) had lengthy and solemn processional interments. They may mark annual holidays, whether seasonal festivals (new year celebrations, *carnival parades, May Day festivities, midsummer games, harvest *rituals), religious feasts (Shiite Muharram processions, Catholic festivals honouring the Virgin Mary), celebrations of ethnic solidarity (St Patrick's Day or Columbus Day parades), or patriotic occasions (Bastille Day in France, Independence Day in the USA, 1 October celebrations in communist *China, 11 October celebrations in the former USSR).

So basic is the need for collective human expression that since the European Enlightenment of the eighteenth century the right to assembly has been regarded as an inalienable prerogative of democratic societies. Already a major issue in the American revolution against Britain in 1776, the 'right to freedom of peaceful assembly and to freedom of association with others' was expressly protected by the European Convention on Human Rights (article 11, Strasbourg, 1966). However, parades and processions that draw large, often emotional crowds pose a threat of disorder. Sometimes they result in random vandalism following sports victories; sometimes because of ideological conflicts, as with religious processions in sensitive areas (Muharram processions in *India or Protestant processions in Northern Ireland); sometimes because the sheer massing of crowds provides an opportunity—or cover— for political subversion (as in the Castro revolution that erupted during new year's celebrations in *Havana, 1959).

The threat to public order may cause authorities to ban parades and processions. Such bans might be expected in oppressive or conflicted societies, as in the slave-owning plantation cultures of the nineteenth-century Americas, or in twentieth-century South Africa, where the ruling groups were in the minority. But they also exist in contemporary democracies at times of crisis. Often ordinances regulate parades and processions, as for instance the Public Processions and Parades Guidelines published by the Parades Commission following the recommencement of public processions in Northern Ireland in 1998.

Parades may be either 'top down', that is, sanctioned by governing authorities, or 'bottom up', that is, generated at street level. Whatever their overt rationale, parades reflect, however subtly, the areas in which they are organized. A prime example is the Macy's Thanksgiving Day parade in *New York, which initiates the Christmas shopping season near the end of each November, on the surface reflecting the commercial preoccupations of the nation and the city that symbolize twentieth-century capitalism. But the parade began in 1924 as a way for first- and second-generation immigrants working at Macy's Department Store to link their memories of festive celebrations in their native lands with the American Thanksgiving holiday. The result was an event that tied the mythos of the United States as an ethnic melting pot directly to the capitalist ethos of New York. Today it has become a national occasion, characterized since 1926 by increasingly massive balloons in the shape of cultural icons like Walt Disney's Mickey Mouse or commercial figures like Ronald McDonald floating high above the crowds.

Televised throughout the United States, Macy's parade draws high-school marching bands and floats from across the country. In crucial years it has served as a patriotic rallying point, notably when it was resumed after a three-year hiatus following the Second World War, or when—in order 'not to disappoint the children'—it was mournfully enacted after the assassination of President Kennedy. Following the 11 September 2001 attack on the World Trade Center, the parade included a replica of the Statue of Liberty and prominently featured policemen and firemen who had become national symbols of resilience. Thus a parade that originated in emigrant memories of Europe, then came to represent the commercial character of the United States and the lure of New York, implicitly has always embodied the ideological underpinnings of the city and the nation.

The more overtly political workers' demonstrations held annually on 1 May, which became a signature event in Bolshevik Russia after 1917, illustrate how parades can become instruments of transnational alliance, often attended by the threat of violence. In seventeenth-century England the maypole had been a virtual symbol of royalist reign, with hundreds erected around the countryside at the restoration of Charles II in 1660. But in the nineteenth century this day of springtime revelry was set aside as a commemorative occasion of unification for labourers, with solidarity parades held throughout Europe and the Americas, extending in the 1920s to China, *Japan, and *India. Officially established in the United States as a day of celebration and demonstration by workers seeking an eight-hour work day in 1886, May Day became the locus for peace rallies in the last years of the First World War. In 1919 the day was celebrated with a parade culminating in Hyde Park in *London; it became the first republican holiday after the abdication of the Kaiser in Germany; and was marked in France by a parade held in defiance of a government prohibition that resulted in the death of one demonstrator and injuries to 428 policemen.

May Day parades (commonly signified by the presence of red flags and often held in defiance of official bans, from Sydney and Lima to South Africa, where they were dubbed 'freedom' parades) have been used as occasions of protest as well as celebration, to make social demands: locally for better working conditions or more political freedom, and internationally for such causes as the withdrawal of foreign troops from China or US troops from Nicaragua and Vietnam. Ironically the May Day parades that had been festive vehicles of resistance to oppression and rallying cries for peace became the symbol of Soviet military power during the Cold War, as masses of tanks were filmed parading past government reviewing stands in Moscow's Red Square.

Though parades can be small as well as large, because of their emphasis on display they tend to a showiness sometimes lacking in processions, which range from the entrances and exits of choirs and clerics in small houses of worship to the ritual entrances of subjects before the emperor in the Forbidden City of Beijing to street events such as saints' day homages. Like parades, processions often establish a complex relationship not only with their immediate viewers but also with religious or secular authority. Religious processions, such as Catholic ones honouring the Virgin, might in one context be an instrument of state authority, as in colonial New Mexico under Spanish rule, and in another serve as vehicles of liberation theology, as in Nicaragua in the latter twentieth century.

Shiite Muharram rites exemplify both the complex relationship with various audiences and the functional fluidity that may characterize processions. Muharram funereal processions commemorate the assassination of Hosain, the grandson of Muhammad, together with his followers and members of his family in the 61st Muslim year (corresponding to AD 680) on the plain of Karbala, outside Baghdad. This is the crucial event that distinguishes Shia as a Muslim sect from the more numerous Sunni sect, whose forerunners, the Umayyads, were the assassins of Hosain. In most countries where Muharram processions are held (*Pakistan, India, Trinidad), Shiites are a minority. Processions in these places establish an embattled relationship with their potential audiences. At times they arouse hostility, as in India; at other times the procession may actually be organized by non-Muslims, as in Trinidad and Tobago, where the Muharram processions, partly organized by Hindus and Christians as well as Shiites, serve as a nostalgic link to the homeland for those of Indian ancestry. In such minority situations, as in the West Indian festival of 'Hosay' in Trinidad, the procession itself is performed by worshippers who are set off from the raucous crowds surrounding them in the streets by rituals of fasting and abstinence, their isolation an emblem of the Shiite situation in the culture at large. When Shiites are in the majority—notably in Iran—these processions have served both to authenticate the authority of the state, when the state apparatus is clerical (eighteenth and nineteenth centuries, and again since 1979), and to

create subversion. During the year leading to the 1979 Iranian revolution against the Shah, the image of Hosain and his embattled family was altered; formerly revered as the intercessor for humanity with God, Hosain was represented as a revolutionary leader against the tyranny of the Shah. After the revolution, a similar displacement took place during the war between Iraq and Iran when Saddam Hussein displaced Yazid, the enemy of the historical Hosain, in processional banners.

Parades and processions do not in themselves serve a single political or sociological function. They may be utilized as instruments of power or protest. They may allow an ethnic or religious population to celebrate its identity within a complex culture. They offer opportunities for subversion. They may be more simply occasions for celebration, or rituals of worship. But whatever the rationale, the impulse to parade or process through the streets or in other public places or areas of private worship seems basic to the human herding instinct. *See also* ENTRIES, ROYAL. MR

Scott, James C., *Domination and the Arts of Resistance: hidden transcripts* (New Haven, 1990)

PARIGI, GIULIO (fl. 1580-1635)

Florentine architect, *scenographer, and stage engineer. In 1608 he succeeded Bernardo *Buontalenti, of whom he may have been a pupil, as principal designer of celebrations and *spectacles to the Medici grand dukes of Tuscany. From then until 1635, after which records of him disappear, he designed a long series of sets, apparatuses, and floats for large-scale *pageants, processions, and entertainments, many of which have been recorded in engravings. His stage designs, as conveyed in these prints, can seem static and over-symmetrical; but he was considerably more inventive in *costume and in stage machinery, producing dramatic effects and transformations. RAA

PARIS see page 1000

PARIS OPÉRA See OPÉRA.

PARKER, STEWART (1941–88)

Irish playwright whose first success was *Spokesong* at the *Dublin Theatre Festival in 1975. His seriously playful dramas, usually involving music, explore the politics, history, and life of Northern Ireland with full-blooded theatricality. He stretched theatrical form to accommodate black *comedy, irony and paradox, and to undermine the clichés of Irish sectarianism. He described his trilogy—*Northern Star* (1984), *Heavenly Bodies* (1986), and *Pentecost* (1987)—as a 'continuing comedy of terrors'. *Northern Star* contains brilliant pastiches of Irish theatrical

(continued on p. 1008)

PARIS

The capital of France, historically one of the major theatre centres of the world.

1. Medieval period; 2. 1500–1700; 3. 1700–1900; 4. Since 1900

1. Medieval period

In France as elsewhere in Europe, *medieval theatre was local and provincial. Paris was not the centre it would later become. This is not to suggest that Paris did not have a lively theatrical culture, only that it was neither unique nor especially influential. In Paris, as elsewhere, the *mystères*, plays with religious subject matter (*see* MYSTERIES; BIBLICAL PLAYS), were first produced by various *guilds of artisans and tradesmen, as were, for instance, the *Miracles de Notre-Dame par personnages*, performed by the goldsmiths' guild on 1 December, the feast day of their patron saint, between 1339 and 1382. Just after the turn of the fifteenth century, however, a lay brotherhood made up of bourgeois men from various *métiers*, the *Confrérie de la Passion, was authorized by Charles VI to perform mysteries and *Passion plays in Paris. This was the only such association in France to receive a royal warrant. The Confrérie performed in the great hall of the Hôpital de la Trinité until 1535, then at the Hôtel de Flandres. Other performances continued to be sponsored by craft guilds, usually in honour of a patron saint. Unlike most other French cities, however, Paris did not invest in the productions or participate in their organization. Nonetheless one of the monuments of the fifteenth-century religious theatre had connections to Paris. This was the *Mystère de la Passion* of Arnoul *Greban, organist and choirmaster of Notre Dame. Written before 1452, this vast canvas of 34,574 lines was a source for many succeeding versions. But whether the Paris Confrérie de la Passion played this particular Passion is another kind of mystery.

Several ambitious performances took place in the sixteenth century; at least three were produced by the Confrérie. One *text of 60,000 lines survives, revealing the size and complexity of such an undertaking. Entitled the *Actes des apôtres* (*Acts of the Apostles*), it opened on 8 May 1541 and continued on Sundays and holidays until 25 September. The venue was the Hôtel de Flandres in a round *amphitheatre with rows of risers and galleries and *boxes above. The production was attacked by the Parlement of Paris for using apocrypha and *farce, for poorly managed stagecraft—'the Holy Spirit did not want to descend'—and for enticing its *audience away from mass. In 1548, when the Confrérie de la Passion applied for the renewal of its privilege, the Parlement denied the brothers the right to play *mystères* in their newly completed *Hôtel de Bourgogne, but awarded them a monopoly of all theatre production. The result was the end of religious drama in Paris.

The Confrérie rented its venue to, among others, an amateur brotherhood of *sots* (fools), the Enfants-sans-Souci. France had a long tradition of *parodic and satiric performance, ranging from court entertainments to the extravagances of *carnival. Again, Paris was no more nor less important to the development of secular theatre than many provincial cities, but the *amateur troupes that specialized in *satire and *burlesque were perhaps more powerful in the capital. The Paris Basoche, a brotherhood of law clerks, participated in the general medieval tendency to turn the world upside down by creating burlesque legal actions to be judged by the High Court during carnival. The *Basochiens then began to write and perform comic plays to be performed publicly. The Enfants sans Souci may have been a branch of the Basoche with the special duty of playing *sotties* and harassing the establishment. Unlike farces, which tend to have stereotypical but realistic *characters and *actions, *sotties* have Le Premier Sot, Le Second Sot, La Mère-Sotte, etc. Dressed in motley, these abstractions engaged in symbolic actions that attacked the social order, using medieval strategies to undermine the medieval social paradigm. Not unnaturally, performances frequently attracted the attention of the Parlement de Paris, which issued warning after warning. Like the Confrérie de la Passion, the Basoche was eventually prevented from presenting the kinds of plays it existed to perform. The actors were forced to submit their *texts to the Parlement and produce the *censored versions. In 1582 a new Act of the Parlement directed them to play only 'eclogues, *comedies, and *tragedies provided there is nothing in them against religion, the king, and the state of the kingdom'. Evidence suggests the actors did not bother.   VS

2. 1500–1700

As the sixteenth century dawned, there were still no theatres or troupes of professional actors in Paris: the revolution of the *early modern period was still to come. *Street theatre dominated, including singers, *acrobats, *puppeteers, farce players, and quack doctors, the most famous of whom was *Tabarin. These performances also found a seasonal outlet in the Paris fairgrounds. Other very different forms of street theatre—which, though held outdoors, were not always for public consumption—included royal *entries and other courtly entertainments like the Carrousel in the place Royale in 1612. Other performances also were aimed at more restricted audiences: when the tragedies and comedies of antiquity were rediscovered and imitated, the plays were read and performed in colleges and at court. Indeed, performances continued to be given in colleges throughout this period, forming an essential part of the education of a gentleman (see UNIVERSITY AND SCHOOL DRAMA). The most popular form of entertainment at court, however, was *ballet, performed by the courtiers themselves. One of the best known was Balthasar de Beaujoyeulx's *Ballet comique de la reine* (*The Queen's Comic Ballet*) at the Salle du Petit Bourbon in the Louvre in 1581. At the same time, there was a continuing interest in the various forms of medieval theatre, as noted above, leading to the construction of Paris's first purpose-built public theatre, the Hôtel de Bourgogne (1548), near what is now Les Halles. But just two years later, the Wars of Religion brought an interruption to the theatrical life of the capital and the Hôtel de Bourgogne stood dark.

Normality returned in 1589 with the accession of Henri IV, and troupes of actors appeared in Paris from the provinces. The Confraternité, though, defended its monopoly and companies were obliged to lease the Hôtel de Bourgogne or perform elsewhere and pay a fine for non-occupation. The venues to which these new troupes turned were mostly indoor *tennis courts, left empty since the vogue for the game had passed. These already had a gallery down one long side; if another was constructed opposite and a trestle *stage erected at one end, they could make quite acceptable temporary theatres. Eventually they were replaced by more permanent installations, but the rectangular form of the tennis court was retained until the last quarter of the seventeenth century, when the rows of *boxes surrounding the *auditorium were frequently remodelled into a horseshoe shape.

Amongst those companies visiting Paris in the early years of the sixteenth century were a number of Italian *commedia dell'arte* troupes. The presence of actresses in these companies, in particular that of Isabella *Andreini, made a significant impact and was probably one of the factors leading to the emergence of the professional actress in France. Other notable occupants of the Hôtel de Bourgogne were Valleran *Le Conte, performing the plays of Alexandre *Hardy, and the trio of celebrated farce actors: *Gros-Guillaume, *Gaultier-Garguille, and *Turlupin.

In 1628, after much coming and going by different troupes, the Hôtel was leased to a company of actors led by *Bellerose, which would henceforth be its sole occupant, eventually becoming known as the Royal Troupe. In 1634 a company led by *Montdory leased a tennis court in the rue Vieille du Temple, later known as the *Marais Theatre, thereby providing Paris with its second permanent *playhouse. In their early years, these theatres were primarily used for the production of *tragicomedy and farce, with Jean *Rotrou as the house playwright of the Hôtel de Bourgogne, and the Marais introducing the works of Pierre *Corneille (see NEOCLASSICISM).

Between 1643 and 1646, *Molière and Madeleine *Béjart attempted to establish a third professional company in Paris, known as the Illustre Théâtre. They adapted two tennis courts, the first in the Saint-Germain area and, when that failed, another on the edges of the Marais. Finally, after having been imprisoned for debt, Molière left Paris and spent the next twelve years *touring the provinces. A third troupe was formed at the *Petit-Bourbon, from 1644 to 1647 and from 1653 onwards, by Italian actors led by Tiberio *Fiorilli who played the role of Scaramouche. This company later featured the celebrated *Harlequin Domenico *Biancolelli. (*See* COMÉDIE ITALIENNE.)

At the same time the trend for courtly entertainments continued and developed with a desire to imitate Italian *opera. It was for such spectacular productions that *Richelieu had a private theatre built in his Palais Cardinal (1641), the first Parisian theatre to possess a *proscenium arch, and the *Salle des Machines was constructed (1662). These differed from the Hôtel de Bourgogne and the Marais in that they did not have a standing pit, but instead featured raked seating areas curving in front of the stage. Molière returned from the provinces in 1658 and, after a trial performance for the King in the Louvre, his company was allowed to share the Petit-Bourbon with the Italians. The latter company performed on the more popular Tuesdays, Fridays, and Sundays, while Molière's troupe had the other days of the week.

Audiences at this time were mixed. A heterogeneous mass of often rowdy men occupied the pit, aristocratic fops sat on either side of the stage, male and female aristocrats and bourgeois occupied the first- and second-row boxes, and lackeys, shop assistants, and members of the lower orders sat on benches in the third-row gallery (see BOX, PIT, AND GALLERY). People frequently caused disturbances by attempting to enter without paying and a series of edicts was issued to prevent this. The practice of whistling to express disapproval also later gave rise to legislation (see BOOING).

In 1660 Molière's troupe was struck a serious blow when without prior warning the Petit-Bourbon was demolished to make way for the Louvre's new colonnade. After a worrying time, during which the company survived by giving private performances, they were eventually allowed to transfer to Richelieu's old theatre in the Palais Cardinal, now known as the *Palais Royal. This was in a state of considerable disrepair, to the extent that, the roof beams being broken, for many years the ceiling consisted of a blue cloth suspended on ropes. Again this theatre was shared with the Italians, although the days on which the two companies performed were reversed.

There were now three companies in Paris: the Hôtel de Bourgogne specializing in tragedy (it was here that the majority of Jean *Racine's works were given), Molière specializing in comedy, and the Marais specializing in a type of spectacular theatre for public consumption known as the machine-play. *Music was significant in the machine-play, and in fact music was popular with all types of audiences both in town and at court, causing Molière to combine his own speciality with ballet to create the new *genre of *comédie-ballet. These were generally first performed at court (which had by now quit Paris and the Louvre for *Versailles and the other royal palaces), before being given in a reduced form for the general public at the Palais Royal.

The craze for stage music also led to the development of a new type of popular theatre when, in 1669, Pierre Perrin was awarded the monopoly on the production of operas in France. He adapted the Bouteille tennis court in Saint-Germain, and it was here that *Pomone*, the first public opera in French, was given in 1671. However, Perrin had chosen his collaborators unwisely, the enterprise failed, and he too was imprisoned for debt. Perrin's monopoly was then awarded to the Italian-born court composer Jean-Baptiste *Lully, who had previously collaborated with Molière on court entertainments. He founded the Royal Academy of Music, which would later be known as the Paris *Opéra. Realizing what an asset stage music was, he immediately took steps to limit the numbers of singers, instrumentalists, and *dancers the other troupes could employ.

The Parisian theatrical scene changed radically with Molière's death in 1673. Four members of his troupe left to join the Hôtel de Bourgogne, leaving the rest apparently unable to perform, and the Palais Royal Theatre was awarded to Lully to house his Academy. It was here that Lully's operas were given for the general public after having been premièred at court. After much negotiation, the remaining members of Molière's troupe took over the lease on the Bouteille tennis court, now known as the Hôtel de *Guénégaud because of the street it faced. They were joined there by the majority of the actors from the Marais to form a new company. This merger might seem surprising, but the Marais troupe, too, had encountered serious difficulties. The axis of Paris had shifted so that Marais area was no longer fashionable. Its streets were muddy and badly lit and people were reluctant to venture there after dark (performances started at five in the afternoon). The centre of social activity was now Saint-Germain where, ironically, the Illustre Théâtre had failed some 30 years before. The new troupe, known as the *Comédiens du Roi (King's Actors), again shared its theatre with the Italians. Now four companies operated in the city: the King's Actors and the Italians at the Guénégaud, the Royal Troupe at the Hôtel de Bourgogne, and the Royal Academy of Music at the Palais Royal.

The Guénégaud troupe did very well, capitalizing on its Molière inheritance and enjoying significant success with a series of highly spectacular machine-plays, despite Lully's continued attempts to restrict its use of stage music. Then in 1679 the company managed to poach Mlle *Champmeslé, the leading tragic actress of the age, from the Hôtel de Bourgogne. Racine had retired from the professional stage in 1677, leaving no one of stature to replace him. Mlle Champmeslé's arrival

enabled the Guénégaud company to add both his masterpieces and those of Corneille to its repertory, while that once-mighty bastion of tragedy, the Hôtel de Bourgogne, was reduced to performing Molière comedies in order to compete. Finally in 1680 the Hôtel de Bourgogne was closed down and its actors were transferred to the Guénégaud, where they were united with the Comédiens du Roi to form the *Comédie-Française. The new company was so rich in actors that it was able to perform seven days a week, although in later years it did find it difficult to satisfy its publics in Paris and at court simultaneously.

A new rhythm of production was effected by the transfer of the Italians to the now vacant Hôtel de Bourgogne. The Italians were not happy with their move, however, complaining that the district of Les Halles was not as full of foreigners as the Saint-Germain area had been. Increasingly they began to incorporate French scenes into their performances until eventually they were giving what amounted to whole plays in French. This attracted the hostility of the Comédie-Française, which was just as desirous of protecting its monopoly on the production of plays in French as Lully was of his onstage music. But when Lully died in 1687, his monopoly passed to his son-in-law and the Opéra increasingly fell into financial disarray.

The Italians had frequently been warned about the obscenity of their performances. In 1697 they were expelled from France, ostensibly for having planned to perform a play satirizing Louis XIV's morganatic wife Mme de Maintenon, although there were doubtless other reasons. The acrobats and puppeteers of the fairgrounds swiftly moved to fill the gap in popular entertainment left by the Italians, but stepped on the toes of the remaining companies by introducing Italian scenes, French scenes, and musical episodes into their performances. The Comédie-Française responded by taking legal action to prevent them from giving true plays (*see also* LEGITIMATE DRAMA). The plan misfired, though, since the strategies the fairground performers employed to evade the various interdictions (using only *monologues, suspending text above the stage and having it recited or even sung by members of the audience) can only have added to the charm of their productions. The Opéra was not in so strong a position as the Comédie-Française and, in 1698, sold to the fairground director Jeanne Godefroy, known as the Widow Maurice, the right to use singers, musicians, and dancers in her troupe's productions in a deal which would eventually give rise to the creation of the *Opéra-Comique.

This period, therefore, saw a transition from royal patronage of the theatres to one of state control, which would culminate in the introduction of *censorship in 1701 (although covert censorship had existed earlier). One feature of this control was the development of monopolies, with theatres first specializing in a given type of drama and later in a given language. At the same time other theatrical forms remained vital. If court theatre was increasingly divorced from Paris, private performances continued in aristocratic town houses, and college theatre thrived throughout. As the century closed, the fairgrounds grew in importance, corrective to the increasing stultification of the established theatres and proving equally popular with the aristocrats and the plebs.   JC

3. 1700–1900

In 1700 the Comédie-Française (Théâtre-Français)—initially so called to distinguish it from the Théâtre-Italien, though the latter company was now in exile—had been in existence for twenty years, and was increasingly to assume the role of a *national theatre. Music theatre was in the hands of the Opéra; while the fairground theatres catered for plebeian taste with their seasonal, and mainly ephemeral, offerings. Harassment of these independent companies by the monopoly theatres was seen at its most extreme in 1706, when the Comédie-Française obtained, and enforced, a decree ordering their *booths to be destroyed. The return of the Italians in 1716 intensified the persecution of the fairground performers, who were repeatedly banned from using spoken *dialogue, and reduced to monologues, placard plays, and puppet shows. However, the tenacity of the directors of the independent companies was rewarded, and their productions were not only established as a popular alternative to the official theatres (Opéra: *opera seria*; Comédie-Française: tragedy and the French comic repertory; Comédie-Italienne: comedy in the Italian tradition—though the Italians played in French from their return to Paris onwards), but also succeeded in attracting a more sophisticated, well-heeled audience drawn from those who were increasingly disenchanted with the established repertory and production styles at the Comédie-Française.

For the first half of the century, France's national theatre can be seen as the most conservative representation of a generally self-satisfied and insular culture. Influences from Spain and Italy were non-existent; Shakespeare was either unknown or (in the case of *Voltaire) mocked as a barbarian; and the only new blood introduced, somewhat unadventurously, was in the form of *comédie larmoyante*, or 'tearful comedy': sentimental and moralizing, the new genre adhered to the formal tradition of five *acts in alexandrine *verse, maintained by most post-Molière comedy. The administration of the Paris theatres was in the hands of the First Gentlemen of the Bedchamber, day-to-day control being exercised by the Superintendent of Royal Entertainments. Formal censorship remained important throughout the century, all plays being required to obtain approval before either performance or *publication. Censors were watchful with regard to philosophical ideas (for example, Voltaire's *Mahomet*), current legislation (for example, plays thought to show approval for duelling), and obscenity (for example, certain plays written for the Italians); while performance of *Beaumarchais's *The Marriage of Figaro* was to be held up for over two years by the personal intervention of King Louis XVI, on account of its allegedly subversive content.

Throughout the century, members of the acting profession remained subject to both civil and ecclesiastical disadvantage, the refusal of Christian burial to Adrienne *Lecouvreur (whose body was thrown on a refuse heap in 1730) producing an eloquent protest from Voltaire, contrasting this treatment with the burial of Anne *Oldfield in Westminster Abbey in the same year in *London. Some 30 years later, Voltaire was to exhort the actors of the Comédie-Française to withhold their labour until their civil rights were restored—but to no avail. However, the most notorious attack on the moral standards of the contemporary theatre came not from a bigoted churchman, but from the self-styled 'citizen of Geneva' Jean-Jacques *Rousseau; while critical comments on the morality of the acting profession on the part of others who themselves wrote for the theatre (such as *Diderot and *Mercier) suggest that such a stance may well have reflected a widespread prejudice on the part of the theatregoing public. On the other hand, actors clearly felt that they had well-founded grievances against the public: cases of refusal to pay, and rowdy and violent behaviour, especially on the part of the military, are well authenticated throughout the century (*see* RIOTS). The presence of a large body of standing spectators in the parterre (no major Paris theatre offered seats in the pit until 1782) naturally encouraged a degree of participation in what was being offered on stage—not only witty sallies, but also disruptive behaviour: the use of whistles was frequently the subject of action by theatre police. It was this period, too, that produced the first recorded appearance of the *claque, a band of spectators hired to ensure the success of a new play.

A different phenomenon, lasting throughout the first half of the eighteenth century, was the presence of scores of spectators on the stage, many no doubt more interested in being seen themselves than in watching the play: the anecdote about Ninus' *ghost in Voltaire's *Sémiramis* elbowing his way through a crowd of fops to cries of 'Make way for the ghost!' shows how fatal the practice must have been to any theatrical *illusion. But the places on stage—seated or standing—paid well, and the company were loath to end the practice, until the generous compensation offered by a patron, the Comte de Lauraguais, enabled them to bring it to an end in 1759. The immediate effect on staging possibilities was enormous: not only in the new freedom acquired in the case of established works—Molière's comedies, the tragedies of Corneille, Racine, or Voltaire—but also the stimulus provided for the writing of new kinds of play requiring greater *realism in stage presentation. Foremost in this respect was the *genre sérieux* or *drame bourgeois, intermediate between tragedy and comedy and pioneered by Diderot as a means of portraying the lives of ordinary people and drawing attention to their problems; the opening scene of his *Le Père de famille* (*Father of the Family*) shows a game of backgammon in progress, with lengthy *dumb show before a word is spoken. No less sentimental than the previous generation's 'tearful comedy', the *drames bourgeois* of Diderot and others were written in a prose which brought the problems they dealt with home to a *bourgeois audience, factors which helped to prepare the way for the subject matter of *fin de siècle* *melodrama. The possibilities of greater realism in staging no doubt gave an impetus to moves towards historical accuracy in *costume, in which Mlle *Clairon and *Lekain had led the way.

Having survived for nearly a century in d'Orbay's premises, opened in 1689 but now inadequate, with a brief interlude at the Tuileries (Salle des Machines), the Comédie-Française moved in 1782 to new premises; the final memorable occasion before the move was the theatre's homage to the aged Voltaire, when he was crowned with a laurel wreath at a performance of his last tragedy *Irène*. The first notable event at the new theatre designed by Peyre and Wailly (the present-day *Odéon) was the performance of *The Marriage of Figaro* in 1784: well advertised by the author's own *publicity after a two-year ban, including a number of well-attended readings of the play by Beaumarchais himself, the première was an unprecedented success, and the play ran for 60 performances. By this time there was greater variety of theatrical entertainment on offer: although the Italian company had lost its separate identity on its merger with the Opéra-Comique in 1762, the first officially sanctioned *boulevard theatres were inaugurated in the 1760s and 1770s, under the direction respectively of Nicolet, Audinot, and L'Écluse.

The three monopoly theatres were to witness some of the first trials of people power in the Revolution of 1789: briefly closed in July in response to popular pressure, they soon lost their elitist identity: the Comédie-Française became the Théâtre de la Nation, the Opéra-Comique became the Théâtre de l'Opéra-Comique National, and the Opéra saw itself under the control of the Municipal Council of the Paris Commune. Legislation put an end to the privilege of the monopoly theatres in 1791; while one of the first achievements of the National Assembly in 1789 had been to abolish the discriminatory prejudice against actors and other minorities. In 1790 the actors of the former Comédie-Française split into two companies on ideological grounds, the Théâtre de la Nation consisting of the more conservative, and the Théâtre de la République of those more committed to the aims of the revolution, led by *Talma. In 1793 the whole body of actors at the Nation was arrested, at Robespierre's instigation, for 'determined opposition to the state', and imprisoned until the end of the Terror. Recriminations and jealousies for a long time prevented a reunion of the two companies, and it was not until 1799 that a rapprochement was sealed by a performance of Corneille's *Le Cid* and Molière's *L'École des maris* (*The School for Husbands*) at the République (the theatre still today occupied by the Comédie-Française in the rue de Richelieu). Under the revolution, new theatres proliferated in Paris, a large proportion of their offerings being politically correct, but artistically mediocre, tributes to republican virtue. However, the 'liberty of the theatres' was brought to an end in 1807 by decree of Napoleon, who limited the number of theatres in the capital to eight; and

as an ongoing result of this dictatorial control, no new theatre was allowed to be opened in France without official sanction until the 1860s.

An important link between the pre- and post-revolutionary years in the Paris theatre is provided by the melodramas of *Pixérécourt: a sentimental and spectacular genre, created on the author's own admission for a new class of 'illiterate' spectators, for whom the theatre was to take the place of the pulpit. However, the repertory of the official theatre for the first quarter of the new century showed little change from what had been on offer at the Comédie-Française before the revolution. *Romanticism, which had a sudden, and quite explosive, impact in the French theatre in the 1830s, owes much to melodrama, a good deal to the young playwrights' knowledge of Shakespeare (stimulated by the year-long visit of an English company headed by *Kemble, *Kean, *Macready, and Miss *Smithson to the Odéon in 1827), and most of all, perhaps, to the determination of *Hugo, *Dumas *père*, *Vigny, and their supporters to challenge the reactionary outlook of actors and spectators, especially at the Comédie-Française. It is for this reason, not because *Hernani* is to be seen as the supreme romantic drama, that the 'bataille d'*Hernani*' (1830; *see* HERNANI RIOTS) stands out as the most important event of this period. Although there was to be a short-lived classical recovery in the 1840s (shown by François Ponsard's *Lucrèce*, which coincided with the failure of Hugo's *Les Burgraves* in 1843, and the success of the actress *Rachel at the Comédie-Française in revivals of Racine and Corneille), there would never be a return to the blinkered acceptance of the neoclassical aesthetic. Although the attempt to conquer the 'citadel' of neoclassical tradition was more or less successful, the more assured romantic successes in the theatre took place away from the Comédie-Française, particularly at the *Porte-Saint-Martin, where both Dumas's *Antony* and Hugo's *Marion de Lorme* were performed in 1831, and the Renaissance Theatre with Hugo's *Ruy Blas* (1838). Henceforward the role of the Comédie-Française was largely—by accident rather than by design—to be the guardian of the national repertory rather than the proving ground for innovation.

The most important developments in mid-century playwriting came about in reaction against the romantic movement. This was seen on the one hand in the deliberate repudiation of the self-indulgent ideology of romanticism by the younger *Dumas and *Augier in their 'théâtre utile', or 'school of common sense'; and more generally in the proliferation of popular genres with few literary pretensions: the *vaudeville, *comédie-vaudeville*, *drame-vaudeville*, *mélodrame, *divertissement*, and other minor forms which filled the boulevard theatres—the most lasting contribution being that of *Labiche and *Feydeau, whose comedies transcend the limitations of genre classification. By the middle of the nineteenth century, the Parisian theatre was rapidly growing into a thriving entertainment industry and, especially during the Second Empire (1852–70), played a major part in a new money-making and pleasure-seeking culture. Some 32,000 titles of plays are recorded during the century, produced in a number of theatres which rose, once controls were lifted by Napoleon III, to over 100. Paris theatres had led the way in the eighteenth century in experimenting with improved stage *lighting (the Argand lamp, or *quinquet*), and the Opéra was to be one of the first European theatres to develop improved gas lighting effects: its new building (the present Opéra Garnier) opened in 1857 with 28 miles of piping, feeding 960 gas jets. Proposals to perform in front of a darkened auditorium consistently met with opposition, not only from women spectators who were more interested in being seen than in watching the play; however, with the advent of electricity at the end of the century, it became the general practice to extinguish house-lights—an interesting side effect of which was the demise of the claque, whose members could no longer follow the signals of their leader in the dark.

If the names of Frédérick *Lemaître and Marie *Dorval stand out from the generation of actors who had supported the romantic drama of Hugo and Dumas, and that of Rachel as the most gifted actress of the mid-century, it was Sarah *Bernhardt who dominated in the closing decades, becoming the first *monstre sacré*, or 'superstar', and a legend in her own time. Triumphing at the Comédie-Française both in roles of Racine and of Hugo, she left for the commercial theatre, founding her own company, where she specialized in the plays of *Sardou and *Rostand, as well as appearing as the male *hero in *Musset's *Lorenzaccio* and as Hamlet.

But the dominance of such superstars was challenged by André *Antoine, often seen as the first modern stage *director. Antoine had begun as a member of an *amateur theatre and his productions always retained an emphasis on ensemble *acting. Between 1887 and 1894 his Théâtre *Libre (Free Theatre) operated as a small experimental theatre club and inspired the founding of others like it across Europe, notably the *Freie Bühne in *Berlin (1889) and the *Independent Theatre in London (1891). On a tiny stage, with an auditorium that held no more than 350, Antoine laid the foundations of stage *naturalism, a form that was to dominate much twentieth-century theatre, especially in English- and German-speaking countries. Supported by Émile *Zola, Antoine promoted the new school of naturalist playwrights by putting on evenings composed of several short plays, and he introduced the work of *Ibsen, *Strindberg, and *Hauptmann to France. He placed great emphasis on presentation of characters shaped by their environment, always tried to have his sets built in time for the actors to *rehearse on, and anticipated a number of the *acting methods now associated with *Stanislavsky. It was no easy task to encourage an intimate, truthful acting style at a time when declamatory speech and flamboyant gestures were all the rage.

Two theatrical events from the 1890s conveniently sum up the close of the century: each in its way isolated, one looking backward, the other forward. Nothing in Rostand's earlier career had forecast the tremendous success of *Cyrano de Bergerac*, performed at the Porte-Saint-Martin in 1897. Running for 400 performances, it stands as the definitive embodiment of Hugo's blueprint for romantic drama: a conventional structure of five acts in verse, but verse in which Rostand's vocabulary, rhyme, and metrical variety go far beyond Hugo's, while his *mise-en-scène is throughout imaginative and exciting. By contrast, the iconoclasm of *Jarry's *Ubu roi* (Théâtre de l'*Œuvre, 1896) is uncompromisingly directed against everything that the French theatre had ever stood for, and the result, ostensibly a *parody of *Macbeth*, although it may look ahead to the theatre of the *absurd, does so with a deliberate offence to good taste which prompted *Yeats's comment: 'After us, the Savage God!'

WDH

4. Since 1900

The twentieth century arrived three years early in Paris, when Pa and Ma Ubu stumbled onto the stage. Although they were dismissed and forgotten at the time, Jarry's creations came to dominate Parisian *avant-garde theatre of the following century. In the years leading up to the outbreak of the First World War, theatre was still a mass medium catering for all classes of Parisian society. These were the glory years of the boulevard and of the *Grand Guignol. Both traded on the naughty associations of theatre as a place where otherwise unavowed pleasures could be indulged, at least at the voyeuristic level. At the Grand Guignol, for example, actors were guillotined, tortured, or raped, and the stage appeared to stream with real blood. The theatres of the Grands Boulevards offered less blatant wish fulfilment, as adulterous males and compliant young women acted out far-fetched situations usually involving marital infidelity. Labiche, Feydeau, Courteline, and their imitators turned out these plays in large quantities and they continued to be the staple of what became known as boulevard comedy throughout the first half of the century. Their main aim was to flatter the newly prosperous *bourgeois audience's sense of its importance and to promote Paris as the centre of all things sophisticated. One of Labiche's most popular comedies, *La Cagnotte*, depicts a group of provincials who have saved up all their money to savour the delights of the capital and depends for its *plot on their eagerness to enjoy all that Paris has to offer.

Jacques *Copeau set himself the task of reforming this theatre of mass entertainment and sex comedies. The theatre's vocation was, he argued, to deal with the great themes of humanity in terms available to all citizens, as in fifth-century BC Athens or Elizabethan London. In 1913 he inaugurated the *Vieux-Colombier Theatre with its attached *training school. His choice of the left bank was deliberate—a location far from the despised boulevards, in a *quartier* where there were, at the time, almost no other theatres. He became part of a movement drawing the centre of the arts world away from Montmartre towards the Montparnasse area, whose brasseries—the Dôme and the Coupole—were to become the accepted meeting point for writers, actors, and artists. During the 1914–18 war, Copeau closed his theatre, but was persuaded to reconvene his company for two seasons in *New York (1917–18). He returned to Paris for four more seasons until, in 1924, a religious crisis led him to convert to Catholicism and to withdraw to a village in Burgundy, accompanied by a few chosen students. Although he ceased to direct in the city, his influence and example continued to dominate the avant-garde theatre in Paris. Two of his former company members, Charles *Dullin and Louis *Jouvet, set up their own theatres, and joined together with Gaston *Baty and Georges *Pitoëff to form the *Cartel des Quatre. The aim of this group, following Copeau, was to reinstate the vision of theatre as great art. Remembered mostly for its lively productions of the classical repertoire, the Cartel also revealed classics then little known, such as Molière's *Don Juan* (revived by Jouvet, 1947). Their work built up an audience for new work as well: *Pirandello's *Six Characters in Search of an Author* had a Parisian triumph in 1923 and new French dramatists such as *Giraudoux and *Anouilh became popular.

Paris had always been the foreign capital of choice for Russian exiles and Pitoëff continued the tradition established by the *Ballets Russes before the war. Sergei *Diaghilev, who had brought the Ballets Russes to Paris, played an important role in stimulating *surrealist performance, especially the early musical extravaganzas involving *Cocteau, *Picasso, and composers of the group Les Six. Perhaps it was the surrealist movement that did the most to make Paris appear a natural haven for artists in the middle years of the twentieth century, but the movement produced little theatre to compare with its innovations in poetry and painting (arguably the greatest surrealist dramatist is *Ionesco, whose work was produced a generation later). The major exception is Antonin *Artaud, who was accepted into the surrealist group in 1924 (though he left in 1926), and contributed to reviving the fortunes of Jarry, naming his first theatre in his honour. Artaud's chief influence came after his death in 1948, when his ideas began to acquire a following, especially after the success of the theatre of the absurd in the 1950s and the rise of the *collectives of the 1960s.

Although most of the theatrical reformers working in Paris between the wars were interested in aesthetics of theatre rather than in its social and political impact, a notable exception was Firmin *Gémier, a man from a poor working-class background, who rose to stardom as an actor of melodrama in the late nineteenth and early twentieth centuries. During the second half of his life, Gémier campaigned vigorously for a broad, popular conception of theatre, not limited to the moneyed audience of the Grands Boulevards, nor to the intellectual Left Bank audience of the Cartel, but capable of speaking to all classes and conditions of people. A scheme to set up a national travelling theatre in a specially designed marquee in 1911 was a failure, but in 1920 Gémier succeeded in establishing the first *Théâtre National Populaire with funds specially voted by the government.

During the German occupation (1940–4), despite the curfew and danger of missing *le dernier métro*, Paris theatres were full night after night. Audiences could at least hope to escape the winter cold by huddling together, and performances in French helped to soothe their sense of national defeat: to hear Racine, Corneille, and Molière restored a sense of national self-respect. After the liberation of Paris, *Huis clos* (variously translated as *No Exit* or *In Camera*) was the first production to reopen to the public in 1944 and its author, Jean-Paul *Sartre, was admired for having kept the flame of philosophical and political freedom burning. The Paris-centred existentialism of Sartre and *Camus was identified with the politics of resistance and freedom. Both authors had worked for the Resistance; both attempted to dramatize extreme situations in which characters were faced with choices through which they could affirm or deny their fundamental freedom.

But soon the political clarity of the immediate post-war years became clouded by the complexities of the Cold War. Sartre and Camus quarrelled publicly and *political theatre gave way to the theatre of the absurd, a different, but deeply felt response to the horrors that so many had been through during the war. The playwrights of this movement were mostly Parisians by choice rather than by birth. Ionesco was Romanian, *Beckett Irish, and *Adamov Armenian. They found in the pocket theatres of the Left Bank a dedicated community of actors and directors, men and women such as Roger *Blin, Jean-Marie *Serreau, Jacques Mauclair, Tsilla Chelton, Delphine Seyrig. Audiences were not always so dedicated, but the theatres were tiny and experimental works such as Ionesco's *The Chairs* (1952) or Beckett's *Waiting for Godot* (1953) could be put on without danger of losing huge sums for their backers. This was just as well: Sylvain Dhomme's production of *The Chairs* was not a commercial success and even though *Waiting for Godot* ran for several months, its relative success could not prevent the Théâtre de Babylone going bankrupt. By the end of the 1950s, however, the plays of these dramatists had achieved worldwide fame and Ionesco received the accolade of a production of his new play *Rhinoceros* by Jean-Louis *Barrault at the *Odéon-Théâtre de France in 1960. The other major new playwright of the 1950s was Jean *Genet. Though French by birth, Genet utterly rejected any allegiance to France, and his last, perhaps greatest play, *Les Paravents* (*The Screens*), used the Algerian War to mount a comprehensive attack on the very concept of French nationhood. This play was written in the late 1950s, when Parisians were enduring regular bomb attacks by supporters of both sides in the struggle to liberate Algeria from colonial control. It was not performed in Paris until 1966, but even then it provoked riots in the streets outside the theatre and questions in the French Parliament.

In the Paris of the 1950s the drive for theatrical reform came mainly from Jean *Vilar, who had founded the *Avignon Festival in 1947 and was appointed director of the Théâtre National Populaire in 1952. Here he produced lively revivals of the classics as well as authors from the modern repertoire, doing much to introduce *Brecht to the Parisian public. His repertoire had a left-wing slant and was supported by a network of other left-oriented directors, notably Serreau, who had opened his theatre to the first production of *Godot* and who established a company specifically aimed at producing African theatre for Parisian audiences. Through his work the plays of Kateb *Yacine and Aimé *Césaire were first seen in Paris. Yacine (from Algeria) and Césaire (from Martinique) both used the French language to write plays of great poetic power exploring the *post-colonial situation. Vilar aroused opposition from the directors of private theatres in Paris, as his state subsidy (*see* FINANCE) was seen as giving him an unfair competitive edge. But with the founding of the Fifth Republic under Charles de Gaulle the subsidized sector developed rapidly and theatre found a new place in the national arts agenda. Gradually Paris strengthened its role as a centre and catalyst both nationally and internationally. A Théâtre des *Nations was founded in 1957 as an annual *festival of international theatre, with the backing of UNESCO but funded by the Parisian municipality and the French government.

In the wake of the near revolution of 1968, many theatre companies adopted the democratic method of *création collective* (collaboratively *devised productions) rather than submit to the authority of authors. The acknowledged leader of this new creative method was the Théâtre du *Soleil, directed by Ariane *Mnouchkine. Their trilogy of *1789*, *1793*, and *L'Âge d'or* brought them worldwide celebrity in the early 1970s, which Mnouchkine has continued to build on, alternating between productions of classic work—Shakespeare, the ancient *Greeks, Molière—and devised work or plays written by Hélène *Cixous. The years immediately following 1968 also saw visits to Paris of major international productions such as those of Tadeusz *Kantor from Poland or Robert *Wilson from the USA. The discovery of this challenging experimental work, relying more on images than on text, helped to strengthen the concept of *total theatre and of a specific *performance language. The Festival d'Automne, founded by Michel Guy in 1972, ensured that outstanding productions from France and abroad were available to audiences in Paris. The visual and emotional appeal of complex mises-en-scène came to be prized in their own right, irrespective of the texts employed, directors often choosing to stage texts not originally written for theatre performance at all.

The attractiveness of Paris to inventive theatre directors did not only serve the interests of mise-en-scène, however; it also served to introduce new plays, especially foreign ones. So, for example, the presence of Jorge *Lavelli meant that *García Lorca's *El público* (*The Audience*) or *Valle-Inclán's *Barbaric Comedies* were seen in Paris long before they were available to audiences in Great Britain. Another striking example is that of Giorgio *Strehler. His work on *Goldoni and Shakespeare never reached London, but was regularly seen in Paris and had a profound influence on many French theatre professionals (his designers Luciano *Damiani and Richard Peduzzi were regularly invited to work in France, Peduzzi eventually heading the main design school). The creation, in 1981, of the Théâtre de l'*Europe, with a large injection of funds from the French government and the appointment of first Strehler then Lluis *Pasqual as its director, is further demonstration of the seriousness with which both the international repertoire and artists who could produce it from inside experience was taken. Another celebrated exile who has contributed to the importance of Paris was Augusto *Boal. When forced into exile from Brazil, he established his Théâtre de l'Opprimé (*see* OPPRESSED, THEATRE OF THE) there in 1974 and the impact of the work it pioneered spread all over the world.

When François Mitterrand was elected president in 1981 and his Socialist Party came to power, subsidies to theatre once more increased, and new money was channelled into a variety of inventive schemes for encouraging and assisting playwrights. It was not a simple matter, however, to persuade writers to return to theatre. In his report *Le Compte rendu d'Avignon* (1987) Michel *Vinaver pointed out that the status of playwrights had changed: they had come to be seen as specialists. Many new playwrights were former actors, and the traditional notion of the play as a literary genre open to any writer, just like the novel or the essay, seemed to be lost. Nevertheless authentic new voices emerged and were encouraged, notably that of Bernard-Marie *Koltès, who was championed by Patrice *Chéreau at his Théâtre des Amandiers, Nanterre. Chéreau's career demonstrates the way in which Paris opens its doors to talent from other regions in France. He grew up in Lyon, and became co-director of Roger *Planchon's Théâtre National Populaire in 1972. But in 1981 he accepted the offer to direct the newly built Nanterre theatre, where he set up a theatre school, directed new work by Koltès, and invited foreign directors such as Luc *Bondy and Peter *Stein. Koltès was among the first of many new playwrights to receive help and encouragement from Théâtre Ouvert, an organization run by Lucien and Micheline Attoun which broadcasts new work regularly on *radio as well as having a studio theatre in Pigalle.

In the second half of the century, Paris theatre became polarized into two sectors: the public and the private. The public includes all subsidized theatre, from the national theatres (four out of five of them are in Paris) to small fringe companies in receipt of project grants. Still pre-eminent among the national theatres is the Comédie-Française. As the oldest company in the world, in which the actors are all shareholders, its history is unbroken since the seventeenth century and its director is still appointed by the head of state. In the first half of the century, it was known chiefly for conservative attitudes and unadventurous approach to the classic repertoire. Its reputation rose during the Occupation, partly because of the outstanding performances and productions of the young Barrault and Madeleine *Renaud. The statutes of the theatre forbade *sociétaires* from performing in any other theatre, a constraint that was too much for the young couple, who left to found their own Compagnie Renaud–Barrault in 1946. Subsequently the rules have been loosened in a series of reforms, and attempts have been made, notably by Mitterrand, to appoint reforming directors who could help restore the company to a position of pre-eminence. The company of *sociétaires* has proved more than a match for such directors, however: Jean-Pierre *Vincent, Antoine *Vitez, and Jacques *Lassalle have been able to do very little to change its ethos. The other national theatres in Paris are the Théâtre de l'Odéon, the home of the Renaud–Barrault company in the 1960s, which has also served as a second stage for the Comédie-Française, and has housed the Théâtre de l'Europe; the Théâtre National Populaire, renamed the Théâtre National du *Chaillot in 1972, when Planchon's theatre in Lyon-Villeurbanne was given the TNP title; and the Théâtre de la Colline, completed in 1988 with a mission to perform new plays. In addition the subsidized sector in Paris includes six large National Dramatic Centres and literally hundreds of other theatres, some large and prestigious like Mnouchkine's Cartoucherie at Vincennes, some much smaller.

The private sector is the inheritor of the boulevard tradition that was so vigorous in 1900. During the middle years of the century, as first *film and then *television began to compete for audiences, the boulevard theatres went into a slow decline. No playwrights emerged who could match Feydeau for wit and ferocity, and boulevard comedy became domesticated. In the 1920s Sacha *Guitry wrote light romantic comedies with just enough wit and sophistication to appear part of the Parisian chic. Between the 1930s and the 1960s others developed this genre, notably Marcel Aymé, André Roussin, Marcel Achard, and Félicien Marceau. In the 1970s Françoise Dorin deliberately took up the challenge of reviving boulevard comedy and enjoyed a great success with middle-class works calculated to be different from the fare at the subsidized theatres. She was followed in this by Loleh Bellon and Yasmina *Reza, both actresses

like herself. Other new talents emerged in the last decades, writing specifically for the private theatres, notably Eric-Emmanuel Schmitt and Jean-Marie Besset.

In the 1990s debates about the role of the author in the theatre acquired added urgency, as writers such as Koltès, Vinaver, Cixous, Xavier Durringer, the team of Agnès Jaoui and Jean-Pierre Bacri, Jean-Luc Lagarce, Olivier *Py, and Noëlle Renaude became known for their expressive use of spoken text. Organizations such as Théâtre Ouvert have received ever more generous funding and have given effective support to many young playwrights. The dominant tone of the new writing for theatre is inward-looking, personal, often expressed in monologue. But although apparently turning their back on the political commitment of earlier plays, many of these writers gave expression to a powerful mood of political disillusion with late capitalism. Theatre in Paris at the start of the twenty-first century is in a position of strength, generating new artistic approaches, new companies, and new playwrights.   DB

BRADBY, DAVID, and DELGADO, MARIA (eds.), *The Paris Jigsaw: internationalism and the city's stages* (Manchester, 2002)

CARLSON, MARVIN, *The Theatre of the French Revolution* (Ithaca, NY, 1966)

COHN, RUBY, *From 'Desire' to 'Godot': pocket theater of post war Paris* (Berkeley, 1987)

HEMMINGS, F. W. J., *The Theatre Industry in Nineteenth-Century France* (Cambridge, 1993)

—— *Theatre and State in France, 1760–1905* (Cambridge, 1994)

HOWARTH, W. D. (ed.), *French Theatre in the Neo-classical Era, 1550–1789* (Cambridge, 1977)

—— *Sublime and Grotesque: a study of French romantic drama* (London, 1975)

KNOWLES, DOROTHY, *French Drama of the Inter-war Years, 1918–1939* (London, 1967)

LOUGH, JOHN, *Seventeenth-Century French Theatre: the background* (Oxford, 1979)

MAZOUER, CHARLES, *Le Theatre Français du moyen-âge* (Paris, 1998)

VIALA, ALAIN (ed.), *Le Théâtre en France des origines à nos jours* (Paris, 1997)

WHITTON, DAVID, *Stage Directors in Modern France* (Manchester, 1987)

WILEY, W. L., *The Early Public Theatre in France* (Westport, Conn., 1972)

styles from *Boucicault to *Behan, as well as dramatizing the tragedy of the 1798 Protestant rebel Henry Joy McCracken. Other plays include *Catchpenny Twist* (1977), *Nightshade* (1985), and works for *radio and *television. The Stewart Parker Trust was established in his memory to support work by young Irish playwrights.   CAL

PARKS, SUZAN-LORI (1963–)

*African-American playwright who first attracted notice in 1990 when *Imperceptible Mutabilities in the Third Kingdom* won an

Obie *award for best new American play. Since then Parks has produced a play every two years or so, staged at leading venues including Yale Repertory Company, the *New York Shakespeare Festival (where a number of her works have been mounted), *Arena Stage, and the *Actors Theatre of Louisville. Fascinated by the play of *history in the contemporary landscape, her *The Death of the Last Black Man in the Whole Entire World* (1990) and *Devotees in the Garden of Love* (1992) work postmodern twists on American myths and icons. This characteristic came to the fore most bravely the next year with *The America Play*, which includes Abraham Lincoln (played by a black actor in

Suzan-Lori **Parks**'s *The America Play*, American Repertory Theatre, Cambridge, Massachusetts, 1994, directed by Marcus Stern. A black Abraham Lincoln watches television, surrounded by the paraphernalia of the USA.

the original production) musing on the 'great hole of history'. *Venus* (1996), about a large African woman exhibited as an anatomical oddity in the nineteenth century, was directed by Robert *Wilson in *New York. *In the Blood* (1999) updated Hawthorne's Hester Prynne from *The Scarlet Letter* into a homeless woman living under a bridge with a ragtag brood of cross-racial children. *Topdog/Underdog*, about sibling rivalry experienced by two black brothers named Lincoln and *Booth, premièred in 2001. BBL

Park burned in 1820 and was rebuilt with a large, well-equipped *stage and seating for 2,500. Managers Stephen *Price and Edmund Simpson supplemented their fine resident company with continual guest appearances by international stars—thus being credited with initiating the star system—and premièred the blockbusters *Metamora* and *Rip Van Winkle*. Its reputation in decline, the Park was not rebuilt after it was destroyed by *fire in 1849. AHK

PARK THEATRE

Originally called the New Theatre, the Park opened in 1798 and became the symbol of *New York's theatrical pre-eminence. Its stone exterior, carpeted lobby, three tiers of *boxes, cushioned seats, and gilded decoration made it the most luxurious American theatre of its time. Its cost had been shared by 113 investors, whose demands, added to those of the actors, defeated two of the original three *managers. *Dunlap, who remained, succeeded with the popular *melodramas of *Kotzebue. The

PARODOS

In Greek, 'side-entrance', used in three distinct senses now and in antiquity: first, the two side entrances into the *orchestra in a Greek theatre; second, the entry of the comic or tragic *chorus; third, the chant (especially anapaestic chant) of a chorus while entering. The meaning 'opening song' is not attested in antiquity, though *parados* has sometimes been confused in criticism with the first choral ode or *stasimon. See* GREEK THEATRE, ANCIENT; ANCIENT THEATRES. WJS

PARODY

Parody mimics human behaviour, and can be the funniest and at the same time the most unscrupulous and wounding form of *satire, a slightly skewed version of its prey. Even when a *puppet and its handler carry out the impersonation, as in the British *television series *Spitting Image*, the moving likeness and distortions of bodily and facial features accentuate, rather than temper, the insults. Meanwhile, the *audience may not be able to repress its tears of joy. In the American *Saturday Night Live* TV series, some actors, under false hair and exaggerated cosmetics, lampoon celebrities, garble political speeches, and smirk shamelessly at their fans. *Monty Python's Flying Circus* levelled its barbs at groups as well as individuals: lumberjacks, hoodlums (the Kray brothers), stubborn salespersons, cranks, and obsessives.

Most parodies are a form of theatricalism (*see* THEATRICALITY), a phenomenon not restricted to theatre productions but subsuming performances about the arts of performing. Theatricalism received a boost in the early 1900s from the sardonic *comedies of *Pirandello, especially *Six Characters in Search of an Author*; but it was implicit in *Molière's *The Versailles Impromptu* (1663); and in *The Rehearsal* (1671), written by *Buckingham and other hands, to make fun of *Dryden's brassy heroic couplets in *The Conquest of Granada* (1670). Henry *Fielding's *Tragedy of Tragedies; or, The Life and Death of Tom Thumb the Great* (1731) parodied almost all aspects of the preceding *heroic drama of the seventeenth century, and most tenaciously its hysterical seriousness. The 28-year-old *Sheridan composed *The Critic; or, A Tragedy Rehearsed* (1779) to parody the *rehearsal process, as Buckingham and Fielding had done, but also to close in on the role of Sir Fretful Plagiary, based on a popular playwright of the time, Richard *Cumberland. Molière called his play, set in the *Versailles chateau's little playhouse, an 'impromptu', but since he wrote out the *text he obviously wanted to offer the impression that the actors made it up as they went along.

A parody can present a community, real or imaginary, in a new and scornful light. John *Gay's *The Beggar's Opera* (1728) turns *London, supremely its police force, real or imaginary, into crooks, and Macheath, a gang leader, into the play's *hero, much as *Brecht would do two centuries later with his adaptation, *The Threepenny Opera* (1928). In the modern era, despite the plethora of parodies, their topics have mostly proved commonplace or their treatments erratic. But Peter *Barnes's tragifarce *Laughter!* (1968) takes place in a concentration camp and ends with a Jewish *vaudeville duo putting on a brief turn, after which 'they die in darkness'. The playlet opens with lines uttered by an 'unnamed author': 'A sense of humour's no remedy for evil. Isn't that why the Devil's always smiling? The stupid are never truly laughed out of their stupidities, fools remain fools, the corrupt, violent, and depraved remain corrupt, violent and depraved. *Laughter's the ally of tyrants. It softens our hatred.' Barnes, pro-

lific writer of comedies and *farces, knows that, in assuaging our grief over fiendishness, parody and its laughter raising take us only so far.   ACB

PARRA, MARCO ANTONIO DE LA (1952–)

Chilean playwright, actor, and novelist. He became known for his play *Lo crudo, lo cocido, lo podrido* (*The Raw, the Cooked, and the Rotten*, written 1978); though banned by the military regime, it became a success once *censorship was lifted. His postmodern works are a mixture of *vaudeville, *cabaret, cartoons, *television shows, and silent movies (*see* MODERNISM AND POSTMODERNISM). Among his most successful plays are *La secreta obscenidad de cada día* (*Our Daily Secret Obscenity*, 1983), *El deseo de toda ciudadana* (*Every Young Woman's Desire*, 1987), *Infieles* (*Beds*, 1988), and *Monogamy* (2000).   MAR

PARRY, LORAE (1955–)

New Zealand performer and playwright. Born in Australia, Parry trained as an actor in New Zealand and has developed as a powerful *feminist playwright and comedian. Early plays such as *Strip* (1983) and *Frontwomen* (1988) use simple *realism and humour to promote women's empowerment and tolerance of *lesbianism, but later plays, especially *Eugenia* (1996), are structurally and thematically more complex in their compassionate examination of the entrapments of history, power, and *gender. Parry also deploys several subversive personae in *television and stand-up comedy presentation, and is active in promoting women's issues in the theatre and play *publishing.   DC

PARSI THEATRE

The dominant form of entertainment in urban *India from the 1860s to the 1930s. Influenced by British travelling companies and *amateur theatricals, Parsi theatre innovatively blended European and South Asian practices of theatrical representation and dramatic construction. Professional *touring companies performed on *proscenium stages decorated with richly painted *curtains. Orchestral *music, declamatory *acting, and mechanical devices created spectacular effects. As a transitional form, Parsi theatre ushered in modern drama and influenced theatre styles throughout South and South-East Asia, and lent its *genres, aesthetics, and economic base to popular Indian *film. Parsi theatre's appeal extended far beyond the Parsi community, and its content had little to do with Parsi religion or culture. Followers of the prophet Zarathustra, the Parsis emigrated from Iran to Gujarat over 1,000 years ago. Settling in Bombay (*Mumbai) in the eighteenth century, prominent families made fortunes as bankers and traders. Social interaction with colonial elites, exposure to English-language theatre, and entrepreneurial skill inclined Parsis to organize the first modern theatrical companies in South Asia. Although companies remained under Parsi management into the twentieth century, actors increasingly were drawn from among Muslims, Hindus, Anglo-Indians, and Baghdadi Jews. Professional writers, musicians, painters, stagehands, and other personnel were often non-Parsis.

Initially companies performed in Gujarati or English and spectators were urban Parsis and Europeans. In 1871 *Urdu-language dramas were introduced and the *audience rapidly expanded to all classes and communities. In the 1910s the Parsi theatre turned towards Hindu audiences through retellings of the Hindu epics in *Hindi. Even while touring in south India and South-East Asia, the companies performed in the languages of north India. The Parsi theatre brought the romantic rhetoric of Urdu poetry and the melodic resonance of Hindustani music to these distant places. It appealed through its performative vocabulary rather than linguistic medium, much like the present-day Hindi cinema. The early repertoire comprised heroic legends from the Persian *Shahnamah*, Indo-Islamic fairy romances (*Indar Sabha*), and adapted Shakespearian *comedies and *tragedies. Later the focus turned to *historical tales, mythological material, and contemporary social dramas. The best-known playwrights, Agha Hashr Kashmiri and Narayan Prasad Betab, wrote work that was adapted for the cinema. Dramatic construction followed the European convention of *acts and *scenes and the use of multiple *plots. The companies themselves *published the plays, and songbooks for the most popular dramas were eagerly sought.

Famous actors included Khurshed Balivala, Kavas Khatau, Jehangir Khambata, Sohrab Ogra, and Fida *Hussain. Women's parts were commonly played by *female impersonators who attracted large followings. Pestan Madan, Edal Mistri, Naslu Sarkari, Darashah Patel, Amritlal, and Narmada Shankar were the most famous of these. Actresses began to appear in the 1870s alongside impersonators. They were Anglo-Indians (Mary Fenton, Patience Cooper) and later Baghdadi Jews (Ruby Myers or 'Sulochana'), Muslims (Kajjan), and Hindus (Munnibai), but never Parsis.

Hundreds of Parsi theatre companies existed, including spin-off troupes outside Bombay. The longest-lived companies were named after British royalty: the Victoria Theatrical Company, the Alfred, and the New Alfred. Some old Bombay *playhouses on Grant Road and near the Victoria Terminus are still in existence as cinema halls (Capitol, Alfred). The advent of sound films in 1931 led to a rapid decline in the Parsi theatre. Most of its personnel found employment in cinema, and audiences too switched loyalties. The Moonlight Theatre of Calcutta, however, continued under the direction of Fida Hussain up to the 1950s.

KH

PASADENA PLAYHOUSE

American company. Founded in 1917 by Gilmor Brown, the Playhouse offered over 40 productions during its first year and moved to its present location, a graceful example of southern California stucco-and-tile design, in 1925. Renowned through the 1950s for presenting world premières as well as the entire Shakespearian canon, its College of Theater Arts *trained such *film actors as Gene Hackman, Dustin *Hoffman, and William Holden. Declared the state theatre of California in 1937, the facility closed in 1969 but reopened in 1986 and now presents an annual season of six plays.

JDM

PÁSKÁNDI, GÉZA (1933–95)

Transylvanian poet and playwright. A member of the Hungarian-speaking minority in Romania, Páskándi was working as a journalist when he was sentenced to six years' imprisonment in 1957 for political reasons. His plays, including the *comedy *Külsö zajok* (*Distant Noises*), were influenced by the theatre of the *absurd and banned in Romania. His polemic drama *Vendégség* (*Guests*) was first staged in Hungary in 1971, followed by the two other pieces of his 'Transylvanian Triptych': *Tornyot választok* (*I Choose a Tower*) and *Szekértől elfutott lovak* (*Horses Running from the Cart*). He moved to Hungary in 1974.

HJA

PASOLINI, PIER PAOLO (1922–75)

Poet, novelist, and filmmaker. Pasolini wrote his first stage work, *I Turcs tal Friúl* (*The Turks in Friuli*), in 1944 in Friulian dialect to commemorate his brother killed in the Resistance. *Nel 46!* (1946) illustrates his enduring taste for *allegory and abstract argumentation. In 1960, he translated *Aeschylus' *Oresteia*, but his desire to reinterpret Greek myth was more amply demonstrated by such *films as *Oedipus* (1967) and *Medea* (1970). Ancient Greece provides the setting for *Pylades*, one of the six *tragedies he wrote in 1966. His polemical *Manifesto for a New Theatre* (1968) advocated a theatre of the word and of ideas.

JF

PASQUAL, LLUIS (1951–)

Spanish-Catalan director. After an apprenticeship with Giorgio *Strehler in *Milan, he was the co-founder (with Fabià *Puigserver) in 1976 of the Teatre Lliure, *Barcelona's leading independent company dedicated to innovative stagings of classical and modern world drama. In 1983 he became director of Spain's national theatre (Centro Dramático Nacional) and in his first season startled *audiences by replacing the orchestra seats of the historic Teatro *Nacional María Guerrero with a vast sandpit for his staging of the *Marlowe/*Brecht *Edward II*. Landmark productions were *Valle-Inclán's *Bohemian Lights* (1984), co-produced with the Théâtre de l'*Europe, Brecht's *Mother Courage* (1985), and *García Lorca's *The Public* (1986), co-produced with the *Piccolo Teatro di Milano. After leaving the CDN in 1989, he directed *opera in Spain, Italy, France, and Belgium and became director of the Théâtre de l'Europe in *Paris. He returned to the

Teatre Lliure in 1998 and was involved in the company's move to a larger space in Barcelona's new Ciutat de Teatre. In 2000, as a farewell to the Lliure's original home, he directed an unconventional staging of *Chekhov's *The Cherry Orchard*, moving the action to encompass the *audience and extend into the lobby as the actors addressed the public directly.   MPH

PASSE MURAILLE, THEATRE

One of *Toronto's first *alternative theatres was founded in 1968 as the theatre wing of Rochdale College, a radical experiment in higher education. Its founder, Jim Garrard, initially produced new American ensemble plays such as Rochelle *Owens's *Futz*, bringing headlines and obscenity charges in 1969. After relocating to a church hall downtown, the company found national fame under Paul Thompson (*artistic director, 1971–82) with *collective creations produced on Canadian themes. These included *The Farm Show* (1972) and *I Love You, Baby Blue* (1975), profits from which enabled the company to buy its present home, which has two small houses.   DWJ

PASSION PLAY

In the strict sense, a play depicting the sufferings of Christ on the cross. A mistaken association of *pascha* with *pascho* (suffer), however, not only linked the Passover Feast to the Passion but also allowed the Resurrection to be included as well. In fact, the need to explain the meaning of the Passion often led to the depiction of other events in human and divine history. The origins of the Passion play are obscure. Possible sources include recitations of the Gospel narratives, as early as the fourth century included in the liturgies of Holy Week, or the *Planctus Mariae* (*Mary's Lament*), a *liturgical ceremony performed during the *Adoratio* on Good Friday; but it is more probable that the real impetus is to be found in the new emphasis during the eleventh and twelfth centuries on the humanity of Christ, so that the Passion play arose in the context of Christocentric mysticism and piety.

Certainly there were fresh expressions of Christ's Passion in the twelfth and thirteenth centuries. A Latin Passion play from the Benedictine monastery in Monte Cassino dates from the twelfth century, and references to other Passion plays throughout the thirteenth century suggest an early tradition of Latin Passions in Italy. In Germany, two Passion plays from the monastery of Benediktbeuren in Bavaria have survived in a thirteenth-century manuscript, but they might actually be even older. Although the Monte Cassino and Benediktbeuren Passions are in Latin, the vernacular was increasingly being used to tell the story of Christ's suffering. In the longer of the German plays, both Mary Magdalene and the Virgin make extensive use of the vernacular. In non-dramatic forms we have the French *Passion des jongleurs* (c.1200), a poem popular among *jongleurs

in both France and England, and the English *Northern Passion* (thirteenth century), both of which were used by later writers in the composition of Passion plays.

By the end of the fourteenth century, the vernacular Passion play was firmly established. The Passion plays performed in Germany and France during the fifteenth and sixteenth centuries were remarkable achievements. Based on the Vulgate Bible, on *The Golden Legend* (a collection of saints lives and short treatises on Christian festivals), and on other works of piety, they furnished dramatic material for some of the most spectacular productions in the history of the theatre. In Germany it has been possible to distinguish at least five regional textual traditions, but expansions, redactions, and alterations were constant, and extant manuscripts represent freeze-frame versions of ever changing *texts. The situation in France is similar, although we know the names of several playwrights. Eustache *Mercadé, Arnoul *Greban, and Jean *Michel were the authors of the most important of the French Passions. Alone or in combination their dramas—cut, combined, adapted to local circumstance— provided the scripts for most of the performances in France for 200 years. These were large, sprawling plays, over 25,000 lines long and requiring anywhere from two to several days to perform. Passion plays for the most part did not long survive the sixteenth century. The Parlement de *Paris banned their performance in 1548; the last recorded performance at Lucerne was in 1616. The tradition carries on, however, at *Oberammergau. *See also* BIBLICAL PLAYS; MEDIEVAL THEATRE IN EUROPE.

RWV

PASTOR, TONY (1837–1908)

American blackface *minstrel and *popular entertainment entrepreneur. Pastor transformed the lower-class entertainment of minstrelsy and *vaudeville into respectable family fare. A New Yorker from birth until death, he began his professional career at P. T. *Barnum's American Museum in *New York in 1846. At 10 he became a blackface minstrel with the Raymond and Waring Menagerie. He also performed in *circus and *variety shows. In 1861 he sang the 'Star Spangled Banner' on the eve of the Civil War, and from then on interspersed all his work with patriotic songs. Pastor is said to have formulated the idea of a vaudeville show, essentially a variety show with a diversity of acts from other forms of American popular entertainment such as minstrelsy, the circus, Shakespeare *burlesques, comedy sketches, and popular *music and *dances. By 1881 Tony Pastor's New Fourteenth Street Theatre opened with the specific purpose of presenting vaudeville 'for the amusement of the cultivated and aesthetic'. The *playhouse was the most popular in New York in the 1880s, and Pastor served as a model for future theatrical impresarios such as Oscar *Hammerstein I.

AB

PASTORAL DRAMA

A form of drama evolved from poetry—particularly the idyll, eclogue, or bucolic—which idealizes nature and the rural life. Ostensibly the pastoral tells stories of shepherds but at root the form problematizes social relationships and ideas of modernization: the purity and simplicity of shepherd life is contrasted with the corruption and artificiality of the court, the town, or the city. The pastoral sometimes uses the device of 'singing matches' between two or more shepherds, and it often presents the poet and his friends in the personae of shepherds and shepherdesses. Classical models are drawn from Theocritus and Virgil and from the idea of a lost golden age, imagined by both Hesiod and Ovid, in which humans lived close to and at one with nature. In Theocritus' idylls the convention and *dramatis personae were established: his verse celebrates the beauty and simplicity of rustic life in Sicily, his *characters including Daphnis, Lycidas, Corydon, and Amaryllis.

The form won renewed significance in the *early modern period. In Italy Poliziano and Beccari set a tone for *Tasso's *Aminta* (1573), generally regarded as the first pastoral play. *Il pastor fido* by Battista *Guarini (c.1597) influenced *Fletcher's *The Faithful Shepherdess* (1608), while *Lyly's *Love's Metamorphosis* (c.1598) borrowed from Spanish and Italian models, also affected by English *folk traditions and mythologies of the forest and Robin Hood. The Spaniard Jorge de Montemayor's *Diana* (c.1560) influenced *Sydney's pastoral prose romance *Arcadia* (1590), which provided a model for *Shirley's play *The Arcadia* (c.1630). In the same period, and in the same manner, perhaps the best known pastoral play, Shakespeare's *As You Like It* (c.1599), found a source in the earlier pastoral romance of *Rosalynde* by Thomas Lodge (1590). Shakespeare's play *parodied the vogue for pastoral *verse while also reimagining the form as a counter-pastoral: despite being a drama of transformation in the woods, it is also full of scepticism about the perceived delights of the rural. Among the lesser dramatists of the end of the Elizabethan period, Anthony *Munday, in his use of Robin Hood stories, provides a further example of the English pastoral and a further contrast with Shakespeare, Lyly, and George *Peele (*The Old Wives Tale*, 1595). Ben *Jonson's pastoral play *The Sad Shepherd* was unfinished at his death in 1637.

Whilst this period saw the pastoral as a *romance form, the eighteenth century began to adapt the convention to more *realistic depictions of rural life. John *Gay ironically subtitled *The Beggar's Opera* (1728) 'a newgate pastoral', while Allan Ramsay's *The Gentle Shephard* (1729), the most popular pastoral drama of the century, made use of the (Pentlands) vernacular, and commented on its contemporary context (the threat of war, status of women, faith and superstition). The success of Ramsay's pastoral inspired a host of imitators, including Theophilus *Cibber's *ballad opera *Pattie and Peggy* (1730). In Kitty *Clive's hugely self-reflexive work *The Rehearsal* (1750), a popular divertissement of *Garrick's late *management, the play-within-the-play is an elaborate pastoral fantasy and the *genre is conceived of as hopelessly outmoded and artificial.

Although the pastoral context remained significant in poetry through the nineteenth and twentieth centuries, the highly conventionalized form of the pastoral drama faded. Dramatists, however, continue to recover from the genre one of its defining features: the dialectic of the rural and the urban, of nature and civilization, simplicity and innocence, and sophistication and artificiality, which remain common themes and sources of narrative and dramatic tension.   AS

PATENT THEATRES

In anticipation of Charles II's return from exile, the remnants of the old *London acting companies began to perform plays in the spring of 1660. Their enthusiasm was understandable but premature, for that summer Charles gave a joint theatrical monopoly to the courtiers William *Davenant and Thomas *Killigrew. They suppressed the extant companies and forced the actors to join their theatres, the King's Company (Killigrew) and Duke's Company (Davenant). Formal patents were granted to them in 1662 and they had eliminated all competition by 1667. The patents were exclusive and granted in perpetuity, creating a dispensation that, although frequently challenged and altered, was to exist for nearly 200 years. When the King's Company collapsed in 1682, the United Company was formed, joining the two patents. After Thomas *Betterton led an actors' revolt against Christopher *Rich in 1695, the rebels operated a rival theatre in *Lincoln's Inn Fields under a licence. Unlike a patent, a licence could be withdrawn at the pleasure of the *Lord Chamberlain; clearly a patent was preferable. However, when the Lord Chamberlain silenced Rich's *Drury Lane Theatre in 1709—technically an illegal move—the two original patents were rendered useless until the order was lifted. For a time London had two theatres but no operative patents.

The situation stabilized in 1714–15 when Rich was allowed to resume operations at Lincoln's Inn Fields, while Richard *Steele was granted a lifetime patent for Drury Lane. By the 1720s the rules about who could legally offer plays had become fuzzy and their enforcement lax. Thomas Odell, Henry Giffard, and Henry *Fielding all established theatres without patent or licence, but the Stage *Licensing Act of 1737 reasserted that only theatres holding royal patents could operate. Not surprisingly, the law had the strong support of the patent houses.

For a brief period (1766–77), Samuel *Foote's *Haymarket Theatre operated under a patent that he received for his lifetime. Foote had run the theatre for several years by virtue of annual licences, and a patent was a great advance, but the old joint monopoly held; Foote was permitted to produce only in the summer and prohibited from competing with the 'winter theatres'. When he died, the *Colmans continued the summer enterprise by virtue of annual licences. John Palmer tried to open the Royalty Theatre without a patent in 1787, but the patentees of Drury Lane and *Covent Garden moved swiftly to have the operation shut down.

In the early nineteenth century the proliferation of small venues and transpontine theatres (*see* MINOR THEATRES) put the old patent system under great stress. While spoken drama was technically limited to the patent houses, other venues began to stretch the boundaries of *melodrama, bringing it closer to the patent house fare. The patent system came to an end with the Theatre Regulation Act of 1843, which lifted the prohibition on spoken drama at non-patent houses. *See also* LEGITIMATE DRAMA; THEATRES ROYAL.   MJK

PATER NOSTER PLAY *See* MORALITY PLAY.

PAULSEN, CARL ANDREAS (1620–?)

German actor who *managed the first important German group of strolling players from 1650 to 1687. Born in Hamburg, Paulsen was probably university educated. The repertoire of his troupe, Charles's High German Company of Players, included 'all manner of New and Well Constructed *Comedies, *Traged-ies, *Pastorals, *Ballets and *Dances' according to a *playbill, as well as 'Beautiful Tableaux'. His actors acquainted German-speaking cities in northern and Eastern Europe with an *early modern English, French, and Spanish repertory, including the plays of *Marlowe, *Kyd, Shakespeare, Lope de *Vega, and *Calderón. *Dr Faustus*, a favourite in the German lands, was staged by the company in Danzig (Gdańsk) in 1669. Strolling companies like Paulsen's were ill-equipped, carrying only rudi-mentary *scenery, *costumes, and *properties, and performed in a variety of makeshift venues with little *rehearsal and (prob-ably) little theatrical discipline.   DLF

PAVLOVSKY, EDUARDO (1933–)

Argentinian playwright, actor, *theorist, and psychoanalyst. Pavlovsky was already an actor when he saw a production of *Waiting for Godot* in the 1950s. He co-founded the *avant-garde theatre group Yenesí and began to write *absurdist plays, such as *We Are* and *The Tragic Wait* (both 1962). The political events of the late 1960s revolutionized his work, resulting in the hugely successful *Mr Galíndez*. Premièred in 1972 (and staged through-out *Latin America), the play violently portrayed an omnipres-ent repressive system led by the invisible Galíndez. *Spiderwebs* achieved notoriety in 1977 when it was officially banned for dis-torting traditional values. Several months later, after his office was invaded by men disguised as gas meter-readers (as *Spider-webs'* two paramilitary agents had been), Pavlovsky escaped to Spain, returning in 1980. In the 1980s his *characters, already

typified by their split condition as the shared subconscious of repressor and victim, began to discard psychological unity, so that *Potestad* (1986) and *Pablo* (1987) display an 'aesthetic of multiplicity'. Two actresses shared the role of 'She' in Laura *Yusem's controversial 1990 staging of *Pas de deux*: one played the naked, raped body, the other the character's ethos which survives to defy her assassin. An 'anti-postmodern' resistance in the face of national and personal physical decay informs such plays as *Red Balloons Red* (1994) and the *monologue *The Death of Marguerite Duras* (2000), which consider the state of late twentieth-century ideologies. Despite extensive *touring as a performer in his own plays, Pavlovsky continues to exert a for-midable presence on the *Buenos Aires scene.   JGJ

PAVY, SALOMON (1590–1603)

English *boy actor. Pavy acted with the Children of the *Chapel Royal, who in 1600 resumed performances at the second *Black-friars Theatre. He specialized in playing old men, and at his death was eulogized by Ben *Jonson (Epigram CXX) as making the Fates believe he was one.   MS

PAXINOU, KATINA (1900–73)

Greek actress and *manager. After studying music and theatre in Geneva, she joined the *Greek National Theatre in 1931 and ap-peared in such memorable productions as Palamas's *Trisevgeni* and *Ibsen's *Ghosts* (as Mrs Alving). In 1942 she made her Broad-way debut with Ibsen's *Hedda Gabler*. She won the Academy award for best supporting actress for her portrayal of Pilar in *For Whom the Bell Tolls* (1943) and appeared in several other *films. In 1950 she returned to the Greek National Theatre and *toured extensively, playing *Greek *tragedy, *García Lorca, and *Dürrenmatt in *New York and *Paris. In 1968 she formed a company with her husband, actor and director Alexis Minotis, and performed in an acclaimed production of *Brecht's *Mother Courage* (1971–2). Paxinou also taught *acting, translated plays, and composed *music for the theatre.   KGo

PAYNE, B. IDEN (1881–1976)

English actor, *manager, director, and educator; awarded an OBE in 1976. Payne began with Frank *Benson in 1899; after a brief term as a manager at the *Abbey Theatre, he worked with Miss *Horniman in 1907 to develop a *regional repertory theatre in *Manchester, not only acting regularly but also serving as gen-eral manager until 1911. In 1913 he moved to the USA where he worked in the *alternative theatre movement in *New York (*Theatre Guild), *Chicago (*Goodman Theatre), and *Phila-delphia (Little Theatre). He served as head of the school of drama, Carnegie Institute of Technology (1914–34). Succeeding *Bridges-Adams in 1934, he became the director of the *Shakespeare Memorial Theatre at Stratford-upon-Avon, staging ten productions. He returned to America in 1943, becoming a professor at the University of Texas in 1946. He also founded and directed the summer *Shakespeare festival at the Old Globe in San Diego in 1949. His memoir was published in 1977.

TP

PAYNE, JOHN HOWARD (1791–1852)

American actor and playwright. Theatrically precocious, Payne began a weekly theatrical journal at the age of 14 and composed his first full-length play at 15. He made his acting debut in 1809 and became the first native-born star on the American (and later English) stage. He was a prolific playwright and adapter. His *Brutus* (1818) was a vehicle for both Edmund *Kean and Edwin *Forrest, while *Thérèse* (1821), *Clari* (1823), *Charles II* (1824), and *Richelieu* (1826) proved that an American could write successfully for English *audiences. He is best remembered as the lyricist of 'Home, Sweet Home' from *Clari*.

GAR

PAZ, ALBIO (1936–)

Cuban playwright, director, and actor, author of *La vitrina* (*The Showcase*, 1971). He directed the Cubana de Acero troupe and later the Mirón Cubano in Matanzas. His play *Huelga* (*Strike*, 1981) won the *Casa de las Américas *award. Other works include *El paraíso recobrao* (*Paradise Regained*, 1973), *El gato de Chinchila* (*The Chinchila Cat*, 1987), and *Don Quijote en una ínsula del Caribe* (*Don Quixote on a Caribbean Island*, 1995).

MMu

PEDRERO, PALOMA (1957–)

Spanish playwright, actress, and director of the post-Franco period. Her first play, *Lauren's Call* (1985), in which she also acted, was a compelling two-*character work that distils a marital crisis and search for sexual identity. Performed in several *Latin American countries and the United States, it remains her signature play. Her most frequently staged work is *The Color of August* (1988), a *one-act piece that depicts a combative reunion between an artist and her model. Longer works include *The Winter of the Happy Moon* (1987), *Wolf Kisses* (1991), and *First Star* (1998). In 1999 she returned with notable success to the shorter single-scene form with *Scowling Cubs*, a disturbing treatment of gratuitous violence in youth culture, which she co-produced with her husband Robert Muro, at *Madrid's alternative Cuarta Pared Theatre.

MPH

PEDRO, ANTÓNIO (1909–66)

Portuguese poet, painter, playwright, director, designer, and critic. After some crucial years abroad (*Paris, 1934–5, *London,

1944–5), participating in major art exhibitions, Pedro's career was divided between *Lisbon and Oporto. After 1953 his experiments with *surrealism and *theoretical work on the theatre came to fruition with the northern TEP (Porto Experimental Theatre). Committed to political resistance, Pedro strove to create a critical *audience, combating the traditionalist, parochial nationalism of mid-century bourgeois taste. He introduced new playwrights, namely Bernardo *Santareno, wrote essays and reviews, a few plays, a treatise on *directing, and pioneered a drama programme for *television.

FM

PEDRO LEAL, ODILE (1964–)

Actor, director, and playwright from French Guiana, the founder and *artistic director of the Guyane Art Théâtre in *Paris and organizer of an annual *festival in Guiana. Her *La Chanson de Philibert* (*The Song of Philibert*, 1996) was first produced in Cayenne. Her Ph.D. thesis, *Théâtre et écritures ethniques de Guyane* (*Theatre and Ethnic Writing in Guiana*), was the first research undertaken on traditional theatre practices in this French *Caribbean department.

AR

PEELE, GEORGE (1558–96)

English playwright. A graduate of Oxford and one of the *university wits, Peele turned his hand to a variety of theatrical composition—court entertainment, *civic pageant, popular *public theatres. *The Arraignment of Paris* (c.1581–4) was performed at court by the Children of the *Chapel; *Anglorum Feriae* (1595) describes a court tilt. *Woolstone Dixie* (1585) and *Descensus Astreae* (1591) were *London civic pageants. Peele's plays for the professional stage are similarly various. *The Battle of Alcazar* (1588–9) is based on contemporary history, *Edward I* (1590–3) on chronicle history, and *David and Bathsabe* (c.1594?) on biblical narrative. All three plays are elaborated by apocryphal and imaginative adventure. Peele's best—and best-known—play, *The Old Wives' Tale* (c.1588–94), is a delightful combination of *folk story and *romance that good-humouredly mocks the conventions of both. Other plays, now lost, may have contributed to his contemporary reputation.

RWV

PEIRANO FALCONI, LUIS (1946–)

Peruvian actor and director. One of the founders of *Ensayo in Lima (1983) and currently dean at Lima's Catholic University, Peirano accomplished major reforms in Peru in *directing, *scenography, and *acting style. A prolific essayist, teacher, theatre and *television *producer, Peirano also took leading roles in *The Resurrection* (1965) and *Death and the Maiden* (1992). He has been directing since 1969; his major work includes *Mrożek's *Emigrés* (1986), Lope de *Vega's *The Dog in the Manger* (1992), *Miller's *Broken Glass* (1997), *Calderón's *The Great*

Theatre of the World (2000), *Hamlet* (2001), and *Brecht's *Galileo* (2001).   LRG

PEKING OPERA *See* JINGJU.

PENHALL, JOE (1967–)

English playwright. With his first major play, *Some Voices* (*Royal Court, 1994), Penhall established himself as a leading figure in a new wave of British dramatists. *Filmed in 2000, the play concerns the misadventures of a young schizophrenic man released into the care of his brother. *Pale Horse* (1995) deepened the melancholy in an investigation of contemporary moral emptiness. *Love and Understanding* (1997) and *The Bullet* (1998) repeated the male double act of *Some Voices*, in their pairs of lawless and conventional male leads. Penhall's breakthrough came with *Blue/Orange* (2000), which centres on the deliberation of two psychiatrists over the diagnosis of a young black man's mental illness. Though he shares with his contemporaries largely urban locations and a sense of underlying violence, there is a delicate compassion in his plays and a sense of impassioned social debate that is his own.   DR

PENNELL, NICHOLAS (1938–95)

Anglo-Canadian actor. Born in Devon, he trained at the *Royal Academy of Dramatic Art, developed a successful stage career, and starred in the acclaimed *television series *The Forsyte Saga*. In 1972 Pennell came to Canada's *Stratford Festival, playing Orlando in *As You Like It* and Marlow in *She Stoops to Conquer*, and remained a pillar of that company for 23 consecutive seasons. While his major roles there included King John, Macbeth, Richard II, Hamlet, Pericles, and Iago, he also excelled in character roles such as Stephano in *The Tempest* and Pisanio in *Cymbeline*, and in modern classics such as *Ghosts* and *The Importance of Being Earnest*. Outside Stratford, Pennell *toured in his own *one-person show, *A Variable Passion*, and appeared at *regional theatres in Canada and the USA.   DWJ

PENNINGTON, MICHAEL (1943–)

English actor. Pennington learned the best traditions of Cambridge undergraduate theatre—fine *verse speaking and a close concern with the meaning of complex *texts—adding to them his rich and cutting voice and lithe stage presence. He soon began working with the *Royal Shakespeare Company, with especial successes as Berowne in *Love's Labour's Lost* (1978), Angelo (1974) and the Duke (1978) in *Measure for Measure*, and Hamlet (1980). Though established as one of the leading classical actors of his generation, he became disillusioned with both the RSC and the *National Theatre and, with Michael *Bogdanov, established the *English Shakespeare Company in 1986 to create a new brash style of Shakespeare production for a popular *audience. In their successful cycles of Shakespeare's *history plays he played Richard II and Prince Henry (later Henry V) as well as a brutal Jack Cade. With the collapse of the ESC's funding in 1994, Pennington left. He joined Peter *Hall at the *Old Vic in 1997 to play Trigorin in *The Seagull* and returned to the RSC in 1999 in the title role of *Timon of Athens*.   PDH

PENNY THEATRES

Also called 'gaffs', penny theatres were common in the poorer districts of many Victorian cities. Documentary evidence, particularly about *London, often comes through religious or temperance tracts, or journalists with an improving agenda, determined to expose their corrupting influence. Gaffs were a permanent feature for the nineteenth-century inhabitants of London's New Cut, Shoreditch, and Whitechapel Road. They were housed in converted factories and warehouses and accommodated thousands, or in dwelling houses or shops with room for only a few spectators. Though children and teenagers probably made up a large portion of the *audience, adults, male and female, were also regularly found in the gaffs. In the larger venues performances were announced on handbills. Shakespeare, *melodramas, and *music-hall programmes were the usual fare, in performances lasting no more than an hour and repeated many times during the evening. Dramas were sometimes performed in *dumb show (in a vain attempt to evade the *licensing regulations), but usually caution was thrown to the wind, and *dialogue, often of a very coarse and lurid nature, was used. Companies varied from the extremely small to a substantial ten or twelve, with individuals *doubling parts, acting as *ticket takers, and running a lottery in the interval.   AF

PEOPLE SHOW

English company, founded in 1966 by jazz pianist/sculptor Geoff Nuttall and other visual artists. The basement of Better Books in Charing Cross Road in *London saw the true birth of the group with the aptly named *People Show No. 1*. All subsequent shows had different titles, but numbers as well, so by 1969 they reached No. 23, playing in key counter-culture venues, including the London Arts Lab, UFO, and Brighton Combination. *Surreal, imagistic, musical, rude, never pandering to the *audience, their shows usually celebrated creative anarchy, often through highly structured *improvisation. At the last count they were up to No. 109—a 2001 revival of the 1980 *People Show Cabaret*.   BRK

PEPPER'S GHOST

A stage illusion invented by Professor John Henry Pepper, first demonstrated in *London in 1862. A ghost appears on the stage, apparently solid and three dimensional but able to walk through real objects. The effect was achieved by placing a large plate of inclined glass across the front of the stage at an angle, so that objects on stage appeared normal, while light from the orchestra pit was strongly reflected into the *audience's line of sight. A facing inclined mirror was placed in the orchestra pit directly under the onstage glass, and an actor (or anything else) in front of the mirror appeared as a virtual image superimposed upon the view of the stage, transparent, and independent of the material reality behind the glass. The effect was popular at Pepper's Polytechnicon, which specialized in popular science entertainment, was used to accompany *Dickens's readings from *The Haunted Man*, had a vogue in *music hall, and appeared in a number of plays written for its use at the Britannia Theatre. Its acoustic and visual limitations were many, however, and it soon passed out of fashion, replaced by simpler techniques like the backlit skrim or gauze. Yet versions of the trick still appear occasionally in theatres that have a strong interest in stage magic—the Antenna Theater in *San Francisco, for example. *See also* ILLUSION; VISION AND THE VISUAL; SPECIAL EFFECTS.

JB

PEPYS, SAMUEL (1633–1703)

English diarist and government official. Pepys's *Diary*, written 1660–9, is a storehouse of information concerning the Restoration theatre. As a regular theatregoer Pepys commented on plays, actors, *costumes, scenes, and *audiences. He inspected stage machinery and visited the *tiring room. He interviewed Thomas *Killigrew, the *manager of the Theatre Royal. Some of his comments on Shakespearian revivals and adaptations are legendary: *Romeo and Juliet* was 'the worst that ever I heard in my life'; *Twelfth Night* was 'a silly play'; *Macbeth* was 'one of the best plays for a stage, and variety of *dancing and *music, that ever I saw'.

RWV

PERAZA, LUIS (PEPE-PITO) (1908–74)

Venezuelan playwright and director. In the late 1930s and 1940s he established a number of companies and theatre societies, and his own *comedy *Cristián* won an important *award in Caracas (1949) while he was director of the Teatro del Pueblo (1942–52). His work was rooted in the *costumbrista* or *folkloric tradition of *costume drama. Of approximately twenty works, he is most remembered for *El hombre que se fue* (*The Man Who Left*, 1938), *Cecilio* (1942), *La gota de agua* (*The Drop of Water*, 1942), and *Manuelita Sáenz* (1960). LCL trans. AMCS

PÉREZ, COSME *See* RANA, JUAN.

PERFORMANCE

A term most commonly used in theatre to refer to the event in which a dramatic *text is physically realized before an *audience. The similar event orientation of music and *dance has caused these to be grouped traditionally with the theatre as the 'performing arts'. This quite straightforward relationship between theatre and performance became much more complex in the late twentieth century due to three related but distinct developments. First, in the artistic world, a type of event called a performance, often connected more with art galleries than theatres, began to appear in the early 1970s. Most early works of performance or *performance art simply displayed the human body in action, usually as a solo piece. Later spoken, often autobiographical material was added, but most performance remained solo, and could often be distinguished from traditional theatre by its rejection of conventional *mimesis. A very important part of performance art throughout the 1970s and 1980s was its use by minority artists, first by feminists and later by gays, lesbians, and members of ethnic minorities, to give voice to their social and cultural concerns (*see* FEMINIST THEATRE; GAY THEATRE; LESBIAN THEATRE).

In the domain of theatre *theory, at about the same time, Richard *Schechner began to call for a study of performance as a very broad range of human activity, of which conventional theatre was only a small part, using critical tools drawn not from aesthetics but from the social sciences. Thus the work of anthropologists like Victor Turner, sociologists like Erving Goffman, and linguists like J. L. Austin were utilized not only to study traditional theatre topics, but to explore a wide variety of other performative activity: *rituals and religious ceremonies, *sports and games, public celebrations and festivals. Eventually Schechner's interests resulted in the establishment of the first programme in *performance studies, at New York University, an annual international conference on the subject beginning in 1994, and major field of study overlapping but generally distinct from traditional *theatre studies.

The third development, related to the other two in complex and sometimes contradictory ways, was the attempt of a number of theorists to develop the concept of performance as a post-structuralist alternative to theatre, which they held is dedicated to the operations of *structuralism. Josette Féral in 1982 placed performance in direct opposition to theatre, undoing and deconstructing the *semiotic codes and competencies upon which theatre is built and thus allowing the free flow of psychic energies and emotional desires. The denial of narrativity, of fixed meanings, even of presence (which the post-structuralists, following Derrida, dismissed as a metaphysical illusion), created a concept of performance opposed not only to theatre but also to the concept of performance in performance art, which emphasized physical presence for phenomenological reasons and narrativity for political ones. Thus, though united in their rejection of theatre, these two ideas of performance created their own opposition, which inspired much theoretical speculation at the end of the twentieth century. *See also* PERFORMATIVITY.   MC

CARLSON, MARVIN, *Performance: a critical introduction* (New York, 1996)

SCHECHNER, RICHARD, *Essays on Performance Theory* (New York, 1977)

PERFORMANCE ART/ART PERFORMANCE *see page 1019*

PERFORMANCE GROUP

American company, founded in 1967 by Richard *Schechner in *New York, an important force in experimental theatre in the 1970s. Schechner was interested in challenging the distinction between *audience and performer and between performance and 'real life'. The goal was an experience of transcendence for all present at the theatre event; Schechner believed in the potential of theatre as *ritual. The Group's pieces were created in collage style and used existing *texts and found material as well as the members' personal contributions. As such the company formed part of a continuum of American *collectives that stretches back to the *Group Theatre of the 1930s. The Performance Group's most famous production was *Dionysus in 69*, based on *Euripides' *The Bacchae*, which they created in 1968–9. The Dionysus actors were encouraged to interact with the audience, and some performances dissolved when the orgiastic experience overtook the theatrical one. The production is now considered one of the prime examples of *environmental theatre, a classification Schechner coined. There were twelve founding members of the Performance Group involved in *Dionysus in 69*; after one other production, *Makbeth* (1970), the original group disbanded. Schechner reformed the Group later that year and continued to create collage-like productions including *Commune* (begun in 1970). Many important experimental theatre artists worked with the Performance Group, including the founding members of the *Wooster Group, who took over the Performing Garage when Schechner's troupe disbanded in 1980.   KF

PERFORMANCE STUDIES

A new discipline which emerged from drama and *theatre studies in the 1970s. The programmatic foundation for performance studies was outlined in 1966 by Richard *Schechner in his essay 'Approaches to Theory/Criticism' (in *Essays on Performance Theory*, 1977). Here the *New York-based academic and director proposed a concept of performance transcending *text-based drama and embracing 'the formal relations between play, games, *sports, theatre and *ritual'. In the following years Schechner demonstrated in numerous publications the interdisciplinary

potential of such a concept. The definition of *performance within the broader parameters of the social sciences implied a departure from aesthetic and historical paradigms which had until then dominated theatre studies. In this understanding dramatic theatre is just one possible manifestation of performance.

Interdisciplinary by nature, performance studies' closest affinities lie with cultural anthropology or at least that branch of anthropology that could be termed 'interpretative'. Seminal texts and concepts include the notion of 'cultural performance', first advanced by Milton Singer in 1959 in his study of modernization in India. This could include weddings, funerals, festivals, and ceremonies. One such cultural performance was analysed by Clifford Geertz in his famous essay 'Deep Play' (1973), a study of cockfighting in Bali. His use of dramatic metaphors to study a social phenomenon made it a crucial text for performance studies. Another influential anthropologist was Victor Turner, whose concept of social drama and studies of ritual further strengthened ties between cultural anthropology and performance studies. Other important *theorists of performance are the folklorist Dell Hymes, who coined the phrase 'breakthrough into performance' to designate a specific, universal mode of behaviour that human beings consciously act out before others, and the sociologist Erving Goffman, who repeatedly used theatrical metaphors to describe social behaviour.

The scope of such research was first demonstrated in the collection *Rite, Drama, Festival, Spectacle: rehearsals toward a theory of cultural performance* (ed. J. MacAloon, 1984). In *Between Theater and Anthropology* (1985) Schechner further elaborated his anthropological understanding of performance studies, introducing several influential concepts, among them the notion that performance is primarily processual rather than product oriented. The area of cultural performances has provided the richest area of enquiry for performance studies and has brought forth a substantial body of research. Phenomena such as tourist performances and theme parks, hitherto ignored by theatre scholars and ethnologists alike, have been recognized and studied as important manifestations of contemporary culture (as in B. Kirshenblatt-Gimblett's *Destination Culture*, 1998). Often this work is undertaken in related disciplines such as cultural anthropology, cultural studies, or *folklore studies and is therefore not specifically declared to be performance studies.

A second branch of enquiry and continued interest is formed by what could be broadly termed *performance art. The new *genres of performance created by *happenings, Fluxus, and later *feminist performance artists, placed themselves initially outside the purview of both art history and theatre studies. Michael Kirby provided the first study with his anthology *Happenings* (1965). The practice of performance artists from the 1960s, the postmodern (*see* MODERNISM AND POSTMODERNISM) experiments of the 1980s (such as the *Wooster Group), and contemporary *media explorations have remained a central focus of

(continued on p. 1023)

PERFORMANCE ART/ART PERFORMANCE

These two terms, and the more general term 'Performance', emerged in the early 1970s to describe contemporary work in Europe, North and South America, Australia, and *Japan which straddled the boundaries of the performing and visual arts. (In this entry the word 'Performance', when capitalized, is intended to convey the category of work covered by 'performance art' and 'art performance'.) That activity of the 1970s and after derived from a long *avant-garde tradition, issuing from experiments in *theatre, visual art, music, poetry, and *dance, and from the various artistic movements in which the separate forms coalesced and cross-fertilized. Performance in this sense seems to defy definition, not only because it comes in so many forms and styles, but because it stakes out its territory, as Michael Kirby has put it, 'at the limits'. This resistance to definition held a particular fascination for historians and *theorists of Performance in the late 1970s; as RoseLee Goldberg wrote, 'performance defies precise or easy definition beyond the simple declaration that it is live art by artists'.

1. Introduction; 2. Art performance; 3. Performance art; 4. Conclusion

1. Introduction

The *Oxford English Dictionary* defines *performance as 'an action, act, deed, operation'. At first one is struck by the active connotations of that definition. Performance suggests something live (and alive), as opposed to something static, like a painting, evoking associations with spontaneity and with the present. And in the 1970s this often suggested further associations with notions of authenticity. Performance seemed to traffic in activity that was real, not fictive, often savouring the materiality of real objects and framing performers as authentic agents in real time, rather than as *characters in another time and place.

But performance also has associations beyond spontaneous activity. We also call the enactment of a ceremony or the rendition of a play or a piece of music a performance (and of course the wider meaning is the one generally used in this encyclopedia). In this sense, to perform is not at all to act spontaneously, but to play a role; performance becomes associated with the metaphor of life as theatre, and the idea of playing out a prefabricated or preordained role, evoking connotations quite opposite to spontaneity and authenticity. Thus over the course of the 1970s and early 1980s, Performance moved from a notion of authenticity, inherited from the culture of the 1960s, to a notion of the death of the self, of human life as a decentred

bundle of roles or *masks, of the individual as a role player with multiple, disjunctive identities.

What differentiates Performance from other arts? Clearly it is not a matter of medium. Music, for instance, might be identified as the art form whose medium is sound, while literature can be identified as the art whose medium is language. But Performance makes use of every available medium, material, or even art form, including *film, music, painting, sculpture, theatre, dance, architecture, photography, and so on. Many Performance pieces employ more than one medium, for instance Laurie *Anderson's use of music with technologically altered instruments and voices, choreographed actions, slide and film projections, video, and holograms. But that does not imply that Performance is necessarily *multimedia. For example, performances by action artists and body artists like Vito Acconci, Chris Burden, Otto Muehl, Joseph Beuys, and Ulay/Abramović in the mid-1970s involved the stark confrontation of bodies and objects in social situations, without extraneous media, creating political metaphors and at times bordering on the violent with the simplest, most elemental of means.

One might think that Performance requires the presence of a performer. But even that broad generalization is thwarted when we consider that a Performance piece may be comprised of the action of *puppets or automata, the movement of objects or machinery (like those of Survival Research Laboratories), or a succession of slide images. Nor does Performance require the presence of an *audience, as Allan *Kaprow's participatory performances, evolving out of *happenings, and Anna Halprin's movement *rituals show. Some have characterized Performance as involving non-professionals, but Eric *Bogosian and Spalding *Gray, as well as the members of *Mabou Mines, are all professional *actors. Can we say that a Performance piece organizes actions and events non-narratively? No, because that would exclude the work of artists like Carmelita Tropicana, Robbie McCauley, and Tim *Miller.

Even though an essential definition may never be found for Performance, there are other ways in which it may be portrayed as an interrelated body of activity. Its unity may be characterized historically or genetically or narratively. The cohesion of recent Performance activity is primarily a matter of inheritance—it is an evolving conversation whose narrative unity is attributable in large measure to the structure and presuppositions of the opening moves of the discourse.

Contemporary Performance seems to emerge from two dominant sources. On the one hand, it was a reaction by certain

painters and sculptors to what they believed to be the fundamental theoretical limitations of gallery aesthetics in the 1960s.
Call this dimension of Performance *art performance*. On the
other hand, at roughly the same time, practitioners of theatre
initiated a revolt against the dominant and prevailing forms of
drama. Call this dimension of Performance *performance art*.
Although art performance and performance art arose in reaction against distinctly different art forms, the two movements
have at times cross-fertilized and overlapped with important
effects. There are differences between Performance practitioners
primarily involved in the gallery-related polemics of art performance and those involved more in the avant-garde theatre
debates of performance art. But the merging of these points of
departure into a generic tradition has become increasingly
salient.

2. Art performance

Art performance is the label for those Performance activities
that originate in the concerns of the fine arts. Many of the European avant-garde art movements of the first half of the twentieth century included para-theatrical auxiliaries, as did both
American and Japanese avant-garde painting and sculpture
during the two decades following the Second World War. Perhaps the stage was set for this post-war activity by some of
the rhetoric used to introduce abstract *expressionism. Harold
Rosenberg dubbed Jackson Pollock's work 'Action Paintings'
and treated his canvases as the tracery of the artist's performative act of painting. Although static, paintings were reconceived
in action terms, rather than object terms, under the category of
performance. Thus in one sense the proponents of art performance literalized the notion that the goal of painting is an activity
or a performance.

But there is another way of charting the emergence of art
performance as a break, rather than a continuity, with art-world
polemics. While abstract expressionism was sometimes characterized as concerned with gesture and action, another interpretation, championed by Clement Greenberg, glossed abstract
expressionism as an exercise in reflexive reductionism which
strove to reveal the essential conditions of painting. In this view,
the abstract expressionist developed the cubist project of acknowledging the surface of the picture plane and asserting
its flatness. Art performance grew out of the repudiation of
this essentialist approach to art, the belief that each art form
has its own delimited nature, fixed by its medium.

While the essentialist paradigm for advanced fine art
gained in stature during the 1950s and 1960s, a counter-
movement of anti-essentialism also gathered strength, often
employing art performance to articulate its anti-essentialist bias.
The most vividly remembered strategy of these 1960s art performances is the happening. One important precedent for happenings was a multimedia event staged by John Cage at Black
Mountain College in 1952, in which a film was shown while

choreographer Merce *Cunningham danced, Charles Olson and
M. C. Richards recited poetry, David Tudor played the piano,
and painter Robert Rauschenberg displayed his work and
played music of his choosing on an old record player. The tenets
of this performance were disseminated in Cage's composition
courses at the New School for Social Research in *New York
during the 1950s, where his students included such figures as
Allan Kaprow, Dick Higgins, Larry Poons, George Brecht, Jackson Mac Low, and Jim Dine. The anti-essentialist message was
that anything could become art. Inspired by Cage, fine artists
displaced their concerns from the canvas and embodied them in
performative *genres like happenings and Fluxus. In a parallel
development, the Japanese groups Gutai Art Association and Hi
Red Centre made art out of actions with objects.

Visual artists looked to performance as a way to break
down distinctions between the arts, to free themselves from
generic rules and boundaries, including restrictive delinea-
tions between the performing and non-performing arts. Their
anti-linear, juxtapositional presentations (rather than *re*-
presentations) putatively trafficked in the real. Their performances were supposedly meant to be real events, rather than
representations of events, and they were related not only
to the anti-illusionism of gallery aesthetics (as in Robert
Rauschenberg's 'combines') but also to the emerging polemics
of avant-garde theatre, in which, as Michael Kirby noted, places
and characters were non-matrixed, non-fictional, and non-
representational. In one way, this view, as articulated by Kirby,
converges on the essentialist view of painting—that a painting
is a real object, paint on a flat canvas. But, in contrast, art performance makers were interested in asserting their works not as
a *special* kind of object but as an object like any other kind of
thing—something ordinary. Hence Fluxus delighted in redis-
covering the world through street tours and mail art. This aspect
of art performance links it to a democratizing impulse in the
arts and culture internationally in the 1960s.

The anti-essentialism of art performance led not only to
a working out of aesthetic concerns in the gallery art world
through *theatricality, but also to alliances with other performing artists—in particular, musicians (like Cage, Robert Ashley,
La Monte Young, Cornelius Cardew, and Pauline Oliveros) and
dancers (especially, in the USA, those associated with the Judson
Dance Theater, including Yvonne Rainer and Steve Paxton). At
the same time, there was cross-fertilization among these fields,
since the visual artists studied with Cage, and the dancers were
influenced by both Cage's and the visual artists' interest in the
real and the ordinary, and later, by minimalism and conceptu-
alism. Their interest in the performative led several visual
artists, such as Rauschenberg, Robert Morris, and Carolee
Schneemann, to make dances, some of which, like Morris's
Site (1964), were concerned with visual perception and aesthetics. This concern finds its parallel in the theatrical performance
art of Richard *Foreman, whose *mise-en-scène has been partly

concerned with framing, *perspective, and perception (see also RECEPTION).

A reaction against another aspect of mainstream gallery aesthetics—its formalism—led, in another way, to 'body art' in the 1970s. Eschewing the flamboyant theatricality of happenings, body artists like Vito Acconi, Chris Burden, Stuart Brisley, and Gina Pane explored issues of risk, death, decision-making, and the psychosexual, often through an existentialist focus on the self through the insistent presence of the body. Also in the 1970s, the closely related movement of conceptual art arose, criticizing the commercial nature of the art world and the commodity status of the art object. For example, in *Catalysis III* (1970), Adrian Piper walked through the streets with 'Wet Paint' printed on her shirt, suggesting the idea 'don't touch' in a way that conflated her rights to sexual autonomy with a gibe aimed at the art world's elevation of the materiality of paint.

As art performance matured in the 1960s and 1970s, it became independent of the movements in the visual art world that spawned it and began to ally itself with other movements. By the 1980s, postmodernism in gallery art, with its programme of exploring and interrogating representations, especially in the *mass media and popular iconography, had a performance component. Laurie Anderson's rock star image had the postmodern quality of both criticizing and participating in contemporary pop culture. And this connected to postmodernism in the theatre, which involved recycling plays, images, and genres, as in the work of director Peter *Sellars. If art performance originally emerged in a cultural moment that valued authenticity and spontaneity, by the 1980s it participated in a cultural moment of anxiety about life as a hollow product of signs and signifying systems (see MODERNISM AND POSTMODERNISM; SEMIOTICS).

An outgrowth or branch of postmodernism in gallery art was the punk movement of the 1980s, which took allusions to popular forms—movies, *television, cartoons, and graffiti—to new heights, while rejecting the polish and expertise of the earlier postmodernists (like Robert Longo). There was an amateur flavour to punk-inspired Performance, a sense of infantile pleasures combined with a feeling of loss, arising, perhaps, from a nostalgia for a post-war period when life seemed simpler and more predictable—a time when many of the younger art performance makers were, in fact, children. The TV talk show, the comedy routine, the *cabaret format were all revived with postmodern irony, not with the loving camp sensibility of the 1960s but with a new sense of cynicism that had a flavour of early *futurist performance. The Kipper Kids' excessive *parody of *music-hall performance, energetically and aggressively assaulting the audience simultaneously with word wit, obscenity, and scatological *props, was a prime example of this branch of art performance, which also overlapped with a parallel emerging sensibility in avant-garde theatre, as in the anti-comedy routines of the Alien Comic.

In the 1970s and 1980s Performance proved a fertile ground for advancing and embodying *feminist politics, allowing an open space for the expression of feelings, fantasies, and political action. In *Los Angeles, Womanhouse, organized by visual artists including Judy Chicago, and the Woman's Building were the site of many installations and performances; during the 1970s, also in California, several women's performance *collectives were founded. In the 1980s and 1990s the French artist Orlan's impossible project of using plastic surgery to mimic images of female beauty in various canonical works by male artists combined feminist social criticism and conceptual art with a new spin on the body art of the 1970s. Janine Antoni's *Loving Care* (1992–6), in which she used her hair as a mop to cover a gallery floor with hair dye, parodically criticized the legacy of male artists like Yves Klein and asserted the female artist's agency. Beginning in 1985, the Guerrilla Girls, a group of anonymous performers wearing gorilla masks, picketed American museums for discriminating against women artists. Their actions connected not only to other feminist movements in visual art, but also to art performances and art-works (for instance, that of Russian artists Komar and Melamid and French artist Daniel Buren) that scrutinized art-world institutions.

By the 1990s American art performance was dominated by identity politics, as not only women but artists of colour asserted their presence in museum exhibitions and in other venues. Coco Fusco and Guillermo *Gómez-Peña underlined the marginalization of Americans of colour and the politics of exhibition when they displayed themselves in art museums and natural history museums as caged exotic specimens of a primitive culture in *Two Undiscovered Amerindians* (1992–4). Toward the end of the twentieth century, new works in art museums were as likely to use new media, such as video and computers, as paint and canvas (see MEDIA AND PERFORMANCE). A number of visual artists have explored the intersection of the possibilities and drawbacks of intensifying technology through live performance. Palestinian-born British artist Mona Hatoum, although known primarily for her video and installation pieces, has worked with video in live performance to explore binaries like live bodies/recorded representations, inside/outside, and private/public, often dealing with themes of suffering and imprisonment, while Australian artist Stelarc works with robotics to extend the capabilities of the human body.

3. Performance art

If art performance emerged out of art-world polemics, performance art was initially a reaction to the polemics and practices of the theatre world in the 1950s and 1960s. Avant-gardists criticized the representationalism of Shakespeare and the modern classics, as well as of popular shows on Broadway and the West End, the spectatorial aspects of mainstream theatre, and its *text-oriented or verbal emphasis. Instead they proposed a theatre that would be presentational, participatory (or at least challenging to the division between spectator and performer), and image oriented as well as kinesthetic. Theatrical performance art brought the performative aspects back to the theatre. One strategy to achieve this goal was to install real events (rather than fictive ones) on stage. So, for different reasons, the art world and the theatre world moved in similar directions, forging a correspondence that has persisted now for over four decades.

The first stage of performance art stemmed from an Artaudian vision of an anti-literary theatre, a view of theatre as a 'concrete physical place', as *Artaud put it, with 'its own concrete language'. This view of theatre reverses the *Aristotelian model that places *spectacle at the bottom of the hierarchy of theatrical elements. According to Artaud and those inspired by his vision, theatre should be emotional and visceral, rather than intellectual (see CRUELTY, THEATRE OF). The *Living Theatre, for example, staged Mysteries and Smaller Pieces (1964) as a series of ritual games without *plot or characters. As in the happenings created by their contemporaries, the Living Theatre breached divisions between spectators and performers in the name of the real. However, there was a difference between the art performance and the performance art of the 1950s and 1960s. While happenings and Fluxus were anti-essentialist, ironically, while employing similar strategies, the Living Theatre, the *Open Theatre, and the 'poor theatre' of Polish director Jerzy *Grotowski were essentialist, searching for the core elements of theatre and theatricality and trying to purify theatre, to strip theatre down to its essence. The actor became a performer rather than a character.

Artaud's emphasis on spectacle led to a consideration of the physicality of the performance space. Not only did the happenings makers and postmodern dancers evince a special interest in articulating space, but so did Foreman, the English director Peter *Brook, and the Hungarian émigré group Squat. Foreman's preoccupation with perspective, perception, and indexical devices, physicalized in production, connected his work in the theatre with the concerns of gallery artists/art performance makers like Michael Snow and Robert Morris. Moreover, the emphasis on the visual generally and hence on the creation of imagery rather than the illustration of texts, moved performance art toward the visual arts, strikingly in the work of Americans Robert *Wilson, Meredith *Monk, and Ping *Chong, and Europeans such as Jan *Fabre (Belgium) and the company La *Fura dels Baus (Spain) in the 1970s and 1980s.

The repudiation of mainstream theatre and even certain strands of avant-garde literary theatre led performance artists in the 1980s to seek out overshadowed, forgotten, or marginalized forms, just as earlier Artaud had been fascinated by Balinese theatre. Performance artists confounded distinctions between high and low culture, reviving forms like *circus, *vaudeville, *magic shows, puppetry, storytelling, comedy routines, and nightclub *variety shows, which converged with the interest in *mass media and popular forms by art performance makers.

Performance artists showed their work in clubs, rather than galleries. Stuart Sherman and Paul Zaloom, each in his own way, created puppet spectacles for avant-garde adult audiences; Spalding Gray appropriated the image of an avant-garde Johnny Carson in Interviewing the Audience, thus mirroring the postmodern turn in art performance.

Perhaps it was a sense of weariness with 1980s performance art as entertainment, divorced from the realities of daily life, that led to the next wave of highly politicized performance art in the 1990s. As in art performance, *feminism had an impact on avant-garde theatre internationally, for instance in the many performances at *WOW Café in New York. In Britain, Rose English and Sally Potter's feminist performances tended toward cinematic imagery, before Potter moved into independent filmmaking. Bobby Baker makes visible and ironic the daily activities of ordinary housewives. Annie Sprinkle, a former *pornographic actress, frankly celebrates women's sexuality with tales and demonstrations of eroticism as well as vulnerability, while Karen *Finley speaks in a Cassandra-like voice of prophecy and possession about women's oppression and abuse.

Feminism was by the 1990s only one branch of multiculturalism, which also included the politics of ethnic identities, sexuality, and ability (see RACE AND THEATRE; GAY THEATRE; LESBIAN THEATRE; QUEER THEORY). Multicultural performance art often took the form of autobiographical confessionals, as in Tim Miller's narratives of gay life in America and Robbie McCauley's stories of her African-American family. This genre was born partly of the widespread use of performance art by feminists (especially in California) in the 1970s, partly of the use of the solo form, which lends itself to autobiography, and partly of the changing, increasingly multicultural demographics of the avant-garde art and theatre worlds, not to mention the world at large. With the expansion of ethnically diverse populations both in the United States and Europe, as well as the intensification of economic and cultural globalization, by the 1990s artists raised questions about who we are, what made us this way, and what is to be done about it. Once again, then, the concerns of art performance and performance art overlapped and intertwined, this time on the terrain of multiculturalism, as they had earlier in the quixotic pursuit of the real.

Not only were ethnic and cultural boundaries interrogated by performance artists of the 1990s, but also the boundaries between media. Video and computer technologies have increasingly attracted performance artists in the 1990s and after, just as they have attracted art performers like Mona Hatoum and Stelarc. New technologies can extend the possibilities of bodies, space, imagery, and point of view in live performance, as well as contrast live and mediated events (see CYBER THEATRE).

In the United States, performance art became notorious and was often censured in the popular press during the 'culture wars', especially when in 1990 the *National Endowment for the

Arts, contravening the recommendations of peer panels, denied funding to four performance artists (Karen Finley, John *Fleck, Holly *Hughes, and Tim Miller), who, over the course of the next several years, pursued their cases through federal courts. In the 1990s US funding shrank for both individual artists and producing organizations, and American performance art was also decimated by the proliferation of cable television and the Internet, which multiplied venues for the subversive acts of social and political criticism that previously had been live performance's domain. In Europe at the turn of the twenty-first century, however, art performance and performance art flourished, often underwritten by state arts funding (see also FINANCE; ARTS COUNCILS).

4. Conclusion

The domain of Performance is marked by a braiding narrative that interweaves art-world and theatre-world issues. In the 1960s a concern with the real made art performance and performance art converge, and in the 1980s a concern with representations (especially ones drawn from popular culture) and their operations also brought fine art and theatre together. By the end of the twentieth century, a concern with political realities as well as political identities (see POLITICS AND THEATRE), often constructed and experienced through a mass media culture and an increasingly virtual culture, once again joined the two strands of Performance in a common bond, a historically contingent united front.   SB/NC

BANES, SALLY, Subversive Expectations: performance art and paratheater in New York, 1976–85 (Ann Arbor, 1998)
CARROLL, NOËL, 'Performance', Formations, 3 (1986)
GOLDBERG, ROSELEE, Performance Art: from futurism to the present, rev. edn. (New York, 2001)
SCHIMMEL, PAUL (ed.), Out of Actions: between performance and the object, 1949–1979 (Los Angeles, 1998)
SHANK, THEODORE, American Alternative Theater (New York, 1982)

research for the discipline. Important publications include Peggy Phelan's Unmarked: the politics of performance (1993), which studies performance art from a feminist perspective, and Judith Butler's Gender Trouble (1990) and Bodies that Matter (1993), which develop the concept of *performativity derived from speech act theory.

A third influence on, and in many respects a development paralleling performance studies, has been cultural studies and the rise of post-structuralist theory (see STRUCTURALISM AND POST-STRUCTURALISM). The centrality of identity politics and marginalized minorities for cultural studies has been echoed in performance studies, underpinned by readings that can be termed ideological. In fact, the areas of interest (particularly in forms of popular culture) are sometimes so close that there seems to be a danger that performance studies could be easily absorbed by cultural studies.

Less developed within performance studies are historical perspectives. This is due, on the one hand, to a suspicion of the traditional historical focus associated with theatre studies, and on the other to the ethnological orientation outlined above. But this too is changing, as recent studies have begun to marry the broader concept of performance with historical phenomena that have been marginalized by theatre studies such as popular entertainment. Particularly influential is Cities of the Dead: circum-Atlantic performance (1996) by Joseph Roach, which moves between *London and New Orleans, the eighteenth and the twentieth centuries, in its analysis of performance, cultural memory, and the slave trade.

Performance studies began as a critical practice. Its main organ was the journal edited by Schechner, Tulane Drama Review, which is today known as TDR: the journal of performance studies and is the most widely read periodical in the field, under his continuing editorship. Other journals are Performing Arts Journal and Performance Research. But most theatre journals now also publish research that owes its methodology to performance studies. In the area of publication the barriers between performance and theatre studies have been largely removed.

The same cannot be said of the institutionalization of performance studies as an independent discipline. In the USA there are still only two departments of performance studies: the graduate programme at New York University (established by Schechner in the early 1980s) and the Department of Performance Studies at Northwestern University, which also offers the subject at undergraduate level. Research and teaching using a performance studies methodology and objects of enquiry are, however, widespread in many theatre departments, especially at graduate level. In Britain, the situation is roughly similar. A low degree of specific institutionalization (the broadest application has been at the University of Aberystwyth) has not prevented a spread of courses and research into the subject. Although it is difficult to provide an accurate international perspective, the rapid growth of the organization Performance Studies International (founded in 1993) has demonstrated vigorous interest in many countries.   CBB

CARLSON, MARVIN, Performance: a critical introduction (1996)
REINELT, J., and ROACH, J. (eds.), Critical Theory and Performance (1992)
SCHECHNER, RICHARD, Performance Studies: an introduction (2002)

PERFORMATIVITY

A term that has come into performance *theory and criticism from philosophy, specifically through the speech act theory of J. L. Austin. Although Austin first presented How To Do Things with Words as a series of lectures at Harvard University in 1955, his work enjoyed a major reconsideration and reformulation at the end of the century in the work of Judith Butler and Jacques Derrida, among others. Performance scholars have come to find the language of performativity useful because it draws on etymological sources shared by *performance while delineating a special attribute which some, but not all, performances may evidence.

Following Austin, certain utterances can be said to be performative when the pronouncement itself makes the action. 'I swear', 'I do' (marry), 'I judge' are typical examples in which it 'seems clear that to utter the sentence (in, of course, the appropriate circumstances) is not to *describe* my doing of what I should be said in so uttering to be doing or to state that I am doing it: it is to do it'. Ironically, Austin excluded theatrical utterances from his original conception of performatives, finding them peculiarly hollow, and 'parasitic' on normal usages. Derrida, on the contrary, recovers the theatre for performatives in his critique of Austin. He insists that the general condition of language is iteration—'iterability'—which makes theatrical utterances not an exception but an instance of the general condition of all utterances, insofar as they are an iteration of a prior linguistic structure. All utterances experience a structural break between the previous form of the utterance and the new iteration. Although this does not guarantee a significant difference, it does guarantee the possibility of difference. Judith Butler, in a pair of books on *gender performances (*Gender Trouble*, 1990; *Bodies that Matter*, 1993), argued that the possibility of intervention and redescription of sexual norms is inherent in the structure of the speech act itself. For while the subject is controlled by certain social norms, the law itself is dependent on being cited and is confirmed in the repetition of its prescriptions. Since performatives can fail (Austin calls failed cases 'infelicities'), the resulting destabilization of law allows an opening for resistance and also for transformation in iteration. However, repeated successful iterations result over time in a kind of sedimentation that makes transformation difficult, even extraordinary.

The usefulness of these theories for performance theory and criticism lies in the enquiry into what 'laws' or norms of social behaviour are reinstituted in various stagings (for example, tropes of the nuclear family, heterosexuality, racial inequality and prejudice, or national myths), and what deviations or transgressions appear to challenge confirmation of the repetition. How much difference in the iteration (the performance) is enough to upset the cultural norm? And how much voluntary power do individual subjects need to alter their habitual citations of the norms of their culture? The force of the performative is precisely its claim to power, thus performances can be seen as sites of struggle over contested social norms.

One way the discourse of performativity operates is to emphasize the making or taking-place of performances. Vivian Patraka, for example, has described how spectators are positioned by the Holocaust Museum in Washington and the *Los Angeles Museum of Tolerance to enter a performative space. In *Spectacular Suffering* (1999), she writes that 'It is the museum-goers (along with the guards) who constitute the live, performing bodies in museums. They are the focus of a variety of performance strategies deployed by museums for the sake of "the production of knowledge taken in and taken home".'

An alternative point of view holds that often in the new theory an overemphasis on the actant-subject has resulted in the neglect of the context of the performative act. This criticism has been raised against Butler's early work: the context may provide more performative force than the performing subject itself. In such cases, performativity is hardly voluntary; it may emerge as accidental or, alternatively, constrained. If performative acts are constrained in some fashion, their iteration is at least partially involuntary, undetermined, and perhaps even unintended by the actant. Repetitions of this type cannot be completely novel or innovative, and in fact may well support or enforce the performance of the law. For example, white performers in blackface may provoke negative reactions because, given the history of *racist uses of blackface by white performers, especially in America, the repetition of the act in the next context still triggers historical associations. Thus, against their intentions, performers may find themselves engaged in racist actions through repetition of past iterations which cannot be displaced. In 1981 the *Wooster Group encountered this problem in *Route 1 & 9*. The group intended a citation to the blackface routine of an actual *African-American entertainer (Pigmeat Markham) in order to redeploy it as an anti-racist parody of Thornton *Wilder's *Our Town*. However, since the Wooster Group was all white, the blackface parody misfired because it could not be read unambiguously, due to the constraints of past iterations of white *minstrel shows. The New York State Council on the Arts had been a major source of funding and withdrew 40 per cent of its subsidy because of 'harsh and caricatured portrayals of a racial minority'. Thus the performative intention of the artists was overwhelmed by historical forces that could not be escaped.   JGR

DIAMOND, ELIN (ed.), *Performance and Cultural Politics* (London, 1996)

PARKER, ANDREW, and SEDGWICK, EVE KOSOFSKY (eds.), *Performativity and Performance* (London, 1995)

PERIAKTOI

*Vitruvius describes a mysterious *Greek theatrical device, not archaeologically attested. In the Hellenistic theatre between each side wing and the outside doors on the stage front there were triangular painted panels (*scaenae*) which could be turned at crucial moments to represent different scenes. The second-century grammarian Pollux asserts that one side illustrated the country, the other the town, especially the harbour; but they also represented gods, streams, and anything too difficult for other mechanisms. This short-lived experiment at stage *realism by the technicians of Hellenistic drama influenced the *early modern imitators of antiquity. *See* SCENOGRAPHY   WJS

PERIPETEIA

An unexpected reversal or a sudden turn of events in the *plot of a *drama that leads to an opposite state of affairs. *Aristotle identified *peripeteia* as an element in a complex plot and linked it with *anagnorisis* (recognition), a new perception or discovery on the part of the *protagonist. Since there can be several instances of *peripeteia* in a play (for instance *Sophocles' *Oedipus the King*) it ought not to be confused with *metabasis*, a general change over the course of a play from prosperity to adversity or vice versa. Aristotle's examples of *peripeteia* underscore the irony of blasted expectation that characterizes this acute form of *metabasis*.   RWV

PERKINS, OSGOOD (1892–1937)

Lean and energetic American comic actor and father of actor Anthony Perkins. After study with George Pierce *Baker at Harvard and military service, Perkins produced and acted in silent *films. He made a belated stage debut in 1924 in *Beggar on Horseback*, and his career caught fire in 1928 with the role of Walter Burns, the wisecracking newspaper editor in *MacArthur and *Hecht's *The Front Page*. In demand for stage and film, he appeared as Sganarelle in *Molière's *School for Husbands*, Astrov in *Chekhov's *Uncle Vanya*, and Johnny Lovo in the film *Scarface* (1932). He died unexpectedly during a preview run in Washington.   MAF

PERLINI, AMELIO ('MEMÉ') (1947–)

Italian actor, director, and cinematographer. In 1973, with the *lighting artist and designer Antonello Aglioti and the musician Alain Curran, Perlini formed Teatro La Maschera, *Rome, and established himself as an important voice in the Italian *avant-garde with the productions of *Pirandello chi?* (*Pirandello Who?*, 1973), *Tarzan* (1975), *Candore giallo (con suono di mare)* (*Yellow Whiteness, with Sounds of the Sea*, 1974), *Othello perche?* (*Why Othello?*, 1975), *Paesaggio n. 5* (*Landscape No. 5*, 1975), and *Locus Solus* (1976). Perlini aimed not to please but to provoke his *audience, to jangle their expectations of theatre as a *spectacle of *scenery and *costumes designed to support a literary *text involving specific *characters. Thus he shrank text to segmented phrases and sounds and, from a position in front of the stage, manipulated lighting in such a way as to reduce actors, objects, and scenery to fragments; the *surreal, *dreamlike atmosphere was heightened by contemporary *music, such as that of Philip *Glass.   JEH

PERRY, JOÃO (1940–)

Portuguese actor and director. He began his career in 1953 at the Teatro *Nacional D. Maria II and became a permanent actor there in 1978, but during the 1960s and 1970s he worked with *alternative companies. Born into a family of actors, his own stage presence and versatility were confirmed by distinguished performances in a wide variety of productions, ranging from drama, *comedy, and *variety to *television and *film. Productions such as *Tango, Equus, Baal*, and *Emigrants* (*Emigranci*) were valued for his meticulous and creative characterization and *Stanislavskian exploration of the psychological dimension of the *actor. He worked with *La Mama Experimental Theatre Club in *New York, where he made his debut as a director in *Stolen Words* (1971). He has since directed Herman Broch, *Marivaux, Shakespeare, and an *opera by Cimarosa.

MJB

PERSPECTIVE

Shortly after the rediscovery of *Vitruvius in the *early modern period, and in accord with the rapid development of perspective in the graphic arts, experiments began in Italy with *painted scenes in perspective in the early sixteenth century. *Serlio's 1545 treatise transmitted the idea to the rest of Europe, where it caught on over the next 100 years, especially in aristocratic theatres under the influence of *neoclassicism. Perspective's ability to create apparent reality (*see* REALISM AND REALITY), provided that the visual angle subtended is kept small, made an important difference: the *audience now seemed to look through a window into the *illusion of another world. Unlike *medieval theatre traditions, which depended on the presence of the actor against a simple or unencumbered ground, in the perspective stage the fictive world is actualized primarily by *trompe l'œil*. Although the visceral impact is greater because the mediation occurs through a less conscious process, the theatre of perspective scenery is limited to what can be convincingly painted and by the necessity to restrict sight lines to a very small range of angles. Staging becomes the task of the scenographer (and eventually in history, of the *director), not the actor. To see the play, the spectators must lose sight of one another. Thus the four-century-long shift of emphasis toward a visual, emotional, and private response has a partial origin in the development of perspective scenery.

Serlio had designed his stage settings with single-point perspective in mind, a natural choice for the streets or squares of an Italian town. But single-point perspective poses severe problems, since it creates an extremely forced perspective that looks cavernous and renders upstage scenery comically small next to actors, requires distortions in the painting of *flats and wings, and is fully effective for only one seat in the house: the 'king's seat', elevated and at the centre of the

Perspective design of Rome by Baldassare Peruzzi from the early sixteenth century, probably for a tragedy. Castel Sant'Angelo and the ruins of the Colosseum are right and left in the upper background, but the single-point perspective is provided by the elegant houses on the stage floor leading to the vanishing point through the archway upstage. In practice scenography such as this would be realized by a series of painted flats.

*auditorium, some distance from the *stage. For everyone else the picture appears distorted. Around 1700, *scena per angolo (two-point perspective with various scenic devices to accommodate it) revolutionized scene painting. In *scena per angolo*, the gentler perspective obtained by placing the two vanishing points far offstage appears less distorted at all distances from the ideal seat. Perspective scenery became easier to do well once Ferdinando *Bibiena disseminated the techniques of *scena per angolo* in 1732, and it remained an expected part of the visual theatre until well into the twentieth century.

Since about the Second World War, perspective scenery has tended to be three dimensional and designers have preferred to use it only for deliberately forced perspective. Perhaps the favourite contemporary device for forced perspective is to place a few structures, intentionally made smaller than life so as to look far away, in silhouette against a *cyclorama (a barn and windmill, or the skyscrapers of a distant city). The full set in painted perspective is now almost never seen, and given that it can never compete with recorded *media, seems unlikely to reappear except as ironic comment. *See also* SCENOGRAPHY; PROSCENIUM; VISION AND THE VISUAL. JB

PETERSON, HORACIO (1926–)

Chilean-born actor and director who moved to Venezuela in 1948. As director of the Ateneo Theatre in Caracas (1952–70) he introduced classical and *avant-garde works, including H. R. *Lenormand's *Time Is a Dream* (1952) and Thornton *Wilder's *Our Town* (1954), which was his first major success. He is best known for the period 1956–8 when he directed *O'Neill, Arthur *Miller, *Camus, and Tennessee *Williams, along with Andrés Eloy *Blanco and Arturo *Uslar Pietri. He was also director of the Teatro del Pueblo (1955–8), but in 1971 turned to commercial theatre, staging fourteen successful plays, and also establishing the Ana Julia Rojas Theatre Workshop. He was *awarded the National Prize for Theatre in 1985.

LCL trans. AMCS

PETHERBRIDGE, EDWARD (1936–)

Lean and poised English actor and director. His early experience was in *regional repertory and on *tour, making his *London debut at the Regent's Park Open Air Theatre in 1962. He began a long association with the *National Theatre in 1964, appearing in *Trelawny of the 'Wells'* (1965), *Rosencrantz and Guildenstern Are Dead* (1967), *Volpone* (1968), *The Way of the World*, and *The White Devil* (both 1969). He was a founder member of the Actors' Company, appearing in *'Tis Pity She's a Whore*, *The Way of the World*, *Tartuffe*, and *King Lear* (all 1972). For the *Royal Shakespeare Company he was a touching Newman Noggs in *Nicholas Nickleby* (1980). He was co-director of the *McKellen/ Petherbridge group at the National (1984–6), acting in *The Duchess of Malfi*, *The Cherry Orchard*, *The Real Inspector Hound*, and *The Critic* (all 1985). He was seen as Cyrano at Greenwich (1990), in *The Seagull* opposite Judi *Dench at the National (1994), and *Cymbeline* at the RSC (1997). On *television he was Dorothy L. Sayers's eponymous detective *hero in *Lord Peter Wimsey* (1987).

AS

PETIT-BOURBON, THÉÂTRE DU

A long vaulted hall, at 54.6 m (179 feet) the longest in *Paris, used intermittently for court entertainments and, from 1577, when the *Gelosi played there, by travelling professional troupes. It had a high, vaulted apse at one end. Its stage was raised above a flat pit, which also served for performance, and it extended, probably forward of the apse, by some 15.6 m (53 feet). Two superimposed galleries of open *boxes ran along the walls of the *auditorium. In 1645, for Strozzi's machine-play *La finta pazza* (*The Counterfeit Madwoman*), Giacomo *Torelli built a new stage on which he installed, for the first time in France, his revolutionary counterweight *scene-shifting machinery. In 1658 the Petit-Bourbon became *Molière's first Paris home, to be shared with Tiberio *Fiorilli's *commedia dell'arte* company.

Two years later, however, it was demolished, to make way for the colonnade of the Louvre, and Molière was transferred to the *Palais Royal.

JG

PETRUSHEVSKAYA, LYUDMILA (1938–)

Soviet/Russian playwright. Petrushevskaya began writing in the 1970s but her plays reached the stage only after glasnost. *Music Lessons* (1972) had been written for the *Moscow Art Theatre but was never staged there; Roman *Viktyuk's *amateur production at Moscow State University (1987) was closed after it caused too much *publicity. Her second play, *Cinzano* (1973), staged at the Studio Chelovek in *Moscow in 1987, was one of the first swallows of glasnost, portraying the squalor of everyday life and addressing openly the issue of alcoholism. By the late 1980s, *Three Girls in Blue* (1983) was in the repertoire of the Lenin Komsomol Theatre, *Columbine's Apartment* (1988) was playing at the *Sovremennik, and the studio production of *Cinzano* was touring European *festivals. Petrushevskaya strikes a neat balance in her plays between everyday life scenes and their absurd, grotesque, and ironic theatricalization. Her plays provide glimpses of mundane existence, spoofs at best; they are void of any development. She uses gossipy, but not vulgar language. Beyond the witty and ironic discourse lies the bleakness of Soviet life: the ordinary problems of women in *Three Girls in Blue*, the drunkenness of the three men in *Cinzano*, the shortage of living space and its crippling effect on human relations in her short play *Love*.

BB

PEYMANN, CLAUS (1937–)

German director. Peymann first attracted national attention with his production of Peter *Handke's *Offending the Audience* (Frankfurt, 1966). After a short period as a co-director at the new *Schaubühne in *Berlin (1971), he worked freelance at major theatres. From 1974 to 1979 he was *artistic director at Stuttgart's State Theatre but was forced to resign in 1979 after a scandal surrounding his alleged sympathies with the terrorist movement the Red Army Faction. He moved with his troupe to Bochum where he remained until 1986, when he assumed control of *Vienna's *Burgtheater. In 1999 he was appointed *artistic director of the *Berliner Ensemble. Peymann is representative of a group of German directors in the late 1960s who tried to reform the established theatre through a combination of collective management and politically inflected productions. His career has always been accompanied by carefully orchestrated controversy, both artistic and political. His productions are characterized by careful *dramaturgical preparation and topical interpretations of the classics. He has developed special relationships with Austrian dramatists such as Handke, Thomas *Bernhard, and Peter Turrini, directing many of the first productions of their plays.

CBB

PHALLUS

A false penis worn by actors in certain forms of classical and classically derived *comedy. Carried also as a serious symbol of regeneration in religious processions, an exaggerated phallus made of leather was sported by some *characters in *Old Comedy and in a variety of local *farces in Greece and Italy. *See* GREEK THEATRE, ANCIENT.   JMW

PHELPS, SAMUEL (1804–78)

English actor and *manager. Phelps began his career as a strolling player, and then joined the York circuit in 1826. In 1837 he first appeared in *London at the *Haymarket, in a series of Shakespearian roles. Except for Iago, Phelps played only supporting roles with *Macready at *Covent Garden (1837–9). In 1844, taking advantage of changes in the law permitting any theatre to perform the *legitimate drama, Phelps leased *Sadler's Wells with the actress Mary Warner. She left after two seasons; Phelps stayed until he resigned the management in 1862. At an entirely unfashionable theatre in north-east London, remote from the West End, Phelps presented 31 of Shakespeare's plays in eighteen seasons (fourteen in the 1856–7 season alone), new plays, and revivals of significant Elizabethan and Jacobean plays then almost unknown. In doing so he attracted a loyal local *audience and some support from West End theatregoers. Lacking Macready's jealousy of potential rivals, Phelps stressed thorough *rehearsals, ensemble, unified productions, and pleasingly illustrative but not lavish *scenery and *spectacle. In this last respect his *Pericles* (1854) and *Midsummer Night's Dream* (1853) were outstanding. After he left Sadler's Wells, Phelps spent his time fishing, returning to the stage in the provinces and in London. His last role was Cardinal Wolsey in *Henry VIII* in 1878. In his large repertory, Phelps was especially admired as Lear and Othello, and although he was not a natural comedian his Bottom and Falstaff were the best of their time.   MRB

PHILADELPHIA

The most populous city in early America, Philadelphia developed an important theatre culture in spite of religious opposition. The first known theatre production occurred in 1749, when *Cato* was performed in a warehouse owned by William Plumstead. The warehouse was used subsequently by the Murray–Kean and *Hallam companies. David *Douglass built the Society Hill Theatre for the Hallam company in 1759, locating it just outside the city in an attempt to avoid protest. A legal challenge was mounted, but the judge in the case attributed 'more moral virtue' to plays than to sermons, and allowed the company to perform. Douglass built the *Southwark Theatre in 1766, considered the first permanent *playhouse in America, and again overcame legal challenges to *acting. The first pro-

fessional production of a play by an American, Thomas *Godfrey's *The Prince of Parthia*, was performed there in 1767. During the revolution, the Southwark served as a hospital until the British occupied Philadelphia and used it for *amateur theatricals.

The ban on theatre enacted at the beginning of the revolution was not rescinded in Pennsylvania until 1789. The Douglass–Hallam company called their theatre 'Opera House Southwark', and disguised plays as moral lectures. When the ban was finally lifted, after a contentious campaign, Philadelphia acquired a second theatre. Thomas *Wignell, who had broken off from Douglass–Hallam, partnered with musician Alexander Reinagle to build the *Chestnut Street Theatre. Opened in 1794, its elegant building and brilliant corps of actors made the Chestnut Street the pre-eminent theatre of its time. Theatrical activity expanded in scope when John B. Ricketts opened the Pantheon, offering *circus and *variety acts.

In the nineteenth century, theatrical pre-eminence shifted to *New York, but Philadelphia maintained a significant level of activity. Native Philadelphians Joseph *Jefferson III and William *Warren became stars, and Edwin *Forrest made the city his home. The Pepin and Breschard Circus built a pavilion, which was converted to a *playhouse in 1811 and renamed the Olympic. This building, remodelled, became the *Walnut Street Theatre in 1820. The *Arch Street Theatre was built in 1828, but competing *managers struggled in a city that seemed unable to support three playhouses. Theatrical renown returned in the 1860s, when Louisa Lane *Drew managed the Arch Street, with an outstanding *stock company. It continued successfully for 30 years, training new actors, including the young Drews and Ada *Rehan, until the rise of the combination system forced its closure.

The twentieth century brought the development of *regional and *community theatre. The Plays and Players Club, begun in 1911, continues to be active, and the Hedgerow Theatre, founded in 1923, was the first theatre *collective in the United States. Occupying an old mill and composed of actors dissatisfied with commercial theatre, it presented year-round repertory through 1958. Theatre for the Living Arts experimented with repertory in the 1960s. Philadelphia restored the Walnut Street Theatre in 1968; it remains the oldest operating theatre in America. Since 1970, the Philadelphia Drama Guild, Philadelphia Theatre Company, and Wilma Theatre have provided professional productions.   AHK

PHILIPE, GÉRARD (1922–59)

French actor. Often considered one of the finest of his generation, and elevated to cult status after his untimely death from cancer, Philipe starred in many acclaimed *films after the Second World War, working with some of the finest directors of French cinema including Claude Autant-Lara, René Clair, Max Ophuls, René Clement, and Roger Vadim. His iconic status in

French culture is also due to Jean *Vilar's vision for the *Théâtre National Populaire, where Philipe attracted large popular *audiences, performing in classical roles for which he became celebrated as a romantic *hero for the modern age: *Corneille's *Le Cid*, *Hugo's *Ruy Blas*, and *Kleist's *Prince of Homburg*.

DGM

PHILIPPINE EDUCATIONAL THEATRE ASSOCIATION

Organization founded in April 1967 by Cecile Guidote-Alvarez. Her pioneering work was continued by PETA's members when she went into exile in 1973 during the Marcos dictatorship. PETA's outreach workshops, conducted in all parts of the *Philippines, have created the foundation for a national theatre and prompted the establishment of a number of theatre groups. Its unique theatre curriculum influenced community theatre movements in Asia, the Pacific, Australia, and Filipino communities in Europe and the United States. PETA's home, the Rajah Sulayman Theatre, rose from the ruins of a Spanish fort in the heart of old Manila in Intramuros. A multi-platform *stage area surrounds the *audience in an *open-air *playhouse by the Pasig River. The Kalinangan Ensemble, PETA's repertory arm, has offered more than 300 productions here, characterized by the 'aesthetics of poverty' for plays which tackle Philippine sociopolitical concerns. Key productions have included Virginia Moreno's *Bayaning Huwad* (*The Straw Patriot*), Orlando Nadres's *Hanggang Dito na Lamang at Maraming Salamat* (*Thank You and Goodbye*, 1975), Malou Jacob's *Juan Tamban* (1979), Eman Lacaba's *May-i, May-i* (1979), Nicanor Tiongson's *Pilipinas Circa 1907* (1982), and Rody Vera's *Radiya Mangandiri* (1993). PETA has also performed in key cities around the world, and some of the Philippines' most celebrated *film and theatre artists have been members. Its numerous programmes include theatre for *youth, teen theatre, women's theatre, playwrights' development, and *theatre-in-education.

RV

PHILIPPINES

Greatly affected by a long period of colonization, first by Spain (1565–1898) and then by America (1901–46), much performance activity since the creation of the Philippine Republic in 1946 continues to show the overlay of imperial cultures on indigenous traditions. Among cultural minorities, indigenous dramas still include *rituals, *dances, and other customs with a mimetic character. Rituals centre on the shaman who, representing the spirit, kills a sacrificial pig or chicken at liminal moments: to ensure good health or fortune at a child's birth, circumcision, or initial menstruation; at the time of courtship, marriage, or sickness; or to pray for a sumptuous harvest or for victory in war. Dances imitate animals (monkeys, birds, butter-flies, squirrels), tribal activities (planting and harvesting of rice, warfare, hunting and gathering), or highlight episodes from ethno-epics. Finally, mimetic customs act out the settlement of bridal dowry, or the preparation of provisions for the 'departure' of the dead. Indigenous dramas of these types are tightly woven into the lives of tribal Filipinos.

The 333 years of Spanish rule witnessed the rise of secular plays like the *komedya, religious dramas like the *sinakulo, and a host of *didactic playlets which enact episodes from Christ's life. Staged during town fiestas, the *komedya* narrates the lives of pueblo patron saints or, more commonly, the epic stories of love and vengeance from medieval kingdoms in Europe and the Middle East. For several days in Lent, the *sinakulo* stages the history of Christian salvation, highlighting Christ's Passion, death, and Resurrection. Traditional *Passion plays (similar to those from *medieval theatre in Europe or the *auto sacramental) feature chanted *dialogue, marches, and *acting conventions which distinguish between the 'holy people' (Christ, the Marys, the apostles) and the *villains (those responsible for Christ's sufferings). During the Christmas season, short plays dramatize the search for an inn by Mary and Joseph on 24 December (*panunuluyan*), the adoration of the shepherds (*pastores*), and the journey of the Three Kings to Bethlehem (*tatlong hari*). During Holy Week, short dramas depict Christ's entry into Jerusalem on Palm Sunday (*osana*), the way of the cross (*via crucis*), the washing of the feet of the apostles (*paghuhugas*), the Last Supper (*huling hapunan*), the Seven Last Words (*siete palabras*), the meeting of Christ and the Virgin on Easter Sunday (*salubong*), and the martyrdom of Longinus (*moriones*). In general theatre underwent a radical reorientation under Spain, mirroring no longer the lives of the indigenous people but the religion and culture of the European overlords, serving to form a mentality that saw the Europeans as superior in race and religion and to create a passivity which made Filipinos accept colonial oppression.

Although introduced by Spanish troupes in the nineteenth century, the *drama* and *sarswela flourished only from 1900 to 1940. The *drama* is a prose play (mostly tragic) about love between typical Filipino *characters. From 1900 to 1905, the *drama*'s love story was allegorized by patriotic playwrights, as in Juan Abad's *Tanikalang Ginto* (*Golden Chain*), in order to protest American occupation of the islands and exhort *audiences to unite against the new colonizer. To avoid further persecution by the American military, *drama* playwrights later had to content themselves with the lachrymose arguments of tragic romances. More comic in spirit is the *sarswela*, a prose play with songs and dances, which used social themes like usury, corrupt politicians, colonial mentality, gambling, drinking, and marital infidelity to fuel its predictable love stories. Both *drama* and *sarswela* presented social conflicts which were resolved through an ending that reaffirmed the values of establishment morality.

American colonial rule affected Philippine theatre in form and content. Rising in the 1920s, *bodabil* was a *variety show which featured American popular dances and songs as well as *magic tricks and comedy skits. During the Japanese occupation (1942–5), an enlarged version of *bodabil* called 'stage show' included the *drama* as its main feature. Meanwhile Western plays in English or English translation were studied and staged in schools. Standard were Shakespeare's *Romeo and Juliet*, *The Merchant of Venice*, and *Hamlet*, as well as the *Greek classics, modern plays (Tennessee *Williams and Arthur *Miller), and Broadway *musicals and *comedies. Both *bodabil* and the plays in English went a long way to reorient Philippine theatre from its Hispanic past to its American present, teaching not only the language of the new overlords but their culture and history as well.

But even as Filipinos began to be Americanized in thought and taste, they were exposed to dramatic *theories and styles that introduced new perspectives and expanded the theatrical vocabulary. In the period of the republic the search for a Filipino cultural identity provided the matter, motive, and styles of significant original plays. Inspired by *Ibsen and other Western writers, the drama of *realism foregrounded the psychological problems of flesh-and-blood characters, as in Nick *Joaquin's *Portrait of the Artist as Filipino* (1952), or social issues that overwhelm the individual, as in Alberto Florentino's *The World is an Apple* (1955). Inspired by Bertolt *Brecht and Augusto *Boal, most of the non-realistic styles of contemporary theatre evolved during the Ferdinand Marcos dictatorship (1972–86) as ways of exposing Marcos's abuses while eluding arrest. Consciously destroying *illusion, these performances often employed symbols, *mime, *dance, song, and stylized *scenery, *costumes, and *props to critique contemporary political, social, or economic ideas. Among the styles used by theatre activists during the time of martial law were the *expressionistic *allegory, the *documentary (with slides and narration), *epic theatre, the *tula-dula* (a poem dramatized for rallies), as well as rock musicals and dance-dramas using ethnic themes, movements, costumes, and instruments. At the start of the new millennium theatre artists continue to reflect and interpret change and the myriad conflicts in Philippine society, as they fuse realistic and non-realistic styles, adapting foreign dramatic *genres to local material, and revitalize traditional forms. *See also* BALTAZAR, FRANCISCO; TOLENTINO, AURELIO; PHILIPPINE EDUCATIONAL THEATRE ASSOCIATION. NGT

PHILIPS, AMBROSE (1675–1749)

English playwright, the author of *The Distressed Mother* (1711), an adaptation of *Racine's *Andromaque* and one of the most popular *neoclassical *tragedies of the eighteenth century. Philips wrote two other tragedies, *The Briton* (1722) and *Humfrey, Duke of Gloucester* (1723), but neither achieved lasting fame. Immortalized by Henry *Carey as 'Namby Pamby', and as a member of *Addison's little senate, Philips also earned the enmity of Pope, who attacked his pastoral poetry. MJK

PHILLIPS, AUGUSTINE (fl. 1593–1605)

English actor who began his career with *Strange's Men but had joined the *Chamberlain's Men by 1594. He was one of the original shareholders in the *Globe *playhouse in 1599 and is listed in many documentary sources pertaining to that company, including the actor lists of 1603 and 1604 and the cast lists of *Jonson's *Sejanus*, *Every Man in his Humour*, and *Every Man out of his Humour*. Phillips performed Sardanapalus in *Tarlton's *The Seven Deadly Sins, Part II*, but his other roles are unknown. He mentioned many celebrated players in his will, including Shakespeare and Henry *Condell. SPC

PHILLIPS, ROBIN (1942–)

Anglo-Canadian director. Born in Surrey, Phillips acted and directed with the *Chichester Festival and *Royal Shakespeare Company, and served as *artistic director of the Greenwich Company Theatre in *London. In 1975 he was appointed artistic director of Canada's *Stratford Festival, which he revitalized with several productions that combined audacious staging with brilliant illumination of *text. Enormously energetic, in six seasons there Phillips directed 29 productions and six revivals, including celebrated versions of *Measure for Measure*, *As You Like It*, and *Richard III*. But his tenure at Stratford began in controversy—a foreigner appointed in nationalistic times— and his departure in 1980 sparked a lengthy struggle over succession. Since then Phillips has served as artistic director of the Grand Theatre in London, Ontario (1983–4), and the Citadel Theatre in Edmonton (1990–5), but has worked mainly as a freelance. Acclaimed productions have included Andrew *Lloyd Webber's *Aspects of Love* (Edmonton, *Toronto, and US *tour, 1991–2), *Schiller's *Don Carlos* (Toronto, 1998), and several productions for the Stratford Festival and the Canadian Opera Company. DWJ

PHILLIPS, STEPHEN (1864–1915)

English playwright. For a brief period Phillips, a cousin of Frank *Benson, was celebrated by the *London theatre community as a new poetic dramatist. Beerbohm *Tree produced *Herod* (1900) and *Ulysses* (1902); George *Alexander produced *Paolo and Francesca* (1902). The praise was excessive, setting up expectations that Phillips was unable to meet. *Nero* (1906) and *Faust* (1908), both produced by Tree, failed, and with that Phillips's career collapsed. His last two plays, *Iole* (1913) and *The Sin of David* (1914), found little support, and he died destitute. TP

PHLYAKES

*Farcical plays from the *Greek cities of southern Italy. The word *phlyakes* can mean either the plays themselves or those who acted in them. Though attributed to Rhinthon in the third century BC, the form may go much further back, offering an unsophisticated alternative to the more literary *New Comedy of Greece and Italy. Because they were performed in makeshift conditions and were free from a formal written *text, their content and nature are largely conjectured from illustrations found on Italian pots and vases. Themes were mythological or domestic, featuring actors in *masks, and with padded *costume including the *phallus.   JMW

PHOENIX THEATRE (LONDON) *See* CURTAIN THEATRE.

PHOENIX THEATRE (NEW YORK)

An early *Off-Broadway theatre, the Phoenix was founded in 1953 by Norris *Houghton and T. Edward Hambleton on lower 2nd Avenue in *New York. Their reputation was established with *The Golden Apple* (1954), an innovative small *musical by composer Jerome Moss and words by John Latouche. The theatre performed an eclectic repertoire of plays including works by *Brecht, *Pirandello, *Chekhov, Shakespeare, and *Schiller, featuring stars such as Zero *Mostel, Irene *Worth, Montgomery Clift, and Uta *Hagen. It also offered new plays such as Arthur *Kopit's *Oh Dad, Poor Dad, Mamma's Hung You in the Closet and I'm Feelin' So Sad* (1964). In 1964 the Phoenix merged with the Association of Producing Artists, founded in 1960 by Ellis Rabb, and the combined companies offered a repertory of classics and revivals of modern plays. Despite their popularity with critics and *audiences, the APA-Phoenix suffered repeated *financial losses and closed in 1970.   MAF

PHYSICAL THEATRE

A relatively new term open to provocative debate. Theatre based on physicality has always existed, ranging from the *circus (using skills like *juggling, *acrobatics, trapeze, and *clowning) and *commedia dell'arte* to *mime, *pantomime, and *dance-theatre. 'Physical theatre', however, attempts to describe a type of hybridized non-traditional theatre which places emphasis on physical virtuosity but is not exclusively dance, and which, although it often uses words, usually does not begin with a written *text (*see also* DEVISING). Its creators often use an image, an object, a movement, or a gesture as a point of departure.

Many early twentieth-century theatre visionaries (*Craig, *Appia, *Jaques-Dalcroze, *Artaud), certainly without knowing it, helped prepare the way for physical theatre, but perhaps none more than Jacques *Copeau. His approach to the playing space required the *actor to exist on stage in a way which was simultaneously revolutionary and traditional. At the Théâtre du *Vieux-Colombier (founded 1913), Copeau covered the orchestra pit and extended the *forestage in a semicircle into the *audi-

torium. His idea was to return the theatre to what he considered its golden ages by eliminating the *proscenium arch and *scenery, which cluttered the space and hampered the actor's movement and the *audience's imagination. Copeau's inspirations—the *Greek theatre, the Elizabethan stage, the *commedia dell'arte*, the circus ring, *Japanese *nō—all had open performing areas which used scenery sparingly, arranging the audience on more than one side.

This open space, Copeau realized, required actors who could occupy it with authority. To achieve this, he began a school which instituted *training in many forms of movement: *ballet, gymnastics, *masked *improvisation, corporeal mime, nō, and clowning, paving the way for a synthesis of physical forms. Exercises from the École du Vieux-Colombier gave rise to the careers of Étienne *Decroux and Jacques *Lecoq, and through them many others: Jean-Louis *Barrault, Marcel *Marceau, Ariane *Mnouchkine, Mummenschanz, Robert *Wilson, Robert *Lepage, Simon *McBurney, and many who, rather than 'saying the text and making appropriate gestures' (*Grotowski's words), relegated the script to a secondary role, created it or adapted it themselves, or treated it unconventionally. Copeau, who was not alone in opening this Pandora's box, would be shocked by what he provoked, since he believed the theatre's task was to serve the *playwright faithfully.

The development of physical theatre also coincided with a growing awareness of Asian forms and the rediscovery of the body through *sport. Western innovators of the early twentieth century were in many cases inspired by glimpses of non-Western forms in which actors were also dancers, singers, and acrobats, and where scenery, when it existed, was sparse and symbolic, allowing space for movement of the actors' bodies and the spectator's imagination (*see* SCENOGRAPHY). This *open stage, like a sports stadium, a boxing ring, or a circus floor, provoked several innovators to find inspiration in boxing (Decroux and *Brecht, among others), gymnastics, and clowning. In 1915 Copeau began to require his students to train physically, first with Dalcroze's exercises and later with the study of Herbertism (gymnastics based on work movements), and in 1924 he produced his own version of a nō play. In 1931 Artaud saw Balinese dancers at the Colonial Exposition in *Paris, and wrote enthusiastically about them. In his 'An Affective Athleticism' (1935) he also asserted that 'French actors now know only how to talk.' Brecht, who saw *Mei Lanfang's Beijing opera (*jingju*) performance in 1936, greatly admired the actors' acrobatic quality.

From the *London Mime Festival's programme for the year 2000, the following description of a performance by No Ordinary Angels reveals one of the forms physical theatre might take: 'Mix the skills and thrills of circus with gymnastics, dance and theatre and you have *Deadly*—a powerfully erotic, multi-award winning portrayal of the Seven Deadly Sins. Set against a background of music from techno to classical, the atmosphere positively crackles with electricity as New Zealander Deborah Pope and Brazilian Rodrigo Matheus create one stunning image after another, and you are left breathless with admiration for the beauty of the human form.' At the beginning of the twenty-first century physical theatre is a hybridized and hyphenated art, relying on the physical skills from the Western tradition and the rigorous physical training of Asian forms, and combining them in an exemplary postmodern fashion to create something that is simultaneously new and old. *See also* MODERNISM AND POSTMODERNISM; PERFORMANCE ART. TL

PIAF, ÉDITH (1915–63)

Famed French singer who supported herself as a child by singing in the *Paris streets. As a *cabaret and *music-hall artist, her intensity, nostalgic lyrics, and strident yet controlled voice greatly moved her *audiences, especially coming from such a tiny, waifish figure. Piaf *toured widely as a singer, and acted in *films as well as stagings of *Cocteau's *Le Bel Indifférent* (*The Indifferent Beau*, 1941) and Marcel Achard's *La P'tite Lili* (*Little Lili*, 1951). Among her famous songs are 'Je ne regrette rien', 'La Vie en rose', and 'Pour deux sous d'amour'. SBB

PICARD, LOUIS-BENOÎT (1769–1828)

French actor and *manager. Picard's early career as a manager in *Paris was peripatetic: the *Odéon burned down in 1799, and his company played in six different theatres before settling at the Louvois in 1801, which he was to manage with considerable success. Meanwhile, he had begun to write *comedies, which range from light-hearted *satires (*La Petite Ville* (*The Little City*, 1801) to *Duhautcours* (1801), whose *realism foreshadows *Scribe, and *Les Capitulations de conscience* (*Capitulations of Conscience*, 1809), a character comedy in the tradition of *Molière. Favoured by Napoleon, Picard was awarded the Légion d'Honneur. Renouncing his acting career, he was elected to the Académie Française in 1807, also becoming manager of the *Opéra. WDH

PICASSO, PABLO (1881–1973)

Spanish painter, sculptor, and ceramist. Throughout his long and extremely varied career Picasso made numerous incursions into the theatre. As early as 1917, in the midst of his cubist phase and at the behest of Jean *Cocteau, he designed the *scenery and *costumes for the *Ballets Russes production of *Parade*. His collaboration with *Diaghilev's company continued in productions of Manuel de Falla's *El sombrero de tres picos*, Stravinsky's *Pulcinella*, and Milhaud's *The Blue Train*, for the *curtain of which Picasso reproduced an enormous version of his own painting *Two Women Running on the Beach*, one of the most striking examples of neoclassical gigantism (1922). Following his last trip to Spain in 1934, he started to write poems and other pieces, the best known of which was the play *Le Désir attrapé par la queue* (*Desire Caught by the Tail*), which was performed privately in *Paris in 1944 with an improvised cast which included Albert *Camus and Jean-Paul *Sartre, but which would have to wait until 1988 for its professional première in *New York. KG

PICCOLO TEATRO DI MILANO

*Milan's Piccolo Teatro was founded in 1947 by Giorgio *Strehler and Paolo *Grassi in the mood of public enthusiasm for reform and renovation which followed the Liberation. The two men ran the theatre jointly, with Strehler *artistic director and Grassi administrative *manager. Under pressure from the 1968 protest movement, Strehler left to found his own troupe, but returned in sole charge in 1972, when Grassi moved to La *Scala. The Piccolo was incorporated into a cross-border European Theatre in 1991, in part to accommodate Strehler who had been working in *Paris at the *Odéon, given the title Théâtre de l'*Europe by the French government. The new venue Strehler and Grassi had been demanding since the 1960s to allow for larger-scale work was opened only in 1998, after the death of both men. The old premises, now used as a *studio theatre, carries the name Sala Grassi, and the new building the Sala Strehler.

The Piccolo was a revolutionary venture in its own time. The ideal was theatre as a 'public service', on a par with transport or health provision, and the necessarily small *audiences were viewed as the vanguard of the informed mass audiences of the future. The company was Italy's first *teatro stabile*, where the adjective serves to distinguish it from the *touring companies which had been the backbone of theatre in Italy, and the model was imitated by other cities. Strehler and Grassi were intent on seeking a new audience and forging a new repertoire, and their success in consolidating the position of the *director changed the nature of theatre in Italy. JF

PICON, MOLLY (1898–1992)

American actress. Born in a New York tenement, she became a child star in theatre and *vaudeville at the age of 5. In 1919 she married her manager Jacob Kalich, who took her to Europe, where she created a sensation in the *Yiddish *operetta *Yankele*. A tiny woman with gamine charm, she became the chief song-and-*dance feature of the Yiddish stage. Her long and rich career included leading roles in Yiddish- and English-language *films, including *Yidl with a Fiddle* (1936), *Little Mother* (1938), *Fiddler on the Roof* (1971), and *For Pete's Sake* (1977). She performed into her eighties, wrote nearly 100 songs and skits, and appeared on *radio and *television. EN

PIÈCE BIEN FAITE *See* WELL-MADE PLAY.

PIERROT

French equivalent of the Italian Pedrolino, a *stock character in *commedia dell'arte, he was an intriguing servant, familiarly *costumed in slack white trousers and blouse with a large ruff. Guiseppe Giaratone popularized Pierrot in the Italian version of *Molière's Don Juan (1665). Pierrot was lazy, outspoken, deliberately stupid, often misinterpreting orders, but later became a more sensitive, lonely, almost mystical figure. The agile Jean-Gaspard *Deburau turned him into a *mime at the Théâtre des *Funambules in early nineteenth-century *Paris, wearing the white costume, collar, *make-up, and black skull cap that now define the role. In the twentieth century *Meyerhold was fascinated by Pierrot.   JTD

PIKE THEATRE CLUB

Small theatre operated in *Dublin by Alan Simpson and his wife Carolyn Swift in a converted coach house from 1953 to 1962. The founders' intention was to shake up the theatrical apathy of post-war Ireland by choosing new and decidedly *avant-garde works. Brendan *Behan's The Quare Fellow and the English-language version of *Beckett's Waiting for Godot premièred there in 1954 and 1955 respectively, both directed by Simpson. The 1957 production of Tennessee *Williams's The Rose Tattoo resulted in police prosecution of the cast and Simpson's imprisonment on grounds of indecency; all were acquitted.

MAS

PILLAI G., SHANKARA (1930–89)

Indian playwright, critic, director, and translator. Pillai studied Malayalam language and literature and taught in various colleges in Tamil Nadu and Kerala before founding the School of Drama of Calicut University (1977) and the School of Letters, Mahatma Gandhi University (1988). Primarily known as an experimental dramatist and teacher, he explored the possibilities of *total theatre in a wide range of forms. In plays like Snehadoothan (Messenger of Love, 1956), Mrugathrishna (Mirage, 1965), Bandhi (The Bond, 1977), Bharatavakyam (Epilogue, 1972), Karutha Daivathe Theddy (In Search of the Black God, 1980), and Poojamurri (Prayer Room, 1966) he focused on conflicts of the inner self and a psychological enquiry into the unknown. His *comedies, closely related to social *satire, include Vivaham Swargathil Nadakunnu (Marriage Happens in Heaven, 1958), Pae Pidicha Lokam (Crazy World, 1969), Rakshapurushan (The Saviour, 1969), Oolappambu (The Artificial Snake, 1969), and Thirumbi Vandhan Thambi (The Younger Brother Returns, 1965). He pioneered the nataka kalari (theatre workshop) movement in Kerala, wrote a number of *one-act and *radio plays for pedagogical purposes, and a major history of Malayalam drama (1980).   JoG

PINAKES

Expensively painted wooden *flats, especially those fitting between the columns of the Hellenistic stage front (see GREEK THEATRE, ANCIENT). At Delos, on a stage with thirteen columns, each of the pinakes would have been 2.5 cm (1 inch) thick, 2.6 m (8.5 feet) high, and 1.5 m (5 feet) wide. There they were called, confusingly, skenai and kept in a neighbouring building when not in use.   WJS

PIÑERA, VIRGILIO (1912–79)

Cuban poet, playwright, and fiction writer. His plays rely on a variety of formal experiments while engaging directly with Cuban culture and society. Electra Garrigó, written in 1941 and premièred in 1948, anticipated existentialism and the theatre of the *absurd on the *Latin American stage. Because it mixed the *Greek tragic model with 'ignoble' symbols and mundane behaviour (Orestes kills 'Clitemnestra Plá' with an obscene poisoned papyrus), its opening met with considerable disruption (see RIOTS). Piñera's lower-middle-class family background is revealed in an autobiographical and *realist play, Aire frío (Cold Air, 1962). The fervent dogmatism of Cuban life from the late 1960s marginalized Piñera from public life, but though over a dozen of his plays remained unproduced, by the 1990s he had became the most frequently staged Cuban playwright. Other work includes Jesus (1950), Falsa alarma (1957), La boda (The Wedding, 1958), El filántropo (The Philanthropist, 1959), El flaco y el gordo (The Thin and the Fat, 1960), Dos viejos pánicos (Two Old Panics, 1968, *Casa de las Américas *award), and Niñita querida (Dear Little Girl, 1993).   MMu

PINERO, ARTHUR WING (1855–1934)

English playwright. Pinero was born in London and began work as a solicitor's clerk, visiting the theatre as often as possible. In 1874 he joined a company in *Edinburgh as a general utility actor, and later played with *Irving and the *Bancrofts. His acting career, though abandoned in 1884, gave him a good grounding in dramatic construction, and he conducted careful *rehearsals of his own plays throughout his life, during which he wrote 54 plays. William *Archer picked him out as promising early, in English Dramatists of Today (1882). Pinero's first real successes in *London were *farces written for the *Royal Court Theatre, notably The Magistrate (1885), The Schoolmistress (1886), and Dandy Dick (1887), which are still regularly revived (The Magistrate at the Royal *National Theatre in 1986). They are tightly plotted and witty, reminiscent in structure of contemporary French farces; but for the English *audience the *plots turn not upon sex but upon social embarrassment—the dean's gambling or the schoolmistress's being a secret star of the comic *opera. His one mild attempt at sexual innuendo in farce, *A Wife without a Smile* (1904), was badly received, though it was successfully revived at the Orange Tree in Richmond in 1998. The 'problem plays', which brought him fame during his lifetime, began with *The Profligate* (1889), in which a man's past almost costs him his wife. His greatest contemporary success, *The Second Mrs Tanqueray* (1893), was generally thought to have improved the status of the English theatre by giving a *realistic and complex picture of the conventional figure of the 'woman with a past'. (*Shaw, of course, thought it thoroughly unrealistic, and wrote *Mrs Warren's Profession* as a corrective.)

Pinero's other plays turning on current social attitudes to women and the double standard of morality, *The Notorious Mrs Ebbsmith* (1895), *Iris* (1901), and *Mid-Channel* (1909), have not survived the problems they dealt with, in spite of a series of strong parts for women. His strongest part, however, Paula Tanqueray, which brought Mrs Patrick *Campbell to fame at the age of 28 and which she played until she was 55, was successfully acted by Felicity Kendal at the National in 1981. A play more often revived (for instance, at the *Old Vic in 1980) is *Trelawny of the 'Wells'* (1898), an affectionate though sentimental tribute to the mid-Victorian theatre of Tom *Robertson. Pinero's social *comedies, such as *The Benefit of the Doubt* (1895) and *His House in Order* (1906), combine an astringent and cynical view of human nature with able plotting. The later plays were not well received, though they include interesting experiments like *The Freaks: an idyll of suburbia* (1918), about a *circus troupe. In spite of Shaw's strictures, Pinero was much less reactionary than Henry Arthur *Jones; he was a close friend of Archer and a founder member of the *Independent Theatre. He wrote little about his views on the theatre but supported the struggle against *censorship and the campaign to set up a *national theatre. He was knighted in 1909.   EEC

PINNOCK, WINSOME (1961–)

English playwright. Most associated with the *Royal Court, she is one of a very small group of black women playwrights to achieve sustained success in Britain. Her work is rooted in the experience of the black communities of England, particularly those of Caribbean extraction. Her plays are often *political, focusing on issues of civil rights, the tensions between traditional cultures and modern society, interracial relationships, and recent black history: all themes that shape or underscore *A Hero's Welcome* (1989), *A Rock in Water* (1989, about the founder of the Notting Hill Carnival), *Leave Taking* (1988), *Talking in Tongues* (1991), and *Mules* (1996).   AS

PINTER, HAROLD (1930–)

English playwright, actor, and director. He acted until September 1960 under the stage name of David Baron (with Anew *McMaster, amongst others), after completing his *training at both the *Royal Academy of Dramatic Art and the Central School of Speech and Drama in *London. It was his second full-length play, *The Caretaker* (1960), which brought him a West End reputation, while Peter *Hall's staging of *The Collection* at the *Aldwych in 1962 began a long association between dramatist and director, first with the *Royal Shakespeare Company and subsequently with the *National Theatre. Pinter's plays were at first variously described as *absurdist, 'comedies of menace', and *Beckettian; but no label aptly fits his unique and constantly changing style. It next became fashionable with critics to define distinct periods of creativity in Pinter's work: black comedies and plays of menace gave place to a lyrical phase where the preoccupation was with dramatizing memory, while his most recent work has been categorized as *political drama. Pinter's enduring popularity has ensured continuing revivals of his works, which has invited regular critical reappraisal of the earlier phases of his creativity. The politics implicit in power play (social and sexual) are now seen to operate as strongly in early plays such as *The Birthday Party* (1958), *The Lover* (1963), or *The Homecoming* (1965) as in *One for the Road* (1984) with its analysis of the evils of absolutism, victimization, and torture. Certainly politics has become a more explicit concern in the plays since his involvement with Amnesty International and PEN, but it is the energizing dynamic of all his plays, even those most preoccupied with intimate relations: *Landscape* (1969), *Old Times* (1971), *Moonlight* (1993), *Ashes to Ashes* (1996), and *Celebration* (2000).

Pinter's style has often been caricatured as overly deploying the pregnant pause. This is a crude reduction, but silence does contribute as powerfully to the rhythm and meaning of his plays as it does to music, allowing *characters momentarily to disguise their motives or hide their intentions, to stave off attack, shield their vulnerability, or sustain an advantage. Simultaneously the pauses allow spectators space in which to reassess characters and situation by exploring the *subtext to the dramatic *action, especially what may be being intimated through the subtle tonal placing of speech and the precise spatial relations of the actors within the setting. Pinter's representations of female characters have been dismissed as chauvinistic by *feminist critics. But women in his plays often emerge as the more powerful (Ruth in *The Homecoming*, Kate in *Old Times*) by exploiting the very dependency implicit within the male characters' gaze and their questionable assertions of superiority; men are frequently the victims or losers for their want of sensitivity. Indeed the shortcomings of what passes for masculinity are relentlessly exposed, particularly in the dramas with all-male casts (*The Caretaker*, and *No Man's Land* of 1975). Betrayal is perhaps Pinter's most enduring theme. There are the subtle betrayals that reap unexpectedly devastating personal consequences (Davies in *The Caretaker*, Spooner in *No Man's Land*); and the casual betrayals of the self that bring spiritual and emotional desiccation, the fate of all three characters in *Betrayal* (1978) and of Deeley and Anna in *Old Times*.

The most notable British actors have been attracted to Pinter's work. Invariably this has resulted in their extending their known techniques: in each case the role to be represented has challenged the performer's conventional stage persona, which in turn has resulted in *audience expectation being challenged in ways that have deeply illuminated the play. Judi *Dench's assumption of a vital, girlish innocence, for example, was tragic in *A Kind of Alaska* when it voiced the inner isolation of a middle-aged woman waking from the nightmarish void that is sleeping sickness, which she had entered as a teenager; and Alan *Bates's customary geniality became a terrifying mask for Nicolas's intricate games of sadism in *One for the Road*. Pinter has himself acted in several of his plays and has directed not only his own work but over twenty plays by such dramatists as Simon *Gray, James Joyce, Noël *Coward, Tennessee *Williams, Jean *Giraudoux, and David *Mamet. Many of Pinter's plays were originally conceived for *radio or *television before being staged; and over ten of his *film scripts have been realized by such directors as Joseph Losey, Elia *Kazan, Karel Reisz, Paul Schrader, and Volker Schlondorff. Losey's project to film Pinter's 1972 adaptation of Proust's *Remembrance of Things Past* was not produced, but the script was staged by Pinter and Di Trevis at the National Theatre in 2000.   RAC

BILLINGTON, MICHAEL, *The Life and Work of Harold Pinter* (London, 1996)

RABEY, PETER (ed.), *The Cambridge Companion to Harold Pinter* (Cambridge, 2001)

PINTILIE, LUCIAN (1933–   )

Romanian director who trained at the Institute of Cinema and Theatre Arts (IACT) in *Bucharest. He directed stage, *television, and *film productions in Romania and was known for varying his style, from the *grotesque to refined lyricism, to suit each production. But his 1972 staging of *Gogol's *The Government Inspector* so inflamed the *censors (who saw in it a *parody of Leonid Brezhnev) that Pintilie was banned from theatre in Romania. In artistic exile, he directed extensively in France, including *opera and theatre for the Théâtre du *Chaillot and Théâtre de la Ville. He also worked at the *Guthrie Theatre in Minneapolis at the invitation of Liviu *Ciulei. His 1979 film of I. L. *Caragiale's *D'ale carnavalului* (*Carnival Doings*) was suppressed by Romanian censors and not released until 1991. After the overthrow of communism in 1989, Pintilie returned to Bucharest to run the government-funded Cinema Creation Studio. His films, notably *Balanta: stejarul* (*The Oak*, 1992), *Un été inoubliable* (*An Unforgettable Summer*, 1994), and *Terminus paradis* (1998) have often been invited to major festivals, including Cannes and Venice.   EEP

PIP SIMMONS THEATRE

English experimental company, named after its founder, which opened at *London Arts Lab in 1968 with two plays by Jean *Tardieu. *Collective *devising created *Superman* (1969), *Do It!* (1971), *The George Jackson Black and White Minstrel Show* (1973), high-energy pop-culture-influenced attacks on liberal values and consumer society. Onstage intensity led to burnout in 1973, but Simmons re-formed the group as an international entity with *An Die Music* (1975). Often causing intense controversy—musical concentration camp scenes are no joke—Simmons never stopped at creative half-measures. Later productions included strong stagings of *The Tempest* and *Woyzeck* (both 1977) but the company disbanded in 1986.   BRK

PIRANDELLO, LUIGI (1867–1936)

Italian playwright, poet, and novelist. Born in Agrigento in Sicily, he studied at the University of Palermo and then in *Rome. Following a quarrel with his professor of classics, he finished his doctorate at Bonn (1891) with a thesis on the origins and the development of sounds in the language of Girgenti, and in 1889 published his first collection of poetry, *Mal giocondo*. In 1894 his father arranged his marriage with Maria Antonietta Portulano, the daughter of a wealthy sulphur merchant. His new financial independence allowed him to live in Rome, but in 1903 his wife's sulphur mine was destroyed by a landslide and Pirandello was forced to earn a living by his pen and by teaching at a teacher-training college. His wife, affected by the family's financial collapse, became seriously ill and was finally removed to a sanatorium, where she died in 1959. The bitter experience may well have prompted Pirandello's increasing interest in the changeable nature of human personality.

Most of his early writing, including an extensive number of works in Sicilian dialect, stems from the tradition of *verismo, the Italian form of *realism established by Giovanni Verga and Luigi *Capuana in the nineteenth century. Success came in 1904 with the novel *Il fu Mattia Pascal* (*The Late Mattia Pascal*), which already reflects the acute psychological observation Pirandello would later develop. Profoundly influenced by Freud and the French psychologist Alfred Binet, the complexity of the human psyche and the split nature of personality are at the core of all of Pirandello's mature fiction, most notably in his novel *Uno nessuna e centomila* (*One, None, and a Hundred Thousand*, 1926).

When he turned to the theatre this fascination was significantly extended. The crucial moment occurred in 1916 when he met the playwright-director Nino *Martoglio and the actor Angelo *Musco, who taught Pirandello how to write for specific actors' abilities. Martoglio drew him into the Sicilian dialect movement and produced his first plays: *Pensaci, Giacuminu!* (*Think It over, Giacomino*, 1916), *Liolà* (1916), and *A' birritta cu* i ciancianeddi (*Cap and Bells*, 1917). Pirandello wrote many roles for Musco, who became a major interpreter of his work. He also wrote plays for several directors, including Virgilio *Talli, who staged *Così è (si vi pare)* in *Milan (*It's So, If You Think So*, or *Right You Are, If You Think So*, 1916) with Ruggero *Ruggeri in the lead, and *Il piacere dell' onestà* in Turin (*The Pleasure of Honesty*, 1917). In 1920 the Compagnia Gemma d'Amora produced *Come prima, meglio di prima*, the same year that Ruggeri was acclaimed for his interpretation in *Tutto per bene* (*All for the Best*).

Pirandello's best-known play, *Sei personaggi in cerca d'autore* (*Six Characters in Search of an Author*), was a flop in Rome in 1921, where *audiences were scandalized by its supposed immorality. A classic work of *metatheatre, calling into question the truth of *performance and the performance of truth, *Six Characters* became one of the most influential plays of the first half of the twentieth century, a complex example of theatre-within-the-theatre which dramatizes the discrepancy between *illusion and reality (*see* REALISM AND REALITY). Its reputation began with a highly successful production in Milan in 1922, which led to numerous European productions of it and other plays, and a season of Pirandello's work at the Fulton Theatre in *New York. His play of that year, *Enrico IV* (*Henry IV*), a subtle investigation of sanity and madness, is also based on concepts of the performance of the self, *acting and honesty, pretence and sincerity. Like much of his work, both of these plays reveal a strong melodramatic undercurrent to the narrative and a pessimistic outlook on life, but these qualities are veiled by a formal *theatricality which is highly accomplished and intriguing.

In 1924 Pirandello joined the Italian Fascist Party by writing a letter to Mussolini, which was published in the newspaper *L'impero*. His decision provoked disdain among fellow intellectuals, and his relationship with the party was strained, but Pirandello remained a member throughout his life. In 1925 he formed the Teatro d'Arte in Rome, founded with his son Stefano and several other writers. An art theatre in the *modernist tradition, Teatro d'Arte became Pirandello's personal project, for which he raised funds, located an appropriate playing space, and chose a company. Though financially supported by the Fascist Party (*see* FINANCE), its purpose was to promote and experiment with new dramatic techniques, which it did with vigour until closing in 1928. In addition to Ruggeri and Lamberto Picasso, the company hired Marta *Abba, who became Pirandello's principal actress and muse, prompting him to write a number of works with female leads, including *Diana e la Tuda* (Zurich, 1926), *L'amica delle mogli* (*The Wives' Friend*, 1927), *La nuova colonia* (*The New Colony*, 1928), *Questa sera si recita a soggetto* (*Tonight We Improvise*, 1930), *Quando si è qualcuno* (*When Somebody Is Somebody*, 1933), *Trovarsi* (*To Find Oneself*, 1932), *Non si sa come* (*No One Knows How*, 1935), and the unfinished *I giganti della montagna* (*The Mountain Giants*, 1937).

In 1934 Pirandello was *awarded the Nobel Prize for Literature, by which time his plays were broadly known and admired.

Starting in the 1960s directors such as Giorgio *Strehler, Luigi *Squarzina, and Gabriele Lavia produced new interpretations which revitalized critical opinion, and the works continue to enjoy a prominent place in the repertoire of Italian theatres. Though their innovation now seems dated and the writing overly philosophical, they are still produced abroad and remain central to the theatre.   DMcM/DK

CAESAR, ANN HALLAMORE, *Characters and Authors in Luigi Pirandello* (Oxford, 1998)

CRUPI, VINCENZO, *L'altra faccia della luna: assoluto e mistero nell'opera di Luigi Pirandello* (Catanzaro, 1997)

PIRANESI, GIOVANNI BATTISTA (1720–78)

Italian architect. Stage design was an indispensable element of the study of architecture in eighteenth-century Venice, and Piranesi is known to have studied design both in his native city and in *Rome, where he moved in 1740. Prisons had been a standard topos of art since *Bibiena's pioneering work on the Piacenza Teatro Ducale in 1687. Piranesi exploited this taste in his *Carceri* (*Prisons*) series of etchings (1749, revised and extended 1761), where the dark images involving criss-crossing staircases, hanging wheels, and pulleys denote a view of life as claustrophobic nightmare in a style clearly reminiscent of contemporary, especially Venetian, stage design.   JF

PIRCHAN, EMIL (1884–1957)

Austrian designer. After training at the Academy of Fine Arts and School of Architecture in *Vienna, Pichan began his career at *Munich's State Theatre. In 1919 he joined Leopold *Jessner at the Staatstheater in *Berlin and collaborated with him until 1932. There followed positions in *Prague (Deutsches Theater) and Vienna where he was head of design at the *Burgtheater from 1936 to 1948. In 1936 he was also appointed professor of stage design at the Vienna Academy and subsequently wrote books on theatre biography and design. Pirchan had a symbiotic relationship with Jessner. Their work included landmark productions such as *Schiller's *William Tell* (1919), *Wedekind's *Der Marquis von Keith* (1920), Shakespeare's *Richard III* (1920); for the last Pirchan created the famous *Jessnertreppen* (Jessner steps), using a giant staircase as the chief scenic element. Pirchan's designs can be characterized as *expressionist with a preference for bold *lighting and symbolic architectural forms.   CBB

PIRON, ALEXIS (1689–1773)

French poet and playwright. Piron's theatrical career began with *parades written for the fairground theatres in *Paris: *Arlequin Deucalion* (1722), for example, a remarkable *tour de force* which circumvented the ban on such theatres employing more than one speaking actor by portraying Deucalion, the sole survivor of the flood. *La Métromanie* (1738), an agreeable *satire on the fashion for amateur versifying, is one of the best examples of French mainline *comic drama to be produced in the century between *Molière and *Beaumarchais. Piron's reputation as author of licentious verse led Louis XV in 1753 to veto his election to the Académie Française.   WDH

PISAREV, ALEKSANDR (1803–28)

Russian dramatist and critic. Considered among the best writers of *comedies and Russian *vaudevilles of his day, Pisarev wrote more than twenty plays, many of which were either translations or adaptations of foreign models. One of his most popular was *The Tutor and the Pupil* (1824) in which Mikhail *Shchepkin proved immensely popular as the pedantic tutor, Schelling, who proves more stupid than his pupil. Shchepkin was also excellent as the landowner with a passion for the sea in Pisarev's *A Trip to Kronstadt*. A typical Pisarev play is *Lukavin*, in which a young man flirts with another man's wife but with his eyes on the daughter's dowry (anticipating *Gogol's *The Government Inspector*). Another is *The Busybody* (1825), in which the obsessional Repeikin (another popular Shchepkin role) is constantly interfering in other people's business. Pisarev was hostile to the poetic style of *Griboedov's *Woe from Wit* and attacked Nikolai Polevoy for believing that the theatre was something more than entertainment.   NW

PISCATOR, ERWIN (1893–1966)

German director who, together with *Brecht, developed the *epic theatre style, although with different emphases. While Piscator's *political theatre sought the large view by amassing documentation, Brecht moved towards parable in order to explore the inner dynamics of capitalism and socialism. Piscator is credited with inventing *documentary drama, the political *revue, and many scenic devices, including the conveyor-belt stage and multiple projection surfaces for *films and slides. Drafted into the German Front Theatre in 1915, he cited the experience of *acting in *Charley's Aunt* amid the bombed ruins of Flanders as sparking the idea of epic theatre. Like many of his generation, Piscator was disillusioned and politically radicalized by the mass destruction and propaganda of the war, as well as by the complicity of capitalist industry, the art establishment, and even the Church. In 1918 he joined the *Berlin *dadaists in several leftist events, then founded the Proletarian Theatre (1920–1), producing plays by *Gorky, Franz Jung, and Upton Sinclair, and *satirical *agitprop works such as *Russlands Tag* (*Russia's Day*, 1920), which combined projections and posters of documentary material, narration, songs, and actors

playing cartoon-like stereotypes, devices he would later identify as epic.

In 1924 Piscator was invited by the Berlin *Volksbühne to direct *Fahnen* (*Flags*) and the *Revue Roter Rummel* (*Rowdy Red Revue*). *Trotz Alledem* (*In Spite of Everything*, 1925) regularly filled the 3,500 seats at the *Grosses Schauspielhaus, re-enacting historical events from 1914 to the 1919 crushing of the German Spartakus Revolution, using film footage from the national archives and other epic devices. Piscator's international reputation was made with four productions in 1927–8 at the new Piscatorbühne: *Hoppla, Wir Leben!* (*Hoppla, We're Alive!*), *Rasputin, Konjunctur* (*Boom*), and *Abenteuer des braven Soldaten Schwejk* (*Adventures of the Good Soldier Schweik*). The last of these was adapted from Jaroslav Hašek's Czech novel by a collective of artists who had often worked together since the days of dada: Brecht helped write the script and George Grosz's graffiti-style animated cartoons, life-size *puppets, and cut-out set pieces appeared with live actors on the conveyor-belt stage. Piscator's *The Political Theatre* (1929) outlines his *theory of epic theatre and the discoveries made in practice.

He fled Germany in 1931, first to Russia, then *Paris, and in 1938 to *New York, where he founded the Dramatic Workshop in the New School for Social Research, and taught, most notably, Tennessee *Williams and Judith *Malina. Although Brecht offered him a position at the *Berliner Ensemble in East Berlin after the war, Piscator instead moved to West Germany in 1951, where he first worked freelance and then became *artistic director of the West Berlin Freie Volksbühne in 1962. He mounted a courageous version of *The Merchant of Venice* the next year that looked forthrightly at Germany's responsibility for the Jewish Holocaust, and highly influential productions in the documentary epic style, including the premières of Rolf *Hochhuth's *Der Stellvertreter* (*The Representative*, 1963), Heinar Kippardt's *In der Sache J. Robert Oppenheimer* (*In the Matter of J. Robert Oppenheimer*, 1964), and Peter *Weiss's *Die Ermittlung* (*The Investigation*, 1965). Besides those pivotal German post-war playwrights, Piscator's work also inspired a new generation of political directors, including Peter *Stein, Joan *Littlewood, Ariane *Mnouchkine, Giorgio *Strehler, and Augusto *Boal. *See also* MATERIALIST CRITICISM.   SBB

PISEMSKY, ALEKSEI (1821–81)

Russian writer of short stories, novels, and fifteen plays. After a successful start in the theatre with his *comedy *The Hypochondriac* (1855, *Aleksandrinsky Theatre, *St Petersburg), Pisemsky wrote his best-known play, *A Bitter Fate*, two years before the Emancipation of the Serfs in 1861 (produced *Moscow and St Petersburg, 1863). The play pits a peasant, Anany, against his owner who, while Anany is away earning money in the city, fathers a child by Anany's wife. On his return, maddened with jealousy, Anany kills the baby, runs away, but ultimately returns to beg forgiveness and accept imprisonment. The play's newly shocking *naturalistic approach in theme and language troubled spectators by its coarse *realism. It acquired a legendary reputation when Polina Strepetova played the wife Lizaveta in 1870, humanizing the presentation of peasant women for the stage. Among Pisemsky's other plays are *Vaal* (1873) and *The Financial Genius* (1876), targeting the materialism of the expanding middle classes.   CM

PITOËFF, GEORGES (1884–1939) AND LUDMILLA (1895–1951)

Russian-French actor, director, designer; and Russian-French actress. First studying law and architecture before becoming an actor and director in *St Petersburg, Georges Pitoëff's early theatrical efforts were greatly influenced by *Meyerhold, *Tairov, and *Komissarzhevskaya, whose troupe he joined in 1908. Later he and his wife Ludmilla founded their own company in Geneva, *touring regularly to *Paris before settling there—first at the Comédie des Champs-Élysées, then at the Théâtre des Arts, and finally at the Théâtre des Mathurins. Throughout the 1920s and 1930s their company produced many modern and contemporary playwrights, including *Wilde, *Shaw, *Strindberg, *Gorky, *Ibsen, *Molnár, *Lenormand, *O'Neill, *Cocteau, and *Anouilh. Their mounting of *Pirandello's *Six Characters in Search of an Author* (1923) was particularly important. While sharing the philosophy of the *Cartel des Quatre, including an emphasis on *mise-en-scène in service of the *text, Pitoëff differed by offering an extremely large repertoire of foreign plays for an insular French public. Responsible for his own *scenography, his geometric visual rhetoric owed much to cubism and *expressionism, and often exploited simple means in concert with experiments in *lighting. Rather than exploring the architectural aspects of mise-en-scène as did *Copeau and *Jouvet, Pitoëff confined his scenographic innovation to the 'empty space' of a given stage, allowing the actor to reign supreme. None more so than Ludmilla, whose virtuosic *acting sustained the ambitions of the company, even after her husband's death.   DGM

PIX, MARY (1666–1709)

English playwright, who had at least thirteen plays on the *London stage between 1696 and 1706. Eight of these were written for Elizabeth *Barry and Anne *Bracegirdle, who performed them at *Lincoln's Inn Fields (1695–1705). Pix's plays anticipated the sentimental reform *comedies of the eighteenth century but clearly present a female perspective on society, particularly on love and marriage. Her complex *plotting and witty *dialogue are apparent in her more successful works *The Innocent Mistress* (1697; revived by Annie Castledine at Derby Playhouse, 1987) and *The Beau Defeated* (1700; revived by Sound and Fury at the White Bear, 1992).   GBB

PIXÉRÉCOURT, RENÉ-CHARLES GUILBERT DE (1773–1844)

French playwright. Born into a noble family, Pixérécourt fought with the French army in exile, but made his way to *Paris and joined the republican cavalry. Having written an anti-Jacobin play, and narrowly escaped with his life, he continued to write for the theatre without success until he made his name with *Victor; ou, L'Enfant de la forêt* (*Victor; or, The Child of the Forest*, 1797). Becoming the principal exponent of le *mélodrame with more than 100 plays to his name, Pixérécourt catered for popular taste for over 30 years. A simplified form of *drame bourgeois for an uneducated public—Pixérécourt himself claimed that he composed plays for 'those who cannot read'—*melodrama offered moral instruction as well as spectacular entertainment; and, profiting from the ending of the ban on independent houses, its authors were to provide the staple fare of the *boulevard theatres.

The standard *plot concerned the persecution of innocence by the unscrupulous wielders of power—political, or more commonly domestic. Pixérécourt's *Coelina; ou, L'Enfant du mystère* (*Coelina; or, The Child of Mystery*, 1800), in spite of its early date, is recognized as exemplary of the new *genre. (It was translated by Thomas *Holcroft and presented at *London's *Covent Garden as *A Tale of Mystery* in 1802.) Coelina's plight as persecuted *heroine is shared with Francisque, her father, whose tongue has been cut out years earlier by the villain Truguelin, to prevent his disclosing the secret of Coelina's birth. The *villain is finally brought to book after a spectacular chase by the forces of justice up a stream and across a waterfall. The sentimental appeal of the mutilated or handicapped became something of a cliché: it is illustrated, for instance, in *La Femme à deux maris* (*The Woman with Two Husbands*, 1802) and in *Valentine; ou, Le Séducteur* (1821), in both of which the heroine's father is a blind old man. The appeal of dumb *animals is illustrated in *Le Chien de Montargis* (*The Dog of Montargis*, 1814), in which the eponymous dog plays a vital role in preventing a miscarriage of justice.

Pixérécourt's *dialogue is turgid and sententious, and reads like a concentrated *parody of the style of eighteenth-century serious drama. He took a close personal interest in the *directing of his plays, and claimed responsibility for the execution of *special effects, such as were required for the finale of *La Tête de mort* (*Death's Head*, 1827), an eruption of Vesuvius, whose lava engulfs the stage: 'The theatre is completely covered by a sea of bitumen and lava; a hail of burning stones and fiery ash falls all around . . . This alarming convulsion of nature forms a horrible sight, worthy to be compared with Hell.' Pixérécourt managed the *Gaîté Theatre in Paris with success from 1825 for ten years, but he lost a considerable fortune when the theatre burned down in February 1835. He suffered a severe stroke, and retired to Nancy, half-blind, to devote the last years of his life to preparing the edition of his selected plays. *See also* SPECTACLE.

WDH

PLACIDE FAMILY

A celebrated Franco-American *family of performers. Scion of the troupe was **Alexandre Bussart Placide** (1750–1812), born in *Paris. He became skilled as a rope dancer, *acrobat, and *mime, whose recorded activities took place at home and in England from 1777. Taking with him a gifted child dancer named **Suzanne Théodore Vaillande** (c.1777–?), he went to Santo Domingo for three years (1788–91), moving to several venues in the eastern United States—notably Charleston, where he presented *ballets, *pantomimes, acrobatics, *operas, and French plays. Suzanne was billed as 'Madame Placide' and bore him two children, though he had left a wife behind in France. Suzanne eloped with an opera singer, and Alexandre in 1796 promptly married (apparently bigamously) the teenage **Charlotte Sophia Wrighten** (c.1780–1823), daughter of a well-known *London actress and herself a prominent player in Charleston at the time. This union produced six children who became active stage personnel, starting with **John Alexander Placide** (1794–1812). **Caroline Placide** (1798–1881), who began performing at the age of 9, wed English actor **Leigh Waring** (d. 1816), by whom she had an actress-daughter **Ann** (1815–?), who married actor **William Sefton** (d. 1839) and then in 1842 theatre *manager James W. *Wallack Jr. **Jane Placide** (1804–35) made a debut in Virginia in 1820, but worked mainly in New Orleans, where she was celebrated for her Cordelia and Lady Macbeth as well as comic roles. **Eliza Placide** (d. 1874) was a utility actress, whose daughter acted for a while under the name **Alice Placide**. **Thomas Placide** (1809–77) was a popular *touring comedian until cancer of the mouth led him to take his life. By far the most distinguished of Alexandre's offspring, however, was the fourth child, **Henry Placide** (1799–1870), widely regarded as the finest comedian America had produced. He made his debut at 8 in Augusta, Georgia, and in 1823 gave the first of countless performances in *New York, where he made his farewell in 1865, having exceeded 500 roles. Able to submerge himself totally in his parts, he excelled in Shakespeare, *Sheridan, sentimental *melodrama, and even opera (*Mozart, Weber, Rossini).

CT

PLACOLY, VINCENT (1946–92)

Haitian playwright and *television writer. Of his fourteen plays only two were published: *Dessalines; ou, La Passion de l'indépendance* (1983) and *Don Juan* (1984). The others include *La Fin douloureuse et tragique d'André Aliker* (*The Sad and Tra-*

gic *End of André Aliker*, 1969), *Vivre ou mourir de la mort de Mara* (*To Live or Die the Death of Mara*, 1988), *Guanahani* (1988), and *Colomb* (1992). His inspiration was fundamentally tragic, and his work is obsessed with history and death. For Placoly the tragedy of the New World is embodied in the slave insurrections that mark the history of the Americas.

MLa trans. JCM

PLANCHÉ, J. R. (JAMES ROBERTSON) (1796–1880)

English playwright. The son of a Huguenot watchmaker, he is described in the old *DNB* as 'Somerset herald and dramatist', reflecting his own order of priorities. An early taste for acting took him to the private theatres; his chief theatrical talent lay in the writing and designing of stage entertainments that met the demand for spectacular but tasteful and even educational amusement. A successful *burlesque, a speaking harlequinade, the translation of a French *melodrama in which a novelty *trap was introduced (*The Vampire*, 1820), and research for Charles *Kemble in 'authentic' *costuming and heraldry for Shakespeare's *King John* (*Drury Lane, 1823) brought him friends in the business, and in 1831 he became a valued member of Madame *Vestris's team in the creation of modern entertainment at the *Olympic. He wrote the spectacular quasi-classical extravaganzas in which she so brilliantly starred (*Olympic Revels*, 1831). He failed *financially as *manager of the Olympic in her absence in 1838 but was retained as designer and occasional writer at *Covent Garden and the *Lyceum. Meanwhile he pursued his (crypto-theatrical?) interests in history and pageantry via the Society of Antiquaries and his gentlemanly appointment to the Herald's Office. He continued to write for the stage, as well as producing a source-book for Victorian historical painting and theatre *spectacle in *The History of British Costumes* (1834). His somewhat self-regarding autobiography, *Recollections and Reflections* (1872), overstates his services to Vestris, but shows clearly how his respectable *antiquarianism and skill in creating amusing fantasies contributed to the genteel rehabilitation of stage entertainment.

JSB

PLANCHON, ROGER (1931–)

French actor, director, and playwright. One of the most influential directors in modern France, and often considered the spiritual successor to Jean *Vilar in espousing the ideals of a decentralized, popular theatre, Planchon is frequently associated with making the *director as important a creative artist as the *playwright. Planchon founded the Théâtre de la Comédie in Lyon in 1953, presenting a repertoire of classic and contemporary plays that would strongly influence his later productions and writing, including *Marlowe (*Dr Faustus*, 1950; *Edward II*,

1954), *Brecht (*The Good Person of Setzuan*, 1954, *Fear and Misery in the Third Reich*, 1956), and *Ionesco (*The Lesson*, 1956). He also began long-standing collaborations with playwrights Michel *Vinaver (*The Koreans*, 1956) and Arthur *Adamov (*Paolo-Paoli*, 1957), as well as with scenographer René *Allio whose work was crucial in defining the Planchon aesthetic: a spectacular, often cinematic, *Brechtian style that attempted to reach a wide popular *audience. In 1957 Planchon became director of the Théâtre de la Cité at Villeurbanne, a working-class suburb of Lyon, where he and Allio collaborated on many important productions, of which the two parts of Shakespeare's *Henry IV* (1957), *Marivaux's *The Second Surprise of Love* (1959), Brecht's *Schweik in the Second World War* (1960), and *Molière's *George Dandin* (1958) and *Tartuffe* (1962) were most celebrated. At this time, when *structuralism was being popularized in French thought, Planchon formulated his idea of 'scenic writing', a concept that he ascribed to Brecht, in which scenic and directorial choices were given equal responsibility to the *text in the determination of meaning. But unlike earlier movements in theatrical aestheticism, scenic writing had the force of *political action, ideological engagement, and epic scope; it became a central concept in French theatre during the 1960s and 1970s.

In the spirit of decentralization and theatre as 'public service', in 1972 Planchon was offered the position of director of the *Théâtre National Populaire at *Chaillot, but declined the move from Villeurbanne. Instead his Théâtre de la Cité was accorded the title of TNP, to be co-*managed with Patrice *Chéreau. At the TNP, Planchon continued to direct Shakespeare, *Racine, Molière, and Marivaux, as well as groundbreaking productions of contemporary plays such as Vinaver's *Overboard* (1973) and *Pinter's *No Man's Land* (1979), and began another successful series of collaborations, this time with *scenographer Ezio *Frigerio.

Throughout his tenure at Villeurbanne, Planchon embarked on a successful career as playwright—or more properly, *auteur* in the parlance of the New Wave *film that he admired—producing many of his own works, which ranged from *musical comedies like *The Three Musketeers* (1958), to modern *comedies like *Patte blanche* (*White Paw*, 1965) and *Dans le vent* (*Trendies*, 1968), to 'provincial plays' such as *La Remise* (*The Return*, 1962), *L'Infâme* (*The Villain*, 1969), *Le Cochon noir* (*The Black Pig*, 1973), *Gilles de Rais* (1976). He considered these latter plays, written and directed in an *epic theatre mode that foregrounded the historical and ideological underpinnings of their *characters' situations, the direct progeny of Brecht's *dramaturgy. In the late 1980s and 1990s Planchon began directing films (*Georges Dandin*, 1987; *Louis, enfant roi*, 1992; *Lautrec*, 1998), creating productions for other companies, including the *Comédie-Française (*Feydeau's *Keep an Eye on Amélie*, 1995), all the while continuing his long association with the TNP where he mounted his own plays, *Fragile Forêt* (*Fragile Forest*) and *Le Vieil Hiver* (*Old Winter*) in 1994.   DGM

DAOUST, YVETTE, *Roger Planchon: director and playwright* (Cambridge, 1981)

PLATA, JORGE (1946–)

Colombian actor, director, and playwright, a founding member of Teatro *Libre in *Bogotá. His production of Esteban *Navajas's *La agonía del difunto* had 3,000 performances in twenty years (1977–97). His own plays include *Un muro en el jardín* (*A Wall in the Garden*, 1987, also in *Paris) and *La boda* (*The Wedding*, 1998, after *Chekhov).   BJR

PLATEA

Deriving from the late Latin *plattus* (a flat area), the term was translated as 'the place' and was used to describe the main acting area in *medieval theatre, particularly when this was within a surrounding circle of *audience and *mansions. By extension it was also used to describe any communal playing place or 'game place' where bull- and bear-*baiting occurred and wrestling contests, and sometimes plays, were presented. *See also* CORNISH ROUNDS.   JWH

PLATT

Meaning plan or scheme, platt was the Elizabethan term for a skeletal outline of the *action of a play, written on a single sheet mounted on pasteboard and posted backstage, for the guidance of actors, 'book holders' (who served as *prompters and *property men), and 'tiremen' (who fitted *costumes and beards). The seven extant examples, all associated with Edward *Alleyn, suggest that a platt typically noted *characters' entrances and exits, indicated the points where properties or *music were required, and listed the *dramatis personae together with the names of the actors playing them.   RWV

PLAUTUS, TITUS MACCIUS (c.254–184 BC)

Roman comic dramatist. The earliest Latin author whose works are preserved, Plautus was the father of *farce and the most successful of all *Roman dramatists. His influence upon later playwrights has been immense. His 21 surviving plays are all believed to have been based on earlier *Greek *New Comedy *texts by such writers as *Menander, Diphilus, and Philemon. But instead of translating them directly into Latin, Plautus, as he freely admitted, 'transformed' them into his 'barbarian' versions that were conditioned by his own abilities and preferences, which, in turn, undoubtedly reflected the taste and pressure of his Roman public. Plautus took the rather urbane and decorous Greek *comedies and injected them with a great deal of vitality, comic fun, and vulgarity. The language of his sometimes grotesque *characters is cruder, more ribald and playful, but also much richer in complex and sometimes fantastical imagery. The intrigues are usually less plausible, and the *plots less thought-provoking than those found in his models, but they are more ingeniously and energetically pursued. For the pleasure of his Roman holiday *audience Plautus greatly increased the amount of song and *dance, adding many references to Roman customs, and often breaking the dramatic illusion entirely to allow his performers to address the audience directly about their own functions as *actors, or even about the play itself. He was fond too, of such devices as *soliloquies and overheard conversations.

Plautus' plots abound in deception and comic conspiracy, and serving as their mischievous agents (and foils) he made extensive use of slave characters, such as Palaestrio in the *Miles Gloriosus* or Pseudolus in the play bearing his name. These slaves are regularly threatened with extreme violence as a consequence of their cleverness and trickery. But the pain, beatings, and threats of torture are not merely a source of fun; they serve as important motivations of plot and *action. There is also a great deal of verbal violence, with characters threatening one another with direst mayhem and torment, while engaging in elaborately abusive insults. Plautus deliberately increased such elements, perhaps to cater to a taste for violent *slapstick in an *audience accustomed to earlier unscripted, knockabout entertainments.

In addition to this violent streak, Plautus' plays are inclined towards coarse and sometimes indecent humour, and a fondness for *disguise and crude deception, a preference for fooling over the development of emotional interest or the advancement of the plot, and a festive conclusion. Less frequently (in for example, the *Rudens* or *Captivi*) the play is informed by more ethical and philosophical concerns while still reaching a happy conclusion. A likely legacy of earlier forms of popular drama may be his extensive use of *music and mastery of a great variety of metrical forms. He strives to create mood and enhance the emotional impact of characters' language through close attention to sound: alliteration, rhyme, assonance, and wordplay are all abundant, and presented in a great variety of both spoken and lyric metres. In performance the songs would probably have been accompanied by heightened gesticulation and dance. Plautus displays in the course of his career a metrical richness and dexterity unmatched by any other Latin author, and these qualities increased, until his later plays might best be characterized as something akin to modern *musical comedy, written in *verse.

One of the recurrent elements of Plautine drama is that characters appear to make up the plot as they go along. Probably this reflects the legacy of a more tentative dramatic fare: improvised, non-literary entertainments (such as *Atellan farce) long favoured by his audience, which the actors are thought to have assembled on the basis of *stock characters and situations, some well-worn but ever popular bits of comic business, and the barest outline of a *scenario. One can trace the influence of such performances in Plautus' deliberate choice to 'make believe' that his own plays are unscripted, taking shape in the presence of an audience which, in turn, assists in their formation.

The chief agent of this *dramaturgical self-consciousness is usually the clever slave who fashions the play around himself to become simultaneously its author and *hero. He fills this role by virtue of his wit and intelligence, triumphing over adversity and the social facts of life in a way that no actual Roman slave could ever have done. Masters are tricked, freedom is won, and the slave enjoys impunity. In fact, Plautus' *protagonists make a point of disdaining and mocking the fates which, but for their success in fashioning unlikely, anti-realist plots, would tumble down upon them. This is one key to his enduring popularity. The audience enjoys the pretence of the *actors'* theatrical improvisation, while in the process admiring and experiencing a mildly subversive and liberating pleasure in the *characters'* ability to salvage something redemptive from their dramatic situation and get away with it. For his original audience the pleasure and release of tension and moral restraint was compounded by the awareness that all the plots and characters are notionally set safely and unthreateningly in Greece: in the time-honoured tradition of ethnic and minority humour, a Plautine play is one extended Greek joke.

Although the changes which Plautus made to his Greek models must have helped to ensure the success of his plays in performance, they did little to endear him to generations of critical classicists, who too often considered him to be at best a hack translator and adaptor of what were believed to be the sublime comedies of the Greek New Comedy playwrights. This is both mistaken (as the discovery of *Menander's texts in the course of the twentieth century has enabled us to perceive), and ironic in the light of the immense influence Plautus has had upon dramatic composition and presentation since the *early modern period. Plautus and *Terence were the first ancient dramatists whose works were revived. The first translation of a Roman comedy, Plautus' *Menaechmi*, was performed at the court of Ferrara in 1486 before an audience of over 10,000. Whereas previously the study and presentation of Roman drama had been the elitist preserve of scholars, the way was now open for its exploitation as vernacular entertainment. Further productions followed, and the earliest Italian comedies, notably *Ariosto's *La Cassaria* of 1513, were closely modelled upon Plautine models. The rebirth of dramatic composition in Italy, and subsequently throughout Europe, was thus directly based on Roman precedent and surviving examples, and in particular upon the works of Plautus. Countless works (including Shakespeare's *Comedy of Errors*) have recycled his plots, characters, theatrical playfulness, and jokes.

In recent decades, to complement the flattery of imitation which theatrical practitioners have, for centuries, provided, classical scholarship has begun to acknowledge Plautus as a superbly gifted comic craftsman who mastered and employed every theatrical skill for the benefit and appreciation of an audience that had already acquired an impressive degree of experience, and some sophistication, in responding to dramaturgical technique. Revivals of his plays are presented with increasing frequency in schools and universities, although relatively few productions have taken place in the commercial theatre. In Italy, however, his works have for many years featured prominently in *festivals of ancient drama, including those taking place in the *ancient theatres of Ostia and Syracuse. In 1991 the J. Paul Getty Museum successfully staged a professional production of *Casina* upon a replica Plautine stage in a translation by Beacham.   RCB

BEACHAM, R. C., *The Roman Theatre and its Audience* (Cambridge, Mass., 1992)

MOORE, T., *The Theater of Plautus* (Austin, Tex., 1998)

SEGAL, E. W., *Roman Laughter: the comedy of Plautus* (New York, 1968)

SLATER, N. W., *Plautus in Performance* (Princeton, 1985)

PLAY

The word that in English describes a dramatic *text also signifies the much larger concepts of pretence and recreation. Major twentieth-century *theorists regarded dramatic *performance as a species of play. In *Homo Ludens: a study of the play-element in culture* (1944), the Dutch cultural historian Johan Huizinga distinguished two basic kinds of play: contests *for* and representations *of*, with dramatic performance exemplifying the latter category. French essayist Roger Caillois, in *Man, Play, and Games* (1958), classified *theatre as a game of mimicry (*see* MIMESIS), which he distinguished from *agons (competitive games), *alea* (games of chance) and *ilinx* (vertigo-inducing movement). The Swiss developmental psychologist Jean Piaget, in *Play, Dreams and Imitation in Childhood* (1946), posited three categories: practice games, games with rules, and symbolic games, with role-playing games belonging to the last category. None of these theorists, however, regarded theatre performed by professional *actors as pure play, since they all defined play as an activity that is pursued freely and for its own sake. Piaget uses the term 'autotelic' to describe this concept, which has its roots in the *romantic notion of aesthetic disinterestedness advanced by Kant and *Schiller.

Other theorists locate play in the *audience's experience rather than the performers'. In *Truth and Method* (1960), hermeneutic philosopher Hans-Georg Gadamer proposed that in theatre, play finds its perfection as an objective, repeatable structure that exists for and in the spectators. In a very different vein, analytic philosopher Kendall Walton, in *Mimesis as Make-Believe* (1990), argued that representational art in general is a 'game of make-believe' for spectators, and theatre in particular is a game in which the actors function as 'props' for the audi-

ence's imaginative play. Scholars such as Glynne Wickham and V. A. Kolve applied the concept of play to the analysis of theatre history. In *The Play Called Corpus Christi* (1966), Kolve proposed that the English word 'play', as applied to dramatic works, derives from the inherently ludic experience of *medieval theatre in Europe. He observed that medieval documents use the words 'play' and 'game' interchangeably to denote works of theatre, and suggested that the idea of theatre as game persisted through the English *early modern period and gave way to a theatre of *illusion after the Restoration.

Many prominent theatre practitioners in the twentieth century also perceived a link between *acting and play, attempting to reform theatre by restoring a spirit of childlike playfulness. In the first half of the twentieth century Evgeny *Vakhtangov in Russia and Jacques *Copeau in France both made extensive use of *improvisation to realize that ideal. The American teacher-director Viola Spolin's *Improvisation for the Theater* (1962) described 'Theatre Games', initially developed for children and subsequently adapted for *Chicago's Second City Company. Spolin inherited the fundamental tenet of her approach from her mentor, sociologist Neva Boyd: that the difference between dramatic acting and playing a game is a matter of degree, not kind. Theatre Games formed the basis of a far-reaching improvisational *genre with broad popular appeal, and profoundly influenced *avant-garde theatre groups such as the *Open Theatre in the 1960s.

In the 1970s and 1980s play became important to the nascent field of *performance studies. Theories of play offered an early precedent for the cross-disciplinary reach of performance studies by situating theatre within the broader field of play activity. Play itself became an object of study for theorists such as Richard *Schechner, who situated both play and theatre within the even broader field of performance. Finally, some performance theorists proposed that a ludic mode of consciousness cut across a wide range of performance practices. For example Victor Turner associated play, theatre, and *ritual with an attitude of 'as-if' that he called the 'subjunctive mood', and also with an experience of intense absorption that, following Mihaly Csikszentmihalyi, he called 'flow'. By the 1990s, theorists of play increasingly began to challenge the long-held assumption that play is insulated from reality. Schechner in *The Future of Ritual* (1993) and Brian Sutton-Smith in *The Ambiguity of Play* (1997) distinguished rigidly bounded play structures from an open-ended attitude of engaged playfulness capable of expanding and destabilizing the boundaries and structures of the real world.   DZS

PLAYBILLS AND PROGRAMMES

In literate societies, the pieces of theatre ephemera distributed to the *audience to provide information considered necessary for understanding the performance; paradoxically, often the most collected of theatre memorabilia. The playbill or pro-gramme often provides invaluable documentation of particular performances, and is also valuable as cultural evidence of what the audience found interesting about a performance, or how the producers hoped the audience would interpret it. The distinc-tion between programme and playbill is elastic and imprecise. The term playbill is somewhat older and originally referred to the advertising handbills which were displayed on the *play-house, stuck to any available surface in the city, and distributed for a small charge at the theatre and by street hawkers. The earli-est extant such handbill in Europe was found among the papers of Charles II and dates from about 1670; it gives a title and a list of scenes but the cast is listed only as 'men and women', pre-sumably because *actresses were still a novelty on the English stage (see WOMEN AND PERFORMANCE). Nothing in any of the earliest playbills indicates novelty, so playbills may have origin-ated as much as a generation earlier.

In the literate Asian theatres, signboards detailing the show were common from the fourteenth century (see POSTERS), and printed copies of the signboards have existed at least since the seventeenth century. In the *kabuki theatre, for example, *banzuke*, printed cast lists with *plot synopses, with strict rules about precedence and positioning of credits, were common be-fore 1800. In all nations the first playbills were in the court or aristocratic theatres, moving down the class ladder with cheaper printing and wider literacy.

Early Western playbills contained a section announcing the cast and often a synopsis by *scene or *tableau; this section was called the 'programme'. The programme initially seems to have been modelled upon the title pages of books, a not-surprising adaptation by printers who dealt with both. Until the mid-nineteenth century the order of the cast tended to be by the social rank of the *character (so the Ghost and Claudius, both being kings, appeared above Hamlet, and the Gravediggers and Players came last), with men listed before women. *Garrick, with his consummate awareness of theatre as a cultural, collect-ible good, and of the value of *publicity, was the first actor to insist on special billing on a playbill; actors' egos assured that the custom would spread quickly.

About 1815, the programme became much more an adver-tisement for the production, on the one hand, and also a col-lectible souvenir on the other. The handbill poster/programme gradually diminished, though it remains common in some poorer countries. The programme itself split into the free pro-gramme intended to help the audience follow the performance, and the souvenir programme, sold at a premium, used to com-memorate a spectator's presence as well as to promote the com-pany and its coming attractions. The souvenir programme, often a handsomely made book, persisted in the continental theatre and has more recently returned to the English-speaking theatre, but the charges assessed for it, as well as its extent and contents, vary considerably by country and theatre. Interestingly, *melo-drama programmes retained their tableaux lists and synopses longer than those for the more serious houses, perhaps pointing to the difficulty in hearing in the former.

About 1870 the programme printed on a long narrow sheet vanished, with the disappearance of the hand presses on which it had been printed, and the modern codex-form programme took its place. Since the 1880s, programme advertising has been a significant source of revenue for many theatres; as the audi-ence has increasingly become middle class and upper middle class, the desirability of theatre patrons as customers has at-tracted advertisers willing to pay high rates. Today the bulk of many programmes around the world is taken up with ad-vertisements for businesses. Because of the need for more pages (on which more advertising can be sold, but which also must draw the attention of theatregoers to be valuable for advert-isers), theatre programmes have generally come to include such matters as *directors' or *dramaturgs' notes, *actor biographies, light treatments of theatre history, and so forth. This body of mediating information helps theatre audiences to form an iden-tity as consumers of high culture, and often influences the reviews and the word-of-mouth a show receives; some contro-versial performances have been 'inoculated' against public outrage by the presentation of the case for the work in the programme.   JB

PLAYBOY RIOTS

J. M. *Synge's *The Playboy of the Western World* elicited noisy protests on its first night in the *Abbey Theatre (26 January 1907) and continued disruption for its following week's run. Nationalists objected to this dramatization of an apparent parri-cide idolized for his deed in a country village because of its alleged obscenity, violence, and misrepresentation of the Irish. The insistence of the Abbey directors—W. B. *Yeats, Lady *Gregory, and Synge himself—on staging the play under police protection increased its provocativeness. Strenuous na-tionalist opposition to the play was repeated by Irish Americans when it was staged by the Abbey company in *New York and *Philadelphia in 1911–12. *See also* RIOTS.   NG

PLAYERS CLUB

Performing arts club located at 16 Gramercy Place, *New York. Founded by actor Edwin *Booth in 1888 on the model of *Lon-don's *Garrick Club, it maintains in its original state the upstairs apartment Booth kept as his residence until his death. Member-ship is open to actors, dramatists, artists, editors, *producers, publishers, musicians, educators, and cartoonists. Its presidents have been theatrical luminaries, such as Booth, Joseph *Jeffer-son III, Walter *Hampden, Dennis King, Alfred *Drake, and José *Ferrer. The Players houses the Walter Hampden Memorial Library, an important source for research on the American

theatre. Originally an all-male domain, the Players has accepted women members since 1989. A continuing tradition is 'Pipe Night', at which a theatrical celebrity is honoured.　　SLL

PLAYFAIR, NIGEL (1874–1934)

English actor, *manager, and director; knighted in 1928. Beginning as an actor with Frank *Benson's company, Playfair appeared in *Shaw's *John Bull's Other Island* (1904) and *Fanny's First Play* (1911). Granville *Barker cast him as Bottom in *A Midsummer Night's Dream* (1914), and with Barker as a model he took up *directing in 1918 when he renovated the *Lyric Theatre Hammersmith. The theatre was launched with Barry *Jackson's production of *Drinkwater's *Abraham Lincoln* (1919). For the next decade the Lyric's stylish productions, especially of Restoration and eighteenth-century drama, delighted *London *audiences. Playfair's major successes included *Gay's *The Beggar's Opera* (1920; 1,463 performances) with designs by Lovat *Fraser, *Congreve's *The Way of the World* (1924) with Edith *Evans, *Farquhar's *The Beaux' Stratagem* (1927) with Evans again, and *Wilde's *The Importance of Being Earnest* (1930) with *Gielgud. Playfair also acted in several of the productions. He retired from directing in 1932.　　TP

PLAYHOUSE

One of the terms given to a building constructed for the purpose of presenting drama to an *audience. The other, more common term in English is *theatre, derived from the Greek *theatron (place for seeing), and was the name given to the first such building erected for the purpose in *early modern England, the *Theatre, in 1576. Although theatre performances have in different times and in different cultures taken place in a wide variety of locations, indoors and out—in churches, private homes, palaces, factories, market-places, town squares, parks, cemeteries—most cultures have developed particular structures devoted to this activity. In classical times (*Greek, *Roman, and Hellenistic) the theatres were large, open-air places of assembly for entire communities, and the remains of many of these still surround the Mediterranean (*see* ANCIENT THEATRES). The Theatre of *Epidaurus has been considered since classic times the outstanding example of the Greek theatre. It is an outdoor structure, with a circular *orchestra in the centre for the movements of the *chorus. Sweeping around this, in slightly more than a half-

Playhouse interior from nineteenth-century London, the Royal Alhambra Palace Music Hall, Leicester Square, in a photo of c.1919. Built as the Royal Panopticon of Science and Art in 1854, it became a music hall four years later, setting the model for the English Moorish style. The building was demolished in 1936 to make way for the Odeon Cinema. As seen here, the pit benches were backed, and considerable decorated space rose above the galleries.

circle, are rows of steps for seating, and facing them was a building for the actors, the *skene. Separating the *skene* from the audience were two passageways through which the chorus entered and exited (*see* PARODOS). The Hellenistic theatre retained many of the features of the classic Greek playhouse, but most notably shifted focus from the orchestra to a raised platform, the *logeion, in front of the *skene* house. The *skene* was also moved forward, taking over part of the circle of the old orchestra. The most fully elaborated Roman theatres carried this process further, reducing the orchestra even more essentially to a half-circle (still surrounded by a half-circle of seats, however), and developing a highly elaborate permanent façade several storeys high for the stage house, the *scaenae frons. The *paradoi* were also roofed over and became part of an architectural element connecting the *stage and *auditorium into a single structure.

After the classical period the great public playhouses of Greece and Rome fell into ruins, and although these ruins were occasionally used for theatrical performances in the late Middle Ages, when theatre appeared again it appeared in a wide variety of performance spaces, but not in buildings created especially for this purpose. Churches, monasteries, town squares, open fields, even cemeteries saw dramatic performances, but in temporary or improvised spaces. Even the elaborate *cycle plays of England were not offered in playhouses, but in a variety of locations in the *open air (*see* MEDIEVAL THEATRE IN EUROPE).

Permanent theatres were not built again in Europe until the early modern period, when the term playhouse becomes more suitable, since these were often more like houses than like the great outdoor places of assembly of classical times, smaller, more intimate, and normally made up of interior spaces. The first such theatres were built in Renaissance Italy during the sixteenth century. The oldest surviving of them is the Teatro *Olimpico, built in Vincenza by Andrea *Palladio on the model of a Roman theatre. After Palladio's death, Vincenzo *Scamozzi, who completed the theatre for its 1585 opening, added street scenes, built in *perspective, behind each of the doors in the Roman-style stage façade. Palladio's Roman stage was soon abandoned for a stage with a single large *proscenium arch, the first surviving example of which is the Teatro *Farnese in Parma.

These first Renaissance theatres were built for academic societies, like the Olimpico, or ruling families, like the Farnese, but alongside them a tradition of public theatres was being established in Venice which reached its full development after the introduction of *opera in the early seventeenth century. The Venetian opera houses utilized what would become the standard pattern for European theatre auditoriums for the next 300 years, according to which an open area on the ground floor (the pit or parterre) provided the least expensive admission, and surrounding it were several tiers of boxes for more affluent spectators, descending in value as one ascended. An area of open seating, the gallery, later commonly replaced the upper

Théâtre du Palais Royal, a private **playhouse** in Paris. Built as the Palais Cardinal by Richelieu in 1641, it passed into royal hands and was used by Molière's company from 1660 and by Lully after 1673. Its design echoed the shape of the tennis-court theatres, with galleries for spectators along the sides, the large floor space reserved for royalty and nobility, who are as visible to the audience as the stage. Here a mythological hunting scene is played before a painted landscape drop behind the proscenium, the lighting provided by hanging chandeliers in the auditorium.

rank of balconies, and the *box, pit, gallery arrangement became standard throughout Europe.

While the inspiration for the first public playhouses of the Renaissance in Italy was primarily from classical sources, inspiration in other countries was often more recent and local. At least nine *public theatres were built in areas neighbouring the city of *London between 1576 and 1642, when all playhouses were officially closed. Public inn yards, used for dramatic performances before the first theatres were built, have generally been considered the primary models for these theatres, which, like the early Italian opera houses, surrounded a pit (without seats) with rows of boxes (see INNS AS PLAYHOUSES). The first permanent playhouses in Spain, the Corral de la *Cruz (1579) and the Corral del *Príncipe (1583), both located in *Madrid, also took their design, as well as their name, from the courtyards

(*corrales) inside of which such playhouses were built. Again, the pit and box arrangement of seating was utilized here. In both England and Spain the first public playhouses of the Renaissance, like the earlier structures upon which they were based, had auditoriums open to the sky. In *Paris, and in a number of other places in Europe, most early public theatres were converted from indoor *tennis courts, which already normally possessed the requisite pit, boxes, and gallery, and often needed only a raised platform for a stage to complete the ensemble. The first French public playhouse was the *Hôtel de Bourgogne, opened in 1548; a royal monopoly protected it until 1625 when a second permanent theatre, the *Marais, opened, also converted from a tennis court.

London's first indoor playhouse, the *Blackfriars, was built in 1576, the same year as its first open-air theatre, but the outdoor houses dominated the scene until 1596, when James *Burbage built the second Blackfriars, which shared the services of Shakespeare's company with the open-air *Globe. During the early seventeenth century indoor playhouses, generally catering to a more aristocratic public, gradually replaced the outdoor theatres (*see* PRIVATE THEATRES; COURT THEATRES). Their exact interior arrangements are not certain, but they did have galleries, some boxes, and a seated pit.

Asian theatrical performances, while often quite elaborate, were offered in temporary and improvised performance spaces until about the time that permanent playhouses began to appear in Europe. In *China, as in Europe, the first permanent theatres were inspired by earlier non-theatrical spaces which had been previously used for theatrical offerings, in this case the popular tea houses. Here the area corresponding to the European pit was filled with tables and chairs where spectators were served tea while watching the play. The poorer spectators were placed not in the pit, but on benches on raised platforms at the sides and back of the auditorium. In larger theatres a balcony might be added for women or wealthier spectators. This style of playhouse remained essentially unchanged in China until the arrival of Western models in the early twentieth century.

*Japan's classic *nō theatre was developed in the late fourteenth and early fifteenth centuries and its arrangements have changed little since that time. Whether located indoors or out, it consists of a square main stage area extending out into the audience with a long walkway, the bridge, at the rear, leading off to the dressing room. Both stage and bridge are covered with their traditional roofs, even when they are erected within an encompassing auditorium. The more popular *kabuki theatre at first used the already established nō stage, but gradually added more and more elements to it. By the 1730s a forestage had appeared, upon which most of the action occurred, and the nō bridge was replaced in importance by the distinctive 'flower path', the *hanamichi, which extended directly out through the audience to the rear of the auditorium. Indeed it was so popular that in the late eighteenth century a second hanamichi was added. By 1830 the traditional nō roof had been abandoned, and the kabuki stage, like its Western counterpart, occupied the full width of the auditorium, without even a proscenium arch, which was introduced under European influence in 1908. The pit was divided into individual boxes and others ran in rows along the sides and back of the auditorium.

When the first new playhouses were created in London in the 1660s after the banning of theatre during the Interregnum, they reflected much more closely the playhouse style of the Continent, and especially France, than that of the public theatres of the Elizabethan and Jacobean periods. The new playhouses, the most important of which were *Lincoln's Inn Fields, *Drury Lane, and *Dorset Garden, were all indoor theatres whose auditoriums were divided into pit (now provided with benches), two or three rows of boxes, and one or two galleries. The stage

differed from continental stages by including in front of the proscenium a substantial *forestage, called the apron, a remnant of the stages that thrust out into the audience in the public theatres of the English Renaissance. This forestage was the main acting area, and was normally entered by doors on either side of the proscenium arch, with small balconies above them. The area behind the proscenium arch was in England used primarily for *scenery, which in this period became an important part of the theatre experience (*see* FLATS AND WINGS; SCENOGRAPHY).

Both in England and on the Continent, the new playhouses built during the seventeenth century were on the whole fairly modest structures, and were not highly visible parts of the urban landscape. In part this was because they were often converted from other equally modest structures, such as the ubiquitous tennis courts, and in part because the most economical space for a structure much larger than a conventional house or shop in the inner city was generally within the open space in the centre of an urban block, with other buildings on all sides facing the surrounding streets. The façade of the theatre was at best a decorated portico the size of which gave little indication of the theatre behind it, as was the case with the *Amsterdam *Schouwburg built in 1637 (an arrangement still to be found today in some of the commercial theatres in London, Paris, and *New York), and often the theatre had no street façade at all, but was reached through a series of narrow passageways, as was the case with both of the leading theatres in London in the early eighteenth century, Drury Lane and *Covent Garden.

The general structure of European playhouses did not change a great deal in the course of the eighteenth century, although the size of theatres gradually increased, especially in the later half of the century, as the population of the major cities rapidly increased. Drury Lane, extensively remodelled several times during the century, began with a seating capacity of about 650 and after the renovations of 1775 could accommodate around 1,800. Covent Garden, when it was built in 1732, had roughly the same seating capacity as the older Lincoln's Inn Fields Theatre which it replaced, about 1,400, but subsequent alterations provided seating for over 2,000 by the 1780s and for 3,000 in 1793, at which time Drury Lane was being enlarged to accommodate 3,600. (*See* illustrations pages 392, 1138.) The stage also grew wider and deeper during this century, and the traditional forestage gradually diminished in size, though it remained, for most of the century, the primary acting area.

The first permanent playhouse built in America was the *Southwark, opening in 1766 in *Philadelphia. The following year the *John Street Theatre opened in New York, though Philadelphia maintained the lead in American theatrical activity through the early years of the nineteenth century. These, and the more elegant and ambitious playhouses that followed in the 1790s, the *Chestnut Street in Philadelphia, the *Park in New York, and the *Federal Street in *Boston, were all designed and *managed by actors with British backgrounds, and they differed in no substantial way from British playhouses of the same period.

Paris theatres, like those in London, gradually increased in size during the eighteenth century while maintaining their basic interior organization. In the later half of the century, however, an interest in theatre architecture grew, encouraged by articles in *Diderot's *Encyclopédie* and Dumont's *Parallèle des plus belles salles de spectacle d'Italie et de France* (1763). Although France dominated the dramatic repertoire of the Continent, Italy, thanks to the genius of the great families of designers—*Bibiena, Mauro, *Quaglio, *Galliari—dominated the field of theatre architecture and scenic design. Late eighteenth-century French works dealing with playhouse architecture invariably considered Italian design superior, in part due to the more capacious stages and in part due to the Italian ovoid auditoriums, which provided better views of the stage than the traditional French rectangular boxes, still reminiscent of the old tennis courts. Among the French architects who imported Italian features, the most influential were doubtless Marie-Joseph Peyre and Charles de Wailly, who designed a handsome new home for the *Comédie-Française in 1782 (renamed the *Odéon, it is still one of the major playhouses of Paris).

Even more important than the internal changes at the new Comédie was the fact that it was a free-standing building with a monumental façade overlooking a public square, in every sense a civic monument. The change from European playhouses tucked away behind other commercial buildings to such highly visible public structures was also a product of eighteenth-century thought. As early as the 1740s *Voltaire called for the cities of Europe to return to the practice of Greece and Rome and create magnificent public edifices for theatre. The first such monumental theatre of modern times was, not surprisingly, erected by Voltaire's friend and disciple Friedrich the Great. In 1745 he created a huge free-standing opera house in an open square in the centre of *Berlin, which Friedrich hoped to make a modern Athens. The example of Friedrich's opera house and the writings of French architectural theorists inspired the two most influential playhouse structures of the late eighteenth century in Europe, the new Comédie in Paris and the Grand Theatre in Bordeaux, designed by Victor *Louis and opened in 1780. Both playhouses were major civic monuments, isolated and elaborate structures, emphasized by converging avenues.

Other major French cities followed these models, and the idea of the playhouse as public monument gradually spread across Europe in the early years of the nineteenth century. The great new *Berlin Royal Theatre, designed by the leading German architect of the period, Karl Friedrich *Schinkel, opened in 1820 and served in turn as a model for city and state theatres all over Germany and Central Europe, where the state theatre building is still in many cities one of the most visible public structures. England's first monumental public playhouse was the rebuilt Covent Garden of 1809 designed by Robert Smirke. On the Continent an important encouragement for the development of the idea of the playhouse as public monument was the close relationship between theatre and the spreading idea of nationalism. In many countries, especially in Central and Eastern Europe, the theatre served as a focus for the display of national myths, legends, and history, presented in the national language. The urban and architectural visibility of the new 'national' theatres of the early nineteenth century reflected their symbolic importance in the building of a national consciousness and memory (*see* NATIONAL THEATRE MOVEMENTS, EUROPE).

Although the inspiration for the erecting of monumental playhouses did not disappear in the later nineteenth century, it was overtaken in importance by another concern, the appropriation of the opera by the new moneyed classes as their central example of high art. Except in Italy, opera had largely been the concern of royalty, and its production very often took place in spaces within princely residences. During this century, however, as the moneyed middle class assumed the dominant position in European society that had hitherto been that of the aristocracy, they became the new patrons of the opera. Perhaps no single architectural feature of the late nineteenth century became so emblematic of high bourgeois culture as the monumental opera house. In the early 1860s, as plans were being developed for what was to become the best known of all such playhouses, Charles Garnier's Paris *Opéra, César Daly, the editor of France's leading architectural journal, wrote a series of articles on the project claiming that the morals and values of every society were echoed in its most prominent public buildings, and that for the late nineteenth century that meant the church, the railway station, and the opera house. The international prestige of opera, and the importance of the opera house as an indication of the cultural aspirations of a community, were particularly clear in America. Here even very modest wooden theatres with no pretensions to the grandeur of their European namesakes, and in which opera was never actually performed, were nevertheless frequently called opera houses, partly to take advantage of the cultural associations of that term and partly to avoid puritanical suspicions of the spoken theatre.

For the next century, from the opening of the Garnier Opéra in 1875 to that of the Opera House in *Sydney in 1976, the monumental opera house remained an obligatory emblem for any city in the world attracted to European high culture, in the Far East, in *Cairo, even in the city of Manaus deep in the Amazonian jungle. Nor were such structures confined to urban centres. *Wagner's 1876 Festspielhaus in *Bayreuth popularized another version of the monumental playhouse, erected, like the great pilgrimage churches of the Middle Ages, as an attraction for a public drawn from great distances. During the twentieth century the most important development of the *festival playhouse outside major urban centres was not in opera but in the spoken drama, for which the first *Shakespeare Memorial Theatre at Stratford, opened just three years after the Bayreuth Festspielhaus, was the first great example. Especially after the Second World War, festival theatres sprang up across Europe and America, where the major sources of inspiration were the Shakespeare Festival Theatre in Stratford, Ontario (*see* STRATFORD FESTIVAL), and the *Guthrie Theatre in Minneapolis.

A common development in the playhouse as public monument in the late twentieth century has been the arts complex, where several playhouses, and perhaps other cultural structures as well, are grouped together into a kind of super-monument or artistic enclave within the city. The most familiar example in New York is *Lincoln Center, which includes performing spaces for dance, opera, and theatre, as well as auxiliary spaces for *films, musical events, and the performing arts collections of the New York Public Library. In London, the South Bank complex similarly combines a wide range of cultural structures, most notably the Royal *National Theatre, a building which itself houses three very different performance spaces.

Wagner's Festival Theatre at Bayreuth was both revolutionary and highly influential not only in its concept and location but in its internal arrangements. His design radically altered the normal interior arrangements of the standard European playhouse for both drama and opera. Instead of the traditional pit surrounded by rows of boxes and galleries variously arranged in a long rectangle as in the French tennis-court plans, or in a half-circle in imitation of classical practice, or in the ellipse favoured by the seventeenth century, or the various ovoid or modified horseshoe patterns of the eighteenth, Bayreuth offered essentially a large fan-shaped auditorium with a single ramp of seats (and a few vestigial boxes at the rear). The side walls were made up of lateral walls that suggested repeated proscenium arches extending into the auditorium, between which were multiple entrances to that space. This more democratic plan was widely adopted in European theatres built during the next century, and its general arrangement came to be known as 'continental seating'.

In the late nineteenth and early twentieth century playhouses felt the effects of the technological revolution, as electricity, steam, and hydraulic power were utilized to make ever more elaborate technical effects (*see* SCENE SHIFTING). The effects of this revolution were first seen in America, Germany, and Central Europe. In New York Steele *Mackaye dazzled audiences at his *Madison Square Theatre and *Lyceum Theatre during the 1880s with hydraulic lifts for the entire stage, an elevator orchestra pit, the latest in electric *lighting effects, and similar marvels. During the same generation, German scenic practice was revolutionized by pioneers like Karl *Lautenschläger, who created the first permanently installed *revolving stage in a Western theatre in *Munich in 1896 (it had long been a feature of the kabuki stage), and Adolf Linnebach, who developed, among many other electrical and technical devices, the modern

*cyclorama and the first successful device for projecting images of scenery (*see* SPECIAL EFFECTS).

The interrelated forces of technological advances, increasing urbanization, and improved public transport all combined at the end of the nineteenth century to make public playhouses ever larger and more elaborate. Improved machinery for lifting or sliding scenery forced the fly-tower over the stage higher and higher and the side wings wider (*see* FLIES AND FLOWN SCENERY). In the auditorium, steel cantilevering, which became general by the 1890s, allowed balconies to become larger and deeper, and reduced the once dominant boxes, in the theatres that still had them, to a few largely vestigial remnants hugging the proscenium arch. The coming of electricity in the 1880s improved illumination both in the auditoriums and onstage, and moreover provided a far safer lighting source than gas, which had been the standard means of illumination during the nineteenth century.

Although gas lighting provided playhouses with more flexible illumination than they had ever previously enjoyed, it was a very dangerous technology, and this, combined with the ever increasing size of theatres in Europe and America, resulted in more and more catastrophic *fires in theatres as the century progressed, culminating in the Ring Theatre fire in *Vienna in 1881, which claimed 450 lives. The result was the enactment of strong fire codes in many countries, which remained in effect even though the coming of electricity somewhat reduced the danger, and which had distinct effects on playhouse design. Stages and auditoriums were now required to be separated by a fireproof safety *curtain, construction material had to be more fire resistant, and multiple exits had to be provided for quick evacuation of the building (*see* SAFETY).

The coming of the First World War and the rise of the cinema finally brought to an end the steady increase in the size, number, and complexity of theatre buildings around the world, particularly in Europe and America, and the pre-war momentum was never really recovered. Nevertheless the years after the Second World War saw a boom in theatre construction and innovation headed by the widespread rebuilding of city centres destroyed by bombing, especially in Germany, and in the 1960s there was a boom in festival, university, and *regional theatre buildings in the United States. The majority of these new playhouses, in both Europe and America, were in the general tradition of the nineteenth-century theatre as civic monument but both exteriors and interiors were distinctly of another era. On the exterior, the columns and pediments of traditional *neoclassical and baroque playhouses were replaced by features more characteristic of high *modernist architecture: open glass façade-walls as in the 1955 State Opera in Hamburg, or sweeping, curved opaque walls in the manner of Le Corbusier in the 1969 Düsseldorf Schauspielhaus.

Equally radical adjustments were seen within these buildings. The rise of experimental theatres and an interest in breaking out of the proscenium arch, both significant turn-of-the-century developments throughout Europe, began to be widely reflected in the design of post-war European and American playhouses. From the early twentieth-century work in experimental theatre came the idea of each national or state theatre having a large theatre for the traditional repertoire and a smaller and generally more flexible auditorium for new and unconventional work (*see* STUDIO THEATRE MOVEMENT). The first major playhouse of the post-war renaissance was the Stadts-theater of Malmö, Sweden, which featured one of the Continent's first glass façades as well as a large and small auditorium under a single roof. In many such theatres the large auditorium was a conventional proscenium theatre, but Malmö's large space was flexible as well, altering its shape by means of false walls and movable stage sections. Its basic pattern, however, reflected the growing interest in breaking out of the proscenium arch (which did not exist here). Provision was made for a large thrust stage to extend out into the audience, seated in sweeping rows on three sides rather like the seating around the orchestra of a classic theatre.

The so-called *thrust stage enjoyed enormous popularity in the late 1950s and through the 1960s, a time of major theatre construction in Europe and America. The playhouse built by Tyrone *Guthrie for the Stratford Festival in Ontario, Canada, in 1957 offered a thrust stage based on a modified Shakespearian public theatre, with surrounding sweeping ranks of seats in the style of Malmö. This design in turn influenced that of the Guthrie Theatre in Minneapolis (1962) and the *Chichester Festival Theatre (1963), both of them in turn inspiring subsequent playhouses in the USA and the UK. Many playhouse designers of the 1960s regarded the thrust stage as the auditorium of the future, a prophecy which has not proven correct; but clear testimony to the power of this belief remains in London's National Theatre, which incorporates under one modernist roof a large theatre of a somewhat modified thrust design, a medium-sized conventional proscenium-arch theatre, and a small experimental theatre which can be arranged in various configurations.

The most innovative playhouse design of the twentieth century occurred in these large civic and festival theatres, but two other basic types of playhouses, with very different sorts of architectural traditions, also contributed significantly to theatrical culture. These were the commercial playhouses and those experimental playhouses not attached to larger theatres. Commercial playhouses were normally found during most of the century clustered near one another in entertainment districts in large cities, and were often generically designated by the name of the district: Broadway theatres in New York, West End theatres in London, *boulevard theatres in Paris. These theatres followed a fairly standard pattern, differing primarily in size and decoration. Their entrance was through a rather narrow decorated façade on a commercial street, with the auditorium fitted in behind small adjacent commercial structures,

and they were almost invariably proscenium-arch theatres with vestigial boxes and one or more wall-to-wall balconies. Due to the space constraints in their expensive and crowded commercial locations, they could also not offer the spacious lobbies, grand staircases, and other impressive public areas that were typical of the free-standing monumental theatres.

The smaller experimental playhouses of the twentieth century, though distinctly different from either the commercial theatres, monumental theatres, or arts complexes, shared a few common features, partly for economic reasons and partly for artistic ones. Economically, experimental playhouses normally lacked the means available to other venues, thus often having to adjust their physical arrangements to a very wide variety of pre-existing spaces. Artistically, many were founded by groups with little interest in replicating the architectural and spatial configurations of the past, and who, to the extent they were able, created playhouses in a great variety of forms. At mid-century, *arena theatre, or theatre in-the-round, with audiences completely surrounding the action, enjoyed a strong vogue in the United States, and a number of playhouses were built in this pattern. Almost every possible type of audience–actor relationship was attempted in one experimental theatre or another; probably the most common and most challenging of all was the so-called 'black box' theatre, which simply provided an open and neutral space for the placement of seating, raised platforms, and lighting, and could accommodate an almost infinite variety of such relationships. In the latter part of the twentieth century, when theatre was often produced in spaces not designed for that purpose—as it had been in the Middle Ages and Renaissance—the interest in a large, open, neutral performance space attracted a number of directors and designers to abandoned industrial buildings. At the end of the century a number of European cities, among them London, Paris, Berlin, and Zurich, converted such spaces into important, and in several cases permanent, new theatrical venues. *See also* ENVIRONMENTAL THEATRE.   MC

BURRIS-MEYER, HAROLD, and COLE, EDWARD C., *Theatres and Auditoriums* (New York, 1948)

CARLSON, MARVIN, *Places of Performance* (Ithaca, NY, 1989)

IZENOUR, GEORGE C., *Theater Design* (New Haven, 1996)

LEACROFT, RICHARD, *The Development of the English Playhouse* (London, 1973)

TIDWORTH, SIMON, *Theatres: an architectural and cultural history* (New York, 1973)

PLAYWRIGHT

A writer of plays, also referred to as a dramatist. The word playwright conjoins the nouns 'wright', meaning craftsman or builder, with 'play', meaning a *text written for *performance. Theatricalized storytelling, including the incorporation of *dialogue, dramatically concentrated *plots, and fictionalized time, is present in many world cultures. This has not always been a written tradition, however, and does not necessarily involve an individual author, often favouring a collective system for organizing and preserving an orally transmitted narrative, as in (perhaps) *The Memphite Drama* (*c*.2500 BC), an Egyptian text thought to have dramatized the passion of the ancient god Osiris (*see* ORIGINS OF THEATRE).

The evolution of the individual playwright in Western culture began with the ancient *Greek dramatic poets who created the great *comedies and *tragedies of fifth-century Athens for competition at religious and civic festivals (*Dionysia). Given the title of teacher (*didaskalos*), these playwrights were responsible for *rehearsing and *training the actors, collaborating with the musicians, choreographing the *dances of the *chorus, and publicly explaining the themes of their plays.

Playwriting as a civic duty and an emerging profession continued to develop during the time of the *Roman Republic as writers, notably the comic masters *Plautus and *Terence, borrowed the structure and plots of extant Greek texts and rebuilt them around contemporary settings, *characters, and themes. A substantial decline in the profession occurred during the late empire period, however, as other, more popular forms of entertainment replaced theatregoing, effectively ending the period of classical drama and the evolution of the profession of playwriting in the West for the next several hundred years.

Extant dramatic texts dating to the eleventh century signal the re-emergence of both collective and individual playwrights in the *medieval period. Clerics began scripting dramatic texts (based in some cases on the *liturgy and in other cases on Greek and Roman plays) for teaching purposes. The first accredited female playwright, *Hrotsvitha, wrote plays based on Terence, though it is unclear whether she wrote for performance; she is possibly an early example of the long-standing tradition of the *closet dramatist engaged in a literary activity unrelated to production and intended for educational, personal enrichment, or even subversive purposes. Anonymous playwriting flourished between the tenth and fifteenth centuries in feudal towns and cities across Europe, producing a feast of outdoor vernacular *religious drama (for example, the English *cycle plays, the Spanish *autos sacramentales*, and the French *Passion plays).

During the *early modern period many leading playwrights, including Shakespeare, *Molière, and Lope de *Vega, were theatre practitioners who also wrote for profit. Ben *Jonson was the first working playwright to publish his collected plays (1616), an act that may have begun the process of foregrounding the playwright as a literary figure. Eric *Bentley, who helped to *theorize the profession in *The Playwright as Thinker* (1946), notes that by the eighteenth century this schism between the literary figure (*Goethe) and the popular entertainer (*Kotzebue) had become entrenched: 'Since then every serious dramatist has had to run the gauntlet between those who feared that he was too theatrical to be poetic and those who feared he was too poetic to be theatrical.'

The nineteenth and twentieth centuries were marked by stylistic and cultural shifts (*romanticism, *realism, *naturalism, *surrealism, *absurdism, postmodernism) linked at least in part by a causal exchange. Playwrights have frequently been at the centre of the dialectic, writing plays that push against the day's *dramaturgical rules (*Hugo's *Hernani*), shove forward social reform (*Ibsen's *Ghosts* and *Shaw's *Widowers' Houses*), engage a *political agenda (*Brecht's *Mother Courage* or *Baraka's *Dutchman*), dramatize a philosophical condition (*Pirandello's *Six Characters in Search of an Author* and *Beckett's *Waiting for Godot*), or render the personal poetic and sublime (*O'Neill's *Long Day's Journey into Night* and Paula *Vogel's *How I Learned to Drive*).

The cultural status of the playwright has varied widely according to place, class, and gender. Female playwrights have struggled with *gender typing since England's first professional female playwright, Aphra *Behn, was accused of being overly bawdy and responded that 'the woman damns the poet'. Playwrights labelled by their ethnic or racial origins have faced similar marginalization, especially in production. During the 1990s August *Wilson responded to the infrequent staging of 'black plays' in the American *regional theatre by calling for a conscious building of a national black theatre dedicated to the production of plays by *African Americans.

Economically the status of the playwright began rising with the concept of the proprietary author in the eighteenth century. The first *Copyright Statute (1710) gave playwrights some control over their writing in England, though as late as 1879 *Gilbert and *Sullivan were forced to produce and stage the *New York première of *The Pirates of Penzance* personally, in order to protect their *royalty income from, ironically, piracy. At the start of the twenty-first century a lack of production opportunity—due in part to the proliferation of other, more popular forms of dramatic entertainment like *television and *film—continues to inhibit the success of emerging playwrights. Yet the moral and intellectual status of major playwrights remains high, ranging from Arthur *Miller to Caryl *Churchill to *Gao Xingjian.   LTC

PLAYWRIGHTS HORIZONS

American *Off-Broadway theatre. Founded in 1971 by Robert Moss to continue the work of Edward *Albee's Playwrights Unit, Playwrights Horizons develops, commissions, and produces new American plays and *musicals. Often perceived, particularly under *artistic director André *Bishop (1981–91), as favouring urban *satire and heightened *realism, its resident playwrights define its changing sensibility. They have included Christopher *Durang, A. R. *Gurney, Jr., Albert Innaurato, and Wendy *Wasserstein. The impressive spectrum of work sustained by Playwrights Horizons, by over 300 writers, includes three Pulitzer Prizes: Stephen *Sondheim and James Lapine's *Sunday in* the Park with George (1984), Alfred Uhry's Driving Miss Daisy (1987), and Wasserstein's The Heidi Chronicles (1988). Other productions include William Finn and Lapine's March of the Falsettos (1981) and Falsettoland (1990), Scott McPherson's Marvin's Room (1991), and Kenneth Lonergan's Lobby Hero (2001)

GAO

PLEASENCE, DONALD (1919–95)

English actor whose professional career began in 1939 in Jersey and was almost immediately interrupted by national service and time as a prisoner of war. Thereafter early work included The Brothers Karamazov at the *Lyric Hammersmith (1946) and productions with the *Birmingham Rep (1948–50), *Bristol Old Vic (1950–1), and *Shakespeare Memorial Theatre (1953). His unusual looks—at once soft and vulnerable and then sinister and vaguely psychotic—as well as his distinctive voice cast him in the classic mould of the British character actor on screen and stage. Although he worked regularly in *London through the 1950s, it was as the tramp Davies in the première of *Pinter's The Caretaker (1960) that his reputation was secured. Two other major roles were in *Anouilh's Poor Bitos (1963) and as Eichmann in Pinter's production of Robert Shaw's The Man in the Glass Booth (1967). All three productions transferred to Broadway. Although most of his subsequent career was on *film, he did return to the stage in Pinter's 1991 revival of The Caretaker.

AS

PLOT

The word commonly used to translate mythos, meaning a fictitious legend or myth, but used in a technical sense by *Aristotle to mean the arrangement of events in the making of a *tragedy. Aristotle preferred that the selection and arrangement of events be consequential, that a plot have a causally related beginning, middle, and end; but other arrangements are possible: plots can be descriptive, showing different aspects of a situation; or didactic, proving a case by example. Whatever its organizing principle, plot is invented by the *playwright in order to express (Aristotle's word is 'imitate'; see MIMESIS) a particular *action. The quality of a plot depends not only upon the arrangement of incident but also upon *characterization and *exposition. It is the combination of incident and circumstance, for example, which allows us to respond to a plot as tragic or comic. Plot should be distinguished from other aspects of *drama, with which it is often confused. As an invented construct it is distinguished from story, which simply relates events in temporal sequence (and may be the dramatist's source). Nor can plot be identified with the dramatic representation, which is neither time bound nor restricted to the presentation of plot incidents. Most importantly, plot is not the equivalent of action, which is the deeper, internal dramatic movement imitated by the plot. A

plot can be simple or complex, single or multiple, loose or tightly knit. In the twentieth century playwrights often abandoned causality as an organizing principle of plot and *theorists complained of its tyranny, but in some form plot remains central to most *dramaturgy.

RWV

PLOWRIGHT, JOAN (LADY OLIVIER) (1929–)

English actress. *Trained at the *Old Vic Theatre School in the late 1940s, Plowright joined the first *English Stage Company, run by her former teacher George *Devine, in the role of Mary Warren in Arthur *Miller's The Crucible in 1956. At the *Royal Court she met Laurence *Olivier while she was playing Margery Pinchwife in her first major commercial success, The Country Wife; she married him in 1961. Her reputation as one of *London's finest actors increased through her virtuosity in several plays of *Ionesco (The Chairs in 1957, The Lesson in 1958, Rhinoceros in 1960 under the direction of Orson *Welles). Through her performance as Beatie Bryant in Arnold *Wesker's Roots (1959), Plowright established herself as a leading actress of her generation. She joined the *National Theatre with Olivier for its first season in 1963, and continued to work there in the following decade. In the 1980s and 1990s Plowright focused more on *film, appearing in such successes as Revolution (1985), Enchanted April (1991), and Tea with Mussolini (1999). The last was directed by Franco *Zeffirelli, who had directed Plowright and Olivier in *de Filippo's Saturday, Sunday, Monday at the National in 1973.

TK

PLUCHEK, VALENTIN (1909–2002)

Russian/Soviet actor and director whose career began at *Meyerhold's theatre in 1926, where he combined work as an actor with organizing the electricians' branch of *TRAM (Young Workers' Theatre) in 1931. In 1939, together with Aleksei *Arbuzov, he organized a theatre *studio in *Moscow and from 1957 until the 1990s headed the Moscow Theatre of Satire. The theatre staged important revivals of *Mayakovsky's *satires The Bedbug and The Bathhouse in the 1950s, and gave the first performance (in the late 1980s) of Nikolai *Erdman's The Suicide, which had been banned since Meyerhold first tried to stage it in 1932.

NW

PLUMMER, CHRISTOPHER (1929–)

Canadian actor. Born in *Toronto, Plummer turned his *amateur beginnings in *Montréal and Ottawa (1945–8) into professional work—and over 100 roles in two years—first with the Canadian Repertory Company and CBC *Radio, then on Broadway (1954–5), most notably in *Anouilh's The Lark and Christopher *Fry's

The Dark Is Light Enough with Katharine *Cornell. Plummer's appearance at the inaugural *American Shakespeare Festival in Connecticut (1955) was largely eclipsed by his career-launching *Henry V* at the 1956 *Stratford Festival in Ontario. Acclaimed for his regal bearing, charismatic stage presence, and compelling, lyrical sense of language, Plummer, a recipient of the Order of Canada (1968), has developed an international reputation for his classical work in Canada as well as with the *Royal Shakespeare Company (1961), the Royal *National Theatre (1981), and in *New York (Iago opposite James Earl *Jones in *Othello*, 1981). His Tony-winning *Barrymore* by William Luce (1996–8) invited inevitable comparisons with John *Barrymore as a classical actor. But Plummer's prolific, versatile canon also includes complex contemporary roles (*Pinter's *No Man's Land* with Jason *Robards, Jr., 1995), *musicals (1973 Tony *award for Anthony Burgess's *Cyrano*, adapted from *Rostand), extensive *television work, and over 50 feature *films including *The Sound of Music* (1965).   MJD

PODESTÁ, JOSÉ JUAN (1858–1936)

Uruguayan-Argentinian *circus performer, actor, director, and *producer. Born in Uruguay to Genoese immigrants, Podestá was the fourth of nine children, with whom he went on to found an Argentinian performance dynasty. He is best known for portraying two *characters: the *clown Pepino the 88 and the outlaw *gaucho Juan Moreira. After *touring Uruguay as clowns and *acrobats, the Podestá brothers established their own circus company in *Buenos Aires in 1880. Because of his physical skill, 'Pepe' was asked to play Juan Moreira in a pantomime based on Eduardo Gutiérrez's eponymous *melodrama. The circus company's production was a great success, the action taking place on a movable stage as well as in the ring itself. In 1886 a spoken version of *Juan Moreira* premièred in Chivilcoy, later playing to record *audiences in *Montevideo and Buenos Aires. In the 1890s Podestá capitalized on the successful *drama gauchesco*, staging *Martín Fierro* and *Leguizamón's *Calandria*, definitively trading the circus ring for the stage, where he continued to perform, direct, and produce, sponsoring Argentina's first three-act play competition in 1903.   JGJ

POEL, WILLIAM (1852–1934)

English actor, director, and playwright, who pioneered the attempt to reconstitute Elizabethan and Jacobean stage conditions for productions of Shakespeare. *London born, Poel was briefly apprenticed in his father's profession, civil engineering, before running away from home to go on the stage. After assorted provincial trials, he returned to London in 1879 and thereafter worked on the fringe and in the interstices of *actor-manager theatre. He was *stage manager of two Shakespearian institutions in their infancies—Emma Cons's Victoria Coffee Palace

(later the *Old Vic) for 26 months from September 1881, and then Frank *Benson's *touring company for the first nine months of 1884. Poel's own approach to Shakespearian production first attracted attention in 1881, when he presented the First Quarto *text of *Hamlet* on a minimally furnished stage surrounded with red *curtains. In 1892 he staged *Webster's *The Duchess of Malfi* for the *Independent Theatre: the production showed both Poel's interest in reviving long-neglected English plays (notably, *Marlowe's *Dr Faustus* in 1896, *Arden of Faversham* in 1897, *Milton's *Samson Agonistes* in 1900, *Everyman* in 1901, Ben *Jonson's *Poetaster* in 1916) and also his tendency to take greater liberties with such texts than he did with Shakespearian ones, which he often cut but rarely rearranged or interpolated. Poel's relative respect for Shakespearian texts was linked to his ongoing attempt to approximate Shakespearian playing spaces and practices. For a production of *Measure for Measure* at the Royalty Theatre in 1893, he devised a portable *stage modelled upon the contract for the *Fortune Theatre. From 1894 he campaigned for the full reconstruction of an Elizabethan *playhouse in London, and formed the *Elizabethan Stage Society in 1895 to further this goal. Unorthodox in his time, Poel's doctrine was popularized by individuals who worked with him early in their careers—notably, Robert *Atkins, Harley Granville *Barker, Lewis *Casson, Edith *Evans, Elsie Fogerty, Lillah *McCarthy, Nugent Monck, Ben Iden *Payne, and Esmé Percy.   MOC

POETIC DRAMA *See* VERSE.

POGODIN, NIKOLAI (1900–62)

Russian/Soviet playwright whose work conformed closely to the *socialist realist norms which were prescriptive for Soviet writing after 1934. His play *Tempo* (1929) already demonstrates a commitment to the cause of rapid industrialization, whilst *Aristocrats* (1934) has the CHEKA, or state security officials, as its heroes. Set in a White Sea Canal construction camp, convicts and political dissidents are shown being re-educated through constructive labour, with the focus on the gangster Kostya who, in this modern *miracle play, is converted into a zealous communist worker. The play was given a remarkable production by Nikolai *Okhlopkov at his Realistic Theatre, deploying minimalist techniques derived from Asian theatre and staged on two platforms, arranged like two hairpins at opposed angles, with the *audience in the round. Pogodin's other major work is a trilogy of plays devoted to Lenin, *The Man with a Gun* (1937), *Kremlin Chimes* (1942), and *The Third Pathetique* (1959).   NW

POISSON, RAYMOND (c.1633–90)

French actor and playwright. Known as Belleroche in *tragedy, his greatest fame came in *comedy as Crispin, a likeable, mumbling, wide-mouthed, scheming valet *costumed in a Spanish-style black jacket, cape, and knee-length boots. This *character, invented by *Scarron in 1654, was taken over by Poisson in 1660 when he arrived in *Paris, and over the next 25 years at the *Hôtel de Bourgogne and the *Comédie-Française he played Crispin in comedies by himself and seven other authors. After his retirement his son Paul and grandson Philippe, known as Crispin II and III, starred in vehicles by *Dancourt, *Lesage, and *Regnard; a second grandson and a great-grandson, Crispin IV and V, exhausted the line.   RWH

POLIAKOFF, STEPHEN (1952–)

English dramatist and *film director. Poliakoff began writing plays whilst still a teenager and in the early 1970s had work produced at the *Royal Court (Lay-By, 1971) and *Bush Theatre (The Carnation Gang, 1973; Hitting Town and City Sugar, both 1975, winners of the Evening Standard's most promising playwright *award). These early plays about post-industrial urban living feature *characters who are lonely, isolated, and under intense pressure. After time as writer-in-residence at the *National Theatre (1976–7), Poliakoff saw his work produced at the *Royal Shakespeare Company; plays from this time include Shout across the River (1978), Breaking the Silence (1984), and Playing with Trains (1989). Coming into Land (1987) and Sienna Red (1992) were less successful and were easily topped by his film and *television screenplays, which include Caught on a Train (1980), She's Been Away (1989), Close my Eyes (1991), and Shooting the Past (1999), which he also directed. The last is archetypal Poliakoff in its intelligence and attention to detail, distinctively televisual in its narrativity, characterization, and its central metaphor of the still photographic image.   AS

POLISH LABORATORY THEATRE

Founded by Jerzy *Grotowski in collaboration with Ludwig Flaszen in Opole, Poland, 1959, initially under the name Theatre of 13 Rows, this sparsely funded experimental ensemble began by staging deconstructed versions of literary classics. Known for its rigorous programme of physical and vocal *training as well as for its 'poor theatre' aesthetic, the company defined itself as a venue for uncompromising investigation of the actor's craft. With its production of Adam *Mickiewicz's Dziady (Forefather's Eve, 1961), the Laboratory began to experiment with altering the spatial relationship between actors and spectators in order to suggest a precisely situated role for the viewer. The style of the Laboratory's productions was non-*naturalistic, featuring highly detailed psychophysical action and extraordinary physical and vocal feats on the part of performers. Rising to international prominence in the mid-1960s following their production of *Marlowe's Dr Faustus, the Laboratory served as a source of inspiration for a generation of theatre artists. Celebrated productions include The Constant Prince (1965, adapted from *Słowacki and *Calderón) and Apocalypsis cum Figuris (1969, *devised from various *texts), both featuring Ryszard *Cieślak in prominent roles that accomplished what Grotowski considered an apotheosis of the actor's craft. Following Apocalypsis, Grotowski announced that he would no longer create new theatrical productions. The Laboratory's emphasis shifted to paratheatrical work that investigated the conditions for a more authentic encounter between actor and spectator. Although various members of the original ensemble chose to pursue independent projects, the Laboratory did not officially dissolve until 1984, after Grotowski emigrated from Poland following the declaration of martial law.   LW

POLITICS AND THEATRE

Discussion of theatre and politics necessitates exploration of several diverse yet frequently interlocking issues. Chief amongst these are: (a) the theatre of politics, the way in which political activities in many societies have been theatricalized; (b) the politics of theatre, evident in the organization, funding, and *censorship of theatrical activity in particular societies and how these are shaped by political structure and practices; and (c) the stances taken in theatrical performances towards political issues and practices, and how these may impact on dramatic and theatrical conventions. Politics will be understood here as the practices and ideologies associated with the formal organization of the social body—although we will also see how the notion of a personal politics evolved in the later twentieth century, with accompanying reconceptions of the relationship between theatre and politics. Particular forms of political organization distinguish themselves by the ideals and principles upon which their legitimacy and authority are secured and order imposed. As such, politics has traditionally referred mainly to processes of governance. However, historically politics has usually been the site of struggle, of contests for power and dominance by various sectors within individual societies. Such struggles inevitably respond to and find reflection in cultural institutions, practices, and ideas: theatre, due to the social and public nature of its production and reception, has often proved to be one of the more significant institutions and practices affected by, and affecting, political struggle.

1. The theatre of politics; 2. Politics of theatre;
3. Theatre engaging with politics

1. The theatre of politics

In many societies power and authority have been effectively communicated and consolidated, or challenged, through theatrical means. The *rituals and processions preceding the Athenian *Dionysia, the triumphal games and processions of Roman generals, the royal *entries and progresses of the Elizabethans, the Nazi Nuremberg rallies, or the Mayday *parades in the Soviet Union, all exemplify large-scale *spectacles where the state and its authorities have been displayed to the public (*see* STATE DISPLAYS; CIVIC FESTIVALS). Such stagings of state power have, in turn, been answered by popular spectacles such as, for example, mass demonstrations against the Vietnam War or the occupation of Beijing's Tiananmen Square by protesters in 1989.

While the theatre of politics is most obvious in such spectacles, the links have also been evident at the level of performance. From *Aristotle through Cicero and Quintilian to Elizabethan handbooks, parallels have been drawn continually between the *actor's art and the ways in which rhetoricians and politicians should perform. We might see a line from such a tradition leading to *Brecht's portrayal of Hitler—in the guise of Arturo Ui, receiving instruction in acting— to the acting coaches brought in to assist presidential candidates in the United States today. In a world of photo opportunities, *television interviews, and staged debates, the modern politician and his or her team might be likened to an *actor-manager, employing *playwright, *stage managers, and supporting cast to mount their performance of power. Beyond this, theorists such as Jean Baudrillard would argue that such performances are simply more obvious symptoms of a wholesale spectacularization of the social in the contemporary world.

2. Politics of theatre

Throughout history theatre has survived *financially due to the patronage of either the state or leading public figures, whether these be *early modern courts, tribal kings and emirs in Nigeria, *Japanese shoguns, or the arts and culture ministries of modern European states (*see* ARTS COUNCILS). As a result theatre has at times served the interests of the people and bodies which fund its presentation. This was quite openly the case, for example, in the courtly *masques of the Renaissance or the organization of *touring *agitprop troupes in the early years of the Soviet Union or the subsequent promotion of *socialist realism as the state-approved style. Or the impact may be less overt but equally recognizable, as in the way the conventions and subjects of *neoclassical French theatre were shaped by political and religious intrigues at the court of Louis XIV.

At a more subtle level, we can recognize how broader political shifts may affect theatre in its location, address, and form. The paradigmatic shifts associated with the Enlightenment led to the emergence of a secular-humanist and democratic social organization and the rise of the bourgeoisie. Dissociated from its functions within the Church or court, theatre played an increasing role in developing *bourgeois cultural activity (and increasingly became dependent on the patronage of this rising class). New forms of drama evolved out of this secular context which succeeded in legitimizing specifically bourgeois values and morals, making these seem natural and spontaneous rather than the product of social conventions and norms. One eventual product of such shifts was the displacement of *heroic tragedy by the sort of domestic *tragedy and *tragicomedy found in authors such as *Ibsen and *Chekhov.

Theatre's dependence upon patronage has always been accompanied by the threat of censure: even within the seemingly liberal atmosphere of classical Athens, where *Aristophanes savagely lampooned leading politicians in outrageously obscene ways, a poet could be prosecuted for attacking the state or the gods, and, indeed, Aristophanes was prosecuted early in his career. In England, the political content of Ben *Jonson's plays led to his imprisonment during Elizabeth's reign, when regulation of the theatre became increasingly strict. The censorship powers of a court official, the *Lord Chamberlain, derived from this period and were formalized under the *Licensing Act of 1737. Until the abolition of his powers in 1968, the Lord Chamberlain's office was responsible for inspecting and enforcing changes to plays before they could be approved for production. Beyond restrictions placed upon representations of the monarchy and God, successive Lord Chamberlains worked without any published standards of taste or moral judgements, although taboo areas included the treatment of living politicians, sexual behaviour (in particular anything to do with homosexuality), and supposedly obscene language.

In societies where strict control of public forms of communication has been the norm, theatrical activity often continued, against great odds, to provide a public space for critical voices. The threat implied in its address to a wide public and the use of public spaces, in turn, produced more severe forms of censorship, as in the imprisonment of many writers under the Nazi and Soviet regimes. It is arguable that the increasing marginalization of theatre within the cultural and political landscape of Western liberal democracies accelerated the dismantling of direct censorship practices (although they were often replaced by more subtle forms, as in decisions over funding taken by public authorities). In contrast, where theatre has had a more public role to play, censorship and worse continue. The well-known case of Václav *Havel turned out happily: in a few months in 1989 he went from banned playwright in Stalinist Czechoslovakia to President of the Czech Republic. The result is rarely so pleasant. In colonial Nigeria the work of playwrights such as Hubert *Ogunde, whose touring theatre supported the anti-colonial struggle, was banned. The situation, however, did not always improve under post-independence governments, with Ogunde a victim again, along with Wole *Soyinka, who was detained by the Nigerian government in 1967–9. Soyinka eventually went into exile, as did Ngugi wa *Thiong'o, a leading Kenyan playwright who was also detained, in 1977–8. In *China, the work of dissident writer, playwright, and recent Nobel laureate *Gao Xingjian has been banned since 1987 for its political references. Paradoxically, such bannings may be seen as indicative of the continuing power of theatre in such societies.

3. Theatre engaging with politics

As the cases of Aristophanes and Jonson illustrate, theatre was used to challenge reigning political realities before the evolution in the twentieth century of political theatre as a distinct tradition of practices and theories. Often staging political resistance to established authority occurred amongst practitioners of less official and more popular performance forms, as with the *medieval *giullari*, from whose popular *satire the modern Italian writer and performer Dario *Fo has drawn much inspiration for his own approaches to developing a more politically challenging theatre. Yet the twentieth century produced some of the most self-consciously political theatre. Diverse movements rose out of a growing desire for theatre to make a more discernible impact on society. Major influences were the spread of Marxist or *materialist analyses of capitalism and bourgeois society, anti-colonial sentiments, and revolutionary struggle in the political and economic spheres, with their accompanying questions about the role of cultural institutions in sustaining capitalist hegemony. These ideas were applied to the structures and institutions of theatre, provoking new debates on its collusion with bourgeois ideology, its function and purpose in society, and questioning the role of the practitioner in these broader struggles.

By its very nature as a public art form, theatre was seen to be valuable for such struggles, possessing the means for delivering complex information and analysis in a simple manner, as well as providing an alternative forum for further debate and discussion. Theatrical forms such as agitprop and the *living newspaper were developed by socialist practitioners as vehicles for delivering a political message with the greatest simplicity and clarity in the context of actual struggles. While agitprop was developed initially in the aftermath of the Soviet Revolution, its immediacy led to its adoption by many other popular theatre movements in Europe and the United States in the 1920s and 1930s (including notably the Workers' Theatre Movement in Germany and in Britain), on to its revival by political theatre activists in the 1960s and 1970s, and its reappearance at anti-globalization demonstrations in the new millennium. Similarly, the living newspaper format, widely practised in Europe and the United States in the 1930s, was revived by various popular movements in subsequent years.

Such initiatives were by no means restricted to liberal-democratic political expressions. In the inter-war years under fascist rule in Hitler's Germany and Mussolini's Italy (as well as in France and Spain), there were similar efforts to exploit the public nature of theatre for right-wing propagandist purposes (*see* FASCISM AND THEATRE). In Italy, theatre was deployed in a set of broad-based campaigns to re-educate the population on the basis of a fascist philosophy. Beyond such measures other theatrical ventures imbued with religious symbolism came to be seen as the very embodiment of fascism—the non-literary cultic spectacles of mass political rallies, liturgies, parades, and so on.

Yet, despite concerted attempts to produce a recognizably fascist aesthetic and a distinctive theatrical tradition, most of these initiatives, limited to a national-popular focus, failed to take root. Unlike socialism, fascism produced no tradition of political theatre which extended beyond national boundaries and cultures. Also notable is the absence of continuity between the initiatives of the inter-war years and after the war. By contrast, socialist-inspired theatre has dominated discourses on political theatre because an evolving tradition can be traced across countries on every continent throughout most of the twentieth century.

The practitioner who was most influential in the development of such a political theatre was the writer and director Bertolt *Brecht. Espousing an *epic theatre, he developed an aesthetic specifically aimed at unmasking or demystifying the *illusions present in reigning bourgeois ideologies which claimed to be natural and spontaneous expressions rather than driven by material interests or the result of historical forces. He used overtly theatrical means to make the familiar strange (the *Verfremdungseffekt* or V-effect), to challenge the habituated and supposedly normal, thus allowing for the imagination of alternative political realities and possibilities. Brecht's use of the V-effect, the adoption of an episodic form of writing, and his promotion of gestic writing and acting—whereby underlying social attitudes and transactions should be brought out in the scripting and playing of *scenes—had an influence on many subsequent writers, directors, and performers well beyond his native Germany.

In many European countries and the United States the 1960s and 1970s witnessed the re-emergence of popular political theatre movements which, while they derived some methods and approaches from Brecht, also drew more consciously on other forms of popular entertainment. Such work aimed to move beyond established theatres and reach working-class *audiences who had lost (or never acquired) the habit of theatre-going. Performances toured to local halls, parks, factories, and *streets. Notable amongst such companies were Red Ladder, *Monstrous Regiment, and *7:84 in Britain, the *San Francisco Mime Troupe and El Teatro *Campesino in the USA, and the work of Dario Fo and Franca *Rame in Italy. Such performances also contributed to the development of radical *community theatre in many countries, with theatre workers involving local communities in addressing immediate issues of concern through *devised theatre.

In many *African and Asian countries theatre played a role in the mid-century anti-colonial struggles. In some places this involved adaptation of local forms for propagandist purposes, as exemplified by *dalangs* who toured subversive *wayang kulit* performances around *Indonesia during the struggles against the Dutch; in others it was through theatrical forms which drew on both Western models and indigenous performance traditions, as in the work of *Bengali writer-directors Utpal *Dutt and Badal *Sircar who founded popular political theatre troupes in *India. While both agitprop and indigenous forms have been used in subsequent government-sponsored theatre for *development work, often aimed at informing rural populations about health or education issues, many countries have also witnessed the development of political theatres which are highly critical of the post-colonial governing elites; from the 1970s on, work by groups such as Kamirithu Community Centre in Kenya, Aranyak Theatre, PROSHIKA in *Bangladesh, and the *Philippine Educational Theatre Association has often encouraged local people to create *community-based performances addressing immediate oppressions. Parallel developments also occurred in *Latin America with the work of the Brazilian Augusto *Boal, whose theatre of the *oppressed (inspired by Paolo Freire's 'pedagogy of the oppressed') is aimed, through various devices such as image theatre, forum theatre, and legislative theatre, at involving audiences as 'spect-actors' who take part in developing the *action initiated by his performers. While Boal saw such work as aimed at 'rehearsing the revolution', during his many years in exile after 1971 his methods were increasingly taken up in Europe and North America by *theatre-in-education companies and others concerned with broader procedures.

Although a transgressive theatre centred on more direct types of economic and political oppression has continued to survive in some countries, in much of the West there was a shift away from such activity towards the end of the twentieth century. This was the result of diverse factors: the rise in political activism based on various identity issues, a concomitant growth of special-interest theatrical activity such as *feminist theatre, black theatre, *gay theatre, *lesbian theatre, and disability theatre; the decline in clear-cut class politics as a whole, itself a product of post-industrialism, globalization, and postmodernity. And linked to all, the dominance of the *mass media, in particular the pace and amount of information and debate which are made available through *television and the Internet. This has led some theorists to argue that, as we enter a new century, theatre's political role is in need of further reconfiguration, with the focus shifting to how it may provide a site of resistance to the wholesale mediatization of experience. *See also* ALTERNATIVE THEATRE. LR

BOAL, AUGUSTO, *Legislative Theatre* (London, 1999)
BRECHT, BERTOLT, *Brecht on Theatre*, trans. John Willet (London, 1964)
STOURAC, RICHARD, and MCCREERY, KATHLEEN, *Theatre as a Weapon: workers' theatre in the Soviet Union, Germany and Britain, 1917–1934* (London, 1986)
VAN ERVEN, E., *Radical People's Theatre* (Bloomington, Ind., 1988)

POLITIS, FOTOS (1890–1934)

One of the first directors in Greece, Politis started his career with *Sophocles' *Oedipus the King* (starring Aimilios Veakis), which he translated and directed for the Society of Greek Theatre in *Athens in 1919. He taught at the Professional Theatre School from 1924, and in 1927 directed *Euripides' *Hecuba* for the theatre company of Marika *Kotopouli. In 1932 he became the first director of the *Greek National Theatre. In the two years before his death he directed 35 productions, including *Aeschylus' *Agamemnon*, Shakespeare's *Othello*, *Ibsen's *Ghosts*, *O'Neill's *Anna Christie*, and *Xenopoulos's *Popolaros*. Politis was noted for his innovative approach to *Greek *tragedy, especially for emphasizing the role of the *chorus, and for introducing platforms on different levels in the settings. He translated several plays and wrote over 1,000 newspaper articles, including theatre *criticism. KGo

POLLOCK, SHARON (1936–)

Canadian playwright and actress. Pollock wrote, 'I think I write the same play over and over again. It's a play about an individual who is directed or compelled to follow a course of action of which he or she begins to examine the morality.' Through this lens she examines events in Canada's past that bring out unresolved issues in the present, for example, racism in *Walsh* (1974) and *The Komagata Maru Incident* (1976), and the legacy of colonialism in *Fair Liberty's Call* (1993). Past and present interweave in plays of private life: in her best-known play, *Blood Relations* (1980), Lizzie Borden, acquitted of the murders of her stepmother and father, challenges her actress friend to come to her own verdict by playing Lizzie as she was, or could have been, at the time of the murders. Past and present overlap also in *Doc* (1984), in which a woman and her father struggle over their conflicting memories of the suicide of her mother. Pollock was *artistic director at Theatre Calgary (1984) and Theatre New Brunswick (1988). RCN

POLLUX, JULIUS, OF NAUCRATIS (second century AD)

Rhetorician and scholar. Pollux's *Onomasticon*, a topically arranged lexicon imperfectly preserved, includes a section on theatrical antiquities. Nevertheless, Pollux's indifference to dates and his preoccupation with terminology makes his discussion of stage machinery, *masks, and *character types more suggestive than truly informative. RWV

PONNELLE, JEAN-PIERRE (1932–88)

French director and designer. After studying music, philosophy, and the history of art at the Sorbonne, as well as studying painting with Fernand Léger, Ponnelle began an extraordinary career in *opera and *ballet by designing for composer Hans Werner Henze (*Boulevard Solitude*, 1952; *König Hirsch*, 1965). He became one of the most important opera directors of his generation, and one of a handful of artists who directed and designed his own productions. He was sought after by major companies throughout the world, including the *Salzburg Festival, where he created renowned productions of Monteverdi and *Mozart (including the often neglected *opera seria*). Re-introducing a taste for the baroque in staging, and with a painstaking attention to visual detail, Ponnelle was one of the first directors to oversee the *filming of his opera productions.

DGM

PON NYA, U (1807–66)

Burmese court playwright. Along with U *Kyin U, he was one of the great nineteenth-century dramatists, though an intensely controversial one. His court-commissioned plays were designed as morality tales. *Paduma* recounts the story of an unfaithful woman who ruthlessly attacks her husband and leaves him for dead. Outrage expressed by court ladies over this unfavourable depiction of women was quelled by his next play, *Wayanthadaya*, which featured a devoted and selfless wife. His last play, *Wizaya*, about an outlaw prince who was banished by the King, proved to be his death warrant. He became a victim in the power struggle over the succession to the throne and was murdered during the revolt of 1866. *See also* MYANMAR.

CRG

POPE, JANE (c.1742–1818)

English actress, singer, and dancer, a protégée of Kitty *Clive and her successor in low comic roles at *Drury Lane. Pope's first appearance came as a young girl, acting in *Garrick's *Lilliput* in 1756. In her early years, she was particularly admired for her pertness and vivacity in roles such as Beatrice in *Much Ado* and the title role in *Colman the Elder's *Polly Honeycomb*. She was the original Miss Stirling in the Colman–Garrick *Clandestine Marriage* and Mrs Candour in *Sheridan's *The School for Scandal*. Later in her career (spent almost entirely at Drury Lane), she excelled in duenna roles.

MJK

POPE, THOMAS (fl. 1593–1603)

English actor who began his career with a troupe of itinerant players in Denmark and Germany (1586–7; *see* ENGLISH COMEDIANS). By 1590 he was playing in *London with Lord *Strange's Men, and took the role of Arbactus in *Tarlton's *The Seven Deadly Sins, Part II*. By 1599 Pope was a member of the *Chamberlain's Men, holding a share in both the old *Curtain Theatre and the new *Globe. His roles are unknown although he appears in the cast lists for *Jonson's *Every Man in his Humour* and *Every Man out of his Humour*. Samuel Rowlands referred to him as 'Pope the clown', but there is no other reason

to associate him with Tarlton, *Kempe, and others who traditionally performed *clown roles.

SPC

POPOV, ALEKSEI (1892–1961)

Russian/Soviet director whose career began at the *Moscow Art Theatre First Studio (1912–18) before he took up a director's post at the Vakhtangov Theatre in 1923, staging plays by emerging Soviet playwrights, including *Olesha's *The Conspiracy of Feelings* (a dramatic reworking of the novel *Envy*) in 1929. Moving to the Theatre of the Revolution in 1930, Popov staged a sequence of plays by *Pogodin, and after 1934, when the climate of Soviet theatre became stagnant, expressed his own creativity in politically safe productions of Shakespeare, including *Romeo and Juliet* (1935) and *The Taming of the Shrew* (1937). From 1935 to 1960, Popov was *artistic director of the Central Red Army Theatre in *Moscow. A talented teacher, Popov learned a great deal from working with *Vakhtangov at the outset of his career, whose legacy he attempted to pass on to his own pupils.

NW

POPOV, OLEG (1930–)

Russian/Soviet *circus artist and *clown whose career began in 1950 as a high-wire trick cyclist, sporting a trademark tow-haired peasant wig and outsize chequered peaked cap. With his mobile features, characterized by minimal *make-up, he developed the persona of the good-natured simpleton who wants to get involved in other circus acts, such as bareback riding or the trapeze, then succeeding in a *parody of the skills of the experts. Popov was inclined to include political comment on home and foreign affairs as part of his act. Among the most popular clowns of his generation, his work was seen widely abroad.

NW

POPOVA, LYUBOV (1889–1924)

Russian/Soviet painter and stage designer who became a prominent member of the Russian *constructivist movement in the early 1920s. She contributed designs to the *Tairov–*Ekster production of *Romeo and Juliet* (1921), but her most important and influential construction was for *Meyerhold's 1922 production of Crommelynck's *The Magnanimous Cuckold*. Set in a flour mill, the scene consisted of an open, skeletal structure of plain latticed wood, comprising levels, inclined planes, ladders, revolving doors, vestigial mill sails, and three painted wheels, one large and enclosed, the other two spoked, all of which revolved in accompaniment to intense emotional moments of action. The whole was mounted on a bare stage against a background of the theatre's plain brick walls. The *biomechanical style of *acting was enhanced by *costumes which established the actors as a workers' collective. To this end, Popova designed acting overalls, called 'prozodezhda', to which individual items of *characterization could be added. Popova later designed stage *properties and propaganda slogans for Meyerhold's 1923 production of *Tretyakov and Martinet's *Earth Rampant*.   NW

POPULAR DE BOGOTÁ, TEATRO

Colombian group founded in 1968 by Jorge Alí Triana, Jaime Santos, and Rosario Montaña. Initially its plays concentrated on national themes, such as the popular *I Took Panama* (1974) by Luis Alberto García, directed by Triana, based on the division of Panama by the USA to build the canal in 1903. Later it complemented new work with productions of Shakespeare, *Molière, Tennessee *Williams, *Brecht, and *Miller, among others, and sponsored alternative *film festivals, storytelling recitals, seminars, and theatre workshops. The theatre closed in 1996.
                                                         BJR

PORNOGRAPHY AND PERFORMANCE

see page 1060

PORQUET, NIANGORAN (1949–98)

Actor, poet, and dramatist from the Ivory Coast. As part of the renewal of the performing arts in Côte d'Ivoire in the early 1980s, Porquet created the notion of the *griotique*: theatrical adaptation of the storytelling techniques of oral performers known as *griots*. For Porquet poetry is meant to be sung and dramatized to the accompaniment of various instruments, particularly the harp-like *cora* and the *balafon* (xylophone), and the central structuring device of his performances is *dance. One of his most notable productions in Abidjan was *Les Zaoulides*, based on the Zaouli *masked dance of the Gouro people of central Côte d'Ivoire.   SVa trans. JCM

PORRES (PORRAS), GASPAR DE (1550–c.1615)

Spanish *actor-manager. Performing between 1585 (when he bought two plays from *Cervantes) and 1608, Porres was probably the most important and prosperous impresario of his day. His company played throughout the country, and employed several actors famous later. A close associate and friend of Lope de *Vega, he bought and first performed dozens of that author's plays, twelve of which he published, with Lope's help, in *Madrid in 1614.   VFD

PORTEOUS, CAMERON (1937–)

Canadian *scenographer. Born in Saskatchewan, Porteous studied design at England's Wimbledon School of Art. He was head of design at the *Vancouver Playhouse (1972–81) and the *Shaw Festival (1979–97), where he designed many productions and championed the company's 'total design' concept. In addition, Porteous has designed many other theatre, *opera, *television, and *film productions, including the Emmy award-winning film *Beethoven Lives Upstairs* (1992). Since 1979 he has been a frequent contributor to the *Prague Quadrenniale, the international exhibition and competition of stage design, and has often curated its Canadian contributions.   DWJ

PORTER, COLE (1891–1964)

American composer and lyricist. Scion of a wealthy Indiana family, Porter began composing in childhood and made his name at Yale (1909–13) by writing music and lyrics for the annual college shows. He co-wrote *See America First* (1916), a patriotic *musical in the manner of *Gilbert and *Sullivan and his first Broadway production. After volunteering with an ambulance corps in the First World War, Porter—having married the even wealthier Linda Lee Thomas—spent much of the 1920s with high society in Paris and Venice. He grew more disciplined about his composing in the 1930s and created a series of successful scores: *Gay Divorce* (1932), in which Fred *Astaire introduced the song 'Night and Day'; *Anything Goes* (1934), a long-running show starring Ethel *Merman and featuring 'I Get a Kick Out of You' and 'You're the Top'; *Leave It to Me!* (1938), in which Mary *Martin sang 'My Heart Belongs to Daddy'; and *Du Barry Was a Lady* (1939), which concluded with Merman and Bert *Lahr singing 'Friendship'. Severely injured and in chronic pain after a 1937 riding accident, Porter grew dependent on medication and alcohol and became less productive. *Kiss Me, Kate* (1948) supplied many hit songs in the context of a soundly constructed *plot (adapted by Sam and Bella Spewack from *The Taming of the Shrew*), while *Can-Can* (1953) and *Silk Stockings* (1955) also saw long commercial runs. Many of Porter's witty songs became popular standards and the shows *Anything Goes* and *Kiss Me, Kate* have seen frequent revivals.   MAF

PORTER, ERIC (1928–95)

English actor whose long stage career was perhaps overshadowed by the celebrity of his *television role of Soames Forsyte in the landmark series *The Forsyte Saga* (1967). Porter made his first professional appearance at the *Shakespeare Memorial Theatre in 1945, and was a member of the *Birmingham Rep (1948–50). In the 1950s he worked for H. M. Tennent, the *Bristol Old Vic, and the *Old Vic in *London, playing roles that included Lear, Vanya, Volpone, Henry IV, and Bolingbroke. In 1957–8 he *toured with the *Lunts, appearing on Broadway in *Dürrenmatt's *The Visit*. Following a celebrated Rosmersholm at the *Royal Court (1959), he joined the *Royal Shakespeare Company, where roles included Malvolio, Leontes (both 1960), Pope

(continued on p. 1062)

PORNOGRAPHY AND PERFORMANCE

The highly contested terms 'pornography' and 'performance' interpenetrate conceptually and historically. About *performance, *theorists seem to agree on two key points: that it entails a double consciousness through which the execution of an *action is mentally compared with a certain model of that action; and that it is done for an *audience, even if that audience is only the self. 'Pornography'—from the Greek *pornei* and *graphos*, meaning, literally, 'whore writing'—refers to representations that are perceived to have sexual arousal as their primary objective. Its definition involves both content and effect and is subject to culturally specific, historically shifting standards of sexual normalcy and deviance. While almost all forms of representation might theoretically be pornographic because it is impossible to limit what every person may find sexually arousing, the most widely recognized forms of pornography intend to incite sexual performance, and in the process create models by which consumers judge themselves and others in the sexual arena. Pornography is thus by common definition highly performative and constitutive of double consciousness. At the same time, part of the *frisson* of pornography is its seeming challenge to this very notion of *performativity by playing to the persistently popular belief that people caught in the grip of sexual climax are beyond artfulness, that is, beyond the capacity knowingly to perform and thus, perhaps, to deceive. The danger and allure of pornography's testing of performativity's limits are arguably more acute in live as opposed to mediatitized performance because of the physical presence of the actors' bodies and their real-time sexual behaviour.

The interpenetrations of pornography and performance are documentable from ancient times, at least since Xenophon's *Symposium* recorded the proffering of nude erotic *dancers who enacted the marriage of *Dionysus and Ariadne at a banquet for the patriarchal intelligentsia in classical Greece. *Feminist, *postcolonial, and *queer studies have radically altered how we understand such representations, emphasizing that they are not just about explicit sexual acts but about circumstantially specific operations of power and identity. Pornographic performance has often reproduced the dynamics of imperial regimes, eroticizing those colonized as Other in terms of sexuality, *gender, *race, ethnicity, and/or class: for example, the re-enactment by slaves of the myth of Pasiphae and the bull for the Emperor Titus in the Roman arena, Byzantine Emperor Justinian's delectation over and then marital containment of Theodora's lewd *circus *acrobatics; brothel performances catering to the eighteenth-century English aristocracy with such exotica as facsimile Tahi-

tian fertility rites; and private erotic theatres for the French nobility and their actress mistresses, including that of the Duc d'Henin featuring plays penned by Delisle de Sales (Jean B. C. Isoard, b. 1745) and performed by priapic athletes. For many feminists, the Marquis de Sade (1740–1814) epitomizes the phallocentric ethos of sex as power over and violence against women. But others, emphasizing the performative aspects of his enterprise, find subversion of that paradigm in the ways his purposefully staged and exaggerated actions—elaborated to still greater excess in his major writings—ultimately *satirized and thus critiqued the excesses of the tyrannous regimes under which he operated. De Sade's obsessive need for his actors to play the roles in which he cast them, as well as his own bisexual desire to switch roles while directing the *ritual, point in microcosm to the fundamental instability of imperial regimes whose status as conquerors relies on specific kinds of performances of Otherness by those conquered.

In Asia, as in Europe, the development of pornography as a distinctive *genre was linked to the spread of printing technology and flowering of literature. If *kunqu* drama espoused Confucian orthodoxy in *China, its performance by prostitute troupes titillated aristocratic audiences who consumed pornography originating in the lower Yang-tze delta during the Ming and Qing dynasties. *Japan's moralistically repressive Tokugawa Dynasty allowed the highly performative, sexually charged culture of the Floating World to appease samurai and rising merchant-class libido. By contrast, native Polynesian culture, while figuring in Western imperialist erotica, did not develop a comparable pornography of its own; sexual mores permitted a wider range of behaviour, including public sexual intercourse during some religious festivals, which mitigated against the pathologizing of sex that drove pornographic production and consumption in other societies.

In Europe and America, official *censorship of pornography intensified in the nineteenth century as the bourgeoisie solidified its political and cultural power. However, far from eliminating the genre, legal repression fostered its subterranean efflorescence in cities such as *London and *New York, creating a bifurcated culture whose highly forbidden and frequented underworld Steven Marcus has termed 'pornotopia'. Graphic depictions of sexual acts in public performance as well as open sexual traffic inside the more respectable theatres were gradually curtailed, but print media that could circulate underground burgeoned, along with fetishization of those bodily extremities that could be glimpsed above ground. Tracy C. Davis has demonstrated that pervasive consumption of pornography (mostly by males) fuelled the continuing association of actresses with prostitutes through the nineteenth and into the twentieth centuries. Actresses were frequently depicted in pornographic novels, serials, and pictures (such as the *carte de visite* photographs that flourished from 1854 to 1880 and allowed for private consumption of performers' images). As spectacular public women, actresses were readily available objects for the projection of male sexual fantasies aroused by the illicit consumption of pornography, whether it explicitly portrayed actresses or not. Theatrical producers and performers became expert at playing to pornographically literate audiences, manipulating sexual codes more boldly in leg shows and *burlesque, and more subtly but no less consciously in performances of *legitimate drama. Sexual desires aroused could be satisfied by prostitutes who remained available outside the theatres and in other venues, like concert saloons. Some of the pornographic codes deployed by stage performers were appropriated by spectators themselves when they attended such public, civic-sponsored events as the annual French Ball masquerade in Madison Square Garden. In the London marriage of Arthur Munby and Hannah Cullwick, sexual intimacies involved elaborate play with pornographic and imperialistic codes as the two switched roles across lines of class, race, gender, and age in private theatricals avidly chronicled in their diaries and Munby's photographs.

In addition to providing an outlet for sexual repression, pornography fed the popular knowledge base about human sexuality that impinged on the institutionalized study and management of the body and emotions, especially of females, undertaken in the interest of maintaining bourgeois respectability. Ideals of normalcy, health, and continent social performance were set, at least in part, against the *spectacles of incontinence elaborated in pornographic representations. Pornography thus needs to be taken into account as a significant frame of reference in analysing the 'scientific' provocation of hysterical female orgasmic performance in gynaecologic clinics and theatres (such as Charcot's) across Europe and the United States, and in Anton Mesmer's less reputable salons. On and behind the scenes of the professional stage, pornographic knowledge also factored into the ways pornophile star makers and impresarios such as David *Belasco provoked and professed to control extreme—and putatively authentic—emotional climaxes by lead actresses, and fetishistic *ballet masters exacted virtuosic, mechanically precise flourishes of exposed extremities from female dancers.

Graphic portrayal of sexual acts generally remained suppressed in public venues until late in the twentieth century, although there is evidence of secret black market erotic theatres, such as those that sprang up in Germany after the First World War. In official culture, widening knowledge of the so-called sexual perversions made imputations of eroticism permissible in a heterosexual context but censorable in a homosexual one, as in the New York productions of Solomon *Asch's *The God of Ven-*geance* (1922), Édouard Bourdet's *The Captive* (1926), and Mae *West's *The Drag* (1927) and *The Pleasure Man* (1928), all shut down under the auspices of the Society for the Suppression of Vice. While Anglo-American censorial standards subsequently shifted (from increased legal crackdowns in the 1930s and their more paranoid enforcement following World War II to the greater liberation of the post-Stonwall, post-*Lord Chamberlain 1970s), overt performances of *lesbian and *gay desire remain more feared for their arousing impact on susceptible audiences and thus more subject to obscene and pornographic classification than heterosexual depictions.

With the so-called sexual revolution that began in the 1960s, more explicit sexual acts became a feature of performances across a wider range of venues. On the legitimate stage at the end of the decade, Fernando *Arrabal incorporated graphic scenes of sadism and bestiality; Kenneth *Tynan celebrated orgasm in *Oh! Calcutta!*; *Hair* glorified free love; and orgies were mounted in Peter *Hall's *opera production of *Moses and Aaron* and Richard *Schechner's *Performance Group's production of *Dionysus in 69*. Meanwhile, performance elements enlivened the expansion of sexual emporia, such as Show World and Playland in Times Square in New York, and the West Village gay bars the Anvil, with its 'Weimar Germany' atmosphere, and the even more strongly s/m-oriented Mineshaft. *Film pornography peaked in the 1970s, working along with ever flourishing and by then more mainstream print media like *Hustler* and *Playboy* to shape the fantasies audiences projected onto performers in all sorts of venues. More cheaply produceable and privately consumable, video supplanted film pornography in the 1980s and enlarged the possibilities of vicarious sexual performance just as the AIDS epidemic called the ethos of lived promiscuity into question.

In *alternative theatre spaces, performers engaged in more self-conscious, critical explorations of pornography. For example, in New York, Elizabeth *LeCompte and the *Wooster Group imitated the 'depthless' performance style of porn films in *Route 1 & 9* (1981). Richard *Foreman's *The Birth of a Poet* (1985) pushed the seminal stereotype of the lust-ridden whore to deconstructive extremes. Karen *Finley, in *performance art works such as *The Constant State of Desire* (1986), thwarted the objectifying gaze with spectacularly obscene defilements of her own body, while 'sex-positive' Annie Sprinkle, appearing in Schechner's *Prometheus Project* (1985) and her own *Post-Post Porn Modernist* (1990), both revelled in and subverted the pornographic economy with elaborate displays of self-commodification on- and offstage. The *San Francisco-based lesbian s/m group Samois (formed in the late 1970s) sought to manipulate traditional gender-coded structures of power for women's pleasure.

At the turn of the millennium, the interpenetrations of pornography and performance proliferate with the mass marketing of computers and the growth of Internet and Web-based technologies (*see* CYBER THEATRE). Redrawing the boundaries of liveness, interactive media allow consumers new voyeuristic and participatory pleasures, including unprecedented ability to access and customize images and sounds and play any role for real-time sexual intercourse in cyberspace, which in turn shape the production and reception of the performing arts, film, and *television. By some estimations, the United States is engaged in a cynical pastiche of Victorian bifurcation as official culture, pushing the rhetoric of church and family, cleans up Times Square and fulminates over the sexual indiscretions of a president while pornography balloons to an industry with a $10 billion to $14 billion annual turnover. From a *performance studies perspective, it is entirely logical that New York's leading theatre critic, Frank *Rich, should have shifted to cover the political arena and in 2001 taken a detour to write a major story on the porn world for the Sunday *New York Times Maga-*zine. Rich reports that pornography is a bigger business than professional football, basketball, and baseball put together, and that Americans, though few will admit it, spend more money per year on porn than they do on other kinds of movies and all the performing arts combined. 'Porn', Rich writes, 'is the one show that no one watches yet miraculously never closes.' *See also* SEX SHOWS AND DANCES. KM

DAVIS, TRACY C., *Actresses as Working Women: their social identity in Victorian culture* (London, 1991)

MARCUS, STEVEN, *The Other Victorians: a study of sexuality and pornography in mid-nineteenth-century England* (New York, 1966)

McCLINTOCK, ANNE, *Imperial Leather: race, gender, and sexuality in the colonial conquest* (London, 1995)

SENELICK, LAURENCE, 'Eroticism in early theatrical photography', *Theatre History Studies*, 11 (1991)

WILLIAMS, LINDA, *Hard-Core: power, pleasure, and the 'frenzy of the visible'*, expanded edn. (Berkeley, 1999)

Pius XII in *The Representative* (1963), Bolingbroke, Henry IV, Shylock (all 1965), Faustus, and Lear (1968). Later stage appearances included an unlikely (but successful) Big Daddy at the Royal *National Theatre in *Cat on a Hot Tin Roof* (1988), Lear for the Old Vic (1989), and Serebriakov in *Uncle Vanya* at the National (1992). AS

PORTE-SAINT-MARTIN, THÉÂTRE DE LA

*Paris *playhouse, erected in 1781 by Lenoir in 75 days as temporary accommodation for the *Opéra, after *fire had destroyed the *Palais Royal. Like the Peyre-de Wailly Théâtre-Français (*see* COMÉDIE-FRANÇAISE), it seated 1,800 in a circular *auditorium with receding tiers of *boxes. Constructed largely of wood with brick vaults, it housed the Opéra until 1794, and stood for 90 years. Between 1802 and 1830 it operated a repertory of *melodramas, *spectacle plays, and *ballets-pantomimes. The major boulevard home of *romantic drama from 1830, the Porte-Saint-Martin was burned down during the Commune in 1871. Rebuilt on the same site in 1873, it remains in operation today. JG

PO SEIN, U (1880–1952)

Burmese actor who modernized the classical *dance-drama *zat pwe*. He was the first *mintha* (male lead) to touch a *minthamee* (female lead) onstage, with the suggestive gesture of placing a flower in her hair and leading her by the hand. Extremely popular, he garnered large and appreciative crowds among the populace and achieved an idol-like status. He added new elements such as *variety acts and *chorus lines, performed on raised *stages (used previously only by the 'higher' order of *puppet theatre), added *lighting, and was the first to charge admission. He died while dancing on stage at the age of 72. *See also* MYANMAR. CRG

POSSART, ERNST VON (1841–1921)

German actor and director. Possart's career is linked to the court theatre in *Munich where he shone as a leading character actor, playing roles such as Shylock, Richard III, and Mephisto. In 1872 he began directing and was appointed *artistic director in 1895, dividing his time between *opera and drama until retirement in 1905. One of the great court actors of the late nineteenth century, he was a master of rhetorical declamation. CBB

POST-COLONIAL STUDIES

The field of post-colonial studies grew out of the study of so-called 'Commonwealth literature' on the one hand and post-colonial theory on the other. The study of English literatures by writers from the former British Empire developed in the 1960s. It was in general regionally organized with emphases determined by the amount and quality of literature emerging from the many different countries once administered by Great Britain. The focus was mainly on writers from Nigeria, *India, and the *Caribbean. Writers from the so-called settler colonies (Australia, New Zealand, Canada, South Africa) had an increasingly ambivalent place as the field became politicized with the advent of post-colonial theory. Post-colonial theory evolved in the 1980s as a response to post-*structuralist theories and can be traced back to the work of Edward Said, Gayatri Spivak, and Homi Bhabha. Although their theoretical orientations are different, they share common ground in their reception of French theory. The foundation text of post-colonial theory is Said's study *Orientalism* (1978) in which he applies Michel Foucault's discourse theory to the history of Western constructions of the 'Orient' to show how 'culture' is inextricably implicated in the political and economic domination of the East. These ideas were further developed in *Culture and Imperialism* (1993). Spivak is more radically deconstructive and combines ideas of Derrida with committed *feminism to interrogate class differences within post-colonial societies (*In Other Worlds*, 1987). Arguably the most influential of post-colonial theorists, Homi Bhabha, has applied psychoanalysis and the theories of Frantz Fanon to examine the dynamics of mutual dependency existing between the colonizers and colonized (*The Location of Culture*, 1994). Post-colonial 'identity' is, according to Bhabha, characterized by ambivalent processes such as imitation (mimicry), alterity, and hybridity. Of particular interest therefore are 'third spaces', such as the emergent *diasporas where creative identity formation takes place outside the conventional matrices of home and tradition.

Post-colonial studies has synthesized these theories to produce a set of concerns and recurrent questions which today can be levelled at any *texts and media products. As a period, post-colonial is understood to be a continuum spanning the colonial past and the post-colonial present. Its geo-cultural orbit is today all-encompassing, embracing not just the former European colonies but also the cultural diasporas established in the Euro-American metropolitan centres. A post-colonial reading will invariably be concerned with the relations of domination and subordination—economic, cultural, and political—existing between and within nations, races, and cultures, which have their roots along the post-colonial continuum.

The place of *theatre and *performance within the wider field of post-colonial studies is a contested one. First, the bulk of research into post-colonial literature has been devoted to fiction. *Drama, by comparison, whether studied as texts or performances, has received relatively little attention. Secondly, theatre, understood as a medium of European provenance, carries by definition the stigma of a Eurocentric 'import'. Nevertheless, the first two post-colonial writers to be awarded the Nobel Prize for Literature, the Nigerian Wole *Soyinka and the Caribbean poet Derek *Walcott, have both dedicated substantial parts of their career to writing and producing plays. Apart from author-centred and local studies, the synthesis of post-colonial theory and theatre studies did not begin until the mid-1990s. Central concerns revolve around rewritings and restagings of the classics, particularly Shakespeare and the *Greeks. Canonical texts include Aimé *Césaire's *Une tempête* (1969) and Soyinka's *The Bacchae of Euripides* (1973). The (re)integration of *ritual into dramatic forms and aesthetic frameworks has been repeatedly explored by Soyinka (*The Road*, 1965; *Death and the King's Horseman*, 1975) and Walcott (*Dream on Monkey Mountain*, 1970) and intensively discussed in recent research (Gilbert-Tompkins and Balme). Ritual and *carnival are studied from the point of view of theatrical elements such as the body, music,

and *costuming. Language, a central concern of post-colonial studies in general, is both one of the basic markers of colonial authority and a specific strategy of resistance in theatre and performance in post-colonial contexts. These strategies include translation from and to indigenous languages as well as mixing indigenous languages and creoles with European ones. Still under-researched but of crucial importance is the integration of *music and *dance, as there are few post-colonial plays that do not utilize these elements to some degree.   CBB

ASHCROFT, BILL, et al., *The Empire Writes Back: theory and practice in post-colonial literatures* (London, 1989)
BALME, CHRISTOPHER, *Decolonizing the Stage: theatrical syncretism and post-colonial drama* (Oxford, 1999)
GILBERT, HELEN, and TOMPKINS, J., *Post-colonial Drama: theory, practice, politics* (London, 1996)

POSTERS

Visual theatre advertising goes back to graffiti found at Pompeii and to the *Chinese *hua-choerh* (Yuan Dynasty advertising banners hung all over the city by *touring companies). For the first centuries of the modern era, *playbills were simply plastered to any available wall, especially those on which they were prohibited, a practice known as 'sniping'. Beginning about 1820, posters (printed on a quarter of a flatbed-press sheet or in a three-sheet format) were differentiated from playbills (one-twelfth or one-sixteenth of a sheet) and became an important aspect of theatre publicity, and a secondary art themselves, due to cheaper printing processes, an increasingly literate population, and an increasingly lower-class *audience (which made theatre *tickets more an 'impulse buy' and thus increased the need for highly motivating pictorial advertisements).

In the 1840s Joseph Morse developed multicolour printing for woodcut *circus posters in New York State; Jules Chéret converted the process for use with lithography in *Paris in 1867, and just as importantly recruited many leading painters to create theatre posters. Chéret's posters were among the first collectable colour lithographs, and because they could be sold as well as posted, their initial high cost was somewhat defrayed. Early theatre posters indicate a *melodramatic approach to advertising the show; they usually feature multiple small panels, often depicting the key effect or sensation scenes or *tableaux, often captioned with key or curtain lines. They attracted spectators by promising excitement, and helped to prime them by directing attention to the distinguishing features of the show and what they were intended to mean.

The late nineteenth-century 'Road' repertoire in the United States was so small and predictable that many printers maintained a stock of standard poster designs for the most popular plays, so that when a company passed through town the venue, time, and date could be slugged and the poster printed immediately. As the star system grew and companies preferred to have their particular production advertised, the Strobridge Lithographing Company of Cincinnati came to specialize in very fast creation and delivery of theatrical posters, and the larger American road companies depended on it. In 1879 Matt Morgan joined the company, rapidly becoming chief artist and designer, and pioneered the single 'selling concept', that is, one large arresting image in place of the old multiple panels. The image might or might not be a scene from the play; rather than a promise Morgan gave the potential audience a single visual motivator to see the show as a whole. Single arresting-image posters immediately swept the United States, leading to a 50-year dominance by Strobridge. The method was picked up by British touring companies, and from Britain spread to the Continent. Within a few years single images had become the standard in theatrical posters.

In general theatrical posters followed advertising style closely, and where the theatre has been closely associated with a broader *avant-garde or bohemia, theatre posters have been strongly influenced by it (for instance the post-Impressionist posters of the Paris avant-garde, the *Bauhaus-influenced posters of the 1920s, and so forth). Possibly the most lasting influence on English-language posters has been the work of Lee *Simonson, Robert Edmond *Jones, and Mordecai *Gorelik in the 1920s and 1930s for the *Theatre Guild in *New York, in which the single arresting image was made extremely simple, often almost a cartoon, and strongly thematic—both catching the eye, and preparing the audience to see the play through predetermined thematic lenses. *See also* PUBLICITY   JB

POSTMODERNISM *See* MODERNISM AND POSTMODERNISM.

POST-STRUCTURALISM *See* STRUCTURALISM AND POST-STRUCTURALISM.

POTTER, DENNIS (1935–94)

English *television dramatist, screenwriter, and director. Born in the Forest of Dean to working-class parents, Potter was one of the 'angry' generation of anti-establishment writers of the 1950s. Unlike most of them, however, he made an early commitment to the new and untried medium of television, and remained loyal to it throughout his working life, producing 43 original plays, series, and adaptations, mostly for the BBC. Widely regarded as the most significant television dramatist, his work was characterized by a concern with the forms and possibilities of television drama, often drawing on, and reworking, *genres of popular culture: *Pennies from Heaven* (BBC, 1978), for example, introduced the device of 'lip-synch' miming to popular music which was to become a Potter trademark. Potter also drew, often controversially, on his own life and obsessions (see, for example, his final plays, *Karaoke* (BBC, 1996) and *Cold*

Lazarus (Channel 4, 1996)). Throughout his life Potter suffered from psoriatic arthropathy, a condition which affects the skin and joints, and which necessitated long periods of hospitalization, an experience dramatized in *The Singing Detective* (BBC, 1986), perhaps his most accomplished work. He also wrote screenplays, and directed for television and the cinema.

SWL

POWADA

*Marathi panegyrical ballad from the state of Maharashtra in *India. From the old Marathi word *pawad*, a chant sung in praise of a deity, the *powada* is composed in a free metre, given buoyancy through internal rhyme and alliteration, and has the vigour of prose and the rhythm of song. *Powadas* are sung by *shahirs* (composer-singers) to the accompaniment of a tambourine. Their companions join them in the refrain, pitching their voices an octave higher. The first extant *powada* dates from the time of Shivaji (1630–80) and commemorates Shivaji's killing of Afzal Khan, the Bijapur ruler Adilshah's agent. Originally sung in Shivaji's court, it was first published in a collection by S. T. Shaligram (1879). In 1891, Shaligram collaborated with Arbuthnot Ackworth, who had served as a government official in Maharashtra for twenty years, on another collection of 58 *powadas*, although both volumes are marred by omission of the impromptu prose passages that *shahirs* customarily added, usually to reflect the views of their patrons.

In the pre-independence period, *shahirs* like Annabhau Sathe and Amar Shaikh sang *powadas* about the struggle of workers and farmers against exploitative mill- and landowners. These rousing compositions would draw *audiences of workers and farmers in the thousands. Today *shahirs* from all over Maharashtra continue to sing about social events and political issues.

SGG

POWER FAMILY

Irish-American acting dynasty. The line begins with (William Grattan) **Tyrone** (1797–1841), born in Kilomacthomas, Ireland. He took to the stage at 14, and played minor roles for some years. From 1826, he was *London's most popular enacter of comic Irish *characters. Between 1833 (when he made his *New York debut in *The Irish Ambassador*) and 1841 he *toured America three times, repeating his acclaim. He also wrote six original plays. Two of his four sons—**Maurice** (d. 1849) and **Harold**—became minor actors. Harold's marriage to actress Ethel Lavenu produced a prominent player, (Frederick) **Tyrone** (1869–1931), born in London. In 1886 he emigrated to Florida, where he made his stage debut in *The Private Secretary*. From 1888 his career was mainly centred in New York, where he acted in many important productions, including the *musical *Chu Chin Chow* (1917). His later years emphasized Shakespeare—Brutus in

Julius Caesar, reprised many times, being his signature role. He wed the actress **Helen Reaume** and sired **Tyrone** (Edmund) (1914–58), born in Cincinnati. The sometimes inaccurately billed Tyrone Power, Jr., acted with his mother at 7 and in 1931 did a Shakespearian season in *Chicago. On Broadway he appeared with Katharine *Cornell in *Romeo and Juliet* (1935) and *St Joan* (1936). After many years as a *film star, he returned to the stage in the 1950s in *Mister Roberts*, *John Brown's Body*, and *Back to Methuselah*. His son **Tyrone** (William) (1959–   ) was born in *Los Angeles, and began his acting career in 1978 as Malcolm in *Macbeth*. *See also* FAMILIES IN THE THEATRE.   CT

PRADO, ANTONIO DE (c.1594–1651)

Spanish *actor-manager. Closely associated with major dramatists like Lope de *Vega and *Calderón, he was himself an outstanding performer. The important company he led from about 1622 until his death employed other leading actors, like Alonso de Osuna and María de Quiñones, but its basis was his own large *family, including his third wife Mariana Vaca and his son Sebastián (1624–85), who was equally famous later.   VFD

PRAGA, MARCO (1862–1929)

Italian playwright and critic. Praga dominated the Italian stage at the turn of the century with his *verismo works. Companies interested in the new *realistic style premièred his plays: Virginia Marini performed *The Virgins* (1889), Eleanore *Duse *The Ideal Wife* (1890), Ermete *Novelli *Alleluja* (1892), Cesare Rossi *L'incanto* (*The Spell*, 1892), Andò-Leigheb *Il bell'Apollo* (1894), and C. Reiter *La crisi* (1904). At the Manzoni Theatre company (1912–15) in *Milan, Praga headed an experimental *playwriting and *directing project. Among other plays, this company premièred his own *The Closed Door* (1913) which became a vehicle for Duse, and *Il divorzio* (1915). Like *Becque, *Strindberg, *Ibsen, and *Chekhov, Praga centred most of his twenty plays on women—*ingénues, wives, and mothers—and while he portrayed seducers in all their rascality, he essentially condemned the 'fallen' or sinful woman and her confused, irrational emotions for destroying the social order.   JEH

PRAGUE

The traditional centre of the Czech state, Prague was the scene of *liturgical plays in the twelfth century (at St George's monastery), of Latin plays in the early sixteenth century (at Prague University, founded in 1348 by Charles IV), and of lavish court festivities under the reign of Rudolf II (1575–1611), especially those conceived between 1568–1585 by Giuseppe Arcimboldo. This promising development was broken with the loss of national independence in 1620. The Habsburg court was moved to *Vienna, the position of Prague as cultural centre was shattered,

and a general Germanizing brought the development of theatre and drama in the Czech vernacular to a standstill for the next century and a half. The first public theatre, built by Count F. A. Špork in 1701, hosted German and Italian *opera and drama companies, as did the Kotce Theatre (1738–83), the first municipal theatre in Prague, where plays in Czech were produced in the 1760s and 1770s. After 1783 it was surpassed by the spacious and elegant Nostitz Theatre (called Theatre of Estates 1798–1864, and again since 1991 after seven years of extensive reconstruction), conceived by Count Nostitz-Rieneck as a 'national theatre' for the population of Czech lands, both German and Czech speaking, putting Prague back on the theatre map of Europe. *Don Giovanni*, conducted by *Mozart himself, had its world première in 1787 there, and after 1785 a modest policy of presenting plays in Czech was followed. The aspirations of the Patriotic Theatre were bolder, in the *playhouse affectionately called Bouda (the Shack, 1786–9); though this was again a bilingual project for the bilingual city, growing nationalist feelings on both sides separated the two communities. In 1851 the Society for Founding a *Czech National Theatre in Prague was established as a significant political act; in 1862 the Provisional Theatre opened, where operas by Bedřich Smetana were the dominant achievements; and finally, in 1883, Czechs had their own National Theatre. In the Theatre of Estates only plays in German were performed between 1862 and 1920, and in 1888 Prague Germans opened the New German Theatre. Eventually the traditional antagonism waned away and German and Czech theatre existed side by side and was beneficial for both linguistic communities. The multi-ethnic character of Prague was lost in the atrocities and holocaust of the Second World War. The Festival of German Speaking Theatres, which since 1996 has brought some half-dozen companies from Germany, Austria, and Switzerland every November, is a proper reminder of this special relationship.

In the Czech National Theatre domestic *realism triumphed in late 1880s, in the written drama and in production style. In the new century, the theatre, under Jaroslav Kvapil's leadership, opened up to the latest European trends. In 1907 a rival appeared: the Vinohrady Theatre (traditionally subsidized by the municipality of Prague), where Karel Hugo *Hilar started his professional career. In the 1920s and 1930s, however, it was the little theatres that indicated future trends. In 1926 the Liberated Theatre had shown in its opening performances an enchantment with clowning and French *modernism. Jindřich Honzl (1894–1953) and Jiří *Frejka were the guiding spirits, and E. F. *Burian their ardent follower as composer and performer. The ways of these leading *avant-gardists soon parted: after a short stay in *Brno, Honzl returned to the Liberated Theatre, and in 1933 Burian founded his own theatre, D34.

After a short period of democracy, the Prague post-war theatre was put under control of the Communist Party/state system, supported by many of the former avant-gardists, including

Honzl and Burian. Every form of private enterprise was explicitly forbidden. (A special theatre regulation Act was the first law passed by the communist-controlled Parliament, in March 1948.) Some theatres in Prague were closed and a process of continuous reorganization was in progress, striving to find the most effective method of control. Nevertheless the young generation took advantage of the first signs of political thaw. Theatre on the *Balustrade was founded in 1958, and other little theatres followed, innovative and different in style: Semafor in 1959, Činoherní Klub (Drama Club) in 1964, and Otomar *Krejča's Theatre beyond the Gate in 1965, all contributing to the international fame of Czech theatre in the 1960s. After the Soviet invasion in 1968, the next two decades were years of general depression, although directors like Ladislav Smoček (1932–) in Drama Club or Evald Schorm (1931–88) in Theatre on the Balustrade maintained uncompromising moral and professional standards. New companies were organized in the professional and *amateur ranks, like Divadlo na Okraji (Theatre on the Fringe, 1969) and Sklep (the Cellar, 1971), and promising talents like Petr Lébl (1965–99) also appeared.

Shortly after the Velvet Revolution of November 1989, directors Jan *Grossman, Krejča, and Jaroslav Vostrý (1931–) returned briefly to the theatres they had been dismissed from, enjoying the satisfaction of moral victory, though only Theatre on the Balustrade under Lébl's management has come to the fore again. A considerable number of new companies emerged; among them, the Kašpar (Joker) Theatre (1990) and CD 94 Theatre Association (1994) seemed to be firmly rooted in Prague's theatre soil by 2001. The majority of the established repertory companies are still administered and subsidized by the municipality, corporate and private sponsorship being subsidiary phenomena, though of growing importance, especially for the new groups. Times have been hard for the resident *mime companies; on the other hand, the musical theatre has flourished. The National Theatre opera company opened up to the world repertoire and its level of production has risen considerably. From 1992 the erstwhile German theatre building housed the competitive and adventurous State Opera. Numerous *musical comedy productions have mushroomed, and some of them erected or adapted new playhouses or *auditoriums to suit their needs. New venues (for international *festivals of *alternative theatre, for example) were also created in derelict industrial halls. *See also* HAVEL, VÁCLAV.   ML

BURIAN, J. M., *Modern Czech Theatre: reflector and conscience of nation* (Iowa City, 2000)
Cultural Guide to Prague (Prague, 2000)

PRAHLADA NATAKA

Literally *The Play of Prahlada*, this traditional Indian form is based on a new theatrical version of the Prahlada and Narasimha narrative (*c.* 1880), in the Oriya language spoken in the eastern state of Orissa in *India. Though commissioned by and credited to Raja Rama Krishna Deva Chhotray, the Zamindar of Jalantara, a tiny princely state now in Andhra Pradesh, the principal author was most likely Goura Hari Paricha. Inspired by Telugu devotional drama, this palace creation combined Carnatic music and chanted Sanskrit passages with theatrical elements drawn from disparate sources, at once classical and *folk. A striking feature of the form is the use of a five-tiered stage on which the performers move up and down. By 1900 the *text was being performed professionally, and today over 50 village-based companies in the Ganjam district of Orissa perform *prahlada nataka*, with gurus and participants drawn from all traditional castes. Usually two troupes vie for the *audience's attention. Originally played over seven evenings, it now starts as early as noon and continues through the night. Sometime after dawn, the priest/performer playing the man-lion avatar of the Hindu god Vishnu appears, usually in violent trance, saving Prahlada from his father's murderous rage, thereby manifesting the protective aspect of the godhead.   JE

PRAMPOLINI, ENRICO (1894–1956)

Italian painter, designer, and *theoretician, a key figure in the *futurist movement. His early manifestos, *Futurist Scenography and Choreography* and *Dynamic Stage Architecture* (both 1915), abolished the traditional divide between *playhouse design and architecture, between *stage and *auditorium, and between *actor and *scenery, and introduced the idea of an 'electro-dynamic luminous stage architecture', which would unfold as a total work of art. He was a prominent exponent of the Futurist Mechanical Theatre through his production of the *puppet plays *Matoum et Tévibar* (1919) and *Night Divers* (1923), the 'mechanical *ballets' *Renaissance of the Spirit, Metallic Night* (both 1922), *Dance of the Propeller* (1923), and *Psychology of the Machines* (1924), and the manifestos *The Aesthetics of the Machine* (1922), *Futurist Mechanical* Art (1923), and *Futurist Scenic Atmosphere* (1924). In 1925 he exhibited a model for a Magnetic Theatre at the Exposition Internationale des Arts Décoratifs in *Paris, which won him the grand prize for theatre. He consolidated his international success by directing and designing a season of futurist *pantomimes in Paris (1927). In the following years he designed over 80 (mainly non-futurist) plays and *operas.   GB

PRASAD, JAISHANKAR (1889–1937)

*Indian playwright, poet, and short-story writer. The scion of a wealthy merchant family of Banaras, Prasad devoted his life to literature and was a key figure of the Chhayavad movement in Hindi poetry that reacted sharply against the puritanical norms preceding it. The *romantic radicalism of this school, which flourished in the 1920s and 1930s, precipitated a new relationship to nature, creating and reflecting the poet's emotional and mental experience. Prasad sought to establish an explicitly Indian point of view in literary and dramatic criticism, and as a consequence rejected *realism, notably in *Ibsen's plays, which he regarded as pessimistic and fatalistic. The poet was to seek the ideal rather than the real, his creative experience finding expression in the depiction of subtle internal states embodied in the experience of *rasa or aesthetic pleasure. In spite of his polemical rejection of the individuation of *character, he nonetheless initiated the exploration of subjectivity, both of the poet and of the characters in his dramatic work.

His thirteen plays, written expressly to counter the commercial *Parsi stage, were written for a small literary coterie, and there is no evidence that they were performed in public in his lifetime. Focusing largely on the glories of the national past, he undertook massive research into historical records, the epics, and the Puranas, in order to lay the groundwork for finely wrought projections of Hindu political power and glory. His four late plays, *Chandragupta* (1931), *Skandagupta* (1918), *Ajatashatru* (1922), and *Dhruvaswamini* (1933), focusing on emperors and conquerors in the projected golden period of Hindu political power, are considered major works in the history of Hindi drama. They are memorable for the personalization of character, the historical blending of the political with the familial and the individual, and most of all for the powerful delineation of rebellious, desiring women who threaten to overstep all bounds of decorum, even though they finally choose to bow to tradition. Devasena and Dhruvasvamini, as epitomes of this new female character type, are fictional women who were given model status for the writers of the 1930s and 1940s. Apart from these plays, Prasad is chiefly remembered today for his ambitious verse epic *Kamayani*, depicting the psychic journey of Manu, the primordial man, through time and an almost futuristic landscape. Prasad's plays, with their glorification of the Hindu past, had revived interest in the 1990s with the rise of the Hindu political right.   VDa

PREHAUSER, GOTTFRIED (1699–1769)

Austrian actor. After his debut in 1716 with an itinerant acting troupe in the Viennese outskirts, he *toured with several companies until in 1720 he played *Hanswurst for the first time in Salzburg. *Stranitzky acknowledged him as his successor and from 1725 Prehauser performed Hanswurst at the Kärntnertortheater in *Vienna, refining this comic *character type into a polished Viennese dandy. Prehauser became known for astounding *costume and character changes as well as for his talent for *farce and improvised sketches.   CBB

PRESTON, THOMAS

Sixteenth-century English dramatist and ballad writer, sometimes identified with the Cambridge scholar Thomas Preston

(1537–98). Like his ballads, his popular *tragedy about a tyrant of antiquity, *Cambyses, King of Persia* (published 1569), glances at contemporary *Reformation politics. It was the first play to feature a central human *character directing the *action performed by *allegorical figures, rather than vice versa as in earlier *morality drama, and is also notable for its use of extraneous comic incidents to mark out the tragic *plot's development. It remained familiar in the mid-1590s, when its rhetoric and mixed *genre were mocked by Shakespeare in *A Midsummer Night's Dream* and *Henry IV*.   MJW

PREVELAKIS, PANTELIS (1909–86)

Greek playwright. Born in Crete, Prevelakis was a devoted student and friend of Nikos *Kazantzakis. In the 1950s he wrote the trilogy *The Sickness of the Century*, produced in its entirety by the *Greek National Theatre, which commented on the loneliness and alienation of the individual. In *The Holy Sacrifice* (1952) the *protagonist walks to his death knowingly, as a result of the debate between the Church and new scientific thought during the Italian *early modern period. *Lazarus* (1954), set during the time of Christ, deals with the quest for the truth beyond the stale institutions of religion. *The Hands of the Living God* (1955), inspired by Dostoevsky and set in the nineteenth century, is a story of guilty conscience and redemption. Prevelakis also wrote *The Volcano* and *The Guests*, as well as poetry, numerous translations, essays on art and literature, and several novels.   KGo

PRÉVILLE (PIERRE-LOUIS DUBUS) (1721–99)

French actor. Arguably the finest comic actor of the eighteenth century, Préville played in the provinces and at the Saint-Laurent Fair before joining the *Comédie-Française in 1753, to assume the Crispin and Sganarelle valet roles. Admired by *Garrick, amongst others, for a naturalness and versatility which enabled him to play both the classic comic repertory and contemporary *drames, in 1775 he created Figaro in *Beaumarchais's *The Barber of Seville*.   JG

PRÉVOST, ROBERT (1927–82)

French-Canadian *designer. His career began with Émile *Legault's *amateur troupe and soon extended to all the major professional theatre, *opera, and *ballet companies in *Montréal. Prévost also designed sets and *costumes for French-language *television from its very beginnings, worked extensively for English Canada's *Stratford Festival in the 1960s and 1970s, and taught set design at the National Theatre School. A recipient of national and international *awards, he is generally recognized as the most creative and most influential designer in the history of the Quebec stage.   LED

PRICE, STEPHEN (1783–1840)

American *manager and producer whose business acumen and commercial sense propelled him to the pinnacle of American theatre in the early nineteenth century. Son of a loyalist New York farmer, Price graduated from Columbia College in 1799. He was licensed to practise law in 1804 and served in the city's criminal courts until 1808 when he bought a management share in the *Park Theatre under the direction of his friend, the actor Thomas A. *Cooper. Price turned the Park into *New York's leading *playhouse by bringing in English stars and signing them to profitable *touring contracts; his successes included G. F. *Cooke, Edmund *Kean, and Charles *Mathews, and he soon had a virtual monopoly on such English imports. From 1826 to 1830 Price was the manager of the *Drury Lane in *London, attesting to his power on both sides of the Atlantic. At the height of his career he was the most powerful manager in North America.
                                                      PAD

PRIESTLEY, J. B. (JOHN BOYNTON) (1894–1975)

English playwright and novelist. Priestley broke into theatre with a successful adaptation of his comic novel about a theatre company, *The Good Companions* (1932). Most of his work was informed by his humanistic socialism, as in *Cornelius* (1935), *They Came to a City* (1943), and *An Inspector Calls* (1946), or his occult theories of time, as in *Dangerous Corner* (1932), *Time and the Conways*, and *I Have Been Here Before* (both 1937). The structure and subject matter of the 'time plays' were influenced by Gurdjieff and Ouspensky, who suggested that our usual linear model falsely represents the ability of time to travel in cycles, for long periods to be apprehended in one moment, and for momentary decisions to open opposing yet parallel time streams. Priestley was also important in bringing European *modernism to West End theatre. *Johnson over Jordan* (1939) reviews the life of an everyman *character, and in production encouraged the use of *expressionist imagery and modernist choreography, *masks, *lighting, and *music. Those elements have continued to fascinate *audiences, most notably in Stephen *Daldry's acclaimed mounting of *An Inspector Calls* at the *National Theatre in 1992, with a design by Ian McNeil which perched the elegant house of the central *characters on stilts lifted above a post-war wasteland.   DR

PRINCE, HAL (HAROLD) (1928–   )

American director and *producer. Native *New Yorker Hal Prince has been one of the most influential forces in *musical theatre, and has won more Tony *awards (twenty) than any other individual. After the University of Pennsylvania, Prince became an apprentice to the noted producer-director George *Abbott, and in 1953 began producing musicals himself. Among his many producing successes in the 1950s were *New Girl in Town*, *West Side Story*, and *Fiorello*. He began *directing in the 1960s, and scored successes with *She Loves Me*, *Zorba*, and *Cabaret*. In the 1970s Prince began collaborating with composer Stephen *Sondheim, a pairing the *London *Times* called 'the most exciting thing to happen to the American musical theatre in the last twenty years'. Sondheim and Prince's productions, including *Company* (1970), *Follies* (1971), *Pacific Overtures* (1976), and *Sweeney Todd* (1979), dealt with topical and sometimes controversial subject matter and often functioned as a layering of ideas and songs rather than through a strong *plot. Prince also directed Andrew *Lloyd Webber's blockbuster musicals *Evita* (1978) and *The Phantom of the Opera* (1986), and in the 1990s a major revival of the classic *Show Boat*. He has also directed *opera at major houses including New York City Opera and the *Metropolitan Opera. In the 1990s Prince became increasingly involved in promoting the work of young composers including Jason Robert Brown, Michael John La Chiusa, and Adam Guettel.   KF

PRINCE OF WALES THEATRE

A *London *playhouse off Tottenham Court Road, originally opened as a theatre in 1810. Before Marie *Wilton took it over in 1865 it had been, variously, the Tottenham Street Theatre, the Regency, the West London, and the Queen's (unofficially the 'Dusthole'), all notably unsuccessful. She renovated the small theatre, aiming directly at the carriage trade, and with her husband Squire *Bancroft reaped a lucrative harvest from the *comedies of Tom *Robertson. The Bancrofts left for the larger *Haymarket in 1880, and the theatre, found structurally unsound, closed in 1882, served as a Salvation Army hostel, and was demolished in 1903.   MRB

PRINCESS OPERA HOUSE

The first purpose-built *playhouse on the Canadian Prairies, it opened in Winnipeg in 1883, hoping to attract American *touring companies by railway by promising a week's stand followed by a two-week circuit to Minneapolis. Although the C. D. Hess Opera Company, Thomas Keene, Hortense Rhéa, Francesca Janauschek, and Sol Smith Russell travelled north, snowbound trains, the Riel Rebellion, and a downturn in Winnipeg's economy curtailed further tours. A resident *stock company (1887–90), *managed by Frank G. Campbell, took over the theatre and toured the immediate area. Reverting to a touring attractions house in 1890, the Princess was destroyed by *fire in 1892.
                                                     PBON

PRINCESS'S THEATRE

A *playhouse in Oxford Street, *London. A converted bazaar, the Princess's began as a venue for concerts and *opera. It became a significant theatre under Charles *Kean (1850–9), who presented a series of well-*rehearsed, pictorially *spectacular, and historically researched Shakespeare plays, as well as 'gentlemanly' *melodrama from French sources—it was here that Queen Victoria saw *Boucicault's *The Corsican Brothers* (1852) eight times. After Kean, and under several managements—Augustus *Harris, Benjamin *Webster, F. B. Chatterton—the theatre never regained its previous eminence, despite a series of great acting performances and striking plays: *Fechter's Hamlet (1861), Boucicault's *The Streets of London* (1864), Joseph *Jefferson's Rip Van Winkle (1875), Charles Warner in *Drink* (1879). Wilson *Barrett (1881–6) staged *Jones's *The Silver King* (1882), and religious spectacles like *Wills's *Claudian* (1883), confirming the Princess's reputation as a melodrama theatre. After 1902 it became a warehouse, and was demolished in 1931. MRB

PRINCIPAL BOY

A female *pantomime performer in men's clothes. Victorian *audiences enjoyed seeing women dressed as men, for example female Romeos and Hamlets, and this pleasure culminated in the principal boy in pantomime. By the 1860s the convention was well established, following its popularity in mid-Victorian extravaganza and *burlesque. As in these forms of drama, pantomime's principal boy—Aladdin, Dick Whittington, Prince Charming, Jack—was dressed in flesh-coloured tights, sang tunefully, and exhibited great dash and spirit. Shapely and imposingly busty at first, she became slimmer and more boyish in the twentieth century. She is still with us. *See also* MALE IMPERSONATION; BREECHES ROLE. MRB

PRÍNCIPE, CORRAL DEL

The second of *Madrid's two permanent *playhouses or *corrales de comedias, the other being the Corral de la *Cruz. The Príncipe opened on 21 September 1583 (on a site now occupied by the Teatro *Español) and lasted, albeit much modified, for over 160 years, being replaced by a *coliseo* (*proscenium theatre) in 1744. Like the Cruz, it was built by two charitable brotherhoods, the Pasión and the Soledad, in an enclosed yard (19 m or 62 feet square) behind a converted house, through which the *audience entered; its rear façade contained a women's gallery, some *boxes above, and a further gallery in the attic. At the far end (east) was a *tiring house with a lower and upper gallery and a machine loft; projecting from this was a roofed *stage (8 m by 4.5 m; 26 by 15 feet; the same size as in the Cruz). There were benches and *gradas* (raked seating) on roofed platforms at the sides of the yard, adjoining the stage. Lateral boxes gradually appeared after 1600 in neighbouring buildings. The yard was roofed in 1713. CD

PRINTING *See* PUBLISHING OF PLAYS.

PRISMA

Venezuelan cultural centre, founded in 1981 by Esther Khon de Cohén and privately run. It aimed to provide *alternative theatre, offering professional productions, *training actors and technicians, and bringing theatre to a wider *audience. Under Martha Candia's direction it offered an aesthetic based on enjoyment and understanding, staging works by *Pirandello, *García Lorca, Tennessee *Williams, Alfonso Vallejo, Manuel Puig, and John *Murrell, among others. The centre received several national and international *awards but closed in 1989. LCL trans. AMCS

PRITCHARD, HANNAH (1709–68)

English actress. Her first recorded performance was in 1733 at *Drury Lane, where she played mostly comic roles and *pantomimes. Greatly admired for her Rosalind in *As You Like It* (1741), by the end of that decade she scored hits in a number of Shakespearian roles, especially Lady Macbeth. Mrs Pritchard was the original Clarinda in Benjamin Hoadly's *The Suspicious Husband* and the title *character in *Johnson's *Irene*. In 1760 she was appointed dresser to Queen Charlotte for her wedding to George III, and she retired from the stage in the year of her death. (*See* illustration p. 1070.) MJK

PRIVATE THEATRES

The indoor *playhouses in *London were always called 'private'. The term appeared after the first ones were built in 'liberties' in London in 1575 and 1576, when it differentiated them from the *public theatres used by the adult professional companies. Although they charged money at the door for public admission, they pretended to give private shows, of the kind that noblemen and the court gave for their friends in private houses. This freed their impresarios from the attentions of the *Master of the Revels, appointed in 1578 to oversee public performances by *censoring playbooks and requiring playing companies to be licensed. It also affirmed the superior social status of the *boys' companies. That the boys staged plays much less often than the adults' daily performances helped the claim that they gave private shows.

When resurrected in 1599 the boy players maintained their claim to higher social status and freedom from control by renewing the word 'private'. The title pages of their playbooks

Mrs **Pritchard** as Lady Macbeth, her most famous role, with David Garrick as Macbeth, Drury Lane, London, 1768, the year of her death. She prepares to return the daggers to the murdered grooms in act II. Though the scenery rendered is medieval, the costumes are eighteenth century.

insistently used it as a mark of their superiority. Even when the King's Men (*see* CHAMBERLAIN'S MEN, LORD) took over the *Blackfriars the title pages of their plays in print proclaimed they had been acted 'publicly' at the *Globe and 'privately' at the Blackfriars. After 1606, when the Master of the Revels secured the right to censor all playbooks, the real advantage of mounting private performances was lost and the claim of 'private' became a complete fiction.

AJG

PROBST, PETER (d. 1576)

German Meistersinger (Mastersinger) and playwright. A contemporary of Hans *Sachs at Nuremberg, Probst wrote at least seven *Fastnachtsspiele, of which the best known is *Von einem Mulner und seinem Weib* (*A Miller and his Wife*).

RWV

PRODUCER

In English this term has a slippery history. Since the early nineteenth century 'production' has consistently meant the mounted performance on stage, yet the person who produces has referred variously to the *manager, the *director, and the financial controller. The confusion probably arose at the beginning of the twentieth century in England and America, when traditional managers were first displaced by businessmen with commercial profit in mind rather than the long-term development of a theatre company. The new breed hired venues and put together casts for specific productions only, and thus were 'producers of product' more obviously than *actor-managers with stable theatres under them. At the same time, however, the first anglophone artists who thought of themselves as directors were appearing, such as Harley Granville *Barker in England and David *Belasco in America. Barker called his directing work producing; his credit on *playbills often read 'the play produced by H. Granville Barker'. The result was that in Britain 'producer' tended to mean director in the first half of the century, and was occasionally used in that sense much longer. In America, perhaps by analogy with Hollywood *film practice, 'director' caught on earlier. But by the last quarter of the century, on both sides of the Atlantic 'producer' had come to be applied to a person responsible for *finance, organization, *publicity, hiring, and the other complex aspects of contemporary production, especially in the commercial sector. Producers may originate, find, or purchase an idea, secure the *licensing rights for a work in *copyright, select an older text for revival, or commission a new play or *musical. Thereafter they will be responsible for the project's administration and supervision, normally hiring the *playhouse, the director, designers, technicians, and publicity, *box office, and clerical staff, as well as overseeing the *casting of the actors. They can wield extraordinary power over the nature of the production like Hugh *Beaumont or Cameron *Mackintosh, involve themselves heavily in promotion like David *Merrick, or allow their creative employees scope like Emanuel *Azenberg. *See also* ARTISTIC DIRECTOR. DK

PROLETKULT

Soviet association, the abbreviated name of the Organization for Proletarian Cultural Enlightenment. Founded in Petrograd (*St Petersburg) in 1917 on the basis of the theories of Aleksandr Bogdanov, who (together with *Gorky) was accused by Lenin of 'God-seeking'. Bogdanov's attempt to establish an independent proletarian culture free from bourgeois contamination was itself considered to be contaminated by 'idealism'. Nonetheless by 1920 Proletkult's influence was widespread, with branches in several centres and some 80,000 members. A significant follower of Bogdanov's ideas was Valerian Pletnev, who later became a target when Proletkult's claim for autonomy was criticized by Lenin himself, in an article 'On Proletarian Culture' (1920) which emphasized the need for the proletariat to inherit the best from the past, pointing out that class's incapacity for cultural creation without foundation in preceding eras. Proletkult theatres were established in Petrograd (1918) and *Moscow (1920), in the latter of which *Eisenstein staged decidedly unproletarian, experimental productions of Jack London's *The Mexican* (1921) and *Ostrovsky's *The Wise Man* (1923). Other Proletkult theatres presented *agitprop plays and, in one case, a production based on Walt Whitman's poem *Europe*. Many important actors and future directors gained early experience with Proletkult groups, including Erast *Garin and the *film director Ivan Pyriev. As the organization began to lose influence, its ideologically purist stance was taken over by RAPP (the Russian Association of Proletarian Writers), which itself was accused of attempting to assume legislative authority

in artistic matters and was summarily abolished in 1932.

NW

PROLOGUE

The opening section of a dramatic performance, presented either as an integral part of the *play or as a dissociated address on a topic unrelated to the dramatic *action. The integrated prologue in *Greek theatre, simply the part of a *tragedy that precedes the *parodos*, devolved into an introductory *monologue, delivered in *Euripides by a *character, in *Seneca often by a non-dramatic supernatural figure, and on the Elizabethan stage by a *chorus figure. These prologues functioned as *exposition or commentary on the ensuing action. The semi-independent or dissociated prologue served a variety of extra-dramatic functions: to defend a particular dramatic *theory or practice, to establish a theatrical 'frame', to comment on current political or social issues; and, of course, to curry *audience favour. The speakers of prologues, whatever their identity, were nevertheless always histrionic, part of the theatrical presentation. Prologues connect the stage world with that of the audience, but they also establish the fictitious nature of the performance. They are therefore shunned in *realistic theatre, although they are occasionally resurrected in modern anti-illusionist theatre. *See* EPILOGUE. RWV

PROMENADE PERFORMANCE

Performance in which the *audience moves between locations, following the action from *scene to scene. The earliest examples are in *rituals and Western *mummers' play traditions, but the technique flourished from the 1960s on. It was a fairly common feature of British *theatre-in-education and some *alternative and *community theatre companies, such as *Welfare State International, in the 1960s and 1970s. It was also popularized by Italian director Luca *Ronconi's staging of *Ariosto's epic poem *Orlando furioso* (1968), and by Ariane *Mnouchkine's direction of Théâtre du *Soleil in *1789* (1970), an epic about the French Revolution. Scottish director Bill *Bryden adopted it for *Lark Rise to Candleford* (1978) and Tony *Harrison's *The Mysteries* (1985) in the Cottesloe at the *National Theatre, while the playwright/director Ann *Jellicoe developed it in the 1980s in staging a series of community plays, usually in school halls and churches. It was further adapted in the 1980s and 1990s by *performance artists and directors making site-specific events and installations, including Suzanne Lacy in the USA and Katie *Mitchell in the UK. The performance mazes of Colombian director Enrique Vargas in the 1990s gave it an especially imaginative twist: audience members journeyed individually through his mazes, often in total darkness, encountering strange scenes in intimate chambers. *See also* ENVIRONMENTAL THEATRE.

BRK

PROMPTER

The person, often culturally assumed to be invisible and silent, who reminds actors of lines and movements; now rare in Western theatre, though surviving in some *opera houses. Until well after 1900, *rehearsal pay was the exception rather than the rule in Western professional theatre, and since most of the theatrical traditions of the world are popular traditions in which the actors are either unpaid or part time, most plays historically have been given by casts who did not fully know their lines and blocking. Images of *medieval theatre occasionally show a man with a *book and a long pointer standing in front of the performers, apparently *directing the actors (*see* illustration p. 908); in the *kabuki in *Japan, the *koken* (the visible *props and *costume assistant assigned to an individual actor) prompts; in *Ram lila* in north *India, prompting is done by the *vyas*, who also comments on the action and talks to the *audience.

The eighteenth- and nineteenth-century European prompter had duties similar to those of the modern *stage manager's 'run' duties. Standing in the prompter's box—partially sunk below the stage down centre—he cued the *lighting operator at the gas table and the crews at the pinrail and machines, made small *sound effects himself, blew a whistle to cue the *act drop, and often read nearly the entire script aloud to the actors on stage. The job was a highly skilled one, and the prompter greatly respected, yet his presence goes virtually unmentioned in documents from the period. In Britain the prompter stood at a desk in the wings stage left ('prompt side'; stage right is OP or 'opposite prompt'). More rehearsal time eventually put an end to continuous need for prompters, though they can still be heard occasionally on opening nights and in some theatres with *repertory playing systems. The prompter's show-running duties were reassigned in the early part of the twentieth century.

Prompting is still essential while actors are learning a script, and so it continues as part of the rehearsal process. Some *film prompting is now done via wireless earpieces. Jeremy Whelan's *Instant Acting* (1994) popularized a system in which actors make an audiotape which is played back as they rehearse on stage, so that they are effectively on continuous prompt, which has shown great promise in getting productions up quickly.   JB

PROPERTIES (PROPS)

Objects visible in the performance space that are not *scenery or *costume. *Personal or hand props* are carried on and off by a particular actor, such as Desdemona's handkerchief. *Set props* are preset on the stage, such as the ladder in *Beckett's *Endgame*. *Dressing props* are set props not textually required, added to the set for *realism or mood, such as portraits on the wall or books in bookcases. Used as an adjective, 'prop' means either 'not fully practical' (prop guns do not fire) or 'revolving around a prop'. Thus a 'prop gag' is a joke that depends on a prop, like the Herald's skytale in *Aristophanes' *Lysistrata*; a 'prop story' is a play whose *plot is built around a prop, such as *Labiche's *An Italian Straw Hat*.   JB

PROSCENIUM

An opening, framed by an arch, through which an *audience views a play, or the arch itself. In ancient *Greek theatre *proskenion* was 'that in front of the *skene', that is, the low platform between the *skene* and the *orchestra on which modern scholars believe most of the *acting took place. *Early modern *perspective scenery made the arched opening essential to restrict the angle of the spectator's view. A form of proscenium arch was first erected for the Teatro *Farnese in 1618. In early baroque theatre the platform of the Renaissance *thrust stages became the apron or *forestage on which the action took place, while behind the proscenium perspective scenery depicted the location (the 'Italian stage'). Actors entered through doors in the arch; proscenia were so wide that three full-sized doors side by side could be accommodated on each side of the arch, which drawings depict as nearly 4 m (13 feet) deep. From about 1680 to 1850, as the *action moved upstage, the forestage and the proscenium shrank while the doors disappeared.

The proscenium arch intensely privileges figure over ground, and suited *romantic theatre well, as *Schlegel pointed out. The *box sets of *realism further benefited from the proscenium, because realism is also dependent on *illusion more than convention. After 1910, as *modernist taste returned toward convention, the proscenium appeared conservative and restrictive, encouraging a private response in each spectator rather than a shared audience experience. To socialist critics the proscenium spoke of a capitalist *bourgeois approach, a feeling still widely current among both practitioners and *theoreticians. *See also* PLAYHOUSE; SCENOGRAPHY.   JB

PROSPECT THEATRE COMPANY

English company, founded in 1961. Based at the Arts Theatre, Cambridge (1964–9), under the direction of Toby Robertson, Prospect *toured both nationally and internationally with a mainly classical repertoire. After seven years without an appropriate base, Prospect found a new home in *London at the *Old Vic in 1977 and two years later became the Old Vic Company. Despite an exemplary record of ensemble playing with actors like Ian *McKellen, Derek *Jacobi, and Dorothy *Tutin, the apparent shift away from touring commitment led to the withdrawal of funding in 1980, after Timothy *West's first season as Robertson's successor.   CEC

PROTAGONIST

From *protos* (first) and *agon* (struggle), meaning 'first contestant'. The term used to designate the leading *actor in a *Greek *tragedy—a performer purported to have been introduced as the *hypocrites* (answerer) by *Thespis in the sixth century BC—after *Aeschylus introduced a second actor (the *deuteragonist*, 'second contestant') and *Sophocles a third (the *tritagonist*, 'third contestant') in the fifth century. By extension, *protagonist* came to refer to the main *character in a tragedy as well as to the main actor. A character in opposition to or in conflict with the protagonist as character was thus the *antagonist*. Three protagonists were customarily selected by the archon and each assigned to one of the three competing tragic poets. The protagonists in turn selected the subordinate deuteragonists and tritagonists and assigned them their roles. (As the number of characters increased the *doubling of parts became necessary.) In the fifth century BC each group of three actors played in all the plays of a single poet; but in the fourth century the system was altered in the interests of fairness so that each actor played in one drama from each of the three poets. In the mid-fifth century the protagonists began to compete for prizes independently of the tragedies in which they performed. In modern usage, 'protagonist' is used to refer to the central character in a play, the one at the centre of the conflicts, and frequently the *hero.   RWV

PROVINCETOWN PLAYERS

American theatre group, operating from 1915 to 1929. Some of the writers and artists who founded the *Washington Square Players in 1915 spent that summer and the next in Provincetown, Massachusetts, then a small fishing village. They staged twelve short plays over two summers, including Eugene *O'Neill's *Bound East for Cardiff* and Susan *Glaspell's *Trifles* (both 1916), then agreed a constitution for a *New York theatre for 'the production of plays by its active members' or other works which interested them. George Cram 'Jig' Cook was elected president and the group created a small theatre on Macdougal Street in Greenwich Village. The Players' productions of O'Neill's *The Emperor Jones* (1920) and *The Hairy Ape* (1922) brought them much attention, and the productions transferred to Broadway. Between 1915 and 1922 they produced 93 new American plays by 47 playwrights. With the departure of Cook and Glaspell for Greece in 1923, a remnant reorganized under O'Neill, Robert Edmond *Jones, and Kenneth *Macgowan. A schism in 1925 had the director James Light and business manager Eleanor Fitzgerald continuing on Macdougal Street and the 'triumvirate' moving to the larger Greenwich Village Theatre. The success of the triumvirate's production of O'Neill's *Desire under the Elms* (1924) helped to bring about its end in that O'Neill was now an established playwright with willing Broad-

way *producers. The Light/Fitzgerald faction, deprived of their leading playwright, struggled on until 1929.   MAF

PROWSE, PHILIP (1937–)

English director and designer. After training at Slade School of Fine Art, Prowse worked at *Covent Garden and Watford during the 1960s, where his highly expressive sets functioned as a dramatic *character. In 1969 he moved to the *Citizens' Theatre in *Glasgow with Watford's director Giles *Havergal, and with writer Robert David MacDonald established a highly successful enterprise. Since directing *Coward's *Semi-Monde* in 1971 he has increasingly worked as a director-designer; at Glasgow his work has included *Genet, *Wilde, *Anna Karenina* (1978), *Phèdre* (1984), *The Duchess of Malfi* (1985), and *Brecht's *Mother Courage* with Glenda *Jackson in the title role (1990). Prowse has directed *Webster at the Royal *National Theatre with mixed success (*Duchess of Malfi*, 1985; *The White Devil*, 1991). In the 1980s he designed widely for *opera (Jonathan *Miller's production of *Don Giovanni*, and his own *The Pearl Fishers*). In the 1990s his authoritarian, *Zeffirelli-inspired productions with rich *costumes and lavish sets have proved successful in the West End: *Lady Windermere's Fan, The Vortex, A Woman of No Importance*.
                                                KN

PRYCE, JONATHAN (1947–)

Welsh actor who trained at the *Royal Academy of Dramatic Art and began his professional career at the Liverpool Everyman and the Nottingham Playhouse. His breakthrough role was Gethin Price in *Comedians* (1975) for which he won his first Tony *award. Through the 1970s he appeared in a succession of *Royal Shakespeare Company productions, including *Measure for Measure, Antony and Cleopatra*, and *The Taming of the Shrew*, while in 1979 he was Hamlet and the Ghost in Richard *Eyre's controversial *Royal Court production. In 1986 he played Macbeth for Adrian *Noble. He created the role of the Engineer in the West End and Broadway productions of *Miss Saigon* (1989, 1991), winning a second Tony for the role, and appeared as Fagin in the West End revival of *Oliver!* (1994). In 2001 he was Higgins in the National Theatre's revival of *My Fair Lady*. For *television he has appeared in *Selling Hitler* (1991) and *Mr Wroe's Virgins* (1993), while his *film roles include Sam in *Brazil* (1985), Perón in *Evita* (1996), and the *villain in the James Bond film *Tomorrow Never Dies* (1997).   AS

PRYNNE, WILLIAM (1600–69)

English *anti-theatrical writer. His *Histriomastix; or, The Actor's Tragedy* (1632), derisively organized like a play into *acts and *scenes, is a torrent of elaborately documented invective against the immorality of the stage. Unfortunately for him, its publication coincided too closely with a high-profile court show starring the Queen, *The Shepherd's Paradise*: his condemnation of female performers as 'notorious whores' was taken as a libel, and his attacks on drama-friendly rulers were construed as referring to King Charles I. He was sentenced to life imprisonment and his ears were cropped, but the Long Parliament released him in 1640.   MJW

PRZYBYSZEWSKA, STANISŁAWA (1901–35)

Polish playwright. Illegitimate daughter of novelist and dramatist Stanisław Przybyszewski, she was educated in France and Germany and lived her last ten years in Danzig (Gdańsk). Between 1925 and 1929 she wrote a trilogy (first published in 1975)—*Ninety-Three*, *The Danton Case*, and *Thermidor*—about the French Revolution based on revisionist French historiography sympathetic to Robespierre. His *character, challenging *Büchner's *Danton's Death* and influenced by *Shaw's *Caesar and Cleopatra*, is portrayed as a brilliant and far-sighted leader. Although only her masterpiece, *The Danton Case*, was staged in her lifetime, since her rediscovery in the 1960s Przybyszewska's plays have been widely staged in Poland and abroad, the most notable being Andrzej *Wajda's *Danton Case* (1975) and his *film version, *Danton*, with Gérard Depardieu (1983). Przybyszewska's extensive correspondence reveals her incisive analysis of the mechanism of revolution and her harrowing life of self-chosen isolation, leading to death from malnutrition and morphine addiction at 34; these letters have served as the basis for several stage and *television dramatizations of her life.   DG

PSYCHOANALYTIC CRITICISM

A set of critical interpretative practices that build upon Sigmund Freud's materialist insights into the unconscious motivations for human action. The potential sources of exchange between psychoanalysis, on the one hand, and *theatre and *performance, on the other, are many. They have some shared keywords (for example, identification and *catharsis) as well as shared interests: language and human symbolization; tensions between reality and fantasy, difference and sameness, me and not-me; and interrelations of speaking and moving bodies in space. These crossings are neither accidental nor recent. What Freud termed 'psychological drama', in which the central struggle is an internal battle fought out in the *hero's own mind, is a concern of much early Western drama, as in the plays of *Euripides or the younger *Seneca. Or, coming forward some 1,500 years, turn to Shakespeare, as Freud so often did, and in *Hamlet*'s titular *character find a walking case study of a self divided against itself. From its earliest origins *drama has been interested in the complex sources of human behaviour, with dramatists, *audiences, and drama critics (Plato and *Aristotle, for starters; *see* THEORIES OF DRAMA, THEATRE, AND PERFORMANCE)

turning to theatre so as to glimpse something of this human complexity, for better and for worse.

Freud's innovation was to stress that mental life is actually overrun, dominated, by unconscious ideas, feelings, and experiences. Out of this 'discovery' of the unconscious Freud elaborated a whole theory of human subjectivity. In a sharp departure from the self-possessed Enlightenment subject, who gives the law unto himself à la Kant, the subject of Freudian psychoanalysis is roiling with conflicting desires, repressed wishes, and aggressive impulses at odds with the demands of civilization. Notably, this divided subject is not given but forged, emerging out of his (or her) history of identifications with others, both real and imagined.

Freud himself described the processes of identification and loss that trace the subject's edge in strikingly theatrical terms. However, theatre was not just a metaphor for Freud; it was also a rich investigative field. In ways similar to dreams, with their mechanisms of displacement, condensation, symbolism, and all-round psychic bait-and-switch, drama too is seen to offer a 'royal road' to the unconscious (*see* DREAMS AND THEATRE). In *The Interpretation of Dreams* (1900) Freud located in *Sophocles' *Oedipus the King* a 'destiny [that] moves us only because it might have been ours'. That *tragedy also lent its name to Freud's much debated 'Oedipus Complex', which refers to the compound of loving and aggressive wishes that characterize an infant's relation to his or her parents.

The first wave of psychoanalytic criticism launched by Freud tended towards biographical criticism, with plays scoured for what they revealed of the author's psychic life. Alternately, attention was focused on the unconscious motivations of a play's *protagonist or upon the hidden meanings—'latent content'— of the play as a whole. But psychoanalytic criticism is more than a matter of applying psychoanalytic concepts to some presumptively known author or predetermined *text, a critical approach that, in the one instance, veers towards biographical fallacy and, in the other, plunges towards reductive criticism. Inspired by Jacques Lacan and post-*structuralism, psychoanalytic criticism has also concerned itself with matters of form—the *how* of a dramatic presentation, which usually includes both body and speech—as well as questions of reception. With Lacan's linguistic turn, the messy (and literal) family relations of mother–son–father that are Freud's Oedipal triangle become structural (and linguistic) positions within the 'symbolic order'. Subjects, if they are to be subjects, must take up positions in language, which is to say, in difference (including terms of sexual difference). Although many feminists have criticized the phallogocentrism in both Freud's and Lacan's bodies of thought, others like Judith Butler, Elin Diamond, and Peggy Phelan have also found in psychoanalysis a conceptual vocabulary for thinking about performance and *politics (*see* FEMINISM). By recasting Freudian psychoanalysis in terms of language, Lacan enables a more socially attuned psychoanalytic criticism, making it possible to see that the unconscious is not some private inner space apart from others. As Terry Eagleton suggests, the unconscious is at once 'within' us and 'outside' us; it is a kind of coming-between that posits an 'I' in relation to, and *as* a relation to, another.

This has important implications for *reception-based theories of drama. Considerations of the audience side of a given performance unsettle presumptions that there is one meaning to any particular play. Instead, spectators are seen as dynamically making meaning out of what they witness. The focus in this instance shifts from the repressed wishes of the author/artist or the *characters on stage to the repressed wishes, aggressions, fantasies, and nightmares shared by the spectators. Performance, from this perspective, is a matter of tapping into and potentially releasing the cultural unconscious.

Live performance offers occasions in which we may behold—in the double sense of seeing and being grasped by—something of the psychic and symbolic processes that launch the subject as such. For example, the explicit body of much 1990s solo *performance art (from the pierced and bleeding body of Ron Athey to the abject yet defiant femininity of Karen *Finley) aims not at activating repressed wishes so much as at exposing and exploding conventional understandings of what it means to have or be some body at all.

The space of performance is thus akin to the 'intermediate area of experience' described by D. W. Winnicott in his important discussion of 'Transitional Objects and Transitional Phenomena' (1953). This intermediate area belongs to a period of human development when the infant is four to twelve months old. Transitional objects, such as blankets and teddy bears, help to open a 'neutral area of experience', in which hard-and-fast distinctions between me and not-me, *illusion and reality, inner and outer, have not yet been made. In adult life, Winnicott suggests, the possibilities for safely testing and negotiating reality, which transitional objects and their intermediate space offered the infant, are re-experienced in such imaginative activities as theatre-making and theatre-spectating. In these activities, the line between illusion and the real is once again blurred and a space is opened for testing the limits of the possible. To think of performance and psychoanalysis side by side, then, is not to invent connections where none exists, so much as to reconceive the history of psychoanalysis as the history of the lived and social body-subject.   AP

CAMPBELL, PATRICK, and KEAR, ADRIAN (eds.), *Psychoanalysis and Performance* (London, 2001)
LAPLANCHE, JEAN, *Life and Death in Psychoanalysis*, trans. Jeffrey Mehlman (Baltimore, 1976)
PHELAN, PEGGY, *Unmarked: the politics of performance* (London, 1993)

PTUSHKINA, NADEZHDA (1949–   )

Soviet/Russian playwright. Ptushkina emerged in the post-Soviet era, and not all of her plays have been published. She writes largely domestic dramas, such as *By the Light of Others' Candles* (Stanislavsky Theatre, 1995), about two women entrapped in their unfulfilled lives. Her plays have been staged in commercial projects and repertory theatres. *As a Lamb* (1996), starring Inna Churikova, created furore for its outspoken eroticism. The play draws on the tale of Jacob's love for Rachel and his enticement by her sister Leah for an exploration of the issue of lust and love.   BB

PUBLICITY

In traditional theatres with *ritual and communal components, publicity consists in merely reminding the usual *audience of the time and place of performance. In societies where entertainment is scarce, it is often only necessary to announce that a play will be available—the function of the trumpets and flags of *early modern theatres, of the parades of nineteenth-century *circuses, and of the barking of the *kido geisha* in front of *kabuki theatres. As Western theatre became more commercial, capitalist, and competitive, a rapid elaboration and development of publicity began after 1700. Aside from direct advertising, innumerable ways were found to promote shows and to keep them and show people before the public eye. In the eighteenth century, increasing literacy and urbanization offered more opportunities for direct advertising, and created an audience of newspaper readers who could be fed a stream of reviews and features. The nineteenth century added cults of celebrity; toward the end of the century, professional publicists began staging publicity stunts, and the rising wages and social prestige at the top of the *acting profession afforded other opportunities to capitalize on stars and their personalities.

Organized modern public relations began with the American Edward L. Bernays (1891–1995)—a fact that he himself ceaselessly publicized—and during his first decade of professional activity, his major clients and the focus of his efforts were theatrical. Successively from 1912 on, he had the promotion contracts for *Brieux's *Damaged Goods* (including a campaign to force it past the *censors), the major Broadway hit *Daddy Long-Legs*, the first American *tour of the *Ballets Russes, Enrico Caruso, and Eugene *O'Neill. When Bernays moved on to other fields in the 1920s, he left behind a professional cadre of *New York theatrical PR people, who carried his strategy, in modified form, to most major theatrical cities.

Bernays took the underlying assumptions of the *modernist agenda and repackaged parts of it into popular commercial appeals. He emphasized that to attract the middle-class audience to the arts in general and live performance in particular, one must stress:

1. 'classiness', especially of canonical works (for instance, the promotion of Caruso's recordings as essential for acquaintance with *opera);

tectum

porticus

sedilia

orchestra

ingressus

mimorum
ædes

proscænium.

planities siue arena.

quintum sed visorio et structura, bestiarum conflicta-
oni destinatum, in quo multi ursi tauri, et stupenda
magnitudinis canes, distinctis caueis et septis aluntur; qui
ad

2. national, regional, and local pride in the artists (analogous to pride in a national *sports team; for instance, Bernays's promotion of O'Neill as the great American playwright fully equal to the best of Europe);

3. relation between the subject matter of the art and the lives of the audience (for instance, the tying of plays to public issues, whether actually important, as in the promoted link between *Damaged Goods*, venereal disease, and *censorship; or manufactured, as in the creation of an 'orphanage issue' to coincide with *Daddy Long-Legs*);

4. the philistine and déclassé nature of indifference to art (Bernays planted hundreds of jokes with comics in *vaudeville and *burlesque, mocking lower-class people for not understanding the Ballets Russes).

Bernays's four appeals are still active at the start of the twenty-first century and have become big business; to a great extent, it was he who demonstrated how to take the programme of theatrical progressives and use it to call an audience into being.   JB

PUBLIC THEATRES

The name given to the *playhouses built in *London from 1576 onwards for professional adult companies to perform in. It referred to open-air amphitheatres such as the *Theatre, the *Curtain, the *Rose, the *Globe, and the *Fortune. They were populist venues, some of them capable of accommodating as many as 3,000 people at a time. Their open structure with only the galleries and the stage roofed, and performances each afternoon, gave the best possible light for viewing the plays, while the two doors for *audience access gave the players a more reliable income than passing a hat around the crowd in an open marketplace. Moreover the disposition of places in the audience favoured the poorest. While the more costly places included seating and a roof overhead, the main crowd stood in the yard around the stage itself. This was the cheapest place from which to see a play, and also the most powerful, in full view of the players. The people whom Hamlet called 'groundlings' had to stand throughout the play and got wet if it rained, but they had the closest access to the show. The roofed *private theatres set the cheapest places at the back of the *auditorium, furthest from the stage.

The Swan Theatre in London in a drawing by the Dutch traveller Johannes de Witt in 1596, the only contemporary illustration of a London **public theatre** of the period. It shows a pit for groundlings, three levels of galleries, three actors performing far downstage, a short stage canopy supported by two large pillars, only two entrance doors on stage, and what are apparently spectators in the stage balcony (the above). Discovered in 1888, the accuracy and meaning of this picture (which is actually a copy made by a friend of de Witt's) have caused considerable debate.

The term 'public' was used dismissively, and such entertainment was thought by many writers to be common and therefore degrading to the gentry, the social rank from which most writers came. The superior term 'private' came to be used as an antonym to 'public'. The 'private' playhouses were those lodged indoors, in halls inside London's liberties. Although the outdoor and indoor theatres both charged admission for their shows, the term 'private' ostensibly meant performances mounted in private houses for invited guests, who did not have to pay for what they saw. This social differentiation of 'public' playing from 'private' was stabilized under the Stuarts. The printed *text of a play stating on its title page that it had been staged at one of the 'private' playhouses was claiming superior quality from its more costly venue. That contrasting status was reflected in the plays chosen to be staged for the court. In Tudor times the *boys' companies, who always used the private theatres, were more favoured than the adults. Once the boy companies had disappeared, from 1616 onwards the *Blackfriars and the *Cockpit companies at their indoor playhouses completely dominated the choice of court plays until the closure of the theatres in 1642. One of the greatest testimonies from the time about the unique valuation given to Shakespeare's plays was that during the years when the boy companies were producing their best work, the Globe's reputation, even though it was a public theatre, gained its company the King himself as its patron and later secured them the Blackfriars playhouse to use every winter from 1608 onwards.   AJG

PUBLISHING OF PLAYS see page 1078

PUCCINI, GIACOMO (1858–1924)

Italian *opera composer. Widely acknowledged as the heir to *Verdi, Puccini's reputation rests primarily on *La Bohème* (Turin, 1896), *Tosca* (*Rome, 1900), *Madama Butterfly* (*Milan, 1904), and *Turandot* (Milan, 1926). Puccini combined a melodic gift and the capacity to write a quasi-*Wagnerian through-composed score with unerring theatrical sense. While his operas characterize *verismo in tone and milieu, his librettists borrowed widely from plays by *Sardou, *Belasco, and *Gozzi. Puccini raised his underprivileged *characters to a genuinely tragic status: Butterfly's death speaks powerfully against the indifference of modern society, and Mimi's death at the end of *La Bohème* achieves a pathos unequalled in operatic theatre. *Tosca*, the most unified of his works, has exceptional momentum and sweeping emotional range. Puccini's versatility is apparent from his final work, *Turandot*, which is the last of the major grand operas. No opera house with an extended season omits Puccini from its repertoire.   SJCW

(continued on p. 1080)

PUBLISHING OF PLAYS

The printing press had many complex effects on Western theatre. The coincidence of a printing industry, a reading public, and a competitive commercial theatre created new channels for theatrical and performative information, strongly influencing *playwrights and theatre *management. Play publishing has also strongly influenced the development of theatre *history itself.

A script is a collapsed, truncated version of what actually happens on a stage (see TEXT); whereas *performance is wildly and simultaneously polysemic, a script is a single array of signs to be read in a fixed order (see SEMIOTICS). 'Orgon hides beneath table' appears in the script, and is not particularly funny, but the *audience of a good production of *Molière's *Tartuffe* generally laugh at that moment, for they see the awkwardness of a tall or stout man in a stiff coat, tight breeches, and stacked-heel shoes trying to hide under a small ornate table. Even if extensive notes are taken at production and incorporated into the printed *stage directions (as has been frequent since about 1880), the script remains a single narrow channel compared with the vast broadband of the performance.

However, exactly because it transmits so little, the script is a kernel of immense potential. Freed of the circumstances of original production, the published text can accrue entirely different interpretations (hence the preference of some literary scholars for reading over performance). Though the ability to use a script as a generative kernel for imagination or performance had always been available to the wealthy, scholarly minority, and to workers in the theatre, the printing press greatly increased the effect of written scripts, because it made copies available in larger numbers at lower prices; this was further enhanced by the development of bookselling as a business in *early modern Europe, so that printed plays could reach readers without the decision or urging (and sometimes without the consent) of playwrights and companies. Thus, for example, though the availability of theatre in eighteenth-century Germany was wildly uneven due to local vagaries of *censorship and patronage (see FINANCE), nearly everyone interested had access to Shakespeare, *Racine, Molière, and *Lessing—play publishing in effect creating a 'theatre of the mind' from which the real theatre of *Schiller and *Goethe was to grow.

Play publishing is a pathway to production and acceptance which does not depend on a first production. This proved essential for the various *modernist movements, as *Ibsen, *Shaw, *Strindberg, and others were often first known to audiences by their published plays, creating a demand sometimes before any production was mounted. Publication can also smooth the way for a technically difficult play (such as Ibsen's *Peer Gynt* or Goethe's *Faust*); preserve and disseminate a work until time and technique are right for it (for instance *Büchner's *Woyzeck*); or make controversial or shocking works available far beyond the tiny houses in which they first played (for instance *Jarry's *Ubu roi*, *Synge's *The Playboy of the Western World*).

Play publishing also furthered the internationalization of theatre. Just before the revolution, Nicolas Barba established the first theatrical bookstore in *Paris. In the following decades he published thousands of scripts for *melodramas, *féeries, equestrian *spectacles (*hippodrama), series *comedies, and many more. Many Barba scripts featured stage directions translated for reading; that is, descriptions of the *action and scene or *scenery rather than actual direction for the stage. It is largely through Barba that we have the works of *Pixérécourt, Cuvelier de Trye, Caignez, and the other early melodramatists, and the production data at the front of a Barba script is generally more reliable than that to be found in the Paris news press of the time.

Barba's major income source, however, was the *romances of Pigault-Lebrun, so wildly popular in the rest of Europe that virtually any bookseller had the Barba catalogue, which meant in turn that French melodrama was available nearly everywhere, and—since no international protection for plays existed, since reading knowledge of French was so common, and since the stage directions were more than enough for local scene *painters and machinists to work from—Barba editions were immediately translated and performed locally all over Europe, helping to inaugurate and sustain the decades-long growth of melodrama.

Though publishing has often allowed popular trends to sweep the globe more easily, it has also allowed works in less-spoken languages and from less-visited nations to find a place on the world stage. Aside from the obvious example of Ibsen, publication and play reading in the industrial nations has been both an income source and a way to reach audiences for many of the playwrights of the new nations of *Africa. Indeed, due to political repression and censorship, many times the bulk of a playwright's career has been sustained by publication abroad, leading to interest from the theatre community and eventual productions. Athol *Fugard and Ken *Saro-Wiwa are merely two of the most prominent examples.

Aside from its value in building audiences, publication has supported playwrights as an alternative source of income. Perhaps the first important case was Oliver *Goldsmith. Thomas

Davies, a one-time actor at *Drury Lane and a member of the circle that included *Garrick, Samuel *Johnson, and Goldsmith himself, seems to have been a theatrical publisher out of charitable or aesthetic motives. He brought out handsome collections of *Lillo and *Massinger, commissioned and published a life of Garrick, and published his own influential commentary on Shakespeare—none of this to much if any profit. The timing of payments and commissions from Davies, coinciding with Goldsmith's many financial crises, suggest that the frequent printings of *The Good Natur'd Man* (1767 and following) and the posthumous, debt-settling printings of *She Stoops to Conquer* were intended primarily to sustain Goldsmith.

Yet another effect of play publishing has been to further the drives toward democracy and hierarchy of the last 150 years, making it possible for more people to practise and share in theatre but also focusing the economic rewards on a smaller and smaller super-class. Although the Copyright Act of 1709 established a fourteen-year *copyright from the date of publication, what production rights were associated with possession of a printed copy was not clear under English copyright until the Copyright Bill of 1833. Following its passage, three publishers—John Dicks, Thomas H. *Lacy, and Samuel French—expanded their play-publishing operations, bringing out many acting editions, prepared mainly from promptbooks. These had the effect of concentrating rewards on the most successful playwrights, for a company could now obtain a popular script in a clear, usable form very easily, and so had less need of an in-house playwright. A few playwrights—*Jerrold, the Brough brothers—did very well under the new system, but the total number of dramatists declined, as income concentrated in fewer hands.

Dicks's Standard Plays, though the strongest of the three series in the early part of the century, later failed to acquire new fashionable properties. In 1849 French acquired Lacy's Acting Editions of Plays series and became a potent competitor, dominating the market by 1870 and effectively driving Dicks out of it within the following decade. French's market domination continues to the present day; in the United States its prime competitor for straight plays is the Dramatists' Play Service, which is an auxiliary cooperative operation of the *Dramatists Guild.

French's editions have had important effects. Because they preserve much information from the original promptbook they have been of great help to the theatre historian. Educational and *community theatres have relied on cheap acting editions for which performance rights are easily acquired, and thus the script in 'community theatre' only rarely reflects the community from which it is drawn, and in *educational theatre, though nearly all of the other theatre crafts will be practised on-site for productions, playwriting remains occasional and auxiliary; in the bulk of *amateur theatre, audiences see the work of actors, designers, technicians, and directors who are their fellow citizens or students, but thanks to French, they hear the words of Neil *Simon or Michael *Frayn. Though drastically reducing

the number of venues available to new playwrights, the widespread distribution of cheap acting editions allowed many playwrights to learn their craft; Henry Arthur *Jones spoke of having 'read my way through the French catalogue', and he was far from the last to have done so.

The publication of plays has also had an extensive influence on theatre history itself. The great bulk of evidence of past performance is contained within scripts, notwithstanding illustrations, letters, diaries, account books, surviving objects, newspaper accounts, etc. Before printing, the survival of any script was highly improbable; it had to acquire enough audience, for one reason or another, to be frequently copied and recopied, if a copy was to reach historians in the future. (Hence, out of at least a half-millennium of *Roman theatrical activity, we have some of *Plautus because he was popular, probably all of *Terence and *Seneca because they were used to teach style, and a thin scattering of other material.) Because even a rare printed edition creates many more copies than a very popular copied manuscript, and because printing spread literacy and hence made texts more likely to be saved by more people, we have far more from any one century since the printing press than we do from the entire two millennia before it. A specialist in any area of ancient or *medieval European theatre often has read every relevant surviving script, but it would be very difficult in one lifetime to read all the surviving scripts in any one major language for the nineteenth century. Thus in theatre history the deployment of the printing press roughly marks the division between interpreting too little information and winnowing too much. (It is frustratingly possible to have both problems at once: the Spanish Golden Age, the English Tudor-Stuart era, the vital period of the *commedia dell'arte, and the great period of French *neoclassical *tragedy all fall within the 150 years when printing had developed but publishing of plays was not yet routine.)

The necessary tendency of theatre history to centre on scripts has had other effects. It was so pronounced in the early years of the twentieth century that much of theatrical scholarship since 1950 has been an attempt to seek a balance with other kinds of evidence (*see* THEATRE STUDIES). A more intractable problem has been that past publishing practices greatly influence the nature and number of plays reaching us, and those practices were in no way influenced by what we would most like to have today. For example, Blayney has effectively refuted the old, still widely repeated, idea that play publishing in Tudor and Stuart England was highly lucrative and active, and that Shakespeare was a best-selling writer within publishing generally—which had allowed us the comforting feeling that what we had from the Elizabethans was probably what mattered. He shows instead that play publishing was an occasional source of reasonable but not large profits, not nearly so important as religious texts, for example; Shakespeare's poem *Venus and Adonis* apparently did far better than any of his plays. Thus we owe much of what we know about the period to publishers, booksellers, and printers who were mainly occupied with other *genres and other business matters; small wonder, then, that so many Elizabethan and Jacobean plays are lost. Theatre history explains what we have; sadly, that may not be what we would like to know.   JB

BLAYNEY, PETER W. M., 'The publication of playbooks', in John D. Cox and David Scott Kastan (eds.), *A New History of Early English Drama* (New York, 1997)

BROOKS, DOUGLAS A., *From Playhouse to Printing House: drama and authorship in early modern England* (New York, 2000)

CHARTIER, ROGER, *Publishing Drama in Early Modern Europe* (London, 1999)

KNUTSON, ROSLYN LANDER, *Playing Companies and Commerce in Shakespeare's Time* (New York, 2001)

MYERS, ROBIN, and HARRIS, MICHAEL, *Economics of the British Booktrade, 1605–1939* (Alexandria, Va., 1985)

PATTEN, ROBERT L., and JORDAN, JOHN O. (eds.), *Literature in the Marketplace: nineteenth century British publishing and reading practices* (New York, 1995)

RAVEN, JAMES, *Judging New Wealth: popular publishing and responses to commerce in England, 1750–1800* (Oxford, 1992)

UNSELD, SIEGFRIED, *Goethe and his Publishers*, trans. Kenneth J. Northcott (Chicago, 1996)

PUIGSERVER, FABIÀ (1938–91)

Catalan designer and director. Although born in Spain, he trained in theatre design at the School of Fine Arts in *Warsaw. Returning to *Barcelona in 1959, he was to revolutionize the Spanish stage with his innovative conceptual *scenography, which moved well beyond the traditions of design. By the time he co-founded the Teatre Lliure in 1976 he was already an internationally recognized designer, having produced the much lauded trampoline-like canvas *scenery for Víctor *García's production of *Yerma* (1971). He also worked with the major Spanish directors of the day: Albert Boadella, Ricard Salvat, Adolfo Marsillach, and José Luis Gómez. His minimalist eye, stripping the stage of superfical decor and astutely providing a visual analogy for the dramatic tension in the *text, provided some of the most impressive designs of the post-war era. He maintained a fifteen-year collaboration with Lluís *Pasqual which provided radical, audacious reimaginings of the Teatro *Nacional María Guerrero's stage for the Spanish premières of *García Lorca's unknown plays *El público* (*The Public*, 1987) and *Comedia sin título* (*Play without a Title*, 1989). While known primarily as a designer, Puigserver's lean, measured productions of works like Per Olov Enquist's *The Night of the Tribades* (1978), presented within the multi-purpose *auditorium of the Teatre Lliure, provided alternative actor–*audience relationships. The new Teatre Lliure building in Barcelona now bears Puigserver's name.   MMD

PULCI, ANTONIA (1452–1501)

Italian dramatist. The wife of Bernardo Pulci and later an uncloistered sister, Antonia wrote plays for performance by nuns or confraternities. Her plays continue the tradition of the *sacra rappresentazione*, but they also point to a sustained dramatic activity in Florentine convents, where the *drammaturga*—a nun responsible for writing and producing plays—became a common figure.   RWV

PULPITUM

A Latin term which designates the simple wooden *stage (Greek *logeion*) of the *Roman theatre, but also any lecturing platform, and has no technical connotation in regard to height. *Proscaenium* (Greek *proskenion*; *see* SKENE) is used in the same sense.   WJS

PUNCH AND JUDY

English *puppet theatre which acquired its present form early in the nineteenth century. The show is a glove-puppet performance of an episodic nature, built around a lord of misrule, whose antisocial behaviour would be intolerable in any other context. Punch's violent fights with his wife Judy are the material of the oldest of *farces, whilst his confrontations with death and the Devil express a fundamental aspect of the human condition. Punch's name originated with the sixteenth-century Neapolitan *commedia dell'arte* figure of Pulcinella. (The puppet, with his big nose, may even have preceded the *masked actor.) Pulcinella wore a pointed hat and a loose-fitting *costume of cheap white fabric, and his performers travelled widely abroad. The *character became Polichinelle in France and Punchinello in England, where he had arrived as a *marionette by the 1660s, probably with Pietro Gimondi. Pulcinella rapidly lost his Italian accent and melded with local characters of *folk farce. In Andalusia he became Don Cristobal, and in the German lands *Hanswurst and, later, *Kasper, whilst in nineteenth-century Russia Petrushka took over his characteristics (as did Jan Klaassen in Holland).

Punch remained a marionette until the end of the nineteenth century, but his significance diminished. From the later eighteenth century his real importance was as a street glove puppet and his white costume had been exchanged for the colourful one of a court jester. From the marionette days Punch retained a squeaker or 'swazzle', which the player put in his mouth to deform the voice. For the street performer, this also served as a form of amplification. Punch as the central figure of a glove-puppet show may have arrived in England with Italian showmen in the late eighteenth century. An Italian called Piccini was performing in *London in the 1820s and his show was recorded pictorially by George Cruikshank and noted down by J. P. *Collier.

The stock show has little plot, but is a series of short and usually violent encounters between Punch and other characters, most notably his wife, death, and the Devil. Most of the episodes occur right across Europe. In England the solo street performer usually had a portable booth or stage and was accompanied by a musician/compère, who also collected the money. Street performances of Punch were popular with the young, but not considered exclusively children's shows: at night the showmen sometimes turned their stages into a shadow or 'galanty' show, and Punch and Judy could be seen at race courses. Once the railways and new concepts of leisure made seaside holidays possible, Punch could be found on beaches and piers and in the parks of seaside towns. Private engagements brought him more and more into middle-class children's parties, with a consequent effect on the content of the show. Nonetheless Punch was generally perceived as subversive and, like many European puppet figures, used for satiric comment on the follies of the day. The magazine *Punch* was named after him.   JMcC

LEACH, ROBERT, *The Punch and Judy Show: history, tradition and meaning* (Athens, Ga., 1985)

PUNJABI THEATRE

With the Partition of the Indian subcontinent in 1947, Punjab was divided, its cultural identity fragmented by the creation of two political states. Inevitably the Punjabi language was victimized by the hegemony of Urdu and Hindi as the official languages of *Pakistan and *India respectively. Despite these linguistic tensions, the long-standing epic and ballad traditions of Punjab, immortalized in the stories of *Heer Ranjha* and *Puran Bhagat*, continued to inspire *folk singing traditions on both sides of the border, and even today the *naqqal* ballad singers in India reach out to larger rural audiences during *melas* (festivals). In addition, popular folk theatrical forms like the *swang* and comic storytellers like the *bhand* continue to entertain the villagers of Punjab in India, along with the vigorous and ever popular dance tradition of the *bhangra*, which has been reinvented in new forms not only in the urban areas of India and Pakistan, but through diasporic interventions in the pop culture of contemporary Britain.

The modern theatre of Punjab in pre-independence India is generally associated with the widespread influence of Norah *Richards, an Irishwoman, who began to direct and organize local theatre work soon after her arrival in Lahore in 1911. Through her efforts I. C. Nanda and Rajinder Lal Sahni emerged as Punjabi playwrights, writing on contemporary issues, using local folk traditions and Western techniques. Through the 1950s, the Punjabi theatre in India fought hard for its survival,

not least through the recognition of Punjabi as a language with a rich literary tradition. In the 1960s Sheila Bhatia and her group Delhi Art Theatre produced lyrical and sophisticated *musicals which were a mixture of folk songs, *dance, and drama. On a different level the populist Sapru House Theatre in Delhi offered coarse productions with salacious titles like *Naram Garam* (*Soft and Hot*), which appealed to the Punjabi *diaspora. Prem Jullundry, Surinder Mathur, and Kimti Anand became celebrities with these crude but money-spinning ventures.

In 1972 the Department of Indian Theatre was established in Punjab University, Chandigarh, with Balwant Gargi as director, soon followed by the Speech and Drama Department in Punjab University, Patiala, with Surjit Singh Sethi as director. These institutions began to free Punjabi theatre from provincialism. Gargi's *Lohakut* (*The Blacksmith*) and *Kanak Di Balli* (*A Stalk of Wheat*) were points of departure, both in form and content; the *protagonists dared to challenge tradition and patriarchy. Sethi's *King Mirza Te Sapera* (*King Mirza and the Snake Charmer*) searched for a new idiom, relying on a symbolic approach, and the playwright Ajmer Aulak, working in Mansa, produced *Ik Ramayana Hor* (*One More Ramayana*) and *Anne Nishanchi* (*Blind Shooters*), poignant studies of Punjabi rural life.

In the 1980s Punjab was in the grip of violent terrorism between Sikhs and Hindus. The Punjabi language became associated with the Sikhs, and non-Sikh performers switched to *Hindi. Actors were thus severed from their language, myths, images, and history. This politicization of language led to a new *political genre, exemplified by Gursharan Singh. Previously identified with *street theatre, he became a cult figure. His bold and evocative plays exposed the disruptive forces that were tearing at the fabric of life; *Tohya* (*The Ditch*) and *Kursiwala teh Manjiwala* (*Man on the Chair, Man on the Cot*) became part of modern Punjabi folklore. Performed mainly in rural areas, his plays still have a mass following. The late 1980s and 1990s saw the emergence of the Company, formed by Neelam Man Singh Chowdhry, using a mix of rural and urban actors. Their repertoire has included *García Lorca's *Yerma*, Doris Lessing's *An Unposted Love Letter*, and *Kitchen Katha* (*The Story of a Kitchen*). Kewal Dhaliwal (Amritsar) and Dr Atamjit (Chandigarh) also remain active despite financial and institutional constraints. *See also* PUNJAB LOK REHAS.   NMSC

PUNJAB LOK REHAS

Theatre *collective, based in Lahore in *Pakistan, that broke away from *Ajoka in 1987. The founders were Mohammed Waseem, Huma Safdar, Lakht Pashi, Mohammed Nadeem, and Idrees Shafqat. To avoid the pressures of commercial theatre, members are volunteers and most productions are free to the public, performed as *street theatre, in villages, schools, and community centres. Performing only in Punjabi in order to reach an *audience of villagers and slum-dwellers, their work is leftist in perspective and invariably serious in tone. Influenced by theatre for *development and Augusto *Boal, their subjects are social issues: the plight of rape victims and general oppression of women, the reasons for and consequences of the Gulf War, the consequences of drug and armament trade with Afghanistan following the martial law regime of Zia-ul-Haque, child labour, bonded labour, and killings of trade union activists. To date, Punjab Lok Rehas has produced about 25 plays.

FAK

PUPPETRY IN INDIA

Allegedly the birthplace of *puppet theatre, *India has many diverse traditions and numerous regional variations. The earliest references to puppets are found in the works of the ancient Sanskrit grammarians Panini and Patanjali, as well as in the Hindu epic of the *Mahabharata* where the puppet Chitrangada is specifically named. The word *sutradhara (the 'holder of strings'), the narrator or director of Sanskrit drama, is closely associated with puppetry. Broadly, we can divide puppetry styles in India into four categories: string (*marionette), rod, glove, and *shadow puppets.

String-puppet traditions are found in Rajasthan (*kathputli*), West Bengal (*tarer putul* and *suto putul*), Orissa (*Gopalila kundhei*), Karnataka (*yakshagana gombeyata*), Tamil Nadu (*bommalattam*), and Maharashtra (*kala sutri bahuliya*). The closest Indian equivalents to the English word 'puppet' are *putul*, *putli*, *kundhei*, *bomma*, all variants of 'dolls' or 'figures'. Prominent among the string-puppet traditions is the Rajasthani *kathputli* (*kath* = 'wood'). Performed by the nomadic Bhat community, this tradition draws heavily on the *folklore surrounding Amar Singh Rathor, a seventeenth-century *hero of the Nagaur district, which remains the base for wandering puppeteers. Interspersing this legendary tale with tricks and skits relating to everyday life, the *kathputli* performers make their own puppets with wooden heads, torsos stuffed and wrapped in cloth, and a long skirt which provides the illusion of flowing movement. The puppeteers hold four to six strings, which they handle manually without the aid of a cross or control. Unlike many of the other string puppet traditions that focus on epic material from the *Ramayana* and the *Mahabharata*, the *kathputli* repertoire remains predominantly in the ballad tradition. Another prominent tradition is *bommalattam* from the Thanjavur district of Tamil Nadu. The puppets are as high as 1.2 m (4 feet) and weigh up to 5 kilograms (11 pounds). They are made from intricately carved wood, adorned with heavy and ornate *costumes. Though controlled by strings, they are jointed and also have iron rods attached to the hands.

Rod-puppet traditions, which flourish in Orissa, Karnataka, Andhra Pradesh, and West Bengal, tend to incorporate string-puppet techniques. In the Bengali tradition of *dangaer putul* (*dangaer* = 'rod') the puppet's body is made of wood, its head sometimes of the white pith of a reed. A central rod is fixed within a hollow bamboo socket tied to the puppeteer's waist, while strings are used to manipulate the puppet's arms and hands. A smaller rod moves the head. The puppeteers perform to a vibrant soundtrack, not unlike the popular *folk opera *jatra* performances in the area.

Glove puppets are found in West Bengal, Orissa, and Kerala. In *beni putul* from West Bengal, for example, the puppeteer performs in full view of the *audience with two puppets in his hands. Sometimes he improvises *dialogue between his puppets, but at other times he functions as a *sutradhara* or narrator, initiating audience participation. Originally the small heads of the puppets were of terracotta, and the wooden hands can make a clapping sound. The small size of the puppets and lack of a stage facilitates itinerant performance: the show over, the puppeteer can pack his gear in a sling bag and walk away. In *sakhi kundhei* from Orissa, the puppeteer sometimes plays a *dholak* (drum) tucked under his thigh. *Pava kathakali* from Kerala was almost extinct when revived in the late 1970s with the support of Kamala Devi Chattopadhyay, a pioneer in the conservation of folk arts. Actively researched by Venu G., this tradition closely resembles the *kathakali *dance-theatre in miniature. The heads and hands of the puppets are carved of wood, vividly painted, and attached to *kathakali* skirts. Two or three puppeteers perform episodes from the epics, accompanied by an orchestra of drums and cymbals.

Shadow puppets exist in Kerala, Andhra Pradesh, Karnataka, and Orissa. *Ravana chhaya* (Ravana's shadow) from Orissa, drawing on episodes from the life of the *villainous yet noble *character Ravana from the *Ramayana*, originally used puppets made from deer and hare skin. A more elaborate form is *tolu bommalatam* from the state of Andhra Pradesh, which uses the largest shadow puppets in the world. At times almost 1.5 m (5 feet) high, the leather is extremely fine so that the colours can be seen through the large screen. The puppeteers in this tradition perform stories from the *Ramayana* and the *Mahabharata* with *family troupes and musicians. In Kerala, *tolpava koothu* (leather puppet play), perhaps the only puppet tradition in India using a permanent *playhouse, is performed within the precincts of Bhadrakali temples and in front of the deity. The puppets are shaped from opaque thick leather that is painted and profusely perforated so as to define elaborate costumes. Much larger in size than *wayang kulit* puppets from *Indonesia, *tolpava koothu* figures nonetheless share some similarities in their use of the silhouette and arm joints. The *lighting provided by oil in coconut shells contributes to the *ritualistic aura.

India's contemporary puppeteers have been influenced by traditional sources and by styles and techniques from abroad. Suresh Datta, for instance, has been affected by the rod-puppet innovations of Sergei *Obraztsov from *Moscow, while Dadi Pudumjee has combined pedagogy derived from Michael Meschke of Sweden with lessons from Meher Rustom Contractor of the Darpana Academy in Ahmedabad. Contractor was among the pioneers of Indian puppetry in the 1950s, such as Raghunath Goswami, Madhulal Master, Devilal Samar, and Haripada Das, whose tradition of rod puppetry in Tripura was continued by his son Prabhitangsu Das. Educational themes, occasionally interspersed with *multimedia, have also inspired the work of puppeteers like Sudip Gupta, Sanjit Ghosh, Ratnamala Nori, Ranjana Pandey, Meena Naik, Mahipat Kavi, Hiren Bhattacharya, and Mansingh Zala. DDP/RB

PUPPET THEATRE

Puppet theatre can range from an approximation to *actors' theatre to an adjunct of storytelling to a form of *performance art. In East and South-East Asia there are strong parallels between repertoires of actors' theatre and puppet theatre, especially in Chinese opera (see, for example, JINGJU) and *Indonesian wayang. The *wayang kulit of Indonesia is thought to have preceded theatre with actors, and we know that in eighteenth-century *Japan *kabuki actors borrowed the repertoire of the ningyo-joruri (puppet theatre, or *bunraku). Even their gestures and acting styles, like those of live performers in Indonesia, were partly based on the puppet theatre. In the West, on the other hand, puppet theatre has often been perceived as an imitation of actors' theatre. Nineteenth-century puppeteers tried to persuade themselves and their *audiences of the *realistic nature of their shows, informing the public that figures 80 cm (2.6 feet) high were 'life-size' (as well as lifelike).

Unlike the human performer the puppet must be animated externally. A puppet in a museum is a material object, in performance it is a channel of communication, but however 'realistic' it may seem to be, its value is purely metonymic. This is one reason why the European *symbolists were attracted to the puppet, and why Maurice *Maeterlinck designated some of his *dreamlike plays as being for puppets. The move towards stylization and simplification in *avant-garde theatre was supported in part by the use of puppets, and as a result the older folk puppeteer was replaced by a new generation of puppet artists. In 1906 Paul Brann opened his Marionette Theatre of the *Munich Artists: no longer a shadow of the live actor, the puppet was now perceived as an expressive performer in its own right. Sergei *Obraztsov (1901–92), the single most influential figure in twentieth-century puppetry, attempted to redefine that which is specific to the puppet. Initially an actor at the *Moscow Art Theatre, he directed the Moscow Central Puppet Theatre from 1931, introducing a new minimalism when he played with his bare hands as puppets, sticking a simple turned wooden ball on one finger to represent a head. In France Yves Joly followed this innovation, giving psychological or behavioural characteristics to gloved hands and endowing simple objects, such as a piece of paper, with life. Performers using part or parts of their own bodies (most commonly the hands) as puppets can be seen in the work of a number of puppet artists and companies, including Hugo and Ines, Teatr 3/4 from Poland, and Philippe Genty.

1. Definition; 2. Origins; 3. Repertoires; 4. Stages; 5. Film and television; 6. Organization and training

1. Definition

What is or is not a puppet depends more on the use the object receives than on what it looks like or how it is made. A reasonable definition of a puppet is an object which a performer is able to invest with a suggestion of life, and into which an audience is prepared to project life. Puppets are mostly anthropomorphic or zoomorphic figures and are usually classified by their mode of operation. The major forms are the *marionette, a fully or partially jointed figure operated from above; the glove puppet, or hand puppet, worn on the hand and operated from below; and the rod puppet, operated, usually from below, and sometimes from the back (as in *China), by rods which both support and permit specific movement. The *shadow-puppet theatre is an extension of the rod puppet, using flat figures against a screen. Japanese bunraku, involving three manipulators standing behind the puppet, which is operated by various rods and levers, is an extension of the rod puppet. Much imitated outside Japan after 1960, this form opened the way for the table-top puppet, where the visible or semi-visible manipulator stands behind the figure whose only control is usually a short rod protruding from the back of the head.

The Chinese counted many different types of puppet, including actors performing like puppets, and a lost tradition of what were known as firework puppets. Water puppets, which survive today in *Vietnam as the national form of puppet theatre (*mua roi nuoc), were also known in China. They are operated from the back by means of long rods under the water. *Africa has some unique puppet forms, amongst which are 2- or 3-m (6.5- or 9.8-foot) high figures of *Mali, surmounted by a tiny head and operated by a puppeteer inside the body. There are also *masks with articulated mobile figures attached (often operated by strings that cause some basic movement), or else large *animals, such as buffalo, that perform dances and then become puppet stages themselves. In this situation the distinction between the puppet and the mask is minimal. Like the mask the puppet has a performer behind it and is a way of presenting a *character or entity. In modern puppetry masks are widely used; in some cases the figure is operated by a puppeteer concealed within it, and in others a full or partial figure, often called a 'body puppet', is attached to the performer.

Automata were long confused with puppets, sometimes deliberately by showmen, who presented and described their theatres as 'mechanical'. Even allowing for modern technology, the distinction remains. A puppet requires a human impulse for each movement, an automaton merely requires the mechanism to be set in motion.

2. Origins

The origins of puppets are uncertain, but much evidence points to shamanistic use. In many cultures dolls or puppets have been used as substitute human beings for magic purposes, and vestiges of this survive today in fetish and *voodoo dolls. In East Asia puppet performances were often given in association with specific religious occasions, such as the anniversary of the dedication of a temple. Puppet shows were also used for such liminal occasions as births and funerals, the performance itself intended to bring good luck or ward off evil spirits. Many such performances were given for the benefit of the gods, and in some cases the puppeteer was himself a priest (the Indonesian dalang, or the itinerant priests of medieval Japan). Even today a Japanese bunraku performance starts with a prayer to Sanbaso, an old puppet representing a god figure, which is kept backstage. Traditional Indian shadow performances begin with a puja, often in the form of an adoration of Ganesh (see PUPPETRY IN INDIA). Vestigial elements of older religious significance can also be found in the white horse of the Burmese theatre (see MYANMAR), which gallops across the stage and represents a constellation that appeared at the creation. Puppets were known to *Native Americans from the north-west coast to Mexico and were used in a religious context, probably to encourage a good harvest. Amongst the Berbers little girls perform with simple stick figures to bring rain, and a very similar custom exists in Turkey.

Nearly everywhere, puppetry was first practised in a religious or cultic context, then going through a process of secularization. In Japan the ningyo-joruri evolved out of religious performances given by itinerant monks, partly to raise funds for their shrine. The medieval Christian Church adopted animated figures to assist in the teaching of the scriptures. The first specific reference to a Christian puppet was the artificial serpent that climbs the Tree of Knowledge in the twelfth-century Anglo-Norman Play of Adam, but animated statues were already known earlier (see MEDIEVAL THEATRE IN EUROPE; LITURGICAL DRAMA). By the end of the sixteenth century, England had a tradition of puppet plays (motions) drawn from biblical material, whilst much of Europe also had puppet plays based on the birth and *Passion of Christ and on the lives of saints. In Spain the decorated altar or retablo gave its name to puppet shows, which were probably animated versions of the scenes with figures which were shown in little boxes known as machinas reales. By the eighteenth century these had fallen into the hands of professional entertainers, and in time developed into purely secular puppet shows. The reference to Bethlehem survived with the Bétièmes of Mons (Belgium) and the Belem of Alcoy (Spain), and nineteenth-century marionette theatres in

Intriguing **puppet theatre** from Mali. The character of Sigi the buffalo appears here as a puppet and as a stage for other puppets, with further puppet figures attached to the horns.

Lyon were known as crèches (cribs). In Eastern Europe, the eighteenth-century Austrian crib rapidly adapted to puppets, becoming the Czech jesle, Polish szopka, and Russian vertep. The szopka was originally taken from house to house by seminarians, who were later replaced by travelling entertainers.

In India and Indonesia puppetry was firmly associated with the religious epics of the Mahabharata and Ramayana. In Karnataka the shadow performer still recites part of the text of the Ramayana and also provides his own glosses and commentaries on it. Rama, an avatar of Vishnu, remains the most popular *hero, whilst Ravana, the hundred-headed demon king of *Sri Lanka (who abducts his bride Sita), is also a key figure—in Orissa, Ravanna gives his name to the show, Ravanchaya. The monkey king Hanuman, presented as a force for good, possesses abundant supernatural powers and comes to the help of Rama. Hanuman may be the monkey figure popular in Chinese theatre and puppet theatre, and the central comic figure of the novel the Journey to the West. Rama is central to puppet shows in *Cambodia, *Thailand, and *Malaysia, whilst in Indonesia his story is but one in a more extensive repertoire, which includes the medieval *Panji cycle, and even some modern pieces. In Indonesia, Semar, the grotesque and hermaphroditic comic figure, possesses extraordinary powers and probably derives from a pre-Hindu deity.

In sub-Saharan Africa puppets were often used during initiation and circumcision rituals. Performances were given in conjunction with the seasons of the agricultural year, encouraging fertility. A popular subject involved a male and female figure, the male provided with an erectile penis. The male sex organ is common to many puppet traditions, even if its religious overtones have made way for comedy. Turkish *Karagöz, Iranian Mobarrak, Japanese Noroma, and Italian Pulcinella all have penises, and often use them to urinate on the audience. Burmese male marionette figures have non-visible genitalia under their clothing, whilst Brazilian Mamulengo puppets, like many African ones (and perhaps owing something to that tradition), indulge in frequent and extensive copulation on stage. Ironically, puppets are now often used in a number of developing nations as a teaching aid in order to promote birth control rather than fertility (see DEVELOPMENT, THEATRE FOR).

Some of the oldest traceable puppets are those of India and China, which may have existed at least a thousand years before Christ, though the earliest documented puppet performances in China date only to the sixth century AD. Idols and oracles with moving mouths and arms were known in classical antiquity. The first name of a puppeteer to survive is the Greek Potheinos, who showed figures known as neurospasta. Puppets followed European colonizers and may have replaced more local puppet forms; a puppeteer accompanied Cortés to Mexico in 1524. In the eighteenth and nineteenth centuries North and South America received many visits from European puppeteers, whilst influences also percolated to India, Japan, and China. European forms of puppetry, notably marionettes, are widespread in Africa today, but are almost certainly an imported tradition.

'Doll' and 'puppet' are interchangeable terms in many languages. It can be argued that the ludic function of the puppet may be as old as the shamanic one. There is a long history of the puppet as a children's toy, going back as far as the miniature jointed figures placed in graves of children in classical antiquity. The jigging doll—a jointed figure held against a board that, when vibrated, makes the figure dance—is found in many cultures and may also have originated as a toy. A variant of this, common in the streets of eighteenth- and early nineteenth-century Europe, was the *planchette* puppet, supported by a string, one end of which was attached to a small post and the other end to the knee of the performer. As he played an instrument, the performer tightened the string to make the puppet dance. Examples have been found in South Africa and Lesotho, but also in twelfth-century Europe.

3. Repertoires

From the medieval *joculatores* of Europe to the Skomorokhi of Russia, popular and secular entertainers combined puppetry with *juggling, *acrobatics, *magic shows, and storytelling. Narrative and storytelling are the starting points for much puppet performance. The *joruri* singer, seated at the side of the stage, provides all the voices for the bunraku theatre. The Indonesian *dalang* works through a gamut of linguistic levels, alternating old court Javanese and vernacular dialect and mixing singing, recitation, narrative, and *dialogue. In Europe the presenter of the show initially provided the voices, a practice depicted by Ben *Jonson in *Bartholomew Fair* (1614), and still employed by a Mr Stretch, whose theatre ran for some 40 years in eighteenth-century *Dublin. *Cervantes, in the Master Peter's Puppet Show episode of *Don Quixote*, has a narrator/showman telling a tale of medieval struggles between Moors and Christians. The most striking survival of this material and style today is the Sicilian Opera dei Pupi, where there are still very clear links with the tradition of the street storyteller or *cantastorie*. The subject matter ranges from Carolingian *romance (much of it concerning the paladins, especially Orlando and Rinaldo) to the lives and deeds of illustrious bandits. In the past the presentation was told in serial form, the episodes being spread over months. Nowadays events are condensed into a single self-contained performance.

Short dialogues, *farces, and knockabout scenes are common to all puppet theatre. Sometimes they are mere interludes, sometimes, in the simple one-man street glove-puppet performance, they are the show itself. A central 'hero' (*Punch, *Kasper, or whoever the local figure may be) goes through a series of encounters, each concluding with a fight. In most traditional puppet theatre, even of the simplest sort, the verbal element is at least as important as the physical batterings and the puppet can become the mouthpiece for the improvisation of the puppeteer. In much of the world, an extra comic effect is provided by a squeaker or 'swazzle' which distorts the voice. In Europe, the swazzle is associated with the glove-puppet theatre today, but earlier was also used for marionettes, especially Pulcinella. Some form of swazzle can be found right across the world, one example being the *kathputli* theatre of Rajastan.

The puppet can give an uncanny imitation of a human being and do things which are inconceivable for the human. Many are designed in terms of the tricks they can perform—expanding and contracting puppets, dismembering skeletons, transforming figures on the one hand, and imitators of acrobats and popular entertainers on the other. Trick marionettes (*fantoccini*) were popular in Italy in the eighteenth century and rapidly were added to the programmes of most European marionette theatres. By the later nineteenth century, as marionettes appeared with ever greater frequency in variety theatres, many companies specialized in *fantoccini*, and the dexterity with which they were handled heralded a new approach to the techniques of the marionette. Chinese puppeteers always placed much emphasis on dexterity. The tradition of Fukien province of southern China, which goes back to the sixteenth century, involves light and highly mobile glove puppets. The celebrated Yang *family can perform remarkable feats of martial arts, even making their puppets somersault in the air and change clothes onstage.

Before 1800 many European performers were both actors and puppeteers, passing from one medium to the other according to the political, social, religious, or economic climate. Masks of the *commedia dell'arte* spread to the puppet stage and generally outlived their stage models. Traces of *commedia* characters, often transformed, re-dressed, and absorbed into local types, can be found in much of Europe. The links between Pulcinella and Kasper in Germany, Petrushka in Russia, and Jan Klaassen in Holland are well documented. Joey *Grimaldi's *Clown joined the English harlequinade (see PANTOMIME, ENGLISH) and almost immediately transferred to the puppet stage. Pulcinella and *Harlequin lingered as *stock presenters in marionette theatres until the twentieth century; whilst in England Scaramouche remained as a lesser figure in the Punch and Judy show, but as a marionette was metamorphosed into a trick expanding one, often endowed with two or three heads. The eighteenth-century European marionette stage presented both *folk and hagiographic plays, and in the nineteenth century *melodrama provided an endless stream of dramatic fodder which was supplemented by adaptations of the popular novels.

Puppets can be perceived as diminutive humans, and as such lend themselves to *parody and *satire. *Bartholomew Fair* introduces a puppet parody of classical mythology, and the fairground theatres of eighteenth-century *Paris frequently resorted to puppets to parody the live theatres that were trying to have them closed down. In the nineteenth century anti-government satire often depicted puppets, whilst Punch,

*Guignol, and other puppet figures gave their names to satirical magazines. Satirical *cabarets of the turn of the twentieth century, such as the Green Balloon in *Cracow, introduced puppet versions of well-known literary and political figures. In the late twentieth century British *television's *Spitting Image* brought wickedly accurate puppet caricatures of political figures and the royal family into the living room.

In every tradition there are clowns who exist to break the dramatic frame and to communicate more directly with the audience, regularly subverting the more serious 'epic' *action. Their scenes allow the highest degree of *improvisation by the performer and often a degree of involvement by the audience. In China clown figures are popular, whilst the character of Monkey causes bedlam. A bunraku programme includes farces, very similar to *kyōgen, alongside the more serious dramas. Indonesia has a rich collection of clowns, including the grotesque but powerful Semar and his sons. Europe had a wide variety of popular comic types, who generally reflect the common man in speech and behaviour and have a basic interest in food, drink, and sex. They appear under many names, but when they figure as servants in such popular dramas as *Faust* and *Don Juan*, their exploits draw these two very serious pieces heavily in the direction of *comedy.

European puppetry from the Middle Ages forward carried a pedagogical or *didactic function. The original religious intention made way for pure entertainment, but in the nineteenth century many puppeteers emphasized the educational value of their work. This was a valuable sales ploy, but helped downgrade the puppet to 'mere' children's entertainment, a position it still largely holds today. In Russia after 1917, puppetry was often absorbed into *agitprop theatre and used to promote the ideals of the revolution. In Nazi Germany, the *Kraft durch Freude* (strength through joy) movement harnessed puppetry for its own propaganda/educational purposes (*see also* FASCISM AND THEATRE). In Czechoslovakia, the modern puppet movement grew out of the educational use of the puppet in the 1920s and 1930s. After the Second World War the socialist countries of Europe saw puppet theatre as a fundamental tool for education and worthy of generous subsidy. Puppet theatres were built on an unprecedented scale, many possessing two, or even three *auditoriums, and a staff of 50 to 100. In the 1960s the agitprop aspect of puppetry was taken up by many politically oriented theatre groups, most notably *Bread and Puppet Theatre in the USA. Puppetry has also become one of the standard means used in Africa and Asia today to convey messages relating to health, AIDS prevention, literacy, and other social issues.

The presenter in front of the stage was common to much traditional puppetry—the bottler for Punch, the musician for Morabbak in Iran or for the Mamulengo performances in Brasil, or the *joruri* singer in Japan. The musician for Russian Petrushka both had dialogues with the puppets and interpreted the unintelligible sounds the puppet produced. The 1950s saw the puppeteer increasingly appear on stage with the puppets, a tendency accelerated with the growing familiarity with the Japanese bunraku after 1960. This freed the puppet from the limitations of the small enclosed stage. Sometimes the puppeteer remained neutral, but often she or he became an actor with the puppet. In the work of the Drak theatre in the Czech Republic the emphasis is on the relationship between the actor and the puppet figure. In some cases the puppet is not even animated but becomes an object onto which the actor projects energy (as in *Circus Unikum*, 1978). Tadeusz *Kantor combined puppetry, visual art, and theatre, using mannequins and machines that operated more like automata, and appeared himself onstage with his creations. From the 1980s there was a growing tendency for self-referential work, the puppeteer becoming the material of the show. Neville Tranter of Stuffed Puppet operates a host of figures, all of which seem to be extensions of himself, whilst he plays a central and manipulative role.

Both the *Bauhaus and the Italian *futurists explored abstract uses of the puppet. Fortunato *Depero created his *Plastic Ballets* (1918), whilst Oskar *Schlemmer experimented with the puppetization of the actor in the *Triadic Ballet* (1912–22) where the performers animated costumes based on geometric forms. In the 1960s and 1970s a new type of theatre known as 'object theatre' emerged, where the emphasis shifted even further away from the dramatic and where the material itself—metal, fabric, wood—and its innate properties became the focus. The notion of endowing matter with human properties began to disappear. What followed was the evolution of an artistic form of expression that merged increasingly with the visual arts. In Philippe Genty's *Dérives* (1989), in which puppetry is only one of the means of representation, the dramatic disappears in favour of a marvellous and *surreal dream world of forms and textures created by the artist. The idea of the puppet fascinated many twentieth-century artists, including Paul Klee. Joan Baixas collaborated with Joan Miró to produce the startling anti-Francoist *Mori el Merma* (1978), which suggested Miró paintings come to life. Other puppeteers have drawn on visual artists for a non-linear and often surrealist style of performance, as Theater Taptoe's Magritte-based *Hemel* (Heaven, 1991).

4. Stages

Puppet stages range from the non-existent to accurately scaled miniature versions of European *opera houses. In India for performances of the *kundhei-nacha* of Orissa and the *pava-kuthu* of Kerala (where the puppets are miniature versions of *kathakali actors), the puppeteers simply squat on the ground in full view of the audience. In eighteenth- and nineteenth-century Iberia a street performer might play an instrument and use his own cloak as a stage (with his puppeteer-assistant inside). Early puppeteers in Japan hung a miniature stage in front of them like a vendor's tray. In parts of Russia, Mongolia, and China the puppeteer would sometimes mount his booth on his head, with a curtain hanging to conceal the body. The simple glove puppet and rod puppets used by the poor itinerant puppeteers in China and Japan require the most minimal screen as a stage, while the traditional glove-puppet stage of south China was an elaborately carved two-storey wooden structure, the upper level being reserved for the 'gods'.

Many puppeteers in Europe and Africa have simply suspended a cloth on a line between two trees (or across a doorway) and popped the figures up over it. In Africa, some puppeteers travel with a light frame construction about a metre (3.3 feet) high, under which they climb and over which they throw cloths to conceal themselves. The traditional Rajasthan stage has a distinctive background of a coloured cloth with a series of arcades cut in it.

In Europe a simple screen, sometimes surmounted by a miniature stage, was a common sight in the streets. A fourteenth-century manuscript of the *Roman d'Alexandre* depicts a stage in the form of a small castle (hence the French term *castelet* for a puppet stage). The court marionette stages of Burma in the late nineteenth century were very wide and the show involved numerous puppets, performers, and an orchestra. The purpose-built bunraku stage can measure over 10 m (33 feet) in width, with a separate side stage for the musician(s) and reciter/singer. Marionette opera in the aristocratic palaces of eighteenth-century Europe allowed for miniaturized versions of baroque performances and employed the greatest scene *painters (for instance Filippo *Juvarra). Nineteenth-century European showmen had elaborate stages that could be set up in available halls or *fairground booths. They created complete theatres in miniature, with *scenery, *lighting, and even an orchestra. Some travelled with their own portable theatres, measuring about 20 by 10 m (65 by 33 feet) and able to accommodate several hundred spectators. Much smaller theatres existed in cellars and living rooms of the poorer areas of industrial towns in Belgium and northern France and in the back streets of *Naples and Palermo.

Today the *scenography of the puppet theatre has often abandoned the conventions of wings and backcloths for a fuller exploration of the space in which the puppet operates. Drak's designer, Petr Matasek, has taken his cue from the Russian *constructivists: all his sets are carefully devised mechanisms with which the puppet can interact. They are placed on the stage and in no sense are mere scenic backgrounds. Philippe Genty likewise eschews the purely scenic and his productions seem to grow organically out of objects and fabrics placed in the centre of the stage.

5. Film and television

Puppet sequences were incorporated into a number of *films of the 1940s—even the voice of Benjamino Gigli was combined with the marionettes of the Yambo company. The art of the pure puppet film was pioneered by Lottie Reiniger, who combined the techniques of shadow puppetry with those of stop-frame animation with *Prince Achmed* (1926). From 1945 the Czech Jiri Trnka produced a series of very beautiful animation films using puppet figures, moving the work away from a filmed puppet show by use of cinematic techniques. His most successful films include the full-length *The Good Soldier Schweik* and *A Midsummer Night's Dream*. From the late 1950s Jan Svankmajer, initially a puppeteer, produced a series of films using *surrealist techniques, abandoning direct storytelling for more allusive means and employing *montage to put over a message about human behaviour. His masterpiece, *Jan Dr Faust*, blends actors, puppets, and techniques of animation.

With the spread of *television in the 1950s and 1960s puppets came to the fore in children's programmes such as the English *Muffin the Mule* and *Thunderbirds*, whose extremely *realistic puppets aimed to imitate humans to perfection. The real breakaway from the filmed puppet show came with Jim Henson in the USA, who treated the televised puppet as if 'real'. Where viewers had been used to the presenter or newsreader, Henson filled the screen with the speaking head of a puppet looking directly into the camera. His most celebrated creation was *The Muppet Show*, and his most endearing characters Kermit the Frog and Miss Piggy.

Video, initially a means of recording puppet performance, has more recently become an integral part of it. Companies often record small items or scenes during the performance and project them on a large screen or part of the set for interaction with actors or other puppets. This has joined the *multimedia arsenal of slide projections and shadow work that are a part of much contemporary puppetry.

6. Organization and training

The international puppetry association UNIMA (Union Internationale de la Marionnette) originated in *Prague in 1929. Its first president was Jindrich Vesely and Czech puppeteers were at the centre of the organization. Initially a European grouping, it was rapidly joined by Japan and the USA. After 1933 political developments cut short activities, which were not revived until 1957. Once more the Czechs were prime movers, and made huge contributions to the spread of the art of modern puppetry in such countries as Iran. Puppetry became increasingly internationalized and festivals multiplied. Whilst local traditions were encouraged and preserved, there was also much cross-cultural fertilization. One consequence was a greater emphasis on the visual nature of the art of puppetry, much of which has shifted from what can be a highly verbal form of entertainment to a performance-based avant-garde.

A further important development of the twentieth century was the rise of schools for the *training of puppet theatre artists. DAMU in Prague and the Institut International de la Marionnette in Charleville-Mézières in France have both inspired directors, including Josef Krofta (director of Drak) and Margareta

Niculescu (founder of the Romanian Tandarica company). Puppetry has found its way increasingly into academic institutions, widening the perception of what constitutes the art, changing deprecatory attitudes towards it, and helping to instil a solid professionalism amongst practitioners. In countries where traditions of puppetry have cultural significance (India and China) there are now puppetry schools, and in Indonesia the now-secularized *dalang* can receive formal training.   JMcC

ADACHI, BARBARA C., *Backstage at Bunraku* (New York, 1985)

BUURMAN, PETER, *Wayang Golek: the entrancing world of classical Javanese puppet theatre* (Oxford, 1988)

DARKOWSKA-NIDZGORSKI, OLENKA, and NIDZGORSKI, DENIS, *Marionnettes et masques au cœur du théâtre africain* (Saint-Maur, 1998)

JURKOWSKI, HENRYK, *A History of European Puppetry*, 2 vols. (Lewiston, 1996–8)

McCORMICK, JOHN, and PRATASIK, BENNIE, *Popular Puppet Theatre in Europe, 1800–1914* (Cambridge, 1998)

McPHARLIN, PAUL, *The Puppet Theatre in America* (Boston, 1969)

PANI, JIWAN, *Living Dolls: story of Indian puppets* (New Delhi, 1986)

SPEAIGHT, GEORGE, *The History of the English Puppet Theatre*, rev. edn. (Carbondale, Ill., 1990)

STALBERG, ROBERTA, *China's Puppets* (San Francisco, 1984)

TILLIS, STEVE, *Towards an Aesthetics of the Puppet* (Westport, Conn., 1992)

PURCĂRETE, SILVIU (1950–   )

Romanian director. Purcărete was director of Teatrul Mic in *Bucharest before going to the National Theatre in Craiova in the late 1980s. His 1989 season, which included *Ubu roi with Scenes from Macbeth, Phèdre, Titus Andronicus*, and D. R. Popescu's *Piticul din grădina de vară* (*The Dwarf in a Summer Garden*) earned him great praise within Romania and many job offers from abroad. Although remaining active at Craiova, he has also directed extensively in France (*Avignon Festival and Limoges), Britain (Nottingham Playhouse, Scottish Opera), Norway, Portugal, and other countries, as well as at the Bulandra Theatre in Bucharest. He assumed the directorship of the Centre Dramatique National du Limousin in 1996. His large-cast, international projects have included the French-Romanian production of *Les Danaïdes* (1995) and the Italian-French production of *De Sade* (1999, co-written by Purcărete and Dick McCaw). *Les Danaïdes*, adapted from *Aeschylus' *The Suppliants*, employed an extravagant but low-tech *theatricality. The cast of 107 used cloth, fire, water, movement, and voice to evoke images and moods. The 50 suitcases carried by the daughters of Danaos became tombstones, temples, beds, city walls, and dominos.
                                                                        EEP

PURIM PLAY

Traditional playlet or *monologue performed on the *carnival-esque holiday of Purim, on which Jews celebrate the events described in the Book of Esther. Purim plays were already popular in Europe in the sixteenth century and were maintained until the Second World War; some Hasidic communities preserve the *genre to this day. The plays began as rhymed *monologues and in the sixteenth century were enlarged to include several performers, with the subject matter drawn from contemporary Jewish life and *folk tales, with biblical themes such as the sacrifice of Isaac introduced in the late seventeenth century. The performances, often compared to the German *Fastnachtsspiel*, were usually presented in private homes during the holiday meal by male students clad in *masks and simple *costumes. Later on, craftsmen, apprentices, and quasi-professional entertainers formed their own holiday troupes. Performances were sometimes characterized by vulgar language and bawdy innuendoes, leading to their occasional banning. The Purim play was the primary theatrical event in traditional European Jewish life and is considered one of the main contributors toward the creation of modern *Yiddish theatre.   EN

PUSHKIN, ALEKSANDR (1799–1837)

Russian writer, the country's greatest poet and one of its greatest prose writers. He is also, ironically, and on the basis of a single play, its greatest tragedian. Not only did his poetry, prose, and drama constitute a complete break with pre-existing Russian models—formal, sentimental, and *neoclassical—but he broke entirely new ground in each *genre and single-handedly invented a new language for Russian literature which became a model for generations to come. Pushkin had become interested in the theatre whilst at school and, following graduation, attempted to write a *tragedy about the uprising of the people of Novgorod against the Varangians, *Vadim*. He then turned for subject matter to the 'time of troubles' at the turn of the seventeenth century. The play which resulted, *Boris Godunov* (1825), written in Shakespearian iambic blank *verse, as opposed to alexandrines, is episodic rather than neoclassical in form, ignores the *unities, and moves freely between Russia and Poland, from a palace to an inn, from moonlit garden to palace square. Making use of Karamzin's *History of the Russian State*, the play charts the rise and fall of Boris and the dubious manner in which he gained the throne, concentrating on the period 1598 to 1604 and the counter-claim to the Russian accession made by a former monk who claims to be the legitimate successor Dmitry, son of Tsar Johann. The play ends with the death of Boris, the offstage murder of his own son and heir to the throne, and the accession of the False Dmitry. The final stage direction has become synonymous with the suppressed and dormant power of the Russian people (the 'narod') who, when called upon to celebrate the accession, 'remain silent'. After a struggle with the *censor, Pushkin managed to have sections of the play published and, in 1830, the play received imperial sanction. The *Maly attempted to stage the 'Fountain Scene' in 1833 but were forbidden and the play had to wait until 1870 for its première, at the Mariinsky Theatre, *St Petersburg.

Pushkin also wrote some 'Little Tragedies' in verse, *The Miserly Knight*, *The Stone Guest* (based on the Don Juan legend), *Mozart and Salieri* (a drama on the distinctions between genius and mere talent), and a play, *Feast in Time of Plague*, set in Elizabethan *London, based on his reading of work by Barry Cornwall and John Wilson. Of these, only *Mozart and Salieri* was staged during Pushkin's lifetime. The poet was also instrumental in furthering *Gogol's career and is popularly believed to have lent him the *plot of *The Government Inspector*, based on incidents in Pushkin's own life. *Boris Godunov* is more famous abroad in Mussorgsky's *operatic version of 1873, although Pushkin's play proved popular during the Soviet period and was given a memorable revival during the 1980s by Yury *Lyubimov, seen at the *Edinburgh Festival in 1989. Declan *Donellan staged a modern-dress version in *Moscow in 2001 with a Russian cast, which had a successful *tour in Britain the same year.   NW

PY, OLIVIER (1965–)

French playwright, director, and actor. A prolific theatrical and cinematic talent, Py founded his own company in 1988, producing close to twenty of his own plays, many of them at the *Avignon Festival during the 1990s, including the *cabaret performance *Miss Knife* (1996) in which he performed the title role. Beginning in 1998 he was director of the Centre Dramatique National at Orléans-Loiret, where he created *Requiem for Srebrenica* (1999), an indictment of the massacre in Bosnia, which later *toured Europe and the United States. In 2001 Stéphane *Braunshweig directed his *L'Exaltation du labyrinthe* at the Théâtre National de Strasbourg.   DGM

Q

QUADRILLE

*Dance of French origin, also called *haute-taille*, introduced to the *Caribbean in the mid-seventeenth century. Accompanied by an orchestra, a *komandè* sets the pace and signals the start of the various figures to the four pairs of dancers. The instruments are a diatonic accordion or a violin, guitar, and varied Caribbean percussion, including *tanboudibas* (oak drum of Basque origin), *siyak* (bamboo scraper), *malakach* (rattles made of calabash), steel triangle, and *tibwa* (two wooden sticks knocked together). The dancers perform four figures—*pantalon, lété, lapoul, pastourèl*—each with different subfigures. At the end of the twentieth century there was a renaissance of quadrille balls. They are most popular in the countryside in Guadeloupe and usually take place on Saturdays and Sundays, except during Lent. In Martinique the quadrille is introduced by a waltz, mazurka, or the local *biguine*.

MRM

QUAGLIO FAMILY

Seven generations of German painters, designers, and architects of Italian descent spanning the seventeenth to the mid-twentieth century. **Lorenzo I** (1730–1805) contributed to the splendour of Carlo Teodoro's court at Mannheim by producing much admired *ballet and *opera *scenery in the late baroque style and designing several *playhouses. His great-nephew **Simon** (1795–1878) produced over 100 sets for the *Munich Hoftheater (1828–60), mostly in the *romantic or pre-*realistic style. Simon's son **Angelo II** (1829–90) was principal set designer for the first productions of *Wagner's *Tristan* (1865), *Die Meistersinger* (1868), *Das Rheingold* (1869), and *Die Walküre* (1870).

JEH

QUAYLE, ANTHONY (1913–89)

English actor and director. An engaging, intelligent, and energetic man, Quayle played supporting roles at the *Old Vic under Tyrone *Guthrie, appearing with *Olivier, *Richardson, *Gielgud, and Edith *Evans. Six years of war service interrupted a promising career, and afterwards he turned down a Hollywood offer in order to run the *Shakespeare Memorial Theatre in Stratford from 1948 to 1956. Without the help of subsidy, he oversaw the theatre's change from a provincial *festival *playhouse to a national institution that could recruit leading directors and actors, including Gielgud, Olivier, Peggy *Ashcroft, and the young Peter *Brook. He directed a version of the Shakespeare *history plays and undertook international *tours. As an actor he was well received in secondary parts such as Aaron, Iago, Pandarus, and Enobarbus, but less well as Othello and Macbeth. He left Stratford to pursue a more varied acting career, and took part in several *films, but was never asked back to the *Royal Shakespeare Company when it assumed control of the SMT. He joined the *Prospect Theatre Company in 1978, and founded his last touring company, Compass Productions, in 1984. He was knighted in 1985.

EEC

QUEEN'S MEN (QUEEN ELIZABETH'S MEN)

Formed in March 1583, by the standards of the time the Queen's Men was an extra-large acting company for *London. Its founders, the Secretary of State Walsingham and the *Master of the Revels, formed it with the twelve best players from the four or five leading companies of the time. It was awarded pre-eminence not only as the chief performer at court but as the only company licensed to play at *public theatres. When on *tour, their chief means of maintaining themselves, towns usually gave them twice what other travelling companies received because they wore the royal livery. Perhaps besides improving playing at court the company was founded to parade the Queen's colours round England, and with them her political and religious ideas. The exceptional size of the Queen's Men prompted the composition of ambitious plays with large casts, like Shakespeare's *King John* and *Richard III*. After the first few years, though, they divided into two groups, one entertaining with tumbling and *juggling as well as plays. Their quality declined once the original players such as the famous *clown Richard *Tarlton died or left, and by 1590 they were outstripped at court by other groups. They still travelled the country, their licence appearing in provincial records as late as 1623.

AJG

QUEER THEORY

Queer theory is best described as an ongoing cultural critique of the heterosexual privileged social order. The term 'queer', popularized in the 1990s, is a comprehensive rubric that embraces gays, lesbians, bisexuals, transsexuals, and, in fact, any who do not perceive themselves as fitting the social norms of *gender and sexuality. It also suggests a political stance that actively resists assimilation. As applied to theatre, queer theory promotes *textual investigations and experiments with performance techniques by which queer experiences can be more overtly addressed. The roots of queer theory can be located in postmodern (*see* MODERNISM AND POSTMODERNISM), post-*structuralist, *psychoanalytic, and *feminist critiques of identity. Joan Riviere, a student of Freud, noted in 1929 that femininity is not ontologically stable, but rather a masquerade. From French historian and philosopher Michel Foucault came the concept of sexuality itself as a product of cultural systems of power and knowledge, while Jacques Lacan hypothesized a hegemonic order of spectator/subject (male, white, heterosexual) over object (female), which permeates cultural production and discourse.

One of queer theory's major objectives is to question anything that has been traditionally accepted as heterosexual in order to discover hidden or coded elements of queer activity. The practice of 'queering' a subject has been applied to theatrical historical periods, dramatic *genres, cultural and *performance practices, as well as individual artists and their work. Queering a topic can sometimes lead to shaky conclusions based more on assumptions and conjectures than on factual evidence, but can also result in skilful and astute scholarship, such as David Savran's study of Arthur *Miller and Tennessee *Williams, *Communists, Cowboys, and Queers* (1992).

Drag and camp as theatrical strategies have been frequently contested sites for queer theory. The definition of camp as an aesthetic style—and whether it is a product of the gay sensibility—has kept theorists busy since Susan Sontag's groundbreaking *Notes on 'Camp'* (1964). More consensus surrounds male and female drag's ability to disrupt gender expect-

ations. Judith Butler, in *Gender Trouble* (1990), states that 'in imitating gender, drag implicitly reveals the imitative structure of gender itself' (*see* FEMALE IMPERSONATION). Camp, though not always a consequence of drag performance, is often associated with it, particularly with male drag. However, the role of camp in female drag (*see* MALE IMPERSONATION) and *lesbian performance has provoked conflicting responses from queer critics. Sue-Ellen Case, one of the foremost scholars of feminist performance, believes that 'butch/femme' role playing can make use of camp's wit and irony 'free from biological determinism, elitist essentialism, and the heterosexist cleavage of sexual difference' (*Towards a Butch–Femme Aesthetic*, 1989). Kate Davy, among others, disagrees and finds that lesbian theatre is 'encumbered' by camp because it cannot help but reinscribe the patriarchal privilege it attempts to critique (*Fe/male Impersonation: the discourse of camp*, 1992).

A good deal of queer theory, rising as it does from feminist discourse, concerns various aspects of lesbian performance. *Film scholar Laura Mulvey, in her 1975 essay 'Visual Pleasure and Narrative Cinema', contends that the 'male gaze' of the *protagonist in Hollywood films shapes the camera's eye as well as the *audience's response. Later queer theorists, adapting Mulvey's examination of distorted female representation on the screen, have taken up visibility issues in live performance. Jill Dolan, Elin Diamond, and Peggy Phelan have vigorously addressed the problem of lesbian representation on the stage, advocating anti-*naturalistic production methods to avoid the influence of patriarchal-heterosexual ideologies. Theatrical performance should reflect the various ethnicities, *races, and economic classes of lesbian audiences. Dolan takes a radical position when she suggests that overt erotic behaviour can be an effective tool of subversion: 'the explicitness of *pornography seems the most constructive choice for practicing cultural disruptions' (*Practicing Cultural Disruptions: gay and lesbian representation and sexuality*, 1992). In a very different but no less provocative vein, Judith Halberstam examines the 1990s phenomenon of drag king performance and argues that female masculinities should not be considered aberrant social behaviour but rather opportunities to demolish constricting gender categories.

To the layperson, *theory can often seem to be an isolated exercise performed by academics for their colleagues and one that has little relevance to actual practice. This charge has often been levelled at queer theoretical writing burdened with difficult terminology that often make it less than approachable even to theatre artists. As a result, many queer theorists, including the ones already mentioned, have made concerted efforts to emphasize the connection between theory and practice. David Román in *Acts of Intervention: performance, gay culture and AIDS* (1998) combines theory, production *criticism, and politics to examine the way AIDS and queer performance interact. At its best, the writing generated by queer theory suggests that it can collaborate and form reciprocally beneficial relationships with theatrical practice rather than segregating itself within its own exclusive sphere. *See also* GAY THEATRE AND PERFORMANCE. RN

JAGOSE, ANNAMARIE, *Queer Theory: an introduction* (New York, 1996)

TURNER, WILLIAM B., *A Genealogy of Queer Theory* (Philadelphia, 2000)

QUEM QUAERITIS TROPE

A literary-musical elaboration of the Easter liturgy consisting of a short *dialogue between the Angel guarding Christ's empty tomb and the three Marys. It begins with the Angel's question, 'Whom do you seek?' (*Quem quaeritis*). The earliest, and simplest, examples date from the tenth century. So long as tropes remained firmly part of the liturgy, they differed little in nature and function from other liturgical ceremonies such as the *Depositio* and the *Elevatio*, but less well-integrated tropes, called *sequences*, could give the appearance of independent compositions. The *Quem Quaeritis* trope preserved in the *Regularis Concordia*, a collection of rules for Benedictine monasteries compiled by Ethelwold, Bishop of Winchester (*c*.970), has traditionally been interpreted as an extra-liturgical ceremony. Moreover, Ethelwold's instructions for its performance suggest a dramatic enactment, and the trope has thus been seen as the seed from which the later, clearly dramatic examples of the *Visitatio Sepulchri* developed. It has been argued with equal force that these tenth-century tropes were liturgical, not dramatic, and that some other catalyst was needed to bring the true *liturgical drama of the eleventh and twelfth centuries into being. The *Quem Quaeritis* trope, considered in isolation, does appear to be *drama; considered in its liturgical context, it appears to be *ritual. The distinction lies less in formal qualities or techniques of presentation than in differences in purpose and perception. As an elaborated figure, this tenth-century trope was not essential to the liturgy, but for its performers and their congregations in monastic churches, neither did it have any significance outside the liturgy. *See* MEDIEVAL THEATRE IN EUROPE. RWV

QUESTORS THEATRE

A leading British *amateur theatre in *London, founded in 1929 by Alfred Emmet, who spent a lifetime fusing it ambivalently to the professional theatre infrastructure of the capital. Distrustful of West End commercialism, Emmet aimed to sidestep its worst effects by creating a mild counter-institution. A converted ex-chapel in Mattock Street was its base from 1933 to the late 1950s, when it built a new 400-seat theatre on the site. Flexible *stage configurations (though its strongest shape is open *thrust, *audience on three sides), plus ample backstage facilities, made it one of the best-resourced amateur groups in the country. It was a founder member of the International Amateur Theatre Association in 1952, hosting amateur productions from Europe, North America, and developing countries. It has a proud history of staging new playwrights, some of whom—like James *Saunders—went on to strengthen professional theatre with challenging plays. In 1969 Emmet retired, having successfully established a 3,000-plus membership, a professional administration, and a school for *actors *training to be professionals. BRK

QUILLEY, DENIS (1927–)

English actor. Quilley began his career while still a teenager at the *Birmingham Rep, later joining the *Old Vic and John *Neville's company at Nottingham. A succession of West End plays and *musicals followed, including the title role in the first *London production of *Bernstein's *Candide* (1959) and *The Boys from Syracuse* (1963). For the *National Theatre he appeared in *Long Day's Journey into Night* (1971) and *School for Scandal* (1972), while for the *Royal Shakespeare Company he was Terri Dennis in Peter *Nichols's *Privates on Parade* (1977, also in the West End and on *film, 1984). He was Sweeney in the first London production of *Sondheim's *Sweeney Todd* (1980), returning to the role in Declan *Donellan's revival at the National in 1993. For the Peter *Hall company at the Old Vic in 1997 productions included *King Lear*, *Waiting for Godot*, and *Waste*. Quilley acted in John *Caird's revival of *Bulwer-Lytton's *Money* (1999) and was Polonius and the First Gravedigger in *Hamlet* (2000). AS

QUIN, JAMES (1693–1766)

English actor, singer, and *manager, the last great actor of the old school before the rise of *Garrick and *Macklin in 1741. Quin began in *Dublin and was performing in *London by 1715, from the start playing parts big and small, comic and tragic. He was a popular Falstaff and Sir John Brute in *Vanbrugh's *The Provok'd Wife*, but he also excelled as Macbeth and as *Addison's Cato. The 'natural' *acting of Garrick and Macklin provided a strong contrast to Quin's more formal, declamatory style, most evident when he played Horatio to Garrick's Lothario in *Rowe's *The Fair Penitent* in 1746. Quin was admired for the force and dignity he lent to tragic roles and the exuberance of his comic ones, but he was criticized for his inability to express the softer passions of pity and delicacy that *audiences increasingly desired. MJK

QUINAULT, PHILIPPE (1635–88)

French dramatist and librettist. Educated and introduced to the theatre by Tristan l'Hermite, he wrote his first *comedy at 18 and produced several successful plays for both the *Hôtel de Bourgogne and *Marais theatres. Oustanding among his successes were *Astrate, roi de Tyr* (1664, a target for *Boileau's satire in *L'Art poétique*) and a *comedy, *La Mère coquette* (Hôtel de Bourgogne, 1665), which challenged Donneau de *Visé's play of the same name at the Marais. Having collaborated with *Molière and *Corneille in the *tragédie-ballet Psyché* (1671), Quinault began a fruitful career as librettist for *Lully's *operas, including *Cadmus et Hermione* (1673), *Alceste* (1674), *Atys* (1676), helping to assure the success of this new *genre with King and court. He was elected to the Académie Française in 1670.

WDH

QUINAULT-DUFRESNE (ABRAHAM-ALEXIS QUINAULT) (1693–1767)

French actor. The most celebrated of the Quinault theatre *family, Quinault-Dufresne joined the *Comédie-Française in 1712. Preferring the simple, unaffected *acting style of *Baron, he created several of *Voltaire's tragic *heroes, Oedipe (*Oedipe*, 1718), Orosmane (*Zaïre*, 1732), and Zamore (*Alzire*, 1736). A man whose extraordinary vanity matched his good looks, he also created the title role in Néricault *Destouches's *Le Glorieux* (*The Egotist*, 1732), a role written for him and which, contemporaries said, he scarcely needed to act.

JG

QUINTERO, HÉCTOR (1942–)

Cuban playwright, director, and actor, whose *comedy *Contigo pan y cebolla* (*Through Thick and Thin*, 1964) is the most frequently produced in Cuba. *El premio flaco* (*The Booby Prize*, 1966) won the *International Theatre Institute (ITI) *award and has been performed widely abroad. Inspired by daily occurrences, Quintero's comedies combine a black humour with tenderness, incorporating *music and *dance in a manner that approaches traditional Cuban *teatro *bufo*. Other work includes *Te sigo esperando* (*Still Waiting for You*, 1996) and *El lugar ideal* (*The Ideal Place*, 1998). He directed the *Havana Musical Theatre (1970–2, 1978–88) and chairs the Cuban centre of ITI.

MMu

QUINTERO, JOSÉ (1924–99)

Panamanian-born American director. After studying at *Chicago's *Goodman Theatre, Quintero began directing the Loft Players, a Woodstock summer *stock company he co-founded in 1949. In 1951 Quintero and Theodore *Mann turned an abandoned Greenwich Village nightclub into the *Circle in the Square, producing in an intimate semi-*arena format. The company moved to a new space in 1960. Quintero had to use a minimalist style, focusing on psychological depth in *characterization. Among his many fine productions were *Dark of the Moon* (1951); *Summer and Smoke* (1952), which made Gerald-

ine Page a star; a landmark revival of *O'Neill's *The Iceman Cometh* (1956), which boosted Jason *Robards's career; *Children of Darkness* (1958), which brought George C. *Scott and Colleen *Dewhurst to prominence; *Our Town* (1959); and *Desire under the Elms* (1963). Noteworthy originals included *The Girl on the Via Flaminia* (1954), which moved to Broadway, and *Plays for Bleecker Street* (1962). New foreign plays included *The Quare Fellow* (1958) and *The Balcony* (1960). Meanwhile he directed outside *New York, did some *film and *television, and freelanced on Broadway, his chief contribution being *Long Day's Journey into Night* (1956). After he left the Circle in the Square in 1963, Quintero confirmed his status as O'Neill's foremost interpreter with numerous productions, including the American première of *Hughie* (1964) and the world première of *More Stately Mansions* (1967). In his later years, despite having to use a voice box after throat surgery, he was mainly involved with university teaching.

SLL

QUINTERO, SERAFÍN AND JOAQUÍN ÁLVAREZ See

ÁLVAREZ QUINTERO, SERAFÍN.

QUINTON, EVERETT (1951–)

American actor and director. Quinton, who describes himself as a 'male actress', joined *New York's *Ridiculous Theatrical Company in 1976 and performed a series of ever larger roles in the company's camp vehicles and travesties (*see* FEMALE IMPERSONATION). With the death of Charles *Ludlam—the Ridiculous's founder, chief playwright, and *artistic director, as well as Quinton's companion—in 1987, Quinton became artistic director. He took on a number of Ludlam's trademark roles, such as Marguerite Gautier in Ludlam's version of *Camille*, and soon emerged as a playwright, writing and performing a *one-person version of *Dickens's *A Tale of Two Cities* (1988). Despite occasional *long-running hits such as Ludlam's *The Mystery of Irma Vep* (performed by Ludlam and Quinton in 1984) and Quinton's one-man *Phaedra* (1996), the Ridiculous was evicted from its Sheridan Square basement theatre in 1996 for unpaid rent. Quinton turned to acting in commercial productions in such roles as the Wicked Stepmother in *Rodgers and *Hammerstein's *Cinderella* (2000) and has directed theatre for *youth, such as C. S. Lewis's *The Lion, the Witch, and the Wardrobe*, at the Omaha Theatre Company for Young People (2000).

MAF

QUOTIDIEN, THÉÂTRE DU

The 'theatre of the everyday', a prominent movement of French dramatic writing in the 1970s that continues to exert influence in the debate about the role of *realism and the relevance of theatre to society. An extension of the *absurdist aesthetic and the *Brechtian engagement of the 1950s and 1960s, *théâtre du quotidien* eschews traditional *plot and *character for a *dramaturgy that foregrounds the socially constructed nature of language and the resulting social alienation in contemporary life. Through their bleak, minimalist depictions of everyday life—often of the lower strata of social hierarchies, or else of the business dealings that determine those hierarchies—playwrights Jean-Paul Wenzel and Michel Deutch (among others) exemplified the post-1968 disillusionment with political and social discourse in France. DGM

·R·

RABE, DAVID (1940–)

American playwright. After dropping out of Villanova University, Rabe was drafted into the army in 1966 and sent to Vietnam. Upon his return he wrote a series of plays exploring the connections between American masculinity and militarism, all produced by Joseph *Papp at the *New York Shakespeare Festival. *The Basic Training of Pavlo Hummel* (1971) described the traumatic effects of the war on a disillusioned draftee, *Sticks and Bones* (1972) is an *absurdist depiction of a blind veteran's homecoming, and *The Orphan* (1973) is about a rural family who lost a son in Vietnam. He returned to the war in *Streamers* (1976), which uses an army barracks as a metaphor for American life in the 1960s. His broader concern with the construction of American masculinity is also evident in *In the Boom Boom Room* (1973), about the misogyny of the strip-club scene, and *Hurlyburly* (1984), a *satire on male rivalry and violence in the world of Hollywood. His most recent play, *A Question of Mercy* (1997), sympathetically portrays a *gay male couple living with AIDS.   JAB

RABER, VIGIL (fl. 1514)

Director and playwright. Raber wrote 26 *Fastnachtsspiele acted at Sterzing. He also directed a performance of the Bozen *Passion play in the town church in 1514, for which he sketched a stage plan. The plan is the only known representation of a church adapted for the performance of a Passion play.   RWV

RABINAL ACHI

The only extant script from the indigenous Maya prior to the conquest. A story of two enemy warriors, one of whom is captured and sacrificed at the end, the play proceeds by a long series of formal challenges interspersed with *dance and *music.   AV

RACE AND THEATRE

The question of 'race', understood here as 'ethnic difference', can be addressed from two broad perspectives. The first and most complex area where race impinges on the theatre is as a theme: the treatment of racially distinct *characters as a source of comic or tragic conflict can be traced back to the beginnings of European drama. The second area comprises the explicitly theatrical presentation of race in a wide variety of performance forms ranging from *circus sideshows to black and white *minstrel shows. The concept of 'race' is, however, extremely contested and should only be applied to theatre history circumspectly. The application of the term 'race' to distinguish different ethnic groups goes back to the efforts of eighteenth-century philosophers and scientists such as Buffon, Linnaeus, and Blumenbach to elaborate anthropological taxonomies commensurate with those of zoology and botany. Their categories, more cultural than biological, did not automatically assume a superiority of particular races over others. The latter idea developed during the nineteenth century when racial concepts were merged with Darwinian biology to ascertain differential degrees of human 'evolution'. The major work to merge cultural and biological theories was Joseph-Arthur Gobineau's *Essay on the Inequality of Human Races* (1853–5). Most treatments of race in drama pre-dating the mid-nineteenth century are framed within questions of cultural rather than biological difference.

1. Race as theme; 2. Presentation of race

1. Race as theme

Racial difference as a theme features throughout both *Greek and *Roman drama. The Greek term *barbaros* to distinguish Greeks from non-Greeks introduced on a linguistic level a concept of difference that was picked up in drama. The oldest surviving *tragedy, *The Persians* by *Aeschylus, thematizes the military and political conflict between the Greek and Persian empires but not primarily as a question of race. It does nevertheless depict the Persians as linguistically and culturally different. The most famous ethnic conflict is that between Jason and Medea, an inhabitant of Colchis, whose attributes of ethnic difference are reinforced by ancillary features such as sorcery. The Roman *comedies of *Plautus feature numerous characters from different parts of the empire, most notably in *Poenulus*, in which the Punic language is actually spoken and where Carthaginians are depicted as a separate race.

In *early modern drama, ethnic difference becomes a major theme. Not only do we find it in the titles of major plays such as Shakespeare's *Othello, the Moor of Venice* and *Marlowe's *The Jew of Malta*, but throughout Elizabethan drama. Shakespeare's plays, particularly *Othello* and *The Merchant of Venice*, but also *The Tempest*, *Titus Andronicus*, and *Antony and Cleopatra*, have provided the focal point for most research into questions of race and ethnicity in the early modern period. Racial questions merge quite often with those of national difference, which attain increasing prominence throughout the sixteenth century. However, Shakespeare's explicit thematization of Welsh-, Scottish- and Irishness in *Henry V* should probably not be considered a problem of race. And to what extent the Egyptian queen Cleopatra was perceived in Shakespeare's time as racially different is difficult to answer. Even Caliban's foreignness, since the 1960s a kind of prototype of the colonized 'other', is, within the argument of the play, less a question of ethnic than anthropological difference, as Trinculo's question—'What have we here, a man or a fish?'— indicates. Othello and Shylock remain, however, the characters who continue to elicit the most intense debates. Although difficult to summarize, there seems to be some consensus that Othello's 'moorishness' and Shylock's Jewish attributes are determined equally by religious as well as cultural factors. Most researchers warn against projecting a post-nineteenth-century perspective of biologically determined racial thinking onto these characters.

The influence of cultural studies and *post-colonial studies has led to a huge upsurge in interest in such questions, often in combination with other categories of alterity such as *gender. Much discussed in this context has been Ben *Jonson's court *masque *The Masque of Blackness* (1605), in which English court ladies, including the Queen, posed as African nymphs with blackened skin. The movement from *Africa to Europe is described as development from blackness to beauty, with the latter figured as antithetical categories. This 'flexibility' was in keeping with Renaissance theories of racial difference which saw skin colour as the result of climatic conditions and therefore ultimately 'reversible'.

With the 'discovery' of the New World in 1492 a new place of interethnic encounter was opened up which was played out chiefly on the *operatic stage. Of the three major actors, Columbus, Pizarro, and Cortés, the last's conquest of Mexico proved the most popular subject by which to explore interracial conflicts. The triad of Cortés, Montezuma, and the interpreter Malinché provided a dramatic configuration which even today sustains interest. John *Dryden's *The Indian Emperor* (1665), which also managed to include Pizarro in its bizarre *plot, was just one of dozens of treatments.

European theatre in the late seventeenth and eighteenth centuries featured racially distinct characters who often fulfil the structural function of the outsider impinging on the harmony of the dramatic status quo. The provenance of such characters is frequently determined by exotic fashion, although the 'Turk' remains the most frequently utilized figure. The Turk as a point of tension has been explained as a response to the expansion of the Ottoman Empire, which remained a serious threat until 1683, and a political and cultural presence on the European continent into the nineteenth century. Examples include *Voltaire's tragedies *Zaïre* (1732) and *Mahomet* (1741) and *Mozart's *Singspiel, The Abduction from the Seraglio* (1782). On the popular stage, the *commedia dell'arte* had already begun to include exotic characters in the late seventeenth century; the *pantomime *Arlequin sauvage* (1721) by Louis François de la Delisle features an indigenous *Harlequin who ridicules the follies of civilization.

European colonialism in the eighteenth century resulted in more plays set in the 'colonies' with a gradual increase in the use of indigenous characters from these countries. Richard *Cumberland's *The West Indian* (1771) features blacks only as servants (the eponymous West Indian is in fact an Englishman), while George *Colman used the same locale for his comic opera *Inkle and Yarico* (1787), a love story between an Englishman and an Indian slave-girl. Perhaps the most spectacular display of ethnic diversity was provided in the pantomime *Omai* (1785), roughly based on James Cook's Pacific voyages, which culminates in a procession of 'discovered' peoples. The most energetic explorer of racial conflict was probably August von *Kotzebue, who repeatedly dramatized conflicts between Europeans and indigenous peoples in sentimental dramas such as *The Indian Exiles* (1790), *La Peyrouse* (1795), and *Pizarro* (1796).

Racially delineated characters become increasingly important on the Anglo-American popular stage where the grinding machines of pantomime (late eighteenth and early nineteenth centuries) and *melodrama (mid- and late nineteenth centuries) accommodated any number of *stock characters, including the famous stage Irishman. In Charles *Reade's *It's Never Too Late to Mend* (1865) even an Australian Aborigine makes an appearance. Perhaps the best-known melodrama of this period is Dion *Boucicault's *Octoroon* (1859), which places a white man in a triangular relationship with an African American and a Native American. Although the public appetite for different stock characters was insatiable, the most consistently portrayed type since the Renaissance was still the Jew, whose depictions ranged from Lessing's paragon of Enlightenment humanism in *Nathan the*

Wise (1779) to demeaning clichés in popular *genres throughout Europe.

The twentieth century has seen in the racial theories of the Nazis the most appalling application of a dubious theory to political practice. Despite the manifest absurdity of such ideas, they remain deeply ingrained in European epistemology and have been intensively interrogated in the context of post-colonialism. An influential text is Frantz Fanon's analysis of European racism *Black Skin, White Masks* (1952), which may have influenced Jean *Genet's play *The Blacks* (1958). Genet explores the theatrical implications of racial representation by insisting that all characters be played by actors of black skin. Many post-colonial dramatists have examined the question of race. Derek *Walcott's *Dream on Monkey Mountain* (1970) refers explicitly to Fanon in its *expressionist depiction of racial humiliation in the *Caribbean. Dennis *Scott's *An Echo in the Bone* (1985) explores a notion of racial memory via a Jamaican *ritual. The most far-reaching exploration of race can be found, not surprisingly, in South African *township theatre, where the brutalities and absurdities of the apartheid system foregrounded the topic in plays such as *Woza Albert!* (1981) and *Asinimali!* (1986). Much of *African-American drama from Lorraine *Hansberry to August *Wilson treats race explicitly or implicitly.

2. Presentation of race

That people of difference races could be a subject of theatrical display was probably discovered by the Romans in their infamous processions of captured and conquered peoples. The early modern period certainly developed an appetite for the real thing, as Trinculo reminds us in *The Tempest*, where the English apparently 'will lay out ten to see a dead Indian'. Henceforth exotic peoples featured intermittently in sideshows, both alive and dead. It was not until the nineteenth century that race began to become a major feature of different genres of theatrical performance. Visiting indigenous peoples were occasionally integrated into pantomimes, while Native Americans began to appear increasingly on the US stage after 1840. Black Americans also began to feature on the stage, ironically enough in the popular mid-nineteenth century minstrel shows which were themselves an important vehicle for perpetuating demeaning racist stereotypes.

After the mid-nineteenth century the major locales for racial display were the unbroken succession of world's fairs and colonial exhibitions which dominated European and North American metropolitan centres well into the twentieth century. They invariably included sections where colonial peoples were on display either as performers or just 'being themselves' in reconstructed villages. A uniquely German variation of this practice was the famous 'Völkerschauen' ethnographical shows, organized in the late nineteenth century by the Hamburg zoo owner and entrepreneur Carl Hagenbeck (1844–1913), which

included people and *animals often in the same act. Although Hagenbeck has earned a place in history for his humane treatment of animals and progressive ideas on zoological architecture, many of the people he imported died while travelling. When not performing, Hagenbeck often lent out performers to anthropologists for study. Nevertheless, these shows provided for millions of Europeans often their only visual contact with colonized peoples. These shows and the colonial exhibitions increasingly stressed the performative aspect of other cultures and occasionally provided theatre artists with access to other performance traditions, as they did famously for W. B. *Yeats and Antonin *Artaud.

See also ASIAN-AMERICAN THEATRE; CHICANO THEATRE; INTERCULTURALISM; NATIVE AMERICAN PERFORMANCE. CBB

ALEXANDER, CATHERINE M., and WELLS, STANLEY (eds.), *Shakespeare and Race* (Cambridge, 2000)

UNO, ROBERTA (ed.), *The Colour of Theatre: a critical source book in race and performance* (London, 2000)

RACHEL (ÉLISA FÉLIX) (1821–58)

French actress. Theatre historians conventionally date the end of the brief success of French *romantic drama at 1843, when three important factors coincided: the failure of *Hugo's *Les Burgraves*, the success of François Ponsard's *tragedy *Lucrèce* at the *Odéon, and the triumph of the young actress Rachel in *Racine's *Phèdre* at the *Comédie-Française. Rachel's rise to stardom might be compared to the fictional career of *Shaw's Eliza Doolittle. Born into an impoverished Jewish family in Switzerland, she was the second of six children of an itinerant pedlar, lacked proper schooling, and on the family's move to *Paris sold oranges in cafés. She was noticed by a retired actor and teacher of elocution, Saint-Aulaire, who arranged her entrance to the *Conservatoire; she stayed only a few months, but was admitted to the Gymnase company, where she attracted the attention of the Comédie-Française actor *Samson, who was a professor at the Conservatoire. It was Samson who really created Rachel, teaching his protégée elocution and *acting technique, as well as the rudiments of the education and culture she lacked, and turning her into the actress who quickly enchanted Paris *audiences by her grace and poise. Making her debut at the Comédie-Française in 1838 as Camille in *Corneille's *Horace*, by the early 1840s she had performed all the leading roles in Racine's tragedies, and in such plays of Corneille's as were still in the active repertoire; contemporary tributes agree that her Phèdre in 1843 was the high point of her career. Jules *Janin in the *Débats*, together with other *critics, gave her enthusiastic notices, and takings at the Comédie increased astonishingly.

Although she captivated audiences, critics, and society hostesses by her charm and talent, there was a downside to her rapid rise to fame: the rapacious attitude of her family, and

Rachel's own greed in financial matters. She was soon earning an unheard-of 60,000 francs a year, but in addition to her work in Paris she began to arrange *tours in the provinces and abroad; and by the late 1840s there were quarrels with the Comédie over contracts and conditions of work, causing resentment on the part of her colleagues. In 1849 she negotiated the termination of her contract as a *sociétaire*, reverting to her status of *pensionnaire* on terms which not only gave her a salary of 42,000 francs but also six months' leave a year, during which she was free to arrange lucrative tours: it is reported that her tour to Russia in 1853–4 brought in 300,000 francs for Rachel herself as well as 100,000 for her brother Raphael as her manager. By 1855, suffering the strain of combining foreign tours with her schedule in Paris—and aware that she was in danger of being eclipsed by the popularity of the new star *Ristori—she resigned from the Comédie-Française altogether, and formed her own company. However, the onset of tuberculosis forced her to dissolve the company in 1856, and she died at the age of 37.

WDH

RACHILDE (MARGUERITE EYMERY) (1860–1953)

French novelist and playwright. Rachilde won notoriety for fiction whose inversion of gender roles caused her to be called 'Mademoiselle Baudelaire'. The risqué image attracted *symbolist writers to her salon, and she wrote her first plays for the Théâtre d'*Art, helping to define its anti-*realist aesthetic; Georgette Camée's performance heightened a *dreamlike scene in *Madame la Mort* (1891). Rachilde advised *Lugné-Poe in his *directing of the Théâtre de l'*Œuvre, persuaded him to produce *Jarry's *Ubu roi*, and concocted misinformation about the opening night in 1897. Her *L'Araignée de cristal* (*The Crystal Spider*, 1894) was the first French play Lugné-Poe produced, but none of her twenty other pieces were performed at the theatre she championed, and she repudiated Lugné-Poe when he attacked the symbolists. An anti-*feminist pamphlet (1928) deepened her isolation from women writers. Other plays include *Volupté* (*Pleasure*, 1896), *La Poupée transparente* (*The Transparent Doll*, 1919), and *Le Rôdeur* (*The Prowler*, 1928). Rachilde's sardonic humour and preoccupation with sexuality make her plays more performable in the twenty-first century than the work of some of her symbolist contemporaries.

FL

RACINE, JEAN (1639–99)

French playwright. Born in La Ferté-Milon and orphaned shortly thereafter, Racine's early religious education by the Jansenists at Port-Royal instilled a rare mastery of Greek and Latin authors, including *Euripides, *Seneca, and Virgil. These would provide the philosophic and stylistic foundation for a series of *tragedies that would come to be regarded as the pinnacle of *neoclassicism in France. Driven to succeed in the teeming literary and theatrical milieu of seventeenth-century *Paris, the young Racine failed in his bid to have two of his early plays performed by the company of actors at the Théâtre du *Marais. But *Molière encouraged Racine's theatrical ambition and it was Molière's company that first performed Racine's *La Thébaïde; ou, Les Frères ennemis* (*The Story of Thebes; or, The Enemy Brothers*, 1664), which was followed by a more successful production of his *Alexandre le Grand* (1665). Unbeknownst to Molière, Racine simultaneously ventured the same play to the rival troupe at the *Hôtel de Bourgogne. This unscrupulous move, coupled with the defection from Molière's company of Racine's presumed mistress, Mlle *Du Parc, and her subsequent triumph in the title role of his *Andromaque* (1667), simultaneously launched Racine's theatrical career and marked a rift between the authors that would continue until Molière's death in 1673. Such rivalries, replete with satiric acrimony that was both published and performed, were a staple of Parisian theatrical life that would punctuate Racine's career as a dramatic author, which continued with productions of his major plays: *Les Plaideurs* (*The Litigants*, his only produced comedy, based on *Aristophanes' *Wasps*, 1668), *Britannicus* (1669), *Bérénice* (1670), *Bajazet* (1672), *Mithridate* (1673), *Iphigénie* (1674), and *Phèdre et Hippolyte* (later published as *Phèdre*; 1677). All were first performed by the troupe of the Hôtel de Bourgogne. During the first performances of *Phèdre*, a cabal ensued when the late Molière's company, now installed at the Hôtel *Guénégaud, directly competed with Racine by performing Jacques Pradon's more successful play on the same subject. As a consequence, Racine retired from the public theatre, married, and assumed the duties of his new appointment, with Nicolas *Boileau, as royal historiographer to Louis XIV. Later, Racine would write two additional tragedies on biblical subjects, *Esther* (1689) and *Athalie* (1691), which were written at the request of Mme de Maintenon to be performed privately by the pupils at the school for girls at Saint-Cyr.

In 1680, the creation of the *Comédie-Française by a royal ordinance, merging the Guénégaud troupe with that of the Bourgogne, began a continuous performance tradition of Racine's plays that ensured their classic status. Between 1680 and 1990 the Comédie-Française offered more than 9,000 performances of Racine. Over the course of three centuries many of France's finest actors have been celebrated for their portrayal of Racinian roles, including *Lecouvreur, *Clairon, *Talma, *Rachel, *Mounet-Sully, and *Bernhardt. Likewise, the study of Racine has always been a fundamental component of actor *training in France, especially at what is now the *Conservatoire National Supérieur d'Art Dramatique.

Racine's plays have been staged by some of the most important French directors of the past century. André *Antoine's production of *Andromaque* at the Théâtre de l'*Odéon (1904) was the first to historicize the action of the tragedy by setting the play in an anteroom at Versailles and *costuming the actors in seventeenth-century dress rather than in traditional costume representing ancient Greece. This interpretative shift would be repeated often, as it was for Jean Meyer's *Phèdre* at the Comédie-Française (1959) and Gildas Bourdet's neorealist *Britannicus* for the Théâtre de la Salamandre (1979). Gaston *Baty's 'Jansenist' *Phèdre* at the Théâtre de Montparnasse (1940) attempted to evoke Knossos, Athens, Versailles, and Port-Royal simultaneously, with a complex interpretation that emphasized the title *character's fear of damnation rather than her incestuous desire. The production marked a trend toward *scenographic abstraction that continued with Jean-Louis *Barrault's well-known *Phèdre* at the Comédie-Française (1946), a production that coincided with the publication of his detailed *mise-en-scène, itself a testament to the painstaking attention that can be lavished on the intricacies of Racinian *verse. With the arrival of *Brecht's ideas in France came several noteworthy productions, many of which carried scenographic minimalism to extremes. These included Jean *Vilar's austere *Phèdre* for the *Théâtre National Populaire at *Chaillot (1957), Roger *Planchon's *Bérénice* for the TNP at Villeurbanne (1963), and Antoine *Vitez's *Andromaque* for the Théâtre des Quartiers d'Ivry (1971), in which the actors, in jeans and T-shirts, self-consciously recounted the story of the play instead of embodying its characters. In the 1990s, directors Yannis *Kokkos, Daniel *Mesguich, Anne Delbée, and Jean-Marie Villégier have also turned their attention to Racine, some producing multiple plays in 'cycles' involving overarching interpretations.

Outside of France, the most notable production of Racine in the twentieth century was the Kamerny Theatre's *Phèdre*, presented in Paris in 1923. Directed by Aleksandr *Tairov and often cited for its cubist design elements, the production demonstrated a unique synthesis of *Stanislavsky's psychological *realism, the *symbolism of *Craig, and the *biomechanics of *Meyerhold. In the Anglo-American theatre, where Racine's plays have suffered from a notorious difficulty in translation, the *Stratford Festival in Ontario and the *Almeida Theatre in *London presented noteworthy productions in the 1990s.

DGM

MASKELL, DAVID, *Racine: a theatrical reading* (Oxford, 1991)
TOBIN, RONALD W., *Jean Racine Revisited* (New York, 1999)

RADIO

A telecommunications medium that broadcasts or receives an audio signal by means of electromagnetic waves.

1. Invention and early history; 2. Types of broadcast systems; 3. Radio theory: revival of oral tradition or a new acoustic art form?; 4. Radio at the end of the century; 5. International broadcasting; 6. Broadcasting and the non-industrialized world

1. Invention and early history

At the dawn of the twentieth century a sense of awe accompanied the mastery of electromagnetic waves for communication over long distances without wires. It seemed as if mankind was decoding the means by which divinity itself became manifest, the means by which the sun communicated with the earth. 'The whole of nature is under wireless control,' wrote A. R. Burrows in the 1918 edition of the *London Yearbook of Wireless Telegraphy and Telephony*. 'This fact, expressed in all reverence, is a natural source of optimism to all engaged in radio research, and strengthens the belief, claiming fresh adherents daily, that radio telegraphy, which even now is still in its infancy, lies but at the fringe of a vast field of discovery.' The first quarter of the twentieth century saw the rapid technical development and distribution of the most pervasive form of mass communication the world has yet known. In London, in 1896, Guglielmo Marconi, the son of an Italian father and an Irish mother, first patented a way to use electromagnetic waves for a wireless telegraph. Though 'the wireless' remains an archaic (and no longer strictly accurate) synonym for radio transmission, the word 'radio' (from Latin 'radius', a spoke or beam emanating from the centre) was formally adopted as the term for the new invention at an international conference in Berlin in 1906. The German translation, 'Rundfunk'—a spark erupting from the centre to the circumference—encodes this meaning even more graphically.

Lee De Forest's invention of the audion tube (*c*.1907), a means of amplifying a minute flow of electricity into an electromagnetic signal, opened the way to extend wireless telegraphy to telephony, the transmission of audio signals such as music or the human voice. In the summer of 1907 he broadcast a phonograph recording from a rooftop aerial in New York. The two-way prototype of wireless telephone or telegraph would evolve into the ham radio, 'walkie talkie', police radio, and cell (or mobile) phone. But greater incentives lay in the one-to-many model signalling from a ship in distress, or later, broadcasting, to anyone who happened to be listening. ('Broadcast' derives from an Old English agricultural word for spreading seeds.) By the end of the twentieth century, 'wirelessness' had dropped out as an essential component of the definition, and now 'radio' has become a catch-all term that includes the general dissemination of audio by cable, carrier current, telephone lines, satellite dish, and the Internet ('webcasting').

In the beginning, broadcasting in America was seen primarily as a means to induce people to buy a radio set by ensuring that the gadget would be supplied with something interesting to listen to once customers took it home. Enthusiastic experimenters and amateur entertainers began sending from 'stations' in garages, attics, churches, university laboratories, department stores, and hotels. Thus began the broadcast of news, weather, election returns, *variety shows, 'sportscasting', concerts, and well-intentioned community service ventures like transmitting music to dance halls too remote to afford a band, or letting a local singer or comic 'audition' to anyone who happened to tune in. One could not sell the stuff put on the air to the *audience since it was available to anyone whether they had paid for it or not. In America it soon became clear that selling the airtime for advertisements amidst the programming was potentially massively more lucrative than selling radio sets. Thus began the sponsorship of radio programmes or commercial broadcast, the dominant form of radio in the United States.

In Europe similar experimentation was severely inhibited by the First World War. Radio broadcasting was taken over by the various militaries, and private broadcasting (with its obvious potential for breaching security) was forbidden. After the war radio expanded rapidly in Europe, with significant inroads into Africa, Asia, and Latin America. Like the invention itself, the development of radio proceeded most rapidly in areas of economic wealth and political stability. The competing signals from proximate countries and different language groups (whose boundaries did not always conform to national ones) threatened to create a tower of Babel in the competition for a place in the broadcast spectrum. The technical perfection of syntropy made it possible for each broadcaster to secure or 'license' a definite place—variously and inconsistently called a frequency, channel, or programme—in the broadcast band.

In 1933 Edwin Armstrong invented FM radio. 'Frequency Modulation' (as opposed to the original AM, or 'Amplitude Modulation') provides a clearer, brighter, static-free broadcast more suited to the subtleties of sound effects and voice, making radio a more desirable medium for music or *drama. Unfortunately the new invention was opposed by the head of the Radio Corporation of America (RCA), David Sarnoff, who saw in it a threat to his plans for the development of *television, thereby putting off access to FM until the late 1940s (and contributing to Armstrong's suicide). With cruel irony, television sound is of high quality because it is broadcast as an FM signal. Meanwhile, radio technology and personnel were developing the music recording industry and contributed not only to the development of television but also were absorbed by the silent movie industry to create the talking *film, because by the mid-1920s people were sometimes choosing to stay at home to listen to radio drama instead of venturing out to see silent movies.

2. Types of broadcast systems

Amid titanic (and still unresolved) battles over its responsibilities, proper use, regulation, and ownership, radio broadcasting developed along national lines, each country having its own system. Broadly speaking, three different (but not necessarily mutually exclusive or internally consistent) approaches to the mission of radio emerged: commercial radio, public service broadcast, and broadcast under direct government control. What

is chosen for broadcast depends upon the manner in which it is underwritten, which in turn depends on the purpose the radio is supposed to serve. These choices have a defining influence on the kind and character of drama and other forms of performative programming that is produced by the broadcast system.

In the United States, the concept of sponsorship (buying airtime for advertising on specific programmes) began in 1922. The massive size of the country led to the creation of networks of stations to extend the reach of sponsorship to nationwide audiences: the National Broadcasting Company (NBC, 1926), the Columbia Broadcasting System (CBS, 1927), the Mutual Broadcasting System (1934–62), and the American Broadcasting Company (ABC, 1947). It was assumed that a certain portion of the broadcast day would be reserved for programmes in the public interest. Among these 'sustaining programmes' underwritten by the networks when no sponsor could be found were notable dramas. Orson *Welles's *Mercury Theatre of the Air (1937–41) began in this way, for example, until it became sponsored by Campbell's Soup.

In the Telecommunications Act of 1934, almost as an afterthought to dispel complaints, a portion of the FM band was reserved for non-commercial broadcasting by churches, educational institutions, and, later, several public radio networks sustained by a mixture of voluntary subscriptions from listeners, government grants, or corporate underwriting. The most significant of these are National Public Radio (NPR), Public Radio International (PRI, formerly American Public Radio), the National Federation of Community Broadcasters (NFCB), and the Pacifica Programme Service (PPS). Despite severe economic limitations, some of the most notable dramatic programmes and series broadcast in America originated here, primarily through the Pacifica Foundation's network of stations. From 1969 to 1977, WHA's 'Earplay' served as the radio drama production centre of NPR, commissioning original radio plays from, among others, Edward *Albee, David *Mamet, Irene *Fornés, Sam *Shepard, and Arthur *Kopit. The last attempt at a nationally distributed non-commercial American drama series in the twentieth century was the Voices International 'SoundPlay' series (1991–5).

Partly in reaction to the limits placed upon American radio by its commercialization, radio began throughout Europe in the early 1920s as public service broadcasting. The British had—to quote one contemporary—'a horror of introducing into England some of the systems of radio advertising' found in the USA. As Asa Briggs remarks in *The Golden Age of Wireless* (1995), 'The BBC conceived of broadcast license holders as a "public" and not as a "market" '. Instead the BBC was established as a public service company in 1922 (and upgraded to a permanent British Broadcasting Corporation in 1927). Advertising on the air is forbidden, though sponsored programmes are allowed (a prerogative not often exercised until the 1980s). The French also baulked at following the Americans in, as one journalist of the

1930s put it, 'treating the audience like imbeciles' and established broadcasting as a state monopoly in 1923, which then both sustained a national broadcasting service and sold broadcast channels to commercial franchises.

Both French national radio and the BBC, like most major national systems throughout Europe, were designed to be supported by licensing fees charged for the use of each home radio receiver, much like the practice of requiring automobiles to be licensed in order to have access to the public roads. Thus, though there is public accountability to ensure that an audience is served responsibly, broadcasters do not have to please and hold an audience on a programme-by-programme basis. By broadcasting on three or four different frequencies or channels ('programmes') at the same time, the national radio system serves several constituencies simultaneously. In general one station (or programme) is reserved for popular music and light entertainment, one for news, analysis, and discussion, and one for intellectual and cultural productions.

In 1922, the BBC went on the air with Shakespeare (an excerpt from *Julius Caesar*). It has more or less continued to think it a patriotic duty to provide opportunities for contemporary authors and to recycle major plays and radio adaptations from the literary tradition from time to time. Drama specifically for radio became a prestigious speciality, with an office devoted to script development. Having commissioned more than 40,000 original radio plays by the end of the twentieth century, virtually no major writer of the period from 1930 to 1990 has not had an opportunity to write for the 'Beeb'. With respect to drama and other cultural programming, throughout the twentieth century, perhaps no other broadcast system has been at once so influential, so prestigious, and so controversial as the BBC.

Non-commercial, public service radio systems have been more congenial to serious and experimental drama, afford better opportunities to employ both established and developing authors, and have been more willing to make room for theatrical productions longer than an hour's duration than systems having to maximize the audience for a sponsor. Funding by sponsor requires performance forms suitable for getting as large an audience as possible to tune in, and holding it hostage to the radio commercial. The commercial is itself a rapid-paced 30- to 60-second 'dramaticule': lucrative, pervasive, influential, innovative, compressed, and effective. Just as the European public service model has strengthened the hand of non-commercial broadcast in the United States, over time the seductively lucrative American commercial model has increasingly crept into European broadcast.

No matter how well insulated, no radio system is immune from government temper tantrums over perceived impertinence. For example, in 1959 French radio blacklisted the 121 signatories of an artists' and intellectuals' manifesto against the war in Algeria, including Simone de Beauvoir, Jean-Paul *Sartre, and Alain Robbe-Grillet. In the 1950s the American networks similarly refused to employ writers and actors accused of harbouring communist sympathies. In the Second World War the radio systems of all combatants were expected to contribute to the war effort by lifting morale and employed drama for this purpose. But in totalitarian countries such as the former Soviet Union and its satellites, the People's Republic of China, dictatorships of Asia, Africa, or Latin America, or Nazi Germany the radio is (or was), officially or unofficially, an extension of the government. Not surprisingly, direct government control typically inhibits free expression in the arts, and drama is either discouraged or enlisted to serve the propaganda interests of the state. In Stalin's Russia radio did not get substantially started until around 1929, and, though *Meyerhold managed to direct some radio drama in the 1930s, it would not be until the 1950s that serious artists had any real access to Radio Moscow.

The actual circumstances, however, are often more complicated than the above profile suggests. Sometimes radio drama and cultural commentaries are encouraged for 'bread and circuses' reasons of prestige, distraction, and morale, or at least permitted so long as they do not transgress into obviously problematic themes. Such was the situation in most of Eastern Europe between the end of the Second World War and 1989, and both Hungary and the former Yugoslavia produced distinguished traditional, ethnic, and *avant-garde radio drama. In the 1960s and 1970s Chinese Red Guard 'cultural workers' broadcast lively performances of traditional Chinese operas modified to convey Maoist themes (*see* GEMING XIANDAI XI). 'Escapist' drama and light comedy is sometimes actively encouraged, as it was in Nazi Germany, such that Günter Eich was able to write soap operas and fantasy dramas of no immediately obvious propaganda value for Hitler's radio throughout the Nazi period.

3. Radio theory: revival of oral tradition or a new acoustic art form?

Compared to visual media like television and film, radio is what Marshall McLuhan identified as a 'hot' medium because it depends upon a consciousness that is prior to the visual privileging occasioned by accessing written language through the eye. Into technically advanced, visual, societies dependent on the written word, radio grafts ancient—even primeval—oral (aural) traditions that have their roots in storytelling and the mesmerizing poetic power of the pure sound—the music—of language. Homer, the singer of tales, is the prototype of the first radio broadcaster, and in order to 'do' radio, remarked Rudolf Arnheim in *Radio: an art of sound* (1936), 'we should feel ourselves back in that primeval age where the word was still sound, the sound still word'. That how the words are said is the key to what they mean is a truism of the theatre, but the essence of radio. The sound, pitch, intensity, inflection, relative degree of calm, passion, indifference, neutrality, and so on not only colour what is said, but are themselves a part of what is said. Delivery must convey *costume, stance, gesture, facial expression, attitude, motive, and *character. 'On your imaginary forces work . . . for'—in radio even more compellingly than on the stage—''tis your thoughts that now must deck our kings' (Shakespeare, *Henry V*).

Evidently all radio is performative and therefore, broadly speaking, theatrical. Even the voice performing what would seem to be the most mundane of tasks such as reading the news and weather or giving the station identification is playing a role. Among the art forms originated by radio must be counted such events as the call-in show, the quiz show, the newscaster (many of whom in many nations established reputations as colourful characters), the pundit or commentator, and the eye-witness reporter.

Like the oral traditions and narrative dramas that preceded it, radio (and radio drama particularly) comes clothed in the magic cloak of audible invisibility. It prompts the mind to conjure its own individual and intimate visual dimension tailored to the auditor's personal experience, giving radio a unique and compelling power to absorb the attention of its audience. It is thus closer to *dream or *romance or fantasy in its ability to take the listeners away from their ordinary circumstances and to allow them the chance to participate vicariously in the pageant of historic or dramatic events. This hypnotic capability persuaded many listeners that a Martian invasion was actually under way when they heard Orson Welles's broadcast of H. G. Wells's *War of the Worlds* as a Hallowe'en programme (30 October 1938). It was this aspect of radio that Marshal McLuhan had in mind when he identified radio as 'a tribal drum' (*Understanding Media*, 1964). Although his racialist essentialism about the German character is problematic, McLuhan is right in observing that Hitler came into such prominence at all 'directly owing to radio and [the extension of its reach via] public-address systems'. All these considerations make radio an ideal medium for drama. Unseen, radio allows greater latitude for the introduction of a narrator than the stage can usually manage (and, not incidentally, brought this innovation into film). But another point of view argues that radio's appropriation of the dramatic or narrative *theories of theatre, or epic poem, or printed novel did not adequately take into account the technical possibilities of the new medium. Radio needed a new acoustic art form rooted in the ventriloquism of electromagnetic waves throwing voices over long distances: recording and mixing, the radical juxtaposition of disparate sources, signal processing, sound alteration, and the like. The true radio author composed ('realized' is the preferred word) with a mixing desk and an edit block, not a pencil or typewriter or *proscenium arch.

At Radio Berlin Kurt *Weill argued for an autonomous 'radio art' that was not 'a reproduction of earlier achievements' because there could be no 'doubt that [in radio] the preconditions for the independent development of an artistic *genre of equal stature are present'. And in 1933 the Italian *futurists F. T.

*Marinetti and Pino Masnata issued a radio manifesto, insisting that 'La Radia must not be theatre because radio has killed the theatre already defeated by sound cinema'. To which BBC radio dramatist and critic Ian Rodger replies in his book on *Radio Drama* (1982): 'It has not been very widely appreciated that radio required the adaptation of existing literary and dramatic forms of expression and that this requirement stimulated experiments which have subsequently had considerable influence upon recent and contemporary writing, in both the new forms of expression and the traditional literary and dramatic forms.'

The technology for the primitive storage and retrieval of sound recording on wax cylinder, lacquered disc, or wire had been improving since the turn of the century. But the leap in the 1940s to audiotape meant that programmes of longer duration (such as dramas of an hour or longer) could be recorded for rebroadcast (at a time convenient to the actors) and easily duplicated for distribution to other radio stations (a distribution process called 'bicycling'), fostering repeat broadcasts and exchanges of programmes, archiving, and the non-broadcast residual uses of programmes (in libraries and educational institutions, for example). Regrettably the acetate, then mylar, audiotape in use from the 1950s to the 1980s deteriorates rapidly and irreplaceable archival material from that period is being lost. With audiotape, radio productions, like film, could also be easily and rapidly edited—a matter of enormous consequence for the production of news and documentaries, but with obvious value to radio drama as well. The producer could now exploit the ability to cut (edit), 'dub' (duplicate), and, finally, 'overdub' (duplicate one sound on top of another, layer) the tape.

These technical innovations inspired acoustic art experimentation, introduced a palette of sound effects into radio drama, and spawned new radio formats such as the 'sound bite' in the news and the radio feature, a personal essay written in sound, dependent upon field recordings of 'actualities'. Dylan Thomas's *Under Milk Wood* is a feature made before the advent of the tape recorder in which a writer is employed to give a sense of life in a Welsh fishing village. With the advent of the tape recorder, it became possible for the village to speak for itself. Peter Leonhard Braun's *Bells in Europe* (1972) or Helmut Kopetzky's *I'm a Beggar* (1994) are notable features of this kind.

Germany has been a congenial home (though by no means an exclusive one) for radiophonic experimentation, such as Kurt Schwitters's *Ur Sonata* (1927) and the text/sound poems of Hugo Ball. This vigorous avant-garde experimentation continued after the Nazi period with, for example, Ernst Jandl and Friederike Mayröcker's *Five Men as All Mankind* (1968), Peter *Handke's *Radio Play No. 1* (1968), the elaborate sound mixes of Mauricio Kagel's *The Inversion of America: epic radio drama* (1969), and John Cage's *Roaratorio: an Irish circus on Finnegans Wake* (1982). Whether emphasizing the avant-garde or literary aspects of radio drama, in the public service radio systems drama departments have generally been moved to induce authors to write original works for the medium. The effort can be traced to the earliest beginnings of radio, but flourished from roughly the end of the Second World War to the 1970s, and continues into the twenty-first century, though increasingly in truncated form.

Perhaps the first specifically radio play ever written, Richard Hughes's *Danger* (BBC, 1924), takes place in a coal mine in which a shaft collapses and causes the lights to go out, thereby leaving the characters, like the audience, in the dark. Bertolt *Brecht and Walter Benjamin saw in radio an opportunity for what they named the *Lehrstück* (instructional or 'learning' play) as a means of political education leading to political engagement or participation in the creative process. Brecht wrote energetically on radio and theory and practice, and collaborated with Weill and Paul Hindemith to produce *The Oceanflight* (first called *The Lindbergh-Flight*) about the transatlantic flight of Charles Lindbergh for the 1929 Baden Baden music festival broadcast by Radio Berlin. During the Second World War and after, Louis MacNeice was employed by the BBC as a scriptwriter and wrote several dozen innovative *verse plays for radio, of which *The Dark Tower* (1946) is perhaps the best known. He also wrote important essays on the art of radio and its particular appropriateness for verse drama.

Wolfgang Borchert's *Outside the Door* (1948) was the first original radio play produced in Germany after the Second World War and, in deliberately assaulting German efforts to airbrush the Nazi period out of history, caused a national shock of recognition. Subtitled 'a play which no theatre wants to produce and no audience wants to see', it tells the story of the universal soldier home from the war. It might well be paired with Norman Corwin's *On a Note of Triumph* (USA, 1945) which also won national acclaim but told the story of the universal soldier returning home victorious. Antonin *Artaud's *To Put an End to the Judgment of God* was commissioned by Radiodiffusion Français for a February 1948 broadcast, but would not actually be aired in France until 30 years later. The 1950s saw the première of such notable radio plays as Günter Eich's *Dreams* (1951) and many other plays, Samuel *Beckett's six radio plays beginning with *All That Fall* in 1956, Harold *Pinter's *A Slight Ache* (1959) and other radio dramas, Tom *Stoppard's *Artist Descending a Staircase* (1972), Ingeborg Bachmann's *The Good God of Manhattan* (1958), and the specifically radiophonic humour of the BBC's long-running *Goon Show*.

With rare exceptions, commercial radio could not rival the achievements of public service broadcasting. The closest approximation were dramatic anthology series which provided one-hour dramatic programmes, sometimes written for radio but more often appropriated from somewhere else. In the USA, Lux Radio Theatre hosted *Screen Guild Players* (1939–51), and NBC Theatre presented *Screen Director's Playhouse* (1949–59), broadcast radio adaptations of feature films, usually with the same cast. Thus at one time or another virtually every Holly-

wood star had a turn on the radio. Half-hour radio dramas were inherited from popular adventure or romantic fiction (*The Adventures of Frank Meriwell*, 1934–49), crime novels (*Ellery Queen*, 1939–48; and *Sam Spade*, extrapolated from Dashiell Hammett's *The Maltese Falcon*, 1930), or comic-book characters (*Adventures of Dick Tracy*, 1935–48; *Blondie*, 1939–50).

The daily fifteen-minute serial (or 'soap opera', after the product often advertised on them) perfectly served the function of commercial radio. Low-mimetic dramas, probably owing something to the serialization, in magazines, of low-mimetic writers such as Charles *Dickens, they were about folk with whom a middle-class audience could easily identify. They would appear daily or weekly, with a *plot that carried over from episode to episode, seducing the listener to tune in to the next one. The first of these was probably *Clara, Lu and Em* (NBC, 1931–3). Other notable examples include *Our Own Ma Perkins*, an enormously popular family drama that ran from 1933 to 1960; and *This Is Nora Drake* (1947–59), featuring a small-town mother raising her family, targeted (successfully) at housewives who were doing precisely that. *The Romance of Helen Trent* (1937–60) set out to prove 'that a woman of thirty-five could still find romance'. Initially designed to convey farming lore and animal husbandry to rural England, the BBC's *The Archers* (piloted 1951) holds the record for the world's longest-running soap opera, and has become a national institution.

A close relative of the soap opera was the weekly (usually half-hour) series in which a regular set of characters had a new and self-contained adventure in each episode, thus providing familiarity and continuity without risk of the audience losing track of the plot. Many of these were adventure stories, combining opportunities for plenty of action and *sound effects. Westerns, or stories set in some highly romanticized version of America's frontier days such as *Gunsmoke* (1952–61), were seen as a particularly American genre (but imitated all over the world). Perhaps the most popular adventure series were mysteries about crime and police, such as *Gangbusters* (1935–57) with its signature police siren. Closely aligned to these were suspense thrillers—mysteries with an element of the supernatural (for which, of course, radio sound effects are perfect). *The Shadow* (1930–54), in which an amateur sleuth 'knows what evil lurks in the hearts of men' and has learned the knack of making himself invisible to thwart crime, sometimes featured the voice of Orson Welles. Other notable examples were the series identified with one of the most skilful radio dramatists, Arch Oboler, *Lights Out* (1935–47). Science fiction and fantasy drama became more popular in the period after the Second World War. *Buck Rogers in the 25th Century* (1932–47) was among the first of the sci-fi dramas.

4. Radio at the end of the century

The last quarter of the twentieth century was a period of astonishing technical development and radical innovation in production and broadcast capabilities. In the face of the anxiety that, like hansom cabs, its time had come and gone, radio modified its formats and programming to justify its survival in an increasingly mediated world. In its 'golden years' when there were fewer alternatives, measurements of the size of the audience were used as one of many factors in making programming decisions and justifying costs to ratepayers or advertisers. In an intensely mediated world with many more alternatives competing to kidnap public attention, the measurement of audience demographics became an obsession, with the quality of programming often sacrificed to the very lucrative business of improving the numbers.

In the 1930s, television had developed as an extension of radio and, in the 1950s, replaced it as the medium of choice for drama and entertainment, appropriating many of the celebrities and programmes that had given radio its golden era. In the 1950s, the replacement of De Forest's tubes by the cheaper, lighter, and less fragile transistors (semiconductors) as a means of amplifying electromagnetic waves made radios portable, durable, and pervasive. Radio now supplied 'sonic wallpaper' (background sound), for companionship, and a vicarious sense of belonging. Short news breaks, sports, weather, traffic information, and pop music went into car radios, battery-powered portable radios, 'boom boxes', the factory floor, the supermarket, and places where teenagers congregated. It both spawned and became the principal marketer and promoter of the popular music recording industry: big bands and Tin Pan Alley in the 1940s, pop music in the 1950s, jazz, folk, and rock in the 1960s, and their descendants (acid, punk, grunge, heavy metal, rap). Music and its performance styles became more and more youth oriented and Dionysian, and, like clothes, went in and out of fashion. Radio added another performance form to the repertory: the Dj ('deejay' or disc jockey) who put the music on the air. A generation later the walkman or personal stereo wrapped the listener in a private, personalized, sound surround—allowing the creation of one's own personal version of what everyone else is listening to. Discrete dramatic or cultural programmes needing an hour or longer were uncongenial to these new uses, and became rarer. Portable radio also penetrated the isolation of the non-industrialized parts of the planet, bringing the seductions and mores of the Western world into remote villages, sometimes creating conflicts with traditional values or indigenous culture.

5. International broadcasting

Radio shrink-wrapped the world into a global village. At the beginning of the twentieth century Marconi transmitted telegraphy across the Atlantic ocean. In 1916, Irish revolutionaries took over the post office in *Dublin because it housed a wireless telegraph, and they hoped it would relay the message of their impending martyrdom to ships bound for America. TELSTAR I, launched in 1962, was intended for television but also included capabilities for trans-oceanic radio broadcasts via satellite which accelerated the international exchange of programmes. By the 1970s a satellite grid was in place that made it possible for any single station or network in Europe or North America to transmit to its entire nation, to the continent, to the world, or any selected subdivision of it. This not only simplified and increased programme distribution and exchange but also brought rural and remote areas into the orbit of an urbanized and mediated world.

By the year 2000, radio was undergoing a digital revolution in recording, production, broadcast, transmission, and distribution. 'Digitalization' allows hitherto unimaginable control over recording and production processes and provides an alternative to 'wireless' transmission. 'Webcasting' is being done by all the major broadcast centres. Web pages cannot only be heard but also inexpensively generated anywhere in the world by anyone with a computer and a telephone—a situation resembling the early days of ham radio. There is no reason why any radio programme made anywhere in the world cannot be heard anywhere else in the world, and at any time. The implications of this for programme formats and content, radio drama and performance, cassette marketing of audio programmes, radio theory, distribution, rights, residuals, government regulation, *censorship, national boundaries, are vast but not now knowable.

6. Broadcasting and the non-industrialized world

Radio has been used to serve the dual purpose of extending the influence, language, and culture of the Western powers into the non-industrial world, and at the same time bringing together and contributing to the education of remote populations. Because it is simpler and cheaper than television (which remains confined to urban centres), it penetrates deeper into the non-Western world and its influence has probably been more pervasive than any other form of intervention. Colonial powers, such as the United Kingdom or France, brought their radio systems with them into Asia, Africa, and Latin America. As early as 1909, in his Nobel Prize acceptance speech, Marconi predicted this use of the wireless: 'However great may be the importance of wireless telegraphy to ships and shipping, I believe it is destined to an equal position of importance in furnishing efficient and economical communication between distant parts of the world and in connecting European countries with their colonies and with America. As a matter of fact, I am at the present time erecting a very large power station for the Italian government at Coltano for the purpose of communication with the Italian colonies in East Africa and with South America.'

International broadcasting was established either as a unit of a national broadcasting system, as with the BBC World Service, or as a government agency, as with the Voice of America or Radio Liberty or Radio Moscow. Often these transmitted via short wave, which travels longer distances than AM or FM radio and, at least in the beginning, was a band less cluttered and less regulated. Initially the intent was to bring something of the news and culture and language of back home to European nationals living abroad. This service was first undertaken in 1927 by the Dutch broadcasting to their citizens in Dutch East India (Indonesia). In 1938 the BBC World Service began broadcasting in indigenous languages as well as English, a practice soon followed by the broadcast services of other countries. During the Second World War and the ensuing Cold War, enemy territory and occupied zones were targeted for propaganda, disorienting the enemy and sustaining the morale of friends. After the war, the superpowers continued to use short wave to invade the airspace of each other's domains. In general, the more democratic and the more developed the country, the less its citizens listened to short wave. By whatever means, indigenous broadcast developed rapidly as a consequence of the Second World War. Wherever the armies went, their radio stations went with them, and remained when they left, bringing Western entertainment into remote villages in Africa and the Pacific.

Generalizations about the development of indigenous or independent radio outside Europe and North America are risky. Usually colonial powers built local radio systems in their territories, and these became the basis of national broadcasting when independence was achieved. But not always. Egypt, for example, developed its own state-run national broadcasting in the 1920s and afterwards established systems to export Radio *Cairo and the Voice of the Arabs throughout the Muslim world. The British reshaped both Gold Coast Radio and the Nigerian Broadcast Service but did not originate either of them. Sometimes, as in Algeria, the independence movement set up outlawed competitive broadcasting, which became the basis of the national radio system. Sometimes the independence movement took over the existing colonial structures and turned them to anti-colonial ends, as in Ghana.

European efforts to bring radio systems to developing nations took place with increasing intensity in the 1950s, and were largely concluded by 1966 when Swaziland and Botswana began broadcasting. Motivations varied, usually inconsistently, from winning the loyalty of the hearts and minds of indigenous populations, to influencing and managing the news, to bringing the language and culture of the host country to a wider audience, to presenting and preserving indigenous languages, cultures, and talents, to contributing to education, social services, and nation building. These efforts were pursued with a mixture of egalitarianism, self-interest, and paternalism, and received with a mixture of gratitude and resentment, but were often supportive of dramatic and other cultural programming, enfranchising national writers, and employing local performance talents. The results are highly problematic. For example, the mere act of employing indigenous writers also privileged them: it was the BBC and not, say, the Nigerians or the Indians who determined who the important writers from these countries were. In Nigeria Chinua Achebe and the Nobel laureate Wole *Soyinka, in India Homi Bhabha and Salman Rushdie, all had their careers advanced via broadcasts on—or employment in—the BBC World Service in their home countries.

On the one hand, there is no doubt that radio has contributed to education (about AIDS, for example), economic development, political enfranchisement, and the survival of indigenous cultures. On the other hand, in intersecting local cultures the radio reframes them. The seductive appeal of Western styles and pop music has proved to be as pervasive as it is gluttonous, shoving (for example) African music into its maw, and disgorging Afro-pop worldwide, a lucrative phenomenon that has proved at once celebratory of and devastating to indigenous performance. Despite well-intentioned official policies calling for 'more authentic self expression' and 'cultural rediscovery and creativity' (Daniel Katz, *Broadcasting in the Third World*, a 1977 UNESCO-sponsored study), the effect has more often been the increasing alienation of people from their own cultural roots. To these quandaries there seems to be no solution.

See also MASS MEDIA; MEDIA AND PERFORMANCE; CYBER THEATRE.   ECF

BARNOUW, ERIK, *A History of Broadcasting in the United States*, 3 vols. (New York, 1966–70)

BRIGGS, ASA, *The History of Broadcasting in the United Kingdom*, 2 vols. (London, 1961–5; 2nd edn. of vol. ii, 1995)

KAHN, DOUGLAS (ed.), *The Wireless Imagination* (Cambridge, Mass., 1992)

KATZ, ELIHU, et al., *Broadcasting in the Third World* (Cambridge, Mass., 1977)

SCHWITZKE, HEINZE, *Das Hörspiel: Form und Bedeutung* (Stuttgart, 1961)

RADIO CITY MUSIC HALL

The world's largest indoor theatre (6,200 seats), occupying an entire city block on West 50 Street in *New York City, opened in 1932. Radio City is part of Rockefeller Center, a complex of fourteen art deco buildings constructed between 1931 and 1939 to house offices of the Radio Corporation of America and studios of their National Broadcasting Company. Conceived on a grand scale by impresario S. L. 'Roxy' Rothafel, Radio City's interiors were designed by Donald Deskey and executed with expensive materials (marble, gold foil, tapestries, carved panels) along with modern industrial materials (Bakelite, permatex, aluminium) and include a series of spacious foyers, lobbies, and smoking rooms. The Hall features a split elevator stage 48 m deep and 30 m wide (160 by 100 feet), with a *proscenium height of 18 m (60 feet). Originally conceived as a headliner house for *vaudeville, the decline of that form caused a rapid change to *film screenings accompanied by lavish stage shows featuring the Rockettes—a female tap-dance ensemble. Since 1933 a Christmas stage show has attracted as many as a million spectators per season.   MAF

RADLOV, SERGEI (1892–1958)

Russian/Soviet playwright and director who received his early training at *Meyerhold's *St Petersburg studios before establishing himself in versatile arenas. At his own Theatre of Popular Comedy he collaborated with the designer Valentina Khodasevich on a number of his own plays (1920–1), whilst directing *mass performances like *Towards the World Commune* (1920). Between 1925 and 1934 he staged *operas at the former Mariinsky Theatre, including Schrecker's *Der Ferne Klang*, Prokofiev's *The Love for Three Oranges*, and Berg's *Wozzeck.* He simultaneously ran his own *Studio Theatre between 1928 and 1942, where he staged *Othello* (a play he returned to several times), *Hamlet, Romeo and Juliet*, and *Ibsen's *Ghosts*, among twenty or so other productions. He directed at the Leningrad *circus in 1927, and at the *Moscow State Yiddish Theatre between 1930 and 1935, including a magnificent *King Lear* starring Solomon *Mikhoels. During the 1950s he worked in Latvia. He staged over 100 productions at more than 30 different venues during his lifetime, including the work of *Aristophanes, *Sophocles, *Plautus, *Calderón, Shakespeare, *Molière, *Goldoni, *Goldsmith, *Lessing, Victor *Hugo, Mérimée, *Pushkin, *Ostrovsky, *Wilde, *Toller, and *Zamyatin. NW

RADOK, ALFRÉD (1914–76)

Czech theatre and film director and playwright, influenced in his youth by E. F. *Burian. The Nazi occupation postponed the start of his professional career, but after the war he staged *operas and *operettas, usually with Josef *Svoboda's *scenography. In 1948 he entered the *Czech National Theatre but was dismissed, for political reasons, the next year; he was readmitted in 1954, and again forced to leave in 1959. The highlights of that period were productions of *Leonov's *Golden Coach*, *Hellman's *The Autumn Garden*, and *Osborne's *The Entertainer*, all in 1957. In the Chamber Theatre (*Prague, 1964), he enlarged *Rolland's intimate *Play on Love and Death* into a social epic with strong contemporary connotations. With Svoboda, he conceived *Laterna Magika for Expo 58 in *Brussels; its second programme was banned, however, and Radok cut off from its future development. He emigrated to Sweden in 1968. Radok had a unique spatial imagination, used music lavishly to create atmosphere, and did not hesitate to adapt the script to his own vision. A perfectionist, he was very demanding with actors, but he enjoyed working with promising young talents like Miloš Forman and Václav *Havel. ML

RADRIGÁN, JUAN (1937–)

Chilean playwright. Since *Testimonio de la muerte de Sabina* (*Testimony of Sabina's Death*, 1979), Radrigán has been recognized for works about marginality. He deals with the under-world and underclass, with drug addicts and prostitutes, and uses black *comedy and colloquial language rich in images and metaphors. Because his stagecraft is simple his work is easily produced by groups with scant resources. Although his plays tend to be specific about the social and political situation of Chile, his *characters struggle for self-respect and search for meaning in their lives in a manner recognizable elsewhere. His most accomplished plays are *El toro por las astas* (*Bull by the Horns*, 1982), *El invitado* (*The Guest*), *Hechos consumados* (*When All Is Said and Done*, 1981, judged by *critics the best production of the year), and *El pueblo del mal amor* (*Destined to Live without Love*, 1986). MAR

RADZINSKY, EDVARD (1936–)

Soviet/Russian playwright. Radzinsky graduated from the *Moscow Institute of Historical Archives, and has displayed a concern for *history in plays and novels about Stalin and Nicholas II (*The Last Tsar* was adapted for the stage as *The Last Night of the Last Tsar*, 1995). His play *Lunin; or, The Death of Jacques* (1974) deals with the last hour of the Decembrist Mikhail Lunin, while *The Seducer Kolobashkin* explores the legend of Don Quixote. Radzinsky has also written non-historical plays, in which he demonstrates a critical attitude to Soviet reality: *A Film Is Being Shot* (1964) addresses film *censorship, and *104 Pages about Love* (1974) involves a stewardess in a romantic *plot though she ultimately dies in a plane crash. Radzinsky has never flattered the regime and has remained a critical voice in post-Soviet Russia. BB

RAIKIN, ARKADY (1911–88)

Russian/Soviet *cabaret artist whose career began in 1938 in a competition for *variety performers, after which his talents as *mime artist and master of ceremonies soon made an impression. His stage persona was that of a disingenuously sympathetic individual overcome with embarrassment whilst trying to impart information of overwhelming importance. From 1939 Raikin was *artistic director of the Leningrad (*St Petersburg) Miniature Theatre where, alongside cabaret, he staged scripted plays of a satirical nature in which, a master of self-transformation, he played multiple roles. One of his most popular creations was the drunk who gives an incoherent lecture on the dangers of alcoholism. NW

RAIMUND, FERDINAND (1790–1836)

Austrian actor and playwright, the major representative of old Viennese popular theatre. His first plays belonged to the 'fairy play' tradition and described in rather sentimental terms aspects of ordinary Viennese life influenced by a benign metaphysical world. Fantastic adventures in the realm of spirits offered scope for magical stage spectacle and fascinating transformations. The main characters' attempts to escape their humble stations are always regretted in the end and they are reconciled to the limits of a modest existence. Raimund's aspiration to write serious drama conflicted with the commercial framework of the Theater in der Leopoldstadt, where he was engaged from 1817 to 1830. Nonetheless he introduced tragic and melancholic aspects in his *allegorical *comedies, as well as good-humoured *satire on popular life in *Vienna. The depth and complexity of his masterpieces, *Der Bauer als Millionär* (*The Peasant as Millionaire*, 1826), *Der Alpenkönig und der Menschenfeind* (*The Alpine King and the Misanthrope*, 1828), and *Der Verschwender* (*The Prodigal*, 1834) ensure that they still occupy a secure position in the German-language repertoire.

GB

RAISONNEUR

In the French nineteenth-century 'théâtre utile' of *Dumas *fils* and *Augier, a play's *didactic message, usually concerning marriage and sexual mores, was commonly underlined (without much subtlety) by a *character whose function was to represent the author's views. The term *raisonneur* is also applied, not always appropriately, to certain characters in *Molière's *comedies.

WDH

RAJATABLA

Venezuelan company founded in 1971 by Carlos *Giménez, who was also its director, and funded by the Ateneo in Caracas. The group, which has a strong international focus, leans toward experimental theatre, spectacular staging, and *ritual motifs, revealing the influence of *Artaud. Its style is idiosyncratic and extrovert, and *text is subservient to *performance. Its best-known production was *El Señor Presidente* (1977), an adaptation of Miguel *Asturias's novel which was performed to high acclaim at the festival in Nancy in France. Equally important were plays about power, *El candidato* (1978) and *El héroe nacional* (1980); José Antonio Rial's *Bolívar* (1982) and *La muerte de García Lorca*; Calderón's *Life Is a Dream* (1985); and *No One Writes to the Colonel*, adapted from García Márquez. Rajatabla started the National Theatre Workshop in 1984 to *train actors, and the Directors' Centre for New Theatre in 1986 to promote study and research.

LCL trans. AMCS

RAKESH, MOHAN (1929–72)

*Indian writer, regarded as one of the major playwrights of modern Indian theatre. Rakesh was the leader of the influential *nayi kahani* or 'new story' movement of the 1950s and 1960s in modern Hindi literature, which introduced a new *realism and a new economy in the presentation of narrative. His experience in writing *one-act plays for All India Radio and his work in films made possible a new professionalism in the handling of voice, *lighting, fine psychological observation, and interplay of *characters. His stories and plays, which focus on the intensity and frustrations of urban relationships in the nuclear family, deal with questions of identity, the limits of communication, and the impossibility of self-definition and self-fulfilment.

The first of his full-length plays, *Asadh ka ek Din* (*A Day in the Month of Asadh*, 1958), which concerns the romantic relationship of *Kalidasa, the foremost classical Sanskrit poet, with his village beloved Mallika, debunked the sacrosanct image of the poet. Viewed in close-up, Kalidasa emerges as vulnerable, self-absorbed, and ultimately exploitative. Directed by Ebrahim *Alkazi on an improvised *open-air stage in 1962 in Delhi, the play established Rakesh as the most promising playwright of the new generation. His final full-length play, *Adhe Adhure* (*Neither Half nor Whole*, 1969), continues to engage urban *audiences. Its central character, Savitri, a working woman and mother of three, is portrayed with initial sympathy but ends as a figure more threatening than threatened, damned to an impossible situation with a hopeless husband. After *Adhe Adhure* Rakesh regarded *dialogue as a dated theatrical convention and experimented with wordless plays just before his early death.

VDa

RAKOTOSON, MICHÈLE (1948–)

Francophone playwright and novelist from Madagascar. She has worked as cultural programme director for the French International Radio service, researched the traditional dramatic form *hira gasy*, and wrote her first plays in Malagasy. Political upheavals sent her into exile in *Paris in the early 1980s and provided the inspiration for her major plays on dictatorship: *Un jour ma mémoire* (*One Day, my Memory*, 1988), *La Maison morte* (*The Dead House*, 1991), and *Elle dansa sur la crête des vagues* (*She Danced atop the Waves*, 1999). Her sister Christiane Ramanatsoa, a director and teacher, staged her new bilingual drama in Madagascar (*Iboniamasiboniamanoro*, 2001).

CJM

RALLI, TERESA (1952–)

Peruvian actress, director, and founding member of *Yuyachkani (1971). One of the most notable and versatile of *Latin American actresses, Ralli excels in roles which combine the tragic and the comic, as in her powerful interpretation of Antigone (2000). She possesses an emotional and intellectual intensity which has been particularly gripping in work such as *The Travelling Musicians* (1983), *Against the Wind* (1989), and *Calderón's *The Great Theatre of the World* (2000). She wrote and directed *The First Supper* (1996) and *Change of Hour* (1998).

LRG

RAMA VI (1880–1925)

King of *Thailand from 1911 to his death, considered the most significant force in Thai theatre history. Involved in court performances from his childhood, he wrote, produced, and directed plays while studying military history and law in England, and started his own *khon (*masked play) troupe soon after he returned to Thailand in 1902. He wrote 151 plays of various types: for traditional, *folk, and modern theatre, adaptations of Western plays, translations of Shakespeare, and dramas in English and French. He also produced, directed, and acted for the court *audience. Many actors, dancers, and comedians were granted noble status during his reign. He established the Royal Department of Performing Arts to assist traditional theatre, then in decline, and founded the Royal School for Performing Arts to nurture young artists. He used theatre to promote nationalism and to counter colonialism. He also wrote many scholarly works on the theatre.   SV

RAME, FRANCA (1929–)

Italian actress and playwright, who came from a *family of travelling players with a history of performance in northern Italy dating from the eighteenth century. Rame made her first appearance on stage when only eight days old, and learned her trade by observing other members of the family. While performing in *Milan with a *variety company she met Dario *Fo, who was in the same show, and the two were married in 1954. Her subsequent career is inseparable from his. She introduced him to popular theatre, to the Italian tradition centred on the actor-author and on *improvisational skills, and she employed her deep, almost instinctive knowledge of theatrical techniques and rhythms to provide him with trenchant criticism of his writing. The two established the Fo–Rame company in 1958 and, at the height of the 1968 movement, they set up a *touring theatrical cooperative, similar to the Rame family company, to perform *political theatre. Her contribution to Fo's plays has been undervalued, and with the rise of *feminism she herself wrote several *one-person shows, such as *All Bed Board and Church*, on the condition of women.   JF

RAM LILA

Dramatization of the epic story about the Hindu deity Ram, which takes place every autumn across northern *India. The story of Ram's birth, marriage, exile, and epic battle to regain his abducted wife Sita has been a foundational narrative of South and South-East Asia for over two millennia. It encapsulates central tenets of kingship, statehood, moral behaviour, and family and *gender relations, and is represented in a variety of styles including *puppetry, singing, *dancing, and *acting. *Ram lila* is based upon Tulsidas's *Ramcharitmanas*, a long poem in the Awadhi dialect of Hindi. Infused with the fervour of devotional poetry, *Ram lila* both inspires reverence for the gods and inculcates an understanding of *dharma* or righteous action. It is also notable for its inclusive public character. *Open-air performances of episodes from Ram's life are played before large crowds for at least ten days leading up to the festival of Dussehra, when the effigy of Ravana, the demon king, is destroyed by burning. Spectators come from all classes and castes, and historically include Muslims and Christians as well as Hindus. In episodes such as the march against Ravana, the crowd falls in behind the monkey-warriors and becomes part of the army. In Varanasi, episodes are associated with and enacted at specific localities identified by their mythic place names. The geography of the *Ram lila* is thereby etched upon the city, and its citizens become inhabitants of sacred space and time.

As in the *ras lila*, the actors are all male, and the roles of Sita, Ram, and his brothers are played by prepubescent boys. The *make-up of these actors and their worship as embodiments of divinity also follow the practice of *ras lila*. Other *characters usually wear *masks, notably Hanuman, Ravana, and Kumbhakarna. But unlike the *ras lila* the performers are *amateurs, and sponsorship through subscriptions is the most common form of patronage. In its most famous and spectacular form at Ramnagar near Varanasi, the *Ram lila* is supported and supervised by the maharaja himself. He attends each performance mounted on an elephant, and the crowds voice a triple allegiance to his person, to the Lord Shiva as protector of Kashi (the ancient name for Varanasi), and to Ram.

The present form of the *Ram lila* began soon after Tulsidas's death in 1624, and according to legend was enacted by his disciple Megha Bhagat. In the nineteenth century the royal house of Banaras established its hereditary sponsorship of the Ramnagar *Ram lila*. In this presentation, passages from Tulsidas's *text are recited by a *vyas* or Brahman specialist, in alternation with chanted passages by a *chorus accompanied by musical instruments. *Dialogue is interspersed between these sung and chanted lines. The style is *ritualistic, highly verbal, and somewhat static, and little emphasis is placed upon mimetic representation. At the end of the twentieth century Hindu nationalists redefined Ram's virtuous kingdom (or *Ram rajya*) to exclude minority communities, notably Muslims and Christians. In the ideology of Hindutva, Ram acquires a militant posture, and his iconography emphasizes physical prowess and musculature. Large public processions and festivals are always susceptible to manipulation by motivated groups (*see* CIVIC FESTIVALS). It remains to be seen whether the pluralistic ambience of the *Ram lila* will be altered by the resurgence of right-wing interest in Ram.   KH

RAMLY, LENIN EL- (1945–)

Egyptian playwright, screenwriter, and *manager. Ramly's *expressionism powerfully interlocks with his flair for popular *comedy (hence his great *box-office appeal), all the while serving to pose topical social and political questions. His best-known play internationally is *Bel-Arabi El-Faseeh* (*In Plain Arabic*, 1991), an unprecedented, devastating *satire of the time-honoured ideal of pan-Arabism. The play also marked the end of Ramly's collaboration with actor-director Mohamed Sobhi, originally a classmate at the Egyptian Theater Institute; the two had founded in 1980 Estudio Tamaneen, a private troupe with justifiable claims to artistic experimentation. As *film writer Ramly received media attention, both at home and abroad, for his attack on Islamist militants in *Al-Erhabi* (*The Terrorist*, 1994), a reworking of sorts of his 1967 short *television drama.

HMA

RAMOS-PEREA, ROBERTO (1959–)

Puerto Rican playwright, director, critic, winner of several national *awards and of the Tirso de Molina award (1992) in Spain for *Miénteme más* (*Lie to Me More*, staged 1993). Author of more than 30 plays, his work alternates between neo-*realism, as in *Módulo 104* (*Module 104*, 1983), and the postmodern, as in *Mistiblú* (1991) and *Morir de noche* (*To Die at Night*, 1995). He often directs his own work, which has been translated into English and French and performed internationally.

JLRE

RANA, JUAN (COSME PÉREZ) (fl. 1622–72)

The most famous Spanish comedian of his day. Having acted in leading companies, by the mid-1630s Pérez was identified with his *clownish persona Juan Rana. This *character, originally a rustic magistrate, appeared in many other guises in over 40 playlets. Advancing years brought infirmity, but he emerged from retirement for major festivals, and rode on a chariot in *Juan Rana's Triumph*, an interlude performed at court in 1672.

VFD

RAND, SALLY (1904–79)

American fan and bubble dancer. Helen Gould Beck was born on a Missouri farm and raised in Kansas City. As Billy Beck, she made her debut at 13 and performed as a *chorus girl at the Garden Theater until graduation from Central High School. After a few years in *vaudeville, she acted in silent *films. Cecil B. DeMille reportedly chose her stage name from his Rand-McNally desk atlas. In 1927 Hollywood's Wampus organization signalled her as a 'baby star'. Rand catapulted to fame in 1933 when she rented a horse and crashed the *Chicago World's Fair midway as Lady Godiva. This led to her engagement as a dancer at the fair, where she developed her celebrated fan *dance: swirling huge ostrich feather fans to conceal ('the Rand is quicker than the eye') her naked body. Her signature melodies were Debussy's 'Clair de lune' and, for her finale, Chopin's 'Valse in C-sharp minor'. Nude dancing with fans or semi-transparent balloons remained central to her career in nightclubs and *burlesque, even as late as 1978, the year before her death. *See also* SEX SHOWS AND DANCES.

FHL

RANDAI

Popular *folk *dance-drama of the Minangkabau ethnic group in west Sumatra (*Indonesia) which evolved at the turn of the twentieth century as a composite art form consisting of martial arts, dance, instrumental music, song, and *acting. Originally an all-male tradition with *female impersonators, most *randai* groups today are mixed. The indigenous martial arts (*silek*) continue to be featured prominently, including circular dances called *galombang*, based on martial arts movements, which are accompanied by songs and flute music. A unique feature of *galombang* is the *tapuak* percussion, performed by dancers slapping their trousers. The *galombang* alternate with acted scenes in performances that typically last three to four hours. Music accompanies the *galombang* as well as portions of the scenes, and lengthy instrumental pieces frame the performance at the beginning and the end. The narratives are derived from traditional Minangkabau tales (*kaba*), the two most famous being *Anggun Nan Tongga* and *Cindua Mato*. Though the form has adopted modern technology (electric *lighting and amplified *sound), more *realistic acting techniques, and an array of modern *costuming, it remains firmly rooted in *silek* and strives to educate its *audiences about Minangkabau customs and tradition.

KP

RASA

Literally 'flavour', *rasa* is one of the most important concepts in *Indian aesthetics. In the world of theatre it refers to the pleasure involved in 'tasting' a particular performance through a heightened experience that transcends temporal, spatial, and personal conditions and constraints. In effect, what one experiences is not just the emotions relating to a *character in a particular *scene, still less the personality of the *actor, but a transpersonal and universalized state of emotions called *sadharanikarana*. Grounded in a spectrum of at least nine distinct emotional registers—*sringara* (erotic), *hasya* (comic), *karuna* (pathetic), *raudra* (furious), *vira* (heroic), *bhayanaka* (terrifying), *bibhatsa* (odious), *adbhuta* (marvellous), and *shanta* (peaceful)—the *rasa* is produced through the exploration of dominant states of emotion (*sthayibhava*), supported by determinant (*vibhava*), consequent (*anubhava*), and transitory states of emotion (*vyababhicari bhava*). Rejecting the cause–effect relationship of *bhava* and *rasa* (as expounded by aestheticians like Bhattalollata), the Kashimiri Saivite seer *Abhinavagupta (AD c.950–c.1025) has offered the most complex *theory of *rasa* in which it prefigures the entire aesthetic experience, rather like the essence underlying the transformation of a seed into a tree. Approximating the *ananda* (bliss) experienced by yogis in touch with the Absolute, the experience of *rasa* falls short of spiritual self-realization. Nonetheless, its consensual and participatory pleasure is made possible to connoisseurs of the arts, who are called *rasika* or *sahridaya*, whose 'consent of the heart' makes the experience of *rasa* at once immediate and indivisible.   RB

RASCÓN BANDA, VÍCTOR HUGO (1948–)

Mexican playwright and novelist. A prominent member of the 'New Dramaturgy', his plays are hard-hitting, dark, and violent explorations of political corruption (*Blue Beach*, 1990), drug trafficking (*Contraband*, 1991), and a social system that has forgotten its poor (*The Fierce Woman of Ajusco*, 1985). Born and raised in the northern state of Chihuahua, he has also written powerful *texts about that region (*Voices on the Threshold*, 1983) and USA–Mexico border issues (*The Illegals*, 1979; *Murder with Malice*, 1994). As a banker, Rascón has his pulse on the law of money in Mexico and the courage to expose its inner machinations in plays such as *The Bank* and *The Executives* (both 1997). His playwriting has evolved from a crude *realism to a more poetical one and, later, to a form of hyper-realism. With *La Malinche* (1998, directed by the Austrian Johann Kresnik), Rascón has ventured into the excesses of the postmodern with a production that both intrigued and outraged Mexican *audiences and critics.   KFN

RAS LILA

Devotional *Hindi-language theatre found in the Braj region of western Uttar Pradesh in *India. It is a specific form of *Krishna lila*, the dramatic telling of miraculous episodes from the life of the Hindu deity Krishna. In *ras lila*, Krishna's consort Radha is prominent and their erotic relationship is celebrated. The circle *dance (*ras*) symbolic of the mystic union between the human Radha and the divine Krishna is the principal medium for the arousal of religious emotion (*bhakti*). Other *genres of *Krishna lila* are the *krishnattam* of Kerala, *ankiya nat* of Assam, and the *gaulan* section of Maharashtra's *tamasha*.

In its present form *ras lila* dates to the sixteenth century when saint-poets disseminated an accessible form of religious faith in Krishna, one of the incarnations of Vishnu, through the common languages of north India. It is performed in temple courtyards by professional *svamis* or *rasdharis*, typically during the monsoon season, before pilgrims and local followers of Vaishnavism. Temple priests are the usual patrons, although affluent devotees may also fill this function. The roles of Krishna, Radha, and the *gopis* (Krishna's girlfriends, who, like Krishna, tend cattle) are played by pre-pubescent boys chosen from local Brahman families. They are worshipped as divine

manifestations (*svarup*) not only during the performance but offstage as well. *Costumes date from the Mughal period, and facial stencils, long black artificial braids, and glittering headgear complete the distinctive look of the actors. Performances are bipartite, comprised of circle dances followed by dramatic episodes, both accompanied by effusive, often enraptured singing and instrumental music. The stage consists of a demarcated circular area (*mandala*) where the dancing and acting take place. Behind it is a throne where Krishna and Radha periodically sit and receive worshippers. Viewers respond through clapping, swaying, and dancing in response to the devotional atmosphere. At significant moments the Radha-Krishna pair assume iconic stances, freezing in a tableau (*jhanki*). Framed by an ornamental border like enshrined deities, the actors become gods and the spectators worshippers as they advance to prostrate themselves and make offerings.

The repertoire of *lila* numbers over 100 episodes. Most popular are the story of Krishna's birth (*Krishna Janam Lila*), the incident of Krishna stealing butter (*Makhan Chor Lila*), the subduing of the serpent Kaliya (*Kaliya Daman Lila*), the tax on the *gopis* selling curd (*Dan Lila*), the stealing of the *gopis'* clothes (*Chir Haran Lila*), the pique of Radha at Krishna's absence (*Man Lila*), and the great circle dance (*Maharas Lila*). The narration of these stories is embellished by verses of famous Hindi poets like Surdas and Nandadas as well as compositions by the performers themselves. The dominant emotion of erotic love, or *shringar ras*, pervades the *ras lila* from beginning to end. However, comic improvisations are also intermixed, particularly through the character Mansukha, who serves as a jester. The dancing in *ras lila* includes virtuoso elements such as rapid spins, twirling on the knees, and acrobatic manoeuvres, and is said to be related to the classical dance style *kathak*. *See also* RAM LILA.   KH

RASTELL, JOHN (c.1475–1536)

English playwright, humanist, and printer. Brother-in-law of Thomas More and father-in-law of the dramatist John *Heywood, Rastell was himself the author of at least one play, *The Nature of the Four Elements* (1517–27), a moral *interlude designed to demonstrate the benefits of Renaissance learning. He may also be the author of *Gentleness and Nobility* and *Calisto and Melebea*, both dated *c.*1517. Rastell is more significant as a printer. He and his son William printed, and thus preserved, a dozen dramas from the early sixteenth century, including plays by Heywood and Henry *Medwall.   RWV

RATTIGAN, TERENCE (1911–77)

English playwright. Rattigan made his name with the long-running West End *comedy, *French without Tears* (1936), followed by the altogether darker *After the Dance* (1939), thereafter largely alternating between comedy and *drama. *The Winslow

Boy (1946), the immaculately wrought tale of a boy expelled from naval college for allegedly stealing a postal order, gained the dramatist new critical respect, while *The Browning Version* (1948), a *one-act about a failed schoolmaster and his wretched marriage, is a miniature masterpiece, its length belying its emotional depth and sophistication. *The Deep Blue Sea* (1952), probably his greatest work, concerns a woman who abandons her rich husband only to find herself trapped in a hopeless relationship with a young airman. Despite taking greater and greater risks in subject matter and form, few of Rattigan's plays were successes after the revolutions in British theatre led by *Osborne's *Look Back in Anger* in 1956. *Ross* (1960) and *Cause Célèbre* (1977) used *filmic, almost epic, structures, while *Variations on a Theme* (1957), *Man and Boy* (1963), and *In Praise of Love* (1973) continued to explore the nature of sexual desire and repression. But Rattigan was dismissed as emotionally repressed, politically conservative, the purveyor of well-made but mechanical potboilers.

Though he is sometimes bracketed with Noël *Coward, who drifted rightward politically, Rattigan was sharply critical of the political and emotional irresponsibility of Coward's generation in *After the Dance* (1939). The charge of emotional repression, sometimes linked to an allegation of cravenly hiding his own homosexuality, also misses the mark, since the plays depict the effects of repression and gives shape to a battle between a repressive society and desire. The final scene of *Separate Tables* (1954), for example, shows a tempestuous battle between judgemental sexual conservatism and liberal decency, conducted entirely through glances and small talk in the dining room of a seaside hotel. A series of successful revivals in the 1990s has changed this perception and Rattigan is increasingly seen as perhaps the finest writer of the English *well-made play tradition, turning its famous mechanics to the service of sexual isolation and longing.   DR

RAUCOURT, MLLE (FRANÇOISE-MARIE-ANTOINETTE-JOSÈPHE SAUCEROTTE) (1756–1815)

French actress. The sensational debut of this tall, handsome 16-year-old at the *Comédie-Française in 1772, as Lefranc de Pompignan's Didon, earned her the generous protection of both Louis XV and his mistress Mme Du Barry, and the mercenary attentions of aristocrats eager for her virginity. Her sexual proclivities, however, were lesbian and, after a series of highly publicized scandals and arrest for debt, she was exiled for three years. Reinstated in 1779 by order of Marie Antoinette, she rebuilt her reputation during the 1780s, starring in tragic-queen roles such as *Racine's Athalie, *Voltaire's Sémiramis, and Hilaire de Requeleyne Longepierre's Médée. In 1782 she appeared cross-dressed as a young soldier, in *Henriette*, a play of

her own composition. Together with other counter-revolutionaries, she was imprisoned in 1793 and narrowly escaped the guillotine. In 1796, dreaming of re-establishing the Comédie-Française in a new home, she formed a 'Second Théâtre-Français' at the Théâtre Louvois. In 1799 she rejoined the reconstituted Comédie. In 1806 she was entrusted by Napoleon with the organization of a company to *tour Italy. She returned seven years later and in 1814 gave her last performance, as Catherine de Médicis in François Raynouard's *Les États de Blois* (*The Blois Parliament*, 1810).   JG

RAUPACH, ERNST (1784–1852)

German dramatist. After studying theology and philosophy in Halle, Raupach worked variously as a teacher and professor of literature and history at *St Petersburg University. In 1824 he settled in *Berlin where he wrote 117 plays, mainly historical and mythological *tragedies in the tradition of *Schiller, as well as *melodramas and sentimental *comedies. Raupach was one of the most performed German dramatists of the late *romantic period. Best known are his play *Der Müller und sein Kind* (*The Miller and his Child*, 1830), for its prevalent death symbolism and fatalistic tone, as well as his skilfully constructed eight-play cycle *The Hohenstaufens* (1837).   CBB

RAVENHILL, MARK (1967–)

English playwright. The title of his first full-length play, *Shopping and Fucking* (1996), may have misled *critics into seeing Ravenhill as celebrating the ecstasy-fuelled, sexually promiscuous lives of his *characters. But the dramatist angrily satirizes the vacuity of his generation's lives and aspirations, a theme which became clearer in *Faust Is Dead* (1997), which pitilessly identified the worst excesses of postmodern thought in a tale of a philosophical guru's journey with a young boy into the American desert. *Some Explicit Polaroids* (1999), lightly influenced by *Toller's *Hoppla, We're Alive!*, places the *satire in a broader context, juxtaposing the empty-headed narcissism of its characters with the unforgiving forces of globalization. *Mother Clap's Molly House* (2001) is a *Brechtian piece, interweaving *scenes set in the early eighteenth century, at the emergence both of a homosexual subculture and of entrepreneurial capitalism, with a contemporary *gay sex party, subtly questioning the relationship between sexual liberation and market economics.   DR

RAVENSCROFT, EDWARD (fl. 1671–97)

English playwright. Ravenscroft wrote a dozen plays, many of them imitations or adaptations of European *comedies, some successful, none of them particularly distinguished. A master of the bedroom *farce, in his first play, *The Citizen Turned Gentle-*

man (1672), he was relatively restrained, but in his later comedies—*The Careless Lovers* (1673), *The Wrangling Lovers* (1676), *The Canterbury Guests* (1694)—he catered shamelessly to Restoration taste. His masterpiece, *The London Cuckold* (1681), spices adulterous *action with smutty *dialogue, and was so popular that it was annually revived on the Lord Mayor's Day until 1751. *The Anatomist* (1697), reduced to an *afterpiece, held the stage for over a century. Ravenscroft also adapted Shakespeare's *Titus Andronicus* (1686), and experimented with *commedia dell'arte* with *Scaramouche a Philosopher* (1677). *The Italian Husband* (1697), a domestic horror play, is an unsentimental examination of a brutal murder.   RWV

RAZNOVICH, DIANA (1945–)

Argentinian playwright and cartoonist, author of some sixteen plays performed throughout Europe and the Americas. After exile in Spain, she reappeared in 1981 with *Disconcerted* (Teatro *Abierto). Works such as *Autumn Garden* (1983), *Dial-a-Mom* (1988), and *Lost Belongings* challenge not only political repression but also ongoing social (especially *gender) regulations.   JGJ

RAZUMOVSKAYA, LYUDMILA (1948–)

Soviet/Russian playwright. Razumovskaya graduated from the Leningrad (*St Petersburg) Theatre Institute and has been writing plays since the mid-1970s. *Dear Elena Sergeevna* (1980, staged 1988, *film by Eldar Ryazanov also 1988) is about a group of pupils who visit their teacher in order to steal exam questions; she does not surrender, but is driven to the brink of suicide by the realization that she has brought up monsters. *Garden without Soil* (1982) explores loveless marriage. The theme of moral corruption caused by the Soviet system runs through Razumovskaya's work.   BB

READE, CHARLES (1814–84)

English novelist and playwright. Reade was better known for his novels, such as *The Cloister and the Hearth* (1861), but wrote some 35 plays, almost all *melodramas. Among them is the popular *comedy *Masks and Faces* (1852), which he wrote with Tom *Taylor, whose liveliest *character is *Garrick's actress Peg *Woffington. *The Courier of Lyons* (1854), a crime drama about mistaken identity, was played with great effect by *Irving at the *Lyceum as *The Lyons Mail* (1877). *It's Never Too Late to Mend* (1864) contained a grim and controversial *scene showing punishment on a prison treadmill, which illustrated Reade's social reformist tendencies. He was responsible for persuading Ellen *Terry to return to the theatre in 1874 to act in one of his own plays. The theatre was not good to Reade: he estimated his total income from the drama at £35 a year.   MRB

REALISM AND REALITY

*Aristotle opens the *Poetics* with a brief discussion of the mimetic arts in general. In contrast to Plato, who raised major questions about the nature, purpose, and success of the mimetic representation of life and truth, Aristotle claims that all arts, despite their different media, subject matter, and modes of *mimesis, are able to represent aspects of the world and reality, including human behaviour and character. The concept of mimesis (or representation) thus serves to connect the artwork to the world; it is the principle of mediation between the two. It provides the means and the purpose of artistic expression. By following the principle of mimesis the artist creates a work that negotiates between the idea of the real (within the artist's imagination) and the nature of the real (existing outside the artist's mind). The artwork is not the idea itself, it is not reality itself, but instead a third thing or condition that somehow connects them. But how well do they correspond? On this question Plato and Aristotle divided. Ever since there has been little agreement, as the histories of both dramatic *theory and theatrical practices reveal.

From the foundational perspective of philosophy, the idea of realism, derived from the primary conception of the Real, presents one of the abiding problems in epistemology and metaphysics. Realism is the generic name for various philosophical arguments through the ages that have been put forward in order to counter the philosophy of idealism (which also has taken various forms). Although the specific terms of idealism and realism did not emerge until the eighteenth and nineteenth centuries, the concepts themselves were central to classical Greek philosophy, and the traditions of Western philosophy have struggled ever since to describe the relation between the Real and the Ideal (or the world and idea). These philosophical debates chart major difficulties in human understanding, including the problem of how the mind, apart from the material world yet still in it, is able to perceive, know, and represent the world accurately and fully. Various oppositional or dialectical terms (for example, reality and appearance, truth and falsehood, essence and existence, materialism and formalism) have been used to articulate this problem.

When the concepts of *reality*, the *real*, and the *realistic* are taken up by *theatre artists, dramatic theorists, and theatre scholars, they are usually anchored in Aristotelian philosophy, specifically the definitions and principles of mimesis or representation. The term mimesis has often been used as a synonym for imitation, the act of reproducing life. Thus, Cicero (as reported in Donatus' essay on *comedy) stated that comedy is 'a copy of life, a mirror of custom, a reflection of truth'. Likewise, imitation has often been used as a synonym for verisimilitude, the appearance or semblance of truth or actuality. The arts, not just theatre, attempt to present—that is, represent—life as it is. As *Voltaire stated in his entry on 'enthusiasm' in the

Philosophical Dictionary, 'Reason consists in constantly seeing things as they really are.' In this sense, the principle of reality can be applied broadly, as George *Lewes did in 1858: 'Art always aims at the representation of Reality, i.e., of Truth.'

In the history of dramatic theory, the appeal to the real or the representative has served to justify the playwright's mission. Dramatic theory in the *early modern period, for example, was an extended commentary on Aristotle, with added flavour provided by *Horace and Cicero. The *neoclassical debate about the three *unities in *drama—time, place, and *action—depended upon assumptions about realistic codes of representation. In turn, the artistic opposition to neoclassicism in the Enlightenment was grounded in the principle of the Real. Thus in 1757 *Diderot proclaimed that 'the perfection of a play consists in the imitation of an action so exact that the spectator, deceived without interruption, imagines he is present at the action itself'. *Strindberg said much the same thing in 1888. In 1830 *Pushkin demanded that the dramatist deliver 'the truth concerning the passions, verisimilitude in the emotions experienced'. And *Ibsen claimed in a letter to Edmund Gosse in 1874 that his decision to write in prose rather than *verse was in order to create 'the *illusion of reality'. Of course, each writer proceeds to define and represent the Real in a specific, even idiosyncratic, manner. For example, *Brecht, though opposed to Ibsen and Aristotle, evoked the principle of reality in defence of his drama.

In rather general terms, the principle of reality has been an abiding justification and mandate for art, as *Shaw announced in 1897: 'When art becomes effete, it is realism that comes to the rescue.' Apparently this basic principle operated in *Greek *tragedy, for Plutarch reports in his *Moralia* that '*Sophocles used to say that having played through the magniloquence of *Aeschylus, and the sharp artificiality of his own manner, he turned finally to the style of ordinary speech [*lexis*], the best and most expressive of character.'

Throughout the history of drama and theatre, then, the relation between art and reality has been negotiated by the general (and often vague) principle of mimesis, defined variously as representation, likeness, imitation, resemblance, and verisimilitude. Yet despite the recurring appeal to some kind of principle of reality, the concept of realism acquired new meanings in modern times, especially between the 1870s and the 1920s. Three interrelated developments are noteworthy.

1. Both theatre artists and theorists put forward a new concept of realism—not just the familiar idea of realistic or representative theatre—to refer to an artistic movement identified with the drama of *Zola, Ibsen, early Strindberg, *Hauptmann, *Chekhov, and *Gorky. In basic accord with the novelists who were already articulating a new realism (such as Balzac, Flaubert, Henry *James, *Tolstoy, George Eliot, and Zola himself), the dramatists sought to produce plays that presented a candid, concrete, and exact picture of contemporary life and society. In this sense realism was an early stage of *modernism,

one of the revolts against not only *romanticism and *melodramatic conventions but also *bourgeois culture and its manifest ideologies. So understood, modern realism is also closely related to *naturalism—a term that Zola used in his essay 'Naturalism in the Theatre' (1881). He called for 'the return to nature and to man, direct observation, correct anatomy, the acceptance and depiction of that which *is*'. Likewise, in the preface to *Miss Julie* (1888) Strindberg spelled out his own version of the naturalistic programme. Ibsen, by contrast, did not write manifestos, but like Chekhov was determined to represent ordinary details in order to capture both the texture of material life and the *subtextual pulse of the *characters' lives—their psychological, social, economic, and moral beings. By representing the illusion of actual experience, realistic drama aimed to reveal not only the social registers of contemporary life but also the sordid, empty, and even tragic nature of modern society.

The aesthetic philosophies of realism and naturalism, influenced by positivism in the sciences, urged writers to be objective in order to dissect society and human character. Both programmes also revealed the influence of Darwinism and the idea of the struggle for survival. Naturalist drama, such as Hauptmann's *The Weavers* (1892) and Gorky's *The Lower Depths* (1902), tended to represent the economic and environmental forces that controlled, even determined, the characters' behaviour. By contrast, realistic drama, such as Ibsen's *Hedda Gabler* (1890) and Chekhov's *The Cherry Orchard* (1904), located the suffering of the characters in their social values and psychological self-deceptions, though a strain of economic, social, and hereditary determinism may operate in these plays as well.

2. The new realistic drama served as a catalyst for *actors and *directors who attempted to develop new realistic methods of acting and staging. Indeed, the figure of the director (e.g. Saxe-*Meiningen, *Reinhardt, Granville *Barker) emerges in this era as a solution, at least in part, to the problem of how to unify the many detailed elements of performance and production in the new realism. New acting companies also emerged at the end of the nineteenth century to perform realist and naturalist drama: *Antoine's Théâtre *Libre in *Paris, *Brahm's *Freie Bühne in *Berlin, the *Independent Theatre Society and the partnership of William *Archer and Elizabeth *Robins in *London, and, most tellingly, the *Moscow Art Theatre, founded in 1897 by *Stanislavsky and *Nemirovich-Danchenko. In addition, some actors and directors, notably Stanislavsky himself, attempted to develop a new system of actor *training and performance.

3. In conjunction with the new acting and directing methods, a new realistic *scenography developed. Although the nineteenth-century stage had already taken up historical *antiquarianism in the production of *historical drama and Shakespeare, thus achieving one kind of realism, the new realistic drama called for a natural or realistic environment, so detailed and accurate that it looked exactly like a Norwegian parlour in *A Doll's House* or a basement lodging in *The Lower Depths*.

*Costumes as well had to be accurate for the time and place of the play, right down to the buttons on Hedda Gabler's dress. And the new stage *lighting, enhanced at the turn of the century by the development of instruments for controlling electric lights, contributed to the aura of a natural environment.

So for a few decades the theatre seemed to achieve a new realism that answered the demands of representing reality. And yet no sooner did realism proclaim itself as the instrument of modernism than a *symbolist—or idealistic—alternative asserted itself. Even the careers of Ibsen and Strindberg show that the dialectic between the Real and the Ideal (that is, between realism and symbolism, naturalism and *theatricality, representation and presentation) is abiding in the theatre. In the early decades of the twentieth century, modernism promoted various non-realistic agendas, from *futurism, *dada, and *surrealism to *expressionism, *constructivism, and *epic theatre. But realism did not disappear from the modern theatre; it continued to be the preferred mode of representation for many *playwrights, actors, designers, and directors. And in *film realism has served as a defining principle of *mise-en-scène and acting.

Advocates for modern realism often claim that it is truer to life—more natural and realistic—than all previous modes of theatrical representation. If so, did it achieve a solution to the debate initiated by Plato and Aristotle? Apparently not, for theatre in every age and locale has developed its particular method for representation; the idea of the natural is in fact an idea of infinite variety. This is why the natural acting of one age, locale, or medium often looks stylized and unnatural to observers from any other age, locale, or medium. Realism is yet one more theatrical style, not a mode of representation without theatrical features. In consequence, it is impossible to define the terms realism and reality in any acceptable manner, especially if we expect them to carry and maintain a shared set of meanings that apply throughout human history, operate across diverse cultures and societies, and fit all art forms. Accordingly, all workable definitions must be local definitions, not only specific to time and place but also particular to a group of people who have agreed upon a set of meanings for the concepts. Change any of these conditions and the meanings also change, sometimes radically.

TP

CARLSON, MARVIN, *Theories of the Theatre*, 2nd edn. (Ithaca, NY, 1993)

CLARK, BARRETT H., *European Theories of the Drama*, rev. Henry Popkin (New York, 1965)

HALLIWELL, STEPHEN, *Aristotle's Poetics* (Chapel Hill, NC, 1986)

REANEY, JAMES (1926–)

Canadian poet and playwright. His most famous work is the 'Donnelly trilogy' about an Irish family destroyed by sectarian violence in nineteenth-century Ontario. Employing a fluid improvisational style and richly poetic language, these plays— *Sticks and Stones*, *The St Nicholas Hotel*, and *Handcuffs*— attracted enormous attention on their premières at *Toronto's *Tarragon Theatre (1973–5) and *toured nationally in 1975. Reaney's other plays include *One Man Masque* (1960), *The Killdeer* (1960), *The Sun and the Moon* (1962), *The Easter Egg* (1962), *Listen to the Wind* (1966), and *Colours in the Dark* (1967). He has also written several plays for *youth, notably *Names and Nicknames* (1963), and his adaptation of *Alice through the Looking Glass* premièred at the *Stratford Festival in 1994. Most of Reaney's plays reflect his upbringing in rural Ontario; his many honours include a Governor-General's Literary award for *The Killdeer and Other Plays* (1962). DWJ

RECEPTION

In *theatre studies reception refers to the response(s) of spectators to a theatrical *performance, conceived in terms of the process by which that response is generated and directed and an aesthetic experience created. The experience is a product of both an immediate cognitive-emotional response to the performance and a long-term intellectualized reflection on the event. The process, usually conceptualized in terms of a communication model, is characterized by several governing factors: the socio-economic-political status of the *audience; the psychological make-up of individual spectators; the socio-psychological dynamics of the audience as a group; and the dramatic and theatrical codes and strategies designed to influence the reception. Taken together, these factors provide the 'theatrical frame' that allows theatrical actions to be interpreted and meaning to be developed. Spectators are not passive recipients of meaning, but active participants in its creation. In critical practice, attention can focus on a particular play, its reception by a particular audience or in a particular period, or its reception by various audiences over a period of time. Attention can also focus on the cognitive and emotional processes whereby an audience comprehends a performance. Theatrical reception as a serious concern in theatre studies and in theatrical *theory dates from the last quarter of the twentieth century. Conventional theorists saw the audience as a passive receiver of messages generated by the performance, which was the prime object of their analyses. Semioticians recognized the role of the spectators but seldom pursued the implications and offered no methodology for investigating audience reception (*see* SEMIOTICS). There were sporadic studies of audience response at the University of Iowa in the 1950s and 1960s, and at Bowling Green State University in Ohio in the 1970s. Also in the 1970s, at the University of Constance in Germany, Robert Jauss and Wolfgang Iser introduced a theory of reception in literary studies that had important implications for theatre studies. Since that time much of the research in theatrical reception has been done in Europe, initially in Germany, later in Belgium, Holland, and Sweden.

Jauss stressed the role of the reader in literary history, suggesting that changing interpretations of literary works are explicable as the result of changing circumstances of reception. He postulated for his 'hypothetical reader' a historically confined 'horizon of expectation' that could be determined by an analysis of the generic, literary, and linguistic contexts of the work itself. A work that broke through this 'horizon of expectation' was aesthetically superior. Iser, although less interested than Jauss in the historical dimension of literary reception, agreed that the reader is co-producer with the *text of meaning. Like his colleague, he found in the literary work an 'implied reader' which he conceived as an authorial construct that forces the actual reader to assume a particular interpretative stance. Jauss's 'hypothetical reader' and Iser's 'implied reader', like the semiotician's 'model reader' or 'model spectator', are both idealized individuals and textual constructs. The responses of actual readers were not analysed. (Iser specifically excluded 'empirical interference'.) Reader-response criticism made a significant shift towards recognizing actual readers by focusing on the social dynamics that condition individual response. The American critic Stanley Fish, for example, writes of a socially defined 'community of readers' whose individual interpretations are governed by group norms.

While literary reception theory has had little direct impact on theatre studies, it has undoubtedly raised the profile of reception research and suggested the possibility of a comparable aesthetics of theatrical reception based on empirical study. The theatrical situation is complicated by the mediating factor of performance, and the 'model spectator' can thus be conceived as a construct of the dramatic work, the performance, or both. Moreover, the spectator normally responds, not simply as an individual, but as a member of an audience—a much more complex entity, whether construct or real. Finally, theatrical theory has moved beyond the notion that theatre consists of the performance of a literary text. Reception theory in particular focuses instead on the interaction of performers and spectators as the essential of theatre. Both performance analysis and reception research are central to the understanding of this interaction. Researchers investigate the background, the competences, and the interpretative framework of spectators—those attributes that allow them to recognize some actions, in some circumstances, as theatre—and they study the implications of these attributes for theatrical reception by examining the actual responses of spectators during and after the performance.

Pre-performance preparation. General concerns of the social and cultural background of spectators are joined by a consideration of mechanisms associated specifically with a particular theatrical culture, designed to influence audience expectations, assumptions, and interpretative frames. These can range from conventional dramatic and theatrical codes that tell the audience what to expect; to performers who are known for particular kinds of roles or *lines of business; to programmes,

*playbills, and pre-performance *publicity; to essays by *dramaturgs and reviews by theatre critics (*see* CRITICISM).

Reception process. The investigation of an audience's immediate response to a performance is more direct—and intrusive. Among the methods used are a 'response machine' on which spectators are asked to push buttons indicating pleasure or displeasure; video recorders to register facial expressions; *applause meters; even cardiograms and encephalograms.

Reception results. When dealing with long-past or historical performances, scholars are largely dependent on occasional written accounts and observations—haphazard evidence at best. For current performances, they depend principally on precoded questionnaires and interviews, both of which risk imposing the investigator's conceptual frame on heterogeneous responses. In Belgium and Sweden, researchers have introduced post-performance 'theatre talks' which bring together different groups of spectators who have attended different performances of the same play. The participants determine the direction of the discussion; the researcher analyses the results.

Reception research in the theatre, even with its strong empirical emphasis, is not innocent of theory. It is concerned, nevertheless, not with aesthetic judgement, but with understanding the spectators' judgements; not with 'stage images and their effects', but with 'the underlying processes'; not with the analysis of formal structures, but with the analysis of theatrical performances as 'events taking place in the socialisation history of the spectators' (Schoenmakers). RWV

JAUSS, H. R., *Towards an Aesthetic of Reception Theory and History of Literature* (Minneapolis, 1982)

SCHOENMAKERS, HENRI (ed.), *Performance Theory, Reception and Audience Research* (Amsterdam, 1992)

RECITATIVE

From the Italian *recitare* (to recite), recitative denotes those passages in *opera, sung by soloists in *dialogue, where the vocal line imitates patterns of spoken language. During the seventeenth century, recitative was difficult to distinguish from formal musical structures, but by the eighteenth century, in *opera seria* especially, the action was furthered by the recitative, which alternated with arias and concerted numbers that articulated the emotions of the *characters. 'Dry recitative' was usually accompanied by a harpsichord alone, while 'accompanied recitative' employed orchestral instruments and was used at moments of growing tension, excitement, or distress. The difference between the two modes can be clearly grasped in *Mozart's mature Italian operas. By the 1810s, distinctions between recitative and musical numbers were breaking down as a more continuous, through-composed musical idiom was sought. Although it is still possible to distinguish between fully scored recitative and arias or duets in *Verdi's work, the scores of his last operas are continuous. In his early mature opera *The Flying*

Dutchman (1843), *Wagner also employed recitative, but by the time he composed *The Rhinegold* (1869), all distinctions have broken down and the music drama is, in essence, pure recitative as the dramatic flow of the words is seamlessly embodied in the music.   SJCW

RECOGNITION *See* ANAGNORISIS.

RED BULL THEATRE

Possibly converted from an inn yard in 1604, the Red Bull was located in Clerkenwell in *London. Constructed as a square building, possibly of brick, it soon became the home for the third of London's resident companies, Queen Anne's Men, who played there until 1617. This company established the reputation that stayed with the *playhouse and its various occupants until the closure of the theatres in 1642. Famous for its plays with battles, it gradually became a 'citizen playhouse', distinct from the indoor *private theatres with their gentlemanly clientele, and performing chiefly to the city's working-class *audiences. *See* INNS AS PLAYHOUSES.   AJG

REDGRAVE, MICHAEL (1908–85)

English actor. His early work at *Liverpool Playhouse (1934–6) was followed in *London by time at the *Old Vic, where he played Orlando to Edith *Evans's Rosalind in *As You Like It* (1936), and Laertes to Laurence *Olivier's Hamlet (1937). In contemporary plays his roles included Harry in T. S. *Eliot's *The Family Reunion* (1939), and Charleston in Robert Ardrey's *Thunder Rock* (1940). Redgrave's imposing height but gentle personal magnetism lent him a striking stage presence. At the *Shakespeare Memorial Theatre he was Richard II (1951), Prospero (1952), King Lear, and Shylock (1953); he also played Antony opposite Peggy *Ashcroft in *Antony and Cleopatra* (1953) and in 1958 he was Hamlet at the age of 50. He appeared as Uncle Vanya at *Chichester in 1962, and directed the opening season of the Yvonne Arnaud Theatre in 1965. He had a lengthy *film career, ranging from Hitchcock's *The Lady Vanishes* (1939) to Losey's *The Go-Between* (1971). Influenced by *Stanislavsky, Redgrave wrote on the craft of *acting in *The Actor's Ways and Means* (1953) and *Mask or Face* (1958), and the autobiographical *In my Mind's Eye* (1983). He was knighted in 1959. From a theatrical *family himself, he married actress Rachel Kempson in 1935; their children Corin, Lynn, and Vanessa *Redgrave have all pursued successful theatrical careers.   VRS

REDGRAVE, VANESSA (1937–)

English actress, the eldest daughter of actors Michael *Redgrave and Rachel Kempson (*see* FAMILIES IN THE THEATRE). After *training in *London she made her professional debut at the Frinton Summer Theatre in 1957. Her London debut followed the next year when she played opposite her father in N. C. *Hunter's *A Touch of the Sun*. She joined the *Shakespeare Memorial Theatre in 1959, appearing as Helena in *A Midsummer Night's Dream* and Valeria in *Coriolanus*. Later roles included Jean Brodie in *The Prime of Miss Jean Brodie* (1966), Gilda in *Design for Living* (1973), Boletta in *The Lady from the Sea* (1976), Arkadina in *The Three Sisters* (1985), Katherine in *The Taming of the Shrew*, Mrs Alving in *Ghosts* (both 1986–7), Lady Torrance in *Orpheus Descending* (1989), and Hesione Hushabye in *Heartbreak House* (1992). In 1994 she played Vita Sackville-West to Eileen *Atkins's Virginia Woolf in the two-woman show *Vita and Virginia* in *New York, and in 1999 she was Carlotta in *A Song at Twilight* in London. In 2000 she was Prospero in *The Tempest* at the new *Globe, and Madame Ranevskaya in Trevor *Nunn's production of *The Cherry Orchard* at the Royal *National Theatre. Her *film appearances have been hugely varied and include Antonioni's *Blow-Up* (1966), Frears's *Prick up your Ears* (1987), and de Palma's *Mission Impossible* (1996).   AS

RED LION THEATRE

Known chiefly from a lawsuit against the builders, the Red Lion was never a tavern, as its name implies, but a purpose-built *playhouse constructed on a site in Stepney just outside the City of *London called Red Lion Yard. Built in 1567 by John *Brayne, brother-in-law of James *Burbage, nothing is known about its use or how long it lasted as a playhouse. Polygonal, with a rectangular *stage 12 by 9 m (40 by 30 feet), and 1.5 m (5 feet) high, its main feature was a turret by the *scaenae frons* rising 9 m (30 feet) from the stage.   AJG

REES, ROGER (1944–)

Welsh actor and director, born in Aberystwyth, and brought up in south *London. He trained at Camberwell Art School and the Slade, and worked as a scenic artist and then *stage manager for a variety of theatres including Wimbledon, where he made his acting debut in the *regional repertory standard *Murder at the Vicarage* (1965). The following year he joined the *Royal Shakespeare Company. Through the 1960s and 1970s he appeared in numerous RSC productions, gradually gaining larger roles. In 1980 he was the eponymous *hero in the company's major production of *Nicholas Nickleby*; the Broadway transfer won him a Tony *award as best actor. Subsequent appearances include Terry Johnson's *Cries from the Mammal House* at the *Royal Court, and Hamlet and Berowne for the RSC (all 1984). Much of his subsequent career has been based in the USA and has included Broadway productions of *Cocteau's *Indiscretions* (1995), *Anouilh's *The Rehearsal* (1996), and *Chekhov's *Uncle*

Vanya (2000), playing Astrov opposite Derek *Jacobi. Rees was a regular in the *television sitcom *Cheers* (1989–90).   AS

REFORMATION AND COUNTER-REFORMATION *see page 1119*

REGIONAL REPERTORY THEATRES, UK

The term repertory theatre (or 'rep') refers to the network of publicly subsidized regional theatres throughout the UK that operate regular seasons of plays produced by a resident *management. Such theatres differ in a number of ways from the major city repertory theatres in continental Europe in that they now rarely maintain a permanent acting company (the Royal *National Theatre and *Royal Shakespeare Company are exceptions), though there may be a nucleus of actors who make frequent appearances; and the pattern of production is seldom true *repertory playing, in which a group of plays will rotate through a season with several changes of bill each week. More usually each production will run for three to four weeks, to be replaced by a new production with a new cast. What has animated the repertory movement throughout its history is the ideal of offering a varied and balanced fare of plays—new and classic, serious and comic—and related artistic events each season that command the interest and feed the imagination of the community. Theatre in this sense is seen as a cultural service rather than a commercial enterprise and justified on the same terms as one would a public library, art gallery, or swimming pool.

The history of the repertory movement in Britain aligns itself almost exactly with the course of the twentieth century. Its seeds lay in the campaigns mounted at the end of the nineteenth century to establish a *national theatre in *London, forcefully articulated by Harley Granville *Barker and William *Archer in their 1904 manifesto, but it effectively began in the regions, which were less constrained by London's major commercial ventures and costly theatre rents. The first repertory theatre in mainland Britain was founded in 1907 in *Manchester by the wealthy theatre enthusiast Annie *Horniman. Having helped found the *Abbey Theatre in *Dublin three years earlier, she was now keen to establish a permanent company dedicated to high standards of production and opposed to commercial practices such as the *long run and the star system. To this end she presented a wide range of high-quality drama and fostered the development of new, home-grown writing. Following hard on the heels of Manchester came reps in *Liverpool (1911) and *Birmingham (1913), and, after the war, smaller but often just as innovative ventures in Northampton, Sheffield, Oxford, *Cambridge, and elsewhere. By 1938 there were over 30 reps in the UK—subsidized not by the state but by wealthy theatre-loving entrepreneurs, charitable trusts, and subscription (*see* FINANCE).

The rebuilding of the cities following the Second World War and the arrival of public subsidy saw an even more rapid and innovative expansion of activity. The ideas, talent, experimentation, and new plays frequently came from Nottingham, *Glasgow, *Manchester, Birmingham, and Bristol, and even the West End came to rely increasingly on product from the reps. *Arts Council subsidy was especially influential: it enabled the rep companies to move out of the straitjacket of weekly repertory (involving a new production every week, usually with one week's *rehearsal), raise production standards by presenting fewer plays per season, and begin to build new *audiences, aided by subsidized *ticket prices. From the mid-1960s, Arts Council money, boosted by contributions from local government and subscription campaigns, became available to fund the long-needed renewal of theatre buildings across the country. From the Belgrade, Coventry (1958), to the West Yorkshire Playhouse, Leeds (1990), there was a surge of new or radically renovated *playhouses which reflected a fresh vision of the repertory theatre and its relationship to its community. Theatres were seen now as arts centres—they incorporated cafés and *studio theatres, ran *youth theatre, *theatre-in-education, and community outreach teams, and hosted *touring companies as well as staging their own productions. By 1980 the number of new theatres (including major conversions) throughout the country totalled 40, of which 34 were outside London. The scale of renewal was all the more remarkable at a time of declining fortunes in the commercial touring sector and the rapidly increasing dominance of *television. Although the early designs were mostly conventional *proscenium-arch affairs, many of the later theatres are impressive for their adventurous exploration of theatre space and actor–audience relationships, notably the *thrust stages of the *Chichester Festival Theatre (1962) and Sheffield's *Crucible Theatre (1971), and the in-the-round *auditoriums (*see* ARENA AND IN-THE-ROUND) at Manchester's *Royal Exchange (1976), Scarborough's Stephen Joseph Theatre (1976), and Stoke-on-Trent's New Victoria Theatre (1986). Some theatres, such as the Everyman in Liverpool (1964), were built deliberately to have a more experimental, *alternative character with the aim of bringing in new, younger audiences, while many of the larger reps (such as the Bolton Octagon and the Birmingham Rep) added small studio theatres and flexible *stage configurations.

A few enterprising reps in this period stand out. The Nottingham Playhouse, especially under Richard *Eyre (1973–8), premièred some of the most penetrating English plays of the 1970s including *Brenton's *Churchill Play*, Stephen Lowe's *Touched*, and Trevor *Griffiths's *Comedians*. The small but lively Victoria Theatre, Stoke-on-Trent, is best known for its *documentary dramas, such as *The Knotty* and *Fight for Shelton Bar*, fashioned out of the region's own history and topical concerns (the building of the local railway, the growth and threatened closure of the local steel industry, among many) and using

(continued on p. 1120)

REFORMATION AND COUNTER-REFORMATION

The religious changes which took place across *early modern Europe, bringing about Protestantism and reviving the Catholic Church, had a wide-ranging impact on *theatre and *performance, as well as on concepts of *theatricality. Most of the popular *religious drama characteristic of *medieval Europe was to die away during this period, faced with Protestant hostility towards the depiction of sacred subjects on stage, as well as a growing feeling amongst Catholics that such performances were indecorous. Some early reformers, such as England's John *Bale, took familiar *genres such as the *morality play and turned them to anti-Catholic propagandist ends. *Marlowe's *Dr Faustus*, a play containing angels and devils but no God, has been seen as demonstrating the transition between medieval and early modern depictions of religious topics on the English stage.

In parts of Europe which became Protestant or were strongly affected by Protestantism, *biblical dramas came to replace *genres like the *mystery play. In Germany and Switzerland, for instance, the Reformation inspired a transition from *Passion plays to biblical drama via such forms as humanist classical drama and Shrovetide *comedy. But in England an initial interest in biblical drama was not kept up, reflecting how attitudes to theatre among the Reformers themselves varied considerably. Some, like Martin Luther and Philip Melanchthon, affirmed the value of drama in providing moral exemplars. Others developed *anti-theatrical ideas from patristic and medieval commentators, arriving at a condemnation of the theatre as inherently deceitful and idolatrous, and of Catholic worship as undertaken for theatrical effect rather than spiritual efficacy. In England, ecclesiastical vestments were given to players to demonstrate contempt for their supposed sacred function, and *character stereotypes drawn from anti-Catholic polemic became especially familiar in English *tragedy; in 1618 a Venetian resident in *London expressed his shock at the level of Protestant prejudice in John *Webster's *The Duchess of Malfi*.

Reformation propagandists, and subsequently their opponents, exploited the permeability of the boundaries between theatre and everyday life. Staged iconoclastic demonstrations were especially characteristic of early Protestantism in Germany, while across Europe, formal disputations between those of rival religious convictions owed much to quasi-theatrical forms such as the *dialogue. Theatrical language was commonplace when describing the demeanour of confessors facing trial for their religious beliefs, or martyrs' final appearances on the scaffold (*see* EXECUTIONS, PUBLIC). The attention paid to public display by some Protestant monarchs—one example being Elizabeth I—was a deliberate attempt to provide a secular alternative to the public religious *spectacles characteristic of Catholicism (*see* STATE DISPLAYS).

Some types of traditional theatre linked to the liturgical year could still be justified in the light of the Reformers' critiques, while others persisted in the face of official disapproval, or in remote regions. But broadly speaking, the Reformation had the effect of limiting the kinds of religious topics which could legitimately receive dramatic treatment, and facilitated in the long term a move away from sacred *plots to secular. Thus it had both an enabling and a constricting effect on playwrights' choice of subject matter. Similarly, while the attrition of *guild drama limited the opportunities available to one kind of *amateur actor, the humanist emphasis on the place of drama within moral education brought about new opportunities for others. The trend for *university and school plays was taken up by both Catholic and Protestant pedagogues, perhaps most systematically in *Jesuit schools and seminaries across Europe; these could become regular civic occasions, even receiving occasional governmental encouragement. Gustav Adolf II of Sweden, asking his bishops in 1572 what he could do to advance learning in the country, was told to foster school drama.

If Protestantism was characterized by an ambivalent relationship to theatricality, Counter-Reformation Catholicism was to use it for explicitly affective and evangelical purposes. The decorative innovations of baroque Catholic churches evolved symbiotically with the increasingly sophisticated art of *scenography. Medieval theatrical traditions could be retained and developed in Catholic countries, wherever they were thought to be edifying. *Sacre rappresentazioni* in Italy, and *Corpus Christi celebrations across Europe, are examples of this. *Autos sacramentales*, the *one-act plays at the centre of Corpus Christi celebrations in Spain, gave concrete and triumphal realization to the abstractions of Catholic eucharistic theology, most famously in the hands of *Calderón.

While the emphasis on predestination in Protestant theology had brought about a new appreciation of fatalism in classical drama, this could be counteracted. The very idea of *tragicomedy was controversial because the genre was a post-classical development, but tragicomedies became a popular Counter-Reformation form because they were suited to demonstrating the benign workings of providence, and endorsing the concept of free will. Battista *Guarini's *Il pastor fido* (*The Faithful Shepherd*, written 1580s, published 1602) was the most influential tragicomedy of the period, while *Tirso de Molina is especially notable for ingeniously subverting the implications of his tragic plots by means of comic endings.

A similar theologically motivated overturning of generic expectation lies behind *tragoediae sacrae* such as Pietro Sforza Pallavicino's *Ermenegildo*. This type of sacred tragedy developed from medieval dramatizations of saints' lives; in them, martyr-*protagonists die in a manner both tragic and triumphant. Enhancing Counter-Reformation Catholicism's encouragement of martyr cults, such plays could celebrate contemporary figures like Sir Thomas More—*hero of several dramas across Europe—or be used to foment nationalistic sen-timent. Plays from nineteenth- and twentieth-century dramatists about *historical individuals embodying the conflicts of the Reformation in their own lives and deaths—as various as *Schiller's *Mary Stuart* (1800), Robert *Bolt's *A Man for All Seasons* (1960), and John *Osborne's *Luther* (1961)—can perhaps be seen as among the legacies of the *tragoedia sacra*.   ASh

ABBÉ, DEREK VAN, *Drama in Renaissance Germany and Switzerland* (Melbourne, 1961)
BROWN, JOHN RUSSELL (ed.), *The Oxford Illustrated History of Theatre* (Oxford, 1995)
ROSTON, MURRAY, *Biblical Drama in England* (London, 1968)
VEEVERS, ERICA, *Images of Love and Religion* (Cambridge, 1989)

theatre to celebrate a community's own stories. The *Citizens' Theatre in Glasgow, under the artistic triumvirate of Giles *Havergal, Philip *Prowse, and Robert David Macdonald, created a visually stunning style and a radical reinterpretation of the classics. The Everyman in Liverpool (1964) signalled the emergence of an alternative to the repertory mainstream; playwrights John *McGrath, Chris Bond, Adrian *Mitchell, Willy *Russell, and Alan *Bleasdale all cut their teeth at the Everyman. The West Yorkshire Playhouse, conceived from the outset as a hub for community arts, is noted for its major productions of *musicals, a series of world premières, creative programmes for youngsters in the summer, and a resident professional schools touring company. Not all repertory has been as adventurous of course: predictable, formula programming has all too often been dictated by the tastes of the predominantly middle-class white (and loyal) audiences that tend to patronize these theatres.

Public arts subsidy came under pressure in the 1970s following the sudden hikes in world oil prices and soaring inflation, accelerated by the arrival in 1979 of the Thatcher administration with its market-forces philosophy. Withdrawals of grant aid began and some of the smaller reps closed. The larger theatres economized by closing down their community outreach teams and drastically reducing studio theatre production. With the trend towards smaller-cast plays, and the commissioning of adaptations rather than wholly new works, the repertoires narrowed. The voices clamouring for a fairer distribution of resources between London and the regions became louder, and in response the Arts Council began to decentralize funding, leading to a wholesale devolution, beginning in 1990, to newly constituted regional arts boards. Only the Royal National Theatre, the Royal Shakespeare Company, and the national touring companies remained funded from the centre.

But decentralization did not counter the unremitting process of underfunding. In 1990 the Arts Council drama panel reported that 31 regional theatres were on the verge of bankruptcy. Some adventurous work continued, but by the end of the twentieth century the British repertory theatre was unsustainable in a great many of the towns and communities it had served for most of the century. Funding was a major factor, but so too, as the Boyden Report (2000) into the future of theatre in England concluded, were the rapidly changing tastes and leisure habits of the communities themselves. If theatres were to respond positively to the needs of a multicultural society and make their programmes accessible to all sections of that society, not least to disaffected urban youth, then the rep, geared primarily to generating its own productions, could no longer be seen as the dominant model for regional theatre. Theatres were needed that could host a variety of work targeted at different facets of the community, respond rapidly to changing interests, and offer far greater opportunity for community involvement. The Boyden recommendations met with a positive response from Arts Council and government alike. Substantial new funding was announced in 2001 for a number of selected, strategically placed regional reps and for more flexible theatre operations that would complement traditional offerings. Perhaps these initiatives will change notions of what regional theatre might be—just as the rep movement itself had done a century earlier.

ARJ

BOYDEN ASSOCIATES, *The Roles and Functions of the English Regional Producing Theatres: a report for the Arts Council of England* (London, 2000)
ELSOM, JOHN, *Post War British Theatre* (London, 1979)
JACKSON, A., 'The repertory theatre movement in England, 1960–1990', in K. P. Müller (ed.), *Englisches Theater der Gegenwart: Geschichten und Strukturen* (Tübingen, 1993)
ROWELL, G., and JACKSON, A., *The Repertory Movement: a history of regional theatre in Britain* (Cambridge, 1983)

REGIONAL THEATRES, USA

As with other countries with dominant cultural capitals, theatre in the United States has been centred in *New York for much of the past 300 years. There have always been theatres elsewhere, of course, but in the second half of the twentieth century the establishment and growth of a network of permanent professional theatres around the country represented a development of lasting significance. Known variously as regional, resident, non-profit, and institutional theatres, they have decentralized American theatre in important ways, though without displacing New York from its primary position.

Following the Revolutionary War, *Philadelphia, New York, *Boston, and Charleston emerged as hubs of four main theatrical circuits, with municipally based companies that *toured the surrounding regions. As the frontier moved west, the pattern was repeated in New Orleans, St Louis, and elsewhere, so that resident troupes expanded from around twenty in 1825 to a peak of 50 around 1865—and then dwindled to near zero by the turn of the century. In 1896 the *Theatrical Syndicate gained an effective monopoly over commercial theatre in New York and around the country; by 1916, the power had passed to the *Shubert brothers, who exercised the same tight control well into the twentieth century. Theatre in the USA was thus established as a national industry based in New York, controlled by a handful of entrepreneurs, who sought profits through the production and distribution of plays that catered to the public taste for *spectacle, sentiment, and star performers.

The resurgence of regional theatres in the twentieth century was generally inspired by European *modernism and a burgeoning desire to create an indigenous American theatre that served artistic and social purposes. In the 1910s the *Little Theatre movement saw small, idealistic, *amateur theatres spring up in Boston, *Chicago, Detroit, Milwaukee, New York, Providence, and other cities. This led to a broadening *community theatre movement, which in some cities, such as Cleveland, prompted a local group of serious amateurs to 'go professional'. In New York during the 1920s and 1930s, a similar impulse resulted in a series of struggling art theatres, including the *Provincetown Players, *Theatre Guild, *Civic Repertory Theatre, and most influentially, the *Group Theatre. Yet at mid-century theatre was still dominated by commercial priorities, even as Broadway openings declined and some touring houses around the country fell idle.

After the Second World War the regional theatre movement was pioneered by three dynamic and determined women. In 1947 Margo *Jones established a resident repertory theatre in Dallas and inspired others to replicate her model with a manifesto, *Theatre-in-the-Round* (1951). That same year Nina Vance marshalled efforts to launch the *Alley Theatre in Houston, which she ran for more than 30 years. In 1950 Zelda *Fichandler co-founded *Arena Stage in Washington, DC, which she led with distinction for 40 years. Other early regional theatres include the Mummers Theatre in Oklahoma City (1949–72), Herbert *Blau and Jules Irving's *Actors Workshop in *San Francisco (1952–66), and the Milwaukee Repertory Theatre (1954). With some variation, these represented a typical pattern: led by a dominant personality, a small, dedicated group of aspiring professionals with limited resources and roots in the community or a local university began to produce in inadequate, rented facilities, often just converted to theatrical use. Another pattern featured a credentialled team of professionals, sometimes alienated by the hit-or-miss ethos of Broadway, who moved to a city and joined with civic and business leaders to establish an institution which aspired to parallel the local symphony and art museum. This pattern was epitomized by the *Guthrie Theatre (1963), founded in Minneapolis after several cities were considered. Its emphasis on a repertory of American and European classics highlighted the shared mission of regional theatres to preserve and refresh past traditions, styles, and playwrights, most obviously Shakespeare. The Guthrie heralded a mid-1960s explosion of regional theatres in cities around the country, including Seattle, Hartford, Baltimore, Louisville, Providence, San Francisco, New Haven, and *Los Angeles.

Whatever their origins and individual differences, the first-generation regional theatres came to share characteristics that set standards for future institutions. Artistic freedom was sought by organizing as tax-exempt, 'not-for-profit' corporations, often led by an *artistic director and *managing director in tandem. Fundraising and subsidy became keys to survival (see FINANCE). Financial crises were chronic as theatres struggled to find or build adequate facilities. On the model of symphony orchestras, stability was sought by programming a season of plays sold in advance to a core subscription *audience of mostly upper-middle-class citizens. The pull between establishing a permanent institution and pursuing artistic goals led to a dynamic and sometimes fiery tension between artists, administrators, and boards of directors. Through it all, a missionary zeal about saving the art of theatre prevailed.

That same mission motivated the concurrent *Off-Broadway movement in New York, equally concerned to establish an alternative to Broadway. Preceded by *Circle in the Square in 1951, the 1960s and 1970s saw such organizations as the Repertory Theatre of *Lincoln Center, the *New York Shakespeare Festival, Roundabout Theatre Company, *Circle Repertory Company, *Manhattan Theatre Club, and *Playwrights Horizons assume the role of producing serious drama, new plays, and classics. While their close proximity to Broadway gave these theatres distinct concerns and unique opportunities, they shared enough common cause with the burgeoning companies elsewhere that the term 'resident theatres' came to be preferred over 'regional theatres' as a comprehensive label for the non-profit professional sector.

The spread of the regional theatre movement in the 1960s was catalysed in large part by one man, W. McNeil Lowry, vice-president for arts and humanities at the Ford Foundation. In 1957 he began a programme which quickly led to generous and sustained support for promising institutions. This initiative led directly to the creation of one agency, the *Theatre Communications Group (1961), and contributed to the establishment of another, the *National Endowment for the Arts (1965). TCG began by providing operational guidance and management models for a core group of regional theatres. Over the years it has sought to nurture both artistic growth and financial stability through conferences, workshops, publications, arts advocacy, and grant making. A federal agency which funds artists and arts organizations, the NEA benefited regional theatres in its first two decades by providing seed money and matching grants that validated a theatre's effort to attract private and corporate philanthropy. In the 1990s its leadership role and annual budgets were greatly diminished following political controversy over a handful of grants.

By 1966, for the first time in the twentieth century, regional theatres in aggregate employed more actors than New York, and this growth continued into the 1970s. The subscription season became a fixture and led to a flexible but standard repertoire that combined classics, modern dramas, American plays, theatrical chestnuts, and new works. A Shakespeare play is often the cornerstone for a season, with *Molière, *Shaw, and *Chekhov making more frequent appearances than *Ibsen, *Pirandello, or *Brecht. The perpetual search for a *comedy to balance the season has prompted frequent revivals of Noël *Coward and *Kaufman and *Hart. Many theatres will mount an American *musical, while others have embraced the holiday tradition of adaptations of *Dickens's *A Christmas Carol*. These cash cows help to offset production of more obscure or challenging work.

At more daring theatres, that work included the development of new plays and playwrights, which led to the occasional practice of transferring a regional production to Broadway. This trend is generally traced to the 1967 Arena Stage production of Howard Sackler's *The Great White Hope*, which won both the Tony *award and the Pulitzer Prize. For the non-profits, success in New York had huge benefits back home for individual artists and the institution as a whole. For Broadway *producers, the provinces became a new source of commercially viable plays. This curious symbiosis was recognized as early as 1976, when an annual special Tony award for outstanding regional theatre was inaugurated. The next year the *Actors Theatre of Louisville launched the Humana Festival of New American Plays, which evolved into a celebrated national showcase. The regional theatres' role in nurturing new American plays seemed to climax in the late 1980s and early 1990s, when no fewer than five of August *Wilson's plays originated at the Yale Repertory Theatre (*see* YALE SCHOOL OF DRAMA) before moving to Broadway. In 1993, after years of development at the Eureka Theatre and the *Mark Taper Forum, Tony *Kushner's *Angels in America* premièred on Broadway to great acclaim.

By this time a national community of professional, institutional theatres was well established, some with permanent endowments but many more with nagging deficits. The demoralizing dominance of finance and institutional priorities led to discussion of a so-called 'artistic deficit'. Even today, while some larger theatres employ a core group of artists year round, more often only a theatre's staff and board of directors live in the local community. Most actors, directors, and designers are jobbed in

from New York or elsewhere, leading to a guest–host relationship between artist and institution. Economic pressures contributed to the formation of in-house conservatories, internship programmes, or alliances with theatre departments at local universities. As part of their professional *training, students appear in secondary roles, rounding out a large cast with minimal impact on salaries. In order to cut costs by sharing them, other companies have experimented with co-productions. While this contributes to abiding concerns about artistic homogenization, it also lends credence to the notion that the regional theatre *en masse* is America's *national theatre movement.

Some regional theatres early recognized a need or obligation to reach beyond their middle-class, middle-aged constituency to find ways to serve the larger community. At larger institutions this led to extensive outreach and educational programmes which attract non-traditional audiences (notably students) or take special creative projects into neighbourhoods and institutions where the arts are missing. A less complimentary aspect of the regional theatre's legacy is its general failure to promote artistic experiment and theatrical innovation of an *avant-garde nature. While structured on a corporate model, few theatres have the equivalent of a research-and-development division; those that do tend to have literary departments which concentrate more on traditional playwriting than alternative strategies for generating new work. This shortcoming stems in part from the innate conservatism of institutions and the widespread difficulty of establishing a permanent second stage which can be used as a laboratory for riskier productions.

A traditional regional theatre is often surrounded by smaller fledgling groups or *alternative theatres, some of which serve special interests or under-represented constituencies (*feminist theatre, *African-American theatre, *gay and *lesbian theatre, etc.) and others which pursue more experimental techniques and agendas. Some of the latter—such as San Francisco's Magic Theatre, Chicago's *Steppenwolf Theatre, Minneapolis's Théâtre de la Jeune Lune—maintained their distinctive identities as they grew into healthy institutions with national reputations. Indeed, what was construed as regional theatre at the start of the twenty-first century was much more diverse than 30 years before, encompassing a wider range of enterprises that include theatre for *youth, upstart ensembles and *collectives, new play laboratories, and summertime *Shakespeare festivals.

A 2000 TCG survey of 262 theatres revealed that they mounted 3,200 productions for an audience of 21.7 million. On average, they financed two-thirds of total expenses from earned income, relying on contributions and subsidy for the other third. As of 2002, TCG counted more than 400 member theatres in 46 states; the majority (58 per cent) had annual budgets under $1 million, while more than a dozen had budgets over $10 million. Though the quality of work varies widely, the sheer quantity testifies to the tremendous significance of the regional theatre movement since 1950. In a new and different way, the movement brought theatre to the nation. It established a network of institutions and professional companies that produced and promoted theatre, old and new, as a vital art form on the local level, enhancing the cultural landscape and decentralizing the American theatre in the process.   STC

BERKOWITZ, GERALD M., *New Broadways: theatre across America, approaching a new millennium* (New York, 1997)

BROCKETT, OSCAR G., 'The American theatre, 1961–1986' and 'The American theatre, 1986–2000', *Theatre History Studies*, 20 (2000)

NOVICK, JULIUS, *Beyond Broadway: the quest for permanent theatres* (New York, 1968)

ZEIGLER, JOSEPH WESLEY, *Regional Theatre: the revolutionary stage* (New York, 1977)

REGNARD, JEAN-FRANÇOIS (1655–1709)

French dramatist and writer of travel romances. During his real-life travels Regnard was captured by corsairs in 1678, and held prisoner at Algiers until ransomed, an experience he was able to exploit in his own fiction. As a playwright, he had perhaps the most personal style of all the members of the talented generation of comic writers following *Molière—due perhaps to the fact that his first plays were composed for the *Comédie Italienne (some in collaboration with *Dufresny), which helped to give him a distinctive approach to the master–servant relationship on stage. From 1695 onwards he wrote for the *Comédie-Française. In *Le Joueur* (1696), the best known of his *comedies, he treats the addiction to gambling in a light-hearted rather than a moralistic manner (though the *hero is punished by losing the girl he has courted); *Le Distrait* (1697) is an amusing treatment of absent-mindedness; while *Le Légataire universel* (1708) uses a gaily amoral story of the 'correction' of an uncle's will in favour of his nephew—and also in favour of the valet Crispin who has impersonated the dying uncle.   WDH

REHAN, ADA (1857–1916)

Irish-American actress. Born Ada Crehan in Limerick, her family emigrated to *New York in 1862. In 1873 she followed several siblings into the theatre, serving a long apprenticeship in regional theatres. In 1879 she joined Augustin *Daly's company in an alliance that would last twenty years. Under Daly's tutelage, Rehan became the company's leading comedienne, playing over 200 roles as varied as Nelly Beers in *Love's Young Dreams* (1879), Miss Lu Ten Eyck in a revival of *Divorce* (1879), Sylvia in *The Recruiting Officer* (1885), and Lady Teazle in *The School for Scandal* (1894). Daly produced numerous Shakespearian *comedies as vehicles for her and she responded with widely praised performances, most notably as Katherine in *Taming of the Shrew*, Viola in *Twelfth Night*, and Rosalind in *As You Like It*. After Daly's death she rarely performed, the last time being on *tour with Otis *Skinner in *The Taming of the Shrew* (1904–5).   GAR

REHEARSAL

The activity of actors and technicians preparing a play or other performance mode for presentation before an *audience. Rehearsal of some type has probably been central since the beginning of theatre as an institution, though what it has meant has varied greatly. We know, for instance, that the *playwright rehearsed his *actors in ancient *Greek theatre (though not the *chorus, who were supervised by the *choregus*, the wealthy citizen who *financed them), and in the *early modern period the author and the owner of the company would have been in charge of preparing the actors for new plays and unexpected changes of bill (*see* COMPANY ORGANIZATION IN EUROPE, 1500–1700). But we know little about how those rehearsals proceeded or how much authority the leader exercised. In succeeding centuries in most countries actors were organized according to *lines of business, playing similar or type roles across a range of plays (*see* STOCK CHARACTER), reducing or eliminating the need for detailed *character investigation. They depended on the *prompter for onstage help with words and movements, and had little incentive for time-consuming practice runs since they were not paid for them. No doubt star actors, whether or not they *managed their own companies, would set the standard for rehearsal, and because most plays were kept in some form of rotating *repertory prior to the rise of the *long run, actors were expected to step into roles they already knew with little or no warning.

But as the technology of theatre—including *lighting, *scenography, and *scene shifting—became more complex in the late nineteenth century, and more concerned with innovative styles like *realism and *naturalism, rehearsal necessarily became more important. The advent of theatrical *modernism solidified the change through the introduction of the *director, who emerged as a functionary separate from actor, playwright, or manager specifically to lead rehearsals, with the goals of textual explication and stylistic unity foremost in mind. *Stanislavsky was the most influential *theorist of rehearsal in the twentieth century, establishing a practice in which actors used solitary and group preparation to delve deeply into the psychology of their characters, often relying on the concept of *subtext under the director's guidance, attempting to explicate and fill in aspects of the characters' natures that are invisible in the *text and outside the narrative of the play. This combination of circumstances—coupled with the contracted payment to actors for rehearsal instituted by *trade unions in the first part of the century in many countries—led to greatly expanded periods of preparation.

Professionals and *amateurs alike now take rehearsal most seriously, knowing that each new production of a play, even of one as well known as *Hamlet*, is considered by Western culture as a new work of art, and aware as well that the audience expects a sophisticated interpretation of even minor characters. What goes on during rehearsal will nonetheless vary enormously, and could range from the complete *devising of a new piece through *improvisation to seemingly endless reiteration of difficult scenes. (The French word for rehearsal, *répétition*, despite its mechanical implication, remains a useful description of an essential element of the practice.) How long a period is devoted to rehearsal is determined by the material and financial conditions of the organization. At the fully subsidized *Moscow Art Theatre, Stanislavsky could take as long as necessary to prepare a text, even as long as a year, and some state theatres in central Europe still have the flexibility to delay opening for months if necessary, as do small self-supporting companies and *collectives. But in contemporary commercial production, three or four dizzying weeks of full-time rehearsal is usually the limit.

In modes dependent on improvisation such as *commedia dell'arte, *agitprop, and *street theatre, preparation before a specific performance may involve only a quick consultation among actors to adapt a stock *scenario to local circumstance. A more *political revision of the process is found in Augusto *Boal's concept of 'rehearsals for revolution', a variation of his theatre of the *oppressed, where the focus is not on the actor–director relationship but on the actor who becomes a spectator and the spectator who becomes an actor, what Boal calls the 'spect-actor'. DK

REICHER, EMANUEL (1849–1924)

Austrian actor. He began his career at provincial theatres in *Vienna, *Munich, and Hamburg before going to *Berlin in 1887, joining the *Berlin Royal Theatre in 1888. A co-founder of the *Freie Bühne, Reicher became a key actor under Otto *Brahm at the *Deutsches Theater from 1894. His *acting broke radically with the declamatory tradition of court theatre performances and established a plainer social style, distinguished by minute psychological accuracy, which was to become emblematic for *naturalist theatre. In 1899 he set up a school of dramatic art and from 1917 directed in *New York. CBB

REID, CHRISTINA (1942–)

Irish playwright. Several of her plays offer female perspectives on Belfast working-class lives, including *Tea in a China Cup* (1983), *Joyriders* (1986), *The Belle of the Belfast City* (1986, George Devine *award), *Did You Hear the One about the Irishman?* (1987), and *Clowns* (1996), a sequel to *Joyriders*. Reid was writer-in-residence at the Lyric Theatre, Belfast (1983–4), moved to *London in 1987, and was playwright-in-residence at the *Young Vic (1988–9). She has written for theatre for *youth and schools, and for *radio and *television. AEM

REID, KATE (1930–93)

Born in London, Reid acted at Hart House Theatre (*Toronto) and had her professional debut in summer stock, CBC *radio and *television, and Toronto's Crest Theatre. Though her formal *training was light, outside lessons with Uta *Hagen in *New York (1951), Reid expanded her classical repertoire at the *Stratford Festival between 1959 and 1965, while her Broadway performances as Martha in *Albee's *Who's Afraid of Virginia Woolf?* (1962) and Caitlin Thomas opposite Alec *Guinness in Sidney Michael's *Dylan* (1964) demonstrated her versatility in contemporary roles. *Williams (*Slapstick Tragedy*, 1966), *Miller (*The Price*, 1968), and Albee (*A Delicate Balance*, *film version, 1973) all wrote roles for her. An exceptional interpreter of tough, complex survivors, whether bawds (Mistress Overdone in *Measure for Measure*, 1992) or queens (Clytemnestra in *Aeschylus' *Oresteia*, 1983), Reid's vulnerable, earthy, compassionate portrayal of Linda Loman in Dustin *Hoffman's 1985 revival of Miller's *Death of a Salesman* remains a highlight of a prolific 40-year career in North American theatre, film, radio, and television. MJD

REIN, MERCEDES (1931–)

Uruguayan writer and translator who has published in a variety of forms, including political *satire and *feminist and children's drama. Imprisoned during the military dictatorship (1974), she lost her teaching position at the University of Uruguay and withdrew to a solitary life. In the theatre she has frequently worked in collaboration with director and dramatist Jorge *Curi; together they wrote *El herrero y la muerte* (*The Blacksmith and Death*, 1981), a long-running coded commentary on the dictatorship. Her most acclaimed play, *Juana de Asbaje* (1993), represents the life of Sor *Juana Inés de la Cruz in baroque counterpoint to *feminist strategies. JCC

REINHARDT, MAX (1873–1943)

Austrian director, one of the most prolific and influential directors of the German-language theatre, too eclectic to be identified strongly with a particular style. His reputation has suffered because, unlike some less significant twentieth-century theatre practitioners, he seldom wrote about his work. Born Max Goldmann near *Vienna of Jewish parentage, Reinhardt began his career as an actor in Austria, but in 1894 moved to *Berlin, where he specialized in playing old men. In 1901 he opened his cabaret 'Schall und Rauch' (later the Kleines Theater), the initial step leading to his domination of Berlin theatre for almost two decades. In his earliest major production, *A Midsummer Night's Dream* at the Neues Theater in 1905, a *revolving stage with a realistic forest was used for the first time in Europe as an element of the performance. In 1906 he acquired the *Deutsches Theater, where he controversially staged *Ibsen's *Ghosts*, with set designs by Edvard Munch, and *Wedekind's *Spring's Awakening*, which had been banned by the *censor since its publication in 1891. In 1910, finding the conventional *proscenium-arch theatre too restricting, he staged the first of his massive productions in a *circus arena, *Sophocles' *Oedipus the King*, using hundreds of extras as the suffering populace of Thebes. In 1911 there followed similar large-scale productions, *The Oresteia* and Hugo von *Hofmannsthal's version of *Everyman*, which was revived many times by Reinhardt, most notably as the centrepiece of the annual *Salzburg Festival from 1920. At the end of 1911 he undertook his most ambitious project when he produced a *mime piece based on a medieval legend, Karl Vollmoeller's *The Miracle*, at the Olympia Exhibition Hall in *London, converted by his favourite designer, Ernst *Stern, to resemble a cathedral. *The Miracle* was later (1924) also performed successfully in *New York and *toured America until 1930. Reinhardt's love of huge performance spaces finally found expression in his plans for the 'Theatre of Five Thousand', the *Grosses Schauspielhaus in Berlin. This building, with its large, horseshoe-shaped *auditorium and *arena stage, was finally opened in 1919 with a revival of *The Oresteia*, but within a few years had run into *financial difficulties and was given over to commercial *revues.

During the First World War, Reinhardt was controversially appointed director of the Berlin *Volksbühne (1915–18), a nominally left-wing foundation, which he saved from probable closure. In 1917 he also launched the 'Young Germany' season at the Deutsches Theater, devoted to work by young writers, himself directing with some success the first piece, Reinhard *Sorge's *The Beggar*. He had little sympathy with the strident images of *expressionism, however, and left the remaining plays to his fellow directors. From 1920 he felt ever more out of tune with the new theatre of the Weimar Republic and was drawn back to his more conservative homeland: with Richard *Strauss, Hofmannsthal, and Bruno Walter he founded the *Salzburg Festival; he moved permanently to his new home, Schloss Leopoldskron, near Salzburg; in 1924 became director of the newly refurbished Theater in der Josefstadt, Vienna; and opened the new Salzburg Festival Theatre in 1925. After further successes in Vienna and Berlin, including the German premières of *Shaw's *St Joan* and *Pirandello's *Six Characters in Search of an Author* in 1924, and having given performances in London, *Manchester, and Oxford, he was dispossessed of his theatres when the Nazis came to power in 1933. He responded by courageously writing an open letter to Goering and Goebbels. In 1934 he went to Hollywood to direct a sugary *film version of *A Midsummer Night's Dream* with James Cagney as Bottom and Mickey Rooney as Puck. Offered by Goebbels the status of 'honorary Aryan' if he agreed to return to Germany to direct, he preferred to emigrate permanently to the United States in 1937 with his wife, the actress Helene Thimig. Here he opened the Max Reinhardt Workshop for Stage, Screen and Radio in Hollywood, and died of a stroke in New York, where he directed for the stage for the last time.

Reinhardt's achievements were many: he staged classics in spectacularly theatrical ways, he discovered elegance and beauty—his so-called 'stylized *realism' or 'impressionism'—in a wide variety of scripts, he paid considerable attention to crowd scenes, he made serious theatre accessible to everyone, and he nurtured the talents of young playwrights and leading actors. Above all, he played a major part in transforming theatre practice from a nineteenth-century craft to a twentieth-century art form.   MWP

STYAN, J. L., *Max Reinhardt* (Cambridge, 1982)

REINSHAGEN, GERLIND (1926–)

German dramatist. Best known as the author of experimental *radio plays, Reinshagen's first theatre piece was *Doppelkopf* (*Rummy*, 1968). Her breakthrough came with *Sonntagskinder* (*Sunday's Children*, 1976), a play about the Third Reich and the war, told in a sequence of 30 *scenes from the perspective of a young girl. Part of a trilogy dealing with German history, it was followed by *Frühlingsfest* (*Spring Festival*, 1980), a critical depiction of the economic 'miracle' in the 1950s, and *Tanz Marie!* (1989), set in the 1980s. She makes innovative use of the *chorus: *dialogue and *characters dissolve into a communal voice that emphasizes the loss of subjectivity. Infrequently performed until the end of the century, her work has had a mixed reception.   CBB

RÉJANE (GABRIELLE RÉJU) (1856–1920)

French actress and *manager. Though Réjane's reputation has remained overshadowed by that of her slightly older contemporary Sarah *Bernhardt, this was only partly due to the personalities and talent of the two rivals; it also reflects the range of plays they performed. Réjane was born into a theatrical *family, both parents working at the Théâtre de l'Ambigu in *Paris (her father, an ex-actor, in the administration, her mother in charge of the bar). She excelled as a student at the *Conservatoire, but chose to make her career for the most part in *boulevard theatres, especially the Théâtre de Vaudeville, appearing there first in 1875. As a result, while the list of her performances includes the leading roles in *naturalist plays like *Germinie Lacerteux* (1888, adapted from the Goncourt novel) and *Becque's *La Parisienne* (1893), as well as in *Ibsen's *A Doll's House* (1894) and *Claudel's *Partage de midi* (*Break of Noon*, 1898), the more typical vehicle for her talent remained drawing-room *comedy and second-rate *well-made plays. She maintained the same tradition as a manager when she took over the Théâtre Nouveau in 1906 and renamed it Théâtre Réjane. Like Bernhardt's, Réjane's career took her abroad, performing for the first time in *London in 1894 and in *New York the following year. Of her *films, the most notable was *Madame Sans-gêne* (1911), based on the *Sardou play she had premièred at the Vaudeville in 1893.   WDH

RELIGION AND THEATRE *see page 1127*

RENAISSANCE *See* Early modern period in Europe.

RENAUD, MADELEINE (1900–94)

French actress. At the *Comédie-Française from 1921 to 1946, she became distinguished for her charm, incisive intelligence, beautiful voice and person, and finely tuned wit and timing, especially in roles in *Molière and *Marivaux. In 1940 she married Jean-Louis *Barrault, who had just joined the company as an actor and director. When the Comédie-Française was re-organized in 1946, the couple left to form their own Compagnie Renaud–Barrault, housed mainly at the Théâtre Marigny from 1946 to 1956. During her long association with Barrault there and at other venues, Renaud continued to expand her repertory to include *Claudel, *Genet, Lope de *Vega, *Chekhov, *Fry, *Anouilh, *Kopit, and Marguerite *Duras, and became world famous as Winnie in *Oh! Les Beaux Jours!* (*Happy Days*, 1963), and in other *Beckett plays, many directed by Roger *Blin. Uneasy with her performance in *Pas moi* (*Not I*, 1975), Beckett did not cast her in *Rockaby*, causing Barrault to break off relationships with the playwright. Barrault noted that Renaud achieved eminence by the direct route of a classically trained artist, while he himself succeeded by trial and error.　　SBB

RENDRA, W. S. (1935–　)

Indonesian playwright, director, and actor, a charismatic Javanese who fought government *censorship and set the stage for a stylized theatre of *political activism in the late 1960s. After study in Yogyakarta and in the United States, he founded Bengkel (Workshop) Teater in 1967. His *minikata* (minimal word pieces), which used stylized chanting of slogans, were a response to the devaluation of language by Suharto's government. Though he produced Western work like *Caligula* and *The Bald Soprano*, he is best known for his own plays. *Mastodon and Condor* (1973) contrasts government aims with the individual spirit and *The Struggle of the Naga Tribe* (1975) shows the resistance of villagers to rapacious foreign development, relying on traditional *gamelan music and a *dalang* (traditional *puppet master) as narrator. *Regional Administrator* (1977) and *Prince Reso* in the 1980s attacked government corruption. Rendra's plays were frequently banned in the Suharto era and he was held under house arrest in the late 1970s. Among those he inspired are playwrights Arifin C. *Noer and Putu *Wijaya.　　KFo

RENE, ROY (1891–1954)

Australian *vaudeville star. After a career as a boy soprano, Rene started wearing whiteface and a black beard in 1916 to play the role of Mo, a stereotyped stage Jew. Mo assumed a range of comic *characters in a high-pitched Jewish accent, relying on Australian colloquialisms, crass vulgarity, and sentimentality. Working as a double act with Nat Phillips, Rene performed 'Stiffy and Mo' routines from 1916 to 1928, after which solo performances of Mo remained phenomenally popular. The Mo *awards were inaugurated in 1975 for achievement by Australian *variety performers.　　EJS

RENÉ D'ANJOU (1409–80)

King of Naples and Sicily in name only, René d'Anjou established a brilliant court at Angers, his birthplace. He is chiefly remembered for his chivalric literary works and his sumptuous dramatic fêtes and *tournaments that brought to life the fantasy world of courtly *romance.　　ARY

RENÉE (1929–　)

New Zealand playwright (formerly known as Renée Taylor). A socialist lesbian *feminist, Renée came to prominence with *Wednesday to Come* (1984), in which four generations of working women respond to the death of the male breadwinner in a relief camp of the 1930s, with clear political implications for a contemporary *audience. Her spare *realism derives from long experience directing rural *amateur drama. A sequel, *Pass It On* (1986), adopts *Brechtian *dramaturgy to anatomize New Zealand's savagely divisive 1951 waterfront dispute. *Jeannie Once* (1990) completes the trilogy. Set in Dunedin in 1879 on the eve of a twenty-year depression (with a jaundiced eye on the similar collapse of New Zealand financial institutions in 1987), it benefits from Renée's feminist *revue experience to incorporate *music hall with audience participation as counterpoint to the serious *political themes. Other plays, stories, and novels similarly affirm working-class and lesbian women, and draw on Renée's *Maori heritage.　　DC

RENGIFO, CÉSAR (1915–80)

Venezuelan painter and playwright. His first work, *Por qué canta el pueblo* (*Why the People Sing*), dates from 1938, though he was not much performed until the 1950s, when the company Máscaras began to stage his work. *Historical themes dominate, as apparent in *Obscéneba* (1958), which deals with the Spanish Conquest, *Soga de Nieve* (*Snow Rope*, 1954), about colonization, and *Lo que dejó la tempestad* (*What the Storm Left Behind*, 1957), about the nineteenth-century civil war. Oil forms the backdrop for *Las torres y el viento* (*The Towers and the Wind*, 1956), which takes issue with social injustice. Rengifo was awarded the National Prize for Theatre in 1980.　　LCL trans. AMCS

(continued on p. 1129)

RELIGION AND THEATRE

This large topic could cover a huge variety of religious experience, but in this entry it will be focused on monotheism. The monotheistic religions initially revealed a deep-rooted prejudice and animosity against theatre. Christianity and Islam followed the Old Testament injunction against cross-dressing (Deuteronomy 22:5), already interpreted in Judaism as a prohibition of theatre practices, the *Talmud* (fourth century AD) being explicit on this (*Avoda Zara*, 18b). For almost 1,000 years the Christian Church conducted a fierce struggle against theatre, with some theologians being particularly outspoken: *Tertullian (*c.*200), Jerome (347–420), and Augustine (354–430). Until the tenth century, *medieval history of theatre is known only from the rulings of the Church, which constantly and consistently denounced and prohibited these 'Satanic' activities. Eventually, starting around 960, theatre practices were welcomed, initially in monasteries and churches. It took an additional 700 years for Judaism and 200 more than that for Islam to tolerate theatre.

Against such a background, the *romantic idea of a fundamental bond between religion and theatre is puzzling. Charles Magnin first advanced the notion in 1838 to suggest a parallel creation of ancient and medieval theatres in Greek and Christian *rituals. This claim has been endorsed by several twentieth-century *theories, with theses ranging from theatre originating in religious ritual to sharing its nature (*see* ORIGINS OF THEATRE). Analysis of the complex relations between religion and theatre, however, might lead to the opposite conclusion.

1. Origin; 2. Re-creation or adoption; 3. Educational policy; 4. Cognitive function; 5. Carnivalesque function; 6. Religious and secular drama

1. Origin

Ritual has been widely considered the source of theatre. In 1912 Émile Durkheim suggested that religions maintain a fundamental distinction between the sacred and the profane and, in contrast to 'religious beliefs' he conceived 'ritual' in terms of 'practices relative to sacred things'. Although recent trends in anthropology have expanded the notion of 'ritual' to apply to certain secular activities, 'religious ritual' remains as delimited by Durkheim. Even if the affinity of theatre to ritual is accepted on the grounds of their shared *'performance' or *performativity, theatre performances are characterized by theatre's particular medium, and not necessarily addressed to the sacred.

From the beginning of the twentieth century attempts have been made to lend scientific support to this romantic intuition, particularly by the Cambridge School of Anthropology. Jane Harrison suggested that in prehistoric societies ritual and theatre reflected their shared nature in the *mimesis (re-doing and pre-doing) of crucial moments in tribal life, such as a successful hunt or a war, even though not all kinds of mimesis are equivalent to theatrical enactment of *characters. Alternatively, Gilbert *Murray and Francis M. Cornford derived all narratives of *Greek *dithyramb, *tragedy, and *comedy from the foundational myth of *Dionysiac ritual. However appealing it may be, this attempt to reduce the wealth of narratives in these *genres to a single narrative formula is clearly contradicted by extant works. Following heavy criticism of this school, Ernest T. Kirby stressed the non-mimetic performative elements of shamanist ritual and claimed that in trance, by assuming the identity of another being (a spirit), the shaman is the prototype of the actor. But trance is not typical of theatre, nor is the shaman enacting a spirit, which is conceived as real and controlled for the cure of a patient.

Richard *Schechner rejected all theories of ritual origin and suggested instead a more fundamental bond, on the grounds of shared performance: theatre and ritual as different manifestations of a basic duality—efficacy and entertainment. Rather than solving the problem of origin, however, he eliminated it by merely postulating a common nature. Moreover, there is a profound difference between performing a real action and enacting a fictional one. Although the origin of theatre in ritual was never demonstrated, the twentieth-century *avant-garde adopted the assumption and often aimed at 'reintroducing' the ritual elements that theatre had allegedly lost. This tendency characterizes such outstanding theatre directors as *Brook, *Mnouchkine, *Grotowski, *Barba, and Schechner himself. The question remains, however: were such ritual elements ever constituents of theatre?

2. Re-creation or adoption

The *Quem Quaeritis trope, the first known theatre performance in medieval Christianity, was definitely created for incorporation in the mass. Was this a case of spontaneous re-creation, after an absolute cessation of the classical tradition, or the adoption of existing surreptitious practices? While 're-creation' postulates a prior extinction of theatrical practices, 'adoption' presupposes that such practices had somehow survived, despite forbidding conditions. This assumption is supported by the increasing frequency of church rulings against theatre toward the end of the ninth century. Although the tangible decline of such rulings in the tenth century can be explained by the Church's ultimate success, it can equally be explained by its eventual acceptance of theatre. Lack of evidence either way prevents the settling of this controversy. However, a close analysis of the *Quem Quaeritis* *stage directions reveals a fair knowledge of existing practices, and thus supports the thesis that the Church adopted them. A thousand years of rejection followed by eventual adoption of theatre probably testifies to the Church having discovered that this art is essentially neutral with regard to the ideas it conveys and is potentially beneficial; only its pagan connotations can explain the bitter animosity in which theatre was held by the Church before the tenth century.

Despite initial rejection, Christianity maintained significant ties with theatre. In some periods, particularly in the sixteenth and seventeenth centuries, religious dramatists reached the pinnacle of art: Shakespeare in a contested Anglican environment, Lope de *Vega, *Calderón, and *Tirso de Molina in a vehemently Catholic one, even the Jansenist Jean *Racine. The Puritans' temporary success in seizing power in England (1642–60), and their rapid move to close the theatres, indicate that the controversy had not been finally settled. Just as the Puritans reinstated earlier Christian attitudes by associating theatre with depravity and paganism, so some extremists of all monotheistic persuasions think to this day, merely awaiting the right political moment to act against the stage.

3. Educational policy

The success of the newly created dramatic genres, such as *mystery, *miracle, and *morality plays, reveals that Christianity had effectively learned to employ theatre as an educational device. In the great *biblical and *cycle plays, dramatization of crucial episodes in the lives (and beyond) of Jesus Christ and other prefigurative biblical characters proved efficient as 'holy script for the poor', or rather the illiterate, a function frequently attributed to images in churches. Morality plays enabled *allegorical personification of difficult and abstract questions of doctrine, such as preparation for the pilgrimage to the next world in *Everyman*. These genres fulfilled a momentous function, not only for monastic *audiences, who underwent meticulous religious preparations, but also for laymen.

Although theatre can be employed both for reaffirmation or refutation of any idea, religious drama adopted a combination of its medium and cathartic fictional structure for fostering dogmas and norms. The *plots of such dramas will question received ideas at the moment of *complication, thereby producing tension, and corroborate their validity at the *denouement, with *catharsis reinforcing the experience by producing abrupt release of tension, that is, pleasure. This can be achieved only under conditions of unified public belief, as when Shakespeare's audience—or most of it—accepted the reality or possibility of the supernatural world in *Macbeth*.

The combination of the medium and a message is an ancient device (*see* DIDACTIC THEATRE). It is widely believed that in *Oedipus the King*, for example, *Sophocles sought reconfirmation of beliefs in the Greek gods by reinstating Oedipus' sacred status, despite the initial suspicion of his crime and the potential implication of the gods' pernicious nature. In contrast, *Euripides inverted the structure by using the same mythical sources for refuting belief. Taking religious conviction to the point of absurdity by exposing the less than human nature of the Greek gods, Euripides implied an alternative and more rational notion of divinity. His absurdist format has been employed in *modernist theatre to promote criticism of the church (*Shaw's *St Joan*) or an atheist position (*García Lorca's *Yerma*). Obviously, all religions shun these procedures, which incidentally demonstrate the neutral and versatile character of theatre.

4. Cognitive function

The prominence of religious themes in various theatrical traditions, East and West, is indicative of audience interests. Why do notions such as theomachy, *hubris, sin, fate, fortune, predestination, and free will, whether or not the intention is to confirm their sway, command such a profound interest in the human mind? Undoubtedly, questioning, reaffirming, and even disproving issues related to spectators' fundamental orientation in the world deserve high status. Because most religions posit divine rule of the world, probing such first principles can bestow upon the audience a sense of understanding the world, as in the numerous plays on the myth of Don Juan. The psychological power of a cognitive control of the world is great, regardless of whether it is genuine or spurious. The tendency of modernist theatre to discredit faith does not contradict but reconfirms this function, as *Ionesco's *Exit the King* can be seen to do.

Accordingly playwrights of the seventeenth century converted mythological narratives to a Christian cognitive and value system. They conceived the pagan gods who people classical works as symbols or prefigurations of Christian divinity or diabolism, as Diane and Venus appear respectively in Racine's *Phèdre*. Some biblical and mythological figures were characterized as harbingers of the Christian fate, as Oedipus is made to seem in *Corneille's *Oedipe*.

5. Carnivalesque function

Using theatre to provide a catharsis of the believers' stress brought on by strict observance of religious precepts has been practised since ancient times in the dramatic *burlesque of gods. In Christianity, this *carnivalesque function was fulfilled in a variety of feasts of *fools. In such anti-rituals, a low-ranking cleric was usually elected to impersonate a high-ranking priest or bishop in celebrating the mass, mocking both officiant and holy ritual. In these temporary inversions of social hierarchy there was a clear element of enactment, which is characteristic of theatre. This type of inversion was also typical of Jewish culture; for example, the Purim-rabbi custom, in which a Yeshiva student was elected to impersonate his real rabbi and perform a mock sermon for the congregation's merriment.

Initially, Judaism permitted theatre performances only for the sake of such a cathartic function, as in the *Purim play, a theatrical *parody of a biblical narrative. Central to this tradition was and still is the Book of Esther, which recounts the deliverance of the Jews of Persia from imminent extermination, some 500 years BC. This book is read seriously in the synagogue on the eve of Purim and mocked theatrically the following day. The conjunction of serious reading and parodic treatment reveals its cathartic function: strict religious observance both creates the tension and necessitates a cultural release valve. In Christian and Jewish cultures this cathartic function aimed not at undermining faith, but at providing an outlet for the release of functional pressure, and thus ultimately reinforcing it.

6. Religious and secular drama

It is usually maintained that modern secular drama developed from religious drama. The temporal precedence of the *Quem Quaeritis* appears to support this thesis. The view has been questioned by Hunningher on the grounds of the greater refinement and complexity of secular drama. Indeed, without the discovery of classical drama and theory in the *early modern period, it is difficult to imagine the rapid development of European secular drama. Moreover, there is no evidence of a religious theatrical tradition preceding ancient Greek theatre either.

All the evidence indicates that there is neither an inherent bond between religion and theatre nor an inherent contradiction between them. But there is a clear contrast between the sense of absolute truth which characterizes most religions, and the neutral and experimental nature of theatre, which can be used for exploring any idea, whether it cements faith or not.

ER

DURKHEIM, ÉMILE, *The Elementary Forms of Religious Life*, trans. J. Ward Swain (1912; New York, 1967)

HUNNINGHER, BENJAMIN, *The Origin of the Theater* (New York, 1961)

NICOLL, ALLARDYCE, *Masks, Mimes and Miracles* (London, 1931)

ROZIK, ELI, 'The adoption of theatre by Judaism despite ritual: a study in the *Purim-shpil*', *European Legacy*, 4 (1999)

WELSFORD, ENID, *The Fool* (1935; London, 1968)

REOG

A Javanese *folk *dance-drama characterized by the use of the *reog* or tiger-peacock *mask (also known as *singabarong*). The form was invented by a former court official of the Majapahit kingdom of Java in the fifteenth century. The essential roles in *reog* are the half-tiger, half-peacock *singabarong*, the fearsome but comic *character *bujangganong* (or simply *ganong*), and women or *female impersonators (*jatilan*) dancing with a hobbyhorse (*kuda kepang*). The cast may be extended to include the *kelana sewandana* (unrefined or rough character), *pentul* and *tembem* (a pair of comic interpreters), and other giant or comic characters. Movements from martial arts, improvised comic turns, and *mime form the basis of *reog* dances, while *music is provided by several drums, gongs, and a pair of *angklung* (bamboo idiophones). *Reog* is popular in both *Indonesia and *Malaysia.

MA

REPERTORY PLAYING

One of the key features of most European *national and regional repertory theatres throughout the twentieth century has been the permanent *acting company, able to deliver a varied programme of plays throughout a season. For actors, the advantages include guaranteed employment for one or more seasons, the opportunity to play a variety of roles, and to be stretched by the challenge of a close-knit ensemble. For *audiences, the system enables them to see different plays within the same week and to catch a popular play at many points through the season. In actuality, however, the pattern has operated with varying degrees of success according to the status and *financial stability of the theatre.

While the repertory ensemble in the aristocratic theatres of eighteenth- and nineteenth-century Europe (such as the *Comédie-Française and the court theatres of the German lands) could lead to productions of the first order, in the UK it had a chequered history. Its seeds lay first in the establishment during the Restoration of semi-permanent acting companies at the *patent theatres, *Drury Lane and (eventually) *Covent Garden, and in the growth during the eighteenth century of the 'circuit' companies which *toured well-defined geographical areas of the country with well-worn plays and entertainments in frequent changes of bill. These *stock companies, as they became known in the next century, were led by *actor-managers who staged stock (or recycled) productions using stock sets and relying on actors trained in playing to type (*see* LINES OF BUSINESS). At their best, they provided a valuable *training ground and a lively, varied fare for their small audiences, while at their worst production standards were shoddy, *rehearsals were almost nonexistent, and stereotyped acting was encouraged. They could not compete in the middle of the nineteenth century with the rising commercial companies, now able, with the aid of the rapidly expanding railway system, to tour major productions of single plays across the country with dedicated casts and *scenery, meeting the increasingly sophisticated demands of their growing, industrialized audiences. The attendant use of the *long run and the *star system soon became common practice and put an end to the repertory company. It was this *box-office-driven theatre that in its turn was challenged by the *regional repertory movement in the UK at the start of the twentieth century.

The virtues of the repertory ensemble, once freed from the straitjacket of 'weekly rep' with the aid of public subsidy, were particularly manifest during the 1960s, 1970s, and 1980s in the UK. There were, for example, the company-*devised productions of Joan *Littlewood's *Theatre Workshop and Peter Cheeseman's *Victoria Theatre (Stoke-on-Trent), the epic-scale productions of the *Royal Shakespeare Company's cycles of Shakespeare's *history plays, the same company's two-play version of *Nicholas Nickleby* (1980), and the Royal *National Theatre's *The Mysteries* (1985, revived several times). All were dependent upon a company of actors working together over many months (sometimes years) and in a variety of plays, each actor able to take an assortment of roles, with stars sometimes playing supporting parts. There may be disadvantages (for example, the loss of wholly convincing *casting in plays from the *naturalistic canon), but for actors and audiences alike the gains often outweigh the losses, particularly with the sense of power and cohesion that a genuine ensemble can achieve.

In the final decades of the century, however, many repertory theatres found themselves increasingly hard pressed to compete with other sectors of the leisure industry, particularly the multiplex cinemas offering unrivalled choice from their own *film repertoires. This together with the cost of keeping a large ensemble company together for a long period of time, and the decline in regular theatregoing, especially among the young, has meant that, in the UK, 'true rep' is kept alive now only by a handful of companies: the large national companies and during the summer season resort theatres such as Keswick's Theatre by the Lake and Scarborough's Stephen Joseph Theatre. In the 1990s even the National Theatre began to abandon the ensemble in its endeavour to create productions that would transfer (cast and all) to the income-generating West End. And in mainland Europe, where the permanent company has been more firmly embedded, the willingness of actors to commit to career-long contracts has severely diminished as lucrative film and *television opportunities beckon. Repertory playing seems destined to become the province of a few specialist and well-subsidized companies rather than the norm.   ARJ

RÉPUBLIQUE, THÉÂTRE DE LA *See* COMÉDIE-FRANÇAISE.

REQUENA, MARÍA ASUNCIÓN (1916–86)

Chilean playwright who wrote mostly historical dramas set in the south of Chile. *Fuerte Bulnes* (*Fort Bulnes*, 1955) drew the largest *audience in the 1950s, while *Ayayema* (1964) depicted the deplorable life of the Alacalufes. Other works include *Pan caliente* (*Hot Bread*, 1967) and *Chiloé, cielos cubiertos* (*Grey Skies*, 1972).   MAR

RESIDENZTHEATER

The present Residenztheater in *Munich, the main stage of the Bavarian State Theatre Company, is a post-war building that replaced the old rococo theatre (Cuvilliés-Theater) destroyed during the Second World War. The ornate interior of the original was rebuilt within the neighbouring royal residence. The old Residenztheater, designed and built by François de Cuvilliés, opened in 1751, serving as Munich's court theatre for *opera, *ballet, and drama. In the late nineteenth century it was used for small-cast plays and operas. Many of *Ibsen's plays received their German-language or even world premières here (for example, *Hedda Gabler*, 1891). In 1882 the first electrical stage *lighting in Germany was installed, and in 1896 Karl *Lautenschläger introduced the *revolving stage. With the end of the monarchy in 1918, the Residenztheater came under state control and was increasingly confined to dramatic works, although large-scale plays were still staged in the neighbouring Nationaltheater until the 1930s.   CBB

REVENGE TRAGEDY

A *genre with roots in classical antiquity that runs a chronological and stylistic gamut that endures to this day. Unlike the classical *de casibus* model of the great figure brought low by fortune and his own 'tragic flaw' (or *hamartia), of which *Sophocles' *Oedipus the King* is the supreme example, revenge tragedy exacts different moral and ethical responses from an *audience, pitting an individual's urge for justice against collective social and religious laws. *Greek *tragedy—*Aeschylus' *Eumenides* or *Euripides' *Medea*—employed bloody retribution to fulfil a social purgative function—at least in *Aristotle's view (*see* CATHARSIS). *Senecan drama became highly influential on the *early modern stage; and was most auspiciously—if inelegantly—adapted in Thomas *Kyd's *The Spanish Tragedy* (*c*.1586), which inaugurated the 'tragedy of blood' that reached its height in the later revenge drama of *Marlowe, Shakespeare, *Webster, *Marston, *Corneille, and *Racine, to name only a few. English revenge tragedy in particular began to constitute its own genre as plays such as *The Spanish Tragedy* and *Middleton's *The Revenger's Tragedy* (1606, once ascribed to *Tourneur) provided models for much of the tone, imagery, and justification explored later in Jacobean revenge drama.

The most notorious Renaissance revenge play, however, is *Hamlet*, which exploits the revenge motif while simultaneously undermining it with a *protagonist who spends the entire play trying to talk himself into avenging his father's murder. Jacobean revenge tragedy offered a disturbing view of the many class and *gender tensions riddling Jacobean society, and expressed a considerable degree of cynicism about the possibility of attaining justice through Judaeo-Christian laws. The thirst for violent individual retribution, often going against the powers of legitimate justice, remains a constant to this day. We are heirs to the imagination of the bloody Jacobean stage (and perhaps its cynicism), as is evident in the phenomenal popularity of contemporary revenge *films such as *Dirty Harry*, *Lethal Weapon*, *Blade Runner*, and *The Terminator*. *See also* GHOST.

LC

REVERSAL *See* PERIPETEIA.

REVIEWING *See* CRITICISM.

REVOLUTIONARY MODERN DRAMA (REVOLUTIONARY MODEL DRAMA) *See* GEMING XIANDAI XI; WUJÜ.

REVOLVING STAGE

A *stage with a permanent turntable big enough to hold more than one set, for near instantaneous scene changes. The revolve was used by Leonardo in *Milan in 1490, and has been standard in *kabuki since 1658 in *Japan. It entered *modernist European theatre with Karl *Lautenschläger's designs in *Munich in 1896, and first appeared in *London at the *Coliseum in 1904. Besides quick changes, revolving stages can be used for *montage effects to show the passage of time, or as treadmills on which an actor appears to be walking while remaining stationary.

JB

REVUE

A programme of light entertainments, largely *musical but including often *satiric sketches, may be called a revue if it focuses on a topical theme or if it is presented in a periodic series. In some instances, the frivolity is intended to throw *censors off the scent of the political gibes. Or the display of beautiful women in gorgeous yet scanty *costumes could be the basic appeal. The visual and thematic unity of a revue lends greater sophistication than one expects of *burlesque or *vaudeville, to which the revue is related. Henry *Fielding's *The Historical Register for the Year 1736* (1737) might be signalled as an early prototype, but the term is French, where it was long used interchangeably with le *music-hall. From the mid-nineteenth century, *Paris enjoyed periodic editions at the *Folies-Bergère and the *Moulin-Rouge, as well as one-time creations like *La Revue nègre* (1925) featuring Joséphine *Baker. The golden age of the revue was on Broadway from the 1890s to the 1920s. Notable series were the lavish *Ziegfeld Follies* (1907–31), the *Shuberts' *Passing Show* (1912–24), *Greenwich Village Follies* (1919–28), George *White's *Scandals* (1919–39), Irving *Berlin's *Music Box Revues* (1921–4), and Earl Carroll's *Vanities* (1923–32). In *London, C. B. *Cochran produced successful revues from the 1910s, followed by André Charlot and, at mid-century, Noël

*Coward and Herbert Farjeon. Greece, Portugal, and Brazil have strong traditions of *political revues.

FHL

REVUELTA, RAQUEL (1926–)

Cuban actress, founder and director of Teatro Estudio. She played major leading roles in *The Good Person of Setzuan* (1959), *Mother Courage and her Children* (1961), *Fuente Ovejuna* (1963), *The Three Sisters* (1972), and *St Joan of the Stockyards* (1978). She also appeared in the *films *Lucía* (1968) and *Cecilia* (1980), and a *televised version of Rómulo Gallegos's novel *Doña Bárbara*.

MMu

REVUELTA, VICENTE (1929–)

Cuban actor and director, a *modernist reformer of the national stage whose work was influenced by *Stanislavsky, *Vilar, *Brecht, *Artaud, and *Grotowski. Revuelta has *trained several generations of theatre artists while maintaining an experimental outlook. A founder of Teatro Estudio in 1958, with his staging of *O'Neill's *Long Day's Journey into Night*, he has also been one of the most versatile and creative actors in Cuba. He has played, among others, Brecht's Galileo, Jerry in *Albee's *Zoo Story* (1965), Lalo in José *Triana's *La noche de los asesinos* (*Night of the Assassins*, 1966), and Feste in *Twelfth Night* (1982). All of those productions were directed by him, and he has also directed *Joan of Lorraine* (1956), *The Good Person of Setzuan* (1959), *Mother Courage and her Children* (1961), Lope de *Vega's *Fuente Ovejuna* (1963), *Chekhov's *Three Sisters* (1972), *Miller's *The Price* (1979), *The Story of a Horse* (1986), and *La zapatera prodigiosa* (*The Shoemaker's Prodigious Wife*, 1998).

MMu

REYES, CARLOS JOSÉ (1941–)

Colombian playwright, screenwriter, and prolific director. He founded or directed a number of independent theatre groups, including Teatro de Arte Popular (1964–5), Casa de la Cultura (1966–68), which later became Teatro la *Candelaria, and Teatro *Popular de Bogotá (1982–92). He served as the first president of the *Corporación Colombiana de Teatro, which he helped to establish. His notable plays include *Soldados* (*Soldiers*, 1966), on the 1928 banana workers' massacre, and *Los viejos baúles empolvados que nuestros padres nos prohibieron abrir* (*The Old Dusty Trunks our Parents Forbade Us to Open*, 1968), a critical look at double moral standards. In 1992 he became the director of the Colombian National Library.

BJR

REYNOLDS, FREDERICK (1764–1841)

English playwright, one of the principal authors of *comedy in the late eighteenth and early nineteenth centuries. Moralistic and sentimental in tone, with strong elements of *melodrama,

Reynolds's comedies resemble those of his contemporary Thomas *Morton and like them had virtually disappeared from the repertory by the mid-Victorian period. Reynolds also wrote librettos for *pantomimes and comic *operas, with music by Henry Bishop. One of his few melodramas, *The Caravan; or, The Driver and his Dog* (1803), created a stir at *Drury Lane with a scene in which a trained Newfoundland dog leapt into a tank of water to save a drowning child, initiating a type of melodrama, lasting until the 1850s, in which dogs saved *heroes and subdued *villains (*see* ANIMALS). Reynolds's best comedies are *How to Grow Rich*, *The Dramatist* (both 1793), *Folly as It Flies* (1801), and *The Delinquent* (1805). In 1827 he claimed to have made £19,000 as a playwright—a sum unimaginable a generation previous.

MRB/MJK

REZA, YASMINA (1959–)

French playwright. Having completed her *theatre studies at the University of Paris and at the Jacques *Lecoq drama school, she began her career as an actress. In 1987 she wrote her first play, *Conversations après un enterrement* (*Conversations after a Burial*), which won the Molière *award for best author. Her next two plays, *La Traversée de l'hiver* (*Winter Crossing*, 1990) and *Art* (1994), also won Molière awards, the latter also taking the 1998 Tony award in *New York. Her fourth play, *L'Homme du hasard* (*The Unexpected Man*, 1995), was equally well received by *audiences in *Paris, *London, and New York. Her screenplay *Le Pique-nique de Lulu Kreutz* (*Lulu Kreutz's Picnic*) was produced in 1998. Her work, which generally consists of witty *dialogues between 'bobos', the French bohemian bourgeois, touches on the tensions between the *characters' true natures and their often artificial social identities.

CHB

RHAPSODY

Ancient *Greek performance form in which a singer recited Homer. The lyre with which performers originally accompanied themselves was later replaced by a staff, so that rhapsody differed from *citharody, in which the singers continued to accompany themselves. Both forms featured elaborately *costumed performers who declaimed from a dais.

RWV

RHONE, TREVOR (1940–)

Jamaican dramatist who *trained at Rose Bruford College in England (1960–3). Frustrated by lack of opportunity, he founded Theatre 77 (later called the *Barn Theatre) in Kingston in 1965, though it was some time before he could quit teaching school to write full time. His early play *The Gadget* (1969) went through many revisions to become the highly successful *Old Story Time* (1979). His concerns are social: a *satire of the tourist industry in *Smile Orange* (1970), a witty treatment of education

in *School's Out* (1975) and of skin shade in *Old Story Time*. *Two Can Play* (1982) is a humorous and disturbing portrait of Jamaicans forced to become infinitely resourceful to save their families amidst the political violence of the late 1970s. His *film scripts include *The Harder They Come* (1972) and *Milk and Honey* (1989). Rhone's ear for vernacular speech, ability to construct character, and his understanding that a people under pressure prefer thoughtfully comic to tragic treatments of social themes made him one of the most important Jamaican playwrights of the 1970s and 1980s.

ES

RIANTIARNO, NANO (1949–)

Indonesian playwright and director, founder of Teater Koma (Coma Theatre). His productions, replete with colour and comedy, have been embraced by the bourgeois intelligentsia who see in them the energy of contemporary *Jakarta. His productions present social issues, including those dealing with income disparity, with a *Brechtian spirit. He has adapted Western work, including *The Threepenny Opera* (1983) and *Animal Farm* (1987), while his own *Cockroach Opera* (1987) satirized the persecutions of Jakarta transsexual prostitutes. *Sam Pek Eng Tay* (1988), a humorous adaptation of a *Chinese *melodrama, was banned in Sumatra and barred from *touring abroad because officials thought the Chinese theme would fan racial tensions. *Primadonna Opera* (1988, 2000), an entertaining story of an ageing star who refuses to yield the stage to a successor, reflected President Suharto's unwillingness to yield power. Teater Koma attracts a young and diverse *audience and is one of the few troupes in *Indonesia that has survived the loss of government subsidy.

KFo

RICCOBONI FAMILY

Italian acting *family. **Luigi** (1686–1753) followed his father **Antonio**, a celebrated Pantalone, into *commedia dell'arte, playing the part of Lelio, the Innamorato. Born in Modena, Lelio, as he became known, worked in Venice from 1702 to 1715, and there married **Elena Balletti**, a writer and actress who took the role of Flaminia, the Innamorata. Like *Goldoni, Lelio aspired to reform contemporary theatre. In *comedy, his aim was to achieve reform of a moral and literary character but his deeper goal was to elevate Italian theatre by reintroducing *tragedy. He translated *Racine, performed tragedies by *Maffei and *early modern playwrights, but had only moderate success with an *audience which demanded lighter fare. Lelio and Flaminia moved their company to *Paris in 1716, when the death of Louis XIV led to the repeal of the 1697 order banning Italian actors. Often performing Lelio's own scripts, the new *Comédie Italienne enjoyed such success at court and in the city as to arouse the resentment of native French companies, but Lelio's ability to imbue the traditional 'masks' with individual *character had a profound influence on French eighteenth-century drama. The young *Marivaux had his early work staged, anonymously, by the Riccoboni company. Lelio's *theoretical and historical writings, especially *Histoire du théâtre italien* (1726), and his *Dell'arte rappresentativa* (1728), helped spread knowledge of Italian culture and stage techniques across Europe. He abandoned the theatre in 1729, but his work was carried on by his son **Francesco** (1707–72), actor-author of around 30 plays and of writings on the art of *acting.   JF

RICE, ELMER (ELMER REIZENSTEIN) (1892–1967)

American dramatist, director, and *producer. The author of more than 50 plays in multiple styles, Rice produced and directed most of his work after 1929 and directed plays by others, most notably *Sherwood's *Abe Lincoln in Illinois* (1938). Trained as an attorney, Rice gave up the law when his flashback courtroom drama *On Trial* (1914) earned him $100,000. His next play, *The Iron Cross* (1917), used *plot and *character as vehicles for an anti-war message. *The Adding Machine* (1923) was not the first *expressionist play on Broadway, but Rice's story of Mr Zero's journey from earthly to eternal monotony was given an unforgettable production by the *Theatre Guild, featuring designer Lee *Simonson's expressionistic *scenery: walls covered with projected numbers, a slanting courtroom, a gigantic adding machine with movable keys. *Street Scene* (1929), a nearly plotless, *naturalistic picture of tenement life, ran for over 600 performances and won Rice his only Pulitzer Prize. During the 1930s, his entertainment vehicles—such as the much revived *Counsellor-at-Law* (1931)—were outnumbered by his brooding, discursive social dramas praising democracy and attacking *fascism. Rice was *New York director for the *Federal Theatre Project (1935–6), resigning in a public fight over government *censorship. In 1938 he joined five other playwrights to form the Playwrights Company. He wrote two successful *comedies—*Two on an Island* (1940) and *Dream Girl* (1945)— both conceived as vehicles for his second wife Betty Field. The memoirs *The Living Theatre* (1959) and *Minority Report* (1963) define Rice's aesthetic.   MAF

RICE, THOMAS D. (1808–60)

American actor and playwright. Little is known of Rice's early life, but by the late 1820s he was appearing in minor roles in a theatre in Louisville, Kentucky. According to legend, Rice observed a crippled black stablehand singing and dancing, learned the song and *dance, and introduced them into his blackface act. When Rice later performed them at *New York's *Bowery Theatre in *The Kentucky Rifle* in 1832, his 'Jim Crow' persona and the song and dance were instantly successful, leading to na-

tional *tours as well as circuits of England. Although Rice is often credited with popularizing blackface performances and laying the groundwork for *minstrel shows, his Jim Crow routine remained a solo act. However, he adapted the Jim Crow persona for several plays and occasionally acted other roles, notably the title *character in the Bowery production of *Uncle Tom's Cabin* (1858).   GAR

RICE, TIM (1944–)

English lyricist and librettist. After working for a record company, he found fame with the lyrics and *books for three *musicals composed by Andrew *Lloyd Webber—*Joseph and the Amazing Technicolor Dreamcoat* (1968), *Jesus Christ Superstar* (1970), and *Evita* (1978). After this collaboration ended, he worked with a number of composers—Stephen Oliver on *Blondel* (1983), Benny Andersson and Bjorn Ulvaeus of ABBA on *Chess* (1985)—before finding a new career scoring Walt Disney animated features. He wrote the score for *Aladdin* (1992) with Alan Menken, with whom he also wrote six new songs for the stage version of Disney's *Beauty and the Beast* (1994). Teaming with composer Elton John, he wrote lyrics for both *film (1994) and stage (1997) versions of *The Lion King*. His latest collaboration with John is another Disney stage production, *Aida* (2000). Rice's typical subject has been the results of sudden fame on the individual.   JD

RICH, CHRISTOPHER (c.1657–1714)

English *manager. Taking control of the ailing *patent company at *Drury Lane around 1693, Rich is cast as the tyrannical villain of theatre history largely because he made the commercial success of the company his first priority. His attempt to cut salaries caused a revolt by the leading players, who formed a rival company at *Lincoln's Inn Fields in 1695. This competition prompted Rich to import foreign and domestic attractions, a device that proved profitable and established the popularity of the mixed bill. Dogged by disagreements, Rich was eventually ousted from Drury Lane. He died before the completion of a new theatre in Lincoln's Inn Fields, which passed into the hands of his *actor-manager son John *Rich.   GBB

RICH, FRANK (1949–)

American critic and journalist. During the 1980s and early 1990s Frank Rich's theatre reviews ruled *New York theatre and earned him the epithet 'the Butcher of Broadway'. Born in Washington, Rich studied at Harvard and started his writing career at *Time* magazine. In 1980 he joined the *New York Times* as theatre critic, and quickly became noted for his tight prose and strongly argued assessments. Many in the theatre community protested the power his reviews had over the survival of productions. He left *criticism in 1993 to become a columnist for the *Times* and has since published two books, including *Hot Seat* (1998), a compendium of his reviews.

KF

RICH, JOHN (LUN) (1692–1761)

English dancer, actor, and *manager. The son of Christopher *Rich, John took over the refurbished theatre in *Lincoln's Inn Fields on his father's death in 1714. The elegant house with mirrored interior became the home of popular adaptations of Italian-style *pantomime in which Rich excelled as *Harlequin. *The Necromancer; or, Harlequin Doctor Faustus* (1723) was his most successful pantomime and he spared no expense in providing spectacular *costumes and *scenery. In 1728 Rich premièred *Gay's *Beggar's Opera*, which ran for an unprecedented 32 nights. By 1730 Rich had built a larger theatre in *Covent Garden in which he mounted a mix of popular plays and pantomime.

GBB

RICHARDS, LLOYD (1922–)

*African-American director who had great influence on the course of American theatre in the second half of the twentieth century. Richards was teaching *acting when one of his students, Sidney Poitier, recommended him as the director of *Hansberry's *Raisin in the Sun* in 1959. Richards thus became the first African American to direct on Broadway, just as he was the first African American to head the Playwrights Conference at the *Eugene O'Neill Theatre Center (1969–99) and to be dean of the *Yale School of Drama (1979–91). One novice dramatist under his wing at the O'Neill Center was August *Wilson, who brought him *Ma Rainey's Black Bottom* in 1984, followed by his next five plays, utterly confident in Richards's ability to bring them to life; in 1987 Richards won a Tony *award for his direction of Wilson's *Fences* (and has received many other awards). He made the Yale Repertory Theatre into a major force in the *regional theatre movement, and steered the early careers of a number of new playwrights in addition to Hansberry and Wilson. Richards has also directed work from *Africa: *A Lesson from Aloes* and other plays by Athol *Fugard, and *The Lion and the Jewel* by Wole *Soyinka. For Richards *directing is analogous to making an indelible print on wet cement, or being 'the first person to make the impression in a placid pool—to start the wave'.

BBL

RICHARDS, NORAH (1876–1971)

Irish director in *India. In 1911 she accompanied her husband, a Unitarian minister, to the Punjab, when he was appointed professor of English at the Dyal Singh College, Lahore. Richards had been a member of the Shakespeare *touring companies of Ben *Greet and F. R. *Benson, and the Lahore students invited her to direct *A Midsummer Night's Dream*, which was followed by a workshop on *acting and *playwriting. She recorded the condition of *Punjabi theatre at the time: 'Plays were very artificial and declamatory with garish and crude sets. Indian theatre had picked up the worst aspects of European theatre.' She introduced the plays of the *Abbey Theatre, *Dublin, whose motto was 'Irish plays by Irish writers for Irish *audiences', and the students responded by substituting Indian for Irish. In 1912 she organized the first of three annual *one-act play competitions which laid the foundation of modern Punjabi theatre. The winners were Shanti Swaroop Bhatnagar's *Urdu play *Karamat* (*Miracle*, 1912), I. C. Nanda's Punjabi *Dulhan* (*The Bride*, 1913), and Rajinder Lal Sahni's Punjabi *Dina Di Janj* (*Dina's Wedding Procession*, 1914). Widowed in 1920, Richards returned to England, but returned once again to Lahore in 1924. When India was partitioned in 1947, she moved to Andretta in Kangra Valley, where she was granted 6 hectares (15 acres) of land by the government. There she created an *amphitheatre, an actor-*training school, and a community centre for artists.

NMSC

RICHARDSON, IAN (1934–)

Scottish actor, born in Edinburgh and *trained in *Glasgow. He joined the *Birmingham Rep in 1958 with a range of roles including Hamlet. At the *Shakespeare Memorial Theatre in 1960 he was Sir Andrew Aguecheek (1960) and Oberon (1961), and for the newly formed *Royal Shakespeare Company he performed leading roles in *The Representative* (1963), *King Lear* (1964), *Marat/Sade* (1964), *Coriolanus* (1966), *Julius Caesar* (1968), *Pericles* (1969), *Measure for Measure* (1970), and *Love's Labour's Lost* (1973). In John *Barton's notable version of *Richard II* he alternated the roles of Richard and Bolingbroke with Richard Pasco (1973). On Broadway he was Higgins in *My Fair Lady* (1976) and played opposite Donald Sutherland in Frank *Dunlop's short-lived production of *Lolita*, adapted by Edward *Albee (1981). For *television he was Bill Hayden, the mole, in the definitive spy thriller *Tinker, Tailor, Soldier, Spy* (1979) and Francis Urquhart, the machiavellian politician, in *House of Cards* (1990), *To Play the King* (1993), and *Final Cut* (1995). He has also appeared at *Chichester in *The Miser* (1995) and *The Magistrate* (1997).

AS

RICHARDSON, RALPH (1902–83)

English actor. With neither the characteristic nobility of John *Gielgud nor the heroism of Laurence *Olivier, Richardson excelled at character roles in classical plays and everyman figures in modern works. While he worked extensively in classical theatre, his pre-war reputation rested on contemporary plays, including Phillpotts's *Yellow Sands* (1926), *Maugham's *Sheppey* (1933), and *Priestley's *Eden End* (1934) and *Johnson over Jordan* (1939). In 1944 Richardson joined Olivier in *managing the *Old

Vic Theatre Company, giving performances which were to become legendary in British theatre: Peer Gynt, Falstaff, Bluntschli, and the original Inspector Goole in Priestley's *An Inspector Calls* (1946). Throughout the 1950s he continued in the classical vein and also appeared in modern work, including Ruth and Augustus Goetz's *The Heiress* (1949), N. C. *Hunter's *A Day by the Sea* (1953), and Robert *Bolt's *Flowering Cherry* (1957). Initially finding himself out of step with the new drama of the 1960s, Richardson rebounded in the 1970s, appearing with John Gielgud in David *Storey's *Home* (1970) at the *Royal Court and Harold *Pinter's *No Man's Land* (1975) at the *National Theatre, where he was also acclaimed in *John Gabriel Borkman* (1975), *The Cherry Orchard* (1978), and *The Wild Duck* (1979). He appeared in two William Douglas *Home plays in the West End: *Lloyd George Knew my Father* (1972) and *The Kingfisher* (1977). Significant *film appearances include *The Fallen Idol* (1948), *The Heiress* (1950), *Richard III* (1955), and *A Long Day's Journey into Night* (1960).

MDG

RICHARDSON, TONY (1928–91)

English director. Although esteemed as a theatre director, it was in *film that Richardson achieved greater recognition. He began as an assistant to George *Devine at the *Royal Court, later directing *Osborne's landmark *Look Back in Anger* (1956), and *The Entertainer* (starring *Olivier, 1957). Both productions transferred to *New York. At Stratford, Richardson directed a notorious *Othello* with Paul *Robeson (1959). Richardson's direction of new writing for the screen was remarkable: *Look Back in Anger* (1959), *The Entertainer* (1960), Shelagh *Delaney's *A Taste of Honey* (1961), *The Loneliness of the Long Distance Runner* (1962). In 1963 he won an Oscar for best direction and best film for *Tom Jones*. From the early 1970s Richardson lived in *Los Angeles and Provence, and spent the rest of his life directing film and *television drama, though his critics claim that he never equalled the successes of the 1960s. His short marriage to Vanessa *Redgrave produced actor-daughters Natasha and Joely. His autobiography, *Long Distance Runner*, was published posthumously in 1993.

KN

RICHELIEU, CARDINAL ARMAND-JEAN DU PLESSIS (1585–1642)

French statesman, chief minister under Louis XIII. In addition to leading military campaigns and solidifying the power of the French monarchy, he was a prominent and interested patron of the arts, employing notable architects, painters, and sculptors to design and decorate his numerous houses. In his *Paris palace, the Palais Cardinal (later the *Palais Royal), he built two theatres which were the first permanent *proscenium *playhouses in France. In these spaces he commanded performances of *tra-

gedies and elaborate spectacular productions. He also established and funded a company of five writers (including *Corneille and *Rotrou) to produce new works for the French stage. One of his most lasting legacies was the creation of the Académie Française in 1634. Controversially, he personally influenced the outcome of the Académie's first official action, which was to condemn Corneille's *Le Cid* for violating *neoclassical standards for tragedy.

CJW

RIDEAU VERT, THÉÂTRE DU

*Montréal company founded in 1948 by actress-director Yvette Brind'Amour. After a difficult period in which it was twice forced to suspend activity and seek to redefine its *audience, it moved in 1960 to a larger venue, the Théâtre Stella (later renamed the Théâtre du Rideau Vert), and has generally prospered since. Its repertoire comprises popular modern authors, classics (its production of *A Midsummer Night's Dream* was a signal success in *Paris in 1965), and well-chosen Québécois plays, notably Michel *Tremblay's epoch-making *Les Belles-Sœurs* (1968) and major works by Antonine *Maillet and Françoise *Loranger.

LED

RIDICULOUS, THEATRE OF THE

Co-founded in 1966 by director John Vaccaro and playwright Ronald Tavel as the Playhouse of the Ridiculous, this company launched the *gay theatre movement in the United States out of a raucous blend of *burlesque, pop culture, and the drag show (*see* FEMALE IMPERSONATION). The success of Vaccaro's wildly irreverent staging is fully embedded in the gay sexuality of Tavel's bawdy and improvisatory *satires like *The Life of Lady Godiva* (1966) and *Gorilla Queen* (1967). The company began to fail after its first season with the departures of Tavel and Charles *Ludlam, who left to become *actor-manager of his own *Ridiculous Theatrical Company. Vaccaro continued to direct Ridiculous productions at *La Mama but with little success, and he pronounced the theatre defunct after a long European *tour in 1972. Despite its brief history, it had a major influence on companies such as *San Francisco's Theatre Rhinoceros and the *lesbian troupe *Split Britches.

JAB

RIDICULOUS THEATRICAL COMPANY

American repertory company dedicated to the work of Charles *Ludlam, who formed it in 1967. The core company included John D. Brockmeyer, Bill Vehr, Susan Carlson, and Lola Pashalinski. The actors all came from Jon Vacarro and Ronald Tavel's Playhouse of the *Ridiculous, where Ludlam's plays *Big Hotel* (1967) and *Conquest of the Universe* (1967) were performed. The *gay camp style of the Ridiculous Theatrical Company appropriated elements of classical plays and Hollywood *film with sexual wordplay and situations and cross-*gender *casting. The roots of the 'Ridiculous' movement can be located in the scatological and political humour of *Aristophanes, the social *comedies of *Molière, and the *avant-garde attack on the bourgeoisie of *Jarry. The camp aesthetic of the movement of the 1960s and 1970s, and its *carnivalesque celebration of tearing down all borders, differs greatly from the queer performance *politics of the 1980s and 1990s and its concern for identity and cultural construction (see QUEER THEORY). In performance the *acting of the Ridiculous Theatrical Company was broad and comic, but played for pathos as well as *laughter. Crossdressing—with Ludlam himself playing many of the women's lead roles—was common. Major productions included *Bluebeard* (1970), *Camille* (1973), and *The Mystery of Irma Vep* (1984). Everett *Quinton, who joined the company in the 1970s, served as *artistic director of the Ridiculous Theatrical Company after Ludlam's death in 1987 until the theatre closed in 1997. *See also* FEMALE IMPERSONATION. MDC

RIGBY, TERENCE (1937–)

Prolific English actor whose bluff persona has been exploited and tempered in a range of classic and modern roles. He was Joey in the Watford revival of *The Homecoming* in 1969, when *Pinter played Lenny, and in 1975 he was Briggs in the première of Pinter's *No Man's Land* at the *National Theatre. He was directed by Peter *Hall in *Macbeth* and *The Cherry Orchard* at the NT (both 1978), where he also appeared in Richard *Eyre's *Richard III* (1992). He was in Hall's revival of *Amadeus* (1999) in *London and *New York, where he also played Agamemnon in the same director's *Troilus and Cressida* (2001). For the *Almeida in 1994–5 he was the *Ghost, Player King, and Gravedigger in Jonathan Kent's *Hamlet* in London and New York, where in 2001 he was Harry in a revival of *Bond's *Saved*. On screen he has appeared in British art cinema (*Accident*, 1967), as the definitive British gangster (*Get Carter*, 1971), in a James Bond film (*Tomorrow Never Dies*, 1997), and in *Elizabeth* (1998). AS

RIGG, DIANA (1938–)

Bold and sexy English actress. She trained at the *Royal Academy of Dramatic Art and initially worked in *regional rep before joining the *Stratford Memorial Theatre in 1959 and the *Royal Shakespeare Company, where early roles included Helena in *Hall's *A Midsummer Night's Dream*, Bianca in *The Taming of the Shrew*, and Cordelia, opposite Paul *Scofield, in *Brook's *King Lear* (all 1962). In the 1960s she was an unforgettable Mrs Peel in the cult British *television series *The Avengers* (1965–7). At the *National Theatre in *London her roles (1972–3) included Dolly in *Stoppard's *Jumpers*, Lady Macbeth, and Célimène in *The Misanthrope*. She starred in *Little Eyolf* at the *Lyric

Hammersmith (1985), *All for Love* at the *Almeida (1991), *Mother Courage* at the National (1995), *Who's Afraid of Virginia Woolf?* at the Almeida (1996), and *Phèdre* and *Britannicus* at the Albery (1998). Having been nominated for a Tony *award on two previous occasions—for *Abelard and Heloise* (1971) and for *The Misanthrope*—Rigg won for Jonathan Kent's Almeida production of *Medea* (London, 1992, *New York, 1994). Later television roles include the eponymous sleuth in *The Mrs Bradley Mysteries* (1998, 2000). She was made DBE in 1994.

AS

RIHANY, NAGUIB EL- (1892–1949)

Egyptian actor, *manager, and director. He collaborated with Badie Khairy and others in reworking French *vaudevilles into purely Egyptian versions, creating memorable interpretations on stage and screen of the Egyptian petite bourgeoisie. After the First World War Rihany moved from comic *folk performance (he won fame as the *commedia-like *character of Kish-Kish Bey, a gullible country mayor) to Western psychological *acting in Egyptian colloquial Arabic (Ammeya). The literary Standard Arabic (Fus'ha) of the Levantine troupes had long been considered essential on the Egyptian stage, but Rihany's status legitimized performing in the colloquial language. HMA

RINGWOOD, GWEN PHARIS (1910–84)

Canadian playwright and *community theatre activist. Raised in Alberta, she wrote her best-known play, the *one-act *tragedy *Still Stands the House* (1938), while a graduate student in North Carolina. Like her subsequent plays *Dark Harvest* (1939), *Jack and the Joker* (1944), and *The Rainmaker* (1946), it reflected her upbringing on the prairie frontier. After moving to central British Columbia in 1953, she continued to write and to produce community theatre. Several later plays, from *Lament for Harmonica* (1959) to *The Furies* (1981), are set among the native people there. *Collected Plays* was published in 1982.

DWJ

RIO DE JANEIRO

The major cultural centre and administrative capital of nineteenth-century Brazil, Rio hosted numerous travelling groups from Europe, principally from France and Portugal. Brazilian theatre began with Martins Pena (1815–48), whose ebullient *comedies provided critical scenes of local life, establishing a tradition of *burlesque type *characters developed further by the *revista* (*revue). Although akin to French and English *vaudeville, *revistas* in Rio reinterpreted the major events of the past year by comic musical sketches, political critique, fantastic *allegorical figures, and the most successful *carnival tunes. By the 1930s *revistas* resembled the polished French and American *musical comedies of the era, but nonetheless were the first significant attempt to create a popular national theatre. In the 1920s and 1930s actors became idols, specializing in light comedies of lower-middle-class suburban life or *satirizing middle-class pretensions. Of the major playwrights of this tendency, Oduvaldo *Viana Filho stands out for his insistence on a Brazilian, rather than Portuguese, diction and *dialogue.

Founded in 1938 by diplomat and impresario Paschoal Carlos Magno, the Brazilian Student Theatre underscored the importance of interchange among *amateur, student, and professional groups which were functioning as *training grounds for actors and writers. These groups organized *festivals and *finance, helping to create an infrastructure that would become an alternative to purely commercial theatre. Among the artists fleeing war-torn Europe, the Polish director Zbigniew Ziembinski mounted Nelson *Rodrigues's *Vestido de noiva* (*Wedding Dress*, 1943) with an amateur group called Os Comediantes. Its *expressionist staging was a landmark in *scenography and ensemble *acting; most critics mark it as the beginning of modern theatre in Brazil.

National industrial growth in the late 1940s and 1950s was paralleled by a fruitful theatrical interchange between Rio and *São Paulo. Viana Filho moved to Rio in 1961 and was instrumental in the creation of the Centros de Cultura Popular (Popular Cultural Centres), whose *Brechtian-Brazilian methods connected to the leftist political movement and became the base of cultural protest against the 1964 military coup (*see* POLITICS AND THEATRE). In 1964 Grupo Opinião's *Opinion Show* interwove song and *documentary testimony through Brazilian popular music, the first of a series of dissident musical performances in a climate increasingly hostile to direct political debate. The government instituted a period of severe *censorship that lasted from 1968 to 1979, which stifled political and artistic expression on the commercial stage. *Alternative theatres took on renewed importance, as directors such as Amir Haddad and João Siqueira pushed the traditions of *street theatre towards a more direct political expression, and other groups created a celebratory, youth-oriented language capable of dodging censorship, as exemplified by Teatro Ipanema's *Hoje é dia de rock* (*Today It's Rock*, 1971).

With the proclamation of general political amnesty in 1979 (the dictatorship ended officially in 1985), small and large theatres worked to recuperate social memory with plays about torture, guerrilla warfare, and cultural amnesia. But with a few notable exceptions like Viana Filho's *Rasga coração* (*Heart Torn Assunder*, 1979), little work surfaced of real dramatic merit—an artistic drain caused by the long-term effects of the dictatorship and the new dominance of *television. At the start of the twenty-first century the commercial stage was dominated by light comedies, often nostalgic in nature, and *monologues presented by TV soap opera stars. The city continues to welcome performers like Denise *Stoklos and directors like Gerald *Thomas, whose

productions travel the Rio–São Paulo axis. Most interesting in a culture that tends to musical expression, biographical plays about national singers and composers have also proved popular, exemplified by *Somos irmãs* (*We're Sisters*, 1997). Scenic experimentation has found expression through directors such as Bia Lessa and Adebal Freire-Filho, whose ambitious environmental production about Brazil's national hero spread over six historic locales in the city (*Tiradentes*, 1992). A younger generation is represented by Moacyr Góes and Moacir Chaves; Paulo Morães's adaptation of *Alice in Wonderland* (2000) was innovative in its use of space. Street experimentation continues with theatre of the *oppressed groups and, more notably, the surge of work in the *favelas* (shanty towns), such as that of the Vidigal Cultural Centre's *Nós do Morro*.   LHD

RIOTS

Riots in and related to theatres have been common in European and American theatres for many centuries, although Marc Baer complains that 'the term *riot* has been over-used by theatre historians'. Nevertheless, in England riots were frequent during the eighteenth and nineteenth centuries. Politics, raised prices, abolition of privilege, xenophobia, feuds between actors were among the causes. Some riots, as in the 1730s, were politically motivated, but *Covent Garden witnessed a violent response to its attempts to raise prices in 1736, while footmen rampaged in 1737 after their privilege of free gallery seats was withdrawn. During a dispute between *Garrick and *Macklin in 1743 'bruisers' were brought in to control the *audience. In 1755 anti-French sentiment led to rioting over several evenings during performances of the *ballet *The Chinese Festival* at *Drury Lane. Internal structures and *scenery were damaged and crowds also smashed the windows of Garrick's house. In 1763 Thaddeus Fitzpatrick organized riots at both Covent Garden and Drury Lane in protest at the abolition of the half-price admission for late arrivals. The rioters rushed onto the stage at Drury Lane, broke woodwork and shattered chandeliers, while at Covent Garden they destroyed the entire fabric of the theatre. Tailors rioted at the *Haymarket Theatre in 1805, on the grounds that a new play, *The Tailors*, mocked their profession. Outside *London the 'Kelly' riot at the *Smock Alley Theatre in *Dublin in 1747 partly resulted from Thomas Sheridan's attempts to prevent spectators going behind the scenes, while in 1767 the *Edinburgh Playhouse 'was demolished, the moveables ransacked, and the fixtures destroyed'.

The most notorious and last major riot in an English theatre was the Old Price or *OP riots at Covent Garden in 1809. The *management had rebuilt the theatre after a fire in 1808, raised the prices of seats in the pit, removed inexpensive seats to accommodate more *boxes, and employed the Italian singer Madame Catalani at great expense. The opening-night performance on 18 September was disrupted by demands for old prices,

Acting MAGISTRATES committing themselves being their first appearance on this stage as performed at the National Theatre Covent Garden Sept. 18. 1809

The OP **riot**, Covent Garden, London, 1809. Magistrates on stage are about to read the Riot Act, in a futile attempt to quell two months of disturbances demanding a return to 'Old Prices' at the theatre. Placards in the house complain of Madame Catalani and the new boxes, as well as castigating the manager J. P. Kemble.

which were finally restored (along with the dismissal of Catalani and a reduction in private boxes) in December, after 67 nights of organized rioting. Throughout the intervening period not a word was heard on stage. Horns, bugles, bells, and rattles, the clatter of sticks, and the display of banners, as well as an 'OP dance', contributed to the disorder. Actors were pelted, fights occurred in the *auditorium, and 'bruisers' hired by the theatre failed to control the crowds (*see* AUDIENCE CONTROL). In many ways the OP riots became an expression of political and social dissent and of national identity, focusing on issues far beyond the immediate circumstances. One other disturbance in nineteenth-century London merits comment. On 12 June 1848, when the Théâtre Historique Company opened at Drury Lane in *Dumas *père*'s *The Count of Monte Cristo*, whistles and shouting drowned out the performance, while protests became more physical on subsequent occasions. Opinion was divided, but it is likely that the riots were orchestrated by elements within the theatrical profession who feared competition from abroad, while further fuelled by nationalism, xenophobia, and chartist dissent.

One year later 31 were killed and 150 wounded by soldiers during the *Astor Place riot in *New York, caused by rivalry between Edwin *Forrest and William *Macready. Supporters of Forrest, who was convinced Macready had been responsible for his poor reception in England, stormed the theatre, but were quelled by the military. As with the William Farren riot in the USA in 1834, social and racial tensions were also behind the disruption.

France's most famous riot was motivated by an assault on tradition. In 1830 riots occurred at the Théâtre-Français (*see* COMÉDIE-FRANÇAISE) after the performance of Victor *Hugo's *Hernani*, which deliberately broke with *neoclassical rules and drew on the influence of Shakespeare, *Schiller, and even contemporary *melodrama. During the first three performances the theatre was stacked with Hugo's friends and supporters, but the play's opponents were equally vociferous. Actors had to 'struggle night after night against a noisy hubbub of jeering, cat-calls, insults, threats and open fighting' (*see* HERNANI RIOTS; illustration, p. 584). On 8 December 1896 another assault on convention provoked strong reaction, when Alfred *Jarry's *Ubu* roi was premièred at the Théâtre de l'*Œuvre, although the greater outcry was on the second night of its performance. Since Jarry may have orchestrated the cabal protesting against the play, this hardly constitutes an authentic riot. *Modernism's assault on convention also triggered violent responses to the world première of *The Rite of Spring* in *Paris in 1913 when the noise of the audience prevented the *dancers from hearing Stravinsky's music, and to *Pirandello's *Six Characters in Search of an Author* on its première in *Rome in 1921.

Among the most notorious riots of the twentieth century were those at the *Abbey Theatre in Dublin after the première of J. M. *Synge's *The Playboy of the Western World* on 26 January 1907. Synge's depiction of his peasant *characters, based on his experiences in the far west of Ireland, as flawed and immoral, inflamed audiences, whose nationalist sensibilities were upset by what they saw (*see* PLAYBOY RIOTS). Police were summoned to the theatre to restore order; Synge's subsequent play *The Tinker's Wedding* (1908) was not produced at the Abbey for fear of further riots. When the Abbey *toured the USA in 1911, *Playboy* again provoked riots at a number of theatres. *Yeats sprang to Synge's defence in 1907, as he did on behalf of Sean *O'Casey, whose irreverent representation of the myths of Easter 1916 in *The Plough and the Stars* (1926) also enraged Abbey spectators. The declining importance of the theatre in the latter half of the twentieth century has meant that it has not been considered as significant a venue as formerly for public protest. Nevertheless, from 15 May to 14 June 1968, student protesters occupied the *Odéon in Paris, which led to the resignation of its director, Jean-Louis *Barrault.   JTD

BAER, MARC, *Theatre and Disorder in Late Georgian London* (Oxford, 1992)

RISTORI, ADELAIDE (1822–1906)

Italian actress and *manager. Statuesque and of a majestic bearing, with a good, clear voice, Ristori was the first Italian actor since the *early modern period to establish an international reputation. Her career paralleled the struggle for freedom from foreign domination and for unification of the Italian states, which was accomplished by 1871; she brought international attention to this cause and served as honorary ambassador abroad. Child of a theatrical family, Ristori was practically born on stage. After a major success playing the title role in Pellico's *Francesca da Rimini* at the age of 14, she joined Turin's prestigious Reale Sarda Company as *ingénue and, from 1837 to 1841, developed her art surrounded by some of the finest Italian actors. Over the next ten years she came to the fore as a leading actress in the Mascherpa company and, opposite a young Tommaso *Salvini, in the Domeniconi–Coltellini company. Her repertory consisted of popular sentimental drama, *Goldonian *comedy, *tragedy, and translations of the French *well-made play. Through marriage to a nobleman she became Marchesa Capranica del Grillo

(1847). In 1853 she rejoined the Reale Sarda and during the company's 1855 *Paris tour, which starred Ristori and Ernesto *Rossi in *Francesca da Rimini*, *Alfieri's *Mirra*, *Schiller's *Mary Stuart*, and Marenco's *Pia de' Tolomei*, she found herself the toast of Parisian critics and literati: *Dumas *père*, *Gautier, George Sand, *Musset, and de *Vigny, among others.

Returning home, the various state authorities considered Ristori's repertory inflammatory and subjected her material to repressive *censorship. Ristori therefore turned to international *touring and, from the late 1850s to 1885, travelled all over the world to great acclaim, even performing sometimes in English and French. Her standard international repertory consisted of exceptional women whom she interpreted as victims of hostile forces. They included four mythical queens—Legouvé's Medea, Alfieri's Mirra, *Racine's Phèdre, Shakespeare's Lady Macbeth—and three historical queens—Schiller's Mary Stuart, and the title roles in *Giacometti's *Elizabeth Queen of England* and *Marie Antoinette*. Ristori dismissed the fixed vocal and gestural conventions of the past and searched for a new *realism of expression. She was noted for her careful study of a *character's moods, inner conflicts, and transitions from one state of mind to the other. As artistic head of her company, she had a fine sense of stagecraft and was renowned for creating dramatic *tableaux and keeping tight control over stage effects.   JEH

RITTNER, RUDOLF (1869–1943)

Austrian actor associated mainly with German *naturalism and Gerhart *Hauptmann. Otto *Brahm employed him from 1894 at the *Deutsches Theater in *Berlin, where he took leading roles in *Ibsen's *Ghosts* and in Hauptmann's *The Weavers* (1892) and *Carter Henschel* (1898). Rittner developed the prototypical naturalistic style: restrained, with careful attention to everyday gestures. In 1907—at the peak of his success—he left the theatre and became a farmer.   CBB

RITUAL AND THEATRE

Since the 1980s increased cooperation between the disciplines of anthropology, with its focus on ethnographic recording of rituals, and *theatre studies, with its *theoretical attention to *performance, has demonstrated the difficulty of separating the modes of ritual from theatrical performances. The field of *performance studies in particular has attempted to establish a theoretical frame for the effectiveness of ritual in a cross-cultural perspective, at the same time considering the larger resonance of theatrical and para-theatrical productions. This development is largely due to the interdisciplinary work of two thinkers. The first is the anthropologist Victor Turner, who applied concepts of drama to ritual processes which remember, refashion, or remedy structures and conflicts of social reality (*Drums of Affliction*, 1968; *The Ritual Process*, 1969; *The Anthropology of*

Performance, 1985). The second is the critic and director Richard *Schechner, who has explored and incorporated non-European rituals and theatrical practices into his practical and theoretical work (especially in his books *Performance Theory*, 1977; *Between Theatre and Anthropology*, 1985; *The Future of Ritual*, 1993). Their fruitful collaboration replays similar innovative theorizing on the *origins of theatre by the Cambridge School of Anthropology, chiefly Jane Harrison, Gilbert *Murray, and Francis Cornford. Inspired by Frazer's *The Golden Bough* (1890–1915), these classicists postulated the derivation of *tragedy from early Greek sacrificial practices and of *comedy from the *Dionysian revels and mystery cults. Their genealogical or 'genetic' method, asserting that theatre derived from the sacred domain in the manner of an evolutionary event, was extremely influential in the twentieth century. It was eventually opposed by a more 'generic' comparison between theatre and ritual, one that saw social action as modelled on the formal element of the performative, a view suggested by the sociologist Helmuth Plessner in the 1920s, evident in *Brecht's notion of 'everyday theatre', and enlarged into a social theory by Erwing Goffman (*The Presentation of the Self in Everyday Life*, 1959).

But the similarity between ritual and theatre does not lie only in formal aspects. More recent anthropological theories have suggested that ritual carries the quality of 'efficacy' (or effectivity) in symbolic communication. In this view the performative possesses not only the traits of conventionality, stereotype, and repetition, but also the power of constituting and reconstituting reality. Borrowing from the 'speech act' theories of J. L. Austin and John Searle, some commentators have claimed that the performative can be an 'illocutionary force' to constitute and change reality, an idea equally applicable to ritual and theatre (*see* PERFORMATIVITY). Traditionally, theatrical performances are assumed to function within the conceptual frame of pretence, of an 'as if' reality, while ritual operates in a mode that has actual effects on lived reality. Since both are staged and *rehearsed practices, the distinction between theatrical performances and ritual actions is somewhat arbitrary, yet some differences remain important. The change of perception of both actor and *audience, for example, depends on the expectations and intentions with which they approach the performance: if, as in ordinary *bourgeois theatre, actors and audience expect to create and derive only entertainment from the event, then the mental and spiritual result is not likely to be the same as that of a ritual ceremony where priest and congregation might well expect immanence and transformation. But even this has been contested. Some theoretical discussions of *acting insist that theatre, just as ritual, can transform experience and therefore transform reality. This assumption has been present from the very beginning of theories of drama, since *Aristotle claimed that *catharsis was central to the experience of tragedy. Another example lies in German classical writings after *Schiller, which asserted the innovative power of *mimesis.

Recent theories on ritual, such as the much discussed and controversial approach by Humphrey and Laidlaw in their work *The Archetypal Actions of Ritual* (1994), imply or even insist that ritual action is 'meaningless', since the intentions of both actor and spectator are unknowable: all that is known is their ritual commitment to perform the act and subscribe to a traditional 'stipulation'. Nonetheless a common denominator can be found in many debates on theatre and ritual—that the efficacy of any performative action depends upon its impact on perception. This calls into question the very idea of framing concepts that distinguish the two practices. Schechner, a leading light of performance theory, has proposed the metaphor of 'porous nets' for expectations, leaving scope for shifting the boundaries of reality and experience, and also allowing for the possibility that both ritual and theatre can change lived reality. Influenced strongly by Turner's studies of ritual processes among the Central African Ndembu, Schechner had previously pointed to the interweaving between the functions of ritual effectiveness and theatrical entertainment, in particular in societies with elaborate theatre traditions and theories about acting such as *India or *Japan.

This kind of intertwining has been claimed by anthropologists like Firth for the *Indonesian *wayang kulit *shadow-puppet play, where before the performance the performer prays to his puppets and offers the sacrifice of the self. Japanese *puppet masters of *bunraku perceive the clothing of the dolls as extensions of the actor's personality and spirit, comparing them to human skin which mediates and transforms the inner and outer. Such notions about 'ritual play' meshed well with *modernist *avant-garde approaches to acting, most famously proposed in Antonin *Artaud's *The Theatre and its Double* (1938) with a call for the revitalization of theatre practice through the 'magic of ritual'.

Performative action—and through it the transformation of performers, contexts, and social functions—connects and merges the domains of theatre and ritual as much as it separates and distinguishes them. Whether transformations will occur as the result of an actual performance is unpredictable. Both ritual and theatre performances, therefore, involve risk for the performer, whose ability to evoke divinities, fictional *characters, the dead or their ghosts, will be judged by criteria known to the culturally conditioned audience. The result of a healing ritual may be the recuperation of the sick person, but failing to achieve this may not diminish the 'success' of the ritual. People like the Kaluli of New Guinea consider performative failure or success according to theatrical elements of stagecraft and acting ability, whether or not the shaman evoked resonance about the divine presence in his audience. The ability of theatrical preparations to clue the audience to expect the unexpected (which is culturally conditioned as the expected) may account for the success of adapting such practices to the healing mode of drama therapy in modern societies.

This applies to theatrical acting in ritual settings in India as well. As the anthropologist-dancer Frédérique Apffel-Marglin explained from her own experiences (*Wives of the God-King: the rituals of the Devadasi of Puri*, 1985), the skill of the *devadasi*, the female ritual *dancer in Indian temples (in this case of the temple of Jagannath in Orissa), consists in evoking the 'taste' (*rasa*) in the devotee of the erotic presence of the divinity, the goddess Lakshmi. Such an effect is only possible through rigorous *training which, according to tradition, empties the body and perception of the performer of all contingent and personal attitudes, desires, and feelings in order for the deity to take possession of her (important in the work of Eugenio *Barba). Similarly, Japanese villagers in the southern Alps of Nagano have claimed to the author that they can dance correctly in honour of the mountain god during the winter solstice ritual because the movements are inscribed and learned 'through the skin', a notion refined in Zen Buddhist influence on the performing arts through the ideal of 'emptying the self'.

Notwithstanding their cosmological reference, such notions can be related to the demands of modern European theatre practitioners like *Grotowski that good acting must be as distant from the falsity of flirting with the audience as from narcissistic self-absorption. In this view actors and spectators are taken up by the 'flow' in a shared experience of ecstatic otherness. Such involvement applies equally to secular and sacred performances, when the donning of *costumes, the holding of *props, or the clueing by music and other stimuli, subjectively transform outer or inner realities. Speaking of the theatricalization of ritual implies nothing about its efficacy, though there may remain a problem if the very theatricality of ritual or the obviousness of its play acting undermines belief in its effectiveness. The problem can be overcome: a ritual leader among the Aborigines of Australia during an initiation ceremony advises the initiates that the bullroarer—a wooden device whirled through the air to make a humming noise—which they previously believed to be a divinity, is just a bullroarer which performs the voice of the deity. But, he admonishes the adepts, this secret should not be divulged and the performance must be honoured and repeated lest the world come to an end. No stronger statement about the performative constitution of the universe through ritual theatre can be imagined.

According to Bruce Kapferer in *The Feast of the Sorcerer* (1997), one of the specific identifiers for ritual action is that it constitutes a sphere of virtuality, a non-contingent reality, which is opposed to that of actuality. If this is so, then theatrical and ritual performances both represent and constitute realities in their own right, worlds of the imagination which evolve according to their own logic. These virtual or imaginary realities become real and transformative for actual life through being bodily performed—even if the body practice is meticulously trained in accordance with (diverse) cosmological ideas. Through performance both theatre and ritual create

and constitute a world which is neither a representation of lived reality nor an ideal model for it, but rather a separate reality.

The creation of what Turner calls 'liminal' space and time enables both theatre and ritual to effect a desired or expected transformation of reality. The virtuality of the performative event relies on the ambiguous nature of its liminal or on-the-threshold reality, which enables it to become creative or constitutive of new forms of perception and cognition. The ambiguity of the performative also makes it dangerous for established powers, secular or sacred, and can make *'play' a matter of life and death. But we should not forget that virtuality can only occur in the liminal and limited space and time of ritual and theatre, for the virtual world they create must feed on the larger, contingent reality of the actual world. We underplay the actual world as source for virtual performances at the risk of stultifying the performative itself. *See also* RELIGION AND THEATRE.   KPK

FIRTH, RAYMOND, 'Ritual and drama in Malay spirit mediumship', *Comparative Studies in Society and History* (1967)

HANDELMAN, DON, 'Is Naven ludic? Paradox and the communication of identity', *Social Analysis*, 1 (1979)

KOEPPING, KLAUS-PETER (ed.), *The Games of Gods and Man: essays in play and performance* (Münster, 1997)

MOORE, SALLY F., and MYERHOOF, BARBARA (eds.), *Secular Rituals* (Assen, 1977)

SCHIEFFELIN, EDWARD, 'On failure and performance', in Carol Laderman and Marina Roseman (eds.), *The Performance of Healing* (London, 1996)

TAMBIAH, STANLEY, 'A performative approach to ritual', *Proceedings of the British Academy*, 65 (1979)

RIVERSIDE STUDIOS

Small-scale arts centre in Hammersmith, *London, previously a BBC *television studio and nicely located by the Thames. Opened in 1975, its first *artistic director was Peter *Gill, who with Jenny Stein and David Gothard launched it as one of the most vibrant *fringe venues in the capital. Gill staged his own productions of classics—*The Changeling* (1978), *The Cherry Orchard* (1978), *Measure for Measure* (1979)—and it has also hosted leading *alternative British *touring groups, such as *Joint Stock, plus major European experimentalists, such as Tadeusz *Kantor's CRICOT 2 and workshops by Dario *Fo and Franca *Rame. When Gill left for the *National Theatre in 1980, the local authorities threatened closure, but David Lefeaux took over in 1982, rescuing it through successful stagings of challenging plays, such as *O'Neill's *A Moon for the Misbegotten*, which transferred to Broadway. Funding reductions in the 1980s forced greater commercialism, but Riverside was relaunched in 1993 by director William Burdett-Coutts with a season that included Twyla Tharp and Robert *Lepage's *Seven Streams of the River Ota*.   BRK

RIX, BRIAN (1924–)

English actor and *manager, who began his career in 1942 and was for a while a member of Donald *Wolfit's company during its *London wartime seasons. He made his reputation, however, as a farceur, performing in and *producing the series of *farces associated with the Whitehall Theatre (1950–69), notably *Reluctant Heroes* (1950), *Dry Rot* (1954), *Simple Spymen* (1958), *Chase Me Comrade* (1964), and *Uproar in the House* (1967). Himself expert in farcical timing, Rix's productions set a style of knowing, sexually based humour entirely different from the earlier *Aldwych farces by Ben *Travers of the 1920s, to which they were compared.   VEE

ROBARDS, JASON (1922–2000)

American actor. Robards's voice and bearing were distinctive and commanding; he was universally acclaimed the greatest interpreter of *O'Neill's tortured *characters. The son of an actor, he studied at the *American Academy of Dramatic Arts. After ten years as an actor and *stage manager (and a stint as a sailor), he won acclaim as Hickey in the historic *Circle in the Square revival of *The Iceman Cometh* (1956), revived on Broadway in 1985. He created the roles of Jamie in *Long Day's Journey into Night* (1956)—also playing in the *film (1962)—and Erie Smith in *Hughie* (1964). Other O'Neill roles included Jim Tyrone in *A Moon for the Misbegotten* (1973), Con Melody in *A Touch of the Poet* (1977), James Tyrone in *Long Day's Journey* (1976 and 1988), and Nat Miller in *Ah, Wilderness!* (1988). Robards also distinguished himself in *Toys in the Attic* (1960) and *After the Fall* (1964). Equally adept at *comedy, he triumphed in *A Thousand Clowns* (1962) and a revival of *You Can't Take It with You* (1983). His career of over 50 films included *Tender Is the Night* (1961), *The Hour of the Gun* (1967), *All the President's Men* (Academy award, 1976), and *Philadelphia* (1993).   TFC

ROBBINS, JEROME (1918–98)

American choreographer, director, and dancer, born Jerome Rabinowitz. Robbins was the foremost American choreographer of the mid-twentieth century, leading a two-pronged creative charge with lyricism, wit, and theatrical invention. While he infused classical *ballet with a modern American spirit, his stage choreography integrated *dance as a fully expressive element. Already performing on Broadway by 1940, Robbins made his mark as a choreographer with Leonard *Bernstein's *Fancy Free* (1944), a jazz-inflected ballet which grew into the Broadway show *On the Town*. In 1948 Robbins was invited by George *Balanchine to join the fledgling New York City Ballet, where he began choreographing in earnest, producing *L'Après-midi d'un faune* (1953), among many others. He kept pace with himself on Broadway, staging dances for several shows before directing and choreographing a string of musical classics. *West Side Story* (1957; he co-directed the film, 1962) used the discipline of classical dance as a scaffold for the expression of ethnicity, street-gang conflict, and forbidden love, using split-stage counterpoint to unprecedented effect. Following *Gypsy* (1959) and *Fiddler on the Roof* (1964), Robbins concentrated on ballet, save for a triumphant reprise of his most popular dance numbers, titled *Jerome Robbins' Broadway* (1989).   EW

ROBERTSON, T. W. (THOMAS WILLIAM) (1829–71)

English dramatist. The eldest of 22 children, Robertson was born in Newark; his father was *manager of the Lincoln circuit and one of his sisters was the actress Madge *Kendal. The Lincoln circuit collapsed in 1849, forcing Robertson to seek work in *London. A theatrical workhorse in Lincoln and London, Robertson was an actor, scene *painter, *prompter, *stage manager, songwriter, and unsuccessful author of sixteen plays before his first success, *David Garrick* (1864), at the *Haymarket. He had been making his living as a journalist writing for *Fun* and the *Illustrated Times*, to which he contributed an interesting series of articles entitled 'Theatrical Types'. In 1865 his *comedy *Society* was staged by Marie *Wilton at the *Prince of Wales's Theatre; it was followed there by *Ours* (1866), *Caste* (1867), *Play* (1868), *School* (1869), and *MP* (1870). During these years Robertson also wrote *melodramas and comedies for other theatres. The Prince of Wales's made a fortune from the enormous success of the Robertson comedies and gave a little of it back to him: he received £1 a night for *Society*, a sum which rose to £5 a night for *MP*. He was also, most unusually for the period, paid for revivals.

Robertson's themes were familiar: social ambition, class antagonism, wealth, the idealizing of young womanhood, and the faith in romantic love as the solution to all problems. Yet he went further than this, at least in technique if not in his socially conservative and rather timid subject matter. He wrote, when he wanted to, with a distinctly un-Victorian delicacy and restraint, especially in love scenes, and glorified the ordinary, the domestic, and the average. A quiet twilight scene of courtship in a West End square in *Society*, the making of a roly-poly pudding in the middle of the Crimean War in *Ours*, a tea party in *Caste* with comic business involving bread and butter and teacups (thus the term 'cup-and-saucer drama' for the plays)—all this contributed to a gentle middle-class domestic verisimilitude that *audiences found greatly appealing. With his stage experience, Robertson ensured both the accuracy and *realism of his domestic interiors and restrained playing by his actors, even of intensely emotional moments (*see* DIRECTING/DIRECTOR). The vogue for his plays abated by 1890, and after about 1910 they were rarely performed. *Caste*, however, eminently actable, is still occasionally revived; *Society* deserves to be.   MRB

ROBESON, PAUL (1898–1976)

*African-American actor, singer, athlete, and political activist. In a 1923 letter, Eugene *O'Neill described the then unknown Robeson as 'a young fellow with considerable experience, wonderful presence and voice, full of ambition and a damn fine man personally with real brains'. O'Neill cast Robeson in the title role of the *Provincetown Players' revival of *The Emperor Jones* as well as Jim Harris, an African-American lawyer who marries a white woman in *All God's Chillun Got Wings* (both 1924–5). Robeson had graduated first in his class at Rutgers University (1919), where he also played four varsity sports, was a champion debater, and was twice named a football All-American athlete. He played professional football (1920–2) while simultaneously studying law at Columbia University, receiving the LLB in 1923. Unenthusiastic about a legal career, he made his professional acting debut on Broadway in *Taboo* (1922), and scored a triumph in a 1925 concert debut as bass-baritone at *New York's Carnegie Hall, with a groundbreaking programme of spirituals and *folk songs. He would make more than 300 recordings, frequent concert *tours, and *radio broadcasts. He was particularly associated with *Kern's 'Ol' Man River', which he sang in revivals of *Show Boat* in *London (1928), New York (1932), and *Los Angeles (1940).

Robeson was among the most admired Othellos of the twentieth century, first performing opposite Peggy *Ashcroft in London (1930). He was the first African American to play the role in the United States (opposite Uta *Hagen in 1943), and repeated the role opposite Mary Ure at Stratford-upon-Avon (1959). His career on stage and *film (*The Emperor Jones*, 1933; *Show Boat*, 1936; *Song of Freedom*, 1936; *King Solomon's Mines*, 1937; *The Proud Valley*, 1940) was interrupted by anti-communist political pressures. Having performed widely in the Soviet Union and supported republican troops in Spain in 1936, Robeson denied under oath in 1946 that he was or had been a member of the Communist Party but refused to retract statements praising the USSR as a model of racial justice. He was intensely investigated and the State Department withdrew his passport in 1950. Unable to work due to blacklisting, his income fell drastically. He completed a short autobiography in 1958 (*Here I Stand*) and, his passport restored, toured the Soviet Union. He returned to the USA in 1961 in poor physical and mental health and went into seclusion until his death. (*See* illustration p. 1144.)   MAF

ROBEY, GEORGE (GEORGE WADE) (1869–1954)

English *music-hall comedian. Known as the 'Prime Minister of Mirth', Robey threw up a career in civil engineering to begin performing as an *amateur, making his professional debut in 1891. Risqué rather than vulgar, he *toured extensively throughout the British Isles and abroad, conspicuous on stage through his bowler hat, large bushy eyebrows, and short, solid figure. A great *pantomime dame, he was also renowned for his songs, delivered in 'a kind of machine-gun staccato rattle through each polysyllabic line, ending abruptly, and holding the pause, while he fixed the *audience with his basilisk stare'. Songs written for him included 'If You Were the Only Girl in the World'. In the 1930s he appeared in C. B. *Cochran's *Helen* (based on *Offenbach's *La Belle Hélène*) and *film versions of *Chu Chin Chow* and *Don Quixote*. In 1935 he played Falstaff in *Henry IV* at *Her Majesty's Theatre, later playing the dying Falstaff in *Olivier's *film of *Henry V*. Almost the last of the great music-hall comedians, he was knighted in 1954.   JTD

ROBIN HOOD PLAY

English *folk play. References to Robin Hood plays date back to the thirteenth century, and in 1473 Sir John Paston noted the loss of a servant who had performed in one. Surviving *texts are difficult to date but show the *hero flouting traditional authority, such as the Sheriff of Nottingham, and stealing from the rich to preserve a greater justice and to provide for the poor. Records indicate parish fundraising fêtes as common performance sites, and criticism has speculated about the power of the plays to express resistance against the growth of a market economy, centralized authority, and economic individualism.   JCD

ROBINS, ELIZABETH (1862–1952)

Anglo-American actress, playwright, journalist, novelist, and *feminist campaigner. Born in Kentucky, she made an acting debut late in 1881 with Junius Brutus *Booth in *New York, then *toured with James *O'Neill and H. M. Pitts, and in 1883 joined the *Boston Museum Company. Marriage early in 1885 to a fellow actor cost Robins her contract with this *stock company, and she returned to touring with O'Neill, playing Mercedes in *The Count of Monte Cristo*. In 1887 her husband drowned himself and, after another nine months touring in Shakespearian roles, Robins went abroad to recover. Taking up residence in England, she figured prominently in *London's belated reception of *Ibsen. In July 1889, a few weeks after Janet *Achurch and Charles Charrington presented *A Doll's House*, Robins played Martha Bernick in a single matinée of *The Pillars of Society*. Over the next decade she appeared in another twelve London productions of plays by Ibsen, most notably the UK premières of *Hedda Gabler* in 1891 (which Robins, who played the title role, presented in tandem with another expatriate American actress, Marion Lea) and *The Master Builder* in 1893 (as Hilde Wangel). With Florence Bell, she was anonymously responsible for *Alan's Wife*: sympathetically representing maternal infanticide as natural selection, this dramatization of a Danish short story was staged by the *Independent Theatre in 1893. After Robins retired

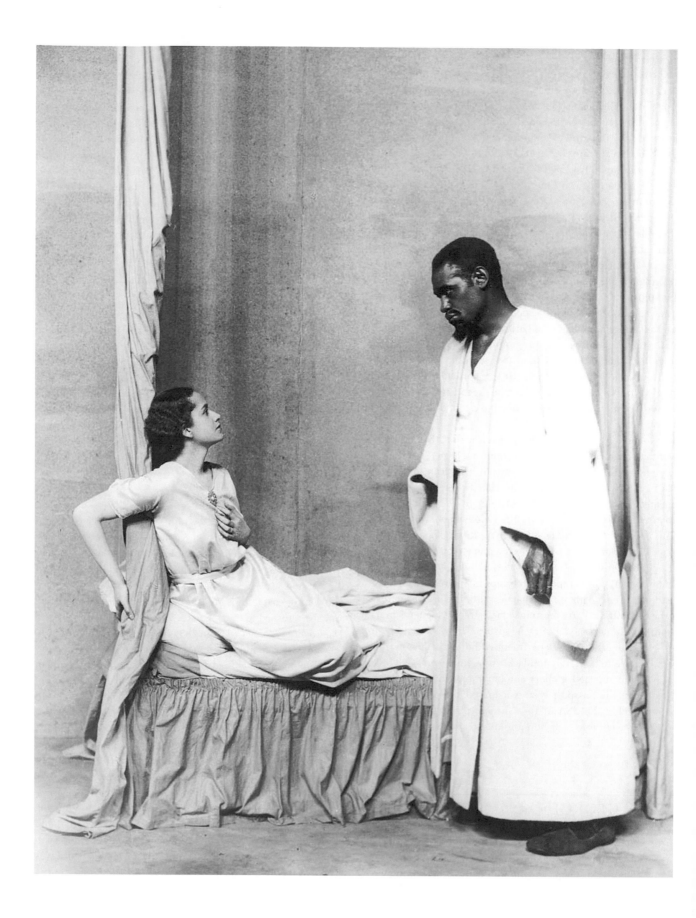

from acting in 1902 and concentrated upon writing, women's issues and feminist objectives became explicit in her work, especially in *Votes for Women*, subtitled 'a dramatic tract in three acts'. The *Vedrenne–Barker management of the *Royal Court Theatre premièred the play in 1907, and Robins recast it as a novel, *The Convert*, published the same year.　　MOC

ROBINSON, BILL ('BOJANGLES') (1878–1949)

*African-American song-and-dance man. An orphan, Bojangles danced on street corners before he was 10, and at the age of 12 joined the *vaudeville troupe headed by the Whitman sisters, in which he was billed as Master Willie Robinson. He expanded his repertory and became a big draw in nightclubs. When he was 50 he made his debut with white *audiences in Lew Leslie's *Blackbirds of 1928*, followed by a series of similar Broadway *musicals. He is best remembered for the roles he performed with Shirley Temple in a series of *films from the 1930s. An inveterate hoofer, Bojangles revolutionized tap *dancing with fast, syncopated footwork.　　BBL

ROBINSON, LENNOX (1886–1958)

Irish playwright and director. Born in Cork, he became *manager of the *Abbey Theatre at *Yeats's invitation in 1910, on the strength of his first play *The Clancy Name* (1908). Except for a few short periods, he remained at the Abbey in a number of capacities until 1956. He directed over 100 productions, among them the premières of *O'Casey's *The Shadow of a Gunman* and *The Plough and the Stars*. He earned immense public affection through his gently ironic and deftly constructed *comedies of provincial life; *The Whiteheaded Boy* (1916), *The Far-Off Hills* (1928), and *Drama at Inish* (1933) stayed in the repertory until the end of the century. Among his other plays are *The Dreamers* (1915), *The Lost Leader* (1918), *The White Blackbird* (1925), *The Big House* (1926), and *Killycreggs in Twilight* (1937). *Ibsen and *Chekhov were his masters, though *Church Street* (1934) is consciously *Pirandellan. He edited *The Irish Theatre* (1939), *Lady Gregory's Journals* (1946), and compiled *Ireland's Abbey Theatre: a History* (1951).　　CFS

ROBINSON, RICHARD (c.1600–48)

English actor. As a *boy actor with the *Queen's Men, Robinson appeared in *Fletcher's *Bonduca* (1611–14) and *Jonson's

Paul **Robeson** and Peggy Ashcroft in *Othello*, Savoy Theatre, London, 1930, directed by Ellen Van Volkenburg, designed by James Pryde. Robeson's first attempt at Shakespeare's Moor, with a cast that included Maurice Browne as Iago, Sybil Thorndike as Emilia, and Ralph Richardson as Roderigo. Thirteen years would pass before Robeson played Othello in America.

Catiline (1611). In *The Devil Is an Ass* (1616), Jonson has a *character praise 'Dick Robinson' as an impersonator of women. After the death of Richard *Burbage in 1619, Robinson, who may have been his apprentice, married Burbage's widow, became a sharer in the company, and ceased acting. Robinson has sometimes been confused with William Robbins (or Robinson), who acted in the 1630s with Queen Henrietta's Men, but did not join the King's company until c.1636.　　RWV

ROBSON, FLORA (1902–84)

English actress. After *training at the *Royal Academy of Dramatic Art, Robson's early opportunities were scarce, with only brief assignments in the 1920s. For four years she worked in a factory to pay the bills, but by the early 1930s she had appeared in *London in plays by *O'Neill, *Pirandello, *Wilde, *Maugham, and Shakespeare, establishing herself as a powerful actress who could both suggest and tap great depths of feeling. In 1933 she joined the *Old Vic–*Sadler's Wells company, taking on more Shakespeare as well as *Chekhov, Wilde, and *Congreve. She played in both London and *New York during the 1940s. By the 1950s her career was well established, with major critical successes in *Gielgud's production of *The Winter's Tale* and Michael *Redgrave's adaptation of *James's *The Aspern Papers*. She also appeared in *Ibsen's *Ghosts* and *John Gabriel Borkman*, and Wilde's *The Importance of Being Earnest*. Toward the end of her career she did some *touring, from *Edinburgh to South Africa. From the mid-1930s she acted regularly in *film, but never achieved the same level of success she attained on stage. She was made DBE in 1960.　　TP

ROBSON, FREDERICK (1821–64)

English actor and *manager. Robson began his career singing comic songs in *London's East End, then moved west in 1850 to act in extravaganza and *burlesque at the *Olympic, where he became co-manager with William Farren. Robson was very short and possessed the capacity to blend the ridiculousness of burlesque with *tragedy. J. R. *Planché, who wrote the *character of the Dwarf for him in *The Yellow Dwarf* (1854), said that his impersonation of the cunning, malignity, passion, and despair of the monster was so powerful that it elevated extravaganza into tragedy. Another *tour de force* was Medea in Robert Brough's burlesque *Medea* (1856). Again Robson's portrayal of grief, rage, and despair in the supposedly light-hearted doggerel *verse of burlesque was extraordinary. He played Shylock and Macbeth in burlesques with similar strength, a strength he carried over to parts written for him in *comedy and *drama which elicited his great powers of pathos and anguish. All he lacked to be a great tragic actor, his contemporaries believed, was height.　　MRB

ROBSON, STUART (1836–1903)

American actor. Born in Annapolis, as Henry Robson Stuart, he made his stage debut in Baltimore in 1852. His first *New York vehicle was *Old Heads and Young Hearts* (1862). His squeaky voice and teetering walk destined him for comic roles, especially Irish policemen. He played for three years in *Philadelphia, three in *Boston, and then three in New York before appearing in several *London productions. Back home, he teamed with William H. *Crane in *Our Boarding House* (1877). The popular pair stayed together for a dozen years—in *Our Bachelors* (1878), *The Comedy of Errors* (1878, revived 1885), *Sharps and Flats* (1880), and most notably in Bronson *Howard's *The Henrietta* (1887), written specifically for them. After an amicable parting, Robson's assignments included *An Arrant Knave* (1889), *She Stoops to Conquer* (1893), *The Meddler* (1898), and a serious drama, *The Gadfly* (1899).   CT

ROCADO ZULU THEATRE

Founded in Brazzaville in Zaire in 1980 by Sony *Labou Tansi, Nicolas Bissi, and Marie-Léontine Tsibanda, its productions included *collective creations in which a *plot was constructed around a myth, a legend, or a scene of daily life. In 1981 it staged Aimé *Césaire's *La Tragédie du roi Christophe* (*The Tragedy of King Christophe*) and its *film and stage adaptations of stories by the Congolese writer Henri Lopes became popular *television shows. It brought *La Rue des mouches* (*Street of Flies*) to the *Limoges Festival in 1981 and subsequently produced *Antoine m'a vendu son destin* (*Antoine Sold Me his Destiny*), directed by Sony and Daniel *Mesguich. The high point of the troupe occurred in 1987 with *Moi, veuve de l'empire* (*I Am the Widow of the Empire*), after which most of its members left.

PNN trans. JCM

RODGERS, RICHARD (1902–79)

American composer. With the librettists Lorenz *Hart and Oscar *Hammerstein II, Rodgers wrote some of the most beloved *musicals in the canon. All together he wrote more than 900 published songs and 40 Broadway musicals. Rodgers was born in *New York and studied at Columbia University, but left before graduating to devote himself to composing. After several *amateur shows with Hart, the pair had their first professional success with *The Garrick Gaieties* in 1925, which featured the groundbreaking jazz *ballet 'Slaughter on 10th Avenue', choreographed by George *Balanchine. Rodgers and Hart worked in Hollywood from 1931–5 and wrote scores for a number of *films. From 1936 to Hart's death in 1943, the duo created a number of well-received Broadway musical comedies including *Babes in Arms* (1937), *The Boys from Syracuse* (1938), and *Pal Joey* (1940). Rodgers and Hammerstein's first collaboration was to change the face of American theatre. *Oklahoma!* (1943), based on Lynn Riggs's play *Green Grow the Lilacs*, ran on Broadway for a record 2,248 performances. The musical revolutionized the form through its emphasis on *plot and *character; before that time musicals tended to string songs together and emphasize entertainment over content. The production was also praised for the seamless integration of Agnes *de Mille's *dances into the story. Other successes in Rodgers and Hammerstein's seventeen-year collaboration were *Carousel* (1945), *South Pacific* (1949), *The King and I* (1951), and *The Sound of Music* (1959). Collectively their musicals earned 34 Tony *awards, fifteen Academy awards, two Pulitzer Prizes, two Grammy awards, and two Emmy awards. After Hammerstein's death in 1960, Rodgers wrote for Broadway, *television, and film. In 1990 the 46th Street Theatre was renamed in his honour.   KF

RODRIGUES, NELSON (1912–80)

Brazilian playwright, internationally known for lacerating studies of lower-middle-class suburban life in *Rio. Rodrigues sought what he called 'an aggressive moralism'; his plays intended to 'transform a simple kiss into an act of eternal degradation', and 'cause typhus and malaria in the public'. Also author of a newspaper column, chronicles of everyday life (in which the absurd and outrageous mesh with the banal), and of pornographic novels under a pseudonym, among his favourite themes were incest, poverty and corruption, soccer and suburban politics, violence, and social and sexual prejudice. Rodrigues's complicated work, often written with a strangely chaste and economic *dialogue, has inspired innovative and varied interpretations on stage, such as Zbigniew Ziembinski's *expressionist production of *Vestido de noiva* (*The Wedding Dress*, 1943), José *Antunes Filho's mythopoetic cycle *Nelson Rodrigues: the eternal return* (1981), *TAPA's social analogies (*The Wedding Dress*, 1994; *The Serpent*, 2000), and José Celso Martinez *Corrêa's sexually explicit and scatological treatment of *Boca de ouro* (*Teeth Made of Gold*, 1999).   LHD

RODRÍGUEZ, JESUSA (1955–)

Mexican director, actor, *performance artist, and *producer. Rodríguez gained international attention with her iconoclastic production of *Donna Giovanna* (1983, with her partner Lilian Felipe and the Grupo Divas), a liberal adaptation of *Mozart's *opera in which roles were played by women whose nudity was meant to deconstruct the traditional discourse of the Don Juan figure. Among her full-length productions are an adaptation of Panizza's *Council of Love* (1988), her original *Yourcenar; or, Marguerite* (1989), *Ambrosio the Monk; or, The Fable of Love* (1990), a three-act opera adapted from Matthew G. *Lewis's Gothic novel *The Monk*, and *The Sky of Below* (1993), a postmodern take on the sacred book of the Maya, the *Popol Vuh*. She is best known for *political sketches that have attracted *audiences from around the world to her *cabaret/bar El Hábito and small chapel/theatre, La Capilla. In these she casts her *satirical net wide to include corrupt politicians, the church hierarchy, machismo, globalization, NAFTA, abortion, and any other current topic that is ripe for debunking.　　KFN

RODWAY, NORMAN (1929–2001)

London-born actor who was brought up in Dublin. After studying classics at Trinity College, Dublin, he taught, and began his career as an *amateur actor. From 1953 he was associated with Globe Theatre, a *Dublin company he ran for some eight years. In *London in 1963 he appeared in one of his celebrated early roles, the title *character in *Stephen D*, an adaptation of James Joyce's *Portrait of the Artist as a Young Man*. From 1966 he was a regular member of the *Royal Shakespeare Company, appearing with the *National Theatre later in his career: he was in Peter *Hall's première of *Pinter's *Silence* (1969); took the title role in Terry *Hands's production of *Richard III* (1970), playing the king as albino blond, heavily hunchbacked, and racked by pain but taut, energetic, obsessed, and mad; and appeared in John *Caird's production of *The Seagull* (1994). Numerous *film roles include Hotspur in Orson *Welles's *Chimes at Midnight* (1966), and *The Empty Mirror* (1999), where he played a Hitler who had survived the war, now ageing and imprisoned. Rodway was also a celebrated *radio actor.　　AS

ROEPKE, GABRIELA (1920–)

Chilean playwright and actress. Most of her output consists of *one-act plays of a psychological nature. She helped to create the Theatre School of the Catholic University of Chile where she has been an actress and teacher. Her most accomplished work is *Una mariposa blanca* (*A White Butterfly*, 1957).　　MAR

ROGERS, WILL (1879–1935)

American humorist and actor. A cowboy from Oklahoma, Rogers entered show business in 1904 as 'lasso-artist' in a *Wild West show. In a 1905 performance at *New York's Madison Square Garden, Rogers was asked to introduce his special trick of simultaneously roping a horse and its rider with two separate ropes. His honesty and charm were immediately apparent when he said in his Oklahoma drawl, 'A rope ain't bad to get tangled up in, if it ain't around your neck.' *Audiences warmed to him at once and he became a *vaudeville headliner for whom the rope tricks were incidental to the real show—his homespun, self-mocking, and hilarious philosophic *monologues. By 1921 he was *touring in a *Shubert *revue at $3,000 per week. Rogers starred in five issues of the *Ziegfeld Follies between 1915 and 1924, but reached larger audiences with his humour column

(1922–35) and *films (24 between 1919 and 1935). He played the father in *O'Neill's *Ah, Wilderness!* in 1934. He was lost in a plane over Alaska.　　MAF

ROJAS, FERNANDO DE (c.1465–c.1541)

Spanish dramatist. Born into a family of *conversos* and possibly under perpetual suspicion for his 'contaminated' Jewish origins, he is credited with the authorship of the vastly influential *La Celestina*, which remains his only literary testament. This 21-act *tragicomedy on the doomed amour of Calixto and Melibea and their go-between or (*celestina*) builds on the classical comic tradition but goes beyond it in both its unforgiving moral resolution and its pithy *dialogue, ranging from the urbane, sophisticated language of court to the downright bawdy. Though probably not intended for the stage and not performed during Rojas's lifetime, *La Celestina* has since been translated and staged in a variety of languages and was the inspiration for *Calisto and Melibea*, the *interlude by the Englishman John *Rastell. The superabundance of dialogue and the absence of explicit *action does not detract from the play's often frenetic pace and cinematic ending, with the accidental fall of Calixto and the suicidal leap of Melibea. In 1994 the play was adapted for *film by Spanish director Gerardo Vega.　　KG

ROJAS ZORRILLA, FRANCISCO DE (1607–48)

Spanish dramatist. Active mainly in the 1630s, he sought to astonish his *audience by presenting unconventional *characters in extraordinary situations. His plays divide, unusually clearly, into *tragedies and *comedies. The former, centred on *revenge and often on classical subjects, were traditionally regarded as the more characteristic, and *Del rey abajo, ninguno* (*No One Lower than the King*), whose *hero believes himself dishonoured by his monarch, enjoyed lasting popularity. He is more admired today, however, for his lighter, *satirical works, like *Entre bobos anda el juego* (*It's a Fool's Game*), an excellent early example of the *comedia de figurón*.　　VFD

ROLLAND, ROMAIN (1866–1944)

French novelist, essayist, and playwright, considered one of the most influential populist intellectuals in France between the two wars. In an age of fervent nationalism, Rolland placed his faith in pacifism and communism, and railed against the elitism of the artistic establishment. With his 1903 essay *Le Théâtre du peuple* (*Theatre of the People*), he emerged as one of the first vocal proponents of the 'théâtre populaire'. His major work for the stage was the monumental *Théâtre de la Révolution*, comprising eight separate plays written between 1898 and 1938. They include *Les Loups* (*The Wolves*, 1898), inspired by the Dreyfus case; *Danton* (1900); and *Le Quatorze juillet* (*The Fourteenth of July*, 1902). His other plays include *Le Temps viendra* (*The Time Will Come*, 1902), a condemnation of imperialism and colonial genocide; and *Liluli* (1919), a biting critique of capitalism. Rolland received the Nobel Prize for Literature in 1915.   CHB

ROLLER, ALFRED (1864–1935)

Austrian painter, architect, and designer. A founding member of the *Vienna Secession, as a set designer he developed the ideas of *Appia and *Craig. In 1903 Gustav Mahler engaged him for the Vienna Court Opera. From 1909 onward he worked with Max *Reinhardt, designing *Goethe's *Faust I and II* (1909, 1911), the première of *Strauss's *Der Rosenkavalier* (1911), *Sophocles' *Oedipus the King* (1910), *Aeschylus' *Oresteia* (1911), and the première of *Hofmannsthal's *Jedermann* (*Everyman*, 1911). In 1920 Roller became a board member of the *Salzburg Festival where he created the famous platform before the cathedral for *Everyman* (1920) and constructed a medieval stage in a church for Hofmannsthal's *The Great Theatre of the World* (1922). Roller was noted for his ability to create simultaneous playing spaces. Best known are the 'Roller Türme', three mobile corner towers which replaced the fixed *proscenium in order to change the look of the scenic space.   CBB

ROMAGNESI, MARC'ANTONIO (1633–1706)

Italian actor who made his career in France. First heard of in Mantua in 1655, he moved to *Paris around 1667, and became one of the most celebrated members of the 'first' *Comédie Italienne, playing lovers' parts (using the name Cintio) until 1694, then switching to the mask of the Dottore. An irascible man, he was involved in documented public quarrels with his colleagues. He retired after the expulsion of the Italian players in 1697.   RAA

ROMAINS, JULES (1885–1972)

French poet, novelist, and dramatist whose plays were huge popular triumphs in the 1920s. His most enduring success was *Knock; or, The Triumph of Medicine*, produced by Louis *Jouvet at the Comédie des Champs-Élysées in 1923, which was much revived and *toured. Jouvet himself played the lead in this *satirical *comedy of trickery and gullibility. Other notable plays feature an eponymous pompous professor in *Monsieur Le Trouhadec saisi par la débauche* (1923) and *Le Mariage de Monsieur Le Trouhadec* (1925), both directed by Jouvet. Earlier his play *Old Crommrdeyre* was directed by *Copeau in his relaunched Théâtre du *Vieux-Colombier, and Romains reworked Stefan *Zweig's adaptation of Ben *Jonson's *Volpone*, creating

one of Charles *Dullin's greatest successes in 1929. He was elected to the Académie Française in 1946 after self-imposed exile in the USA during the Second World War, after which his creative energies were directed to politics.   BRS

ROMANCE

By the fifteenth century, English drama had appropriated the popular literary *genre of chivalric romance as a source of narrative material. The *action of such plays is rarely confined to a single location: rather they are loosely structured around travel through an exotic landscape, often pseudo-classical or pseudo-Mediterranean; sometimes the chronological limits are similarly wide, with generations passing in the space of the performance. The story often deals with a heroic knight's adventures, fighting giants and monsters, encountering enchanters, and rescuing damsels in distress; there is a premium on valiant deeds and the honourable treatment of women. Events develop towards the reunion of separated lovers or families, frequently effected by distinctive *props which enable them to recognize one another after long, transforming absence. The lack of geographical or historical authenticity is to the point: the genre appeals to notions of a past that is better and more exciting than the *audience's daily lives, but avoids asserting its literal truth. There are records of dramatic romances being performed in England from 1444 until the middle of the seventeenth century, and they were especially popular during the 1570s and 1580s, but relatively few *texts survive. Much of the genre's knowable history perforce concerns its impact on other types of drama rather than its development in its own right. It was familiar coin by the 1540s, when John Redford cast one of the earliest secular *morality plays, *Wit and Science*, in the form of a chivalric quest. Later in the century, romance in turn assimilated elements from the morality tradition, notably the use of *allegorical shorthand and the *character of the Vice.

Perhaps the most startling appropriation came in 1587, towards the end of romance's vogue, when its emphasis on travel, military adventure, and winning the love of a fair lady became part of the deep structure of *Marlowe's *Tamburlaine the Great*. The *tragedy's disruption of the familiar structures of rank, by elevating a shepherd to royal status, also affected romance proper, which typically concerns itself primarily with aristocratic characters, who may temporarily assume a meaner status but are always restored to their birthright; the symbolic aspects of high rank make knights and princes figures with whom anyone can identify. From the 1590s, however, *London audiences were shown the exploits of demotic characters, while more traditional romances, such as *Mucedorus* (*c*.1591), actively demonized social climbers as upstart *villains. The trend for heroic apprentices was later *satirized in *Beaumont's *The Knight of the Burning Pestle* (1607). Never entirely missing from the repertory, romances again became fashionable around 1609, a development reflected in the late plays of Shakespeare and the *tragicomedies of Beaumont and *Fletcher. In part this was driven by a self-consciously sophisticated nostalgia for bygone dramatic modes: old plays were successfully revived, notably *Mucedorus*, and new ones presented themselves as if they were antiquated 'winter's tales'. But another factor was growing official disapproval of the stage's engagement in matters of state: hard political points were more acceptably made on the seacoast of Bohemia than nearer home.   MJW

ROMAN THEATRE

A great variety of theatrical activity flourished at Rome from at least the fourth century BC to the end of the sixth century AD. The occasion, content, and manner of theatrical presentation varied enormously over this vast period of time, and discerning the evolution and nature of such activity is difficult, requiring a good deal of guess work and generalization. By convention, and for convenience, the history of Roman theatre can be divided into the republican period (lasting until the mid-first century BC), and the imperial period, which continued to the end of antiquity.

1. The republican period; 2. The imperial period

1. The republican period

During the republican period, ample opportunity existed for Romans to participate in a variety of public theatrical entertainments. Most of these were centred on the formal religious festivals and the public games (*ludi*) that marked them. By the mid-fourth century stage shows (*ludi scaenici*) had been introduced (initially at the Ludi Romani), and occasions for these at annual official games multiplied to amount to perhaps some 60 or 70 days of performances each year by the middle of the first century BC. In addition to these formal state holidays, it was also the practice for victorious Roman generals to dedicate games, and for noble families to stage funeral games to honour their deceased relatives.

The provision and management of the official state games was the responsibility of the elected magistrates, most commonly the aediles, although other officials also occasionally acted as patrons. In the beginning, the Senate voted a fixed sum for use by the appropriate official for particular holidays, but by the second century BC the individual had considerable latitude, leading to a situation in which, to ensure splendour and win popularity, the magistrate supplemented the state funds with his own wealth, to promote a successful political career. By the late republic, this factor had become an indispensable instrument for political advancement.

Admission to the games was probably open to all: citizens and slaves, men, women, and foreigners. The diversity of the *audience was reflected by the variety of theatrical entertainments offered it. Both the evolution and nature of these is difficult to trace in detail. Traditionally, theatrical performance was said to have been introduced by Etruscan performers invited to appear at Rome in 363 BC, in the hope of propitiating the gods during a pestilence. These imported scenic performances seem subsequently to have been combined with certain native Roman ribald satiric entertainments, the 'fescennine verses' into what might be thought of as medleys of music, *dance, jokes, *improvisation; a sort of *variety show, which the Romans termed *satura*. In addition, it seems likely that early unscripted drama at Rome was probably influenced by performances taking place in the areas south of Rome settled by the Greeks, who built numerous theatres in southern Italy and Sicily (*see* GREEK THEATRE, ANCIENT). The presentation of the first scripted drama at Rome was said to have been the work of a former Greek slave, Livius *Andronicus, who migrated to Rome, and in 240 BC staged there his translation of a Greek play at the Ludi Romani.

Judging from the titles of his plays, Andronicus (who presented both *tragedies and *comedies) created Latin versions of original Greek works refashioned to entertain a relatively unsophisticated audience. He enjoyed great success, and by the end of the third century he and his acting and playwriting colleagues were allowed to form a professional *Collegium*, an indication of the popularity and importance which dramatic art had attained. There were good political reasons for granting such formal recognition to the profession. The Roman authorities had recognized the importance of maintaining civic morale during the dark days of the second Punic War (218–201 BC), and had established additional games to satisfy the popular demand for more numerous and spectacular entertainments. These games enjoyed a particular status by virtue of their religious basis, but at the same time their content and performance were severely circumscribed and subject to tight control, exercised over them by the Roman aristocracy. This tended, it seems, more towards the restriction of any potentially subversive political or social content, while considerable latitude was allowed for ribaldry, and sexual jesting (*see* CENSORSHIP).

In the case of comedy, because the Roman playwrights based their *plots on Greek works of *New Comedy, and these were notionally set in Greece, the Roman audience could enjoy watching the 'foreign' *characters' scandalous or ridiculous behaviour without any directly implied criticism of Roman customs or values. Nevertheless the early comic authors, *Plautus, *Terence, and *Naevius, faced the challenge of having to entertain a demanding popular audience whose prior experience of theatre was conditioned by *satire and ribald abuse and who would have been quick to pick up (or even misconstrue) political references, while simultaneously avoiding giving offence to religious or political interests. Moreover, the playwrights faced the need to balance native and Greek traditions in composing new works or translating old ones.

Writers of tragedy, including Ennius, *Pacuvius, and *Accius, also based their works upon Greek models, although because of the absence of any complete surviving example of republican tragedy it is difficult to determine with any precision the relationship, and in particular, whether such adaptations or imitations were for the most part based upon the 'greats' of the classical Greek tragic theatre, *Aeschylus, *Sophocles, and *Euripides, or may have looked to contemporaneous Hellenistic tragedians for their inspiration and guidance. The evidence of titles and a few scraps of *text suggests that the playwrights (and their audience) tended to favour flamboyant emotion, *spectacle, violence, and rhetorical display in tragic fare.

The composition of both comedy and tragedy appears to have diminished and eventually virtually died out by the mid-first century BC, although revivals of earlier works continued to appear on the stage. But this dearth of new writing does not appear to reflect a commensurate decline in theatrical performance. Alongside comedy and tragedy other *genres had appeared, and older ones continued and grew in popularity. The venerable *Atellan farces that had preceded Roman scripted comedy continued to hold the stage. Prior to the construction of a permanent and enclosed theatre (55 BC), spectators could freely move from one attraction to another at holiday entertainments, and the short sketches comprising such *farces may have had better success in holding their attention than did the development and nuanced meaning of a longer and complex plot. By the mid-first century BC, the Atellan farces had acquired literary form, and were widely performed in Latin, although at least occasionally still presented in the original Oscan language as well.

Long before the introduction of scripted comedy, Romans were probably familiar with the *mime, which had originated in Greece and been imported into southern Italy by Greek colonists. Initially it was not even essentially dramatic: *acrobatics, song and dance, jokes, conjuring—every type of broad entertainment in fact—were grafted onto the flimsiest of impromptu *scenarios to create a kind of variety show. The mime may have influenced early Roman comedy; in any case, from at least the early second century BC, it was formally incorporated into the Roman holiday calendar, and was the chief ornament of the Floralia festival whose festivities were noted for their licence and merriment, and, in particular, for naked female performers. One of the reasons for the great popularity of the mime was that it could be presented at any time on its own, as an interlude or afterpiece with other drama, or in conjunction with any other form of public or private entertainment. It lasted to the end of antiquity and beyond; undoubtedly owing its popularity and longevity to its adaptability and minimal staging requirements.

During the first few centuries of Roman theatrical practice, no permanent theatres were constructed. From the introduction of drama at Rome until more than a century after the death of Plautus, all theatres at Rome were temporary structures, built for particular occasions and then dismantled. Such wooden *stages were erected in the city frequently during the period, and continued to be built in the imperial period as well. Because these early stages shaped Roman drama, including the surviving plays of Plautus and Terence, it is possible in turn to determine a good deal about their nature by identifying the elements necessary to stage such plays. They were performed upon a raised wooden stage. The scene building, called the *scaena*, backed this. The front façade of this building, facing onto the stage, had three openings that could be fitted with serviceable, possibly folding, doors. In addition, entrance onto the stage was afforded from either side, and used by characters when they referred to coming or going to offstage areas (the harbour, the forum) other than through the doors. The area in front of the three doors was thought of, conventionally, as an open street. The doorways (which sometimes had a small raised porch, the *vestibulum*, attached to them) functioned as entrances to houses thought of as located along the street. In addition, the plots of the plays frequently make use of a passageway conceived as being behind the houses, which appears to have been thought of as an open area affording access to the rear of the houses (or to the gardens, often referred to as behind them).

From literary sources we know that from the beginning of the second century BC these temporary stages and the performances taking place upon them were increasing lavish—sometimes astonishingly so. In addition to a variety of theatrical genres and the use of many *costumed performers, attention was focused on the embellishment and scenic requisites of the temporary theatre structures themselves. The officials sponsoring the games commissioned elaborate, multi-storeyed and multicoloured structures, decorated with *perspective painting, *skenographia*, and every sort of architectural embellishment, hoping that their popularity and future electoral success might benefit from such ostentatious munificence. This was an important defining aspect of theatrical activity at Rome. Elaborate public entertainments simultaneously validated personal power, while contributing to the public's sense of being paid the honour and enjoying the splendour that was its due. Thus the bestowal and reception of theatrical presentations was viewed as an exchange of gifts that established a socially significant transaction between both parties, as patron and client. After the end of the republic, similar factors conditioned the relationship between the Emperor and the Roman people.

2. The imperial period

The construction of the first permanent theatre at Rome by the victorious general Pompey the Great in 55 BC represented an extension of this concept. The attraction of such an edifice to Pompey was its provision of a convenient site where he and later politicians and rulers could appear before a huge crowd to display and validate the popular basis for their authority. Pompey's theatre (which served as architectural prototype for numerous theatres subsequently constructed throughout the Roman Empire) may have held as many as 20,000 spectators. With a stage almost 90 m (300 feet) in width, it was probably the largest of all Roman theatres, and also one of the most sumptuous. The three-storey façade of its scene building (the *scaenae frons*) was adorned with stone and stucco and embellished with fine decorative detail, and numerous statues. The *auditorium (cavea)* was covered with a huge coloured linen awning (the *vela*), attached to masts located around the perimeter wall, to shade the spectators from the sun. The most striking element in Pompey's edifice was a temple to Venus Victrix at the top and rear of the auditorium, directly opposite the stage. It was said that when Pompey's political rivals objected to a permanent theatre, he claimed that he was merely building a temple beneath which steps (the semicircular rows of seating) would be provided for watching the games honouring the gods. For six centuries this splendid theatre was one of Rome's foremost cultural and political monuments; complemented but never surpassed in importance by two subsequent theatres, those of Balbus (13 BC) and of Marcellus (11 BC). *See* ANCIENT THEATRES.

Under the emperors, presentations in the theatre (together with those in the Circus Maximus and Colosseum; *see* CIRCUS, ROMAN) were of major political significance, since they provided one of the few occasions in which the rulers and the people could see and communicate directly, through proclamations by the former, and acclamations (or occasionally chanted expressions of discontent) and petitions from the latter. Not just at Rome, but throughout the empire, the emperor was responsible for the provision of municipal buildings, and reserved for himself the right to sponsor public entertainments. By the end of the first century AD, often even the smallest towns had acquired a theatre. The theatres and performances were symbolic of Roman prestige and imperial glory. Inside the theatres the population was presented with dazzling spectacles calculated to impress and to cast reflected glory upon the rulers or their local representatives. The games increased in frequency and splendour; at Rome the emperor and his people might spend as much as a third of the year together at shows.

By the end of the first century BC, the composition of new plays for the theatre had virtually ceased, as alternative forms of scenic entertainments gradually displaced scripted comedy and tragedy. Theatrical activity, however, thrived and steadily increased in popularity and importance. In addition to revivals of old plays, and the perennially popular mime, in the early imperial period the new art of *pantomime appeared (often in spectacular and lavish stagings), and performances of it rapidly spread throughout the empire, attracting huge, partisan, and enthusiastic audiences. Pantomime was presented by a single non-speaking actor (accompanied by a *chorus and musicians) who enacted an entire plot, drawn from mythology or earlier dramatic compositions, performing all the roles himself and seeking to represent characterization, emotion, and narrative entirely through the movements and gestures of his body. Despite the skill and sophistication demanded of such performers (many of whom acquired star status) they were, like all Roman actors, officially considered disreputable, subject to severe legal restrictions, denied Roman citizenship, and from time to time banned altogether because of the scandals and frequent public disorders associated with their behaviour. Nevertheless, pantomime held the stage until the end of antiquity, its character and the responses to it displaying remarkable continuity.

The fact that a number of emperors, notably Caligula and Nero, were avid and ostentatiously generous supporters of scenic presentations (which increasingly encompassed spectacles like *gladiatorial contests, *animal fights, *damnatio, and *naumachia enacted in the arena) did not enable the theatre to overcome the residual antipathy felt towards it by Roman moralists, whose traditional hostility was joined by the opprobrium of the emergent Christian Church. For Christian leaders the games themselves were an affront and an annoyance, and morally repugnant; the pagan religion, however (of which, from earliest times, the theatre was an expression), was a present danger to the very survival of the Church. Christians were urged to avoid the games, and during the last centuries of the Roman Empire in the West, as Christian influence and political power grew, theatrical performance was increasingly subjected to various regulations, restrictions, and at different times and places outright prohibition. Although placed under pressure by the systematic suppression of paganism, throughout the fourth and fifth centuries AD the spectacles continued, their variety and scale still impressive. Despite the ascendancy of the new religion and increasingly massive social and political disruption throughout the empire, at the end of antiquity we can discern the same mixture of sophistication and vulgarity, the same conjunction of diverse entertainments, that were first evident in Roman theatrical practice seven centuries before.

Eventually the combination of Christian antipathy, social disruption, economic crisis, and political disintegration destroyed the infrastructure that had enabled the games and the spectacles performed at them to continue. The last recorded scenic entertainments at Rome were given in 549, and the formal presentation of theatre at Rome appears to have ceased within a few decades. In the *Byzantine Empire some vestige of the traditional games continued, but in general official theatrical activity, including the mimes and pantomimes, appears to have withered, and was officially banned by the Trullan Council in 692. Yet the legacy of the Roman theatre is immense. Although, as in so many areas, the heritage of the Greeks has tended to overshadow—at least in the popular conception of things—that of the Romans, in fact the modern theatre as formulated and practised since the *early modern period owes far more in virtually all its manifestations to Roman custom and achievement than to Greek. Our critical *theory, our *drama, and our *playhouses are hugely in its debt.   RCB

BEACHAM, R. C., *The Roman Theatre and its Audience* (Cambridge, Mass., 1992)

—— *Spectacle Entertainments of Early Imperial Rome* (New Haven, 1999)

BEARE, W., *The Roman Stage*, 3rd edn. (London, 1968)

ROMAN PLAYHOUSES *See* ANCIENT THEATRES.

ROMANTICISM

A movement that transformed the arts, literature, and intellectual culture of Europe and America at the end of the eighteenth and beginning of the nineteenth centuries. A highly complex phenomenon, romanticism articulated the ideals and aspirations of radical forces that had been unleashed by the French Revolution. In its early phases, romantic culture was optimistic, reflecting confidence that the utopia sought for by revolution was achievable; in its latter phases, especially after the fall of Napoleon in 1815, romanticism was marked by deep pessimism as reactionary governments were installed throughout Europe. Romantic art has many characteristics, among them the prizing of subjective vision above objectively verifiable truths; the elevation of feeling above reason, in particular the emotions aroused by romantic love; the worship of nature as the proper environment for human life; and the understanding of the individual human soul as the site of universal conflicts.

Although ultimately the theatre was as altered by romanticism as were the other arts, the process of change took much longer. There were several reasons for this. Technically, in all aspects of performance and production, the theatre of the late eighteenth century was not capable of representing adequately the romantic vision. It was also ill-prepared as an institution. Until the latter part of the nineteenth century, both commercial and state-sponsored theatre in Europe and America largely sustained the ideology of the Enlightenment that insisted theatre promote and preserve social harmony. Consequently it is impossible to identify in theatre a coherent romantic movement. Nevertheless, from the earliest days theatre did respond to different aspects of the movement, so that in the course of the nineteenth century the romantic transformation took place piecemeal.

In playwriting, the romantic impetus was first apparent in the work of the German *Sturm und Drang (1770–84). Inspired by *Rousseau's natural philosophy, Gothic literature, and Enlightenment humanism, the drama of *Sturm und Drang* set forth themes of social and familial alienation and was often centred around *characters who experience severe mental conflict. The episodic structure of these plays owed much to Shakespeare and decisively rejected the *neoclassicism of Enlightenment drama. Few *Sturm und Drang* plays were performed, however, and when they were it was in versions adapted to the conventions of the theatre. Both *Goethe and

*Schiller began in *Sturm und Drang*, with *Götz von Berlichingen* (*Berlin, 1774) and *The Robbers* (Mannheim, 1782) respectively, but much of their mature drama, performed at the *Weimar Court Theatre, represents a culmination of Enlightenment theatre rather than an embodiment of romanticism (*see* WEIMAR CLASSICISM). At best, Schiller's *William Tell* (Weimar, 1804), with its romantic setting in the Swiss Alps, can be regarded as a play *about* a romantic personality and different modes of romantic experience; it does not use the stage to materialize the subjective romantic experience. The one play of Goethe's that does, *Faust I* (Brunswick, 1829), was considered by its author to be unsuitable for theatrical representation, and, when it was staged, the most unconventional, romantic aspects of the work, in particular everything to do with witchcraft, were cut.

Romantic poets throughout Europe aspired to write drama that would incorporate subjectivism on stage, but their works remained stubbornly *closet drama. Some achieved a minor success: Coleridge's *Remorse* (1813) had a surprising run at *Drury Lane, *Byron wrote several plays, some of which—*Marino Faliero, Werner, Manfred*, and *Sardanapalus*—were successful when revived by *Macready and Charles *Kean, and Ludwig *Tieck's *Bluebeard* was produced in Düsseldorf in 1835. But most of the romantic poets' works never saw the stage and only a few have been revived in the modern era, never with lasting success. In the German-speaking theatre, only the Viennese playwright Ferdinand *Raimund successfully achieved a sustained romantic ambience in his attractive fairy plays, *The Alpine King and the Misanthrope* (*Vienna, 1828) and *The Spendthrift* (1834). There was, however, one extended period of romantic playwriting in *Paris, in the liberal environment following the Revolution of 1830. Under the leadership of Victor *Hugo and Alexandre *Dumas *père*, for a little more than a decade the Parisian theatre staged a series of plays that flouted the neoclassical *unities that had traditionally moulded French drama by setting their frequently violent and irregular *actions in the colourful ambience of the Middle Ages and Renaissance. Hugo's *Hernani* was a *succès de scandale* when it was staged at that bastion of neoclassicism the *Comédie-Française in 1830 (*see* HERNANI RIOTS); his later successes, in particular *Lucrèce Borgia* (1833) and *Ruy Blas* (1838), were staged in commercial theatres devoted mainly to *melodrama. A strong case can be made for the ubiquitous *genre of melodrama as the one abiding response of the popular theatre to romanticism. While melodrama retained the ethos of eighteenth-century sentimentalism, its Gothic landscapes and the tendency to focus the conflict of the action within the souls of either the *hero or the *villain show the distinct influence of romantic culture.

The immediate impact of any performance is substantially dependent on the *actor. At the turn of the century, the most admired style of acting was that practised in England by John Philip *Kemble and Sarah *Siddons or in Germany by Pius Alexander *Wolff and August Wilhelm *Iffland, which presented elevated or idealized characters, reminiscent of the Enlightenment theatre. However, in the first decades of the nineteenth century, some actors came to the fore who powerfully represented the agony of the romantic hero, most frequently in the drama of the past, especially Shakespeare. Notable in this regard was the German Ludwig *Devrient, who uncannily brought to life the unconscious of his characters, the English Edmund *Kean, who raised melodramatic acting to a sensational tragic level, and the American Edwin *Forrest, who strove to corporealize the idea of America as a land of untrammelled nature. The impact of the romantic actor was ephemeral, however, as romantic acting is inimitable and can never be developed into a tangible discipline, the principles of which can be handed down from generation to generation.

By their very nature, *scenography and *costuming responded more immediately to romanticism. They readily accommodated demands for historically accurate environments with an abundance of local and period colour (see ANTIQUARIANISM), and had no difficulty in providing the wild and rugged landscapes so characteristic of melodrama in the first half of the nineteenth century. By the middle of the century, romantic *realism, which was consummated in the productions of Charles *Kean, Franz von *Dingelstedt, and Richard *Wagner, had become the dominant scenic style of the European theatre.

In some ways *opera was more compatible with romanticism than the spoken theatre. Music could convey with immediacy the volatile emotions of characters. The bel canto operas of Bellini, Donizetti, and Rossini memorably explore extreme states of mind and the intricacies of sexual desire, usually in exotic or historical settings that lie beyond the everyday world of the *audience. In Germany Marschner and Weber did the same with operas set partly in the realm of the supernatural. But perhaps it was Wagner who most fully recognized the essence of Romantic theatre. From his Byronic music drama *The Flying Dutchman* on, he was acutely aware of the potential the stage setting possessed to serve as a metaphor for the inner life of his characters; in this way the stage could materialize the subjective vision of the romantic hero and the universal forces at war within the hero's soul. His great hymn to romantic love, *Tristan and Isolde*, cannot be coherently staged without embracing the principle of romantic scenography. Unfortunately, when it came to directing his own works Wagner's entirely conventional visual sense did not allow him to put his ideas into practice.

It remained to later generations to fulfil the potential of the romantic stage. The introduction of electric *lighting allowed for infinitely more subtle gradations in mood and atmosphere. It enabled Adolphe *Appia, in his *symbolist designs for Wagner's music dramas, to demonstrate how abstract form and pure space could be used to embody characters' inner worlds, though his ideas would not be successfully applied until the mid-twentieth century. While Henrik *Ibsen was rigorously anti-romantic in his view of the world, the manner in which he closely tied all scenic elements to his characters' volitional being and to the symbolic structure of the play represents a fulfilment of both romantic scenography and *dramaturgy. This also applies to *Chekhov's work, while *Strindberg, a more overtly experimental dramatist, perhaps realized the potential of romanticism both in theme and form in his symbolist drama *A Dream Play*. The German *expressionists were strongly influenced by Strindberg, and their 'ego-centred' dramas have customarily been seen as the consummation of the romantic ideal in the German theatre. Thus while romanticism arose from the revolutionary consciousness of the late eighteenth century, it was only in the twentieth that the theatre could rise fully to the challenges it offered.   SJCW

ROMBERG, SIGMUND (1887–1951)

American composer. Born in Hungary and educated in *Vienna, where he learned Viennese *operetta, he emigrated to *New York in 1909 and tried his hand at writing American music. In 1913 he was hired by the *Shuberts as a staff composer, for whom he cranked out serviceable, undistinguished scores for more than 30 *revues and *musical comedies. Frustrated and threatening to quit, he was given a chance to write a few original operettas, several of which—*Maytime* (1917), *Blossom Time* (1921)—established him as a leading composer of the form. In 1924 he wrote perhaps the most enduring American operetta, *The Student Prince*, which was the longest-running Broadway show of the 1920s, followed by *The Desert Song* (1926) and *The New Moon* (1928). Romberg's work was enhanced by his introduction of a contemporary popular idiom amid the conventions of traditional *romantic operetta. When the age of the 1920s operetta passed, Romberg continued to evolve his style, leading a popular dance band and finding late-career success in 1945 with *Up in Central Park*.   JD

ROME, MEDIEVAL AND MODERN

(For ancient Rome, see ROMAN THEATRE.) Integral to the development of theatre in this Mediterranean city are its legacy, first, as capital of the western Roman Empire (sacked AD 410 by Visigoths, and the last emperor deposed in 476); and, second, its position as Holy See of the Pope, head of the Christian Church, and as capital of the Papal States (755–1870), the Pope's extensive temporal domain, which gave Rome an important position in the struggle for balance of power between France and the Habsburg Empire from about 1700 to 1870, when Italy was unified. In the feudal society of the *medieval period, ancient pagan festivals and fertility and mystic rites existed side by side with, and were gradually subsumed by, Christian festivals (Christmas, *carnival, Easter, saints' days). The theatrical arts of *playwriting, *scenery, and *costume manifested themselves in these religious events beginning with the responses of the

Easter vigil in Gregorian chant. The Archconfraternity of Gonfalone, a charitable organization of aristocrats and wealthy merchants recognized by the Pope in 1264, produced plays with religious subjects, including several in the Colosseum: *Conversione di S. Paolo* (1440), *Resurrezione* (c.1500), and a sumptuous *Passion play, complete with *music and *chorus (c.1500).

Beginning around 1450, a growing admiration of antiquity created a longing for a new classic era. The revival of classical theatre was spurred by the rediscovery of twelve lost plays by *Plautus (1429); the transfer of many ancient manuscripts to Italy after the fall of Constantinople (1453); the establishment of the first printing office in Rome (1467); and the publication in Latin (1498) of *Aristotle's *Poetics* which, as reinterpreted by *theorists such as *Castelvetro into *neoclassical rules, would govern dramatic *genres in Europe until the nineteenth century (*see* EARLY MODERN PERIOD IN EUROPE). The Roman Academy, founded in the late 1450s, promoted production in the Forum, the Colosseum, and elsewhere of classical *Roman *tragedy (*Seneca) and *comedy (Plautus, *Terence). Private performances of classical plays and their contemporary imitations took place in the palace halls of wealthy aristocrats and ecclesiastics. At the Vatican, the Medici Popes Leo X and Clement VII enjoyed Bibbiena's *Calandria* (1514); *Ariosto's *Suppositi* (1519), and *Machiavelli's *Mandragola* (1525). The new *perspective scenery for these productions was designed by Rome's foremost painters and architects (Raphael, Peruzzi), who relied on *Vitruvius' treatise *De Architectura* (c.15 BC, rediscovered 1414, printed 1486) for advice (*see* SCENOGRAPHY). Sumptuous papal processionals, jubilees, royal *entries, and banquets featuring pagan *characters in *allegorical plays, wild *animals, music, and *dance, also promoted the power of the Church and its cardinals. The period also saw the rise of the *pastoral and *ballet.

The sack of Rome in 1527 put an end to the Renaissance papacy and, with the growing threat of Protestantism, led to the repressive measures of the Counter-*Reformation. In the realm of religious drama the newly founded *Jesuits applied the rules of classical theatre to biblical subjects and developed scene design and *intermedii, while convents and monasteries continued the *sacra rappresentazione tradition. From 1623 to 1669, under the Barberini popes, Roman *opera developed its own particular form, and while a papal edict prohibited *women performers in the Papal States until 1798, the *commedia dell'arte tradition lived on in the librettos of Giulio Rospigliosi, later Pope Clement IX, and women's parts were sung by *castrati. Lavish productions during carnival and on state occasions were performed for *audiences of 3,000 or more men (women were usually excluded) in the great halls of Palazzo Barberini and the Cancelleria, and in royal courts.

In 1671 Christina of Sweden, patroness of Scarlatti and Corelli, established the first public opera house, Teatro Tordinona. By 1756 Rome had eight public theatres, all of them horseshoe shaped with a seated parterre and rows of surrounding *boxes. The central box was reserved for the Governor of Rome and others were leased by the aristocracy for the season (7 January to the beginning of Lent, or 26 December to Mardi Gras). To avoid competition in the presentation of operas, the Argentina alternated years with the Alibert, which was enlarged in 1720 by Francesco Galli da *Bibiena.

The Arcadian Academy (1690) had little success in developing an Italian neoclassical literary tradition similar to that of France, and when important Italian playwrights did appear, Roman theatre lacked the professionalism with which to perform their works. In 1758 at the Tordinona, *Goldoni was shocked to find actors playing his modern renditions of the ancient *commedia* in the traditional *masks, his female parts interpreted by men, and his lines not adequately memorized. He fared better at the Capranica and wrote *Pamela maritata* (1769) for that company after the success of their performances in *Pamela nubile* (1758). In 1781 *Alfieri leapt on stage to protest at the changes to his *Orestes. One of the best companies was the Vestri-Venier, which performed *Maffei's *Merope* in 1818 at Teatro Apollo (once Tordinona). Among other worthy visitors to Rome with their companies in the mid-nineteenth century were *Ristori, *Bellotti-Bon, and Ernesto *Rossi. It is hardly surprising that operas and concomitant ballets remained the dominant form of entertainment in Rome during the late baroque period and through the Enlightenment and the age of *romanticism. Among the set designers were the Bibiena family; among the librettists, Pietro *Metastasio, whose *melodramas were quickly set to music (*Didone abbandonata* was a success at Teatro Alibert, 1726); among the composers, Scarlatti, Pergolesi, Paisiello, Donizetti, Bellini, Rossini, and *Verdi. In the peninsula, the Italian romantic movement manifested itself around 1815 in a yearning for political independence from Austria and freedom from the French neoclassical literary tradition, and called for the development of a new national literature. Verdi's works were particularly revolutionary in appeal. In *La battaglia di Legnano* (Teatro Argentina, 1849) the theme of defeat of the German invader led to shouts of 'Viva Verdi!' The Austrians viewed Alfieri's tragedies such as *Orestes* and *Saul*, which were in the repertory of Gustavo *Modena and *Salvini, as dangerous and *censored them regularly.

In 1870 the Papal States were annexed to a unified Italy, of which Rome became the capital in 1871. Efforts were made to turn the city into a theatre centre like *Milan, and a *repertory theatre for opera and ballet was created at Teatro Constanzi (renamed Teatro dell'Opera in 1928). However, the new government refused to subsidize theatre even in Rome, Milan, or *Naples and stars like *Duse, *Novelli, and *Zacconi *toured abroad, following in the footsteps of Ristori, Rossi, and Salvini. In an effort to create a theatre like the *Comédie-Française, Roman aristocrats subsidized Teatro Drammatico Nazionale, directed by Paolo *Ferrari, in 1886. Novelli made a similar attempt with Casa di Goldoni, established at Rome's former Teatro Valle in 1900. Both were short-lived. By the turn of the century, *naturalist playwrights from abroad (*Zola, *Becque, *Hauptmann) and from Italy (Verga, *Capuana, *Giacosa, *Bracco) had been successfully introduced in productions featuring *Talli, Duse, Zacconi, and the *Gramatica sisters. A reaction to *realism between 1895 and 1925 arrived in the works of *D'Annunzio and *Benelli, in *futurism (a futurist evening was held in 1913 at Teatro Constanzi), in the post-First World War *teatro grottesco* (*see* GROTESQUE, THEATRE OF THE), and in Luigi *Pirandello. Anton *Bragaglia played a vital role in introducing to Rome Italian and foreign *avant-garde works and new ideas in staging.

In 1935, under the *fascist regime, Silvio D'Amico obtained government support for a National Academy of Dramatic Art to *train actors and directors. After the Second World War, Orazio Costa, one of the Academy's graduates, became *artistic director of the Piccolo Teatro della Citta di Roma, Rome's first successful repertory theatre for prose works (1948–54). In the wake of the 1968 socio-cultural revolution, experimental artists, such as Leo *de Berardinis, Memé *Perlini, Carlo *Cecchi, and Giorgio *Barberio Corsetti, attempted to reach a different class of people and experimented with theatrical forms. The official theatres opened up to this work. Vito Pandolfi, Luigi *Squarzina, Maurizio *Scaparro, and Luca *Ronconi are among the artistic directors that have led the Teatro di Roma, established as the repertory theatre of the city of Rome in 1964, which supports its productions of spoken drama and dance events with socio-cultural activities that reach out to its wide audience.

JEH

CARLSON, MARVIN, *The Italian Stage* (London, 1981)
KIMBELL, DAVID, *Italian Opera* (Cambridge, 1991)
STINGER, CHARLES L., *The Renaissance in Rome* (Bloomington, Ind., 1985)

ROMERIL, JOHN (1945–)

Australian playwright. A founding member of the *Australian Performing Group, Romeril has remained committed to its ideals of collaboration, socialism, and focus on Australian subject matter. He is best known for *The Floating World* (1974), which confronts Australia's post-war relationship with Japan, and *Marvellous Melbourne* (1970, written with Jack Hibberd), a *revue inspired by the nineteenth-century Australian play of the same name. Romeril has also worked extensively in *community theatre and has a sustained interest in *Japanese theatre techniques.

EJS

ROMERO, MARIELA (1949–)

Venezuelan playwright, actress, and *television writer. Her debut play was *Algo alrededor del espejo* (*Something around* the Mirror, 1967), though recognition only came with *El juego* (*The Game*, 1976), concerned with young beggar girls. *El inevitable destino de Rosa de la Noche* (*The Inevitable Destiny of Rosa of the Night*, 1980) deals with child prostitution, *El vendedor* (*The Seller*, 1984) is about the sale of women, and *Esperando al italiano* (*Waiting for the Italian*, 1988) about mature women who prostitute themselves. Her recurrent themes are the disadvantaged position of women, solitude, and the impossibility of human relationships, which she expresses through colloquial and direct *dialogue layered with meaning.

LCL trans. AMCS

RONCONI, LUCA (1933–)

Italian director. Born in Tunisia, Ronconi was an actor with a number of Italian companies before his unsuccessful debut as director in 1963 with *Goldoni's *La buona moglie* (*The Good Wife*), which was criticized for its *naturalistic excess. He soon overcame this shaky start with an intensely theatrical approach to *early modern drama, particularly in subversive productions of Shakespeare's *Measure for Measure* and *Richard III* (both 1967). Ronconi's use of space and movement, amplified by complicated mechanical devices and *scenography, created a strong visual impression that was paralleled by an *acting style aimed at undercutting conventional interpretations and strengthening the actor–spectator relationship. Clearly influenced by *Artaud's Theatre of *Cruelty, Ronconi's major productions of the late 1960s and early 1970s included *Middleton and *Rowley's *The Changeling*, Middleton's *A Game at Chess* and *The Revenger's Tragedy* (previously ascribed to *Tourneur; in Ronconi's production all the roles were played by women), and Giordano Bruno's *Il candelaio* (*The Candle Maker*, 1968). International acclaim greeted his *environmental version of *Ariosto's epic *Orlando furioso* (1968), written with Eduardo Sanguineti. Designed by Uberto Bertacca, the scenography allowed for simultaneous staging of multiple scenes: performers and *audience interacted on an equal basis and spectators were asked to shift *scenery and move retractable platforms with actors riding on them.

During the political and cultural upheaval of the 1970s, Ronconi's productions aimed at further subverting the theatrical canon, with an environmental production called *XX* at the *Odéon in *Paris (1971), *Kleist's *Die Kätchen von Heillbron* on barges on the lake in Zurich, and *Aeschylus' *Oresteia* at the 1972 Belgrade Festival with the audience extremely close to the action. Disappointed by the response to his work in his own country, he turned more and more to *opera, directing many productions in Italy and abroad, and worked for *television as well. In 1975 he was named director of the Venice Biennale *festival, mounting seven *comedies by *Aristophanes updated to the present in a single show. During this period he also formed his own *studio in Prato where actors tested new performance styles; the results included productions of *Euripides' *The Bacchae* and *Calderón's *Life Is a Dream*. In the 1980s Ronconi turned his attention to Austrian theatre by staging *Schnitzler's *The Tower* and Arno Holz's *Ignorabimus*. In 1989 he was named director of the Teatro Stabile in Turin. Despite frequent hostility to his work in Italy, Ronconi persisted with experimental theatre in Turin, with productions of works by Botho *Strauss, *Pirandello, Ariosto, and *Ibsen. Notable were Karl *Kraus's *The Last Days of Mankind* (1990), *O'Neill's *Strange Interlude* (1991), and radical remakes of *Measure for Measure* (1991) and *Tasso's *Aminta* (1994).   DMcM/DK

RONFARD, JEAN-PIERRE (1929–)

Québec playwright and director. Born in France, he came to Canada in 1960 as *artistic director of the National Theatre School in *Montréal. After some time with the Théâtre du *Nouveau Monde he opted for less traditional dramatic values and forms than the TNM offered, helping to found in 1975 what has become the Nouveau Théâtre Expérimental de Montréal. Typical of Ronfard's outrageous, abundant *dramaturgy is the seven-play cycle *Vie et mort du roi boiteux* (*Life and Death of the Lame King*, 1981–2), a vaguely Shakespearian *parody of Western myths and values. *Hitler*, another controversial, cartoon-like portrayal, played to packed houses in 2001.   LED

ROSCIUS GALLUS, QUINTUS (c.120–62 BC)

*Roman comic actor. Roscius was born a slave, but his success caused him to be freed by Sulla, who in 82 BC admitted him to the equestrian order, an unprecedented honour for an actor at Rome. He subsequently acquired great wealth and prestige, and his name became proverbial for excellence and popularity. He instructed his close friend Cicero in elocution, and was defended by him in a lawsuit; the oration defending him survives. Roscius was admired for his grace and style. He was meticulous in the perfection of his roles, noted for his observation and careful *rehearsal of gestures and vocal delivery, as well as his skill at *improvisation. Although he occasionally played *tragic roles, he excelled in *comic parts and was particularly noted for his impersonation of parasites, and famous for the perfection of his realization of Ballio, the maniacal pimp in *Plautus' *Pseudolus*.   RCB

ROSE, BILLY (1899–1966)

American *producer. Born William Samuel Rosenberg, he began his career as a Tin Pan Alley lyricist, writing the words for a wide range of popular songs, among them 'It's Only a Paper Moon'. In 1925 he opened the first of his several Manhattan nightclubs. He was brought into the theatre when Fanny *Brice, who had performed several of his songs, asked to meet

him. They were married in 1927, and in 1930 he produced his first Broadway *revue, featuring Brice. His productions were typically lavish, vulgar, and spectacular—none more spectacular than *Jumbo* (1935), a *circus-cum-*musical in *New York's *Hippodrome with aerialists and a menagerie of *animals, including the titular elephant. After producing expositions and aquacades in the late 1930s, he returned to musicals and plays in the 1940s and 1950s. He also owned two Broadway theatres—the Ziegfeld and the National on 41st Street, which he renamed the Billy Rose. The foundation which he established in the late 1950s generously funded the New York Public Library's theatre collection, which is named after him and housed in *Lincoln Center.   JD

ROSENCOF, MAURICIO (1933–)

Uruguayan playwright and journalist. The son of Jewish immigrants, Rosencof was a political activist and a journalist early in life, forming the Union of Communist Youths and being instrumental in the Tupamaros national liberation movement. Before he was imprisoned by the military dictatorship in 1972, he wrote a number of plays for El *Galpón, including *El gran Tuleque* (*The Great Tuleque*, 1960), *Las ranas* (*The Frogs*, 1961), and *Los caballos* (*The Horses*, 1967). From 1973 until 1984 he was in isolation, but his guards paid him with cigarettes and extra food for writing poems and letters for them; he used the cigarette papers to write *dialogue, which was eventually smuggled out. Although he composed about eight plays during his imprisonment, he was able to remember and reassemble only four of them. The best known is *El combate en el establo* (*Fight in the Stable*, *Montevideo, 1985), in which two men are jailed in a stable until they become cows. The younger man resists complete transformation by crafting a crude flute, resisting oppression by holding onto humanity.   EJW

ROSENTHAL, JEAN (1912–69)

American *lighting designer. A pioneer in the art of theatrical lighting, Rosenthal began her study with George Pierce *Baker at Yale during the early 1930s. In 1935 she found employment with the *Federal Theatre Project's *New York-based Project 891, run by John *Houseman and Orson *Welles. Rosenthal became their principal lighting designer after the two left the FTP in 1937 to found the *Mercury Theatre. By the early 1950s Rosenthal was in high demand. Some of her most original designs were achieved in collaboration with the Martha *Graham Dance Company, and she also designed for some of the biggest Broadway *musicals of the 1950s and 1960s, including *West Side Story* (1957), *The Sound of Music* (1959), *A Funny Thing Happened on the Way to the Forum* (1962), *Fiddler on the Roof* (1964), and *Cabaret* (1966). Her work was also seen at the American Ballet Theatre, the New York City Opera, and the *American

Shakespeare Theatre. Her book on theatrical lighting, *The Magic of Light*, was published posthumously in 1972.   JAB

ROSE THEATRE

The third amphitheatre *playhouse built in *London after the *Theatre and the *Curtain in Shoreditch, and the only one to be extensively excavated. The Rose was paid for by Philip *Henslowe, a businessman, in collaboration with a local grocer who was to sell food and drink there. Built on *Bankside in 1587 near the bear- and bull-*baiting houses, the Rose became, along with the Theatre, one of the two playhouses licensed in 1594 by the *Master of the Revels for use by a resident playing company. The Rose's residents were the *Admiral's Men; their leading player, Edward *Alleyn, married Henslowe's step daughter in 1592. Depicted in engravings as a six-sided polygon, when its remains were excavated in 1989 the Rose turned out to be a fourteen-sided structure, 22.5 m (74 feet) in diameter, with a stage on the northern flank. The excavation showed that it was enlarged in 1592, when Henslowe spent £108 on it, by extending two sides of the previously symmetrical polygon towards the north, making a tulip shape, with the stage in the newly built section. In 1600 Henslowe replaced the Rose with the *Fortune Theatre, and put in another company which used it till 1604.
                                                                    AJG

ROSHCHIN, MIKHAIL (1933–)

Soviet/Russian playwright who has supplied the *Sovremennik and *Moscow Art Theatre with ample material. He offers an ironic view of the petty concerns of modern life. *Old New Year* (1967), which *satirizes Soviet traditions, was staged and turned into a *film by Oleg *Efremov, while *Valentin and Valentina* explores young people's relationships. Roshchin's plays concern interesting themes but offer little potential for the theatre. Together with Aleksei *Kazantsev he founded a centre for young dramatists and directors in *Moscow.   BB

ROSSET, CACÁ (1954–)

Brazilian director, actor, and *television personality. With Luiz Roberto Galizia and Alice Vergueiro, Rosset founded Teatro Ornitorrinco (Platypus Theatre) in 1977. He became known for his manic adaptations of *Brecht (*Mahagonny Songspiel*, 1982), *Jarry (*Ubu-Folias Physicas*, 1985), Shakespeare (*A Midsummer Night's Dream*, also staged at the *New York Shakespeare Festival, 1990), and *Molière. Using an irreverent aesthetic based in *circus and *carnival, combined with the most libertine side of Brazilian humour, these spectacles ran to full houses nationally and internationally.   LHD

ROSSI, ERNESTO (1829–1906)

Italian *actor-manager. Rossi *trained and acted with Gustavo *Modena (1846–8), who instilled in him the desire to create characters 'with blood running through their veins' and taught him the value of long *rehearsals, careful *textual study, and psychological analysis. Modena also introduced him to Shakespeare, as yet little known in Italy. In 1852 Rossi joined Turin's prestigious Reale Sarda Company, displaying his versatility in Italian and French *comedies, *tragedies, and sentimental works and playing opposite *Ristori in *Francesca da Rimini* during the company's 1855 *Paris *tour. Now in possession of new *verse translations by Giulio Carcano, Rossi successfully performed *Othello* and *Hamlet* at Teatro Re, *Milan (1856). Tommaso *Salvini followed suit shortly thereafter and their interpretations of Shakespearian roles were often compared. Short of stature and burly, Rossi had a flexible face, a body capable of supple movement and expressive gesture, and a voice that shifted volume and tone with facility. The tempestuous and unpredictable nature of his passions earned him the title of a *'romantic' actor as compared to Salvini, who was described as 'classical' because of his more studied style.

From 1864 until his death, Rossi performed under the aegis of the Ernesto Rossi Company in a repertory of Italian (*Alfieri, *Giacometti, *Ferrari) and foreign playwrights (*Corneille, *Hugo, *Scribe, *Goethe, *Iffland, *Laube, *Byron, *Calderón) as well as Shakespeare. By 1864 he had added *The Merchant of Venice*, *Romeo and Juliet*, *Macbeth*, *King Lear*, *Julius Caesar*, *Coriolanus*, and *Antony and Cleopatra* to his repertory and in 1866 Paris welcomed him as the 'Italian *Talma' in *Hamlet*, *Othello*, and three acts of *Le Cid*. After 1868, in an age of the international star, Rossi spent much of his time touring throughout the world like his two Italian compatriots, Ristori and Salvini. All three experimented with bilingual productions, but Rossi relied on a Shakespearian repertory more than they. Although lauded elsewhere, particularly in Spain, Portugal, South America, and Romania, his Shakespearian performances in *London met with a cold reception. In 1906 he fell ill while performing *King Lear* in Odessa and returned home to die.
                                                                    JEH

ROSTAND, EDMOND (1868–1918)

French playwright. Rostand is an outstanding case of the happy conjunction of the man and the hour, for his *historical drama *Cyrano de Bergerac* (1897) filled a national need, felt far outside the theatre. His earliest plays suggested a lightweight talent, but *Cyrano*, written at the invitation of Constant *Coquelin, the best-known actor of the day, who had been impressed by the imaginative quality shown in *La Princesse lointaine* (*The Far Princess*, 1895), at once took the theatregoing public by storm, at a time when national spirit had still not recovered from the humiliation of defeat in the Franco-Prussian War. The bizarre *character with whom the *Paris public identified at the *Porte-Saint-Martin Theatre for an unprecedented 600 performances was the Poet as *Hero: but a swashbuckling poet able to disarm a bully while composing a ballad, before entertaining us with a fantasy about travel to the moon; and whose courage inspires the French troops at the siege of Arras before his pathetic death moves us to tears in the final *act. Often scorned by the critical intelligentsia at the time and since, *Cyrano de Bergerac* is a striking example of pure theatre, captivating *audiences by brilliant stagecraft and verbal virtuosity, and illustrating that juxtaposition of the sublime (the poet with the exalted imagination) and the *grotesque (the ugly lover handicapped by his long nose) in which Victor *Hugo had seen the essence of *romantic drama. Rostand was elected to the Académie Française in 1901 on the strength of *Cyrano* and of *L'Aiglon* (1900), in which Sarah *Bernhardt played Napoleon's ill-fated son.   WDH

ROSWITHA *See* Hrotsvitha of Gandersheim.

ROTE SPRACHROHR, DAS

Literally 'The Red Mouthpiece', the most important German *agitprop theatre during the Weimar Republic. Founded by M. Vallentin and members of the Communist Youth Organization, the company's performances consisted initially of spoken *choruses. These were followed by *didactic plays and *revues. Their work regarded art as an ideological weapon in the class struggle, in direct support of the Communist Party. After 1930 the group experimented with *epic theatre techniques, using short scenes that could be performed in factory halls and on the streets (*see* STREET THEATRE). Rote Sprachrohr dissolved after 1933 as its members were imprisoned or forced into exile.
                                                                  CBB

ROTHENSTEIN, ALBERT *See* Rutherston, Albert.

ROTIMI, OLA (1938–2000)

Nigerian playwright and director. His first play, a robust indictment of political charlatans, was *Our Husband Has Gone Mad Again* (1966). Three years later *The Gods Are Not to Blame* established him more widely, a bold but somewhat clumsy adaptation of *Oedipus the King*, which he directed with characteristic panache and *toured extensively. For the next 35 years, Rotimi was a major figure in Nigerian theatre, writing a series of strong, sometimes *melodramatic, occasionally broadly comic plays that contributed to the reappraisal of Nigerian history and to debate about *politics, often combining *dialogue, *music, song, and *dance. *Kurunmi* (1969) and *Ovonramwen Nogbaisi* (1971) began as examinations of episodes from Nigerian history. *Hold-

ing Talks (1977), subtitled 'an *absurdist drama', took a *satirical approach to contemporary events. These 'Ife plays' were presented by the Ori Olokun Players (later called Awovarsity Players), a group that Rotimi hoped would become the first fully professional English-speaking theatre in Nigeria. Rotimi responded to the shift to the left on Nigerian campuses in *If* (1983), which he described as 'a full-length socio-political *tragedy', and the *historical drama *Hopes of the Living Dead* (1988). Productions were particularly effective in the *open-air Crab Theatre, Port Harcourt, which furthered Rotimi's determination to break down rigid barriers between actors and *audiences. He worked abroad for several years from 1991, and died in Ife while on a mission to establish a new theatre company.
                                                                  JMG

ROTROU, JEAN (1609–50)

French playwright. After Pierre *Corneille, Rotrou was the most significant French dramatist of the 1630s and 1640s. His first effort was staged in 1628 at the *Hôtel de Bourgogne, where by 1632 he had succeeded *Hardy as salaried playwright. Fourteen of his plays were in the Bourgogne's repertory in the early 1630s. Protected by Cardinal *Richelieu, Rotrou was enlisted as one of the five authors who wrote plays under Richelieu's direction. By the mid-1630s he claimed authorship of 30 plays. Largely *tragicomedies and *comedies drawn from Spanish, Italian, and Latin sources, and composed in the exuberantly melodramatic manner of the day, without regard for the *neoclassical rules, these were mostly, as *Mahelot's *Mémoire* illustrates, intended for an elaborate multiple *scenography. In 1639 Rotrou purchased a legal post in his native Dreux and retired there to produce his most durable work, in particular three plays that illustrate the impact that the new, regular aesthetic was beginning to have upon early-century baroque *dramaturgy: *Venceslas* (1647), a tragicomedy adapted from Francisco de *Rojas Zorrilla, which was played at the *Comédie-Française until 1857; *Cosroès* (1648), a regular *tragedy that remained in the Comédie's repertory until the early eighteenth century; and *Le Véritable Saint Genest* (1645), a quasi-regular baroque tragedy inspired by Lope de *Vega and influenced by Corneille's *L'Illusion comique* and *Polyeucte*, about the conversion of the Roman actor Genest whilst playing the role of the martyr St Adrian. Currently regarded as Rotrou's best play, it was revived successfully by the Comédie-Française in 1988.   JG

ROUND HOUSE

Converted in 1968 from a Victorian engine shed in Camden in *London, the Round House became an unusual and exciting performance venue. Arnold *Wesker hoped to make it a home for Centre 42, an 'arts community for the people'. The first outstanding year included *Brook's *Themes on the Tempest*, *Arden and

*D'Arcy's *The Hero Rises Up*, Nicoll *Williamson in *Hamlet*, the *Living Theatre, and *Berkoff's *Metamorphosis*. Wesker resigned in 1970 after the failure of his play *The Friends*, and George Hoskins then ran the theatre as a receiving house until 1979. His first success was *Tynan's *Oh! Calcutta!*, and though his programme varied in quality, it included *Barrault's *Rabelais*, *Mnouchkine's *1789* with the Théâtre du *Soleil, the *Grand Magic Circus, the Red Buddha Theatre, and *La Grande Eugène*, as well as small *circuses, rock *musicals, and contemporary *ballet. Hoskins also ran popular Sunday rock concerts, but they led to a drug-ridden reputation that the producer Thelma Holt found difficult when she took over in 1977. She converted the acting space to an *arena arrangement in order to import plays from the *Royal Exchange Theatre, *Manchester, and also brought in other *regional and overseas companies; her greatest success was probably Robert *Sturua's *Richard III* from *Tbilisi. The theatre closed in 1983 for lack of subsidy; occasional subsequent performances included a residency by the *Royal Shakespeare Company in 2002.   EEC

ROUSSEAU, JEAN-JACQUES (1712–78)

French philosopher, writer, and composer. Although author of the *anti-theatrical polemic known as the *Lettre à M. d'Alembert*, in the 1740s and 1750s Rousseau sought success as a playwright and composer. He began seven plays, one of which, *Narcisse*, was produced but failed at the *Comédie-Française. His 'heroic *ballet' *Les Muses galantes* was *rehearsed by the *Opéra, but withdrawn before performance. Only his *operetta *Le Devin du village* was successful when produced in 1753. Rousseau considered himself a musician and supported himself as a musical copyist. He was a gleeful participant in the war of the *buffons*, when he and other *philosophes* defended the Italian *opera buffa* against Jean-Philippe Rameau and his French *tragédie lyrique*. Five years after the success of *Le Devin*, however, Rousseau broke with *Paris, the *philosophes*, and the theatre, which he then attacked as a symbol of the corruption of a hypocritical urban society.   VS

ROUTLEDGE, PATRICIA (1929–)

Popular English actress, known for her skills as a comedienne but equally equipped for darker roles. She was educated at the University of Liverpool and trained at *Bristol Old Vic and the Guildhall School. Early engagements include *A Midsummer Night's Dream* at the *Liverpool Playhouse (1952), *The Duenna* in *London (1954), *Virtue in Danger* at the *Mermaid (1963), and *The Caucasian Chalk Circle*, *The Country Wife*, and *The Magistrate* at *Chichester (all 1969). On Broadway she appeared in *How's the World Treating You?* (1966), *Darling of the Day* (1968), and as the President's Wife in the ill-fated *1600 Pennsylvania Avenue* (1976). In the 1980s, and paralleling a successful *tele-vision career, she appeared in *Noises Off* (1981), *Richard III* for the *Royal Shakespeare Company (1984), Nicholas *Hytner's revival of *Carousel* for the *National (1992), *The Rivals* at the Albery (1994), and in Chichester's *The Importance of Being Earnest* (1999).   AS

ROUX, JEAN-LOUIS (1923–)

French-Canadian actor, director and playwright. Trained as an actor in France, he returned to *Montréal in 1950 and the following year founded, with Jean *Gascon (who had also studied in *Paris), the Théâtre du *Nouveau Monde, which soon became the foremost company in French Canada. For the next 30 years Roux was associated with it, directing and acting in plays from the classical French canon while gradually introducing more modern works by French and Québécois authors. Equally at home in French and English (he has had major roles in productions of Shakespeare at the *Stratford Festival and has translated and directed several of Shakespeare's plays), he is recognized as one of the finest actors of his generation. Roux has also had a distinguished career as actor and writer for *radio, national *television, and *film. The recipient of many *awards, he has played a major role at the centre of Canadian cultural activity.

LED

ROVINA, HANNA (1889–1980)

Russian-Israeli actress admired for her regal appearance and impressive voice. Rovina originally trained as a Hebrew kindergarten teacher. In 1917 she became a founding member of the *Moscow *Habima company and was associated with it throughout her life. Her role as Leah in the Habima's production of *The Dybbuk* (1922) made her into a visual icon and earned her a reputation as the Hebrew theatre's leading actress. She settled in Palestine with the rest of the company in 1928. Her repertoire was wide, but she was especially admired for her mother roles, notably in Pinsky's *The Eternal Jew* (1923), *Gordin's *Mirele Efros* (1939), *Čapek's *Mother* (1939), *Sophocles' *Oedipus the King* (1947), *Brecht's *Mother Courage* (1950), *Euripides' *Medea* (1955), Meged's *Hannah Szenesh* (1958), and *O'Neill's *Desire under the Elms* (1958).   EN

ROVINSKI, SAMUEL (1932–)

Costa Rican playwright, novelist, and essayist. His plays include *Las fisgonas de Paso Ancho* (*The Nosy People of Paso Ancho*, 1971) and *Un modelo para Rosaura* (*A Model for Rosaura*, 1975). While most of his work contains elements of political *satire, he has also written serious *political theatre in *El martirio del pastor* (*The Martyrdom of the Pastor*, 1987) about the murder of Archbishop Romero. Rovinski has also written for *film and *television.   EJW

ROVNER, EDUARDO (1942–)

Argentinian playwright and critic. His more than twenty plays—including *Anniversary Concert* (1983), *Castaway Dreams* (1985), and *She Returned One Night* (1993)—combine *realist theses with concentrated, *absurdist stagings, often built upon *sainete and *grotesco models. Rovner was *artistic director of the Teatro *Municipal San Martín (1991–4).   JGJ

ROWE, NICHOLAS (1674–1718)

English writer. Although Rowe was Poet Laureate (from 1715) and the author of important *tragedies, he is now remembered for his six-volume edition of Shakespeare (1709), which contained the first biography of Shakespeare, introduced *act and *scene divisions still in use, and began an industry of Shakespeare editing that continued without cease. In Rowe's own day, he was best known for extremely popular 'she-tragedies' like *The Fair Penitent* (1703), *Jane Shore* (1713), and *Lady Jane Grey* (1715). The plays feature a strong enunciation of female subjectivity, but ultimately focus on the pity, distress, and death of the female *protagonists. The rebellious *heroines either become admirably penitent or are excluded from their social worlds, so that the plays tend to side with bourgeois patriarchal values, often revealing a Whig bias. In any event, they provided excellent roles for actresses from Anne *Oldfield to Sarah *Siddons.   MJK

ROWLEY, SAMUEL (c.1575–c.1624)

English actor and dramatist, possibly brother to fellow actor-playwright William *Rowley. Philip *Henslowe's accounts show he was an important member of the *Admiral's Men by 1597, and he was still with them in 1613. Although Henslowe paid Rowley for writing scripts—including additions to *Marlowe's *Dr Faustus* in 1602—the company's terms may have precluded their publication: only one Rowley play certainly survives, *When You See Me, You Know Me* (printed 1605). This engaging (if inaccurate) portrait of Henry VIII—which influenced Shakespeare's *Henry VIII* (1613)—includes lively episodes in which the incognito King meets a *London gangster, and in which his son Edward chooses Protestantism after comparing letters from his half-sisters Mary and Elizabeth.   MD

ROWLEY, WILLIAM (c.1585–1626)

English actor and dramatist. Nothing is known of his life before 1607, when he collaborated with John Day and George Wilkins to write the topical play *The Travels of the Three English Brothers* for Queen Anne's Men, but it is likely that he was already working as an actor, always the principal strand of his career. He specialized in comic roles, especially rotund *clowns, raising *laughter by exploiting his ungainly physique; one of his *characters was said to move like a great tub of porridge. By 1609, he was acting with the Duke of York's Men, and soon became a leading member with especial responsibility for the company's *finances. In the 1620s, he transferred to the King's Men (*see* CHAMBERLAIN'S MEN, LORD), in accordance with their policy of filling vacancies by buying in the best talent from other companies, rather than by internal promotion; for them he played, among others, the Fat Bishop in *Middleton's *A Game at Chess* (1624).

As a dramatist Rowley mainly worked in collaboration, notably on *A Fair Quarrel* (1616) and *The Changeling* (1622) with Middleton, *The Witch of Edmonton* (1621) with *Dekker and *Ford, *The Birth of Merlin* (1622) with an unknown collaborator, and *A Cure for a Cuckold* (1624) with *Webster; his role seems to have been to script the comic subplots. *The Changeling* was frequently and *The Witch of Edmonton* occasionally revived in the twentieth century; an adapted version of *The Birth of Merlin* was a success for Theatr Clwyd in 1989.   MJW

ROYAL ACADEMY OF DRAMATIC ART

Founded in 1904 by Beerbohm *Tree at His (*Her) Majesty's Theatre, RADA has been a premier source of *London *training for British theatre ever since. Established in Gower Street, its first principal (1909–55), Sir Kenneth Barnes, ensured success through constantly improving facilities. In 1921 a new theatre was built; in 1927 a new administrative/teaching building was added; but both were virtually destroyed in 1941 by a bomb. Post-war reconstruction included three *playhouses, notably the Vanbrugh Theatre (1954). In the late 1990s everything was completely rebuilt with the help of a £22.7 million National Lottery grant. George Bernard *Shaw was a key supporter. As a council member, in 1912 he signed over the royalties of *Pygmalion* to the Academy, and his 1950 bequest added one-third of all royalties due to his estate. Its training constantly responding to theatre industry developments, it has produced generations of stellar alumni, including Charles *Laughton, Glenda *Jackson, and Kenneth *Branagh.   BRK

ROYAL ALEXANDRA THEATRE

Designed by architect John Lyle for Cawthra Mulock, the Royal Alex opened in *Toronto in 1907, at a cost of $700,000, as a venue for *touring American and British shows. Such stars as John, Ethel, and Lionel *Barrymore, Jessica *Tandy and Hume *Cronyn, John *Gielgud, John *Martin-Harvey, Helen *Hayes, Al *Jolson, and Paul *Robeson performed on its stage. Purchased from the Mulock estate and saved from demolition in 1963 by Edwin 'Honest Ed' Mirvish, the Alex continues to import shows on a subscription basis augmented with mega-hit *musicals like

The infamous baby-stoning scene in Edward Bond's *Saved*, **Royal Court Theatre**, London, 1969. The play was banned by the Lord Chamberlain in 1965, despite the theatre company's attempts to evade the prohibition, and was seen publicly only after the abolition of British censorship in 1968.

Hair, A Chorus Line, Les Misérables, Rent, and *Mamma Mia!*
PBON

ROYAL COURT THEATRE

Small, unprepossessing *playhouse, opened in 1888 in Sloane Square in *London, home to two of the most influential ventures in twentieth-century British theatre. The first occurred from 1904 to 1907, when Harley Granville *Barker and his business *manager J. E. Vedrenne presented a series of matinée and evening performances, the *Vedrenne–Barker seasons. *Maeterlinck, *Yeats, *Schnitzler, and *Hauptmann were seen alongside *Galsworthy, St John *Hankin, Elizabeth *Robins, and, most prominently, *Shaw, whose plays were recognized for the first time as stageworthy and commercially viable. Barker also established the role of the *director as a creative force in British theatre. Despite some success housing the *Abbey Theatre's first London productions, and seasons by J. B. *Fagan and Barry *Jackson, the Court struggled between the wars, eventually suffering the twin misfortunes of conversion into a cinema in 1934 and bombing in 1940. Four years after its renovation, the *English

Stage Company began residency in a season that included John *Osborne's *Look Back in Anger* (1956). George *Devine, the company's first *artistic director, remodelled the venue in imitation of the *Berliner Ensemble's home at the Theater am *Schiffbauerdamm in *Berlin: he ripped out the gilt *proscenium arch and added a *forestage, converting two of the lower *boxes into downstage entrances. The production of Osborne's play helped bring about a revolution in theatrical tastes, re-establishing the importance of challenging, socially conscious writing, and bringing a minimal visual aesthetic to British *mise-en-scène and *scenography. In 1971 a *rehearsal room at the top of the building was converted to a small experimental space, the Theatre Upstairs. The building was extensively renovated between 1997 and 2000, and reopened with new leather seating, greatly improved backstage and administrative space, an enlarged Theatre Upstairs, and a new restaurant and bar area cut out of the mud beneath Sloane Square, though the architects altered nothing of the basic *stage–*auditorium relationship. The grandeur of the high unadorned stage opening and the intimacy of the vertically stacked auditorium has proved an ideal setting, visually and financially, for theatrical experiment. DR

ROYAL EXCHANGE THEATRE

Three-tiered, 700-seat *playhouse of tubular steel and glass built within a Victorian cotton exchange in *Manchester, with an in-the-round configuration (*see* ARENA AND IN-THE-ROUND). It opened in 1976 under the collaborative *artistic directorship of Michael *Elliott, Caspar Wrede, Braham Murray, Richard Negri, and James Maxwell. The performance space, which can utilize up to seven gangways through the *auditorium at stage level, and two levels of vertical space, promotes an intimate and engaging relationship between actors and *audience. Notable productions include Adrian *Noble's *The Duchess of Malfi* (1980), Nicholas *Hytner's *Edward II* (1986) and *Don Carlos* (1987), Murray's concentration camp *Macbeth* (1988) featuring David Threlfall, James Macdonald's *Richard II* with Linus Roache, and Gregory Hersov's *Look Back in Anger* (1995) with Michael Sheen. A number of world premières, including Ronald *Harwood's *The Dresser* (1980) and Shelagh Stephenson's *An Experiment with an Air-Pump* (1998), demonstrate a strong commitment to new writing. Structural damage caused by an IRA bomb in 1996 necessitated extensive repair work and a temporary relocation (until 1998) to the theatre's *touring structure; a 120-seat *studio was incorporated into the refurbished complex.

VRS

ROYAL LYCEUM THEATRE

The first building constructed for exclusive theatrical use in Ontario, the Lyceum in *Toronto provided a space for drama, *opera, *minstrel, and *variety shows between its opening in 1848 and its destruction by *fire in 1874. Only two lessees met with success: John Nickinson (1853–60), an English-born *actor-manager, whose *stock company featured *family members augmented by such travelling stars as William E. *Burton, Matilda *Heron, Lola *Montez, and James W. *Wallack; and George Holman (1867–72), whose stock company featured currently successful *New York and *London plays and English operas.

PBON

ROYAL NATIONAL THEATRE *See* NATIONAL THEATRE OF GREAT BRITAIN.

ROYAL SHAKESPEARE COMPANY

From the opening of the *Shakespeare Memorial Theatre in 1879 until 1960, performances in Stratford were a summer *festival season. In 1958 Fordham Flower, chairman of the board, and Peter *Hall, as the new *artistic director, planned a strikingly different future. Hall proposed a permanent company on the European model with actors on long contracts (though never as permanent members of an ensemble), a second home in *London, and a wider repertory, with the Stratford shows of Shakespeare and his contemporaries transferring to London to join productions of other classical drama and new plays. Hall also conceived of the new model as a national company with substantial state support. In 1961 the enterprise was renamed the Royal Shakespeare Company and Hall's model was adopted, with the *Aldwych Theatre as the London base. Hall involved young directors like Peter *Brook and John *Barton but also Michel *Saint-Denis, whose non-British perspective was crucial to the company's development.

Hall's company became known for its innovative Shakespeare productions, like Brook's *King Lear* (1962) and Hall and Barton's *The Wars of the Roses* (based on the *history plays, 1963), but also for its exploration of the European repertory in work such as *Brecht's *The Caucasian Chalk Circle* (directed by William *Gaskill, 1962) and *Weiss's *Marat/Sade* (directed by Brook, 1964). The RSC commissioned new plays (such as John *Whiting's *The Devils*, 1961) and brought controversial plays like *Hochhuth's *The Representative* (1963) to Britain. Its willingness to experiment was typified by a season at the *Arts Theatre in London in 1962 and the Theatre of *Cruelty season at the *London Academy of Music and Dramatic Art in 1964 exploring *Artaud. In 1966 the RSC became more visibly radical in its politics with Brook's *US*, attacking American involvement in Vietnam. Where *Olivier's *National Theatre was emphatically an *actors' theatre, Hall's RSC was a *directors' theatre—but also a *playwrights' theatre, with new work encouraged and with Shakespeare's plays treated as if newly written.

In Stratford the RSC made underrated Shakespeare plays popular (such as *Troilus and Cressida*, 1960), popular plays contemporary (such as Hall's *Hamlet* with David *Warner, 1965), as well as placing Shakespeare among his contemporaries, for example by playing *Marlowe's *The Jew of Malta* beside *The Merchant of Venice* (1965). Hall was encouraged to take the company's work on the road: Theatregoround was created for small-scale *touring, primarily of Shakespeare, in 1965, eventually closing in the 1970s, though the emphasis on its form of work continues.

In 1968 Hall handed the company over to Trevor *Nunn who, like Hall, was 28 when given the responsibility. Nunn made Barton, Terry *Hands, and David *Jones his associates and continued Hall's model, creating two companies to alternate between Stratford and London. The Shakespeare repertory continued to gather praise, especially Brook's *A Midsummer Night's*

Peter Brook's milestone version of *A Midsummer Night's Dream* for the **Royal Shakespeare Company**, Stratford-upon-Avon, 1970, one of its most famous productions. The joyful union of Titania (Sara Kestelman) and Bottom (David Waller) was accompanied by Mendelssohn's famous wedding march, which the composer intended for the final act. Bottom, hoisted aloft by the fairies and provided with an improvised phallus, is observed by other fairies at the top of the white box that constituted Sally Jacobs's innovative set.

Dream (1970), with the influence of the London repertory (including *Pinter, *Ibsen, and *Barnes) on the Shakespeare productions increasingly marked. The commitment to new drama continued in London with seasons at the Place and the *Donmar Warehouse. In Stratford Buzz *Goodbody established a *studio theatre in a tin shack that opened as the Other Place in 1974 with her *King Lear*, followed by her modern-dress *Hamlet* in 1975. The exploration of small-scale Shakespeare continued with Nunn's *Macbeth* (1976), which underscored the increasing difficulty for designers, directors, and actors of finding a contemporary style for Shakespeare in the Royal Shakespeare Theatre (as the main house has been called since 1961). The Other Place was also used for new drama by David *Edgar, David *Rudkin, Pam *Gems, and others. Nunn also began in 1977 the practice of taking the entire Stratford season to Newcastle-upon-Tyne, ensuring the company's work was accessible to *audiences in the north of England.

In 1978 Nunn made Hands associate director. The RSC had grown into a massive enterprise, by far the largest theatre institution in the world. In 1979 the company mounted 33 productions with 175 actors, playing in Stratford and London and touring in the UK and to Broadway. Best known for its large-scale shows—for example, in 1980 both Barton's ten-play Greek cycle and Edgar's eight-hour adaptation of *Nicholas Nickleby*—the RSC also developed other modes: *The Dillen* (1983), for instance, used local *amateur actors and the audience journeyed through Stratford to follow the *action.

In 1982 the company finally opened its London home at the *Barbican with productions of *1* and *2 Henry IV* directed by Nunn, echoing the first productions at the Shakespeare Memorial Theatre in 1932. The Pit provided a substandard small venue to continue the studio tradition. The poor design of the Barbican complex and the struggles to secure funding from the City of London made the venture a continual burden, and the RSC finally announced its intention to leave the Barbican in 2001. Yet in 1986 Frederick Koch's benefaction enabled the RSC to build the *Swan Theatre in the shell of the old Victorian house in Stratford as a 450-seat space, to explore *early modern and Restoration drama in a brilliant design that echoes Renaissance *playhouses without any attempt at authenticity. The Swan's exhilarating dynamics encouraged some of the RSC's finest work and most intriguing revivals. Nunn's production of *Les Misérables* (1985) showed that the RSC could make a commercial as well as artistic success of a *musical, providing a much needed source of revenue for many years.

Nunn left the RSC in 1986 and under Hands it flourished along similar, if increasingly predictable, lines. The Other Place was closed in 1989 and rebuilt to include much-needed *rehearsal space in 1991. *Financial constraints and inadequate subsidies led to the closing of the Barbican for four months in 1990, for the company was always disproportionately reliant on *box office compared with the National Theatre's subsidies.

In the same year Hands resigned and Adrian *Noble became artistic director. The range of work continued, though in an even less politicized mode. The Newcastle residency was briefly paralleled by one in Plymouth in the late 1990s but the company also began looking to the USA as a major source of income with regular visits to *New York. In 2001 Noble announced radical plans to restructure the enterprise, abandoning the Barbican and the tradition of a large-scale ensemble in favour of small ad hoc companies to tour increasingly in the USA, and planning two new theatres in Stratford by demolishing the RST, closing the Other Place, and keeping only the Swan. (Michael Boyd is expected to replace Noble in 2003.) As the RSC continues to adapt to changing economic, political, and cultural climates, it maintains its position as the world's largest theatre company and the major site for contemporary Shakespeare production.

PDH

BEAUMAN, SALLY, *The Royal Shakespeare Company: a history of ten decades* (Oxford, 1982)

BROCKBANK, PHILIP, et al. (eds.), *Players of Shakespeare*, 4 vols. (Cambridge, 1985–98)

KENNEDY, DENNIS, *Looking at Shakespeare: a visual history of twentieth-century performance*, 2nd edn. (Cambridge, 2001)

ROYAL SHAKESPEARE THEATRE *See* SHAKESPEARE MEMORIAL THEATRE.

ROYALTIES

A percentage of *box-office receipts paid to the author of a play. They became standard in France in the late eighteenth century and 100 years later in England and America. From 1791 playwrights in France received royalties on the night's receipts at every theatre in the country. The percentages varied according to the importance of the theatre and the number of *acts in the play: after the deduction of one-third for house charges, $12\frac{1}{2}$ per cent for four or five acts at top theatres, $8\frac{1}{3}$ per cent for two or three acts, $6\frac{1}{4}$ per cent for one act, and more if the author's work constituted the whole *playbill. Popular dramatists lived handsomely on this system. In England dramatists had done reasonably well early in the nineteenth century from substantial fees for the *copyright of a *published play and fixed payments of £33 6s. 8d. for each performance (replacing the old *benefit system on the third, sixth, ninth, and twentieth nights of a new play). However, by the 1830s and 1840s, with the slump in theatre attendance and economic depression, dramatists were paid derisory sums: usually—with some generous exceptions—£50 an act at West End theatres, far less at *minor theatres, and almost nothing for the copyright. Indeed, there was no copyright whatever in a performed play until the Dramatic Authors Act of 1833. Royalty and sharing agreements were not common until the 1880s. International and American copyright agreements in 1886 and 1891 respectively further strengthened the royalty position of the published dramatist. *See also* Society of Dramatic Authors and Composers; Society of Authors; Dramatists Guild; licensing of plays.

MRB

ROZENMACHER, GERMÁN (1936–71)

Argentinian playwright, short-story writer, and critic. A cantor's son, Rozenmacher is perhaps best known for *Requiem for a Friday Evening* (1964), about a Jewish family's intergenerational conflicts. He also wrote *Simon Brumelstein, Knight of the Indies* (1970, staged posthumously 1982) and co-authored, with three other 'neorealist' dramatists, *The Black Aeroplane* (1970).

JGJ

RÓŻEWICZ, TADEUSZ (1920–)

Polish poet, short-story writer, and playwright. Blurring distinctions of *genre and using *stage directions to challenge artistic convention, Różewicz's poetic *realism questions the assumptions of *mimesis and produces an 'open *dramaturgy' that regards the *text as a work in progress to be completed by actors and director. His first performed play, *The Card Index* (1959), introduced a new theatrical language of fragmented structure and imagistic collage made from the scrap heap of modern civilization. In the wake of Auschwitz, his antihero's (*see* HERO AND ANTIHERO) experiences of alienation and loss cannot be communicated through ideologies, moral judgements, or intellectual speculations, but only through the bare facts of human existence and ultimately silence. Różewicz has been a restless experimenter with form. Following a path leading from *Chekhov through Kafka to *Beckett, he has moved toward an interior drama played out in the empty spaces between events. *The Old Woman Broods* (1968) contemplates the persistence of life amidst post-apocalyptic rubble. *White Marriage* (1974) is a pastiche of *fin de siècle* sexual obsession seen through the eyes of two pubescent girls; and *The Trap* (1982) reveals Franz Kafka's sexual and familial entanglements. Różewicz the playwright has been silent since then.

DG

ROZOV, VIKTOR (1913–)

Soviet/Russian playwright. Rozov's plays focus on children on the way to adulthood, and became the main source for the repertoire of Anatoly *Efros and Oleg *Efremov. In his *In Search of Joy* (1957) the *hero demolishes a piece of furniture, symbol of the petty bourgeoisie, with his father's sabre; the gesture accompanying this act became symbolic for the break with tradition. *Alive Forever* (1943, 1956) deals with the compromising moral values of the immediate post-war years, and formed the basis for Mikhail Kalatozov's *film *The Cranes Are Flying*.

BB

ROZOVSKY, MARK (1937–)

Russian/Soviet playwright and *artistic director of the Nikitsky Gate Theatre in *Moscow. His credo, 'Theatrical Circles Arranged in a Spiral', appeared in 1972. Rozovsky is best known outside Russia for a stage adaptation of *Tolstoy's *Kholstomer* as *The Story of a Horse*, which was given a memorable production by *Tovstonogov in Leningrad (*St Petersburg). It was seen at the *Edinburgh Festival in 1987 and also in English-language productions in *New York and *London (1984, the latter directed by Michael *Bogdanov). In 1989 Rozovsky was responsible for staging *Tretyakov's controversial play on sexual mores, *I Want a Baby*, banned since *Meyerhold first attempted to produce it in 1930.

NW

RUBIO, MIGUEL (1951–)

Peruvian director, *theorist, and founder of *Yuyachkani (Lima, 1971). A member of Eugenio *Barba's International School of Theatre *Anthropology, Rubio's theatre research includes mounting international symposia and working in Andean-marginal communities. An active and gifted director, he has dealt with historical and social themes by combining scenic *realism with a personal poetic and magical Andean vision. His productions include *The Travelling Musicians* (1983), *Encounter of Foxes* (1985), *Against the Wind* (1989), *Goodbye, Ayacucho* (1990), *Do Not Play That Waltz for Me* (1990), *Antigone* (2000), and *Santiago* (2000).

LRG

RUDKIN, DAVID (1936–)

English playwright, who achieved success with his first play, *Afore Night Come* (1963), staged in an experimental season by the *Royal Shakespeare Company. It is a characteristic work in its examination of the relation between violence and *ritual, its sympathy for an outsider figure casually welcomed into a closed community and as casually killed, and its deployment of a carefully sustained network of imagery linking *dialogue and *action. *Ashes* (1978) elides a Belfast couple's infertility with the political impasse in Northern Ireland. *The Sons of Light* (1981), *The Triumph of Death* (1981), and *The Saxon Shore* (1986) show Rudkin increasingly working with mythopoeic material, often of his own invention, to illuminate the relation between history, place, and contemporary life and to show how *ritual is often the means whereby the seemingly incommunicable and the darkest of human tendencies can find expression. Not surprisingly, Rudkin has both been attracted to creating a *scenario for *dance (Darrell's *Sun into Darkness*), and proved a fine translator of classical drama (*Hippolytus*), *Ibsen's plays (*Peer Gynt, When We Dead Awaken, Rosmersholm*) and *opera librettos (*Moses and Aaron* for the Solti/*Hall staging at *Covent Garden in 1965), a form of music theatre for which he has himself created original work (*Broken Strings, Inquest of Love*). RAC

RUDMAN, MICHAEL (1939–)

American director working in Britain. Known for his easy movement between commercial and subsidized theatre, Rudman has frequently directed revivals of modern drama. From the mid-1960s to the 1970s, he worked in *regional repertory theatres, and was *artistic director of the *Hampstead Theatre Club until 1979. Subsequently he became director of the Lyttelton Theatre at the *National Theatre in *London, where he mounted *Death of a Salesman* (1979) with Warren Mitchell (a play he revisited with Dustin *Hoffman in *New York in 1984), *For Services Rendered* (1979), *Measure for Measure* (1980), *The Browning Version/ Harlequinade* (1980), and *The Magistrate* (1986). His work at the National made him seem a natural choice as the new artistic director of the *Chichester Festival Theatre in 1990, but he was dismissed after a year following the commercial failures of an adaptation of *Greene's *The Power and the Glory* and a *musical version of *Ionesco's *Rhinoceros*. In 1993 he directed *Frayn's *Donkey's Years* at the Sheffield *Crucible and in 2000 he directed his ex-wife, Felicity Kendal, in a revival of *Coward's *Fallen Angels*. MDG

RUEDA, LOPE DE (c.1512–1565)

Spanish playwright and *actor-manager who, as leader of a troupe of travelling players, performed a variety of religious and secular plays at religious festivals, in private houses and courtly halls before aristocratic *audiences, and in city squares, courtyards, fairs, etc., on simple board-and-trestle stages. The repertory consisted of *autos sacramentales*, religious plays in honour of the feast of *Corpus Christi; *comedias*, full-length secular plays; and—Rueda's own contribution—*pasos*, short, comic pieces usually played in conjunction with *comedias*. His four *comedias* and two ('*pastoral colloquies' were published in 1576, his two collections of *pasos* in 1567 and 1570. RWV

RUGANDA, JOHN (1941–)

Ugandan director and playwright. A founding member of the Makerere Travelling Theatre, Ruganda left Idi Amin's Uganda in 1973 for Kenya, where he founded the Nairobi *University Free Travelling Theatre. His early plays, *The Burdens* (1972), *Black Mamba* (1973), and *The Floods* (1980), deal with the social and political upheavals in Uganda since independence. His dramatic style was influenced by *Brecht's *epic theatre. While *The Burdens* and *The Floods* figure on school and university curricula, the later plays like *Echoes of Silence* (1986) and *The Glutton* (1989) gained little critical attention although they are more sophisticated, merging elements of the theatre of the *absurd

with *Serumaga's *allegorical style. Since the 1990s Ruganda has taught at the University of Swaziland. He received a Ph.D. from New Brunswick. EB

RUGGERI, RUGGERO (1871–1953)

Italian actor who gained international notoriety during a career of 65 years. He performed an extensive repertoire of Italian and European plays and led various theatrical companies. In 1925 he was invited by *Pirandello to join his company, Teatro d'Arte, which included Marta *Abba. Ruggeri *toured with Teatro d'Arte in *London and *Paris, where he performed in *Enrico IV* (*Henry IV*) and in *Sei personaggi in cerca d'autore* (*Six Characters in Search of an Author*). He became one of the best interpreters of Pirandello's work, noted in particular for his portrayal of Henry IV. In his later years he performed under the direction of both Giorgio *Strehler and Luchino *Visconti, including Jaques in the latter's *As You Like It* (translated as *Rosalinda*). ATS

RUHR VALLEY

Named after the River Ruhr and situated in the west of Germany, the Ruhr Valley covers an area of about 4,500 square km (about 2,800 square miles) on the east bank of the Lower Rhine. One of Germany's most densely populated urban regions, the valley was a coal-mining and industrial centre well into the twentieth century; in 1928 the critic Herbert Ihering declared that the area, with its working-class population, was an ideal subject for a topical social play. The Ruhr Valley has a long history of civic culture, manifested in the many theatres subsidized by its cities, often in the face of their financial difficulty, a circumstance which has continued with the restructuring of the region into hi-tech and service industries after the Second World War. Its *playhouses cover a broad range of the performing arts, including *opera, *operetta, *musicals, *dance, drama, and *cabaret. Some theatres have organized first-rate *festivals, and a triennial festival covering the whole Ruhr Valley is planned for 2003; but generally the established municipal theatres remain the centres of performance.

Bochum. For some generations the Bochum Schauspielhaus has been one of the leading stages in the German-speaking world. Its rise began in 1918 with Saladin Schmitt (*Intendant 1918–49) who, with his successor Hans *Schalla (1949–72), staged the entire Shakespeare canon at the Schauspielhaus. Peter *Zadek, the next director (1972–7), continued this Shakespeare tradition with daring experimental productions of *The Merchant of Venice* (1972) and *Hamlet* (1977). His successor Claus *Peymann (1979–86) favoured a more restrained style, counterpoised by Frank-Patrick Steckel's emphasis on the socio-political dimensions of drama (1986–93), while Leander *Haussmann (1993–9) advocated an aesthetics of pleasure

(*Spasstheater*) and mounted a number of new German plays. The tradition of director's theatre gave way to an actor-centred approach with the appointment of Mathias Hartmann in 2000. Bochum's other playhouse, the Prinz Regent Theater, which originated in the washroom of a former coal mine, opened in 1991 as the home of an independent theatre group mounting unconventional performances of rarely staged plays.

Dortmund, situated on an old trading road, looks back upon a theatrical tradition that began with religious plays in the *medieval period and humanist plays in the *early modern period. The nineteenth century was marked by a reliance on temporary venues for a broad repertory of popular operas from *Mozart's *The Magic Flute* to Weber's *Freischütz*), and of plays by *Schiller, Shakespeare, and *Kotzebue. In 1904 the Stadttheater Dortmund opened with a permanent ensemble, producing opera, drama, and *ballet. After its destruction in the Second World War, a large new building in the *Bauhaus style was erected with an opera house, a playhouse, and a *studio theatre.

Duisburg, situated at the confluence of the Ruhr and the Rhine, has had a theatre since 1912, in use mainly for opera and concerts. In 1995 Duisburg joined forces with its neighbouring city Düsseldorf to create Deutsche Oper am Rhein with two orchestras and shared opera and ballet companies. In 1977 the Akzente theatre festival began to present visiting companies, often accompanied by *films, exhibitions, and lectures. The first festival was dedicated to Shakespeare.

Essen, the metropolis of the Ruhr Valley, has a long theatrical tradition, from *religious plays in the local convent in the Middle Ages to humanist and *Jesuit dramas and a range of popular pieces (*carnival plays, *farces, buffooneries) in the *early modern period. From the seventeenth to the nineteenth centuries the city's theatre was dominated by licensed *touring companies with repertories of popular operas and plays. In 1878 a local industrialist, Friedrich Grillo, constructed a playhouse for his native city. Built in the Wilhelminian style by the *Berlin architect Heinrich Seeling, the house opened in 1892 and continued to offer the standard repertoire. In the 1920s and 1930s its reputation attracted important artists, such as the designer Caspar *Neher and the legendary choreographer Kurt Jooss (1901–79). Destroyed in 1944, it was rebuilt in 1950 and soon regained its pre-war importance by engaging guest directors like Erwin *Piscator and Jean-Louis *Barrault. A striking new opera house, the Aalto-Theater (named after its designer, Alvar Aalto), opened in 1988 and has achieved a national reputation. Several private playhouses enrich the city's cultural life, and Essen holds an annual festival of ballet and modern dance.

Mülheim's Theater an der Ruhr, one of the best-known ventures in the region, owes its existence to a triumvirate composed of the Italian Roberto Ciulli (director), Helmut Schäfer (*dramaturg), and Gralf-Edzard Habben (designer). Starting in 1981 a small ensemble on a low budget mounted 49 productions in eighteen years, many of them focusing on social and political issues. Transgressing normal linguistic, textual, and cultural conventions, unconventional works like the collage *Pinocchio Faust* (1997) by Collodi/*Goethe, or the *Silkroad Project* (1997–9) with actors of various nationalities, gained considerable local acclaim and were invited to tour to Syria, Iran, and Turkey. Theater an der Ruhr has organized 'landscape of theatre' festivals which have brought companies from Yugoslavia (1986–8), Poland (1989–91), and Russia (1993–4). One of these, a troupe from Skopje called Pralipe, chose to stay in Mülheim in 1991 and has staged several productions annually, often intercultural experiments. Each year the city organizes the Mülheimer Theatertage, a competition of the best new German plays.

Recklinghausen has been the scene of the annual Ruhrfestspiele since 1948. In 1947 the Hamburg state theatres, which suffered from lack of fuel, received spontaneous support from the city's coal mines, and in gratitude staged performances of various kinds. The slogan 'Kunst für Kohle' (art for coal) captured the post-war determination to keep theatre alive in a time of great deprivation, and ultimately led to an annual festival and a Festspielhaus, which opened in 1965. In 1991 Hansgünther *Heyme became its manager and reorganized the Ruhrfestspiele as a European festival of all the performing arts. Since then noted artists such as Maurice Béjart, Peter *Brook, Ariane *Mnouchkine, Michel Piccoli, and Robert *Wilson have made appearances on Recklinghausen's 'green hill'. Each festival is themed, and performances occur in many alternative spaces, including former coal mines and factories now converted to industrial museums.   HFP

RUIZ DE ALARCÓN Y MENDOZA, JUAN
(*c*.1581–1639)

Dramatist who wrote in Spain though born in Mexico, and who differed in many ways from his coevals. A 'colonial', a much mocked hunchback, and a lawyer, in 1626 he abandoned *playwriting after only a single decade, having written fewer than 30 works, which rarely foreground conventional themes like romantic love or honour. *El Anticristo* (*The Antichrist*) mixes *spectacle and theology, three others centre on magic, and a few are heroic dramas, but quite the most characteristic are his supposedly moralistic *comedies. His moralizing, however, is less otherworldly than ethical and *satirical; the virtues he celebrates are integrity, truthfulness, loyalty, and friendship. That his messages are clear is a consequence of his technique. His *plots are precisely constructed, his *characters sharply etched, and his language direct, almost excessively devoid indeed of lyricism or rhetoric. In his masterpece, *La verdad sospechosa* (*The Truth is Suspect*), a compulsive liar is defeated in love by a truthful rival, though his fabrications are so inventive that one feels tempted to forgive him (especially since his society seems almost as mendacious); in *Corneille's adaptation, *Le Menteur*, he is indeed allowed to get the girl. In *Las paredes oyen* (*Walls Have Ears*) a rich and handsome slanderer similarly loses out to a poor but honourable hunchback. But Alarcón's most original creation is the *hero of *Don Domingo de don Blas*, who defends with engaging logic his comfort-seeking lifestyle; when duty calls, however, both he and a thieving ne'er-do-well prove nobly patriotic.   VFD

RUMAN, MIKHAIL (1922–73)

Egyptian playwright. Influenced by Tennessee *Williams and Arthur *Miller, and having translated some of their plays into Arabic, Ruman made his playwriting debut at the age of 40 with *Al-Dokhan* (*Smoke*, 1962). Most writers in Nasser's Egypt sought to establish the middle-class intellectual as the seer of the emerging 'revolutionary' society, implicitly blaming the authorities for failing to heed the advice of that class. By contrast, Ruman persistently portrayed the bourgeois visionary as a painfully quixotic antihero (*see* HERO AND ANTIHERO). Dismissed by his contemporaries as an eccentric, Ruman was equally unpopular with the *censors, and fewer than half of his eighteen plays were staged during his lifetime.   HMA

RUSH, GEOFFREY (1951–)

Australian actor and director. Despite his mesmerizing and Oscar-winning performance as David Helfgott in the *film *Shine* (1996), Rush trained with *Lecoq and is a highly theatrical actor with a great ability to transform himself. His particular strengths are in broad *comedy and in working an *audience, but he is equally powerful in mannered roles. Of his many Australian performances his Proposhkin in Neil *Armfield's production of *Diary of a Madman* was particularly acclaimed, and *toured Russia and Georgia. Rush's fondness for irreverence and clowning were much in evidence in his direction of *The Popular Mechanicals* and its sequel *Pop Mex 2*, plays inspired by the workmen in *A Midsummer Night's Dream*, which began in *Sydney and became cult hits throughout Australia. Although he is now a film star, Rush continues to work in theatre, particularly in collaboration with Armfield.   EJS

RUSSELL, ANNIE (1864–1936)

Anglo-American actress. Born in Liverpool, she moved at five to *Montréal, where she made her stage debut at 8 in *Miss Multon*. Her first *New York appearance was in *HMS Pinafore* (1879), but it was the title role in *Esmeralda* (1881) that brought her acclaim—a portrayal she repeated almost 900 times in New York and on *tour. Ill-health kept her offstage for a time (1891–4), after which she recaptured her popularity, notably in Bret Harte's *Sue* (1896). In *London she originated the title role

in *Shaw's *Major Barbara* (1905) in the *Vedrenne–Barker seasons. Back in New York, she appeared in Shakespeare (Puck, Viola, Beatrice) and other classic parts. After touring two years in a thriller, *The Thirteenth Chair*, she retired from the professional stage in 1918 to teach theatre at Rollins College in Florida. She was most admired for her beautiful voice and natural style.
                                                            CT

RUSSELL, LILLIAN (1861–1922)

American singer and actress. Born Helen Louise Leonard in Iowa, Russell made her stage debut in *Chicago at 16 in *Time Tries All*. Moving to *New York, she toyed with the idea of grand *opera, but opted for a career in *operetta. In 1879 she was a *chorus girl in *HMS Pinafore*, and had her first major role in *The Grand Mogul* (1881). From then until 1899 she starred in nearly 30 works—many written for her—including *Polly* (1884), *La Cigale* (1891), and *An American Beauty* (1896). From 1899 to 1904 she appeared in the *revues of *Weber and Fields, notably *Twirly-Whirly* (1902), in which she introduced John Stromberg's sentimental song 'Come Down, ma Evenin' Star', thereafter her trademark number (and the only song she ever recorded). Although her offstage behaviour was far from exemplary, her unsurpassed beauty and onstage charm rendered her the reigning queen of light opera.   CT

RUSSELL, WILLY (1947–)

English playwright. Russell's commercially popular plays and *musicals frequently focus on *characters struggling to escape the confines of class or *gender roles in his native Liverpool. His first successful play, the musical *John, Paul, George, Ringo . . . and Bert* (1974), was commissioned by Alan Dossor of the Liverpool Everyman Theatre and later transferred to the West End. After several other plays for the Everyman, Russell's next hit was *Educating Rita* (1980), commissioned by the *Royal Shakespeare Company and directed by Mike Ockrent. It transferred to the West End where it ran for over two years and was later *filmed. *Blood Brothers*, another musical, again examines emergent class-consciousness, although through the providential theme of twins separated at birth who are destined to meet. The musical began life at the *Liverpool Playhouse in 1983 and after revisions and false starts became a West End hit in 1988, running for several years. *Shirley Valentine*, a one-woman play, premièred at the Liverpool Everyman in 1986 before moving to the West End and Broadway. It was subsequently filmed in 1989.   MDG

RUTEBEUF (fl. 1250–80)

Professional entertainer (*trouvère*), author of *The Miracle of Theophilus* (*c*.1261), based on an *exemplum* concerning the

Virgin. The play hints at multiple staging, but its brevity (663 lines) and the dominant role of Theophilus may imply that it was intended to be recited by Rutebeuf himself.   RWV

RUTHERFORD, MARGARET (1892–1972)

English actress. Although principally remembered after 1936 as a performer on *film of deceptively eccentric English ladies like Agatha *Christie's Miss Marple, Rutherford had a long stage career. Originally trained as a piano and elocution teacher, she began at the *Old Vic in 1925. She played Miss Prism in the celebrated 1939 production of *Wilde's *The Importance of Being Earnest* (opposite Edith *Evans), and was the original Madame Arcati in *Coward's *Blithe Spirit* (1941).   VEE

RUTHERSTON (ROTHENSTEIN), ALBERT (1884–1953)

English designer and painter, whose small theatre output was chiefly for Granville *Barker: *costumes for *The Winter's Tale* (*Savoy, 1912), which were reproduced as illustrations to Barker's acting edition of the play; the whole scheme for *Shaw's *Androcles and the Lion* (Savoy, 1913); a permanent setting comprising four tower-like houses with doorways opening onto a square with fountain and distant vista for *Molière's *The Forced Marriage* (*St James's, 1913). Barker later commissioned from Rutherston illustrations for *Cymbeline* for the Players Edition of Shakespeare (1923). Rutherston's style tended to stress *theatricality: the structures grouped about the playing space for the Molière were simply functional set pieces creating four distinct means of entry as deployed in *Roman *comedy; the work on *Cymbeline* consisted mainly of swirling drapes printed with airily sketched designs suggestive of a particular locality but left to fall into obvious folds. There was no pretence at *realism, only an aesthetic simplicity with some feeling for period. His *Sixteen Designs for the Theatre* (1938) is a useful visual record.   RAC

RUZANTE (c.1495–1542)

Stage name of the Paduan actor and playwright Angelo Beolco. Scholars of the twentieth century have re-established Ruzante as a unique comic genius, no longer unsung. In his earlier surviving sketches he explored and impersonated the world of Paduan peasants, rather than the urban scene which *commedia erudita* took from *Plautus. His farcical but persuasive evocations of the underdog and the loser draw a fine line between mocking derision on the one hand, and subversive sympathy on the other, a line which critics have been trying to pin down ever since—his *Conversation of Ruzante Returned from the Wars* (c.1529) is the only Italian *text of the whole century to present war in a *realistic manner. He eventually accepted the five-*act format of *commedia erudita*, and even openly imitated Plautus, but always retained his own inimitable voice. In his use of a mixture of different Italian dialects, in his totally performance-oriented *dramaturgy, and in his semi-professional merging of his own identity in his stage role, he is seen as a precursor of *commedia dell'arte*.   RAA

RYGA, GEORGE (1932–87)

Canadian *radio and *television writer, playwright, and novelist. Born and raised in an immigrant Ukrainian community in Alberta, he achieved sudden prominence with *The Ecstasy of Rita Joe* (*Vancouver Playhouse, 1967), a lyrical *tragedy about a Native Canadian woman seeking unsuccessfully to return from the city to her reserve. Appearing in Canada's centennial year, it had a galvanizing effect, marking the arrival of a major Canadian drama. Later plays fared less well. The scheduled 1971 Vancouver Playhouse production of *Captives of the Faceless Drummer* was cancelled due to the board's discomfort with its references to the hostage-taking in *Montréal which provoked a declaration of martial law in October 1970. Other plays include *Sunrise on Sarah* (1972), *Ploughmen of the Glacier* (1976), *Seven Hours to Sundown* (1976), and *Paracelsus* (1986). Foremost among his many television scripts is *Letter to my Son* (1978).   RCN

·S·

SABBAN, RAFIK AL- (1933-   )

Syrian director and scriptwriter. After an apprenticeship with Jean *Vilar in France in the late 1950s he returned to Damascus and launched a semi-professional troupe, introducing Greek *tragedy, Shakespeare, and *Molière to Syrian *audiences accustomed to a stream of low *comedies. He became an important force in the National Theatre and Syrian Television, both founded in 1960. His productions include: *Sophocles' *Antigone* and *Electra*, Tawfik el-*Hakim's *Praxagora* and *Al-Sultan'l-Ha'er* (*The Sultan's Dilemma*), Shakespeare's *The Merchant of Venice, Twelfth Night*, and *Much Ado About Nothing*, Molière's *Tartuffe*, *Calderón's *Life Is a Dream*, *Brecht's *Señora Carrar's Rifles*, Nazem Hikmat's *A Love Story*, and Alfred *Farag's *Al-Zeer Salem*. He emigrated to Egypt in the early 1970s, where he became a professor of drama and cinema, besides establishing a major career in *film and *television writing.

RI

SABBATINI, NICCOLÒ (1574-1654)

Italian architect, *scenographer, and stage engineer. He was a native of Pesaro on the Adriatic, which made him a subject of the dukes of Urbino until that state reverted to the papacy in 1638. It was around that date that he created the large Teatro del Sole for his home city, and at the same time published his influential *Practice of Building Sets and Machines in the Theatre*: the *theory and practice of the two projects went hand in hand. His manual reduced the technique of building theatres and sets to simple principles available to ordinary artisans and builders. This implicitly rejected the excessively elaborate and ambitious practices of the expensive baroque theatres of the largest Italian cities, and so made theatre potentially accessible to smaller centres and a wider public.

RAA

SABBIONETA

An ideal town constructed by Vespasiano Gonzaga outside Mantua in the late sixteenth century. It contained a small, self-contained *playhouse erected by *Scamozzi between 1588 and 1590. On a raked stage (11 by 7 m; 36 by 23 feet) he placed a fixed scene in lattice and stucco, similar to the central alleyway of the Teatro *Olimpico in Vicenza. This *perspective urban setting was not architecturally separated from the narrow acting space of the *proscenium, which faces a semicircular *auditorium with five wooden tiers of seating and an imposing colonnade.

GB

SACCO, ANTONIO (1708-88)

Italian *actor-manager (surname sometimes recorded as Sacchi). He perfected the *Harlequin-type role of Truffaldino, importing material from recognizable literary sources which were pleasingly attributed to this improvised mask. He began his career in Florence, and *toured widely even as far as *Lisbon, but is most associated with occupancies of theatres in Venice. *Goldoni's early *commedia dell'arte *scenarios, including *The Servant of Two Masters* which was later written out in full, were composed around his favoured mask. Later his company realized the very differently oriented theatrical 'Fables' of Carlo *Gozzi, starting with *The Love for Three Oranges* (*Pomegranates* in the original Italian) in 1761.

RAA

SACHS, HANS (1495-1576)

German poet, dramatist, and Meistersinger. A prolific writer in several *genres, Sachs himself listed over 4,000 titles, including more than 200 dramas. His reputation, however, rests on his humorous depictions of everyday life, on the farcical anecdotes called *Schwanke*, and especially on the more than 80

Fastnachtsspiele originally performed in his home town of Nuremberg at Shrovetide as part of the *carnival revelry. Sachs also wrote more than 60 non-carnival *comedies and an equal number of *tragedies. His plays were performed at a variety of locations within the city: at taverns, public houses, guildhalls, churches, and cloisters.   RWV

SACKVILLE, THOMAS (1536–1608) AND THOMAS NORTON (1532–84)

English politicians and dramatists. As young barristers, they wrote *Gorboduc* (1562) for the Inner Temple's Twelfth Night revels. The *tragedy of a legendary British monarch who divides his kingdom, it made a covert *political statement in favour of Elizabeth I's establishing the succession by marriage. It is notable for its formal and stylistic innovations in the use of blank *verse and *allegorical *dumb shows, and inaugurated a fashion for *Senecan tragedy at the *Inns of Court. Much admired in the sixteenth century as a literary work, it was revived theatrically in *Dublin in 1601.   MJW

SACRA RAPPRESENTAZIONE

A form of Italian popular drama, without division into *acts or change of *scenery, based on religious themes and stories from the scriptures. It differed from *religious theatre in Spain and France in that it did not originate with the clergy. It is presumed to have evolved from the *lauda drammatica* and it was the foundation of the *dramma sacro*. Begun in Umbria in the thirteenth century as part of a movement of religious renewal, it spread to the rest of Italy, and is still practised in some rural communities. *See* MEDIEVAL THEATRE IN EUROPE.   GGE

SADDIKI, TAYEB (1930–)

Moroccan actor, director, playwright, and *manager, the most important force in modern Moroccan theatre. Interested in experimentation from the start of his career in the late 1950s, he led a number of companies as *artistic director, from his own People's Theatre to the Casablanca Municipal Theatre (1964–76). At first he directed plays from the world repertory, such as *Gogol's *Revizor* (1958), *Aristophanes' *Ecclesiazusae* (1959), *Jonson's *Volpone* (1960), *Beckett's *Waiting for Godot* (1960), and *Ionesco's *Amédée* (1964). He then devoted himself to Moroccan and Arabic work, including Saghrouchni's *Last Act* (1962), Chakroun's *Hammad and Hamid* (1964), Kenfaoui's *Sultan Attoulba* (1965), al-*Eulj's *The Rams Involve Themselves* (1969), and *Madani's *Forgiveness* (1976). Searching for forms that would resonate in his country, he staged experimental adaptations drawn from the Arab classics (*Meetings of Hamadhani*, 1971) and others from the Moroccan popular trad-

ition (*Al Harraz of Chraïbi*, 1970; *The Caftan of Love Crimped by Passion*, 1999).   MMe

SADLER'S WELLS THEATRE

A *playhouse in Finsbury, *London. Sadler's Wells grew out of a late seventeenth-century pleasure garden and was opened as a theatre building in 1765. Unable to perform the *legitimate drama, it concentrated on dancing, performing *animals, *pantomime—Joseph *Grimaldi was the theatre's great pantomime *clown—and *spectacle entertainments like the sea battles in a stage water tank (fed by the New River) from 1804 to 1815. The best years of Sadler's Wells in the nineteenth century were during the managerial tenure of Samuel *Phelps (1844–62), which saw the production of 31 of Shakespeare's plays—carefully *rehearsed, stressing unity and ensemble, pictorially pleasing but not spectacular—a high-water mark of the Victorian theatre. Sadler's Wells then went through a lean period for many years. After presenting *melodrama, boxing, skating, and *music hall, it closed in 1906 and became derelict. In 1931 Lilian *Baylis erected a new theatre on the site, intended as a northern counterpart to the *Old Vic. It was later used for *opera, *ballet, and performances by visiting companies, becoming the home of Sadler's Wells Royal Ballet in 1977. It has recently been extensively renovated for *dance, opera, and experimental theatre.   MRB

SADOVSKY, PROV (1818–72)

Russian actor and senior member of a famous acting *family. Sadovsky made his *Moscow debut at the *Maly Theatre in 1839, where he developed into a first-rate character actor especially in the plays of *Ostrovsky. Graduating from the role of simpleton in Russian *vaudevilles, he made his mark as the Fool in *King Lear* (1843) and as Podkolyosin in *Gogol's *Marriage* the same year. He next triumphed in *Molière as M. Jourdain in *The Would-Be Gentleman* (1844) and Argan in *The Imaginary Invalid* (1846). He also acted the role of the servant Osip in Gogol's *The Government Inspector* (1845) but offended some with the *realistic coarseness of his interpretation, which was also true, to an extent, of his Gravedigger in *Hamlet*. During the 1850s and 1860s he appeared in 26 different roles in plays by Ostrovsky, as well as in plays by *Turgenev, *Pisemsky, and *Sukhovo-Kobylin. Comparing his talent with that of his great contemporary *Shchepkin, the critic Apollon Grigoriev wrote: 'Shchepkin portrays passions which are separable from the individual; Sadovsky plays the individual himself.'   NW

SADUR, NINA (1950–)

Soviet/Russian playwright. Sadur graduated from the Institute of Literature in 1983. *The Marvellous Old Woman* (1982) is composed of two short plays, drawing on themes of Russian *folklore that run through her work. Lidia encounters an old woman in the field, who plays a game that sends her down a dark hole from which she is reborn, but subsequently she is unable to discern this world from the other. *Drive On* (1983) deals with a peasant who attempts suicide on a railway line, while the train driver tries to stop him to no avail; an old woman comes along and simply walks off with the peasant. Sadur combines reality with the *surrealism of Russian folklore, using language sparsely and poetically. She has also written stage adaptations of *Gogol, Leskov, Dostoevsky, and *Lermontov.   BB

SAFETY

Safety hazards in even the best-run theatre are abundant and diverse. Heavy objects, including massive live electrical circuits, hang by temporary rigging. Large heavy *scenery moves at high speeds over considerable distances, steered by operators whose view may be obstructed. Flammable materials, numerous sources of heat, and large volumes of air inside high windowless walls invite sudden catastrophic *fires in theatres. Jury-rigged machinery and structures are put together in one-of-a-kind configurations. A full set of modern industrial tools offers all their familiar dangers. Commercial, visual, and *lighting considerations dictate that exits are few, and the crowd sits closely packed in the dark. Human factors aggravate everything. Unfamiliarity breeds unpredictability; because every shop project is unique, the worker on any given table saw or drill press is not as practised as workers in other industries. Many of the devices being constructed, tested, and perfected will be new to the worker. Performers learn, practise, and perform *dance, gymnastic stunts, and mock combat in spaces which are rarely as systematically safe as a dance studio, gym, or dojo. Production run crew are frequently hired at the last minute and rarely given a complete understanding of the machinery they operate; *choruses may be dancing on stages and around machinery which they first saw only days before opening. Technical and dress *rehearsals are often held at, or during, the end of periods of frantic construction, so that technicians may be exhausted and impaired in judgement, and often communicate poorly about devices they have just succeeded in working. Because theatres—whether commercial, subsidized, or *amateur—operate on tight margins, *financial pressure to cut corners on safety is constant.

The proliferation of the *proscenium end-stage, developed in the *early modern period, made fire the greatest danger in Western theatre. The contrast with older styles of staging is striking. No *Greek source even refers to deaths by fire in the theatre. The huge *Roman Colosseum suffered several major fires with no more than a dozen deaths at any time. When the *Globe in *London burned to the ground in 1613, there were no deaths and few injuries. Yet in 1615 in Seville, at the new proscenium-style Teatro Ataranzanas, a fire killed scores of people. For the first time Europe heard a story that was to become familiar: too few exits, too hard to get to; a fire of amazing energy and speed; a large enclosed space that channelled air flow against flammable materials, producing an effect like that in a blast furnace; doorways choked with bodies, partially incinerated by the intense heat.

By 1780 there had been more than twenty theatre fires with death tolls greater than 50. In 1781, Boullet, machinist at the *Palais Royal in *Paris, saw about twenty members of the company killed on stage when a back door opened and a smouldering fire suddenly erupted. In the next year he analysed the dangers of theatre fire into component processes:

1. *very rapid ignition* when flames, too close to combustible material, touched off scenery. Airflow over suspended or stretched vertical fabric is extremely fast and spreads the fire upward, producing high temperatures and tall flames. Within a minute or two this leads to:

2. the *foredraught*, a powerful rush of air through the *auditorium toward the *stage, heating and feeding the fire. This occurs simultaneously with:

3. *panic* in the house, leading to violence, pressing and trampling to death, blocked exits, and falls from galleries. Panic is generally the second-leading cause of deaths. During the panic, there is a

4. *collapse of the *flies*, in which the wooden *grid and any rope-hung scenery drop onto the fire on stage, creating the fuel for the

5. *flashover* (this is the modern term; in the eighteenth and nineteenth centuries it was called the backdraught, because the first rush of air was the foredraught). Much of the material on stage, though well above kindling temperature, would not have oxygen enough to ignite; but when a door was opened backstage by escaping actors or technicians, the added airflow would ignite tons of material at once, and the strong draught would drive a wave of flame to the back wall of the auditorium. This generally caused the majority of deaths.

In the reconstruction of the Palais Royal in 1782, Boullet introduced the fire *curtain. When the rapid ignition started, if the fire curtain were dropped into place, it would prevent the foredraught, giving the crew much more time to cut down and extinguish the burning scenery and to douse lamps. Further, it would conceal the fire from the *audience, helping to prevent the panic. With the extra time, the fire could often be stopped before it spread far into the flies, but even if it did, and the theatre were lost, the greatly lengthened escape time would save many lives. And if the fire curtain stayed in place—hence the importance of making it of flameproof materials and hanging it on metal cables and battens—flashover would be much smaller, occur much later, and vent upward into the flies instead of outward into the house. In the next twenty years the fire curtain at the Palais Royal proved its merits at least three times.

In 1801 Boullet published an essay outlining nearly every modern method of fire and *audience control. While nothing could make a flame-lit theatre with fabric scenery wholly safe, the fire curtain, shielded gas jets, proper safety architecture, and the presence of firefighting staff with proper equipment for every performance should have greatly reduced the death tolls from theatre fires. Instead, the nineteenth century was the era in which the very worst fires in theatres occurred most often. Commercial theatres deliberately limited external access, to reduce the number of ushers needed to prevent unpaid admission; they also limited aisle widths, in order to pack in more paying customers per area. Gas in tubes leading to lighting jets throughout the stage and house created a new and previously unimagined danger. Fire codes were weak, unenforced, or non-existent; for example, though it was nominally illegal almost everywhere, many doors were constructed opening inward as late as 1900.

The deadliest fires tended to occur on holidays, when theatres were filled with audiences of *women and children and when performances had a maximum of *special effects, *limelight, and flown scenery. Disasters at Richmond (1811), Lehman's Theatre (*St Petersburg, 1836), the Ring Opera House (*Vienna, 1881), Conway's (Brooklyn, 1876), the Front Street (Baltimore, 1895), and the Iroquois (*Chicago, 1903) were all at holiday season performances and resulted in many dead children and mothers.

For decades these holocausts recurred, but little action was taken until two theatre fires captured the imagination of popular culture. The 1876 fire at Conway's Theatre, prompting songs, poems, and books memorializing the suffering of the young audience, and the heroic conduct of actress Kate Claxton who calmed the crowd into evacuating in an orderly way, until a disorderly patron triggered a last-minute panic that cost hundreds of lives. Nascent American popular culture had learned how to dramatize such an event. When the next major US theatre fire occurred, on 30 December 1903, publishers, composers, and the yellow press were ready. At a children's matinée at the newly built (and widely advertised as fireproof) Iroquois Theater, fire killed hundreds of young children and their mothers in less than fifteen minutes. Subsequent investigation revealed that though Chicago had an almost model fire code for theatres, corruption had allowed nearly every safety measure to go ignored; the most egregious was a fire curtain hung on manila lines with wooden battens with enclosing cloth not flameproofed; this jammed, burned, and fell early in the fire, allowing a full backdraught.

Worldwide publicity of the event nearly equalled that later given to the sinking of the *Titanic*. The profit-motivated neglect of safety, the horror of the manner of death, the large number of sentimentalizable victims, the arrogant confidence of engineers that all-electric theatres did not need the safety precautions that gas had required, were all trumpeted in Marshall Everett's *The Great Chicago Theater Disaster* (1904), a bestseller for years afterward. Everett's work featured tender, *Dickensian descriptions of child and mother victims, titillating material about the chorus girls, stirring accounts of heroic actors, stagehands, and firefighters—everything needed to arouse Edwardian sentimentality. By June 1904, most major cities worldwide had toughened fire codes and enforcement, demanding most of what is still prevalent 100 years later, and what Boullet had recommended in 1801: wide and unimpeded aisles, emergency lighting, clearly marked outward-opening unlocked doors, well-maintained fire axes and firefighting equipment everywhere, codes on minimum seat spacing and limits on the number of seats in a row, regular inspections, and of course the fire curtain, hung on metal cable and never tied off. Sprinklers, water curtains, and remote central electric shut-offs are the only features that would not have been familiar to Boullet.

Other dangers in the theatre have been met by a mixture of *trade union work rules, insurance company pressure, legislation, and craft customs. They range from taping down cables and marking them with glow tape, to posting warnings around strobe lights, to training young technicians never to move a batten during construction without shouting a warning. In many cases the safety concerns and practices are exactly those one might find in any modern industrial facility, for example, the correct use of such extremely dangerous tools as the joiner and bandsaw.

Three additional areas of safety concern in recent years have been stage combat, artificial fogs, and chemical hazards generally. Mock combat was always dangerous and has become more so, since the audience, trained by *film stuntmen who need only get something to look right once, demands that actors get as close as feasible to real danger nightly. Beginning in the USA and now in most nations, stage violence is carefully planned and rehearsed separately for safety considerations. (This practice is not new; it was common in *kabuki before 1800.) Fight choreographers are increasingly licensed and certified, and that speciality is growing quickly.

The glycerol fogger was at first thought to have solved many of the problems associated with stage fog; it was much less harsh to mucus membranes than sal ammoniac smoke, and, unlike dry ice fog, it did not vanish under bright lights and did not leave floors dangerously slick with water. However, in recent years a pattern of respiratory injury and illness has become associated with the glycerol fogger and various unions have demanded that it not be used. Safety studies are under way, and as of 2001 some glycerol foggers are still on the market and in use. It seems unlikely that they will remain so much longer, given how widely they are distrusted.

Finally, paint, pigment, and dyes used in scenery are increasingly coming under scrutiny. Many colouring agents are toxic in large amounts and their effects in small doses over long periods of time are often poorly understood. Some human pathogens can incubate and grow in latex acrylic paints, with the potential for disease among painters and stagehands exposed while the paint is wet. There is abundant anecdotal evidence for the occurrence of 'multiple chemical sensitivity' (MCS) in a disproportionate ratio among long-term theatre technicians. MCS somewhat resembles an allergic reaction in which dozens or hundreds of different organic chemicals (usually dyes and solvents) can serve as the allergen. But exactly what constitutes MCS, and any generally accepted medical or safety advice about it, are still open questions. It seems reasonable to forecast, however, that it will be a major area of contention in theatrical safety in the early twenty-first century.

JB

GILLETTE, J. MICHAEL, *Theatrical Design and Production*, 3rd edn. (Mountain View, Calif., 1997)

WALNE, GRAHAM (ed.), *Effects for the Theatre* (London, 1995)

SAFETY CURTAIN *See* CURTAIN.

SAHRIDAYA

The ideal spectator in Sanskrit drama. Literally 'one of similar heart', the *sahridaya* identifies closely with the representation of particular states of emotion (*bhava*) in a performance. A connoisseur who is capable of savouring the *rasa* ('juice' or 'taste') of a performance, he or she is sometimes identified as a *rasika*—one who has been initiated into the full enjoyment of an aesthetic experience. According to the *Natyasastra*, the *sahridaya* must be noble, learned, virtuous, impartial, and critically responsive to the structure of emotion in a work of art. *See also* AUDIENCE.

LSR/RB

SAINETE

Short, generally *one-act, mode of Spanish *comedy, originally performed in the interval or at the end of a more serious piece or as the finale to a series of entertainments. An eighteenth-century derivation of the traditional *early modern forms of the *paso* and the *entremés*, popularized among *Madrid *audiences and given generous amounts of *costumbrismo* or local colour by established authors such as Ramón de la Cruz, the *sainete* continued to evolve in the nineteenth century and reached its pinnacle in the early twentieth, especially at the hands of Carlos Arniches and the *Álvarez Quintero brothers, where it was used as a lively evocation of popular culture in the lowlife quarters of Madrid and Andalusia. Many *sainetes* were intended as *parodies of, and were often produced at the same theatres as, plays of a more serious and established kind by both Spanish and foreign playwrights. An Argentinian variant of the *genre is the *sainete criollo*.

KG

SAINETE CRIOLLO

A *one-act play popular in the South American River Plate region (1890–1930). Derived from nineteenth-century Spanish *sainetes* ('tasty morsels', more or less) and *zarzuelas*, the *sainete criollo* was characterized by the encounter of local creole and immigrant cultures, resulting in a Babel of dialects, picturesque characters, songs and celebrations, and *melodramatic, often violent *plots. The writer Alberto Vacarezza summarized the typical plot: 'A *conventillo* [tenement] patio/ an Italian *encargao* [manager]/ a leathery Spaniard/ a broad, a smooth talker/ two thugs with knives/ flirtatious words, a love affair/ obstacles, jealousies, arguments/ a duel, a knifing/ uproar, shooting/ help, cops . . . curtain.' Turn-of-the-century immigration and urbanization led to the proliferation of multi-family dwellings in *Buenos Aires' southern suburbs, and the *conventillo*'s shared inner patio became the *sainete criollo*'s setting, carnivalizing the locale in direct contrast with the dominant *naturalism of the period. Nemesio Trejo, Carlos Mauricio Pacheco, and Vacarezza stand out as playwrights, along with the actors José *Podestá, Elías Alippi, and Florencio Parravicini.

JGJ

ST CHARLES THEATRE

James H. *Caldwell opened America's largest and finest *playhouse on St Charles Street in New Orleans in 1835, with a capacity of 4,100 spectators and lit entirely by gas (*see* LIGHTING). The excellent *stock company included for a time the young Charlotte *Cushman. The theatre also hosted such traveling stars as Edwin *Forrest, J. B. *Booth, and the ballerina Fanny Elssler. Destroyed by *fire in 1842, a smaller replacement opened on the site the next year, remained important until the Civil War, and continued as a minor roadhouse and *vaudeville theatre until it succumbed to flames in 1899.

DLR

SAINT-DENIS, MICHEL (1897–1971)

French actor, director, and teacher. Nephew and student of Jacques *Copeau, Saint-Denis later headed the Compagnie des Quinze, for which he directed several noteworthy productions at the Théâtre du *Vieux-Colombier, including four major plays by André *Obey. Instrumental in bringing the ideas of Copeau to the Anglo-American theatre, he took the troupe to *London where it made a huge impression before disbanding. There he established the London Theatre Studio (1935–9), coming into contact with major figures of the British theatre including *Guthrie, *Gielgud, and *Olivier. From 1946 to 1952 he founded and ran the *Old Vic Centre, which included a *training school and a *touring company of young professionals, the *Young Vic, and where his idea of an organic theatre institution, replete with a comprehensive programme to connect training to the profession, was fully articulated. Returning to France in 1953, he headed the Centre Dramatique de l'Est in Strasbourg, where he continued to develop this organic model, later continued in the development of curriculum for both the National Theatre School of Canada and the *Juilliard School in *New York. His two books, *Theatre: the rediscovery of style* (1960) and *Training for the Theatre* (1982), solidified his reputation.   DGM

ST DENIS, RUTH (1879–1968)

Pioneer American dancer. Ruth St Denis was the first American dancer to incorporate the traditions and practices of the *vaudeville and *legitimate stages into the emerging indigenous concert *dance movement. Beginning with *Radha*, her 1905 self-described 'dance translation', St Denis combined popular and ethnic dance steps with a visually entertaining, fully theatricalized *mise-en-scène to innovative effect, winning her acceptance in the United States and Europe as a 'classic' dancer in the same category as Isadora *Duncan. In 1916 she and husband Ted Shawn founded Denishawn, a *Los Angeles-based dance school and *touring company. A watershed experiment in dance pedagogy and performance, Denishawn was responsible for several generations of influential dance and theatre artists, among them Hollywood starlets Louise Brooks and Lillian *Gish and the modern dancers Martha *Graham and Doris Humphrey.   LTC

ST JAMES'S THEATRE

Built near Piccadilly by John Braham in 1835, the St James's initially served as a venue for popular entertainment such as *farces, adaptations of *Dickens, and wild *animal shows. In the 1840s and 1850s it featured French drama, including several visits by *Rachel. The *Bateman daughters performed Shakespeare here in the 1850s, while Henry *Irving gave his first *London performance here in 1866. Mrs John Wood took over the theatre, renovating it in 1869; John *Hare and W. H. *Kendal took control in 1879, again renovating it, and staging a number of fashionable *comedies in the 1880s. In 1891 George *Alexander became the *actor-manager, turning the *playhouse into a leading West End outlet for social dramas and comedies, *costumed *melodrama, and romantic *verse drama. After the First World War, the venue featured a number of leading actors, including *Forbes-Robertson, Sybil *Thorndike, Edith *Evans, Noël *Coward, George Arliss, Michael *Redgrave, Paul *Scofield, Laurence *Olivier, Vivien *Leigh, Madeleine *Renaud, and Jean-Louis *Barrault. The theatre was closed in 1957, then torn down.   TP

ST JAMES THEATRE

*New York *playhouse on West 44th Street that opened as Erlanger's Theatre in 1927 with George M. *Cohan in *The Merry Malones*. This 1,600-seat venue, which cost Abraham Erlanger $1,500,000 to build, was lost in 1932 to the Astor estate, which reopened it that year as the St James. It was later owned by the *Shubert Organization but in 1956, when the government ordered the organization to divest itself of many of its theatres, the St James became the first acquired by the Jujamcyn Organization, which completely redesigned and renovated it. Although this playhouse has hosted some important new dramas, as well as several significant Shakespeare productions (including America's first uncut *Hamlet*, starring Maurice *Evans, 1938), its bread and butter has been *musicals and *revues. These include such landmark shows as *Oklahoma!* (1943), *The King and I* (1951), *The Pajama Game* (1954), *Hello, Dolly!* (1964), and *The Producers* (2001).   SLL

ST MARTIN'S THEATRE

A small *playhouse in *London (550 seats), built in 1916, which served often as a venue for serious modern drama, including plays by *Galsworthy, *Lonsdale, *Priestley, and *Synge. It also has featured a mixed bag of popular plays which occasionally attained decent *long runs. It had real success in 1970 with Anthony Shaffer's *Sleuth*, which ran for three years before transferring to the Garrick. In 1974 Agatha *Christie's *The Mousetrap*, which had been playing at the Ambassador's Theatre since 1952, moved into St Martin's and proceeded to run for further decades, the longest-running production in London history.

TP

ST PETERSBURG

Built by Peter the Great during the early eighteenth century, St Petersburg (called Petrograd 1914–24, and Leningrad 1924–90) is now the Russian Federation's second cultural and theatrical centre after *Moscow. As early as 1714 Peter's sister, Natalya Alekseevna, commissioned the construction of a theatre to stage religious plays designed to be free to all-comers. A visiting German troupe performed there in 1719. In 1723 Peter ordered the construction of a theatre near the Admiralty building especially for foreign *touring groups. In 1756 the Empress Elizaveta inaugurated the first state public theatre in Russia, situated on Vasilevsky Island; its troupe included actors who had trained in Yaroslavl with Fyodor *Volkov, generally considered the founding father of Russian theatre. The company was initially headed by the *neoclassical dramatist Aleksandr *Sumarokov, and then by Volkov himself. In 1779 one Karl Knipper established the Free Russian Theatre in a former riding school on Tsaritsyn Meadow which the classical actor Ivan *Dmitrevsky led until 1783, the year in which the theatre was renamed the *Maly (Small) to distinguish it from the Bolshoi (Big) Kamenny Theatre, built in 1783 and which, like its Moscow counterpart, tended to house *opera and *ballet. In 1828 the Italian architect

Rossi was commissioned to build a large theatre just off Nevsky Prospekt, which opened in 1832 as the *Aleksandrinsky, an imperial theatre designed to rival its Muscovite counterparts. However, the theatregoing public was comparatively unsophisticated and a diet of sentimental *comedies, *melodramas, and Russian *vaudevilles tended to be the order of the day. *Censorship also played its part in banning more significant work, such as *Pushkin's *Boris Godunov* and *Lermontov's *Masquerade*.

A major breakthrough came in 1836 when, in the presence of Tsar Nicholas I himself, the première of *Gogol's *The Government Inspector* was given at the Aleksandrinsky and a new era in Russian drama was inaugurated. This period was dominated by the *acting talents of Aleksandr Martynov, who had the kind of creative influence at the Aleksandrinsky that Mikhail *Shchekpin had at the Moscow *Maly. Martynov was instrumental in popularizing the plays of Gogol, *Turgenev, and *Ostrovsky, in which he made famous appearances. The Mikhailovsky Theatre was opened in 1833, first as a concert hall and then, from the 1870s onwards, as the permanent headquarters of a company performing exclusively in French for the Russian aristocracy. The Mariinsky Theatre (renamed the Kirov in the 1930s) was a *circus arena before being destroyed by *fire and rebuilt in its present baroque splendour in 1860. It became St Petersburg's equivalent of the Moscow *Bolshoi, with first performances of operas by Tchaikovsky, Rimsky-Korsakov, Mussorgsky, and Borodin, in addition to founding a school of Russian ballet and offering works choreographed by Marius Petipa and Mikhail Fokin (Michel *Fokine).

The theatrical life of the city during the latter half of the nineteenth century was dominated by the Aleksandrinsky Theatre and a host of fine actors, including Konstantin *Varlamov, Maria Savina, Vasily Dalmatov, Vladimir Davydov, and Vera *Komissarzhevskaya, who starred in the ill-fated first performance of *Chekhov's *The Seagull* in 1896. With the rescinding of the imperial monopoly in 1882, a number of private theatrical enterprises sprang up. Komissarzhevskaya opened her own small theatre on Ofitserskaya Street in 1904, where she tried to emulate the *Moscow Art Theatre by staging the new *naturalist and *symbolist drama of the age. Her brother Fyodr (Theodore *Komisarjevsky) and Nikolai *Evreinov set up the Merry Theatre for Grown-up Children here during the 1908–9 season; Evreinov also established his own Theatre of Antiquity (1907–12) in tandem with Aleksandr Kugel's *satirical *Krivoe Zerkalo (Crooked Mirror) Theatre, where Evreinov also directed between 1910 and 1917. Meanwhile *Meyerhold had been appointed head of the imperial theatres and between 1908 and 1917 staged a range of dramas and operas in sumptuous style. At the same time he was evolving an alternative theatrical persona, 'Doctor Dapertutto', at *fringe venues in the city, and producing the theatre journal *The Love for Three Oranges*.

The 1917 Revolution brought about a transfer of power from the court to the Theatrical Section of the Petrograd branch of the Commissariat for Enlightenment (Narkompros) and in 1919 Aleksandr *Blok, together with Maxim *Gorky and the actress Maria Andreeva, established the Bolshoi Drama Theatre, which has occupied its present premises on the Fontanka since 1920. Here actors of the calibre of Yury Yuriev and Nikolai Monakhov put on a range of powerful classical dramas between 1919 and 1923 with themes in tune with the revolutionary moment. From the 1950s until the 1980s the theatre was headed by Georgy *Tovstonogov and became familiar to European and American *audiences as a result of successful world tours. The Aleksandrinsky (renamed the Pushkin Theatre in 1937) staged a range of new Soviet plays during the 1920s and 1930s, securing the services of actors with pre-revolutionary reputations alongside a new generation which included Nikolai Cherkassov, star of *Eisenstein's *films *Aleksandr Nevsky* and *Ivan the Terrible*. Nikolai *Akimov is especially associated with Leningrad, where he ran the Theatre of Comedy on Nevsky Prospekt from the late 1930s until the 1960s and directed notable productions of plays by Evgeny *Shvarts during the 1940s. Apart from Tovstonogov's work at the Bolshoi Drama Theatre, little of note was seen in the city during the last quarter of the twentieth century until Lev *Dodin assumed control of the Maly in 1983 and promptly created a troupe that gained a worldwide reputation. The Kirov produced the choreographic talents of Yury Grigorovich during the 1960s, who later went on the become *artistic director of the Moscow Bolshoi and, at the end of the century, audiences worldwide thrilled to the orchestral and operatic performances of the Kirov company under the baton of Valery Gergiev. St Petersburg, now under its original name once more, has a Theatre Institute, with a research centre and library on St Isaac's Square and an actor-*training school on Mokhovaya Street.   NW

SAINT PLAY

*Medieval drama based on the lives of saints, either biblical or extra-biblical, featuring conversion, miracle, and martyrdom. The treatment of biblical saints in the *liturgical drama was confined largely to single scenes. The only Latin saint plays that anticipate the later vernacular versions are several on the extra-biblical St Nicholas. Saint plays were produced in England, Spain, and Italy, but the bulk of those extant are French. The saints featured were, like St Nicholas, extra-biblical figures around whom legends had accumulated. While conversion, either of or by the saint, continued as a theme, the emphasis of saint plays gradually shifted to miracle and martyrdom. Martyrdom in particular afforded opportunity for grisly scenic *special effects, as saints were mutilated, grilled, boiled in lead, beheaded, or drowned. Later writers occasionally essayed the form: *Dekker and *Massinger in *The Virgin Martyr* (1620) and Jean *Rotrou in *Saint Genest* (1646).   RWV

SAJER, FAWAZ AL- (1948–88)

Syrian director. Trained in *Moscow, mostly under Yury *Zavadsky and M. O. Kneple, he came to attention at Damascus University when he directed three *one-acts by Riad Ismat, Osvaldo *Dragún, and Mamdouh Adwan entitled *An Nakoun Aw La Nakoun* (*To Be or Not to Be*, 1975), followed by *Rasoul Min Qaryet Tamera* (*A Messenger from Tamera Village*, 1976), by the Egyptian Mahmoud *Diab. For the new Experimental Theatre he directed *Gogol's *Diary of a Madman* (1977), performed by Assad *Fudda, his colleague at the Academy of Dramatic Arts, and Sadallah *Wannous's adaptation of a Peter *Weiss work, which was entitled *Rihlet Hanzala Min'l-Ghaflah Ila'l-Yaqazah* (*The Voyage of Hanzala from Ignorance to Awareness*). His last production was William *Saroyan's *The Cave Dwellers* (1988). His Ph.D. thesis was on *Stanislavsky *training in the Arab world.   RI

SAKATA TŌJŪRŌ (1647–1709)

*Kabuki actor, *manager, and playwright. Born in Echigo in north-west *Japan, Tōjūrō became the most famous exponent of *wagoto*, or the 'gentle style', associated with *Kyoto and *Osaka. He was famous for his lover roles, particularly those of wealthy, effeminate men who lose their positions due to profligacy or the machinations of others and must go into disguise. *Chikamatsu Monzaemon wrote kabuki plays for Tōjūrō: *Letter from the Pleasure Quarter* is a magnificent example that reveals something of Tōjūrō's manner. He emphasized *realism in *acting and was known for his witty declamatory style, and his legacy of realism and depiction of fallen figures lives on in Chikamatsu's domestic plays. His ideas on acting are preserved in the treatise *Yakusha rongo* (*The Actors' Analects*), a fascinating collection of writings by actors from Tōjūrō's era.   CAG

SAKS, GENE (1921–)

American director and actor. After graduating from Cornell University in 1943, Saks studied at the Dramatic Workshop of the New School for Social Research (*New York). He appeared *Off-Broadway in *Juno and the Paycock* in 1947, then in a series of Broadway productions, and emerged as a director in 1963 with *Enter Laughing* by Carl Reiner. He established a reputation as an inventive director of *comedies and *musicals, among them Jerry *Herman's *Mame* (1966) and Bernard Slade's *Same Time, Next Year* (1975). Saks's outstanding accomplishment may be his direction of Neil *Simon's plays, especially the autobiographical trilogy—*Brighton Beach Memoirs* (1983), *Biloxi Blues* (1985), and *Broadway Bound* (1986)—and Simon's Pulitzer Prize-winning *Lost in Yonkers* (1991). Saks has directed such notable *films as *Barefoot in the Park* (1967), *The Odd Couple* (1968), and

Cactus Flower (1969). In 1997, he directed Christopher Plummer in the *one-person show *Barrymore*.   MAF

SALAZAR BONDY, SEBASTIÁN (1924–65)

Peruvian playwright, teacher, poet, and critic. He studied in the University of San Marcos and at the *Paris Conservatoire, obtaining the Peruvian National Theatre *award for *Love, the Great Labyrinth* (1947), a satirical middle-class *farce. Inspired by European models, he also wrote *historical plays such as *Rodil* (1952) and *Flora Tristán* (1958). Using *Brechtian techniques of *satire, humour, and social commentary, Salazar explored the contradictions of Lima's traditional bourgeois class in *The Debt Arranger* (1962), *The Diviner* (1965), and several *one-act plays.   LRG

SALCEDO, HUGO (1964–)

Mexican playwright. He won national and international recognition with *The Singers' Trip* (1990; Tirso de Molina *award in Spain for best Spanish-language play), based on the real-life tragic fate of Mexicans who suffocated in a train car as they tried to enter the United States illegally. Border themes and types are recurrent in Salcedo's plays, with depiction of gratuitous violence in *The Desert Burns with Winds from the South* (1990) and *Boulevard* (1995), both of which use myth and *tragedy in journeys through the labyrinthine and often dangerous world of Tijuana, where Salcedo resides.   KFN

SALEM, ALI (1936–)

Egyptian playwright. A *puppeteer by training, Salem creates *characters resembling those of popular *comedy in spirit and form (hence his ability to cross over to commercial theatre), but also living in a pseudo-*realistic world that, as the play unfolds, takes on fantastical and Kafkaesque dimensions. Calling Salem 'the most distinguished *satirist of his generation', M. M. Badawi identified three targets of Salem's attacks: bureaucracy, corruption, and despotism. *Enta Elli Qattalt El-Wahsh* (*You Killed the Beast*, 1970), subtitled 'the comedy of Oedipus', was a daring criticism of Nasser, represented by Oedipus.   HMA

SALISBURY COURT THEATRE

A hall *playhouse built in 1629 by Richard Gunnell in the Whitefriars precinct, south of Fleet Street in *London. Gunnell was an actor hoping to emulate the two other hall theatres of the time, the *Blackfriars and the *Cockpit. A brick barn converted into a playhouse about 13 m (42 feet) square externally, with an interior built in the round, it was smaller than its peers and in its twelve years of life never matched them. King Charles had to ban the practice of gallants sitting on stage to watch the plays. For its last five years it housed Queen Henrietta's Men.

AJG

SALLE DES MACHINES

*Paris *playhouse, built for Louis XIV to replace the demolished *Petit-Bourbon as a private court theatre for spectacular entertainments. It was inaugurated in 1662 with Cavalli's *opera *Ercole amante*. The theatre, a long rectangle some 78 m (256 feet) in depth, took up the entire north wing of the Tuileries Palace. Its most impressive feature, however, was its *stage, which was designed and equipped with machinery by the *Vigarani *family, Gaspare and his sons Carlo and Lodovico. It was the deepest in Europe: behind a *forestage 4.5 m (15 feet) deep and reserved exclusively for actors and *dancers, a vista stage stretched back an additional 38.4 m (126 feet) in order to accommodate infinite *perspective effects. Because of its appalling acoustics, the theatre was little used, though in 1671 it did see performances of *Psyché*, by *Corneille and *Molière, with a finale in which one of Vigarani's cloud machines carried 300 divinities. It was the ideal venue for the annual mute *spectacles devised by *Servandoni in the eighteenth century. From 1764, after *fire destroyed the *Palais Royal, the *Opéra was temporarily relocated in the Salle des Machines—or rather onto its stage, for such were Vigarani's dimensions that Soufflot's provisional opera house was installed in its entirety, stage and *auditorium, within the shell of his stage house alone. When the Opéra vacated in 1770, the *Comédie-Française spent twelve damp, draughty years there.

During 1789, at the outbreak of the revolution, the Salle des Machines briefly housed the Théâtre de Monsieur, an enterprise under the patronage of Louis XVI's brother. In 1792, however, it was deprived of its theatrical function in order to become, first, the seat of the Convention, and then, under the Directory, the Conseil des Anciens. In 1809 Napoleon ordered architects Percier and Fontaine to redesign the Théâtre des Tuileries on the site of the Salle des Machines. Further modifications were effected in 1862. The Salle des Machines was destroyed under the Commune in 1871, when the entire north wing of the Tuileries was burned down.

JG

SALMAWY, MOHAMMED (1945–)

Egyptian journalist, playwright, and novelist. In 1984, only three years after the assassination of President Sadat, Al-Talia Theatre presented a double-bill of two *one-act plays by this activist-journalist: *Foot Alaina Bukra* (*Come Back Tomorrow*) and *Welli Ba'du* (*Who's Next*). Ideologically, their indictment of *Infitah*, Sadat's notoriously corrupt version of capitalism, marked the return of the long-repressed voice of his predecessor President Nasser. Salmawy's style has ranged from *expressionism (with an *absurdist slant) to *realism, yet all his plays attempt to depict (too transparently, some would argue) the Egyptian socio-political condition. Thanks, perhaps, to their topical nature, Salmawy's plays are widely endorsed by the media and frequently performed and translated.

HMA

SALTYKOV-SHCHEDRIN, MIKHAIL (1826–89)

Russian satirical novelist, dramatist, polemicist, and editor. His first work for the stage, *Dramatic Scenes and Monologues*, an adaptation of his *Provincial Sketches* (1856) and a *satire on bureaucratic rule, was prohibited by the *censor. His first staged work was *Mrs Muzovkin's Story*, also adapted from *Provincial Sketches* and staged at the *Aleksandrinsky Theatre, *St Petersburg, in 1857. In the same year his *comedy *The Death of Pazukhin*, about a family of repulsive legacy hunters, appeared in print but was not staged until 1893 and next revived at the *Moscow Art Theatre in 1914 by *Nemirovich-Danchenko. Saltykov's major claim to fame is his saga of provincial family life *The Golovlyovs*, which chronicles the decline of a family as a consequence of alcoholism and material greed. It was dramatized as *Little Judas* and staged at Anna Brenko's private theatre in 1880, then revived in more complete versions in 1910 and 1931. Another prose work which lent itself to dramatization is his *History of a Town* (1869), a bitter *parody of Russian history in the form of a chronicle of the town of Glupov (Dumbtown). The work is a satire on Count Arakcheev, whose name was a byword for the imposition of military discipline and strict order under Alexander I. In this work, Saltykov mocks social planners and warns factions of both left and right against social regimentation. It was staged (in a dramatization by Andrei Globa) at the *Moscow Theatre of Satire in 1932.

NW

SALVINI, TOMMASO (1829–1915)

Italian *actor-manager. Salvini was tall of stature and had a powerful physical presence and expressive features; his superb melodious voice and beautifully articulated speech could reflect many shades of meaning. Critics described him as a classical actor because he shaped his roles very carefully, exerting great control over his *character's emotional life and gestures, and usually repeating a part exactly each performance. Salvini learned his approach to *acting from the great Italian *actor-manager Gustavo *Modena, with whom he apprenticed (1843–5), showing the first signs of his exceptional abilities as David in *Alfieri's *Saul* and Nemours in *Delavigne's *Louis XI*. From 1846 to 1860, except for a break in 1849 when he volunteered for the National Guard to fight the Austrians in defence of the newly established Roman Republic, Salvini furthered his reputation at home. He acted first opposite *Ristori in several plays, including *Francesca da Rimini*, and then opposite Clementina Cazzola, his beloved companion until her death in 1868, in *Voltaire's *Zaïre*, Alfieri's *Saul*, and Shakespeare's *Othello* and *Hamlet*. His Othello also triumphed in *Paris in 1857, Salvini's first venture abroad. From 1864 to 1867, during the political upheavals of unification, Salvini directed the Fiorentini company in *Naples, bringing in 40 new plays and adding several roles to his permanent repertory—King Lear (which he studied for five years), the suffering husband in *Giacometti's *La Morte civile*, and the title role in D'Aste's *Samson*. Thereafter he would add to his permanent repertory only *Macbeth*, *Coriolanus*, and A. Soumet's *Gladiator*.

Having discovered the profitability of performing abroad during an 1869 *tour to Spain and Portugal, and finding little state support for theatre in a newly unified Italy, from 1871 to 1889 Salvini alternated long tours to South America, the USA, England, Scotland, Ireland, Germany, Austria, France, Russia, Eastern Europe, and Egypt with short stays at home. His interpretations, especially of Othello, on these journeys served as compelling models to influential actors, directors, and writers. William *Poel attributed to him his decision to have a career in the theatre, *Stanislavsky was deeply impressed by the two hours of preparation Salvini devoted each night to his role, *Zola lauded both his performance in *Morte civile* and the play itself as *realistic masterpieces, and an admiring Edwin *Booth appeared with him in *Hamlet* and *Othello*.   JEH

SALZBURG FESTIVAL

Austrian *festival of the performing arts, founded by Hugo von *Hofmannsthal, Max *Reinhardt, and Richard *Strauss in 1920. The Salzburg Festival was intended to vitalize the cultural vacuum of the modern world by reviving the glories of Central European high and *folk art. From the start, however, it failed to attract popular *audiences because of high prices. Subsequently it has become the most exclusive of European festivals, a feature that one long-standing director (1964–87), Herbert von Karajan, did little to discourage. Artistic standards are of the highest, and all major *opera stars, leading actors and directors of the Austrian and German theatres, and international symphony orchestras have performed there. Under Gerard Mortier (*artistic director, 1991–2001), the conservative image of the festival has, controversially, been challenged by innovative productions of classic opera and drama and by the successful presentation of experimental works.   SJCW

SAMBANDHA (PAMMAL SAMBANDHA MUDDIYAR) (1873–1967)

*Tamil playwright, *producer, director. Growing up in Chennai (Madras), he was inspired by the *proscenium theatre culture of the city, having little exposure to the traditional and *ritual theatre of rural Tamil Nadu. A lawyer by profession, Sambandha started his own theatre group, the Suguna Vilasa Sabha (1891), involving lawyers and other professionals from the middle class. Under his leadership *amateur theatre acquired a new respectability in educated upper-caste and middle-class circles. Strongly influenced by Shakespeare and *Kalidasa, Sambandha wrote 80 plays, starting with *Pushpavalli* (1891). He went on to write, produce, and direct *Amaladitya* (an adaptation of *Hamlet,* 1906); a social critique of the caste system in *Brahman and Shudra* (1933); a tear-jerking *melodrama *Manohara* (1895); the *farce *Chandra Hari* (written in 1923 to recover from the death of his fellow actor Vadivelu, who played female roles in his plays); and at least two highly successful Tamil *films adapted from *Sabhapathy* (1937) and *Sarangadhara* (1896). While experimenting with a wide variety of forms, Sambandha retained a certain formality in his treatment of social messages. Responsible for reducing the performance time of Tamil plays from eight to three hours, he is perhaps remembered less as a radical than as a reformer, who attempted to introduce *Stanislavskian *acting to his company.

PR/RB

SAMSA (SAMI VENKATADRI IYER) (1898–1939)

Indian dramatist of *Kannada theatre. Self-taught, he became proficient in Sanskrit, old Kannada, and English. After travel throughout *India and short stints of work in Quetta, Burma, Natal, and the Fiji Islands, he returned to Karnataka in 1915. Isolated in Mysore, and with a developing persecution complex, he conceived a master plan of writing 23 plays on the kings of the Mysore Dynasty; he completed far fewer, and only six have survived. Though Mysore in the early twentieth century was a progressive princely state, with an upwardly mobile, English-educated middle class, Samsa turned to the past for his material and chose to write in archaic old Kannada.

His work was part of a new school of *historical drama that included playwrights like Jaishankar *Prasad in *Hindi and D. L. Roy in *Bengali. They shared a desire to invent a glorious past for India in opposition to its colonial histories, but, unlike Prasad and Roy, Samsa did not reconstruct the histories of pan-Indian empires and focused instead on the tiny kingdom of Mysore. His six surviving plays trace the lineage of its dynasty from the 1550s to the 1650s, depicting an array of kings—brave and cowardly, graceful and ugly, benevolent and power-hungry. Within a bleak picture of the medieval monarchy, he celebrates the emergence of Ranadheera, an idealized king, more legendary than historical. Ranadheera appears first in Samsa's *Vigadavikramaraya* (*Vikramaraya, the Villain*) as a promising rebel, slowly acquires the qualities of kingship in *Vijayanarasimha* (the name of the royal sword), and finally emerges as a mature statesman in his last play, *Mantrashakti* (*The Power of Strategy*). The series provides a complex depiction of the dynasty, a strange blend of the real and the ideal, the factual and the fictional. Though Samsa produced some of his plays with *amateur actors in the 1920s, they were neglected after his death. Only in 1985 did his plays receive professional recognition in the repertory of *Ninasam Tirugata.

KVA

SAMSON, JOSEPH-ISIDORE (1793–1871)

French actor and playwright. A long-time star and *sociétaire* of the *Comédie-Française, where he made his debut in 1826, he excelled in *comedies by *Molière and dramas by *Scribe, notably in the roles of Bertrand de Rantzau in *Bertrand et Raton* (1833) and the doctor in *L'Ambitieux* (*The Ambitious Man*, 1834). As a student at the *Conservatoire he had been told to avoid classical tragic roles because of his nasal voice and undistinguished appearance. He returned to the Conservatoire as a professor in 1829, where later *Rachel was one of his students. He helped found the Society of Dramatic Artists with Baron Taylor. In addition to acting, he wrote several *vaudevilles and situational dramas, of which the most successful were *La Famille Poisson* (1846) and *La Dot de ma fille* (*My Daughter's Dowry*, 1854); also an extended didactic poem on the art of theatre, *L'Art théâtral* (1865).

CHB

SAM S. SHUBERT THEATRE

Named after the founder of the *Shubert chain of theatres, it was built by Lee and J. J. Shubert in *New York not only as a memorial to their brother but as the flagship and headquarters of the chain (as it remains today). Designed by noted architect Henry B. Herts, it shares the western wall of Shubert Alley with its sister theatre, the *Booth. It opened in 1911 with the *Forbes-Robertson Repertory Company production of *Hamlet* and has housed many successes, none more notable than the *musical *A Chorus Line*, which ran for more than 6,000 performances.

MCH

SÁNCHEZ, FLORENCIO (1875–1910)

Uruguayan playwright. Born in *Montevideo, Sánchez was the River Plate region's first great playwright, producing at least sixteen plays during the golden age of theatre in the area. Before his untimely death while on a scholarship in Italy, Sánchez saw his plays sell out in Montevideo and *Buenos Aires. He also worked as a journalist for both literary and anarchist weekly papers. Although most of his plays take place in the city, he is best known today for his rural gaucho *tragedies: *M'hijo el dotor* (*My Son the Doctor*, 1903), *La gringa* (*The Immigrant's Daughter*, 1904), and *Barranca abajo* (*Down the Ravine*, 1905). He wrote *naturalistic *thesis plays about conflicts between the old creole populace and new immigrants. Designed for an urban, bour-

geois *audience, his plays reinforced official policy about the benefits of foreign immigration to the region. Despite his anarchist, bohemian, and socially critical tendencies, Sánchez ironically served to consolidate the theatre of *realism as the region's dominant model.

JGJ

SÁNCHEZ, LUIS RAFAEL (1936–)

Puerto Rican playwright and novelist, the island's most renowned contemporary writer. His first play, *La espera* (*Waiting*, 1958), inaugurated the University of Puerto Rico Experimental Theatre. *La farsa del amor compradito* (*The Farce of Commercial Love*) and *13 Sol, Interior* (both 1961) were well received, but *La pasión según Antígona Pérez* (*The Passion According to Antigone Pérez*, 1968) gained him universal critical acclaim. Its staging (by Pablo Cabrera) was noteworthy for the use of *Brechtian techniques to convey *tragedy in a tale about a Latin American dictator. *Quíntuples* (1984), Sanchez's most recent play, was an international success in Brazil, Venezuela, Colombia, Mexico, Dominican Republic, Spain, and several North American cities.

JLRE

SANCHEZ-SCOTT, MILCHA (1953–)

American playwright of Indonesian, Chinese, Dutch, and Colombian heritage who spent her early years in Colombia, Mexico, and London. Sanchez-Scott attended Catholic school in La Jolla, California, and graduated from the University of San Diego where she studied literature, philosophy, and theatre. When she moved to *Los Angeles to pursue an acting career she was discouraged by the paucity of roles for Hispanics and turned to playwriting. Her first play, *Latina* (1980), was based on her experiences working as a receptionist in a maid's agency in Beverly Hills. Sanchez-Scott's most produced play to date is *Roosters* (1987), which explores relationships in a rural Chicano household through a style of magical *realism infused with heightened language, a poetic interpretation of the way working-class Chicanos speak. *Roosters* has been produced by professional theatres as well as by colleges, universities, and community-based Hispanic companies. *See also* CHICANO THEATRE; HISPANIC THEATRE, USA.

JAH

SANCHIS SINISTERRA, JOSÉ (1940–)

Spanish playwright, director, and *dramaturg. Founder of *Barcelona's independent Teatro Fronterizo and author of its manifesto in 1977, he became a guiding force in the resurgence of Catalan-language drama in the post-Franco period. His early plays, written in Spanish, were often postmodern stage adaptations of novels or stories. *The Night of Molly Bloom* (1979) was based on the final chapter of *Ulysses* and *The Great Natural Theatre of Oklahoma* (1982) on Kafka texts. *Ay, Carmela!* (1986), an original play about an acting couple caught behind the lines during the Spanish Civil War, was his first major success. In 1999, Catalonia's new National Theatre staged his *The Hired Reader*, a brilliant, enigmatic play in which excerpts from Conrad, Faulkner, and Durrell are integrated into the dramatic *text.

MPH

SANDIWARA

Popular Malay theatre in the 1950s and 1960s in *Malaysia and *Indonesia. The emergence of *sandiwara* after the decline of the *bangsawan (Malay opera) marked the beginning of a modern Malay theatre in which written scripts and *directing became essential. The need for good scripts, as opposed to the *improvised *dialogues of the *bangsawan*, encouraged many literary figures to write plays for the first time. *Acting techniques shifted from the vocalist-actor-dancer routine of the *bangsawan* to a *naturalistic mode, and scenes were changed behind *curtains rather than by a retinue of *dancers and singers in full view. In place of mystical and legendary scenes on *painted backdrops, *properties and *scenery were now designed to provide a *realistic ambience. *Sandiwara* stories were linear and centred around issues of social class and social conflicts, both romantic and melodramatic. Plays by well-known writers became classics of the *sandiwara* era, such as Kala Dewata's *Tile and Thatched Roofs*, Awang Had Salleh's *To Wipe away Tears*, Kalam Hamidy's *Child Pledged to the Seven Saints*, and Osman Awang's *Guest at Kenny Hill*. Before *sandiwara* gave way to modern Malay theatre and *television dramas in the 1970s, it also had a large impact through *radio broadcasts.

MA

SANDOW, EUGEN (ERNST FRIEDRICH MÖLLER) (1876–1925)

German strongman and actor. Known as the 'Mighty Monarch of Muscle', Sandow appeared in 1889 at the Royal Aquarium, *London, wrestling and lifting weights (including a carthorse). In 1893 he was brought to America but received little attention until he came to the notice of Florenz *Ziegfeld, who engaged Sandow for the 1898 *Chicago Columbian Exposition. Ziegfeld's promotion launched both his own and Sandow's international career. After they fell out Sandow continued to perform in *vaudeville acts until his vogue waned. His performances combined feats of strength with an aestheticization and eroticization of the male body. Wealthy women reputedly paid up to $300 to feel his biceps backstage. As an advertiser of cosmetic aids such as corsets and health oils, he was one of the first promoters and popularizers of physical culture, developing a system of body building based on classical statuary.

CBB

SAN FRANCISCO

Before the US annexation of California in 1846, theatre in the San Francisco Bay area consisted of Spanish *Passion plays, shepherds' plays, religious *processionals, and traditional festival entertainments. After the gold rush of 1849, San Francisco became the theatrical capital of the west coast. David G. 'Doc' Robinson founded one of the first theatres in 1850 with profits from his pharmacy: the 280-seat Dramatic Museum on California Street. His *playhouse was soon rivalled by Thomas Maguire's Jenny Lind Theatre, which was managed by Junius Brutus *Booth, Jr. Within the year, Junius had secured the services of his younger brother Edwin *Booth, one of the greatest American actors of the nineteenth century. Despite drinking problems, Edwin achieved success in *comedies and *burlesques, in addition to numerous Shakespearian roles, many of them opposite Catherine Sinclair (former wife of Edwin *Forrest). Booth moved to the Metropolitan Theatre with his new co-star Laura *Keene, eventually leaving the city to make his *New York debut after a benefit performance of King Lear in 1856. Lola *Montez, another fixture of the 1850s, became famous for her signature spider *dance.

San Francisco witnessed rapid expansion after the Civil War as the terminus of the transcontinental railway. Thousands of Chinese labourers were imported for its construction, making San Francisco an early centre for *Asian-American theatre. Soon after the railway's completion in 1869, the city became a major hub for *touring productions. The city's famous playhouses of this era were the Baldwin, the California, and the Tivoli Opera House. Local talent, such as the playwright and *manager David *Belasco and actress Maxine Elliott, were nurtured by the vibrant theatre scene before achieving national success. Although the Great Earthquake of 1906 destroyed many of San Francisco's theatres, most were quickly rebuilt, and during the 1920s and 1930s the city continued to play host to touring stars like Katharine *Cornell and Alfred *Lunt and Lynne Fontanne.

The performing arts experienced another boom after the Second World War. The *Actors Workshop, founded in 1952 by Herbert *Blau and Jules Irving, gained national attention for its pioneering productions of *avant-garde playwrights like *Brecht, *Pinter, *Beckett, and *Genet. Three important theatre companies emerged during the ferment of the 1960s: the *San Francisco Mime Troupe and two *regional theatres, the *American Conservatory Theatre and the Magic Theatre. Founded by William *Ball in 1964, ACT took up residence at the Geary Theatre in 1966, where it established a reputation for producing classical and established modern European drama. It is also home to an important actor-*training programme. The more adventurous Magic Theatre, based at Fort Mason, achieved national attention during the 1970s when Sam *Shepard served as resident playwright working in collaboration with director Robert *Woodruff, especially for *Buried Child* (1979). Since then, the

1181

city has continued to provide a congenial atmosphere for theatre and *performance art, and has a particularly strong presence of *gay and *lesbian companies. JAB

SAN FRANCISCO MIME TROUPE

Founded by R. G. Davis in the late 1950s, the company flourished in the counter-cultural environment of *San Francisco of the 1960s as an outdoor *agitprop theatre committed to the *political causes of the New Left. The aesthetic ideology of the troupe is characterized by *Brechtian appropriations of *popular entertainment forms. In 1965 Davis staged *A Minstrel Show*, a daring deconstruction of *minstrelsy and an attack on American racism. The troupe began a sustained engagement with the gestic possibilities of *commedia dell'arte in Joan Holden's adaptation of *Goldoni's play *L'amante militare* (*The Soldier Lover*), which *satirized the Vietnam War (1967). The troupe became a *collective after Davis resigned as director in 1970. Thereafter, the group solidified its identity by making *musical theatre a permanent part of its stage vocabulary, and by establishing a pattern of performing original scripts by Holden in Bay Area parks in the summer while *touring other times of the year. It was a paradox of the 1980s that the company received *National Endowment for the Arts funding to attack American conservatism during the Reagan era in shows like *Factwino versus the Moral Majority* (1983). In the 1990s the company broadened its political concern to include issues of multiculturalism, immigration, and the environment. JAB

SANGEET NATAK AKADEMI

Cultural institution supporting the performing arts in *India, established in 1953. Encouraged by Jawaharlal Nehru as part of a larger attempt to build a modern, secular nation-state, the Akademi conducted a series of national seminars and *festivals in theatre, *dance, and music between 1954 and 1958. The *National School of Drama in New Delhi, founded by the Akademi in 1959 in collaboration with the existing Asian Theatre Institute, was an outcome of the recommendations of the First Drama Seminar (1956). Apart from its annual *awards to outstanding national artists, the Akademi has contributed to the cultural life of the country by sponsoring and funding activities such as *folk theatre, workshops, research, and publications. Its mandate to cover all the performing arts of a vast and culturally diverse country, however, along with an acute dearth of financial resources, has understandably affected its ability to succeed comprehensively. KJ

SANGER, 'LORD' GEORGE (1827–1911)

English *circus proprietor. His father owned a travelling peepshow, and George established his own show of trained mice and canaries, after which he opened a tent circus with his brother John in 1853. He bought *Astley's Amphitheatre in 1871, giving command performances before Queen Victoria in 1885 and 1898. His circus *toured Europe as well as America. Sanger claimed the title 'Lord' in response to Buffalo Bill's advertising hype as the 'Honourable' William *Cody. In 1911, Sanger was murdered by a man who had worked as a labourer on his farm—and who was bequeathed £50 in Sanger's will. His reminiscences in *Seventy Years a Showman* (1910) provide a fascinating insight into the travelling shows of the nineteenth century. AF

SANGHYANG

Various types of Balinese exorcistic trance-*dances involving spirit possession. The best-known form is *sanghyang dedari*, in which two pre-pubescent girl dancers enter a trance in which they are believed to become possessed by spirits of heavenly nymphs. Other forms of *sanghyang* possession trance are associated with animal spirits, such as *sanghyang jaran*, *sanghyang celeng*, *sanghyang monyet*, and *sanghyang lelipi*, in which male dancers are possessed by the spirits of horses, pigs, monkeys, or snakes respectively. These trance *rituals are intended for purification, healing, or protection of the village community from epidemics, bad harvests, or evil spirits; generally to prevent misfortune. Trance induction begins in the innermost temple ground and is facilitated by incense smoke, chanting by female (*kidung*) and male (*cak*) *choruses, and prayers spoken by the head priest (*pemangku*). Once in a trance state, the dancers take on the character of the invoked celestial or animal spirits, often performing feats such as dancing on burning coconut husks. In *sanghyang dedari*, the young girls are sometimes lifted onto the shoulders of attendants, where they perform delicate dance movements while their eyes are closed. Thus they are often paraded through the village to purify and bless the area. The trance state is sustained by continued chanting and/or *gamelan music. While in trance, the *sanghyang dedari* dancers often prescribe ritual remedies required for purification or healing. At the conclusion of the ritual, holy water is sprinkled on the dancers by the priest to guide them out of trance. Several aspects of these trance rituals have influenced the development of more recent secular performance *genres; for instance, the dance of the *sanghyang dadari* is re-created and refined in *legong, and the male *cak* chorus is a central feature of *kecak. *See also* INDONESIA. KP

SANNU, YACUB (1839–1912)

Egyptian playwright, actor, *manager, and director. In 1870 Sannu founded the first Egyptian theatrical troupe, in response to the visiting European companies that performed under the auspices of Khedive Ismail, Egypt's westernizing Ottoman viceroy. Sannu drew upon the *comedies of *Molière, *Goldoni, and *Sheridan, as well as on indigenous spectacles (such as *Karagöz and other *shadow theatre). Sannu's overriding interest was to communicate with the Egyptian *audience, for both aesthetic and political reasons, and eventually he sacrificed many of the traditions of European theatre he initially held as sacrosanct. Encouraging audience participation, he allowed spectators to change the *plot of the play while in progress; often they even determined its ending. Actors' *improvisations sanctioned by the audience routinely became part of the performance on subsequent nights. With the closing down of Sannu's theatre in 1872 (when the socio-political implications of some of his plays incurred the wrath of Ismail), the preference for populist performance died away. The Levantine troupes, travelling to Egypt from 1876 onwards, consolidated a *text-oriented tradition that established literary Arabic (Fus'ha) as the standard language on stage.   HMA

SANO, SEKI (1905–66)

Japanese-Mexican director. His early work in *Japan was strongly influenced by Marxist *politics and proletarian theatre activists. Forced into exile in 1931, he went to Europe, via Hollywood, *Chicago, and *New York, where he met important leftist artists. In Germany he met *Piscator and *Brecht, whose theatre experiments with factory workers made a deep and lasting impression. In 1932 he travelled to the Soviet Union, and his training in the *Stanislavsky system would be a major influence on his subsequent work. In 1937 he was expelled from the Soviet Union along with many other foreigners, finally arriving in Mexico in 1939, where he stayed until his death. Sano continued to advocate a people's theatre and worked closely with the Mexican League of Revolutionary Writers and Artists. In 1941 he staged Clifford *Odets's *Waiting for Lefty* in support of striking tramcar conductors. An ardent anti-fascist and impressed by the *Federal Theatre Project in the United States, Sano staged an operatic, *open-air production of *The Rebellion of the Hanged* in 1942, based on a novel by Bruno Traven. Sano's most lasting legacy has been as a teacher of more than 6,500 students, many of whom went on the become major actors, and for his rigorous *training and *directing in *Method *acting, which produced the now legendary production of *A Streetcar Named Desire* (1952), which, it was rumoured, Tennessee *Williams found superior to the Broadway version.   KFN

SANQUIRICO, ALESSANDRO (1777–1849)

Italian artist, designer, and machinist. In 1806, after a *neoclassical apprenticeship, Sanquirico began to work regularly at *Milan's La *Scala. As sole designer from 1817 to 1832, he prepared hundreds of settings for *opera and *dance and conceived the redecoration of the theatre's interior (1829–30), including its magnificent chandelier. His name is particularly linked with the *romantic tradition of opera (Rossini, Bellini, Donizetti, Pacini) and the dramatic *ballets of Taglioni and *Viganò. The chief characteristics of his style were asymmetrical architectural design, historical verisimilitude, suggestive *lighting and a lively sense of colour, 'pavilions' with richly decorated *curtains, drapes, friezes, and mouldings, and spacious cellars or subterranean spaces with suggestively lit vaulted ceilings. Sanquirico also designed gardens, funerals, and Ferdinando I's coronation ceremony *See also* SCENOGRAPHY.   JEH

SANSKRIT THEATRE AND DRAMA *See* ABHINAYA; AHARYA; ANGIKA; BHASA; BHAVABHUTI; HASTA; KALIDASA; MAHENDRAVIKRAMAVARMAN; NATYASASTRA; SATTVIKA; SUDRAKA; VACIKA; VISAKHADATTA.

SANTANA, RODOLFO (1944–)

Venezuelan playwright who received recognition with *La Muerte de Alfredo Gris* (*The Death of Alfredo Gris*, 1964). In 1965 he was appointed director of Casa de La Cultura in Petare, and his experiences there led to *Algunos en el islote* (*Some on the Island*, 1965) and experimental works such as *Los tiempos modernos* (*Modern Times*, 1966) and *Paz y aviso* (*Peace and Warning*, 1966). *El sitio* (*The Place*, 1967) is about social revolution. Other plays include *Nuestro Padre Drácula* (*Our Father Dracula*, 1968), *Barba Roja* (*Red Beard*, 1970), *La empresa perdona un momento de locura* (*The Company Forgives a Moment of Madness*, 1976), which was highly acclaimed internationally, and *Gracias por los favores recibidos* (*Thank You for the Favours Received*, 1977). Santana has won a number of national *awards.
                                            LCL trans. AMCS

SANTANDER, FELIPE (1934–)

Mexican playwright. Drawing on his training as an agricultural engineer, Santander had a resounding success with *The Extension Agent* (1978), a critique of ill-conceived agrarian reform and social injustice in rural Mexico. Using *Brechtian techniques adapted to Mexican culture with *corridos* or sung ballads, Santander has his singing narrator (the *cancionero*) ask theatregoers to provide the play's *denouement, a tactic which added greatly to the play's popularity. *The Extension Agent* *toured throughout Mexico and was staged in various *Latin American countries, as well as in the United States; it played for over six years in *Mexico City, and in 1980 it won the prestigious Cuban *Casa de las Américas prize. While its companion piece, *The Two Brothers* (1984), had some success at home and was performed professionally in the United States, it did not bring Santander the acclaim or attention that he enjoyed with *The Extension Agent*.   KFN

SANTARCANGELO FESTIVAL

The medieval town Santarcangelo on the Adriatic coast of Italy hosts an international summer *festival of experimental theatre, Santarcangelo dei Teatri. The events, which come in many forms besides drama—*circus events, *puppet theatre, *clowning, *dance, *nō theatre, Greek funeral rites—take place in the piazzas, courtyards, and houses of the town and in the surrounding countryside. Pietro Patino and his Teatro Politico, an outgrowth of the 1968 cultural revolution, inaugurated the festival with *street performances in 1971. Over the following years, *artistic directors Roberto Bacci and Antonio Attisani brought in young, international, experimental groups, and well-known artists. More lately led by Leo *de Berardinis (1994–7) and Silvio Castiglioni (1998–2001), the festival has encouraged conversation about the theatre—its organization, *acting, technology, *criticism, poetics, and *theory—from Shakespeare to *commedia dell'arte, with a view to creating new directions for performance and new relationships with the *audience.   JEH

SANTARENO, BERNARDO (1957–81)

Portuguese playwright, pseudonym of António Martinho do Rosário, a doctor and psychiatrist, whose work registers the upheavals in the theatrical scene before and immediately after the Revolution of 1974. Led by the search for a national subject matter that is not devoid of universal appeal, his *tragedies deal with love (lyrical, violent, wasted) regulated by social constrictions, jealousy, sex, the flesh, and the instincts. They include *A promessa* (*The Promise*, 1957), *O crime da aldeia velha* (*Murder in the Old Village*, 1959), and *Português. Escritor. 45 anos de idade* (*Portuguese. Writer. 45 Years Old*, 1974). In these and other works religion is represented in its most reactionary form, as an obsessive mystical experience; his *characters alternate between the extremes of symbolic good and satanic evil. Santareno reveals a Portuguese society that left citizens in ignorance in order to continue an obscurantist form of power. He developed dramatic structures in line with European tendencies, such as *Brecht's and *Piscator's *didacticism and *García Lorca's *folk lyricism.   JOB

SANTIAGO DE CHILE

Theatrical activities in Santiago started in colonial times with performances largely religious in nature. At the beginning of the independence period, Fray Camilo *Henríquez wrote (1812) that theatre was an effective tool to propagate the idea of independence among common people and thereby develop a national identity, and wrote a play (*Camila; or, The Patriot of South America*, 1817) to bolster his idea. With this in mind, Bernardo O'Higgins, Chile's liberator, saw to it that a theatre was built in Santiago, opening in 1818. The first play by a Chilean author was staged in 1823: Manuel Magallanes's *La hija del sur; o, La independencia de Chile* (*Daughter of the South; or, The Independence of Chile*). Thereafter until the end of the nineteenth century, authors such as Juan Rafael Allende, Daniel Caldera, Alberto Blest Gana, and Daniel Barros Grez wrote *romantic dramas intended to develop allegiance to the emerging nation. In the first half of the twentieth century several theatres were operating in Santiago, the most important being the Teatro Municipal, where a middle-class *audience saw performances by European companies. A number of major dramatists emerged—Armando *Moock, Antonio Acevedo Hernández, and Germán Luco Cruchaga, for example—whose plays were staged with some success in Santiago theatres. In 1915 the Chilean Society of Playwrights was created to defend the members' rights and publish and circulate their work. Most of the plays produced in this period were *melodramas or light *comedies staged by commercial companies with actors like Rafael Frontaura, Elena Puelma, Alejandro Flores, Américo Vargas, and Pepe Rojas.

A visit in 1937 by Margarita *Xirgu's contemporary theatre company performing *García Lorca's poetic plays, and the election of President Pedro Aguirre Cerda, an educator and promoter of the arts, set the stage for a new era in Santiago theatre. The state now subsidized the arts through the universities, and the main impulse for change came from the theatres of the University of Chile and Catholic University, founded in 1941 and 1943 respectively. They *trained actors and theatre technicians and promoted classic and contemporary plays. Stimulated by this favourable atmosphere, young dramatists began to write psychological and *surrealist plays, turning away from the *realistic and *naturalistic conventions that had prevailed in Chile. In the 1950s the plays of Isidora *Aguirre, Luis Alberto *Heiremans, María Asunción *Requena, and Egon *Wolff were produced by the university theatres. In the 1960s theatrical activities in Santiago were enriched by the creation of the Theatre of the Technical University and by several repertory companies like *Ictus and Los Cuatro that were receptive to experimental approaches or deeply concerned with social issues.

In the wake of the Cuban Revolution and in reaction to the foreign policy of the USA, a strong leftist movement emerged in Chile that culminated in the election of the Marxist Salvador Allende as President in 1970. University theatres and independent groups attempted to meet the needs of the new government. Professional and *amateur theatre flourished, producing plays accessible to the populace. Groups created original works to address social issues such as alcoholism, the class struggle, and family problems, making use of *Brechtian techniques combined with humour and *melodrama. This invigorating atmosphere ended abruptly with the military coup in 1973. Many artists and intellectuals were sent into exile, incarcerated, or killed. Amateur groups were banned. Dramatists and directors tried using a metaphorical and ambiguous language to criticize Pinochet's regime, though covert methods did not always succeed: Marco

Antonio de la *Parra's play *Lo crudo, lo cocido, lo podrido* (*The Raw, the Cooked, and the Rotten*) was forcibly cancelled the day before opening at the Catholic University theatre (*see* CENSORSHIP). But this situation did not prevent many groups—such as Ictus, Teatro de Fin de Siglo, Teatro Imagen, and Teatro de la Memoria—from challenging the dictatorship. Ictus, for example, was able to produce David *Benavente's *Pedro Juan y Diego* (*Tom, Dick and Harry*, 1976), dealing with effects of the government's economic policies on the poor. When the dictatorship ended, theatre in Santiago experienced a revitalization and by the late twentieth century was flourishing. Theatres like *Gran Circo Teatro, La Feria, La Memoria, and La *Troppa, and dramatists like de la Parra, *Griffero, *Radrigán, and Margarita Inés Stranger, received positive international attention.   MAR

HURTADO, MARÍA DE LA LUZ, *Teatro chileno y modernidad: identidad y crisis social* (Santiago de Chile, 1997)

SÃO PAULO

From the beginnings of *Jesuit drama in Brazil in the sixteenth century (*see also* EVANGELICAL THEATRE IN LATIN AMERICA), the most notable 'Paulista' movements have been concerned with *politics and social change. A small town until the major waves of immigration in the late nineteenth century, São Paulo had a limited but expressive regional theatre, though it mainly imported productions from *Rio de Janeiro. Immigration, especially of Italian anarchists, brought a certain nuance to neighbourhood and workers' theatres, and the growth of student groups, along with the economic expansion of industrialization in the 1940s, paved the way for a cosmopolitan urban theatre, as exemplified by the Brazilian Comedy Theatre (TBC). Founded by the Italo-Brazilian industrialist Franco Zampari, the TBC became the prototype of professional theatre in Brazil and was São Paulo's most successful company from 1948 to 1964. The other major group of that period, the Arena Theatre, was formed in 1953 by José Renato as an alternative to the *proscenium-based and costly productions of the TBC. With the inclusion of activists Gianfrancesco *Guarnieri, Oduvaldo *Viana Filho, and Augusto *Boal, Arena began to search for a dramatic form that would speak to the social problems of the nation, and the Dramatic Seminar of 1958 dealt directly with the problem of finding national texts. Guarnieri's *They Don't Wear Black-Tie* and Viana Filho's *Chapetuba Futebol Clube* (both 1958), the two major plays of the seminar, reflect the social *realism of this tendency, emphasizing Brazilian linguistic and gestural codes.

The military coup of 1964 underscored the need for a new theatrical approach that could assess the dictatorship and the failure of the left. Under the direction of Boal, Arena developed the joker (*coringa*) system, in which tales of national heroes were told through *music and *verse (*see also* OPPRESSED, THEATRE OF THE). A significant development came from the director José Celso Martinez *Corrêa (Zé Celso) with Teatro Oficina

(Workshop Theatre, founded 1958). His production of Oswald de Andrade's *O rei da vela* (*Candle King*, 1967) proposed an aesthetic of aggression similar to that of the *Living Theatre, one which emphasized Brazilian stereotypical images, a *grotesque caricature of the exotic and erotic. Complementing the offerings of Oficina and Arena, impresario Ruth *Escobar opened a space for the daring work of Víctor *García (*Arrabal's *The Automobile Graveyard*, 1968; *Genet's *The Balcony*, 1969), and the São Paulo production of Zé Celso's *Roda viva* (1968).

The profile of the movement now emphasized independent and *amateur companies, and by the early 1970s *collective creation and the traditions of popular theatre were utilized for both political and artistic questioning. Teatro União Olho Vivo (Awake and United), under the direction of its principal playwright César Vieira, maintained a militant profile in the working-class neighbourhoods of São Paulo away from the watchful eye of *censorship, while the groups Pod Minoga and Ornitorrinco relied on collective corporeal expression. Gerald *Thomas made his appearance on the Paulista stage in the 1980s, and after a year's intensive work with Grupo de Arte Pau-Brasil, veteran director José *Antunes Filho produced the hallmark *spectacle *Macunaíma* in 1978. This effervescence of collective experimentation with corporeality also helped to prepare for the performance experimentation that characterized the late 1970s and 1980s with solo works by Marilena Ansaldi and Denise *Stoklos. A strong group of women playwrights emerged in São Paulo during this period, exemplified by Maria Adelaide *Amaral, Consuelo de *Castro, Leilah *Assunçao, Hilda Hirst, and Renata Pallottini.

The emphasis on visual and corporeal expression, sometimes tending to aestheticism, continued beyond the official end of the dictatorship in 1985. But the corruption scandals of democratization in the early 1990s, and a growing mistrust of neo-liberal social and cultural policies, shifted the theatre toward the political again; even commercial *comedies like Juca de Oliveira's *Caixa dois* (*Falsified Accounts*, 1999) have examined these issues. The group *TAPA has continued its investigation of specific political moments in Brazilian history; Antunes Filho, Zé Celso, and Stoklos were still active at the start of the twenty-first century; Antônio Nobrega, a composer-singer-dancer-actor originally from Pernambuco, uses popular culture as a historical memory to confront *mass-media culture. Significant new groups insist on the social utility of art, returning to collective creation through *improvisation. Companhia do Latão has dedicated itself since 1996 to the study of *Brechtian poetics, while Grupo Folias d'Arte emphasizes the *cabaret aspects of the Brechtian aesthetic. Teatro da Vertigem (Vertigo Theatre), active since 1995, creates apocalyptical *environmental pieces using site-specific locales such as an abandoned hospital wing, a police torture station, and a prison.

Despite this renewal of theatrical plurality, at the turn of the millennium theatre in São Paulo was seriously hampered by the privatization of *finance and an economic and social violence that keeps *audiences away. A loose confederation of theatre artists began the 'Art against Barbarism' movement in 1999, to pressure the government into changing its market-driven cultural policies. A renewed social commitment can also be detected in the Paulista revival of attention to the playwright Plínio *Marcos, who since the late 1960s has been a barometer of how Brazil perceives its crisis of urban violence; at the start of 2002 there were at least six commercial stagings of his work.

LHD

SARCEY, FRANCISQUE (1827–99)

French journalist. Beginning as a teacher dismissed for liberal beliefs, Sarcey became the leading theatre critic of the second half of the nineteenth century, succeeding Sainte-Beuve in his Monday column at Le Temps; his reviews were collected in book form as Quarante ans de théâtre after his death. 'Uncle Sarcey', as he was affectionately called by actors, was eclectic in his views, the main criteria of his critical approach always being common sense and theatrical effectiveness. He was enthusiastic in his appreciation of revivals of *romantic masterpieces belonging to an earlier generation: Ruy Blas in 1879, Antony in 1884; he saluted Balzac's La Marâtre (1848) as the dawning of a new *realism in the theatre; and while he dismissed *Maeterlinck's *symbolist drama as untheatrical, he was able to recognize a quite different talent for poetic drama in *Rostand, even before the success of Cyrano de Bergerac. See CRITICISM.   WDH

SARDOU, VICTORIEN (1831–1908)

French dramatist. Sardou carried on from where his predecessor *Scribe had left off, exploiting the formula of the *well-made play, with its mechanical contrivances and its *scènes à faire, in plays performed with success from 1860 until well after the turn of the century—sometimes at the *Comédie-Française, but more often in independent *boulevard theatres such as the Gymnase or the *Palais Royal. He was also much performed on the *London stage and in the United States. His subject matter ranged from *farce and light *comedy, such as Les Pattes de mouche (A Scrap of Paper), his first success, in 1860; Divorçons! (Let's Get a Divorce, 1880), through *comedy of manners (La Famille Benoîton, 1865), political comedy (Rabagas, 1872), and comedy in a *historical setting (Madame Sans-gêne, 1893) to *historical drama with more serious pretensions (Thermidor, 1891). In London the works were the butt of *Shaw's *criticism, in the essay 'Sardoodledom', or in his devastating analysis of Fedora; but Sardou's well-developed sense of theatre and meticulous craftsmanship made him the most successful dramatist of his day.

One of the most fruitful collaborations in the latter half of his career was with Sarah *Bernhardt, for whom he wrote plays to be performed in her own theatre, including Fedora (1882),

Théodora (1884), La Tosca (1887), and Gismonda (1894); while his Robespierre was premièred by *Irving, in English translation, at the *Lyceum (1899). Examples of Sardou's work as a more serious dramatist must include Thermidor, in which he sought to redress the balance of national feeling towards the history of the revolution by going against the revisionist tide of pro-Robespierre sentiment. After a successful opening at the Comédie-Française, the second performance was the occasion of a *riot by left-wing students outraged by condemnation of the Terror; further performance was vetoed, Clemenceau defending this action with his phrase 'La Révolution est un bloc': that is, a historical event that republican Frenchmen must accept in its totality. Compared with this attempt to enlist the theatre in the service of historiography, Robespierre offers a sentimental rehabilitation of its subject in the sort of historical *melodrama (with 69 speaking parts and 250 supernumeraries) of which *Dumas père might have been proud. The end of Sardou's career was marked by protracted litigation, when he sued the librettists of *Puccini's Tosca for plagiarism; the case was resolved (in his favour) only in the year of his death.   WDH

SARKI

Title for a Hausa regional chief in Niger and northern Nigeria and his investiture *ritual. The ceremony occurs a week after the chief's election and 40 days after the death of his predecessor. The setting is the new leader's house, and the *audience the entire village community. Two performers are involved: the sarki himself and the official conducting the ceremony, the doka. The precisely regulated action, accompanied by praise singing, involves *dance movements around a white mat during which the officiant consecrates the sarki by investing him with his new robes and insignia of office. A modern 1973 Hausa-language play derived from this ancient practice and translated into English is Gado K'Arhin Allaa's Inheritance, Strength from God (1977).   PNN trans. JCM

SARO-WIWA, KEN (1941–95)

Nigerian dramatist. After involvement as a student with the Ibadan's *university travelling theatre, Saro-Wiwa devoted himself, by turn, to administration, business, publishing, *television production, politics, the environment, and writing. He did everything with formidable energy and with an intense sense of the theatrical. During the early 1970s he reworked an undergraduate *revue sketch, The Transistor Radio, as a *radio play, and subsequently developed it as the pilot for what became a television sitcom with attitude, Basi and Company. He wrote dozens of scripts for this phenomenally successful series, which he produced during the mid-1980s. The *farce and *satire of Transistor Radio can also be found in (unpublished) later plays; an adaptation of *Gogol's The Government Inspector, The Supreme Commander, was staged shortly after the Nigerian Civil War; *Eneka* was so provocative that the group that staged it in Port Harcourt (*c.*1971) was disbanded. In commenting on events at the tribunal that sentenced him to death, Saro-Wiwa, a thorn in the side of a ruthless regime, quoted Shakespeare, creating yet again an extraordinary fusion between the actual and the theatrical.　JMG

SAROYAN, WILLIAM (1908–81)

American writer. When his most successful play, *The Time of your Life* (1939), was awarded the Pulitzer Prize, Saroyan returned the award and $1,000 cheque with a note explaining that art and business do not mix. The subjectivity, whimsy, and optimism of his work anticipated attitudes cultivated by the Beat Generation writers. Responding in 1942 to suggestions that his work was *surreal, Saroyan wrote, 'No one could possibly create anything more surrealistic and unbelievable than the world which everyone believes is real and is trying hard to inhabit . . . The job of art, I say, is to make a world which can be inhabited.' The author of some 45 plays, 22 volumes of short stories, eleven novels, and six volumes of memoirs, Saroyan was content to work in his own way and professed indifference to commercial or critical acceptance. Born to Armenian-American parents in Fresno, California, Saroyan left school and home at 15 and found work as a message boy in *San Francisco. He moved to *New York in 1928 and reached national attention in 1934 when the short story 'The Daring Young Man on the Flying Trapeze' appeared in *Story* magazine. The long *one-act play *My Heart's in the Highlands* (1939) was produced by the *Group Theatre for an 'experimental' five performances and was continued by the *Theatre Guild as part of their subscription season. Saroyan offered the Group *The Time of your Life*, but director Harold *Clurman declined it, a move he soon regretted. The play is a loosely structured fable about a gathering of likeable eccentrics who find refuge in a San Francisco saloon, a utopian retreat for misfits. When this paradise of acceptance is threatened by the interventions of a brutish police detective, a comic eccentric takes action to eliminate the threat and restore sanctuary, at least temporarily. Saroyan's other plays tend toward a similar mood, philosophy, and outcome. *Love's Old Sweet Song* (1940), *The Beautiful People* (1941, directed by Saroyan), *Across the Board on Tomorrow Morning* and *Talking with You* (1942, directed by Saroyan), and *The Cave Dwellers* (1957) all saw brief Broadway runs. Saroyan's one-act *Hello, Out There* (1942) has been admired by critics as the playwright's most disciplined work and a small masterpiece; it has been more widely produced than any but *The Time of your Life*.　MAF

SARSWELA

*Musical play from the *Philippines in one or three *acts which features typical Filipino *characters and situations within the framework of a romantic love story. Whether performed by commercial troupes or community actors, the play uses a *proscenium stage and painted backdrops. Descended from the *zarzuela, which was introduced by a Spanish troupe around 1879, the new form was hailed by the Filipino intelligentsia as more enlightened and refined than the *komedya (a play on Moors and Christians) which the *sarswela* eventually supplanted. From 1890 to 1940, the *sarswela* reigned supreme in the theatres of Manila as well as in public plazas during fiestas in the Tagalog, Pampango, Cebuano, Ilocano, Hiligaynon, Waray, Bicol, and Pangasinan regions. After the Second World War old *sarswela* were regularly revived in Manila while new ones continue to be written in the Ilocos. At the turn of the twentieth century many *sarswela* depicted Spanish oppression of the Filipinos and the anti-colonial struggle which climaxed in the 1896 Revolution. From 1910 onward, however, most examples avoided political controversy (especially with the American colonizer), concentrating on safe social issues, such as gambling, drinking, marital infidelity, social climbing, the colonial mentality, and usury. Conflicts built on such issues were developed through tortuous *plots, that invariably came to a 'correct' ending—a conclusion that reaffirmed the morality of the establishment, which preaches that gamblers, drunkards, philanderers, social climbers, and usurers should mend their ways. Predictably the conflict between rich and poor was resolved with the marriage of the landlord's son to the peasant's daughter. Through such endings the *sarswela* convinced *audiences that the ruling status quo deserved continuing faith and support.　NGT

SARTRE, JEAN-PAUL (1905–80)

French philosopher, novelist, and playwright, who in 1964 rejected the Nobel Prize. Sartre worked as a teacher in his early life and spent a formative year as a prisoner of war, which helped him link his existentialism with political struggle. After his release he began to write for the theatre. His plays, termed the 'theatre of situations', feature *characters locked in combat with one another, struggling for supremacy. His first play, *The Flies* (directed by Charles *Dullin in 1943), is an updated version of the Electra myth and was read at the time as a call to resist the Nazi occupation, reflecting Sartre's own experience as an active member of the Resistance. *Huis clos* (*No Exit*, or *In Camera*, 1944), his most famous play, is a post-death *ménage à trois* featuring a woman and her male as well as lesbian lover, both of whom vie for her affection while vilifying each other. One of Sartre's most famous lines (and, indeed, of modern French theatre), 'hell is other people', sums up both his philosophy and his *dramaturgy.

Les Mains sales (*Dirty Hands*, 1948) features a young intellectual who fails as a revolutionary through self-doubt. Revolution (as well as drama) can only come about, Sartre suggests, through choices and actions. The *hero in his sequel, *Le Diable*

et le bon Dieu (*The Devil and the Good Lord*, directed by *Jouvet, 1951), manages to break out of a cycle of inaction and wreaks havoc around him, but this action is tinged with limitations since it is accomplished in a quest to define his own existence. Other notable plays include an adaptation of *Kean* by *Dumas père* (1954) and *Les Séquestrés d'Altona* (*The Condemned of Altona*, 1959). Sartre's final theatrical work was an adaptation of *Euripides' The Trojan Women* at the *Théâtre National Populaire in 1965. He wrote a major study of Jean *Genet entitled *Saint-Genet, Actor and Martyr* (1952), but his own drama differed from Genet's in that it was limited by a mid-nineteenth-century concept of drawing-room dramaturgy.   BRS

SASTRE, ALFONSO (1926–   )

Spanish playwright, essayist, and critic. Largely outlawed by the Francoist regime, his work developed as a critical response to the *bourgeois dramas of Jacinto *Benavente, Adolfo Torrado, and Eduardo Marquina, and as a defence of the theatre as an instrument for social mobilization and transformation, crystallized in the frustrated attempt in 1950 to found the Teatro de Agitación Social. Thereafter Sastre embarked on a wide-ranging investigation of theatrical *realism, both theoretically (in articles, manifestos, and book-length studies) and practically (through the foundation of the Grupo de Teatro Realista). In Sastre's view, the 'definitive' start of his theatrical career occurred in 1953 with the première of *Escuadra hacia la muerte* (*The Death Squad*), a series of six bleak tableaux linked by blackouts, a 'cry of protest against the threatening prospect of a new world war', and *La mordaza* (*The Gag*, 1954). His work developed with the 'complex *tragedies' of the late 1960s and 1970s, slices of Spanish social reality collected in his *Teatro penúltimo* (1972). To this 'penultimate' phase should be added an 'ultimate' one in which Sastre produced powerful revisions of *Rojas's *La Celestina* and *Plautus' *Amphitruo*.   KG

SATIRE

One of the two most common forms of mockery, the other being *parody. Satire is literary, parody an enactment. But the line of separation wavers and at times disappears. Both boast a range of weapons: irony or saying more or less the opposite of what is meant ('He's a real genius!'), sarcasm or saying something in an uncomplimentary or hurtful way ('What idiot told you that?'), understatement, hyperbole, and assorted other figures of speech. All may be aimed at individuals, groups, institutions, or abstractions like trendiness (fashionable practices, rumour-mongering, slang of the day). Neither is quite a *genre; rather, they send cross-currents of morality, acerbity, and topical additions through three of the formal genres—*comedy, *tragicomedy, *farce—complicating those genres and sometimes enriching them.

Ever since *Aristophanes applied himself to satire in the *drama, and subsequently *Horace and Juvenal gave their names to satirical prose and verse, satire has defended its occasional savagery as a cleansing function. Persons of sensitive taste will recognize the social desirability of giving trash its rightful name. A doctoral student once wrote in a class paper: 'Satire as corrective when couched in invective is seldom effective.' Writing satire, though, may confer satisfaction on a critic, especially when it is brutal and he or she is blessed enough not to call forth a brutal retort. Strict Freudians—if any are left—might think of callous satire as an incomplete, sublimated death wish.

Aristophanes assailed his targets with what might be called smiling distaste. He expressed disappointment with the bluster of Athenian statesmen, compared with a principled (but fictitious) community founded above Earth by the *Birds*; contempt for the self-righteous teaching and philosophy attributed by him to Socrates in *Clouds*; men addicted to legal cases and law courts in *Wasps* (adapted 2000 years later in *Racine's *Les Plandeurs* (*The Litigants*, 1668). He disparaged other poets' plays (*Frogs*) and advised women to defeat war by denying sex to their partners (*Lysistrata*). He dared to imagine women snatching legal and parliamentary power from men in *Thesmophoriazusae* (411 BC) and subsequently in *Ecclesiazusae*.

The scope of his mockery and the gallery of his laughing stocks are nearly matched by those of another monumental exponent of satire, *Molière, more than two-thirds of whose 33 plays rely on some of the most instructive, pointed, entertaining dramatic satire written. Over and over in his comedies and tragicomedies Molière depicted extreme examples of what Ben *Jonson called humours, roles dominated by one characteristic (*see* COMEDY OF HUMOURS). Molière's list takes in Harpagon in *The Miser* (1668); his opposite, Monsieur Jourdain, the extravagant spender in *The Would-Be Gentleman* (1670); the hypocritical priest-cum-cadger, and his mark, Orgon, in *Tartuffe* (1668–9); Argan in *The Imaginary Invalid* (1673), a patient starved for medicines who gobbles prescription drugs like fast food; Zeus the triumphant seducer in *Amphitryon* (1668), now considered a dig at Molière's patron Louis XIV; the less-than-effective seducer who is the *protagonist of *Don Juan* (1665); the snobbish girls in *The Affected Damsels* (1659); and the ageing pretender in *The Seductive Countess* (1671). Alceste, the verbally violent social critic of *The Misanthrope* (1666), and no fewer than six leading male parts, bring misery into their lives by marrying or coveting much younger women, as the author himself did—Le Barbouillé in *The Jealous Husband* (n.d.), Sganarelle in *The Imaginary Cuckold* (1660), a second Sganarelle in *The School for Husbands* (1661), a third Sganarelle in *The Forced Marriage* (1664), Arnolphe in *The School for Wives* (1662), and George Dandin in the play with the same name (1668). These portraits have become types for all time. In Philaminte, a middle-aged lady, and her daughter Henriette, Molière created a mother and daughter who announce their intention to set up a women's academy, which shall rule over French language and manners; this is often taken to be a skit on women, but it is rather a veiled, comic assault on the French Academy and, indeed, the futility of founding an academy in the first place. (In *Love's Labour's Lost* Shakespeare earlier had the King of Navarre and three of his male courtiers talk about giving up the pursuit of women in favour of pursuing learning in a new academy.) Molière's most direct impersonation takes place in *The Versailles Impromptu* (1663), in which, playing himself, he mimicked five actors from his rivals at the *Hôtel de Bourgogne company. In his performance, then, the author, as actor, turned his satire into parody.

Encouraged by Molière's examples, scores of playwrights all over Europe tried their hands at satirical theatre. Restoration authors in *London, from *Dryden and *Wycherley to *Congreve and *Farquhar, purloined Molière's plots; they also attempted something like his ferocity in plays that aimed at marquesses and other high-society panhandlers. (Congreve could sporadically equal Molière's controlled rage.) In Denmark the Norwegian-born Ludvig *Holberg wrote more than twenty comedies streaked with satire; in Italy (and later Paris) Carlo *Goldoni sustained Molière's satirizing of *petits commerçants*; and in Russia the outstanding theatre satirist of the nineteenth century, Nikolai *Gogol, wrote *Revisor* (*The Government Inspector*, 1836), a sceptical look at tax chicanery in a remote Russian community. In the production Vsevolod *Meyerhold directed nearly a century later (1926) in *Moscow, that venturesome artist reasserted his stage skills with satire in a portrait of communist apparatchiks. The twentieth century was crammed with satirical scenes and plays by Bertolt *Brecht (*Mahagonny*, 1930; *Arturo Ui*, 1941), Friedrich *Dürrenmatt (*The Visit*, 1956), Jean *Genet (*The Balcony*, 1956), Boris *Vian (*The Knacker's ABC*, 1950), and many worthy others. Among them is the most striking American drama since *O'Neill's death in 1953, Tony *Kushner's two-part *Angels in America* (1993), with its devastating picture of Roy Cohn's anti-Semitism, homophobia, anticommunism, and influence in Washington, as well as the loathing of everyone who passed through his tawdry life. ACB

CHARNEY, MAURICE, *Comedy High and Low* (Oxford, 1978)
KERNAN, ALVIN B., *Modern Satire* (New York, 1962)

SATŌ MAKOTO (1943–)

Japanese director and playwright. A veteran of the 1960s underground (*angura*) theatre movement, Satō was instrumental in forming what is now called the Black Tent Theatre in *Tokyo. His *Brechtian, *politically committed theatre is apparent in such plays as *Ismene* (1966), *My Beatles* (1967), *Nezumi Kozō: The Rat* (1969), and *The Dance of Angels Who Burn their Own Wings* (1970, a radical revision of Peter *Weiss's *Marat/Sade*). His trilogy *The Comic World of Shōwa* (1975–9) cast a sharply critical gaze on the ultra-nationalist ideology of pre-war *Japan. Satō's company have toured *Japan with their trademark black tent since the 1970s, and have linked with other leftist theatre groups like the *Philippine Educational Theatre Association on projects such as *Journey to the West* (1980). Since then, Satō has been increasingly active as a director, notably of *Brecht, but also of *avant-garde Japanese playwrights like *Kara Jūrō and *Terayama Shūji. He has also distinguished himself as a director of *opera, including a production of *Wozzeck* at *Avignon in 1995. CP

SATRIYA

A highly *ritualized *dance form performed in the monasteries (*satra*) of Assam in the north-east of *India. Evolving between 1469 and 1580, in correspondence with the propagation of Vaishnavism by saint-poets like Sankaradeva and Madhavadeva, it represents a particularly heightened form of worship in the form of a dance. Performed by monks, with female roles played by boys—the tradition has only begun to accept women as performers in more secular contexts—*satriya* is associated with vigorous movements accompanied by strong gestures, stamping of feet, and quick turns of the body. Punctuated by the rhythmic beats of the *khol* (drum) and *tal* (cymbal), the dance includes both *nritta* (pure) and *nritya* (expressive) elements. While the former includes abstract and stylized movements, including *nadu-bhangi*, *jhumura*, *chali*, *natua*, *bahar*, the latter focuses on the emotional states underlying dramatic situations. As in other classical dance traditions in India, there is a strong martial base underlying the fundamentals of *satriya* movement, as embodied in the *ora* (stance), *zap* (jump), *pak* (turn), and other elements constituting the *mati-akhara*, or basic techniques of the tradition. Increasingly secularized since the 1950s and formally acknowledged as a classical art by the *Sangeet Natak Akademi, *satriya* is now studied by young people across communities, irrespective of caste and gender restrictions.

AMB

SATTVIKA

One of the most subtle components in the psychophysical dimensions of *acting in classical *Indian performance traditions. Inadequately described as 'sentiments', *sattvika* originates in a pre-expressive inner state of being called *sattva*, which stimulates the production of heightened emotional states. Registering through symptoms of paralysis (*sthamba*), perspiration (*sweda*), trembling (*kampa*), weeping (*asru*), among other infinitesimal signs of psychophysical expression like a change of colour (*vaivarnya*) and the breaking of voice (*swarabheda*), the acting that emerges out of these inner states of being (*sattvikabhinaya*) is understandably regarded as a rare achievement. Combining a rigorous *training in specific techniques of breathing, along with

Attic volute krater by the Pronomos Painter, in a drawing by E. R. Malyon. The vase shows the cast of a **satyr-play** in the Sanctuary of Dionysus in Athens, *c*.400 BC. Most of the chorus members (extreme right and left) hold satyr masks and wear the typical costume of a hairy loincloth with short horsetail and erect phallus. Dionysus (above centre) lies on a couch embracing a woman, while actors in costume hold masks representing characters that include an oriental king, a young woman, Heracles (with club), and the father of the satyrs. In the lower band centre sits Pronomos, the most famous piper of his day, with Charinos (probably the chorus trainer) holding a lyre.

a nurturing of the imagination, this mode of acting dwells extensively on minute movements of the eyes, eyebrows, nostrils, and even the facial muscles of the cheek. *See also* ABHINAYA.

LSR/RB

SATYR-PLAY

An ancient *Greek drama aimed primarily at characterizing the *chorus of satyrs and motivating its conventionally lively *dances. Satyrs, or more properly *silens*, were half-horse, half-human mythical companions of *Dionysus. Satyr costume consisted of a *mask with equine ears, a snub nose, and unkempt hair and beard, and a girdle (*perizoma*) fitted with a horse tail and invariably erect human male genitals (*phallus). Wide use of satyr *costume in Dionysiac *ritual, sometimes in processions and mummeries with mythological themes, led *Aristotle and others to suppose that *tragedy originated in 'satyr-play-like performances'. The satyr-play was integral to the original programme of the City *Dionysia. *Aeschylus regularly added a satyr-play (often thematically connected) to each tragic trilogy. It soon declined in popularity, however; omitted from the dramatic contests, it was added to the *Lenaea and to various Rural Dionysia in and after 440 BC. *Euripides is the first dramatist known to have substituted a fourth tragedy for a satyr-play, with *Alcestis* in 438. Because *Alcestis* is short, humorous, fantastic, and ends happily, many scholars think it generically mixed. Some freely assign other plays containing such (by no means unusual) qualities to a supposed 'prosatyric' *genre. By 341 BC tragic poets competed at the City Dionysia with three tragedies only, while a single 'old' satyr-play was performed outside the competition. The satyr-play enjoyed a revival when the *audiences of the largely urban, Hellenistic monoculture (third century BC to second century AD) embraced it as a quaint, *folkloric, classic, and then somewhat bucolic relic. The *plots of the earliest satyr-plays employ myths strictly speaking (unlike tragedy which mainly employs 'legend'), and typically evoke those critical moments when humanity progressed from savagery to civilization. Euripides' *Cyclops* is the only complete satyr-play, but substantial fragments of others survive.

EGC

SAUNDERS, JAMES (1925–)

English playwright. Saunders's early work, such as *Alas, Poor Fred* (1959) was in the *Ionesco-inspired style of English *absurdism. His first major success was *Next Time I'll Sing to You* (1962) in which actors *rehearsing a play about 'the Hermit of Canfield' discover that their lives are similarly marked by social alienation. Although his next important play, *A Scent of Flowers* (1964), opened in the West End, Saunders has more frequently worked with *London's smaller theatre companies, such as the *Questors Theatre. Another small theatre, Sam *Walters's Orange Tree, originated *Bodies* (1977), which played in the West End in 1984.

MDG

SAVARY, JÉRÔME (1942–)

French director. Born in Buenos Aires, Savary emigrated to *Paris and co-founded the anarchic 'anti-movement' called Panique, which began *touring *fringe *festivals with the intention of creating a popular theatre by ridiculing the cultural establishment. In 1966 his production of *Arrabal's *The Labyrinth* as a *happening *toured to Frankfurt, *London, and *New York. His company, now called the *Grand Magic Circus, created a sensation with *Zartan* in 1970. In 1988 he succeeded Antoine *Vitez as director of the Théâtre National du *Chaillot, where he was successful in creating a large popular theatre that alternated classics (Shakespeare, *Molière, *Rostand) with new works, especially *musical *spectacles that forged popular culture with myth, such as *Zazou* (1990), based on popular *chansons* of the 1940s and 1950s. In 2000 he became director of the beleaguered *Opéra-Comique, where his intention was to create a truly popular musical theatre. His opening production was a reworking of his first full-blown spectacle, a reinterpretation of *Offenbach's *La Périchole*.

DGM

SAVITS, JOCZA (1847–1915)

Hungarian actor, director, and scholar, and a co-founder of the German stage employees' union (Deutsche Bühnengenossenschaft; *see* TRADE UNIONS). From 1885 to 1906 he was director at the *Munich Court Theatre, where he worked with Karl *Lautenschläger to construct a 'Shakespeare stage'. First used in 1889 for *King Lear*, this 'reform' stage devoid of decor enabled performances of the complete *texts of Shakespeare's plays without the usual lengthy pauses for scene changes. The stage consisted of three parts: a *curtain which divided the main *stage from a *forestage; a raised upstage area behind a closed backdrop; and wing curtains on both sides of the stage for entrances and exits. For over two decades Savits presented Shakespeare to a Munich *audience which he demanded 'accept the dramatist-poet's call for imaginary settings' rather than elaborate *scenery. Savits enumerated his ideas in a major work on Shakespearian *dramaturgy, *Shakespeare und die Bühne des Dramas* (1917). *See also* OPEN STAGE.

CBB

SAVOY THEATRE

Built in 1881 by C. J. Phipps for Richard *D'Oyly Carte as the home for *Gilbert and *Sullivan *operettas, which were performed there until 1896 (capacity 986). It was the first public building in *London to be illuminated entirely with electric incandescent lamps (*see* LIGHTING) and the first to introduce a queuing system for pit and gallery seating. The building of the Savoy Hotel forced renovations undertaken by A. Bloomfield Jackson in 1903, at which time the entrance was moved from Embankment to its current location off the Strand. Harley Granville *Barker staged influential productions of Shakespeare there in 1912 and 1914. It was rebuilt in 1929 by architect Frank Tugwell (with an art deco interior by Basil Ionides), for Rupert D'Oyly Carte (capacity 1,130). The interior was destroyed by *fire in 1990 but was painstakingly restored by William Whitfield, and the theatre reopened in 1993.

FJH

SAXE-MEININGEN *See* MEININGEN PLAYERS.

SCAENAE FRONS

In the *Roman theatre, the decorated architectural façade of the *scaena* (Greek *skene*) which served as the background to the playing area. In *early modern Italy, attempts to incorporate the *scaenae frons* into *playhouse architecture failed in the face of the demands of *perspective scenery. The Teatro *Olimpico (1580–4), featuring a raised stage backed by a decorated *scaenae frons*, proved a dead end. The Teatro *Farnese (1618) signalled the end of the *scaenae frons*, reduced to a frame for a scenic vista, as an integral part of theatre architecture.

RWV

SCALA, FLAMMINIO (1552–1624)

Venetian *commedia dell'arte* *actor-manager and dramatist. As well as directing the *Confidenti and *Desiosi, he published a unique collection of *scenarios, *The Theatre of Performed Stories* (1611). His *prologue to the 1618 *comedy *The Pretended Husband* assesses the relative importance of dramatist and actor in theatrical creation.

RAA

SCALA, LA

The Teatro alla Scala in *Milan was built on the orders of the Empress Maria Theresa to replace the earlier Teatro Regio which had been destroyed by *fire. It opened in 1778 with Salieri's *Europa riconosciuta*, and quickly established itself as Italy's premier *opera house. The theatre was damaged by Allied bombing of Milan in 1943, but reopened in 1946 with a concert conducted by Arturo Toscanini, who had left the theatre in 1929 in protest at *fascist rule in Italy. The rebuilding respected architect Piermarini's structure of *stalls and six tiers of plush *boxes in a horseshoe pattern, all topped by a grand chandelier. It was made a civic theatre in 1921, a smaller chamber theatre was added in 1955, and in 1997 its statute was changed to make it a foundation. Every figure of note in Italian music has had some association with La Scala. Rossini was closely identified with it, and premières included Donizetti's *Lucrezia Borgia* (1833), *Verdi's *Nabucco* (1842), and *Puccini's *Madame Butterfly* (1904).

JF

SCAMOZZI, VINCENZO (1552–1616)

Italian architect and stage designer. He received his formative training in Vicenza, studied in *Rome (1578–80), and settled in Venice, where in 1582 he won a competition for the completion of Sansovino's Biblioteca Marciana. Frequent travels in Italy and abroad rounded off his learning, which he demonstrated in his *Discourses on the Antiquities of Rome* (Venice, 1583) and *The Idea of a Universal Architecture* (Venice, 1616). He designed some temporary festive decor for the royal *entry of Maria of Austria in Vicenza (1581) and the coronation of Morosina Grimani in Venice (1597). He is best known for the completion of the Teatro *Olimpico in Vicenza and the construction of the Teatro Olimpico in *Sabbioneta.   GB

SCAPARRO, MAURIZIO (1932–)

Italian director. Scaparro began as a *critic for a number of theatre journals and in 1961 advanced to the editorship of *Teatro nuovo*. In 1963 he switched to practice, becoming *artistic director of the Teatro Stabile in Bologna and making his directing debut in 1964 with *Festa grande di aprile*. In 1965 in Spoleto he presented *La Venexiana* (an anonymous play of the sixteenth century), which established him as a major director. Scaparro has mounted more than 60 productions in his career, among them *Sagra del Signore della Nave* (*Our Lord of the Ship*) by *Pirandello (1967), *Chicchignola* by Ettore Petrolini (1969), Shakespeare's *Hamlet* (1972), *Rostand's *Cyrano de Bergerac* (1977, 1985, 1995), and *Brecht's *Galileo*. He has also managed the theatre *festival at the Venice Biennale. In *Rome (Teatro di Roma) he directed *Camus's *Caligula*, an adaptation of *Cervantes's *Don Quixote* (both 1983), and Pirandello's *Il fu Mattia Pascal* (*The Late Mattia Pascal*, 1986), often incorporating *multimedia devices.   DMcM

SCARPETTA, EDUARDO (1853–1925)

Italian *actor-manager and playwright. After an apprenticeship with Antonio Petito, the famous Neapolitan Pulcinella, in 1880 Scarpetta began presenting adaptations of such French *boulevard authors as Hennequin, *Feydeau, and Halévy (*see* MEILHAC) at *Naples' San Carlino Theatre in an attempt to bring recognizable contemporary *characters to the dialect theatre. He became identified with the new 'mask' of Felice Sciosciammocca, the *protagonist for many of his Neapolitan *farces. The finest of these are *Miseria e nobilità* (*Misery and Nobility*, 1888) and *O miedeco d'e pazze* (*Doctor for the Mad*, 1908). He was the father of Vincenzo Scarpetta, who acted in his plays and succeeded him as actor-manager, and of Eduardo, Titina, and Peppino *de Filippo.   JEH

SCARRON, PAUL (1610–60)

French writer of burlesque poetry, novelist, and dramatist. Seriously disabled by rheumatism throughout his adult life, Scarron was the husband of Françoise d'Aubigné, the future Mme de Maintenon. He achieved considerable success with his *comedies *Jodelet; ou, Le Maître valet* (1645) and *Dom Japhet d'Arménie* (1652), which were still in the repertory of *Molière's company in the 1660s. His most important legacy in a theatrical context is his novel *Le Roman comique* (1651–7), based on the travels of an itinerant company of actors. In spite of the burlesque extravagance of its plot, the novel contains considerable historical interest as to the conditions in which *touring companies lived and performed in the mid-seventeenth century.   WDH

SCENA PER ANGOLO

Early *perspective scenery was *painted in a single-point perspective. At the time of its introduction (probably by Ferdinando Galli-*Bibiena, around 1695–1705) *scena per angolo* meant *painting scenery in the two-point perspective already common in architectural drawings. The practice of positioning wings for the advantage of the perspective (rather than in parallel rows) thus began with settings that had been painted in *scena per angolo*. By 1720 the term effectively meant 'two-point perspective with asymmetric *flat placement'. After 1750 it also implied the alignment of the edges of flats with the lines to the vanishing points, instead of parallel to the *proscenium line. *See* SCENOGRAPHY.   JB

SCENARIO

One of the terms used by Italian *commedia dell'arte* actors for the *plot summary which they used instead of a written script: other words were *soggetto* and *canovaccio*. The great majority of such documents which have survived are in unpublished manuscripts, since one reason for working from a scenario rather than a script was that a company retained control of its own material and did not allow it to pass into the public domain. Just one practitioner, Flaminio Scala, chose to publish a collection of 50 scenari in 1611, for reasons which are still being debated by scholars. A scenario took the form of a *scene-by-scene account of the essential events or business which needed to take place between *characters in order to advance the *plot. Each entrance of a new character was signalled by a name in the left-hand margin, so the actors could quickly spot the moment at which they would next be needed, and one has the impression of a document which could be posted backstage for consultation by the company. At the beginning were listed the characters and their relationships (grouped in family units), and the essential *properties needed. What tends to be missing from scenarios, from the point of view of a modern student, is precise information about jokes or comic effects (when *lazzi* are mentioned, no details are given), or about the balance between ridiculous and sentimental tones in scenes involving more 'serious' characters. Concrete facts about methodology and comic content have therefore to be deduced from other sources.   RAA

SCENE

A unit of segmentation in *drama, normally involving a change in the configuration of *characters on stage. A partial change is marked by exit or entrance: so long as at least one character continues into the next scene, there is a *liaison des scènes*, common in French *neoclassical theatre. A total change is marked by the exit of one complete set of characters and the entrance of another (considered an *act change in seventeenth-century France). A total change in character configuration accompanied by a change in setting or time may signal either a scene or an act change. Though obviously related, scene should not be confused with *scenery; sometimes scene is used synonymously with 'setting'.

RWV

SCÈNE À FAIRE

French term, usually applied to the nineteenth-century *well-made play, for a *scene that is dramatically necessary for the resolution of the *action. Commonly translated as 'obligatory scene', the *scène à faire* is a large-scale and emotionally fraught confrontation between opposing forces that clarifies relationships and reveals, often in a public forum, previously hidden desires of the chief *characters, leading to the *denouement. Much used by *Scribe and *Sardou in *Paris, the *scène à faire* was despised by *Ibsen, the *naturalists, and *Shaw, though all of them resorted at times to big scenes of a similar type, as Ibsen did in the final act of *Hedda Gabler* and Shaw did, albeit ironically, in *The Devil's Disciple* and *Pygmalion*.

DK

SCENE DESIGN *See* SCENOGRAPHY.

SCENERY

Stage decoration that creates a setting (or set or decor) for dramatic *action. Scenery may range from the highly emblematic to the precisely mimetic (*see* MIMESIS). In the former case, conventional signs are employed to represent a stage environment (such as a demon-mouth to represent 'hell' as in the *hell mouth of *medieval theatre). Emblematic scenery has been particularly associated with classical and medieval Western stages, as well as certain traditional practices of Asia. It might also be thought to include playing spaces that have a permanent or semi-permanent architectural façade behind the actors, as many *playhouses did in the *early modern period in Europe. In the case of mimetic scenery, on the other hand, the designer attempts to create a stage imitation of an objective or subjective reality. Scenery that attempts to imitate precisely a perceived objective reality has been especially associated with the *naturalist movement in Western theatre, while that which attempts to imitate a perceived subjective reality has been particularly associated with the *symbolist and *expressionist movements of *modernism. Emblematic and mimetic set pieces need not be mutually exclusive, however, and many scenic practices (such as *Japanese *kabuki) employ both forms in the creation of stage

space. Finally, some designers (such as the Russian *constructivist Lyubov *Popova) have largely sidestepped the emblematic/mimetic divide by creating stage decorations that almost entirely forgo representation. In its most extreme form, scenery of this type is intended to refer to nothing outside the autonomous *semiotic system of the play-world. For theoretical and historical treatment of scenery and stage design, *see* SCENOGRAPHY.

MWS

SCENE SHIFTING

Theatre is 'the seeing place' (*theatron*) and a performance will be seen against a background of some sort—the setting or scene (*see* SCENOGRAPHY). Historically the possibilities are that there may be a single conventional setting for all works given at a *playhouse, there may be a unit set for each play, or there may be *scenery which changes during the play; scene shifting is the process by which it changes. There are many ways in which scenery can be changed on an end-*stage, but they reduce to three basic forms: (*a*) changing the scenery in view or out of view of the *audience; (*b*) allowing technicians and workers (or actors) to be seen moving scenery; (*c*) hiding or not hiding scenery before and after it is in play.

The most illusionistic way is to change scenery out of view of the audience, with technicians invisible, to and from fully hidden locations. Of the major theatre traditions in the world, only the Western has shown any marked preference for maximal *illusion; several Asian theatre traditions use changeable scenery but it is nearly always shifted by visible workers, usually in full view of the audience, and only rarely is it concealed before and after use. Documents pertaining to the Sanskrit theatre (*see* INDIA) seem to describe something rather like the mechanically changed shutter and groove systems of the nineteenth century, and there seems to be little question that wagons were dragged onto the stage by ropes, but little else is known.

Scene shifting in Western theatre was always a trade-off between time and illusion. Illusionistic scene changes enforce delays; concealment from the audience is apt to consume space and time (for example, a *curtain must be lowered, or crews are slowed by working on a darkened stage), and the enforced delay can itself destroy illusion. During the seventeenth, eighteenth, and nineteenth centuries, Western theatre worked its way toward ever more rapid and ever more concealed changes. In 1619 *Aleotti introduced scenery sliding from the wings at the Teatro *Farnese. This became and remained the standard until late in the nineteenth century. Though the scene changed in full view of the audience, the change was very rapid—the surviving system at the *Drottningholm Court Theatre (1766) can execute a complete change in slightly less than ten seconds. Technicians and scenery are fully hidden in the wings and in the winch cellar.

The two principal ways of changing the scene were generally referred to as the shutter-and-groove and the chariot-and-pole systems. In a shutter-and-groove system, wings ('shutters'; *see* FLATS AND WINGS) slid or rolled on casters in tracks cut into the floor, sometimes with a stabilizing overhead rail or rope guide. In cheaper theatres they were moved by technicians, either walking behind them or pushing and pulling at their offstage edges; in more expensive houses, the flats sat on floor trucks or were hung from overhead trolleys which were moved by winch-and-pulley systems. In the chariot-and-pole system, trucks with flanged wheels ('chariots') ran on wooden tracks or in grooves in the basement under the stage, with long wooden frames or towers ('poles') mounted on the trucks, protruding through slots in the stage, to which scenery could be attached. In cheaper and smaller systems the chariots were either pushed by hand or temporarily rigged with block and tackle, but in more elaborate systems windlasses turned wooden drums which pulled the chariots into place. *Torelli and other Italian designers developed some endless-line chariot-and-pole systems in which turning the crank would cause the scenery alternately to close and open, without a need for reconnection, but in practice this more elaborate rigging was uncommon; it was simpler and more reliable to move the running lines and rerig during the scenes, before each change.

It has often been said that the shutter-and-groove system was 'English' or 'Anglo-American' and the chariot-and-pole system 'continental', but examples of both systems can be found on both sides of the supposed dividing line. A better explanation is economic; a chariot-and-pole system was far more expensive than shutter-and-groove, though it produced better results; the court theatres of Europe were subsidized and could afford the better system, whereas the English-speaking theatres were commercial and chose the cheaper system.

The significance of scene shifting was first elucidated by Richard Southern in *Changeable Scenery*, one of the half-dozen most influential works in theatre history. Southern established the viability and importance of the theatrical, performance-reconstruction approach to history (as opposed to the older dramatic or script-centred methods), helping to give theatre history both a subject matter and a methodology of its own (*see* HISTORIOGRAPHY). He systematically examined and analysed surviving shutter-and-groove equipment, accumulated many eyewitness accounts (mostly fragmentary and embedded in letters, diaries, articles, and books about other subjects), and carefully compared scripts and promptbooks, showing that, from about the Restoration until as late as 1870, scene shifting was performed in front of the audience *not* as an unavoidable expediency (or because our ancestors did not understand curtains, as some historians before the Second World War actually appeared to suggest), but as a part of the attraction—something for the audience to enjoy. To some extent eighteenth- and nineteenth-century plays were actually *about* scene changes (in the sense that a big modern science fiction movie is about *special effects, or that some car races

seem to be about wrecks—they are what the audience comes to see).

The very rapid scene changes of the period from 1670 to 1870 were exciting because large mechanical systems were unusual and hardly seen outside theatres, but also because they allowed a swiftness of storytelling that older, more verbal theatres only rarely touched in a few deliberately breakneck plays (such as *Marlowe's *Tamburlaine*, *Calderón's *Life Is a Dream*, *Corneille's *Le Cid*). The motion of the scenery, the constant appearances of new views and effects, must have had an effect rather like rapid camera cuts in *film, creating a sense that something exciting was going on, pulling the audience forward through a breathless stream of events. This is utterly consistent with the sensational tone of the scripts for *melodrama, for which either shutter-and-groove or chariot-and-pole scenery was used, and with the descriptions of the *acting that took place in front of it.

Once Southern had established that scene shifting was more than just a convenience—that it was, in fact, a part of what the theatre as a whole communicated to its audience—his perspective was rapidly applied to many other kinds of scene shifting. Unfortunately, what we actually know of scene shifting in more ancient theatres limits the amount of light that can be cast on them in this way. No hardware survives and we have no drawings or paintings of *Greek *periaktoi in use. We do not know if paintings were hung on each *periakton* (for an unlimited number of possible scenes), or painted directly on it (three possible scenes). A few of the surviving *tragedies are set in more than one location (notably *Sophocles' *Ajax*), and several of *Aristophanes' *comedies could be staged so as to use more than one location, but since they also include *text referring to changed locations, perhaps the *periaktoi* were not expected to give such information. We know, if anything, less of *Roman scene shifting than we do of the Greek; only that there are references to its having happened, and that at least some of it seems to have involved pulling scenery up from below the stage. Some rearrangement of scenes happened in *medieval theatre in Europe, but it was probably not rapid and not in full view of the audience—redecorating an upright pole from the Tree of Life to the Cross might be an example.

It is primarily in the Western *modernist theatre that we can see the *semiotic implications of scene changes, and compare them with those of earlier systems. As a greater *realism in scenery became more and more the rule, and better *lighting combined with the shrinking of the *forestage moved *action upstage, scene shifting from the wings became more problematic. The shift to flown scenery (*see* FLIES) did not necessarily require that scene shifts take place out of view of the audience, but since the act *drop and/or the oleo were themselves flown, it was visually consistent with closing the curtain between scenes.

Quite possibly the greater 'seriousness' of the theatre from 1860 forward may have motivated both the rise and the fall of the act drop. If an audience is supposed to consider seriously what they have just seen, as it is clear that playwrights from T. W. *Robertson forward expected them to do, then lowering the curtain divides the evening into alternating 'witnessing times' and 'contemplating times', a kind of discussion format well suited not only to the cup-and-saucer comedies but to *Shaw, *Ibsen, *Strindberg, and *Chekhov; as the *well-made play transformed into the *thesis play, and theme trumped *plot, time to think about, and even to discuss, the theme became valuable to the audience, and rushing on to the next part of the story was less urgent.

But if modernist theatre at first embraced the covered scene shift, it shortly discovered the disadvantages; mentally the audience was allowed to escape from the stage back into the *auditorium and had to be retrieved at every 'curtain up'. The ironic detachment this bred was too much for the fusion of passion and contemplation that was the ultimate rationale and justification for the single, unified effect. Thus various ways of changing the scenery, and of using less illusionistic scenery, evolved in the early twentieth century. *Craig suggested the use of large screens on neutral, unit sets; *Piscator used projections which changed in full view of the audience; *constructivism and various descendants of *expressionism put large, sometimes functional machinery directly on stage and made its shifts part of the action, not as a method of narration as in the older theatre, but as an expression of the image of human beings trapped in a world too large and powerful for them. After the Second World War, making use of the sorts of innovations in lighting that had developed in the experimental theatres of the 1930s, designers like Jo *Mielziner created unit sets that were used piecemeal, with lights accomplishing changes of location and time; unity of effect no longer required *unity of time or place.

More recently, the use of electric winches in large *musicals, and for scripts which require rapid movement through many times and places, has brought back swift scenery changes in full view of the audience as a part of the entertainment; many of the large Euro-musicals of the late twentieth century relied on very swift changes of great quantities of flown scenery (in addition to rapid lighting changes), which would have been impossibly expensive when there had to be one technician for every line set, but can now be controlled by a single operator at the winch board. It is interesting to note that in their delight in *spectacle, lack of interest in theme, and enjoyment of the show as an occasion rather than as 'art', the contemporary musical audience is very like the nineteenth-century melodrama audience, which also delighted in scenes changing before their eyes.

JB

SOUTHERN, RICHARD, *Changeable Scenery: its origin and development in the British theatre* (London, 1952)

SCENOGRAPHY see page 1196

SCHALLA, HANS (1904–83)

German actor and director. Schalla began as an actor in 1922 in Hamburg, followed by engagements at Wrocław, Darmstadt, Kassel, and Essen. In 1940 he directed at the *Berlin State Theatre (*Berlin Royal Theatre), meeting Gustav *Gründgens, who employed him after the war in Düsseldorf until 1949. From 1949 to 1972 Schalla was *artistic director of the Schauspielhaus, Bochum, where he directed 114 productions. His repertoire emphasized unconventional interpretations of the classics, and his productions were characterized by staccato speech rhythms, *scenery reminiscent of abstract painting, and *costumes usually dominated by a single strong colour. He was awarded the Otto *Brahm Medal in 1971.

CBB

SCHAUBÜHNE

*Berlin theatre. Founded in 1962 by the students Jürgen Schitthelm and Klaus Weiffenbach, the history of the Schaubühne can be roughly divided into four phases. The first, extending until 1969, saw a number of innovative productions at the Schaubühne am Halleschen Ufer in West Berlin which did not attract significant *critical attention. The second and most important phase began in 1970 when Schitthelm and Weiffenbach invited the director Peter *Stein and a group of actors, directors, designers, and *dramaturgs to form a new company based on democratic principles. The constitution provided (and still provides) for participation of all members of the theatre in the production process. From the outset the theatre included political offerings (*Brecht's *The Mother*, 1970) and artistically complex works without explicit political orientation (*Kleist's *The Prince of Homburg*, 1971). The production process was characterized by long *rehearsal periods, intensive research into the social and historical background of the plays, and substantial dramaturgical intervention. Major productions included *Ibsen's *Peer Gynt* (1972), *Gorky's *Summerfolk* (1974), *Shakespeare's Memory* (1976), and *Aeschylus' *Oresteia* (1980). Together they established the Schaubühne as the leading German-speaking theatre, assuming the position once held by the *Berliner Ensemble in East Berlin.

The second phase culminated in 1981 with the opening of a new building at Lehninger Platz (on Kurfürstendamm), a three-stage complex with variable seating facilities, and ended in August 1985 with Stein's departure. The third phase (1985–99) was marked by a succession of *artistic directors (Luc *Bondy, Jürgen *Gosch, Andrea *Breth, among others) and a gradual decline in the status of the theatre. The fourth phase began with a new artistic board consisting of Sascha Waltz (choreographer), Thomas *Ostermeier (director), Jens Hillje (dramaturg), and Jochen Sandig. Although its pre-eminent position is now contested, the Schaubühne—with over 30 invitations to Berlin

(continued on p. 1209)

SCENOGRAPHY

The accumulation of spatial signs that creates a stage setting. Scenography (literally, painting of the *skene) thus is a category of signs that includes stage architecture, *scenery, machines, and *lighting, but does not include such elements as speech, non-verbal acoustic signs, *actors' actions, actors' appearance, and actors' *properties, or the non-ludic areas of the *playhouse such as lobbies and bars.

1. Introduction

Though scenographic sign systems can vary widely, it is possible to identify some general characteristics. The first major element in scenography is the architectural form of the *stage itself and the location of the stage in relation to the *audience. Stage forms can vary in terms of size, shape, elevation, acting surface, and distance from the audience. Differences in stage forms will affect the *semiotics of a *performance as a whole, often signalling to the audience the type of drama that is about to be presented. In contemporary Western societies, for example, a 'black-box' stage (small, square, zero elevation, concrete surface, very close to the spectators) generally prepares audiences to receive a more experimental production than would a large, elevated stage. Similar clues can be given in terms of the behaviour and *reception that is expected of the audience. A small stage that the audience can approach and circle, such as that used for Javanese *shadow puppetry (see WAYANG KULIT), may signal that the audience is permitted to view from all sides. A *proscenium stage, on the other hand, generally indicates that the audience should remain in their seats and observe from afar.

Stage architecture limits and defines the possibilities of stage movement. A large oblong space, for example, permits movements different from a small rectangular one, and a *thrust stage permits movements different from an *arena. While a proscenium stage encourages actors to 'cheat out' by facing toward the audience even while moving, an arena stage eliminates this problem while introducing new ones. Similarly, possible movements on a raked stage are not the same as those on a flat one, and possible movements on sand are rather different from those on wood. In addition to determining potential movements within a stage space, stage architecture helps to determine the signification of the movements themselves. On a raked proscenium stage, for example, upstage is generally read as a more dramatically 'powerful' position than downstage, while on a flat thrust stage such a signification would largely lose its meaning.

A second major element in scenography is scenery or stage decoration. Scenery can range from the highly stylized and emblematic (such as a single branch to represent 'forest') to the utterly *illusionistic (such as a woodland scene re-created down to the last bramble). It may be a three-dimensional imitation of a two-dimensional painting, as in much *early modern and baroque (or *neoclassical) scenery, or it may choose to emphasize the three-dimensionality of the stage space, as in the designs of Adolphe *Appia. It may offer one ideal audience viewpoint (front row centre, perhaps, or the royal *box), or it may offer multiple sight lines of more or less equal value. Some stage decorations remain uniform throughout, while others change repeatedly. In the case of a uniform stage decoration, changes of setting may still occur, but must be indicated by other means, through the use of props, lighting, gestures, *costumes, or *sound effects. In the case of changing stage decoration, *scene shifting may be quick or slow, hidden or intentionally explicit. In many cases (such as Japanese *kabuki or Italian baroque theatre), scene shifting in and of itself could be a highly visible and greatly appreciated aspect of the performance.

Like stage architecture, stage decoration helps to determine possible stage movements. The movement of actors on an Elizabethan stage, for example, could be horizontal but rarely vertical. With the increase in the nineteenth century in the use of vertical stage elements such as stairs, turrets, hills, and rocks, the proscenium stage encouraged more complex movement along a vertical axis. In some cases, actors' movements can also be severely limited by the scenery employed. The actor on a stage that uses forced-perspective scenery, for example, increasingly reveals the illusion of the *perspective *painting as he or she moves upstage. While this limiting condition is avoided by the employment of frankly non-illusionistic scenery, new stage limitations may be thereby introduced.

Scenery helps to locate the drama geographically and historically, and serves to define the *characters of the drama. Scenic choices in the representation of Elsinore, for example, may indicate that we are in medieval Denmark, but may also signify a great deal about the characterization of Hamlet (dark or bright, towering or mundane, *naturalistic or stylized) within the specific production. Similarly, scenery helps to create and define the atmosphere of a production. Thus the fairy-tale woodlands of Beerbohm *Tree's or Max *Reinhardt's productions of *A Midsummer Night's Dream* in *London and *Berlin at the start of the twentieth century, for instance, bear with them a vast range of significations (both aesthetic and ideological) that contrast sharply with the bare white walls and acrobat's swings of Peter *Brook's production of the same play (1970). The extraordinary richness of such significations has made scenery the crucial scenographic element in most Western theatre since the early modern period, as well as in certain Asian theatres such as kabuki.

Stage machinery is a third element in scenography. Stage machines have often been used to change sets quickly, allowing a more or less uninterrupted performance. Machines such as the Roman *periaktoi, the baroque carriage-and-frame system, and the kabuki *revolving stage have all been developed for this purpose. Stage machines may also be used to transgress limitations imposed by stage architecture and decoration. In one of the earliest instances of a stage machine, a crane with a rope and pulley called a *mechane was used to *'fly' gods, animals, and *heroes above the *skene, thus adding a vertical axis to the otherwise largely horizontal field of ancient *Greek stagecraft. On the other hand, a mechanical device such as the Victorian vampire *trap (which could allow characters to ascend or descend from the stage floor) created a vertical axis beneath rather than above the stage space. In some instances, such as English court *masques and nineteenth-century disaster *spectacles, the illusions produced by stage machines have been the central scenographic elements of performance. More typically, however, machinery complements lighting, stage architecture, and especially scenery in the creation of a setting.

Though machinery has been an important part of Western theatre since the Greeks, it did not flower until the seventeenth century, through the craftsmanship of Italian designers such as Giacomo *Torelli. Innovations in machinery since then have tended to be developmental rather than revolutionary. Even the most elaborate of modern stage machines, while they can accomplish far more due to electricity and hydraulics, are generally refinements of baroque effects that operate on the same principles as their ancestors.

The same cannot be said of lighting, the scenographic element that owes the most to modern innovation. Stage lighting may be artificially or naturally produced, and may have both a practical function (that is, making the production space visible to the audience) and a scenographic one. Throughout most of theatre history, the use of natural light predominated. Artificial lighting first became essential during the Italian Renaissance with the construction of the first indoor theatres, and the practice later spread to the rest of the Continent and to England. *Footlights were used by the early seventeenth century, often accompanied by a row of lights along the rear of the acting area for the illumination of the backdrop. Concealed lights from above and to the sides of the stage were also used, as well as exposed lights such as chandeliers. Though artificial lighting prior to the nineteenth century was largely a practical affair of mere stage illumination, lighting did occasionally have a scenographic function. As early as the mid-sixteenth century, Sebastiano *Serlio wrote of using coloured lights for the illumination of stage space, and coloured lights were occasionally employed for the enhancement of stage settings throughout the neoclassical and *romantic periods.

Until the nineteenth century, however, lighting technology was insufficiently advanced to allow light to be an important element in scenography. London's *Lyceum Theatre installed the first gaslit stage in 1817, and gas lighting became standard in theatres by 1850. Though dangerous, gas lighting allowed far greater control and therefore greatly enhanced the scenographic possibilities of light. This control was increased, and the dangers reduced, with the introduction of electric lighting to the theatre around 1880. Subsequent technological innovations such as spotlights and gels would have great impact on the development of the art, as would the design experiments of Henry *Irving, the Duke of Saxe-*Meiningen, and Appia. By the twentieth century, lighting was widely considered a major aspect of scenography, though its usage has varied enormously. Some modern designers, following Appia, have made it the central element of stage design, while others, following the *Berliner Ensemble, have de-emphasized its dramatic role. Between these two poles, however, lies a century's worth of wide experimentation with the semiotics of light.

2. Non-Western traditions

Most traditional performance styles both East and West have placed relatively little emphasis on scenography. Stage decoration, for example, is rarely used in the traditional performance *genres of Asia, *Africa, and the Middle East. While certain genres of Indian, Chinese, and Japanese theatre have relatively complex scenic styles, scenery has not received the emphasis in these traditions that it has in the mainstream European theatre since the early modern period. The major exception is Japanese kabuki, for which scenography is a highly developed art that plays a central role in the performance as a whole. After a brief survey of several non-Western traditions, kabuki will be examined in greater detail.

While neither scenery nor stage properties are important to most traditional performance in *India, there is some evidence of scenery in the Sanskrit dramas of the first millennium AD. Because very little visual evidence of ancient Indian theatres has survived, we are almost entirely reliant upon the *Natyasastra of *Bharata. Bharata writes that one-half of the ideal playhouse was to be devoted to spectators, the other to the actors. The space devoted to the actors was halved again, with one part constituting the stage and the other the backstage. The stage was divided into separate zones (kaksya), although it is not clear how this was achieved. While it is possible that different parts of the stage were conventionally associated with different locales, it is also possible that scenery was used to designate places, much as in the conventions of *medieval *mansion staging. Bharata also suggests, in chapter 14 of the *Natyasastra*, that stage doors were used for performance, possibly in a symbolic manner.

We are forced to rely on almost as much guesswork when reconstructing the possible scenery of *zaju performances of Yuan (1260–1368) and Ming (1368–1644) Dynasty *China. A 1324 mural gives some evidence that these early dramas took place before a painted backdrop on a tiled stage. On other occasions, however, a red carpet may have been employed as a more flexible means of indicating stage space. Though scenery and stage properties were usually absent, a few zaju extravaganzas seem to have employed elaborate stage effects. One three-day performance, for instance, depicted a journey to hell that included saws, grinding stones, boiling cauldrons, mountains of knives, trenches running blood, trees sprouting swords, and ghostly guardians of the underworld. These horrors were depicted convincingly enough to provoke screams from the audience; on one occasion, the local prefect was awakened from his sleep by the cries and immediately suspected that the town was under pirate attack. Though such spectaculars suggest a refined art of scenic illusion, it should be noted that they came late in the Ming Dynasty (and therefore late, too, in the development of zaju) and do not seem typical of the genre as a whole.

One of the many dramatic forms to follow zaju was Beijing opera (*jingju), which originated and grew to maturity during the Qing Dynasty (1644–1911). The city stage for Beijing opera is an intimate space, generally consisting of a square platform, raised a few feet above the ground, open on three sides, and topped by a canopy. A wooden railing surrounds the platform, and lacquered columns hold up the canopy at the four corners. Actors enter and exit through two doors in the rear wall (stage right for entrances, stage left for exits), and a large embroidered *curtain hangs between the two doors. A carpet, a wooden table, and a few chairs comprise the major set pieces. This relatively spartan scenography allows for an extremely flexible scenic space. The table and chairs are used to represent a wide variety of settings, and can be quickly transformed into a royal pavilion, a law court, a bridge, a hill, or a door. At times other properties are also used to clarify a specific setting: a bamboo pole for a soldier's tent, or four pieces of cloth carried by a running actor to signify the wind. To a degree unusual for Western theatre, space in the Beijing opera is also suggested through the movements of the actors. Gestures can indicate the opening and closing of doors, and can divide and subdivide playing areas of the stage.

The *nō theatre of *Japan also makes use of a sparsely decorated stage. The stage itself is a platform of polished cypress wood, about 6 m square (about 19 feet) which rises less than a metre (2 feet 7 inches, to be exact) off the ground. It is open on three sides and covered by a wooden roof supported by four pillars. An aged pine tree is painted on the back wall. A long railed bridgeway (hashigakari) extends to the left of the stage, leading to a curtained doorway. The bridgeway leads to the actors' dressing room and is the entrance and exit route for all the principal characters. It is decorated by three small trees, which stand at intervals alongside it. At the beginning of a play, four musicians enter along the hashigakari and seat themselves at the back of the stage, where they are visible to the audience throughout. Simple stage properties such as bamboo poles and coloured cloth may be used to represent wagons, boats, houses, and other scenic elements. Otherwise, props and scenery are almost entirely absent.

Scenery is far more essential to the performances of the Japanese *bunraku *puppet theatre. Standing roughly 11 m wide, 8 m deep, and 4.5 m high (36 by 25 by 15 feet), the bunraku stage is divided into levels by three raised partitions which partially hide the bodies of the puppet masters and serve as platforms on which the puppets stand. Exits are generally made through a doorway upstage centre. Scene settings are represented by realistically painted backdrops, which are regularly changed to reflect new scenes. Long-distance travel is indicated by rolling a long backdrop painted with changing landscape panels behind a stationary puppet, a technique that appears to have been in use as early as 1715. About thirteen years later (1727), trap-lifts were introduced in order to raise and lower scenic elements through the floor. Stage properties generally appear only when crucial to the *action, and are oversized so as to be visible to the entire *auditorium.

The spectacle of Japanese kabuki overshadows that of bunraku and stands in stark contrast to the serenity and simplicity of nō. Kabuki was originally performed on the same stage as the nō drama, but by the end of the seventeenth century the bridgeway had been widened, a curtain added to conceal the performing area, and a dance floor (shosabutai) occasionally used. The result of this last innovation is that the kabuki stage developed the use of two stage floors. The first is a permanent floor made of wide, unpainted boards; the second is the dance platform made of polished cypress, which is laid atop the permanent stage floor and the bridgeway. A second distinguishing feature of the kabuki, the *hanamichi, was introduced at some point between 1724 and 1735. A walkway approximately 1.5 m (5 feet) wide, the hanamichi begins at stage right and extends through the audience to the back of the auditorium. It is used for entrances, exits, and as an extension of the stage space (illustration, p. 660). The increase in the importance of the hanamichi led inexorably to the decline of the hashigakari, and a further step away from the nō stage. While a curtained passage at the side of the stage continued to be used for entrances, exits, and scenery changes, by the late eighteenth century the hanamichi had become the 'strongest' route for exits and entrances. By

1830, the vestigial remains of the *hashigakari* had disappeared. By about this time the kabuki theatre had also widened to roughly its current dimensions, which, by Western standards, are extraordinarily broad and shallow: an auditorium 18 m (60 feet) deep and 27 m (90 feet) wide is by no means unusual.

The kabuki stage exhibits a mixture of conventional and illusionistic scenography. Coloured floor cloths, for instance, may represent distinct settings by obeying a highly conventional symbology: blue for water, grey for earth, and white for snow. At other times, settings are far more illusionistic. One-half of the stage might contain an entire interior of a house, complete with furnishings and working doors, while the other half holds a garden or wilderness scene complete with trees, bushes, rocks, and a backdrop depicting a vista. Since roughly the 1760s, in response to the influence of Western illustration, kabuki scenographers began to design such houses and paint accompanying backdrops by using techniques of perspective. Even in such cases, however, it should be noted that kabuki designers refrain from thoroughgoing stage illusions: cracks between individual *flats, for example, are left exposed, and conventional iconography is often used alongside the perspective painting. Set pieces, which are frequently employed, may be elaborate but are generally more conventional than illusionistic. The braces holding up a tree, or the two-dimensionality of scenic stones, bushes, or walls, are all generally left exposed. As in the nō drama, musicians remain in view during the performance, usually seated to the extreme left of the stage.

One of the hallmarks of kabuki performance is a sudden transformation of the stage space. Techniques for achieving this include trap-lifts, revolving stages, wagon platforms, curtain drops, and the unusual *gandogaeshi*. The trap-lift (*seridashi*) was borrowed from the puppet theatres of *Osaka and first used for a kabuki in 1736. Its function continues to be the raising and lowering of scenery. In 1748 the *seridashi* was enlarged and could raise large pieces such as walls and gates. In 1759 an elaborate *seridashi* was constructed that emerged from the stage floor at an angle. After 1744 the *seridashi* began to raise and lower not only scenery but actors as well, and later productions would utilize the trap-lift to raise as many as twenty performers at once. Like the trap-lift, the revolving stage was imported to kabuki from the puppet theatres of Osaka, where it had been in use since 1758. Its importation to the kabuki stage in 1793, for the play *History of Azuma*, is the first instance of a fully installed (rather than temporary) revolving stage in theatre history. In order to produce a simultaneous transformation on both vertical and horizontal planes, the revolving stage is often used simultaneously with one or more trap-lifts. Unlike their Western counterparts, kabuki stage designers never place more than two stage settings on a rotating stage. Occasionally one setting alone will suffice; rather than rotate the stage to produce a new setting, a single setting is rotated simply to provide a new perspective.

Of all the various techniques of transforming the stage space quickly, perhaps none is simpler or more effective than the sudden curtain drop. Night can suddenly fall by the drop of a black curtain, or, as in one kabuki play (*The Forest of Suzu*), dawn can arrive when a black curtain hung at the back of the stage drops to reveal a painted morning vista. Small wagon platforms, another technique for changing scenes, were first introduced in the early eighteenth century to bring set pieces and performers on- and offstage quickly. On the modern kabuki stage, these wagons are generally used to carry performers only for *dance pieces, and to reorganize set pieces on the stage rather than entirely change a set. Finally, the *gandogaeshi* needs to be mentioned, if only because it is the scene-changing method most peculiar to kabuki, though it bears some resemblance to the Renaissance *scena versatilis*. Also borrowed from the puppet theatre, the *gandogaeshi* is a technique whereby one piece of scenery is turned to expose another, differently painted or differently constructed surface. The rooftop setting of one scene might be folded back to reveal, for example, a temple interior, which then becomes the principal set for the following scene. The evolution of kabuki scene design rivals, in complexity, that of the evolution of European scene design during roughly the same period. That other non-Western traditions have laid similar emphasis on scenography seems doubtful, but much research in the area remains to be done.

3. Ancient Greece to the sixteenth century in Europe

The study of ancient Greek performance is always a speculative affair, and scene design is no exception. *Aristotle dates the origin of scenography with the plays of *Sophocles, but the philosopher is contradicted by the anonymous *Vita* of *Aeschylus, which credits Aeschylus with the first use of stage decoration. Writing in the first century BC, *Vitruvius calls Agatharchus of Samos the first scenographer, and claims that he painted scenes for Aeschylus, a statement that does not precisely contradict either of the Greek sources. While Aeschylus' *Oresteia* (458 BC) is the first play to use a building as a background, it may have been inspired by Sophocles' own use of stage decoration, and thus does not settle the issue. Some scholars, comforted by consensus, have therefore placed the origin of Western scenography between 468 and 456, when Sophocles and Aeschylus were both working.

Vitruvius' account (suspect as it is, coming roughly four centuries after the fact) supplies us with a number of interesting insights. Agatharcus, Vitruvius writes, inspired Anaxagoras and Democritus to use perspective in stage design 'so that, by this deception, a fruitful representation of the appearance of buildings might be given in painted scenes'. Since Vitruvius defines scenography as 'the shading of the frontal parts and receding sides whereby all lines are related to the centre of the circle', some scholars have further credited Agatharcus with the discovery of the principle of perspective with a central vanishing point. Whether or not this is so, it seems that Greek scenography by the last third of the fifth century BC at least involved foreshortening techniques and chiaroscuro effects.

While most *tragedies are set in a single location, some (such as Aeschylus' *Eumenides*) change locations, as do many *comedies. If the Greeks really had developed illusionistic scenography, then they may have developed a means to change scenes within plays as well. Two basic devices have been suggested for this purpose: *pinakes* (painted panels much like modern flats) and *periaktoi* (triangular prisms that could be rotated to change scenes). Evidence of *pinakes* is provided by the fact that grooves have been found in the columns of the *skene* of some later theatres; precisely how they might have been changed (if, indeed, they were changed at all) remains a matter of informed guesswork. While the use of *pinakes* as early as the fifth century has been well established, that of *periaktoi* is largely speculative.

By the beginning of the fourth century BC, two stage machines were in use in comedies and presumably in tragedies as well: the *mechane* (a stage crane) and the *ekkyklema* (a wheeled platform). The *mechane* was chiefly used to show a character in flight, either in a chariot, on the back of a beast, or suspended alone in a harness, and was most likely placed to the side and behind the *skene* to lift the character over the top of the playing space. The *ekkyklema* was used for revealing tableaux, and was probably wheeled out from the inside of the *skene*. In tragedies it most often displayed the bodies of characters killed offstage; in comedies it might reveal stage furnishings, surprising characters, or other comic discoveries. (*See also* ANCIENT THEATRES.)

Though strongly influenced by Greek theatrical practices, *Roman scenography developed its distinctive style by the beginning of the first century BC, when the plain wooden platform of the Roman stage gave way to a performing space before an elaborate architectural façade. This façade, or *scaenae frons*, was often three storeys high, with between three and five doors and numerous niches, frescos, statues, and pediments. In tragedy, the *scaenae frons* represented a temple or royal palace; in comedy it stood for a city street. According to Vitruvius, setting was also provided by means of *periaktoi*, which illustrated one of three settings: tragic (exemplified by columns, pediments, statues, and other royal objects), comic (marked by private dwellings with windows and balconies), and satyric (involving trees, caverns, mountains, and other rustic areas). Though how the *periaktoi* indicated these settings is still debated, it seems that either illusionistic or emblematic scenes were painted upon the *periaktoi*, which were then rotated to indicate a change in setting.

After the collapse of the Roman theatre in the early sixth century AD, European performing arts largely survived through popular entertainments, state spectacles, and church liturgy. Owing to the effects of the iconoclastic struggle and the sack of Constantinople, it is especially difficult to say anything with certainty about the scenic designs of Byzantium. Nevertheless, it appears that sermons in *dialogue were performed in *Byzantine churches from the seventh to the eighth centuries, and that these led to full *liturgical dramas by the mid-Byzantine period. Scene design for these liturgical dramas appears to have involved a 'house' (*mansion) on one side of the stage, and a curtain through which the actors entered. Of Western Europe we know somewhat more, though here too a certain amount of informed guesswork is called for. By the beginning of the thirteenth century, largely through the gradual separation of the *Quem Quaeritis* trope from the liturgy as a whole, religious drama emerged as a mode of performance in its own right. Indoor theatre generally took place in churches, where scenic requirements included benches or low platforms (*sedes*) and simple 'houses' (also referred to by the Latin *domus* or later by the French *mansion*), as well as a stage area (*locus) that might be raised from the floor and furnished. For early *medieval dramas, small crowds of spectators were able to move from area to area to follow the action. As crowds grew, benches mounted on platforms were provided for some spectators (particularly the nobility), and the actors began to perform atop the *sedes*, which could be placed at dramatically significant areas throughout the church. This design may have been the origin of the most common form of medieval scene design, whether indoor or outdoor: mansion staging.

Mansion staging consisted of two basic elements: mansions and an open playing area (*platea). Mansions served to locate the scene (Daniel's house, the lion's den) and store any required properties, and were generally equipped with curtains and open on four sides. The number of mansions varied according to the production, but heaven and hell were almost always included, and usually placed at opposite ends of the performing space (with a fixed stage, heaven may have been placed in the east and hell in the west). Heaven (or the *heavens) was usually a two-storey structure, large enough to house many characters, topped by a celestial 'wheel'. Hidden torches were often used to light the structure, and stage machinery was used in more elaborate productions to enable angels to fly between heaven and earth. As impressive as heaven was, hell may have been the spectacular highlight of the medieval stage. A gaping, bestial mouth of teeth, fire, smoke, screaming sinners, and flying demons, and often surmounted by the fortified towers of the damned city of Dis, *hell mouth made use of the full range of medieval stage effect. While the mansions were the focus of medieval scenic design, the *platea* was a more generalized space often representing a rural road, a town street, or a journey between mansions.

Most European performances occurred on fixed stages, but *pageant wagons were used for Spanish *autos sacramentales* and English *mystery plays (*see also* BIBLICAL PLAYS). Though there is some debate as to how these mobile stages operated, most scholars now agree that each play was mounted on a separate wagon, that the wagons were wheeled to a series of predetermined points around town, and that the play was performed anew at each point. Over the course of the festival, an audience member standing at one of the points could therefore witness the full cycle of plays. Outside concessions to the necessities of transportation, the decorations of the pageant wagons were probably similar to those of the fixed stage.

By the sixteenth century, permanent companies with distinctive regional traditions had established themselves in Germany (the Meistersinger theatre), Holland (the *Chambers of Rhetoric), and England (the Elizabethan stages). But the most important innovations in scenography would come from Italy, where stage design would attract some of the greatest artists of the age. Vitruvius' treatise on Roman architecture, *De Architectura* (rediscovered 1414, printed 1486), had become by 1500 a central authority on theatre architecture and scenography. In 1521 an especially influential edition of the book was printed in Italian translation with illustrations. Pomponius Laetus, the leader of the Roman Academy at the end of the fifteenth century, borrowed heavily from Vitruvius in his attempt to re-create the classical stage. For his stage, Laetus apparently created a platform backed by a façade; the façade was divided into a series of curtained doorways, each housing a different character. Widely illustrated in editions of *Terence's plays, Laetus' 'Terence stage' may have spread through Europe in the sixteenth century, though evidence of its actual use is unclear and it is possible that the Terence stage remained largely if not totally an iconographic invention.

However influential the Terence stage may have been for early modern scenography, the development of perspectivism would clearly surpass it in importance. Perspective illustration evolved slowly in Italy during the fourteenth and fifteenth centuries, and by the sixteenth century had begun to make its way into the playhouse. The chronicles of Ferrara offer the first official description of a perspective setting (for *Ariosto's *The Casket* in 1508), but Italian scenographers may have used such techniques as early as the 1480s. By the 1530s Italian stage settings regularly featured geometrical perspective with a single central vanishing point, and Baldassare Peruzzi had emerged as one of the premier stage designers of Europe, combining perspective techniques with Vitruvian design.

Peruzzi's pupil Sebastiano Serlio systematized the innovations of the previous decades in his *Second Book of Architecture* (1545), the first early modern work to include a chapter on the theatre. Inspired by Vitruvius' descriptions, Serlio used perspective techniques to create an influential series of illustrations of tragic, comic, and satyric settings, consisting of a painted backdrop and three pairs of angled side wings receding symmetrically at right angles to the front of the stage. The wings closest to the audience were richly decorated, with many three-dimensional details to enhance the illusion. The stage was level in the front, where the actors performed, but steeply raked toward the back, where the scenery was placed. Finally, and significantly, the vantage point of the ruler was made the organizing principle of the stage as a whole, with the height of the platform raised to the ruler's eye level and the ruler's chair placed directly in line with the vanishing point of the scenery.

Though scenery on a Serlian stage was not meant to be changed, designers lost little time finding ways to create a more flexible stage. Drawing from Vitruvius' descriptions in *De Architectura*, several designers returned to the classical *periaktoi*, expanding them in some cases from conventional three-sided form to four, five, and even six sides. Some designers experimented with mobile angled wings, while still others found ways to throw painted canvas coverings over immobile wings in order to change scenes more quickly. But of all these innovations, it was the *flat wing that would prove most effective, and it was the flat wing alone that would outlive the Renaissance. The technical difficulties in painting scenes in perspective on flat wings proved far more complicated than on angled wings, but these difficulties were largely solved in 1600, with the publication of Guido Ubaldus' *Six Books of Perspective*. In the first decade of the seventeenth century, scenes made up entirely of flat wings begin to appear in drawings by the designer Giovani Battista *Aleotti. Fifty years later, flat wings would become the dominant scenic element on the Italian stage.

A further innovation of sixteenth-century Italian stage design was the proscenium arch, which seems to have originated around 1560. Its precise origin is still debated, though its form may have been derived from the Renaissance picture frame or the public triumphal arch, or perhaps from the Roman *scaenae frons*. The proscenium arch also answered a desire to hide the increasingly complex machinery of the baroque stage, and thereby enhance stage illusion. Whatever its roots, however, its effect has been clear: the proscenium arch hid offstage space and significantly deepened the separation between stage and auditorium, spectacle and spectator. Particularly when combined with the elaborate stage machinery developed at the same time —machinery which included flying devices, *traps, rotating platforms, wave simulators, and collapsible walls—the proscenium arch reinforced the emerging conception of a theatrical performance as a moving painting. It is difficult to overstate the importance of early modern Italian innovation for the history of scenography. Roughly a century after the first printing of Vitruvius' treatise, a radically new visual style emerged, developed, and won wide acceptance. Not until the end of the nineteenth century would such a fundamental break again occur.

4. The seventeenth and eighteenth centuries

Most of the changes in the next two centuries were extensions and refinements of Italian Renaissance discoveries. The importance of Ubaldus' groundbreaking work on perspective became more and more apparent during the first half of the seventeenth century, as flat wings made possible systems for quick scene

Sheridan's *The School for Scandal*, Drury Lane, London, 1777. This famous engraving of the 'screen scene' reveals major elements of neoclassical **scenography**: the main action on the forestage out beyond the proscenium, a practical screen and chair corresponding to those in use in contemporary life, the perspective interior setting, painted books in painted bookcases on the upstage drop, and a perspective painted landscape outside the window.

shifting. Scene changes became so enjoyable in and of themselves that they were often executed for no reason beyond the simple pleasure of the metamorphosis. The art and science of Renaissance stage machines, meanwhile, flowered into the extraordinary mechanical contrivances of the baroque stage spectacle. Some of the machines created during the baroque period for the simulation of rolling seascapes, fluttering angels, collapsing castles, and thundering snowstorms have not been surpassed for their combination of technical expertise and artistry.

Of all the many skilled scenographers of seventeenth-century Italy, none contributed more than Giacomo Torelli. A student of Aleotti's, Torelli designed the Teatro Novissimo in Venice, where his experiments with stage design earned him the nickname *il gran stregone*, 'the great sorcerer'. Between 1641 and 1645, he introduced to the Teatro Novissimo the carriage-and-frame (or 'chariot-and-pole') method. There is some question as to whether Torelli may have invented the system, since another scenographer may have used a form of it at the Teatro *Farnese as early as 1628, but at any rate Torelli appears to have

perfected and popularized it. The system worked by mounting flat wings on rectangular frames, which passed through long slits in the stage floor to wheeled platforms (or 'chariots') running on rails in the cellar. The carriage-and-frame contraption was duplicated on either side of the stage, with all of the carriages connected by a complex system of ropes and pulleys to a single winch. When the winch was turned, one set of flats would be moved into the proscenium while its double was simultaneously drawn off. The offstage frame could then be fitted with a new wing, and the entire process could be repeated for the next scene change. A very effective method of changing scenes, it was soon adopted by theatres throughout Europe, with the exception of England and the Netherlands, though English stage designers would later adopt a modified type of carriage-and-frame construction in order to change revolving wings.

The speed and fluidity thus achieved allowed Torelli to conceive of a new relationship between scene shifting and the entertainment as a whole. Several sixteenth-century treatises had suggested ways of temporarily distracting an audience in order to divert attention from complicated scene changes (extreme examples include suddenly blowing trumpets from one side of the stage, or raising a commotion at the rear of the auditorium). Moreover, sixteenth-century scene changes were generally reserved for breaks in the entertainment as a whole—between, say, an *act of the play and the *intermezzi* (see INTERMEDIO)—which would further minimize the disruption they might cause. All this changed with Torelli. Instead of hiding or minimizing the commotion of scene changes, Torelli made them part of the spectacle as a whole, frequently changing settings within rather than between scenes for the sheer pleasure of visual discovery. This use of scene shifting as entertainment, a hallmark of baroque scenography, would have been virtually unthinkable without the carriage-and-frame invention.

Torelli went to *Paris in 1645 to design productions for the *Petit-Bourbon and the *Palais Royal, both of which he remodelled with techniques from the Teatro Novissimo. His staging of *Corneille's *Andromède* at the Petit-Bourbon in 1650 started a lengthy vogue for 'machine-plays', performances that featured little outside the spectacle of elaborate stage machines and scene-shifting techniques. Machine-plays did much to popularize baroque scenography and became the stock-in-trade of several theatres in Paris, including the Théâtre du *Marais and the *Salle des Machines. Gaspare *Vigarani, the builder of the Salle des Machines and a jealous rival of Torelli, claimed for his theatre all the scenery and machinery Torelli had designed for the Petit-Bourbon. These works—judging from contemporary evidence, some of the finest creations of the baroque stage—Vigarani promptly and entirely destroyed.

While most of the innovations of the seventeenth century continued to come from Italy, during this century England first emerged as an important centre for scene design. Queen Elizabeth had been rather frugal in her entertainments, but James I and Charles I opened their purse strings to a variety of spectacles, especially for the court *masque, closely identified with the architect and designer Inigo *Jones. Jones visited Italy at least twice and Paris once between 1600 and 1615, and the influence of the Italian style is clearly apparent in his work.

Jones introduced perspective scenery to England for *The Masque of Blackness* (written by Ben *Jonson, 1605). Learning from the Italians, Jones placed the King at the centre point of the perspective and level with the horizon line. *The Masque of Blackness* featured an array of stage machines (most of which were used to depict a seascape with sea monsters) far surpassing anything yet seen on the English stage, though scene changes were entirely absent and the proscenium arch not yet introduced. Early steps toward both developments may be found in *Hymenaei*, staged the following year. For this show, Jones placed enormous statues at either side of stage and suspended a curtain between them, an early step toward the proscenium that he would refine and enlarge in subsequent masques. Jones also designed a version of the neoclassical *scena versatilis* (a set piece

that turns to expose a new scene on the reverse) by creating a convex globe that revolved to reveal eight performers on the concave side. Later Jones employed the neoclassical *scena ductilis*, in which a large painted shutter was removed from the stage to reveal a new scene behind. More versatile than the *scena versatilis*, the *scena ductilis* became the most popular method of scene shifting on the English stage until it was gradually replaced by a system of grooves.

The first step toward the new method may be found in the pastoral *Florimène* (1635), for which Jones and John *Webb designed a series of grooves along which the back shutters could be slid on- and offstage. The groove system was further developed for the last masque of all, William *Davenant's *Salmacida Spolia* (c.1640). Jones used grooves for the side wings as well as the back shutters, thus allowing the entire stage space to change scene without great interruption. Four scene changes were possible in this configuration. As with Torelli's spectacles in Italy and France, Jones featured these scene changes as entertainments in and of themselves, relying on new stage machines that replicated Italian and French effects. Though never quite so lavish as their continental counterparts, English theatres such as Jones's *Whitehall Banqueting House (1622) were well equipped with machinery, including multiple cloud devices and large traps through which whole scenes could rise. It was partially due to the increasing focus on scenery and stage machinery that Ben Jonson ceased writing for the masque. Complaining bitterly of 'the Machines and the showes' that had banished 'prose, or *verse, or sense' from the stage, Jonson broke off his collaboration with Jones and fired the opening salvo in the battle between *text and spectacle that has consumed theatre *theory ever since.

After the restoration of the monarchy in 1660, English stage machinery became increasingly sophisticated and extravagant, allowing for faster and more changes, deeper perspectives, and more convincing simulations. But in the English manner this was development by evolution rather than revolution. By the late nineteenth century, the system of grooves and flats that had typified English scenography since Jones had largely disappeared, replaced in many cases by the more efficient carriage-and-frame method of the continental stage.

For the next major development of baroque scenography we must turn, again, to Italy. Around 1703 the scenographer and architect Ferdinando Galli-*Bibiena introduced angled perspective (*scena per angolo*) to a theatre in Bologna. Previous designers had organized their perspective illustrations around a single vanishing point at the centre of the picture, with architectural features often marching in lockstep along either side toward a central vista. Bibiena broke with this convention by establishing two or more vanishing points, often placing the architectural features in the middle of the painting with the vistas out to the sides. Though the mathematics of *scena per angolo* are significantly more complex than those of traditional perspective illustration, the result is a looser, less static image, one that strives for harmony through asymmetry. The implications of the *scena per angolo* are highly significant. Unlike conventional perspective painting, the *scena per angolo* extends the eye beyond the visible stage, forcing the spectator to complete the stage picture in his or her imagination. Moreover, the avoidance of strict symmetry disperses the spectatorial gaze across the stage picture, allowing for greater visual autonomy. One result of this dispersal is the diminution of the symbolic power of the king or prince, who had previously occupied the position of the ideal spectator; with the *scena per angolo*, fixing the ideal spectatorial position becomes a more subjective affair.

Another of Bibiena's innovations was to enlarge greatly the scale of the architectural features in his settings. Previously the architecture displayed in a scene setting could be encompassed by the eye of the spectator; one can always see the tops of Torelli's buildings, for instance. But Bibiena's royal interiors, courtyards, and cathedrals seem to loom up far beyond the spectator's vision, as though only a small portion of the entire structure could be framed by the proscenium arch. In Bibiena's designs the imaginary extension of the design beyond the visible stage is therefore achieved by a combination of *scena per angolo* and architectural magnitude.

Bibiena popularized many of his theories in his volume *L'architettura civile* (*Civil Architecture*,1711), which became an important work for baroque scenography. His aesthetics were further spread through the wide-ranging accomplishments of his *family, whose name became virtually synonymous with theatre architecture and stage design in the eighteenth century. Crucial, too, for the dissemination and development of *scena per angolo* and other baroque innovations throughout the Continent were scenographers such as Filippo *Juvarra, Jean-Nicholas *Servandoni, the *Quaglio family, the Mauro family, and the *Galliari family. With the work of these and other designers, baroque scenography adopted its characteristic features of opulence, grandiosity, asymmetry, and, increasingly, an attention to mood that drew heavily on chiaroscuro effects. The culmination of the style, however, would be achieved by an artist not directly associated with the theatre at all: Gianbattista *Piranesi, who drew heavily from the stage designers of his time and influenced them in turn, introducing a dark subjectivity into the increasingly ruined landscape of the late baroque. In the long shadows of Piranesi's labyrinthine structures, baroque scenography would reach its apex and its end.

5. The nineteenth century and the beginnings of modernism

Reaction to the opulence of baroque stage design had already begun in the mid-eighteenth century when simpler forms were advocated, principally in the German lands. The fruits of German neoclassicism can be seen in nineteenth-century stages such as that of the new *Berlin Royal Theatre (1818–24), where the stringently neoclassical designer Karl Friedrich *Schinkel placed all action on the proscenium before a bare stage; the only form of scenery that remained was a painted backdrop framed in a proscenium arch. But neoclassical restraint was not to be the norm of the nineteenth century. In France, England, and Germany as well, nineteenth-century stage design would move in a variety of directions: toward increasing spectacle and illusion, toward *romantic fantasy and exoticism, toward *realism and historical accuracy, and toward a greater concern for a unified *mise-en-scène. Out of the tangled enthusiasms of the century three designers would emerge—the Duke of Saxe-Meiningen, Adolphe Appia, and Edward Gordon *Craig—who would shape the landscape of the modern stage.

In the years following the revolution, French audiences exhibited an extraordinary appetite for stage spectacle. In much French *melodrama of the period, dramatic action featured less prominently than did natural disaster, with volcano eruptions, floods, and fires drawing large crowds. Exotic locales, antique historical periods, and supernatural happenings proved equally popular. The increasing demand for spectacle, particularly after about 1820, put great pressure on theatre *managers to develop ever more elaborate stage machines, and continued the alliance between science and stagecraft that had first emerged in the Renaissance. No one embodied this alliance better than Louis Daguerre, best known today as inventor of the daguerreotype, an early form of photograph. Much like Serlio and Bibiena before him, Daguerre combined an interest in optics with an interest in scene design. He began his career rather traditionally, painting scenes at the Paris *Opéra, though he may have assisted as well in the painting of panorama theatres. In these theatres, the audience was seated in the middle of a circular auditorium and surrounded by an enormous, continuous landscape painting. In 1822 Daguerre introduced an offshoot called a *diorama. In Daguerre's version, the audience sat on a platform in front of an enormous painting, the cloth of which was often translucent in order to allow light to filter through one layer of painted cloth to the next, thus making the scene appear three dimensional. Though the diorama itself was stationary, the platform on which the audience was seated would turn every quarter-hour to face a new painting, which would often depict the same landscape at a different time of day or a different season of the year. Other diorama theatres used two long canvases on rollers, one set behind the other in order to give a three-dimensional impression of a moving landscape. Both panorama and diorama theatres proved enormously popular in Paris, with playhouses such as the Panorama-Dramatique established to meet the demand.

By the second decade of the nineteenth century, *box sets —an arrangement of flats forming three walls and a ceiling— were being used to stage household interiors. The use of box sets indicated a desire to represent intimate domestic spaces with the same attention to illusion as had previously been paid to Gothic castles, battle scenes, and erupting volcanoes.

It was therefore the first step toward the hyper-illusionistic stage of French *naturalism. The development of the imaginary 'fourth wall' may have originated in 1853 with Adolphe *Montigny, who appears to have arranged his actors around a table in the middle of the box set rather than in a semicircle around the *prompter's box, as was customary. André *Antoine continued the development with his Théâtre *Libre (1887), for which he insisted that all interior sets be designed so as to give the impression that the fourth wall had simply disappeared. The interiors of these box sets Antoine filled with all of the quotidian bric-a-brac necessary to complete the simulation; for a scene in a butcher's shop, Antoine famously hung chunks of real meat.

Similar enthusiasms for exotic spectacle, historical accuracy, and hyper-illusionism characterize the Victorian stage. As in France, panorama and diorama exhibitions were popular in England, and panoramic techniques entered conventional theatre productions toward the middle of the century. In order to satisfy a demand for Gothic thrills, stage techniques such as gauze (for creating mists and vapours) were combined with special effects such as the 'vampire trap' of 1820 (a trap with springs that allowed a supernatural figure suddenly to appear or disappear through the stage floor) or *Pepper's ghost of 1862 (a mirror trick for making a ghost appear on stage). At the same time, the movement toward more 'realistic' and historically accurate scenography, which had begun already in the late eighteenth century, gained momentum as the nineteenth century advanced. For a number of productions at *Drury Lane and *Covent Garden between 1794 and 1817, the *actor-manager John Philip *Kemble and the designer William *Capon introduced the use of historically accurate sets and dress. The innovations of Kemble and Capon set the stage for such theatre artists as James Robinson *Planché, Lucia *Vestris, Charles *Mathews, and Charles *Kean. Planché's *costume designs for Charles Kean's 1823 production of King John emphasized historical accuracy, and his 1834 stage set for Alfred *Bunn's The Minister and the Mercer utilized, for apparently the first time on an English stage, a full box set. Vestris and Mathews, meanwhile, shocked London audiences with their 1841 production of Dion *Boucicault's London Assurance, which featured, according to one contemporary account, 'not stage properties, but bona fide realities'. The movement probably reached its apex with the Shakespeare productions of Kean, whose enthusiasm for historical accuracy extended even to the plants featured on stage (see ANTIQUARIANISM).

Some of the greatest innovations of the late nineteenth-century English stage, however, must be attributed to Henry Irving. As manager of the Lyceum in 1881, Irving ceased using the groove system of scene shifting that had characterized the English stage for over two centuries. In its place he introduced 'free plantation', meaning scenery could be placed anywhere on the stage. Free plantation enabled greater flexibility in the placement of scenery and encouraged the development of an additional innovation: three-dimensional set pieces. Though stairs, platforms, bridges, and boulders had already become common by the 1870s, the elimination of the groove system greatly facilitated their manipulation. Commanding an army of well over 100 set changers, Irving was able to move toward a truly plastic, three-dimensional stage space, and significantly decrease the reliance of stage design on the flat surfaces of perspective painting.

As daring as it was, Irving's transformation of the Lyceum stage was surpassed in novelty and influence by the experiments of the Meiningen company at the court of Georg II, Duke of Saxe-Meiningen. Duke Georg, who founded the company in 1874, directed all of the productions (alongside his *stage manager Ludwig *Chronegk) and designed all the scenery, properties, and costumes himself. He brought to these productions an antiquarianism more thoroughgoing than any other on the nineteenth-century stage, insisting upon historical accuracy not only in costumes, scenery, and properties but in speech, gesture, and bearing. He was able to unify all of these elements into a single vision through his wide range of talents (in addition to his directing abilities, he was an accomplished painter and draughtsman) and dictatorial control over all aspects of production. His innovations in stage design were considerable. Like Irving, Georg used three-dimensional set pieces alongside painted flats and wings, but went further than Irving in the development of the plastic possibilities of scenography. His scene designs were multi-level landscapes in which vertical movement was as important as horizontal. For Fiesko he designed a grand double stairway, for William Tell a mountain crag criss-crossed with Alpine trails, for Hermannschlacht a German forest broken up by fallen trees, boulders, and crevasses. He may have been the first to consider not only what his settings would look like, not only how his actors would look in them, but also how settings control actor movement. A lover of 'organic' asymmetry, Georg designed settings that forced his actors to move at oblique angles to one another and to the proscenium, and to arrange themselves with carefully planned haphazardness about the stage. The movement of actors, whether as individuals or—more famously—in the form of enormous crowds, was inseparable from the conception of the setting as a whole. As a result of several successful European *tours, the impact of the Meiningen company far exceeded its relatively brief lifespan, counting Antoine and *Stanislavsky among its many admirers. Without the Meiningen company, the Théâtre Libre and the *Moscow Art Theatre may have been unimaginable.

If the Duke of Saxe-Meiningen has not become a household name among contemporary theatre artists it is largely because his reputation has been overshadowed by that of the two men who followed him: Adolphe Appia and Edward Gordon Craig. Of the two the older by ten years was Appia, a passionate Wagnerite who argued that music was the apex of the arts and wrote a study of scene designs for imaginary productions of *Wagner's *operas. The work, entitled *La Mise en scène du drame wagnérien* (*The Staging of Wagner's Music Dramas*, 1895), was followed by a more complete expression of his theories, *Die Musik und die Inszenierung* (*Music and Stage Design*, 1899). Taken together, these two volumes laid out a comprehensive programme for the fundamental transformation of stage design. Much like Duke Georg, Appia regarded the movement of the actor as essential to stage design, and wanted to free the stage from the conventions of painting it had drawn upon since the Renaissance. Appia argued that, since the actor was three dimensional, the entirety of the stage set should also be three dimensional. Instead of attempting to simulate depth through techniques learned from perspective painters, Appia believed that stage designers ought to exploit the three-dimensionality already inherent in the stage space itself. Though much of this line of argument had already been explored by the Meiningen company, Appia exceeded the Duke in the purity of his approach. Where Irving and the Duke had combined three-dimensional elements with two-dimensional painted simulations, Appia banished all forms of scenic painting and painted architecture from his stage.

The greater distinction, however, between Appia and the entire tradition of Western scenography that preceded him was his emphasis on abstraction and on lighting. Although Wagner had insisted on conventional, highly illusionistic stage sets for his productions, Appia felt that the true spirit of Wagner's music called for stark, sculptural abstractions on a minimally decorated stage. 'We need not try to represent a forest,' he wrote in support of his designs for *Siegfried*, 'what we must give the spectator is man in the atmosphere of a forest.' And what this atmosphere called for, especially, were landscapes formed of light and shadow. Appia was not the first to use light creatively as a designer—the scenographer Philip de *Loutherburg, for example, had used lighting for atmospheric effect as early as the 1770s, and artists such as Irving and Duke Georg were making great use of atmospheric lighting by the late nineteenth century. Appia was, however, the first to give lighting such centrality in his overall aesthetic system and to explore its potential for the stage so thoroughly. Appia distinguished between several forms of light, particularly emphasizing chiaroscuro effects, and argued that light possessed a unique ability to unify the various elements of the stage space and bring forth the essence of each object on stage. He drew attention to the plasticity of stage lighting, arguing that it should be used as a moving, dramatic force in its own right. For Appia, stage lighting should be a protean force, creating, shaping, and unifying the stage space in a manner similar to that of music, as 'only light and music can express "the inner nature of all appearance" '. Fortunately, such idealist musings were given ballast by means of Appia's illustrations, which revealed for the first time the abstractions of form and shadow that became hallmarks of twentieth-century scenography. Light in these designs was used not merely to illuminate a scene or to give a moment a certain atmosphere or mood, but actually to construct and define stage space. Such an aesthetic idea could not have been conceived without nineteenth-century developments in stage lighting, and would not be realized fully until the arrival of electricity. Such technological developments also allowed the extensive use of stage projections (as, for example, in the productions of Erwin *Piscator), another innovation Appia predicted and espoused.

Gordon Craig, who has probably received more scholarly attention than the Duke of Saxe-Meiningen and Appia combined, deserves more credit as a popularizer than as an innovator in his own right. A much more able self-promoter than the introverted Appia, Craig developed a programme that drew broadly from the innovations of his forebears. Like Duke Georg, Craig insisted that productions be guided by a single artistic will, who would forge staging and scenic design into a unified work of art. Like Appia, he believed that the illusionistic stage inspired by conventions of painting ought to be entirely replaced by a kinetic stage of abstract architectural masses, darkness, shadows, and light. Never one to be pinioned by the practical demands of the theatre, Craig at one point called for a stage filled with great moving cubes, rising and falling like the tones of an organ, while folding screens furled and unfurled and coloured lights continuously played. One aspect of this dream in particular, the use of great numbers of folding screens, he experimented with his entire life, though never with much success.

Whatever their differences, Saxe-Meiningen, Appia, and Craig fought for a theatre based on fundamentally new conventions of stage design. Scenographers after them would increasingly abandon the use of illusionistic techniques borrowed from painting, and utilize instead the inherent depth of the stage space to give a sense of three-dimensionality. Though few scenographers would simultaneously direct their productions, the general *modernist principle of a unified production would lead to much closer collaboration between designers and *directors. Following Saxe-Meiningen and Appia, many scenographers would take their starting point from the movement of actors upon the stage. Others would find ways to make actors as malleable as Craig's *Über-marionetten, or else search for ways to eliminate them entirely. Finally, scenographers throughout Europe and America would explore varieties of non-representational stage design, making use of abstract forms, stage projections, and the creation of stage space through light and shadow. Given the radical nature of these innovations, the period from roughly 1880 to 1920 may be said to mark the most significant break in Western scenography since the Renaissance.

6. The twentieth century

While the revolt against realist scenography in Western Europe was being led by Appia and Craig, in Russia the call to arms was first sounded by a periodical entitled *World of Art*, begun in 1898 by Sergei *Diaghilev. Diaghilev's theatrical vision began to reach a wide European audience after the first Paris performance of the *Ballets Russes in 1909, and would continue to evolve until the director's death in 1929. Working with a company of designers that included Leon *Bakst, Natalya *Goncharova, Alexandre *Benois, and Mikhail Larionov, Diaghilev developed an immediately recognizable and widely imitated scenographic style. Though strikingly traditional in many ways (the sets generally consisted of little besides a large painted backdrop), the scenography was unambiguously anti-realist and tended toward abstraction. Unlike most of Appia's and Craig's designs, those of the Ballets Russes embraced an exotic opulence, revelling in bold colour combinations and rich ornamentation. Bakst introduced intense silvers, oranges, reds, pinks, and golds into his stage paintings, accenting the oriental dress of the Ballets Russes dancers. Later, under Goncharova and Larionov, the group began to employ flat, richly painted images reminiscent of Byzantine iconography and Russian *folk painting. Such designs suggested a mood at once modern and primal, decadent and holy, and thus provided an evocative if painterly setting for the latter-day rites of Igor Stravinsky and Vaslav Nijinsky.

While many artists of the Ballets Russes never returned to their homeland after 1917, some of the greatest innovations of twentieth-century scenography would be made by the artists of post-revolutionary Russia. Associated at the outset with *futurism, Russian *constructivism emerged around 1920 and quickly made its presence felt on the stage. A 1921 production of *Romeo and Juliet*, directed by Aleksandr *Tairov and the Kamerny Theatre in *Moscow, featured a cubist-influenced design of swirling, abstract forms by Aleksandra *Ekster that anticipated the more daring innovations to come. The central features of constructivist design emerged more distinctly the same year in *Meyerhold's production of *Mayakovsky's *Mystery-Bouffe*, designed by Anton Lavinsky and Vladimir Khrakovsky. Here the painterly gave way entirely to the architectural. Rather than curtains, backdrops, or illusionary set pieces, the stage featured platforms of differing levels criss-crossed by ladders, and catwalks, and a ramp stretching deep into the auditorium. The following year constructivist design truly came of age with Lyubov *Popova's design for Meyerhold's production of *The Magnanimous Cuckold*. Popova's creation was an autonomous stage machine that could conceivably be placed anywhere or used for almost any production. Multifunctional and almost entirely non-representative (to a small degree it referred to a windmill in the play), it resembled a cross between a jungle gym and the interior workings of some gigantic clock, a combination perfectly suited to the *biomechanical practices of Meyerhold's troupe. With Popova's design, the stage was realized as a 'machine for acting'.

Constructivist scenography did not only use the latest mechanics of lighting and stage design; it celebrated the power of mechanics itself. In this respect, the movement was a significant departure from the early modernist vision of Appia, who saw the use of technology as a potential path back to lost ancient *rituals and the lost regions of the inner self. Far more consistent with the heritage of Appia was *expressionism. Though difficult to characterize broadly, expressionist scenography tended to emphasize formal abstraction, simplification of colour, exaggeration of central images, and heavy chiaroscuro effects. Instead of attempting to present an objective picture of a setting, expressionist scenography aimed to re-create the mood of a setting, or else to envision how a setting might appear as mediated through a (usually extreme) mental state. Lighting played a particularly important role on the expressionist stage, employed not only (as in Appia) to emphasize the abstract and subjective nature of the setting, but also as a solution to the problem of rapid-fire scene changes. Innovations in the use of light proved the ideal complement to the stream-of-consciousness writing style so typical of expressionist writing. Settings established largely through lighting could be changed in the blink of an eye, creating a fluid or staccato stage space that mirrored, in new ways, the process of thinking itself. Such designs had a significant impact upon, and were in turn influenced by, the *montage methods of *film. Particularly in Germany and northern Europe, expressionist techniques were adopted so broadly that it is difficult to associate the movement with a single artist or group of artists, but the German directors Jürgen *Fehling and Leopold *Jessner did exert particular influence over the style. The latter, working primarily with designers Emil *Pirchan and Cesar Klein, was especially well known for his creative use of *Jessnertreppen* (Jessner steps), large staircases that changed form through light and shadow, which were widely adopted throughout Europe. The central scenographic use of steps was also adopted at about the same time by the influential French director and designer Jacques *Copeau.

By the mid-1920s, expressionism was already beginning to decline in Germany, and a new movement was rising to replace it. *Epic theatre found its first major practitioner in the director-designer Erwin *Piscator. Borrowing elements of expressionism as well as constructivism, Piscator presented sharply critical visions of mass mechanization that made use of functional and mechanistic stage designs. His scenography aimed to engage the critical functions of the audience through a collage of effects: revolving stages, elevators, conveyor belts, transparent screens, projections, dramatic lighting changes. Particularly provocative was Piscator's use of film alongside stage events. For Ernst *Toller's *Hoppla, wir leben!* (*Hoppla, We're Alive!*, 1927), for example, Piscator used two movie screens, one behind the other, occasionally making the front screen transparent. The production opened with a newsreel account of the previous nine years of world events, and film clips alternated with live action throughout the performance. The setting for *Rasputin* in the same year was even more ambitious, using three film projectors and 2,000 m (c.6,500 feet) of film. The production featured a revolving stage on top of which sat an enormous globe that opened in sections; next to the globe was a continuous film chronicle of the events of the First World War, including occasional superimposed commentary.

Piscator's functional use of stage devices and openly *didactic approach to scenography had a great influence on the development of epic theatre, though the most famous inheritor of that tradition often took pains to distance himself from his forebear. While arguing that the practices of such *avant-garde directors as Piscator and Meyerhold were 'passive and reproductive' and therefore 'anti-revolutionary', Bertolt *Brecht developed a theory of scenography that in fact owed much to them. According to Brecht, disparate stage effects should be combined not (as Appia and Craig believed) for the purpose of creating a unified theatrical space, a harmonious *Weltanschauung*, and an all-consuming spectacle, but for precisely the opposite end. Epic scenography should aim to show the constructed nature of stagecraft and the independent function of each theatrical element, and should encourage the audience to pay critical attention to the performance. Moreover, it should be considered an integral component of *dramaturgy as a whole, a consideration that should lead directors and scenographers to work closely together throughout the entirety of the *rehearsal process. Although developed in unprecedented ways by Brecht and his collaborators, many of these principles found their roots in constructivism and in earlier epic experiments.

Of the three scenographers with whom Brecht worked over the course of his career (Caspar *Neher, Teo *Otto, and Karl von *Appen), Neher had the longest and closest professional relationship with Brecht, collaborating with him from 1923 to 1953. Neher considered the scenographer's art inseparable from the production process as a whole, and attended rehearsals whenever possible, frequently developing his stage designs from performance patterns that would emerge during this process. Brecht in turn often relied on Neher's design sketches for inspiration in his direction. Like Brecht, Neher might use any stage device whatsoever if it suited the dramatic purpose, and screen projections, placards, painted scenery, platforms, curtains of all types, folding screens, and rolling carts were mixed with the same abandon as highly stylized imagery was combined with naturalistic stage properties. The entirety was generally lit with a bright, uniform light that eschewed atmospheric effect and refused to direct the attention of the spectator to any particular part of the stage. The effect of such designs on the scenography of the late twentieth century has been enormous, with numerous contemporary director-designers (such as Pina *Bausch, Ariane *Mnouchkine, Richard *Foreman) and theatre companies (such as *Cheek by Jowl, Theatre de *Complicité, the *Wooster Group) owing a heavy debt to Brecht's *Berliner Ensemble.

While Russia and Germany occupied central positions in the development of modernist stage design, the century also saw the emergence of the United States as an aesthetic innovator. In the early part of the century, American scenography was largely defined by David *Belasco, whose style of 'Belasco realism' was highly naturalistic. The first major challenge to the style was issued by Robert Edmond *Jones, who was commissioned to design a set for Harley Granville *Barker's 1915 production of *The Man Who Married a Dumb Wife* at the *New York Stage Society. At the time of his commission, Jones had recently returned from Europe, where he had studied many of the recent trends, and his new design would reflect this experience. His set was extremely simple, consisting entirely of right angles and a flat background out of which an oversized door and window had been cut. The façade was painted with a simple palette of black, white, and grey and geometric designs of the sort that would soon be associated with art deco. Here was the birth of American 'New Stagecraft', an abstract, minimal, and modern style first associated with Jones, Lee *Simonson, and Norman *Bel Geddes. Its techniques were further developed by a second generation of American scenographers, a group that includes Oliver *Smith, Donald *Oenslager, Boris *Aronson, Howard *Bay, and Jo *Mielziner. Mielziner in particular became a central figure, giving shape to the peculiarly American scenographic style of 'poetic realism'. Well suited to plays such as *Williams's *The Glass Menagerie* and *A Streetcar Named Desire* and *Miller's *Death of a Salesman* (all of which Mielziner designed, 1945–9), the scenography of 'poetic realism' emphasized the dreamy, half-remembered quality of otherwise workaday reality, creating subjective moods through the employment of scrims, hazy lighting, partially deconstructed set pieces, and other such devices. More recently, Mielziner's former assistant Ming Cho *Lee has been responsible for many American scenographic developments since the 1960s. Reflecting the influence of the Berliner Ensemble among others, Lee's designs largely discarded the still essentially pictorial style of New Stagecraft in favour of a more sculptural notion of stage space.

Perhaps the most influential scenographer of the late twentieth century, however, has been Josef *Svoboda, who was appointed chief designer and technical director of the *Czech National Theatre in *Prague in 1948. Influenced by Meyerhold, Piscator, the Czech pre-war avant-garde tradition, and the *multimedia experiments of E. F. *Burian and Miroslav *Kouřil, Svoboda has developed a greatly versatile body of work over a long career. He is perhaps best known for his discovery and application of innovative stage technology, particularly in the realm of film and slide projection. Taking advantage of the thawing of Soviet *socialist realism in the late 1950s, Svoboda and the director Alfréd *Radok introduced two new theatre forms at the Brussels World's Fair in 1958. The first, which they called Polyekran, was a spectacle in which slides and films were projected onto static, variously angled screens. The second, *Laterna Magika, fused the projection spectacle of Polyekron with live actors, dancers, singers, and musicians. These two forms have since led to further developments, including Diapolyekran (first seen at the Montréal Expo in 1967), in which computerized projection screens composed a wall of 112 cubes, each flashing changing slides at varying rates. Svoboda used such forms either as *total theatres in and of themselves or as aspects of more conventional theatre design (a 1966 production of *Gorky's *The Last Ones*, for example, used Laterna Magika techniques to great effect). Such designs have significantly advanced the avant-garde tradition of breaking down barriers between the arts, and even (given the obvious influence of *television on the Diapolyekran) challenged distinctions between high art and *mass media. For these reasons, Svoboda is often seen as a pioneer in the fields of multimedia performance and *cyber theatre. Svoboda's integration of performance and technology has also proved an ideal medium for his recurring aesthetic of collage and quotation—an aesthetic that can be called postmodern and that has exerted great influence over contemporary scenography.

The styles of contemporary scenography are too highly varied to permit many generalizations. Particularly in the 1960s and 1970s, many directors and designers were influenced by the theories and practices of *environmental theatre. An insistence on the integration of spectacle and spectator, environmental theatre is a radicalization of the avant-garde attack on the proscenium stage. The scenographic possibilities of such a theatrical space have been explored by numerous director-designers, including Peter Brook, Richard *Schechner, Ariane Mnouchkine, Jerzy *Grotowski, and Josef Szanja, and companies such as the Red Tent Theatre and the Hamidashi Gekijo in Japan. While environmental scenography has received some international attention, it remains largely an avant-garde phenom-

enon, and most of the innovation in contemporary scenography continues to occur in relatively conventional theatre spaces. Designers such as Richard Hudson in Great Britain, John *Conklin in the United States, Erich Wonder in Germany, and Richard Peduzzi in France, among countless others, have continued to expand the possibilities of indoor stage space. Most recently, the American director-designer Julie *Taymor has proved not only the artistic potential of scenographic experimentation but its potential mass appeal as well, in her staging of Disney's *The Lion King*. See also VISION AND THE VISUAL; MEDIA AND PERFORMANCE.

MWS

BABLET, DENIS, *Esthétique générale du décor de théâtre de 1870 à 1914* (Paris, 1965)
—— *The Revolutions of Stage Design in the 20th Century* (New York, 1977)
BJURSTROM, PER, *Giacomo Torelli and Baroque Stage Design* (Stockholm, 1961)
GUNJI, MASAKATSKU, *Kabuki* (New York, 1985)
HOWARD, PAMELA, *What Is Scenography?* (London, 2002)
IZENOUR, GEORGE, *Theater Technology*, 2nd edn. (New Haven, 1996)
KENNEDY, DENNIS, *Looking at Shakespeare: a visual history of twentieth-century performance*, 2nd edn. (Cambridge, 2001)
LARSON, ORVILLE K., *Scene Design in the American Theatre from 1915 to 1960* (Fayetteville, Ark., 1989)
NICOLL, ALLARDYCE, *The Development of the Theatre*, 5th edn. (New York, 1967)
OENSLAGER, DONALD, *Stage Design: four centuries of scenic invention* (New York, 1975)
RISCHBIETER, HENNING, and STORCH, WOLFGANG, *Art and Stage Design in the 20th Century: painters and sculptors work for the theatre* (Greenwich, Conn., 1968)
ROSENFELD, SYBIL, *A Short History of Scene Design in Great Britain* (Oxford, 1973)
SOUTHERN, RICHARD, *Changeable Scenery: its origin and development in the British theatre* (London, 1952)

*Theatertreffen and 44 television broadcasts—has secured itself a place in Western theatre history.

CBB

SCHECHNER, RICHARD (1934–)

American director, scholar, and teacher. Schechner was among the first to appreciate and discuss the dimension of *performance beyond the strict confines of theatre. He was instrumental in developing the discipline of *performance studies during the 1960s and 1970s with his groundbreaking investigations of the links among performative behaviour, daily life, *play theory, and anthropology. His interests in the latter led to a series of *intercultural studies of performance as well as his influential definition of it as 'restored' (that is, 'twice behaved') behaviour. Among his books, *Performance Theory* (1988), *Between Theater and Anthropology* (1985), and *The Future of Ritual* (1993) continue to be highly influential, as does his editorship of *The*

Drama Review (*TDR*), which he returned to in 1985 after a first period as editor from 1962 to 1969. He founded the Department of Performance Studies at New York University, where he continues to hold a professorship.

Schechner is as much a man of the theatre as a scholar. He began his directing career with the Free Southern Theater (1963–6) and the New Orleans Group (1965–7) prior to founding the *New York-based *Performance Group in 1967, where he mounted numerous innovative productions, including *Dionysus in 69*, *Makbeth*, and a notable *environmental production of *Shepard's *The Tooth of Crime*. In keeping with his interest in the relationship between *theory and practice, during his years with the Performance Group (1967–80) Schechner also championed experiments in performer *training, *collective creation, environmental theatre, and various forms of *audience participation. He continues to direct and conduct workshops around the world.

IDW

SCHIARETTI, CHRISTIAN (1955–)

French director. A student of philosophy as well as theatre, Schiaretti eventually enrolled at the *Conservatoire in *Paris, where he studied under Antoine *Vitez, Jacques Lasalle, and Claude Régy. In 1991 he was named director of the Comédie de Reims, becoming the youngest director ever to administer a national theatre in France. There he established a permanent resident troupe, the first since the decentralization of the French theatre. He has staged a great variety of works, ranging from *Greek classics to twentieth-century European *avant-garde. He has also collaborated with contemporary writers on new creations, such as the *Ahmed* suite (1994–6) with Alain Badiou and *Stabat Mater Furiosa* (1999) with Jean-Pierre Siméon. He has also staged several *operas, including *Puccini's *Madame Butterfly* (1997), and *Strauss's *Ariadne on Naxos* (2001). In 2001 he succeeded Roger *Planchon as director of the *Théâtre National Populaire. CHB

SCHICKSALSTRAGÖDIE

A *genre popular in the early nineteenth century in Germany, 'fate tragedy' describes plays in which there can be no escape, often for a whole family, from the tragic outcome. While in most *tragedy the *hero behaves as though free to make moral choices, here, as in *Seneca, fate is inexorable, the hero defeated from the start. Although sometimes used to describe *Schiller's *The Bride of Messina* (1803), *Schicksalstragödie* more properly defines romantic pieces (*see* ROMANTICISM) like Zacharias *Werner's *The 24th of February* (1810) or *Kleist's *The Schroffenstein Family* (1804), in which a whole family is gradually destroyed by a fated feud. MWP

SCHIFFBAUERDAMM, THEATER AM

German *playhouse, built in 1890 in the centre of *Berlin, since 1954 the home of the *Berliner Ensemble. Its first period of prominence was from 1928 until 1931 under the management of Ernst Josef Aufricht (1898–1971), who opened with *Brecht and *Weill's *The Threepenny Opera* (1928). Directed by Erich *Engel and designed by Caspar *Neher, the *musical play became an immediate success. Other important premières of critical plays followed in 1929: *Giftgas über Berlin* (*Poison Gas over Berlin*) by Peter Martin Lampel, which was banned after its première; *Pioneers in Ingolstadt* by Marieluise *Fleisser (directed by Brecht, set by Neher); *Happy End*; and in 1931, *Italian Night* by Ödön von *Horváth. Aufricht employed many leading directors—among them Karl Heinz *Martin and Leopold *Jessner—and some of the finest actors as well, including Lotte *Lenya, Carola Neher, Ernst *Deutsch, Heinrich George, Gustav *Gründgens, Heinz Rühmann, and Heinz Schweikart. Between 1933 and 1945 the theatre provided mainly light entertainment. After the war, with the theatre now under the control of the German Democratic Republic, in what had become East Berlin, Fritz Wisten put together a repertoire of *comedy and premièred new Communist Party plays (1946–50). In 1950 the company consolidated with the *Volksbühne until the reopening of that theatre at Rosa Luxemburg-Platz in 1954, when the Berliner Ensemble arrived. CBB

SCHIKANEDER, EMANUEL (1751–1812)

Austrian actor, director, *manager, dramatist, and singer. A central figure in *Viennese popular theatre, Schikaneder was director of an itinerant theatre group until 1789 when he became director of the Wiener Vorstadttheater auf der Wieden. In 1801 he founded the Theater an der Wien and remained director until 1806. As an actor Schikaneder was a successor to Felix *Kurz, firmly rooted in the tradition of Viennese broad comedy. He wrote numerous light *comedies, *burlesques, and *musical plays. Having met *Mozart in Salzburg in 1780, Schikaneder became famous as librettist for *The Magic Flute* (1791) and performed Papageno on opening night. CBB

SCHILLER, FRIEDRICH (1759–1805)

German dramatist, poet, aesthetician, director, and professor of history, author of arguably the finest *verse *tragedies in the German language. Born in Marbach, he began writing plays while still at his military academy in Württemberg, from which he was expelled in 1780. In 1782 he fled from the repressive regime in Stuttgart and eventually was appointed theatre poet at the *Mannheim Court Theatre. Here his revolutionary *Sturm und Drang* prose drama *The Robbers* (1782) caused a sensation at its première ('The theatre resembled a madhouse: rolling eyes, clenched fists, stamping feet, hoarse shouts in the *auditorium! Complete strangers embraced each other in tears, women staggered almost fainting towards the exits'). Karl Moor, cheated of his inheritance by his evil brother Franz, leads a robber band to seek restitution. He defeats Franz but finally recognizes the dangers of his own violent idealism. Despite its *melodramatic language and incidents, *The Robbers* has remained popular in the German repertoire, most famously in *Piscator's controversial staging at the *Volksbühne in *Berlin in 1926. On a set heavily influenced by *Eisenstein's *Battleship Potemkin*, Piscator transformed the violent robber Spiegelberg into the *hero of the piece and had him made up to resemble Trotsky. Schiller's next plays, *The Conspiracy of Fiesco in Genoa* (1783) and *Intrigue and Love* (1784), have been called the first *political plays in German. The former, 'a republican tragedy', is set in Genoa in 1547 and describes a failed revolution against the Doge. The latter, a 'bourgeois tragedy', shows the impossibility of love between a young nobleman and a middle-class girl. *Don Carlos* (1787), a long and complex verse tragedy, on which *Verdi's opera is loosely based, portrays two young idealists, Don Carlos and the Marquis of Posa, whose attempt to end Spanish tyranny in the Netherlands is crushed by reactionary forces in sixteenth-century Spain.

In 1789 Schiller became professor of history at Jena University, not far from the cultural centre of Weimar, and in 1794 he began a deep friendship with *Goethe. Having for ten years devoted himself to historical and philosophical studies, he began to write once more for the stage. In 1799 he moved permanently and directed for the *Weimar Court Theatre, the work including Goethe's *Iphigenia* in 1802 and the première of his own epic trilogy about the Thirty Years War, *Wallenstein* (1798–9). The *action traces the career of the hugely successful general Wallenstein: his idealistic aspiration to restore Europe to peace by deserting the Emperor and joining with the Swedish army leads to his death through his own indecision and the machinations of his would-be successor. In 1800 the Weimar Court Theatre premièred *Mary Stuart*, Schiller's finest play, depicting the final days and execution of Mary on the orders of Elizabeth I. While ostensibly the tragic heroine, Mary attains sublimity in her death, and Elizabeth has to live on, isolated and unable to escape from the contamination of political life. Schiller also invented a meeting between the two queens, a powerful scene in which Elizabeth is dismayed to encounter the beauty of her cousin, who is here still 27 years old.

There followed *The Maid of Orleans* (1801), in which Joan of Arc dies heroically on the battlefield, and *The Bride of Messina* (1803), a classical piece employing a *chorus, about the enmity of two brothers. Schiller's last completed play, *William Tell* (1804), sets the legendary hero against the background of the Swiss War of Independence against the Austrians, contrasting his moral freedom in assassinating the cruel governor Gessler with the brutality of the political struggle waged by his countrymen. The play has subsequently been a great favourite in revolutionary situations, most memorably being the production with which Leopold *Jessner reopened the former Kaiser's theatre in *Berlin after the First World War, and also the play with which the Volksbühne in East Berlin reopened in the recently founded German Democratic Republic in 1954. Ironically, its staging by Christoph Schroth in Schwerin in 1989, a few months before the tearing down of the Berlin Wall, was read by the *audience as a protest against Soviet dominance in East Germany. However, the image of Tell as a strong nationalist individual could also be appropriated by fascist elements, a line from *Tell*, 'The strong man stands mightiest alone', being the title of one of the chapters of Hitler's *Mein Kampf*, and the play, together with Goethe's *Faust*, being the favourite classic of Nazi Germany (*see* FASCISM AND THEATRE).

In addition to his playwriting and work as a director in Weimar, Schiller published important *theoretical essays about the theatre, including *The Stage Regarded as a Moral Institution* (1784), a document that helped to raise the theatre to become an important element in German culture; *On Pathos* (1793), which argued that tragedy delivers no moral lessons but inspires by its examples of moral strength in the face of suffering; and *On the Sublime* (1793), arguing that tragedy reinforces our sense of moral freedom by showing how heroes can rise above their fate and, like Mary Stuart, achieve 'sublimity'. By watching tragedies, we become 'inoculated against the unavoidable fate' of our own death and so learn to achieve ascendancy over it. *See* WEIMAR CLASSICISM; HISTORICAL DRAMA.   MWP

PATTERSON, MICHAEL, *The First German Theatre* (London, 1990)
PRUDHOE, JOHN, *The Theatre of Goethe and Schiller* (Oxford, 1973)

SCHILLER, LEON (1887–1954)

Polish director, composer, and *manager. Schiller studied theatre with *Craig in *Paris and composition in *Vienna before his debut as director in 1917. He headed the Bogusławskiego Theater in *Warsaw (1924–6), the Theatre of the Army in Łódź (1946–9), and the Teatr Polski in Warsaw (1949–50), among others, and founded a department of directing at the Institute of Theatre Art in Warsaw. A committed socialist, he joined the Communist Party after the Second World War and was a member of the Polish parliament, but in 1950 he was disgraced by the regime, fired from his positions, and marginalized. Schiller was a man of sharp contradictions: he first promoted the *avant-garde but in old age accepted Soviet *socialist realism, and he oscillated between Catholicism and Marxism. He directed about 150 productions, the core being in the tradition of Polish *romanticism, including *Słowacki's *Kordian* (1930, 1935, 1939), *Mickiewicz's *Forefathers' Eve* (1932, 1933, 1934, 1938), and *Wyspiański's *Achilles* (1925). He also directed Shakespeare and other classics. He sought a 'monumental theatre' or a 'theatre greater than life', often collaborating with *modernist *scenographers on work based in anti-*illusionism, *symbolism, or *expressionism, creating grand and complex *spectacles with an abundance of crowds and *music, elaborate *lighting, and expressive *acting. Schiller also wrote and staged plays with *music using traditional Polish songs, and directed several *documentary theatre productions.   KB

SCHILLER THEATER

Conceived in 1894 by Raphael Löwenfeld as a people's theatre and designed by Max Littmann, the Schiller Theater in *Berlin was opened in 1907. In 1923 it became part of the state-subsidized national theatre under Leopold *Jessner. After a period as a private venture, in 1938 it was renamed Schiller-Theater der Reichshauptstadt with the actor Heinrich George as director. Totally destroyed by bombing in 1943, after its reopening in 1951 it quickly became West Berlin's major theatre under the director Boreslaw Barlog, who collected a superb ensemble and major directors. After Barlog's departure in 1971 it lost its pre-eminent position to the *Schaubühne. With its expensive infrastructure and vague artistic profile, it was a target for *financial restructuring after reunification, and the Berlin Senate closed it down in 1993. CBB

SCHINKEL, KARL FRIEDRICH (1781–1841)

Painter, designer, and one of the most famous architects of the nineteenth century. He developed a style which combined the utopian potential of French revolutionary *neoclassicism with a convincing functionality. He studied in Italy and *Paris, and after 1805 he worked under *Iffland at the *Berlin Royal Theatre where he designed *scenery for about 40 productions (most notably The Magic Flute, 1816; *Schiller's Maid of Orleans, 1817; Faust II, 1832). Between 1818 and 1824 Schinkel rebuilt the Royal Theatre at the Gendarmenmarkt, one of the most famous examples of neoclassical *playhouse architecture. He broke with the baroque conventions by trying to bridge the gap between *stage and *audience, thus anticipating the fin de siècle reforms of theatre architecture. Unlike the traditional *illusionist stage of the time, his strongly symbolic sets emphasized three-dimensional space. CBB

SCHLEGEL, AUGUST WILHELM (1767–1845)

German literary historian and translator. A congenial poet-translator, Schlegel remains best known for his part in the translation of Shakespeare with Ludwig *Tieck (1797–1820). Schlegel translated seventeen of the plays for the series completed by Dorothea Tieck and Wolf von Baudissin in 1833. Although now sounding dated, this translation is still the most widely performed in Germany and regarded by some as highly faithful to the original. Schlegel did much to publicize *romanticism, especially in his Lectures on Dramatic Art and Literature. First given in *Vienna in 1808, they deal with the whole field of Western drama, claiming the importance of the theatre of the past, an ideal shared by many romantics. The lectures also insist that drama is a *text for *performance, not to be valued for its literary merit alone. Although harshly criticized by later romantic writers, perhaps because his perspective was more international than national, as a scholar Schlegel made major contributions to German, Sanskrit, and romance philology. CBB

SCHLEGEL, JOHANN ELIAS (1719–94)

German playwright and aesthetician. In opposition to *Gottsched's notions of drama as a vehicle of moral improvement, Schlegel developed a dramatic *theory focused on the individual *character, with Shakespeare and *Sophocles as his models. He stressed the importance of the comic aspects of drama as a reflection of the *bourgeois life of his time. Although

known as the 'German *Racine' for his earlier *neoclassical plays, Schlegel's writing prepared the ground for *Lessing and the *Sturm und Drang movement. CBB

SCHLEMMER, OSKAR (1888–1943)

German artist, director, and *theorist. Schlemmer directed the theatre department of the *Bauhaus from 1923 to 1929, where he created his Triadic Ballet (1922) based on ideas expressed in his essay 'Man and Art Figure' (1925). For theatre to become a true art form, Schlemmer argued, the human performer must be transformed into an abstract figuration. In the Triadic Ballet actors disappeared beneath all-encompassing *masks and *costumes, the performance made of *dance movement along geometrical lines. He also worked as a designer in the conventional theatre for *Piscator, among others. Schlemmer's work was highly influential on post-war dance and *performance art. CBB

SCHMIDHUBER DE LA MORA, GUILLERMO (1943–)

Mexican playwright and scholar. An early success was the *award-winning The Heirs of Segismundo (1980), about imaginary beings descended from *Calderón's *hero in Life Is a Dream. In 1987 Schmidhuber won the Golden Prize of the University of Miami for the best Spanish-language play written by someone in the United States, for In the Lands of Columbus. With productions in the USA (1989), *Mexico City (1989), and Spain (1994), In the Lands of Columbus is the first part of a trilogy about Columbus in America. Columbus's Fifth Voyage (1992) concerns a trip that Columbus should have taken, while Goodbye to Columbus (1992) deals with the loss of culture and language among Latinos in the United States. KFN

SCHMIDT, DOUGLAS (1942–)

American designer. Born in Cincinnati, he began his career by designing *scenery in 1961 for four plays at the summer repertory theatre in Monmouth, Maine. From 1964 to 1968 he designed twenty productions for the Cincinnati Playhouse in the Park, and from 1969 to 1973 a dozen for *Lincoln Center's Beaumont Theatre. Of the latter, Enemies (1972) brought him the Joseph Maharam *award. In 1974 the Drama Desk honoured him for Over Here! and Veronica's Room. In 1977 he won an Obie for The Crazy Locomotive, and another Maharam for Agamemnon. He has designed scenery for *opera in *New York, Washington, *San Francisco, *Los Angeles, and Tanglewood (Massachusetts), including two major New York revivals of Porgy and Bess (1983, 2000). Among his *musicals are Damn

Yankees (1994 revival), *Band in Berlin* (1999), and *The Civil War* (1999). He has occasionally designed *costumes. CT

SCHNEIDER, ALAN (1917–84)

American director. Born Abram Leopoldovich Schneider in Kharkhov, Ukraine, he went to the USA as a child. After study at the University of Wisconsin and Cornell University, he embarked on a peripatetic career in both regional and commercial theatre, achieving early success on Broadway with *The Remarkable Mr Pennypacker* (1953) and *Anastasia* (1954). He directed many productions for *Arena Stage, where he was *artistic director for one season (1952–3). He staged the historic American première of *Waiting for Godot* at Miami's Coconut Grove Playhouse in 1956, which led to a long-standing friendship with *Beckett. Schneider directed the American premières of most Beckett plays, as well as *Film* (1964) with Buster Keaton. In the 1960s he also became associated with Edward *Albee and Harold *Pinter, directing world or American premières of many of their works, including *Who's Afraid of Virginia Woolf?* (1963), for which he won a Tony *award. Known as a playwright's director, he was scrupulous in placing the demands of the script ahead of his own interpretative impulses. He was widely respected at the time of his death in *London, after being struck by a passing motorcycle. STC

SCHNITZLER, ARTHUR (1862–1931)

Austrian dramatist and novelist. His youth as a medical student in *Vienna was characterized by erotic adventures, gambling, and intellectual debates in coffee houses. His first play, *Anatol* (written 1889–92), describes a bourgeois youth like himself who has no orientation and drifts through a life of endless, superficial pleasures. In 1891 he established his career with a performance of *The Adventure of his Life*, but attempts to stage *Anatol* in Vienna led to *censorship problems, and when *The Fairy Tale* opened in 1893 it caused such a scandal that performances had to be cancelled after two nights. *Liebelei* (*Love Games*, 1895), which premièred at the *Burgtheater with Adele Sandrock in the lead, was an enormous success and was immediately produced in ten German theatres, and a *publishing contract with S. Fischer Verlag made Schnitzler an established writer at the age of 33. The trouble did not stop, however: *Überspannte Person* (*The Eccentric*, published 1896 but not acted until 1932), *Freiwild* (*Fair Game*, *Berlin, 1896), and most of all *Der Reigen* (*La Ronde*, 1900, produced 1920) brought notoriety and charges of immorality. Nonetheless in the years preceding the First World War he wrote a string of highly successful works and became one of the most widely performed dramatists in the German-speaking countries.

Schnitzler's plays are an accurate reflection of life and atmosphere in Vienna at the turn of the century. He was an acute observer of the disintegration of the Habsburg Empire. With a mixture of melancholy and humorous grace, sentimentality, and gentle irony he delineated the social changes following the Industrial Revolution, and has often been called the *Doppelgänger* of Sigmund Freud. His plays are subtle studies of human nature, characterized by elegant, charming *dialogue and a *dramaturgy of apparent formlessness that hides a precise and musical structure. His sophisticated psychological *realism and the impressionist form of his plays were brought out most clearly in productions by Otto *Brahm and *Reinhardt, while the Vienna Burgtheater preferred his *historical dramas. Following a court case against *La Ronde* in 1921, Schnitzler withdrew the performing rights as he feared that the play and his intentions behind it were not properly understood or appreciated by contemporary *audiences. When the ban was lifted in 1982 it was performed in a large number of major playhouses (in Britain for example, by the *Royal Shakespeare Company at the *Aldwych) and its notoriety soon evaporated. Other plays still regularly performed, albeit rarely outside the German-speaking countries, are *Der grüne Kakadu* (*The Green Cockatoo*), *Der einsame Weg* (*The Lonely Way*), *Der Ruf des Lebens* (*Life's Calling*), *Komtesse Mizzi* (*Countess Mizzi*), *Das weite Land* (*Undiscovered Country*), and *Professor Bernhardi*. GB

SCHOENAERTS, JULIEN (1925–)

Greatest Flemish actor of the post-war period. After his studies at the Studio Herman Teirlinck in *Antwerp, Schoenaerts joined the Royal Dutch Theatre (National Theatre) in Antwerp, acted in The Netherlands, and set up several impressive solo productions. His most creative work was in collaboration with Walter *Tillemans, who directed some of his greatest performances: Kaspar in Peter *Handke's eponymous play, Davies in *Pinter's *The Caretaker*, Hamm in *Beckett's *Endgame*, and Vladimir in *Waiting for Godot*. Schoenaerts possesses a uniquely energetic theatrical presence. His *acting is characterized by the utmost control of expression and by an impressive talent for exploring the emotional value of sound and rhythm in the *text.

JDV

SCHÖNBERG, CLAUDE-MICHEL *See* BOUBLIL, ALAIN.

SCHÖNEMANN, JOHANN FRIEDRICH (1704–82)

German actor, remembered chiefly for his part in the Leipzig reform project of Caroline *Neuber and J. C. *Gottsched. He performed the part of *Harlequin in the 1730s before the *character was banned by Neuber. He *managed his own troupe in the 1740s and 1750s, which included Konrad *Ekhof, Sophie

*Schröder, and *Ackermann. His financial incompetence forced him to dissolve his troupe and retire in 1757. CBB

SCHOOLS OF DRAMA See TRAINING FOR THEATRE.

SCHOUWBURG

The first municipal theatre of *Amsterdam, located on the Keizersgracht, inaugurated on 3 January 1638. The architect Jacob van Campen used stone for the building after the merger in 1632 of the two Amsterdam *Chambers of Rhetoric and the demise of the first Dutch Academy, on whose site the theatre was erected. The Schouwburg opened with Joost van den *Vondel's *Gijsbrecht van Aemstel*, written especially for the occasion; until the late twentieth century this play, combining local history with abundant praise of marriage, was performed almost annually during the Christmas season. The original *playhouse on Keizersgracht was soon redesigned in the Italian style with *proscenium arch and stage machinery. Destroyed by *fire in 1772, a wooden structure was built two years later, which lasted until a fire of 1890 when it was replaced by the present edifice (1894). In the later twentieth century, in spite of increasing competition from smaller, experimental theatrical ventures and the construction of the new Amsterdam *opera house (Muziektheater, 1986), the Schouwburg has maintained a vital role in the capital's theatre scene. It has three in-house companies (Toneelgroep Amsterdam, Het Toneel Speelt, Courage), and hosts four theatre *festivals as well as numerous premières each year. TH

SCHREYVOGEL, JOSEPH (1768–1832)

Austrian *dramaturg and director. As secretary of the *Burgtheater in *Vienna from 1814 to 1832 Schreyvogel shaped a repertoire of high literary standards, staging Shakespeare, *Calderón, *Molière, *Corneille, *Goethe, *Schiller, *Kleist, and *Grillparzer. He built up a fine ensemble and constantly fought against *censorship. Under the pseudonym of Karl August West he wrote, among many other works, an influential adaptation of Calderón's *Life Is a Dream*. CBB

SCHRÖDER, FRIEDRICH LUDWIG (1744–1816)

German actor and director. The son of Sophie Charlotte *Schröder and stepson of Konrad *Ackermann, Friedrich joined his stepfather's group in Switzerland in 1759 and followed him to Hamburg in 1764, first as a *dancer, later as an actor. Under the tutelage of Konrad *Ekhof he performed in comic parts and in larger character roles including King Lear, Philip (*Schiller's *Don Carlos*), Othello, Richard II, and Shylock. Together with his mother he took over the *management of the Hamburg Comödienhaus am Gänsemarkt after Ackermann's death in 1771, which they directed until 1780. During a much celebrated *tour to Mannheim he helped establish the new progressive drama. He was a member of the *Burgtheater in *Vienna (1781–5), and again became director of the Hamburg theatre (1785–98).

Schröder encouraged contemporary drama, especially authors of the *Sturm und Drang* movement: *Lessing's *Emilia Galotti* (1772), *Goethe's *Clavigo* and *Götz von Berlichingen* (1774), Schiller's *The Robbers* and *Love and Intrigue*, and *Klinger's *The Twins* (1776) were among those he mounted. He also contributed to the breakthrough of Shakespeare on the German stage, first in adaptations, later in versions closer to the original; his production of *Hamlet* (1776) was particularly significant. His influential *acting style was based on a *realist aesthetic of 'truth and naturalness' and featured strong emotional contrasts, which served as the antithesis for Goethe's more restrained *Weimar classicism. Goethe portrayed Schröder as the *actor-manager Serlo in *Wilhelm Meister's Apprenticeship* (1795–6). CBB

SCHRÖDER, SOPHIE (1781–1868)

German actress, a leading exponent of *romantic acting. In a career spanning 45 years and many major German theatres, Schröder achieved greatest acclaim for her performance of tragic roles at *Vienna's *Burgtheater from 1815 to 1829. She was particularly associated with *Grillparzer's drama (*Sappho*, 1818; *Medea*, 1821) but also excelled as Lady Macbeth, Portia, and Phèdre. CBB

SCHRÖDER, SOPHIE CHARLOTTE (ACKERMANN) (1714–93)

German actress and *manager. After a short-lived marriage to the *Berlin organist J. D. Schröder, she joined the *Schönemann troupe in 1740. In 1741 she founded her own acting company in Hamburg, which was dissolved in 1744. In 1747 she joined the Theater Danzig and followed Konrad E. *Ackermann on his *tour through Russia, and married him in *Moscow in 1749. The couple founded the renowned Ackermannsche Gesellschaft, which travelled throughout the German-speaking countries. As the company's teacher and leading actress she was noted for her intellect and energy as well as for a refined *acting style. CBB

SCHUMANN, PETER (1934–   )

German-born American director and puppeteer. Schumann moved permanently to the United States in the late 1950s to work as a sculptor before founding the *Bread and Puppet

Theatre Company in 1961. Combining elements of *Brecht, medieval mysticism, *puppetry, and pageantry, he created a distinctive synthesis of *avant-garde performance and guerrilla theatre. Schumann also bakes loaves of bread that he distributes to *audiences before shows in order to emphasize their communal and *ritual nature. He came to prominence in the late 1960s for his protest works against the Vietnam War. *The Cry of the People for Meat* (1969), for example, movingly depicted a Vietnamese village bombed by American fighter jets. The company increasingly took to the *streets by the end of the decade, often leading processions with haunting puppet madonna figures, or 'Grey Ladies', requiring multiple operators. Schumann's interest in outdoor performance received a boost when his company was invited to become the theatre-in-residence at Goddard College in 1971, an experimental university located in Vermont. There he began an annual outdoor summer pageant featuring enormous puppets called the Domestic Resurrection Circus. The Circus eventually became a major counter-cultural event, attracting over 40,000 people by the time he discontinued it in 1998. JAB

SCHWAB, WERNER (1958–94)

Austrian dramatist and prose writer. Educated in fine arts, Schwab was among the most provocative and successful young dramatists of the mid-1990s. His plays are primarily interested in language, dialect-inflected speech presented as verbal attacks, playing freely with word associations, paradoxes, and misspellings. His *characters find themselves in extreme situations: murder, rape, incest, and cannibalism are among the atrocities that often end in *grotesque and comic travesty. Schwab died of an alcohol overdose in 1994. Notable plays include *Die Präsidentinnen* (*The Lady Presidents*, 1990) and *Volksvernichtung; oder, Meine Leber ist sinnlos: eine Radikalkomödie* (*Genocide; or, My Life Is Blameless: a radical comedy*, 1992). CBB

SCHWARTZ, MAURICE (1890–1960)

Ukrainian-American actor, director, playwright, and *manager. 'Mr Second Avenue' was the defining figure of the inter-war *Yiddish theatre in *New York. He joined David Kessler's company in 1912 and became known for his passionate *acting and outstanding entrepreneurial skills. In 1918 he became partner in the Irving Place Theatre, and shortly afterwards established the *Yiddish Art Theatre, which survived until 1950. Dedicated to artistic productions that appealed to educated Jewish *audiences, in the 1920s he experimented with various forms, including a *constructivist rendition of *Goldfaden's *The Tenth Commandment* (1926), designed by Boris *Aronson. His most successful productions were *Yoshe Kalb* (1932) and *The Brothers Ashkenazi* (1937), which made extended national and inter-

national *tours. Schwartz starred in two important Yiddish *films, *Uncle Moses* (1932) and *Tevye* (1939). EN

SCHWARZ-BART, SIMONE (1938–   )

Guadeloupean novelist and playwright. In *Ton beau capitaine* (*Your Handsome Captain*, 1987), a *monodrama in the tradition of *Beckett's *Krapp's Last Tape*, Wilnor is an exploited Haitian worker in Guadeloupe. Alone on stage he plays and answers a tape-recorded letter from his wife in Haiti. Schwarz-Bart portrays a drama of love, separation, exile, and resistance through detailed *stage directions. The songs, *dances, music, silences, ancestral *rituals, and *voodoo set up Wilnor's spiritual evolution to a liberated Christ figure who grows to understand his wife's infidelity. This precise and poetic *text has been performed at the *Limoges Festival, in *New York, and elsewhere. MRM

SCOFIELD, PAUL (1922–   )

English actor. After training at Croydon Repertory Theatre and the *London Mask School, he established his reputation at the *Birmingham Repertory Company before moving to Stratford in 1946. He played a wide variety of roles at the *Shakespeare Memorial Theatre over the next three seasons, from the Clown in *The Winter's Tale* to Henry V. He demonstrated that his intelligence and his extraordinary voice—described by one *critic as 'a mountain voice, rifted, charmed, that can glitter on the peak and fall, sombre, in the sudden crevasse'—could turn parts thought almost unactable, like Don Armado in *Love's Labour's Lost*, into deeply humane studies of individuals. His Hamlet (1948) was, for Kenneth *Tynan, simply 'the best Hamlet I have seen'. As Thomas More in *Bolt's *A Man for All Seasons* (1960), Scofield created a study of conscience that gained him a wider international reputation. But it was his King Lear (1962), directed by Peter *Brook for the *Royal Shakespeare Company, which marked his greatness; its searching of Lear's rigidity at the opening made the transition to mad outsider painful and colossal in a nihilistic universe which drew Shakespeare close to *Beckett. Scofield returned to the role for Brook's *film (1971) and in a new *radio production in 2002.

As Timon of Athens in 1965 he charted a similar collapse to Lear's, described as 'declining from a sunny mellifluousness to an unhinged vengefulness with impeccable logic'. After the comparative failure of his Macbeth in 1967, he left Stratford and became carefully selective about his performances, never playing a role unless fully committed to it and to the production. As *Chekhov's Vanya (*Royal Court, 1970), Salieri (*Shaffer's *Amadeus*, 1979), or *Ibsen's John Gabriel Borkman (Royal *National Theatre, 1996), he showed his fascination with failures. But he was also gifted in *comedy: as the delicately drunk Khlestakov in *Gogol's *The Government Inspector* (*Aldwych, 1965),

*Zuckmayer's Captain of Köpenick (*Old Vic, 1971), or *Jonson's Volpone (National, 1977). Scrupulously private and deeply committed to his art and the actor's responsibility to the dramatist, Scofield has never been a conventional star actor but has been admired as one of the most provocative actors of his age. He was made a Companion of Honour in 2001.   PDH

SCOTT, CLEMENT WILLIAM (1841–1904)

English critic for the *Daily Telegraph* for more than 25 years from 1872, and editor of *Theatre* magazine (1877–89; *see* CRITICISM). Scott was a true theatre lover, but his conventional morality led him to oppose *Ibsen and the 'New Drama', and he is best remembered for his intemperate attack on the *Independent Theatre's production of *Ghosts* (1891), for which he was castigated by *Archer and *Shaw. Scott wrote several plays, often in collaboration and adapted from the French; the most successful was *Diplomacy* (1878) from *Sardou's *Dora*. His book *From 'The Bells' to 'King Arthur'* (1896), a record of first nights at the *Lyceum from 1871 to 1895, drew some praise from his old adversary Shaw.   EEC

SCOTT, DENNIS (1939–91)

Jamaican playwright, poet, director, *dancer, and actor. He joined the National Dance Theatre Company of Jamaica in 1965, and won prizes in 1966 and 1969 for his early plays *Chariots of Wrath* and *The Passionate Cabbage*. *The Crime of Anabel Campbell* (1970) transposed the *character of Clytemnestra to contemporary Jamaica. The remarkable *Echo in the Bone* (1974) relates the story of the murder of a white plantation owner, and the man who may have killed him, in a non-linear and highly theatrical form, using elements of surviving African *rituals taken from *Caribbean spirit possession and the 'Nine Night Ceremony' for the dead. *Dog* (1978) is a disturbing Orwellian fable about rich and poor. In 1977 Scott became director of the Jamaica School of Drama, and from 1983 taught *playwriting and *directing at the *Yale School of Drama. In the USA he also worked with the *Eugene O'Neill Theatre Center and the National Theatre of the Deaf, which commissioned his adaptation of *Sir Gawain and the Green Knight*. He acted regularly on the US *television series *The Cosby Show*, before his early death.
                    AS

SCOTT, GEORGE C. (1927–99)

American actor. Scott served in the US Marines (1945–9) and began acting while studying journalism at the University of Missouri. Making his *New York debut as Richard III with the *New York Shakespeare Festival (1957), he subsequently appeared in *The Andersonville Trial* (1959), *Desire under the Elms* (1963), *The Little Foxes* (1967), *Uncle Vanya* (1973), as Willy Loman in his own production of *Death of a Salesman* (1975), and in *Sly Fox* (1976). At the *Circle in the Square, he directed and acted in *Present Laughter* (1982) and *On Borrowed Time* (1991). Best known as a *film actor, his prominent roles included Claude Dancer in Otto Preminger's *Anatomy of a Murder* (1959), the zany General Buck Turgidson in *Dr Strangelove* (1964), the crafty Mordecai Jones in *The Flim-Flam Man* (1967), and the powerful title role in *Patton* (1970). On *television he played leading parts in adaptations such as *Winterset* (1959), *The Crucible* (1967), *The Price* (1971), *Oliver Twist* (1982), and *Inherit the Wind* (1999).
                    JDM

SCOTT, JANE (1779–1839)

English playwright, *manager, and performer, a founder of *London's West End. In 1804 John Scott built a theatre, the Sans Pareil (*Adelphi), for his daughter and her pupils; by 1807 she had a full dramatic company with whom she performed her work, tailored for the new middle-class and tourist *audiences of the imperial capital. Of her more than 50 plays only one, *The Old Oak Chest* (1816), was printed, and played in illegal theatres for its radical suggestions; her work was highly various, mediating contemporary trends—Gothic and *romantic as well as the radical—to an audience seeking entertainment.   JSB

SCRIBE, AUGUSTIN-EUGÈNE (1791–1861)

French dramatist and librettist. Originally trained as a lawyer, Scribe had his first play performed in 1815, and at his death he had written nearly 500 plays, mostly in collaboration with less well-known authors (towards whom he had a reputation for generosity). Many of his plays were produced for the Gymnase Theatre, where he was appointed house dramatist in 1821; an early attempt to gain acceptance at the *Comédie-Française (with *Le Mariage d'argent*, 1827) seems to have been an undeserved failure. Scribe specialized to begin with in *vaudeville*, or light *comedy, a *genre in which he was able to create a reputation for effective dramatic construction. His name soon became synonymous with the term *well-made play which was to be so important in nineteenth-century theatre history, in Britain and the USA as well as in France, even if it was later ridiculed by *Shaw. The tight logic of *plot, the subordination of *character to situation, the contrived or mechanical creation of suspense, and the inevitable resolution in a *scène à faire* were appropriate to the *comédie-vaudeville*, and the *farces of *Labiche or *Feydeau. But the formula of the well-made play had the effect in more serious drama of turning characters into puppets controlled by chance—for instance, in the historical plays with which Scribe did succeed in establishing himself at the Comédie-Française.

Le Verre d'eau (*The Glass of Water*, Comédie-Française, 1840) is designed to illustrate the supposition that important historical events can be related to the most trivial of causes. Set in England under Queen Anne, the play features a power struggle between the Duchess of Marlborough and Bolingbroke, who champions the young couple Masham (desired by both the Queen and the Duchess) and Abigail, whom Masham is able to marry, once the machinations of the Duchess have been defeated. The *denouement depends on the request for a glass of water at a court reception, which reveals to both women their sexual rivalry. A similar causation, this time leading to a tragic outcome, is seen in the *historical drama *Adrienne Lecouvreur* (Comédie-Française, 1849), when the young actress's misinterpretation of the behaviour of her lover Maurice de Saxe leads to her death after inhaling poison from a bouquet sent by her rival.

Both of these plays retained their popularity up to the end of the nineteenth century. *Adrienne Lecouvreur* in particular, written in collaboration with Legouvé as a vehicle for *Rachel, was frequently revived by Sarah *Bernhardt, who played in it in *London as well, where it was also one of the great successes of Janet *Achurch. Scribe, who was elected to the Académie Française in 1834, enjoyed a distinguished parallel career in the field of *opera. Not only was his play to be the basis for Cilea's opera *Adriana Lecouvreur* in 1902, but throughout his active life he was himself the librettist for some of the most successful operas and *opéras-comiques* of his day, from Rossini's *Le Comte Ory* (1828) and Boieldieu's *La Dame blanche* (1825) to several operas by Meyerbeer, including *Robert the Devil* (1831) and *L'Africaine* (1865). He was the librettist for *Verdi's *Sicilian Vespers* in 1855; and his libretto for Auber's *Gustave III; ou, Le Bal masqué* formed the basis for Verdi's more distinguished *Masked Ball*. WDH

SCRIPT *See* TEXT.

SCUDÉRY, GEORGES DE (1601–67)

French playwright. Brother of the novelist Madeleine (to the writing of whose popular romances he contributed), Scudéry was an ambitious as well as a prolific author of *tragedies, *tragicomedies, and *comedies. The most interesting of these is perhaps *La Comédie des comédiens*, one of two plays with this name staged during the 1632–3 *Paris season showing a theatre company at *rehearsal and in performance: Scudéry's features *Montdory's company at the *Marais Theatre, while the alternative by Gougenot presents their rivals at the *Hôtel de Bourgogne. Scudéry played a prominent role in the 'Querelle du *Cid*', his hostile *Observations* (1637) containing a pedantic commentary on *Corneille's play. *See also* NEOCLASSICISM. WDH

SEATTLE REPERTORY THEATRE

American *regional theatre. Founded in 1963 by Stuart Vaughn and a local committee of prominent Seattle citizens, SRT survived *financial instability in its early years to become the leading institutional theatre of the Pacific north-west. A 1971 production of *Richard II* starring Richard Chamberlain first brought SRT to national attention. Daniel Sullivan became *artistic director in 1981 and earned a reputation for premièring new mainstream plays that went on to successful commercial runs in *New York, such as Herb *Gardner's *I'm Not Rappaport* and Wendy *Wasserstein's *The Heidi Chronicles*. In 1997 Sullivan left to pursue his freelance career and was replaced by Sharon Ott. STC

SECK, DOUTA (1919–91)

Senegalese actor and singer, born in Mali, educated in Senegal at the *École William Ponty. In *Paris he studied architecture from 1946, but abandoned it for training as a singer under Marcelle Gérar. His acting career began in 1949 when he played the Congo Witch-Doctor in *O'Neill's *Emperor Jones*. In 1955 and 1956 he played the Coolie and the Merchant respectively in *Brecht's *The Exception and the Rule*. But it was in 1964 in Salzburg that he achieved fame with his powerful performance as Christophe, the visionary King of Haiti, in Aimé *Césaire's *La Tragédie du roi Christophe*, a role he played regularly in Europe, *Africa, and the *Caribbean until 1978. Seck's temperament appeared to match the intense, romantic, and haughty *character of Christophe, and the actor became known as Seck-Christophe to his colleagues. Other important Parisian assignments included roles in John Berry's adaptation of Prosper Mérimée's novel *Tamango* (1954), Yves Jamiaque's *Negro Spiritual* (1955), and Peter *Brook's *Mahabharata* (1985). Seck also acted in more than ten *films. He returned to Dakar in 1972 and worked at the Daniel Sorano National Theatre until 1984, going abroad occasionally on short-term acting contracts. JCM

SEDAINE, MICHEL-JEAN (1719–97)

French dramatist. Sedaine's reputation rests on *Le Philosophe sans le savoir* (*A Philosopher without Knowing It*, 1765), a *bourgeois *drame which earned the admiration of *Diderot, the *theorist of the new *genre. However, the greater part of Sedaine's output for the theatre was as author of librettos for the *Opéra-Comique. He was elected to the Académie Française in 1789, and *Le Philosophe sans le savoir* remained in the repertory of the *Comédie-Française well into the nineteenth century.

WDH

SÉGA

Traditional song-and-dance form of the francophone islands of the Indian Ocean: Mauritius, Réunion, and the Seychelles. It evolved from the music of slaves brought there to work on the plantations. With a typical 6/8 tempo, it initially used only percussion as accompaniment, but gradually European harmonic instruments were incorporated, such as the guitar, violin, and accordion. Now often commercially performed in tourist hotels, its purer traditional form was undergoing a revival at the end of the twentieth century. Well-known exponents of the genre include Ti-Frère from Mauritius, Jean-Claude Volcy from the Seychelles, and Maxime Laope and Jules Arlanda from Réunion.   PGH

SEGAL, ZOHRA (1912–)

Indian dancer and actress of Indian and British *radio, theatre, *film, and *television. Of aristocratic Muslim Pathan parentage, Segal broke *gender norms and pioneered a career in performing arts. After study in Lahore, she travelled to Germany to pursue *dance at Mary Wigman's school. In 1935 she joined Uday Shankar's *ballet company and as a principal dancer performed throughout the world. She taught dance at Shankar's India Culture Centre in Almora and later at her own Zoresh Dance Institute in Lahore. From 1945 to 1959 she was a member of Prithvi Theatres, serving as dance director and acting alongside Prithviraj *Kapoor and her sister Uzra Butt. The company gave some 2,000 performances by *touring over 100 towns in *India. In the 1960s she moved to *London, working for the BBC, the *Old Vic, and the *British Drama League. She achieved acclaim in two Merchant–Ivory films, *The Guru* and *Courtesans of Bombay*, in the television serial *Jewel in the Crown*, and in two films about the Indian *diaspora, *Bhaji on the Beach* directed by Gurinder Chadha and *Masala* directed by Krishna Srinivas. Segal continued to perform in her eighties, notably in the *Ajoka Theatre production of *Ek Thi Nani* in Lahore. Among other *awards, *India honoured her with the Padma Shri in 1998.   KH

SEKYI, KOBINA (1892–1956)

Gold Coast playwright. The Cosmopolitan Club at Cape Coast, a meeting place for the educated and miseducated, is one of the targets of Sekyi's *satire in *The Blinkards*, yet this organization produced the play in 1917. Sekyi was a young Gold Coaster with a philosophy degree from London University and an acute sense of how ridiculous his countrymen and -women made themselves by aping European ways. A loosely structured piece that moves effectively between English and Fanti, *The Blinkards* was published only in 1974. Since then it has been produced in Ghana and Nigeria by directors delighted to find such a lively early text.   JMG

SELDES, MARIAN (1928–)

American actress and teacher, who made her Broadway debut as a servant in *Euripides' *Medea* (1947). She originated roles in Tennessee *Williams's *The Milk Train Doesn't Stop Here Anymore* (1964) and Edward *Albee's *A Delicate Balance* (1967), among others. While a teacher at *New York's *Juilliard School from 1968 to 1990, she played in the Broadway *long runs of *Equus* (1974) and *Deathtrap* (1978). Seldes has dabbled in *television and *film, but her reputation as a consummate stage actress has continued to grow with New York performances in Albee's *Three Tall Women* (1994) and *The Play about the Baby* (2001).   EW

SELLARS, PETER (1957–)

American director. Using eclectic staging techniques derived from European and American *avant-garde theatre and non-Western performance, Sellars's modern-dress productions of the classics always address the culture and politics of contemporary America. He apprenticed at Pittsburgh's Lovelace Marionette Theatre at the age of 11 and staged *puppet shows throughout his teens. At Andover and Harvard he directed scores of productions, culminating in his first professional assignment, *Gogol's *Inspector General* at the *American Repertory Theatre in 1980. As *artistic director of the Boston Shakespeare Company (1983–4) and later of the American National Theatre at Washington's Kennedy Center (1985–6), Sellars developed a performance style that juxtaposes psychological *realism with precisely choreographed physicality. Strongly influenced by Vsevelod *Meyerhold and Yury *Lyubimov, *music always plays a central role in Sellars's theatre. In the late 1980s he focused exclusively on *opera, most notably the *Mozart–*da Ponte trilogy which he set in *New York City. In collaboration with composer John Adams, Sellars developed a repertoire of new opera that combines national politics with intense spiritual yearning, evident in works like *Nixon in China* (1987), *The Death of Klinghoffer* (1991), and *El Niño* (2000). In the 1990s this spiritual theme dominated his productions of Messiaen's *St François d'Assise* (1992), *Handel's *Theodora* (1996), *Tang Xianzu's *Peony Pavilion* (1998), and Stravinsky's *Biblical Pieces* (1999). He was the director of the *Los Angeles Festivals of 1990 and 1993, teaches at the University of California, Los Angeles, and has directed a number of productions with community groups.   MPB

SEMIOTICS *see page 1219*

SEMYONOVA, EKATERINA (1786–1849)

Russian actress. The daughter of a peasant mother, Semyonova rose from rags to riches to become one of the finest tragic actresses of her day. A pupil of *Dmitrevsky and *Shakhovskoy and blessed with a powerful temperament, she starred in plays by *Ozerov, *Racine, *Voltaire, and *Schiller before abandoning

(continued on p. 1220)

SEMIOTICS

The study of signs, cultural traces (verbal, pictorial, plastic) that express, represent, or communicate meanings. Semiotics was first significantly applied to theatre by members of the Prague Linguistic Circle in the 1930s, drawing upon the methodologies of Russian formalism and the linguistic theories of Ferdinand de Saussure (1857–1913). Petr Bogatyrev (1893–1970), Jindřich Honzl (1894–1953), and Jan Mukařovský (1891–1975) considered theatre as a complex communicative instrument, employing a system of visual signs (such as *scenography, *costume, bodies) and aural signs (such as voice, *sound, *music) that are in constant flux, both in relationship to each other and in shifting of function.

This first generation of semiotic writing on theatre ended in the early 1940s, and although after the Second World War semiotics was again applied to literature, and then to painting, music, and the cinema, it was not until the late 1960s that it again became important in theatre theory. The lead this time was taken by French scholars, working in the tradition of modern French *structuralism. Articles by Roland Barthes and Steen Jansen prepared the way for the first book-length study of semiotics and theatre, published by Tadeusz Kowsan in 1970. From France, interest in theatre semiotics spread to Belgium, where André Helbo founded in 1972 a semiotics review, Degrés, and later published several books on the semiotics of theatre, and to Italy, where the leading Italian semiotician Umberto Eco wrote several important essays on theatre, and where Marco de Marinis soon emerged as a leader in the new field. A more formal and mathematically oriented semiotic analysis of dramatic *texts was developed in the 1960s in Romania by Solomon Marcus.

In France, studies of semiotics and theatre by Patrice Pavis and Anne Ubersfeld appeared in the late 1970s, although the primarily literary approach represented by their work was challenged in 1978 in two major articles entitled 'Lo spettacolo come testo' ('The Spectacle as Text') by de Marinis. In these articles de Marinis argued that theatre semiotics should not be oriented toward the written dramatic text, but should rather focus, as the Prague School had done, upon the 'spectacle text' as it operated in the theatre. Thus defined, semiotics provided a grounding analytic methodology that has influenced practically every subsequent analytic approach to *performance, whether these approaches were directly semiotic or not.

A few translated articles in the late 1970s introduced semiotics to English-speaking theorists of theatre, followed by the first English-language book on the subject, Kier Elam's The Semiotics of Theatre and Drama in 1980. Three years later Erika Fischer-Lichte's three-volume Semiotik des Theaters provided a comprehensive summary of what might be called the first generation of modern theatre semiotic theory, discussing its operations on three levels: as system (involving all possible signs in the theatre), as norm (involving the sign systems of a particular historical *genre or mode), and as individual speech (involving the sign systems operating in a particular production).

In that same year de Marinis also published a review of the discipline, where he once again presciently called for a reorientation of semiotics, this time stepping back from analysis of the sign systems on stage to one of how those signs operated in a particular social context. De Marinis's article was part of a general shift taking place in semiotic analysis at the beginning of the 1980s. Achim Eschbach in his 1979 Pragmasemiotik und Theater explained the shift in relation to the two founding theorists of semiotics, Saussure and the American Charles Peirce. Modern semiotics, suggested Eschbach, had almost universally followed the Saussure model, which was built upon the concept of the sign as an arbitrary symbol (the signifier) that had been culturally united with some particular meaning (the signified). Basically, this system assumed that the production of the sign, uniting signifier and signified by a sender, would automatically communicate the appropriate meaning to a receiver. The signifier–signified model, noted Eschbach, ignored a necessary third element in the process that was far more important to Peirce, the interpretant, the 'meaning' actually stimulated in the mind of the receiver, which Peirce was careful to distinguish from the signified. Instead of being a mere passive receiver of someone else's signs, in this model the recipient, as interpreter of those signs, becomes a partner in the production of meaning.

The relatively minor attention given to the *audience's contribution by the first generation of modern theatre semioticians is demonstrated by the fact that Elam's book devotes only nine of its 210 pages to this subject, but during the 1980s audiences became a major area of semiotic investigation, resulting in a convergence of an important part of semiotic analysis with modern *reception theory. Typical of the new orientation was a special issue of the Italian semiotic journal Versus in 1985 devoted to 'the semiotics of theatrical reception'. Although semiotics continued to provide an analytic approach for many different aspects of the theatre experience, in general it was applied more and more to an understanding of the social and cultural context of theatre, an area which was also becoming a central interest in *theatre studies in general. Significantly, both Pavis and

Fischer-Lichte, the leaders in the field of theatre semiotics in France and Germany, published collections of essays at the beginning of the 1990s on *interculturalism and theatre. Semiotics here still served as a grounding methodology, but the focus was much more upon the cultural dynamics themselves.

As the twentieth century ended, this seemed the general situation of theatre semiotics. It was no longer widely regarded as a global system for theatre analysis of the future, as it had been a generation earlier, but more as an important stage in the development of modern performance analysis, providing a fundamental analytic strategy upon which would be built or against which would be defined such major subsequent areas of exploration as post-structuralism, *gender studies, and cultural studies. *See also* THEORIES OF DRAMA, THEATRE, AND PERFORMANCE; STRUCTURALISM AND POST-STRUCTURALISM.

MC

CARLSON, MARVIN, *Theatre Semiotics: signs of life* (Bloomington, Ind., 1990)

DE MARINIS, MARCO, *The Semiotics of Performance*, trans. Aine O'Healy (Bloomington, Ind., 1993)

FISCHER-LICHTE, ERIKA, *The Semiotics of Theatre* (Bloomington, Ind., 1992)

the professional stage and marrying a prince. Her first appearance was as the eponymous *heroine in Voltaire's *comedy *Nanine*, in 1803, whilst still at the dramatic school to which her landowner father had sent her. After graduation she became one of the highest-paid actresses of her day and very popular with aristocratic men of letters as well as with *audiences. Gnedich, for example, translated *King Lear* from the French especially for her. *Pushkin was also an admirer. Not only did she learn a great deal from studying her roles with Shakhovskoy and Gnedich but she made a point of observing and then imitating *touring performers, such as Mlle *George. The tables were turned, in 1809, when she found herself performing Gnedich's version of *Tancred* with George herself in the audience. The 'Russian George', as she became known, competed with her rival in 1811 when they found themselves playing the same role in *Moscow. *Box-office receipts during this period soared to a remarkable 400,000 roubles. Her status as classical tragedienne was affected by the advent of *romantic drama but Pushkin declared that 'When one speaks of Russian *tragedy, one mentions Semyonova—and, perhaps, her alone.'

NW

SENDA KOREYA (1904–94)

*Japanese director and actor from a hugely talented family, born Itō Kunio. His brother Itō Michio (1893–1961) was a famous dancer who began his career performing in *At the Hawk's Well* by *Yeats in 1916. A second brother, Itō Kisaku (1899–1967), was the foremost stage designer of his generation for the modern theatre (*shingeki*). Senda joined the *Tsukiji Little Theatre as an actor in 1924, then left to pursue his interests in *political theatre in Germany from 1927 to 1931. On his return to *Tokyo he staged the first Japanese production of *Brecht's *Threepenny Opera* and performed often as an actor, most notably as Hamlet. Imprisoned during the war for his political views, Senda founded a new company, Haiyûza (the Actors' Theatre), in 1945, dedicated to improving the standards of Japanese performance. During his long tenure he mounted memorable productions of Shakespeare, Brecht, *Chekhov, and such Japanese playwrights as *Abe Kōbō. A major figure in post-war Japanese theatre, Senda's high artistic standards and progressive political stance helped define the accomplishments of the entire period.

JTR

SENDRATARI

A modern Javanese *dance-drama without *dialogue, now spread more widely in *Indonesia. The first *sendratari* was created in 1961 by R. T. Kusumokesowo as a series of six works portraying episodes from the *Ramayana* epic. *Sendratari Ramayana* was designed as a tourist attraction and staged during consecutive full moons from June to October at an *open-air theatre in front of the Hindu-Javanese temple Prambanan in central Java. Two years later, the new Candrawilwatikta open-air theatre in east Java staged a semi-historical fourteenth-century story (*Damarwulan*) of the Majapahit kingdom. The form was then adopted by Balinese artists and since 1980 a new *sendratari*, with the role of the narrator (*dalang*) highlighted, has been staged annually at the Bali Arts Festival. The city of Yogyakarta also organized an annual *sendratari* festival featuring regional work, while smaller versions of *sendratari Ramayana* continue to be performed widely in Java and Bali as tourist attractions.

SM

SENECA, LUCIUS ANNAEUS (5/4 BC–AD 65)

Roman philosopher and tragic playwright, who in addition to his extensive literary activities also played a prominent role in the political life of Rome. He served as a senator under Caligula and Claudius. The Empress Agrippina the Younger entrusted him with the education of her son, the future Emperor Nero. During the first years of his reign, Nero was greatly influenced by his tutor's advice and political philosophy; indeed Seneca served as virtual ruler of Rome. But later, perhaps jealous of Seneca's wealth and prestige, Nero ordered him to commit suicide, for, allegedly, supporting a conspiracy against the Emperor's life.

Seneca's Latin *tragedies are based loosely on *Greek originals. These include *Hercules Furens*, *Hercules Oetaeus*,

Troades, Phoenissae, Medea, Phaedra, Oedipus, Agamemnon, and *Thyestes*. A tenth tragedy, *Octavia*, based on events in the reign of Nero, is sometimes attributed to Seneca (almost certainly erroneously). It is a matter of great scholarly debate whether they were written primarily for recitation, or intended to be staged (*see* CLOSET DRAMA). Although such problematic elements as unannounced changes of setting, sudden entries and exits, *dumb shows, and the like do not absolutely preclude ancient staging (the plays have been presented to modern *audiences with considerable success), they may argue against it. Unlike surviving specimens of Greek tragedy, and the fragments of earlier Roman works, there are no implicit *stage directions, and little felt sense of practical *dramaturgy. Seneca does not aim at subtle or consistent *character delineation and still less at effective stage *actions. He seems concerned instead with immediate rhetorical impact and the excitement of raw emotion through lurid descriptive passages.

The works contain highly effective set speeches, and some stirring *choral odes, as well as numerous examples of precepts and 'lessons' based on Seneca's stoic philosophy. Whatever his influence or the theatrical use of his plays in ancient Rome, they later greatly appealed to *early modern playwrights and their audiences. The sensational violence and melodramatic horror, the prevalence of *ghosts and black magic, the evocation of direst woe and *catastrophe, and even the recourse to rant and bombast: these elements compelled attention and excited first admiration and then widespread imitation. Moreover, the dark mixture of court intrigue, deception, and pervasive anxiety that Seneca's troubled works distil from the ago of Nero was not too foreign or exotic for Renaissance taste. His themes and philosophy were readily intelligible, the stories were sensational, and at times he created moments of genuine emotion, poetic beauty, or thrilling drama. His Latin was accessible, and his five-*act format easy to emulate.

The first English translation of Seneca appeared in 1559, and the Elizabethan stage was soon strewn with his demons, tyrants, fustian, and corpses. If *Senecan *revenge tragedy spawned such offspring as Shakespeare's *Titus Andronicus*, it also deeply influenced *Richard III* and left more than its mark on *Hamlet*. Nor was the influence felt only in violent action and passionate rhetoric; Seneca's ideas absolutely permeate Elizabethan drama (with particular prominence in the works of *Kyd and *Marlowe) and decisively colour its mood and morality. His impact on the great dramatic works of that age was fundamental and, through it, he has never ceased to influence our own. It is deeply ironic that of all the tragic works of antiquity, Greek or Roman, the most profound influence upon early modern practice was exercised by plays that may never have been performed in their own time.

In recent years, although not numerous, prominent revivals of Seneca's plays have taken place. The most significant and influential of these was Ted Hughes's translation of *Oedi-

pus*, staged by Peter *Brook for the *National Theatre at the *Old Vic in *London (1968) as part of Brook's Theatre of *Cruelty season. Oedipus was played by John *Gielgud, Jocasta by Irene *Worth, in a *total theatre production conceived as a primitive rite. The chorus mingled with the audience while emitting inarticulate wails, cries, and hisses, to enmesh and engage the spectators in what was essentially a strange and frightening ceremonial of human sacrifice and shamanistic obsession. In 1994 Caryl *Churchill's translation of *Thyestes* was directed by James Macdonald, and *toured by the *English Stage Company of the *Royal Court Theatre. This too used the Senecan *text as the occasion for an intensely experimental production: a variety of *media, including most prominently video, was employed to evoke the disturbing imagery and powerful rhetorical qualities of the language and the emotional intensity of the *plot. *See also* ROMAN THEATRE. RCB

BOYLE, A. J. (ed.), *Seneca Tragicus* (Clayton, 1983)
PRATT, N., *Seneca's Drama* (Chapel Hill, NC, 1983)
SUTTON, D., *Seneca on the Stage* (London, 1986)

SENECAN DRAMA

The ten *tragedies attributed to the Roman writer *Seneca were not only read, translated, and acted in sixteenth-century England, but also taken as models for new plays in both Latin and English. Starting with *Sackville and Norton's *Gorboduc* (1562), the *genre was mainly performed at the two universities and the *Inns of Court, where drama was considered a valuable adjunct to a student's rhetorical training. The vogue lasted about 30 years, though Latin Senecan plays continued to be acted in the English *Jesuit colleges in Europe throughout the seventeenth century.

Drama modelled on Seneca is characterized by the juxtaposition of classical literariness with sensationalism. Using *stock characters like the tyrant, the servant, and the vindictive *ghost, the plays deal with the high passions aroused by extreme events such as adultery, incest, and murder; these emotions are expressed at length in bombastic speeches and introspective *soliloquies, but the violent *action itself is usually kept off the stage and described in detail by a lamenting messenger. The genre influenced some of the thematic preoccupations of Elizabethan and Jacobean tragedy. MJW

ŞERBAN, ANDREI (1943–)

Romanian-born director whose career has chiefly been in the USA. *Fragments of a Trilogy: Medea, Electra*, and *The Trojan Women* (*La Mama, *New York, 1974) established his reputation as a leading director of the *avant-garde. Visually daring, emotionally potent, *Fragments* remains a landmark staging of *Greek *tragedy. Controversial productions of other classics followed: *Good Woman of Setzuan* (La Mama, 1975); *The Cherry

Orchard (*Lincoln Center, 1977); *Ghost Sonata* (Yale Rep, 1977), and *Happy Days* (*New York Shakespeare Festival, 1979). In *Sganarelle*, based on *Molière, the director explored a new theatrical language anchored in the musicality of words (Yale, 1978). As in all his experiments, Şerban sought to recover the visceral power of theatre by reinventing tradition, in this case the tradition of *commedia dell'arte*. The interest in *commedia* led him to *Gozzi's theatrical fables: *King Stag* (1984) and *The Serpent Woman* (1988), both at the *American Repertory Theatre in Cambridge. Using *masks, *puppets, *dance, and Asian performance styles, *King Stag* exploded with high-voltage physicality that served Gozzi's spiritual *allegory. With *Puccini's *Turandot*, also based on Gozzi (*Los Angeles Olympic Arts Festival and *Covent Garden, 1984), Şerban scored another international success. These spectacular productions, however, should not overshadow Şerban's ability to create chamber theatre. His *Three Sisters* (ART, 1982) stripped the *realistic claptrap from *Chekhov's masterpiece to forge a haunting memory play. A search for the transcendent runs throughout his work.

From 1990 to 1993 he headed the Romanian National Theatre in *Bucharest, and he has increasingly turned his attention to *opera: Philip *Glass's *The Juniper Tree* (ART, 1985), *Lucia di Lammermoor* (Lyric Opera, *Chicago, 1990), *Strauss's *Elektra* (*San Francisco Opera, 1991), *Offenbach's *Tales of Hoffmann* (*Vienna State Opera, 1993), *Khovanshchina* (*Opéra Bastille, *Paris, 2001), and *Verdi's *Falstaff* (planned for Vienna, 2003). Starting in the late 1980s, a series of radical stagings put Şerban in the forefront of Shakespeare interpreters: *Twelfth Night* (ART, 1989), *Cymbeline* (NYSF, 1998), *The Merchant of Venice* (*Comédie-Française, 2001), *Hamlet* (NYSF, 1999), *Richard III* (La Mama, 2001). *The Taming of the Shrew* (ART, 1998) was a startling rediscovery. The enormous range of Şerban's artistic palette distinguishes him from other contemporary directors. 'Directing a play', he says, 'I lose myself. I search for its essence, so I, Andrei Şerban, have no signature.' Şerban has been a most scrupulous reader of *texts, and his assiduous attention to words has produced dazzling stage images that illuminate rather than illustrate the script. He now heads the Hammerstein Center for Theatre Studies at Columbia University.   ACH

SERF THEATRE

The status of Russian peasants during the eighteenth and nineteenth centuries was little better than that of slaves until the Emancipation Act of 1861 brought some improvement. Despite this, enlightened estate owners who took their responsibilities seriously created circumstances which were not just exploitative and demeaning but, although often self-interested, raised the cultural level of those who were their property. One important method was the creation of theatres in which serfs were taught the arts of *acting, singing, music, and *ballet.

Serf theatres first began to appear towards the end of the seventeenth century and reached their apogee at the end of the eighteenth and beginning of the nineteenth centuries, when they numbered about 170. Conditions under which serfs performed varied considerably, with actresses treated as little more than concubines in the worst cases or with acting talents 'collected' as extensions of already existing acquisitions of fine art. Among the most significant theatres were those on the Sheremetev estates, the first of which was formed during the 1760s. A theatre survives at Ostankino (now a museum) which in its day was a typical eighteenth-century structure along the lines of *Drottningholm with complex stage machinery and a machine house for producing elaborate transformation scenes. The 200-strong troupe was taught by European specialists drafted in for the purpose. Decor was provided by some of the best designers of the age. Prince Yusupov's theatre at Arkhangelskoe vied with that at Ostankino for supremacy. Built in 1818, the *auditorium housed 400 and the troupe consisted of twenty to 25 dancers, ten singers, and 25 musicians. Count Vorontsov, another progressive and enlightened serf owner, placed particular emphasis on theatrical performance and even paid his serf actors wages. Serf theatres proved an important source for the development of professional theatre in Russia, the Imperial Ballet acquiring an entire serf troupe in 1800; another was seconded to the *Bolshoi in 1828 with a serf orchestra of 27 members. Among the outstanding actors of the imperial theatres whose careers began in serf theatres were Ekaterina *Semyonova, Mikhail *Shchepkin, and the father of Pavel *Mochalov.   NW

SERLIO, SEBASTIANO (1475–1554)

Italian architect, painter, and theorist, born in Bologna. He pursued a deep scholarly interest in humanist-inspired archaeology, which was intended to guide and inform contemporary architectural practice. His only known commission in stage design was to build a temporary theatre in Vicenza, probably in 1539. On the *theoretical side, however, he became a fundamental source for later historians of theatre, on the basis of just six chapters of his *Second Book of Architecture*, published in French translation in 1545 and then in Italian in 1560. His printed designs for three standard stage settings, for *Comedy, *Pastoral, and *Tragedy, are constantly reproduced in modern studies. There was probably little that was innovative in what he proposed: on the contrary his importance lies in having drawn together in a simple theoretical model the practices which were already regarded as canonical, and which can be read about in contemporary chronicles and even in theatre *prologues. In fact he summarized, at a crucial moment, everything which had been done in classical-style static *scenography, just before the vogue for elaborate machinery and scene changes took over.

Serlio's recommended design for a theatre was based as much as he could manage on interpretations of classical theatre ruins, and on the Roman author *Vitruvius. However, it can also be seen that this revival was not truly authentic, because it was adapted to the kinds of indoor space which court and academic theatres used in the early sixteenth century. Raked seats, in semicircle or horseshoe plan, faced a platform stage; seating areas were divided and assigned to different sexes and social classes. The stage itself did not yet involve a genuine *proscenium arch, but nevertheless hinted at a picture-frame effect because of the assumption that the *scenery should always involve illusionistic *perspective, with a receding panorama painted on a *flat backcloth and practicable buildings at each side. For tragedy, the setting evoked would be palatial and aristocratic; for comedy, urban and domestic; for the new *genre of pastoral (intriguing to see presented at all as early as 1545), rustic and Arcadian.   RAA

SERREAU, JEAN-MARIE (1915–73)

French director. Trained by *Dullin, Serreau was partly responsible for the discovery and success of the theatre of the *absurd in France. Closely associated with the *avant-garde, he directed plays by *Adamov, *Arrabal, *Beckett, and *Ionesco, as well as new works by *Genet and *Duras. He is credited with introducing *Brecht to *Paris, with *The Exception and the Rule* at the Noctambules in 1947. In the 1960s and 1970s, Serreau became one of the most important French directors of non-European and post-colonial theatre, with productions of works by Kateb *Yacine (*Le Cadavre encerclé*, 1964; *Les Ancêtres redoublent de férocité*, 1967), Aimé *Césaire (*La Tragédie du roi Christophe*, 1963; *Une tempête*, 1969), and Bernard *Dadié (*Béatrice du Congo*, 1971). Desiring to fuse technology and poetry, he often experimented with *multimedia techniques. In 1970 he founded the Théâtre de la Tempête at the Cartoucherie.   CHB

SERULLE, HAFFE (1947–)

Novelist and playwright from the Dominican Republic, who has served as director of the theatre at the Universidad Autónoma de Santo Domingo and as director of the National School of Dramatic Art. His plays, which rely upon a symbolic approach to social issues, include *Prostitución en la casa de Dios* (*Prostitution in the House of God*, 1978), *Duarte* (National Prize for Theatre, 1981), and *Leyenda de un pueblo que nació sin cabeza* (*Legend of a People Born without Heads*).   EJW

SERUMAGA, ROBERT (1939–81)

Ugandan director, playwright, and novelist. Serumaga read economics at Trinity College, Dublin, and trained with the BBC *radio drama department. Informed by *Beckett's theatre of the *absurd and *Stanislavsky's concept of *training actors, he returned to Uganda in 1966 and founded the semi-professional Abafumi Players. His published plays, *A Play* (1967), *The Elephants* (1970), and *Majangwa* (1971), follow the absurdist mode but address the political and social disintegration in Uganda under Obote and Amin. With *Renga Moi* (1972) and *Amerykitti* (1974) he created a new style of abstract *dance-drama representing the political atrocities in visual images and movements. *Amerykitti* was performed at the Organization of African Unity meeting in Kampala and described by Idi Amin as 'gymnastics'. Serumaga joined the liberation army that ousted Amin, but died mysteriously in Nairobi. His innovative theatre found no direct followers in Uganda, but actors trained at the Abafumi Academy still figure prominently in *Africa.   EB

SERVANDONI, JEAN-NICOLAS (1695–1766)

Italian designer. Servandoni worked principally in *Paris, where he designed settings for the *Opéra from 1726 to 1735, and for his own mute spectaculars at the *Salle des Machines between 1738 and 1758. Reacting against the more painterly style, he introduced into France the full baroque *scenography of Ferdinando *Bibiena's *scena per angolo*: replacing central one-point *perspective settings with oblique and diagonal arrangements of wing-*flats, he sought to create a more three-dimensional stage picture, into which the dramatic *action might be fully integrated.   JG

SESENTA, TEATRO DEL

'Theatre of the Sixties', Puerto Rican theatre company founded in 1963. The group has won many national and international *awards and has produced over 80 plays, ranging from *Weiss's *Marat/Sade* (1974), *Decameron* (1986), and *Chekhov's *The Seagull* (1990), to Puerto Rican plays such as *La verdadera historia de Pedro Navaja* (*Peter Blade's Real Story*, 1980), Luis Rafael *Sánchez's *The Passion According to Antigone Pérez* (1992), and Ramos Escobar's *¿Puertorriqueños?* (*Puerto Ricans?*, 1999). The company has participated in major *festivals, including Latino festivals in *New York (1985–6) and the World Festival at Nancy (1975).   JLRE

SET/SETTING *See* SCENERY; SCENOGRAPHY.

SETTLE, ELKANAH (1648–1724)

English playwright. Settle was active in the *London theatre for nearly 50 years, producing a score of plays at both *patent theatres, *drolls at the fairs, and civic pageants as City Poet. His first success, *The Emperor of Morocco* (1673), provoked a quarrel with *Dryden, a pattern that continued with John Crowne, *Shadwell, and *Otway. Settle's plays were characterized by stage violence, extravagant machine effects, and, in the case of *The Fairy Queen* (1692, with Henry Purcell), spectacular scenes of *music and *dancing. He died a pauper.   RWV

7:84

*Touring socialist theatre companies established in 1971 (in England) and 1973 (Scotland) by the writer, director, and cultural activist John *McGrath and his actor wife Elizabeth McLennan. The companies, which performed predominantly to working-class *audiences outside established theatres, took their name from a statistic published in *The Economist*—that 7 per cent of the population owned 84 per cent of the wealth. Productions include (for 7:84 England) McGrath's *Trees in the Wind* (1971) and *Six Men of Dorset* (1984), and (for 7:84 Scotland) *The Cheviot, the Stag and the Black, Black Oil* (1973) and *Blood Red Roses* (1980). Like their founders, the troupes fell foul of the right-wing cultural politics of the 1980s; public funding for the English company was withdrawn in the mid-1980s, and McGrath was forced to resign from 7:84 (Scotland) in 1988. The latter company is still in existence.   SWL

SEWELL, STEPHEN (1953–)

Australian playwright who studied physics at Sydney University. Sewell's plays are uncompromising and conscientious Marxist critiques with a broad interest in the political, economic, and social life of contemporary citizens, particularly Australians. Grand in style, often requiring large casts, his plays have won much critical acclaim. Nineteen fifties working-class conservatism is examined in *The Father We Loved on a Beach by the Sea* (1977), and *Traitors* (1979) explores human relationships to socio-political processes. While his most ambitious play, *Dreams in an Empty City* (1986), further engages with the relationship of morality to capitalism, later smaller-scale works, such as *The Garden of Granddaughters* (1993), focus on the *politics of family relationships.   SBS

SEX SHOWS AND DANCES

Performance and performative activities that provide entertainment and a point of entry for the selling and buying of sex. Evidence of theatricalized sexual activity and the exhibition of the body through dance-like movement is extant in wall paintings and pottery and in erotic literature from a range of ancient Eastern and Western cultures. A form of sexual hospitality and commodity, these performances routinely took place in commercial settings like brothels, but also in the homes of the wealthy and elite, and may have been associated with the *ritualized activities of various religious cults. Despite the frequency of performative sexuality, however, there is clear evidence of a disapproving public even before the Christian era. Ovid, for example, speaks disapprovingly of 'adulteries of the stage', not-

ing that *mimes were using sexualized language and imagery to entertain the Roman public ('Nor is it enough that the ear is outraged with impure words; the eyes grow accustomed to more shameful sights . . .'). Twentieth-century histories of sexuality and culture link the economy of sex (both political and material) with the presence of theatricalized sexuality in a variety of public celebratory activities (*carnivals and masquerades, for example), and the emergence of a sexual subculture in modern capitalism.

A good example of the latter is the evolution of *burlesque in the United States. In the mid-nineteenth century, the term 'burlesque' was used to describe imports like Lydia Thompson and her British Blondes (a satirical *music-hall *revue), and somewhat later the American-born 'spectacle-extravaganza' (a hybrid *dance entertainment using flimsy melodramatic *plots to showcase the legs of young female *chorus dancers). At their economic height during the 1880s and 1890s, burlesque shows featured a variety of legitimate entertainments (song-and-dance teams, for instance, as well as skit comedians like Abbott and Costello) in addition to the lowbrow, sexualized comedy of male comics and the 'leg dancing' routines of the female chorus. By the early twentieth century, however, the new family-oriented *vaudeville *variety format appropriated many burlesque acts, leaving only the more extreme components—like the strip-teases and the sexual innuendo of the male comics—and thus marginalizing the form. By the mid-twentieth century burlesque was relegated to the realm of live *pornography under the mantle 'strip-club'.

Contemporary sex shows range from live sexual activity to a series of dances performed in adult fantasy clubs, including pole dancing, table dancing, and lap dancing—forms of eroticized movement that simulate sexual activity and can include physical contact with the *audience. The term 'live' must be redefined in the digital age, since the Internet has the capacity to create a liminal place where real-time links signify liveness by establishing the sense of a transgeographical reality (*see* CYBER THEATRE; MEDIA AND PERFORMANCE). Though much contemporary *feminist scholarship attempts to theorize the *gender politics of sex shows, disagreement abounds about the relationship between male objectification and sexual exploitation of women versus the validity of choosing sex work as a profession.   LTC

SEYDELMANN, KARL (1793–1843)

German actor. Despite a relatively brief career, Seydelmann performed at many major theatres—including *Prague, Cassel, Stuttgart, and finally the *Berlin Royal Theatre—taking the major character parts of the time. He was particularly renowned for his interpretation of classical roles such as Carlos in *Goethe's *Clavigo*, Mephisto, Shylock, Richard III, Othello, and King Philip in *Don Carlos*. An accomplished virtuoso actor with a magnetic presence, he was a pioneer of *realist *acting who opposed unfocused and exaggerated declamation. His emphasis on the delineation of *character made him a forerunner of *naturalism.   CBB

SEYLER, ATHENE (1889–1990)

English actress. Seyler's career was primarily in *comedy, at which she excelled—from Shakespeare, *Congreve, and *Wycherley to *Sheridan, *Shaw, and *Wilde. She first demonstrated her skills in Restoration comedy when she played Cynthia in Congreve's *The Double Dealer* (1916). Her Shakespearian roles began in 1920 with Rosalind in *As You Like It*, and over the next four decades she was a beloved comic actress on the *London stage, appearing in Restoration plays and Shakespeare on a regular basis. She also played a few more serious roles, including Emilia in *Othello*, the Nurse in *Romeo and Juliet*, and Madame Ranevskaya in *The Cherry Orchard*. Her last role in 1966 was in *Arsenic and Old Lace*. In 1944 she published *The Craft of Comedy*, a valuable guide to comic *acting. In 1950 she was elected president of the council of the *Royal Academy of Dramatic Art, where she had studied in 1907–8.   TP

SHADOW-PUPPET THEATRE

Performance with light projections of *puppets that ranks in importance with live *acting in parts of Asia. The *Indonesian tradition reached Mameluke Egypt by the twelfth century, brought by traders, and shadow theatre subsequently spread through the Ottoman Empire and North Africa. Shadows are often classified separately from puppets because the *audience sees a shadow, not an object. This distinction made performances possible during Lent in nineteenth-century Catalonia, when no other theatre was allowed. If the shadow has no substance, the object that casts it does, and is operated in a manner similar to many rod puppets. Some are highly articulated, some not at all. In Indonesian *wayang kulit, part of the audience is on the same side of the screen as the flat figures employed to project the shadows. In *Thailand the large leather *nang talung figures show complete scenes and are held in front of a screen by dancers. Sometimes a single performer handles a huge number of figures (Indonesia), but the main puppeteer, who generally provides all the speech, may have a number of assistants (Kerala). Musicians vary from a single instrument to an orchestra, and singing may be provided by one of the musicians (*Karagöz) or by the puppeteer himself (as the Indonesian *dalang* does).

The screen, usually of cotton, varies from barely a metre (3 feet) in width (Karagöz) to several metres (Indonesia). Figures range from under 30 cm (12 inches) in *China to nearly 2 m (6 feet) in Andhra Pradesh. Leather is the traditional material, but poor puppeteers have used paper or anything else available. Indonesian puppets are coloured but opaque, whereas Chinese ones are generally translucent and highly coloured. Andhra Pradesh and Karnataka have coloured shadows, but in Orissa they are black. Karagöz is coloured, but earlier Turkish shadows may not have been. The screen, usually lit from the back by a lamp hung above and behind the performer, can also be lit by a row of lights placed at the base. With the former, the size of the image can be modified according to the proximity of the figure to the light source, a tactic that can give a sense of depth and perspective.

Shadow performance using the hands existed in Europe long before 'Italian' or 'Chinese' shadows with animated silhouette figures became popular through Dominque Séraphim in *Paris in 1784. His most celebrated piece, *The Broken Bridge*, prompted wide imitation abroad. Henri Rivière at the Chat Noir *Cabaret in the same city (1885–97) developed an art shadow theatre involving projected and coloured *scenery from two magic lanterns. The figures were cut in zinc. New materials have been introduced to shadow theatre, including fabric, wire mesh, and plastics. In the 1970s Gioco Vita (Piacenza, Italy) freed shadow theatre from a single fixed screen, introducing a large variety of light sources in *Gilgamesh* (1982). The company also combined shadows with puppets and live actors.

See also NANG; NANG SBEK THOM; LAKHON FON.   JMcC

BORDAT, DENIS, and BOUCROT, FRANCIS, *Les Théâtres d'ombres* (Paris, 1956)
REUSCH, RAINER, *Schattentheater* (Schwäbisch Gmünd, 1997)
TILAKASIRI, JAYADEVA, *The Asian Shadow Play* (Ratmalana, 1999)

SHADWELL, THOMAS (c.1642–1692)

English playwright. The son of a prominent Norfolk royalist, Shadwell attended Cambridge and pursued a legal career, but turned to playwriting in 1668 with *The Sullen Lovers*. Most of the twenty plays that he wrote over the next 23 years were *comedies, acted at *Lincoln's Inn Fields (1668–71), *Dorset Garden (1672–81), and *Drury Lane (1682–92). Shadwell was experimental in comedy and at his best was able to exploit the titillation of sex and *satirize its participants simultaneously. *The Virtuoso* (1676) is equally mocking of libertinism, romantic love, and science. *The Squire of Alsatia* (1688), an extraordinarily successful play that held the stage for 80 years, presents an unsettling reversal of the theme of *Terence's *The Brothers* by contrasting the praise of a liberal education with its ambiguous results. Shadwell's *tragedies, a rewriting of *Timon of Athens* (1678) and a Don Juan play, *The Libertine* (1675), are both satirical attacks on the libertine moral code of contemporary comedy. Shadwell also tried his hand at *opera with adaptations of *Davenant's *Tempest* (1674) and *Lully's *Psyche* (1675), admitting in the preface to the latter that 'the great design was to entertain the town with variety of music, curious *dancing, splendid scenes and machines'. Shadwell was himself satirized in *Dryden's *MacFlecknoe* (1678), but undoubtedly took some

satisfaction in his succession to Dryden as Poet Laureate ten years later.   RWV

SHAFFER, PETER (1926–   )

English dramatist. After working as a coal miner, librarian, and music critic, and studying at Cambridge, Shaffer achieved his first success as a dramatist with *Five Finger Exercise* (1958). Two *one-act plays, *The Private Ear* and *The Public Eye* (1962), were also successful, but *The Royal Hunt of the Sun*, staged by the *National Theatre in 1964, was the first of his plays to reveal epic theatrical qualities, in both its staging and its physical demands. Through its opposition of Atahualpa, sun King of the Incas, and Pizarro, leader of the Spanish conquistadores, it explored the relationship of man and God, a recurrent theme in Shaffer's subsequent work. *Black Comedy* (National Theatre, 1965) depended on the simple trick of reversing light and dark, so that a play taking place in pitch blackness is clearly seen by the *audience. It was revived as a double bill with another Shaffer play, *White Lies* (1968). *The Battle of Shrivings* (*London, 1970) was less successful, but *Equus* (National Theatre, 1973) effectively explored issues of faith, belief, and sexuality through the story of a psychiatrist treating a stable boy who has blinded six horses. The theme of man and God resurfaces in *Amadeus* (National Theatre, 1979), which depicts *Mozart through the eyes of his jealous rival Salieri, whose fight with Mozart becomes a fight against God and divine inspiration. Such concerns are echoed in *Yonadab* (1985). *Lettice and Lovage* was staged in 1987. Shaffer has also written for *radio and *television, and completed several thrillers with his brother Anthony.
                                                                JTD

SHAFTESBURY THEATRE

Built in 1911 by Bertie Crewe for Walter and Frederick Melville in *London, it was originally the New Prince's Theatre (capacity 1,250), became the Prince's Theatre in 1914, and the Shaftesbury in 1963. Sarah *Bernhardt played here in 1921, and *Diaghilev's *Ballets Russes performed in 1921 and 1927. A 1926 *Macbeth* starred Sybil *Thorndike and Henry *Ainley, and the *musical *Funny Face* (1928–9) starred the *Astaires. Michael *Redgrave and Peggy *Ashcroft staged a remarkable *Antony and Cleopatra* in 1953. *Hair* opened at the Shaftesbury the day after *censorship ended in Britain in 1968 and ran for nearly 2,000 performances, closing only when the ceiling collapsed (July 1973). In 1974 the *playhouse was designated a building of Special Architectural or Historical Interest to protect it from demo-

Peter **Shaffer**'s *Equus*, National Theatre, London, 1973, directed by John Dexter, designed by John Napier. Peter Firth as the stable boy Alan Strang ecstatically rides a symbolic horse in the middle of a playing space that resembled a show ring or debating chamber.

lition. In 1984 it was purchased by the Theatre of Comedy Company founded by Ray Cooney with the support of 30 leading actors, writers, and directors, was renovated in 1986, and renamed the Shaftesbury Theatre of Comedy. Peter *O'Toole, Tom Conti, Donald *Sinden, Eric Sykes, and Michael Williams are some of the performers whose appearances have helped keep the theatre viable in recent years.   FJH

SHAKESPEARE, WILLIAM *see page 1228*

SHAKESPEARE FESTIVALS

The practice of celebrating the work of William Shakespeare with a *festival—setting aside a special time and place for seeing a couple of his plays and participating in related activities—may be said to have originated with David *Garrick's 1769 Shakespeare Jubilee, a three-day programme of events that initiated the long association of Stratford-upon-Avon with popular bardolatry. Theatre companies dedicated primarily to Shakespeare production have continued to enrich the English cultural scene since the late nineteenth century, among them William *Poel's *Elizabethan Stage Society, Lilian *Baylis's *Old Vic, the *Royal Shakespeare Company, the *English Shakespeare Company. The Shakespeare festival, however, is a distinct phenomenon—even though the term 'festival' is often used loosely (for example, as part of the name of theatre companies like Ontario's *Stratford Festival, *Oregon Shakespeare Festival, Alabama Shakespeare Festival, and others). Strictly speaking, a festival involves a short period of intense activity, usually in summer, when it can occur outdoors. These seasonal festivals with their pre-performance greenshows, refreshment stands, and other family-oriented amenities have maintained their strongest presence in the United States and Canada. Since the 1970s there has been a remarkable proliferation of annual community festivals of Shakespeare in public parks. Some have lasted only a few seasons, but new ones appear each summer. Since 1990 the total number of North American Shakespeare festivals (and companies calling themselves festivals) has held steady at about 125. (*See also* OPEN AIR PERFORMANCE.)

*London's Open Air Theatre in Regent's Park began as a festival on the green in 1932. Although it now operates as a company, presenting four plays each summer (at least two by Shakespeare), its setting along with its *cabaret and children's attractions perhaps qualify it also as a festival. The two longest-running American Shakespeare company/festivals both began in 1935. Oregon Shakespeare Festival, Ashland, is usually credited as the first, because its opening season's two plays were fully staged. The Old Globe Theatre, San Diego, came into existence because the public petitioned not to raze a replica of Shakespeare's Globe (*see* GLOBE RECONSTRUCTIONS) that had been built in 1935 as a temporary structure to showcase one-hour

(continued on p. 1232)

SHAKESPEARE, WILLIAM (1564–1616)

English actor, playwright, *manager, poet, and landowner.

1. Career; 2. Shakespearian drama; 3. Theatrical afterlives

1. Career

The most popular and influential dramatist in world history was baptized in provincial Stratford-upon-Avon on 26 April 1564, and it is a mark of his canonization as Britain's national writer that his birthday (which may have taken place at any time over the preceding few days) has been celebrated since the eighteenth century on the feast day of England's patron saint George, 23 April. As the eldest son of a local glover who rose to be alderman and town bailiff, Shakespeare was entitled to be educated at the local grammar school (traces of its standard syllabus in Latin literature and rhetoric are visible throughout his works), and he may also have enjoyed privileged access to performances by the acting companies which passed through Stratford on *tour. Whatever else he may have done immediately after leaving school he was married locally at 18 to Anne Hathaway, who was 26 and already pregnant with their daughter Susanna, but at some point after the birth of their twins Judith and Hamnet in 1585 Shakespeare left Stratford to enter the *London-based theatrical profession. (The theory that he was already a player before his marriage, in the Lancashire Catholic household of Alexander Houghton, is based on very slender evidence.)

Shakespeare probably began his stage career as an actor, but, to judge by the style of his first play, the *Lyly-influenced *The Two Gentlemen of Verona*, he was already writing by the late 1580s. (Few of his plays can be dated with absolute certainty, although there is a broad consensus among scholars: the chronology which follows is based on that of the Oxford edition, as documented in Wells and Taylor.) Within a short time the scope and power of Shakespeare's plays about the Wars of the Roses (three parts of *Henry VI*, 1591–2) were unnerving established university-educated playwrights such as Robert *Greene: the earliest printed allusion to him is an anxious attack on 'Shake-scene' as 'an upstart crow' in *Greene's Groatsworth of Wit* (1592). This first sequence of English chronicle plays (a *genre Shakespeare practically invented; *see* HISTORICAL DRAMA) culminated in *Richard III* (*c*.1592–3), and by then Shakespeare was not only writing under the influence of his contemporary Christopher *Marlowe (especially visible in *villain-*hero roles such as Richard III himself, and the glamorously barbaric Aaron of *Titus*

Andronicus, *c*.1592–3) but was influencing him in turn, to judge by Marlowe's turn to native subject matter in his last play, *Edward II* (1593). Furthermore, the young Shakespeare's self-evident literary ambition extended across history and *tragedy and into one genre Marlowe never touched, *comedy: the assured pursuit of a single theme across the interwoven *plots of *The Taming of the Shrew* (*c*.1590–1), for example, marks an immense technical advance on all its English forebears in this mode. This thirst for new artistic territory combined happily with Shakespeare's social aspirations when, during the closure of the theatres by plague in 1593–4, he dedicated two narrative poems to the Earl of Southampton, *Venus and Adonis* and *The Rape of Lucrece*. The former, an urbane erotic tragicomedy in the mode of Marlowe's *Hero and Leander*, would be Shakespeare's most popular published work in his own time.

A more decisive event in Shakespeare's career, however, took place after the theatres reopened, when the dramatist became a member of the Lord *Chamberlain's Men, initially formed to play at Elizabeth's court during the Christmas season of 1594–5 and destined to become the official royal company, the King's Men, on the accession of James I in 1603. Shakespeare would remain with them—not just as actor and writer but as a managing shareholder—for the rest of his working life, the only contemporary playwright to enjoy so settled a working relationship with a single company (and thus with particular actors, among them Richard *Burbage, who created many of his leading roles). It was apparently a lucrative arrangement: in 1596 Shakespeare obtained a grant of arms for his father (giving the Shakespeares the status of gentlemen, which the likes of Greene and Marlowe had obtained with their university degrees), and in 1597 he bought the second-largest house in Stratford, New Place, for his family. His escape from the uncertain, freelance conditions under which his rivals worked may have allowed Shakespeare to spend more time there than would otherwise have been possible: he never seems to have had a permanent London home (investing in a London property only in 1613, at the very end of his writing career, before which metropolitan tax assessments and minor lawsuits find him only in rented lodgings), and he may even have done some of his composing in Stratford rather than the capital.

Wherever he was writing, Shakespeare's *dramaturgy entered a more lyrical phase after the narrative poems, with *The Comedy of Errors* and *Love's Labour's Lost* (*c*.1594–5), and this lyricism found bravura expression in the three plays he gave the Chamberlain's Men in 1595–6, each surpassing all previous

English achievements in its genre: *Romeo and Juliet*, *Richard II*, and *A Midsummer Night's Dream*. Through the later 1590s he concentrated on pursuing and even reconciling the history and comedy of the latter two. He produced four more chronicles, first *King John* (1596) and then the three plays which extend the story of *Richard II* to make up a second tetralogy depicting the dynastic events which preceded the first, the two parts of *Henry IV* (*c*.1596–8) and their sequel *Henry V* (1599). These last three—the first two starring Shakespeare's greatest comic creation, Falstaff, and the latter culminating in a marriage—bring tragic history into dialogue with comedy, and they are contemporary with four mature romantic comedies, *The Merchant of Venice* (1596–7), *The Merry Wives of Windsor* (1597–8), *Much Ado About Nothing* (1598) and *As You Like It* (1599). By now printers were placing Shakespeare's name on title pages to advertise quarto editions of his plays, and his literary achievements were being hymned by the likes of Francis Meres, whose *Palladis Tamia* (1598) praises Shakespeare's 'sugared sonnets among his private friends' and hails him as a reincarnation of Ovid and a master of both comedy and tragedy.

For whatever reasons (biographically inclined critics sometimes point to the deaths of his son Hamnet in 1596 and of his financially embarrassed father in 1601), Shakespeare turned decisively to the latter at the turn of the seventeenth century. His remaining comedies grow ever more bitter, from the exquisite *Twelfth Night* (1601) to the intellectual 'problem plays' *Measure for Measure* (1603) and *All's Well That Ends Well* (1604–5), which seem deliberately to test how much suffering and moral conflict a comedy can dramatize without renouncing the conventions of the happy ending altogether. But for the best part of a decade most of Shakespeare's energies were devoted to writing tragedy proper. *Julius Caesar* (1599) may have been the first play staged at the *Globe on Bankside, and it would in time be followed by two further dramatizations from Plutarch of the lives of doomed Romans, the expansive *Antony and Cleopatra* (1607) and the concertedly political *Coriolanus* (1608). In between came *Hamlet* (*c*.1600), *Troilus and Cressida* (1602), *Othello* (1603–4), *Timon of Athens* (co-written with Thomas *Middleton around 1605), *King Lear* (1605–6), and *Macbeth* (1606). By now Shakespeare had apparently given up acting (a late seventeenth-century tradition, seconded by recent statistical extrapolations from the assumption that actor-playwrights are more likely to repeat rare words found in the speeches they memorize for performance, assigns him the role of the Ghost in *Hamlet*, which may have been his last), and investments in land and tithes suggest that he was spending more time in Stratford. His remaining plays, composed after his daughter Susanna and her physician husband John Hall had made him a grandfather (to Elizabeth, born in 1607), look at once to the fashionable present and to the archaic past. *Pericles* (1607–8), probably co-written with George Wilkins, dramatizes a medieval *romance in an affectingly simple mock-medieval style, and its successors, though belonging to the courtly

vogue for sophisticated *tragicomedy initiated by Shakespeare's junior colleagues Francis *Beaumont and John *Fletcher (and written with the company's exclusive new indoor theatre, the *Blackfriars, in mind), also echo much earlier and more naive works in their pursuit of wonderful reconciliations between fathers and daughters, politics, and magic. *The Winter's Tale* (1609) adapts a twenty-year-old prose romance by Shakespeare's first critic, Greene; *Cymbeline* (1610), a tour de force of multiple narrative, offers an astonishing mix and match of motifs drawn from nearly all of Shakespeare's earlier plays at once; and his last unassisted play, *The Tempest* (1611), achieves a visionary, lyrical fusion of elements drawn from accounts of a contemporary shipwreck in the Bermudas, from Montaigne, from Ovid, and from his own earlier explorations of usurpation and paternity. After these came three collaborations with Fletcher, rapidly replacing him as the King's Men's chief dramatist: an adaptation of a subplot from *Cervantes' newly translated *Don Quixote*, *Cardenio* (1612–13, now tantalizingly lost, as is an earlier Shakespearian comedy *Love's Labour's Won*); the sceptical pageant history *Henry VIII* (1613); and a tragicomedy based on Chaucer's *Knight's Tale*, *The Two Noble Kinsmen* (1613–14). Shakespeare was in Stratford involved in disputes over land enclosures during the next two years, and on 25 March 1616 he was there altering his will to make it more difficult for his daughter Judith's new husband (convicted of fornication with another woman during their engagement) to gain access to her share of his estate. The signature on this document looks shaky, as if the testator were ill, and only a month intervened before the will was put into effect: the playwright died on 23 April, probably his 52nd birthday.

2. Shakespearian drama

Many of the qualities which have enabled Shakespeare's plays to dominate the anglophone theatrical repertory (and many others) over most of the ensuing four centuries are already acknowledged in the preliminary materials to the collected edition, now known as the First Folio, compiled by his fellow actors John *Heminges and Henry *Condell (1623). Strikingly, it signals their generic variety in its very title, *Mr William Shakespeares Comedies, Histories and Tragedies*, which recognizes the unclassical, mixed form of the English *history play (crucial to Shakespeare's subsequent promotion as national writer) as a central part of his oeuvre. Ben *Jonson, who had acted in Shakespeare's plays (as Shakespeare had in his), contributed a justly celebrated memorial poem which accurately prophesies the extent to which the Shakespeare corpus would establish the international standing of the English stage, proclaiming that Shakespeare so thoroughly outshines his chosen native models (specifically Lyly, *Kyd, and Marlowe) that his achievements equal those of the classical theatre and excel those of its continental successors.

Both here and elsewhere Jonson's poem expresses a sense that Shakespeare's works miraculously exceed their own time and place ('He was not of an age, but for all time'), an effect they owe in part to their profound commitment to *early modern humanism. If they are Christian in their underlying ethics and in the apparently limitless range of their compassion, Shakespeare's plays, though willing to accommodate witches, *ghosts, fairies, and classical deities (and a few meddling priests), nonetheless feature no angels and no devils, with the exception of Joan La Pucelle's non-speaking fiends in the early *1 Henry VI*—itself part of a cycle which adapts aspects of the *medieval *biblical plays to a secular subject. The Folio preliminaries, accordingly, never mention *religion at all, and the very fact that it is possible to argue about whether or not Shakespeare was (like his father) a secret Catholic suggests how thoroughly his plays—even *King John* and *All Is True* (*Henry VIII*)—sidestep the controversies of the *Reformation altogether. Indeed their scrupulous evasion not just of ecclesiastical disputes but of most forms of local topicality (in favour of dramatic patternings rooted in the slower-changing structures of the family) looks almost like a calculated long-term marketing strategy. But this celebrated impartiality goes well beyond the merely non-committal, and reflects a deep-seated habit of mind and world-view rather than just a desire not to offend any potential patrons or *censors. Outside the Roman plays and the English histories, Shakespeare does not just disdain to reflect explicitly on his own immediate context but refuses to be tied down by history and geography at all, and even his depictions of the classical and medieval past have their share of calculated anachronisms and *metatheatrical jokes. In the more openly *dream-oriented comedies and romances, indeed, Shakespeare positively flaunts this independence from superficial consistency and plausibility—as when *The Winter's Tale* includes a visit the Delphic oracle, a discussion of the Renaissance painter Giulio Romano, and a shipwreck on the sea-coast of Bohemia. Jonson, recognizing Shakespeare as a peer of *Aeschylus, *Euripides, and *Sophocles in tragedy, saw quite clearly that there were no classical precedents to which he could possibly liken Shakespearian comedy, the genre in which Shakespeare's career began and ended. Eschewing the minute depiction of contemporary vices and follies undertaken by exponents of *city comedy in favour of an Ovidian interest in metamorphosis (most often expressed through cross-dressing, with heroines such as Julia, Portia, Rosalind, Viola, and Imogen all transformed by male *disguise; *see* MALE IMPERSONATION), the comic Shakespeare is no more willing to be limited to the historical circumstances of Elizabethan and Jacobean London than he is to any others. His plays, consequently, have often been as much (and as little) at home on the stages of other times and other places as they were on those of the Globe and the Blackfriars.

Shakespeare's plays owe something of this continuing availability to successful appropriation, though also to their sheer range of dramatic techniques. Voraciously incorporating methods and materials drawn from high and low culture alike

(from the *masque to the *morris dance, from the classical *chorus to the indigenous *clown, from literary *pastoral to seasonal *folk drama: some of the tragic heroes, allowed to reflect in *soliloquy on the plays in which they are involved, even recognize a kinship between their own *spectacles and those offered by bear-*baiting), Shakespearian drama provides such a plenitude of possible modes of entertainment that it can be assimilated to an immense variety of theatrical tastes and circumstances. Indeed Shakespeare's plays have always had to be adapted, to some extent, for performance, since they are on average about 25 per cent longer than the scripts produced by his peers, and some early editions (such as the Folio texts of *Hamlet* and *King Lear*) suggest that they were only acted in customized, cut forms even in Shakespeare's lifetime. They are verbally generous in texture as well as in length, their poetic richness catering to a less visually oriented theatre than those which have followed it, and this trait—which some critics blame for a general tendency among Shakespeare-trained English actors to concentrate on voice at the expense of the rest of the physique—has allowed them to thrive just as importantly as literary *closet drama as they have on the stage. But whether performed or only read, the appeal of Shakespeare's plays has usually centred on their extraordinary feats of characterization, their knack of making the speaking subject-positions that people them seem at once as instantaneously recognizable and as irreducibly mysterious as real human beings. Where his sources (whether in Holinshed's chronicles, in Plutarch, in Chaucer, or in the Italian novella) tend to explain away characters' behaviour by supplying simple motivations, Shakespeare invariably complicates and obscures those motivations, and where his sources make *character something fixed and given he prefers to open it out to mutual redefinition, as fluent and protean as his metaphors. Roles such as Richard III, Bottom, Shylock, Hamlet, Iago, Rosalind, Cleopatra, Prospero—to name only a handful of the ones for which generations of actors have vied—consequently give themselves to performers, and respond to performers' gifts in their turn, as few others do.

3. Theatrical afterlives

It was in part this unclassical sense of character, combined with the increasingly outdated linguistic density of the plays, which encouraged later seventeenth-century dramatists such as *Davenant, *Dryden, *Tate, and *Cibber to rewrite Shakespeare's works to make them approximate more closely to *neoclassical notions of the self, of verbal *decorum, and of poetic justice—though such adaptations were also shaped by a desire to rewrite female roles written for performance by *boy actors in order to provide greater opportunities for the display of the Restoration theatre's most exciting innovation, the professional actress (*see* WOMEN AND PERFORMANCE). As Jonson's commendatory poem points out, Shakespeare's plays remained staples of the London theatre into the 1620s (and would continue to do so to the closing of the playhouses in the 1640s), but after the Restoration, though a handful were revived in their pre-war forms (notably *Hamlet*, *Othello*, and *1 Henry IV*), some of what are now Shakespeare's most valued plays—*The Tempest*, *Macbeth*, *King Lear*—reappeared only in heavily modified versions (the latter, for example, was supplied by Nahum Tate with a happy ending, instinctively restored from Shakespeare's more straightforward and conventional source). Even so, the great Shakespearian tragic roles stayed the touchstones of serious *acting—as with Burbage, so with *Betterton—and their rewritten variants were gradually replaced, as the patriotic celebration of Shakespeare (harnessed and promulgated in particular by the great eighteenth-century *actor-manager David *Garrick) increasingly made adapting the national poet's works seem like a treasonous surrender to French critical dogmas. (Even so, on Garrick's *proscenium-arch stage at *Drury Lane, equipped with cumbersome *perspective scenery inimical to the fluent stagecraft of the Elizabethans, Shakespeare's works could still only be seen in truncated and transposed forms, some of them prepared by Garrick himself.) This British canonization of Shakespeare as solid middle-class antitype to all things French paved the way for his pan-European adoption as the archetypal *romantic artist during the early nineteenth century, when the French translations of, in particular, *Ducis (which substantially rewrote the plays to ennoble their diction and to avoid their barbarous profusions of onstage deaths) gave place to those produced by enthusiastically anti-classical Germans such as *Schlegel and *Tieck (on which translations into many other European languages were soon based). In Germany, indeed, Shakespeare was adopted as honorary father of the national theatre; in France, his plays inspired the romantic drama of *Dumas *père*, and in Italy gave rise to the three great Shakespearian *operas of *Verdi (*Macbeth*, *Otello*, *Falstaff*); but in Britain, although a line of heroic Shakespearian actors continued to shine on increasingly elaborate pictorial sets (from *Siddons and the *Kembles to the *Keans, *Macready, *Irving, and *Terry), Shakespeare's influence was often more successfully incorporated in literature than on the stage. The novels of Sir Walter Scott, for example, mediated the social, generic and linguistic scope of Shakespearian history for the nineteenth century far more effectively than did the sub-Shakespearian *verse dramas of *Byron and Tennyson. Byron, indeed, recognized that Shakespeare was 'the worst of models—though the most extraordinary of writers', and in dramatic writing proper it may be that Shakespeare substantially exhausted the particular forms he developed: his influence on subsequent playwrights has been more often (and more safely) registered in pervasive allusion (as in the works of *Chekhov or, more parasitically, *Stoppard) than in direct imitation.

A backlash against pictorial *realism in Shakespearian staging at the end of the nineteenth century, led in part by the zealous antiquarian William *Poel and his more pragmatic disciple Harley Granville *Barker, coincided with the rise of the individual *director, and opened up Shakespearian performance the world over to the aesthetics of *modernism. This movement was comparatively slow to take hold in Britain: through the 1930s and 1940s figures such as Laurence *Olivier, John *Gielgud, and Donald *Wolfit were still working in modes inherited from the actor-managers of the Victorian age, and anglophone *directors have in any case been held back from some of their continental colleagues' wilder flights by the necessity to work with Shakespeare's now partly archaic language rather than fresh modern translations. In stage design, the Royal Shakespeare Theatre in Stratford (which replaced the original 1879 *Shakespeare Memorial Theatre, and has been the headquarters of the *Royal Shakespeare Company since the Stratford festival theatre was refounded as such in 1960) was built with a Victorian-style proscenium arch as recently as 1932 (even though some of the first productions mounted there featured what were then *avant-garde sets by *Komisarjevsky). But elsewhere new theatres were increasingly given *open, *thrust stages with the non-*illusionistic, *flat-free production of Shakespeare in mind (Tyrone *Guthrie's experiments at the *Stratford Festival in Ontario in the early 1950s were much imitated), and it would be fair to say that theatregoers arriving to see a new production of a Shakespeare play anywhere have since about 1950 been substantially unable to predict what it will look like. Performances in modern dress, in attempted re-creations of Elizabethan dress, in *costumes chosen from some period in between, in costumes borrowed from other cultures, and in costumes drawn from some eclectic blend of all these are only a few among the many options with which post-war designers have experimented (*see* SCENOGRAPHY). Just as they have been the obligatory test-cases for every new school of literary *criticism since the eighteenth century, so Shakespeare's plays have provided occasions for the development of each successive movement in the modern and postmodern theatre (and, increasingly, *film): *Artaud, *Stanislavsky, *Brecht, *Welles, *Brook, *Mnouchkine, *Zadek, *Lepage, *Ninagawa, all have had careers shaped to a large extent by their encounters with Shakespeare. To look a little way downmarket, even the through-composed large-cast *musicals which at the start of the millennium occupy so many West End theatres owe much of their style at least indirectly to Shakespeare: their baleful progenitor *Les Misérables* (itself based on *Hugo's Shakespeare-influenced novel) was originally produced by the Royal Shakespeare Company (using techniques pioneered in the RSC's stage adaptation of *Dickens's Shakespeare-influenced novel *Nicholas Nickleby*, a show which had itself adapted them from productions of Shakespeare's histories), and the most long-running of them all—*Cats*—was directed by the former RSC *artistic director Trevor *Nunn. Highbrow and low, the post-Renaissance theatre has as much evolved around the playing of Shakespeare as life on earth has evolved around the breathing of oxygen. Giving up the former would be almost as difficult—and just as undesirable—as giving up the latter.

MD

BATE, JONATHAN, and JACKSON, RUSSEL (eds.), *Shakespeare: an illustrated stage history* (Oxford, 1996)

DOBSON, MICHAEL, with WELLS, STANLEY (eds.), *The Oxford Companion to Shakespeare* (Oxford, 2001)

DE GRAZIA, MARGRETA, and WELLS, STANLEY (eds.), *The Cambridge Companion to Shakespeare* (Cambridge, 2001)

KENNEDY, DENNIS, *Looking at Shakespeare: a visual history of twentieth-century performance*, 2nd edn. (Cambridge, 2001)

SCHOENBAUM, SAMUEL, *Shakespeare: a compact documentary life* (Oxford, 1978)

WELLS, STANLEY, TAYLOR, GARY, et al., *Shakespeare: a textual companion* (Oxford, 1987)

abridgements of the plays during a world's fair in Balboa Park. Not until 1949 did full-length Shakespeare plays become the staple of the Old Globe.

The 1950s brought two highly visible and influential festivals with seasons extending well beyond the summer months: the Stratford Festival of Canada in Stratford, Ontario (1952), and the *American Shakespeare Festival, Stratford, Connecticut (1955). The former continues as a 'destination festival' for hundreds of thousands of theatregoers who come for a few days each year to see several plays in rotating repertory in three different theatres. The latter offered star-studded productions for 27 years, but *financial problems caused its demise in 1982. The *New York Shakespeare Festival, founded by Joseph *Papp, also had its origins (as the Shakespeare Workshop) in the 1950s. Papp presented his first summer Shakespeare at the Emmanuel Presbyterian church in 1955, moved outdoors in 1956, and *toured the city using a flatbed truck as a stage in 1957. The decision to settle in Central Park and offer admission-free Shakespeare productions was unprecedented and not easily achieved. By 1962 Papp's energetic fundraising and pursuit of federal and state grants came to fruition with the opening of the *Delacorte Theatre, a permanent outdoor facility in Central Park. Today the New York Shakespeare Festival functions as a year-round producing organization for a variety of work, some of which has moved to Broadway, while its signature venture, Shakespeare in Central Park, remains outdoors in summer and free to the public.

Beautiful outdoor settings distinguish some long-running festivals. American Players Theatre, founded in 1979 near the small farm community of Spring Green, Wisconsin, requires its *audience to follow a narrow path up a steep hill to reach the *amphitheatre nestled on the other side of the mountain. Kentucky Shakespeare Festival began in a carriage house in 1960, but has made Louisville's shady Central Park its production site since 1962. An endless green vista beyond the stage of Nebraska Shakespeare Festival (1986) in Omaha's Elmwood Park makes this an exceptionally lovely, free festival, enhanced by founder Cindy Phaneuf's Shakespeare garden at the entrance. Westerly Shakespeare in the Park, founded in 1990, incorporates the natural beauty of pond, grassy slope, and trees into its productions in Westerly, Rhode Island's Wilcox Park. In Kansas City, Heart of America Shakespeare Festival has flourished in beautiful Southmoreland Park since 1993.

While park settings are used by many outdoor festivals, other formats vary widely. Georgia Shakespeare Festival (1985) performs in a permanent tent on the campus of Oglethorpe University in Atlanta. Bard on the Beach (1990) of *Vancouver, British Columbia, also uses a tent and boasts a view of city, sea, and mountains. Atlanta Shakespeare Festival (1979) for many years presented Shakespeare in the back room of a tavern. William T. Brown's Shakespeare on Wheels, based at the University of Maryland-Baltimore County for a decade from 1985, toured with a truck whose fold-out panels converted it into an Elizabethan stage. Utah Shakespearean Festival (1961), like Oregon, employs both indoor and outdoor facilities.

California, New York, and Texas lead the United States in numbers of Shakespeare festivals. Dallas and Fort Worth both offer free outdoor Shakespeare only a short distance apart. The growing numbers of organizations devoted to producing Shakespeare led Sidney Berger, founding *artistic director of Houston Shakespeare Festival, to call a meeting of artistic directors in Washington, DC, in 1991, at which was born the Shakespeare Theatre Association of America. The association holds an annual conference, publishes a newsletter and directory, and tracks trends in Shakespeare festival production.

FHL

ENGLE, RON, LONDRÉ, FELICIA HARDISON, and WATERMEIER, DANIEL J. (eds.), *Shakespeare Companies and Festivals: an international guide* (Westport, Conn. 1995)

LONEY, GLENN, and MACKAY, PATRICIA, *The Shakespeare Complex* (New York, 1975)

SHAKESPEARE MEMORIAL THEATRE

The first Shakespeare Memorial Theatre, designed by Dodgshun and Unsworth, was completed in 1879, a Victorian extravaganza of mixed Gothic and Tudor styles. It was the first *playhouse in history dedicated to a single dramatist. It burned down in 1926; *Shaw announced that 'Stratford-on-Avon is to be congratulated . . . It is very cheerful news.' He hoped that 'a proper modern theatre' would be built but 'I don't expect an ideal theatre'. The competition for the new theatre was won by Elisabeth Scott, aged only 29; she was the first woman architect to design a major public building in the country. It opened in 1932, to mockery of its exterior (described as 'a jam-factory' and as a crematorium), admiration for its elegant foyer, and anxiety about the relationship of *stage to *auditorium. The distance between *actors and *audience was difficult: Baliol Holloway commented that 'it is like acting to Calais from the cliffs of Dover', while *Bridges-Adams complained that 'what we eventually got . . . was the theatre . . . in which it is hardest to make an audience laugh or cry'. The original capacity of 1,000 seats was progressively increased by expanding the back of the gallery and adding cantilevered side slips for the gallery and side *boxes in the circle to connect the audience to the stage until, by the 1990s, there were 1,500 places (including standing room). The theatre was renamed the Royal Shakespeare Theatre in 1961 upon the formation of the *Royal Shakespeare Company by Peter *Hall. There have been repeated attempts to remodel the stage to solve the problems and reduce the divisive effect of the *proscenium arch, including placing some of the audience at the back of the stage in 1976 and bringing the stage further into the *stalls in 1999. With backstage space increasingly cramped, and the need to create more room for the *Swan Theatre (opened in the shell of the Victorian theatre in 1986), the RSC announced in 2001 that it wished to demolish the building completely.

PDH

SHAKHOVSKOY, PRINCE ALEKSANDR
(1777–1846)

Russian dramatist, teacher, and director. A member of the imperial theatre committee, Shakhovskoy was sent to France in 1802 to study European methods. On his return he became head of a *St Petersburg theatre and wrote about 100 plays. His *The New Sterne* (1805), a polemical *comedy aimed at the vogue for sentimentalism, brought him to public notice, as did plays on Russian *historical subjects and *vaudevilles with a patriotic slant, such as *Lomonosov; or, The Poet Recruit* (1814) and *The Cossack Poet* (1812). His comedy *A Lesson for Coquettes; or, The Lipetsk Spa* (1815) *satirized Gallomania and romantic poetry in the person of the poet Fialkin, a thinly disguised portrait of Zhukovsky. In the 1820s and 1830s he adapted Walter Scott and Shakespeare and wrote plays incorporating songs and *dances, sieges, and conflagrations, suggesting compromise with the popular taste for *romantic subject matter; his *The Bigamous Wife* (1830) is typical. He was a successful teacher, numbering *Semyonova and *Karatygin among his pupils, and also wrote articles on the history of Russian theatre.

NW

SHANGE, NTOZAKE (PAULETTE WILLIAMS)
(1948–)

*African-American playwright and novelist. Shange created enormous excitement with her first play, *for colored girls who have considered suicide / when the rainbow is enuf* (1974), a 'choreopoem' which moved from small venues in California and the Lower East Side of *New York to the *New York Shakespeare Festival and Broadway. It greatly moved *audiences with its unconventional language and self-celebratory female postures, and caused a storm cloud of commentary, some of it charging that the play castigated African-American males. *From Okra to Greens* followed in 1978, along with *A Photograph: Lovers in Motion* (the title was revised at least twice) and with *Spell # 7*, another cross-*genre choreopoem, this one relying on *dance, *masks, and song. *Boogie Woogie Landscapes* was produced in 1979. She won an Obie in 1982 for her adaptation of *Brecht's *Mother Courage*, and *Crossroads Theatre staged *The Love Space Demands* in 1992. To commemorate the twentieth anniversary of *for colored girls*, it was revived in 1994 at Woodie *King's New Federal and a number of other theatres across the USA, introducing the work to a new generation of women. (*See* illustration p. 1234.)

BBL

SHANGHAI

The largest city in *China and the theatrical centre of the south. Historically Shanghai had extensive contact with the West and was instrumental in the development of Western-style 'spoken drama' (*huajü) in China. As early as 1889 missionary colleges in Shanghai were staging plays, some written by the students themselves. Inspired by the *Chunliu She (Spring Willow Society) production of *Uncle Tom's Cabin* in Tokyo in 1907, theatres in Shanghai began to put on regular productions of new drama known as *wenming xi (civilized drama). In 1910 Ren Tianzhi created the first professional troupe devoted to new drama, the Evolutionary Troupe, and in 1912 Lu Jingruo, a veteran of the Spring Willow Society, returned from *Japan and organized the New Drama Society which performed under the name of Chunliu Juchang (Spring Willow Theatre). Although *wenming xi* declined after 1918, it laid the foundation for the more mature *huajü*. The new drama movement spread to other parts of China in the 1920s and 1930s, but Shanghai continued as its centre. Some of the most important playwrights, including *Tian Han, Xia Yan, and Hong Shen, were based there, while the city's status as the centre of China's *film industry drew further writers, directors, and actors.

Shanghai is also an important city for traditional theatre. Apart from hosting prominent troupes of several local operas, including *yueju* (Shaoxing opera), *huju* (Shanghai opera), and the classical *kunqu, Shanghai has also been the centre of Beijing opera (*jingju) in the south, known for its often lavish and showy 'Shanghai style'. In the 1960s and 1970s Shanghai played a pivotal role in the creation of revolutionary model plays (*geming xiandai xi). When Jiang Qing, wife of Mao Zedong and former Shanghai movie star, ran into opposition in Beijing to her radical plan of using Beijing opera to portray contemporary revolutionary heroes, she found an ally in the mayor of Shanghai, Ke Qingshi. In 1963 Ke organized the East China Drama Festival in Shanghai; in the opening speech Ke echoed Jiang's and Mao's desire to place more revolutionary plays on

New York performance of Ntozake **Shange**'s choreopoem entitled *for colored girls who have considered suicide / when the rainbow is enuf*, 1976 (first produced 1974). Based in African-American speech, the play presents the individual stories of seven women in poetic form melded with song and dance.

the Chinese stage. When the eight model plays became the only permissible dramatic works in 1967, Shanghai contributed three to the list: two Beijing operas, *Taking the Tiger Mountain by Strategy* and *On the Docks*, and the *wujü (dance-drama) The White-Haired Girl.*   SYL

staged. He also acted in the *television series *La manivela* (*The Crank*) and remains an important TV celebrity. His recent theatre roles have been in *Einstein* (1995) and *Sostiene Pereira* (*Pereira's Statement*, 1997), an adaptation of Antoni Tabucchi's novel on the Salazar dictatorship in Portugal.   MAR

SHARÍM, NISSÍM (1932–)

Chilean actor and director, the senior member of the theatre company *Ictus. He joined the group in 1962 as an actor and later worked as a director and producer. In 1969, along with Delfina *Guzmán, he redefined the goals of Ictus to emphasize a form of *collective creation that would better reflect the socio-political context of Chile and *Latin America, and he played a leading role in the challenges to Pinochet's regime the group

SHARMAN, JIM (1945–)

Australian director. A graduate of the National Institute of Dramatic Art, *Sydney, Sharman's first shows were non-*naturalistic productions with fellow graduates at the Jane Street Theatre. In 1969 his Sydney production of the *musical *Hair* was seen by 1.3 million people, and after the success of his 1972 version of *Jesus Christ Superstar* he went on to direct the premi-ère in *London (1973), later also mounting David *Williamson's

The Removalists and *The Rocky Horror Show*. He also directed the cult *film of that piece, *The Rocky Horror Picture Show* (1975), for which he is best known. Sharman's *directorial style is big, bold, and very visual. Apart from a dazzling international *box-office success in musicals, he was responsible for encouraging Patrick *White back to the theatre. While he ran the Lighthouse Company in Adelaide, Sharman also encouraged the work of director Neil *Armfield and playwrights Louis *Nowra and Stephen *Sewell. Sharman wrote and directed *The Burning Piano* (1993), a *television tribute to Patrick White.   SBS

SHATROV (MARSHAK), MIKHAIL (1932–   )

Soviet/Russian playwright. Shatrov came from a Bolshevik family killed during the purges, which partly explains his repeated concern with the theme of Lenin and the revolution. His plays are ideologically challenging and highly *theatricalized, using narrators, documents, posters, and a *chorus. Frequently *characters from the present comment about the past in a *Brechtian manner. *The Peace of Brest-Litovsk* (1963, staged 1987) tackled too openly the figures of Bukharin, Trotsky, and Zinoviev and was banned. *Day of Silence, Sixth of July*, and *The Bolsheviks* form Shatrov's Lenin trilogy, staged by *Efremov at the *Sovremennik Theatre (1965–6). *Blue Horses on Red Grass* (1979), a play about the Third Youth League Congress, was directed by Mark *Zakharov. During the period of glasnost Shatrov gained major attention with *Thus We Shall Conquer* (*Moscow Art Theatre, 1984) and *The Dictatorship of Conscience* (Theatre of the Lenin Komsomol, 1988). *Dictatorship* draws on non-contemporaries and fictional characters to support Lenin's case, and Zakharov's bold staging brought the director to the fore-front of theatre *politics. *Onward, Onward, Onward* (1987) was the last of Shatrov's glasnost plays before he turned his attention to the construction of a cultural centre.   BB

SHAW, FIONA (1958–   )

Irish actress, working primarily on the classic English stage. After a degree from University College, Cork, she trained at the *Royal Academy of Dramatic Art, *London, where she won a gold medal. She joined the Royal *National Theatre immediately after to play Julia in *Sheridan's *The Rivals*, and subsequently learned her craft in a four-year stint with the *Royal Shakespeare Company, playing such roles as Celia in *As You Like It* and Kate in *The Taming of the Shrew*. Work with director Deborah *Warner raised much international *critical attention, including lead roles in *Brecht's *Good Person of Setzuan* (RNT, 1988), Sophocles' *Electra* (RSC, 1988), a highly agitated Hedda Gabler (*Abbey Theatre, *Dublin, 1991), a cross-dressed Richard II (RNT, 1995), and a very raw and moving Medea (Abbey, 2000). Her style combines *Method acting with a personal,

highly charged emotionalism, which deconstructs and challenges preconceived notions of *character and *text.   BRS

SHAW, GEORGE BERNARD (1856–1950)

Irish novelist, playwright, journalist, cultural critic, political theorist, pundit, and public personality. Born in Dublin, the second child of George Carr Shaw and of Lucinda Elizabeth Gurly, into the class he called the 'downstarts', downwardly mobile Anglo-Irish Protestants, he never attended university but started work as a clerk at the age of 15. Escaping to *London in 1876, he never returned to live in Ireland. A prolonged period of unemployment, self-education, and unsuccessful novel writing, was ended by work as a journalist, reviewing successively art, books, music, and theatre for London journals and newspapers. A zealous convert to socialism in the 1880s, he became a leading member of the left-wing, middle-class Fabian Society and a well-known lecturer and political publicist.

Shaw came to playwriting in the 1890s as a convinced socialist and a crusader for *avant-garde theatre, both evident in his doctrinaire *Quintessence of Ibsenism* (1891). His first play, *Widowers' Houses* (1892), written for J. T. *Grein's *Independent Theatre, was a polemic *Ibsenian problem play, designed to accuse its middle-class *audience of capitalist complicity in slum-landlordism. Even more scandalous was *Mrs Warren's Profession* (written 1893), exposing the cash–sex nexus of prostitution as the unspeakable counterpart of respectable marriage. *Mrs Warren* was denied a public licence in Britain for over 30 years, and provoked a prosecution for immorality when staged in *New York in 1905 (*see* CENSORSHIP). Shaw's technique was to borrow *plots, *characters, and situations from the conventional nineteenth-century theatre, which he knew intimately from his experience as a reviewer, and to overturn and subvert all of the audience's expectations of such theatre. So his *Arms and the Man* (1894) mocked military romance with its unromantic Swiss mercenary soldier Bluntschli; *Candida* (1897) was written as a counterpart to *A Doll's House* to illustrate the proposition that in the standard Victorian family it was the male who was the petted doll. Shaw's piquantly playful versions of familiar *genres were designed for the theatres and actors of his time. *The Devil's Disciple* (1897) was intended as an *Adelphi *melodrama, *You Never Can Tell* (1899) a *farce for the *Haymarket, *Caesar and Cleopatra* (1901) a *historical epic vehicle for leading actors Johnston *Forbes-Robertson and Mrs Patrick *Campbell. But in nearly every case they proved too different, too difficult for contemporary theatre *managements. Shaw was forced to collect and *publish two volumes of *Plays Pleasant and Unpleasant* (1898) and *Three Plays for Puritans* (1901) in default of satisfactory productions. His one major success in the nineteenth century was the American staging of *The Devil's Disciple* by the British *actor-manager Richard *Mansfield.

The money made from this production and his marriage in 1898 to the wealthy Irishwoman Charlotte Payne-Townshend enabled Shaw to retire as theatre critic for the *Saturday Review*, a position he had held since 1895. His collected theatre *criticism, published as *Our Theatre in the Nineties* (1930), is a monument to his achievement in this genre. Ironically, it was not long after he had completed *Man and Superman* (published 1903), a 'comedy and a philosophy' intended to be gargantuanly beyond staging, that Shaw found a theatre able to do justice to his work.

The *Vedrenne–Barker management at the *Royal Court Theatre (1904–7), and collaboration with Harley Granville *Barker, brought the production of eleven Shaw plays, both new and earlier works. Shaw's reputation was made, in particular, by *John Bull's Other Island* (1904), a treatment of the 'Irish question' *satirically transposing stereotypes of Irishman and Englishman. The Court productions showed that Shaw's new form of *comedy of ideas, apparently so full of talk, so little corresponding to conventionally plotted drama, could nonetheless grip audiences. This was true even of plays such as *Man and Superman*, which took time out from its battle of the sexes *action for a philosophical *dialogue, 'Don Juan in Hell', and of *Major Barbara* (1905) with its hard-hitting analysis of philanthropy, power, and moral responsibility. Shaw's dialectic skills, his musical management of long speeches as prose arias, his immense gifts of comic characterization, produced theatre unlike anything that had gone before.

Though his discussion plays *Getting Married* (1908) and *Misalliance* (1910) were less well received, Shaw was to achieve one of his greatest and most popular successes with *Pygmalion* (1914), written for Mrs Patrick Campbell. The Cinderella story of the flower-girl turned into a lady by a professor of phonetics resulted in a lifelong struggle by Shaw, first with the theatre director Beerbohm *Tree, and then with *film producers, to prevent it being returned to stock with a 'happy' ending. This was a battle Shaw was to lose posthumously when the sugar-coated *musical comedy adaptation, *Lerner and Loewe's *My Fair Lady* (1956), went on to make more money for the Shaw estate than all his plays put together.

The First World War brought Shaw intense unpopularity in Britain for his unseasonably cool *Common Sense about the War* (1914) and the disillusionment expressed in *Heartbreak House* (written 1916–17). This (most un-Chekhovian) experiment in the *Chekhovian style—'a fantasia in the Russian manner on English themes'—indicted the irresponsibility of the intelligentsia that had led to the war in its ship-shaped country house drifting onto the rocks. Considered dated in Britain in the immediate post-war period, but with a major international reputation, Shaw's plays were increasingly premièred abroad. Both *Heartbreak House* (1920) and the immense 'metabiological pentateuch' *Back to Methuselah* (1922), dramatizing Shaw's religion of Creative Evolution, were produced by the *Theatre Guild in New York.

Shaw's theatrical fortunes were once again revived by *St Joan* (1923), an enormous success particularly for Sybil *Thorndike, who created the part in Britain. Although some critics objected to the jokiness of the *epilogue, in which the revived saint debates with her former friends and enemies, the central character, no-nonsense mystic, Protestant and nationalist before her time (as Shaw saw her), has become one of the classic roles for women actors in the modern period. The play helped to win Shaw the Nobel Prize for Literature for 1925. In the 25 remaining years of his life Shaw continued to be immensely productive in the theatre, with *The Apple Cart* (1929), *Too True to Be Good* (1932), and a dozen further plays, often on political themes with fantastic or futuristic settings. Few of these had much commercial success, but the *Malvern Festival, founded by Barry *Jackson, provided a dedicated space for Shaw productions in the 1930s. In spite of his politically irresponsible championship of dictatorial government, he continued to be much admired and much courted, his opinions on all matters sought and publicized to the end of his long life.

Shaw, arguably the most important English-language playwright after Shakespeare, produced an immense oeuvre, of which at least half a dozen plays remain part of the world repertoire. In the English-speaking world they are often staged as part of a classic middlebrow repertoire, generally in conservative, period-style productions, and works such as *Heartbreak House* and *St Joan* are periodically revived as star vehicles by London West End managements. The specialist *Shaw Festival in Niagara-on-the-Lake, Ontario, mounts much more imaginative and innovative productions, notably *Misalliance* (1990) and *The Doctor's Dilemma* (2000), both directed by Christopher *Newton, and Jim Mezon's *John Bull's Other Island* (1998). Academically unfashionable, of limited influence even in areas such as Irish drama and British political theatre where influence might be expected, Shaw's unique and unmistakable plays keep escaping from the safely dated category of period piece to which they have often been consigned. *See also* POLITICS AND THEATRE.

NG

GRENE, NICHOLAS, *Bernard Shaw: a critical view* (Basingstoke, 1984)
HOLROYD, MICHAEL, *Bernard Shaw*, 5 vols. (London, 1988–92)
MEISEL, MARTIN, *Shaw and the Nineteenth-Century Theater* (Princeton, 1963)

SHAW, GLEN BYAM (1904–86)

English actor and director. His substantial *acting experience, which included playing Horatio to John *Gielgud's Hamlet (1939), rendered him sympathetic but authoritative in his later *directing work. His productions, often designed by *Motley, were clear and unobtrusive, allowing actors space for *characterization. He was co-director of the *Shakespeare Memorial Theatre with Anthony *Quayle (1953–6), and then sole director (1956–9) during a phase of glamorous casts and celebrated productions. In 1953 Shaw controversially but successfully cast Peggy *Ashcroft against type as the Egyptian Queen in *Antony and Cleopatra*, with Michael *Redgrave as Antony; Laurence *Olivier and Vivien *Leigh featured in Shaw's *Macbeth* and also in Peter *Brook's *Titus Andronicus* in 1955. Peter *Hall emerged as Shaw's protégé; he directed *A Midsummer Night's Dream* in 1959, and succeeded to the directorship in 1960. Shaw's later work in *opera included *The Rake's Progress* (*Sadler's Wells, 1962) and *The Ring* (*Coliseum, 1973). VRS

SHAW FESTIVAL

Canadian company, founded in 1962 in the historic town of Niagara-on-the-Lake, Ontario. Lawyer and playwright Brian Doherty wished to salute George Bernard *Shaw as 'a great playwright—a great prophet of the twentieth century'. From small beginnings the Shaw Festival has evolved into an internationally renowned enterprise featuring an ensemble of 80 actors in three theatres—the Court House Theatre (1962, 324 seats), the Festival Theatre (1973, 861 seats), and the Royal George Theatre (1980, 328 seats). Offering a season of almost 800 performances of eleven plays to *audiences of almost 320,000 on a large annual budget, the Shaw has become increasingly adept at interpreting its original classical mandate to allow greater scope in Canada's expanding theatre culture. In the first festival two plays were performed by non-professional actors for eight weekends but in 1963 the Shaw joined the earlier *Stratford Festival as Canada's second professional summer theatre dedicated to celebrating a major English-language playwright, while advancing the development of the arts in the nation. Under Andrew Allan (1963–5) and Barry Morse (1966–7) only one of the fourteen plays was outside the Shaw canon. Paxton Whitehead (1967–77) built on Morse's initiatives to give the Festival a national profile by expanding the season, increasing production values, and attracting name actors to the company. The Festival began to *tour and included *Ibsen and other English, American, and Canadian writers deemed stylistically compatible with Shaw.

Under Christopher *Newton (1980–2002), the Shaw consolidated its claim to be the only *festival in the world devoted to the production of Shaw and his contemporaries, taking Shaw's life (1856–1950) as the period of its concern. The Festival developed a strong ensemble company around established and new actors, and expanded its off-season activities to include national tours, co-productions with regional theatres, play development workshops with small *Toronto theatres, and lecture, *radio, and concert series. The summer festival also expanded to include a wider range of Shaw's canon, often in innovative and sometimes controversial productions, to increase his accessibility to modern *audiences. It also produced American classic plays, series devoted to J. B. *Priestley and Harley Granville *Barker (directed by Neil Munro), and the works of Shaw's European contempor-

aries (*Andreev, *Erdman, *Wedekind, *Witkiewicz). Period *musicals, *farces, and thrillers have become a feature of the repertoire, and educational programmes for students and others have been remarkably successful. In 2000 the mandate was broadened again to include plays written about the 1856–1950 period. Jackie Maxwell succeeded Newton as *artistic director in 2002. MJD

SHAWN, WALLACE (1943–)

American playwright and actor. After pursuing an extensive education in history and politics at Harvard and Oxford, Shawn won an Obie *award for his first play, *Our Late Night* (1975), which was produced by director Andre *Gregory's theatre company, the Manhattan Project. His next play, *A Thought in Three Parts* (1977), created a scandal for its graphic sexual depictions when it was performed by *Joint Stock in *London. Shawn collaborated with Gregory again to create the *film *My Dinner with Andre* (1981). The centre of the piece, assembled from actual conversations, is Shawn's sceptical interrogation of Gregory's rationale for leaving the theatre in order to explore para-theatrical experiments with *Grotowski. Returning to England to work with the *Royal Court Theatre, Shawn's writing took a strong *political turn in *Aunt Dan and Lemon* (1985), a play about the legacy of Nazism. The Royal *National Theatre subsequently produced *The Fever* (1991), a single-*character play affirming a Marxist critique of Third World poverty, and *The Designated Mourner* (1996), a *monologue-driven play for three actors that explores the failure of democracy in an unspecified South American country. He has also appeared in a number of films. JAB

SHCHEPKIN, MIKHAIL (1788–1863)

Russian actor, the David *Garrick of his day who introduced *realistic methods of *acting to the Russian stage. Rising from the ranks of the *serf theatres, Shchepkin brought about important changes in Russian theatrical tradition which would have lasting effects. He made his debut on the *Moscow imperial stage in 1822, proving himself an outstanding and popular actor, and becoming the close friend of writers and intellectuals such as *Pushkin, *Lermontov, *Griboedov, *Gogol, Stankevich, Belinsky, Herzen, *Turgenev, as well as the famous Aksakov family of Slavophiles. Shchepkin's importance lay not only in the qualities of psychological verisimilitude which he brought to his acting roles, but also in his attitude to the theatre as a serious art form. The examples he set by way of a strict professionalism, attention to detail, *rehearsal procedures, questions of ensemble and *mise-en-scène were crucial for both playwriting and play production. Those who were immediately affected included Turgenev and Gogol; others who inherited his tradition were, notably, *Ostrovsky, *Stanislavsky, and *Nemirovich-Danchenko.

According to Herzen, Shchepkin 'created truth on the Russian stage; he was the first to become non-theatrical in the theatre'. Belinsky admired his performances, especially as the mayor in Gogol's *The Government Inspector*. His playing in Turgenev's *The Bachelor* (1850) and *The Parasite* (1862) served to establish that writer's reputation as a successful dramatist, whilst his own observations on the Russian theatre were, in Stanislavsky's words, those of Russian theatre's 'great legislator'.   NW

SHCHUKIN, BORIS (1894–1939)

Russian/Soviet actor who joined *Vakhtangov's Studio in 1920, acting in the latter's famous productions of *The Miracle of St Anthony* (1921) and *Princess Turandot* (1922). His subsequent career was spent at the Vakhtangov Theatre, where his command of the theatrical *grotesque made him an excellent Shapiro in *Olesha's *The Conspiracy of Feelings* (1929), directed by Aleksei *Popov, and Polonius in Nikolai *Akimov's controversial production of *Hamlet* (1932). His greatest claim to fame in Soviet times was as the eponymous capitalist Egor Bulychov in *Gorky's play, and as various incarnations of Lenin, both on stage and on screen.   NW

SHEAN, AL *See* GALLAGHER, ED.

SHELDON, EDWARD (1886–1946)

American playwright. Sheldon's *Salvation Nell* (1908) was produced soon after his graduation from Harvard, where he studied playwriting with George Pierce *Baker. The production, starring Minnie Maddern *Fiske, was admired for its eventful script, convincing *acting, and *naturalistic *scenery. Sheldon saw himself as a craftsman more than an artist and sought out subjects likely to become hits. *The Nigger* (1909, about a southern governor who discovers his own black ancestry) and *The Boss* (1911, a labour play) surged with *melodramatic power and controversial *dialogue and *actions. *The High Road* (1912) and *Romance* (1913) turned toward more whimsical topics. Stricken by severe arthritis in 1917 and bedridden for the rest of his life, Sheldon became a *New York institution. Visited regularly by writers and actors, he was considered a benevolent sage on *dramaturgical questions. He was credited as co-author with Sidney *Howard for *Bewitched* (1924) and with Charles *MacArthur for *Lulu Belle* (1926).   MAF

SHELLEY, PERCY BYSSHE (1792–1822)

English poet. Shelley is the author of four weighty *verse dramas, the best known being *The Cenci* (1819). Since this excessively poetic (rather than dramatic) Elizabethan-style *tragedy dealt with a real case of incest and parricide in sixteenth-century Italy, it could not be licensed for performance and was first done privately by the Shelley Society in 1886 (*see* CENSORSHIP; LORD CHAMBERLAIN). In the twentieth century it was seen with Sybil *Thorndike (1922, 1926) and Barbara *Jefford (1959, at the *Old Vic) as Beatrice Cenci. A 1935 version by *Artaud in *Paris represented one of his few actual productions.   MRB

SHELVING, PAUL (1888–1968)

English designer. He studied fine art at the beginning of the twentieth century, winning prizes for model and outline drawing, and was greatly influenced by Edward Gordon *Craig's *Much Ado About Nothing* (1903). Small acting roles and pageant designs were interrupted by military service in France. On discharge he became the resident designer and scene *painter at the *Birmingham Repertory Theatre under Barry *Jackson, and designed *Shaw's *Back to Methusaleh* (1923) and the famous modern-dress Shakespeare productions (1925–8). For a decade from 1929 he was resident designer at the new *Malvern Festival with Shaw and Jackson, and after the Second World War he returned to Birmingham for *Man and Superman*, *King John*, and *Ibsen's *Lady from the Sea* with the young Peter *Brook as director. Shelving's personal signature was simplicity of colour and line, with bold colourful patterns and great attention to ornamental detail.   PH

SHEN JING (SHEN CHING) (1553–1610)

*Chinese playwright and prosodist for *kunqu. Ranked with *Tang Xianzu as a genius of the late Ming dynasty, Shen's reputation subsequently declined because of his formalism. Six of seventeen plays are extant, the most popular of them being *Yixia ji* (*The Altruistic Knight-Errant*), based on the exploits of Wu Song in the novel *Shuihu zhuan* (*Water Margin*). Six of its 36 *scenes were performed as highlights throughout the Qing Dynasty. Shen's *Nan jiugong shisandiao qupu* (*Manual of Nine Modes and Thirteen Keys for Southern Drama*) codifies 652 tunes for the *kunqu* musical style, responding to and further enabling its emergence as the pre-eminent form, until Beijing opera (*jingju) replaced it in the eighteenth century. Shen's concern with performability distinguished him from contemporary *chuanqi playwrights. He wrote shorter plays (of about 30 scenes), more actor friendly, some consisting of ten two-to-four-scene playlets linked by a theme (filial piety, *satire of contemporary mores). He was among the first to write Wu dialect for the *jing* (painted-face actor who depicts *villainous or comical *characters) and *chou* (comic actor who performs using dialect), and featured those roles in playlets that depict inept magistrates, thugs, monks and priests, and merchants. Both innovations marked a departure from the 'scholar–beauty' romances favoured heretofore.   CS

Warren Clarke as Blue Morphin and Richard O'Brien as Willie the Space Freak in *The Unseen Hand*, Royal Court Theatre Upstairs, London, 1973, directed by Jim Sharman, designed by Brian Thomson. First produced at La Mama in New York, 1969, **Shepard**'s short play confronts American cowboy myths with the myth of outer space, set in and around a ruined Chevrolet on the dividing strip of a California freeway.

SHEPARD, SAM (1943–   )

American playwright, actor, and director, born Samuel Shepard Rogers. A prominent figure of *Off-Off-Broadway's upsurge in the 1960s, Shepard became one of the most widely admired and produced American playwrights in the later twentieth century. His work is regarded as unmistakably American in its energies, jargons, and pop-culture trappings. At the same time, however, it harbours the existential undertow of *Beckett, whose *Waiting for Godot* inspired Shepard as a teenager in southern California. Shepard's avalanche of early works exposed the raw patchwork of inner experience at the expense of conventional *character and *plot; the plays take place in real time, incorporating jagged 'verbal arias' and bold stage images. During this period he met Joseph *Chaikin, with whom he would establish a lifelong creative relationship. Like many of his plays of this period, *The Tooth of Crime* reflects his passion for rock and roll—he wrote the original music for its songs. Shepard disagreed openly with aspects of Charles *Marowitz's première production at the Open Space in *London (1972), and even more so with Richard *Schechner's reconceptualized, *environmental staging at *New York's Performing Garage (1973). The play's rocky production beginnings aside, however, it is usually seen as a first major work to harness Shepard's vision and vitality. An updated version, with new music composed by T-Bone Burnett, opened in New York in 1996.

Returning to California in 1974, Shepard found an artistic home at *San Francisco's Magic Theatre where he came under the influence of director Robert *Woodruff. Here he would produce his breakthrough 'family' plays, beginning with *Curse of the Starving Class* (1977) and *Buried Child* (1978), for which he received the Pulitzer Prize. The honour—along with his debut as a *film actor in *Days of Heaven*—swept the fiercely individualistic playwright into the mainstream of American theatre.

True West (1980) renewed his ascendancy, thanks to a comically enhanced *Steppenwolf Theatre revival in 1982 starring John *Malkovich and Gary *Sinise. *Fool for Love* (1983) earned one of many Obie *awards for Shepard as a playwright, but his first such acknowledgement as a director. These pieces lay bare dysfunctioning family bonds and the betrayed promises of American mythic narratives, drawing on a roughly hewn *realism which unfolds amid scruffy Western landscapes and hinges on reversible images of the mundane and the apocalyptic. Although any Shepard work has been anticipated eagerly—whether new, like *The Late Henry Moss* (2000), or revised, like *Buried Child* (1995)—his plays have come sporadically since the mid-1980s. His latter-day cowboy persona has won popularity as a film actor and drawn him closer to the screen as writer and director. EW

SHER, ANTONY (1949–)

South African actor. After leaving apartheid South Africa, Sher went to drama school in *London and worked in *regional repertory companies and on the *fringe (including in Caryl *Churchill's *Cloud Nine* for *Joint Stock and in Mike *Leigh's *Goosepimples*). His *absurdist *music-hall *clown Fool in *King Lear* (*Royal Shakespeare Company, 1982) and spider-like Richard III (1984) established him as a viscerally exciting and dangerous classical actor, physicalizing *characters in new ways that dominated the stage (often at the expense of other actors). A novelist and painter as well, he documented the experience of playing Richard III in *The Year of the King* (1985). He returned to South Africa to play Titus Andronicus (*Market Theatre, 1995) as a grizzled Boer. Refusing a narrow definition of range, his roles have been deliberately spread wide: Tartuffe and Shylock, *Marlowe's Tamburlaine and *Rostand's Cyrano, the painter Stanley Spencer and the composer Mahler, *Brecht's Arturo Ui and *Stoppard's Henry Carr, and his *film career has further expanded his scope. His thorough research work before *rehearsal includes psychological analysis, for example interviewing murderers before playing Macbeth (1999). He was knighted in 2000. PDH

SHERIDAN, RICHARD BRINSLEY (1751–1816)

Irish playwright and *manager, the son of the actor Thomas Sheridan and the novelist and playwright Frances Sheridan. Sheridan was born in *Dublin and educated at Harrow. He married the singer Elizabeth Linley whilst they were both still minors and fought two duels with a rival suitor on her behalf; throughout his career, Sheridan retained a lively talent for transforming the incidents of his life into the raw material of theatre. His first play was *The Rivals* (1775), a light-hearted *burlesque of

sentimental *comedy, set in *Bath and featuring the inimitable Mrs Malaprop. *St Patrick's Day* (a *farce) and *The Duenna*, a comic *opera described by William *Hazlitt as 'a perfect work of art', were performed the same year. In 1776 Sheridan bought *Garrick's half-share in *Drury Lane Theatre in *London. The theatre's *finances were already in disarray; as manager, Sheridan's reckless extravagance further exacerbated the situation.

Sheridan created sparkling dramas which combined the *stock characters and conventions of Restoration comedy with topical humour and subtle moral *satire. In 1777 he produced *A Trip to Scarborough*, a moralized adaptation of *Vanbrugh's play *The Relapse*. Later that year saw the first performance of his best-known comedy, *The School for Scandal*. Witty repartee, a colourful cast of scandalmongers, together with Sheridan's ingenious exploitation of *proscenium effects, combined to create one of the most enduring and cherished plays in the history of British comedy. This success was followed by a topical entertainment entitled *The Camp* (1778) and *The Critic* (1779), an *afterpiece satirizing contemporary drama and the prevailing fashion for spectacular scenic effects.

In 1780 Sheridan became a Member of Parliament and proceeded to combine his theatrical career with the drama of politics. He was appointed Secretary to the Treasury in 1783 and played an important role in the impeachment of Warren Hastings for his maladministration as governor-general of India. Sheridan's intense opposition to colonial tyranny also provided the inspiration for *Pizarro*, his controversial adaptation of *Kotzebue's play about the Spanish conqueror of Peru, starring John Philip *Kemble as Rolla, the Peruvian *hero. Between 1791 and 1794 Sheridan presided over the demolition of Wren's Drury Lane, and its replacement by a huge and luxurious new theatre designed by Henry Holland. But after Drury Lane was destroyed by *fire in 1809 Samuel Whitbread barred Sheridan from the management; the playwright lost his parliamentary seat in 1811 and was arrested for debt two years later. He was buried close to Garrick in Westminster Abbey. JM

SHERRIFF, R. C. (ROBERT CEDRIC) (1896–1975)

English playwright and screenwriter. Sherriff began writing for an *amateur company but his seventh play, *Journey's End* (1928), propelled him into professional theatre. The script had been turned down by every *management in *London, who believed that its subject matter, the behaviour of a group of soldiers in a dugout trench on the Western Front towards the end of the First World War, was inherently uncommercial. Produced by the *Stage Society for two nights, with *Olivier in lead, the *critic James *Agate devoted his entire weekly *radio broadcast to the play. A hit production soon followed, inspiring a revival of serious dramatic writing about the war. Sherriff never repeated this success, though his well-crafted thrillers *Miss Mabel* (1948), *Home at Seven* (1950), and *The White Carnation* (1953) chimed with the mood of post-war *audiences. After the rise of *Osborne and the *Royal Court, Sherriff's last play, *A Shred of Evidence* (1960), was denounced by the critics as from a time gone by.

DR

SHERWOOD, ROBERT E. (1896–1955)

American playwright. A thoughtful, intellectual writer attuned to his times, Sherwood won three Pulitzer Prizes between 1936 and 1940. A graduate of Harvard University, Sherwood was wounded in the First World War. He became *film reviewer (1920–4) and later editor of the original *Life* magazine (1924–8). *Reunion in Vienna* (1931), a *comedy about the lost world of pre-war Europe written to feature Alfred *Lunt and Lynn Fontanne, was a major success and established Sherwood as a mainstay of the *Theatre Guild and the Lunts. In a move that would become habitual, Sherwood *published the play along with a brooding philosophical preface, describing it as 'an escape mechanism' from economic depression and the rise of totalitarianism. The end of civilization continued in *The Petrified Forest* (1935), ostensibly a gangster drama, starring Humphrey Bogart as a desperate killer and Leslie Howard as a spiritually exhausted poet, but intended as a parable about civilization's self-hatred and seeming desire for destruction by brutes (*filmed the next year with the same actors). *Idiot's Delight* (Pulitzer, 1936) is a complex mixture of *comedy, *musical, and *drama and ends with an imagined beginning of the Second World War. *Abe Lincoln in Illinois* (Pulitzer, 1938) chronicles Lincoln's transition from innocent idealist to practical man of action. *There Shall Be No Night* (Pulitzer, 1940) uses the Soviet invasion of Finland as the setting for a didactic drama on the necessity of fighting against totalitarian expansion. Sherwood served as speech writer for Franklin Roosevelt during the war and later won a fourth Pulitzer for his book *Roosevelt and Hopkins* (1948). He won an Academy award in 1946 for his script of the film *The Best Years of our Lives*.

MAF

SHIELDS, ELLA (1879–1952)

American singer and comedienne. In the USA Shields began as a 'coon singer', drawing upon the traditions of *minstrelsy. She went to *London in 1904 and began a long, successful career in *music-hall entertainment. She became famous in *male impersonation, in the mode of Vesta *Tilley. Dressed in top hat and tails, she sang various songs, including 'If You Knew Susie', while 'Burlington Bertie from Bow' was performed in tattered clothes. In the 1920s she returned to America, appearing in various cities. Although she retired in 1929, she occasionally reprised her act in the 1930s and 1940s.

TP

SHIELS, GEORGE (1886–1949)

Irish dramatist. Paralysed in a railway accident in Canada, Shiels returned to Ireland in 1913, and settled into a confined life in a wheelchair. He became a mainstay of the *Abbey Theatre in *Dublin between 1921 and 1948, writing two dozen popular *comedies. Despite his personal difficulties, his plays are mostly light-hearted, teasing the Irish with a constrained *satire. His popular work includes *Paul Twyning* (1922), *Professor Tim* (1925), *The New Gossoon* (1930), *The Passing Day* (1936), and *Tenants at Will* (1945). In a more serious mode, *The Rugged Path* (1940) and *The Summit* (1941) reveal a darker critique of Irish self-deceptions.

TP

SHIMIZU KUNIO (1936–   )

Japanese playwright. Born in Niigata, Shimizu began his career as a student radical during the 1960s, working closely with the young director *Ninagawa Yukio. After graduation Shimizu wrote for the small *avant-garde companies that proliferated in *Tokyo, his greatest early success being *The Dressing Room* (1977), a *metatheatrical piece mixing a whimsical vision of *Chekhov with contemporary Japanese politics. Among his later works are *Older Sister Burning Like a Flame* (1978), in which a Shakespearian actor from Tokyo falls prey to dark forces in his past, and a second play about memory and the theatre, *Tango at the End of Winter* (1984), successfully produced in *London in 1991 with a British cast, directed by Ninagawa. Unlike some of his contemporaries, Shimizu continues to place the *text at the centre of theatre. His plays are among the most eloquent and unsettling written in *Japan in the latter half of the twentieth century.

JTR

SHIMPA

The first movement to create a modern theatre in *Japan. *Shimpa* (new school) set itself as distinct from the 'old school', *kabuki. The fathers of *shimpa*, Sudō Sadanori (1867–1907) and Kawakami Otojirō (1864–1911), began as political activists for democratic rights in the 1880s using theatre as *agitprop, but as *shimpa* became more professional its political message waned. By the 1890s Kawakami in particular had created a popular form of contemporary theatre whose repertory was based largely on sensational treatments of news items like the Sino-Japanese War or adaptations of melodramatic novels by writers like *Izumi Kyōka. Kawakami and his wife, Sadayakko (1872–1946) were the most colourful and enterprising figures in early twentieth-century Japanese theatre. On their American and European *tours, Sadayakko (who became Japan's first modern professional actress) was compared favourably to Eleanore *Duse and Sarah *Bernhardt. With their pastiches of kabuki, the troupe pandered to Western *audiences hungry for *Japonisme*, but Kawakami and his wife introduced Western scenic and *lighting effects to Japan, as well as plays by Shakespeare, *Maeterlinck, and *Sardou. Even so, Japanese scholars and critics have slighted their efforts as amateurish and opportunistic. Other troupes such as the Seibidan ensured that *shimpa*'s stagecraft, music, and *acting—particularly the use of *female impersonators (*onnagata)—remained essentially kabuki inspired. By 1910 *shimpa*'s melodramatic repertory and reliance on kabukiesque conventions made it fall increasingly out of favour with reformers like *Osanai Kaoru, though it remained popular thanks to the work of *onnagata* like Kitamura Rokurō (1871–1961) and Hanayagi Shōtarō (1894–1965), and actresses like Mizutani Yaeko (1905–79). *Shimpa* celebrated its 100th anniversary in 1988 to sold-out houses, indicating that there was still a place for good *melodrama. Newer plays by *shingeki (new theatre) writers like Kubota Mantarō (1889–1963) and *Inoue Hisashi, and guest appearances by kabuki stars like Kataoka Nizaemon XV and *Bandō Tamasaburō V, have helped keep *shimpa* alive, but at the end of the twentieth century it generally suffered from a lack of fresh material and good acting.

CP

SHINGEKI

'New theatre', the leading movement in modern Japanese theatre until the 1960s. For much of the twentieth century the modernization of theatre in *Japan basically meant its westernization, a project that created its own internal tensions and contradictions. In its attempt to emulate European stagecraft, *acting techniques, repertory, and *dramaturgy, *shingeki* rejected traditional Japanese theatre, especially *kabuki. Where traditional theatre focused on the sensual qualities of a performance (including *music and the physical appeal of the actor), *shingeki* appealed to the *audience's intellect; spoken drama thus came to replace music and *dance. Kabuki's presentational style of acting was abandoned in favour of greater *realism; at the same time, innovations in theatre architecture, such as the *proscenium arch, helped create the illusion of a fourth wall between actors and audience. Japanese theatre was slow to modernize, in large part because of the popularity and technical brilliance of kabuki, which as late as the 1890s still boasted excellent actors and playwrights. By the beginning of the twentieth century, however, it was clear that kabuki had become impervious to change. 'New' became the buzzword. Various attempts to reform Japanese theatre, such as *shimpa* (new school), *shin-kabuki* (new kabuki), and *shinkokugeki* (new national theatre), nonetheless retained many kabuki conventions like the *hanamichi* runway and the female impersonator (*onnagata).

In Japan the cult of the *director was promoted before a dramatic literature could develop fully. Both *Tsubouchi Shōyō and *Osanai Kaoru attempted to introduce Western plays, staging, and acting techniques to Japanese theatre, and to raise the

literary standards of the dramatic *text, but these were not easy tasks. Tsubouchi founded the Literary Society (Bungei Kyōkai) in *Tokyo in 1906 to train *amateur actors and stage European works; Osanai established the Free Theatre (Jiyū Gekijō), modelled after *Antoine's Théâtre *Libre, in 1909. Their productions of European drama had enormous impact. The repertoire was eclectic, reflecting changes in contemporary European theatre: Shakespeare, *Ibsen, *Chekhov, and *Gorky were favourites, but productions of *Hauptmann, *Maeterlinck, *Strindberg, and *Wedekind also excited much debate. Though the Free Theatre staged original Japanese drama, translated plays continued to dominate *shingeki* until well into the 1930s. Tsubouchi and Osanai focused their attentions on developing modern directorial and acting skills, but kabuki mannerisms were hard to shake. Though he was a more radical reformer than Tsubouchi, Osanai worked with the kabuki actor Ichikawa Sadanji II (1880–1941) in training actors from that theatre. The Literary Society disbanded in 1913, and after the closing of Osanai's Free Theatre in 1919, there were practically no attempts at collaboration between the traditional and modern theatres again until the 1960s.

In 1924 Osanai joined with *Hijikata Yoshi to open the state-of-the-art *Tsukiji Little Theatre. Osanai idolized *Stanislavsky, but Hijikata's models were *Piscator, *Reinhardt, and *Meyerhold; their tastes indicated the polarization between apolitical *naturalism and leftist *expressionism that was to last in *shingeki* until the 1960s. The TLT became a fertile training ground for actors and directors like Sugimura Haruko (1909–97) and *Senda Koreya, but Osanai's reluctance to stage Japanese plays was a blow to native playwrights. After his untimely death in 1928, the TLT split into two camps. The leftists, led by Hijikata, spawned one of the major works of *socialist realism in Japan, *Kubo Sakae's *Land of Volcanic Ash* (1937). The Literary Theatre (Bungakuza), organized around playwrights like Kubota Mantarō (1889–1963) and *Kishida Kunio, concerned itself with purely aesthetic criteria and with the development of a Japanese repertory. Proletarian theatre flourished before the war until it was crushed by the militarists. The Literary Theatre fared better, in part due to Kishida's collaboration with the authorities; it was one of the few theatres allowed to perform throughout the Second World War.

Two leftist *shingeki* troupes emerged soon after the war, the Mingei (People's Theatre) founded by Kubo, and the Haiyūza (Actors' Theatre) led by Senda. The Rōen (Workers' Council on Theatre), founded in the 1950s by progressive labour unions, ensured large audiences for *shingeki* troupes through its sales of subscription tickets. American and European drama dominated the post-war Japanese stage, with Senda responsible for the interest in *Brecht. Several excellent Japanese playwrights appeared, however, including Miyoshi Jūrō (1902–58), *Tanaka Chikao, Fukuda Tsuneari (1931–), and *Kinoshita Junji. Two prominent novelists, *Abe Kōbō and *Mishima Yukio, also distinguished themselves in the 1950s as *shingeki* playwrights; their works were among the first to be translated from post-war Japanese drama. By the 1960s, however, the rise of *absurdism, the discrediting of the Stalinist Old Left, and the quest for more native sources of theatrical inspiration led to the demise of *shingeki*'s artistic and political dominance over modern Japanese theatre. *See* ANGURA. CP

SHINGŬK

Modern Korean theatre in the Western mould, parallel to *Japanese *shingeki*. *Shingŭk* (literally, 'new drama') began to emerge when modern commercial theatre (*shinp'agŭk*) dominated the stage in *Korea. Two theatre groups were influential in its creation. In 1921, under the leadership of *Kim U-jin, Korean students studying in *Tokyo formed the *Tongwuhoe* (Society of Comradeship) and developed the first Korean modern drama. They *toured Korea in the summer vacation, performing works such as Cho Myŏng-hŭi's *The Death of Kim Yŏng-il* (1921) and introduced plays by *Ibsen, *Shaw, *O'Neill, *Čapek, and *Pirandello. In 1931, a team of intellectuals led by *Yu Ch'i-jin founded the *Kŭgyesul Yŏnguhoe* (Theatre Arts Research Society) to promote *realistic theatre through performance, playwriting, *criticism, *audience education, and the translation of foreign plays. Despite the dissolution of these two groups by the Japanese police, they made significant contributions to Korean modern theatre. They established the first serious modern theatre, raised the quality of production, taught the audience new ideologies, and produced notable young playwrights. Today *shingŭk* still implies modernity, Western values (democracy, individualism, socialism), and Korean nationalism. JOC

SHINP'AGŬK

The commercial theatre of *Korea popular from 1910 through the 1930s. *Shinp'agŭk* (literally, 'new school drama') was heavily influenced by *Japanese *shimpa, and was first performed by Hyŏkshin Troupe in Seoul, a theatrical company founded by the prominent actor and *producer Im Sŏng-ku (1887–1921). Despite the popularity of productions like *The Pistol-Robber* (1912), his work was modelled on the third-rate Japanese *shimpa* groups seen in Korea and depended on improvised *dialogue. As *shinp'agŭk* grew in popularity, new theatre companies developed better techniques. One of the most important artists was *Pak Sŭng-hŭi, the leader of *Towolhoe* (the Earth and Moon group), and the first playwright and director to use completely developed scripts for the form.

Most *shinp'agŭk* plays dealt with subjects that could move contemporary *audiences emotionally, and fell into three main types. (*a*) Military plays evoked patriotism through stories in which patriotic soldiers fight invaders to defend the Korean nation and are praised as national heroes. (*b*) Detective plays promoted virtue and reproved vice, usually designating a policeman as the *hero, who implacably traces and finally arrests the robber who had earlier wounded him. (*c*) Domestic plays, the most popular type, dealt with love, revenge, injustice, filial piety, and conflicts between men and women. Domestic plays were *melodramas with a pedestrian sentimentality that often consoled the audience for the suppression endured under Japanese colonialism. Although Korean audiences of the time responded enthusiastically, reflecting their personal sufferings and the nation's tragedy, *shinp'agŭk* was restrained by its inherent sentimentalism from developing a modern *dramaturgy. Revivals of the form, such as Pak Sung-hui's *Arirang Pass*, were occasionally produced at the end of the century for the benefit of the older generation. JOC

SHIPENKO, ALEKSEI (1961–)

Soviet/Russian playwright, almost a classic among contemporary Russian dramatists. *The Observer* (1984), an anthology of rock music in the Soviet Union, was directed by Boris Yukhananov in 1986 at the School of Dramatic Art, and *Van Halen's Death* (1987), also dealing with rock culture, was still in several theatre repertoires in 2000. *Natural Housekeeping in Shambale* (1989) explores a journey into the other world, reflecting Shipenko's preoccupation with archaic and Eastern culture; it was staged by the Formal Theatre (*St Petersburg) and Omsk Drama Theatre. Other plays include two from 1988, *Archeology* and *La Funf in der Luft* (a macaronic nonsense phrase muttered by the *protagonist, more or less meaning 'la five in the sky'). BB

SHIRLEY, JAMES (1596–1666)

English playwright and schoolmaster. Born in *London, he graduated from Cambridge, took holy orders, and became headmaster of St Alban's grammar school before turning to the theatre in 1623. A member of Gray's Inn, he was resident dramatist for the Queen's Men (for whom he wrote the majority of his plays) from 1625 to 1636. He then moved to *Dublin, where he played a crucial role in establishing the first Irish *playhouse, the Werburgh Street Theatre. Upon his return to London in 1640 he became attached to the King's Men (*see* CHAMBERLAIN'S MEN, LORD), remaining with them until the closure of the theatres in 1642. After the Civil War (he took the royalist side) he went back to teaching, setting up a school and publishing a Latin grammar. Rumoured to be a Catholic, his connection with the court circle (he was Valet of the Chamber of Queen Henrietta Maria), together with his attempts to seek the patronage of prominent aristocrats, gave him a reputation as a royalist only partially justified by his work. Although his plays rarely take a *political stance as openly as those of other Caroline dramatists, such as *Massinger or *Brome, they often engage in topical commentary and *satire of court life.

Among Shirley's best-known works are *Hyde Park* (1632) and *The Lady of Pleasure* (1635), witty *comedies of London life and manners which foreshadow in many respects the drama of the Restoration, albeit displaying a much stricter moral strain. Also well known is *The Cardinal*, a *revenge tragedy written in 1641 in which reference is made to the trial of Cardinal Laud and the growing dissension between the King and his Parliament. Less well known, despite representing the bulk of his work, are his *tragicomedies and romantic comedies. Of the handful of plays he wrote for Dublin, *St Patrick for Ireland* (1639) deserves special mention as an example of English colonialist propaganda thinly disguised as a tribute to Irish *folklore. Shirley is also the author of *The Triumph of Peace*, a *masque presented by the *Inns of Court to Charles I in 1634.

PCR

SHITE

The main, and only absolutely essential, role in a *nō or *kyōgen play. In some plays the *shite* plays a different *character in each of the two *acts. *Shite* also refers to the actors who perform *shite*, take the companion and children's roles, comprise the *chorus, and serve as stage attendants. Nō *shite* actors belong to five professional schools: Hōshō, Kanze, Kita, Komparu, Kongō; kyōgen actors are not divided by roles. The actor playing the *shite* role controls the visual design of a performance (*costumes and *props), selects the other performers, chooses the variant *texts, and conducts the single *rehearsal. *See also* WAKI.

KWB

SHOWBOATS

Also called floating theatres, American showboats were flat-bottomed barges which carried a theatre and living quarters for the owner and his *family, all of whom contributed to the presentation of shows for *audiences who would come on board wherever the boat docked. Without power of their own, the early 'floaters' travelled only downstream at the mercy of currents and winds. Later showboats operated in tandem with steam towboats, which housed additional performers and crew. The tow steamer enabled the floating palace to better avoid sandbars, to travel upstream, and to venture along tributary rivers and bayous, as well as providing steam for the calliope whose melody announced the showboat's arrival from as far as 11 km (7 miles) away.

Some scholars surmise that as early as 1817 Noah *Ludlow might have offered performances on the boat on which he transported his players through Tennessee. The first documented use of a riverboat as a theatre is the Chapman family's Floating Theatre, which left Pittsburgh in July 1831 and reached New Orleans in the spring; there they sold the boat, travelled by land back to Pittsburgh, and started again, taking their English repertoire of classic plays down the Ohio and Mississippi. The Chapmans were able to sustain the business for a decade, because William Chapman's close-knit family served as a model of domesticity in an era when itinerant entertainers tended to be regarded with suspicion. Many less scrupulous operators followed in their wake, offering *variety entertainment regarded as lowering of artistic quality and moral tone. Floating theatre ceased to exist during the Civil War.

In 1878 Augustus Byron French and his wife Callie (Leach) French revived the dormant practice of showboating when they launched *French's New Sensation*, the first of five boats to bear that name under their ownership during the next 30 years. French initiated the scheduling that became standard practice: leaving the northern base in the spring to play the southern regions after the autumn harvest. French and his partner James McNair presented only wholesome family entertainment at landings sometimes only 8 or 16 km (5 or 10 miles) apart, serving small communities with little access to cultural events. Others sustained that tradition for a time: Edwin A. Price's *Water Queen*, Ralph Emerson's *Cotton Blossom*, E. E. Eisenbarth's *Eisenbarth-Henderson Temple of Amusement*. With W. R. Markle's launching of the *Sunny South* in 1905 and the *Golden-rod* in 1909, showboating was transformed from small family-run enterprises to big business. Larger, more opulent boats docked at big cities, playing longer runs and gearing their offerings to city folk who already had numerous entertainment options. Over the next three decades the numbers of showboats dwindled rapidly. The Bryant family kept *Bryant's New Show-boat* going until 1942 by presenting old *melodramas for laughs.

It was an Atlantic coastal showboat, the *James Adams Floating Theatre*, that incongruously served as the model for the Mississippi River boat in Edna *Ferber's 1926 novel *Show Boat*, on which the 1927 Jerome *Kern *musical is based. All surviving showboats (notably, the *Goldenrod* at St Charles, Missouri, and the *Majestic* at Cincinnati) and reconstructions of showboats for use as performance spaces (University of Minnesota, University of Washington) are permanently moored.

FHL

BRYANT, BETTY, *Here Comes the Showboat!* (Lexington, Mass., 1994)
GRAHAM, PHILIP, *Showboats: the history of an American institution* (Austin, Tex., 1976)

SHUBERT BROTHERS

American *managers, *producers, and theatre owners. **Lee** (1873–1953), **Sam S.** (1876–1905), and **J. J.** ('Jake') (1878–1963), born in Lithuania, were raised in Syracuse, New York. The first brother to succeed was Sam, who began as a paper boy outside Syracuse's Wieting Theatre, and worked himself up to theatre treasurer. In 1894 the brothers co-produced a profitable north-east *touring production of Charles *Hoyt's *A Texas Steer*, followed by another Hoyt work. Before long, the trio gained control over the Syracuse theatre, expanded their growing empire to Utica, and then moved on to Broadway in *New York, where they leased the reputedly jinxed Herald Square Theatre on 35th Street. Several special matinées of new plays produced by Sam were such failures that the Shuberts decided to stay away from unknown playwrights henceforth. Between the time of their finest regular production, *The Brixton Burglary* (1901), at the Herald Square Theatre, and their final production before Lee's death, *The Starcross Story* (1954), they produced over 520 shows. At one point, they controlled the booking in more than 1,000 national theatres, and owned 31 Broadway theatres, 63 elsewhere in America, and held part ownership in five *London theatres. They possessed a huge stock of *costumes and *scenery, and had numerous designers, writers, and performers under contract.

After Sam's early death in a train crash his brothers divided the firm's many responsibilities, although Sam's will, giving Lee his holdings, sharply split them. In 1916 the Shuberts successfully defeated the *Theatrical Syndicate in their rivalry for control of the American theatre. The brothers split their responsibilities, with J. J. overseeing all matters relating to *musical productions, while Lee managed the firm's straight plays as well as all its New York and national bookings. They fought often with the press, even barring certain *critics from productions. Notoriously secretive, penny-pinching (they refused all refund requests), and humourless, the Shuberts engaged in ruthless, even devious business methods, which helped them to overcome bankruptcy during the Depression. Eventually they were responsible for almost one-quarter of all Broadway productions and two-thirds of all ticket sales. In 1956 the Supreme Court found the firm guilty of monopolistic practices and forced divestiture of various holdings and the abandonment of its booking business.

The Shuberts introduced many managerial innovations, including the hiring in 1908 of Broadway's first women ushers, and the provision of *box-office wall racks for tickets, although their money-saving tactics included failing to provide hot water in their theatres' *toilets. The Shuberts' prolific production history was focused mainly on ephemera aimed at escape-hungry *audiences. One of their rare new straight plays of some importance was *Dark of the Moon* (1945), while their most significant musical productions included the *operettas *Maytime* (1917), *Blossom Time* (1921), and *The Student Prince* (1924); the *revues *The Show Is On* (1936) and *At Home Abroad* (1935); the Olsen and Johnson musical farce *Hellzapoppin'* (1938); and two versions of the *Ziegfeld Follies* (1936, 1943) following *Ziegfeld's death.   SLL

SHUMANG LILA

A popular theatre tradition from the north-eastern state of Manipur in *India. Derived from the words for 'courtyard' and 'play', *shumang lila* has its roots in three traditions of performance. Maharaja Chandrakirti Singh (1851–86) encouraged his court jesters to give public performances that later became known as *fagee lila*. In the early twentieth century two forms arose that belonged to the *fagee* *genre but contained an undercurrent of protest against the British masters and their bureaucracy: the *kabul pala* (chorus of *kabul*) and *fadibee pala* (chorus of the tattered clothes). Together these forms gave rise to *shumang lila*, which is marked today by its satiric humour and a *subtext that deals with the unrecognized grievances of common people relating to insurgency, the violence of the Indian army, and social injustice. Initially, the *dialogue was improvised, as in the first full-length *shumang lila* *text, *Harishchandra* (1918). Scripts were not written until the 1950s, the pioneers being Ningombam Angonon and Nongmaijing Sharma. Later G. C. Tongbra contributed significantly to the genre, and among contemporary playwrights Chana Lukhoi is prominent.

Generally, *shumang lila* performance takes place in an open space with the *audience close to the performers seated on three sides. There is no *scenery or elaborate *props. Male troupes predominate, men taking the women's roles (*see* FEMALE IMPERSONATION), though some all-women troupes exist as well. The performance begins with a patriotic song, followed by another saluting the audience, a tradition that reflects the nationalist origins of the *shumang lila* tradition. Shows normally begin after sunset and continue late into the night, testifying to the enormous popularity of this form with large sections of the population, whose lives resonate deeply with the social and *political content of the performance. *See also* MANIPURI THEATRE.   SR

SHUSHERIN, YAKOV (1753–1813)

Russian actor. Beginning his career in minor roles at the Medoks Theatre in *Moscow, Shusherin transferred to *St Petersburg in 1786 where he won fame and favour both with *audiences and with Catherine the Great, in two of whose plays he appeared. Returning to Moscow in 1793, he made successful appearances in plays by *Kotzebue and *Ozerov, and as King Lear in a version by Nikolai Gnedich. A role which won him wide popularity was as a Negro slave, Xury, in Kotzebue's *The Parrot*. He also scored a great success as Oedipus in Ozerov's version.   NW

SHUTER, NED (c.1728–1776)

English actor and singer, a favourite low comedian during the mid-eighteenth century. In an age when spectators enjoyed humbling actors they considered insufficiently solicitous of favour, *audiences relished Shuter's banter and mock chastisement of them. He began acting in his early teens and quickly learned a number of comic roles, including Polonius. Throughout his career he never moved far from low comic *characters, and while he did create Hardcastle in *Goldsmith's *She Stoops to Conquer* (1773) and Sir Anthony Absolute in *Sheridan's *The Rivals* (1775), he was best loved for his occasional comic productions like *The Cries of London* and his work at *fairground booths.

MJK

SHUTTERS *See* SCENE SHIFTING.

SHVARTS, EVGENY (1896–1958)

Russian/Soviet dramatist who specialized in plays for children and 'fairy tales for adults'. His first play, *Underwood* (1929), is about a witch who steals a typewriter but who is brought to book by a Young Pioneer. His most important plays were based on the stories of Hans Christian Andersen—*Little Red Riding Hood* (1937), *The Snow Queen* (1938), *The Shadow* (1940), and *The Naked King* (1938, staged 1960). His best-known work is probably *The Dragon*, first directed by Nikolai *Akimov in 1944, now seen as a powerful *allegory of totalitarianism.

NW

SICHUAN OPERA *See* DIFANGXI.

SIDDONS, SARAH (1755–1831)

English actress. The eldest daughter of Roger *Kemble, she made an early marriage while working in her father's *family troupe. A first *London debut failed, but a second, in 1782, was a triumph. For the next 30 years Siddons was regarded as the leading tragic performer of her time, and comparison with her was the severest test any aspiring actress had to undergo. She specialized in roles which required tenderness, sorrow, indignation, remorse, resolution, and heroic dignity. When young she was acclaimed for her beauty and in later years her impressiveness was not diminished. The parts for which Siddons was famous included Isabella in *Southerne's *The Fatal Marriage*, Belvidera in *Otway's *Venice Preserv'd*, Euphrasia in Arthur *Murphy's *The Grecian Daughter*, Zara in *Congreve's *The Mourning Bride*, Lady Randolph in John *Home's *Douglas*, Calista in *Rowe's *The Fair Penitent*, and the title role in his *Jane Shore*. Her greatest Shakespearian *characters were Constance, Lady Macbeth, Volumnia, and Queen Katherine. Siddons also excelled as Mrs Beverley in Edward *Moore's prose *tragedy *The Gamester* and as Mrs Haller in *Kotzebue's *The Stranger*. In many of these roles she was partnered by her brother John Philip *Kemble. Her private life was at times unhappy but her public life off the stage was conducted with intelligence and propriety. She had unbending good manners which discouraged presumption and innate good taste which she cultivated by mingling with distinguished people from the world of arts and letters. She

loved her profession and retired from it with reluctance, causing a good deal of mirth by the number of her farewells.

FD

SIDJA, I MADE (c.1930–)

Balinese puppet master, considered the most knowledgeable living exponent of *wayang parwa*, the *shadow theatre of Bali in *Indonesia. Versed in all the traditional Balinese performing arts, including *mask dance (*topeng*) and opera (*arja*), he leads Paripurna Arts Group and is in demand for performances that are religiously motivated. In the late 1990s he collaborated with Shadowlight Theatre in *San Francisco on an experimental production titled *Sida Karya*.

KFo

SIDNEY, PHILIP (1554–86)

English poet and critic. One of the outstanding figures of the English *early modern period, Sidney wrote his *Defense of Poesy* (1583, published 1595) in answer to *anti-theatrical polemics by John Northbrooke and Stephen *Gosson. The English theatre of the time provided few models for Sidney's classically derived poetic which, filtered through Italian commentaries that fused *Aristotelian and *Horatian precepts, stressed instruction and delight, *decorum, and the dramatic *unities, mentioned in the *Defense* for the first time in English *criticism. Despite the eloquence of Sidney's argument, it had no effect on Elizabethan practice.

RWV

SIERRA, GREGORIO MARTÍNEZ *See* MARTÍNEZ SIERRA, GREGORIO.

SIEVEKING, ALEJANDRO (1935–)

Chilean playwright, actor, and director. His first plays were psychological in nature, such as *Mi hermano Cristián* (*My Brother Christian*, 1957) and *Los hermanastros* (*The Stepbrothers*, 1960). Thereafter he turned to Chilean tradition, myths, and *folklore, and avoided the conventions of *naturalism. In this category are *Animas de día claro* (*Spirits by Daylight*, 1962) and the well-received *melodrama *La remolienda* (*The Rave*, 1965). *Todo se irá, se fue, se va al diablo* (*Everything Will Go, Has Gone, Is Going to the Dogs*, 1968), an incisive *satire of the upper middle class, was hailed by the *critics for its original stage setting. He and the Teatro del Ángel, a group he created with his wife Bélgica Castro, remained in political exile in Costa Rica from 1974 to 1984.

MAR

SILVA, ANTÓNIO JOSÉ DA (1705–39)

Portuguese playwright. Born in Rio de Janeiro, he grew up and studied in *Lisbon during the reign of D. João V (1707–50), the heyday of the Portuguese baroque. Known as the Jew (he was a

'New Christian' through enforced conversion), his was a short literary career: imprisoned in 1726, he suffered with the whole of his family the heavy rigour of the Inquisition and was finally condemned and burned at the stake (*see* EXECUTIONS, PUBLIC). Between 1733 and 1738 he wrote eight *tragicomic *operas: *Don Quixote, The Life of Aesop, The Wars between Rosemary and Marjoram, Medea's Charms, Metamorphoses of Proteus, Phaeton's Fall, Amphitryon,* and *Crete's Labyrinth.* A high point in the history of Portuguese playwriting, his work is the national model of *neoclassical drama, resulting from a cross-fertilization of Spanish and Italian influences, appropriating themes with wide European currency. He combined borrowed motifs with topical references to Portuguese culture and society that could easily be grasped by the popular *audiences at the theatre in Bairro Alto, where his plays were performed by *puppets (*bonifrates*). His work was rediscovered in the early twentieth century, though infrequently performed until the 1960s.

JOB

SIM, ALASTAIR (1900–76)

Scottish actor and director. His eccentric and sometimes lugubrious style, mixing pathos and irony with subtlety and assurance, was particularly suited to James *Bridie's morally ambiguous *characters such as the eponymous *Dr Angelus* (1947). Beginning his career as late as 1930, when he appeared as the Messenger in *Othello*, he progressed swiftly to Banquo in 1932 and two seasons with the *Old Vic in *London. In parallel with his *film career he was a West End regular, making frequent appearances as Hook in *Peter Pan*, where his ability to convey irascible foolishness, bemused humiliation, and wheedling and malicious *villainy was particularly appropriate. Later in life he appeared in critically acclaimed seasons at *Chichester. His film roles include Inspector Cockerill in *Green for Danger* (1946), the headmaster pitched against Margaret Rutherford in *The Happiest Days of your Life* (1950), Scrooge in *A Christmas Carol* (1951), and Miss Fritton in *The Belles of St Trinian's* (1954).

AS

SIMON, BARNEY (1933–95)

South African director and playwright. In the 1970s Simon worked in Zululand and the Transkei running workshops. With Mannie *Manim he formed the Company and the *Market Theatre, which opened in 1976 with Simon as *artistic director. Shaped by the workshop process, his collaborative plays include *Hey Listen!* (1974, adapted from his *Jo'burg, Sis!* stories), *Cincinnati* (1979), *Woza Albert!* (1981, with Percy *Mtwa and Mbongeni *Ngema), *Black Dog/Inj'emnyama* (1984), *Outers* (1985), *Born in the RSA* (1985), *Score Me the Ages* (1989), and *Silent Movie* (1992). Influenced by Joan *Littlewood, Athol *Fugard, and his own experiences in America in the 1960s, Simon's

plays focus on the experience of the individual and the restoration of dignity for those on the social margins.

YH

SIMON, JOHN (1925–)

American arts critic. Yugoslavian-born Simon has written *criticism for *New York Magazine* since 1969. He was also drama critic for the *Hudson Review* (1960–81) and *film critic for *Esquire* (1973–5). Proudly politically incorrect about the theatre, Simon often disparages actresses' looks and *auteur* *directing like that of Peter *Sellars. He believes theatre should have intellectual substance, and his own writing is sharply entertaining and discerning. Notoriously hard to please, Simon thinks a critic should have a vision of the theatre, be open but not too flexible, and promote theatre's literary as well as performance values. His books include *Singularities: essays on the theatre* (1976) and *Dreamers of Dreams* (2001).

GAO

SIMON, NEIL (1927–)

American playwright and screenwriter. Simon's many Broadway hits and screenplays have made him one of the most successful playwrights of all time. Until his autobiographical trilogy (*Brighton Beach Memoirs*, 1983; *Biloxi Blues*, 1985, *film, 1988; *Broadway Bound*, 1986) *critics often dismissed his plays as glib domestic *comedies that substituted one-liners for *character development. *Lost in Yonkers* (Tony and Pulitzer, 1991), dealing with abandonment as well as love, proved Simon could use his comic sensibility to serve a painful story as well as smooth it out.

Simon began his career as part of a comedy-writing team with his brother Danny for several *television *variety shows (including the *Phil Silvers Show*, 1958–9, and Sid Caesar's *Show of Shows*, 1957–8), experiences that encouraged quick gags and stock situations. His first Broadway play, with brother Danny, was *Catch a Star!* (1955), and *Come Blow your Horn* (1961) was his first original Broadway play. *Barefoot in the Park* (1964; film, 1967), about a newly-wed free spirit and her conservative husband, typifies Simon's motifs of attraction and compromise, as well as quirky characters and *New York settings. *The Odd Couple* (1965), about two divorced men attempting to room together, one messy, one neat, was later filmed (1968) and became a long-running television series. Other hits include *Plaza Suite* (1968; film, 1971), *The Prisoner of Second Avenue* (1972; film, 1974), and *The Sunshine Boys* (1972; film, 1975). Simon also wrote the *books for *Sweet Charity* (1966; film, 1969) and *Promises, Promises* (1967).

The death of his first wife in 1973 led to attention to serious issues in his work. *The Gingerbread Lady* (1970) had portrayed an alcoholic actress, but it was *Chapter Two* (1977; film, 1978), about a widower's sudden remarriage, based on his own remarriage to actress Marsha Mason, that impressed critics as an honest exploration of pain. Mason starred in that and many other of his works, including the film *The Goodbye Girl* (1977; Broadway *musical, 1993). Simon's adaptations include *Fools* (1981), based on Sholem *Aleichem's tales, and *God's Favorite* (1976), a modern-day retelling of the Book of Job; both received mixed reviews. Simon increasingly experimented with style and darker themes: *Jake's Women* (1992) attempts *surreal stream-of-consciousness; *Laughter on the 23rd Floor* (1993), recalling his days writing for Sid Caesar, is a comedy addressing McCarthyism. *Proposals* (1997), unusually opening *Off-Broadway, is a nostalgic romance narrated by a black maid, while *The Dinner Party* (2000) is an attempt at a *farce that turns serious. Simon has written two volumes of autobiography, *Rewrites* (1996) and *The Play Goes On* (1999). Now the author of 31 plays, as early as 1975 he received a special Tony *award for lifetime contribution to the theatre, and in 1983 he became the only living playwright with a New York theatre named after him.   GAO

SIMONOV, KONSTANTIN (1915–79)

Russian/Soviet dramatist, novelist, and poet who came to prominence during the Second World War. Among a dozen or so plays his best known outside Russia is *The Russian People* (1941), a sequel to his Stalin Prize play *A Lad from our Town* (1940), and set in a Russian town under German occupation. The play was adapted by Clifford *Odets for an American production, and by Tyrone *Guthrie as *The Russians*, staged at *Old Vic in *London (1943). *The Russian Question* (1946) has a *New York setting and presents the Soviet view of the emerging Cold War conflict.   NW

SIMONOV, RUBEN (1899–1968)

Russian/Soviet actor and director who became head of the Vakhtangov Theatre in 1939. Prior to this he had worked as an actor, appearing in *Vakhtangov's own productions of *The Miracle of St Anthony* (1921) and *Princess Turandot* (1922). Excelling in *comedy, Simonov was a notable Benedick in *Much Ado About Nothing* (1936), and a grotesque Claudius in *Akimov's *expressionistic *Hamlet* (1932). He also starred as the spirited gangster Captain Kostya in an experimental production of *Pogodin's *Aristocrats* (1935), and as Cyrano de Bergerac (1942), both directed by *Okhlopkov. His directorial career was solid, but less distinguished in comparison.   NW

SIMONSON, LEE (1888–1967)

American designer. After studying with George Pierce *Baker at Harvard, Simonson's first professional set designs were for the *Washington Square Players in *New York. After service in the First World War, he helped found and direct the *Theatre Guild, for which he created many of the most important designs of the

1920s, including *RUR* (1922), *Peer Gynt* (1923), *The Adding Machine* (1923), *Marco Millions* (1928), *Roar China* (1930), and *Dynamo* (1930). He also designed for *opera, including *Wagner's *Ring* cycle and Stravinsky's *Le Pas d'acier* at the *Metropolitan Opera in the 1940s. Simonson garnered early praise for his ability to create effective *scenery across a range of styles from *realism and *naturalism to *expressionism and *constructivism. Often compared with Robert Edmond *Jones and Samuel *Hume, Simonson's designs were associated with the 'New Stagecraft' movement. He clarified his own vision for *scenography in a number of books. *The Stage Is Set* (1932) distanced him from the *theories of *Craig while championing many practical applications of *modernist design. His autobiography, *Part of a Lifetime* (1943), is an important document of the American theatre of the 1920s and 1930s. He also wrote an influential primer entitled *The Art of Scene Design* (1950).   JAB

SIMOV, VIKTOR (1858–1935)

Russian designer. After graduating from the Moscow Institute of Painting, Sculpture, and Architecture in 1882, Simov worked as an artist and architect. He designed sets for Savva *Mamontov's private *opera and *ballet company, and for the Society for Art and Literature, before joining the *Moscow Art Theatre at its inception in 1898. He remained chief designer until 1912, when he joined the Svobodny (Free) Theatre set up by Konstantin *Mardzhanov, but returned to MAT in 1925 and remained until his death. Simov was responsible for the designs of many key MAT productions such as Aleksei *Tolstoy's *Tsar Fyodor Ioannovich* (1898) and the four groundbreaking *Chekhov productions (1898–1904). Working closely with *Stanislavsky, he initiated the practice of field research, visiting a *Moscow dosshouse for *Gorky's *The Lower Depths* (1902) and Rome for *Julius Caesar* (1903). Simov brought three-dimensional *realism and historical and location accuracy to Russian stage *design, contributing much to the MAT reputation for authenticity.

CM

SINAKULO

A theatrical rendition of the life, death, and resurrection of Jesus Christ performed annually during Holy Week in lowland *Philippines, especially in provinces around Manila, and (under alternative names) in the region of Bicol, the town of Iloilo, and the island of Leyte. Traditional *sinakulo* is staged over eight nights (Palm Sunday to Easter Sunday). Abridged versions, which start in the Garden of Gethsemane and culminate with the Crucifixion, take place on Good Friday, often in a church plaza. Stylized forms of chanting, marching, and *acting distinguish holy *characters (*banal*), notably Jesus and the Virgin Mary, from the evil *hudyo* (soldiers) and *hari* (Herod, Pilate). Participation in the *sinakulo* is a form of *religious devotion and sacrifice, involving a vow (*panata*), pledged as supplication or thanksgiving. The first *sinakulo* followed publication in 1704 of the *pasyon*, a vernacular narrative in *verse of the life of Christ by Gaspar Aquino de Belen, although a revised version, the *Pasyong Genesis* (1814), proved more influential. The traditional *Passion play declined after independence in 1946, but successfully evolved in the last two decades of the twentieth century. The inclusion of corporeal self-mortification (*ritual self-flagellation and crucifixion) both attracted and distracted *audiences, while in Manila political *sinakulos* emerged as a form of social activism.   NHB

SINDEN, DONALD (1923–)

English actor, celebrated and *parodied in equal measure for his distinctive and rather plummy vocal quality. He joined the *Shakespeare Memorial Theatre company in 1946, was later with the *Bristol Old Vic and from 1963 the *Royal Shakespeare Company. An assured and sophisticated actor, Sinden has been particularly successful in high *comedy: he was a definitive Lord Foppington in *The Relapse* (1967) and Sir Peter Teazle in *The School for Scandal* (1983). His darker roles include Romeo (1947), and for the RSC, Richard Plantagenet in *The Wars of the Roses* (1963), Malvolio in *Twelfth Night* (1969), Lear (1977), and Othello (1979). In the modern repertoire he appeared at *Chichester in *Rattigan's *In Praise of Love* (1973), Stockman in *Ibsen's *An Enemy of the People* (1975), and the Duke of Altair in Christopher *Fry's *Venus Observed* (1992). More recently he was with Peter *Hall's company in *She Stoops to Conquer* (1993) and *Hamlet* (1998) and in the première of Ronald *Harwood's elegy on ageing, *Quartet* (1999).   AS

SINGAPORE

With the close of the colonial era in 1963, the performing arts were limited to a small number of *amateur groups vying for limited resources. Expatriate players continued to present *London hits, but Singaporean groups in the main language groups (English, Chinese, Malay, and Tamil) gradually expanded to fill the vacuum. Malay theatre, centred in Singapore prior to separation from Malaysia in 1965, was sustained at a less active level. Modern Chinese theatre, developed in the 1950s by the Singapore Amateur Players, found itself under intense government surveillance during and after the Chinese Cultural Revolution (1966–76). Playwright-director Kuo Pao Kun exerted an important influence before his detention with other leftists in 1976.

The nation's rise to 'First World' economic status in the 1980s influenced a burgeoning of performance, underpinned by government sponsorship. Significant writers and directors include Lim Chor Pee, Goh Poh Seng, Stella Kon, Robert Yeo, Max Le Blond, Haresh Sharma, Alvin Tan, Elangovan, and Malaysians, Krishen Jit, and Leow Puay Tin. *Intercultural theatre has found expression in productions by the Singapore Repertory Theatre, Action Theatre, TheatreWorks, the Theatre Practice, Theatre Ox, and the Asia-in-Theatre Research Centre, among others. In particular, *Ong Keng Sen's Flying Circus Project (TheatreWorks) and Kuo Pao Kun's Theatre Training and Research Programme (Practice Performing Arts School) have sponsored an influx of regional traditional performance. The earlier Mandarin theatre trend of using theatre to debate local social issues has been continued by the Necessary Stage (TNS), Drama Box, and Agni Kootthu.

*Performance art also gained a foothold in Singapore, primarily among visual artists involved with the Artists' Village group (1988). Tang Da Wu, Cheo Chai-Hiang, Vincent Leow, Lee Wen, Amanda Heng, Chandrasekaran, Jason Lim, and Noor Effendy Ibrahim have produced significant work. Performance art has become one of the most dynamic of cultural fields, and its influence in Singapore theatre and *dance and movement can be seen in TheatreWorks, Zai Kuning's Metabolic Laboratory, Teatre Ekamatra, and Jeff Chen's productions with TNS. Lim Tzay Chuen, Matthew Ngui, and Suzann Victor have explored the performative edge of environmental installation and a new generation of Artists' Village has been exploring curatorship as performance. In 1994, Josef Ng performed *Brother Cane*, a work critical of the legal persecution and caning of homosexual men. Sensationalist press coverage provided the government with an opportunity to proscribe not only performance art but also Augusto *Boal's forum theatre (*see* OPPRESSED, THEATRE OF THE), as deployed by TNS. This suppression echoed the earlier 'Marxist conspiracy' crackdown on Third Stage in 1987 and Chinese-language theatre during the 1970s. Continued government pressures for normative worker 'performance' on the job, to sustain a 'performance edge' over economic rivals, have accompanied tight regulation of participatory theatre, ethnic, religious, sexual, and political themes. But the emergence of an educated, Internet-savvy middle class, with higher expectations of democratic enfranchisement, can be expected to lead to increasing cultural liberalization. *See also* CENSORSHIP.   WRL

KRISHNAN, SANJAY (ed.), *Nine Lives: ten years of Singapore theatre, 1987–1997* (Singapore, 1997)

SINGSPIEL

'Song play', a popular form of *musical drama in the second half of the eighteenth century in Germany, is distinguished from *opera, mainly because the *dialogue is spoken not sung. *Singspiele* have a light touch, tuneful songs, often about love, in a bucolic or magic setting. *Goethe wrote a number of them, staged by the *amateur theatre at the *Weimar court, sometimes in the *open air. The highest achievements of the *genre were *Mozart's *Abduction from the Seraglio* (1782) and *The Magic Flute* (1791). The nineteenth-century *operetta and *mélodrame reveal the influence of the *Singspiel*.   MWP

SINISE, GARY (1955–)

American actor. He co-founded the *Steppenwolf Theatre Company in *Chicago in 1974 and directed its 1982 *New York debut, *Shepard's *True West*, featuring himself and John *Malkovich as the warring brothers. He made his *film debut with *A Midnight Clear* (1991), then produced, directed, and played George in a film version of *Of Mice and Men* (1992); subsequent film roles include Lieutenant Dan in *Forrest Gump* (1994) and Ken Mattingly in *Apollo 13* (1994). His *television credits include Tom Joad in *The Grapes of Wrath* (1991) and the title roles in *Truman* (1995) and *George Wallace* (1997). He returned to Steppenwolf to play Stanley in *A Streetcar Named Desire* (1997) and McMurphy in their Broadway production of *One Flew over the Cuckoo's Nest* (2001).   JDM

SIRCAR, BADAL (1925–)

Bengali director, dramatist, and actor. Trained as a civil engineer, Sircar started writing *comedies in his leisure time. In 1962 he composed the *absurdist *Evam Indrajit*, about identity and conformity in the metropolitan jungle; published and staged in 1965, it created a sensation across *India and was translated into many Indian languages. Meanwhile Sircar had gone on official work to Nigeria (1964–7), where he wrote a string of plays, including *Baki Itihas* (*Remaining History*), *Tringsa Satabdi* (*Thirtieth Century*), and *Pagla Ghora* (*Mad Horse*), which highlight existential meaninglessness in an inhuman world. On returning to Calcutta (*Kolkata) he started his own group, called Satabdi, and soon was experimenting with a form of theatre-in-the-round which he called 'Third Theatre'—as opposed to the urban and rural varieties. In 1973 he finally rejected the *proscenium, dramatizing Howard Fast's novel *Spartacus* in a bare room with the *audience seated in clusters on the floor. His original scripts for this flexible theatre included *Michhil* (*Procession*, 1974), *Bhoma* (1976), and *Basi Khabar* (*Stale News*, 1979). He often theatricalized real-life incidents, sometimes the specific experiences of peasants. His plays are characterized by socially conscious themes, a wry sense of humour, pithy *dialogue, and simple, direct language which attains an aphoristic, even poetic quality.

In 1977 Sircar resigned his job to devote himself entirely to theatre and write an important book on his work (*The Third Theatre*, 1978). Satabdi presented his plays both indoors and outdoors in Calcutta parks and in villages where theatre had never been seen. He attempted to break the divide between actor and spectator and to arouse socio-political awareness, often through one-hour performances with minimal theatrical trappings. Sircar's commitment and workshops created many Third Theatre disciples all over India. For the first time in *Bengali theatre, a troupe was *touring Bengal's villages and liberating theatre from a *box-office economy. Despite Sircar's influence and international recognition, however, his brand of theatre continues to be thought marginal by Calcutta's mainstream groups. On the other hand, Third Theatre must reinvent itself in order to regain some of the subversive edge that it has lost through repetitive devices.   AL

SISSLE, NOBLE (1889–1975)

*African-American performer who teamed with Eubie *Blake in 1915 and helped revolutionize *musical comedy. They met in Baltimore playing in a band, formed a *vaudeville team called the Dixie Duo, and created an all-black Broadway musical in 1921, *Shuffle Along*, a show so popular it stopped traffic outside the theatre. Blacks and whites shared their amusement in public together. Sissle, who played one of the lead roles, had an eye for talent: he recommended Josephine *Baker for the *chorus line and Florence *Mills was added to the show on his advice. With Blake he wrote *The Chocolate Dandies* (1924) and reincarnations of *Shuffle Along* in 1932 and 1952. Sissle was one of the founding members of the Negro Actors' Guild in the 1930s, and served as its first president.   BBL

SISTREN

Jamaican women's *collective, founded in 1977. Designed to create *improvisatory theatre with a group of working-class women in the Manley government's emergency employment programme, Sistren was a part of the vibrant *Caribbean women's movement of the 1970s and 1980s (*see* FEMINISM). Its work, usually directed by Honor Ford-Smith, was based on oral histories of the women participants, and dealt also with broad social issues such as *gender, violence, sexuality, family roles, poverty, and women's work and education. Ford-Smith's edition of the life stories of Sistren members, *Lionheart Gal* (1986), records what she calls 'the gamut of language used in Jamaican society and its relationship to class'. The company's best-known work was *Bellywoman Bangarang* (1978); other notable plays include *QPH* (1981) and *Domestick* (1982).   ES

SJÖBERG, ALF (1903–80)

Swedish actor and director. Despite numerous offers to direct theatre and *films internationally, Sjöberg rarely worked outside the Royal Dramatic Theatre in *Stockholm. In his more than 50-year tenure at *Dramaten, he was lauded for visually evocative productions of *Ibsen, *Strindberg, and contemporary writers, and his innovative modern Shakespeare productions created a new tradition for playing the classics. His *directing was always vital, often poetic, and frequently committed to social issues. Sjöberg strove to balance a keen inner *realism with a richer outer visual image: he treated *audiences to stunning visual compositions and a fluid, rhythmic pacing of ensemble and *text. He introduced the contemporary international repertory to Sweden, the foremost being the work of *Brecht and *Sartre, but extending to new writers from South Africa, *Latin America, and Eastern Europe. His film version of Strindberg's *Miss Julie* won a Palme d'Or at Cannes in 1951.　　DLF

SKARMETA, ANTONIO (1940–)

Chilean dramatist, novelist, and *film director who played an important intellectual and artistic role in the Allende government. He lived in exile in Germany from 1975 to 1989, where he participated in an international movement opposing the military regime in Chile. In 1983 his play *Ardiente paciencia* (*Burning Patience*) was performed with great success in Europe, and in 1986 was staged in Chile by El *Nuevo Grupo under the direction of Héctor *Noguera. It was translated into Basque for the group Masakarada (1998), and has been twice adapted for film.
　　MAR

SKELTON, JOHN (c.1464–1529)

English poet and dramatist. Skelton's only drama, *Magnificence* (1515–16), is a *morality play in which the *allegorized Magnificence is brought to ruin and despair through the bad advice of evil counsellors, but is ultimately restored to a wiser though less opulent happiness by good counsellors. The language is commendable; the characterization, structure, and thematic focus less so. *Magnificence* seems to reflect the necessity of *doubling (the eighteen *characters could be played by five *actors), and there are over 50 *stage directions in English and Latin; but we know nothing of an original performance.　　RWV

SKENE

Originally Greek 'hut', meaning the simple building before which ancient *Greek drama was performed. The early addition of a *proskenion*, the low construction supporting the stage 'before the hut', and accessible by a short wooden stair from the *orchestra, created a true stage building. The classical theatre of 400 BC (Theatre of *Dionysus) could use the roof as well as the stage and orchestra levels simultaneously with machinery (especially the *ekkyklema and *mechane), and had the capacity to simulate effects such as fire and thunder. Though one door was perhaps usual, it could be converted quickly to a cave and other doors or windows could be created if required. Projecting wings enclosing the stage, found after 330 BC, are thus *paraskenia* ('things beside the *skene*') even though they may be only access doorways. About 300 BC the classical stage proper was raised to c. 2.5 m (8 feet), with access from below only from the sides, and a *proskenion* was thereby created with a pillared façade into which flats (*pinakes*) were fitted. This required that the entire building then be raised to two storeys, with the upper façade also consisting of pillared openings with *paraskenia*. The term *skene* (Latin *scaena*) never applied to the seating area.
　　WJS

SKINNER, CORNELIA OTIS (1901–79)

American actress and playwright. The daughter of actors Maud and Otis *Skinner, she was best known for the *one-person evenings of *character sketches and *monologues which she created and performed in *New York, *London, and on *tour between 1925 and 1961. Of her plays, *The Pleasure of his Company* (with Samuel Taylor, 1958) was most successful, and her memoir, *Our Hearts Were Young and Gay* (with Emily Kimbrough, 1942), became a popular 1944 *film. Among her one-woman creations were *The Wives of Henry VIII* (1931), *The Loves of Charles II* (1933), *Mansion on the Hudson* (1935), and *Paris '90* (1952). Also a respected character actress in plays, Skinner appeared in Broadway productions which included Lillian *Hellman's *The Searching Wind* (1944), *Wilde's *Lady Windermere's Fan* (1946), and as Lady Britomart in *Shaw's *Major Barbara* (1956).
　　MAF

SKINNER, OTIS (1858–1942)

American actor. Born in Cambridge, Massachusetts, he gained his early experience with a *Philadelphia troupe in which he played 92 roles in his first season (1877–8). Following his *New York debut in 1879, he had important supporting roles with major companies, eventually heading his own *touring troupe from 1894. A rather flamboyant actor, he scored a success with the blustering ex-soldier in *The Honor of the Family* (1908), and his greatest triumph as the beggar Hajj in *Kismet* (1911), which he played for four years. After some 325 roles, his Broadway valedictory came in *A Hundred Years Old* (1929). He published an autobiography, *Footlights and Spotlights* (1924). His daughter was the actress Cornelia Otis *Skinner.　　CT

SLABOLEPSZY, PAUL (1948–)

South African actor and playwright, born in England to an English mother and Polish refugee father who emigrated to Pietersburg when Paul was 3 years old. After study at the University of *Cape Town, he founded the Space Theatre in 1972 with Athol *Fugard, Yvonne *Bryceland, and her husband Brian Astbury. Later he joined the Company at the *Market Theatre in *Johannesburg. His plays include *Saturday Night at the Palace* (Market, 1982), *Over the Hill* (*Grahamstown Festival, 1985), *Boo to the Moon* (1987), *Fordsburg's Finest* (Market, 1988); *Smallholding* (1989), *Mooi Street Moves* (Grahamstown Festival, Market Theatre, 1992), *The Return of Elvis du Pisanie* (1992, which won more *awards than any other production in the history of South African theatre), *Victoria Almost Falls* (1994), and *Life's a Pitch*

(2001). His work focuses on the dreams, unease, and insularity of the lower-middle-class white male in South Africa.   YH

SLAPSTICK

Literally a *prop paddle used for meting out punishment in *music hall or *vaudeville, but more generally a term embracing exaggerated or knockabout comedy and its stylistic features. The slapstick derives from Arlecchino's *batocchio* and *Harlequin's *batte* in *commedia dell'arte*. Its two slats of wood hinged together at one end make a sharp crack upon contact with, for example, a victim's posterior. The brand of physical, comic extravagance conjured by the slapstick label can be traced to ancient Western *comedy and seen in other cultures—for example, a comparable comic weapon is described in accounts of thirteenth-century Chinese variety plays (*zaju*).   EW

SLAVKIN, VIKTOR (1935–)

Soviet/Russian playwright. Slavkin's plays offered genuinely new themes (the subculture of stagnation) in a collage of various sources new to the theatre. *A Young Man's Grown-up Daughter* (1979) deals with the meeting of old university friends, who were once jazz fans and 'teddy boys'. *Cerceau* (1985) uses a collage of texts to treat the midlife crisis of a group of 40-year-olds, who lead lives of tragic isolation and cannot share feelings. At the end they see a glimpse of hope in the possibility of living together, yet at this point they all leave.   BB

SŁOWACKI, JULIUSZ (1809–49)

Polish poet and playwright. Like *Mickiewicz, Słowacki was educated in *Vilnius, lived in *Warsaw, and eventually settled in *Paris. He wrote some fifteen plays indebted to Shakespeare and the *romantic movement, with subjects that range from legendary Poland (*Balladyna, Lilla Weneda, Mindowe*) to Polish and European *history (*Samuel Zborowski, The Golden Skull, Mazepa, Beatrix Cenci, Mary Stuart*) to the 1830s and 1840s (*Kordian, Fantasy*). They offer rich, complex, and imaginative material for spectacular stagings and excellent roles for actors. Prohibited by the *censor in the early nineteenth century, Słowacki's dramas were gradually mounted in Poland after 1851, though *Kordian*, his most politically explosive play, a biography of a romantic *hero who plots the assassination of the Russian Tsar, had to wait until the end of the century for production (*Cracow, 1899). Thereafter Słowacki's works became part of the Polish national repertoire, regularly encountered by major directors (including Leon *Schiller) and performed by famous actors. *The Constant Prince*, based on *Calderón, was notably directed and acted by Juliusz Osterwa, who treated it as a *morality play in an *open-air *spectacle with dozens of extras on horseback (Vilnius, 1926, and *tours all over Poland). Jerzy

*Grotowski's condensed 'poor theatre' study, with Ryszard *Cieślak in the lead, which forced the *audience to peer on the events as if at a *ritual or in an operating theatre, is considered one of the finest achievements of the *Polish Laboratory Theatre (Wrocław, 1965).   KB

SLY, WILLIAM (fl. 1590–1608)

English actor. Sly performed with *Strange's Men or the Lord *Admiral's Men when he played two roles (Porrex, and a lord) in *Tarlton's *The Seven Deadly Sins, Part II*. From around 1598 until his death he performed with the *Chamberlain's Men. He is listed amongst the cast members for three of *Jonson's plays (*Sejanus, Every Man in his Humour*, and *Every Man out of his Humour*), although the roles he took are unknown, and his name also appears in the list of 'principall actors' in the First Folio of Shakespeare's plays (1623). Sly was on the King's Livery list in 1604, and four years later bequeathed to actor Robert *Browne his share in the *Globe.   SPC

SMITH, ALBERT (1816–60)

English performer and writer who began his career as a journalist, contributor to *Punch*, and author of theatrical extravaganzas. His 1850 performance *The Overland Mail* initiated a series of humorous travelogues that included panoramas, songs, and *special effects. Smith's second production, *The Ascent of Mt Blanc* (1852), was one of the most successful theatrical events of its time, running for over 2,000 performances at the Egyptian Hall in *London. It provided a fast-paced, ironic account of Alpine travel that exploited contemporary interest in that region. Smith further developed the genre in *Mt Blanc to China* (1858).   SF

SMITH, ANNA DEAVERE (1950–)

*African-American actor and playwright. In the late 1970s, through experiments with re-enacting recorded interviews as an *acting exercise, she developed a unique form of *documentary theatre that combines mimicry, journalism, and oral history. She created solo performance pieces that portrayed a real-life community or conflict by interviewing dozens of people, editing the interviews, and then performing them verbatim as a series of *character sketches, retaining the subject's speech patterns and vocal intonations. Two pieces in particular earned nationwide acclaim and made Smith a major cultural figure. *Fires in the Mirror: Crown Heights, Brooklyn and Other Identities* (1992) depicted 26 people connected to *racial disturbances that erupted between blacks and Jews in a *New York neighbourhood in 1991. In a similar vein, *Twilight: Los Angeles, 1992* (1993) investigated the explosive aftermath of the Rodney King verdict. In each piece, the strategic juxtaposition of numerous voices and the virtuosity of Smith's chameleonic performance yielded a powerful portrait of racial identity in the USA. In *House Arrest* (1997), first staged with a cast of fifteen before reverting to a solo piece, Smith broadened her focus to examine the US presidency and the media, with less success. For three summers at Harvard (1998–2000), with major funding from the Ford Foundation, Smith ran the Institute on the Arts and Civic Dialogue, which gathered artists, scholars, and a 'core *audience' to explore how art and performance can shape and promote social discourse between disparate communities. Smith has appeared in the *films *Dave*, *Philadelphia* (both 1993), and *The American President* (1995) and the *television series *The Practice* and *The West Wing*.   STC

SMITH, DODIE (1896–1990)

English playwright, screenwriter, novelist, and actress. Smith is well known as the author of the children's novel *The Hundred and One Dalmations* (1956), but had been a very successful playwright in the 1930s. After *training as an actress at the *Royal Academy of Dramatic Art, she wrote a series of popular plays under the alias of C. L. Anthony, beginning with *Autumn Crocus* (1931, starring Jessica *Tandy), followed by *Service* (1931), *Touch Wood* (1934), and *Call It a Day* (1935). Abandoning the pseudonym, *Dear Octopus* (1938), her most successful play, featured Marie *Tempest and John *Gielgud in *London, Lillian *Gish in *New York. It typifies her finely crafted structure, sensitive female *characters, and preference for domestic settings—the 'octopus' of the title is the loving, sometimes suffocating, embrace of family. She lived in the United States during the Second World War, where she wrote screenplays (*The Uninvited*, 1944) and the novel *I Capture the Castle* (1949), subsequently turned into a play (1954). Late in life she wrote four volumes of autobiography.   GAO

SMITH, JOE (1884–1981) AND CHARLIE DALE (1881–1971)

American *vaudeville team. *New York was the birthplace of both Smith (Joseph Sultzer) and Dale (Charles Marks). The two boys met in 1898 when their rented bicycles collided. Their comic squabbling so convulsed the owner that he said they reminded him of *Weber and Fields and urged them to become friends. Sharing an interest in singing and dancing, they at once began a partnership that lasted for 73 years until the elder's death. Working in a restaurant kitchen by day, the pair began performing in bars at night. For a few cents they bought some misprinted business cards, and thus Sultzer and Marks became Smith and Dale in 1900. The first classic sketch they developed was 'The Schoolroom'. But their most popular skit, introduced in 1906, was 'Dr. Kronkhite', in which the tall, moustachioed

Smith was the patient, and the smaller Dale the Yiddish-flavoured doctor who said, 'Take off dee coat, my boy'. This became the most performed comedy act of all time, and was still regaling *audiences 60 years later.   CT

SMITH, MAGGIE (1934–   )

English actress who started her career as Viola for the Oxford University Dramatic Society in 1952. She made her *New York debut in the *New Faces of 56 Revue* (1956), and her *London debut the next year with *Share my Lettuce* with Kenneth Williams. She was a member of the *Old Vic company in 1959–60, appearing as Lady Pliant in *Congreve's *The Double-Dealer*, Celia, the Queen in *Richard II*, and Maggie Wylie in *Barrie's *What Every Woman Knows*. In 1963 she joined the *National Theatre to play Desdemona to *Olivier's Othello. Subsequent roles included Hilde Wangel, Myra in *Hay Fever*, Beatrice, and Miss Julie. She was already recognized as a talented comedienne and dramatic actress specializing in eccentric English women of a certain age when she won her first Oscar for the *film *The Prime of Miss Jean Brodie* (1968). In the 1970s she was a regular at the *Stratford Festival in Canada, appearing as Cleopatra, Millamant, and Lady Macbeth (all 1976), Titania, Hippolyta, Judith Bliss, and Rosalind (1977). Later stage work includes *Virginia* (1980), *Lettice and Lovage* (1987), and Lady Bracknell in *The Importance of Being Earnest* (1993). She received a further Oscar for her role in *California Suite* (1977). Among her numerous *television roles, her appearance in Alan *Bennett's *Talking Heads* (1989) was exceptional. In 1989 she was made DBE.   AS

SMITH, OLIVER (1918–94)

American designer and *producer. In a career that lasted half a century, he designed *scenery for more than 400 shows, many of which he also produced or co-produced. His early work emphasized *ballet—*Saratoga* (1941), *Rodeo* (1942), *Fancy Free* (1944)—but he soon added straight plays, *operas, and big Broadway *musicals. He won eight Tony *awards: *My Fair Lady* (1956), *West Side Story* (1957), *The Sound of Music* (1959), *Becket* (1960), *Camelot* (1960), *Hello, Dolly!* (1964), *Baker Street* (1965), and a special 1965 Tony for sustained achievement. He also won four Donaldson awards (1947–52), four New York Drama Critics' awards (1956–60), the Sam S. Shubert award for distinguished contributions to the theatre (1960), and New York City's Handel Medallion for the arts (1975). He was co-director of the American Ballet Theatre (1945–80).   CT

SMITH, SOL (1801–69)

American *actor-manager. A pioneering *manager on the United States frontier for some 40 years, Smith apprenticed with the

*Drake Company along the Ohio River and into Kentucky before organizing his own troupe in 1823. He joined Noah *Ludlow in a management partnership in 1835, which dominated the theatrical scene in St Louis until 1853, controlled the theatre in Mobile, Alabama, until 1840, and in the mid-1830s challenged the major producer in New Orleans, James *Caldwell, eventually forcing him into bankruptcy. Ludlow and Smith produced a wide range of popular *melodrama, classic drama, and *musical entertainments for their circuit of theatres along the Mississippi, often importing major actors, singers, and dancers. Although Smith's early career took place under frequently wretched conditions, at their height his theatres in New Orleans and St Louis compared favourably with major theatrical centres on the East Coast. The joint management of Ludlow and Smith collapsed over a financial quarrel. Smith's memoirs, published shortly before his death, are an invaluable source for theatre on the American frontier, and reflect his genial personality.

AW

SMITH, WILLIAM H. (1806–72)

English and American actor, *manager, and playwright. Smith came to the United States in 1827, acted in *Philadelphia and *Boston, and managed the stage company of the *Boston Museum in the 1840s. He attracted Bostonians of all classes to the theatre with a mix of Shakespeare, *melodrama, and sentimental *comedy, featuring guest stars such as Edwin *Booth, Fanny *Davenport, and George Vandenhoff. Smith scored a major success with his temperance melodrama *The Drunkard* at the Boston Museum in 1844. After its 100-night initial run, it drew crowds wherever it played and was performed continually into the twentieth century.

AHK

SMITHSON, HARRIET CONSTANCE (1800–54)

Irish actress and muse. She made her *Dublin debut at 14 and her *Drury Lane debut at 17, after which she stayed in *London playing roles which required grace and beauty. She was a useful performer but not a contender for the most demanding tragic *characters. She went with an English company to *Paris in 1827 and was required to play Ophelia: she had an immense success and thereafter played leading roles including Juliet, Desdemona, and *Rowe's Jane Shore. For the first time French *audiences, accustomed to the rules of *neoclassical *tragedy, were deeply moved by Shakespeare. Miss Smithson's image was incorporated into every young poet's *romantic fantasies. An unlucky accident in 1833 lamed her and more or less ended her career. Hector Berlioz married her and paid her debts, and for a time they were happy. Her finest performances live on in his music and in pictures by Delacroix.

FD

SMOCK ALLEY THEATRE

The first Irish post-Restoration theatre was built in 1662 by John Ogilby in East Essex Street, *Dublin. At 9.4 m (31 feet) deep, its stage was smaller than the main *London theatres, but it shared their basic configuration of a large apron, *proscenium arch, *boxes, pit, and two rows of galleries. Initially, the theatre had strong links with nearby Dublin Castle, the administrative centre for British rule in Ireland, and many early actors held commissions in Castle regiments, though these ties weakened over time. Rebuilt in 1735, its *management was assumed by Thomas Sheridan in 1745. Sheridan (the father of Richard Brinsley *Sheridan) introduced a number of reforms, including banning spectators from the stage. In spite of a *riot that almost destroyed the building in 1754, Smock Alley remained among the most important theatres of the period in the British Isles, launching the careers of Thomas Sheridan, Spranger *Barry, and Peg *Woffington, among others. Competition forced its closure in 1788; the building was converted into a church, and is now used as a Viking adventure centre.

ChM

SMOKTUNOVSKY, INNOKENTY (1925–94)

Russian/Soviet actor who first came to prominence as Prince Myshkin in Georgy *Tovstonogov's production of Dostoevsky's *The Idiot* (1957), seen at the 1966 World Theatre Season in *London. He also won international acclaim as Hamlet in Kozintsev's 1964 *film, before joining the *Moscow Art Theatre a decade later. Among his many great performances, his *Chekhovian roles stand out—as Ivanov, Uncle Vanya, Dorn in *The Seagull*, and Gaev in *The Cherry Orchard*. His Vanya was seen at the Royal *National Theatre (London, 1989). An actor of outstanding temperament, he tended to subdue his charismatic personality in deference to ensemble.

NW

SOBEL, BERNARD (1936–)

French director. Strongly influenced by the *Berliner Ensemble, Sobel's early work included assisting both Benno *Besson and Jean *Vilar. With Jacques Roussillon, he founded and co-directed the Théâtre Gérard-Philipe at Saint-Denis, and in 1964 he founded the group that would become the Théâtre de Gennevilliers, which became a Centre Dramatique National under his leadership. Over those two decades and beyond, Sobel's productions of German works (by, for example, *Lessing, *Schiller, *Lenz, *Kleist, *Müller), as well as his approach to Shakespeare and *Molière, have assured his legacy as one of the most committed exponents of a *Brechtian aesthetic in France.

DGM

SOBOL, JOSHUA (1939–)

One of Israel's foremost playwrights, known for *politically provocative work. Sobol was a member of a left-wing kibbutz from 1957 to 1965, studied philosophy at the Sorbonne, and had his first play produced in 1971 by the Haifa Municipal Theatre, where he served as playwright in residence and *artistic director from 1984 to 1988. He is the author of nearly 40 plays, including *The Night of the Twenty* (1976), *The Soul of a Jew* (1982), *Ghetto* (1984), *The Palestinian* (1985), *The Jerusalem Syndrome* (1987), and *Village* (1996). His work has been produced internationally and has received prestigious *awards in Israel, Britain, and Germany.   EN

SOCIALIST REALISM

A prescriptive term for socialist artistic practice, which emerged from the First Soviet Writers' Conference in 1934, used in opposition to 'formalism'. Socialist realism required adherence to four basic principles. The first was *narodnost*, and implied that whatever an artist wrote, painted, or composed must be recognizable by or intelligible to the people (*narod*). This excluded anything elitist, abstract, *modernist, or aesthetically remote from ordinary experience. The second principle was *ideinost*, which meant that a work of art should be ideologically sound and reflect a progressive, socialist view of history and social development. The third principle, *partiinost*, required that literature serve the interests of the Communist Party; this demand was based on a probable misunderstanding of Lenin's essay 'On Party Organization and Party Literature', which was interpreted as if his edicts applied to creative literature as well. The fourth principle was *tipichnost* (typicality), and meant not what is typical of the present (which is necessarily susceptible to criticism) but what will be typical of the socialist future. Therefore every artwork needed to contain some promise of that likely future, usually an idealized version of the man or woman who will constitute it—the 'positive' *hero or heroine—who may be shown as opposed or even destroyed by negative forces, but only if coupled with the assurance that his or her virtues will eventually triumph. This last scenario can be seen, typically, in Vsevolod *Vishnevsky's classic socialist realist play *An Optimistic Tragedy*, where the self-sacrifice and eventual death of a female commissar represents triumph over the forces of anarchy and the welding together of collective forces that will construct the future in her name, and in the name of the Party. *See also* REALISM.   NW

SOCÍETAS RAFFAELLO SANZIO

Contemporary Italian *collective, named after the painter Raphael. Under the direction of Romeo Castellucci, the company has presented a series of performances whose *mise-en-scène includes the use of complex imagery, dense audio scores, technological apparatus, performing objects, *animals, and children in linguistically minimal works devised from deconstructed classic *texts. The company has gained notoriety for its use of special performers with various conditions of advanced anorexia, morbid obesity, and post-operative conditions of tracheotomy and mastectomy. Raffaello Sanzio's *Giulio Cesare* (1997) based in part on Shakespeare's *Julius Caesar*, was a performative meditation on the power of rhetoric, and *Genesi: from the Museum of Sleep* (1999), which explored the relations of creation and destruction in myth and science, included young children of company members as performers. Earlier productions of the company include *La discesa di Inanna* (*The Fall of Inanna*, 1989), *Gilgamesh* (1990), and *Masoch* (1993). The company is also active in developing children's theatre, such as *Buchettino* (2001), directed by Chiara Guidi, which attempts to mine the dangerous creativity of the child.

Castellucci has *theorized his stage work as employing an aesthetic of the 'dis-human' and the 'dis-real', which acts as an erasure of traditional constructions of human-ness and identification on stage. The stage of the dis-human incorporates non-human performers such as machines and animals, and non-traditional performers such as children and disabled adults. The supplements of the performing machine, animal, child, and the 'disabled/perfect' actor establish an aesthetic that resists *acting, metaphor, and narrative in favour of performative embodiment, metonymy, and image.   MDC

SOCIETY FOR THEATRE RESEARCH

British organization, founded in 1948 by Ifan Kyrle Fletcher, Sybil Rosenfeld, and Richard Southern. It aims to promote knowledge and appreciation of the theatre and theatre history, to foster research, and to provide a meeting point for all who are interested in the history and technique of the British stage. The Society publishes at least one book a year for distribution to its members, and offers a prize for the year's outstanding book on British theatre. It presents the annual *Poel Festival featuring drama school students (*see* TRAINING FOR THEATRE). An ongoing series of lectures in *London is open to the public. Research awards are made for the support of specific projects in theatre history undertaken by amateur or academic workers. *Theatre Notebook*, a refereed journal, publishes articles, reviews, notes, and queries. Distinguished actors connected with the Society have included Edith *Evans, Robert Eddison, and Timothy *West, its current president. *See also* THEATRE STUDIES.   FD

SOCIETY OF AUTHORS

Founded in the United Kingdom in 1884 with Alfred Tennyson as its first president, the Society of Authors seeks to protect the rights and interests of writers, both generally and individually.

The Society, an independent *trade union, lobbies government for increased protection for literary works through changes in national laws, such as those concerned with *copyright protection. It also acts as an advice bureau for its members, giving them guidance on *publishing and *film contracts and on relations with agents, theatre *managers, and broadcast organizations. It provides writers with information on *licensing, accountancy, and tax matters, as well as acting on complaints against publishers and others perceived as exploiting writers, even going so far as to initiate legal proceedings on behalf of its members. In addition to these functions, the Society serves as the literary and dramatic agent for the estates of such notables as G. B. *Shaw, and T. S. *Eliot. There are subdivisions within the Society for the writers and illustrators of works for children, educational writers, medical writers, and translators, and the Society publishes a quarterly journal, *The Author*. Its membership numbers in the thousands. Societies of authors organized along similar lines are found in many other countries, such as the *Society of Dramatic Authors and Composers in France and *SOGEM in Mexico. The American Society of Composers, Authors, and Publishers (ASCAP) is concerned primarily with performing rights, while the *Dramatists Guild in the USA fulfils many of the functions of the Society of Authors in the UK.

A predecessor of the Society, the Dramatic Authors' Society, served the interests of playwrights throughout the 1800s and its members were instrumental in the passage of the Dramatic Authors' Act in 1833, which gave dramatic authors control over the public performances of their works and allowed for the collection of performance-based *royalties. TEH

SOCIETY OF DRAMATIC AUTHORS AND COMPOSERS

The first association of dramatic authors in France was founded in 1777 by *Beaumarchais as a legislative instrument to define and defend the creative and proprietary rights of dramatic writers. Under the presidency of Victor *Hugo, the society expanded internationally to provide protection to authors outside of France, and in 1926 it created the International Confederation for Societies of Authors. Today, the essentially francophone organization (Société des Auteurs et Compositeurs Dramatiques, or SACD) has offices in *Paris, *Brussels, and *Montréal, and counts over 30,000 members from multiple disciplines, including theatre, music, *dance, *film, *television, and *radio. The society is governed by a representative administrative council, which serves to negotiate contracts between its authors and professional organizations, monitor rights of performance and reproduction of material in different countries, and administer financial assistance and grants to contemporary authors. CHB

SOFOLA, ZULU (1938–95)

Nigerian playwright, director, and teacher. Educated in Nigeria and the USA, Sofola was a pioneering woman dramatist and academic who made provocative public interventions in politics, religion, and theatre. Some of her plays, such as the farcical *Wizard at Law* and the sombre *Ivory Tower* (1991), draw very obviously on European originals. Others, like *Queen Omu Ako of Oligbo* (1988), for which she carried out extensive research into local conventions, were deliberately Afrocentric in approach. Always relevant, sometimes reactionary, her plays often comment on *gender issues and topical concerns. *Ivory Tower* was significantly subtitled 'a new spirit of African womanhood' and confronted the secret cults that were disrupting life on Nigerian campuses. JMG

SOGEM

Spanish acronym for General Society of Mexican Writers. Established in the 1960s, SOGEM is Mexico's national writers' guild, charged with protecting its members' rights, with providing medical insurance and retirement pensions, and with ensuring that writers receive their *royalties. SOGEM owns various writers' houses (Casa del Escritor) which offer free room and board to writers from around the world. Among the most active members of the SOGEM are writers for *film, *television, and theatre. SOGEM also operates three small theatres in *Mexico City whose purpose is to promote Mexican theatre. KFN

SOIRÉE (VEILLÉE DE CONTES)

Traditional *Caribbean funeral *ritual of storytelling, led by a 'tirè-kont', which has been transformed into public *performance. Often accompanied by a *gwo ka*, a percussion instrument, these examples of storytelling in the French islands have taken a number of theatrical forms. In the hands of Élie Pennont the *soirée* has become a *monologue accompanied by movement which indicates the surrounding universe; in the work of Joby *Bernabé, José Égouy, and Lucette Salibur it is a poetic *text about the world of myth; while for Arthur *Lerus it is an updated version of the traditional story form. In some cases the *soirée* has been applied to classic European plays as a *post-colonial strategy of subversion. Reworked by Pennont and Serge Ouaknine, for example, *Othello* was performed by a single actor-storyteller (Théâtre de la Soif Nouvelle, Martinique, 1998). Except for Desdemona, he assumed all the roles, becoming a creole-speaking guide to the plight of the Moor in a non-European context. AR

SOLDENE, EMILY (1840–1912)

English actress and singer. Trained in *opera and oratorio, she made her debut at *Drury Lane in *Verdi's *Il trovatore* (1865).

Shakespeare's *Richard II*, **Théâtre du Soleil**, Paris, 1981, directed by Ariane Mnouchkine, designed by Guy-Claude François, Jean-Claude Barriera, and Nathalie Thomas. Georges Bigot as the King (kneeling, in white) in the company's intercultural production that drew on the vocal, gestural, and visual methods of classical Japanese theatre, creating an estranged idea of the English medieval court.

Her theatrical career, however, began on the *variety stage in *music halls like the Canterbury, Oxford, and Alhambra. From 1871 her reputation was based on her performances in the *opéra bouffe* of *Offenbach and Hervé, beginning with *The Grand Duchess of Gerolstein*. Her greatest success was as Drogan in *Geneviève de Brabant* (1871) and as Mlle Lange in Lecoq's *La Fille de Madame Angot* (1873). Her splendid voice and dramatic vivacity made her the most popular female singer of light opera in the 1870s, performing in theatres like the Alhambra and *Gaiety as well as in America and Australia.   VEE

SOLEIL, THÉÂTRE DU

French theatre company founded in *Paris by Ariane *Mnouchkine (and ten former Sorbonne students) in 1964, modelled on their student theatre *collective, formed with socialist principles of equality of responsibilities. The company's third production, a version of Arnold *Wesker's *The Kitchen* (1967), brought them international attention, particularly for its opening *mime sequence of kitchen labour. *A Midsummer Night's Dream* (1968) featured two dancers from the Béjart *ballet company, an innovation which broke with the company's principles of equal status and pay. Both productions were performed in the Cirque Médrano, a suitable space for their goal of a people's theatre. The events of May 1968 saw the company members turn political activists, developing an association with trade unions, a rejection of the classical repertoire, and the beginnings of a *devised form called 'collective creation'. Four works were created in this style: *The Clowns* (1969), two on the French Revolution, *1789* and *1793* (1970 and 1972), and a play of contemporary life, *L'Âge d'or* (*The Golden Age*, 1975). The process of devising, the plays' *dramaturgy, and the multi-focused performances helped these theatre workers come to terms with their impotence as political activists. *1789; or, The*

Revolution Must Stop at the Perfection of Happiness, the first production in what was to become their permanent home, a disused munitions factory (Cartoucherie) in the Vincennes forest, was created by the actors playing fairground workers who told their personal histories of the revolution. Thus ordinary workers became recorders of macro-history and their own personal experiences. The final collective creation, *L'Âge d'or*, was a *commedia dell'arte*-inspired story of a North African immigrant worker falling victim to the corruption and inequalities of contemporary society.

In 1979 Mnouchkine's adaptation of Klaus Mann's novel *Méphisto* marked a turning point in the company's history. The more conciliatory *politics of the piece outraged the left and the unions withdrew their support. A period of experimentation with the forms of various Eastern theatres followed, applied to the canonical *texts of the European stage (three plays by Shakespeare, 1981–4; a tetralogy of plays by *Euripides and *Aeschlyus, *Les Atrides*, 1990–3; and *Molière's *Tartuffe*, 1995). These lavish, highly physicalized, and *interculturalist *spectacles were enormously successful. The same approach to commissioned plays set in Asia by Hélène *Cixous (*The Terrible but Unfinished History of Norodom Sihanouk, King of Cambodia* in 1985, and *The Indiade; or, India of their Dreams* in 1987) retained the pictorialism of the Orient but the hybridized *acting style was absent. This was rectified in 1999 in *Drums on the Dyke*, an imagined Chinese fable in which live actors were manipulated as *bunraku puppets. From the beginning of this orientalist period the Soleil came to resemble a global village of ethnicities, and the stage a mêlée of accents and bodies. Though the company no longer operates as a cooperative, the original collective ethos is still visible in the multiple tasks company members undertake, including Mnouchkine, who can be seen at times gathering dirty dishes and taking *tickets at the door.

BRS

SOLILOQUY

Literally 'single speech', the Latin-derived eqivalent of the Greek-derived *monologue, soliloquy is most often used of a form of monologue in which a speaker, alone on the stage, or believing himself to be alone, delivers an extended speech within the context of the dramatic fiction. A soliloquy cannot go beyond the competence and knowledge of the *character, and, as the speaker is alone, cannot be intended to deceive. A soliloquy is either 'conventional', a function of the theatrical code (the Elizabethan practice), or 'motivated', a function of dramatic characterization (the *realistic practice). It tends to be (*a*) an introspective revelation of character, (*b*) a reflective commentary on the dramatic *action, or (*c*) a deliberation of future action. A soliloquy can be addressed to the *audience (*Richard III*) but it is more often an interior monologue (*Hamlet*). RWV

SOLOGUB, FYODOR (1863–1927)

Russian poet, novelist, and playwright, whose best-known work is his novel *Melky bes* (*The Little Demon*), dramatized in 1910 and revived in a version by Roman *Viktyuk in the 1980s. Its theme of madness, decadence, sullied innocence, and perversity were typical of the so-called Decadent movement to which Sologub belonged. The conflict between the material and the spiritual is a persistent feature of his work and finds expression in plays such as *The Triumph of Death*, staged by *Meyerhold in 1907, and *The Gift of the Wise Bees*, his treatment of the Laodameia legend borrowed from Innokenty *Annensky's reworking of *Euripides. A *theorist of *symbolist theatre, his influential essay 'The Theatre of a Single Will' (1908) advocated stylized modes of writing and performance. In the spirit of Edward Gordon *Craig, Sologub was hostile to the actor's living presence and wished to return the theatre to the poet and the *Über-marionette, declaring: 'One man wills in drama—the author. One performs the *action—the actor.' His *Nocturnal Dances* (1908) is a version of a fairy tale presenting the triumph of the aesthetic over the commonplace. Sologub's ideas were unpopular during the Soviet period and his work neglected.

NW

SOLÓRZANO, CARLOS (1922–)

Mexican playwright, director, scholar, educator. Born in Guatemala, his adult life has been spent in Mexico. A self-described *expressionist, Solórzano's plays are heavily influenced by the myths of Mesoamerican culture, as well as by French existentialism, as in his blending of Christian and indigenous Easter *rituals with existentialist philosophy in *The Doll Puppets* (1958). The oppression of the poor is the main theme of *The Hands of God* (1958), a kind of modern *mystery play which inverts notions of good and evil. In *The Crucified One* (1958), a Pontius Pilate-like priest symbolically washes his hands when the young actor playing Christ in a local *Passion play is killed by drunken celebrants. Solórzano was fundamental in establishing the professional University Theatre of the National Autonomous University of Mexico in 1952; in 1973 he was named head of the department of dramatic literature and theatre of that university. An ex-honorary president of the *International Theatre Institute, Solórzano is the author of important studies of Mexican and *Latin American theatre. KFN

SOMIGLIANA, CARLOS (1932–87)

Argentinian playwright and director who figured prominently in the development of a critical neorealism (*see* REALISM AND REALITY). From *Yellow* (written 1959, produced 1965) to *Lavalle, the Story of a Statue* (1983) his works stand out for their crisp *dialogue and focus on historical conflict. *Official Number One* (presented in Teatro *Abierto's 1982 *festival) buried the stage in corpses in one of the first explicit representations of the disappeared.   JGJ

SOMMI, LEONE DE' (1525–92)

Italian Jew from Mantua who was a semi-professional theatre practitioner: his company, protected by the dukes of Mantua, functioned in the context of an 'Israelite University'. His *Wedding Comedy*, in Hebrew, is a precious testament of the extent to which the Jewish community was prepared to adopt the formats of Italian humanist culture; he also left a number of Italian dramatic compositions in manuscript, which have still not been published. His *Four Dialogues on Stage Performance* (composed between 1556 and 1565) are an important source for sixteenth-century theatre practice, though perhaps not influential or even known in their own time. As well as offering standard humanist views about the classical origins and *genres of drama, they give a thorough survey of *dramaturgy, *acting, and staging, with a particularly high concentration on the practical artisan aspects of *scenography, *lighting, and stage construction.   RAA

SONDHEIM, STEPHEN (1930–   )

American composer-lyricist. Considered the pre-eminent *musical theatre songwriter of his generation, Sondheim's work embodies and further extends the *genre's emphasis on narrative-driven songs and *characters. Often labelled misanthropic, his sharp, unsparing wit and carefully crafted lyrics most frequently grace shows that go beyond the light romantic fare typical of musical comedy. As a teenager he befriended James Hammerstein, whose father, Oscar *Hammerstein II, was then writing *Oklahoma!* with Richard *Rodgers. The elder Hammerstein took an interest in Sondheim's aspirations and encouraged him to pursue music. After studying with composer Milton Babbitt, Sondheim made his Broadway debut as lyricist for *Bernstein's *West Side Story* (1957), and in 1959 wrote the words for Jule *Styne's *Gypsy*, which starred the great Ethel *Merman.

He began writing both words and music with *A Funny Thing Happened on the Way to the Forum* (1962), a broad *farce based on *Plautus that featured Zero *Mostel in the lead role. After an unsuccessful collaboration with Richard Rodgers on *Do I Hear a Waltz?* (1965), Sondheim came into his own with *Company* (1970), one of the most innovative musicals of its time. Working with director Harold *Prince and choreographer Michael *Bennett, he fashioned an uncompromising look at modern relationships with an inventive, unsentimental score that captured the restless ambivalence of urban life in the 1970s. That decade was to be his most productive. *Follies* (1971), considered by many his most remarkable score, used a reunion of former showgirls to explore the myths of show business glamour and the potent memories and regrets they engender. *A Little Night Music* (1973), composed in 3/4 time, featured Sondheim's most popular song, 'Send in the Clowns'. In 1976 he offered the unusual *Pacific Overtures*, based on the opening of Japan to the West in 1853. Despite one of his most adventurous scores and a stunning set design by Boris *Aronson, the work was unsuccessful.

Sweeney Todd (1979) was Sondheim's most theatrically effective production. Based on the gruesome 1847 play by George Dibdin Pitt (adapted by Christopher Bond in 1973), it blended *operetta, *melodrama, and horror with Prince's fluid staging. The tale of a vengeful barber in mid-nineteenth-century London was performed with great verve by Len *Cariou and Angela *Lansbury as Mrs Lovett, who bakes Sweeney's victims into meat pies. After the failure of *Merrily We Roll Along* (1981), Sondheim won the Pulitzer Prize in 1984 for *Sunday in the Park with George*, a visually striking musical about the painter Georges Seurat. *Into the Woods* (1988) was a novel examination of fairy tales and their archetypal motifs. *Assassins* (1991) presented the killers of American presidents in a *revue. It was scheduled for a Broadway revival in 2001, cancelled as a result of the World Trade Center attack.

Passion (1994), based on Ettore Scola's *film *Passione d'amore*, had a solid critical reaction and a bravura performance by Donna Murphy as the spurned lover Fosca, but struggled to find an *audience. Its *operatic feel and intermission-less, largely sung-through style made for a demanding evening. On the occasion of his 70th birthday, Sondheim reflected on the state of musical theatre at the new millennium with Frank *Rich: 'You have two kinds of shows on Broadway', he said, 'revivals and the same kind of musicals over and over again, all spectacles. . . . You get tickets for *The Lion King* a year in advance, and essentially a family comes as if to a picnic, and they pass on to their children the idea that that's what the theater is—a spectacular musical you see once a year, a stage version of a movie. . . . We live in a recycled culture.' Although he never had the commercial success of Andrew *Lloyd Webber, Sondheim's brilliant lyrics, unconventional subjects, sparkling wit, and uncompromising vision of musical theatre make him the most original composer-lyricist of the late twentieth century.   SN

ZADAN, CRAIG, *Sondheim & Company* (New York, 1989)

SONNENFELS, JOSEF VON (1733–1817)

Austrian critic. A dominant figure in Austrian Enlightenment circles, Sonnenfels gained considerable influence over the theatre when appointed Censor of German Theatre in 1770. Heavily influenced by *Gottsched's emphasis on morally uplifting drama on the French model (*see* NEOCLASSICISM), his ideas on theatre reform were formulated in *Letters on the Viennese Stage* (1768). He combated the local popular theatre by strict *censorship, but was unable to dent its popularity. At the same time he made a major contribution to the establishment of the *Burgtheater and its elevation to the status of a *national theatre in 1776.   CBB

SOPHOCLES (c.495–406 BC)

Athenian *tragic dramatist. During his long and supremely successful career Sophocles was said to have introduced the third actor (see PROTAGONIST) and scene painting to the *Greek theatre. Of more than 120 plays (with which he won at least twenty victories, eighteen of them at the City *Dionysia), only seven survive. We cannot attempt to trace any development in Sophocles' dramatic technique because the chronology of his works is so uncertain. *Philoctetes* was definitely performed in 409 and *Oedipus at Colonus* in 401 (posthumously), but there is no evidence at all for the dates of *Ajax, Electra, Oedipus the King*, or *Women of Trachis*, and very unreliable evidence for *Antigone*, though it and *Ajax* are usually thought to be comparatively early plays.

Perhaps because of *Aristophanes' description of him in *Frogs* as a model of good temper, or *Aristotle's high regard for *Oedipus the King* in his influential *Poetics*, or possibly because we know he had a highly respectable political career, Sophocles has often been seen as an 'establishment figure' in contrast with *Euripides the *enfant terrible*. Both views are flawed. Even the surviving plays of Sophocles (and the extant selection probably does not do justice to his versatility and range) are challenging and uncomfortable in the extreme. His *heroes often suffer terribly despite being, or indeed just because they are, fundamentally good: Oedipus is the obvious example, but the gentle Deianeira in *Women of Trachis* is another. More unexpectedly, perhaps, Sophocles can be seen as challenging some of the most cherished assumptions of his society. For example, Neoptolemus in *Philoctetes* is faced with a complex choice between personal morality and the public good when he is instructed to trick Philoctetes into accompanying the Greek army to Troy. Eventually Neoptolemus refuses to abandon the wronged hero on his deserted island and insists on restoring his bow, without which the Greeks cannot sack Troy, despite the protests of his commander Odysseus. The play has a remarkably seamless structure which reflects its moral tensions and produces tremendous suspense: will Troy ever be taken? Eventually Heracles, now a god, appears and orders Philoctetes and Neoptolemus to Troy, and the mythological equilibrium is restored, but not before the *audience has become convinced that personal morality is sometimes more important even than the good of the city (represented in the play by the Greek army), an uncomfortable message in Athens in the final stages of the Peloponnesian War.

Philoctetes' bow is one of a series of significant *properties used in Sophocles' plays which become the focus of the audience's attention and articulate the progress of the *plot. The sword with which Ajax kills himself is another; and after Ajax's suicide, his dead body becomes the visual and thematic focus of the last part of the play. In *Electra* the focus similarly shifts from an object to a corpse, but in a way which emphasizes this play's multiple bitter ironies: the disguised Orestes presents his sister, who believes him dead, with an urn he says contains Orestes' ashes. She laments wildly over it, and refuses to be parted from it even as Orestes tries to make himself known to her. At the play's shocking climax, the corpse of Clytemnestra (only in Sophocles is she murdered before her lover Aegisthus) is brought out on the *ekkyklema* and is misidentified as that of Orestes by the deluded Aegisthus before he is killed. So Orestes is falsely presumed dead twice, and twice a visual symbol is used to convince those on stage that false is true, and simultaneously to illustrate the irony for the audience. Related to this is Sophocles' interweaving of metaphorical and actual blindness in the Oedipus plays: in *Oedipus the King*, when Oedipus has sight he is blind, unlike the blind Teiresias; only when he re-enters in his bloodied and blinded *mask can he see clearly.

The power of Sophocles' plays, and their beauty of language, ensured their continued performance after his death: a number of famous actors in the fourth century BC were known for their interpretations of his roles (Timotheus of Zacynthus, for example, was famous for his Ajax, particularly in the suicide scene, and Polus of Aegina played Electra using his own son's ashes to guarantee the emotional impact of his performance). In the modern world, particularly after the *early modern period, Sophocles has been the most popular of the ancient dramatists. *Oedipus the King* and *Antigone* in particular have been constantly performed, translated, and adapted, and it was specifically Sophocles' Oedipus and Electra after whom Freud named his complexes. In 1585 at the Teatro *Olimpico in Vicenza, *Oedipus the King* was the first Greek tragedy to be performed in modern times. This was exceptional, and it was not until the nineteenth century that regular performances of Greek tragedy took place. In 1841 a production of *Antigone* with music by Mendelssohn was produced at Potsdam under the aegis of Friedrich Wilhelm IV, and proved to be the first of many across Europe. Later an extremely influential *Oedipus the King*, with Jean *Mounet-Sully as Oedipus, was performed at the *Comédie-Française in 1881 in *Paris. In the nineteenth and early twentieth centuries the play was banned from the professional stage in Britain and considerable pressure at the highest levels had to be brought to bear before it could be performed (see CENSORSHIP; LORD CHAMBERLAIN). Eventually it was performed in 1912 to public acclaim, with John *Martin-Harvey as Oedipus and Lillah *McCarthy as Jocasta, directed by Max *Reinhardt. Laurence *Olivier probably remains the most famous of many postwar Oedipuses, playing opposite Sybil *Thorndike at the *Old Vic in 1945, in the version by W. B. *Yeats first performed at the *Abbey Theatre, *Dublin, in 1926. The play has been adapted by such diverse talents as *Corneille (1659), *Voltaire (1718), *Gide (1930), and *Cocteau (*La Machine infernale*, 1932), among many others. There are also numerous versions of *Antigone*, notably that of Jean *Anouilh (1944), performed under the Nazi occupation of France and using the Sophoclean story to negotiate the moral tensions between idealism and pragmatism in the face of *force majeure*. More recent important adaptations include Seamus Heaney's version of *Philoctetes*, called *The Cure at Troy*, which strongly emphasizes the impetus of the play towards peace and reconciliation, an interpretation heavily influenced by the author's Northern Irish background. JMM

EASTERLING, P. E., *The Cambridge Companion to Greek Tragedy* (Cambridge, 1997)

SEALE, DAVID, *Vision and Stagecraft in Sophocles* (London, 1982)

TAPLIN, OLIVER P., *Greek Tragedy in Action* (London, 1978)

SORESCU, MARIN (1936–96)

Romanian poet and dramatist. Sorescu's *Iona* (*Jonah*), a *monodrama, was first produced by Andrei *Şerban in *Bucharest in 1969 to great praise. Although the *censors' distrust of Sorescu's poetic ambiguity limited production of his works in Romania prior to 1989, *Jonah* received numerous stagings in Europe, *India, and the United States, as did a companion piece, *Matca* (*The Matrix*, 1974). Since 1989 many of his works, including the *history plays *Răceala* (*A Cold*, 1977) and *A treia ţeapă* (*A Third Stake*, 1979, also translated as *Vlad Dracula the Impaler*), have become key elements in the national repertory. EEP

SORGE, REINHARD JOHANNES (1892–1916)

German dramatist. A victim of the First World War, Sorge is remembered chiefly for his play *The Beggar* (1912), which was staged posthumously by *Reinhardt at the *Deutsches Theater in 1917. Both play and production epitomized *expressionism. The episodic structure, focus on a single *protagonist, father–son conflict, and theme of spiritual renewal are paradigmatic for expressionist drama. Reinhardt's production, with a star-studded cast including Ernst *Deutsch and Emil *Jannings, marked a departure to new staging techniques through symbolic *lighting and the use of a bare *stage. CBB

SORMA, AGNES (1865–1927)

German actress. After work in various provincial theatres, Sorma came to the *Deutsches Theater, *Berlin in 1883, where she performed under first Adolf *L'Arronge, then Ludwig *Barnay at the Berliner Theatre. From 1894 to 1898 she was a member of Otto *Brahm's ensemble at the Deutsches Theater. She worked freelance at various Berlin theatres and went on many international *tours, often performing next to Josef *Kainz. Important parts included Nora in *Ibsen's *A Doll's House* (1892) and Portia in *The Merchant of Venice* (1905) directed by *Reinhardt. She was a principal actress of *naturalism

in the plays of *Hauptmann, Ibsen, and *Shaw, as well as a passionate and intense interpreter of the classical roles. It was often remarked that her finely nuanced, psychological *acting style became increasingly superficial after she left Brahm's ensemble to become a star performer. CBB

SOTHERN, E. A. (EDWARD ASKEW) (1826–81) AND E. H. (EDWARD HUGH) (1859–1933)

Anglo-American actors, father and son. E. A. was born in Liverpool and made a name for himself as a comic actor in provincial theatres. He moved to the USA in 1852, working first in *Boston and later in *New York, where he joined *Wallack's company in 1854. His signature role came in 1858 when he reluctantly agreed to play Lord Dundreary in Laura *Keene's production of Tom *Taylor's *Our American Cousin*, a performance celebrated as one the funniest on the American stage, and he furthered his reputation playing a relative of Dundreary's in *Brother Sam* (1862). He also attempted more serious roles with varying degrees of success, including the title part in *David Garrick* (1864) and Fitzaltamont in the 1877 production of *The Failed Tragedian*.

E. H. Sothern was born in New Orleans and studied art in London before returning to the USA. Unlike his tall and lanky father, E. H. was small and handsome, and developed into an important serious actor. His first role was a cabin-boy in his father's production of *Brother Sam* in 1879. For the next ten years he *toured with several famous troupes, including John *McCullough's, becoming a popular leading man. In 1887 E. H. joined Daniel *Frohman's company at the *Lyceum in New York where he took some of his most famous roles, including *The Prisoner of Zenda* (1895), adapted from Anthony Hope's novel, in which E. H. portrayed both Prince Rudolf and his lookalike nemesis. But it was his work with his second wife, Julia *Marlowe, that defined his reputation. Together they acted in a series of hallmark Shakespeare productions beginning in 1904 and continuing until Marlowe's retirement in 1924. PAD

SOTTIE

A form of French *farce played in the fifteenth and sixteenth centuries by *sots* or *fools in their traditional *costume of motley coat, ass's ears, and marotte (bauble). *Sotties* were associated specifically with the Enfants-sans-Souci, a sub-group of the Parisian *Basochiens, a society of law clerks. RWV

SOUBRETTE

A specialized female role within a *stock company. The pert, clever, and scheming female servant of *Molière's *comedies, helping her mistress to the hand of the *hero and outwitting father, guardian, or rival, passed quickly into English theatre and became a *stock character type in the eighteenth century. *See* LINES OF BUSINESS.   MRB

SOUGOUNOUGOU

Performance in the Odienné province of Upper Côte d'Ivoire consisting of men *masked as animals. The performing group is made up of a *chorus and *stock characters: Nanzégé, the hero-hunter, his wife Niofolityé, and various animal *characters. These are identifiable by their detailed *costuming, with Niofolityé, played by a male actor (*see* FEMALE IMPERSONATION), sporting a headscarf and coral necklace, and the animal impersonators wearing stylized skin-masks and reproducing animal movements. A typical show consists of sketches on the adventures of Nanzégé. Constantly ridiculing fellow hunters, or secular or clerical figures of village authority, he is usually saved *in extremis* from severe punishment by his wife's magical intervention. His *mimed, sung, or *danced reactions to his self-created fate constitute the high point of the performance.   JCM

SOUND AND SOUND EFFECTS

Sight and hearing are the two theatrical senses because they work reliably at a distance and can be shared by an indefinite number of people simultaneously. Yet non-verbal sound has historically not been as highly valued as sight in Western theatre, and to a great extent in global theatre as well. Scientific, historical, aesthetic, and ethnographic understanding of sound in the theatre is rudimentary compared with our understanding of *lighting, *scenography, rhetoric, speech, or theatrical *music.

1. A new craft; 2. Acoustics of performance spaces;
3. What sound means; 4. Sound design begins, 1850–1950;
5. Improvements and challenges, 1950–present

1. A new craft

In the social ladder of theatre crafts and specialities, the most recent usually rank lowest—*scenery and *costumes clearly taking precedence over lights in most theatre organizations, for example. Though sound effects have been present since *Greek theatre, sound design as a recognized speciality has only been around since the 1960s, and thus it ranks very low. Its newness also means that 'sound people' live with fuzzy boundaries and confusing responsibilities. A technician or designer who says that his or her speciality is 'theatrical sound' might be referring to a speciality in the acoustics of *playhouses, in making sound effects, in mixing and mastering speciality recordings, in audio playback equipment, or in incidental music and music history; but more likely, the person who 'does the sound' does all of those, and more. In addition it is often customary for the 'sound person' to be given such tasks as making intercom systems work.

This jurisdictional problem is complex and often results in sound designers and sound technicians being held responsible for things over which they have no control. Actors who have been miked (equipped with wireless microphones) are heard through the same sound system and speakers as the sounds selected or created by the sound designer, and the wireless-mike system itself is the sound person's responsibility, but a sound designer has no say about actors' voices. A music director may choose to control all of the music, all of the music except the incidental music, or all of the music except the pre-curtain, incidental, entr'acte, and post-show music; whatever is not the music director's domain will be 'sound', as will the system through which the *audience hears the music.

Very often the set or the theatre architecture will have important (sometimes negative) acoustic consequences. In practice, most theatres in the modern industrial world are constructed with at least the consultation of an acoustic engineer, but very few scene designers pay much attention to acoustics. If a *special effects specialist is called in, sounds connected with the special effects are often removed from the responsibilities of the sound designer (though they will probably still be executed by the sound operator). It might be fair to say that theatrical sound is the field of everything to do with sound that has not already been decided by someone else.

It is perhaps indicative that where a lighting or set designer uses 'effect' to refer to something unusual, the entire job of the sound person is often described as 'sound effects'. The very division between 'sound' and 'sound effects' is difficult to map; if, for example, a scene on stage depicts a party, then additional recorded party noise played through speakers in the wings is generally called a sound effect; if the music of a band in the next room is added, it may or may not still be a 'sound effect' depending on the significance of the music to the play.

2. Acoustics of performance spaces

The *stage itself was probably among humanity's first acoustic devices. As soon as people performed for a crowd of any size, it was surely noticed that certain natural places—an elevated hard surface with a rear wall, or a central flat area at the bottom of a natural depression—were aurally 'alive', giving performers greater resonance, clarity, and volume than other places. As the places were reused, modification and improvements would have led to noticeably better sound: removing rubble and brush, putting stone benches in the seating areas, paving the performance area with stone or planking, smoothing the rear walls. Presumably when deliberately constructed theatres began to develop, the improved natural theatres were copied at first, and thus many of their acoustic qualities were incorporated into theatre architecture at its beginning.

End-stage and *thrust configurations can naturally amplify sound by up to 10 decibels—roughly the difference between a voice that is intelligible and one that can be easily followed without concentration, or the difference between a raised voice and a shout. Since, without amplification or shaping, sound volume falls off approximately with the square of distance, this means a theatre that takes full advantage of mechanical amplification can have a back row almost 75 per cent further away from the stage, which translates into seating two to three times as many people. The *arena stage can produce a roughly 6-decibel amplification, with a 40 per cent increase in seating with acceptable audibility. It is important to remember that although audibility is physical, acceptability is cultural; natural amplification will increase the distance at which a given signal-to-noise ratio and volume will occur, but whether the audience wants to be able clearly to understand a *Chekhovian whisper or is happy to perceive a *Boucicaultian cannon fire is determined historically and culturally. Of the commonly used configurations for staging, only the traverse or alley stage has little natural amplification; this, and the fact that it tends acoustically to a more pronounced 'ring' than other configurations, may partly account for its transcultural unpopularity.

The natural amplification of a theatre space is caused by sound reflection. Echoes which arrive within 50 milliseconds (one-twentieth of a second) of the primary sound increase clarity of the spoken word; if an echo is comparable in energy to the original sound (less than about 6 decibels different), and arrives more than 50 milliseconds later, it will make the sound 'muddy' or 'unclear'. Sound travels about 16 m (52 feet) in 50 milliseconds; thus for clarity, no echo pathway should be more than 16 m longer than a straight line from the stage to a seat. For example, a back wall should not be more than 8 m (26 feet) behind the actor. The side walls should be damped with sound-absorbing material (since, if they are reflective, they will create too-long pathways and muddying echoes in all but the smallest houses). If there is a roof, the ceiling should be sound reflective and not much more than 10 m (32 feet) above the spectators' heads, angled so that one hears the echo from the surface almost directly overhead (this produces the shortest path).

Sound quality—the ability to discern timbre and the resonance that makes sound seem more significant—is largely a matter of resonance, which is usually measured by 'reverberation time', the time after the instantaneous cut-off of a sound at which its echoes are 60 decibels quieter, a drop in volume about equal to that from a shout to a whisper. Theatres with too short a reverberation time sound 'flat', 'thin', 'dry', or 'dead' so that resonant voices become reedy and thin, pistol shots sound like hand claps, and thunder machines grind mechanically; theatres with too long a reverberation time ('too lively', 'wet', or 'rich') make actors unintelligible, turn every door slam into a cannon, and lose the larger effects in booming, thundering, white noise. For spoken performance, reverberation times of about 1 to 1.25 seconds are preferred (this corresponds closely to the 50-millisecond rule for clarity), and for music about 1.8 to 2 seconds.

Despite the scientific measurement of acoustics, sound designers constantly work in spaces with major problems, and architects continue to design many acoustic follies. Everything from sound machines to speakers must be constantly adjusted for them; an effect which is brilliant in the 'home' house may be an utter failure on *tour because of the differing acoustics of spaces, and sound technicians have to be able to make adjustments very quickly.

Though not quantified by modern instruments, all of these principles were familiar to the architects of the *ancient theatres and performance spaces of Greece, *India, *China, and Mesoamerica—Chinese and Roman architects alike could tell when a theatre 'sounded right' and knew what to do to make it sound better. For example, the very wide and shallow stages of some *Roman theatres compensated for the loss of floor reflectance by using a very high (up to 25 m; 80 feet), hard-surfaced *scaenae frons. The relatively deep, *dance-oriented stages of Mesoamerica, on the other hand, were backed by stepped surfaces to give long reverberation times. One of the most common ways in which archaeologists identify a performance space is that it is a raised or depressed platform, hard surfaced, with a sound-reflecting back wall, with a reverberation time in the spoken word or the music range. This can lead to over-identification; one reason that we believe that performance spaces have been shaped like this throughout history is that any space shaped like this, if found by an archaeologist, tends to be identified as a performance space.

3. What sound means

Leonard lists five reasons for sound effects:

1. to give information which is needed but not given in the *dialogue, especially time and place, such as battle noises indicating wartime, city traffic indicating a city;
2. to supply sounds referred to in the *text;
3. to affect audience mood, often with sounds serving other purposes as well; for instance, a textually required creaking door can be made 'creepy' for a thriller or funny for a *comedy;
4. to provide an emotional stimulus in connection with an offstage action; for instance, the first reviews described the drum roll leading up to the offstage hanging at the end of *Miller's The Crucible as 'sickening' and 'horrifying';
5. to reinforce an onstage *action, for instance, crackling sounds for fire effects, crashes for things being broken—what is being reinforced is the *illusion of reality.

All five of these uses can be found in Western and in non-Western theatre. But the way in which sound accomplishes these purposes—that is, how sound means what it means—varies greatly from culture to culture. These variations are often parallel to differences in cultural tradition, with more conventional theatres using non-*realistic expressive sounds and more illusionistic theatres seeking verisimilitude. For example, in the *nautanki drama of northern India, the nagara (a large skin-covered drum) is used in full view of the audience at every entrance and exit, reinforcing the onstage action just as a Western sound designer might amplify a door slam or add a creak, but the nagara in no way resembles a door; the Western theatre uses the sound illusionistically, as an index, where the nautanki theatre uses it as a symbol.

Conventional and illusionistic sounds overlap in most traditions. There is a marked preference for onstage sound to be realistic in many cultures. Offstage sounds are often conventionalized symbols. Sounds may stand for events, such as the centa drums for entrances and exits of male *characters and the itaykka drums for female in the *kathakali theatre. Or sounds may stand for sounds, as in the production of more than 100 conventional sounds in the geza ('noise room' or 'music room') of the *kabuki, many of which bear only a slight resemblance to the actual sounds they represent.

The Western theatre was illusionistic with regard to sound from at least the *early modern period forward. The plays of Shakespeare and *Calderón were accompanied by a wide variety of realistic sound and it is clear that most of these—horns, gunshots, bells, etc.—were supplied by direct use of the device itself. Frances Ann Shirley points out that while the dialogue of Shakespeare's plays includes innumerable descriptions of offstage sights, offstage sounds appear almost entirely in the *stage directions. However, in both the English and Spanish early modern theatre, some sounds—notably cannon, horses' hooves, and the clash of weapons—are often 're-inforced by the text' with an identifying tag in the dialogue immediately after the effect, suggesting that imitations may have been imperfect and therefore needed textual identification.

Though it was always one of the most illusionistic traditions, Western theatre also had its own conventional tradition in sound. Simultaneously with the use of illusionistic sound in the European theatres, there was also a use of 'punctuation' sound in *commedia dell'arte, generally accompanying *lazzi—the cowbell when a character shook with rage or excitement, the slide whistle for fainting, the triangle or chime for a happy thought. (This survived into stand-up comedy in almost pure form, as the drum 'rimshot' after a punch line.)

Incidental music had been common in the West since *medieval theatre, but when *melodrama was added to the repertoire of Western *genres late in the eighteenth century, it brought with it an additional expressive range in sound design, using bits of familiar melodies and various instruments to underscore and elaborate scenes (for example in Rossini's overture for William Tell: flute and oboe for birdsong, reeds for wind, plucked strings for raindrops on a lake, and horns for the call to battle, all both imitative of the natural sound and expressive of the desired emotion).

4. Sound design begins, 1850–1950

By the middle of the nineteenth century, the illusional, the conventional, and the musical traditions in Western theatrical sound began to fuse, and before 1900 there was close to one tradition mingling the methods and goals of all three. The nineteenth century also saw the construction of more and more elaborate backstage sound machines for particular effects, for instance the 'thunder run' (a series of sheet-metal or wooden ramps with resonators down which cannonballs could be rolled for thunder effects), the 'wind machine' (a wide canvas belt between rollers, which rubbed against a steel pipe to make the sounds of wind howling past the eaves), and such familiar devices as rice sprinkled on a snare drumhead for rain, coconut halves banged on a box for hoofbeats, and so on. W. S. *Gilbert and Henry *Irving, among many others, wrote frequent notes for their productions asking that particular machines be adjusted for realism or emotional impact.

*Stanislavsky's *Moscow Art Theatre production of Chekhov's The Seagull (1898) showed some of what might be done; the sounds of a lakeside town at dusk on a summer evening vividly created the offstage environment, both realistically and expressionistically. The effect required many stagehands, each making one of the component sounds, and was too complicated for most productions. But the design of ambient sound for a quiet moment, at a time when theatrical sound was dominated by cavalry charges, fire engines, and the like, made this an influential production. The transforming idea was that sound should be realistic but its timbre, pitch, and rhythm should enhance the mood. The brutal gunshot that kills Hedda Gabler should not be the same as the comic ineffectual attempted murder in Uncle Vanya.

At the *Old Vic in *London in the late 1920s and early 1930s, Frank Napier formulated influential principles and methods that pointed the way to later sound designs. The director Tyrone *Guthrie said that Napier 'could could give you the hoofbeat realistic . . . or . . . the hoofbeat *surrealistic—the Inner Meaning of the hoofbeat'. Napier's Noises Off advocated that sounds be instantly recognizable, emotionally coloured to suit the play, and as if they all originated in the same world. He described the ideal way of evolving a sound design at a time when audio playback was of relatively poor quality and always noticeably scratchy, so that mechanical effects were preferable.

According to Napier, nearly all stage sounds were complex, made up of several overlapping and differing sounds, and the first step was analysis into component simple sounds. For example, a cuckoo clock sounding consisted of continued ticking, the whirr of the spring mechanism, the door opening, the hammer-and-diaphragm that supplied air to the whistle, the in-and-out whistle itself, and the door closing. Even a simple door slam might involve a hinge squeak, the rattle of hardware on the door as it was set in motion, the impact, a reverberation, and the rattle after impact. Once a list of simple sounds and their timings had been worked out, the next step was to decide how each simple sound ought to be coloured, making it louder or softer, shriller or more melodious, higher or lower, than the real sound. Then for each sound, a source, which might well *not* be the real thing, should be devised. Finally a means would be found for sequencing the simple sounds to produce the desired complex sound.

An overall sound or an orchestration for the whole play could be created by using a common set of simple sounds in the building up of complex sounds, and by establishing patterns in the colouring. For example, one might establish a pattern of using more reverberation than natural for important sounds that punctuated the action, so that the flames of the manuscript and the suicidal gunshot both echo longer than they naturally would in *Hedda Gabler*, or one might make sounds for a comedy faster and busier than natural (such as the title character's repeated falls in *Kaufman's *The Man Who Came to Dinner*). The last step in orchestration was to adjust the sound for the acoustics of the theatre. If one needed a flat snap in a concert hall, for example, one had to restrict sound paths so that the natural reverberation would not enrich the sound; on the other hand, in a dry house thunder machines would require extra resonators to be effective.

Napier's principles, though they produced excellent results, were time consuming and labour intensive. Few theatres employed anyone specializing in sound and almost none allowed enough time to make it possible. Perhaps the closest to Napier's ideal ever realized was in the original production of *Wilder's *Our Town* (1938), in which the conscious decision to *rehearse with live sounds from an early stage led to uniquely rich aural work. Ultimately, *Noises Off* was far more influential on *radio and early *television. After the Second World War, BBC sound effects recordings, still some of the best available, which had been built up by Napier's methods, became widely available and were used for broadcast; their superiority to other products led competitors and eventually theatres to learn Napier's methods, the letter in particular if not the spirit in general.

5. Improvements and challenges, 1950–present

In 1951 for the first time sound quality was no longer a given for a space: electronic reverberation was installed to improve sound quality in the Royal Festival Hall in London. The technique led to general improvements in sound quality as many second-rate houses could buy better acoustics out of a box. Electronic reverberation also made it possible to 'tune' a theatre or concert hall, so that multi-purpose spaces (particularly municipal and educational *auditoriums) could have optimal acoustics for several different functions, adjusting reverberation time with the twist of a knob. Such systems are still not common except in new spaces where classical music must alternate with lectures, the two common functions that require the most different tunings.

Reel-to-reel tape recorders in the 1950s made for easier cueing, and produced sound with much less hiss than that found in phonograph records, so a greater diversity of sounds could be used in greater numbers. Sound boards, modelled on light boards, became common in the 1960s, allowing an operator in the booth to cue in ambient noise and to mix it on the fly, so that, for example, a single operator could create the sounds of a car pulling up on a gravel driveway on a summer evening, and a light rain starting as a couple got out of the car, just as in a *film, but timing everything to coincide with the not-altogether-regular actions of the live actors. Sound boards also gave most theatres a way to mix purchased recordings with their own recorded sounds to make new effects.

The existence of better tools and thus better control of sound led rapidly to expanded use of sound, and to the recognition of sound as a genuine theatrical design discipline like lighting, set, and costumes. Dan Dugan of the *American Conservatory Theatre in *San Francisco seems to have been the first person given the title 'sound designer' (in 1968), though he was clearly far from the first person to have the function, and by the mid-1970s the title was commonly found in professional programmes throughout the English-speaking world.

In recent decades the far superior quality of cinema sound has strongly influenced both what is attempted by, and what is demanded of, theatrical sound. Cinemas are deliberately acoustically dead; they have reverberation times as close to zero as can be managed, so that all sound is primary, emerging from speakers around the room. Movies do not sound acoustically dead because the echoes needed for reverberation are recorded in the soundtrack itself; films, unlike theatre performance, need not rely on the building to make sounds work. Since volume in cinema can be arbitrarily high, it is then possible to produce near perfect clarity at all seats by proper adjustment of speaker volumes. Sound quality is very nearly as good as it would be if all the listeners wore headphones.

It is difficult for playhouses without electronic amplification to match this; even in the best theatres, film-like clarity is possible for audiences of no more than 300 (in an excellent *proscenium theatre) to 500 (in a fine arena). A person with normal hearing and good concentration, in a hall with good acoustics, can clearly distinguish speech in a room with a volume of about 2,800 cubic metres (c.100,000 cubic feet), and performance spaces as big as 4,000 cubic metres (c.140,000 cubic feet) were common before the twentieth century (though one might wonder how well anyone in the back row could hear). Yet contemporary spectators complain of inability to hear in most spaces larger than 1,200 cubic metres (42,000 cubic feet). *Musicals are now all but universally miked, and even realistic stage plays are sometimes miked as well. This creates a subtly different quality in the sound, for the primary sound now originates from speakers out in the house, echoes are not proportional to the distances from the actors and the walls, and thus the aural cues imply that one is not watching live actors so much as three-dimensional film without close-ups.

As hearing continues to deteriorate from cumulating loud music and noisy environments, as people grow less accustomed to concentrating while listening, and as headphones and good home stereo systems raise expectations, we might doubt that we will hear another Laurence *Olivier or John *Barrymore, or even a Mary *Martin or Ethel *Merman. When audiences demand to be able to hear as well as they do with headphones in their living rooms, natural projection withers in the face of artificial amplification. This subtly blurs the distinction between live and recorded performance; seemingly the audience no longer must behave as if they are in a room with a living person, who must speak so that they can hear, and to whom they must listen. 'Live cinema' sound also redefines the job of *acting; the clear diction and resonant projection that were once major parts of *training can be largely dispensed with for film. But the trained voice was more than just a necessity for audibility; it had a wider range and a greater precision of emotional expressiveness, and the best playwrights wrote to take advantage of the exactitude with which a trained voice could touch the whole realm of human psychological possibility. If trained voices are no longer needed for audibility, a much more subjective and interior style of acting will be enabled, and the 'liveness' of theatre will further deteriorate.

Although digital sound has made it easy to use many more effects by improving cueing and decreasing noise, and multiple compact disc players have allowed more complex mixes, oddly the digital revolution at first was something of a setback for the sound designer. Sound direct from a CD required that one take what was available (and of course if the sound were mixed and transferred to tape the acoustic advantages would be lost). It was easier to pull a steam train off a recording than to imagine the right steam train and construct its sound. This will certainly be only a temporary setback for design; by 2000 it was common for special sound effects to be made up again, as CD writers or 'burners' became ordinary consumer goods, allowing any theatre to create and alter sound digitally.

Digital sampling, enabling the digital editing of sound, is a great convenience and will make major differences as technicians become more experienced with it. In addition to performing all the tricks formerly done with mixing boards, electronic delays and repeats, and cut and spliced tape, the sampler offers important new capabilities. Simple software which runs on desktop computers can analyse sound digitally, so that one can subtly speed up or slow down music without changing its pitch, sweeten a flute, add reverberation to an explosion, alter the timbre of a machine's noise, and so forth. The sound designer is gradually being freed from searching for an actual sound that corresponds to the imagined sound, now that it is possible to create almost any sound directly. Electronic cueing, in which onstage sensors can be used to trigger direct-from-memory sound effects, makes it possible to coordinate effects with precision that was previously impossible; James Lebrecht describes the coordination of a breaking-bottle sound recording with the shattering of a nearly soundless stage bottle, for example, which was extremely difficult to do before the advent of electronic cueing.

As sound systems rapidly become more capable, as designers and technicians learn to exploit them, and as sound people become more established in theatrical practice and custom, sound will win a larger role in the theatre; it seems likely that the sort of improvement lighting underwent from 1945 to 1960 may well occur for sound early in the twenty-first century.

See also MEDIA AND PERFORMANCE; MULTIMEDIA PERFORMANCE; CYBER THEATRE. JB

KAYE, DEENA, and LEBRECHT, JAMES, *Sound and Music for the Theatre*, 2nd edn. (Boston, 2000)

LEONARD, JOHN, 'Sound effects', in Graham Walne (ed.), *Effects for the Theatre* (London, 1995)

—— *Theatre Sound* (New York, 2001)

LORD, PETER, and TEMPLETON, DUNCAN, *The Architecture of Sound: designing places of assembly* (London, 1986)

NAPIER, FRANK, *Noises Off: a handbook of sound effects* (London, 1936)

RETTINGER, MICHAEL, *Handbook of Architectural Acoustics and Noise Control: a manual for architects and engineers* (Blue Ridge Summit, Pa., 1988)

SHIRLEY, FRANCIS ANN, *Shakespeare's Use of Off-Stage Sound* (Lincoln, 1963)

SOUTH-EAST ASIA *See* CAMBODIA; INDONESIA; LAOS; MALAYSIA; MYANMAR; PHILIPPINES; SINGAPORE; THAILAND; VIETNAM.

SOUTHERNE, THOMAS (1660–1746)

Irish playwright. Southerne's first play, *The Loyal Brother* (1682), was performed at *Drury Lane with a *prologue and *epilogue written by his friend John *Dryden. The successful mingling of *heroic and sentimental *tragedy was repeated in his dramatic adaptations of Aphra *Behn's novels *The Fatal Marriage* (1694) and *Oroonoko* (1695). Southerne's unusually sympathetic treatment of a female perspective of the world is most obvious in his three *comedies of manners. The most popular of these, *Sir Anthony Love* (1690), directly *satirizes male behaviour through the witty and skilful intrigues of the heroine Lucia, who dominates the *action of the play disguised as the titular Sir Anthony: a *breeches role written for Susannah Mountfort. William *Congreve contributed a song to Southerne's comedy *The Maid's Last Prayer* (1693) and Southerne was instrumental in revising Congreve's first play, *The Old Bachelor* (1693), performed a few weeks later. Southerne was a commercial playwright, seeking to please an *audience in transition between Restoration libertinism and eighteenth-century sentiment, but, unlike many, his writing also attracted *critical praise. GBB

SOUTHWARK THEATRE

The first permanent *playhouse in America, the Southwark was built in 1766 by David *Douglass in *Philadelphia. Though located outside the city limits, its opening brought a lengthy *anti-theatrical campaign. It was roughly constructed of brick and wood, painted red, and lit by oil lamps. In 1767 it presented Thomas *Godfrey's *The Prince of Parthia*, the first play by an American to be professionally produced. It served the American Company throughout the 1790s. Following a *fire in 1821, it became a distillery, prompting *Dunlap's comment, 'Once pouring out a mingled strain of good and evil, it now dispenses purely evil.'
AHK

SOVREMENNIK THEATRE

The Sovremennik opened in 1957 in *Moscow with *Rozov's *Alive Forever*. Oleg *Efremov and his class of the *Moscow Art Theatre School (including Galina Volchek and Oleg *Tabakov) left the MAT, which was unable to resolve problems of collective leadership or make contact with its contemporaries. The name *Sovremennik* (contemporary) signalled that *audience, *actors, and *playwrights belonged to the younger generation; productions were designed to create a psychological bond with the audience through the exploration of shared concerns such as the nature of truth and responsibility. The Sovremennik's relationship with the authorities, however, was not an easy one. Productions were often criticized, and the repertoire of contemporary plays was looked on with great suspicion. When Efremov left the Sovremennik to become *artistic director of the MAT in 1970, he took along many actors and broke up the Sovremennik ensemble. During the 1970s and 1980s Galina Volchek developed an interesting repertoire and welcomed talented young directors, including Valery *Fokin and Roman *Viktyuk.
BB

SOWANDE, BODE (1948–   )

Nigerian playwright, director, and *manager. Best known in Nigeria for his *television scripts, Sowande's plays include *The Night Before* (Ibadan, 1972), *A Sanctus for Women* (produced as *The Angry Bridegroom*, Sheffield, 1976), and *Farewell to Babylon* (Ibadan, 1978). His international reputation is partly based on *Circus of Freedom Square* (1985) and *Ajantala-Pinocchio* (1992), both produced in Italy. A graduate in French, he received a commission for a play to mark the bicentenary of the French Revolution (*Tornadoes Full of Dreams*, Lagos, 1989), and the next year wrote a localized version of *Molière's *The Miser* called *Arelu*. As part of his engagement with Yoruba material, in 1995 he adapted Amos Tutuola's *My Life in the Bush of Ghosts*. Convinced that the playwright must contribute to raising *political awareness, Sowande's work has often confronted social and political

issues. He frequently mixes fact with fiction, explores the relationship between anarchy and revolution, and draws attention to the process that changes idealists into cynics. His productions are often complex, sometimes sprawling, his focus blurred by political rhetoric and his conclusions characterized by loose ends. The richness of his mixture of Yoruba and European elements, together with his religious preoccupations—mostly clearly seen in *Barabas and the Master Jesus* (1980)—mean that he is out of step with the more radical of the second generation of Nigerian dramatists.
JMG

SOWERBY, GITHA (1876–1970)

English playwright whose best-known work is the powerful *Rutherford and Son* (1912). Set in the north Yorkshire home of the oppressive patriarch, the portrayal of a father's obsession with his glass manufacturing business and his tyranny over the wrecked lives of his family was influenced by *Ibsen and Granville *Barker. The play was revived to acclaim at the Royal *National Theatre by Katie *Mitchell in 1994. Sowerby's other work includes *Ruth* and *Before Breakfast* (both 1912), *A Man and Some Women* (1914), *Sheila* (1917), *The Stepmother* (1924), and *The Policeman's Whistle* (1935). She also wrote several children's books with her sister Millicent.
AS

SOYINKA, WOLE (AKINWANDE OLUWOLE SOYINKA) (1934–   )

Nigerian actor, playwright, novelist, theorist, and political activist. Winner of the Nobel Prize for Literature in 1986, Soyinka is commonly regarded as *Africa's greatest playwright. His confrontational approach has kept his work and his person in controversy. The anti-colonial stance of his early work persisted from *The Lion and the Jewel* (1959) to *Death and the King's Horseman* (1976). But he is also a *post-colonial writer, forging in the 1960s a distinctive local theatre that, while written in English, drew basic structural elements from Yoruba *rituals and festivals, as in *A Dance of the Forests* (1960), *The Strong Breed* (*film, 1963; staged in Ibadan, 1966), *The Road* (*London, 1965), and *Kongi's Harvest* (Lagos, 1965). In the 1970s Soyinka turned to European models and handled them distinctively, particularly in *The Bacchae of Euripides* at the *National Theatre in London (1973) and *Opera Wonyosi* (Ile-Ife, 1977). The latter, based on *The Threepenny Opera* and incorporating a wide range of *musical styles, indicates Soyinka's high regard for *Brecht and his familiarity with European and African composers. Less obvious was the response to Jean *Genet in *A Play of Giants* and a reworking of *The Blacks* (unperformed).

Soyinka has long been involved in the practical aspects of theatre. After study at Leeds University (1954–7), he was a play reader at the *Royal Court Theatre in London before his return

World première of Wole **Soyinka**'s *Beatification of Area Boy*, West Yorkshire Playhouse, Leeds, 1995, directed by Jude Kelly, with Susan Aderin as Mama Put and Anthony Ofoegbu as the Military Governor's ADC.

to Nigeria in 1960, where he established immediately the 1960 Masks, and in subsequent years the Orisun Theatre. From *Swamp Dwellers* (London, 1958), which was triggered by the announcement that oil had been found in the Niger Delta, Soyinka demonstrated passionate responses to Nigerian events, notable especially in his writing for *radio, *television, and his satirical *revues, including *The New Republican* (Ibadan, 1964), *Before the Blackout* (Ibadan, 1965), and *Before the Deluge* (Abeokuta, 1991). His contributions to national debates in these formats has fed into the longer plays: the anti-authoritarianism of the revue sketch 'Babuzu Lion of Malladi' can be seen as a precursor to *Kongi's Harvest* (1967), while the popular *Jero Plays* (*The Trials of Brother Jero*, Ibadan, 1960; *Jero's Metamorphosis*, Bristol, 1974), together with *Requiem for a Futurologist* (1983, based on a radio play), came from a compulsion to comment on current situations.

The major works of the 1990s had a similar genesis. *From Zia, with Love* (Siena, 1992) was written partly because the Nigerian military junta had introduced the death sentence for offences connected with drug trafficking and made it valid retroactively. Soyinka's reaction was first heard in a radio play, *A Scourge of Hyacinths* (BBC, 1991); the stage response, which tells the story from a different perspective, incorporates several revue-style episodes and a number of songs. *Beatification of Area Boy* (Leeds, 1995), another major play of the later period, drew on material that had been presented in a revue (*Before the Deluge*) and included songs from a record Soyinka had released entitled *Unlimited Liability Company* (1983).

As his international reputation grew, Soyinka's situation at home worsened. He was detained in 1967 during the Biafran War, released two years later, going into exile in Ghana and Britain, and not returning until 1976. Despite the Nobel Prize—*Africa's first for literature—and his high public profile, his opposition to the repressive military dictatorship forced him into exile again in 1994. He was charged with treason in 1997, eventually returning after the charges were lifted in 1998, though he chose to remain based outside Nigeria.

His 1990 *satire on American political correctness, *1994*, was presented at Emory University in Atlanta when Soyinka took up a chair there in 1996. He responded to a request for a play for young British actors with *Travel Club and the Boy Soldier* (1997), which confronted 'First World' youths with 'Third

World' issues. About the same time events affecting members of the playwright's family prompted a new radio play: escaping from the tightening noose of Sani Abacha's oppressive regime, Soyinka's daughter had flown with her family to London where, after giving birth, she found herself in a tangle of red tape. *Document of Identity* (BBC, 1999) takes the family's dilemma as its starting point. Much of Soyinka's writing during the 1990s was polemical; almost all was in prose, some of it bilious. Lacking direct contact with his primary *audience and in touch with only a few trusted companions, his recent plays have lacked the resonance of the earlier ones. The best works, however, *From Zia* and *Area Boy*, exhibit a continuing interest in mixing the music and conventions found in popular Nigerian theatre. This was also apparent in the international production of *King Baabu* (Lagos, 2001), a radical reworking of *Jarry's *Ubu roi*. Directed by Soyinka, with a cast from Nigeria and Britain, and crew members from Switzerland, it subsequently *toured nationally and abroad. *See also* AFRICA, ANGLOPHONE.   JMG

SPANISH GOLDEN AGE *See* EARLY MODERN PERIOD IN EUROPE.

SPEAIGHT, ROBERT (1904–76)

English actor, director, and writer. After Oxford and his professional debut in 1926 with the *Liverpool Repertory Company, Speaight's first major role was as the war-shattered Hibbert in *Sherriff's *Journey's End* (1929–30). A relatively short, stocky actor with a rich voice, he created the role of Becket in the 1935 première of T. S. *Eliot's *Murder in the Cathedral*, a part he would play in many revivals but which also led to typecasting problems. Roles in other modern *verse drama included Antony in Ronald Duncan's *The Way to the Tomb* (1945–6) and Sir Claude Hulhammer in Eliot's *The Confidential Clerk* (1954). As a director his work included French-language productions of *Antony and Cleopatra* (1947) and *Romeo and Juliet* (1950), and *King Lear* in *Los Angeles (1960) in which he also played the lead. A writer of wide-ranging interests, he published several novels and biographies, together with a number of theatre studies, including *William Poel and the Elizabethan Revival* (1954), *Shakespeare on the Stage* (1973), and his memoirs, *The Property Basket* (1970).   CEC

SPECHT, KERSTIN (1956–)

German dramatist and *film director. After studying German literature and theology at Munich University, she worked as an assistant director for the Bavarian broadcasting company. This was followed by further study at the Munich Film and Television School where she produced three short films: *Die stille Frau* (*The Silent Woman*); *Africa*; *Wilgefort*. As a stage writer she came into prominence in 1990 with *Das glühend Männle*

(*The Radiant Mannikin*, Bonn, 1990) and *Amiwiesen* (*Yankee Fields*, 1990). Further plays include *Carceri* (1996) and *Die Froschkönigin* (*The Frog Princess*, 1998). Her earlier plays are written in the tradition of critical *folk theatre, relying on dialect and containing references to fairy tales and folk songs); in *Carceri* she deals with the French philosopher Althusser, who killed his wife in 1980.   CBB

SPECIAL EFFECTS

As with *pornography, *comedy, and overacting, almost any two people can agree on examples of special effects, but no one rule identifies them. Walne's *Effects for the Theatre*, one of the best contemporary discussions of the subject, omits any definition. Commonly a special effect:

1. presents something that is not actually happening, either because it is physically impossible (people disappearing, a man turned into an animal), or because it is impossible in a theatre (a sinking ship, a helicopter landing);
2. hopes to make a strong impression upon the *audience;
3. is an unusual or unique event;
4. is executed by methods that cross normal craft and operational boundaries (for instance a trick *prop wired to pick up a sound that activates a special light);
5. relies on distraction of the *audience (for example, actors fencing downstage left, pulling the attention of spectators just as another actor enters through a vampire *trap upstage right);
6. uses concealed or deceptive devices (such as traps, false bottoms, hidden wires);
7. creates *illusions which are mutually reinforcing by concealed coordination (a black powder charge set off in a steel drum in the wings, timed with the flash of special *lighting instruments, followed by the shaking of a stage wall, a picture dropping from the wall, the rumble of a thunder run, and the fall of fake debris from a 'snow bag', designed to create the impression of a bomb because the component effects appear to be causing each other).

Theatrical traditions around the world embrace special effects for the moment of sacrament, when the spectator sees concepts become material with an immediacy that *text alone cannot match. Special effects bypass *Diderot's paradox of *acting: the actor playing Hamlet can sustain the sacrament only by keeping his *acting invisible, and if we are emotionally engaged we do not simultaneously judge his acting or contemplate Shakespeare's philosophy of action. But a really good *ghost effect can chill the blood, and confront us with our fear of what follows death, even though we know at that moment exactly how it is done (*see* PEPPER'S GHOST). When a concept central to a culture is enacted and embodied convincingly, we touch the heart of theatre.

For example, in one Yoruban *ritual in *Africa, the night *dance of the Olua festival, many conventions of Yoruban performance have been altered to make a key effect possible. The performance is given at night by flickering firelight, with most lighting from the rear, and electric lighting has not been added though it has been readily available for many years. An end-stage configuration replaces the more usual in-the-round (*see* ARENA AND IN-THE-ROUND), and the audience is kept far back rather than brought up close. The two dancers perform in a space in which *scenery is of different sizes. The effect is a greatly exaggerated version of the one produced by actors walking upstage in *perspective scenery; unable to obtain parallax to accurately estimate distance (and thus size), the human eye falls back on comparison with the objects to which the dancer appears to be closest. Since these objects are of misleading sizes, the dancers appear to abruptly grow and shrink by a factor of more than three, sometimes apparently half a metre (almost 2 feet) tall, sometimes more than 6 metres (20 feet) tall. The performance is built around, and for the effect of, a recurring motif in West African mythology, that of beings who change their size at will. A culturally vital metaphor is brought to immediate material life in the presence of the entire community.

Special effects may have large conventional components but they are illusionistic at heart. Even though a Chinese *parade dragon does not look 'real' in the way that a computer-generated animated dragon in a modern special effects *film does, the dragon still relies on a combination of illusions—that smoke shot from a bellows through the nostrils looks as if it had been exhaled, that the dragon itself is a single organism rather than a team of operators, and that the jaws open and close volitionally. The illusion is more or less participatory depending on the limits of technology and audience convention; culture and tradition determine whether the audience is to see or not to 'see' the crane (*mechane*) and cables needed for Medea to depart into the heavens or the wires that allow Peter Pan to *fly.

Often special effects owe their sacramental power to the coincidence of convention and illusion. For example, in *kabuki one finds the *bukkaeri*, a sort of 'drop top' *costume in which a few threads pulled from the shoulders cause the upper part of the costume to fall, inside out, over the lower; the inside lining matches the undergarment, so the result is an instantaneous change of colour and cut, an apparent complete recostuming. If this change is covered by a distraction elsewhere on the stage, it can appear to have happened instantly. It is often used for the moment when a ghost masquerading as a living person is suddenly revealed; we understand the suddenness by the illusion but the revelation by convention. The reverse can happen as well; in several kabuki plays the combination of conventions of a wave cloth with a boat on wheels, pushed by the 'invisible' stagehands, produces an illusion of a boat at sea.

From its beginnings Western theatre has been biased against special effects, usually associating them with popular entertainment and often relegating them to lower-status theatres. In *Aristotle's *Poetics*, *spectacle is made the last and least of the six elements of *tragedy. The tendency can be traced through the disputes between Inigo *Jones and Ben *Jonson; the rivalries between actors, *playwrights, and machinists in the baroque courts; the denigration of *melodrama, *féerie, *pantomime, and stage *magic by the 'serious' artists of the nineteenth century; the eagerness with which the American *musical shed its fantastic roots as it became 'serious' (compare *The Black Crook* with *Show Boat*); and the critical disapproval of big, popular, spectacle-centred shows, a tradition that runs from *Uncle Tom's Cabin* (1852) and *Around the World in Eighty Days* (1876) to *Les Misérables* (1980) and *The Phantom of the Opera* (1986).

Because Western theatre has been so enamoured of illusion for the last few centuries, many theatrical legends surround effects that were somehow 'too real'. These range from the pursuit by wolves of a woman tied to a horse in *Mazeppa* (the horse was led by the halter, and walked across the stage; the wolves were hand puppets worked from behind a *ground row), which was supposed to have induced women to faint, to the various apocryphal attempts by spectators to rescue the *heroines of melodramas from drowning (in a sea of waving cloth), burning to death in buildings (which had gas jet flames in their windows), or being run over by locomotives (which were mostly canvas). The heyday of such *realistic special effects was the nineteenth century, from which all these examples come, and behind many a famous figure there was a machinist of distinction—the melodramatist *Pixérécourt admits, on the first page of his memoirs, his debt to A. Moench in *Paris, and Charles *Kean's years at the *Princess's Theatre in *London would have been very different without his designer Frederick *Lloyds.

Many fine illusionistic effects were seen in pantomime; unfortunately we have almost no detailed descriptions of exactly how they were executed, but from notes on standard practices and what is known of the favourite tricks of machinists, we can make plausible guesses. For example, *Planché's *Beauty and the Beast* (1841) might have used a transformation trap, concealed behind a *ground row, to simultaneously drop the beast through the floor and raise the prince immediately behind where he had been standing; a flash bomb behind the same ground row, to momentarily deafen and blind the audience and thus cover the sound of the trap and the motions of the actors; a deliberately too-large costume on the prince identical to the one worn by the beast, so that the prince would appear to be much smaller; a *firework on the good fairy's wand and a bright, suddenly unshuttered arc light or *limelight on her, to make the audience glance her way just as the effect went off; and a set of tubular bells struck at the moment of transformation. The wand firework and the fairy limelight would pull the eye far to the other side of the stage; the bomb would be set off as the trap crew switched the two actors; an instant later when the audience looked back, still somewhat confused by the bomb, they would see that the beast had become the prince.

The late nineteenth century was the last great age of the special effect on stage, the age in which audiences flocked to *The Bells* (1871) not just for *Irving but also for the gauze effect, *The Corsican Brothers* (1852) not so much for Kean as to see the ghost glide, *Uncle Tom's Cabin* (see TOM SHOW) for Eliza crossing the ice, and Augustin *Daly's *Under the Gaslight* (1867), in which the heroine was tied to railway tracks with the train stopping barely in time. The Paris stage was known for its extraordinary technical feats, the most admired of which were in the Verne and d'Hennery collaborations. In *A Trip to the Moon* (1875), a strikingly realistic (for the time) space launch was shown on stage from the astronaut's point of view, by means similar to the 'bridge trick' in *Boubil and Schönberg's *Les Misérables* more than a century later. *Around the World in Eighty Days* was to play on and off in Paris for over 50 years, during which the major effects (advertised as *tableaux) increased from eighteen to 42, with new effects (usually new means of transportation) added each season, and the show lengthened from between two and three hours to almost five.

The end of the special effects era has been attributed to a number of circumstances. Electric lights banished the flickering shadows of gaslight, in which many effects looked better. The seriousness of early *modernism undermined the idea of visual amusement for the audience (though surely *Ibsen's *Peer Gynt* and *Brand* were written with a keen awareness that there were stock methods of performing all of the special effects). Above all, the cinema set a standard with which onstage special effects could not compete.

If Joe Aveline (in Walne) is correct that modern Western audiences see special effects almost entirely ironically, then that is another symptom of the isolation of and resistance to the sacrament at the heart of special effects, and theatre in the West is less theatrical than ever. Nowadays, special effects are notable for being 'things you can't do on stage', which is mediated knowledge available only to well-informed theatregoers. For example, we know that a movie camera illusion can keep a man in close-up all the way from a bridge rail down to the water below; when the same thing is made to happen on stage in *Les Misérables* (by using a counterweighted bridge that flies up when the man steps off) it is interesting not because we have not seen it before but because we thought it was impossible on stage.

This mediated aspect of special effects extends as far as letting the audience in on the trick. Programmes (see PLAYBILLS AND PROGRAMMES) for the *touring company of *Miss Saigon* (opened 1989) explain that for the helicopter landing, the blade is a rubber ball on a piece of cotton rope (and that it took many experiments to find something safe that would make the proper sound and look right under the lights), that one of the flight crew is a lightweight dummy, and that the soldiers rushing in and out are actually passing through the helicopter into a concealed door to the backstage. Yet when the effect works well, the audience still sees the working helicopter

and not the collection of tricks; ironic mediation and postmodern knowledge seem to collapse in the face of fundamental *theatricality. See also MEDIA AND PERFORMANCE; CYBER THEATRE.

JB

FINKEL, ALICIA, *Romantic Stages: set and costume design in Victorian England* (London, 1996)

MOYNET, M. J., *L'Envers du théâtre* (Paris, 1873), trans. Allan S. Jackson with M. Glen Wilson as *French Theatrical Production in the Nineteenth Century* (New York, 1976)

OGUNBA, OYIN, 'Stage and staging in Yoruban ritual drama', in Dele Layiwola (ed.), *African Theatre in Performance* (Amsterdam, 2000)

WALNE, GRAHAM (ed.), *Effects for the Theatre* (London, 1995)

SPECTACLE see page 1272

SPECTATOR See AUDIENCE.

SPERR, MARTIN (1944–   )

German dramatist. After training as an actor in *Vienna, Sperr came to prominence in the late 1960s with his *Bavarian Trilogy*. *Hunting Scenes from Lower Bavaria* (1966) deals with social behaviour in a Bavarian village, exposing the ignorant dumbness of villagers hounding a young homosexual in 1949. *Tales from Landshut* (1967) shows two rural entrepreneurs fighting for control of a local monopoly and reveals brutal scheming, mendacity, and anti-Semitic behaviour. The last and least accomplished of the three plays, *Münchener Freiheit* (1971), deals with unscrupulous profit making in Munich real estate. *Hunting Scenes from Lower Bavaria* inaugurated the so-called *Volkstück revival of the 1960s with a simultaneous rediscovery of the plays by *Horváth and *Fleisser. Sperr also wrote a version of Edward *Bond's *Saved* for Munich Kammerspiele (directed by Peter *Stein, 1966), as well as a translation and adaptation of Shakespeare's *Measure for Measure* for Peter *Zadek (1967, Bremen). Sperr also works as an actor and translator.   CBB

SPIDERWOMAN THEATER

Oldest continually performing women's theatre company in North America, founded in 1975. Composed of three Kuna/Rappahannock sisters, Lisa Mayo, Gloria Miguel, and Muriel Miguel, this *Native American *feminist theatre group capitalizes upon traditional Native philosophies of humour. Their plays, such as *Sun Moon and Feather*, *Women in Violence*, *Rever-ber-berations*, and *Winnetou's Snake Oil Show from Wigwam City*, use an improvisational style of *clowning that disarms the *audience through *laughter while developing serious investigations of ethnicity, *gender, age, and sexuality. The group takes its name from the Hopi creation goddess who taught her people how to weave. Through a technique they call 'storyweaving', the artists create plays that intertwine

(continued on p. 1273)

SPECTACLE

From the Latin *speculatum* (show, stage play), spectacle has two related meanings in modern *theatre studies. First, it can refer to the visual element of a complex theatrical presentation, wherein it functions (*a*) as a system of codified signs signalling spectators that they are witnessing a *performance, something distinguished from ordinary life, and (*b*) as one of the ways by which a dramatic *action is represented (*Aristotelian *opsis*). Second, spectacle can denote a specific kind of performance, characterized by a primary if not exclusive reliance on (usually elaborate) visual effects. Spectacle in the second sense can be either *mimetic or non-mimetic. A *ballet, for instance, is a visual representation of a dramatic fiction; a tumbling act is a demonstration of human skill and strength. Moreover, spectacle as visual display need not involve direct human participation at all: a *fireworks display only indirectly attests to the human ingenuity of its devising, as does an elaborate scene change (*see* SCENE SHIFTING) that in itself draws spectators' approbation. Of course, every spectacle, both mimetic and non-mimetic, conveys a symbolic political, cultural, or religious message. A Roman triumph (*trionfi*) celebrated a victorious campaign, reinforced Roman superiority over foreign adversaries, and furthered political ambitions. The pyrotechnic displays of Bernardo *Buontalenti in Renaissance Italy and the elaborate Shakespearean productions of Charles *Kean in Victorian England were both testaments to technical innovation and progress. The scenic miracles of the *medieval theatre reflected God's power as well as the machinist's ingenuity.

The two meanings of spectacle cannot in practice be clearly distinguished. Spectacle is essential to all *theatre, is indeed its defining characteristic. It has functioned historically on a continuum ranging from the pure display of the *circus to a barely noticed or acknowledged element in chamber theatre. Even among those performance forms in which spectacle draws attention to itself as a major element, its role has been variable, its relationship to other elements indeterminate, reflecting changing tastes, values, and perceptions.

Ancient Greece. In Greek *mousike* spectacle, primarily in the form of *dance and *costume, was intimately linked with music and poetry. The *dithyramb and choral drama (*tragedy, *comedy, *satyr-play) evolved from and continued to feature costumed, dancing *choruses. The 'spectacle' for which *Aeschylus was famous was achieved mainly through choric dance and costume, and through large numbers of supernumeraries, rather than through scenic effect. *Sophocles, on the other hand, was credited with introducing scene *painting, and dramatists

made use of stage machines such as the *ekkyklema and the *mechane. (*See* GREEK THEATRE.)

Rome. Spectacle for the Romans was a subspecies of *voluptates* (pleasures), but by imperial times, elaborate, often bloody spectacles also served important public functions. *Gladiatorial combat demonstrated manly prowess; *venationes (*animal fights) illustrated imperial power; mass executions helped maintain law and order. The circus, where chariot racing provided the spectacular pleasure, was a microcosm of the Roman state, with ranks and classes arranged in due order (*see* CIRCUS, ROMAN). In some instances, there were theatrical additions: condemned criminals were forced to play roles in dramatized fictions and myths (*see* DAMNATIO); *naumachia re-enacted actual sea battles, functioning as kinds of historical pageant; even gladiatorial combat was theatricalized through costuming. (*See also* ROMAN THEATRE.)

Middle Ages. Wonders and marvels, evidence of God's presence in the world, were staples of *medieval stage presentation. Angels descended in clouds of glory; martyrs were mutilated; blood flowed; fountains gushed water, blood, or milk. The emblems of religious art and architecture were reproduced in processions and *tableaux vivants*, in the scenic *mansions and symbolic costumes of theatrical presentations of human and divine history. Emblematic scenic devices and costumes served similar *allegorical functions in *tournaments and court entertainments.

Early modern Italy. The roots of Renaissance spectacle were in medieval pageantry and display, but now, under court aegis, spectacle affirmed the authority and status of court and prince. The wonders and marvels of elaborate scenic effects reflected less on God's power than on the prince's magnificence and the scene designer's technical brilliance. This Renaissance theatre was in fact a theatre of spectacle in which the dramatist and the actor played subordinate roles. The development of *perspective, changeable *scenery, stage machinery, and the *proscenium stage contributed to a pictorial and painterly theatre wherein a static stage picture, punctuated by surprising scenic effects, replaced dynamic stage action. The sixteenth-century architect-designer inaugurated a 300-year era of scene painting as an essential of stage production (*see* SCENOGRAPHY).

Victorian England. Spectacle is associated with the shows, *pageants, and processions of Elizabethan and Jacobean England, with the court *masque, and with the *opera, *ballet, and *pantomime of the eighteenth century; but it reached a zenith in stage production of the nineteenth century, propelled by pictorialism and *realism, and by a desire for historical accuracy; made possible by technological advances, especially in *lighting; and fuelled by the conviction that *audiences, lacking the imagination of their forebears, could no longer be satisfied or adequately informed by the spoken word. Thus we find the 'archaeological exactitude' of Charles *Kean (*see* ANTIQUARIANISM), and a 'spectacular Shakespeare' that saw real rabbits in Beerbohm *Tree's *A Midsummer Night's Dream*, and Shakespeare's 30-line description of the entry into London of Bolingbroke and Richard in *Richard II* translated into a spectacle featuring several hundred extras and lasting an estimated 40 minutes.

Twentieth century. In the twentieth century, spectacle as visual display has for the most part become the province of the *musical, the ballet, the opera, and the epic *film. Otherwise, perhaps in reaction to the extravagances of the nineteenth century, the twentieth was a century of scenic minimalism.

Theoretical speculation concerning spectacle has been limited mainly to its role in dramatic theatre. Aristotle listed *opsis* as the least among the six parts of tragedy, and treated the realization of the tragic in performance as incidental to the drama, unnecessary, and usually tasteless. Attempted justifications of Victorian spectacle notwithstanding, most discussions have followed Aristotle in decrying spectacle as not only the least among the parts of drama, but as actually antipathetic to dramatic art. Spectacle was resurrected in the last half of the twentieth century in the more neutral senses of (*a*) the object of the audience's gaze, (*b*) the visible part of a dramatic performance, (*c*) the *mise-en-scène; and in these senses it has been subjected to *semiotic analyses of varying degrees of complexity. There have been sporadic attempts to revive the Greek *opsis* as a theoretical concept linking *dramaturgy and performance, but the English word 'spectacle' seems destined to remain less precise in its application. *See* VISION AND THE VISUAL.   RWV

---

personal narratives with traditional Native American storytelling and elements of pop culture. Their *multimedia productions present a non-linear view of time and celebrate the connections between generations.   CLS

SPLIT BRITCHES

American *lesbian-*feminist performance group. Peggy Shaw, Lois Weaver, and Deborah Margolin formed the company after their successful collaboration on a play by the same name for the *WOW Café in 1980. The group draws on *cabaret, *satirical *revue, and the drag show to create often campy performances about lesbian sexuality and, particularly, butch–femme role playing. By the late 1980s the *collective began to create longer dramatic performances like *Belle Reprieve* (1991), a queer deconstruction of Tennessee *Williams's *A Streetcar Named Desire*. Many noted academic feminists have described the group as a model of *gender-subversive performance. *See* QUEER THEORY; FEMINISM.   JAB

SPOKEN CHINESE THEATRE *See* HUAJÜ.

SPORT

The spectacular nature of athletic contests has been apparent at least since the fifth century BC. The Greek Olympiads, which offered competitions of physical speed, strength, and accuracy, were directly parallel to the dramatic contests presented annually in the *Dionysia *festivals in Athens (*see* GREEK THEATRE, ANCIENT). Like the arts of war, sporting events can be pleasing in themselves to watch and exciting in terms of outcome. In one

sense sport is *ritualized, sublimated, or regulated fighting—performed fighting, we might say—closely allied to the tactics of classical warfare. Both require physical stamina and aggression; the events of the Olympiad (running, jumping, wrestling, throwing the javelin, discus, and hammer) were directly modelled on the techniques of land battle common in the Greek experience. Both war and sport are inherently teleological or end-directed (like the *plot of a *tragedy, we might also say): the conclusion will mean glory for the victor and embarrassment, disgrace, or death for the vanquished. Both warfare and sport can be adapted or ceremonialized into entertainment events, and the two modes can also blend easily, as they did in *Roman *gladiatorial contests, *animal fights, *naumachia, and *circus races, in the *tournaments of the *medieval period in Europe, or the game played in the ball courts in ancient Mesoamerica. The presence of spectators not only theatricalizes, it also transforms the purpose of an athletic contest, moving sport from the realm of pure *play to the realm of display.

In the modern period, the rise of professional sports in the latter half of the nineteenth century commodified the bodies of competitors for the sake of entertainment and laid the groundwork for the adulation of celebrity athletes in the twentieth century. English Association Football ('soccer' is a nickname derived from 'association'), which began as a gentleman's sport, soon was vigorously appropriated by the working classes, partly because it required so little specialized equipment. A series of parliamentary Acts after 1847 gradually released British industrial workers on Saturday afternoons, which were often used to play or watch football, establishing the game as part of what Guttmann calls 'proletarian leisure'. By the end of the century local clubs were common, matches and leagues became regulated, and some payments were made to players. The stage was set for the huge commercial development of professional sport that spread globally and incorporated many other amateur games: baseball, boxing, American football, basketball, tennis, rugby, ice hockey, and so on down to roller derby and *television wrestling.

The aesthetic and dramatic implications of sport are magnified by the relationship that usually develops between fans ('fanatics') and a home team. We might expect fans to maintain an intense loyalty to school games, but allegiance passes on to professional sports as well. Despite the fact that in the early twenty-first century many sports are big businesses operated for profit, *audiences regularly take a passionate interest in the fortunes of their side, assuming a pride of ownership in the civic or national team. The absorption of a sporting match, amplified by rivalry, gambling, or alcohol, sparks a febrile excitement among spectators that no theatrical or *filmed show can hope to equal. The *spectacle of men or women engaging all their cunning and strength to achieve a clear victory is an appealing release from the ambiguities of contemporary life, and no doubt is one of the reasons for the ardour of supporters. But since a clear victory for one side always means a clear defeat for the other, the emotion of fans, especially male fans, whether in celebration or despair, can easily spill over into violent expression, as it did so often in British football in the latter twentieth century. The soccer riot, parallel in some ways to *riots in the theatre, which also fed upon the proximity of numerous spectators in an agitated state, is merely one example of how large-scale sport creates unique opportunities for audience participation.

By the end of the twentieth century spectator sports had become intensely commodified through celebrity tours, corporate sponsorship, and a growing demand for televised matches. The development embraced games that generally were amateur as late as the mid-century like golf, tennis, and foot racing. Big-time sport became big-time entertainment, and first-rank athletes often became indistinguishable from film stars—or from *opera stars, considering the popularity of the 'three tenors' concerts that began as part of the 1990 soccer World Cup. The modern Olympics, started in 1896 as a celebration of amateurism and international understanding, have been most notably altered as cultural attitudes to sport changed. The Nazi Party attempted to control them for propaganda purposes in *Berlin in 1936, and in the Cold War period they became a site for ideological confrontation between the superpowers. In 1980 the games were boycotted by 62 nations because they took place in *Moscow, and four years later the Soviet Union and most Soviet-bloc countries boycotted them because they were in *Los Angeles. As the pretence of the amateur standing of Olympic athletes was gradually abandoned, and the number and nature of events included greatly expanded, the quadrennial meeting became more and more a product manufactured by a multinational firm called the International Olympic Committee. In such a marketable environment—an example of how the con-

ditions of postmodernity allow the commodification of almost all areas of life—it is not surprising that some members of the committee were corrupted by gifts and bribes in choosing host cities (which can reap enormous rewards in trade and tourism). Nor is it surprising that the spectacularization of sport has reached a high point with the Olympic opening ceremonies in the 1990s and beyond. Often designed by leading stage *scenographers, these gigantic demonstrations of *dance, music, *fireworks, and other live events, globally televised, have contextualized Olympic sport as a form of theatre.   DK

GUTTMANN, ALAN, *Sports Spectators* (New York, 1986)
KENNEDY, DENNIS, 'Sports and shows: spectators in contemporary culture', *Theatre Research International*, 26 (2001)

SPRECHSTIMME

German term, literally 'speech-voice', used interchangeably with *Sprechgesang* (literally, 'speech-song'). Used in connection with the *operas of serial German composers of the early twentieth century, *Sprechstimme* indicates a form of articulation that has the tonal qualities of speech but the rhythmic regularity of music. It was used most strikingly by Alban Berg in his opera *Wozzeck* (1925) and in Schoenberg's *Moses and Aaron* (1930–2), where the part of Moses is composed entirely in *Sprechgesang*. This highly anti-romantic style of delivery has not, however, been widely adopted due to the narrow range of emotion it can communicate.   SJCW

SPRING WILLOW SOCIETY *See* CHUNLIU SHE.

SQUARZINA, LUIGI (1922–   )

Italian playwright and director. Squarzina was one of the brilliant generation of people, like *Strehler and *Visconti, who introduced the new director-led theatre to Italy. He worked with Vittorio *Gassman in the Teatro d'Arte Italiano, producing the first complete Italian *Hamlet* (1952) and taking works by *Pirandello to South America. He is most closely associated with the Genoa Teatro Stabile, but later worked in *Rome. His own plays, which include *Three Quarters of the Moon* (1955) and *The Five Senses* (1987), show Squarzina to be an acute, disenchanted observer of his own time.   JF

SRI LANKA

A country in South Asia with two major linguistic traditions, Sinhala, an Indo-European language, and Tamil, a Dravidian one. Although today the supremacy of one over the other is a matter of intense controversy and conflict, the two have coexisted on the island since antiquity, have developed distinctive literatures, and have influenced one another. Sinhala is spoken by roughly 75 per cent of the island's population, Tamil by about 25 per cent concentrated mainly in the north and east. The linguistic boundaries are fluid, however, and subject to changing political and economic realities. Plantation agriculture introduced in British colonial times resulted in an influx of Indian Tamil labour to the central hill country, and a substantial Tamil-speaking population now resides there. Similarly, the twenty-year civil war, starting in the early 1980s, has resulted in significant movements of Tamil populations away from the war zones into the south. The influence of the Indian subcontinent on the literature and performance traditions of both languages has been considerable.

1. Sinhala; 2. Tamil

1. Sinhala

Sri Lanka has a rich tradition of Sinhala *ritual performances that hark back to a pre-Buddhist past. Deities and demons propitiated to prevent sickness, famine, and other hazards were later integrated into a pantheon with the Buddha as head, and singing, *dancing, drum music, *masked performances, and dramatic enactments of origin myths became part of popular Buddhism. Comic prose interludes which punctuated these rituals later generated more secular forms of dramatic entertainment. *Kolam* performances in the coastal villages of south Sri Lanka, for example, were patterned on exorcism rites. A narrator introduced each *costumed and masked actor, who danced a role. While women were part of the *audience, the performers were always male. *Kolam* plays were a masquerade of motley *characters, with caricatures of village authority figures, a dramatic event sometimes spliced in.

Two ritual dramas are especially interesting. The first, *sokari*, a *folk performance found mainly in the central hill country, uses a story about marital infidelity to satirize important village type characters (the crafty physician, the exploitative trader, the village headman, a Brahman, the village virago, the exorcist). Sokari, the beautiful but barren wife of the ritualist Guruhamy, runs off with a village physician but is reconciled with Guruhamy when she convinces him that she was the innocent victim of a spell. The *gam maduva* rituals enact the myth of the goddess Pattini. Palanga, Pattini's husband, has squandered their wealth on a courtesan. Accused of stealing the Queen's bracelet, he is killed by the King of Madurai. Pattini discovers his body, resurrects him by the power of her virtue, tears off one of her breasts and flings it at the city of Madurai, which is destroyed by fire. Both *gam maduva* and *sokari* are performed after harvest as fertility rituals. The one seems to *parody the other: Pattini is chaste, faithful, and long-suffering, while Sokari is young, attractive, and unfaithful.

External influences affected a number of traditions, starting with the *nadagam*, a folk opera with stylized dance, which was popular in the eighteenth and nineteenth centuries in south-western Sri Lanka. It may be derived from the *Tamil *nattukuttu* plays and spread by Christian missionaries, though others argue *nadagam* goes back to a pre-fifteenth-century Sinhala poetic drama tradition which absorbed the performance tradition of south Indian immigrants who settled there between the twelfth and fifteenth centuries. The extant *texts were the first written versions of an already established tradition, and the Christian themes the result of colonial missionary contact. As *nadagam* performances lost popularity, *puppet plays took their place, performed at secular and religious festivals, using the same texts. The *Passion play originated in Catholic areas of the north and spread to the west coast; today the most famous performance is held on the island of Duwa during Holy Week. By the late nineteenth century performers of *Parsi theatre from Bombay (*Mumbai) had introduced *nurti*, a form of secular entertainment for urban audiences. Soon Sinhala plays based on the *nurti* format of music, song, dance, elaborate sets, and a fourth-wall *proscenium stage became popular. Dramatists like John de Silva used *nurti* as a vehicle for nationalist anti-colonial sentiments. Two hundred years of British colonialism created an English-speaking elite who, in the early twentieth century, introduced Western theatre and performance traditions to Sri Lanka. The plays were in English and played to small city audiences, but by the 1940s experiments in adapting and translating European plays for the Sinhala theatre grew.

After independence attempts to create a modern, secular, national drama led to considerable experimentation. In 1956 E. R. Sarachchandra produced *Maname*, a poetic drama based on Buddhist legend, blending the stylized dance of the *nadagam* with *nurti* music. It became instantly popular. Thereafter Sarachchandra's poetic dance-dramas broke the barrier that had existed between urban and rural audiences and influenced generations of younger dramatists. Socialism was the political ideology of the 1970s. Plays with a socialist polemic thrust, and translations or adaptations of European dramatists like *Ibsen, *Brecht, and *Sartre, dominated the theatres. *Street theatre, introduced by actor-directors such as Gamini Hathotuwegama, was another expression of political activism. Though the civil war with the Tamil separatist movement did not directly affect most people living in the south, the increasingly authoritarian governments of the 1980s and early 1990s resulted in strict *censorship of the press and almost all forms of literary activity. The theatre surprisingly remained immune from censorship, perhaps because performances were seen as ephemeral, or distanced from political reality like traditional ritual performances, where similar criticism had been permitted or ignored. Satirical *political plays critical of the government and focusing on the pervasive atmosphere of violence became very popular. There was an unprecedented rise in theatre attendance. Playwrights made money, their work was performed around the country, and good actors became household names. By the late twentieth century the rapid penetration of *television into villages and the popularity of serialized tele-dramas had undermined the position of the theatre. Traditional folk performances also have been dying but new religious rituals such as the Saibaba cult and cults to new deities have been taking their place.

2. Tamil

The theatrical tradition of Sri Lankan Tamils combines, as in other Asian traditions, a rich coexistence of pre-modern, pre-literate performance cultures with the conflicting legacies of modernity. Traditional performances include dramatic re-enactments of rituals in religious centres, as well as storytelling traditions of the *kuttu*, which can be found in almost all locations where Tamils predominate, as in Batticaloa, Trincomalee, Vanni, Jaffna, Mannar, and the Tamil neighbourhoods of Colombo. The Tamils living on tea plantations have their own forms, *kamankuttu* and *ariccunan tapacu*. Generally, *kuttu* (resembling *terukkuttu of Tamil Nadu, *India) is performed on a circular stage, with stylized rhythmic movements accompanied by the beats of the *maddalam* (drum) and the directions of the *annavi* (presenter), who guides the performance. The *kuttu* repertoire consists of Hindu epics, myths, and legends, which are treated differently according to specific styles of performance, costume, and choreography, as embodied in two distinct types of *kuttu*: *vadamodi* and *tenmodi*. The *kattavarayan kuttu* of Jaffna is a *genre by itself.

From the late nineteenth century onwards, professional troupes from Tamil Nadu entertained audiences in Sri Lanka with their own versions of *Parsi theatre with songs in the south Indian classical tradition as well as popular songs performed with histrionic flair. This tradition inspired Sri Lankan Tamils to develop their own versions of popular musical entertainment, which were successful till 1970. In the 1930s and 1940s there were more 'serious' interventions in proscenium theatre, represented by Chornalingan (1889–1983), who modelled himself on *Sambandha Mudaliyar of Tamil Nadu by adapting English plays and focusing on *dialogue rather than music. The other important playwright was Kanapathipillai (1903–68), who regaled his audiences with *Shavian socio-political *satires written in the Jaffna dialect. The rediscovery of *kuttu* as an effective form of contemporary theatre constituted an important advance. Inspired by Sarachchandra's seminal Sinhala plays, Vithiananthan (1928–88) adapted the *kuttu* form in productions like *Karnan* and *Ravanesan*, and continued to revive the tradition of *kuttu* with the assistance of the state, especially in schools between 1956 and 1966. Yet another development in theatre was the spate of modern plays influenced by theatre in Tamil Nadu, many of which merged with socially radical Tamil *films (as in Tamil Nadu itself).

The 1970s saw the emergence of young directors like Sundaralingam, Tarcissius, Balendra, Zuhair Hameed, and Mownaguru, who had been influenced by Western theatrical developments within the traditional matrix of *kuttu*. With the escalation of ethnic conflicts and civil war in Sri Lanka by the 1980s, there was a clampdown on all national media and local entertainment in Jaffna, but theatre continued to survive as a powerful medium of social and political criticism. With Shanmugalingam's path-breaking plays theatre continued to flourish in schools and at Jaffna University. Street theatre was used for the propagation of political messages in distant villages. Sithamparanathan, who directed Shanmugalingam's plays, used *Boal's model of forum theatre to extend socio-political discussion among the spectators (*see* OPPRESSED, THEATRE OF THE), and later as a means for rehabilitating war victims. In spite of these political interventions, it is still not uncommon to see plays that are largely an extension of the formulas adopted in south Indian Tamil cinema, a feature that has been discernible since the 1960s.   RO/KS

OBEYESEKERE, RANJINI, *Theater in a Time of Terror: satire in a permitted space* (New Delhi, 1999)

SARACHCHANDRA, E. R., *The Folk Drama of Ceylon* (Colombo, 1966)

SRIMPI

A Javanese court *dance performed by four female dancers to honour visiting royalty. Created by Prince Mangku Nagara I (1757–95), the *Srimpi Anglirmendung* from Surakarta was originally a small *bedoyo performed by seven dancers, later reduced to four. In the Yogyakarta tradition, the four dancers symbolize the four winds. One *srimpi* (*Renggawati*) from Yogyakarta has five dancers, and describes the story of Princess Renggawati catching a white bird that is the animal form of her beloved King Anglingdarma. Many other *srimpis* were created by noblemen to commemorate important events and usually named after the *gamelan melody accompanying them. *Srimpi* compositions are now taught to and performed by dance students in *Indonesia outside the courts.   SM

SRIRANGA (ADYA RANGACHARYA) (1904–86)

Indian dramatist, director, and scholar who worked in *Kannada theatre. Born in Karnataka in the south of *India, Sriranga studied Sanskrit in Pune and *London, which provided the foundation for his contribution to theatre scholarship. He wrote extensively on Sanskrit drama and translated the *Natyasastra, the classical Indian treatise on *dramaturgy, into English and Kannada. Starting in 1930 he wrote more than 40 plays in Kannada. *Harijanvara*, one of his earliest, depicts the social tensions created within a traditional society during Gandhi's anti-untouchability movement. Later his social critique turned ironic, as in *Shokachakra* (*The Wheel of Grief*, 1952), where a Gandhian politician faces moral anguish over the reversal of traditional values in modern times. After the 1950s Sriranga often employed the model of a play-within-a-play, as in *Kattale Belaku* (*Darkness and Light*, 1959) and *Rangabharata*

(1965). He was also an active theatre practitioner, directing many of his own plays and spearheading the *amateur theatre movement in Karnataka. His plays have been widely translated into other Indian languages. KVA

STAFFORD-CLARK, MAX (1943–)

English director, particularly associated with new writing. After study at Trinity College, Dublin, he was connected with *Edinburgh's *Traverse Theatre from 1966 to 1974 (*artistic director, 1968–71), then founded *Joint Stock (with David *Hare and David Aukin, 1974), a company which involved actors in the writing process and developed many of Caryl *Churchill's works. He has directed six Churchill premières, including *Cloud Nine* (1979), *Serious Money* (1987), and *Blue Heart* (1999). As artistic director of *London's *Royal Court (1979–93), his premières included Michael Hastings's *Tom and Viv* (1985) and Timberlake *Wertenbaker's *Our Country's Good* (1987), which ran in *repertory with *Farquhar's *The Recruiting Officer*. His book *Letters to George* (1989) is a series of letters to Farquhar about the *rehearsal process. He co-founded the *touring company Out of Joint with Sonia Friedman in 1993, developing and directing Sebastian *Barry's *The Steward of Christendom* (1995), Mark *Ravenhill's *Shopping and Fucking* (1996), and Alistair Beaton's political *farce *Feelgod* (2001), among other works. Stafford-Clark's direction is considered lively and nuanced. GAO

STAGE

The space, specified by the conventions of the particular theatrical tradition, within which the *audience will assume that people are performing and that objects, clothing, space, and light are designed; the place where the *actors act; where the play is played. This spatial locus of sacramental process is so fundamental to theatre that 'stage' often means 'theatre' in English idiom, a metonym common to theatre language (or stage talk) since at least a generation before Shakespeare. Modern usage classifies stages by the position they occupy relative to the audience. An *end-stage* stands at one end of the hall or room, with the audience seated on just one side. If the stage is framed by an arch, it may also be called a *proscenium, picture-frame, picture, or keyhole stage. An *alley or traverse stage* is situated between two facing banks of seating, and is much the least common arrangement. A *thrust stage* has seating on three sides. In *arena* or *in-the-round* seating, the audience completely surrounds the stage.

It has been conventionally held in the twentieth century that the more an audience surrounds a stage, the more intimate will be the connection with the actors and the more communal the experience; conversely, an audience all facing in the same direction, separated from the stage, has a less involving, more distant, private experience that emphasizes visual effect. Whether or not this is true, through most of the twentieth century theatrical conservatism was associated with the end-stage and radicalism with thrust and arena stages. JB

STAGE DESIGN *See* SCENOGRAPHY.

STAGE DIRECTIONS

Sometimes also called *didascalia*, stage directions consist of all *text in a play not spoken by actors. Many *theorists since the 1980s have followed semiotician Anne Ubersfeld in regarding even *character headings, and *act and *scene divisions, as *didascalia*. Stage directions were sparse or non-existent in plays throughout most of Western theatre history and in most non-Western traditions. The earliest extant manuscripts of classical *Greek plays lack even character headings, using dashes to mark shifts in speaker. With a few notable exceptions, stage directions in plays from the *medieval and *early modern periods in Europe indicate little beyond entrances and exits; over the centuries editors have added most other stage directions typically included in modern editions. The use of stage directions increased gradually until the end of the nineteenth century. By that time, stage directions, such as the door slam that ends *Ibsen's *A Doll House*, were often pivotal to a play's *plot and impact. Playwrights such as *Shaw and, slightly later, Eugene *O'Neill composed stage directions spanning several pages. Some *futurist and *dada plays, as well as several plays by Samuel *Beckett, consist wholly of stage directions.

A number of factors contributed to the increased use of stage directions: (*a*) the breakdown of clear performance conventions dictating stage movement and *scenography; (*b*) a growing demand for novel stage *spectacles, a trend most evident in nineteenth-century *melodrama; (*c*) a quasi-scientific fascination with the effect of environment on behaviour, articulated most explicitly in the doctrines of *naturalism; (*d*) the development of psychology in the late nineteenth century, which encouraged playwrights to convey motivations and emotions not expressed directly through *dialogue; and (*e*) an expanded market for *published plays that had to communicate effectively to a reading public.

As the use of stage directions increased, *directors were assuming a new role as the primary authority in the production process and began to view stage directions as an impingement on their creative prerogative. At the turn of the twentieth century Edward Gordon *Craig insisted that competent directors had nothing to learn from stage directions. Similarly, some *acting textbooks in the second half of the century enjoined actors to strike out all stage directions before beginning to study their parts. Theatre theorists toward the end of the century such as Patrice Pavis, Marco de Marinis, and Marvin Carlson echoed this attitude, arguing that stage directions have the force of optional suggestions rather than binding requirements. Meanwhile, some playwrights insisted on their right to have their plays performed exactly as written. In the 1980s this controversy erupted into a series of highly publicized disputes in which playwrights such as Beckett, Edward *Albee, and Arthur *Miller objected to or threatened legal action against productions that flouted their stage directions.   DZS

STAGE DOOR

The door between the street and the backstage areas of a *playhouse, to be used by theatre professionals and their invited guests, traditionally monitored by the 'stage-door keeper'. A 'stage-door Johnny' (Edwardian *London) was an upper-class man who waited at the stage door—in popular fiction, because he was in love with an actress, in reality because some of the badly underpaid *chorus girls depended on quasi-prostitution to survive.   JB

STAGE LIGHTING *See* LIGHTING.

STAGE MANAGER

A complicated term that changes meaning according to historical and traditional circumstances. In England and America it was sometimes used to refer to *actor-managers of the nineteenth or early twentieth centuries, or to a functionary delegated by them to organize actor movement on stage, a prototype of the *modernist *director. In translating certain Asian theatre roles into English, the stage manager could be an onstage performer separate from the *action of the play, who may variously serve as narrator, master of ceremonies, coordinator of the stage crew, *prompter, onstage *acting coach, cheerleader, or effects person, who may be conventionally visible or invisible and may or may not interact with the *characters, *audience, or actors-as-actors. Functionaries as different as the *kyogen kata* of *kabuki in *Japan, or the *Adhikari* of *jatra and the *Vyas* of *Ram lila in *India, have become the 'stage manager' in some English translations.

In the modern Western theatre, the stage manager is the chief operations officer for a production, and the liaison between the artistic, technical, and production management teams. In the Anglo-American tradition, the stage manager is the director's assistant, secretary, and executive officer; she or he schedules and arranges *rehearsals and conducts the business side of them; records movements, stage business, and cues in the promptbook (*see* BOOK); facilitates at meetings of the design and technical staff; heads the production crew; maintains the director's version once the show is running; and calls the cues during the show's run, in addition to numerous other duties.

Normally the stage manager will have a number of assistants. Because of the complexities of technology and production, stage management is almost indispensable in modern theatre, among its most highly honoured crafts, and the most consistently employable.   JB

STAGE SOCIETY

The longest-lived of the late Victorian and Edwardian play-producing societies in *London. Founded in 1899 and incorporated in 1904, it presented productions for 40 years and was not formally wound up until 1948. It was also the largest of the British independent theatres, with membership initially held to 300 but eventually rising as high as 1,500. While the founders and subscribers were *amateurs, Stage Society performers were professionals acting for little or nothing, and its venues were commercial theatre buildings on dark nights. Consequently, productions were given only one or two performances in the interstices in West End schedules, usually Sunday evenings and Monday matinées. A notable handful of Stage Society productions were of plays which had been refused a licence (*see* CENSORSHIP) and were therefore given nominally private performances, including *Shaw's *Mrs Warren's Profession* (1902), Granville *Barker's *Waste* (1907), and *Pirandello's *Six Characters in Search of an Author* (1925). On the other hand, performances could prove to be try-outs for the commercial theatre: Stanley *Houghton's *Hindle Wakes* (1912) and R. C. *Sherriff's *Journey's End* (1928) were instances of Stage Society works that moved on to West End *managements. *See also* INDEPENDENT THEATRE; VEDRENNE–BARKER SEASONS.   MOC

STALLS

Individual seats with arm rests, 'orchestra seats' in some American usage; also that section of a modern theatre on the main *audience floor in front of the *stage. *Wycherley's pit, *Calderón's 'stewpots', and *Molière's parterre were entirely bench seating, giving the best view and audibility to rowdy lower-class patrons (*see* BOX, PIT, AND GALLERY). Stalls first appeared at the front of the pit in the 1820s; from there they spread to the front of the first circle, then gradually backward through the theatre so that since the 1920s stall seats have been universal everywhere but in boxes. The trend to stalls throughout the late nineteenth century is often taken as evidence of the continuing *embourgeoisement* of the theatre, since they provided a more private, orderly experience, the convenience of reserved seats, and coordination of prices with audibility and visibility.   JB

STANFIELD, CLARKSON (1793–1867)

English designer, influential at the Royal Coburg (*see* OLD VIC THEATRE) and *Drury Lane theatres. From the early 1820s he also enjoyed considerable success as an easel artist and after 1840 this became his principal occupation. Benefiting from the development of gas *lighting on stage, he was most admired for the clarity of his *painting in scenes of landscape and Eastern exoticism. He also painted *dioramas of great splendour and accuracy for Drury Lane *pantomimes during the 1830s. His panoramic scene of the Agincourt battlefield for *Macready's *Henry V* at *Covent Garden (1839), and his designs for *Acis and Galatea* at Drury Lane (1842), were his last significant theatre works.

CLB

STANISLAVSKY, KONSTANTIN (1863–1938)

Russian actor and director, perhaps the most influential *theorist of *acting in the twentieth century. Stanislavsky changed his name from Alekseev in 1885 when he began to perform in the *amateur theatre movement in *Moscow. Along with Aleksandr Fedotov and others, he founded an amateur group called the Society of Art and Literature in 1888, where his acting and *directing reached professional standards. Ten years later he founded his first professional theatre company, this time with Vladimir *Nemirovich-Danchenko: the *Moscow Art Theatre (MAT), which became one of the most famous troupes of the age. The company was drawn both from the amateur society and from the Music and Drama Institute of the Moscow Philharmonic Society where Nemirovich-Danchenko taught. Their joint agenda for the theatre focused on ensemble, modern standards of *scenography, authenticity in sets and *costumes, discipline and dedication to art, in-depth *rehearsal, and creating a contemporary repertoire of high quality. Stanislavsky's role was to act and direct, while Nemirovich-Danchenko was to be literary manager (*dramaturg) and organizer, as well as direct. In the early years Stanislavsky created a number of major roles, including those in the four major *Chekhov plays: Trigorin (*The Seagull*, 1898), Astrov (*Uncle Vanya*, 1899), Vershinin (*Three Sisters*, 1901), and Gaev (*The Cherry Orchard*, 1904). Other notable parts were Stockmann in *Ibsen's *An Enemy of the People* (1900), the title role in *Hauptmann's *Michael Kramer* (1901), and Satin in *Gorky's *The Lower Depths* (1902). Stanislavsky co-directed some of these productions with Nemirovich-Danchenko (the Chekhov plays, for example), while others he directed alone (*Death of Ivan the Terrible*, 1899; *The Power of Darkness*, 1902) or with another colleague (*Tsar Fyodor Ioannovich*, with A. Sanin, 1898). Tall, attractively built, imaginative, disciplined, and self-critical, Stanislavsky excelled as an actor. His natural introspection led him to dissect his roles in the minutest detail and relate their every aspect to the overall production, a practice he encouraged among the members of the young company and which led him to the notion that acting could be systematically taught.

After an experimental studio headed by *Meyerhold failed (in Stanislavsky's view) in 1905, he reached a crisis in his own

technique and began subsequently to record his observations towards the creation of what eventually became known as the 'system'. This period of development coincided with a difficult time at MAT, particularly in his relationship with Nemirovich-Danchenko, and they had begun to move in opposite directions. Resigning from the board in 1908, Stanislavsky embarked on an experimental journey, rehearsing *Turgenev's *A Month in the Country* (1909). An intimate psychological drama, the play gave opportunity for Stanislavsky to work on his theories about imagination, memory, and the emotions. The key was an idea garnered from the French psychologist Ribot that it is possible to retrieve the emotional impact of memories given an appropriate external stimulus. This led to the central principle of the system, that by using 'affective memory' or 'emotional memory' an actor can create fusion between his or her own self and the *character being created by stimulating emotions the actor has experienced. A strong imagination is paramount, as well as a willingness to create, as if true, the external circumstances for the character on stage (the 'magic if'). Such a use of the imagination and emotions would prevent the mechanistic repetition of roles which Stanislavsky had experienced, and would ensure vitality on stage. The fusion of the actor's self with the role also implied immense self-control, concentration, and discipline, and a willingness to believe in the truth of what is being created at the expense of a conscious awareness of its *theatricality. Physical training to establish complete control over the actor's body, and exercises to sustain concentration, became necessary requisites. Stanislavsky allied this psychological approach to close study of the structure of the *text to establish a 'through-line of *action' to which all the analyses of the individual roles would cohere. Crucial to this development was his work on Chekhov's plays, which led Stanislavsky to assert that a latent drama or *subtext operated under the spoken *dialogue, revealing hidden desires and 'objectives' of the characters, who were treated as psychological mechanisms. Such an agenda was particularly appropriate to the *realistic plays in *naturalistic productions he favoured, which also called for the establishment of a 'fourth wall', the pretence that the audience is not present, in order to preserve the semblance of reality. In 1912 Stanislavsky set up a studio at MAT with Leopold *Sulerzhitsky as a *training centre for young actors to develop his system.

After the 1917 Revolution, Stanislavsky took on the world of music theatre. He introduced his demanding standards of acting into *opera at the Bolshoi Opera Studio in 1918, which subsequently became the Stanislavsky Opera Theatre. He was in demand as a teacher, especially in the various studios connected with MAT. He managed MAT's European and American *tour (1922–4), returning to a company newly reorganized by Nemirovich-Danchenko which integrated the older generation with those now emerging from the studios. Stanislavsky staged with particular success two plays reflecting the mixed politics of the period: *Bulgakov's *Days of the Turbins* (1926) and Vsevolod

*Ivanov's *Armoured Train 14–69* (1927). A heart attack in 1928 left him debilitated and housebound but with time to record his system. He had already published a hasty autobiography (*My Life in Art*, 1924) in connection with the foreign tour. The results of his efforts, which continued into the 1930s, were *An Actor Prepares* (1936), *Building a Character* (published posthumously, 1950), and *Creating a Role* (1961), the last being a collection of remaining writings rather than a work created by Stanislavsky himself.

Stanislavsky's collected works were published in Russia in eight volumes between 1954 and 1961 and form the core of the system, which became enshrined in drama training in Soviet Russia for decades after Stanislavsky's death. One of his pupils, Richard *Boleslavsky, imported the ideas to America in the 1920s, where they were notably taken up by Lee *Strasberg and developed as the 'Method' at the *Actors Studio in *New York. The fundamental difference between the two is that the Method ignores Stanislavsky's changes to the system in later years, when he recognized the dangers of excessive concentration on the actor's emotional memory, and conceded that bodily actions worked out under intense scrutiny could stimulate the required emotional states ('method of physical action'). Stanislavsky continued tutoring and training in the 1930s, and worked on new opera and drama productions, his last being *Molière's *Tartuffe*, begun in 1935 but produced in 1939, a year after his death. His legacy is immense and has affected vast areas of theatre training, rehearsal practice, and approaches to acting. Through the influence of Michael *Chekhov, Boleslavsky, and especially Strasberg, Stanislavsky's principles, in one form or another, have also been enormously important in Hollywood and other commercial *films, where they are particularly suited to the psychological intimacy of the camera. *See also* STUDIO THEATRE MOVEMENT. CM

BENEDETTI, JEAN, *Stanislavski and the Actor* (London, 1998)
MITTER, SHOMIT, *Systems of Rehearsal* (London, 1992)

STAPLETON, MAUREEN (1925–)

American actress. Having dropped out of college to pursue an acting career in *New York, Stapleton studied at the *Actors Studio and made her debut in the 1946 Broadway revival of *Synge's *The Playboy of the Western World*. Her breakthrough performance came as the earthy Serafina delle Rose in Tennessee *Williams's *The Rose Tattoo* (1951). Stapleton, who over the course of her career demonstrated a formidable emotional range as well as a knack for *comedy, played in Broadway premières of *The Crucible* (1953), *Orpheus Descending* (1957), *Toys in

Stanislavsky as the down-and-out Satin (centre) in the Moscow Art Theatre production of Gorky's *The Lower Depths*, Moscow, 1902, directed by Nemirovich-Danchenko and Stanislavsky.

the Attic (1960), and *The Gingerbread Lady* (1970). Her last notable stage performance came as Birdie in the acclaimed 1981 revival of Lillian *Hellman's *The Little Foxes*. Stapleton also has worked in *television and *film; her screen appearances include *Airport* (1970), *Interiors* (1978), and *Reds* (1981). EW

STATE DISPLAYS

Public displays which show off the power and affirm the authority of any sovereign entity, determined more by territoriality than kinship and in which the central governing agency supersedes local authority. These include autonomous city-states, kingdoms, monarchies, empires, republics, nation-states, and totalitarian regimes. State displays may be graphic or emblematic, taking the form of authorized art (for example, the Soviet *socialist realism of the 1930s), royal coats of arms or emblems of state (flags, insignia, symbols like the American eagle), coins stamped with an image of a head of state—an emperor backed by figures of gods or personified imperial attributes (as in Rome), a monarch (as in England), or a president (as in the United States).

Such displays may be worn as clothing, regulated by sumptuary laws that restrict fabrics (European royal ermine worn only by kings), prescribe status decorations (purple stripes on the togas of Roman senators or aediles), or limit methods of construction (sewn clothing restricted in eleventh-century Ghana to the king and crown prince). They may be manifest in monuments, like the great funeral pyramids of Egypt or the Washington or Lincoln Memorials in the United States, or reflected in imposing buildings of state, such as the eighteenth-century palace of *Versailles in France or the imperial palace at the heart of the Forbidden City behind the Tiananmen 'Gate of Heavenly Peace' in Beijing, *China (initially built in the 1420s, restored in 1651). They may take the form of state ceremonies (inaugurations, burials, elaborate dinners), *parades, or processions.

State processions and massed gatherings may both symbolize and reflect historical changes in the nature of government. By decreeing the founding of the Communist People's Republic from the rostrum of the Tiananmen Gate on 1 October 1949, Chairman Mao declared an end to the imperial Chinese order. Subsequently, Tiananmen Square was built in the 1950s as a gigantic official space (nearly 40 hectares or 100 acres) for a million people to gather. The amassing of large crowds in rallies designed both to affirm the power of the state and to reduce citizens to subjects may also be seen in Nazi gatherings, as for instance the 1934 Sixth Party Congress in Nuremberg staged for and documented in Leni Riefenstahl's *film *Triumph of the Will*, in which military spotlights illuminated the insignia-draped parades of farmers (the 'land warriors') from many German regions marching with their shovels in military formations past the enshrined Nazi elite (*see* FASCISM AND THEATRE). Though such displays characterize autocratic governments and totalitarian regimes, massed gatherings are also the tools of democracy, illustrated by the elaborate 1981 state wedding of Prince Charles, heir to the British throne, and Lady Diana Spencer, and the funeral of then divorced Princess Diana in 1997.

Whatever their form and despite their differences, state displays in cultures ranging from ancient Egypt, Greece, Persia, China, *India, and Rome through the Sudanese Ghanian and Malian empires (northern Africa, eleventh to fourteenth centuries) to modern European, Asian, and American nation-states have certain features and functions in common. Because they manifest power, state displays tend to be large in size; they often confer status on privileged participants; they frequently use a glorified concept of the past to justify the present. Such a past may be recalled emblematically (engravings on Roman triumphal arches), in inscriptions (funerary monuments that link dead rulers to illustrious ancestors), in nostalgic symbols (the riderless horse that represents a fallen leader even in modern democracies, as in the funeral for slain US president John F. Kennedy in 1963), or as narrative forms (authorized historical chronicles). Chronicles may be written, as in the case of the *Rex Gestae* glorifying the reign of Augustus, the first Roman Caesar, after his death in AD 14, or the histories by Tudor apologists Halle and Holinshed in sixteenth-century England. Or they may be preserved as oral narratives: thus, the importance of the *dyeli*, that is, the *griot* (bard and spokesman), who in fourteenth- and fifteenth-century Malian courts both instructed the emperor in the traditions of his African ancestors and validated his power throughout a far-flung, trade-dependent empire, in which Islamic influences cohabited closely with traditional *African cultural and religious practices.

As suggested by the example of the Malian Empire, the ways in which a state displays its power are tied closely to the religion, the political ideology, the economy, and the degree of hybridity in the state. When there is a state religion (as in Catholic Europe before the sixteenth century or in contemporary Islamic states), ceremonies of state coincide with religious *ritual observances, festivals, and rites of passage that often differentiate *gender roles, frequently involving restrictions of clothing and public access for women. Religious ceremonies may be used as state displays by nations establishing colonial empires, as for instance by the Spanish, who legitimized their rule throughout the Americas by using both language and ceremony. Under the Bourbon kings of the eighteenth century, for instance, the Spanish established New Spain (in Mexico) as their most powerful colony by reordering and reclaiming public spaces, converting local festivals into Catholic religious ceremonies, and imposing a language of state in such places as San Felipe el Real de Chihuahua, some 1,600 km (1,000 miles) north of Mexico City.

As evidenced in empires that encompass diverse peoples, state displays play a role in building as well as maintaining power. The imperial centre may be both the capital and the symbol of the empire, designed like Rome, Ovid's 'urbs et orbis' (the city and the world), to overawe visitors by its grandeur, its architecture, and its triumphal processions (*trionfi*). The Diamond Jubilee commemorating 60 years of Queen Victoria's reign in 1897 presented a similar *spectacle showcasing the exotic in the streets of *London, echoed in celebrations throughout the empire 'on which the sun never set'. Faced with the need to consolidate eleven republics into one Soviet state, communists similarly used Red Square, a reconfigured centre of Muscovite power, as a locus for vast political demonstrations, military drills, and parades that drew participants from various parts of the Soviet conglomerate state, replacing religious (and local) holidays with state displays such as the Pageants of Youth of the 1930s, or the annual May Day and October Revolution celebrations. Like other states encompassing both ethnic and linguistic diversity, the Soviets too created an official language as part of the apparatus of displaying, building, affirming, and symbolizing sovereign power.   MR

ANDERSON, BENEDICT, *Imagined Communities: reflections on the origins and spread of nationalism*, rev. edn. (London, 1991)

STATIONERS' COMPANY

The incorporation of the *London Company of Stationers in 1557 legitimized the authority of the association of scriveners, bookbinders, limners, and stationers which had existed since the beginning of the fifteenth century. The company was given a monopoly on the printing and selling of books, although the licence to print remained a government prerogative. The arrangement provided economic benefit to the printers and stationers, and ease of *censorship to the government. Members of the company were required to enter licensed books that they intended to print in the company's Register, which functioned both as a fee book and as a notice of *copyright. The power to license the printing of books was vested in various officials, but from 1607 it appears that for plays it was exercised by the *Master of the Revels. One difficulty arises from the fact that not all *published plays were registered; between 1584 and 1615, for instance, one-quarter were not registered. Nevertheless, the Register provides important information concerning the printing and dating of plays. The company's charter expired in 1694, and was replaced by the Copyright Act of 1709.   RWV

STEELE, RICHARD (1672–1729)

Irish writer, editor, and *manager. Best known for his collaborations with *Addison on the *Tatler* and the *Spectator*, Steele was deeply involved with the theatre for much of his life. His first play, *The Funeral* (1701), was a great success and remained in the repertory throughout the eighteenth century. Produced in the same year as his pious tract *The Christian Hero*, the play expresses both Steele's piety and his humane sense of good theatre. His next plays, *The Lying Lover* (1703) and *The Tender Husband* (1705), also show him attempting to accommodate Jeremy *Collier's strictures against immorality into comic drama. Unlike Collier, Steele was genuinely interested in the moral reformation (not abolition) of the stage. Upon the accession of George I, Steele became governor of *Drury Lane, and in 1715 its patentee. The wording of the *patent reflects the prevailing moral concerns of the Collier controversy (*see* ANTI-THEATRICAL POLEMIC) and charges Steele to address them. While Steele left the business affairs of his *playhouse to the *actor-managers, he considered himself its moral arbiter. He even experimented with a semi-private theatrical venture called 'The Censorium', which was part theatre, part concert hall, part self-improvement seminar. His dramatic masterpiece *The Conscious Lovers* (1721) was an instant hit and an enduring success for the remainder of the century. More often criticized than read nowadays, it artfully blends exemplary virtue and low *comedy.

MJK

STEIN, GERTRUDE (1874–1946)

American writer. A central organizing presence in *modernism, Stein sought to apply principles of fragmentation and simultaneity evident in paintings by *Picasso, Braque, and other artists to drama and theatre. Her 77 'plays' and *'operas' (identified as such by Stein but bearing no *character names or distinctions between *stage direction, *dialogue, or texts for singing) were composed between 1913 and 1946. They have been staged only rarely. Stein wrote that theatre was the appropriate literary form for the modern era in that, unlike a novel, theatre happens in a continuous physical present. 'What is a play?', Stein asked; and answered, 'A play is *scenery'. Narratives were right for earlier times, when people moved from place to place on sequential journeys; but modern experience is epitomized by air travel, during which one sees many things at once. Her theatre attempted to render the 'actual present' and so was without *plot or *action. The critic Stark *Young captured Stein's objective when he wrote of John *Houseman's production of her most-produced work, *Four Saints in Three Acts: an opera to be sung* (1934, music by Virgil Thomson), 'the opera turns itself in one's hand, like a melon or a flower'. Stein's *Dr Faustus Lights the Lights* (1938) saw *New York stagings by the *Living Theatre (1951), Maxine Klein at *La Mama ETC (1972), Richard *Foreman and the *Ontological Hysteric Theatre (1982), and Robert *Wilson at *Lincoln Center (1992).

MAF

STEIN, PETER (1937–   )

German director, arguably the most important of his generation. His work is characterized by great intellectual rigour and attention to detail, without any of the dryness that this might imply. He studied literature and fine art at Munich University, where he took part in student productions. In 1964 he joined the Munich Kammerspiele under Fritz *Kortner, who, together with *Brecht, was to provide a major influence. His direction of a Bavarian dialect version of Edward *Bond's *Saved* in 1967 was a remarkable professional debut, being named as production of the year by *Theater heute*. It was distinguished by the *realism of its performances, its shocking contemporary content, and its imaginative staging. His career in *Munich came to an abrupt end in 1968, when the Kammerspiele banned his production of Peter *Weiss's *Vietnam-Discourse*, a virulent attack on US policy in South-East Asia. Stein worked in Bremen until he once again resigned in protest at the infringement of artistic freedom, debating this problem in his production of *Goethe's *Torquato Tasso* (1969). In his portrayal of the court poet Tasso, Stein explored the position of a hired performer in capitalist society. This *Brechtian appropriation of a classic was amplified by political statements read out by the actors in the interval.

In 1970 Stein relocated to *Berlin and was a driving force in the founding of a theatre *collective at the *Schaubühne am Halleschen Ufer. This was set up on an idealistically democratic basis, with every employee having an equal say in the running of the theatre. In the long term this proved unworkable, but established the practice of inviting the participation of actors and backstage staff in the selection of plays for the repertoire and in other decision making. Provocatively, the new collective opened with Stein's production of Brecht's *The Mother*, in which a simple woman is converted to communism. This was to prove one of the many sources of ongoing conflict between Stein and the West Berlin Senate, concerned about subsidizing left-wing attacks on the so-called Free World. So strong did Stein's international reputation become that he needed only to threaten to leave Berlin for the Senate to concede ever greater subsidies. His next major production was *Ibsen's *Peer Gynt*, staged over two nights in 1971, which challenged the bourgeois concept of the individual, revealing Peer as an infinitely reproducible nonentity. There followed original stagings of *Kleist's *Prince of Homburg* (1972), *Gorky's *Summerfolk* (1974), and *As You Like It* (1977). For Shakespeare's *comedy, which was staged in a film studio with the Forest of Arden created with real trees and a pond, Stein worked with his ensemble for six years, presenting the results of their research in a spectacular living exhibition, *Shakespeare's Memory* (1976). After *Aeschylus' *Oresteia* (1980), and *Chekhov's *Three Sisters* (1984), Stein left the Schaubühne to work internationally as freelance director of *opera, of *O'Neill's *The Hairy Ape* (1987), Chekhov's *The Cherry Orchard* (1989), and on a 21-hour staging of Goethe's *Faust* (2000).

MWP

STEPANOVA, VARVARA (1894–1958)

Russian/Soviet painter, designer, and founder member of the Working Group of Constructivists. Her stage designs for

*Meyerhold's 1922 production of *Sukhovo-Kobylin's *Tarelkin's Death* consisted of *constructivist items made out of wooden slats in the shape of crates large enough to contain individual actors (when functioning as prison cells, for example), plus exploding and collapsing stools. The central crate was designed to resemble a giant mincing machine and stood as a metaphor for tsarist Russia. Her *costume designs, like working overalls, were intended to tone in with the decor. She also worked briefly on *film set design in 1926.

NW

STEPHENS, ROBERT (1931–95)

English actor. At the *Royal Court his dashing good looks saw him veer between heroic leads and languid ne'er-do-wells in *Miller's *The Crucible* (1956), and *Osborne's *The Entertainer* (1957) and *Epitaph for George Dillon* (1958). Joining *Olivier's *National Theatre at the *Old Vic in 1963, his reputation as a weighty and significant actor was won in *Hamlet* (as Horatio in the inaugural production), *Farquhar's *The Recruiting Officer* (1963), *Shaffer's *The Royal Hunt of the Sun* (1964), *Arden's *Armstrong's Last Goodnight*, and *Pinero's *Trelawny of the 'Wells'* (both 1965). Although his star waned somewhat, he returned to the NT in *The Cherry Orchard* and *Brand* (both 1978). A high-profile *film and *television career never quite translated into commercial stardom. Towards the end of his life his reputation as an actor of power and pathos was secured when he appeared at the *Royal Shakespeare Company as Falstaff (1992) and as Lear, his last stage role (1993). He was knighted in 1995.

AS

STEPHENSON, ELIE (1944–)

Guianese writer who became French Guiana's first playwright with *O Mayouri* (1974). All his plays, whether *tragedies, *satires, or *historical dramas, interrogate Guianese society, weaving French and *creole scenes as a representation of French Guiana's socio-linguistic condition and to communicate more readily with the creole-speaking *audience. They include *Un rien de pays* (*A Speck of a Country*, 1976), *Les Voyageurs* (1977), *La terre* (*The Earth*, 1979), *Les Delinters* (1979), and *La Nouvelle Légende de d'Chimbo* (*A New Legend of d'Chimbo*, 1984). Stephenson's plays have been performed in French Guiana and in numerous *festivals throughout the francophone *Caribbean.

LEM

STEPPENWOLF THEATRE

American *regional theatre. Founded in 1974 in the *Chicago suburb of Highland Park by actors Terry Kinney, Jeff Perry, and Gary *Sinise, the company played a major role in Chicago's 'off-Loop' theatre movement of the 1970s and 1980s. Steppenwolf attracted international attention for its dedication to ensemble productions, detailed *character work, and a rugged, muscular

*acting style, a reputation that was magnified when many members went on to celebrity in *film and *television. These include Sinise, John *Malkovich, John Mahoney, Joan Allen, and Laurie Metcalfe. Landmark productions which went on to success in *New York include Sam *Shepard's *True West* (1982) with Malkovich and Sinise, which won two Obie *awards; Frank Galati's adaptation and staging of *The Grapes of Wrath* (1988), which won two Tony awards; and Tug Yourgrau's *The Song of Jacob Zulu* (1992), featuring the South African a capella group Ladysmith Black Mambazo.

STC

STERN, ERNST (1876–1954)

The most important stage designer of the early twentieth century in Germany. Born in *Bucharest of German-Hungarian origin, he became Max *Reinhardt's main collaborator in *Berlin from 1906 and, like Reinhardt, possessed a chameleon-like ability to find a style suited to each play and its production. This style, which usually produced delicately charming sets, was normally characterized by stylized *realism, sometimes referred to as 'impressionistic' (*see* SCENOGRAPHY). He designed several of Reinhardt's Shakespeare productions, notably *Twelfth Night* (1907), *Hamlet* (1909), and *A Midsummer Night's Dream* (1913). He helped Reinhardt's production of *The Miracle* (1911) to be an international success, first at the Olympia in *London, which he transformed into a massive cathedral, and later in *New York. When Reinhardt founded the 'Young Germany' season to stage new works in Berlin, Stern became the principal designer of Berlin *expressionism, even though his more serene style was not wholly suited to the stridency of expressionist images. His most successful collaboration with Reinhardt was on the first piece of the season, *Sorge's *The Beggar* (1917). His design for *Goering's *Naval Encounter* (1918) was less suited to 'ecstatic' expressionism by reproducing a wholly realistic gun turret on stage, and in Felix Hollaender's production of *Kaiser's *From Morning to Midnight* (1919) he used a laughable mechanical device to create the skeleton that appears in a tree. A more successful collaboration in expressionist style was with Paul Leni on his silent *film *The Waxwork Collection* (1924), where the sets are strikingly *surreal and *dreamlike. But in general Stern was more comfortable with the classics, as in *Büchner's *Danton's Death* (1916) and *Ibsen's *John Gabriel Borkman* (1917). Significantly, when Stern began to work mainly in London from the late 1920s, he designed sets for Noël *Coward's *Bitter Sweet* (1929) and other popular *musicals like *White Horse Inn* (1931). In 1937 he was even in charge of Selfridge's designs for the coronation of George VI. During the Second World War, by which time he had changed his first name to Ernest, he returned to Shakespeare, working on Donald *Wolfit's productions between 1943 and 1945.

MWP

ERNEST STERN, *My Life, my Stage* (London, 1951)

STERNHAGEN, FRANCES (1930–)

American actress who began her professional career at the age of 18 playing Laura in a summer *stock production of *The Glass Menagerie*. She went on to take a drama degree from Vassar College and attended classes at *New York's *Neighborhood Playhouse, before spending several years at Washington's *Arena Stage. Her Broadway breakthrough won her the 1973 Tony *award for playing multiple *characters in Neil *Simon's *The Good Doctor*. She is best known for her creation of indefatigable, mature female characters, most notably Dora in the Broadway production of *Equus* (1974) and Ethel Thayer in *On Golden Pond* (1979). She has received several Drama Desk and Obie awards for an expansive range of roles, and another Tony for the revival of *The Heiress* with Cherry Jones (1995).   SBM

STERNHEIM, CARL (1878–1942)

German dramatist. Sternheim is best known for his dramatic cycle *Aus einem bürgerlichen Heldenleben* (*From a Bourgeois Hero's Life*), satiric *comedies portraying Wilhelmenian Germany through the fictional Maske family on the eve of the First World War. Plays such as *Die Kassette* (*The Cash Box*, 1911), *Die Hose* (*The Underpants*, 1911), and *Der Snob* (1914) created scandals because of their 'immorality' and were banned during the war. Other works include *Bürger Schippel* (1913) and *Die Marquise von Arcis* (1919, translated as *The Mask of Virtue*, 1935). Sternheim was initially deemed *expressionist for stylistic reasons but his plays are formally quite traditional, owing more to *Molière than to Ernst *Toller. His career declined during the Weimar Republic and, banned by the Nazis, he died in Brussels during the German occupation. His work was rediscovered in the 1970s in Germany and is increasingly produced in other languages.   CBB

STEVENS, ROGER L. (1910–98)

American *producer and impresario. After an impoverished youth, Stevens built a fortune in real estate. Starting with a production of *Twelfth Night* (1949), he became one of Broadway's most prolific and successful producers over the next 30 years. He championed the works of Harold *Pinter and William *Inge, among others, and was noted for his good taste and business regularity. He actively mentored a number of young producers with both material and advisory help. In 1961 President John F. Kennedy invited Stevens to help create a national cultural arts centre in Washington. The Kennedy Center was due almost entirely to Stevens's political acumen in negotiating with Congress, and his legendary fundraising skills. As its head until his retirement in 1988, he created a non-profit producing centre, forging alliances with national as well as local artists. He also helped establish the *National Endowment for the Arts, serving as its first chairman.   AW

STEVENSON, JULIET (1956–)

English actress who trained at the *Royal Academy of Dramatic Art. With the *Royal Shakespeare Company her repertoire included Titania and Hippolyta in *A Midsummer's Night's Dream* (1981), Isabella in *Measure for Measure* (1983), Rosalind in *As You Like It*, Cressida in *Troilus and Cressida* (both 1985), and Mme de Tourvel in *Les Liaisons dangereuses* (1985). At the *Royal Court she was Paulina in Ariel Dorfman's *Death and the Maiden* (1992), while at the Royal *National Theatre she played Hedda Gabler in 1989 and Amanda in *Private Lives* in 1999. Her screen appearances have been less frequent but she was a touching Nina in the delightful *Truly, Madly, Deeply* (1990) and a satisfyingly pompous Mrs Elton in *Emma* (1996). Her *métier* is intelligent, rather introspective *characters edged with steel or mild eccentricity.   AS

STEWART, ELLEN (1920–)

American *manager and director. Since 1962 Stewart has been one of the most important *producers of *avant-garde drama in the world. Believed to have been born in Louisiana, Stewart eventually moved to *New York to study fashion design in 1950. After working for Saks 5th Avenue she opened Café La Mama in 1962, a clothing boutique that doubled as an experimental performance space called *La Mama Experimental Theatre Club. She quickly became the premier presenter of *Off-Off-Broadway theatre and her work was emulated widely. An extravagant personality, Stewart regularly rang a bell on a pushcart to open productions, welcoming the *audience to La Mama, 'dedicated to the playwright and all aspects of the theatre', and more than a generation of influential American playwrights, directors, and performers have been nurtured by her support. She has received numerous *awards and citations, including a MacArthur 'genius' Fellowship. Her personal visibility became a material boon during the *National Endowment for the Arts funding cuts of the 1990s when she consistently used her award money to keep the doors of La Mama open. A documentary *film about her life in theatre, *Mama's Pushcart*, appeared in 1995.   JAB

STEWART, NELLIE (1858–1931)

Australian actor and singer, daughter of actors Richard Stewart and Theodosia Yates Stirling. She made her debut aged 5 with Charles *Kean in *The Stranger* in *Melbourne in 1864, and as an adult was a versatile actor and singer, appearing for J. C. *Williamson's company in a variety of comic and dramatic operatic starring roles. She left Williamson's in 1887, establishing a permanent professional and personal partnership with George Musgrove. In 1902 she played the first non-singing role of her career, as Nell *Gwynn in *Sweet Nell of Old Drury*, which established her as Australia's leading comedy actress, known as 'Australia's idol'.   KMN

STEWART, PATRICK (1940–)

English actor. Joining the *Royal Shakespeare Company in 1966, Stewart was associated with the company for almost three decades, appearing in a large number of productions, including *The Revenger's Tragedy*, *Henry V*, *Titus Andronicus*, and *A Midsummer Night's Dream*. His distinctive voice and commanding presence made him equally attractive for BBC *television, where he played Sejanus in *I, Claudius* (1976) and Karla, John le Carré's master spy, in the serializations of *Tinker, Tailor, Soldier, Spy* (1978) and *Smiley's People* (1982). But international celebrity came with the role of Captain Jean-Luc Picard in *Star Trek: The Next Generation* (on television 1987–94 and in *films 1994, 1996, 1998). Other film appearances include *Excalibur* (1981), *Dune* (1984), *Jeffrey* (1995), and *X-Men* (2000), which pitted his Professor Xavier against fellow RSC alumnus Ian *McKellen's Magneto. Stewart's later stage work includes Prospero on Broadway, a celebrated *one-person dramatization of *Dickens's *A Christmas Carol* (from 1991), *Othello* (Washington, 1997), *Miller's *The Ride down Mount Morgan* (2000), and J. B. *Priestley's *Johnson over Jordan* (West Yorkshire Playhouse, 2001).   AS

STOCK CHARACTER

A *character of the same general type appearing in a number of different plays. Perhaps the best-known theatrical tradition relying heavily upon stock characters was the Italian *commedia dell'arte*, which offered not only traditional general types—the young lovers, the comic servants, the foolish old men—but much more specific stock characters that were also endlessly repeated: the flamboyant but cowardly Spanish captain, the foolish pedant, the elderly lover of the young wife. The comic tradition has continued through the centuries to make much use of this device, but stock characters have also been important in serious drama, every historical period developing certain type characters that were often repeated, such as the dashing heroes of the Spanish *early modern 'cape and sword' plays or the darker and more introspective machiavels or revengers of the English stage of that era (*see* REVENGE TRAGEDY). During the English Restoration the stock comic characters of the fops, the witty couples, and the country bumpkins had their stock parallels in the noble leading figures of the *heroic dramas, influenced by *Corneille.

The most familiar use of stock characters in more recent times is probably in the nineteenth-century *melodrama, with its noble *heroes, persecuted maidens, aristocratic *villains, stalwart British sailors, and so on, but long before the rise of melodrama actors throughout the European tradition specialized in noble fathers, male romantic leads, tyrants, *soubrettes, and *ingénues, since most companies hired, *trained, and *cast actors according to certain general stock types that were called *emplois* in France and *lines of business in England. Nor was this a peculiarly European phenomenon. In *India, the classic Sanskrit theatre manual, the *Natyasastra*, contains lengthy descriptions of a great array of traditional stock character types, and *Japanese *kabuki contains similar carefully delineated traditional role categories.

The rise of modern *realism with its emphasis upon the originality and uniqueness of each new drama, has muted (though by no means terminated) theatrical reliance upon stock types, but the early and mid-nineteenth-century stage was particularly rich in stock characters, not only because the repetition of predictable character types and situations was more acceptable, but also because the traditional *stock company itself, the dominant type of theatre enterprise of the period, was organized according to the standard lines of business. The 'stage Yankee', for example, became as familiar to American theatregoers of the early nineteenth century as a figure like the Spanish Capitano had been to audiences of the *commedia* three centuries before, and other racial, ethnic, and social stock characters were widely utilized. During the twentieth century, as *radio, *film, and *television attracted much of the public that had earlier sought entertainment in the theatre, stock characters became more associated with these new media. They appear, for example, in the widely circulated series television shows—either serious like soap operas, or comic, where the average sitcom (like the *commedia*) continues to rely heavily upon contrasting but familiar character types.   MC

STOCK COMPANY

A means of organizing a resident acting company into specialist *lines of business, dating from the Elizabethan period. Each actor, such as the *clown in the Elizabethan company, would play many parts, but all within his own range as clown. By the nineteenth century this system had been codified, and actors were hired as a Light Comedian, a First Old Man, or a Female Juvenile Lead. Such a company could handle anything in the *repertory: *tragedy, *comedy, *farce, or *melodrama. The stock company was the resident company in a theatre, although *touring companies, which appeared in the middle of the nineteenth century, were also organized according to lines of business. The stock company had an extensive repertory, which changed frequently, and therefore very little time or necessity for *rehearsals, since each actor in the company was already in the possession of a large number of parts, which he or she could play at a moment's notice without rehearsals—except for a handful of new pieces, to break a new actor into an existing play, or to arrange exits and entrances. With the advent of the *long run and the *casting of actors for every play, and with the touring company taking its own plays on a single long-run hit out of *London or *New York, the stock company disappeared rapidly in the 1870s and 1880s. A nostalgic and charming picture of a minor stock company appears in *Pinero's comedy *Trelawny of the 'Wells'* (1898). MRB

STOCKHOLM

Founded in 1252, Stockholm in 2002 contained more *playhouses than many larger European cities. Until professional companies arrived in the eighteenth century, *Reformation schoolmasters had reserved theatre for select *audiences. In 1572, for example, a church ordinance recommended the performance of *comedies and *tragedies for the sake of moral instruction, and in 1620 Lutheran bishops proposed that Swedish rhetoricians teach classical plays to advance learning. As a result, Gustav II invited the first professional actor to the Swedish court in 1628, and the German comedian Christian Thum later became the director of Sweden's first court theatre. The teaching of translated works spurred the writing of native drama, including the first published play, *Tobie Comedie* (1550). Professor Johannes Messenius' comedy *Disa* (1611) about the Queen of Sweden was the nation's first *historical drama; it was performed in Stockholm until late in the eighteenth century. Uppsala university students performed original dramas such as *Apollo*, *Darius*, and *Hippolytos* in the Lejonkulan, Sweden's first permanent playhouse, from 1686 to 1691.

Though detractors called his reign 'a twenty-year masquerade', the ascension of Gustav III in 1771 brought the European Enlightenment to the country. The goal of this prolific writer-actor-king was to inspire a Swedish artistic renaissance by importing French culture to his court. In 1771 he permitted Petter Stenborg's company to perform light popular drama in Swedish, and the following year established the Royal Opera of Sweden. The first Swedish national *opera, *Thetis och Pelée*, was performed in 1773, followed by a version of *Acis and Galatea* and *Gluck's *Orpheus and Eurydice*. A new Royal Opera building opened in 1782 with the performance of *Cora and Alonzo*. Realizing the need of Swedish *actors for *training, Gustav III summoned Jacques Monvel and fifteen *Comédie-Française actors to Stockholm in 1781. He also brought *scenographers such as Carlo *Bibiena to design *scenery. In 1787 Gustav licensed A. F. Ristell to establish the first private dramatic theatre, the Svenska Dramatiska Teatern. Bankrupt after one season, Ristell fled the country, leaving 21 of his actors to found the Royal Dramatic Theatre (*Dramaten) in May 1788, its inaugural performance being Gyllenborg's tragedy *Sune Jarl*. After Gustav's death, subsequent monarchs established a royal monopoly until 1842, purchasing theatres and transferring *financial responsibility to the government. A new opera house was built in 1898; Dramaten's current home was opened in 1908.

Dominating the late nineteenth-century stage were star actors such as Gustaf Frederickson and Nils Personne, who borrowed French techniques. By the late 1880s, however, advanced artists such as August Lindberg, Ludvig Josephson, Harald Molander, and August *Strindberg were complaining about the star system and Dramaten's lack of vision. In 1900 its repertory still consisted primarily of light comedies, *well-made plays, and *historical romances. Independent theatres in Stockholm, like Josephson's Nya Teatern, began to attract patrons away from Dramaten with a progressive repertoire of foreign writers including Shakespeare, *Goethe, *Schiller, *Scribe, *Dumas *fils*, and the Norwegians *Ibsen and Bjørnstjerne *Bjørnson. With the rise of the *director during the 1880s, stylistic breakthroughs were made with productions of Shakespeare (Lindberg's *Hamlet*, 1884), Ibsen (Lindberg's *The Wild Duck* and *Ghosts*, 1883–4), and Strindberg (H. Molander's *Gustav Vasa*, 1889). The 'theatre king' Albert Ranft created a powerful syndicate that ruled the independent theatre scene for over 30 years.

In the 1920s directors Per Lindberg and Olof *Molander brought *modernist methods to Sweden, ushering in ideas from *Appia, *Fuchs, and *Craig, a strategy that solidified the pre-eminence of the director. Other important directors such as Alf *Sjöberg, Mimi Pollack, Bengt Ekerot, and Ingmar *Bergman emerged in mid-century and later. A brilliant Shakespeare interpreter, Sjöberg also brought *Sartre, *Brecht, and *Buero-Vallejo to Stockholm audiences. Bergman's interpretations of Ibsen, *Molière, Strindberg, Shakespeare, *Witkiewicz, and contemporary works by *Mishima, *Gombrowicz, and *Fugard established him as one of the foremost stage directors of the twentieth century, equalling his fame as a *film director. He was still active at the age of 84, opening a production of Ibsen's *Ghosts* at Dramaten in 2002. Rickard Günther, Thorsten Flinck, Susan Osten, Peter Oskarson, Åse Kalmér, Pia Forsgren, and Staffan Valdemar Holm (the *artistic director of Dramaten from 2002) have continued the Stockholm directing tradition. Gifted twentieth-century actors have included Tora Teje, Lars Hanson, Inga Tidblad, Jarl Kulle, Alan Edwall, Anita Björk, Sif Ruud, Stina Ekblad, Bibi Andersson, Pernille August, Maria Göranzon, Jan Malmsjö, and Ernest Josephson.

Despite the achievements of Strindberg and August Falck at their *Intima Teatern (1907–10), Max *Reinhardt was the first successful Strindberg interpreter. His dark, *expressionist *touring productions of *The Dance of Death*, *Storm Weather*, *The Ghost Sonata*, and *A Dream Play* at Dramaten in 1921 set the standard for twenty years. Later Olof Molander's Strindberg cycle at Dramaten from 1935 to 1963—including *A Dream Play* (1935, 1955), *To Damascus I* (1937), *The Ghost Sonata* (1942, 1960), and *The Great Highway* (1949)—became a new starting point for a national Strindberg tradition. Bergman rejected Molander's biographical, *surrealistic approach, and his powerful versions have been hallmarks for 50 years, including Stockholm performances of *A Dream Play* (1970), *The Ghost Sonata* (1973, 2000), and *Miss Julie* (1985). New interpreters such as Stefan Valdemar Holm have also made their mark with Strindberg's works.

In the 1940s theatre for *youth began to appear, culminating in the company Unga Klara, founded by Susan Osten in 1975. Commercial Swedish theatre is also concentrated in Stockholm, competing for audiences alongside the independent and royal theatres. In addition, the city's cultural life is enriched by a strong *folk theatre movement; since the 1950s, Parkteatern has staged free theatrical productions in Stockholm city parks.   DLF

MARKER, FREDERICK, and MARKER, LISE-LONE, *A History of Scandinavian Theatre* (Cambridge, 1996)
ENGLUND, CLAES, and JANZON, LEIF, *Theatre in Sweden* (Stockholm, 1997)

STOKLOS, DENISE (1950–)

Working as playwright, director, and performer in solo performance pieces since 1979, Brazilian artist Stoklos has won a large international *audience. Her pieces, such as *Mary Stuart* (1987), *500 Years: a fax to Christopher Columbus* (1992), and *Civil Disobedience* (1997), are generally grounded in historical reference. Though often produced in languages other than Portuguese, her work remains rooted in Brazilian life. A consummate *mime, dependent on Brazilian gestural codes, her *actor-based *theory of 'essential theatre' opts for a utopian humanism in response to cultural, political, and sexual repression. Many of her pieces have been created while visiting artist with *New York's *La Mama Theatre, including *Louise Bourgeois: I do, I undo, I redo* (2000), a *monologue with *text taken from Bourgeois's autobiography, and *Deconstructing and Reconstructing the Father*, which was visually enriched by a sculpture set designed by Bourgeois herself.   LHD

STOLL, OSWALD (1866–1942)

British theatre owner and *manager, knighted 1919. Born in Australia, Stoll began his career as the co-manager of the Parthenon Music Hall, Liverpool. He took over Leveno's Music Hall in Cardiff in 1889, and introduced the two-houses-per-night system that became standard for late nineteenth-century *music halls. In 1900 he helped establish the Moss Empires circuit, and worked to promote the social respectability of music-hall entertainment. From 1904 he managed the London *Coliseum, staging spectacular shows alongside *variety bills. He took over the London Opera House in 1916 and converted it into a cinema, characteristically exploiting new possibilities in popular entertainment.   SF

STONE, JOHN AUGUSTUS (1801–34)

American actor and playwright. Born in Concord, Massachusetts, Stone made his stage debut as Old Norval in *Home's *Douglas*, continuing during his career to portray old men and eccentric comic figures. Stone's fame derives not from acting but from his only successful play. Written in response to Edwin *Forrest's call for a play about a Native American, *Metamora* (1829) earned the contest's $500 prize. Its stirring actions, noble central *character, and elevated language provided Forrest with a star vehicle and earned him hundreds of thousands of dollars over the next twenty years. A penniless Stone committed suicide.   GAR

STOPPARD, TOM (1937–)

Playwright. Born in Czechoslovakia, Stoppard grew up in Singapore before moving to England in 1946. His first major play, *Rosencrantz and Guildenstern Are Dead* (1966–7), retold *Hamlet* through the eyes of its two unfortunate courtiers, reconceived as a *Beckettian double act, only faintly aware of their position as meaningless puppets in a wider drama. It established several characteristics of Stoppard's *dramaturgy: his word-playing intellectuality, audacious, paradoxical, and self-conscious *theatricality, and preference for reworking and adapting pre-existing narratives. In *Jumpers* (1972) a professor of moral philosophy is placed alongside radical gymnasts in a murder-mystery thriller. *Travesties* (1974), based on the fact that Lenin, Joyce, and Tristan Tzara were all in Zurich during the First World War, exploits the dazzling possibilities of their incongruous encounter in a *Wildean context.

Stoppard's ability to turn the lead of intellectual abstruseness into theatrical gold has attracted *criticism. His plays have been dismissed as pieces of clever showmanship, lacking in substance, social commitment, or emotional weight. It is true that his theatrical surfaces serve more to conceal than reveal their author's views, and his fondness for vertiginous towers of paradox spirals away from social comment. This is seen most clearly in his *comedies *The Real Inspector Hound* (1968) and *After Magritte* (1970), which create their humour through highly formal devices of reframing and juxtaposition. Stoppard has eloquently defended his refusal of commitment, and his tentative advocacy of art as a value in itself, with increasing sophistication. He has confessed to political conservatism, but his plays about *censorship, human rights, and state repression—notably *Every Good Boy Deserves Favour*, 'a play for actors and orchestra' (1977), and two *television works, *Professional Foul* (1977) and *Squaring the Circle* (1984)—are unmistakably engaged politically.

Many of Stoppard's later works bring a profound emotional depth to his characteristic intellectual sparkle. *The Real Thing* (1982) uses a *metatheatrical structure to consider the pain of an adulterous relationship, and in *Arcadia* (1993), perhaps his best play, a dual time scheme, flashing between the present and the early nineteenth century, produces a real and surprising pathos lurking within its investigation of chaos theory, *historiography, and landscape gardening. *The Invention of Love* (1997) has a similar effect with an exploration of love and passion, through a debate on classical translation conducted between the older and younger A. E. Housman. Other works include *Night and Day* (1978), *Undiscovered Country* (adapted from *Schnitzler's *Das weite Land*, 1979), *On the Razzle* (from *Nestroy's *Einen Jux will er sich machen*, 1981), and *Hapgood* (1988). *Radio plays, some subsequently adapted for the stage, include *If You're Glad I'll Be Frank* (1966), *Albert's Bridge* (1967), and *Artist Descending a Staircase* (1972). Stoppard has been a mainstay of the *National Theatre and is one of the most internationally performed dramatists of his generation.

DR

STOREY, DAVID (1933–)

English writer. Although he considers himself first a novelist (he won the Booker Prize for *Saville* in 1976), Storey earned great critical acclaim for a number of plays that appeared in quick succession between 1967 and 1975. Like fellow Yorkshire dramatist David *Mercer, several of Storey's works refract elements of his 'split' life as the rugby-playing son of a miner and a Slade School of Art graduate and writer. His first play, *The Restoration of Arnold Middleton* (1967), about the mental breakdown of a schoolteacher, was produced at the *Royal Court and transferred to the West End. With his second play for the Royal Court, *In Celebration* (1969), Storey teamed up with Lindsay *Anderson, who had previously directed the *film version of Storey's novel, *This Sporting Life* (1963). Anderson directed all of Storey's subsequent major plays: *The Contractor* (1969), *Home* (1970), *The Changing Room* (1971), *Life Class* (1974), and *Early Days* (1980). Storey's work divides into *character pieces (*Middleton*, *In Celebration*, *Home*) and work pieces (*The Contractor*, in which a wedding marquee is erected on stage; *The Changing Room*, about a rugby team). The plays are united, however, by a spare, *Chekhovian style and are often organized around an absence: offstage events in *The Contractor* and *The Changing Room*; absent figures, such as the missing title character of *Cromwell* (1973); or non-events such as the pretended rape in *Life Class*.

MDG

STORM AND STRESS *See* Sturm und Drang.

STRANGE'S MEN

Late Tudor *London playing company, mainly formed from *Leicester's Men. Several of its members joined the *Chamber-lain's Men with Shakespeare, when its patron Ferdinando, Lord Strange, younger brother of the Earl of Derby, died in 1594. It played at court in 1590, an unprecedented six times in the 1591–2 season, and three more in 1592–3, probably because Edward *Alleyn had joined it, although he kept the livery of the *Admiral's Men. Lord Strange was put up to lead a Catholic plot in 1593, but reported it to the government. Shakespeare's early career as a player is thought by some to have started with Strange's Men.

AJG

STRANITZKY, JOSEPH ANTON (1676–1726)

Austrian comic actor. Stranitzky began as an itinerant comedian in southern Germany in 1699 and moved to *Vienna in 1705, where he set up as a dentist and fair *booth actor in Johann Baptist Hilverding's troupe and later *managed. He developed the part of the Salzburg peasant *Hanswurst, which was to become his leading role. In 1711–12 he assumed control of the new Kärntnertor Theatre, the first permanent German language theatre. Plays came from a variety of sources but all were laced with Stranitzky's earthy Hanswurst *improvisations. Stranitzky established the tradition of Viennese *folk theatre which continued into the mid-nineteenth century.

CBB

STRASBERG, LEE (1901–82)

American *acting teacher and director. As acting teacher for the *Group Theatre (1931–7) and the *Actors Studio (1948–82), Strasberg was identified as the pre-eminent teacher of his day and—through his work with *film actors such as Marlon *Brando and James Dean—helped to shape the notion of *realistic acting around the world. The productions he directed for the Group Theatre, especially *The House of Connelly* (1931) and *Men in White* (1933), were admired by critics for their ensemble acting and graceful staging. Born in Galicia, Strasberg emigrated with his parents at the age of 7 and was immersed in the cultural life of the *Yiddish-speaking community of *New York's Lower East Side. He enrolled in 1924 at the *American Laboratory Theatre, studying with Richard *Boleslavsky and Maria *Ouspenskaya, alumni of the *Moscow Art Theatre and the studios of Konstantin *Stanislavsky and Eugene *Vakhtangov. Strasberg later described his own system—known as the *Method—as a blending of Stanislavsky and Vakhtangov techniques. Strasberg joined Harold *Clurman and Cheryl *Crawford in forming the Group Theatre in 1930. His intense belief in the rightness of his views and the truthful performances that his techniques fostered led many in the Group to revere him, while others resented his authoritarianism and the psychological strain of the 'affective memory' technique he adapted from Vakhtangov. Strasberg resigned from the Group in 1937 and directed freelance until he began teaching at the Actors Studio in 1948, and was named its *artistic director in 1951. Late in his

Stratford Festival Theatre in Canada, in its original configuration of 1957. The main floor and balcony seating, modelled on ancient Greek amphitheatres like that at Epidaurus, extends 220 degrees around the open stage. The stage and permanent backdrop, designed by Tanya Moisewitsch and Tyrone Guthrie, constitute a modernist reinvention of the Elizabethan stage, placing the actors in the literal centre of the playhouse and providing acting areas on three levels.

life, Strasberg emerged as a notable film actor himself, and was nominated for an Academy award for his portrayal of a mobster in *The Godfather, Part II* (1974).   MAF

STRATFORD FESTIVAL

Located in Stratford, Ontario, the Stratford Festival is the largest classical repertory theatre in North America and in many ways the flagship of Canadian theatre. It produces a dozen or more plays per year, plus a wide range of concerts, lectures, and ancillary events, in a season that stretches from April to November. While centred on Shakespeare and other classics, its mandate also encompasses twentieth-century classics and new plays. The company was created at the urging of Tom Patterson (1920–   ), a local journalist with virtually no theatre experience. In 1952 Patterson persuaded an organizing committee to invite

the English director Tyrone *Guthrie to give advice, and the committee in turn persuaded Guthrie to be the company's first *artistic director. (Patterson was its first general manager, but held the position for only one year.) Guthrie directed both productions in the first season, *Richard III* and *All's Well That Ends Well*, which ran in repertory for six weeks in the summer of 1953. Guthrie and his designer Tanya *Moisewitsch created a revolutionary *thrust stage which influenced *playhouse architecture for decades, housed initially in a *circus tent and then in a new building that opened in 1957.

At first the acting company consisted of international stars supported by a predominantly Canadian ensemble. Famous names at Stratford have included Alec *Guinness and Irene *Worth (1953), James Mason (1954), Siobhán *McKenna (1957), Jason *Robards (1958, 1969), Julie Harris (1960), Paul *Scofield (1961), Alan *Bates (1967), Maggie *Smith (1976–8,

1980), and Peter *Ustinov (1979–80). But the company also developed its own Canadian stars, such as William *Hutt, Douglas Rain, Frances Hyland, Christopher *Plummer, Martha *Henry, Colm Feore, and Cynthia Dale, and more recently has brought in Canadian *television celebrities such as Paul Gross and Al Waxman. In addition, many actors who originally came from abroad remained to make Stratford their home, including Douglas *Campbell, Pat Galloway, Tony *van Bridge, Brian *Bedford, and Nicholas *Pennell.

Guthrie's hand-picked successor, Michael *Langham, was also its longest-serving artistic director (1956–67). Langham brought international fame to the company with his devotion to the classics and his mastery of the Festival's thrust stage, and took productions to *New York, *London, and *Edinburgh. Perhaps his most famous production was *Henry V* (1956), featuring Plummer in the title role and several celebrated Québécois actors as the French court, and Langham returned several times to direct such productions as *Arms and the Man* (1982) and *Love's Labour's Lost* (1983–4). Subsequent artistic directors have all been Canadians, either native born or naturalized: Jean *Gascon (1968–74), Robin *Phillips (1975–80), John *Hirsch (1981–5), John *Neville (1986–9), David William (1990–3), and Richard Monette (1994–). Further *tours have included Europe (1973), Australia (1974), and New York (frequently).

Stratford's Festival Theatre is one of the most recognizable playhouses in the world. Major renovations in 1996–7 reduced both its seating capacity (from 2,276 to 1,824) and the span of its fan-shaped *auditorium. In 1956 the company began using a second playhouse, the Avon Theatre, a former touring house and cinema built in 1901, which now seats about 1,100. A third space was added in 1971, a fit-up thrust stage in a local community centre, seating 487 and named the Tom Patterson Theatre. In 2002 the company celebrated its 50th season by opening a fourth stage, the 246-seat Studio Theatre, a scaled-down replica of the Festival Theatre, in a former scene shop. In 50 years the Festival's *audience has grown from 68,000 to over 600,000 annually.   DWJ

HUNTER, MARTIN, *Romancing the Bard: Stratford at fifty* (Toronto, 2001)

PATTERSON, TOM, and GOULD, ALLAN, *First Stage: the making of the Stratford Festival* (Toronto, 1987)

STRAUSS, BOTHO (1944–)

German dramatist. Strauss first came to prominence as a *critic for *Theater heute*. In 1970 he joined Peter *Stein at the *Schaubühne in *Berlin as a *dramaturg, but became a freelance writer in 1975 and has since been acknowledged as one of the most significant contemporary German dramatists. His first plays *Die Hypochonder* (1972) and *Bekannte Gesichter, gemischte Gefühle* (*Well-known Faces, Mixed Feelings*, 1975) were moderately successful, but his breakthrough came with

Trilogie des Wiedersehens (*Three Acts of Recognition*, 1977) with its technique of fluid, interlocking conversation that exposed the vapidity of a provincial arts society. *Gross und Klein* (*Great and Small*, 1980) is a kind of latter-day *expressionist *Stationendrama* featuring a woman *protagonist on a journey through the indifference of West German society; *Kalldewey Farce* (1982) is a rare example of German intellectual *farce. Other plays include *Der Park* (1984), a very free adaptation of *A Midsummer Night's Dream*, *Die Fremdenführerin* (*The Tour Guide*, 1986), *Besucher* (*Visitors*, 1988), *Sieben Türen* (*Seven Doors*, 1988), and *Die Zeit und das Zimmer* (*The Time and the Room*, 1989). *Schlusschor* (*Final Chorus*, 1991) refers to German reunification. Strauss's work is grounded on a fine ear for contemporary speech and a keen satirical eye for emotional and intellectual posturing. Despite often hilarious *dialogue the plays are philosophically inflected; the mythical themes and figures are married with the trivia of quotidian middle-class existence. Strauss has been sharply criticized for his neo-conservative essay 'Anschwellender Bocksgesang' (lit. 'Swelling Song of a Billy Goat', 1993), in which he argued for an aesthetic restoration of conservative metaphysics; his play *Ithaka* (1996) was attacked for similar arguments.   CBB

STRAUSS, RICHARD (1864–1949)

German composer. Although Strauss never fully liberated himself from Wagnerian leitmotif, his *operas inhabit a stage-world different from *Wagner's. In *Salome* (Dresden, 1905), based on Oscar *Wilde's play, and *Elektra* (Dresden, 1909), to a *text by Hugo von *Hofmannsthal, Strauss for the first time introduced modern themes of pathological sexuality to the operatic stage. As Strauss's celebrated partnership with Hofmannsthal developed, they looked more to the past for their material. *Der Rosenkavalier* (Dresden, 1911) recalls Habsburg Vienna, while *Ariadne on Naxos* (Stuttgart, 1912) is a charming exercise in the mixture of tragic and comic *genres, set in the eighteenth century. Of their later collaborations, the elaborate *symbolist *allegory *Die Frau ohne Schatten* (*The Woman without a Shadow*, *Vienna, 1924) has met with much acclaim in recent years. After Hofmannsthal's death Strauss collaborated with many librettists, but among his late works only his last opera, *Capriccio* (*Munich, 1942), is still regularly performed. The serenity of this conversation piece, about the relative merits of music and words, acquires a strange intensity when one considers that it was composed at the height of the Second World War.

                                                                          SJCW

STREET THEATRE

Many street entertainments probably had their genesis in the skills of the shaman— *juggling, *magic acts, *acrobatics, skills that took *audiences on a journey out of the everyday with minimal means of production—and street theatre is surely as old as the most ancient of crossroads. Street theatre also connects with *carnival, festival, revels and riotous assemblies, popular gatherings that disrupt routine with rudeness, insert the miraculous into the mundane, challenge authority with the cheapest of jokes, and give power a poke in the eye. With historic antecedents stretching back well beyond the Greeks, it is not surprising that later manifestations were global in reach, such as in the Spanish *género chico—the generic term for short secular popular plays of the sixteenth and seventeenth centuries, which includes the Spanish peso, Cuban *bufo, and Argentinian *zarzuela—and in the many types of *folk play in Asia and the Pacific Islands, such as the mani-rimdu of *Nepal, the sandaegŭk in *Korea (see KAMYŎNGŬK), and *Indonesia's kuda kepang. The *mimes, minstrels, and strolling players that peopled every fair and market-place in *medieval Europe were simply one aspect of a vast and enduring transcultural web of often illicit pleasures enjoyed by millions at street level. Given such traditions, and the raw, high-risk nature of its territory, street theatre can be both sublime and ridiculous, sophisticated and crude, seductive and provocative—sometimes all at once. It is therefore—contrary to contemporary critical convention—extremely difficult to do well.

The accelerating urbanization of Western societies in the final two centuries of the last millennium ensured that street theatre increasingly was a regular and widespread trade. It had its gruesome dimensions in public *executions and tortures everywhere, in the nineteenth-century reflected in Britain in the comic grotesque *puppet shows of *Punch and Judy, and in America in the sidewalk shenanigans of blackface *minstrelsy. In the mid-twentieth-century it served a widening range of purposes, from entertainment that pretended a pristine innocence—say, in the between-wars *pierrot shows of English seaside towns—through intense participation in *political struggle and upheaval—say, in the *agitprop of the 1930s European Workers' Theatre Movement, or the unbuttoned provocations of theatrical demonstrations in 1960s American civil rights and anti-Vietnam War protests (*Bread and Puppet Theatre leading the way). Later it engaged with more or less ambivalence in the international *festivals, in the competition between 'cultural capitals', and in the merry-go-round of special events (including the Olympic Games) mounted for transcultural tourists, all tending to place it in service to capitalist globalization as the millennium drew to a close (see INTERCULTURALISM). Yet its original rebellious spirit survived, and even sometimes thrived, in the uncontainable invention of thousands of street theatre groups around the world. The specialist festivals of street performers at Stockton-on-Tees in the UK, Aurillac in France, Arkangel in Russia, and elsewhere, frequently proved that the shape-shifting magic of the shaman was still alive and well, even in the most secular of circumstances. See also STREET THEATRE IN INDIA. BRK

STREET THEATRE IN INDIA

Predominantly left-wing *open-air theatre, described by Safdar *Hashmi, one of its chief artists, as 'a militant *political theatre of protest [whose] function is to agitate the people and to mobilize them behind fighting organizations'. Its history is broken and sporadic, coinciding with periods of political upheaval. Its origins are undocumented but go back to the anti-British struggle of the 1940s. Chargesheet (1951), performed in Calcutta (*Kolkata) by the *Indian People's Theatre Association (IPTA), is among the earliest known street plays. After the Communist Party campaign in the 1952 general elections street theatre declined, except in West Bengal where Utpal *Dutt continued using it till the 1980s. Contemporary street theatre began in the turbulent 1970s, and is normally produced in any open space like parks or at factory gates or in office compounds for residents and workers of the area. Calcutta saw hundreds of street performances by radical groups. After giving up mainstream theatre, Badal *Sircar experimented with open-air theatre and foregrounded the discontent of the rootless urban middle class. In north *India, street theatre was pioneered by Jana Natya Manch (Janam, formed 1973) and in south India by Samudaya (formed 1975, with many units all over Karnataka). Janam's first street play Machine (1978) is a classic of the *genre. Janam logged about 6,500 performances of 55 street plays by June 2000, and many of these have been extensively translated and adapted, including in *Pakistan and *Bangladesh. Aurat (Woman, 1979), Halla Bol (Attack!, 1988), and Aartanaad (on child sexual abuse, 1996) are fine examples of popular political theatre that combine a directness of address with aesthetic vigour. Though Samudaya's Belchi (1978), about a real-life massacre of lower castes in Bihar, was performed about 2,500 times, its overall street theatre output has declined. The year 1989 was a high point for street theatre, when, after Hashmi's murder, 30,000 performances marked his birthday on 12 April. *Feminist groups have turned to street theatre since the early 1980s, and have done some excellent plays. In the 1990s non-governmental organizations have also taken up street theatre, espousing a number of causes like environmentalism, AIDS, and family planning. Unlike left-wing street theatre, which relies on voluntary contributions at the end of the performance, NGO street theatre has been largely funded by the state and foreign agencies. On the whole, however, street theatre's role in providing a voice to the voiceless has been considerable. SD

STREHLER, GIORGIO (1921–97)

The outstanding Italian director of the post-war years. His achievements helped change the course of theatre in Italy, enabling the *director to replace the *actor as the central figure in the production process. The performer, in his various guises from the capocomico in *commedia dell'arte to the *actor-

Street theatre in India by the Delhi company Jana Natya Manch (People's Theatre Front), a scene from an agitprop play about the bungling of the Delhi Transport Company. Prepared in five hours in response to a rise in fares announced the same day, the piece was first performed in New Delhi in 1979. This photo shows a revival in the mid-1980s in Punjab. As in many street performances, the audience has arranged itself in a rough circle, those nearer the action sitting on the ground.

manager or so-called 'great actor' of Victorian and pre-war days, had enjoyed a position of dominance in Italian theatre which the writer had never enjoyed. The director was an unfamiliar figure who made a tentative entrance in Italy only in the early years of the century. With the restoration of democracy, there were calls for him to be jettisoned together with other supposed relics of *fascism. Strehler in *Milan, together with *Visconti and *Squarzina, ensured that the organizing vision of the director was considered indispensable. He did not arrive at that position gradually. In an article in *Posizione* in 1942, he wrote: 'to cloak the director's role in some run-of-the-mill modesty is a sign only of uncertainty, compromise and inability'. He never ran that risk.

Strehler was born in the village of Barcola, near Trieste, into a family of musicians and artists. His father died when Giorgio was 2 and the family moved to Milan, where he studied drama. In the years of fascism, he made his debut as an actor, was enlisted in the army but fled to Switzerland where, in a refugee camp, he gained his first experience of directing. He had

already made the acquaintance of Paolo *Grassi before the war, and in liberated Milan the two decided to establish a theatre of a new type. They chanced on an ex-cinema which had been used as a torture chamber by the Nazis, and had it converted into a theatre which became the *Piccolo Teatro. The first production, directed by Strehler, was *Gorky's *The Lower Depths*, presented in May 1947. While later in his career Strehler would produce few works but keep them on in *repertory for many years, in the early years the Piccolo produced a total of 80 plays, the vast majority directed by Strehler. *Pirandello and *Goldoni, authors who were to figure prominently in his output, appeared in the first season. In 1947 he also produced *Verdi and Prokofiev at La *Scala, and would all his life move between drama and *opera. The cinema held no attraction. Strehler and Grassi divided roles at the Piccolo, but in the 1960s, as part of a diffuse malaise affecting Italian theatre, the Piccolo itself, once in the vanguard, was viewed as stale and conservative. Strehler was criticized so heavily by the militant student movement that he resigned to set up a new company, Gruppo Teatro e Azione, whose aim was to present work with a *political theme. While in the same year Dario *Fo chose to perform in alternative venues and to write popular theatre on conflicts featured in the headlines of the day, Strehler performed work by *Brecht, *Gorky, and *Weiss in conventional theatres. The experiment ended in 1972, when Strehler returned to the Piccolo, assuming sole charge of the operation. In 1982 Jack Lang, Minister for Culture in the Mitterrand government, offered Strehler the position of *artistic director of both the *Comédie-Francaise and the *Odéon in *Paris. Since it seemed that his hopes of seeing a newer, larger home for the Piccolo were about to be realized—in the event the new venue opened only after his death—he refused the offer but accepted a newly created post at the Odéon alone as director of Théâtre de l'*Europe. He held the position in conjunction with his post with the Piccolo, and in 1991, the Piccolo, together with theatres in *Madrid and Paris, became part of one overarching Theatre of Europe. His last years were spent defending himself, successfully, from a charge of having embezzled European Union funds.

Strehler's style has been analysed exhaustively in books, articles, and interviews, but the results of this effort are meagre. Strehler published an influential book, *Per un teatro umano* (*Towards a Human Theatre*, 1974), and the adjective 'humanist' or the equally unhelpful 'eclectic' has been attached to his directing. He was not an experimentalist, he did little to encourage new writing in Italy, and preferred to work and rework a few scripts from the classical canon. He refused to be associated with one school or tradition, and probably any quest for a constant aesthetic standard in a career which lasted several decades is futile. His genius was in his ability to release an energy in an individual script by meticulous critical analysis and by attention to the individual *scene, but it is worth underlining that, having reduced the power of the actor, he held to the collaborative notion of production, first outlined in the manifesto of the Piccolo. 'The word in the first place, the gesture in the second in a process which reaches completion only in front of an *audience.' He had a privilege granted to few directors, of returning time and again to a few plays. The first production of Goldoni's *Arlecchino, Servant of Two Masters* was in 1947, and it remained in his repertoire over 40 years through six separate productions. In it he harnessed the acrobatic talents of Marcello Moretti, his first Arlecchino, to produce a unique synthesis of the words of Goldoni the theatrical reformer and the styles of *commedia dell'arte* Goldoni had tamed. Pirandello, Shakespeare (most notably *The Tempest*, 1978), and Brecht were the other authors who dominated his portfolio. His first Brecht production was *The Threepenny Opera* in 1956, but although the meeting between the two came relatively late, the contact with Brecht's methods was a watershed, even if, idiosyncratically, he blended Brecht with *Stanislavsky. In his last decade, he directed only the Promethean spirits of European theatre, mounting his sixth production of Pirandello's enigmatic myth *The Mountain Giants*

in 1993, and between 1987 and 1992, he produced a version of *Goethe called *Fragments of Faust I and II*, returning to the stage himself in the title role. JF

HIRST, DAVID L., *Giorgio Strehler* (Cambridge, 1993)
RONFANI, UGO, *Io Strehler: conversazioni con Ugo Ronfani* (Milan, 1986)

STRINDBERG, AUGUST (1849–1912)

Swedish playwright. Strindberg's father was a shipping administrator who had married his former domestic servant. Strindberg never completely came to terms with his mother's lowly station; he called his autobiography *The Son of a Serving Woman* (1886). After brief experience of student life in 1872, he tried his hand at journalism. Finally he took up a post as assistant librarian at the Royal Library in *Stockholm in 1874 and worked there until 1881. During this period he wrote his first major *historical drama, *Master Olof* (1876); a much acclaimed novel on contemporary artistic life in Stockholm, *The Red Room* (1879); and works of cultural history, *Old Stockholm* (1882) and *The Swedish People* (1882). In 1877 he married the divorced actress Siri von Essen, with whom he was to have three children. Their tempestuous marriage lasted twelve years. In 1883 he left Sweden for a period of self-imposed exile until 1897, though he returned briefly in 1884 to face a trial for blasphemy for his collection of stories *Married Life*. The Stockholm jury acquitted him.

During the 1880s Strindberg wrote a series of plays inspired by the *naturalist movement: *The Father* (1887), *Miss Julie* (1888), and *Creditors* (1888). These depicted the kind of warfare between the sexes that he had experienced in his marriage with Siri. Living in Denmark at the time, he established the Scandinavian Experimental Theatre in Copenhagen to facilitate productions of his plays, but the venture collapsed within a week. Following an acrimonious divorce from Siri, Strindberg moved to *Berlin and married a young Austrian journalist, Frida Uhl, in 1893. After a year of misery together, they divorced at the end of 1894. Strindberg then moved to *Paris to pursue experiments in alchemy, where a successful production of *The Father* in 1894 brought him public recognition. But the repeated failures he had suffered in his personal life precipitated a severe mental crisis during 1895–6, a time he called the 'Inferno period'. Remarkably, even at the height of his anguish, he was able to make precise notes that permitted him to write a novel about his suffering called *Inferno* (1897) and an *expressionist dream play, *To Damascus* (1898), in which he attempted to come to terms with his failed marriages.

In 1897 he returned to Sweden, moved back to Stockholm in 1899, and remained there until his death. The production of *To Damascus* at *Dramaten in November 1900 led to his meeting Harriet Bosse, a young actress who became his third wife in 1901. Their marriage was even more tempestuous than his previous two and resulted in a pattern of separation and reconciliation until 1904 when they divorced. Despite the upheavals in his emotional life, these were enormously productive years. He wrote a cycle of historical dramas to bring alive Swedish history, from *Gustav Vasa* (1899) to *Gustaf III* (1902). He wrote an *absurdist black *comedy, *The Dance of Death* (1900), two further parts of *To Damascus*, and completed *A Dream Play* (1901). He wrote the major novels *Gothic Rooms* (1904) and *Black Banners* (1904). He founded *Intima Teatern (Intimate Theatre) with the actor August Falck in 1907 and wrote his chamber plays for that company: *The Storm, The Ghost Sonata*, and *The Pelikan*. Intima presented 24 of his plays from 1907 until it closed in 1910. In *Open Letters to the Intimate Theatre* (1909) Strindberg set down his advice on *acting and staging. In the final years of his life he wrote *The Great Highway* (1909) and a series of works of cultural history. This brief listing gives only a taste of the range and scope of his creative genius.

Miss Julie is the most frequently performed of all Strindberg's plays but in its own time evoked shocked horror. It was refused by Strindberg's *publisher and frequently banned by theatre *censors across Europe. It offered *audiences a brutally frank insight into the naturalist world that Zola had depicted in his novels, while the preface stressed the kind of complex motivation for the *characters' behaviour suggested by thinkers such as Hippolyte Taine. Jean and Miss Julie are shown to be amoral predators, using sex as a weapon in their struggle for mutual domination. Further to the naturalist cause, the *stage directions insist on a real kitchen, with real utensils and furniture, in place of the painted *scenery of the *illusionist stage.

Equally revolutionary were Strindberg's dream plays written after his Inferno crisis: *To Damascus* and *A Dream Play*. In these works Strindberg conjures up a spiritual landscape in which his own sufferings are the starting point for a theatrical meditation upon life and relationships, hope and despair. Settings blend and merge, as the figures strike out on a quest for the meaning of existence. The inevitable failures that confront the characters are shown with the certainty of one who has looked into the abyss and is no longer terrified of the emptiness he has seen. Running through the late plays also is a strong sense of solidarity and compassion for human beings in their confused and frightened state. Above all, the works represent the aesthetic transcendence of absurdity, the sensitive creation of dreamlike beauty out of the chaos of darkness and despair.

In his ideas on theatre practice Strindberg wrote in advance of his age, as the contemporary theatre lacked the technological resources to project onto the stage the *dream images he suggested in his *texts. Long after his death, directors in Sweden such as Olof *Molander in the 1930s and Ingmar *Bergman in the 1970s were finally able to create the dreamlike atmosphere Strindberg had envisaged. Throughout the twentieth century Strindberg's dramas and his ideas on theatre practice

have proved fruitful inspiration for playwrights and directors in Europe and America.   DT

VALENCY, MAURICE, *The Flower and the Castle* (London, 1963)
MEYER, MICHAEL, *Strindberg: a biography* (London, 1985)

STRIPTEASE *See* PORNOGRAPHY AND PERFORMANCE; SEX SHOWS AND DANCES.

STRNAD, OSKAR (1879–1935)

Austrian designer. Trained as an architect in *Vienna, Strnad worked mainly in this field until 1919 when he began to design for the theatre. In 1924 Max *Reinhardt engaged him for the Theater in der Josefstadt as well as for his *Berlin and Salzburg productions. From 1926 he worked together with Bruno Walter at the *Salzburg Festival, where he designed for *opera as well as for the *films *Maskerade* and *Episode*. He also designed for theatres in Dresden, Berlin, and *Paris. Despite a number of projects to construct *playhouses, most of his plans were not realized.   CBB

STROUSE, CHARLES (1928–)

American composer. After studying with Aaron Copland and Nadia Boulanger, Strouse turned to popular music, playing in dance bands and as a *rehearsal accompanist. He began writing theatre *music for stock productions at an upstate New York resort, where he first met lyricist Lee Adams. In 1960 they made their joint Broadway debut with the successful *Bye Bye Birdie*, integrating traditional Broadway sound with satirical rock and roll rhythms. He and Adams wrote four more Broadway *musicals together, ending their exclusive collaboration in 1970 after *Applause*, a powerful vehicle for Lauren Bacall. They reunited only twice, both times with disastrous results. Strouse continued to write for the musical theatre in *New York and *London with new lyricists, finding his greatest success with *Annie* (1977), written with Martin Charnin. He also wrote scores for several *films and the theme song for the popular *television series *All in the Family*.   JD

STRUCTURALISM AND POST-STRUCTURALISM

Important branches of twentieth-century European and American *theory and criticism in the arts. The array of approaches collectively labelled post-structuralist theory, or simply 'theory', which derived from other fields (including literature, *film studies, and anthropology), dominated the fields of *theatre studies and *performance studies, especially in North America, beginning in the 1980s. While structuralism may be seen as a modernist critical movement, post-structuralist theory and criticism are closely aligned with postmodernist practice in the arts (*see* MODERNISM AND POSTMODERNISM).

Structuralism emerged as a school of thought in Prague in the 1930s, where a group of Czech literary scholars and Russian émigrés, including Roman Jakobson, further elaborated ideas about language and literary techniques taken up by the Russian formalists in the 1920s. However, it was the work of the French anthropologist Claude Lévi-Strauss, expanding upon the earlier ideas of the Swiss linguist Ferdinand de Saussure, that built a foundation for structuralism in various intellectual disciplines in France in the 1940s and 1950s; these theories travelled to England and America in the 1960s and early 1970s, as works by Lévi-Strauss were translated into English, along with those of the literary theorist Roland Barthes and others. Finding in linguistics a model for a more rigorous and scientific approach to anthropology than was currently employed, Lévi-Strauss sought to analyse the internal structures of social relations and cultural practices (including language, *myth, *ritual, marriage and kinship rules, and art) by isolating what he saw as the systematic patterns of binary oppositions that constitute them and the interrelations of their component parts.

In his well-known essay 'The Structural Study of Myth', for instance, Lévi-Strauss examines the Oedipus myth, showing how its recurring patterns of overrating and underrating blood relations, men killing monsters, and men unable to walk normally, may be interpreted as a cultural attempt to come to terms with the problem of whether humans are born from earth (i.e. autochthonously), as ancient Greek cosmology held, or from the union of man and woman, as social experience indicates. Lévi-Strauss teases out the recurrence and interrelations of seemingly random elements of the myth—without regard for chronological sequence—from Homer's epics to *Sophocles' play to Freud's psychoanalytic theories. He argues that this myth (and myths in general) serve as a tool for coping with cultural contradictions, and he maintains that thinking in binary oppositions is an invariant structure of the human mind. For Lévi-Strauss structuralism can thus account for and explain the underlying patterns of all human thought and culture, and structuralist analysis shows that there is no difference between archaic or 'primitive' thought and the modern mind, or between structures of thought across cultures.

A number of the Prague School structuralists wrote about *theatre and *drama, including Jan Mukařovský, whose study of Charlie Chaplin applied structuralist principles to understanding the actor's technique (and gesture in particular), and Otakar Zich, who proposed a proto-structuralist analysis of plays, including not only the written *texts but other components of staging (both studies were published in 1931). Working separately in France, in 1950 Étienne Souriau proposed a model of dramatic structure (similar to Vladimir Propp's earlier investigation of the morphology of the Russian fairy tale), working out over 200,000 dramatic situations, in all possible combinations and repetitions of six 'functions' (related to roles or *characters) in the drama of all periods and geographical areas. Though not identical to it, structuralism is closely related to *semiotics, a system of analysing signs and their meanings that also partly derives from Saussure's linguistic theories. Thus a number of theatre and performance theorists have worked in both structuralism and semiotics, for instance Petr Bogatyrev, who in 1938 identified the signifying aspects of various elements of *folk theatre, and Paul Bouissac, whose 1976 analyses of the *circus often rely on polarities like culture/nature, animal/human, wild/tame, big/small, female/male, elegant/sloppy.

As structuralist theories flourished in various fields of intellectual enquiry, objections to its tenets arose from several directions, giving rise to various schools of thought including deconstruction (Jacques Derrida), psychoanalysis (Jacques Lacan), and some brands of Marxist analysis (Louis Althusser; *see* MATERIALIST CRITICISM), while also influencing certain strands of *feminism, *queer theory, new *historicism, and *post-colonial studies. On the one hand, all of these approaches may be seen as post-structuralist, in that they follow and argue with the structuralist method, but on the other hand they are not necessarily allied with each other. Post-structuralists of various stripes have raised three prime objections to structuralist principles: the human mind does not possess invariant or essential structures, but rather is constructed by culture, including language, in which the subject is always enmeshed; the system of determinate binary oppositions cannot be sustained; and meaning is not always fixed, but is uncertain and unstable. Indeed many post-structuralists would argue that meaning is always in flux, always open to further interpretation and negotiation.

Some theorists who initially embraced structuralism, such as Barthes, Lacan, and the intellectual historian Michel Foucault, turned from what they saw as the reductionism of the earlier framework to approaches that could account for uncertainties, incoherencies, indeterminacies, and unresolvabilities. The work of Derrida, whose deconstruction is most closely identified with post-structuralism, has been concerned to break down binary oppositions, showing that they are not natural or inevitable products of the human mind but discursive constructions—indeterminate ones that inevitably collapse under interpretative pressure. In fact, reality itself is a construct of representations, of signs and *texts. For the deconstructionist, there is nothing outside the texts, be they written, spoken, or gestural. Indeed, for Derrida, each of those textual modes is 'always already' dependent on and contained within each of the others. Although Derridean deconstruction, like structuralism, also derives from Saussure's ideas to a large extent, it emphasizes the arbitrariness of the sign/signifier relationship rather than the systematicity of language as a set of signs.

A number of French post-structuralists have written about theatre, *theatricality, and *performance, in particular about the problematic of *Aristotelian *mimesis. As early as 1966, in 'The

Theatre of Cruelty and the Closure of Representation', Derrida analysed *Artaud's ruminations on the theatre of *cruelty, suggesting that it is precisely in non-mimetic theatre that one could achieve 'pure presence as pure difference', because it would be 'neither a book nor a work, but an energy . . . expenditure without economy, without reserve, without return, without history'. Jean-François Lyotard's 1977 essay 'The Tooth, the Palm' is a wide-ranging consideration of the theatre theories of *Zeami, Artaud, and *Brecht; he ultimately celebrates as 'energetic' the *dance-theatre of Merce *Cunningham, John Cage, and Robert Rauschenberg, with its separation of elements, its discontinuity, and its refusal of representation. In 'Modern Theatre Does Not Take (a) Place', Julia Kristeva, also writing in 1977, praises the work of Robert *Wilson, Yvonne Rainer, and Richard *Foreman as 'a radically new locus of representation'. Josette Féral has argued that *performance art breaks down the symbolic codes that theatre preserves and thus rejects codes and even representation itself.

Since the early 1980s many American and Canadian theatre theorists have turned to deconstruction and other forms of post-structuralism in considering various aspects of theatre and performance, as well as theatre studies as a discipline. For example, in several books, Herbert *Blau takes up issues of concern to post-structuralism, asserting that theatre vanishes even as it is created and that its meanings exceed representation. In *Liveness*, Philip Auslander challenges the cherished binary opposition between live theatre, *sports events, music concerts, and legal proceedings, on the one hand, and performances in various cultural domains that are recorded or broadcast on film, video, and *television (*see* CYBER THEATRE; MEDIA AND PERFORMANCE). In ' "Just Be Your Self": logocentrism and difference in performance theory', Auslander deconstructs theories of *acting (like *Stanislavsky's) that rely on mimesis and presume the existence of an unmediated, essential, stable self. A number of feminist theorists in Europe and America, including Hélène *Cixous, Sue-Ellen Case, Peggy Phelan, Elin Diamond, and Féral, have engaged with deconstruction and French feminist *psychoanalytic criticism, derived from or departing from Lacan.

For the most part, however, post-structuralism is not so much a uniform theory of theatre or even a set of theories as it is a resource for critical interpretation. Theatre critics and scholars apply post-structuralist ideas by looking for post-structuralist themes in the work they analyse—whether it is canonical theatre, contemporary theatre, or postmodern theatre that may, itself, have been influenced by deconstruction and Lacanian feminism. For instance, Elinor Fuchs discusses the sense of dislocation, decentredness, and absence in much postmodern theatre, from the *Wooster Group to the plays of Suzan-Lori *Parks and Des McAnuff, and David McDonald sees David *Hare's *Fanshen* as embodying a 'two-faced dance of undecidability' in regard to justice during the Chinese Cultural Revolution. SB

AUSLANDER, PHILIP, *Liveness: performance in a mediatized culture* (London, 1998)
BLAU, HERBERT, *The Audience* (Baltimore, 1990)
CASE, SUE-ELLEN (ed.), *Performing Feminisms: feminist critical theory and theatre* (Baltimore, 1990)
MURRAY, TIMOTHY (ed.), *Mimesis, Masochism, & Mime: the politics of theatricality in contemporary French thought* (Ann Arbor, 1997)
REINELT, JANELLE G., and ROACH, JOSEPH R. (eds.), *Critical Theory and Performance* (Ann Arbor, 1992)

STUDIO THEATRE MOVEMENT

Formal innovation and aesthetic experiment were the hallmarks of studio theatres during the past century or so. Often their work furthered social (and occasionally *political) critique, and sometimes they developed new approaches to *training for, and research into, *performance. Primarily a Western phenomenon to begin with, the history of studio theatres combined the opening of new kinds of performance space (*see* PLAYHOUSE) with ideas about investigative creativity in performance. As part of the various *avant-garde and *alternative theatre movements of the late nineteenth and twentieth centuries, studio theatre is best described as a series of overlapping trends and contrasting strands of practice. Hence, studio theatre produced high-intensity nodes of experimental energy in the great *modernist movements of twentieth-century art in *naturalism, *symbolism, *futurism, and so on; it cross-fertilized with the between-wars *community-oriented art theatre and *Little Theatre movements on both sides of the Atlantic; it was essential to the post-1960s blossoming of *fringe, alternative, and independent theatre and performance, as well as eventually becoming incorporated into the emporia of *national theatre complexes. It also provided a source for much sought after cultural commodities in the commercialized circuits of international theatre *festivals.

The first studio theatres were founded in 1880s Europe by directors enthusiastic about naturalism. André *Antoine opened the Théâtre *Libre as a small experimental theatre club in *Paris, from 1887 to 1894 staging plays by *Ibsen, *Strindberg, and other naturalist writers. In Germany Otto *Brahm set up the *Frei Bühne in *Berlin in 1889, producing plays by Ibsen and Gerhart *Hauptmann, while in *London J. T. *Grein created the *Independent Theatre in 1891, putting on plays by Ibsen and *Shaw. The Parisian symbolists reacted against Antoine, and in 1890 the poet Paul *Fort opened the Théâtre d'*Art, which in 1892 was renamed Théâtre de l'*Œuvre by the actor-director Aurélien *Lugné-Poe, who produced *Maeterlinck, *D'Annunzio, and *Jarry, whose *Ubu roi* ran for just two nights in 1896.

In the following year *Stanislavsky founded the *Moscow Art Theatre with Vladimir *Nemirovich-Danchenko. In the first fifteen years MAT experimented with a widening range of styles, leading Stanislavsky to create its First Studio in 1912, a training forum set to develop his system for naturalistic *acting. Further studios followed up until 1931, in a linking of pedagogy and practical research that many subsequent studio theatres emulated. Vsevolod *Meyerhold, under the pseudonym of 'Dr Dapertutto', paralleled his official role as director of the *St Petersberg imperial theatres (1908–18) with experimental work in small studio theatres—the House of Interludes, the Tower, and Strand Theatres—which became the basis of his systems for actor training. In France in 1913 Jacques *Copeau founded a theatre company in the *Vieux-Colombier, with an associated training school, aimed at nothing less than a total renewal of theatre art. In Germany theatre experimentation was literally imported into the studio at the *Bauhaus in *Weimar, where in the 1920s and 1930s Walter *Gropius and Oskar *Schlemmer designed *constructivist *costumes and *scenery and a new kind of *total-theatre building. But alongside such research programmes, studio theatres in Europe and the USA continued to spawn unpredictably challenging and sometimes mischievous performances. These ranged from Strindberg's 'chamber plays', written for the tiny *Intima Teatern in *Stockholm, which he founded in 1907, to the *surrealist-*dada mayhem of performative provocations at the Cabaret Voltaire in Zurich from 1916. Historical coincidence plays a part in this rich theatrical *diaspora: *New York's première studio theatre, Daly's 63rd Street Theatre, opened in 1922 and mounted provocative new work till 1936, when the *Federal Theatre Project took over. In exactly the same period the highly compressed 'synthetic theatre' of futurism had its heyday at the Teatro degli Independenti in *Rome.

In the second half of the twentieth century the idea of studio theatre was stretched to breaking by a plethora of experimental building-based initiatives. In Europe in the immediate aftermath of the Second World War, makeshift studio-like stages were a necessity born of disaster until the 1950s, when a wave of new theatre building began in many countries. But it was in the 1960s that the studio theatre blossomed with the beginnings of the international alternative theatre movement. In effect, any space could be transformed into a theatre and limited funds meant that generally such spaces were likely to be small. The slender means and experimental aims—aesthetic and cultural—of some key studio theatres were signalled in their titles: the Polish director Jerzy *Grotowski led the way in 1959 when he founded the Teatr 13 Rzedow (Theatre of 13 Rows) in Opole, followed by the *Polish Laboratory Theatre in Wrocław in 1965, both devoted to rigorous actor training. In New York the first *Off-Off-Broadway venue was created in 1959 by Joe Cino in his *Caffe Cino, quickly followed by the Judsons Poets' Theatre in 1961 and Café *La Mama in 1962. In the UK, the first fringe studio theatre, the *Traverse Theatre Club in *Edinburgh, was started by the American Jim Haynes in 1963; he also opened the London Arts Laboratory in a small warehouse in 1968. In *Japan the post-*shingeki movement, started in 1959 by the Youth Art Theatre (Seigei), in the 1960s spawned two companies that perform in tents, *Kara Jūrō's Situation Theatre (Jōkyō gekijō) and *Satō Makoto's Black Tent Theatre 68/71

(Kuro Tento 68/71). By the late 1970s and 1980s, when the UK's annual Alternative Theatre Directory was listing over 250 small-scale venues, many countries had an equivalent proliferation of studio theatres.

Against this background, it is not surprising that studio theatre became, in part, increasingly institutionalized as the millennium drew to a close. Many universities and training colleges had 'black-box' studios, so called because the open space that could adapt to any stage configuration was defined by black-painted walls. Older theatres added experimental spaces to their main house and as new theatres were built it became customary to include a studio theatre. The growing number of experimental theatre festivals around the world created an exciting trade in studio theatre productions, risking the commodification of art even as it radically challenged the status quo. Hence, both as a nuts-and-bolts practical resource and as a utopian vision of free creative space, the studio theatre became an icon of progressive experiment, with a significance far beyond the meagre means of production which had shaped most of its history.

BRK

ARONSON, ARNOLD, *American Avant-Garde Theatre* (London, 2000)
BRAUN, EDWARD, *The Director and the Stage: from naturalism to Grotowski* (London, 1982)
COUNSELL, COLIN, *Signs of Performance: an introduction to twentieth-century theatre* (London, 1996)

STURM UND DRANG

'Storm and stress', an influential literary movement in late eighteenth-century Germany, took its name from the title of a play of 1776 by one of its leading exponents, Friedrich Maximilian *Klinger. The period began with *Goethe's youthful drama set in medieval Germany *Götz von Berlichingen* in 1773, and ended with *Schiller's contemporary domestic *tragedy *Intrigue and Love* in 1784. *Sturm und Drang* plays were strongly influenced by Shakespeare, who had been upheld by *Lessing as a model to replace the stultifying effect of French *neoclassicism. The resulting works were characterized by a focus on a powerful central figure, usually in revolt against a corrupt and flaccid society. In his *Observations on the Theatre* (1774) the most representative member of the movement, Jakob *Lenz, argued that a piece of theatre should no longer be restricted by the neoclassical *unities of time, place, and *action, but should instead seek its unity in the central figure. Emulating the epic sweep of Shakespeare, the portrayal of vibrant *heroes was achieved by tracing their progress through many locations and across several years. Such extravagant technical demands for multiple settings, together with the provocative subject material and charged, occasionally obscene, language of the plays, made the staging of most of them virtually impossible in the theatre of the day. Thus the major pieces of the period, Lenz's *The Tutor* (1774) and Schiller's *The Robbers* (1781), could be performed only in bowdlerized versions, while Lenz's *The Soldiers* (1776) had to wait a century before reaching the stage. Only Heinrich Leopold Wagner (1747–79), who was less demanding of stage resources, had modest contemporary success with *Remorse after the Deed* in 1775 and with his most famous play, *The Child Murderess* (1777; performed in a version with a happy ending in 1778). Nevertheless the works of the *Sturm und Drang* had a powerful influence on *romanticism, and the episodic character of their plays re-emerged in *expressionist drama and in *Brecht, who wrote an adaptation of Lenz's *Tutor*.

MWP

STURUA, ROBERT (1938–)

Georgian director, and head of the Rustaveli Theatre in *Tbilisi since 1978. Sturua first came to international attention in the late 1970s, when his productions of *Brecht's *The Caucasian Chalk Circle* and Shakespeare's *Richard III* were seen abroad to great critical acclaim. Sturua drew inspiration from his teacher Tumanishvili, and from Georgian *folk theatre, popular music, cinematic *montage, and the formalist *theories of Bakhtin. He has staged drama and *opera abroad, mainly in Germany and England, including productions in the 1990s of *Hamlet* with Alan Rickman, *Three Sisters* with Vanessa, Lynn, and Jemma *Redgrave, and *The Seagull*. None was especially well received, *The Seagull* being restricted to provincial venues, *Three Sisters* attracting hostile *criticism. If Sturua tends not to travel well, work with his own company has been outstanding and his leading actor, Ramaz Chkhikvadse (known as the Georgian *Olivier), has played an important part in his success. Sturua's Vakhtangov Theatre production of *Shatrov's *The Treaty of Brest* was also seen in *London in the late 1980s during the period of glasnost, when excerpts from his production of *King Lear* were staged in Leicester. His revelatory *The Merchant of Venice* was in *Moscow in 2000.

NW

STYNE, JULE (1905–94)

American composer. Born in London, Styne grew up in Chicago and became a prolific and pre-eminent composer of Broadway *musicals in the post-war era. A child prodigy at the piano, he honed his ability as a tunesmith on the popular charts of the 1920s and 1930s. He was playing for dance bands, conducting, and coaching vocalists in 1930s *New York when he was brought to Hollywood to work with singers like Shirley Temple and Mary *Martin. In the 1940s he struck up a partnership with lyricist Sammy Cahn, scoring the *film *Anchors Aweigh* (1945) and writing the Oscar-winning title song for *Three Coins in the Fountain* (1954). Despite a comfortable life in Hollywood, Styne longed for Broadway success, and in 1944 bucked the customary traffic pattern by going east. He and Cahn had their first Broadway hit in 1947 with *High Button Shoes*. Styne went on to compose scores for more than 25 shows, among them *Bells Are Ringing* (1956), with lyrics by his frequent collaborators Betty *Comden and Adolph Green. Styne, who once observed, 'without the rendition there is no song', endowed several singers with their signature tunes, including Carol *Channing's 'Diamonds Are a Girl's Best Friend' from *Gentlemen Prefer Blondes* (1949), and Barbra Streisand's 'People' from *Funny Girl* (1964). Still composing in relative anonymity at the time, Styne gained overdue recognition with Ethel *Merman's powerhouse performance in *Gypsy* (1959), which indelibly associated her clarion pipes with 'Everything's Coming up Roses'.

EW

SUASSUNA, ARIANO (1927–)

One of Brazil's best-loved playwrights. His comic parables about society and religion mix the forms of Iberian *religious plays with Portuguese-Brazilian *folk legends. *Auto da compadecida* (*The Rogue's Trial*, 1956) uses the *auto sacramental* to present the trials of two tricksters who appeal to the Virgin Mary and a black Jesus for help against social injustice. The co-founder of important regional theatre groups in Recife in the 1940s, in 1970 Suassuna organized the Armorial movement, encouraging north-eastern artists and writers to study and preserve the roots and living traditions of popular culture.

LHD

SUBSIDY *See* FINANCE.

SUBTEXT

A *Stanislavskian concept, subtext suggests, on the most basic level, that the written words of a play (the *text) are incomplete in and of themselves, and that there is meaning to be found beneath them. Underlying what a *character says is the subtext, the inner life which motivates and informs speech, *action, and even silence. The notion that an *actor must locate and/or create the subtext of a script, then convey it onstage, is central to the practices of both Stanislavsky's system and its descendant, the American *Method. On a larger level, subtext can also refer to the ineffable contribution actors make to the performance of scripted material, offering *audiences readings of plays which may be deeper and psychologically more complex than the plays themselves; the meaning of a script is therefore dependent upon actors' performance of both text and subtext. By filling in what is not written, actors become, in effect, co-authors of the *performance event.

The development of the idea of subtext is linked historically to psychological *realism, and specifically to Stanislavsky's work on *Chekhov's plays at the *Moscow Art Theatre at the turn of the twentieth century. In *My Life in Art* (1924), Stanislavsky hints at the essence of subtext when he says of Chekhov's plays: 'Their charm does not lie in the *dialogue; it lies in the meaning behind this dialogue, in the pauses, in the looks of the actors, in the way they display emotions.' Stanislavsky holds that it is not the *plots of Chekhov's plays that make them effective, but their 'complex inner activity'. These observations opened up a whole world of theatrical experimentation for Stanislavsky, as he discovered how much could be revealed by actors through 'rays' of communication. He sought ways for actors to take characters from the written page and make them appear to audiences as 'real' human beings, who listen, think, reflect, react, and speak from an ongoing inner life (see REHEARSAL).

As part of the terminology of both the system and the Method, one assumption about subtext is that there can be a marked difference between what characters say and what they mean; the meaning is dependent upon the given circumstances. The phrase 'I love you', for example, has an utterly different effect when rendered with sarcasm rather than sincerity; its purpose is altogether different when spoken to an enemy instead of a friend. This notion of subtext does not devalue the text, but invites close reading and careful interpretation. Script analysis is the means by which an actor determines character intentions and 'actions', often in collaboration with a *director. Following Stanislavsky, Sonia Moore taught actors to 'own' scripted words by learning why authors wrote them. Stella *Adler also privileged the *playwright's contribution, telling students that script analysis was their primary obligation. Both approaches hold that the text offers actors clues to the subtext and provides a psychological map for character speech and action.

Other Method acting teachers, however, placed a higher value on the subtext than the text. Lee *Strasberg, for example, spoke very little about script analysis and far more about the actor's work on the self. His belief in the power of subtext was so great, he asserted that a prepared actor might theoretically perform the meaning of a *scene without speaking. Similarly, Sanford *Meisner likened the text of a play to a canoe, and the actor's emotion to the river on which the text 'floats'. The implication in these branches of Stanislavsky-based *training is that emotional availability and expressiveness are more important to an actor's work than analysis and interpretation of texts (which may, perhaps, be left to directors).

In the late twentieth century subtext was seized by some *politically active artists, such as *feminist practitioners, as a means of subverting rather than supporting canonical texts. Actors may provide ironic commentary or resistant strains beneath the surface of the lines, altering both authorial 'intent' and traditional interpretations of a play. Such is the power that subtext affords the actor. Perhaps the most important aspect of subtext, in the end, is the way in which its discovery shifted the status of both actor and text. Through the use of subtext, the actor is understood to be no less important than the playwright; the actor becomes co-creator. A play is 'dead' on the page, but 'comes to life' onstage through the artistic contributions of the actor.
RM

BENEDETTI, JEAN, *Stanislavski: an introduction* (London, 1982)
STANISLAVSKI, CONSTANTIN, *An Actor's Handbook* (New York, 1963)

SUDERMANN, HERMANN (1857–1928)

German playwright. After studying literature and history in Königsberg and *Berlin, Sudermann first worked as a teacher and journalist. His debut as a dramatist came in 1889 with *Die Ehre* (*Honour*). He attained prominence along with *Hauptmann and was the most performed German playwright at the turn of the century, thought to be as powerful as *Ibsen. His *naturalistic plays deal with social problems and the threat of an increasingly oppressive environment. *Honour* projects the classical seduction motif into a Berlin working-class milieu, while *Sodom's End* (1890) deals with the conflict between emancipated artists and conservative bourgeoisie, a theme that he further developed in *Heimat* (*Homeland* or *Magda*, 1893). His *comedy *Der Sturmgeselle Sokrates* (*The Tempestuous Fellow Socrates*, 1903), about the 1848 democrats, provoked both aesthetic and political attack. Sudermann was strongly influenced by Nietzsche, Flaubert, *Zola, and Fontane. Despite his skill (he wrote about 35 plays) his work is now dated and very seldom revived.
CBB

SUDRAKA

Ancient *Indian playwright associated with only one work—*Mricchakatika* (*The Little Clay Cart*). Hagiographic references in the *prologue to the play identify Sudraka as a Kshatriya king with expertise in the *Vedas*, mathematics, elephant lore, and the arts relating to courtesans. A devotee of Siva, he is said to have lived for 100 years, though the exact dates of his life remain nebulous (c. second century BC–c. fifth century AD). Allegedly derived from *Bhasa's four-act play *Charudatta*, *Mricchakatika* deals with the love of a noble Brahman, Charudatta, for the courtesan Vasantsena, in a broad canvas of epic action involving intrigue, murder, reconciliation through justice, and a robust subplot dealing with the overthrow of a despotic ruler by a shepherd rebel. Cast in the *prakarana* category of Sanskrit drama, this ten-act blockbuster draws on real life rather than on a classical tale or legend, incorporating a large number of low-class characters, who speak a wide range of Prakrit dialects. Pungent in its social commentary, Sudraka's masterpiece was one of the earliest Sanskrit plays, following *Kalidasa's *Shakuntala*, to attract European attention. At least two celebrated productions were staged in *Paris in the nineteenth century—Gérard de Nerval and Méry's highly *romanticized rendering of *Le Chariot d'enfant* in 1850, and Victor Barrucand's more 'anarchist' interpretation of *Le Chariot de terre cuite*, produced by the Théâtre de l'*Œuvre in 1895.
LSR/RB

SUID, GUSMIATI (1942–2001)

*Indonesian dancer and director who founded the Gumarang Sakti Dance Company in 1982, now recognized as a prolific and innovative choreographer. Her work was inspired by the traditional dance forms of her own Minangkabau ethnic group of West Sumatra, noted for movement styles derived from martial arts. Her narrative and thematic works included *Bulan Maraok* (*Lustrous Moon*), *Api Dalam Sekam* (*Fire in the Rice Husk*), and *ASA* (*Origin*). She *toured with her troupe extensively in Europe, Asia, and the USA and created several piece in collaboration with international artists, such as *Face to Face* with the German choreographer Joachim Schlomer in 1999.

KP

SUJO, JUANA (1913–61)

Argentinian actress and director who moved to Venezuela in 1948. She founded the Dramatic Studio (1949), the School of Performing Arts (1950), and the National School of Performing Arts (1952). She balanced her *training activity with a professional career, staging classics and modern work to great acclaim. In 1954 the dictatorship withdrew funding from her school, on the grounds that theatre was an outdated art form. As a result she set up the Sociedad Venezolana de Teatro to provide a stable base, premièring Román *Chalbaud's *Caín adolescente* (*Cain as an Adolescent*, 1955). Thanks to support from the actor Carlos Márquez in 1958, she opened an independent theatre, Los Caobos, with the première of *Chúo Gil* by Arturo *Uslar Pietri. Hugely successful, the play was followed by pieces by Carlos *Gorostiza, Ben *Jonson, and Isaac *Chocrón.

LCL trans. AMCS

SUKHOVO-KOBYLIN, ALEKSANDR (1817–1903)

Russian playwright and philosophy scholar. Having studied in Moscow, Heidelberg, and Berlin between 1834 and 1842, his career was cut short when he was accused in 1850 of the murder of his mistress, a Frenchwoman. The criminal investigation included two spells in prison before he was finally acquitted in 1857. His trilogy of plays reflects these experiences. *Krechinsky's Wedding* (1855, *Maly Theatre) is a *comedy modelled on the French *well-made play which attacks the pretensions and moral bankruptcy of the bureaucracy. Several *characters are carried over into *The Case* (written 1861 but *censored until 1882, Maly), which spells out the fate of the duped *heroine of the first play, whose father now attempts to bribe her out of the clutches of two corrupt officials. *Tarelkin's Death* (1869, banned until an *amateur performance in *St Petersburg, 1900) follows one of the corrupt officials as he adopts the identity of a dead neighbour and attempts to blackmail his colleague. He is caught and tortured by the police until he confesses. The last two plays contain an element of the *grotesque inspired by actors such as the French Pierre Levassor, who was able to distort his appearance so as to act several roles in the same play. The trilogy was given *avant-garde productions by *Meyerhold starting in 1917, the most memorable being *Tarelkin's Death* (*Moscow, 1922) which turned Sukhovo-Kobylin's *grotesque vision of nineteenth-century Russia into a political tool. The works resurfaced as *films in the 1960s and as *musicals in the 1970s and 1980s.

CM

SULERZHITSKY, LEOPOLD (1872–1916)

Russian director, trusted colleague of *Stanislavsky. Trained as an artist, and a follower of *Tolstoy's religious beliefs, Sulerzhitsky was introduced to the *Moscow Art Theatre by *Gorky and *Chekhov before commencing work as a director in 1905, assisting Stanislavsky with productions of Hamsun's *The Drama of Life* (1907), *Andreev's *The Life of Man* (1907), *Maeterlinck's *The Blue Bird* (1908), and the *Craig–Stanislavsky *Hamlet* (1911). Before his premature death in a boating accident, 'Suler', as he was affectionately known, spent the last period of his life nurturing the spiritual atmosphere of the Art Theatre's First *Studio where, in close collaboration with *Vakhtangov, he attempted to put Stanislavsky's *acting *theories into practice. Prolonged and often agonizing *rehearsal periods culminated in productions of Herman *Heijermans's *The Wreck of 'The Hope'* (1913), a dramatized version of *Dickens's *The Cricket on the Hearth* (1914), and Johann Henning Berger's *The Flood*. The lighter side of Sulerzhitsky's nature was expressed through participation in the evening *kapustniki*, or 'cabbage parties', during which members of the company let their hair down as light relief from the rigours of a day's work on the 'system'.

NW

SULLIVAN, ARTHUR (1842–1900)

English composer of comic *operas or *operettas. As a young man Sullivan made a considerable mark as a choral and orchestral composer and conductor. But by the time he embarked on his first collaboration with William Schwenck *Gilbert, *Thespis* (*London, *Gaiety, 1875), it was clear that his talents were best suited to the composition of light music. Over the following 25 years Gilbert and Sullivan collaborated on thirteen stage-works, the so-called Savoy Operas (produced at the *Savoy Theatre by Richard *D'Oyly Carte), which stand at the apex of English operetta and light opera. Sullivan's skill at imitating the idiom of Italian lyric and French grand opera complemented Gilbert's *parodies of *melodrama and *satires of London life. His music is noted for its good humour and its capacity to set the atmosphere of the stage. It is distinguished by a sweetness of melody and tone, which expresses perfectly the winsome innocence that the British at this time considered to be expressive of the national character. Sullivan wrote one grand opera, *Ivanhoe* (*Covent Garden, 1891), but although this achieved a remarkable run of over 160 performances, it has disappeared from the repertoire. The Savoy operas, however, have maintained their popularity throughout the English-speaking world.

SJCW

SULLIVAN, BARRY (1821–91)

Irish actor. Sullivan played in Ireland, Scotland, and the English provinces before appearing in *London in 1852 at the *Haymarket as Hamlet. He was a tragedian of the old school, never especially popular in London, and spent a great deal of time touring in the provinces, America, and Australia. His Benedick opposite Helen *Faucit's Beatrice opened the *Shakespeare Memorial Theatre in Stratford-upon-Avon in 1879. Sullivan was not strong in *comedy and made his reputation in Shakespearian *tragedy and *romantic drama. His Hamlet was much praised for its grace, restraint, clarity, elocutionary power, and careful study, and it stood comparison with the Hamlet of Edwin *Booth. The young *Shaw greatly admired it, and considered Sullivan, 'a splendidly monstrous performer', to be the last exponent of the tradition of superhuman *acting. Sullivan also played Iago, Lear, Cassius, Richard III, Shylock, Hotspur, and Falstaff in a 50-year career, but it was as Hamlet that he was remembered.

MRB

SUMAROKOV, ALEKSANDR (1717–77)

Russian dramatist, poet, journalist, and critic. The first writer to break with the linguistic tradition of church Slavonic, Sumarokov laid the foundations of a European-centred Russian culture founded on French *neoclassical principles. The first writer of *tragedy and *comedy in the history of the Russian stage, Sumarokov was also its first *theorist, his 'Epistle on Poetry' (1748) being the equivalent of *Boileau's *L'Art poétique*. Of his nine tragedies and twelve comedies, the latter tend to be imitative of *Molière and the former pale versions of *Racine. His first tragedy, *Khorev* (1747), was followed by *Hamlet* (1748) and a range of eminently worthy but largely forgettable work whose themes were taken from ancient and more recent Russian history. It was not until he wrote *The False Dmitry* (1771) that Sumarokov discovered an original voice within the straitjacket of neoclassical form, in a play which went so far as to suggest that even an illegitimate successor could be legitimized by good rule. The play provided an example for Russian *historical drama which was later developed along Shakespearian lines by *Pushkin in *Boris Godunov* (1825). Pushkin, rather disparagingly, called Sumarokov 'a weak child of other people's vices' and Belinsky was even more condescending. Nevertheless, like *Gogol, Sumarokov regarded the stage as a 'rostrum' for the expression of social views which, in his case, were generally progressive. He considered tragedy a means of social education and was among the first to champion women's right to an independent emotional life.

NW

SUMNER, JOHN (1924–)

English director. Although Sumner worked mostly in Australia, he was always regarded there as English and during the nationalistic 1970s was criticized for his Anglocentric programming and unadventurous productions by partisans of the *Australian Performing Group, among others. He began his career working for H. M. Tennent, the *London *producing agency, but in 1952 became manager of the Union Theatre at the University of *Melbourne, which eventually became the Melbourne Theatre Company. Sumner made the troupe a flourishing institution and remained with it until his retirement in 1987. He supported Australian playwriting, his most conspicuous success being the 1955 première of Ray *Lawler's *Summer of the Seventeenth Doll*, and also worked at various times for the Elizabethan Theatre trust, which sought to promote professional Australian theatre. Sumner's autobiography is entitled *Recollections at Play* (1993).

EJS

SUNARYA, ASEP SUNANDER (1953–)

Sundanese *dalang* (puppet master) of *Indonesia. Descended from a noted line of *dalang*, Sunarya is the foremost performer in a family renowned for *wayang golek purwa*, the rod-*puppet theatre of West Java. He began his career in the 1970s, won the Binojakrama (biennial contest of Sundanese puppetry) in the early 1980s, and developed into the most innovative performer of the genre. Ogres with heads that split or who vomit spaghetti were among the new breed of figures he introduced. Musical innovations include a *gamelan which can play in different scales.

KFo

SUNDARI, JAISHANKER (1889–1975)

Legendary Indian actor of Gujarati theatre, who enthralled his *audiences as a *female impersonator from 1901 to 1932. Later he made his mark as a director of plays like *Ibsen's *A Doll's House* and *The Lady from the Sea* in Gujarati adaptation. He joined Dadabhai Ratanji Thuthi's professional theatre Thanthania Natak Mandali at the age of 9 in Calcutta (*Kolkata); at 11 he joined Bapulal Nayak's Natak Mandali and achieved instant stardom as Sundari (Desdemona) in *Saubhagya Sundari*, a loose adaptation of *Othello*. His performance achieved such fame that he became known as Sundari. Like his contemporary *Balgandharva of the *Marathi stage, Sundari played female roles with so much grace and style that women were inspired to imitate his mannerisms, *costumes, and style in real life.

With his good looks, *acting talent, and extremely melodious voice, he became the prototype of the ideal Indian woman. Owing to some misunderstanding with his company, he retired from playing female roles in 1932, but continued to direct. His autobiography, *Thoda Ansu Thoda Ful* (*Some Tears, some Flowers*, 1976) is of special interest because it deals with his career as an actor (as 'woman') and as a director (as man).

KJ

SUPPLE, TIM (1962–   )

British director. Supple is best known for his work on classic drama and *comedies and adaptations of multicultural stories. Under his *artistic directorship from 1993 to 1999 the *Young Vic Theatre flourished. His Christmas production, a visual retelling of *The Grimm Tales* (1994), subsequently transferred to Broadway (1998). Productions such as *OMMA: Oedipus and the Luck of Thebes* (1994), *The Jungle Book, Blood Wedding* (1996), and *Twelfth Night* demonstrated a range of interests. His innovative staging methods integrate organic, *physical *acting with strongly atmospheric staging and *music. Since leaving the Young Vic, Supple has taken his visual staging to the *Royal Shakespeare Company (*The Comedy of Errors*, 1996; *Tales from Ovid, A Servant of Two Masters*, both 1999) and the Royal *National Theatre (*Haroun and the Sea of Stories, The Epic of Gilgamesh*).

KN

SURABHI THEATRES

Professional theatre groups in Andhra Pradesh, *India, all belonging to one *family. Going back more than 100 years, the Surabhi troupes continue to *tour the villages of rural Andhra with a repertoire of approximately 25 plays, including extravaganzas and mythologicals like *Maya Bazar, Krishna Leelalu, Chintamani, Balanagamma*, and *Sati Anasuya*. Founded by the veteran theatre personality Vanarasa Govinda Rao (c.1868–1953), the Surabhi theatres got their names from the village Surabhi in Cuddapah district, where the families eventually settled down. Hailing originally from Maharashtra, these performers belonging to the *aare* community were first associated with *puppetry, after which they performed *actors' theatre. With the help of Raptati Subba Das, Rao started the first Surabhi group—Sarada Manovinodini Sabha—around 1891–2. Within the next ten years, the productions toured extensively to the Madras presidency, Mysore, the Nizam's territory, Burma (*Myanmar), and even the Malay archipelago (*Malaysia). Backed by veteran singer-actors like China Ramaiah, Anjanamma, Papabai, and Venkubai, and using the latest techniques of 'trick scenes' and other devices borrowed from *Parsi companies, Surabhi theatres became highly popular. In the course of time, the families increased in number and Rao saw to it that all his sons and daughters owned a company of their own. There were 36 such independent Surabhi companies in 1960, only to be reduced to four by the end of the century. Rao was a great philanthropist and was responsible for starting the cultural organization of the Andhra Nataka Kala Parishath (1929).

MNS

SURREALISM

European movement of the early twentieth century which emphasized chance and automatism, along with irrational modes of cognition and creativity, in order to activate or represent a liberation of the self and culture from the restrictions of rationality. Surrealism began in *Paris with a group of artists, poets, and theatre practitioners such as Antonin *Artaud, Philippe Soupault, and Paul Éluard, led by André Breton (1896–1966) and Tristan Tzara (1896–1963). Tzara arrived in Paris in 1920 from Zurich where he had led the *dada movement during the First World War. The dadaists demonstrated an iconoclastic approach to art production, aggressively antagonizing the public in a battle against bourgeois values of style, taste, conformity, and rational argument. Surrealism drew from a similar rejection of bourgeois norms, but through Breton's interest in Freud, in particular *The Interpretation of Dreams* (1900), turned more towards liberatory change through techniques of the irrational. The first *Manifesto of Surrealism* was written by Breton in 1924 and set forth the primary strategies of automatism, which attempted to bring forth pure thought and creativity without the control normally exercised by the conscious mind. However, it was Guillaume Apollinaire (1880–1918) who much earlier coined the term 'surrealism' in the preface to his play *The Breasts of Teiresias*, which was written in 1903 and revised for production in 1917. According to Apollinaire surrealism would bring a new and striking aesthetic to the theatre. The structure of Apollinaire's *text is deeply indebted to *Jarry's *Ubu roi* (1896), following a comparable self-reflexive, *satiric, and imagistic style. A *verse drama, the play's *characters and *action are liquid with sudden transformations of subjects and illogical shifts in *plot. Teiresias begins as a woman, Thérèse, with balloon breasts attached to strings, but soon manifests a beard and moustache as the balloons are bounced to the *audience. Typical surrealist *dramaturgy is exemplified in *Cocteau's *The Wedding on the Eiffel Tower* (1921), a *dialogue of clichés between two phonographs, and Artaud's *The Jet of Blood* (1925), a nightmarish scenario of lust and apocalypse.

Surrealist staging practice was not discrete but a convergence of *symbolist, *futurist, dadaist, and cubist aesthetics and *theory. Major productions included Cocteau's *Parade* (1917) with *music by Erik Satie and *costumes by *Picasso, performed by *Diaghilev's *Ballets Russes; *The Breasts of Teiresias* at the Conservatoire Renée Maubel; and Cocteau's *The Wedding on the Eiffel Tower* at the Théâtre des Champs-Élysées. *Masks and costumes were used to alter the performer's body through cubistic fragments with caricatured and cartoonish emblems. The stage was likewise distorted in fantastic imagery, bold colours, and a general sense of play. Surrealism continued to exert a wide influence in twentieth-century theatre and performance. The post-war theatre of the *absurd (*Beckett, *Genet, *Ionesco), the chance strategies of John Cage, and the theatre of images of Robert *Wilson and Richard *Foreman borrow heavily from the early surrealist experiments. *See also* AVANT-GARDE; DREAMS AND THEATRE.   MDC

SURUR, NAGUIB (1932–78)

Egyptian poet, playwright, actor, and director. Surur used a simple but colourful colloquial Arabic that admirably complemented his epic-like reworkings of *folkloric material in his plays. The pride that he took in his career as a professional actor and director made him even more distinctive, standing in sharp contrast to most Egyptian playwrights, who aspire to the status of men of letters and often treat performance considerations with an indifference that borders on disdain. Surur's turbulent life and untimely death perpetuated his image as a tortured, unsung genius.   HMA

SUTHERLAND, EFUA (1927–96)

Ghanaian playwright and director, a leading figure in Ghanaian theatre from the end of the 1950s until her death. Her ideas about narrative drama continue to exert an influence. Emerging from an education at Cambridge and London, Sutherland was acutely aware that she was cut off from Ghanaian village communities and the artistic conventions they fostered. A great collaborator, she used her national and international position to develop a performance tradition that, while being open to influences from the rest of the world, drew its strength from the local. She secured funds for a drama *studio in Accra whose construction was inspired by the architecture of local compounds, and at Atwia Ekumfi she had a 'Story House' built in which the community kept alive performance traditions. She also established a professional theatre company, Kusum Agoromba, that produced both the home-grown and adaptations of the foreign (such as *Everyman*). The company performed throughout the country in both English and Akan. Although Sutherland was responsible for several important initiatives and wrote or *devised a number of important *texts, it was *The Marriage of Anansewa* (1975), which draws on Ananse storytelling traditions, that has made an enduring mark on Ghanaian playwriting.   JMG

SÜTŐ, ANDRÁS (1927–)

Transylvanian playwright. His first work, *Mezítlábas menyasszony* (*The Barefooted Bride*), written with Zoltán

Hajdú, was one of the most frequently performed plays in Kolozsvár in the late 1940s. *Pompás Gedeon* (*Gorgeous Gideon*, 1968), a *tragicomedy more elaborate dramatically and stylistically, consolidated his position as a leading Hungarian-speaking writer in Romania, and his fame was further ensured by a tetralogy of plays staged in Kolozsvár under the direction of György Harag from 1975 to 1981. Sütő strongly opposed the nationalistic communist regime of Romania in the 1980s; much of his work concerns the violent destruction of Transylvanian villages and the plight of their residents.   HJA

SUTRADHARA

Literally the 'holder of strings', the *sutradhara* is the *stage manager and *director of Sanskrit drama, though his presence has been conventionalized in other performance traditions in *India as well. In classical Sanskrit plays, he first orchestrates the *rituals and prayers of the opening *nandi*. Assisted by an attendant and the jester-like *character of the *vidushaka*, he performs various dance steps and gestures during the purvaranga, the ritualistic preliminaries of the play. Later he enters once more in the *prologue to the play, which is announced and introduced. More than a character, the *sutradhara* is supposed to be, according to the dictates of the *Natyasastra*, not only knowledgeable in all aspects of music, song, and *dance, but in geography, astrology, medicine, and the other *shastras* (disciplines) as well.   LSR/RB

SUZMAN, JANET (1939–)

South African actress. Born in Johannesburg, she was educated at the University of Witwatersrand and *trained at the *London Academy of Music and Dramatic Art. She is the niece of anti-apartheid campaigner Helen Suzman and herself a prominent human rights campaigner. Suzman made her debut in a production of Keith *Waterhouse and Willis Hall's *Billy Liar* at Ipswich in 1962, joining the *Royal Shakespeare Company in the same year. Over the next decade she appeared in many of the major Shakespearian roles, including Viola (1962), Lady Anne (1963), Rosaline, Portia, Ophelia (all 1965), Katherine and Celia (1967), Beatrice and Rosalind (1968), and Lavinia and Cleopatra (1972). In the 1970s and 1980s Suzman acted in many *London productions, including *Hedda Gabler* (1977) and *Andromache* (1987). In 1991 she appeared in *The Cruel Grasp* at the *Edinburgh Festival. Her *film appearances include *A Day in the Death of Joe Egg* (1970), *Nijinski* (1978), and *Leon the Pig Farmer* (1992). She returned to South Africa to make her debut as a director at the *Market Theatre in Johannesburg, of which she was a founding member, with a production of *Othello* with Bantu actor John *Kani in the title role. She also directed a *television version of *Othello* in 1988. Suzman has appeared in many TV productions, including *Robin Hood* for CBS (1983) and *The Singing Detective* (1986) for the BBC.   AS

SUZUKI TADASHI (1939–)

Japanese director. Co-founder with *Betsuyaku Minoru of the Waseda Little Theatre in 1966, Suzuki's innovative stagings of works by Betsuyaku, *Satō Makoto, and *Kara Jūrō were crucial to the breakaway from orthodox *shingeki* (new theatre) *realism. Suzuki's experience of seeing the *nō actor *Kanze Hisao perform in *Paris in 1972 made him reappraise classical Japanese theatre. His direction of Kanze and actress Shiraishi Kazuko in productions of *The Trojan Women* (1974) and *The Bacchae* (1978) defined the Suzuki style: an intense synthesis of traditional Japanese theatre and the *avant-garde. He is also famous for the 'Suzuki method' of *actors' *training, a series of physical exercises aimed to reinvest performance with an 'animal energy' he feels has been lost in modern civilization. Inspired by Jerzy *Grotowski's Poor Theatre, Suzuki moved the WLT in 1976 to Toga, a remote mountain village in Toyama prefecture, where he held the first of his annual international theatre *festivals in 1982. He officially changed the name of his company to SCOT (Suzuki Company of Toga) in 1985. He regularly *tours abroad, directing *Greek *tragedies, Shakespeare, and *Chekhov. He frequently collaborates with Anne *Bogart and others in workshops on his Suzuki exercises, and his book, *The Way of Acting*, was translated into English in 1985. (*See* illustration p. 1306.)   CP

SVOBODA, JOSEF (1920–2002)

Czech stage designer, architect, and teacher. He made his debut as a *scenographer in 1943 and by 1946 was already in charge of stage design in *Prague's biggest *opera house, a flexible partner of the provocative directors Alfréd *Radok and Václav Kašlík (1917–89). In the *Czech National Theatre, which he entered in 1948, Svoboda passed through a short period of obligatory *realism, but his talent flourished in Radok's productions of the late 1950s. Fascinated by the possibilities of modern technology, as Radok and his brother Emil were, Svoboda developed with them *Laterna Magika and a system of simultaneous projection, which he used for the first time on a regular stage in 1959 in *Krejča's production of Topol's *Their Day*. Radok's dismissal ended this promising collaboration and restricted the development of Laterna Magika. Svoboda was Krejča's partner at the National Theatre and the Theatre Beyond the Gate from 1958, where his famous designs for *Chekhov were seen for the first time (*The Seagull*, 1960 and 1972; *Three Sisters*, 1966; *Ivanov*, 1970). He also worked abroad frequently, for drama and opera, where he enjoyed more artistic freedom, better technical resources, and perhaps less control from directors. This might be the reason why the principles of his scenography sometimes

showed better in his sets for an opera by *Wagner in *Bayreuth, or for Luigi Nono's opera *Intoleranza* in *Boston (1965)—where he used live telecast long before doing so more extensively in Prague for Laterna Magika (Antonín Máša's *A Night Rehearsal*, 1981). Svoboda always strived for a scenography able to express movement, rhythm, and even *action. He believed theatre must allow modern technology to invade it, including holography and new synthetic fabrics, which can appear transparent or solid under light. Thus *characters on the stage may appear and disappear almost unnoticed, as if they moved from being to nonbeing, from the real to the virtual world, as in his production of his own piece *The Trap* (Laterna Magika, 1999). Svoboda, an elegant purist, was the great beneficiary of *Craig's legacy, but also an ardent follower of the magic baroque designs of the *Bibienas. Widely recognized as one of the world's greatest scenographers, his unremitting experimentation and artistic achievement were the model for generations of designers and directors in the second half of the twentieth century.

See illustration p. 1308.   ML

SWANN, DONALD *See* FLANDERS, MICHAEL.

SWANSTON, ELLIARD (d. 1651)

English actor. Swanston was a member of Lady Elizabeth's company until 1622, but joined the King's Men (*see* CHAMBERLAIN'S MEN, LORD) in 1624 and remained in a prominent position in that company until 1642. He professed Puritan sympathies during the Civil War and became a jeweller after the closing of the theatres. He appears to have played a variety of roles, some *villainous, but including the major parts of Othello, Richard III, and Bussy D'Ambois. A *character in *Shadwell's *The Virtuoso* (1676) refers to 'Swanstead' as 'a brave roaring fellow! would make the house shake again'.   RWV

SWAN THEATRE

Built in 1595 by Francis Langley as the second *amphitheatre *playhouse on *London's *Bankside, at Paris Garden, the original Swan was never a success as a theatre. Used in 1597 by a group called Pembroke's Men who broke away from the nearby *Rose company, the Privy Council ordered it to be demolished, and although it survived it seems never to have been used regularly for playing. The only play known to have been performed there is *Middleton's *A Chaste Maid in Cheapside* (1611). Otherwise it was used for fencing matches and other shows, and one spectacular con-trick in 1602, when an *audience was enticed by a printed *playbill to a show, 'England's Joy', that never happened.

It was built on a polygonal frame, with about twenty bays and three levels of galleries, external stair towers, and access from the yard to the lowest gallery. Its square stage had two

large pillars supporting its cover. The Swan's main claim to fame is the drawing of it discovered in 1888 in the University Library at Utrecht by K. T. Gaedertz. Made by Johannes de Witt, a Dutch visitor to London in 1596, it survives in a copy made by a friend, along with a Latin text describing the four theatres of London at the time. De Witt's drawing is the only surviving picture of the interior of an *open-air London playhouse. Its accuracy, or the accuracy of the copy, has been extensively disputed.

The name 'Swan' was reused at Stratford-upon-Avon in 1986 for a third theatre to supplement the *Royal Shakespeare Company's two other spaces. It was built behind the main house on the site of the old Victorian *Shakespeare Memorial Theatre, which had burned down in 1926. Conceived chiefly to stage neglected Elizabethan, Jacobean, and Restoration plays, its wooden *auditorium seats 460 people on three sides, using a *thrust stage. AJG

SWINARSKI, KONRAD (1929–75)

Polish director and designer. Bilingual in Polish and German, Swinarski studied theatre and fine arts and made his theatrical debut in 1954. He was at the *Berliner Ensemble from 1955 to 1957 and for a while was one of *Brecht's assistants. On his return to Poland he worked at the major *Warsaw theatres, at the Stary in *Cracow (where he created a remarkable *acting ensemble), and began to develop a major international reputation, directing in Europe, Israel, the USA, and the Soviet Union. His range was eclectic, taking in modern drama, classics, and *opera. He directed more than a dozen of Brecht's plays (among them *The Threepenny Opera* and *Puntila and his Man Matti*) and work by *Dürrenmatt, *Genet, *Kopit, and *Weiss. He returned frequently to the Elizabethans, mounting Shakespeare's *Twelfth Night, Hamlet, All's Well That Ends Well, A Midsummer Night's Dream, Richard III*, *Marlowe's *Edward II*, and the anonymous *Arden of Faversham*. He directed a number of Polish classic works at the Stary, including Zygmunt Krasiński's *The Undivine Comedy* (1965), *Słowacki's *Fantasy* (1967), *Wyspiański's *The Judges* and *The Spell* (1968), *Mickiewicz's *Forefathers' Eve* (1973), and Wyspiański's *Deliverance* (1974). In general Swinarski sought to blend the *romantic, spiritual, and anarchic Polish heritage with German structured and practical culture, often relying on *Verfremdung and other *epic theatre methods yet creating a distinctive and spectacular *theatricality. He died in a plane crash. KB

Suzuki Tadashi's adaptation of *The Bacchae* by Euripides for the Waseda Little Theatre, Tokyo, 1978, directed by Suzuki. The nō actor Kanze Hisao as Pentheus, one of his last roles, with Shiraishi Kayoko as Agave. Her legs and feet are in a posture typical of Suzuki's physical method, which involves a distinctive form of stamping with the feet.

SYDNEY

The Sydney Theatre Company (STC), a major subsidized theatre, not only performs in one of Australia's most famous icons, the Sydney Opera House, but since 1984 has also occupied the Wharf Theatre, with stunning views of the harbour. When Sydney was first settled by the British as a convict colony, however, theatre was not encouraged, despite the famous 1789 performance of *Farquhar's *The Recruiting Officer* depicted in Thomas Kenneally's novel *The Playmaker* and Timberlake *Wertenbaker's play *Our Country's Good*. Though the first *playhouse was opened by Robert Sidaway in 1796, the establishment of Sydney's professional theatre was the unlikely work of Barnett Levey, a man with no theatrical experience, who opened the Theatre Royal in 1833. During the nineteenth century Sydney was dominated by overseas imports, particularly after the gold rushes of the 1850s, when there was much money to be made by overseas stars visiting Australia. The first localized Australian *comedy, *The Currency Lass*, premièred in 1844 at the Royal Victoria Theatre, and later successful plays included Alfred Dampier's and Thomas Somers's *For the Term of his Natural Life* (1886) and Bert Bailey's *On our Selection* (1912), both adaptations of popular prose writing. Otherwise the repertoire generally consisted of *melodramas, Shakespeare, and *pantomimes. By the end of the nineteenth century Sydney, like *Melbourne, was dominated by the *management policies of J. C. *Williamson, no admirer of Australian drama, who built a theatre empire throughout Australia and New Zealand.

Alternatives began to emerge in the early twentieth century, mostly based around *amateur theatre movements, although these enterprises often included professionals; for example, Doris Fitton's Independent Theatre fostered the talents of Peter Finch who, like many performers of the time, earned his keep from *radio work. The politically committed, left-wing New Theatre also had a repertoire which was very different from Williamson's. Highlights of the mid-twentieth century included the Mercury Theatre (founded immediately after the Second World War by a group including Finch and Sydney John Kay), the John Alden company, which specialized in Shakespeare, and the Phillip Street *Revues, which ran from the mid-1950s to the early 1960s. In 1954 the Australian Elizabethan Theatre Trust, based in Sydney, was founded to foster and develop Australian theatre. Both the Trust's name and the appointment of an Englishman, Hugh *Hunt, to run it indicated a compromised stance in some nationalists' eyes; however, the Trust helped to promote much important Australian theatre, including Ray *Lawler's *Summer of the Seventeenth Doll* (1955) and Alan Seymour's *The One Day of the Year* (1960).

In 1958 the National Institute of Dramatic Art was founded to educate theatre workers at home, eliminating the necessity for aspirants to travel overseas for *training as predecessors such as Michael *Blakemore and Keith *Michell had done.

Svoboda's off-centre scenography for Dürrenmatt's *The Anabaptists*, Czech National Theatre, Prague, 1968, directed by Miroslav Macháček. Svoboda's signature style is apparent in the integration of lighting, a ramp, and wooden scaffolding resembling a giant spider or an early scientific instrument.

NIDA went on to found the Old Tote Theatre in 1962, a company which concentrated on classical and major modern works. After overextending itself during the 1970s, when it ran three theatres, Old Tote crashed in 1978 and reinvented itself in 1979 as the Sydney Theatre Company. The 1970s also gave birth to the Nimrod theatre, founded in 1970 by John *Bell and Ken Horler as an alternative to the more traditional Old Tote. Nimrod was particularly committed to presenting Australian plays and to fostering the careers of Australian theatre workers, and it built on the success of productions like *The Legend of King O'Malley* (by Bob Ellis and Michael Boddy, 1970) to create a distinctly Australian theatrical style: larrikin, anti-authoritarian, energized, upfront, and confrontational. When this style was applied to the classics, especially to Shakespeare, a palpably Australian inflection was achieved. Later on Nimrod became increasingly mainstream (one of its leading directors, Richard Wherrett, left to head the newly formed STC) and the company went bankrupt in 1987. A large group of ex-Nimrod theatre workers then formed a syndicate to buy the Belvoir Street Theatre and founded Company B, which has flourished since 1994 under the artistic directorship of Neil *Armfield. The Nimrod Street Theatre, where much of Nimrod's best work appeared, was renamed the Stables Theatre and from 1980 was occupied by the Griffin Theatre Company, dedicated to promoting Australian playwriting. Sydney also hosts a major annual theatrical event, the Gay and Lesbian Mardi Gras, which attracts visitors from all over the world. EJS

SYMBOLISM

European movement of the late nineteenth and early twentieth centuries, which promoted the use of art, music, theatre, and writing to uncover the 'hidden realities' of metaphysics. The basic strategy of symbolism—the use of signs to deliver meanings otherwise unavailable—has always been present in most aspects of theatre aesthetics. Nonetheless the specific theatre movement began in *Paris in the late nineteenth century. Symbolist artists, such as playwright Maurice *Maeterlinck, director and *manager Paul *Fort of the Théâtre d'*Art, and actor, director, and manager Aurélien-Marie *Lugné-Poe of the Théâtre de *l'Œuvre, sought to create new theatre forms based on representations of metaphysical realms depicted through occult and spiritual material. Precursors of symbolist theatre included the poets and playwrights Charles Baudelaire (1821–67), Paul Verlaine (1844–96), Arthur Rimbaud (1854–91), Villiers de l'Isle Adam (1838–89), and Stéphane Mallarmé (1842–98). Their early use of symbolism to express the inexpressible, and the theory of the correspondences and synaesthesia, became critical elements in later symbolist *dramaturgy and practice. *Wagner's notions of a total artwork (*Gesamtkunstwerk*), tone-speech, and the spiritual content of his *operas, along with Friedrich Nietzsche's (1844–1900) philosophy of a *Dionysian primordial unity at-

tainable through the Apollonian structure of art, were likewise influential on the practice of symbolist theatre.

Symbolist theatre developed, in part, through a reaction to the objective and scientific representations of *naturalism as exemplified in the *theories and dramaturgy of Émile *Zola and the practice of André *Antoine at the Théâtre *Libre. As an antithetical response to and rejection of naturalism, symbolism can be understood as beginning the structure of thesis and antithesis of the historical *avant-garde. However, it is important to note that the repertory at the Théâtre Libre, Théâtre d'Art, and Théâtre de l'Œuvre contained a mix of plays that can be considered as exemplary of both movements. Symbolist productions of quasi-*realist plays such as the Théâtre de l'Œuvre's *Rosmersholm* and *The Master Builder* by *Ibsen further upset any neat portioning of naturalism and symbolism.

Symbolist performance theory developed preceding any actual productions through the writings of Mallarmé, Maeterlinck, and Gustave Kahn, whose 'Theatre of the Future: The Profession of Faith of a Modernist' (1889) is considered the first manifesto of theatrical symbolism. Kahn's article called for a theatre and drama that intimately connected with the arts of music and poetry, and he advocated *spectacles of textless form and colour, poetic drama, and *circus techniques. Mallarmé and Maeterlinck were both concerned about the possibilities of the material stage to present the abstract truths of the metaphysical realm. Maeterlinck suggested the use of *puppets in place of the actor, whose bodily materiality would always confine the theatre to naturalist representations. The problem of the body of the actor on a stage of abstraction would later be developed in the theory of E. Gordon *Craig, the Italian *futurists, and Oskar *Schlemmer's work at the *Bauhaus.

Symbolist dramaturgy, such as Maeterlinck's *The Intruder* and *The Blind*, first produced in 1891 by Fort, developed *characters and *plots of a generalized or eternal nature. Instead of naturalism's materialist concerns of economics and class represented through detailed psychological depictions, symbolism used representations of imagined psychic states between life and death to establish difference and dramatic flow. The symbolist plays, some of which used *verse and *mime, were often static and inactive, with long pauses added in an attempt to evoke a reverie in the spectator necessary for the contemplation of the higher realms of existence.

In 1890, at the age of 18, Fort founded the Théâtre d'Art, dedicating it in part to symbolist drama, and many of the elements that make up symbolist *mise-en-scène were first put into practice there. Symbolist *scenography attempted to depict a space of mystery that would lead to representations of the unknown phenomena of the metaphysical. Designers such as Pierre Quillard, Paul Sérusier, and Édouard Vuillard rejected scenic realism and foregrounded an often dark and obscuring stage in which the *action was sometimes seen through gauze scrims. The theatre also employed synesthesia, attempting to engage all of the senses; during some performances scents were delivered across the *auditorium from atomizers controlled by actors standing in the aisles. Paul Napoleon in his scenario for *Song of Songs*, developed a typical symbolist performance strategy by calling on each scene to carry different emblematic and structural qualities. The first scene called for music to be played in the key of C, and the dominant colour to be purple, while the actors would emphasize the vowels of 'i' and 'o' in their speech. Frankincense was to be the aroma.

The Théâtre d'Art closed in 1892, but members of the company, including Lugné-Poe, established the Théâtre de l'Œuvre that same year, and continued producing symbolist drama, including Maeterlinck's *Pelléas and Mélisande* (1893) and symbolist stagings of works by Ibsen, *Strindberg, and *Bjørnson. In 1896, the theatre presented Alfred *Jarry's *Ubu roi*, which proved to be a landmark production in the history of the avant-garde. It also marked a closure of sorts to French symbolism, with a move away from the *romantic exploration of metaphysics toward the *satiric, confrontational, and agonistic modality of the later avant-gardes of futurism and *dada. Although symbolist theatre in France did not survive after the 1890s, with the possible exception of Paul *Claudel's early plays, the movement continued to be an important force in the theatre of Poland, Russia, Spain, Portugal, and Ireland, often operating as a tool for the representation of national identity, as in *Yeats's *Cathleen Ni Houlihan* (1903).

Symbolist aesthetics continued to exert an influence on European and American theatre practice throughout the twentieth century. The designs of *Appia and Craig extended the use of a symbolic and ahistorical mise-en-scène, creating stages that represented a timeless space of interiority and mysticism. In contemporary theatre practice symbolist strategies are often quoted by such artists as Robert *Wilson and *Socíetas Raffaello Sanzio. Their use of scrims and abstracted spaces with performers distorting movement and vocal patterns create a nonspecific time and space of metaphor and sign that would not have been out of place in the Théâtre d'Art. *See also* MODERNISM AND POSTMODERNISM; DREAMS AND THEATRE. MDC

CHOTHIA, JEAN, *André Antoine* (Cambridge, 1991)

DEAK, FRANTISEK, *Symbolist Theater: the formation of an avant-garde* (New York, 1993)

SYNGE, JOHN MILLINGTON (1871–1909)

Irish playwright, poet, essayist. Born near *Dublin, from a middle-class Anglo-Irish Protestant family, he was educated at Trinity College, Dublin, and spent several years studying music in Germany, and languages and literature in *Paris, before an 1898 visit to the Aran Islands off the west coast of Ireland provided him with a subject and style for drama. Having met W. B. *Yeats in Paris in 1896, he was encouraged to participate in the Irish literary revival, and Yeats was subsequently to dramatize

Synge's discovery of Aran as a symbol of the cultural nationalist enterprise. Certainly, over his five visits to Aran 1898–1902, as reflected in his travel book *The Aran Islands* (1907), he gathered *folk tales, observed customs and incidents, and heard a dialect of English heavily influenced by the Irish language, all of which contributed to the creation of his plays. So, for example, his *one-act *tragedy *Riders to the Sea* (1904) used Aran omens of death to give theatrical force to the struggle for survival against the sea, centred on the old mother mourning the last of her sons.

Synge's plays, with their inspiration in rural Irish speech and folklore, corresponded to the aspirations of the Irish *national theatre movement, and when the *Abbey Theatre was founded in 1904, he joined with Yeats and Augusta *Gregory as one its three directors. However, his dramatic vision clashed with the expectations of the nationalist *audiences. His first produced play, the one-act *tragicomedy *The Shadow of the Glen* (1903), provoked protests for its representation of an unhappily married countrywoman going off with a tramp. *The Well of the Saints* (1905), a fable-like drama of blind beggars who prefer blindness to sight, was almost equally unpopular, and *The Playboy of the Western World* (1907) was received with *riots (*see* PLAYBOY RIOTS). Synge's ironic vision of the Irish country community, the sophistication of his generically unstable dramatic form, puzzled and outraged Dublin audiences who looked for more idealizing and traditional representations of Ireland in the Irish *national theatre. His two-act *comedy *The Tinker's Wedding*, which showed a priest attacked by tinkers, was judged to be too dangerous to stage, and he did not live to complete his last play, *Deirdre of the Sorrows*, a dramatisation of old Irish saga material, produced posthumously in 1910.

Synge's work was controversial in Ireland in his lifetime, not least for his highly wrought stage dialect of Irish English, which many Irish people judged inauthentic. Yet this poetic speech, combining the syntax of the Irish language with archaic fossils of older English vocabulary, helped to win Synge's drama an early and lasting international reputation. Already translated into Czech and German within his lifetime, Synge went on to be recognized as a classic figure of modern drama, an influence on *O'Neill, *Brecht, and Derek *Walcott. *The Playboy of the Western World* has ironically become one of the most frequently revived plays in Ireland, and holds its place in the repertoire of world theatre. NG

SZAJNA, JÓZEF (1922–)

Polish designer and director who was a prisoner in Auschwitz in his youth. After establishing himself as a designer of *scenery, *costumes, and *lighting, he became head of Teatr Ludowy in Nowa Huta (1963–6), where he started directing, followed by a decade as director of the Studio Theater in *Warsaw (1972–82), where he also taught design. In the 1970s he *toured Europe and the USA with his productions and since the 1980s he has directed, designed, exhibited paintings, and lectured all over the world. His best productions, some of which he wrote as well as directed and designed, include *Replika* (1972, 1995), *Gulgutiera* (1973), *Dante* (1974, 1992), and *Cervantes* (1976). As a *director, Szajna exercised control over every aspect of production, using space in an innovative way and incorporating found objects into the *scenography.   KB

SZYFMAN, ARNOLD (1882–1967)

Polish *manager and director. Szyfman organized and supervised the construction of Teatr Polski in *Warsaw, which opened in 1913 with Zygmunt Krasiński's *Irydion*. One of the most beautiful *playhouses in Europe, it was equipped with a *revolving stage and up-to-date *lighting, and was under Szyfman's management from 1913 until 1939, except for his two-year internment in Russia in the First World War. In hiding during the next war, Szyfman resumed management of the Polski in 1945, was fired by the communist authorities in 1949, and returned a final time from 1955 to 1957. He also was manager of other Warsaw theatres and companies. At the Polski he employed the best artists and directed numerous memorable productions himself, including *Mickiewicz's *Forefathers' Eve* (1934, 1955) and other national masterpieces, 22 Shakespeare plays, eighteen by *Shaw (one was the world première of *The Apple Cart*, 1929), and many contemporary plays, domestic and foreign.   KB

·T·

TABAKOV, OLEG (1935–)

Soviet/Russian actor and director. After graduating from the *Moscow Art Theatre School Tabakov began his career as an actor at the *Sovremennik under Oleg *Efremov, and followed him in 1983 to the MAT. With his graduate students of the MAT School, Tabakov founded the Theatre Studio, which gained official status in 1986 and is one of the most popular theatres in *Moscow, including leading theatre and *film actors in the troupe. In 1987 he became dean of the MAT School, and in 2000 succeeded Efremov as *artistic director of the theatre.

BB

TABARIN (ANTOINE GIRARD) (d. 1626)

French street performer and mountebank. With his wife Francisquine and brother Mondor he performed a *medicine show on the Pont Neuf and adjacent Place Dauphine in *Paris, providing free entertainment and expensive nostrums and thus competing both with the medical establishment, which was outraged, and with the great *farce players of the *Hôtel de Bourgogne, who seem to have been cordial. He *published his comic *monologues and *dialogues and a few short farces; the humour is boisterous and often obscene. He was famed for his large hat which could be bent into an endless variety of shapes, and his performances remained legendary for many decades after his death.

RWH

TABLEAU VIVANT

The 'living picture' was usually created by arranging a person or group of persons to represent a scene from a painting or sculpture. The form may have originated as an *allegorical or narrative representation of episodes of the Gospels or classical mythology, and was common at feasts and religious festivals in Europe from the *medieval to the *early modern periods. In eighteenth-century polite society, *tableaux vivants* became popular entertainments, genteel 'charades' with detailed imitation of well-known paintings and sculpture groups in private theatres and salons. By the mid-nineteenth century, the subject matter had been extended to embrace literary episodes 'illustrative of Shakespeare, *Dickens, Tennyson, and of the historic scenes of the French revolutionary period', as a source from 1882 put it. In *London, *Astley's Amphitheatre promoted Andrew *Ducrow as the 'Living Model of Antiques' in 1829, but the male *poseur*'s appeal was short-lived. The notorious 'Judge and Jury' clubs and the Coal Hole in the Strand had female performers in 'fleshings' (flesh-coloured tights) posing as classical statuary. James Greenwood described, with some disappointment, 'a trio of bold-faced women, with noses snub, Roman, and shrewish, with wide mouths and eyes crowsfooted', representing the Graces on a revolving pedestal (*The Wilds of London*, 1876). Ever sensitive to popular demand, the *music hall also imported the *tableau vivant*. The Canterbury Hall, with a change of subjects every Monday, produced *tableaux* after popular or epic paintings in 1873, such as H. Bielfield's *The Rainbow Nymphs* and Titian's *Venus Rising from the Sea*. Opposition became fierce as proprietors dared more, and stage 'realization' of pictures became a barely disguised excuse for the exhibition of female nudity. In the early twentieth century the *variety theatre saw the rise of 'adagio' acts such as the Ganjou Brothers and Juanita and Gaston and Andree. In the 1930s the Windmill Theatre offered copies of Victorian *tableaux vivants*, protected from prosecution because they were classical pictures in frozen poses (*see* CENSORSHIP; PORNOGRAPHY AND PERFORMANCE).

It is not surprising that living pictures also appeared in the regular theatres. From the early nineteenth century, representations of the passions and of moral positions or dilemmas were realized in frozen attitudes, with accompanying *music. In 1832 painting combined with drama in Douglas *Jerrold's play *The*

Rent Day and David Wilkie's painting of the same name. The *Spectator* described the *Drury Lane performance where 'the rising of the *curtain discloses an animated realization of the picture . . . and at the end of the first act, it falls upon another of "The Distraining for Rent" '. Dramatic tableaux became a feature of *act endings in *melodrama as a means of getting performers off the stage and, more particularly, of freezing a frame of emotions and attitudes, giving added weight to the dramatic *crisis or climax rather than animating a narrative or allegorical image.

AF

TABORI, GEORGE (1914–)

Hungarian-English dramatist and director. Born in *Budapest into a Jewish family, Tabori studied in *Berlin in the early 1930s before emigrating to England in 1936 where he assumed British nationality and worked as a journalist and intelligence agent and saw military service. His father was murdered in Auschwitz, while his mother narrowly escaped transportation. Tabori moved to the USA in 1947 where he wrote for the screen (scripting films for Hitchcock, Litvak, and Losey) and the stage with *Brecht, Elia *Kazan, and Lee *Strasberg. After moderate success in *New York Tabori began working in Germany in the late 1960s where he established a major reputation as a dramatist and experimental director, mainly of his own work. Influences include Brecht, the *Living Theatre, *Beckett, Kafka, psychoanalysis, and gestalt therapy. The dominant theme in Tabori's writing is the Jewish experience seen from a variety of perspectives: familial (*My Mother's Courage*, 1979; *Cannibals*, 1968); historical (*Jubilee*, 1983; *Mein Kampf*, 1987; *Masada*, 1988); theological (*Goldberg Variations*, 1991); literary (*Shylock*, 1978; *Nathan's Death*, 1991). Although the Holocaust is explicit or implicit in almost all his work, Tabori's plays are shaped by Jewish humour and witty *dialogue. Written in English, most of his plays have been premièred and published in German translation. His undisputed place in contemporary German theatre rests equally on his reputation as writer and director.

CBB

TAGANKA THEATRE

The Theatre of Drama and Comedy (on Taganka Square) in *Moscow was founded in 1946 by Aleksandr Plotnikov, who staged mainly mediocre plays. The repertoire was in a lamentable state and the theatre in deficit. In 1963 Yury *Lyubimov staged *Brecht's *The Good Person of Setzuan* with his students, which established him as a director of note, and he was subsequently appointed *artistic director of the Theatre of Drama and Comedy. Lyubimov added the designation *na Taganke* to the name, derived from its location in a proletarian area: a red-flame square henceforth formed the emblem of the theatre. Though the new name was not officially acknowledged, supporters referred only to 'the Taganka'. In the next twenty years (1964–84)

Lyubimov formed a new ensemble and created his own repertoire of more than 30 productions, which included plays and adaptations of works in prose and poetry, ranging from the classical to the most contemporary. He drew upon all elements of performance—*lighting, set design, music, choreography, *mime, song, *dance, and *acting—and established the Taganka as a major venue of *avant-garde and dissident art in Moscow. Lyubimov never engaged in *political theatre as such; he was preoccupied with ideas of the time, with the establishment of a direct link to the *audience, and with *collective creation (ideas often emerged from meetings with the intelligentsia). Nonetheless, the Taganka catered largely for the dissident intelligentsia and existed in frequent conflict with officials.

In the late 1970s construction began on a new building, one of the few in Moscow to have been designed especially for a particular director. When Lyubimov was exiled in 1983, Anatoly *Efros was appointed director. Efros maintained his predecessor's policies as much as possible but also developed his own repertoire, and the Taganka's role changed. After Efros's death in 1987, Nikolai *Gubenko took charge and, in his function as Minister of Culture, invited Lyubimov back. After his return Lyubimov began to demand Western discipline from the company and made salaries performance related. The troupe split up in 1993, half of the ensemble going with Gubenko to the new stage (called Comradeship of Taganka Actors), leaving the old and small stages on Taganka Square to Lyubimov.

BB

TAGORE, RABINDRANATH (1861–1941)

Bengali writer, director, choreographer, composer, educator, and artistic icon of modern *India. Tagore's worldwide fame, after he became the first non-European to win the Nobel Prize for Literature (1913), focused on his poetry and his other literary work in fiction, essays, and philosophical discourses. His innovations in other arts, such as his songs and paintings, were also recognized. But scholars have largely neglected his pathbreaking and prolific output of drama (over 60 plays), central to the evolution of modern Indian theatre. Born into an aristocratic and cultured Calcutta (*Kolkata) family, Tagore participated in home theatricals, composing his first drama, *Valmiki Pratibha* (*Valmiki's Genius*, 1881), as a *musical on the genesis of the Hindu epic *Ramayana*. He wrote, directed, scored, and acted the lead in it—a common procedure for virtually all his plays. He composed two more musicals by 1888, next returning to this form in his sixties. Between 1884 and 1900, he favoured *verse drama in complex metres and varying lengths, from short *dialogues in one *scene to sprawling *tragedies in five *acts. Some of these became hits on Calcutta's professional stage, though without his creative involvement. He also wrote several *comedies and *farces during this period.

In 1902 his outlook on theatre changed radically. His essay 'The Stage' rejected Western *illusionism outright. He exhorted

Indian artists to forget *realism and return to the imaginative vision of classical Sanskrit theatre and the *improvisation of Indian *folk forms. Meanwhile he left Calcutta and made the village of Santiniketan his base for an experimental school which eventually grew into his international university, Visva-Bharati. To encourage unity with nature, the school held classes under trees. This environmental awareness led him in 1908 to create a new kind of drama for the students: 'season plays' which celebrated the natural cycle, performed by the children under his direction, with *rehearsals open to all for their educational value. Tagore insisted that theatre, *dance, music, and art form compulsory parts of the curriculum. Productions often coincided with religious or secular festivals, and frequently took place in the *open air.

Tagore moved to more thematically elaborate plays, which he premièred at Santiniketan and were often seen publicly in Calcutta. Three masterpieces followed. The allegorical *Raja* (1911) is about spiritual quest; the moving story of a boy's death, *Dakghar*, was given its world première as *The Post Office* by his friend and admirer W. B. *Yeats at the *Abbey Theatre (*Dublin, 1913); and *Achalayatan* (*Immovable Institution*, 1914) is a scathing attack on religious orthodoxy. For circumstantial reasons, Tagore did not himself stage his finest works of the early 1920s: the ecologically conscious *Muktadhara*, opposing the damming of rivers, and the exposé of materialistic totalitarianism in *Rakta-karabi* (*Red Oleander*). He did direct the all-women *Natir Puja* (*The Dancer's Puja*, 1926), about egalitarian reforms of Buddhism, and *Tapati* (1929), a strong statement about female independence. Toward the end of his life he created a hybrid dance-drama inspired by visits to South-East Asia. Adapting traditional Indian dance idioms, he developed a lyrical style in a musical text composed by him and sung by a *chorus on stage. The three major productions in this mode, about the varying emotional registers of love, *Chitrangada* (1936), *Chandalika* (1938), and *Shyama* (1939), *toured triumphantly through many Indian cities and *Sri Lanka. Music remained central to his work—the final version of *Raja* (*Formless Jewel*, 1935) contains 25 songs—with melodies based on classical ragas or folk tunes.

A perfectionist *director, Tagore was never satisfied with his plays, changing the scripts between rehearsals, extensively revising printed *texts for revivals. Progressively he simplified *scenery and *costume designs, advocated smaller theatres, and, for his dance-dramas, sat visibly in a downstage corner as their author-director. Tagore influenced the course of Indian theatre directly, through translations of his plays into other South Asian languages, by *casting respectable young ladies at a time when society found actresses questionable, and by reinventing traditional forms to stretch the imaginative boundaries and grammar of the theatre.   AL

LAL, ANANDA, *Rabindranath Tagore: three plays* (Calcutta, 1987)

TAIROV, ALEKSANDR (1885–1950)

Russian/Soviet director whose career began as an actor in 1905. During a season at *Komissarzhevskaya's theatre in *St Petersburg (1906–7), he played minor roles for *Meyerhold, whose work he at first admired but later rejected. This was followed by a period with Pavel Gaideburov's *touring company, during which he directed *Hamlet* and *Uncle Vanya* (1908), the latter *rehearsed almost entirely to musical accompaniment in the manner of *Vakhtangov. Tairov's first important post was at Mardzhanov's Free Theatre in 1913, where he directed his future wife Alisa *Koonen in *Schnitzler's *The Veil of Pierrette*, in a production which revealed a debt to Meyerhold and the traditions of harlequinade and *commedia dell'arte*. In 1914 Tairov and Koonen established their own venue in *Moscow, the Kamerny (Chamber) Theatre, which they ran jointly until 1950. It was here that Tairov staged a number of outstanding productions in accordance with the general principles set out in his theatrical manifesto, *Zapiski rezhissera* (*Notes of a Director*, 1921). Tairov's was essentially an aesthetic theatre of what he called 'emotionally saturated form', which insisted on a completely unified aesthetic experience for the spectator, involving the actor's movement, the designer's unified concept of decor and *costume (*see* SCENOGRAPHY), as well as the role played by *music and rhythm. The entire production was to be under the overall control of a *director who ensured the aesthetic unity of the whole. Hostile to *Stanislavskian 'psychologism' and Meyerholdian *biomechanics, Tairov created a 'universal' theatre based on the 'universal' actor, who combined expertise as singer, dancer, *acrobat, and theatrical performer with an all-round ability to act in a variety of *genres from *operetta to classical *tragedy. The ideal exponent of these principles proved to be Alisa Koonen who, for the 36 years of the theatre's active life, performed leading roles in most of Tairov's productions, commencing with *Kalidasa's Shakuntala and *Wilde's Salome and concluding with Emma Bovary and *Chekhov's Nina in *The Seagull*.

During the 1920s Tairov worked with some of the leading *avant-garde designers of the age, including Pavel Kuznetsov, Aleksandra *Ekster, Natalya *Goncharova, Aleksandr Vesnin, and Georgy Yakulov, as well as the Stenberg brothers and Vadim Ryndin. The theatre's resident composer during its early years was Henri Forterre, but Tairov also used the music of established composers, such as Debussy, Dohnányi, Prokofiev, Lev Knipper, and, in the late 1920s, that of Aleksandr Medtner.

Among Tairov's most memorable productions were *Romeo and Juliet* (1921), *Racine's *Phèdre* (1922), and three plays by Eugene *O'Neill, *The Hairy Ape* and *Desire under the Elms* (in 1926), and *All God's Chillun Got Wings* (1929). He also made significant contributions to *constructivist theatre production with Innokenty *Annensky's *Thamira Kitharides* (*Famira Kifared*, 1916), said by some to be the first production staged according to constructivist principles, as well as a dramatic version of G. K. Chesterton's *The Man Who Was Thursday* (1923) with decor by Vesnin, which even exceeded the scale of Meyerhold's innovations during the early 1920s. Characteristically, Tairov also staged French *operetta—*Girofle-Girofla* (1922) in a constructivist-cum-*circus environment designed by Yakulov—and brilliantly imaginative extravaganzas, such as E. T. A. *Hoffmann's *Princess Brambilla* (1920) complete with conjuring feats, disappearing acts, and *masked actors doubling as animals in exotic *carnival parades. He also staged pioneering versions of *Shaw's *St Joan* (1924) and the first foreign production of *Brecht's *The Threepenny Opera* (1930). Despite being well received abroad, Tairov's essentially apolitical theatre inevitably fell foul of authority (his production of *Bulgakov's *The Crimson Island* was banned shortly after opening). This outside pressure had mainly negative effects, but did produce one outstanding production, in 1933, of *Vishnevsky's Soviet Civil War classic, *An Optimistic Tragedy*, with imaginative decor by Vadim Ryndin, in which Koonen excelled in the unlikely role of the woman commissar who quells a group of anarchist sailors. Even this success was not enough to appease the authorities, who closed the Kamerny in 1938 and merged it with *Okhlopkov's Realistic Theatre. The situation was rescued, ironically, by the outbreak of war and the evacuation of the Kamerny company to the east, where they were able to resume their work before returning to Moscow following the cessation of hostilities. With Stalinist paranoia at its height, however, and anti-Semitism once more on the political agenda (Tairov's real name was Aleksandr Yakovlevich Kornblit), he and Koonen were removed from control of their theatre in 1950. NW

TAKARAZUKA REVUE (TAKARAZUKA KIGEKIDAN)

A famous Japanese company of all-female performers founded in 1913 in the hot-spring resort of Takarazuka, about 25 kilometres (15 miles) from the city of Osaka in central *Japan, created by the railroad magnate Kobayashi Ichizō (1873–1957) to attract patrons to the area. The company now maintains an additional theatre in *Tokyo, and both venues continue to provide *spectacle and entertainment to an enormous circle of fans and admirers. *Kabuki, the most popular form of Japanese theatre until the early twentieth century, used only male actors. The few actresses who performed in the modern forms of *shimpa and *shingeki in the early 1900s were looked down upon socially, whatever their talents. Kobayashi's troupe was thus a daring and highly successful attempt to place female performers on the stage. Dedicated to 'wholesome family entertainment', the romantic stories performed, with women in both male and female parts, range in subject matter from adaptations of classical Japanese tales to European stories of royalty and

occasional Broadway *musicals. Potential performers are chosen by examination and *train for two years at the troupe's academy, where they perfect singing and *dancing skills. Performers are divided into five troupes; once they begin their professional careers, they may perform for a limited number of years only. The cultural significance of the show is described well in Jennifer Roberts's *Takarazuka: sexual politics and popular culture in modern Japan* (1998). *See also* WOMEN AND PERFORMANCE; MALE IMPERSONATION. JTR

TAKEDA IZUMO II (1691–1756)

Japanese playwright and *manager. Son of the manager-playwright Takeda Izumo I, he used the name Takeda Koizumo until his father's death in 1747. He contributed to the writing of 28 works produced at the *Osaka Takemoto-za *bunraku *puppet theatre, the most famous of which are in collaboration with *Namiki Sōsuke (Senryū). These include three outstanding plays: *Sugawara and the Secrets of Calligraphy* (1746), *Yoshitsune and the Thousand Cherry Trees* (1747), and *Chūshingura: the treasury of loyal retainers* (1748). Works such as *The Rise and Fall of the Heike* (1739), *Summer Festival and the Mirrors of Osaka* (1745), and *Two Sumo Wrestlers and their Pleasure Quarter Diaries* (1749) are also still regularly performed on the bunraku and *kabuki stages. CAG

TAKEMOTO GIDAYŪ (1651–1714)

*Bunraku chanter. Born the son of a farmer from Tennōji outside *Osaka, he was the most famous chanter of his age, his name *gidayū* becoming the term for bunraku singing. He was granted the honorary court title of Chikugonojō in 1701. Initially an apprentice to Kaganojō in *Kyoto, he founded his own theatre, Takemoto-za, in Osaka in 1684, and invited *Chikamatsu Monzaemon to write plays for him the next year. After the success of *Love Suicides at Sonezaki* in 1703, Chikamatsu gave up writing for *kabuki and became the Takemoto-za staff playwright in 1705. Gidayū was known for his powerful voice. He wrote several short treatises on the art of bunraku chanting which were important for Chikamatsu and show a master actor's sense of how to capture and keep attention. In his view, entertaining the *audience meant leading them into the depths of *tragedy and suffering to show the nobility of ordinary men and women, and then out again into a brighter world of hope. CAG

TALESNIK, RICARDO (1935–)

Argentinian playwright, screenwriter, and performer. Talesnik's 1967 debut, *La fiaca* (*Don't Wanna*), was an immediate success, inspiring a 1969 hit *film and productions in 30 countries. In 1970 he co-authored *The Black Plane* and wrote *A Hundred Times I Shouldn't*. In addition to his dramatic writing, Talesnik performs comic sketches.   JGJ

TALIPOT, THÉÂTRE

Réunionese theatre company. Founded by the French writer-director Philippe Pelen Baldini in 1986, the company has developed a multicultural and multilingual form of theatre, probably inspired by Peter *Brook, which reflects the diverse cultural heritage of Réunion island and the Indian Ocean region. Yet it has remained accessible and popular with international *audiences through its emphasis on *mime, *music, and *dance. Based in Saint-Pierre, its major *touring productions celebrate mythical themes with universal resonances, such as *Mâ* (1996), *Les Porteurs d'Eau* (*The Water Carriers*, 1997), and *Passage* (2000).   PGH

TALLER DE ARTES DE MEDELLÍN

Colombian group (*taller* means 'workshop') founded in 1975 by Samuel Vásquez, Mario Yepes, and Jorge Iván Grisales, among others. From the beginning the company rejected a *naturalistic approach to concentrate on creating reality itself (*see* REALISM AND REALITY), and to act upon it. 'Teatro de cámara' (chamber theatre) is the term used by Vásquez, its director, to describe settings in which the physical proximity of actors to *audience is of utmost importance, to promote a sharing of the event. Among its outstanding productions have been *Los hampones* (*The Outlaws*, 1979), by Jorge Gaitán Durán; *The Architect and the Emperor of Assyria* by Fernando *Arrabal (produced 1985); and *El bar de la calle Luna* (*The Luna Street Bar*, 1979) by Vásquez. *See also* STUDIO THEATRE MOVEMENT.   BJR

TALLER DE COLOMBIA, TEATRO

Colombian *street theatre founded in 1972 by Jorge Vargas and Mario Matallana, which has staged more than 25 productions. Most of its works are *collective creations, though it has occasionally worked with playwrights such as Juan Carlos Moyano and Fernando González Cajiao for dramas based on indigenous myth. It has invited outside directors such as Peter *Schumann from the *Bread and Puppet Theatre, who co-directed with Matallana *Aicneloiv; o La sombra del olvido* (*Aicneloiv; or, The Shadow of Oblivion*, 1998), on the daily violence that afflicts Colombia. Taller's expert use of stilts, giant *masks, colourful *costumes, artful machinery, *dance, and live *music has earned them rave reviews over much of the Americas, Europe, and *Korea.   BJR

TALLI, VIRGILIO (1858–1928)

Italian director and *actor-manager. A great supporter of *realist drama, Talli was the first to stage *Becque in Italy (*La Parisienne*, 1890; *Les Corbeaux*, 1891). From 1900 to 1928 he directed over 300 plays of both foreign—*Brieux, *Chekhov, *Andreev, *Shaw—and Italian origin, including *D'Annunzio's *Daughter of Jorio* (1904, with Irma *Gramatica), *Giacosa, *Bracco, *Praga, *Benelli, *Chiarelli, and *Pirandello's *It's So, If You Think So* (1917), *Henry IV* (1922), and *The Life I Gave You* (1923). In *Rome he co-directed Teatro Argentina with Chiarelli (1918–21) and headed the National Company (1921–3).   JEH

TALMA, FRANÇOIS-JOSEPH (1763–1826)

French actor. Reared in *London on English theatre, he *trained under *Molé at the newly established École Royale de Déclamation (*see* CONSERVATOIRE NATIONAL SUPÉRIEUR D'ART DRAMATIQUE) before making his debut at the *Comédie-Française in *Voltaire's *Mahomet* in 1787. He made a name for himself in 1789 by playing the title role in Marie-Joseph *Chénier's inflammatory anti-monarchical play about the St Bartholomew's Day massacre, *Charles IX*, a role turned down by his colleagues on political grounds. The scandal aroused by Chénier's play eventually split the Comédie both ideologically and physically, and in 1791, after the liberation of the theatres made their once exclusive classical repertoire freely available, the radical faction, led by Talma, defected to the newly built Variétés-Amusantes (later Théâtre de la République) in the rue de Richelieu. There, alongside plays by *Corneille and *Racine, he staged work by authors with whom he collaborated closely—five more plays by Chénier, three of *Ducis's Shakespearian *tragedies, and new plays by Gabriel Legouvé, Népomucène Lemercier, and Antoine-Vincent Arnault, all of which challenged the conservatism of his former colleagues. Although never active in politics, Talma was republican in his sympathies, and his first marriage, to Julie Careau, a former *dancer who hosted a revolutionary salon frequented by moderately progressive politicians, brought the actor into contact with Napoleon Bonaparte in 1795. A friendship and mutual admiration quickly developed between the two men.

In 1799 Talma rejoined the reintegrated Comédie-Française. While he remained a company member until his death, however, for most of the next two decades he was only a part-time *Paris actor. Not only was he required, for the greater prestige of France and its Emperor, to supply entertainment at court at home (Saint-Cloud, Fontainebleau, La Malmaison) and abroad (*Brussels, 1803; Mainz, 1804; Erfurt, 1808; Dresden, 1813), but also the debts incurred as a result of his generosity and extravagance forced him frequently to undertake highly lucrative provincial and foreign *tours. Talma was revolutionary in more senses than one: not only did his career span the decades from the outbreak of revolution to the Bourbon restoration, but he helped effect a radical transition from a *neoclassical to a *romantic aesthetic in both *acting and *costume. His playing was described as 'a combination of *Racine and Shakespeare' (Mme de Staël). To the declamatory formality of traditional *verse speaking he brought a new English conversational naturalism, plus a liberal use of expressive gesture and business when he was not speaking. No *hero, knight, or lover, his talent was for the portrayal of intense, manic, doom-laden passion: of the 247 roles he played at the Comédie-Française, Oreste (Racine's *Andromaque*), Manlius (Antoine de La Fosse's *Manlius Capitolinus*), Néron (Racine's *Britannicus*), and Hamlet (Ducis's *Hamlet*) were amongst his most celebrated. From the outset of his career he followed *Lekain and *Larive in the pursuit of historical authenticity of dress: in 1790 he scandalized co-actors by playing the fifteen-line role of Proculus, in Voltaire's *Brutus*, wearing a costume designed by the painter David—Roman toga and sandals, bare arms and legs, and no *wig. Talma was the undisputed leader of his profession for almost 40 years and such was the extent of his celebrity, that his death, of intestinal cancer, was reported as far away as *Sydney, Australia.   JG

TAMAHNOUS THEATRE

Canadian company. Chilcotin Indian for 'magic', Tamahnous was founded in *Vancouver (1971) by John Gray and others to strike theatrical magic out of the voices and bodies of a tightly knit *collective. Between 1971 and 1986 Tamahnous was Vancouver's leading *alternative theatre, featuring visceral re-examinations of classical *texts (*The Bacchae*, 1971; *Medea*, 1973; *Haunted House Hamlet*, 1986), *devised work (*Nijinsky*, 1972; *Vertical Dreams*, 1979), and premières of Canadian plays. Tamahnous phased out its collective principle in 1984 and left its permanent space, the East Cultural Centre, for smaller venues in 1986. Despite some excellent work, it ceased production in 1994.   MJD

TAMASHA

A form of *folk theatre performed in Maharashtra, *India. The Urdu word *tamasha* (spectacle) entered Marathi during Aurangzeb's occupation of Maharashtra from 1680 to 1707. It referred to the songs and *dances performed by the low-caste Mahar and Mang communities for the entertainment of soldiers in the Mughal army. By the mid-eighteenth century, *tamasha* evolved into a more structured form under the patronage of the Peshwas, administrators to the Maratha kings. The *gan* (invocation to Ganapati, the deity of the Peshwas) and the *gaulan*, the milkmaid's song to Lord Krishna, were followed by erotic songs, known as *lavanis*, danced by *nachas* (*female impersonators). With the collapse of Maratha rule in 1818, *tamasha* lost its urban upper-caste patronage and turned for support to rural

*audiences, who were primarily attracted to *lavanis*. Consequently, women's troupes called *sangeet baris*, specializing in *lavani* performances, developed to meet this demand. The practice of *daulatjada*, in which a patron showed appreciation of a dancer's skill by offering a coin that she had to fetch from him, emerged at this time. Its sexual implications became even more explicit when women dancers from the Mahar and Kolhati communities replaced the *nachas* in *dholki baris*, which performed full-fledged *tamashas*.

By the 1920s *tamasha* had settled into its present five-part structure, in which the *gan* is followed by the *gaulan*, in which a dancer dressed in a gold-bordered silk sari, pulled up tight between the legs and tucked in at the waist, dances tantalizingly with her back to the audience. She then assumes the role of Lord Krishna's beloved Radha and calls out to her aunt Maushibai—a role played hilariously by the *songadya*, or *clown. Their repartee with Krishna is followed by the third part of the *tamasha* performance, the *lavani* dances. Next, the *shahir* (composer-singer) introduces the theme of the *vag* (narrative), assisted by the *songadya* who comments satirically on current affairs. The *vag* itself is a full-fledged play drawn from historical or legendary sources with *satire and *slapstick humour. At the end comes the *mujra*—a dance in which the performers call upon the saints and great *shahirs* of the past to bless them. The strong *musical accompaniment for the entire performance is provided by the *dholki* (two-faced drum), the *tuntuney* (one-stringed drone), the *sambal* (tambourine), and, at times, the harmonium.

While the *dialogue of earlier *tamasha* performances is lost on account of its *improvisatory nature, the formal compositions of the *lavanis* have been preserved through oral transmission. Indeed, many of their tunes were borrowed by Annasaheb *Kirloskar, the founder of *sangeet natak* (musical theatre), and his followers. During the independence struggle, the cultural wings of political parties used the *tamasha* to raise consciousness against British rule. From the 1960s onwards, the *tamasha* was staged in a sanitized form for urban audiences by city-based *shahirs* like Vasant Sabnis, whose *Viccha Majhi Puri Kara* (*Fulfil my Desire*, 1965) was a *box-office hit. C. T. Khanolkar used the *tamasha* form in his adaptation of *Brecht's *Caucasian Chalk Circle* (1973), directed by Vijaya Mehta. After 1955 a *lavani* dance sequence became almost obligatory for every Marathi *film, with live *tamashas* imitating them in their performances. Despite its adaptability, however, the full-fledged *tamasha* has been dying a slow death, while glamourized *sangeet baris* are doing lively business in urban centres. *See also* SEX SHOWS AND DANCES; MARATHI THEATRE.   SGG

TAMIL THEATRE

Concentrated in the south-eastern state of Tamil Nadu in *India, Tamil theatre has a long and varied history whose origins can be traced back almost two millennia to *dance-theatre forms like *kotukotti* and *pandarangam*, which are mentioned in an ancient anthology of poems entitled the *Kalingathu Parani*. In the legendary narrative poem *Silappathikaram* (*c.*fifth–sixth centuries AD) as well, there are references to the three components of dance-theatre—*geetham* (song), *nrittam* (dance), and *vadhyam* (music). Along with these classical inscriptions, there are strong *folk and *ritual components in a multitude of 'living traditions'. These include *terukkuttu (literally 'street theatre'), which dramatizes episodes from the *Mahabharata*; the *kaniyankkutu*, drawing on folk tales and stories of *Sudalai Maadan* (the god Shiva as worshipped by outcastes); and the upper-caste *ritual performance of *Radha Kalyanam* celebrating the union of Radha and Krishna.

As in the other states of India, these subaltern, folk, and ritual theatre forms have survived the processes of modernization and secularization out of which 'modern' Tamil theatre has developed. By the late nineteenth century, professional drama companies like the Manamohana Nataka company (1880) and the Kalyanarama Iyer company (1890) emerged, influenced by *Parsi theatre in Maharashtra. By 1891, Pammal *Sambandha Muddiyar started the Suguna Vilasa Sabha, the first *amateur theatre group, made up of lawyers, doctors, and other professionals. By 1910 the enormously active Sankaradas Swamigal formed the Samarasa Sanmarga Nataka Sabha, under whose auspices he produced legendary *musicals. Most of the *plots were drawn from mythological narratives, with immensely popular songs composed by Swamigal himself, including national freedom songs that were often unrelated to the play but received encores from a rapturous *audience. Such was his popularity that by 1918 he had established a second company, the Madurai Thathuva Meenalochani Vithuva Bala Sabha in Madurai, whose full-scale musicals were in a class apart. Other trendsetters included T. K. Shanmugam and T. K. Bhagavathy, who staged *historical, mythological, and social plays with musical interludes. T. K. Sahasranamam trained under them and later adapted their theatrical model. Significantly, there were also a number of women's theatre troupes like Shrimati Balamani, Shrimati Balambai, and Shrimati Rajambai, all of which received the support of Sankaradas Swamigal.

An important development in the 1930s and 1940s was the emergence of *sabha* culture, a distinctive feature of Tamil life, which involves the paid membership of individuals, generally from the urban middle class, in musical, dramatic, and literary societies. These forums continue to accommodate *farces and *comedies by amateur groups, which are supported by the same urban middle class clientele that provide the core audience for traditional dance and music. As in other language traditions of modern Indian theatre, the musical tradition of Tamil theatre was affected by the advent of the talkies in the 1930s. Indeed, Tamil *film continues to provide one of the richest sources of entertainment in the state of Tamil Nadu, whose leading political personalities have doubled as movie stars and as advocates of a people-oriented, pro-Tamil, Dravidian politics. At least one Chief Minister of Tamil Nadu, C. N. Annadurai, wrote trenchant, hard-hitting plays on the evils of the caste hierarchy, social injustice, hypocrisy, and inequality. His enormously popular *Velaikkari* (*Maidservant*, 1947) and *Oor Iravu* (*One Night*, 1948) *toured throughout Tamil Nadu in the early 1960s.

The post-independence Tamil theatre has seen multiple trends—the spectacular historical extravaganzas of *Manohar, whose National Theatre (1954) was one of the last representatives of 'Company Nataka', specializing in mythologicals and stage effects, though without the rich musical repertoire of earlier times. In a more satirical register, the director Cho (Ramasamy), a lawyer by profession, regaled audiences in the 1970s by taking potshots at politicians in general. While Cho's *political *satires like *Muhammad bin Tughluq* (1968) and *Nermai Urangum Neram* (*When Honesty Sleeps*, 1981) were highly entertaining, there were more committed and textured plays from a leftist perspective offered by Komal Swaminathan, notably *Chekku Maadugal* and *Thanneer . . . Thanneer* (*Water . . . Water*). These plays provided a middle ground between the upper-caste maverick politics of Cho and the remnants of *company theatre.

From the late 1970s onwards, a few Tamil theatre practitioners have attempted to recontextualize traditional theatre within contemporary forms and narratives. Some useful experiments in this mode have been made by the director and theatre academician S. Ramanujam, who has staged memorable productions of Shankara *Pillai's *Karuta Theyvathai Theri* (*In Search of a Black God*) and Srigantan Nair's *Kanchana Sita* (*Golden Sita*) in Malayalam, as well as *Purancheri* (*Outer Slum*) and *Veriyattam* (an adaptation of *The Trojan Women*) in Tamil. Through his organization of workshops conducted by Badal *Sircar (from West Bengal) and B. V. *Karanth (from Karnataka), a number of Tamil theatre workers were inspired to seek new directions, including Gnani Sankaran and Veerasamy, who started the first *street theatre movement in Tamil, now represented by active groups like Chennai Kalai Kuzhu (1984) under Pralayan's leadership. Sankaran also formed and directed the Madras-based group Pareeksha, which was active in the 1980s, and known for many Tamil adaptations of Badal Sircar's texts. Another participant, the actor, director, and academician Mu. Ramasamy, has organized theatre *festivals and staged successful adaptations of *Antigone* and Badal Sircar's *Spartacus* with his group Nija Nataka Iyakkam, formed in Madurai in 1979. K. S. Rajendran has also contributed as a director with his adaptations of *Brecht's *The Caucasian Chalk Circle* and Vijay *Tendulkar's *Silence! The Court Is in Session*. In the 1990s Tamil Nadu also saw the growth of a women's theatre movement, with an increasingly *feminist orientation through the interventions of Jeeva, Prasanna Ramaswamy, and Mangai, who has organized women's festivals.

Two leading contemporary Tamil playwrights are Indira Parthasarathy and N. *Muthuswamy, who is also the *artistic director of Tamil Nadu's most prominent *avant-garde theatre group, Koothu-p-pattarai. While both playwrights deal broadly with changing social values in the modern world, Parthasarathy's plays like *Nandhan Kathai* (*The Story of the Outcaste Nandhan*), *Pasi* (*Hunger*), and *Porvai Porthiya Udalgal* (*Covered Bodies*) are cast in a more *realist mode, contrasting sharply with the *absurdist linguistic registers and non-linear narrative structures of Muthuswamy's plays. A younger generation of playwrights is represented by Murugabhoopathy, Muthukumarasamy, Prem-Ramesh, and Gunasekaran, a *dalit theatre actor, director, and academician who focuses on *dalit* (oppressed castes) themes among other social issues, in collaboration with his group Tannaney Kalai Kuzhu. At the start of the twenty-first century there are new political and aesthetic concerns in Tamil theatre that go beyond formal experimentation, supplemented by *training programmes conducted in theatre departments in Thanjavur and Pondicherry. *See also* SRI LANKA. PR/RB

TAMIRIS, HELEN (1905–66)

American *dancer and choreographer. Helen Becker took the exotic stage name Tamiris while dancing with the *Metropolitan Opera Ballet in the early 1920s. In her 1927 independent concert debut, she embraced the emerging *modernist aesthetic by freely experimenting with traditional notions of musical accompaniment and by addressing difficult contemporary social problems, most notably in *Three Negro Spirituals* (1928) and *How Long Brethren* (1937). In the mid-1930s she helped form the Dance Unit of the *Federal Theatre Project. Tamiris later achieved considerable success as a Broadway choreographer, winning the 1949 Tony *award for her work in *Touch and Go*. LTC

TANAKA CHIKAO (1905–95)

Japanese playwright and director. Tanaka had a success with his first play, *Ofukuro* (*Mother*, 1933), but wrote little of note until after the end of the Second World War. His career flourished after he joined the Haiyū-za (Actors' Theatre) company as director and regular playwright in 1951. Of Tanaka's many plays the most famous are marked by an intense metaphysical concern for the soul (probably due to his long connection with Nagasaki and his interest in Catholicism) and a preoccupation with stage language. Early noted for his fluent, *realistic but not commonplace *dialogue, in his mature plays, such as *Kyōiku* (*Education*, 1954), originally written as an exercise for young Haiyū-za actors, and *Maria no Kubi* (*The Head of Mary*, 1959), the *audience approaches near to souls yearning for salvation as prose heightens into poetry. The quest for spiritual peace also

informs *Chidori* (1960), whose egoistic *hero—common in Tanaka's plays—finds redemption after an elusive emotional relationship with his granddaughter Chidori, expressed though prose and poetic language, *music, and flashbacks into memory. BWFP

TANBOU LIBÈTE

Haitian exile company founded by Michel-Rolph Trouillot, Guy Gerald Ménard, and other anti-Duvalier activists based in *New York. Between 1971 and 1975 they mounted shows on the model of the *Living Theatre. Their two greatest successes were *Si kacho pran pale* (1972) and *Malere tou patou* (1973), long poems in *creole sung to several voices.

MLa trans. JCM

TANDY, JESSICA (1909–94)

English actress who became a naturalized American citizen in 1954. Tandy joined the *Birmingham Repertory Theatre in 1928, and the next year made her West End debut at the *Royal Court as Lena Jackson in *The Rumour*. Her reputation as one of the leading ladies of her generation was established when she appeared as Manuela in *Children in Uniform* in 1934 to rave reviews. Thereafter she played in most of the major venues in *London, receiving greatest recognition for her Shakespearian roles, which included Ophelia to John *Gielgud's 1934 Hamlet at the New Theatre; Viola and Sebastian in *Twelfth Night* and Katherine in *Henry V* at the *Old Vic in 1937 under Tyrone *Guthrie; Cordelia to Gielgud's Lear (a production supervised by Granville *Barker) and Miranda to his first Prospero in 1940. During the war she went to the United States and a Broadway career, which culminated in her performance as Blanche in *A Streetcar Named Desire*, for which she won her first Tony *award. She won a second Tony as Fonsia Dorsey in *The Gin Game* (1978) and a third as Annie Nations in *Foxfire* (1983). In 1989 she became the oldest actress to win an Academy award for best actress as Daisy Werthen in the *film of *Driving Miss Daisy*. She married Hume *Cronyn in 1942, and they appeared in a number of stage and film productions together. TK

TANGO

South American popular music and *dance genre from the late nineteenth century, first brought to the stages through *sainetes (local comic theatre). The dance vocabulary (tight embrace and entanglement of legs) and the lyrics' topics (love betrayals and revenge) provoked scandal and fascination among the higher classes locally and abroad. Tango often evokes fatal men and women in a dangerous partnership, where obscure desires become spectacularly stylized. Depictions of tangos in theatre and *film (*The Four Horsemen of the Apocalypse*, 1921; *Last Tango in*

Paris, 1973; *Tango*, 1998), tango portrayals and metaphors in advertisement and literary fiction, and to some extent tango lyrics, have made these overtones a worldwide cliché. But to Argentines and Uruguayans, and specially to *rioplatenses* (inhabitants of the harbour cities of *Buenos Aires and *Montevideo), the tango originally expressed national dislocations, tense racial and ethnic miscegenations, and class struggles, as well as *gender and sexual tensions. Tango practice, often held in lowlife clubs and *cabarets, was a site of illicit encounters between upper-class men and prostitutes; gigolos and aristocratic women; people of colour, mestizos, and whites; and locals and immigrants. They all competed with each other by improvising tango dance steps.

The tango has developed differently for social clubs than for the stage in the Río de la Plata, as well as abroad. On stage the tango tends to emphasize flashy, aggressive figures, relying on the contrast between aerial and heavily grounded movements and on sharp changes in trajectory. Club tango styles show greater north–south variations. *Rioplatense* club styles place emphasis on the 'tango walk', improvised footwork, and serenity of performance, while European and North American ballroom styles tend to exhibit set figures and dramatic gestures centred in the upper body. In contemporary film, theatre, and choreography, the tango often conveys impending conflict, suspense, or danger, frequently of a psychological or ethical nature: transgression and its pitfalls are encoded in the sexualized terms of the dance. Tangos are by now a civilized tradition, conservative, with a touch of wildness. In tangos imperialism and class conflicts seem to be long over, assimilated, and forgotten.

MES

TANG XIANZU (T'ANG HSIEN-TSU) (1550–1617)

Widely considered *China's greatest pre-modern playwright. He left five plays, of which the most famous is *The Peony Pavilion*, also known as *The Return of the Soul* (1598), about a young girl from a respectable family who sees a scholar in a dream. Although she has never actually met the young man, she pines with love for him and dies. Her desire is so deep, however, that she visits him as a ghost and makes love to him; she then conquers death, returns to her mortal form, and marries him. The play caused a sensation in its time, its *heroine seen an icon of passionate self-determination, and continues to be one of the most popular in the Chinese opera repertoire. *The Purple Flute* and *The Purple Hairpin* were written earlier; both tell the story of the ill-fated romance between the Tang Dynasty courtesan Huo Xiaoyu and Li Yi. Two later plays, *The Story of Handan* and *The Story of Southern Branch*, also based on Tang classical tales, concern the vanity of earthly rewards, good fortune, and honour. Tang Xianzu himself had been a loyal civil servant who criti-

cized corruption in his youth and was exiled to present-day Canton. He retired from office in 1598 to write plays.

SYV

TANVIR, HABIB (1929–)

Indian playwright, poet, and director, pioneer of a movement that sought to close and politicize the urban–rural divide in the arts. Joining the *Indian People's Theatre Association a few years after its formation in 1943, he became aware of the vitality of *'folk' forms, particularly *nacha* and *pandavani*, which were native to the state of Madhya Pradesh in central *India, where he was born and brought up (in Raipur). A multilingual artist, Tanvir has worked in *Urdu, *Hindi, and, most inventively, in Chhattisgarhi, the language spoken by the predominantly tribal group of actors who make up the Naya Theatre and with whom he has been associated since 1958.

Even before his connection with Chhatisgarhi folk theatre, Tanvir wrote and produced the legendary *Agra Bazar* (1954). Earthy and replete with robust *characters and the songs and cries of vendors in a bazaar, it was to become a classic of its kind, focusing on the writing, rather than the life, of the nineteenth-century Urdu poet Nazir Akbarabadi. Another of Tanvir's famous productions, *Mitti ki Gadi*, a fluid adaptation of *Sudraka's classic Sanskrit play *Mricchakatika* (*The Little Clay Cart*), was conceptualized while he was *touring Europe in 1956–7, following his short stints as a student at the *Royal Academy of Dramatic Art and the *Old Vic Theatre School. Ultimately, however, Tanvir is remembered for one phenomenal production, *Charanadas Chor*, which continued to draw packed houses long after it was first produced in 1974. A somewhat *Brechtian adaptation of a Rajasthani folk story, this play narrates the trials of a charismatic thief (*chor*), the representative of a common man, who makes good in spite of himself, and who ultimately gets entrapped within his own vows. While the Queen pressures him to lie, the thief remains true to himself and pays the price with his own life. Since its widely acclaimed international exposure at the *Edinburgh Festival in 1982, *Charanadas Chor* has played all over the world and continues to be a favourite at Indian drama *festivals. Tanvir has produced many other plays that question the complacency and corruption of post-independence India. Despite his nationwide status—he was for a time a member of the upper house of the Indian Parliament—Tanvir has not been able to consolidate the future of his group, which remains economically vulnerable.

VDa/RB

TAPA (TEATRO AMADOR PRODUÇÕES ARTÍSTICAS)

Founded in *Rio de Janeiro in 1974 as an *amateur troupe (thus the name, Amateur Theatre of Artistic Productions), TAPA chose professional status in 1979 and moved to *São Paulo in 1986, where it remains one of the most significant companies in Brazil. With some twenty artists under contract in 2002, it offers an international repertoire including *Chekhov, *Molière, and *Shaw, along with Brazilian work by Nelson *Rodrigues, Jorge *Andrade, and Plínio *Marcos. Its *artistic director, Eduardo Tolentino de Araújo, stipulates that the *text should be the basis of production and 'have theatrical and analogical potential', expressing a relation with 'the anguish of the moment' yet be in touch with the Brazilian situation 'either in theme or theatrical treatment'. Tolentino's clean *directorial style, influenced by *Strehler and *Brook, promotes a lyrical estrangement (see VERFREMDUNG) and provides moments for reflection, which extended even to a production of Rodrigues's *The Wedding Dress* with Polish actors in Łódź (2000). TAPA's much admired production of Shaw's *Major Barbara* (2001–2) proposed an astute critique of Brazilian neo-liberalism.   LHD

TARA ARTS GROUP

Asian-British theatre company. Founded in 1976 in response to the racist murder of Gurdip Singh Chaggar during the Southall riots, Tara wished to express the British-Asian experience and its negotiation of diverse cultures. The group aims for a distillation of the performance traditions of the Indian subcontinent, East Asia, and Western actor *training. Its distinctive fusion of drama, *music, *dance, and *mime draws inspiration from the *dramaturgy of *Bharata's *Natyasastra, the classical *Indian theatre treatise. Tara's first production, *Tagore's *Sacrifice* (1977), was followed by *devised, *agitprop plays on *racism and cultural adjustment, as well as ones from the Sanskrit tradition such as *The Little Clay Cart* and *The Broken Thigh* (both 1986). In 1989 Tara extended its focus to a revision of European classics from a *post-colonialist stance: *The Government Inspector* satirized a post-independence India that still kowtows to the English. In 1990, Jatinder Verma became the first British Asian to direct at the Royal *National Theatre: his acclaimed *Tartuffe*, set in Aurangzeb's court, drew on Indian *folk theatre. In 1991 Wandsworth funding cuts threatened Tara's existence. Recent productions such as *Exodus* (1998) and *Journey to the West* (2001) explore the Indian *diaspora.   RVL

TARDIEU, JEAN (1903–95)

French poet and playwright. He came from an artistic and musical family and was an established poet and writer on modern art before the Second World War. Afterwards he worked for French *radio and *television for many years, commissioning *avant-garde plays and directing programmes for France-Culture. He published four volumes of plays. Those most frequently performed are from the first two, *Théâtre de chambre* (1955) and *Poèmes à jouer* (1960); his later plays were mostly for

radio or librettos for chamber *operas. All his plays are short and experimental: the longest and most ambitious, *Les Amants du métro* (*The Underground Lovers*, 1952), lasts for an hour at most. They often imitate the structure of musical forms in words (*Conversation-sinfonietta*), play complicated linguistic games, or *parody the conventions of traditional theatre; some foreshadow or echo in miniature the themes of ontological insecurity and the techniques found in *Beckett and especially *Ionesco. His work was frequently performed in the 1950s and 1960s by *fringe companies in France and Britain, and remains popular with student groups.   EEC

TARKINGTON, BOOTH (1869–1946)

American playwright and novelist. A prolific writer from Indianapolis, Tarkington was educated at Purdue and Princeton universities. Along with his Purdue classmates George Ade and George Barr McCutcheon, Tarkington was part of the 'Indiana school' of writers whose plays, novels, and essays saw wide popularity between 1900 and 1925. He wrote more than 21 plays, most adapted by him from his own novels. Though he first came to theatrical attention in 1901 by adapting his *historical romance *Monsieur Beaucaire* for the leading man Richard *Mansfield, Tarkington was at his best in coming-of-age stories about charming and precocious Midwestern teenagers, such as *Seventeen* (1917), which featured Ruth *Gordon, and *Clarence* (1919), written for the comic abilities of Alfred *Lunt. Orson *Welles adapted the Pulitzer Prize-winning novel *The Magnificent Ambersons* (1918) into a highly regarded *film in 1942.   MAF

TARLTON, RICHARD (d. 1588)

English actor, first mentioned as an actor by Gabriel Harvey in 1579 and as the author of a ballad about 1570. From 1583 to his death, Tarlton acted with the *Queen's Men, a troupe of the best English actors chosen by the *Master of the Revels. He played at the *Curtain, in several *London *inns licensed for theatrical performance, and wherever the company stopped on *tour. Whatever the play, Tarlton inhabited his usual persona of stage rustic, such as Derick in *The Famous Victories of Henry V*. Dressed in a theatricalized version of peasant attire and playing on the tabor and pipe, Tarlton was the company's *clown, that is, both its chief comic actor and a country bumpkin, often transposed to urban settings as a displaced farmworker forced to find employment as apprentice or domestic servant. Despite this demeanour of rustic simplicity, his *character usually bested others in verbal combat. He was celebrated for his skill at *improvisation, not only within plays, where he was famous for retaliating to spectators' rhymed taunts with clever verses of his own, but also in *jigs, the short *afterpieces of song and *dance improvised in response to suggestions from spectators. He wrote a play entitled *The Seven Deadly Sins*, which survives only in abbreviated form. He was often hired to attend banquets at court or aristocratic homes as a kind of professional jester. Some of his exploits on and off the stage are described in *Tarlton's Jests* (1600). MS

TARRAGON THEATRE

*Toronto's most prestigious producer of new Canadian plays, translations of Québec plays, and intriguing new works and modern classics from abroad. Its well-equipped warehouse space north of the centre contains two theatres, seating about 210 and 100, as well as a *rehearsal hall, offices, and a teaching studio. Founded in 1971 by director Bill Glassco, Tarragon quickly gained national prominence as a producer of new Canadian drama, especially with its critically acclaimed premières of plays by David Freeman, David *French, and James *Reaney, and English-language premières of Michel *Tremblay and other Québécois writers. After Glassco resigned as *artistic director in 1982, his hand-picked successor, former theatre critic Urjo *Kareda, continued to provide important first and second productions of plays by Canadian writers such as John Murrell, Judith *Thompson, Joan MacLeod, Morris Panych, and Jason Sherman. DWJ

TASSO, TORQUATO (1544–95)

Italian poet and dramatist. Born in Sorrento, he found his most continuous patronage from the Este dukes of Ferrara, in whose court he composed his major epic poem *Gerusalemme liberata*. It was here also that (it is believed) the professional *Gelosi company performed in 1573 Tasso's five-*act *pastoral drama *Aminta*, which was read and translated all over Europe for many generations afterwards. The *plot is simple: suspense about whether the nymph Silvia will surrender herself to the love of the shepherd Aminta, before he commits suicide out of desperation. In the end she does make the rite of passage from celibacy to love. Some highly dramatic and emotional events precede this happy ending, but they are all narrated rather than enacted, and it is notorious that the two lovers never appear on stage together even for a final *tableau of union. The work is thus as much a *text to be read and brooded over as to be performed, and its influence on pastoral theatre was in fact minimal in terms of plot construction and dramatic technique. Its highly charged but oblique eroticism nevertheless created a poetic tone which was to be attached ever more to the pastoral *genre, whether literary or dramatic. More linked to the theatrical occasion were the passages of barely veiled allusion to the Ferrarese court which was watching the play: they contain a good deal of predictable flattery, but also some elements of personal vendetta. Tasso also wrote a *tragedy, eventually entitled *Torrismondo*, completed and published in 1587. Although set in a romanticized Scandinavia, this story of incest and gradual revelation is clearly based heavily on *Sophocles' *Oedipus the King*. The *comedy *Intrigues of Love* was begun in the 1570s and completed after his death by academic colleagues. It involves a complex circular chain of unrequited loves on the one hand, and a series of caricatured buffoons on the other—in both elements showing the clear influence which *commedia dell'arte* was beginning to exert on *commedia erudita*. RAA

TATE, NAHUM (1652–1715)

Irish playwright. A graduate of Trinity College, Dublin, Tate moved to *London in 1672 and began his career with two *tragedies, *Brutus of Alba* (1678) and *The Loyal General* (1679). His adaptation of *Richard II* (1680) was banned for political reasons (*see* CENSORSHIP), and his attempt to title the play *The Sicilian Usurper* was similarly unsuccessful. The following year, Tate produced *The Ingratitude of a Commonwealth*, based on *Coriolanus*, and a version of *King Lear* that eliminated the Fool, made Edgar and Cordelia lovers, and restored Lear to his throne. His *Lear* replaced Shakespeare's *text on the English stage for the next 157 years. Tate scored a success with *A Duke and No Duke* (1684), a *farce based on Aston Cokain's *Trappolin Supposed a Prince* (1633), but fared less well with *Cuckold's Haven* (1685), derived from *Eastward Hoe* (1605). Tate's defence of farce in the 1693 edition of *A Duke and No Duke* was taken, not surprisingly, from an Italian treatise. He wrote *The Island Princess* (1687) and the libretto for Henry Purcell's *Dido and Aeneas* (1689), but thereafter ceased playwriting. RWV

TAVIRA, LUIS DE (1948–)

Mexican director. As a young Jesuit priest, he was sent on a secular mission to study at the School of Drama at the National Autonomous University of Mexico in 1968. Coming into contact with radical figures in Mexican theatre, de Tavira left the order and quickly became Mexico's most celebrated and controversial director. A champion of the *director as *auteur*, de Tavira has thrilled and outraged critics and *audiences with his highly idiosyncratic, free adaptations of *texts by Shakespeare, Lope de *Vega, *Calderón, *Büchner, *Brecht, among many others. He has worked closely with the Mexican playwright Vicente *Leñero on productions which have attracted great attention for their bold staging and *politics, as in *The Martyrdom of Morelos* (1982), *No One Knows Anything* (1988), and *The Night of Hernán Cortés* (1992). With echoes of his Jesuit past, he considers the theatre to be a mystical space where actors should overcome their inherent narcissism to dominate their intellect. The much debated results can be surprising and make stunning, if sometimes excessive, use of stage effects. He has held important administrative positions (director of the University Theatre Centre, the Experimental Centre of Theatre at the National

Institute of Fine Arts, the experimental Casa de Teatro), where controversy has followed him.   KFN

TAYLOR, C. P. (CECIL PHILIP) (1928–81)

Scottish dramatist born into an immigrant Jewish family in Glasgow. His first professional production was *Aa Went to Blaydon Races* in 1962 at Newcastle Playhouse, and in 1965 began a productive relationship with the *Edinburgh *Traverse Theatre with *Happy Days Are Here Again*. Subsequent plays include *Of Hope and Glory* (1965), *Allergy* (1966), *Lies about Vietnam/Truth about Sarajevo* (1969), *Bread and Butter* (1969), *Passion Play* (1971), *The Black and White Minstrels* (1972), *Schippel* (1974), *Me* (1976), and *Walter* (1977). Taylor worked extensively with *community theatre groups, the mentally handicapped, and theatre for *youth. He died shortly after the opening of *Good*, which was premièred by the *Royal Shakespeare Company in 1981. Set in Germany, the play shows the fall of a liberal professor whose moral and physical cowardice leads him to join the Nazi Party and work in Auschwitz. A major retrospective at the *Edinburgh International Festival in 1992 did little to inspire the recovery of his plays and reputation by scholars or practitioners, but did underline the quality and complexity of *Good* in a stylish production by Michael Boyd for the *Glasgow Tron Theatre.   AS

TAYLOR, JOSEPH (1586–1652)

English actor. Already a seasoned actor with the Duke of York's company, Lady Elizabeth's company, and Prince Charles's company, Taylor in 1619 replaced Richard *Burbage as leading actor of the King's Men (*see* CHAMBERLAIN'S MEN, LORD). After John *Heminges's death in 1630, Taylor, together with John *Lowin, assumed *management of the company. Taylor specialized in heroic and handsome young lovers or dashing *villains. He last acted in 1648.   RWV

TAYLOR, LAURETTE (COONEY) (1884–1946)

American actress. Taylor began acting in 1903 and developed a technique markedly different from her peers in commercial theatre; Brooks *Atkinson described it as 'spontaneous and eloquent'. The *critic John Corbin wrote that Taylor had 'the greatest talent, the greatest spirit of our times', but that her ability was wasted in poor dramatic material. In 1911 she married the English playwright J. Hartley Manners and starred in a series of immensely popular plays by him, most notably *Peg o' my Heart*. Taylor performed more than 1,000 times the role of the plucky young Irishwoman who inherits a fortune and wins the heart of London society. After Manners's death in 1928, Taylor became an alcoholic and was frequently out of work. She emerged to acclaim in 1938 in a revival of Sutton Vane's *Outward Bound*

and again in 1944 as Amanda Wingfield in Tennessee *Williams's *The Glass Menagerie*.   MAF

TAYLOR, TOM (1817–80)

English playwright. Taylor gained degrees from Glasgow and Cambridge before becoming first a barrister, then a journalist and dramatist, and was a civil servant for 21 years in the Department of Health. Later he was art critic of *The Times*, editor of *Punch* (1874–80), and professor of English at University College London. He was an enthusiastic *amateur actor and knew *Dickens personally, joining him in private theatricals, and supported the campaign for a *national theatre which was active in the early 1870s. He wrote or adapted around 80 plays, often based on novels, historical biographies, or foreign originals. His adaptations show an acute understanding of dramatic narrative, a good example being *A Tale of Two Cities* (1860), which he wrote in consultation with Dickens. The *comedy *Our American Cousin*, featuring the absurd *character Lord Dundreary, is famous for establishing E. A. *Sothern's reputation in 1858; it is infamous for being performed at Ford's Theatre in Washington when Abraham Lincoln was assassinated by John Wilkes *Booth in 1865.

The *Ticket-of-Leave Man* (1863) had a long and popular life throughout the nineteenth century, and was even recast in *fairground booth theatres as *The Ticket-of-Leave Woman*. The play demonstrates Taylor's awareness of technical developments in Victorian stagecraft. It conveys the atmosphere of place not through spectacular effects but through the precise detail of its 'cup-and-saucer' scenes in a drawing room, a kitchen, a city office, and the Bellevue Tea Gardens, all of which suggest a close familiarity with *London life. Taylor collaborated with Charles *Reade on *Masks and Faces* (1852) and with Augustus Dubourg on *New Men and Old Acres* (1869), both sentimental comedies, but he also turned his hand to *pantomimes and a *hippodrama, *Garibaldi*, at *Astley's Amphitheatre (1859). His more serious dramas were often derived from French sources. They include *Still Waters Run Deep* (1855) and *The Fool's Revenge* (1859, from *Rigoletto*). Taylor's ability to imbue foreign *plots with English familiarity and sentiment were important factors in his continuing popularity. His last play was *Love and Life* (1878).   AF

TAYMOR, JULIE (1952–)

American director, designer, and *mask and *puppet maker. At the age of 16 she spent a year in *Paris studying *mime at the *Lecoq school. As an undergraduate at Oberlin College, she joined Herbert *Blau's experimental ensemble KRAKEN. In the mid-1970s, she spent four years in Asia, mostly in Java and Bali, studying and experimenting with traditional forms of mask and puppet theatre (*see* INDONESIA). Back in the USA, she designed *costumes, masks, and puppets for directors such as Elizabeth

Swados and Andrei *Şerban until she began directing her own productions, many of them with *music composed by her partner Elliot Goldenthal. These included an original piece titled *Juan Darien: A Carnival Mass* (1988), which was later remounted and *toured extensively. In the 1990s her innovative fusion of movement, music, and design led to a major grant, invitations to direct *opera around the world, and her crucial creative role in the transformation of Disney's *The Lion King* into a Broadway *musical (1997). That success earned her two Tony *awards, catapulted her to fame, and provided the opportunity to pursue less commercial projects, such as a *film adaptation of *Titus Andronicus* (1999).　　　　　　　　　　　　　　STC

TA'ZIEH

The Ta'zieh (consolation) plays of Persia (present-day Iran) are similar in both structure and function to the *Passion plays of *medieval Europe. The early history of the form is obscure, but most scholars assume that it developed out of a variety of traditional performative religious observances. Its historical basis was the heroic martyrdom of Husayn, grandson of the prophet Muhammad and the redemptive figure of the Shiite branch of Islam. His death on the plains of Karbala in 680 is the central episode of any Ta'zieh cycle, but like the European Passion plays, each Ta'zieh cycle contains a wide variety of closely and more distantly related material. As early as the tenth century, elaborate processions mourning the death of the martyr were a standard feature of the commemorative festivals held during the month of Muharram, when his death occurred. These festivals received royal encouragement in the sixteenth century, when the Shiite Safavid dynasty came to power, and many reports by merchants and envoys mention the elaborate Muharram pageants, with *costumed processions, tableaux, and mock battles. During this same period another Muharram performative tradition developed, the recitation of the life and deeds of Shiite martyrs by professional storytellers, a major performative art in many Islamic nations. These two traditions, one largely visual, the other largely auditory, are generally thought to have provided the basis for the elaborate Ta'zieh cycles, which seem to have first appeared in the eighteenth century and had their period of greatest flourishing under the Kajar kings (1786–1926). Performances were and are still presented by both *amateur and professional companies both in small improvised theatres and in elaborate, permanent structures. The most famous of the latter was the State Tekya, built in Tehran in the late nineteenth century and seating up to 20,000 spectators.　　　　　　　　　　　　　　MC

TBILISI

Capital and theatrical centre of the Republic of Georgia, with a population in 2000 of c.1,000,000. Forms of theatrical activity in Tbilisi have been traced to the fifth century and the era of Tsar Vakhtang Gorgasal, when Georgia developed its native forms of theatre known as *sakhioba*, combining *music and *dance with speech. Buildings for theatrical performances known as *sakhli satamasho* were constructed at court between the eleventh and thirteenth centuries, showing various kinds of entertainment including the erotic *simger sigodat*. In addition there was the popular theatre of *masks, the *berikaoba*, and the *keenoba*, a form of popular *carnival depicting the struggle of the Georgian people against foreign occupation during the seventeenth century. Following union with Russia in 1801, *amateur groups began to perform work by the Georgian national poet Shota Rustaveli, but it was not until 1821, when the Russian dramatist *Griboedov went to live in Tbilisi (Tiflis), that a professional theatre began to emerge, one of its early leaders, Abishadze, having been a student at the *Moscow *Maly Theatre. A national theatre was founded in Tbilisi during the 1880s but its first dramatic work, *Khanuma* by Avksenty Tsagareli, was not performed until 1901. In 1921 the theatre was christened the Rustaveli after the romantic poet who lived in the reign of Queen Tamar (1184–1213), and whose epic masterpiece *The Knight in the Panther's Skin* makes him the Georgian equivalent of Dante or *Milton. The other main theatre in Tblisi is the Mardzhanishvili, named in honour of the Soviet Georgian Kote Mardzhanishvili (Konstantin *Mardzhanov), whose production of Lope de *Vega's *Fuente Ovejuna* at the Rustaveli Theatre in 1922 inaugurated a new period in Georgian theatre and starred a number of outstanding actors, including Vera Andzhaparidze, Akaky Khorava, Tamara Chavchavadze, and Ushangi Chkheidze. During the Soviet period, of the 25 state-subsidized theatres in Georgia eleven were located in Tbilisi, including the Griboedov Theatre, the Abashidze Theatre of *Musical Comedy, the Palishavili Theatre of *Opera and *Ballet, the Theatre of Young Spectators, and the Georgian Film Actors' Studio. The greatest mark on Georgian and world theatre during the twentieth century was made by Mikhail Tumanishvili at the Rustaveli and at the Film Actors' Studio and, subsequently, by his pupil Robert *Sturua, who took over the directorship of the Rustaveli during the 1970s and introduced the company's work to an international *audience.　　　　　　　　　　　　　　NW

TCHELITCHEW, PAVEL (1898–1957)

Russian stage designer. A student of Aleksandra *Ekster in *Kiev, he designed several *ballets for Boris Kniaseff and Viktor Zimin in Istanbul (1920–1) before going to *Berlin where he designed for the Blaue Vogel *cabaret (1921–3) and then in *New York when it moved there as the Blue Bird. Tchelitchew settled in *Paris in 1923 and developed an interest in *surrealism and the occult. He designed *Ode* for *Diaghilev (1928) and *Orfeo* for *Balanchine (1936). His designs were often constructed according to a spiral or circular scheme dependent on exotic colour contrasts and with a sense of vital movement.   NW

TEIRLINCK, HERMAN (1879–1967)

Flemish novelist, playwright, and *theorist, born in *Brussels, where his *expressionist plays were performed in the Royal Flemish Theatre. *De vertraagde film* (*Film in Slow Motion*, 1922) is located in a modern city with a middle *act underwater, showing what passes through the heads of a young couple who commit suicide by drowning. *Ik dien* (*I Serve*, 1924) is a secularized version of the medieval *Beatrijs* legend, while *De man zonder lijf* (*The Man without Body*, 1925) gives concrete shape to a split personality. Teirlinck promoted a new theatrical style marked by varying rhythms and the inclusion of *masks and *acrobatics. After the Second World War he became the founder of the National Theatre, based in *Antwerp. Strongly influenced by Gordon *Craig, he initially emphasized the role of the *director, but in his major theoretical work *Wijding voor een derde geboorte* (1956) he saw the *actor as the autonomous creator of theatre art.   JDV

TELBIN, WILLIAM (1813–73)

English designer. His first major commission was for *Macready's *King John* at *Drury Lane (1842), fourteen designs for which are preserved in the Folger Shakespeare Library. He joined Charles *Kean's scene *painting team at the *Princess's Theatre in 1856, contributing designs for *The Winter's Tale*, *The Tempest*, and *King John*. He designed Charles *Fechter's *Hamlet* (1861) at the *Lyceum, creating a very effective disappearance for the *Ghost. He also worked in the provinces and at *Covent Garden. His son W. L. Telbin designed for *Irving and wrote articles on scenic design.   JTD

TELEVISION *see page 1326*

TÉLLEZ, FRAY GABRIEL *See* TIRSO DE MOLINA.

TELUGU THEATRE

The theatre of Andhra Pradesh, south *India, where Telugu is the dominant language. Sculptural and inscriptional evidence suggests that the performing arts flourished in Andhra by the second century BC, even though the first written evidence of dramatic performances by Palkuriki Somanatha is from the thirteenth century AD. The only extant play of the medieval period is *Kridabhiramam*, translated from Sanskrit by Vinukonda Vallabharayudu. In the fourteenth and fifteenth centuries, Sanskrit dramas were translated in poetic form as *kavyas*. Later the

Nayaka (1565–1673) and Maratha (1674–1855) kings of Thanjavur chose Telugu as their court language and patronized drama through song-and-*dance *yakshaganas, performed both in the court and village squares.

With the advent of English education in the second half of the nineteenth century, modern Telugu drama came into being with translations from Sanskrit and English. Kokkonda Venkataratnam Pantulu's translation of *Narakasura Vijaya Vyayogamu* (1872) from Sanskrit is regarded as the first modern play in Telugu; it was followed by translations of *Kalidasa's *Abhijnana Sakuntala* by Paravastu Rangacharyulu (partly completed, 1872) and Kandukuri Veeresalingam (1872/1883). Vavilala Vasudeva Sastry's *Sizaru Charitramu* (*Julius Caesar*, 1875) was the first English play translated. He also wrote the first social drama, *Nandaka Rajyam* (*The Reign of Nandaka*, 1880), which deals with the enmity between two Brahman sects. All of these early attempts were *closet dramas.

Veeresalingam, a reforming man of letters, was the first to stage modern Telugu productions, such as his own *Vyavahara Dharmabodhini* (*A Primer of Legal Practice*, 1880), an indictment of the legal profession. In the same year Dharwada Nataka Samajam toured Andhra with its *Hindi productions and inspired several Telugu playwrights to start *amateur groups. Veeresalingam, Kondubhotla Subrahmanya Sastry, and Nadendla Purushothama Kavi wrote and staged plays on the Dharwada model between 1880 to 1886 in Rajahmundry, Guntur, and Machilipatnam respectively. Influenced by the *Parsi theatre and *company theatre productions from other parts of India, Dharamavaram Ramakrishnamacharyulu of Bellary initiated the tradition of *padya natakam*—literally, a play with metrical stanzas sung to an elaborate raga, like *Chitranaleeyam* (*The Curious Story of Nala*, 1887). With the popularity of this *genre, singers became stars and poets became playwrights overnight. Even though poetry dominated dramatic writing, without adequate characterization and *plot development, a few playwrights of *padya natakam* stand out for their happy blending of poetry and dramatic technique, including Panuganti Lakshmi Narasimharao, Balijepalli Laxmikantham, and Tirupti Venkatakavulu.

Gurazada *Apparao's *Kanyasulkam* (*Bride Price*, 1892; published in 1897) was a major breakthrough in exploring the social problem play, while Vedam Venkataraya Sastry's *Pratapurudriyam* (*The Story of Prataparudra*, 1897) set a model for the *historical play, which inspired Kolachalam Srinivasarao to write several works in this patriotic mode, notably *The Fall of Vijayanagar* (1907), which had a memorable production history with the illustrious Bellary Raghava in the lead role of a Pathan. It was during 1891–2 that Vanarasa Govindarao founded his *Surabhi theatre, which grew into several troupes as his family multiplied. All these groups mainly staged mythological musicals and occasional historical plays.

(continued on p. 1337)

TELEVISION

The major mass communications invention of the twentieth century. Although its technological and aesthetic development was pre-dated by *film and *radio, television fused the multiple forms of radio (with which it shares its electronic means of transmission) and the visual immediacy of film (from which it differs in terms of its electronic rather than photographic image). Until 1929, film lacked the sound dimension contemporaneously available on the 'blind medium' radio; radio's visual 'lack' was eventually supplied to a mass *audience by television after the Second World War. In television, sound and vision have a parallel importance, and in content terms the factual is as prominent as fiction. As a result, television has arguably had the greatest social impact of all the twentieth-century media (see MASS MEDIA). In his monumental history of the British Broadcasting Corporation (BBC) Asa Briggs remarked that anyone born after 1922 (when the British Broadcasting Company, as it was called at first, was formed) 'could hardly conceive of a pre-broadcasting age'. It would be similarly difficult for anyone born after 1945 to conceive of a pre-television age, so saturated are we with information and images derived from this powerful medium.

Television must be understood first and foremost as a major industry whose development, running in tandem with technological change, has moved from the national to the international. The industry still reflects contrasting ideologies worldwide, positioned within and inflected by national cultures and histories. The most rapid initial development took place mid-century within the cultures of the most powerful industrial nations, mainly but not exclusively anglophone. Although the UK and USA were at the forefront, France, Germany, *Japan, and Russia made important contributions. The post-war consumer boom was beneficial to television; then Japanese technological innovation late in the twentieth century ensured further expansion. Television services outside the developed world were slower to establish themselves, and were often partly conditioned by exported organizational models. By the beginning of the twenty-first century television had become a global industry, dominated by Japanese and American technology/entertainment corporations. But whatever the level of foreign domination, there was never total exclusion of national cultures; in large societies with powerful senses of themselves like *India and *China, and in *Latin American and *African nations, there are healthy broadcasting environments in which the forces of American (and to a lesser extent British or European) cultural imperialism are in lively conflict with indigenous forms.

Because broadcasting industries worldwide have been dominated by the originary models offered by Britain and America, what follows will concentrate on development within these two cultures, and on their dynamic overlapping. To suggest a universal sense of what television 'is' would be an empty exercise, but to consider these founding structures critically is to posit a means of calibrating crucial developments and changes, a means through which specific national cultures can at least be considered if never totally defined. In broad terms, then, this account concentrates on two dominant traditions of television illustrated through British and American histories. It examines how they interacted during the 'television century', and offers a view of their apparent polarization into conflict as the twenty-first century heralded a corporate age in which an aggressive globalization drove national cultures into more and more defensive modes and in which concepts of the national and the international interacted and were reformulated.

The British model involves state or quasi-state ownership of broadcasting networks and a concept of 'public service', a recognition that a mass medium has a duty of care towards the people in a society. At its worst, this can mean patriarchal and elitist programming policies; at its best, it can ensure high-quality information and sophisticated levels of debate as well as entertainment. A 'public service network' is paid for from taxes, and such networks are integral parts of many national cultures, both democratic and non-democratic. In Europe, they are found in the Scandinavian nations, the Netherlands, Germany, France, Spain, and Italy, and elsewhere they are found in, for example, countries of the former British Empire. Public service television makes a real contribution to public life in many of these cultures. In contrast, when networks have been constrained meekly to toe the party lines of a dominant ideology in totalitarian states (as in the old communist bloc) transmitters frequently become key targets for takeover when such regimes collapse (as occurred in Belgrade in 2000). This is because, first, the outright lies peddled by such networks are deeply resented, and secondly because a 'free' network is normally part of any reform process.

In the American commercial tradition, networks are also defined as 'free', but free of government and its overt interference. Freedom of this kind means that, while networks are organized as businesses and largely driven by commercial considerations, they are also subject to laws and regulations. In the USA, since 1933, this has been the task of the Federal Communications Commission (FCC). The American model tends to lay greater stress on entertainment as a means of delivering mass audiences to the advertisers who ultimately pay for programmes in the system. But the model is not without a concept of the 'social', if only because social concerns press so heavily upon the audiences engaged in viewing, and because regulating bodies like the FCC often exist to monitor output. The British tradition has tried earnestly to legislate for 'what people need' for a full and responsible social life whilst being mindful of 'what they want'; the American tradition has proclaimed openly its desire to give people what they want without necessarily ignoring what they need in social terms. The systems are united in a recognition of television as pre-eminently a mass medium with a dual role: to inform and to entertain.

By the end of the twentieth century, television had become far more important in terms of the size of its audience and the apparent range of its influence than its sister mass medium radio, which dominated the period between the two world wars. Television's flexibility and its gradual release from the time-bound schedules of its first phase of mass development (roughly 1945–65) may have begun with production technologies like better cameras and greater transmission coverage, but the real breakthrough occurred when technology at the viewer end of the communication chain multiplied choice of what and when to view. In a second phase of development (approximately 1965–85), the ability to record transmissions off-air on video recorders and the degree of active choice in viewing offered by the hand-held channel changer gave greater flexibility than was available in the 1945–65 period. As multi-channel environments became the norm in a third phase (from the mid-1980s), with cable, satellite, and digital systems supplementing terrestrial modes of transmission, patterns of viewing once apparently fixed to immutable schedules were disaggregated in ways unimaginable to the television pioneers. In a future further fragmented by multifarious digital options, it seems likely that consumers will have literally hundreds of stations to view and the increased possibility of direct interaction with the screen.

As the twenty-first century began, the viewer was already technically free to choose and bombarded with choice. In reality, this choice was (and is) heavily conditioned, especially by economic factors. But television is certainly characterized by the variety of its output and the ubiquity of its opportunities for viewing; unlike theatre and cinema, many different kinds of programme are transmitted on television over much longer periods of time to much larger audiences in a greater variety of locations. Some programmes, like news and current affairs, are factual; others, like soaps, serials, and situation *comedies, are fictional; still others, like *documentary dramas and 'docusoaps', mix factual and dramatic elements. Television is still primarily a domestic entertainment, but cheaper sets leading to multiple ownership have increased the number of sets in many modern houses, while larger screens and better image definition have led to its presence at special occasions of many kinds (for example, offering 'action replays' on giant screens at sporting events). In cinemas and theatres, by contrast, individuals activate their choice in a direct financial transaction but are largely powerless to determine the time and place that together constitute them as an 'audience' for a 'performance'. All these factors combine to make television a heavily consumed medium more obsessively regulated and monitored than cinema, theatre, or even radio.

To abstract television *drama from television itself, as this account will now do, is to focus on one substantial and significant, but by no means comprehensive, part of the medium's overall output. Nonetheless, since at least the 1960s, far more people have derived their experience of drama from television than from the ancient medium of theatre, or from the newer media of cinema and radio. The notion that the only real 'national theatre' in any society is on television would be hard to disprove in terms of audience numbers alone. For makers of drama (*playwrights, *actors, technicians, designers, *producers, *directors) television offers a tempting access to huge audiences; but it also constrains those makers with its relatively rigid generic patterns, its commercially driven unwillingness to take the risk of experimentation, and the relatively heavy surveillance of regulators. It should be said, too, that drama programming is at the most expensive end of TV production and therefore vulnerable to the cost-cutting endemic to large industries in hard economic times. In concentrating primarily on the histories and development of British and American television drama, it is important to remember that the developmental influence of the two templates adduced above has been reinforced by the fact that the anglophone output of these two nations has become a major factor in an international market dominated by the English language. Amidst technological and cultural change, drama in all its forms—and from a variety of sources—has been a staple for network heads and schedulers the world over. Because it can address emotional as well as intellectual wants and needs in its audiences, because it confronts the private and the public in interesting—even unique—ways, this is likely to remain so through changes still to come.

1. Early television drama: the 'photographed stage play';
2. The 'golden age' in America; 3. Britain's 'golden age';
4. Popular dramatic forms;
5. Late twentieth-century industrial changes;
6. Writers and producers; 7. The globalized future

1. Early television drama: 'the photographed stage play'

Initially, very few people anywhere in the world had access to TV, let alone to TV drama. The 1930s was a pre-development period interrupted by the Second World War. Early transmissions were confined to a very few countries (principally, Britain, America, and Germany). Although radio was the dominant mass medium, and radio drama far more significant, TV drama was produced experimentally as early as 1928 in the USA and 1930 in Britain. With the new medium rather cut off from the world of cinema, because the electronic camera was far less flexible than its photographic counterpart, theatre remained the dominant influence until the mid-1950s. From 1936 (when the BBC began regular transmissions) to the outbreak of the Second World War, the BBC's flagship drama programme was *Theatre Parade*, a programme mainly presenting excerpts from West End productions of the period. For example, in 1938 J. B. *Priestley's *When We Are Married*, then running at *London's *St Martin's Theatre, was transmitted. 'High-art' plays by classic authors such as Shakespeare, *Shaw, and *Sheridan were mixed with popular hits just as they were on Shaftesbury Avenue. The public service imperatives of the BBC's first director-general, the charismatic John (later Lord) Reith, ensured a high premium on the educative and the socially cohesive throughout the TV schedule, and drama was no exception. So *Journey's End*, R. C. *Sherriff's classic Great War play of 1929, was transmitted on Armistice Day 1937. Significantly, it was shortened to one hour, if for no other reason than that drama was but one kind of programming amongst many in an abbreviated schedule. There were a few plays written especially for television, for example the innovative *Condemned to be Shot* by R. E. J. Brooke. In this 1939 play, the camera point of view supplied the dramatic role of *protagonist (the programme makers eschewing the shot-reverse-shot grammar already the staple of popular cinema). In 1938 there was the first serial, *Ann and Harold*; it was about a London society couple, its upper-middle-class situation a real clue as to its expected audience of London-based set owners. In 1936–9, there were only 20,000 TV sets in Britain, concentrated in the London area where the only transmitter was situated.

Television in Britain was halted altogether during the war, the single-channel service going off-air in 1939 in the middle of a Mickey Mouse cartoon. It resumed transmission of this cartoon at the end of hostilities at the exact same point, a vivid symbol of the value television networks have placed historically on the continuousness of their coverage. In the USA, the broadcasting environment of commercial television networks began to form during the war. Commerce dominated American television as it had its radio, and both major broadcasters NBC (National Broadcasting Company, founded 1926) and CBS (Columbia Broadcasting System, founded 1927) began TV transmissions in 1939. But TV drama started in earnest with NBC's *Kraft Television Theater* from 1947, and this type of anthology series became the dominant form. Like its pre-war British equivalent it was heavily dependent upon theatre for both material and personnel—simply substituting *New York and Broadway for London and the West End. In 1947, the BBC head of drama Val Gielgud (the brother of John *Gielgud) referred to the kind of production common on both sides of the Atlantic as a 'photographed stage play'. With the television screen a duplicate *proscenium arch, studio settings replicating wood-and-canvas

*stage sets, actors grouped as if on an end-stage (and often in danger of projecting too much for the always more intimate medium), TV drama was but a reflection of theatrical art. As camera technology improved (and especially with multi-turret cameras and multi-camera set-ups), television began to exploit some of the potential for visual selection which it shared with cinema. The power of the close-up and the cramped nature of domestic settings, combined with the intimacy of viewing arrangements in the early days (families grouped around receivers in living rooms), meant that TV drama focused increasingly on individual relationships amongst a few *characters in intimate settings. These conditions of production and *reception helped define the differences between theatre, cinema, and television in artistic terms. Improvements in production and reproduction technologies happened so quickly after the Second World War that by the mid-1950s a truly mass audience became available to programme makers. Television drama was now in a position to establish itself as something culturally and aesthetically different, and it came of age in this period.

However, its personnel were still being trained mainly for the theatre, and viewing early material now it is impossible not to be struck by the staginess of writing, acting, and production. *Training for the theatre was primarily training in *realist modes of performance with an emphasis on the psychological. *Brechtian-style television drama was, and still is, a rarity; paradoxically (in view of *Brecht's *politics), styles disruptive of surface realism are far more frequently found in comedy and in advertisements than anywhere else. The synergy with realist or *naturalist theatre was increased by the fact that not only were plays studio-bound, they went out live. Getting a play onto the small screen entailed careful studio *rehearsal not only of actors, but also of camera and microphone operators, and an army of supporting technical staff. Cameras were bulky and unwieldy, attached umbilically to heavy cables which had to be manhandled by studio assistants. Location filming was rare, and rapid cutting between scenes (the norm in cinema) was more constrained in the TV studio since complicated camera set-ups could only be achieved by a combination of intricate manoeuvres across the studio floor and dextrous on-the-spot editing in the control room. Film inserts were possible, and offered some visual respite, but American technicians did not perfect the telerecording process until 1953 (even then there was still an obvious difference in picture quality between electronic and photographic images).

For the actor, a *costume change would often have to be done on the run between one part of the studio and another. It was all much more like the wings of a proscenium stage during a performance than a movie location or sound stage between shots. All these constraints gave rise to one major advantage which can be detected in the energy of some plays of the period: a quasi-theatrical real-time sense of controlled emergency existed in the studio; and there was a readiness to improvise if things went wrong. This gave some productions an edge in performance comparable to the best theatre performances. Television drama was in almost all senses more like theatre than film at this time; in some ways it was even more dependent on the adrenalin of the moment because personnel felt themselves to be special. They were pioneers in a new medium beginning to express new possibilities.

2. The 'golden age' in America

In the USA, the anthologies of the early 1950s, sponsored by major manufacturing companies like Kraft, Philco, and Goodyear, developed into a 'golden age' of drama. Watching plays from these series today, a striking factor is that programme sponsorship meant that one company alone occupied all the available advertising time. Instead of the fragmentary ad-break of later times, there is a rather tedious saturation by one-company advertising (sometimes amounting to product mini-lectures). With an individual sponsor, the right of veto on material was undoubtedly a problem for programme makers, and eventually such monopolies were discontinued. The words *'theatre' and *'playhouse' symbolize the anthologies' high-art aspirations, and like the BBC's pre-war *Theatre Parade* some included classics in the repertoire. But the Americans branched out more and more into new drama designed for the new medium.

In so doing they introduced many new actors, designers, writers, and directors. *Marty*, the hit of 1953, was broadcast on *Goodyear TV Playhouse*, and made stars of both writer Paddy *Chayefsky and lead actor Rod Steiger. Filmed in 1955, *Marty* was equally successful on the big screen, winning Oscars for Chayefsky, director Delbert Mann, and Ernest Borgnine, who replaced Steiger. Other actors (Paul Newman, Joanne Woodward), writers (Rod Serling, Gore Vidal), and directors (Sidney Lumet, Arthur Penn) showed that television could be an alternative means of career advancement. Chayefsky's founding concept of the 'marvellous world of the ordinary' was built on the anthology drama's inevitable emphasis on *dialogue, close-ups, and scene development rather than *mise-en-scène, rapid cutting, and location. Intimate studio dramas about ordinary people offered the speaking actor and his or her face a performance mode qualitatively different from the increasingly elliptical, more visual, mode of film and the more declamatory mode of theatre. Writing about *Marty* in 1954, Chayefsky defined the post-war period as 'an age of savage introspection'; he claimed, presciently, that television was the dramatic medium through which 'new insights into ourselves' would be exposed to view in the modern world.

Rapid expansion of drama programming in America soon brought about sub-genre specialization—for example, *The Armstrong Circle Theatre* series, which ran throughout the 1950s, specialized in documentary dramas. One, shown in January 1957, dramatized the very recent events of the Hungarian Uprising of October–November 1956, thus fusing drama

with television's other real-time strength, the dissemination of news. There is a strong link here with British television, where dramatic realism was founded on current affairs. The documentary dramas of Robert Barr and Caryl Doncaster in the late 1940s and early 1950s were educative programmes about social organizations (for example, the fledgling health service, the probation service, the justice system). The educative thrust of the public service remit can be discerned, too, in the prestige literary adaptation—something that was later to become a trademark British television output. In 1947 Daphne du Maurier's *Rebecca* was presented; in 1951 Sherlock Holmes made his first television appearance in a six-part series. But there were more populist outputs, too, like the first 'soap operas', their dramatic practices like their generic name grounded upon the original pre-war American daytime radio dramas literally advertising soap powders. *The Appleyards* (1952–7) and *The Grove Family* (1954–7), as the titles suggest, were centred on individual families rather than the streets, areas, pubs, or workplaces now more usually chosen for their greater potential for multiple storylines.

But even as the studio drama experienced its heyday in the USA, change was in the air. Series such as *I Love Lucy*, *Dragnet*, and *Cheyenne* (beginning in 1952, 1953, and 1955 respectively) fundamentally changed the nature of television drama. For one thing, they shifted the centre of gravity of the American industry from the live to the filmed drama, from theatre to cinema, and from *New York (with TV studios intimately connected to Broadway theatre) to California (with its opportunities for location filming in good light and connections with Hollywood). Industrially, the change occurred through two connected factors: first, the break-up of NBC led to the creation of a new American network—the American Broadcasting Company (ABC); secondly, the movie studios (led by Warner Brothers) decided to join the television revolution rather than fight it. Using ABC in particular, the film studios began to exploit the new market by making TV drama. The above list of groundbreaking series includes a domestic comedy (with connections to Hollywood 'screwball' comedy), a police procedural drama (with connections to 'social films'), and a western. Thus rooted in a combination of Hollywood *genre branding and movie company entrepreneurialism, and financed by big studios with the resources to retain high-quality writers, directors, and performers, these series set trends that are still running (with the possible exception of the western, which now exists mainly in variant form). Not only were such programmes cheap to make (for *Cheyenne*, which ran for seven years, each 50-minute episode took only five days to make) they were also easy to sell, capitalizing upon audiences' prior familiarity with the look and content of well-defined film genres. Television drama was thus taken out of the intimate rooms upon which studio plays had focused into a wider world, out of the claustrophobic, stagy, 'setting' into the real-life 'location'. Because film was the medium throughout, the differences in image quality between studio and location were not so easy to spot (though they now seem obvious—as the actors' multiple shadows on early TV films clearly demonstrate). But at the time, these popular programmes made on film moved the industry in a new direction.

3. Britain's 'golden age'

Change followed elsewhere in the wake of the arrival of commercial television in Europe in the mid-1950s. American companies began to sell material in this expanded overseas market; recovering their costs in the USA, they could sell abroad for pure profit. When Britain's second channel began transmitting in 1955, both *I Love Lucy* and *Dragnet* were among the earliest hits of the Independent Television (ITV) schedules. The second channel was crucial to the industrial development of British television. Institutionally, the BBC had been suspicious of the junior medium right up until the early 1950s. This was something of a negative Reithian inheritance, and it meant that senior managers continued to believe that radio would still be the major broadcasting form in the post-war world. They even tried to prove it by tempting ITV's first-night audience in 1955 with the counter-attraction of a sensational episode of a radio soap, *The Archers*.

But ITV was a success partly because it immediately set out to exploit the wider set ownership of the 1950s. The class aspect of pre-war set ownership was reversed by a combination of cheaper sets, better transmission coverage nationwide, and populist forms. The live coverage of the 1953 coronation had indicated the huge possibilities of the medium by the sheer size of its audience (estimated at 20 million in Britain alone). ITV rode the wave of a consumer boom in electrical goods, and was instrumental in turning British television into a truly mass medium. Drama departments' stock-in-trade from now on was to include most of the later range of TV drama forms—soaps, series, serials, films, and adaptations (classic and popular), as well as single plays. Some of these forms had initially been developed through film and radio, but television was the only medium able to utilize the full gamut of possibilities on a regular, scheduled, basis. The new ITV stations quickly established both an element of regionality, and an ability to network innovative programming when expedient to do so. Over the years, the effect of the regular contract-tendering process has left only one of the original franchise holders still transmitting (Granada), but regional/national balance is still an aim.

Facilities for video editing from 1958 increased TV's flexibility, and further rang the death knell for live drama as a staple. Indeed, live production subsequently tended only to occur as a one-off publicity gimmick (the hospital series *ER* made a live episode in 1999, and *Coronation Street*'s 40th anniversary was celebrated with a nostalgic live edition in 2000). British TV drama up until the late 1950s was in many ways a clone of the American drama anthologies, making heavy use of theatre trends and personnel. The advantage was not only one way: John *Osborne's *Look Back in Anger* would arguably never have become the revolutionary drama it did if an excerpt from the play had not been broadcast by Granada a couple of months into its run at the *Royal Court in 1956. Harold *Pinter, too, endorsed a growing belief in the theatre community that television was now an important opinion-former. As part of ABC's *Armchair Theatre* series in 1960 his play *A Night Out* was viewed by over 6 million people; Pinter calculated that another of his plays (*The Caretaker*, running concurrently in the West End) would have had to run for 30 years to reach as large an audience through theatrical means alone.

Armchair Theatre (1956–68) was a mould-breaker in British television drama to set alongside the American anthologies; like them its extension of the 'social real' in content made it an innovator; like them it also brought influential individuals (like its producer Sydney Newman) to prominence. Writing in 1959, Newman put his philosophy succinctly: 'If television drama expresses the times it will flourish.' His policy put a high premium on new work by young writers portraying contemporary themes, and this led to a British 'golden age' of plays intended specifically for the small screen, many of which were on film. Significantly, Newman's apprenticeship had not been a theatrical one, as it had for so many other producers of his time; he had worked in his native Canada and in the USA in documentary film and TV drama. His guiding concept of 'agitational contemporaneity' was in tune with the 'angry young man' times. Post-war Britain was less deferential, more critical of its various establishments than ever before. The political landscape was changing in general in the West, and the 1960s became a decade of revolution. Television drama in Britain found popular modes for dramatizing key social and political issues of the times. Amongst the *Armchair Theatre* dramatists articulating the first stirrings of this realist spirit were Alun *Owen, whose trilogy of plays about working-class life *No Trams to Lime Street* (1959), *After the Funeral*, and *Lena, Oh my Lena* (both 1961) set new standards in realist dialogue and characterization. Significantly, Owen's innovative 1961 attempt to break out of realism, with the magic realism of *The Rose Affair* (a variation on 'Beauty and the Beast'), was largely disliked by audiences and critics; the demand for realism was even stronger than in theatre and cinema.

With the BBC's *Wednesday Play* (1965–70) and its successor *Play for Today* (1970–84), Newman went on to take British television drama into new realms of success and controversy. The hard-hitting social subject matter of plays like Nell Dunn's *Up the Junction* (1965) and Jeremy Sandford's *Cathy Come Home* (1966) was intensified by a technological breakthrough—the sync-sound, hand-held film camera. This allowed directors like Kenneth Loach to operate in actual locations, much closer to the apparent surface of real life. The subjects treated by these filmed plays—sex and abortion in the former, housing problems and the poverty trap in the latter—had a bleak seriousness that took them more into the sober territory of the current affairs documentary than into the frivolity of entertainment. *Cathy Come Home*, in particular, was received by contemporary audiences as if it actually were a documentary. There were debates in local and national political assemblies, and even a special screening at the Houses of Parliament in December 1966 for government ministers who had missed it first time round. There was a repeat transmission in January 1967, such was the interest generated; arguably, the film exerted leverage on subsequent local and national housing policies.

Television dramas like these were a world away both from the photographed stage play of the earliest period and the intimate studio drama of the American golden age. Their single-camera working methodology contrasted with the multi-camera studio, and was much more akin to film studio/location environments. This model went on to dominate the serious TV drama of the Newman period, and the partnership between Loach and the producer Tony Garnett could fairly claim to have set the trend for the next quarter-century. The movement towards the cinema rather than the theatre was typified by the fact that *Up the Junction* was developed into a film in 1967, and David *Mercer's 1967 TV play *In Two Minds* (about mental illness) was filmed as *Family Life* in 1972. Committed directors like Loach (who directed both these films and their TV originals), producers like Garnett, and writers like Sandford, Mercer, and Dennis *Potter ensured a high level of controversial material at a time when the post-war consensus in Britain was being reformulated under extreme pressure from a younger generation. These 'telefilms' also betrayed the professional ambitions of their young producers and directors—towards the film industry rather than theatre, with television as a means to that end. Writers like Sandford and Potter had little in the way of theatre ambitions (indeed, both were journalists before they wrote plays). But more important than this was the political will to change articulated in the films and endorsed by their audiences.

In the 1970s Loach and Garnett went on to work with another writer, Jim Allen. Their collaboration on *Days of Hope* in 1975 caused more controversy because of its provocative portrayal of twentieth-century British history from a committed left-wing perspective. Following this, Loach found himself frozen out in the 1980s, before returning triumphantly with film successes in the 1990s. Controversies like those caused by Loach's politics were partly about what you could and could not say in a mass medium, and he was not the only one to fall foul of television regulation. This regulation could sometimes be turned into a subtle form of political *censorship. The biggest controversy of this kind occurred over a documentary drama intended for *Monitor*, an arts magazine programme: Peter Watkins's 1965 film *The War Game*.

Watkins already had a reputation as an innovative programme maker before the *War Game* controversy. Like both Potter and Loach, he was an Oxbridge graduate who came to the BBC trailing promise and harbouring an animus against the old British establishment; he too wanted social change. His 1964 *Culloden* was greeted warmly by the BBC establishment, viewers, and critics alike. The use he made of the new flexible camera technology was similar to Loach's, but his practice went one step further towards documentary and one step away from scripted drama. He got *amateur actors to re-create the 1746 battle of Culloden for a camera crew who roved around the action like a twentieth-century film/TV news unit. Meanwhile, a documentary-style voiceover emphasized the battle tactics, glossed the politics of the situation, and emphasized the cruel, colonialist behaviour of the English authorities and their brutal army. At this time, many former British colonies were taking their first steps towards independence, and this film was as much about reassessing Britain's colonialist past as it was about reappraising Scottish history. But because the political comment was masked by an eighteenth-century setting, this documentary drama did not make waves in the way *The War Game* did.

Here, in a similar style, amateur performers improvised reactions to an imagined nuclear strike on south-east England. Much contemporary political opposition to government defence policies was focused on Britain's strategic dependence on a nuclear deterrent. The Campaign for Nuclear Disarmament (CND, founded 1958) brought together a wide spectrum of people on the political left, disseminated a good deal of information about the negative effects of nuclear weapons, and focused popular discussion about weapons of mass destruction. But the people in Watkins's film were not so much proselytizing CND activists as ordinary people playing the very roles that the authorities expected them to play in a real nuclear war. They were Civil Defence volunteers, fire crews, police, local government administrators. Some scenes were simple *improvisations based on how people were supposed to behave in such an eventuality according to the government's own 'Protect and Survive' Civil Defence pamphlet; others asked them to react to realistic situations (having their property commandeered, for example). Dramatic impact derived more from the visual grammar of the documentary or current affairs programme than from any acting skill on the part of the on-screen performers. Voiceover and captions adduced facts and statistics taken directly from UK and US government scientific sources; 'vox-pop' and 'expert' interviews punctuated what appeared often to be (and sometimes was) news footage.

The film was a chilling insight into the distance warfare had travelled from a 'Spirit of the Blitz' human scale to a post-Hiroshima reality. The British establishment balked at the mere prospect of a mass audience seeing people unable to cope in a nightmare scenario so much at variance with soothing propaganda that nuclear war was survivable. So much was this the case, that under some official pressure the governors of the BBC took the unusual step of banning the film's transmission, causing a huge furore in the press. It was, in fact, twenty years before the BBC felt able to transmit *The War Game* at all (though it had been released to private film clubs and societies). When finally shown in 1985, it entered a world in which (rightly or wrongly) the nuclear debate was widely perceived to be less pressing, following the gradual rapprochement between the USSR and the USA that brought the Cold War period to an end in the late 1980s. America also confronted this subject for the first time in TV drama in the same period (in ABC's *The Day After*, 1983).

4. Popular dramatic forms

Sydney Newman's decision to split his BBC Drama Department into three sections, separating single play production from serials and series, demonstrated the sheer volume of drama production by the mid-1960s. Differing demands at the levels of production and reception were now part of the television landscape, and the emergence of 'long forms' (like soaps, series, and mini-series) reshaped further the TV drama of the late twentieth century. But it is important not to lose sight of the generality of TV drama during a period rightly remembered for controversial and boundary-breaking single dramas. Although British circumstances were neither dominant nor universal, the policies of British public service television towards 'serious' drama can usefully be seen as something of a counterweight to the commercializing (some would say, trivializing) tendencies of popular drama forms led principally but not exclusively by American models. But just as the serious is not always the most effective, the popular should not be seen as always trivial.

If the 1950s was the decade in which television still did not know whether it was theatre-in-disguise or movies-on-the-cheap, the 1960s was the decade in which its confidence in itself as a medium in its own right burgeoned, and in which distinctive popular forms established certain tones of the medium's distinctive voice. There had always been so many things television could do that other media either could not do, or no longer wanted to do; as well as news, current affairs and documentary in all its forms, live programmes (special events and sport), children's programmes, religious broadcasting, even systematic advertising should not be ignored. But theatre and cinema (to a lesser extent radio) could claim drama was better done in these older media. In the 1960s, however, the gradual development of forms that were all its own took television drama into expressive territory beyond theatre and cinema. During the 1960s the film-on-TV and the film-for-TV were also developed, giving the industry additional purchase on the means of making drama. The series, the serial, the sitcom, the soap opera, the 'made-for-TV-movie', and boundary-blurring forms like the documentary drama gave the makers of television drama a more varied palette by which a range of contemporary subjects could be treated and through which audiences could perceive a complex articulation of contemporary concerns.

The soap opera offers a good example of popular drama: its American origins ensured both its entertainment provenance and its tendency to run its *plots in parallel with newsworthy issues. Britain's longest-running TV soap, *Coronation Street*, which began on ITV in 1960, is a case in point. The early episodes look now like a watered-down *Look Back in Anger* but at the time they signalled a similar willingness to treat the social issue of a 'New Britain' seriously. The difference was that *Coronation Street* was doing this for a mass, prime-time audience, several times a week. While its style changed over time, it continued to treat current affairs issues (in 2001, rape and cervical cancer, for example). The best of subsequent British soaps (for example, Channel 4's *Brookside* from 1982; the BBC's *EastEnders* from 1985) were similarly intent on ventilating social issues—especially women's issues—in the public sphere. British soaps tend to be downwardly mobile, as it were, exploring issues adjacent to the lives of the popular audience. American TV, by contrast, perfected rather glossier, upwardly mobile soaps in which capitalist entrepreneur characters (melo)dramatized aspects of the American Dream in series like *Dallas* (1978–91) and *Dynasty* (1981–9). These prime-time soaps indulged the dreams of wealth that constitute the bedrock of the fantasy life of populations in capitalist countries. Both were exported, but the traffic in soaps was not all one way. *Neighbours* (made first in 1985 by the Australian independent Grundy) has been a huge hit worldwide. And Portuguese- and Spanish-language 'telenovelas', an ingenious inflection of the basic melodramatic premises of soap opera, projected Brazil's TV Globo and Mexico's Televisa companies into the world market from the late 1960s. Telenovelas were formally innovative; tending to run over a finite number of programmes unlike Anglo-American and Australian soaps, they sometimes treated national historical subjects. Telenovelas have been widely dubbed into other languages (for example, Chinese, Russian, and German).

The police procedural series, again American in origin, also advanced in the 1960s, building on the treatment of social reality evident in American models such as *Dragnet* and *Highway Patrol* (1955–9). *Z Cars* (1962–5, 1967–78), like *Highway Patrol*, was a series that recognized new complexities in modern, more mobile, urban societies. While British series like *Dixon of Dock Green* (1955–76) were guilty of portraying a cosy, pre-war image of policing, *Z Cars* showed a Britain trying to come to grips with social change, its police force working in an urban no man's land. Scripts (Troy Kennedy Martin, Alan Plater), acting (Brian Blessed, Colin Welland), and direction (John *McGrath, Ken Loach) were of a high enough standard to command a mass audience consistently. ITV led the way with that other staple of television scheduling, the hospital series. *Emergency—Ward 10* (ATV, 1957–67) was, like *Coronation Street*, initially regarded as a documentary-style drama, and was equally studio-bound. The American film series *Ben Casey* (ABC, 1961–6) and *Dr Kildare* (NBC, 1961–6) had a different visual aesthetic, but at their best had a generic quality that enabled important social issues to be debated, and allowed space for the reflection on mortality that the hospital situation inevitably evokes. At their worst (and such series often move to this level the longer they run) they can become a sub-romance genre fixated on relationships between glamorous doctors and nurses. The BBC's *Casualty* (1986–), which began as a counterblast to Thatcherite health service cuts, is an example of this kind of deterioration.

It is important to remember that, unlike American series, most British output continued to be recorded and edited electronically. In the second phase of development the electronic image still lagged far behind film in terms of clarity and definition, and this made the export of such series unlikely (especially given their often parochial content). There were exceptions; *The Adventures of Robin Hood* (1955–9), for example, made a successful transition to American TV but this was a series made on film. The classic serial, however, offered a different model: post-war, staple (mainly BBC) productions characteristically used *Dickens, the Brontës, and Jane Austen (*Pride and Prejudice*'s first adaptation was as early as 1952). The BBC adaptation of John *Galsworthy's *The Forsyte Saga* in 1967, however, set new standards. Not only did this 26-episode series regularly garner audiences of almost 16 million in Britain, it also made a breakthrough in other countries and established the BBC as an international player. It was exported to a new American network, the Public Broadcasting Service (PBS), in 1969–70 and to more than twenty other countries worldwide. It blazed a trail for subsequent adaptations and costume dramas, amongst these Andrew Davies's 1995 adaptation of *Pride and Prejudice*, the fifth adaptation of this classic novel and the most successful internationally.

British television was very successful in exporting the 'high-art' adaptation following *The Forsyte Saga*. 'Heritage series' like *The Six Wives of Henry VIII* (BBC2, 1971) and *Upstairs, Downstairs* (London Weekend Television, 1971–5) made successful transitions to the American commercial networks. Quality adaptations like *Brideshead Revisited* (Granada, 1981) and *Jewel in the Crown* (Granada, 1984) were sold successfully around the world. The 'quality' in such programmes stems from a number of factors. There is the host *text—normally either a recognized classic (Evelyn Waugh, Jane Austen) or a novel at the point of achieving classic status (the Paul Scott series). Second, there tend to be crucial features of content that can be underlined, even brought up to date, through the adaptation. Both *Brideshead Revisited* and *The Jewel in the Crown* engaged in revaluations of national histories but achieved international appeal through their treatments of class, *race, and *gender. Thus powerful cultural links were forged between historical and current social and political concerns. Third, the writers

of the adaptations (the likes of Dennis Potter, John *Mortimer, Andrew Davies) tend to have higher profiles, and therefore more impact on the final product, than Hollywood screenwriters. Fourth, such series attract high-quality performers with international reputations. Fifth, there is always a high level of aesthetic 'finish' to the mise-en-scène and design aspects. Finally, co-production deals between British, European, and American companies have more recently ensured that the resource-base needed for such projects is available in the new more competitive environment, and classic adaptations have become part of the multinational market.

Another important popular TV form is the situation comedy. Here, too, the early examples successful worldwide were American film series like *I Love Lucy* and *I Married Joan* (1952–5). These series were essentially continuous family and marriage narratives. *The Mary Tyler Moore Show* (1970–7), with a star already established through *The Dick Van Dyke Show* (1961–6), even launched one of the most successful American production companies, MTM Enterprises. British television scored two particular successes with *Steptoe and Son* (1962–5; 1970–4) and *Till Death Us Do Part* (1966–8; 1972–5). Both regularly featured writing that mixed pathos with humour; both featured small-screen acting of the highest calibre; both dared to use the sitcom to confront social issues. Both were also successful in the export market, mirror-image formats appearing in other cultures. *Steptoe* was popular in both the USA and the Netherlands (in America it was called *Sanford and Son*, featured an African-American cast, and ran on NBC 1972–7). *Till Death* also had its format adapted for the American market, becoming the highly acclaimed CBS series *All in the Family*, which ran over two decades (1971–92). The lead characters of *Till Death/All in the Family* achieved semi-mythical status in their respective cultures as archetypes for bone-headed but hilarious right-wing populist cant (Alf Garnett in Britain, Archie Bunker in America). The American comedy drew audiences of 50 million in its heyday. In the suffocating atmosphere of turn-of-the-century transatlantic political correctness, such programmes could neither be made nor openly enjoyed, perhaps, but these older programmes were generally excused and continued to be enjoyed in repeats and on 'heritage' networks like UK Gold. Format-adaptation was to become a familiar part of the global TV industry in the latter years of the twentieth century; if series could not be exported directly, their basic structures were simply replicated and sold on for 'translation'.

'Straight comedy' and science fiction programming has also been both innovative and exportable. In the minor but important area of developing dramatic modes in TV that are not reliant on naturalism, *Monty Python's Flying Circus* (1969–74) was both a successful British export to America and a mould-breaker, tapping a rich vein of surrealist aesthetics unavailable to realist drama. The antecedents for *Monty Python* lay not in theatre or film but in radio comedy like *The Goon Show*

(1951–60). Science fiction, too, enabled fantasy to permeate writing, performance, and direction; brand leaders here included the American *Star Trek* (original series 1969–71) which in subsequent development lasted over four series. In Britain, *Dr Who* (1963–89) exhibited similar tendencies, and the quasi-sci-fi drama series *The Prisoner* (1967–8) became a cult programme as a result of its Orwellian futurist vision of an individual fighting a surveillant culture. If in reviewing the early examples of these series we are struck by the datedness of their special effects, this should only alert us to the essentially time-bound nature of all performance codes and conventions. A combination of the possibilities available to special effects through digital technology and commercial pressures to produce at lower cost began to threaten even the evidential status of the documentary by the 1990s.

The realism of TV drama in all its forms is heavily coded, as a result not only of increased technological possibility but also of what the cultural theorist Raymond Williams called 'structures of feeling' (or modes of perception common to large groups of people within specific historical conjunctures). TV realism has played its part in structuring its audiences' means of perceiving external realities; its guiding structural principles, its ways of nominating and narrating, are now embedded in our audio-visual culture, and television has taken over the role of explaining ourselves to ourselves, once the province of the theatre, the novel, the radio programme, or even the film. As a dramatic mode, it has begun to feed back in the opposite direction, such that modern documentary forms (the docu-soap, 'Reality TV') have become heavily narrativized and dramatized in programmes like *Driving School* (1997) and *Big Brother*—the worldwide hit of 2000 that originated in the Netherlands.

5. Late twentieth-century industrial changes

If television drama's important synergies were first with the theatre and then with the cinema, the feedback loop started to move emphatically in the opposite direction in the 1980s. The relationship with theatre remained largely based on human resources, but the shift towards cinema went beyond the small-screening of classic movies evident even in early times (for example, the BBC screened D. W. Griffith's *Birth of a Nation* as early as 1947). The release of 'back-catalogue' movies to television in the 1950s signalled the burgeoning interest the studios were taking in television. The next stage was the acquisition of prestige feature films for prime-time transmission by American networks in the early 1960s. From 1961 the lead programme in the field was NBC's *Saturday Night at the Movies* series. This can be compared to the pre-war *Theatre Parade* in terms of its significance as an aesthetic trend in television. By 1966 the programme had become popular enough to feature in the Top Twenty of the Neilsen ratings (the American statistical barometer of success) and the values of movie-making could be said to have been implanted in American TV.

In the 1970s a further move towards film in TV drama occurred through the pervasive influence of the 'made-for-TV movie'. Hollywood studios were now as prepared to make films specifically for the small screen as they became in the 1980s to release film material 'straight to video'. In America there was a good deal of time to fill on network schedules, and the made-for-TV movie exploited this. Material was characteristically *melodramatic, and often utilized real-world stories and events. In common with earlier American models, these films could recoup costs on the American domestic market, then be sold on to foreign network buyers for pure profit. Sometimes a very popular example like *Brian's Song* (about an American footballer's battle with cancer, 1971) was even released to cinema. Made-for-TV movies have 'long legs' in industry parlance (they get lucrative multiple repeats on cable and satellite networks). Films made-for-television joined Hollywood movies as yet another arm of American cultural expansion (not to say imperialism). In Britain, such material was taken up by all the networks, but especially the populist ITV companies.

By the end of the 1960s there had been a number of changes in the broadcasting environment in Britain. A third channel—BBC2—was founded in 1964 resulting in increased choice for viewers and a more experimental output. BBC2 broadcast on VHF 625 lines instead of the older UHF 405; the result was improved picture quality and 625 ultimately replaced the other wavelength. Worldwide, 525 and 625 lines became the industry standard for the twentieth century (although further change towards high-definition image and screen formats more like the cinema took place by its end). There was also a shift from black and white to colour transmission from 1968 onwards (anyone born after this date, perhaps, cannot conceive of a pre-colour television world). Further new channels followed in Britain—Channel 4 from 1982, Channel 5 from 1997—and Channel 4 particularly had a decisive influence on drama.

Channel 4 typifies the dual interests manifested on both sides of the Atlantic by the end of the third developmental phase. Its 'Film on Four' initiative, whereby films were made for virtually simultaneous cinema and television release, arguably boosted an ailing British film industry. In the 1990s it was generating international successes like *Four Wedding and a Funeral* (1994) and *Trainspotting* (1996). Workers moved between the two media as easily as they moved between theatre and television in the 1960s, and the elliptical filmic mode of scripting and shooting dominated television drama from the late 1980s onwards. The visual element became more and more important in supplying the narrative drive to realist television drama, and it has come more and more to resemble film. Single-camera and location production for prestige TV drama, multi-camera video and studio for the cheaper, soap, end of the market: these became the industrial realities of making TV drama at the end of the twentieth century.

6. Writers and producers

As with theatre and cinema, creating anything for television is a collective project. But the temptation to discern the irreducible core of significant work in the visions of particular individuals is still common to commentary on all three media. Whereas the director and writer have been key in the histories of both the cinema and the stage, writers and producers have been the important figures in television. Paradigmatic cases from the first two phases of development are two writers, the American Paddy Chayefsky and Britain's Dennis Potter. Both have a history of publication which marks them out in a largely ephemeral medium; both thought and commented in depth about television drama; most important of all, both focused on television to the virtual exclusion of other forms of dramatic writing.

If Chayefsky's mature work established the single TV play as a category to be reckoned with, Potter's work within long-form TV drama, beginning with *Pennies from Heaven* in 1978, is more significant. His groundbreaking anti-realist formal techniques and *genre pastiche meant that, for example, popular music could become a Brechtian commentator-on-the-action in his work. In *Pennies from Heaven* popular culture was the double-edged sword of modern consciousness, mediating simultaneously the dream world and its critique. Made into a cinema feature by MGM in 1981, the subtle satirical edge of the BBC series was lost in the transposition to an American setting and to the larger-scale medium. There was a similar Brechtian edge to Potter's single play *Blue Remembered Hills* (1979), where the adult actors playing children were always in visible excess to the characters they were portraying. The world of childhood was distanced (*see* VERFREMDUNG) in several ways, with the protagonists remote in place (the Forest of Dean), in time (the Second World War), and literally remote from childish bodies (in their all-too evident maturity of physique).

Subsequent series like *The Singing Detective* (1986) and *Lipstick on your Collar* (1993) made Potter into a figure impossible to ignore, as did his railing against late twentieth-century media ownership in lectures and in his valedictory dual series *Karaoke* and *Cold Lazarus* (1996—broadcast on both public service BBC and commercial Channel 4). Potter's career straddled the shift in television drama between the electronic world of the television studio and the photographic world of the film camera, and between the public service ideal and the new organization of all television on commercial lines. The fact that his television dramas, like Chayefsky's, could and did create cultural turbulence is an indication of two things: the importance of the writer and the developing maturity of the medium.

If it is more difficult to single out American examples, it is not because there has ever been a dearth of excellent writers for American TV drama but because the important shows are often inspired by a producer-writer, like *All in the Family*'s Norman Lear. Such producers then use 'schools of writers' for series such as *Hill Street Blues* (1981–7), *ER* (1994–), *NYPD Blue* (1993–), *Ally McBeal* (1997–2002), *Seinfeld* (1990–8), and *The Sopranos* (1999–). The writer-collectives for these series are presided over by people like Steven Bochco, David Kelley, and David Chase. Producers of this stature (James MacTaggart, Kenith Trodd, and Tony Garnett are British examples) are the prime movers of TV drama. Amongst the witty (and sometimes Potter-esque) innovations demonstrated in the American dramas are memory/fantasy sequences, intertextual references, and elliptical story-arcs that compress and reverse chronology. Bochco's groundbreaking *Hill Street Blues* set new standards for the police procedural, edging it even closer towards documentary styles; Kelley's *Ally McBeal* yoked screwball film comedy with a post-feminist sexual ethic, and added in elements of fantasy; Chase's *The Sopranos* mixed debates about modern masculinity with the gangster movie. Producers like these have made significant marks on their culture and shifted television drama towards postmodern forms (*see* MODERNISM AND POSTMODERNISM).

The 'long-form' formats used in Potter's best work developed significantly in the late 1970s and 1980s. Television drama, having left theatre aesthetics behind in the early 1960s and moved away from a pure cinema aesthetic, established the serial/series as its most distinctive form. While the look of the film was still sought, the capacity for historical sweep, thematic range, and character development without the telescoping necessary in film was open to the series and mini-series in ways otherwise available only to the novel. The mini-series (two to four separate programmes) was added to the arsenal of forms as a compromise means of retaining some of the focus of the single play while having most of the potential for plot and character development over time. The American writer Alex Haley's *Roots* (1977) is a key example that broke several boundaries. Most importantly it dramatized an aspect of American history, its treatment of African slaves in the earliest phase of its formation as a nation-state, at a moment when the race debate had reached a crucial stage in contemporary history. It did this in the epic manner, following the descendants of the West African character Kunte Kinte through American history over a twelve-hour drama. ABC chose to broadcast the mini-series on successive evenings, something revolutionary in scheduling terms (and, as it turned out, hugely successful with audiences). Although Haley's history and ethics have both been questioned subsequently, the series achieved great success at home and abroad. The NBC four-part drama *Holocaust* (1978) was similarly successful; most significantly, it was well received and much debated in what was then West Germany. Its treatment of the Nazi Final Solution was condemned in some quarters because of its soap-like structure (a group of characters involved in multiple storylines, with inevitable simplifications), but it opened debate and ventilated opinion on a serious issue in much the same way claimed for soaps.

In British television, history was used in a rather more ironic, postmodern way in Richard Curtis and Ben Elton's comic series *Blackadder* (four series between 1983 and 1989). The series took the character Blackadder through key phases of English history (the Crusades, the Elizabethan era, the eighteenth century, the Great War), reshaping in its comic portrayal classic concepts of Englishness. The transhistorical, cowardly conniver Blackadder (played by Rowan Atkinson) always survived the comic vagaries of history, along with three or four other character types, whose names changed but whose characteristics and function in British history remained the same (a time-server, a bumbling but vicious aristocrat, an empty-headed public school enthusiast, a put-upon but idiotically cheerful worker). A poignant slow-motion final sequence in the final series, *Blackadder Goes Forth*, finished off both *'hero' and comrades, unable to cheat their way out of death at the effective endpoint of British imperialism (slaughter in the trenches). The series referenced British history in a playful, intertextual way, counting on a degree of knowingness in its audience. So Good Queen Bess (Elizabeth I), far from being the Virgin Queen icon of English heroism and enterprise, was played as a capricious psychopath, likely at any moment randomly to order the eponymous hero's death.

In Britain, some writers continue the Potter tradition: Alan *Bleasdale, for example, who made his reputation with *Boys from the Blackstuff* (1982). His *GBH* (1991) was interesting for many reasons, not least for the fact that the writer first conceived the idea (the battle between an unscrupulous left-wing politician and an ethical activist in a local political situation not unlike the Liverpool of the 1980s) as a film. He then considered developing it as a novel, before finally settling on the TV series that allowed him to develop character and situation at length (as in a novel) but also have the visual impact of screen performance. Bleasdale, like Potter before him, turned TV drama into a kind of twentieth-century Victorian novel. The dominance of formats allowing long-run developments was evident on both sides of the Atlantic at the end of the twentieth century: in, for example, series as diverse as the American *ER* and *NYPD Blue*, the British *Holding On* (1997), and *Clocking Off* (2000–1). Increasingly, writers chose to begin their careers in soap and series forms, rather than writing for the theatre then moving into television and film as people did in the 1950s and 1960s. For example, Jimmy McGovern became a leading British writer in the late 1990s. His career began as a writer on the Channel 4 soap *Brookside*; he then made his name with the police/psychological series *Cracker* (1993), going on to one-off dramadocs (*Hillsborough*, 1996, about the 1989 football stadium disaster). So dominant have these television forms become that the docudrama/dramadoc and its American equivalent the made-for-TV movie have become the last refuge for the 'single play' so famous between the 1950s and 1970s.

At the end of the twentieth century, playwrights no longer expected to be the primary writers for television. There are always exceptions: Alan *Bennett's *Talking Heads* series (1988) was unusual for its *dramaturgy, *monologue plays not being common in the medium. David *Hare (in, for example, his 1982 *Licking Hitler*) also wrote occasionally for television, and had his stage plays adapted for the small screen. But overall the theatre stopped being a profound influence on television in the 1980s. Television drama is now a vital branch of an important entertainment industry, with an aesthetic deriving from film but qualitatively different from it. New technology, including DVD video cameras, discs, and receivers, has brought television sound and image quality ever closer to celluloid. Series like *This Life* (1996–8) and *The Cops* (1999–2001), made for the BBC by Tony Garnett's independent company World Productions, use lightweight digital cameras to very similar effect to the American lawyer and police dramas made by Steven Bochco and others on film.

7. The globalized future

By the 1990s, the new ecology of broadcasting in Britain consisted in independent production companies selling work to networks eager to maximize audience share (whether the history of those networks was 'commerical' or 'public service'). The model is the film, not the theatre company, and it owes more to the American industry than the British (adapting late to new commercial realities from the time of the Thatcher government). The success of the American cable company Home Box Office (HBO) may be taken as paradigmatic of the third phase of television's development. America's most successful cable network was launched as early as 1972, but took some time to establish itself as a major force in television. Although its initial reputation was as a purveyor of Hollywood films, it consolidated its success by moving into production of films and series. By the mid-1990s, it had 18 million subscribers in the USA and subsidiaries all over the world. It had also established co-production agreements of various kinds with national and independent companies (for example, with Granada, BBC Lionheart, and World Productions in Britain). By the end of the twentieth century, it also had a reputation for quality one-off dramas like *And the Band Played On* (1993) and for series like *The Sopranos*.

The emergence, too, of media moguls such as Rupert Murdoch (whose Sky TV company became the significant non-terrestrial broadcaster in Britain in the 1990s) served to reshape an industry now firmly geared to film rather than theatre imperatives and methodologies. Writers pitch ideas, work up 'treatments', draft scripts, and (just as in the movies) are seen more as hired hands than artists. Directors construct narratives that are visual before they are aural. Actors work through 'non-matrixed performance' (that is, they just 'behave' on camera for discrete scenes, rather than look for their characters' 'through-line' in the theatrical manner of *Stanislavsky). Perhaps the biggest difference between film and television drama lies in the director's role. The industrialized processes of TV production ensure that the director is more of a hired hand than an *auteur*, required to deliver product on time and within costs like the old time B-movie makers. It is less likely that they can acquire either the status of certain film directors or the cultural authority of some theatre directors. Nonetheless, many film directors made their initial mark on the small screen in drama productions or advertising (Ridley Scott is one example).

Finally, it is worth remembering that the dominance of the Anglo-American industrial models has had grave consequences for cultures slower to develop the necessary technologies and lacking the economic power. A country like New Zealand had no television service at all until the 1960s, and its public service networks were commercial in all but name (and heavily dependent upon Anglo-American imports) by the late 1990s. Although most countries in the world had fully-fledged TV services by the 1970s, most were also ripe for exploitation by a perennially dominant group of powerful nations. A relative lack of infrastructure resulted in their dominance by Anglo-American (and particularly American) industrial power, amounting to cultural imperialism by the 1990s. Because American TV companies could rely on recouping production costs in their own vast domestic market, there was widespread exporting of programmes and American TV culture became ubiquitous.

In the ecology of the twenty-first century, however, even American companies need co-production deals with foreign programme makers in order to survive. TV drama is an expensive item, and terrestrial broadcasters in all nations had to look over their shoulders once international cable and satellite companies like Sky and HBO began production towards the end of the twentieth century. But, as in the agora of ancient Greek city-states, national cultures are still formed and re-formed in the market-place of television broadcasts and, as in those ancient times, the drama can still only be successful when it ventilates issues of public importance (however transient those issues may be). Although the third stage of television's development saw an inexorable shift all over the world towards more commercial models, an established global marketplace does not necessarily mean less or weaker drama in the future. But the need for vigilance from a critical public is unlikely to diminish in the era of the transnational TV drama.   DJP

BARNOUW, ERIK, *Tube of Plenty: the evolution of American television* (Oxford, 1975)

CAUGHIE, JOHN, *Television Drama: realism, modernism, and British culture* (Oxford, 2000)

ELLIS, JOHN, *Seeing Things: television in the age of uncertainty* (London, 2000)

GITLIN, TODD, *Inside Prime Time* (London, 1994)

SMITH, ANTHONY (ed.), *Television: an international history* (Oxford, 1995)

WILLIAMS, RAYMOND, *Television: technology and cultural form* (London, 1992)

The next 30 years (1901–30) saw the rise and fall of the commercial theatres. *Zamindars* (landlords) interested in promoting theatre activities founded companies and produced extravagant productions. Three such prominent companies include the Hindu Nataka Samajam (Rajahmundry), the Mylavaram Company (Bezwada), and the Mote Company (Eluru). The directors employed the best talent available in the Telugu-speaking region. The Parsi models of trick scenes and roller paintings dominated. In the hub of this commercial activity rose two distinguished theatre groups—Ramavilas Sabha (Tenali) and Indian National Theatrical Company (Machilipatnam)—which staged well-crafted plays with dedication and disciplined artistry. However, with *film attracting the best talent, the downfall of the commercial theatres was inevitable, and the earlier popularity of the *padya natakam* was seriously affected.

The nationalist movement from the 1920s onwards brought into focus chronicle and historical plays reflecting contemporary events, and some of these plays were proscribed (*see* CENSORSHIP). Translations of Western plays and original plays with a romantic aura dominated the amateur stage. Simultaneously, Bhamidipati Kameswararao's adaptations of *Molière and *Sheridan were popular with college groups. By 1930 *realism became the prominent mode of dramatic writing. P. V. Rajamannar's *Tappevaridi* (*Whose Fault Is It?*, 1930), a problem play in prose on the conflict between the generations about love and marriage, was a trendsetter. While Rajamannar's thrust was on the familial conflicts in an urban community, Narla Venkateswararao wrote on changing rural life.

By 1943 theatre activity increased, with the Andhra Nataka Kalaparishath organizing annual *festivals and competitions; Praja Natya Mandali produced powerful plays on rural inequalities; and Andhra University promoted experimental theatre through drama competitions. These activities provided a firm ground for the next 30 years when products of these institutions enlivened the theatre. Natya Sangham (1954) remained, for a short time, the primary forum for theatre activities under Abburi Ramakrishna Rao and A. R. Krishna. It produced Telugu classics like *Kanyasulkam* and *Prataprudriyam*, alongside modern Indian plays in translation like Girish *Karnad's *Hayavadana* and Badal *Sircar's *Evam Indrajit*. Between 1960 and 1980, competitions (*parishaths*) were very much in vogue and produced some outstanding plays exemplifying social critique, such as N. R. Nandi's *Maro Mohenjodaro* (*Another Mohenjdaaro*, 1964) and Rachakonda Viswanatha Sastry's *Nizam* (*Truth*, 1962) on the exploitation of the poor. By 1972 as many as 106 associations were conducting annual competitions, with dramatists like Bhamidipati Radhakrishna, Gollapudi Maruthirao, Yendamuri Veerendranath, Ganesh Pathro, and Haranathrao exploring contemporary problems relating to inter-caste marriage, social inequality, and the oppression of women. Divakarbabu, Patibandla Anandarao, Bharani, and Valluri Siva Prasad have continued the tradition of social critique in their condemnation of the exploitation of the depressed classes.

The theatrical scene at the start of the new century offers mixed fare. While the *verse play finds occasional *audiences, the social problem play is more popular. *Street theatre is emerging as a viable alternative for social protest beyond the strictures of the realist, *proscenium play, while university theatres devote time and energy to producing experimental plays and occasionally classics.   MNS

TEMPEST, MARIE (1862–1942)

English actress. A popular performer and vocalist at the turn of the century, she appeared at *London theatres in *musical comedies such as *The Geisha* (1896) and *San Toy* (1899), and *comedies such as *Robertson's *Caste* (1902) and *The Marriage of Kitty* (1903) by her husband Cosmo Gordon Lennox. Her association with the *manager George *Edwardes during *San Toy* was terminated when, playing a Chinese boy, she insisted on wearing the more flattering shorts instead of trousers. Her considerable talent was rarely exploited, and she was often *cast as a charming, beautiful, but essentially decorative addition to the cup-and-saucer *comedies with which she was generally associated. At the end of her career, Dodie *Smith's *Dear Octopus* (1938) provided a vehicle for her considerable talent.   AF

TENDULKAR, VIJAY (1928–   )

Marathi writer. Born in Bombay (*Mumbai), he was one of the leaders of the new theatre movement that began in the 1950s (*see* MARATHI THEATRE). His *Shrimant* (*The Wealthy*, 1955) questions the middle-class values of marriage, family, and human relationships. *Manus Navacha Bait* (*An Island Called Man*, 1958) subverts the cosy drawing-room setting of mainstream plays by portraying the reality of unemployed middle-class youth facing homelessness; the crisp, ironic *dialogue stands in stark contrast to the sentimental overwriting of mainstream theatre. In *Shantata Court Chalu Ahe* (*Silence! The Court Is in Session*, 1968) Tendulkar used a play-within-the-play to reveal the psychological violence the middle class can wreak on those who contravene its hypocritical social conventions. *Gidhade* (*Vultures*, 1971) is a raw depiction of a middle-class family ready to shed blood for family property, while the eponymous *protagonist of *Sakharam Binder* (1972) rejects marriage in favour of mutually beneficial contracts with destitute women. Both these plays became controversial because of their alleged obscenity. Even more provocative, Tendulkar's most notable play, *Ghashiram Kotwal* (*Police Chief Ghashiram*, 1973), was condemned in orthodox circles for its anti-Brahmanism. Drawing on *folk the-atre traditions of song, *dance, and actor deployment, he turned a historical event into an *allegory of the prevailing political situation, depicting ordinary men growing into monsters under the patronage of self-serving politicians. Tendulkar has written 29 plays in all, many of which have been widely translated and produced in other Indian languages.   SGG

TENNIS-COURT THEATRES

As the medieval French sport of 'real tennis' declined in popularity during the seventeenth century, the availability of the indoor courts in which it was played grew, as either temporary or permanent *playhouses. Essentially a tennis court was a long, rectangular structure with a flat stone floor, a covered, ground-level spectator gallery running around three walls, and a tiled roof. The installation of a raised *stage at one end, the division of the side gallery into *boxes, the addition of a second tier above it, and a similar construction against the opposite side were sufficient to convert it into a theatre—one that was easily dismantled when the tenant actors moved on. Although unsatisfactory from the point of view of sight lines, the essential geometry of the tennis court—approximately 33 m (108 feet) by 12 m (39 feet), or a length-to-width ratio of 3:1—was enormously influential in France, tyrannizing the development of theatre architecture until the mid-eighteenth century.

The nation's first two permanent public theatres were both constructed in *Paris according to the tennis-court model. Whilst the *Hôtel de Bourgogne had not literally been a tennis court when it was built in 1548, it had broadly similar internal dimensions. The *Marais, on the other hand, had been a tennis court until *Montdory undertook its permanent conversion in 1634. Moreover, the first home of *Molière's company, the Illustre Théâtre, in 1643 was the Mestayers tennis court. The first Paris *opera house was a former tennis court: having leased the Bouteille tennis court, Sourdéac and Champeron installed boxes, an *amphithéâtre*, and a stage equipped with machinery for their opera, *Pomone*, in 1671. Renamed the *Guénégaud theatre in 1673, this was also the initial home of the *Comédie-Française from 1680 to 1689.

Whilst tennis was imitated outside France, only in England did tennis-court theatres play any significant role. The first *London tennis court converted for permanent use as a theatre was Gibbons's tennis court, opened in 1660 by Thomas *Killigrew. The following year Lisle's tennis court in *Lincoln's Inn Fields was leased by Sir William *Davenant for his *The Siege of Rhodes*, the first play to employ changeable *scenery in a permanent *public playhouse in England.   JG

TENT SHOW

A form of itinerant theatre especially popular in nineteenth-century America. While tents had been used to house theatres under various circumstances during the early century, including by religious evangelical movements like the Millerites, much of the impetus for *touring tent shows came from the itinerant demands of the California gold rush. Sacramento's Eagle Theatre (1849–50) was a temporary canvas-sided structure under the *management of leading actor J. B. Atwater. Similarly, theatres in *San Francisco in the early 1850s were often crude, temporary structures combining *circus and other para-theatrical amusements with *legitimate theatre. Among the first tent entrepreneurs was D. G. Robinson (fl. 1849–60, also known as 'Yankee' or 'Dr' Robinson). His career began among the temporary canvas neighbourhoods of San Francisco in 1850 and soon carried over to regular tent circuits in the Midwest, performing *burlesques of Shakespeare and other classic dramas. With the rise of railways and the expansion of the country, tent shows grew in popularity, particularly among the smaller and more isolated communities of the Midwest and south, where permanent *playhouses were impractical. Following crude circuits and irregular schedules, companies performed a variety of skits, scenes, and lectures designed to appeal to a broad and largely unsophisticated *audience. The financial depression of the early 1870s also contributed to the tent show's popularity, as managers sought more economical means to tour.

Among the forms that prospered during the 1870s was the *Chautauqua, which expanded beyond its original religious content to include *vaudeville skits, lectures, and dramatic readings or scenes. Over 1,000 independent Chautauqua companies were touring the United States by 1915. By the turn of the twentieth century tent companies had become a major performance outlet. In some cases their popularity was the direct result of increasingly restrictive and monopolistic practices by the leading *producers, especially the *Theatrical Syndicate after 1895. One famous case was that of Sarah *Bernhardt, who defied the Syndicate in 1905 and successfully toured the USA, primarily in tents. By the early 1920s there were as many as 400 tent companies playing to as many as 75 million spectators. But the popularity of *radio and *film, as well as the growth of vaudeville circuits, soon undercut the economic advantages that tent companies enjoyed. The ravages of the Great Depression put an end to most of them by the end of the 1930s, although a form of the practice was revived by shows for US troops overseas during the Second World War and the Korean War.   PAD

TER-ARUTUNIAN, ROUBEN (1920–92)

Armenian-American designer. Born in Tiflis, Soviet Georgia (*Tbilisi), he was educated in *Berlin, *Vienna, and *Paris. His first professional assignments (1943–4) were *costumes for the Berlin State Opera, Dresden Opera, and Vienna State Opera. In 1951 he emigrated to *New York, where he was soon designing important productions for the New York City Ballet (notably *Balanchine's The Nutcracker, 1964), American Ballet Theatre, and Martha *Graham's modern *dance company. For the *American Shakespeare Theatre in Connecticut, he designed *scenery and costumes for numerous productions from 1956 to 1960. His Broadway debut came with New Girl in Town (1957), followed the next year by scenery for Who Was That Lady I Saw You With?, which brought him the Outer Critics Circle *award. Nominated five times for a Tony award, he won for his costumes in the *musical Redhead (1959).   CT

TERAYAMA SHŪJI (1935–83)

*Japanese director and writer. A seminal figure in *avant-garde culture during the 1960s and 1970s, Terayama's short but productive life was plagued by ill-health. A published poet at 16, he went on to a distinguished and diverse career as a writer and director for stage, *television, *radio, and *film, as well as photographer and television commentator. His first play, Blood Sleeps Standing Up, was staged in 1960. In 1967 he founded his own theatre company, Tenjō Sajiki (Les Enfants du Paradis), which, inspired by Antonin *Artaud, carried out radical experiments with dramatic *text, *performance, venue, and *audience relationships. A poet with visual images as well as words, the look of a Terayama production defined Japanese counter-culture: *grotesque, *surrealistic, sexy, violent, rebellious yet strangely nostalgic. He was famous for *street performances like Man-Powered Airplane Solomon (1970) and Knock (1975). Other plays include Mink Marie (1967), Lessons for Servants (1978), and Lemmings (1980). Terayama and his company frequently *toured Europe and the USA. Though the company disbanded on his death, some former members continue his legacy.   CP

TERENCE (195/185–159 BC)

Roman comic playwright. Terence came to Rome as a slave, probably brought from North Africa by a Roman senator who educated and eventually freed him. Little is reliably known about his life, although it seems likely that he enjoyed the friendship and patronage of prominent and sophisticated aristocrats who encouraged and supported his work. A leading actor, Lucius Ambivius Turpio, advised him and promoted his career. Terence wrote six plays: Andria, Hecyra, Heauton Timoroumenos, Eunuchus, Phormio, and Adelphi. He based them upon *Greek originals (primarily by *Menander; see NEW COMEDY), while attempting (not always successfully) to present such *fabulae palliatae in a manner that would appeal to a less sophisticated *Roman theatre.

Terence was born either some ten years before or at the time of *Plautus' death. Yet in almost every way the surviving works of Rome's two greatest comic playwrights display a radically different approach to their craft and, by implication, to their Roman *audience as well. Unlike Plautus, Terence appears to have been relatively faithful to the *plots, characterization, and atmosphere of his models while rendering them more acceptable to the conditions of performance at Rome. He re-worked them, in the process bringing his own dramatic sensibility to bear, not to diminish their subtlety or transform them into bawdy *farces, but rather to enhance and make the works accessible to a Roman audience whose taste and sophistication he evidently sought to educate. Terence created more realistically drawn *characters, with greater emphasis given to individual psychology, and rarely resorted to the *stock figures used by Plautus. Terentian characters are not required to be single-minded types but are instead motivated in more complex and ambiguous ways. This in turn enhances the ethical relevance of the plays. The situations test and expose the characters in a manner closer to what we now think of as *realistic.

This loosening of dramatic stereotype and conventional comic morality is accompanied by greater sobriety in language. There is none of the wordplay, indecencies, irrelevant jokes, extravagant fantasies, or sudden outbursts of song characteristic of Plautine drama. There is no rhetorical emphasis on punishment and torture, no extravagant flights of verbal fantasy, alliteration, assonance, or invented words. Instead Terence sought to write pure and elegant Latin, which was simple, flexible, and concise, but also capable of irony and wit: the language spoken perhaps by the cosmopolitan circle with which he is thought to have associated. Staging conventions are more realistically employed. The *plot is rarely interrupted for comic asides, or for audience address, topical allusion, or *slapstick.

Like other Roman dramatists, Terence presented his works to holiday audiences who were looking to be entertained. It is not surprising that these spectators were at times distracted by the attractions of rival entertainments. The first performance of Terence's Hecyra, for example, was abandoned by the audience in favour of a tightrope walker and boxers; the second attempt to stage the play suffered a similar fate caused by a competing *gladiatorial display. Evidently at least a portion of the audience had little regard for the relatively sophisticated, complex, and restrained *comedies Terence offered them, or for the *prologues that he employed to lecture on dramatic technique, argue with his critics, defend his craft, and plead for a fair hearing. Terence also suffered the taunts of a rival dramatist, Luscius Lanuvinus, who claimed that he had taken liberties in translating and adapting his Greek originals.

Terence seems to have been less concerned with accurate translation than with creating careful reconceptions of the original *texts. His Eunuchus evidently marked a turning point in the development of his craft, in which he managed to achieve a balance between catering to the taste and expectations of his audience, respecting the dramatic integrity of his Greek model, and exploring his own themes and ideas. Terence added extra characters and scenes from another play (one which Plautus had

himself translated) and the result was extremely successful, winning for Terence the largest fee ever paid for a comedy. In his subsequent plays, the Phormio and Adelphi, he continued to employ a judicious mixture of traditional farcical elements and familiar characters while retaining (and arguably extending) the naturalism, ethical complexity, and intelligence of the original works.

The plays of Terence are the most intricately plotted of all surviving ancient drama, creating complex patterns of *action with careful attention to plot symmetry, while often creating technically brilliant parallels between the patterns of onstage action and the thoughts and frequently ironic misapprehensions of his characters. He evidently sought to induct his audience into a more sophisticated appreciation of dramatic nuance and the manner in which often ambiguous relationships and attitudes can be presented and examined theatrically. Menander's emphasis upon patience, tolerance, and a fair-minded and reasonable approach to human relationships (and in particular, the expression and pursuit of love) were adapted to Roman ideals of family obligations, propriety, and public duty.

Terence's influence upon European drama has been immense. His works were widely admired and discussed in antiquity, extensively copied, annotated, and analysed in the *medieval period, and published in numerous editions during the *early modern period. Many of these were illustrated, and examples produced in the last decade of the fifteenth century contain important visual evidence of the earliest attempts by scholars to understand and to stage ancient drama. In turn, such experiments led to new plays composed in direct imitation of Terence and of Plautus. Thus the *dramaturgy, representation of character, and wit and elegance of Terence's *dialogue left an indelible mark upon subsequent practice, providing, most notably, the models for the modern *comedy of manners.

Masked performances of Heauton Timoroumenos, Andria, and Adelphi were presented at the *Weimar Court Theatre of *Goethe and *Schiller in the first decade of the nineteenth century. The experimental production of Adelphi in 1802 (in which close attention was paid to the historical accuracy of *costuming and the use of the *masks) was particularly successful, and marked a turning point for the development of the Weimar theatre, the education of its audience, and, beyond this, the presentation of ancient drama in the contemporaneous theatre. Somewhat surprisingly, revivals of Terence's plays have been infrequent in the modern era, despite his outstanding virtues as a skilled playwright. Translators (and in their turn directors) have found it difficult to determine an appropriate style for his language and its enactment.   RCB

ARNOTT, W. G., Menander, Plautus, and Terence (Oxford, 1968)
BEACHAM, R. C., The Roman Theatre and its Audience (Cambridge, Mass., 1992)
GOLDBERG, S. M., Understanding Terence (Princeton, 1986)
KONSTAN, D., Roman Comedy (Ithaca, NY, 1983)

TERENTIEV, IGOR (1892–1941)

Russian/Soviet theatre practitioner and exponent of the eccentric *grotesque, in a tradition established by Grigory Kozintsev and Leonid Trauberg, who published their *'Eccentrism' manifesto in 1922 on the basis of work at the Factory of the Eccentric Actor (FEKS). Sergei *Eisenstein and *Meyerhold also produced work in this vein during the early 1920s. Terentiev's 1927 production of *Gogol's *The Government Inspector* (*surreally cubist *costume design by Andrei Sashin) attempted to upstage Meyerhold's 1926 version in terms of its grotesque and eccentric features and included five free-standing cubicles, one of them a privy, in place of Meyerhold's fifteen doors, and live mice.

NW

TERRISS, WILLIAM (1847–97)

English actor. His early career as a tea planter and sheep farmer added to his reputation for athletic and vigorous roles, which he assumed with ease, and he was universally known as 'Breezy Bill' for his devil-may-care demeanour and association with the *heroes of *nautical melodrama, notably William in *Jerrold's *Black-Ey'd Susan*. He played athletic heroes at *Drury Lane (Captain Molyneux in *Boucicault's *The Shaughraun* in 1875) and with *Irving (whom he called 'Guv'nor') at the *Lyceum. Though he played Shakespeare—Edgar in *King Lear*, Laertes in *Hamlet*, Mercutio in *Romeo and Juliet*—he had difficulty with the *verse, complaining of *King Lear* that it was 'a damned dull play you know. Damned dull. Heavy as anything.' At the *Adelphi from 1885 he was more comfortable, playing the popular soldier-sailor heroes in *melodramas like *Harbour Lights* (Sims and Pettitt, 1885) and *The Swordsman's Daughter* (Thomas and Scott, 1895). He married the actress Isabel Lewis in 1870. Attacked in a fit of madness and stabbed to death outside the Adelphi by Richard Prince, an ambitious young actor, Terriss's funeral procession to Brompton Cemetery was lined by an estimated 50,000 mourners, and the list of those sending flowers was headed by the Prince of Wales.

AF

TERRY, ELLEN (1847–1928)

English actress. Ellen Terry's family was a notable theatrical dynasty (*see* TERRY FAMILY): her parents ran their own company, her elder sister Kate was initially considered a more promising actress than Ellen, both Terry's children, Edith *Craig and Edward Gordon *Craig, became important theatrical innovators, and Kate's grandson John *Gielgud carried on the tradition. Ellen began acting professionally as a child, playing such roles as Mamillius in *The Winter's Tale* (1856) and Arthur in *King John* for Charles *Kean. Yet she took some time before achieving serious success and her career was stalled for several years on account of her private life. First she left the stage to marry the much older painter G. F. Watts in 1864. Although Watts's painting of Terry (*Choosing*, National Portrait Gallery, London) is deservedly famous, the marriage soon collapsed and Terry returned to the stage. In 1868 she suddenly disappeared and her family believed she was dead. In fact she had eloped with the architect Edwin Godwin, by whom she had two children: the *feminist theatre director Edith (Edy) Craig, and the *designer, *director, and *theorist Edward Gordon Craig. Terry's career began again in earnest in 1874 when Charles *Reade persuaded her to act in *The Wandering Heir*, and in 1875 she played her first Portia in a *Merchant of Venice* sumptuously mounted by Marie (*Wilton) and Squire *Bancroft. In 1878 Terry played the title role in W. G. *Wills's *Olivia*, based on *Goldsmith's *The Vicar of Wakefield*. Later that year she joined forces with Henry *Irving (who had previously played alongside her in 1867 in *Garrick's adaptation of *The Taming of the Shrew*) and began a twenty-year partnership with him based at the *Lyceum Theatre. Here Terry starred as Beatrice in *Much Ado About Nothing*, Portia, Queen Katherine in *Henry VIII*, and Imogen in *Cymbeline*. Despite the dramatic painting by John Singer Sargent of Terry as Lady Macbeth, this was not one of her best roles. Terry's forte was in charming the public with her Pre-Raphaelite good looks, merry laugh, and appearance of spontaneity, which is why her Beatrice was so successful. But she never played the part that seemed tailor made for her, Rosalind in *As You Like It*, presumably because there was not a significant enough role for Irving. She also had success with less classical plays, such as *Bulwer-Lytton's *The Lady of Lyons*, and she was popular in the role of Marguerite in *Faust*.

Irving and Terry *toured America several times and their partnership flourished. But while Irving was knighted in 1895, and Terry dubbed 'Our Lady of the Lyceum' by Oscar *Wilde, Terry, partly because of the Godwin scandal, had to wait until 1925 before, in failing health, she received the equivalent of Irving's accolade, Dame of the British Empire. In 1892 she began an extended correspondence with George Bernard *Shaw (published by Edith Craig, 1931). Shaw, who as a *critic frequently mocked the Lyceum aesthetic, encouraged Terry to branch out on her own and wrote the role of Lady Cicely Waynflete in *Captain Brassbound's Conversion* for her. In 1902 she played in Shakespeare away from the Lyceum, as Mistress Page in Beerbohm *Tree's *Merry Wives of Windsor* at His (*Her) Majesty's Theatre, and in 1903 she moved into *management with *Much Ado About Nothing* and *Ibsen's *The Vikings*, starring herself in productions directed by her son and designed by him and her daughter. Despite this formidable array of theatrical talents the project was a *financial failure. In 1906 the Golden Jubilee of her first appearance on the stage was celebrated in an all-star matinée at *Drury Lane. From 1910 to 1921 Terry toured England, Australia, and the USA, lecturing on Shakespeare, a format that also allowed her to recite favourite speeches without relying on her failing memory for lines (although by now her sight was also failing); *Four Lectures on Shakespeare* (1931) reveal her as a lively and important critic. Late in life Terry appeared in five silent *films. Although she had made several fortunes during her career, her habit of giving money away left her financially insecure. Her home at Smallhythe in Kent is now a museum and archive. Terry's autobiography *The Story of my Life* (1908) was edited and annotated in 1933 by Christopher St John (Christabel Marshall), Edy Craig's partner.　　　EJS

AUERBACH, NINA, *Ellen Terry: player in her time* (London, 1987)

TERRY, MEGAN (1932–)

American playwright, best known for her work with the *Open Theatre in *New York (1963–8) and the *Omaha Magic Theatre. Trained as a designer at the University of Washington and the Banff School of Fine Arts, Terry began to write in Seattle during the late 1950s. She moved to New York where she co-founded the Open Theatre in 1963 with Joseph *Chaikin. As director of the company's playwriting workshop, she rejected psychological *realism and created scripts that would allow actors to undergo 'transformation' in performance. Transformation-plays, like *Calm down Mother* (1965) and *Comings and Goings* (1966), require actors to undergo rapid shifts in time, place, and persona. *Viet Rock* (1967), a protest piece about the Vietnam War, also achieved recognition as the first rock *opera. After leaving the Open Theatre, she wrote *Approaching Simone* (1970), a play about the French religious philosopher Simone Weil, produced at the *La Mama Theatre. In 1971 she became playwright-in-residence at the Omaha Magic Theatre. Her concern with issues of *feminism and American *politics is reflected in such plays as *Babes in the Bighouse* (1974) and *Mollie Bailey's Traveling Family Circus, Featuring Scenes from the Life of Mother Jones* (1983). *See also* FEMINIST THEATRE, USA.　　　JAB

TERRY FAMILY

The most significant and enduring *family dynasty in modern British theatre, embracing the children and descendants of the English provincial actors **Benjamin Terry** (1818–96) and **Sarah Ballard** (1817–92). Usually the successes of this family are measured by the careers of their daughter the actress Ellen *Terry, the influence of her son Edward Gordon *Craig and her daughter Edy *Craig on *scenography and *directing, and the world-renowned work of Ellen's great-nephew the actor and director John *Gielgud. This measurement, however, has tended to obscure the careers of the other children of the family founders, **Fred** (1866–1933), **Marion** (1852–1930), and **Kate** (1844–1924), let alone those of their grandchildren. Fred Terry, for example, pursued a successful acting career and together with his wife Julia Neilson (1868–1957) embarked from 1900 on a 30-year association in romantic *melodramas such as *The Scarlet*

Pimpernel and *Sweet Nell of Old Drury* which endeared them to English provincial *audiences in particular. Their daughter **Phyllis Neilson-Terry** (1892–1977) followed in her parent's footsteps playing the roles made famous by her mother, though her career was more varied. She had extensive experience with Shakespeare, taking Viola and Juliet at *Her Majesty's under *Tree (1910–12), and *toured the American *vaudeville circuit. Her brother **Dennis Neilson-Terry** (1895–1932) began his career as a Shakespearian actor with the *Benson company before the First World War. Thereafter he toured the English provinces and South Africa in mainly commercial vehicles like *The Honourable Mr Tawnish* (1920) and Edgar Wallace's *The Terror* (1927).

Kate Terry retired in 1867 after a relatively short acting career. She was equally adept at Shakespeare and leading parts of the Victorian repertoire like *Bulwer-Lytton's *Money* and *The Lady of Lyons* or Sheridan *Knowles's *The Hunchback*. In these she was directly compared to Helen *Faucit. Marion Terry possessed, according to Ruskin, 'the serenity of effortless grace'. She was in the *Bancrofts' first season at the *Haymarket (1880–1), replaced her sister Ellen as Viola in *Irving's *Twelfth Night* (1884), toured extensively with him as Marguerite in his adaptation of *Faust* (1884) and as Portia in *The Merchant of Venice* (1894). Her greatest successes occurred during her two years with George *Alexander at the *St James's Theatre (1891–3). She was the original Mrs Erlynne in *Wilde's *Lady Windermere's Fan*, a role she revived as late as 1911.

Others who pursued successful acting careers include **Beatrice** (1890–?) and **Minnie** (1882–?); **Hazel Terry** (1918–74), the daughter of Dennis Neilson-Terry; **Olive** (1884–1957); and **Mabel Terry-Lewis** (1872–1957), the daughter of Kate Terry. The entire dynasty, especially the female line, appeared to share many of the same qualities: charm, creative energy, and flair as well as individual distinctiveness.　　　VEE

STEEN, MARGUERITE, *A Pride of Terrys* (London, 1962)

TERTULLIAN (QUINTUS SEPTIMUS FLORENS TERTULLIANUS) (c.160–c.225)

Carthaginian church father. After training in literature and law, Tertullian converted to Christianity about 195 and thereafter exercised his considerable talents as a Latinist and rhetorician on behalf of his new faith. An uncompromising moralist, he was especially concerned to keep Christianity free of pagan pollution. In *De Spectaculis* (*On Spectacles, c.*200), Tertullian argued (a) that all *spectacle, whether at the theatre, the *amphitheatre, or the *circus, was rooted in pagan idolatry and was therefore injurious to faith, and (b) that such activities excite the passions and thereby undermine moral discipline. He nevertheless understood the attractions of spectacle and pointed the way to a possible accommodation when he noted that similar pleasures were available in Christian literature and song. Later church policy concerning theatrical presentation was deeply influenced by Tertullian, as were the assumptions and arguments of later *anti-theatrical tracts.   RWV

TERUKKUTTU

A traditional *dance-theatre form from Tamil Nadu in the south of *India. Literally translating as 'street theatre', terukkuttu is generally performed in the *open air in front of the shrines of the goddess Draupadi, the dominant female *character of the Mahabharata epic, several episodes of which form the core narrative of the repertoire. Enacted by specific *families located in the districts of north and south Arcot in Tamil Nadu (the last name of these families is Thambiran, an ancient Tamil word meaning 'respected master'), terukkuttu functions simultaneously as a religious activity and as entertainment for local communities. Organized by one or a cluster of villages, a performance can last from ten to 40 days, depending on the *financial resources of the sponsoring communities. In the afternoon before each performance, a traditional storyteller narrates the episode of the evening's enactment. The actors spend many hours painting their faces, wearing *costumes with elaborate headgear and wooden shoulder pads decorated with pieces of glass. At about 10.00 p.m. the *kattiyakkaran, or jester-like character who serves as a commentator, announces the play to the accompaniment of a small orchestra (harmonium, percussion, a wind instrument, and a *chorus of five or six voices). Though a written *text containing songs and *spoken words has been handed down through many generations, each group also has a vadhyar (master) who collaborates with the actors in rewriting their parts. Generally the actors train for specific roles rather than for the entire play, the lines for the narrative being distributed between the kattiyakkaran and the primary characters, who engage in animated *dialogue, often improvised. All female characters are played by male actors (see FEMALE IMPERSONATION). Vigorous *dance movements in circular patterns (kirikai), interspersed with intricate footwork, characterize the rough immediacy of the performance, punctuated by the high-pitched singing and musical accompaniment.

Apart from the performance itself, the terukkuttu event includes participatory *rituals. The most memorable one accompanies the death of Duryodhana, marking the end of an all-night performance. The actors playing Duryodhana (who caused the war by disrobing Draupadi) and Bhima (the strongest of the Pandava brothers) leap out of the acting space and chase each other through the streets of the village, all the villagers following them. The chase ends at an enormous reclining figure of Duryodhana, made out of mud by traditional potters while the performance was in progress. After a series of heightened speeches and vigorous dances around the mud figure, the actor playing Duryodhana stands on it and is killed by Bhima, who breaks the thigh of the Duryodhana clay figure, releasing stage blood in spurts. A lamentation by Duryodhana's wife is joined by all the women of the village, mourning their own dead. Ceremonies like this make the relationship between ritual and performance explicit. Apart from its traditional enactment, terukkuttu has also been reinvented by experimental *Tamil theatre groups like Na. *Muthuswamy's Koothuppattarai troupe, which presents stylized narratives on social and *political themes. The convention of the kattiyakkaran has also been adapted by *street theatre groups performing political work relating to communalism and corruption.   PR/RB

FRASCA, RICHARD ARMAND, The Theatre of the Mahabharata: terukuttu performance in south India (Honolulu, 1990)

TEXT

It is normally thought that the text of a play is comprised of *dialogue and *stage directions. Contemporary playtexts usually include both; however, playtexts comprised exclusively of either are also extant. Typically nowadays the playtext is written down, though a text might be passed on orally, existing in the memory of a troupe or a culture. Characteristically, in texts that contain dialogue and stage directions, the dialogue is the largest part; nevertheless, even in such plays the stage directions can bulk quite large, as in the case of *O'Neill's Strange Interlude.

For *Aristotle, the text was by far the most important element of *drama. In his Poetics, Aristotle argued that the primary cognitive value of drama was that it revealed what in human affairs 'is possible in accordance with probability and necessity'. That is, drama discloses regularities in human life—it shows what is likely to happen, for example, when strong-willed people like Creon and Antigone face off. Moreover, since this knowledge is already available from the *plot, not only did Aristotle regard the plot as primary, but he also went on to demote radically the relevance of *performance to drama. He says, 'Spectacle is attractive, but is very inartistic and is least germane to the art of poetry. For the effect of *tragedy is not dependent on performance and actors.' Aristotle thinks that the elements of *spectacle, performance, and *acting are effectively dispensable, since he believes that the knowledge to be had from drama and its characteristic emotional impact, the *catharsis of pity and fear, are essentially carried by the plot. Thus, that which is of central value in drama can be had simply by reading the text. The performance of the text is, at best, icing on the cake and, at worst, a distraction.

This privileging of the text spurred a predictable revolt in the twentieth century, most vociferously expressed by Antonin *Artaud. The priority of the text, and of text-based theatre, was challenged by the practice of the theatre of images, such as Robert *Wilson's The Life and Times of Joseph Stalin. However, it is arguable that this ostensible debate over the priority of the text or performance rests on a misunderstanding of the nature

of theatre which itself encourages confusion over the nature of the playtext. Though we speak of theatre as a single art, it may be more fruitful to think of it as two arts, or as one art with two ontologically different aspects. On the one hand, theatre is a literary art. On the other hand, it is a performing art. As a literary art, it is a verbal construction, one that can be appreciated and evaluated by being read, just as one might read a novel. As a performing art, it belongs to the same family as music and *dance, and can only be appreciated and evaluated through enactment.

The play as a literary work is created by a *playwright, who is an author. That is, the primary artist in this respect is a *creator*. As a performing art, in contrast, the primary artists are *executors*, the *directors, actors, designers, *music directors, and so on who make the text manifest. Of course, the same person could be both the creator of a play, its author, and one of its executors, its director or an actor, for example. Nevertheless, the roles of creator and executor are distinguishable. As the choreographer is to the dancers, and the composer to the conductor-cum-orchestra, so the author of a playtext normally is to the director, actors, designers, and so on. In these cases, there are two different arts: the art of composition and the art of performance. The creation of the author—the text—is fixed by her intentions. The art of the performance is variable. Just as we expect different violinists to bring out different qualities in a score, so we expect actors and directors to disclose different aspects of the text. We prize texts for the singularity of their design, but performances are valued for their variability and diversity.

In this we are making a virtue out of necessity. No text, no matter how elaborate, is determinate regarding every feature relevant to its manifestation or implementation in performance. There are always some questions unanswered by the text, about matters like how a *character looks, how she expresses herself, how the space is to be shaped, what motivates a line reading, and so on. Different performances make different choices concerning these questions. We evaluate performances in terms of the choices they make—in terms of their insight, profundity, and inventiveness—often comparing and contrasting the performance at hand with other variations on the same text. Though there are significant debates about the latitude or degree of compliance performers should respect in filling in the unavoidable indeterminacies of the text (see COPYRIGHT), no one can deny that all performances involve interpretations of playtexts in the sense that performances must go beyond what is given by the text.

As literary art, playtexts are types from which copies are derived, just as your copy of the novel *Ulysses* and my copy of the novel are tokens of the type that James Joyce created. But what kind of types are they? From the perspective of theatre as a performing art, given their inevitable indeterminacy, playtexts are recipes. They are sets of instructions to be filled in and executed by actors, directors, and so on. Playtexts specify the ingredients of the performance—such as lines of dialogue and *props—as well as the range of global emotional tones or flavours appropriate to the work. But just as a culinary recipe calls for the cook to interpret how much salt a 'pinch' is, so the executors of the playtext must exercise judgement in arriving at, for instance, the precise tempo of a performance. This does not allow the executors of the playtext to do anything they wish with the text, just as the cook cannot legitimately 'interpret' 'a pinch of salt' as an instruction to add a slice of orange.

Nevertheless, the playtext as recipe permits a healthy space for variations and inventions—as do recipes in the culinary arts and scores in the musical arts—within the bounds of its indeterminate instructions, though exactly where those bounds may be are subject to debate (for example, must performative variations be constrained by the author's, such as Shakespeare's, original intention, or by the hypothetical intention Shakespeare would have, were he alive today, or is the constraint presented by the text even looser?). And certain playtexts are expressly designed to accommodate more *improvisation than others, such as Megan *Terry's script for *Comings and Goings*.

Moreover, it is because the playtext is somewhat indeterminate, in the way that a culinary recipe is, that it makes sense that we savour different performances of it as we do different preparations by different chefs of the same sauce. Each variation of the same recipe brings out different dimensions or aspects of the recipe-type. Hence, the debate over the priority of text over performance can be dissolved, once one realizes that drama is ontologically two arts rather than one. As a literary art, the text is evidently primary. But as a performing art, the relation of the text to the performance is not adversarial but reciprocal and mutually supportive. The text is a recipe for its performance. But one does not eat recipes for apple pies; one eats pies.

See also PERFORMANCE STUDIES. NC

TEYYAM

A colloquial expression meaning god, *teyyam* refers to the spirits, deified heroes, lineage ancestors, and pan-Indian deities propitiated in *ritual performances in northern Kerala state, *India. *Teyyam* is unique to this region, and is the primary form of popular Hinduism. It may date from as early as the first century AD when heroes killed in battle were deified by erecting stones to be worshipped in their honour. Today over 300 different *teyyams* are propitiated at special festivals in community or lineage shrines on schedules that range from annual to once every twelve years. Each *teyyam* is unique, has its own story of

A ritual performance of one of the heroic warriors in **teyyam**, before a fire at a village shrine near Kannur, Kerala, India, 1977.

origin, and can serve quite different functions. Some are worshipped exclusively by a joint family, or an individual household, while others are worshipped by a specific caste. Worship may benefit an individual, an extended family, or entire community.

Performances in community shrines are on fixed dates, some set by astrological calculations. Some propitiate a single *teyyam* and are modest affairs involving the central performer accompanied by drummers and assistants. Others may propitiate as many as twelve or 32 gods in a single festival lasting up to seven days and nights, and include feeding the entire community. Occasionally an individual may commission a new *teyyam* as a 'vow to god'—as did one householder who, cured of leprosy, built a shrine to the *teyyam* Visnumurti for annual propitiation.

Teyyam performances are organized in a series of stages through which a low-caste dancer (*kolakarran*) is eventually transformed into the deity, becoming a vehicle for visitation by the god who interacts with his devotees. The performance sequence begins with preliminary rituals (consecration of the space, purification of the performer, paying respects to the patrons), progresses through the chanting of songs about the origin and history of the deity invoked, may include a special *dance representing the deity in its youthful stage, and culminates in the full visitation of the performer *costumed and *made up as the deity. The event concludes when the deity, led by assistants, interacts with the devotees present by answering questions, offering prophecies, giving blessings, and receiving offerings, which often include palmwine or the sacrifice of cocks. Make-up helps transform the performer as the deity is 'painted' into his face. As the make-up is prepared, the ingredients are charged with the god's 'power' (*sakti*) by breathing into the mixture, and through repetition of sacred phrases (*mantra*). The performer receives the deity's full power at the moment when he looks in a mirror, witnessing and manifesting his transformation.

Society in Kerala was transformed in the twentieth century. Where caste rules once regulated a hierarchically ordered society, today democratically elected governments in the area often include communists. Not surprisingly *teyyam*'s role and function has changed radically for many performers, patrons, and devotees of the gods.

PZ

THACKER, DAVID (1950–   )

English director. Since the mid-1980s Thacker has been a leading proponent of Arthur *Miller's work in Britain, directing the world premières of *Two-Way Mirror* (1989) and *The Last Yankee* (1993). Thacker's emotional and psychological explorations of *texts places an emphasis on clarity of *acting, a style suitable for Miller's work, which also found success with *Ibsen (*Ghosts*, 1986, with Vanessa *Redgrave; a BBC *television version of *A Doll's House*, 1994). Thacker's clear readings have led to numerous successful productions of Shakespeare; as *artistic director of the *Young Vic from 1984 to 1993 he directed *Othello*, *Macbeth*, *Hamlet*, *Measure for Measure*, *Julius Caesar*, and *Romeo and Juliet*. In 1986 he hosted a symposium to mark Jan *Kott's book *Shakespeare our Contemporary*. Since 1993 he has been with the *Royal Shakespeare Company, where he directed an *award-winning *Pericles* (1989), and innovative productions of *Two Gentlemen of Verona* (1991), *The Merchant of Venice*, *Julius Caesar* (both 1993), *Coriolanus*, and *Measure for Measure* (both 1994).

KN

THAILAND

Since Thailand lies on a major trade route its performance traditions have been strongly influenced by the cultures of *India and *China, as well as by conflicts with its neighbours in South-East Asia. Some forms of music and *dance were established well before the birth of the nation, originally known as the Sukhothai kingdom (1235–1350). *Rong ram tampleng* is an ancient phrase, literally meaning singing, dancing, and playing music, and it is at the core of Thai theatrical expression. *Len pleng*, an early form of village folk singing usually performed by professionals, contained a question-and-answers session on religious and secular subjects; this evolved into a short play with two men arguing over a woman, or two women arguing over a man, and the structure of much Thai theatre has followed this pattern. The chants of monks portraying *characters in the tales of Buddha were another major influence. Finally, the phrase *rabam ram ten* found in stone relics describes three forms of dance which have become important features in Thai theatre: group dance, dance with hand movements, and dance with steps alone.

During the Ayudhya kingdom (1350–1767) many pageants and other forms of theatre were staged to dramatize the divinity of the monarchs. Among them were the *nang *shadow play, the *chaknak dukdamban* pageant for immortality, various dances, and martial arts. The rich heritage of the Ayudhaya theatre laid foundations for *khon, a style of performance marked by the wearing of *masks. *Rabam*, a *ritual court dance performed by women to ensure the annual rainfall, was developed into a dance-drama with elements from *khon* and *lakon. The new form was later named *lakon nai* or the 'inside palace' theatre, as opposed to its predecessor, *lakon nok* or the 'outside palace' style. In the eighteenth century a royal decree prohibited women from performing except in the king's own productions. The move was taken to stop the drafting of young women into noble households as mistresses under the guise of dancers. In 1767 Ayudhya was captured by the Burmese for the second time, and hundreds of thousands of Thais were marched off to Burma as prisoners. The Burmese subsequently adopted Thai theatre styles and called them Ayudhya or Yodia dance, still common in *Myanmar. After regaining independence, King Taksin and his successors in the kingdom of Bangkok revived the performance styles of the Ayudhya period, taking the cultivation of theatre as one of their most important tasks. The *Ramayana* and other lost Ayudhya plays were rewritten by the monarchs, their relatives, and the court poets. Many royal families and noblemen had their own *khon* or *lakon* troupes for private and state functions.

By the 1860s a new hybrid theatre style, *lakon pantang* or 'thousand ways theatre', broke from earlier traditions by borrowing theatre and dance elements from immigrants in Bangkok. Stories and characters were chiefly foreign and allowed artists to create independent styles; closer contact with Europe brought *realistic *scenery, *acting, *costume, and *make-up. Many new forms were created such as *lakon pood*, or Western spoken drama; *lakon dukdamban*, or dance-drama with realistic sets; *lakon rong* or sung drama. Entrance fees were introduced when noble patronage declined. Theatre began to cater to public tastes, which gave rise to several distinct regional popular theatre *genres such as *likay*, in central Thailand, *mohlam* in the north-eastern region, and *nora* in the south. *Likay* is *improvised drama with songs and comic devices. *Mohlam roung* is similar to *likay*, while *mohlam pluen* is a sung dance-drama accompanied by traditional tunes played by a Western orchestra. A dance troupe in the local style is an integral part of the show, which is usually based on *Sang Sin Chai* or other famous local stories. Actors in both types wear *likay* costumes, but actresses wear local traditional dress. *Lakon saw* comes from the north and has a mixed cast singing traditional music, dressed in both traditional and modern costumes. The repertoire includes local legends and modern plays. (*See also* HUN.) Despite the decline of court patronage, King *Rama VI played an active role in preserving and promoting both Thai and Western theatres at the start of the twentieth century.

The constitutional monarchy, formed in 1932, brought theatre from the royal court into the hands of the government. Traditional forms, considered the legacy of the absolute monarchy, were abandoned for newer styles which promoted nationalism. Though the National College of Dramatic Arts was established in 1934, it was not until 1945 that *khon* performance was brought back into life. Today Thailand is scattered with colleges and schools which offer degrees, diplomas, and certificates in traditional and modern theatre and dance. Government policies on culture and tourism have encouraged further exploration—more than 300 new dance pieces have been choreographed between 1970 and 2000—so that Thai theatre has brought both tradition and innovation into the twenty-first century.
SV

THALBACH, KATHARINA (1954–)

German actress and director. The daughter of a theatre family, her debut at the *Berliner Ensemble in 1968 immediately established Thalbach as a major acting talent. In 1977 she began working in West Germany, and has performed in a large variety of classical and contemporary roles ranging from Shakespeare to *Kleist to *Brecht. She is also a *film actor, perhaps best known in *The Tin Drum* (1979). Her performances are noted for their original and often unorthodox readings of roles. Her interest in discovery and experiment led her into *directing, in which she showed the same talent for unconventional readings of classical plays. Most noteworthy were her *Macbeth* (*Berlin, 1987) and Brecht's *A Man's a Man* (Hamburg, 1989).
CBB

THANG-TA

Armed and unarmed fighting techniques of the Meitei people from the state of Manipur in *India. *Thang-ta* (sword-spear) is the popular name for a martial arts system known as Huyen Lallong (Art of Warfare). The history of the Meiteis is characterized by interclan and intertribal warfare and conflicts with neighbouring kingdoms, but also by long periods of stable government. With its long and energetic practice sessions, *thang-ta* allowed Meitei warriors to hone their combat skills in times of peace as well as war. According to Meitei myth, the limbs and bones of the community's progenitor, Tin Sidaba, turned into the swords and tools used in *thang-ta*. The art flourished during the reign of King Khagemba in the late fifteenth and early sixteenth centuries; *Chainarol*, a manuscript written in the sixteenth or seventeenth century, contains glimpses of the prevailing warrior customs. After the Anglo-Manipuri war in 1891 (resulting in Manipur's annexation by the British Empire), the British immediately outlawed the region's martial arts. *Thang-ta* went underground and was kept alive only because a few expert practitioners continued the tradition in secrecy.

After the independence of India in 1947—Manipur became a territory of the Indian Union in 1949—*thang-ta* slowly re-emerged, and is now popular in Manipur as a martial art and a technique used in theatre and *dance. Across the state a number of martial arts academies educate men and women in *thang-ta*, and some choreographers like Th. Chaotombi and directors like Ratan *Thiyam and Heisnam *Kanhailal have incorporated it into their productions. The traditional repertoire of *thang-ta* is divided into four broad categories: *ta-khousarol* (art of spear dance), *thanghairol* (art of sword play), *sarit-sarat* (unarmed combat), and, most importantly, *thengkourol* (art of touch and call). While the first three are commonly practised, *thenkourol* is rarely encountered. Not a technique of a direct combat, it is a magical practice whereby a particular series of movements accompanied by *rituals ensures victory in battle. *See also* MANIPURI THEATRE.
SR

THEATERTREFFEN

German theatre *festival. Founded in 1964, this showcase of the German theatre takes place annually in May in *Berlin, assembling ten notable productions from Germany, Austria, and Switzerland (invitations were not extended to East German theatres before Germany's reunification). The productions are selected by a jury of seven theatre *critics from work which premièred over the past year. The selected plays are to show an 'extraordinary collaboration between dramatic *text, *dramaturgy, *direction, *actors' performance, and design'. The jury's work and judgement have been controversial throughout the festival's existence for a tendency to focus on the director's theatre of Peter *Stein, Peter *Zadek, Claus *Peymann, and others. Neglected smaller theatres and troupes frequently complained that the jury was biased and the meeting a showcase for the highly subsidized public theatres. The Theatertreffen is accompanied by a programme of international productions and a seminar for younger theatre practitioners. CBB

THEATRE For most topics beginning with some form of the word 'theatre', see the next significant word of the item's title or name. For example, for 'theatre of the absurd' *see* ABSURD, THEATRE OF THE; for 'Teatro Nacional D. María II' *see* NACIONAL D. MARÍA II, TEATRO.

THEATRE

Derived from *theatron, the ancient Greek word for 'seeing place' (cognates in *theates* 'spectator', *theama* 'show'), 'theatre' has over the centuries lost much of its optic precision, and through a series of inflations and associations is now commonly used to refer to (a) a building designed for the *performance or exhibition of plays, *operas, or *film (see PLAYHOUSE); (b) the art of producing plays; (c) the institution of theatre generally. (Other, more obviously metaphoric usages do not concern us here.) Sensing particularly the loss of point of view implicit in the Greek word, and mindful of the historical and cultural limitations of modern definitions, theoreticians are re-examining *theatron* and postulating definitions that are simultaneously tentative and heuristic. It is urged, for instance, that for a performance to be 'theatre' requires two sets of participants—*audience and performers—and an organized spatial relationship between them. A theatrical event, a collaboration between spectators and performers, is a construct of its participants. The reintegration of the spectator into the idea of theatre re-establishes 'gaze' both optically and metaphorically at its centre.

The tentative nature of any definition of theatre, however abstract or general, is made necessary by the great variety of theatrical traditions and forms that have flourished throughout the world and continue to expand in their diversity. Moreover, definitions of theatre, like its formal characteristics, are culturally and historically determined. Richard *Schechner places theatre in a continuum 'that reaches from the *ritualizations of animals (including humans) through performances in everyday life—greetings, displays of emotion, family scenes, professional roles, and so on—through to play, *sports, theatre, *dance, ceremonies, rites, and performances of great magnitude' (*Performance Theory*, rev. edn., 1988). The performances in Schechner's continuum that qualify as 'theatre', however, can shift with time and place. (*See* PERFORMANCE STUDIES.)

The ever changing complexity of theatre can to some extent be conceptualized in terms of the arts and techniques available to it. Indeed, a conventional ontological issue is whether theatre is a single autonomous art, a unified synthesis of various arts (*Wagner's *Gesamtkunstwerk*, 'total artwork'; *see* TOTAL THEATRE), or a contradictory amalgam of conflicting arts (*Brecht's *Theaterarbeit*, 'theatre-product'). Gesture and movement, singing and speaking, poetry, costume and decor, *scenography and stage technology—as one or more of these resources is emphasized, the performance veers to forms that we sometimes distinguish from theatre: dance, gymnastics, athletics; oratory, oratorio, opera; recital; *spectacle, *tableau. Moreover, the centrifugal force that accompanies the foregrounding of these various arts and skills leads outward into independent areas of study: kinesiology, musicology, art and architecture, literary study.

In spite of widespread recognition that in the widest sense theatre defies definition, Western *theory in general clings to the intersection of *drama and performance as the locus of theatre. That is, together with spectators, performers, and organized space, *action or the representation of an action (*Aristotelian *mimesis) is deemed indispensable to theatre. Thus Patrice Pavis: 'A *text (or an action), an *actor's body, a *stage, a spectator—this would seem to be the necessary sequence of all theatre communication' (*Dictionary of the Theatre*, 1998). The mimesis test nevertheless excludes many forms that both practitioners and scholars regard as theatre. The notion of mimetic theatre is undoubtedly useful, but it cannot be allowed more than tentative and temporary status. 'Theatre' is no more limited by its function as a medium for drama than 'drama' is limited to the single medium of theatre. *See also* THEATRE STUDIES. RWV

THEATRE, THE

Built by James *Burbage in 1576 in Shoreditch, on the main road north out of the city, the Theatre was the first successful custom-built *playhouse in *London. It was the second attempt by Burbage, once a player with *Leicester's Men, after the *Red Lion of 1567. A large twenty-sided polygon, its design and its name were meant to be reminders of the D-shaped classical *Roman theatres. Its stage thrust out halfway into the open yard. In 1594 it became the home to a new playing company, the Lord *Chamberlain's Men, whose leader was Richard *Burbage, James's son, and whose chief writer was William Shakespeare. When the lease of the land it was built on expired in 1597, the landlord closed it down. Two years later it was dismantled and its timbers were taken for reuse as the frame for the *Globe on the other side of the river.   AJG

THEATRE BUILDINGS *See* PLAYHOUSE.

THEATRE COMMUNICATIONS GROUP

Service organization for non-commercial American theatre. Established in 1961 by a Ford Foundation grant, TCG's mission is 'to strengthen, nurture and promote the not-for-profit American theatre'. Serving over 400 theatres and 17,000 individual members, most associated with *regional theatres, TCG is central to virtually all not-for-profit producers. Its activities include advocacy, grant programmes, conferences, surveys, and publications, including *American Theatre*, a monthly trade magazine *publishing selected new plays, nationwide programme schedules, and yearly theatrical statistics. Other publications include an employment bulletin, translations, plays, and reference books. TCG is now the US centre of the *International Theatre Institute.   GAO

THEATRE DESIGN *See* PLAYHOUSE; SCENOGRAPHY.

THÉÂTRE-FRANÇAIS *See* COMÉDIE-FRANÇAISE.

THEATRE GUILD

American art theatre that emerged from the *Washington Square Players in 1918. The Players were reconstituted as the Guild through the efforts of Lawrence Langner (who maintained his day job as a patent attorney) and so began life with a clean *financial slate. Benefiting from the Players' experience the Theatre Guild chose to become fully professional. It made other significant decisions: to produce only full-evening plays 'which should be great plays', to lease or build a theatre building accommodating 500–600 persons and thus 'larger than the usual *Little Theatre', to organize on a subscription basis, and to produce no plays written by its board members. These principles propelled the Guild during the years 1919 to 1939 to succeed as an art theatre in the Broadway environment. By 1930 the original subscription list of 135 had grown to 35,000 in *New York and 45,000 in 132 cities and towns around the country. The introducer of numerous plays by *Shaw to the United States, meticulous productions of key works by Eugene *O'Neill, Elmer *Rice, Robert E. *Sherwood, Philip *Barry, and S. N. *Behrman added to its enormous prestige, attracting the talents of the *Lunts, among others. After the loss of some younger members (and some cultural currency) to the *Group Theatre in 1931, of major playwrights to the Playwrights Company in 1938, and their *playhouse in 1943, the Guild ex-

isted largely as a commercial enterprise under the direction of long-time *manager Theresa Helburn.   MAF

THEATRE-IN-EDUCATION

Most usefully thought of as an English educational movement characterized by its aims and working methods, rather than as a theatrical form. TIE uses theatre as part of the educational process, focusing on contemporary social and political issues. After the Belgrade Theatre, Coventry, established a TIE company in 1965 to develop its links with the community, the *Arts Council of Great Britain agreed to fund various forms of Young People's Theatre (*see* THEATRE FOR YOUTH) for the first time, a key factor in the rapid early expansion of TIE. Actor-teachers took specially *devised work into local schools, often working with small numbers of children. Collaborative working practices are at the heart of the TIE movement. Plays are rarely self-contained, stand-alone entities: interactive workshops are usually an important part of the educational process. The performance elements of a TIE programme are thus often no less collaborative than the devising process itself. Much TIE can be seen as a development of *Brechtian practice, with an emphasis on making an *audience active and reflexive. In its heyday, in the late 1970s and early 1980s, TIE tended to be oppositional and *political in the sense of posing questions about power structures. *Peacemaker*, for example, a programme for 5- to 8-year-olds, written by David Holman in collaboration with Theatre Centre in 1982, focused on the first meeting of two people from either side of an impenetrable wall and aimed to examine issues around conflict resolution. When initially performed it created a storm of controversy: a senior Conservative government minister (Norman Tebbit) condemned the play and the company without having seen it or read it. In spite of his intervention there have been numerous subsequent productions of the play.

At that time many *regional theatres had an associated TIE company, with funding from a variety of sources. Some companies received support in kind (use of local authority buildings and access to infrastructures, for example); some were closely tied to the development of regional theatres' *community programmes. By the mid-1980s, *financial cutbacks had forced the closure of some of the less well-established TIE companies. After the 1988 Education Act, which introduced Local Management of Schools (and devolution of budgets from Local Education Authorities to individual schools), most authorities cut off their financial support to TIE companies, many of which had prided themselves on being able to *tour programmes without charging schools, seeing their work as an essential part of the educational process and a necessary counterbalance to the institutionalization of education. By the end of the twentieth century only a few companies were operating, none of them as securely funded as they had been in the heyday. The idealistic impetus of the movement seemed (perhaps temporarily) to have been stifled by lack of finance and the increasing demands of the National Curriculum within schools. *See also* EDUCATIONAL THEATRE; OPPRESSED, THEATRE OF THE.   BGW

JACKSON, ANTHONY (ed.), *Learning through Theatre* (London, 1993)

THEATRE-IN-THE-ROUND *See* ARENA AND IN-THE-ROUND.

THÉÂTRE NATIONAL POPULAIRE

Theatre company founded by Firmin *Gémier in 1920 at the old Trocadéro Theatre in *Paris, across the Seine from the Eiffel Tower. This was to fulfil his dream for a popular state-subsidized theatre, a vision he shared with other theatre practitioners of the early twentieth century, in particular Romain *Rolland (*see* FINANCE). He received only limited support from the French government, and the nineteenth-century *proscenium stage and compartmentalized house of the Trocadéro did not lend themselves easily to Gémier's idea of a communal theatre experience; he died in 1933 never having fully realized his project. In 1935 the Trocadéro was demolished to make room for a larger modern performance space in the Palais du Chaillot, which opened in 1937. Over the next two decades, the Théâtre du *Chaillot was run successively by Paul Abram and Pierre Aldebert, although the TNP remained essentially dormant until Jean *Vilar stepped in as director in 1951. Vilar transformed the Chaillot into the focal point of a vision, like Gémier's, to popularize and decentralize the arts in France, which he felt had become enslaved to antiquated notions of class hierarchy and social elitism. He abolished *footlights and front *curtains, and suppressed all superfluous *scenery in favour of minimalist scenery and stylized, colourful *costumes. His reforms were not limited to the stage performance, however. In the house, he abandoned the traditional codes of evening dress (*see* AUDIENCE DRESS) and tipping, and he substituted expensive glossy programmes with the playtext and photos from the production. He also instituted a new system of *ticket subscriptions, special theatre weekends and galas, as well as open debates and discussions with authors, actors, and directors. For the first time, the TNP functioned successfully as a venue for high-quality productions at an affordable price. Vilar's repertoire was an eclectic mix of French classics, German *romantics, and European moderns, many of which were unfamiliar to Parisian *audiences at the time, and his company attracted some of the most talented actors of the era, notably Gérard *Philipe, María *Casares, and Daniel Sorano. For many years, the TNP was associated with the *Avignon Festival, which Vilar inaugurated in 1947, so for nearly twenty years the mainstage productions of the Chaillot were recreated each summer under the stars in the courtyard of the medieval papal palace on the Rhône River. After Vilar left the Chaillot in 1963, Georges Wilson took over the direction of the TNP. Wilson attempted to continue

building on Vilar's legacy, expanding the repertoire to include more works by contemporary European authors. In the increasingly politicized decade that followed, however, Wilson was unable to attract the younger audiences to the Chaillot, and by the late 1960s, the *financial situation of the TNP was dire.

Consequently, in 1972 the title of the TNP was transferred to the company run by Roger *Planchon in Villeurbanne, near Lyon. Over the next 30 years the company was a vehicle for Planchon's distinctive *directorial style, where a creative *mise-en-scène stands on equal footing to the author's *text. Inspired by *Brecht and the new wave cinematographers of the 1950s and 1960s, Planchon staged a series of spectacular productions depicting the personal torment of individual *characters as metaphors for greater ideological conflicts. His 1983 creation *Ionesco* supplemented *Ionesco's last play, *Journeys among the Dead*, with other texts and material so as to compose a total image of the isolation of a Romanian in exile during the Cold War. Planchon's own plays, such as *Le Cochon noir* (*The Black Pig*, 1973), *Gilles de Rais* (1976), and *Le Radeau de la Méduse* (*The Raft of the Medusa*, 1996), similarly adhere to a *Brechtian model for presenting an individual's relationship with history. In addition to his own creations, Planchon mounted new works by contemporary authors, including *Vinaver, Dubillard, and *Pinter. Planchon left the TNP in 2001, and was succeeded by Christian *Schiaretti, formerly the director of the Comédie de Reims.   CHB

THEATRE NETWORK

Canadian company. Founded in Edmonton in 1976 as a *collective 'to mirror prairie life through drama', and to create 'a network of common awareness among people who share a cultural heritage', Network soon adopted a regular season format (1980) and renovated a 1938 cinema into a permanent theatre (1990). While developing western Canadian playwrights and other artists remains a priority, its mainstage mandate has progressively expanded to include new Canadian work and, through its 1997 amalgamation with Phoenix Theatre, the best of world contemporary theatre.   MJD

THEATRE ROYAL, MONTRÉAL

Opened in 1825, it was the first building devoted exclusively to theatre in *Montreal. Its *manager arranged an overly ambitious first season of professional theatre (including a series of performances by Edmund *Kean), resulting in insolvency. More humble fare followed, much of it *amateur, in English and occasionally in French. Closed in 1844, it was reborn in 1847 as a second, much larger building which was destroyed by *fire in 1862. A third *playhouse, seating 1,500, opened the same year and remained in operation until 1913. For most of its history the

Royal, in its three embodiments, was the principal venue for professional theatre.   LED

THEATRES ROYAL

*Playhouses in Britain which operated under direct warrant or *patent issued by the crown. Originally such patents were awarded to individuals who were empowered to form companies and to erect buildings. In 1660 Charles II granted the first patents to Thomas *Killigrew and William *Davenant, giving them an effective monopoly of all dramatic performances in *London. Killigrew built his first theatre royal in 1663, and after its destruction by *fire in 1672, the new Theatre Royal *Drury Lane opened in 1674. Davenant built his in 1661 at *Lincoln's Inn Fields. The site and the theatre were leased by Christopher *Rich in 1714 and the Theatre Royal, *Covent Garden, was erected in 1732. These were supplemented by the patents to perform *opera granted to John *Vanbrugh at the Queen's Theatre, *Haymarket (1709), and to Samuel *Foote at the Little Theatre, *Haymarket (Theatre Royal), during the summer months (1766). The draconian 1737 *Licensing Act prevented the performance of plays by theatre companies unless protected by letters patent issued by an Act of Parliament or by the licence of the *Lord Chamberlain. The value of such protection was soon perceived by those who wished to build theatres elsewhere. Parliamentary Enabling Acts awarded letters patent to theatres outside London throughout the eighteenth century, thus entitling them to be called theatres royal. The first was in *Edinburgh (1767), followed in 1768 by *Bath and Norwich. Similar acts were passed for York and Kingston upon Hull (1769), Liverpool (1771), *Manchester (1775), Chester (1777), Bristol (1778), Margate (1786), Newcastle-upon-Tyne (1787), *Glasgow (1803), and Birmingham (1807).

The monopoly granted to these theatres royal to perform the *legitimate repertoire was contested throughout the eighteenth and early nineteenth centuries. As the populations of the major centres (especially London) began to increase, the monopoly of legitimate drama by the patent theatres, and their resolute opposition to increasing the numbers of theatres permitted to perform this drama, became irksome to entrepreneurs less interested in the preservation of a 'national drama' than in making money. The struggle to free the stage in London intensified in the period after 1808, especially after the destruction by fire of Drury Lane and Covent Garden in the first decade of the nineteenth century. Although the letters patent continued to be passed down by *managements, their significance, together with the title 'theatre royal', became merely decorative when the Theatre Regulation Act removed all restrictions on repertoire in 1843.   VEE

HUME, ROBERT D., *The London Theatre World 1660–1800* (Carbondale, Ill., 1980)

THEATRE STUDIES

As an academic discipline recognized in universities and characterized by organized research, theatre studies was conceived during the early years of the twentieth century, but received relatively widespread acceptance only after 1950. Even at the end of the century its epistemology remained uncertain. Two long-standing assumptions inhibited the development of theatre studies as a distinct field of study. First, art associated with high culture was conceived as monumental and permanent, available for repeated access in a way that ephemeral and popular performance was not. Second, as a consequence, *theatre was identified with *drama and its study seen as a branch of literary studies. The earliest discussions of theatre reflect these assumptions. *Aristotle's *Poetics* has historically provided theoretical justification for treating the dramatic *text as the essence of theatre, and most ancient and medieval scholarship concerned itself with textual matters, largely ignoring the world of *performance. *Early modern *theorists remained for the most part innocent of theatrical concerns, and again paid little heed to the popular theatres of Shakespeare or Lope de *Vega. A growing interest in classical *playhouse architecture was later joined by a concern with *scenography and *acting technique. Nevertheless, attempts to distinguish drama and theatre, to understand performance, were based on the idea that, although knowledge of the theatrical circumstances attending the initial production of a dramatic text was valuable for understanding it, once written the play provided the blueprint for its own performance. The essence of theatre remained in the text; a performance was at best an interpretation—usually imperfect—of the text.

This idea underlay the initial introduction of theatre studies (or drama) into American universities. Drama had been part of the educational programmes of humanists and *Jesuits since the sixteenth century, but until early in the twentieth century dramatic performance in American education was little more than an approved extracurricular activity. Nevertheless, the practical exigencies of performing the classics of dramatic literature led logically to classroom instruction in the techniques of theatrical production. Precisely when and where this occurred is not clear. George Pierce *Baker introduced a playwriting course at Harvard in 1903, followed in 1912 by a 'workshop' course in which plays were performed. Thomas Wood Stevens established a degree programme in theatre at the Carnegie Institute of Technology in Pittsburgh in 1914. By 1925, when Baker became head of drama at Yale, colleges and universities throughout the United States included the practical study of theatre in their curricula, usually complemented by historical and theoretical studies that continued to stress dramatic literature.

In continental Europe, theatre studies developed differently, as a result of a conscious reconceptualization of the object of study. In Germany, Max Herrmann drew a sharp distinction between drama and theatre: 'A drama is the word-based artistic creation of an individual; theatre is the product of an *audience and those who serve it.' No longer simply a mediating form for dramatic literature, theatre was considered an autonomous 'spatial art' whose essence lay in performance, in the activities whereby an aesthetic event is created. The Institute for Theatre Studies (*Theaterwissenschaft*) that Herrmann founded in *Berlin in 1923 served as a model for the academic study of theatre throughout most of Europe. European institutes differ from American departments—and some British and Irish departments—in their exclusion of the practical *training of actors, *directors, and designers, which is normally carried out in dedicated conservatories.

Theatre studies nevertheless struggled for the next 35 years. The notion that drama was literature and theatre merely its mediating form persisted. Herrmann maintained academic respectability by avoiding the empirical investigation of contemporary performance and concentrating, at least initially, on the reconstruction of past styles of performance, an emphasis continued at Yale by A. M. Nagler. In the 1930s, also in Germany, Carl Niessen advocated the study of performance far beyond the limits of conventional theatre, but the idea made so little impact on theatre studies generally that its reintroduction in 1973 by the American Richard *Schechner was considered innovative. In Britain, the reluctance of departments of literature to relinquish their proprietary rights to drama delayed the academic recognition of theatre studies until after the Second World War. A Department of Drama was established at the University of Bristol in 1946, which generally followed the American model but left professional training to the *Bristol Old Vic Theatre School. Such departments nevertheless did not become common in British universities and polytechnics until after 1960.

Even the advocates of theatre studies continued to conceive of their discipline in terms of classic dramatic theatre—a fact made apparent at an international conference convened in *London by the *Society for Theatre Research in 1955. That same conference, however, led to the formation two years later of the *International Federation for Theatre Research, which marked the beginnings of an internationalization of theatre research as the contours of the new discipline began to emerge. Contemporary performance became a legitimate object of study, and there was a fresh impetus in both Europe and America on studies in scenography and iconology, on *reception and audience research, and on performance analysis and *theory. Theatre history continued as a major interest, but with a heightened historiographical and methodological sophistication. The study of traditional dramatic theatre also continued, but it no longer monopolized research. American universities sometimes trained theatre practitioners, but American doctoral programmes shared with European institutes an emphasis on theoretical and historical research. National professional organizations promoted research, and professional journals published the results.

Still, as the twentieth century ended, theatre studies remained an evolving discipline, plagued by 'epistemological chaos' and 'endemic structural difficulties' (Patrice Pavis), with no clearly defined theoretical basis. Drama and theatre remained confused; theatre and practice remained disjoined; historical and empirical methodologies remained isolated; institutional organization and support remained fragmented and uncertain. Moreover, a kind of centrifugal force had spun off drama studies, theatre studies, media studies, *performance studies, and cultural studies. But such seeming chaos can mark intellectual vigour as well as confusion. There is promise in the replacement of the dramatic text with performance at the centre of theatre studies, in the reconceptualization of theatrical text and practice in terms of a wider culture that is itself performative, that theatre studies may finally take its place as a central humane discipline. *See also* HISTORIOGRAPHY. RWV

FISCHER-LICHTE, ERIKA, 'From text to performance: the rise of theatre studies as an academic discipline in Germany', *Theatre Research International*, 24 (1999)

JAMES, D. G., ed., *The Universities and the Theatre* (Bristol, 1952)

THEATRE WORKSHOP

Highly influential English company, based (1953–78) at the *Theatre Royal, Stratford East, *London. Established in 1945, Theatre Workshop was the last in a long line of troupes set up by Joan *Littlewood (director) and Ewan MacColl (folk musician), committed to *touring to working-class *audiences in non-theatrical spaces. The Workshop specialized in new, company-*devised plays and productions of the classics (including the first British production of *Brecht's *Mother Courage*, in 1955). By the late 1950s Theatre Workshop (minus MacColl) had become an important part of the new wave of British theatre, largely through a series of remarkable productions of new plays, notably Brendan *Behan's *The Quare Fellow* (1956) and *The Hostage* (1958), Shelagh *Delaney's *A Taste of Honey* (1958), and the *collectively written *Oh! What a Lovely War* (1963). All the Workshop's productions were shaped by Littlewood's distinctive personality and *directorial methods (which included the extensive use of *improvisation and the rewriting of plays in *rehearsal). The company's radical ethos was eventually compromised by systematic underfunding, which caused Littlewood to leave the professional theatre altogether. Although the title Theatre Workshop was dropped in 1978, a company continues to thrive at the Theatre Royal. SWL

THEATRICALITY

Presentational mode of *performance that draws attention to its own status as *theatre and as artifice. Performances can acquire a quality of theatricality through the use of *puppets and *masks, displays of vocal or physical virtuosity, and conventions such as the aside. Theatricality has little meaning in contexts where virtually all dramatic performance is overtly theatrical, such as most non-Western theatre, or Western theatre prior to the nineteenth century. Theatricality opposes attempts to absorb an *audience fully within the fictional world of the play and to conceal or repress the world of the performance. While Denis *Diderot's eighteenth-century notion of the imaginary 'fourth wall' anticipates the anti-theatricality ideal, that ideal did not gain wide currency until the end of the following century with the advent of realistic drama and production, and, most significantly, the new medium of *film. In the early twentieth century, in reaction to the newly dominant aesthetic of *realism and *naturalism, a counter-aesthetic of vigorous theatricality sprang up. Russian director Vsevolod *Meyerhold was at the forefront of this trend, and slightly later Bertolt *Brecht's *theory of *epic theatre provided its most fully articulated and influential ideological rationale. As a metaphor outside of theatre, theatricality suggests the self-conscious construction of a public persona, as in the example of drag (*see* FEMALE IMPERSONATION; MALE IMPERSONATION). One of the most famous and controversial applications of the concept of theatricality outside theatre is critic Michael Fried's attack on the 'theatricality' of art styles, such as minimalism, that emphasize the objecthood of the artwork and acknowledge the presence of the viewer. *See also* METATHEATRE.   DZS

THEATRICAL SYNDICATE

An association or 'trust' comprised of six businesses (booking agencies and theatre owners) that joined together in 1896 to control most American theatrical production, until outmanoeuvred and eclipsed by the *Shubert Organization after 1910. The period of Syndicate dominance was the most centralized ever in the history of American theatre and offers a case study in monopolistic business practices. The Syndicate consisted of the Klaw and Erlanger Exchange; Samuel Nixon and J. Fred Zimmerman; Al Hayman; and Charles *Frohman. The trust owned or controlled booking for nearly all 'first-class' theatres in the United States and so was in a position to dictate script choices, production styles, salaries, *royalty agreements, *ticket prices, and even advertising rates. The Syndicate built upon economic trends under way since the Civil War. The expansion of the railways and the absence of government regulation made it possible for entrepreneurs to buy theatre buildings along a transportation route, dissolve the local *stock company housed there, and substitute a series of 'combination' productions that were *cast, built, and *rehearsed in *New York. Competitors were eliminated through outright purchase or by the use of temporarily low ticket prices which drove them out of business. With an unchecked ability to drive down costs and set prices, the Syndicate flourished *financially, fighting off challenges from independent theatre owners, booking agents, playwrights

such as David *Belasco, or recalcitrant actors such as Minnie Maddern *Fiske, who *toured the country performing in gymnasiums, *tents, and skating rinks to avoid Syndicate control.

The Syndicate was blamed for much that ailed American theatre and drama. Conceived as a purely business enterprise, the Syndicate had no interest in theatre as an art form. Plays, actors, and designs were valued strictly in economic terms. Playwrights and composers, if they wished to sell their work, were required to produce standardized *comedies, *melodramas, and *operettas that conformed to proven formulas. Actors were regarded as interchangeable commodities and allowed little or no range, expected to play the same type or even the same role for years on end. Though the Shuberts finally overwhelmed the Syndicate between 1910 and 1920, they substituted a new monopoly for the old. Soon after *film and *radio overwhelmed theatre as popular entertainment and 'the road' was largely converted to movie theatres. Theatre as a locally produced professional enterprise did not recover across the United States until it saw a partial revival in the *regional theatre movement of the 1960s and 1970s. *See also* LITTLE THEATRE MOVEMENT; COMMUNITY THEATRE, USA; TRADE UNIONS, THEATRICAL.   MAF

THEATRON

Greek 'viewing place'. The architecture of the *Greek *ancient theatre distinguished *skene* (the stage building) from *theatron* (the seating), but since the stage building was in origin often temporary, both in the East and the West, the word came to imply our *'theatre', which is the usual meaning of Latin *theatrum*. Seating was at first on a hillside, then by about 500 BC on wooden scaffolding, increasingly with stone seating fronting the *orchestra for distinguished priests or magistrates (*prohedria*). But it is also possible, as in *Roman festivals, that occasionally the steps of temples were designed as seating with temporary *stages erected before them. After *c.*330 BC the Athenian model (*see* DIONYSUS, THEATRE OF) of semicircular stone seating became standard, but with many variants based on different geometric models, such as those described by the architect *Vitruvius. The different 'wedges' (Greek *kerkides*, Latin *cunei*) separated by gangways could vertically demarcate social or political groupings; under Roman influence a very complex hierarchy from front to back developed, with horizontal divisions enforced by walkways (Greek *diazoma*, Latin *praecinctio*), barriers (Latin *balteus*), and special ticketed entrances (Latin *vomitorium*), the orchestra now being reserved for the elite. Seats were always narrow (*c.*41 cm; 16 inches).   WJS

THEOBALD, LEWIS (1688–1744)

English author, immortalized as the king of the dunces in the first versions of Pope's *The Dunciad* (1728), a reward for attacking Pope's edition of Shakespeare (1725) in his *Shakespeare Restor'd* (1726). At *Lincoln's Inn Fields Theatre, Theobald wrote and produced *pantomimes with John *Rich. While these works—such as *Harlequin a Sorcerer* (1725), *Apollo and Daphne* (1726), and *The Rape of Proserpine* (1727)—were performed hundreds of times, his serious plays, such as his adaptation of *Richard II* (1719) and his more popular *Double Falsehood* (1727), were produced much less frequently.   MJK

THEORIES OF DRAMA, THEATRE, AND PERFORMANCE *see page 1355*

THESIS PLAY

A translation of the French term *pièce à thèse*, a thesis play investigates controversial social and moral issues in order to stimulate discussion and direct debate. Usually identified with the work of *Augier and *Dumas *fils* it found its most developed form in the works of *Brieux, especially *Les Avariés* (*Damaged Goods*, 1902), which dealt directly with the problem of syphilis; *Ibsen's work between 1879 and 1882, especially *Pillars of Society*, *A Doll's House*, *An Enemy of the People*, and *Ghosts*; and some of *Shaw's early plays like *Widowers' Houses* (1892). The first thesis play is usually identified as Dumas's *The Natural Son* (1858), dealing with the difficulty faced by illegitimate children. Augier and Brieux focused on social problems and attitudes, specifically the effects of science, law, and politics upon society.   VEE

THESPIS (fl. 534 BC)

Semi-mythical inventor of Athenian *tragedy. *Aristotle, later sources say, believed that Thespis added the *prologue and speech to *choral performance, creating a new *genre. This may accurately represent the development of *drama from choral lyric (*see* DITHYRAMB), but attributing that development to one man probably owes more to the Greek love of finding causes than to fact. *See also* GREEK THEATRE, ANCIENT.   JMM

THIONG'O, NGUGI, WA (1938–)

Kenyan dramatist. Although better known as a novelist, Thiong'o has had an influential drama career. In the early 1960s at Makerere University he wrote, produced, and *published a *melodrama, *Black Hermit*, and several short *realistic plays. In 1975 he co-authored with Micere *Mugo an epic, nationalist play, *The Trial of Dedan Kimathi*. One of the first Kenyan productions at the National Theatre in Nairobi, it reached an even wider *audience through travelling theatre performances in Kiswahili. In 1976 Thiong'o, invited along with his

cousin Ngugi wa *Mirii to write a play for the Kamariithu Community Educational and Cultural Centre (KCECC), created *Ngaahiika Ndeenda* (*I Will Marry When I Want*), a popular, class-conscious attack on neocolonialism. The play's licence for performance was withdrawn and Thiong'o jailed without trial (*see* CENSORSHIP). The experience made him realize the need to work closely with subaltern classes and through indigenous languages and cultures. After his release in 1978 he returned to KCECC but the resultant play, *Maitu Njugira* (*Mother Weep for Me*), was refused a licence. Controversial *rehearsals in 1982 provoked the Kenyan government into destroying Kamariithu Theatre and Thiong'o fled into exile. He continued to advocate anti-imperialist literature and theatre in African languages through such polemical essay collections as *Decolonising the Mind* (1986) and *Moving the Centre* (1993). *See also* POST-COLONIAL STUDIES.   DaK

THIYAM, RATAN (1948–)

*Artistic director of Chorus Repertory Theatre in Imphal, *Manipur. As *India's most internationally recognized director with considerable exposure within the subcontinent, Thiyam is known for his visually spectacular productions that reflect the state of global and national violence through a *modernist reading of the epics. At least three of his major productions—*Urubhanga* (1981), *Chakravyuha* (1984), and *Karnabhara* (1991)—deal with critical events from the *Mahabharata*, within which Thiyam has attempted to trace historical affinities to contemporary Manipur, a military state ridden with insurgency and intertribal conflicts. The search for peace has taken Thiyam beyond polemical productions on corruption and civic decay like *Imphal Imphal* and *Imphal Karusi*, towards more meditative reflections on violence, like Dharamvir *Bharati's *Andha Yug* (*The Blind Age*) and Agneya's Hindi poem *Uttarapriyadarshi*. Elaborating on this poem in a highly layered and *surreal *mise-en-scène, Thiyam's production depicted the aftermath of the Kalinga war in which the Emperor Ashoka (Priyadarshi) survives a nightmarish vision of hell to embrace the eightfold path of the Buddha. The hell was contemporary, made up of modern instruments of torture and human limbs cooked in the kitchen of a five-star hotel, a metaphoric evocation of Manipur today. While some critics regard Thiyam's productions as export-quality *spectacles, which decontextualize martial arts traditions like *thang-ta* for sensational effects, others claim he is reinventing tradition meaningfully. Based in Manipur, where his actors live together on a 1-hectare (2-acre) farm, Thiyam is nonetheless strongly linked to the international *festival circuit and to the cultural agencies of the Indian state. In 1987–8 he served a brief term as the director of the *National School of Drama in New Delhi, where, between 1974 and 1977, he had been exposed as a student to the professionalism of theatre by his mentor, Ebrahim *Alkazi.   RB

(continued on p. 1361)

THEORIES OF DRAMA, THEATRE, AND PERFORMANCE

Although *performance as a type of human activity unquestionably dates far back beyond any historical records (*see* ORIGINS OF THEATRE), *drama and *theatre possess at least relatively clear historical records, though these have come down to us with a certain mixture of legend and myth. In each of the world's three major classic theatre traditions, the classic *Greek theatre, the Sanskrit theatre of *India, and the *nō theatre of *Japan, theoretical writings about this art form appear virtually from the beginnings of the art form itself.

From the classic Greek stage indeed we have one important work which is both drama and theory, *Aristophanes' *Frogs* (405 BC), which includes extended critical commentary on as well as *parodies of the major Greek tragic dramatists who were the author's contemporaries. The major theoretical work in the Greek tradition, however, was the *Poetics* of *Aristotle (384–322 BC), which has served from the *early modern period onward as the grounding work of theatrical theory in the West. Aside from Aristotle, the most influential Western theorist from the classic period was the Roman author *Horace, whose famous formulation of the purpose of poetry, 'to delight and to instruct', added to dramatic theory a dimension of social utility that was often repeated in subsequent theory. The major concepts and lines of argument in Aristotle and Horace set the pattern for much subsequent theory, which generally followed them in dividing the drama into distinct *genres, particularly into *comedy and *tragedy, and in privileging the latter as the superior form, with a particular pattern of *action, type of *hero, and anticipated effect. Perhaps most significant was their emphasis upon the poetic *text, with almost no commentary upon the production of that text in the theatre, an emphasis maintained in Western dramatic theory until quite recently.

Classic Asian dramatic theory is very different in orientation. The key work of Sanskrit poetics, the *Natyasastra* of *Bharata, even in the badly preserved form which has survived, is vastly longer and more comprehensive than the *Poetics* of Aristotle, dealing not only with different types of play and elements of their construction, but with the architecture of the theatre, its *scenery (*see* SCENOGRAPHY), the *costumes, *make-up, and *properties of the *actors, their movements, gestures, and modes of delivery, the *casting of roles, the use of *dance and *music, and the arrangement of emotions and sentiments. Bharata dominated Sanskrit poetics to perhaps even a greater extent than Aristotle did those of the West. The first well-preserved treatises and commentaries on the *Natyasastra* come (as for Aristotle) from long after its writing, but from the ninth century until the seventeenth it remained the bedrock of Indian dramatic theory. Many commentators stressed its literary concerns, but the comprehensive scope of the *Natyasastra* provided Indian poetics with an interest in all aspects of theatre largely lacking in Western theory.

The drama theory of Japan provides an even sharper contrast to the Western tradition, since its focus is not at all on the literary and poetic drama but upon the work of the actor. The two major theoretical traditions are the *geidan* (artistic words), which together with the secret oral *hiden* have been handed down within the acting profession, and the *hyōbanki* (critical writings), discussing the actors from the spectator's point of view. The first great dramatic theorist of Japan was also its first great dramatist, *Zeami, the founder of the classic nō theatre. The works of Zeami and his followers on nō have parallels in each of the other traditional Japanese forms, the writings of Okura Toraakira on *kyogen, those of *Chikamatsu Monzaemon on the *puppet theatre (*bunraku), and the four-volume collection of *geiden*, *The Actors' Analects*, on *kabuki, edited by Hachimonjiya Jishō II in 1776.

The *medieval period in the West generated very little in the way of dramatic theory, but there was a great flowering of such writing in the Renaissance, led by the Italians Francesco Robortello, Julius Caesar Scaliger, and Lodovico *Castelvetro, all of whom wrote extensive commentaries on Aristotle, reinterpreted according to their own interests and experience. Their writings formed the basis of *neoclassical dramatic theory, represented by such theorists as Sir Philip *Sidney and Ben *Jonson in England and François d'*Aubignac and Nicholas *Boileau in France. The title of Sidney's work, *A Defense of Poesy* (1595), indicates another continuing concern of dramatic theorists, countering the ongoing suspicion of theatre (*see* ANTITHEATRICAL POLEMIC) in the West comprehensively discussed in Jonas Barish's excellent study *The Antitheatrical Prejudice* (1981).

The neoclassical tradition, which dominated European dramatic theory and practice until the coming of *romanticism at the beginning of the nineteenth century, emphasized the strict separation of genres, the elevation of tragedy (in both subject matter and poetic form), a consistent tonality within each work, and adherence to the famous 'three *unities'. The unity of time required action limited in scope, preferably to a single day or less; the unity of space required a single setting or at least an action confined to a limited area; the unity of action forbade subplots or auxiliary centres of interest within the play. For most of Europe, the most familiar articulation of these neoclassical principles was Boileau's *Art poétique* (1674).

On the whole the dramatists most successful in following these regulations were the French, with *Racine as the most praised example, and the dramatic theory and practice of France provided the model for most of Europe in the seventeenth and early eighteenth centuries. By the middle of the eighteenth century, however, a certain uneasiness with the strict regulations of the neoclassical tradition could be detected even in the leading theorists working in that tradition, Gotthold *Lessing in Germany, Samuel *Johnson in England, and even *Voltaire in France. For each of these writers, although in the case of Voltaire with profound ambivalence, the example of Shakespeare provided the most powerful challenge to neoclassicism's insistence upon the traditional unities and the strict adherence to genre and tonality.

The practices and assumptions of neoclassical drama were also eroded during this century by a drama reflecting the values, concerns, and tastes of an increasingly important bourgeois public. A new emotionality entered comedy, resulting in the sentimental comedy championed by Richard *Steele, and an emphasis on moral values, represented by John *Dennis's concept of 'poetic justice', so changed the view of serious drama that even the tragedies of Shakespeare were altered so that evil was clearly punished and good rewarded. Theorists and dramatists like George *Lillo in England, Lessing in Germany, and Denis *Diderot in France called for a drama in which middle-class heroes in realistic situations would replace the elevated kings and heroes of classic tragedy (*see* BOURGEOIS THEATRE; DRAME, LE).

The other significant development in eighteenth-century European theory was the appearance of a tradition of performance-oriented theory, opening at last an aspect of critical discourse on theatre that had been present in Asian theory from the beginning. The eighteenth century is sometimes called the age of actors, and the appearance of well-known and highly admired actors in a number of European countries during this period doubtless inspired the application of theoretical tools to this art. The most famous actor of the era, David *Garrick, was himself the author of one of the first such treatises in 1744, and he did much to inspire subsequent writings, including the most famous of the century, Diderot's *Paradox of the Actor* (written about 1773).

Although literary romanticism began in England and Germany, in dramatic theory the Germans dominated the early years of the movement, and the writings of August *Schlegel were particularly influential. Against the neoclassical goals of unity and harmony, Schlegel championed a romantic vision delighting in the mixing of seemingly disharmonious, even contradictory elements, united in a single work not by mechanical means but by a more natural and spiritual apprehension, organic unity, a product of nature and genius as opposed to the art and artifice of neoclassicism. The resistance to romantic theory

was most pronounced in France, long the centre of neoclassicism, but eventually the new approach, championed among others by Stendhal and by Victor *Hugo in the preface to his play *Cromwell* (1827), triumphed there also.

Although romanticism rejected the rigid genre distinctions of neoclassicism, opening the way to the plays of mixed tonality that are typical of the modern theatre, the German romantic theorists also produced a remarkable body of writing upon the traditional genres of comedy and especially tragedy. The writings of Schlegel, Arthur Schopenhauer, G. W. F. Hegel, Friedrich *Hebbel and Friedrich Nietzsche, taking the theory of tragedy into the new directions opened by the German philosophic tradition, maintained that genre in the central position it had held since Aristotle.

Although the realist dramatists and theorists of the later nineteenth century tended to define themselves in opposition to the romantics, they in fact shared many of the same concerns, including an interest in mixed genres, local colour, and the historical context of the work. This latter concern fitted particularly well with the scientific spirit of such early realists as Hippolyte Taine and Émile *Zola. This spirit, however, led *realism away from the metaphysical concerns of romanticism to seek an apparently objective observation of the actions of everyday reality, what theorist Jean Jullien called a 'slice of life'.

Realism became, in the theory and practice of the late nineteenth and much of the twentieth century theatre, the new classicism, against which a whole series of new, more subjective and abstract romanticisms would react. The first such reaction was *symbolism, looking back to the German romantic tradition primarily through the work of Richard *Wagner. The interest of the symbolist on sensual impressions rather than discursive thought gave new impetus to theorizing about the non-discursive elements of the theatre, and thus other theatre arts, besides those of the dramatist and the actor, began to receive theoretical attention. Adolphe *Appia, inspired by the challenge of creating proper visual settings for Wagner, wrote the first major Western theatre treatise devoted to theatre scenery and space (*see* SCENOGRAPHY) and to the function of *light in relation to both. Sharing Appia's influence was another theorist and stage designer, Edward Gordon *Craig, who broke even more sharply with the literary tradition of the theatre and championed in both theory and practice a separate art of the stage, where the controlling artist would be not the *playwright but the *director, thus anticipating one of the major developments of the twentieth-century theatre.

During the first half of the twentieth century a series of *avant-garde reactions to realism appeared, each accompanied by its own body of theoretical speculation which often rivalled the work itself in its effect. First came Italian *futurism, dedicated to speed, technology, and the violent overthrow of established forms and works. Its founder and chief theorist was Filippo *Marinetti. The related *dadaists, headed by Tristan

Tzara, were even more anarchistic, while the *surrealists, whose critical spokesman was Guillaume Apollinaire, pursued a more positive programme, seeking a deeper truth behind surface reality. The Russian futurists, like Vladimir *Mayakovsky, had much more in common with this surrealist goal than with those of Italian futurism. Yet another anti-realistic direction was suggested by the Polish artist and theorist Stanisław *Witkiewicz, who called for a theatre of 'pure form', the performance equivalent of abstract painting.

The metaphysical strain found in surrealism and Russian futurism provided one of the major theoretical orientations developed during the twentieth century as a reaction to the dominance of realism. From the surrealist movement came Antonin *Artaud. Though he died in 1948, Artaud emerged in the 1950s through his book *The Theatre and its Double* as one of the most influential theorists of the century, his rejection of discursive language echoing the symbolists and surrealists, and his quest for the turbulent heart of existence echoing German romanticism. The interest in an ecstatic theatre that inspired such major theorists and directors of the 1960s and 1970s as Jerzy *Grotowski and Peter *Brook owed much to the writings of Artaud.

Artaud's major theoretical rival for influence in the late twentieth-century theatre was Bertolt *Brecht, who countered the metaphysical concern of Artaud with a central interest in the theatre as an instrument of social and *political action. Dramatic theorists from the Renaissance onward had touched upon the political use of theatre, but almost invariably as an instrument in the service of making spectators better citizens. Romanticism, with its interest in challenging existing systems, saw theatre as an instrument of this endeavour, and so theorists and artists like Victor Hugo and Richard Wagner specifically linked their artistic experiments to political revolutions. During the nineteenth century the relationship between art and its surrounding society was stressed by the Russian civic critics like Nikolai Chernyshevsky and positivists like Hippolyte Taine, and social commentary and critique became one of the central concerns of the developing realist theatre as may be seen, for example, in the plays and theoretical essays of George Bernard *Shaw. The tie between realism and socially engaged drama, in both theory and practice, was most firmly established in Soviet Russia, where in 1932 Stalin declared *'socialist realism' to be the official artistic standard of the state.

A struggle had been going on in Russia since the beginning of the revolution between artists and theorists, who agreed about a close relationship between the theatre and revolution but who disagreed about its implementation. In the early years of the revolution the leading figures in this debate were Konstantin *Stanislavsky and Vsevolod *Meyerhold. Stanislavsky, whose theoretical writings on the art of acting would dominate that field for much of the twentieth century, was strongly committed, especially in his early years, to the doctrine of real-

ism, and in his later years was enshrined by the state as a champion of that favoured approach. Meyerhold, much influenced by symbolist thought, felt that a revolutionary new society required a revolutionary new theatre, a position that led him into direct conflict with Stalin's artistic doctrine and eventually to his arrest and execution in 1940.

A variation of this same struggle was played out in the 1930s when Brecht, the most influential political dramatist of the century, championed in his plays and theory a proudly anti-realistic socialist theatre to which he gave the name *'epic', referring to Aristotle's distinction between epic and dramatic narratives and claiming a new approach that rejected not only conventional realism, but the whole dramatic tradition since the Greek theorist. Not surprisingly, Brecht's rejection of realism was in turn attacked by more traditional socialist theorists, most notably Georg Lukács, and for most of his career Brecht maintained a precarious balance politically and personally between a West which regarded him, especially during the years of the Cold War, as a covert communist, and an East which distrusted his Western interest in artistic experimentation. His theories and practice were, however, widely influential on both sides of the Iron Curtain.

The conflict between social and metaphysical theory, in various forms, has fuelled much debate within dramatic theory during the twentieth century. Jean-Louis *Barrault, the noted French director, is reported to have remarked during the 1950s that the theatre of the future 'would have to choose between Brecht and Artaud', and many theorists and practitioners at mid-century saw the theatre in just those bipolar terms. There were, of course, other theoretical alternatives in the increasingly complex world of twentieth-century intellectual speculation, and at least one approach, dating back to Artistotle, continued to produce a body of theory as extensive and significant as either metaphysical or social theory. This was the tradition of formal criticism, receiving new impetus in the late nineteenth century when scientific analysis was applied not only to playwriting by *naturalists like Zola, but to dramatic theory and play analysis by theorists such as Gustav *Freytag, who sought to discover the 'rules' of dramatic construction by empirical analysis of the world's great dramas, George Polti, who claimed to reduce all dramatic literature to 36 basic situations, and Ferdinand Brunetière, who attempted to make Schopenhauer's concept of the conflict of wills into a regularizing 'law of theatre'.

During the first half of the twentieth century, formal and social orientations dominated the dramatic theory of England and America, where Anglo-Saxon pragmatism and empiricism have traditionally discouraged metaphysical speculation. Brander *Matthews at Columbia University, the first professor of dramatic literature at an English-speaking university, provided a body of critical writing based on theorists like Freytag and Brunetière that was highly influential among American theorists in the early twentieth century. While Matthews insisted upon a close relationship between the written drama and its performance, an alternative theoretical tradition developed among American literary scholars that, in the name of a more rigorous formal analysis of texts, excluded all extraneous social and cultural concerns, including the conditions of physical performance. This was particularly the case with New Criticism, an approach which dominated American theory from the emergence of T. S. *Eliot just after the First World War until the work of Northrop Frye, W. K. Wimsatt, and Cleanth Brooks in the late 1950s. Like the earlier Russian formalists, the New Critics sought to discover specific rules that governed the operations of literary language by close study of the structure and operating principles of individual works. A similar attempt to create an approach to literary analysis based upon objective formal principles, in this case heavily under the influence of Aristotle, was undertaken by the Chicago School of criticism, which flourished in the middle years of the twentieth century, inspiring such works as Elder Olson's studies of comedy and tragedy.

Although the rise of romanticism and realism tended to discourage the theoretical study of particular genres, except for tragedy, the twentieth century's new interest in formal analysis brought with it a new interest in genre, so that book-length studies like Olsen's and major anthologies of critical writings now appeared not only on the hitherto comparatively neglected genre of comedy, but also on genres with even less academic credentials, such as *melodrama. Tragedy, however, remained as always the favoured genre for theoretical study. The highly influential Cambridge School of Anthropology in the early years of the century brought new perspectives to both tragedy in the work of Gilbert *Murray and comedy in that of F. M. Cornford by applying the insights of modern anthropological research to the study of Greek drama. Tragedy theorists of the 1920s like W. M. Dixon and F. L. Lucas still viewed this form as drama's highest achievement, but near the end of the decade Joseph Wood Krutch in America and Water Benjamin in Germany argued from rather different theoretical perspectives that the loss of a metaphysical centre and a belief in the human ability to apprehend this centre had made tragedy impossible in the modern world. This argument stimulated a lively debate over the possibility of tragedy in America during the next several decades, with the negative evaluation of Krutch carried into writings on the subject in the early 1960s by Murray Krieger and George Steiner and the possibility of modern tragedy defended both by professional theorists like Mark Harris and Francis Fergusson and by leading dramatists like Maxwell *Anderson and Arthur *Miller.

An alternative to this debate was proposed in the 1950s by the Swiss dramatist Friedrich *Dürrenmatt, who, while agreeing that pure tragedy was no longer possible, suggested that an equivalent depth of expression more suitable to the modern consciousness was available through comedy, particularly a dark comedy that approached tragic depths through the *grotesque.

During the 1960s a number of theorists produced studies of this significant modern genre, called 'dark comedy' by J. L. Styan and modern *tragicomedy by Karl Guthkie.

The most important development in formal theory in the later twentieth century was the rise of *semiotics, which launched, first in Europe and then in America, a revolution in theoretical practice. It became the grounding for a formidable expansion of theoretical work, initiating what was often called an 'age of theory' in both literary and *theatre studies. Semiotics, the study of the nature and functions of signs in human culture, is closely related to philosophical study and as such can be traced back to Greek thought, but the modern European and American development of this approach was essentially inspired by the pioneering work of the Swiss linguist Ferdinand de Saussure and the American philosopher Charles Sanders Peirce. The first systematic development of semiotic analysis was undertaken by the group of Czech scholars known as the Prague Linguistic Circle in the 1920s and 1930s. Theatre was a particular interest of several members of this group, but their work was not widely recognized until semiotics appeared later as a major international theoretical concern. After the Second World War semiotic analysis was applied first to literature, then to painting, music, and *film, but it was not until the late 1960s that it again became important in theatre theory. The lead this time was taken by French scholars, working in the tradition of modern French *structuralism and largely under the influence of literary and cultural theorists like Roland Barthes. For this reason most of the first modern works in theatre semiotics, unlike those of the earlier Prague School, were concerned primarily with analysis of the literary text, as may be seen in the work of Patrice Pavis, Anne Ubersfeld, and Kier Elam, author of the first book-length study of the subject in English, in 1980.

Politically oriented drama and theatrical theory were relatively uncommon in America after a wave of interest in the 1930s and 1940s, but these concerns dominated much of the theatrical culture in the late 1960s and early 1970s as a result of the Vietnam War and the social issues raised by unequal treatment of such groups as blacks, women, and *Chicanos. This period saw the emergence in *Latin America of one of the leading theorists of the century, Augusto *Boal, who built upon Brecht's work to create a distinctive theory and model of a theatre of commitment for the contemporary world. In North America, however, the theoretical writing of this period of political upheaval, by engaged writers like LeRoi Jones (who later took the name Amiri *Baraka) and Luis *Valdez, was on the whole of less importance than their dramas and political activities.

On the other hand, modern *feminism, which had important parallels to the struggle for equality and recognition in the *African-American community, became a major source of theoretical writing in all fields from the 1970s onward. As has been the case with many modern movements, the groundwork for feminist theory was laid in literary studies before being applied to theatre and performance. Feminist theory by the mid-1970s had become an important new area of interest in literary studies, and the early 1980s saw a number of feminist studies of Shakespeare, preparing the way for a more general application of feminist theory to theatre and drama, which first appeared near the end of this decade.

Since an important concern of feminist analysis was the process by which meanings are created in cultural products (such as Shakespeare's plays), semiotics provided an extremely important tool, and as feminist theory was being developed the field of semiotics was shifting in ways that would make it an even more useful tool for feminist analysis of the theatrical event. Instead of remaining focused on the written text, semioticians by the end of the 1970s were broadening their interest, first to look at the realization of the play on the stage, what Italian semiotician Marco de Marinis called the 'spectacle text', and then to consider the contributions of the *audience to the process, introducing the techniques and concerns of modern social analysis and *reception theory into the analytic process. Thus at the end of the 1980s Jean Alter and Fernando de Toro laid out principles of what they called a 'sociosemiotics' of theatre while Susan Bennett and Herbert *Blau in the 1990s devoted books entirely to studies of the audience.

Scarcely had semiotics become established as an important new approach to theoretical analysis, however, than it was challenged—most directly by deconstruction, the analytic approach brought into the international literary scene by French philosopher Jacques Derrida in the late 1960s and early 1970s. Deconstruction drew upon the same philosophical and linguistic roots as semiotics and structuralism, but sought to move beyond them by rejecting their tendency, typical of Western thought, to seek stable, self-authenticating, definite systems of meaning based upon some primary reality reflected in writing. In literary studies, deconstruction returned to the very close textual analysis that had characterized New Criticism, but with an almost opposite goal in mind, seeking the disjunctures and contradictions that disrupted the totalizing and unifying meanings sought by earlier generations of scholars.

As an analytic tool, deconstruction was far less important in theatre and drama theory than in literary analysis, but certain of the concerns that it introduced had enormous effect on subsequent writing in these fields. Artaud was a major target of Derrida's attack on a mystic fundamental unity as a source of meaning and plenitude. Artaud called for a theatre that would look beyond its thralldom to discourse and language to a more basic reality, the reality of true presence. As Elinor Fuchs noted in an important article in 1985, the avant-garde tradition in theatre, which had often, especially in the 1960s and 1970s, stressed the bodily presence of the actor, tended after Derrida to turn from presence to absence, destabilizing meanings and displacing the subject. This theoretical tension between an Artaudian metaphysics of presence and a Derridian metaphysics of absence has echoes in much late twentieth-century theatrical theory, which often provoked a skirmish between the structuralist and semiotic concept of theatre as a site of messages and meanings and a post-structuralist concept of performance as a site of desire. The first extended exploration of this tension occurred in writings of the 1980s by theorists like Josette Féral and Richard *Foreman, who asserted that performance served to deconstruct theatre's representational messages, opening the experience to unstructured flows of desire. The theorist who has been the most successful and influential in applying the concerns of post-structuralist theory to the theatre has been Blau, particularly in a series of books and articles appearing during the 1980s attempting to articulate the psychic origins of the theatrical act itself and the drives which sustain it.

A number of theorists during the 1980s saw the apparently irreconcilable differences between semioticians and post-structuralists as in fact involving an interest in two quite different but equally important aspects of the theatre experience. André Helbo, for example, suggested that theatre is a 'site of confrontation' between the voice, preoccupied with meaning and communication, and the body, the site of flows of pleasure and desire; it is an art equally devoted to signs and energies. Similarly in the United States, Bert O. States, although primarily interested in the phenomenological operations of theatre, saw these concerns as working in tandem with the operations of semiotics, and Jean Alter suggested that theorists should take a 'binocular view' of theatre, recognizing both its 'referential function', concerned with information and meaning, and its more phenomenological 'performant function', seeking to please or amaze an audience by a display of exceptional achievement.

Performance emerged as a major critical term in theatre theory during the 1970s and 1980s, particularly in America, from two quite different sources. On the one hand, in the wake of post-structuralism it was utilized by a variety of post-structuralist, semiotic, and phenomenological theorists to open an area of theoretical discourse about theatre that dealt with the experiential as opposed to the discursive side of the art; on the other hand, and more significantly, it was utilized by theorists interested in the social and cultural aspects of theatre. The most important of this latter group was Richard *Schechner, who early in the 1970s began to call for the study of performance rather than of theatre, performance being a much more inclusive term involving, in addition to traditional theatre, *sports, *ritual, *play, and any sort of public or private behaviour consciously produced to make an impression on an audience. For critical tools to analyse these phenomena Schechner looked to the social sciences, and under his influence theatre and performance theory, which had traditionally borrowed methods and critical terms from literary and art theory and from philosophy, now turned to the social sciences as well. Particularly important was anthropologist Victor Turner, who saw in the drama a model for certain recurring patterns of social action and who collaborated with Schechner, developing an interest in theatre theory as Schechner was developing one in anthropology. Turner's concept of theatre operating in a fluid, 'liminal' area where cultural meanings are formed or renegotiated was extremely influential on subsequent theorists, particularly as it reinforced the also popular notion of the *'carnivalesque' world of fluid cultural meanings seen as operative in art by Russian theorist Mikhail Bakhtin.

Another social scientist whose influence on the development of performance theory was considerable was the sociologist Erwin Goffman, who like Turner applied the metaphor of theatre to work in his own field, developing concepts that were in turn taken back into the field of theatre and performance theory by Schechner and others. Goffman's best known work considers the performative quality of everyday life, and this work not only encouraged performance theorists like Schechner to broaden considerably their domain of interest but also provided important critical methodologies for the analysis of performance of all types, as for example, the concept of the 'frame', the context of performance which allows an audience to recognize it as performance.

During the 1980s the increasing concern of semiotic theory with the role of the audience, and the rise of modern performance theory with its interest in the social and cultural placement of the performed act, both encouraged a greater attention to the entire social, cultural, and political positioning of the theatre event. Feminism emerged as an important new direction in theatre theory in 1988 with the publication of the first two book-length studies in this area, by Sue-Ellen Case and Jill Dolan. Both remarked on the wide range of possible theoretical approaches already being utilized in this field, which Dolan grouped under three general categories: liberal, cultural, and materialist feminisms. The first, seeking equal treatment for women artists under already established rules, has been extremely important politically, but less so theoretically, since it works within these already established critical assumptions. Cultural or radical feminism has sought a special, unique voice for women artists and audiences different from that developed within the predominantly male tradition. Rosemary K. Curb and Linda Walsh Jenkins sought a women's semiotic system, based on women's signs, while French feminist theory, closely allied with French post-structural thought, and particularly with the theory of the neo-Freudian Jacques Lacan and Julia Kristeva (see PSYCHOANALYTIC CRITICISM), sought to develop a specifically feminist theory and practice that would deny the logical and discursive language developed by a patriarchal tradition. Hélène *Cixous in France and Gerlind *Reinshagen in Germany pursued this goal as both dramatists and theorists.

Materialist feminism, which has produced the largest and most varied body of theatrical theory, emphasizes the social construction of gender, rather than the innate differences of women and men or the universals of humanity. Neo-Marxist

thought and the work of Brecht have been particularly useful to materialist theorists, as may be seen, for example, in the influential work of Elin Diamond, who has reworked Brecht's attack on Aristotelian mimesis in feminist terms. Materialist feminism has also opened theory and practice to previously silenced minorities within feminism itself, such as women of colour in the work, for example, of Yvonne Yarbro-Bejarno and Glenda Dickerson, and lesbians in the writings of, for example, Sue-Ellen Case and Kate Davy. Male homosexual theatre (see GAY THEATRE AND PERFORMANCE) has stimulated less theoretical discussion, but important contributions have been made by David Savran in his study of American drama in the 1940s and 1950s and David Román in more recent *performance art. Although she has written little directly concerning theatrical performance, the social theorist Judith Butler was extremely influential during the 1990s in the study of *gender and performance, in her argument that gender is not a given social or cultural attribute but is a category constructed through performance (*performativity) by which the subject enters the social domain. A central concern for gender and performance theorists after Butler was to develop strategies by which the subject could find alternatives to unsatisfactory performative roles.

The growing importance of performance theory in the late twentieth century opened an important new area of theoretical investigation dealing with the performing body. The century had already proven to be the most important in the Western tradition in terms of theoretical writing about acting, beginning with the great Russian pioneers Stanislavsky and Meyerhold, and continuing with some of the most influential theorists of the century, Brecht, Artaud, and *Grotowski, followed by a host of lesser but important writers on this art. The new concerns about performance further encouraged this interest, so that by the end of the century studies of the performing body rivalled and perhaps surpassed in number and importance more traditional studies of theatrical production. Aside from the many gender- or ethnic-oriented studies, theorists like Peggy Phelan, Philip Auslander, and Rebecca Schneider produced important new work on the performing body in general and its relationship to its audience and culture.

The theoretical interest in the social and political implications of performance also reflects a general trend in late twentieth-century theory toward the social and cultural contextualization of theatre. Once again literary studies opened the way, and Shakespeare provided the bridge by which this theoretical orientation entered theatre studies. The two leading schools of this new social orientation were British cultural materialism, led by Raymond Williams, who included the drama in his very broad range of cultural studies, and American new *historicism, a term coined by one of its leaders, Stephen Greenblatt, whose primary concern has been drama, and especially Shakespeare. Under the influence of these schools, and drawing upon a wide variety of neo-Marxist, anthropological, and social theorists, in particular the studies of social power by Michel Foucault, many theatre and performance theorists at the end of the twentieth century were studying how the theatre operated in relation to its surrounding culture, how it affirmed or subverted the values and assumptions of that culture, or how it negotiated relationships between different cultures. The multicultural and *intercultural operations of theatre in particular received new theoretical prominence. Significantly, both Patrice Pavis and Erika Fischer-Lichte, leaders of the field of theatre semiotics in France and Germany in the 1970s, published at the beginning of the 1990s collections of essays on interculturalism, and major new studies on this subject were contributed by, among others, Joseph Roach in America and Chistopher Balme in Germany. The increasingly rich and complex interaction of cultural traditions around the globe as the twenty-first century began suggested that theoretical studies of this type will surely play a more and more important role in theatre theory in the years to come. *See also* HISTORIOGRAPHY; MATERIALIST CRITICISM; MODERNISM AND POSTMODERNISM; MYTH STUDIES; POST-COLONIAL STUDIES; QUEER THEORY.

MC

BARISH, JONAS, *The Antitheatrical Prejudice* (Berkeley, 1981)

CARLSON, MARVIN, *Theories of the Theatre* (Ithaca, NY, 1993)

CLARK, BARRETT H., *European Theories of the Drama* (New York, 1965)

DUKORE, BERNARD, *Dramatic Theory and Criticism from the Greeks to Grotowski* (New York, 1974)

GEROULD, DANIEL, *Theatre/Theory/Theatre: the major critical texts from Aristotle and Zeami to Soyinka and Havel* (New York, 2000)

THOMAS, AUGUSTUS (1857–1934)

American playwright. Born in St Louis, Thomas was, according to his autobiography, *Print of my Remembrance* (1922), drawn to the theatre from an early age. He read law and worked on the railway and as a journalist before becoming a playwright. His insistent focus on American themes was evident from *Alabama* (1891), his first original success, which deals with the reconciliation of an old Confederate and his nationalistic son. Subsequently, *In Mizzoura* (1893), *Arizona* (1900), and *Copperhead* (1918) revealed Thomas's talent for constructing compelling American *characters and drawing distinctly American locales. Thomas was also interested in topical themes, evident in *The Witching Hour* (1907), a study of the occult, and *As a Man Thinks* (1911), an examination of hypnotism. He also wrote *comedies, the best being *The Earl of Pawtucket* (1903). Thomas served for many years as president of the Society of American Dramatists.

GAR

THOMAS, BRANDON (1856–1914)

English actor, playwright, and songwriter. Thomas composed songs for the *music halls, acted in *farces, *comedies, *melodramas, and an occasional Shakespeare, and wrote a dozen or so popular plays, but he is best known for writing and starring in the amazingly successful farce *Charley's Aunt* (1892), which ran for four years in *London. Thomas revived it successfully in the following decade. The play was frequently performed by professional and *amateur companies in the twentieth century. Translated into several dozen languages, it has few to rival it in popularity.

TP

THOMAS, GERALD (1954–)

Brazilian director. A polemical figure in Brazilian theatre since his 1985 staging of *Quatro vezes Beckett* (*Four Times Beckett*, produced, like most of his work, in *São Paulo and *Rio), Thomas was born in Brazil of English-German parents, educated in Europe, and resides mainly in *New York. Epitomizing the *director as *auteur*, he has been both criticized and admired for his striking imagery and *metatheatrical productions. His work consistently refers to *operas and literary classics, *Beckett and Kafka being constants. He offers pastiches of quotations, psychoanalytical *dream images woven together by musical references, and autobiographical commentary (he refers to himself as a 'wandering Jew'). In the 1990s Thomas produced a series of *happenings and musical rave parties in Rio and São Paulo, and has since turned his attention to media critique. He returned to his favourite subject in *Esperando Beckett* (*Waiting for Beckett*, 2000), in which the incisive *television interviewer Maria Gabriela conducted a *'monologic' interview with Beckett, played by the immobile back of an 'actor-ghost'.

LHD

THOMPSON, JUDITH (1954–)

Canadian playwright. While at the National Theatre School, she realized that the *monologues she composed as *acting exercises indicated her true vocation. The materiality of the voice is the defining characteristic of her *dramaturgy. Her *characters are driven to speak by unconscious impulses; the border between conscious and unconscious is (in her words) a 'screen door'. Her plays have a surface *naturalism through which erupts language that is violently poetic, disorienting, and darkly comic. Likewise the past erupts into the present with hallucinatory intensity. Memory, one character says, is 'carved in the palm of my hand'. Religious imagery pervades her work: the presence of evil in the world is set against redemptive impulses. She has also written for *radio, *television, and *film. Her stage plays include *The Crackwalker* (1980), *White Biting Dog* (1984), *I Am Yours* (1987), *Lion in the Streets* (1990), *Sled* (1997), and *Perfect Pie* (2000).

RCN

THOMPSON, LYDIA (1836–1908)

English dancer and actress. Thompson had a successful career as a dancer and comic at the *Haymarket before travelling to the USA in 1868 at the head of her own company. Billed as the 'British Blondes', Thompson and company performed *Ixion; or, The Man at the Wheel*, a satirical *farce filled with jokes, impersonations, revealing *costumes, and suggestive *dances, based loosely on Greek mythology. Combining *parody with the leg show, she helped establish the *genre of *burlesque on the American stage; though considered risqué by many, her productions were extremely successful. In 1891 Thompson made her fifth and final US *tour. She continued to perform in *London until retiring in 1904.   PAD

THOMPSON, MERVYN (1935–92)

New Zealand director and playwright. Trained by Ngaio *Marsh, the working-class Thompson rebelled against her Anglocentrism and championed cultural nationalism of the left, both as an *artistic director (of Christchurch's Court Theatre and Wellington's Downstage) and as a charismatic university teacher and director. He was also a significant writer, notably of *documentary plays with music, including *O! Temperance!* (1972) on the temperance and women's suffrage movement, *Songs to Uncle Scrim* (1976) about the Depression, and *Songs to the Judges* (1980) championing Maori rights against a century of New Zealand colonial injustice. A passionate and controversial advocate of New Zealand plays, he was an outstanding developmental director for Greg *McGee, *Renée, and emerging women playwrights at national workshops in the 1980s. His vulnerably autobiographical plays, the *expressionist and *Brechtian *First Return* (1974) and his *one-person show *Passing Through* (1991), are moving retrospectives of three decades in New Zealand theatre.   DC

THORNDIKE, SYBIL (1882–1976)

English actress who worked first with Ben *Greet's company, and then at the *Gaiety Theatre, *Manchester. There she married Lewis *Casson in 1908, and acted, often under his direction, for the next 60 years. She played leading Shakespearian parts at the *Old Vic (1914–18), including Beatrice, Portia, and Imogen, and also Prince Hal and the Fool in *King Lear*. As an actress she was intense, intelligent, quick to take direction, somewhat androgynous in youth, with a deeply musical voice, and was capable of playing an amazing variety of strong parts, from Hecuba, Medea, and Candida to Mistress Quickly and the working-class *heroines of the Gaiety. She triumphed in *St Joan*, which *Shaw wrote for her (1922). She was a high Anglican and lifelong socialist, with a belief in the civilizing mission of theatre. In later life she took some character parts in *films and *television, and her distinctive voice was often heard in *radio plays. She was made a Dame of the British Empire in 1931.   EEC

THROCKMORTON, CLEON (1897–1965)

American scene and *lighting designer. A founding member of the *Provincetown Players in 1915, Throckmorton used simple materials and backlit silhouettes to create the haunting *expressionist environments for *O'Neill's *The Emperor Jones* (1920) and collaborated with Robert Edmond *Jones in designing O'Neill's *The Hairy Ape* (1922). Throckmorton provided *scenery for the *Group Theatre's first production—*The House of Connelly* (1931)—and became a major commercial designer. He designed 66 productions during the decade of the 1930s, ranging from the stifling Midwestern interiors for Sidney *Howard's *Alien Corn* (1933) to the elegantly simple unit set for the *Federal Theatre Project production of *Auden's poetic *dance and *choral *satire *The Dance of Death* (1936).   MAF

THRUST STAGE

A *stage surrounded on three sides by the *audience, with actor entrances chiefly through or along a back wall. The thrust was the primary stage of ancient, *medieval, and English and Spanish *early modern theatre. Permanent architectural features of the back wall are significant in the *dramaturgy of each place and period—the *Greek *ekkyklema, the balconies of the *Roman *scaenae frons, the Elizabethan *discovery space. The back wall or rear space of modern thrust staging is usually designed specifically for each production.   JB

TIAN HAN (T'IEN HAN) (1898–1968)

Chinese playwright. After six years in Japan, Tian returned to *China in 1922 and became an avid proponent of Western-style drama, giving it the now accepted name of *huajü in 1927. Apart from writing, translating, and critiquing new plays, he produced theatre work with his Nanguo She (South China Society) in *Shanghai, Nanjing, and Guangzhou. The performances included new *one-act plays (like his own *Death of a Famous Actor* in 1929) and translations ranging from the *Japanese new school (*shimpa) to European plays like *Wilde's *Salome*. He became a member of the Communist Party in 1931 and was actively involved in the left-wing dramatic movement. Some of his better-known *huajü plays of this period are *The Rainy Season* (1931), *The Moonlight Sonata* (1932), and *The Charming Ladies* (1947). He was a prominent figure in reforming traditional theatre, partly by writing new scripts for *jingju (Beijing opera) and regional forms. In 1949 he became president of the All-China Dramatists Association but continued to write influential work, including the Beijing operas *The White Snake* (1952) and *Xie

Yaohuan (1961), and the *huajü* play *Guan Hanqing* (1958).

SYL

TIBETAN THEATRE

Performance native to the Tibetan Autonomous Region in *China, as well as to Tibetan communities in western China and in *India, employs song, *dance, *dialogue, elaborate *costumes, and an instrumental *musical ensemble. At the start of the twenty-first century 'Tibetan theatre' is a hotly contested arena, as groups within the Tibetan Autonomous Region argue with Tibetans in exile over whose performances are more authentic. The Tibetan forms have roots in *religion and popular storytelling. Religious *ritual in Tibet has in itself always been highly theatrical: eleventh-century travellers described exorcism plays by *masked performers in which monks vanquished the minions of hell in ritual battles much like those seen at Tibetan temples today. These ritual battles, or echoes of them, are typical elements in the *prologues of contemporary Tibetan performances, which, after purifying the space, provide an outline of the *plot. The play proper often dramatizes events from Buddhist *sutras*, though love stories and historical romances are among the narratives shared with traditional storytellers. Performers were exclusively male until the modern period.

Tibetan theatre was not conceived as an entertainment for passive spectators but as part of social and religious life. Plays were performed on temple grounds or in other open spaces, and the *audience could on occasion be incorporated into the *action. The function of drama has been changing, however, both for residents of the Tibetan Autonomous Region and for the Tibetan community in exile. Within the Autonomous Region, the Chinese government attempted to use Tibetan theatre as it used local performance traditions everywhere in China, to make government policy palatable to the masses. This approach appears to have been roundly rejected, but Chinese performance styles have left their mark in the raised *stages that now separate audience from actors and in the enlargement of the orchestra to include the Western instruments that had already been incorporated into Chinese troupes. The government-sponsored Tibetan Troupe of the Autonomous Region performs in this style, and is criticized by exile organizations such as the Tibetan Institute of Performing Arts in Dharamsala, India. TIPA performances, however, infuse their own nationalist content into the dramas they perform. Within the Autonomous Region, smaller temple-based and *amateur troupes are said to be keeping older traditions alive. *See also* DIASPORA.

KC

TICKETS

The purchase of a ticket is generally required for admission to formal theatres. A piece of paper, stipulating the name of the show, the venue, the date and time of the performance, the price of admission, and (usually) the location of the seat represents the contract between the theatre and the spectator, a promise that the theatrical performance will take place and that the spectator will be admitted. Some tickets may provide more limited information and some may include rules of the performance (no photography permitted, no refunds or exchanges, and so on). The price of a ticket can vary according to the time of performance (a matinée may be less expensive than an evening performance), the location of the seat (the better the seat the more expensive), and the status of the *audience member (reductions may be available for students, children, seniors, and the un- or under-waged). A 'hot' ticket describes a ticket for a show that is hard to come by—a performance sold out for that night or for several nights, weeks, or months ahead. In this instance, theatre patrons may try to acquire tickets either through agencies, where a significant commission will be added to the published price, or through scalpers or touts found outside the theatre selling tickets, often at hugely inflated prices, in the hour or so before the performance. In most countries the scalping of tickets is illegal, but the practice is common when tickets are in high demand.

It is customary for theatres to assign a number of tickets for shows as complimentary. For opening night, 'comps' go to theatre reviewers so that a show will garner appropriate attention by the media. More generally, 'comps' go to members of the production as well as other key people (representatives from funding agencies, sponsors, donors). In eighteenth-century France, assignment of complimentary tickets became highly codified. Clause 57 of the *règlement* of 1757 prescribed six balcony seats in the Théâtre-Français (*see* Comédie-Française) for the playwright of a five-act play, fewer for a shorter play, during a play's first run. This was extended in 1774 to 60 free tickets for the first three shows and twenty for subsequent performances. *See also* BOX OFFICE.

SBe

TIECK, LUDWIG (1773–1853)

German playwright, critic, and translator. After studying theology and philology, Tieck moved to *Berlin in 1794 where he worked as a freelance writer. In 1799 he joined the early *romantics in Jena, including Novalis, A. W. *Schlegel, and F. Schlegel. During a visit to England in 1817 he gathered materials on the Elizabethan stage, an important event in a lifelong preoccupation with Shakespeare. In 1825 Tieck became *dramaturg at the Dresden Court Theatre and had a significant impact on its repertoire during the 1820s and 1830s, with productions of Shakespeare, *Calderón, Lope de *Vega, *Kleist, and *Grillparzer. In 1843 he produced his legendary *A Midsummer Night's Dream* in Berlin, utilizing many features of the Elizabethan stage and accompanied by Mendelssohn's *music.

As a dramatist Tieck is the most influential German representative of romantic *comedy: his plays *Puss in Boots* (1797)

and *The World Upside Down* (1799) are distinguished by their
*parody of prevailing dramatic *genres and styles. Typical are
anti-*illusionistic devices such as a play-within-a-play with interaction between author, actors, and *audience. More intellectual
discussion than effective stage pieces, even at the time of writing Tieck's plays were ignored by the larger theatres in Germany, and have rarely been performed. Tieck was a tireless
theatre reformer, promulgating progressive ideas such as ensemble *acting and an abstract stage. Equally important are his
critical writings and translations of *Cervantes. He (and his
daughter Dorothea) helped to finish A. W. Schlegel's monumental translation of Shakespeare, which became the standard version in German-speaking lands.   CBB

TILLEMANS, WALTER (1932–)

Flemish director. Soon after his studies at the Studio Herman
Teirlinck in *Antwerp, Tillemans was employed by the Royal
Dutch Theatre (KNS) in the same city. His work has been
marked by a rough, popular style, social commitment, and a
sense of pure *theatricality. Convinced of the community value
of theatre, he was the first director to introduce an authentic
*Brechtian style in Flanders; notable *Brecht productions in the
1960s were *The Good Person of Setzuan*, *The Life of Galileo*, and
A Man's a Man, which he daringly transposed to Vietnam. He
has also been an important Shakespeare director, and in 1979 he
founded the Raamtheater in Antwerp which introduced writers
such as David *Mamet and Pavel Kohout.   JDV

TILLEY, VESTA (MATILDA POWLES) (1864–1952)

*Male impersonator and *music-hall artiste. Encouraged by her
father, Harry Ball, a musician and music-hall chairman, she
made her stage debut aged 3 or 4. Moving to Nottingham, the
precocious 'Great Little Tilley' performed at miners' galas and
pub music halls, wearing male *costume to sing songs written by
her father. She was always immaculately tailored, whether as a
'masher', soldier, or curate, playing on the pretensions of the
rising middle classes in carefully chosen songs such as 'The
Seaside Sultan' and 'The Afternoon Parade'. Best known for
'Burlington Bertie—the Boy with the Hyde Park Drawl' and
'Algy—the Piccadilly Johnnie with the Little Glass Eye', she married her own 'young swell', theatrical entrepreneur Walter de
Frece, in 1890. He became her *manager, furthering her career
on the music-hall and *variety stages, in *film, and in America.
                                                         AF

TIMONEDA, JOAN (c.1520–1583)

Spanish writer and publisher. An influential Valencian publisher, Timoneda used his workshop to print his own creative

work, narrative, poetic, and dramatic. Of his *comedias,
Amphitrion and *Menechmos* (both adaptations of *Plautus)
and *Cornelia* (inspired by *Ariosto) are the best known, though
Timoneda also experimented with other *genres, such as the
*entremés, the *farsa*, and the *auto sacramental*. The *autos* performed and *published in the 1550s and 1570s, with their lively
reworking of biblical themes and religious motifs, are generally
considered to be precursors of the *genre popularized in the
seventeenth century by *Calderón.   KG

TIPTON, JENNIFER (1937–)

American *lighting designer. Tipton set out to be a dancer but
an apprenticeship with lighting designer Tom Skelton in the
early 1960s led to a lifelong affiliation with choreographer Paul
Taylor and a career as one of the USA's busiest and most respected lighting designers for *dance, theatre, and *opera. She
has collaborated with many innovative choreographers and directors, including Twyla Tharp, Jerome *Robbins, Mikhail Bar-
yshnikov, Mark Lamos, Peter *Sellars, JoAnne *Akalaitis,
Elizabeth *LeCompte, and Robert *Wilson. Her designs are
noted for a subtle, cerebral, and sculptural quality that serves
the needs of the individual production without attracting undue
attention. At *Yale School of Drama since 1981, she is mentor to
a new generation of lighting designers. She is the recipient of
numerous *awards.   STC

TIRING HOUSE

The dressing room, or 'attiring house', in Shakespearian
theatres. It was a small space, where actors dressed and awaited
their cues. At a *playhouse like the *Globe, it occupied three or
five bays of the circle of twenty. All the actors had to keep their
clothing and *properties there ready for use. It was where all
backstage activity went on, including the noises 'within' of trumpets and drums. The company's special *costumes were stored
on the upper level.   AJG

TIRSO DE MOLINA (GABRIEL TÉLLEZ) (1579–1648)

Spanish dramatist. In 1600 he entered the Order of Mercy as a
novice, in whose ranks he would hold several posts and whose
history he would complete in 1639. But by 1610 he was also
known as a playwright, and in the early 1620s was Lope de
*Vega's outstanding rival. In 1625, however, a Committee for
Reform set up by Olivares required him to leave *Madrid and
write no more plays, and thereafter his output was small. He
nevertheless claimed in 1634 to have written over 400
*comedias, of which some 80 survive. Like Lope, whose innov-
ations he staunchly defended, he had a rather more comic than
tragic sense of life, but though he lacked Lope's spontaneity and

genius as a poet, his mindset was more intellectual and satirical and his outlook more broadly humane. Like Lope's, his plays are uneven, but their range is extremely wide. Whether he was truly more feminist than his coevals is debatable, but certainly he portrayed some strikingly strong and intelligent women, like the eponymous *Antona García* (c.1623) and *La gallega Mari-Hernández*, or Queen María de Molina, who personifies, in one of his many political *comedias*, *La prudencia en la mujer* (*Prudence in Woman*, c.1623). His reputation for psychological insight is similarly open to question, but his works are full of unusual *characters carefully portrayed, like David's son Amnon in *La venganza de Tamar* (c.1621–4), one of several *biblical plays.

Some of his finest works are urban *comedies, like *Marta la piadosa* (*Martha the Pious*, c.1615) or *Don Gil de las calzas verdes* (*Don Gil of the Green Breeches*, 1615); the latter exploits more ingeniously than any of its time the extremely popular *plot motif of the woman who regains her faithless lover by dint of deceit and *disguise. *El vergonzoso en Palacio* (*The Shy Man at Court*, 1609–13), remarkable for its multiplicity of interwoven plots, its exploitation of role play, and the characterization of one of its *heroines, the narcissistic Serafina, is by contrast a model of that other comic *genre, the *comedia palatina*.

His *religious plays include some notable *autos sacramentales*, but above all two *comedias* (though his authorship of both has been questioned) whose *protagonists merit the unusual fate of damnation. *El condenado por desconfiado* (*Damned for Despair*, c.1624), a powerfully visual drama, tells, in counterpoint with the tale of a double-dyed *villain who is ultimately saved, that of a doubt-driven hermit, whose paranoia is harrowingly portayed. By contrast, Don Juan Tenorio's fundamental error, in *El burlador de Sevilla* (*The Trickster of Seville*, c.1622), is that he can indulge an obsessive delight in deceit (a vice which almost his whole society shares), but indefinitely postpone the reckoning the Stone Guest eventually brings. Reworkings from *Molière to *Mozart to *Shaw have made his character and story a universal myth, very variously interpreted, but Tirso's seminal drama is in essence a dynamic, colourful sermon.   VFD

TOBY

Popular *character from American *tent shows. Usually portrayed as a gap-toothed, red-haired, freckle-faced boy, Toby was a stereotypical country bumpkin much beloved by rural *audiences in the late nineteenth and early twentieth centuries. Invariably slow-witted and bumbling, he managed to resolve impossible *plot complications despite himself, usually by uncovering some long-lost treasure or property at the end. The figure may well have derived from the earlier 'Yankee' *character. Tradition holds that Fred Wilson solidified the features of the role before 1910 while travelling the Midwest with Horace

Murphy's Comedians. Other notable Toby performers included Haley Sadler, Neil Schaffner, and Rose Melville, who portrayed a female version known as Suzy. Among the last troupes to perform traditional Toby shows was Hank Martin's Tent Show, based in Iowa during the Great Depression, and renowned for its use of Elviry, a female counterpart and comic love object.   PAD

TOILETS *see page 1366*

TOKYO (EDO)

*Japan's capital and largest city, situated on the central Pacific coast of Honshu Island, at the head of Tokyo Bay. Settlement dates back to about 10,000 BC, and a village called Edo (literally, 'Rivergate') appears in twelfth-century records. In 1590 the national military ruler, Toyotomi Hideyoshi (1536–98), ordered his chief vassal, Tokugawa Ieyasu (1542–1616), to relocate to Edo. When Ieyasu emerged supreme in Japan, taking the title of shogun in 1603, he established the national military government (shogunate) in Edo, which ruled the country from Edo Castle until 1867. These two and a half centuries are known as the Edo or Tokugawa Period. The Tokugawa shogunate required all of Japan's feudal lords (*daimyō*) to maintain palaces in Edo. *Daimyō* wives and heirs were obliged to live permanently in Edo and the *daimyō* themselves to reside there for alternate two-year periods. This residence policy sparked a century of unprecedented urban growth as commoners flocked to the city to provide goods and services for the large samurai population. By the early eighteenth century Edo was Japan's largest city, and by the nineteenth century one of the largest cities in the world. After 1700 Edo emerged as the nation's cultural centre, overtaking the great western metropolises of *Kyoto and *Osaka. In the performing arts, the Shogun and *daimyō* were the primary patrons of *nō and *kyōgen in the Tokugawa Period. The vast majority of nō/kyōgen performances were held at *daimyō* residences and were forbidden to commoners, but some 21 large-scale, four-to-fifteen-day-long subscription performances open to the public were held in Edo. Many men and women of the samurai and commoner classes studied nō singing and instruments as *amateurs.

The dominant form of drama in Edo was *kabuki, the pride of Edo commoners. The three or four licensed theatres presented dawn-to-dusk shows almost every day. The samurai presence in the city coloured the spirit of Edo kabuki. *Historical dramas, *Ichikawa Danjūrō's bravura *acting, and combative chivalrous townsmen populated the Edo kabuki stage. Kabuki became associated with the religious life of the city thanks to theatre *festivals and the *Danjūrōs' linking of Buddhist practice and kabuki. Numerous small theatres sprang up and temples and shrines sponsored theatres on their grounds. Small theatres

(continued on p. 1367)

TOILETS

Confine human beings in a particular place for more than an hour or two, especially if food and drink are available, and it is likely that some of them will need to urinate or excrete. Theatrical performances which can last for many hours can make the problem acute, and across the history of British theatre there have been a variety of solutions on offer. In ancient Rome, there is evidence that *audiences brought chamber pots to public entertainments, but there is no comparable evidence for *early modern theatres in *London. Spectators may have used a resource like Win Littlewit in Ben *Jonson's Bartholomew Fair, who, needing to urinate in the midst of the Fair, had to be helped out with 'a dripping-pan or an old kettle'. While members of the upper classes in their *boxes in eighteenth-century theatres might also have used chamber pots (especially since they used them in church, dining rooms, and drawing rooms), the rest of the audience probably urinated wherever they were seated or left the *playhouse, either to make use of corridors or stairs or the facilities available at nearby taverns, but risking thereby losing their place in an *auditorium without numbered seats. Certainly there is no sign of *managers or their architects at the time making any provision for audience conveniences.

The invention of the flushing water closet in 1596 by Sir John Harington had no immediate effect on public buildings, but the patent of 1775 spurred change. Flushing water closets are included in the 1778 plans for the *Haymarket; the first documented case of their installation, however, is at the Pantheon in 1793. In 1795–6, a plumber's bill indicates repairs to 21 water closets and nine urinals at *Drury Lane. Elsewhere, older practices persisted. The system of providing passes so that patrons could retreat to a public urinal, privy, or tavern then return to their seats was widely instituted, but abuses on the part of patrons and management were legion. In the *Theatre Royal Newcastle, a lead lining was ordered in 1837 for 'the Floor between the front seat and front of the Gallery . . . to prevent Nuisances', referring to the habit of theatregoers to urinate in situ and thereby not lose their place in the gallery on a crowded night.

In 1864 the *Lord Chamberlain acknowledged the importance of providing properly ventilated water closets and urinals on every tier of London theatres, but there was no way to enforce this. The Canterbury Hall, built in 1854, in 1893 still had neither toilets nor a system of passes to allow patrons to use the drained enclosure in the yard. In the 1890s, after performances at *Sadler's Wells an inspector 'found that there was hardly any place where some one or the other had not committed a nuis-

ance' in the theatre's vicinity, women urinating opposite Rosebery Avenue and dozens of men relieving themselves against the wall of the New River Company, despite the lessee's claim of ample urinal provision within the theatre.

Not even in the early 1900s could it be taken for granted that both sexes could be accommodated in all parts of the highly class-stratified theatres, never mind accommodated adequately in proportion to their numbers. At the Manor Theatre in Hackney, just one toilet for women and another for men plus two urinal stalls accommodated up to 680 patrons. Overall, the more expensive portions of auditoriums tended to be better provided in proportion to the number of their patrons, male and female. Access to toilets was often directly off the auditorium aisles, thus the segregation of one kind of *ticket holder from another was not just a matter of class stratification in viewing the performance, but also to ensure that when theatregoers withdrew to relieve themselves the classes did not mingle. The stench percolated freely back into the auditorium, but elite audiences seemed unconcerned as long as they breathed only their own kind's emanations.

In all likelihood, especially in the hot weather of summer or the sultry humidity that built up during a packed house even in midwinter, theatres reeked of more than just coal gas (see LIGHTING) and sweating humanity. At the large and prestigious *Covent Garden, which had at least some flushing water closets, the other privies were emptied only twice a year in the 1820s. At the Royal Lyceum Theatre in Macclesfield, the 'night soil' was removed at most once a year in the 1850s and 1860s. The wooden trough urinals or earthen-pit closets were gradually replaced by slate-lined facilities and water closets but these were often under-pressurized, had drains that were not trapped, sewers that did not drain, or sewers that were shared with noxious neighbours such as the slaughterhouse adjoining Marylebone Theatre in the 1860s. Cleanliness was the exception. By 1886, civic regulations at Exeter firmly stipulated that 'the several Lavatories and Urinals in the Theatre shall be properly and effectually cleansed once at least in each and every week during which the building is used for public performances', which gives an indication as to how often the task was performed before the ordinance. Annual inspections consistently complained that water, odour-neutralizing lime or zinc, and fresh air would benefit most of London's facilities.

At the end of the nineteenth century *Shaw complained about the interminable intervals in *Irving's productions, 'during which the women in the audience sat in silent boredom whilst the men wandered about the corridors and refreshment bars'. In Shaw's description men leave the auditorium—not least, though unstated, to smoke—and women remain, since middle-class women were assumed not to need lavatory facilities in public places like theatres and were trained from childhood to observe such proprieties.

The provision of WCs became a highly regulated matter in the twentieth century, with *gender needs and gender balance in the composition of the audience playing a major part. In the Greater London Council's 1968 technical regulations for 'Places of Public Entertainment', it was assumed that 'the public . . . consists of equal numbers of males and females' and, for an audience of 1,000, required two WCs and twenty urinals for men but only three WCs for women. Current advice in technical handbooks is more generous to women, though not to men, one manual recommending two WCs and ten urinals for men and eleven WCs for women, while another suggests two WCs and sixteen urinals for men and thirteen WCs for women. But current advice does nothing to alter the provision in earlier buildings and the consequential queues.

The needs of modern audiences can have effects on the plays themselves. When *Stoppard's *Travesties* was about to open in *New York, he found that the play had to be cut to accommodate the criterion of what he dubbed '"Broadway Bladder" (a term . . . which refers to the alleged need of a Broadway audience to urinate every 75 minutes)'. It was with the same thought in mind that a review of John *Barton's *Hamlet* for the *Royal Shakespeare Company (1980) noted that 'the RSC decided to give us two intervals instead of what had seemed to be becoming the statutory one. Without, I hope, betraying too much unseemly enthusiasm, may I say that even with a production as splendidly absorbing as this—"for this relief, much thanks".'

Stoppard was producing a non-gendered generalization: the 75-minute rule is not a need for all members of a Broadway audience but primarily for middle-aged men with prostate problems. For many women at almost any theatre, whenever it was built, the failure of architects to recognize the differences in the sexes and the time taken to use the toilet facilities means that the interval can usually be entirely taken up with standing in a queue for the lavatory. Darkened auditoriums and patterns of audience decorum also mean that people leaving during the performance will be seen as signally disruptive and may find it impossible to return to their seats until a suitable break. Modern anxieties about the body can thus produce significant and unwelcome tension in spectators' experience of a performance.

TCD/PDH

Davis, Tracy C., 'Filthy—nay—pestilential: sanitation and Victorian theatres', in Della Pollock (ed.), *Exceptional Spaces: essays in performance and history* (Chapel Hill, NC, 1998)

imitated kabuki to the extent allowed by legal restrictions and financial resources. Amateurs enthusiastically took up the arts of kabuki: *shamisen* playing and singing in various styles, *dance, and amateur theatricals. Throughout the period the shogunate sought to limit the power and prestige of kabuki, attempting to control theatre buildings, the sumptuousness of productions, the mixing of social classes at shows, and homosexual prostitution near the theatres. In 1840 the government ordered the kabuki theatres torn down and rebuilt in a distant north-eastern suburb, but the form continued to flourish. Other centres of entertainment in Edo included the Yoshiwara licensed brothel district and restaurant districts around the city where professional women entertainers played songs and danced for small groups of customers. *Puppet theatres were located near kabuki theatres. Sumo wrestling was the major spectator *sport of the period, with frequent public matches held at large arenas in temples from the 1780s.

In the Meiji Restoration of 1867 the shogunate was overthrown and the Emperor established his official residence in newly renamed Tokyo (Eastern Capital). The centre of Japan's political, cultural, and economic life, Tokyo was the birthplace of all of the new developments in theatre and performance from the Meiji Restoration until today. Freed from legal restrictions, theatres were built all over the city. In the early Meiji Period women's *gidayū* recitation and various storytelling arts enjoyed burgeoning popularity. In the 1890s *shimpa* challenged kabuki's popularity and the cinema was introduced to Tokyo. The 1,700-seat Imperial Theatre was built in 1911 to showcase kabuki and other performing arts. The European-inspired theatre reform movement that culminated in *shingeki* was centred at Waseda University and the *Tsukiji Little Theatre in Tokyo.

Tokyo and its performance life survived two major disasters—the Great Earthquake of 1923 and the devastating fire bombings of 1945—and today it is one of the great theatre cities of the world. Three national theatre complexes support performances of kabuki, *bunraku, nō/kyōgen, and contemporary drama. On any given day literally thousands of venues, great and small, offer live performances, from jazz ensembles to symphonies and *koto* recitals; from ballet to *buyō* and *butoh; from grand kabuki to Western-style plays and *musicals to hundreds of *avant-garde experimental performances in converted basements and warehouses; from professional sumo to professional baseball and soccer and myriad public matches between college sports teams; from cinemas to school recitals and karaoke bars.

LRK

TOLENTINO, AURELIO (1867–1915)

Filipino revolutionary writer. In 1896 Tolentino was an avid member of the Philippine revolutionary movement called the

Katipunan, headed by Andres Bonifacio. Throughout the revolution against Spain and the war against the American colonizers, Tolentino wrote articles for several revolutionary papers, and was in and out of jail for seditious activities. He produced a total of 69 literary works, most of them plays and novels written in three languages: Spanish, Tagalog, and Pampango. His most famous play—which earned him several incarcerations for sedition under the American regime—was *Kahapon, Ngayon at Bukas* (*Yesterday, Today, and Tomorrow*), a fierce *allegory on colonization and the revolutionary response. Among his other plays are *Bagong Cristo* (*The New Christ*), *Sumpaan* (*Oaths*), and *Dalawang Sarong Ginto* (*Two Golden Jugs*). RV

TOLLER, ERNST (1893–1939)

German playwright. One of the most influential exponents of *expressionism, Toller came to attention with his 1919 play *Die Wandlung* (translated as *Transfiguration*), a personal and general treatment of the transformation of German society from patriotism to pacifism during the First World War. His involvement with the abortive Munich Soviet Republic in 1919 led to five years in prison from 1919 to 1924. After his release Toller moved to *Berlin and, while avoiding direct political activism, channelled his radical socialist convictions into writing. His exile to the USA in 1933 led to depression, an increasing sense of failure, and finally to suicide. His plays revolve around a number of central concerns. The experiences of the war form the background of *Die Wandlung* and most notably *Hinkemann* (1923). Political activism is explored in almost all the plays in a variety of styles and settings, ranging from choral works performed by *amateur working-class actors to *scenarios for *mass performances and expressionist works featuring *dream sequences; heightened staccato speech rhythms and an episodic structure. Important plays include *Masse Mensch* (*Masses and Men*, 1920), in which *realistic scenes alternate with dream interludes in a debate on violence and left-wing *politics. *Die Maschinenstürmer* (*The Machine Wreckers*, 1922) deals with the Luddite revolt. *Hoppla, wir leben!* (*Hoppla, We're Alive!*, 1927) shows a cross-section of Berlin society; *Piscator's production featured a famous set with simultaneous playing areas. Despite his narrow ideological focus, Toller was one of the most significant playwrights of his time, epitomizing the politically committed dramatist. CBB

TOLSTOY, ALEKSEI (KONSTANTINOVICH) (1817–75)

Russian poet, novelist, and historical playwright. Well known in literary circles for his short stories, poetry, and a novel, he retired from the civil service in 1861 to concentrate on literary work. Several 'dramatic ballads' were followed by a trilogy of *historical dramas set in the late sixteenth century: *The Death of Ivan the Terrible* (1866), *Tsar Fyodor Ioannovich* (1868), and *Tsar Boris* (1870). Good contacts at court facilitated funding for the landmark première of the *Death of Ivan the Terrible* at the *Aleksandrinsky Theatre (*St Petersburg, 1867). Regarding the dramatist as central to the theatre, Tolstoy wanted to retain control of all aspects of performance. His lavish budget ensured that production standards were unusually high: historical *realism arrived on the Russian stage affecting *design, *costume, and *acting style. The other two plays were severely *censored for performance because of their implicit discussion of Russian autocracy. *Tsar Fyodor Ioannovich* premièred in 1898 (Petersburg), and was also the opening production of the *Moscow Art Theatre in 1898. A censored version of *Tsar Boris* (*Moscow, 1881) was followed by full versions at the Aleksandrinsky (1898) and the *Maly Theatre, Moscow (1899), and the first two parts of the trilogy were given new productions at MAT in 1927 and 1936 respectively. Tolstoy's final play, *The General*, set in thirteenth-century Novgorod, written in 1870, was performed posthumously at the Aleksandrinsky in 1877 and later received a notable production at the Maly (1918) in the new style brought by the revolution. CM

TOLSTOY, LEV (LEO) (1828–1910)

Russian novelist, dramatist, essayist, and moral educator. Count Tolstoy's best plays, written towards the last quarter of his life, are generally in a *naturalistic vein and have a *didactic slant. His views on drama and the theatre can be gleaned from his essay *What Is Art?* (1897–8), which identifies him as an early *socialist realist in that he believed art should be accessible to people in general and not just composed for an elite. He was particularly scathing about *opera and singled out *Wagner's *Ring* cycle, which he anatomized and anathematized in detail, as he did Shakespeare's *King Lear*, which he read in English and found to be incomprehensible and of little use to anybody. He famously said of *Chekhov's plays that they were bad, but not as bad as those of Shakespeare. Nevertheless he considered the drama 'probably the most influential province of art' and wrote sixteen plays, none of which is as memorable as *War and Peace* or *Anna Karenina* but at least two of which will probably survive, *The Power of Darkness* (1886) and *The Fruits of Enlightenment* (1889). The former was based on an actual case of murder of a newborn child by its peasant father who, racked by a guilty conscience, eventually made a public confession of his crime. It was banned from performance until 1895 (*see* CENSORSHIP). The latter was a *satire directed at the inability of the landowning class to understand the peasantry. By the time he wrote *The Fruits of Enlightenment*, Tolstoy had broken with the Orthodox Church and invented his own brand of Christianity based on peasant toil, non-resistance to evil, pacifism, and the simple life. He dressed himself in a peasant blouse and tried to give up his property which, as it included landed estates, was resisted by his family. His first play, *A Contaminated Family*, dates from as early as the 1860s, as does *The Nihilist*, performed in 1866, and he only resumed playwriting after a twenty-year gap with *The First Distiller* (1886), a comic fantasy on temperance themes based on his short story, 'The Imp and the Crust'. Most of his other plays were published posthumously, including *The Living Corpse* (1900), which exposes the laws governing marriage and divorce, and *The Light Shines in Darkness* (1900), a clearly autobiographical work about an aristocrat at odds with his family. *The Cause of It All* (1910) is another temperance play and, in featuring a worker, proved popular in Soviet times. A four-act play set in third-century Syria, *Peter the Baker*, appeared in 1918 and was staged the same year by *Meyerhold at the *Aleksandrinsky Theatre, *St Petersburg. Other noteworthy productions of Tolstoy's plays include the première of *The Fruits of Enlightenment*, with Vera *Komissarzhevskaya and directed by *Stanislavsky (1891), and the latter's revival of *The Power of Darkness*, in grimly naturalistic mode, at the *Moscow Art Theatre (1902).   NW

TOLU BOMMALATAM

Popular *shadow-puppet theatre form prevalent in Andhra Pradesh in south *India. Though its legendary origin takes it back to AD 200, reliable sources indicate that *tolu bommalatam* (leather-puppet performance) took its distinct shape during the sixteenth century. The *puppets are two-dimensional, translucent cut-outs with elaborate designs, made from processed goatskin. Each performance uses a large number of puppets, and sometimes several for a single *character. The puppeteers speak the *dialogue, provide *sound effects, and manipulate the articulated puppets with thin bamboo sticks. The *audience watches the colourful shadows of the puppets cast on a backlit white screen. A performance could last the entire night, with *plots normally derived from epics such as the *Ramayana* and the *Mahabharata*. The variants of this form are popular in parts of Karnataka and elsewhere in south India, and have obvious similarities to the shadow-puppet theatres of South-East Asia, such as the Indonesian *wayang kulit*. *See also* PUPPETRY IN INDIA.   KVA

TOMASHEFSKY, BORIS (c.1866–1939)

Ukrainian-American *Yiddish actor. Tomashefsky arrived in *New York in 1881, in possession of a melodious voice and good looks, and in 1882 participated in the first Yiddish performance in America, *The Witch* by Abraham *Goldfaden. Increasing competition forced him to play on the road beginning in 1893, where he became popular and began to write and compose for the stage. In Baltimore he met his actress wife Bessie (1873–1962), and in 1891 the Tomashefskys returned to New York, where he cultivated a career as the ultimate matinée idol of the Yiddish stage. Though he excelled in *musical comedy and *melodrama—he was said to have the best pair of legs on the Yiddish stage—he was also committed to a more serious repertoire in Yiddish adaptations of classics and in literary Yiddish drama.   EN

TOM SHOW

George L. *Aiken's adaptation of Harriet Beecher Stowe's 1851 novel *Uncle Tom's Cabin* appeared in Troy, New York, in 1852, and quickly became as sensationally popular as the novel. In various forms *Uncle Tom's Cabin* held the stage for the next 90 years, spawning a distinct *genre, the Tom show. *Touring groups, often playing in *tents and accompanied by a *parade and brass band, crossed North America, performing in tiny rural communities as well as in urban centres. Forty-nine Tom shows were on the road in 1879; by the end of the century, the number had reached nearly 450. Connections to the Stowe novel were often tenuous, but the *spectacle (Eliza crossing the ice; the bloodhounds) and sentimentality (Little Eva's death and apotheosis) remained intact. Although Tom shows lingered on until the 1940s, most had disbanded a decade early, under pressure from *radio, sound *films, and the Depression.   AW

TOPENG

Derived from two Old Javanese roots signifying 'to press against the face', the term *topeng* has described various forms of *masked *dance in Java, Bali (*see* INDONESIA), and even *Malaysia. Roving companies of masked players appear in administrative records by 850 in Java and 882 in Bali, though little is known of these early traditions. In Java and Malaysia, the term *wayang topeng* is now most frequently used to describe masked dance-dramas based on the romantic tales of Prince Panji, which, though set in earlier times, seem to have emanated from the Majapahit courts in eastern Java from the fourteenth to sixteenth centuries. In the several regional variants of this tradition, *characters present a continuum of human behaviour, from the extremely refined Panji to the lustful and crude Klana.

As Islam became the dominant religion of Java during the sixteenth century, performance *genres underwent radical conversions in style, often becoming more abstract and contemplative. The central Javanese courts of Surakarta and Yogyakarta maintained an active masked dance rivalry, while the regions of Sunda, Cirebon, Malang, and Madura all developed distinctive variations of *wayang topeng*, with a narrator (*dalang*) providing the *dialogue. Cirebon has a reputation for having the most refined and abstract tradition, unique in its extensive use of women as masked dancers. With the dissolution of the Majapahit kingdom, many members of its Hindu elite migrated to Bali, where masked dance genres continued to develop. The present tradition of *topeng* in Bali seems to have originated in the late seventeenth century and uses stories drawn from the *Babad Dalem*, or *Chronicles of the Kings*. These genealogical narratives relate struggles within the Majapahit Empire and between later Balinese principalities. As in Javanese *wayang topeng*, a continuum of human types is presented, with dance and storytelling accompanied by the distinctive gong-chime orchestras (*gamelan) of the region.

In the oldest form of Balinese *topeng* (*topeng pajegan*), one man portrays all the characters—alternating full-faced masks used for dancing with half-masks that allow greater scope for improvised storytelling and commentary. *Topeng pajegan* is commonly presented at temple anniversaries and at life-cycle events (tooth filings, marriages, cremations) celebrated by Balinese families; its performances end with a public offering. Near the end of the nineteenth century, it became more common to present *topeng* with troupes of players. The less sacred *topeng panca* (five-person *topeng*) encouraged more extensive comic byplay among the performers, as well as a more theatrical depiction of dramatic confrontations. More recently, the conventions of *topeng* have been combined with those of *arja to create *topeng prembon*. This popular syncretic form has given more scope to singing and has encouraged the inclusion of women as (non-masked) performers. JE

TORELLI, GIACOMO (1608–78)

Italian architect and stage designer, born to an aristocratic family in Fano on the Adriatic. He worked first of all in the early 1640s in Venice, where he left behind detailed illustrations of his work in what has been interpreted as an act of self-publicity. Invited by Cardinal Mazarin to France in 1645, he designed a number of *spectacles, *dances, and weddings under royal patronage, and also mounted productions of plays. He first of all repeated his design for Strozzi's *La finta pazza* (*The Counterfeit Madwoman*), first mounted in Venice in 1641: to conform to French royal taste it was performed with comic *ballet interludes. He was then involved in mounting the first *opera produced in *Paris: in collaboration with the composer Luigi Rossi, he helped mount the latter's *Orfeo* at the Palais Cardinal (later *Palais Royal) in 1647. Possibly influenced by *Sabbatini, he was known for his dramatic *special effects—flights through the air, sudden spectacular appearances, all the *illusionistic surprises of baroque theatre, which led to his being known in Paris as 'the miracle-worker' or the 'Great Sorcerer'. He staged *Molière's *Les Fâcheux* (*The Bores*) in 1661; but by this time the *Vigarani family had been summoned to Paris and were working to supplant him. Gaspare Vigarani burned all Torelli's sets from the *Petit-Bourbon in 1660, though the drawings survived and eventually reappeared in the entry 'Machines de Théâtre' in *Diderot's *Encyclopédie* (1772), indicating substantial continuing

influence in French theatre practice. Sent away from Paris, Torelli returned to his home town of Fano, where he enjoyed renewed success with an Italian public with whose tastes he had arguably always been more in tune. *See* SCENOGRAPHY.

RAA

TORONTO

The largest city in Canada and one of the most important theatre centres in the English-speaking world. It is home to the country's largest *opera, *ballet, and regional theatre companies, and its *audiences also support a wide range of smaller and *alternative theatre companies, large-scale *touring productions, locally produced commercial theatre, and many performances by universities and theatre *training programmes.

Toronto was founded in the 1790s as a British port garrison on Lake Ontario, and its earliest recorded performances were typical of such outposts: either *amateur theatricals or ragtag tours from the United States. As steamship and rail links grew, Victorian Toronto became an important stop for international stars such as Henry *Irving and Sarah *Bernhardt, and also served as a base for some Canadian touring companies. Although there were earlier temporary theatres, Toronto's first purpose-built *playhouse was the *Royal Lyceum (1848), squeezed awkwardly between storefronts on King Street; of the many others built between 1870 and 1910, only the *Royal Alexandra Theatre (1907) is still standing. The busiest years of American *vaudeville prompted another flurry of construction: a splendid example is the Elgin and Winter Garden complex on Yonge Street, a double-decker theatre built in 1913, derelict for many years but renovated in the 1980s.

By 1930, with the rise of *film and the onset of the Depression, professional theatre virtually disappeared in Canada, though touring productions at the Royal Alex remained a notable exception. Many amateur companies arose to take their place; in Toronto, the flagship of this movement was Hart House Theatre, a 500-seat state-of-the-art *'little theatre' that opened in 1919 in the University of Toronto. Hart House hosted many local and regional drama *festivals, including the Dominion Drama Festival, a national competition founded in 1932. In the 1940s, Hart House Theatre under resident director Robert Gill (1911–74) became an important training centre for a new generation of Canadian theatre professionals, so that when new theatres sprang up after the war there was a body of trained and experienced Canadians to supply the talent—and the audiences. The first of these companies in Toronto was the New Play Society, founded in 1946 by Mavor *Moore and his mother Dora Mavor Moore, who as a young woman had played leading roles in England with the Ben *Greet company. (Toronto's annual *awards for theatre excellence are named in her honour.) The city's other post-war companies included the Jupiter Theatre (1951–4) and the Crest Theatre (1953–66), while summer *stock companies such as the Straw Hat Players (founded 1948) and the Red Barn (founded 1949) entertained seasonal residents in 'cottage country' north of the city. When Tyrone *Guthrie came to Canada in 1953 to create the *Stratford Festival, he had no trouble *casting most of the roles from Canadian talent.

In 1960 a combination of civic and private interests built a new theatre dubbed the O'Keefe Centre (later renamed the Hummingbird Centre). The first production there was a try-out for the Broadway-bound *musical *Camelot*, but though the 3,200-seat *auditorium proved uncongenial for theatre production, it is still used heavily for opera, ballet, and touring concerts. Inspired by *New York's *Lincoln Center, the city then embarked on another project next door, the St Lawrence Centre for the Arts, for which a new resident company was created called Toronto Arts Productions (now the *Canadian Stage Company). By the time the St Lawrence Centre opened in 1970, however, a new small-theatre movement had begun. The most prominent of these companies were Theatre *Passe Muraille, the *Factory Theatre Lab, *Tarragon Theatre, and Toronto Free Theatre (later merged with Canadian Stage Company). Like their precursor Toronto Workshop Productions, all these alternative companies converted disused warehouses or church halls into well-equipped *studio theatres of 100 to 300 seats. Their success was due in part to finding a mandate that had not been well served by mainstream companies: the production of new Canadian plays. In the ensuing decade, a second wave of alternative companies explored other agendas: these included Nightwood Theatre, a *feminist company founded in 1978 by a women's *collective, and Buddies in Bad Times Theatre, founded by Sky Gilbert in 1979 to specialize in *gay and *lesbian themes.

While touring productions still visit Toronto, most commercial theatre is locally produced. The most successful of these *producers has been Ed Mirvish, a prominent local retailer who in 1963 purchased the Royal Alex to save it from demolition, then renovated it and initiated an eclectic subscription series that included both local and touring productions. In 1993 Mirvish Productions, by then run by his son David Mirvish, opened a new purpose-built theatre nearby, the Princess of Wales, for *long-running musicals such as *Beauty and the Beast* and *The Lion King*. The Mirvishes also expanded their Royal Alex subscription series into several other large downtown playhouses. Another commercial production company, Garth Drabinsky's Livent, created and exported original musicals such as *Ragtime* and *The Kiss of the Spider Woman* before collapsing from over-expansion. A new *repertory company called Soulpepper, founded in 1998 by a group of prominent Toronto actors, has brought summer classical theatre to Toronto, an activity previously the domain of the nearby Stratford Festival and *Shaw Festival. The variety of commercial offerings has attracted many tourists from Canada and the northern USA to the city as an alternative to Broadway. Such productions—along with the vital experimental and *performance art scene—

have shown that the work of Canadian artists and craftspeople is among the best in world theatre.   DWJ

JOHNSTON, DENIS W., *Up the Mainstream* (Toronto, 1991)
SADDLEMYER, ANN (ed.), *Early Stages* (Toronto, 1990)
—— and PLANT, RICHARD (eds.), *Later Stages* (Toronto, 1997)

TORONTO FREE THEATRE *See* CANADIAN STAGE COMPANY.

TORONTO WORKSHOP PRODUCTIONS

Important precursor to *Toronto's *alternative theatre movement. The *artistic director for almost all its history was George Luscombe (1926–99), a Canadian who trained with Joan *Littlewood in *London. The company's first home in 1959 was a 100-seat *arena theatre in an East End basement, where its first productions were *one-acts by *Chekhov and *García Lorca. Its first critical success was *Hey Rube!* (1961), a *collective piece about a ragtag group of *circus performers. In 1967 the company opened a new 300-seat arena in a former car showroom downtown and significantly expanded its production schedule. Its greatest success was *Ten Lost Years* (1974), based on an oral history of the Depression, which *toured extensively and was remounted several times. After Luscombe was replaced as artistic director in 1986, the company fell prey to conflicting interests, and it closed in 1989. A critical biography, Neil Carson's *Harlequin in Hogtown*, appeared in 1995.   DWJ

TORRE, GUILLERMO DE LA (1933–)

Argentinian designer. Torre is equally at home in *Buenos Aires's state-run, commercial, and independent theatres. Albeit rather conventional, his *award-winning *designs are highly regarded for their careful and complete attention to detail. He has taught design at the National School of Dramatic Art since 1969.   JGJ

TORRES, MIGUEL (c.1940–)

Colombian actor, playwright, poet, and director. In 1970 he founded the group El Local in *Bogotá, where he has remained director. Among its most popular productions are *El tunel que se come por la boca* (*The Tunnel That Is Eaten by its Mouth*, 1971), written by Alejandro Jorodowski, in which he used *Grotowski's techniques; *La cándida Eréndira* (*Innocent Eréndira*, 1977), an adaptation of the García Márquez novella using popular and regional theatre forms from La Guajira; *El círculo de tiza caucasiano*, a version of *Brecht's *The Caucasian Chalk Circle*; and *The Trial* (1991), an adaptation of Kafka's story through *Weiss. His play *La siempreviva* (*The Everlasting*), based on the 1985 government takeover of the Palace of Justice in the centre of Bogotá, was widely acclaimed by *critics and public. In 2000 Torres opened El Local's new *playhouse with his own *En carne propia* (*In one's Own Flesh*), which he also directed.   BJR

TORRES MOLINA, SUSANA (1946–)

Argentinian writer and director. Her most frequently staged plays emphasize role playing, from her first, *Strange Plaything* (1977), to the cross-gendered *. . . y a otra cosa mariposa* (*That's Enough of That*, 1981), which she directed after returning from political exile. Later works, inspired by *Japanese *butoh, *dance-theatre, and image-theatre, are more lyrical and improvisational. *Amantissima* (1988) explores mother–daughter relationships, and *Unio mystica* (1991) pioneered Argentine theatrical exploration of the effects of the AIDS epidemic.   JGJ

TORRES NAHARRO, BARTOLOMÉ DE
(c.1485–c.1530)

Spanish playwright. Ordained a priest in Italy and heavily influenced by Italian writers of the *early modern period, he was the author of a collection of comedies together with some poems and a theoretical treatise on *comedy, published as *Propalladia* (1517). The book was banned in 1559 and later republished in an expurgated form. The *Comedia Himenea* (*Hymeneal Comedy*), his best-known play, owes something to *Rojas's *La Celestina*. The earliest surviving 'cape and sword' (*capa y espada*) play on the theme of honour, it introduced such conventional Spanish *characters as the lover (*galán*), the lady (*dama*), and the comic servant (*gracioso*).   KG

TOTAL THEATRE

Term much used in the twentieth century to describe *performance that uses—or, more often, aspires to use—numerous artistic elements to create a powerful or overwhelming experience for the *audience. The urge to draw upon and exploit the totality of performative devices—*music, *dance, *acting, *scenography and the plastic arts, *costume, *masks, *lighting, *playhouse architecture, the configuration of the *stage and *auditorium, and spectator *environment—is particularly *modernist, rising from *Wagner's intention to produce a *Gesamtkunstwerk* or 'total work of art' in his music dramas (*see* OPERA) and *Craig's attempt to elevate the *director-designer into the prime artist of the theatre. The major *theoretical proponent of total theatre was *Artaud, who in the 1930s demanded that the stage abandon its logocentric history in favour of a theatre of *cruelty: a sensory, kinetic, and visceral strategy that would invoke the darker or Dionysiac side of human life. Artaud's influence, combined with the innovations of the theatre of the *absurd, led to major experiments in total theatre in the West in the 1960s.

Notable examples included the season of theatre of cruelty by *Brook with the *Royal Shakespeare Company in *London, especially his highly memorable production of *Weiss's *Marat/Sade* (1964); the *ritualistic work of *Schechner's *Dionysus in 69* with the *Performance Group in *New York and the *Living Theatre's *Paradise Now* (both 1968); and in *Paris, the *carnivalesque approach of *Barrault's *Rabelais* (1969) and of *Mnouchkine's *1789* with Théâtre du *Soleil (1970). Despite the radical politics of many of these groups, and the reliance by some of them on *collective creation, in important ways the movement has been chiefly aestheticist, standing in opposition to the clarity and simplicity demanded by earlier *political theatre movements of the century, exemplified in the *epic theatre of *Piscator and *Brecht. Postmodern examples of total theatre include a number of the large-scale operas of Robert *Wilson, such as *Einstein on the Beach* (music by Philip *Glass, 1976), the marathon *intercultural work of Brook (*The Mahabharata*, 1985) and Mnouchkine (*Les Atrides*, 1990–3), and the globalized *festival productions of Robert *Lepage (*The Seven Streams of the River Ota*, 1994).   DK

TOURING

Moving a show from one venue to another, generally over a planned route. Despite its tendency to move into permanent *playhouses, the acting profession is essentially mobile, requiring only 'two boards and a passion' for performance. We know that ancient *Greek actors journeyed widely throughout the Mediterranean under the protection of the *Artists of Dionysus, and professional players of all types in *medieval Europe lived a life of continuous travel. Within easy distance of any location there is a fixed population, of whom only some will be interested in seeing the performance. In a modern commercial setting, when the *long run is the economic norm (as opposed to *repertory playing), once the local *audience is exhausted the company must mount a new play if it wishes to stay in business. One way to evade this constraint is to tour, taking the production to fresh audiences. The decision to tour will probably be made on narrow but precisely calculated margins; for example, the effective addition of something like a 25 per cent greater population in the *New York area, due to the commuter railways, appears to have doomed the 'road' in the twentieth century, while nineteenth-century *managers calculated to the day when to pick up a show from a major city and tour it in the provinces.

When the decision to tour is not economic, it is often political: it might be wise to get away from the politically volatile capital, as French royalist actors (1791–5) and Jacobin actors did (1795–8), and theatre companies sometimes left *London for months to avoid association with endemic *rioting. Or touring might be a career move, as *Molière's company allowed the memory of its first disastrous *Paris performance to die, or as some

*Chinese companies would tour extensively while another company's actor was the Emperor's favourite. Technologies of transport are clearly relevant. The extension of the railways to most parts of Britain in the second half of the nineteenth century vastly increased the economic viability of theatrical touring, and rock shows at the start of the twenty-first century can tour extensively by relying on large motorized trucks that are effectively houses on wheels, which carry all the equipment needed and are comfortable for the performers.

Whatever the cause, touring has had profound effects upon the theatre. First and foremost, by broadening the scope of competition, it forces improvements in quality and the rapid transfer of artistic techniques and of technology. If the provinces receive tours, they become more capable, as provincial technicians and actors measure themselves by higher standards. Henry *Irving's first tours of the United States (1883–4), for example, had to travel with nearly every piece of equipment, but by the time of his last tours (1903–4) he could count on finding most of what he needed, and the technicians to operate it, in almost any large city. Even today, many young theatre technicians get their first look at new innovations by working as casual labour for touring *musicals or for rock concerts. Secondly, in many parts of the world, touring encouraged the emergence of professional theatre; the economic advantages of touring were enough to allow full-time performers to make a living and the professional theatres of many European and Asian nations have their origins in touring. Finally, touring has fostered a tradition of portability, reusability, and flexibility in theatrical equipment which persists to this day; much of the way that things are done backstage is predicated on the assumption that everything must be packed up and moved soon, whether this is true or not.

JB

TOURNAMENT

In the Middle Ages, the term referred to mock combat and specifically to cavalry combats between opposing groups of antagonists, but eventually it was used to refer to any meeting at which mock combats were held. In its fully developed form, the tournament might include various types of combat, including jousts between individuals, cavalry combats between groups, single combats with swords, and combats between individuals on foot. The medieval origins of the tournament are obscure, but it probably originated in France or Germany during the ninth or tenth centuries and spread from northern France in the twelfth century throughout Christendom. During its early development the warlike features of the original form of the tournament were radically altered by the restrictions imposed by religious and secular authorities, the introduction of various safety features, the addition of rules, the supervision by heralds, and the restriction of participants to those of high birth. An equally significant agent of change was the impact of chivalric

ideals. By the early thirteenth century, tournaments began to conform to the whole apparatus of courtly love, offering occasions for the display of individual gallantry, usually in supposed service to the knight's lady. Women consequently came to be accorded an important role as spectators and as presenters of prizes. Inevitably, the courtly and chivalric character of such occasions was matched by accompanying feasts, *dances, minstrelsy, and sumptuous *costumes. From a brutal form of mock warfare, the tournament thus developed into a courtly diversion and the means of bringing chivalric romance to life.

From the fourteenth century, the tournament, along with other court entertainments, served as a major instrument of political propaganda. As a regular part of the celebrations of coronations, knightings, dynastic marriages, and state visits, the tournament provided opportunities for extravagant *state display on a grand scale of power and magnificence. It became an agent of political policy, a means to impress foreign observers and a means to encourage the loyalty of both the nobility who participated and the common people who might be present for at least some of the *spectacle. Tournaments were not, however, the exclusive preserve of the court. They were often civic ventures (though never in England), and in the Low Countries and Germany they were frequently sponsored by jousting societies. As the tournament became established as a form of courtly entertainment, it was inevitable that mimetic elements should be introduced. Disguises (characters from Arthurian romance were favourite choices), speeches, music, scenic devices and locations, and complex *allegorical subject matter, often in imitation of literary romance, all played a role in the creation of events in which feats of arms often seem to have taken second place to the production of pageants and spectacles. At the same time, the venues for tournaments, once undefined tracts of land over which combatants would fight for an unspecified length of time, became fixed arenas, surrounded in many instances by specially erected staging for spectators. This might be multi-tiered in structure, and, in the case of the viewing stands for royalty and the nobility, it might be elaborately decorated and furnished. A cross between allegorical pageantry and heroic drama, tournaments became increasingly like a form of theatre, especially when a single controlling intelligence created a unified thematic and artistic design governing the entire event. Such sophistication is evident in the tournaments held at the courts of René d'Anjou and Philip the Good, Duke of Burgundy, in the fifteenth century. Close links between the Burgundian and English courts then contributed to the great spectacle tournaments held in England during the reigns of Edward IV, Henry VII, and Henry VIII, forging a tradition that continued up to the seventeenth century during the reigns of Elizabeth I and James I.

During the seventeenth century tournaments were largely superseded by other forms of court entertainment. They occurred sporadically during the eighteenth century (though not in England). In the nineteenth century revived interest in

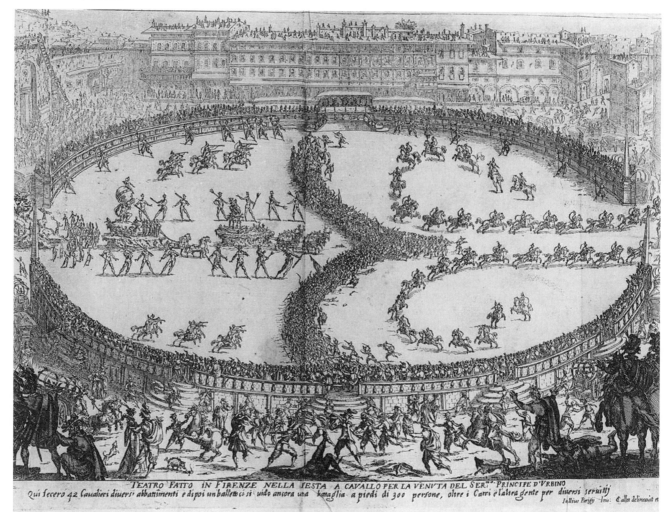

Magnificent **tournament** for the Duke of Urbino's visit to the Grand Duke of Tuscany in Florence, 1616, scenography by Giulio Parigi. The original caption claims that 42 horsemen and 300 persons on foot took part in this festival performance. The poetic text by Angelo Salvadori, with engravings by Jacques Callot, was published as *Guerra di belleza* in the year of the event.

the Middle Ages, together with the influence of Walter Scott's novels, helped keep the form alive. In the United States, ante-bellum southern culture, with its agrarian aristocracy of slave-owners, its love of horses, and its chivalric code of manners and related worship of women, gave rise to a number of tourna-ments. Since then tournaments have continued in Europe and elsewhere, though generally without their former literary and theatrical trappings, either as demonstrations of medieval com-bat or as pastimes presented at 'fayres' celebrating the Middle Ages or the Renaissance.   ARY

attributed to him in 1656. His only extant play is *The Atheist's Tragedy* (1609), an overtly Christian treatment of some common Jacobean *tragic themes: here, in contrast to Shakespeare's *Hamlet*, a murdered father's *ghost recommends that his son 'leave revenge unto the King of kings', and providence inter-venes to destroy the Machiavellian *villain at the very climax of his schemes. Despite this apparent ideological closure, the play can achieve considerable tragic power in performance; there was a notable revival at *Birmingham Repertory Theatre in 1994.   MJW

TOURNEUR, CYRIL (*c*.1575–1626)

English dramatist. His traditional reputation rests on a play he did not write, *Middleton's *The Revenger's Tragedy*, erroneously

TOVSTONOGOV, GEORGY (1915–89)

Soviet/Russian director. Appointed *artistic director of the Bol-shoi Drama Theatre in Leningrad (*St Petersburg) in 1957,

Tovstonogov merged the approaches of *Stanislavsky and *Meyerhold, mixing figurative stylization with psychological analysis. His productions sought a harmony of historical and contemporary meaning, the objective and the subjective, the political and the personal. Relying on cinematic devices to maintain narrative, his repertoire included contemporary and classical Russian plays as well as prose adaptations. A remarkable example was the version of *Tolstoy's *The Story of a Horse* (1975, directed with Mark *Rozovsky), which achieved wide international success. Set on a stage veiled in sackcloth, with *costumes of the same material, Tovstonogov interpreted the condition of the horse as a tragic metaphor for human life, creating at the same time an *allegory about how we deform nature by claiming it as property. His work tended to stay 'universal' or general rather than make explicit social criticism, echoing his neutral position in the *politics of Soviet theatre.

BB

TOWNSHIP MUSICALS

South African *musical theatre characterized by multilingual *dialogue, dynamic vocal and *physical theatre, which blends Western dramatic structure with township music and performance styles. In the 1920s and 1930s urban African communities in South Africa expanded rapidly. Slum yards became the focus of black recreational life and the 'shebeen society' of informal (and illegal) pubs became the centre for entertainment. Miners and contract workers brought African, Afro-Western, and Afrikaans *folk music together in a syncretic urban musical style called *marabi*, widely adopted by the working class. By the 1950s African-American performance culture had been identified with urban cultural autonomy, and Sophiatown was the black cultural centre. Other influential forms were *tsaba-tsaba*, a local adaptation of American jive; *kwela*, or penny-whistle players, which in turn fused into *mbaqanga*, the people's own jazz. Union Artists was established to protect the professional rights of black artists, and organized the African Music and Drama Association. Ian Bernhardt promoted the Township Jazz Concerts, which culminated in *King Kong* (1959). Influenced by that piece, Athol *Fugard's collaboration with the Serpent Players, and Alan Paton's *musical *Mkumbane*, Gibson *Kente revolutionized urban African popular theatre during the 1960s by incorporating gospel, jazz, and local music to create a syncretic *spectacle of township life in song and *dance. Sam Mhangwane and the Sea Pearls Drama Society produced these township musicals in Sowetan Tsotsitaal (a street slang), including *Crime Does Not Pay* (1963), *Unfaithful Woman* (1964, which *toured continuously for twelve years), *Blame Yourself* (1966), and *Thembi* (1978). Though the form is no longer vital, older examples are occasionally revived and new pieces written in a nostalgic mode.

YH

TOY THEATRE

In *London in 1811 William West issued sheets of engraved *characters from popular plays. By 1812 multiple sheets were on sale, together with *proscenium stage fronts and wooden stages. Sheets were plain or coloured and, once mounted on cardboard, the characters were cut out and fitted on slides. The pieces were performed in front of painted scenes, usually by children. West published 140 plays between 1811 and 1843, printing sheets etched on copper plates and employing carpenters to make the little stages. In the first half of the nineteenth century many firms were engaged in publishing plays or portraits and about 300 plays were published for toy theatre performance. After 1835 cheaper sheets were produced by Skelt, Green, and Pollock, the latter surviving in a small shop in Hoxton until the Second World War. A perennial favourite was the *melodrama *The Miller and his Men*. *Dickens refers to his fascination with toy theatres in *A Christmas Tree*, while Robert Louis Stevenson popularized the toy theatre in his essay 'A Penny Plain and Twopence Coloured', although some of his assertions are inaccurate. An interest in toy theatres developed on the Continent a little later than in England. Germany was especially prolific, its first major publisher of toy theatres being Winkelmann in *Berlin around 1830, and its last Schreiber, in business until 1939. Heavier in style than the English equivalents, the sheets were later lithographed in colour. In Austria, Trentsensky, established about 1840, was the outstanding publisher, producing some of the most imposing toy sets ever seen. Denmark developed toy theatre publications later in the nineteenth century, while toy theatres were also produced in Czechoslovakia, France, and Spain. For William *Archer the working of the toy theatre remained a mystery. He could not conceive how anyone could 'find pleasure in pasteboard figures'.

JTD

TRADE UNIONS, THEATRICAL

In most industrial nations, theatre is heavily unionized. For most backstage and technical unions, the pattern of unionization will depend upon the national pattern and the organization of the theatre. For example, in the United States, the dominance of the *Theatrical Syndicate and the *Shubert brothers' organization, and the predominance of craft unions in the early twentieth century, led to a structure of many small, narrowly focused unions active only in a few major theatrical cities: stagehands, electricians, carpenters, *painters, musicians, dressers, *ticket-sellers, movers, truck drivers, custodians, press agents, and ushers are all separately unionized. In Germany, the predominance of large state theatres and a stronger early model of industrial organization concentrated theatre workers into large umbrella organizations. British stagehands, within the federal structure of the Trades Union Congress, and facing many small operators in provincial cities, tend to participate actively in fragmented, locally democratic, and largely independent locals. French stagehands, facing an industry centred in *Paris with a few directly or indirectly subsidized giants, concentrate power at the national level and accept direction from above.

The core problem of artistic unions, notoriously, is that many people would like to do creative work even in poor conditions for very little pay or benefits. Consequently artists' labour organizations seek as much of a closed shop as possible to prevent a bidding-down of wages. At the same time, their memberships often include many people who do not see what they do as primarily an income-producing job, but as a profession. Thus member discomfort with industrial-style unionization dissipates much of the potential power of artists' unions.

This can be clearly seen in the history of British Actors' Equity, which began as an *actor-manager-led Actors' Association in 1891, intending to improve conditions in general and promote theatre, then split off an Actors' Union which excluded actor-managers and focused narrowly on wages and working conditions. The two remerged in 1910 in the face of mounting losses by both organizations, and resplit in the post-First World War prosperity, forming a Stage Guild that was essentially a benevolent association for the affluent actor, and an Actors' Association that was a kind of genteel craft union. Only an outbreak of appalling *management aggression, including the stranding of one distinguished company on the road in the late 1920s, finally pushed them back together to form British Actors' Equity, and even then the new organization did not seek TUC membership until 1940.

The real strength of any artists' organization is its few prominent members; only the willingness of top designers, directors, or actors to strike in support of unknowns exerts any pressure. The American Actors' Equity strikes of 1919 revealed this; where earlier organizations such as the White Rats had secured virtually no contracts, when prominent headliners walked offstage in mid-performance in a wildcat strike in August 1919, theatre management caved in on all points in less than a month. But the circumstances of that strike—a tradition of unpaid *rehearsals running many weeks, a management 'right to strand' a road company, added performances without added pay especially on holidays—were so egregious, and endured so far into even very successful careers, that, as one anonymous *chorus girl put it, 'If we can rehearse for half a year for no pay, we can strike for half a year if we need to, for the same wages.'

Since the Second World War, in the English-speaking countries auxiliary functions of labour unions have become more important. In the USA many teachers of design in university *training institutions hold a United Scenic Artists card not because they intend to work professionally but as a résumé booster. Both American and British Equity represent actors at many provincial houses only because the headliners are Equity

members; in effect the union becomes part of the certification process for quality. Unions promote a generally higher standard and have high entry barriers; a *producer who must hire a union actor in a bit part at three times the pay is apt to insist on a highly competent, experienced actor in even the smallest roles, thus raising the bar for everyone. At the start of the twenty-first century, to a great extent unions are a means of distributing the income the theatre earns in a way that ensures the continuing presence of an adequate supply of artists and craftspeople; labour relations in the theatre, while sometimes fractious day to day, are mostly harmonious because management and labour collude.   JB

TRAGEDY

Few plays called tragedies have been written for theatre performance since the two world wars and yet the word 'tragedy' is heard almost daily as real events are presented on *television and in newspapers. Individual lives, the future of the globe, politics, *sports, and humanitarian issues bring before us many of the constituents of stage tragedies: violence, suffering, endurance, a sense of inevitability. In the actions of exceptional persons and numbers of anonymous witnesses commenting on events, the tragic *heroes and *choruses are reborn in actuality for us to see on screens and in newsprint. What are missing are dramatists to manipulate the action, create the *characters, and with eloquent, sensitive, arresting speeches record how these events have come to pass and how men and women confront them. In presentation of our everyday tragedies many opinions about cause and effect are given, faces are transformed by emotion and resolution, and mangled bodies seen, but no author assumes authority and controls events.

Nevertheless tragedies written for theatre performance in earlier ages are still honoured in *criticism and performed alongside plays of our own time. Nostalgia for theatre of the past may be partly responsible, a desire to see 'gorgeous Tragedy, | In scepter'd pall come sweeping by' (*Milton, 1632). Ruins of theatres built to stage these plays are witness to the large *audiences they once attracted and the *texts remain an enduring and irresistible challenge to critics, scholars, and teachers and, almost equally, to actors, directors, and whole theatre companies. The old tragedies have not died in European culture and are increasingly finding new life in theatres around the world.

From its earliest times, in Athens of the fifth century BC, when tragedy was the dominant dramatic form (*see* GREEK THEATRE, ANCIENT), its attractions and significance have been much discussed. The retelling of ancient stories, multiple sources, and complex texts may well have given both authority and mystery to performances. Among tragedy's *origins were the public assemblies and debates which were the foundation of Athenian democracy and, in keeping with tradition, the plays were written to provoke questions and demand judgement. Tragedy also derived from choral singing, enacted narratives, and civic and religious ceremonies. The philosopher *Aristotle wrote the first sustained analysis of the form in his *Poetics* and his judgements, expressed in notes rather than a finished treatise, have influenced scholars and practitioners ever since.

That tragedy is 'an imitation of an *action' is Aristotle's central idea, which he illustrated with reference to *Sophocles' *Oedipus* and other plays known to him. This action must be 'serious, complete, and of a certain magnitude' and the handling of it in the *'plot' is the dramatist's primary task. Second and third in importance are the creation of 'characters' and provision of the tragedy's 'thought' or argument. The action should present a change of fortune (*peripeteia*) from prosperity to adversity in a way that both satisfies moral sensibility and 'arouses pity and fear' in its audience. In consequence, the *protagonist cannot be entirely evil or entirely good: if the *hero were evil, Aristotle argued, the misfortune would call for no pity; if good, there would be no fear. By arousing both these feelings, a tragedy purged them from spectators. (This concept of purgation, or *catharsis, has far-reaching implications for aesthetic theory and has been much debated.) The misfortune must derive, Aristotle concluded, not from vice or depravity, but from 'some error or frailty' within a good man, later to be called the hero's 'tragic flaw' (*hamartia*). From his basic concept of art as imitation (*mimesis), Aristotle also required characters to be true to life and consistent in thought and feeling, however conflicting they might be. In plot, the dramatist should always aim 'either at the necessary or the probable' and, in imitating what he found in life, should seek to make it more noble.

Not all the tragedies known to Aristotle followed his formulation in all respects and after his time, as theatre practice and writing changed, other *theories about what constitutes a tragedy were offered. While continuing to emphasize seriousness, consistency (or unity), and magnitude, most of these required the action to end with the death of the principal character or characters. In *Roman times, when *comedy had become the dominant dramatic form, *Seneca's tragedies emphasized the influence of passion and fate and showed how injustice motivates violent and cruel actions; perhaps never intended for performance, their claim for attention lies in the fear and horror provoked, rather than in the arousal of pity. In *medieval theatre, the central tenets of Christianity were represented in *religious dramas that replaced wayward fortune with a provident God in charge of human lives and demonstrated how the death of Jesus Christ brought blessing and not misfortune. Tragedy did not thrive in this culture except in moral narratives; according to Boethius (480–524), in Chaucer's translation, 'tragedy is to say a "dite" [story] of prosperity for a time that endeth in wretchedness'. Only with a rebirth of classical learning were tragedies again written for the stage, in Elizabethan and Jacobean times regaining much of the acclaim

and prestige they had originally enjoyed (*see* EARLY MODERN PERIOD IN EUROPE).

Shakespeare and his *London contemporaries, having read Seneca attentively, developed their own 'tragedy of blood'. Horatio's account of the action of *Hamlet* is applicable to many other tragedies then playing. He speaks:

> Of carnal, bloody, and unnatural acts;
> Of accidental judgments, casual slaughters,
> Of deaths put on by cunning and forc'd cause;
> And in this upshot, purposes mistook
> Fall'n on th' inventor's heads.

One variant is today called *revenge tragedy, the hero of which seeks justice or restitution of honour by violent means; Thomas *Kyd's *Spanish Tragedy* (1590) and Shakespeare's *Hamlet* (1600–3) are examples famous in their own day. Other variants were the tragedies of ambition, such as *Marlowe's *Tamburlaine* (c.1587) and Shakespeare's *Macbeth* (1606), and of passion, such as *Othello* (c.1602) and *Webster's *White Devil* (1612). Like the medieval narratives, they customarily showed the rise and fall of great men and the punishment of evil.

These tragedies differ from classical example in being peopled by many distinctive characters, some of them simple folk or *fools. These interact with the protagonists and help to define their natures by demonstrating contrasting motives, abilities, and feelings, in the analogical manner of earlier *miracle plays. An audience gains an ever increasing and deepening knowledge of the hero or heroine as their inner thoughts and feelings are progressively exposed by what they say and do, and by what happens to them. In Shakespeare's tragedies, their inner resources seem to grow as they face disaster; Webster, who followed in his footsteps, summed up this effect in *The White Devil*: 'Adversity | Expresseth virtue, fully, whether true, | Or else adulterate.' With its attention held by increasing terror and fear of consequences, an audience can find that empathy with the protagonists increases, despite any crimes they have committed.

After a few decades tragedy lost popular favour in England while in another form it grew to prominence in France, playing to smaller audiences. The nine tragedies that Jean *Racine wrote between 1664 and 1676 were carefully and consistently modelled on classical example, excluding the minor characters and comic interludes of Elizabethan and Jacobean practice. The mental and emotional dilemmas of their leading characters, especially the women, are expressed in lengthy speeches of great sensitivity. Action turns on violent feelings and intractable conflicts that reflect the politically troubled and unsettled times, with civil war threatening and intellectual controversy and scepticism increasing. The main characters of *Andromaque* (1667), for example, are Hector's widow, the sons of Achilles and Agamemnon, and Helen's daughter, young persons who have inherited the aftermath of the sack of Troy, a war they did not choose but whose horrors still obsess them and bind their actions. Sexual passion, pride, guilt, jealousy, and revenge drive the plot; marriage, murder, suicide, and madness are its consequences, accompanied by recognition of previously unsuspected emotions. This tragedy was Racine's first triumph, the passionate clarity of its language and remorseless interlocking of its action helping to establish a new and *neoclassical form of tragedy. Pierre *Corneille had written his first tragedy, Médée (1635), almost 30 years before Racine's, and he continued writing others until, after a considerable interval, he was competing with his much younger rival. In contrast to Racine's doomed protagonists, Corneille's are noble and virtuous, his audiences roused to amazement and admiration rather than pity.

After this sustained triumph in *Paris, tragedies have never regained dominance. In their place during the eighteenth century, *melodramas and *romantic dramas became popular successes. In England, George *Lillo's London Merchant (1731) was an unusual throwback to Elizabethan domestic tragedies that had considerable influence in France as a model for a brief vogue of *bourgeois tragedy. *Voltaire wrote numerous neoclassical tragedies which were respectfully received but none of them has been thought worthy of revival. In Germany, where leading poets wrote for the theatre, neoclassical tragedy found most favour, *Schiller's Mary Stuart (1800) having a long and varied stage history.

Tragedy's prestige was to be reaffirmed by Friedrich Nietzsche in The Birth of Tragedy, published in 1872 when he was professor of classical philology at Basle. This short book asserted that the earliest tragedies were informed by a *Dionysian freedom of spirit and enquiry that had later been stifled, in art as in life, by an Apollonian order and sobriety imposed by philosophers, teachers, and lawmakers of all kinds: *Aeschylus and Sophocles are seen in opposition to *Euripides and Socrates, *music as a direct expression of tragedy's affirmation of life. Nietzsche's arguments have raised many objections but his enthusiastic endorsement of *Wagner's music dramas as the true inheritors of tragedy has the facts of history on its side in that *operas composed by *Verdi, *Puccini, Berg, Britten, and many others have presented tragic actions and expressed them through orchestral music and roles requiring amazing vocal technique in performance. When considering the birth of tragedy, Nietzsche was also announcing that it had died as a text-based drama.

In the twentieth century, tragedies have occasionally been written, though seldom in classical, Elizabethan, or any other consistent tradition. One discernible tendency has been to set tragic action in rural communities; for example, *Synge's Riders to the Sea (1904), *O'Neill's Desire under the Elms (1924), and *García Lorca's Blood Wedding (1933). In these plays, an inherited morality and way of life bring intolerable burdens on the principal characters, leading to death. Some of *Ibsen's nineteenth-century dramas set in close-knit families with inherited ideals that the characters cannot or will not sustain have some of the features of tragedies—misfortune, necessity, error, commanding characters—for example, Ghosts (1881) and John Gabriel Borkman (1896)—and later dramatists have, more or less consciously, followed his lead. In the USA, O'Neill wrote a trilogy in imitation of Greek predecessors, Mourning Becomes Electra (1929–31), and slowly developed his own, more Ibsen-like, tragic form, notably in Long Day's Journey into Night (written 1939–41; produced and published 1956). Arthur *Miller has also, very consciously, brought social drama and tragedy together in A View from the Bridge (1955).

In twentieth-century tragic dramas, an audience is led to follow a group of persons in a recognizable and familiar contemporary setting, rather than witness the misfortune of one exceptionally gifted protagonist at one particular time of crisis. Its perception of an entire society is called in question, as well as its judgement of individual persons. If the term tragedy is widened to include all such plays, then it could be argued that this form of drama has not died but found new life. Tragedies in a strict sense belong to the past and, in modern times, are performed as exceptional survivals that can awaken audiences to moral issues and instinctive feelings that might otherwise be forgotten.

See also GENRE; TRAGICOMEDY; FARCE.   JRB

BROWN, JOHN RUSSELL, Shakespeare: the tragedies (London, 2001)
NUTTALL, A. D., Why Does Tragedy Give Pleasure? (Oxford, 1996)
STEINER, GEORGE, The Death of Tragedy (London, 1961)
WILES, DAVID, Tragedy in Athens: performance space and theatrical meaning (Cambridge, 1997)

TRAGICOMEDY

In a preface to his Faithful Shepherdess (1608–9), John *Fletcher reports that it had failed on the stage because its *audience failed to recognize a tragicomedy. Such a play, he explains, lacks deaths, 'which is enough to make it no *tragedy, yet brings some near it, which is enough to make it no *comedy'. Fletcher's title alludes to Giovan Battista *Guarini's Il pastor fido (written 1580s; performed 1595) and his defence of it seems indebted to Il compendio della poesia tragicomica in which Guarini explained that this form of drama should take 'great persons' from tragedy 'but not great *action; a *plot which is life-like but not true . . . the danger, not the death'; and from comedy should come 'a feigned complication, a happy reversal, and above all, comic order'. Guarini cited the Amphitrion that *Plautus had called a tragicomedy and broadened the ground of his argument by quoting *Horace's defence of *satyr-plays, in which a god or semi-god 'that late was seen to wear | A royal crown and purple, be made hop | With poor base terms, through every baser shop' ('Ars Poetica', trans. Ben *Jonson).

Leaving the *pastoral setting and collaborating with Francis *Beaumont, Fletcher went on to write a number of tragicomedies, notably *Philaster* (1608–10), their first public success, and *A King and No King* (1611). A vogue had been started that lasted in England until *Dryden's *The Secret Love; or, The Maiden Queen* of 1667. While *characters are natural in manners, they are remote from ordinary experience and involved in an intricate plot that often rests on improbable circumstances. Strong passions, horror, unmitigated evil, improbable *disguise, and moral transformation are all present and expressed in lively and often florid language. To latter-day readers, the style can seem superficial. T. S. *Eliot objected that 'the evocative quality of the *verse of Beaumont and Fletcher depends upon a clever appeal to emotion and associations which they have not themselves grasped; it is hollow.' But Thomas Stanley's commendatory verses to the 1647 folio edition of Beaumont and Fletcher's plays testify that, in performance in their own day, such writing 'could beget | A real passion by a counterfeit' to such effect that audiences wept openly. An enjoyment of these tragicomedies depends on an ability to admire virtuosity of expression and dramatic construction and, at the same time, to be moved by the sentiments of the characters.

Tragic and comedic elements have often been found within a single play, but without that sustained and equal attention to both that justifies calling it a tragicomedy. In Philip *Sidney's posthumous *Apology for Poetry* (1595), dramatists who 'thrust in the *clown by head and shoulders to play a part in majestical matters, with neither decency nor discretion' are censored for the 'gross absurdities' of 'their mongrel tragicomedy'. But clowns in tragedies had long been sanctioned by ancient and popular tradition in many countries. In the English *biblical plays, torturers occupied in crucifixion or soldiers slaughtering innocent babies make jokes as they engage in their familiar business. In practice there was no fixed line between tragedy and comedy. The two appear side by side in separate plots in Greene's *Friar Bacon and Friar Bungay* (*c.*1589). A tragic action is presented with comic irony and its *hero possesses a keen comic awareness in *Marlowe's *Jew of Malta* (*c.*1589) and Shakespeare's *Richard III* (1593) and *Titus Andronicus* (1594). The Porter's appearance in *Macbeth* (*c.*1606) to make jokes about damnation and drunkenness is a famous example of a comic incident in a tragedy. Shakespeare had earlier taken comedy close to tragedy in *The Merchant of Venice* (1597) when Shylock voices his passion for revenge and Antonio faces death. At about the same time as Fletcher wrote his first tragicomedy, Shakespeare was moving towards a closer fusion of comedy and tragedy in *Cymbeline* and *The Winter's Tale*, both with two offstage deaths and an apparent death onstage.

The mingling of modes was found throughout *early modern Europe, especially in the *comedias* of sixteenth-century Spain, where comedy and disaster are often close together, their complicated plots giving rise to intense emotions and ending with unexpectedly happy reversals of fortune (*see* PERIPETEIA). Italian and Spanish example was followed in France during the early decades of the seventeenth century, among others by the prolific Alexandre *Hardy and, in his earlier years, Pierre *Corneille. But as tragedy ceased to be a dominant form, its boundary with comedy became much less marked and tragicomedy dropped out of favour. As stage characters and speech became closer to those of real life, tragicomedy's obviously artificial style became increasingly unacceptable. The term, however, continued to be used on occasion. After seeing a production of *The Wild Duck* (1884) acted in a farcical style, *Ibsen complained that his play should 'be tragi-comedy or else Hedvig's death is incomprehensible'.

Many plays that contain a mixture of moods might be called tragicomedies but they do not approach the artificial and sophisticated manner that the term traditionally implies. The deaths, ironies, and jesting present in *Chekhov's *Seagull* (1896), *Gorky's *The Lower Depths* (1902), *O'Casey's *Juno and the Paycock* (1924), and *Beckett's *Endgame* (1957) would entitle them tragicomedies if the term were used loosely; what they lack are the great persons, feigned complications, and, above all, the comic ordering that takes pleasure in danger while avoiding death. These and many other plays that are both serious and comic are so far from those of the early modern Europe that established tragicomedy as a dramatic form, that almost all meaning would be drained from that term if applied to them. The playwrights of the theatre of the *absurd of the mid-twentieth century might lay the best claim to it: *Ionesco entitled *The Chairs* (1952) a 'Tragic Farce'. Only when a play provokes *laughter, tears, and amazement does it come close to the original tragicomedies.

See also GENRE; FARCE.   JRB

WAITH, EUGENE M., *The Pattern of Tragicomedy in Beaumont and Fletcher* (New Haven, 1952)

TRAINING FOR THEATRE

Training for theatre and performance internationally, until the twentieth century, was focused primarily on the *actor. In some cultures training is embedded in community processes, as in the indigenous forms of *Africa or, say, the samba schools of Brazil. Where performance has been a profession many formal training approaches have emerged, but two main tendencies broadly correspond to dominant practices in the East and West. These principally derive from key differences between body-based and script-based performance.

Traditional Asian theatre training concentrated mainly on the performer's physical skills, so that direct transmission from master to student artist was the norm. In traditions which involve scripts—such as *Japanese *nō theatre or Sanskrit drama in *India—textual conventions were highly formalized, encoding *genres and forms in notations for an established repertoire of physical and vocal actions. But also in non-textual traditions the emphasis fell on the highly disciplined acquisition of technical skills appropriate to the demands of particular forms. Frequently this was a lifelong task, with training starting in childhood or youth and continuing into adulthood, and usually falling into two major phases. The first phase was not so much a training in how to 'act', but rather a rigorous induction into becoming an artist. The childhood of the Indian *kathakali actor is spent making the body pliable and inscribing it with the many minutely controlled movements and gestures which constitute the form's expressive repertoire. Equivalent training existed for controlling the movements of *Malaysian and *Indonesian *shadow puppets, for reproducing the melodies of the *gamelan in Javanese theatre or the tunes of Thai theatre (see THAILAND), for executing the acrobatics of Beijing opera (*jingju). The neophyte artist is schooled in the grammar of particular aesthetic languages, each passed down through generations of practitioners. Hence, the fifteenth-century Japanese theorist of nō acting *Zeami insisted that the arts of chanting and *dance should be learned between 7 and 17, before the study of role play, or acting itself, began. This is the second phase of the artist's life work. The roles of traditional Asian theatre are invariably generic types—*stock characters like old male king, young male hero, young woman, *villain, *clown—with relatively fixed codes of conduct, transmitted through demonstration and imitation by teacher and student. Often roles are studied and perfected over a lifetime, so the student becomes a master of the tradition. Thus, the general method has been one of apprenticeship to a master, sometimes within *families, sometimes in hereditary clans, sometimes in schools. Today, however, state-funded academies also teach young performers in traditional forms in many countries of Asia, as the demand of theatre—more popular there than in the West—has outstripped the supply of the apprenticeship system.

Dominant theatre traditions in the West have been *text based and logocentric, so that training mostly has used codes that do not have to be directly transmitted from master to apprentice. Until about the mid-nineteenth century the main repository for training was the theatre company, so that performance skills were generally acquired in the process of production itself. Ancient *Greek dramatists instructed performers and were known as 'teachers'; *Roman actor-managers employed professional actors who developed skills through the staging of plays; in *medieval European drama the players were mostly *amateur, though membership of trades *guilds with responsibility for particular plays probably provided for informal training; in sixteenth-century Italy the troupes of the *commedia dell'arte, sometimes bound together by *family ties, passed skills on through quasi-apprenticeships; in Elizabethan England *boy actors were trained for female roles until puberty, before graduating to male parts in the company of stock-holding actors; in the eighteenth and nineteenth centuries *actor-managers schooled the performers they employed in the formal styles of the times (see LINES OF BUSINESS). Hence, the discontinuous history of training in Western theatre to the nineteenth century is a product of the changing styles of drama as interpreted by producing companies.

The first European conservatoires and private academies were founded in the early nineteenth century. In France the *Conservatoire d'Art Dramatique was created in 1808 (though it dates back to the École Royale de Déclamation of 1786) and in 1812 a special class for *Comédie-Française actors was added. In England the *London Academy of Music and Dramatic Art began in 1861 and the Guildhall School of Music and Drama started in 1880. The Russian Academy of Dramatic Art was started in 1878. But the twentieth century saw a sustained evolution of formalized training institutions for the theatre in most countries. In London the *Royal Academy of Dramatic Art was founded in 1904, quickly followed in 1906 by the Central School of Speech and Drama. In Finland the Finnish School of Drama was established in 1920, though the *Finnish National Theatre had a school for actors between 1906 and 1920. The inter-war years saw the creation of many training centres in the West, but the major growth took place in the second half of the twentieth century, when training in state institutions for all types of theatre professions besides actors became the norm internationally. This expansion was a response to a widening professionalization of the theatre, so that the majority of institutions were producing artists conventionally geared to theatre as an aspect of the global cultural industries.

Alongside the formal institutes, training was intimately bound up with the rise of the *director and the creation of *studios to develop particular innovations. The first attempt in Western theatre to create a quasi-scientific approach to performer training was undertaken by *Stanislavsky at the *Moscow Art Theatre from 1897. Subsequently, training in Western theatre was linked closely to innovations in theatre style, so pedagogic methods and curriculum structures varied a great deal. In Russia Stanislavsky's former pupil, Vsevolod *Meyerhold, rejected *naturalism's focus on the inner life of the *character to concentrate on the actor's body in a system he called *biomechanics. In France Jacques *Copeau, reacting against the dominance of the Comédie-Française, created an intensive three-year programme which centred on physical skills, but also included craft skills (drawing, modelling), voice work, *improvisation, and dramatic *theory. In Germany Bertolt *Brecht incorporated actor training in the extended *rehearsal processes of the *Berliner Ensemble, developing skills that would enable the actor to demonstrate the social status of the character. In America, Richard *Boleslavsky taught the Stanislavsky system at the *American Laboratory Theatre. After the Second World War, Lee *Strasberg, as director of the *Actors Studio in *New York, extended the system to create *Method acting, a style of training which was especially suited to *film: Strasberg's students included Marlon *Brando, Ann Bancroft, and Paul Newman. Major training centres developed at the *Yale School of Drama and the *Juilliard School. Subsequent directors who have greatly influenced approaches to actor training include Peter *Brook, Jerzy *Grotowski, Eugenio *Barba, and *Suzuki Tadashi.

BRK

HODGE, ALISON (ed.), *Twentieth Century Actor Training* (London, 2000)

ZARRILLI, PHILIP B. (ed.), *Acting (Re)Considered: theories and practices* (London, 1995)

TRAM

Acronym of Teatr Pabochei Molodezhi (Young Workers' Theatre), a mainly *amateur organization which flowered in the Soviet Union in the latter half of the 1920s and at the beginning of the 1930s. Closely allied with the Komsomol (Communist Youth League), TRAM staged *agitprop productions serving Communist Party policy in improvisatory styles influenced by *Proletkult and the *Blue Blouse troupes. The first TRAM was based in Leningrad (*St Petersburg), in 1925, followed by one in *Moscow in 1927, and then in some twelve or more cities. In 1932 a plenum of the Central Committee of the Soviet Communist Party recommended 'reconstruction' of TRAM organizations, which were henceforth to be affiliated to trade unions and given specific tasks, based on the need to acquire a greater understanding of formal dramatic composition and *Stanislavskian performance techniques. The Moscow and Leningrad branches were turned into regular theatres, while others were transformed into 'Theatres for Young Spectators'. NW

TRAPS

Openings in the *stage floor, or in the *scenery, normally concealed by a cover, and used for entrances and exits as well as various scenic functions. Theatrical *spectacle often depends upon surprise. At least since the *medieval *cycle plays, when devils would emerge from traps in the stage, the surprising appearance and disappearance of actors and objects has been part of the pleasure of theatrical *illusion. A trap can surprise an *audience with an entrance in an apparently solid floor or wall, a *character using an unexpected entrance or exit, or a mysterious appearance, disappearance, or transformation. The *romantic theatre and *melodrama generally brought the craft of the trap to its pinnacle, and many stages were equipped with a large number of traps as standard equipment. Traps have been too numerous in history to detail entirely, but here is a brief (and highly incomplete) glossary.

Banquo trap: the downstage centre trap, named after its use in *Macbeth*.

Bristle trap: a trap covered with radial bristles or birch twigs, attached at the edge and free in the centre, flush with the stage, through which an actor can pop up or down very suddenly.

Cauldron trap: the upstage centre trap, named after its use in *Macbeth*.

Corsican trap or *ghost glide*: a shoulder-width trap running across the stage with a sliding cover set flush with the stage and a moving platform under the floor on inclined rails. When the platform is pulled forward the actor is moved across the stage while simultaneously rising until his or her feet are flush with the stage floor. Named after its use in *Boucicault's *The Corsican Brothers* (1852), a play so popular that nearly all melodrama houses acquired a ghost glide as standard equipment and many other melodramas were written to use it.

Diaphragm trap: covered by a slit rubber diaphragm, painted the colour of the stage or wall, used for very fast entrances and exits.

Footlight trap, floats trap: a long narrow trap used for candle and later gas footlights, which allowed *lighting to be dimmed and wicks and mantles to be trimmed by lowering the footlights further into the stage.

Grave trap: the grave-sized trap, centre stage, named after its use in *Hamlet*.

Slider trap: a trap in which the covering door, normally flush with the stage floor, drops just below floor level and slides sideways on rails; the platform on which the rising actor stands then locks into place to become part of the stage floor.

Star trap: a circular trap whose cover is a set of adjoining triangles hinged at the outer edge, set flush with the stage. A person rising or descending through it can appear or disappear rapidly.

Vampire or *vamp trap*: a trap whose cover is two quick-acting, close-fitted sprung leaves. With a distraction at the moment of the exit or entrance, the actor can appear to pop through a solid wall or out of the floor. Named after its use for the sudden appearances and disappearances in *The Vampire*. JB

TRAVERS, BEN (1886–1980)

English playwright and novelist who enjoyed two periods of great popular success, the second 50 years after the first. From 1925 to 1933 he wrote nine *'Aldwych farces' tailored to a team of talented actors including Tom Walls (unscrupulous *hero), Ralph Lynn (silly-ass hero's friend), Robertson *Hare (bullied husband), and Mary Brough (formidable female). The plays rely heavily on these carefully constructed *characters; they play better than they read, but need careful timing and conviction. *A Cuckoo in the Nest* (1925), *Rookery Nook* (1926), *Thark* (1927), and *Plunder* (1928) are those most often revived by both professionals and *amateurs. They rely on the usual British fear of scandal and sexuality, though *Plunder* does take burglary and murder in its stride. *Plunder* did well at the *National Theatre in 1976, as did Travers's late success *The Bed before Yesterday*

(1975); the last shows a post-*censorship explicitness about the heroine's late-flowering sexual satisfaction.   EEC

TRAVERSE THEATRE

Beginning in 1963 in a former Edinburgh brothel converted into a 60-seat theatre, the Traverse's early focus was on introducing the European and American *avant-garde to Scottish *audiences. Along with work by *Arrabal, *Duras, Paul Foster, and Scottish writers such as Stanley Eveling and C. P. *Taylor, many early counter-cultural figures appeared, including Lindsay *Kemp and the *People Show. Despite a rapid turnover of *artistic directors (including Max *Stafford-Clark, Michael *Rudman, and Mike Ockrent, who all gained early experience there), its prolific output won an international reputation. Its role in promoting Scottish drama increased under Chris Parr, who between 1975 and 1981 fostered a new generation of writers including Tom McGrath and John Byrne. Having moved to a 100-seat venue in 1969, the company acquired a new two-theatre complex in 1992. Especially at *Edinburgh Festival time, when it never seems to shut, the Traverse continues to facilitate a two-way exchange between Scottish and world theatre.   GJG

TRAVESTY (TROUSER) ROLE

Male *character written for the female voice and sung by a female performer: for example, Siebel in Gounod's *Faust* (1859), Prince Orlofsky in Johann Strauss's *Die Fledermaus* (1874), Nicklaus in *Offenbach's *Tales of Hoffmann* (1881), Octavian in Richard *Strauss's *Der Rosenkavalier* (1911), and the Composer in his *Ariadne on Naxos* (1916). The term does not, strictly speaking, apply to those roles originally written for *castrati performers that are now performed by women, nor to the cross-dressing, *breeches part of the Restoration stage and after, nor to other instances of *male impersonation by women performers in drama or on the *variety stage. *See also* OPERA.   AS

TREADWELL, SOPHIE (1885–1970)

American writer, who worked variously as a journalist, novelist, and dramatist, Treadwell's reputation rests on *Machinal* (1928), a sensational example of American *expressionism. While working as a journalist, Treadwell wrote more than 30 plays, most of which were never produced. The *naturalistic *Gringo* (1922) was staged by Guthrie *McClintic, and the romantic *comedy *Oh Nightingale* (1925) had a brief run and was optioned by Hollywood. Treadwell's 1927 investigation of the Ruth Snyder–Judd Gray murder case (Snyder was the first woman executed in the electric chair) provided material for *Machinal*, an economically crafted play depicting in nine hypnotic *scenes the Young Woman's journey from office girl to boss's wife to victim of the chair. Apart from the play's topicality (it was staged only

eight months after Snyder was put to death), it endures as a prototypical expressionistic story of the human being's destruction by the machine of modern life (business systems, social systems, legal systems, the absence of love and compassion). The play was rediscovered in a 1990 *New York Public Theatre production, directed by Michael Greif.   MAF

TREE, ELLEN (1806–80)

English actress, who married Charles *Kean in 1842. She was a strikingly beautiful young woman who first appeared on stage at *Covent Garden in 1823, acting Olivia for the *benefit of her sister, the singer Maria Tree; all four sisters went on the stage. After a spell at *Edinburgh and *Bath she was engaged at *Drury Lane, and at Covent Garden in 1829. For her *benefit in 1832 she played Romeo to Fanny *Kemble's Juliet, and in 1836 created the male part of Ion in Thomas Talfourd's coldly classical *tragedy *Ion*. After *touring America between 1836 and 1839 she played Rosalind and Viola in *London. Following her marriage to Kean, she was his leading lady, playing more matronly parts as her figure filled out. The Fool in *King Lear* was a peculiar piece of *casting; she played Hermione in *The Winter's Tale*, the Chorus in *Henry V* as the Muse of History, Katherine in *Henry VIII*, Constance in *King John*, Ophelia, and Lady Macbeth, but she was not outstanding in the great tragic parts.   MRB

TREE, HERBERT BEERBOHM (1853–1917)

English actor and *manager; knighted in 1909. Against parental opposition, Tree chose to become an actor, making his debut in *London in 1878. In 1884 he had a notable success in Charles *Hawtrey's *farce *The Private Secretary*. In 1887, aided by his wife Helen Maud Hope, who was accomplished as an actress and in business, Tree became a manager, briefly at the Comedy Theatre, then at the *Haymarket, where he began to distinguish himself in both *melodrama and Shakespeare. For the rest of his career he would follow the model of Henry *Irving, staging grand *spectacles of Shakespeare while also producing a range of melodramas, *comedies, and social dramas that allowed him to display his flamboyant *acting skills. In the 1890s, when Tree became one of the leading *actor-managers of the West End, his mix of plays included *The Merry Wives of Windsor* (1891), *Wilde's *A Woman of No Importance* (1893), and Paul Potter's *Trilby* (1895), based on George Du Maurier's novel. The profits of *Trilby* allowed him to build *Her Majesty's Theatre, which opened in 1897. For the next two decades he produced major West End successes, including Stephen *Phillips's *Herod* (1900) and *Ulysses* (1902), *Belasco and Long's *The Darling of the Gods* (1903), and Phillips and Comyns Carr's *Faust* (1908). In 1914 he appeared with Mrs Patrick *Campbell in *Shaw's *Pygmalion*. During his career he staged eighteen of Shakespeare's plays, reviving some of them often. Though he did not excel in the major tragic roles of Hamlet, Macbeth, and Othello, usually he was successful in the *character roles of Falstaff, Caliban, Bottom, Malvolio, and Cardinal Wolsey. Most tellingly, he was a threatening *villain: the Devil in H. A. *Jones's *The Tempter*, Svengali in *Trilby*, Fagin in *Oliver Twist*, Nero in Phillips's *Nero*, and Shylock. The run of Jewish characters suggests, perhaps, the uneasy relation between ideas of the diabolical and anti-Semitism in Victorian and Edwardian society. In 1904 Tree developed an actor-*training programme that became the *Royal Academy of Dramatic Art. His annual *Shakespeare festival, begun in 1905, proved to be the training ground for many promising actors. He had three children, including Viola Tree who acted with Tree and his wife. A notorious womanizer, Tree had at least seven other children from extramarital affairs. He was the half-brother of Max *Beerbohm, the dramatic *critic and caricaturist.   TP

TREMBLAY, MICHEL (1952–)

Québec dramatist and novelist. His *Les Belles-Sœurs* (*Sisters-in-Law*, 1968) was a watershed for francophone *dramaturgy. The furore aroused by its use of *joual*, *Montréal's working-class French, hitherto considered too vulgar for public display, diverted attention from the play's formal innovations, its stylized *monologues and *choruses, pervaded by an intense, sometimes startling poetry. Now a modern classic, it has been performed in more than twenty languages and dialects as diverse as Japanese, Yiddish, and Yorkshire English. Drawing on many of the same *characters but expanding the claustrophobic universe of *Les Belles-Sœurs*, some 30 plays have followed, most of them critical and popular successes, notably *A toi, pour toujours, ta Marie-Lou* (*Forever Yours, Marie-Lou*, 1971), a *tragedy transcending scenic time/space; *Hosanna* (1973), where homosexual identity, central to much of Tremblay's work, is examined; *Albertine, en cinq temps* (*Albertine, in Five Times*, 1984), where one female character, portrayed by five actresses, relives critical stages of her long, troubled life; and *Marcel poursuivi par les chiens* (*Marcel Pursued by Hounds*, 1992), exploring, not for the first time, the world beyond sanity.

Tremblay has been deeply influenced by classic *Greek authors (*Aeschylus in particular) and by his abiding love of *opera (his *Nelligan*, with music by André Gagnon, was performed by the Montréal Opera in 1990). His translations of authors as diverse as *Aristophanes, *Chekhov, and Tennessee *Williams have also been staged with considerable success. Since the mid-1990s he has turned his attention mainly to the novel.   LED

TREMONT THEATRE

There were two *Boston *playhouses in Tremont Street. The first was built by Isaiah Rogers in 1827. Featuring a heavy gran-

ite façade, three tiers of *boxes, and a gallery circling a pit, it was the first Boston theatre lit by gas (*see* LIGHTING), though its small size meant it could never offset the cost of maintaining its elegant appointments. With the decline of the *Federal Street Theatre the Tremont became the city's leading venue, but continued to lose money and was purchased by a Baptist congregation in 1843, who renamed it the Tremont Temple and continued to occupy it at the start of the twenty-first century. The second Tremont opened a few blocks down the street in 1889 with a capacity of 1,700 and a large *stage. After housing a number of notable productions, in 1915 it was given over to a *long run of *The Birth of a Nation*. In 1949 it was remodelled as the Astor Cinema, and demolished in 1983.   TFC

TRENYOV, KONSTANTIN (1876–1945)

Russian/Soviet dramatist, short-story writer, and putative founder of the *socialist realist school of Soviet playwriting. His main plays are *Pugachev Times*, about the Pugachev peasant revolt (*Moscow Art Theatre, 1925), and *Lyubov Yarovaya* (1926), a Civil War drama depicting the tragedy of family members on opposed sides of the conflict—in this case, a Bolshevik wife, Lyubov Yarovaya, at war with her White husband. In a poignant finale, he is led away to be shot whilst she turns her attention, with minimal remorse, to the task of defeating the enemy. The play went through several revisions and received a Stalin Prize in 1936. Of his later plays, *On the Banks of the Neva* (1937) is set during the revolution and offers a theatrical portrait of Lenin. This play also required revision in response to critics who demanded a more expansive treatment of the Soviet leader.   NW

TRETYAKOV, SERGEI (1892–1939)

Russian/Soviet poet, playwright, theorist, and translator associated with the modernist *avant-garde LEF (Left Front of the Arts) movement. An advocate of *agitprop theatre, he adapted *Ostrovsky's *Enough Stupidity in Every Wise Man* as a *political 'montage of attractions' for *Eisenstein's famous production at the Proletkult Theatre (1923). His own propaganda plays, *Are You Listening, Moscow?!* and *Gas Masks* (1923), were both staged by Eisenstein, the latter in a *Moscow gas plant. Tretyakov's adaptation of Marcel Martinet's First World War novel *La Nuit* as a revolutionary drama, *Earth Rampant*, was staged by *Meyerhold in 1923, deploying Tretyakov's notion of 'speech montage' (propagandist, choric declamation) in a production lit by military headlights, with a real army lorry onstage and a dispatch rider on a motorbike hurtling through the *auditorium. His schematic, anti-imperialist play *Roar, China!* was staged at Meyerhold's theatre in 1926, and by agitprop groups in the West. His next play, *I Want a Baby*, designed to provoke discussion on the theme of socially controlled reproduction, was banned before the première (directed by Meyerhold, *construct-ivist design by El Lissitsky). Tretyakov met *Brecht during a *Berlin tour and had become his Russian translator before being arrested in 1937. Following torture, he avoided implicat-ing others by committing suicide in prison.   NW

TRIANA, JOSÉ (1931–)

Cuban playwright and poet, author of *La noche de los asesinos* (*Night of the Assassins*, 1965), the most widely produced Cuban play internationally. Concerned with a symbolic ceremo-nial staged by three adolescent brothers about to murder their parents, the play was directed by Vicente *Revuelta, who also played the role of Lalo, and won the *Casa de las Américas *award in *Havana. In 1967 the production was seen at the Théâtre des *Nations and *Avignon Festival during an extensive European *tour. Triana resided in Spain from 1954 to 1959, when he returned to Cuba. In 1960 he premièred *El mayor gen-eral hablará de Teogonía* (*The Major General Will Speak on Teogony*) and *Medea en el espejo* (*Medea in the Mirror*); in 1963, *El parque de la fraternidad* (*Fraternity Park*), *La casa ardiendo* (*The House on Fire*), *La visita del ángel* (*The Visit of the Angel*) and *La muerte del Ñeque* (*Death of Ñeque*). Since 1980 he has lived in *Paris, where his output has included *Revolico en el Campo de Marte* (*A Mess in the Champ de Mars*, 1985); *Palabras comunes* (*Common Words*, 1986), a free adaptation of Miguel de Carrión's novel *Las honradas*, produced by the *Royal Shakespeare Company; *Cruzando el puente* (*Crossing the Bridge*, 1992), directed by Ricardo Salvat in Valencia; and *La fiesta* (*The Party*, 1995).   MMu

TRICICLE

Catalan *mime group formed in 1979 by Carles Sans, Joan Gracia, and Paco Mir. Initial productions were academic and self-reflexive in character, consisting largely of the reinterpret-ation of techniques by masters such as Marcel *Marceau. Grad-ually the group evolved a more subjective approach that incorporated gags, *masks, gestures, and clowning. Their inter-national reputation was assured with shows like *Manicòmic* (1982), *Exit* (1984), and *Slàstic* (1986). *Terrífic* (1992) was a manic and interactive spoof on the *genre of the terror movie, and *Entretrès* (1997), a compound of the Spanish theatrical term *entremés and *entre tres* (between three), of the Anglo-American sitcom. The group produced several pieces for *television and *toured throughout Europe, America, and *Japan, though their most widely viewed performance was at the closing ceremony of the 1992 Olympic Games in *Barcelona. Exploiting both bod-ily and facial tics, voiceover, and elaborate *scenery and *light-ing, Tricicle's mimes have played a variety of roles, including statues, babies, dogs, chain-saw assassins, and Olympic athletes.   KG

TRICYCLE THEATRE

Opened in 1980 as a 200-seat fringe theatre in Kilburn High Road in *London. Originally created as a base for Kenneth Chubb's *touring company of the same name, it subsequently presented a mixed programme of new plays—especially with multicultural and *feminist themes—plus shows and work-shops for *youth. In 1999 it staged a recreation of the Stephen Lawrence inquiry, *The Colour of Justice*, which transferred to the West End. More recently it has concentrated on community-oriented projects with children and young people.   BRK

TRINIDAD THEATRE WORKSHOP

Company founded in Port of Spain by Derek *Walcott. It be-came the driving force in developing new *Caribbean theatrical vocabularies, using *improvisation, ensemble *acting, and ex-periments with *total theatre. It was most energetic for about a decade from 1966, during Walcott's most sustained engage-ment. After he resigned in 1976, the company was intermit-tently important during the 1980s and into the 1990s, most significantly during periods when Walcott returned. The Work-shop was the crucible for his most important work, in associ-ation with many of the finest Caribbean theatrical and musical talents, such as Wilbert Holder, Slade Hopkinson, Albert Laveau, Errol Jones, Helen Camps, and Andre Tanker.   ES

TRINITY REPERTORY COMPANY

American *regional theatre in Providence, Rhode Island. Launched by local citizens as a *community theatre in 1964, its rapid growth and professionalization were catalysed by a major federal grant to provide performances for high-school students. Founding *artistic director Adrian Hall brought the theatre to national attention with a vigorous, muscular style of *epic theatre, which often featured rough-hewn *environmental *scenery by resident designer Eugene *Lee and *musical scores by resident composer Richard Cumming. A number of these productions were original adaptations of novels or other works. After 25 years, Hall was succeeded by experimental director Anne *Bogart, who left after one controversial season (1989–90), long-time company actor Richard Jenkins (1990–4), and then Oskar Eustis (1994–   ), who brought new life and stability to the theatre by erasing a substantial deficit, producing more new plays, and strengthening ties with community, city, and state leaders.   STC

TRIONFI

From the Latin word *triumphus*, in ancient Rome the highest honours accorded a victorious general. An elaborate proces-sion featured the triumphant general on a chariot, preceded by senators and followed by prisoners and troops. The *ritual inspired Petrarch's poem *Trionfi*, a description of a series of triumphal processions of *allegorical figures such as Love, Chastity, Death, Fame, Time, and Eternity. These and similar allegorical representations found frequent expression in the paintings of the fourteenth century and during the *early modern period, especially in Italy, and led to the creation of festive *spectacles in the form of processions. *See* PARADES AND PROCESSIONS. GGE

TRISSINO, GIAN GIORGIO (1478–1550)

Italian humanist and playwright, born in Vicenza. His *Sofonisba* (1515) was the first original attempt to write a classical-style *tragedy in the *early modern period. It deals with a defeated Numidian queen who chooses death rather than slavery; and its structure was more based on *Greek tragedy than on the *Roman models which eventually found more favour. It remained unperformed until 1556: the first tragedies actually staged were by Giovan Battista *Giraldi. RAA

TROPPA, LA

Chilean theatre created in 1987 by Juan Carlos Zagal, Laura Pizarro, and Jaime Lorca after graduating from the Catholic University Theatre School. Early productions like *El santo patrono* (*The Patron Saint*, 1987) and *Voodoo* (1988) defined their method: using *puppets and scale models they created multi-*perspective *scenography to depict *characters embarked upon an exterior or interior journey to understand the world and themselves. Their most successful works have been *Pinocchio* (1991), *Viaje hacia el centro de la tierra* (*A Journey to the Centre of the Earth*, an adaptation of Jules Verne's novel), and *Twins* (1999), based on *The Notebook* by the Hungarian Agota Kristof. MAR

TRÖSTER, FRANTIŠEK (1904–68)

Czech designer, architect, and teacher. After study in *Prague and *Paris, he began his career in the early 1930s in Prague and *Bratislava. His work matured in collaboration with the director Jiří *Frejka (Lope de *Vega's *Fuente Ovejuna* in 1935, *Gogol's *The Government Inspector* and Shakespeare's *Julius Caesar* in 1936, *Pushkin's *Boris Godunov* in 1937). Tröster developed what *Hofman had begun: his *scenography was subjective but markedly multidimensional. Whereas Hofman was basically a painter, Tröster was an architect, creating phantasmal structures out of new materials, which provided unusual as well as *realistic details. His ingenious *lighting and chiaroscuro turned ordinary objects into 'unreal reality'. According to Oscar Niemeyer, Tröster's 'sculptural scenic architecture' marked the beginning of modern stage design. From 1950 until his death he was head of stage design at the Prague Academy of Performing Arts. ML

TROTTER, CATHERINE (COCKBURN) (1679–1749)

English playwright. Trotter's first play was an adaptation of Aphra *Behn's novel *Agnes de Castro* and was performed at *Drury Lane (1696). A friend and contemporary of Delarivière Manley and Mary *Pix, Trotter largely escaped the personal attacks that other female playwrights endured. Her four plays (*tragedy and *tragicomedy) avoid topical references and contemporary settings although, like Behn, her female *characters challenge the social mores that promote marriage as a financial contract and preclude female sexual expression. *Love at a Loss*, first performed at Drury Lane in 1700, was revived at a *London *fringe venue, the Link, in 1992. GBB

TSUBOUCHI SHŌYŌ (1859–1935)

Japanese playwright, director, and translator. Born in Gifu prefecture, he discovered Western literature after the opening of *Japan in 1868 and developed a strong interest in Shakespeare, eventually translating the entire corpus of plays into Japanese for the first time. Wishing to stage Shakespeare as well, Shōyō, by then a professor at Waseda University in *Tokyo, formed Bungei Kyôkai (the Literary Society) in 1905, using student performers, both male and female. In 1911 the group performed *Hamlet* in his translation and *A Doll's House*, which made *Ibsen, as well as the leading lady *Matsui Sumako, famous in Japan. Matsui ran off with her lover, Shōyō's colleague Shimamura Hōgetsu, and the company was dissolved in 1913. Deeply discouraged, Shōyō retired from active involvement in the stage. His play *The Hermit*, chosen by *Osanai Kaoru as the first Japanese drama to be performed at the *Tsukiji Little Theatre in 1926, is the story of a master betrayed by his disciple. Shōyō's various accomplishments are chronicled in the collections of Japan's finest theatre museum, dedicated to him, on the campus of Waseda University. JTR

TSUKIJI LITTLE THEATRE (TSUKIJI SHŌGEKIJŌ)

A Japanese theatre company founded in 1924 by *Osanai Kaoru. The *financial aid of *Hijikata Yoshi made it possible to build a new theatre in the Tsukiji district in the centre of *Tokyo for the company after the devastating earthquake of 1923. The first truly professional modern theatre company in *Japan, Osanai and his colleagues were determined to educate playgoers to the best of contemporary European theatre and lift standards of performance by Japanese actors. The repertory was mostly Western until the company was dissolved shortly after Osanai's death in 1928. Many in the next generation of important actors, writers, and directors, including *Senda Koreya and *Kubo Sakae, trained with the company, which lifted both standards and expectations for modern theatre in Japan. *See* SHINGEKI.

JTR

TSURUYA NANBOKU IV (1755–1829)

*Kabuki playwright. Born in the centre of Edo (*Tokyo) in a merchant house, he began his apprenticeship in 1776 and became senior playwright in 1803. He was involved in many aspects of theatrical life and wrote under several names for various actors and theatres, finally as Nanboku IV from 1812. As senior playwright he wrote 120 plays; he also published 25 books of illustrated fiction. He is known for theatrical innovation, using frequent stage tricks and effects such as stage blood. He is also famous for his ghost plays, in particular *Yotsuya Ghost Stories* (1825), which revel in depictions of the *grotesque. One recurring theme is the fall of high-born figures into Edo low life; *Princess Sakura and Letters from the East* (1817) is a fine example, often revived for the contemporary stage. His first great success was *The Foreign Adventures of 'India' Tokubei* (1804), in which the theme of a rebel who tries to overthrow the government proved be fascinating for his *audience.

CAG

TSYPIN, GEORGE (1954–)

Russian-born, *New York-based designer. Layers of visual references, *multimedia technology, and an architectural approach to space characterize the work of Tsypin, one of the most prominent postmodern *scenographers. His career in theatre began when he won a French set design competition while still a student at *Moscow's Architectural Institute. He moved to the USA in 1979 to work as an architect, but was drawn back to theatre and studied set design at New York University with John *Conklin. Influenced by *constructivism, Tsypin realized his desire to 'explode the box' in a series of productions with Peter *Sellars in the mid-1980s (*Dumas *père's* Count of Monte Cristo, *Sophocles' *Ajax*, *Mozart's *Don Giovanni*, *Wagner's *Tannhaüser*) which juxtaposed *realistic architectural fragments with abstract conceptual structures. In the 1990s his work assumed a minimalist character, his designs often resembling gallery installations (Messiaen's *St. François d'Assise*, *Handel's *Theodora*, Wagner's *Ring*, Prokofiev's *War and Peace*). Besides Sellars he has worked for many years with Julie *Taymor, Robert Falls, JoAnne *Akalaitis, and Andrey Konchalovsky.

MPB

TUCKER, SOPHIE (1884–1966)

American *vaudeville singer and dancer. Born (probably) in Poland to emigrating Russian-Jewish parents, Tucker began life on the road and never stopped. In her teens she worked her way to *New York and the famous *Yiddish theatre strip of 2nd Avenue. Her first professional appearance was at the 116th Street Musical Hall, and she spent much of her early life in small houses. Guided by the theatrical agent William Morris, Tucker eventually became a headline act on the vaudeville circuit with songs such as 'Who Paid the Rent for Mrs. Rip Van Winkle (When Rip Van Winkle Went Away)?' (1914). In her autobiography (*Some of These Days*, 1945), Tucker credits herself with developing the shimmy *dance and perfecting 'coon shouting' (blackface comic ballads) in vaudeville. She left vaudeville in 1918 to perform blues music in the *cabarets in New York and *London. She also performed in six *films and two Broadway shows. Her funeral in New York was attended by 3,000 mourners.

AB

TUILERIES, THÉÂTRE DES *See* SALLE DES MACHINES.

TUNE, TOMMY (1939–)

American dancer, singer, director, and choreographer. Arriving in *New York from his native Texas in 1965, he appeared in the *choruses of several Broadway *musicals before landing his first featured role in *Seesaw* (1973). While remaining active as a performer, he branched into directing and choreography, beginning *Off-Broadway with *The Club* (1976) and moving to Broadway with *The Best Little Whorehouse in Texas* (1978). Other directing efforts followed, including the non-musical *Cloud 9* (1981) before he entered the ranks of master director/choreographers with *Nine* (1982), *Grand Hotel* (1989), and *The Will Rogers Follies* (1991)—conceptual musicals marked by great creative vision and a cinematic fluidity. In the midst of this streak, he also earned a best actor in a musical Tony *award for *My One and Only* (1983), tap *dancing about the stage with his gangly 2-m (6-foot 6-inch) frame. In the 1990s he returned to performing, both on *tour and in a spectacular Las Vegas extravaganza, *EFX*. With nine Tonys, he is the only person ever to have won the award in four different categories.

JD

TUNIS

Capital of Tunisia and successor city to ancient Carthage. Located on the straits of Sicily, Tunis has been a place of meeting and passage since ancient times. Well before the installation of a French protectorate, separate French, Italian, and Maltese districts existed within the European city, bordering the Arab

Médina. Here showmen presented the *li'bat of Karakouz* (*shadow puppets; *see* KARAGÖZ) and the *li'bat Ismail Pacha* (*puppet theatre) to eager *audiences gathered around the *fedâwî* (storytellers) and *meddâh* (singer-reciters). In the European districts Italian and French *touring companies were active by the early nineteenth century, and a number of European *playhouses were constructed after 1840. *Verdi's *La traviata* was presented in 1856, three years after its première in Venice, and *A Masked Ball* in 1859, the same year it was first seen in *Rome. French became more widely understood throughout Tunis as more of the elite attended French universities, and plays enacted in French by Tunisians were seen by some factions in the colonial administration as a means of integrating Tunisians into Western civilization. A concerted move to develop a Tunisian national theatre resulted in 1908 in the creation of En-Najma (the Star), the first Tunisian theatre company, followed in 1945 by the Tunisian Theatre Defense Committee, which developed *training and gave Tunisians and Arabs access to municipal subsidies. A favourite venue for Egyptian companies in the first half of the twentieth century, many of *Cairo's theatre artists found a new home in Tunis and influenced the growth of Tunisian theatre.

The local passion for European work was manifested by the large number of companies—no fewer than twenty have existed at any time since the early twentieth century—and their evolution marks the periods in the city's theatrical history. Ash-shahâma and Al-adâb, founded in 1910 and 1911, merged in 1921 into At-tamthîl Al-arabî (the Arabian Theatre), which dominated the scene for a quarter-century. The Theatre Union (1936) and Al-Kawkab At-tamthîlî (Theatre Star, 1942) then rose to prominence, succeeded by the TVT (the company of the city of Tunis), the first indigenous troupe to be officially granted professional status since 1954. After independence, the TVT, under the direction of Ali *Ben Ayed from 1962 and resident in the municipal theatre, was the leading company. The municipal theatre continued to offer a regular programme by European companies, especially light French *comedies.

In the 1960s a counter-movement gained force, and by 1976 Al-*Masrah al-Jadid led the way for a professional theatre independent of state control, creating a new dynamic in the city's artistic life. A growing number of independent companies emerged, some of them receiving public assistance and their own playhouses (often abandoned cinemas). The New Theatre Company was the first, opening in the former cinema Lido with its cult piece *Autumn Rain* (1979), and the Organic Theatre Company, directed by Izzeddin Gannoun, still plays in the Cinema Al-Hamrâa. Directors Moncef Saym and Rajah Ben Ammar converted the Carthage Cinema for their Phou Theatre Company, while Tawfiq Jbali adapted the ballroom of a large hotel into El-Teatro. The Earth Theatre Company, created by playwright-director Noureddine Ouerghi and actress Nejia Ouerghi in the city of Jendouba, moved to Tunis in the 1980s, where it

has shared the task of promoting new work with the Familia Production Company, founded by director Fadhel Jaibi, actress Jalila Baccar, and producer Habib Belhédi. Some 30 Arab and *African companies visit Tunis during the biennial Festival International des Journées Théâtrales de Carthage, developed by the Tunisian National Theatre in 1983, giving Tunis a claim to be the capital of Arab and African theatre.   MMe

TURGENEV, IVAN (1818–83)

Russian novelist and playwright. Drama dominated the early part of Turgenev's writing career, novels the latter half. Though he wrote ten plays of varying length and quality, only *A Month in the Country* (1850) is responsible for his international status as a dramatist. Influenced by *Gogol, the early *satires suffered heavily from *censorship (especially in the difficult years after the 1848 disturbances in Europe), often waited years for production, and some were not performed: *Indiscretion* (1843), *Penury* (1845, produced 1852), *The Parasite* (1849, produced 1862), and *An Evening in Sorrento* (1852, produced 1885). A frequent visitor to France, Turgenev fell foul of the Russian authorities on a visit home in the early 1850s for his views on serfdom, contacts with radicals, and publication of a forbidden obituary for Gogol; as a result *A Month in the Country* languished for 22 years (written 1850, produced *Moscow, 1872). Only *The Bachelor* (1850), *Lunch with a Marshal of the Nobility* (1849), and *The Provincial Lady* (1851) reached the stage near the date of their composition.

Turgenev's drama raised little interest among *audiences in the early 1850s and the delay to his masterpiece may well have helped its reception, as did the performance of Maria Savina in one of the two main female roles in the 1879 production in *St Petersburg. *A Month in the Country* marks a move away from Gogol towards the *realism of Turgenev's contemporary Aleksandr *Ostrovsky, and also towards the topography and subtlety of his own novels and of *Chekhov nearly half a century later. A psychological drama with little overt *action, it examines the turbulence in relationships caused by the arrival of a young tutor at a country estate for the summer. Mother and young ward compete for his affections, creating a model for a series of triangular relationships and examining women in love from different angles. Such a passionate but *plotless structure demanded a new style of *acting and staging only fully achieved in *Stanislavsky's production (*Moscow Art Theatre, 1909). This interpretation dominated the twentieth century until Anatoly *Efros disturbed it with his 1977 version of passionately and physically expressed despair. Like Chekhov, Turgenev has been regarded as a writer in the European mould, and there have been many notable productions of the play outside Russia, including a *ballet version by Frederick Ashton (*London, 1977).
                                                                              CM

TURKKA, JOUKO (1942–   )

Finnish director and playwright. His period at the Helsinki City Theatre (1975–82) is remembered for his exciting interpretations of Finnish classics, such as Minna Canth's *folk *comedy *The Burglary* (1881), which dispensed with *dialogue and provoked his *audience with coarse, neorealistic (*see* REALISM AND REALITY) descriptions of the common people, shattering romantic clichés. He used simultaneous staging to create an overview of the Finnish Civil War of 1918 in Hannu Salama's *Where There's a Deed There's a Witness*. As head of the Finnish Theatre Academy in *Helsinki (1982–5) he emphasized physicality in *training. His methods are considered both oppressive and inspiring, and his passionate outlook is also evident in his own plays: *Lies* (1992), *Dear Deceptions in Love* (1996), and *Connecting People* (2000).
LIB

TURLUPIN (HENRI LEGRAND) (1587–1637)

French actor, called Belleville when acting in *tragedy. The youngest member of the famous *farce trio at the *Hôtel de Bourgogne, Turlupin is first mentioned there in 1615. In contrast to the rotund *Gros-Guillaume and the spidery *Gaultier-Garguille, he was well built and handsome; he played the knavish member of the trio, with a *mask that resembled the Italian *character Brighella's (*see* COMMEDIA DELL'ARTE). His stage name, which dates back to the fifteenth century, became a generic synonym for buffoon, and his comic speciality of low puns, or *turlupinades*, was still in vogue 40 years after his death among the idle younger courtiers of Louis XIV.
RWH

TURRINI, PETER (1944–   )

Austrian dramatist. His first play, *Rozznjogd* (*Rat Hunt*, 1971), established Turrini as one of a group of dramatists writing dialect plays, along with Wolfgang *Bauer, Franz Xaver *Kroetz, and Martin *Sperr. Six other plays immediately followed. With *Die Minderleister* (*Low Achievers*, 1988), on unemployment in the steel industry, Turrini blended social *realism with *surrealistic sequences and heightened language to achieve a modern-day *Passion play. His innovative combination of *folk theatre and experimental forms makes him one of the most interesting contemporary Austrian dramatists. Since the mid-1970s Turrini has also written for the *television series *Alpensaga*, dealing with life in a small village community from the beginning of industrialization in 1900 to the end of the Second World War.
CBB

TUSSAUD, MADAME *See* WAXWORKS.

TUTIN, DOROTHY (1931–2001)

English actress who trained at RADA and made her professional debut in 1950. Considered a leading young actress in the 1950s, her reputation was confirmed by her vivacious Cecily in Anthony Asquith's *film adaptation of *Wilde's *The Importance of Being Earnest* (1952). After working with the *Old Vic in *Bristol and *London, she joined the *Shakespeare Memorial Company at Stratford, where her major roles included Ophelia, Viola, and Juliet. In the West End she was a great success in Graham *Greene's *The Living Room* (1953), and the next year she was equally celebrated as Sally Bowles in *I Am a Camera*. In 1971 and 1972 she starred as Peter Pan at the London *Coliseum. Her screen appearances were less frequent but included the *film of *A Tale of Two Cities* (1958), Anne Boleyn in the BBC *television series *The Six Wives of Henry VIII* (1970), Goneril in *King Lear* (1984), and Alan *Bleasdale's *Jake's Progress* (1995). She was also a regular at the *Chichester Festival. Tutin was made DBE in 2000.
AS

TYL, JOSEF KAJETÁN (1808–56)

Czech playwright, actor, novelist, journalist, and *manager. He began as an actor with a German *touring company in 1829, but his efforts to perform plays in Czech increased after his return to *Prague (1831), where he soon became the leading figure of Czech theatre and ardent organizer of Czech cultural life in general. His *amateur company produced plays in Czech, and between 1846 and 1851 Tyl was the *dramaturg responsible for the Czech repertory in the Theatre of Estates. He wrote his most important plays in those years, both 'dramatic *folk tales' and 'scenes from life', moving from late *romanticism to early *realism, but always with strong patriotic and sentimental touches. As a result of his political activities he was forced to leave Prague and tour the Czech regions, where he died in poverty. Some of Tyl's plays still appear on the repertory of Czech theatres, including *The Bagpiper of Strakonice* (1847), *The Bloody Trial* and *Jan Hus* (both 1848), and *A Stubborn Woman* (1849).
ML

TYLER, ROYALL (1757–1826)

American jurist and playwright. Born in Boston and educated at Harvard, Tyler served briefly during the Revolutionary War but returned to Harvard to finish his legal studies (1779) and be admitted to the bar (1780). During a 1787 trip to *New York, he saw a production of *Sheridan's *School for Scandal* and within weeks had written *The Contrast*. Mounted by Thomas *Wignell's American Company in 1787 at the *John Street Theatre in New York, *The Contrast* became the first professionally produced American *comedy. The play introduced the *character of the Yankee, laying the groundwork for a comic line that lasted generations.
GAR

TYNAN, KENNETH (1927–80)

British critic and *dramaturg. For a decade Tynan was the most influential theatre critic in Britain, working 1954 to 1963 at the *Observer* (*see* CRITICISM). His elegant prose made him standard-bearer for the new theatres of the 1950s and 1960s, an early champion of *Brecht, *Beckett, Peter *Brook, Joan *Littlewood, and the *Royal Court dramatists. Of John *Osborne, he wrote famously that he doubted he 'could love anyone who did not wish to see *Look Back in Anger*'. Tynan always retained his youthful love of what he called 'high-definition performance' and charismatic stars like Noël *Coward, Orson *Welles, and Laurence *Olivier, for whom he worked between 1963 and 1969 as literary manager of the new *National Theatre. There he persuaded Olivier to play Othello and Shylock, brought in directors like Franco *Zeffirelli and Jacques Charon, and commissioned major plays, including Peter *Shaffer's *Black Comedy* (1965) and Peter *Nichols's *The National Health* (1969). A long-standing opponent of *censorship, he celebrated its abolition by producing the erotic *revue *Oh! Calcutta!* (1968). After his early death he was described by Tom *Stoppard, one of his discoveries, as 'part of the luck we had'. CDC

·U·

ÜBER-MARIONETTE

Term devised by Edward Gordon *Craig to describe the ideal performer in his revolutionary theatre. These dolls (replacing *actors, whom he found unacceptable in their reliance on physical and facial mannerisms) would be life-sized, exquisite, carved by expert sculptors, and moved mechanically with a *dancer's ritualized grace. The vision was part of Craig's desire to control all elements of a performance within one aesthetic concept and under the mastery of one individual: the designer-as-*director (*see* SCENOGRAPHY). The marionette was a compound of Craig's fascination with the *masks of *nō theatre, and with *puppets of the Italian tradition and of *Japanese *bunraku. The term *Über-marionette* is sometimes used to describe a living actor who is under the dictatorial control of a director.   RAC

UDALL, NICHOLAS (c.1505–1556)

English playwright. One-time headmaster of Eton College and later master of Westminster School, Udall probably wrote *Ralph Roister Doister* (c.1550), the only play that can be attributed to him with any certainty, for a school performance. Modelled on *Roman *comedy, the play balances comic inventiveness with pedagogical design. The parasite Merrygreek's mispronunciation of Roister Doister's love letter to Christian Custance leads to Roister Doister's rejection and a terrific mock battle in which the braggart soldier is routed. The play deliberately avoids scurrility and seeks to teach decency and modesty.   RWV

UKALA, SAM (1948–)

Nigerian playwright, director, and teacher. A resolute supporter of decolonization, Ukala set out to explore African traditional aesthetics and progressively subvert Western *dramaturgy. His plays, including *Akpaland* and *The Placenta of Death*, explore the contemporary possibilities of *folk styles. Building on a shared concern with popular theatre, Ukala worked with Bob Firth's UK-based Horse and Bamboo Theatre Company to create *Harvest of Ghosts*, a wordless piece of *festival theatre that took the 'judicial murder' of Ken *Saro-Wiwa and eight Ogoni activists as a starting point. It made use of *masked figures in a carefully choreographed production that was successfully performed in Britain in 1999.   JMG

ULISES, TEATRO DE

Mexican company. A group of writers, visual artists, and musicians, Ulises stood out for creating theatre for the elite at a time of revolutionary nationalism in Mexico. Lasting for only seven months in 1928, the theatre gained notoriety for its foreign (mostly European) repertoire and its abstract, minimalist productions, which outraged traditionalists who accused it of being snobbish and unpatriotic. Ulises established the model for future *alternative groups by its professional and intellectual approach, and by its casual, although sometimes combative, attitude to detractors.   KFN

ULIVE, UGO (1933–)

Venezuelan director, playwright, and *film producer, born in Uruguay. He learnt his trade with the El *Galpón de *Montevideo with Atahualpa *del Cioppo. From 1961 to 1965 he was director of the National Theatre of Cuba in *Havana, where he staged works by *García Lorca and *Brecht. In 1968 he was invited to direct for El *Nuevo Grupo in Caracas, where he achieved his greatest successes, particularly with productions of Harold *Pinter and Heiner *Müller. He made his debut as a playwright with *Prueba de fuego* (*Test of Fire*, 1981), for which he won an *award and much public acclaim; the play was also staged in *London. *Reynaldo* followed the next year, *Baile de máscaras* (*Masked*

Ball) in 1983, and *El dorado y el amor* (*El Dorado and Love*) in 1986. His work, highly conceptual, imaginative, and full of critical *realism, is nonetheless very personal.

LCL trans. AMCS

ULLMAN, LIV (1939–)

Norwegian actress who made her debut in Oslo in 1957 in the role of Anne Frank. Her *acting in a number of classical roles was characterized by intuitive intensity, though working with Peter *Palitzsch on *Brecht in 1961 she added distancing (*Verfremdung*) techniques. She is best known for Ingmar *Bergman's *films. In *Persona* (1966), *Cries and Whispers* (1972), *Scenes from a Marriage* (1974), and *Face to Face* (1976), she offered searing interpretations of *characters at breaking points in their lives. In 1975 she played Nora in an acclaimed production of *A Doll's House* in *New York. She turned to directing films at the end of the twentieth century: the family saga *Sofie* (1992), and *Faithless* (2000), scripted by Bergman.   DT

UNDERSTUDY

An actor, usually an apprentice or a junior member of the company, who prepares a role in which a major player has been cast, in order to (*a*) further her *training, (*b*) assume the role should the original actor be unable to do so. The practice is venerable, but is most common where companies are stable and training institutionalized. The understudy who blossoms into a star when the opportunity arises is a cliché of the American *musical. The requirement for understudies has been standardized in many professional theatres by *trade union negotiations.

RWV

UNITI

An Italian *commedia dell'arte* troupe of this name is recorded at intervals between 1578 and 1640: over this period it is unlikely that it maintained a continuous character or identity. Like other companies it received the protection of the dukes of Mantua, and performed in northern and central Italy.   RAA

UNITIES

Theoretical considerations which formed the basis for *neoclassical *tragedy, and whose practical application was to provide an important set of prescriptive 'rules' for the *genre. The three unities—of time, place, and *action—were often traced back to *Aristotle, though the text of the *Poetics* specifically recommends only that of *action* as a binding condition; the unity of *time* is noted merely as Aristotle's practical experience of theatrical performance: 'tragedy endeavours, as far as possible, to confine itself to a single revolution of the sun . . .' From this

far from magisterial statement was to develop a dogmatic assertion of the rules for dramatic composition, which were to retain their importance, especially in France, for over 200 years. The unity of *place* was deemed (by J.-C. Scaliger, writing on Aristotle in 1561) to follow, as a logical consequence, from that of time; and the theory of the three unities, once established in Italy by *Castelvetro's edition of the *Poetics* (1570), followed in France by Jean de *La Taille in *De l'art de la tragédie* (1572), lost little time in assuming the character of an immutable doctrine. In practice, the new doctrine was largely ignored both in the Spanish Golden Age theatre and in the Elizabethan age of Shakespeare, *Marlowe, and others (in spite of its favourable formulation by *Sidney in his *Defense of Poesy*, c.1580; *see* EARLY MODERN PERIOD IN EUROPE). In France, however, after a rearguard action fought on behalf of 'irregular' tragedy and *tragicomedy by François Ogier in 1628, there is little sign of dissension among dramatists or their critics about the basic doctrine of the unities: even during the aftermath of *Corneille's success with *Le Cid* in 1637 his adversaries criticized him, not for non-observance of the unity of time, but for crowding too many events into the single day of the play's action. By the time of the publication of his *Discours des trois unités* in 1660 Corneille was almost as orthodox in his commentary on the 'rules' as his critic *Aubignac. Perhaps his most notable innovations are the definition of unity of action as 'unité de péril' (the *hero should not be exposed—as Rodrigue in *Le Cid* had manifestly been —to a multiplicity of dangers), and with regard to the unity of place, the idea of a 'fictional' setting, that is, a space onto which the private apartments of the *dramatis personae, the kings and queens, would open.

*Racine was masterful in handling the unities, whether in the case of a mythological subject like *Phèdre* (1677) or a subject from Roman history such as *Bérénice* (1670). Theorists paid less attention to *comedy than to tragedy in this respect; but it would be difficult to find a play in which the three unities are more completely (and unobtrusively) observed than *Molière's *The Misanthrope* (1666). It was *Boileau, a contemporary of Molière and Racine, who formulated in his *Art poétique* (1674) what has remained the neatest encapsulation of the doctrine:

> Qu'en un lieu, qu'en un jour, un seul fait accompli
> Tienne jusqu'à la fin le théâtre rempli.

('In a single place, and a single day, the working-out of a single event must hold the *audience captive.') Among diehard champions of the neoclassical formula in the eighteenth century —by which time the challenge of Shakespeare had to be reckoned with—the name of *Voltaire must be given pride of place, though it is true that defence of the unities formed only one part of his campaign. Even earlier than this, in the days of Corneille and Racine, the formal technicalities of composition according to the three unities were often subsumed in what has been called the 'fourth unity': the unity of tone, or overall aesthetic coherence, together with that other pillar of neoclassical doctrine, the *bienséances* (*decorum). In the early nineteenth century the historian Guizot was to write that the partisans of neoclassicism were wrong to insist exclusively on the unities; what mattered, he declared, was the 'unité d'impression', which Shakespeare had achieved by quite different means. The conservatism of the *Comédie-Française, however, still succeeded not only in preserving the repertoire of the past, but in encouraging new playwrights to adhere to the neoclassical formula; and it was left to Victor *Hugo, by argument in his *Préface de Cromwell* (1827) and by demonstration in his play *Hernani* (1830), to prove the viability on the French stage of a radically different *dramaturgy. *See also* THEORIES OF DRAMA, THEATRE, AND PERFORMANCE.   WDH

UNITY THEATRE

An influential and long-lasting left-wing company in *London. Its first success was *Odets's *Waiting for Lefty* (1936), and though much of its material was written by members and its actors were usually *amateur, it had an important international output, including *Señora Carrar's Rifles*, which was the first *Brecht play in Britain (1937), *O'Casey's *The Star Turns Red* (1940), *Sartre's *Nekrassov* (1956), and *Adamov's *Spring 71* (1962). Its actors and directors included Paul *Robeson, Ted Willis, Lionel *Bart, Alfie Bass, and Bob Hoskins, who presented and *toured *living newspapers, *documentary dramas, *satire, and political *pantomimes. Its rented base in Goldington Street was burnt out in 1975, and the theatre did not recover. *See also* POLITICS AND THEATRE.   EEC

UNIVERSITY AND SCHOOL DRAMA

Although the reading and perhaps the recitation of plays for the purposes of moral and rhetorical instruction occurred as early as the tenth century in Europe, dramatic performance as part of an organized educational curriculum was the work of *early modern humanist scholars at the end of the fifteenth century. The repertory consisted of (*a*) classical plays in their original languages, (*b*) new plays composed in Latin, and (*c*) new plays in the vernacular, based on classical models. Its purpose was to teach rhetorical and grammatical eloquence, sound moral precepts, and a civilized imperturbability.

*Roman drama, especially the *comedy of *Terence, was central to both *medieval and Renaissance academic theatre. In the tenth century *Hrotsvitha modelled six plays on Terence. In the twelfth century, the authors of the Latin *comoedia* from the Loire Valley combined Terence with Ovid. In fourteenth-century Italy humanistic writers, including Petrarch, wrote plays of university life based on Terence. Notions of staging were confused, however, and even in the fifteenth century humanist imitations of classical comedy and *tragedy retained a

medieval structure. Students may or may not have performed Latin plays before the fifteenth century, but they had certainly acted in medieval *farces and *moralities, and some of their teachers tapped this enthusiasm for educational purposes. Julius Pomponius Laetus (1425–98) exploited the new availability of Latin texts at his Roman Academy, where *Plautus and Terence were regularly performed; and Ravisius Textor (*c*.1476–1524) wrote a number of farces, morals, and *dialogues for his pupils at the University of *Paris. By the early sixteenth century the acting of classical plays and of imitations in Latin (and later the vernacular) was firmly established in schools and universities throughout Europe. In France, dramatists of the Pléiade found actors and *audiences in colleges. In England, academic playwrights wrote plays for performance at schools, at the universities, and for the *Inns of Court.

The potential for *religious instruction was recognized at an early date by both Protestants and Catholics. The publication in 1501 of Hrotsvitha's plays inspired what has become known as the 'Christian Terence', in which Terentian *dramaturgy was united with edifying subject matter, usually biblical, reflecting Christian values. The Christian Terence was a staple of schoolmasters in the Protestant areas of northern Europe, but similar academic plays were also acted at English universities. *Abraham sacrifiant*, a 'tragedy' by the Calvinist Théodore de *Bèze, was acted by students in Lausanne in 1550. Although Calvinist reformers were critical of public entertainments, and at the Synod of Nîmes (1572) banned all plays, they specifically excepted 'those of a strictly educational character'. Two Latin tragedies by the Scottish scholar George Buchanan—examples of the 'Christian *Seneca'—were acted at Bordeaux 1540–3 by the author's pupils, including Montaigne, who recalled the occasions with pleasure. The Catholic equivalent of the Protestant Christian Terence was provided by the *Jesuits who, at their colleges throughout continental Europe, produced, between 1551 and 1773, an estimated 100,000 plays, initially in Latin but by the seventeenth century increasingly in the vernacular. *See also* REFORMATION AND COUNTER-REFORMATION.   RWV

UNIVERSITY TRAVELLING THEATRE

Social and artistic movement, chiefly in anglophone regions of *Africa, designed to take plays from academic centres to provincial or rural areas, that helped solve problems of patronage in post-colonial Africa. At the University of Ibadan, Nigeria, between 1961 and 1967 students such as Alfred Opubor and Dapo Adelugba, supported by expatriate academics Martin Banham and Geoffrey Axworthy, created a theatre modelled on indigenous travelling forms such as *alarinjo* and Yoruba opera. Other West African universities followed suit, including Legon (Ghana) and Fourah Bay (Sierra Leone). A major 1965 *tour by Uganda's Makerere Free Travelling theatre of East Africa inspired many regional institutions, including Zambia's

*Chikwakwa Theatre and the Universities of Nairobi (Kenya), Dar es Salaam (Tanzania), Malawi, and Botswana. University travelling theatre normally mixes plays in English with those in local African languages, though some universities tried to push beyond the ideology of 'taking theatre to the people' by linking the tours to workshops in theatre skills or to participatory *development work with community groups. Since the 1960s the movement has provided a seedbed for many African dramatists and directors.

DaK

UNIVERSITY WITS

Culturally inclined to favour evolutionary models of historical development, Victorian literary scholars were struck by what seemed to be a quantum leap in the sophistication of English drama in the 1580s. In 1887, George Saintsbury proposed that this was caused by the emergence of a group of university-educated dramatists, notably *Lyly, *Peele, *Greene, and *Marlowe, whom he called 'the university wits'. The theory is now discredited (the *London theatres had employed university graduates as scriptwriters since at least the mid-1570s), but the phrase is still used as a convenient term for Shakespeare's immediate professional predecessors.

MJW

UNRUH, FRITZ VON (1885–1970)

German playwright and novelist. Of aristocratic Prussian background, Unruh came to the fore with his poetic *expressionist dramas *Vor der Entscheidung* (*Before the Decision*, 1914), a discussion of *Kleist, and *Offiziere* (*Officers*, 1911), a play that treats the conflict between military discipline and self-determined action. Recipient of the prestigious Kleist *award in 1915 and celebrated as the 'new Kleist', von Unruh's significance was partly dependent on his position as a representative of the military class who turned to pacifism around the time of the First World War. The poetic *tragedy *Ein Geschlecht* (*A Race*, 1918) is an expressionist work in which the horror of war is transcended by a utopian vision of a new race of mankind. His later plays treat mainly *historical themes in a variety of dramatic styles. Despite continued output, his work after the First World War never attained the pre-eminence of the early plays. After a short political career in the 1920s, von Unruh moved to Italy and France in the 1930s. After internment in France, he escaped to *New York, and returned to Germany in 1962.

CBB

URBAN, JOSEPH (1872–1933)

Austrian-American designer. At first an architect in Germany and Austria, Urban began to work with the *Vienna *Burgtheater in 1905 and was quickly in demand as an *opera designer all over Europe. In 1912 he moved to the USA, collaborating with the *modernist directors R. E. *Jones, Lee *Simonson, and Norman *Bel Geddes, as well as designing for major opera houses, the *Ziegfeld Follies*, and *musicals. An important influence in American theatre, Urban belonged to the first generation who put the theories of *Appia and *Craig into practice. Innovative both technically and aesthetically, Urban applied pointillist techniques to scene *painting, thus allowing for parts of the scenic image to appear or disappear under different coloured lights; also he was one of the first to use platforms and portals which generated a frame and focus on the stage while providing continuous elements for unit sets.

CBB

URDU THEATRE IN INDIA

Urdu is the sister language to *Hindi, possessing the same grammar and syntax with elevated diction borrowed from Arabic and Persian instead of Sanskrit. Urdu emerged as a language of the stage in the nineteenth century, when it was sometimes termed Hindustani, helping to spread popular musical theatre throughout South and South-East Asia. In the twentieth century, it became a vehicle of modern drama primarily among urban north *Indian Muslims. Urdu continued in a larger capacity, however, as the medium of Bombay (*Mumbai) *film, *radio dramas, and *television serials.

The first major theatrical work in Urdu was Amanat's *Indar Sabha* (1853), a product of the cultural renaissance at the Lucknow court. Combining elements from romance tales (*masnavi*), Urdu *ghazal*s, and Braj Bhasha poetry, this pageant of song and *dance was popular for a century. Its success stemmed from its hedonistic atmosphere and spectacular productions by *Parsi theatrical companies. Companies recognized the potential of Urdu not only as a lingua franca but as a repository of north India's rich poetic and musical traditions. From the 1870s professional writers penned hundreds of Urdu dramas for the Parsi companies. At first these were rough translations of Gujarati dramas by Parsis (Marazban's *Khurshid*, Aram's *Nurjehan* and *Benazir Badr-e Munir*). Soon the Urdu medium came into its own, and it remained the Parsi theatre's preferred language. Raunaq published plays based on old Indo-Islamic tales, legends of the Punjab, historical themes, and social problems such as drunkenness. The next generation, Murad, Habab, and Abdullah, were north Indians recruited to the Bombay companies. Their dramas followed the same types, although Indic (Sanskritic) stories like *Shakuntala* also appeared (see KALIDASA). Shakespearian adaptations dominated the output of Ahsan and the early Agha Hashr Kashmiri (1879–1935), the most renowned playwright of the period. Later Hashr specialized in 'socials' (*Silver King*, *Yahudi ki Ladki*) and Hindu mythological material (*Bilwa Mangal*, *Bhagirath Ganga*). Talib and Betab were other important playwrights. All were attached to prominent companies like the Victoria, the Alfred, the New Alfred, or the

Madan Theatres, whose owners commissioned their dramas and published them.

Literary playwriting in Urdu dates to Taj's *Anarkali* (1927), a well-constructed historical romance, followed by other dramas written along European lines by academics. With the founding of the *Indian People's Theatre Association, a stronger nationalist voice entered Urdu theatre. Eminent poets like Ali Sardar Jafri and Khwaja Ahmad Abbas wrote *realistic plays dealing with contemporary and historical issues. Radio plays by well-known Urdu novelists Manto, Bedi, Krishan Chandar, and Upendranath Ashk were also important during the 1940s. One early IPTA member was Habib *Tanvir, whose *Agra Bazar, Mitti Ki Gadi*, and *Charandas Chor* have invested Urdu theatre with new vitality. Working with performers from the Chhattisgarh region, Tanvir has bridged the urban–rural divide with his hybrid style of production. *See also* PAKISTAN.

KH

URE, ALBERTO (*c.*1940–)

Controversial Argentinian director, noted for his psycho-dramatic techniques and emphasis on perversion and cruelty. Eduardo *Pavlovsky calls him a 'master at tautening *texts without breaking them'. In 1977 Ure directed Pavlovsky's *Spiderwebs*, the first play officially prohibited by the military junta. His 1984 restaging of Griselda *Gambaro's *The Camp* had Emma, concentration camp prisoner-henchwoman, wear a French-maid's uniform instead of a burlap smock, and tiptoe on invisible pumps.

JGJ

URE, MARY (1933–75)

Scottish actress, born and *trained in *Glasgow. Her rather vulnerable beauty made her an effective Ophelia in Peter *Brook's 1955 *Hamlet* with Alec *Clunes and Paul *Scofield. In 1956 she was again in Brook's company for *The Visit* with Anthony *Quayle, and she made her most celebrated stage appearance as Alison in the première of John *Osborne's *Look Back in Anger* at the *Royal Court that year. Also in 1956 she appeared on Broadway opposite Vivien *Leigh in Robert *Helpmann's production of *Duel of Angels* (1960). She was first married to Osborne and later to the actor Robert Shaw.

AS

USIGLI, RODOLFO (1905–79)

Mexican playwright. Self-proclaimed father of the modern Mexican stage, he championed a *national theatre that would hold up a mirror to Mexico's social and political realities. A harsh critic of those who betrayed the revolution for personal gain, Usigli gained notoriety with *The Impostor*, an exploration of the psychology of political demagoguery. Written in 1938, its première ten years later elicited strong protests from the political left and right, who both objected to the central delusional

*character, César Rubio, a failed history professor who comes to believe that he is the military hero of the same name who was murdered during the revolution. The character also dies at the hands of the man who betrayed the real César Rubio. The author of some 40 plays, Usigli believed the theatre to be a place of self-discovery, no matter how painful the process. In *historical plays, such as the trilogy *Crown of Shadows* (1947), *Crown of Fire* (1961), and *Crown of Light* (1964), he looked to Mexico's past in order to understand its painful entry into modernity. Other work focused on private lives, revealing the psychological effects of sexual repressions and social hypocrisies; *Jano Is a Woman* remains one of the best. Usigli is generally recognized as the major figure in twentieth-century Mexican drama; the most important theatre research centre in Mexico, the CITRU, is named in his honour.

KFN

USLAR PIETRI, ARTURO (1906–)

Venezuelan writer whose plays include *El ultraje* (*The Insult*, 1927), *La llave* (*The Key*, 1928), *El día de Antero Albán* (*Antero Albán's Day*, 1957), directed by Nicolás Curiel at the Teatro Universitario, and *El Dios invisible* (*The Invisible God*, 1958). The Los Caobos theatre opened with *Chúo Gil*, directed by Albio *Paz to much critical acclaim. Other plays include *La Tebaida* (*The Story of the Thebans*) and *La fuga de Miranda* (*Miranda's Escape*). He was awarded the National Prize for literature in 1955.

LCL trans. AMCS

USTINOV, PETER (1921–)

English actor, director, writer, raconteur, and broadcaster, the London-born son of White Russian émigrés. Ustinov was educated at Westminster School and trained under Michel *Saint-Denis at the London Theatre School, He made his debut in 1938 in *Chekhov's *The Wood Demon* and his *London debut at the Players' Theatre in his own *Late Joys* (1939). Although he has performed a variety of plays, Ustinov is more closely associated with productions of his own work. He has appeared in or directed *Fishing for Shadows* (1940), *The Love of Four Colonels* (1951), and *Romanoff and Juliet* (1957), and acted in, directed, and produced the latter's *film version in 1961. Lear at the *Stratford Festival, Ontario (1979), was his first Shakespearian role. Later plays include *Photofinish* (1962), *The Unknown Soldier and his Wife* (1967), *Who's Who in Hell* (1974), *Overboard* (1981), and *Beethoven's Tenth* (1983). Film appearances of note include *Spartacus* (1960), *Topkapi* (1964)—both of which brought him Academy awards—*Logan's Run* (1976), and *Death on the Nile* (1978). His autobiography is *Dear Me* (1977).

AS

U'TAMSI, TCHICAYA (GÉRARD FÉLIX) (1931–88)

Born in Mpili, U'Tamsi went to France in 1946, abandoned his studies, and led a bohemian life with a series of jobs. Encouraged by Aimé *Césaire to pursue a literary career, he published several volumes of poetry in the 1950s. As a journalist with the overseas broadcasting station La France d'Outre-Mer, he adapted and dramatized African *folk tales as well as writing his own serials. In 1960 he went to Kinshasa to cover the independence celebrations centring around Patrice Lumumba, and subsequently worked for UNESCO in Paris until his retirement. U'Tamsi came to the theatre through the air waves but once said, 'if I owned a hall, had actors and money, all I would do is theatre'. His two-play sequence *Le Zulu* and *Vwène le fondateur* (*The Zulu* and *Vwene, the Founding Hero*, 1977), about a *clownish president who commits grotesque horrors, is similar to *Macbeth* in the destructive and tragic passion that grips the *hero. After *Le Destin glorieux du Maréchal Nnikon Nniku Prince qu'on sort* (*The Glorious Destiny of Marshal Nnikon Nniku, the Presentable Prince Consort*, 1979), he returned to the events of the Congo in *Le Bal de Ndinga* (*Ndinga's Dance*), a lament in several voices. Produced by Théâtre International de Langue Française (Paris, 1987) to the strains of the song 'Indépendance Cha-Cha' by the African Jazz band, the play explored the hopes and disillusionment of an entire (de)colonized society.

PNN trans. JCM

·V·

VACA, JUSEPA (fl. 1602–34)

The most famous actress of early seventeenth-century Spain. In 1602 she married the *actor-manager Juan de Morales Medrano, and the company they led was one of the most important until 1632, when their daughter Mariana married Antonio de *Prado and they joined his. Jusepa's dynamic talent, especially in mannish and transvestite roles, was displayed in dramas written for her by playwrights like Lope de *Vega and *Vélez de Guevara.

VFD

VACIKA

A fundamental category in classical *Indian theatre, incorporating all aspects of speech and voice in performance. Verbal *acting—*vacikabhinaya*—demands the most rigorous discipline at multiple levels: speech, diction, pronunciation, enunciation, intonation, modulation, knowledge of metrical patterns, and appropriate modes of address. In Sanskrit drama, Sanskrit is spoken by the upper-caste *characters, while different dialects of Prakrit are assigned to characters from the lower sections of society, including women. Speech traditions in classical theatre such as *kutiyattam* cannot be entirely separated from song and chanting, or, more precisely, an understanding of the musical component of each word that can be used to register particular emotions through specific breathing techniques. In *folk theatre traditions such as *yakshagana*, the *vacika* of the actors is improvised at crucial points in the narrative, thereby interrupting the musical structure of the performance. *See also* ABHINAYA.

LSR/RB

VAKHTANGOV, EVGENY (1883–1922)

Russian actor, *theorist, and director who played minor roles at the *Moscow Art Theatre before being identified by *Stanislav-sky as a likely exponent and teacher of the emerging 'system'. Sensing that the established Art Theatre actors were not prepared to devote themselves to the task of assimilating new methods, Stanislavsky established the First *Studio in 1912 as a breeding ground for younger members of the company under the tutelage of Vakhtangov, *Sulerzhitsky, and Boris Sushkevich. It was here that Michael *Chekhov, Boris *Zakhava, Yury *Zavadsky, and others were initiated into the emotional and intellectual disciplines required by the new approaches to *acting, which assumed forms of quasi-religious, spiritual, and emotional intensity. Having acquired his first experiences as a director at the First Studio, Vakhtangov came into his own when he moved out to what became known as the Third Studio of the Moscow Art Theatre (after 1926, the Vakhtangov Theatre). Already he was beginning to tire of the overcharged and slightly incestuous atmosphere of the First Studio. He had been excited by *Meyerhold's pre-revolutionary experiments at various fringe locations in *St Petersburg, and had become interested in notions of the theatrical *grotesque and more overt forms of stage expressiveness. In fact, he was working towards his own concept of 'fantastic *realism', which he put into effective practice with productions of *Maeterlinck's *The Miracle of St Anthony*, *Chekhov's *The Wedding*, *Gozzi's *Princess Turandot*, and Solomon *Anski's *The Dybbuk* in an intense flourish of creativity during the early 1920s before his untimely death from stomach cancer. The two most significant productions of this period were undoubtedly those of *Princess Turandot* at the Third Studio, which he *rehearsed whilst terminally ill, and a guest production at the *Habima Theatre of *The Dybbuk*, rehearsed in Russian but acted in Hebrew. It is interesting to note that Vakhtangov's changing views of the nature and purpose of theatre were almost in direct response to the Russian Revolution. Putting aside his original doubts, he accepted the revolution and incorporated its implications in his work, even going so far as to contemplate staging a *mass performance.

His post-revolutionary productions tended to be either ironic commentaries on a superannuated social and religious past (Chekhov, Maeterlinck) in productions which deployed all the resources of the comic and fantastic grotesque or, as with Gozzi's play, celebrated a new-found expressive freedom, endorsed through the élan of improvisatory discovery, which synthesized popular forms with sophisticated artistry. The première of *Turandot* was a festive occasion, the exoticism of an Eastern fairy tale, supported by the ornately cubist design by Ignaty Nivinsky, merging with styles of popular Western acting and staging traditions which harked back to the medieval *mummers' play, the *pantomime, the harlequinade, the *puppet show, and *commedia dell'arte. The production is rightly considered one of the most memorable and influential in Soviet and Russian theatre. NW

VALDEZ, LUIS (1940–)

American playwright, director, actor, and filmmaker. Born in rural California to Mexican farmworker parents, Valdez wrote his first play, *The Shrunken Head of Pancho Villa*, in 1964 while an undergraduate at California State University, San Jose. In 1965 he founded the Teatro *Campesino (Farmworkers' Theatre), a *touring troupe that inspired other young *Chicanos to create their own *teatros*. Valdez's play with music *Zoot Suit* (1978) exposes the racial discrimination suffered by Chicanos in Los Angeles in the 1940s. Co-produced by Teatro Campesino, it was first seen at the *Mark Taper Forum in *Los Angeles and was the first (and only) play by and about a Chicano to be produced on Broadway (1979). Valdez adapted and directed this play for the screen in 1981; he also wrote and directed the *film *La Bamba* (1987), about the 1950s rock singer Richie Valens. He directed his play *I Don't Have to Show You No Stinking Badges!* (1986), a *satire about Hollywood stereotyping, at the Taper. His most recent play, *The Mummified Deer* (2000), tells the story of a dying 80-year-old Mexican woman whose family becomes a metaphor for the Chicanos' history in the south-west. Valdez's career has been an eclectic mixture of *actos* (sketches), plays, videos, films, and essays. He remains the most visible Chicano playwright, director, and filmmaker, and continues to dedicate his work to the experiences of the Chicanos. JAH

VALENTIN, KARL (1882–1948)

German comedian, author, and *filmmaker. A product of the local *vaudeville and *cabaret tradition, together with his partner Liesl Karlstadt, he raised Bavarian *folk comedy to a high level by creating a comic world comprised of the recalcitrance of inanimate objects, cross-purpose language, and the malignity of human nature, prefiguring in many respects the theatre of the *absurd. He was admired by *Brecht, who compared him to Chaplin as an artist able to bridge the gap between the popular and the *avant-garde. CBB

VALLE-INCLÁN, RAMÓN DEL (1866–1936)

Spanish playwright, novelist, and *theorist. Although his first play was staged in 1899, his fame as a dramatist is largely based on plays written in the 1920s. *Bohemian Lights* (1921–5) is his undisputed masterpiece and the first of his *esperpentos*. As described in the play's *dialogue, the term represents an aesthetic of *grotesque deformation such as occurs in the concave mirrors of a funhouse. *Divine Words* (1922), a grotesque exploration of superstition and debauchery in rural Galicia, was staged by Margarita *Xirgu in 1933, under the playwright's close supervision, and was not seen again until José Tamayo circumvented *censorship to produce it in *Madrid in 1961. *Barbaric Plays*, an epic trilogy comprising two early plays of 1907 and 1908 and the later *Silver Face* (1922), was finally staged in its entirety in 1974 at Frankfurt's Stadt Schauspielhaus. In 1991 it received productions at Jorge *Lavelli's Théâtre National de la Colline and at Spain's National Theatre Centre. *Dublin's *Abbey Theatre staged the first production in English in 2000, directed by Calixto *Bieito, in a translation by Frank *McGuinness called *Barbaric Comedies*. Seen as a precursor of *Artaud, *Brecht, and *Ionesco, Valle-Inclán is now ranked with *Garcia Lorca in the hierarchy of modern Spanish theatre. MPH

VALLEJO, MANUEL DE (fl. 1619–44)

Spanish *actor-manager. Taking over his father's company in 1621, he led it successfully until his death. In 1631 its members, who included then his famous but short-lived wife María de Riquelme and the star performer Damián Arias de Peñafiel, joined the Cofradía de la Novena, the important actors' guild newly formed by himself and others. His similarly named son was also a leading actor-manager, especially in the 1670s. VFD

VAMPILOV, ALEKSANDR (1937–72)

Soviet/Russian playwright. Vampilov studied philology at Irkutsk University and completed his studies at the Institute of Literature, *Moscow. His plays challenged a social type of his time, the egoist and materialist who lacks moral values. *Farewell in June* (1966) investigates corruption, *The Elder Son* (1970) explores self-betrayal of a materialistic nature, while *Duck-Hunting* (1970) and *Last Summer in Chulimsk* (1973) continue the concern with egoism. Vampilov's *dramaturgy is informed by a critical view of Soviet society: he attacks the corruption allowed by the system, bureaucracy that takes no account of individuals,

One of David Garrick's most effective comic roles was Sir John Brute in drag, in his revised version of **Vanbrugh**'s *The Provok'd Wife*, Drury Lane, London, 1768. In Vanbrugh's original text Brute appears in this scene dressed as a bishop.

and the suspiciousness that infects those who are themselves subjected to suspicion.   BB

VAN BRIDGE, TONY (1917–   )

Canadian actor and director. Born in England, he studied at the *Royal Academy of Dramatic Art, acted in weekly *repertory, and, after the war, spent seven years with the *Young Vic and *Old Vic companies. In 1954 he emigrated to Canada where he became a leading classical actor, appearing with the *Stratford Festival (fifteen seasons), the *Shaw Festival (22 seasons), and many *regional theatres in Canada and the USA. At Stratford he excelled in comic parts such as Bottom (1960) and Falstaff (1965–7), and at the Shaw Festival directed three J. B. *Priestley plays in successive years (1988–90). He was an award-winning *television actor (*Judge*, 1981–4) and for several years *toured as G. K. Chesterton in a *one-person play he also wrote. An autobiography appeared in 1995.   DWJ

VANBRUGH, JOHN (1664–1726)

English playwright and architect. After an early ten-year career in royal service and the military, Vanbrugh established his dramatic credentials with two successful *comedies, *The Relapse* (1696), a sequel to and a rebuttal of Colley *Cibber's *Love's Last Shift* (1696), featuring Cibber himself as Lord Foppington, and *The Provok'd Wife* (1697), an uncompromising look at the marital discord as well as the bliss that defines marriage. Vanbrugh replied to Jeremy *Collier's attack on his immorality and profanity (see ANTI-THEATRICAL POLEMIC) in *A Vindication of the Relapse and the Provok'd Wife* (1698). The bulk of Vanbrugh's remaining plays were adaptations and translations of French work, while *The Pilgrim* (1700) is an adaptation from *Fletcher. These adaptations were nevertheless more than hack work, and in some cases represent improvements on the originals. As an architect, Vanbrugh designed Castle Howard (1701), Blenheim Palace (1705), and the *Haymarket Opera (1703), which he co-managed with *Congreve in 1705-6. His last play, *The Provok'd Husband*, left unfinished at his death, was completed by Cibber in 1728.   RWV

VANCOUVER

Canada's third-largest city, founded in 1886 as the terminus of the first national railway. Its many theatrical venues include three city-owned theatres: the 2,900-seat Queen Elizabeth Theatre (opened 1959) which hosts local *opera and *ballet productions as well as *touring *musicals and concerts; the 670-seat *Vancouver Playhouse next door; and the Orpheum, a 2,800-seat former *vaudeville house and cinema beautifully restored as a concert hall. A second mainstream theatre company, the Arts Club, emerged in the 1960s and now produces, under long-time *artistic director Bill Millerd, about fifteen productions per year in three venues. Another company, Bard on the Beach, presents Shakespeare each summer in a tent overlooking English Bay. Fed by theatre schools at local universities and colleges, *alternative professional theatre flourishes at several smaller venues such as the Firehall Arts Centre and the Vancouver East Cultural Centre, as well as an annual *fringe festival. The Playwrights Theatre Centre, founded in 1970 as the New Play Centre, is the oldest of Vancouver companies devoted to developing new Canadian plays. Despite all this activity, however, Vancouver's mild climate and spectacular setting sometimes seem to weaken *audience commitment by providing many other attractions.

In its early years, Vancouver saw limited professional theatre due to its distance from other theatre centres. Its first important companies were *amateur: the University of British Columbia's Players' Club (founded 1915) and the Vancouver Little Theatre (founded 1921). In the 1930s the UBC Extension Department began offering theatre instruction throughout the province, and its teacher Dorothy Somerset later established a summer theatre school and a theatre department at UBC. The extension work inspired Vancouver's first post-war professional company, Everyman Theatre, founded in 1946 by Somerset's colleague Sidney Risk. Everyman started with a bus tour across western Canada, then performed in a storefront theatre before backers took it to a larger playhouse downtown, where it closed after a 1953 production of *Tobacco Road* brought police action. Another professional venture, Totem Theatre (1951-4), started as outdoor summer stock, but achieved its greatest success with winter seasons on an intimate *arena stage. Much theatre talent at the time was groomed in musicals, notably at Theatre under the Stars, which presented lavish summer productions in Stanley Park beginning in 1940. The success of such seasonal companies led to a major initiative, the Vancouver International Festival (1958-68), which featured emerging international music, opera, and theatre stars alongside local talent.
                                      DWJ

VANCOUVER PLAYHOUSE

The regional theatre of Canada's third-largest city. It was founded in 1963 to be the resident company of a new community-based, city-owned theatre, and now produces about six plays each season in that 650-seat space. In its early years the company's most celebrated productions were new plays that reflected local issues and values such as Eric Nicol's *Like Father Like Fun* (1966) and George *Ryga's *The Ecstasy of Rita Joe* (1967). *Artistic directors have included Christopher *Newton (1973-9), Larry Lillo (1988-93), and Glynis Leyshon (1997-). An important recent production was *The Overcoat*, an original movement piece based on the story by *Gogol, premièred in 1997 and *toured nationally in 2000.   DWJ

VAN DRUTEN, JOHN (1901-57)

Anglo-American playwright and director. Born in London, Van Druten studied and briefly taught law, but soon embraced writing full time. After a 1926 lecture tour in America, he moved to California and in 1944 became a US citizen. His total output for the stage—sometimes adapted from other sources, and often directed by him—comes to 29 works. The cast of his first play, *The Return Half* (1924), was headed by the then unknown John *Gielgud. After a few problem plays, he devoted himself largely to escapist middle-class *comedies, starting with *There's Always Juliet* (1931). His two greatest successes were the sophisticated three-character *The Voice of the Turtle* (1943), which chalked up 1,557 performances in *New York, and the folksy 23-person *I Remember Mama* (1944), which ran for 714. His *I Am a Camera* (1951) was the basis of the *musical *Cabaret* (1966), which ran for 1,165 performances. He wrote two autobiographies, *The Way to the Present* (1938) and *The Widening Circle* (1957).   CT

VAN ITALLIE, JEAN-CLAUDE (1936-)

Belgian-born American playwright. Van Itallie moved to the United States when he was 4 years old and was educated at Harvard. After briefly studying *acting at the *Neighborhood Playhouse in *New York, he became playwright-in-residence for the *Open Theatre (1963-8). His plays for the company were characterized by a break with psychological *realism and an exploration of 'transformations', depictions of *characters undergoing rapid shifts of persona. *America Hurrah* (1966), a trilogy of *one-acts, was written as an *absurdist *satire of American culture. His next major work, *The Serpent* (1968), broke new aesthetic ground and established Van Itallie as one of the premier playwrights of his generation. Written for an ensemble, the play interweaves the biblical story of Genesis with disturbing re-enactments of the Zabruder *film of President Kennedy's assassination. During the 1970s he became an important adaptor of *Chekhov. Frequently working with directors Joseph *Chaikin and Andrei *Şerban, his adaptations of *The Seagull* (1973), *The Cherry Orchard* (1977), *Three Sisters* (1979), and *Uncle Vanya* (1983) received numerous productions in New York and major *regional theatres. He revisited the style of the Open Theatre with his ambitious adaptation of *The Tibetan Book of the Dead* for *La Mama in 1983. The project reflected the playwright's increasing engagement with Buddhism as a way to conceive of 'the healing power of theatre', especially towards issues of war, poverty, and disease. Van Itallie remained a prolific playwright during the 1980s and 1990s while holding a number of influential teaching positions at Yale, Princeton, Columbia, and New York universities.   JAB

VARIETY

Variety entertainment or variety theatre consists of a collection of individual acts—such as song, *dance, comic *monologue, *acrobatics, *clowning, trained *animals, *magic shows—performed in succession on a bill. Long a staple of the English *music halls and American concert saloons (also known as 'free-and-easies' or 'honky-tonks'), variety was associated with a heavy-drinking male clientele. Beginning in the 1880s in *New York, Tony *Pastor's success in presenting variety programmes without vulgarity in facilities more like *legitimate theatres than saloons transformed it into *vaudeville, which appealed to a broader *audience that included women and children. Meanwhile, variety continued to be presented in various venues, including dime museums. Thus all vaudeville is composed of variety acts, but not all variety could be called vaudeville.

In England the term 'variety' continued to be used, often disparagingly, while music-hall entertainment gained some respectability as it began to be formalized into twice-nightly programmes instead of the earlier continuous cycles of acts. Whatever the nomenclature, forms of variety entertainment can be found in most cultures: in *Paris on the nineteenth-century boulevard du Temple and the twentieth-century *Folies-Bergère, in the 1920s Russian *Chauve-Souris* that *toured internationally, in the *carpas* of Mexico, and at the *concert parties of Ghana. Variety is quintessentially popular entertainment, because its rationale is to provide something for everyone. By the mid-twentieth century American stage variety shows had blended into related forms like *cabaret and *revues, as popular audiences turned to *radio, *film, and *television. On television the long-popular *Ed Sullivan Show* epitomized variety via the *mass media. England's BBC kept radio variety alive into the 1950s with programmes like *Variety Bandbox* and *Take It from Here*.

A 'variety turn' is an act or routine used to bridge intervals in longer shows.

Variety is also the name of the 'Bible' of American show business. Founded in 1905 by Sime Silverman (1873–1933) as a trade newspaper for all forms of show business, *Variety* continues weekly publication.   FHL

VARLAMOV, KONSTANTIN (1848–1915)

Russian actor who excelled in comic *character roles. Extremely popular throughout his career and familiarly known as Dyadya Kostya (Uncle Kostya), Varlamov joined the *Aleksandrinsky Theatre in *St Petersburg in 1875. Here he proved a superb comic improviser in Russian *vaudevilles, *farces, and *operettas, but his principal successes were in work by *Gogol and in 29 *Ostrovsky roles. From the 1880s onwards he suffered increasingly from elephantiasis, to the point of immobility. He still continued to appear on stage and was remarkably successful as a totally static Sganarelle in *Molière's *Don Juan*, directed by *Meyerhold in 1910.   NW

VASARI, GIORGIO (1511–74)

Italian artist, *scenographer, and biographer, attached to the court of the Medici grand dukes of Tuscany. He organized and designed *spectacles and *pageants of all kinds for his princely patrons between 1536 and 1566. He also created some stage designs elsewhere—as in the case of the well-documented set for *Aretino's *Talanta* in Venice in 1542. This offered a panoramic view of the monuments of Renaissance *Rome, and may have involved some elements of moving *scenery. His *Lives of the Artists* is also a source of information for other artists and episodes of stage history and design.   RAA

VASILIEV, ANATOLY (1942–)

Soviet/Russian director. Vasiliev studied under Maria *Knebel and worked at the *Moscow Art Theatre during the 1970s. His production of Viktor *Slavkin's *A Young Man's Grown-up Daughter* (1979) at the Stanislavsky Theatre was spectacular for its use of jazz *music, condemned as decadent in the Soviet Union. For several years Vasiliev *rehearsed Slavkin's *Cerceau* (1985), a landmark in Russian theatrical history, a combination of lived experience and collated literary material about the mid-life crisis of a group of 40-year-olds. In 1987 Vasiliev founded his own theatre, the School of Dramatic Art, and worked with *improvisation based on rigid textual structures. Since *Amphitryon* (1995) and *The Stone Guest* (1998) he has been experimenting with *text by depriving it of narrative function and reducing it to a pure sign system to enhance the meaning of the word, a technique best demonstrated in *Mozart and Salieri: Requiem* (2000).   BB

VAUDEVILLE

The name given to American *variety entertainment that sought to be dissociated from the male-oriented fare in the concert saloons, 'honky-tonks', and 'free-and-easies'. The adoption of a classy-sounding French term (used in France to mean light *comedies incorporating snatches of popular tunes) along with the move into venues free of drink and smoke allowed variety entertainment to expand its *audience by attracting respectable women to matinée and evening performances. Tony *Pastor led the way, first using the word 'vaudeville' in 1875 for his variety shows at the Metropolitan Theatre on Broadway. After the 1881 opening of his New 14th Street Theatre 'catering to the ladies', vaudeville soared in popularity. Koster and Bial soon adopted the format at their hall on 34th Street. B. F. *Keith advanced the *genre with the creation of the vaudeville circuit and the introduction of continuous performances, so that a spectator could enter at any time and stay until that act came around again. In partnership with E. F. *Albee from 1883, Keith's vaudeville venues began with *New York's Union Square Theatre (1893) and *Boston's Colonial (1894). By 1920 the Keith–Albee circuit controlled over 400 *playhouses. So rigorous were the partners about clean language and wholesome material that theirs was dubbed the 'Sunday school circuit'. Albee was a ruthless businessman whose exploitation of performers was epitomized in the monopolistic practices of his United Booking Office, which he created in 1906 and which maintained control of *publicity, bookings, and facilities until vaudeville lost its audiences to talking *films and motorcars.

F. F. Proctor (1851–1929) began acquiring theatres in 1880, notably Proctor's Pleasure Palace (1895) and the 5th Avenue Theatre (1900), both in New York. *Hammerstein's Victoria Theatre dominated New York vaudeville from 1904 to 1914. Martin Beck (1867–1940) covered the Midwest and west with over 250 theatres on his Orpheum circuit, and opened the *Palace Theatre in New York in 1913. To play the Palace was regarded as the apogee of any career in vaudeville. The Palace was a two-a-day house until 1932, which meant that performers did their acts only twice a day there, as opposed to as many as six turns a day on the small-time circuits.

*African-American vaudevillians had their own southern circuit, the Theatre Owners Booking Association (TOBA, euphemistically known as 'Tough On Black Actors'). However, the vaudeville stage was better integrated than other aspects of American society between 1890 and the 1920s, with numerous black musical groups, *monologists like Charlie Case, singer-comedians like Bert *Williams, *opera singers like Sissieretta Jones, ventriloquists, and song-and-dance teams on the bill at top theatres. The legendary tap-dancing Nicholas brothers enlivened vaudeville's last two decades.

As the dominant American entertainment form, vaudeville generated a wealth of talent and it is difficult to do justice to the variety and inventiveness of such acts as regurgitators, singing *animals, contortionists, quick-change and sleight-of-hand artists, clog *dancers, and midget *acrobats. Specialists in ethnic or national humour included the Scottish Harry *Lauder, *Weber and Fields with their 'Dutch' act, Jewish comedienne Fanny *Brice, blackface duo Montgomery and Stone (see MINSTREL

SHOWS), and Irish pairs like *Gallagher and Shean. Other major stars included the comic monologuists Frank Fay, Will *Rogers, and Ed *Wynn ('The Perfect Fool'), and the comic team George *Burns and Gracie Allen. Comedy, song, and dance teams were particularly memorable, such as the *Marx Brothers, the Three Keatons, the Four *Cohans, Eddie *Foy and the Seven Little Foys, as were the singers Nora Bayes, the Dolly Sisters, Anna Held, Lillian *Russell, and Fay Templeton. The list goes on, with singer-comedians Eddie *Cantor, Marie *Dressler, and Mae *West; singer-dancers Marilyn *Miller and Ann Pennington; dancers Ray 'Rubberlegs' *Bolger, Bill 'Bojangles' *Robinson, Vernon and Irene Castle; and dancer-comedians like Joe Frisco. *Magicians included Harry *Houdini and Harry *Kellar; a 'tramp act' brought W. C. *Fields to fame; body cultist Eugen *Sandow had an international reputation; and *female impersonator Julian *Eltinge had a New York playhouse named after him.

Unquestionably the greatest star in vaudeville—indeed, 'the world's greatest entertainer'—was Al *Jolson, though he devoted most of his career to *musical comedy, movies, and *radio, and never played the Palace. Jolson's electrifying voice and engaging comic banter could hold an audience for hours while other performers waited their turn that might not come. Entertainers who acknowledged the influence of Jolson included Eddie Cantor, Bing Crosby, and Judy Garland, who carried vaudeville traditions into the early *television variety shows. *See also* MUSIC HALL.   FHL

VAUGHAN, KATE (c.1852–1903)

English actress and dancer. She started her career at the Grecian Theatre, *London (1870), but made her name in *burlesque under John *Hollingshead. She performed at the *Gaiety Theatre from 1873 where she was identified as a member of 'the Gaiety Quartette' with Edward Terry, Nellie *Farren, and Edward Royce. From 1883 she *toured the English provinces playing in School for Scandal, She Stoops to Conquer, Tom *Taylor's Masks and Faces, and H. A. *Jones's The Dancing Girl. Her career was plagued by illness and she died in South Africa.   VEE

VAUTHIER, JEAN (1910–92)

Belgian playwright, born in Liège. An *absurdist contemporary of *Beckett, *Genet, and *Ionesco, Vauthier distrusted rational discourse and relied on fantasy and *dream, which in his plays clash with trite reality. But he created a distinct poetic diction in which the French language expresses emotion by its physical quality. The eponymous *hero of Capitaine Bada (*Paris, 1952) is a pathetic, *clown-like poet and emblematic of Vauthier's work. Jean-Louis *Barrault acted Bada in a sequel, Le Personnage combattant (The Fighting Character, 1956), and Marcel *Maréchal revived the original play in 1966 and commissioned Le Sang (Blood, 1970). Vauthier also wrote French adaptations of some of Shakespeare's plays and of *Marlowe's *The Massacre at Paris*. JDV

VAUXHALL

In 1732 Jonathan Tyers opened the New Spring Gardens at Vauxhall in *London. Seeking an affluent clientele, Tyers established an orchestra and later introduced popular singers from the theatres, side shows, and a rotunda in the roccoco style. Decorated supper boxes were available and some clients arrived by river, although from 1750 the Gardens were accessible via Westminster Bridge. *Fireworks were first recorded in 1798. The Gardens, which spawned and outlived numerous imitators, abandoned their fashionable image in the nineteenth century, reducing admission prices in the 1830s and introducing a *diorama, *variety concerts, *tableaux vivants, and *acrobatics. They closed in 1859. JTD

VEDRENNE–BARKER SEASONS

The joint management of the *Royal Court Theatre in *London by John Eugene Vedrenne (1867–1930) as business *manager and Harley Granville *Barker as director was a gradual extension of the practices of play-producing societies. A veteran of *Stage Society productions and a friend of *Shaw, Barker agreed to stage a production of Shakespeare's *The Two Gentlemen of Verona* at the Court Theatre in 1904 on condition that he could also present some matinée performances of Shaw's *Candida*. The autumn brought a programme of thrice-weekly matinées enacted by professionals between their regular West End performances; and in the following year Vedrenne and Barker took over the lease and, having engaged a *stock company, went to an evening bill, plus matinées. Presented in short runs and revived as demand warranted, productions were distinguished by careful *casting, ensemble *acting, and coherent *directing. Across three seasons between October 1904 and June 1907 the Court presented 32 plays, 28 of them for the first time, including work by John *Galsworthy, St John *Hankin, John *Masefield, Elizabeth *Robins, Laurence *Housman, and Barker himself. Shaw, however, dominated the list of Court playwrights: he effectively directed his own plays, which overall accounted for about three-quarters of performances. In addition to being the main moneymaker for Vedrenne and Barker, Shaw was also their chief *financial backer and lost heavily when they moved into the much larger *Savoy Theatre for the 1907–8 season, after which the venture foundered. MOC

VEERESALINGAM, KANDUKURI (1848–1919)

*Telugu dramatist, novelist, editor and social reformer from Andhra Pradesh, *India. Concerned primarily with women's education and widow remarriage, he is also remembered for his seminal translation of *Kalidasa's *Abhijnana Sakuntalam* (1871–83), which served as a model for later translations. His *Vyavahara Dharmabodhini* (*A Primer of Legal Practice*, 1880), an indictment of the legal profession, was the first modern play staged in Andhra. *Brahma Vivaham* (*A Brahman Wedding*, 1880) on child marriage inspired many playwrights, including Gurazada *Apparao. Veeresalingam was the author of several *farces, including ten based on English originals. All of them criticized the blind beliefs prevalent in society. He also translated *Malavikagnimitram* (1885), *Prabodhachandrodayam* (1885–91), and *Ratnavali* (1880) from Sanskrit, and *Chamatkara Ratnavali* (*Comedy of Errors*, 1880), *Ragamanjari* (*Sheridan's *Duenna*, 1885), and *Kalyana Kalpavalli* (Sheridan's *The Rivals*, 1894) from English. His original plays include mythologicals such as *Prahlada* (1885) and *Satya Harischandra* (1886), and *allegorical plays like *Tiryag–Vidwan Mahasabha* (*The Assembly of Demented Scholars*, 1889) on the mercenary attitude of brahman priests, and *Maharanya Puradhipatyam* (*A Sovereign of the Forest Kingdom*, 1889) on the dubious ethics of people in power. His *Viveka Deepika* (*A Torch of Wisdom*, 1880) on the social neglect of young widows makes a strong plea for widow remarriage. MNS

VEGA CARPIO, LOPE DE *see page 1403*

VÉLEZ DE GUEVARA, LUIS (1579–1644)

Spanish dramatist. Popular and prolific, he claimed to have written 400 plays. Some 100 survive, largely on heroic themes, and notable both for their lyricism and exploitation of visual effect. His *melodramatic *La serrana de la Vera* (*The Mountain Maid of La Vera*) depicts the life and death by execution of a bloodthirsty female outlaw. *Reinar despúes de morir* (*Queen after Death*) is by contrast a moving *tragedy on the Inés de Castro legend. VFD

VERANNA, GUBBI (1890–1972)

*Actor-manager of the well-known Gubbi Theatre Company in Karnataka, south *India. Born at Gubbi, a small town in southern Karnataka, Veranna joined the local theatre group at an early age as a junior stagehand and later was promoted to actor. With large entrepreneurial skills and *acting talent, he soon became an indispensable member of the troupe and eventually its owner in 1917. The company rose to fame rapidly in Karnataka by consolidating the innovations made by the *company theatre movement. Veranna brought actors like Subbaiah Naidu and G. Sundaramma and playwrights such as Bellave Narahari Shastry and B. Puttaswamaiah into the troupe, and incorporated innovations in contemporary stagecraft, including

(continued on p. 1404)

VEGA CARPIO, LOPE DE (1562–1635)

Spanish dramatist. Born in Madrid, the son of an embroiderer, he attended a Jesuit school and probably the University of Alcalá. Before and after brief naval experience in the 1580s, when he was already known as a poet and playwright, he served a long series of noble masters, especially the Duke of Sessa, but though idolized by the public he never gained due recognition at court, and his last decade was overshadowed by disappointment and distress. Though sincerely devout, especially after a mid-life religious crisis, Lope de Vega was notoriously active sexually; he fathered eleven offspring by two wives and some of his (at least) six lovers. Of the latter the most important were Elena Osorio, who in 1587 provoked savage libels for which he was exiled to Valencia, but 45 years later inspired his masterly prose play *La Dorotea*; Micaela de Luján, who bore him five children; and (after his ordination as a priest in 1614) Marta de Nevares, to whom he remained devoted for sixteen years.

His literary activity was more extraordinary still. In addition to innumerable works in every *verse and prose *genre of his day, Lope (as he is known) was said to have written 1,800 *comedias (as well as over 400 *autos sacramentales). Since fewer than 400 survive, 600 or 700 is a likelier but still prodigious total; over half a century, roughly one a month. This productivity, his closeness to his public, and his genius as both a playwright and a poet gave him the dominant role in the evolution of Golden Age drama. Antecedents can be found for most of the elements of his art, but those he incorporated became the norm, and little in later plays had not been foreshadowed in his. He gave the 'New Comedy' its fixed but flexible form, as well as unrestricted content, and outlined his method mid-career in his confident (though superficially shamefaced) *Arte nuevo de hacer comedias en este tiempo* (1609). Rejecting as unacceptable to the *audience the rigidity of the *neoclassical rules, he insisted on modifications, which though restrained by *Horatian ideas of *decorum were in practice very far-reaching. The works of so fluent a dramatist are inevitably uneven, but even his weakest have flashes of startling originality, and most reveal more calculation than he is often credited with. His sources were of necessity very diverse. Some plays draw for instance on classical mythology, the Bible, or the lives of saints. Untypical of the latter is his astonishingly *metatheatrical *Lo fingido verdadero* (*What's Feigned Is True*, c.1608): two plays performed before Diocletian by Genesius, the patron saint of actors, are subverted by real emotions; before and during the second, he is miraculously converted and baptized, and his last role is that of a martyr.

Very many more or less *historical plays are set in a huge range of countries and periods, but especially in late medieval Spain. *Fuente Ovejuna* (1612–14), the most frequently performed, dramatizes the murder of a nobleman by villagers he had tyrannized, and the solidarity under torture that won them a royal pardon. Like the eponymous *heroes of his *Peribáñez* (c.1605) and *El villano en su rincón* (*The Peasant in his Corner*, c.1611), they clearly have Lope's sympathy, but he insists that they are loyal to the crown, and he is often seen in general as a political conformist, or even an establishment propagandist. Though many of his plays were commissioned as publicity by noblemen, the Church, or the court, and though he never questioned monarchy as a system, he must often have fuelled debate about its functioning in practice, and many of his rulers are badly flawed. One such is the paranoid King of Portugal who slays exemplary nobles in *El Duque de Viseo* (*The Duke of Viseu*, 1608–9). Another is the lecherous Duke of Ferrara in Lope's masterpiece *El castigo sin venganza* (*Punishment without Revenge*), performed by *Vallejo in 1632. Though based on an account by Bandello (who like other *novellieri* provided many of Lope's *plots) of a historical occurrence, this almost neoclassical *tragedy can be seen as Lope's *Phèdre*, except that here the Hippolytus succumbs to his stepmother's advances, and they consummate a guilty but genuine love. Apprised of this, the Duke (with unhistorical secrecy) punishes both with death, but claims that, having himself reformed, he does so solely as heaven's instrument. His true motivation is problematic, but Lope provokes both condemnation and compassion for all three. A more characteristically lyrical tragedy is *El caballero de Olmedo* (*The Knight of Olmedo*, 1620–5), based in part on the *Celestina*, but mainly on a well-known semi-historical tale. Until well into the final *act, life seems to be smiling on two young lovers, but their idyll is undermined by reminders of the fate we know awaits them.

Far more frequently, however, Lope's optimistic nature gives love a happy outcome. His best *comedies are in the 'cloak and sword' mould, like *La discreta enamorada* (*The Shrewd Girl in Love*, 1606), *Las bizarrías de Belisa* (*Belisa's Extravagances*, 1634), or the metatheatrical *La noche de San Juan* (*Midsummer's Eve*, 1631). *La dama boba* (*The Dumb Belle*) contrasts a bluestocking with her initially stupid sister, who nevertheless proves the cleverer when educated by love, though ironically the gallant who effects the transformation is more intent on getting her larger dowry. Another comic but mildly subversive masterpiece is *El perro del hortelano*. Its 'Dog in the Manger' is a Countess who vacillates throughout between love for her secretary and regard for her noble rank. Eventually a triple *anagnorisis enables them to marry; he too is revealed to be nobly born, but when he reveals to her that this is a fabrication she reveals that for her, as for society, appearances are enough, and the audience is invited to keep their secret.

Many of Lope's plays were performed worldwide in the twentieth century. In particular, *Fuente Ovejuna*, often heavily adapted, was frequently mounted as political propaganda. A balanced production by the Royal *National Theatre (directed by Declan *Donellan, 1989) was extremely well received in Britain. In Spain, that play, *El castigo sin venganza*, and numerous comedies have been successfully performed by the Compañía Nacional de Teatro Clásico. *See also* EARLY MODERN PERIOD IN EUROPE. VFD

lavish *scenery, difficult scene changes, glittering *costumes, electric *lighting, and projectors. With this technology at its disposal, the Gubbi Company mounted several spectacular productions on mythological subjects like *Kurukshetra* (1934), *Krishnalila* (1944), and *Dashavatara* (1958), which made a deep popular impression. With three branches and more than 300 employees, the Gubbi *toured extensively in Karnataka, Andhra Pradesh, and Tamil Nadu. Veranna himself is remembered especially as a comedian. Through elaborate improvisations he transformed minor roles into memorable comic *characters, like the thief in his popular hit *Sadarame*. He moved *comedy from the subplot into the main *action of the play; the King of Mysore, Krishnaraja Wodeyar, conferred on him the title of 'Versatile Comedian'. The Gubbi Company continued after his death—though without the same level of fame—and is the only troupe in Karnataka to have survived for more than a century. *See also* KANNADA THEATRE. KVA

VERDI, GIUSEPPE (1813–1901)

Composer who dominates Italian *opera. He was internationally celebrated in his day and, while there was a temporary decline in popularity after his death, well over half of his 28 operas are now in the repertoire of all major opera houses. Verdi combines the lyricism of bel canto and the *spectacle of grand opera in dramas that centre on conflicts between individuals of often heroic proportions. He used his formidable melodic gift both to craft *characters of great power and psychological complexity and to give the dramatic *action a momentum unequalled in opera. His early works, of which *Nabucco* (*Milan, La *Scala, 1842), *Ernani* (Venice, *Fenice, 1844), and *Macbeth* (Florence, 1847) are the most revived, became popular for their rousing drama and stirring *choruses; in the 1850s they became briefly associated with growing Italian nationalism. *Rigoletto* (Fenice, 1851), *Il trovatore* (*Rome, 1853), and *La traviata* (Fenice, 1853) are the most popular of his works, as these terse but moving dramas display Verdi's distinctive qualities at their best. In the latter part of his career he wrote more in the style of French grand opera, in which the *action is not worked out as economically as in Italian opera. Not all these works were instantly successful, but in recent years *Simon Boccanegra* (Fenice, 1857), *A Masked Ball* (Rome, 1859), *The Force of Destiny* (*St Petersburg, 1862), *Don Carlos* (*Paris, *Opéra, 1867), and the perennially popular *Aida* (*Cairo, 1871) have achieved widespread popularity. After a silence of almost sixteen years, Verdi completed his career with *Otello* (Scala, 1887) and *Falstaff* (Scala, 1893), works that are widely considered to be equal to the Shakespearian plays upon which they are based. SJCW

VERDON, GWEN (1925–2000)

American dancer and actress. Some years after her childhood debut as 'Baby Alice, the Fastest Little Tapper in the World' in *Los Angeles in the late 1920s, Verdon began dancing with the Jack *Cole Dancers at Columbia Pictures and in nightclub *revues around the country. Her astonishing *dance technique and vibrant, sexually charged stage presence helped her to win the first of her four Tony *awards for *Can-Can* in 1953. Verdon began her long personal and professional partnership with choreographer-director Bob *Fosse in the 1955 production of *Damn Yankees*, where her *acting, singing, and dancing crystallized her reputation as the most formidable 'triple threat' in *musical comedy. In later years she pursued straight *film and *television roles, including parts in the film *Cocoon* and in the television series *Magnum PI*. LTC

VERFREMDUNG

Since Bertolt *Brecht's first use of the term in 1936, the German word has been translated variously as 'disillusion', 'alienation', 'de-alienation', 'distanciation', 'estrangement', and 'defamiliarization', each of which alludes to a relevant feature of this concept. In his 1948 'Short Organum for the Theatre' Brecht described *Verfremdung* as aiming 'to free socially conditioned phenomena from that stamp of familiarity which protects them against our grasp today' through a defamiliarizing representation 'which allows us to recognize its subject, but at the same time makes it seem unfamiliar'. On occasion Brecht applied the term to the strategies of diverse artists down the ages who have sought to arouse new or revitalize old perceptions through a process of 'making strange'. However, Brecht remained critical of those *Verfremdungseffekten* ('defamiliarization effects', or 'V-effects'), which he felt made the objects represented seem incomprehensible, given, or unchangeable. It is precisely his insistence on the social task of mastering life which distinguishes

Brecht's concept of *Verfremdung* from Viktor Shklovsky's theory of 'defamiliarization', a Russian formalist idea which is alleged to have influenced Brecht during a visit to *Moscow in 1935. In his essay 'Art as Technique' (1917), Shklovsky described *ostranenie* (defamiliarization) as a device which, by making objects 'unfamiliar' through increasing the difficulty and length of perception, could combat habitualization and reimpart the sensation of things as they are perceived. But whereas Shklovsky's aim was to recover a naive sensation of life, Brecht wished to expose habitualized behaviour as the product of a socio-economic condition that is alterable.

A major component of Brecht's political aesthetic, *Verfremdung* is underpinned by his engagement with the Marxist tradition. Due in part to his use of the term *Entfremdung* (alienation) prior to, and in some theoretical writings from the 1930s alongside *Verfremdung*, the latter has been associated with Marx's theory that under capitalism people are alienated from one another and from the products of their own activity, creating a world of objects which has power over and above them. However, to translate *Verfremdung* as 'alienation' is misleading insofar as it gives undue emphasis to only one of Brecht's thematic concerns, and, even more problematically, can encourage the misinterpretation that Brecht's theatre involves purely non-empathetic or even hostile relations between *actors, *characters, and *audience. More central to the practice of *Verfremdung* is Marx's idea that social reality is not timeless and universal but an ever changing, man-made construct. Brecht defamiliarized those conventions of *illusionist theatre which he believed inhibited the appreciation of that idea: hence his overt display of human productivity and technology—making *lighting apparatus and musicians visible, or *scene shifting behind a half-*curtain—and his interruption of the flow of *action by inserting narration, song, and direct address. In addition Brecht introduced historicizing devices such as scene titles, projections, and summary reports which present the action played out as a critical recreation of past events. For performers, he devised a method of distancing actor from character through the *rehearsal technique of 'quoting' *text and turning it into the past tense. Most importantly, Brecht asserted that the realization of a socialist *Verfremdung* was dependent upon a historicizing method of interpretation. For instance, in the case of Shakespeare's *Othello* he advocated that the fatalist tendency to interpret Othello's jealousy as eternal should be estranged by showing instead how the character's behaviour is a product of the battles for property and position specific to the *early modern context.

As a method of intervention, *Verfremdung* bears the traces of Brecht's interest in modern science and dialectics. When describing the inquisitive attitude necessary for the achievement of *Verfremdung*, Brecht often referred to the analytical method of turning a familiar phenomenon, like Galileo's swinging chandelier, into something strange and incomprehensible by observing it with astonishment. In turn, this state of excited detachment makes the phenomenon more comprehensible and controllable, just as Galileo's amazement at the pendulum motion enabled him to discern the rules by which it is governed. While Brecht initially argued that *Verfremdung* required the minimizing of familiarizing processes such as empathy, he later modified this position and placed greater emphasis on the dialectical interplay of empathy and detachment. In the Western world many of the playful and visually striking techniques employed by Brecht to create V-effects, such as non-illusionist stylization and overt displays of technology, have been adapted by the commercial theatre and *mass media industry, where they are often disconnected from Brecht's socialist project and used to promote the consumption of pleasurable wit and *spectacle. However, interventionist theatre critics and practitioners worldwide continue to find the interruptive, *historicizing, and denaturalizing potential of *Verfremdung* an important source of inspiration. *See also* EPIC THEATRE; BRECHTIAN; MATERIALIST CRITICISM; POLITICS AND THEATRE.

MM

BRECHT, BERTOLT, *Brecht on Theatre*, ed. and trans. John Willett (London, 1964)

BROOKER, PETER, *Bertolt Brecht: dialectics, poetry, politics* (London, 1988)

VERGERIO, PIER PAOLO (1370–1445)

Italian humanist and playwright. The title of Vergerio's only play, *Paulus: a comedy for the correction of youthful morals* (1390), attests to its author's humanist ideals. Written in Latin, *Paulus* has the trappings of *Roman *comedy—five *acts arranged as *protasis*, *epitasis*, and *catastrophe*; the *stock characters of young master, servant, bawd, courtesan—but the setting in a university town, the episodic *plot, and the freely shifting *scenes reflect the play's late *medieval milieu. *Paulus* is the earliest of several plays on Italian university life.   RWV

VERISMO

A movement in Italian literature and *opera (literally, *'realism') that parallels and was influenced by the *naturalism of Émile *Zola. Verismo was introduced to Italy through the prose writings of Giovanni Verga (1840–1922), whose short story set among Sicilian peasants, 'Cavalleria rusticana' ('Rustic Chivalry'), provided the basis for the celebrated opera of the same name (*Rome, 1890) by Pietro Mascagni (1863–1945). This, along with Ruggiero Leoncavallo's *Pagliacci* (*Players*, *Milan, 1892), is the most enduring product of verismo, but it did inspire a number of operas, mainly by minor composers, set among the peasantry and, occasionally, the urban proletariat of contemporary Italy, thus providing an alternative to the ubiquitous historicist settings of Italian opera. Verismo introduced the common people to the operatic stage, characteristic details of local colour were caught in the *scenography and the music, and the action, usually terse and brutal, was driven by the passions of greed, revenge, and lust. The term has also been applied to the operas of *Puccini, Umberto Giordano (1867–1948), and Francisco Cilea (1866–1950). While these composers frequently chose historical or exotic settings, the intimacy and frequent lack of heroic dimension in their *characters create a characteristically verist atmosphere. Verismo enjoyed some currency outside Italy as well, particularly in the late operas of the French composer Jules Massenet (1842–1912), especially *La Navarraise* (*London, 1894), and the German Eugen d'Albert (1864–1932), in whose *Tiefland* (*The Lowlands*, *Prague, 1903) the Italian veristic idiom is used skilfully to dramatize violent sexual intrigue among the peasants of Catalonia.   SJCW

VERSAILLES

Originally built as a hunting retreat by Louis XIII, this modest country house was completely redesigned and landscaped by order of Louis XIV beginning in 1661. The gardens designed by André Le Nôtre complemented the architecture by Louis Le Vau and Jules Hardouin-Mansart: together, grounds and chateau formed a magnificent whole which exemplified baroque architecture at its height. In 1682 Louis completed the transfer of the French government to Versailles from the Louvre in Paris; from that time until the revolution, Versailles functioned as the artistic and political centre of French culture. Under Louis XIV, Versailles became the home of the King's troupes of musicians, dancers, and singers: these performers entertained on a daily basis as well as at the magnificent state festivals of 1664, 1668, and 1674. However, there was no formal theatre space at Versailles until 1770 when the Opéra was built for the wedding of Louis XVI and Marie Antoinette; before that, sites in and around the chateau were transformed into stages for *operas, court *ballets, carousels, *comédies-ballets, and other events. The 1664 festival of *Les Plaisirs de l'île enchantée*, for example, used the intersections of garden paths, the old moat, and the pond which was later converted into the Apollo fountain. The 1674 *Divertissement* included a performance of *Molière's *The Hypochondriac* in the outdoor Marble Court. Today, Versailles's gardens are the location for summer laser shows which celebrate the performance history of the chateau and grounds.

GES

VERSE

Speech on stage in modern times has many of the qualities of contemporary prose, but more speakable and more like actual offstage speech. In the past, however, in many countries and for long periods, verse was the normal form in which *dialogue for theatre performances was written: prose was not sufficiently

sustained, witty, pungent, clear, sensational, memorable. And, for much the same reasons, verse has remained in use on occasions when a play is not intended to imitate life but to re-create and boldly refashion it. The *tragedies and *comedies of ancient *Greece were invariably written in verse that was both spoken and sung. Various verse forms were used, ranging from the apparently simple to the resonant, subtle, or complex. *Roman comedy followed this practice and, quite independently, so did the refined and meditative *nō plays of Japan from the fourteenth century onwards. Throughout Europe in *medieval times, religious *mystery and *morality plays continued to use verse, often shaped in stanzas with ingenious rhyme schemes and lines of different length. Verse served quick repartee and broad comedy as well as formal prayer, invocation, and sustained *soliloquy. Secular *folk plays used simpler and altogether cruder verse.

At first in *early modern Europe, verse remained the staple for stage dialogue. In Spain, Lope de *Vega used a variety of verse forms along with quick-moving octosyllabics taken from traditional ballads. In England, *Marlowe and other Elizabethans used prose only occasionally, usually to comic effect or for episodes of madness; but already there were exceptions, John *Lyly regularly and Ben *Jonson occasionally adopting prose for entire plays. Shakespeare wrote predominantly in verse, sometimes abandoning it for swift-moving wit or the lumbering talk of *clowns. In *King Lear* (c.1606), the *hero turns to prose in his madness but for him, towards the close of the tragedy, Shakespeare wrote verse so simple in its elements, so carefully modulated in tone and pitch, that no artifice seems involved as he speaks words burdened with great emotion.

Elizabethan 'blank verse'—an unrhymed iambic line of ten syllables alternately unstressed and stressed—could be adapted for a great variety of subjects, moods, persons, and situations, by modifying the basic stresses and varying syntax. In the words of the poet Sir Philip *Sidney, such verse enabled each syllable of each word to be weighted 'by just proportion according the dignity of the subject'. Dramatists took pride in verse: Thomas *Dekker claimed that the 'melody' of a play's dialogue could, 'with golden chains' draw members of an *audience:

> Forg'd out of the hammer, on tiptoe to reach up
> And, from rare silence, clap their brawny hands,
> To applaud what their charm'd soul scarce understands.
>
> (*If It Be Not Good*, 1612)

Less than 100 years later, verse was not so universally used and honoured, nor would it be again. *Molière wrote comedies either wholly in prose or wholly in verse; *Goethe and *Lessing also used both. For tragedies, however, it was for longer the usual choice: for example, in France, by *Racine and *Corneille; until well into the nineteenth century in Germany and Austria, by *Schiller, *Kleist, and *Grillparzer. Poets who turned to the theatre had only limited success with verse plays. In England, among *Byron's numerous attempts, his *Cain* (1821), with flexible, quick-moving verse, has received occasional twentieth-century productions. Although not written for stage enactment, so has *Milton's *Samson Agonistes* (1671), the closest to Greek example of any tragedy in English, in verse form as in structure and theme.

In the twentieth century some poets have made the crossover to theatre: in Spain, triumphantly, Federico *García Lorca; in Ireland, for small *audiences, W. B. *Yeats; in England, reaching the West End and Broadway, T. S. *Eliot, and to smaller audiences, poets from the political left, including W. H. *Auden and Stephen Spender; in the United States, Archibald MacLeish and Robert Lowell. Exceptions to the neglect of verse kept recurring. *Ibsen started to write *Brand* (1875), his first major success, as a long narrative poem; here, as in *Peer Gynt* (1877), verse is used throughout, bringing echoes of *folk tales and church hymns. In England after the Second World War, when theatre dialogue was tending towards *filmic *realism, Christopher *Fry wrote a sequence of verse plays that, with *The Lady's Not for Burning* (1948), reached the West End; some were ecclesiastical in origin, like Eliot's *Murder in the Cathedral* (1935), but most were verbally ingenious reinventions of an earlier style of patently artificial comedy.

During the twentieth century, the nature of poetry changed radically as, once again, poets sought a closer relationship to the mood and language of the times. Without regular rhymes or constant metrical form, the new free verse could maintain the rhythms of speech and poets began to recite, or at least read, their self-revealing poems in public, as bards had done centuries before. They performed in bars and public squares of cities: for example, in *New York, Allen Ginsberg and others of the Beat Generation; in *Moscow, Eugeni Yevtushenko and other anti-Stalinist poets. With occasional impersonations and hand-held *properties, a minimal form of theatre performance was reborn and, by the twenty-first century, sponsored poetry readings had become common in community centres and classrooms. Some dramatists never wholly deserted verse. They were mostly those who sought a wider, less elitist public than the audiences at established theatre houses. In prose plays *Brecht used verse to grip attention, make short phrases memorable, or move the narrative forward without elaborate scenes or time-consuming detail. This lead was followed by other *politically motivated dramatists: in Britain, for example, by John *Arden in *Workhouse Donkey* (1963). But at the start of the twenty-first century, verse is no longer common in the theatre except for songs, *burlesque, or pastiche, and in revivals of old plays.

Whether old or new, plays in verse make special demands on *actors. They must shape their entire performances to its varying metre, sustained cadences, and words with exceptional resonance and carefully controlled emphasis. In times when actors work frequently for *film and *television, which almost always call for lifelike behaviour and speech, 'verse speaking' has come to be regarded as a specialist skill whereas, formerly, it was a necessary accomplishment, essential to the imaginative experience that was expected and enjoyed by large popular audiences.   JRB

VESTRIS, MME (FRANÇOISE-MARIE-ROSETTE GOURGAUD) (1743–1804)

French actress. Sister-in-law of the *dancer-*ballet master Gaetano Vestris, Mme Vestris joined the *Comédie-Française in 1768, and specialized in tragic princesses. Her major successes included roles such as de Belloy's Gabrielle de Vergy (1777) and *Voltaire's Irène (1778). However, one English tourist thought her 'all art and rant'. Although protected by the Duc de Duras, a Gentleman of the Bedchamber, Mme Vestris's politics were anti-royalist: she was a friend of Marie-Joseph *Chénier and in 1789 triumphed alongside *Talma in his revolutionary *Charles X*.   JG

VESTRIS, MADAME (LUCIA ELIZABETH BARTOLOZZI, LATER MATHEWS) (1797–1856)

English actress, singer, *manager, theatrical innovator, born into a cosmopolitan artistic family in *London. In 1813 she married Armand Vestris, and made her debut in 1815 at the King's Theatre where he was *ballet master. In 1816 they went to *Paris; she returned in 1819, alone. The *succès de scandale* of her famous *breeches performance in *Giovanni in London* at *Drury Lane in 1820 made her a star. Vestris's appearances in breeches always emphasized feisty femininity, showing off her fabulously perfect legs. In 1830 she took a burletta licence for the little *Olympic, near the struggling *patent houses, remodelling her theatre as a modern, feminine alternative to their discomforts. In an intimate 'drawing-room' space, she offered pretty musical pieces and undemanding *farces, finishing by eleven. The standard was reliable and the class-segregated *auditorium, with no free admissions and no tipping, offered no unpleasant surprises. These simple changes made her theatre fashionable. Behind the scenes Vestris copied the best French *boulevard theatres, with fresh *scenery, good working conditions and contracts, and adequate *rehearsal. She attracted loyal workers, including *Planché, *Liston, and Benjamin *Webster, and regularly appeared herself in Planché's *metatheatrical extravaganzas.

In 1835 she hired Charles *Mathews, Jr., and they developed a light *comedy partnership; in 1838 they married and unsuccessfully *toured America. In 1839 they took over *Covent Garden. Despite the disapproval of *Macready, Vestris's artistic practices transferred well to the *legitimate stage, and her scrupulous professionalism was more effective in the revival of 'the national drama' than his hectoring moralism had been. For three seasons she staged classic comedy and new writing, such as *Boucicault's *London Assurance* (1841), and notable Shakespearian productions, including the previously unrevived *Love's Labour's Lost* (1839) and a *Merry Wives of Windsor* (1840) set in Shakespeare's time. But the expenses of the old theatre meant little profit, and Mathews declared bankruptcy in 1842. In 1847, after a period of unremitting work at the *Haymarket under Webster and in provincial touring, they took on the *Lyceum. There the John Morton *farce *Cox and Box* prefaced eleven Planché extravaganzas, with scenery by William *Beverley. From 1849 modern French plays translated by G. H. *Lewes were used to develop their cool modern comedy style. Vestris took her farewell *benefit in 1854.

Madame Vestris brought to the British stage a European perspective, which deployed virtuoso talent, *training, and elegant taste to flatter a fashionable *audience. She managed the problems that beset the London stage in her time by innovation, finding original solutions to a range of issues. At the Olympic she successfully negotiated the opposition between the antique practices of the theatre under aristocratic patronage and rising middle-class aspiration and self-definition through propriety. As performer she exploited and at the same time excused and made acceptable her sexual appeal and scandalous reputation, turning her sexuality into an asset that connoted good taste and luxury. She was one of the most important practitioners of her generation.

JSB

VIAN, BORIS (1920–59)

French novelist, poet, singer, jazz musician, and playwright. The *enfant terrible* of post-Second World War France, his anti-militarist writing condemned his nation's involvement in the Indo-Chinese and Algerian conflicts. A member of the *avant-garde movement the College of Pataphysicians, he wrote seven plays, all vigorously iconoclastic. These include *L'Équaririssage pour tous* (*The Knacker's ABC*, 1950), a *satire of the Normandy invasion and the only one of his plays to be produced in his lifetime; *Les Bâtisseurs d'empire* (*The Empire Builders*, 1959), a *monologue recounting the progressive degeneration of a middle-class family, and *Le Goûter des généraux* (*The Generals' Tea-Party*, 1965), an anti-military *vaudeville. Like fellow pataphysician Eugène *Ionesco, Vian believed in the incommunicability of language and the absurdity of social institutions.

CHB

VIANA FILHO, ODUVALDO (VIANINHA) (1936–74)

Brazilian playwright and actor. An astute theoretician whose critical writings offer a complex dialogue between *theory and practice, Viana Filho's history as a playwright and leftist activist is inextricably tied to the *political theatres of the 1950s and 1960s. Although he wrote *Brechtian *musical sketches and rural political *satire, his major theme was the alienation of the lower middle class in *Rio. His varied theatrical styles sought to renew the Brazilian popular traditions of *street theatre, *revue, and *boulevard theatre. *Rasga coração* (*Heart Torn Asunder*, 1974), his major play, is a collage of historical fact and interpretation, created by using a *realist basis intercut with flashbacks, *Verfremdung* techniques, and the conventions of musical *revues.

LHD

VIAU, THÉOPHILE DE (1590–1626)

French poet and playwright. Repeatedly imprisoned, and banished, for his free-thinking views and allegedly obscene verse, Théophile may have been a member of an itinerant acting company. The *tragedy *Pyrame et Thisbé*, his one surviving play (though he is likely to have written others), still figured in the repertory of the *Hôtel de Bourgogne some ten years later, the stage design used for it being one of the most interesting in the sketchbook of decors left by Laurent *Mahelot.

WDH

VICENTE, GIL (c.1465–c.1536)

Portuguese poet and playwright. The history of his life is elusive; before becoming the court's 'master of the rhetoric of play-making' he may have been a goldsmith. His career began in 1502, when, as part of the court's celebration of the birth of the royal prince, he staged a short secular piece in the mode of Juan del *Encina's Christmas *pastorals. Vicente worked almost exclusively for the royal courts of Manuel I and João III until 1536, either commissioned by the sovereign or putting on plays 'of his own invention'. The most significant personality in early sixteenth-century Iberian drama, Vicente wrote in Portuguese and Castilian rhymed stanzaic *verse, often using both languages in the same play. His work has been regarded as a forerunner of the *auto sacramental* and the *comedia*, two of the main *genres of the Spanish Golden Age (see EARLY MODERN PERIOD IN EUROPE). His accomplishments were not confined to playwriting but embraced theatre in a wider sense: *directing, *rehearsing, finding ways to interact with the structure and acoustics of the venue, exploring or devising staging patterns, finding or designing *costumes and *props, selecting or composing the *music for the play.

His theatrical entertainments were not produced for the *playhouse. Yuletide plays were usually performed in chapels, churches, and monasteries, while those written to honour the birth of royal children were presented in the palace chambers, great halls, and gardens. Taking advantage of the venues, the characteristics of the *audience, and of the occasion, Vicente at first exploited the coincidence between the performance location and the fictional locale of the play. Although he would often revert to this 'circumstantial theatre' throughout his career, a closer study of his work shows a gradual deviation from this practice. If in the earlier plays the *characters stepped into the *audience's normal places of congregation, sometimes speaking directly to a few chosen spectators and involving them in the *action, a new understanding of theatrical space allowed him to move toward the Renaissance division between performers and audience.

The Vicente canon consists of 50 plays that have survived chiefly in the *Copilaçam de todalas obras*, published posthumously in 1562 by his son and daughter, and organized in four books. Works of devotion include *Visitation, Castilian Pastoral, The Magi, The Sibyl Cassandra, Portuguese Pastoral, Fair, Soul, Ship of Hell, Purgatory, Ship of Heaven, History of God, Resurrection*, and *St Martin*; while *comedies include *Rubena, The Widower, The Crest of Coimbra*, and *Forest of Deceits*. *Tragicomedies consist of *Amadis of Gaul, Ship of Love, Forge of Love, Exhortation to War, Temple of Apollo*, and *Pilgrimage of the Aggrieved*. *Farces include *Who Has Bran?, The Old Man of the Orchard, Fairies, The Judge of Beira, Gypsies, The Priest of Beira, Lusitania*, and *The Physicians*. The *Minor Works*, the final book, is composed of assorted poems, a paraphrase of Psalm 50, and his own epitaph.   JCa

VICHEKESHO

East *African form of comic drama, roughly translatable as 'things which are ridiculous'. It probably originated on the island of Zanzibar and was popularized by *tarab* singer and entertainer Siti binti Said. *Vichekesho* performances usually consist of short comic skits in which a clever man is contrasted with a fool who ultimately suffers for his stupidity. Under British colonial rule *vichekesho* was used to promote modern Westernized styles of living, but after independence the Tanzanian Peter Saimanga used it for political *satire. It remains a popular form with many commercial theatre companies in the region.   JP

VICTORIA THEATRE

The first permanent theatre in-the-round (*see* ARENA AND IN-THE-ROUND) in the UK, seating 389, it was converted from a cinema in Stoke-on-Trent by Stephen *Joseph in 1962. Its first *manager, Peter Cheeseman, took over as *artistic director in 1966 and continued until retirement in the early 1990s. His company became famous for its verbatim *documentary plays about local issues, such as the town's branch-line railway (*The Knotty*, 1966) and the threat to close the steelworks (*Fight for Shelton Bar*, 1974). It was also a *training ground for distinctive practitioners, such as Alan *Ayckbourn, Stephen Lowe, and Alan Dosser. In 1986 it was replaced by a new 600-seat purpose-built theatre-in-the-round.   BRK

VIDUSHAKA

Comic *stock character in classical Sanskrit drama. A privileged jester who has the licence to ridicule social norms, the *vidushaka* is the sounding board and alter ego of the *hero, who could be a god, a king, a minister, or a Brahman. Functioning as a surrogate minister for humour and love affairs, he intervenes in the *plot only to complicate matters. The *Natyasastra*, among other treatises on ancient Indian *dramaturgy, specifies the physical deformities of the *character—protruding teeth, a bald pate, red eyes, a limp, a dwarf-like stature, supplemented by his crooked stick and even more twisted face. This grotesquerie is matched by his gluttony and vulgar language in Prakrit dialect, which exposes his degraded Brahman status. Apart from being a character in specific plays, the role of the *vidushaka* can also be conventionalized, as in his appearance in the *ritualistic preliminaries (*purvaranga*) to Sanskrit plays. In performances of *kutiyattam in Kerala, the *vidushaka* continues to play a significant role through his critical commentary in colloquial Malayalam on the learned Sanskrit *dialogues used by the main characters. In an even more virtuosic display of verbal *parody, the *vidushaka* holds the stage for a number of nights in a non-stop solo improvisation that ridicules the foibles of society and contemporary politics through veiled references and satirical comments, at times directed at the spectators in the *audience. *See also* KATTIYAKKARAN.   LSR/RB

VIENNA

Capital city of Austria, formerly of the Habsburg, then of the Austro-Hungarian Empire. Like other central European cities, during the Middle Ages Vienna developed a rich tradition of *religious theatre (*see* MEDIEVAL THEATRE IN EUROPE). Its university was a centre for the performance of humanistic drama during the Renaissance and, with the coming of the Counter-*Reformation, the city saw much *Jesuit drama. In the course of the seventeenth century, the Habsburg court became internationally noted for its lavish operatic entertainments, especially the production of Cesti's *Il pomo d'oro* (*The Golden Apple*) in 1668, which was unprecedented in the scale of its *spectacle. From the baroque period on, Vienna has been particularly associated with the production of *opera, which is followed by a significant proportion of the city's population.

Vienna came into its own as a theatre city in 1711, when the Styrian improviser Joseph Anton *Stranitzky set up his troupe of travelling players as a permanent company in the Kärntnertortheater. At this time, Vienna was the only German-speaking city large enough to support a regular commercial theatre, and the improvised *comedy flourished. After Stranitzky's death in 1726, his company continued to perform under the direction of other improvisers, notably Gottfried *Prehauser and Joseph Felix von *Kurz, giving rise to the most vigorous urban comic tradition in eighteenth-century Europe. This popular theatre was unusually eclectic; its sources can be traced to Stranitzky's *Hanswurst comedies, *commedia dell'arte, *Haupt- und Staatsaktionen, and even the Jesuit drama and court opera. Its multifaceted nature is fully apparent from its one universally acknowledged masterpiece, *Mozart and *Schikaneder's *The Magic Flute*, first performed at the Theater an der Wieden in 1791.

By the time of Mozart, however, the popular theatre had been placed on the margins of the city's culture. The critic and man of letters Josef von *Sonnenfels had attacked the popular theatre in his *Letters on the Viennese Stage* (1768), claiming that its coarse comedy and *improvisation did nothing to educate and elevate the morals of the citizenry. Accordingly, the players were expelled from their theatre in the centre of the city and forced to play in the suburbs. To raise the level of theatrical performance, in 1776 the Habsburg Emperor Josef II changed the *Burgtheater, which had been operating for some decades as a court theatre, into a national theatre (*see* NATIONAL THEATRE MOVEMENTS, EUROPE). The Burgtheater constitutes the most complete realization of Enlightenment ideology in theatre. Josef intended the theatre to serve as a conduit for his power: its dramatic offerings were to reflect the rational principles he was using to transform his feudally structured empire into a modern bureaucracy, and its actors were to serve as models of social grace and deportment for the citizens of the empire to emulate. The enterprise was remarkably successful. To this day Burgtheater actors enjoy an uncommon respect in Viennese society and, though the theatre's repertoire is not bound by the policies of the city or national government, its productions are often considered to provide important perspectives on matters of national significance. The Burgtheater has traditionally been celebrated for the seamless quality of its ensemble.

The popular theatre was not subdued by its expulsion to the suburbs. On the contrary, it gained renewed strength from it. For much of the nineteenth century, this sector of the Viennese theatre was dominated by a handful of institutions. The Theater in der Leopoldstadt (1781–1847), known as the 'laugh-theatre of Europe', was famed for its broad comedy and for its seemingly inexhaustible repertoire of *Volksstücke; it also premièred most of the romantic comedies of Ferdinand *Raimund. The Theater in der Josefstadt (1788–present) developed a mixed repertoire that included much drama also seen at the Burgtheater, while in the latter half of the century most of the *operettas of Johann Strauss, Millöcker, Lehár, and others received their premières at the Theater an der Wien (1801–present). The Carltheater (1847–1928) was distinguished for some years by the direction of Johann Nepomuk *Nestroy, the last of the improvisatory actors and a satiric writer of *Aristophanic impact.

Early in the twentieth century the centre of gravity in German-language theatre shifted from Vienna to *Berlin, as the Viennese theatre adapted less readily to the changes in theatrical modes of representation and organization that were occasioned by the experimental drama of the time. For example, soon after the turn of the century the major Viennese playwright Arthur *Schnitzler ensured his plays, all set in Vienna, were actually premièred in Berlin. Nevertheless, Vienna has remained a major theatre centre. Throughout the century, it has produced important actors and directors, among them Max *Reinhardt, Fritz *Kortner, and Maximilian Schell, who have gone on to major careers in the German-speaking theatre as a whole. Furthermore, there has been little decrease in theatrical activity. Opera is still the most highly prized *genre. The Staatsoper, on the site of the old Kärntnertortheater, is one of the world's pre-eminent opera houses, while operetta and modern opera flourish at the Volksoper. The Theater an der Wien continues to be the home of *musical comedy and operetta, as does the Raimundtheater. The Theater in der Josefstadt and the Deutsches Volkstheater perform a repertoire of traditional and contemporary drama, while the Burgtheater continues to be the most highly regarded theatre in Central Europe. Its repertory is primarily classical, but it has recently staged works, particularly those of Thomas *Bernhard, which have been highly critical of the Austrian establishment and of the perceived cultural complacency of the country. These have caused immense controversy in a city where the past is prized with particular intensity. The modern revival of the important plays of Ödön von *Horváth has taken place, in part, in Vienna, while the plays of Wolfgang *Bauer and Peter *Handke have been staged in a variety of Viennese theatres. So while Vienna still employs its theatres to maintain an image of itself as a comfortably cosmopolitan but essentially old-world city, on its stages the values of its society do not go entirely unquestioned.   SJCW

VIETNAM

A South-East Asian country with a long theatre tradition. The northern part of what is now Vietnam was ruled by China until AD 939, while Hindu civilizations dominated the south, partly explaining the extensive Chinese and (much less) Indian influences on Vietnamese culture. During French colonial rule (1862–1945) Vietnam experienced powerful French cultural influence, and thereafter the Americans exerted large impact in the south (1954–75). Still the Vietnamese retain an age-old pride in their cultural independence, identity, and achievements.

*Folk performances, including temple seance ceremonies, courting songs, and small-scale popular theatricals, are very ancient in Vietnam. Besides the folk opera *hat cheo, water *puppetry (*mua roi nuoc) was a popular form by the early twelfth century. This involved brief comic or fighting scenes staged on ponds, the hidden puppeteers using long rods. Having conquered China, the thirteenth-century Mongols tried unsuccessfully to subjugate Vietnam. In 1285 a Chinese actor captured in

Vietnam was persuaded to teach his art, an event marking a steep increase in Chinese influence over Vietnamese court theatre. The particular theatrical form taught was *zaju, and many of its performance features became part of Vietnamese theatre, including complex *make-up, relative lack of stage *properties, *costumes, movements, and gestures of the actors, and the language and *plots of the plays.

Emperor Gia Long (ruled 1802–20) of the Nguyen Dynasty, a great theatre lover, had the first theatre built in Hué's imperial palaces. Under Minh Manh (ruled 1820–41) the Chinese actor Kang Konghou (Vietnamese: Can Cung Hau) contributed to *training the court troupe, bringing to Vietnam the styles of nineteenth-century *Chinese theatre, including Beijing opera (*jingju). Vietnamese theatre underwent modernization during the French period. Apart from introducing the purely spoken theatre *kich, the French built a large theatre in Hanoi in 1911, which was renovated in the 1990s and remains in active use. The popular hat cheo became urban: previously an *open-air form, it was now sometimes seen in theatres with *stages, *scenery, *lighting, and stage properties.

The fact that the Vietnamese revolutionary Ho Chi Minh (1890–1969) was a lover of French culture did not prevent him from leading a very long, intense, and ultimately successful nationalist movement based on Marxism-Leninism. Ho held that the arts should be politicized and function as propaganda for socialism and for Vietnamese patriotism. The communists have continued this policy, although much more flexibly since Vietnam's reunification in 1976, and especially since they began a policy of reform in 1986. The trend towards theatrical modernization gathered force since the defeat of the French in 1954, especially in the south. Many urban professional theatre companies have been established and new theatres built. At the same time, traditional dramas and patterns of performance survive with official encouragement, and many actors still believe in their traditional protective spirits. Although not all genres are equally appealing to *audiences, theatre remains a vital force in Vietnamese society.   CPM

VIEUX-COLOMBIER, THÉÂTRE DU

Formerly the Athénée Saint-Germain, the Vieux-Colombier was founded by Jacques *Copeau in 1913 to put into practice his aim of purifying the theatre and creating 'le tréteau nu' (the bare stage). Notable first-season productions included L'Échange by the then unknown Paul *Claudel, and a much revived production of Shakespeare's Twelfth Night (La Nuit des rois). In 1917 the company decamped to the Garrick Theatre, *New York, for two seasons to escape the war. When Copeau's most celebrated disciple, Louis *Jouvet, left the company in 1924 the theatre was converted into a cinema, only to be restored in 1930 by Copeau's ex-pupils, the Compagnie des Quinze. The theatre then hosted many memorable productions including the première of

*Sartre's Huis clos (1944), became the *training ground for Jean *Vilar, and hosted *Artaud's infamous fundraising lecture for his rehabilitation in 1947. The theatre is a registered historical monument owned by the state and managed by the *Comédie-Française.   BRS

VIGANÒ, SALVATORE (1769–1821)

Italian dancer, choreographer, and composer. The nephew of Boccherini, Viganò learned from Jean Duberval a practice of choreography demanding mimic talent. After working principally in *Vienna, Venice, and *Milan, he became *ballet master in 1811 at La *Scala. He invented the coreodramma, a highly theatrical work based on mythology, history, or a Shakespeare play that synthesized *dance patterns with *mime. He created over 40 dances; among the greatest were The Creatures of Prometheus (1801), with music especially composed for him by Beethoven; Othello (1818); the mock heroic Gli strelizzi (The Guards, 1809); and The Titans (1819).   JEH

VIGARANI FAMILY

Italian *family of architects and *scenographers. Gaspare (1588–1663) built a long, successful career designing large-scale *scenery and apparatuses in his native duchy of Modena, for public *spectacles organized both by the court and by the religious authorities: in 1654 he constructed a theatre holding 3,000 spectators. Invited to *Paris, he created the *Salle des Machines at the Tuileries in 1662; in the process he opposed and supplanted the previous influence of Giacomo *Torelli, to the extent of confiscating and burning his sets from the *Petit-Bourbon. His son Carlo (1623–93) returned to Paris after his father's death and created major royal pageants and spectacles for Louis XIV between 1664 and 1675, in collaboration with his younger brother Ludovico. Carlo received French nationality and patents of nobility, after the signature in 1672 of his 'act of association' with the composer *Lully (also Italian by birth) which launched the foundation of the *Opéra in Paris.   RAA

VIGNY, ALFRED DE (1797–1863)

French playwright. In the early 1830s, when *romantic drama was becoming established in the *Paris theatres, Vigny stood out as the intellectual among the leading dramatists. His theatrical debuts were marked by translations from Shakespeare (Le More de Venise, *Comédie-Française, 1829); while his masterpiece Chatterton (Comédie-Française, 1835), which treats the last hours of the Bristol boy-poet's life with real pathos (notably contributed by Vigny's mistress Marie *Dorval in the role of Kitty Bell), was conceived as a philosophical plea on behalf of the sufferings of genius in a hostile, materialist society, in what the author defined as a 'drama of ideas'.   WDH

The curtain call in Jean **Vilar**'s production of *Richard II*, Avignon Festival, 1953, seen every summer from 1947 to 1953 with Vilar in the lead. Staged outdoors in the Court of Honour of the Palais des Papes, a building that dates from the same period as the play's setting, the dark brown walls of the palace formed a massive backdrop for Shakespeare's investigation of kingship.

VIKTYUK, ROMAN (1936–)

Russian director. Viktyuk took over the Theatre of Moscow State University in the mid-1970s, where he successfully directed *Petrushevskaya's *absurd play *Music Lessons* (1980). He also worked at the *Sovremennik Theatre in *Moscow but his breakthrough came with a dance-show production of Jean *Genet's *The Maids* (1988), for which he *cast male actors in the parts of the maids. For Viktyuk things morally wrong and socially not permissible are ornamented until sin becomes so beautiful that it is unrecognizable as sin. In the late 1990s cracks began to appear in his aestheticized world; Viktyuk's homosexuality dominated the artistic discourse, his productions bordered on vulgarity, and his popularity diminished.   BB

VILALTA, MARUXA (1932–)

Mexican playwright and director. The winner of ten *awards for best play of the year, many of her pieces are concerned with social issues. *Number 9* (1965) is an *expressionist piece about the dehumanization of factory workers, while *Together Tonight, Loving Each Other So Much* (1970) is a dark, *absurdist *comedy about middle-class self-centredness. In *A Woman, Two Men and a Gun Shot* (1981) and *A Small Tale of Horror and Unbridled Love* (1985) Vilalta *parodies *melodrama and *gender identity. Subsequent plays, such as *A Voice in the Desert: the life of St Jerome* (1990), are religious in theme.   KFN

VILAR, JEAN (1912–71)

French director and *actor-manager. As founding director of the *Avignon Festival and *manager of the *Théâtre National Populaire, Vilar transformed the state-supported theatre from an elitist to a popular institution through several innovations: freedom of repertory, reform of technology and management policies, decentralization, and creation of new *audiences. After attending university and Charles *Dullin's theatre school in *Paris, Vilar completed military service and joined a *touring company. Returning to Paris in 1942, he acted his first major role in *Synge's *The Well of the Saints*, and directed his first play, *Strindberg's *Dance of Death*. As founding director of the Compagnie des Sept, he won acclaim for productions of Strindberg, *Molière, and T. S. *Eliot. Expanding *Copeau's philosophy of popular theatre, Vilar directed the Avignon Theatre Festival from 1947 until his death, with the aim of bringing together troupes and spectators, especially young people, from all over Europe in a July holiday atmosphere to heal the bitterness of the war and discover the shared heritage of the European classics. Vilar believed that theatre could bring culture and thus social enlightenment to all classes, strengthen democracy, and make wars and tyranny less likely. He was the first in post-war France to direct German works, including *Büchner's *Danton's Death* (1948), *Brecht's *Mother Courage* (1951), and *Kleist's *Prince of Homburg* (1951), while his anchors remained *Molière, *Corneille, and Shakespeare. In Avignon Vilar abandoned Italianate theatre, and built an *open-air wooden *stage in the courtyard of the ancient Palais des Papes, which accommodated thousands of spectators.

A fine actor himself, as a director Vilar emphasized *character and *textual clarity over *spectacle, and demanded that *actors be highly disciplined in preparation for a role, but then allowed them to improvise and reinterpret, so long as they made strong, intimate contact with the audience. At the Théâtre National Populaire, which he managed from 1951 to 1963, Vilar remodelled the Palais de *Chaillot, removing the orchestra pit, galleries, *curtain, *proscenium, and *footlights, which greatly enlarged the *auditorium. 'To bring together the shopkeeper with the high court judge . . . the postman with the professor', he lowered *ticket prices, eliminated tips to ushers, provided good inexpensive food, free programmes and buses, performances for school classes and workers, public symposia, and a journal for theatre patrons. Performances started on time and *critics' previews were eliminated, which meant that premières belonged to the public, without the critics' mediation.

Although not a radical, Vilar often produced plays that provoked critical reflection on political events. In the era of the Algerian War and Gaullist nationalism, he staged an antimilitarist *Ubu roi*, and produced Brecht's *Galileo* to protest against French tests of the atom bomb. As Barthes noted, Vilar's was a theatre of civic awareness carrying the moral gestus of its time. His vision of theatre as community was challenged at the 1968 Avignon Festival when the *Living Theatre led protests condemning Vilar as reactionary and the festival as 'a marketplace of culture'. Nonetheless, Vilar's innovations were emulated worldwide, and opened the way for decentralization and the founding of national theatres in Saint-Étienne, Strasbourg, Lyon, and other cities.   SBB

VILLAIN

A *character who energizes dramatic *action by desiring or performing what the play represents as culturally evil. Directly opposed to the *hero or *protagonist, a villain is distinguished from a morally acceptable antagonist only by his or her wickedness, and the term might be applied equally to Clytemnestra in *Aeschylus' *Agamemnon* (458 BC), Iago in Shakespeare's *Othello* (1603–4; in the cast of characters of the First Folio he is called 'a villain'), and Hannibal Lecter in the *film *The Silence of the Lambs* (1990)—even though each of them could also be considered in part noble, attractive, or even heroic. Ravana in the *Indian epic the *Ramayana* (upon which much South Asian and South-East Asian performance depends) is parallel: on one level he is a villain, but he is also heroic and artistic. The word, deriving from medieval French and English *villein*, originally meant a tenant feudal peasant, and thus a base or low-born person, suggesting a class-based definition of the villain that has been prevalent since *early modern drama.

The nineteenth century was heyday of the villain in the West. Once *romanticism had insisted that the hero of *tragedy need not be high-born, or that he might be alienated from society, an opposing figure was needed to clarify the protagonist's virtue. The dramatic usefulness of this strategy was abundantly clear in popular *melodrama, where the opposition between abstract good and evil was normally enacted over the body of a young, beautiful, and defenceless female character, the villain attempting to take advantage of his superior financial position to work his evil ways. Since his power had been gained improperly or illegally, often depriving the hero or the heroine of a rightful inheritance, the *action of most melodramas consisted in exposing not so much the villain's iniquity as his imposture.

The presence of a villain in drama raises complicated issues about the nature of evil, which are often left unresolved. Coleridge famously gave up on explaining Iago, calling his actions 'motiveless malignity', though since Freud playwrights and critics have been more likely to posit a root cause in (fictional) childhood development that twisted the character into malevolence (see PSYCHOANALYTIC CRITICISM). *Modernist theatre in general, consciously moving away from the incredible bad boys of melodrama, has tended to lessen the out-and-out evil of antagonists, but the villain has remained a powerful type figure in popular cinema, from the black hats of westerns to the *femmes fatales* of film noir. Villains are especially notable in Hollywood action films, where a master criminal, perverted politician, unscrupulous businessman, or megalomaniacal terrorist threatens worldwide horror and devastation that only the physically attractive hero can prevent or undo. DK

VILLAURRUTIA, XAVIER (1903–50)

Mexican playwright and poet. His first efforts at drama were short, playful pieces notable for their symbolism, like *It Seems a Lie* (1933) and *What Are You Thinking About?* (1934). After studying at Yale in 1936, Villaurrutia wrote longer, more complex plays though they tended towards the abstract and the symbolic. *The Ivy* (1942) is a rendition of the Phaedra myth told through the lives of an aristocratic family just prior to the Mexican Revolution of 1910. Villaurrutia's legacy has been more literary than theatrical. KFN

VILLEGAS, OSCAR (1943–)

Mexican playwright and director, whose work is testimony to the social and political unrest of the 1970s. *Renaissance* (1971) is about Beatlemania, sexual liberation, and political repression; *Marlon Brando Is Someone Else* (1977) tells of gratuitous crime among alienated youth. The explicit treatment of sexual prom-

iscuity in *The Pyre* (1983) caused something of a commotion with local authorities. Villegas is best known for *Santa Catarina* (1980), about same-sex encounters in a school for young boys, and for *Atlantida* (1977), which takes place among the lumpenproletariat. KFN

VILLIERS, GEORGE *See* BUCKINGHAM, GEORGE VILLIERS, 2ND DUKE OF.

VILNA TROUPE

*Yiddish theatre established in German-occupied *Vilnius in 1915, committed to high art and to ensemble *acting in the *Stanislavsky tradition. The troupe catered to the Jewish intelligentsia, specializing in serious Yiddish drama by *Asch, Hirshbein, *Gordin, Pinski, and translations of *Molière, *Schnitzler, *Sudermann, and *O'Neill. In 1917 the Vilna Troupe arrived in *Warsaw, where Kobrin's *realistic drama *Yankl Boyle* met with great critical success. In 1920 their world première of *Anski's *The Dybbuk* gained them enormous prestige in Warsaw, but *critical success and clashing egos caused the group to break into smaller troupes that *toured Europe. A fragment of the original group, including Joseph *Buloff, was invited to America in 1923, where their success could not overcome competition with the *Yiddish Art Theatre, and they disbanded in 1924. EN

VILNIUS

Capital of Lithuania. Lithuanian theatre emerged in the first instance from popular theatre, since Lithuanian was not the official language of the country under prolonged periods of foreign domination. In the late eighteenth century the first professional town theatre was established in Vilnius. Performances were in Russian, though, since Lithuania was under Russian rule. When the Jewish Theatre (*Vilna Troupe) was established in 1908, it was just as much an ethnic minority theatre as the Lithuanian performances put on at the Town Theatre. After Lithuania's independence in 1918 plays and productions in Lithuanian were encouraged, and Lithuanian theatres opened in a number of cities. In Vilnius, the Lithuanian State Theatre existed alongside the Russian Drama Theatre. The Theatre for the Young Spectator was founded under Soviet rule, and a *puppet theatre followed in 1958. Although many artists and directors trained at the Vilnius Conservatory, a number perfected their *training in *Moscow or Leningrad (*St Petersburg). Juozas Miltinis, who headed the Panevežys State Theatre from 1940 to 1994, placed emphasis on expressive movement and influenced the Conservatory teacher Dalia Tamulevičiute.

In the 1990s the Vilnius theatre scene was dominated by three directors: Rimas Tuminas, who works at the Academic Theatre and has formed a markedly poetic and visual style

(*Lermontov's *Masquerade*, Shakespeare's *Richard III*); Oskaras Koršunovas, who has specialized in works of the 1920s and 1930s, and has excelled with experimental productions (Kharms's *The Old Woman*); and Eimuntas Nekrošius, who began at the Young Spectator's Theatre in the 1980s and in 1992 joined the LIFE *festival (1993–7), where he directed *Mozart and Salieri* (1994), *Three Sisters* (1995), and *Hamlet* (1997). In 1998 LIFE was disbanded and Nekrošius formed his own theatre, Menofortas, where he continued his Shakespeare cycle with *Macbeth* (1999) and *Othello* (2000).   BB

VIÑAS, DAVID (1929–   )

Argentinian scholar, novelist, and playwright, one of the country's most respected intellectuals, noted for questioning oligarchic violence and domination. Most of his plays are historically based, including *Lisandro* (1972), *Tupac-Amarú* (1973), and *Dorrego* (1976, performed 1986). Exiled during the military dictatorship, Viñas rejected a 1992 Guggenheim award in memory of his two 'disappeared' children.   JGJ

VINAVER, MICHEL (1927–   )

French playwright. A successful international businessman, Vinaver became one the most important French dramatists of the post-1968 generation, his plays exemplifying the trend toward post-*structuralism and deconstruction in French critical thought. After the promise of his early works, *The Koreans* (1956) and *Hotel Iphigenia* (1959), Roger *Planchon's production of the monumental *Overboard* (1973) solidified Vinaver's reputation. While often cited as exemplifying the *théâtre du* *quotidien*, his plays experiment freely with dramatic structure and time, providing a mine for directorial interpretation. Like *Overboard*, the later works, including *Situation Vacant* (1971), *A Smile on the End of the Line* (1977), and *The Television Programme* (1988), often deal with the intrusion of larger economic and sociopolitical forces on the construction of personal life, language, and thought. His *dramaturgical technique is often considered 'juxtapositional' or deconstructive, resisting traditional narrative closure and seeking fragmentation and possibility in a *Brechtian vein. A champion of the work of younger playwrights, Vinaver has been instrumental in the resurgence of government and institutional support for emerging talent, composing an influential government report in 1987 on the challenges and concerns of those who write for French theatre. His play *11 September 2001* (2002) is a fascinating response to the terrorist attacks on the USA.   DGM

VINCENT, JEAN-PIERRE (1942–   )

One of the leading French directors of the post-1968 generation, Vincent began his career co-directing the Théâtre de Sartrouville with Patrice *Chéreau. From 1975 to 1983 he headed the Théâtre National de Strasbourg, where he championed the work of younger authors, including Serge Rezvani and Jean-Claude *Grumberg, and where his collaboration with playwrights Michel Deutch and Bertrand Chartreux brought about notable interpretations of modern French history and society, including *Vichy-Fictions* (1980) and *Le Palais de Justice* (1981). Greatly influenced by *Brecht, whose minor works he championed early in his career, Vincent's deconstructive approach to the classical repertoire, akin to that of Peter *Stein, foregrounds a *text's ideological underpinnings as well as its contemporary relevance. Briefly (and turbulently) heading the *Comédie-Française (1983–6), and then teaching at the *Paris *Conservatoire, he succeeded Chéreau as director of the Théâtre des Amandiers at Nanterre in 1990.   DGM

VIRAHSAWMY, DEV (1942–   )

Mauritian poet and dramatist. He is best known for his prolific output of plays in creole, often freely adapted from Shakespeare (*Zeneral Makbef*, 1981; and *Toufann*, a version of *The Tempest*, 1991), but also from *Molière (*Tartuffe* became *Tartchif froder*, 1993). Others include Indian stories such as *Dropadi* (1982) and even *musicals such as *Zozef ek so palto larkensiel* (*Joseph and his Technicolor Dreamcoat*, 1981, a free-wheeling version of *Lloyd Webber's work). His early poetry (*Disik salé*, 1976) was politically committed and popular in form, and like his early plays, such as *Bef dâ disab* (*Ox in the Sand*, 1980), was *published in trilingual versions (French, Mauritian, and Réunionese creole).   PGH

VISAKHADATTA

Author of the Sanskrit *Mudrarakshasa* (*The Signet Ring of Rakshasa*), the only play attributed to him. From the *text itself we learn that he was the grandson of Vateswaradatta and the son of Bhaskaradatta, who held the title of maharaja. The playwright assumed the title of *deva*, and his patron king, acknowledged in the concluding verse of one manuscript of the work as Chandragupta, happens to be the *hero of *Mudrarakshasa*. This has led some scholars to identify the patron with Chandragupta II, or Vikramaditya of the Gupta dynasty of Magadha (reigned 375–413), which means that Visakhadatta could have been a younger contemporary of *Kalidasa.

Breaking with the tradition of lyrical or romantic plays with metaphysical associations, *Mudrarakshasa* is exceptional in Sanskrit drama for its explicit political focus. Robust and worldly in its representation of everyday life and realpolitik, and forceful in its diction, this seven-act play concerns the astute diplomacy of Chanakya, the minister of the Maurya king Chandragupta, whose pragmatism in controlling the affairs of the state has sometimes been described as machiavellian. The scheming Chanakya defeats the ruling Nanda kings and shifts the loyalty of their efficient minister Rakshasa to Chandragupta himself.   KNP

VISCONTI, LUCHINO (1906–76)

Italian director with parallel careers in theatre, *opera, and *film. There were almost two souls in Visconti, one which laid bare harsh social reality (he was a communist) and one which relished the opulence of style and splendour (he belonged to the nobility). He made his theatrical debut with Jean Cocteau's *Les Parents terribles* (1945), but his strong directorial stance, his insistence on imposing his own vision, was a novelty which made him unpopular with actors, who complained of his dictatorial ways. In 1954 he moved to opera, directing Spontini's *La Vestale*, and thereafter working with Maria Callas on *Gluck, Bellini, and Donizetti. In cinema he served an apprenticeship as assistant to Jean Renoir, and made his own debut in 1943 with *Ossessione*. The term neorealism was first used for this film, and in the post-war period he was one of the principal exponents of this approach. Later his vision widened, and he directed for the screen such literary masterpieces as *Death in Venice* (1971) and *The Leopard* (1963).   JF

VISÉ, JEAN DONNEAU DE (1638–1710)

French playwright. Donneau de Visé's chief claim to literary fame is as the founder in 1672 of the pioneering periodical *Le Mercure galant* (which was later to become *Le Mercure de France*); but he had already established a place in theatre history by his intervention in the 'Querelle de l'*École des femmes*', the controversy surrounding *Molière's play of 1662 which produced hostile attacks from rival actors and playwrights, courtiers, and opportunist publicity-seekers (the last category including the young de Visé). Having made his peace with Molière, de Visé continued to write for the theatre, specializing in machine-plays (*see* SALLE DES MACHINES) and *comedies on topical subjects.   WDH

VISHNEVSKY, VSEVOLOD (1900–51)

Russian/Soviet dramatist who served with the cavalry during the Civil War and wrote a play (*The First Cavalry Army*, 1929) based on his experiences. In 1921 he had organized an eight-hour outdoor epic about the Kronstadt sailors' revolt, but his revolutionary zeal is seen to best effect in *Optimistic Tragedy* (1932), staged memorably by *Tairov in 1933 on a spiralling tiered setting by Vadim Ryndin, and with Alisa *Koonen as the commissar sent by the Party to discipline a group of anarchist sailors. His *Unforgettable 1919* (1949) is a shameless, and factually dubious, celebration of Stalin.   NW

VISION AND THE VISUAL

The centrality of vision for the theatrical medium is evident in the etymology of the word *'theatre' as has often been noted: *theatron* is literally a place to see. Visuality is thus an all encompassing question and precondition for the functioning of theatre. Yet in the realm of *theory we detect a long-standing feud between the dominance of the dramatic *text and the visual aspects of production. The philosophical suspicion of the visual, although particularly observable since the eighteenth century, can of course be traced back to *Aristotle's *Poetics* where he relegates *opsis* (*spectacle, or *scenery and *costume) to the most lowly and superfluous aspects of theatre.

From a historical perspective it is necessary to ask what and how spectators see and under what conditions. Theatre research today does not generally regard the visual as an ahistorical cognitive given, but rather as contingent on many aesthetic, ideological, and social factors. It is of course much easier to ascertain what spectators saw (the fields of *scenography and *playhouse architecture) than how they saw it; attempts to treat the latter based on art history records are fraught with methodological problems. One area that has been intensively discussed is the introduction of *perspective scenery during the *early modern period. It has been demonstrated, for example, that the perspective stage with its privileging of a particular point of view is ideologically loaded and linked to questions of power. Thus seeing in the theatre is by no means a neutral, purely cognitive activity.

Towards the end of the eighteenth century theatre became increasingly divided into two categories: the dramatic, a generally highbrow theatre dominated by the word; and popular forms stressing *music and spectacle (*pantomime, and *special effect). This division was enforced by licensing restrictions on dramatic theatre in many countries (*see* LICENSING ACTS; PATENT THEATRES) and reinforced by wider philosophical and pedagogical developments which increasingly derogated the visual. The popular forms developed into the pictorialism characteristic of the nineteenth-century theatre with astonishing *trompe l'œil* effects, designed to deceive and delight the eye (*see* ILLUSION). In reaction to such emphasis on pictorialism, the anti-*naturalistic reform movement of the early twentieth century redefined the visual by stressing allusion rather than depiction, with abstract stage pictures designed to stimulate the spectator's internal images.

The twentieth century has seen various developments leading to a reassertion of theatre as a visual medium. These include the dominance of *directors, many of whom realize their reinterpretation of texts through striking images; and the influence of *film, including the integration of film sequences (for instance *Piscator) and filmic devices such as *montage to structure stage *action (Robert *Lepage). Since the 1960s the influence of visual and *performance art (Robert *Wilson) has led increasingly to a redefinition of theatre and of our critical vocabulary. As early as 1970 German critics coined terms such as *Bildertheater* ('designer's theatre', more or less) to describe a shift from the dominance of the spoken word to the visual image. Nevertheless the tension between word and image endures. The fact that the first Festival of Visual Theatre was organized in 1999 in *London as a category separate from conventional theatre suggests that a general perception remains that theatre is not a visual art.   CBB

VITEZ, ANTOINE (1930–90)

French actor, director, teacher, and author. The most intellectual director of his era, Vitez was able to work in Russian, German, and Greek, and was inspired by contemporary critical *theory. The work of *Brecht and *Meyerhold was foundational for Vitez, who began acting at 18, joined the Communist Party in 1957, was secretary to the poet Louis Aragon, and taught *acting at the *Lecoq School and the *Conservatoire National. He began as a director in 1966 with his own adaptation of *Sophocles' *Electra* at Caen, and gained recognition *directing in the communist suburbs ringing *Paris, including the Théâtre des Quartiers d'Ivry, which he led from 1971 to 1980. With his productions of *Electra* (1971), Brecht's *Mother Courage* (1973), and *Catherine* (1976), he attained an international reputation. Believing that 'theatre can be made from anything', Vitez adapted *Catherine* from an Aragon novel, staging it with a group of actors who passed a book around and read passages as they ate a complete dinner. In 1978–9 he produced four *Molière plays in repertory, using only the *props and furniture listed by Molière's *stage manager.

His signature approach was to help actors develop gestures, movement, vocalizations, and breathing to render the intrinsic rhythm and music of the *text with their bodies and voices in space. The *scenography of his long-time collaborator Yannis *Kokkos lent an epic dimension to the spatial imagery of the actors' movement. As *artistic director of the Théâtre National du *Chaillot from 1981 to 1988, and of the *Comédie-Française from 1988 until his unexpected death, he tried, like *Vilar, to democratize the theatre, offering a wide range of classical and modern works. Vitez's important productions of later years included *Hugo's *Hernani* (1985), *Claudel's *The Satin Slipper* (1987), and *Rojas's *La Célestine*, starring Jeanne Moreau (1989). At his death Vitez was working on *Galileo* by Brecht, the playwright who was, like Vitez himself, a relentless questioner.   SBB

VITRAC, ROGER (1899–1952)

French dramatist. Born in Lot (south central France), Vitrac went to Paris with his parents in 1911. The bourgeois provincialism of his childhood infused his writing, which often apprehended the adult world through the sensibility of a child, as in his best-known play *Victor; ou, Les Enfants au pouvoir* (*Victor; or, Children Take Over*, 1928). After founding the literary journal *Aventure* in 1922 and publishing *dada poetry, Vitrac joined the *surrealists and signed the 1924 manifesto, but was dismissed apparently for his obsession with theatre over poetry. He and Antonin *Artaud started their own theatre, the Alfred Jarry (1926–9), which produced two of Vitrac's plays: *Les Mystères de l'amour* (1927) and *Victor*. Attacking middle-class institutions and hypocrisy in a mix of *farce, *dream elements, risqué humour, Artaudian *'cruelty', and often *tragedy, Vitrac honed his *dramaturgical skills through sixteen plays that were largely unappreciated during his lifetime. He was a big man with ready laughter or tears, mystified but never resentful that success eluded him. *Le Sabre de mon père* (1951) scandalized *critics by its military *satire, but won posthumous acclaim.   FHL

VITRUVIUS (first century BC)

Roman author of *De Architectura*, an architectural treatise in ten books. Little or nothing is known of his life beyond what is reported in *De Architectura*. He was a practising architect and military and civil engineer under Julius Caesar and Augustus. His treatise (c.31 BC, with later revisions) is of interest to theatre historians because book 5 includes a discussion of the siting, consolidation, and functional design of theatres in both the *Roman and *Greek style. The planimetric design prescribed by Vitruvius is demonstrably based on actual practice, not mere theoretical abstraction. Rediscovered in the *early modern period, Vitruvius' book influenced the construction of a number of sixteenth- and seventeenth-century *playhouses.   EGC

VIVIAN BEAUMONT THEATRE *See* Lincoln Center for the Performing Arts.

VIVIANI, RAFFAELE (1888–1950)

Italian actor, composer, and playwright. Viviani taught himself to read and write and became a nationally known *variety performer by the age of 24. In 1917 he formed his own company and, building on his variety character sketches and songs, he wrote the *dialogue and composed the lyrics and music for over 40 *musical plays—many of them panoramic dramas that take place in specific areas of *Naples. Among these are *Via Toledo by Night* (1918), *Il scugnizzo* (*Street Urchin*, 1918), *Circo equestre Sgueglia* (*Sgueglia's Equestrian Circus*, 1922), and *Nullatenenti* (*Have-Nots*, 1929). He painted genuinely compassionate and often humorous portraits of the Neapolitan working class, the poor, and the disenfranchised. His *realistic depictions and his use of Neapolitan led to fascist *censorship from the late 1920s until the end of the Second World War.   JEH

VIVIESCAS, VICTOR (1958–)

Colombian playwright, director, and essayist. He won first prize in the National Playwriting Contest for *Crisanta sola, soledad Crisanta* (*Crisanta Alone, Loneliness Crisanta*, 1986) and for *Ruleta rusa* (*Russian Roulette*, 1993). One of the most important playwrights of his generation, his other works include *Aníbal es un fantasma que se repite en los espejos* (*Anibal Is a Ghost Who Repeats Himself in the Mirrors*, 1986), *Prométeme que no gritaré* (*Promise Me That I Will Not Scream*, 1988), *Lo obsceno* (*The Obscene*, 1997), and a version of *Chekhov's *Platonov* (1999). He is one of the co-authors of *La cruzada de los niños de la calle* (*The Crusade of the Street Children*), staged in *Madrid by José *Sanchis Sinisterra (2000). He explores solitude, memory, intimacy, and betrayal in a language rich in connotation and metaphor, and his lyrical pessimism has been compared to Heiner *Müller and Bernard-Marie *Koltès. Viviescas taught movement and *acting at University of Antioquia in Medellín (1985–92), and directs the Dramatists' Workshop at the Teatro *Nacional's Casa in *Bogotá.   BJR

VLAAMSE VOLKSTONEEL (FLEMISH PEOPLE'S THEATRE)

*Modernist Flemish company, operating from 1920 to 1932. The central figure was Jan Oskar de Gruyter, who thought theatre an important educational and emancipatory tool. Though he considered the *director primary, de Gruyter promoted a literary repertoire and insisted that language be used as an instrument of culture. The company often took its message to remote parts of Flanders. De Gruyter was succeeded in 1924 by the Dutchman Johan de Meester, Jr., who had been influenced by *Tairov and *Meyerhold, and who moved in the direction of the *expressionist *avant-garde, drawing on medieval and traditional subjects to suit the company's purpose of emancipating the Flemish people. Anton Van de Velde's *Tyl* (1925), a play written in close consultation with de Meester, was particularly successful and was invited to *Paris by Firmin *Gémier. A highly imaginative political *satire, it featured several legendary *characters and a *constructivist setting by René Moulaert. With ever increasing tempo, the actors played like *acrobats on narrow sloping platforms and staircases. Another typical production was *Hamlet* (1927), in which de Meester took the title role. The French-speaking Belgian playwright Michel de *Ghelderode also cooperated with the Vlaamse Volkstoneel.   JDV

VODANOVIC, SERGIO (1926–2001)

Chilean playwright and lawyer. A master of *parody and *satire, Vodanovic usually targeted the Chilean upper middle class but also focused on the inner conflicts of individuals. His most accomplished play is *Viña: tres comedias en traje de baño* (*Viña:*

Three Comedies in Bathing Suits, 1964). During the 1970s his plays dealt with social and political unrest during the Allende regime and the Pinochet dictatorship. Representative of this period are *Nos tomamos la universidad* (*We Occupied the University*, 1971) and *La mar estaba serena* (*The Sea Was Calm*), produced by *Ictus in 1978, a metaphorical reference to the dictatorship.   MAR

VOGEL, PAULA (1951–)

American playwright. Like Caryl *Churchill and Maria Irene *Fornés, Vogel's plays focus on women and women's issues. Through a mix of scatological humour, fantasy, and rage Vogel addresses such issues as incest and domestic violence. *How I Learned to Drive* (1998), about a young girl's sexually charged driving lessons with her uncle, evokes erotic confusion and healing rather than victimhood. *The Baltimore Waltz* (1992), inspired by her brother's death, likewise stands apart from other AIDS plays through its *allegory about 'Acquired Toilet Disease', including, as Frank *Rich described it, 'erotic jokes, movie kitsch and medical nightmare'. As head of the playwriting programme at Brown University from 1984 to 1999, Vogel used innovative exercises for her students, including writing complete plays in 48 hours and the same scene three different ways. Other plays include *Desdemona* (1979), a revisioning of *Othello*; *The Oldest Profession* (1981), about ageing prostitutes; *And Baby Makes Seven* (1984), about lesbian mothers of imaginary children; *Hot n' Throbbing* (1992), about *pornography; and *The Mineola Twins* (1997), about extremism. *See also* FEMINIST THEATRE.   GAO

VOKES FAMILY

English actors and *dancers. **Fred** (1846–88), **Jessie** (1851–84), **Victoria** (1853–94), and **Rosina** (1854–94) were the son and daughters of **Frederick Vokes** (1816–90), a *costumier. Herbert Fawdon, known as **Fawdon Vokes** (d. 1904), was adopted into the troupe. An extraordinarily talented *family, they were professional performers as children. Fred and Fawdon were *acrobatic dancers, Jessie *danced, taught, and *managed the troupe, Victoria sang and acted, and Rosina was a witty comedienne. Between 1869 and 1879 they dominated the *Drury Lane *pantomime, moving in 1880 to *Covent Garden. They *toured extensively in America, where they were enthusiastically received as 'pleasing, chaste and exceedingly comical' entertainers.

AF

VOLKOV, FYODOR (1729–63)

Russian actor, christened 'the father of the Russian Theatre' by Vissarion Belinsky. Peter the Great's daughter, the Empress Elizaveta Petrovna, learned of the existence of a group of *amateurs, including Volkov, his brother Grigory, and Ivan *Dmitrevsky, who were performing plays to a high standard in the town of Yaroslavl. In 1750, keen to found a national theatre, the Empress summoned the troupe to *St Petersburg where they gave a private performance for her of a *comedy, *A Sinner's Repentance*. Satisfied with this, Elizaveta proceeded to provide for the troupe's education and in 1756 an act was promulgated granting them fully-fledged status as a theatre company under the directorship of Aleksandr *Sumarokov, thus laying the foundation for the imperial theatres which followed. Volkov became the leading actor and, after 1761, took over the *management from Sumarokov. Volkov was a highly intelligent performer, blessed with a powerful temperament, which found expression in a number of roles in Russian classical *tragedies such as Sumarokov's *Hamlet* and his *Khorev*. Fonvizin described him as 'a person of great learning . . . who could have become a statesman'. Volkov actually took part in the *coup d'état* against Peter III which brought the Empress Catherine to the throne, for which she offered him the post of cabinet minister and the Order of St Andrew, both of which he refused. He also officiated at her coronation, staging a street masquerade in her honour, *Minerva Triumphant*. At his death management of the troupe was assumed by Dmitrevsky.   NW

VOLKSBÜHNE (PEOPLE'S THEATRE)

German term to describe a theatre movement and the buildings that emerged from it. The cultural movement was founded in 1890 by Franz Wille in *Berlin as a subscription organization, the Freie Volksbühne (Free People's Theatre). Disputes over programming led to a split in 1892. The social democratic journalist Franz Mehring took over the organization and Wille founded the Neue Freie Volksbühne. The two organizations eventually merged in 1927 with a nationwide membership of half a million. Meanwhile a *playhouse had been built in 1914 as the 2,000-seat Volksbühne am Bülowplatz. The movement became a crucial forum for politically committed theatre during the Weimar Republic and is most closely associated with Erwin *Piscator's directorship of the theatre (1924–7) and that of K. H. *Martin (1929–32). In 1933 the Nazi regime took over the Volksbühne, renaming it Theater am Horst-Wessel-Platz. After the war the movement was reconstituted in a divided Germany, each eventually with its own Volksbühne. The original reopened in 1954 as the Volksbühne am Rosa-Luxemburg-Platz. After 1969 it achieved renown under Benno *Besson and again after 1992 under the controversial directorship of Frank *Castorf. The West Berlin Freie Volksbühne, in a new building from 1963, had a series of major *artistic directors, starting with Piscator, who staged important *documentary and *historical drama, including the work of Rolf *Hochhuth. It lost its public subsidy in 1992 after reunification and was closed.   CBB

VOLKSSTÜCK (PEOPLE'S PLAY)

A broad term encompassing German-language dramas that portray the life of common people, usually designed for popular consumption. These range from light-hearted dialect *comedies, which entertained *audiences in *Vienna throughout the eighteenth and for most of the nineteenth centuries, to present-day serious studies of the contemporary lower class. Major exponents of the former were Ferdinand *Raimund and Johann *Nestroy. Twentieth-century writers of the more politically oriented *Volksstück* are Marieluise *Fleisser, whose *Pioneers in Ingolstadt* (1929) explored the narrow lives of the working class, and Ödön von *Horváth, who, in plays like *Tales from the Vienna Woods* (1931), sets traditional 'folksy' sentimentality against the harsh reality of ordinary lives. The most successful recent writers in this vein have come from Austria (Peter *Turrini, Wolfgang *Bauer) and Bavaria (Martin *Sperr, Franz Xaver *Kroetz). Kroetz's *Farmyard* (1972) describes the doomed relationship between a farmer's retarded daughter and an inarticulate farm labourer. In many respects the *Volksstück* has now been appropriated, superseded, and sanitized by *television soap operas.   MWP

VOLLARD, THÉÂTRE

Réunionese theatre company, 1979–99. Named after the *avant-garde art dealer Ambroise Vollard, it was launched by Emmanuel Genvrin and Jean-Luc Trulès with a production of *Jarry's *Ubu roi*. The company went on to create a successful popular theatre in Réunion island, using creole and French in ambitious productions reflecting the history of the French colony, written by Genvrin and Pierre-Louis Rivière, often staged in unconventional environments and involving creole food and music. The growth of a sense of community and identity in the island was reflected in plays such as *Marie Dessembre* (1981), *Nina Ségamour* (1982), *Étuves* (1984), and *Lepervenche chemin de fer* (1990), all by Genvrin. His *satirical adaptation of Vollard, *Votez Ubu Colonial* (1994), provoked the hostility of the island's political establishment and caused the withdrawal of the company's state subsidies, leading to its eventual closure.

                                    PGH

VOLODIN (ALEKSANDR LIFSHITS)
(1919–2001)

Soviet/Russian playwright. Volodin trained at the State Institute for Cinematography, graduating in 1949. His plays are cinematic in structure, with frequent flashbacks and parallel actions, and many have served as scripts for *films (for instance, *Five Evenings*, 1957; film by Nikita Mikhalkov, 1978). Volodin was always critical of appearances: in *The Factory Girl* (1956) he targets a factory about to be filmed for its pretence that working conditions are perfect. He explored the personal lives of ordinary people, often treating relationships and failed romances with a touch of irony. For Volodin happiness had to be found by the individual, despite social and ideological constraints.

BB

VOLONAKIS, MINOS (1925–99)

Greek director. Born in Athens, he studied theatre with Karolos *Koun. He directed for private companies starting in 1960, as well as for the State Theatre of Northern Greece in Thessaloniki, including the first Greek production of *Beckett's *Waiting for Godot*. Between 1975 and 1978 he was *artistic director of the State Theatre of Northern Greece. His memorable productions included *Brecht's *Mr Puntila and his Man Matti* and *Euripides' *Medea* with Melina *Mercouri. In 1982 he directed *Sophocles' *Oedipus the King* for the *Greek National Theatre and that same year, in an attempt to bring theatre closer to the working classes, he inaugurated the Festival of the Rocks in *Athens, an annual event that featured performances in *open-air spaces. Volonakis is remembered for the visual aspects of his productions as well as for his numerous translations of ancient *Greek and American plays.

KGo

VOLTAIRE (FRANÇOIS-MARIE AROUET) (1694–1778)

French philosopher, historian, polemicist, and poet. Devoting a great part of his creative energy to the theatre, Voltaire was placed by contemporaries on a level with his predecessors *Corneille and *Racine as a writer of *tragedy. Many of his best-known plays were based on subjects from classical antiquity: *Oedipe* (1718), *Mariamne* (1725), *Mérope* (1743), *Sémiramis* (1748) among others; but *Zaïre* (1732), his tragedy with most lasting appeal, is set in Jerusalem during the Crusades, and *Alzire* (1736) in South America at the time of the Spanish Conquest. In exile in *London from 1726 to 1729, Voltaire acquired a good working knowledge of English, partly at least by attending London theatres. His serious acquaintance with Shakespeare dates from this period; and *Zaïre* and *La Mort de César* (1731) show the influence of *Othello* and *Julius Caesar* respectively; while the appearance of a *ghost on stage (not seen in French drama for several generations) represents in both *Ériphile* (1732) and *Sémiramis* an explicit borrowing from *Hamlet*. An important innovation in the field of tragedy was Voltaire's creation of a 'sub-genre' of philosophical tragedy, in which the harmful effects of religious fanaticism are shown, as in *Zaïre*, *Alzire*, *Mahomet* (1741), and *L'Orphelin de la Chine* (1755). Another was the choice of subjects from national history (*Zaïre*; *Adélaïde du Guesclin*, 1734; *Tancrède*, 1760) as an alternative to the legacy of classical antiquity.

But Voltaire was very much a traditionalist in aesthetic matters; and although he had out-Shakespeared Shakespeare in *La Mort de César* by producing a tragedy without women *characters, he later became hostile to the English influence, denouncing Shakespeare in intemperate terms on grounds of taste, especially in his 'Lettre à l'Académie' (1776). In the field of *comedy, Voltaire was equally hostile to the new *genre of 'tearful comedy' (*comédie larmoyante), frequently castigating *La Chaussée for his pernicious influence; though in his own comic drama, the insipid attempt at a more traditionalist formula is often redeemed only by a concession to sentiment. The fact that *L'Écossaise* (1760) was written in prose, as well as containing a virulent attack on his enemy Fréron, makes this play by far the most acceptable of his comedies. Voltaire played a prominent part in campaigns concerning the religious and civil status of the *acting profession: when Christian burial was refused to Adrienne *Lecouvreur (1730) and again in the 1760s when he exhorted actors like *Lekain and Mlle *Clairon to put pressure on the authorities by 'withdrawing their labour'. He had a close relationship with Lekain, who acted (as Voltaire himself did) in his private theatricals at Ferney. Elected to the Académie Française in 1746, he was paid a remarkable tribute shortly before his death, when he was crowned with a laurel wreath during a performance of his tragedy *Irène* at the *Comédie-Française. *See also* NEOCLASSICISM; THEORIES OF DRAMA, THEATRE, AND PERFORMANCE.

WDH

VONDEL, JOOST VAN DEN (1587–1679)

Dutch playwright and poet. Influenced by the *Chambers of Rhetoric, Vondel began with mock poems and patriotic poetry. He wrote *Gijsbrecht van Aemstel* for the opening of *Amsterdam's new municipal theatre, the *Schouwburg (1638), a *religious play that was performed there annually on New Year's Day until 1968. A founder of the Netherlands' national drama and its main representative of humanist drama, Vondel combined the classical with *characters that belonged to the *medieval tradition. His *biblical plays, such as *Lucifer* (1654) and *Adam in Exile* (1664), were still performed occasionally at the end of the twentieth century.

CBB

VON SYDOW, MAX (1929–)

Swedish actor. Soon after he started his career in the 1950s he joined Ingmar *Bergman's company in Malmö, and subsequently performed in many of Bergman's *films. His portrayal of a knight returning from the Crusades in *The Seventh Seal* (1957) brought him international acclaim. Further probing performances in *The Virgin Spring* (1959), *Through a Glass Darkly* (1962), and *Shame* (1968) confirmed his ability to portray emotionally tormented *characters. On stage he worked with Bergman on a gallery of equally complex roles, starting with *The Misanthrope* (Malmö, 1957), in which he played Alceste as a defiant and confused idealist. He gave an emblematic performance of the role of the embittered Lawyer in Bergman's production of *Strindberg's *A Dream Play* (1970), and went on to portray an emotionally stunted Gregers Werle in *Ibsen's *The Wild Duck* (1972). He has had a substantial Hollywood career, but was especially noted in Bille August's *Pelle the Conqueror* (1988) and as the Norwegian writer in Jan Troell's *Hamsun* (1996). DT

VOODOO

Haitian *ritual practice with large performative elements. A voodoo ceremony takes place at the request of a devotee of a *loa* (spirit), and culminates with the trance of the possessed through whose mouth the spirit speaks. The possessed (medium) is assisted by the *oungan*, who is both *actor and *stage manager. By drawing *vêvês*, the symbolic designs of the *loas*, he prepares the decor, and by leading the participants in a round *dance he marks the performance space—a circle in the middle of which the *poto-mitan*, a column that supports the roof, symbolizes communication between earth and sky. The *oungan* performs prescribed gestures for ablutions, libations, or sacrificial offerings, using accessories like the *ason* (a ritual rattle), and a scarf to wipe the faces of the participants. The colours of the scarf and the sacrificial animal are also prescribed, and the *ounsis* (the temple servants) must be dressed in white. The ceremony involves intensely visual and auditory dimensions, as songs and dances are accompanied by insistent drumbeats that punctuate various stages of the action. Voodoo is a game of doubles, suggesting a performative universe of doubles: the *loa* spirits double as God, the devotee doubles as the *oungan* and the possessed, the possessed is doubled by the possession trance crisis. MLa trans. JCM

VOSKOVEC, JIŘÍ (1905–81) AND JAN WERICH (1905–80)

Czech actors, playwrights, and *managers, a pair of intellectual *clowns known as V+W. Their *Vest Pocket Revue* (opened 1927) was a highly entertaining series of jazz and political *revues that were in principle *burlesques, but their sharp, semantically dense humour, based on puns, was highly sophisticated. The Liberated Theatre was under their management from 1929 and became the most popular stage in *Prague until 1938, when Voskovec was deprived of the licence. They both emigrated to the United States, where their composer Jaroslav Ježek (1906–42) died. In 1945–6 they were back again, but Voskovec emigrated permanently to the USA in 1950. Werich stayed in Prague, out of favour for a couple of years,

then in the middle 1950s was put in charge of the Satirical (ABC) Theatre, where he revived some of V+W's revues: his bold *improvisations encouraged the new little theatre movement. No other Czech actor has won such respect as a national guru. ML

VOSS, GERT (1941–)

German actor. Particularly linked with Claus *Peymann since 1974, Voss has performed a range of classical and contemporary roles. In 1986 he moved with Peymann to *Vienna's *Burgtheater and starred in the opening production of *Richard III*. Under Peter *Zadek Voss played Shylock, the title role in *Chekhov's *Ivanov*, and Antony in *Antony and Cleopatra* (*Berliner Ensemble, 1994). He also acted Othello in George *Tabori's production (1990). One of the most celebrated performers in German theatre, Voss's *acting is distinguished by keen intelligence and ironic wit. *Theater heute* named him actor of the year four times, and he has received many prestigious *awards. CBB

VYCHODIL, LADISLAV (1920–)

Slovak *scenographer and teacher. After study in *Prague and *Brno, he became a designer of the Slovak National Theatre in 1945, and in 1951 head of its scenographic studios. In 1952 he established the department of scenography at the Academy of Performing Arts in *Bratislava, and in 1968 was one of founders of International Organization of Scenographers, Theatre Architects, and Technicians. An ardent follower of František *Tröster and a student of the Czech inter-war *avant-garde, he worked for the unity of space, light, colour, and actors' presence. Despite his perfectionism, Vychodil was sometimes restrained by resources, often using an *open and minimally furnished stage. In the early 1960s, while working in Prague with Alfréd *Radok, he acquired a more complex and playful style, using in an ironic way the *surrealist methods of *montage and collage. He developed this further in 1990s in Josef Bednárik's lavish productions of *opera and *musicals, in both Prague and Bratislava. ML

VYSOTSKY, VLADIMIR (1938–80)

Russian actor and bard. Vysotsky trained at the *Moscow Art Theatre Studio and in 1964 joined the *Taganka Theatre, where he soon emerged as a leading actor. He played the parts of *Brecht's Galileo, Dostoevsky's Svidrigailov, and Esenin's Khlopusha in *Lyubimov's productions. Most important was his performance as Hamlet: he turned the Danish prince into a man from the street, allowing ordinary people to understand Hamlet's ethical dilemma, and recited to guitar accompaniment Pasternak's poem 'Hamlet' (then unpublished).

Vysotsky's fame as an actor was complemented by his reputation as bard. His songs and poems dealt with themes incompatible with *socialist realism: alcoholism, the real street life, prostitution. They were very popular and circulated illegally on tape. In 1966 he married the French actress Marina Vlady. His death in 1980 was a great loss to the Taganka Theatre, which paid homage with a production devoted to his life.

BB

·W·

WAGNER, RICHARD (1813–83)

German *opera composer, librettist, theorist, conductor, and theatre *director. Born in Leipzig, Wagner began his career by composing operas in the characteristic styles of his day, conducting in minor German opera houses, and, for three years, pursuing journalism in *Paris. He made his name with *Rienzi* (Dresden, 1842), a grand opera in the French style, which led to his appointment as musical director of the Dresden Court Opera, where he did much to improve performance standards. His first mature opera, *The Flying Dutchman* (Dresden, 1843), was not initially successful, but *Tannhäuser* (Dresden, 1845) and *Lohengrin* (Weimar, 1850), grand operas based on German material, established him as the leading opera composer of his generation.

Wagner's career was interrupted by his involvement in an abortive uprising against the Saxon monarchy in May 1849. A warrant for his arrest led to an eleven-year exile from German states in Switzerland. Here he wrote three major *theoretical essays, *Art and Revolution* (1849), *The Artwork of the Future* (1850), and *Opera and Drama* (1852), in which he argued that each art can only fulfil itself when it works in cooperation with all the others. In history this only happened once, at the Festival of Dionysus (*see* DIONYSIA) in ancient Athens; since then the arts have fragmented into separate forms and have been exploited by the Church, absolutist princes, and, in the nineteenth century, commerce. Wagner intended to unite the arts once again, in works that would allow the people—the 'Volk'—to discover their own identity and would become the central events of their social life. He also conducted a detailed exploration as to how music can become a dramatic language. All this was preparatory to the composition of the central work of his career, *The Ring of the Nibelung*, a tetralogy based upon medieval German romances and Norse sagas, which took him 25 years to complete. The music dramas of *The Rhinegold*

(*Munich, 1869), *The Valkyrie* (Munich, 1870), *Siegfried*, and *Twilight of the Gods* (both Bayreuth, 1876), which take over fourteen hours to perform, are unified by Wagner's resourceful use of the leitmotif, a musical fragment, phrase, or melody that is given specific and frequently multiple dramatic meanings. The score for each act is continuous, so that musical and dramatic form are identical.

For professional, aesthetic, and personal reasons, Wagner could not sustain work on the *Ring* without interruption, and in 1857 he broke off composition for twelve years in order to complete *Tristan and Isolde* (Munich, 1865), a hymn to romantic love, and *The Mastersingers of Nuremberg* (Munich, 1868), his only comedy, centring on the power of art as a vitalizing force in society. Wagner was notoriously improvident and had little business sense so his life was bedevilled by debt. In 1864, however, he came under the patronage of Ludwig II of Bavaria, whose largesse relieved Wagner of his main financial burdens. Ludwig also helped finance the building of the *Bayreuth Festival Theatre, where the first complete performance of the *Ring* was staged in 1876. The acoustics and sight lines of this theatre, with its sunken orchestra pit, wedge-shaped seating, triple *proscenium arch repeated on the sides of the *auditorium, and wooden walls, have never since been equalled (*see* PLAYHOUSE). Wagner intended the theatre as a site for an annual *festival, but *finances dictated that in his lifetime there would only be one other production, that of his final music drama, *Parsifal* (1882), a quasi-religious work based on Buddhism, Schopenhauer, and ascetic Christian doctrines.

Perhaps no figure in the history of opera has aroused such rancorous dispute as Wagner. Only a few question that his music dramas, which require massive orchestras, have unusual power and beauty and his use of the leitmotif and his theories of the *Gesamtkunstwerk* or 'total work of art' have been immensely influential among musicians and theatre people alike (*see* TOTAL THEATRE). But Wagner's egoism and ambition, coupled with his

The Bayreuth centennial production of **Wagner**'s *The Rhinegold*, Bayreuth Festival, 1976, directed by Patrice Chéreau, designed by Richard Peduzzi. This landmark version of the *Ring* cycle, conducted by Pierre Boulez, resituated Wagner's heroic and mythic characters in the nineteenth-century Industrial Revolution.

extravagance and unconventional private life, made him a controversial figure in his time. Since then, his works have been reviled successively for their decadence, militant nationalism, and, since 1980 or so, anti-Semitism. Nevertheless, Wagner's dramas are informed by a powerful tragic sense that addressed the political, economic, and social problems of his day and reintroduced the European theatre to the abiding themes of ancient drama. Today they play to packed houses whenever they are performed. *See also* ROMANTICISM. SJCW

MAGEE, BRYAN, *Aspects of Wagner* (Oxford, 1988)

MÜLLER, ULRICH, et al., *The Wagner Handbook*, trans. John Deathridge (Cambridge, Mass., 1992)

WILLIAMS, SIMON, *Richard Wagner and Festival Theatre* (Westport, Conn., 1994)

WAGNER, ROBIN (1933–)

American designer. After beginning in the 1950s in his native *San Francisco, Wagner moved to *New York and began to design *Off-Broadway. Switching to Broadway as an assistant to Ben Edwards and Oliver *Smith, he entered the first rank of scene designers with the production of *Hair* (1968). Often associated with large spectacular sets (*Jesus Christ Superstar, On the Twentieth Century, 42nd Street*), many of his best designs have featured a choreographic resculpting of space (*Dreamgirls, Chess*). One of his most famous sets, for *A Chorus Line* (1975), was one of his most minimal. His designs can also display a sense of humour, as in *The Producers* (2001). A designer of *opera and rock concerts as well as theatre, Wagner has taught at Columbia University. JD

WAGNER, WIELAND (1917–66)

German designer and stage *director. As the grandson of Richard *Wagner, Wieland was born with the family's expectation that he would direct the *Bayreuth Festival. He trained in a theatre dominated by romantic *realism, with some knowledge of the quasi-expressionist designs of Emil Preetorius and Alfred

*Roller. He reopened the Bayreuth Festival in 1951 with a production of *Parsifal*, which rejected the styles in which he had worked before the war. Instead, in a *symbolist manner that owed much to the ideas of Adolphe *Appia, *scenery was abstract and staging sparse (*see also* SYMBOLISM; SCENOGRAPHY; ROMANTICISM). Over the next fifteen years, when he co-directed the festival with his brother Wolfgang (1919–   ), Wieland restaged the entire canon of his grandfather's work, highlighting both mystical dimensions and, paradoxically, the less-than-heroic aspects of the *action. His greatest achievement was the production of *Tristan and Isolde* (1962) in which symbols combining erotic and Celtic themes were bathed in subtly changing *lighting that evoked perfectly the *dreamlike action of the work. Wieland Wagner also directed elsewhere in Germany, notably Stuttgart, where he applied his symbolist style to the *operas of Richard *Strauss, Beethoven, *Verdi, *Gluck, and others. His work had a profound impact on the design and direction of opera as a whole, decisively moving it away from realism.   SJCW

WAGONS *See* PAGEANT.

WAHBA, SAAD EDDIN (1923–97)

Egyptian playwright, screenwriter, and journalist. Motivated by a socialist suspicion of larger-than-life *heroes, Wahba built his plays around a large gallery of *characters, each with a story and voice interesting in its own right. His early plays, all set in the countryside, were clever apologies for the 1952 Revolution satirizing the feudal society under the *ancien régime*. The second phase in his career showed a determination to expose the corruption and opportunism which then boded ill for the new socialist utopia. After 1970 he devoted more attention to *film, and was for a time the president of the *Cairo International Film Festival. But he also wrote a handful of plays *satirizing the consumerism and anti-intellectualism of contemporary Egypt.
                                             HMA

WAJDA, ANDRZEJ (1926–   )

Polish director and designer, one of the world's major filmmakers. After studing fine arts in *Cracow (1946–9) and *film in Łódź (1949–53), Wajda made his debut as a film director with *The Generation* (1955) and as a theatre director with *A Hat Full of Rain* at Teatr Wybrzeże in Gdańsk (1959). Since then he has directed many films and *television plays and dozens of theatre productions, the majority at the Old Theatre in Cracow. In 1980 he allied himself with the Solidarity movement, and during the martial-law period of the 1980s he directed illegal productions in churches. In 1989 he was elected as a senator on the Solidarity ticket.

In his films he has been keenly interested in national history and the national ethos (the remarkable *Ashes and Diamonds*, 1958), as well as contemporary struggles with communism (*Man of Marble*, 1978; *Man of Iron*, 1981). In the theatre Wajda, a painter himself, created productions as if painting vast, colourful, and visionary moving canvases on the stage. His best works in this mode include his own adaptations of Dostoevsky novels: *The Possessed* (Cracow, 1963, 1971, 1975; New Haven, 1974), *Nastasya Filipowna*, based on *The Idiot* (Cracow, 1977; *Tokyo, 1989), and *Crime and Punishment* (Cracow, 1984, 1986, 1987). Among Polish classics he focused on *Wyspiański, directing *The Wedding* (Cracow, 1963, 1991; filmed 1962) and *November Night* (Cracow, 1974; filmed 1977), and staged *Przybyszewska's *The Danton Case* (*Warsaw, 1975; Gdańsk, 1980; filmed 1982). Wajda has also directed other classical and contemporary plays: *Hamlet* (1960, 1980, 1989), *Antigone* (1984), *Romeo and Juliet* (1990), *Mrożek's *The Emigrants* (1976), and Kazimierz Moczarski's *Dialogues with the Executioner* (1977). Wajda designed the *scenery for several of his productions and developed the complete *scenography for others. He has won the Palme d'Or at Cannes (1982), an Academy lifetime achievement award (2000), and many other prizes.
                                             KB

WAKI

The secondary role in a *nō play and the actors (*waki-kata*) who perform both the *waki* and the *waki-zure* (*waki* companion) roles. The *waki* represents a living, male *character (for instance priest or courtier) and never wears a *mask. Although usually secondary in dramatic importance to the *shite*, the *waki* generally begins and ends a play; setting the scene, engaging the *shite* in *dialogue, and watching him exit. In a few plays, such as *Rashōmon*, the *waki* is the main *character, and in rare plays (such as *Kosode Soga*) no *waki* appears. *Waki* actors belong to three professional schools: Fukuō, Hôshō, and Takayasu.
                                             KWB

WALCOTT, DEREK (1930–   )

St Lucian playwright, poet, director, and actor. Walcott is the towering figure of anglophone *Caribbean theatre, though outside the region his poetry has received more attention. He began to write plays while still at secondary school, and in 1950 directed his *Henri Christophe* for the St Lucia Arts Guild, which he had co-founded the same year. His first important play, *The Sea at Dauphin* (1954), a revision of *Synge's *Riders to the Sea*, was produced by the same company. He studied in the USA in 1958–9, and upon returning founded the *Trinidad Theatre Workshop, which would be the focus for his work for a number of years, in the Caribbean territories and further abroad. Walcott has written more than 40 plays, *musicals, and screenplays, which attempt as a whole to bring together different cultural influences to create a new language of Caribbean performance. Most notable in this respect are *Malcochon* (1959), *Ti-Jean and his Brothers* (1958), *Dream on Monkey Mountain* (1967), *The Joker of Seville* (commissioned by the *Royal Shakespeare Company, 1974), and *Pantomime* (1978), a brilliant variation on the Robinson Crusoe story. Also important are the more *realist *Remembrance* (1977), the adroit *farce *Beef, No Chicken* (1981), and a moving exploration of the difficulties of being an artist in the Caribbean, *A Branch of the Blue Nile* (1983). His work has been widely performed internationally. Starting in 1981 he taught creative writing at *Boston University. He received the Nobel Prize for Literature in 1992.   ES

WALCOTT, RODERICK (1930–2001)

St Lucian playwright, director, and twin brother of Derek *Walcott. Roderick led the Arts Guild when his brother went to university, and began to write and direct his own plays with three *one-acts of 1957: *The Harrowing of Benjy* (1957), the steel-band drama *Shrove Tuesday March*, and *The One-Eye Is King*. He also directed his brother's work (*Ti-Jean and his Brothers*, 1957). He was a *carnival band leader and designer, which contributed to his theatrical vocabulary in plays such as the *musical *The Banjo Man* (1958), *Malfinis* (1962), *A Flight of Sparrows*, and *Education of Alfie* (both published 2000).   ES

WALKER, GEORGE F. (1947–   )

Canadian playwright, whose career began in 1972 at the newly formed *Factory Theatre in *Toronto, which sought to produce new Canadian plays, then a bold step. He remains associated with that theatre. His plays, whose first productions he often directs, have the pace and absurdity of tragic *farce; his *characters live on the edge of disaster, against which they struggle desperately, inventively, and (almost) hopelessly. The plays of the 1970s, such as *Beyond Mozambique* (1974) and *Gossip* (1977), are ironic fantasias on themes from popular culture. *Criminals in Love* (1984) began a series set on his home turf, the working-class East End of Toronto, inhabited by characters whose lives are constricted by the power of wealthy elites and impersonal bureaucracies. Other notable plays include *Nothing Sacred* (1988), based on *Turgenev's *Fathers and Sons*, *Love and Anger* (1989), the six-play cycle *Suburban Motel* (1999), and *Heaven* (2000). His works have had many productions across Canada, including several in French translation in Québec. They are also widely produced abroad.   RCN

WALKLEY, ALFRED BINGHAM (1855–1926)

English critic, educated at Oxford. Walkley reviewed for the *Star* and the *Speaker* in the 1890s, then served as drama critic of *The Times* (1902–26). He provided a cultured voice, usually well measured, in the assessment of West End theatre. He was often sympathetic to the new drama, yet not an advocate, as was his colleague William *Archer. He published several collections of his *criticism, and he served as president of the Society of Dramatic Critics.   TP

WALL, MAX (1908–90)

English comedian and actor. Wall began his career in the 1920s as 'Max Wall and his Independent Legs', establishing a distinctive style of *grotesque and sometimes menacing *clowning. He achieved success in *variety and *revue, appearing in the 1930 Royal Variety Performance, and was popular on *radio and *television in the 1940s and 1950s. After a period of obscurity, Wall pursued a second career in theatre, appearing at the *Royal Court in *London in *Jarry's *Ubu roi* (1966), *Osborne's *The Entertainer* (1974), and in *Beckett's plays. His *one-person show *Aspects of Max Wall* (1974) revived his earlier variety acts.
SF

WALLACE, NELLIE (1870–1948)

Scottish vocalist and comedienne. 'The Essence of Eccentricity', Glasgow-born Wallace appeared as a child actress in plays (Little Willie in *East Lynne*), graduating to clog *dancing with the Three Sisters Wallace, and finally to a solo act in the *music halls. With her lanky frame, buck teeth, and generally unprepossessing appearance, described by Wilson Discher as 'an expanse of lurid wallpaper', suggestive and bizarre asides became her trademark—'If you're fond of anything tasty, what price me?'—along with similarly outrageous songs such as 'Let's Have a Tiddley at the Milk Bar' and 'The Blasted Oak'.
AF

WALLACK FAMILY

Anglo-American theatrical *family. In 1787 actor-singer William H. Wallack (1760–1850) married actress Elizabeth Field Granger (c.1760–1850). Both were *Londoners who had successful careers in England, Scotland, and Ireland. They had four children who took to the stage: Mary (d. 1834); Elizabeth (dates undetermined), who wed an actor named Pincott, a union that produced Leonora (1805–84), an actress who married actor Alfred Wigan (1814–78); Henry John (1790–1870); and James William (c.1795–1864). Henry went to America in 1819, playing in Baltimore and *Philadelphia before making his *New York debut in 1821 as Norval in *Douglas*. He was a respected actor (and occasionally *manager) on both sides of the Atlantic, playing in all *genres, including a dozen Shakespearian roles. By his first wife, dancer Fanny Jones, he sired four performers: Julia, George, Fanny, and—most notably—James William (1818–73; called 'the Younger', or incorrectly 'Jr.', to distinguish him from his uncle). As a child of 4, James appeared in Philadelphia in *Pizarro*, and at 17 began a serious career at *Covent Garden in his father's company. His range was large, though his forte was *tragedy and serious *melodrama. In 1842 he married the tragedienne Ann Sefton (1815–79), and they co-starred in numerous productions. He *toured widely in America and Australia, acclaimed for his Fagin in *Oliver Twist* and Mathias in *The Bells*, as well as Iago, Richard III, Mercutio, Macbeth, Othello, Hotspur, and Jaques. Henry Wallack's younger brother James ('Wallack the Elder') began his adult career as Laertes in 1812 at *Drury Lane, where he went on to win praise as Petruchio, Mercutio, and Benedick. With his new wife Susan Johnstone, in 1818 he went to New York, where he made his debut as Macbeth and added Hamlet, Romeo, and Richard III to his repertoire. He frequently moved back and forth between England and America, managing for a time the National in New York and the *Haymarket in London. In 1852 he opened Wallack's Lyceum in New York, and *Wallack's Theatre in 1861. He established what would become the reigning American company for 35 years. In later years he received accolades for his Shylock and bade farewell to the stage as Benedick in 1859. Of his four children, one became a major force in the theatre: John Johnstone Wallack (1820–88), who acted under the name Allan Field, then styled himself John Lester, and finally settled on the name Lester Wallack in 1861. Though born in New York, he was raised in England, where he had the lead in *Pizarro* at 15, and at 19 began touring the provinces, playing Macduff and Richmond to his father's Macbeth and Richard III. In 1847 he made his New York debut in *Boucicault's *Used Up*. He both acted and managed at his father's Lyceum, and even mounted some plays of his own (notably *The Veteran*, 1859). He opened a third Wallack's Theatre in 1882, acting only occasionally. After a career of more than 300 roles, he said goodbye to acting as Marlow in *She Stoops to Conquer* (1886), and retired completely from the theatre in 1887. He left an autobiography, *Memories of Fifty Years* (1889).

CT

WALLACK'S THEATRE

*New York *playhouse at the corner of Broadway and 13th Street. From its construction in 1861 until the *Wallacks moved uptown to 30th Street in 1881, it was the city's most fashionable and elegant venue. Founded by the *actor-manager James W. Wallack, of a distinguished English-American theatrical *family, it was taken over in 1864 by his son, the actor Lester Wallack. The company, presenting mostly English works that included Shakespeare, *Sheridan, and *romantic drama, continued at 30th Street until Lester's death in 1888. The 13th Street theatre (in what was then an increasingly immigrant

neighbourhood) was renamed the Star in 1881 and demolished in 1901.

MAF

WALLER, LEWIS (1860–1915)

English actor and *manager. Waller made his debut in 1883 at Toole's Theatre, *London, in a *farce, *Uncle Dick's Darling*. Handsome, exuding virility, with a splendid physique and a powerful voice, he was the prototypical romantic *hero, especially as D'Artagnan in *The Three Musketeers* (1898) and Monsieur Beaucaire (1902) in the play of that name. The heroic patriotism of his Henry V was never exceeded. Waller also played Hotspur, Brutus, Othello, and the Bastard in *King John*, and a wide variety of parts in modern *comedies and *dramas, including *Ibsen. He acted in *New York in Robert Hichens's *The Garden of Allah* (1911). His good looks and manly nobility of bearing caused a great flutter among his female *audience, and his more fervent admirers wore badges at the theatre proclaiming that they were KOW, keen on Waller. Much to his embarrassment, he had become a matinée idol.

MRB

WALNUT STREET THEATRE

Opened in 1809, the Walnut Street in *Philadelphia is the oldest American theatre still in use. Originally housing Pepin and Breschard's *Circus, it was converted to a *playhouse in 1811 and renamed the Olympic. It served various companies, including that of *Warren and *Wood when the *Chestnut Street Theatre was being rebuilt after a fire. It underwent numerous changes as successive *managers strove to make it financially profitable. Joe Cowell removed its dome and restored its name to the Walnut Street in 1820, then hired noted architect John Haviland to design a makeover, including a new façade, in 1828. Cowell featured Thomas Hamblin, J. B. *Booth, and *Cooper as guest performers, but moved on because of competition from other theatres. Francis C. *Wemyss, Charlotte *Cushman, and John Sleeper Clarke served terms as manager. Though often closed, the theatre remained standing until 1968, when it was declared a national landmark and restored.

AHK

WALSER, MARTIN (1927–)

German writer. One of the foremost contemporary German novelists, Walser wrote intermittently for the stage between 1960 and 1982. In *The Rabbit Race* (1962), a nonconformist is declared insane. *The Black Swan* (1964), in which a young student discovers that his father was formerly a concentration camp doctor, was discussed as a parable of West German society and its unwillingness to face up to the Nazi past. *Überlebensgross Herr Krott* (*Larger than Life Mr Krott*, 1963) frames the story of a dying industrialist as a parable of the moribund state of capitalism. Walser also translated plays by Christopher *Hampton, Howard *Brenton, and Edward *Albee.

CBB

WÄLTERLIN, OSKAR (1895–1961)

Swiss actor and director. Born and educated in Basel, Wälterlin directed *opera and drama there in the 1920s (including *Wagner's *Ring* with Adolphe *Appia, 1924–5). From 1938 until his death he was the *Intendant* of the *Zurich Schauspielhaus, which between 1933 and 1945 became a meeting place for exiled German theatre practitioners, including *Brecht, Therese *Giehse, Wolfgang Langhoff, and Leopold Lindtberg. In the 1950s Wälterlin systematically promoted German-Swiss drama and directed the premières of many plays by Max *Frisch and Friedrich *Dürrenmatt. Altogether he directed 125 plays for the Zurich Schauspielhaus, of which approximately 100 were designed by Teo *Otto.

CBB

WALTERS, SAM (1939–)

British director and actor. After *training in *London, Walters performed in *regional repertory theatre before turning to directing in 1967 (Swan Theatre, Worcester). In 1971 he began producing unusual revivals and new writing in a room above a pub in Richmond in Surrey. The high standards of production turned his Orange Tree Theatre into an *award-winning small theatre, and in 1991 a significant sum was raised to build a permanent theatre-in-the-round (see ARENA AND IN-THE-ROUND). The Orange Tree has commissioned new writing by Martin *Crimp, David Cregan, James *Saunders, Fay Weldon, and Olwen Wymark. It has also produced revivals of D. H. *Lawrence plays, French *farce, obscure *musicals, Susan *Glaspell, and Granville *Barker. The theatre has premièred work by Václav *Havel since the 1970s. Walters is married to the actress-director Auriol Smith.

KN

WALTON, TONY (1934–)

Anglo-American designer. English born, Walton first worked on the *New York stage in 1957. His early reputation was made primarily in *musicals requiring wit and flexibility, and he has worked regularly with conceptual directors like Bob *Fosse (*Pippin*, *Chicago*) and Tommy *Tune (*Grand Hotel*, *The Will Rogers Follies*) for whom his cinematic visual sense was vital. Primarily a scenic designer, he has also designed *costumes, especially for *opera and *dance. He began his *film work in 1964 as costume designer for *Mary Poppins*, starring his then-wife Julie Andrews, and has since worked as designer and art director for a wide range of films, including musicals (*The Boy Friend*, *All That Jazz*). Comfortable in theatre, film, and *television, Walton

has won all of the major *awards—Tony, Oscar, and Emmy.

JD

WANAMAKER, SAM (1919–93)

American actor and director. Wanamaker trained at the *Goodman Theatre, *Chicago, and briefly acted on Broadway after the Second World War. He visited *London in 1952, playing alongside Michael *Redgrave and Googie Withers in his own production of Clifford *Odets's *The Country Girl* (renamed *Winter Journey*), and stayed, preferring post-war England to the McCarthyism of America. Wanamaker's experience with the *Group Theatre in *New York ideally placed him to introduce *Method *acting to Britain, which he explored in Odets's *The Big Knife* (1954) and Richard Nash's *The Rainmaker* (1956). In 1957 he became director of the New Shakespeare Theatre in Liverpool, which he ran as a prototype arts centre with numerous outreach activities. His lifelong fascination with Shakespeare was kindled by his (poorly received) Iago to Paul *Robeson's Othello (Stratford, 1959) and his appearance as Macbeth on a return visit to the Goodman in 1964. In 1970 he founded the Playhouse Trust and World Centre for Shakespeare, where his vision and tireless fundraising overcame huge obstacles (such as a High Court battle with Southwark Council) to reconstruct the *Globe Theatre near its Elizabethan site (see GLOBE RECONSTRUCTIONS). Sadly he died a few months after the unveiling of the first building works. Wanamaker's work for *opera, *film, and *television further demonstrated his versatility. His production of Prokofiev's *War and Peace* opened the *Sydney Opera House in 1973. His *film acting included *The Spy Who Came in from the Cold* (1966) and *Private Benjamin* (1980), his directing included *Custer* (1967), and he appeared in TV programmes such as *Columbo* and *Hawaii Five-O*. British actress Zoe Wanamaker is his daughter.

KN

WANG SHIFU (WANG SHIH-FU) (probably mid- to late thirteenth century)

Chinese dramatist of *zaju*, the four-act plays characteristic of the Yuan Dynasty. The author of *China's best-loved romantic drama *Xixiang ji* (*The Romance of the Western Chamber*), Wang remains a shadowy figure. The earliest biographical details are found in Zhong Sicheng's fourteenth-century drama catalogue *A Register of Ghosts*, where Wang is credited with a total of fourteen *zaju*, of which only two others are extant: *Lichun tang* (*The Hall of Beautiful Spring*) and *Poyao ji* (*The Tale of the Dilapidated Kiln*). Given the sensuous poetic diction of *Xixiang ji*, the greatest loss may well be Wang's *Jiao hong ji* (*The Tale of Jiaoniang*), a well-known story that was dramatized again by the late Ming Dynasty playwright Meng Chengshun. As a cycle of five linked *zaju*, *The Romance of the Western*

Chamber is almost unique in the Yuan *zaju* repertoire, nearly all of which consists of single four-act plays. Wang was dramatizing a love story already popular in a twelfth-century version, and five more of his plays are known to have shared *plots with other *zaju*. This apparent angling after popular success suggests to some critics that Wang was an educated professional in the first great age of Chinese theatre.   KC

WANNOUS, SADALLAH (1941–97)

Syrian playwright. Drama study in *Paris exposed him both to the theatre of the *absurd and the student uprisings of the late 1960s. Shattered by the 1967 Arab defeat by Israel, on his return to Syria he wrote in 1969 a politically daring play, *Haflet Sammar Min Ajel Khamsah Huzairan* (*An Entertainment on the Occasion of the 5th of June*), which was *published and produced in Beirut before it was licensed in Damascus in 1971. His other works include *Al-Feelo Ya Maleka'l-Zaman* (*The Elephant, Oh Lord of Ages*, 1969) and *Mughamaret Raes'l-Mamlouk Jaber* (*The Adventure of Slave Jaber's Head*, 1972), both deeply influenced by *Brecht. He collaborated with Fawaz al-*Sajer in launching the government-subsidized Experimental Theatre, and wrote adaptations from *Gogol, *Weiss, and *Buero-Vallejo. Diagnosed with cancer in 1992, Wannous feverishly wrote plays praised by the *critics, and which had successful productions in *Cairo, Damascus, and Beirut: *Munamnamat Tarikhiah* (*Historical Miniatures*), *Tuqus'l-Isharat wal-Tahawolat* (*Rituals of Signs and Transformations*), *Al-Ayamo'l-Makhmourah* (*The Drunken Days*), and *Malhamatu'l-Sarrab* (*The Epic of Mirage*).   RI

WARD, DOUGLAS TURNER (1930–   )

*African-American actor, director, and playwright. Ward acted *Off-Broadway and had a small part in the original cast of *Hansberry's *Raisin in the Sun* (1959), but his contributions in 1965–6 set in motion the rest of his life. First, he wrote and acted in two *one-act *comedies, *Day of Absence* and *Happy Ending*, which *satirized white supremacy and had an extended run Off-Broadway. Second, he published an article in the *New York Times* that changed the lives of hundreds of African-American Theatre workers. 'American Theatre: for whites only?' was a call for a permanent African-American theatre, fashioned along lines set out by W. E. B. DuBois in the 1920s. Ward's timing was good; US cities were racially explosive and social countermeasures were urgently needed. With a large grant from the Ford Foundation, Ward established the *Negro Ensemble Company in 1967 (run initially by a triumvirate of Ward, Robert Hooks, and Gerald Krone), and continued as its *artistic director. He acted in or directed many of the company's major productions, including Lonnie *Elder's *Ceremonies in Dark Old Men* (1969), Joseph Walker's *The River*

Niger (1972), Samm-Art Williams's *Home* (1979), and Charles *Fuller's *A Soldier's Story* (1981).   BBL

WARD, GENEVIÈVE (1838–1922)

American-born actress. As a young woman Ward travelled to Europe with her mother and settled in Italy, where, after a brief marriage to Russian Count Constantine de Guerbel, she pursued an *operatic career as Madame Guerrabella. When her voice failed she shifted to stage roles in England, first appearing as Lady Macbeth (1873) at the *Manchester Theatre Royal, a part she later played in French in *Paris. Admired in *London for Portia, Antigone, and Belvidera in *Otway's *Venice Preserv'd*, among others, she made her biggest mark in *Forget-Me-Not* (1879) by Herman Merivale and F. C. Grove, which she eventually *toured internationally. She played with *Irving at the *Lyceum as Eleanor in Tennyson's *Becket* (1893) and Morgan le Fay in *King Arthur* (1895). An *acting teacher and coach from 1890 to 1905, she appeared on stage rarely. She was the first actress honoured as Dame of the British Empire (1921).
                                                                    LQM

WARD, NICK (1962–   )

Anglo-Australian playwright and director. After winning *Edinburgh Festival *Fringe First *awards for student adaptations of Kafka and D. H. *Lawrence, Ward established an intense, elliptical style with the Fenland *tragedy *Apart from George* (1987). The East Anglian landscape reappeared in *Trouble Sleeping* (1995). This reworks two *characters, a mother and son, from *The Strangeness of Others* (1988), in which an atypically large cast of disparate Londoners hides a very domestic story about two estranged brothers. After a period writing for the screen, Ward returned with *The Present* (1995), about a British-based Australian (the author's own background) going home to a world of sexual tension and uncertain reality. Ward also cowrote the libretto for *The Cenci* (1998), a *music drama based on *Artaud.   CDC

WARDLE, IRVING (1929–   )

English drama critic for the *Observer* (1959–62), *The Times* (1963–89), and the *Independent on Sunday* (1990–5). In the 1970s he branched out from judicious middle-of-the-road reviewing. His play *The Houseboy* (1974)—about his dishwashing career while a student at the Royal College of Music—was produced at *London's Open Space Theatre, and he edited the offbeat theatre journal *Gambit* (1973–5). In 1978 he published a useful biography, *The Theatres of George Devine*. In a brisk account of his calling, *Theatre Criticism* (1992), he described it as 'a marginal life, at home neither in theatres nor newspaper offices'. See CRITICISM.   BRK

WARFIELD, DAVID (1866–1951)

American actor. Born David Wohlfeld in *San Francisco, in 1888 he had his first speaking role in *Taylor's *The Ticket-of-Leave Man*. Moving to *New York in 1890, he did small parts until *Weber and Fields hired him in 1898 as the company's Jewish-dialect comedian. His stature was established when David *Belasco starred him as the rags-to-riches Jewish pedlar in *The Auctioneer* (1901), which he took on *tour for two years. Still more popular was the sentimental *The Music Master* (1904), whose 627-performance run was a straight-play record at the time, and kept Warfield busy for three years. His last new play was *The Return of Peter Grimm* (1911), in which the title *character returns from the dead. Thereafter Warfield reprised his earlier hits. Finally he achieved his ambition of playing Shylock, which he toured for two years (1922–4); at that point he retired completely from the stage at 57.   CT

WARNER, DAVID (1939–)

English actor. Warner trained at the *Royal Academy of Dramatic Art, and subsequently joined the *Royal Shakespeare Company where he began fruitful collaborations with Peter *Hall and Tony *Richardson. He was Lysander in Hall's *A Midsummer Night's Dream* (1962), Henry VI in *The Wars of the Roses* (1963), the King in *Richard II* (1964), and Valentine Brose in Henry Livings's *Eh?* (1964). In 1965 he was one of the decade's definitive Hamlets in Hall's production, which failed with *critics but captured the imagination of its young *audience. Subsequently he appeared in *Gogol's *The Government Inspector* (1970) and in David *Hare's *The Great Exhibition* (1971). An eclectic catalogue of *film roles veers from the extraordinary to the journeyman: among the most interesting are the title part in *Morgan: A Suitable Case for Treatment* (1966), Lance Bombardier Evans in *The Bofors Gun* (1968), and the father in *The Company of Wolves* (1984).   AS

WARNER, DEBORAH (1959–)

English director. She *trained in *stage management at the Central School of Speech and Drama in *London, founding Kick Theatre in 1980. Specializing in Shakespeare, Kick won an *Edinburgh Fringe First for *King Lear*. Warner was resident director at the *Royal Shakespeare Company 1987–9, where her *Titus Andronicus* and *King John* were praised for their clarity and energy. Warner's long collaboration with actress Fiona *Shaw began when she directed her in *Electra* (1988) and *Good Person of Setzuan* (Royal *National Theatre, 1989). Her 1990 appointment as associate director for the RNT (along with Nicholas *Hytner and Declan *Donellan) established her as one of a new generation of innovators. That year she directed Brian Cox and Ian *McKellen in *King Lear*, and in 1991 directed Shaw in *Hedda Gabler* (*Abbey Theatre, *Dublin) and in *Electra*, this time set in Ireland (*Riverside Studios, London). RSC director Terry *Hands notes that Warner 'strips away all the falsity and discovers the true shape of the play underneath'. Recently her direction has extended beyond classical *texts. She has directed site-specific work (*see* ENVIRONMENTAL THEATRE) in the St Pancras Chamber Project (1995) and Euston Tower Project (1999), *The Waste Land* (1995), Britten's *The Turn of the Screw* (1995), the *St John Passion* (2000), and a *film, *The Last September* (2000), based on Elizabeth Bowen's novel.   RVL

WARNER, EARL (1952–98)

Barbadian director and actor. In 1977 the formerly conservative Green Room Players produced the first *African play in Barbados, Wole *Soyinka's *Death and the King's Horseman*, with Warner in the lead. Later he studied and taught theatre in *Manchester, and came back from England to become a full-time director, creating new work and revising old all over the *Caribbean as well as in the USA and the UK. Among his important productions were three plays by Derek *Walcott: *Remembrance* (1982), the première of *A Branch of the Blue Nile* (1983), and *Beef, No Chicken* (1985). Other directing work included the multi-authored *Lights* (1985), about women's lives in Barbados, and Trevor *Rhone's *Smile Orange* (1986). Warner ran the Caribbean Lab of the Jamaica School of Drama for almost three years, where he developed new strategies for Caribbean performance.   ES

WARNER, JACK (1944–)

American Jesuit who graduated from the *Goodman School of Drama in *Chicago before moving to Progreso in Honduras in 1979. He founded a people's theatre company, La Fragua, to create a forum for local peasants to rediscover Honduran culture, explore religious themes, and educate other rural Hondurans. Warner uses *Brecht and *Grotowski to develop performance pieces that are chiefly physical and incorporate *dance, *mime, and *music. Works are based on stories from the Bible, on Central American literature (*Los motivos del lobo*, *The Wolf's Motives*), or indigenous legends (*El origen del maiz*, *The origin of corn*). *See also* OPPRESSED, THEATRE OF THE.   EJW

WARREN, MERCY OTIS (1728–1814)

American playwright and historian. Warren was intimately involved in American revolutionary pamphleteering before and during the War of Independence. Plays attributed to her, printed anonymously in periodicals and as pamphlets, include *The Adulateur* (1772), *The Defeat* (1773), and *The Group* (1775), all of which criticized Massachusetts Governor Thomas Hutchinson and British colonial policies, and encouraged revolutionary activity. After the war she wrote (among others) *The Sack of Rome* and *The Ladies of Castile* (*published together, 1790). She also completed a three-volume history of the United States in 1805. SEW

WARREN, WILLIAM (THE ELDER) (1762–1832)

English-born actor and *manager. He began his career in 1784 as Young Norval in *Douglas*, and joined Tate *Wilkinson's company in 1788 where he supported Sarah *Siddons. Emigrating to America in 1796, Warren was hired by Thomas *Wignell for *Philadelphia's *Chestnut Street Theatre, where his first role was Friar Laurence in *Romeo and Juliet*, followed by Bundle in *The Watermen*. An instant success, he devoted the remainder of his career to Philadelphia and Baltimore. With William *Wood he took over the management of the Chestnut Street and ran it successfully until his retirement in 1829, along the way discovering Edwin *Forrest. Primarily a comic actor, Warren was noted for his Anthony Absolute, Toby Belch, Falstaff, and Peter Teazle. With his third wife Esther Fortune (Joseph *Jefferson's sister-in-law) he had six children, all of whom worked in the theatre, the most famous being William Warren the Younger. TFC

WARSAW

The capital of Poland since 1596, located in the geographical centre of the country and of Europe. The city's performance history began in earnest with *The Dismissal of the Greek Envoys* by Jan Kochanowski (1530–84), produced in 1578 at Queen Anna's palace. The author, educated in *Cracow and Padua, used Italian production methods in staging his *tragedy. The court sought companies from Western Europe, including the *English Comedians in the 1610s, who probably played Shakespeare. King Władysław IV built a *proscenium theatre in the Royal Castle (1637) to house Italian *opera, and toward the end of the seventeenth century French companies performed *Molière, *Racine, and *Corneille.

By the time that August III erected a free-standing opera house in 1748, Enlightenment notions had encouraged the growth of academic drama (*see* UNIVERSITY AND SCHOOL DRAMA), which had been present in the country since the early sixteenth century, and the development of a nationalist drama. King Stanisław August created the first Polish public theatre, subsidized and professional, which was inaugurated with *The Intruders* by Józef Bielawski in 1765, a date that marks the birth of the Polish National Theatre. Interrupted by the First Partition of Poland (1772), it moved to a new building in 1779. Wojciech Bogusławski, 'the father of the National Theatre', an excellent actor and singer, prolific playwright and translator, and dexterous entrepreneur, led the National for three periods between 1782 and 1814. His repertoire of patriotic works, classics, and

adaptations of new foreign plays made the enterprise into an instrument of political and social reform, a source of opposition to the Russian occupation (after the Second Partition, 1793), a basis of patriotism during the Kosciuszko Uprising (1794), and a stronghold of resistance after the Third Partition (1795).

Theatre in Warsaw in the nineteenth century saw brief moments of freedom in the Napoleonic era (1807–13) and during the November Uprising (1830–1), and long periods of Russian control. In the persecution following the uprising even the name 'National Theatre' was prohibited. Its third building (1832), one of the largest in Europe, a jewel of *neoclassical architecture, was called the Wielki (Grand) Theatre and used for opera; spoken drama was given a wing in the structure in 1836, called the Rozmaitości (Variety) Theatre. The whole institution, known as the Warsaw State Theatres, eventually contained seven stages and 800 employees performing opera, *ballet, drama, *farce, and *operetta. The chairman, personally appointed by the Tsar, was usually the retired Russian chief of police for the city—an irony of great symbolic resonance for the freedom-loving Poles. The institution had excellent actors and singers. The Wielki produced the best European operas as well as Polish works by Stanisław Moniuszko (1819–72), including *Halka* (1858) and *The Haunted Manor* (1865). The Rozmaitości ensemble was particularly strong between 1865 and 1885; an age of stars produced Modrzejewska as leading lady (who later conquered American stages as Helena *Modjeska), accompanied by a first-rate troupe. The repertoire consisted of classical tragedies and contemporary *comedies and *dramas, but the best national plays were banned by Russian *censorship. In the late 1860s, competition arrived from temporary summer or garden theatres, built in public parks or as annexes to cafés, which provided popular entertainment from travelling companies. The *modernist epoch began with the introduction of private art theatres in the early 1900s. The most important of them, the Polski Theatre, built by Arnold *Szyfman in 1913, had a spacious stage, up-to-date equipment (a *revolving stage and modern *lighting), luxurious foyers and *auditorium, and strong *acting company; it became the flagship of Polish culture in Warsaw, which was still under Russian rule.

After Poland's political resurrection in 1918, Warsaw enjoyed a renewed theatre life. Four theatres made the most important contributions. The Polski produced a varied repertoire, invited the best directors and designers, and had excellent actors. Its memorable productions included Zygmunt Krasiński's *Irydion* (1913), Stanisław *Wyspiański's *The Deliverance* (1918), Adam *Mickiewicz's *Forefathers' Eve* (1934), fifteen plays by Shakespeare, and eighteen by *Shaw (including the world première of *The Apple Cart*, 1929). The Reduta Theatre, created in 1919 by the actor and director Juliusz Osterwa, promoted Polish plays in *realist productions; when he became head of the Rozmaitości he renamed it the National Theatre in 1924.

The Bogusławski Theatre was headed in 1924–6 by Leon *Schiller, the leading director of the time, while the Athenaeum was under the *management of the excellent actor Stefan Jaracz (1883–1945) from 1930 to 1933 and again from 1935 to 1939. About 200 theatrical institutions of various types operated in Warsaw in the period between 1918 and 1939, including fifteen permanent *playhouses and those devoted to opera, operetta, and *cabaret.

The interruptions of the Second World War were as severe as anywhere in Europe. During the war many theatre people took part in both armed and civilian resistance. Many perished, were imprisoned, or sent to Auschwitz. The National was bombed and burned. The German occupiers forbade theatrical activity, except for a few censored comedy and cabaret stages. These were boycotted by Polish artists, who instead organized illegal, underground productions performed secretly in private apartments, schools, and monasteries. Warsaw was almost completely destroyed during the 1944 Uprising and a systematic demolition by Germans afterwards. At the end of the war all of the city's theatres were in ruins except the Polski, which Szyfman reopened in 1946. As the capital was rapidly rebuilt, theatre life blossomed again, though curtailed by the Soviet-installed communist regime. A rigid Stalinist repression imposed a *socialist-realistic repertoire and aesthetics from about 1948 to 1955. With few exceptions, the national classics were prohibited, along with Western plays and works by Catholic writers. Even after the 1956 'Thaw' in Soviet policy, theatres were controlled by the Party and strictly censored; though well subsidized, they were expected to conform to official ideology.

But the national repertoire was again permitted, along with new Polish work and plays from the West, while young, experimental groups were pushing the boundaries of censorship. Warsaw again became a major centre: its repertoire and production styles were diverse, the playhouses full, and their work admired by foreign visitors. The Współczesny (Contemporary) Theatre presented mostly foreign plays, while the Dramatyczny (Dramatic) focused on new Polish work, including premières of *Witkiewicz, *Gombrowicz, *Mrożek, and *Różewicz. The Polski successfully continued under Szyfman, and then under Stanisław Balicki (1958–64), when it produced Forefathers' Eve (1955) and plays by *Słowacki, among others. A special niche was carved out by Józef *Szajna, *avant-garde designer and director, head of the Studio Theatre (1972–82). Younger *audiences admired the postmodern productions of Adam Hanuszkiewicz, head of the Popular (1963–8), the National (1968–82), and the New (Nowy, from 1994). 1965 witnessed the reopening of the rebuilt Wielki and the inauguration of the annual *festival of the country's best productions. *Politics became the dominant force again with the imposition of martial law in 1981, which resulted in the boycott of *mass media by theatre artists, who created a network of underground, illegal,

uncensored, independent productions in churches and private homes.

The fall of communism in 1989 and Poland's re-emergence as an independent country did not at first revitalize theatre in Warsaw, because—like so much theatre in Eastern Europe—it lost its energizing purpose of fighting for freedom and was subjected to a shrinking of state subsidies; audiences demanded entertainment above all. The most important event was the re-opening (after a 1985 *fire) of the National in 1996, with Jerzy Grzegorzewski as *artistic director. He focused on formal concerns; after years of *politically oriented work he represented an apolitical, aestheticist approach. He was followed by a generation of young directors who introduced new attitudes and styles: they scornfully turned their backs on history and enthusiastically embraced modern mass culture. At the beginning of the twenty-first century Warsaw had about 30 permanent professional theatres. The Theatre Academy, programmes at universities, a theatre *museum, periodicals, and festivals—all contributed to making the city once again a leading force in Polish culture and world theatre.   KB

WARSAW YIDDISH ART THEATRE (VYKT)

*Yiddish theatre established in 1921 in *Warsaw by Ida *Kamińska and her first husband Zygmund Turkow. The group performed modern and classical Yiddish plays, including adaptations of *Goldfaden and Etinger, European plays ranging from *Molière to *Rolland and *Andreev, and occasional commercial pieces. VYKT was constantly on the road, *touring throughout Poland, often under dire circumstances, and in 1928 a *financial crisis led to the company's collapse. In 1939 Turkow revived VYKT with several quality productions, but it crumbled under the German invasion of Warsaw.   EN

WARSHA THEATRE COMPANY, AL-

Egyptian troupe, founded in 1987 by Hassan El-Geretly (its *artistic director). Al-Warsha (Arabic for 'workshop') was the first and most financially secure of the non-commercial, independent companies not reliant upon state funding. It experiments with a new approach to indigenous performance traditions, through the adaptation of foreign *texts (Dayern Maydour, 1992, based on *Jarry's Ubu cycle), or through the reconstruction or deconstruction of *folk narratives (Ghazl Al-A'mar (Spinning Lives), 1998, based on the Hilaliya folk epic). While the troupe enjoys media attention both home and abroad, its work has occasionally been accused of orientalism for using exotic folk material to cater to foreign acceptance and sponsorship. Nonetheless its success ushered the 'free' theatre troupes of the 1990s. But while most of those companies eventually lost their autonomy to state funding or *censorship, Al-Warsha continues to enjoy independence and systematic growth, witnessed by its innovative public relations activities, outreach educational programmes, and professional development workshops, all of which involve collaboration with international cultural institutions based in Egypt.   HMA

WASAN-KARA

Among the Hausa of pre-colonial Niger and northern Nigeria, a feast of harvest, hence its literal meaning, a 'game of cornstalks'. Nowadays it is organized by theatre groups (*samariyas*) in the Zinder region in Niger to comment on social or political events, like important visits by foreign dignitaries, by re-creating them onstage. A performance is considered successful if the actors are able to imitate the real-life personalities, their gait, speech habits, tics, and mannerisms, with such *realism that the *audience immediately recognizes them. Such performances tend to caricature and *satire, and it sometimes happens that those who are satirized are present, always an occasion for some *laughter at their expense.   PNN trans. JCM

WASHINGTON SQUARE PLAYERS

American theatre group operating 1914–18, reorganized in 1919 to form the *Theatre Guild. Like the *Provincetown Players, the Washington Square Players emerged from a group of intellectuals, artists, and political radicals who frequented the Liberal Club, near Washington Square in Greenwich Village. They produced 62 *one-act plays and six longer plays over the course of three and a half years and pushed the *Little Theatre movement toward a semi-professional state while mounting acclaimed productions of modern plays. In late 1914 Lawrence *Langner, Helen Westley, and others pledged 'to bring about the birth and healthy growth of an artistic theatre in this country'. Operating on a subscription basis and *managed by a five-member committee, the group rented the Bandbox Theatre (299 seats) and offered a season in 1915, mixing short plays by *Maeterlinck, *Chekhov, and *Wedekind with new American drama. The WSP expanded operations in 1916 to include *tours and moved to the larger Comedy Theatre. The loss of personnel to the draft and an overwhelming debt forced them to close in 1918.   MAF

WASSERSTEIN, WENDY (1950–)

American playwright whose commercially successful *comedies show women trapped between modernity and convention. Raised in a well-off Jewish family, Wasserstein graduated from Mt. Holyoke College, studied creative writing at City University of New York, and received an MFA from the *Yale School of Drama. *Uncommon Women and Others* (*New York, 1977) uses her undergraduate experience to critique the possibilities for women. In *Isn't It Romantic* (1981) two young women grapple

with the pressure to marry. *The Heidi Chronicles* (1988) follows the *feminist movement and its disillusions through one woman's life; it won both the Pulitzer Prize and the Tony *award. In *The Sisters Rosensweig* (1992) three middle-aged sisters support and struggle with one another and come to terms with their Jewish heritage, while *An American Daughter* (1997) suggests pitfalls for women in public office. The last three plays were developed at the *Seattle Repertory Theatre and directed by Daniel Sullivan. Among Wasserstein's other plays are *When Dinah Shore Ruled the Earth* (1975, with Yale classmate Christopher *Durang), *Tender Offer* (1983, *film adaptation 1998), and *Miami* (1986). The Phoenix Theatre and *Playwrights Horizons provided early artistic homes.   FL

WATERHOUSE, KEITH (1929–)

English novelist, dramatist, humorist, and journalist. Much of his theatre, *film, and *television writing has been in collaboration with Willis Hall. Their early successes include the adaptation of Waterhouse's own novel *Billy Liar* (1960), *Celebration* (1961), and *All Things Bright and Beautiful* (1962), which established their reputation as wry and astute observers of British provincial, and in particular Yorkshire, mores. In contrast their saucy hit play *Say Who You Are* (1965) tells of a *ménage à trois* in Knightsbridge. Independently and in partnership with Hall, Waterhouse has adapted several foreign plays for the British stage including Eduardo de *Filippo's *Saturday, Sunday, Monday* (1973) and *Filumena* (1977); adaptations of novels include *Mr and Mrs Nobody* (1986, from *The Diary of a Nobody*), *Bookends* (1990, from *The Marsh Marlowe Letters*), and *Our Song* (1992, from his own work). One of Waterhouse's most popular pieces is *Jeffrey Bernard Is Unwell* (1989), based on the rather louche writing of the eponymous *Spectator* columnist.

AS

WATERS, ETHEL (1896–1977)

*African-American singer and actress who began her career in *Philadelphia, literally stopping the show with her rendition of 'St Louis Blues'. Eight years later she was billed as 'Sweet Mama Stringbean' in *New York. She soon appeared in *revues such as *Africana, Paris Bound, Blackbirds of 1928*, and in Irving *Berlin's *As Thousands Cheer* (1933), where she sang 'Suppertime'. She launched her acting career in 1939 with *Mamba's Daughters*, and appeared in *Member of the Wedding* (1950), which was made into a *film. In her later years she toured with the evangelist Billy Graham.   BBL

WATERSON, SAM (1940–)

American actor. Educated at Yale and the Sorbonne, Waterson first appeared on Broadway as Jonathan in Arthur *Kopit's *absurdist Oedipal tale *Oh Dad, Poor Dad, Mamma's Hung You in the Closet and I'm Feelin So Sad* (1963), and then worked almost exclusively *Off-Broadway. He originated the roles of Kent in Sam *Shepard's *La Turista* (1967) and Thomas Lewis in *The Trial of the Catonsville Nine* (1968). The turning point of his career occurred when Joe *Papp cast him as Benedick in the *New York Shakespeare Festival's *Much Ado About Nothing* (1971). Waterston received Obie, Drama Desk, and New York Critics Circle *awards for his performance, and played major roles for the festival throughout the 1970s, appearing in *The Tempest* (1974), *A Doll's House* (1975), *Hamlet* (1975), *Henry V* (1976), and *Measure for Measure* (1976). His portrayal of Tom Wingfield in a teleplay of *A Glass Menagerie* (1973) was well received, and thereafter he worked increasingly in *television and *film, most notably as the journalist Sydney Schanberg in *The Killing Fields* (1984). JAB

WAXWORKS

Popular amusement form consisting of wax sculptures and figures, usually of famous or infamous people. The display of wax figures dates to ancient cultures. The Egyptians, Greeks, and Romans all used wax models of gods and ancestors, primarily for funeral processions. Wax votives appeared during the *medieval period when wax *masks of monarchs and other important persons were displayed during public celebrations. In the *early modern period wax portraits and figurines were carved by artists to make medallion casts and rough models for larger works. Polychromatic wax figures developed in the seventeenth century and were especially popular in Italy and Spain. Among the most famous wax artists was Guido Zumbo of Sicily, who, in addition to making wax portrait medallions, collaborated with French physician Guillaume Desnoues to create wax anatomical models. Desnoues, in a breach of medical ethics and public good taste, put the models on display in public exhibitions in *London and *Paris. His wax museums were an instant sensation and remained so until his death in 1735.

The French remained at the forefront of wax sculpting during the eighteenth century, though two English artists, Isaac Gosset and John Flaxman, were recognized as leading proponents of the art. Their works were among the first in Europe to receive popular acclaim in public exhibitions and imitators were numerous. Some even made it to the New World: George Washington reported viewing a wax exhibit in Annapolis in 1772. In Paris, Philippe Curtius owned two major wax museums during the late eighteenth century and was the most famous wax sculptor of his time. His niece Marie Grosholtz, who had studied with him since childhood, inherited his collections and museums in 1794 and continued his legacy as Mme Tussaud. Much of her notoriety came from the wax death masks she was ordered to make of those executed during the Reign of Terror. In 1802 she divorced her husband and moved to London; she

spent 33 years *touring the provinces with her collections. She opened a permanent exhibit in Baker Street in 1835. In 1884 the exhibit moved to its current location on Marylebone Road. Madame Tussaud's remains the most famous and successful of the wax museums with venues in Europe, North America, and Asia. PAD

WAYANG GOLEK

*Puppet theatre of Sunda and Java in *Indonesia. A single *dalang* or puppet master manipulates three-dimensional rod puppets to tell stories from the *Mahabharata* and *Ramayana* in Sundanese-speaking areas. Accompanied by a *gamelan orchestra and one singer, performances last from nine in the evening through the night. Based on *wayang cepak*, which treats historical episodes or stories of Amir Hamzah, the uncle of Muhammad, *wayang golek* originated in the eighteenth century as puppet masters from the north coast of Java migrated into the highlands. It is now seen at weddings, circumcisions, or other life-cycle ceremonies, presented on a temporary stage outside the home of the host family. *Ritual performances continue, but most spectators now are seeking entertainment; indeed the biting *political critique of performers sometimes evokes government *censorship. Thousands of spectators gather to enjoy the lifelike manipulation and raucous humour of top *dalang* such as Asep Sunander *Sunarya, Ade Sunarya, and Dede Amung Sutarya. Traditionally a hereditary art, since the 1970s it has been taught at SMKI, the Indonesian High School of Performing Arts in Bandung. The older *wayang cepak*, itself derived from the shadow theatre (*wayang kulit*), continues to be presented in some areas of north, central, and east Java. KFo

WAYANG KULIT

*Shadow-puppet theatre of *Indonesia. *Wayang*, commonly translated as *puppet, is the traditional theatre of Java and Bali in which a *dalang* (puppet master) uses puppets, *masks, or people to narrate a story to the percussive music of a *gamelan orchestra. *Wayang kulit* (literally, 'hide puppet') uses figures made of water buffalo skin. The single puppeteer-narrator sits behind a white screen, using a lamp to create the shadows. The puppets are displayed on a horizontal banana tree board which sits atop wooden legs, where they lie ready for use. A set includes about 100 puppets on Bali and over 300 puppets on Java, and as many as 50 figures can be used in a single performance. Delicate manipulation, complex formulas in archaic language, virtuoso singing, dexterous vocal technique, intricate *plot patterns, and bawdy humour are combined in a remarkable performance by the *dalang*, who improvises inside a pattern of formulaic songs and narratives. His presentations, which are hired by a family or village for a rite of passage celebration,

A *dalang* manipulating figures behind a screen for ***wayang kulit***, Yogyakarta, Java, Indonesia, 1996. The bright light bulb, mounted in a reflector hanging in the centre, creates the shadow puppet images for the audience on the opposite side of the screen.

may last up to eight hours. *Wayang kulit* relies on stories from the *Mahabharata* and *Ramayana*, while *wayang gedog* dramatizes the escapades of the amorous east Javanese Prince *Panji. Local histories and contemporary tales may also be performed.

Played on Java since at least the ninth century, *wayang kulit* was probably first introduced in the Hindu-Buddhist period which began in AD 78. Early Javanese models influenced shadow-puppet genres throughout all of *South-East Asia (*see* NANG SBEK THOM; NANG TALUNG). When the court of Majapahit, the last Javanese Hindu-Buddhist dynasty, moved to Bali at the end of the fifteenth century, some *dalang* followed, laying the framework for *wayang parwa*, the popular shadow-puppet theatre of that island. At the same time Islam brought innovations to Java, including an elaboration of music, expansion of the orchestra, changes in the performance structure, and a greater stylization of the figures. These alterations are credited to the Wali, the saints who converted the island to Islam from whom Javanese *dalang* say they are descended. It seems likely that the sufistic Wali used the arts in a programme of religious conversion. Philosophical developments of the art were made in the Dutch colonial period also, as Javanese aristocrats, disenfranchised from political pursuits, invested enormous energy in court performance.

On Bali the form is simpler. *Mahabharata* stories are presented in five-hour performances, musically accompanied by four *gender* (percussion instruments with metal keys that are hit with brass hammers), for tooth filings, marriages, cremations, and the like. There are currently about 300 Balinese *dalang*, with I Wayan Wija the most popular performer and I Made *Sidja acknowledged as the master in interpretation of religious material. Although in the past Balinese puppeteers came only from lineages of *dalang*, today students can study the art at the High School of Performing Arts and at the Indonesian University of the Arts, in Denpasar.

Contemporary Javanese *wayang* has three *pathet* (keys or musical modes) regulated by the dominant note of the gamelan used. The style of *wayang kulit purwa* established in the court city of Surakarta is followed all over Java. A long opening mantra precedes the first court scene, in which a kingdom is introduced and its ruler sends out an army; a second monarch then dispatches troops which clash with the first forces. Around midnight a *clown scene called the *goro-goro* (world in chaos) intervenes with extensive jokes and popular songs. The *hero then receives advice from a hermit and kills a series of ogres in the forest in the 'flower battle' scene. The story culminates in a major battle which resolves the plot. The three-part structure is said to symbolize the human life from birth (court scene) through adolescence (flower battle) to death (final battle).

Despite its traditional nature, Javanese *wayang kulit* has undergone numerous alterations. In the second half of the twentieth century the *dalang* *Nartosabdho was a major innovator, while Anom Suroto and Ki Mantep, popular at the end of the century, continued to adapt the form. It has also been influenced by *radio and *television, which have tended to make performance less ritualistic and more entertaining. But *wayang kulit* remains important in the life of the nation, and performers can now train at the Indonesian University of the Arts in Surakarta or the Indonesian Institute of the Arts in Yogyakarta.   KFo

WAYANG WONG

An elaborate performance tradition of Javanese court *dance-drama, the origin of which is traditionally ascribed to Sultan Hamengku Buwono I (1755–92) of Yogyakarta and Mangku Nagara I (1757–95) of Surakarta in central Java. *Wayang* means shadow; *wong* (or *orang* in Indonesian) means human being. The form borrows many of its conventions from the earlier shadow play (*wayang purwa*), including the *dialogue, singing, narration, *characterization, and the aesthetic ideal of Javanese dance. As in the *shadow play, *wayang wong* is also accompanied by a *gamelan orchestra and divided into three sections defined by the modal designations of gamelan music. Episodes from the Indian epics *Ramayana* and *Mahabharata* and local legends are its main repertoire. In Surakarta, Susuhunan Paku Buwono X (1893–1939) established the Sri Wedari recreation park in the early 1900s, where non-court artists performed commercialized *wayang wong* nightly for a popular *audience on an elevated *stage with *curtains and *props. In Jakarta, choreographers Sardono W. Kusumo and Retno Maruti have revitalized and successfully rechoreographed *wayang wong* for the educated audience of metropolitan *Jakarta. *See* WAYANG KULIT.   SM

WAYLETT, HARRIET (1798–1851)

English actress, born into the stage *family of Cooke. She made an early debut; when she ran away with an officer, her father sued for loss of her services. She married but soon left the actor Waylett. She made her reputation singing fashionable ballads, including 'Home Sweet Home', in *soubrette and *breeches roles at Birmingham *Theatre Royal before moving to *Drury Lane in 1824 with Alfred Bunn, provoking scandal. G. A. Lee composed many of her songs, and with him she entered the

*management free-for-all of the 1830s, assuming control of the unlicensed Strand in 1834; by 1840 she was free to marry Lee.
                                                                    JSB

WEAVER, FRITZ (1926–)

American actor. Raised in Pittsburgh, he did conscientious objector service in the Second World War, then attended the University of Chicago. He was soon a success on stage in *New York, compiling impressive credits, most notably in classics at the *Phoenix Theatre (1955–60) and *American Shakespeare Festival in Connecticut (1955–8). 'I don't think I would have become an actor if not for Shakespeare', he said; 'contemporary *realism wouldn't have attracted me.' His career total is 22 Shakespeare plays, including title roles in *Hamlet*, *Macbeth*, *King Lear*, *Richard II*, and *Henry IV*. Modern plays in which he excelled include *The Chalk Garden* (1955), *The Power and the Glory* (1958), *Childs Play* (revival, 1970) and *Angel's Fall* (1983). He was never a juvenile: from the start, his craggy, gaunt appearance conveyed patrician authority, and his strongest feature is his dusky, saw-toothed voice.   CR

WEBB, JOHN (1611–72)

English architect and designer. Educated at the Merchant Taylors' School, *London, Webb became Inigo *Jones's assistant in 1628 and later married into his family; some architectural plans for Jones's court *masques are in his hand, but may be later copies. In 1656 he designed the production of William *Davenant's *The Siege of Rhodes* at Rutland House, which saw the English public stage's first use of the *proscenium arch and *painted *scenery, strategies that had been pioneered by Jones in the *court theatre of the 1630s and before. In 1665 Webb designed the Hall Theatre, Whitehall, as a replacement for the *Cockpit-in-Court.   MJW

WEBBER, ANDREW LLOYD *See* LLOYD WEBBER, ANDREW.

WEBER, JOSEPH (1867–1942) AND LEW FIELDS (1867–1941)

American comedians and *producers. Joseph Moishe Weber was born in *New York to an immigrant Polish family. Moses Schoenfeld was born in *Warsaw, came to New York as a child, and took the name Lewis Maurice Shanfield. The two became childhood friends and, sharing a passion for performing, began appearing at the age of 10 in *variety halls and beer gardens with their own song, *dance, and *slapstick acts— sometimes in Irish or German dialects. In 1881 they created their signature characters of Mike (the short, padded Weber) and Meyer (the lanky Fields), which they *toured across the country. By the 1890s they headed three touring companies. In

1896 they leased the Imperial Theatre and renamed it the Weber & Fields Music Hall, where they played and presented such talent as De Wolf *Hopper, Lillian *Russell and David *Warfield. Following a disagreement, the pair separated in 1904, but reconciled in 1912 with shows titled *Hokey Pokey* and *Roly Poly*. From 1914 to 1927 they appeared in a series of silent *films, including *Mike and Meyer*, and in the sound films *Blossoms on Broadway* (1937) and *Lillian Russell* (1940).

CT

WEBSTER, BENJAMIN (1797–1882)

English actor, *manager, playwright, and member of a theatrical *family. Webster started his career playing *Harlequin and Pantaloon in *pantomime before joining *Vestris's company at the *Olympic Theatre in 1830. Most of his theatrical life, however, was spent as an *actor-manager: first at the *Haymarket (1837–53) and then at the *Adelphi (1844–76), reopening it as the New Adelphi in 1859. The Adelphi, well run, remained principally a *melodrama house; Webster's management of the Haymarket was more significant. He introduced *stall seats to the theatre in 1843 and put backs on the pit benches. But it was on the stage that his management distinguished itself. He secured the services of leading playwrights, like Sheridan *Knowles and *Bulwer-Lytton, and engaged first-rank actors in good productions: the *Keans in *As You Like It*, Bulwer-Lytton's *The Lady of Lyons*, and in Knowles's new play *The Rose of Aragon* (1842); *Macready in the first performances of Bulwer-Lytton's *Money* (1840); Tom *Taylor's and Charles *Reade's *Masks and Faces* (1852), with himself as the penurious poet Triplet. He also staged a revolutionary *Taming of the Shrew* in 1844 on an approximation of an Elizabethan stage. As a dramatist Webster wrote some 50 plays, mostly melodramas and adaptations of novels. A versatile performer, he played *comedy and pathos with equal effect; in his later years he became an excellent character actor. Webster's Petruchio and Malvolio were much praised, and he was a sinister and malignant Tartuffe.

MRB

WEBSTER, JOHN (c.1580–c.1633)

English dramatist. The son of a coach-maker, he was born in London and educated at the Merchant Taylors' School. He first worked in the theatre in 1602 as a contributor to three syndicate-written plays for the *Henslowe companies. In 1604 the King's Men (*see* CHAMBERLAIN'S MEN, LORD) hired him to adapt *Marston's *The Malcontent* for adult actors, a task which entailed adding an induction and a role for the company *clown, and in 1604–5 he collaborated with *Dekker on two *city comedies, *Westward Hoe* and *Northward Hoe*. It may have been Dekker who induced him to offer his first solo play, *The White Devil* (1612), to the *Red Bull, the most downmarket of the *London amphitheatres. Although Webster felt the production

had been well *acted, notably by the rising star Richard Perkins (who probably played Count Lodovico), it proved unsuccessful with the house's plebeian *audience constituency, possibly because the *tragedy's allusive language and dense, exposition-light storytelling demanded a level of attention beyond that required by the typical Red Bull repertory. It was, however, successfully revived in the 1620s and 1660s. Webster's next play, *The Duchess of Malfi* (1613), has a similar style but a simpler narrative, and is more ambitious in its use of stage *spectacle. A dark tragedy about the conflict between sexual desire and social honour, it was produced by the King's Men with John *Lowin and Richard *Burbage in the leading male roles; it remained in their repertory until the 1630s. It was revived in the later seventeenth century, and in 1733 Lewis *Theobald produced an adaptation, *The Fatal Secret* (published 1735).

These two tragedies are widely known for their gruesome qualities, a preconception that influenced productions in the twentieth century, which were frequent. This is increasingly considered a misleading emphasis which obscures their other concerns: their attention to latent psychological states, their treatment of the experience of disempowered figures like women and servants, and the *characters' almost indestructible human vitality in defiance of law and convention. The plays are also noted for the political sophistication with which they address the workings of early seventeenth-century European societies at many levels: in *The White Devil*, the institutions of the state—notably the law and the Church—are shown to serve the interests of rich and powerful men rather than any abstract ideal of justice, and in *The Duchess of Malfi* individual freedom of action is delimited not only by codes of private behaviour but also by geopolitical events.

Webster's later *tragicomedy *The Devil's Law-Case* (1619) is less often seen, but proved eminently stageworthy when produced at the *Royal Academy of Dramatic Art in 2001; it offers one of Jacobean drama's best roles for an older woman. During the 1620s he returned to collaboration, working with *Middleton (*Anything for a Quiet Life*, 1621), *Rowley (*A Cure for a Cuckold*, 1624), and *Heywood (*Appius and Virginia*, c.1627); he was also employed by the King's Men, along with *Massinger and *Ford, to finish off *Fletcher's last play, *The Fair Maid of the Inn* (1626). Thereafter he virtually disappears from view; he was dead by 1634.

MJW

WEBSTER, MARGARET (1905–72)

English director. She began as a performer for Ben *Greet's company and at the *Old Vic, where her roles included Lady Macbeth and Toinette in *Molière's *Tartuffe*. Her first major directorial triumph was *Richard II* in New York, starring Maurice *Evans (1937, 132 performances on Broadway). Another notable success with Shakespeare was *Othello* in 1942, which achieved 296 performances on Broadway; controversially, she

*cast the African-American Paul *Robeson in the lead. Webster also directed many classical productions for Marweb, her bus and truck company which toured America in the late 1940s, and she was the first woman to direct at the *Metropolitan Opera House. Webster liked bustle, crowds, energy, and visual detail. She did significant research for her productions, and wrote about her work as a director in *The Same Only Different* (1969), which includes the history of her theatrical dynasty, and in *Don't Put your Daughter on the Stage* (1972). Webster's career in America was disrupted after she was investigated by Senator Joseph McCarthy and subsequently she found it easier to find directing work within the university system and in the UK (for example, at Stratford in 1956 and the Old Vic in 1957).

EJS

WEDEKIND, FRANK (1864–1918)

German playwright and actor. Born in Hanover, son of a doctor and an actress, he grew up in Switzerland, where he worked with a Zurich firm. After visiting Paris in 1892 he turned to the theatre, appearing as an accomplished performer in satirical *cabaret in *Munich. His performance style anticipated the intensity of *Artaud: Hugo Ball spoke of the convulsions that shook Wedekind's body and described his acting as 'flagellant, hypnotic, and as gruesome as hara-kiri'. Influenced by *naturalism, he began writing social dramas, but without the same level of *realism. His best-known play, *Spring's Awakening*, translated by Edward *Bond in 1974, was written in 1891 but first performed in 1906, directed by *Reinhardt. Containing scenes of homosexual love, masturbation, and flagellation, the piece is a disturbing condemnation of the way in which an oppressive society deals with puberty. Its provocative content, episodic structure, abrupt language, and two-dimensional and symbolic *characters, like the Man-in-the-Mask played at its première by the author, all anticipate *expressionism. Wedekind thus provides a link in the chain from the *Sturm und Drang* through *Büchner to modernist playwriting (see MODERNISM AND POSTMODERNISM). His 'Lulu plays', *Earth Spirit* (1898) and *Pandora's Box* (1904), have as their central figure Lulu, memorably played by Louise Brooks in Pabst's silent *film version (1929), a purely sexual creature who drives men to ruin. Finally she meets her nemesis by being murdered by Jack the Ripper, one creature of instinct destroyed by another. At the Leipzig première of *Earth Spirit* Wedekind played the male lead, Dr Schön. In both these plays, which deliberately sought to outrage contemporary bourgeois society, Wedekind reflects

Helene **Weigel** singing in her greatest role, Mother Courage in Brecht's *Mother Courage and Her Children*, Berliner Ensemble at the Deutsches Theater, Berlin, 1949, directed by Brecht, designed by Teo Otto and Heinrich Kilger. Courage's supply wagon is here hauled by her children.

the concern of the time with sexuality and with the perceived threat of powerful women. His other major plays, while still satirical, are gentler in tone. *The Marquis of Keith* (1901), which was one of *Jessner's outstanding *Berlin productions in 1920, deals with an amoral confidence trickster, a man whose antisocial behaviour is celebrated by Wedekind in preference to the stultified bourgeoisie. Wedekind was repeatedly in trouble with the *censor and in 1899 was imprisoned for political *satire, a theme he addressed in his *one-act play *Censorship* (1908). It is his legacy as a challenger of conventional morality rather than his plays themselves that make Wedekind now so memorable.

MWP

WEIGEL, HELENE (1900–71)

Austrian actress and *manager. After training in *Vienna, Weigel began her career in Frankfurt. She moved to *Berlin in 1922, working with various directors, including Leopold *Jessner and Erich *Engel. She met *Brecht in 1923, and they married in 1929. Weigel's influence was almost certainly a major cause of Brecht's increasing interest in strong proletarian female *characters, particularly mother figures. Weigel was developing a reputation for performing working-class characters when she met Brecht, which was enhanced by her performance as the title character in Brecht's *The Mother* in 1932.

Weigel, Brecht, and their two children fled Nazi Germany in 1933. Weigel performed the title role in the première of Brecht's *Señora Carrar's Rifles* (*Paris, 1937), repeated in the Danish première (1938). That year she also performed in an early version of *Fear and Misery of the Third Reich*. She did not appear on stage again until 1948, when she played the title role in Brecht's adaptation of *Antigone* in Chur, Switzerland. The following year she played the title role in Brecht's *Mother Courage* in East Berlin, where its success helped win state support for the *Berliner Ensemble, which Brecht founded in 1949 with Weigel as *Intendant. The Ensemble *toured a 1951 restaging of *Courage* to *Paris (1954) and to *London (1956). Weigel's performance, informed by a powerful simplicity and an emotional intensity made more vibrant by understatement, won recognition as one of the greatest in twentieth-century European theatre. Weigel led the Ensemble through a critical transition after Brecht's death in 1956, turning it into a company defined by Brecht's ideas rather than his ongoing work. She also continued to organize tours exhibiting old and new successes. These included Brecht's 1954 production of *The Caucasian Chalk Circle* with Weigel as Natella Abashvili and a 1964 production of *Coriolan* in which she played Volumnia. These tours secured the company an international reputation and helped provoke widespread interest in the principles and practices of *epic theatre.

JR

WEI LIANGFU (WEI LIANG-FU) (fl. 1522–73)

Chinese music master, entertainer, and sometime physician; revered as the 'Sage of Song' by lovers of *kunqu. Wei was active in the Suzhou hinterland, where the Kunshan style of music originated. By 1600 he was a semi-legendary figure, reputed to have remained in a room for ten years while he forged a refined style of Kunshan music from *folk forms (fixed tunes referred to as qupai), which he found chaotic and vulgar. More likely he was one of several musicians who refined Kunshan music in a period from 1506 to 1566, establishing it as the pre-eminent style of southern drama (referred to as kunqu). His Qulü (Rules for Songs), also disseminated as Nanci yinzheng (Adducing Correct [Forms] for Southern Lyrics), instructs composers to distinguish each song's mode (gong) and key (diao) and master each word's tone and articulation ('clear' or 'turbid'), so that tune and *text will harmonize. Other passages instruct performers to place beats accurately, so that qupai are rhythmically proportionate and transitions between them smooth. Aesthetically, Wei sought to place southern opera on a par with that from the north. He believed that the slow and expressive southern songs, accompanied by woodwinds, complemented the taut and urgent northern songs, which were sung to stringed accompaniment.   CS

WEILL, KURT (1900–50)

German composer. The son of a cantor, Weill began performing and composing as a child. After advanced study in *Berlin, he established himself as a composer of instrumental music before devoting himself to music theatre. For his first *opera, The Protagonist (1926), he worked with Georg *Kaiser, beginning a lifelong practice of collaborating with first-class playwrights and lyricists. He initially collaborated with *Brecht in 1927 when the two created the 'Songspiel' Mahagonny around Brecht's poems. Weill complemented the dark, socially critical *texts with *music that powerfully combined the *modernist idiom with popular traditions and contemporary 'low-art' music, especially jazz and ragtime. The resulting succès de scandale encouraged the team to develop the piece into a full-scale opera, Rise and Fall of the City of Mahagonny (1930). Meanwhile, they capitalized on their distinctive popular songwriting style with a work for singing actors, the wildly successful The Threepenny Opera (1928). A hurriedly completed follow-up project, Happy End (1929), was much less successful. Weill also helped Brecht develop the overtly *political, didactic Lehrstücke (learning plays) he began writing in the late 1920s. Weill provided music for the 'school opera' He Said Yes/He Said No (1930) and, with Paul Hindemith, for the cantata Lindbergh's Flight (1928).

Weill married the actress and singer Lotte *Lenya in 1926; they divorced in 1933 when Weill left Nazi Germany but remarried in 1937. Emigrating to the USA after two years in

*Paris, he began a successful second career composing *musicals. Of his eight Broadway shows, the two biggest successes were Lady in the Dark (1941, *book by Moss *Hart, lyrics by Ira *Gershwin) and One Touch of Venus (1943, Ogden Nash and S. J. Perelman). Perhaps his most influential American work was his 'Broadway Opera' Street Scene (1947, Elmer *Rice and Langston *Hughes). Street Scene and Mahagonny remain in the operatic repertory. Weill's more popular music enjoyed a tremendous resurgence during the 1980s and 1990s, when his songs began to be featured by a new generation of *cabaret singers and pop musicians.   JR

WEIMAR CLASSICISM

A movement in literature and theatre associated with the culture of the Weimar court at the turn of the eighteenth century, especially with the work of *Goethe and *Schiller. Weimar classicism was the final and most exalted phase of the German Enlightenment in which human capacity for reason, forbearance, fortitude, and acceptance of one's fate were raised to almost godlike stature. In theatre, the values of Weimar classicism were best expressed in Goethe's dramas Iphigenia in Tauris (1787) and Torquato Tasso (1790), in Schiller's Wallenstein Trilogy (1799) and Mary Stuart (1800), and in Schiller's concept of the Sublime, a state of consciousness that he argued should be the end of tragic *action. Goethe's 'Rules for Actors', which he wrote for the *Weimar Court Theatre, describe how *tragedy should be represented on stage, with attention to the formal demeanour required for the representation of noble feeling. These 'Rules', like the ideas of Weimar classicism, dominated the German theatre for much of the nineteenth century. See also NEOCLASSICISM; ROMANTICISM.   SJCW

WEIMAR COURT THEATRE

Under the direction of *Goethe from 1791 to 1817, the court theatre at Weimar became the model for German repertory theatres during the nineteenth century. Its repertoire balanced classics, modern dramas, and light entertainment, its *acting company developed an ensemble approach to performance, and, during the years Goethe and *Schiller worked together (1799–1805), some basic principles of stage *directing were explored. In the performance of *tragedy the company was guided by Goethe's 'Rules for Actors', which encouraged a noble demeanour on stage, reminiscent of classical statuary, a style emulated by German actors throughout the nineteenth century (see WEIMAR CLASSICISM). Only one Weimar actor, Pius Alexander *Wolff, achieved national fame, when he left the company in 1816 to become leading tragic actor at the *Berlin Royal Theatre. Goethe, who never greatly appreciated the position of director, resigned in 1817 when the Duke of Weimar insisted a dog be introduced on stage.   SJCW

WEI MINGLUN (WEI MING-LUN) (1941–)

Chinese playwright of *chuanju*, the regional music drama of Sichuan. The son of a *chuanju* drummer and scriptwriter, Wei's career as an actor started at the age of 9 with the Zigong City *Chuanjü* Troupe of Sichuan province. He gradually learned directing and playwriting. He received nationwide recognition in the early 1980s when his *chuanju* scripts *Bold Yi*, *The Fourth Daughter*, and *The Scholar of Sichuan* won national *awards. His 1986 play *Pan Jinlian: the history of a fallen woman* sparked national controversy because of its *modernist style and revisionist views of sex and women. Wei's combining of a modernist *semiotics and the aesthetic code of traditional Chinese theatre—a style the dramatist himself called 'chuanju of the *absurd'—was thought by some critics to herald the future of Chinese drama. *Pan Jinlian*'s revisionist approach to the archetypal 'bad woman' of traditional Chinese literature and theatre made it appear to advocate sexual liberation. In the 1990s his plays (*Evening Glow on Mount Qi*, *Changing Faces*, and *Du Landuo, the Chinese Princess*) continued to attract critical attention, so that Wei is now regularly known by the nickname 'genius from Sichuan'.   SYL

WEISS, PETER (1916–82)

German playwright, novelist, *filmmaker, and painter. Weiss left Nazi Germany with his parents in 1934. The family lived in London and Prague, where Weiss studied painting, before emigrating to Sweden in 1939. He initially pursued a career in painting, began publishing in 1946, and moved to *avant-garde *film during the 1950s. After 1960 he turned exclusively to writing, first in Swedish, then German. He became known in Germany for his fiction and his *puppet play *Night with Guests* (1963), then achieved international recognition with *The Persecution and Assassination of Jean-Paul Marat as Performed by the Inmates of the Asylum of Charenton under the Direction of the Marquis de Sade* (1964). Reflecting Weiss's own developing *political concerns, *Marat/Sade* sets Marat's arguments for political revolution, however bloody, against Sade's endorsement of extreme individual liberation. The play does not resolve this debate, however, complicating it further by setting it within a post-revolutionary, madhouse world. Weiss creates this world by combining an aggressive treatment of the spectator inspired by *Artaud's theatre of *cruelty with framing techniques and a use of song drawn from *Brecht's *epic theatre. The work was immediately recognized as a major reconsideration of the relationship between these two seeming antipodes of twentieth-century theatre, thanks in part to the international success of Peter *Brook's *London production (1964). Weiss felt that Brook's exuberant *theatricality overemphasized Sade and Artaud; he preferred the more soberly epic East German première, which favoured Marat.

The Investigation (1965) used a *montage of transcripts from the 1964 West German investigation into war crimes at Auschwitz to show how the death camp's organization embodied values still central to post-war capitalism. An important contribution to the *documentary theatre movement, the play premièred in a West *Berlin production directed by *Piscator, and simultaneously at thirteen other East and West German theatres. *Song of the Lusitanian Bogey* (1967) and the *documentary drama *Vietnam Discourse* (1968) were both informed by Weiss's increasing commitment to Marxism. Responding to the criticism that he had begun to substitute *politics for art, Weiss explored the role of the revolutionary writer in *Trotsky in Exile* (1970) and the relationship between political liberation and artistic vision in *Hölderlin* (1971). During the 1970s he devoted his energies to a massive three-part novel, *Ästhetik des Widerstands* (1975–81). He finished one more play before his death, *The New Investigation* (1981).   JR

WEKWERTH, MANFRED (1929–)

German director. Wekwerth joined *Brecht as assistant director at the *Berliner Ensemble in 1951 and remained connected with that theatre throughout his career. After Brecht's death in 1956 and Helene *Weigel's assumption of command, Wekwerth became the company's chief director from 1960 to 1969. His most famous production was Brecht's adaptation of *Coriolanus*, which *toured to *London in 1965 and which he restaged at the *National Theatre in 1973. After a falling out with Weigel, he left the Ensemble in 1969 and wrote a dissertation in *theatre studies. The ensuing book, *Theatre and Science* (1975), was widely discussed; it advanced the *theory that the spectator was the most important part of the theatrical equation. In 1977 he was reappointed to the board of the Berliner Ensemble and fought to maintain Brecht's heritage and performance tradition. A staunch supporter of the German Democratic Republic, Wekwerth fell into disfavour after reunification and lost his official positions.   CBB

WELFARE STATE INTERNATIONAL

British company, founded in 1968 by John Fox and Sue Gill, that has worked across many hybrid forms of public art, incorporating *clowning, *puppetry, fire sculpture, lantern-making, and diverse *performance art practices. Along with performances, processions, and installations, they devise *rituals for a post-religious society for such moments as birth, naming, partnerships, and death, working with figures and myths from around the world which they see as archetypal. Such postmodern eclecticism paradoxically derives from a desire to challenge aspects of postmodernity, often harking back to pre-modern artistic forms and notions of community (*see* MODERNISM AND POSTMODERNISM). After a nomadic decade in caravans, in 1979 Fox and

Gill settled in Ulverston, Cumbria, which has become the base for a loose association of artistic collaborators and for annual summer schools which have influenced many community arts workers and theatre-makers. While developing longer-term projects with local communities, the company also undertakes large-scale commissions elsewhere, such as *Raising the Titanic* (1983), a performance in *London's Docklands involving 150 people, in which the *Titanic* figured as a Ship of Fools and an image of capitalism, and *Glasgow All Lit Up!* (1990), in which 10,000 people carried lantern sculptures through the streets of *Glasgow.   GJG

WELLER, MICHAEL (1942–)

American playwright. Educated at Brandeis University, Weller's early work was produced at the *Edinburgh Fringe Festival and in *London at the *Royal Court Theatre and *Marowitz's Open Space. His 1970 London success *Cancer*, a drama of leave-taking about a group of college seniors, established his career at home when it received its American première at Washington's *Arena Stage under the title *Moonchildren* (1972). Directed by Alan *Schneider, the production transferred to *New York where critics hailed Weller as a spokesman for the 1960s generation. Many of his later plays chronicle the progress of the counter-culture through the personal and political disillusionments of the 1970s and 1980s. Notable among this group are *Fishing* (1975), *Loose Ends*, which won the American Theatre Critics Association *award for best play (1979), and *Split*, a drama about divorce in two parts (*Abroad*, 1978, and *At Home*, 1980). He also wrote the screenplays for the *musical *Hair* (1979) and *Ragtime* (1980), and has continued to write prolifically for *Off-Broadway and *regional theatres.   JAB

WELLES, ORSON (1915–85)

American director and actor. A polymathic original, Welles's stage productions of the 1930s and 1940s explored the limits of theatre technology and staging techniques. He often starred in his own productions and even designed *scenery, *costumes, and *special effects. Welles made his professional debut in *Dublin at the *Gate Theatre in 1931 and *toured the USA with Katharine *Cornell in *Romeo and Juliet* (Mercutio), *Candida* (Marchbanks), and *The Barretts of Wimpole Street* (Octavius Barrett) in 1933–4. Welles made an immediate mark as director in 1936 with his Haitian-inflected (or 'voodoo') *Macbeth*, staged at the Lafayette Theatre in Harlem in *New York. The production inaugurated Welles's partnership with producer John *Houseman and their sponsorship by the 'Negro People's Theatre' unit of the *Federal Theatre Project. The pair soon moved on to found a classically based unit for the FTP (Project 891), with Welles staging and starring in visually striking, innovative productions of *Horse Eats Hat* (adapted

from *Labiche, 1936) and *Marlowe's *Dr Faustus* (1937). Welles reworked and cut *texts, exploited the *auditorium as an acting area, and used *puppets as actors. When in 1937 the Welles–Houseman production of Marc *Blitzstein's leftist *opera *The Cradle Will Rock* was banned by the FTP due to political pressures, the pair founded their own *Mercury Theatre and continued a remarkable string of productions. Welles set his heavily cut and rearranged *Julius Caesar* (1937) in a fascist state often eerily lit from below and against a blood-red upstage wall. In 1938 the Mercury staged *The Shoemaker's Holiday*, *Heartbreak House*, and *Danton's Death*, after which the company dissolved as Welles was lured to Hollywood where he began work on his heralded *film *Citizen Kane* (1940). Welles's stage direction decreased from this point, but his New York productions of *Native Son* (1941), *Around the World* (with music by Cole *Porter, 1946), and *King Lear* (1956), and his *London productions of *Moby Dick* (1955) and *Rhinoceros* (1960), showed his abiding, if undisciplined, talent as director and (in all but *Native Son* and *Rhinoceros*) centrifugal leading actor. Beset by repeated artistic and commercial failures in his later years, Welles was best known to *audiences after 1960 as a commercial spokesman for supermarket wines.   MAF

WELL-MADE PLAY (*la pièce bien faite*)

A dramatic structure pioneered by French playwright Eugène *Scribe and perfected by his successor Victorien *Sardou. The aim was to provide a constantly entertaining, exciting narrative which satisfyingly resolved the many complications and intrigues that drove the story. A well-made play is characteristically based on a secret known only to some of the *characters and usually shared with the *audience, one character trying to keep it hidden or another trying to uncover it. Initial *exposition is normally followed by ups and downs in the characters' fortunes, and will lead to the *scène à faire (usually translated as 'obligatory scene') in which the characters confront each other with this information. The chains of events and the *denouement must all be logical and plausible. The overall structure should also be repeated in each act.

The term has always been a controversial one, *Shaw famously describing it as 'Sardoodledum'. Those for whom writing is a matter of inspiration and sensibility denounce the suggestion of soulless mechanics in the notion of making a play. The tight internal logic of the structure, sharply framed by exposition and denouement, is also anathema to dramatists who look to social and *political realities. Further, the idea that there is a universal way of structuring a play 'well' is deeply problematic given the mercurial nature of audience tastes, expectations, and desires. Indeed, Scribe's and Sardou's ruthlessly plausible endings have not survived such changes, and the resolutions of many of their plays can seem ludicrous to contemporary spectators less concerned with neatness and more attuned to irresolution and moral ambiguity. Nonetheless the form has influenced many playwrights, including *Labiche, *Feydeau, and *Augier. In Britain, *Robertson, H. A. *Jones, and *Pinero were among its early importers, and even *Ibsen, often thought to be its fiercest opponent, uses elements of the well-made play in many of his early prose plays, if only to *parody them. *Rattigan and *Priestley were often acclaimed and just as often condemned as masters of the well-made play, though in fact they drift far from its precepts. Traces of the form continue to be found in writers like David *Hare, and it also survives in the rigid rules for screenwriting promoted by Robert McKee in *Story* (1997).   DR

WEMYSS, FRANCIS COURTNEY (1797–1869)

American actor, *manager, and historian. Following his acting debut at *New York's Chatham Theatre in 1824, he soon turned to management. In *Philadelphia he managed the *Chestnut Street and the *Walnut Street theatres in succession during the 1830s, and opened the Pennsylvania Theatre in 1836. He also managed theatres in Baltimore, Pittsburgh, and Washington. In 1849 he became stage director at *Barnum's American Museum in New York. He contributed to American theatre history by editing a series of early American plays, publishing his memoirs in 1847, and compiling *Chronology of the American Stage from 1752–1852* (1852).   AHK

WENMING XI (WEN MING HSI)

'Civilized drama', an early form of Western-style theatre in *China, the precursor of *huajü. At the turn of the twentieth century China was forced to modernize after suffering repeated military defeats from Japan and the West. Western-style theatre was viewed as an educational tool for the masses, a task considered impossible for the traditional theatre; the name followed the fashion of calling new things 'civilized'. As early as 1899 students at St John's missionary school in *Shanghai performed a play of their own creation called *Ugly Scenes of Officialdom* and by 1907 school performances were widely popular in the city, producing well-known *wenming xi* actors such as Wang Zhongxian. Another source for *wenming xi* was *shizhuang xinxi* (modern *costume new drama), plays of contemporary stories performed by actors from traditional theatres in modern costume. Both these forms followed in the traditional mould, however, mixing speech with singing and *mime. The model for purely spoken drama came from *Japanese *shimpa, when in 1907 the Chinese student group *Chunliu She (Spring Willow Society), with the help of Japanese actors, staged an adaptation of *Uncle Tom's Cabin* in *Tokyo. All important *wenming xi* activities were concentrated in Shanghai. In 1910 Ren Tianzhi created the Evolutionary Troupe, the first professional new drama company in China. Two years later,

Lu Jingruo, a veteran of the Spring Willow Society, returned to Shanghai where he organized the New Drama Society, performing under the name of Spring Willow Theatre.

Although some *wenming xi* had finished scripts, either original compositions or adapted from translations, the majority of the repertoire belonged to *mubiao xi* (outline plays) which contained mere sketches of scenes and relied heavily on *improvisation. In performance many troupes adopted the practice of *muwai xi* (out-of-curtain plays), scenes performed in front of the *proscenium *curtain during set changes, in an attempt to placate an *audience accustomed to the non-stop *action of traditional theatre. *Wenming xi* also kept the traditional practice of using only male actors whose role assignments followed strict divisions of *character or performer types. An unusual category created for the form was *wenming zhengsheng* (civilized principal male), known for his improvisational propaganda speech advocating democracy and Western civilization. After reaching a peak in 1917, the major *wenming xi* troupes lost their appeal in Shanghai. Smaller groups carried on in *touring shows until the genre died out in 1924, eventually giving way to *huajü.   SYL

WERFEL, FRANZ (1890–1945)

Austrian dramatist, novelist, and poet. Although primarily known as a novelist, Werfel wrote consistently for the stage. His first phase was *expressionist, with an adaptation of *Euripides' *The Trojan Women* (1916) as an anti-war statement. *The Mirror Man* (1921) is a Faustian story of man's temptation to self-deify, his fall, and his salvation, while *The Goat Song* (1922) is based on the idea of the unredeemed animal in man. In the 1920s Werfel turned to *historical themes with *Juarez and Maximilian* (1925), dealing with the execution of the Habsburg Emperor in Mexico, followed by *God's Kingdom in Bohemia* (1930). *The Goat Song* and his '*comedy of a *tragedy', *Jacobowsky and the Colonel*, were both produced by the *Theatre Guild in *New York in 1926, the latter taken to Broadway in 1944. *The Eternal Road*, a play about the persecution of the Jewish people, with music by Kurt *Weill, was directed by *Reinhardt in New York (1937).   CBB

WERKTEATER (WERKTHEATER)

*Amsterdam company which began as a laboratory for theatre research in 1970. The objective of the *collective, founded by twelve actors including Peter Faber and Shireen Strooker, was to produce personal and *politically committed work. Inspired by the *Living Theatre and Jerzy *Grotowski, Werkteater ('work theatre') performances were created through *improvisation and *devising and were intended to initiate discussion with the *audience about current affairs. The company worked in alternative locations like a former factory building, as well as psychiatric and penal institutions, and nursing homes. Sets were bare and *costumes simple. The company rejected the glitter of opening nights and the satisfaction of *applause. In representing *characters, actors delved into their own selves, eventually attempting to convey how the fate of the social underdog affected the committed actor, a method which generated intense post-production discussions with spectators. The collective began to disintegrate in the late 1970s, some actors leaving to pursue careers elsewhere, and small-scale ventures replacing grander work, ultimately leading to a schism in 1985 and loss of state subsidy in 1988 (*see* FINANCE). Thereafter the Werkteater prepared tailor-made productions for trade, industry, government institutions, and other social organizations, which it has continued since 1997 as a foundation.   TH

WERNER, ZACHARIAS (1768–1823)

German playwright. Zacharias is remembered chiefly for his *one-act play *Der vierundzwanzigste Februar* (*The 24th of February*, 1810), which established the popular and much maligned *genre of the *Schicksalstragödie* (tragedy of fate), a special form of trivial drama in which fatalistic forces, in this case a family curse, bring about the resolution. In 1942 *Camus took up the play's *plot for his novel *The Stranger*, as well as for his drama *Le Malentendu*. Werner also wrote a successful play about Martin Luther, *The Consecration of Power* (1807).   CBB

WERTENBAKER, TIMBERLAKE (1951–)

Anglo-French playwright, American born, often associated with the *Royal Court Theatre in *London and director Max *Stafford-Clark. Much of her work, beginning with *New Anatomies* (1981) and *Abel's Sister* (1984), has focused upon history, mythic and documented, and analysed the relationship of language, *gender, and authority. Several of her plays use reflexive, theatrical forms to rework another literary *genre: *The Grace of Mary Traverse* (1985) is the picaresque journey of an eighteenth-century woman from innocence to experience; *The Love of a Nightingale* (1988) retells the Greek myth of Philomel and Procne; and *Our Country's Good*, based on Thomas Keneally's novel *The Playmaker*, traces the experience of mounting a theatrical production by the first convicts in Australia. The transformational experience of theatre is a theme she returns to in *After Darwin* (1998), while *The Break of Day* (1995) was written as a *fin de siècle* response to *Chekhov's *Three Sisters*. *Three Birds Alighting on a Field* (1991) explores the art world as a metaphor for contemporary Britain, while *Credible Witness* (2001) returns to loss and cultural identity. She has translated works by *Sophocles, *Euripides, and *Marivaux, as well as *Mnouchkine's *Mephisto* (1986).   LT

WESKER, ARNOLD (1932–)

British dramatist. Born in east *London (Stepney), the son of Jewish émigrés, Wesker worked in a variety of jobs (including pastry chef, carpenter's mate, and farm labourer) and completed a film course before achieving success with his first play, *Chicken Soup with Barley* (1958). His early works drew on his own experiences for their subject matter, combining autobiography and *naturalist dramatic form with a strong cultural radicalism, making him well suited to the label of 'working-class realist' that was applied to many writers in the late 1950s. Championed by George *Devine and the *English Stage Company, Wesker found a home at the *Royal Court Theatre, forming a strong and creative alliance with the director John *Dexter, and helping to fix the image of the Court as the home of contemporary social *realism. *The Kitchen* (1958) dramatized Wesker's experiences as a chef in a London restaurant, and is one of the few plays in the period to be set in the workplace. The *Trilogy* (comprising *Chicken Soup*, *Roots*, and *I'm Talking about Jerusalem*) was performed in 1960 to critical and popular acclaim. Wesker was also politically and culturally active at this time, was briefly imprisoned for anti-nuclear activities, and was prominent in the activities of Centre 42, an organization that attempted to involve the labour movement in supporting the arts. His work was of a piece, and the intellectual passion and hostility to post-war popular culture that inflamed Beatie Bryant, the protagonist of *Roots*, also informed the arts *festivals he organized with Centre 42. In the 1970s Wesker disowned his earlier radicalism and began experimenting with non-naturalist forms, seen, for example in *The Merchant* (1977, an adaptation of *The Merchant of Venice*), *Caritas* (1981), *Mothers* (1982), and *Annie Wobbler* (1983)—the last two plays being dramatic *monologues. Despite a successful revival of *The Kitchen* in 1994, Wesker was not a significant presence in Britain after 1980 and, like his near contemporary Edward *Bond, has been more popular abroad.   SWL

WEST, MAE (1893–1980)

American actress, singer, and playwright. Born to a corset model and prizefighter in Brooklyn, West would one day remark, 'I used to be Snow White, but I drifted.' Winning amateur contests and *stock roles from the age of 8, she performed in *vaudeville and Broadway *revues from 1911 to 1921. West shocked *New York in 1926 by writing, *producing, and starring in *Sex*, a story of a prostitute that was closed by the police and landed her in jail. Undeterred, *The Drag* (1927) explored male homosexuality and transvestism. The wit and daring of *Diamond Lil* (1928) provided a perfect showcase for her stage personality, while *Pleasure Man* (1928) was also closed by police. After entering *film in 1932, she appeared on stage less frequently: in her 1944 play *Catherine Was Great*, in a revival tour of *Diamond Lil* (1947–51), and in a nightclub act (1954–9) in which she was worshipped by male bodybuilders.   MAF

WEST, TIMOTHY (1934–)

Versatile English actor whose classical stage work contrasts with his screen comedy. He began his career as an assistant *stage manager at Wimbledon (1956) and made his first *London appearance in *Caught Napping* in 1959. He was a member of the *Royal Shakespeare Company (1964–6) and of the *Prospect Theatre (1966–72), where roles included Prospero, Boling-broke, and Lear. He was Shpigelsky in *A Month in the Country* for the RSC (1975), Iago at Nottingham (1976), and Shylock at the *Old Vic (1980). For *Bristol Old Vic he appeared in the title roles of *The Master Builder* (1989) and *Uncle Vanya* (1990) and as James Tyrone in *A Long Day's Journey into Night* (1991). He was Willie Loman for Theatre Clwyd in 1993, Gloucester opposite Ian *Holm in the Royal *National's *King Lear* in 1997, and Falstaff, with his son Sam West as Hal, in the English Touring Theatre's *1 and 2 Henry IV* (1996).   AS

WEST END *See* LONDON.

WHALEY, ANDREW (1958–)

Zimbabwean playwright, director, and actor. Whaley was one of the first white theatre artists who tried to establish multiracial theatre in post-independence Zimbabwe. His plays have won major *awards at the festivals of the National Theatre Organization, and include *Chef's Breakfast*, *The Nyoka Tree*, and *Platform 5*. *The Rise and Shine of Comrade Fiasco* is set in a Zimbabwean prison cell in 1986 and shows four characters, among them an enigmatic former guerrilla fighter, confronted with their country's and their individual histories. First performed in Harare in 1990, it was won the Fringe First *award at the *Edinburgh Festival the same year. Whaley has also worked with the Harare-based Sundown Theatre and with Daves Guzha's Theatre in the Park.   MRo

WHITE, GEORGE (1890–1960)

American *dancer, actor, and *producer. Born George Weitz in *New York, he danced in *music halls for pennies as a child, and started as a song-and-dance man in *burlesque at 14, appearing prominently in the *Ziegfeld Follies* of 1915. He is best known for producing *George White's Scandals*, a series of *revues that ran through thirteen editions from 1919 to 1939. He had a gift for discovering talented showgirls and promising comedians, many of whom went on to stardom. He often contributed his own words and music, staged and performed numbers himself, and popularized such dances as the Charleston, Black Bottom, and Turkey Trot.   CT

WHITE, JANE (1922–)

*African-American actress. She first appeared on Broadway in 1945 in Lillian Smith's *Strange Fruit*, followed by *Dark of the Moon* (1949), *Take a Giant Step* (1953), and *Once upon a Mattress*. In 1956 she had the title role in *Lysistrata*, and during the 1960s she performed in other *Greek and Shakespearian plays in *regional theatres and *Off-Broadway, several of which were directed by Michael Cacoyannis, including *Coriolanus*, *Iphigenia in Aulis*, *King Lear*, and *Troilus and Cressida*. In 1999 she appeared as a teacher in the *film *Beloved*.   BBL

WHITE, PATRICK (1912–90)

Australian novelist and playwright, Nobel laureate, 1973. While best known as a novelist, White's first play, *The Ham Funeral*, was written in 1947. First seen at the Adelaide Festival in 1962, it was followed by *The Season at Sarsaparilla* (1962), *A Cheery Soul* (1963), and *Night on Bald Mountain* (1964). His non-*naturalistic style separated his work from the surge of nationalist playwriting that began in the late 1960s. However, from the late 1970s White forged important creative relationships with a new generation of Australian directors and actors. Jim *Sharman directed revivals of *Season at Sarsaparilla* (1976) and *A Cheery Soul* (1979), the premières of *Big Toys* (1982) and *Netherwood* (1983), and the *film *The Night, the Prowler*. Neil *Armfield directed first productions of *Signal Driver* (1982) and *Shepherd on the Rocks* (1987), and revivals of *Season at Sarsaparilla* (1983) and *The Ham Funeral* (1989).   KMN

WHITEFRIARS THEATRE

A hall *playhouse in *London used through 1607–8 and perhaps later by *boys' companies. The King's Revels Children performed there, with an early *Beaumont and *Fletcher play, *Cupid's Revenge*, and perhaps *Ram-Alley*, a play staged in 1610, when the King's Children may have merged with the former Blackfriars Boys. Two entrepreneurs were imprisoned in 1608 for staging a play at Whitefriars during a ban because of the plague. The theatre's exact location is unknown. The later *Salisbury Court Theatre was sometimes called the Whitefriars because it was built in the same neighbourhood.   AJG

WHITEHALL BANQUETING HOUSE

The principal site for staging court plays in *London in the Christmas season from Elizabeth's time. The Elizabethan structure was built in three weeks in 1582, as a wooden frame covered by canvas, shaped like a Tudor great hall, with a wooden dancing floor for staging Elizabethan *masques. A new brick and stone structure was constructed 1606–9, with a wooden interior with columns carved and painted in the Doric and Ionic modes, and elaborate decorative plasterwork. Again it was made to look like a theatre, although its chief role was to stage the elaborate masques of the Jacobean court. The third Banqueting House in Whitehall still survives. Designed by Inigo *Jones, it was completed in 1622. Its interior a perfect double cube, it is a brilliant example of the Palladian courtly style of the time. When the Rubens ceiling was installed in 1635, King Charles feared damage from candle smoke and banned the production of plays and masques. *See also* COURT THEATRES.   AJG

WHITELAW, BILLIE (1932–)

English actress who is particularly celebrated as a performer of *Beckett's plays, and often was his actress of first choice. Her work in this repertoire began in 1964 with *Play* for the *National Theatre, and continued with *Not I* (*Royal Court, 1973), *Footfalls* (1976), *Happy Days* (1979), and *Rockaby* and *Enough* (1982). She began her career as a child actor on *radio and worked as a *stage manager in provincial theatre. She made her *London debut in 1954 in *Feydeau's *Hotel Paradiso*. She then appeared in the *Theatre Workshop's *Progress to the Park* (1960), the *revue *England, our England* (1962), and *O'Neill's *A Touch of the Poet* (1962). From 1965 she appeared at the *Chichester Festival and the *Old Vic as well as at the *Royal Shakespeare Company where she played Clare in David *Mercer's *After Haggerty* (1971). More recent successes have included Martha in *Who's Afraid of Virginia Woolf?* at the RSC in 1987. Her screen career has been extensive, if never of the first order, including roles in *Lena, Oh my Lena* (1960), *Charlie Bubbles* (1968), *The Dressmaker* (1988), and *Jane Eyre* (1996).   AS

WHITING, JOHN (1917–63)

English playwright. Whiting was a rarity in the pre-1956 British theatre: his plays were cerebral, experimental in form, and challenging in subject matter. Only *A Penny for a Song* (1951, revised 1962) was unreservedly successful. When *Saint's Day* (1951) won a playwriting competition at the *Arts Theatre, *London, the *critics were scandalized by its symbolic textures, *allegorical resonances, and strange clashes of register. *Marching Song* (1954), a meditation on the Nuremberg trials, achieves richness through layering classical allusions. Though in difficulty with critics and *audiences, he had fervent admirers. *Guthrie, *Devine, *Brook, and *Ashcroft wrote in defence of *Saint's Day* and Peter *Hall commissioned *The Devils* for the *Royal Shakespeare Company's first *Aldwych Theatre season in 1961. Loosely based on Aldous Huxley's *The Devils of Loudon* (1952), the play is a thrillingly ragged blending of history and desire that prefigures Howard *Barker. In the uncompromising austerity of his

vision and the flinty poeticisms of his *dialogue, Whiting provided a glimpse of the complex British playwriting that began to unfold around the time of his premature death.
                                    DR

WHITTAKER, HERBERT (1910–)

Canadian theatre *critic. Trained in design, he began reviewing for the *Gazette* in his native *Montréal, and from 1949 to 1975 was lead critic at *Toronto's *Globe and Mail*, 'Canada's national newspaper'. Whittaker's encouragement of new professional ventures was vital to the establishment and growth of Canada's post-war theatre. He also continued as a theatre practitioner: in 1951 he was named best director at the Dominion Drama Festival, and in 1961 designed a celebrated 'Eskimo' *King Lear* for the *touring Canadian Players. Critical collections and memoirs by Whittaker were published in 1985, 1993, and 1999.
                                    DWJ

WIGNELL, THOMAS (1753–1803)

English and American actor and *manager. A member of *Garrick's company in England, Wignell joined his cousin Lewis *Hallam's American Company in 1774. Because theatres closed during the Revolutionary War, his American stage debut was delayed until 1785. A small, stooped man with twinkling blue eyes, he became highly successful as a comic actor. After he played the role of Jonathan in Royall *Tyler's *The Contrast* and financed *publication of the play, Wignell became associated with the stock 'Yankee' character in American plays, but Dunlap described his subtle comic style as more English than American. Disagreements with Hallam led Wignell to break off and form the New American Company in 1792, in partnership with the prominent *Philadelphia musician Alexander Reinagle. Together they built the elegant *Chestnut Street Theatre and assembled a brilliant acting company that initially included Mrs Oldmixon, James *Fennell and Mrs Whitlock, and later included Thomas A. *Cooper, William H. *Warren, and Anne Brunton *Merry. Wignell and Reinagle concentrated on presenting popular classics and became particularly well known for comic *opera, performed with a full orchestra. They expanded to Washington, where they opened the capital's first *playhouse, Baltimore, and Alexandria, Virginia. After Reinagle's death, Warren became co-manager of the company. Wignell married Merry in 1803, but he died less than two months after the marriage. In the almost ten years of his career as a manager, Wignell substantially raised the level of theatrical quality in early America.   AHK

WIGS

Coverings for the head intended to simulate hair, either *realistically or stylistically, and to indicate *character and/or period.

Wigs, beards, and other hairpieces, however crude the fibre or construction, are a cheap and easy way of effecting a transformation. In *medieval religious dramas Christ wore a gilt wig; cross-dressed *heroines in Restoration *comedy removed a male wig to reveal their identity; David *Garrick's trick wig for Hamlet stood on end when the Ghost appeared. Traditional *Chinese and *Japanese performers use ornate, stylized wigs which are particular to the role being played. In Europe professional wig-makers have constructed fashionable, professional, and theatrical wigs since the seventeenth century.   VLC

WIJAYA, PUTU (1944–   )

*Indonesian playwright, director, and actor. A prolific writer and leader of post-1968 theatre, Wijaya is known for mixing Western and traditional Indonesian performance aesthetics and spirituality. Balinese born, he performed with both W. S. *Rendra and Arifin C. *Noer before heading his own theatre company, Teater Mandiri, in *Jakarta in 1972, where he was exclusive playwright and director. Irreverently mixing fantasy and reality, he strives to invoke 'mental terror' in *audiences as an attack against the monotonous rhythms of daily life. His work includes *Aduh* (*Ouch*, 1973), *Edan* (*Crazy*, 1976), *Aum* (*Roar*, 1982), and *Yel* (1991).   CRG

WILBRANDT, ADOLF VON (1837–1911)

German playwright and director who worked at the *Burgtheater in *Vienna in the 1870s and 1880s; he was *artistic director from 1881 to 1888. He maintained the Burgtheater's tradition of performing the classics but added *Raimund, *Gogol, and *Bjørnson to the repertoire. A playwright of considerable renown in his time, he wrote in the tradition of *Schiller for *tragedy and *Freytag for *comedy. *The Master of Palmyra* (1889), written after he had retired from the Burgtheater, is often thought his best work.   CBB

WILDE, OSCAR (1854–1900)

Irish playwright, poet, journalist, and fiction writer. Born in *Dublin, the elder son of the well-known eye-surgeon and antiquarian Sir William Wilde and his poet wife 'Speranza' (Jane Elgee), he was a distinguished student at Trinity College, Dublin, and at Oxford. Influenced by Walter Pater and the aesthetic movement, Wilde first established himself in *London as a public personality, a fame increased by his lecture tour of the United States (1882). Throughout the 1880s Wilde was prominent in London literary circles as a wit, essayist, and prolific journalist. His novel *The Picture of Dorian Gray* (1891), though highly controversial for its supposed decadent immorality, was enormously popular and influential. Wilde had written two unsuccessful plays early in his career, the Russian *historical

drama *Vera; or, The Nihilists*, and the neo-Elizabethan *verse *tragedy *The Duchess of Padua*. But it was not until he turned to society *comedy with *Lady Windermere's Fan* (1892) that he found his mode as a playwright. Produced by the *actor-manager George *Alexander (who had originally commissioned the play) in the fashionable *St James's Theatre, it was hugely successful. *Lady Windermere* drew upon the French nineteenth-century tradition of the 'woman with a past' play going back to *Dumas *fils*'s *La Dame aux camélias*. While staying within this conventional form as adapted for the more puritanical English theatre, Wilde played subversively with its implied ethics. With its subtitle 'a play about a good woman', *Lady Windermere* challenged an *audience to choose between the witty, cynical, but ultimately self-sacrificing Mrs Erlynne, the woman with the past, and her severely moralistic 'good' daughter.

With this social comedy, Wilde established a formula he was to repeat with equal success in his next two plays, *A Woman of No Importance* (1893) and *An Ideal Husband* (1895). In each the sentimental architectonics of the *well-made play were retained, while a Wildean dandy voiced the epigrams that punctured and inverted traditional Victorian morality. In his last comedy *The Importance of Being Earnest* (1895), Wilde gave the play over to the dandies and turned the *plot into *farce. This 'trivial play for serious people', with its deadpan concentration on muffins, cucumber sandwiches, and the need to be named Earnest, joyously *satirized the surfaces of a society without depth or meaning. Much loved and continually revived throughout the English-speaking world, *Earnest* has sometimes been seen as a forerunner of the modern theatre of the *absurd. (*See also* COMEDY OF MANNERS.) Wilde was always prepared to court controversy: his *symbolist drama *Salome*, written in French and translated by his lover Lord Alfred Douglas, was refused a licence by the British censor (*see* CENSORSHIP; LORD CHAMBERLAIN). Produced by *Lugné-Poe at the Théâtre de *l'Œuvre (*Paris, 1896), it was to prove influential in a European tradition of symbolist theatre. A series of trials in 1895 led to Wilde's imprisonment for homosexual offences. While in prison, he wrote his most important poem, 'The Ballad of Reading Gaol', and his passionate apologia *De Profundis*, but he was never able to re-establish his career as a writer, dying in Paris three years after his release.   NG

WILDENBRUCH, ERNST VON (1845–1909)

German playwright. Wildenbruch spent most of his professional career as a diplomat, employed at the Berlin office of foreign affairs. He wrote several popular nationalistic plays with *historical settings, which were performed by the *Meiningen Company. *The Quitzows* (1888), a play about the Hohenzollerns, was his most acclaimed work. He also wrote a trilogy about the Emperor Henry IV (1896) which was a tremendous success at the time.   CBB

WILDER, CLINTON (1920–86)

American *producer. Wilder managed a wide range of commercial productions in both *New York and *London in the 1950s and early 1960s, with such works as Marc *Blitzstein's *opera *Regina* (1949) and Gore Vidal's *Visit to a Small Planet* (1956). With his partner Richard *Barr, Wilder championed the early work of Edward *Albee, and presented Albee's first Broadway play, *Who's Afraid of Virginia Woolf?* (1961). With the profits from that production, Wilder, Barr, and Albee formed the Playwrights Unit to encourage writers and to present their work in the emerging *Off-Off-Broadway scene; among the writers they introduced to American *audiences were Adrienne *Kennedy, Sam *Shepard, Lanford *Wilson, Paul Zindel, Jean-Claude *Van Itallie, and Amiri *Baraka. Wilder was a leader in seeking innovative ways to *finance and make new work possible, helping to create the Theatre Development Fund and otherwise supporting the burgeoning non-profit and *regional theatre movement of the 1960s and 1970s.   AW

WILDER, THORNTON (1897–1975)

American playwright. Sometimes ranked with *O'Neill, *Miller, and *Williams as one of America's best dramatists, Wilder's critical reputation is controversial. Harold Bloom described Wilder as 'the grand exception' to American drama's obsession with domestic *realism and the nightmarish potentialities of family life, and Travis Bogard praised Wilder as America's great comic playwright in the medieval sense: he saw a comic order in the workings of the universe. At the same time, *critics—especially those from the political left—have dismissed Wilder as a sentimentalist (Harold *Clurman), the 'prophet of a genteel Christ' (Michael Gold), and 'a minor writer' who represents 'The Library' (Ernest Hemingway). Born in Madison, Wisconsin, Wilder spent much of his childhood in China, where his father held a series of diplomatic posts. Wilder completed high school in California and attended Oberlin College and Yale University, served in the Coast Guard, and received an MA in French from Princeton University (1926). His play *The Trumpet Shall Sound* (written 1917) was performed by the *American Laboratory Theatre in *New York. *The Bridge of San Luis Rey* (1927) became a best-selling novel and won the Pulitzer Prize. A collection of experimental short plays, *The Angel That Troubled the Waters*, was published in 1928 and a group of theatrically challenging but stageable short works, *The Long Christmas Dinner and Other Plays*, in 1931. Wilder's theatrical reputation was secured when *Our Town* (1938) ran for more than a year and won the Pulitzer Prize. Now regarded by many as a classic, the play employs virtually no *scenery and uses the *Stage Manager as a narrator who introduces and controls the *action in a simple telling of daily life, love, marriage, and death in a small New Eng-

land town. *The Merchant of Yonkers* (1938) was Wilder's first treatment of a Johann *Nestroy *comedy that was better received in *The Matchmaker* (1954) and wildly successful when adapted by Michael Stewart and composer/lyricist Jerry Herman as the *musical *Hello, Dolly!* (1964). Wilder's *The Skin of our Teeth* (1942, Pulitzer Prize) has entered the American repertory, beginning with a long-running Broadway production directed by Elia *Kazan and starring Tallulah *Bankhead as a temptress and Fredric *March and Florence Eldridge as a long-suffering couple who represent the human race's perseverance across millennia. Wilder's later plays, such as *The Alcestiad* (1955) and *Plays from Bleecker Street* (1962), received respectful reviews but have been rarely revived.

                                                                                MAF

WILDGRUBER, ULRICH (1937–99)

German actor. After training at the Max-Reinhardt Seminar in *Vienna, Wildgruber performed at various theatres throughout the 1960s. His breakthrough came in 1976 in Peter *Zadek's legendary production of *Othello* in Hamburg, performing the title role as a mixture of King Kong and *clown coated in black *make-up. This led to an intense collaboraton between the two artists. He also performed in *films and *television. Wildgruber was a controversial actor, celebrated as a talented extrovert and often criticized for the same quality. He took his own life.

                                                                                CBB

WILD WEST SHOWS

Late nineteenth-century phenomenon that attempted to re-create the American west with displays of riding and shooting and the dramatization of famous frontier incidents. Although P. T. *Barnum and others had previously staged demonstrations of frontier life, Buffalo Bill *Cody assembled a huge company in an outdoor arena in 1883, and over the next few years his show gained enormous popularity. It featured prominent frontier personages, including Sioux Chief Sitting Bull, dramatizations of frontier incidents, such as Custer's Last Stand, and exhibitions of shooting and riding by performers like Annie *Oakley. Cody's Wild West became such a success in the United States and Europe that it spawned over a 100 imitators. His one-time partner William F. Carver launched his own Wild America company. Gordon W. 'Pawnee Bill' Lillie proved an able Wild West *manager, and his show eventually merged with Cody's. Other influential Wild West companies included the Miller Brothers' 101 Ranch Real Wild West, which developed from the huge Oklahoma ranch of George W. Miller, and Col. Zach Mulhall's Wild West, which starred Will *Rogers, who began as an expert roper before moving on to political commentary. The Wild West shows were a short-lived phenomenon, as the First World War and the Great Depression brought an end to most of the frontier enterprises.   RAH

WILKINSON, NORMAN (1882–1934)

English designer and artist. Trained in art, Wilkinson began as a *costume designer for the Charles *Frohman *repertory season in 1910 at the *Duke of York's Theatre in *London. Granville *Barker tapped him as scene designer for *The Winter's Tale* (1912) and for *scenery and costumes for *Twelfth Night* (1912) and *A Midsummer Night's Dream* (1914). These beautiful, symbolic designs have become classics of *modernist Shakespeare, especially the decorated *curtains and the colourful, eclectic costumes. Of special note were the gilded fairies in *Dream* and the geometric set and costumes for *Twelfth Night*. In the 1920s Wilkinson worked for Nigel *Playfair at the *Lyric Theatre Hammersmith, where he continued to work in a non-*realist, impressionist mode. He also worked for the Phoenix Society. In 1932 he redesigned *Dream* for the *Shakespeare Memorial Theatre at Stratford-upon-Avon.   TP

WILKINSON, TATE (1739–1803)

English actor and *manager. A highly skilled mimic, Wilkinson was sacked from John *Rich's company because of his indiscreet imitations on stage of Peg *Woffington. Lacking sensitivity—and possessing an overblown ego—he further irritated *Garrick by a similar performance. Fleeing north, he took joint ownership in 1763 of the York theatre (a *theatre royal from 1769; his house still adjoins this venue), and seven years later became sole manager of the York circuit, which included Leeds, Pontefract, Wakefield, Doncaster, and Hull. Wilkinson brought a full company to these *playhouses, and gave many successful actors and actresses their first roles, including J. P. *Kemble and Sarah *Siddons. His blustering account, *The Wandering Patentee* (1795), gives valuable insight into provincial management in the eighteenth century.   AF

WILKS, ROBERT (c.1665–1732)

Irish actor and *manager, one of the most important actors of the early eighteenth century and a member of the famous triumvirate (along with Colley *Cibber and Barton *Booth) that ruled *Drury Lane from 1718 to 1732. He began acting in *Dublin in 1691 and may have acted in *London as early as 1693. He had an amazing memory and soon mastered a vast array of parts, many of them principal ones, such as Plume in *Farquhar's *The Recruiting Officer*, Sir Harry Wildair in Farquhar's *The Constant Couple*, and Sir Charles Easy in Cibber's *The Careless Husband*. In *comedy he excelled in genteel roles, in *tragedy pathetic ones.   MJK

WILLIAMS, BERT (1876–1922)

*African-American performer. In the 1890s Williams formed a partnership with George Walker and for over ten years they produced and starred in popular shows including *In Dahomey*, *Abyssinia*, *Sons of Ham*, and *Bandana Land*. Williams and Walker productions were a *training ground for many early African-American performers, such as Charles *Gilpin, Florence *Mills, and Ada Overton Walker. Williams forged an important connection between black *musical comedy and the mainstream stage when he joined the *Ziegfeld Follies* in 1910, singing his signature tune 'Nobody', and submerging his eloquence under the veneer of the *clown, the man who was and had nothing.   BBL

WILLIAMS, CLIFFORD (1926–)

Prolific Welsh director, particularly associated with the *Royal Shakespeare Company, where he was associate director from 1963 to 1991. His career has been significantly international and has encompassed a distinguished record of *opera and *musical theatre. He began as an actor in *London and in *regional repertory (1945–8), was the founder and director of the Mime Theatre Company (1950–3), and director of the Marlowe Theatre, Canterbury (1955–6). As director at the *Arts Theatre his work included *García Lorca's *Yerma* (1957) and *O'Neill's *Moon for the Misbegotten* (1960). In 1963 he mounted Rolf *Hochhuth's *The Representative* for the RSC at the *Aldwych, opening one day after the première in Basel. Perhaps his most influential Shakespeare production was a voguish all-male version of *As You Like It* (1967) for the *National Theatre, where he also directed *Shaw's *Back to Methuselah* (1969). Popular hits from this time include Anthony Shaffer's *Sleuth* (1970) and *Tynan's *Oh! Calcutta!* in both London and *Paris (1970). In 1975 he directed Shaw's *Too True to Be Good* at the Aldwych with Ian *McKellen and Judi *Dench. Following the Broadway revival of Frederick *Lonsdale's *Aren't We All?*, in 1986 he directed Derek *Jacobi in *Breaking the Code* for the West End and Broadway. His musical work has included *The Flying Dutchman* (London, 1966), *Dido and Aeneas* (Windsor Festival, 1969), *The Rise and Fall of the City of Mahagonny* (Aalborg, 1984), and *Bellman's Opera* (*Stockholm, 1990; London, 1992). In 1996 he mounted *Strindberg's *The Father* for the Roundabout Theatre in *New York.   AS

WILLIAMS, EMLYN (1905–87)

Welsh playwright, actor, and *monologuist. Williams ran parallel careers as playwright and actor, scoring an early success opposite Charles *Laughton in Edgar Wallace's *On the Spot* (1930). His plays are characterized by his lyrical Welsh-speaker's English, *well-made construction, and a lifelong preoccupation with criminal psychology, most successfully expressed in *Night Must*

Fall (1935). Centring on a young murderer who carries his victim's head in a hat-box and exerts a sexual attraction on the young woman who discovers his secret, the play has been frequently revived, usually as a star vehicle for handsome Welshmen like Hywel Bennett, Richard *Burton, and the author himself. Williams also played the lead role in his *The Corn Is Green* (1938), a sentimentalized retelling of his own story as the working-class boy led to an Oxford scholarship by a formidable schoolmistress. Its Welsh village location reappeared in *The Druid's Rest* (1944), a witty self-*parody in which a mysterious stranger, this time an Englishman in Wales, arrives carrying a hat-box (it turns out to be full of books), and in *The Wind of Heaven* (1945), which skilfully locates the Second Coming in the Victorian valleys. Like many playwrights of his generation, Williams was wrong-footed by the *Royal Court revolution, and he wrote only two original plays after 1950, concentrating on prose, including two excellent volumes of autobiography. He also toured *one-person shows based on the writings of Charles *Dickens (1951), Dylan Thomas (1955), and H. H. Munro or 'Saki' (1977).   CDC

WILLIAMS, HARCOURT (1880–1957)

English actor and director. Williams joined Frank *Benson's company in 1898, remaining for five years. In 1903 he *toured with Ellen *Terry, and in 1906–7 toured America with H. B. Irving (Henry *Irving's son). Upon returning to *London, he played Valentine in a revival of *Shaw's *You Never Can Tell*, and from 1908 to 1916, when he joined the war effort, appeared in three more plays by Shaw and acted in Shakespeare, *Ibsen, and Granville *Barker. After the war he returned to *acting, but he also began to *direct. Influenced by Barker, he directed innovative productions of Shakespeare at the *Old Vic, where he served as director from 1929 to 1933, and also staged Shaw. He later wrote a memoir about his experiences, *The Old Vic Saga* (1949). Much of the rest of his career was dedicated to acting in Shakespeare; he also performed in Barker, *Chekhov, *Pinero, *Ibsen, and Shaw.   TP

WILLIAMS, TENNESSEE (THOMAS LANIER WILLIAMS) (1911–83)

American playwright. Born to a minister's daughter and travelling salesman in Columbus, Mississippi, Williams would mine his southern upbringing, the sufferings of his fragile sister, and later experiences of world travel and sexual exploration to write some 60 plays, two novels, eight volumes of short stories, three volumes of poetry, and a memoir sensational in its degree of self-revelation. The depth and quality of his dramatic canon have secured him a supreme stature in American theatre, rivalled only by *O'Neill and *Miller. From the beginning, Wil-

liams was unapologetic about the autobiographical sources of his writing. After winning a *Group Theatre contest with some short plays in 1939, Williams vowed to write 'a picture of my own heart . . . a passionate denial of *sham* and a cry for beauty'. Williams's childhood formation in an Episcopalian rectory (the home of his maternal grandparents) coupled with his growing awareness of his homosexual inclinations (a forbidden orientation in that place and time) seems to have instilled in him an Augustinian fascination with the human split between spirit and body, transcendent desires and animal instincts coexistent in one organism. Prevented by social strictures from writing openly about homosexual *characters throughout most of his career, Williams transfigured his experiences into those of female characters who, in some of the outstanding plays of the twentieth century—*A Streetcar Named Desire* (1947, Pulitzer Prize), *Summer and Smoke* (1948), *The Night of the Iguana* (1961)—suffer the conflicting urges for spiritual transcendence and sexual desire for absolute masculinity, represented through a series of sleek, muscular, self-assured male figures. In some plays, like *Battle of Angels* (1940, revised as *Orpheus Descending*, 1957) and *Sweet Bird of Youth* (1959), an older female is the sexual aggressor and the younger man a stud-for-hire who by story's end is horribly punished by the community for the danger he represents. In other plays, the desirable man is unavailable to the woman due to probable homosexuality (*Cat on a Hot Tin Roof*, 1955, Pulitzer Prize; *Suddenly Last Summer*, 1958; *Period of Adjustment*, 1960), or a surpassing spirituality that has moved the male toward chastity (*The Milk Train Doesn't Stop Here Anymore*, 1962). In rare works, such as *The Rose Tattoo* (1951), the frustrated woman and lusty male accommodate one another and the play ends happily.

Another category of Williams play centres on the struggle of a sensitive artist to cope with life and create art from experience. Such a play began Williams's fame in *The Glass Menagerie* (1945) and he returned to the theme obsessively in later works such as *The Two-Character Play* (1967, later as *Out Cry*, 1973) or *Vieux Carré* (1977). A few plays describe the artist's struggle through biography, such as *I Rise in Flame Cried the Phoenix: a play about D. H. *Lawrence* (1959) or *Clothes for a Summer Hotel* (1980) about Scott and Zelda Fitzgerald. Beginning around 1960, Williams entered what he called his 'Stoned Age', a period of some fifteen years during which he was a heavy user of alcohol, amphetamines, and barbiturates. Despite these dependencies, Williams maintained a strict working schedule (stimulated by strong coffee and amphetamines), but the quality of the work was denigrated by *critics and did not attract large *audiences. Following the death of his long-time companion Frank Merlo from lung cancer in 1963, Williams suffered a series of psychological and physical breakdowns and hospitalizations. By the time of his *Memoirs* (1975), he claimed to have his addictions under control; but his 1983 death due to choking on the cap of a pill bottle cast doubt upon this claim.

Williams was associated with some of the outstanding productions of twentieth-century American theatre. His emergence in post-war *New York coincided perfectly with the careers of designers such as Jo *Mielziner, directors such as Elia *Kazan and José *Quintero, and the flourishing of the *Method among a generation of American *actors expertly equipped to enact the poetic *realism of his psychologically complex stage creations. That said, Williams's breakthrough production—*The Glass Menagerie*, directed by Eddie Dowling in 1945—reflected a previous generation. Laurette *Taylor, the coquettish star of the 1910s, gave a legendary comeback performance as Amanda Wingfield, but Eddie Dowling at 56 was far too old for the autobiographical *character, Tom Wingfield. Kazan's 1947 direction of *A Streetcar Named Desire*, the multi-layered Mielziner set, and the Method performances of Marlon *Brando as Stanley Kowalski and Kim Hunter as Stella combined with Williams's *text to form a unity so satisfying as to define a new American style. Much of that magic was captured in Kazan's screen version (1951), which added the fascination of British actress Vivien *Leigh as the tormented Blanche Dubois. Kazan's productions of *Cat on a Hot Tin Roof* and *Sweet Bird of Youth*, and Paul Newman's performances as the sexually charged young men who animated them, were archetypal creations of the realistic theatre of the 1950s. Though *Summer and Smoke* was unsuccessful in its original Broadway staging, Quintero's *arena-style revival at *Circle in the Square in 1952 was a landmark in its proof of the value of intimate staging in the burgeoning *Off-Broadway movement. In 1998, a previously unknown Williams play—the prison drama *Not about Nightingales* (1938)—was directed by Trevor *Nunn in an acclaimed production by the Royal *National Theatre in *London and the *Alley Theatre in Houston.   MAF

DEVLIN, ALBERT J. (ed.), *Conversations with Tennessee Williams* (Jackson, Miss., 1986)

LEVERICH, LYLE, *Tom: the unknown Tennessee Williams* (New York, 1995)

MURPHY, BRENDA, *Tennessee Williams and Elia Kazan: a collaboration in the theatre* (Cambridge, 1992)

WILLIAMSON, DAVID (1942–)

Australia's most popular and successful playwright, Williamson has an international profile and many of his plays have become *films. After study at Monash and Melbourne universities, he established his reputation as a witty satirist dissecting the dilemmas and pretensions of the middle classes in a distinctive Australian vernacular, with plays such as *The Removalists* and *Don's Party* (both 1971). Primarily a *realist writer, Williamson's observations of Australian manners and mores, coupled with incisive social criticism delivered in a comic but confrontational style, saw him rapidly graduate from *alternative to mainstream theatre, writing full time from 1972. In plays such as *A Handful*

of Friends (1976), *Travelling North* (1979), *The Perfectionist* (1982), *Emerald City* (1987), *Money and Friends* (1991), *Dead White Males* (1995), and *The Great Man and Sanctuary* (2000), Williamson has charted the evolution of Australia's baby-boomer sensitivies to great commercial and critical acclaim. He regularly engaged in high-profile disputes with his *critics in the newspapers and remains Australia's most prominent playwright.   SBS

WILLIAMSON, J. C. (JAMES CASSIUS) (1844–1913)

American *actor-manager. After an apprenticeship in provincial theatre, Williamson joined Lester *Wallack's *New York company in 1863, remaining until 1871. Williamson then moved to *San Francisco, where he produced *Struck Oil* as a vehicle for himself and his first wife Maggie Moore (1851–1926). The Williamsons were engaged by George Coppin for a highly successful Australian *tour of *Struck Oil* in 1874, and the next year toured *India, Britain, and the USA. They returned to Australia in 1879 after which Williamson became a major theatrical *manager. His policy was based on importing lavish British and American productions to Australia, with little reference to local conditions. He also acquired the Australasian performing rights to all *Gilbert and *Sullivan works. J. C. Williamson Ltd., established in 1911 and known as 'the Firm', dominated Australian commercial theatre, particularly in the presentation of *musicals, until its demise in 1976.   KMN

WILLIAMSON, NICOLL (1938–)

Scottish actor who began at Dundee Rep in 1960 before joining the *Royal Court and appearing in *That's Us* and *Arden of Faversham* (both 1961). At the *Royal Shakespeare Company he appeared in Henry *Livings's *Nil Carborundum* and *Gorky's *The Lower Depths* (both 1962). In 1964 the role of Maitland in John *Osborne's *Inadmissible Evidence* won him the Evening Standard best actor *award, and the New York Drama Critics award for the Broadway version. Through the 1960s he appeared as Vladimir in *Waiting for Godot* (1964), Sweeney in *Sweeney Agonistes* (1965), and Poprichtchine in *Diary of a Madman* (1967). In 1969 his performance as *Hamlet* as a rasping antihero (*see* HERO AND ANTIHERO) divided *audiences and critics. At the same time his reputation as self-destructive, self-critical, mad, bad, and dangerous to know saw his stage career falter. An eclectic catalogue of *film roles includes Gunner O'Rourke in *The Bofors Gun* (1968), based on John *McGrath's play *Events While Guarding the Bofors Gun* (1966)—McGrath recording that the self-destructive sociopath O'Rourke was written 'for and in some minute manner about Nick'—Merlin in *Excalibur* (1981), and Badger in *The Wind in the Willows* (1996).   AS

WILLIAMSTOWN THEATRE FESTIVAL

American repertory theatre. The festival was conceived in 1955 as a way of boosting summer tourism to the Berkshire Mountains of western Massachusetts. Nikos Psacharopoulos became *artistic director the next year, and its resident company came to include Mildred *Dunnock and E. G. Marshall. Under Psacharopoulos the festival grew in ambition and stature during the 1960s and early 1970s, staging, for example, a legendary production of *Chekhov's *The Seagull* and sprouting supplementary and experimental creative venues. Psacharopoulos's 33 years, which ended with his death in 1989, established the festival as a flagship American summer *regional theatre for production and theatre apprenticeship, while retaining an informal, holiday ambiance. Williamstown's proximity to *New York has drawn a steady stream of leading American directors and headline performers from stage and screen. The festival has produced a number of American and world premières by established playwrights.   EW

WILLS, W. G. (1828–91)

Irish playwright and painter. Wills was a man of eccentric habits and bohemian lifestyle. He wrote 40 plays, mostly *romantic dramas. His first successful piece, *Olivia* (1878), at the *Royal Court in *London, a version of *Goldsmith's novel *The Vicar of Wakefield*, gave Ellen *Terry a great hit. A religious drama, *Claudian* (1884), had a good run for Wilson *Barrett at the *Princess's. Wills wrote several poetic dramas for *Irving, notably *Charles the First* (1872) and *Faust* (1885), which Irving performed 792 times at the *Lyceum, in the provinces, and in America—his greatest managerial success.   MRB

WILSON, AUGUST (1945–)

American playwright. Though born Frederick August Kittel in Pittsburgh, to Daisy Wilson, daughter of North Carolina sharecroppers, and Frederick Kittel, a German immigrant, he changed his name to confirm his *African-American heritage. A precocious reader, he left school at 15 when a teacher refused to believe him capable of an essay he submitted. His education thereafter was in the public library and on the streets of the Hill District, the bustling black community where seven of his eight major plays are set. He discovered the history and power of black culture through the blues: 'I got Bessie Smith one day and Malcolm X the next, and I was ready,' he said. In 1978 he moved to St Paul, Minnesota, and in that northern city of Scandinavian immigrants (like Seattle, where he moved in 1990) he found the distance to write about Pittsburgh. The first play in his authentic voice was *Jitney* (1979), using a gypsy cab office as the setting for a torrent of aspiration, conflict, and often comic storytelling. His breakthrough came in 1982 when the *Eugene O' Neill Theatre Center accepted *Ma Rainey's Black Bottom* for development. That began his collaboration with famed black director Lloyd *Richards, who helped shape his first six plays. *Ma Rainey* went quickly to Broadway (1984), where it won the first of Wilson's unprecedented seven consecutive New York Critics Circle *awards for best new American play.

From the start Wilson planned to set a play about black life in each decade of the twentieth century; as of 2002, he had just two to go, having completed *Ma Rainey*, *Fences* (1985), *Joe Turner's Come and Gone* (1986), *The Piano Lesson* (1989), *Two Trains Running* (1990), *Seven Guitars* (1995), *Jitney* (revised, 1996) and *King Hedley II* (1999). These dates are first professional stagings, usually following initial workshops at the O'Neill Center. After changes at several *regional theatres, each *text achieved its final version when mounted on Broadway. There, only *Fences* and *Piano Lesson*, both Pulitzer Prize-winners, proved immediately profitable, but all went on to be widely staged by the non-profit regional companies. In the process Wilson pioneered a path for serious drama free of Broadway's commercial tyranny. He has provided a showcase for an unexpected wealth of black *acting talent, and in controversial public pronouncements, such as his 1997 debate with *critic Robert *Brustein, he has become a vigorous spokesman for a black theatre characteristically either marginalized or co-opted by the establishment.

Wilson is no structural innovator, but his fluent, allusive, and poetic vernacular rises to incantatory lyricism, as in the messianic vision in *Joe Turner* of the carnage of the Atlantic slavers. A frequent theme is the search for the individual 'song', the true self that reweaves a culture ravaged by *diaspora and oppression. He finds spiritual resource in historic imagination, such as the ghost at the climax of *Piano Lesson* or the 366-year-old prophet Aunt Esther, born the year African slaves were first forced to Virginia. Sometimes ribald, he can rise to bleak *tragedy. His rank is with Eugene *O'Neill and Tennessee *Williams as a quintessential American voice.   CR

WILSON, LANFORD (1937–)

American dramatist. His more than 45 plays have won important *awards and have been widely produced. Raised in Missouri, Wilson's first work was seen *Off-Off-Broadway at *Caffe Cino and *La Mama; early plays included *The Madness of Lady Bright* (1964), *Balm in Gilead* and *Ludlow Fair* (1965), and *The Rimers of Eldritch* (1966). He co-founded the *Circle Repertory Theatre and served as resident playwright. Starting in 1970 most of his plays opened there, usually directed by Marshall *Mason and designed by John Lee *Beatty, and the team continued after the theatre's demise in 1996. *The Hot l Baltimore* (1973) was highly successful and later became a *television series. *The Fifth of July* (1978), with William *Hurt as Ken Talley, startled *audiences with Wilson's caustic picture of post-

Einstein on the Beach, music by Philip Glass, text by Robert **Wilson**, Metropolitan Opera, New York, 1976, directed and designed by Wilson. In this four-hour dreamlike work, lacking plot and consistent character, the repetition of musical phrases and visual imagery worked to deny narrative expectations, to slow time, and to encourage the audience to approach the action in a non-rational manner.

Vietnam disillusion. *Talley's Folly* (1979), starring Judd *Hirsch, and *A Tale Told* (1981), revised as *Talley and Son* (1985), completed the Talley family trilogy. In *Burn This* (1987) a relationship erupts between two people who should stay apart. *Redwood Curtain* (1993), a failure on Broadway despite the play's lyricism and Beatty's magical *scenery, has nonetheless seen several revivals, while *Sympathetic Magic* (1997) won the Obie for best play. One of the first openly *gay playwrights to depict gay relationships as part of ordinary life, Wilson shows sympathy to a variety of outcasts. He has also written for television and *film, and translated *Chekhov's *Three Sisters*.

FL

WILSON, ROBERT (fl.1572–1600)

English actor and playwright. Noted for his 'extemporal wit' with *Leicester's company and the *Queen's Men from 1572 through 1588, Wilson probably ceased acting in the early 1590s and concentrated on playwriting. Between 1598 and 1600 he collaborated in the writing of fourteen plays for the *Admiral's Men. His extant plays—*The Three Ladies of London* (c.1581), *The Three Lords and the Three Ladies of London* (c.1589), and *The Cobbler's Prophecy* (c.1594)—owe a debt to the older moral *interlude in their emphasis on public ethics and the health of the body politic. RWV

WILSON, ROBERT (1941–)

American director, designer, playwright, performer, and visual artist, one of the most influential and controversial of theatre artists. He was born in Waco, Texas, and dropped out of a business administration course at the University of Texas in 1962 to move to *New York and pursue the arts. He received a degree in interior design from the Pratt Institute in 1966, became interested in the works of pioneering choreographers Merce *Cunningham, George *Balanchine, and Martha *Graham (*see* DANCE), and in 1968 set up an experimental theatre company, the Byrd Hoffman School of Byrds, in downtown Manhattan. His first major productions were *The King of Spain* and *The Life and Times of Sigmund Freud* (both 1969). His works were praised and decried for their novel approach to the notion of the theatre event: *dreamlike and indebted to *symbolism, they often took many hours to unfold, seemingly in slow motion, and seldom featured conventionally defined *plot, *characters, or *dialogue.

In the early 1970s Wilson worked closely with a deaf-mute boy, Raymond Andrews, whom he had adopted, and in 1971 the 'silent opera' he created with Andrews, *Deafman Glance*, became an international sensation. Some of Wilson's major pieces in the 1970s included *KA MOUNTain and GUARDenia Terrace*, in Shiraz, Iran (1972), and *A Letter to Queen Victoria* in Europe and America (1974–5). This period exhibited a new interest in the deconstruction of language, prompted by a writing and performing collaboration with an autistic young man, Christopher Knowles. Wilson's now legendary collaboration with composer Philip *Glass, *Einstein on the Beach*, premièred in France in 1976 and was also presented at the *Metropolitan Opera that year. Wilson's career flourished in Europe in the next decades, when he created original works such as *Death, Destruction, and Detroit* at *Berlin's *Schaubühne (1979) and *The Black Rider* (with Tom Waits) at the Thalia Theater in Hamburg (1991). Wilson's most ambitious project remains unrealized: *the CIVIL warS: a tree is best measured when it is down*. This *opera was planned as a collaboration with many international artists and was to première in its entirety at the Olympic Arts Festival in *Los Angeles in 1984, but organizational concerns, *finance, and internal politics prevented its completion. Several sections of the production, including its 'Knee Plays' (vignettes which fit between the major sections of action, with music by David Byrne), were produced in international locations.

Wilson has directed for many international opera companies including La *Scala, the Metropolitan, Houston Grand Opera, and the Zurich Opera. He has also collaborated with a number of acclaimed rock composers and *avant-garde artists, including playwright Heiner *Müller (*Hamletmachine*, 1986), dancer Lucinda Childs (*Einstein on the Beach* and others), *performance artist Laurie *Anderson (*Alcestis*, 1986), writer Susan Sontag (*Alice in Bed*, 1993), and musician Lou Reed (*Time Rocker*, 1996; *POE-try*, 2000). In 1995 he took to the stage himself in a solo adaptation of *Hamlet*, which opened in Texas and *toured around the world. His second collaboration with Waits, an adaptation of *Büchner's *Woyzeck*, premièred in Copenhagen in 2001. Wilson is the recipient of numerous international honours, and his designs and drawings are often exhibited. In the summers he develops his work at the Watermill Centre for the Arts in New York.   KF

WILTON, MARIE (1839–1919)

English actress and *manager. She began her career in the provinces and became a star in *burlesque in the 1850s at the Strand Theatre in *London. Lively and petite, she was also cast in saucy boys' parts, being much admired by *Dickens in H. J. *Byron's *The Maid and the Magpie* (1858). Tiring of typecasting, she borrowed £1,000 in 1865 and leased the run-down Queen's Theatre in Tottenham Street, known locally as the 'Dusthole', renaming it the *Prince of Wales's. Deliberately excluding the ginger-beer drinking, orange-eating *melodrama *audience, she renovated the theatre, put white lace antimacassars on the *stalls seats, flowers in the *auditorium, carpets in the aisles, raised the seat prices, and successfully set out to attract the carriage trade. A small theatre by London standards, seating only 814, the now elegant Prince of Wales's was thought to resemble a comfortable, well-appointed drawing room. Drawing-room plays, therefore, replaced the burlesques of Byron, who withdrew from the co-management in 1867. This largely meant the *comedies of Tom *Robertson, in which Wilton played his sunnier and more spirited *heroines, like Mary Netley in *Ours* (1866), Polly Eccles in *Caste* (1867), and Naomi Tighe in *School* (1869). After her marriage to Squire *Bancroft in 1867, she took a back seat in the management, but all the good work had been done. So lucrative were the Robertson comedies that the Bancrofts were able to retire in 1885, after five years at the *Haymarket.   MRB

WING AND GROOVE *See* SCENE SHIFTING.

WINGE, STEIN (1940–   )

Norwegian director. Winge's father was a well-known *expressionist artist who designed the *scenery for his son's first major production, an experimental *Antigone* in 1970. Shortly thereafter Winge became a director at the National Theatre in Oslo, where he astonished *audiences throughout Norway with unconventional stagings of *Ibsen, *Strindberg, *Brecht, *Verdi, and *Mozart. His reputation for controversial work grew after 1979, when he became director of the National Theatre's experimental space, Torshov, especially with his 'poor theatre' *Shakespeare Project* (1983–4). His international career began with an irreverent *Three Sisters* at the *Los Angeles Theatre Center in 1985, where he returned annually during the rest of the decade. In 1990 he was named director of the Norwegian National Theatre and inaugurated an annual international Ibsen Festival. In the 1990s he was acknowledged as one of Europe's leading experimental directors of both drama and *opera, outraging some spectators but dazzling others by his unconventional *casting, his visual and narrative originality, and his imaginative use of crowds.   MC

WINTER, WILLIAM (1836–1917)

American critic who reviewed for the *New York Tribune* from 1865 until 1908, and was widely regarded as the doyen of American drama critics by the 1890s. A prolific writer, he published more than 50 volumes of work, encompassing *criticism, biography, travelogues, poetry, and reminiscences. His background in theatre *theory and history and his wide reading in several languages were major factors in his success. He formed close personal friendships with many actors, most notably Edwin *Booth, and was most important for his critical emphasis on performance: he regarded the *actor as the central element in theatre art. Winter's traditional approach became increasingly outdated as the new *realistic drama, and the performance style it demanded, appeared. He railed against the work of *Ibsen, *Shaw, *Pinero, and *Maeterlinck, and was eventually forced to resign his post at the *Tribune* in 1908, though he continued to publish widely in periodicals until his death.   AW

WINTER GARDEN

*New York theatre at 50th Street and Broadway. Designed to suggest an English garden, it opened with a *revue, *La Belle Paree* (1911), starring Al *Jolson, who was long associated with the venue. A 1912 show, *The Whirl of Society*, featured a bridgeway that ran down the centre of the orchestra, something like a *Japanese *hanamichi*, which allowed stars, especially Jolson and scantily dressed showgirls, to get much closer to the *audience. Editions of *The Passing Show*, a *Shubert-produced revue, were its chief occupants from 1912 to 1924, with the era's greatest musical performers. The theatre's present appearance dates from its redesign in the 1920s, when it also received its first marquee. Live shows were abandoned for *films from 1928 to 1933. After reverting to theatrical performance, it presented a series of outstanding revues. Films returned in 1945, but revues, *musicals, and the occasional play were back in 1948. It subsequently housed such landmark shows as *West Side Story* (1958), *Funny Girl* (1964), *Mame* (1966), *Follies* (1971), *Pacific Overtures* (1976), *42nd Street* (1980), and *Cats* (1982).   SLL

WISE, ERNIE *See* MORECAMBE, ERIC.

WITKIEWICZ, STANISŁAW IGNACY (1885–1939)

Polish playwright, novelist, painter, and philosopher, known as Witkacy. Educated at home by his father to be an artist, Witkacy went to Australia in 1914 with Malinowski and later served in the tsarist army, witnessing the 1917 Revolution. Returning to Poland, he worked as a formist painter while earning his living as a portraitist. Between 1918 and 1926 he wrote over 30 plays—mostly unpublished and unperformed—that illustrate his *theory 'Pure Form in the Theatre' (1920), an anti-*realist doctrine that sought to liberate drama from storytelling and psychology and make it an autonomous formal construction

akin to modern painting and music. Characterized by grotesque humour, drug-induced *dream logic, hyper-vivid colours, and spectacular stage effects, his plays are both social and existential, portraying the growing mechanization of life and loss of the metaphysical feeling of the strangeness of existence. They include *They* (1920), *Water Hen* (1921), *Crazy Locomotive* (1923), *Madman and the Nun*, *Mother* (both 1924), *Beelzebub Sonata* (1925), and *Shoemakers* (1934).

Witkacy's flamboyant life, uncompromising individualism, and desperate suicide made him a hero to post-war intelligentsia, who used his works to battle Russian-imposed *socialist realism. Following *Kantor's revival of *The Cuttlefish* in 1956, premières of Witkacy's plays became major events of modern Polish theatre, his works gradually assimilated into popular culture, *cabaret performance, and rock *musicals. Now recognized as Poland's leading playwright-theorist of the twentieth century, Witkacy's self-referential *parody of *modernism, pastiche of different styles, blending of theory and practice, and mixture of high and low *genres also make him postmodern.   DG

WODEHOUSE, P. G. (PELHAM GRENVILLE) (1881–1975)

English humorist and lyricist. Although chiefly remembered for his Bertie Wooster stories, Wodehouse was a prolific lyricist for *musicals between the wars. He collaborated with librettist Guy *Bolton and composer Jerome *Kern on the Princess Theatre shows in *New York, notable for reorienting musical theatre towards an American idiom. Their work together includes *Have a Heart* (1917), *Oh, Boy!* (1917), *Leave It to Jane* (1917), and *Oh, Lady! Lady!* (1918). Wodehouse also contributed the words to the song 'Bill' in Kern's *Show Boat* (1927). His other musical collaborations with Bolton include *Oh, Kay!* (1926) with the *Gershwins and *Anything Goes* (1934) with Cole *Porter. Wodehouse also contributed lyrics to musicals by Irving *Berlin and Ivor Novello. Comparatively less successful were his straight plays, including *A Damsel in Distress* (1928), *The Play's the Thing* (1926), an adaptation from *Molnár, and *Leave It to Psmith* (1930).   MDG

WOFFINGTON, PEG (c.1720–60)

Irish actress, of uncertain origins: her childhood was indigent but many unsustainable myths surround her *training for the stage in *Dublin. Factual evidence dates her earliest appearances with Madame Violante's Lilliputians from 1731, and later as a dancer at the Aungier Street Theatre in 1735, where she appeared at random intervals in roles that included Ophelia. *London *audiences first saw her in the *breeches role of Silvia in *Farquhar's *The Recruiting Officer* in 1740 at *Covent Garden, but she moved to *Drury Lane the next year and remained for seven seasons, notably playing Cordelia to *Garrick's Lear (1742). Their relationship flourished during a shared *tour to Dublin that summer. She returned to Covent Garden in 1748 after breaking with Garrick (now managing Drury Lane), but was enticed by Thomas Sheridan to join him at the *Smock Alley Theatre in Dublin (1751–4). When she rejoined Thomas Rich's Covent Garden company in 1754, it was at a salary of £800 a year, making Woffington one of the highest-paid actresses of her day. Three years later she collapsed with a stroke while performing the *epilogue to *As You Like It*, retired to her home in Teddington, and died in London. During her short career Woffington excelled more in comic than tragic roles. Fine strong features within a neatly shaped face offset brilliantly expressive eyes, while her well-proportioned figure was ideal for breeches roles (her celebrated impersonation as Sir Harry Wildair was preferred to any contemporary male actor's).

RAC

WOLF, FRIEDRICH (1888–1953)

German dramatist. A trained doctor and member of the Communist Party, during the Weimar Republic he was a leading representative of *Zeitstück*, works on timely issues. Prominent examples include his widely performed *tragedy *Zyankali* (*Cyanide*, 1929), arguing against the anti-abortion law. Forced into exile in 1933 (which he spent in the Soviet Union), his most important play of this period is *Professor Mamlock*, which deals with anti-Semitism. Wolf played an important role after 1945 in the German Democratic Republic where until his death he was the most prominent playwright after *Brecht.

CBB

WOLFE, GEORGE (1954–)

American playwright, director, and producer. Born in Kentucky, Wolfe attended Pomona College and New York University, and first received widespread attention for his 1986 play *The Colored Museum*, a series of eleven vignettes satirizing stereotypical depictions of *African Americans. Originally produced at *Crossroads Theatre, *The Colored Museum* transferred to the *New York Shakespeare Festival, where Joseph *Papp became Wolfe's early champion. Other successes included the 1992 *musical *Jelly's Last Jam*, about jazz legend Jelly Roll Morton, which Wolfe wrote and directed; and Tony *Kushner's *Angels in America*, which earned Wolfe the Tony *award for direction in 1993. In that year, Wolfe succeeded JoAnne *Akalaitis as *producer of the NYSF Joseph Papp Public Theatre and pursued an artistic policy of cultural inclusiveness (Wolfe is African American and openly gay). He co-created the musical *Bring in 'da Noise, Bring in 'da Funk*, a history of African Americans told through tap *dancing and rap music, for which he won his second Tony for direction in 1996. Under Wolfe the Public

produced a number of new plays and musicals by emerging and established writers, including Anna Deavere *Smith, Suzan-Lori *Parks, and Michael John La Chiusa, and continued the tradition of free outdoor Shakespeare. At the same time Wolfe was criticized for promoting his own work, and in particular for opening the musical *The Wild Party*, a collaboration with La Chiusa, directly on Broadway in 2000 rather than at the Public; the production made a considerable loss.

KF

WOLFF, EGON (1926–)

Chilean playwright. His first plays were psychological, for instance two dramas from 1958, *Los discípulos del miedo* (*Disciples of Fear*) and *Mansión de lechuzas* (*Mansion of Owls*). Along with others of his generation he produced his best work during the 1960s, when he continued to be interested in the psychology of insecure, obsessive, or victimized *characters, but also treated the social forces that prevented them from living normal lives. He abandoned *naturalist conventions for a *surrealist style, depicting an ambiguous and *dreamlike world where reality and fiction mingled. *Los invasores* (*The Invaders*, 1963), staged by the School of Theatre of the University of Chile, is representative: in dealing with middle-class fears of losing social and economic power, it anticipated the social conflicts of the Allende regime. *Flores de papel* (*Paper Flowers*, 1970), considered his most accomplished play, is also centred around the clash of social classes and mirrors the violence then escalating in most of *Latin America. Although *La balsa de la Medusa* (*The Raft of the Medusa*, 1980) reiterates the subjects of earlier plays, the impact on the *audience was heightened because the country was in thrall to a dictatorship that had deepened the gap between rich and poor. Wolff's other plays include *Kindergarten* (1977), *José* (1980), and *Háblame Laura* (*Laura, Talk to Me*, 1988).

MAR

WOLFF, PIUS A. (1782–1828)

German actor. Called *Goethe's most talented disciple, Wolff became a celebrated exponent of the Weimar style (*see* WEIMAR CLASSICISM), in contrast to the more *naturalistic acting of the time. From 1816 until his death he worked at the *Berlin Royal Theatre.

CBB

WOLFIT, DONALD (1902–68)

The quintessential English *actor-manager of the twentieth century, he *toured indefatigably and was always the most important person in his company. Wolfit was solidly built and somewhat moon-faced, but had undeniable power and stage presence, and a rich and versatile vocal technique; this can fortunately still be assessed in a number of *films (including *Room at the Top*, 1959; *Decline and Fall*, 1968). He acted from 1920 with Matheson *Lang's company, at the *Old Vic, and also at the *Shakespeare Memorial Theatre; in 1937 he founded his own company, and toured Britain and the USA for 30 years, giving regular *London seasons, and putting on lunchtime Shakespeare performances during the Blitz. He was happy in strong 'heavy' parts, including Tamburlaine, Lear, Oedipus, and the Wandering Jew, but he also played in *Ibsen, *Galsworthy, *Barrie, *Sheridan, and *Shaw, and excelled as Long John Silver. He was sometimes criticized for using less than adequate supporting players, *costumes, and *scenery, but his dedication to performing Shakespeare and the classics throughout the country was admirable. He was knighted in 1957. Ronald *Harwood's *The Dresser* (1980) gives an affectionate though apocryphal picture of Wolfit at work.   EEC

WOMEN AND PERFORMANCE

Western theatre dates to 500 BC, but while women performed as *dancers, *mimes, musicians, and in early Greek religious rites, they were excluded from formal appearance as actors in the *Greek and *Roman theatres. Greek social conventions confined women to the home, and as the Athenian *Dionysia festivals became more theatrical, they became a male preserve. Women of course were excluded from most professional or artisan occupations in Europe, and were excluded from other theatrical cultures as well. They never appeared in *Indian *kathakali* or *Japanese *nō, and while *kabuki was created in 1601 by a woman named *Okuni, and originally performed by women, actresses were banned in 1623. In England, women were prohibited from appearing on the professional stage in the *medieval and *early modern periods. Consigned to the streets and market-places of Europe, women *mimes began a tradition of popular performance that foreshadowed *commedia dell'arte*. Drawing on *physical theatre skills and *improvisation, they were integral to the success of these bawdy performances in Italy, France, and Spain. An Italian *commedia* troupe that included women performed in Lyon as early as 1548, and Isabella *Andreini established a respectable reputation as a *commedia* actress in the later part of the century. The impact of *commedia dell'arte* on seventeenth-century theatre, particularly on *Molière's work, ensured the gradual acceptance of women on stage.

In England, however, all-male performances continued until the closing of the theatres in 1642 (*see* BOY ACTOR; BOYS' COMPANIES; FEMALE IMPERSONATION). A troupe of professional French actresses in England in 1629 met with public disapproval, though English noblewomen performed in court theatricals and Queen Anne and her ladies appeared in the court *masques of Ben *Jonson and Inigo *Jones. Elizabeth Howe has claimed that the word 'actress' was first used in English to describe the earliest court performance of Queen Henrietta Maria (wife of Charles I) on Shrove Tuesday 1626. After the monarchy was restored in 1660 and the theatres reopened, Charles II decreed that women performers were necessary for 'useful and instructive representations of human life', and the monopoly *patents granted to William *Davenant and Thomas *Killigrew gave them the right to use professional actresses. Interestingly, women playwrights also began to be successful in this period: Aphra *Behn had eighteen plays staged in *London, and Susannah *Centlivre had twenty plays produced between 1660 and 1720.

But although the stage was one of the few activities available for women to support themselves, actresses were considered disreputable in England since they were thought to display themselves to please the predominantly male *audience of the Restoration period. Although some formed relationships with members of the nobility—Nell *Gwynn became one of Charles's mistresses—many others were subject to sexual harassment from *managers and the public. The *Licensing Act of 1737 raised the status of the theatrical profession as a whole by separating professional performers from the category of rogues and vagabonds, and the development of women's roles in sentimental *comedy (*see* COMÉDIE LARMOYANTE) in the mid-1700s contributed to an elevation in the social status of actresses. But the presence of prostitutes in theatres continued to taint them, and although Sarah *Siddons, Eliza *Vestris, Fanny *Kemble, Charlotte *Cushman, and others were financially successful, actresses were regarded as threats to middle-class notions of femininity.

Women's performance has often played a significant political role. The visible self-sufficiency of the actress as a working woman led a number of British and American women to use the stage as a platform for social issues in the early 1900s. Elizabeth *Robins and Cecily *Hamilton wrote and performed in suffrage plays, and took an active role in the suffrage movement. The Actresses' Franchise League was formed in Britain in 1908 to support the enfranchisement of women, performing *monologues and plays and presenting pageants on women's history. Post-1968 *feminism also used theatre as a strategy for raising awareness of *gender inequalities. Theatre *collectives and feminist writers, including Caryl *Churchill and Sarah *Daniels, addressed issues of *race, sex, gender equity, and violence against women. In the USA, At the Foot of the Mountain, the Women's Interart Theater, *Spiderwoman, and *Split Britches brought audiences images of new roles for women. In Britain, the Women's Theatre Group (1974) and *Monstrous Regiment (1975) created and performed work that challenged conventional attitudes toward women (*see* FEMINIST THEATRE, UK; FEMINIST THEATRE, USA).

Writers and practitioners subsequently experimented with developing a feminist idea of performance, drawing on feminist *theories based around *psychoanalysis, *semiotics, and the body. Hélène *Cixous in *Portrait of Dora* (1976) illustrates *écriture féminine*, a form of writing that is poetic and elliptical, fragmented and ambiguous. Her work, together with the theoretical and critical writings of Luce Irigaray and Julia Kristeva, has influenced new forms of performance designed to liberate women from traditions of theatre that excluded them. In the late twentieth century women's *performance art became a vital form, from the video art of French artist Orlan's operations to the lecture format of the British performer Bobby Baker's *How to Shop* (1993). Exhibited in galleries or at site-specific locations, the artist's body became both the subject and the object of the work, as in Carolee Schneeman's *Interior Scroll* (1975) and Karen *Finley's *Constant State of Desire* (1987). *See also* WOMEN IN AUDIENCES; QUEER THEORY; LESBIAN THEATRE; MALE IMPERSONATION; BREECHES ROLE. LT/LM

DAVIS, TRACY C., *Actresses as Working Women* (London, 1991)
HOWE, ELIZABETH, *The First English Actresses* (Cambridge, 1992)

WOMEN IN AUDIENCES

Demographic data on theatre *audiences is not often available and this has led to much speculation about their social composition, especially for distant historical periods. For example, received histories of English theatre in the late sixteenth and early seventeenth centuries stated that only aristocratic women and prostitutes were in the audience. Late twentieth-century theatre scholarship has suggested, however, that this is an oversimplification of actual attendance patterns and the audience was much more diversified in terms of both *gender and class (particularly in the significant presence of citizens and their wives). In certain situations, women bring particular specialist knowledge to the act of viewing. Some women who go to *kathakali theatre also come together socially to sing kathakali *texts and thus bring an expertise in the vocal styles and words of the performance they are watching. More broadly, twentieth-century *feminist theatre has assumed to address an audience that is predominantly (and occasionally only) female and with a distinct and shared understanding of women's experience.

Feminist performance *theory (*see* FEMINISM) has attempted to account for the experience of women both on stage and in the audience. Jill Dolan's landmark *The Feminist Spectator as Critic* (1988) drew the conclusion that mainstream theatre addressed an audience that was resolutely white, heterosexual, and male. This left the feminist spectator alienated from the representational mode and ideology of dominant types of performance. Feminist theatres in the late twentieth century often experimented with radically different strategies of engagement with women audiences—making them the active subjects of the performance rather than the passive objects of desire typical of nineteenth-century *realist theatre.

In some cultures, theatre audiences are segregated according to aspects of identity. For example, the audience for *kutiyattam at Kerala temples in *India is organized by caste and sex. Brahman men occupy the seating area in front of the

stage; non-Brahmans and women can only sit or stand in the passageways surrounding that area. SBe

WOMEN'S PROJECT AND PRODUCTIONS

American *Off-Broadway theatre dedicated to women's writing. Julia Miles, associate director of *New York's *American Place Theatre, founded the Women's Project in 1978 after a survey revealed that only 7 per cent of plays produced in not-for-profit American theatres were written by women and only 6 per cent directed by them. In 1986 a million-dollar grant from playwright Sallie Bingham enabled WPP to become independent, and it moved to Brooklyn Heights in 1998. The Women's Project provides its members with readings, workshops, and full productions. Though sometimes perceived as insular, WPP has supported many of America's most celebrated women in theatre, including playwrights Anna Deavere *Smith, Emily Mann, Paula *Vogel, Wendy *Wasserstein, and Constance Congdon, and directors Anne *Bogart and Carey Perloff. It has also published seven anthologies of women's plays. GAO

WOOD, CHARLES (1932–)

English playwright. Having served in the military, Wood made the absurdity and brutality of warfare a recurring theme in his drama. *Dingo* (1967), a bitter play attacking romantic notions of the Second World War, was written for the *National Theatre but withdrawn because of *censorship problems. He succeeded with his next play for the National, the spectacularly theatrical *H: being monologues at the front of burning cities* (1969), about the Lucknow campaign. During the 1960s Wood wrote the screenplays *The Knack . . . and How to Get It* (1965), *Help!* (1965), *How I Won the War* (1967), and, with John *Osborne, *The Charge of the Light Brigade* (1968). The *filming of the last of these was the subject of Wood's *comedy *Veterans* (1972), which starred John *Gielgud at the *Royal Court. His other plays include *Cockade* (1963), *Meals on Wheels* (1965), *Fill the Stage with Happy Hours* (1966), *Jingo* (1975), *Has Washington Legs?* (1978), *Across from the Garden of Allah* (1986), and an adaptation of Shakespeare's first tetralogy, *The Plantagenets* (1988), for the *Royal Shakespeare Company. MDG

WOOD, JOHN (1930–)

Lean and elegant English actor, born in Derbyshire, whose career began at Oxford University where he was president of the Oxford University Dramatic Society. At the *Old Vic from 1954 he was part of the company's cycle of Shakespeare productions using First Folio *texts. At the *Royal Shakespeare Company from 1971 his career developed with a series of diverse roles. He was also closely associated with the work of Tom *Stoppard: in 1974 he won an *Evening Standard* best actor *award and in 1976 the Tony for his performance as Carr, the put-upon minor diplomat and Foreign Office official in *Travesties*. Stoppard directed him in *Schnitzler's *Undiscovered Country* at the *National Theatre (1979), where he also appeared in *The Provok'd Wife* (1980) and *Richard III* (1992). Later appearances at the RSC included Prospero in *The Tempest*, Solness in *The Master Builder*, Sheridan Whiteside in *The Man Who Came to Dinner* (all 1989), and the title role in Nicholas *Hytner's production of *King Lear* in 1990, for which he again won the *Evening Standard* award. *Film and *television appearances include *Nicholas and Alexandra* (1971), *The Purple Rose of Cairo* (1985), *Shadowlands* (1993), and *Chocolat* (2000). AS

WOOD, MATILDA VINING (MRS JOHN WOOD) (1831–1915)

English and American actress and *manager. Wood came to the United States with her husband in 1854, and achieved great popularity in *musical comedy and *burlesque, performing in *New York, other eastern cities, and California. After the Woods divorced in 1858, she managed her own company and continued *touring. In 1859 she managed the Forrest Theatre in Sacramento and the American Theatre in *San Francisco for brief periods. She temporarily managed Laura *Keene's Varieties in 1863, and then assumed the lease, redecorating it and renaming it the Olympic. Wood excelled in the presentation of *spectacles and short burlesques in which she performed. At the height of her popularity in 1866, she gave up the Olympic to return to *London, where she managed the *St James's for eight years, transforming it from a chronic failure to a successful theatre. She also managed the *Royal Court Theatre for a few seasons. Wood toured to the United States occasionally until she retired from the stage in 1905. AHK

WOOD, PETER (1925–)

English director of theatre and *opera, with an elegant, witty, and eminently sophisticated style. He was educated at Cambridge and was director of the Arts Theatre there (1956–7) before working for both the *Royal Shakespeare Company and the *National Theatre from their earliest days. Major productions include the première of *The Birthday Party* for the *Arts Theatre, *London (1958), *The Master Builder* with *Olivier as Solness (1964), and *The Prime of Miss Jean Brodie* (1966). From the 1970s he has been associated with premières of *Stoppard's work, including *Jumpers* (1972), *Travesties* (1974), *Night and Day* (1978), *On the Razzle* (1981), and *Indian Ink* (1995). International productions include *Design for Living* (1971) and *Macbeth* (1975) in *Los Angeles and *Così fan tutte* for Santa Fe Opera

(1977). He has also directed *The Abduction from the Seraglio* for Glyndebourne (1980) and *Don Giovanni* at *Covent Garden (1981). Further particular successes at the National include *The Provok'd Wife* with John *Wood as Sir John Brute (1980), *The Threepenny Opera* (1982), *The Rivals* (1983), and *The Beaux' Stratagem* (1989). He also directed the revival of *The Silver King* at *Chichester in 1990 with Alan *Howard. AS

WOOD, WILLIAM (1779–1861)

American actor and *manager. Following a theatrical apprenticeship in *Philadelphia, where he gained a local reputation for genteel *comedy, Wood became the assistant to the manager of the *Chestnut Street Theatre and assumed joint management responsibilities with William *Warren the Elder in 1804. For the next two decades, Warren and Wood's management of the Chestnut company, which also *toured to theatres they controlled in Baltimore and Washington, prospered. In the mid-1820s, however, competition among several Philadelphia theatres and the emerging star system challenged their paternalistic management policies. Wood split with Warren and briefly managed another theatre, but the new stars now had the upper hand and Wood's eighteenth-century policies were no longer feasible. Wood continued to act in Philadelphia until 1846 and published a memoir, *Personal Recollections of the Stage*, in 1855. BMC

WOODRUFF, ROBERT (1947–)

American director. A native of Brooklyn, Woodruff's career began in *San Francisco, where he was co-founder and *artistic director of the Eureka Theatre (1973–8) and the Bay Area Playwrights Festival (1976–84). He achieved early fame as the director of Sam *Shepard's plays, including the world premières of *Buried Child* (1979) and *True West* (1980) at the Magic Theatre in San Francisco. He also collaborated with the Flying Karamazov Brothers on several productions, including a zany treatment of *The Comedy of Errors* (1983) at the *Goodman Theatre in *Chicago. In later years he became better known for his radical and visually stunning interpretations of classic *texts by Shakespeare, *Brecht, and others, including a controversial mounting of *Webster's *The Duchess of Malfi* (1992) at the *American Conservatory Theatre that featured graphic images of violence and sex. After decades as an *avant-garde journeyman at major American *regional theatres and in Israel, Woodruff became artistic director of the *American Repertory Theatre in Cambridge, Massachusetts, in 2002. STC

WOODWARD, HENRY (1714–77)

English actor, author, and *manager, who spent nearly his entire life on the stage. He first appeared in a juvenile production of

*Gay's *The Beggar's Opera* in 1729 and ended his career as Stephano in *The Tempest* just before his death. He excelled in physical *comedy and *pantomime, and for a time he was advertised as 'Woodward' for spoken roles and 'Lun Jr.' for pantomime ones. His physicality was sometimes criticized, as were his facial contortions, but along with mimicry they were also his strengths. Apart from his money-losing venture as co-manager of the Crow Street Theatre, *Dublin, in the early 1750s, he spent most of his career in London.   MJK

WOODWORTH, SAMUEL (1785–1842)

American journalist, poet, and playwright. Born in Massachusetts, Woodworth displayed a youthful talent for poetry but undertook a varied journalistic career, writing and publishing several different types of periodicals. He co-founded and quickly abandoned the New York *Mirror* (1823), for years the city's leading literary journal. He wrote in several genres and is widely remembered as the lyricist of 'The Old Oaken Bucket', a song popular into the twentieth century. His most important play was *The Forest Rose* (1825), a *'pastoral *opera', which transformed Royall *Tyler's Jonathan into the physically graceless but economically shrewd stage Yankee.   GAR

WOOLLCOTT, ALEXANDER (1887–1943)

American drama critic, among the best-known cultural personalities during the 1920s in New York. In his drama *criticism from 1914 to 1928 (for the *Times*, the *Herald*, the *Sun*, and the *World*), Woollcott wrote in a witty, sometimes flowery manner that heavily favoured certain performers but also rigorously advocated journalistic freedom, as in a 1915 dispute with the *Shubert brothers over his right to review in their theatres. His fame grew after he launched the Vicious Circle, a group of writers who met for lunch and conversation at the Algonquin Hotel. In 1929 he began writing a column for the *New Yorker* and hosting a weekly *radio show, *The Town Crier*, that continued until 1942. Woollcott acted occasionally, including a run as Sheridan Whiteside in *Kaufman and *Hart's *The Man Who Came to Dinner* (1939), a *character widely understood to have been modelled on Woollcott himself.   LTC

WOOSTER GROUP

American performance ensemble, based in *New York, which creates dense and challenging theatre works that have sparked praise and controversy around the world. Director Elizabeth *LeCompte and performer Spalding *Gray, among others, founded the company in 1980, out of the remnants of the *Perfomance Group. They are now resident at the Performing Garage on Wooster Street in SoHo. Their first piece, *The Rhode Island Trilogy*, was inspired by events in Gray's life; gradually

the group established a practice of layering *text, *performance, *sound effects, *music, and technical elements including live and recorded video. The company create their performances on a long-term basis, *improvising around ideas and research material. Often the base is an existing text, but one distorted or reshaped; playwright Arthur *Miller tried to block the Wooster Group's 1983 production *LSD (. . . Just the High Points . . .)*, because it included a cut-down and sped-up version of his play *The Crucible* alongside depictions and discussions of drug use; the production was forced to close early. The Group's more recent works, which have gained increasing international attention, include *Brace Up!* (based on *Chekhov's *The Three Sisters*) and a comparatively traditional staging of *O'Neill's *The Hairy Ape*, which played at a disused Broadway theatre in 1997. The members of the Wooster Group, several of whom had no previous experience in theatre before joining the company, are Jim Clayburgh, Willem Dafoe, Gray, LeCompte, Peyton Smith, Kate Valk, and Ron Vawter (who died in 1994). *See also* MEDIA AND PERFORMANCE; MULTIMEDIA PERFORMANCE.   KF

WORTH, IRENE (1916–2002)

American actress. Worth left a teaching career to make her professional debut in 1942 in *Escape Me Never*. In 1944 she left New York for *London, where she spent the next 30 years, in order to act and to study *acting under Elsie Fogerty. Her portrayal of Celia Copplestone in *Eliot's *The Cocktail Party* at the *Edinburgh Festival in 1949 established her as one of the most commanding and sensitive actresses of her generation. In the early 1950s she joined the *Old Vic company, where she played Desdemona (1951), Helena in *A Midsummer Night's Dream* (1951), and Lady Macbeth (1952). She opened the *Stratford Festival in Ontario with Alec *Guinness, playing Helena in Tyrone *Guthrie's production of *All's Well That Ends Well* (1953), and was with the *Royal Shakespeare Company for a season in 1962. She won three Tony *awards—for Alice in *Albee's *Tiny Alice* (1965), for Princess Kosmonopolis in *Williams's *Sweet Bird of Youth* (1975), and for Grandma Kurnitz in *Simon's *Lost in Yonkers* (1991)—received an honorary CBE in 1975, and an Obie award for sustained achievement in 1989.   TK

WOW CAFÉ

Founded in Greenwich Village in *New York in 1980 by *performance artists Peggy Shaw and Lois Weaver, the Women's One World performance space has served a key role in nurturing experimental work by *lesbian playwrights and performance artists in America. The women-only *collective is characterized by a strong community ethos and a playful, tongue-in-cheek aesthetic, as well as an egalitarian organizational structure that emphasizes inclusivity and operates on a policy of 'sweat equity', requiring that performers volunteer time and labour in maintaining and operating the space. Noted performers who have long-standing associations with WOW Café include Holly *Hughes, Carmelita Tropicana, and the company *Split Britches.

LW

WRIGHT, GARLAND (1946–98)

American director. Wright moved east from Texas in 1969 to act at the *American Shakespeare Festival in Stratford, Connecticut, where he made his directing debut in 1973 with *Julius Caesar*. In 1974 he founded the Lion Theatre Company in Manhattan where he defined his artistic style: collaborative script development, precise ensemble *acting, and minimalist staging. In 1976 Wright gained national attention with his production of Jack Heifner's *Vanities*, setting a new record for *longest-running non-musical *Off-Broadway. Wright won an Obie *award in 1977 for his adaptation and production of *K*, based on Kafka's *The Trial*. He was associate *artistic director of the *Guthrie Theatre in *Minneapolis from 1980 to 1983, and directed at *regional theatres around the United States. His production of Eric Overmeyer's *On the Verge* won Wright a second Obie when staged by the *Acting Company in 1987.

MAF

WUJÜ (WU CHÜ)

Modern Chinese 'dance-drama'. Although *dance holds a prominent place in traditional theatrical forms, *wujü* took inspiration from Western *ballet. After the Second World War Dai Ailian, who had studied at Dartington Hall, introduced English ballet to *China. Dai became the head of the Beijing School of Dance in 1949 and engaged Russian choreographers to introduce the Russian method, until they were forced to leave China in 1960 when relations with the Soviet Union cooled. Works such as *Le Corsaire*, *Swan Lake*, and *Giselle* helped produce a new generation of Chinese dancers. At the same time, attempts to mix ballet with traditional Chinese dance resulted in the creation of the first *wujü* in 1959, *The Maid from the Sea*, a story about the love of a mermaid for a young hunter. In the 1960s revolutionary themes combined with ballet and traditional dance to create *geming xiandai wujü* (revolutionary modern dance-drama); two of these were included in the original eight revolutionary model plays (*geming xiandai xi*). Staged by the Beijing School of Dance, the first, *Red Detachment of Women*, was about the struggle between a communist company of women soldiers and a local tyrant on a southern island in the 1920s. The second, *The White-Haired Girl*, produced by the Shanghai School of Dance, told the story of a girl being rescued by the communist army after living for years in the mountains to avoid the brutality of a landlord. Although they relied on ballet for their basic form, both *wujü* made considerable efforts to stress the theme of class struggle and the Chinese traditions of choreography, *costume, and *music, including the use of offstage songs. In the mid-1970s two more revolutionary *wujü* were created according to this model: *Ode to Yimeng* and *Children of the Grassland*. After the Cultural Revolution *wujü* based on Chinese *folk dance were developed, a prominent example being *Legend of the Silk Road*. Produced by the Gansu Province Dance Troupe in the mid-1980s, the work depicted the adventures of a father and daughter on the Silk Road in the Tang Dynasty, its choreography inspired by the flying figures on murals in the caves of Dunhuang, at the western end of the ancient Silk Road.

SYL

WYCHERLEY, WILLIAM (1641–1715)

English playwright. A native of Shropshire, Wycherley was privately educated. He lived in France 1655–9, and subsequently served five years as a soldier and diplomat. His theatrical career was short and eventful. His first play, *Love in a Wood* (1671), earned him the friendship of *Buckingham and the favours of the Duchess of Cleveland. *The Gentleman Dancing-Master* (1672), like *Love in a Wood* based on a play by *Calderón, brought him the patronage of the King. Wycherley's two masterpieces, *The Country Wife* (1675) and *The Plain Dealer* (1676), were his last efforts in drama, and his subsequent life was the stuff of his own *comedy. He fell ill, recovered in France, married against the King's will and thus lost royal favour, engaged in lengthy litigation, was jailed for debt, and had his royal pension rescinded. Seldom debt free and encumbered by a bankrupt estate, Wycherley was tricked into marriage eleven days before his death. *The Country Wife* was controversial in its own time and remains open to a variety of interpretations. Wycherley's view of social behaviour appears degrading, but it is difficult to take anything very seriously. None of the *characters is admirable, all are mocked: romantic love, rural virtue, the city rake's triumph—all are suspect. What we do find is lots of ridicule, lots of sex, lots of fun. (*The Country Wife* was later played in a watered-down version as *The Country Girl*, 1766.) *The Plain Dealer*, a dark and disturbing comedy, combines sex, sword-play, and intrigue in a bleak version of *Molière's *Misanthrope*. The title character's savage and sardonic commentary makes him simultaneously a comic misanthrope and a serious satiric spokesman.

RWV

WYNDHAM, CHARLES (1837–1919)

English actor and *manager. Wyndham trained as a doctor and served as a surgeon with the Federal Army in the American Civil War. He turned to the stage, and after acting and *touring in America he went into management at the new Criterion Theatre in *London in 1876. He succeeded with *The Pink Dominos* (1877), *Albery's adaptation of a risqué French *farce. *Robertson's *David Garrick*, which he revived in 1886 and 1888, portraying *Garrick himself, was his biggest hit.

Wyndham played the leading characters of the older *comedy, such as Charles Surface in *Sheridan's *The School for Scandal*, and Dazzle in *Boucicault's *London Assurance*, with dash and polish. In the 1890s he took serious *raisonneur roles in the society dramas of Henry Arthur *Jones, especially *The Case of Rebellious Susan* (1894) and *The Liars* (1897), also playing the fearsome judge Sir Daniel Carteret in *Mrs Dane's Defence* (1900). With the profits of the Criterion he built the Wyndham Theatre (1899) and the New Theatre (1903). He was knighted in 1902, and in 1916 married Mary Moore, for years his leading actress. Handsome and distinguished, Wyndham was an actor of great charm and impeccable timing, a light comedian without peer who could also play stronger roles.   MRB

WYNN, ED (ISAIAH EDWIN LEOPOLD) (1886–1966)

American actor and comedian. Wynn entered *vaudeville as a child, taking his stage name in 1904 while *touring in a sketch called 'The Freshman and the Sophomore'. By 1910, he was appearing in *musical comedy and in 1914 became a regular in the *Ziegfeld Follies. With a lisping, lilting voice, wispy hair, and bulbous nose, Wynn developed a devastating knack for absurd statements and the incongruous use of *props. Wynn was blacklisted by *producers for his support of the *Actors' Equity strike, and henceforward became his own producer for such vehicles as *Wynn's Carnival* (1920), *The Perfect Fool* (1921), and *The Grab Bag* (1924). Wynn's career gradually moved to *radio during the 1930s, an exception being the *long-running Broadway musical *Hooray for What?* (1937). In the 1950s, Wynn became a *television regular and appeared in serious roles in the television production of *Requiem for a Heavyweight* (1956) and the *film *The Diary of Anne Frank* (1959). His last major appearance was as the lovable Uncle Albert who 'loves to laugh' in Disney's *Mary Poppins* (1964).   MAF

WYNYARD, DIANA (DOROTHY ISOBEL COX) (1906–64)

English actress. Best known for her physical beauty and delicacy of performance, Wynyard spent much of the 1920s on *tour or with the *Liverpool Playhouse. During the early 1930s she established herself as a commercial star in West End theatre, but moved on to the *Shakespeare Memorial Theatre in Stratford, where she played a wide range of roles including Gertrude in *Hamlet* (1948), Portia in *The Merchant of Venice* (1948), Katherine in *The Taming of the Shrew* (1949), and Lady Macbeth (1949). Her Hermione in *The Winter's Tale* (1948) and Beatrice in *Much Ado* (1949) were considered by critics to be particularly engaging and were reprised opposite John *Gielgud in 1951 and 1952. Her last performance was as Gertrude in *Hamlet* for the *National Theatre's opening season in 1963.   TK

WYSPIAŃSKI, STANISŁAW (1869–1907)

Polish playwright, designer, director, *theorist, as well as painter and poet. Educated in *Cracow and *Paris, he paralleled *Appia and *Craig in creating a *modernist *scenography. After his production of *Mickiewicz's *Forefathers' Eve* (1901) Wyspiański was viewed as the *romantic poet's successor. His own plays, including *The Wedding* (1901), *Deliverance* (1903), *Akropolis*, and *November Night* (both written in 1904, produced posthumously), combine *naturalism with *symbolism and historical truth with imaginative poetry. Wyspiański influenced and inspired Polish theatre throughout the twentieth century, his *texts providing complex material for directors, designers, and actors. His early major follower was Juliusz Osterwa, who directed and performed in *Deliverance* several times after 1918. After the Second World War Jerzy *Grotowski mounted *Akropolis* as a shocking and moving metaphor of Auschwitz (*Polish Laboratory Theatre, 1962), while Mieczysław Kotlarczyk treated it as a glorification of culture and freedom and a hymn of hope (Cracow, 1966). Andrzej *Wajda's production of *November Night* (Cracow, 1974) was simultaneously the most faithful and the most imaginative interpretation of Wyspiański's work in the second part of the twentieth century. Wajda, a painter and *filmmaker, presented the play as a vast multi-layered canvas with astonishing images, expressive crowd scenes, and sung *soliloquies.

KB

·X·

XENOPOULOS, GREGORIOS (1867–1951)

Greek playwright, born in Constantinople (Istanbul) and raised on the Ionian island of Zakynthos. His first play, *The Soul Father*, was produced by Nikolaos Lekatsas in 1895, followed by *The Third*, which shows *Ibsen's influence in its structure and *characters. In 1904 Constantine Christomanos directed *The Secret of Contessa Valeraina* for the New Stage, and thereafter Xenopoulos wrote over 40 dramas and *comedies, several novels and short stories, as well as essays on *realism and *naturalism. His plays, written in demotic, deal with the psychology and relationships of middle-class *characters in the changing Greek society of the early twentieth century. They include *Stella Violanti* (produced in 1909 by both *Kyveli and *Kotopouli), *The Temptation* (1910), *The Students* (1919), and *Popolaros* (*Greek National Theatre, *Athens, 1933). KGo

XIRGU, MARGARITA (1888–1969)

Catalan actress and director. Beginning her career in the Catalan language in *Barcelona, where Oscar *Wilde's *Salome* premièred in 1910, Xirgu moved into Castilian-language theatre after 1912. She dominated *Madrid's stage with performances that merged the styles of *melodrama with more *realistic practice. Nurturing and promoting the work of living dramatists, including *García Lorca, Rafael Alberti, and Alejandro *Casona, and staging radical foreign plays, Xirgu helped cultivate the rich theatrical climate of pre-Civil War Spain. *Touring in *Latin America when the Civil War broke out, she chose to remain there until her death. She presented world premières in *Buenos Aires of seminal works like Alberti's *El adefesio* (*The Absurdity*, 1944) and García Lorca's *The House of Bernarda Alba* (1945), which could not be officially staged in the censorious climate of Francoist Spain (*see* CENSORSHIP). She initiated various teaching methods in Chile and Uruguay which had a large impact on actor *training in both countries. MMD

·Y·

YABLOCHKINA, ALEKSANDRA (1866–1964)

Russian actress from an acting family, whose first stage appearance was at the age of 6. Her entire career after 1888 was spent at the *Moscow *Maly Theatre, where she acted alongside some of the greats of nineteenth-century Russian theatre—Ermolova, *Lensky, Yuzhin, and Olga Sadovskaya. Among her roles were Beatrice in *Much Ado About Nothing*, Ophelia, Cordelia, Lady Anne in *Richard III*, Desdemona, Lady Sneerwell in *Sheridan's *The School for Scandal*, and Anne Boleyn in Shakespeare's *Henry VIII*. Her final stage appearance, when in her nineties, was as Miss Crawley in a dramatization of Thackeray's *Vanity Fair* (1961).   NW

YACINE, KATEB (1929–89)

Algerian novelist, poet, and playwright. He established his literary reputation with the experimental novel *Nedjma* in 1957, but the following year produced his first play, *Le Cadavre encerclé* (*The Surrounded Corpse*), and subsequently devoted himself primarily to theatre. Partly under the influence of *Brecht, whom he met in *Paris in 1955, he turned from a *surrealistic to a more *epic theatre style with strong political engagement. After the independence of Algeria in 1962 he lived primarily in that country, though he wrote in French, and his plays were presented in Paris by Jean-Marie *Serreau, Alain Ollivier, and Marcel *Maréchal. In 1971 he turned to creating plays in colloquial Arabic, performed in Algeria by his own troupe, Action Culturelle des Travailleurs d'Alger. The Troupe also performed in Paris in 1975, and *toured the Arabic play *Mohammed, Take your Suitcase* and others to communities of Algerian workers in France. His best-known French play, the *farce *Poudre d'intelligence* (*Intelligence Powder*), has also been presented in *New York, by the Ubu Repertory.   MC

YAKSHAGANA

A generic term referring chiefly to a traditional theatre form in coastal Karnataka in south *India, with variants in other parts of the region. The name literally means 'the song (*gana*) of demi-gods (*yakshas*)' and its origin is obscure. During the Vijayanagara Empire in the sixteenth century the term probably referred only to a literary form. In the course of the next 300 years, it gradually evolved into a robust theatre *genre meant for feudal entertainment. The form of *yakshagana* suggests that the pan-Indian *bhakti* devotional movement (a form of worship which personalized the divine) provided an ideological framework for its transmission. More certainly, the *ritual theatre genres in coastal Karnataka, especially *bhutaradhane* (the devil worship traditions), contributed to *yakshagana*'s theatrical conventions.

Traditionally, *yakshagana* troupes are attached to temples but the context of their performances is not strictly religious. Financed by the village community, performances are held virtually in any open space and last the whole night. The stage is normally a square of 6 m (20 feet.) demarcated on the ground, with the *green room (*chouki*) at the back and the *audience sitting on three sides. The musicians—one singer (*bhagavata*) and two instrumentalists—sit on a table at the far end of the stage while the actors make entrances and exits from the corners on either side. There are no *props except for a makeshift stool, which might represent a chariot or a throne. A small hand-held *curtain (*tere*) often signals the entrance of *characters and there are stock *dances for typical actions, like the 'war-dance pattern' (*yuddhada kunita*) and the 'journey-dance pattern' (*prayanada kunita*). A typical *yakshagana* performance opens with an invocation by the *bhagavata* and his dialogic exchange with the comedian, followed by ornate dance pieces by Balagopala and Streevesha (the female roles). This is followed by the enactment of a specific script (*prasanga*), which is normally based on epic stories. The story is presented in a fast-paced, episodic narrative, mingling songs with improvised *dialogue. It usually climaxes with combat and concludes with a marriage, and thus most of the traditional *prasangas* are called either *Kalaga* (battle) or *Kalyana* (wedding).

Yakshagana underwent major changes in the twentieth century through exposure to modernity. It began to include *plots from history and its performances became commercial. Since the 1950s new *yakshagana* troupes have popularized the form with travelling shows which incorporate modern equipment such as tents, chairs, and power generators, affecting both *acting and presentation. In a counter-movement, there have been attempts to salvage *yakshagana* from crude commercialization by well-known impresarios like Shivarama *Karanth, who created his own repertory and training institute to teach and reinvigorate the tradition. *See also* KANNADA THEATRE.

KVA

YALE SCHOOL OF DRAMA

Yale University in New Haven, Connecticut, founded a drama department within its School of Fine Arts in 1924, hired George Pierce *Baker from Harvard, and enrolled the first students in 1925. Yale established a separate graduate school, the Yale School of Drama, in 1955. A premier American institution of professional theatre *training, Yale offers three-year programmes leading to advanced degrees and certificates in *acting, *directing, design (*scenography), *dramaturgy and dramatic *criticism, *playwriting, *stage management, and theatre *management. The School and its professional affiliate, the Yale Repertory Theatre, have been led by Robert *Brustein, Lloyd *Richards, and Stan Wojewodski, Jr. James Bundy assumed leadership in 2002.

RM

YAMIN, MOHAMMED (1903–62)

*Indonesian playwright and poet. Along with several other Sumatra-born intellectuals, such as Sanusi Pane, Yamin was linked to the nationalist struggle against Dutch colonialism. He is regarded as one of the country's first modern writers because of his quest for a unifying Indonesian language and culture. Rather than using Dutch or a local language, as was customary at the time, his plays were written in Malay, which was adopted as the Indonesian national language at the National Youth Congress in 1928. *Ken Angrok dan Ken Dedes*, staged at the Congress, was set in thirteenth-century Java, and extols Indonesia's glorious past.

CRG

YARTEY, NII (FRANCIS) (1946–)

Ghanaian choreographer who since 1976 has developed new concepts of *African *dance as an art form. Named *artistic

director of the National Theatre, Accra, in 1992, his sensitively choreographed dance-dramas include *Bukom* (1986) and *Solma* (*To Tell a Story*, 1994). The second of these became part of the Africa '95 *festival in *London, and *Musu: saga of the slaves* (1996) had great impact at the Images of Africa festival in Denmark. Co-choreographed with Monty Thompson of the *Caribbean Dance Company, *Musu* reflected a move towards internationalism as a means of escaping the severe artistic constraints imposed by the economy of Ghana; it was subsequently presented in London and Hanover. In 2000 Yartey choreographed sequences for the opening ceremony of the African Cup of Nations Football Tournament (Accra) and for the Miss Universe competition (Ghana).

JMG

YASSIN, MUSTAPHA KAMIL (1925–)

Malaysian playwright, also known as Kala Dewata. Emergent in the post-independent *Malaysia of the 1960s, he was a leading proponent of modern drama based on Western *naturalistic theatre. He criticized the popular Malaysian theatre of *bangsawan* and *sandiwara* as old-fashioned because of their poetic language, painted backdrops, and intricate or fantastical *plots, advocating instead *realism in *dialogue and story. Often set in a living room, his plays tackle social issues such as intergenerational conflict, urban versus rural values, and interethnic disparities. His signature work is *Atap Genting Atap Rembia* (*Tile Roof, Thatched Roof*, 1963).

CRG

YATES, MARY ANN (1728–87)

English actress, the greatest tragedienne between Susannah *Cibber and Sarah *Siddons. Yates quickly came to *Garrick's attention and was employed at *Drury Lane starting in 1754. Her forte was haughty, imperious roles, but her repertory was varied. In *tragedy she played *Rowe's Jane Shore, Monimia in *Otway's *The Orphan*, and Cleopatra; in *comedy she ranged from Indiana in *Steele's *The Conscious Lovers* to Silvia in *Farquhar's *The Recruiting Officer*. Apart from a failed attempt to establish a third winter company at the King's Theatre (*Haymarket) in the 1770s, she acted mainly at Drury Lane and *Covent Garden.

MJK

YATES, RICHARD (1706–96)

English actor and sometime *manager. Though he acted at *Drury Lane and *Covent Garden at the height of his power, he began at *Fielding's *Haymarket in 1736 and often performed at lesser venues and *fairground booths. His most famous roles were Ben in *Congreve's *Love for Love*, the lying valet in *Garrick's *farce of that name, and Shakespeare's *clowns. He was occasionally criticized for overacting and for forgetting his lines. He entered in the management of the theatre in

Birmingham and the King's Theatre, Haymarket, for a time in the 1770s.   MJK

YEATS, WILLIAM BUTLER (1865–1939)

Irish poet, dramatist, *manager, and director, who grew by experiment, shrewd self-criticism, and acute observation to be a complete man of the theatre. Awarded the Nobel Prize for Literature in 1923, he devoted his speech of acceptance to his work not as poet but as playwright and founding director (1904) with Augusta *Gregory and J. M. *Synge of *Dublin's *Abbey Theatre, home of what by then had become the National Theatre Society (see NATIONAL THEATRE MOVEMENT, IRELAND). Though *The Land of Heart's Desire* was staged in *London in 1894, Yeats did not become an activist for a theatre that would be a wholly Irish enterprise until he found kindred spirits in Lady Gregory and Edward *Martyn in 1898. The *Irish Literary Theatre was founded to promote the concept further through three seasons of plays (1899–1901), after which Yeats worked for four further seasons (1902–4) with W. G. *Fay's *amateur company, before the Abbey was achieved with the *financial assistance of Annie *Horniman. Yeats generally became the apologist for the Abbey's aesthetic principles, programming, and social and political values in the press and through the house magazine, *Samhain*. There and throughout a range of essays one can trace the evolution of his concept of a theatre that might be distinctively Irish and devoid of English cultural influence.

In his dramas, mostly in *verse, Yeats sought to break away from the Shakespearian model, taking variously *Maeterlinck, *Sophocles, *Racine, the *morality tradition, and ultimately *Japanese *nō as his models. He required a play to demonstrate clarity, simplicity, and refinement; and meticulously revised his works after observing them staged until he achieved such qualities. For subject matter he turned to Irish sagas about Cuchulain, Deirdre, or Congal, to the Gospels and the life of Jonathan Swift, to Greek myth and Jungian archetypes. But always Yeats's focus was on a heroic life caught at an instant in time when its particular individuality most clearly defines itself through a momentous choice. He devised uniquely personal stage conventions, deploying *masks, *choric utterance, *ritual, or *dance, as ways of conveying his *audiences through the deeply psychological experience his *characters undergo. His was a 'drama of the interior'. What impresses is the variety of moods (comic, farcical, ecstatic, tragic) that Yeats can bring to such explorations of the 'deeps of the mind'.

Staging such revolutionary drama required, Yeats realized, a revolution in theatre practice, a new kind of concentration and focus. Disliking what he considered the *melodramatic, egocentric, or fussy mannerisms of English *acting style, Yeats espoused Fay's method of confining movement to the current speaker. This focused audience attention on speech, so vital in performing verse drama. He sought a similar concentration in

*scenography. Initially inspired by Sturge Moore and Charles Ricketts, he evolved a system of *curtained hangings of one colour to offset a contrasting colour in the *costumes. After 1911 he deployed a set of Gordon *Craig's screens to achieve architectural settings where a necessary monumentality was realized by sharply angled and unusually positioned *lighting. For the dance-plays this system was reduced to a single screen and carpet, the simplest way of indicating a playing space. Stylization was to prevail in all aspects of the staging, the better to focus awareness on the actor as conveyor of meaning. From the time of his nō-inspired dance-plays (especially after Ninette de Valois began to choreograph these works in 1926), the body of the actor became as important a medium of expression as the voice, particularly when a mask limited facial movement. Yeats's ideas about theatre, his *dramaturgy, his practice as director, have remained powerful forces in Irish theatre.   RAC

YEVREINOV, NIKOLAI *See* EVREINOV, NIKOLAI.

YEW, CHAY (1965–)

American playwright. Born in 1965 in Singapore, Yew moved to Los Angeles in 1988 to attend Pepperdine University. He staged his first play in *Singapore in 1987, only to run afoul of government *censors who rejected the work because it included a gay *character. When a professor in America refused to *cast him in a production because of his Asian appearance, Yew resisted by turning to writing and within a few years emerged as an important new voice in *Asian-American playwriting. *Porcelain* (1992) won the 1993 *London Fringe *award for best play. This piece, along with *A Language of their Own* (1994) and *Half Lives* (1996), comprise his 'Whitelands' trilogy which focuses on gay Asian life, especially the interracial difficulties encountered in the age of AIDS. Yew is the director of the Asian Theatre Workshop at the *Mark Taper Forum in *Los Angeles.   JSM

YIDDISH ART THEATRE

American company, founded in *New York by Ukrainian-born *actor-manager Maurice Schwarz at the Irving Place Theatre in 1918, moving to Second Avenue in 1925. Unlike the left-wing *ARTEF Theatre, the Yiddish Art Theatre embraced traditional *Yiddish emotionalism, achieving successful *tours and transfers to Broadway in English, while maintaining art theatre values of *rehearsed and scripted productions. Schwarz promoted adaptations of Sholem *Aleichem, playwrights Israel Joshua Singer (*Yoshe Kalb* in 1932–3 transferred to Broadway), Peretz Hirshbein (who had founded a short-lived Yiddish Art Theatre in Odessa), Halper *Leivick (*The Golem*), and Shakespeare in translation. Artists nurtured there included the *Adler *family

(Jacob, Celia, and Stella), Muni Weisenfreund (Paul *Muni), and designers Boris *Aronson and Mordecai *Gorelik. The 1930s brought the Depression and the beginning of the decline in spoken Yiddish, and the Yiddish Art Theater ceased production in 1949.   GAO

YIDDISH THEATRE

Yiddish is a vernacular that has been spoken by Jews in Western and Central Europe since about 1000, and in Eastern Europe since the fourteenth century. It is based on Middle High German, with structural elements of post-biblical Hebrew and borrowings from the Slavic languages, and almost always using a Hebrew script.

1. Europe; 2. North America

1. Europe

Modern Yiddish theatre emerged during the last quarter of the nineteenth century from two distinct sources: *folk traditions such as *Purim plays and traditional quasi-professional entertainers, and playwriting efforts that began at the very end of the eighteenth century. The first performance of a Yiddish play, Solomon Etinger's *Serkele*, took place in 1862 in Zitomir in the Ukraine at a modern rabbinical seminary. The female lead was played by the 22-year-old student Abraham *Goldfaden, who would become the father of Yiddish theatre. From the start *music played a large role in its development. Music was the only performing art for which traditional Jewish culture had trained personnel (cantors) and, because of its non-representational nature, provoked the least cultural resistance. The first secular Yiddish entertainers were itinerant musicians, the Broder Singers, organized in 1860 in the Polish town of Brod. The group, along with similar troupes, travelled to the towns and villages of Eastern Europe with comic songs and ballads for working-class *audiences, occasionally adding bits of *dialogue, *make-up, and *props for dramatic flavour. Eventually cantors and choirboys would become an important source for skilled performers in Yiddish theatre, and music remained central.

In 1876 Goldfaden joined forces with Israel Gradner, the leader of the Broder Singers, who was then performing in a wine cellar in Jassy, Romania, on the eve of the Russo-Turkish War. Goldfaden imposed a simple dramatic framework on Gradner's musical material and created a theatrical form that combined a fixed *scenario with improvised dialogue and stage business. Goldfaden enlarged the troupe, introduced women performers, and produced *musical plays for which he wrote the *book, lyrics, and music, and also supervised the sets, *costumes, and staging. His musicals *The Witch* (1879), *The Two Kuni-Lemls* (1880), and *Shulamith* (1880) became immediate classics of the Jewish stage, and were copied by a number of emerging troupes.

The 1883 tsarist ban on theatrical performances in Yiddish encouraged most Yiddish actors to immigrate to the West, though some travelling companies continued to function in the Russian Empire in a semi-clandestine manner. At first *London became a new centre of the young Jewish stage, though the poor immigrant community of the East End could not support the influx of East European Jewish thespians, and most of the actors moved on to the United States. Nonetheless, until the Second World War London and *Paris maintained Yiddish theatre activity, supporting both local talent and guest performers. The Yiddish theatre followed the Jewish *diaspora to other places as well, with significant centres in Argentina (*see* JUDÍO, TEATRO) and South Africa.

In 1908 the lifting of the tsarist ban led to the renewal of popular Yiddish theatrical activity in Russia and to the formation of an art theatre movement. A Yiddish Theatrical Society was organized in *Warsaw as a joint effort of the distinguished writer Y. L. Peretz and A. Vayter, an activist and playwright. Soon afterwards, writer Peretz Hirshbein founded in Odessa the first professional Yiddish art theatre, hoping to emulate *Stanislavsky's *Moscow Art Theatre, and the *Vilna Troupe was established in Warsaw. It was estimated that before the First World War there were sixteen Yiddish theatrical troupes in the Russian Empire. A steady growth in *amateur theatrical activity occurred after the 1917 Revolution, particularly in the Ukraine and Belarus. The Jewish Theatrical Society of *St Petersburg (1916) would later develop into the *Moscow State Yiddish Theatre, directed by Alexander Granovsky, a student of Max *Reinhardt who developed a *modernist style that merged Jewish folk traditions with *carnivalesque *parody and *constructivist principles. Following Granovsky's move to the West in 1928, the theatre was led by the actor Solomon *Mikhoels, whose acting in *Radlov's production of *King Lear* received international acclaim.

In the 1930s Poland became a centre of activity with twenty active Yiddish troupes, five of them in Warsaw. They included the *Warsaw Yiddish Art Theatre (VYKT), Yung Teater (a theatre for *youth), and satirical and *cabaret *revues. This bustling theatrical scene ended with the outbreak of the Second World War. Most of the 350 Yiddish actors in Poland were killed in the Holocaust, with the exception of about 80 who fled to the USSR. In 1946 Ida *Kamińska revived the Yiddish theatre in Warsaw. She carried on for 30 years, when increasingly anti-Jewish policies forced her to emigrate, marking the end of Yiddish theatre in Eastern Europe.

2. North America

Yiddish theatre arrived in America in 1882, gaining immense popularity with the 3.5 million Jews who settled in the United States between 1881 and 1925. By 1900 *New York had become the world capital of the Yiddish stage with four flagship theatres presenting 1,100 performances a year for some 2 million patrons. The theatres, all in the Bowery area, were large houses with seating capacities ranging from 2,000 to 3,500. In 1927, two years after mass immigration had ceased, there were 24 Yiddish theatres across America, eleven of them in New York, and ten years later, when the movement was already in decline, some 1.75 million tickets to Yiddish shows were sold in New York City alone.

The first Yiddish production in the United States, an unauthorized version of Goldfaden's *operetta *The Witch*, was enacted in 1892 at Turn Hall on East 4th Street by the Golubok *family troupe, recently arrived from London. It featured a local youngster, Boris *Tomashefsky, who would become one of the great stars of the Yiddish stage. At the end of the year the troupe was playing at the Old Bowery Garden, a narrow beer hall with a small stage that mostly hosted American *vaudeville acts. The Yiddish shows, regularly presented on Friday nights and Saturday matinées, offered pirated versions of works by Goldfaden and by Shomer Shaykevitch (1849–1905), one of the first playwrights to follow Goldfaden's formula. Goldfaden himself arrived in 1887, hoping to capitalize on his fame, but returned to Europe in failure. Jacob P. *Adler also failed on his first visit that same year, though his second attempt in 1890 ultimately led to his becoming the greatest dramatic actor of the Yiddish stage in America.

Two prolific dramatists monopolized the early phase: Joseph Lateiner (1853–1937) and the self-proclaimed 'professor' Moyshe Hurwitz (1884–1937). Together they manufactured several hundred plays, specializing in quasi-historical extravaganzas, heart-wrenching *melodramas, and *tsaybilder*, *spectacles depicting recent events of national or sensational significance. The working-class audience flocked to these stirring concoctions of *tragedy and *comedy, music and spectacle, which were full of plagiarized scenes and historical inaccuracies. Many of the plays included religious *rituals such as the lighting of the Sabbath candles or a wedding ceremony, enactments which reflected communal nostalgia. The actors delivered their lines in *Daytshmerish*, an artificially Germanized Yiddish, and played in an operatic, broad, intense style. Often working with unfinished scripts and constantly learning new parts, they *improvised, lifted lines from other *texts, and interpolated song-and-*dance numbers with little relation to the *plot. Admiration for Yiddish performers reached fanatical proportions with the *patriyotn*, passionate fans of a particular star who regularly crowded the gallery. The *auditorium itself was a homey space with pedlars promoting their wares in the intervals and patrons eating and drinking during the performance.

The growing intellectual elite disliked this common atmosphere, and dreamed of a Yiddish theatre of ideas. Jacob *Gordin, a Russified intellectual, was their torch bearer. The sensational success of his first play, *Siberia* (1891), marked the beginning of the literary Yiddish stage. Gordin rejected escapist spectacles, introducing *realistic domestic melodramas that dealt with serious social and moral issues. He also reformed stage practice by insisting that actors learn their lines, give up trademark *shticks* and *improvisations, and discard affected pronunciation. General prosperity and the decline of the Bowery area led to the formation of a new Yiddish theatre district on 2nd Avenue. The first houses to open were the 2nd Avenue Theatre (1911) and the National (1912), elegant constructions that cost nearly $1 million apiece. Built respectively for *actor-managers Kessler and Tomashefsky, each had a seating capacity of 2,000. The last two *playhouses to be constructed were completed in 1926: Maurice *Schwartz's *Yiddish Art Theatre, with 1,236 seats, and the Public, with 1,752 seats. Both had posh interiors that attested to the upward mobility of their patrons. 2nd Avenue became synonymous with the great stars of the 1920s and 1930s. The first lady of the *musical theatre was Molly *Picon, and other popular performers included Menashe Skulnik, Herman Yablokoff, Aaron Lebedeff, Ludwig Satz, and Mikhel Mikhelsco, with Jenny Goldstein reigning supreme as queen of melodrama and musical tearjerkers.

The art theatre movement marked the period after the First World War. Strongly influenced by developments in Europe and America, the trend was supported by post-1905 immigrants, many of them radicals with a serious commitment to Yiddish culture. They joined *amateur dramatic clubs that prepared the ground by encouraging young dramatists and actors. One of the major clubs developed into the *Folksbiene, an amateur company that was still in existence at the start of the twenty-first century. Maurice Schwartz, then actor-manager of the Irving Place Theatre, staged Peretz Hirshbein's *The Forsaken Nook* in 1918. With its simple mode of production, the play was the antithesis of the bravura of the popular Yiddish stage, and was the beginning of a second golden epoch; Schwartz—actor, director, *producer, and occasional playwright—defined its shape between the wars. Though he followed a realistic *acting style, in the 1920s he experimented with lavish modernist shows, notably a constructivist production of Goldfaden's *The Tenth Commandment* (1926) designed by Boris *Aronson, a recent arrival from the Soviet Union.

In 1925 the three great Yiddish playwrights of the period, Hirshbein, David Pinsky, and H. Leivick, united in the creation of Unzer Teater, a small non-commercial institution in the Bronx, which lasted but one season. The same fate befell the Shildkraut Theater in 1930, and a number of other ambitious projects in the next decade. Only one small company thrived during the 1930s, the communist-affiliated *ARTEF, influenced by the Russian *avant-garde and directed by Benno Schneider, a disciple of Evgeny *Vakhtangov.

The Yiddish theatre reached its artistic zenith in the 1930s, while at the same time losing its audience. As the foreign born became more acculturated and the number of the American-born rose, Yiddish was losing its position as the primary language of the Jewish community. The production of serious drama declined rapidly after the Second World War; Yiddish seasons became shorter, the elegant playhouses were abandoned, and the actors, ageing with their audiences, resorted to *touring, not unlike the wandering players of a century before. Yiddish theatre, influenced by the American experience, also had a lasting influence on the American stage, with a number of its most important figures moving uptown to Broadway. Interest in the tradition has been rekindled among young American Jewish artists, and playwrights such as Tony *Kushner and David Marguelis have worked on English-language adaptations of the Yiddish classics.   EN

LIFSON, DAVID S., *The Yiddish Theatre in America* (New York, 1965)
NAHSHON, EDNA, *Yiddish Proletarian Theatre: the art and politics of the Artef, 1915–40* (Westport, Conn., 1988)
ROSENFELD, LULLA, *Bright Star of Exile: Jacob Adler and the Yiddish theatre* (New York, 1977)
SANDROW, NAHMA, *Vagabond Stars: a world history of Yiddish theatre* (New York, 1977)
VEIDLINGER, JEFFREY, *The Moscow State Yiddish Theater: Jewish culture on the Soviet stage* (Bloomington, Ind., 2000)

YING RUOCHENG (YING JO-CH'ENG)
(1929–   )

Chinese performer and director of *huajü (spoken drama), the self-consciously modern form that developed in reaction to older operatic styles. A Beijing native of Manchu descent, Ying graduated in 1948 from the foreign languages department of Qinghua University. In 1949 he became one of the founding members of the Peking People's Art Theatre, recognized as an ensemble devoted to a *realist *acting style. His performances in *Lao She's *Teahouse* and *Cao Yu's *Thunderstorm* made him a national star. Widely read in Western literature, he played Hamlet and translated *Stanislavsky into Chinese and twentieth-century masterworks of Chinese drama into English. The Cultural Revolution interrupted Ying's career, but by 1979 he was able to travel with Cao Yu to the United States where the two avidly caught up on developments in Western theatre. During this visit Ying himself acted in American *films and *television (all Chinese sources note his role as Khubilai Khan in the American TV production of *Marco Polo*). In 1983 Ying brought Arthur *Miller to *China to direct the People's Art Theatre in a production of *Death of a Salesman*, which Ying had translated, and in which he starred as Willie Loman. In 1986 he was appointed Vice-Minister of Culture.   KC

YOKTHE PWE

*Puppet theatre developed over centuries in Burma (*Myanmar), performed by a troupe of puppeteers, singer-actors, and musicians. Skilful manipulation of *marionettes is accompanied by spoken *dialogue, song, and orchestral *music. A traditional puppet set consists of 28 jointed, carved wooden figures, dressed in elaborate silk *costumes, which range in size between 30 and 35 cm (12 and 14 inches) and are manipulated by twelve to sixteen strings. The puppeteers stand behind a screen or painted backdrop and hold the puppets over the top and in front of the screen so that the puppets stand on the stage floor. Shows, which might last an hour or all night, begin with an invocation by the *nat-kadaw*, a votaress puppet; after offering prayers to the spirit gods, she dances happily. Routines with wild animals, ogres, and alchemists follow; these lively episodes are referred to as the 'Himalayan scenes' and symbolize the chaos of creation. Then one or two puppet dramas will be performed. Their stories are often based on ancient tales of the Buddha's incarnations and include humorous improvised scenes with *clown puppets, and love scenes with a prince and princess, which display the puppeteer's mastery of the art. *Yokthe pwe* is thought to have been the inspiration for classical Burmese *dance and drama and was most popular in the eighteenth and nineteenth centuries. Since the late 1980s there has been renewed interest in the form and performances can be seen at pagoda festivals, art academies, and tourist sites.

                                                         MSh

YORUBA POPULAR THEATRE

Three major Nigerian *actor-managers of the mid-twentieth century, Hubert *Ogunde, Duro *Ladipo, and Kola *Ogunmola, drew on tradition to create versions of popular modern performance. Despite the difficulties of establishing professional *touring companies in *Africa, they created groups willing to face the rigours of the road, presenting work normally developed from narratives they selected themselves. The *plots were worked up through *improvisation by performers who tended to specialize in role types (*see* STOCK CHARACTER), relying on Western-influenced methods and Yoruba traditions. Their approaches differed. Ladipo was concerned with authenticity and initially played in cultural centres and on university campuses rather than for the large-scale public attracted by Ogunde's showman tactics. For his part, Ogunmola cultivated an extraordinary rapport with his *audiences through his talents as an *actor. Other popular groups have followed: at one point nearly 100 companies were members of the Union of Nigerian Dramatists and Playwrights, led by figures such as the comic actor Moses Olaiya (or 'Baba Sala'), Oyin Adejobi, Ojo Ladipo (or 'Baba Mero'), and Lere Paimo (or 'Eda', Everyman, the part with Lapido's company that made him famous).   JMG

YOSHIZAWA AYAME I (1673–1729)

Japanese *kabuki actor. Famous as the founder of the *onnagata (*female impersonator) role in kabuki, he performed in *Kyoto and *Osaka. He was renowned for his realistic portrayal of women and perfected the role of the high-class courtesan (*keisei*). We know about his style from published 'actor critiques' (*yakusha hyōbanki*) and from his own ideas recorded in the treatise 'Ayamegusa' ('The Words of Ayame') in *Yakusha rongo* (*The Actors' Analects*), where he provides considerable detail on his philosophy of *acting. He maintained the pose and mannerisms of a woman even offstage, and refused to let others see him eating. This concern for *realism (*jitsu*) was common to Kyoto-Osaka kabuki of the early era (*see* SAKATA TŌJŪRŌ). Two of Yoshizawa's sons became *onnagata* actors and took his name. Another son performed as a male lead, establishing the name Nakamura Tomijūrō I, which still exists today.   CAG

YOUNG, CHARLES MAYNE (1777–1856)

English actor. Young first appeared at Liverpool in 1798, and became a leading actor there and at *Edinburgh, making his debut in *London at the *Haymarket in 1807 as Hamlet. After that he played only leading parts at the *patent theatres, acting Othello to Edmund *Kean's Iago and staying with the Shakespearian and established repertory rather than the modern drama. On stage he was graceful, dignified, stately, and solemn, somewhat lacking in passion and tenderness. He was often compared to *Kemble, whom he much admired. He retired in 1832 with a farewell performance of Hamlet at *Covent Garden.
                                                                                                 MRB

YOUNG, STARK (1886–1963)

American *critic, playwright, and director. A native of Mississippi, Young was a lifelong advocate of the gracefulness and appreciation for beauty that he saw in southern culture. Graduating from the University of Mississippi in 1901, he studied with Brander *Matthews at Columbia, earning an MA (1902). Young taught at the universities of Mississippi and Texas and at Amherst College. At the age of 40, he moved to *New York and became an editor at *Theatre Arts Magazine* (1921–40) as well as theatre critic for the *New Republic* (1922–42). A friend and adviser to the *Provincetown Players, his play *The Saint* was staged by them in 1925; in the same season, he directed *O'Neill's *Welded*. Young was a respected translator of *Chekhov and his six books on theatre emphasize the power of art to provide meaning by giving form to truth and beauty.   MAF

YOUNG PEOPLE'S THEATRE *See* YOUTH, THEATRE FOR.

YOUNG VIC THEATRE

*London *playhouse in the Cut, near the *Old Vic. Built quickly in 1970, largely of breezeblock, it was an offshoot of the *Na-

tional Theatre but became independent in 1974. It holds 450 people (with a 100-seat *studio for experimental work); it has a *thrust stage and wooden benches, and is an exciting and adaptable space offering close contact with the *audience. Frank *Dunlop founded it to present classics for young people at affordable prices; his actors included Nicky Henson, Denise Coffey, and Jim Dale. They opened with an immediate hit, *Scapino* from *Molière, which transferred to Broadway—the first of many *tours—and continued with straightforward but imaginative productions from *Oedipus the King* to *Charley's Aunt*. Dunlop was succeeded as *artistic director by Michael *Bogdanov, then from 1984 to 1993 by David *Thacker, who introduced more mainstream productions of classics such as *Ibsen's *Ghosts* with Vanessa *Redgrave, and solved the theatre's considerable *financial problems; he was succeeded by Tim *Supple and then by David Lan. The theatre runs workshops with local schools, and its Christmas shows are usually excellent. It has also housed important visits, such as Trevor *Nunn's *Macbeth* (1978), Peter *Brook's *Ubu* (1978) and *Hamlet* (2001), and residencies by the *Royal Shakespeare Company.
                                                                                                 EEC

YOUTH, THEATRE FOR

An umbrella term that encompasses two age-related categories of performance work. *Theatre for children* means professionally produced plays aimed at children up to about the age of 12; *theatre for young people* refers to professional work designed for older age groups. Another term, *youth theatre*, generally refers to non-professional work performed by young people, rather than for them.

Theatre for children has for long been accorded a much higher status in continental Europe than in the UK. Most of the larger European cities, and several cities in North America (such as Minneapolis, Seattle, and *Toronto), possess specialist children's and/or young people's theatre companies operating in their own well-equipped buildings. Many have long and impressive histories: the *Moscow Theatre for Children was established as early as 1918. The work varies enormously, from the usual adaptations of fairy tales and classic novels to stylistically inventive plays dealing with contemporary social issues. *Grips Theater in *Berlin, Green Thumb in *Vancouver, and Theatre Centre in *London have been notable pioneers in this field. In the UK in general, however, *touring predominates and only two building-based children's theatres exist: the Unicorn (central London) and Polka (south London). Just one theatre, Contact in *Manchester, caters exclusively for the older age range.

Theatre for and with young people. Various examples have existed in British history, from the Elizabethan *boy actors to *university and school drama to teach rhetoric, enliven the classics, and develop confidence and articulacy. But the real beginnings of professional theatre for youth were during the early years of the twentieth century. J. M. *Barrie's *Peter Pan* proved an extraordinary West End success with family *audiences in 1904, while matinée productions of Shakespeare for school audiences were given at Lilian *Baylis's *Old Vic during and immediately after the First World War. Bertha Waddell formed the pioneering Scottish Children's Theatre in 1927, giving performances of plays written and compiled especially for younger children; and Peter Slade founded the Parable Players in 1935 to perform in schools and other venues. Meanwhile, in the USA there was a parallel growth of interest in theatre for youth and its educational benefits, before and after the First World War, led by pioneers such as Alice M. Herts and Winifred Ward; the establishment of the short-lived Federal Theatre for Children (1936–9), part of the *Federal Theatre Project, stimulated a longer-lasting interest in the field among writers amd directors.

The end of the Second World War triggered renewed activity. In the USA, several dedicated professional companies were formed and children's theatre programmes were established in a number of universities, providing *training as well as expanding the range and volume of productions for children and raising the status of the genre. In the UK, several specialist companies were founded, notably the London Children's Theatre (which became Theatre Centre), the West of England Children's Theatre (in which Brian Way began to experiment with participatory forms), the *Young Vic, and Caryl Jenner's Mobile Theatre Company, Amersham, later to transfer to London as Unicorn Theatre. Poorly funded, most companies struggled to survive, but a boost to the work came with the *Arts Council's injection of new money into both children's theatre of the more traditional kind after 1966, and the burgeoning *theatre-in-education (TIE) movement. Many companies (such as Greenwich & Lewisham Young People's Theatre (GYPT), Nottingham Roundabout, Rochdale's M6 Theatre and Tiebreak) have their roots in participatory TIE, while others (such as Theatre Centre, Merseyside Young People's Theatre, Cleveland Theatre Company, and Quicksilver) have always been more performance oriented. The boundary lines between TIE and young people's theatre became increasingly blurred through the 1980s and 1990s, due to funding pressures and a greater emphasis on production values and stylistic experimentation with *physical theatre and *mime. The scarcity of funds and dedicated buildings continued to be a major obstacle to artistic development and public recognition of the work in the UK, and by 1990 had led to closures of many companies. Occasional commercial productions of popular children's plays and adaptations of the classics continue to tour the larger theatres, and the *regional reps often cater for young people on a seasonal basis, but, despite new money released by the Arts Council in 2001, the general provision remains well below that of continental European countries.

Youth theatre flourishes in most large cities across Europe and in the USA and Canada, variously fostered by *regional theatres as part of their 'outreach' programmes, by local education authorities, and by community arts centres. In the UK, the *National Youth Theatre, founded in 1956, has been a focal point in the development and raising of standards of performance by young people, while the National Association of Youth Theatres promotes training, *festivals, and networking. *See also* COMMUNITY THEATRE. ARJ

ENGLAND, ALAN, *Theatre for the Young* (London, 1990)

McCASLIN, NELLIE (ed.), *Theatre for Young Audiences* (New York, 1978)

SWORTZELL, LOWELL (ed.), *International Guide to Children's Theatre and Educational Theatre* (New York, 1990)

WAY, BRIAN, *Audience Participation* (Boston, 1981)

YU CH'I-JIN (1905–74)

Director, *manager, and playwright of modern *Korean theatre (*shingŭk). With Hong Hae-sŏng (1893–1957), who acted in various productions of the *Tsukiji Little Theatre in *Japan, he founded the Drama-Cinema Club in 1931 and organized an exhibition of over 4,000 modern theatrical objects, including the Tsukiji's photographs, scripts, programmes, and ground plans. The same year he became a founding member of the Theatre Arts Research Society (Kŭgyesul Yŏnguhoe), a group that popularized Western *realistic theatre. His 30 plays, ranging from tragedy to comedy, made him the most influential playwright of the 1930s and 1940s, and he dealt courageously with the social and political implications of Japanese colonialism. His first play (*The Earthen Hut*, 1931) allusively exposed the Korean farmer's suffering under harsh military rule. He was appointed the first director of the National Theatre in 1950 and the first director of the Drama Centre in 1962. His representative plays are *The Cow* (1935), *Prince Maŭi* (1936), *The Fatherland* (1946), and *Wonsulrang* (1950). JOC

YUEJU See DIFANGXI.

YUNG, DANNY (1943–)

*Hong Kong playwright, director, producer, installation and visual artist, and cultural critic. After completing his studies in America, Yung returned to Hong Kong and in 1979 presented his first theatre work, *Broken Record #1*. In 1982, he founded Zuni Icosahedron, a performing and visual arts *collective, and he has been *artistic director since 1985. His productions—provocative in their interrogation of different aspects of Chinese culture and uncompromising in their defiance of traditional theatre conventions—have become synonymous with the *avant-garde theatre in Hong Kong. Controversial successes include the *One Hundred Years of Solitude* series, the *Chronicle of Women* series, the *Opium Wars* series, and the *Deep Structure of Chinese Culture* series. Since the mid-1990s, he has become increasingly interested in cross-cultural, cross-region collaboration and, in productions such as the *Journey to the East* series and *King Lear—Experimental Shakespeare* (2000), experimented with cross-media and new art forms and concepts. He has directed and produced over 70 stage productions and his works have *toured *Japan, Taiwan, Belgium, Britain, Germany, and the United States. He also curates *multimedia exhibitions and organizes forums on cultural policy issues.

MPYC

YUSEM, LAURA (1939–)

Argentinian director. Ten years after staging her first play, Yusem achieved recognition in the 1980 *Buenos Aires theatre season for *Różewicz's *White Wedding*. Noted for her collaborations with Griselda *Gambaro (*Antígona furiosa*, 1986) and Eduardo *Pavlovsky (*Pas de deux*, 1990), Yusem has also staged the plays of other Argentinians like Oscar Viale, Roberto *Cossa, Jorge *Goldenberg, and Ricardo *Monti, as well as European classics. Yusem's *dance training is evident in choreographed high-concept productions set in unconventional spaces, or in unconventionally used traditional spaces, as when she closed off the house of the Teatro *Cervantes, forcing the *audience to join *Antígona furiosa*'s actors onstage.

JGJ

YUYACHKANI

Peruvian company, founded in 1971 in Lima by Miguel *Rubio, Ana Correa, Teresa *Ralli, and others. Yuyachkani is internationally recognized for incorporating *music, *dance, *ritual traditions, *masks, symbols, and other *folkloric elements in its

performances. Its reflections on the nationalization of mining, agrarian reform, political violence, migration, and the marginalization or displacement of social or racial groups has resulted in plays such as *Copper Fist* (1972), *Allpa Rayku* (*For the Land*, 1978), *The Travelling Musicians* (1983), *Against the Wind* (1989), *Until When, my Heart* (1994), and *Serenade* (1995). *Return* (1997), *Angels and Demons* (1999), *Subdue, Atahualpa* (1999), and *Santiago* (2001) re-created religious festivals and historical events in attempts to recover a collective national memory.

LRG

YU ZHENFEI (YÜ CHEN-FEI) (1902–93)

Chinese *kunqu* and *jingju* (Beijing opera) actor of the *xiaosheng* (young man) category. As the son of a distinguished authority on *kunqu*, the dominant lyrical form prior to Beijing opera, Yu received intensive *training from the age of 6. Though he had over 200 *kunqu* scenes in his repertory he remained an *amateur until an invitation from the Beijing opera actor *Cheng Yanqiu prompted him to resign his teaching post at Jinan University in 1931. His literary and *kunqu* background helped him create many exquisite *xiaosheng* *characters opposite Cheng's *heroines, including Li Jing in *The Story of Hongfu*, Emperor Xuanzong in *Princess Mei*, and Wang Hui in *Dream of a Maiden*. He also performed opposite such well-known Beijing opera actors as *Mei Lanfang, Ma Lianliang, and Zhang Junqiu, and was considered one of the most distinguished interpreters of the genre. He lived in *Hong Kong in the 1940s but returned to Beijing in 1955. Two years later he became president of the *Shanghai City School of *Jingju* and *Kunqu* Drama and *artistic director of Shanghai Youth *Jingju* Troupe in 1960.

SYL

·Z·

ZACCONI, ERMETE (1857–1948)

Italian *actor-manager. An exponent of *realism, Zacconi became known as an actor with a natural and elegant delivery who slowly revealed his *character's psychological depth. Taking *Antoine's Théâtre *Libre as a model, he formed his own company and presented the new realistic canon at *Milan's Manzoni Theatre (1894–5), including works by *Ibsen, *Maeterlinck, *Tolstoy, *Turgenev, *Hauptmann, *Giacometti, *Giacosa, and *Praga. Foreign *tours made him an international star by 1897; *Duse and he toured her *D'Annunzio repertory (1900, 1901, 1906) as well as Ibsen and Praga (1921). Among his major successes were Oswald in Ibsen's *Ghosts*, the title role in *Musset's *Lorenzaccio*, and, in his mature years, the title role in Testoni's *Cardinal Lambertini*. Critics accused him of misinterpreting some authors, particularly Shakespeare, and of placing too much emphasis on a character's neuroses.   JEH

ZADEK, PETER (1926–)

German director. Born in *Berlin, he came to Britain with his Jewish parents in 1933. In 1943 he went to Oxford University, where he was influenced by Nevill Coghill and studied alongside Kenneth *Tynan and Richard *Burton. Leaving Oxford without a degree, he took the *directing course at the *Old Vic Theatre School, and had his first professional engagement in 1949. In 1957 he staged the world première of *Genet's *The Balcony* (1957) at the *Arts Theatre Club, prompting Genet to leap onto the stage to threaten Zadek with a revolver—the first of many scandals to accompany Zadek throughout his career. He directed for BBC Television and worked in weekly repertory in Swansea 1954–5. After 1960 he worked almost exclusively in Germany, producing Shakespeare's *Measure for Measure* in Ulm, where he began his long-term collaboration with the designer Wilfried *Minks. Zadek's background in British theatre

reveals itself in the inventive wit and spontaneity of his productions, a contrast to the much more precise work of a more typical German director like Peter *Stein, who has described Zadek's productions as 'Shakespeare in underpants'.

Zadek has no political philosophy or defined aesthetic, he frequently directs the same *text in entirely different ways, and often chooses texts that are buoyant and fun. Thus one of his earliest German productions in Ulm was of *Behan's *The Hostage* (1961). In 1962 he went to Bremen, where he became *artistic director in 1964. Here he directed *Wedekind's *Spring's Awakening* and Behan's *The Quare Fellow*, but went freelance again in 1967. In his spectacular 1967 production of *O'Casey's *The Silver Tassie* in Wuppertal he introduced a *chorus of dancing football players set against the horrors of the Great War. As director of the Schauspielhaus Bochum (1972–5) he staged novels by Hans Fallada, notably *Little Man, —What Now?* (1972, adapted with Tankred *Dorst). His production of *The Merchant of Venice* (1972) provocatively challenged German guilt about the Holocaust by presenting Shylock as a repulsive Yid. *King Lear* (1974) was presented in *vaudeville style, built up from improvisations with his ensemble. In 1976 his Othello (Ulrich *Wildgruber) wore a *minstrel blackface, and a naked Desdemona (Eva *Mattes) was violently murdered, her corpse slung over a curtain. *The Winter's Tale* in Hamburg (1978) was performed on two tons of green slime, a powerful visual image of the morass into which Leontes' jealousy drags the *action. In 1985 he became director of the Schauspielhaus Hamburg, where he made a particular effort to attract a wider *audience with productions of *As You Like It* (1986) and a popular *musical, *Andi* (1987). In his third staging of *The Merchant of Venice*, in *Vienna in 1988, Shylock was played as a Wall Street broker. In 1989 he left Hamburg to be replaced by Michael *Bogdanov. After further entertaining productions as a freelance director, he joined the *Berliner Ensemble in 1992, presenting *Antony and Cleopatra* with the Ensemble in Vienna (1994) and *Pinter's

Moonlight in Hamburg (1995). Zadek has also directed for *opera, *film, and *television.   MWP

ZAJU (TSA-CHÜ)

Chinese variety play. Although no longer part of the repertoire, *zaju* had a seminal impact on later theatrical forms and on the modern conception of drama in *China. Arising in the Song (960–1279) and Yuan (1279–1360) periods, *zaju* was the first major musically based theatrical form. Combining tunes derived from a variety of sources—court music, lyrical poetry, *folk song—*zaju* had a tight four-act structure and featured a single singing role, making vocal artistry primary. In some plays different *characters assumed the singing role, but typically a single *protagonist would expand upon a subjective point of view in the arias. Role types outlined and controlled characterization, a feature that would mark all subsequent operatic forms. *Zaju* role types were rather simply based on gender, relative prominence in the play, age, and the character's moral tone. From the extant tomb tiles, murals, and paintings, it appears that *make-up, *costume, gait, and movements provided visual cues for the *audience about the role types, which included the male lead (*zhengmo*), the female lead (*zhengdan*), and the *clown or *villain of either gender (*jing*). Each of these categories had supporting roles (old man and woman, painted female, etc.).

Zaju was performed on temporary or permanent stages in temples, at court, and in the urban entertainment quarters. Temple and court performances were often tied to specific *ritual or seasonal occasions, whereas the large urban theatres, which could accommodate as many as 1,000 spectators, operated year-round as commercial undertakings. Performance spaces were largely devoid of *realistic *scenery, and symbolic *props served various purposes. Musical accompaniment included string, wind, and percussion instruments such as the Chinese lute, flutes, clappers, and drums. By the late sixteenth century the original musical tradition was defunct and no scores have survived.

From the beginning *zaju* was based on plausible artifice rather than *mimesis. The earliest records of actresses note that some specialized in both female and male roles, and later theatrical forms—such as *kunqu, *jingju (Beijing opera), and *yueju (see DIFANGXI)—commonly featured cross-gender performance. Judging from the list of several hundred opera titles, the *zaju* repertoire featured many stories about exalted personages—emperors and their relatives, for instance—as well as humble denizens of the realm. The ghosts of chamber pots, drunken pedlars, and muddleheaded courtesans all appear as characters. Moreover, based on the 30 printed opera texts that have survived from the Yuan period, playwrights such as *Guan Hanqing and *Gao Wenxiu were irreverent toward the rich and powerful and often sympathetic to the lower orders.

The Ming court was fond of *zaju* but considerably less enamoured of such unflattering and unpredictable portrayals. A number of early fifteenth-century edicts proscribed the appearance of emperors and imperial relatives on stage. As *zaju* manuscripts had to be handed over to the court, the princely theatre enthusiasts Zhu Quan (1378–1448) and Zhu Youdun (1379–1439), together with the staff of the court entertainment bureau, had the opportunity to overhaul the repertoire thoroughly. They revised most extant plays or improved upon plays (such as *Ma Zhiyuan's) with elaborate *spectacles celebrating Confucian virtues and Taoist notions of immortality.

Zaju ceased to be a vital performance tradition by the middle of the sixteenth century but became significant textually. Having attained to the status of 'ancient plays', the Yuan *zaju* encouraged writers to adopt a looser form as a vehicle for self-expression, and the original Yuan texts were published in both popular and literary versions. One such collection, *The One Hundred Yuan Plays*, extensively redacted by the scholar-official Zang Maoxun (1615/16), reinvented *zaju* definitively. Zang projected the image of an orderly world governed by poetic rhyme and Confucian reason, and made *zaju* available in a compact and aesthetically appealing form for subsequent generations. Twentieth-century critics and cultural functionaries seized upon *zaju* to secure a place for China in the world literary order, claiming certain examples as classical *tragedies.   PS

ZAKHAROV, MARK (1933–)

Soviet/Russian director. Zakharov came to the Theatre of the Lenin Komsomol in 1973 and developed a wide-ranging repertoire, including *musical productions (*Troubadour and his Friends* and Grigorii Gorin's *Till*, both 1974), *political plays by Mikhail *Shatrov, contemporary plays by Aleksei *Arbuzov and Lyudmila *Petrushevskaya, and classics in modern interpretation. His troupe contained some of the most popular *film actors, including Inna Churikova, Aleksandr Abdulov, Oleg Yankovsky, and Dmitry Pevtsov. Zakharov created a reputation by political engagement in the early perestroika era when he was one of the first to support the course of reform, challenging in his articles the interference of bureaucrats. In his productions he tackled historical issues with a hitherto unknown openness, as in Mikhail Shatrov's *The Dictatorship of Conscience* (1986), which for the first time mentioned figures such as Bukharin and Trotsky who had been blotted out of Soviet history books. Zakharov caught the spirit of the time, attracting young *audiences with productions such as the rock *opera *Perchance* by Voznesensky and Rybnikov (1981). In subsequent years he continued to add visually stunning and psychologically convincing productions to the repertoire, always in collaboration with his set designer Oleg Sheintsis.   BB

ZAKHAVA, BORIS (1896–1977)

Russian/Soviet actor, director, and teacher, whose first acting experience was with *Vakhtangov at the latter's Mansurov *Studio and then at the *Moscow Art Theatre's Third Studio, where he appeared in Vakhtangov's productions of *Maeterlinck's *The Miracle of St Anthony* (1921) and *Gozzi's *Princess Turandot* (1922). In 1923 Zakhava worked simultaneously at *Meyerhold's theatre, appearing in three productions (1924–5). He went on to direct a number of productions at the Vakhtangov Theatre, including two last plays by *Gorky (1932–3). He was also head of the Vakhtangov (later Shchukin) Theatre School and wrote *theoretical and autobiographical books on *acting and theatre.   NW

ZAKS, JERRY (1946–)

German-born American director and actor, known mainly for his staging of *comedies and *musicals. After appearing on Broadway as an actor in several musicals, Zaks began directing *Off-Off-Broadway in the 1970s. He moved to *Off-Broadway in 1981 with Christopher *Durang's *Beyond Therapy, Sister Mary Ignatius Explains It All for You*, and *The Actor's Nightmare*. His later Off-Broadway credits include *Baby with the Bathwater* (1984), *The Foreigner* (1984), *The Marriage of Bette and Boo* (1985), *Wenceslas Square* (1988), and *Assassins* (1991), while among his Broadway credits are *The House of Blue Leaves* (1986), *The Front Page* (1986), *Anything Goes* (1987), *Lend Me a Tenor* (1989), *Six Degrees of Separation* (1990), *Guys and Dolls* (1992), *Laughter on the 23rd Floor* (1993), *Smokey Joe's Café* (1995), *A Funny Thing Happened on the Way to the Forum* (1996), and *The Civil War* (1999). Four of these were for *Lincoln Center, which made him a resident director, but he left in 1990 to become 'director at large' for the Jujamcyn *producing organization.   SLL

ZAMYATIN, EVGENY (1884–1937)

Russian/Soviet novelist, essayist, short-story writer, and dramatist who studied naval engineering in Newcastle. His first play, *The Society of Honorary Bell Ringers* (1925), was based on his novella *The Islanders* and *satirizes the English middle class. He is best known for his dystopian novel *We* (1920–1); a dramatized version was prepared for *Foregger's Mastfor Theatre, with designs by *Eisenstein, but was never staged. His other work includes a play in defence of heresy, *The Fires of St Dominic* (1922), and *The Flea* (1925), a dramatized version of Leskov's *Story of the One-Eyed Craftsman from Tula and the Steel Flea* which, written in the style of a popular *balagan*, or *clown show, pokes fun at the backwardness of tsarist Russia and the philistine limitations of bourgeois England. It was staged at the Second *Moscow Art Theatre and proved very popular, unlike his *tragedy *Attila*, which casts a favourable light on the notorious marauder and was banned in *rehearsal during 1928. Increasingly persecuted after 1929, Zamyatin applied to Stalin for permission to emigrate and, amazingly, this was granted. He settled in Paris in 1932 and spent the remaining five years of his life working on a novel, *The Scourge of God*, which parallels the fourth-century conflict between Russia and Attila to the twentieth-century conflict between Russia and the West. An essay on 'The Modern Russian Theatre' (1932) considers the merits and demerits of *Stanislavsky and *Meyerhold and reviews various examples of contemporary Soviet theatre.

NW

ZANNI

Stereotype mask—i.e. *character—in Italian *commedia dell'arte*. When the professionals took over the *Plautine *plot formulas of *commedia erudita*, they needed a standard identity for the role of the ignorant *clownish servant. This was found in the figure of the peasant from the Bergamo area who had migrated to the city to find work, a phenomenon based in the social reality of the sixteenth century. The name Zani, or Zanni, is a Lombard version of Giovanni; and the Bergamo dialect is still seen within Italy as particularly impenetrable and comic. The master–servant confrontation between the Venetian merchant Pantalone and the Bergamask servant Zani became one of the core elements of 'Italian comedy'. Individual actors multiplied their versions of the role, adding extra names to identify themselves, such as Zan *Ganassa, Zan Fritella, etc.; and the 'zany' contribution of these masks became so important that the whole *genre was sometimes called simply 'commedia degli zanni'. Zannis were usually dressed in the roughest undyed material, with broad-brimmed hats and a dark, wolfish half-*mask. The notion that stage servants had to speak Bergamask lasted for two centuries on the Italian stage, and the initially intrusive alien mask of *Harlequin, dressed very differently, was quickly assimilated to this convention.   RAA

ZAOUROU, BERNARD ZADI (1938–)

Dramatist from the Ivory Coast. Educated at home and at the University of Strasbourg, he wrote his first play, *Sory Lambé* (1967), while still a student in France. On his return home he became a lecturer at the university and studied the oral performance traditions of his Bété culture. The result of this work was *La Termitière* (*The Anthill*, 1981), which marked a break with the conventions of French drama and set the stage for a renewal of Ivorian theatre. The founding of the Cercle d'Animation (later to become the Didiga) marked his rise as a dramatist, and between 1980 and 1985 he wrote eight experimental plays, including *Les Rebelles du bois sacré* (*Rebels in the Sacred Wood*, 1982), *L'Œuf de pierre* (*Egg of Stone*, 1983) and *Le Secret des dieux* (*The Secret of the Gods*, 1985). The essence of his drama lies in its use of gesture, speech, and *music as theatrical languages, and his appropriation of the techniques of an ancient art form known as the *didiga. His other works for the stage are Les Sofas and L'Œil (published 1975).   SVA trans. JCM

ZAPOLSKA, GABRIELA (1857–1921)

Polish actor, *manager, playwright, and novelist. Married at 19 but soon divorced, she embarked on a precarious career as an actor. Appearing as Nora in A Doll's House, she introduced *Ibsen in Russia while on *tour in 1883. From 1889 to 1895 Zapolska studied *acting in *Paris, appearing in minor roles at the Théâtre *Libre. Returning to Poland as a proponent of *naturalism with socialist sympathies, she wrote plays and novels about alcoholism, prostitution, class and ethnic conflicts, and oppression of women, embroiling her in scandal and controversy. She established a theatre school and, with her second husband, ran a company bearing her name. Her satirical dramas and *comedies containing outstanding roles for women have constantly held the stage in Poland. Malka Szwarcenkopf (1895) depicts *Warsaw Jewish life; Miss Maliczewska (1910) portrays a poor young actress battling against sexual exploitation. Zapolska's masterpiece, The Morality of Mrs Dulska (1906), exposes the hypocrisy of bourgeois family life (*film scenario by the author, 1912). Many productions since the fall of communism have revealed Zapolska's *satire of the nouveaux riches to be more timely than ever.   DG

ZARZUELA

Spanish musical *genre, similar to the *operetta, which emerged in the seventeenth century as part of the musical entertainment organized for the court at the Palacio de la Zarzuela. The first known zarzuelas were by *Calderón, with *music by Juan de Hidalgo, combining witty librettos with melodies of high quality and great diversity. With the coming of Italian *opera in the eighteenth century, the popularity of the zarzuela began to wane. But the hybrid nature of the *genre, with its brew of sophisticated musical ensembles and arias, *verse and prose *dialogue, popular songs, and lowlife comic *characters, appealed to nineteenth-century tastes and prompted the construction of a specialized venue, the Teatro de la Zarzuela, which opened in *Madrid in 1856. In its related forms as género grande, long and operatic in scope, and *género chico, short and often gently titillating *one-act *farces, mostly set in the poorer quarters of *Madrid, the zarzuela has survived to the present. See also SARSWELA.   KG

ZAT PWE

Classical theatre of Burma (*Myanmar) combining traditional and modern plays, song and *dance, and comic skits in all-night performances. Burmese court theatre emerged during the end of the Nyaugyan Dynasty (1599–1751), based on Buddhist *jataka tales, and possibly influenced by pre-existing religious theatre. The first documented full-fledged court drama, Manikhet, dates from 1733. Refined literary court drama peaked during the reign of King Mindon in the works of dramatists U *Kyin U (1819–53) and U *Pon Nya (1807–66). With the annexation of Burma by the British in 1886, court patronage vanished and was replaced by popular support. The focus shifted from refined dramatic scripts back to song, dance, and comic scenes in a performer-centred style reminiscent of an older *folk form called anyein pwe, performed by female dancers and male *clowns. A famous performer of the emerging popular style, *Po Sein, further modernized it by adapting Western staging methods, creating new dance and song routines, and reintroducing *Jataka tales. Since independence in 1948, modern plays (pya zat) have increasingly replaced or augmented classical stories. Popular during local pagoda festivals, these *variety shows prominently feature comic skits, pop songs, and dance numbers in the all-night entertainment. Despite modernization, a performance always begins with a solo dance by the female natkadaw (spirit medium), related to animistic *nat pwe. Traditional zat pwe is accompanied by the saing waing orchestra which consists of the leading pat waing, a unique circular set of 21 tuned drums, the kyi waing, a circular set of bronze kettles, several other drums, gongs, clappers, cymbals, and wind instruments. A Western orchestra is often added in contemporary performances.

                                                                   KP

ZAVADSKY, YURY (1894–1977)

Russian/Soviet actor and director who was *Vakhtangov's leading actor at the Third Studio of the *Moscow Art Theatre, which he joined in 1915, performing the role of the saint in *Maeterlinck's The Miracle of St Anthony (1920) and Calaf in *Gozzi's Princess Turandot (1922). He played the Count in *Stanislavsky's 1927 production of *Beaumarchais's The Marriage of Figaro. He organized his own *studio in *Moscow during the 1920s, before becoming director of the Moscow Mossoviet Theatre in 1940, a post he held for the remainder of his career. He also taught at the State Institute of Theatrical Art, where he numbered Jerzy *Grotowski among his students.

                                                                   NW

ZEAMI (KANZE MOTOKIYO) (1363–1443)

*Japanese *nō actor, *manager, playwright, and *theorist. In 1374 Zeami and his father *Kan'ami performed before the young shogun Ashikaga Yoshimitsu (1358–1408), thereby winning military and aristocratic patronage. Taking advantage of the education and tastes he acquired from these patrons, Zeami transformed the popular sarugaku of his talented father into an elegant art form known today as nō. In addition to performing before varied *audiences, Zeami wrote over 50 innovative, poetic plays, many of which are considered masterpieces today, and twenty extraordinary treatises about theatre. At the death of Kan'ami in 1384, Zeami took over the management of the Yūzaki (later Kanze) troupe, relinquishing leadership in 1422 to his son Motomasa, who died in 1432. Headship went to his nephew Onnami, but his son-in-law *Komparu Zenchiku was Zeami's artistic heir. What little is known about Zeami's performances is intriguing: for example, in 1405 he performed for the retired shogun Yoshimitsu at Daigoji temple and in 1410 for his son Yoshimochi at a private mansion; in 1412 he was hired to perform nō in *Kyoto to placate a deity who was possessing a merchant, and in Bungo (northern Kyushu) for seven days for the public.

Zeami's treatises, written between 1400 and 1433, remained the protected property of acting troupes until 1909 when a manuscript was discovered in a second-hand bookshop. The earliest treatise, *Fushikaden* (*Teachings in Style and the Flower*, 1400–18), includes descriptions of age-appropriate *training, types of *miming (*monomane*), the interactions between actor and *audience and between movement and *text, and his aesthetic concept of *hana* (flowering). *Kyuui* (*Nine Levels*, c.1427) describes levels of *acting ability and relates them to the *training and development of actors; *Kakyoo* (1424) analyses six principles of acting, including mind–body interaction, auditory and visual effects, and effective stage presence, as well as ideas about *yūgen* (mysterious beauty), *myō* (the wondrous), and *shoshin* (beginner's heart). *Sarugaku dangi* (*Conversations about Sarugaku*, 1430), a collection of Zeami's sayings and descriptions of events by his son Motoyoshi, includes anecdotes, comments on performers, and descriptions of performance practices, plus issues of theoretical concern. Other treatises deal with music, voice production, composing plays, the two basic arts (song and *dance) and three modes (aged, martial, feminine), and strategies for managing a troupe.

Exactly which plays Zeami wrote and the order of their composition is a matter of scholarly debate as playwrights' names were not attached to texts and rewriting older works and joint composition were common. Many of the plays attributed to Zeami are *mugen* nō, plays which feature deities (*Unoha, Takasago, Oimatsu*), spirits of plants (*Saigyōzakura*), or ghosts (*Tadanori, Izutsu*), who appear as commoners in Act I and reveal their true natures in Act II. Themes of salvation, love, war, art, obsession, and celebration are expressed in densely beautiful poetry which is sung and danced on stage.

KWB

HARE, THOMAS BLENMAN, *Zeami's Style: the noh plays of Zeami Motokiyo* (Stanford, Calif., 1986)

RIMER, THOMAS, and YAMAZAKI MASAKAZU (trans.), *On the Art of the Nō Drama: the major treatises of Zeami* (Princeton, 1984)

ZEFFIRELLI, FRANCO (1923–)

Italian designer and director. An architect by training, Zeffirelli began as an actor in 1945 but soon dedicated himself to design, working in the 1940s and 1950s on *films with Vittorio de Sica, Roberto Rossellini, Michelangelo Antonioni, and Luchino *Visconti. For Visconti's stage productions in 1949 he designed *scenery or *costumes for *A Streetcar Named Desire*, *As You Like It*, and *Troilus and Cressida*. He began directing and designing his own productions of *opera in 1951, working over the next five decades on more than 50 productions in major houses around the world, from La *Scala in *Milan to *Covent Garden in *London to the *Metropolitan in *New York. His *directing was marked by emotional and sexual energy and a comic sense almost manic in intensity, while his designs relied on sumptuous materials and visual luxury, using twentieth-century methods to create a nineteenth-century *scenography. Often accused of empty formalism because of his insistence on details, Zeffirelli, claiming he was a populist, always dismissed his critics and frequently expressed disdain for the entire Italian cultural establishment.

His work in the theatre began in earnest in 1960 when he was invited to design and direct *Romeo and Juliet* at the *Old Vic in London, a production of intense and overheated mood that established the style for the play for the next generation. Relying on *verismo strategies borrowed from *Verdi, Zeffirelli created a passionate and sentimental interpretation with youthful actors and youthful energy. His other theatre work was also primarily in England, including *Othello* for the *Royal Shakespeare Company (1961), *Hamlet* (1964), *Much Ado About Nothing* and *The Taming of the Shrew* (both 1965), and seminal productions of Eduardo *de Filippo's *Saturday, Sunday, Monday* (1973) and *Filumena* (1977), most of these for the *National Theatre. Even when he approached more modern *texts, Zeffirelli never abandoned his taste for the spectacular: painstaking attention to the aesthetics of the scene was evident in *Albee's *Who's Afraid of Virginia Woolf?* (*Paris, 1964; Milan, 1965), *Miller's *After the Fall* (*Rome, 1964), Giovanni Verga's *La Lupa* (Rome, 1965) with Anna *Magnani in the title role, and *Musset's *Lorenzaccio* at the *Comédie-Française (Paris, 1978).

He worked with some of the major performers of the second half of the twentieth century, from Maria Callas and Placido Domingo to Laurence *Olivier, Richard *Burton, and Elizabeth Taylor. His films of Verdi and Shakespeare were widely received, if sometimes criticized for excess. They include *The Taming of the Shrew* (1966), *Romeo and Juliet* (1968), *La traviata* (1982), *Otello* (1986), and *Hamlet* (starring Mel Gibson, 1990). A self-acknowledged supporter of the political right wing, Zeffirelli entered politics as a candidate for Forza Italia in 1994. His autobiography is *Zeffirelli by Zeffirelli* (1986).

DMcM/DK

ZEMACH, NAHUM (1887–1939)

Russian pioneer of Hebrew theatre. His efforts began in his native Bialystock in 1912, where he organized Habima Ha'Ivrit (Hebrew Stage), which produced a Hebrew version of Ossip Dymow's *The Eternal Wanderer*, presented in 1913 at the Eleventh Zionist Congress in *Vienna. Although the company disbanded, it was a precursor to the *Habima Theatre founded by him in *Moscow in 1917. Zemach interested *Stanislavsky in the fledgling troupe, which became incorporated into the *Moscow Art Theatre as an independent *studio. Zemach stood at the helm of the Habima until 1927, when, during its American *tour, the company split because of internal rifts. Zemach stayed in *New York, his theatrical efforts faltering, and his later efforts to rejoin the Habima rejected.   EN

ZIEGFELD, FLORENZ (1869–1932)

American *producer and theatre owner. Emerging from a career as agent and *manager for *vaudeville performers, Ziegfeld left a lasting mark on American show business with the creation of his *Follies* in 1907, a *revue of comedy, song, *dance, and female *choruses that enlivened Broadway theatre in successive annual editions until 1931. The *Follies* were built upon four principles: glamour (Ziegfeld's motto was 'glorifying the American girl'); pace (a calculated build to a big first-*act *curtain and overwhelming finale); decency (exotic and exposing *costumes, but avoidance of overt sexual humour or display); and *spectacle (expanses of three-dimensional functional *scenery and painted sets by Joseph *Urban and other noted designers). The first-act ending of the 1927 edition featured a vast, semicircular staircase on which fourteen grand pianos and two complete orchestras slowly revolved as the entire enormous cast, spectacularly attired in evening clothes and satin gowns, fringe, and plumed headdresses, entered singing and arranged themselves as elegant *scenery. An artistically ambitious and perfectionist impresario, Ziegfeld spent ever larger sums to achieve novelty and surprise and to surpass his previous editions. Punctuating the *spectacle were vaudeville performers such as Will *Rogers, Fanny *Brice, W. C. *Fields, Eddie *Cantor, and Ed *Wynn. Ziegfeld was a major customer for American songwriters, commissioning more than 500 songs from a stable of composers including Irving *Berlin, Jerome *Kern, and Victor *Herbert. He also produced *book *musicals and was a force behind the landmark production of *Show Boat* (1927).
                                                        MAF

ZIEGFELD THEATRE

At the corner of 6th Avenue and 54th Street in *New York, it was built by Florenz *Ziegfeld to house his *Follies* and other productions. Opened in 1927 with the *musical *Rio Rita*, only one edition of *Follies* was presented in the theatre, in 1931–2. Sumptuously decorated throughout, it was designed in an unconventional ellipse by Joseph *Urban and Thomas Lamb. The landmark *musical *Show Boat* (1927) premièred in the house, which was converted to a cinema in 1933. In 1944 Billy *Rose returned it to legitimate theatre, but eventually leased it to NBC *television. Between 1963 and 1966 it again presented live fare, but was demolished in 1966.   MCH

ZIMBABWE ASSOCIATION OF COMMUNITY THEATRE

Established in 1986, ZACT is one of the two major official theatre bodies in Zimbabwe, together with the National Theatre Organization. ZACT's objectives are to promote community theatre groups nationwide, provide professional skills through seminars and workshops, and work for standardized wages for theatre artists. Ngugi wa *Mirii, formerly involved in the Kamariithu Theatre in Kenya and exiled to Zimbabwe, has been the national coordinator from the beginning. ZACT has developed the Kamiriithu project, following its basic ideological principles and relying on collective playwriting and staging.
                                                        MRo

ZINSOU, SENOUVO (1946–)

Togolese dramatist. After early acting work in school and university drama troupes in Lomé, Zinsou became a writer of political, social, and moral *satire. The best known of his many plays are *On joue la comédie* (*We Are Acting*, 1984) and *La Tortue qui chante* (*The Singing Tortoise*, 1987). Based on *folk tales and the *concert party—a popular form of *improvised performance—he breaks with Western tradition to create a theatre rooted in traditional culture. Using animal *characters, and relying on the fantasy world of folk tales, he has converted the concert party into a written form, incorporating elements like the verbal exchanges between actor and *audience, with spectators sometimes taking part in the *action.
                                                  SA trans. JCM

ZIPPRODT, PATRICIA (1925–98)

American designer who learned clothing construction in the workrooms of leading fashion designers, but found her niche in theatrical *costume. In 1957 she launched her career by designing the costumes for Gore Vidal's *A Visit to a Small Planet*. Thereafter she worked almost constantly for established Broadway and *Off-Broadway companies, and was a favourite of some of the leading directors and *producers of her time, designing costumes for *Fiddler on the Roof*, *Cabaret*, *1776*, *Chicago*, *The Crucible* by Arthur *Miller, *Brighton Beach Memoirs* and *Plaza*

Suite by Neil *Simon, *Period of Adjustment* by Tennessee *Williams, and *The Gang's All Here* by *Lawrence and Lee, among many others. She also added *opera, *ballet, *television, and *film credits to her résumé.   MCH

ZOLA, ÉMILE (1840–1902)

French novelist, dramatist, and critic whose *theories of *naturalism were to alter radically theatre production in France in the late nineteenth century. From the outset he was deeply aware of the relationship between art and its economic production. His first major novelistic success was *Thérèse Raquin* (1867), which he later adapted as a four-act play, first performed in 1873 at the Renaissance *operetta house. Despite its short run in an inappropriate theatre, it became the template for the naturalist play. Zola's magnum opus, however, was a twenty-volume series of novels entitled *Les Rougon-Macquart* (1871–93), a magnificent social history of Second Empire France fictionalized in the lives of two branches of the one family, the petit bourgeois Rougons and the poacher-smuggler-alcoholic Macquarts. One novel in particular made him the most talked-about writer of his generation: *L'Assommoir*, a hard-hitting indictment of the social conditions of working-class Parisians, especially those conditions that bred alcoholism. It had a lucrative run on stage in 1879 in a version by the *melodramatist William Busnach, who was also responsible for adaptations of *Nana* and *Pot Bouille*. Zola's connection to the theatre extended to *Antoine's Théâtre *Libre, which staged Léon Hennique's version of his short story *Jacques Damour* in its first season (*Paris, 1887).

Zola's second major drive was as a literary and theatrical critic (*see* CRITICISM). In his reviews for *Bien public* and *Voltaire*, he sought to reform French theatre of its penchant for contrived *plots of the *well-made play, two-dimensional *scenery, and performances in which actors' personae substituted for *characters. He called instead for representation of all sections of society in scientific experiments. These essays were published subsequently in *Le Naturalisme au théâtre* (*Naturalism in the Theatre*) and *Nos auteurs dramatiques* (*Our Playwrights*) in 1881. They were clarion calls for naturalism, a theory based on 'scientific' principles of observation and 'slice-of-life' representation, the inner workings of human and social development, the ability of heredity to determine behaviour, and on verisimilitude and accuracy. In his early career Zola had been an avid reader of modern scientific theories: Prosper Lucas's *Treatise on Natural Heredity* (1847–50), Charles Darwin's *Origin of the Species* (translated into French in 1862), and particularly Claude Bernard's concept of homeostasis, published in his 1865 *Introduction to Experimental Medicine*. Zola's mantra for literature and theatre thus ran, 'Determinism dominates everything'.

All his work had social and *political implications, as it spanned the gamut of French society and exposed weaknesses and vices at all levels, incurring the wrath of extreme right-wing politicians. Fame turned to notoriety with his public intervention in what was to become known as the Dreyfus Affair. He was convicted of libel for his open letter to the President, *J'accuse*, in which he exposed institutional anti-Semitism. He was stripped of his national honours and forced into exile to London in 1898 to escape prison. When Dreyfus was pardoned in 1899, Zola was free to return. Three years later in Paris he died in bed of carbon monoxide poisoning from a faulty stove. The death was recorded as accidental, though there were suspicions he had been murdered.   BRS

ZORIN, LEONID (1924–   )

Russian/Soviet dramatist who received encouragement, when still a small boy, from no less a figure than *Gorky. He first came to international notice with his play *Guests* (1954), which deals with a new upper class spoiled by power and which places the blame squarely on Soviet society. *Friends and Years* (1962) was among the first attempts to deal frankly with the facts of Stalinist oppression, whilst a satirical *comedy, *Dion* (1965), set during the time of the Roman Emperor Domitian, was removed from the stage in Leningrad (*St Petersburg) when critics noted contemporary political *allegories. Probably his most popular play is *Warsaw Melody* (1967), described as 'a lyrical drama in two parts', which reflects a major swing, during the 1960s, from the social to the personal in the wake of revelations about the legacy of Stalinism. Basically a love story, it concerns a Russian boy and Polish girl (both students) whose relationship is frustrated, first by laws which forbid Soviet citizens to marry foreigners, and subsequently by other factors which come between them. The play was performed 4,000 times in its first year alone at various venues throughout the country and on 150 separate occasions between 1967 and 1977.   NW

ZORRILLA, JOSÉ (1817–93)

Spanish playwright, poet, and journalist. His most celebrated play, *Don Juan Tenorio* (1844), was an adaptation of *Tirso de Molina's *The Trickster of Seville* with a *romantic overlay and a final redemption scene that appealed to conservative *audiences. Although less than a success at its première, it became immensely popular and was staged yearly in Spanish-speaking countries to coincide with All Saints' Day (1 November). A new production at *Madrid's Teatro *Español in 2000 updated the *action with effective *mise-en-scène to attract younger *audiences. Zorrilla's own favourite among his more than 30 works for the stage was *Traitor, Unconfessed, and Martyr* (1849), which is considered the last major work of Spanish romantic theatre.   MPH

ZUCKMAYER, CARL (1896–1977)

German dramatist and novelist. After service in the First World War, Zuckmayer's first play, *Kreuzweg* (1920), was an exercise in *expressionism. His breakthrough came in 1925 with his *Volkstück* or folk *comedy *Der fröhliche Weinberg* (*The Merry Vineyard*), a new form of critical *realism in the tradition of *Anzengruber and *Hauptmann. The play was both an immediate success and a scandal for its satirical portayal of conservatives. His next major success was *The Captain of Köpenick* (1931), a *satire of the Prussian hierarchy and its cult of the uniform, a German classic that has been made into several *films. In 1938 Zuckmayer emigrated to the USA where he settled as a farmer and writer in Vermont. He returned to Germany in 1946 and achieved his last major success with *The Devil's General*, written in exile in 1943. His post-war plays were less successful. CBB

ZURICH SCHAUSPIELHAUS

Leading Swiss municipal theatre. Founded in Zurich in 1837, a city suspicious of theatre, it was initially *managed by the dramatist Charlotte Birch-Pfeiffer for a bourgeois *audience conscious of its own good reputation. Under Alfred Reucker's direction from 1901 to 1921 the theatre achieved its first period of prominence, and after 1933 began to profit from the many exiled German theatre practitioners, becoming perhaps the most important German-speaking theatre. In 1938 Oskar *Wälterlin became the new director; he gathered a first-class ensemble of actors, directors, and designers, and his premières of *Brecht's wartime plays were major European events. After the war this extraordinary ensemble dissolved, yet Wälterlin managed to find new talent in the local playwrights Max *Frisch and Friedrich *Dürrenmatt. Since then the theatre has maintained its position as an important German-speaking stage, although it has been somewhat eclipsed in recent years by Theater Basel. Christoph *Marthaler became *artistic director in 2000. CBB

ZWEIG, STEFAN (1881–1942)

Austrian biographer, novelist, dramatist, and librettist. Zweig's early work includes a *tragedy in blank *verse, *Tersites* (1907), a *comedy in the style of *Marivaux, *Der verwandelte Komödiant* (*The Actor Transformed*, 1912), and the *naturalist *Das Haus am Meer* (*The House by the Sea*, 1912). Zweig himself regarded his early plays as a stepping stone for his more mature essays and novels. In 1917 he emigrated to Switzerland, where his *tragedy *Jeremiah* (1917) premièred, an anti-war play pleading for reconciliation among the warring nations (produced again in *New York in 1939). Between the wars he became one of the most widely read and translated German authors. As a dramatist he was noted for his version of Ben *Jonson's *Volpone* (1925) and he also wrote the libretto for Richard *Strauss's *opera *Die Schweigsame Frau* (*The Silent Woman*, also based on Jonson). In 1941 Zweig and his second wife Lotte Altmann emigrated to Brazil where they committed suicide the following year. CBB

TIMELINE

PREPARED BY DIANE DeVORE

HISTORICAL/CULTURAL EVENTS

BC

c.3000–1500	Indus Valley Civilization
c.1600–1028	Shang Dynasty in China
c.1500	Aryans invade India; Brahmanism develops
776	Traditional date for first Olympic Games in Greece
630	Greek colony of Naukratis in Egypt
508	New democratic constitution in ancient Greece
c.500	Buddhism and Jainism develop in India
490	Invasion of Greece repulsed by Athenians at Marathon
478	Beginnings of Athenian empire
461	Era of Pericles begins in Athens
431–429	Peloponnesian War between Athens and Sparta; death of Pericles (429)
404	Athens loses war against Sparta
338	King Philip of Macedon defeats Thebes and Athens and takes over mainland Greece
336–323	Alexander the Great rules Macedon; invades Asia 334
311	Division of Alexander's territories into the Hellenistic kingdoms
279	Celts invade Greece
218	Hannibal invades Italy
c.206–AD 220	Han Dynasty in China

THEATRE AND PERFORMANCE EVENTS

BC

c.2600	First evidence of Egyptian ritual performances
c.1500	Evidence of importance of dance, ritual, and music in China
after 508	Greek tragedies at City Dionysia in Athens (traditional date is 534)
c.500	Theatre of Dionysus built in Athens
486	Prize for comedy introduced at City Dionysia
472	Aeschylus' *The Persians*
458	Aeschylus' *Oresteia*
456	Death of Aeschylus
431	Euripides' *Medea*
424	Aristophanes' *Knights*
411	Aristophanes' *Lysistrata*
409	Sophocles' *Philoctetes*
406	Deaths of Sophocles and Euripides
401	Sophocles' *Oedipus at Colonus* (produced posthumously)
c.380	Death of Aristophanes
363	Traditional date for first Etruscan performances in Rome
336–210	Hellenistic period: rise of New Comedy
326	Theatre of Dionysus rebuilt in stone
c.300	Artists of Dionysus in existence
292	Death of Menander
191	Plautus' *Pseudolus*

THEATRE AND PERFORMANCE EVENTS

BC

184 Death of Plautus

159 Death of Terence

c.200–100 Sanskrit dramas in India

c.200–AD 200 *Natyasastra* composed in India, a compendium on drama and acting for Sanskrit theatre

55 First permanent Roman theatre

AD

65 Death of Seneca

c.300–400 Possible dates for Indian Sanskrit playwrights Bhasa, Sudraka, and Kalidasa

c.500 Opposition to Roman entertainments begins by Christians in western and eastern empires

526 Theatre and worship of Dionysus banned in Byzantium

549 Last recorded scenic entertainments in Rome

679 Council of Rome orders English Church to ban plays

714 Emperor Xuan Zong establishes school to train singers, dancers, and other court entertainers in China

c.900s *Quem Quaeritis* tropes introduced in Easter services in Europe

c.960–70 Hrotsvitha of Gandersheim composes six Christian plays modelled on Terence

c.1000 End of classical Sanskrit drama and reformation of *kutiyattam*

c.960–1270 Oldest extant Chinese drama, *The Doctor of Letters*

c.1150 Hildegard of Bingen's *Ordo virtutum* (*The Way of the Virtues*)

c.1160 Allegorical play *Antichristus* in Austria

HISTORICAL/CULTURAL EVENTS

BC

168 Rome conquers Macedon

30 Roman republic ends when Octavian (Augustus) assumes monarchical power

AD

64 First persecutions of Christians in Rome

79 Vesuvius erupts, buries Pompeii and Herculaneum

c.300–500 Northern India united under Gupta dynasty; reign of Guptas ends with defeat by White Huns and India plunges into anarchy

330 Constantine, first Christian Roman emperor, renames Byzantium as Constantinople and makes it his capital

407 Germanic tribes invade Western Europe

410 Sack of Rome by Visogoths

476 The last Roman emperor in the West is deposed

618–907 Tang Dynasty in China

711 Muslims seize Spain

772–814 Charlemagne's reign over European empire

960–1279 Rule of Song Dynasties in China

c.1000 Leif Eriksson lands on North American continent

1066 Norman conquest of England

1085 Christian reconquest of Spain begins (completed 1492)

HISTORICAL/CULTURAL EVENTS

1204	Western Crusaders seize Constantinople from Byzantines
1226	Death of St Francis of Assisi
1236–40	Mongols conquer Russia
1264	Feast of Corpus Christi instituted
1279–1368	Rule of Yuan Dynasty in China
1287	Mongols invade Burma
1291	Muslims take Acre, last Crusader state in Palestine
1305–77	'Babylonian Captivity' of popes at Avignon
1338–1453	The Hundred Years War
1348	The Black Death begins in Europe
1368	Rule of Ming Dynasty in China
1431	Fall of Angkor to the Thais
1453	Ottoman Turks take Constantinople
1462–92	Lorenzo the Magnificent rules Florence
1492	Columbus lands in the New World
1497	Leonardo da Vinci completes *Last Supper* in Milan
1498	Vasco da Gama reaches India
1501	First African slaves to Caribbean
1508–12	Michelangelo paints the Sistine Chapel in Rome
1517	Protestant Reformation begins with the posting of Luther's 95 theses
1519	Cortés takes Mexico City for Spain
1520–2	Magellan circumnavigates the globe
1527	Troops of the Holy Roman Emperor Charles V sack Rome
1533	Ivan IV the Terrible reigns as the first Russian tsar
1534	Henry VIII made supreme head of Church in England; Society of Jesus (Jesuits) formed in Counter-Reformation
1543	Copernicus refutes prevalent theory of universe
1559	Publication of Spain's first *Index of Prohibited Books*
1561	Capital of Castile established at Madrid

THEATRE AND PERFORMANCE EVENTS

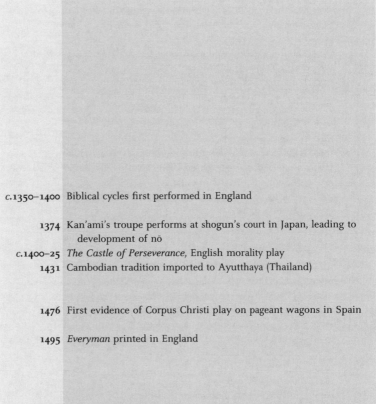

c.1350–1400	Biblical cycles first performed in England
1374	Kan'ami's troupe performs at shogun's court in Japan, leading to development of nō
c.1400–25	*The Castle of Perseverance*, English morality play
1431	Cambodian tradition imported to Ayutthaya (Thailand)
1476	First evidence of Corpus Christi play on pageant wagons in Spain
1495	*Everyman* printed in England
1508	Perspective used in painted scenery for Ariosto's *La Cassaria*
1515	First recorded performance of *khon* masked drama in Thai court
c.1518	Machiavelli's *The Mandrake*
1539	Last carnival at Nuremberg
1545	First document of Italian *commedia dell'arte* company
1547	Valenciennes Passion play
1548	Mystery plays banned in Paris; Confrérie de la Passion acquires Hôtel de Bourgogne for secular plays, first permanent theatre in Paris
1564	Birth of William Shakespeare
1567	First London playhouse, the Red Lion, built in Stepney by John Brayne; two *comedias* performed at a Spanish mission in Florida
1570s	*Commedia dell'arte* troupes touring in England, France, and Spain
1573	Tasso's pastoral drama *Aminta* in Ferrara

THEATRE AND PERFORMANCE EVENTS

1574 Queen Elizabeth of England issues patent to Leicester's Men
1576 James Burbage builds the Theatre in Shoreditch, London
1579 Corral de la Cruz in Madrid
1583 Queen's Men founded in London; Corral del Príncipe in Madrid
1585 Teatro Olimpico at Vicenza
1587 Marlowe's *Tamburlaine the Great* in London
1594 Shakespeare becomes shareholder in the Chamberlain's Men
    (known after 1603 as the King's Men)
1599 Chamberlain's Men build the Globe
1600 Shakespeare's *Hamlet*
1600–1800 Continued development of rural forms of Indian drama
1603 In Japan, the female dancer Okuni gives public performances in
    Kyoto, early form of kabuki
1605 *The Masque of Blackness* by Ben Jonson and Inigo Jones at the
    English court
1607 Monteverdi's opera *Orfeo* in Mantua

1613 The Globe burns
1616 Death of Shakespeare; last performance of the Lucerne Passion play

1619 Teatro Farnese constructed in Parma with proscenium arch
1622 First certain date of plays at the Alcázar
1629 Women banned from the stage in Japan; first permanent company
    at Hôtel de Bourgogne in Paris
1637 Corneille's *Le Cid* in Paris
1641 Richelieu's Paris theatre, the Palais Cardinal (later the Palais Royal)
1642 Parliament closes theatres in England

1644–51 Various restrictions on public performances of *comedias* in Spain

1658 Molière's company performs in Paris
1660 Charles II grants two theatre patents for London; professional
    actresses first appear on the English stage
1661 Louis XIV establishes Académie Royale de Danse
1665 William Darby's *Ye Bear and ye Cub* in Virginia, first English play
    recorded in the American colonies

1673 Death of Molière
1674 King's Company opens Drury Lane Theatre in London
1677 Dryden's *All for Love* in London; Racine's *Phèdre* in Paris
1680 Comédie-Française founded in Paris
1684 Takemoto Gidayu founds bunraku company in Osaka
1685 Alessandro Scarlatti founds the Neapolitan school of opera

HISTORICAL/CULTURAL EVENTS

1603 Takugawa shogunate established in
    Japan
1605 Cervantes' *Don Quixote*, part I (part II
    in 1615)
1607 Jamestown, first permanent Virginia
    settlement
1609 Galileo invents telescope

1618–48 Thirty Years War

1637 Descartes's *Discourse of Method*

1642 Rembrandt paints *Night Watch* in
    Amsterdam; Civil War in England;
    death of Cardinal Richelieu
1643–1715 Rule of Louis XIV in France
1644 Descartes's *Principles of Philosophy*
1644–1911 Rule of Qing Dynasty in China (last
    of dynastic rulers)
1649 Charles I of England beheaded
1652 Dutch settlement in South Africa
1653 Taj Mahal built in Agra, India

1660 Restoration of English monarchy with
    Charles II

1666 Great Fire of London
1672 Royal African Company for slave
    trade founded

1687 Newton's law of gravity
1694 La Fontaine's *Fables* completed
1701–4 War of Spanish Succession

HISTORICAL/CULTURAL EVENTS

1710	St Paul's Cathedral completed in London
1719	Daniel Dafoe's *Robinson Crusoe*
1726	Jonathan Swift's *Gulliver's Travels*
1729	Bach's *St Matthew Passion*
1742	Handel's *Messiah*
1750	Death of Bach
1751–65	Diderot and d'Alembert's *Encyclopédie*
1756–63	Seven Years War between England and France
1759	Cook claims New Zealand for England
c.1760	Beginning of Industrial Revolution in England
1765	James Watts invents the steam engine
1767	Fall of Thai capital, Ayutthaya, to Burmese
1773	Boston Tea Party
1775–83	American Revolution
1776	US Declaration of Independence
1787	US Constitution drafted; Russia begins second war with Ottoman Empire
1788	First British settlers in Australia
1789	Storming of Bastille marks beginning of French Revolution
1791	Death of Mozart
1792	Mary Wollstonecraft's *Vindication of the Rights of Women*
1793	Louis XVI of France beheaded
1793–4	Reign of Terror in France, ending with Robespierre's fall

THEATRE AND PERFORMANCE EVENTS

1703–21	Chikamatsu's best-known bunraku plays
1716	Playhouse opens in Williamsburg, Virginia
1722	Ludvig Holberg's *The Pewterer Who Wanted to be a Politician* in Copenhagen
1724	First acting company in Philadelphia
1728	John Gay's *The Beggar's Opera* in London
1731	George Lillo's *The London Merchant* in London; Voltaire's *Zaire* in Paris
1737	Stage Licensing Act in England
1745	Goldoni's *The Servant of Two Masters* in Venice
1746	David Garrick assumes management of Drury Lane
1748	Takeda Izimo's bunraku play *Chushingura*
1752	First theatre company formed in Russia
1767	Lessing's *Minna von Barnhelm* in Hamburg; first permanent playhouse in New York, John Street Theatre, opens with Farquhar's *The Beaux' Stratagem*
1774	In North America, Continental Congress discourages theatre performance
1777	Sheridan's *School for Scandal* in London; Klinger's *Sturm und Drang* published
1779	Death of Garrick
1782	Schiller's *The Robbers* in Mannheim
1785	Mozart's *The Marriage of Figaro* in Vienna
1787	Mozart's *Don Giovanni* in Prague
1788	Dramaten (Royal Dramatic Theatre) founded in Stockholm
1789	William Dunlap's *The Father; or, American Shandyism* in New York
1790	Anhwei Troupes arrive in Beijing, starting movement towards *jingju* (Beijing opera)
1791–1817	Goethe director of court theatre at Weimar

THEATRE AND PERFORMANCE EVENTS

1800–1900 Development of modern urban theatre in India

1809 In London, Drury Lane Theatre burns, enlarged Covent Garden Theatre opens

1816 Gas used in stage lighting for first time, at Chestnut Street Theatre, Philadelphia

1828 Start of development of minstrelsy in USA
1830 Hugo's *Hernani* causes riots at the Comédie-Française
1831 First American showboat
1833 Dramatic Copyright Act in England; foundation of Dramatic Authors' Society

1840 Karl Immerman's open-stage production of *Twelfth Night* in Düsseldorf
1843 In England Theatre Regulation Act abolishes stage monopoly and extends censorship powers

1849 Debut of Edwin Booth, in Boston

1864 Abolition of the monopoly of Comédie-Française on classic French drama
1865 Tony Pastor opens the first variety theatre in New York

1871 Verdi's *Aida* premières in Cairo

HISTORICAL/CULTURAL EVENTS

1796 Buddhist revolt against Manchu rule in China

1801 Alexander I becomes emperor of Russia
1803–15 Napoleonic Wars
1808 Goethe's *Faust*, part I

1811 Jane Austen's *Sense and Sensibility*
1815 Napoleon defeated at Waterloo; French monarchy restored
1816 Samuel Taylor Coleridge's 'Kubla Khan'

1818 Mary Shelley's *Frankenstein*
1819 John Keats's 'Ode to a Grecian Urn'
1820 Austria subdues revolt in Italy
1821 Greeks rise against Turkish rule
1824 Beethoven's Ninth Symphony in Vienna
1827 Death of Beethoven

1831 Pushkin's *Eugene Onegin*

1836 Dickens's *Oliver Twist*
1837–1901 Reign of Queen Victoria

1840 Start of Opium War in China

1845–51 Famine in Ireland
1847 Charlotte Brontë's *Jane Eyre*; Emily Brontë's *Wuthering Heights*
1848 Marx and Engels's *The Communist Manifesto*; revolutions in Europe; California gold rush

1851 Napoleon III founds Second Empire in France
1854–6 Crimean War
1859 Darwin's *Origin of Species*
1861–5 Civil War in USA
1862 Bismarck Chancellor of Prussia
1863 Manet's *Déjeuner sur l'herbe* exhibited in Paris

1865 Assassination of Abraham Lincoln; Tolstoy's *War and Peace*
1867 Canada becomes a dominion; end of shogun rule in Japan and beginning of modernization
1870–1 Franco-Prussian War
1871 German unification complete; the Paris Commune

HISTORICAL/CULTURAL EVENTS

1874	First Impressionist exhibition in Paris
1876	Victoria proclaimed Empress of India; battle of Little Bighorn in the USA; Bell patents the telephone
1876–8	Famine in India
1880	Edison develops light bulb
1885	Indian National Congress founded as focus for nationalism
1889	Eiffel Tower built in Paris; Rodin's *The Thinker*
1895	Tchaikovsky's *Swan Lake* in St Petersburg
1898	Spanish-American War
1900	Freud's *The Interpretation of Dreams*
1900–1	Boxer Rebellion in China
1901	Australia becomes a dominion
1902	Conrad's 'Heart of Darkness'; Méliès's film *A Voyage to the Moon*
1903	Wright brothers' first flight
1905	First Russian revolution
1907	Picasso's *Les Demoiselles d'Avignon*
1908–12	Cubism in Paris
1912	Chinese Republic proclaimed; *Titanic* sinks
1913	Stravinsky's *Rite of Spring* in Paris
1914–18	First World War
1915	Einstein's general theory of relativity; Kafka's 'The Metamorphosis'
1916	Easter Rising in Dublin
1917	Bolshevik Revolution
1919	Ezra Pound begins the *Cantos*

THEATRE AND PERFORMANCE EVENTS

1872	Japanese government places actors under the control of the Ministry of Religious Instruction in attempt to improve public morals
1876	Wagner opens Bayreuth Festival with *The Rhinegold*
1878	Irving becomes manager of Lyceum Theatre, London
1879	Ibsen's *A Doll's House* premières in Copenhagen
1880s	Establishment of *bangsawan* performance style in Malaysia and Indonesia
1881	First modern cabaret, Le Chat Noir, in Paris; Savoy Theatre in London reopens with all-electric lighting
1882	Monopoly of imperial theatres abolished in Russia
1883	Metropolitan Opera House opens in New York
1884	Buffalo Bill's first open-air Wild West show, in Nebraska
1887	Antoine's Théâtre Libre in Paris
1888	New Burgtheater opens on the Ring in Vienna; Strindberg's *Miss Julie*
1889	Braham's Freie Bühne in Berlin opens with Ibsen's *Ghosts*
1891	Fort's Théâtre d'Art in Paris; Grein's Independent Theatre in London opens with *Ghosts*
1893	Lugné-Poe's Théâtre de l'Œuvre opens in Paris
1895	Irving becomes first actor to be knighted
1896	Jarry's *Ubu roi* at Théâtre de l'Œuvre
1898	Stanislavsky and Nemirovich-Danchenko's Moscow Art Theatre founded
1904	Gregory and Yeats found Abbey Theatre in Dublin
1904–7	Vedrenne–Barker seasons in London
1905	Reinhardt takes over the Deutsches Theater, Berlin; Isadora Duncan's first school of modern dance, Berlin
1906	Final full-scale court performance of *gambuh* dance-drama in Bali; death of Ibsen
1907	First Chinese spoken drama (*The Black Slave's Cry to Heaven* in Chinese in Tokyo); *Playboy* riots in Dublin
1909	Ballets Russes in Paris
1912	Craig–Stanislavsky production of *Hamlet* at Moscow Art Theatre
1913	Jacques Copeau's Théâtre du Vieux-Colombier opens in Paris; *Darktown Follies* opens in Harlem in New York

THEATRE AND PERFORMANCE EVENTS

1920 Salzburg Festival founded; O'Neill's *The Emperor Jones* in New York

1921 Pirandello's *Six Characters in Search of an Author* opens in Rome

1923 Meyerhold Theatre founded in Moscow; The Cotton Club opens in Harlem

1924 Stanislavsky's *My Life in Art*; Tsukuji (Little) Theatre in Tokyo

1925 Pirandello's Teatro d'Arte founded in Rome; Shaw wins Nobel Prize for Literature

1926 Martha Graham's dance troupe appears in New York

1927 Piscator takes over Volksbühne in Berlin

1928 Brecht–Weill *The Threepenny Opera* in Berlin

1931 Group Theatre founded in New York

1932 Artaud's 'First Manifesto of the Theatre of Cruelty'

1933 Brecht, Reinhardt, Piscator, and many other artists escape Nazi Germany

1934 Pirandello wins Nobel Prize for Literature

1935 Federal Theatre Project in USA; Gershwin's *Porgy and Bess*

1936 O'Neill wins Nobel Prize for Literature

1940 Meyerhold executed

1942 Mao Zedong's 'Talks at the Yan'an Forum on Literature and Art'

1943 Rodgers and Hammerstein's *Oklahoma!* in New York

1946 New York City Ballet established

1947 Strehler and Grassi's Piccolo Theatre in Milan; Actors Studio founded in New York

1950 Korean National Theatre founded

1952 First All-China Festival of traditional operas in Beijing

1953 Beckett's *Waiting for Godot* in Paris

1954 Joseph Papp's New York Shakespeare Festival founded; National School of Drama in New Delhi

HISTORICAL/CULTURAL EVENTS

1920 Gandhi begins non-cooperation movement against British rule in India; Irish Civil War; League of Nations founded

1921 Irish Free State established

1922 Joyce's *Ulysses*; Elliot's *The Waste Land*; Mussolini in power in Italy

1925 Hilter's *Mein Kampf*; Fitzgerald's *The Great Gatsby*

1927 First talking film, *The Jazz Singer*; Monet's *Water Lilies* in Paris

1928 First television in USA; Alexander Fleming discovers penicillin

1929 Wall Street crash starts Great Depression

1933 Hitler becomes Chancellor of Germany

1935 Italy invades Ethiopia; German rearmament

1936 Spanish Civil War; Margaret Mitchell's *Gone with the Wind*

1937 Picasso paints *Guernica*

1939–45 Second World War

1940 Fall of France; Battle of Britain

1941 Germany invades USSR; Orson Welles's film *Citizen Kane*; Japan bombs Pearl Harbor

1945 Newsreels of Nazi death camps as war in Europe ends; atomic bombs dropped on Hiroshima and Nagasaki; Japanese surrender

1947 Indian Independence and Partition

1947–90 The Cold War

1948 First Arab–Israeli War; Gandhi assassinated

1949 People's Republic of China established under Mao

1950–1 Korean War

1952 Ralph Ellison's *Invisible Man*

1953 Death of Stalin

1954 Viet Minh victory at Dien Bien Phu

1954–62 Algerian War

c.1954–68 Civil Rights movement in America

HISTORICAL/CULTURAL EVENTS

*c.*1955–62	Beatnik movement
1956	De-Stalinization in USSR; Allen Ginsberg's poem *Howl*
1957	USSR launches Sputnik I and II
1958–69	De Gaulle president of France
1959	Alan Resnais's film *Hiroshima mon amour*
1960	Independence of African nations begins; Hitchcock's *Psycho*; Fellini's *La dolce vita*
1961	Foucault's *Madness and Civilization*
1962	Cuban Missile Crisis
1963	John Kennedy assassinated
1965	Vietnam War begins
*c.*1965–73	Hippie counter-culture movement
1967	Six Day War in Middle East; the 'summer of love'
1967–70	Nigerian Civil War
1968	Worldwide student unrest and protest; Warsaw Pact invades Czechoslovakia; Martin Luther King and Robert Kennedy assassinated
1969	Neil Armstrong is first man on moon; Woodstock Music Festival
1973	Watergate; Yom Kippur War
1974	Nixon resigns as US president; start of the punk movement
1975	Khmer Rouge takeover in Cambodia
1981	IBM launches the personal computer
1982	Falklands War
1984–5	Ethiopian famine

THEATRE AND PERFORMANCE EVENTS

1956	Osborne's *Look Back in Anger* produced in London
1957	O'Neill posthumously awarded Pulitzer Prize for *A Long Day's Journey into Night*; Efua Sutherland's open-air theatre, the Drama Studio, in Ghana
1958	Off-Off-Broadway movement begins at Caffe Cino, New York
1961	Death of Mei Lanfang; Royal Shakespeare Company founded in Stratford-upon-Avon
1962	Ngugi wa Thiong'o's *The Black Hermit* in Kenya
1963	Tawfiq el-Hakim's *The Tree Climber*, in Cairo
1964	Mnouchkine's Théâtre du Soleil founded in Paris; Imamu Amiri Baraka's *Dutchman* in New York
1968	End of British stage censorship; Dario Fo and Franca Rama found Nuova Scena in Milan; *Hair!* on Broadway; Living Theatre's *Paradise Now* on tour in Europe and USA
1969	Beckett wins Nobel Prize for Literature
1970	Peter Brook founds International Centre for Theatre Research in Paris; Brook's *A Midsummer Night's Dream* for Royal Shakespeare Company; Laurence Olivier becomes first actor raised to peerage
1971	Yury Lyubimov's *Hamlet* in Moscow (for ten years); Lloyd Webber's *Jesus Christ Superstar*
1975	Khmer Rouge regime destroys performance traditions and executes performers in Cambodia; the Wooster Group founded in New York; National Theatre of Great Britain moves to new South Bank building in London; *A Chorus Line* in New York
1976	Robert Wilson–Philip Glass *Einstein on the Beach* in New York; Market Theatre founded in Johannesburg; centennial production of Wagner's *The Ring* by Pierre Boulez and Patrice Chéreau opens at Bayreuth
1980	Ninagawa Yukio's *Ninagawa Macbeth* in Tokyo
1982	Suzuki Tadashi's Toga International Arts Festival founded in Japan; Lloyd Webber's *Cats* in New York; Fugard's *Master Harold and the Boys* at Yale Repertory Theatre
1983	Laurie Anderson's performance art piece *United States*
1985	Peter Brook's production of *The Mahabharata* at Avignon Festival

THEATRE AND PERFORMANCE EVENTS

1986   Wole Soyinka wins Nobel Prize for Literature; Karen Finley's performance art piece *The Constant State of Desire*

1990s   Drastic reductions of state subsidy for theatres in former socialist countries in Europe

1992   Derek Walcott wins Nobel Prize for Literature

1993   Tony Kushner's *Angels in America* on Broadway

1997   The Globe Theatre opens in London; Dario Fo wins Nobel Prize for Literature

2000   Gao Xingjian wins Nobel Prize for Literature

HISTORICAL/CULTURAL EVENTS

1989   Berlin Wall comes down; protests in Tiananmen Square; death of Japanese Emperor Hirohito; Václav Havel elected president of Czechoslovakia

1990   Collapse of Soviet Union and satellite states in East Europe; Cold War ends; Nelson Mandela freed in South Africa

1990s   The rise of the Internet

1991   The Gulf War

2001   Terrorist attacks on the World Trade Center in New York and Pentagon in Washington; USA invades Afghanistan and starts 'War on Terrorism'

FURTHER READING

An exhaustive bibliography of theatre and performance would clearly be impossible. This list contains a selection of some of the most important and useful books in English on various general aspects of the subject. Works on individual artists (playwrights, actors, directors, etc.) have not been included unless they deal with larger issues. Most of the longer entries in the Encyclopedia contain brief bibliographies.

**1. Reference Works and Theatre Histories | 2. Theoretical and General Works | 3. Ancient Europe | 4. Medieval Europe
5. Europe 1500–1700 | 6. Europe 1700–1900 | 7. Europe since 1900 | 8. Russia and Soviet Union | 9. Africa | 10. South Asia
11. South-East Asia | 12. East Asia | 13. North America | 14. Latin America and Caribbean | 15. Journals**

1. Reference Works and Theatre Histories

BANHAM, MARTIN (ed.), *The Cambridge Guide to Theatre* (Cambridge, 1995).
—— HILL, ERROL, and WOODYARD, GEORGE (eds.), *The Cambridge Guide to African and Caribbean Theatre* (Cambridge, 1994).
BRANDON, JAMES R. (ed.), *The Cambridge Guide to Asian Theatre* (Cambridge, 1993).
BROCKETT, OSCAR G., and HILDY, FRANKLIN, *History of Theatre*, 9th edn. (Boston, 2003).
BROWN, JOHN RUSSELL (ed.), *The Oxford Illustrated History of Theatre* (Oxford, 1995).
CHAMBERS, COLIN (ed.), *The Continuum Companion to Twentieth Century Theatre* (London, 2002).
Enciclopedia dello spettacolo, 10 vols. (Rome, 1954–66).
GASCOIGNE, BAMBER, *World Theatre* (Boston, 1968).
HARTNOLL, PHYLLIS (ed.), *The Oxford Companion to the Theatre*, 4th edn. (Oxford, 1983).
HAWKINS-DADY, MARK, and PICKERING, DAVID (eds.), *International Dictionary of Theatre*, 3 vols. (London, 1992–6).
LEECH, CHRISTOPHER, et al. (eds.), *The Revels History of Drama in English*, 8 vols. (1976–83; reprinted London, 1996).
LONDRÉ, FELICIA HARDISON, *The History of World Theatre: from the Restoration to the present*, 2 vols. (New York, 1991).
MOLINARI, CESARE, *Theatre through the Ages*, trans. Colin Hamer (New York, 1974).
NAGLER, A. M. (ed.), *A Source Book in Theatrical History* (New York, 1952).
NICOLL, ALLARDYCE, *World Drama*, rev. edn. (London, 1976).
PAVIS, PATRICE, *Dictionary of the Theatre: terms, concepts, and analysis*, trans. Christine Shantz (Toronto, 1998).
RUBIN, DON, et al. (eds.), *The World Encyclopedia of Contemporary Theatre*, 5 vols. (London, 1994–8).
SOUTHERN, RICHARD, *Seven Ages of the Theatre* (London, 1964).
THOMSON, PETER and SALGADO, GAMINI, *The Everyman Companion to the Theatre* (London, 1987).
TRUSSLER, SIMON, *The Cambridge Illustrated History of British Theatre* (Cambridge, 1994).
WYCKHAM, GLYNNE, *A History of the Theatre*, 3rd edn. (Oxford, 1985).

2. Theoretical and General Works

ABERCROMBIE, NICHOLAS, and LONGHURST, BRIAN, *Audiences: a sociological theory of performance and imagination* (Thousand Oaks, Calif., 1998).
AUSLANDER, PHILIP, *Liveness: performance in a mediatized culture* (London, 1999).
BARBA, EUGENIO, and SAVARESE, NICOLA, *The Dictionary of Theatre Anthropology: the secret art of the performer*, trans. Richard Fowler (London, 1991).
BENNETT, SUSAN, *Theatre Audiences: a theory of production and perception*, 2nd edn. (New York, 1997).
BENTLEY, ERIC, *The Playwright as Thinker: a study of drama in modern times* (New York, 1946).
BHARUCHA, RUSTOM, *The Politics of Cultural Practice: thinking through theatre in an age of globalization* (Hanover, New Hampshire, 2000).
—— *Theatre and the World: performance and the politics of culture* (London, 1993).
CARLSON, MARVIN, *Performance: a critical introduction* (New York, 1996).
—— *Places of Performance: the semiotics of theatre* (Ithaca, NY, 1989).
—— *Theories of the Theatre: a historical and critical survey, from the Greeks to the present*, 2nd edn. (Ithaca, NY, 1993).
CASE, SUE-ELLEN, *Feminism and the Theatre* (New York, 1987).
CHAUDHURI, UNA, *Staging Place: the geography of modern drama* (Ann Arbor, 1995).
CLARK, BARRETT H., *European Theories of the Drama* (New York, 1965).

Cole, Toby, and Chinoy, Helen K. (eds.), *Actors on Acting*, rev. edn. (New York, 1980).

Diamond, Elin (ed.), *Performance and Cultural Politics* (London, 1996).

Dolan, Jill, *The Feminist Spectator as Critic* (Ann Arbor, 1991).

Dukore, Bernard, *Dramatic Theory and Criticism from the Greeks to Grotowski* (New York, 1974).

Elam, Keir, *The Semiotics of Theatre and Drama*, 2nd edn. (London, 2002).

Gerould, Daniel, *Theatre/Theory/Theatre: the major critical texts from Aristotle and Zeami to Soyinka and Havel* (New York, 2000).

Goffman, Erving, *The Presentation of Self in Everyday Life* (Garden City, New York, 1959).

Huxley, Mike, and Witts, Noel (eds.), *Twentieth Century Performance Reader* (New York, 1996).

Kirshenblatt-Gimblett, Barbara, *Destination Culture: tourism, museums, and heritage* (Berkeley, 1998).

Leacroft, Richard, and Leacroft, Helen, *Theatre and Playhouse: an illustrated survey of theatre building from ancient Greece to the present day* (New York, 1984).

Pavis, Patrice (ed.), *The Intercultural Performance Reader* (New York, 1996).

—— *Languages of the Stage: essays on the semiology of the theatre* (New York, 1982).

—— *Theatre at the Crossroads of Culture* (London, 1992).

Phelan, Peggy, *Unmarked: the politics of performance* (London, 1993).

Postlewait, Thomas, and McConachie, Bruce (eds.), *Interpreting the Theatrical Past: essays in the historiography of performance* (Iowa City, 1989).

Reinelt, Janelle G., and Roach, Joseph R. (eds.), *Critical Theory and Performance* (Ann Arbor, 1992).

Roach, Joseph R., *Cities of the Dead: circum-Atlantic performance* (New York, 1996).

—— *The Player's Passion: studies in the science of acting* (Ann Arbor, 1993).

Rozik, Eli, *The Roots of Theatre: rethinking ritual and other theories of origin* (Iowa City, 2002).

Schechner, Richard, *Between Theatre and Anthropology* (Philadelphia, 1985).

—— *Essays on Performance Theory* (New York, 1977).

—— *Performance Studies: an introduction* (London, 2002).

Senelick, Laurence, *The Changing Room: sex, drag and theatre* (London, 2000).

Sidnell, Michael J. (ed.), *Sources of Dramatic Theory*, 2 vols. (Cambridge, 1991–4).

Turner, Victor, *From Ritual to Theatre* (New York, 1982).

3. Ancient Europe

Beacham, R. C., *The Roman Theatre and its Audience* (Cambridge, Mass., 1992).

—— *Spectacle Entertainments of Early Imperial Rome* (New Haven, 1999).

Beare, W., *The Roman Stage*, 3rd edn. (London, 1968).

Csapo, E. G., and Slater, W. J., *The Context of Ancient Drama* (Ann Arbor, 1995).

Easterling, P. E., and Hall, E. (eds.), *Actors and Acting in Antiquity* (Cambridge, 2002).

Goldhill, Simon, *Reading Greek Tragedy* (Cambridge, 1986).

Green, J. R., *Theatre in Ancient Greek Society* (London, 1994).

Gruen, Erich S., *Studies in Greek Culture and Roman Policy* (Leiden, 1990).

Herington, C. J., *Poetry into Drama: early tragedy and Greek poetic tradition* (Berkeley, 1985).

Hunter, Richard L., *The New Comedy of Greece and Rome* (Cambridge, 1985).

Knox, Bernard M. W., *The Heroic Temper* (Berkeley, 1964).

—— *Word and Action* (Baltimore, 1979).

Pickard, A., *The Dramatic Festivals of Athens*, 2nd edn., rev. J. Gould and D. Lewis (Oxford, 1968, addenda 1988).

Simon, Erika, *The Ancient Theatre* (London, 1982).

Taplin, Oliver, *Greek Tragedy in Action* (London, 1978; rev. edn. 1985).

Vernant, Jean-Pierre, and Vidal-Naquet, Pierre, *Myth and Tragedy in Ancient Greece* (New York, 1988).

Wiles, David, *The Masks of Menander* (Cambridge, 1991).

Winnington-Ingram, R., *Studies in Aeschylus* (Cambridge, 1983).

4. Medieval Europe

Axton, R., *European Drama of the Early Middle Ages* (London, 1974).

Bevington, David (ed.), *Medieval Drama* (Boston, 1975).

Burke, Peter, *Popular Culture in Early Modern Europe* (London, 1979).

Eckehard, Simon (ed.), *The Theatre of Medieval Europe: new research in early drama* (Cambridge, 1991).

Elliott, John R., *Playing God: medieval mysteries on the modern stage* (Toronto, 1989).

Harris, John Wesley, *Medieval Theatre in Context* (London, 1992).

Nicoll, Allardyce, *Masks, Mimes, and Miracles* (London, 1935).

Rossiter, A. P., *English Drama: from early times to the Elizabethans* (Folcroft, 1978).

Segal, Erich (ed.), *Roman Laughter: the comedy of Plautus*, 2nd edn. (New York, 1987).

Stevens, Martin, *Four Middle English Mystery Cycles* (Princeton, 1987).

Tydeman, William, *The Theatre in the Middle Ages* (Cambridge, 1978).

Wickham, Glynne, *Early English Stages, 1300–1660*, 5 vols. (London, 1959–).

—— *Medieval Theatre*, 3rd edn. (Cambridge, 1987).

5. Europe 1500–1700

Allen, John J., *The Reconstruction of a Spanish Golden Age Playhouse: El Corral del Principe 1583–1744* (Gainesville, Florida, 1983).

Andrews, Richard, *Scripts and Scenarios: the performance of comedy of Renaissance Italy* (Cambridge, 1993).

Bentley, G. E., *The Jacobean and Caroline Stage*, 7 vols. (Oxford, 1941–68).

—— *The Profession of Player in the Shakespeare's Time* (Princeton, 1984).

BRANDT, GEORGE W., and HOGENDOORN, W. (eds.), *German and Dutch Theatre 1600–1848* (Cambridge, 1992).

CAIRNS, CHRISTOPHER (ed.), *The Commedia dell'Arte from the Renaissance to Dario Fo* (Lewiston, NY, 1989).

CHAMBERS, E. K., *The Elizabethan Stage*, 4 vols. (London, 1923).

CLUBB, LOUISE GEORGE, *Italian Drama in Shakespeare's Time* (New Haven, 1989).

COHEN, WALTER, *Drama of a Nation: public theater in Renaissance England and Spain* (Itaca, NY, 1985).

COX, JOHN D. and KASTAN, DAVID (eds.), *A New History of Early English Drama* (New York, 1997).

DAWSON, ANTONY, and YACHNIN, PAUL, *The Culture of Playgoing in Shakespeare's England* (Cambridge, 2001).

GREENBLATT, STEPHEN, *Renaissance Self-Fashioning* (Chicago, 1980).

GURR, ANDREW, *Playgoing in Shakespeare's London*, 2nd edn. (Cambridge, 1996).

—— *The Shakespearean Stage 1574–1642*, 3rd edn. (Cambridge, 1992).

HERRICK, MARVIN, T., *Italian Comedy in the Renaissance* (Urbana, Ill., 1965).

HOLLAND, PETER, *The Ornament of Action: text and performance in Restoration comedy* (Cambridge, 1979).

HOWARD, JEAN, *The Stage and Social Struggle in Early Modern England* (London, 1994).

HOWARTH, W. D., *Molière: a playwright and his audience* (Cambridge, 1982).

HUNTER, G. K., *English Drama 1586–1642* (Oxford, 1997).

JEFFERY, BRIAN, *French Renaissance Comedy, 1552–1630* (Oxford, 1969).

LOUGH, JOHN, *Seventeenth-Century French Drama: the background* (Oxford, 1979).

MCKENDRICK, MELVEENA, *Theatre in Spain 1490–1700* (Cambridge, 1989).

—— *Women and Society in the Spanish Drama of the Golden Age* (Cambridge, 1974).

ORGEL, STEPHEN, *The Illusion of Power: political theatre in the English Renaissance* (Berkeley, 1975).

—— and STRONG, ROY, *Inigo Jones: the theatre of the Stuart Court*, 2 vols. (Berkeley, 1973).

POWELL, JOCELYN, *Restoration Theatre Production* (London, 1984).

RICHARDS, KENNETH, and RICHARDS, LAURA, *The Commedia dell'Arte: a documentary history* (Oxford, 1990).

SCOTT, VIRGINIA, *The Commedia Dell'Arte in Paris, 1644–1697* (Charlottesville, Virginia, 1990).

THOMSON, PETER, *Shakespeare's Professional Career* (Cambridge, 1992).

—— *Shakespeare's Theatre*, 2nd edn. (London, 1992).

VINCE, RONALD W., *Renaissance Theatre: a historiographical handbook* (Westport, Conn., 1984).

WICKHAM, GLYNNE, *Early English Stages, 1300–1660*, 5 vols. (London, 1959–   ).

WIKANDER, MATTHEW H., *Princes to Act: royal audience and royal performance, 1578–1792* (Baltimore, 1993).

WILSON, EDWARD M., and MOIR, DUNCAN, *The Golden Age: drama 1492–1700* (London, 1971).

6. Europe 1700–1900

BAILEY, PETER (ed.), *Music Hall: the business of pleasure* (Milton Keynes, 1986).

BAKER, MICHAEL, *The Rise of the Victorian Actor* (London, 1978).

BEVIS, RICHARD W., *English Drama: Restoration and eighteenth century, 1660–1789* (London, 1988).

BOOTH, MICHAEL R., *Theatre in the Victorian Age* (Cambridge, 1991).

—— *Victorian Spectacular Theatre 1850–1910* (London, 1981).

BRATTON, J. S. (ed.), *Music Hall: performance and style* (Milton Keynes, 1986).

BROWN, FREDERICK, *Theatre and Revolution: the culture of the French stage* (New York, 1980).

BRUFORD, WALTER H., *Theatre, Drama and Audience in Goethe's Germany* (London, 1957).

CARLSON, MARVIN, *The French Stage in the Nineteenth Century* (Metuchen, NJ, 1972).

—— *The German Stage in the Nineteenth Century* (Metuchen, NJ, 1972).

—— *Goethe and the Weimar Theatre* (Ithaca, NY, 1978).

—— *The Italian Stage from Goldoni to D'Annunzio* (London, 1981).

DAVIS, TRACY, *Actresses as Working Women: their social identity in Victorian culture* (New York, 1991).

—— *The Economics of the British Stage, 1800–1914* (Cambridge, 2000).

—— and DONKIN, ELLEN (eds.), *Women and Playwriting in Nineteenth-Century Britain* (Cambridge, 1999).

DONKIN, ELLEN, *Getting into the Act: women playwrights in London, 1776–1829* (London, 1994).

DONOHUE, JOSEPH, *Theatre in the Age of Kean* (Oxford, 1975).

HEMMINGS, F. J. W., *The Theatre Industry in Nineteenth-Century France* (Cambridge, 1993).

—— *Theatre and State in France, 1790–1905* (Cambridge, 1994).

HUME, ROBERT D. (ed.), *The London Theatre World, 1660–1800* (Carbondale, Ill., 1980).

INNES, CHRISTOPHER (ed.), *A Sourcebook on Naturalist Theatre* (London, 2000).

JACKSON, RUSSELL (ed.), *Victorian Theatre* (London, 1989).

KRUGER, LOREN, *The National Stage: theatre and cultural legitimation in England, France, and America* (Chicago, 1992).

MARKER, FREDERICK J., and MARKER, LISE-LONE, *A History of Scandinavian Theatre* (Cambridge, 1996).

MEISEL, MARTIN, *Realizations: narrative, pictorial, and theatrical arts in nineteenth-century England* (Princeton, 1983).

MORASH, CHRISTOPHER, *A History of Irish Theatre, 1601–2000* (Cambridge, 2002).

NICHOL, ALLARDYCE, *The Garrick Stage* (Manchester, 1980).

ODELL, G. C. D., *Shakespeare from Betterton to Irving*, 2 vols. (New York, 1920).

OSBOURNE, JOHN, *The Meiningen Court Theatre, 1866–1890* (Cambridge, 1988).

PATTERSON, MICHAEL, *The First German Theatre: Schiller, Goethe, Kleist, and Büchner in performance* (London, 1990).

POWELL, KERRY, *Women and Victorian Theatre* (Cambridge, 1997).

REES, TERENCE, *Theatre Lighting in the Age of Gas* (London, 1978).

ROWELL, GEORGE, *The Victorian Theatre, 1792–1914*, 2nd edn. (London, 1979).

SCHUMACHER, CLAUDE (ed.), *Naturalism and Symbolism in European Theatre, 1850–1918* (Cambridge, 1996).

SENELICK, LAURENCE (ed.), *National Theatre in Northern and Eastern Europe, 1746–1900* (Cambridge, 1991).

SHAW, GEORGE BERNARD, *Our Theatre in the Nineties*, 3 vols. (London, 1932).

SOUTHERN, RICHARD, *Changeable Scenery: its origin and development in the English theatre* (London, 1952).

WIKANDER, MATTHEW H., *Princes to Act: royal audience and royal performance, 1578–1792* (Baltimore, 1993).

WILLIAMS, SIMON, *German Actors of the Eighteenth and Nineteenth Centuries: idealism, romanticism, realism* (Westport, Conn., 1985).

7. Europe since 1900

APPIA, ADOLPHE, *Texts on Theatre*, ed. Richard C. Beacham (London, 1993).

ARTAUD, ANTONIN, *Theatre and its Double*, trans. Mary Caroline Richards (New York, 1958).

ASTON, ELAINE, and REINELT, JANELLE (eds.), *The Cambridge Companion to Modern British Women Playwrights* (Cambridge, 2000).

BABLET, DENIS, *The Revolution in Stage Design in the Twentieth Century* (Paris, 1977).

BARKER, CLIVE, and GALE, MAGGIE B. (eds.), *British Theatre Between the Wars, 1918–1939* (Cambridge, 2000).

BOOTH, MICHAEL R., and KAPLAN, JOEL H. (eds.), *The Edwardian Theatre: essays on performance and the stage* (Cambridge, 1996).

BRADBY, DAVID, *Modern French Drama 1940–1990*, 2nd edn. (Cambridge, 1991).

—— and WILLIAMS, DAVID, *Director's Theatre* (New York, 1988).

BRAUN, EDWARD, *The Director and the Stage: from naturalism to Grotowski* (New York, 1982).

BRAUN, KAZIMIERZ, *A History of Polish Theatre, 1939–1989* (Westport, Conn. 1996).

BRECHT, BERTOLT, *Brecht on Theatre*, ed. John Willett (New York, 1964).

BROOK, PETER, *The Empty Space* (New York, 1968).

—— *The Shifting Point, 1946–1987* (New York, 1987).

BURIAN, JARKA M., *Leading Creators of Twentieth-Century Czech Theatre* (London, 2002).

CRAIG, EDWARD GORDON, *On the Art of Theatre* (London, 1911).

ESSLIN, MARTIN, *The Theatre of the Absurd*, new edn. (London, 2001).

GOLDBERG, ROSELEE, *Performance Art: from futurism to the present*, rev. edn. (New York, 2001).

GOODMAN, LIZBETH, *Contemporary Feminist Theatres: to each her own* (London, 1993).

GRENE, NICHOLAS, *The Politics of Irish Drama: plays in context from Boucicault to Friel* (Cambridge, 1999).

GROTOWSKI, JERZY, *Towards a Poor Theatre* (New York, 1968).

HAINAUX, RENÉ (ed.), *Stage Design throughout the World*, 4 vols. (New York, 1956–76).

HOLROYD, MICHAEL, *Bernard Shaw*, 4 vols. (London, 1988–92).

HORTMANN, WILHELM, *Shakespeare on the German Stage: the twentieth century* (Cambridge 1998).

INNES, CHRISTOPHER, *Avant-Garde Theatre: 1892–1992* (London, 1993).

JELAVICH, PETER, *Munich and Theatrical Modernism, 1890–1914* (Cambridge, Mass., 1985).

KAPLAN, JOEL H., and STOWELL, SHEILA, *Theatre and Fashion: Oscar Wilde to the suffragettes* (Cambridge, 1994).

KENNEDY, DENNIS, *Granville Barker and the Dream of Theatre* (Cambridge, 1985).

—— *Looking at Shakespeare: a visual history of twentieth-century performance*, 2nd edn. (Cambridge, 2001).

KOTT, JAN, *Shakespeare Our Contemporary*, trans. Boleslaw Taborski (New York, 1966).

MACGOWAN, KENNETH, and JONES, R. E., *Continental Stagecraft* (New York, 1922).

McGRATH, JOHN, *A Good Night Out: popular theatre, audience, class and form* (London, 1981).

MORASH, CHRISTOPHER, *A History of Irish Theatre, 1601–2000* (Cambridge, 2002).

PATTERSON, MICHAEL, *The Revolution in German Theatre, 1900–1933* (London, 1981).

REBELLATO, DAN, *1956 and All That: the making of modern British drama* (London, 1999).

ROBERTS, PHILIP, *The Royal Court Theatre and the Modern Stage* (Cambridge, 1999).

ROUSE, JOHN, *Brecht and the West German Theatre: the practice and politics of interpretation* (Ann Arbor, 1989).

SAUNDERSON, MICHAEL, *From Irving to Olivier: a social history of the acting profession, 1880–1983* (New York, 1985).

SENELICK, LAURENCE (ed.), *Cabaret Performance: Europe, 1890–1940* (Cambridge, 1993).

SHANK, THEODORE (ed.), *Contemporary British Theatre* (London, 1994).

TYNAN, KENNETH, *A View of the English Stage, 1944–1965* (London, 1984).

WILLETT, JOHN, *Theatre of the Weimar Republic* (New York, 1988).

8. Russia and Soviet Union

BAKSHY, ALEXANDER, *The Path of the Modern Russian Stage and Other Essays* (London, 1916).

BRAUN, EDWARD, *Meyerhold: a revolutionary theatre*, 2nd edn. (London, 1995).

CARTER, HUNTLY, *The New Spirit in the Russian Theatre* (London, 1929).

GREGOR, JOSEPH, and FÜLOP-MILLER, RENÉ, *The Russian Theatre* (London, 1930).

KARLINSKY, SIMON, *Russian Drama from its Beginnings to the Age of Pushkin* (Berkeley, 1985).

KLEBERG, LARS, *Theatre as Action* (London, 1993).

LEACH, ROBERT, *Revolutionary Theatre* (London, 1994).

—— and BOROVSKY, VICTOR (eds.), *A History of Russian Theatre* (Cambridge, 1999).

MAGARSHACK, DAVID, *Stanislavsky: a life* (London, 1950).

—— *Chekhov, the Dramatist* (London, 1980).

RUDNITSKY, KONSTANTIN, *Russian and Soviet Theatre: tradition and the avant-garde* (London, 1988).

RUSSELL, ROBERT, and BARRATT, ANDREW (eds.), *Russian Theatre in the Age of Modernism* (London, 1990).

SAYLER, OLIVER, *The Russian Theatre* (New York, 1922).

SEGEL, HAROLD, *Twentieth Century Russian Drama* (Baltimore, 1993).

SLONIM, MARC, *Russian Theatre from the Empire to the Soviets* (Cleveland, 1961).

SMELIANSKY, ANATOLY, *The Russian Theatre after Stalin* (Cambridge, 1999).

STANISLAVSKY, KONSTANTIN, *My Life in Art*, trans. J. J. Robbins (1924; New York, 1956).

VAN NORMAN BAER, NANCY (ed.), *Theatre in Revolution: Russian avant-garde stage design, 1913–1935* (London, 1992).

WORRALL, NICK, *Modernism to Realism on the Soviet Stage* (Cambridge, 1989).

9. Africa

BANHAM, MARTIN, and PLASTOW, JANE (eds.), *Contemporary African Plays* (London, 1999).

BARBER, KARIN, COLLINS, JOHN, and RICARD, ALAIN, *West African Popular Theatre* (Bloomington, Ind., 1997).

BLAIR, DOROTHY, *African Literature in French* (London, 1976).

BREITINGER, ECKHARD (ed.), *Theatre and Performance in Africa: intercultural perspectives* (Bayreuth, 1994).

DUNTON, CHRIS, *Make Man Talk True: Nigerian drama in English since 1970* (London, 1992).

ETHERTON, MICHAEL, *The Development of African Drama* (London, 1982).

GRAHAM-WHITE, ANTHONY, *The Drama of Black Africa* (New York, 1974).

GUNNER, LIZ (ed.), *Politics and Performance: theatre, performance and song in southern Africa* (Johannesburg, 1994).

JEYIFO BIODUN, *The Yoruba Popular Travelling Theatre of Nigeria* (Lagos, 1984).

KACKE, GÖTRICK, *Apidan Theatre and Modern Drama* (Stockholm, 1984).

KAMLONGERA, CHRISTOPHER, *Theatre for Development in Africa: with case studies from Malawi and Zambia* (Bonn, 1989).

KERR, DAVID, *African Popular Theatre from Pre-colonial Times to the Present Day* (London, 1995).

KRUGER, LOREN, *The Drama of South Africa: plays, pageants and publics since 1910* (London, 1999).

MDA, ZAKES, *When People Play People: development communication through theatre* (Johannesburg, 1993).

OGUNBA, OYIN, and IRELE, ABIOLA (eds.), *Theatre in Africa* (Ibadan, 1978).

OGUNBIYI, YEMI, *Drama and Theatre in Nigeria: a critical sourcebook* (Lagos, 1981).

OKPEWHO, ISODORE, *African Oral Literature: backgrounds, character and continuity* (Bloomington, Ind., 1992).

ORKIN, MARTIN, *Drama and the South African State* (Manchester, 1991).

OWOMOYELA, OYEKAN, *African Literatures: an introduction* (Waltham, Mass., 1979).

—— (ed.), *A History of Twentieth-Century African Literatures* (Lincoln, Nebr., 1993).

—— *Visions and Revisions: essays on African literature and criticism* (Washington, 1991).

PETERSEN, BHEKIZIZWE, *Monarchs, Missionaries and African Intellectuals: African theatre and the unmaking of colonial marginality* (Johannesburg, 2000).

PLASTOW, JANE, *African Theatre and Politics: the evolution of theatre in Ethiopia, Tanzania and Zimbabwe. A comparative study* (Amsterdam, 1996).

SCHIPPER, MINEKE, *Theatre and Society in Africa* (Johannesburg, 1982).

SOYINKA, WOLE, *Art, Dialogue and Outrage: essays on literature and culture* (Ibadan, 1988).

—— *Myth, Literature, and the African World* (Cambridge, 1976).

THIONG'O, NGUGI WA, *Penpoints, Gunpoints, and Dreams: the performance of literature and power in post-colonial Africa* (New York, 1998).

—— *Decolonising the Mind: the politics of language in African literature* (Oxford, 1986).

WALTER, HAROLD, *Black Theatre in French: a guide* (Québec, 1978).

10. South Asia

AHMED, SYED JAMIL, *Acin Pakhi Infinity: indigenous theatre of Bangladesh* (Dhaka, 2000).

BAUMER, R., and BRANDON, JAMES, (eds.), *Sanskrit Drama in Performance* (Honolulu, 1981).

BHARUCHA, RUSTOM, *Theatre and the World: performance and the politics of culture* (London, 1993).

—— *The Theatre of Kanhailal: Pebet and memoirs of Africa* (Calcutta, 1992).

—— *The Politics of Cultural Practice: thinking through theatre in an age of globalization* (London, 2000).

BYRSKI, M. CHRISTOPHER, *Concept of Ancient Indian Theatre* (New Delhi, 1974).

DUTT, UTPAL, *Towards a Revolutionary Theatre* (Calcutta, 1982).

FRASCA, RICHARD ARMAND, *The Theatre of the Mahabharata: terukuttu performance in south India* (Honolulu, 1990).

GHOSH, MANMOHAN (ed. and trans.), *The Natyashastra Ascribed to Bharat Muni* (Calcutta, 1967).

GOKHALE, SHANTA, *Playwright at the Centre: Marathi drama from 1843 to the present* (Calcutta, 2000).

HANSEN, KATHRYN, *Grounds for Play: the nautanki theatre of north India* (Berkeley, 1992).

HASHMI, SAFDAR, *The Right to Perform* (Delhi, 1989).

KAPUR, ANURADHA, *Actors, Pilgrims, Kings and Gods: the Ramlila at Ramnagar* (Calcutta, 1990).

LAL, ANANDA, *Rabindranath Tagore: three plays* (Calcutta, 1987).

MUKHERJEE, SUSHIL KUMAR, *The Story of the Calcutta Theatres: 1753–1980* (Calcutta, 1982).

OBEYESEKERE, RANJINI, *Theater in a Time of Terror: satire in a permitted space* (New Delhi, 1999).

PANCHAL, GOVERDHAN, *Kuttampalam and Kutiyattam* (New Delhi, 1984).

RANADE, ASHOK D., *Stage Music of Maharashtra* (New Delhi, 1986).

RICHMOND, FARLEY P., SWANN DARIUS L., and ZARRILLI, PHILLIP (eds.), *Indian Theatre: traditions of performance* (Honolulu, 1990).

SCHECHNER, RICHARD, *Performative Circumstances from the Avant Garde to Ramlila* (Calcutta, 1983).

SIRCAR, BADAL, *The Third Theatre* (Calcutta, 1978).

VATSYAYAN, KAPILA, *Traditional Indian Theatre: multiple streams* (New Delhi, 1980).

ZARRILLI, PHILLIP B., *When the Body Becomes All Eyes: paradigms, practices and discourses of power in Kalarippayattu* (New Delhi, 1998).

—— *When Gods and Demons Come to Play: Kathakali dance-drama in performance and context* (London, 2000).

11. South-East Asia

General

BRANDON, JAMES R., *Theatre in Southeast Asia* (Cambridge, Mass., 1967).

GHULAM-SARWAR, YOUSOF, *Dictionary of Traditional Southeast Asian Theatre* (Oxford, 1994).

MIETINNEN, YUKKA, *Classical Dance and Theatre in Southeast Asia* (Oxford, 1992).

PONG, CUOA SOO (ed.), *Traditional Theatre in Southeast Asia* (Singapore, 1995).

Burma

SINGER, NOEL, *Burmese Theatre and Dance* (Oxford, 1995).

Cambodia

KRAVEL, PECH T., *Yike and Bassac: theatre of Cambodia* (Phnom Penh, 1997).

Indonesia

BANDEM, I MADÉ, and DEBOER, FREDERIK E., *Kaja and Kelod: Balinese dance in transition* (Oxford, 1982).

BRANDON, JAMES R. (ed.), *On Thrones of Gold: three Javanese shadow plays* (Honolulu, 1993).

EMIGH, JOHN, *Masked Performance: the play of self and other in ritual and theatre* (Philadelphia, 1996).

Malaysia

GHULAM-SARWAR, YOUSOF, *Panggung Semar: Aspects of Traditional Malay Theatre* (Trumbull, 1995).

SWEENEY, AMIN, *Malay Shadow Puppets: the Wayang Siam of Kelantan* (London, 1980).

Philippines

TIONGSON, NICANOR G., *Komedya* (Quezon City, 1999).

—— *Sinakulo* (Quezon City, 1999).

Thailand

RUTNIN, MATTANI MOJDARA, *Dance, Drama, and Theatre in Thailand: the process of development and modernization* (Toyo Bunko, 1993).

12. East Asia

China

BIRCH, CYRIL, *Scenes for Mandarins: the elite theatre of the Ming* (New York, 1995).

CHEUNG, MARTHA P. Y., and LAI, JANE C. C. (eds.), *An Oxford Anthology of Contemporary Chinese Drama* (Hong Kong, 1997).

CRUMP, JAMES IRVING, *Chinese Theatre in the Days of Kublai Khan* (Tucson, Ariz., 1980).

DOLBY, WILLIAM. *A History of Chinese Drama* (London, 1976).

LOPEZ, MANUEL D., *Chinese Drama: an annotated bibliography of commentary, criticism, and plays in English translation* (Metuchen, NJ, 1991).

MACKERRAS, COLIN, *Chinese Drama from its Origins to the Present Day* (Honolulu, 1988).

—— *The Performing Arts in Contemporary China* (London, 1981).

—— and TUNG, CONSTANTINE (eds.), *Drama in the People's Republic of China* (Albany, NY, 1987).

RILEY, JO, *Chinese Theatre and the Actor in Performance* (Cambridge, 1997).

SCOTT, ADOLPHE C., *The Classical Theatre of China* (London, 1957).

SHIH CHUNG-WEN, *The Golden Age of Chinese Drama* (Princeton, 1976).

YAN HAIPING (ed.), *Theatre and Society: an anthology of contemporary Chinese drama* (Armonk, 1998).

YU SHIO-LING (ed.), *Chinese Drama after the Cultural Revolution 1979–1989* (Lewiston, 1997).

YUNG, BELL, *Cantonese Opera: performance as a creative process* (Cambridge, 1989).

Korea

CHO, OH-KON, *Korean Puppet Theatre: Kkoktu Kaksi* (East Lansing, Mich., 1979).

—— *Traditional Korean Theatre* (Berkeley, 1988).

KARDOSS, JOHN, *An Outline History of Korean Drama* (New York, 1966).

KOREAN ITI (ed.), *The Korean Theatre, Past and Present* (Seoul, 1981).

LEE, DUHYUN, *Korean Performing Arts: drama, dance, and music theater* (Seoul, 1997).

Japan

BRANDON, JAMES R., *Nō and Kyōgen in the Contemporary World: brilliance and bravado, 1697–1766* (Honolulu, 1997).

—— and LEITER, SAMUEL L. (eds.), *Kabuki Plays on Stage*, 4 vols., (Honolulu, 2002–3).

FRALEIGH, SONDRA HORTON, *Dancing into Darkness: Butoh, Zen, and Japan* (Pittsburgh, 1999).

GOODMAN, DAVID, *Japanese Drama and Culture in the 1960s: the return of the gods* (London, 1988).

KLEIN, SUSAN BLAKELEY, *Ankoku Butoh: the premodern and postmodern influences on the dance of utter darkness* (Ithaca, NY, 1989).

KOMINZ, LAWRENCE R., *The Stars Who Created Kabuki: their lives, loves, and legacy* (New York, 1997).

KOMPARU KUNIO, *The Noh Theatre: principles and perspectives* (New York, 1983).

LEITER, SAMUEL L., *New Kabuki Encyclopedia* (Westport, Conn., 1997).

—— *The Art of Kabuki: famous plays in performance* (Berkeley, 1979).

ORTOLANI, BENITO, *The Japanese Theatre: from shamanistic ritual to contemporary pluralism* (Princeton, 1995).

POWELL, BRIAN, *Japan's Modern Theatre: a century of change and continuity* (London, 2002).

RIMER, J. THOMAS, *Towards a Modern Japanese Theatre: Kishida Kunio* (Princeton, 1974).

—— and MASAKAZU, YAMAZAKI, *On the Art of the No Drama: the major treatises of Zeami* (Princeton, 1984).

ROBERTSON, JENNIFER, *Takarazuka: sexual politics and popular culture in modern Japan* (Berkeley, 1998).

SENDA AKIHIKO, *The Voyage of Contemporary Japanese Theatre*, trans. J. Thomas Rimer (Honolulu, 1997).

SHAVER, RUTH, *Kabuki Costumes* (Rutland, Vt., 1966).

SUZUKI TADASHI, *The Way of Acting: the theatre writings of Suzuki Tadashi*, trans. J. Thomas Rimer (New York, 1986).

THORNBURY, BARBARA E., *Sukeroku's Double Identity: the dramatic structure of Edo Kabuki* (Ann Arbor, 1982).

TSUBIOKE, EIKO (ed.), *Theatre Japan*, 2nd edn. (Tokyo, 1993).

13. North America

ALLEN, ROBERT C., *Horrible Prettiness: burlesque and American culture* (Chapel Hill, 1991).

AUSLANDER, PHILIP, *Presence and Resistance: postmodernism and cultural politics in contemporary American performance* (Ann Arbor, 1994).

BENSON, EUGENE, and CONOLLY, L. W. (eds.), *The Oxford Companion to Canadian Theatre* (Oxford, 1989).

BIGSBY, C. W. E., *A Critical Introduction to Twentieth-Century American Drama*, 3 vols. (Cambridge, 1982–5).

BRASK, PER (ed.), *Contemporary Issues in Canadian Drama* (Winnipeg, 1995).

CLURMAN, HAROLD, *The Fervent Years: the story of the Group Theatre and the thirties* (New York, 1957).

DOUCETTE, LEONARD E., *Theatre in French Canada: laying the foundations 1606–1867* (Toronto, 1984).

DUDDEN, FAYE E., *Women in the American Theatre: actresses and audiences, 1790–1870* (New Haven, 1994).

DURHAM, WELDON (ed.), *American Theatre Companies, 1888–1930* (Westport, Conn. 1987).

—— *American Theatre Companies, 1931–1986* (Westport, Conn., 1989).

ENGLE, RON, and MILLER, TICE L. (eds.), *The American Stage: social and economic forces from the colonial period to the present* (Cambridge, 1993).

FEARNOW, MARK, *The American Stage and the Great Depression: a cultural history of the grotesque* (New York, 1997).

FILEWOD, ALAN, *Collective Encounters: documentary theatre in English Canada* (Toronto, 1987).

GILBERT, DOUGLAS, *American Vaudeville* (New York, 1940).

GOLDBERG, ROSELEE, *Performance Art: from futurism to the present*, rev. edn. (New York, 2001).

GOLDSTEIN, MALCOLM, *The Political Stage: American drama and theater of the Great Depression* (New York, 1974).

GRIMSTED, DAVID, *Melodrama Unveiled: American theater and culture 1800–1850* (Chicago, 1968).

HARRIS, ANDREW B., *Broadway Theatre* (London, 1993).

HART, LINDA, and PHELAN, PEGGY (eds.), *Acting Out: feminist performances* (Ann Arbor, 1993).

HAY, SAMUEL A., *African American Theatre: a historical and critical analysis* (Cambridge, 1994).

HILL, ERROL (ed.), *The Theatre of Black Americans*, 2 vols. (Englewood Cliffs, NJ, 1980).

HIRSCH, FOSTER, *A Method to their Madness: the history of the Actor's Studio* (New York, 1984).

JOHNSTON, DENIS W., *Up the Mainstream: the rise of Toronto's alternative theatres 1968–1975* (Toronto, 1991).

KNOWLES, RIC, *The Theatre of Form and the Production of Meaning: contemporary Canadian dramaturgies* (Toronto, 1999).

LARSON, ORVILLE K., *Scene Design in the American Theatre from 1915 to 1960* (Fayetteville, Arkansas, 1989).

LEITER, SAMUEL L., *The Encyclopedia of the New York Stage*, 3 vols. (Westport, Conn., 1985–92).

LEVINE, LAWRENCE W., *Highbrow/Lowbrow: the emergence of cultural hierarchy in America* (Cambridge, 1988).

LONDRÉ, FELICIA HARDISON, and WATERMEIER, DANIEL J., *The History of North American Theater: the United States, Canada, and Mexico from pre-Columbian times to the present* (New York, 1998).

McARTHUR, BENJAMIN, *Actors and American Culture, 1880–1920* (Philadelphia, 1984).

McCONACHIE, BRUCE A., *Melodramatic Formations: American theatre and society, 1820–1870* (Iowa City, 1992).

MARRA, KIM, and SCHANKE, ROBERT A. (eds.) *Staging Desire: queer readings of American theater history* (Ann Arbor, 2002).

MARRANCA, BONNIE (ed.), *The Theatre of Images* (New York, 1977).

MASON, JEFFREY D., *Melodrama and the Myth of America* (Bloomington, 1993).

MESERVE, WALTER J., *An Emerging Entertainment: the drama of the American people to 1828* (Bloomington, 1977).

—— *An Outline History of American Drama* (New York, 1994).

NORTON, RICHARD C., *A Chronology of American Musical Theatre*, 3 vols. (Oxford, 2002).

O'CONNOR, JOHN, and BROWN, LORRAINE, *Free, Adult, Uncensored: the living history of the Federal Theatre Project* (London, 1980).

ODELL, C. C. D., *Annals of the New York Stage*, 15 vols. (New York, 1927–49).

RICHARDSON, GARY A., *American Drama: from the colonial period through World War I* (Boston, 1993).

RUBIN, DON (ed.), *Canadian Theatre History: selected readings* (Toronto, 1996).

SADDLEMYER, ANN (ed.), *Early Stages: theatre in Ontario 1800–1914* (Toronto, 1990).

—— and PLANT, RICHARD (eds.), *Later Stages: essays in Ontario theatre from the First World War to the 1970s* (Toronto, 1997).

SHAFER, YVONNE, *American Women Playwrights, 1900–1950* (New York, 1995).

SMITH, WENDY, *Real-Life Drama: the Group Theatre and America, 1931–40* (New York, 1990).

TOLL, ROBERT C., *Blacking Up; the minstrel show in nineteenth century America* (Oxford, 1974).

WAINSCOTT, RONALD H., *The Emergence of the Modern American Theater, 1914–1929* (New Haven, 1997).

WILMETH, DON B., and BIGSBY, CHRISTOPHER (eds.), *The Cambridge History of American Theatre*, 3 vols. (New York, 1998–2000).

ZEIGLER, JOSEPH WESLEY, *Regional Theatre: the revolutionary stage* (New York, 1977).

14. Latin America and Caribbean

ALBUQUERQUE, S., *Violent Acts: a study of contemporary Latin American theatre* (Detroit, 1991).

BOYLE, CATHERINE, *Thematic Development in Chilean Theatre since 1973: in search of the dramatic conflict* (Madison, 1992).

DAUSTER, FRANK (ed.), *Perspectives on Contemporary Spanish American Theater* (Cranbury, NJ, 1997).

DE COSTA, ELENA, *Collaborative Latin American Popular Theatre: from theory to form, from text to stage* (New York, 1992).

ELLIS, LORENA, *Brecht's Reception in Brazil* (New York, 1995).

GEORGE, DAVID, *Flash and Crash Days: Brazilian theater in the post-dictatorship period* (New York, 1999).

—— *The Modern Brazilian Stage* (Austin, Tex., 1992).

GLISSANT, EDOUARD, *Caribbean Discourses: selected essays* (Charlottesville, Va., 1993).

GRAHAM-JONES, JEAN, *Exorcising History: Argentine theater under dictatorship* (Cranbury, NJ, 2000).

JONES, BRIDGET DICKSON, and LITTLEWOOD, SITA E., *Paradoxes of French Caribbean Theatre: an annotated checklist of dramatic works: Guadeloupe, Guyane, Martinique from 1900* (London, 1997).

LARSON, CATHERINE, and VARGAS, MARGARITA, *Latin American Women Dramatists: theater, texts, and theories* (Bloomington, Ind., 1998).

LEON-PORTILLA, MIGUEL, *Pre-Columbian Literature of Mexico* (Norman, Okla., 1969).

LUZIARAGA, GERARDO (ed.), *Popular Theater for Social Change in Latin America: essays in Spanish and English* (Los Angeles, 1978).

MARTIN, RANDY, *Socialist Ensembles: theater and state in Cuba and Nicaragua* (Minneapolis, 1994).

TAYLOR, DIANA, *Disappearing Acts: spectacles of gender and nationalism in Argentina's dirty war* (Raleigh, NC, 1997).

—— *Theatre of Crisis: drama and politics in Latin America* (Lexington, NC, 1991).

—— and VILLEGAS, JUAN (eds.), *Negotiating Performance: gender, sexuality, and theatricalism in Latin/o America* (Durham, 1994).

VERSÉNYI, ADAM, *Theatre in Latin America: religion, politics, and culture from Cortes to the 1980s* (Cambridge, 1993).

WEISS, JUDITH, et al., *Latin American Popular Theatre* (Albuquerque, N. Mex., 1993).

15. Principal Journals

American Theatre
Asian Theatre Journal
Comparative Drama
Essays in Theatre
Gestos
Journal of American Drama and Theatre
Journal of Dramatic Theory and Criticism
Latin American Theatre Review
Modern Drama
New Theatre Quarterly
Nineteenth Century Theatre
Performance Research
Performing Arts Journal
Shakespeare Quarterly
Shakespeare Survey
Slavic and Eastern European Performance
TDR (The Drama Review)
Theater (formerly Yale/Theater)
Theatre Annual
Theatre Arts (1939–64)
Theatre Arts Magazine (1916–39)
Theatre Design and Technology
Theatre History Studies
Theatre Journal
Theatre Notebook
Theatre Quarterly (1970–81)
Theatre Research International
Theatre Survey
Western European Stages
Women and Performance

SELECTIVE INDEX OF DRAMATIC TITLES

PREPARED BY SARAH WILLIAMS

References to dramatic titles in the Encyclopedia are here catalogued by entry headword. Operas, musicals, revues, pantomimes, films, radio or television shows are normally so indicated, and identical titles of works by different hands are divided by the authors' names. Works written in languages other than English are listed under their most common English title when they are well established (e.g. *Cherry Orchard, The* or *Oedipus the King*), while lesser-known works are normally registered by their original titles in strict alphabetical order (e.g. *Der Drang* or *Un jour ma memoir*). Section numbers are indicated in the case of entries with numbered parts (e.g. 'scenography 6').

AA: le théâtre d'Arthur
Adamov: Adamov, Arthur
Aa Ooru Ee Ooru: Kannada theatre
Aartanaad: street theatre in India
Aa Went to Blaydon Races: Taylor, C. P.
Abbaracadabra: Boublil, Alain and Claude-Michel Schönberg
Abdala: Martí, José
Abduction from the Seraglio,The (opera): Mozart, Wolfgang Amadeus; *Singspiel*; race and theatre 1; Wood, Peter
Abelard and Heloise: Rigg, Diana
Abe Lincoln in Illinois: Beatty, John Lee; Holbrook, Hal; Massey, Raymond; Rice, Elmer; Sherwood, Robert E.
Abel's Sister: Wertenbaker, Timberlake
Abenteuer des braven Soldaten Schwejk see *Adventures of the Good Soldier Schwejk, The*
Abhijnanashakuntala (*Shakuntala Recognized*): Kalidasa; Kirloskar, Annasaheb; Marathi theatre; Telugu theatre; Veeresalingam, Kandukuri; see also *Shakuntala*

Abie's Irish Rose: film and theatre 5
Abigail: Blanco, Andrés Eloy
Abigail's Party: Leigh, Mike
Abingdon Square: Fornés, Maria Irene
'*A birritta cu' i cianpanedi* see *Cap and Bells*
Abou Al-Hassen: Algiers
Abraham: Hrotsvitha of Gandersheim
Abraham Lincoln: Drinkwater, John; Gilpin, Charles; Playfair, Nigel
Abraham sacrifiant: Bèze, Theodore de
Abramo e Isaaco: Belcari, Feo
Abroad: Weller, Michael
Absence of War, The: Hare, David
Absent Friends: Ayckbourn, Alan
Absolute Hell (TV): Dench, Judi
Absolute Signal: Gao Xingjian; Lin Zhaohua
Absurdity, The (*El adefesia*): Xirgu, Margarita
Absurdos en soledad (*Absurdities in Solitude*): Casas, Myrna
Absurd Person Singular: Ayckbourn, Alan
Abufar; ou, La Famille arabe: Ducis, Jean-François
Abundance: Henley, Beth
Abyssinia: African-American theatre; Williams, Bert
Accident (film): Merchant, Vivien; Rigby, Terence
Accidental Death of an Anarchist: Fo, Dario; Meng Jinghui

Accidental Tourist, The (film): Hurt, William
Accident at the North Station: Betti, Ugo
Accompaniment, The: Gorostiza, Carlos
Accountant Wawah: Musinga, Victor Elame
AC/DC: Hirsch, John
Acharnians, The: Aristophanes
Achilles: Schiller, Leon
Achilles and Polyxena: Hooft, Pieter Corneliszoon
Acis and Galatea: Stockholm
Acis and Galatea (opera): Craig, Edward Gordon; Gay, John
A civilizátor (*The Civilizer*): Madách, Imre
A Corda (*Tug of War*): Africa, lusophone
Across from the Garden of Allah: Jackson, Glenda; Wood, Charles
Across the Board on Tomorrow Morning: Saroyan, William
Acting Shakespeare: McKellen, Ian
Acto cultural (*Cultural Act*): Cabrujas, José Ignacio
Actor's Nightmare, The: Zaks, Jerry
Acts of the Apostles (*Actes des apôtres*): Paris 1
Acts without Words I and II: farce 4
Adamant Eve, The: McLaren, Robert
Adam in Exile: Vondel, Joost van den
Adam's Opera (musical): Dane, Clemence

Adam's Rib (film): Gordon, Ruth; Kanin, Garson
Adam the Creator: Čapek, Karel
Adam Zero (ballet): Benthall, Michael
Adaptation: May, Elaine
Addams Family, The (film): Julia, Raul; Malina, Judith
Adding Machine, The: Rice, Elmer
Adélaïde du Guesclin: Voltaire
Adelchi: Milan
Adelphi: Terence
Adhe Adhure (*Halfway House*; *Neither Half nor Whole*): Hindi theatre; Rakesh, Mohan
Admirable Crichton, The: Barrie, J. M.; Gillette, William Hooker
A doktor úr (*The Doctor*): Molnár, Ferenc
Adrea: Carter, Mrs Leslie
Adrienne Lecouvreur: Scribe, Augustin-Eugène
Aduh (*Ouch*): Wijaya, Putu
Adulateur, The: Warren, Mercy Otis
Adúltera (*Adulterous*): Martí, José
Adultery Punished: Głowacki, Janusz
Adventure of his Life, The: Schnitzler, Arthur
Adventures of Dick Tracy, The (radio): radio 3
Adventures of Frank Meriwell, The (radio): radio 3
Adventures of Robin Hood, The (TV): television 4
Adventures of the Good Soldier Schwejk, The (*Abenteuer des braven Soldaten Schwejk*):

Pallenberg, Max; Piscator, Erwin
Advise and Consent: Hughes, Barnard
Aeroplanes: Gorostiza, Carlos
Affairs of Anatol, The (film): film and theatre 4
Affected Damsels, The (*Les Précieuses ridicules*): Molière; satire
A flor da pele (*Nerves on Edge*): Castro, Consuelo de
Afore Night Comes: Daniels, Ron; Rudkin, David
Africa (film): Specht, Kerstin
Africa and God: Ogunde, Hubert
Africana (revue): Waters, Ethel
African Millionaire: Cape Town
Africapolis: censorship 8
After Aida: Mitchell, Julian
After Dark: Boucicault, Dion; Brady, William Aloysius
After Darwin: Wertenbaker, Timberlake
After Haggerty: Mercer, David; Whitelaw, Billie
After Magritte: Stoppard, Tom
Aftermath: Murray, T. C.
After Pilkington (TV): Gray, Simon
After Sorrow: Chong, Ping
After the Dance: Rattigan, Terence
After the Fall: Holbrook, Hal; Miller, Arthur; Robards, Jason; Zeffirelli, Franco
After the Funeral: Owen, Alun
After the Lions: Harwood, Ronald

H

J

K

SELECTIVE INDEX OF DRAMATIC TITLES

T

PICTURE ACKNOWLEDGEMENTS

The publisher wishes to thank the following who have kindly given permission to reproduce illustrations as identified by the page numbers. While every effort has been made to secure permissions, we may have failed in a few cases to trace the copyright holder. We apologise for any apparent negligence.

© Agence de Presse Bernand 272, 1257; Agnès Varda/Agence Enguérand, Paris 1412; Akademie der Künste, Berlin 646; Ancient Art & Architecture Collection 57; Anglo-Chinese Educational Institute 507; Archives of the National Theatre, Prague (photo: Jaromir Svoboda) 219, 1308; © Mary Jo Arnoldi 1084; © Catherine Ashmore 966; Bayreuther Festspiele/Wilhelm Rauh 1424; photograph courtesy Rustom Bharucha 615; Biblioteca Nazionale Centrale, Florence 1374; Bibliothèque nationale de France 831; Eckhard Breitinger 19, 220, 1268; Musée Condé, Chantilly, France/Lauros/Giraudon/Bridgeman Art Library 908; British Library 147, 807, 926; The British Museum, London 660, 705; Bulloz 1046; William Burdett-Coutts 797; courtesy Neelam Man Singh Chowdhry (photo: Simon Annand) 619; from *Shakespeare's England: An Account of the Life and Manners of his Age*, edited by Sidney Lee, 1916, Clarendon Press, Oxford 1076; Photograph by Donald Cooper © Photostage 127, 357, 424, 435, 451, 489, 508, 515, 834, 1161, 1163, 1239; © Bettmann/Corbis 1234; © Dean Conger/Corbis 264; © Macduff Everton/Corbis 934; © Lindsay Hebberd/Corbis 1435; © Bob Krist/Corbis 115; © Michael S. Yamashita/Corbis 648; © Ruphin Coudyzer 806; Dr Eric Csapo 1190; Sue Cunningham/SCP 717; Deutsches Archaeologisches Institut 426; © T. Charles Erickson 1009, 1453; © Richard Feldman 531, 892; © John Haynes 1226; Herzog Anton Ulrich Museum, Braunschweig (photo: B.P. Keiser) 171; Hulton Archive 89, 474, 604, 634, 1044; Index, Firenze 1026; © Jana Natya Manch (photo: Rathin Das) 1293; Photograph Janice Te-fen Lo 700; Gianfranco Mantegna/University of California, Davis 754; Martin von Wagner Museum, University of Würzburg (photo: K. Oehrlein) 75; © Jukka O. Miettinen 496, 682, 912, 913; The Museum of London 392; photo courtesy National School of Drama Archives, India 151; The National Swedish Art Museum (photo: Statens Kunstmuseer, Stockholm) 299; Nogami Memorial Noh Theatre Research Institute, Hosei University 946; © Photothèque des musées de la ville de Paris (photo: Jean-Yves Trocaz) 584; © Sonja Rothweiler 131; Photograph courtesy Sangeet Natak Akademi, New Delhi 149; Scottish National Portrait Gallery, Collection the Earl of Rosebery 433; SCR Photo Library 307, 525, 850, 1280; Shakespeare Centre Library, Stratford-upon-Avon 1144; Shizuoka Performing Arts Center 1306; © Ronald T. Simon 183; Peter Smith 1290; Stadtarchiv Zurich (photo © W.E. Baur) 986; © Oda Sternberg 896; © Point Tokyo Co. Ltd. 945; Sveriges Teatermuseum, Stockholm (photo: Beata Bergstöm) 385; Taganka Theatre 776; Teatremuseet, Copenhagen 739; Theaterwissenschaftliche Sammlung, Universität zu Köln 1438; University of Bristol Theatre Collection 158; © The Board of Trustees of the Victoria & Albert Museum 178, 1070, 1138, 1202, 1398; Phillip Zarrilli 672, 1344.